Hoover's MasterList of U.S. Companies

2024

Hoover's MasterList of U.S. Companies is intended to provide readers with accurate and authoritative information about the enterprises covered in it. The information contained herein is as accurate as we could reasonably make it. We do not warrant that the book is absolutely accurate or without error. Readers should not rely on any information contained herein in instances where such reliance might cause financial loss.

The publisher, the editors, and their data suppliers specifically disclaim all warranties, including the implied warranties of merchantability and fitness for a specific purpose. This book is sold with the understanding that neither the publisher, the editors, nor any content contributors are engaged in providing investment, financial, accounting, legal, or other professional advice.

Mergent Inc., provided financial data for most public companies in this book. For private companies and historical information on public companies prior to their becoming public, we obtained information directly from the companies or from third-party material that we believe to be trustworthy. Hoover's, Inc., is solely responsible for the presentation of all data.

Many of the names of products and services mentioned in this book are the trademarks or service marks of the companies manufacturing or selling them and are subject to protection under US law. Space has not permitted us to indicate which names are subject to such protection, and readers are advised to consult with the owners of such marks regarding their use. Hoover's is a trademark of Hoover's, Inc.

Copyright © 2024 by Hoover's, Inc. All rights reserved. No part of this book may be reproduced or transmitted in any form or by any means, electronic or mechanical, including by photocopying, facsimile transmission, recording, rekeying, or using any information storage and retrieval system, without permission in writing from Hoover's, except that brief passages may be quoted by a reviewer in a magazine, in a newspaper, online, or in a broadcast review.

10 9 8 7 6 5 4 3 2 1

Publishers Cataloging-in-Publication Data

Hoover's MasterList of U.S. Companies 2024,

    Includes indexes.

    ISBN: 979-8-89251-053-0

    ISSN 1549-6457

    1. Business enterprises — Directories. 2. Corporations — Directories.

HF3010 338.7

U.S. AND WORLD BOOK SALES

Mergent Inc.
28 Liberty ST
58th Floor
New York, NY 10005
Phone: 704-559-6961

e-mail: skardon@ftserussell.com
Web: www.mergentbusinesspress.com

Mergent Inc.

Executive Managing Director: John Pedernales

Publisher and Managing Director of Print Products: Thomas Wecera

Director of Print Products: Charlot Volny

Quality Assurance Editor: Wayne Arnold

Production Research Assistant: Davie Christna

Data Manager: Allison Shank

MERGENT CUSTOMER SERVICE-PRINT PRODUCTS
Support and Fulfillment: Stephanie Kardon

Phone: 704-559-6961
email: skardon@ftserussell.com
Web: www.mergentbusinesspress.com

ABOUT MERGENT INC.

For over 100 years, Mergent, Inc. has been a leading provider of business and financial information on public and private companies globally. Mergent is known to be a trusted partner to corporate and financial institutions, as well as to academic and public libraries. Today we continue to build on a century of experience by transforming data into knowledge and combining our expertise with the latest technology to create new global data and analytical solutions for our clients. With advanced data collection services, cloud-based applications, desktop analytics and print products, Mergent and its subsidiaries provide solutions from top down economic and demographic information, to detailed equity and debt fundamental analysis. We incorporate value added tools such as quantitative Smart Beta equity research and tools for portfolio building and measurement. Based in the U.S., Mergent maintains a strong global presence, with offices in New York, Charlotte, San Diego, London, Tokyo, Kuching and Melbourne. Mergent, Inc. is a member of the London Stock Exchange plc group of companies. The Mergent business forms part of LSEG's Information Services Division, which includes FTSE Russell, a global leader in indexes.

Abbreviations

AFL-CIO – American Federation of Labor and Congress of Industrial Organizations
AMA – American Medical Association
AMEX – American Stock Exchange
ARM – adjustable-rate mortgage
ASP – application services provider
ATM – asynchronous transfer mode
ATM – automated teller machine
CAD/CAM – computer-aided design/computer-aided manufacturing
CD-ROM – compact disc – read-only memory
CD-R – CD-recordable
CEO – chief executive officer
CFO – chief financial officer
CMOS – complementary metal oxide silicon
COO – chief operating officer
DAT – digital audiotape
DOD – Department of Defense
DOE – Department of Energy
DOS – disk operating system
DOT – Department of Transportation
DRAM – dynamic random-access memory
DSL – digital subscriber line
DVD – digital versatile disc/digital video disc
DVD-R – DVD-recordable
EPA – Environmental Protection Agency
EPROM – erasable programmable read-only memory
EPS – earnings per share
ESOP – employee stock ownership plan
EU – European Union
EVP – executive vice president
FCC – Federal Communications Commission
FDA – Food and Drug Administration
FDIC – Federal Deposit Insurance Corporation
FTC – Federal Trade Commission
FTP – file transfer protocol
GATT – General Agreement on Tariffs and Trade
GDP – gross domestic product
HMO – health maintenance organization
HR – human resources
HTML – hypertext markup language
ICC – Interstate Commerce Commission
IPO – initial public offering
IRS – Internal Revenue Service
ISP – Internet service provider
kWh – kilowatt-hour
LAN – local-area network
LBO – leveraged buyout
LCD – liquid crystal display
LNG – liquefied natural gas
LP – limited partnership
Ltd. – limited
mips – millions of instructions per second
MW – megawatt
NAFTA – North American Free Trade Agreement
NASA – National Aeronautics and Space Administration
NASDAQ – National Association of Securities Dealers Automated Quotations
NATO – North Atlantic Treaty Organization
NYSE – New York Stock Exchange
OCR – optical character recognition
OECD – Organization for Economic Cooperation and Development
OEM – original equipment manufacturer
OPEC – Organization of Petroleum Exporting Countries
OS – operating system
OSHA – Occupational Safety and Health Administration
OTC – over-the-counter
PBX – private branch exchange
PCMCIA – Personal Computer Memory Card International Association
P/E – price to earnings ratio
RAID – redundant array of independent disks
RAM – random-access memory
R&D – research and development
RBOC – regional Bell operating company
RISC – reduced instruction set computer
REIT – real estate investment trust
ROA – return on assets
ROE – return on equity
ROI – return on investment
ROM – read-only memory
S&L – savings and loan
SCSI – Small Computer System Interface
SEC – Securities and Exchange Commission
SEVP – senior executive vice president
SIC – Standard Industrial Classification
SVP – senior vice president
USB – universal serial bus
VAR – value-added reseller
VAT – value-added tax
VC – venture capitalist
VP – vice president
VoIP – Voice over Internet Protocol
WAN – wide-area network
WWW – World Wide Web

CONTENTS

Volume 1

Company Lists 2a-14a
    Top 500 Companies By Sales 2a
    Top 500 Companies By Employees 7a
    Top 500 Companies by Net Profit 12a

Company Listings A – L 2

Volume 2

Company Listings M – Z 819

Indexes 1555
    By Company 1557
    By Headquarters Location 1599

Hoover's MasterList
of U.S. Companies

Company Listings

M & F BANCORP INC
NBB: MFBP

2634 Durham Chapel Hill Blvd., Suite 101
Durham, NC 27707
Phone: 919 687-7800
Fax: 800 433-8283
Web: www.mfbonline.com

CEO: James H Sills III
CFO: Randall C Hall
HR: –
FYE: December 31
Type: Public

M&F Bancorp strives to be the mother and father of lending in the Tar Heel State. It's the holding company for Mechanics and Farmers Bank (M&F Bank), which serves urban markets in central North Carolina from seven branch locations. Established in 1907, the bank provides standard products and services including savings and checking accounts, IRAs, and CDs. M&F Bank is a Community Development Financial Institution, a US Treasury-designation for organizations that provide services to low-income communities. Its loan portfolio is dominated by real estate loans and mortgages, largely written for faith-based and not-for-profit organizations. In 2016 the bank cut some 11% of its workforce to cut costs.

	Annual Growth	12/14	12/15	12/16	12/20	12/21
Assets ($mil.)	2.9%	298.4	298.3	256.4	309.1	365.1
Net income ($ mil.)	15.0%	1.0	0.3	(3.9)	1.1	2.8
Market value ($ mil.)	6.0%	9.4	6.3	8.4	7.7	14.2
Employees	–	–	70	70	–	–

M & T BANK CORP
NYS: MTB

One M&T Plaza
Buffalo, NY 14203
Phone: 716 635-4000
Fax: –
Web: www.mtb.com

CEO: Rene F Jones
CFO: Darren J King
HR: –
FYE: December 31
Type: Public

M&T Bank Corporation (M&T) is a bank holding company with a total assets of $200.7 billion and deposits of $131.5 billion. Its wholly owned bank subsidiaries are Manufacturers and Traders Trust Company (M&T Bank) and Wilmington Trust, National Association (Wilmington Trust, N.A.). The banks offer deposit, loan, trust, investment, brokerage, mortgage, and insurance services to individuals and small- and mid-sized businesses. Its lending is largely focused in those states, but it originates from its loans via offices in other states and Canada. The firm also manages a proprietary line of mutual funds through Wilmington Funds Management. M&T was founded in 1856 as Manufacturers and Traders Trust in Buffalo, New York. In early 2022, M&T acquired People's United Financial for approximately $8.3 billion.

	Annual Growth	12/19	12/20	12/21	12/22	12/23
Assets ($mil.)	14.8%	119,873	142,601	155,107	200,730	208,264
Net income ($ mil.)	9.2%	1,929.1	1,353.2	1,858.7	1,991.7	2,741.0
Market value ($ mil.)	(5.2%)	28,202	21,149	25,515	24,100	22,774
Employees	5.7%	17,773	17,373	17,569	22,808	22,223

M V M, INC.

44620 GUILFORD DR STE 150
ASHBURN, VA 201476063
Phone: 571 223-4500
Fax: –
Web: www.mvminc.com

CEO: Kevin P Marquez
CFO: Joseph D Stanton
HR: Julie Geery
FYE: December 31
Type: Private

Need a secret agent, man? Founded in 1979 by three former US Secret Service agents, MVM provides security staffing and consulting services, primarily to US government entities. Along with security guards, MVM also offers executive protection, risk assessment, cultural training, analytical support, program management, and technical services. Its language support offerings include transcription, translation, and summarization services. The company has provided security services in Iraq during reconstruction efforts in that nation. Among MVM's customers are the Department of Justice, Internal Revenue Service, and the Department of Energy. Chairman and CEO Dario Marquez, one of the company's founders, controls MVM.

M. A. MORTENSON COMPANY

700 MEADOW LN N
MINNEAPOLIS, MN 554224837
Phone: 763 522-2100
Fax: –
Web: www.mortenson.com

CEO: Daniel L Johnson
CFO: Lois Martin
HR: Jim Olson
FYE: December 31
Type: Private

M. A. Mortenson Company is a general contractor company that performs construction, development, planning, and design-build services for a variety of projects in the aviation, data center, performing arts, healthcare, hospitality, manufacturing, public, and the federal government sectors. The company also has groups devoted to federal contracting, sports venues, and renewable energy, including wind farms, water/wastewater, and biofuel facilities. Some of its notable projects include the DaVita Office Building Expansion, Hilton Garden Inn, Arlene Schnitzer Concert Hall Acoustical Enhancement, QTS Data Center, Hillsboro Hops Ballpark, and UW Health Eastpark Medical Center. Founded in 1954, the company has offices across the US.

M. B. KAHN CONSTRUCTION CO., INC.

101 FLINTLAKE RD
COLUMBIA, SC 292237851
Phone: 803 736-2950
Fax: –
Web: www.mbkahn.com

CEO: William H Neely
CFO: –
HR: –
FYE: December 31
Type: Private

One of the largest construction companies in the southeastern US, M. B. Kahn Construction Co. works on commercial, institutional, and industrial projects including hospitals, airports, shopping centers, and manufacturing plants. Additionally, it is rated as one of the top builders in the nation's education market. The company provides general contracting and design/build delivery services, as well as construction management and program management services. Russian immigrant Myron B. Kahn founded the company in 1927. It is now chaired by Alan Kahn, his grandson. The group operates through divisions in South Carolina and Georgia.

	Annual Growth	12/14	12/15	12/16	12/17	12/18
Sales ($mil.)	7.0%	–	322.7	310.1	–	394.9
Net income ($ mil.)	–	–	7.1	–	–	–
Market value ($ mil.)	–	–	–	–	–	–
Employees	–	–	–	–	–	513

M. J. BRUNNER INC.

11 STANWIX ST FL 5
PITTSBURGH, PA 152221312
Phone: 412 995-9500
Fax: –
Web: www.brunnerworks.com

CEO: –
CFO: –
HR: –
FYE: December 31
Type: Private

Independent ad agency Brunner, formerly known as Blattner Brunner, provides advertising, design, marketing, and public relations. Specific services include brand strategy, research and planning, mobile and shopper marketing, and social media. Its Brunner Digital unit (formerly bbdigital) offers services such as Web site design and development, digital marketing, and media planning. The agency's clients include Zippo Manufacturing Company, H.J. Heinz Company, DeVry University, and GlaxoSmithKline. Chairman and CEO Michael Brunner, who helped found the agency in 1989, has been its controlling shareholder since 2003.

	Annual Growth	12/05	12/06	12/07	12/08	12/09
Sales ($mil.)	(6.4%)	–	–	55.5	48.6	48.6
Net income ($ mil.)	28.3%	–	–	1.0	1.6	1.6
Market value ($ mil.)	–	–	–	–	–	–
Employees	–	–	–	–	–	100

M.A. PATOUT & SON LIMITED, L.L.C.

3512 J PATOUT BURNS RD
JEANERETTE, LA 705447122
Phone: 337 276-4592
Fax: –
Web: www.mapatout.com

CEO: Craig Caillier
CFO: Randall K Romero
HR: –
FYE: July 31
Type: Private

For M. A. Patout & Son, family tradition means processing sugarcane into raw sugar, blackstrap molasses, and cane syrup. Founded in 1825, the company is owned and operated by descendants of the founding Patout family. It operates the oldest working sugar mill in the US (the Enterprise Factory in Patoutville, Louisiana), and is one of the oldest family-owned sugar businesses in the nation. The company also owns two additional factories in southern Louisiana (in the towns of Franklin and Raceland) through subsidiaries Sterling Sugars and Raceland Raw Sugars. The company owns 43,000 acres of cane fields and its mills have the capacity to process approximately 4.6 million tons of cane per year.

	Annual Growth	07/14	07/15	07/16	07/18	07/19
Sales ($mil.)	1.8%	–	–	288.8	306.0	304.9
Net income ($ mil.)	(0.3%)	–	–	11.6	27.6	11.4
Market value ($ mil.)	–	–	–	–	–	–
Employees	–	–	–	–	–	413

M.C.A. COMMUNICATIONS, INC.

483 W 38TH ST
HOUSTON, TX 770186603
Phone: 281 591-2434
Fax: –
Web: www.mcacom.com

CEO: Richard Cortez
CFO: –
HR: –
FYE: December 31
Type: Private

MCA Communications makes sure its clients are wired for sound -- and for video, data, and security. The company designs, builds, and maintains voice and data telecommunications systems and provides related consulting services for businesses. It also installs wiring, provides technical support, and implements video-conferencing and security systems, using access card readers, closed-circuit video, and sound reinforcement material. MCA serves such clients as financial institutions, energy companies, correctional facilities, educational institutions, and commercial office building operators. MCA Communications was founded in 1983 by president and CEO Richard Cortez.

	Annual Growth	12/10	12/11	12/12	12/13	12/14
Sales ($mil.)	0.7%	–	–	26.0	34.8	26.4
Net income ($ mil.)	67.9%	–	–	0.4	2.1	1.3
Market value ($ mil.)	–	–	–	–	–	–
Employees	–	–	–	–	–	115

M.D.C. HOLDINGS, INC.   NYS: MDC

4350 South Monaco Street, Suite 500
Denver, CO 80237
Phone: 303 773-1100
Fax: –
Web: www.mdcholdings.com

CEO: David D Mandarich
CFO: Robert N Martin
HR: –
FYE: December 31
Type: Public

Operating through its Richmond American Homes subsidiary and several other units, M.D.C. Holdings (MDC) is one of the largest homebuilders in the US, and is active in Arizona, California, Colorado, Florida, Maryland, New Mexico, Nevada, Pennsylvania, Tennessee, Texas, Utah, Virginia, and Washington. The homebuilder targets first-time and first-time move-up buyers with single-family detached homes that sell for an average price of around $597,500. Subsidiary HomeAmerican Mortgage provides loans to buyers of MDC's homes. MDC also has subsidiaries that offer home and title insurance.

	Annual Growth	12/19	12/20	12/21	12/22	12/23
Sales ($mil.)	9.0%	3,293.3	3,901.2	5,254.7	5,718.0	4,642.9
Net income ($ mil.)	13.9%	238.3	367.6	573.7	562.1	401.0
Market value ($ mil.)	9.7%	2,849.1	3,628.5	4,168.4	2,359.3	4,125.0
Employees	1.5%	1,656	1,773	2,080	1,643	1,760

M/I HOMES INC   NYS: MHO

4131 Worth Avenue, Suite 500
Columbus, OH 43219
Phone: 614 418-8000
Fax: 614 418-8080
Web: www.mihomes.com

CEO: Robert H Schottenstein
CFO: Phillip G Creek
HR: –
FYE: December 31
Type: Public

M/I Homes is one of the nation's leading builders of single-family homes, having sold over 143,400 homes since commencing homebuilding activities in 1976. The company's homes are marketed and sold primarily under the M/I Homes brand. It delivers homes to first-time, move-up, empty-nest, and luxury buyers at prices ranging from about $200,000 to $800,000 and sizes ranging from 1,000 to 5,500 sq. ft. M/I Homes also builds attached townhomes in select markets. It caters to more than 15 markets located in ten states. Its M/I Financial mortgage banking subsidiary provides title and mortgage services. M/I Homes is founded by cousins Melvin and Irving Schottenstein in 1976.

	Annual Growth	12/19	12/20	12/21	12/22	12/23
Sales ($mil.)	12.7%	2,500.3	3,046.1	3,745.9	4,131.4	4,033.5
Net income ($ mil.)	38.2%	127.6	239.9	396.9	490.7	465.4
Market value ($ mil.)	36.8%	1,092.4	1,229.5	1,726.2	1,282.0	3,823.8
Employees	3.5%	1,401	1,515	1,657	1,663	1,607

MAC BEATH HARDWOOD COMPANY

320 N KYLE ST
EDINBURGH, IN 461241200
Phone: 812 526-9743
Fax: –
Web: www.macbeath.com

CEO: –
CFO: –
HR: –
FYE: July 31
Type: Private

This MacBeath doesn't want to get the spot out. MacBeath Hardwood Company specializes in spotted and striped specialty hardwoods from the US, Mexico, Panama, India, Brazil, and several African nations. With wood from its 300,000 board feet-capacity drying kiln, the company makes furniture squares, lumber, veneer, plywood, maple countertops, and specialty products like hand rails, marine plywood, and wood "blanks" to be used for baseball bats. MacBeath has five distribution centers in California, Indiana, and Utah; it also ships large loads worldwide. It also operates an online store. The company was founded in the early 1950s by K.E. MacBeath.

	Annual Growth	07/04	07/05	07/06	07/07	07/08
Sales ($mil.)	(0.7%)	–	–	–	26.1	25.9
Net income ($ mil.)	(70.7%)	–	–	–	0.5	0.2
Market value ($ mil.)	–	–	–	–	–	–
Employees	–	–	–	–	–	90

MACALESTER COLLEGE

1600 GRAND AVE
SAINT PAUL, MN 551051899
Phone: 651 696-6000
Fax: –
Web: www.macalester.edu

CEO: –
CFO: David Wheaton
HR: Bob Graf
FYE: May 31
Type: Private

Macalester College provides a private, liberal arts education experience in St. Paul, Minnesota. The four-year school serves about 2,000 students. It offers more than 800 courses in 60 areas of study, giving it about 40 major programs in fields including natural science, social science, fine arts, and humanities. Macalester has a student-to-faculty ratio of 10:1 and a staff of about 170 full-time faculty members. It was founded in 1874 by the Rev. Edward Duffield as a Presbyterian-related but non-sectarian college, and was named after Charles Macalester, a prominent Philadelphia businessman and philanthropist.

	Annual Growth	05/18	05/19	05/20	05/21	05/22
Sales ($mil.)	1.7%	–	127.1	116.8	113.0	133.6
Net income ($ mil.)	–	–	(16.8)	(60.9)	177.8	(3.4)
Market value ($ mil.)	–	–	–	–	–	–
Employees	–	–	–	–	–	750

MACALLISTER MACHINERY CO INC

6300 SOUTHEASTERN AVE
INDIANAPOLIS, IN 462035828
Phone: 317 545-2151
Fax: –
Web: www.macallister.com

CEO: Pershing E Macallister
CFO: David Baldwin
HR: James Keough
FYE: December 31
Type: Private

MacAllister Machinery is Indiana's leading heavy equipment supplier. The company sells and rents new and used Caterpillar equipment including tractors, loaders, handlers, pavers, compactors, drills, and excavation equipment. MacAllister's Power Systems division handles the sales and service of Caterpillar electric power, electric power generation, industrial, marine power systems, and oil and gas. It also offers equipment from some 50 other manufacturers (including Kubota, Stihl, and AGCO). Based in Indiana, MacAllister Machinery was founded in 1945 by E.W. MacAllister and is still controlled by the MacAllister family.

MACATAWA BANK CORP.   NMS: MCBC

10753 Macatawa Drive
Holland, MI 49424
Phone: 616 820-1444
Fax: –
Web: www.macatawabank.com

CEO: Ronald L Haan
CFO: Jon W Swets
HR: –
FYE: December 31
Type: Public

Macatawa Bank Corporation is the holding company for Macatawa Bank. Since its 1997 founding, the company has grown into a network of more than 25 branches serving western Michigan's Allegan, Kent, and Ottawa counties. The bank provides standard services, including checking and savings accounts, CDs, safe deposit boxes, and ATM cards. It also offers investment services and products through an agreement with a third-party provider. With deposit funds, the bank primarily originates commercial and industrial loans and mortgages, which account for nearly 75% of its loan book. Macatawa Bank also originates residential mortgages and consumer loans.

	Annual Growth	12/19	12/20	12/21	12/22	12/23
Assets ($mil.)	7.4%	2,068.8	2,642.0	2,928.8	2,906.9	2,748.7
Net income ($ mil.)	7.8%	32.0	30.2	29.0	34.7	43.2
Market value ($ mil.)	0.3%	382.4	287.6	303.1	379.0	387.6
Employees	(1.7%)	364	355	330	341	340

MACE SECURITY INTERNATIONAL, INC.   NBB: MACE

4400 Carnegie Avenue
Cleveland, OH 44103
Phone: 440 424-5321
Fax: 216 361-9555
Web: www.mace.com

CEO: Sanjay Singh
CFO: Mark Barrus
HR: –
FYE: December 31
Type: Public

Mace Security International (MSI) aims to secure your person and your property. The firm makes a variety of security products, including electronic surveillance and access control products, cameras, monitors, alarms, and Kindergard brand childproof locks. It also sells Mace brand defense sprays for consumers and law enforcement officers, as well as tear gas and animal repellents. While security products account for two-thirds of sales, MSI also operates an e-commerce division that sells its own products and those of third parties. MSI is exiting the car wash business, which at its peak operated some 60 car and truck washes, to focus on its security and e-commerce activities. MSI was founded in 1993.

	Annual Growth	12/18	12/19	12/20	12/21	12/22
Sales ($mil.)	(6.6%)	11.5	10.5	15.4	13.1	8.8
Net income ($ mil.)	–	(1.9)	(1.7)	1.7	0.6	(1.7)
Market value ($ mil.)	(14.6%)	18.2	16.2	25.5	17.4	9.7
Employees	–	–	–	–	–	27

MACERICH CO (THE)   NYS: MAC

401 Wilshire Boulevard, Suite 700
Santa Monica, CA 90401
Phone: 310 394-6000
Fax: –
Web: www.macerich.com

CEO: Thomas E O'Hern
CFO: Scott W Kingsmore
HR: Annette Cameron
FYE: December 31
Type: Public

Macerich provides the infrastructure that houses top retail shops throughout the US. The self-administered real estate investment trust (REIT) acquires, develops, leases, and manages shopping and strip malls. Its portfolio consists of about 45 regional shopping centers and some five community shopping centers totaling approximately 47 million sq. ft. of gross leasable space. The properties are located in the US, with top markets in Arizona, California, and the New York metropolitan area. Macerich's tenants include some of the country's leading retailers, including Victoria's Secret, Gap, Dick's Sporting Goods, American Eagle Outfitters, and Foot Locker.

	Annual Growth	12/19	12/20	12/21	12/22	12/23
Sales ($mil.)	(1.2%)	927.5	786.0	847.4	859.2	884.1
Net income ($ mil.)	–	96.8	(230.2)	14.3	(66.1)	(274.1)
Market value ($ mil.)	(13.0%)	5,814.1	2,304.5	3,732.1	2,431.9	3,332.5
Employees	(2.9%)	737	670	640	651	655

MACH 1 GLOBAL SERVICES, INC.

950 W ELLIOT RD STE 212
TEMPE, AZ 852841145
Phone: 480 921-3900
Fax: –
Web: www.mach1global.com

CEO: –
CFO: –
HR: –
FYE: December 31
Type: Private

It doesn't ship goods at the speed of sound, but Mach1 Global Services does like to think fast. The freight forwarder provides domestic and international air, ground, ocean, and rail shipping services by buying transportation capacity from carriers and reselling it to customers. It also offers a variety of logistics services, including project management and supply chain management. Most of Mach1's customers come from the retail, automotive, high-tech, entertainment, health care, and manufacturing industries. The company has offices in the US, Mexico, and Asia (mostly China); it operates in other regions via network partners. CEO Michael Entzminger formed Mach1 in 1988.

	Annual Growth	12/03	12/04	12/05	12/06	12/08
Sales ($mil.)	14.4%	–	57.1	69.7	86.1	97.8
Net income ($ mil.)	(29.6%)	–	1.2	3.1	1.8	0.3
Market value ($ mil.)	–	–	–	–	–	–
Employees	–	–	–	–	–	210

MACHADO/GARCIA-SERRA PUBLICIDAD, INC.

1790 CORAL WAY FL 3
CORAL GABLES, FL 331452785
Phone: 305 444-4647
Fax: –
Web: www.mgscomm.com

CEO: –
CFO: –
HR: –
FYE: December 31
Type: Private

Machado|Garcia-Serra Publicidad provides integrated communications specializing in bridging the cultural gap between US consumer product manufacturers and the Hispanic market. The agency -- which does business as Machado Garcia-Serra Communications or MGSCOMM -- offers expertise in advertising, public relations, promotion, and event marketing, serving clients in the automotive, health care, and retail industries. The agency maintains three offices in Florida, New York, and Mexico. It was established in 2003 by public relations and advertising veterans Manual Machado and Al Garcia-Serra.

	Annual Growth	12/03	12/04	12/05	12/06	12/07
Sales ($mil.)	82.3%	–	–	–	32.2	58.8
Net income ($ mil.)	(20.2%)	–	–	–	0.7	0.6
Market value ($ mil.)	–	–	–	–	–	–
Employees	–	–	–	–	–	22

MACIAS GINI & O'CONNELL LLP

500 CAPITOL MALL STE 2200
SACRAMENTO, CA 958144759
Phone: 310 277-3373
Fax: –
Web: www.mgocpa.com

CEO: –
CFO: –
HR: Penny Auterson
FYE: December 31
Type: Private

Grateful clients might say, "Gracias, Macias!" Accounting and consulting firm Macias Gini & O'Connell (MGO) provides services through more than half a dozen California offices. The company (formerly Macias, Gini & Company) is a member of the BDO Seidman Alliance. MGO targets companies in such industries as manufacturing, real estate, health care, and technology; other clients include governmental, educational, and not-for-profit organizations. Services include internal auditing, tax planning and preparation, SEC filings, and merger and acquisition services. Its Macias Consulting Group specializes in performance evaluation and financial and technology management. MGO was founded in 1987 by Kenneth Macias.

	Annual Growth	12/05	12/06	12/11	12/12	12/20
Sales ($mil.)	11.8%	–	16.6	30.1	36.2	78.5
Net income ($ mil.)	2.6%	–	4.2	6.4	7.6	6.0
Market value ($ mil.)	–	–	–	–	–	–
Employees	–	–	–	–	–	700

MACK & ASSOCIATES LTD.

100 N LA SALLE ST STE 2110
CHICAGO, IL 606022448
Phone: 312 368-0677
Fax: –
Web: www.mackltd.com

CEO: –
CFO: –
HR: –
FYE: December 31
Type: Private

Mack & Associates knows how and where to find the right people for the administrative job. The firm provides direct-hire, temp-to-hire, and temporary staffing services to Chicago-area businesses. The company recruits, screens, checks references, and provides skill assessments for all its candidates and also offers payroll administration services. It fills primarily clerical, administrative, and professional support positions. The company serves clients in such industries as real estate, banking, architecture, construction, legal, and advertising industries. Mack & Associates was founded in 1984 and is owned by CEO Charlene Gorzela.

	Annual Growth	12/09	12/10	12/11	12/12	12/16
Sales ($mil.)	10.0%	–	3.1	3.6	3.6	5.6
Net income ($ mil.)	6.0%	–	0.0	0.1	(0.1)	0.1
Market value ($ mil.)	–	–	–	–	–	–
Employees	–	–	–	–	–	13

MACOM TECHNOLOGY SOLUTIONS HOLDINGS INC   NMS: MTSI

100 Chelmsford Street
Lowell, MA 01851
Phone: 978 656-2500
Fax: –
Web: www.macom.com

CEO: –
CFO: –
HR: –
FYE: September 29
Type: Public

M/A-COM Technology Solutions (aka MACOM) designs and manufactures semiconductor products for Telecommunications (Telecom), Industrial and Defense (I&D) and Data Center industries. The holding company makes analog semiconductors used in wireless and wireline applications across the radio-frequency (RF), microwave, and millimeter wave spectrum. Its portfolio encompasses some 3,500 standard and custom integrated circuits (IC), multi-chip modules (MCM), and subsystems across dozens product lines. Richardson RFPD, Gateway Tech, and Pangaea are among its top customers. More than 45% of sales come from customers in the US.

	Annual Growth	09/19*	10/20	10/21*	09/22	09/23
Sales ($mil.)	6.7%	499.7	530.0	606.9	675.2	648.4
Net income ($ mil.)	–	(383.8)	(46.1)	38.0	440.0	91.6
Market value ($ mil.)	39.3%	1,539.1	2,399.5	4,638.5	3,676.6	5,791.4
Employees	8.1%	1,100	1,050	1,100	1,200	1,500

*Fiscal year change

MACOMB-OAKLAND REGIONAL CENTER, INC.

15600 19 MILE RD
CLINTON TOWNSHIP, MI 480383502
Phone: 586 263-8700
Fax: –
Web: www.morcinc.org

CEO: –
CFO: –
HR: –
FYE: September 30
Type: Private

Michigan's disabled citizens have more than a friend in MORC. The Macomb-Oakland Regional Center (MORC) advocates for adults and children with developmental, physical, or psychiatric disabilities, hoping to improve the lives of its clients. In addition to finding homes and jobs and coordinating recreational activities for the disabled, the not-for-profit organization helps connect customers with support services including psychology, nursing, and medical care. It also holds community education seminars, and it provides home health visitation and rehabilitation therapy services through its MORC Home Care and MORC Rehab divisions. Founded in 1972, MORC serves over 4,000 clients in the state.

	Annual Growth	09/16	09/17	09/19	09/20	09/21
Sales ($mil.)	(15.7%)	–	172.6	93.3	92.5	87.1
Net income ($ mil.)	–	–	(0.0)	1.8	2.0	0.5
Market value ($ mil.)	–	–	–	–	–	–
Employees	–	–	–	–	–	300

MACROGENICS, INC   NMS: MGNX

9704 Medical Center Drive
Rockville, MD 20850
Phone: 301 251-5172
Fax: –
Web: www.macrogenics.com

CEO: Scott Koenig
CFO: James Karrels
HR: –
FYE: December 31
Type: Public

MacroGenics is a biopharmaceutical company focused on developing and commercializing innovative monoclonal antibody-based therapeutics for the treatment of cancer. The company has a pipeline of product candidates being evaluated in clinical trials sponsored by MacroGenics or its collaborators. These product candidates include six immuno-oncology programs, some of which were created primarily using the company's proprietary, antibody-based technology platforms. In 2021, the company and its commercialization partner commenced US marketing of MARGENZA (margetuximab-cmkb), a human epidermal growth factor receptor 2 (HER2) receptor antagonist indicated, in combination with chemotherapy, for the treatment of adult patients with metastatic HER2-positive breast cancer who have received two or more prior anti-HER2 regimens, at least one of which was for metastatic disease.

	Annual Growth	12/19	12/20	12/21	12/22	12/23
Sales ($mil.)	(2.2%)	64.2	104.9	77.4	151.9	58.7
Net income ($ mil.)	–	(151.8)	(129.7)	(202.1)	(119.8)	(9.1)
Market value ($ mil.)	(3.0%)	675.3	1,418.9	996.2	416.5	597.1
Employees	(3.1%)	384	370	427	357	339

MADDEN (STEVEN) LTD.   NMS: SHOO

52-16 Barnett Avenue
Long Island City, NY 11104
Phone: 718 446-1800
Fax: –
Web: www.stevemadden.com

CEO: Edward R Rosenfeld
CFO: Zine Mazouzi
HR: –
FYE: December 31
Type: Public

Steven Madden designs, sources and markets fashion-forward branded and private label footwear, accessories and apparel for women, men and children. Its wholesale business boasts some brands such as Madden Girl, Steve Madden, and Betsey Johnson as well as Superga, and Anne Klein under license. The company's direct-to-consumer business mainly consists of about 230 brick-and-mortar retail stores, including about 165 Steve Madden full-price stores, about 65 Steve Madden outlet stores and one one Dolce Vita full-price store, as well as six e-commerce websites. Steven Madden distributes its products throughout the US, Canada, Mexico, and Europe, and other international markets. Steven Madden generates almost 85% of revenue from its domestic markets.

	Annual Growth	12/19	12/20	12/21	12/22	12/23
Sales ($mil.)	2.6%	1,787.2	1,201.8	1,866.1	2,122.0	1,981.6
Net income ($ mil.)	5.0%	141.3	(18.4)	190.7	216.1	171.6
Market value ($ mil.)	(0.6%)	3,169.0	2,602.4	3,424.0	2,354.8	3,094.6
Employees	1.2%	4,000	2,800	3,500	4,000	4,200

MADISON AREA TECHNICAL COLLEGE DISTRICT

1701 WRIGHT ST
MADISON, WI 537042599
Phone: 608 246-6100
Fax: -
Web: www.madisoncollege.edu

CEO: -
CFO: -
HR: -
FYE: June 30
Type: Private

Madison Area Technical College (MATC) is a technical and community college that offers courses in liberal arts and sciences, adult basic education, and technical training. Students often enter careers in biotechnology, broadcast captioning, internet development, mechanics, or law enforcement. The college, which is the largest member of the Wisconsin Technical College System, provides education to more than 40,000 students each year. Many students go on to transfer to the University of Wisconsin or other UW system schools. MATC has 10 college facilities spread among five campuses in south central Wisconsin.

	Annual Growth	06/15	06/16	06/17	06/18	06/19
Sales ($mil.)	(3.2%)	-	77.4	71.4	70.5	70.1
Net income ($ mil.)	-	-	(2.9)	11.6	20.0	(2.4)
Market value ($ mil.)	-	-	-	-	-	-
Employees	-	-	-	-	-	3,500

MADISON ELECTRIC COMPANY

31855 VAN DYKE AVE
WARREN, MI 480931047
Phone: 586 825-0200
Fax: -
Web: www.madisonelectric.com

CEO: -
CFO: Benjamin Rosenthal
HR: -
FYE: January 31
Type: Private

Founded by Morris and Max Blumberg, Madison Electric broke ground in a rented room in Detroit in 1914. The company has grown from pushing light bulbs, fuses, wire, and conduit, to rival the top 200 electrical and electronics distributors in the US. Joined by affiliate Standard Electric Co., Madison Electric distributes electrical supplies, industrial automation, commercial lighting, and network communication components. Branches dotting Michigan cater to a swath of commercial, industrial, utility, and defense activities. Supply options tout brands by 3M, Brady, Federal Signal, Leviton, Panduit, Square D/ Schneider Electric, and Thomas & Betts. The family-owned company is led by the Blumberg's fourth generation.

	Annual Growth	01/08	01/09	01/10	01/11	01/12
Sales ($mil.)	20.7%	-	-	53.0	66.1	77.2
Net income ($ mil.)	-	-	-	(1.5)	(0.4)	1.0
Market value ($ mil.)	-	-	-	-	-	-
Employees	-	-	-	-	-	200

MADISON HUNTSVILLE COUNTY AIRPORT AUTHORITY

1000 GLENN HEARN BLVD SW STE 20008
HUNTSVILLE, AL 358242107
Phone: 256 772-9395
Fax: -
Web: www.flyhuntsville.com

CEO: -
CFO: -
HR: -
FYE: June 30
Type: Private

If you're flying into northern Alabama, you might very well be landing at a facility operated by the Huntsville-Madison County Airport Authority. The agency operates the Huntsville International Airport, which handles about 100 flights daily. In addition, the Huntsville-Madison County Airport Authority oversees the International Intermodal Center, a US Customs Port of Entry which is equipped to handle cargo arriving by airplane, train, or truck. The agency also maintains the 4,000-acre Jetplex Industrial Park, which offers air, rail, and truck transportation.

	Annual Growth	06/17	06/18	06/19	06/20	06/21
Sales ($mil.)	(14.3%)	-	33.1	37.0	31.4	20.8
Net income ($ mil.)	(0.6%)	-	17.6	14.5	25.6	17.3
Market value ($ mil.)	-	-	-	-	-	-
Employees	-	-	-	-	-	115

MADIX, INC.

500 AIRPORT RD
TERRELL, TX 751605200
Phone: 214 515-5400
Fax: -
Web: www.madixinc.com

CEO: -
CFO: -
HR: Brooke Boddie
FYE: December 31
Type: Private

Madix has become a fixture in the retailing world and beyond. Through its handful of factories in Texas, Alabama, and Massachusetts, Madix manufactures more than 65,000 products, including store fixtures, point-of-purchase displays, workstations, heavy-duty racking, and storage products. The company operates distribution centers throughout the US and the UK. Selling its products worldwide, its customers include airports, hospitals, retailers, Internet cafes, and government agencies. Madix was established in 1982 through the merger of Dixie Craft Manufacturing and Maytex Store Fixtures.

MADONNA REHABILITATION HOSPITAL

5401 SOUTH ST
LINCOLN, NE 685062150
Phone: 402 413-3000
Fax: -
Web: www.madonna.org

CEO: Paul Dongilli Jr
CFO: -
HR: Mark Pankoke
FYE: June 30
Type: Private

Madonna Rehabilitation Hospital finds a rapt audience in recovering patients living in and around Lincoln, Nebraska. The hospital has more than 250 beds and provides acute and long-term rehabilitation, as well as subacute care. The hospital treats patients with a variety of orthopedic, musculoskeletal, and neurological conditions such as brain and spinal cord injury, stroke, cancer, cerebral palsy, arthritis, and multiple sclerosis. Patients have access to a full team of physicians to help integrate and treat all symptoms. Madonna Rehabilitation Hospital was founded as a geriatric hospital by the Benedictine Sisters of Yankton, South Dakota, in 1958.

	Annual Growth	06/18	06/19	06/20	06/21	06/22
Sales ($mil.)	3.2%	-	166.6	174.0	182.8	183.3
Net income ($ mil.)	-	-	11.6	10.6	39.1	(4.8)
Market value ($ mil.)	-	-	-	-	-	-
Employees	-	-	-	-	-	1,400

MADRIGAL PHARMACEUTICALS INC

NMS: MDGL

Four Tower Bridge, 200 Barr Harbor Drive, Suite 200
West Conshohocken, PA 19428
Phone: 267 824-2827
Fax: -
Web: www.madrigalpharma.com

CEO: -
CFO: -
HR: -
FYE: December 31
Type: Public

Madrigal Pharmaceuticals is focused on developing novel small-molecule drugs for the treatment of cardiovascular-metabolic diseases and nonalcoholic steatohepatitis (nonalcoholic fatty liver disease, or NASH). Its lead candidate is MGL-3196, an oral drug for the treatment of NASH and hypercholesterolemia. Looking to enter new areas of development, Synta Pharmaceuticals merged with private firm Madrigal in 2016 and took the latter's name. Prior to the merger, Synta's preclinical research efforts included potential therapies for autoimmune diseases, transplant acceptance, respiratory conditions, and cancerous tumors. In late 2015 it terminated trials for its then-lead program, oncology candidate ganetespib.

	Annual Growth	12/19	12/20	12/21	12/22	12/23
Sales ($mil.)	-	-	-	-	-	-
Net income ($ mil.)	-	(83.9)	(202.2)	(241.8)	(295.4)	(373.6)
Market value ($ mil.)	26.2%	1,810.9	2,209.6	1,684.2	5,768.8	4,598.8
Employees	-	29	42	71	92	-

MAGEE REHABILITATION HOSPITAL FOUNDATION

1513 RACE ST
PHILADELPHIA, PA 191021125
Phone: 215 587-3000
Fax: –
Web: mageerehab.jeffersonhealth.org

CEO: Jack Carroll
CFO: Patricia Underwood
HR: Cindy Payne
FYE: June 30
Type: Private

Part of Pennsylvania's Jefferson Health System, The Magee Memorial Hospital for Convalescents (operating as Magee Rehabilitation) is a not-for-profit health organization that provides inpatient and outpatient rehabilitative care to patients disabled by stroke, arthritis, spinal cord and brain injuries, or other conditions. With 96 beds, it also offers rehabilitation for patients recovering from amputation, orthopedic surgery, and joint replacements. In addition, it provides wellness programs for muscular, neurological, and neurodegenerative disorders. Outpatient services include physical therapy, speech therapy, and emotional support.

	Annual Growth	06/18	06/19	06/20	06/21	06/22
Sales ($mil.)	(3.5%)	–	81.2	63.7	82.2	73.0
Net income ($ mil.)	–	–	11.9	(9.6)	9.4	(3.9)
Market value ($ mil.)	–	–	–	–	–	–
Employees	–	–	–	–	–	600

MAGNECO/METREL, INC.

740 WAUKEGAN RD STE 212
DEERFIELD, IL 600154400
Phone: 630 543-6660
Fax: –
Web: www.magneco-metrel.com

CEO: –
CFO: Susan Malloy
HR: –
FYE: December 31
Type: Private

Magneco/Metrel makes ceramics, but you won't find any artistic pieces at this company's plant! Magneco/Metrel uses the world's largest blast furnace to produce high-temperature refractory ceramics. The lineup serves as a lining in pipes and molds carrying molten iron and steel. The heat of molten steel would erode the pipes and molds without the ceramic barrier. Magneco/Metrel also makes a spray-on nano-particulate refractory line that can be used to create a liner for constructing or repairing steel-making molds and pipe. Its ceramics line is sold largely to steel foundries; other applications include ironmaking, glass, and copper. Magneco/Metrel was established in 1979 and is owned by CEO Charles Connors.

	Annual Growth	12/06	12/07	12/08	12/10	12/11
Sales ($mil.)	1.5%	–	–	63.4	62.0	66.4
Net income ($ mil.)	68.4%	–	–	0.7	2.3	3.4
Market value ($ mil.)	–	–	–	–	–	–
Employees	–	–	–	–	–	145

MAGNETEK, INC.

N49W13650 CAMPBELL DR
MENOMONEE FALLS, WI 530517051
Phone: 262 783-3500
Fax: –
Web: www.cmco.com

CEO: Peter M McCormick
CFO: Marty J Schwenner
HR: –
FYE: December 29
Type: Private

In the world of electrical equipment, Magnetek is a power player. Among the largest, the company makes digital power and motion-control systems. The systems comprise radio remote controls, programmable drives, and collision-avoidance devices used in overhead cranes and hoists. Its DC drives and integrated subsystems are used to control high rise, high speed elevators. Magnetek also offers power inverters, which direct AC power from generator to utility grid, for wind turbines and other renewable energy projects. In late 2015, Magnetek was acquired by material handling products maker Columbus McKinnon Corporation for roughly $189 million.

MAGNITE INC

NMS: MGNI

1250 Broadway, 15th Floor
New York, NY 10001
Phone: 212 243-2769
Fax: –
Web: www.magnite.com

CEO: Michael G Barrett
CFO: David L Day
HR: –
FYE: December 31
Type: Public

The Magnite, formerly known as The Rubicon Project, Inc., provides technology solutions to automate the purchase and sale of digital advertising inventory. The company provides a full suite of tools for sellers to control their advertising business and protect the consumer viewing experience. These controls are particularly important to CTV sellers who need to ensure a TV-like viewing and advertising experience for consumers. Its clients include many of the world's leading buyers and sellers of digital advertising inventory. About 80% of the company's total sales are generated from the US.

	Annual Growth	12/19	12/20	12/21	12/22	12/23
Sales ($mil.)	41.1%	156.4	221.6	468.4	577.1	619.7
Net income ($ mil.)	–	(25.5)	(53.4)	0.0	(130.3)	(159.2)
Market value ($ mil.)	3.4%	1,130.8	4,255.7	2,425.1	1,467.5	1,294.3
Employees	19.7%	444	569	876	947	911

MAGNUM CONSTRUCTION MANAGEMENT, LLC

6201 SW 70TH ST FL 2
SOUTH MIAMI, FL 331434718
Phone: 305 541-0000
Fax: –
Web: www.mcm-us.com

CEO: –
CFO: –
HR: –
FYE: December 31
Type: Private

Munilla Construction Management (formerly Magnum Construction Management) was founded in 1983 and is owned by the Munilla family whose background in construction dates back more than five decades. MCM provides a range of design-build and construction management services to public- and private-sector clients in South Florida. The company contracts for a variety of construction projects, including commercial, institutional, educational, residential, and health care facilities; airports; and such civil construction projects as roads and railway stations.

MAGYAR BANCORP INC

NMS: MGYR

400 Somerset Street
New Brunswick, NJ 08901
Phone: 732 342-7600
Fax: –
Web: www.magbank.com

CEO: John S Fitzgerald
CFO: Jon R Ansari
HR: –
FYE: September 30
Type: Public

Magyar doesn't mean "bank" in Hungarian, it means "Hungarian" in Hungarian. Magyar Bancorp is the holding company for Magyar Bank, which serves central New Jersey individuals and businesses through about a half-dozen offices. The bank offers standard deposit products including checking and savings accounts, NOW accounts, and CDs. It uses these funds to originate loans and invest in securities. Magyar Bank focuses on real estate lending, including construction loans, residential and commercial mortgages, and home equity loans, which altogether account for about 90% of its loan portfolio. Mutual holding company Magyar Bancorp, MHC, owns 56% of Magyar Bancorp.

	Annual Growth	09/19	09/20	09/21	09/22	09/23
Assets ($mil.)	9.5%	630.3	754.0	774.0	798.5	907.3
Net income ($ mil.)	26.7%	3.0	2.2	6.1	7.9	7.7
Market value ($ mil.)	–	–	–	76.4	83.0	68.4
Employees	(3.1%)	110	104	101	94	97

MAHWAH BERGEN RETAIL GROUP, INC.

933 MACARTHUR BLVD
MAHWAH, NJ 074302045
Phone: 551 777-6700
Fax: –
Web: www.ascena.com

CEO: –
CFO: –
HR: –
FYE: August 03
Type: Private

Mahwah Bergen Retail Group (formerly known as Ascena Retail Group) is primarily in the business of retail-apparel, shoes, and accessory stores. The national specialty retailer previously owns Ann Taylor, Lane Bryant, Loft, and Lou & Grey and has a network of associates who work in its stores, home offices, distribution centers, and international locations. In 2021, the retailer of women's clothing changed its name from Ascena Retail Group to Mahwah Bergen Retail Group. Also in 2021, a bankruptcy court has approved the company's Chapter 11 plans.

MAIMONIDES MEDICAL CENTER

4802 10TH AVE
BROOKLYN, NY 112192916
Phone: 718 581-0598
Fax: –
Web: www.maimo.org

CEO: Kenneth Gibbs
CFO: Robert Palermo
HR: Delia Kenningtonlynch
FYE: December 31
Type: Private

Maimonides Health is Brooklyn's largest healthcare system, serving over 350,000 patients each year through the system's three hospitals, approximately 2,000 physicians, and more than 80 community-based practices and outpatient centers. The system is anchored by Maimonides Medical Center, one of the nation's largest independent teaching hospitals and home to centers of excellence in numerous specialties; Maimonides Midwood Community Hospital (formerly New York Community Hospital), a 130-bed adult medical-surgical hospital; and Maimonides Children's Hospital, Brooklyn's only children's hospital and only pediatric trauma center. Maimonides' clinical programs rank among the best in the country for patient outcomes, including its Heart and Vascular Institute, Neurosciences Institute, Bone and Joint Center, and Cancer Center. Maimonides is an affiliate of Northwell Health and a major clinical training site for SUNY Downstate College of Medicine.

	Annual Growth	12/16	12/17	12/19	12/21	12/22
Sales ($mil.)	8.7%	–	958.4	1,304.9	952.3	1,451.2
Net income ($ mil.)	–	–	19.6	7.5	(144.8)	(65.3)
Market value ($ mil.)	–	–	–	–	–	–
Employees	–	–	–	–	–	7,195

MAIN LINE HEALTH SYSTEM

240 N RADNOR CHESTER RD
RADNOR, PA 190875170
Phone: 610 225-6200
Fax: –
Web: www.mainlinehealth.org

CEO: –
CFO: –
HR: –
FYE: June 30
Type: Private

Main Line Health is a not-for-profit network that includes four acute care hospitals, a drug and alcohol recovery treatment center, home care, outpatient centers, a physician network, and a biomedical research organization, all serving the greater Philadelphia area. Its hospitals -- Lankenau Medical Center, Bryn Mawr Hospital, Paoli Hospital, and Riddle Hospital -- are accredited as primary stroke care centers, comprehensive breast centers, and chest pain centers. Other specialties include diabetes and endocrinology, orthopedics, and cardiovascular care. Bryn Mawr Hospital offers residency programs in family practice, radiology, and surgical podiatry. Main Line Health was founded in 1985.

	Annual Growth	06/16	06/17	06/18	06/19	06/20
Sales ($mil.)	1.1%	–	–	1,742.0	1,769.2	1,781.7
Net income ($ mil.)	–	–	–	267.6	21.3	(17.8)
Market value ($ mil.)	–	–	–	–	–	–
Employees	–	–	–	–	–	17,485

MAIN LINE HOSPITALS, INC.

130 S BRYN MAWR AVE
BRYN MAWR, PA 190103121
Phone: 610 526-3000
Fax: –
Web: www.mainlinehealth.org

CEO: Jack Lynch
CFO: Michael J Buongiorno
HR: Debra Fedora
FYE: June 30
Type: Private

Bryn Mawr Hospital, a member of the Main Line not-for-profit health network, is an acute care facility providing a variety of inpatient and outpatient services in the western suburbs of Philadelphia. With some 320 beds, Bryn Mawr Hospital is recognized nationally for its orthopedic program. Founded in 1893 by Dr. George Gerhard, the teaching hospital also provides cancer, cardiac, surgical, pediatric, reproductive health, diagnostic imaging, psychiatric, bariatric, and wound care services. The hospital also operates the Main Line Health Center outpatient facility (which includes a comprehensive breast center) in Newtown Square.

	Annual Growth	06/18	06/19	06/20	06/21	06/22
Sales ($mil.)	5.7%	–	–	–	1,485.3	1,569.7
Net income ($ mil.)	–	–	–	–	194.7	(160.1)
Market value ($ mil.)	–	–	–	–	–	–
Employees	–	–	–	–	–	5,840

MAINE & MARITIMES CORPORATION

209 STATE ST
PRESQUE ISLE, ME 047692663
Phone: 207 760-2499
Fax: –
Web: –

CEO: Brent M Boyles
CFO: Michael I Williams
HR: –
FYE: December 31
Type: Private

Maine & Maritimes (MAM, formerly Maine Public Service) is the consumer's main hope for smooth sailing in the waters of regional electricity supply. A holding company formed by electric utility Maine Public Service (MPS), which is now Maine & Maritimes' primary subsidiary, it transmits and distributes electricity to customers in a service area that encompasses 73,000 people in northern Maine. MAM originally operated a range of energy-related businesses but has since refocused on its utility operations (MAM Utility Services). In 2010 the company was acquired by Canadian energy and services firm Emera.

MAINE COAST REGIONAL HEALTH FACILITIES INC

50 UNION ST STE 2
ELLSWORTH, ME 046051534
Phone: 207 664-5311
Fax: –
Web: –

CEO: Charlie Therrien
CFO: Kevin Sedgwick
HR: Noah Lundy
FYE: September 30
Type: Private

Maine Coast Memorial Hospital provides medical services to the residents of Ellsworth, right on the Maine coastline. The community hospital has about 60 acute care beds. Its specialty service offerings include emergency medicine, cancer treatment, rehabilitation, orthopedics, surgery, and mental health care. Maine Coast Memorial Hospital also operates a maternity and family birthing center, senior services, and a center for adolescent health, as well as diagnostic and medical laboratory facilities. The hospital is part of Maine Coast Health Care.

	Annual Growth	09/18	09/19	09/20	09/21	09/22
Sales ($mil.)	8.4%	–	85.0	67.8	92.2	108.3
Net income ($ mil.)	31.8%	–	2.1	(5.5)	(0.8)	4.8
Market value ($ mil.)	–	–	–	–	–	–
Employees	–	–	–	–	–	658

MAINEGENERAL HEALTH

35 MEDICAL CENTER PKWY STE 202
AUGUSTA, ME 043308160
Phone: 207 626-1000
Fax: –
Web: www.mainegeneral.org

CEO: Charles Hays
CFO: Michael Koziol
HR: Ashley Semones
FYE: June 30
Type: Private

If you're aching or ailing within shouting distance of the Kennebec River in Maine, then MaineGeneral Health is the place to head. The comprehensive health care organization features acute care hospitals, outpatient clinics and physicians' practices, long-term care centers, and home health and hospice agencies. Its flagship facilities are the three main campuses (in state capital Augusta and Waterville farther north) of MaineGeneral Medical Center, together featuring about 290 inpatient beds. MaineGeneral Health also runs nursing homes with some 270 beds in all, as well as senior living apartments, lab and imaging centers, and inpatient rehabilitation and mental health facilities.Operations

	Annual Growth	06/16	06/17	06/20	06/21	06/22
Sales ($mil.)	132.0%	–	10.4	575.1	632.2	702.1
Net income ($ mil.)	61.1%	–	1.5	31.9	1.6	16.7
Market value ($ mil.)	–	–	–	–	–	–
Employees	–	–	–	–	–	3,800

MAINEHEALTH

22 BRAMHALL ST
PORTLAND, ME 041023134
Phone: 207 662-0111
Fax: –
Web: www.mainehealth.org

CEO: Andrew T Mueller
CFO: –
HR: –
FYE: September 30
Type: Private

Maine Medical Center (MMC) is the flagship hospital of MaineHealth, which is an integrated health network comprising a dozen local hospital and other health facilities that touch central, southern, and western Maine and eastern New Hampshire. MMC is a not-for-profit medical center consists of a tertiary care community hospital, The Barbara Bush Children's Hospital, and outpatient clinics. Specialty services include cancer care, geriatrics, emergency medicine, cardiovascular care, rehabilitation, neurology, orthopedics, and women's health. Through its partnership with the Tufts University School of Medicine, the 640-bed teaching hospital provides a variety of medical education and training programs. MMC also conducts research through the Maine Medical Center Research Institute. The medical center was founded in 1874.

	Annual Growth	09/18	09/19	09/20	09/21	09/22
Sales ($mil.)	8.2%	–	2,717.3	2,884.9	3,451.7	3,440.3
Net income ($ mil.)	169.0%	–	5.6	283.1	492.8	109.5
Market value ($ mil.)	–	–	–	–	–	–
Employees	–	–	–	–	–	2,000

MAINEHEALTH SERVICES

110 FREE ST
PORTLAND, ME 041013576
Phone: 207 661-7010
Fax: –
Web: www.mainehealth.org

CEO: –
CFO: –
HR: Amy Malloy
FYE: September 30
Type: Private

MaineHealth provides health care to residents of central, southern, and western Maine. The health system's facilities include Maine Medical Center, Spring Harbor Hospital, and Stephens Memorial Hospital (part of Western Maine Health). MaineHealth also operates long-term care facilities, a home health care service, physician practices, medical laboratories, and other health care service units. The company's Synernet subsidiary provides administrative and group purchasing services for MaineHealth's members and other health care organizations.

	Annual Growth	09/07	09/08	09/19	09/20	09/22
Sales ($mil.)	43.5%	–	23.5	2,717.3	36.4	3,705.9
Net income ($ mil.)	–	–	(0.1)	5.6	(4.8)	(200.2)
Market value ($ mil.)	–	–	–	–	–	–
Employees	–	–	–	–	–	7,000

MAJOR LEAGUE BASEBALL PLAYERS ASSOCIATION

12 E 49TH ST FL 24
NEW YORK, NY 100178207
Phone: 212 826-0808
Fax: –
Web: www.mlbplayers.com

CEO: –
CFO: –
HR: –
FYE: December 31
Type: Private

The Major League Baseball Players Association (MLBPA) is for big leaguers only. The organization is the collective bargaining representative for Major League Baseball's 1,200 players. The union negotiates salaries, arbitrates grievances, ensures the on-field safety of its players, controls the license for MLB and distributes licensing revenues. The MLBPA also certifies player agents. All players, coaches, managers, and trainers who have signed with the league are eligible to pay dues of $50 per day during the 183-day season for membership in the association. MLBPA was organized in 1966 and negotiated the first collective bargaining agreement with team owners in 1968.

	Annual Growth	12/14	12/15	12/16	12/17	12/18
Sales ($mil.)	(5.3%)	–	52.7	56.8	36.6	44.7
Net income ($ mil.)	(14.4%)	–	31.0	31.6	12.6	19.4
Market value ($ mil.)	–	–	–	–	–	–
Employees	–	–	–	–	–	36

MAKE-A-WISH FOUNDATION OF AMERICA

1702 E HIGHLAND AVE STE 400
PHOENIX, AZ 850164664
Phone: 602 279-9474
Fax: –
Web: www.wish.org

CEO: Richard Davis
CFO: Trevor Vigfusson
HR: Doug Klein
FYE: August 31
Type: Private

The Make-A-Wish Foundation of America's mission is to grant the wishes of children with life-threatening medical conditions. The charitable organization grants wishes to ailing kids between the ages of two-and-a-half and 18 from more than 60 chapters in the US and its territories. Funded through donations, in-kind contributions, grants, chapter fees, and corporate donations, the not-for-profit foundation boasts a volunteer network of some 25,000 people and has granted more than 226,000 wishes to children since its creation in 1980. The foundation was originally named the Chris Greicius Make-A-Wish Memorial, after the first boy to receive his wish: becoming an honorary Arizona state trooper.

	Annual Growth	08/15	08/16	08/19	08/21	08/22
Sales ($mil.)	5.2%	–	94.7	104.7	113.7	128.6
Net income ($ mil.)	21.7%	–	4.4	4.3	0.4	14.3
Market value ($ mil.)	–	–	–	–	–	–
Employees	–	–	–	–	–	200

MALDONADO NURSERY & LANDSCAPING INC.

16348 NACOGDOCHES RD
SAN ANTONIO, TX 782471005
Phone: 210 599-1219
Fax: –
Web: www.mnlsa.com

CEO: –
CFO: Neomal Ratnayeke
HR: Rachelle Garzacadena
FYE: December 31
Type: Private

The Maldonado family wants to keep San Antonio green and beautiful. Maldonado Nursery & Landscaping operates a retail garden center and provides services such as commercial and residential landscape design, installation, and maintenance. The firm also offers professional irrigation installation and maintenance, designed to ensure efficient watering for customers in municipalities with strict water restrictions. Maldonado Nursery & Landscaping is owned and operated by brothers Jerry, Oscar, and Roy, and their father, Rogelio Maldonado, who founded the company in 1987.

	Annual Growth	12/00	12/01	12/02	12/08	12/19
Sales ($mil.)	(7.2%)	–	154.2	9.1	24.4	39.9
Net income ($ mil.)	74.8%	–	0.0	(0.1)	0.6	2.7
Market value ($ mil.)	–	–	–	–	–	–
Employees	–	–	–	–	–	337

MAMMOTH ENERGY SERVICES INC
NMS: TUSK

14201 Caliber Drive, Suite 300
Oklahoma City, OK 73134
Phone: 405 608-6007
Fax: -
Web: www.mammothenergy.com

CEO: Arty Straehla
CFO: Mark Layton
HR: -
FYE: December 31
Type: Public

Mammoth Energy Services (Mammoth) is an integrated, growth-oriented energy services company focused on the construction and repair of the electric grid for private utilities, public investor-owned utilities and co-operative utilities through its infrastructure services businesses. The company also provides products and services to enable the exploration and development of North American onshore unconventional oil and natural gas reserves. Its complementary suite of services provides the company with the opportunity to cross-sell its services and expand its customer base and geographic positioning.

	Annual Growth	12/19	12/20	12/21	12/22	12/23
Sales ($mil.)	(16.1%)	625.0	313.1	229.0	362.1	309.5
Net income ($ mil.)	-	(79.0)	(107.6)	(101.4)	(0.6)	(3.2)
Market value ($ mil.)	19.3%	105.5	213.3	87.3	414.7	213.8
Employees	(17.8%)	1,607	820	783	1,037	733

MANAGEMENT & TRAINING CORPORATION

500 N MARKET PLACE DR STE 100
CENTERVILLE, UT 840144900
Phone: 801 693-2600
Fax: -
Web: www.mtctrains.com

CEO: Scott Marquardt
CFO: Mary Calvin
HR: Becky Packer
FYE: December 31
Type: Private

Management & Training Corporation (MTC) is the nation's leading operator of federal Job Corps centers and one of the nation's leading contractors providing rehabilitation, education, and vocational programs at correctional facilities and immigrant processing centers. As part of its services, MTC operates more than 20 Job Corps centers, about 25 correctional facilities, more than 10 prison and detention medical departments, four community release centers, six detention centers, two workforce development sites, and two outpatient behavioral health programs worldwide.

	Annual Growth	12/18	12/19	12/20	12/21	12/22
Sales ($mil.)	(2.9%)	-	-	907.3	857.1	854.8
Net income ($ mil.)	(23.4%)	-	-	54.4	59.6	32.0
Market value ($ mil.)	-	-	-	-	-	-
Employees	-	-	-	-	-	9,500

MANATEE MEMORIAL HOSPITAL, L.P.

206 2ND ST E
BRADENTON, FL 342081000
Phone: 941 746-5111
Fax: -
Web: www.manateememorial.com

CEO: Tom McDougal
CFO: Mark Tierney
HR: -
FYE: December 31
Type: Private

Docile aquatic mammals will have to seek medical care elsewhere. Manatee Memorial Hospital provides general medical, surgical, and community health services to land-dwelling humans in southwestern Florida. The 320-bed hospital has about 400 affiliated physicians and offers acute primary and specialty care services including emergency, cancer, cardiovascular, neurology, rehabilitation, and women's health care services. It also operates FirstCare urgent care clinics and provides community health screenings with partner Life Line Screenings. A subsidiary of Universal Health Services, Manatee Memorial is part of the Manatee Healthcare System, which also includes the 120-bed Lakewood Ranch Medical Center.

	Annual Growth	12/13	12/14	12/15	12/16	12/17
Sales ($mil.)	7.0%	-	244.3	249.8	268.5	299.1
Net income ($ mil.)	42.4%	-	11.5	2.4	7.1	33.3
Market value ($ mil.)	-	-	-	-	-	-
Employees	-	-	-	-	-	1,450

MANHATTAN ASSOCIATES, INC.
NMS: MANH

2300 Windy Ridge Parkway, Tenth Floor
Atlanta, GA 30339
Phone: 770 955-7070
Fax: 770 995-0302
Web: www.manh.com

CEO: Eddie Capel
CFO: Dennis B Story
HR: -
FYE: December 31
Type: Public

Manhattan Associates develops, sells, deploys, services, and maintains software solutions and designed to manage supply chains, inventory, and omnichannel operations, for retailers, wholesalers, manufacturers, logistics providers, and other organization. The Atlanta-based company provides customers in retail, consumer goods, food and grocery, logistics service providers, industrial and wholesale, high technology and electronics, life sciences, and government. Manhattan also offers three distinct areas to assist customers such as supply chain, omnichannel, and inventory. It sells third-party hardware such as bar code printers and scanners, and other peripherals. The company generates the majority of its revenue in the Americas.

	Annual Growth	12/19	12/20	12/21	12/22	12/23
Sales ($mil.)	10.7%	617.9	586.4	663.6	767.1	928.7
Net income ($ mil.)	19.8%	85.8	87.2	110.5	129.0	176.6
Market value ($ mil.)	28.2%	4,909.9	6,475.5	9,572.9	7,474.1	13,256
Employees	7.7%	3,400	3,400	3,600	4,150	4,580

MANHATTAN BRIDGE CAPITAL, INC.
NAS: LOAN

60 Cutter Mill Road
Great Neck, NY 11021
Phone: 516 444-3400
Fax: 212 779-2974
Web: www.manhattanbridgecapital.com

CEO: Assaf Ran
CFO: Vanessa KAO
HR: -
FYE: December 31
Type: Public

Manhattan Bridge Capital (formerly DAG Media) knew that when it came to a bridge it had to cross it. In 2008 it renamed itself when its DAG Funding Solutions commercial lending subsidiary, which the company started in 2007, became its most profitable unit. The company offers short-term, secured, commercial loans to small businesses. It also offers an online service, Nextyellow.com, that lets consumers search for a product or service. The consumer's request is matched with appropriate businesses, and the matched businesses then call or email the customer. Vendor partners pay the company monthly fees to be featured in the matching process.

	Annual Growth	12/19	12/20	12/21	12/22	12/23
Sales ($mil.)	7.5%	7.3	7.0	6.8	8.6	9.8
Net income ($ mil.)	5.1%	4.5	4.2	4.4	5.2	5.5
Market value ($ mil.)	(6.0%)	72.8	59.6	62.9	61.0	56.9
Employees	-	5	5	6	5	5

MANHATTAN COLLEGE CORP

4513 MANHATTAN COLLEGE PKWY
BRONX, NY 104714004
Phone: 718 862-8000
Fax: -
Web: www.manhattan.edu

CEO: -
CFO: Matthew S McManness
HR: -
FYE: June 30
Type: Private

A trip to Manhattan College doesn't take you to that well-known borough, but instead to the Riverdale section of the Bronx. With its campus overlooking Van Cortlandt Park, Manhattan College is a private Catholic university with about 3,200 undergraduate and graduate students studying a wide range of topics, from engineering to the arts to biotechnology. The school grants about 40 undergraduate degrees and graduate degrees in education and engineering. Founded in 1853 by the Brothers of the Christian Schools, the college was originally located on Canal Street in Manhattan, then later moved to a rural location at 131st Street and Broadway, before settling into its present campus in 1922.

MANHATTAN SCHOOL OF MUSIC INC

120 CLAREMONT AVE
NEW YORK, NY 100274698
Phone: 212 749-2802
Fax: –
Web: www.msmnyc.edu

CEO: Peter Robbins
CFO: –
HR: –
FYE: June 30
Type: Private

Music is on the minds of students at the Manhattan School of Music in New York. The school is dedicated to the study of jazz and classical music. Majors range from orchestral instruments and voice to piano, composition, and jazz. It has more than 800 students and nearly 275 faculty. The school provides undergraduate, graduate, and doctoral programs. Manhattan School of Music also offers distance learning and a Global Conservatory, which provides video conferencing to institutions throughout the world. Famous alumni include Harry Connick, Jr., Herbie Hancock, and Yusef Lateef. Pianist and philanthropist Janet D. Schenck founded the Manhattan School of Music as as the Neighborhood Music School in 1917.

	Annual Growth	06/16	06/17	06/20	06/21	06/22
Sales ($mil.)	3.5%	–	61.2	62.4	63.9	72.5
Net income ($ mil.)	5.9%	–	4.6	0.8	5.4	6.1
Market value ($ mil.)	–	–	–	–	–	–
Employees		–	–	–	–	450

MANHATTANVILLE COLLEGE

2900 PURCHASE ST
PURCHASE, NY 105772132
Phone: 914 694-2200
Fax: –
Web: www.mville.edu

CEO: –
CFO: –
HR: Asma Alirahi
FYE: June 30
Type: Private

Manhattanville College is a private liberal arts institution offering undergraduate and masters degree programs in more than 50 fields. Manhattanville is home to about 1,700 undergraduate students and 1,000 graduate students. In addition to college degree programs, the school also offers in-house and on-site corporate training programs in such areas as business writing, project management, and diversity. Manhattanville was founded in 1841 in New York City by the Religious of the Sacred Heart. It relocated in 1847 to an area just north of New York City on a hill overlooking the village of Manhattanville. The school has been coeducational and non-denominational since 1971.

	Annual Growth	06/13	06/14	06/20	06/21	06/22
Sales ($mil.)	(0.2%)	–	97.6	95.2	90.7	96.0
Net income ($ mil.)	(21.6%)	–	3.0	(3.6)	(0.3)	0.4
Market value ($ mil.)	–	–	–	–	–	–
Employees		–	–	–	–	420

MANITEX INTERNATIONAL INC   NAS: MNTX

9725 Industrial Drive
Bridgeview, IL 60455
Phone: 708 430-7500
Fax: –
Web: www.manitexinternational.com

CEO: Michael Coffey
CFO: Joe Doolan
HR: –
FYE: December 31
Type: Public

Manitex International makes products that are uplifting -- literally. One of the largest manufacturers of lifting equipment in North America, Manitex makes and sells boom trucks and sign cranes used in industrial jobs, as well as energy exploration, construction, and commercial building. Through Liftking, the company makes rough terrain forklifts, heavy handling transports, and military specialty vehicles. The Manitex family also includes Badger Equipment (cranes and material handling). A Crane & Machinery unit distributes Manitex, Terex, and Fuchs equipment.

	Annual Growth	12/19	12/20	12/21	12/22	12/23
Sales ($mil.)	6.7%	224.8	167.5	211.5	273.9	291.4
Net income ($ mil.)		(8.5)	(13.6)	(4.6)	(4.9)	7.4
Market value ($ mil.)	10.1%	120.5	104.5	128.8	81.0	177.1
Employees	4.2%	598	480	526	608	705

MANITOU AMERICA HOLDING, INC.

1 GEHL WAY
WEST BEND, WI 530953463
Phone: 262 334-9461
Fax: –
Web: www.gehl.com

CEO: William D Gehl
CFO: Malcolm F Moore
HR: Sylvain Andre
FYE: December 31
Type: Private

Manitou Americas (formerly known as Gehl Company) is primarily engaged in manufacturing heavy machinery and equipment of a type used primarily by the construction industries, such as skid loaders, track loaders, articulated loaders, and telescopic handlers. It is a producer of GEHL, Manitou, and Mustang-branded equipment for construction, agriculture, industry, and beyond. It is also a leader in the designs, manufactures, and distributions of compact equipment worldwide. Manitou Americas is a wholly-owned subsidiary of Manitou BF S.A. It was founded in 1859 by Louis Lucas when he built a foundry to supply the local area with farm implements and machines.

MANITOWOC COMPANY INC (THE)   NYS: MTW

11270 West Park Place, Suite 1000
Milwaukee, WI 53224
Phone: 414 760-4600
Fax: –
Web: www.manitowoc.com

CEO: Aaron H Ravenscroft
CFO: David J Antoniuk
HR: Ashley Barkdoll
FYE: December 31
Type: Public

The Manitowoc Company is one of the world's leading providers of engineered lifting solutions. The company design and manufactures lifting equipment such as tower cranes, mobile hydraulic cranes, lattice-boom crawler cranes, and boom trucks. Its products are used in a variety of applications, including energy production and distribution; petrochemical and industrial; infrastructure, such as road, bridge, and airport construction; and commercial and residential construction. Brands include Aspen Equipment, Grove, MGX Equipment Services, National Crane, Potain, Shuttlelift, and Manitowoc. Most of its revenue originates outside the US. Manitowoc traces its historical roots back to 1902.

	Annual Growth	12/19	12/20	12/21	12/22	12/23
Sales ($mil.)	5.0%	1,834.1	1,443.4	1,720.2	2,032.5	2,227.8
Net income ($ mil.)	(4.2%)	46.6	(19.1)	11.0	(123.6)	39.2
Market value ($ mil.)	(1.2%)	614.2	467.1	652.4	321.5	585.7
Employees	(0.5%)	4,900	4,200	4,600	4,800	4,800

MANN+HUMMEL FILTRATION TECHNOLOGY INTERMEDIATE HOLDINGS INC.

1 WIX WAY
GASTONIA, NC 280546142
Phone: 704 869-3300
Fax: –
Web: www.wixfilters.com

CEO: Keith A Wilson
CFO: Steven P Klueg
HR: Tim Zorn
FYE: December 31
Type: Private

Affinia Group Intermediate Holdings caters to car drivers with a natural affinity for parts. The company is a leading designer, manufacturer, and distributor of aftermarket vehicular components. Affinia's slew of products -- primarily oil and air filters, ball joints, idler arms, steering components, and suspension parts -- are made for passenger cars; SUVs; light, medium, and heavy trucks; and off-highway vehicles. Its well-known brand names, including McQuay-Norris, Nakata, ecoLAST, Raybestos, and WIX, are sold in 70 countries. It primarily serves the US and South American markets.

	Annual Growth	12/10	12/11	12/12	12/13	12/14
Sales ($mil.)	(2.0%)	–	–	1,453.0	1,361.0	1,396.0
Net income ($ mil.)		–	–	(102.0)	10.0	82.0
Market value ($ mil.)		–	–	–	–	–
Employees		–	–	–	–	5,574

MANNATECH INC
NMS: MTEX

1410 Lakeside Parkway, Suite 200
Flower Mound, TX 75028
Phone: 972 471-7400
Fax: –
Web: www.mannatech.com

CEO: Alfredo Bala
CFO: David A Johnson
HR: –
FYE: December 31
Type: Public

Mannatech is a global wellness solution provider that develops and sells innovative, high-quality, proprietary nutritional supplements, topical and skin care and anti-aging products, and weight-management products that target optimal health and wellness. Harper's Biochemistry, a leading and nationally recognized biochemistry reference, has recognized that these molecules are found in human glycoproteins, and are believed to be essential in helping to promote and provide effective cell-to-cell communication in the human body. Its products are distributed through a network of approximately 145,000 active associates. The company also operates a non-direct selling business in mainland China. Majority of its revenue is generated from outside its Americas operation.

	Annual Growth	12/19	12/20	12/21	12/22	12/23
Sales ($mil.)	(4.4%)	157.7	151.4	159.8	137.2	132.0
Net income ($ mil.)	–	3.3	6.3	9.8	(4.5)	(2.2)
Market value ($ mil.)	(15.8%)	29.9	34.6	71.3	33.3	15.1
Employees	(0.2%)	215	226	247	228	213

MANNING & NAPIER, INC.

290 WOODCLIFF DR
FAIRPORT, NY 144504298
Phone: 585 325-6880
Fax: –
Web: www.manning-napier.com

CEO: –
CFO: –
HR: –
FYE: December 31
Type: Private

Manning & Napier is an independent investment management firm that provides its clients with a broad range of financial solutions and investment strategies for both wealth and asset management. The firm serves high-net-worth individuals and large institutions, including corporations, endowments, 401(k) plans, pension plans, Taft-Hartley plans, and foundations. Its Wealth Management private clients are primarily composed of individual investors and families, small businesses and business owners, and small- to mid-sized non-profit organizations, endowments, and foundations. Manning & Napier offers its products through a direct sales force and through financial intermediaries and investment consultants. Formed in 1970, the company went public in 2011. It was acquired by Callodine Group in late 2022, for $12.85 per share in cash.

MANNKIND CORP
NMS: MNKD

1 Casper Street
Danbury, CT 06810
Phone: 818 661-5000
Fax: –
Web: www.mannkindcorp.com

CEO: Michael E Castagna
CFO: Steven B Binder
HR: –
FYE: December 31
Type: Public

MannKind is a biopharmaceutical company focusing on developing and commercializing therapeutic products to treat patients with endocrine and orphan lung diseases. Its signature technologies?Technosphere dry-powder formulations and Dreamboat inhalation devices?offer rapid and convenient delivery of medicines to the deep lung where they can exert an effect locally or enter the systemic circulation. In its endocrine business unit, the company currently commercialize two products: Afrezza (insulin human) Inhalation Powder, an ultra-rapid-acting inhaled insulin indicated to improve glycemic control in adults with diabetes, and the V-Go wearable insulin delivery device, which provides continuous subcutaneous infusion of insulin in adults that require insulin. Mannkind is the solely responsible for the commercialization of Afrezza and V-Go in the US. It also include a novel inhalation profiling apparatus, known as BluHale, which uses miniature sensors to assess the drug delivery process at the level of an individual inhaler.

	Annual Growth	12/19	12/20	12/21	12/22	12/23
Sales ($mil.)	33.3%	63.0	65.1	75.4	99.8	199.0
Net income ($ mil.)	–	(51.9)	(57.2)	(80.9)	(87.4)	(11.9)
Market value ($ mil.)	29.6%	348.3	845.2	1,180.1	1,423.1	982.9
Employees	15.7%	233	241	349	395	417

MANOR CARE, INC.

333 N SUMMIT ST
TOLEDO, OH 436041531
Phone: 419 252-5500
Fax: –
Web: www.promedicaseniorcare.org

CEO: Paul A Ormond
CFO: Steven M Cavanaugh
HR: –
FYE: December 31
Type: Private

HCR ManorCare is a lord of the manor in the nursing home kingdom. The company operates about 500 nursing homes, assisted living centers, and rehabilitation facilities in more than 30 states. Its facilities, which operate under the names Heartland, ManorCare Health Services, and Arden Courts, provide not only long-term nursing care, but also rehabilitation services and short-term, post-acute care for patients recovering from serious illness or injury. Many of its facilities house special units for Alzheimer's patients. In addition to its nursing and assisted-living facilities, HCR ManorCare offers hospice and home health care through offices across the US. It is owned by private equity firm The Carlyle Group.

MANPOWERGROUP INC
NYS: MAN

100 Manpower Place
Milwaukee, WI 53212
Phone: 414 961-1000
Fax: 414 332-0796
Web: www.manpower.com

CEO: Jonas Prising
CFO: John T McGinnis
HR: Diane May
FYE: December 31
Type: Public

ManpowerGroup's portfolio of services includes recruitment for permanent, temporary, and contract professionals, as well as administrative and industrial positions. In addition to recruitment and assessment, the company also offers training and development, career management, outsourcing, and workforce consulting services. Its Experis brand specializes in IT, engineering, and finance jobs, while its Right Management brand offers career development and coaching. ManpowerGroup operates a global network of over 2,200 owned or franchised offices in about 75 countries and territories. ManpowerGroup was founded 1948 by attorneys Elmer Winter and Aaron Scheinfeld.

	Annual Growth	12/19	12/20	12/21	12/22	12/23
Sales ($mil.)	(2.4%)	20,864	18,001	20,724	19,828	18,915
Net income ($ mil.)	(33.9%)	465.7	23.8	382.4	373.8	88.8
Market value ($ mil.)	(4.9%)	4,702.0	4,366.9	4,713.1	4,029.4	3,848.3
Employees	(0.1%)	28,000	25,000	30,000	30,900	27,900

MANTECH INTERNATIONAL CORPORATION

2251 CORPORATE PARK DR STE 600
HERNDON, VA 201716005
Phone: 703 218-6000
Fax: –
Web: www.mantech.com

CEO: Matthew A Tait
CFO: Judith L Bjornaas
HR: –
FYE: December 31
Type: Private

ManTech International provides security-focused IT services to agencies, primarily US government intelligence entities, such as the National Geospatial-Intelligence Agency, the Department of Homeland Security, the Missile Defense Agency, the Federal Bureau of Investigation, US Army Intelligence & Security Command, the US Air Force. Its solution sets, which include full-spectrum cyber; secure mission and enterprise IT; advanced data analytics; software and systems development; intelligent systems engineering; intelligence mission support; and mission operations, are aligned with the long-term needs of the company's customers. In late 2022, ManTech was acquired by Carlyle, a global investment firm, in an all-cash transaction representing a total enterprise value of approximately $4.2 billion.

MANUFACTURED HOUSING ENTERPRISES, INC.

9302 US HIGHWAY 6　　　　　　　　　　　　CEO: Mary J Fitzcharles
BRYAN, OH 435069516　　　　　　　　　　　　　　　　　　CFO: -
Phone: 419 636-4511　　　　　　　　　　　　　　　　　　　HR: -
Fax: -　　　　　　　　　　　　　　　　　　　FYE: December 31
Web: www.mheinc.com　　　　　　　　　　　　　　　Type: Private

Manufactured Housing Enterprises builds modular, sectional, and singlewide homes as well as commercial and retail developments for clients in the Midwest. The company is the largest manufactured home builder in Ohio and among the 20 largest in the country. It offers more than 80 floor plans for singlewide homes as well as two-story homes of more than 3,000 sq. ft. The company has delivered homes to Illinois, Indiana, Indiana, Kentucky, Michigan, Missouri, Tennessee, West Virginia, and Wisconsin. Manufactured Housing Enterprises was established in 1965, when being "mod" was fab.

	Annual Growth	12/14	12/15	12/16	12/17	12/18
Sales ($mil.)	31.0%	–	15.0	18.9	28.1	33.8
Net income ($ mil.)	25.8%	–	1.5	1.7	2.6	2.9
Market value ($ mil.)	–	–	–	–	–	–
Employees	–	–	–	–	–	26

MAQ, LLC

2027 152ND AVE NE　　　　　　　　　　　　　　　　　　CEO: -
REDMOND, WA 980525521　　　　　　　　　　　　　　　　CFO: -
Phone: 425 526-5399　　　　　　　　　　　　　　　　　　HR: -
Fax: -　　　　　　　　　　　　　　　　　　　FYE: December 31
Web: www.maqsoftware.com　　　　　　　　　　　　Type: Private

MAQ makes software, but you won't find it in a box. Specializing in design and development, MAQ builds Web, Windows, and Smartphone applications for corporate clients. Experts in Web 2.0 applications, the company's development and testing services include application development, migration, and maintenance; as well as applications for mobile phones and PDAs; data warehousing and business intelligence; and enterprise resource planning and customer relationship management. MAQ works primarily with Microsoft related technology including .NET, Visual Studio, and Microsoft SQL Server 2005. The company offers onsite services or a blended model, mixing onsite and offshore development (through operations in India).

MAR-JAC POULTRY, INC.

1020 AVIATION BLVD　　　　　　　　　　　　　　CEO: Joel Williams
GAINESVILLE, GA 305016839　　　　　　　　　　CFO: Mulham Shbeib
Phone: 770 531-5000　　　　　　　　　　　　　　HR: Malorie Bishop
Fax: -　　　　　　　　　　　　　　　　　　　　　　FYE: April 27
Web: www.marjacpoultry.com　　　　　　　　　　　　Type: Private

From farm to table, Mar-Jac Poultry's business is "poultry in motion." The company is one of the major processors of chicken sold to the domestic fast-food restaurant and foodservice market. Its operations include a hatchery to raise birds and a feed mill that churns 8,500 tons of feed a week for some 200 farmers in Georgia who contract with the company to grow its chicks and broilers. Mar-Jac's plant processes about two million chickens a week, which are vacuum-packed in its cold storage facility prior to shipment to mostly local distributors in the US, and some international export customers. Mar-Jac was started by brothers Marvin and Jackson McKibbon in 1954, and later acquired by a group of poultry farmers.

	Annual Growth	04/08	04/09	04/10	04/11	04/12
Sales ($mil.)	3.9%	–	–	262.9	257.1	284.0
Net income ($ mil.)	(47.9%)	–	–	29.9	11.2	8.1
Market value ($ mil.)	–	–	–	–	–	–
Employees	–	–	–	–	–	1,200

MARATHON OIL CORP.　　　　　　　　　　　NYS: MRO

990 Town and Country Boulevard　　　　　　　CEO: Lee M Tillman
Houston, TX 77024-2217　　　　　　　　　　CFO: Dane E Whitehead
Phone: 713 629-6600　　　　　　　　　　　　　　　　　　HR: -
Fax: -　　　　　　　　　　　　　　　　　　　FYE: December 31
Web: www.marathonoil.com　　　　　　　　　　　　Type: Public

Marathon Oil is an independent exploration, development and production company primarily operates in the oil and gas industry. It has proved reserves of about 1.3 million barrels of oil equivalent. Marathon Oil's major focus of production is the US: Eagle Ford in Texas, the Bakken in North Dakota, STACK and SCOOP in Oklahoma and Northern Delaware in New Mexico. The company explores for, produces and markets crude oil and condensate, NGLs and natural gas in the US and outside of the US. In addition to its operations in the Equatorial Guinea, the company generates about 95% of sales from the US.

	Annual Growth	12/19	12/20	12/21	12/22	12/23
Sales ($mil.)	6.6%	5,190.0	3,086.0	5,467.0	8,036.0	6,697.0
Net income ($ mil.)	34.1%	480.0	(1,451.0)	946.0	3,612.0	1,554.0
Market value ($ mil.)	15.5%	7,835.7	3,848.6	9,474.3	15,619	13,940
Employees	(4.3%)	2,000	1,672	1,531	1,570	1,681

MARATHON PETROLEUM CORP.　　　　　　NYS: MPC

539 South Main Street　　　　　　　　　　　　　　　　CEO: -
Findlay, OH 45840-3229　　　　　　　　　　　　　　　　CFO: -
Phone: 419 422-2121　　　　　　　　　　　　　　　　　HR: -
Fax: -　　　　　　　　　　　　　　　　　　　FYE: December 31
Web: www.marathonpetroleum.com　　　　　　　Type: Public

Marathon Petroleum Corporation is a leading, integrated, downstream energy company. It operates the nation's largest refining system with approximately 2.9 million barrels per day of crude oil refining capacity and believes it is one of the largest wholesale suppliers of gasoline and distillates to resellers in the US. The company distributes its refined products through one of the largest terminal operations in the US and one of the largest private domestic fleets of inland petroleum product barges. In addition, its integrated midstream energy asset network links producers of natural gas and NGLs from some of the largest supply basins in the US to domestic and international markets.

	Annual Growth	12/19	12/20	12/21	12/22	12/23
Sales ($mil.)	4.8%	124,813	69,032	120,930	179,952	150,307
Net income ($ mil.)	38.4%	2,637.0	(9,826.0)	9,738.0	14,516	9,681.0
Market value ($ mil.)	25.3%	22,172	15,220	23,548	42,832	54,596
Employees	(26.1%)	60,910	57,900	17,700	17,800	18,200

MARBRIDGE FOUNDATION, INC.

2310 BLISS SPILLAR RD　　　　　　　　　　　　　　　　CEO: -
MANCHACA, TX 786524400　　　　　　　　　　　　　　　CFO: -
Phone: 512 282-1811　　　　　　　　　　　HR: Courtney Nuttall
Fax: -　　　　　　　　　　　　　　　　　　　　　　FYE: June 30
Web: www.marbridge.org　　　　　　　　　　　　Type: Private

The Marbridge Foundation provides long-term care for more than 240 adults with cognitive disabilities such as Alzheimer's, cerebral palsy, mental retardation, and Parkinson's disease. Located on a 170-acre campus, the foundation's activities include several classrooms, recreational facilities, horse stables, computer labs, and an art studio. The Marbridge Foundation's goal is to train and educate residents with cognitive challenges so that they can reach the peak of their potential abilities. Residents stay for several years or their entire lives. The foundation was founded in 1953 by the Bridges family.

	Annual Growth	06/15	06/16	06/17	06/21	06/22
Sales ($mil.)	5.8%	–	16.0	–	20.3	22.4
Net income ($ mil.)	39.0%	–	0.6	–	2.8	4.5
Market value ($ mil.)	–	–	–	–	–	–
Employees	–	–	–	–	–	200

MARCH OF DIMES INC.

1550 CRYSTAL DR STE 1300
ARLINGTON, VA 222024144
Phone: 571 257-2324
Fax: –
Web: www.marchofdimes.org

CEO: –
CFO: David Damond
HR: Teresa Imperati
FYE: December 31
Type: Private

The March of Dimes has been on the march, lending a hand, since 1938. Established by President Franklin Roosevelt to fight polio, the organization has evolved into an advocate for the prevention of birth defects and infant mortality. Its focus areas include genetic birth defects, premature birth, parent education, and expanding access to health care. March of Dimes provides information and support services for research and professionals. To help babies get a healthy start, March of Dimes partners with Publix Super Markets, Macy's, HCA Healthcare, Pampers, Philips, and Northrop Grumman, among others.

	Annual Growth	12/08	12/09	12/13	12/14	12/16
Sales ($mil.)	(3.3%)	–	214.7	202.8	195.9	169.3
Net income ($ mil.)	–	–	35.3	(9.7)	(7.9)	(8.7)
Market value ($ mil.)	–	–	–	–	–	–
Employees	–	–	–	–	–	1,200

MARCHEX INC

1200 5th Ave, Suite 1300
Seattle, WA 98101
Phone: 206 331-3300
Fax: –
Web: www.marchex.com

NMS: MCHX
CEO: Russell C Horowitz
CFO: Holly Aglio
HR: –
FYE: December 31
Type: Public

Marchex's conversational intelligence platform, that incorporates AI functionality to help with sales engagement and marketing solutions, helps businesses turn strategic insights into the actions that can drive their most valued sales outcomes. Its multichannel voice and text capabilities help enable sales and marketing teams to deliver the buying experiences that improves their customer experiences. Marchex provides its' conversational intelligence solutions for market-leading companies in numerous industries, including several of the world's most innovative and successful brands. Most of its sales come from the US.

	Annual Growth	12/18	12/19	12/20	12/21	12/22
Sales ($mil.)	(11.6%)	85.3	106.1	51.2	53.5	52.2
Net income ($ mil.)	–	(2.7)	(4.0)	(38.4)	(4.4)	(8.2)
Market value ($ mil.)	(11.9%)	114.4	163.1	84.6	107.0	69.1
Employees	(6.6%)	254	291	245	187	193

MARCHON EYEWEAR, INC.

35 HUB DR
MELVILLE, NY 117473500
Phone: 631 755-2020
Fax: –
Web: www.marchon.com

CEO: Claudio Gottardi
CFO: Phil Hibbert
HR: –
FYE: December 31
Type: Private

One of the world's largest eyewear designers, distributors and manufacturers, Marchon distributes eyeglasses and sunglasses in more than 100 countries and sells 20 million pair of glasses annually. It sells its eyewear collections under the Marchon brand and those of approximately 25 designers and brand names, including Calvin Klein, DKNY, Victoria Beckham, Lacoste, and NIKE. The company manufactures eyewear in Italy and also has satellite design offices located in Hong Kong, Tokyo, Sweden, and Southern California. Founded by three friends in 1983, Marchon is owned by the vision-care provider Vision Service Plan.

MARCO'S FRANCHISING, LLC

5252 MONROE ST
TOLEDO, OH 436233140
Phone: 419 885-7000
Fax: –
Web: www.marcos.com

CEO: Jack Butorac
CFO: Ken Switzer
HR: –
FYE: December 28
Type: Private

Pizza company Marco's Franchising is on the rise. The operator of the Marco's Pizza chain, the company has more than 200 franchised and company-managed pizza restaurants located in 17 states and the Bahamas. Its restaurants, many of which are located in mid-western and southern states, offer Italian-style pizza, as well as hot subs, salads, and meatballs. The company also manages its own distribution operations that serve about half of the chain's restaurants. Marco's Pizza was founded by Italian immigrant Pasquale "Pat" Giammarco, who opened the first Marco's location in Ohio in 1978 and then worked to expand the business until 2004, when current CEO Jack Butorac bought the rights to the franchise.

MARCUM LLP

730 3RD AVE FL 11
NEW YORK, NY 100173216
Phone: 212 485-5500
Fax: –
Web: www.marcumllp.com

CEO: –
CFO: –
HR: Laura Carusone
FYE: December 31
Type: Private

Marcum LLP (formerly MarcumStonefield) is making a mark on the world of accounting and consulting. With more than 20 offices in the US, China, and the Caribbean, Marcum offers a full range of business and personal financial services including accounting, auditing, and tax and investment consulting. It also offers professional services such as mergers and acquisitions planning, family office services, forensic accounting, and litigation support. The firm serves multiple industries such as construction, health care, real estate, media and entertainment, and financial services. Founded in 1951, Marcum is a member of the Marcum Group.

	Annual Growth	12/14	12/15	12/16	12/17	12/18
Sales ($mil.)	(8.1%)	–	273.1	320.1	341.0	212.2
Net income ($ mil.)	16.0%	–	15.7	11.2	14.3	24.6
Market value ($ mil.)	–	–	–	–	–	–
Employees	–	–	–	–	–	2,500

MARCUS CENTER FOR THE PERFORMING ARTS, INC.

929 N WATER ST STE 1
MILWAUKEE, WI 532023122
Phone: 414 273-7206
Fax: –
Web: www.marcuscenter.org

CEO: –
CFO: –
HR: –
FYE: December 31
Type: Private

Marcus Center for the Performing Arts brings Broadway to the brewers. The center anchors Milwaukee's downtown theater district and offers opera, symphonies, ballet, and national touring Broadway and off-Broadway productions. Marcus Center also hosts cultural celebrations, craft fairs, lectures, and other public and private events (weddings and parties with catering). It offers outreach and educational programs to the city's school children as well. Founded in 1967, the theater took its current name in 1997 when benefactors Ben and Ciel Marcus gave more than $10 million to the Marcus Center's parent, Milwaukee County War Memorial, for its renovation.

MARCUS CORP. (THE)   NYS: MCS

100 East Wisconsin Avenue, Suite 1900
Milwaukee, WI 53202-4125
Phone: 414 905-1000
Fax: 414 905-2879
Web: www.marcuscorp.com

CEO: Gregory S Marcus
CFO: Chad M Paris
HR: Desiree Ingermann
FYE: December 28
Type: Public

The Marcus Corporation is a leader in the lodging and entertainment industries, with significant company-owned real estate assets. It owns or operates around 85 theaters boasting more than 1,065 screens at roughly 85 locations in more than 15 states in the US under the Marcus Theatres, Movie Tavern by Marcus, and BistroPlex brands. It also owns a family entertainment center, Funset Boulevard, adjacent to its movie theatre in Appleton, Wisconsin. The company's lodging division, Marcus Hotels & Resorts, owns and/or manages about 15 hotels, resorts and other properties in roughly 10 states. The Marcus Corporation was founded in 1935 by Ben Marcus.

	Annual Growth	12/19	12/20	12/21	12/22	12/23
Sales ($mil.)	(2.9%)	820.9	237.7	458.2	677.4	729.6
Net income ($ mil.)	(23.0%)	42.0	(124.8)	(43.3)	(12.0)	14.8
Market value ($ mil.)	(18.1%)	1,034.1	427.6	569.4	452.0	466.0
Employees	(7.2%)	10,500	4,200	7,500	8,050	7,780

MARGATE MEDICAL STAFF, INC.

2801 N STATE ROAD 7
MARGATE, FL 330635727
Phone: 954 974-0400
Fax: -
Web: www.hcafloridahealthcare.com

CEO: -
CFO: -
HR: -
FYE: December 31
Type: Private

Northwest Medical Center is an acute care hospital serving residents in the northwestern area of Florida's Broward County. The comprehensive medical center is part of the HCA system of health care providers. Founded in 1984, the hospital provides services including pediatrics, surgery, orthopedics, sleep diagnostics, and cardiovascular care. Northwest Medical Center houses more than 220 patient beds and 600 doctors. Specialty centers located on hospital grounds include birthing, minimally invasive surgery, pelvic health, and bariatrics units.

	Annual Growth	12/02	12/03	12/04	12/05	12/13
Sales ($mil.)	1.7%	-	-	0.0	129.4	0.1
Net income ($ mil.)	1.3%	-	-	0.0	(1.3)	0.0
Market value ($ mil.)	-	-	-	-	-	-
Employees	-	-	-	-	-	800

MARIAH MEDIA, INC.

400 MARKET ST
SANTA FE, NM 875017300
Phone: 505 989-7100
Fax: -
Web: www.outsideinc.com

CEO: -
CFO: -
HR: -
FYE: June 30
Type: Private

Mariah Media goes for the outdoorsy type. Publisher of Outside magazine, the company targets readers who have an active lifestyle and enjoy outdoor sports, travel, and adventure. Content includes gear reviews, travel guides, photo galleries, and "ask the experts" columns. Its Web site, Outside Online, features blogs, online videos, and podcasts. The magazine is perhaps best-known for publishing the first-hand account of one of its writers who survived an ill-fated trip up Mount Everest in which several people died. (Writer Jon Krakauer later wrote the best-selling book Into Thin Air detailing the trip.) The company was founded in 1977.

MARIAN UNIVERSITY, INC.

3200 COLD SPRING RD
INDIANAPOLIS, IN 462221960
Phone: 317 955-6000
Fax: -
Web: www.marian.edu

CEO: -
CFO: -
HR: -
FYE: June 30
Type: Private

Marian College is a Franciscan Catholic and liberal arts institution offering undergraduate and graduate programs through academic departments such as business, nursing, education, and sport studies. The school has an enrollment of more than 2,000 students and boasts a student-to-teacher ratio of just over 12 to 1. Marian College was founded in 1851 by the Sisters of St. Francis as a teacher training institution for German Catholics in southern Indiana.

	Annual Growth	06/17	06/18	06/19	06/20	06/22
Sales ($mil.)	6.5%	-	105.7	107.2	105.9	135.9
Net income ($ mil.)	-	-	16.5	9.5	(0.5)	(9.0)
Market value ($ mil.)	-	-	-	-	-	-
Employees	-	-	-	-	-	305

MARIETTA CORPORATION

6710 RIVER RD
HODGKINS, IL 605254310
Phone: 607 753-6746
Fax: -
Web: www.fluentbyvoyant.com

CEO: Donald W Sturdivant
CFO: Perry Morgan
HR: -
FYE: September 25
Type: Private

Marietta makes miniatures -- those little personal care amenities found in hotels and bed-and-breakfast inns. The manufacturer specializes in soaps, shampoos, lotions, and other necessities. Products are distributed to hospitality and institutional customers, including hotels, spas, military bases, and correctional facilities. Using its sample-size packaging know-how, Marietta also provides contract manufacturing for consumer products companies. It has worked with top firms, such as Est e Lauder, Procter & Gamble, and Pfizer. Marietta's manufacturing and warehousing network spans the US, Canada, Europe, and Asia. Founded as Marietta Packaging Company in 1976, it has been owned by Ares Management since 2004.

MARIN GENERAL HOSPITAL

250 BON AIR RD
KENTFIELD, CA 949041784
Phone: 415 925-7000
Fax: -
Web: www.mymarinhealth.org

CEO: David Bradley
CFO: Theresa Daughton
HR: Garrett Yee
FYE: December 31
Type: Private

Serving Northern California's Marin County, Marin General Hospital is the county's largest acute-care health care facility with some 235 beds. Opened in 1952, Marin General Hospital has been a member of Sutter Health since 1996. It operates the Marin Cancer Institute, the Haynes Cardiovascular Institute, the Surgery Center of Marin, and The Institute for Health & Healing which provides holistic care within the hospital setting. Other services include adult psychiatric care, a level III trauma center, a family birthing center, neonatal intensive care, pediatrics, and a cardiac catheterization lab.

	Annual Growth	12/16	12/17	12/18	12/21	12/22
Sales ($mil.)	7.9%	-	371.0	470.1	429.1	541.7
Net income ($ mil.)	(2.9%)	-	17.8	4.1	(5.9)	15.3
Market value ($ mil.)	-	-	-	-	-	-
Employees	-	-	-	-	-	1,100

MARIN SOFTWARE INC
NMS: MRIN

149 New Montgomery Street, 4th Floor
San Francisco, CA 94105
Phone: 415 399-2580
Fax: –
Web: www.marinsoftware.com

CEO: Christopher Lien
CFO: Robert Bertz
HR: –
FYE: December 31
Type: Public

Marin Software is a leading provider of digital marketing software for search, social and eCommerce advertising channels, offered as a unified software-as-a-service, or SaaS, advertising management platform for performance-driven advertisers and agencies. The company markets and sells its solutions to advertisers directly and through leading advertising agencies, and its customers collectively manage billions of dollars in advertising spend on its platform globally across a wide range of industries. Its software works with ad publishers Amazon, Apple, Baidu, Bing, Criteo, and Yahoo! and integrates with enterprise applications.

	Annual Growth	12/19	12/20	12/21	12/22	12/23
Sales ($mil.)	(22.5%)	49.0	30.0	24.4	20.0	17.7
Net income ($ mil.)	–	(12.4)	(14.1)	(12.9)	(18.2)	(21.9)
Market value ($ mil.)	(28.2%)	24.9	36.5	67.0	18.1	6.6
Employees	(17.1%)	229	162	156	177	108

MARINE PRODUCTS CORP
NYS: MPX

2801 Buford Highway, Suite 300
Atlanta, GA 30329
Phone: 404 321-7910
Fax: –
Web: www.marineproductscorp.com

CEO: Ben M Palmer
CFO: –
HR: –
FYE: December 31
Type: Public

Marine Products manufactures fiberglass motorized boats distributed and marketed through its independent dealer network. Marine Products' product offerings include Chaparral sterndrive, outboard and jet pleasure boats and Robalo outboard sport fishing boats, ranging from 16 feet to 36 feet. The company designs, manufactures and sells recreational fiberglass powerboats in the sport boat and sport fishing boat markets. Marine Products sells its products to a network of about 210 domestic and 90 international independent authorized dealers. The company intends to remain a leading manufacturer of recreational powerboats for sale to a broad range of consumers worldwide. The US generates the majority of the company's revenue.

	Annual Growth	12/19	12/20	12/21	12/22	12/23
Sales ($mil.)	7.1%	292.1	239.8	298.0	381.0	383.7
Net income ($ mil.)	10.2%	28.2	19.4	29.0	40.3	41.7
Market value ($ mil.)	(5.7%)	496.3	501.1	430.8	405.7	392.9
Employees	0.6%	673	823	880	935	690

MARINE TOYS FOR TOTS FOUNDATION

18251 QUANTICO GATEWAY DR
TRIANGLE, VA 221721776
Phone: 703 640-9433
Fax: –
Web: www.toysfortots.org

CEO: Robert M Shea
CFO: –
HR: –
FYE: December 31
Type: Private

The Marine Toys for Tots Foundation wears a Santa hat every year. A not-for-profit charity organized by the United States Marine Corps, Toys for Tots collects and distributes new toys at Christmas to children in need. Campaigns in some 650 communities distributed more than 16.2 million toys to 7.6 million children in 2008. About 70 corporations are national sponsors, collecting an average of $60 million in toys each year. Big Lots, ESPN, Starbucks, Neopets, and Ford Motor Company are among them. Major Bill Hendricks started Toys for Tots in 1947 after he couldn't find an organization to give away a Raggedy Ann doll that his wife had made for needy children.

	Annual Growth	12/15	12/16	12/19	12/20	12/22
Sales ($mil.)	5.6%	–	274.3	263.3	298.3	379.6
Net income ($ mil.)	–	–	2.2	23.8	41.8	(8.7)
Market value ($ mil.)	–	–	–	–	–	–
Employees	–	–	–	–	–	12

MARINEMAX INC
NYS: HZO

2600 McCormick Drive, Suite 200
Clearwater, FL 33759
Phone: 727 531-1700
Fax: –
Web: www.marinemax.com

CEO: William B McGill
CFO: Michael H McLamb
HR: –
FYE: September 30
Type: Public

MarineMax is the largest recreational boat and yacht retailer selling new and used recreational boats, yachts, and related marine products and services. It has over 120 locations worldwide, including about 80 retail dealership locations, some of which include marinas. The company sells related marine products, including engines, trailers, parts, and accessories. The company also arranges related boat financing, insurance, and extended service contracts; provides boat repair and maintenance services; offers yacht and boat brokerage sales; and, where available, offers slip and storage accommodations. MarineMax is the largest retailer of Sea Ray and Boston Whaler.

	Annual Growth	09/19	09/20	09/21	09/22	09/23
Sales ($mil.)	18.0%	1,237.2	1,509.7	2,063.3	2,308.1	2,394.7
Net income ($ mil.)	32.0%	36.0	74.6	155.0	198.0	109.3
Market value ($ mil.)	20.7%	342.2	567.5	1,072.7	658.6	725.6
Employees	22.3%	1,754	1,736	2,666	3,410	3,928

MARINUS PHARMACEUTICALS INC
NMS: MRNS

5 Radnor Corporate Center, Suite 500, 100 Matsonford Road
Radnor, PA 19087
Phone: 484 801-4670
Fax: –
Web: www.marinuspharma.com

CEO: Scott Braunstein
CFO: Steven E Pfanstiel
HR: –
FYE: December 31
Type: Public

Marinus Pharmaceuticals is ready to put an end to epileptic seizures. The biopharmaceutical company is developing a drug candidate, ganaxolone, to be used as an add-on therapy for the treatment of partial onset seizures in people with epilepsy. (Epilepsy affects some 50 million people globally, and over 5 million people are under treatment in the US, Europe, and Japan.) The company is also developing ganaxolone to treat conditions associated with Fragile X Syndrome, which causes intellectual disability, behavioral, and learning challenges. Founded in 2003 by former CEO Henry Penner, Marinus went public in 2014, raising $45 million in its IPO. It plans to use the proceeds to further develop and commercialize ganaxolone.

	Annual Growth	12/19	12/20	12/21	12/22	12/23
Sales ($mil.)	–	–	1.7	15.3	25.5	31.0
Net income ($ mil.)	–	(54.1)	(67.5)	(98.8)	(19.8)	(141.4)
Market value ($ mil.)	49.8%	117.9	665.9	648.4	217.2	593.3
Employees	40.2%	43	72	113	153	166

MARION COMMUNITY HOSPITAL INC

1431 SW 1ST AVE
OCALA, FL 344716500
Phone: 352 401-1000
Fax: –
Web: www.hcafloridahealthcare.com

CEO: Chad Christianson
CFO: –
HR: –
FYE: August 31
Type: Private

With a giant like hospital operator HCA behind it, residents of Marion County, Florida can count on Ocala Regional Medical Center (ORMC) to be there to keep them healthy. The 200-bed acute care hospital and its sister facility, the 94-bed West Marion Community Hospital, provide a full spectrum of health care services to residents of the Sunshine State. ORMC specializes in bariatrics, cancer care, heart and vascular ailments, neuroscience, and women's care. West Marion operates a joint care center for orthopedic surgeries and physical therapy. Locals also have access to 24-hour health advice through HCA's Consult-A-Nurse telephone service.

	Annual Growth	09/02	09/03	09/04	09/05*	08/15
Sales ($mil.)	81.0%	–	–	–	0.8	301.5
Net income ($ mil.)	145.5%	–	–	–	0.0	50.1
Market value ($ mil.)	–	–	–	–	–	–
Employees	–	–	–	–	–	1,100

*Fiscal year change

MARIST COLLEGE

3399 NORTH RD
POUGHKEEPSIE, NY 126011387
Phone: 845 575-3000
Fax: -
Web: www.marist.edu

CEO: -
CFO: John Pecchia
HR: Carol Koogen
FYE: June 30
Type: Private

Marist College is a gem among small private US colleges. The liberal arts college has a enrollment of more than 6,300 students and a student-faculty ratio of 16-to-1. It offers more than 40 bachelor's and a dozen master's programs, as well as some 20 certificate programs. It seven schools specialize in communication and the arts, computer science and math, continuing education, liberal arts, management, science, and social and behavioral sciences. In addition to its main 210-acre campus along the shores of the Hudson River, the college has several off-campus extension sites that mainly cater to adult students. Marist was founded in 1929 to train new members in the Marist Brothers order of Catholic priests.

	Annual Growth	06/18	06/19	06/20	06/21	06/22
Sales ($mil.)	12.9%	-	227.0	219.9	319.4	326.9
Net income ($ mil.)	(8.7%)	-	36.3	26.2	46.8	27.7
Market value ($ mil.)	-	-	-	-	-	-
Employees	-	-	-	-	-	1,300

MARITZ HOLDINGS INC.

1375 N HIGHWAY DR
FENTON, MO 630990001
Phone: 636 827-4000
Fax: -
Web: www.maritz.com

CEO: David Peckinpaugh
CFO: Holly Francois
HR: Erin Dunstan
FYE: March 31
Type: Private

Maritz Holdings designs employee incentive and reward programs, including incentive travel rewards, corporate gifts, employee recognition programs and awards, and customer loyalty programs. The company also plans corporate trade shows and events and offers traditional market research services such as the creation of product launch campaigns. Its programs are designed to help its clients improve workforce quality and customer satisfaction. The company operates through several subsidiaries, including Maritz Motivation (services for marketing, sales, and HR), Maritz Automotive (helping clients and partners' sales), Maritz Global Events (meeting and event industry professionals), and Maritz Travel (planners, sales operations and procurement). The company is owned by Steve Maritz.

	Annual Growth	03/18	03/19	03/20	03/21	03/22
Sales ($mil.)	(30.2%)	-	-	1,303.2	362.4	634.2
Net income ($ mil.)	(43.2%)	-	-	54.3	10.8	17.5
Market value ($ mil.)	-	-	-	-	-	-
Employees	-	-	-	-	-	2,500

MARK MASTER, INC.

11111 N 46TH ST
TAMPA, FL 336172009
Phone: 813 988-6000
Fax: -
Web: www.markmasterinc.com

CEO: Kevin A Govin
CFO: -
HR: Katie Govin
FYE: December 31
Type: Private

Sometimes you can't go where everybody knows your name. To remedy that situation, Mark Master makes nameplates, name badges, rubber stamps, daters, banners, and other signage and identification products. Its brand portfolio includes Eco-Mark, MasterLine, and StampWizard, among others. Products can be ordered online or over the phone. Mark Master has served companies in the financial services, health care, transportation, food and beverage, and real estate industries. Founded in 1933 by Armand and Virginia Govin, the company is still owned by the Govin family, including CEO Ron Govin.

	Annual Growth	12/06	12/07	12/09	12/10	12/14
Sales ($mil.)	(33.8%)	-	172.8	-	10.7	9.6
Net income ($ mil.)	-	-	0.0	-	0.8	(0.2)
Market value ($ mil.)	-	-	-	-	-	-
Employees	-	-	-	-	-	85

MARKEL GROUP INC

NYS: MKL

4521 Highwoods Parkway
Glen Allen, VA 23060-6148
Phone: 804 747-0136
Fax: -
Web: www.markel.com

CEO: Thomas S Gayner
CFO: Brian Costanzo
HR: -
FYE: December 31
Type: Public

Markel Corporation is a diverse financial holding company serving a variety of niche markets. It is a holding company for insurance, reinsurance, and investment operations around the world which was founded in 1930. The company provides customized direct and facultative placements in the US and abroad, as well as treaty reinsurance. Markel International provides specialty insurance internationally from its base in the UK, while investment management is provided by Markel CATCo and Nephila Holdings. Subsidiary Markel Ventures invests in non-insurance companies.

	Annual Growth	12/19	12/20	12/21	12/22	12/23
Assets ($mil.)	10.1%	37,474	41,710	48,449	49,791	55,046
Net income ($ mil.)	2.8%	1,790.5	816.0	2,425.0	(214.1)	1,996.1
Market value ($ mil.)	5.6%	15,012	13,569	16,205	17,301	18,646
Employees	3.8%	18,600	18,900	20,300	20,900	21,600

MARKER 29 PRODUCE, INC.

4 NORTH ST
ONANCOCK, VA 234171920
Phone: 757 787-1000
Fax: -
Web: -

CEO: -
CFO: -
HR: -
FYE: December 31
Type: Private

Marker 29 plants its "Carrots for Sale" signpost in the southeastern region of the US. The company is an agent and broker for the fresh produce industry. Its primary product is carrots; Marker 29 also offers a variety of other fruits and vegetables. The company's principal partner is Coggins Farms & Produce, which has produce growing and packing operations in Georgia. Marker 29 provides storage, packing, and delivery services and offers private-label packaging. Its products can be found in retail stores such as Albertson's, SUPERVALU, and Winn Dixie.

	Annual Growth	12/03	12/04	12/05	12/06	12/07
Sales ($mil.)	(6.8%)	-	-	3.6	2.9	3.1
Net income ($ mil.)	(18.4%)	-	-	1.7	1.0	1.1
Market value ($ mil.)	-	-	-	-	-	-
Employees	-	-	-	-	-	13

MARKER THERAPEUTICS INC

NAS: MRKR

350 Kirby Drive, Suite 300
Houston, TX 77054
Phone: 713 400-6400
Fax: -
Web: www.markertherapeutics.com

CEO: Peter Hoang
CFO: -
HR: Edmund Cheung
FYE: December 31
Type: Public

TapImmune taps into the immune system to take out autoimmune disorders. Its research is primarily focused on the biological TAP system, which triggers an immune system response in cells. The TAP system shuts down in many cancer tumor cells, but the company is developing a vaccine to restore the immune function. TapImmune is also researching a vaccine adjuvant product designed to enhance the effectiveness of existing and new infectious disease vaccines. The company also has technologies that could be used to identify or screen drugs for potential effectiveness in treating cancers and viral and infectious diseases.TapImmune is buying Marker Therapeutics to add that firm's portfolio of T cell therapies for blood cancers.

	Annual Growth	12/19	12/20	12/21	12/22	12/23
Sales ($mil.)	98.5%	0.2	0.5	1.2	9.0	3.3
Net income ($ mil.)	-	(21.4)	(28.7)	(41.9)	(29.9)	(8.2)
Market value ($ mil.)	17.6%	25.6	12.9	8.5	2.4	49.0
Employees	(18.4%)	18	44	56	67	8

MARKET & JOHNSON, INC.

2350 GALLOWAY ST
EAU CLAIRE, WI 547033472
Phone: 715 834-1213
Fax: –
Web: www.market-johnson.com

CEO: Dan Market
CFO: –
HR: –
FYE: December 31
Type: Private

Market & Johnson provides commercial construction and general contracting services in western Wisconsin. It offers a full range of services ranging from the planning and preliminary design stages through delivery and maintenance. The company operates in the industrial, commercial, government, health care, religion, and education markets. Projects range from large buildings to small remodeling jobs. Juel Market and Milt Johnson founded the company as a home builder in 1948. Today Market & Johnson is owned by a group of five principal managers including CEO Dan Market.

	Annual Growth	12/09	12/10	12/11	12/12	12/13
Sales ($mil.)	11.1%	–	–	84.6	107.3	104.4
Net income ($ mil.)	80.4%	–	–	1.5	6.2	5.0
Market value ($ mil.)	–	–	–	–	–	–
Employees	–	–	–	–	–	250

MARKET AMERICA, INC.

1302 PLEASANT RIDGE RD
GREENSBORO, NC 274099415
Phone: 336 605-0040
Fax: –
Web: www.marketamerica.com

CEO: Ridinger
CFO: –
HR: Kelley Rood
FYE: December 31
Type: Private

Calling itself a cross between Amazon and QVC, Market America is an Internet marketer and broker of products and services from a variety of categories, including apparel, beauty and personal care, electronics, entertainment, nutrition, and sports. Market America sells more than 2,500 of its own branded products (such as Isotonix, Motives, and Snap) and spotlights the offerings of more than 3,000 other retailers (including Sears, Staples, and Wal-Mart) on its SHOP.COM web site (acquired in 2010). In addition, the company manages UnFranchise, a network marketing business with more than 180,000 independent shopping consultants. The company was founded in 1992 by president and CEO James "JR" Ridinger.

	Annual Growth	12/07	12/08	12/09*	10/16*	12/19
Sales ($mil.)	4.9%	–	229.0	224.5	412.0	385.8
Net income ($ mil.)	15.6%	–	3.5	15.8	23.3	17.2
Market value ($ mil.)	–	–	–	–	–	–
Employees	–	–	–	–	–	650

*Fiscal year change

MARKETAXESS HOLDINGS INC.   NMS: MKTX

55 Hudson Yards, 15th Floor
New York, NY 10001
Phone: 212 813-6000
Fax: 212 813-6390
Web: www.marketaxess.com

CEO: Richard M McVey
CFO: Antonio L Delise
HR: –
FYE: December 31
Type: Public

MarketAxess operates leading electronic trading platforms delivering greater trading efficiency, a diversified pool of liquidity and significant cost savings to its clients across the global fixed-income markets. Almost 1,900 institutional investor and broker-dealer firms are active users of the company patent trading technology. The company also provides real-time the ability to view indicative prices from its broker-dealer clients' inventory available on its platform, access to real-time pricing information and analytical tools available through its Corporate BondTicker service. The majority of its revenue accounts in US. The company was incorporated in the year 2000.

	Annual Growth	12/19	12/20	12/21	12/22	12/23
Sales ($mil.)	10.1%	511.4	689.1	699.0	718.3	752.5
Net income ($ mil.)	5.9%	204.9	299.4	257.9	250.2	258.1
Market value ($ mil.)	(6.3%)	14,368	21,624	15,587	10,570	11,099
Employees	13.7%	527	606	676	744	881

MARKETING ANALYSTS INC.

2000 SAM RITTENBERG BLVD STE 3007
CHARLESTON, SC 294074629
Phone: 843 797-8900
Fax: –
Web: www.marketinganalysts.com

CEO: –
CFO: –
HR: –
FYE: December 31
Type: Private

Not surprisingly, Marketing Analysts Incorporated (known as MAi) is into a little market research. The firm provides custom market research services primarily in such areas as the automotive industry, consumer goods, health care, and technology. It also offers research on brand equity and the effectiveness of branding efforts. Studies cover such topics as concept testing, product testing, satisfaction studies, and segmentation. Founded in 1982 by president Rob Pascale, the firm conducts its quantitative and qualitative research in thirty countries, across six continents. In late 2008, MAi agreed to merge with Data Development Worldwide, another independent market research firm based in New York.

MARKETO, INC.

901 MARINERS ISLAND BLVD STE 200
SAN MATEO, CA 944041592
Phone: 650 376-2303
Fax: –
Web: –

CEO: Allison Blais
CFO: Keith S Felipe
HR: Caitlin Brundrett
FYE: December 31
Type: Private

A recognized leader in the industry by Gartner, Forrester, and SiriusDecisions, Marketo helps transform its customers' digital marketing with constant product innovation, a vibrant community of marketers, and a robust partner ecosystem. Its Marketo Engage product offers content personalization, experience automation, and marketing impact analytics, among others. In addition, its Cross-Channel Engagement features include email marketing, personalize web campaigns, paid media, event and webinar, dynamic chat, SEO expertise, social media, mobile push, and SMS text messaging. The company serves enterprise customers in healthcare, manufacturing, higher education, financial services, and technology industries. Among Marketo's customers are Charles Schwab, Fujitsu, Roche, Panasonic, and CenturyLink.

MARKMONITOR INC.

5335 GATE PKWY
JACKSONVILLE, FL 322563070
Phone: 208 389-5740
Fax: –
Web: www.markmonitor.com

CEO: –
CFO: –
HR: –
FYE: August 31
Type: Private

MarkMonitor can not only help you make your mark, it can help you protect it. The company provides software used to manage intellectual property on the Internet, including applications for brand protection and trademark management, as well as securing website domains and enterprise DNS information. MarkMonitor also provides fraud protection applications used to detect, analyze, and combat phishing and malware attacks. In addition to hosted software, it offers managed services such as consulting, enforcement lifecycle management, and brand threat reporting. The company was founded in 1999, and has been an ICANN-accredited domain registrar since then. It has offices in the US and Europe.

MARKS PANETH LLP

685 3RD AVE FL 4
NEW YORK, NY 100178408
Phone: 212 503-8800
Fax: –
Web: www.cbiz.com

CEO: –
CFO: Brian L Fox
HR: Meredith Hauptman
FYE: December 31
Type: Private

Marks Paneth (formerly Marks Paneth & Shron) wants to show you the money. The firm offers accounting and wealth management services to high-net-worth individuals and its families, businesses, not-for-profit organizations, and professional practices. It offers a broad range of tax, auditing, litigation, and corporate financial advisory services for its clients. Other areas of expertise include bankruptcy and restructuring advise. Marks Paneth helps not-for-profits with organizational and board development, funding, marketing, program development, evaluation, and executive searches. The company was founded in 1907.

	Annual Growth	12/02	12/03	12/04	12/05	12/12
Sales ($mil.)	(70.2%)	–	–	–	49.5	0.0
Net income ($ mil.)	(68.7%)	–	–	–	19.2	0.0
Market value ($ mil.)	–	–	–	–	–	–
Employees	–	–	–	–	–	575

MARKWEST ENERGY PARTNERS, L.P.

1515 ARAPAHOE ST STE 1-600
DENVER, CO 802023150
Phone: 303 925-9200
Fax: –
Web: www.markwest.com

CEO: –
CFO: –
HR: –
FYE: December 31
Type: Private

MarkWest Energy Partners (a wholly owned subsidiary of MPLX LP) is engaged in the gathering, processing, and transportation of natural gas; the transportation, fractionation, storage and marketing of NGLs; and the gathering and transportation of crude oil. Its Northeast segment includes Antrim Shale, and Huron/Berea Shale. It also has facilities in the Marcellus Shale and Utica Shale basin, as well as operations in the Southwest including Cana and Arkoma Woodford Shale, Granite Wash Formation, Barnett Shale, and more.

MARKWINS BEAUTY BRANDS, INC.

22067 FERRERO
CITY OF INDUSTRY, CA 917895214
Phone: 909 595-8898
Fax: –
Web: www.markwinsbeauty.com

CEO: Lina Chen
CFO: Lina Chen
HR: Christy Simpson
FYE: December 31
Type: Private

Markwins International believes beauty comes in all shades and ages. It makes and markets cosmetics and personal care products, including lipstick, nail polish, and bath collections, for tweens and adults. Its ethnic-designed cosmetic lines include Black Radiance (for African-Americans) and Tropez (for Hispanic and Asian women). Markwins also makes the value-priced Wet 'n' Wild cosmetics, and packages beauty kits under The Color Workshop and Spa Institute labels. Through partnership agreements, the company produces cosmetics under licensed brands. Markwins, which owns Physicians Formula Holdings, is buying the Bonne Bell and Lip Smacker brands from Aspire Brands.

MARLIN BUSINESS SERVICES CORP.

300 FELLOWSHIP RD
MOUNT LAUREL, NJ 080541201
Phone: 888 479-9111
Fax: –
Web: www.peacsolutions.com

CEO: Jeffrey A Hilzinger
CFO: Michael R Bogansky
HR: –
FYE: December 31
Type: Private

Marlin Business Services provide customers services which include loans and leases for the acquisition of commercial equipment and working capital loans, it leases more than 100 categories of commercial equipment to about 68,000 small and mid-sized businesses -- and it provides the financing for the deals, in part through its Marlin Business Bank subsidiary. Copiers makes up over 20% of Marlin's lease portfolio, but its customers also can get products as diverse as computer hardware and software, security systems, telecom equipment, dental implant systems, water filtration systems, and restaurant equipment. The company primarily operates through its main subsidiary, Marlin Leasing.

MARQUETTE LUMBER COMPANY, INCORPORATED

3201 CARDINAL DR STE 5
VERO BEACH, FL 329631976
Phone: 772 231-5252
Fax: –
Web: www.marquettelumber.com

CEO: Daniel Downey
CFO: –
HR: –
FYE: December 31
Type: Private

Marquette Lumber Co. makes its mark in wood. The company processes American hardwoods (Northern, Southern, and Appalachian), used mostly for furniture and flooring, and wholesales it to manufacturing and construction companies. The firm operates two lumberyards and offices in Norwalk, Ohio; Sandown, New Hampshire; St. Louis; and Vero Beach, Florida. Russel H. Downey founded Marquette Lumber Co. in 1919 in South Bend, Indiana. The company moved to Vero Beach, Florida in 1972; the founding Downey family still runs it.

	Annual Growth	12/03	12/04	12/05	12/06	12/07
Sales ($mil.)	(14.5%)	–	10.4	10.5	8.8	6.5
Net income ($ mil.)	–	–	0.0	0.0	0.0	(0.0)
Market value ($ mil.)	–	–	–	–	–	–
Employees	–	–	–	–	–	10

MARQUETTE UNIVERSITY

1250 W WISCONSIN AVE
MILWAUKEE, WI 532332225
Phone: 414 288-7250
Fax: –
Web: www.marquette.edu

CEO: Paul J Jones
CFO: John C Lamb
HR: –
FYE: June 30
Type: Private

A member of the Association of Jesuit Colleges and Universities, Marquette University provides undergraduate, graduate, and professional courses and programs. It specializes in business, engineering, arts and sciences, nursing, law, dentistry, and other fields. The university offers undergraduates some 75 majors and 65 minors and post-graduate students about 50 doctoral and master's degree programs. With an enrollment of more than 11,700 students, Marquette University boasts a student/faculty ratio of 14:1. Its student population consists of students from all 50 US states and nearly 70 countries. Founded in 1881, the university is named after French missionary explorer Father Jacques Marquette.

	Annual Growth	06/17	06/18	06/20	06/21	06/22
Sales ($mil.)	12.2%	–	463.4	679.5	725.4	733.4
Net income ($ mil.)	13.2%	–	57.6	53.7	106.2	94.6
Market value ($ mil.)	–	–	–	–	–	–
Employees	–	–	–	–	–	3,000

MARRIOTT INTERNATIONAL, INC. — NMS: MAR

7750 Wisconsin Avenue
Bethesda, MD 20814
Phone: 301 380-3000
Fax: –
Web: www.marriott.com

CEO: Anthony G Capuano
CFO: Kathleen K Oberg
HR: Jennie Perez
FYE: December 31
Type: Public

Marriott International is one of the world's leading hoteliers, that operates, franchises, and licenses hotel, residential, timeshare, and other lodging properties under numerous brand names. The company has more than 6,100 franchised and licensed properties. Its hotel portfolio, which comprises nearly 1.5 million guest rooms, includes the premium Delta Hotels and Renaissance Hotel brands and its flagship Marriott Hotels & Resorts as well as the Ritz-Carlton, W Hotels, The Luxury Collection, and JW Marriott luxury brands. Additionally, the company operates the selectservice and extended-stay brands Courtyard and Fairfield Inn. North America accounts for 75% of Marriott International's revenue.

	Annual Growth	12/19	12/20	12/21	12/22	12/23
Sales ($mil.)	3.1%	20,972	10,571	13,857	20,773	23,713
Net income ($ mil.)	24.7%	1,273.0	(267.0)	1,099.0	2,358.0	3,083.0
Market value ($ mil.)	10.5%	43,990	38,323	48,002	43,253	65,511
Employees	(4.0%)	174,000	121,000	120,000	377,000	148,000

MARRIOTT VACATIONS WORLDWIDE CORP. — NYS: VAC

9002 San Marco Court
Orlando, FL 32819
Phone: 407 206-6000
Fax: –
Web: www.marriottvacationsworldwide.com

CEO: –
CFO: –
HR: –
FYE: December 31
Type: Public

Marriott Vacations Worldwide, formerly part of hotel giant Marriott International, is one of the world's leading timeshare companies, operating more than 120 resorts. Its properties are in prime vacation destinations in the US (such as California, Colorado, Florida, Hawaii, and South Carolina) and a handful of other countries (Aruba, France, Spain, the West Indies, and Thailand). The villas are jointly owned by about 420,000 people who have exclusive use of the properties for limited periods of time. Marriott spun off Marriott Vacations as a separately-traded company in 2011.

	Annual Growth	12/19	12/20	12/21	12/22	12/23
Sales ($mil.)	2.1%	4,355.0	2,886.0	3,890.0	4,656.0	4,727.0
Net income ($ mil.)	16.5%	138.0	(275.0)	49.0	391.0	254.0
Market value ($ mil.)	(9.9%)	4,547.7	4,846.5	5,968.3	4,753.6	2,998.3
Employees	–	–	22,000	18,000	20,300	21,400	22,000

MARSH & MCLENNAN COMPANIES INC. — NYS: MMC

1166 Avenue of the Americas
New York, NY 10036
Phone: 212 345-5000
Fax: 212 345-4809
Web: www.marshmclennan.com

CEO: John Q Doyle
CFO: Mark C McGivney
HR: Claudia Ullivarri
FYE: December 31
Type: Public

Marsh & McLennan Companies (Marsh McLennan) is the world's leading professional services firm in the areas of risk, strategy and people. The company operates across four global businesses – Marsh, Guy Carpenter, Mercer and Oliver Wyman. Marsh provides data-driven risk advisory services and insurance solutions to commercial and consumer clients. Guy Carpenter is the company's reinsurance intermediary and advisor. Mercer delivers advice and technology-driven solutions that help organizations redefine the future of work, shape retirement and investment outcomes, and advance health and well-being for a changing workforce. Oliver Wyman Group provides management consulting to private sector and governmental clients. Serving in over 130 countries, Marsh McLennan generates about 50% of total revenue from its US customers.

	Annual Growth	12/19	12/20	12/21	12/22	12/23
Sales ($mil.)	8.1%	16,652	17,224	19,820	20,720	22,736
Net income ($ mil.)	21.2%	1,742.0	2,016.0	3,143.0	3,050.0	3,756.0
Market value ($ mil.)	14.2%	54,814	57,565	85,521	81,417	93,220
Employees	2.8%	76,000	76,000	83,000	85,000	85,000

MARSHALL MARKETING & COMMUNICATIONS, INC.

2600 BOYCE PLAZA RD STE 210
PITTSBURGH, PA 152413949
Phone: 412 914-0970
Fax: –
Web: www.marshallmarketingusa.com

CEO: Craig A Marshall
CFO: Ann Butler
HR: –
FYE: December 31
Type: Private

Marshall Marketing & Communications provides marketing research and analysis to clients in the retail and media industries. The company provides a complete market intelligence program (known as the Marshall Plan) consisting of needs analysis, questionnaire development, survey design, data collection, data delivery, analysis, and strategic consulting. Chairman and CEO Craig Marshall founded the company in 1985.

	Annual Growth	12/98	12/99	12/00	12/01	12/07
Sales ($mil.)	4.7%	–	3.0	3.5	3.4	4.4
Net income ($ mil.)	6.3%	–	0.4	0.7	0.8	0.7
Market value ($ mil.)	–	–	–	–	–	–
Employees	–	–	–	–	–	25

MARSHALL UNIVERSITY

1 JOHN MARSHALL DR
HUNTINGTON, WV 257550003
Phone: 304 696-2385
Fax: –
Web: www.marshall.edu

CEO: –
CFO: –
HR: –
FYE: June 30
Type: Private

If "You Are Marshall," you know that Marshall University is a state-supported, non-profit educational institution serving about 14,000 students, including 3,500 graduate and medical students. The university offers about 55 baccalaureate and more than 50 graduate programs through more than a dozen colleges and schools. It also offers two Associate Programs, two Ed.S, four Doctoral Degree Programs and three First Professional programs. Marshall students attend classes either at the university's main campus in Huntington, West Virginia; at its regional campuses; or online.

	Annual Growth	06/17	06/18	06/20	06/21	06/22
Sales ($mil.)	0.9%	–	192.9	193.8	198.8	200.2
Net income ($ mil.)	–	–	5.1	(16.2)	38.7	(16.9)
Market value ($ mil.)	–	–	–	–	–	–
Employees	–	–	–	–	–	1,632

MARSHFIELD CLINIC HEALTH SYSTEM, INC.

1000 N OAK AVE
MARSHFIELD, WI 544495702
Phone: 715 387-5511
Fax: –
Web: www.marshfieldclinic.org

CEO: Susan Turney
CFO: –
HR: Barb Burr
FYE: December 31
Type: Private

Marshfield Clinic Health System (MCHS) is a private group medical practice that operates more than 60 medical locations across Wisconsin. The network has more than 1,600 providers comprising over 170 specialties, and subspecialties, in Wisconsin. MCHS's primary operations include Marshfield Medical Center, Flambeau Hospital, and Marshfield Children's Hospital and clinics; other parts of the network include Marshfield Labs and the Security Health Plan of Wisconsin, medical education and research organizations. MCHS was founded in 1916.

	Annual Growth	09/18	09/19*	12/20	12/21	12/22
Sales ($mil.)	4.0%	–	2,613.3	–	2,796.1	2,943.8
Net income ($ mil.)	–	–	107.7	–	26.7	(477.5)
Market value ($ mil.)	–	–	–	–	–	–
Employees	–	–	–	–	–	8,377

*Fiscal year change

MARSHFIELD CLINIC, INC.

1000 N OAK AVE
MARSHFIELD, WI 544495702
Phone: 715 387-5511
Fax: –
Web: www.marshfieldclinic.org

CEO: –
CFO: Gary Jankowski
HR: Kathy Mitchell
FYE: September 30
Type: Private

Marshfield Clinic is a private group medical practice that operates more than 50 medical locations across Wisconsin. The network provides primary and tertiary care through its more than 700 physicians who represent about 80 medical specialties. Through two hospitals -- the 25-bed Flambeau Hospital and the 40-bed Lakeview Medical Center -- and dozens of clinics Marshfield annually serves roughly 380,000 patients and handles 3.8 million patient encounters. Other parts of the network include Marshfield Laboratories and Security Health Plan of Wisconsin, as well as medical education and research organizations.

	Annual Growth	06/05	06/06*	09/08	09/09	09/15
Sales ($mil.)	4.5%	–	813.9	102.3	1,062.8	1,211.1
Net income ($ mil.)	0.5%	–	23.2	6.0	78.8	24.4
Market value ($ mil.)	–	–	–	–	–	–
Employees	–	–	–	–	–	363

*Fiscal year change

MARTEN TRANSPORT LTD

129 Marten Street
Mondovi, WI 54755
Phone: 715 926-4216
Fax: –
Web: www.marten.com

NMS: MRTN
CEO: Timothy M Kohl
CFO: James J Hinnendael
HR: Nancy Nelson
FYE: December 31
Type: Public

Marten Transport is a multifaceted business offering a network of refrigerated and dry truck-based transportation capabilities across the company's five distinct business platforms ? Truckload, Dedicated, Intermodal, Brokerage and MRTN de Mexico. Marten is one of the leading temperature-sensitive truckload carriers in the US, specializing in transporting and distributing food, beverages and other consumer packaged goods. The company offers service in the US, Canada and Mexico, concentrating on expedited movements for high-volume customers. Additionally, the Wisconsin-based also hauls dry freight. The company's fleet includes more than 3,660 tractors and over 5,750 trailers. Marten Transport's largest customers were Wal-Mart.

	Annual Growth	12/19	12/20	12/21	12/22	12/23
Sales ($mil.)	7.6%	843.3	874.4	973.6	1,263.9	1,131.5
Net income ($ mil.)	3.6%	61.1	69.5	85.4	110.4	70.4
Market value ($ mil.)	(0.6%)	1,747.4	1,401.0	1,395.3	1,608.4	1,705.9
Employees	0.8%	4,087	4,162	4,007	4,575	4,213

MARTHA JEFFERSON HEALTH SERVICES CORPORATION

500 MARTHA JEFFERSON DR
CHARLOTTESVILLE, VA 229114668
Phone: 434 654-7000
Fax: –
Web: www.marthajefferson.org

CEO: James E Haden
CFO: –
HR: –
FYE: December 31
Type: Private

Virginians who take a fall while scaling the Mountain State's many cliffs might seek help from Martha Jefferson Health Services (operating as Martha Jefferson Hospital). The hospital cares for the residents of an eight-county region in central Virginia, including the city of Charlottesville. With more than 175 beds and a staff of 450 doctors, it offers most medical specialties including maternity care, cancer treatment, pain management, cardiology, and home health care. The hospital also has fertilization, outpatient surgery, and urgent care centers, as well as primary and specialty care practices. Martha Jefferson Hospital, which was founded in 1903, joined the Sentara Healthcare network in 2011.

	Annual Growth	09/04	09/05	09/06*	12/13	12/14
Sales ($mil.)	(67.0%)	–	–	174.2	0.0	0.0
Net income ($ mil.)	–	–	–	10.4	–	–
Market value ($ mil.)	–	–	–	–	–	–
Employees	–	–	–	–	–	1,600

*Fiscal year change

MARTHA STEWART LIVING OMNIMEDIA, INC.

601 W 26TH ST RM 900
NEW YORK, NY 100011101
Phone: 212 827-8000
Fax: –
Web: www.marthastewart.com

CEO: –
CFO: –
HR: –
FYE: December 31
Type: Private

Martha Stewart Living Omnimedia (MSLO) seems to prove the old adage that all publicity is good publicity. Legendary lifestyle maven Martha Stewart and her company, MSLO, have embraced the media spotlight, including Stewart's much ballyhooed sentence on federal criminal charges related to insider trading of stock. The domestic guru has her fingers in many revenue-generating pies that center around three business segments: publishing (magazines, books, websites), broadcasting (TV programs, satellite radio), and merchandising. The majority of MSLO's business comes from publishing activities, which are driven by its flagship magazine, Martha Stewart Living.

MARTIN & BAYLEY, INC.

1311A W MAIN ST
CARMI, IL 628211389
Phone: 618 382-2334
Fax: –
Web: www.hucks.com

CEO: –
CFO: –
HR: –
FYE: March 27
Type: Private

Martin & Bayley (dba Huck's Food and Fuel) operates 115 Huck's convenience stores and a number travel centers in mostly in Illinois and Indiana, but also in Missouri, Kentucky, and Tennessee. Half of its outlets are in Illinois. The company operates a commissary at its warehouse in Carmi, Illinois to supply sandwiches, chicken, and other food items to its stores. Some stores sell Godfather's Pizza. Family-owned since its inception, Martin & Bayley became a 100% employee-owned firm, when the Martin and Bayley families sold their stakes in the company.

	Annual Growth	03/08	03/09	03/10	03/11	03/18
Sales ($mil.)	–	–	(1,579.4)	466.2	528.9	523.3
Net income ($ mil.)	193.4%	–	0.0	5.3	7.5	8.2
Market value ($ mil.)	–	–	–	–	–	–
Employees	–	–	–	–	–	1,500

MARTIN MARIETTA MATERIALS, INC.

4123 Parklake Avenue
Raleigh, NC 27612
Phone: 919 781-4550
Fax: –
Web: www.martinmarietta.com

NYS: MLM
CEO: C H Nye
CFO: James A Nickolas
HR: –
FYE: December 31
Type: Public

Martin Marietta Materials, Inc. (Martin Marietta) is a natural resource-based building materials company. The company supplies aggregates (crushed stone, sand and gravel) through its network of approximately 350 quarries, mines and distribution yards in nearly 30 states, Canada, and The Bahamas. Martin Marietta also provides cement and downstream products, namely, ready mixed concrete, asphalt and paving service. The company's heavy-side building materials are used in infrastructure, nonresidential and residential construction projects. Nearly all of the company's revenue comes from the US.

	Annual Growth	12/19	12/20	12/21	12/22	12/23
Sales ($mil.)	9.4%	4,739.1	4,729.9	5,414.0	6,160.7	6,777.2
Net income ($ mil.)	17.6%	611.9	721.0	702.5	866.8	1,168.9
Market value ($ mil.)	15.6%	17,288	17,555	27,234	20,894	30,843
Employees	–	8,846	8,700	10,000	9,400	–

MARTIN MIDSTREAM PARTNERS LP
NMS: MMLP

4200 Stone Road
Kilgore, TX 75662
Phone: 903 983-6200
Fax: –
Web: www.mmlp.com

CEO: –
CFO: –
HR: –
FYE: December 31
Type: Public

Martin Midstream Partners moves petroleum products. The company gets most of its sales from the distribution of natural gas liquids (NGLs). Its NGL customers include retail propane distributors, industrial processors, and refiners. Martin Midstream owns more than 720 miles of natural gas gathering and transmission pipelines. Martin Midstream also manufactures sulfur and sulfur-based fertilizer products and provides marine transportation (through a fleet of more than 50 inland barges and push boats and four offshore tug barges) and the storage of liquid hydrocarbons (at about 50 terminals). The company, an affiliate of Martin Resource Management operates primarily in the Gulf Coast region of the US.

	Annual Growth	12/19	12/20	12/21	12/22	12/23
Sales ($mil.)	(1.5%)	847.1	672.1	882.4	1,018.9	798.0
Net income ($ mil.)	–	(174.9)	(6.8)	(0.2)	(10.3)	(4.5)
Market value ($ mil.)	(12.2%)	156.8	55.6	103.5	116.7	93.4
Employees	–	–	–	–	–	1,619

MARTIN RESOURCE MANAGEMENT CORPORATION

4200 STONE RD
KILGORE, TX 756626935
Phone: 903 983-6200
Fax: –
Web: www.themartincompanies.com

CEO: –
CFO: Bob Bondurant
HR: Jamie Graham
FYE: December 31
Type: Private

Martin Resource Management likes to push around petroleum products. The employee-owned company's flagship affiliate, Martin Midstream Partners, offers transportation, storage, marketing, and logistics management services for petroleum products, including sulfur, sulfur derivatives, fuel oil, liquefied petroleum gas, asphalt and other bulk tank liquids, primarily in the southern US. Martin Resource also manufactures and markets fertilizer and other processed sulfur products. Through its Martin Energy Services unit the company offers inland marine fuel supply and offshore support services. Other units include The Brimrock Group (sulfur), Cross Oil Refining & Marketing, and Martin Asphalt.

	Annual Growth	12/07	12/08	12/09	12/11	12/15
Sales ($mil.)	(2.1%)	–	2,903.0	1,537.6	2,985.1	2,493.9
Net income ($ mil.)	24.9%	–	5.8	23.2	37.7	27.3
Market value ($ mil.)	–	–	–	–	–	–
Employees	–	–	–	–	–	2,300

MARVELL TECHNOLOGY INC
NMS: MRVL

1000 N. West Street, Suite 1200
Wilmington, DE 19801
Phone: ( ) 302 295-4840
Fax: –
Web: www.marvell.com

CEO: Matthew J Murphy
CFO: Jean Hu
HR: –
FYE: February 3
Type: Public

Marvell Technology is a leading supplier of infrastructure semiconductor solutions, spanning the data center core to network edge. The company is a fabless semiconductor supplier of high-performance standard and semi-custom products with core strengths in developing and scaling complex System-on-a-Chip architectures, integrating analog, mixed-signal and digital signal processing functionality. Leveraging leading intellectual property and deep system-level expertise, as well as highly innovative security firmware, its solutions are empowering the data economy and enabling the data center, carrier infrastructure, enterprise networking, consumer, and automotive/industrial end markets. About 90% of Marvell's revenue comes from outside of the US.

	Annual Growth	02/20*	01/21	01/22	01/23*	02/24
Sales ($mil.)	19.5%	2,699.2	2,968.9	4,462.4	5,919.6	5,507.7
Net income ($ mil.)	–	1,584.4	(277.3)	(421.0)	(163.5)	(933.4)
Market value ($ mil.)	29.5%	20,807	44,539	57,400	38,298	58,447
Employees	3.9%	5,633	5,340	6,729	7,448	6,577

*Fiscal year change

MARVIN ENGINEERING CO., INC.

261 W BEACH AVE
INGLEWOOD, CA 903022904
Phone: 310 674-5030
Fax: –
Web: www.marvingroup.com

CEO: Howard Gussman
CFO: Ariel Lechter
HR: Christina Schallig
FYE: January 31
Type: Private

Marvin Engineering helps missiles get from Point A to Point B. The company manufactures missile launchers, ejector racks, test equipment, and other hardware for military customers and companies in the aerospace and defense industries. Customers include branches of the US military and major US defense contractors, as well as the governments of Australia, Canada, and Israel. Marvin Engineering is part of the Marvin Group, which also includes Aerospace Dynamics International, Flyer Defense, Marvin Land Systems, Geotest-Marvin Test Systems, and Clean Water Technologies.

	Annual Growth	01/05	01/06	01/07	01/08	01/09
Sales ($mil.)	8.0%	–	–	114.9	105.7	133.8
Net income ($ mil.)	–	–	–	22.8	0.6	(3.4)
Market value ($ mil.)	–	–	–	–	–	–
Employees	–	–	–	–	–	750

MARY WASHINGTON HEALTHCARE

2300 FALL HILL AVE STE 418
FREDERICKSBURG, VA 224013343
Phone: 540 741-2507
Fax: –
Web: www.marywashingtonhealthcare.com

CEO: Michael P McDermott
CFO: Sean T Barden
HR: –
FYE: December 31
Type: Private

Health care is Mary Washington Healthcare's realm in the Old Dominion State. The medical provider offers a comprehensive range of health services to residents of Fredericksburg and surrounding communities in central Virginia through its not-for-profit regional system of two hospitals and 28 healthcare facilities. The hub of this system is Mary Washington Hospital, a 437-bed acute care medical center that provides services including emergency/trauma care and surgical procedures. The health system also includes outpatient care programs and facilities providing primary care and specialty care services for women, seniors, and children.

	Annual Growth	12/18	12/19	12/20	12/21	12/22
Sales ($mil.)	(43.9%)	–	764.5	778.4	148.0	135.0
Net income ($ mil.)	(70.9%)	–	82.0	69.6	8.0	2.0
Market value ($ mil.)	–	–	–	–	–	–
Employees	–	–	–	–	–	4,000

MARYLAND AND VIRGINIA MILK PRODUCERS COOPERATIVE ASSOCIATION, INCORPORATED

13921 PARK CENTER RD STE 200
HERNDON, VA 201713236
Phone: 703 742-6800
Fax: –
Web: www.mdvamilk.com

CEO: –
CFO: Jorge Gonzalez
HR: Maura Ruane
FYE: December 31
Type: Private

Milk is "Mar-VA-lous" for the members of the Maryland & Virginia Milk Producers Cooperative Association. Known as Maryland & Virginia, the co-op processes and sells milk for nearly 1,500 member/farmers with dairy herds in the southeastern US and mid-Atlantic region. Maryland & Virginia produces fluid milk, ice cream, and cultured dairy products for retail sale under the Marva Maid, Maola, and Valley Milk brands. Its butter, condensed milk, and milk-powder products are sold primarily to food manufacturers. As a co-op, it also offers agricultural supplies to its members. Maryland & Virginia operates three fluid-milk processing plants, a manufacturing plant, and an equipment-supply warehouse.

	Annual Growth	12/08	12/09	12/10	12/11	12/12
Sales ($mil.)	3.1%	–	–	1,219.2	1,362.5	1,296.4
Net income ($ mil.)	(20.4%)	–	–	8.7	(2.8)	5.5
Market value ($ mil.)	–	–	–	–	–	–
Employees	–	–	–	–	–	550

MARYLAND DEPARTMENT OF TRANSPORTATION

7201 CORPORATE CENTER DR
HANOVER, MD 210761415
Phone: 410 865-1037
Fax: –
Web: mdot.maryland.gov

CEO: –
CFO: –
HR: –
FYE: June 30
Type: Private

Traveling in Maryland? You can thank (or curse) the Maryland Department of Transportation (MDOT). MDOT is responsible for building, operating, and maintaining a safe and seamless transportation network that includes highway, transit, maritime, and aviation facilities. The Department of Transportation is organized along various administrative groups including the Maryland Motor Vehicle Administration, Transit Administration, Port Administration, Aviation Administration, and Highway Administration. MDOT annual budget of about $1.5 billion is funded through the state's Transportation Trust Fund and federal aid.

	Annual Growth	06/18	06/19	06/20	06/21	06/22
Sales ($mil.)	6.4%	–	4,609.5	4,792.0	5,058.3	5,547.0
Net income ($ mil.)	15.4%	–	229.6	(210.7)	232.0	353.1
Market value ($ mil.)	–	–	–	–	–	–
Employees	–	–	–	–	–	1,000

MARYLAND SOUTHERN ELECTRIC COOPERATIVE INC

15065 BURNT STORE RD
HUGHESVILLE, MD 206372699
Phone: 888 440-3311
Fax: –
Web: www.smeco.coop

CEO: –
CFO: Sonja M Cox
HR: Beth Kennedy
FYE: December 31
Type: Private

Historic Southern Maryland gets it power via the South Maryland Electric Cooperative (SMECO), which distributes electricity to about 154,000 residential, commercial, and industrial customers in four counties, via about 11,360 miles of power line and 54 electric substations. One of the ten largest electric cooperatives in the US, the member-owned enterprise gets its wholesale power supply through its membership in wholesale energy trading and risk management service company ACES Power Marketing. Overseen by a board of directors, SMECO's single mission is to provide reliable, competitively priced energy and related services to its members.

	Annual Growth	12/18	12/19	12/20	12/21	12/22
Sales ($mil.)	21.1%	–	–	–	461.1	558.2
Net income ($ mil.)	14.1%	–	–	–	5.7	6.5
Market value ($ mil.)	–	–	–	–	–	–
Employees	–	–	–	–	–	375

MARYMOUNT MANHATTAN COLLEGE

221 E 71ST ST
NEW YORK, NY 100214532
Phone: 212 517-0400
Fax: –
Web: www.mmm.edu

CEO: James Buckman
CFO: –
HR: –
FYE: June 30
Type: Private

Marymount Manhattan College is a four-year, undergraduate liberal arts college in the middle of New York City with an enrollment of more than 2,000 students. Marymount Manhattan offers 17 major programs of study in fields including media, technology, and performing arts. The college has a student-to-teacher ratio of 12:1. It was originally was founded in 1936 by the Religious of the Sacred Heart of Mary in Tarrytown, New York; it was independently chartered in 1961 as Marymount Manhattan College.

	Annual Growth	06/14	06/15	06/20	06/21	06/22
Sales ($mil.)	6.2%	–	66.5	102.6	88.0	101.0
Net income ($ mil.)	30.8%	–	2.0	18.3	6.5	13.2
Market value ($ mil.)	–	–	–	–	–	–
Employees	–	–	–	–	–	630

MARYVILLE CONSULTING GROUP, INC.

7777 BONHOMME AVE STE 2300
SAINT LOUIS, MO 631051911
Phone: 636 519-4100
Fax: –
Web: www.maryville.com

CEO: –
CFO: William T Jerry
HR: –
FYE: December 31
Type: Private

Maryville Data Systems wants to improve your company's data systems. The company, doing business as Maryville Technologies, is an information technology and engineering services firm that designs and builds complex corporate computer systems, primarily in the Midwest. The company's offerings include computers, servers, networking equipment, and software from more than 50 suppliers. Maryville also provides remote monitoring for computer systems, and it operates technology training centers. Customers have included State Farm, Union Pacific Railroad, Cargill, and the Federal Reserve Bank. The employee-owned company was founded in 1994.

	Annual Growth	12/09	12/10	12/11	12/12	12/13
Sales ($mil.)	2.2%	–	29.1	30.8	37.0	31.0
Net income ($ mil.)	(8.5%)	–	3.5	4.2	5.6	2.7
Market value ($ mil.)	–	–	–	–	–	–
Employees	–	–	–	–	–	136

MASCO CORP.

NYS: MAS

17450 College Parkway
Livonia, MI 48152
Phone: 313 274-7400
Fax: –
Web: www.masco.com

CEO: Keith J Allman
CFO: John G Sznewajs
HR: Andrea Carr
FYE: December 31
Type: Public

Masco Corporation is a global leader in the design, manufacturing, and distribution of home improvement and building products. These products are sold primarily for repair and remodeling activity and, to a lesser extent, new home construction. It sells its products through home center retailers, online retailers, wholesalers, distributors, mass merchandisers, hardware stores, direct to the consumer, professional contractors, and homebuilders. Well-known brands include Delta and Peerless (plumbing), Behr (paints and stains), Hot Spring (spas), and Kichler (decorative and outdoor lighting). While most of its sales are within North America, Masco has a major presence in the UK, mainland Europe, and China.

	Annual Growth	12/19	12/20	12/21	12/22	12/23
Sales ($mil.)	4.4%	6,707.0	7,188.0	8,375.0	8,680.0	7,967.0
Net income ($ mil.)	(0.7%)	935.0	1,224.0	410.0	844.0	908.0
Market value ($ mil.)	8.7%	10,587	12,118	15,491	10,295	14,776
Employees	–	18,000	18,000	20,000	19,000	18,000

MASHANTUCKET PEQUOT TRIBAL NATION

2 MATTS PATH
MASHANTUCKET, CT 063383804
Phone: 860 396-6500
Fax: –
Web: www.mptn-nsn.gov

CEO: Jason Guyot
CFO: –
HR: Honey Carter
FYE: September 30
Type: Private

Mashantucket Pequot Tribal Nation has propelled itself from the depths of poverty to its lofty position as the wealthiest Native American tribe in the US. With roughly 900 members and a seven-member government council, the tribe owns and operates Foxwoods Resort Casino in Connecticut. Foxwoods comprises six casinos, with a total of more than 6,200 slot machines and 380 gaming tables, plus four hotels (including the MGM Grand at Foxwoods) and the world's largest Bingo hall. Through its Foxwoods Development Company, the tribe develops and manages various hospitality-related enterprises, from a luxury spa hotel and golf courses to a museum and research center dedicated to the tribe's life and history.

MASIMO CORP.

NMS: MASI

52 Discovery
Irvine, CA 92618
Phone: 949 297-7000
Fax: –
Web: www.masimo.com

CEO: Joseph E Kiani
CFO: Micah Young
HR: –
FYE: December 30
Type: Public

Masimo is a global medical technology company that develops, manufactures, and markets a variety of noninvasive monitoring technologies. Its patient monitoring solutions generally incorporate a monitor or circuit board, proprietary single-patient use or reusable sensors, software and/or cables. The company provides its products to hospitals, emergency medical service (EMS) providers, home care providers, long-term care facilities, physician offices, veterinarians and consumers through its direct sales force, distributors and original equipment manufacturers (OEM) partners. Its US market generates the majority of the company's sales. Joe Kiani founded Masimo in 1989 as a private "garage start-up" company.

	Annual Growth	12/19*	01/21	01/22*	12/22	12/23
Sales ($mil.)	21.6%	937.8	1,143.7	1,239.2	2,035.8	2,048.1
Net income ($ mil.)	(19.7%)	196.2	240.3	229.6	143.5	81.5
Market value ($ mil.)	(7.4%)	8,421.1	14,170	15,459	7,811.8	6,188.7
Employees	(8.0%)	5,300	6,200	6,200	9,900	3,800

*Fiscal year change

MASS GENERAL BRIGHAM HEALTH PLAN, INC.

399 REVOLUTION DR
SOMERVILLE, MA 021451484
Phone: 617 772-5500
Fax: –
Web: www.massgeneralbrighamhealthplan.org

CEO: Deborah Enos
CFO: Garrett Parker
HR: –
FYE: December 31
Type: Private

Mass General Brigham Health Plan, previously known as AllWays Health Partners, Inc. serves commercial and Medicaid members. As a member of Mass General Brigham, it is advancing innovative value-based care models that center on the health needs of its members and enable seamless and affordable care. Mass General Brigham offers health plans for small businesses, large groups, and families and individuals. The company offers Value HMO for Boston employees and retirees, ensuring access to the highest quality care. The Value HMO networks include Massachusetts General Hospital, Brigham and Women's Hospital, Beth Israel Deaconess Medical Center, Lahey Clinic, Spaulding Rehab, Mass Eye and Ear, and more.

	Annual Growth	12/11	12/12	12/13	12/14	12/15
Assets ($mil.)	15.4%	–	–	349.2	434.4	465.3
Net income ($ mil.)	–	–	–	(68.1)	(108.7)	(22.8)
Market value ($ mil.)	–	–	–	–	–	–
Employees	–	–	–	–	–	488

MASS GENERAL BRIGHAM INCORPORATED

399 REVOLUTION DR STE 327
SOMERVILLE, MA 021451495
Phone: 617 278-1000
Fax: –
Web: www.massgeneralbrigham.org

CEO: Anne Klibanski
CFO: Niyum Gandhi
HR: Deborah Wanzer
FYE: September 30
Type: Private

Mass General Brigham is an integrated academic healthcare system. Mass General Brigham connects a full continuum of care across a system of academic medical centers, community and specialty hospitals, a health insurance plan, physician networks, community health centers, home care, and long-term care services. It is a non-profit organization that is committed to patient care, research, teaching, and service to the community. In addition, Mass General Brigham is one of the nation's leading biomedical research organizations and a principal teaching affiliate of Harvard Medical School.

	Annual Growth	09/06	09/07	09/08	09/10	09/15
Sales ($mil.)	54.7%	–	–	551.0	8.1	11,666
Net income ($ mil.)	–	–	–	(44.1)	(0.1)	(916.1)
Market value ($ mil.)	–	–	–	–	–	–
Employees	–	–	–	–	–	67,000

MASSACHUSETTS DEPARTMENT OF TRANSPORTATION

10 PARK PLZ STE 4160
BOSTON, MA 021163979
Phone: 857 368-4636
Fax: –
Web: www.mass.gov

CEO: Stephanie Pollack
CFO: –
HR: –
FYE: June 30
Type: Private

The Massachusetts Department of Transportation (MassDOT) oversees the operations essential for the massive job of moving people and goods throughout the Commonwealth. In 2009 the former Massachusetts Executive Office of Transportation merged with other state agencies to form MassDOT. The unified organization operates in four divisions: highway; transit; aeronautics; and the registry of motor vehicles. In addition to its regulatory responsibility, MassDOT also provides research, planning, and information services relevant to the state's transportation system.

	Annual Growth	06/17	06/18	06/20	06/21	06/22
Sales ($mil.)	(81.3%)	–	2,957.8	3,114.7	3,500.7	3.6
Net income ($ mil.)	(46.6%)	–	2.0	58.4	13.9	0.2
Market value ($ mil.)	–	–	–	–	–	–
Employees	–	–	–	–	–	6,100

MASSACHUSETTS HIGHER EDUCATION ASSISTANCE CORPORATION

33 ARCH ST STE 2100
BOSTON, MA 021101442
Phone: 617 728-4507
Fax: –
Web: www.asa.org

CEO: –
CFO: –
HR: –
FYE: December 31
Type: Private

Don't know how you're going to pay for college? You might want to consult ASA, ASAP. The Massachusetts Higher Education Assistance Corporation, which does business as American Student Assistance (ASA) is a non-profit student loan collection agency that helps students understand, finance, and repay their higher education loans to prevent student loan default. Its SALT program boosts collection rates by offering students a variety of online tools to help them learn repayment options through blogs and videos, track payment progress, and find scholarships and careers/internships. Founded in 1956, ASA partners with 300-plus higher education institutions, nonprofits, and corporations nationwide, serving over one million borrowers.

	Annual Growth	06/14	06/15*	12/19	12/21	12/22
Assets ($mil.)	10.5%	–	471.2	751.9	1,090.7	945.2
Net income ($ mil.)	(14.5%)	–	37.8	41.7	44.2	12.6
Market value ($ mil.)	–	–	–	–	–	–
Employees	–	–	–	–	–	580

*Fiscal year change

MASSACHUSETTS INSTITUTE OF TECHNOLOGY

77 MASSACHUSETTS AVE
CAMBRIDGE, MA 021394307
Phone: 617 253-1000
Fax: –
Web: web.mit.edu

CEO: –
CFO: –
HR: Leslie West
FYE: June 30
Type: Private

Massachusetts Institute of Technology (MIT) is an academic community for undergraduate and graduate for education, research, and innovation. MIT is providing its students with an education that combines rigorous academic study and discovery of support of intellectual stimulation of a diverse campus community. MIT has around 11,860 students from all 50 states and the District of Columbia, four territories, and about 135 foreign nations in the academic year ending 2022-2023. The school's student-to-faculty ratio is 3:1 (undergraduates). Founded in 1865, MIT is integral part of host city Cambridge.

	Annual Growth	06/18	06/19	06/20	06/21	06/22
Sales ($mil.)	2.7%	–	3,931.9	3,950.6	3,945.1	4,265.2
Net income ($ mil.)	–	–	1,252.2	1,447.9	12,229	(3,215.8)
Market value ($ mil.)	–	–	–	–	–	–
Employees	–	–	–	–	–	12,000

MASSACHUSETTS MEDICAL SOCIETY INC

860 WINTER ST
WALTHAM, MA 024511411
Phone: 781 893-4610
Fax: -
Web: www.massmed.org

CEO: -
CFO: -
HR: -
FYE: June 30
Type: Private

The Massachusetts Medical Society (MMS) is a professional organization of physicians and medical students with more than 24,000 members. The organization, an advocate for patients and physicians, promotes a code of ethics for medical professions, as well as the training, research, and continuing education of physicians and other health care professionals. It also helps to develop health care policy and publishes the New England Journal of Medicine, a leading medical journal. The Massachusetts Medical Society was founded in 1781 and is the oldest continuously operating medical society in the nation.

	Annual Growth	05/12	05/13	05/16*	06/19	06/20
Sales ($mil.)	(64.9%)	-	118.5	135.2	0.0	0.0
Net income ($ mil.)	(58.5%)	-	12.2	12.4	0.0	0.0
Market value ($ mil.)	-	-	-	-	-	-
Employees		-	-	-	-	700

*Fiscal year change

MASSACHUSETTS MUNICIPAL WHOLESALE ELECTRIC COMPANY

327 MOODY ST
LUDLOW, MA 010561246
Phone: 413 589-0141
Fax: -
Web: www.mmwec.org

CEO: Ronald Decurzio
CFO: -
HR: Michelle Izquierdo
FYE: December 31
Type: Private

A massive power resource, Massachusetts Municipal Wholesale Electric Company (MMWEC) provides power supply services to its members -- 23 of the state's 40 municipal utilities (28 utilities are also participants in MMWEC power supply projects). The power supplier has about 715 MW of generating capacity from interests in fossil-fueled and nuclear power plants in the northeastern US, and it negotiates bulk electricity purchases from other generators for its members. MMWEC is the operator and principal owner of the Stony Brook Energy Center, a 520 MW, combined-cycle intermediate and peaking generating station in Ludlow, Massachusetts.

	Annual Growth	12/18	12/19	12/20	12/21	12/22
Sales ($mil.)	10.2%	-	228.3	227.9	242.1	305.2
Net income ($ mil.)	-	-	-	-	-	-
Market value ($ mil.)	-	-	-	-	-	-
Employees	-	-	-	-	-	70

MASSACHUSETTS MUTUAL LIFE INSURANCE CO. (SPRINGFIELD, MA)

1295 State Street
Springfield, MA 01111
Phone: 413 744-8411
Fax: -
Web: www.massmutual.com

CEO: Roger W Crandall
CFO: Elizabeth Ward
HR: -
FYE: December 31
Type: Public

Massachusetts Mutual Life Insurance, known as MassMutual, is a leading mutual life insurance company that is run for the benefit of its members and participating policy owners. The company provides individual and group life insurance, disability insurance, individual and group annuities and guaranteed interest contracts (GIC) to individual and institutional customers in all 50 states, the District of Columbia and Puerto Rico. Its US and International affiliates include Barings LLC, C.M. Life Insurance Company and MML Bay State Life Insurance Company, Haven Life, MassMutual Trust Company, FSB, and MML Investment Advisers. MassMutual was founded in 1851.

	Annual Growth	12/07	12/08	12/09	12/10	12/11
Assets ($mil.)	3.1%	131,491	125,086	132,943	141,102	148,600
Net income ($ mil.)	22.9%	201.0	(1,060.0)	(283.0)	594.0	459.0
Market value ($ mil.)	-	-	-	-	-	-
Employees		-	-	-	-	-

MASSACHUSETTS PORT AUTHORITY

1 HARBORSIDE DR STE 200S
BOSTON, MA 021282905
Phone: 617 561-1600
Fax: -
Web: www.massport.com

CEO: Lisa S Wieland
CFO: John Pranckevicius
HR: David M Gambone
FYE: June 30
Type: Private

Massachusetts Port Authority (Massport) operates three airports: Boston Logan International, Hanscom Field, and Worcester Regional. Logan is home to 50 airlines and is New England's largest airport and the first port of call for many international flights entering the US. (It accounts for the majority of Massport's revenues.) Hanscom Field operates as the region's main aviation airport and offers niche commercial services, while Worcester Regional primarily supports commercial flight services. Massport also oversees various waterfront properties of the Port of Boston. The agency was created by the Commonwealth of Massachusetts in 1956. The governor of Massachusetts appoints the agency's board members.

	Annual Growth	06/12	06/13	06/14	06/15	06/20
Sales ($mil.)	4.5%	-	-	-	662.9	824.5
Net income ($ mil.)	(0.6%)	-	-	-	107.4	104.3
Market value ($ mil.)	-	-	-	-	-	-
Employees		-	-	-	-	1,102

MASTEC INC. (FL)

NYS: MTZ

800 S. Douglas Road, 12th Floor
Coral Gables, FL 33134
Phone: 305 599-1800
Fax: -
Web: www.mastec.com

CEO: Jose R Mas
CFO: Paul Dimarco
HR: -
FYE: December 31
Type: Public

MasTec specializes in building underground and overhead distribution systems, including trenches, conduits, cell towers, cable, and power lines, which provide wireless and wireline/fiber communications; clean energy infrastructure; electrical power generation, transmission, and distribution systems; heavy industrial plants; compressor and pump stations and treatment plants; water and sewer infrastructure, including water pipelines; and other civil construction infrastructure. The company is one of the leading renewables contractors in North America, with expertise in wind, solar and biomass, waste-to-energy (WtE) and biogas, cogeneration or combined heat and power projects and gas-fired power projects. It is also a leading infrastructure construction company operating mainly throughout North America across a range of industries.

	Annual Growth	12/19	12/20	12/21	12/22	12/23
Sales ($mil.)	13.7%	7,183.2	6,321.0	7,951.8	9,778.0	11,996
Net income ($ mil.)	-	392.3	322.8	328.8	33.4	(49.9)
Market value ($ mil.)	4.2%	5,086.6	5,405.3	7,316.0	6,765.0	6,003.1
Employees	-	21,000	18,000	25,000	32,000	-

MASTECH DIGITAL INC

ASE: MHH

1305 Cherrington Parkway, Building 210, Suite 400
Moon Township, PA 15108
Phone: 412 787-2100
Fax: -
Web: www.mastechdigital.com

CEO: Vivek Gupta
CFO: John J Cronin Jr
HR: -
FYE: December 31
Type: Public

Mastech provides outsourced staffing services primarily for businesses in need of contract information technology (IT) personnel. The company provides systems integrators and other IT staffing companies with temporary technical staff on a wholesale basis. It also serves companies in other industries directly. The company mainly serves customers in the US, but it has international recruiting operations in India. Apart from finance, clients come from such industries as consumer products, health care, retail, technology, and telecom. Formerly a subsidiary of IGATE Corporation, Mastech was spun off to its parent company's shareholders in 2008.

	Annual Growth	12/19	12/20	12/21	12/22	12/23
Sales ($mil.)	1.0%	193.6	194.1	222.0	242.2	201.1
Net income ($ mil.)	-	11.1	9.9	12.2	8.7	(7.1)
Market value ($ mil.)	(6.6%)	128.4	184.4	198.0	127.7	97.8
Employees	(5.4%)	1,745	1,671	2,014	2,019	1,397

MASTERCARD INC
NYS: MA

2000 Purchase Street
Purchase, NY 10577
Phone: 914 249-2000
Fax: –
Web: www.mastercard.com

CEO: Michael Miebach
CFO: Sachin Mehra
HR: Tom Gorzkowski
FYE: December 31
Type: Public

Mastercard is a technology company in the global payments industry that connects consumers, financial institutions, merchants, governments, digital partners, businesses, and other organizations worldwide, enabling them to use electronic forms of payment instead of cash and checks. The company provides a wide range of payment solutions and services using its family of well-known brands, including Mastercard, Maestro, and Cirrus. Mastercard provides its services in more than 210 countries and territories and more than 150 currencies. Mastercard generates about 35% of its revenue in North America.

	Annual Growth	12/19	12/20	12/21	12/22	12/23
Sales ($mil.)	10.4%	16,883	15,301	18,884	22,237	25,098
Net income ($ mil.)	8.4%	8,118.0	6,411.0	8,687.0	9,930.0	11,195
Market value ($ mil.)	9.3%	278,883	333,382	335,605	324,780	398,360
Employees	15.8%	18,600	21,000	24,000	29,900	33,400

MASTERCRAFT BOAT HOLDINGS INC
NMS: MCFT

100 Cherokee Cove Drive
Vonore, TN 37885
Phone: 423 884-2221
Fax: –
Web: www.mastercraft.com

CEO: Frederick A Brightbill
CFO: Timothy M Oxley
HR: –
FYE: June 30
Type: Public

MasterCraft Boat Holdings (formerly MCBC Holdings) -- which operates through subsidiaries MasterCraft Boat Company, NauticStar, and Crest Marine -- manufactures sport boats used for water skiing and wakeboarding as well as pure powerboating pleasure. Its primary brands include the premium Star and X-Series (XStar, ProStar, X22, X24, X26) lines, as well as the entry-level NXT (NXT22 and NXT20) line. MasterCraft boats are wholly manufactured in Tennessee; the US is its largest market, but it has dealers in some 40 countries. Founded in 1968, the company went public in 2015.

	Annual Growth	06/19	06/20	06/21	06/22	06/23
Sales ($mil.)	9.2%	466.4	363.1	525.8	707.9	662.0
Net income ($ mil.)	34.0%	21.4	(24.0)	56.2	58.2	68.9
Market value ($ mil.)	11.8%	339.2	329.8	455.2	364.4	530.6
Employees	(3.0%)	1,195	884	1,500	1,750	1,060

MASTERSPAS, LLC

6927 LINCOLN PKWY
FORT WAYNE, IN 468045623
Phone: 260 436-9100
Fax: –
Web: www.masterspas.com

CEO: –
CFO: –
HR: –
FYE: December 31
Type: Private

Master Spas is heating things up as a leading manufacturer of portable spas and hot tubs. The company sells its products in the US and Europe through its network of hot tub dealerships and contract service centers. Its products include a range of spas that filter water, conserve energy, and feature hydrotherapeutic jets. Master Spas also offers accessories, such as remote controls, LED lighting, and flatscreen TV theater systems for outdoor entertainment. The company runs a manufacturing plant and a distribution center in Fort Wayne, Indiana. Its London-based Aegean Master Spas also operates a distribution center and sells through an extensive network of branches and dealers throughout the UK.

	Annual Growth	12/03	12/04	12/05	12/06	12/08
Sales ($mil.)	(3.1%)	–	–	–	51.6	48.5
Net income ($ mil.)	(7.0%)	–	–	–	3.1	2.6
Market value ($ mil.)	–	–	–	–	–	–
Employees	–	–	–	–	–	286

MATANUSKA TELECOM ASSOCIATION, INCORPORATED

1740 S CHUGACH ST
PALMER, AK 996456796
Phone: 907 745-3211
Fax: –
Web: www.mtasolutions.com

CEO: Michael Burke
CFO: Laurie Browning
HR: Rachel Jaime
FYE: December 31
Type: Private

One of the the largest telephone cooperatives in the largest state, the Matanuska Telephone Association, better known as MTA, offers telecommunications services to the residents of south-central Alaska. Established in 1953, the co-op provides local and long-distance voice service and cell phone service (MTA Wireless), Internet access, and digital cable television. It also offers telecommunications systems (provided by third-party companies such as Avaya), as well as Internet and wireless plans, to businesses.

	Annual Growth	12/10	12/11	12/12	12/13	12/14
Sales ($mil.)	(0.4%)	–	–	57.6	58.0	57.1
Net income ($ mil.)	–	–	–	5.0	(0.6)	(1.3)
Market value ($ mil.)	–	–	–	–	–	–
Employees	–	–	–	–	–	300

MATERION CORP
NYS: MTRN

6070 Parkland Blvd.
Mayfield Heights, OH 44124
Phone: 216 486-4200
Fax: 216 383-4091
Web: www.materion.com

CEO: Jugal K Vijayvargiya
CFO: Shelly M Chadwick
HR: Terry Cyran
FYE: December 31
Type: Public

Materion is an integrated producer of high-performance advanced engineered materials used in a variety of electrical, electronic, thermal, and structural applications. It sells products to a number of markets, semiconductor, industrial, aerospace and defense, energy, defense, automotive, consumer electronics, telecommunications and data centers. It manufactures a variety of precious and specialty metal products, including frame lid assemblies and clad and precious metal pre-forms, high temperature brazes materials, advanced chemicals, microelectronics packaging, precious metal, non-precious metal, and specialty metal products. Other products include precision optics and thin film coatings, inorganic chemicals and powders, specialty coatings, specialty engineered beryllium, copper-based alloys, and beryllium composites; ceramics, engineered clad and plated metal systems. Materion gets almost 50% of its revenue from US customers.

	Annual Growth	12/19	12/20	12/21	12/22	12/23
Sales ($mil.)	8.9%	1,185.4	1,176.3	1,510.6	1,757.1	1,665.2
Net income ($ mil.)	17.2%	50.7	15.5	72.5	86.0	95.7
Market value ($ mil.)	21.6%	1,227.4	1,315.6	1,898.2	1,806.7	2,686.7
Employees	7.0%	2,600	3,072	3,443	3,723	3,404

MATIV INC
NYS: MATV

100 Kimball Pl, Suite 600
Alpharetta, GA 30009
Phone: 800 514-0186
Fax: –
Web: www.swmintl.com

CEO: –
CFO: –
HR: –
FYE: December 31
Type: Public

Mativ Holdings (formerly Schweitzer-Mauduit International) is a global leader in specialty materials headquartered in Alpharetta, Georgia, USA. The Company offers a wide range of critical components and engineered solutions to solve customers' most complex challenges, targeting premium applications across diversified and growing end-markets. Combined with global manufacturing, supply chain, innovation, and material science capabilities, its broad portfolio of technologies combines polymers, fibers, and resins to optimize the performance of customers' products across multiple stages of the value chain. Mativ generates approximately 50% of its sales in the US.

	Annual Growth	12/19	12/20	12/21	12/22	12/23
Sales ($mil.)	18.6%	1,022.8	1,074.4	1,440.0	2,167.4	2,026.0
Net income ($ mil.)	–	85.8	83.8	88.9	(6.6)	(309.5)
Market value ($ mil.)	(22.3%)	2,276.3	2,179.8	1,620.9	1,133.0	830.0
Employees	12.3%	3,400	3,600	5,100	7,500	5,400

MATLEN SILVER GROUP, INC.

72 E MAIN ST
SOMERVILLE, NJ 088762312
Phone: 908 393-8600
Fax: –
Web: www.matlensilver.com

CEO: –
CFO: –
HR: –
FYE: December 31
Type: Private

The Matlen Silver Group knows the value of providing a sterling set of information technology (IT) services. The company provides a wide range of IT-related services to companies in the financial, pharmaceutical, and insurance industries. It develops and implements customized software and IT infrastructures and also provides such services as IT staffing, support, project management, and business consulting. In addition, the company licenses custom software to clients through its LTech Consulting subsidiary, a provider of software as a service (SaaS) and platform as a service (PaaS) technologies. The Matlen Silver Group's customers have included Bank of America, Pfizer, and ADP. The company was founded in 1980.

	Annual Growth	12/03	12/04	12/05	12/06	12/20
Sales ($mil.)	6.0%	–	44.5	42.8	52.8	113.7
Net income ($ mil.)	13.4%	–	0.9	1.6	4.2	6.8
Market value ($ mil.)	–	–	–	–	–	–
Employees	–	–	–	–	–	450

MATRIX SERVICE CO.

15 East 5th Street, Suite 1100
Tulsa, OK 74103
Phone: 918 838-8822
Fax: –
Web: www.matrixservicecompany.com

NMS: MTRX
CEO: John R Hewitt
CFO: Kevin S Cavanah
HR: Lou Stevens
FYE: June 30
Type: Public

Matrix Service Company provides engineering, fabrication, construction, and maintenance services to support critical energy infrastructure and industrial markets. It maintains regional offices throughout the US, Canada, and other international locations, and operate through separate union and merit subsidiaries. It is licensed to operate in all 50 states, in four Canadian provinces and in other international locations. Its segments have included Process and Industrial Facilities, Storage and Terminal Solutions, and Utility and Power Infrastructure. Founded in 1984, the majority of its sales were generated in the US.

	Annual Growth	06/19	06/20	06/21	06/22	06/23
Sales ($mil.)	(13.4%)	1,416.7	1,100.9	673.4	707.8	795.0
Net income ($ mil.)	–	28.0	(33.1)	(31.2)	(63.9)	(52.4)
Market value ($ mil.)	–	–	–	–	–	–
Employees	–	5,000	2,900	2,717	2,810	–

MATSON INC

1411 Sand Island Parkway
Honolulu, HI 96819
Phone: 808 848-1211
Fax: –
Web: www.matson.com

NYS: MATX
CEO: Matthew J Cox
CFO: Joel M Wine
HR: –
FYE: December 31
Type: Public

Matson transports freight between the continental US and ports in Hawaii, Guam, Micronesia, and China. Besides containerized freight, cargo carried by Matson vessels includes automobiles, foods and beverages, retail merchandise, and building materials. Subsidiary Matson Logistics provides logistics and multimodal transportation services (arrangement of freight transportation by combinations of road, rail, and air). Other subsidiaries specialize in container stevedoring and related services for Matson and other carriers in Honolulu. The company traces its historical roots all the way back to 1882, when Captain William Matson sailed a schooner that transported goods from San Francisco to Hawaii.

	Annual Growth	12/19	12/20	12/21	12/22	12/23
Sales ($mil.)	8.9%	2,203.1	2,383.3	3,925.5	4,343.0	3,094.6
Net income ($ mil.)	37.7%	82.7	193.1	927.4	1,063.9	297.1
Market value ($ mil.)	28.0%	1,403.5	1,959.8	3,097.0	2,150.3	3,770.2
Employees	21.4%	1,988	4,149	4,259	4,288	4,315

MATTEL INC

333 Continental Blvd.
El Segundo, CA 90245
Phone: 310 252-2000
Fax: –
Web: www.mattel.com

NMS: MAT
CEO: Ynon Kreiz
CFO: Anthony Disilvestro
HR: –
FYE: December 31
Type: Public

Mattel is a leading global toy company and owner of one of the strongest catalogs of children's and family entertainment franchises in the world. Its products include Barbie and Polly Pocket dolls, Fisher-Price and Thomas & Friends toys, Hot Wheels and Matchbox cars, and American Girl dolls and books. Mattel also sells action figures and toys based on Walt Disney, Warner Bros., and NBCUniversal movies, WWE Wrestling, Nickelodeon characters, and the popular Minecraft video game. Other products include games (UNO), educational toys, and puzzles. Mattel's biggest customers have included Walmart, Amazon, and Target. The North America region accounts for nearly 60% of sales. The company was founded by Ruth and Elliot Handler, and Harold "Matt" Matson in 1945.

	Annual Growth	12/19	12/20	12/21	12/22	12/23
Sales ($mil.)	4.8%	4,504.6	4,583.7	5,457.7	5,434.7	5,441.2
Net income ($ mil.)	–	(213.5)	126.6	903.0	393.9	214.4
Market value ($ mil.)	8.6%	4,722.2	6,081.3	7,513.7	6,217.2	6,579.7
Employees	8.3%	24,000	32,100	36,300	33,900	33,000

MATTERSIGHT CORPORATION

200 W MADISON ST STE 3100
CHICAGO, IL 606063498
Phone: 877 235-6925
Fax: –
Web: –

CEO: –
CFO: –
HR: –
FYE: December 31
Type: Private

Mattersight has an eye for important data. The company (formerly eLoyalty) provides behavioral analytics software used by companies to collect and analyze customer data generated from sources including e-mail, call centers, as well as field sales and Internet channels. It also offers systems designed to measure financial and operating metrics associated with CRM programs and tools to help insurance companies, banks, and brokerages to identify instances of identity or financial fraud.

MATTESON-RIDOLFI, INC.

14450 KING RD
RIVERVIEW, MI 481937939
Phone: 734 479-4500
Fax: –
Web: www.penpoly.com

CEO: –
CFO: –
HR: –
FYE: December 31
Type: Private

Matteson-Ridolfi distributes chemicals such as catalysts, pigments, resins, solvents, surfactants, and thickening agents to companies in the adhesives and sealants, automotive, glass and refractory, paints and coatings, pharmaceuticals, pulp and paper, and soaps and detergents industries. The company maintains facilities in Cleveland; Detroit; and Louisville, Kentucky. Customers include Cabot and other major chemical manufacturers. The family of company president Scot Westerbeek owns Matteson-Ridolfi, which was founded in 1932.

	Annual Growth	12/06	12/07	12/08	12/09	12/10
Sales ($mil.)	1.4%	–	–	33.4	28.7	34.4
Net income ($ mil.)	42.0%	–	–	1.5	1.9	3.0
Market value ($ mil.)	–	–	–	–	–	–
Employees	–	–	–	–	–	18

MATTHEWS INTERNATIONAL CORP — NMS: MATW

Two Northshore Center
Pittsburgh, PA 15212-5851
Phone: 412 442-8200
Fax: –
Web: www.matw.com

CEO: Joseph C Bartolacci
CFO: Steven F Nicola
HR: –
FYE: September 30
Type: Public

Matthews International is a global provider of brand solutions, memorialization products, industrial technologies, and brand solutions. Brand solutions consists of brand management, pre-media services, printing plates and cylinders, engineered products, imaging services, digital asset management, merchandising display systems, and marketing and design services primarily for the consumer goods and retail industries. The company is also one of the nation's leading makers of cremation equipment and urns, bronze and granite memorials, metal and wood caskets, and commemorative products; it builds mausoleums as well. Additionally, Matthews International makes and sells marking and coding equipment, industrial automation products, and order fulfillment systems. The diverse company has operations in more than 30 countries across North America, Europe, Asia, Australia, and Central and South America, but North America accounts for approximately 70% of sales.

	Annual Growth	09/19	09/20	09/21	09/22	09/23
Sales ($mil.)	5.2%	1,537.3	1,498.3	1,671.0	1,762.4	1,880.9
Net income ($ mil.)	–	(38.0)	(87.2)	2.9	(99.8)	39.3
Market value ($ mil.)	2.4%	1,078.3	681.3	1,057.0	682.8	1,185.6
Employees	2.2%	11,000	11,000	11,000	12,000	12,000

MATTINGLY FOODS, INC.

302 STATE ST
ZANESVILLE, OH 437013200
Phone: 740 454-0136
Fax: –
Web: www.mattinglycold.com

CEO: Rick Barnes
CFO: Rusty Deaton
HR: –
FYE: December 29
Type: Private

Mattingly Foods is a leading regional foodservice supplier that distributes food products and other goods to chain restaurant operators in more than a dozen states. It delivers a variety of dry goods, along with frozen and refrigerated foods. In addition to its distribution business, Mattingly Foods operates a cash & carry store where customers can purchase wholesale goods. Robert Mattingly started the family-owned business as Mattingly Seafood with his wife, Bette, in 1947.

	Annual Growth	12/03	12/04	12/05	12/06	12/07
Sales ($mil.)	(5.2%)	–	309.2	301.3	290.9	263.4
Net income ($ mil.)	(11.0%)	–	1.6	3.1	1.0	1.1
Market value ($ mil.)	–	–	–	–	–	–
Employees	–	–	–	–	–	240

MATTRESS FIRM HOLDING CORP.

10201 MAIN ST
HOUSTON, TX 770255229
Phone: 713 923-1090
Fax: –
Web: www.mattressfirm.com

CEO: –
CFO: –
HR: –
FYE: February 02
Type: Private

Mattress and bedding retailer Mattress Firm operates or franchises more than 2,300 stores across the US. It is one of the largest mattress retailers in the country, operating primarily through its namesake locations. The company sells conventional and specialty mattresses under a host of best-selling brands (Simmons, Tempur-Pedic, Stearns & Foster, Sleepy's, tulo, Tuft & Needle, and Serta), as well as bed frames and accessories. The company's Sleep.com website provides expert advice and helps people explore the health benefits of quality sleep, and the Sleep.com app provides free sleep tracking and personalized insights to improve sleep.

MATTSON TECHNOLOGY, INC.

47131 BAYSIDE PKWY
FREMONT, CA 945386517
Phone: 510 657-5900
Fax: –
Web: www.mattson.com

CEO: Allen Lu
CFO: –
HR: Carla Zhao
FYE: December 31
Type: Private

Mattson Technology supplies plasma and thermal processing equipment used in the process to make computer chips. Its systems include equipment that deposit materials onto silicon wafers, prepare wafers for photoresist, and etch patterns onto wafers. Top customers Global Foundries (a contract manufacturer of semiconductors) and Samsung Electronics (an OEM) together account for more than two-thirds of sales. Mattson has been purchased for $300 million by E-Town Dragon Semiconductor Industry Investment Center, a private equity firm based in Beijing.

	Annual Growth	12/11	12/12	12/13	12/14	12/15
Sales ($mil.)	(44.1%)	–	–	552.6	–	172.5
Net income ($ mil.)	54980.2%	–	–	0.0	–	10.3
Market value ($ mil.)	–	–	–	–	–	–
Employees	–	–	–	–	–	370

MAUI LAND & PINEAPPLE CO., INC. — NYS: MLP

200 Village Road, Lahaina
Maui, HI 96761
Phone: 808 877-3351
Fax: –
Web: www.mauiland.com

CEO: Warren H Haruki
CFO: Tim T Esaki
HR: –
FYE: December 31
Type: Public

Aloha! Maui Land & Pineapple (ML&P) invites you to live and play on its Hawaiian island -- Maui. Through its Kapalua Land Company subsidiary, the company operates the 1,650-acre Kapalua Resort on Maui's northwest coast. The resort includes a minority-owned Ritz-Carlton hotel, as well as tennis and spa facilities, residential homes and condos, and shops and restaurants. ML&P also develops residential and commercial property on its 23,000 acres surrounding the resort. Its Kapalua Realty Company is a general brokerage real estate firm located within the resort. The company additionally owns forest and nature preserves on the island. Formerly one of Hawaii's largest pineapple producers, the company exited that business in 2009.

	Annual Growth	12/18	12/19	12/20	12/21	12/22
Sales ($mil.)	17.4%	11.0	10.0	7.5	12.4	21.0
Net income ($ mil.)	37.6%	0.5	(10.4)	(2.6)	(3.4)	1.8
Market value ($ mil.)	(1.3%)	193.2	219.1	224.6	194.0	183.5
Employees	(10.5%)	14	11	17	9	9

MAVENIR, INC.

55 WALKERS BROOK DR STE 402
READING, MA 018673272
Phone: 781 246-9000
Fax: –
Web: www.mavenir.com

CEO: Philippe Tartavull
CFO: Jacky Wu
HR: –
FYE: January 31
Type: Private

From 5G application/service layers, to packet core and RAN, Mavenir Systems (formerly Xura Inc.) leads the way in evolved, cloud-native networking solutions enabling innovative and secure experiences for end users. Mavenir is the industry's only end-to-end, cloud-native Network Software and Solutions/Systems Integration Provider for 4G and 5G, focused on accelerating software network transformation for Communications Service Providers. It also offers a comprehensive end-to-end product portfolio across every layer of the network infrastructure stack. Leveraging innovations in IMS (VoLTE, VoWiFi, Advanced Messaging (RCS)), Private Networks as well as Converged Packet Core and OpenRAN vRAN, Mavenir accelerates network transformation for over 250+ CSP customers in more than 120 countries. Mavenir was founded in 2005.

MAXCYTE INC
NMS: MXCT

9713 Key West Avenue, Suite 400
Rockville, MD 20850
Phone: 301 944-1700
Fax: 301 944-1703
Web: www.maxcyte.com

CEO: Douglas Doerfler
CFO: Ron Holtz
HR: –
FYE: December 31
Type: Public

MaxCyte will put your blood cells to work. Its cell-loading technologies use blood cells instead of traditional chemical methods to transport medical gene therapies to targeted sites, increasing their safety and efficacy. The company partners with drugmakers to help them develop more effective therapies in a shorter amount of time. MaxCyte's partners have included biotech firms Geron, MediNet, and Northern Therapeutics. The company works to develop immune system therapies in a variety of fields, including oncology and cardiology. MaxCyte was founded in 1999.

	Annual Growth	12/18	12/19	12/20	12/21	12/22
Sales ($mil.)	27.7%	16.7	21.6	26.2	33.9	44.3
Net income ($ mil.)	–	(8.9)	(12.9)	(11.8)	(19.1)	(23.6)
Market value ($ mil.)	–	–	–	–	1,043.4	559.1
Employees	–	–	65	–	84	125

MAXIM HEALTHCARE SERVICES, INC.

7227 LEE DEFOREST DR
COLUMBIA, MD 210463236
Phone: 410 910-1500
Fax: –
Web: www.maximhealthcare.com

CEO: –
CFO: William Butz
HR: Jade Young-Rizzo
FYE: December 31
Type: Private

Maxim Healthcare Services aims to promote good health by offering home health care and related services in over 35 states in the US. The company offers private duty nursing, skilled nursing, physical rehabilitation, companion care, respite care, and behavioral care for individuals with chronic and acute illnesses and disabilities. It delivers patient care through private-duty nursing, at-home behavioral health care, and personal caregiving services. While the company specializes in caring for medically-fragile pediatric patients, it is expanding its focus on Applied Behavioral Analysis (ABA) therapy and companion care services, as well as launching technology to enable its nurses to document notes electronically. The company, which operates from more than 150 locations nationwide, was established in 1988.

	Annual Growth	12/11	12/12	12/13	12/14	12/15
Sales ($mil.)	6.2%	–	–	1,226.9	1,269.3	1,382.9
Net income ($ mil.)	–	–	–	(1.4)	4.7	11.7
Market value ($ mil.)	–	–	–	–	–	–
Employees	–	–	–	–	–	35,000

MAXIMUS INC.
NYS: MMS

1600 Tysons Boulevard
McLean, VA 22102
Phone: 703 251-8500
Fax: –
Web: www.maximus.com

CEO: –
CFO: –
HR: –
FYE: September 30
Type: Public

MAXIMUS is a leading operator of government health and human services programs worldwide. The company's primary portfolio of work is tied to business process services (BPS) in the health services and human services markets. The company provides Medicaid enrollment services in the US, as well as Children's Health Insurance Program (CHIP) services and state-based health insurance exchange operations. MAXIMUS partners with government agencies in the US, Australia, Canada, Saudi Arabia, Singapore, Italy, Sweden, South Korea, and the United Kingdom. MAXIMUS was founded in 1975. The company generates the majority of its sales in the US.

	Annual Growth	09/19	09/20	09/21	09/22	09/23
Sales ($mil.)	14.2%	2,886.8	3,461.5	4,254.5	4,631.0	4,904.7
Net income ($ mil.)	(9.5%)	240.8	214.5	291.2	203.8	161.8
Market value ($ mil.)	(0.8%)	4,712.7	4,172.9	5,075.0	3,530.0	4,555.3
Employees	7.5%	29,600	34,300	35,800	39,500	39,600

MAXITROL COMPANY

23555 TELEGRAPH RD
SOUTHFIELD, MI 480334176
Phone: 248 356-1400
Fax: –
Web: www.mertik.net

CEO: Bonnie Kern-Koskela
CFO: Christopher Kelly
HR: –
FYE: December 31
Type: Private

Maxitrol is a recognized international manufacturer of electronic gas modulation systems, gas pressure regulators/governors, combination gas control valves, gas safety devices, and gas filters under brand names including EXA Electronics and Selectra Electronics. Other products include combination, ball valves, air filters and air control system. Maxitrol's continues to develop innovative technology for the natural gas industry. In addition, the company continue to create and produced inventive products including the 325 series regulators and or use with 2 psi and 5 psi piping systems, the Selectra electronic gas flame modulation systems for direct and indirect fired heaters. Maxitrol was founded by Frank Kern Jr. in 1946, when he acquired Detroit Regulator Co., a small firm making gas pressure regulators.

MAXLINEAR INC
NMS: MXL

5966 La Place Court, Suite 100
Carlsbad, CA 92008
Phone: 760 692-0711
Fax: –
Web: www.maxlinear.com

CEO: Kishore Seendripu
CFO: Steven G Litchfield
HR: Kersten Rodriguez
FYE: December 31
Type: Public

MaxLinear is a provider of communications systems-on-chip (SoC) solutions used in broadband, mobile and wireline infrastructure, data center, and industrial and multi-market applications. It is a fabless integrated circuit design company whose products integrate all or substantial portions of a high-speed communication system, including integrated radio-frequency (RF), high-performance analog, mixed-signal, digital signal processing, security engines, data compression and networking layers, and power management. Its products are used in Television, set-top boxes, cable modems, automobiles, and personal computers. Its highly integrated semiconductor devices and platform-level solutions are primarily manufactured using low-cost CMOS process technology The company sells to electronics distributors, module makers, OEMs, distributors, and original design manufacturers (ODMs). Majority of its sales were generated from Asian customers.

	Annual Growth	12/19	12/20	12/21	12/22	12/23
Sales ($mil.)	21.6%	317.2	478.6	892.4	1,120.3	693.3
Net income ($ mil.)	–	(19.9)	(98.6)	42.0	125.0	(73.1)
Market value ($ mil.)	2.9%	1,736.2	3,124.6	6,168.3	2,777.7	1,944.8
Employees	26.0%	697	1,420	1,503	1,844	1,759

MAXOR NATIONAL PHARMACY SERVICES LLC

320 S POLK ST STE 900
AMARILLO, TX 791011429
Phone: 806 324-5400
Fax: –
Web: www.maxor.com

CEO: –
CFO: –
HR: –
FYE: December 31
Type: Private

Maxor National Pharmacy Services provides health care and pharmacy services including retail and mail order prescriptions (Maxor Pharmacies), pharmacy benefits management (MaxorPlus), pharmacy consulting (Maxor Pharmacy Consulting Services), and infusion and injection services (IVSolutions). The company operates about a dozen Maxor Pharmacy stores, mostly in Texas and Washington, but also in Colorado and New York. Its correctional division provides services to more than 330,000 offenders in more than 250 correctional facilities in 26 states through direct management contracts or via its pharmacy services division. Founded in 1926 as a single pharmacy in Amarillo, Maxor put itself up for sale in 2013.

	Annual Growth	12/04	12/05	12/06	12/07	12/09
Sales ($mil.)	17.2%	–	118.5	–	176.3	223.9
Net income ($ mil.)	–	–	–	–	–	–
Market value ($ mil.)	–	–	–	–	–	–
Employees	–	–	–	–	–	481

MAXUS REALTY TRUST INC
NBB: MRTI

104 Armour Road, P.O. Box 34729
North Kansas City, MO 64116
Phone: 816 303-4500
Fax: 816 221-1829
Web: www.mrti.com

CEO: David L Johnson
CFO: John W Alvey
HR: –
FYE: December 31
Type: Public

Maxus Realty Trust believes in the value of maximizing housing space. The real estate investment trust (REIT) invests in income-producing properties, primarily multifamily residential properties. It owns a portfolio of approximately 10 apartment communities in the Midwest US. Maxus Realty Trust was originally established to invest in office and light industrial facilities, but switched gears and began focusing on residential real estate in 2000. The REIT de-registered with the SEC and stopped trading on the NASDAQ in 2008.

	Annual Growth	12/17	12/18	12/19	12/20	12/21
Sales ($mil.)	10.8%	89.2	113.7	118.8	120.3	134.3
Net income ($ mil.)	1.7%	14.0	6.4	13.1	11.3	14.9
Market value ($ mil.)	10.7%	119.0	133.3	143.9	155.9	178.5
Employees	–	–	–	–	361	354

MAXX SPORTS TV INC
NBB: AMXX

444 West Fairmont
Tempe, AZ 85282
Phone: 480 968-1772
Fax: 480 894-1907
Web: www.resy.net

CEO: Dirk D Anderson
CFO: Kerrie Janik
HR: –
FYE: March 31
Type: Public

Banged up desks and broken filing cabinets get new lives through Reconditioned Systems. The company purchases used office furniture and workstations from brokers, dealers, manufacturers, and end users, and then refurbishes them for sale (both retail and wholesale). Reconditioned Systems, which specializes in reviving Haworth workstations, saves more than 1,000 tons of office furniture from landfills each year. In addition to its restoration activities, the firm offers furniture installation services. It supplies both the private sector and government agencies.

	Annual Growth	03/99	03/00	03/01	03/02	03/03
Sales ($mil.)	1.0%	11.0	10.9	14.3	8.3	11.5
Net income ($ mil.)	(53.2%)	1.1	0.7	0.9	(0.3)	0.1
Market value ($ mil.)	(7.7%)	3.4	4.1	3.8	2.8	2.5
Employees	8.9%	64	81	74	73	90

MAYER ELECTRIC SUPPLY COMPANY, INC.

3405 4TH AVE S
BIRMINGHAM, AL 352222300
Phone: 205 583-3500
Fax: –
Web: www.mayerelectric.com

CEO: Nancy C Goedecke
CFO: –
HR: –
FYE: January 02
Type: Private

Mayer Electric Supply helps to light up those southern nights. The company is one of the nation's largest distributors of electrical supplies, with about 50 branch locations in the southeastern US. It offers some 40,000 items made by leading manufacturers, such as 3M, GE, Littelfuse, and Schneider Electric. Products include conduit, circuit breakers, controls and switches, fire and safety products, LED and low-voltage lighting systems, motors, power tools, transformers, and wire and cable. Mayer Electric supplies customers in the construction, datacomm, government, industrial, and utility industries. The Collat family, including CEO Nancy Collat Goedecke, owns Mayer Electric.

	Annual Growth	12/16	12/17	12/18	12/19*	01/21
Sales ($mil.)	4.0%	–	911.4	1,072.0	1,138.1	1,067.0
Net income ($ mil.)	0.7%	–	11.2	11.6	14.1	11.5
Market value ($ mil.)	–	–	–	–	–	–
Employees	–	–	–	–	–	900

*Fiscal year change

MAYO CLINIC HEALTH SYSTEM - NORTHWEST WISCONSIN REGION, INC.

1221 WHIPPLE ST
EAU CLAIRE, WI 547035270
Phone: 715 838-3311
Fax: –
Web: www.mayoclinichealthsystem.org

CEO: –
CFO: –
HR: –
FYE: December 31
Type: Private

Cheeseheads experiencing blocked arteries or high cholesterol have Luther Midelfort - Mayo Health System on their side. The organization serves western Wisconsin, including Eau Claire and surrounding communities, through its Luther Hospital, Midelfort Clinic, and other facilities. The health care system has been part of the Mayo Clinic since 1992. Luther Hospital, founded in 1905, maintains more than 300 beds and specializes in comprehensive cardiac, trauma, and intensive care. The adjacent Midelfort Clinic houses more than 200 primary and specialty doctors' offices. The Luther Midelfort system also includes nearly a dozen community family care clinics, and provides pharmacy and home health services.

	Annual Growth	12/06	12/07	12/08	12/12	12/13
Sales ($mil.)	(9.8%)	–	–	514.6	253.5	307.7
Net income ($ mil.)	–	–	–	(4.4)	45.7	44.9
Market value ($ mil.)	–	–	–	–	–	–
Employees	–	–	–	–	–	1,290

MAYO CLINIC HEALTH SYSTEM-FRANCISCAN HEALTHCARE, INC.

700 WEST AVE S
LA CROSSE, WI 546014783
Phone: 608 785-0940
Fax: –
Web: www.mayoclinichealthsystem.org

CEO: Robert Nesse MD
CFO: Tom Tiggelaar
HR: Beth Dittbenner
FYE: December 31
Type: Private

St. Francis, friend to all living things, was also a caretaker of body, mind, and spirit, a philosophy still espoused at Franciscan Skemp Healthcare. Dually sponsored by Mayo Clinic and the Franciscan Sisters of Perpetual Adoration, the company operates as Mayo Clinic Health System Franciscan Healthcare. The community health system serves residents of northeastern Iowa, southeastern Minnesota, and western Wisconsin. Three hospitals in Wisconsin comprise the main facilities of the healthcare network -- the La Crosse campus, Sparta campus, and Arcadia campus. It also operates primary care clinics. Services include home healthcare, nursing homes, and tertiary care.

	Annual Growth	12/00	12/01	12/02	12/04	12/13
Sales ($mil.)	(53.4%)	–	–	321.3	250.6	0.0
Net income ($ mil.)	(36.3%)	–	–	9.6	9.9	0.0
Market value ($ mil.)	–	–	–	–	–	–
Employees	–	–	–	–	–	3,445

MAYO CLINIC HOSPITAL-ROCHESTER

200 1ST ST SW
ROCHESTER, MN 559050002
Phone: 507 284-2511
Fax: –
Web: www.mayoclinic.org

CEO: –
CFO: Dennis Dahlen
HR: Renae Syverson
FYE: December 31
Type: Private

Multidisciplinary teamwork with coordinated care is Mayo Clinic's secret sauce. The not-for-profit Mayo Clinic provides health care, most notably for complex medical conditions, through its clinics in Rochester, Minnesota, Arizona, and Florida. The clinics' multidisciplinary approach to care attracts more than a million patients a year from around the globe. For less specialized care, the Mayo Clinic Health System operates a regional network of affiliated community hospitals and clinics in Minnesota, Iowa, and Wisconsin. Mayo Clinic also conducts research and trains physicians, nurses, and other health professionals. The Mayo Clinic is named for Dr. William Worrall Mayo, who settled in Rochester in 1863.

MAYO CLINIC JACKSONVILLE (A NONPROFIT CORPORATION)

4500 SAN PABLO RD S
JACKSONVILLE, FL 322241865
Phone: 904 953-2000
Fax: –
Web: www.mayoclinic.org

CEO: Kent R Thielen
CFO: Mary J Hoffman
HR: Jorida M Mha
FYE: December 31
Type: Private

With more than 370 doctors and scientists on staff, Mayo Clinic Jacksonville offers a broad range of medical, surgical, and research services. The clinic, part of the larger Mayo Clinic network and one of its four major campuses, offers specialty services such as organ transplantation, neurology, and oncology therapy. Most patients provided care from the clinic are treated on an outpatient basis; those who require hospitalization are admitted to the adjacent Mayo Clinic Hospital, a 214-bed acute care facility. The Jacksonville campus also includes the Birdsall Medical Research center and the Griffin Cancer Research building.

	Annual Growth	12/08	12/09	12/13	12/15	12/16
Sales ($mil.)	6.2%	–	340.8	657.6	457.3	520.3
Net income ($ mil.)	–	–	(4.3)	(0.4)	65.3	94.8
Market value ($ mil.)	–	–	–	–	–	–
Employees	–	–	–	–	–	5,500

MAYS (J.W.), INC. — NAS: MAYS

9 Bond Street
Brooklyn, NY 11201
Phone: 718 624-7400
Fax: 718 935-0378
Web: www.jwmays.com

CEO: Lloyd J Shulman
CFO: –
HR: –
FYE: July 31
Type: Public

J. W. Mays can get you space in Brooklyn, as long as you're interested in offices and not bridges. The company owns and leases about 10 properties in and around New York City -- mostly former MAYS department stores -- and a warehouse in central Ohio. It leases its properties to retail, restaurant, commercial, and other tenants. The MAYS department store chain, founded in 1924 by Russian immigrant Joe Weinstein, closed in 1989 when management realized the New York real estate it occupied was worth more than the struggling discount retail business. Weinstein's descendants, including CEO Lloyd Shulman, control more than half of the company, although relations among the heirs have not always been harmonious.

	Annual Growth	07/19	07/20	07/21	07/22	07/23
Sales ($mil.)	2.5%	20.5	19.5	20.2	21.4	22.6
Net income ($ mil.)	–	1.5	(0.9)	0.4	(0.7)	(0.1)
Market value ($ mil.)	6.7%	70.7	39.9	77.3	90.3	91.5
Employees	0.9%	29	29	29	31	30

MAYVILLE ENGINEERING CO INC — NYS: MEC

715 South Street
Mayville, WI 53050
Phone: 920 387-4500
Fax: –
Web: www.mecinc.com

CEO: Jagadeesh A Reddy
CFO: Todd M Butz
HR: Andrea Norman
FYE: December 31
Type: Public

Sometimes it's all right to get loaded. Mayville Engineering Company (MEC) manufactures shotshell reloading machinery and equipment, used by hunters, sport shooting enthusiasts, and sporting goods stores. MEC also provides coating, welding, riveting, painting, manufacturing, prototyping, and mechanical assembly services. Its operations are divided across the main divisions of MEC Tube, MEC Coatings, MEC Fabrication, and MEC Shooting Sports. Overall, these divisions cater to the agricultural, construction, military, medical, and industrial markets.

	Annual Growth	12/19	12/20	12/21	12/22	12/23
Sales ($mil.)	3.2%	519.7	357.6	454.8	539.4	588.4
Net income ($ mil.)	–	(4.8)	(7.1)	(7.5)	18.7	7.8
Market value ($ mil.)	11.4%	190.5	272.6	302.8	257.1	292.9
Employees	(1.0%)	2,600	2,150	2,200	2,300	2,500

MBC HOLDINGS, INC.

1613 S DEFIANCE ST
ARCHBOLD, OH 435029488
Phone: 419 445-1015
Fax: –
Web: www.mbcholdings.net

CEO: –
CFO: –
HR: –
FYE: December 31
Type: Private

These are brothers heavy in the midwestern construction business. MBC Holdings is the parent company of heavy and civil construction firm Miller Bros. Construction (also known as Team Miller). The firm specializes in highway contracting, commercial and industrial construction, and paving, as well as earthwork and excavation, working primarily in Ohio, Michigan, Indiana, and Kentucky. Other subsidiaries include aggregates specialists Cardinal Aggregate; and steel contractors Sawyer Steel Erectors, Wymer Steel, and DeWitt Rebar. Brothers Dale and Floyd Miller started the family-owned company in 1945.

	Annual Growth	12/03	12/04	12/05	12/06	12/09
Sales ($mil.)	6.3%	–	–	69.8	97.0	89.2
Net income ($ mil.)	–	–	–	0.8	6.0	(1.7)
Market value ($ mil.)	–	–	–	–	–	–
Employees	–	–	–	–	–	721

MBI, INC.

501 MERRITT 7 FL 4
NORWALK, CT 068517002
Phone: 203 853-2000
Fax: –
Web: www.mbi-inc.com

CEO: Peter Maglathlin
CFO: Michael Wilbur
HR: –
FYE: December 31
Type: Private

Privately-owned MBI aims to hit the heartstrings of America in easy-to-arrange monthly installments. The direct marketing company offers a multitude of collectible items that range from porcelain Betty Boop figurines and plush teddy bears to official First Day of Issue covers for new US stamps, die-cast sports cars, jewelry, and leather-bound book collections. The items are generally accompanied by monthly payment plans. MBI creates and markets more than 500 new products each year under its Danbury Mint, The Easton Press, and PCS Stamps & Coins divisions. It is one of the leading magazine advertisers in the US and has a mailing list of more than 10 million names. MBI was founded in 1969 by chairman Ted Stanley.

MBIA INC. — NYS: MBI

1 Manhattanville Road, Suite 301
Purchase, NY 10577
Phone: 914 273-4545
Fax: –
Web: www.mbia.com

CEO: William C Fallon
CFO: Anthony McKiernan
HR: –
FYE: December 31
Type: Public

MBIA's operating subsidiaries are focused on running off their insured portfolios. The holding company's independent subsidiary, National Public Finance Guarantee Corporation, is a provider of insurance for municipal bonds and stable corporate bonds, including tax-exempt and taxable indebtedness of US political subdivisions and territories, as well as utilities, airports, health care institutions, higher educational facilities, housing authorities, and other similar agencies and obligations issued by private entities that finance projects that serve a substantial public purpose. Separately, its MBIA Insurance Corporation's insured portfolio consists of policies that insure various types of international public finance and global structured finance obligations that were sold in the new issue and secondary markets.

	Annual Growth	12/19	12/20	12/21	12/22	12/23
Assets ($mil.)	(22.7%)	7,284.0	5,751.0	4,696.0	3,375.0	2,606.0
Net income ($ mil.)	–	(359.0)	(578.0)	(445.0)	(195.0)	(491.0)
Market value ($ mil.)	(9.9%)	473.0	334.7	803.1	653.6	311.3
Employees	(10.0%)	93	89	87	75	61

MCAFEE CORP.

6220 AMERICA CENTER DR
SAN JOSE, CA 950022563
Phone: 866 622-3911
Fax: –
Web: www.mcafee.com

CEO: Peter Leav
CFO: Jennifer Biry
HR: –
FYE: December 25
Type: Private

Mcafee Corp. is a worldwide leader in online protection. Its solutions adapt to its customers' needs and empower them to confidently experience life online through integrated, easy-to-use solutions. The company delivers comprehensive protection to safeguard people's privacy and identity in addition to its award-winning antivirus. Its smart technology helps people effortlessly navigate risks, make smarter decisions, and take charge of their personal information. Its technology can be purchased online and from retail stores or through cell phone carriers, internet service providers (ISPs), device makers, or other McAfee partners. The company provides its products to roughly 110 million customers on their over 600 million devices.

	Annual Growth	12/17	12/18	12/19	12/20	12/21
Sales ($mil.)	(33.9%)	–	–	–	2,906.0	1,920.0
Net income ($ mil.)	–	–	–	–	(289.0)	2,688.0
Market value ($ mil.)	–	–	–	–	–	–
Employees	–	–	–	–	–	2,262

MCAP INC (NEW)

108 Village Square, Suite 315
Somers, NY 10589
Phone: 914 669-5333
Fax: –
Web: www.mangosoft.com

NBB: MCAP
CEO: Dennis M Goett
CFO: Charles Montecino
HR: –
FYE: December 31
Type: Public

MCAP Inc. is focused on technology-driven financial services. The company has three subsidiaries, such as MCAP Technologies LLC, MBIT LLC and MCAP LLC. MCAP Technologies LLC is a financial technology company that develops software utilized in various financial markets. It also provides institutional customers with customized trading solutions and global market access. MBIT LLC is a digital asset company focused on crypto-currency, Decentralized Finance (DeFi) protocols and blockchain integration in the global financial markets. The company's subsidiary MCAP LLC is a broker-dealer focused on electronic securities market making. In addition, the subsidiary connects institutional investors, broker-dealers and companies to the global equity and fixed income markets.

	Annual Growth	12/06	12/07	12/08	12/09	12/10
Sales ($mil.)	–	0.3	0.3	2.6	0.1	–
Net income ($ mil.)	–	0.1	(0.8)	0.6	(0.1)	(0.4)
Market value ($ mil.)	–	–	–	–	–	–
Employees	68.2%	1	1	1	1	8

MCCARTHY BUILDING COMPANIES, INC.

12851 MANCHESTER RD
SAINT LOUIS, MO 631311802
Phone: 314 968-3300
Fax: –
Web: www.mccarthy.com

CEO: Raymond Sedey
CFO: Kristin Newman
HR: Emily Willard
FYE: December 31
Type: Private

McCarthy Building Companies is one of the top privately-held builders in the US. It has a long history of building facilities that drive greater value. From exceptional levels of quality and safety ? to ease of maintenance over time, it is firmly committed to helping its clients and partners achieve the short- and long-term strategic goals of every project it does. Contracts include heavy construction projects and transportation expertise (bridges and highways and road construction), commercial projects (retail and office buildings), and more. Founded by Timothy McCarthy in 1864, the company is 100% employee owned.

	Annual Growth	12/18	12/19	12/20	12/21	12/22
Sales ($mil.)	5.7%	–	4,513.1	4,706.4	4,374.3	5,334.7
Net income ($ mil.)	–	–	–	–	–	–
Market value ($ mil.)	–	–	–	–	–	–
Employees	–	–	–	–	–	6,465

MCCLOSKEY MECHANICAL CONTRACTORS, INC.

445 LOWER LANDING RD
BLACKWOOD, NJ 080125110
Phone: 856 784-5080
Fax: –
Web: www.mccloskeymechanical.com

CEO: Dennis McCloskey Sr
CFO: –
HR: –
FYE: December 31
Type: Private

McCloskey Mechanical knows how to duct and cover. Running duct work and laying pipe are only a couple of the tasks performed by the plumbing and HVAC contractor that works for commercial customers in seven northeastern states. Working from offices in Massachusetts and New Jersey, it does remodel and design/build work on everything from parking garages and hospitals to hotels and shopping malls. McCloskey Mechanical has worked on projects for Temple University, Gucci, Apple, the US Air Force, and Swarovski. CEO David McCloskey Sr. formed the company in New Jersey in 1985; it expanded into Maryland in 2007.

MCCORMICK & CO INC

24 Schilling Road, Suite 1
Hunt Valley, MD 21031
Phone: 410 771-7301
Fax: 410 771-7462
Web: www.mccormickcorporation.com

NYS: MKC
CEO: Lawrence E Kurzius
CFO: Michael R Smith
HR: Lisa Corona
FYE: November 30
Type: Public

McCormick & Company is one of the world's leading spice makers that offers a broad assortment of herbs, spices, seasonings, flavorings, sauces, and extracts. McCormick distributes and markets its products under brands including Lawry's, Club House, and McCormick, as well as ethnic labels Zatarain's, Thai Kitchen, and Simply Asia and regional brands Ducros and Schwartz. Its products are sold to customers spanning the entire food industry, from food retailers to food service businesses and industrial food manufacturers. McCormick operates in some 160 countries throughout the world but generates more than 70% of sales in the Americas region.

	Annual Growth	11/19	11/20	11/21	11/22	11/23
Sales ($mil.)	5.6%	5,347.4	5,601.3	6,317.9	6,350.5	6,662.2
Net income ($ mil.)	(0.8%)	702.7	747.4	755.3	682.0	680.6
Market value ($ mil.)	(21.3%)	45,376	50,129	23,008	22,837	17,381
Employees	2.7%	12,400	13,000	14,000	14,200	13,800

MCCOY-ROCKFORD, INC.

6869 OLD KATY RD
HOUSTON, TX 770242105
Phone: 713 862-4600
Fax: –
Web: www.mccoyrockford.com

CEO: Stan Bunting
CFO: –
HR: Crystal Arevalo
FYE: December 31
Type: Private

McCoy-Rockford (formerly known as McCoy Workplace Solutions) is the premier, single source provider of products and services for commercial interior spaces in a variety of sectors throughout Texas, including corporate, education, small business, and healthcare. It supplies desks, chairs, tables, lighting, architectural and demountable walls, and floor coverings. Carries over 200 product lines, the company's primary furniture manufacturing partner, Steelcase, is the global leader in commercial office furniture. McCoy also provides services such as furniture rental, installation, maintenance and repair, and project management.

	Annual Growth	12/04	12/05	12/06	12/07	12/08
Sales ($mil.)	14.4%	–	–	92.5	102.3	121.1
Net income ($ mil.)	29.9%	–	–	1.8	1.0	3.1
Market value ($ mil.)	–	–	–	–	–	–
Employees	–	–	–	–	–	275

MCDANIEL COLLEGE, INC.

2 COLLEGE HL
WESTMINSTER, MD 211574390
Phone: 410 848-7000
Fax: –
Web: www.mcdaniel.edu

CEO: –
CFO: –
HR: –
FYE: May 31
Type: Private

McDaniel College's predecessor school was a true pioneer, being the first coeducational institution south of the Mason-Dixon Line, and among the first in the nation. McDaniel College is a four-year private university offering undergraduate and graduate studies in liberal arts and sciences. Its 1,600 undergraduate students may choose from 23 majors, and can even opt to study abroad at its campus in Budapest, Hungary. McDaniel College has a faculty of 149 professors; 96% hold the most advanced degrees in their disciplines. Some 90% of undergraduate classes are taught by full-time faculty with Ph.D.s.

	Annual Growth	06/15	06/16	06/17	06/18*	05/19
Sales ($mil.)	(6.5%)	–	–	74.0	74.3	64.7
Net income ($ mil.)	(43.7%)	–	–	9.5	10.2	3.0
Market value ($ mil.)	–	–	–	–	–	–
Employees	–	–	–	–	–	500

*Fiscal year change

MCDONALD'S CORP

NYS: MCD

110 North Carpenter Street
Chicago, IL 60607
Phone: 630 623-3000
Fax: –
Web: www.mcdonalds.com

CEO: Christopher Kempczinski
CFO: Ian Borden
HR: –
FYE: December 31
Type: Public

McDonald's Corporation franchises and operates McDonald's restaurants, which serve a locally relevant menu of quality food and beverages in communities across more than 100 countries. The company has over 40,000 restaurants at the end of 2022. The popular chain is well-known for its Big Macs, Quarter Pounders, McDonald's Fries, McFlurry desserts and Chicken McNuggets. The company's main market includes Australia, Canada, France, Germany, Italy, the Netherlands, Russia, Spain and the U.K. More than half of revenues are generated outside the US.

	Annual Growth	12/19	12/20	12/21	12/22	12/23
Sales ($mil.)	4.9%	21,077	19,208	23,223	23,183	25,494
Net income ($ mil.)	8.9%	6,025.4	4,730.5	7,545.2	6,177.4	8,468.8
Market value ($ mil.)	10.7%	142,813	155,077	193,734	190,453	214,288
Employees	(7.5%)	205,000	200,000	200,000	150,000	150,000

MCDONOUGH COUNTY HOSPITAL DISTRICT

525 E GRANT ST
MACOMB, IL 614553313
Phone: 309 833-4101
Fax: –
Web: www.mdh.org

CEO: Kenny Boyd
CFO: Bill Murdock
HR: Christina Brown
FYE: June 30
Type: Private

It may be small, but that doesn't keep McDonough District Hospital (MDH) from serving the health care needs of patients throughout west-central Illinois. The not-for-profit MDH is an acute care facility with 48 beds. The hospital provides general medical, emergency, and surgical services, as well as specialty care including behavioral health, cancer, cardiopulmonary, dialysis, nutritional, pediatric, and women's health services. The hospital also offers home health and hospice programs. It has a medical staff of physicians representing a range of specialties. MDH opened its doors in 1958 with 25 beds.

	Annual Growth	06/17	06/18	06/19	06/20	06/21
Sales ($mil.)	13.1%	–	–	0.6	0.8	0.7
Net income ($ mil.)	–	–	–	(3.2)	0.0	0.3
Market value ($ mil.)	–	–	–	–	–	–
Employees	–	–	–	–	–	600

MCG-HJT, INC.

510 S GRAND AVE STE 300
GLENDORA, CA 917414207
Phone: 626 564-2227
Fax: –
Web: www.mcgarchitecture.com

CEO: Scott Hoffland
CFO: –
HR: –
FYE: June 30
Type: Private

MCG Architects (which does business as MCG Architecture) specializes in designing and planning shopping centers and other retail buildings, as well as urban renewal projects and hotels. The firm provides consulting, surveying, site analysis, cost control, computer-aided design, and project management services; it also offers interior and graphic design services. Projects include the Centennial Centre in Las Vegas; Independence Corporate Center in Cleveland; and Natomas Town Center in Sacramento, California.

	Annual Growth	06/96	06/97	06/98	06/99	06/08
Sales ($mil.)	4.1%	–	–	14.5	24.2	21.6
Net income ($ mil.)	–	–	–	1.4	0.1	(0.0)
Market value ($ mil.)	–	–	–	–	–	–
Employees	–	–	–	–	–	53

MCGOUGH CONSTRUCTION CO., LLC

2737 FAIRVIEW AVE N
SAINT PAUL, MN 551131307
Phone: 651 633-5050
Fax: –
Web: www.mcgough.com

CEO: Thomas McGough Jr
CFO: –
HR: Andrea Malloyjohnson
FYE: December 31
Type: Private

McGough Construction Company is a full-service, full-solution construction resource company that provides support at every level of development. The nationally recognized general contractor in commercial construction provides construction services ranging from site acquisition to post-construction facility management. McGough Construction concentrates on commercial, residential, and civic projects through its five primary units: construction; preconstruction; strategic planning; development (logistics, project management, zoning); and facility management. Peter McGough and his six sons incorporated the family-owned and operated company in 1956.

MCGRATH RENTCORP

NMS: MGRC

5700 Las Positas Road
Livermore, CA 94551-7800
Phone: 925 606-9200
Fax: –
Web: www.mgrc.com

CEO: –
CFO: –
HR: –
FYE: December 31
Type: Public

McGrath RentCorp is a diversified business-to-business rental company with four rental divisions: relocatable modular buildings, portable storage containers, electronic test equipment, and liquid and solid containment tanks and boxes. Through subsidiaries, the company rents and sells electronic equipment. Its largest segment is Mobile Modular, which rents portable buildings used as classrooms, field offices, health care clinics, or rest rooms. Other subsidiaries such as TRS-RenTelco rents and sells electronic test equipment used in the aerospace, defense, communications, semiconductor, and manufacturing industries, while Enviroplex makes and sells modular buildings used in California public schools. Adler Tank Rentals provides containers used for storing hazardous and nonhazardous materials. The company traces its roots back to 1979.

	Annual Growth	12/18	12/19	12/20	12/21	12/22
Sales ($mil.)	10.2%	498.3	570.2	572.6	616.8	733.8
Net income ($ mil.)	9.7%	79.4	96.8	102.0	89.7	115.1
Market value ($ mil.)	17.7%	1,255.5	1,866.7	1,636.4	1,957.4	2,408.1
Employees	3.4%	1,066	1,099	1,061	1,184	1,218

MCKEE WALLWORK & COMPANY, LLC

701 SPUR ST NE STE B
ALBUQUERQUE, NM 871026001
Phone: 505 821-2999
Fax: –
Web: www.mckeewallwork.com

CEO: –
CFO: –
HR: –
FYE: December 31
Type: Private

Ad agency McKee Wallwork Cleveland specializes in providing advertising and marketing services for growing companies. The agency offers planning, creative ad development, and media services for companies such as The Albuquerque Convention and Visitors Bureau; Heritage Hotels & Resorts; the University of New Mexico, and Mr. Rooter. Its portfolio includes work in television, radio, print, outdoor ads, Web marketing, and direct mail. The company changed its name from McKee Wallwork Henderson in 2005 after the departure of creative director Carol Henderson.

MCKESSON CORP

6555 State Highway 161
Irving, TX 75039
Phone: 972 446-4800
Fax: –
Web: www.mckesson.com

NYS: MCK
CEO: Brian S Tyler
CFO: Britt J Vitalone
HR: –
FYE: March 31
Type: Public

McKesson is a top global pharmaceutical distributor. The company delivers prescription and generic drugs, as well as health and beauty care products, to retail and institutional pharmacies worldwide. The company is also a major medical supplies wholesaler, providing medical and surgical equipment to alternate health care sites such as doctors' offices, surgery centers, and long-term care facilities. In addition to distribution, McKesson offers management, consulting, and technology services that help customers navigate supply chain, clinical, administrative, and financial operations. McKesson was founded in 1833.

	Annual Growth	03/19	03/20	03/21	03/22	03/23
Sales ($mil.)	6.6%	214,319	231,051	238,228	263,966	276,711
Net income ($ mil.)	219.9%	34.0	900.0	(4,539.0)	1,114.0	3,560.0
Market value ($ mil.)	32.1%	15,920	18,395	26,525	41,634	48,423
Employees	(10.6%)	80,000	80,000	76,000	75,000	51,000

MCLANE COMPANY, INC.

4747 MCLANE PKWY
TEMPLE, TX 765044854
Phone: 254 771-7500
Fax: –
Web: www.mclaneco.com

CEO: Anthoney Frankenberger
CFO: Chad Rice
HR: Doreen Shuta
FYE: December 30
Type: Private

McLane Company is one of the largest wholesale suppliers of grocery and food products in the US, serving 46,000 retail locations. It buys, sells, and delivers more than 50,000 consumer products to customers and nearly 110,000 locations across the US, such as convenience and discount stores, mass merchandisers, wholesale clubs, and drug stores. Through McLane Grocery and McLane Foodservice, the company operates over 80 distribution centers and is one of the nation's largest private fleets. In addition, McLane provides spirits, wine, beer, and nonalcoholic beverages distribution through its subsidiary, Empire Distributors, Inc. McLane is a wholly owned unit of Berkshire Hathaway Inc.

	Annual Growth	01/08	01/09*	12/12*	01/16*	12/16
Sales ($mil.)	7.1%	–	29,800	37,390	48,145	48,016
Net income ($ mil.)	–	–	–	–	–	–
Market value ($ mil.)	–	–	–	–	–	–
Employees	–	–	–	–	–	25,000

*Fiscal year change

MCLAREN BAY REGION

1900 COLUMBUS AVE
BAY CITY, MI 487086880
Phone: 989 894-3000
Fax: –
Web: www.mclaren.org

CEO: Darrell Lentz
CFO: Sean Fischer
HR: –
FYE: September 30
Type: Private

McLaren Bay Region provides a full range of medical services for the residents at the tip of Saginaw Bay in eastern Michigan. A part of McLaren Health Care, the hospital's main campus has more than 400 beds and provides general medical and surgical care, as well as specialty care in areas such as cardiovascular disease, neuroscience, oncology, rehabilitation, orthopedics, and women's health. It also features an emergency room and Level II trauma center, and provides home health and hospice care. A second campus, McLaren Bay Special Care Hospital, is a long-term acute care hospital serving patients requiring hospital stays of longer than 25 days. The regional provider also provides outpatient and home health services.

	Annual Growth	09/18	09/19	09/20	09/21	09/22
Sales ($mil.)	1.7%	–	351.9	292.8	317.9	369.8
Net income ($ mil.)	6.6%	–	22.0	15.5	64.6	26.7
Market value ($ mil.)	–	–	–	–	–	–
Employees	–	–	–	–	–	1,800

MCLAREN HEALTH CARE CORPORATION

1 MCLAREN PKWY
GRAND BLANC, MI 484397471
Phone: 810 342-1100
Fax: –
Web: www.mclaren.org

CEO: Philip A Incarnati
CFO: David Mazurkiewicz
HR: Kim Matelski
FYE: September 30
Type: Private

McLaren Health Care is where people in The Auto State go for repairs. The health care system includes some 300 facilities, including a dozen regional hospitals and a network of cancer, dialysis, imaging, and surgery centers across the state of Michigan. Combined, its facilities have about 2,900 beds and serve more than 50 counties. Through its subsidiaries, McLaren manages a primary care physician network, commercial and Medicaid HMOs, and assisted living facilities, and provides visiting nurse/home health care and hospice services. Its Great Lakes Cancer Institute provides cancer research and treatment with partner Michigan State University.

	Annual Growth	09/07	09/08	09/15	09/21	09/22
Sales ($mil.)	10.8%	–	84.5	187.1	329.0	353.2
Net income ($ mil.)	(0.3%)	–	4.1	19.6	(16.4)	3.9
Market value ($ mil.)	–	–	–	–	–	–
Employees	–	–	–	–	–	10,003

MCLAREN MACOMB

1000 HARRINGTON ST
MOUNT CLEMENS, MI 480432920
Phone: 586 493-8000
Fax: –
Web: www.mclaren.org

CEO: Thomas M Brisse
CFO: –
HR: –
FYE: September 30
Type: Private

Mount Clemens Regional Medical Center (doing business as McLaren Medical Center-Macomb) is an general acute care hospital serving the Macomb County area of suburban Detroit. With about 290 beds, the hospital offers such specialties as cardiac and cancer care, family practice services, home and hospice care, and emergency care. The McLaren Health Care-controlled company also operates three prompt care centers in nearby townships as well as a wound treatment clinic. Of the more than 420 physicians on staff at the hospital, more than 100 are family medicine and internal medicine specialists who provide primary care.

	Annual Growth	09/18	09/19	09/20	09/21	09/22
Sales ($mil.)	0.8%	–	410.3	323.8	361.4	420.0
Net income ($ mil.)	(18.9%)	–	46.6	46.8	69.4	24.9
Market value ($ mil.)	–	–	–	–	–	–
Employees	–	–	–	–	–	2,249

MCLOONE METAL GRAPHICS, INC.

75 SUMNER ST
LA CROSSE, WI 546033132
Phone: 608 784-1260
Fax: –
Web: www.mcloone.com

CEO: –
CFO: –
HR: –
FYE: December 31
Type: Private

Mcloone Metal Graphics (MMG) designs and prints specialty marketing and labeling materials such as nameplates, decals, overlays, and signs. MMG (aka Mcloone) provides graphic design and fulfillment services in addition to its custom printing services. The company was founded in 1954 by James E. Mcloone and is now a subsidiary of JSJ Corporation.

	Annual Growth	12/05	12/06	12/07	12/08	12/09
Sales ($mil.)	(8.7%)	–	13.4	15.0	12.9	10.2
Net income ($ mil.)	(21.3%)	–	1.2	1.5	0.8	0.6
Market value ($ mil.)	–	–	–	–	–	–
Employees	–	–	–	–	–	130

MCMASTER-CARR SUPPLY COMPANY

600 N COUNTY LINE RD
ELMHURST, IL 601262081
Phone: 630 834-9600
Fax: –
Web: www.mcmaster.com

CEO: Robert Delaney
CFO: –
HR: Allison Thomas
FYE: November 16
Type: Private

McMaster-Carr Supply distributes mechanical, electrical, and utility products, including air conditioners, clamps and drills, exhaust fans, generators, light bulbs, pipes, pumps, saws, switches, and valves. McMaster-Carr operates five regional branches in Atlanta, Chicago, Cleveland, Los Angeles, and New Jersey, which provide customer service and sales. More than 95% of its items ship from stock and most orders arrive same or next day. The company offers its products through its website and mobile app.

MCNAUGHTON-MCKAY ELECTRIC CO.

1357 E LINCOLN AVE
MADISON HEIGHTS, MI 480714126
Phone: 248 399-7500
Fax: –
Web: www.mc-mc.com

CEO: Mark C Borin
CFO: John D Kuczmanski
HR: Adrienne Myrand
FYE: December 31
Type: Private

McNaughton-McKay is a wholesale distributor of electrical supplies serving markets in Michigan, Ohio, Georgia, North Carolina and South Carolina. One of the 100% employee-owned companies in the US, McNaughton-McKay distributes an array of product lines from manufacturers such as nVent Hoffman, Sylvania, Panduit, Appleton, Sola HD, and Rockwell Automation, to name a few. It is a full-line electrical distributor of products ranging from pipe and wire to complex automation control systems for everyone from small electrical contractors to large-scale manufacturers. It sells to the construction, lighting, motion, networking, and industrial automation markets.

	Annual Growth	12/18	12/19	12/20	12/21	12/22
Sales ($mil.)	13.0%	–	1,515.3	1,335.2	1,651.5	2,186.2
Net income ($ mil.)	–	–	–	–	–	–
Market value ($ mil.)	–	–	–	–	–	–
Employees	–	–	–	–	–	1,800

MCNEESE STATE UNIVERSITY

4205 RYAN ST
LAKE CHARLES, LA 706054500
Phone: 337 475-5000
Fax: –
Web: www.mcneese.edu

CEO: –
CFO: –
HR: –
FYE: June 30
Type: Private

Founded in 1939 as Lake Charles Junior College, McNeese State is one of nine schools in the University of Louisiana System. Its more than 7,285 enrolled students can choose from more than 250 majors, minors and certificate programs, as well as nearly 20 graduate programs offered at colleges of business, education, science, engineering and mathematics, liberal arts, agricultural science, nursing and & health professions, the Division of General and Basic Studies, and the William J. Dor , Sr. School of Graduate Studies. Its campus consists of nearly 80 buildings over approximately 1,560 acres. The roughly 120-acre main campus features approximately 50 buildings, including the three original structures ? Kaufman Hall, Ralph O. Ward Memorial Gym (the Arena), and Francis G. Bulber Auditorium. The university is named for Louisiana educator John McNeese.

	Annual Growth	06/17	06/18	06/19	06/21	06/22
Sales ($mil.)	1.3%	–	58.4	61.6	46.9	61.5
Net income ($ mil.)	14.5%	–	19.4	15.1	71.5	33.4
Market value ($ mil.)	–	–	–	–	–	–
Employees	–	–	–	–	–	894

MCNICHOLS COMPANY

2502 N ROCKY POINT DR STE 750
TAMPA, FL 336071421
Phone: 877 884-4653
Fax: –
Web: www.mcnichols.com

CEO: –
CFO: Craig A Stein
HR: –
FYE: December 31
Type: Private

McNichols Company manufactures metal products that are full of holes ... by design. Its products include perforated and expanded metals, wire mesh, bar and plank gratings, fiberglass grating, floorings, handrail components, ladder rungs, and mattings. Its perforated metal (aka "hole") products are sold under the brand names Eco-Mesh, Grate-Lock, Perf-O-Grip, Safplate, and Vinylmesh, among many others. The company also provides custom fabrication services. McNichols operates is business through some 20 service centers nationwide. It was founded in 1952 by the late Robert McNichols, grandfather of current president Scott McNichols. The McNichols family runs the firm based on Christian principles.

	Annual Growth	12/05	12/06	12/07	12/08	12/09
Sales ($mil.)	(13.0%)	–	–	185.8	209.4	140.8
Net income ($ mil.)	–	–	–	7.8	3.7	–
Market value ($ mil.)	–	–	–	–	–	–
Employees	–	–	–	–	–	400

MCPHEE ELECTRIC, LTD

505 MAIN ST
FARMINGTON, CT 060322912
Phone: 860 677-9797
Fax: –
Web: www.phalconusa.com

CEO: Michael McPhee
CFO: John Conroy
HR: –
FYE: December 31
Type: Private

McPhee Electric is energized about its work. The company, which is a unit of Phalcon, provides electrical construction and data and communications installation services (including cellular towers) throughout New England. Services include conceptual planning, feasibility studies, budgeting, design development, installation, maintenance, and service. McPhee Electric's clients come from a wide variety of industries including education, financial services, government, health care, manufacturing, pharmaceuticals, retail, and utilities. The company's projects include utility substations, Foxwoods Resort Casino, a Bristol-Myers Squibb research facility, and Cordon Bleu Culinary Institute.

	Annual Growth	12/15	12/16	12/17	12/18	12/19
Sales ($mil.)	0.7%	–	142.0	148.4	114.6	144.9
Net income ($ mil.)	(5.4%)	–	17.2	19.4	20.6	14.6
Market value ($ mil.)	–	–	–	–	–	–
Employees	–	–	–	–	–	500

MCRAE INDUSTRIES, INC.

NBB: MCRA A

400 North Main Street, P.O. Box 1239
Mount Gilead, NC 27306
Phone: 910 439-6147
Fax: –
Web: www.mcraeindustries.com

CEO: D Gary Mc Rae
CFO: Kelly Franklin
HR: –
FYE: July 29
Type: Public

McRae Industries has interests ranging from bar codes to boots. The company's footwear segment, consisting of subsidiaries McRae Footwear and Dan Post Boot Co., makes combat boots for the US and foreign militaries, Western boots, and work boots. Dan Post Boot markets and distributes boot brands Laredo, Dingo, John Deere, and Dan Post. A third subsidiary, Compsee, makes bar code readers, printers, and optical data-collection equipment. Compsee also licenses and sells computer software worldwide. McRae Industries makes most of its money from the Western and work boot segment. The McRae family controls more than 50% of the company's voting power.

	Annual Growth	08/19	08/20*	07/21	07/22	07/23
Sales ($mil.)	11.0%	82.2	69.3	82.2	124.8	124.7
Net income ($ mil.)	39.7%	2.1	(0.1)	3.4	10.2	8.1
Market value ($ mil.)	13.6%	59.3	41.0	72.1	90.4	98.9
Employees	–	–	–	–	–	–

*Fiscal year change

MCSHANE CONSTRUCTION COMPANY LLC

9500 BRYN MAWR AVE STE 200
ROSEMONT, IL 600185257
Phone: 847 292-4300
Fax: –
Web: www.mcshaneconstruction.com

CEO: James McShane
CFO: –
HR: Colleen Magruder
FYE: September 30
Type: Private

Design/build construction firm McShane Construction Company plans, executes, and closes out construction projects in the Midwest, Southeast, Southwest, and the West Coast of the US. The firm specializes in building for markets including health care, hospitality, industrial, institutional, multi-unit residential, office, and retail. Best known for its education and industrial process facilities, McShane has worked for clients such as Notre Dame, Ford, and General Mills. Established in 1984 by CEO James McShane, the company is a part of The McShane Companies, which also includes Texas-based Cadence McShane Construction.

MCSHANE DEVELOPMENT COMPANY LLC

9500 BRYN MAWR AVE STE 300
ROSEMONT, IL 600185211
Phone: 847 292-4300
Fax: –
Web: www.mcshanerealestate.com

CEO: James McShane
CFO: –
HR: Jennifer Werneke
FYE: December 31
Type: Private

McShane Development Company invests in and develops office, health care, and industrial real estate throughout the US. It offers build-to-suit development as well as redevelopment and turnkey projects; most of its portfolio is located in Illinois. McShane Development also plans multifamily and business park projects. The company is the investment arm of The McShane Companies, which also includes McShane Construction and Cadence McShane Construction. McShane Corporation has offices in Austin and Houston, Texas; Chicago; Irvine, California; and Phoenix. CEO James McShane founded the company in 1988.

	Annual Growth	09/01	09/02	09/03	09/05*	12/08
Assets ($mil.)	(44.4%)	–	26.9	22.4	27.5	0.8
Net income ($ mil.)	–	–	–	–	–	–
Market value ($ mil.)	–	–	–	–	–	–
Employees	–	–	–	–	–	300

*Fiscal year change

MDU RESOURCES GROUP INC

NYS: MDU

1200 West Century Avenue, P.O. Box 5650
Bismarck, ND 58506-5650
Phone: 701 530-1000
Fax: –
Web: www.mdu.com

CEO: David L Goodin
CFO: Jason L Vollmer
HR: Bonnie Taylor
FYE: December 31
Type: Public

MDU Resources provides essential products and services through its regulated energy delivery and construction materials and services businesses. The company, through its wholly owned subsidiary, MDU Energy Capital, owns Montana-Dakota, Cascade and Intermountain. The electric segment is comprised of Montana-Dakota while the natural gas distribution segment is comprised of Montana-Dakota, Cascade and Intermountain. The company, through its subsidiary, Centennial, owns WBI Energy, Knife River, MDU Construction Services and Centennial Capital. WBI Energy is the pipeline segment, Knife River is the construction materials and contracting segment, MDU Construction Services is the construction services segment, and Centennial Capital is reflected in the Other category.

	Annual Growth	12/18	12/19	12/20	12/21	12/22
Sales ($mil.)	11.4%	4,531.6	5,336.8	5,532.8	5,680.7	6,973.9
Net income ($ mil.)	7.8%	272.3	335.5	390.2	378.1	367.5
Market value ($ mil.)	6.2%	4,854.4	6,049.7	5,363.5	6,279.8	6,177.9
Employees	6.1%	11,797	13,359	12,994	12,826	14,929

MEALS ON WHEELS AMERICA

1550 CRYSTAL DR STE 1004
ARLINGTON, VA 222024142
Phone: 703 548-5558
Fax: –
Web: www.mealsonwheelsamerica.org

CEO: Ellie Hollander
CFO: Don Lermer
HR: Teresa Carpenter
FYE: December 31
Type: Private

Meals on Wheels Association of America (MOWAA) helps to fuel programs throughout the US that deliver meals to people who are elderly, homebound, disabled, or otherwise at risk of going hungry. It provides information, via conferences and newsletters, and tools, including bulk purchasing services, to Meals on Wheels programs that are members of the association. MOWAA also works to obtain government grants and distribute money to local meal delivery programs. The Meals on Wheels concept was developed in the UK during WWII and introduced in the US in 1954.

	Annual Growth	12/18	12/19	12/20	12/21	12/22
Sales ($mil.)	21.0%	–	12.0	71.3	23.8	21.3
Net income ($ mil.)	174.8%	–	0.0	24.0	0.1	0.5
Market value ($ mil.)	–	–	–	–	–	–
Employees	–	–	–	–	–	32

MECHANICS' INSTITUTE

57 POST ST FL 3
SAN FRANCISCO, CA 941045002
Phone: 415 393-0117
Fax: –
Web: www.milibrary.org

CEO: –
CFO: –
HR: –
FYE: August 31
Type: Private

Don't expect to find someone to fix your car at The Mechanics Institute. Dedicated to cultural and educational advancement, the Mechanics' Institute provides members with a variety of services, activities, and resources from its San Francisco location. The Institute maintains the oldest library on the West Coast and one of the oldest chess clubs in the US. It was founded in 1855 when San Francisco was a frontier town. The institute served as a social hub and center for adult education for a community with no established technical education system; holding vocational classes for local mechanics and manufacturers.

	Annual Growth	08/12	08/13	08/15	08/16	08/22
Sales ($mil.)	(12.2%)	–	4.4	2.5	2.5	1.4
Net income ($ mil.)	–	–	1.7	(0.4)	(0.4)	(0.9)
Market value ($ mil.)	–	–	–	–	–	–
Employees	–	–	–	–	–	22

MECKLERMEDIA CORP

50 Washington Street, Suite 902
Norwalk, CT 06854
Phone: 212 389-2000
Fax: –
Web: –

CEO: –
CFO: –
HR: –
FYE: December 31
Type: Public

If your brand isn't on the Web, WebMediaBrands wants to help. The company provides digital content, education, job listings, events, and other resources for media, creative, and design professionals. Its flagship Mediabistro network of websites targets the media industry, including digital and print publishing, advertising, television, and public relations markets. Its AllCreativeWorld reaches creative and design professionals through websites such as Graphics.com and Creativebits. WebMediaBrands also offers community, membership, and e-commerce offerings such as a freelance listing service and a marketplace for designing and purchasing logos. Chairman and CEO Alan Meckler owns about 40% of WebMediaBrands.

	Annual Growth	12/10	12/11	12/12	12/13	12/14
Sales ($mil.)	(20.7%)	9.0	12.4	14.0	12.5	3.6
Net income ($ mil.)	–	(3.0)	(11.9)	(8.7)	(5.7)	(3.8)
Market value ($ mil.)	(27.3%)	9.8	2.9	12.2	19.2	2.7
Employees	(28.5%)	69	74	121	94	18

MEDAILLE COLLEGE FOUNDATION, INC.

18 AGASSIZ CIR
BUFFALO, NY 142142601
Phone: 716 880-2000
Fax: –
Web: www.medaille.edu

CEO: –
CFO: –
HR: Bobbie Bilotta
FYE: June 30
Type: Private

Medaille College is a private New York State liberal arts college that provides career-oriented education. With a student enrollment of more than 2,500, the school offers bachelor's, master's, and associate degrees in a range of subjects through day, evening, and weekend programs. Fields of study include business, biology, communication, criminal justice, education, psychology, and veterinary technology. Medaille traces its roots to 1875, when it was founded by the Sisters of St. Joseph as an institute to educate teachers. In 1937 the institute received a charter from New York State and was named Mount St. Joseph Teachers College. The school expanded its mission and earned its current name in 1968.

	Annual Growth	06/18	06/19	06/20	06/21	06/22
Sales ($mil.)	2.3%	–	–	36.7	36.3	34.9	39.4
Net income ($ mil.)	–	–	–	(0.6)	(2.3)	(0.4)	(1.5)
Market value ($ mil.)	–	–	–	–	–	–
Employees	–	–	–	–	–	693

MEDAIRE INC

80 East Rio Salado Parkway, Suite 610
Tempe, AZ 85281
Phone: 480 333-3700
Fax: 480 333-3592
Web: www.medaire.com

CEO: Bill Dolny
CFO: –
HR: –
FYE: December 31
Type: Public

MedAire can help you in a medical emergency in the air, on land, or at sea. The firm provides emergency medical training, equipment and remote medical advice for the aviation and maritime industries. It also provides medical kits and training for non-medical professionals -- such as flight and maritime crews -- that includes CPR certification, as well as practice with wound management, IV fluids, injections, and other medical emergencies in remote situations. MedAire's Global Response Center provides logistics support for medical evacuations, prescription replacement, and other services to commercial airlines and business travelers. The company is owned by global medical services firm International SOS.

	Annual Growth	12/03	12/04	12/05	12/06	12/07
Sales ($mil.)	15.1%	17.5	25.4	28.4	30.1	30.7
Net income ($ mil.)	–	(1.2)	(1.1)	(0.4)	(1.6)	2.8
Market value ($ mil.)	2.8%	49.0	27.1	35.8	36.4	54.8
Employees	–	–	–	–	173	–

MEDALLION FINANCIAL CORP

NMS: MFIN

437 Madison Avenue, 38th Floor
New York, NY 10022
Phone: 212 328-2100
Fax: –
Web: www.medallion.com

CEO: –
CFO: –
HR: –
FYE: December 31
Type: Public

Medallion Financial turns taxicab licenses, or "medallions," into gold. The specialty finance company makes loans for the purchase of medallions, which are usually limited in number per city by law. It targets mainly New York City, but also finances medallions in Boston and Cambridge, Massachusetts; Chicago; and Newark, New Jersey. (A NYC taxi medallion costs more than $1 million.) Subsidiary Medallion Bank funds its taxi and commercial lending activities by issuing certificates of deposit to clients; it also originates loans for boats, trailers, motorcycles, and RVs. Other subsidiaries, including Medallion Capital and Freshstart Venture Capital, offer commercial loans ranging from $200,000 to $5 million.

	Annual Growth	12/19	12/20	12/21	12/22	12/23
Assets ($mil.)	13.8%	1,541.7	1,642.4	1,873.1	2,259.9	2,587.8
Net income ($ mil.)	129.2%	2.0	(34.8)	54.1	43.8	55.1
Market value ($ mil.)	7.9%	170.5	114.9	136.0	167.4	231.0
Employees	(3.0%)	191	187	136	158	169

MEDIA SCIENCES INTERNATIONAL, INC.

203 RIDGE RD
GOSHEN, NY 109245307
Phone: 201 236-1100
Fax: –
Web: –

CEO: –
CFO: Denise Hawkins
HR: –
FYE: June 30
Type: Private

Media Sciences International supports the art, science, and business of printing. The company makes printing supplies for color business printers. Its products include solid ink sticks designed for printers from a variety of manufacturers, including Brother, Dell, Konica Minolta, Oki Data, Ricoh, Samsung, Seiko Epson, and Xerox. Through its INKlusive program, Media Sciences supplies customers with color printers for a monthly fee that covers the price of ink supplies; the program requires a multiyear commitment. Media Sciences sells directly and through reseller channels, primarily in the US.

MEDIA STORM, LLC

160 VARICK ST FL 10
NEW YORK, NY 100131220
Phone: 212 941-4470
Fax: –
Web: www.mediastorm.biz

CEO: –
CFO: –
HR: –
FYE: December 31
Type: Private

Media Storm is a rainmaker looking to bring a deluge. The company provides media planning and buying services for television, radio, print, and interactive channels. Media Storm creates showers of customers primarily for clients in the entertainment industry; it specializes in audience acquisition for broadcasters, cable networks, pay-per-view companies, and television program syndicators. Customers have included such big names as HBO, NBCUniversal, Food Network, Twentieth Century Fox, and the NFL. The company also drives traffic and memberships for e-commerce client Shopzilla. Managing partners Tim Williams and Craig Woerz created Media Storm in 2001.

	Annual Growth	12/03	12/04	12/05	12/06	12/07
Sales ($mil.)	50.5%	–	36.5	80.9	114.4	124.3
Net income ($ mil.)	40.8%	–	3.8	7.1	10.1	10.6
Market value ($ mil.)	–	–	–	–	–	–
Employees	–	–	–	–	–	170

MEDIANEWS GROUP, INC.

101 W. Colfax
Denver, CO 80202
Phone: 303 954-6360
Fax: 303 894-9327
Web: www.medianewsgroup.com

CEO: Steve Rossi
CFO: Michael Koren
HR: –
FYE: June 30
Type: Public

MediaNews Group counts some notable newspapers among its fold. The company operates some 60 daily newspapers, serving markets in about a dozen states. Its portfolio includes The Denver Post, the St. Paul Pioneer Press, and the San Jose Mercury News. Altogether, MediaNews publications boast a combined daily circulation of 2.3 million; Sunday circulation is about 2.5 million. It operates websites for all of its newspapers, hosted and supported by its MediaNews Group Interactive division. As part of its business, it owns a CBS affiliate TV station in Anchorage, Alaska, and four radio stations in Texas. Holding company Affiliated Media, which owns MediaNews, entered then later emerged from bankruptcy in 2010.

	Annual Growth	06/03	06/04	06/05	06/06	06/07
Sales ($mil.)	15.8%	738.6	753.8	779.3	835.9	1,329.8
Net income ($ mil.)	(3.3%)	40.8	27.6	39.9	1.1	35.6
Market value ($ mil.)	–	–	–	–	–	–
Employees	4.4%	10,700	10,000	10,000	10,100	12,700

MEDICAL INFORMATION TECHNOLOGY, INC.

7 BLUE HILL RIVER RD
CANTON, MA 020211001
Phone: 781 821-3000
Fax: –
Web: ehr.meditech.com

CEO: Howard Messing
CFO: Barbara A Manzolillo
HR: –
FYE: December 31
Type: Private

Medical Information Technology (MEDITECH) develops electronic healthcare record (EHR) software for hospitals, clinics, physician practices, and other medical care providers. The company's software interacts with other functions including scheduling and billing. Its web-based MEDITECH Expanse platform allows an organization to gather information about patients from throughout the care continuum including specialties such as oncology. It also has the capability to gather data about patient groups to improve care.

MEDICAL PROPERTIES TRUST INC   NYS: MPW

1000 Urban Center Drive, Suite 501
Birmingham, AL 35242
Phone: 205 969-3755
Fax: 205 969-3756
Web: www.medicalpropertiestrust.com

CEO: Edward K Aldag Jr
CFO: R S Hamner
HR: –
FYE: December 31
Type: Public

Hospitals Trust Medical Properties is a self-advised real estate investment trust (REIT) formed in 2003 to acquire and develop net-leased healthcare facilities. It has investments in more than 435 facilities and approximately 46,000 licensed beds in over 30 states in the US, in six countries in Europe, across Australia, and in Colombia in South America. Its facilities consist of more than 205 general acute care hospitals, 110 inpatient rehabilitation hospitals (IRFs), about 20 long-term acute care hospitals (LTACHs), more than 40 freestanding ER/urgent care facilities (FSERs), and nearly 60 behavioral health facilities.

	Annual Growth	12/19	12/20	12/21	12/22	12/23
Sales ($mil.)	0.5%	854.2	1,249.2	1,544.7	1,542.9	871.8
Net income ($ mil.)	–	374.7	431.5	656.0	902.6	(556.5)
Market value ($ mil.)	(30.6%)	12,645	13,052	14,154	6,672.8	2,941.0
Employees	–	–	86	106	112	119	–

MEDICINOVA INC   NMS: MNOV

4275 Executive Square, Suite 300
La Jolla, CA 92037
Phone: 858 373-1500
Fax: –
Web: www.medicinova.com

CEO: Yuichi Iwaki
CFO: Edward C Stepanow Jr
HR: –
FYE: December 31
Type: Public

MediciNova has medicine all over the map. The biopharmaceutical company has a diverse pipeline of products in development that aim to treat everything from asthma and cancer to anxiety and insomnia. Two of its core candidates are being clinically tested for use in the treatment of severe asthma and multiple sclerosis. Others are being developed for preterm labor, interstitial cystitis (urinary frequency and bladder pain), and urinary incontinence. MediciNova has been building its development portfolio through licensing agreements, acquiring product rights primarily from midsized Japanese pharmaceutical companies such as Kissei Pharmaceutical, Kyorin Pharmaceutical, and Mitsubishi Tanabe Pharma Corporation.

	Annual Growth	12/19	12/20	12/21	12/22	12/23
Sales ($mil.)	–	–	–	4.0	–	1.0
Net income ($ mil.)	–	(12.9)	(13.9)	(10.1)	(14.1)	(8.6)
Market value ($ mil.)	(31.3%)	330.6	258.0	131.4	100.5	73.6
Employees	12.9%	8	9	11	13	13

MEDIDATA SOLUTIONS, INC.

350 HUDSON ST
NEW YORK, NY 100144504
Phone: 212 918-1800
Fax: –
Web: www.medidata.com

CEO: Tarek A Sherif
CFO: Rouven Bergmann
HR: Allison Falzone
FYE: December 31
Type: Private

Medidata Solutions has electronic remedies to help clinical trials run smoothly. The company is leading the digital transformation of life sciences, creating hope for millions of patients. Medidata assists to generate the evidence and insights to help pharmaceutical, biotech, medical device, diagnostic companies and academic researchers to accelerate value, minimize risk and optimize outcomes. In addition, the company serves more than 2,000 customers. Tarek Sheriff, Glen de Vries, and Dr. Edward Ikeguchi founded the company in 1999. Medidata is a wholly owned subsidiary of Dassault System.

MEDIFAST INC   NYS: MED

100 International Drive
Baltimore, MD 21202
Phone: 410 581-8042
Fax: –
Web: www.medifastinc.com

CEO: Daniel R Chard
CFO: James Maloney
HR: Faith U Ms
FYE: December 31
Type: Public

Medifast is the global company behind one of the fastest-growing health and wellness communities called OPTAVIA, which offers Lifelong Transformation, One Healthy Habit at a Time. Medifast help clients to achieve their health goals through a network of more than 60,900 independent OPTAVIA Coaches, approximately 90% of whom were clients first, and have impacted almost 2.0 million lives to date. OPTAVIA Coaches introduce clients to a set of healthy habits, in most cases starting with the habit of healthy eating, and offer exclusive OPTAVIA-branded nutritional products, or Fuelings. Fuelings are nutrient-dense, portion-controlled, nutritionally interchangeable and simple to use.

	Annual Growth	12/19	12/20	12/21	12/22	12/23
Sales ($mil.)	10.7%	713.7	934.8	1,526.1	1,598.6	1,072.1
Net income ($ mil.)	6.3%	77.9	102.9	164.0	143.6	99.4
Market value ($ mil.)	(11.5%)	1,194.0	2,139.3	2,281.9	1,256.9	732.4
Employees	3.6%	550	713	984	874	634

MEDISYS HEALTH NETWORK INC.

8900 VAN WYCK EXPY
JAMAICA, NY 114182832
Phone: 718 206-6000
Fax: –
Web: www.jamaicahospital.org

CEO: Bruce Flanz
CFO: Mounir F Doss
HR: –
FYE: December 31
Type: Private

Feeling queasy in Queens? MediSys Health Network's got a cure for what ails you. The health system encompasses two not-for-profit general hospitals located in the New York City borough of Queens: Jamaica Hospital Medical Center and Flushing Hospital Medical Center. The hospitals collectively house some 700 acute care beds and 300 long-term care and psychiatric beds. The system features level I trauma, brain injury, psychotherapy, stroke, transition, and rehabilitation units. MediSys also operates a network of family health care clinics and home health agencies.

	Annual Growth	12/13	12/14	12/17	12/21	12/22
Sales ($mil.)	3.6%	–	5.2	3.9	4.6	6.8
Net income ($ mil.)	(5.6%)	–	1.5	0.4	0.2	1.0
Market value ($ mil.)	–	–	–	–	–	–
Employees	–	–	–	–	–	3,000

MEDIVATION, INC.

525 MARKET ST STE 2800
SAN FRANCISCO, CA 941052736
Phone: 415 543-3470
Fax: –
Web: www.pfizer.com

CEO: David T Hung
CFO: Jennifer Jarrett
HR: –
FYE: December 31
Type: Private

Medivation motivates medicine makers. The company acquires, develops, and sells (or partners with companies working on) biopharmaceuticals. Medivation initiates drug development programs, seeking out candidates that address unmet medical needs and have the potential to rapidly enter clinical development and marketing stages. The firm typically develops its drug candidates through early-stage clinical trials, and then determines whether to conduct further studies or to seek a partner or buyer to continue later-stage trials. Medivation's lead product, the blockbuster Xtandi, treats certain forms of prostate cancer; the drug was developed in partnership with Astellas. Pfizer bought Medivation for $14 billion in 2016.

MEDLER ELECTRIC COMPANY

2155 REDMAN DR
ALMA, MI 488019313
Phone: 989 463-1108
Fax: –
Web: www.medlerelectric.com

CEO: –
CFO: –
HR: –
FYE: December 31
Type: Private

No meddlers here; this company just wants to help customers. Medler Electric Company is a distributor of electrical parts and supplies; it gets the majority of its business from companies in the construction market. Medler Electric carries products (ranging from motors and heaters to lighting and much more) from such manufacturers as 3M, Cooper Lighting, Daniel Woodhead, Ferraz Shawmut, Littelfuse, and Square D Company. The employee-owned company was established in 1918 by W. W. Medler and operates through 14 branch offices in the state of Michigan.

	Annual Growth	12/13	12/14	12/15	12/16	12/17
Sales ($mil.)	3.5%	–	–	45.7	43.3	49.0
Net income ($ mil.)	(8.8%)	–	–	0.0	0.0	0.0
Market value ($ mil.)	–	–	–	–	–	–
Employees	–	–	–	–	–	111

MEDLEY STEEL AND SUPPLY, INC.

9925 NW 116TH WAY
MEDLEY, FL 331781101
Phone: 305 863-7480
Fax: –
Web: www.medleysteel.com

CEO: –
CFO: –
HR: –
FYE: December 31
Type: Private

Service center Medley Steel and Supply processes and distributes steel products such as angles, beams, channels, flat bars and strips, pipe, plate and sheets, and tubing. The company's inventory includes products made from aluminum, alloys, stainless steel, and tool steels. Medley Steel and Supply distributes its products in South Florida, the Caribbean, and Latin America. The company was founded in 1978.

	Annual Growth	12/07	12/08	12/09	12/10	12/11
Sales ($mil.)	(6.6%)	–	16.1	9.3	11.0	13.1
Net income ($ mil.)	(16.3%)	–	1.4	0.6	0.4	0.8
Market value ($ mil.)	–	–	–	–	–	–
Employees	–	–	–	–	–	29

MEDLINE INDUSTRIES, LP

3 LAKES DR
NORTHFIELD, IL 600932753
Phone: 847 949-2645
Fax: –
Web: www.medline.com

CEO: –
CFO: –
HR: –
FYE: December 31
Type: Private

Medline is a healthcare company; a manufacturer, distributor, and solutions provider focused on improving the overall operating performance of healthcare. Partnering with healthcare systems and facilities across the continuum of care, Medline provides the clinical and supply chain resources required for long-term financial viability in delivering high-quality care. The company has a fleet of more than 1,600 trucks and does business in more than 125 countries worldwide including locations in the Americas, Caribbean, Europe, Asia, Africa and the Middle East. The company was founded in 1966.

MEDLINK INTERNATIONAL INC

NBB: MLKN A

1 Roebling Court
Ronkonkoma, NY 11779
Phone: 631 342-8800
Fax: –
Web: www.medlinkus.com

CEO: –
CFO: –
HR: –
FYE: December 31
Type: Public

MedLink helps bridge the communication gap for hospitals. The company offers answering services and access to an Internet-based network (called the MedLink VPN) that gives small and medium-sized medical facilities quick access to medical records, test results, and scheduling applications. Its electronic health record service (MedLink EHR) offers automated patient-centric data, while its K-Rad Konsulting unit handles IT consulting services. The company provides direct-to-consumer testing through its LabTestPortal business. MedLink depends on a handful of customers, including New York-based New Island Hospital and several radiology centers in California. Chairman and CEO Ray Vuono owns 29% of MedLink.

	Annual Growth	12/06	12/07	12/08	12/09	12/10
Sales ($mil.)	379.3%	0.0	0.3	0.5	0.5	6.0
Net income ($ mil.)	–	(1.6)	(2.5)	(4.4)	(3.8)	0.2
Market value ($ mil.)	29.7%	16.7	71.4	46.6	24.3	47.1
Employees	32.6%	11	29	25	34	34

MEDSTAR HEALTH, INC.

10980 GRANTCHESTER WAY
COLUMBIA, MD 210446097
Phone: 410 772-6500
Fax: -
Web: www.medstarhealth.org

CEO: Kenneth A Samet
CFO: Michael J Curran
HR: Ashley Handwerk
FYE: June 30
Type: Private

MedStar Health is a not-for-profit, regional healthcare system based in Columbia, Maryland, and one of the largest employers in the region. MedStar Health runs ten hospitals and about 35 other health-related businesses across Maryland and the Washington, DC area. MedStar Health has one of the largest graduate medical education programs in the country, training about 1,150 medical residents annually, and is the medical education and clinical partner of Georgetown University. With more than 31,000 physicians, nurses, and many other clinical and non-clinical associates, MedStar has a comprehensive service offering, including emergency services, home health care, and rehabilitation.

	Annual Growth	06/18	06/19	06/20	06/21	06/22
Sales ($mil.)	8.6%	–	5,690.4	5,788.6	6,725.5	7,279.2
Net income ($ mil.)	–	–	187.9	136.4	774.9	(199.3)
Market value ($ mil.)	–	–	–	–	–	–
Employees	–	–	–	–	–	33,000

MEDSTAR-GEORGETOWN MEDICAL CENTER, INC.

3800 RESERVOIR RD NW
WASHINGTON, DC 200072113
Phone: 202 444-2000
Fax: -
Web: www.medstarhealth.org

CEO: –
CFO: Pipper Williams
HR: Mary J Schweickhardt
FYE: June 30
Type: Private

Medstar-Georgetown Medical Center (dba as Medstar Georgetown University Hospital as a part of MedStar Health) is a 609-bed acute care teaching hospital serving residents of the greater Washington, DC, area, including Maryland and Virginia. The hospital's staff of more than 1,100 physicians represents a wide range of medical specializations including cardiology, oncology, neurology/neurosurgery, and surgical transplantation. Medstar Georgetown provides a comprehensive array of inpatient, outpatient, surgical, and rehabilitative care services. The hospital is part of a local network of affiliated primary care providers.

	Annual Growth	06/09	06/10	06/11	06/15	06/16
Sales ($mil.)	0.4%	–	782.5	809.1	774.6	801.8
Net income ($ mil.)	15.0%	–	45.4	43.7	98.1	104.8
Market value ($ mil.)	–	–	–	–	–	–
Employees	–	–	–	–	–	4,000

MEGA MATRIX CORP

ASE: MPU

3000 El Camino Real, Bldg. 4, Suite 200
Palo Alto, CA 94306
Phone: 650 340-1888
Fax: -
Web: www.megamatrix.io

CEO: Michael G Magnusson
CFO: Harold M Lyons
HR: –
FYE: December 31
Type: Public

With a high-flyin' inventory, AeroCentury leases used turboprop aircraft and engines to domestic and foreign regional airlines and other commercial customers. The company buys equipment from an airline, and then either leases it back to the seller, buys assets already under lease and assumes the obligations of the seller, or makes a purchase and then immediately enters into a new lease with a third-party lessee (when it has a customer committed to a lease). Typically, lessees are responsible for any maintenance costs. AeroCentury owns over 40 aircraft, mainly deHavilland and Fokker models. Almost 90% of the company's lease revenues come from airlines headquartered outside the US.

	Annual Growth	12/20*	09/21*	12/21	12/22	12/23
Sales ($mil.)	(85.6%)	16.2	5.6	0.5	1.9	0.0
Net income ($ mil.)	–	(42.2)	18.8	(4.2)	(8.5)	(4.1)
Market value ($ mil.)	(49.2%)	341.0	2,091.9	1,894.0	55.8	44.7
Employees	–	–	9	–	4	–

*Fiscal year change

MEGATECH CORP.

NBB: MGTC

555 Woburn Street
Tewksbury, MA 01876
Phone: 978 937-9600
Fax: 978 453-9936
Web: www.megatechcorp.com

CEO: Vahan V Basmajian V
CFO: –
HR: Phil Ferguson
FYE: December 31
Type: Public

When auto mechanics need to tune up their skills, they turn to Megatech Corporation. The company offers automotive instructional programs and training equipment for students and professional technicians to schools, training centers, and the US military. Courses consist of computer-based instruction and hands-on practice. The company provides programs in areas such as gasoline automobile engines, diesel truck engines, diesel marine engines, alternative fuel engines, hydraulics, electronics, and transmissions, among others. Megatech was founded in 1971.

	Annual Growth	12/99	12/00	12/01	12/02	12/03
Sales ($mil.)	15.3%	1.8	2.1	1.8	3.1	3.2
Net income ($ mil.)	150.9%	0.0	0.0	0.0	0.1	0.0
Market value ($ mil.)	17.7%	0.5	0.3	0.3	0.6	0.9
Employees	(5.4%)	15	–	9	16	12

MEHERRIN AGRICULTURAL & CHEMICAL CO

413 MAIN ST
SEVERN, NC 278779901
Phone: 252 585-1744
Fax: -
Web: www.meherrinag.com

CEO: G D Barnes Jr
CFO: Jeff Vinson
HR: –
FYE: July 31
Type: Private

Meherrin Agricultural & Chemical sells farmers what they need to produce peanuts, which the company's subsidiaries then buy, process, and sell. Farm supplies offered by Meherrin Agricultural & Chemical include seeds, fertilizers, crop protectants, and other agricultural chemicals. The company also offers seeds for a variety of other crops. The company also offers services such as field services, fertilizer application, seed treatment, and financing. Meherrin Agricultural & Chemical was founded in 1958.

MEIJER, INC.

2929 WALKER AVE NW
GRAND RAPIDS, MI 495449428
Phone: 616 453-6711
Fax: -
Web: www.meijer.com

CEO: Hank Meijer
CFO: Brad Freiburger
HR: Sue Kitzmiller
FYE: January 31
Type: Private

Meijer (pronounced "Meyer") is a retail giant in the Midwest. With more than 600 varieties of high-quality fresh produce, including organic and exotic fruits delivered straight from the farm, the company also offers over 220,000 products at affordable prices, including fresh groceries, housewares, apparel, sporting goods, seasonal items and more. The company's in-store pharmacies offer free prescription programs, clinical services, walk-in immunizations, and diabetes specialists. Most stores also sell gasoline, offer banking services, and have multiple in-store restaurants. Meijer operates supercenters in six states. Founder Hendrik Meijer opened his first store in 1934; the business is still family owned and run.

MELALEUCA, INC.

4609 W 65TH S
IDAHO FALLS, ID 834026003
Phone: 208 522-0700
Fax: -
Web: www.melaleuca.com

CEO: Frank L Vandersloot
CFO: -
HR: Renee Meier
FYE: December 31
Type: Private

Melaleuca is one of the largest online retailers in North America. Manufactures and sells more than 400 health and wellness products, the company reaches more than 2 million households each month in about 20 countries and territories. Its exclusive household products span the categories of nutrition, personal care, eco-friendly home cleaners, cosmetics, and more. These products are marketed through a global network of independent sales representatives and through Melaleuca's website. It has business primarily across North America, and also in Europe, the Middle East, and Asia Pacific. The company was founded in 1985 to market a tea tree oil formulation called Melaleuca Oil.

MELINTA THERAPEUTICS, LLC

389 INTERPACE PKWY STE 450
PARSIPPANY, NJ 070541132
Phone: 844 633-6568
Fax: -
Web: www.melinta.com

CEO: -
CFO: -
HR: -
FYE: December 31
Type: Private

Melinta Therapeutics, LLC provides innovative therapies to people impacted by acute and life-threatening illnesses. Its portfolio currently includes six commercial-stage products: Baxdela (delafloxacin), Kimyrsa (oritavancin), Minocin (minocycline) for Injection, Orbactiv (oritavancin), TOPROL-XL (metoprolol succinate) and Vabomere (meropenem and vaborbactam). Melinta also has a licensing agreement in place with Cidara Therapeutics securing the rights to market and distribute development candidate rezafungin in the US. TOPROL-XL is a registered trademark of the AstraZeneca group of companies.

MELROSEWAKEFIELD HEALTHCARE PARENT CORPORATION

170 GOVERNORS AVE
MEDFORD, MA 021551643
Phone: 781 979-3000
Fax: -
Web: www.hallmarkhealth.org

CEO: Pamela Whelton
CFO: -
HR: -
FYE: September 30
Type: Private

Hallmark Health sends its very best -- health care -- to residents living in the suburbs north of Boston. The system includes the Lawrence Memorial and Melrose-Wakefield hospitals, which together have about 324 beds. The hospitals provide a full range of health services including primary, diagnostic, surgical, and rehabilitative care. The Hallmark network (which has more than 700 physicians) also includes the Malden Medical Center (radiology, laboratory, and dialysis services), family health clinics, physician offices, long-term health care facilities, and home health services. Physicians-in-training are supported through a family practice residency program offered in association with Tufts University.

	Annual Growth	09/12	09/13	09/14	09/15	09/20
Sales ($mil.)	(19.3%)	-	-	-	6.3	2.2
Net income ($ mil.)	-	-	-	-	(2.3)	(0.3)
Market value ($ mil.)	-	-	-	-	-	-
Employees	-	-	-	-	-	2,700

MEMORIAL BEHAVIORAL HEALTH CENTER IN SPRINGFIELD

701 N 1ST ST
SPRINGFIELD, IL 627810001
Phone: 217 788-3000
Fax: -
Web: www.memorial.health

CEO: -
CFO: -
HR: -
FYE: September 30
Type: Private

If you've lost the spring in your step and need a little care, Memorial Medical Center will be there. As the flagship facility for Memorial Health System in Springfield, Illinois, this acute care and teaching hospital provides a wide range of medical and surgical services as well as emergency medicine and outpatient care. Its myriad specialties include cardiovascular, maternity, cancer care, behavioral health, orthopedic, rehabilitation, and burn treatment services. The hospital, which sees 25,000 inpatients per year, also has special surgical divisions for bariatric procedures and organ transplants. The 500-bed hospital is a teaching affiliate of the Southern Illinois University (SIU) School of Medicine.

	Annual Growth	09/17	09/18	09/19	09/20	09/21
Sales ($mil.)	-	-	711.3	734.8	647.7	710.6
Net income ($ mil.)	31.9%	-	58.8	(13.0)	39.7	135.0
Market value ($ mil.)	-	-	-	-	-	-
Employees	-	-	-	-	-	1,311

MEMORIAL HEALTH SERVICES

17360 BROOKHURST ST STE 160
FOUNTAIN VALLEY, CA 927083720
Phone: 714 377-2900
Fax: -
Web: www.memorialcare.org

CEO: -
CFO: Aaron Coley
HR: Darcel Noble
FYE: June 30
Type: Private

Memorial Health is a community-based, not-for-profit organization that provides a full range of inpatient, outpatient, home health, hospice, behavioral health and primary care physician services. It has affiliations with Decatur Memorial Hospital, Jacksonville Memorial Hospital, Lincoln Memorial Hospital, Memorial Behavioral Health, Memorial Care, Memorial Health care, Springfield Memorial Hospital and Taylorville Memorial Hospital. Memorial Health was founded in 1897, with the opening of the Springfield Hospital and Training School. The institution was founded by a group of German Lutherans.

	Annual Growth	06/18	06/19	06/20	06/21	06/22
Sales ($mil.)	3.3%	-	2,438.8	2,556.1	2,580.9	2,688.5
Net income ($ mil.)	-	-	209.0	(52.4)	770.4	(249.2)
Market value ($ mil.)	-	-	-	-	-	-
Employees	-	-	-	-	-	6,000

MEMORIAL HEALTH SYSTEM

701 N 1ST ST
SPRINGFIELD, IL 627810001
Phone: 217 788-3000
Fax: -
Web: www.memorial.health

CEO: Edgar J Curtis
CFO: -
HR: Adele Long
FYE: September 30
Type: Private

Memorial Health System provides the people of Central Illinois with health care services through three community-based, not-for-profit hospitals, as well as home health and primary care operations. Flagship facility Memorial Medical Center in Springfield, with some 500 licensed beds, provides comprehensive inpatient and outpatient acute-care services and conducts medical education and research programs. Two smaller hospitals -- Taylorville Memorial Hospital and Abraham Lincoln Memorial Hospital -- each with 25 beds serve the communities of Taylorville and Lincoln. Other operations include a hospice and home health care services provider, a mental health organization, and a primary care physician network.

	Annual Growth	09/18	09/19	09/20	09/21	09/22
Sales ($mil.)	9.8%	-	85.3	-	82.6	112.8
Net income ($ mil.)	-	-	(2.7)	-	(17.6)	(5.7)
Market value ($ mil.)	-	-	-	-	-	-
Employees	-	-	-	-	-	2,400

MEMORIAL HEALTH SYSTEM OF EAST TEXAS

1201 W FRANK AVE
LUFKIN, TX 759043357
Phone: 936 634-8111
Fax: –
Web: www.stlukeshealth.org

CEO: Bryant H Krenek Jr
CFO: Ken Miller
HR: –
FYE: June 30
Type: Private

Memorial Health System of East Texas operates deep in the heart of East Texas. The system is anchored by the 270-bed Memorial Medical Center-Lufkin, a full-service general acute care hospital offering everything from rehabilitative and diabetes care to specialized centers in heart disease and cancer treatment. The Lufkin hospital also includes Memorial Specialty Hospital, a long-term ward for critically ill patients. In addition, Memorial Health System of East Texas features two critical access hospitals with limited services including emergency care and diagnostic imaging; it also has a clinic network. It is part of non-profit health care systems operator Catholic Health Initiatives (CHI).

	Annual Growth	06/18	06/19	06/20	06/21	06/22
Sales ($mil.)	1.3%	–	161.5	157.4	154.3	168.0
Net income ($ mil.)	–	–	(2.9)	1.9	(8.9)	(0.4)
Market value ($ mil.)	–	–	–	–	–	–
Employees	–	–	–	–	–	940

MEMORIAL HERMANN HEALTHCARE SYSTEM

929 GESSNER RD STE 2600
HOUSTON, TX 770242593
Phone: 713 242-3000
Fax: –
Web: www.memorialhermann.org

CEO: –
CFO: Stacey Bevil
HR: Garrett Chelsey
FYE: June 30
Type: Private

Memorial Hermann Healthcare System is an integrated health system and known for excellent clinical expertise, patient centered care, leading edge technology for innovation. As Houston's largest not-for-profit health care system, it includes 17 hospitals with more than 4,386 beds and seven convenient care centers. The system also has joint ventures with three hospitals in the Greater Houston metropolitan. Memorial Hermann provides medical training in affiliation with The University of Texas Health Science Center Medical School. Other services and programs include home health services, air ambulances, and imaging; it also offers retirement community and nursing home. Memorial Health Provides HMO and PPO for employers group and Advantage HMO plan.

MEMORIAL HOSPITAL

1101 MICHIGAN AVE
LOGANSPORT, IN 469471596
Phone: 574 753-7541
Fax: –
Web: www.logansportmemorial.org

CEO: –
CFO: Barret Rhoads
HR: –
FYE: December 31
Type: Private

If your Eel River boat has been sunk by a Wabash cannonball, you're probably a short crawl from a hospital. Logansport Memorial Hospital is a 80-bed acute care regional medical center serving the residents of Cass County and the surrounding communities in north central Indiana. The hospital offers a full range of medical services and programs, including primary and emergency care, and specialized services in areas such as diabetes, cardiac rehabilitation, medical imaging, respiratory therapy, and mammography. Logansport Memorial Hospital has about 40 physicians on its active medical staff. The hospital opened in 1925 as the Cass County Hospital and changed its name to Memorial Hospital in 1947.

	Annual Growth	12/15	12/16	12/17	12/18	12/21
Sales ($mil.)	7.5%	–	69.7	70.4	82.0	100.1
Net income ($ mil.)	–	–	1.7	2.1	1.4	(0.8)
Market value ($ mil.)	–	–	–	–	–	–
Employees	–	–	–	–	–	650

MEMORIAL HOSPITAL AUXILIARY, INC.

4500 13TH ST
GULFPORT, MS 395012515
Phone: 228 867-4000
Fax: –
Web: www.gulfportmemorial.com

CEO: Gary G Marchand
CFO: Jennifer Dumal
HR: –
FYE: December 31
Type: Private

Formed by the southern Mississippi county of Harrison, Memorial Hospital at Gulfport is an acute care facility with some 440 beds. The hospital provides medical, surgical, and emergency services, as well as diagnostic imaging, comprehensive cancer care, rehabilitation programs, and cardiac care. It also operates mobile, walk-in, and outpatient clinics for minor injuries, rehabilitation, and behavioral health services, and it offers hospice, senior care, and support groups. The hospital's medical staff includes nearly 300 physicians with some 40 specialties. The not-for-profit hospital was established in 1946.

	Annual Growth	12/13	12/14	12/15	12/19	12/20
Sales ($mil.)	7.8%	–	–	0.2	–	0.3
Net income ($ mil.)	–	–	–	(0.0)	–	(0.0)
Market value ($ mil.)	–	–	–	–	–	–
Employees	–	–	–	–	–	2,500

MEMORIAL SLOAN-KETTERING CANCER CENTER

1275 YORK AVE
NEW YORK, NY 100656007
Phone: 212 639-2000
Fax: –
Web: www.mskcc.org

CEO: Craig B Thompson
CFO: Michael P Gutnick
HR: –
FYE: December 31
Type: Private

Memorial Sloan-Kettering Cancer Center (MSK) one of the oldest and largest private cancer center for patient care, innovative research, and outstanding educational program. The center includes about 500 inpatient beds, more than 1,455 physicians, 4,000 nurses, 24,100 inpatient stays, and 732,700 outpatient visits. Memorial Hospital specializes in bone-marrow transplants, radiation therapy, and chemotherapy. It also offers programs in cancer prevention, diagnosis, treatment, research, and education. As the experimental research arm of Memorial Sloan Kettering Cancer Center, The Sloan Kettering Institute hosts more than 100 laboratory investigators, 900 pre- and postdoctoral trainees. Memorial Sloan Kettering Cancer Center was founded in 1884 as New York Cancer Hospital.

	Annual Growth	12/16	12/17	12/19	12/21	12/22
Sales ($mil.)	8.1%	–	4,499.1	5,561.9	6,398.4	6,630.4
Net income ($ mil.)	–	–	314.4	302.7	1,480.8	(1,050.4)
Market value ($ mil.)	–	–	–	–	–	–
Employees	–	–	–	–	–	9,325

MENDOCINO BREWING CO INC

NBB: MENB

1601 Airport Road
Ukiah, CA 95482
Phone: 707 463-2627
Fax: –
Web: www.mendobrew.com

CEO: Yashpal Singh
CFO: Mahadevan Narayanan
HR: –
FYE: December 31
Type: Public

Mendocino Brewing Company operates breweries in Ukiah, California, and Saratoga Springs, New York, that produce beers under the names Red Tail Ale, Blue Heron Pale Ale, Black Hawk Stout, Eye of the Hawk Select Ale, and Butte Creek Brewing Porter. The company's beers are available throughout the US, as well as in Europe and Canada through the company's subsidiary, United Breweries International. Mendocino's products are distributed in its European territory by UK brewer Shepherd Neame. It also opeates two brew pubs -- one in Hopland, California, and one in Saratoga Springs, New York. Billionaire Vijay Mallya owns more than 70% of the company.

	Annual Growth	12/11	12/12	12/13	12/14	12/15
Sales ($mil.)	(7.4%)	–	39.2	35.6	34.0	31.2
Net income ($ mil.)	–	–	0.6	(0.9)	(1.5)	(1.1)
Market value ($ mil.)	3.2%	–	2.5	3.9	1.3	2.8
Employees	–	–	–	73	91	89

MENDOCINO COAST DISTRICT HOSPITAL

700 RIVER DR
FORT BRAGG, CA 954375403
Phone: 707 961-1234
Fax: –
Web: www.mcdh.org

CEO: Jonathan Baker
CFO: Mark Smith
HR: –
FYE: December 31
Type: Private

Mendocino Coast District Hospital provides medical care for residents of the rural communities in the coastal region near Fort Bragg, California. Its services include emergency medicine, occupational and physical therapy, obstetrics, respiratory care, hospice, and cardiology. The nearly 50-bed hospital also offers health education classes and support groups. Mendocino Coast District Hospital was founded in 1971.

	Annual Growth	06/18	06/19	06/20*	12/21	12/22
Sales ($mil.)	10.0%	–	59.1	59.6	58.7	78.7
Net income ($ mil.)	–	–	3.1	2.8	(6.2)	(1.5)
Market value ($ mil.)	–	–	–	–	–	–
Employees	–	–	–	–	–	320

*Fiscal year change

MENIL FOUNDATION, INC.

1533 SUL ROSS ST
HOUSTON, TX 770064729
Phone: 713 525-9400
Fax: –
Web: www.menil.org

CEO: –
CFO: –
HR: –
FYE: June 30
Type: Private

The Menil Foundation controls the renowned art collection of the late John and Dominique de Menil. The collection was opened to the public in 1987 with the founding of a gallery in Houston. Key elements of the Menils' collection include African and tribal art, Byzantine era pieces, as well as 20th-century paintings (especially those done by surrealists, including Max Ernst and Ren Magritte). The war chest for this impressive collection was funded mainly from stock in Schlumberger, the oil services firm founded by Dominique's father. (The oil connection explains how the French-born couple found their way to Houston.)

	Annual Growth	06/06	06/07	06/08	06/10	06/13
Sales ($mil.)	37.4%	–	–	12.2	49.6	59.8
Net income ($ mil.)	–	–	–	(8.0)	35.2	44.6
Market value ($ mil.)	–	–	–	–	–	–
Employees	–	–	–	–	–	70

MENLO COLLEGE

1000 EL CAMINO REAL
MENLO PARK, CA 940254306
Phone: 650 543-3927
Fax: –
Web: www.menlo.edu

CEO: –
CFO: –
HR: Emma Gordon
FYE: June 30
Type: Private

Menlo College is a co-educational baccalaureate institution focused on business management, mass communications, and liberal arts. The college is located just south of San Francisco in a residential community near the cities of Menlo Park and Palo Alto. Some 700 students are enrolled, and tuition costs about $24,000 per year. Menlo College was founded in 1927.

	Annual Growth	06/18	06/19	06/20	06/21	06/22
Sales ($mil.)	17.3%	–	42.7	51.5	52.0	68.8
Net income ($ mil.)	–	–	(1.1)	1.7	7.2	18.0
Market value ($ mil.)	–	–	–	–	–	–
Employees	–	–	–	–	–	471

MENNO TRAVEL SERVICE, INC.

203 S MAIN ST STE 1
GOSHEN, IN 465263770
Phone: 800 635-0963
Fax: –
Web: www.mennotrav.com

CEO: Michael Bedient
CFO: Ron Parent
HR: –
FYE: September 30
Type: Private

For travelers with more of a mission than sipping fruit drinks poolside in some tropical locale, there's Menno Travel Service, which does business as MTS TRAVEL. The company provides travel and tour services to religious and not-for-profit groups through nine offices in the US. MTS focuses on supporting Christian organizations in carrying out their missions worldwide with airfare, accommodations, and other travel arrangements. It also books religious and pilgrimage tours for groups and individuals; standard vacation tours, packages, and cruises; and business and meeting travel. MTS was acquired by Raptim Travel, a provider of missionary, humanitarian, and religious travel services, in 2009.

	Annual Growth	09/03	09/04	09/05	09/06	09/07
Sales ($mil.)	8.1%	–	95.2	101.6	111.7	120.2
Net income ($ mil.)	3.0%	–	0.2	0.0	(0.6)	0.2
Market value ($ mil.)	–	–	–	–	–	–
Employees	–	–	–	–	–	156

MENTOR GRAPHICS CORPORATION

8005 SW BOECKMAN RD
WILSONVILLE, OR 970707777
Phone: 503 685-7000
Fax: –
Web: www.new.siemens.com

CEO: –
CFO: –
HR: –
FYE: January 31
Type: Private

Mentor Graphics lends a hand to guide engineers who design electronic components. The company is a leading global developer of electronic design automation (EDA) software and systems used by engineers to design, simulate, and test electronic components, such as integrated circuits (IC's), wire harness systems, and printed circuit boards (PCBs). Products include PADS (PCB design), Nucleus (operating system), and Calibre (IC design). Its software is used to design components for such products as computers and wireless handsets. Clients come from the aerospace, IT, telecommunications, and, increasingly, transportation industries. Mentor Graphics was acquired by Siemens for $4.5 billion in 2017.

	Annual Growth	01/13	01/14	01/15	01/16	01/17
Sales ($mil.)	3.5%	–	1,156.4	1,244.1	1,181.0	1,282.5
Net income ($ mil.)	0.3%	–	153.6	145.2	94.2	154.9
Market value ($ mil.)	–	–	–	–	–	–
Employees	–	–	–	–	–	5,700

MERA PHARMACEUTICALS, INC.

NBB: MRPI

18331 Pines Blvd., Suite 273
Pembroke Pines, FL 33029
Phone: 855 845-5274
Web: –

CEO: –
CFO: –
HR: –
FYE: October 31
Type: Public

Algae... It's got to be good for something, and Mera Pharmaceuticals aims to find out what that might be. The company has developed the technology to cultivate microalgae on a large scale, and is working to identify and extract substances it hopes can be used in nutritional supplements, vitamins, pharmaceuticals, and cosmetics. The company's nutritional supplement products AstaFactor and Salmon Essentials contain astaxanthin, which acts as an antioxidant and anti-inflammatory agent. Mera Pharmaceuticals also provides private label and bulk astaxanthin sales.

	Annual Growth	10/07	10/08	10/09	10/10	10/11
Sales ($mil.)	(10.4%)	0.5	0.6	0.6	0.3	0.3
Net income ($ mil.)	–	(0.3)	(1.9)	(0.2)	(0.5)	(0.2)
Market value ($ mil.)	(29.3%)	4.4	2.7	2.7	1.6	1.1
Employees	(5.4%)	5	6	5	4	4

MERAKEY USA

620 GERMANTOWN PIKE
LAFAYETTE HILL, PA 194441810
Phone: 610 260-4600
Fax: -
Web: www.merakey.org

CEO: -
CFO: Derek Yacovelli
HR: -
FYE: June 30
Type: Private

Merakey USA is a not-for-profit developmental, behavioral health, and education provider. Founded in 1969, the system primarily offers a variety of behavioral health care services that include mental health and drug and alcohol rehabilitation, emotional support, mental retardation services, juvenile justice, autism, special education, foster care, and elder care to individuals and communities across the country. The system offers these services to more than 50,000 people annually at about 700 locations. In addition to its approximately 35,260 consumers by division, the system offers approximately 990 programs.

	Annual Growth	06/14	06/15	06/20	06/21	06/22
Sales ($mil.)	3.0%	-	49.4	6.1	59.2	60.7
Net income ($ mil.)	-	-	1.3	0.1	(1.0)	(2.3)
Market value ($ mil.)	-	-	-	-	-	-
Employees	-	-	-	-	-	6,500

MERCANTILE BANK CORP. NMS: MBWM

310 Leonard Street N.W.
Grand Rapids, MI 49504
Phone: 616 406-3000
Fax: -
Web: www.mercbank.com

CEO: -
CFO: -
HR: -
FYE: December 31
Type: Public

Mercantile Bank Corporation is the bank holding company for Mercantile Bank, which provides banking services to businesses, individuals, and governmental units. It has assets of approximately $5.1 billion and operates about 45 branches in central and western and central Michigan. The bank's primary deposit products are checking, savings, and term certificate accounts, and its primary lending products are commercial loans, residential mortgage loans, and installment loans. It owns about 20 automated teller machines and about 20 video banking machines. Real estate loans make up about 60% of the bank's loan portfolio. Outside of banking, the subsidiary Mercantile Insurance Center sells insurance products. Mercantile was founded in 1997 by directors and bankers.

	Annual Growth	12/19	12/20	12/21	12/22	12/23
Assets ($mil.)	10.2%	3,632.9	4,437.3	5,257.7	4,872.6	5,353.2
Net income ($ mil.)	13.5%	49.5	44.1	59.0	61.1	82.2
Market value ($ mil.)	2.6%	588.1	438.1	564.9	539.9	651.2
Employees	(0.7%)	683	665	656	669	665

MERCHANTS BANCORP (INDIANA) NAS: MBIN

410 Monon Blvd.
Carmel, IN 46032
Phone: 317 569-7420
Fax: -
Web: www.merchantsbancorp.com

CEO: Michael F Petrie
CFO: John F Macke
HR: Laura Dane
FYE: December 31
Type: Public

Merchants Bancorp in Carmel, Indiana provides credit for a variety of commercial endeavors. It focuses on Federal Housing Administration multi-family housing loans, healthcare facilities financing, and agricultural lending. It performs its business through several subsidiaries, including Merchants Bank of Indiana. It acquired Joy State Bank, located in Joy, Illinois, in early 2018.

	Annual Growth	12/19	12/20	12/21	12/22	12/23
Assets ($mil.)	27.7%	6,371.9	9,645.4	11,279	12,615	16,953
Net income ($ mil.)	37.8%	77.3	180.5	227.1	219.7	279.2
Market value ($ mil.)	21.2%	852.3	1,194.8	2,046.7	1,051.7	1,841.3
Employees	17.1%	329	404	481	556	618

MERCK & CO INC NYS: MRK

126 East Lincoln Avenue
Rahway, NJ 07065
Phone: 908 740-4000
Fax: 908 735-1500
Web: www.merck.com

CEO: Robert M Davis
CFO: Caroline Litchfield
HR: -
FYE: December 31
Type: Public

Merck & Co is a global health care company that delivers innovative health solutions through its prescription medicines, vaccines, biologic therapies and animal health products. The pharmaceutical giant's top products include cancer drug Keytruda, diabetes drugs Januvia and Janumet, HPV vaccine Gardasil, a pediatric combination vaccines ProQuad, M-M-R II, Varivax. In addition, Merck makes childhood and adult vaccines for such diseases as measles, mumps, rubella and varicella and pneumonia, as well as veterinary pharmaceuticals through Merck Animal Health. In addition, the company offers an extensive suite of digitally connected identification, traceability and monitoring products. The US market accounts for about 45% of revenue.

	Annual Growth	12/19	12/20	12/21	12/22	12/23
Sales ($mil.)	6.4%	46,840	47,994	48,704	59,283	60,115
Net income ($ mil.)	(56.1%)	9,843.0	7,067.0	13,049	14,519	365.0
Market value ($ mil.)	4.6%	230,252	207,088	194,024	280,885	275,999
Employees	0.4%	71,000	74,000	68,000	69,000	72,000

MERCURY GENERAL CORP. NYS: MCY

4484 Wilshire Boulevard
Los Angeles, CA 90010
Phone: 323 937-1060
Fax: -
Web: www.mercuryinsurance.com

CEO: Gabriel Tirador
CFO: Theodore R Stalick
HR: -
FYE: December 31
Type: Public

Mercury General Corporation (Mercury General) is primarily engaged in writing personal automobile insurance. The company is the parent of a group of insurers, including Mercury Casualty Company that writes automobile insurance for all risk classifications in about a dozen states. Private passenger automobile insurance accounts for a majority of premiums written. However, Mercury General also sells commercial vehicle insurance and a bit of homeowners, mechanical property, and umbrella insurance. The company is a California automobile insurer founded in 1961 by George Joseph, the company's chairman of the Board of Directors.

	Annual Growth	12/19	12/20	12/21	12/22	12/23
Assets ($mil.)	4.8%	5,889.2	6,328.2	6,772.5	6,514.2	7,103.4
Net income ($ mil.)	(25.9%)	320.1	374.6	247.9	(512.7)	96.3
Market value ($ mil.)	(6.5%)	2,698.2	2,890.9	2,938.0	1,893.7	2,065.9
Employees	(2.3%)	4,500	4,300	4,300	4,300	4,100

MERCURY SYSTEMS INC NMS: MRCY

50 Minuteman Road
Andover, MA 01810
Phone: 978 256-1300
Fax: -
Web: www.mrcy.com

CEO: William L Ballhaus
CFO: David E Farnsworth
HR: Cristina Spence
FYE: June 30
Type: Public

Mercury Systems is a technology company that delivers processing power for the most demanding aerospace and defense missions. As a leading developer of essential components, products, modules, and subsystems, it sells to defense prime contractors, the US government, and original equipment manufacturers (OEM) commercial aerospace companies. Its products and solutions are deployed in more than 300 programs with over 25 different defense prime contractors and commercial aviation customers. Its customers utilize its mission-critical solutions for a variety of applications including command, control, communications, computers, intelligence, surveillance and reconnaissance ("C4ISR"), electronic intelligence, mission computing avionics, electro-optical/infrared ("EO/IR"), electronic warfare, weapons and missile defense, hypersonic, and radar. The US accounts for the vast majority of revenue. The company was founded in 1981.

	Annual Growth	06/19*	07/20	07/21	07/22*	06/23
Sales ($mil.)	10.4%	654.7	796.6	924.0	988.2	973.9
Net income ($ mil.)	-	46.8	85.7	62.0	11.3	(28.3)
Market value ($ mil.)	(16.3%)	4,007.3	4,572.3	3,759.5	3,645.5	1,970.3
Employees	11.8%	1,661	1,947	2,384	2,386	2,596

*Fiscal year change

MERCY CARE

4500 E COTTON CENTER BLVD
PHOENIX, AZ 850408840
Phone: 602 263-3000
Fax: –
Web: www.mercycareaz.org

CEO: Mark Fisher
CFO: –
HR: –
FYE: June 30
Type: Private

Mercy Care is a not-for-profit provider of managed health care services in Arizona. The Mercy Care Plan provides these services under a contract with the Arizona Health Care Cost Containment System, the state of Arizona's Medicaid program. The plan provides health coverage and prescription drug benefits to some 300,000 members. The company, founded in 1985, is affiliated with St. Joseph's Hospital & Medical Center (which is part of Catholic Healthcare West), Dignity Health, and Carondelet Health Network. The plan is administered by health care management firm Schaller Anderson.

MERCY CHILDREN'S HOSPITAL

2401 GILLHAM RD
KANSAS CITY, MO 641084619
Phone: 816 234-3000
Fax: –
Web: www.childrensmercy.org

CEO: –
CFO: Dwight Hyde
HR: –
FYE: June 30
Type: Private

Children's Mercy Kansas City is a not-for-profit health system and a leading independent children's health organization dedicated to holistic care, translational research, breakthrough innovation, and educating the next generation of caregivers. It transforms the health, wellbeing, and potential of children, with unwavering compassion for those most vulnerable. Among its specialized services are diabetes and endocrinology, genetics, cardiovascular surgery, neonatology, and rehabilitation. Children's Mercy also offers several research education opportunities for healthcare professionals, researchers, and students.

	Annual Growth	06/15	06/16	06/20	06/21	06/22
Sales ($mil.)	10.9%	–	1,020.2	1,614.1	1,754.1	1,894.0
Net income ($ mil.)	19.3%	–	36.0	91.8	175.7	104.0
Market value ($ mil.)	–	–	–	–	–	–
Employees	–	–	–	–	–	7,000

MERCY CORPS

45 SW ANKENY ST STE 200
PORTLAND, OR 972043500
Phone: 503 796-6800
Fax: –
Web: www.mercycorps.org

CEO: Alexandra Gandolf
CFO: Chad Snelgar
HR: Allissa Schuster
FYE: June 30
Type: Private

Mercy Corps is dedicated to helping the poor and oppressed in developing countries. The not-for-profit organization offers emergency relief and economic support, as well as assistance in building sustainable communities. It also develops curriculum guides to introduce students to various topics ranging from Kurdish history and Afghan henna art to the worldwide clean water campaign. Since its founding, Mercy Corps programs have provided about $1.5 billion in assistance to people in 106 nations. Originally the organization was named Save the Refugees Fund when it was founded by Dan O'Neill in response to the plight of Cambodian refugees in 1979.

	Annual Growth	06/18	06/19	06/20	06/21	06/22
Sales ($mil.)	10.8%	–	311.7	324.5	357.0	423.5
Net income ($ mil.)	–	–	(9.6)	4.1	7.6	29.2
Market value ($ mil.)	–	–	–	–	–	–
Employees	–	–	–	–	–	543

MERCY GWYNEDD UNIVERSITY

1325 SUMNEYTOWN PIKE
GWYNEDD VALLEY, PA 194370010
Phone: 215 646-7300
Fax: –
Web: www.gmercyu.edu

CEO: –
CFO: –
HR: –
FYE: June 30
Type: Private

Gwynedd-Mercy University (GMercyU, formerly Gwynedd-Mercy College) is a private Catholic school founded in 1948 by the Sisters of Mercy. It offers about 40 associate and bachelor's, degree programs at schools of allied health, arts and sciences, business, education, and nursing. The college also offers graduate programs in business, education, and nursing. GMercyU has an enrollment of nearly 3,000 students and a student-to-faculty ratio of 13 to 1. In addition to its main campus, the college operates centers for life-long learning (as part of its business school) in Philadelphia and Fort Washington, Pennsylvania, that cater to working adults. GMercyU was founded in 1948.

	Annual Growth	06/15	06/16	06/17	06/19	06/21
Sales ($mil.)	1.3%	–	47.0	74.5	82.9	50.3
Net income ($ mil.)	–	–	(0.5)	3.0	3.8	2.7
Market value ($ mil.)	–	–	–	–	–	–
Employees	–	–	–	–	–	300

MERCY HEALTH

615 S NEW BALLAS RD
SAINT LOUIS, MO 631418221
Phone: 314 579-6100
Fax: –
Web: www.mercy.net

CEO: Lynn Britton
CFO: Shannon Sock
HR: Jodie Rayborn
FYE: June 30
Type: Private

Mercy Health, formerly known as the Sisters of Mercy Health System, provides a range of health care and social services through its network of facilities and service organizations. The organization operates some 35 acute care hospitals (including four specialty heart hospitals and two children's hospitals) with more than 4,200 licensed beds, as well as 700 clinics and outpatient facilities in four Midwestern states. Its hospital groups include facilities for nursing homes, medical practices, and outpatient centers. Mercy Health also operates Resource Optimization & Innovation (ROi), its industry-leading health care supply chain organization, and health outreach organizations in Louisiana, Mississippi, and Texas.

	Annual Growth	06/18	06/19	06/20	06/21	06/22
Sales ($mil.)	4.7%	–	6,509.3	6,519.5	7,422.8	7,469.5
Net income ($ mil.)	–	–	(33.0)	(325.8)	1,330.2	(231.3)
Market value ($ mil.)	–	–	–	–	–	–
Employees	–	–	–	–	–	8,800

MERCY HEALTH

12621 ECKEL JUNCTION RD
PERRYSBURG, OH 435511304
Phone: 513 639-2800
Fax: –
Web: www.mercy.com

CEO: John M Starcher Jr
CFO: –
HR: –
FYE: December 31
Type: Private

Mercy Health (formerly Catholic Health Partners) performs acts of healing in Kentucky and Ohio. One of the nation's largest not-for-profit health systems, Mercy Health offers health care services through about 450 facilities, including 23 hospitals, eight homes for the elderly, five hospice programs, and seven home health agencies. It also operates more than 150 clinics, a number of physician practices, and a health insurance plan. The system is co-sponsored by the Sisters of Mercy South Central and Mid-Atlantic communities; the Sisters of the Humility of Mary; the Franciscan Sisters of the Poor; and Covenant Health Systems. Mercy Health merged with Maryland-based Bon Secours Health System to create the 43-hospital system Bon Secours Mercy Health in 2018.

	Annual Growth	12/14	12/15	12/16	12/17	12/18
Sales ($mil.)	2.6%	–	–	–	4,737.9	4,860.1
Net income ($ mil.)	–	–	–	–	457.0	(978.8)
Market value ($ mil.)	–	–	–	–	–	–
Employees	–	–	–	–	–	2,500

MERCY HEALTH - ST. RITA'S MEDICAL CENTER, LLC

730 W MARKET ST
LIMA, OH 458014602
Phone: 419 227-3361
Fax: -
Web: www.mercy.com

CEO: Steve Walter
CFO: John Renner
HR: -
FYE: December 31
Type: Private

St. Rita's Medical Center is all about healing. The general medical-surgical hospital serves west central Ohio. The not-for-profit facility provides health care services in a number of medical specialties, including trauma and emergency care, orthopedics, cancer, pediatrics, women's health, and cardiovascular disease. It also has physical rehabilitation, mental health, and outpatient care facilities and works to improve community health through disease screenings, smoking cessation programs, and other outreach initiatives. Established in 1918 by the Sisters of Mercy, the hospital is a member of Catholic Healthcare Partners.

	Annual Growth	12/15	12/16	12/17	12/18	12/21
Sales ($mil.)	3.6%	-	408.6	427.7	442.5	488.6
Net income ($ mil.)	10.5%	-	91.4	120.1	59.1	150.5
Market value ($ mil.)	-	-	-	-	-	-
Employees	-	-	-	-	-	2,850

MERCY HEALTH FOUNDATION OF SOUTHEASTERN PENNSYLVANIA

3805 WEST CHESTER PIKE # 10
NEWTOWN SQUARE, PA 190732329
Phone: 610 567-6000
Fax: -
Web: www.trinityhealthma.org

CEO: David Clark
CFO: -
HR: -
FYE: June 30
Type: Private

Mercy Health System of Southeastern Pennsylvania serves a portion of the state, but covers practically the entire continuum of care. The health system operates four acute-care hospitals, as well as community health care centers and home health care agencies. The system's hospitals include Mercy Philadelphia Hospital (210 beds), Mercy Fitzgerald Hospital (220 beds), Mercy Suburban Hospital (130 beds), and Nazareth Hospital (200 beds). It also offers a managed health care plan to individuals who qualify for Medicaid or Medicare coverage through an affiliation with Gateway Health Plan. Mercy Health System is part of Catholic Health East.

	Annual Growth	06/13	06/14	06/15	06/19	06/20
Sales ($mil.)	(50.2%)	-	94.5	2.4	1.6	1.4
Net income ($ mil.)	-	-	18.9	-	-	-
Market value ($ mil.)	-	-	-	-	-	-
Employees	-	-	-	-	-	8,000

MERCY HEALTH NETWORK, INC.

1449 NW 128TH ST STE 300 # 6
CLIVE, IA 503257425
Phone: 515 247-3121
Fax: -
Web: www.mercyone.org

CEO: -
CFO: -
HR: -
FYE: June 30
Type: Private

Mercy Health Network tends to the hearts (and other body parts) of the Heartland through its collection of hospitals, clinics, nursing homes, and other health care operations. The integrated health network, formed through a joint operating agreement between Catholic Health Initiatives and Trinity Health, manages hospital systems in five Iowa cities: Clinton, Des Moines, Dubuque, Mason City, and Sioux City. The network also includes several rural hospitals and affiliated facilities. The largest hospital group is Mercy Medical Center-Des Moines, which consists of three campuses (including a mental health facility) with more than 900 inpatient beds. All together, Mercy Health Network has more than 2,000 beds.

	Annual Growth	06/12	06/13	06/14	06/15	06/20
Sales ($mil.)	17.7%	-	8.7	14.4	14.7	27.2
Net income ($ mil.)	-	-	(0.1)	(0.2)	0.2	0.0
Market value ($ mil.)	-	-	-	-	-	-
Employees	-	-	-	-	-	7,500

MERCY HEALTH NORTH LLC

2200 JEFFERSON AVE
TOLEDO, OH 436047101
Phone: 419 251-1359
Fax: -
Web: www.mercy.com

CEO: -
CFO: -
HR: -
FYE: December 31
Type: Private

Mercy, mercy me: Mercy Health Partners Northern Region is deeply involved with caring for the health of its community members. The not-for-profit company is a system of hospitals that provide medical services to residents of northwestern Ohio and southeastern counties of Michigan. Founded by the Grey Nuns and sponsored by the Sisters of Mercy, the Catholic faith-based system includes seven hospitals with a combined total of more than 1,000 beds. Areas of specialty include cancer treatment, diabetes care, pediatric, neurological services, cardiovascular care, trauma treatment, and critical care transportation. Mercy Health Partners Northern Region is part of the Catholic Healthcare Partners network.

MERCY HOSPITAL

175 FORE RIVER PKWY
PORTLAND, ME 041022779
Phone: 207 879-3000
Fax: -
Web: www.northernlighthealth.org

CEO: Eileen F Skinner
CFO: Stephen McDonnell
HR: -
FYE: September 30
Type: Private

Mercy Health System of Maine provides medical services to the people of Portland and other residents of Cumberland County. The health system operates two hospital campuses, as well as primary and specialty care centers. It boasts a total of 230 beds. The system also operates a substance abuse treatment program, a women's shelter, a home health and hospice program, and a hospitality home for families of patients undergoing treatment. Mercy Health System of Maine, which includes Mercy Hospital and VNA Home Health Hospice, is a part of Eastern Maine Healthcare Systems.

	Annual Growth	09/14	09/15	09/16	09/21	09/22
Sales ($mil.)	2.8%	-	213.7	220.1	253.3	258.9
Net income ($ mil.)	-	-	(22.9)	(21.5)	10.7	(10.0)
Market value ($ mil.)	-	-	-	-	-	-
Employees	-	-	-	-	-	1,200

MERCY HOSPITAL AND MEDICAL CENTER

2160 S 1ST AVE RM 1
MAYWOOD, IL 601533328
Phone: 312 567-2000
Fax: -
Web: www.mercy-chicago.org

CEO: John Capasso
CFO: -
HR: Nancy Davis
FYE: June 30
Type: Private

Chicagoans in the loop know Mercy Hospital and Medical Center is the place to go for health care. The Catholic hospital, located near Chicago's Loop (the historic downtown commercial district), has about 480 beds and operates a network of community clinics and occupational health facilities that provide employment-related services, such as drug screening, executive physicals, and physical therapy. Other services include a cancer treatment center, inpatient hospice care unit, eye care center, heart and vascular center, diabetes treatment center, stroke treatment center, and inpatient and outpatient chemical dependence recovery programs. Chicago's first teaching hospital, it is owned by Ohio-based system Trinity Health.

MERCY HOSPITAL SOUTH

10010 KENNERLY RD
SAINT LOUIS, MO 631282106
Phone: 314 525-1000
Fax: −
Web: www.mercy.net

CEO: −
CFO: −
HR: −
FYE: June 30
Type: Private

St. Anthony's Medical Center applies its skills to medical cases in the Midwest. The hospital serves residents in the areas surrounding St. Louis, Missouri, as well as portions of southwestern Illinois. With about 770 beds and some 800 affiliated physicians, the hospital provides a comprehensive offering, including inpatient and outpatient medical, surgical, diagnostic, and behavioral health care. The hospital operates a level II trauma center, cancer and chest pain units, and a pediatric emergency center, as well as several urgent care facilities. It also offers home health, hospice, laboratory, and pharmacy services. St. Anthony's Medical Center was founded in 1900 by the Franciscan Sisters of Germany.

	Annual Growth	06/17	06/18	06/19	06/21	06/22
Sales ($mil.)	6.0%	−	−	517.6	573.6	617.2
Net income ($ mil.)	34.3%	−	−	12.1	58.6	29.4
Market value ($ mil.)	−	−	−	−	−	−
Employees	−	−	−	−	−	3,900

MERCY HOSPITAL SPRINGFIELD

1235 E CHEROKEE ST
SPRINGFIELD, MO 658042203
Phone: 417 820-2000
Fax: −
Web: www.mercy.net

CEO: Steve Mackin
CFO: −
HR: −
FYE: June 30
Type: Private

Mercy Hospital Springfield is an 890-bed acute-care hospital in the Mercy Health system. The facility provides health care to southwestern Missouri and northwestern Arkansas and includes the Mercy Children's Hospital Springfield. Other hospital specialties include cardiology and stroke care, as well as women's and seniors' health, cancer, emergency, trauma, burn, neuroscience, rehabilitation, and sports medicine. In addition to its hospital in Springfield, Mercy Hospital Springfield operates a number of community clinics and specialty care centers in the area.

	Annual Growth	06/14	06/15	06/16	06/21	06/22
Sales ($mil.)	1.4%	−	948.2	1,024.7	1,115.7	1,048.7
Net income ($ mil.)	(22.0%)	−	93.4	104.7	165.3	16.4
Market value ($ mil.)	−	−	−	−	−	−
Employees	−	−	−	−	−	4,400

MERCY MEDICAL CENTER

1000 N VILLAGE AVE
ROCKVILLE CENTRE, NY 115701000
Phone: 516 594-6470
Fax: −
Web: www.catholichealthli.org

CEO: Alan Guerci Dr
CFO: William Armstrong
HR: Barbara Geiger
FYE: December 31
Type: Private

Overlooking Long Island's Hempstead Lake State Park, Mercy Medical Center offers healthcare services to patients just east of Manhattan. The not-for-profit Catholic hospital has expertise in weight loss and orthopedic surgeries, mammograms and breast health, and women's health services. It also provides outpatient services, such as family and mental health care. With about 380 beds, the medical center employs some 700 physicians who deliver about 1,300 babies each year. Its acute care facilities include a suburban branch of Memorial Sloan-Kettering Cancer Center. Mercy Medical Center, established in 1913 by the Sisters of the Congregation of the Infant Jesus, is part of Catholic Health Services of Long Island.

	Annual Growth	12/14	12/15	12/17	12/19	12/21
Sales ($mil.)	4.9%	−	195.3	234.0	257.4	260.3
Net income ($ mil.)	−	−	6.7	0.7	0.9	(18.2)
Market value ($ mil.)	−	−	−	−	−	−
Employees	−	−	−	−	−	1,610

MERCY SHIPS INTERNATIONAL

15862 STATE HIGHWAY 110 N
LINDALE, TX 757715932
Phone: 903 939-7000
Fax: −
Web: www.mercyships.org

CEO: Myron E Ullman III
CFO: −
HR: −
FYE: December 31
Type: Private

Mercy Ships brings floating medical care to areas of the world that need it most. The Christian-based not-for-profit serves more than 50 developing nations around the world from its ship Africa Mercy, which has six operating rooms and nearly 500 berths, and a land-based clinic in Sierra Leone. Staff and volunteers perform cleft lip and cleft palate surgeries, cataract and tumor removals, and other medical procedures. The organization also distributes water purification kits, prescription eyeglasses, and prescriptions, and offers a variety of training and education programs for local workers. Mercy Ships was founded in 1978 by Don and Deyon Stephens (who still serve as president and company VP, respectively).

	Annual Growth	12/07	12/08	12/09	12/15	12/19
Sales ($mil.)	(53.7%)	−	49.1	52.9	68.7	0.0
Net income ($ mil.)	−	−	(1.0)	1.1	16.4	0.0
Market value ($ mil.)	−	−	−	−	−	−
Employees	−	−	−	−	−	650

MERCY UNIVERSITY

555 BROADWAY
DOBBS FERRY, NY 105221186
Phone: 914 674-7600
Fax: −
Web: www.mercy.edu

CEO: −
CFO: −
HR: Karen Sheer
FYE: June 30
Type: Private

Mercy College is a private Catholic school founded by the Sisters of Mercy in 1950. The college provides higher education to some 9,000 undergraduate and graduate students in the New York City area. Mercy College offers 90 degrees in fields including business, accounting, civic and cultural studies, computer science, education, health professions, literature, language, communication, natural sciences, and social sciences. The institution also provides some online courses, as well as professional certification programs. Mercy College employs some 200 full-time faculty members.

	Annual Growth	06/16	06/17	06/18	06/19	06/22
Sales ($mil.)	2.5%	−	151.5	146.7	145.0	171.6
Net income ($ mil.)	−	−	38.1	20.6	10.0	(15.1)
Market value ($ mil.)	−	−	−	−	−	−
Employees	−	−	−	−	−	500

MEREDITH ENTERPRISES INC

3000 Sand Hill Road, Building 2, Suite 120
Menlo Park, CA 94025
Phone: 650 233-7140
Fax: −
Web: −

CEO: Allen Meredith
CFO: Charles P Wingard
HR: −
FYE: December 31
Type: Public

Meredith Enterprises merrily invests in and manages commercial real estate, with a focus on properties in the west, southeast, and Hawaii. Properties include office, industrial, and retail space; Meredith Enterprises has a portfolio of properties containing around 500,000 sq. ft. of leasable space; most of its holdings are in California, but the real estate investment trust (REIT) also has holdings in suburban Atlanta, Georgia, and Kona, Hawaii. Chairman and CEO Allen Meredith owns 100% of the REIT, which he took private in 2005.

	Annual Growth	12/00	12/01	12/02	12/03	12/04
Sales ($mil.)	12.1%	5.0	4.6	4.2	7.7	7.9
Net income ($ mil.)	(28.0%)	3.2	(2.5)	1.1	2.4	0.9
Market value ($ mil.)	−	−	−	12.6	14.0	16.0
Employees	−	−	3	4	4	4

MEREO BIOPHARMA 5 INC

800 W EL CAMINO REAL STE 180
MOUNTAIN VIEW, CA 94040
Phone: 650 995-8200
Fax: –
Web: www.mereobiopharma.com

CEO: Denise Scots-Knight
CFO: –
HR: –
FYE: December 31
Type: Private

OncoMed Pharmaceuticals is a development-stage biotech company working to produce pharmaceuticals targeting cancer cells. Like a growing group of pharma firms, its work is focused on cancer stem cells (CSCs), which are believed to be the root cause of cancer tumors. Traditional chemotherapy may kill the tumors but leaves the CSCs to grow more tumors. OncoMed's antibody drugs target both CSCs and the tumors they produce. The company has three candidates in development; it has strategic alliances with major pharma companies Celgene, GSK, and Bayer in conjunction with its product development. OncoMed was acquired by UK-based rare disease specialist Mereo BioPharma in 2019.

	Annual Growth	12/13	12/14	12/15	12/16	12/17
Sales ($mil.)	21.4%	–	–	25.9	25.2	38.2
Net income ($ mil.)	–	–	–	(85.4)	(103.1)	(39.1)
Market value ($ mil.)	–	–	–	–	–	–
Employees	–	–	–	–	–	56

MERIDIAN BIOSCIENCE, INC.

3471 RIVER HILLS DR
CINCINNATI, OH 452443023
Phone: 513 271-3700
Fax: –
Web: www.meridianbioscience.com

CEO: –
CFO: –
HR: –
FYE: September 30
Type: Private

Meridian is a fully-integrated life science company with principal businesses in the development, manufacture, sale and distribution of diagnostic testing systems and kits, primarily for certain gastrointestinal and respiratory infectious diseases, and elevated blood lead levels; and the manufacture and distribution of bulk antigens, antibodies, immunoassay blocking reagents, specialized Polymerase Chain Reaction (PCR) master mixes, and bioresearch reagents used by other diagnostic test manufacturers and researchers in immunological and molecular tests for human, animal, plant and environmental applications. Majority of its sales were generated in Americas.

MERIDIAN PARTNERS, LLC

1000 5TH ST STE 200
MIAMI BEACH, FL 331396510
Phone: 305 444-1811
Fax: –
Web: www.mp.team

CEO: –
CFO: –
HR: –
FYE: December 31
Type: Private

Meridian Partners tends to get SAPpy when it comes to consulting. That's because the firm specializes in helping government agencies, public school districts, and companies that use SAP's business software (an enterprise resource planning product that manages human resources, supply chain, customers, and products). Meridian Partners offers project management, upgrades, implementation, and technical maintenance, as well as training and staffing services to clients that include South Florida Water Management District, Miami Dade County Public Schools, and RailAmerica. Managing partners Wilberto Martinez and Jose Aleman co-founded the company in 2000.

MERIDIAN TECHNOLOGY GROUP, INC.

90 LA PAZ LOOP
SANTA FE, NM 875082284
Phone: 503 697-1600
Fax: –
Web: www.meridiangroup.com

CEO: –
CFO: –
HR: –
FYE: December 31
Type: Private

Meridian Technology Group provides businesses with a map for the path to technological success. The company provides a variety of IT consulting and software engineering services such as project management, systems integration, network design, and application design. It specializes in technology which enables clients to transition into Web-based business processes, for example. Meridian Technology Group's customers come from a wide range of industries including financial services, manufacturing, and health care. The company operates throughout the western US from offices in Oregon, Washington, and Texas. President Richard Creson founded Meridian Technology Group in 1990.

	Annual Growth	12/04	12/05	12/06	12/07	12/08
Sales ($mil.)	(4.0%)	–	–	13.9	13.0	12.8
Net income ($ mil.)	–	–	–	0.1	0.0	(0.2)
Market value ($ mil.)	–	–	–	–	–	–
Employees	–	–	–	–	–	135

MERIT MEDICAL SYSTEMS, INC.

NMS: MMSI

1600 West Merit Parkway
South Jordan, UT 84095
Phone: 801 253-1600
Fax: –
Web: www.merit.com

CEO: Fred P Lampropoulos
CFO: Raul Parra
HR: Mike Voigt
FYE: December 31
Type: Public

Merit Medical Systems is a leading manufacturer and marketer of proprietary medical devices used in interventional, diagnostic and therapeutic procedures, particularly in cardiology, radiology, oncology, critical care and endoscopy. The company's products include catheters, guide wires, needles, and tubing used in heart stent procedures, and angioplasties, as well as products for endoscopy, dialysis, and other procedures. Merit Medical sells its products as stand-alone items or in custom-made kits to hospitals and other health care providers as well as to custom packagers and equipment makers worldwide. The majority of the company's revenue comes from the US. Merit was founded in 1987 by Fred P. Lampropoulos, Kent W. Stanger, Darla Gill and William Padilla.

	Annual Growth	12/19	12/20	12/21	12/22	12/23
Sales ($mil.)	6.0%	994.9	963.9	1,074.8	1,151.0	1,257.4
Net income ($ mil.)	104.0%	5.5	(9.8)	48.5	74.5	94.4
Market value ($ mil.)	24.9%	1,806.3	3,211.7	3,604.6	4,085.9	4,394.9
Employees	2.3%	6,355	5,989	6,446	6,846	6,950

MERITAGE HOMES CORP

NYS: MTH

18655 North Claret Drive, Suite 400
Scottsdale, AZ 85255
Phone: 480 515-8100
Fax: –
Web: www.meritagehomes.com

CEO: Phillippe Lord
CFO: Hilla Sferruzza
HR: –
FYE: December 31
Type: Public

Meritage Homes is a leading designer and builder of single-family homes and builds houses in high-growth areas of the western, eastern, and central US. Targeting first-time, and first-move up homebuyers, the builder constructs single-family homes in Arizona, California, Colorado, Texas, Florida, Georgia, North Carolina, South Carolina, Utah, and Tennessee. Sold under the Meritage Homes, its houses are priced from approximately $250,000 to $1,400,000 and at an average of approximately $440,100 and $446,900, respectively. Founded in 1985, about around 35% of the builders' home sales are made in the western and eastern US each.

	Annual Growth	12/19	12/20	12/21	12/22	12/23
Sales ($mil.)	13.7%	3,666.9	4,501.2	5,141.3	6,292.2	6,138.3
Net income ($ mil.)	31.2%	249.7	423.5	737.4	992.2	738.7
Market value ($ mil.)	29.9%	2,225.9	3,016.7	4,446.0	3,358.4	6,345.2
Employees	5.0%	1,510	1,570	1,773	1,921	1,838

MERITAGE HOSPITALITY GROUP INC
NBB: MHGU

45 Ottawa Ave SW, Suite 600
Grand Rapids, MI 49503
Phone: 616 776-2600
Fax: 616 328-6925
Web: www.meritagehospitality.com

CEO: Robert Schermer Jr
CFO: Tracey Smith
HR: –
FYE: January 1
Type: Public

This company is really big on the beef in Michigan. Meritage Hospitality Group is a leading franchisee of Wendy's fast food hamburger restaurants, with about 70 locations operating mostly in western and southern Michigan. The units, franchised from Wendy's/Arby's Group, offer a menu of burgers and other sandwiches, fries, and other items. In addition to its quick-service operations, Meritage runs four franchised O'Charley's casual dining restaurants in Michigan near Grand Rapids and Detroit. The company was founded in 1986 as Thomas Edison Inns. The family of chairman Robert Schermer, Sr., including CEO Robert Schermer, Jr., controls Meritage.

	Annual Growth	12/18	12/19*	01/21	01/22	01/23
Sales ($mil.)	9.5%	435.3	467.5	516.2	577.1	626.0
Net income ($ mil.)	(10.1%)	13.0	12.1	14.9	17.4	8.5
Market value ($ mil.)	2.4%	113.8	128.8	124.9	139.8	125.2
Employees	2.4%	10,000	11,000	11,000	11,000	11,000

*Fiscal year change

MERITER HEALTH SERVICES, INC.

202 S PARK ST
MADISON, WI 537151507
Phone: 608 417-5800
Fax: –
Web: www.unitypoint.org

CEO: Sue Erickson
CFO: Beth Erdman
HR: Mary Jones
FYE: December 31
Type: Private

Meriter Health Services believes that the health concerns of its patients merits its careful attention. A teaching affiliate of the University of Wisconsin, the Madison-based system serves residents of southern Wisconsin and northwestern Illinois. Its flagship facility is the 450-bed Meriter Hospital, a not-for-profit community hospital providing general medical and surgical care, as well as pediatric mental health services through its Child and Adolescent Psychiatric Hospital unit. Meriter Health Services also operates primary care clinics, a home health care provider, and clinical laboratories. It owns two-thirds of Physicians Plus Insurance, a regional HMO.

	Annual Growth	12/10	12/11	12/12	12/15	12/22
Sales ($mil.)	(37.9%)	–	773.6	775.0	4.2	4.1
Net income ($ mil.)	–	–	(16.4)	12.8	1.2	0.4
Market value ($ mil.)	–	–	–	–	–	–
Employees	–	–	–	–	–	3,330

MERITUS HEALTH, INC.

11116 MEDICAL CAMPUS RD
HAGERSTOWN, MD 217426710
Phone: 301 790-8000
Fax: –
Web: www.healthmart.com

CEO: –
CFO: –
HR: –
FYE: June 30
Type: Private

Meritus Health provides a wide range of medical services to patients living in western Maryland, southern Pennsylvania, and adjacent portions of West Virginia. The system's Meritus Medical Center has 250 beds and 40 bassinets and offers acute, tertiary, and long-term care, including inpatient behavioral health services, cardiac care, obstetrics, cancer treatment, rehabilitation, and trauma care. Meritus Health also operates the for-profit Meritus Enterprises, a provider of outpatient health care, including diagnostic imaging, laboratory services, and ambulatory surgery. In addition, it provides general practice care at the Robinwood Professional Center.

	Annual Growth	06/08	06/09	06/10	06/11	06/12
Assets ($mil.)	–	–	–	–	9.9	542.5
Net income ($ mil.)	2040.9%	–	–	0.0	–	7.5
Market value ($ mil.)	–	–	–	–	–	–
Employees	–	–	–	–	–	3,105

MERLE NORMAN COSMETICS, INC.

9130 BELLANCA AVE
LOS ANGELES, CA 900454772
Phone: 310 641-3000
Fax: –
Web: www.merlenorman.com

CEO: Jack B Nethercutt
CFO: Michael Cassidy
HR: Kathy Axelrod
FYE: December 31
Type: Private

Merle Norman Cosmetics has built a foundation by offering samples to customers through its "try before you buy" concept. Founded by a young woman named Merle Nethercutt Norman, the company opened its first shop in Santa Monica, California, in 1931. The family owned company makes and markets primarily skin care products and color cosmetics that are sold through some 2,000 independently owned and operated retail outlets operating under the name Merle Norman Cosmetic Studios. Reaching from the US to Canada, Mexico, and the United Arab Emirates, its studios are typically located in malls. Brand names include Automatic Definitive, Inspirations, Luxiva, and Only Natural, among others.

	Annual Growth	12/08	12/09	12/10	12/12	12/13
Sales ($mil.)	(0.9%)	–	–	78.7	79.2	76.6
Net income ($ mil.)	(4.0%)	–	–	4.3	0.4	3.8
Market value ($ mil.)	–	–	–	–	–	–
Employees	–	–	–	–	–	529

MERRIAM-WEBSTER, INCORPORATED

47 FEDERAL ST
SPRINGFIELD, MA 011051230
Phone: 413 734-3134
Fax: –
Web: www.merriam-webster.com

CEO: –
CFO: –
HR: –
FYE: September 30
Type: Private

Merriam-Webster is never at a loss for words. The reference publisher's offerings include vocabulary builders such as Merriam-Webster's Collegiate Dictionary and Webster's Third New International Dictionary, Unabridged . Merriam-Webster also publishes CD-ROMs for some of its publications. The company was founded in 1831 by brothers George and Charles Merriam. They bought the rights to Noah Webster's 70,000-entry reference opus, An American Dictionary of the English Language, Corrected and Enlarged (considered by many to be the first American dictionary), in 1843 and published revised editions of the book. Merriam-Webster is a subsidiary of Encyclop dia Britannica.

MERRIMACK PHARMACEUTICALS INC
NMS: MACK

One Broadway, 14th Floor
Cambridge, MA 02142
Phone: 617 720-8606
Fax: –
Web: www.merrimack.com

CEO: Gary L Crocker
CFO: Jean M Franchi
HR: Corey Mathison
FYE: December 31
Type: Public

Merrimack Pharmaceuticals takes a technological approach to fighting cancer. A biopharmaceutical company based in Cambridge, Massachusetts. The company do not have any ongoing research or development activities and are seeking potential acquirers for the remaining preclinical and clinical assets. Merrimack traces its roots back to the early 1990s.

	Annual Growth	12/19	12/20	12/21	12/22	12/23
Sales ($mil.)	–	–	–	–	–	–
Net income ($ mil.)	–	(17.3)	(3.0)	(2.5)	(1.5)	(1.2)
Market value ($ mil.)	43.6%	45.2	98.9	56.1	164.5	192.4
Employees	–	–	–	–	–	–

MERRIMAN HOLDINGS INC.
NBB: MERR

250 Montgomery Street, 16th Floor
San Francisco, CA 94104
Phone: 415 248-5603
Fax: –
Web: www.merrimanco.com

CEO: –
CFO: –
HR: –
FYE: December 31
Type: Public

Merriman Holdings (formerly Merriman Curhan Ford Group) sees funds in its clients' futures. The company provides investment banking, venture and corporate services, asset management, and investment research services, with a focus on fast-growth sectors such as clean technology, media, and consumer services. Offerings include strategic advisory, restructuring, and private placements of stock, warrants, and convertibles. The company is also active in the emerging China market. Merriman Holdings has offices in New York City and San Francisco.

	Annual Growth	12/10	12/11	12/12	12/13	12/14
Sales ($mil.)	(15.1%)	30.7	21.9	12.9	10.0	15.9
Net income ($ mil.)	–	(5.3)	(7.9)	(6.9)	(4.0)	(1.6)
Market value ($ mil.)	0.6%	9.9	1.9	0.3	0.6	10.2
Employees	(20.3%)	77	35	32	29	31

MESA AIR GROUP INC
NMS: MESA

410 North 44th Street, Suite 700
Phoenix, AZ 85008
Phone: 602 685-4000
Fax: –
Web: www.mesa-air.com

CEO: Jonathan G Ornstein
CFO: Michael J Lotz
HR: –
FYE: September 30
Type: Public

Mesa Air Group, Inc. is the holding company of Mesa Airlines, Inc., a regional air carrier operating as as American Eagle and United Express Airlines. The company provides scheduled passenger service to more than 105 cities in about 40 states, the District of Columbia, Cuba, the Bahamas, and Mexico as well as cargo services out of Cincinnati/Northern Kentucky International Airport. It operates a fleet of about 145 aircraft with approximately 640 daily departures and currently operates out of domiciles in Phoenix, Arizona (PHX), Dallas, Texas (DFW), Houston, Texas (IAH), Sterling, Virginia (IAD), and Louisville, Kentucky (SDF). Founded in 1982 by Larry and Janie Risley, "Mesa Air Shuttle" launched service between Farmington and Albuquerque, New Mexico on a five-seat Piper Saratoga aircraft.

	Annual Growth	09/19	09/20	09/21	09/22	09/23
Sales ($mil.)	(8.9%)	723.4	545.1	503.6	531.0	498.1
Net income ($ mil.)	–	47.6	27.5	16.6	(182.7)	(120.1)
Market value ($ mil.)	(40.3%)	276.1	120.8	313.6	67.6	35.2
Employees	(10.4%)	3,576	3,200	3,241	2,454	2,303

MESA LABORATORIES, INC.
NMS: MLAB

12100 West Sixth Avenue
Lakewood, CO 80228
Phone: 303 987-8000
Fax: –
Web: www.mesalabs.com

CEO: Gary M Owens
CFO: John Sakys
HR: –
FYE: March 31
Type: Public

Mesa Laboratories is a multinational manufacturer, developer, and seller of life sciences tools and critical quality control products and services, many of which are sold into niche markets driven by regulatory requirements. The company develops, manufactures, markets, sells and maintains life sciences tools and quality control instruments and related software, consumables, and services. Hardware include physical products such as instruments used for molecular and genetic analysis, protein synthesizers, medical meters, wireless sensor loggers, and data loggers. The company has manufacturing operations in the US and Europe, and its products are marketed by its sales personnel in North America, Europe, and Asia Pacific, as well as by independent distributors in these areas and throughout the rest of the world. The company generates almost 55% of total revenue.

	Annual Growth	03/19	03/20	03/21	03/22	03/23
Sales ($mil.)	20.7%	103.1	117.7	133.9	184.3	219.1
Net income ($ mil.)	(40.6%)	7.5	1.3	3.3	1.9	0.9
Market value ($ mil.)	(6.7%)	1,237.7	1,214.0	1,307.5	1,368.6	938.2
Employees	19.1%	347	460	506	681	698

MESABI TRUST
NYS: MSB

c/o Deutsche Bank Trust Company Americas, Trust & Agency Services, 1 Columbus Circle, 17th Floor, Mail Stop: NYC01-1710
New York, NY 10019
Phone: 904 271-2520
Fax: –
Web: www.mesabi-trust.com

CEO: –
CFO: –
HR: –
FYE: January 31
Type: Public

In the Iron Range of Mesabi the stockholders trust. Mesabi Trust collects royalties and bonuses from the sale of minerals that are shipped from Northshore Mining's Silver Bay, Minnesota, facility. The mining company is a wholly owned subsidiary of Cliffs, a supplier of iron ore products to the steel industry. Northshore Mining pays royalties to Mesabi Trust based on production and sales of crude ore pulled from the trust's property; it has curtailed its extraction efforts, citing lack of demand. Independent consultants track production and sales for Mesabi Trust. Deutsche Bank Trust Company Americas is the corporate trustee of Mesabi Trust.

	Annual Growth	01/19	01/20	01/21	01/22	01/23
Sales ($mil.)	(36.4%)	47.3	32.0	26.0	71.5	7.7
Net income ($ mil.)	(41.6%)	45.6	30.1	23.4	68.8	5.3
Market value ($ mil.)	(4.3%)	360.0	267.8	326.6	367.1	302.2
Employees						

MESQUITE ENERGY, INC.

711 LOUISIANA ST
HOUSTON, TX 770022716
Phone: 713 756-2700
Fax: –
Web: www.mesquite-energy.com

CEO: Antonio R Sanchez III
CFO: Cameron W George
HR: –
FYE: December 31
Type: Private

Mesquite Energy (formerly Sanchez Energy) is a privately held independent oil and natural gas exploration and production company focused on the development of its properties in the western portion of the Eagle Ford Shale in South Texas. The company constructs one of the largest positions in Texas, comprising more than 400,000 gross acres, and operates one of the most active drilling programs in the region. Headquartered in Houston, with field offices in Catarina and Carrizo Springs, Texas, it has a broad set of approximately 2,300 mature producing wells. In 2020, the company has completed its financial restructuring and emerged from Chapter 11 bankruptcy protection.

MESSER CONSTRUCTION CO.

643 W COURT ST
CINCINNATI, OH 452031511
Phone: 513 242-1541
Fax: –
Web: www.messer.com

CEO: Tim Steigerwald
CFO: –
HR: –
FYE: September 30
Type: Private

Messer Construction provides unmatched leadership of complex, commercial construction projects. The builder provides commercial construction services (including design/build and project management) for projects in Indiana (Indianapolis), Kentucky (Louisville and Lexington), Ohio (Cincinnati, Columbus, and Dayton), North Carolina (Charlotte and Raleigh), and Tennessee (Knoxville and Nashville). It has clients in the life sciences, higher education, senior living, manufacturing/industrial, public, and healthcare sectors, among others. Its projects have included the renovation of Michaelman, Inc., Advanced Materials Collaboration Center & Corporate Campus, and Cook Regentec Build-Out & Renovations. Founded in 1932, employee-owned Messer became employee-owned in 1990.

	Annual Growth	09/12	09/13	09/14	09/15	09/17
Sales ($mil.)	(3.3%)	–	–	–	1,167.1	1,092.0
Net income ($ mil.)		–	–	–	–	–
Market value ($ mil.)		–	–	–	–	–
Employees		–	–	–	–	1,390

MESSIAH UNIVERSITY

1 UNIVERSITY AVE
MECHANICSBURG, PA 170556706
Phone: 717 796-1800
Fax: –
Web: www.messiah.edu

CEO: –
CFO: David Walker
HR: –
FYE: June 30
Type: Private

As its name implies, Messiah College is a private Christian college that offers bachelor's degrees in the liberal and applied arts and sciences. Accredited by the Middle States Association of Colleges and Secondary Schools, the institution serves more than 3,000 students across more than 80 undergraduate majors. Messiah College, with 200 full-time faculty members, boasts a student/faculty ratio of 13:1. The institution's main campus, located 12 miles southwest of Harrisburg, Pennsylvania, partners with a satellite campus in Philadelphia associated with Temple University. Previously named the Messiah Bible School and Missionary Training Home, Messiah College was founded by the Brethren in Christ Church in 1909.

	Annual Growth	06/18	06/19	06/20	06/21	06/22
Sales ($mil.)	0.6%	–	97.8	96.9	95.3	99.5
Net income ($ mil.)	–	–	(4.8)	(10.5)	6.8	(15.6)
Market value ($ mil.)	–	–	–	–	–	–
Employees	–	–	–	–	–	800

MESTEK INC.

NBB: MCCK

260 North Elm Street
Westfield, MA 01085
Phone: 413 568-9571
Fax: –
Web: www.mestek.com

CEO: Stuart B Reed
CFO: –
HR: Joanne Berwald
FYE: December 31
Type: Public

Mestek is a family of more than 45 specialty manufacturers serving many facets of the HVAC equipment and building envelope industries including HVAC, metal forming, and architectural building envelopes. HVAC equipment group and controls group is a leading manufacturer of heating, ventilation, and cooling products including residential and commercial hydronic heating equipment with intelligent controls and air conditioning. The metal forming segment under Mestek Machinery focuses on coil handling and metal forming machinery while its Architectural group manufactures glass skylights, sunshades, louvers, and ornamental metal products. John Reed founded Mestek in 1946.

	Annual Growth	12/17	12/18	12/19	12/20	12/21
Sales ($mil.)	1.6%	329.3	350.7	341.7	310.9	350.8
Net income ($ mil.)	(4.7%)	15.0	18.5	32.0	45.0	12.4
Market value ($ mil.)	2.4%	220.5	218.2	234.6	213.7	242.5
Employees	–	–	–	–	–	–

META PLATFORMS INC

NMS: META

1 Meta Way
Menlo Park, CA 94025
Phone: 650 543-4800
Fax: –
Web: www.facebook.com

CEO: Mark Zuckerberg
CFO: Susan Li
HR: –
FYE: December 31
Type: Public

Meta Platforms builds useful and engaging products that enable people to connect and share with friends and family through mobile devices, personal computers, virtual reality headsets, and in-home devices. Meta, which allows outside developers to build apps that integrate with Facebook, boasts 3 billion monthly active users. Facebook owns photo and video sharing site Instagram, messaging applications Messenger, and WhatsApp. The company generates more than 55% of total revenue from outside the US.

	Annual Growth	12/19	12/20	12/21	12/22	12/23
Sales ($mil.)	17.5%	70,697	85,965	117,929	116,609	134,902
Net income ($ mil.)	20.6%	18,485	29,146	39,370	23,200	39,098
Market value ($ mil.)	14.6%	525,645	699,563	861,392	308,191	906,492
Employees	7.7%	49,942	58,601	71,970	86,482	67,317

METALDYNE PERFORMANCE GROUP INC.

1 DAUCH DR
DETROIT, MI 482111115
Phone: 248 727-1800
Fax: –
Web: www.aam.com

CEO: –
CFO: Mark Blaufuss
HR: –
FYE: December 31
Type: Private

Metaldyne designs and supplies a slew of products for engine, transmission, and driveline applications. The company focuses on powertrain products, such as balance shaft modules, differential assemblies, clutch modules, and exhaust components. Other business units make vibration control (dampers, isolation pulleys), sintered (connecting rods, bearing caps), and forged parts. Customers have included OEMs Chrysler, Ford, GM, and Toyota. Metaldyne in 2017 was acquired by American Axle & Manufacturing (AAM) for $3.3 billion.

	Annual Growth	12/12	12/13	12/14	12/15	12/16
Sales ($mil.)	1.3%	–	–	2,717.0	3,047.3	2,790.7
Net income ($ mil.)	15.0%	–	–	73.3	125.7	96.9
Market value ($ mil.)	–	–	–	–	–	–
Employees	–	–	–	–	–	12,000

METALICO, INC.

135 DERMODY ST
CRANFORD, NJ 070163217
Phone: 908 497-9610
Fax: –
Web: www.metalico.com

CEO: –
CFO: –
HR: –
FYE: December 31
Type: Private

No, dude, it's not a heavy metal band, but Metalico is into metal – specifically, scrap metal recycling and lead fabrication. The company collects ferrous and nonferrous metal at about 30 facilities in the eastern, midwestern, and southern US and recycles it into usable scrap. Recycled ferrous metal (iron and steel) is sold mainly to steelmakers, including operators of electric arc furnace minimills and steel mills. Metalico's nonferrous scrap includes aluminum, which is sold to makers of aluminum products. Metalico engages in lead fabrication at four US facilities. Its lead products include sheet (for roofing) and shot (for reloading).

METALLUS INC

NYS: MTUS

1835 Dueber Avenue SW
Canton, OH 44706
Phone: 330 471-7000
Fax: –
Web: www.timkensteel.com

CEO: Michael S Williams
CFO: Kristopher R Westbrooks
HR: –
FYE: December 31
Type: Public

TimkenSteel is the leading manufacturer of special bar quality (SBQ) large bars (6 inches in diameter and greater) and seamless mechanical steel tubing. Its business model is unique in the industry, focusing on creating tailored products and services for its customers' most demanding applications. In addition, TimkenSteel manages raw material recycling programs, which are used internally as a feeder system for its melt operations and allow the company to sell scrap not used in its operations to third parties. Customers include manufacturers in automotive, oil and gas, industrial equipment, mining, construction, rail, defense, heavy truck, agriculture, and power generation. The US accounts for 90% of revenue.

	Annual Growth	12/19	12/20	12/21	12/22	12/23
Sales ($mil.)	3.0%	1,208.8	830.7	1,282.9	1,329.9	1,362.4
Net income ($ mil.)	–	(110.0)	(61.9)	171.0	65.1	69.4
Market value ($ mil.)	31.4%	338.8	201.3	711.2	783.1	1,010.7
Employees	(7.4%)	2,500	2,000	1,850	1,700	1,840

METALS RECOVERY HOLDINGS LLC

3000 GSK DR STE 201
CORAOPOLIS, PA 151081383
Phone: 724 774-1020
Fax: –
Web: www.befesa.com

CEO: Michael Griffin
CFO: Andrew Repine
HR: –
FYE: December 31
Type: Private

Bearing out the adage that one person's trash is another's treasure, through Horsehead Corporation, Horsehead Zinc Powders, INMETCO, and Zochem, Horsehead Holdings turns zinc-containing dust and discarded batteries into value-added zinc and nickel-based products. Key raw materials for the company include dust from the electric-arc furnaces used at steel minimills and residue from the galvanizing of metals. Besides zinc metal, Horsehead's products include zinc oxide, zinc dust (used in corrosion-resistant coatings), and nickel-based metals (used as a feedstock to produce stainless and specialty steels). The company filed for Chapter 11 bankruptcy protection in 2016.

METHES ENERGIES INTERNATIONAL LTD   NBB: MEIL

1208 Celebration Ave
Las Vegas, FL 34747
Phone: 321 214-4039
Fax: –
Web: www.methes.com

CEO: –
CFO: Edward A Stoltenberg
HR: –
FYE: November 30
Type: Public

Methes Energies International lives and breathes biodiesel. Okay, maybe the company doesn't breathe fuel, but it resells biodiesel produced by third-party companies, sells a line of biodiesel processors under the Denami brand, and offers an array of services to biodiesel producers. The company also produces biodiesel through two facilities in Ontario and markets and sells its products throughout Canada and the US. Other offerings include selling feedstock (e.g. vegetable oils and animal fats used in biofuel production), installing and commissioning its Denami processors, and licensing related proprietary software used to operate the processors. Founded in 2007, Methes Energies filed to go public in mid-2012.

	Annual Growth	11/13	11/14	11/20	11/21	11/22
Sales ($mil.)	–	8.9	5.5	–	–	–
Net income ($ mil.)	–	(5.7)	(6.3)	(0.1)	(0.1)	(0.1)
Market value ($ mil.)	(41.3%)	194.2	86.3	0.7	18.8	1.6
Employees	–	44	23	–	–	–

METHODE ELECTRONICS INC   NYS: MEI

8750 West Bryn Mawr Avenue, Suite 1000
Chicago, IL 60631-3518
Phone: 708 867-6777
Fax: –
Web: www.methode.com

CEO: Donald W Duda
CFO: Ronald L Tsoumas
HR: –
FYE: April 29
Type: Public

Methode Electronics is a leading global supplier of custom engineered solutions with sales, engineering, and manufacturing locations in North America, Europe, Middle East, and Asia. The company designs, engineers, and produces mechatronic products for OEMs utilizing its broad range of technologies for user interface, LED lighting system, power distribution, and sensor applications. Its solutions are found in the end markets of transportation (including automotive, commercial vehicle, e-bike, aerospace, bus and rail), cloud computing infrastructure, construction equipment, consumer appliance, and medical devices. Its business is managed on a segment basis, with its four segments being Automotive, Industrial, Interface and Medical. The US accounts for about 40% of the total revenue.

	Annual Growth	04/19*	05/20	05/21*	04/22	04/23
Sales ($mil.)	4.2%	1,000.3	1,023.9	1,088.0	1,163.6	1,179.6
Net income ($ mil.)	(4.2%)	91.6	123.4	122.3	102.2	77.1
Market value ($ mil.)	8.7%	1,050.6	1,022.0	1,609.4	1,598.0	1,468.3
Employees	2.0%	6,187	6,044	7,200	7,000	6,700

*Fiscal year change

METHODIST HOSPITALS OF DALLAS INC

1441 N BECKLEY AVE
DALLAS, TX 752031201
Phone: 877 637-4297
Fax: –
Web: www.methodisthealthsystem.org

CEO: Stephen L Mansfield
CFO: Michael J Schaefer
HR: –
FYE: June 30
Type: Private

Methodist Hospitals of Dallas, which does business as Methodist Health System, one of the leading healthcare providers in North Texas. It has more than 2,500 physicians at its facilities. Methodist Health System provides services including cancer care, brain and spine, heart care, emergency and trauma services and transplant. The 592-bed teaching and referral hospital boasts a Level I trauma center and an organ transplant program. Other facilities include the 42-bed Methodist Midlothian Medical Center, the 262-bed Methodist Mansfield Medical Center, and the 443-bed Methodist Richardson Medical Center.

	Annual Growth	06/15	06/16*	09/19*	05/20*	06/20
Sales ($mil.)	(90.2%)	–	431.7	1,554.2	0.0	0.0
Net income ($ mil.)	–	–	35.6	141.1	(0.1)	(0.0)
Market value ($ mil.)	–	–	–	–	–	–
Employees	–	–	–	–	–	2,300

*Fiscal year change

METHODIST LE BONHEUR HEALTHCARE

1211 UNION AVE STE 700
MEMPHIS, TN 381046600
Phone: 901 516-7000
Fax: –
Web: www.methodisthealth.org

CEO: Gary S Shorb
CFO: –
HR: Carla Robbins
FYE: December 31
Type: Private

Methodist Le Bonheur Healthcare (Methodist Healthcare) is a not-for-profit health care system serving the Memphis area with four hospitals; multiple minor medical, surgical, and diagnostic health centers; and surgery centers. In addition to traditional health services, Methodist Healthcare offers extended care services, sleep disorder centers, and wound healing centers. It also operates physician practices and a physician referral service. The system's flagship hospital, Methodist University Hospital has more than 615 beds and is a teaching hospital affiliated with the University of Tennessee Health Science Center. It was founded in 1918 by The United Methodist Church to help meet the growing needs for quality healthcare in the Mid-South.

	Annual Growth	12/15	12/16	12/17	12/21	12/22
Sales ($mil.)	12.8%	–	152.7	162.9	218.7	315.2
Net income ($ mil.)	–	–	(5.1)	(0.1)	17.1	123.0
Market value ($ mil.)	–	–	–	–	–	–
Employees	–	–	–	–	–	11,459

METLIFE INC   NYS: MET

200 Park Avenue
New York, NY 10166-0188
Phone: 212 578-9500
Fax: –
Web: www.metlife.com

CEO: Michel A Khalaf
CFO: John D McCallion
HR: –
FYE: December 31
Type: Public

MetLife is a leading global provider of insurance, annuities, and employee benefit programs. MetLife companies offer life, accident, and health insurance, retirement, and savings products through agents, third-party distributors such as banks and brokers, and direct marketing channels. It holds leading market positions in the US (where generates about 60% of the company's revenue), Japan, Latin America, Asia, Europe, and the Middle East. It is also one of the largest institutional investors in the US with a general account portfolio invested primarily in fixed-income securities (corporate, structured products, municipals, and government and agency) and mortgage loans, as well as real estate, real estate joint ventures, other limited partnerships and equity securities.

	Annual Growth	12/19	12/20	12/21	12/22	12/23
Assets ($mil.)	(1.8%)	740,463	795,146	759,708	666,611	687,584
Net income ($ mil.)	(28.1%)	5,899.0	5,407.0	6,554.0	2,539.0	1,578.0
Market value ($ mil.)	6.7%	37,250	34,312	45,669	52,890	48,329
Employees	(2.1%)	49,000	46,500	43,000	45,000	45,000

METRIC & MULTISTANDARD COMPONENTS CORP.

120 OLD SAW MILL RIV RD
HAWTHORNE, NY 105321515
Phone: 914 769-5020
Fax: –
Web: www.metricmcc.com

CEO: Ivo Peske
CFO: –
HR: –
FYE: December 31
Type: Private

Having trouble screwing in that fastener? Don't get a hammer; it may be a metric component. If so, Metric & Multistandard Components (MMCC) touts the largest metric inventory in the US -- over 48,000 items. The company distributes an array of metric fasteners and industrial components, from dies and drills to flange bushings, hanger bolts, nuts, rods, and screws. More than 98% of its efforts are business-to-business; sales offices in New York, Chicago, Atlanta, Dallas, and Reno cater to resale stores, original equipment manufacturers, and maintenance, repair and overhaul companies. An office in Germany handles European purchasing and shipping. MMCC is held by its founding families, Voves, Peske, and Hacaj.

METRO PACKAGING & IMAGING INC

5 HAUL RD
WAYNE, NJ 074706624
Phone: 973 709-9100
Fax: –
Web: www.metroymcas.org

CEO: –
CFO: –
HR: –
FYE: December 31
Type: Private

Metro gives its customers the full printing package. Metro Packaging and Imaging prints product packaging including folding cartons, flexible packaging, paper bags, and curved cups, as well as prints directly onto CDs. The company, founded as Metro Litho in 1964, uses gravure, flexographic, dry offset (letterpress), and silkscreen methods and offers a full range of digital imaging services. The company expanded its operations and menu of services in 2006 by adding full prepress capabilities. Metro's clients include Kraft Foods, Revlon, and Hartz. Metro Packaging boasts operations in California, Georgia, Minnesota, New Jersey, North Carolina, and Ohio.

	Annual Growth	12/04	12/05	12/06	12/09	12/10
Sales ($mil.)	(60.6%)	–	–	1,312.6	26.6	31.5
Net income ($ mil.)	609.3%	–	–	0.0	0.7	1.2
Market value ($ mil.)	–	–	–	–	–	–
Employees	–	–	–	–	–	120

METRO-NORTH COMMUTER RAILROAD CO INC

420 LEXINGTON AVE FL 12
NEW YORK, NY 101701200
Phone: 212 878-7000
Fax: –
Web: new.mta.info

CEO: –
CFO: –
HR: –
FYE: December 31
Type: Private

Part of New York's Metropolitan Transportation Authority, Metro-North Commuter Railroad carries passengers between New York City and its New York and Connecticut suburbs. The company, known as MTA Metro-North Railroad or Metro-North, covers 795 miles of track and serves a ridership of about 83 million. Three of the company's lines operate from Grand Central Terminal in New York City; the other two operate from Hoboken, New Jersey. MTA Metro-North Railroad serves more than 120 stations in seven counties in New York State (Bronx, Dutchess, New York, Orange, Putnam, Rockland, and Westchester) and two in Connecticut (Fairfield and New Haven). The railroad 2014 operating annual budget was $1.4 billion.

	Annual Growth	12/03	12/04	12/05	12/06	12/08
Sales ($mil.)	5.6%	–	433.1	470.2	490.5	538.6
Net income ($ mil.)	(6.7%)	–	247.0	226.4	152.6	186.9
Market value ($ mil.)	–	–	–	–	–	–
Employees	–	–	–	–	–	5,564

METROPLEX ADVENTIST HOSPITAL, INC.

2201 CLEAR CREEK RD
KILLEEN, TX 765494110
Phone: 254 526-7523
Fax: –
Web: www.adventhealth.com

CEO: Kevin Roberts
CFO: Robert Brock
HR: Kenneth Finch
FYE: December 31
Type: Private

Because the Texas towns of Belton, Killeen, and Lampasas aren't large, they share a large health system between them. Metroplex Health System includes Metroplex Adventist Hospital, with 148 beds in Killeen, a behavioral health unit with 60 beds, and Rollins Brook Community Hospital with 25 beds in Lampasas. The system, part of Adventist Health System and served by Scott & White, provides all the basics of general medical care including physician office buildings, home health services, and other outpatient services. Metroplex Adventist Hospital also serves the needs of nearby Ft. Hood, making it the largest community healthcare provider to the military in the US.

	Annual Growth	09/17	09/18*	12/19	12/21	12/22
Sales ($mil.)	12.1%	–	104.2	142.4	182.1	164.7
Net income ($ mil.)	–	–	(2.0)	8.1	20.2	(2.5)
Market value ($ mil.)	–	–	–	–	–	–
Employees	–	–	–	–	–	779

*Fiscal year change

METROPOLITAN AIRPORTS COMMISSION

6040 28TH AVE S
MINNEAPOLIS, MN 554502701
Phone: 612 726-8100
Fax: –
Web: www.metroairports.org

CEO: Brian Ryks
CFO: –
HR: James Laurent
FYE: December 31
Type: Private

When you fly to the Twin Cities, you'll most likely fly into a facility operated by the Metropolitan Airports Commission. The agency operates Minneapolis-St. Paul International Airport (MSP), along with six smaller, reliever airports in the Twin Cities area. The smaller airports handle general aviation traffic and support military aircraft operations, thus reducing potential congestion at MSP. The Metropolitan Airports Commission is considering other non-aeronautical uses for areas of the reliever airports such as business or commercial land development. The agency was created in 1943 by the Minnesota Legislature.

	Annual Growth	12/18	12/19	12/20	12/21	12/22
Sales ($mil.)	(4.1%)	–	400.9	228.1	294.1	353.0
Net income ($ mil.)	(3.6%)	–	109.5	0.4	63.1	98.2
Market value ($ mil.)	–	–	–	–	–	–
Employees	–	–	–	–	–	575

METROPOLITAN BANK HOLDING CORP

NYS: MCB

99 Park Avenue
New York, NY 10016
Phone: 212 659-0600
Fax: –
Web: www.mcbankny.com

CEO: Mark R Defazio
CFO: Anthony J Fabiano
HR: –
FYE: December 31
Type: Public

Metropolitan Bank Holding has a niche in the New York City commercial real estate market. Targeting middle market firms needing less than $20 million in credit, the holding company, through its Metropolitan Commercial Bank, lends to real estate entrepreneurs serving construction, multi-family, retail, mixed-use, nursing home, and other industries. Most of the properties against which it provides credit are located in the New York City metropolitan area, with a few situated in New Jersey and other nearby states. The bank went public in 2017, raising more than $100 million to help with organic growth endeavors.

	Annual Growth	12/19	12/20	12/21	12/22	12/23
Assets ($mil.)	20.5%	3,357.6	4,330.8	7,116.4	6,267.3	7,067.7
Net income ($ mil.)	26.5%	30.1	39.5	60.6	59.4	77.3
Market value ($ mil.)	3.5%	533.6	401.2	1,178.5	649.1	612.7
Employees	13.5%	167	189	202	241	277

METROPOLITAN COLLEGE OF NEW YORK

60 WEST ST 8TH FL
NEW YORK, NY 100061735
Phone: 212 343-1234
Fax: –
Web: www.mcny.edu

CEO: –
CFO: Thomas Berke
HR: Elaine Robles
FYE: December 31
Type: Private

Metropolitan College of New York (MCNY) offers an alternative to traditional higher education models. The school's curriculum strives to integrate classroom learning with workplace experience so that students can more immediately see the purpose of their studies. The MCNY system encourages students to work full-time or participate in internships while attending school. Students can earn associate's, bachelor's, and master's degrees in the areas of business, human services, education, and public administration. MCNY was founded in 1964 by social activist Audrey Cohen.

	Annual Growth	12/16	12/17	12/19	12/21	12/22
Sales ($mil.)	(2.4%)	–	31.7	31.0	30.1	28.0
Net income ($ mil.)	32.8%	–	0.0	(0.0)	0.0	0.3
Market value ($ mil.)	–	–	–	–	–	–
Employees	–	–	–	–	–	310

METROPOLITAN EDISON COMPANY

76 S MAIN ST
AKRON, OH 443081812
Phone: 800 736-3402
Fax: –
Web: www.firstenergycorp.com

CEO: –
CFO: Mark T Clark
HR: –
FYE: December 31
Type: Private

Metropolitan Edison is an electric company, and it knows a thing or two about serving cities and surrounding communities. The company, a subsidiary of holding company FirstEnergy, provides electric services to a population of 1.3 million in a 3,300-sq. ml. service area in south central and eastern Pennsylvania. Metropolitan Edison, or Met-Ed as it is sometimes referred to, operates almost 16,500 miles of power transmission and distribution lines. Although the company's primary source of electricity is derived from oil-and gas-fired units, its York Haven Power Company generates hydroelectric power.

	Annual Growth	12/08	12/09	12/10	12/16	12/17
Sales ($mil.)	(8.4%)	–	1,689.0	1,818.5	865.4	837.2
Net income ($ mil.)	7.3%	–	55.5	58.0	87.8	97.3
Market value ($ mil.)	–	–	–	–	–	–
Employees	–	–	–	–	–	678

METROPOLITAN GOVERNMENT OF NASHVILLE & DAVIDSON COUNTY

100 METRO COURTHOUSE
NASHVILLE, TN 37201
Phone: 615 862-5000
Fax: –
Web: www.nashville.gov

CEO: –
CFO: –
HR: Kent Minich
FYE: June 30
Type: Private

Memphis may have the blues but Nashville has that country sound. Tennessee's second-largest city (with about 600,000 people) is home to many recording studios, music labels, and thousands of working musicians. The city also has a large health care community, with two Fortune 500 companies - HCA and Community Health Systems- employing thousands of people.

	Annual Growth	06/18	06/19	06/20	06/21	06/22
Sales ($mil.)	11.3%	–	2,605.4	2,572.6	3,170.0	3,593.3
Net income ($ mil.)	(40.7%)	–	416.6	(315.7)	830.2	86.9
Market value ($ mil.)	–	–	–	–	–	–
Employees	–	–	–	–	–	18,000

METROPOLITAN GROUP PROPERTY & CASUALTY INSURANCE CO.

700 Quaker Lane
Warwick, RI 02886-6669
Phone: 401 827-2400
Fax: –
Web: –

CEO: William Moore
CFO: –
HR: Hara John
FYE: December 31
Type: Public

Because MetLife is practically bigger than life, it is able to offer property/casualty insurance for the stuff that fills our lives. Its subsidiary Metropolitan Property and Casualty Insurance (MPC) operates under the MetLife Auto & Home brand and is a leading provider of property/casualty insurance for automobiles, boats, and homeowners insurance. Its products are sold through workplaces and directly to individuals in the US. Auto insurance accounts for 70% of premiums and includes both standard and non-standard policies. Homeowner's and other coverage, including personal excess liability, make up the remaining 30% of the company's premiums.

	Annual Growth	12/97	12/98	12/99	12/00	12/01
Assets ($mil.)	1.6%	500.1	514.3	681.3	731.0	533.2
Net income ($ mil.)	45.7%	12.6	10.3	1.5	95.2	56.8
Market value ($ mil.)	–	–	–	–	–	–
Employees	–	–	–	–	–	–

METROPOLITAN OPERA ASSOCIATION, INC.

30 LINCOLN CENTER PLZ
NEW YORK, NY 100236980
Phone: 212 799-3100
Fax: –
Web: maintenance.metoperafamily.org

CEO: William Morris
CFO: –
HR: –
FYE: July 31
Type: Private

Italians and Germans alike desire an American debut at the Met. Well, their operas do, anyway. The Metropolitan Opera Association manages The Metropolitan Opera company, which presents more than 200 performances every year in its residence at the Lincoln Center for the Performing Arts. The Met is known for performing most works in their original languages and for producing regular Saturday radio broadcasts, which are aired throughout North America and in South America, Europe, and the Asia/Pacific region. In association with sponsors, the Met makes video and CD recordings of the performances and distributes them worldwide. The Met was founded in 1883.

	Annual Growth	07/07	07/08	07/09	07/15	07/19
Sales ($mil.)	(0.1%)	–	309.4	223.5	335.3	307.5
Net income ($ mil.)	–	–	34.9	(71.2)	26.2	(5.9)
Market value ($ mil.)	–	–	–	–	–	–
Employees	–	–	–	–	–	1,500

METROPOLITAN PROPERTY & CASUALTY INSURANCE CO.

700 Quaker Lane
Warwick, RI 02886-6669
Phone: 401 827-2400
Fax: –
Web: –

CEO: William Moore
CFO: –
HR: Hara John
FYE: December 31
Type: Public

Because MetLife is practically bigger than life, it is able to offer property/casualty insurance for the stuff that fills our lives. Its subsidiary Metropolitan Property and Casualty Insurance (MPC) operates under the MetLife Auto & Home brand and is a leading provider of property/casualty insurance for automobiles, boats, and homeowners insurance. Its products are sold through workplaces and directly to individuals in the US. Auto insurance accounts for 70% of premiums and includes both standard and non-standard policies. Homeowner's and other coverage, including personal excess liability, make up the remaining 30% of the company's premiums.

	Annual Growth	12/97	12/98	12/99	12/00	12/01
Assets ($mil.)	21.9%	2,013.4	2,136.8	3,072.7	3,319.5	4,450.9
Net income ($ mil.)	–	–	72.1	149.5	90.3	22.7	(112.3)
Market value ($ mil.)	–	–	–	–	–	–
Employees	–	–	–	–	–	–

METROPOLITAN SECURITY SERVICES, INC.

100 E 10TH ST STE 400
CHATTANOOGA, TN 374024218
Phone: 423 702-8200
Fax: –
Web: www.waldensecurity.com

CEO: Amy S Walden
CFO: Scott Cochran
HR: Brenda Armstrong
FYE: December 31
Type: Private

Walden Security is something of a right-hand man -- or in this case, woman -- to businesses and government. Majority owned and operated by women (the company is controlled by co-founder, chairman, and CEO Amy Walden), the security services contractor recruits, trains, and manages uniformed security professionals to guard such sites as airports, auto dealerships, manufacturing facilities, museums, office buildings, residences, schools, and shopping malls. It is also contracted by the US General Services Administration to provide alarm monitors, clerks, court security officers, and police officers. Walden Security has operations in about 15 states.

	Annual Growth	12/05	12/06	12/07	12/08	12/09
Sales ($mil.)	–	–	–	(1,277.6)	85.7	95.9
Net income ($ mil.)	10535.9%	–	–	0.0	0.2	0.9
Market value ($ mil.)	–	–	–	–	–	–
Employees	–	–	–	–	–	2,500

METROPOLITAN ST. LOUIS SEWER DISTRICT

2350 MARKET ST STE 300
SAINT LOUIS, MO 631032517
Phone: 314 768-6200
Fax: –
Web: www.msdprojectclear.org

CEO: –
CFO: –
HR: Carmen Tisdale
FYE: June 30
Type: Private

Business is draining for The Metropolitan St. Louis Sewer District (MSD), which provides wastewater collection and treatment services for a population of about 1.3 million in the St. Louis area. The district operates nearly 10,000 miles of sewer lines and seven wastewater treatment plants that process an average of 370 million gallons of sewage per day. MSD serves about 425,000 residential and commercial/industrial customers. It has a budget of more than $470 million and is governed by a six-member board, divided equally between appointees of the mayor of St. Louis and of the St. Louis County executive. The district was created by voters in 1954 and began operations two years later.

	Annual Growth	06/08	06/09	06/11	06/12	06/16
Sales ($mil.)	3.6%	–	249.7	219.4	226.0	319.9
Net income ($ mil.)	(4.8%)	–	68.8	(10.6)	21.3	48.9
Market value ($ mil.)	–	–	–	–	–	–
Employees	–	–	–	–	–	976

METROPOLITAN STATE UNIVERSITY OF DENVER

890 AURARIA PKWY
DENVER, CO 802041804
Phone: 303 556-5740
Fax: –
Web: www.msudenver.edu

CEO: –
CFO: –
HR: Elizabeth Wellington
FYE: June 30
Type: Private

Metropolitan State University of Denver serves students from the Mile High City and beyond. The public university offers bachelor's and master's degrees through its three schools: Business; Professional Studies; and Letters, Arts and Sciences. It offers 55 major and 90 minor degree programs from its main Denver campus, as well as satellite campuses in Northglenn and Greenwood Village. Students can take classes during the day, at night, on weekends, or through correspondence or online. Some 23,000 students attend MSU Denver, which changed its name from Metropolitan State College of Denver (Metro State) in 2012.

	Annual Growth	06/01	06/02	06/03	06/05	06/16
Sales ($mil.)	1.9%	–	121.9	66.1	2.1	157.8
Net income ($ mil.)	–	–	(81.6)	1.2	(0.5)	8.9
Market value ($ mil.)	–	–	–	–	–	–
Employees	–	–	–	–	–	2,300

METROPOLITAN TRANSIT AUTHORITY OF HARRIS COUNTY

1900 MAIN ST
HOUSTON, TX 770028130
Phone: 713 739-4834
Fax: –
Web: www.ridemetro.org

CEO: –
CFO: –
HR: –
FYE: September 30
Type: Private

The Metropolitan Transit Authority of Harris County (known as METRO in its hometown) is the region's largest public transit provider. METRO's transit network includes local bus, METRORail, which includes the Red Line (Main Street and Northline), the Green Line (East End) and the Purple Line (Southeast), Park & Ride commuter buses, METROLift paratransit service, HOV/HOT Express Lanes, curb2curb microtransit service and METRO Star Vanpool. METRO's service are covers more than 1,300 square miles across the City of Houston, major portions of unincorporated Harris County, and about 15 smaller, surrounding cities.

	Annual Growth	09/18	09/19	09/20	09/21	09/22
Sales ($mil.)	(19.8%)	–	75.3	42.8	26.7	38.9
Net income ($ mil.)	–	–	(116.6)	119.1	408.7	(86.9)
Market value ($ mil.)	–	–	–	–	–	–
Employees	–	–	–	–	–	3,916

METROPOLITAN TRANSPORTATION AUTHORITY

2 BDWY
NEW YORK, NY 100042207
Phone: 212 878-7000
Fax: –
Web: new.mta.info

CEO: –
CFO: Jaibala Patel
HR: –
FYE: December 31
Type: Private

Metropolitan Transportation Authority (MTA) is North America's largest transportation network, serving a population of 15.3 million people across a 5,000-square-mile travel area surrounding New York City through Long Island, southeastern New York State, and Connecticut. The MTA network comprises the nation's largest bus fleet and more subway and commuter rail cars than all other US transit systems combined. The MTA's operating agencies are MTA New York City Transit, MTA Bus, Long Island Rail Road, Metro-North Railroad, and MTA Bridges and Tunnels.

	Annual Growth	12/18	12/19	12/20	12/21	12/22
Sales ($mil.)	(8.2%)	–	9,043.0	4,728.0	5,775.0	7,004.0
Net income ($ mil.)	148.8%	–	498.0	532.0	4,160.0	7,667.0
Market value ($ mil.)	–	–	–	–	–	–
Employees	–	–	–	–	–	67,457

METROPOLITAN UTILITIES DISTRICT OF OMAHA

7350 WORLD COMMUNICATIONS DR
OMAHA, NE 681224041
Phone: 402 554-6666
Fax: –
Web: www.mudomaha.com

CEO: Jack Frost
CFO: Debra A Schneider
HR: Cherie Funkhouser
FYE: December 31
Type: Private

The Metropolitan Utilities District (MUD) distributes natural gas and water in the Omaha, Nebraska, metropolitan area. The company serves some 220,000 natural gas customers and more than 200,000 water customers. It also collects sewer and trash fees for municipalities. Customer-owned MUD, which claims to be the fifth-largest public gas utility in the nation, is a political subdivision of the State of Nebraska. Its board members are elected by residents of its service territory.

	Annual Growth	12/09	12/10	12/11	12/12	12/16
Sales ($mil.)	(1.3%)	–	–	311.9	292.8	291.7
Net income ($ mil.)	15.8%	–	–	15.3	46.2	31.8
Market value ($ mil.)	–	–	–	–	–	–
Employees	–	–	–	–	–	852

METROPOLITAN WASHINGTON AIRPORTS AUTHORITY

1 AVIATION CIR
WASHINGTON, DC 200016000
Phone: 703 417-8600
Fax: –
Web: www.mwaa.com

CEO: John E Potter
CFO: Andrew Rountree
HR: –
FYE: December 31
Type: Private

The Metropolitan Washington Airports Authority operates Washington Dulles International and Ronald Reagan Washington National airports, the primary airports serving the nation's capital. The airports generate revenue from aircraft landing fees, concessions, and space rental. The agency also oversees the Dulles Toll Road. A public agency, the Metropolitan Washington Airports Authority was created in 1987 by the District of Columbia and the Commonwealth of Virginia with the consent of the US Congress.

METROSTAR SYSTEMS, LLC

1856 OLD RESTON AVE STE 100
RESTON, VA 201903329
Phone: 703 481-9581
Fax: –
Web: www.metrostar.com

CEO: Ali Manouchehri
CFO: –
HR: –
FYE: December 31
Type: Private

MetroStar Systems makes information shine. The company provides information technology services and consulting primarily to government clients. Among its services are software development and integration, Web and sales portal development, network operations support, and program management. Public sector customers have included the US Department of Defense and the State Department; it has also served such commercial clients as Computer Sciences Corporation and CACI. MetroStar was founded by CEO Ali Reza Manouchehri in 1999.

	Annual Growth	12/09	12/10	12/11	12/12	12/13
Sales ($mil.)	11.1%	–	–	20.2	24.6	24.9
Net income ($ mil.)		–	–	0.0	(0.1)	(1.3)
Market value ($ mil.)	–	–	–	–	–	–
Employees		–	–	–	–	215

METTERS INDUSTRIES, INC.

1011 ARLINGTON BLVD # 11
ARLINGTON, VA 222093925
Phone: 703 527-7345
Fax: –
Web: www.metters.com

CEO: –
CFO: –
HR: –
FYE: March 31
Type: Private

Service matters to Samuel Metters. Metters founded, owns, and leads systems integrator and combat simulation specialist Metters Industries. The company, which he started in 1981 after retiring from the US Army, provides IT consulting services including network design and integration, database development, systems migration, training, and engineering support. It also develops custom software and provides network security services. Metters largely serves various branches of the Department of Defense and other civilian federal agencies. Clients have included all branches of the US military and the US Department of State; commercial clients have included Booz Allen Hamilton, United Defense, and Raytheon.

	Annual Growth	03/02	03/03	03/04	03/09	03/12
Sales ($mil.)	12.1%	–	16.5	15.7	26.9	45.9
Net income ($ mil.)	4.3%	–	0.0	0.2	1.9	0.0
Market value ($ mil.)	–	–	–	–	–	–
Employees		–	–	–	–	176

METTLER-TOLEDO INTERNATIONAL, INC. NYS: MTD

1900 Polaris Parkway
Columbus, OH 43240
Phone: 614 438-4511
Fax: 614 438-4646
Web: www.mt.com

CEO: –
CFO: –
HR: –
FYE: December 31
Type: Public

Mettler-Toledo International is one of the top suppliers of precision instruments and services in the world. It is recognized as an innovation leader and its solutions are critical in research and development, quality control, and manufacturing processes for its customers. It makes a range of bench and floor scales that precisely weigh materials as little as one ten-millionth of a gram to more than 60 kilograms. It's main markets are laboratory, industrial, and food retail, among others. Mettler-Toledo also makes analytical instruments and software for life science, engineering, and drug and chemical compound development. The US accounts for about a third of the company's revenue.

	Annual Growth	12/19	12/20	12/21	12/22	12/23
Sales ($mil.)	5.9%	3,008.7	3,085.2	3,717.9	3,919.7	3,788.3
Net income ($ mil.)	8.9%	561.1	602.7	769.0	872.5	788.8
Market value ($ mil.)	11.2%	17,076	24,533	36,534	31,115	26,110
Employees	1.7%	16,200	16,500	17,800	18,000	17,300

METWOOD INC

721 Rossiter Street
Mount Dora, FL 32757
Phone: 800 323-4130
Fax: –
Web: –

CEO: Keith M Thomas
CFO: –
HR: –
FYE: June 30
Type: Public

Metwood is shaping the future of construction. The company manufactures light-gauge steel building materials, usually combined with wood, for use in residential and commercial construction in lieu of conventional wood products. The combination increases load strength and structural integrity, allowing for durable designs that can't be produced with wood alone. Products include girders and headers; floor joists; roof and floor trusses and rafters; metal framing; structural columns; and garage, deck, and porch concrete pour-over systems. The company primarily sells to lumber yards and home improvement stores, mainly in Virginia. Affiliate Providence Engineering provides civil engineering services.

	Annual Growth	06/15	06/16	06/17	06/18	06/19
Sales ($mil.)	–	1.7	1.8	1.9	1.9	–
Net income ($ mil.)	–	(0.0)	(0.7)	(0.4)	(0.5)	(3.8)
Market value ($ mil.)	(30.7%)	15.2	7.0	2.3	3.5	3.5
Employees		13	14	13	14	–

MEXCO ENERGY CORP. ASE: MXC

415 West Wall Street, Suite 475
Midland, TX 79701
Phone: 432 682-1119
Fax: –
Web: www.mexcoenergy.com

CEO: Nicholas C Taylor
CFO: Tamala L McComic
HR: –
FYE: March 31
Type: Public

Mexco Energy gets most of its energy not from present day Mexico, but from its close neighbor -- what once was Old Mexico, West Texas. The oil and gas exploration and production independent has proved reserves of 6.3 billion cu. ft. of natural gas and 659,700 barrels of oil. While the company owns oil and gas properties in other states (including Louisiana, New Mexico, North Dakota, and Oklahoma), the majority of its activities take place in Texas. Holly Frontier Refining & Marketing is Mexco Energy's top customer. Mexco Energy president Nicholas Taylor owns about 44% of the company.

	Annual Growth	03/19	03/20	03/21	03/22	03/23
Sales ($mil.)	37.3%	2.7	2.7	2.8	6.6	9.6
Net income ($ mil.)	–	(0.0)	(0.1)	0.2	2.9	4.7
Market value ($ mil.)	23.1%	10.6	4.7	18.9	34.6	24.3
Employees	4.7%	5	6	5	5	6

MEXICAN AMERICAN OPPORTUNITY FOUNDATION

401 N GARFIELD AVE
MONTEBELLO, CA 906402901
Phone: 323 890-9600
Fax: –
Web: www.maof.org

CEO: –
CFO: –
HR: –
FYE: June 30
Type: Private

The Mexican American Opportunity Foundation (MAOF) works to increase and improve opportunities for the largest and fastest-growing Hispanic group in the US. One of the largest Latino not-for-profit organizations in the nation, MAOF serves more than 100,000 Californians. It provides funding for a wide variety of advocacy programs, including nutrition and health awareness, childcare centers, and literacy initiatives. The East Los Angeles-based group also offers computer classes and other career training at no cost to qualified individuals. Sometimes referred to as an "urban Cesar Chavez," Dr. Dionicio Morales founded MAOF in 1963; Morales died in September 2008.

	Annual Growth	06/18	06/19	06/20	06/21	06/22
Sales ($mil.)	5.7%	–	99.0	109.4	119.4	116.7
Net income ($ mil.)	–	–	0.3	0.3	(0.7)	(2.1)
Market value ($ mil.)	–	–	–	–	–	–
Employees	–	–	–	–	–	710

MEYER & WALLIS, INC.

117 N JEFFERSON ST # 204
MILWAUKEE, WI 532026160
Phone: 414 224-0212
Fax: –
Web: www.meyerwallis.com

CEO: Robert L Meyer
CFO: –
HR: –
FYE: December 31
Type: Private

Meyer & Wallis provides full service advertising and marketing for clients across the US. Services include strategic development, advertising, design, public relations, and interactive marketing with a strong background in serving retail clients. The agency also serves companies in health care and consumer products. Its portfolio includes work for such clients as the American Heart Association, Quad/Graphics, and Vectren Energy. The agency has offices in Indianapolis and Milwaukee. Meyer & Wallis was founded in 1967 by industry veteran CEO Bob Meyer.

	Annual Growth	12/04	12/05	12/06	12/07	12/08
Sales ($mil.)	19.4%	–	9.8	9.8	17.3	16.7
Net income ($ mil.)	–	–	(0.1)	(0.1)	0.7	(0.1)
Market value ($ mil.)	–	–	–	–	–	–
Employees	–	–	–	–	–	25

MFA FINANCIAL, INC.

One Vanderbilt Ave., 48th Floor
New York, NY 10017
Phone: 212 207-6400
Fax: 212 207-6420
Web: www.mfafinancial.com

NYS: MFA
CEO: Craig L Knutson
CFO: Michael Roper
HR: –
FYE: December 31
Type: Public

MFA Financial (formerly MFA Mortgage Investments) has three good buddies: Fannie, Freddie, and Ginnie. This self-advised mortgage real estate investment trust (REIT) was incorporated in 1997 to invest in mortgage-backed securities and mortgages such as those guaranteed by government-related entities Fannie Mae, Freddie Mac, and Ginnie Mae. The REIT's investment portfolio mainly consists of agency mortgage-backed securities, AAA-rated mortgage-backed securities, corporate and government bonds, and cash. MFA Financial buys its securities and loans from the banks, savings and loans, investment banks, and mortgage banking institutions that originate them. Its portfolio weighs in at approximately $8 billion.

	Annual Growth	12/19	12/20	12/21	12/22	12/23
Assets ($mil.)	(5.6%)	13,567	6,932.3	9,139.7	9,112.4	10,773
Net income ($ mil.)	(32.1%)	378.1	(679.4)	328.9	(231.6)	80.2
Market value ($ mil.)	10.2%	779.7	396.5	464.7	1,003.9	1,148.6
Employees	54.6%	66	58	298	349	377

MFA INCORPORATED

201 RAY YOUNG DR
COLUMBIA, MO 652013599
Phone: 573 874-5111
Fax: –
Web: www.mfa-inc.com

CEO: Ernie Verslues
CFO: –
HR: Amanda Cooper
FYE: August 31
Type: Private

Agricultural cooperative MFA brings together 45,000 farmers in Missouri and adjacent states. It is a primary manufacturer of livestock feed, holding a major market share within its trade territory. It is also a supplier and marketer of plant food and crop protection products. The co-op also provides its members with animal feeds, animal-health products, and farm supplies. The company's some 145 company-owned MFA Agri Services Centers combined with nearly 25 locally owned MFA affiliates and approximately 400 independent dealers. The company was founded in 1914.

	Annual Growth	08/14	08/15	08/16	08/17	08/18
Sales ($mil.)	7.1%	–	–	1,192.7	1,373.3	1,367.9
Net income ($ mil.)	30.1%	–	–	4.1	14.1	6.9
Market value ($ mil.)	–	–	–	–	–	–
Employees	–	–	–	–	–	1,393

MFA OIL COMPANY

1 RAY YOUNG DR STE 1
COLUMBIA, MO 652013506
Phone: 573 442-0171
Fax: –
Web: www.mfaoil.com

CEO: Jon Ihler
CFO: Jeff Raetz
HR: Beth Bartlett
FYE: August 31
Type: Private

Many farmers appreciate MFA Oil. The energy cooperative, controlled by its 40,000 farmer-members, produces fuel and lubrication products and manages bulk petroleum and propane plants in the Central and Western US. Operating 140 propane plants, the company sells more propane for farm use and home heating than any other company in Missouri. It also operates nearly 100 oil and lubricant bulk plants and serves customers in Arkansas, Iowa, Kansas, and Oklahoma. Additionally, the company operates 76 convenience stores under the Break Time brand (in Arkansas and Missouri), more than 160 Petro-Card 24 fueling locations, and owns 10 Jiffy Lube and a dozen Big O Tire franchises.

	Annual Growth	08/13	08/14	08/15	08/16	08/17
Sales ($mil.)	(7.2%)	–	–	1,045.1	800.3	900.0
Net income ($ mil.)	(58.4%)	–	–	48.1	24.7	8.3
Market value ($ mil.)	–	–	–	–	–	–
Employees	–	–	–	–	–	2,110

MGE ENERGY INC

133 South Blair Street
Madison, WI 53788
Phone: 608 252-7000
Fax: –
Web: www.mgeenergy.com

NMS: MGEE
CEO: Jeffrey M Keebler
CFO: –
HR: –
FYE: December 31
Type: Public

MGE Energy is an investor-owned public holding company distributes electricity to approximately 161,000 customers in Dane County, Wisconsin, including the city of Madison, and purchases and distributes natural gas to approximately 173,000 customers in the Wisconsin counties of Columbia, Crawford, Dane, Iowa, Juneau, Monroe, and Vernon. MGE owned some 840 miles of overhead electric distribution line and 1,315 miles of underground electric distribution cable. These electric distribution facilities are connected by more than 50 substations, installed with a capacity of over 1.2 million kVA. MGE's gas facilities include some 3,045 miles of distribution mains, which are all owned by MGE.

	Annual Growth	12/19	12/20	12/21	12/22	12/23
Sales ($mil.)	5.0%	568.9	538.6	606.6	714.5	690.4
Net income ($ mil.)	7.9%	86.9	92.4	105.8	111.0	117.7
Market value ($ mil.)	(2.1%)	2,850.4	2,532.5	2,974.4	2,545.9	2,614.9
Employees	(0.4%)	731	723	706	701	719

MGIC INVESTMENT CORP. (WI)   NYS: MTG

250 E. Kilbourn Avenue
Milwaukee, WI 53202
Phone: 414 347-6480
Fax: –
Web: www.mgic.com

CEO: Timothy J Mattke
CFO: Nathaniel Colson
HR: –
FYE: December 31
Type: Public

MGIC Investment is a holding company and provides private mortgage insurance, other mortgage credit risk management solutions, and ancillary services through its wholly-owned subsidiaries. MGIC owns Mortgage Guaranty Insurance Corporation (MGIC), and was licensed in the US, Puerto Rico, and Guam. Such coverage allows otherwise-qualified buyers who aren't able to scrape up the standard about 20% down payment to get mortgages. MGIC writes primary insurance on individual loans; its customers include banks, mortgage brokers, credit unions, and other residential mortgage lenders. MGIC had about $1.2 billion in primary insurance in force.

	Annual Growth	12/19	12/20	12/21	12/22	12/23
Assets ($mil.)	1.2%	6,229.6	7,354.5	7,325.0	6,213.8	6,538.4
Net income ($ mil.)	1.4%	673.8	446.1	635.0	865.3	712.9
Market value ($ mil.)	8.0%	3,861.2	3,419.8	3,929.4	3,542.4	5,256.4
Employees	(3.5%)	724	739	711	683	627

MGM RESORTS INTERNATIONAL   NYS: MGM

3600 Las Vegas Boulevard South
Las Vegas, NV 89109
Phone: 702 693-7120
Fax: –
Web: www.mgmresorts.com

CEO: William J Hornbuckle
CFO: Jonathan S Halkyard
HR: –
FYE: December 31
Type: Public

MGM Resorts International is a global gaming and entertainment company with domestic and international locations featuring best-in-class hotels and casinos, state-of-the-art meeting and conference spaces, incredible live and theatrical entertainment experiences, and an extensive array of restaurant, nightlife and retail offerings, and sports betting and online gaming operations. It operates 17 domestic casino resorts and, through its 56% controlling interest in MGM China Holdings Limited, operates two casino resorts in Macau. It also has global online gaming operations through our consolidated subsidiary LeoVegas AB and our unconsolidated 50% owned venture, BetMGM, LLC.

	Annual Growth	12/19	12/20	12/21	12/22	12/23
Sales ($mil.)	5.8%	12,900	5,162.1	9,680.1	13,127	16,164
Net income ($ mil.)	(13.6%)	2,049.1	(1,032.7)	1,254.4	1,473.1	1,142.2
Market value ($ mil.)	7.7%	10,864	10,290	14,656	10,949	14,590
Employees	(2.6%)	70,000	42,000	59,000	64,000	63,000

MGP INGREDIENTS INC (NEW)   NMS: MGPI

100 Commercial Street, Box 130
Atchison, KS 66002
Phone: 913 367-1480
Fax: –
Web: www.mgpingredients.com

CEO: Augustus C Griffin
CFO: Brandon Gall
HR: Erika Lapish
FYE: December 31
Type: Public

MGP Ingredients is a leading producer and supplier of premium distilled spirits and specialty wheat protein and starch food ingredients. By-products from this process are mixed with corn and made into a variety of alcohol additives, used in distilled beverages, foods, and pharmaceuticals. MGP also produces fuel grade alcohol which is sold primarily for blending with gasoline to increase the octane and oxygen levels of the gasoline that can serve as a substitute for lead and petroleum-based octane enhancers. In addition, the company is also a supplier of premium spirits, including gin, bourbon, and rye whiskeys. Founded in 1941, MGP has evolved from a pure-play commodities provider to a maker of value-added ingredients.

	Annual Growth	12/19	12/20	12/21	12/22	12/23
Sales ($mil.)	23.2%	362.7	395.5	626.7	782.4	836.5
Net income ($ mil.)	29.0%	38.8	40.3	91.3	109.5	107.5
Market value ($ mil.)	19.4%	1,066.7	1,036.1	1,871.1	2,342.1	2,169.0
Employees	19.9%	341	360	672	690	705

MGT CAPITAL INVESTMENTS INC   NBB: MGTI

150 Fayetteville Street, Suite 1110
Raleigh, NC 27601
Phone: 914 630-7430
Fax: –
Web: www.mgtci.com

CEO: Robert B Ladd
CFO: Robert B Ladd
HR: –
FYE: December 31
Type: Public

MGT Capital Investments is looking for ROI, no matter if it's in American dollars or British sterling. The holding company is focused on medical imaging technology. It owns a 55% stake in Medicsight, a publicly traded company that develops medical imaging software to help detect cancer. The company narrowed its investments in 2010 when it divested its holdings in Medicexchange, XShares, HipCricket, and Eurindia. The following year it sold its stake in UK financial advisory firm Moneygate. Virtually all of MGT Capital's revenues now stem from Medicsight. Originally listed on the NYSE Amex in 1996, the company began trading on the London Stock Exchange's AIM exchange in 2011.

	Annual Growth	12/18	12/19	12/20	12/21	12/22
Sales ($mil.)	(20.5%)	2.0	0.5	1.4	0.9	0.8
Net income ($ mil.)	–	(23.8)	(8.8)	(3.9)	(1.5)	(6.0)
Market value ($ mil.)	(47.0%)	37.6	12.7	28.2	11.6	3.0
Employees	(15.9%)	4	3	2	2	2

MIAMI JEWISH HEALTH SYSTEMS, INC.

5200 NE 2ND AVE
MIAMI, FL 331372706
Phone: 305 751-8626
Fax: –
Web: www.miamijewishhealth.org

CEO: Jeffrey P Freimark
CFO: –
HR: Laura G Phr
FYE: June 30
Type: Private

With age comes experience, and Miami Jewish Health Systems is plenty experienced when it comes to geriatric care. The not-for-profit 460-bed nursing home and 30-bed hospital provides services to southern Florida residents of all ages, with a focus on the elderly. It also operates independent and assisted-living centers for seniors, as well as an ambulatory health center for general health care services. Its facilities provide a variety of services, such as care for Alzheimer's patients, assisted and independent living, rehabilitation, hospice, and home health care.

	Annual Growth	06/17	06/18	06/19	06/20	06/21
Sales ($mil.)	(6.5%)	–	68.6	64.0	69.2	56.2
Net income ($ mil.)	–	–	(1.4)	(34.4)	(12.2)	8.9
Market value ($ mil.)	–	–	–	–	–	–
Employees	–	–	–	–	–	1,100

MIAMI UNIVERSITY

501 E HIGH ST
OXFORD, OH 450561846
Phone: 513 529-1809
Fax: –
Web: www.miamioh.edu

CEO: –
CFO: –
HR: –
FYE: June 30
Type: Private

Not that Miami, the other one. Named for the Miami Indian Tribe that inhabited the area now known as the Miami Valley Region of Ohio, Miami University emphasizes undergraduate study at its main campus in Oxford (35 miles north of Cincinnati) as well as at commuter campuses in Hamilton, Middletown, and West Chester, Ohio, and a European Center in Luxembourg. The school offers bachelors, masters, and doctoral programs in areas including business administration, arts and sciences, engineering, and education. Its student body includes more than 15,000 undergraduates on the Oxford campus; 2,500 graduate students; and another 5,700 students attending satellite campuses. Miami University was established in 1809.

	Annual Growth	06/11	06/12	06/16	06/17	06/18
Sales ($mil.)	3.8%	–	440.5	522.2	544.6	551.7
Net income ($ mil.)	33.3%	–	32.9	65.1	83.7	184.5
Market value ($ mil.)	–	–	–	–	–	–
Employees	–	–	–	–	–	4,925

MIAMI VALLEY HOSPITAL

1 WYOMING ST
DAYTON, OH 454092711
Phone: 937 208-8000
Fax: –
Web: www.premierhealth.com

CEO: Jenny M Lewis
CFO: Lisa Bishop
HR: Gretchen L MBA
FYE: December 31
Type: Private

Don't go to Florida looking for this hospital! Miami Valley Hospital (MVH) is an acute care facility serving the residents of Dayton, Ohio and surrounding areas through two campuses. MVH and MVH South have roughly 950 beds and offer 50 primary and specialty care practices through its Regional Adult Burn Center, the MVH Cancer Center, MVH Sports Medicine Center, and behavioral health units for outpatient and inpatient chemical dependency therapy and other psychiatric services. MVH also offers Level I trauma services, Level III-B NICU, adult burn center, an air ambulance program, and blood, marrow, and kidney transplant services. The hospital is part of the Premier Health Partners network.

	Annual Growth	12/18	12/19	12/20	12/21	12/22
Sales ($mil.)	5.4%	–	–	–	1,279.5	1,349.1
Net income ($ mil.)	(36.2%)	–	–	–	300.0	191.3
Market value ($ mil.)	–	–	–	–	–	–
Employees	–	–	–	–	–	8,403

MICHAEL ANTHONY JEWELERS INC

115 South MacQuesten Parkway
Mt. Vernon, NY 10550-1724
Phone: 914 699-0000
Fax: 914 699-2335
Web: www.michaelanthony.com

NBB: MAJJ
CEO: –
CFO: –
HR: –
FYE: February 1
Type: Public

Most of what glitters is gold at Michael Anthony Jewelers. The company spins gold into upscale chains (which account for the majority of its sales), charms, earrings, and bracelets bearing diamonds, colored gemstones, and pearls. It also makes engagement and wedding rings in classic and fashion-forward styles. Michael Anthony sells its jewelry through two mall stores in New Jersey. The company is part of the Richline Group, a wholly owned subsidiary of Berkshire Hathaway, with substantial holdings in the jewelry business. It was founded by brothers Michael and Anthony Paolercio in 1977.

	Annual Growth	01/99	01/00	01/01*	02/02	02/03
Sales ($mil.)	(3.5%)	137.0	144.5	124.7	141.9	118.6
Net income ($ mil.)	–	2.1	2.6	(1.4)	1.0	(4.2)
Market value ($ mil.)	(15.8%)	0.0	0.0	0.0	0.0	0.0
Employees	1.0%	683	663	639	742	712

*Fiscal year change

MICHAEL BAKER INTERNATIONAL, INC.

500 GRANT ST STE 5400
PITTSBURGH, PA 152192523
Phone: 412 269-6300
Fax: –
Web: –

CEO: Brian A Lutes
CFO: Chris Statham
HR: –
FYE: December 31
Type: Private

Michael Baker Jr. is the first-born subsidiary of engineering and construction consulting group Michael Baker. Michael Baker Jr. focuses on engineering design for civil infrastructure and transportation projects, which include highways, bridges, airports, busways, corporate headquarters, data centers, correctional facilities, and educational facilities. The unit also provides planning, geotechnical, and environmental services in the water/wastewater, pipeline, emergency and consequence management, resource management, and telecommunications markets. Recent projects include facilities for the US government.

	Annual Growth	12/04	12/05	12/06	12/07	12/09
Sales ($mil.)	8.3%	–	–	329.2	351.9	418.5
Net income ($ mil.)	–	–	–	(12.4)	10.2	15.5
Market value ($ mil.)	–	–	–	–	–	–
Employees	–	–	–	–	–	3,200

MICHAEL FOODS GROUP, INC.

9350 EXCELSIOR BLVD STE 300
HOPKINS, MN 553433455
Phone: 952 258-4000
Fax: –
Web: www.michaelfoods.com

CEO: James E Dwyer Jr
CFO: –
HR: –
FYE: December 29
Type: Private

It's not meat and potatoes, but poultry and potatoes and some dairy foods at Michael Foods Group. The group operates through Michael Foods, Inc., one of the top US producers and distributors of value-added egg products (frozen, liquid, pre-cooked, and dried). Its Egg Products division, comprised of four subsidiaries, supplies egg products to food service, retail grocery, and food ingredient customers. The group's business includes Crystal Farms, a distributor of cheese, butter, and other dairy case items to US groceries, and Northern Star, a supplier of refrigerated potato products to North American food service operators and grocery stores. The company was acquired by cereal maker Post Holdings in mid-2014.

MICHAEL MERGER SUB LLC

717 TEXAS ST STE 2900
HOUSTON, TX 770022836
Phone: 918 748-3370
Fax: –
Web: www.midconenergypartners.com

CEO: –
CFO: –
HR: –
FYE: December 31
Type: Private

Mid-Con Energy Partners is a Delaware limited partnership that owns, operates, and develops producing oil and natural gas properties in North America. With a focus on the Mid-Continent region of the US, in particular Oklahoma and Colorado, the company's operations primarily consist of enhancing the development of mature, producing oil properties through an oil recovery method called waterflooding. It has total estimated proved reserves of about 8 million barrels of oil equivalent, a majority of which is oil. Managed by Mid-Con Energy GP, Mid-Con Energy Partners was formed in July 2011 and went public in December 2011.

MICHELS CORPORATION

817 MAIN ST
BROWNSVILLE, WI 530061444
Phone: 920 583-3132
Fax: –
Web: www.michels.us

CEO: Patrick D Michels
CFO: Jason Kozelek
HR: –
FYE: December 31
Type: Private

Michels Corporation is one of the largest, most diversified energy and infrastructure contractors in North America. The family-owned company fulfills needs for energy, transportation, distribution, and communications customers in the US and Canada. Michels is a full-service engineering procurement, and construction contractor. It serves its customers with pipe fabrication, pipeline construction, electric utility construction, hot work construction, OPGW cable installation, overhead power line construction, microtunneling, trenchless pipe repair and lining, directional drilling, direct pipe, deep foundations, aggregate piers, soldier piles and lagging. It provides bridge construction, highway and road construction, construction aggregates, concrete crushing, recycled concrete aggregates and are paving contractors. Michels was founded in 1959.

MICHIGAN CONSOLIDATED GAS CO

2000 2nd Avenue
Detroit, MI 48226-1279
Phone: 313 235-4000
Fax: -
Web: www.michcon.com

CEO: Anthony F Earley Jr
CFO: David E Meador
HR: -
FYE: December 31
Type: Public

DTE Gas warming homes for those living in the land of the Spartans and Wolverines. The company is a utility subsidiary of DTE Energy and provides natural gas to 1.3 million residential, commercial, and industrial customers in some 500 communities throughout Michigan. DTE Gas owns storage properties in four underground natural gas storage fields with an aggregate capacity of approximately 140 Bcf. It acquires gas from producers along the US Gulf Coast, US Mid-Continent, and Canada.

	Annual Growth	12/09	12/10	12/11	12/12	12/13
Sales ($mil.)	(4.8%)	1,765.0	1,628.0	1,483.0	1,293.0	1,448.0
Net income ($ mil.)	11.0%	93.0	130.0	109.0	114.0	141.0
Market value ($ mil.)	-	-	-	-	-	-
Employees	-	-	-	-	-	1,100

MICHIGAN MILK PRODUCERS ASSOCIATION

41310 BRIDGE ST
NOVI, MI 483751302
Phone: 248 474-6672
Fax: -
Web: www.mimilk.com

CEO: John Dilland
CFO: -
HR: Kelly Kerrigan
FYE: September 30
Type: Private

Ice cream and other dairy products might be missing a major ingredient without Michigan Milk Producers Association (MMPA). The dairy cooperative, which serves more than 2,100 farmers in Michigan, Ohio, Indiana, and Wisconsin, produces some 3.9 billion pounds of milk each year. Milk products include sweetened condensed milk, instant nonfat milk, and dried buttermilk, as well as other items the likes of cream, cheese, butter, and ice-cream mixes. With no consumer brands or products, MMPA sells its products as ingredients to food makers who sell baby formulas, candy, ice cream, and yogurt. Founded in 1916, the co-op operates a pair of Michigan plants and a merchandise facility.

	Annual Growth	09/07	09/08	09/09	09/10	09/11
Sales ($mil.)	25.1%	-	-	556.7	698.8	870.9
Net income ($ mil.)	3.2%	-	-	6.0	6.8	6.4
Market value ($ mil.)	-	-	-	-	-	-
Employees	-	-	-	-	-	200

MICHIGAN STATE UNIVERSITY

426 AUDITORIUM RD
EAST LANSING, MI 488242600
Phone: 517 355-1855
Fax: -
Web: www.msu.edu

CEO: Seth Ciabotti
CFO: -
HR: Carol B Noud
FYE: June 30
Type: Private

Founded in 1855, Michigan State University (MSU) was the model of a land-grant institution made into law in 1862. MSU and its nearly 50,025 students cover a lot of land in East Lansing. The university offers more than 400 academic programs of study through more than 15 colleges and unrivaled opportunities for undergraduate research. It has extensive programs in core fields including education, physics, psychology, medicine, and communications. It is also a leading research university with top-ranked international studies programs. As a highly ranked research university, MSU is awarded millions of dollars in research grants each year from public and private entities.

	Annual Growth	06/14	06/15	06/16	06/17	06/18
Sales ($mil.)	4.7%	-	-	1,811.1	1,931.6	1,986.9
Net income ($ mil.)	-	-	-	71.0	481.9	(246.3)
Market value ($ mil.)	-	-	-	-	-	-
Employees	-	-	-	-	-	11,100

MICHIGAN TECHNOLOGICAL UNIVERSITY

1400 TOWNSEND DR
HOUGHTON, MI 499311200
Phone: 906 487-1885
Fax: -
Web: www.mtu.edu

CEO: -
CFO: -
HR: Kyllonen Patricia
FYE: June 30
Type: Private

Michigan Technological University trains techies in the Wolverine State. A premier research university, the school, affectionately known as Michigan Tech, offers a range of programs in computing, engineering, technology, business and technology, forest resources and environmental science, social work, sciences and arts, and non-departmental sponsored educational programs. Based in Houghton, the school has an enrollment of about 7,000 undergraduate and graduate students, and a faculty of almost 480 instructors. The company is considered to be a discrete component unit of the State of Michigan because its Board of Control is appointed by the Governor.

	Annual Growth	06/10	06/11	06/13	06/17	06/22
Sales ($mil.)	(34.0%)	-	147.5	155.4	173.7	1.5
Net income ($ mil.)	-	-	(0.9)	3.0	(1.9)	0.3
Market value ($ mil.)	-	-	-	-	-	-
Employees	-	-	-	-	-	1,939

MICRO IMAGING TECHNOLOGY INC

970 Calle Amanecer, Suite F
San Clemente, CA 92673
Phone: 949 388-4546
Fax: -
Web: www.micro-imaging.com

NBB: MMTC
CEO: Jeffrey G Nunez
CFO: Victor A Hollander
HR: -
FYE: October 31
Type: Public

Micro Imaging Technology (formerly Electropure) is developing laser-based technology that detects microbes and microorganisms in water. Micro Imaging Technology hopes to commercialize its products for applications such as food inspection and water testing, but the company hasn't had enough money to do so. In 2005 the company sold the assets of its Electropure EDI subsidiary, a maker of ion-permeable membranes and deionization devices; Electropure then changed its name to Micro Imaging Technology, effective 2006. In 2007 the company sold and installed two bacteria identification systems in Tokyo. Former US Postmaster General Anthony Frank owns a 45% stake in Micro Imaging Technology.

	Annual Growth	10/09	10/10	10/11	10/12	10/13
Sales ($mil.)	-	0.0	-	-	-	-
Net income ($ mil.)	-	(3.5)	(2.9)	(1.4)	(1.2)	(0.9)
Market value ($ mil.)	18.9%	1.3	1.3	0.0	0.0	2.6
Employees	(4.5%)	6	5	5	7	5

MICROBLEND, INC.

543 COUNTRY CLUB DR
SIMI VALLEY, CA 930650637
Phone: 330 998-4602
Fax: -
Web: www.microblend.com

CEO: John E Tyson
CFO: Jon Steging
HR: -
FYE: June 30
Type: Private

No more inventory! Product on demand! Revolution! Sounds like the sales pitch that came from countless dot-coms circa 1999. But MicroBlend Technologies aims to change the way paint is manufactured and sold through just those heady fin de siecle promises. Its Automated Paint Machine system manufactures paint at the point of sale, as it's been ordered (interior/exterior, flat/gloss, color, and amount), reducing the need for a huge retail space devoted to hundreds of gallons of already-made paint. MicroBlend has licensing agreements with several manufacturers to produce its equipment and component sauces. The company has also formed a co-branding partnership with DuPont's coatings unit.

MICROBOT MEDICAL INC NAS: MBOT

25 Recreation Park Drive, Unit 108
Hingham, MA 02043
Phone: 781 875-3605
Fax: –
Web: www.microbotmedical.com

CEO: Harel Gadot
CFO: Rachel Vaknin
HR: –
FYE: December 31
Type: Public

For Microbot Medical (formerly StemCells), success stems from reinvention. Formerly focused on the discovery of cell-based therapies to treat diseases of the central nervous system (CNS), the company faced a major setback in mid-2016 when its unsuccessful Pathway Study in spinal cord injury was terminated. StemCells' initial response was to begin winding down operations. However, within months the company merged with private firm Microbot. The merged company is now focused on the development of robotic medical devices such as a titanium miniature robot that can clean artificial drainage plants implanted in the body. It is hoped that those devices will eventually be used to clean plaque from blood vessels to prevent heart attack or stroke.

	Annual Growth	12/19	12/20	12/21	12/22	12/23
Sales ($mil.)	–	–	–	–	–	–
Net income ($ mil.)	–	(7.2)	(9.2)	(11.3)	(13.2)	(10.7)
Market value ($ mil.)	(36.6%)	119.1	80.7	87.8	35.2	19.2
Employees	–	12	14	17	21	–

MICROCHIP TECHNOLOGY INC NMS: MCHP

2355 W. Chandler Blvd.
Chandler, AZ 85224-6199
Phone: 480 792-7200
Fax: 480 792-7790
Web: www.microchip.com

CEO: Ganesh Moorthy
CFO: J E Bjornholt
HR: –
FYE: March 31
Type: Public

Microchip Technology develops, manufactures and sells smart, connected, and secure embedded control solutions used by its customers for a wide variety of applications. The semiconductor maker offers a variety of embedded devices, including eight-, 16-, and 32-bit microcontrollers (it's a leading producer worldwide). With over 30 years of technology leadership, its broad product portfolio is a Total System Solution (TSS) for its customers that can provide a large portion of the silicon requirements in their applications. TSS is a combination of hardware, software, and services which help its customers increase their revenue, reduce their costs and manage their risks compared to other solutions. The company's solutions serve more than 120,000 customers across the industrial, automotive, consumer, aerospace and defense, communications and computing markets. Microchip gets about 70% of sales from customers outside the US.

	Annual Growth	03/19	03/20	03/21	03/22	03/23
Sales ($mil.)	12.1%	5,349.5	5,274.2	5,438.4	6,820.9	8,438.7
Net income ($ mil.)	58.4%	355.9	570.6	349.4	1,285.5	2,237.7
Market value ($ mil.)	0.2%	45,251	36,982	84,666	40,986	45,699
Employees	5.4%	18,286	18,000	19,500	21,000	22,600

MICROFINANCIAL INCORPORATED

200 SUMMIT DR STE 100
BURLINGTON, MA 018035274
Phone: 781 994-4800
Fax: –
Web: www.timepayment.com

CEO: –
CFO: James R Jackson Jr
HR: –
FYE: December 31
Type: Private

MicroFinancial thinks big when it comes to leasing small-ticket items to small and midsized businesses. Through TimePayment, MicroFinancial leases items that are generally valued between $500 and $15,000. Although the "microticket" leaser provides financing for a variety of office and commercial equipment, the majority of the contracts in its portfolio are for POS authorization systems for debit and credit cards. It doesn't lease and rent equipment directly, but through a network of independent dealers across the US. TimePaymentDirect processes applications and approves credit online; Insta-Lease does the same via telephone, fax, and e-mail. Funds managed by Fortress Investment are buying MicroFinancial.

MICRON SOLUTIONS INC (DE) NBB: MICR D

25 Sawyer Passway
Fitchburg, MA 01420
Phone: 978 345-5000
Fax: 978 342-0168
Web: www.micronsolutionsinc.com

CEO: Salvatore Emma Jr
CFO: Derek T Welch
HR: –
FYE: December 31
Type: Public

It's all about heart for Arrhythmia Research Technology (ART). The company offers signal-averaging electrocardiographic (SAECG) software that collects data and analyzes electrical impulses of the heart in an effort to detect potentially lethal heart arrhythmias. The company plans to sell the products through licensing agreements with equipment makers. Until it finds a marketing partner, however, ART is relying on sales from its Micron Products subsidiary, which makes snaps and sensors used in the manufacture and operation of disposable electrodes for electrocardiographic (ECG) equipment. Micron Products has acquired assets of several companies that enhance its metal and plastics molding capabilities.

	Annual Growth	12/18	12/19	12/20	12/21	12/22
Sales ($mil.)	3.6%	19.6	17.5	20.8	20.4	22.6
Net income ($ mil.)	–	(1.1)	(2.1)	1.1	1.7	(1.3)
Market value ($ mil.)	(4.1%)	8.4	7.6	10.6	9.5	7.1
Employees	6.0%	88	86	112	108	111

MICRON TECHNOLOGY INC. NMS: MU

8000 S. Federal Way
Boise, ID 83716-9632
Phone: 208 368-4000
Fax: –
Web: www.micron.com

CEO: –
CFO: –
HR: –
FYE: August 31
Type: Public

Micron Technology is one of the largest memory chip makers in the world. It makes DRAM (Dynamic Random Access Memory), NAND Flash, and NOR Flash memory, and other memory technologies. Its memory and storage solutions enable disruptive trends, including artificial intelligence, 5G, machine learning, and autonomous vehicles, in key market segments like mobile, data center, client, consumer, industrial, graphics, automotive, and networking. Micron's products are offered under the Micron, Crucial, and Ballistix brands, as well as private labels. Micron generates more than 50% of revenue from the US.

	Annual Growth	08/19*	09/20	09/21	09/22*	08/23
Sales ($mil.)	(9.7%)	23,406	21,435	27,705	30,758	15,540
Net income ($ mil.)	–	6,313.0	2,687.0	5,861.0	8,687.0	(5,833.0)
Market value ($ mil.)	11.9%	49,048	50,870	81,241	62,926	76,794
Employees	3.8%	37,000	40,000	43,000	48,000	43,000

*Fiscal year change

MICROPAC INDUSTRIES, INC. NBB: MPAD

905 E. Walnut
Garland, TX 75040
Phone: 972 272-3571
Fax: –
Web: –

CEO: Mark King
CFO: Patrick S Cefalu
HR: –
FYE: November 30
Type: Public

Micropac Industries makes hybrid microelectronic circuits and optoelectronic components/assemblies, as well as solid-state relays, power controllers and amplifiers, Hall-effect sensors, light-emitting diodes (LEDs) and displays, and high-temperature products. The company also offers contract manufacturing and packaging services, with plants in Mexico and the US. Micropac's customers include industrial and medical markets, as well as contractors for the US Department of Defense and NASA, which account for more 70% of sales. Director Heinz-Werner Hempel owns more than three-quarters of the company. Micropac's products are marketed in the US and Europe.

	Annual Growth	11/19	11/20	11/21	11/22	11/23
Sales ($mil.)	4.7%	25.5	22.3	27.3	27.8	30.6
Net income ($ mil.)	(35.8%)	3.7	1.5	3.1	2.8	0.6
Market value ($ mil.)	(5.7%)	34.1	30.9	42.3	36.1	27.0
Employees	2.0%	132	143	153	147	143

MICROSEMI CORPORATION

11861 WESTERN AVE
GARDEN GROVE, CA 928412119
Phone: 949 380-6100
Fax: –
Web: www.microsemi.com

CEO: Steve Sanghi
CFO: Eric Bjornholt
HR: Kimberley Connell
FYE: October 01
Type: Private

Microsemi offers a comprehensive portfolio of semiconductor and system solutions for communications, defense and security, aerospace and industrial markets. The company's power management semiconductors regulate and condition electricity to make it more usable by electrical and electronic systems. Other products include high-performance and radiation-hardened analog mixed-signal integrated circuits, FPGAs, SoCs and ASICs; timing and synchronization devices and precise time solutions, voice processing devices; RF solutions; discrete components; enterprise storage and communication solutions, security technologies and scalable anti-tamper products; Ethernet solutions; Power-over-Ethernet ICs and midspans; as well as custom design capabilities and services. The company is a wholly owned subsidiary of Microchip Technology Inc.

MICROSOFT CORPORATION — NMS: MSFT

One Microsoft Way
Redmond, WA 98052-6399
Phone: 425 882-8080
Fax: –
Web: www.microsoft.com

CEO: Satya Nadella
CFO: Amy E Hood
HR: –
FYE: June 30
Type: Public

Microsoft is one of the world's leading technology companies with products that include the Windows operating system, cross-device productivity and collaboration applications, and Azure cloud services. The company offers licensing and support for its wide portfolio of software products; designing, selling, and delivering devices (including PCs, tablets, gaming and entertainment consoles, other intelligent devices, and related accessories) and delivering relevant online advertising to a global audience. LinkedIn, its business-oriented social network, is used by millions to make connections. Microsoft's customers range from consumers and small businesses to the world's biggest companies and government agencies. Geographically, Microsoft's revenue is evenly split between the US and the other countries, and about 70% of its revenue comes from services and other. Microsoft was founded in 1975.

	Annual Growth	06/19	06/20	06/21	06/22	06/23
Sales ($mil.)	13.9%	125,843	143,015	168,088	198,270	211,915
Net income ($ mil.)	16.5%	39,240	44,281	61,271	72,738	72,361
Market value ($ mil.)	26.3%	995,591	1,512,486	2,013,329	1,908,761	2,530,893
Employees	11.3%	144,000	163,000	181,000	221,000	221,000

MICROSTRATEGY INC. — NMS: MSTR

1850 Towers Crescent Plaza
Tysons Corner, VA 22182
Phone: 703 848-8600
Fax: 703 848-8610
Web: www.microstrategy.com

CEO: Phong Q Le
CFO: Andrew Kang
HR: –
FYE: December 31
Type: Public

MicroStrategy is a global leader in enterprise analytics software and services. Its vision is to enable Intelligence Everywhere by providing world-class software and services that provide enterprise users with actionable insights. Its MicroStrategy Platform is an enterprise analytics software platform that incorporates a comprehensive suite of software offerings that are packaged and configured to meet customer requirements. Its customers include leading companies from a wide range of industries, including retail, consulting, technology, manufacturing, banking, insurance, finance, healthcare, telecommunications, as well as the public sector. MicroStrategy also offers consulting, education, and support services. Majority of its sales were generated from its domestic markets.

	Annual Growth	12/19	12/20	12/21	12/22	12/23
Sales ($mil.)	0.5%	486.3	480.7	510.8	499.3	496.3
Net income ($ mil.)	88.0%	34.4	(7.5)	(535.5)	(1,469.8)	429.1
Market value ($ mil.)	45.1%	2,405.9	6,554.1	9,184.5	2,388.0	10,654
Employees	(5.2%)	2,396	1,997	2,121	2,152	1,934

MICROTECHNOLOGIES LLC

8330 BOONE BLVD STE 600
VIENNA, VA 221822658
Phone: 703 891-1073
Fax: –
Web: www.microtech.net

CEO: Anthony R Jimenez
CFO: Jeff Langhan
HR: –
FYE: December 31
Type: Private

MicroTechnologies is a US small business dishing up tech services to some big clients. Also known as MicroTech, the Hispanic- and veteran-owned company delivers IT reseller products, technical support, systems integration, and management consulting services to clients ranging from Fortune 500 companies to the federal government. It has added virtualization and cloud computing to its service portfolio. It also serves state, city, and local agencies. For the US General Services Administration, it has provided and set up personal computers, Web access, data, voice, and video communications, and teleconferencing systems for President Obama's staff.

	Annual Growth	12/05	12/06	12/07	12/08	12/10
Sales ($mil.)	(64.7%)	–	–	2,124.0	39.0	93.5
Net income ($ mil.)	667.5%	–	–	0.0	2.5	7.4
Market value ($ mil.)	–	–	–	–	–	–
Employees	–	–	–	–	–	80

MICROVISION INC. — NMS: MVIS

18390 NE 68th Street
Redmond, WA 98052
Phone: 425 936-6847
Fax: –
Web: www.microvision.com

CEO: Sumit Sharma
CFO: Anubhav Verma
HR: –
FYE: December 31
Type: Public

Microvision thinks tiny images have big potential. The company's PicoP display technology can be used to create high-quality video and image displays using an ultra-miniature projector that is embedded into mobile devices such as cell phones, DVD players, gaming devices, and laptops. The projector enables users to display images and data onto a variety of surfaces from mobile products. Microvision's first product -- the SHOWWX accessory projector -- connects via cable to a video-out connection on a mobile device. It is sold directly and through distributors in Asia and Europe. The company also produces prototypes based on its light scanning technology under government and commercial development contracts.

	Annual Growth	12/19	12/20	12/21	12/22	12/23
Sales ($mil.)	(4.9%)	8.9	3.1	2.5	0.7	7.3
Net income ($ mil.)	–	(26.5)	(13.6)	(43.2)	(53.1)	(82.8)
Market value ($ mil.)	38.6%	140.2	1,047.7	975.6	457.6	518.0
Employees	83.5%	30	52	96	350	340

MICROWAVE FILTER CO., INC. — NBB: MFCO

6743 Kinne Street
East Syracuse, NY 13057
Phone: 315 438-4700
Fax: 315 463-1467
Web: www.microwavefilter.com

CEO: Carl F Fahrenkrug
CFO: Richard L Jones
HR: –
FYE: September 30
Type: Public

Microwave Filter Company (MFC) can improve your powers of reception. The company's electronic filters process TV, radio, and other signals, and prevent unwanted signals from interfering with transmissions. Its Fastrap filters are used by cable TV operators either to allow or to prevent viewing of pay-per-view broadcasts and premium programming. MFC sells more than 1,700 products to the broadcasting, cable television, defense, and mobile radio industries. Subsidiary Niagara Scientific makes material handling equipment for the cosmetics, food processing, and pharmaceutical industries. Sales are primarily in the US.

	Annual Growth	09/19	09/20	09/21	09/22	09/23
Sales ($mil.)	(0.5%)	3.9	3.1	5.2	5.2	3.8
Net income ($ mil.)	–	0.2	(0.3)	0.6	0.7	(0.2)
Market value ($ mil.)	9.3%	1.1	1.2	1.4	1.9	1.5
Employees	–	–	–	–	–	–

MICROWAVE TRANSMISSION SYSTEMS, INC

1751 JAY ELL DR
RICHARDSON, TX 750811835
Phone: 972 669-0591
Fax: –
Web: www.mtsi.com

CEO: Preston D Spurling
CFO: –
HR: –
FYE: December 31
Type: Private

Microwave Transmission Systems (MTSI) constructs and maintains wireless communications transmitting and receiving facilities. In addition to building and erecting microwave towers and installing and testing cellular equipment, the company's services include planning related to feasibility studies and FCC radio frequency licensing. It also provides site and project management services. Founded in 1987, MTSI has offices and subsidiaries in Florida, New Mexico, North Carolina, Ohio, Tennessee, and Texas. Affiliated companies include Viper Communications and Site Communications.

	Annual Growth	12/13	12/14	12/15	12/16	12/17
Sales ($mil.)	5.7%	–	53.9	49.5	40.8	63.6
Net income ($ mil.)	–	–	(1.1)	(1.2)	(2.0)	4.6
Market value ($ mil.)	–	–	–	–	–	–
Employees	–	–	–	–	–	656

MID AMERICA CLINICAL LABORATORIES LLC

2560 N SHADELAND AVE STE B
INDIANAPOLIS, IN 462191706
Phone: 877 803-1010
Fax: –
Web: www.questdiagnostics.com

CEO: Dianne Vanness
CFO: –
HR: –
FYE: December 31
Type: Private

Let's hope the Hoosiers at Mid America Clinical Laboratories don't suffer from test anxiety. The company operates more than 30 specimen collection and laboratory sites in Indianapolis and the surrounding central Indiana region. The company processes more than 4.5 million tests every year, and its labs are equipped to perform a variety of medical testing, including biopsies, PAP tests, urinalyses, and blood tests. Mid America Clinical Laboratories is a joint venture company owned by Ascension Health's St. Vincent Hospital, Community Hospital, and Quest Diagnostics.

	Annual Growth	12/05	12/06	12/07	12/08	12/09
Sales ($mil.)	60.4%	–	18.3	67.3	70.9	75.5
Net income ($ mil.)	41.1%	–	3.3	9.2	8.9	9.2
Market value ($ mil.)	–	–	–	–	–	–
Employees	–	–	–	–	–	525

MID PENN BANCORP INC

NMS: MPB

2407 Park Drive
Harrisburg, PA 17110
Phone: 866 642-7736
Fax: –
Web: www.midpennbank.com

CEO: Rory G Ritrievi
CFO: Allison S Johnson
HR: –
FYE: December 31
Type: Public

Mid Penn Bancorp is the holding company for Mid Penn Bank, which operates more than a dozen branches in central Pennsylvania's Cumberland, Dauphin, Northumberland, and Schuylkill counties. The bank offers full-service commercial banking, insurance, and trust services. Its deposit products include checking, savings, money market, and NOW accounts. Commercial real estate, construction, and land development loans account for nearly 80% of the company's loan portfolio; the bank also writes residential mortgages and business, agricultural, and consumer loans. Mid Penn is a descendant of Millersburg Bank, founded in 1868. Trust company CEDE & Co. owns about a third of Mid Penn Bancorp.

	Annual Growth	12/18	12/19	12/20	12/21	12/22
Assets ($mil.)	21.3%	2,078.0	2,231.2	2,998.9	4,689.4	4,498.0
Net income ($ mil.)	50.8%	10.6	17.7	26.2	29.3	54.8
Market value ($ mil.)	6.8%	365.7	457.5	347.9	504.2	476.1
Employees	10.8%	406	444	466	619	611

MID VENTURES INC.

2001 BUTTERFIELD RD STE 1500
DOWNERS GROVE, IL 60515
Phone: 630 719-0211
Fax: –
Web: –

CEO: Donald Slivensky
CFO: –
HR: –
FYE: December 31
Type: Private

Mid Ventures, doing business as MicroTek, operates classroom facilities that companies rent for off-site employee training sessions. In addition to classrooms, each location offers amenities such as break rooms, conference rooms, and e-learning capabilities. MicroTek also consults on course design, site selection, and instructor services. The firm has campuses in about a dozen US cities but operates worldwide. It also has international locations. In addition to classroom training, it offers virtual sessions and provides event management services. Founded in 1991, MicroTek and has served clients such as Dell, E*Trade, and PeopleSoft.

	Annual Growth	12/99	12/00	12/01	12/02	12/07
Sales ($mil.)	30.1%	–	7.8	11.3	14.5	49.6
Net income ($ mil.)	24.4%	–	1.5	0.4	0.9	7.0
Market value ($ mil.)	–	–	–	–	–	–
Employees	–	–	–	–	–	100

MID-AM BUILDING SUPPLY, INC.

1615 OMAR BRADLEY RD
MOBERLY, MO 652709406
Phone: 660 263-2140
Fax: –
Web: www.midambuilding.com

CEO: –
CFO: –
HR: –
FYE: December 31
Type: Private

Mid-Am Building Supply is a wholesale distributor of building materials in Middle America. The company sells windows, doors, siding, roofing materials, cabinets, and other interior supplies from National Gypsum, Owens Corning, Schlage, and Bostitch, among other manufacturers. It also operates four door-fabrication warehouses, offers tool repair, and provides estimates for cabinet and window installation. Mid-Am's trucks deliver the goods to lumber dealers through about a half dozen locations in Illinois, Iowa, Kansas, and Missouri. The third-generation family-owned business was founded in 1967 by Joe and Hildegarde Knaebel.

	Annual Growth	12/03	12/04	12/05	12/06	12/07
Sales ($mil.)	1.8%	–	131.2	139.6	–	138.6
Net income ($ mil.)	102.6%	–	4.2	3.9	–	34.8
Market value ($ mil.)	–	–	–	–	–	–
Employees	–	–	–	–	–	31

MID-AMERICA APARTMENT COMMUNITIES INC

NYS: MAA

6815 Poplar Avenue, Suite 500
Germantown, TN 38138
Phone: 901 682-6600
Fax: 901 682-6667
Web: www.maac.com

CEO: –
CFO: –
HR: –
FYE: December 31
Type: Public

Mid-America Apartment Communities (MAA) is a self-administered, self-managed real estate investment trust (REIT) that focuses solely on buying multifamily residences. MAA owns or has interests in more than 100,000 apartment units in more than 15 states, primarily located in the South West, Southeast and Mid-Atlantic regions of the US. Its largest markets, wherein about 70% of the company's apartment units offered are located in Georgia, Texas, North Carolina, and Florida. MAA, which has an average property occupancy rate of about 95%, targets large and midsized markets.

	Annual Growth	12/19	12/20	12/21	12/22	12/23
Sales ($mil.)	7.0%	1,641.0	1,678.0	1,778.1	2,019.9	2,148.5
Net income ($ mil.)	11.8%	353.8	255.0	533.8	637.4	552.8
Market value ($ mil.)	0.5%	15,387	14,784	26,774	18,320	15,691
Employees	(0.9%)	2,513	2,530	2,429	2,387	2,427

MIDAS MEDICI GROUP HOLDINGS INC

445 Park Avenue, 20th Floor
New York, NY 10022
Phone: 212 792-0920
Fax: –
Web: –

CEO: Nana Baffour
CFO: Johnson M Kachidza
HR: –
FYE: December 31
Type: Public

Midas Medici has some very regal aspirations for its holdings. The company formed in 2009 to purchase UtiliPoint International, a consultant and research services provider to the energy and utility industries. In March 2011 Midas Medici bought IT services company Consonus Technologies in exchange for 4.9 million shares of stock. Consonus provides IT infrastructure, data center, and managed services to businesses of all sizes. Midas Medici is branding its two energy and technology subsidiaries as "green IT" services that focus on smart grid and cloud computing capabilities. CEO Nana Baffour and president Johnson Kachidza control 57% of Midas Medici's stock.

	Annual Growth	12/07	12/08	12/09	12/10	12/11
Sales ($mil.)	190.4%	–	3.7	3.0	1.1	89.7
Net income ($ mil.)	–	–	(0.3)	(1.5)	(2.5)	(10.0)
Market value ($ mil.)	–	–	–	–	19.8	25.7
Employees	–	–	–	23	16	347

MIDCOAST ENERGY PARTNERS, L.P.

1100 LOUISIANA ST STE 3300
HOUSTON, TX 77002
Phone: 800 755-5400
Fax: –
Web: www.midcoastenergy.com

CEO: –
CFO: –
HR: –
FYE: December 31
Type: Private

Midcoast Energy Partners was formed by Enbridge Energy Partners in 2013 as an investment vehicle to own and grow its natural gas and NGL midstream business. It has minority stakes in Enbridge's network of natural gas and natural gas liquids (NGLs) gathering and transportation systems, natural gas processing and treating facilities, and NGL fractionation plants in Texas and Oklahoma. Organized as a limited partnership, Midcoast Energy Partners is exempt from paying income tax as long as it distributes quarterly dividends to shareholders. It went public in 2013, raising $333 million. In 2017 Enbridge Energy Partners agreed to acquire control of Midcoast Energy Partners.

	Annual Growth	12/12	12/13	12/14	12/15	12/16
Sales ($mil.)	(29.4%)	–	5,593.6	5,894.3	2,842.7	1,966.0
Net income ($ mil.)	–	–	–	53.9	144.3	(284.5)	(157.0)
Market value ($ mil.)	–	–	–	–	–	–
Employees	–	–	–	–	–	1,250

MIDCONTINENT INDEPENDENT SYSTEM OPERATOR, INC.

720 CITY CENTER DR
CARMEL, IN 460323826
Phone: 317 249-5400
Fax: –
Web: www.misoenergy.org

CEO: John R Bear
CFO: –
HR: Dennis C Hetletved
FYE: December 31
Type: Private

Midcontinent Independent System Operator (MISO) is an independent, not-for-profit, member-based organization that monitors and coordinates the operation of an electric transmission system with more than 68,000 miles of transmission lines across some 15 US states and Manitoba, Canada. MISO operates one of the world's largest energy markets with more than $40 billion in annual gross market energy transaction. In addition to managing the power grid within its region, MISO administers the buying and selling of electricity, and partners with members and stakeholders to plan the grid of the future. MISO became the nation's first FERC-approved Regional Transmission Organization (RTO) in 2001.

MIDCONTINENT MEDIA, INC.

3600 MINNESOTA DR STE 700
MINNEAPOLIS, MN 554357918
Phone: 952 844-2600
Fax: –
Web: –

CEO: Patrick McAdaragh
CFO: –
HR: –
FYE: June 30
Type: Private

Midcontinent Media operates primarily through its main subsidiary (Midcontinent Communications) which it co-owns with cable giant Comcast. Midcontinent Communications provides cable television, local and long-distance digital telephone service, and high-speed Internet access to more than 300,000 consumers and businesses in more than 335 communities in four Midwestern and Plains states. Midcontinent Media also provides outsourced call center services to such retailers as The Wine Enthusiast and Woolrich through its Midco Call Center Services subsidiary. Midcontinent Media's also oversees charitable programs through the Midcontinent Media Foundation which administers funds for regional health care, social, educational, and arts programs.

MIDDLE TENNESSEE STATE UNIVERSITY

1301 E MAIN ST
MURFREESBORO, TN 371320002
Phone: 615 898-2300
Fax: –
Web: www.mtsu.edu

CEO: –
CFO: –
HR: –
FYE: June 30
Type: Private

Middle Tennessee State University (MTSU), founded in 1911 as a school for teacher training, offers bachelor's and master's degrees through its eight university colleges. The educational institution boasts basic and applied sciences, business, education and behavioral science, honors, liberal arts, mass communication, and graduate studies. The school bestows master's degrees in eight areas, including business and education. MTSU also confers a Specialist in Education degree and doctorate degrees. It has an enrollment of more than 25,000 students. MTSU is part of the State University and Community College System of Tennessee.

	Annual Growth	06/05	06/06	06/12	06/13	06/14
Sales ($mil.)	54.2%	–	5.7	218.3	190.3	183.0
Net income ($ mil.)	–	–	–	18.4	46.8	35.0
Market value ($ mil.)	–	–	–	–	–	–
Employees	–	–	–	–	–	2,400

MIDDLEBY CORP

NMS: MIDD

1400 Toastmaster Drive
Elgin, IL 60120
Phone: 847 741-3300
Fax: –
Web: www.middleby.com

CEO: –
CFO: –
HR: –
FYE: December 30
Type: Public

Middleby makes a slew of commercial and institutional foodservice equipment for restaurants, retailers, and hotels worldwide. Middleby operates through three segments: Commercial Foodservice Equipment, Food Processing Equipment, and Residential Kitchen Equipment. The largest, Foodservice, makes machines for most types of cooking and warming activities. Products are sold under about 70 brands ? Anets, Blodgett, Southbend, and TurboChef, among others. Residential Kitchen makes ovens, refrigerators, dishwashers, microwaves, and other related products, and Food Processing makes cooking, mixing, slicing, and packaging machines. Over 70% of sales come from the US and Canada.

	Annual Growth	12/19*	01/21	01/22*	12/22	12/23
Sales ($mil.)	8.1%	2,959.4	2,513.3	3,250.8	4,032.9	4,036.6
Net income ($ mil.)	3.3%	352.2	207.3	488.5	436.6	400.9
Market value ($ mil.)	7.6%	5,881.9	6,910.6	10,547	7,177.5	7,888.8
Employees	2.3%	9,778	9,289	10,624	11,268	10,722

*Fiscal year change

MIDDLEFIELD BANC CORP.   NAS: MBCN

15985 East High Street   CEO: Thomas G Caldwell
Middlefield, OH 44062-0035   CFO: Donald L Stacy
Phone: 440 632-1666   HR: –
Fax: –   FYE: December 31
Web: –   Type: Public

Here's your cash, stuck in the Middlefield Banc with you. The firm is the holding company for Middlefield Bank, which has about 10 offices in northeast and central Ohio. The community bank offers standard deposit services such as checking and savings accounts, CDs, and IRAs. Investments, insurance, and brokerage services are offered through an agreement with UVEST, a division of LPL Financial. Residential mortgage loans comprise more than 60% of the company's loan portfolio; commercial and industrial loans make up about 20%. The bank also offers commercial mortgages, construction loans, and consumer installment loans. Middlefield Banc is buying Liberty Bank, which operates three branches in northeast Ohio.

	Annual Growth	12/19	12/20	12/21	12/22	12/23
Assets ($mil.)	11.4%	1,182.5	1,392.0	1,331.0	1,687.7	1,822.9
Net income ($ mil.)	8.1%	12.7	8.3	18.6	15.7	17.4
Market value ($ mil.)	5.5%	211.2	182.1	200.8	221.8	262.0
Employees	7.2%	194	–	185	238	256

MIDDLESEX WATER CO.   NMS: MSEX

485C Route 1 South, Suite 400   CEO: Dennis W Doll
Iselin, NJ 08830   CFO: A B O'Connor
Phone: 732 634-1500   HR: –
Fax: –   FYE: December 31
Web: www.middlesexwater.com   Type: Public

Like all gardens, the Garden State needs water to thrive. Middlesex Water provides water and wastewater services to residential, business, and fire protection customers in New Jersey through its Middlesex, Pinelands, and Bayview systems. It also distributes water in Delaware through its Tidewater system. All told, the utility's subsidiaries have nearly 140,000 customers, and serve a retail population of about 200,000. The company also is engaged in municipal contract operations and public/private partnerships, and provides line maintenance services. Middlesex Water's nonregulated Utility Service Affiliates (Perth Amboy) unit operates the municipal water and wastewater systems in Perth Amboy, New Jersey.

	Annual Growth	12/19	12/20	12/21	12/22	12/23
Sales ($mil.)	5.4%	134.6	141.6	143.1	162.4	166.3
Net income ($ mil.)	(1.8%)	33.9	38.4	36.5	42.4	31.5
Market value ($ mil.)	0.8%	1,132.9	1,291.5	2,143.9	1,402.0	1,169.4
Employees	0.2%	352	348	347	350	355

MIDLAND CAPITAL HOLDINGS CORP   NBB: MCPH

8929 South Harlem Avenue   CEO: Paul M Zogas
Bridgeview, IL 60455   CFO: –
Phone: 708 598-9400   HR: –
Fax: 708 598-5445   FYE: June 30
Web: –   Type: Public

Midland Capital is the holding company for Midland Federal Savings and Loan Association, which serves southwest Chicago and its suburbs through about five branches. The savings and loan offers a variety of deposit products, including checking and savings accounts, money market accounts, CDs, and IRAs. Its loan portfolio is almost completely made up of residential mortgages. The company sells life, health, property/casualty, and business coverage through subsidiary Midland Insurance Services. Chairman and CEO Paul Zogas and his family own more than half of Midland Capital Holdings' stock.

	Annual Growth	06/03	06/04	06/05	06/06	06/07
Assets ($mil.)	(6.0%)	160.0	153.6	139.0	130.8	124.9
Net income ($ mil.)	0.3%	0.7	1.0	1.2	1.0	0.7
Market value ($ mil.)	7.7%	11.6	13.9	15.3	15.7	15.6
Employees	0.3%	89	87	82	90	90

MIDLAND COGENERATION VENTURE LIMITED PARTNERSHIP

100 E PROGRESS PL   CEO: Doyle N Beneby Jr
MIDLAND, MI 486408900   CFO: Laurie Valasek
Phone: 989 839-6000   HR: –
Fax: –   FYE: December 31
Web: www.midcogen.com   Type: Private

Midland Cogeneration Venture has the power to go all the way (and the reputation to get away with it). The company, formerly Midland Nuclear Power Plant, operates one of the largest cogeneration power plants in the US (at one time the largest gas-fired steam recovery power plant in the world). Midland Cogeneration Venture, with a generating capacity of more than 1,560 MW, is responsible for about 10% of the electricity used in Michigan's lower peninsula. It also produces up to 1.35 million pounds per hour of process steam for industrial use. Swedish private equity firm EQT Infrastructure (70%) and US energy investment group Fortistar (30%) bought Midland Cogeneration Venture in 2009.

	Annual Growth	12/12	12/13	12/14	12/15	12/16
Sales ($mil.)	(0.2%)	–	–	0.3	0.3	0.3
Net income ($ mil.)	(16.3%)	–	–	0.3	0.1	0.2
Market value ($ mil.)		–	–	–	–	–
Employees		–	–	–	–	112

MIDLAND STATES BANCORP INC   NMS: MSBI

1201 Network Centre Drive   CEO: Jeffrey G Ludwig
Effingham, IL 62401   CFO: Eric T Lemke
Phone: 217 342-7321   HR: –
Fax: –   FYE: December 31
Web: www.midlandsb.com   Type: Public

Midland States Bancorp is a diversified financial holding company. It is the $7.4 billion-asset holding company for Midland States Bank, a community bank that operates branches in Illinois and Missouri. The bank provides a full range of commercial and consumer banking products and services, business equipment financing, merchant credit card services, trust and investment management, and insurance and financial planning services. Subsidiary Midland Wealth Management provides wealth management services. Midland States Bancorp went public in 2016.

	Annual Growth	12/19	12/20	12/21	12/22	12/23
Assets ($mil.)	6.6%	6,087.0	6,868.5	7,443.8	7,855.5	7,866.9
Net income ($ mil.)	7.8%	55.8	22.5	81.3	99.0	75.5
Market value ($ mil.)	(1.2%)	624.1	385.1	534.3	573.7	594.0
Employees	(4.5%)	1,100	904	907	935	914

MIDMARK CORPORATION

10170 PENNY LN STE 300   CEO: John Baumann
MIAMISBURG, OH 453425014   CFO: Robert Morris
Phone: 937 528-7500   HR: Cathy Winner
Fax: –   FYE: December 31
Web: www.midmark.com   Type: Private

Midmark Corporation is the only clinical environmental design company that enables a better care experience for the medical, dental and animal health markets. For the medical market, Midmark provides a unique offering of clinical workflow solutions, Midmark real-time locating system technology, medical equipment, diagnostic devices and design assistance, resulting in improved efficiency within health systems. Within the animal health market, the company offer solutions that serve the full care continuum of animal healthcare?from boarding and containment to preventive and procedural care. It provides customers a single source for high-quality and innovative equipment, technology, clinical training and services. Midmark was founded in 1915 as a manufacturer of cement mixers.

MIDNITE EXPRESS INC.

448 7TH ST NW
WEST FARGO, ND 580781150
Phone: 701 281-2511
Fax: –
Web: www.midnitexpress.com

CEO: –
CFO: –
HR: –
FYE: December 31
Type: Private

Truckload hauler Midnite Express, whose drivers have been known to be on the road in the middle of the day as well as at night, delivers freight throughout the US. The company also provides logistics and freight brokerage services, matching customers' cargo with carriers' capacity. Midnite Express is owned by MME, which also operates less-than-truckload carrier Midwest Motor Express.

	Annual Growth	12/14	12/15	12/16	12/17	12/18
Sales ($mil.)	3.8%	–	15.8	15.9	16.6	17.7
Net income ($ mil.)	40.9%	–	0.4	0.5	1.4	1.0
Market value ($ mil.)	–	–	–	–	–	–
Employees	–	–	–	–	–	80

MIDSTATE MEDICAL CENTER

435 LEWIS AVE
MERIDEN, CT 064512101
Phone: 203 694-8200
Fax: –
Web: www.midstatemedical.org

CEO: Lucille A Janatka
CFO: Ralph Becker
HR: –
FYE: September 30
Type: Private

MidState Medical Center serves patients across the Nutmeg State. The acute care hospital serves central Connecticut and has some 155 beds (including six psychiatric beds). It offers patients a range of services including cardiac, emergency medicine, and maternity care. MidState Medical Center also has centers dedicated to diabetes, cancer treatment, digestive health, nutrition, and women's health. The hospital manages satellite facilities in Cheshire, Wallingford, and Southington, and it operates an emergency center and the MidState Medical Services Building for outpatient care. MidState Medical Center is part of the Hartford HealthCare network.

	Annual Growth	09/18	09/19	09/20	09/21	09/22
Sales ($mil.)	8.7%	–	320.1	351.5	324.8	411.0
Net income ($ mil.)	(71.7%)	–	28.8	23.9	60.1	0.7
Market value ($ mil.)	–	–	–	–	–	–
Employees	–	–	–	–	–	900

MIDWAVE WIRELESS, INC.

11700 PLAZA AMERICA DR STE 900
RESTON, VA 201904751
Phone: 703 483-7993
Fax: –
Web: www.terrestar.com

CEO: Jeffrey W Epstein
CFO: Vincent Loiacono
HR: –
FYE: December 31
Type: Private

TerreStar's business can't seem to get off the ground. The company is developing an IP-based satellite and terrestrial mobile broadband network through its majority-owned TerreStar Networks unit that will provide wireless voice and data services to customers in the US and Canada (basically, the first satellite smartphone). In addition, the company is developing an equivalent service for Europe through TerreStar Global. As a wholesale service provider, TerreStar plans to offer communications services through partners and service providers. In 2010, TerreStar Networks filed for Chapter 11 bankruptcy, followed in 2011 by TerreStar Corporation. DISH Network has agreed to buy TerreStar Network's assets for $1.4 billion.

MIDWAY FORD TRUCK CENTER, INC.

7601 NE 38TH ST
KANSAS CITY, MO 641619409
Phone: 816 455-3000
Fax: –
Web: www.midwayfordtruck.com

CEO: –
CFO: –
HR: –
FYE: December 31
Type: Private

You can take a train, a plane, or hoof it to Kansas City, Missouri, but once you get there, you can buy some big wheels at Midway Ford Truck Center. From its two locations, Midway Ford Truck Center sells new and used Ford and Freightliner (Sterling, Western Star) heavy trucks, as well as tractors, light trucks, and SUVs. The company also provides parts, service, and collision repair for over-the-road and light trucks. Midway Ford Truck Center was founded in 1961 by Ford.

MIDWEST AIR TECHNOLOGIES, INC.

6700 WILDLIFE WAY
LONG GROVE, IL 600475319
Phone: 847 821-9630
Fax: –
Web: www.midwest-air.com

CEO: –
CFO: –
HR: Mary Hake
FYE: December 31
Type: Private

Midwest Air Technologies (MAT) is a leading producer of quality fencing products, lawn and garden accessories, and pet accessories. It manufactures and distributes quality products such as residential, chain link, and agricultural fencing under the YardGard and FarmGard brands, trellis's, shepherds hooks, and other lawn and garden accessories under the Gilbert & Bennett brand, and a line of pet containment and other pet accessories. The company is a unit of MAT Holdings, a privately-held, globally diversified manufacturing, marketing, and distribution company, which was founded by Dr. Steve Wang in 1984.

MIDWEST ENERGY, INC.

1330 CANTERBURY DR
HAYS, KS 676012708
Phone: 785 625-3437
Fax: –
Web: www.mwenergy.com

CEO: –
CFO: –
HR: –
FYE: December 31
Type: Private

Some rural residents of the Sunflower State rely on Midwest Energy for their power and gas needs. The multi-utility serves approximately 48,000 electricity customers and 42,000 natural gas customers in central and western Kansas. It also has some power generation operations; it purchases most of its electric supply from wholesale marketers. The company's Midwest United Energy subsidiary is a competitive natural gas supplier in four states, and its WestLand Energy unit sells propane to Kansas consumers. Midwest Energy has seen its power sales grow by 23% since 2006, and its natural gas sales by 17%.

	Annual Growth	12/18	12/19	12/20	12/21	12/22
Sales ($mil.)	5.6%	–	208.9	191.8	236.1	245.8
Net income ($ mil.)	4.7%	–	19.0	15.8	19.7	21.8
Market value ($ mil.)	–	–	–	–	–	–
Employees	–	–	–	–	–	274

MIDWEST GAME SUPPLY COMPANY

1119 N JEFFERSON ST
KEARNEY, MO 640608393
Phone: 816 628-2299
Fax: –
Web: www.midwestgamesupply.com

CEO: Linda Sohm
CFO: –
HR: –
FYE: December 31
Type: Private

The business might be dicey but things couldn't be better for Midwest Game Supply. The company manufactures and distributes casino quality table game equipment including dice, wool and synthetic layouts, chips, chairs, and the multitude of accessories used by dealers and players of poker, blackjack, roulette, and craps. The company's distribution services provide everything necessary for the gaming floor of a casino, from chip spacers to slot machines. The company sells more than 50,000 pairs a month of its signature product, "Certified Perfects" dice, serving casinos across the US. The company was founded in 1945 by John (Mac) McMenamy who sold the company to Chuck and Linda Sohm in 1986.

	Annual Growth	12/09	12/10	12/11	12/12	12/13
Sales ($mil.)	(5.3%)	–	4.8	4.6	4.2	4.1
Net income ($ mil.)	–	–	–	(0.1)	0.0	0.0	(0.2)
Market value ($ mil.)	–	–	–	–	–	–
Employees	–	–	–	–	–	27

MIDWESTERN STATE UNIVERSITY

3410 TAFT BLVD
WICHITA FALLS, TX 763082096
Phone: 940 397-4000
Fax: –
Web: www.msutexas.edu

CEO: –
CFO: –
HR: –
FYE: December 31
Type: Private

Founded in 1922 as Wichita Falls Junior College, Midwestern State University (MSU) became a full university in 1946. The north-central Texas school, accredited by the Southern Association of Colleges and Schools Commission on Colleges, offers 45 undergraduate programs and nearly 30 graduate programs to nearly 6,000 students. The university's largest study programs include education, health sciences, and business. MSU is the only Texas university to become a member of the Council of Public Liberal Arts Colleges, which focuses on liberal arts education. With a student/faculty ratio of 18:1, MSU boasts a full-time faculty of 230, half a dozen residence halls, and more than 100 student organizations.

	Annual Growth	12/19	12/20	12/21*	08/22*	12/22
Sales ($mil.)	7.5%	–	0.1	0.0	57.3	0.2
Net income ($ mil.)	–	–	(0.0)	(0.1)	(14.9)	(0.1)
Market value ($ mil.)	–	–	–	–	–	–
Employees	–	–	–	–	–	800

*Fiscal year change

MIDWESTONE FINANCIAL GROUP, INC.

102 South Clinton Street
Iowa City, IA 52240
Phone: 319 356-5800
Fax: –
Web: www.midwestone.com

NMS: MOFG
CEO: Charles N Reeves
CFO: Barry S Ray
HR: –
FYE: December 31
Type: Public

MidWestOne Financial Group is the holding company for MidWestOne Bank, which operates about 35 branches throughout central and east-central Iowa. The bank offers standard deposit products such as checking and savings accounts, CDs, and IRAs, in addition to trust services, private banking, home loans and investment services. More than two-thirds of MidWestOne Financial's loan portfolio consists of commercial real estate loans, and commercial mortgages and industrial loans. Founded in 1983, MidWestOne has total assets of $4.65 billion.

	Annual Growth	12/19	12/20	12/21	12/22	12/23
Assets ($mil.)	8.4%	4,653.6	5,556.6	6,025.1	6,577.9	6,427.5
Net income ($ mil.)	(16.8%)	43.6	6.6	69.5	60.8	20.9
Market value ($ mil.)	(7.2%)	568.6	384.5	508.0	498.3	422.3
Employees	(1.3%)	771	780	760	811	732

MIKART, LLC

1750 CHATTAHOOCHEE AVE NW
ATLANTA, GA 303182112
Phone: 404 351-4510
Fax: –
Web: www.mikart.com

CEO: –
CFO: –
HR: –
FYE: December 31
Type: Private

In the art of making pills and capsules Mikart pays attention to the details. The company offers contract pharmaceutical manufacturing services, specializing in oral capsule and tablet formulations. Tablets and capsules can be immediate or time-release; the company also makes liquid formulations and provides specialty packaging, including laminated foil, blister, and pouches. Mikart's facilities have the capacity to produce everything from small pilot-scale batches all the way up to full-scale commercial production. Other services include drug development, feasibility studies, and product testing. Mikart will also walk customers through all the required regulatory processes. Private equity firm Nautic Partners acquired Mikart in 2018.

	Annual Growth	06/04	06/05	06/06*	12/08	12/10
Sales ($mil.)	7.1%	–	–	24.3	26.5	32.0
Net income ($ mil.)	–	–	–	(0.6)	0.5	1.7
Market value ($ mil.)	–	–	–	–	–	–
Employees	–	–	–	–	–	200

*Fiscal year change

MILAEGER'S, INC.

4838 DOUGLAS AVE
RACINE, WI 534022447
Phone: 262 639-2040
Fax: –
Web: www.milaegers.com

CEO: –
CFO: –
HR: –
FYE: December 31
Type: Private

Milaeger's has the difficult task of keeping things green on the banks of Lake Michigan. The company operates two nurseries in Racine and Sturtevant, Wisconsin, selling seeds, soil, plants, mulch, as well as apparel, Christmas collectibles, figurines, folk art, outdoor furniture, and home decor. It also offers landscape services including lawn, tree, and shrub care along with design services. Milaeger's regularly hosts shows by collectibles merchants, local fashion shows, and gardening workshops. The company's Java Garden Cafe, onsite at both locations, offers hot and cold beverages, dessert, and light lunch and dinner items. Milaeger's was founded in 1960 by Dan and Joan Milaeger.

	Annual Growth	12/14	12/15	12/16	12/17	12/18
Sales ($mil.)	3.9%	–	14.1	13.7	14.0	15.8
Net income ($ mil.)	(27.8%)	–	0.3	0.1	0.2	0.0
Market value ($ mil.)	–	–	–	–	–	–
Employees	–	–	–	–	–	125

MILBANK MANUFACTURING CO.

4801 DERAMUS AVE
KANSAS CITY, MO 641201180
Phone: 816 483-5314
Fax: –
Web: www.milbankworks.com

CEO: Katrina Henke
CFO: James A Fitts
HR: Kim Thomey
FYE: December 31
Type: Private

Milbank Manufacturing will keep the power turned on, at home and at work. The family owned company is one of the largest designer and manufacturer of electrical meter mounting equipment, including sockets, enclosures, power outlets and pedestals. Its lineup of more than 16,000 items also offers circuit breakers, test switches, and safety switches. Manufactured at five plants, Milbank's products are channeled through a network of manufacturer's representatives to electric utility companies, contractors, industrial distributors, and OEMs across North America.

MILBERG LLP

1 PNNSYLVANIA PLZ FL 49 FLR 49
NEW YORK, NY 10119
Phone: 212 594-5300
Fax: –
Web: www.milberg.com

CEO: –
CFO: –
HR: Claudia Hach
FYE: October 31
Type: Private

Milberg (formerly Milberg Weiss) has made its reputation -- and drawn its share of controversy -- representing plaintiffs in class-action lawsuits against some leading corporations. It also practices in areas such as antitrust, consumer protection, and mass torts. The firm has more than 65 lawyers in offices in Los Angeles, New York, Tampa, and Detroit. In June 2008 Milberg agreed to pay a $75 million fine in exchange for the dismissal of a 2006 indictment in which federal prosecutors alleged the firm paid kickbacks to get people to serve as plaintiffs. Earlier in 2008, firm co-founder Melvyn Weiss pleaded guilty to a related conspiracy charge and resigned from the firm, which changed its name to Milberg.

MILES COLLEGE, INC.

5500 MYRON MASSEY BLVD
FAIRFIELD, AL 350642697
Phone: 205 929-1000
Fax: –
Web: www.miles.edu

CEO: –
CFO: –
HR: Irshad Khan
FYE: June 30
Type: Private

A private, historically black, liberal arts school, Miles College is affiliated with the Christian Methodist Episcopal Church. The college offers bachelor's degrees in such subjects as accounting, biology, chemistry, environmental science, political science, and social work, along with several education-related majors. Miles College was founded in 1905.

	Annual Growth	06/18	06/19	06/20	06/21	06/22
Sales ($mil.)	15.8%	–	29.6	33.3	42.6	46.0
Net income ($ mil.)	67.3%	–	0.0	3.2	7.2	0.2
Market value ($ mil.)	–	–	–	–	–	–
Employees	–	–	–	–	–	300

MILES HEALTH CARE, INC

35 MILES ST
DAMARISCOTTA, ME 045434047
Phone: 207 563-1234
Fax: –
Web: www.mainehealth.org

CEO: James Donavan
CFO: –
HR: –
FYE: September 30
Type: Private

Miles Health Care provides acute and specialty health care service to the residents of Maine's Lincoln County. The not-for-profit company operates Miles Memorial Hospital -- known as LincolnHealth Miles Campus -- a rural medical center with about 40 beds and has emergency, intensive care, surgery, and birthing departments. In addition, Miles Health Care operates outpatient and specialty practice clinics, physician practice offices, and home health, rehabilitation, and hospice programs. It also provides long-term senior care through its nursing, assisted, and independent living facilities. Miles Health Care is a member of Lincoln County Healthcare (LincolnHealth), which is part of the MaineHealth network.

	Annual Growth	09/04	09/05	09/06	09/08	09/09
Sales ($mil.)	111.6%	–	52.0	59.0	14.2	1,043.0
Net income ($ mil.)	–	–	(0.3)	3.5	0.6	12.7
Market value ($ mil.)	–	–	–	–	–	–
Employees	–	–	–	–	–	800

MILESTONE CONSTRUCTION SERVICES, INC.

8604 PILGRIM CT
ALEXANDRIA, VA 223082441
Phone: 703 406-0960
Fax: –
Web: –

CEO: –
CFO: –
HR: –
FYE: December 31
Type: Private

Milestone Construction Services specializes in construction management, consulting, and general contracting. Founded in 1998 the company started out exclusively building facilities for the Metropolitan Washington Airport Authority in the nation's capital, but has branched out into commercial projects such as office buildings, retail space, restaurants, industrial facilities, and high-end residential development. It maintains a staff of technical experts, including professional construction managers, superintendents, architects, engineers, cost estimators, inspectors, and construction scheduling professionals. Milestone Construction Services operates throughout the US from offices in Virginia and Maryland.

	Annual Growth	12/05	12/06	12/07	12/08	12/10
Sales ($mil.)	(10.5%)	–	–	29.1	26.2	20.9
Net income ($ mil.)	(79.8%)	–	–	0.3	0.2	0.0
Market value ($ mil.)	–	–	–	–	–	–
Employees	–	–	–	–	–	27

MILESTONE SCIENTIFIC INC.

425 Eagle Rock Avenue, Suite 403
Roseland, NJ 07068
Phone: 973 535-2717
Fax: –
Web: www.milestonescientific.com

ASE: MLSS
CEO: Jan A Haverhals
CFO: –
HR: –
FYE: December 31
Type: Public

Trips to the dentist might never be pain-free, but they could be less painful if Milestone Scientific has its way. The company develops and markets dental injection devices (based on its CompuFlo technique) that cause less pain than a traditional syringe. Its primary product, CompuDent, and its accompanying accessory The Wand, is a computer-controlled local anesthetic delivery unit that can be used in routine treatments, including root canals, crowns, fillings, and cleanings. CompuDent is also marketed as CompuMed to the medical industry for use in dermatology and orthopedics. Milestone sells its products through a global distributor network to dental and medical professionals in more than 25 countries.

	Annual Growth	12/19	12/20	12/21	12/22	12/23
Sales ($mil.)	4.1%	8.4	5.4	10.3	8.8	9.8
Net income ($ mil.)	–	(7.5)	(7.3)	(6.8)	(8.7)	(6.9)
Market value ($ mil.)	(16.1%)	105.4	160.8	156.2	36.4	52.3
Employees	1.5%	16	19	26	20	17

MILFORD REGIONAL MEDICAL CENTER, INC.

14 PROSPECT ST
MILFORD, MA 017573003
Phone: 508 473-1190
Fax: –
Web: www.milfordregional.org

CEO: Edward Kelly
CFO: Beth Cadle
HR: –
FYE: September 30
Type: Private

Medical treatment in south central Massachusetts and northern Rhode Island is the main affair of Milford Regional Medical Center. The 145-bed hospital provides acute medical services to the residents of Milford, Massachusetts, and surrounding areas. Specialty services include emergency medicine, home health care, diagnostic imaging, physical therapy, obstetrics, and cancer treatment. It also has an affiliated physician practice group, the Tri-County Medical Associates. The Medical Center, which employs about 200 physicians, is a teaching hospital affiliated with the University of Massachusetts.

	Annual Growth	09/18	09/19	09/20	09/21	09/22
Sales ($mil.)	(2.2%)	–	298.9	299.2	231.3	279.5
Net income ($ mil.)	6.7%	–	5.4	(0.3)	(9.3)	6.5
Market value ($ mil.)	–	–	–	–	–	–
Employees	–	–	–	–	–	1,159

MILKEN FAMILY FOUNDATION

1250 4TH ST FL 1
SANTA MONICA, CA 904011418
Phone: 310 570-4800
Fax: –
Web: www.mff.org

CEO: –
CFO: –
HR: –
FYE: November 30
Type: Private

Former investor Michael Milken is behind the foundation that helps to give back. The Milken Family Foundation funds awards and grants in the areas of education and medical research. Its $25,000 Milken Educator Award is given to up to 80 teachers, specialists, and principals annually. Other initiatives include the Teacher Advancement Program, a teacher recruitment and development program, and the Milken Festival for Youth, which funds community service opportunities for primarily disadvantaged students. Brothers Lowell Milken (the organization's chairman) and Michael Milken (a trustee; also famously indicted on racketeering charges in 1989 after amassing a fortune on junk bonds) started the foundation in 1982.

	Annual Growth	11/12	11/13	11/15	11/21	11/22
Sales ($mil.)	(21.6%)	–	115.3	27.9	8.5	12.9
Net income ($ mil.)	(31.9%)	–	95.5	11.2	1.5	3.0
Market value ($ mil.)	–	–	–	–	–	–
Employees						200

MILLENNIAL MEDIA, INC.

2400 BOSTON ST STE 300
BALTIMORE, MD 212244781
Phone: 410 522-8705
Fax: –
Web: www.millennialmedia.com

CEO: –
CFO: –
HR: –
FYE: December 31
Type: Private

"There's an app for that" is music to the ears of Millennial Media. Using a proprietary data and technology platform called MYDAS, the independent mobile-advertising company connects app developers and major advertisers by buying space in apps to display highly targeted banner and video ads. MYDAS gives developers a way to deliver ads from Warner Bros, Patagonia, Porsche, GM, and others to more than 7,000 different types of mobile devices. Supported apps come from small developers, content providers (New York Times, CBS Interactive), and major developers (Zynga, Pandora). Millennial Media, the nation's second-largest mobile advertiser, was formed in 2006 and went public in 2012. It was acquired in 2015 by AOL.

MILLENNIUM PRIME INC

6538 Collins Avenue, Suite 382
Miami Beach, FL 33141
Phone: 786 309-5549
Fax: –
Web: www.millenniumprime.com

NBB: MLMN
CEO: –
CFO: –
HR: –
FYE: September 30
Type: Public

Genio Group has decided that playing cards just isn't in the cards. Until 2005 the company designed and marketed entertainment products including the Genio Cards card collection, which consisted of 360 cards spanning 30 different educational categories, such as endangered animals, man-made landmarks, and space travel. The game-playing cards used popular Marvel super heroes to promote learning. Citing lack of sufficient funding, Genio Group exited that business. Steven Horowitz succeeded Matthew Cohen as CEO in mid-2006. The firm is currently searching for new operations.

	Annual Growth	09/18	09/19	09/20	09/21	09/22
Sales ($mil.)	–	0.0	0.0	0.0	–	–
Net income ($ mil.)	–	(0.1)	0.9	(0.1)	(0.3)	(0.3)
Market value ($ mil.)	18.9%	5.8	7.9	7.7	25.4	11.5
Employees	–	–	–	–	2	2

MILLER & CHEVALIER CHARTERED

900 16TH ST NW
WASHINGTON, DC 200062915
Phone: 202 626-5800
Fax: –
Web: www.millerchevalier.com

CEO: Anthony F Shelley
CFO: Pamela Bernstein
HR: –
FYE: December 31
Type: Private

The law firm of Miller & Chevalier will make sure you have all your government affairs in order. The company specializes in tax, employee benefits, litigation, white collar crime, international trade, and yes -- government affairs. Despite being one of the smaller firms, Miller & Chevalier has served over 40% of the Fortune 100 and approximately 30% of the Global 100, a list highlighting global corporations proactive in managing environmental and social issues. Miller & Chevalier was founded in 1920 and its practice areas and expertise are the natural consequence of its Washington, DC location.

MILLER ELECTRIC COMPANY

6805 SOUTHPOINT PKWY
JACKSONVILLE, FL 322166220
Phone: 904 388-8000
Fax: –
Web: www.mecojax.com

CEO: Henry K Brown
CFO: Susan A Walden
HR: Karen Anderson
FYE: September 30
Type: Private

Miller Electric Company flips the switch for projects primarily in the Southeast. The Florida-based electrical contractor provides services including construction, installation, renovation, and maintenance of electrical systems. Industries the company serves include: communications, construction, health care, and transportation. Outside of Florida, the company has offices in Alabama, Arizona, Arkansas, Georgia, North Carolina, Virginia, Tennessee, Texas, and Wisconsin. Clients have included Anheuser Busch, Bank of America, Blue Cross and Blue Shield, EverBank Field, and the University of North Florida. Miller Electric was founded by Henry G. Miller in 1928 and remains a family business.

	Annual Growth	09/17	09/18	09/19	09/20	09/21
Sales ($mil.)	13.7%	–	336.4	381.0	399.2	494.0
Net income ($ mil.)	24.4%	–	11.5	11.3	17.6	22.2
Market value ($ mil.)	–	–	–	–	–	–
Employees	–	–	–	–	–	703

MILLER ELECTRIC CONSTRUCTION, INC

1800 PREBLE AVE
PITTSBURGH, PA 152332242
Phone: 412 487-1044
Fax: –
Web: www.millerelectric.com

CEO: Richard R Miller
CFO: –
HR: –
FYE: June 30
Type: Private

If you're looking for an electrical contractor, then it could be Miller Electric Construction time for you. Miller Electric Construction specializes in industrial and commercial electrical construction projects in western Pennsylvania and nearby portions of Ohio and West Virginia. The company constructs lighting, data communication, and power distribution systems for general construction contractors, construction managers, and area businesses, institutions, and attractions. Dick Miller founded the company in the early 1960s.

	Annual Growth	06/06	06/07	06/08	06/09	06/10
Sales ($mil.)	(1.6%)	–	–	26.8	34.1	26.0
Net income ($ mil.)	(5.9%)	–	–	0.2	0.4	0.2
Market value ($ mil.)	–	–	–	–	–	–
Employees	–	–	–	–	–	150

MILLER INDUSTRIES INC. (TN) NYS: MLR

8503 Hilltop Drive
Ooltewah, TN 37363
Phone: 423 238-4171
Fax: 423 238-5371
Web: www.millerind.com

CEO: Jeffrey I Badgley
CFO: Deborah L Whitmire
HR: David Taylor
FYE: December 31
Type: Public

Miller Industries is the world's largest manufacturer of towing and recovery equipment. It makes bodies of wreckers and car carriers, which are installed on truck chassis manufactured by third parties. Its multi-vehicle transport trailers are specialized auto transport trailers with upper and lower decks and hydraulic ramps for loading vehicles that carry 6 to 7 vehicles. Miller Industries' US brand names include Century, Challenger, Champion, Chevron, Eagle, Holmes, Titan, and Vulcan. The company's European brands are Jige and Boniface. About 90% of the company's revenue comes from North America.

	Annual Growth	12/19	12/20	12/21	12/22	12/23
Sales ($mil.)	9.0%	818.2	651.3	717.5	848.5	1,153.4
Net income ($ mil.)	10.5%	39.1	29.8	16.3	20.3	58.3
Market value ($ mil.)	3.3%	425.0	435.2	382.3	305.1	484.0
Employees	8.6%	1,310	1,280	1,450	1,450	1,821

MILLER TRANSPORTATION SERVICES, INC.

5500 HIGHWAY 80 W
JACKSON, MS 392093507
Phone: 601 856-6526
Fax: –
Web: –

CEO: –
CFO: –
HR: –
FYE: December 31
Type: Private

No beer here. Tank truck carrier Miller Transporters hauls bulk commodities such as chemicals and petroleum products from a network of more than 20 terminals in the eastern half of the US. The company operates a fleet of some 500 tractors and 1,100 trailers and carries cargo domestically as well as between the US and Canada and Mexico. A sister company, Miller Intermodal Logistics, arranges the transportation of liquid bulk cargo worldwide. The company that became Miller Transporters was founded in 1942 by Harold Dewey Miller. Its founder's family still owns Miller Transporters.

	Annual Growth	12/13	12/14	12/15	12/16	12/17
Sales ($mil.)	3.0%	–	108.2	102.0	104.2	118.2
Net income ($ mil.)	292.4%	–	0.0	0.3	1.0	4.2
Market value ($ mil.)	–	–	–	–	–	–
Employees	–	–	–	–	–	1,000

MILLER WASTE MILLS, INCORPORATED

580 E FRONT ST
WINONA, MN 559874256
Phone: 507 454-6906
Fax: –
Web: www.millerwastemills.com

CEO: Hugh L Miller
CFO: Brian Evenson
HR: Genelle G Beck
FYE: December 31
Type: Private

Miller Waste Mills (doing business as RTP) is a custom compounder of engineering thermoplastics. The family owned global company manufactures specialty compounds from more than 60 engineering resins that can affect color, level of conductivity, high-temperature performance, and wear resistance in engineered plastics. Its compounding starts with a base resin or polymer. Miller Waste Mills also produces engineered bioplastic specialty compounds that use resins derived from renewable sources, not petroleum. Subsidiary Wiman Corp. makes specialty plastic film. Miller Waste Mills' products are used in a wide array of markets, including electronics, automotive, consumer, medical, industrial, and sports.

MILLER ZELL, INC.

6100 FULTON INDUSTRIAL BLVD SW
ATLANTA, GA 303362853
Phone: 404 691-7400
Fax: –
Web: www.millerzell.com

CEO: –
CFO: –
HR: –
FYE: December 31
Type: Private

Miller Zell helps companies design their retail stores in ways that will make consumers want to spend more. Its services include the integrated design of a retail environment from the ground up -- from layout to lighting to signage. The company also designs, distributes, and installs promotional retail programs designed to drive sales. Miller Zell's clients have included quick-serve restaurants (Blimpie, Honey Baked Ham), retail outlets (Wal-Mart, Rite Aid), and car dealerships (Infiniti, Lexus). Miller Zell also offers warehousing and logistics services.

MILLERKNOLL INC NMS: MLKN

855 East Main Avenue
Zeeland, MI 49464
Phone: 616 654-3000
Fax: –
Web: www.hermanmiller.com

CEO: Andrea R Owen
CFO: Jeffrey M Stutz
HR: Anarella Wagers
FYE: June 3
Type: Public

MillerKnoll (formerly known as Herman Miller) is one of the largest and most influential modern design companies worldwide. A top US maker of office furniture, the company is known for developing designs for corporate, government, home office, residential and health care environments. MillerKnoll's products include ergonomic devices, filing and storage systems, freestanding furniture, seating, textiles and wooden casegoods. It manufactures its products in the US, the UK, China, Brazil, Mexico, and India, and sells them worldwide through its sales staff and dealer network, as well as through independent dealers and online. Most of the company's revenue are generated in the US.

	Annual Growth	06/19*	05/20	05/21	05/22*	06/23
Sales ($mil.)	12.3%	2,567.2	2,486.6	2,465.1	3,946.0	4,087.1
Net income ($ mil.)	(28.4%)	160.5	(9.1)	173.1	(27.1)	42.1
Market value ($ mil.)	(20.4%)	2,686.5	1,742.6	3,618.4	2,320.2	1,077.9
Employees	8.0%	8,000	7,600	7,600	11,300	10,900

*Fiscal year change

MILLINOCKET REGIONAL HOSPITAL INC

200 SOMERSET ST
MILLINOCKET, ME 044621298
Phone: 207 723-5161
Fax: –
Web: www.mrhme.org

CEO: Bob Peterson
CFO: Catherine Lemay
HR: Carolyn Bouchard
FYE: June 30
Type: Private

Millinocket Regional Hospital provides medical services to the residents of Millinocket, Maine and its surrounding areas. The hospital has 25 critical access beds and offers specialized services such as orthopedics, surgery, pediatrics, emergency medicine, cancer care, and cardiac rehabilitation. It also provides a long term care unit, as well as an occupational wellness center. The hospital is a founding member of the Maine Health Alliance and employs a medical staff including nearly 20 physicians.

	Annual Growth	06/18	06/19	06/20	06/21	06/22
Sales ($mil.)	0.1%	–	32.3	30.9	34.2	32.4
Net income ($ mil.)	–	–	(1.4)	0.1	3.8	0.7
Market value ($ mil.)	–	–	–	–	–	–
Employees	–	–	–	–	–	220

MILLS-PENINSULA HEALTH SERVICES

1501 TROUSDALE DR
BURLINGAME, CA 940104506
Phone: 650 696-5400
Fax: –
Web: www.mills-peninsula.org

CEO: –
CFO: –
HR: –
FYE: December 31
Type: Private

With health facilities south of San Francisco, Mills-Peninsula Health Services provides care to communities in and around Burlingame, California. The not-for-profit health care group includes the 240-bed Mills-Peninsula Medical Center, an acute-care hospital in Burlingame; Mills Health Center, an outpatient diagnostic, surgery, and rehabilitation facility in San Mateo; and physician practice offices in surrounding areas. The facilities provide specialty services such as cancer care, cardiovascular therapy, behavioral health, radiology, respiratory care, and senior services. Mills-Peninsula Health Services is part of the Sutter Health network.

	Annual Growth	12/00	12/01	12/02	12/09	12/13
Sales ($mil.)	3.6%	–	398.5	274.0	533.8	609.9
Net income ($ mil.)	172.8%	–	0.0	18.0	56.7	54.5
Market value ($ mil.)		–	–	–	–	–
Employees		–	–	–	–	2,200

MILTON HERSHEY SCHOOL

1201 HOMESTEAD LN
HERSHEY, PA 170338818
Phone: 717 520-2000
Fax: –
Web: www.mhskids.org

CEO: Maria T Krau
CFO: –
HR: –
FYE: July 31
Type: Private

For students at the Milton Hershey School, receiving a quality education is very sweet, indeed. Founded in 1909 by chocolate mogul Milton S. Hershey and his wife Catherine, the Milton Hershey School is a residential private school for low-income children. About 1,800 students -- from pre-kindergarten through 12th grade -- are enrolled; more than three-quarters are from Pennsylvania, and the remainder hail from around 30 other states. The school has a student-teacher ratio of about 7:1. Applicants must demonstrate social and financial need. Students attend school, live in one of the campus's residences under the guidance of houseparents, receive health care services, and much more, free of charge.

MILTOPE CORPORATION

3800 RICHARDSON RD S
HOPE HULL, AL 360434017
Phone: 334 284-8665
Fax: –
Web: www.mymiltope.com

CEO: Dianne Howells
CFO: Robert Maddox
HR: –
FYE: December 31
Type: Private

Miltope is the leading manufacturer of rugged computer, server/mass storage and network peripheral equipment solutions for military, industrial, and commercial aviation applications that call for reliable performance under demanding environmental conditions. Its rugged computing products have included handhelds/tablet (RTCU-4, RTHD-2, and RTHD-3), laptops (PLC-4G, RCLC-1-G2, SRNC-14, SRNC-17-G2), supernet (VECOM), and communications (Voyager Flat Panel MP, and Voyager Parabolic MP). These products are designed and tested to work under the most rigorous conditions. The company, headquartered in Alabama, was founded in 1975.

MILWAUKEE AREA TECHNICAL COLLEGE FOUNDATION, INC.

700 W STATE ST
MILWAUKEE, WI 532331419
Phone: 414 297-6792
Fax: –
Web: www.matc.edu

CEO: –
CFO: –
HR: Laquitha Bonds
FYE: June 30
Type: Private

Milwaukee Area Technical College (MATC) is not just for techies. The two-year college offers more than 170 degree, diploma, certificate, and apprentice programs to more than 30,000 students. The school also offers pre-college education for students seeking a high school diploma or preparing for college-level studies, and short-term, entry-level occupational training. Academic divisions include business, liberal arts and sciences, graphic arts, television/video production, culinary and hospitality, and health occupations. MATC has four campuses in and around Milwaukee, Wisconsin.

	Annual Growth	06/13	06/14	06/15	06/20	06/22
Sales ($mil.)	12.6%	–	7.1	7.0	10.6	18.3
Net income ($ mil.)	26.4%	–	1.4	1.0	0.4	8.8
Market value ($ mil.)		–	–	–	–	–
Employees		–	–	–	–	2,800

MILWAUKEE BUCKS, LLC

1543 N 2ND ST FL 6
MILWAUKEE, WI 532124036
Phone: 414 227-0500
Fax: –
Web: www.bucks.com

CEO: –
CFO: Patrick McDonough
HR: –
FYE: June 30
Type: Private

A herd of basketball fans gather around these Bucks. The Milwaukee Bucks professional basketball franchise joined the National Basketball Association in 1968 and earned a championship title just three years later with the help of Hall of Fame player Lew Alcindor (later Kareem Abdul-Jabbar). The team has made one other appearance in the NBA Finals in 1974. Hometown fans support the Bucks at Milwaukee's aging Bradley Center. Local businessmen Wesley Pavalon and Marvin Fishman were originally awarded the basketball franchise. Wisconsin Senator Herb Kohl, whose family started the Kohl's department store chain, has owned the Bucks since 1985.

MILWAUKEE COUNTY WAR MEMORIAL, INC.

750 N LINCOLN MEMORIAL DR # 315
MILWAUKEE, WI 532024018
Phone: 414 273-5533
Fax: –
Web: www.warmemorialcenter.org

CEO: –
CFO: –
HR: –
FYE: December 31
Type: Private

Bringing culture to the brewery town, the Milwaukee County War Memorial (MCWM) supports arts and cultural activities throughout the city. To that end, its operations include the War Memorial Center, the Marcus Center for the Performing Arts, the Milwaukee Art Museum, the Charles Allis Museum (19th century French and American paintings), and the Villa Terrace Decorative Arts Museum. Most of the locations support local and traveling performing arts and exhibits and offer space to rent for corporate and private events. MCWM was formed by a group of Milwaukee women at the end of WWII "to honor the dead by serving the living."

	Annual Growth	12/18	12/19	12/20	12/21	12/22
Sales ($mil.)	6.1%	–	2.0	2.4	2.0	2.4
Net income ($ mil.)		–	(0.1)	(0.4)	(0.2)	(0.1)
Market value ($ mil.)		–	–	–	–	–
Employees		–	–	–	–	92

MIND TECHNOLOGY INC
NAS: MIND P

2002 Timberloch Place, Suite 550
The Woodlands, TX 77380
Phone: 281 353-4475
Fax: –
Web: www.mind-technology.com

CEO: –
CFO: –
HR: –
FYE: January 31
Type: Public

Here's a shocker: Mitcham Industries has few rivals that can match 'em when it comes to the leasing and sales of seismic equipment to the global seismic industry. The company's equipment offerings include channel boxes, geophones, earth vibrators, various cables, and other peripheral equipment. Through short-term leasing (three to nine months) from Mitcham Industries, oil and gas companies - a major customer group -- can improve their chances of drilling a productive well and reduce equipment costs. The company also manufactures marine seismic equipment under the Seamap brand.

	Annual Growth	01/19	01/20	01/21	01/22	01/23
Sales ($mil.)	(4.9%)	42.9	42.7	21.2	23.1	35.1
Net income ($ mil.)	–	(19.8)	(11.3)	(20.3)	(15.1)	(8.8)
Market value ($ mil.)	(36.3%)	5.5	3.9	3.0	1.9	0.9
Employees	(0.4%)	193	232	204	200	190

MINDBODY, INC.

651 TANK FARM RD
SAN LUIS OBISPO, CA 934017062
Phone: 877 755-4279
Fax: –
Web: www.mindbodyonline.com

CEO: Richard Stollmeyer
CFO: Brett White
HR: –
FYE: December 31
Type: Private

The goal of many fitness programs is to help the mind and body work together. The goal of Mindbody Inc. is to help fitness and wellness companies integrate front and back office functions into a smooth operation. The company offers a Software-as-a-Service platform for small businesses gathered under the wellness umbrella (yoga, massage, fitness centers, pilates, spin-cycling studios, spas, salons, and more) to schedule appointments and manage billing and payments. Mindbody counts more than 42,000 local business subscribers. It went public with a stock offering in June 2015 and was later acquired by investment firm Vista Equity Partners in 2019 for $1.9 billion.

MINERALS TECHNOLOGIES, INC.
NYS: MTX

622 Third Avenue
New York, NY 10017-6707
Phone: 212 878-1800
Fax: –
Web: www.mineralstech.com

CEO: Douglas T Dietrich
CFO: Matthew E Garth
HR: Erin N Cutler
FYE: December 31
Type: Public

Minerals Technologies, one of the top producers of bentonite and precipitated calcium carbonate (PCC), supplies a broad range of specialty mineral, mineral-based, and synthetic products to primarily the paper, foundry, steel, construction, environmental, energy, polymer, and consumer products industries. With about 1,900 trademarks, the company's technologically advanced product lines include VOLCLAY, PANTHER CREEK, PREMIUM GEL, ENERSOL, RAFINOL and VitaLife. Majority of the company's sales come from the US. Minerals Technologies Inc. (MTI) has a history dating back to 1992, when the company became a publicly traded company, through an initial public offering from Pfizer.

	Annual Growth	12/19	12/20	12/21	12/22	12/23
Sales ($mil.)	4.9%	1,791.0	1,594.8	1,858.3	2,125.5	2,169.9
Net income ($ mil.)	(10.8%)	132.7	112.4	164.4	122.2	84.1
Market value ($ mil.)	5.5%	1,867.5	2,013.0	2,370.4	1,967.6	2,310.8
Employees	2.6%	3,628	3,566	3,961	4,070	4,027

MINERS INCORPORATED

5065 MILLER TRUNK HWY
HERMANTOWN, MN 558111442
Phone: 218 729-5882
Fax: –
Web: www.superonefoods.com

CEO: James A Miner Sr
CFO: –
HR: –
FYE: June 24
Type: Private

Miner's is a family-owned chain of about 30 grocery stores in Michigan, North Dakota, northern Minnesota, and Wisconsin. Most of the company's stores fly the Super One Foods banner, but there are a few under the U-Save Foods and Marketplace Foods names. Following the acquisition of seven Jubilee and Festival Foods stores in Minnesota from Plaza Holding Co., Miner's converted the stores to its Super One Foods banner, most of which are located in Minnesota. Miner's also has a wholesale grocery operation in Duluth. Miner's was founded by Anton and Ida Miner, who started out selling groceries out of their tavern in Grand Rapids, Michigan in the 1930s. In 1943 they built the family's first store, Miner's Market.

	Annual Growth	06/09	06/10	06/11	06/12	06/17
Sales ($mil.)	2.4%	–	463.6	475.6	501.5	548.9
Net income ($ mil.)	(0.5%)	–	27.1	30.2	31.8	26.1
Market value ($ mil.)	–	–	–	–	–	–
Employees	–	–	–	–	–	2,300

MINERVA NEUROSCIENCES INC
NMS: NERV

1500 District Avenue
Burlington, MA 01803
Phone: 617 600-7373
Fax: –
Web: www.minervaneurosciences.com

CEO: Marc D Beer
CFO: Frederick Ahlholm
HR: –
FYE: December 31
Type: Public

Minerva Neurosciences has had enough of people not wanting to take their meds because of the side effects. The company is developing psychiatric pharmaceuticals designed to treat schizophrenia, depression, insomnia, and Parkinson's. While there are plenty of therapies already on the market for neuropsychiatric diseases, Minerva is focused on developing meds that don't leave patients with the typical side effects of lethargy, weight gain, sleep problems, and decreased sex drive. Its lead drug candidate is for schizophrenia, and while the company conducted a small Phase II trial, it needs further study. Minerva Neurosciences went public in 2014 and raised $32 million, which it plans to use to further fund its drug candidates.

	Annual Growth	12/19	12/20	12/21	12/22	12/23
Sales ($mil.)	–	–	41.2	–	–	–
Net income ($ mil.)	–	(72.2)	1.9	(49.9)	(32.1)	(30.0)
Market value ($ mil.)	(3.6%)	49.7	16.4	5.6	11.1	43.0
Employees	(8.8%)	13	11	9	9	9

MINES MANAGEMENT, INC.

6500 N MINERAL DR STE 200
COEUR D ALENE, ID 838159408
Phone: 509 838-6050
Fax: –
Web: –

CEO: Glenn M Dobbs
CFO: Nicole Altenburg
HR: –
FYE: December 31
Type: Private

Mines Management explores and develops silver and copper properties in the US. The company's primary property is the Montanore project in northwestern Montana, which was operated between 1988 and 2002 by Falconbridge. Mines Management would like to further develop the Montanore property, and it is working to complete the required environmental and engineering studies and to determine an economically viable way to conduct mining operations. Its preparation of the property for study was expedited in 2006, and underground testing took up most of 2007 through 2009. Silver Wheaton owned 11% of Mines Management, while US Global Investors owned just over 7%. In 2016 the company was acquired by Hecla Mining.

MINI-SYSTEMS, INC.

20 DAVID RD
NORTH ATTLEBORO, MA 027602102
Phone: 508 695-1420
Fax: –
Web: www.mini-systemsinc.com

CEO: Glen E Robertson
CFO: –
HR: –
FYE: December 31
Type: Private

Mini-Systems, Inc. (MSI) manufactures thin-film and thick-film chip resistors and capacitors for marine, military, aerospace, communications, cryogenics, and implantable medical device applications. The company also produces multichip modules. Its Electronic Package division turns out custom hybrid microelectronic packages, including alumina/glass sidewall packaging, an alternative to plastic packages. Customers include Northrop Grumman. It also had a hand in developing Voyager's One's Golden Record (a sample of human sounds and images) for NASA. Mini-Systems was established in 1968 by Glen Robertson, the company's president. The company is owned by its officers and outside investors.

	Annual Growth	12/14	12/15	12/16	12/17	12/18
Sales ($mil.)	3.2%	–	12.8	15.4	13.4	14.0
Net income ($ mil.)	19.3%	–	2.1	3.5	3.8	3.5
Market value ($ mil.)	–	–	–	–	–	–
Employees						200

MINIM INC

848 Elm Street
Manchester, NH 03101
Phone: 617 423-1072
Fax: –
Web: www.zoomtel.com

NAS: MINM
CEO: Jeremy Hitchcock
CFO: –
HR: –
FYE: December 31
Type: Public

Even though it offers a variety of communications products, Zoom Telephonics' primary mode is modems. Selling under its Hayes and Global Village brands, the company specializes in the design and production of hardware used to move data over the Internet, including DSL, cable, and dial-up modems, as well as VoIP (Voice over Internet Protocol) and Bluetooth products. It sells its products in the US, Europe, South America, and other markets through retailers like Best Buy, Staples, and Wal-Mart; it also sells through distributors and to OEMs (original equipment manufacturers). Founded in 1977, Zoom Telephonics was spun off from Zoom Technologies in 2009.

	Annual Growth	12/18	12/19	12/20	12/21	12/22
Sales ($mil.)	11.9%	32.3	37.6	48.0	55.4	50.6
Net income ($ mil.)	–	(0.1)	(3.3)	(3.9)	(3.6)	(15.5)
Market value ($ mil.)	(40.5%)	2.8	2.2	6.8	2.3	0.4
Employees	29.6%	33	38	61	83	93

MINISTRY HEALTH CARE, INC.

400 W RIVER WOODS PKWY
MILWAUKEE, WI 532121060
Phone: 414 359-1060
Fax: –
Web: www.ministryhealth.org

CEO: Nicholas F Desien
CFO: –
HR: Tammy Weiman
FYE: June 30
Type: Private

Part of the Marian Health System, Ministry Health Care is a network of hospitals, clinics, and other health facilities serving all of Wisconsin and eastern Minnesota. The network includes 15 acute and tertiary care hospitals (such as the 500-bed Saint Joseph's Hospital of Marshfield), as well as about 50 physician clinics, long-term and assisted living facilities, home health agencies, hospices, and other community health programs and services. Ministry Health Care's flagship facility was founded in 1890 by the Sisters of the Sorrowful Mother as a Catholic health care system to contribute to the well-being of the community. Ministry Health Care and Marian Health System merged with Ascension Health in 2013.

	Annual Growth	06/12	06/13	06/14	06/15	06/22
Sales ($mil.)	(15.7%)	–	–	–	281.0	84.8
Net income ($ mil.)	–	–	–	–	(31.5)	46.9
Market value ($ mil.)	–	–	–	–	–	–
Employees		–	–	–	–	5,000

MINITAB, LLC

1829 PINE HALL RD
STATE COLLEGE, PA 168013008
Phone: 814 238-3280
Fax: –
Web: www.minitab.com

CEO: Jeff Slovin
CFO: William J Vesnesky
HR: –
FYE: December 31
Type: Private

Minitab is a market leader in data analysis, predictive analytics and process improvement. By unlocking the value of data, Minitab enables organizations to improve performance, develop life changing innovations and meet their commitments of delivering high quality products and services and outstanding customer satisfaction. Thousands of businesses and institutions worldwide use Minitab Statistical Software, Minitab Connect, Real-Time SPC Powered by Minitab, Salford Predictive Modeler, Minitab Workspace, Minitab Engage, and Quality Trainer. Minitab Solutions Analytics is Minitab's proprietary integrated approach to providing software and services that enable organizations to make better decisions that drive business excellence.

	Annual Growth	12/05	12/06	12/07	12/08	12/09
Sales ($mil.)	(5.2%)	–	–	59.8	63.6	53.7
Net income ($ mil.)	(47.9%)	–	–	10.5	3.8	2.8
Market value ($ mil.)	–	–	–	–	–	–
Employees		–	–	–	–	296

MINN-DAK FARMERS COOPERATIVE INC

7525 RED RIVER RD
WAHPETON, ND 580759705
Phone: 701 642-8411
Fax: –
Web: www.mdf.coop

CEO: Kurt Wickstrom
CFO: Rick Kasper
HR: –
FYE: August 31
Type: Private

Minn-Dak Farmers Cooperative serves sugar beet growers in the Red River Valley of Minnesota, North Dakota, and South Dakota. Headquartered in Wahpeton, North Dakota, the co-op processes its sugar beets into sugar as well as products the likes of molasses and beet pulp pellets (used in animal feed). Minn-Dak's products are then marketed through agents worldwide. The co-op's Minn-Dak Yeast segment produces fresh bakers' yeast. The cooperative is owned by its farmer/members, which consist of a group of some 500 sugar beet growers. Founded in 1972, its customers include industrial users, including confectioners, breakfast-cereal manufacturers, and bakeries.

MINNESOTA STATE COLLEGES AND UNIVERSITIES

30 7TH ST E
SAINT PAUL, MN 551014914
Phone: 800 456-8519
Fax: –
Web: www.minnstate.edu

CEO: –
CFO: Laura M King
HR: Renee Hogoboom
FYE: June 30
Type: Private

The Minnesota State Colleges and Universities (MnSCU) system is made up of 31 universities and community and technical colleges, including two dozen two-year colleges and seven state universities. The colleges and universities operate 54 campuses in 47 Minnesota communities and serve about 310,000 students in credit-based courses. Overall, the system produces nearly 42,000 graduates each year. The system was created in 1995 through the merger of the state university system, the community college system, and the technical college system. The student-teacher ratio is 19:1. MnSCU is separate from the University of Minnesota.

	Annual Growth	06/13	06/14	06/15	06/16	06/19
Sales ($mil.)	(47.9%)	–	–	–	835.4	118.1
Net income ($ mil.)	(51.1%)	–	–	–	118.0	13.8
Market value ($ mil.)	–	–	–	–	–	–
Employees		–	–	–	–	15,000

MINNESOTA WILD HOCKEY CLUB, LP

317 WASHINGTON ST
SAINT PAUL, MN 551021609
Phone: 651 602-6000
Fax: –
Web: www.nhl.com

CEO: Craig Leipold
CFO: –
HR: –
FYE: August 31
Type: Private

Fans of this team are Wild about hockey, you might say. Minnesota Wild Hockey Club owns and operates the Minnesota Wild professional hockey franchise. The team joined the National Hockey League in the expansion of 2000 (along with the Columbus Blue Jackets), filling the void left after the Minnesota North Stars moved to Texas in 1993 to become the Dallas Stars. An investment group led by Robert Naegele Jr. helped bring hockey back to the Twin Cities. Former Nashville Predators owner Craig Leipold acquired control of the team from Naegele in 2008.

MINNKOTA POWER COOPERATIVE, INC.

5301 32ND AVE S
GRAND FORKS, ND 582013312
Phone: 701 795-4000
Fax: –
Web: www.minnkota.com

CEO: Robert McLennan
CFO: –
HR: Jeff Franck
FYE: December 31
Type: Private

The Minnkota Power Cooperative keeps the juice flowing to power users in northwestern Minnesota and eastern North Dakota. The generation and transmission cooperative supplies electricity to its 11 member-owner distribution cooperatives, and, as operating agent for the Northern Municipal Power Agency, to 12 municipal systems, to serve more than 118,000 retail customers in a 34,500-sq.-mi. region. Minnkota owns and operates the 235 MW lignite coal-fired generation Unit 1 of the Milton R. Young plant in Center, North Dakota and 30% of the 400 MW lignite coal-fired Coyote Station near Beulah. The company also has wind power assets.

	Annual Growth	12/17	12/18	12/19	12/20	12/21
Sales ($mil.)	(25.7%)	–	406.4	402.2	162.5	167.0
Net income ($ mil.)	(35.4%)	–	10.1	11.7	2.7	2.7
Market value ($ mil.)	–	–	–	–	–	–
Employees	–	–	–	–	–	355

MINUTEMAN PRESS INTERNATIONAL, INC.

61 EXECUTIVE BLVD
FARMINGDALE, NY 117354710
Phone: 631 249-1370
Fax: –
Web: www.minutemanpress.com

CEO: Robert Titus
CFO: Stanley M Katz
HR: –
FYE: December 31
Type: Private

Minuteman Press International wants to be the first in line for your printing business. The company franchises full-service quick printing centers, offering graphic design, typesetting, and printing. It provides franchisees with equipment, supplies, training, marketing services, and site selection, as well as start-up financing options. Minuteman Press International has more than 950 printing centers worldwide, with locations in Australia, Canada, South Africa, the UK, and the US. The company was founded by Roy Titus in 1973. His son, Bob, leads the firm as president.

	Annual Growth	12/10	12/11	12/12	12/13	12/14
Sales ($mil.)	3.4%	–	–	20.8	23.5	22.3
Net income ($ mil.)	24.8%	–	–	1.2	3.6	1.8
Market value ($ mil.)	–	–	–	–	–	–
Employees	–	–	–	–	–	120

MIRACLE SOFTWARE SYSTEMS INC.

45625 GRAND RIVER AVE
NOVI, MI 483741309
Phone: 248 233-1100
Fax: –
Web: www.miraclesoft.com

CEO: –
CFO: –
HR: –
FYE: June 30
Type: Private

For businesses who feel that it might take divine intervention to solve their IT problems, Miracle Software Systems offers a more down-to-Earth alternative. The company provides IT services such as enterprise application development and integration, consulting, network design, legacy systems migration, and training. The service-oriented architecture (SOA) specialist primarily installs, customizes, and supports software from IBM, but it also offers products from Oracle, and SAP, among others. Customers have included businesses in the health care (Pfizer), insurance (Premera Blue Cross), finance, logistics (Menlo Worldwide), manufacturing (John Deere), and retail (Target) industries.

	Annual Growth	06/08	06/09	06/10	06/11	06/17
Sales ($mil.)	13.0%	–	29.9	26.0	27.0	79.6
Net income ($ mil.)	–	–	(0.3)	(0.0)	(0.0)	3.0
Market value ($ mil.)	–	–	–	–	–	–
Employees	–	–	–	–	–	435

MIRACOSTA COMMUNITY COLLEGE DISTRICT

1 BARNARD DR
OCEANSIDE, CA 920563820
Phone: 760 757-2121
Fax: –
Web: www.miracosta.edu

CEO: –
CFO: –
HR: Rachel Garcia
FYE: June 30
Type: Private

MiraCosta College is a public, two-year community college serving northern San Diego County in southern California. The college offers associate degrees, certificates of achievement and proficiency, and professional certification in approximately 70 academic disciplines including nursing, education, psychology, oceanography, music, and business. MiraCosta College has an annual enrollment of some 14,500 credit students and 2,500 noncredit students. Originally known as Oceanside-Carlsbad Junior College, the school was established in 1934; it relocated and became MiraCosta College in 1964.

	Annual Growth	06/18	06/19	06/20	06/21	06/22
Sales ($mil.)	17.7%	–	29.7	28.1	38.3	48.4
Net income ($ mil.)	28.6%	–	10.0	7.1	(0.7)	21.3
Market value ($ mil.)	–	–	–	–	–	–
Employees	–	–	–	–	–	780

MIRATEK CORP.

8201 LOCKHEED DR STE 218
EL PASO, TX 799252558
Phone: 915 772-2852
Fax: –
Web: www.miratek.us

CEO: –
CFO: Arturo Herrera
HR: –
FYE: April 30
Type: Private

MIRATEK has a vision for technology. The company provides a variety of information technology support and consulting services for government and commercial clients in the US and Mexico. Areas of specialty include computer network systems engineering and integration, testing, and hardware and software maintenance. It also provides such environmental services as energy studies, remote sensing, and hazardous waste site management. Clients have included defense contractors (Lockheed Martin), utilities companies (El Paso Electric Company), and government agencies (National Nuclear Security Administration). MIRATEK was founded by owner and CEO Joe Diaz. It has satellite offices in New Mexico, Texas, and Washington, D.C.

	Annual Growth	04/04	04/05	04/06	04/07	04/08
Sales ($mil.)	(42.6%)	–	89.2	18.8	14.2	16.8
Net income ($ mil.)	(55.7%)	–	5.3	1.9	0.4	0.5
Market value ($ mil.)	–	–	–	–	–	–
Employees	–	–	–	–	–	102

MIRENCO INC

206 May Street, P.O. Box 343
Radcliffe, IA 50230
Phone: 515 899-2164
Fax: –
Web: www.mirenco.com

CEO: Dwayne L Fosseen
CFO: Glynis M Hendrickson
HR: –
FYE: December 31
Type: Public

MIRENCO would like to see bus fumes consigned to the scrap heap of history. The company's signature product, D-Max, is an electronic throttle control for heavy-duty start-and-stop vehicles such as buses and garbage trucks that is designed to improve fuel efficiency and reduce environmental emissions. MIRENCO's HydroFire product adds technology to reduce nitrogen-oxide emissions to the D-Max system. The company's EconoCruise product uses GPS technology to read the road ahead and adjusts the vehicle's cruise control to better manage throttle and emissions. Chairman and CEO Dwayne Fosseen owns about 35% of MIRENCO.

	Annual Growth	12/06	12/07	12/08	12/09	12/10
Sales ($mil.)	(27.7%)	–	–	0.8	0.3	0.4
Net income ($ mil.)	–	–	–	(0.4)	(0.6)	(0.5)
Market value ($ mil.)	47.2%	–	–	1.9	1.0	4.2
Employees	–	–	–	–	10	10

MISONIX OPCO, INC.

1938 NEW HWY
FARMINGDALE, NY 117351214
Phone: 631 694-9555
Fax: –
Web: www.bioventussurgical.com

CEO: Stavros G Vizirgianakis
CFO: Joseph P Dwyer
HR: –
FYE: June 30
Type: Private

Did you hear that Misonix is on the cutting edge of ultrasonic medical equipment? The development and manufacturing company makes ultrasonic devices to cut bone, remove tumors, and clean wounds. Its LySonix system is used to remove soft tissue during liposuction surgery. Subsidiary Hearing Innovations is developing devices to treat deafness and tinnitus. In addition to its therapeutic products, Misonix manufactures the Aura line of fume hoods used in scientific and forensic laboratories. The company manufactures its products at its facility in Farmington, New York. Misonix markets its products in the US and internationally through a direct sales force and wholesale distributors.

MISSION BROADCASTING, INC.

4822 KEMP BLVD STE 300
WICHITA FALLS, TX 763085273
Phone: 440 526-2227
Fax: –
Web: www.missionbroadcastinginc.com

CEO: Dennis Thatcher
CFO: –
HR: –
FYE: December 31
Type: Private

TV is the purpose of this company. Mission Broadcasting owns broadcasting licenses for 16 television stations serving small and medium-sized markets mostly in Texas, Missouri, and Pennsylvania. It generates most of its revenue through local service agreements with TV stations owned by Nexstar Broadcasting under which Nexstar operates the stations and provides programming, sales, and other services. The company's portfolio of stations includes affiliates of all the major broadcasting networks, as well as a couple stations affiliated with mini-network MyNetworkTV. President David Smith, who owns the company, started Mission Broadcasting in 1998.

	Annual Growth	12/15	12/16	12/17	12/18	12/19
Sales ($mil.)	2.5%	–	104.2	107.1	109.2	112.2
Net income ($ mil.)	–	–	19.5	5.6	(5.8)	(28.7)
Market value ($ mil.)	–	–	–	–	–	–
Employees	–	–	–	–	–	38

MISSION HOSPITAL, INC.

509 BILTMORE AVE
ASHEVILLE, NC 288014601
Phone: 828 213-1111
Fax: –
Web: www.missionhealth.org

CEO: Chad Patrick
CFO: –
HR: –
FYE: September 30
Type: Private

Its mission is clear and bold: Improve the health of all in western North Carolina. Mission Hospital is a 760-bed regional referral center serving the western quarter of North Carolina and portions of adjoining states. A not-for-profit community hospital system, Mission is located in Asheville on two adjoining campuses: Memorial and St. Joseph's. It provides tertiary-level services in neurosciences, cardiac care, trauma care, surgery, pediatric medicine, and women's services and has a medical staff of more than 540. It also includes the Mission Children's Hospital. Mission Hospital is the flagship hospital of Mission Health System, which is being acquired by HCA Healthcare for $1.5 billion.

	Annual Growth	09/11	09/12	09/13	09/14	09/15
Sales ($mil.)	5.8%	–	861.0	942.3	936.2	1,019.5
Net income ($ mil.)	2.0%	–	86.3	71.9	64.8	91.5
Market value ($ mil.)	–	–	–	–	–	–
Employees	–	–	–	–	–	10,000

MISSION PHARMACAL COMPANY

10999 W INTERSTATE 10 STE 1000
SAN ANTONIO, TX 782301300
Phone: 210 696-8400
Fax: –
Web: www.missionpharmacal.com

CEO: Neill B Walsdorf Sr
CFO: Tom Dooley
HR: –
FYE: April 30
Type: Private

Mission Pharmacal's purpose, objective, and undertaking, if you will, is to make you feel better. The company makes prescription and over-the-counter (OTC) remedies for infection, kidney stones, and arthritis, as well as nutritional supplements. Mission's products include kidney stone preventer Urocit-K, dermatitis ointment Texacort, bacterial infection fighter Tindamax, and CitraNatal prescription prenatal vitamins. The company also offers third-party OTC, nutritional, and prescription manufacturing, packaging, and inventory management to pharmaceutical companies. Mission is owned and run by the founding Walsdorf family.

	Annual Growth	04/13	04/14	04/15	04/16	04/17
Sales ($mil.)	5.9%	–	152.0	157.2	138.4	180.5
Net income ($ mil.)	–	–	(1.6)	7.6	0.9	(0.8)
Market value ($ mil.)	–	–	–	–	–	–
Employees	–	–	–	–	–	225

MISSISSIPPI COUNTY ELECTRIC COOPERATIVE, INC.

510 N BROADWAY ST
BLYTHEVILLE, AR 723152732
Phone: 870 763-4563
Fax: –
Web: www.mceci.com

CEO: –
CFO: –
HR: –
FYE: December 31
Type: Private

Like much of the rest of the state of Arkansas, people in Mississippi County get their electricity from a cooperative. Mississippi County Electric Cooperative (MCEC) serves customers in the northeast corner of Arkansas about 60 miles north of Memphis. The area is home to two steel mills owned by Nucor Corporation that are powered by MCEC power; most customers are industrial or agricultural. The coop also offers Internet service via rural satellite broadband provider WildBlue, and provides its customers with energy audits and information on saving energy. It is a member of Touchstone Energy, a national alliance of electric cooperatives in nearly 40 states. MCEC was formed in 1938.

	Annual Growth	12/16	12/17	12/18	12/21	12/22
Sales ($mil.)	6.4%	–	161.5	172.3	213.6	219.8
Net income ($ mil.)	–	–	(1.6)	(1.5)	(2.2)	(13.9)
Market value ($ mil.)	–	–	–	–	–	–
Employees	–	–	–	–	–	16

MISSISSIPPI POWER CO

2992 West Beach Boulevard
Gulfport, MS 39501
Phone: 228 864-1211
Fax: –
Web: www.mississippipower.com

CEO: Anthony L Wilson
CFO: Moses H Feagin
HR: –
FYE: December 31
Type: Public

Mississippi Power provides electric services to about 186,680 residential, commercial, and industrial customers in the Magnolia State. The utility, operates more than 6,890 miles of transmission and distribution lines, and it generates nearly 3,160 MW of capacity from its power plants (of which 1,450 MWs are coal-fired). Mississippi Power also sells wholesale electricity to several Florida municipal and cooperative utilities, and it offers energy conservation services and sells electrical appliances. Mississippi Power is a subsidiary of utility holding firm Southern Company.

	Annual Growth	12/19	12/20	12/21	12/22	12/23
Sales ($mil.)	3.9%	1,264.0	1,172.0	1,322.0	1,694.0	1,474.0
Net income ($ mil.)	7.8%	139.0	152.0	159.0	164.0	188.0
Market value ($ mil.)	–	–	–	–	–	–
Employees	(0.7%)	1,030	1,000	1,000	1,000	1,000

MISSISSIPPI STATE UNIVERSITY

245 BARR AVE MCARTHUR HALL
MISSISSIPPI STATE, MS 39762
Phone: 662 325-2302
Fax: –
Web: www.msstate.edu

CEO: –
CFO: –
HR: –
FYE: June 30
Type: Private

While agriculture is at its roots, Mississippi State University's (MSU) is today a four-year university offering approximately 150 undergraduate majors and pre-professional programs, as well as master's, educational specialist, and doctorate degree programs at a dozen colleges and schools. It confers more than 4,300 degrees annually and has an enrollment of more than 20,870 students at its main campus in Starkville and a regional campus in Meridian. More than three-quarters of its student body hail from Mississippi. MSU was created by the Mississippi Legislature in 1878 as The Agricultural and Mechanical College of the State of Mississippi.

	Annual Growth	06/18	06/19	06/20	06/21	06/22
Sales ($mil.)	5.7%	–	525.2	547.5	572.6	619.8
Net income ($ mil.)	5.5%	–	71.2	68.9	58.9	83.5
Market value ($ mil.)	–	–	–	–	–	–
Employees	–	–	–	–	–	4,500

MISSOURI CITY OF KANSAS CITY

414 E 12TH ST STE 105
KANSAS CITY, MO 641062705
Phone: 816 513-1313
Fax: –
Web: www.kcmo.gov

CEO: –
CFO: –
HR: Bruce Beatty
FYE: April 30
Type: Private

You may not be in Kansas anymore, but you could still be in Kansas City . Situated opposite Kansas City, Kansas, is the city of Kansas City, Missouri, the state's largest city, with a population of about 460,000. Its council-manager form of government is made up of 12 members presided over by the mayor. The city manager serves and advises the council and prepares the annual budget for council consideration, as well as enforces municipal laws and ordinances and manages city operations. With more than 200 fountains within 320 square miles, its official nickname is the "City of Fountains." Incorporated in 1850, it is home to the Chiefs and Royals and is famous for barbeque.

	Annual Growth	04/18	04/19	04/20	04/21	04/22
Sales ($mil.)	6.7%	–	1,150.0	1,150.1	1,171.4	1,398.0
Net income ($ mil.)	–	–	(22.9)	42.0	28.4	339.7
Market value ($ mil.)	–	–	–	–	–	–
Employees	–	–	–	–	–	8,000

MISSOURI DEPARTMENT OF TRANSPORTATION

105 W CAPITOL AVE
JEFFERSON CITY, MO 651016811
Phone: 573 751-2551
Fax: –
Web: www.modot.org

CEO: –
CFO: –
HR: –
FYE: June 30
Type: Private

Missouri has come a long way since its first byway, Three Notch Road, was built in 1735, and MoDOT has had a lot to do with the progress. The Missouri Department of Transportation (MoDOT) overseas one of the nation's largest state highway systems. Specifically, it designs, builds, and maintains the 32,000-plus miles of highway and some 10,000 bridges, and administers federal and state programs that affect public transit and air, water, and rail transportation throughout the state. MoDOT is governed by the six-member Missouri Highways and Transportation Commission. The agency that became MoDOT got its start when the Missouri Legislature established a job for a state highway engineer in 1907.

MISSOURI HIGHER EDUCATION LOAN AUTHORITY

633 SPIRIT DR
CHESTERFIELD, MO 630051243
Phone: 636 733-3700
Fax: –
Web: www.mohela.com

CEO: –
CFO: Scott Gailes
HR: Christine Ellinger
FYE: June 30
Type: Private

From the "Show Me" state comes Missouri Higher Education Loan Authority, one of the country's top holders and servicers of student loans. The not-for-profit organization helps borrowers obtain education financing such as Federal Stafford, alternative or supplemental, and consolidation loans through lending institutions such as Bank of America and U.S. Bancorp. It also offers a "Rate Relief" program that can lower a borrower's interest rate by up to 3%, as well as deferment and forbearance options that either postpone or reduce a borrower's monthly payment. The authority also manages loan servicing for lending institutions nationwide.

	Annual Growth	06/17	06/18	06/19	06/21	06/22
Assets ($mil.)	(3.6%)	–	1,727.5	1,549.7	1,611.8	1,491.1
Net income ($ mil.)	–	–	18.9	17.1	24.6	(31.8)
Market value ($ mil.)	–	–	–	–	–	–
Employees	–	–	–	–	–	550

MISSOURI STATE UNIVERSITY

901 S NATIONAL AVE
SPRINGFIELD, MO 658970001
Phone: 417 836-5000
Fax: –
Web: www.missouristate.edu

CEO: –
CFO: –
HR: –
FYE: June 30
Type: Private

When Missouri students say "show me", Missouri State University happily obliges. It is the state's second-largest university (after University of Missouri) with an enrollment of 23,800 students. The school offers about 85 undergraduate majors, 133 undergraduate minors, and 50 graduate majors, including 14 masters, 3 doctoral degrees (audiology, physical therapy, and nurse practitioner), and one specialist degree. The university' coursework includes accounting, biology, criminology, and physical geography. Missouri State awarded almost 4,000 degrees in 2013. It also hosted some 16 NCAA Division One sports teams that year.

	Annual Growth	06/16	06/17	06/18	06/20	06/22
Sales ($mil.)	(27.3%)	–	216.2	223.4	43.6	44.0
Net income ($ mil.)	–	–	(16.0)	(7.0)	24.9	12.1
Market value ($ mil.)	–	–	–	–	–	–
Employees	–	–	–	–	–	2,066

MISTRAS GROUP INC   NYS: MG

195 Clarksville Road   CEO: –
Princeton Junction, NJ 08550   CFO: –
Phone: 609 716-4000   HR: –
Fax: –   FYE: December 31
Web: www.mistrasgroup.com   Type: Public

Mistras is a leading one-source multinational provider of integrated technology-enabled asset protection solutions, helping to maximize the safety and operational uptime for civilization's most critical industrial and civil assets. The company's core capabilities also include non-destructive testing (NDT) field inspections enhanced by advanced robotics, laboratory quality control and assurance testing, sensing technologies and NDT equipment, asset and mechanical integrity engineering services, and light mechanical maintenance and access services. Mistras technology-enabled asset protection solutions are used to evaluate the safety, structural integrity, and reliability of critical energy, industrial and public infrastructure. Mistras leads clients are in the oil and gas, petrochemical, aerospace and defense, renewable and non-renewable energy, civil infrastructure, and manufacturing industries. The US accounts for about 70% of total revenue.

	Annual Growth	12/19	12/20	12/21	12/22	12/23
Sales ($mil.)	(1.5%)	748.6	592.6	677.1	687.4	705.5
Net income ($ mil.)	–	6.1	(99.5)	3.9	6.5	(17.5)
Market value ($ mil.)	(15.4%)	436.6	237.4	227.3	150.8	224.0
Employees	(3.3%)	5,500	5,400	5,400	5,400	4,800

MITCHELL SILBERBERG & KNUPP LLP

2049 CENTURY PARK E FL 18   CEO: –
LOS ANGELES, CA 900673120   CFO: –
Phone: 310 312-2000   HR: Won Park
Fax: –   FYE: September 30
Web: www.msk.com   Type: Private

Legally representing folks from the entertainment industry may not sound like your cup of tea, but somebody's got to do the job -- turns out Mitchell Silberberg & Knupp is up for the challenge. Founded in 1908, the law firm provides a variety of business law services with an emphasis on intellectual property and the entertainment industry. Other practice areas include technology; immigration; corporate law and homeland security; tax, trust, and estates; and international trade. Mitchell Silberberg & Knupp employs about 125 attorneys with three US offices located in Los Angeles, New York, and Washington, D.C.

	Annual Growth	09/08	09/09	09/10*	12/10*	09/15
Sales ($mil.)	(27.5%)	–	0.2	0.2	68.3	0.0
Net income ($ mil.)	–	–	0.0	0.0	32.9	(0.2)
Market value ($ mil.)	–	–	–	–	–	–
Employees	–	–	–	–	–	300

*Fiscal year change

MITEK SYSTEMS, INC.   NAS: MITK

600 B Street, Suite 100   CEO: Scipio Carnecchia
San Diego, CA 92101   CFO: David Lyle
Phone: 619 269-6800   HR: –
Fax: –   FYE: September 30
Web: www.miteksystems.com   Type: Public

Mitek is a global leader in mobile capture and digital identity verification solutions built on the latest advancements in AI and machine learning. Mitek's identity verification solutions enable an enterprise to verify a user's identity during a digital transaction, which assists financial institutions, payments companies and other businesses operating in highly regulated markets in mitigating financial risk and meeting regulatory requirements while increasing revenue from digital channels. Mitek also reduces the friction in the users' experience with advanced data prefill and automation of the onboarding process. Mitek's innovative solutions are embedded into the apps of more than 7,500 organizations and used by more than 80 million consumers for mobile check deposit, new account opening and more. International revenue account for more than 25% of the company's total revenue.

	Annual Growth	09/19	09/20	09/21	09/22	09/23
Sales ($mil.)	19.5%	84.6	101.3	119.8	143.9	172.6
Net income ($ mil.)	–	(0.7)	7.8	8.0	3.0	8.0
Market value ($ mil.)	2.7%	440.0	580.8	843.4	417.6	488.7
Employees	19.2%	284	360	448	588	573

MITEL NETWORKS, INC.

1146 N ALMA SCHOOL RD   CEO: –
MESA, AZ 852013000   CFO: –
Phone: 613 592-5660   HR: –
Fax: –   FYE: June 30
Web: www.mitel.com   Type: Private

ShoreTel's internet protocol-based telephony hardware and software offers small and midsized businesses, government agencies, and schools an alternative to standard phone service. It provides voice, video, data, and mobile communications with products that include phones and switches, as well as messaging and systems management software. The company provides a cloud-based subscription service and licenses its software for use in customers' data centers. It also offers communications service for call centers. ShoreTel generates most of its sales in the US. The company counts about 40,000 customers in the financial services, health care, manufacturing, nonprofit, and technology industries, among others.

MJB WOOD GROUP, LLC

1585 HIGH MEADOWS WAY   CEO: Scott Griggs
CEDAR HILL, TX 751048413   CFO: –
Phone: 972 401-0005   HR: Annie Gray
Fax: –   FYE: October 31
Web: www.mjbwood.com   Type: Private

MJB Wood Group, a Coors family-owned company, is a global leader in sourcing, manufacturing, and distributing wood products. Its diverse selection of panel products, wood components, millwork, and specialty products are carefully sourced both domestically and internationally to meet the unique needs of its customers throughout North America and beyond. Its network of logistics partners throughout the US and Mexico makes it easy to service a single location or multiple locations. MJB has a highly-skilled sales team whose expertise focuses on sourcing from South America, Europe, Asia, and other emerging international markets.

MKS INSTRUMENTS INC   NMS: MKSI

2 Tech Drive, Suite 201   CEO: John T Lee
Andover, MA 01810   CFO: Seth H Bagshaw
Phone: 978 645-5500   HR: –
Fax: –   FYE: December 31
Web: www.mksinst.com   Type: Public

MKS Instruments deliver foundational technology solutions to leading-edge semiconductor manufacturing, electronics and packaging, and specialty industrial applications. MKS applies its broad science and engineering capabilities to create instruments, subsystems, systems, process control solutions, and specialty chemicals technology that improve process performance, optimize productivity and enable unique innovations for technology and industrial companies. Top customers include Applied Materials and Lam Research. It also developed product strategies, including Surround the Wafer and Surround the Workpiece. The company generates some 40% of its sales from customers in the US. The company was founded in 1961.

	Annual Growth	12/19	12/20	12/21	12/22	12/23
Sales ($mil.)	17.5%	1,899.8	2,330.0	2,949.6	3,547.0	3,622.0
Net income ($ mil.)	–	140.4	350.1	551.4	333.0	(1,841.0)
Market value ($ mil.)	(1.7%)	7,359.7	10,065	11,652	5,668.4	6,882.0
Employees	16.1%	5,500	5,800	6,400	10,900	10,000

MMC CORP

7801 W 110TH ST
OVERLAND PARK, KS 662102305
Phone: 913 469-0101
Fax: –
Web: www.mmccorp.com

CEO: Tim Chadwick
CFO: Dave Cimpl
HR: –
FYE: December 31
Type: Private

MMC Corp serves as a holding company for Midwest Mechanical Contractors, MW Builders, and other units. The group of eight independently operated companies provide preconstruction, construction, HVAC, and plumbing services throughout the US including Kansas, Texas, Nevada, Nebraska, and New Jersey. It specializes in mechanical work for commercial, health care, industrial, pharmaceutical, and power generation facility projects. Employee-owned MMC is ranked as one of the top specialty contractors in the US and its division have completed projects for the University of Kentucky, AT&T, and Wal-Mart. Claude Sanders founded Midwest Mechanical Contractors as a residential plumbing company in 1932.

MMC MATERIALS, INC.

133 NEW RAGSDALE RD
MADISON, MS 391101803
Phone: 601 898-4000
Fax: –
Web: www.mmcmaterials.com

CEO: –
CFO: –
HR: Arlene King
FYE: December 31
Type: Private

MMC Materials wants to cement its footprint firmly in the Southeast US. The company manufactures and distributes concrete, aggregates (gravel, sand, limestone), concrete mixes and accessories, and precast products such as steps and bumpers. MMC also offers decorative concrete flooring and driveways. It serves a variety of customers in the industrial, infrastructure, highway, commercial, and residential construction industries. With more than 60 plant locations, MMC Materials and its affiliate, Bayou Concrete, operates in Arkansas, Louisiana, Tennessee, Alabama, and Mississippi. The company was founded as Mississippi Concrete and Material Company in 1927. MMC is part of the Dunn Construction Company group.

	Annual Growth	12/02	12/03	12/04	12/05	12/07
Sales ($mil.)	11.4%	–	99.2	98.3	–	152.7
Net income ($ mil.)	(9.1%)	–	19.2	7.2	–	13.1
Market value ($ mil.)	–	–	–	–	–	–
Employees	–	–	–	–	–	450

MMR GROUP, INC.

15961 AIRLINE HWY
BATON ROUGE, LA 708177412
Phone: 225 756-5090
Fax: –
Web: www.mmrgrp.com

CEO: –
CFO: –
HR: Christy Linder
FYE: December 31
Type: Private

That murmur you hear could be the gentle hum of a properly functioning power system. MMG Group provides electrical and instrumentation construction, maintenance, management, and technical services for clients in the oil and gas, manufacturing, chemical, and power generation industries around the world. It also offers services in offshore marine and platform environments. Its Power Solutions division constructs onsite power-generation systems in industrial plants and other facilities. The group primarily operates in the Gulf of New Mexico. Founded in 1990, MMG is 100% management owned and has served such clients as Chevron, Shell, BP, Merck, Air Liquide, DuPont, and 3M.

	Annual Growth	12/18	12/19	12/20	12/21	12/22
Sales ($mil.)	6.4%	–	783.9	564.2	687.6	945.1
Net income ($ mil.)	58.1%	–	23.7	36.1	35.8	93.7
Market value ($ mil.)	–	–	–	–	–	–
Employees	–	–	–	–	–	4,000

MMRGLOBAL INC

4401 Wilshire Blvd., Suite 200
Los Angeles, CA 90010
Phone: 310 476-7002
Fax: –
Web: www.mymedicalrecords.com

CEO: Robert H Lorsch
CFO: Bernard Stolar
HR: –
FYE: December 31
Type: Public

MMRGlobal aims to ride the worldwide digitizing wave as more physicians and consumers switch to digital medical record systems. Its products in development include online professional record storage systems and personal document management systems under the brands MyMedicalRecords Pro and MyEsafeDepositBox. The company's technology allows patient information to be stored securely, but be shared with physicians, pharmacies, or insurance providers through the Internet. Previously operating as a biopharmaceutical development company, in early 2009 the company completed a reverse merger with privately held MyMedicalRecords.com, eventually changing its name to MMRGlobal in 2010.

	Annual Growth	12/11	12/12	12/13	12/14	12/15
Sales ($mil.)	(39.4%)	1.4	0.8	0.6	2.6	0.2
Net income ($ mil.)	–	(8.9)	(5.9)	(7.6)	(2.2)	(3.0)
Market value ($ mil.)	(50.8%)	9.0	3.9	7.0	2.3	0.5
Employees	(46.3%)	48	19	19	17	4

MNP CORPORATION

44225 UTICA RD
UTICA, MI 483175464
Phone: 586 254-1320
Fax: –
Web: www.mnp.com

CEO: Terri Chapman
CFO: Craig L Stormer
HR: Anne Ventimiglio-Ess
FYE: November 30
Type: Private

If you are fascinated with fasteners, then MNP will galvanize your senses. MNP manufactures a plethora of precision fasteners and cold formed components, including screws, rivets, washers, small stampings, as well as screw machine parts. Its services range from plating to annealing, flat-rolling, pickling, hot-dip galvanizing, and coatings. General Fasteners, Cadon Plating & Coatings, Marathon Metals, and Ohio Pickling & Processing are a few of MNP's affiliated companies that produce a medley of metal parts, and jointly operate the GFC/MNP Engineering Center in Michigan. The company serves the automotive, heavy truck, military, and industrial markets.

	Annual Growth	11/17	11/18	11/19	11/20	11/21
Sales ($mil.)	(1.6%)	–	232.7	218.5	171.5	222.0
Net income ($ mil.)	(17.7%)	–	22.6	23.9	14.5	12.6
Market value ($ mil.)	–	–	–	–	–	–
Employees	–	–	–	–	–	746

MOBILE AREA NETWORKS INC

2772 Depot Street
Sanford, FL 32773
Phone: 407 333-2350
Fax: –
Web: www.mobilan.com

CEO: –
CFO: –
HR: –
FYE: December 31
Type: Public

Mobile enough to move from wireless to plastic, Mobile Area Networks provides custom plastic injection molding services. The company originally installed wireless LANs in hotels, office buildings, and convention centers, but in 2002 it moved into plastics manufacturing. Mobile Area Networks focuses on developing proprietary products and custom molding. The company makes air conditioner parts, archery bow parts, consumer and novelty products, high-tech military parts, irrigation devices, non-invasive medical device parts, roofing construction items, snow ski equipment parts, sporting rifle parts, and other specialty applications. CEO George Wimbish controls Mobile Area Networks.

	Annual Growth	12/09	12/10	12/11	12/12	12/13
Sales ($mil.)	(75.7%)	0.3	0.3	0.2	0.0	0.0
Net income ($ mil.)	–	(0.3)	(0.4)	(0.3)	0.3	(0.1)
Market value ($ mil.)	8.8%	0.2	1.0	1.5	0.4	0.3
Employees	(26.9%)	7	6	4	2	2

MOBILEIRON, INC.

10377 S JORDAN GTWY STE 110
SOUTH JORDAN, UT 840953972
Phone: 650 919-8100
Fax: –
Web: www.ivanti.com

CEO: –
CFO: –
HR: –
FYE: December 31
Type: Private

MobileIron was founded in 2007 by Ajay Mishra and Suresh Batchu as the industry's first mobile-centric, zero trust platform built on a unified endpoint management (UEM) foundation. MobileIron's mobile-centric, zero trust approach ensured that only authorized users, devices, apps and services could access business resources. The MobileIron platform was built to secure and manage corporate data in a world where people access cloud data using mobile devices and modern endpoints. Its technical representatives stand ready to help clients' keep their end-users productive and deliver information that provides easy-to-find answers to common questions.

MOBILEPRO CORP.

6100 OAK TREE BLVD # 200
INDEPENDENCE, OH 441316914
Phone: 216 986-2745
Fax: –
Web: –

CEO: Jay O Wright
CFO: –
HR: –
FYE: March 31
Type: Private

MobilePro has slimmed down, divesting its telecommunications and broadband businesses. The company is left with a subsidiary called ProGames Network, which is developing online gaming products. In 2007 MobilePro agreed to merge ProGames with Winning Edge International, a sports handicapping firm, with ProGames owning more than 80% of the combined company. The deal fell apart, however, due to a lack of financing. MobilePro is considering strategic alternatives in order to maximize shareholder value. The company is vague on what forms those alternatives may take, but says its goals are to eliminate debt and to return value to shareholders.

	Annual Growth	03/04	03/05	03/06	03/07	03/08
Sales ($mil.)	(67.3%)	–	–	99.0	89.1	10.6
Net income ($ mil.)	–	–	–	(10.2)	(45.9)	(18.4)
Market value ($ mil.)	–	–	–	–	–	–
Employees	–	–	–	–	–	64

MOCON, INC.

7500 MENDELSOHN AVE N
MINNEAPOLIS, MN 554284045
Phone: 763 493-6370
Fax: –
Web: www.ametekmocon.com

CEO: James O Davis
CFO: Elissa Lindsoe
HR: –
FYE: December 31
Type: Private

MOCON makes precision instruments that help you look before you leak. Its products include permeation and packaging instruments that measure the rate at which oxygen, carbon dioxide, and water vapor penetrate packaging. The company also makes materials analyzers that measure the thickness of coatings and thin films. Such products are used by packagers in the food and beverage, pharmaceuticals, and chemical industries, and by paper, plastics, and coatings manufacturers. MOCON also makes pharmaceutical capsule and tablet weighing and sorting devices, automatic sample preparation systems, and offers related consulting and development services. MOCON agreed to be bought by Ametek for about $180 million in 2017.

MOD-PAC CORP.

1801 ELMWOOD AVE
BUFFALO, NY 142072496
Phone: 716 898-8480
Fax: –
Web: www.modpac.com

CEO: Daniel G Keane
CFO: David B Lupp
HR: Geraod Bogacz
FYE: December 31
Type: Private

Brown paper packages tied up with strings, these are a few of MOD-PAC's favorite things. MOD-PAC makes folding carton packaging for big brand and private-label manufacturers of personal and healthcare products, as well as candy, food and beverage, and even auto parts. Over 70% of its income comes from custom folding carton sales. MOD-PAC also boasts personalized printing of special-occasion paper goods for bridal and gift shops and Internet resellers. Chairman Kevin Keane and his son, CEO Daniel Keane, together own more than 40% of the company.

MODEL N, INC

NYS: MODN

777 Mariners Island Boulevard, Suite 300
San Mateo, CA 94404
Phone: 650 610-4600
Fax: –
Web: www.modeln.com

CEO: Jason Blessing
CFO: John Ederer
HR: –
FYE: September 30
Type: Public

Model N is a leading provider of cloud revenue management solutions for life sciences and high tech companies. Its software helps companies drive mission critical business processes such as pricing, quoting, contracting, regulatory compliance, rebates and incentives. With deep industry expertise, Model N supports the complex business needs of the world's leading brands in pharmaceutical, medical technology, semiconductor, and High Tech manufacturing across more than 120 countries, including Johnson & Johnson, AstraZeneca, Novartis, Microchip Technology and ON Semiconductor.

	Annual Growth	09/19	09/20	09/21	09/22	09/23
Sales ($mil.)	15.3%	141.2	161.1	193.4	219.2	249.5
Net income ($ mil.)	–	(19.3)	(13.7)	(29.7)	(28.6)	(33.9)
Market value ($ mil.)	(3.2%)	1,076.1	1,367.6	1,298.6	1,326.9	946.2
Employees	10.4%	733	781	982	1,035	1,089

MODERN WOODMEN OF AMERICA

1701 1ST AVE
ROCK ISLAND, IL 612018779
Phone: 309 793-5537
Fax: –
Web: www.modernwoodmen.org

CEO: –
CFO: –
HR: John Lovelady
FYE: December 31
Type: Private

One of the largest fraternal benefit societies in the US, Modern Woodmen of America provides annuities, life insurance, and other financial savings products to nearly 730,000 members through more than 1,000 agents. The organization, founded in 1883, is organized into "camps" (or chapters) that provide financial, social, recreational, and service benefits to members. Founder Joseph Cullen Root chose the society's name to compare pioneering woodmen clearing forests to men using life insurance to remove the financial burdens their families could face upon their deaths.

	Annual Growth	12/03	12/04	12/05	12/06	12/07
Assets ($mil.)	4.9%	–	–	–	7,928.9	8,318.2
Net income ($ mil.)	(2.6%)	–	–	–	99.2	96.6
Market value ($ mil.)	–	–	–	–	–	–
Employees	–	–	–	–	–	480

MODERNA INC   NMS: MRNA

200 Technology Square
Cambridge, MA 02139
Phone: 617 714-6500
Fax: –
Web: www.modernatx.com

CEO: Stephane Bancel
CFO: James Mock
HR: –
FYE: December 31
Type: Public

Moderna is a biotechnology company pioneering messenger RNA (mRNA) therapeutics and vaccines to create a new generation of transformative medicines to improve the lives of patients. It has transformed from a research-stage company advancing programs in the field of messenger RNA (mRNA), to an enterprise with a diverse clinical portfolio of vaccines and therapeutics across six modalities, a broad intellectual property portfolio in areas including mRNA and lipid nanoparticle formulation, and an integrated manufacturing plant that allows for both clinical and commercial production at scale. Moderna maintains alliances with a broad range of domestic and overseas government and commercial collaborators. The US accounts for about 35% of revenue.

	Annual Growth	12/19	12/20	12/21	12/22	12/23
Sales ($mil.)	226.6%	60.2	803.4	18,471	19,263	6,848.0
Net income ($ mil.)	–	(514.0)	(747.1)	12,202	8,362.0	(4,714.0)
Market value ($ mil.)	50.2%	7,471.9	39,908	97,020	68,615	37,990
Employees	61.2%	830	1,300	2,700	3,900	5,600

MODESTO IRRIGATION DISTRICT (INC)

1231 11TH ST
MODESTO, CA 953540701
Phone: 209 526-7337
Fax: –
Web: www.mid.org

CEO: –
CFO: –
HR: Michelle Kincanon
FYE: December 31
Type: Private

Modesty notwithstanding, Modesto Irrigation District (MID) does much more than irrigate almost 58,000 acres of land in and around Modesto, California. The state-owned not-for-profit utility also generates, transmits, and distributes electricity. In 2012 the company reported that it distributed electricity in a 260-sq.-mi. area to about 94,120 residential and 12,265 commercial and industrial customers and some 7,547 other customers. MID also markets wholesale power and treats and provides drinking water to the city of Modesto for distribution purposes. In 2012 the organization had 103,733 irrigated acres (and more than 3,100 customer accounts) in its service area.

	Annual Growth	12/18	12/19	12/20	12/21	12/22
Sales ($mil.)	1.9%	–	425.8	430.9	441.5	450.1
Net income ($ mil.)	(66.3%)	–	75.0	71.4	40.5	2.9
Market value ($ mil.)	–	–	–	–	–	–
Employees	–	–	–	–	–	440

MODINE MANUFACTURING CO   NYS: MOD

1500 DeKoven Avenue
Racine, WI 53403
Phone: 262 636-1200
Fax: 262 636-1424
Web: www.modine.com

CEO: Neil D Brinker
CFO: Michael B Lucareli
HR: –
FYE: March 31
Type: Public

Modine Manufacturing specializes in providing innovative thermal management solutions to diversified global markets and customers. It is a leading provider of engineered heat transfer systems and high-quality heat transfer components for use in on- and off-highway original equipment manufacturer (OEM) vehicular applications. Products include powertrain cooling, heat transfer modules, on-engine cooling, auxiliary cooling, and battery thermal management systems. With manufacturing operations in more than 15 countries and technical centers in the US, Spain, Germany, and Italy, among others, about 50% of Modine's revenues are generated outside of the US. The company was founded in 1916.

	Annual Growth	03/19	03/20	03/21	03/22	03/23
Sales ($mil.)	0.9%	2,212.7	1,975.5	1,808.4	2,050.1	2,297.9
Net income ($ mil.)	15.9%	84.8	(2.2)	(210.5)	85.2	153.1
Market value ($ mil.)	13.5%	722.6	169.3	769.5	469.4	1,200.9
Employees	(1.9%)	12,200	11,300	10,900	11,100	11,300

MODIVCARE INC   NMS: MODV

6900 E Layton Avenue, 12th Floor
Denver, CO 80237
Phone: 303 728-7030
Fax: 520 747-6605
Web: www.modivcare.com

CEO: L H Sampson
CFO: L H Sampson
HR: –
FYE: December 31
Type: Public

ModivCare is a technology-enabled, healthcare services company, which provides a suite of integrated supportive care solutions for public and private payors and their patients. Its value-based solutions address the social determinants of health, or SDoH, connect members to care, help health plans manage risks, reduce costs, and improve health outcomes. It is the nation's largest manager of NEMT programs for state governments and MCOs, a leading in-home personal care services provider in the seven eastern states where it provides those services, and a leading provider of remote patient monitoring and medication management solutions.

	Annual Growth	12/19	12/20	12/21	12/22	12/23
Sales ($mil.)	16.2%	1,509.9	1,368.7	2,002.3	2,511.7	2,751.2
Net income ($ mil.)	–	1.0	88.8	(6.6)	(31.8)	(204.5)
Market value ($ mil.)	(7.1%)	840.6	1,969.1	2,106.3	1,274.5	624.8
Employees	53.7%	3,800	17,500	20,200	20,000	21,200

MODIVCARE SOLUTIONS, LLC

6900 E LAYTON AVE STE 1200
DENVER, CO 802373656
Phone: 404 888-5831
Fax: –
Web: www.modivcare.com

CEO: –
CFO: –
HR: –
FYE: December 31
Type: Private

LogistiCare is a go-between for getting from your house to the doctor's office and back. The company brokers non-emergency transportation services for commercial health plans, government entities (such as state Medicaid agencies), and hospitals throughout the US. Using its nearly 20 call centers and a network of some 1,500 independent, contracted transportation providers, the company coordinates the medical-related travel arrangements of its clients' members. In addition, it contracts with local school boards to coordinate transportation for special needs students. The company provides more than 26 million trips each year for clients in some 40 states. LogistiCare is a subsidiary of Providence Service.

	Annual Growth	12/13	12/14	12/15*	04/17*	12/17
Sales ($mil.)	14.2%	–	884.3	1,083.0	1,234.4	1,318.2
Net income ($ mil.)	(21.0%)	–	71.7	40.5	44.8	35.4
Market value ($ mil.)	–	–	–	–	–	–
Employees	–	–	–	–	–	3,128

*Fiscal year change

MOHAWK INDUSTRIES, INC.   NYS: MHK

160 S. Industrial Blvd.
Calhoun, GA 30701
Phone: 706 629-7721
Fax: –
Web: www.mohawkind.com

CEO: Jeffrey S Lorberbaum
CFO: Clifford Suing
HR: Christina V Dusen
FYE: December 31
Type: Public

Mohawk Industries is the world's largest maker of commercial and residential flooring products. The company's vertically integrated manufacturing and distribution processes provide competitive advantages in carpet, rugs, ceramic tile, laminate, wood, stone, luxury vinyl tile (LVT) and sheet vinyl flooring. The company's brands are among the most recognized in the industry and include American Olean, Daltile, Durkan, Eliane, Feltex, Godfrey Hirst, IVC, Karastan, Marazzi, Mohawk, Pergo, Quick-Step and Unilin. The company sells its products worldwide. Most of its revenue is generated in the US (about 55%), and it has a strong market position in Brazil.

	Annual Growth	12/19	12/20	12/21	12/22	12/23
Sales ($mil.)	2.8%	9,970.7	9,552.2	11,201	11,737	11,135
Net income ($ mil.)	–	744.2	515.6	1,033.2	25.2	(439.5)
Market value ($ mil.)	(6.7%)	8,685.5	8,976.5	11,602	6,510.0	6,591.5
Employees	0.9%	41,800	42,000	43,000	40,900	43,300

MOHEGAN TRIBAL GAMING AUTHORITY

1 MOHEGAN SUN BLVD
UNCASVILLE, CT 063821355
Phone: 860 862-8000
Fax: –
Web: www.mohegansun.com

CEO: Mario C Kontomerkos
CFO: –
HR: Crystal Bourez
FYE: September 30
Type: Private

The sun also rises at Mohegan Sun, a gaming and entertainment complex run by the Mohegan Tribal Gaming Authority for the Mohegan Indian tribe of Connecticut. The Native American-themed Mohegan Sun complex includes three casinos (Casino of the Earth, Casino of the Sky, and Casino of the Wind) that feature slot machines, game tables, horse race wagering, an arena, a cabaret, stores, restaurants, and a luxury hotel. The company also owns Pocono Downs, a horse racetrack in Pennsylvania. Gambling revenues go to the Mohegan Tribe, and are used for cultural and educational programs. The tribe has lived as a community for hundreds of years in what is today southeastern Connecticut, and has about 1,900 members.

	Annual Growth	09/18	09/19	09/20	09/21	09/22
Sales ($mil.)	4.6%	–	1,388.8	1,115.0	1,228.8	1,590.5
Net income ($ mil.)	–	–	(2.4)	(162.0)	7.4	75.2
Market value ($ mil.)	–	–	–	–	–	–
Employees	–	–	–	–	–	11,000

MOISTURESHIELD INC.

801 JEFFERSON ST
SPRINGDALE, AR 727643401
Phone: 479 756-7400
Fax: –
Web: www.moistureshield.com

CEO: –
CFO: –
HR: –
FYE: December 31
Type: Private

MoistureShield (formerly Advanced Environmental Recycling Technologies, or AERT) specializes in processing and converting scrap plastic and wood fiber waste into outdoor decking and fencing systems and window and door components. Its products are mainly used in residential renovation and remodeling by homeowners, homebuilders, and contractors as a greener alternative to traditional wood and plastic products. AERT markets its products under such names as ChoiceDek and MoistureShield; ChoiceDek is sold to home improvement retailers such as Lowe's through an agreement with distributor BlueLinx. H.I.G. Capital acquired 80% of AERT in 2011.

	Annual Growth	12/12	12/13	12/14	12/15	12/16
Sales ($mil.)	7.5%	–	68.8	76.0	82.7	85.3
Net income ($ mil.)	–	–	(0.1)	0.4	0.7	3.9
Market value ($ mil.)	–	–	–	–	–	–
Employees	–	–	–	–	–	380

MOLECULAR TEMPLATES INC   NAS: MTEM

9301 Amberglen Blvd., Suite 100
Austin, TX 78729
Phone: 512 869-1555
Fax: –
Web: www.mtem.com

CEO: Eric E Poma
CFO: –
HR: David Oelrich
FYE: December 31
Type: Public

By targeting next-generation immunotoxins, Molecular Templates (formerly Threshold Pharmaceuticals) hopes to develop drugs that are effective at fighting cancer. These immunotoxins, called Engineered Toxin Bodies (ETBs), are able to forcefully enter cells and can target cancer cells for direct attack. The company's MT-3724 candidate is being studied for the treatment of leukemia and lymphoma, while Evofosfamide is in trials to treat solid tumors and bone marrow cancer. In mid-2017 Threshold Pharmaceuticals merged with Austin, TX-based Molecular Templates.

	Annual Growth	12/18	12/19	12/20	12/21	12/22
Sales ($mil.)	10.4%	13.3	22.3	18.8	38.7	19.8
Net income ($ mil.)	–	(30.3)	(69.4)	(104.9)	(83.0)	(92.7)
Market value ($ mil.)	(46.6%)	15.2	52.5	35.3	14.7	1.2
Employees	–	68	168	236	261	–

MOLINA HEALTHCARE INC   NYS: MOH

200 Oceangate, Suite 100
Long Beach, CA 90802
Phone: 562 435-3666
Fax: 562 437-1335
Web: www.molinahealthcare.com

CEO: Joseph M Zubretsky
CFO: Mark L Keim
HR: –
FYE: December 31
Type: Public

Molina Healthcare, a FORTUNE 500 company, provides managed healthcare services under the Medicaid and Medicare programs, and through the state insurance marketplaces. Molina Healthcare serves approximately 5.3 million members eligible for Medicaid, Medicare, and other government-sponsored healthcare programs for low-income families and individuals, including Marketplace members, most of whom receive government premium subsidies. Molina Healthcare was founded in 1980.

	Annual Growth	12/19	12/20	12/21	12/22	12/23
Sales ($mil.)	19.3%	16,829	19,423	27,771	31,974	34,072
Net income ($ mil.)	10.3%	737.0	673.0	659.0	792.0	1,091.0
Market value ($ mil.)	27.7%	7,870.0	12,335	18,449	19,153	20,956
Employees	15.8%	10,000	10,500	14,000	15,000	18,000

MOLLER INTERNATIONAL INC

1222 Research Park Drive
Davis, CA 95618
Phone: 530 756-5086
Fax: –
Web: www.moller.com

CEO: –
CFO: –
HR: –
FYE: June 30
Type: Public

Meet George Jetson…well, not quite, but Moller International is working on a Vertical Take-off and Landing (VTOL) aircraft that bears more than a passing resemblance to George's daily ride. The company is testing a prototype of its M400 Skycar in preparation for seeking FAA certification. The forecasted specs on the Skycar are intended to make traffic-jam veterans giddy: four passengers (including the pilot), maximum speed of 375 mph, cruising speed of 275 mph, and a range of 750 miles. No Skycars have been sold, though, and the resulting lack of revenue has caused Moller International's auditors to question whether the company can stay in business.

	Annual Growth	06/11	06/12	06/13	06/14	06/15
Sales ($mil.)	–	0.0	0.0	–	–	–
Net income ($ mil.)	–	(2.3)	(1.7)	(1.9)	(1.7)	(3.1)
Market value ($ mil.)	(31.5%)	24.9	13.9	24.9	9.0	5.5
Employees	6.5%	7	7	7	7	9

MOLLOY COLLEGE

1000 HEMPSTEAD AVE
ROCKVILLE CENTRE, NY 115701135
Phone: 516 678-5733
Fax: –
Web: www.molloy.edu

CEO: Daniel T Henry
CFO: –
HR: Lilian Osorio
FYE: June 30
Type: Private

Molloy College is a Catholic school on the South Shore of Long Island. In addition to a variety of undergraduate majors, the college offers graduate degrees in business, criminal justice, education, nursing, and social work. Molloy College has an enrollment of 3,500 undergraduate and 1,000 graduate students. About 45% of incoming freshmen are first-generation college students. More than 68% of the educational institution's full-time faculty have doctoral degrees. Through its global learning program, Molloy College students have studied abroad in a wide variety of locations, including Australia, Belgium, China, Italy, France, India, Thailand, and the UK.

	Annual Growth	06/18	06/19	06/20	06/21	06/22
Sales ($mil.)	3.4%	–	149.2	128.1	158.4	165.0
Net income ($ mil.)	(49.3%)	–	6.4	5.2	6.9	0.8
Market value ($ mil.)	–	–	–	–	–	–
Employees	–	–	–	–	–	700

MONARCH CASINO & RESORT, INC.   NMS: MCRI

3800 S. Virginia Street
Reno, NV 89502
Phone: 775 335-4600
Fax: –
Web: www.monarchcasino.com

CEO: John Farahi
CFO: –
HR: Rheena Razon
FYE: December 31
Type: Public

Monarch Casino & Resort operates tropical-themed Atlantis Casino Resort Spa in Reno, Nevada, includes nearly 820 hotel rooms, a 61,000-sq.-ft. casino, restaurants, a health club, retail outlets, and a family entertainment center. The company also owns and operates the Monarch Casino Black Hawk in Black Hawk, Colorado. Casino operations, which account for more than half of revenue, include gaming tables, slot and video poker machines, keno, and a race and sports book. The company was incorporated in 1993.

	Annual Growth	12/19	12/20	12/21	12/22	12/23
Sales ($mil.)	19.1%	249.2	184.4	395.4	477.9	501.5
Net income ($ mil.)	26.9%	31.8	23.7	68.5	87.5	82.4
Market value ($ mil.)	9.2%	926.9	1,168.8	1,411.8	1,467.9	1,320.2
Employees	6.0%	2,300	2,300	2,650	2,700	2,900

MONARCH CEMENT CO.   NBB: MCEM

449 1200 Street, P.O. Box 1000
Humboldt, KS 66748
Phone: 620 473-2222
Fax: 620 473-2447
Web: www.monarchcement.com

CEO: Walter H Wulf Jr
CFO: Debra P Roe
HR: John Bilby
FYE: December 31
Type: Public

Monarch's chrysalis is made of stone. The Monarch Cement Company quarries clay, limestone, and gypsum near its Kansas plant to make portland cement, ready-mixed concrete, and other building materials. It can produce more than 1 million tons of cement annually and serves customers in Kansas, Iowa, southeast Nebraska, western Missouri, northwest Arkansas, and northern Oklahoma. Its Monarch-brand portland cement is used in the production of ready-mixed concrete for constructing highways, bridges, and buildings. Chairman and president Walter Wulf Jr. and vice chair Byron Radcliff respectively control about 9% and 10% of the company.

	Annual Growth	12/19	12/20	12/21	12/22	12/23
Sales ($mil.)	11.2%	172.1	188.8	211.8	232.6	262.8
Net income ($ mil.)	22.1%	33.1	33.9	60.4	40.9	73.7
Market value ($ mil.)	26.6%	221.8	254.8	385.5	396.6	569.1
Employees	–	–	–	–	–	–

MONARCH SERVICES INC.   NBB: MAHI

4517 Harford Road
Baltimore, MD 21214-3122
Phone: 410 254-9200
Fax: 410 254-0991
Web: www.monarchservices.com

CEO: –
CFO: –
HR: –
FYE: April 30
Type: Public

Monarch Services (formerly Monarch Avalon) is making life changes. The company closed its printing and envelope division and sold its board games business and Girls' Life magazine. In addition, the company sold its Peerce's Plantation restaurant, based in Lutherville, Maryland. It closed its tobacco shop, Adam's Leaf & Bean, in 2004. Monarch Services has experienced negative operating cash flow since 2002, and its ability to continue as a going concern remains in doubt. Chairman A. Eric Dott and his son, president and CEO Jackson Dott, own about 40% of the company.

	Annual Growth	04/02	04/03	04/04	04/05	04/06
Sales ($mil.)	2.3%	4.6	4.4	5.4	5.6	5.0
Net income ($ mil.)	–	(0.8)	(1.0)	(1.1)	(0.8)	(1.4)
Market value ($ mil.)	(33.2%)	3.7	2.1	2.2	4.5	0.7
Employees	8.2%	43	38	94	77	59

MONDELEZ INTERNATIONAL INC   NMS: MDLZ

905 West Fulton Market, Suite 200
Chicago, IL 60607
Phone: 847 943-4000
Fax: –
Web: www.mondelezinternational.com

CEO: –
CFO: –
HR: –
FYE: December 31
Type: Public

One of the world's largest snack companies, Mondelez International owns a pantry of billion-dollar brands such as Oreo, Ritz, LU, Clif Bar, and Tate's Bake Shop biscuits and baked snacks, as well as Cadbury Dairy Milk, Milka, and Toblerone chocolate. It also has additional businesses in adjacent, locally relevant categories, including gum & candy, cheese & grocery, and powdered beverages. Biscuits (cookies, crackers, and salted snacks) and chocolate account for most of the company's revenue. Mondelez, which operates in approximately 80 countries and sells its products in more than 150 countries around the world, generates most of its revenue outside the US.

	Annual Growth	12/19	12/20	12/21	12/22	12/23
Sales ($mil.)	8.6%	25,868	26,581	28,720	31,496	36,016
Net income ($ mil.)	6.4%	3,870.0	3,555.0	4,300.0	2,717.0	4,959.0
Market value ($ mil.)	7.1%	74,274	78,846	89,418	89,876	97,671
Employees	3.3%	80,000	79,000	79,000	91,000	91,000

MONGODB INC   NMS: MDB

1633 Broadway 38th Floor
New York, NY 10019
Phone: 646 727-4092
Fax: –
Web: www.mongodb.com

CEO: Dev Ittycheria
CFO: Michael Gordon
HR: –
FYE: January 31
Type: Public

MongoDB is a developer data platform company. The foundation of the company's offering is the leading, modern-general purpose database, which is built on a unique document-based architecture. The company's robust platform enables developers to build and modernize applications rapidly and cost-effectively across a broad range of use cases. The company offers the best of both relational and non-relational databases. Geared to work with large amounts of data, offerings run on-premise, hybrid, and in the cloud environments, including those from Amazon, Microsoft, and Google. Developers can download MongoDB's Community Server product at no charge. From there, customers can move up to MongoDB Enterprise Advanced or use its MongoDB Atlas, a database-as-a-service product. The company offers its products through subscriptions. About 60% of revenue comes from the Americas.

	Annual Growth	01/20	01/21	01/22	01/23	01/24
Sales ($mil.)	41.3%	421.7	590.4	873.8	1,284.0	1,683.0
Net income ($ mil.)	–	(175.5)	(266.9)	(306.9)	(345.4)	(176.6)
Market value ($ mil.)	25.0%	11,923	26,886	29,468	15,582	29,134
Employees	29.1%	1,813	2,539	3,544	4,619	5,037

MONITRONICS INTERNATIONAL, INC.

1990 WITTINGTON PL
FARMERS BRANCH, TX 752341904
Phone: 972 243-7443
Fax: –
Web: www.brinkshome.com

CEO: William E Niles
CFO: Fred A Graffam III
HR: Liz Flores
FYE: December 31
Type: Private

Monitronics International, doing business as Brinks Home Security, provides alarm system monitoring services to residential and commercial customers in the US, Canada, and Puerto Rico. Authorized independent dealers sell, install, and service its security systems and related equipment through its dealer channel. The company also has a direct-to-consumer sales channel. Monitronics monitors client accounts from its central supervising station in Dallas. In 2018 the firm signed a licensing agreement with Brinks Co. to use the Brinks name for all Monitronics' home security offerings. Monitronics filed for Chapter 11 protection in 2019 and emerged from bankruptcy reorganization about two months later.

	Annual Growth	12/15	12/16	12/17	12/18	12/19
Sales ($mil.)	(45.9%)	–	–	553.5	540.4	162.2
Net income ($ mil.)	–	–	–	(111.3)	(678.8)	(33.3)
Market value ($ mil.)	–	–	–	–	–	–
Employees	–	–	–	–	–	1

MONJE, INC.

20393 SW AVERY CT STE 100   CEO: -
TUALATIN, OR 970628638   CFO: -
Phone: 503 746-5072   HR: -
Fax: -   FYE: November 30
Web: www.monje.com   Type: Private

Monje Forest Products is a wholesale distributor of building materials, including lumber and plywood, electrical supplies, and plumbing supplies. Its selection of timber consists of Douglas fir, hemlock, and redwood, among other varieties. Though the company is based stateside, it primarily serves construction firms and contractors in South Africa, Japan, and throughout the Pacific Rim, including the islands of Hawaii, Guam, and Saipan. President Hank Monje and secretary Jim Monje founded Monje Forest Products in 1983.

MONMOUTH MEDICAL CENTER INC.

300 2ND AVE   CEO: Eric Carney
LONG BRANCH, NJ 077406395   CFO: David McClung
Phone: 732 222-5200   HR: Gail Russell
Fax: -   FYE: December 31
Web: www.rwjbh.org   Type: Private

Monmouth Medical Center is a 530-bed, tertiary care teaching hospital providing comprehensive health care to residents of central New Jersey. The not-for-profit medical center offers services ranging from orthopedics, diagnostics, and obstetric care to surgery, dentistry, and geriatric services. The medical center campus also includes a children's hospital, a cancer center, a neuroscience institute, an outpatient care clinic, and hospice and home health facilities. Monmouth Medical Center is a teaching affiliate of the Rutgers-Robert Wood Johnson Medical School. The hospital is part of the RWJBarnabas Health network.

	Annual Growth	12/16	12/17	12/18	12/19	12/21
Sales ($mil.)	(4.5%)	-	529.8	546.9	556.8	440.7
Net income ($ mil.)	(49.7%)	-	53.0	43.8	5.6	3.4
Market value ($ mil.)	-	-	-	-	-	-
Employees	-	-	-	-	-	2,400

MONMOUTH UNIVERSITY INC

400 CEDAR AVE   CEO: -
WEST LONG BRANCH, NJ 077641898   CFO: -
Phone: 732 571-3400   HR: -
Fax: -   FYE: June 30
Web: www.monmouth.edu   Type: Private

Students looking for a monumental education might want to head to Monmouth University. The private institution offers more than 30 undergraduate and 20 graduate programs through eight schools that include business administration, education, humanities and social sciences, and nursing and health sciences, as well as graduate and honors schools. Founded in 1933 as the Monmouth Junior College, Monmouth University has an enrollment of roughly an 6,500 graduate and undergraduate students. The school's student-teacher ratio is about 14:1.

	Annual Growth	06/14	06/15	06/20	06/21	06/22
Sales ($mil.)	2.4%	-	227.9	261.8	255.7	269.0
Net income ($ mil.)	(26.0%)	-	13.2	1.7	(0.4)	1.6
Market value ($ mil.)	-	-	-	-	-	-
Employees	-	-	-	-	-	1,000

MONMOUTH-OCEAN HOSPITAL SERVICE CORPORATION

4806 MEGILL RD   CEO: Vincent Robbins
WALL TOWNSHIP, NJ 077536926   CFO: Brian Hector
Phone: 732 919-3045   HR: Stephanie McClintock
Fax: -   FYE: December 31
Web: www.kennardnj.com   Type: Private

"Share and share alike" could be the motto of this hospital services cooperative. The not-for-profit Monmouth-Ocean Hospital Service, also known as MONOC, is comprised of more than a dozen acute care hospitals in New Jersey that share the costs and resources associated with the provision of pre-hospital emergency care. MONOC provides mobile intensive and critical care, ambulance transport, helicopter services, and advanced life support to nearly 3 million residents in the Garden State. The organization also provides continuing medical education to EMTs and other medical professionals, police officers, and the general public. All of MONOC's emergency services are coordinated by the statewide 911 dispatch center.

	Annual Growth	12/99	12/00	12/12	12/15	12/19
Sales ($mil.)	2.2%	-	20.4	44.0	38.3	30.9
Net income ($ mil.)	-	-	1.9	0.8	(2.6)	(0.5)
Market value ($ mil.)	-	-	-	-	-	-
Employees	-	-	-	-	-	400

MONOGRAM FOOD SOLUTIONS, LLC

2330 E 5TH ST   CEO: -
CHARLOTTE, NC 282044337   CFO: -
Phone: 901 685-7167   HR: Abigail Garcia
Fax: -   FYE: December 28
Web: www.monogramfoods.com   Type: Private

Monogram Food Solutions is focused on M, E, A, and T. As a manufacturer of meat and meat snack products, the company produces beef jerky, sausage, hot dogs, bacon, and other processed food items. Its brands include Circle B, King Cotton, and Trail's Best Meat Snacks. Through several special licensing agreements, Monogram Food Solutions also sells Jeff Foxworthy Jerky Products, NASCAR Jerky and Steak Strips, and Bass Pro Uncle Buck's Licensed Products. The company, which distributes its products nationwide, operates facilities in Minnesota, Indiana, and Virginia. Founded in 2004, Monogram Food Solutions was formed through the merger of assets (King Cotton and Circle B) previously owned by Sara Lee Corp.

	Annual Growth	12/15	12/16	12/17	12/18	12/19
Sales ($mil.)	8.0%	-	-	640.8	647.8	747.9
Net income ($ mil.)	-	-	-	2.6	11.1	(4.2)
Market value ($ mil.)	-	-	-	-	-	-
Employees	-	-	-	-	-	790

MONOLITHIC POWER SYSTEMS INC   NMS: MPWR

5808 Lake Washington Blvd. N.E.   CEO: Michael R Hsing
Kirkland, WA 98033   CFO: Bernie Blegen
Phone: 425 296-9956   HR: -
Fax: -   FYE: December 31
Web: www.monolithicpower.com   Type: Public

Monolithic Power Systems (MPS) is a global company that provides high-performance, semiconductor-based power electronics solutions. The fabless semiconductor company offers digital, mixed-signal and analog microchips ? especially DC-to-DC converters for powering networking and telecommunication infrastructure, wireless access points, notebook computers, and other consumer electronic devices. Its core strengths include deep system-level and applications knowledge, strong analog design expertise and innovative proprietary process technologies. The company was founded in 1997. It generates the majority of its sales outside the US.

	Annual Growth	12/19	12/20	12/21	12/22	12/23
Sales ($mil.)	30.5%	627.9	844.5	1,207.8	1,794.1	1,821.1
Net income ($ mil.)	40.8%	108.8	164.4	242.0	437.7	427.4
Market value ($ mil.)	37.2%	8,549.9	17,589	23,694	16,983	30,295
Employees	15.5%	2,002	2,209	2,700	3,247	3,564

MONONGAHELA POWER CO

1310 Fairmont Avenue
Fairmont, WV 26554
Phone: 304 366-3000
Fax: –
Web: www.firstenergycorp.com

CEO: Paul J Evanson
CFO: Jeffrey D Serkes
HR: –
FYE: December 31
Type: Public

Electricity flows from Monongahela Power (Mon Power) just like the river the utility was named after. The company services approximately 388,000 residential and commercial customers in a service area of 13,000 sq. mi. in West Virginia. Mon Power, along with West Penn Power and Potomac Edison, comprise the Allegheny Power arm of Allegheny Energy, which is now part of FirstEnergy. In 2013 Mon Power owned or controlled 3,580 MW of generating capacity. The company is contractually obligated to supply Potomac Edison with sufficient power to meet that company's power load obligations in West Virginia.

	Annual Growth	12/02	12/03	12/04	12/05	12/06
Sales ($mil.)	(4.2%)	917.0	987.7	683.8	789.9	773.7
Net income ($ mil.)	–	(81.7)	80.7	2.5	10.2	69.1
Market value ($ mil.)	13.8%	329.9	446.2	534.6	556.7	553.8
Employees	–	–	–	–	–	–

MONOTYPE IMAGING HOLDINGS INC.

600 UNICORN PARK DR
WOBURN, MA 018013343
Phone: 781 970-6000
Fax: –
Web: www.monotype.com

CEO: Ninan Chacko
CFO: Christopher Brooks
HR: Dana Sheehan
FYE: December 31
Type: Private

Monotype Imaging provides the design assets, technology and expertise and its fonts and technologies are designed to enable creative expression and give brands a distinct global voice. Providing customers over 40,000 fonts, the product of the world's most celebrated and gifted type designers ? while making it easier to license, deploy, and manage usage of all fonts across the enterprise.

MONRO INC

NMS: MNRO

200 Holleder Parkway
Rochester, NY 14615
Phone: 585 647-6400
Fax: 585 647-0945
Web: www.monro.com

CEO: Michael T Broderick
CFO: Brian J D'Ambrosia
HR: –
FYE: March 25
Type: Public

Monro is a leading nationwide operator of retail tire and automotive repair stores in the US. It offers replacement tires and tires related services, automotive undercar repair services, and a broad range of routine maintenance services, primarily on passenger cars, light trucks, and vans. The company also provides other products and services for brakes, mufflers and exhaust systems, and steering, drive train, suspension, and wheel alignment. Operates in more than 30 states, its retail tire and automotive repair stores operate primarily under the brands Monro Auto Service and Tire Centers, Tire Choice Auto Service Centers, Mr. Tire Auto Service Centers, Car-X Tire & Auto, Tire Warehouse Tires for Less, Ken Towery's Tire & Auto Care, Mountain View Tire & Auto Service, Tire Barn Warehouse, and Free Service Tire & Auto Centers. Monro services approximately 5.0 million vehicles in the recent fiscal year.

	Annual Growth	03/19	03/20	03/21	03/22	03/23
Sales ($mil.)	2.5%	1,200.2	1,256.5	1,125.7	1,359.3	1,325.4
Net income ($ mil.)	(16.4%)	79.8	58.0	34.3	61.6	39.0
Market value ($ mil.)	(13.3%)	2,717.2	1,256.5	2,080.3	1,385.6	1,536.7
Employees	1.3%	8,183	8,184	7,800	8,750	8,600

MONROE MEDICAL FOUNDATION INC

529 CAPP HARLAN RD
TOMPKINSVILLE, KY 421671808
Phone: 270 487-9231
Fax: –
Web: www.mcmccares.com

CEO: Vicky McFall
CFO: Ricky Brown
HR: –
FYE: February 28
Type: Private

Monroe County Medical Center provides both medical and behavioral health services for the residents of Monroe County, Kentucky. The medical center includes an acute-care hospital, home health and adult day care, and an emergency center. The nearly 50-bed facility also offers nutrition counseling, CPR classes, diabetes education, and a cancer support group.

	Annual Growth	02/16	02/17	02/18	02/20	02/22
Sales ($mil.)	1.1%	–	18.3	19.1	19.6	19.4
Net income ($ mil.)	79.9%	–	0.1	(0.1)	(0.4)	1.9
Market value ($ mil.)	–	–	–	–	–	–
Employees	–	–	–	–	–	240

MONSTER BEVERAGE CORP (NEW)

NMS: MNST

1 Monster Way
Corona, CA 92879
Phone: 951 739-6200
Fax: –
Web: www.monsterbevcorp.com

CEO: Rodney C Sacks
CFO: Thomas J Kelly
HR: –
FYE: December 31
Type: Public

Monster Beverage develops, markets, sells and distributes energy drink beverages and concentrates for energy drink beverages. In addition, the company serves up a variety of "alternative" beverage category combines non-carbonated, ready-to-drink iced teas, lemonades, juice cocktails, single-serve juices and fruit beverages, ready-to-drink dairy and coffee drinks, energy drinks, sports drinks, single-serve still waters, and sodas in about 155 countries worldwide. With more than 17,500 registered trademarks and pending applications in various countries around the world, the company sells most of its products in the US and Canada through a distribution network, and also directly to retailers such as grocery chains and mass merchandisers, among others. The US and Canada account for about 65% of the company's sales.

	Annual Growth	12/19	12/20	12/21	12/22	12/23
Sales ($mil.)	14.2%	4,200.8	4,598.6	5,541.4	6,311.1	7,140.0
Net income ($ mil.)	10.2%	1,107.8	1,409.6	1,377.5	1,191.6	1,631.0
Market value ($ mil.)	(2.4%)	66,192	96,324	100,032	105,751	60,005
Employees	14.2%	3,529	3,666	4,092	5,296	6,003

MONTANA STATE UNIVERSITY

216 MONTANA HALL
BOZEMAN, MT 59717
Phone: 406 994-4361
Fax: –
Web: www.montana.edu

CEO: –
CFO: –
HR: –
FYE: June 30
Type: Private

Montana State University helps develop young minds in Big Sky Country. The university, located in Bozeman, serves more than 14,500 students, most of whom are undergraduates from Montana. The school offers baccalaureate degrees in 60 fields, master's degrees in 45 fields, and doctoral degrees in about 20 fields. The school offers primarily a liberal arts education, though it is also strong in agriculture and the fine arts. The university provides courses in fields ranging from English to political science to engineering. It has a teaching staff of more than 1,150, including 781 full-time and 373 part-time faculty and department heads. Tuition and fees for a resident student is $6,705; a non-resident, $20,062.

	Annual Growth	06/18	06/19	06/20	06/21	06/22
Sales ($mil.)	5.3%	–	411.2	421.2	431.7	479.9
Net income ($ mil.)	51.5%	–	16.8	12.8	57.6	58.5
Market value ($ mil.)	–	–	–	–	–	–
Employees	–	–	–	–	–	2,500

MONTCLAIR STATE UNIVERSITY

1 UNIVERSITY AVE 1
MONTCLAIR, NJ 070431624
Phone: 973 655-4000
Fax: –
Web: www.montclair.edu

CEO: –
CFO: –
HR: –
FYE: June 30
Type: Private

With its roots as a teaching college, it's fitting that today Montclair State University (MSU) is one of a handful of universities in the US offering a doctorate in pedagogy (the art and science of teaching). For more than 100 years MSU has provided a comprehensive curriculum for future educators, as well as other students studying a variety of subjects. With an enrollment of some 20,000 students, MSU operates through six schools and colleges: College of the Arts, College of Education and Human Services, College of Humanities and Social Sciences, College of Science and Mathematics, School of Business, and the Graduate School.

	Annual Growth	06/18	06/19	06/20	06/21	06/22
Sales ($mil.)	0.1%	–	324.3	310.4	284.2	325.3
Net income ($ mil.)	–	–	(15.8)	(11.5)	30.1	26.7
Market value ($ mil.)	–	–	–	–	–	–
Employees	–	–	–	–	–	2,000

MONTEFIORE MEDICAL CENTER

111 E 210TH ST
BRONX, NY 104672401
Phone: 718 920-4321
Fax: –
Web: www.montefiore.org

CEO: Steven M Safyer
CFO: –
HR: –
FYE: December 31
Type: Private

The primary teaching hospital of the Albert Einstein College of Medicine, Montefiore offers medical education programs. Montefiore Medical Center attends to the health care needs of residents across the Bronx, Westchester and the Hudson Valley. Montefiore Einstein Center for Cancer Care, a Montefiore Center of Excellence, delivers advanced patient-centered, multidisciplinary care designed to maximize treatment outcomes while optimizing the quality of life for each patient. Children's Hospital at Montefiore (CHAM), a premier academic children's hospital, nationally renowned for its clinical excellence, innovative research and commitment to training the next generation of pediatricians and pediatric subspecialists. Montefiore Medical Center was founded in 1884 by Jewish philanthropists.

	Annual Growth	12/14	12/15	12/16	12/17	12/21
Sales ($mil.)	1.8%	–	–	2,690.3	3,762.8	2,948.5
Net income ($ mil.)	–	–	–	42.2	43.4	(313.7)
Market value ($ mil.)	–	–	–	–	–	–
Employees	–	–	–	–	–	11,000

MONTEFIORE NYACK HOSPITAL FOUNDATION, INC.

160 N MIDLAND AVE
NYACK, NY 109601912
Phone: 845 348-2000
Fax: –
Web: www.montefiorenyack.org

CEO: Mark Geller
CFO: –
HR: –
FYE: December 31
Type: Private

Nyack Hospital rocks when it comes to providing medical services in New York's Rockland and Bergen counties. The not-for-profit hospital is a 375-bed acute care medical and surgical facility with a staff of more than 650 doctors and surgeons. Nyack Hospital houses specialty centers for cancer care, stroke, pediatrics, joint replacement, sleep studies, wound care, and women's wellness. In partnership with Touro College of Osteopathic Medicine, it also provides training programs for medical students. Nyack Hospital is a member of the New York-Presbyterian Healthcare System and is affiliated with the Columbia University College of Physicians and Surgeons.

	Annual Growth	12/14	12/15	12/16	12/17	12/19
Sales ($mil.)	8.6%	–	216.2	224.1	229.9	300.6
Net income ($ mil.)	–	–	(2.8)	(8.8)	(11.3)	10.9
Market value ($ mil.)	–	–	–	–	–	–
Employees	–	–	–	–	–	1,300

MONTEREY MUSHROOMS, LLC

260 WESTGATE DR
WATSONVILLE, CA 950762452
Phone: 831 763-5300
Fax: –
Web: www.montereymushrooms.com

CEO: –
CFO: –
HR: –
FYE: September 30
Type: Private

Monterey Mushrooms is proud to provide fresh, locally grown mushrooms. The company started with a single farm in 1971 and has since grown into an international giant. Monterey Mushrooms maintains nine North American farms. The company's bulk and packaged fresh mushrooms are available at food retailers and foodservice operators, and as ingredients for food manufacturers. In addition to fresh mushrooms, the company offers mushroom products packed in cans, jars, and frozen sauces. The company's biotech business serves other mushroom growers through its spawn supplier, Amycel, and nutritional supplement provider Spawn Mate.

MONUMENT HEALTH RAPID CITY HOSPITAL, INC.

353 FAIRMONT BLVD
RAPID CITY, SD 577017375
Phone: 605 719-1000
Fax: –
Web: www.monument.health

CEO: Charles Hart
CFO: –
HR: –
FYE: June 30
Type: Private

Mt. Rushmore sightseers, bikers, and locals alike can seek medical care at Rapid City Regional Hospital. The medical facility is a general and psychiatric hospital with some 330 acute care beds and 50 psychiatric beds located in the Black Hills region of western South Dakota. In addition to emergency and acute care, the not-for-profit hospital also offers a behavioral health center, a rehabilitation facility, a cancer care institute, and women's and children's departments. Rapid City Regional Hospital is part of Regional Health, a network of regional hospitals, medical clinics, and senior care centers.

	Annual Growth	06/12	06/13	06/14	06/15	06/22
Sales ($mil.)	7.6%	–	–	517.9	437.5	927.3
Net income ($ mil.)	(11.5%)	–	–	56.7	39.4	21.4
Market value ($ mil.)	–	–	–	–	–	–
Employees	–	–	–	–	–	4,200

MOODY'S CORP.

NYS: MCO

7 World Trade Center, 250 Greenwich Street
New York, NY 10007
Phone: 212 553-0300
Fax: –
Web: www.moodys.com

CEO: Robert Fauber
CFO: Mark Kaye
HR: –
FYE: December 31
Type: Public

Moody's Corporation is a global integrated risk assessment firm that empowers organizations and investors to make better decisions. It has two primary segments: Moody's Investors Service (MIS) and Moody's Analytics (MA). MIS publishes credit ratings provides assessment services on a wide range of debt obligations and the entities that issue such obligations, and structured finance securities. MA provides financial intelligence and analytical tools to assist businesses in making decisions. Moody's has operations in more than 40 countries and generates the majority of the company's from the US. John Moody founded Moody's in 1900.

	Annual Growth	12/19	12/20	12/21	12/22	12/23
Sales ($mil.)	5.2%	4,829.0	5,371.0	6,218.0	5,468.0	5,916.0
Net income ($ mil.)	3.1%	1,422.0	1,778.0	2,214.0	1,374.0	1,607.0
Market value ($ mil.)	13.3%	43,321	52,961	71,270	50,840	71,266
Employees	8.3%	11,000	11,490	13,460	14,426	15,151

MOOG INC

NYS: MOG A

400 Jamison Road, East Aurora
New York, NY 14052-0018
Phone: 716 652-2000
Fax: –
Web: www.moog.com

CEO: Patrick Roche
CFO: Jennifer Walter
HR: –
FYE: September 30
Type: Public

Moog makes precision-control components and systems used in aerospace products, defense, and industrial markets. Hydraulic components include high-performance servo valves with mechanical or electronic feedback, high-dynamic performance hydraulic servo pumps, energy-efficient electro hydrostatic actuators and complex hydraulic manifold systems. It also makes infusion therapy pumps, CT scan medical equipment, ultrasonic sensors, and surgical handpieces and motors used in devices for sleep apnea. Customers in the US make up about two-thirds of its sales. Moog traces its roots back to 1951 when Bill Moog, Art Moog, and Lou Geyer pooled $3,000 and opened Moog Valve.

	Annual Growth	09/19*	10/20	10/21	10/22*	09/23
Sales ($mil.)	3.4%	2,904.7	2,884.6	2,852.0	3,035.8	3,319.1
Net income ($ mil.)	(1.2%)	179.7	9.2	157.2	155.2	171.0
Market value ($ mil.)	8.4%	2,755.7	2,253.5	2,649.4	2,372.6	3,809.6
Employees	1.3%	12,809	12,623	14,000	14,000	13,500

*Fiscal year change

MOORE & VAN ALLEN PLLC

100 N TRYON ST STE 4700
CHARLOTTE, NC 282024003
Phone: 704 331-1000
Fax: –
Web: www.mvalaw.com

CEO: –
CFO: –
HR: –
FYE: December 31
Type: Private

Moore & Van Allen is a full-service law firm that serves international, national, regional, and local clients in a wide range of industries and areas of focus, including corporate, financial services, commercial real estate, health care, manufacturing, retail, individual wealth management, and technology. It is one of the largest law firms in the Southeast with nearly 400 lawyers and professionals and offices in Charlotte and Charleston. It is founded by Robert Lassiter, Jr. and James Moore. William Van Allen joined the firm in 1950.

MOOREFIELD CONSTRUCTION, INC.

600 N TUSTIN AVE STE 210
SANTA ANA, CA 927053781
Phone: 714 972-0700
Fax: –
Web: www.moorefieldconstruction.com

CEO: –
CFO: –
HR: –
FYE: September 30
Type: Private

Moorefield Construction wants to be more than just another big-box store builder. The company provides general contracting services for retail projects throughout Arizona, California, Colorado, Idaho, Nevada, New Mexico, Oregon, Utah, and Washington. Clients have included Lowe's, Best Buy, and Walgreen. The company operates from offices in Santa Ana and Sacramento. Moorefield Construction was founded in 1957 by the late Harold Moorefield, and continues to be owned and operated by his family, including his wife Ann (CEO) and their sons, Mike (president), Larry (VP), and Hal (VP).

	Annual Growth	09/12	09/13	09/14	09/15	09/16
Sales ($mil.)	17.2%	–	70.0	118.5	112.8	112.7
Net income ($ mil.)	62.4%	–	0.0	0.0	0.2	0.3
Market value ($ mil.)	–	–	–	–	–	–
Employees	–	–	–	–	–	95

MORAVIAN UNIVERSITY

1200 MAIN ST
BETHLEHEM, PA 180186614
Phone: 610 861-1300
Fax: –
Web: www.moravian.edu

CEO: –
CFO: –
HR: Elaine Schmidt
FYE: June 30
Type: Private

Moravian College, America's sixth-oldest college, was founded in Pennsylvania by the Moravian Church in 1742. The private school offers undergraduate coursework in the liberal arts and sciences, with more than 50 programs including the arts, chemistry, business, music, and physics. It enrolls about 1,600 students from 24 states and 14 countries with a student to teacher ratio of 11:1. Moravian College also includes the Moravian Theological Seminary, an ecumenical graduate school offering master's degrees in divinity, pastoral counseling, and theological studies. Tuition and fees for the college total about $35,000 per year.

	Annual Growth	06/18	06/19	06/20	06/21	06/22
Sales ($mil.)	22.0%	–	76.0	78.9	77.5	138.0
Net income ($ mil.)	–	–	(3.2)	(0.5)	36.2	9.6
Market value ($ mil.)	–	–	–	–	–	–
Employees	–	–	–	–	–	450

MOREHEAD MEMORIAL HOSPITAL INC

117 E KINGS HWY
EDEN, NC 272885201
Phone: 336 623-9711
Fax: –
Web: www.uncrockingham.org

CEO: –
CFO: –
HR: –
FYE: September 30
Type: Private

Morehead Memorial Hospital is a not-for-profit community hospital that provides health care services to residents of North Carolina's Rockingham County. The hospital has about 110 acute care beds and provides general medical-surgical care, including emergency services, obstetrical care, outpatient surgery, and cancer treatment. It also provides home health care services and operates several ancillary facilities, such as a freestanding diagnostic imaging facility and a physical rehabilitation center. The hospital's main campus (built in 1960) includes Morehead Nursing Center, a long-term care facility with about 120 beds. Morehead Memorial Hospital traces its origin back to 1924.

	Annual Growth	09/13	09/14	09/15	09/16	09/17
Sales ($mil.)	(4.8%)	–	81.2	77.6	72.5	70.1
Net income ($ mil.)	–	–	(7.1)	(6.0)	(6.7)	(5.8)
Market value ($ mil.)	–	–	–	–	–	–
Employees	–	–	–	–	–	850

MOREHOUSE COLLEGE (INC.)

2900 LAUREL RIDGE WAY APT 5107
ATLANTA, GA 303446209
Phone: 404 681-2800
Fax: –
Web: www.morehouse.edu

CEO: John S Wilson Jr
CFO: Gwendolyn Sykes
HR: Adrian Cheatham
FYE: June 30
Type: Private

Morehouse College is the largest private liberal arts college for African-American men. Located three miles from downtown Atlanta, the college has an enrollment of more than 2,500 students. Facilities include the Leadership Center at Morehouse College, Morehouse Research Institute, and Andrew Young Center for International Affairs. The school has courses of study in business and economics, humanities and social sciences, and science and mathematics. It also offers a degree in engineering in conjunction with Georgia Institute of Technology. Notable alumni include civil rights activist Dr. Martin Luther King Jr., filmmaker Shelton "Spike" Lee, and actor Samuel L. Jackson.

	Annual Growth	06/14	06/15	06/20	06/21	06/22
Sales ($mil.)	5.0%	–	105.4	205.8	206.0	148.3
Net income ($ mil.)	–	–	(2.1)	61.0	101.7	8.6
Market value ($ mil.)	–	–	–	–	–	–
Employees	–	–	–	–	–	700

MORGAN STANLEY   NYS: MS

1585 Broadway
New York, NY 10036
Phone: 212 761-4000
Fax: -
Web: www.morganstanley.com

CEO: Edward N Pick
CFO: Sharon Yeshaya
HR: -
FYE: December 31
Type: Public

One of the world's top investment banks, Morgan Stanley is a global financial services company that, through its subsidiaries and affiliates, advises, and originates, trades, manages and distributes capital for governments, institutions and individuals. It offers everything from advising corporate clients on mergers & acquisitions to raising capital for large companies to managing real estate investments for wealthy individuals. Morgan Stanley has more than $1.3 trillion of assets under management. Majority of the company's revenue comes from the US. The company was originally incorporated in 1981, and its predecessor companies date back to 1924.

	Annual Growth	12/19	12/20	12/21	12/22	12/23
Assets ($mil.)	7.5%	895,429	1,115,862	1,188,140	1,180,231	1,193,693
Net income ($ mil.)	0.1%	9,042.0	10,996	15,034	11,029	9,087.0
Market value ($ mil.)	16.2%	83,163	111,487	159,689	138,313	151,702
Employees	7.3%	60,431	68,000	75,000	82,000	80,000

MORGAN, LEWIS & BOCKIUS LLP

1701 MARKET ST STE CON
PHILADELPHIA, PA 191032987
Phone: 215 963-5000
Fax: -
Web: www.morganlewis.com

CEO: -
CFO: James M Diasio
HR: Jeri Papa
FYE: September 30
Type: Private

Long a leading Philadelphia law firm, Morgan, Lewis & Bockius is home to more than 2,200 lawyers and other legal professionals, such as patent agents, employee benefits advisors, regulatory scientists, and other specialists in more than 30 offices throughout the US, Europe, and Asia. The firm's multiple practice areas include corporate, finance and investment management, intellectual property, labor, employment and benefits, and litigation, regulation, and investigation. Providing services to clients of all sizes, the firm donates more than 125,000 hours to pro bono work annually. Morgan, Lewis & Bockius was founded in 1873.

MORNINGSTAR INC   NMS: MORN

22 West Washington Street
Chicago, IL 60602
Phone: 312 696-6000
Fax: -
Web: www.morningstar.com

CEO: Kunal Kapoor
CFO: Jason Dubinsky
HR: -
FYE: December 31
Type: Public

Morningstar is a leading global provider of independent investment insights. It offers variety of products and solutions that serve market participants of all kinds, including individual and institutional investors in public and private capital markets, financial advisors, asset managers, retirement plan providers and sponsors, and issuers of securities. Its customers have access to a wide selection of investment data, research, credit, ESG, and fund ratings, and indexes directly on its proprietary desktop or web-based software platforms, or through subscriptions, data feeds, and third-party distributors. The company also provides investment-management services, investment analysis platforms, and portfolio management and accounting software tools to advisors and financial institutions. The US is the company's largest market; it provides roughly 70% of its revenue.

	Annual Growth	12/19	12/20	12/21	12/22	12/23
Sales ($mil.)	14.7%	1,179.0	1,389.5	1,699.3	1,870.6	2,038.6
Net income ($ mil.)	(1.8%)	152.0	223.6	193.3	70.5	141.1
Market value ($ mil.)	17.3%	6,465.2	9,894.6	14,613	9,254.5	12,231
Employees	13.9%	6,737	7,979	9,556	12,224	11,334

MORO CORP.   NBB: MRCR

841 Worcester St, #511
Natick, MA 01760
Phone: 484 367-0300
Fax: 484 667-9915
Web: www.morocorp.com

CEO: -
CFO: James McKay
HR: -
FYE: December 31
Type: Public

The Moro Corporation is an industrial holding company that owns multiple construction businesses that provide a range of materials and services for the commercial construction industry. Its J.M. Ahle, J&J Sheet Metal, and Whaling City Iron subsidiaries fabricate and distribute sheet metal products, and reinforcing and structural steel, in addition to other construction accessories. Titchener Iron Works specializes in architectural and ornamental metal. Its Rado Enterprises and Appolo Heating units provide plumbing and HVAC services, while Rondout Electric provides electrical contracting services.

	Annual Growth	12/18	12/19	12/20	12/21	12/22
Sales ($mil.)	(0.9%)	54.7	54.3	50.5	58.4	52.8
Net income ($ mil.)	(15.0%)	0.8	(0.0)	3.4	1.7	0.4
Market value ($ mil.)	7.2%	6.7	6.1	5.0	6.4	8.9
Employees	-	-	-	-	-	-

MORRE-TEC INDUSTRIES, INC.

1 GARY RD
UNION, NJ 070835527
Phone: 908 688-9009
Fax: -
Web: www.morretec.com

CEO: -
CFO: -
HR: -
FYE: December 31
Type: Private

Depending on the situation, Morre-Tec Industries can bring home the bacon or fry it up in the pan. (If, by bacon, you mean bromine- and chlorine-based chemicals.) Not only does the New Jersey company distribute chemicals through its partnerships with ICL Industrial Products and others, but Morre-Tec also manufactures its own line of specialty chemicals. Through it divisions Extracts & Ingredients, JEDCO Adhesives, and Repackaging Services Corporation, Morre-Tec also manufactures adhesives and solvents and imports chemicals for the food and cosmetics industries. The company was formed in 1987.

	Annual Growth	02/04	02/05	02/06*	12/08	12/11
Sales ($mil.)	13.3%	-	-	6.5	-	12.2
Net income ($ mil.)	76.9%	-	-	0.0	-	0.6
Market value ($ mil.)	-	-	-	-	-	-
Employees	-	-	-	-	-	24

*Fiscal year change

MORRIS BUSINESS DEVELOPMENT CO

220 Nice Lane #108
Newport Beach, CA 92663
Phone: 949 444-9090
Fax: -
Web: www.morrisbdc.com

CEO: George Morris
CFO: George Morris
HR: -
FYE: March 31
Type: Public

Morris Business Development hopes to get more out of life as an investment firm. The company, formerly Electronic Media Central, previously provided CD and DVD replication, duplication, and packaging services. However, in 2007 the firm changed its name to Morris Business Development and became a managed investment company, providing early stage capital, strategic guidance, and operational support to other businesses.

	Annual Growth	03/10	03/11	03/12	03/13	03/14
Sales ($mil.)	11.5%	0.0	0.0	0.0	0.0	0.0
Net income ($ mil.)	-	(0.0)	(0.0)	(0.0)	(0.0)	(0.0)
Market value ($ mil.)	18.9%	0.9	0.3	0.4	0.9	1.7
Employees	-	-	1	1	-	-

MORRIS COLLEGE

100 W COLLEGE ST
SUMTER, SC 291503599
Phone: 803 934-3200
Fax: –
Web: www.morris.edu

CEO: –
CFO: –
HR: –
FYE: June 30
Type: Private

The mission of Morris College is to prepare its students for the real world. The historically black college awards baccalaureate degrees in the arts and sciences, with an emphasis on liberal arts, career-based programs, and teacher education. Morris primarily serves students from the Northeastern and Southeastern US and cultivates an ethical and religious environment to complement the total development of its students. The Baptist Educational and Missionary Convention of South Carolina founded Morris College in 1908 to provide educational opportunities for Black students who had been denied under the existing educational system. The college's founding body continues to oversee Morris College.

	Annual Growth	06/18	06/19	06/20	06/21	06/22
Sales ($mil.)	9.7%	–	17.7	18.0	16.2	23.4
Net income ($ mil.)	186.3%	–	0.2	(0.8)	2.0	3.7
Market value ($ mil.)	–	–	–	–	–	–
Employees	–	–	–	–	–	220

MORRIS HOSPITAL

150 W HIGH ST
MORRIS, IL 604501463
Phone: 815 942-2932
Fax: –
Web: www.morrishospital.org

CEO: Mark Steadham
CFO: –
HR: Colleen Bosco
FYE: December 31
Type: Private

Feeling a little green in Grundy? Morris Hospital & Healthcare Centers will fix you right up! The system operates the 90 bed Morris Hospital as well as a handful of primary care physician practices and eight health care centers (the Braidwood, Channahon, Dwight, Gardner, Marseilles, Minooka, Morris, and Newark Healthcare Centers) scattered throughout Grundy and four neighboring counties in northwest Illinois. Specialized services at Morris Hospital include neurology, oncology, pediatrics, rehabilitation, pain management, and occupational health. It has a level II trauma center and a level II obstetrical unit. Not-for-profit Morris Hospital employs some 200 physicians across most medical specialties.

	Annual Growth	12/15	12/16	12/17	12/21	12/22
Sales ($mil.)	6.2%	–	157.1	167.1	198.1	225.5
Net income ($ mil.)	(7.1%)	–	9.8	10.1	13.7	6.3
Market value ($ mil.)	–	–	–	–	–	–
Employees	–	–	–	–	–	525

MORRIS PUBLISHING GROUP, LLC

725 BROAD ST
AUGUSTA, GA 309011336
Phone: 706 724-0851
Fax: –
Web: www.morrispublishinggroup.com

CEO: William S Morris IV
CFO: Delinda Fogel
HR: Sally Roberts
FYE: December 31
Type: Private

No news would be bad news for Morris Publishing Group. The newspaper company has a portfolio of about a dozen daily newspapers serving small and midsized markets. Papers include The Augusta Chronicle (Georgia), The Florida Times-Union (Jacksonville), and The Topeka Capital-Journal (Kansas). The company also publishes several non-daily papers, shoppers, and regional interest magazines. Morris Publishing is controlled by the family of chairman William Morris through their Shivers Trading & Operating Company. The Morris family also owns affiliate Morris Communications, which has book publishing, outdoor advertising, and radio broadcasting operations.

MORRISTOWN STAR STRUCK LLC

8 FRANCIS J CLARKE CIR
BETHEL, CT 068012850
Phone: 203 778-4925
Fax: –
Web: www.starstruckllc.com

CEO: –
CFO: –
HR: –
FYE: October 31
Type: Private

Jewelers can set their watches by Star Struck. The company distributes batteries, repair tools, testing machines, cleaning agents, and other supplies for jewelry and watchmaking. Besides its batteries for timepieces, Star Struck carries batteries for calculators, cameras, and hearing aids from major brands (Energizer, Rayovac) as well as its own private label. The company serves more than 17,000 customers, including jewelers, watch repairmen, electronics professionals, and hobbyists. Its products are sold via phone or online. Star Struck was founded in 1981.

MORSE OPERATIONS, INC.

2850 S FEDERAL HWY
DELRAY BEACH, FL 334833216
Phone: 561 276-5000
Fax: –
Web: www.edmorse.com

CEO: –
CFO: Dennis Macinnes
HR: –
FYE: December 31
Type: Private

Morse Operations (dba Ed Morse Automotive Group) has been selling cars and trucks long enough to know the code of the road. It owns about a dozen new car dealerships across Florida, most of them operating under the Ed Morse name. Dealerships house more than 15 franchises and 10 domestic and import car brands, including Cadillac, Fiat, Chevrolet, Buick, GMC, Scion, Honda, Mazda, and Toyota. The company's Bayview Cadillac in Fort Lauderdale is one of the world's largest volume sellers of Cadillacs. Morse Operations also sells used cars, provides parts and service, and operates a fleet sales division. Founder and auto magnate, the late Ed Morse, entered the automobile business in 1946 with a 20-car rental fleet.

	Annual Growth	12/14	12/15	12/16	12/17	12/18
Sales ($mil.)	(8.2%)	–	–	1,334.8	1,019.2	1,125.5
Net income ($ mil.)	–	–	–	9.4	4.4	(0.7)
Market value ($ mil.)	–	–	–	–	–	–
Employees	–	–	–	–	–	950

MOSAIC

4980 S 118TH ST
OMAHA, NE 681372200
Phone: 402 896-3884
Fax: –
Web: www.mosaicinfo.org

CEO: Linda Timmons
CFO: Cindy Schroeder
HR: –
FYE: June 30
Type: Private

Mosaic creates color in the lives of the disadvantaged. The not-for-profit organization provides individualized support and advocacy services, living facilities, education, and employment for people with disabilities. The Christian organization serves some 3,500 clients through 40 agencies across the US, as well as select international locations. Services include case management, foster care, vocational training, and supervised living arrangements. Mosaic also offers senior independent living services and support at select facilities. The organization is affiliated with the Evangelical Lutheran Church in America.

	Annual Growth	06/18	06/19	06/20	06/21	06/22
Sales ($mil.)	9.7%	–	257.8	264.9	281.6	340.4
Net income ($ mil.)	44.9%	–	7.4	14.2	9.4	22.4
Market value ($ mil.)	–	–	–	–	–	–
Employees	–	–	–	–	–	5,000

MOSAIC CO (THE)   NYS: MOS

101 East Kennedy Blvd., Suite 2500
Tampa, FL 33602
Phone: 800 918-8270
Fax: 763 577-2990
Web: www.mosaicco.com

CEO: –
CFO: –
HR: –
FYE: December 31
Type: Public

The Mosaic Company ranks as one of the world's largest producers of phosphate and potash, which are used for crop nutrition and as input to animal feed. Mosaic products account for more than 40% of the company's revenue, followed by phosphates and potash. The company mines its phosphate in Florida, Brazil and Peru. About 75% of Mosaic's sales are from international customers. The company was incorporated in 2004 and serves the top four nutrient-consuming countries in the world, which includes China, India, the US, and Brazil. The company serves customers in about 40 countries.

	Annual Growth	12/19	12/20	12/21	12/22	12/23
Sales ($mil.)	11.4%	8,906.3	8,681.7	12,357	19,125	13,696
Net income ($ mil.)	–	(1,067.4)	666.1	1,630.6	3,582.8	1,164.9
Market value ($ mil.)	13.4%	7,013.6	7,457.6	12,734	14,218	11,580
Employees	(4.8%)	12,600	12,617	12,525	13,570	10,352

MOSAIC HEALTH SYSTEM

5325 FARAON ST
SAINT JOSEPH, MO 645063488
Phone: 816 271-6000
Fax: –
Web: www.mymlc.com

CEO: Mike Poore
CFO: John Wilson
HR: –
FYE: June 30
Type: Private

Heartland Health provides medical care in the heart of the Midwest. The integrated health care system serves residents of northwest Missouri, as well as bordering areas of Kansas and Nebraska. Its flagship facility is Heartland Regional Medical Center, a 350-bed acute-care hospital that features an emergency room and Level II trauma center, as well as specialty care programs in heart disease, cancer, and obstetrics. Heartland Health also provides primary care through a multi-specialty medical practice (Heartland Clinic), and it offers home health, hospice, and long-term care services from the primary medical center facility. The company's Community Health Improvement Solutions unit is an HMO health insurer.

	Annual Growth	06/18	06/19	06/20	06/21	06/22
Sales ($mil.)	6.0%	–	688.2	778.5	780.3	820.6
Net income ($ mil.)	–	–	85.3	75.0	221.8	(104.9)
Market value ($ mil.)	–	–	–	–	–	–
Employees	–	–	–	–	–	32,000

MOSAIC IMMUNOENGINEERING INC   NBB: CPMV

1537 South Novato Blvd, #5
Novato, CA 94947
Phone: 657 208-0890
Fax: –
Web: www.ptsc.com

CEO: Steven King
CFO: Paul Lytle
HR: –
FYE: December 31
Type: Public

Patriot Scientific proudly designs microprocessors for licensing to other parties. Advanced Micro Devices, which has an equity investment in the company, licenses Patriot's microprocessor patent portfolio. AMD also has the rights to manufacture and sell Patriot's Ignite 32-bit stack microprocessor. CASIO COMPUTER, Fujitsu, Hewlett-Packard, Hoya, NEC, Nokia, Philips, Sharp, and Sony, among others, have licensed technology from Patriot. The company also owns part of Scripps Secured Data, Inc. (SSDI) and Talis Data Systems, both network security software suppliers.

	Annual Growth	05/19	05/20*	12/20	12/21	12/22
Sales ($mil.)	–	–	–	–	–	–
Net income ($ mil.)	–	(0.8)	(1.1)	(0.8)	(3.7)	(2.4)
Market value ($ mil.)	326.2%	0.0	0.0	23.5	7.4	7.2
Employees	41.4%	2	1	7	7	8

*Fiscal year change

MOSSY HOLDING COMPANY, INC

12150 OLD KATY RD
HOUSTON, TX 77079
Phone: 281 558-9970
Fax: –
Web: www.mossynissanhouston.com

CEO: –
CFO: –
HR: –
FYE: December 31
Type: Private

Mossy Holding Company gathers plenty of rolling stock. The company operates the Mossy chain of nearly 20 auto dealerships in the San Diego, New Orleans, and Houston markets, including locations that are part of its Mossy Nissan franchise. The company's dealers also sell new cars and trucks made by Ford, Toyota, Honda, Volkswagen, BMW, Buick, and Fiat, and offer used cars as well as parts and repair services. Owned by the Mossy family, the company began when Wiley Mossy bought his first Oldsmobile dealership in New Orleans in 1934.

MOTHER MURPHY'S LABORATORIES, INC.

2826 S ELM EUGENE ST
GREENSBORO, NC 274064435
Phone: 336 273-1737
Fax: –
Web: www.mothermurphys.com

CEO: –
CFO: Timothy Hansen
HR: –
FYE: October 31
Type: Private

This Mother Murphy does her cooking in an industrial-strength kitchen. Mother Murphy's Laboratories develops and manufactures dry and liquid, natural and synthetic flavorings and extracts for the bakery, beverage, dairy, tobacco, confectionery, pharmaceutical, tobacco, pet product, confectionery, and snack food industries. The company specializes in vanilla and vanilla variations, offering a wide array of product types of everyone's favorite baking flavoring. Family owned and operated Mother Murphy's Laboratories was founded in 1945 by Kermit Murphy, Sr., who named the company after his mother. Murphy died in 2008.

	Annual Growth	10/14	10/15	10/16	10/17	10/18
Sales ($mil.)	43.9%	–	–	50.9	63.9	105.3
Net income ($ mil.)	99.0%	–	–	11.6	17.2	46.0
Market value ($ mil.)	–	–	–	–	–	–
Employees	–	–	–	–	–	120

MOTHERS AGAINST DRUNK DRIVING INC

511 E JOHN CARPENTER FWY STE 700
IRVING, TX 750623958
Phone: 214 744-6233
Fax: –
Web: www.madd.org

CEO: –
CFO: –
HR: –
FYE: December 31
Type: Private

MADD wants to convince everyone that drunk driving and underage drinking don't mix. Mothers Against Drunk Driving (MADD) is an activist group that offers education, court and legislative advocacy, and other volunteer services in an effort to curb drunk driving. It boasts more than 3,500 people and organizations nationwide. Programs encompass adults, college students, youth, and law-enforcement professionals. About half of its funding comes from donors; the rest is from corporate donations and the Victim of Crimes Act, which distributes money seized from criminals to victim services groups. MADD was founded in 1980 by mothers who were upset when a repeat drunk driver killed a teenage girl in California.

	Annual Growth	06/08	06/09	06/10*	12/13	12/14
Sales ($mil.)	(3.1%)	–	41.0	40.9	33.4	35.0
Net income ($ mil.)	–	–	(3.5)	2.8	(0.9)	(1.2)
Market value ($ mil.)	–	–	–	–	–	–
Employees	–	–	–	–	–	320

*Fiscal year change

MOTION COMPUTING, INC.

8601 RANCH ROAD 2222 BLDG II
AUSTIN, TX 787302304
Phone: 512 637-1100
Fax: -
Web: www.motioncomputing.com

CEO: Philip S Sassower
CFO: Michael J Rapisand
HR: -
FYE: December 31
Type: Private

Motion Computing serves those who are on the move -- literally. The company designs and sells tablet PCs, as well as mobile accessories such as keyboards, docking stations, storage drives, cases, and power supplies, for the healthcare, retail, government, construction, and manufacturing industries, among others. For example, its dashboard-mounted computers are used by police officers and EMS drivers. Motion Computing also offers a line of semi-rugged tablet computers aimed at mobile workforce sectors such as construction and field services. Its products are sold directly, as well as through an extensive network of software vendors, resellers, and distributors.

MOTION PICTURE ASSOCIATION, INC.

1600 I ST NW
WASHINGTON, DC 200064010
Phone: 818 995-6600
Fax: -
Web: www.motionpictures.org

CEO: Christopher Dodd
CFO: David England
HR: -
FYE: December 31
Type: Private

The Motion Picture Association (MPA) is rated "E" for entertainment. The trade association represents the interests of major US film, TV, and home-entertainment companies in the nation's capital of Washington, DC. It is best known as the entity that provides the G, PG, PG13, R, and NC-17 motion-picture ratings. It also leads the fight against piracy and copyright violations and provides TV-show ratings. MPA's board of directors includes the studio heads of the six major movie companies, including Walt Disney Studios, Sony Pictures, Paramount Pictures, Netflix, Universal Studios, and Warner Bros.

	Annual Growth	12/97	12/98	12/99	12/00	12/19
Sales ($mil.)	(10.9%)	-	-	-	45.5	5.1
Net income ($ mil.)	(21.0%)	-	-	-	4.4	0.0
Market value ($ mil.)	-	-	-	-	-	-
Employees	-	-	-	-	-	200

MOTOR CITY ELECTRIC CO.

9440 GRINNELL ST
DETROIT, MI 482131151
Phone: 313 921-5300
Fax: -
Web: www.mceco.com

CEO: -
CFO: -
HR: Courteney Zagacki
FYE: December 31
Type: Private

Although still a motor city mad man, Motor City Electric Co. has driven outside of its home state of Michigan to spark growth of its business operations. With offices in Indiana, Nevada, Florida, Texas, and Ontario, Canada, the company has become one of the largest electrical contractors in the US. Motor City Electric provides electrical construction and its divisions specialize in automotive, industrial, emergency, public works and steel, technology, and excavation services. The company and its group of subsidiaries have installed electric systems in office complexes, correctional facilities, manufacturing plants, casinos, water treatment facilities, and data centers.

MOTORCAR PARTS OF AMERICA INC

NMS: MPAA

2929 California Street
Torrance, CA 90503
Phone: 310 212-7910
Fax: -
Web: www.motorcarparts.com

CEO: Selwyn Joffe
CFO: David Lee
HR: -
FYE: March 31
Type: Public

Motorcar Parts of America (MPA) is a leading supplier of automotive aftermarket non-discretionary replacement parts and test solutions and diagnostic equipment. The company's hard parts products include light-duty rotating electrical products, wheel hub products, brake-related products, and turbochargers. MPA sells the remanufactured products to retailers and warehouse distributors, which sell to do-it-yourself (DIY) consumers and to repair shops (DIFM or do-it-for-me) market. MPA also maintains a special order shop that can facilitate quick turnarounds on parts too rare for large-quantity remanufacturing. Although most of MPA's products are sold under its customers' private labels, the company does market alternators and starters with its Quality-Built, Pure Energy, D&V Electronics, Dixie Electric, DelStar, and DelStar brands. MPA was founded in 1968. Almost all of the company's revenue was generated in North America.

	Annual Growth	03/19	03/20	03/21	03/22	03/23
Sales ($mil.)	9.6%	472.8	535.8	540.8	650.3	683.1
Net income ($ mil.)	-	(7.8)	(7.3)	21.5	7.4	(4.2)
Market value ($ mil.)	(20.8%)	367.9	245.2	438.6	347.6	145.0
Employees	9.7%	3,868	4,012	5,700	5,800	5,600

MOTOROLA SOLUTIONS INC

NYS: MSI

500 W. Monroe Street
Chicago, IL 60661
Phone: 847 576-5000
Fax: 847 576-3477
Web: www.motorolasolutions.com

CEO: Gregory Q Brown
CFO: Jason J Winkler
HR: -
FYE: December 31
Type: Public

Motorola Solutions is one of the leading companies in public safety and enterprise security. The company's radios and wireless broadband products are used by government, public safety, and first-responder agencies for communications and personnel deployment. Commercial and industrial customers use products from Motorola to stay in touch with the mobile workforces. Besides two-way radios, the company makes vehicle-mounted radios, fixed and mobile video cameras and accessories. It serves more than 100,000 public safety and commercial customers in over 100 countries. Some 70% of sales are to customers in the US. Motorola Solutions goes back to the late 1920s.

	Annual Growth	12/19	12/20	12/21	12/22	12/23
Sales ($mil.)	6.1%	7,887.0	7,414.0	8,171.0	9,112.0	9,978.0
Net income ($ mil.)	18.5%	868.0	949.0	1,245.0	1,363.0	1,709.0
Market value ($ mil.)	18.1%	26,781	28,264	45,157	42,831	52,036
Employees	5.4%	17,000	18,000	18,700	20,000	21,000

MOTT MACDONALD GROUP INC.

111 WOOD AVE S STE 5
ISELIN, NJ 088302700
Phone: 973 379-3400
Fax: -
Web: -

CEO: -
CFO: -
HR: -
FYE: December 31
Type: Private

Mott MacDonald is a global engineering, management and development firm. It was formed in 1989 with the merger of two long-established and well-known international engineering consultancies: Mott, Hay & Anderson, renowned for its contribution to transportation engineering. Mott MacDonald operates from 180 principal offices in 50 countries across over 10 core sectors: buildings, communications, education, environment, health, industry, international development, oil and gas, power, transport, urban development, and water. Its expertise have included air services advisory, building design, business, improvement, and more.

	Annual Growth	12/08	12/09	12/10	12/11	12/12
Sales ($mil.)	13.0%	-	-	374.2	440.6	478.0
Net income ($ mil.)	14.8%	-	-	20.7	25.4	27.2
Market value ($ mil.)	-	-	-	-	-	-
Employees	-	-	-	-	-	2,500

MOUNT CARMEL HEALTH SYSTEM

1039 KINGSMILL PKWY
COLUMBUS, OH 432291129
Phone: 614 234-6000
Fax: –
Web: www.mountcarmelhealth.com

CEO: Michael Englehart
CFO: Andy Priday
HR: Kathryn Smith
FYE: June 30
Type: Private

Mount Carmel Health System cares for the sick in the greater Columbus area and central Ohio. The health care system boasts 1,500 physicians at three general hospitals and a specialty surgical hospital, offering a comprehensive range of medical and surgical services including cardiovascular care. Mount Carmel Health also operates outpatient centers including primary care and specialty physicians' practices, and it offers home health care services. The hospital group is part of Trinity Health, one of the largest Catholic health care systems in the US.

	Annual Growth	06/17	06/18	06/20	06/21	06/22
Sales ($mil.)	(7.7%)	–	1,911.4	1,345.0	1,427.6	1,389.7
Net income ($ mil.)	–	–	157.2	1.4	59.1	(35.6)
Market value ($ mil.)	–	–	–	–	–	–
Employees	–	–	–	–	–	8,000

MOUNT OLIVE PICKLE COMPANY, INC.

1 CUCUMBER BLVD
MOUNT OLIVE, NC 283651210
Phone: 919 658-2535
Fax: –
Web: www.mtolivepickles.com

CEO: –
CFO: –
HR: –
FYE: April 30
Type: Private

Mount Olive Pickle Company makes pickled products preferred by persnickety people. The company's pickles are the #1 selling brand in the southeastern US and a top seller across the nation. Every year, it produces more than 110 million jars of condiments -- offering some 80 styles of processed and fresh-pack pickles, relishes, and peppers. The company procures its yearly supply of more than 160 million pounds of cucumbers and peppers from farmers in North Carolina, as well as nine other states and Mexico. Mount Olive Pickle Company, which boasts more than 1,200 brine vats, was founded in 1926 by Lebanese immigrant Shickrey Baddour.

MOUNT SINAI MEDICAL CENTER OF FLORIDA, INC.

4300 ALTON RD
MIAMI BEACH, FL 331402948
Phone: 305 674-2121
Fax: –
Web: www.msmc.com

CEO: Steven Sonenreich
CFO: Alex Mendez
HR: Paul Katz
FYE: December 31
Type: Private

Mount Sinai Medical Center is the largest private independent not-for-profit teaching hospital in South Florida. The medical center, which boasts more than 670 licensed beds, provides general medical and surgical care, as well as specialty care in cardiology (Mount Sinai Heart Institute), neuroscience, oncology, orthopedics, pulmonology, radiology, and other fields. It also participates in clinical research studies and drug trials with an emphasis on cancer, heart, and lung conditions. It maintains an inpatient behavioral health unit and houses the Wien Center for Alzheimer's disease and memory disorders diagnosis and research, the largest such facility in the region.

	Annual Growth	12/15	12/16	12/20	12/21	12/22
Sales ($mil.)	9.6%	–	560.3	648.5	847.3	968.6
Net income ($ mil.)	10.6%	–	19.7	(3.6)	37.3	35.9
Market value ($ mil.)	–	–	–	–	–	–
Employees	–	–	–	–	–	3,225

MOUNTAIN MERGER SUB CORPORATION

2 BETHESDA METRO CTR # 12
BETHESDA, MD 208146319
Phone: 301 968-9220
Fax: –
Web: www.mtge.com

CEO: –
CFO: –
HR: –
FYE: December 31
Type: Private

When reading its name, it's not difficult to figure out what MTGE Investment (formerly American Capital Mortgage Investment) does. The newly formed real estate investment trust (REIT) invests in and manages a portfolio of residential mortgage-backed securities, mostly fixed-rate pass-through certificates guaranteed by Fannie Mae, Freddie Mac, or Ginnie Mae. The company, which is externally-managed by American Capital MTGE Management, also plans to invest in adjustable-rate mortgages (ARMs) and collateralized mortgage obligations (CMOs). American Capital Mortgage was formed and went public in 2011.

MOUNTAIN STATES HEALTH ALLIANCE

400 N STATE OF FRANKLIN RD
JOHNSON CITY, TN 376046035
Phone: 423 431-6111
Fax: –
Web: www.balladhealth.org

CEO: Dennis Vonderfecht
CFO: Marvin Eichorn
HR: Brooke Graham
FYE: June 30
Type: Private

Mountain States Health Alliance (MSHA) believes in teamwork when it comes to providing health care to the good people living in Tennessee and Virginia. Along with MSHA's 13 acute care and specialty hospitals, the system operates more than 20 primary and preventive care centers and numerous outpatient care sites, including First Assist Urgent Care, MedWorks, Same Day Surgery, and Rehab Plus. It also operates the Mountain States Medical group of about 180 doctors who administer care at dozens of locations throughout the region. Formed in 1998, MSHA is home to roughly 1,700 beds; its largest facility is the Johnson City Medical Center with 445 beds. MSHA plans to merge with Wellmont Health System.

MOUNTAIN STATES PIPE & SUPPLY CO, INC

7765 ELECTRONIC DR
COLORADO SPRINGS, CO 809221546
Phone: 719 634-5555
Fax: –
Web: www.msps.com

CEO: –
CFO: –
HR: –
FYE: December 31
Type: Private

These supplies can measure what your pipes use. Mountain States Pipe & Supply distributes pipes, valves, and related products for natural gas and water in Arizona, California, Colorado, Ohio, and Texas. It offers meter boxes, backflow kits, and similar goods through its US Metering and Technology division. The company carries products from manufacturers such as Elster American Meter, Febco, Pacific Pipe, and Tyler Pipe. It also provides meter installation, equipment rental, and utilities billing. Customers have included Global Water Resources, Kinder Morgan, and PG&E. Mountain States Pipe & Supply was founded in 1955.

	Annual Growth	12/09	12/10	12/11	12/12	12/13
Sales ($mil.)	(4.0%)	–	–	21.1	19.6	19.4
Net income ($ mil.)	–	–	–	0.2	(0.2)	(0.4)
Market value ($ mil.)	–	–	–	–	–	–
Employees	–	–	–	–	–	130

MOUNTAINWEST PIPELINE, LLC

333 S STATE ST
SALT LAKE CITY, UT 841112302
Phone: 801 324-5173
Fax: –
Web: –

CEO: –
CFO: –
HR: –
FYE: December 31
Type: Private

Dominion Energy Questar Pipeline operates a 2,500-mile long natural gas pipeline system that spans across Colorado, Utah, and Wyoming. It owns and operates the Overthrust Pipeline in southwestern Wyoming and a 50% stake in the White River Hub. The company also owns the Clay Basin storage facility with is capable of holding about 120 billion cu. ft. of natural gas. Dominion Energy Questar Pipeline is a subsidiary of energy distribution giant Dominion Energy.

MOVADO GROUP, INC.

NYS: MOV

650 From Road, Ste. 375
Paramus, NJ 07652-3556
Phone: 201 267-8000
Fax: –
Web: www.movadogroup.com

CEO: Efraim Grinberg
CFO: Sallie A Demarsilis
HR: Michelle Kennedy
FYE: January 31
Type: Public

Movado is a leader in the design, development, marketing, and distribution of watch brands in the industry. Its watch brands include Movado, Concord, Ebel, Olivia Burton, and MVMT as well as the licensed Coach, Tommy Hilfiger, Hugo Boss, Lacoste, and Calvin Klein which are sold worldwide. While its watches range in price from about less than $75 to mass market to over $10,000 for luxury designs. Movado sells its watches to major jewelry stores and department store chains (including Nordstrom and Macy's), as well as to independent jewelers and online retailers. The company operates a growing chain of more than 50 outlet centers across the US and four outlet centers in Canada. Most of the company's revenue come from outside the US.

	Annual Growth	01/20	01/21	01/22	01/23	01/24
Sales ($mil.)	(1.0%)	701.0	506.4	732.4	751.9	672.6
Net income ($ mil.)	2.3%	42.7	(111.5)	91.6	94.5	46.7
Market value ($ mil.)	12.5%	381.6	457.8	821.4	783.5	611.1
Employees	6.6%	1,145	2,412	2,594	2,914	1,476

MOVE SOLUTIONS, LTD.

2201 CHEMSEARCH BLVD
IRVING, TX 750626400
Phone: 214 630-3607
Fax: –
Web: www.movesolutions.com

CEO: –
CFO: –
HR: Donnita Herbert
FYE: December 31
Type: Private

Move Solutions, Ltd. (MSL) helps make it easy for office transplants. Focused on providing office relocation services, offerings include furniture installation, inventory management and storage, project management, relocation analysis, and interstate and intrastate transportation. MSL also provides packing equipment and offers cleaning services when clients must return vacated lease space to the landlord. MSL primarily serves clients located in Texas. Customers have included federal and state agencies, as well as businesses in the private sector. Move Solutions is a unit of Total Office Solutions, a Dallas-based supplier of office furniture and equipment.

	Annual Growth	12/07	12/08	12/16	12/17	12/18
Sales ($mil.)	3.7%	–	14.2	15.4	20.3	20.4
Net income ($ mil.)	(3.2%)	–	0.5	0.0	1.3	0.4
Market value ($ mil.)	–	–	–	–	–	–
Employees	–	–	–	–	–	300

MOZILLA FOUNDATION

149 NEW MONTGOMERY ST
SAN FRANCISCO, CA 941053740
Phone: 650 903-0800
Fax: –
Web: www.mozilla.org

CEO: Mark Surman
CFO: –
HR: Michael Aukland
FYE: December 31
Type: Private

Microsoft's Internet Explorer (IE) may have subdued Netscape in the "browser wars" of the 1990s, but Mozilla's Firefox rose from the ashes with renewed vigor. Firefox has clawed market share away from IE over the years (now at about 25%) only to now be harassed itself by the meteoric rise of Google's Chrome, being overtaken by the browser in usage share at the end of 2011. The Mozilla Foundation was created in 2003 to carry on the open-source development work of the mozilla.org project (spun off from Netscape in 1998). For-profit subsidiary Mozilla Corporation (spun off in 2005) oversees product development, marketing, and distribution.

	Annual Growth	12/13	12/14	12/15	12/19	12/21
Sales ($mil.)	6.8%	–	19.3	421.3	28.4	30.7
Net income ($ mil.)	11.4%	–	3.5	57.1	6.5	7.3
Market value ($ mil.)	–	–	–	–	–	–
Employees	–	–	–	–	–	588

MPHASE TECHNOLOGIES INC.

NBB: XDSL

1101 Wootton Parkway, #1040
Rockville, MD 20878
Phone: 301 329-2700
Fax: –
Web: www.mphasetech.com

CEO: –
CFO: –
HR: –
FYE: June 30
Type: Public

mPhase Technologies has lots of plans for potential profits. mPhase, a development-stage company, designed broadband communications equipment that lets telephone companies provide television over DSL lines. It has since shifted its development to middleware that allows telephone companies to deliver voice, Internet, and television service over Internet protocol (IP). It plans to market its systems to phone companies in areas with relatively little multi-channel television access, such as international markets and the rural US. It is also developing power cells that utilize nanotechnology through its AlwaysReady subsidiary.

	Annual Growth	06/17	06/18	06/19	06/20	06/21
Sales ($mil.)	–	–	–	2.5	30.3	30.7
Net income ($ mil.)	–	(0.3)	0.3	(2.0)	(14.1)	1.7
Market value ($ mil.)	710.0%	0.0	0.0	66.8	6.3	33.8
Employees	101.0%	3	4	4	90	49

MPLX LP

NYS: MPLX

200 E. Hardin Street
Findlay, OH 45840
Phone: 419 421-2414
Fax: –
Web: www.mplx.com

CEO: Michael J Hennigan
CFO: C K Hagedorn
HR: –
FYE: December 31
Type: Public

MPLX is a diversified master limited partnership formed in 2012 by Marathon Petroleum Corporation (MPC) to own, operate, develop and acquire midstream energy infrastructure assets. It gathers, processes, and transports natural gas; gathers, transports, fractionates, stores and markets natural gas liquids (NGLs); and transports, stores and distributes crude oil and refined petroleum products. Headquartered in Findlay, Ohio, MPLX's assets consist of a network of crude oil and products pipeline assets located in the Midwest and Gulf Coast regions of the United States. It owns and operates light-product terminals, an inland marine business, storage caverns, crude oil and product storage facilities (tank farms), a barge dock facility, and gathering and processing assets. MPLX went public in 2012. Marathon Petroleum Corporation and MPLX completed another large drop-down deal in 2017, whereby MPLX paid $8.1 billion to obtain refining logistics assets and fuels distribution services from MPC. The transaction increased by 50% the size of MPLX's balance sheet.

	Annual Growth	12/19	12/20	12/21	12/22	12/23
Sales ($mil.)	5.7%	9,041.0	7,569.0	10,027	11,613	11,281
Net income ($ mil.)	28.6%	1,434.0	(720.0)	3,077.0	3,944.0	3,928.0
Market value ($ mil.)	9.6%	25,549	21,726	29,694	32,955	36,848
Employees	–	–	–	–	5,811	5,810

MPM CAPITAL LIMITED PARTNERSHIP

450 KENDALL ST
CAMBRIDGE, MA 021421227
Phone: 617 425-9200
Fax: –
Web: www.mpmcapital.com

CEO: –
CFO: –
HR: –
FYE: December 31
Type: Private

MPM Capital might be behind that latest medical breakthrough. The investment firm targets biotechnology, specialty pharmaceutical, and medical technology companies. With more than $2 billion of committed capital in four funds, it invests in all stages of a firm's development, typically offering between $5 million and $50 million per transaction, and takes a long-term approach. MPM Capital's portfolio includes about 60 firms, including Affymax, AVEO Pharmaceuticals, Oxagen, and Surface Logix. Most of MPM Capital's investments are in US concerns, but the company also seeks opportunities in Europe, and more recently, Asia and Australia. The company has offices in Boston and San Francisco.

MPM HOLDINGS INC.

260 HUDSON RIVER RD
WATERFORD, NY 121881910
Phone: 518 233-3330
Fax: –
Web: www.momentive.com

CEO: Jack Boss
CFO: Erick R Asmussen
HR: –
FYE: December 31
Type: Private

Momentive Performance Materials is a leading global high-performance silicones and specialties company that provides silicone and specialty solutions to a wide range of industries, including, automotive, electronics, personal care, consumer products, aerospace and building and construction. The company offers an extensive portfolio of additives, including silanes, specialty fluids and urethane additives. The company also offers extensive offering of formulated products, including elastomers and coatings. With a diverse customer base of more than 4,000 customers on more than 100 countries around the world, the company's major manufacturing sites are located in Brazil, China, India, Italy, Korea, Japan, Thailand, the UK, and the US.

MR COOPER GROUP INC   NAS: COOP

8950 Cypress Waters Blvd.
Coppell, TX 75019
Phone: 469 549-2000
Fax: –
Web: www.mrcoopergroup.com

CEO: –
CFO: –
HR: –
FYE: December 31
Type: Public

Mr. Cooper Group Inc. is a leading servicer and originator of residential mortgage loans. Company's purpose is to keep the dream of homeownership alive, and Mr. Cooper do this by helping mortgage borrowers manage what is typically their largest financial asset, and by helping its investors maximize the returns from their portfolios of residential mortgages. The company performs operational activities behalf of investors and originates residential mortgages.

	Annual Growth	12/19	12/20	12/21	12/22	12/23
Assets ($mil.)	(6.2%)	18,305	24,165	14,204	12,776	14,196
Net income ($ mil.)	16.2%	274.0	305.0	1,454.0	923.0	500.0
Market value ($ mil.)	51.0%	808.1	2,004.5	2,688.0	2,592.4	4,206.7
Employees	(7.0%)	9,100	9,800	8,200	6,600	6,800

MR. GOODCENTS, INC.

8997 COMMERCE DR
DE SOTO, KS 660188428
Phone: 913 583-8400
Fax: –
Web: www.goodcentssubs.com

CEO: David Goebel
CFO: –
HR: –
FYE: December 31
Type: Private

This chain has a proposition for those hungering for a sound investment in lunch. Mr. Goodcents Franchise Systems operates a chain of more than 100 sandwich shops under the name Mr. Goodcents Subs & Pasta. The eateries offer a selection of hot and cold subs, including the Centsable Sub and the Penny Club, along with a variety of pasta dishes, soups, and sides. In addition to quick-service dining, many locations offer party trays and box lunches for carry-out. Mr. Goodcents has franchised locations in nearly 10 states, primarily in Kansas and Missouri. Former McDonald's executive Joe Bisogno opened the first Mr. Goodcents in 1989.

MRC GLOBAL INC   NYS: MRC

1301 McKinney Street, Suite 2300
Houston, TX 77010
Phone: 877 294-7574
Fax: –
Web: www.mrcglobal.com

CEO: Robert J Saltiel Jr
CFO: Kelly Youngblood
HR: –
FYE: December 31
Type: Public

MRC Global Inc. is the world's top distributor of pipes, valves, fittings (PVF), and other infrastructure products catering primarily to the energy industry. It has over 250,000 PVF and other oilfield products that help oil and gas companies in the construction and maintenance of complex equipment that is used in extreme operating conditions (pressure, temperature, corrosion). MRC Global's customers include oil exploration and production companies, natural gas utilities, crude oil refiners, and petrochemical manufacturers. It also provides services like multiple deliveries and zone store management. With more than 200 service locations, the company serves some 10,000 customers around the world, though most of its revenue comes from the US (nearly 80%).

	Annual Growth	12/19	12/20	12/21	12/22	12/23
Sales ($mil.)	(1.8%)	3,662.0	2,560.0	2,666.0	3,363.0	3,412.0
Net income ($ mil.)	30.8%	39.0	(274.0)	(14.0)	75.0	114.0
Market value ($ mil.)	(5.2%)	1,150.1	559.0	580.1	976.4	928.3
Employees	(3.3%)	3,200	2,600	2,600	2,800	2,800

MRIGLOBAL

425 DR MARTIN LUTHER KING JR BLVD
KANSAS CITY, MO 641102241
Phone: 816 753-7600
Fax: –
Web: www.mriglobal.org

CEO: Tom Bowser
CFO: R T Fleener
HR: Monica D Agostino
FYE: September 30
Type: Private

MRIGlobal provides contract research services for government and private-sector clients in fields such as agricultural and food safety, analytical chemistry, biological sciences, energy, engineering, environment, health sciences, information technology, and national defense. The institute operates laboratories and agricultural research centers in Florida, Kansas, Maryland, Missouri, North Carolina, and Washington, DC. MRIGlobal also manages the US Department of Energy's National Renewable Energy Laboratory in Golden, Colorado. Work related to biological and chemical defense accounts for most of MRIGlobal's sales. The not-for-profit organization was founded in 1944.

	Annual Growth	09/13	09/14	09/15	09/21	09/22
Sales ($mil.)	(14.9%)	–	466.8	90.7	116.1	128.6
Net income ($ mil.)	21.5%	–	1.6	(4.4)	8.5	7.4
Market value ($ mil.)	–	–	–	–	–	–
Employees	–	–	–	–	–	2,547

MRV COMMUNICATIONS, INC.

20520 NORDHOFF ST
CHATSWORTH, CA 913116113
Phone: 818 773-0900
Fax: –
Web: –

CEO: –
CFO: –
HR: –
FYE: December 31
Type: Private

MRV Communications puts the buzz in optical communications. MRV supplies the switching, routing, Ethernet, optical transport, and console management equipment used in voice, data, and video traffic by telecommunications carriers, data centers, and labs. It also provides network system design services, as well as integrated network products and services. It sells to cable operators, networking services providers, Internet and telecom companies, and governments worldwide. About two-thirds of sales are outside the US, mostly in Europe.

MS FOUNDATION FOR WOMEN INC

1 WILLOUGHBY SQ
BROOKLYN, NY 112017615
Phone: 212 742-2300
Fax: –
Web: www.forwomen.org

CEO: –
CFO: –
HR: –
FYE: June 30
Type: Private

The Ms. Foundation for Women is dedicated to helping women and girls by providing grants, public education, and training in the areas of health and safety, leadership, and economic security. It established the Take Our Daughters To Work (which became Take Our Daughters and Sons To Work in 2003), an annual event targeting children ages eight to twelve. Most of the organization's revenues come from grants and gifts, but it also earns funds through special events, publication and product sales, and various special events. The Ms. Foundation for Women was established in 1973.

	Annual Growth	06/15	06/16	06/17	06/19	06/20
Sales ($mil.)	(12.1%)	–	7.0	4.3	14.5	4.2
Net income ($ mil.)	–	–	(0.3)	(2.8)	6.3	(4.7)
Market value ($ mil.)	–	–	–	–	–	–
Employees	–	–	–	–	–	19

MSC INDUSTRIAL DIRECT CO INC

515 Broadhollow Road, Suite 1000
Melville, NY 11747
Phone: 516 812-2000
Fax: 516 349-7096
Web: www.mscdirect.com

NYS: MSM
CEO: –
CFO: –
HR: –
FYE: September 2
Type: Public

MSC Industrial Direct is one of the largest US direct suppliers of industrial products. It distributes fasteners and measuring instruments, cutting tools, and plumbing supplies to customers in metalworking and maintenance, repair, and overhaul (MRO) businesses. MSC Industrial stocks more about 2 million products. The company also serves Fortune 1000 manufacturing companies through its 6,500 associates. The company sells -- mainly to small and mid-size firms -- through its master catalog (which runs to several thousand pages), promotional mailings and brochures, as well as via telemarketing and the Internet.

	Annual Growth	08/19	08/20	08/21*	09/22	09/23
Sales ($mil.)	4.5%	3,363.8	3,192.4	3,243.2	3,691.9	4,009.3
Net income ($ mil.)	4.4%	288.9	251.1	216.9	339.8	343.2
Market value ($ mil.)	10.7%	3,752.8	3,698.4	4,736.8	4,361.0	5,643.1
Employees	2.4%	6,700	6,315	6,571	6,994	7,377

*Fiscal year change

MSCI INC

7 World Trade Center, 250 Greenwich Street, 49th Floor
New York, NY 10007
Phone: 212 804-3900
Fax: –
Web: www.msci.com

NYS: MSCI
CEO: Henry A Fernandez
CFO: Andrew C Wiechmann
HR: –
FYE: December 31
Type: Public

MSCI, formerly Morgan Stanley Capital International, manages more than 278,000 daily equity, fixed income, and hedge fund indices used by large asset management firms. Its leading, research-enhanced products, and services include indexes; portfolio construction and risk management analytics; environmental, social, and governance (ESG) and climate solutions; and real estate benchmarks, return analytics, and market insights. MSCI has over 6,600 clients across more than 95 countries. The Americas accounts for about half of the company's total sales.

	Annual Growth	12/19	12/20	12/21	12/22	12/23
Sales ($mil.)	12.9%	1,557.8	1,695.4	2,043.5	2,248.6	2,528.9
Net income ($ mil.)	19.5%	563.6	601.8	726.0	870.6	1,148.6
Market value ($ mil.)	21.7%	20,420	35,317	48,458	36,791	44,738
Employees	14.3%	3,396	3,633	4,303	4,759	5,794

MSG NETWORKS INC.

11 PENNSYLVANIA PLZ
NEW YORK, NY 100012006
Phone: 212 465-6400
Fax: –
Web: www.msgnetworks.com

CEO: Andrea Greenberg
CFO: Bret Richter
HR: –
FYE: June 30
Type: Private

MSG Networks is an industry leader in sports production, and content development and distribution. MSG owns sports teams the New York Knicks of the NBA and the NHL's New York Rangers. The company owns regional sports networks MSG, MSG+, and streaming platform MSG Go offering games for basketball's Knicks and New York Liberty and hockey's Rangers, New York Islanders, New Jersey Devils, and Buffalo Sabres.

MSGI SECURITY SOLUTIONS INC

575 Madison Avenue
New York, NY 10022
Phone: 212 605-0245
Fax: –
Web: www.msgisecurity.com

CEO: J J Barbera
CFO: –
HR: –
FYE: June 30
Type: Public

MSGI Technology Solutions Solutions (formerly Security Solutions) invests in companies that make equipment and software for security, safety, and surveillance applications. It typically acquires controlling interests in early-stage, early growth technology and software development businesses. Majority-owned Innalogic develops software applications that combine biometric, sensor, text, and/or video data for wireless mobile devices to aid in emergency response. The company's Future Developments America subsidiary makes audio and video electronic surveillance equipment. MSGI Technology Solutions has licensing agreements with Hyundai Syscomm and Apro Media through which it aggregates and configures security systems.

	Annual Growth	06/06	06/07	06/08	06/09	06/10
Sales ($mil.)	–	0.1	0.2	4.0	0.3	–
Net income ($ mil.)	–	(15.2)	(12.4)	(20.2)	(8.0)	(13.4)
Market value ($ mil.)	(23.1%)	190.1	66.3	66.3	66.3	66.3
Employees	(30.7%)	13	13	7	3	3

MSX INTERNATIONAL, INC.

500 WOODWARD AVE STE 2150
DETROIT, MI 482263417
Phone: 248 829-6300
Fax: -
Web: www.msxi.com

CEO: Fred Minturn
CFO: Todd Hauser
HR: Carole I Freeman
FYE: January 02
Type: Private

MSX International (MSXI) is all revved up to provide outsourced business services. The company provides engineering, human resources services, and other outsourced business services (including marketing, document management, and purchasing) to clients primarily from the auto industry. Its offerings, which are designed to make businesses more efficient, cost-effective, and profitable, also include temporary and permanent staffing, executive search, career management, training, product engineering, and supply chain management. The company was established in 1996.

MT SAN ANTONIO COMMUNITY COLLEGE DISTRICT

1100 N GRAND AVE
WALNUT, CA 917891341
Phone: 909 594-5611
Fax: -
Web: www.mtsac.edu

CEO: -
CFO: Michael D Gregoryk
HR: -
FYE: June 30
Type: Private

Mt. San Antonio College broadens the horizons of students in the Land of Milk and Honey. The junior college east of Los Angeles serves about 20 San Gabriel Valley communities including the cities of Pomona, Irwindale, Walnut, and Covina. Established in 1946, the school is the largest single-campus community college in California, offering more than 200 academic degree and vocational certificate programs in areas ranging from the arts to business to social sciences to technology. The college's student enrollment is about 60,000, of whom some 35,000 are full-time.

	Annual Growth	06/18	06/19	06/20	06/21	06/22
Sales ($mil.)	14.6%	-	75.0	72.9	88.1	112.8
Net income ($ mil.)	-	-	(31.4)	(26.9)	(5.3)	9.8
Market value ($ mil.)	-	-	-	-	-	-
Employees	-	-	-	-	-	1,500

MTD PRODUCTS INC

5965 GRAFTON RD
VALLEY CITY, OH 442809329
Phone: 330 225-2600
Fax: -
Web: www.mtdparts.com

CEO: Robert T Moll
CFO: Jeffery Deuch
HR: Janeen Jackson
FYE: October 31
Type: Private

MTD Products is a leader in the design and manufacture of outdoor power equipment with award-winning products and powerful brands such as Cub Cadet, Rover, WOLF-Garten, Robomow, Troy-Bilt, and Yard Machines. The outdoor power equipment manufacturer produces lawnmowers and snow blowers for both the residential and commercial markets. Its Cub Cadet brand is the fastest-growing riding mower brand in the US, and is hailed across the globe for its world-class sports turf equipment. Each brand is backed by a strong network of the company's sales, service, and support. The company has facilities located in Europe, North America, Asia, and Australia. The company was founded in 1932 by Theo Moll, Emil Jochum, and Erwin Gerhard.

MTM TECHNOLOGIES, INC.

507 N STATE RD
BRIARCLIFF MANOR, NY 105101511
Phone: 866 383-2867
Fax: -
Web: www.mtm.com

CEO: Marcus Holloway
CFO: Rosemarie Milano
HR: -
FYE: March 31
Type: Private

When it comes to business technology, MTM Technologies has all sorts of technological bases covered. The company is a disruption solution and managed services provider with more than 30 years of experience giving clients nationwide the tools to become market disruptors in their fields. Its clients are US Bank and USDA. Among MTM Technologies' specialties are virtualization, cloud and digital infrastructure, security and managed services. The company handles products from a variety of suppliers, including Cisco Systems, Citrix, EMC, VMware, Microsoft, and NetApp. Columbia Partners, an investment firm, bought MTM in 2015. The company was founded 1986.

	Annual Growth	03/05	03/06	03/07	03/07	03/08
Sales ($mil.)	(11.7%)	-	-	275.0	275.0	242.7
Net income ($ mil.)	-	-	-	(32.0)	(32.0)	(14.4)
Market value ($ mil.)	-	-	-	-	-	-
Employees	-	-	-	-	-	64

MTR GAMING GROUP, INC.

STATE ROUTE 2 S
CHESTER, WV 26034
Phone: 304 387-8000
Fax: -
Web: www.cnty.com

CEO: Gary L Carano
CFO: Robert M Jones
HR: -
FYE: December 31
Type: Private

Gamblers looking beyond casino games can climb the summit of MTR Gaming Group. The company operates three regional casino hotels in the US. Its Mountaineer Racetrack and Gaming Resort in Chester, West Virginia includes horse racing and wagering, in addition to some 2,500 slot machines, 25 poker tables, and approximatelu 60 additional table games. The Mountaineer resort also boasts a hotel and convention center, as well as a fitness center, a theater, and several restaurants. Its Presque Isle Downs & Casino in Erie, Pennsylvania also has horse racing and wagering, as well as about 2,000 slot machines, 50 table games, and dining options. MTR also owns Scioto Downs, the operator of a harness racetrack in Ohio.

MUELLER (PAUL) CO

1600 West Phelps Street
Springfield, MO 65802
Phone: 417 575-9000
Fax: -
Web: www.paulmueller.com

NBB: MUEL
CEO: David T Moore
CFO: -
HR: Chris Dickerson
FYE: December 31
Type: Public

Paul Mueller Company manufactures stainless-steel industrial storage tanks and processing equipment and is a world-leading producer of dairy farm equipment, such as heat recovery equipment. Paul Mueller's industrial equipment unit makes processing equipment for food, beverage, chemical, and pharmaceutical applications. Its Mueller Transportation unit delivers the company's products and components. Paul Mueller makes around 65% of its net sales in its home country, the US. The company traces its roots back in 1940.

	Annual Growth	12/19	12/20	12/21	12/22	12/23
Sales ($mil.)	3.8%	197.2	201.1	184.6	191.5	229.2
Net income ($ mil.)	-	6.6	(2.6)	7.0	3.6	(9.9)
Market value ($ mil.)	20.0%	30.4	36.0	44.5	52.1	63.0
Employees	-	958	785	878	848	-

MUELLER INDUSTRIES INC — NYS: MLI

150 Schilling Boulevard, Suite 100
Collierville, TN 38017
Phone: 901 753-3200
Fax: –
Web: www.muellerindustries.com

CEO: Gregory L Christopher
CFO: Jeffrey A Martin
HR: –
FYE: December 30
Type: Public

Mueller Industries is a leading manufacturer of copper tubes and fittings, lines sets, plastic tube and fittings, steel nipples, bars and rods, forgings, extrusions, pipes, valves, vessels, heat exchangers, and duct systems. Mueller also resells a myriad of products, including brass and plastic plumbing valves, plastic fittings, malleable iron fittings, faucets, and plumbing specialty products. Its operations are divided among three divisions: Piping Systems, Industrial Metals, and Climate. The company's products are used in a wide range of applications including transportation, automotive, and industrial applications. With operations in North America, Europe, Asia, and the Middle East, Muller Industries generate most of its sales in the US.

	Annual Growth	12/19	12/20	12/21	12/22	12/23
Sales ($mil.)	8.9%	2,430.6	2,398.0	3,769.3	3,982.5	3,420.3
Net income ($ mil.)	56.3%	101.0	139.5	468.5	658.3	602.9
Market value ($ mil.)	10.4%	3,624.5	3,985.3	6,679.4	6,735.3	5,382.5
Employees	(2.4%)	4,964	5,007	5,337	5,137	4,509

MUELLER WATER PRODUCTS INC — NYS: MWA

1200 Abernathy Road N.E., Suite 1200
Atlanta, GA 30328
Phone: 770 206-4200
Fax: –
Web: www.muellerwaterproducts.com

CEO: Marietta E Zakas
CFO: Steven S Heinrichs
HR: –
FYE: September 30
Type: Public

Mueller Water is one of the largest manufacturers and marketers of hydrants, as well as valves and pipe couplings in North America. Its flow control products are used in new and upgraded municipal infrastructure, industrial, and residential and non-residential construction projects, such as water distribution networks, water and wastewater treatment facilities, fire protection systems, and gas distribution. Mueller Water Products brands include Mueller, Echologics, Hydro Gate, Hydro-Guard, HYMAX, Jones, Krausz, Mi.Net, Milliken, Pratt, Pratt Industrial, Singer, and U.S. Pipe Valve & Hydrant.

	Annual Growth	09/19	09/20	09/21	09/22	09/23
Sales ($mil.)	7.1%	968.0	964.1	1,111.0	1,247.4	1,275.7
Net income ($ mil.)	7.6%	63.8	72.0	70.4	76.6	85.5
Market value ($ mil.)	3.1%	1,752.0	1,619.5	2,372.4	1,600.8	1,976.5
Employees	0.8%	3,100	3,100	3,400	3,600	3,200

MUHLENBERG REGIONAL MEDICAL CENTER, INC.

1200 RANDOLPH RD
PLAINFIELD, NJ 070603361
Phone: 908 668-2000
Fax: –
Web: www.hackensackmeridianhealth.org

CEO: –
CFO: –
HR: –
FYE: December 31
Type: Private

Muhlenberg Hospital is breathing life anew. The 355-bed facility was shut down by former owner JFK Health System in 2008, but was sold to Community Healthcare Associates (CHA) in mid-2018. CHA plans to redevelop the hospital in a $57 million project that will establish a 186,000-sq.-ft. medical arts complex and some 120 upscale residential apartments. Included in the new development will be primary and specialty care offices, a women's health center, a diagnostic lab, an ambulatory surgical center, and a behavioral health center, among other care facilities. It will also feature a fitness center and a business center.

	Annual Growth	12/13	12/14	12/15	12/16	12/17
Sales ($mil.)	12.9%	–	0.7	0.5	2.5	1.0
Net income ($ mil.)	285.1%	–	0.8	2.0	0.7	44.2
Market value ($ mil.)	–	–	–	–	–	–
Employees	–	–	–	–	–	181

MULESOFT, INC.

50 FREMONT ST STE 300
SAN FRANCISCO, CA 941052231
Phone: 415 229-2009
Fax: –
Web: www.mulesoft.com

CEO: –
CFO: –
HR: –
FYE: December 31
Type: Private

MuleSoft is a leader in integration and API platform connecting the world's applications, data, and devices. The company replaced donkey with mule and began selling software that uses application programming interfaces (APIs) to connect applications, data, and devices into a network of applications. MuleSoft's Anypoint Platform enables an infrastructure so companies can conduct business using mobile, cloud, software-as-a-service, and Internet of Things technologies. MuleSoft serves thousands of companies, including Cisco, VMware, HSBC, AstraZeneca, Wells Fargo, Verizon, IBM, and Audi. Founded in 2006, the Salesforce company is trusted by more than 175,000 developers and leading companies in almost every industry.

	Annual Growth	12/13	12/14	12/15	12/16	12/17
Sales ($mil.)	57.9%	–	–	–	187.7	296.5
Net income ($ mil.)	–	–	–	–	(49.6)	(80.0)
Market value ($ mil.)	–	–	–	–	–	–
Employees	–	–	–	–	–	841

MULTI-COLOR CORPORATION

4053 CLOUGH WOODS DR
BATAVIA, OH 451032587
Phone: 513 381-1480
Fax: –
Web: www.mcclabel.com

CEO: Kevin Kwilinski
CFO: –
HR: Amy Malzhan
FYE: March 31
Type: Private

Multi-Color Corporation is a global label solution supporting a number of the world's most prominent brands including leading producers of home and personal care, wine and spirits, food and beverage, healthcare and specialty consumer products. The company serves international brand owners in the North American, Latin American, EMEA and Asia Pacific regions with a comprehensive range of the latest label technologies. With operations in more than 25 countries worldwide, Multi-Color also provides specialized label solutions including pressure sensitive shack, cut and stack, and heat transfer.

	Annual Growth	03/15	03/16	03/17	03/18	03/19
Sales ($mil.)	25.6%	–	870.8	923.3	1,300.9	1,725.6
Net income ($ mil.)	–	–	47.8	61.4	71.9	(28.7)
Market value ($ mil.)	–	–	–	–	–	–
Employees	–	–	–	–	–	8,400

MULTI-FINELINE ELECTRONIX, INC.

101 ACADEMY STE 250
IRVINE, CA 926173035
Phone: 949 453-6800
Fax: –
Web: www.mflex.com

CEO: Reza Meshgin
CFO: Tom Kampfer
HR: –
FYE: December 31
Type: Private

Multi-Fineline Electronix (MFLEX) is one of the largest flexible printed circuit manufacturers, assemblers and suppliers across the globe. The company manufactures a variety of flexible printed circuit boards (FPC), Flexible Circuit Assemblies, and Module Assembly. Its FPC products include adhesive and adhesive-less materials, thin dielectric materials, thin copper, and more. Current applications for its products include computer/data storage, portable bar code scanners, personal computers, wearables, medical, automotive, industrial and other consumer electronic devices. In addition, it also offers services such as application engineering, modeling and simulation, and manufacturing support. MFLEX is managed by Suzhou Dongshan Precision Manufacturing Co., Ltd. (DSBJ). The company traces its roots back to 1984.

MULTI-MEDIA TUTORIAL SERVICES, INC.   NBB: MMTS

1214 East 15th Street
Brooklyn, NY 11230
Phone: 718 951-2350
Fax: –
Web: www.tutorialchannel.com

CEO: –
CFO: –
HR: –
FYE: February 29
Type: Public

Math may be easy for Multi-Media Tutorial Services, but making a profit is not. The financially struggling company produces and markets Math Made Easy educational DVDs, a series of more than 100 titles that teach basic arithmetic, word problems, and other math skills. Its products can be purchased on its MathMadeEasy.com Web site, which also provides online tutorial programs. Multi-Media Tutorial Services also offers the Reading Made Easy series of literacy and reading comprehension tapes. The company targets grade school, middle school, high school and college learners.

	Annual Growth	02/04	02/05	02/06	02/07	02/08
Sales ($mil.)	(6.1%)	0.8	0.9	1.1	0.8	0.7
Net income ($ mil.)	–	–	(0.5)	(0.4)	(0.4)	(0.8)	(1.5)
Market value ($ mil.)	(33.7%)	7.4	3.2	4.2	5.9	1.4
Employees	5.7%	20	22	26	20	25

MULTI-SHIFTER, INC.

11110 PARK CHARLOTTE BLVD
CHARLOTTE, NC 282738859
Phone: 704 588-9611
Fax: –
Web: www.multi-shifter.com

CEO: –
CFO: Kelly Minchener
HR: –
FYE: December 31
Type: Private

Few companies can multi-task like Multi-Shifter, Inc. The company manufactures industrial battery handling equipment, including battery changing vehicles, storage, washing, and wastewater filtration systems. Its products are distributed largely to companies that operate electrically powered forklift trucks. Since its founding in 1974, Multi-Shifter has installed more than 2,000 battery handling systems across North America, Australia, and Europe; over 200 of these workhorses are touted to be 15 to 20 years old, and still operating. Multi-Shifter garners the business of blue chip companies, such as Apple, Ford Motor, General Electric, and Michelin. Multi-Shifter is owned and led by its founder's son, John Pratt.

	Annual Growth	12/06	12/07	12/08	12/09	12/11
Sales ($mil.)	(9.2%)	–	–	5.3	3.4	4.0
Net income ($ mil.)	20.8%	–	–	0.2	0.2	0.3
Market value ($ mil.)	–	–	–	–	–	–
Employees	–	–	–	–	–	15

MULTI-STATE LOTTERY ASSOCIATION

13001 UNIVERSITY AVE
CLIVE, IA 503258225
Phone: 515 725-7900
Fax: –
Web: www.musl.com

CEO: Terry Rich
CFO: –
HR: –
FYE: June 30
Type: Private

It takes a lot of MUSL to produce some of the largest jackpots in the world. Made up of 30 state lotteries, as well as those of the District of Columbia and the US Virgin Islands, the Multi-State Lottery Association (MUSL) operates the popular Powerball drawing, which has produced some of the world's largest jackpot prizes. Through MUSL, states can combine their buying power to achieve large jackpots and drive lottery sales. The not-for-profit association, which pays out half of its ticket sales in prizes and uses the other half to help fund each member/state's legislature's projects, allows the member/states to share the cost of lottery operation.

MULTICARE HEALTH SYSTEM

315 MARTIN LUTHER KING JR WAY
TACOMA, WA 984054234
Phone: 253 403-1000
Fax: –
Web: www.multicare.org

CEO: William G Robertson
CFO: James Lee
HR: –
FYE: December 31
Type: Private

MultiCare Health System is a not-for-profit health system that serves the residents in the southern Puget Sound region and southwestern Washington. Altogether, the system's eight hospitals have more than 1,895 beds. The largest facility, Tacoma General, boasts more than 435 beds and provides specialized cancer, cardiac, orthopedic, trauma care, general medical and surgical care. Other medical centers include Good Samaritan Hospital (with approximately 375 beds), Allenmore Hospital (some 130 beds), Auburn Regional Medical Center (approximately 195 beds), and Mary Bridge Children's Hospital (more than 80 beds). Wellfound Behavioral Health Hospital is an independently operated joint venture of MultiCare and CHI Franciscan Health.

	Annual Growth	12/18	12/19	12/20	12/21	12/22
Sales ($mil.)	7.4%	–	3,234.1	3,367.4	3,824.2	4,003.7
Net income ($ mil.)	–	–	336.3	311.4	352.6	(515.0)
Market value ($ mil.)	–	–	–	–	–	–
Employees	–	–	–	–	–	6,510

MULTICELL TECHNOLOGIES INC   NBB: MCET

68 Cumberland Street, Suite 301
Woonsocket, RI 02895
Phone: 401 762-0045
Fax: –
Web: www.multicelltech.com

CEO: W G Newmin
CFO: –
HR: –
FYE: November 30
Type: Public

MultiCell Technologies is working on multiple therapeutics, but still sells liver cells on the side to help pay the rent. It is developing drug candidates to treat degenerative neurological diseases. Its MCT-125 candidate is being developed as a treatment for the fatigue that comes with multiple sclerosis while MCT-175 is intended to slow the progression of the disease. Two other candidates are targeting breast and cervical cancers. MultiCell also produces liver cells (hepatocytes) and a serum-free culture medium for research. Larger firms, including Corning and Pfizer, have licensed the company's liver cell lines.

	Annual Growth	11/10	11/11	11/12	11/13	11/14
Sales ($mil.)	(16.0%)	0.0	0.0	0.0	0.0	0.0
Net income ($ mil.)	–	(1.2)	(1.8)	(1.3)	(1.2)	(0.4)
Market value ($ mil.)	(40.5%)	18.2	22.3	5.9	3.2	2.3
Employees	–	2	2	2	2	2

MUNCY COLUMBIA FINANCIAL CORP   NBB: CCFN

232 East Street
Bloomsburg, PA 17815
Phone: 570 784-1660
Fax: –
Web: www.firstcolumbiabank.com

CEO: Lance O Diehl
CFO: Jeffrey T Arnold
HR: –
FYE: December 31
Type: Public

CCFNB Bancorp knows the ABCs of banking. It is the holding company for First Columbia Bank & Trust, a community institution serving Pennsylvania's Columbia, Montour, Northumberland, and Luzerne counties from some 15 locations. The bank offers standard products and services as well as wealth management and trust services. It uses funds from deposits to write a variety of loans; real estate loans account for more than 80% of its loan portfolio. The bank also offers consumer and construction loans. CCFNB Bancorp owns a 50% stake in Neighborhood Group (dba Neighborhood Advisors), an insurance and financial products agency. CCFNB Bancorp merged with Columbia Financial Corporation in 2008.

	Annual Growth	12/19	12/20	12/21	12/22	12/23
Assets ($mil.)	21.9%	742.7	855.1	952.7	944.0	1,639.8
Net income ($ mil.)	(21.5%)	8.9	9.3	9.4	9.5	3.4
Market value ($ mil.)	(7.6%)	173.9	157.1	186.2	171.4	126.7
Employees	19.4%	133	139	138	130	270

MUNICIPAL ELECTRIC AUTHORITY OF GEORGIA

1470 RIVEREDGE PKWY
ATLANTA, GA 303284640
Phone: 770 563-0300
Fax: –
Web: www.meagpower.org

CEO: –
CFO: –
HR: –
FYE: December 31
Type: Private

With more juice than a ripe Georgia peach, the Municipal Electric Authority of Georgia (MEAG Power) supplies wholesale electric power. The authority has a generating capacity of 2,069 MW through its interests in nuclear and fossil-fueled plants. Some 49% of the energy MEAG Power delivered in 2012 came from its nuclear plants. MEAG Power transmits electricity to 48 municipal and one county distribution systems across Georgia that in turn serve some 600,000 consumers. It utilizes a transmission network that is co-owned by all the power suppliers in Georgia, although it is considering joining a regional transmission organization (RTO) to further defray costs.

	Annual Growth	12/17	12/18	12/19	12/20	12/21
Sales ($mil.)	1.6%	–	681.3	648.9	639.7	714.2
Net income ($ mil.)	–	–	(4.1)	17.7	23.1	77.0
Market value ($ mil.)	–	–	–	–	–	–
Employees	–	–	–	–	–	150

MUNICIPAL UTILITIES BOARD OF DECATUR, MORGAN COUNTY, ALABAMA

1002 CENTRAL PKWY SW
DECATUR, AL 356014848
Phone: 256 552-1400
Fax: –
Web: www.decaturutilities.com

CEO: –
CFO: –
HR: –
FYE: September 30
Type: Private

Decatur Utilities (the operating name of the Municipal Utilities Board of Decatur) caters to the power, gas, water, and wastewater needs of more than 30,000 residents (including 14,600 gas customers) of the city of Decatur, and Morgan County, in Alabama. In an area that experiences heavy rain, Decatur Utilities spends approximately $1 million each year to repair clay sewer pipe and brick manholes and other aging infrastructure. The Municipal Utilities Board of Decatur was created by the Alabama Legislature in 1939 to provide safe and reliable utility services to the city of Decatur.

	Annual Growth	06/99	06/00	06/01	06/02*	09/09
Sales ($mil.)	(25.8%)	–	–	1,538.4	–	141.3
Net income ($ mil.)	150.7%	–	–	0.0	–	0.4
Market value ($ mil.)	–	–	–	–	–	–
Employees	–	–	–	–	–	173

*Fiscal year change

MUNROE REGIONAL MEDICAL CENTER, INC.

1500 SW 1ST AVE
OCALA, FL 344716559
Phone: 352 351-7200
Fax: –
Web: www.munroeregional.com

CEO: –
CFO: –
HR: –
FYE: September 30
Type: Private

Munroe Regional Health System operates the Munroe Regional Medical Center and affiliated facilities serving residents of north central Florida's Marion County and surrounding areas. Munroe Regional Medical Center is a 500-bed acute care hospital that offers comprehensive medical, surgical, and emergency care, along with programs devoted to cardiovascular care, stroke prevention and care, orthopedics, and women's health. The system also provides home health services and operates outpatient clinics providing primary care, diagnostic, and rehabilitation therapy services. Adventist Health System subsidiary Florida Hospital acquired the hospital's lease and operations from Community Health Systems in mid-2018.

	Annual Growth	09/05	09/06	09/08	09/09	09/17
Sales ($mil.)	(0.3%)	–	263.0	312.1	313.6	254.5
Net income ($ mil.)	–	–	4.1	(3.3)	(7.4)	(19.3)
Market value ($ mil.)	–	–	–	–	–	–
Employees	–	–	–	–	–	2,179

MUNSON HEALTHCARE

1105 SIXTH ST
TRAVERSE CITY, MI 496842345
Phone: 800 252-2065
Fax: –
Web: www.munsonhealthcare.org

CEO: Ed Ness
CFO: –
HR: –
FYE: June 30
Type: Private

Munson Healthcare is a not-for-profit health care system serving residents in northern Michigan. Its flagship facility is Munson Medical Center in Traverse City, a regional referral hospital with about 390 beds offering specialty services including cancer treatment, behavioral health, cardiac care, and orthopedics. Munson Healthcare also has management agreements and other types of affiliations with about a dozen other hospitals in the region. In addition, Munson Healthcare operates urgent care and community clinics, home health care and hospice agencies, an ambulance service, and the Northern Michigan Supply Alliance, a supply chain management group co-owned with Trinity Health.

	Annual Growth	06/17	06/18	06/20	06/21	06/22
Sales ($mil.)	5.4%	–	1,039.2	1,144.5	1,258.3	1,284.2
Net income ($ mil.)	–	–	142.6	39.1	260.3	(48.6)
Market value ($ mil.)	–	–	–	–	–	–
Employees	–	–	–	–	–	4,000

MURPHY COMPANY MECHANICAL CONTRACTORS AND ENGINEERS

1233 N PRICE RD
SAINT LOUIS, MO 631322303
Phone: 314 997-6600
Fax: –
Web: www.murphynet.com

CEO: James J Murphy Jr
CFO: Robert L Koester
HR: –
FYE: March 31
Type: Private

Keeping Murphy's Law from plaguing construction projects is a task handled by Murphy Company Mechanical Contractors and Engineers. One of the nation's top mechanical contractors, Murphy Company provides energy, HVAC, plumbing, piping, and design/build services to the commercial, industrial, heavy industrial, and institutional markets. Its projects range from new and retrofit construction to clean manufacturing (for biotechnology or microelectronics clients). The company, which offers 24-hour service, became LEED-certified in mid-2011. Clients have included Harrah's and Pfizer. The Murphy Company was founded in 1907 and continues to be controlled and managed by members of the founding family.

MURPHY OIL CORP

NYS: MUR

9805 Katy Fwy, Suite G-200
Houston, TX 77024
Phone: 281 675-9000
Fax: –
Web: www.murphyoilcorp.com

CEO: Roger W Jenkins
CFO: Thomas J Mireles
HR: –
FYE: December 31
Type: Public

Murphy Oil Corporation is a global oil and natural gas exploration and production company, with both onshore and offshore operations and properties. It produces crude oil, natural gas, and natural gas liquids primarily in the US and Canada, and explores oil and gas in target areas worldwide. The company partially or wholly owns almost 970 oil wells and nearly 350 gas wells worldwide, with proved reserves of about 715.4 million barrels of oil equivalent. Murphy Oil's major holdings include fields in the Eagle Ford Shale area, the deep-water Gulf of Mexico, and the Hibernia and Terra Nova in Canada. About 80% of sales were generated in the US.

	Annual Growth	12/19	12/20	12/21	12/22	12/23
Sales ($mil.)	5.2%	2,829.1	1,967.3	2,299.3	3,932.7	3,460.1
Net income ($ mil.)	(12.9%)	1,149.7	(1,148.8)	(73.7)	965.0	661.6
Market value ($ mil.)	12.3%	4,093.7	1,848.3	3,988.3	6,569.7	6,516.3
Employees	(3.1%)	822	675	696	691	725

MURPHY USA INC

NYS: MUSA

200 Peach Street
El Dorado, AR 71730-5836
Phone: 870 875-7600
Fax: –
Web: www.murphyusa.com

CEO: –
CFO: –
HR: –
FYE: December 31
Type: Public

Former operating unit of Murphy Oil Corporation, Murphy USA (MUSA) markets refined products through its network of branded gasoline stations and convenience stores customers and unbranded wholesale customers in more than 25 Southeast, Southwest and Midwest US states. The company's around 1,150 retail gas stations (almost all of which are in close proximity to Walmart stores) sell gas under the Murphy USA brand. It also operates about 405 Murphy Express locations and sells some 4.8 billion gallons of motor fuel through retail outlets.

	Annual Growth	12/19	12/20	12/21	12/22	12/23
Sales ($mil.)	11.3%	14,035	11,264	17,361	23,446	21,529
Net income ($ mil.)	37.7%	154.8	386.1	396.9	672.9	556.8
Market value ($ mil.)	32.1%	2,438.0	2,727.0	4,151.6	5,824.9	7,429.8
Employees	12.0%	9,900	9,900	14,615	15,100	15,600

MUSCULAR DYSTROPHY ASSOCIATION, INC.

222 S RIVERSIDE PLZ STE 1500
CHICAGO, IL 606065808
Phone: 520 529-2000
Fax: –
Web: www.mda.org

CEO: Lynn O Vos
CFO: Michael Kennedy
HR: –
FYE: December 31
Type: Private

The Muscular Dystrophy Association (MDA) is a not-for-profit national voluntary health agency supporting worldwide research at hundreds of universities and hospitals to find effective treatments and cures for neuromuscular diseases. Through more than 150 association-supported, hospital-affiliated care centers and its field offices nationwide, the association offers comprehensive medical services, education, and support to patients and their families. The association produces and distributes educational information about neuromuscular diseases in the form of publications and seminars for the medical and scientific community and the general public. It receives the vast majority of its revenue from individual contributors. The association has strong partnerships with Citgo, Kroger, Acosta, Harley Davidson, and Casey's General Store. Founded in 1950, MDA is funded by private contributions.

	Annual Growth	12/12	12/13	12/14	12/15	12/22
Sales ($mil.)	(9.4%)	–	153.0	139.8	126.0	63.2
Net income ($ mil.)	(15.6%)	–	19.7	(15.0)	5.2	4.3
Market value ($ mil.)	–	–	–	–	–	–
Employees	–	–	–	–	–	950

MUSEUM OF FINE ARTS

465 HUNTINGTON AVE
BOSTON, MA 021155597
Phone: 617 267-9300
Fax: –
Web: www.mfa.org

CEO: Richard Lubin
CFO: –
HR: Maureen O'Reilly
FYE: June 30
Type: Private

In a city known for its erudite inhabitants, the The Museum of Fine Arts (MFA), Boston is one of the most comprehensive art museums in the world. The MFA offers a wide range of collections such as Art of Americas, Art of Europe, Art of the Ancient World, Contemporary Art, Textile and Fashion Arts, and Musical Instruments. The museum also provides public programs for children and adults, including art classes and workshops. With over 70,000 member households, the MFA attracts some 1.4 million visitors annually. Founded in 1870 the museum, through a partnership, moved to Huntington Avenue in 1909.

	Annual Growth	06/08	06/09	06/10	06/13	06/15
Sales ($mil.)	13.9%	–	69.2	122.8	131.5	151.0
Net income ($ mil.)	–	–	(49.8)	7.2	(8.9)	13.8
Market value ($ mil.)	–	–	–	–	–	–
Employees	–	–	–	–	–	1,000

MUSEUM OF THE CITY OF NEW YORK, INC.

1220 5TH AVE
NEW YORK, NY 100295221
Phone: 212 534-1672
Fax: –
Web: www.mcny.org

CEO: –
CFO: –
HR: Candace Washington
FYE: June 30
Type: Private

You wouldn't think a city as quiet and unassuming as New York would go in for tooting its own cultural and historical horn, but that it does at the corner of Fifth Ave. and 103rd. The Museum of the City of New York (MCNY) is modestly dedicated to preserving the history of the City So Nice They Named It A Second Time. MCNY can boast -- not that it would, being from New York and all -- strong collections in photography, theater history, and of Currier and Ives hand-colored lithographs. The MCNY also awards the Gotham Giant award to "New Yorkers whose contributions to the life of the city stand out and merit recognition." The museum was founded in Gracie Mansion in 1923, and moved to its current location in 1932.

	Annual Growth	06/17	06/18	06/20	06/21	06/22
Sales ($mil.)	7.2%	–	12.1	13.8	13.9	15.9
Net income ($ mil.)	–	–	(3.5)	0.5	3.4	3.4
Market value ($ mil.)	–	–	–	–	–	–
Employees	–	–	–	–	–	85

MUSTANG FUEL CORPORATION

9800 N OKLAHOMA AVE
OKLAHOMA CITY, OK 731147406
Phone: 405 884-2092
Fax: –
Web: www.mustangfuel.com

CEO: Carey Joullian IV
CFO: –
HR: Stephanie McCarty
FYE: December 31
Type: Private

Like a good mustang, Mustang Fuel is independent -- an independent oil and gas exploration, production, transportation and marketing company, that is. The company owns and operates 200 properties and owns non-operated interests in more than 1,300 other properties. It also controls more than 100,000 net undeveloped leasehold acres in a four-state service region. Mustang Fuel also owns natural gas gathering and transporting pipelines, operates one of the largest gas processing facilities in Oklahoma, and has a fleet of trucks that transports petroleum products. It also markets gas. Subsidiaries include Mustang Fuel Marketing Company and Mustang Gas Products, LLC.

	Annual Growth	12/03	12/04	12/05	12/08	12/09
Sales ($mil.)	(5.2%)	–	313.7	441.4	482.2	240.7
Net income ($ mil.)	52.7%	–	1.7	24.6	43.4	13.7
Market value ($ mil.)	–	–	–	–	–	–
Employees	–	–	–	–	–	124

MUSTANG MACHINERY COMPANY, LLC

12800 NORTHWEST FWY
HOUSTON, TX 770406302
Phone: 713 460-2000
Fax: –
Web: www.mustangcat.com

CEO: Bradford Tucker
CFO: –
HR: –
FYE: January 31
Type: Private

Mustang CAT is a privately-held Cat dealership that sells and leases new and used Caterpillar brand construction machinery and power systems to its customers in Southeast Texas. Mustang CAT provides Caterpillar construction equipment and a selected group of allied lines, and Caterpillar engines as well as the design, engineering, and fabrication of engine packages in a wide range of power ratings. The Cat Rental Store offers Caterpillar and allied lines of large and small equipment for the building construction industry. Other services include engine repair, scheduled oil sampling, and performance analysis reports. Mustang Cat has served the local community as a family-owned business since 1952.

MUTUAL OF OMAHA INSURANCE CO. (NE)

Mutual Of Omaha Plaza
Omaha, NE 68175
Phone: 402 342-7600
Fax: –
Web: www.mutualofomaha.com

CEO: Jeffrey R Schmid
CFO: David A Diamond
HR: Mark Saldivar
FYE: December 31
Type: Public

Founded in 1909, Mutual of Omaha Insurance Company is a mutual life, accident and health insurance company. It provides individual, group, and employee benefits products through a range of affiliated companies. It offers Medicare supplement, disability, illness, and long-term care coverage, as well as life insurance and annuities through its United of Omaha Life Insurance. Its Mutual of Omaha Investor Services offers brokerage services, pension plans, and mutual funds.

	Annual Growth	12/11	12/12	12/13	12/14	12/15
Assets ($mil.)	5.1%	29,198	30,993	5,795.4	6,426.8	35,629
Net income ($ mil.)	26.5%	130.1	283.8	105.8	30.4	333.0
Market value ($ mil.)	–	–	–	–	–	–
Employees	–	–	–	–	–	–

MV OIL TRUST

NYS: MVO

The Bank of New York Mellon Trust Company, N.A., Trustee, Global Corporate Trust, 601 Tr
Houston, TX 77002
Phone: 713 483-6020
Fax: –
Web: –

CEO: –
CFO: –
HR: –
FYE: December 31
Type: Public

Call it what you will, black gold, Texas tea, or the black blood of the earth, MV Oil Trust is wringing out the value from each drop and distributing it to shareholders. MV Oil Trust receives royalty interests from the mature oil and gas properties of MV Partners located in Kansas and Colorado. The properties have proved reserves of 9.5 million barrels of oil from 922 net wells. The trust receives royalties based on the amount of oil (and gas) produced and sold and then distributes virtually all of the proceeds to shareholders on a regular basis. MV Partners, a private company engaged in the exploration, production, gathering, aggregation, and sale of oil and natural gas, has the rights to 80% of net proceeds.

	Annual Growth	12/19	12/20	12/21	12/22	12/23
Sales ($mil.)	8.6%	13.0	6.8	12.1	27.2	18.1
Net income ($ mil.)	8.6%	12.1	5.6	11.3	25.5	16.8
Market value ($ mil.)	17.7%	72.1	35.9	101.5	187.8	138.2
Employees	–	–	–	–	–	–

MV TRANSPORTATION, INC.

2711 N HASKELL AVE STE 1500
DALLAS, TX 752042911
Phone: 972 391-4600
Fax: –
Web: www.mvtransit.com

CEO: Thomas A Egan
CFO: Erin Niewinski
HR: Dan Abfalter
FYE: December 31
Type: Private

Need to supply transportation by bus? MV Transportation will run your bus system so you don't have to. The company operates more than 200 contracts to offer fixed-route and shuttle bus services, as well as paratransit (transportation of people with disabilities) and transportation of Medicaid beneficiaries. Its customers consist primarily of transit authorities and other state and local government agencies responsible for public transportation. MV Transportation operates in more than 130 locations spanning 28 US states and in British Columbia, Canada and Saudi Arabia; overall, the company maintains a fleet of about 7,000 vehicles. MV Transportation was founded in 1975.

	Annual Growth	12/05	12/06	12/07	12/08	12/09
Sales ($mil.)	29.3%	–	–	422.6	646.0	706.5
Net income ($ mil.)	–	–	–	–	(3.0)	23.5
Market value ($ mil.)	–	–	–	–	–	–
Employees	–	–	–	–	–	20,000

MVP HEALTH PLAN, INC.

625 STATE ST
SCHENECTADY, NY 123052260
Phone: 518 370-4793
Fax: –
Web: www.mvphealthcare.com

CEO: David Oliker
CFO: Mark Fish
HR: Jan Cozzy
FYE: December 31
Type: Private

MVP Health Plan, also know as MVP Health Care, provides health insurance and employee benefits to its more than 700,000 members in upstate New York, New Hampshire, and Vermont. MVP, a not-for-profit organization, offers a variety of plans including HMO, PPO, and indemnity coverage, as well as dental plans, health accounts, and Medicare Advantage plans. Subsidiary MVP Select Care provides third-party administration (TPA) services for self-insured employers. MVP Health Care was founded in 1983 as Mohawk Valley Physicians' Health Plan.

	Annual Growth	12/11	12/12	12/13	12/14	12/15
Assets ($mil.)	9.2%	–	–	–	540.3	589.9
Net income ($ mil.)	–	–	–	–	(26.3)	11.1
Market value ($ mil.)	–	–	–	–	–	–
Employees	–	–	–	–	–	1,500

MW BUILDERS, INC.

18725 W 109TH ST
LENEXA, KS 662154137
Phone: 913 469-0101
Fax: –
Web: www.mwbuilders.com

CEO: –
CFO: David Cimpl
HR: –
FYE: December 31
Type: Private

MW Builders, a subsidiary of MMC Corp., provides construction management and general contracting services in the US. The group focuses on commercial construction projects for sectors including entertainment, higher education, hospitality, health care, and senior living. MW Builders was incorporated in 1971. The employee-owned company operates from offices in Overland Park, Kansas; and Salado, Texas.

MWH GLOBAL, INC.

370 INTERLOCKEN BLVD STE 300
BROOMFIELD, CO 800218009
Phone: 303 533-1900
Fax: –
Web: www.mwhconstructors.com

CEO: Alan J Krause
CFO: David G Barnes
HR: Darrell Gallo
FYE: January 01
Type: Private

MWH Global is an environmental engineering, construction, and management firm that specializes in water-related projects or "wet infrastructure." The company's typical projects include building water treatment or desalination plants, water transmission systems, or storage facilitates. MWH also provides general building services for transportation, energy, mining, ports and waterways, and industrial projects. The company is active in some 35 countries and serves governments, public utilities, and private sector clients. Affiliates of the employee-owned company include software provider Innovyze, and business and government relations firm mCapitol. Canadian Engineering firm Stantec acquired MWH Global for $795 million in May 2016.

	Annual Growth	12/00	12/01*	01/03*	12/05*	01/16
Sales ($mil.)	3.6%	–	774.5	975.9	946.0	1,318.2
Net income ($ mil.)	4.0%	–	19.8	942.3	–	35.9
Market value ($ mil.)	–	–	–	–	–	–
Employees	–	–	–	–	–	6,700

*Fiscal year change

MYERS INDUSTRIES INC. NYS: MYE

1293 S. Main Street
Akron, OH 44301
Phone: 330 253-5592
Fax: 330 761-6156
Web: www.myersindustries.com

CEO: Michael McGaugh
CFO: Sonal P Robinson
HR: Brandi Buescher
FYE: December 31
Type: Public

Myers Industries is a leading manufacturer of plastic reusable material handling containers and pallets, and plastic fuel tanks as well as the largest distributor of tools, equipment and supplies for the tire, wheel and under vehicle service industry in the US. Material Handling offers portable plastic fuel tanks and water containers and storage totes. Myers' Distribution segment engaged in the distribution of tools, equipment, and supplies used for tire, wheel and under-vehicle service. International net sales accounted for approximately 5% of its total net sales. Myers Industries was founded in 1933.

	Annual Growth	12/19	12/20	12/21	12/22	12/23
Sales ($mil.)	12.1%	515.7	510.4	761.4	899.5	813.1
Net income ($ mil.)	19.0%	24.3	36.8	33.5	60.3	48.9
Market value ($ mil.)	4.0%	614.6	765.7	737.3	819.1	720.4
Employees	11.1%	1,640	2,400	2,725	2,500	2,500

MYMD PHARMACEUTICALS INC NAS: MYMD

855 N. Wolfe Street, Suite 601
Baltimore, MD 21205
Phone: 856 848-8698
Fax: –
Web: www.mymd.com

CEO: Chris Chapman
CFO: Ian Rhodes
HR: –
FYE: December 31
Type: Public

When there's no time to send a sample off to the lab, Akers Biosciences (ABI) steps up. The company manufactures a variety of point-of-care rapid diagnostic tests. It has produced diagnostic tests for the detection of allergic reactions to Heparin and BreathScan Alcohol Detectors for on- and off-the-job alcohol safety initiatives. In addition, it also has particle immuno-filtration assay (PIFA) Technology platform. PIFA technology is a patented immunoassay method which rapidly and accurately detects target antigens or antibodies. ABI customers include health care providers (hospitals) as well Medicare and Medicaid programs, and private payors, such as indemnity insurers and managed care plans. The company entered into a membership interest purchase agreement (MIPA) with the members of Cystron Biotech, LLC. Almost all of its revenue accounted in the US.

	Annual Growth	12/18	12/19	12/20	12/21	12/22
Sales ($mil.)	–	1.7	1.6	–	–	–
Net income ($ mil.)	–	(10.8)	(3.9)	(17.6)	(29.9)	(15.2)
Market value ($ mil.)	0.4%	1.5	4.2	2.6	8.0	1.5
Employees	(8.8%)	13	12	4	9	9

MYR GROUP INC NMS: MYRG

12121 Grant Street, Suite 610
Thornton, CO 80241
Phone: 303 286-8000
Fax: –
Web: www.myrgroup.com

CEO: Richard S Swartz Jr
CFO: Betty R Johnson
HR: –
FYE: December 31
Type: Public

MYR Group is a holding company of specialty electrical construction service providers that was established in 1995 through the merger of long-standing specialty contractors and constructs transmission and distribution lines for the electric utility infrastructure, commercial, and industrial construction markets. The company also installs and maintains electrical wiring in commercial and industrial facilities and traffic and rail systems. The company operates nationwide through subsidiaries, including The L.E. Myers Co., Harlan Electric, Sturgeon Electric, MYR Transmission Services, and Great Southwestern Construction.

	Annual Growth	12/19	12/20	12/21	12/22	12/23
Sales ($mil.)	15.2%	2,071.2	2,247.4	2,498.3	3,008.5	3,643.9
Net income ($ mil.)	24.6%	37.7	58.8	85.0	83.4	91.0
Market value ($ mil.)	45.1%	543.7	1,002.7	1,844.5	1,536.1	2,413.1
Employees	6.1%	7,100	7,200	7,600	8,500	9,000

MYREXIS, INC. NBB: MYRX

c/o Xstelos Holdings, Inc., 630 Fifth Avenue, Suite 2260
New York, NY 10020
Phone: 801 214-7800
Fax: –
Web: www.myrexis.com

CEO: –
CFO: Jonathan M Couchman
HR: –
FYE: June 30
Type: Public

Myrexis hoped to convince cancer cells to stop dividing and die with the destabilizing agent drugs in its pipeline. The pharmaceutical development firm's pipeline consisted of oncology compounds in clinical and preclinical R&D stages, including drugs aiming to treat solid tumors and relapsed cancers. However, the company restructured its operations and slashed its workforce in 2011 after deciding to halt clinical trials on its leading candidate, Azixa (a metastatic tumor drug), in order to focus on its more promising early stage development compounds. Then, in early 2012, it halted all remaining development activities and began exploring strategic alternatives. In November 2012 Myrexis announced plans to liquidate.

	Annual Growth	06/09	06/10	06/11	06/12	06/13
Sales ($mil.)	–	5.5	0.0	0.2	–	–
Net income ($ mil.)	–	(58.1)	(47.0)	(38.7)	(31.2)	(11.6)
Market value ($ mil.)	(64.4%)	160.3	129.6	123.4	90.0	2.6
Employees	(72.7%)	181	152	81	10	1

MYRIAD GENETICS, INC. NMS: MYGN

322 North 2200 West
Salt Lake City, UT 84116
Phone: 801 584-3600
Fax: –
Web: www.myriad.com

CEO: Paul J Diaz
CFO: R B Riggsbee
HR: Angela Conde
FYE: December 31
Type: Public

Myriad Genetics is a leading genetic testing and precision medicine company dedicated to advancing health and well-being for all. Myriad discovers and commercializes genetic tests that determine the risk of developing disease, assess the risk of disease progression, and guide treatment decisions across medical specialties where critical genetic insights can significantly improve patient care and lower healthcare costs. Myriad Genetics markets its products in the US (which accounts for more than 85% of total revenue) through its own sales force and uses collaborations to sell them elsewhere.

	Annual Growth	06/20*	12/20	12/21	12/22	12/23
Sales ($mil.)	4.2%	638.6	299.8	690.6	678.4	753.2
Net income ($ mil.)	–	(199.5)	(53.1)	(27.2)	(112.0)	(263.3)
Market value ($ mil.)	14.0%	1,019.5	1,777.8	2,481.2	1,304.4	1,720.7
Employees	–	2,700	2,700	2,400	2,600	2,700

*Fiscal year change

N-VIRO INTERNATIONAL CORP

2254 Centennial Road
Toledo, OH 43617
Phone: 419 535-6374
Fax: –
Web: www.nviro.com

CEO: Timothy R Kasmoch
CFO: James K McHugh
HR: –
FYE: December 31
Type: Public

Wastewater sludge smells like money to N-Viro International. The company's patented process converts sludge and other bio-organic waste into a better-quality soil by treating it with alkaline byproducts. The treated N-Viro Soil is used in agriculture and as a landfill cover material, among other applications. N-Viro has licensed its recycling process to more than 25 wastewater treatment plants around the world. Outside the US, the company's process is marketed through a network of agents. N-Viro International itself manages two facilities that use the process, under a contract with the City of Toledo, Ohio, and another in Florida.

	Annual Growth	12/11	12/12	12/13	12/14	12/15
Sales ($mil.)	(32.1%)	5.6	3.6	3.4	1.3	1.2
Net income ($ mil.)	–	(1.6)	(1.6)	(1.6)	(1.8)	(2.3)
Market value ($ mil.)	(10.8%)	10.0	8.2	11.8	23.3	6.3
Employees	(22.7%)	28	18	19	12	10

NACCO INDUSTRIES INC
NYS: NC

5875 Landerbrook Drive, Suite 220
Cleveland, OH 44124-4069
Phone: 440 229-5151
Fax: –
Web: www.nacco.com

CEO: J C Butler Jr
CFO: Elizabeth I Loveman
HR: –
FYE: December 31
Type: Public

NACCO Industries brings natural resources to life by delivering aggregates, minerals, reliable fuels, and environmental solutions through its robust portfolio of NACCO Natural Resources businesses. The company conducts its businesses through three segments: Coal Mining, North American Mining (NAMining), and Minerals Management. The Coal Mining segment operates surface coal mines for power generation companies. The NAMining operates mines in Florida, Texas, Arkansas, Indiana, Virginia, and Nebraska and will serve as exclusive contract miner for the Thacker Pass lithium project in northern Nevada. The company's operating coal mines include Bisti Fuels Company, Coteau, Coyote Creek Mining Company, Demery Resources Company, Falkirk, Mississippi Lignite Mining Company, and Sabine. In addition, the company also has a business providing stream and wetland mitigation solutions.

	Annual Growth	12/19	12/20	12/21	12/22	12/23
Sales ($mil.)	11.1%	141.0	128.4	191.8	241.7	214.8
Net income ($ mil.)	–	39.6	14.8	48.1	74.2	(39.6)
Market value ($ mil.)	(6.0%)	348.8	195.9	270.3	283.0	271.9
Employees	(8.3%)	2,400	2,000	1,600	1,600	1,700

NAISMITH MEMORIAL BASKETBALL HALL OF FAME, INC

1000 W COLUMBUS AVE
SPRINGFIELD, MA 011052518
Phone: 413 781-6500
Fax: –
Web: www.hoophall.com

CEO: –
CFO: –
HR: –
FYE: December 31
Type: Private

The Naismith Memorial Basketball Hall of Fame is dedicated to promoting and preserving the history of the game of basketball. It boasts the Edward J. and Gena G. Hickox Library, which documents the sport as played by men and women at all levels from high school to professional, not only in the US but also internationally. The Hall of Fame's more than 285 inductees include the game's most prominent figures, such as college coaching legend and player John Wooden, professional players Wilt Chamberlain and Julius "Dr. J" Erving, and the inventor of the game, James Naismith, for whom the Hall of Fame is named.

	Annual Growth	12/00	12/01	12/05	12/06	12/13
Sales ($mil.)	–	–	(1,296.6)	6.7	4.8	6.6
Net income ($ mil.)	74.5%	–	0.0	(1.1)	0.7	0.2
Market value ($ mil.)	–	–	–	–	–	–
Employees	–	–	–	–	–	7

NAMI-MAINE

3803 FAIRFAX DR STE 100
ARLINGTON, VA 222035860
Phone: 703 524-7600
Fax: –
Web: www.nami.org

CEO: –
CFO: Peggy Stedman
HR: Blythe Laney
FYE: December 31
Type: Private

When you can't trust the stuff in your own head, who can you trust? The National Alliance for the Mentally Ill (NAMI) helps the millions of people in the US who have severe mental illnesses such as autism, bipolar disorder, major depression, obsessive-compulsive disorder, and schizophrenia, and their families. NAMI's Veterans Resource Center supports veterans, soldiers, and their families. NAMI's mission is to provide support and education, help combat stigmas, and improve the quality of life for mentally ill people. It also advocates for better care and jobs as well as more research funding. The organization operates through more than 1,100 local affiliates in all 50 states. NAMI was founded in 1979.

	Annual Growth	12/14	12/15	12/19	12/20	12/21
Sales ($mil.)	20.6%	–	10.4	19.4	26.5	31.9
Net income ($ mil.)	–	–	(0.9)	1.4	7.1	9.2
Market value ($ mil.)	–	–	–	–	–	–
Employees	–	–	–	–	–	72

NAN YA PLASTICS CORPORATION, AMERICA

9 PEACH TREE HILL RD
LIVINGSTON, NJ 070395702
Phone: 973 992-1775
Fax: –
Web: www.npcusa.com

CEO: –
CFO: –
HR: –
FYE: December 31
Type: Private

Where do artificial Christmas trees come from? It's Nan Ya business. More specifically, it's Nan Ya Plastics Corporation USA's business. A subsidiary of Taiwanese firm Nan Ya Plastics-- itself a unit of Formosa Plastics Corporation-- the company produces rigid PVC film that is used in the making of such products as artificial trees, packaging material, stationery, water treatment panels and baffles, and shrink wrap. Established in 1983, Nan Ya Plastics Corporation USA is based in New Jersey and also operates a PVC manufacturing plant in Wharton, Texas.

	Annual Growth	12/13	12/14	12/15	12/16	12/17
Sales ($mil.)	(3.3%)	–	124.9	120.3	116.7	113.1
Net income ($ mil.)	(25.2%)	–	4.9	7.0	10.3	2.0
Market value ($ mil.)	–	–	–	–	–	–
Employees	–	–	–	–	–	1,300

NANO MAGIC INC
NBB: NMGX

31601 Research Park Drive
Madison Heights, MI 48071
Phone: 844 273-6462
Fax: –
Web: www.nanomagic.com

CEO: Tom J Berman
CFO: Leandro Vera
HR: –
FYE: December 31
Type: Public

Applied Nanotech Holdings hopes to make it big by thinking small. The company conducts research on carbon nanotubes -- molecular-sized cylindrical structures that could be used in making electronic displays and other products. Applied Nanotech derives most of its revenues from contracts with agencies of the US government or by doing research on a contract basis with other entities. The company is developing nanomaterials for use in epoxies, glass fibers, and nylons. Other applications of carbon nanotube technology are in conductive inks (used in communications instrumentation, flexible electronics, printed circuit boards, and radio-frequency identification tags), sensors, and thermal management.

	Annual Growth	12/18	12/19	12/20	12/21	12/22
Sales ($mil.)	(12.2%)	4.3	2.4	4.8	5.0	2.6
Net income ($ mil.)	–	(0.1)	(1.0)	(0.8)	(1.6)	(2.1)
Market value ($ mil.)	2.6%	2.4	6.3	10.7	1.7	2.7
Employees	10.0%	13	12	21	35	19

NANOPHASE TECHNOLOGIES CORP.
NBB: NANX

1319 Marquette Drive
Romeoville, IL 60446
Phone: 630 771-6708
Fax: –
Web: www.nanophase.com

CEO: Jess A Jankowski
CFO: Jess A Jankowski
HR: –
FYE: December 31
Type: Public

Nanophase Technologies sweats the small stuff. The company is commercializing its nanocrystalline materials (molecular-size ceramic and metallic materials in powder form) for applications in advanced materials technology, such as conductive and antistatic coatings for computer monitors. It also develops abrasion-resistant coatings (with uses from coated vinyl flooring to contact lenses), environmental catalysts, health care products (sunscreen), and advanced ceramics (cutting tools and ceramic bearings). Chemicals maker BASF accounts for more than half of Nanophase's sales.

	Annual Growth	12/18	12/19	12/20	12/21	12/22
Sales ($mil.)	27.3%	14.2	12.5	17.1	29.5	37.3
Net income ($ mil.)	–	(2.1)	(3.0)	1.0	2.3	(2.6)
Market value ($ mil.)	11.5%	36.0	13.8	41.9	217.0	55.7
Employees	11.0%	54	53	54	58	82

NANOSTRING TECHNOLOGIES INC
NBB: NSTG Q

530 Fairview Avenue North
Seattle, WA 98109
Phone: 206 378-6266
Fax: –
Web: www.nanostring.com

CEO: R B Gray
CFO: K T Bailey
HR: –
FYE: December 31
Type: Public

NanoString Technologies develops, manufactures and markets technologies that unlock scientifically valuable and clinically actionable information from minute amounts of biological material. The company makes a complex genomic analysis device called the nCounter Analysis System, the device uses tissue extracted from a tumor to analyze up to 800 genes in a single experiment. These tests can help researchers understand the molecular basis of some diseases, such as cancer. In addition, the company has installed approximately 1,120 nCounter systems. The company makes some 65% of its sales in Americas.

	Annual Growth	12/18	12/19	12/20	12/21	12/22
Sales ($mil.)	4.5%	106.7	125.6	117.3	145.1	127.3
Net income ($ mil.)	–	(77.4)	(40.7)	(110.1)	(115.3)	(159.5)
Market value ($ mil.)	(14.4%)	692.8	1,299.7	3,124.6	1,972.9	372.4
Employees	10.2%	476	551	579	766	703

NANTHEALTH INC
NBB: NHIQ

760 W. Fire Tower Rd., Suite 107
Winterville, NC 28590
Phone: 855 949-6268
Fax: –
Web: www.nanthealth.com

CEO: –
CFO: –
HR: –
FYE: December 31
Type: Public

NantHealth uses Big Data to make cancer treatment personal. The company's employ precision medicine, data, and software-as-a-service (SaaS) solutions give physicians, payers, pharma, and patients actionable information that drives improved patient outcomes and economics across the healthcare ecosystem. Its diagnostic tool GPS Cancer (genomic proteomic spectrometry) collects molecular data to predict a patient's response to treatments. The company's cloud-based system is to help providers improve decision-making to reach better patient outcomes. NantHealth aims to catch the industry switch to reimbursements based on quality of care rather than quantity. Billionaire founder Dr. Patrick Soon-Shiong controls 59% of the company.

	Annual Growth	12/18	12/19	12/20	12/21	12/22
Sales ($mil.)	(7.0%)	89.5	96.0	73.2	62.6	67.0
Net income ($ mil.)	–	(192.2)	(62.8)	(56.3)	(58.3)	(67.8)
Market value ($ mil.)	60.9%	4.2	7.9	24.9	8.1	28.1
Employees	(8.5%)	543	398	356	340	380

NAPCO INTERNATIONAL LLC

9200 75TH AVE N STE 140
MINNEAPOLIS, MN 554282684
Phone: 952 931-2400
Fax: –
Web: www.napcointl.com

CEO: –
CFO: Gerald Theisen
HR: –
FYE: December 31
Type: Private

NAPCO modern tanks keep rollin' along. The company makes and distributes spare parts and retrofit packages for military vehicles, communication systems, and electronic systems for the US military and foreign governments in over 60 nations around the world. Most sales stem from spare and replacement parts for wheeled and tracked vehicles such as tanks, trucks, reconnaissance, and armored personnel carriers, as well as aircraft parts. NAPCO's communications and electronics products support telephone, telecommunications, radio, avionics, and transportable shelters. NAPCO is owned by JATA LLC. NAPCO began as Northwestern Auto Parts Company in 1918.

	Annual Growth	12/01	12/02	12/03	12/05	12/07
Sales ($mil.)	(5.7%)	–	–	29.1	22.6	23.0
Net income ($ mil.)	16.8%	–	–	3.1	0.2	5.8
Market value ($ mil.)	–	–	–	–	–	–
Employees	–	–	–	–	–	65

NAPCO SECURITY TECHNOLOGIES, INC.
NMS: NSSC

333 Bayview Avenue
Amityville, NY 11701
Phone: 631 842-9400
Fax: –
Web: www.napcosecurity.com

CEO: Richard L Soloway
CFO: Kevin S Buchel
HR: –
FYE: June 30
Type: Public

Crime pays for Napco Security Technologies. If you're trying to prevent it, Napco manufactures a slew of security products used in commercial and residential buildings, as well as government and institutional facilities. Products include burglary and fire alarm systems, exit alarm-locks and digital-access control locks, video surveillance systems such as cameras and monitors, and emergency communications systems. Napco also buys and resells security devices made by third-party manufacturers. The company sells its products worldwide mainly through independent distributors, dealers, and installers of security equipment.

	Annual Growth	06/19	06/20	06/21	06/22	06/23
Sales ($mil.)	13.4%	102.9	101.4	114.0	143.6	170.0
Net income ($ mil.)	22.1%	12.2	8.5	14.9	19.6	27.1
Market value ($ mil.)	3.9%	1,091.3	860.1	1,337.3	757.1	1,274.1
Employees	1.7%	1,076	1,161	1,102	1,149	1,150

NAPROTEK, LLC

90 ROSE ORCHARD WAY
SAN JOSE, CA 951341356
Phone: 408 830-5000
Fax: –
Web: www.naprotek.com

CEO: –
CFO: –
HR: –
FYE: December 31
Type: Private

When it comes to making the newest new gizmo, you won't find Naprotek napping. Founded in 1995, the company provides a range of printed circuit board (PCB) engineering and contract manufacturing services to electronics makers. Engineering services include circuit design, material and component sourcing, and PCB layout, while manufacturing operations include low volume PCB production, ball-grid array assembly and rework, and box build assembly services. Naprotek also offers prototype assembly, testing, and product upgrades and repair services. Customers have included Cisco Systems, IBM, Intel, and Tellabs. CEO Najat Badriyeh is the majority owner. The company targets customers in the semiconductor, telecommunications, defense, gambling, aerospace, security, instrumentation, and computer markets.

NASB FINANCIAL INC
NBB: NASB

12498 South 71 Highway
Grandview, MO 64030
Phone: 816 765-2200
Fax: –
Web: www.nasb.com

CEO: David H Hancock
CFO: Rhonda Nyhus
HR: Barbara Cornwell
FYE: September 30
Type: Public

NASB Financial is the holding company for North American Savings Bank, which operates about 15 branches and loan offices in the Kansas City and Springfield, Missouri areas. Established in 1927, the bank offers standard deposit products to retail and commercial customers, including checking and savings accounts and CDs. Mortgages secured by residential or commercial properties make up most of the bank's lending activities; it also originates business, consumer, and construction loans. Subsidiary Nor-Am sells annuities, mutual funds, and credit life and disability insurance. Chairman David Hancock and his wife Linda, who is also a member of the company's board of directors, own about 45% of NASB Financial.

	Annual Growth	09/19	09/20	09/21	09/22	09/23
Assets ($mil.)	1.9%	2,605.2	2,552.2	2,359.4	2,644.4	2,814.1
Net income ($ mil.)	(15.8%)	43.2	103.5	73.7	32.1	21.6
Market value ($ mil.)	(9.5%)	326.4	443.1	465.3	397.8	219.3
Employees	–	–	–	–	–	–

NASCO HEALTHCARE INC.

16 SIMULAIDS DR
SAUGERTIES, NY 124775067
Phone: 920 563-2446
Fax: -
Web: www.nascohealthcare.com

CEO: Ken Miller
CFO: John Bohrman
HR: -
FYE: December 31
Type: Private

Students can learn a thing or two from The Aristotle Corporation -- from geometry and sewing to CPR and beekeeping. Through its Nasco International division, the firm makes educational materials for grades K-12 that cover more than a dozen subject areas, including art, math, health, science, and vocational agriculture. It also produces medical teaching aids (such as CPR mannequins, simulation kits), farm supplies, lab bags, and senior care products. Aristotle sells more than 65,000 items under brands such as Life/Form, Simulaids, Whirl-Pak, and Triarco through catalogs and an independent dealer network in more than 100 countries. It also has two retail stores. Aristotle is a subsidiary of Geneve Corporation.

NASDAQ INC

NMS: NDAQ

151 W. 42nd Street
New York, NY 10036
Phone: 212 401-8700
Fax: -
Web: www.ir.nasdaq.com

CEO: Adena T Friedman
CFO: Ann M Dennison
HR: -
FYE: December 31
Type: Public

Nasdaq, Inc. (Nasdaq) is a global technology company. The company's global offerings are diverse and include trading and clearing across multiple asset classes, trade management services, fixed income and commodities trading and clearing (FICC), and Cash Equity Trading. There were nearly 4,200 total listings on The Nasdaq Stock Market, including some 440 ETPs. The combined market capitalization was approximately $28.2 trillion. In Europe, the Nasdaq Nordic and Nasdaq Baltic exchanges, together with Nasdaq First North, were home to some 1,235 listed companies with a combined market capitalization of approximately $2.6 trillion. The US accounts for majority of Nasdaq's revenue.

	Annual Growth	12/19	12/20	12/21	12/22	12/23
Sales ($mil.)	9.2%	4,262.0	5,627.0	5,886.0	6,226.0	6,064.0
Net income ($ mil.)	8.2%	774.0	933.0	1,187.0	1,125.0	1,059.0
Market value ($ mil.)	(14.2%)	61,600	76,347	120,789	35,286	33,440
Employees	18.2%	4,361	4,830	5,814	6,377	8,525

NASH PRODUCE, LLC

6160 S NC HWY 58
NASHVILLE, NC 278568642
Phone: 252 443-6011
Fax: -
Web: www.nashproduce.com

CEO: -
CFO: -
HR: -
FYE: December 31
Type: Private

Nash Produce is a leading producer of fresh vegetables serving wholesalers and retailers around the country. With growers in North and South Carolina, Florida, Georgia, and Virginia, the company harvests, packs, and ships cantaloupes, pumpkins, sweet potatoes, and watermelons. It is also one of the leading producers and processors of pickling cucumbers in the US. Nash Produce was started by Dale Bone in 1977 as a cucumber-grading station. It was purchased by a group of North Carolina growers in 2006.

	Annual Growth	12/13	12/14	12/16	12/17	12/18
Sales ($mil.)	6.5%	-	44.0	57.6	56.5	56.5
Net income ($ mil.)	(21.1%)	-	2.1	2.8	1.6	0.8
Market value ($ mil.)	-	-	-	-	-	-
Employees	-	-	-	-	-	50

NASLAND ENGINEERING

4740 RUFFNER ST
SAN DIEGO, CA 921111520
Phone: 858 292-7770
Fax: -
Web: www.nasland.com

CEO: Don K Nasland
CFO: -
HR: -
FYE: December 31
Type: Private

Nasland Engineering provides civil engineering, surveying, and land planning services to private land developers and government agencies in Southern California and Arizona. It offers services for developing subdivisions, commercial/industrial sites, apartments and condominiums, and streets and highways. It also offers flood-control planning, utilities system design, hydrology studies, assessment district engineering, and consulting services. Projects include work for Sea World, the San Diego River Improvement Project, and the redesign of National City, California's "Mile of Cars" auto dealer district. In 1959 Don Nasland founded the company; his two sons, Don and Steven, now own and operate Nasland Engineering.

	Annual Growth	12/14	12/15	12/16	12/17	12/18
Sales ($mil.)	9.7%	-	5.5	5.7	5.3	7.3
Net income ($ mil.)	-	-	(0.2)	0.1	0.2	1.6
Market value ($ mil.)	-	-	-	-	-	-
Employees	-	-	-	-	-	43

NASSAU HEALTH CARE CORPORATION

2201 HEMPSTEAD TPKE
EAST MEADOW, NY 115541859
Phone: 516 572-0123
Fax: -
Web: www.numc.edu

CEO: Megan Ryan
CFO: John Maher
HR: -
FYE: December 31
Type: Private

Nassau Health Care (NuHealth) keeps residents healthy in the suburbs of the Big Apple. The health system operates Nassau University Medical Center, which has some 530 beds, as well as the A. Holly Patterson Extended Care Facility, a skilled nursing center with 590 beds. Other operations include about a half-dozen community family health centers and a home health care agency serving the people of Long Island. Nassau University Medical Center's specialized services include trauma, burn care, orthopedics, psychiatry, and obstetrics. NuHealth is a public benefit company governed by a representative board appointed by state and county officials.

	Annual Growth	12/17	12/18	12/19*	05/20*	12/21
Sales ($mil.)	(10.8%)	-	587.6	0.0	0.0	416.8
Net income ($ mil.)	-	-	(53.3)	0.0	(0.0)	(113.6)
Market value ($ mil.)	-	-	-	-	-	-
Employees	-	-	-	-	-	3,500

*Fiscal year change

NATHAN'S FAMOUS, INC.

NMS: NATH

One Jericho Plaza, Seconf Floor - Wing A
Jericho, NY 11753
Phone: 516 338-8500
Fax: -
Web: www.nathansfamous.com

CEO: Eric Gatoff
CFO: Ronald G Devos
HR: -
FYE: March 26
Type: Public

Patrons of this restaurateur are in the dog house. Nathan's Famous is a leading franchisor of quick-service restaurants with a chain of about 300 Nathan's outlets known for all-beef frankfurters served with a variety of toppings. The eateries, located in about 25 states and a half dozen other countries, also serve hamburgers, crinkle-cut fries, and breakfast sandwiches. More than 50 Nathan's units also feature fish and chips under the Arthur Treacher's brand. In addition to restaurants, the company sells Nathan's branded products through vending machines, Subway units at Wal-Mart stores, and Auntie Anne's pretzel shops. Specialty Foods Group makes Nathan's hot dogs for retail sale under a licensing deal.

	Annual Growth	03/19	03/20	03/21	03/22	03/23
Sales ($mil.)	6.5%	101.8	103.3	75.8	114.9	130.8
Net income ($ mil.)	(2.2%)	21.5	13.4	11.1	13.6	19.6
Market value ($ mil.)	1.5%	279.1	226.6	272.9	224.3	295.9
Employees	(1.9%)	149	120	146	131	138

NATIONAL ACADEMY OF RECORDING ARTS & SCIENCES, INC.

3030 OLYMPIC BLVD
SANTA MONICA, CA 904045073
Phone: 310 392-3777
Fax: –
Web: www.grammy.com

CEO: Neil Portnow
CFO: Wayne J Zahner
HR: Gaetano Frizzi
FYE: July 31
Type: Private

The National Academy of Recording Arts and Sciences, better known as The Recording Academy, provides arts advocacy, outreach and education, and support services to professionals in the recording industry. The membership organization boasts some 18,000 members served by a dozen regional chapters throughout the US. The Recording Academy acknowledges outstanding work by musicians, producers, engineers, and recording professionals with its annual GRAMMY Awards ceremonies. Its first international venture, The Latin Academy of Recording Arts & Sciences (which produces The Latin GRAMMY Awards), was formed in 1997. The Recording Academy was established in 1957.

	Annual Growth	07/13	07/14	07/15	07/21	07/22
Sales ($mil.)	1.8%	–	77.6	83.0	73.7	89.3
Net income ($ mil.)	(23.2%)	–	7.1	8.8	(6.2)	0.9
Market value ($ mil.)	–	–	–	–	–	–
Employees		–	–	–	–	110

NATIONAL AMERICAN UNIVERSITY HOLDINGS INC.   NBB: NAUH

5301 Mt. Rushmore Road
Rapid City, SD 57701
Phone: 605 721-5200
Fax: –
Web: www.national.edu

CEO: Ronald L Shape
CFO: Thomas Bickart
HR: –
FYE: May 31
Type: Public

National American University Holdings believes in the power of continuing education. Through subsidiary Dlorah, the for-profit company owns National American University (NAU), which has more than 20 campuses in eight states and offers classes online. Some locations are considered hybrids, offering both in-class and online courses. Targeting working adults and other non-traditional students, NAU offers associate's, bachelor's, and master's degrees, as well as certification in business, criminal justice, and health care disciplines. The university was founded in 1941 as the National School of Business; the holding company, which was formed in 2007 to acquire an education company, purchased Dlorah in 2009.

	Annual Growth	05/19	05/20	05/21	05/22	05/23
Sales ($mil.)	(26.6%)	37.3	24.4	15.5	12.6	10.8
Net income ($ mil.)	–	(25.1)	1.1	(6.1)	5.3	5.6
Market value ($ mil.)	0.3%	2.0	9.2	3.7	2.3	2.0
Employees	(18.3%)	469	396	312	249	209

NATIONAL AMUSEMENTS, INC.

846 UNIVERSITY AVE
NORWOOD, MA 020622631
Phone: 617 461-1600
Fax: –
Web: www.showcasecinemas.com

CEO: Sumner M Redstone
CFO: Michael Kszystyniak
HR: Giselle Martinez
FYE: December 31
Type: Private

National Amusements operates Showcase SuperLux, Cinema de Lux, Showcase Cinemas, and Multiplex Cinemas branded theaters in the US, the UK, and Latin America. The Showcase Cinemas is a world leader in the motion picture exhibition industry, operating more than 810 movie screens in the US, UK, Argentina and Brazil. With roughly 25 theater locations in the US, Showcase Cinemas delivers the finest entertainment experience, offering the best in viewing, comfort and dining.

NATIONAL ASSOCIATION FOR STOCK CAR AUTO RACING, INC.

1 DAYTONA BLVD
DAYTONA BEACH, FL 321141212
Phone: 386 310-5000
Fax: –
Web: www.nascar.com

CEO: Brian Z France
CFO: James C France
HR: Jaime Lewis
FYE: December 31
Type: Private

In the race for riches in the sports world, NASCAR is on the right track. The National Association for Stock Car Auto Racing serves as the sanctioning body for stock car racing, one of the most popular spectator sports in the US. It runs more than 100 races each year in three circuits: the Nationwide, Camping World Truck, and its signature Sprint Cup Series. Featuring popular drivers such as Jeff Gordon and Tony Stewart, the Sprint Cup draws millions of fans to the tracks each year. In addition to organizing and promoting the races, the association negotiates broadcast rights and licenses the NASCAR brand for merchandise. NASCAR was founded in 1948 by Bill France Sr. and is still owned by the France family.

NATIONAL ASSOCIATION FOR THE ADVANCEMENT OF COLORED PEOPLE

4805 MOUNT HOPE DR
BALTIMORE, MD 212153206
Phone: 410 580-5777
Fax: –
Web: www.naacp.org

CEO: Leon W Russell
CFO: Junko Kobayashi
HR: –
FYE: December 31
Type: Private

The NAACP (National Association for the Advancement of Colored People) strives to ensure that all people are represented and have equal rights in American society and culture, regardless of race. The nation's oldest and largest civil rights organization, the group works via advocacy, education, and research, and it publishes the magazine Crisis and a quarterly newsletter The NAACP Advocate . It registers African Americans to vote, encourages academic achievement among high school students, and works with inmates to promote education and reduce recidivism. Sources of support include contributions and membership dues. The NAACP was founded in 1909 by a group that included W.E.B. Du Bois and Ida B. Wells-Barnett.

NATIONAL ASSOCIATION OF BROADCASTERS

1 M ST SE
WASHINGTON, DC 200035125
Phone: 202 429-5300
Fax: –
Web: www.nab.org

CEO: Innocent Nahabwe
CFO: Ken Almgrem
HR: –
FYE: December 31
Type: Private

The National Association of Broadcasters (NAB) represents on-the-air talkers, ranging from local radio reporters to TV network news anchors. The trade group serves as its members' eyes, ears, and, of course, voice before Congress, the courts, and federal regulatory agencies in Washington, DC. NAB priorities have included spectrum management, retransmission consent, political advertising rates, and limiting content regulation. The NAB predates television and goes back to the early days of radio -- the organization was founded in 1923.

	Annual Growth	03/13	03/14	03/15	03/17*	12/22
Sales ($mil.)	(0.2%)	–	57.9	64.1	70.9	57.1
Net income ($ mil.)	–	–	4.5	(15.3)	9.7	(6.7)
Market value ($ mil.)	–	–	–	–	–	–
Employees	–	–	–	–	–	173

*Fiscal year change

NATIONAL ASSOCIATION OF CREDIT MANAGEMENT, INC.

8840 COLUMBIA 100 PKWY
COLUMBIA, MD 210452100
Phone: 410 740-5560
Fax: –
Web: www.nacm.org

CEO: –
CFO: Kelly Gilmartin
HR: –
FYE: December 31
Type: Private

This group gives credit where credit is due, but it takes it away when it's past due. The National Association of Credit Management (NACM) provides an array of information and services to the business, credit, and financial industries in the US and Canada. NACM provides credit education, certification, and lobbying on behalf of its members. Its affiliated associations offer credit reports, collections, and business liquidation services. Its subsidiary Finance Credit and International Business (FCIB) serves exporters and multinational corporations. The association was formed in 1896.

	Annual Growth	12/16	12/17	12/18	12/19	12/21
Sales ($mil.)	0.3%	–	–	–	0.3	0.3
Net income ($ mil.)	–	–	–	–	(0.0)	(0.0)
Market value ($ mil.)	–	–	–	–	–	–
Employees	–	–	–	–	–	47

NATIONAL ASSOCIATION OF MUSIC MERCHANTS INC.

5790 ARMADA DR
CARLSBAD, CA 920084608
Phone: 760 438-8001
Fax: –
Web: www.namm.org

CEO: Joe Lamond
CFO: Larry Manley
HR: Mary Brown
FYE: September 30
Type: Private

At the International Music Products Association, all the world's a band. Known as the National Association of Music Merchants (NAMM), it's a non-profit group of more than 9,000 musical equipment and products makers, distributors, and retailers in 100-plus countries. NAMM boasts a pair of annual trade shows (one each in Southern California and Nashville) that attract key players from the music products industry. It also lobbies government, publishes a product review and a magazine, and offers seminars and other educational opportunities. It also funds music-related outreach programs, as well as several charities. NAMM was founded in the early 1900s as the National Association of Piano Dealers of America.

	Annual Growth	09/14	09/15	09/16	09/19	09/22
Sales ($mil.)	(14.3%)	–	21.2	24.5	26.2	7.2
Net income ($ mil.)	–	–	0.0	1.4	0.9	(11.2)
Market value ($ mil.)	–	–	–	–	–	–
Employees	–	–	–	–	–	62

NATIONAL ASSOCIATION OF WHOLESALER-DISTRIBUTORS, INC

1325 G ST NW STE 1000
WASHINGTON, DC 200053134
Phone: 202 872-0885
Fax: –
Web: www.naw.org

CEO: –
CFO: –
HR: –
FYE: November 30
Type: Private

The National Association of Wholesaler-Distributors (NAW) works to influence public policy, conduct research, and provide group purchasing programs for about 40,000 member wholesale-distribution companies and about 85,000 people who work in the industry. It encompasses about 80 national wholesale-distribution trade associations and about 30 state, regional, and local associations. Members operate in a wide range of industries but share an interest in getting goods to market efficiently. NAW was formed in 1946.

	Annual Growth	11/16	11/17	11/18	11/21	11/22
Sales ($mil.)	7.3%	–	6.4	6.1	6.5	9.1
Net income ($ mil.)	(15.0%)	–	0.7	0.5	(0.8)	0.3
Market value ($ mil.)	–	–	–	–	–	–
Employees	–	–	–	–	–	20

NATIONAL AUDUBON SOCIETY, INC.

225 VARICK ST FL 7
NEW YORK, NY 100144396
Phone: 212 979-3000
Fax: –
Web: www.audubon.org

CEO: David Yarnold
CFO: Mary B Henson
HR: –
FYE: June 30
Type: Private

Audubon has gone to the birds. The National Audubon Society is a not-for-profit organization dedicated to preserving birds and other wildlife, and their habitats, by conserving and restoring their natural ecosystems. The society operates programs and educational centers in every US state, and in several South American and Caribbean countries, to encourage grassroots conservation and promote environmental public policy reform. Projects have included saving habitats in the Everglades, Arctic Wildlife Refuge, Long Island Sound, and Mississippi River basin. Audubon also publishes Audubon Magazine. A precursor to the society formed in 1886 but disbanded when it grew too quickly. The current society began in 1905.

	Annual Growth	06/07	06/08	06/09	06/10	06/16
Sales ($mil.)	4.8%	–	–	74.0	80.1	102.6
Net income ($ mil.)	–	–	–	–	(1.8)	(19.2)
Market value ($ mil.)	–	–	–	–	–	–
Employees	–	–	–	–	–	600

NATIONAL AUTOMOBILE DEALERS ASSOCIATION

8484 WESTPARK DR STE 500
TYSONS, VA 221023588
Phone: 800 557-6232
Fax: –
Web: www.nada.org

CEO: Mike Stanton
CFO: Joseph Cowden
HR: –
FYE: December 31
Type: Private

The National Automobile Dealers Association (N.A.D.A.) has been around almost as long as there have been cars. Founded in 1917, N.A.D.A. represents more than 16,000 new car and truck dealers in the US and abroad. Through its more than 32,500 franchises, N.A.D.A. offers a range of services including: government relations (lobbying of Congress, education of dealers), legal and public affairs, dealership operations and other courses through N.A.D.A University, insurance and retirement benefits, IT training, and convention and exposition support. N.A.D.A. also publishes AutoExec magazine (it sold The N.A.D.A. Official Used Car Guide). Membership is open to any dealer with a new car or truck sales and service franchise.

	Annual Growth	12/13	12/14	12/17	12/21	12/22
Sales ($mil.)	1.7%	–	60.8	90.2	140.1	69.5
Net income ($ mil.)	–	–	10.6	14.8	85.5	(3.4)
Market value ($ mil.)	–	–	–	–	–	–
Employees	–	–	–	–	–	300

NATIONAL BANK HOLDINGS CORP

NYS: NBHC

7800 East Orchard Road, Suite 300
Greenwood Village, CO 80111
Phone: 303 892-8715
Fax: –
Web: www.nationalbankholdings.com

CEO: –
CFO: –
HR: –
FYE: December 31
Type: Public

National Bank Holdings is the holding company for NBH Bank, which operates over 95 branches located primarily in Colorado and the greater Kansas City region under various brands, including Bank Midwest and Bank Midwest Mortgage in Kansas and Missouri; Community Banks of Colorado and Community Banks Mortgage in Colorado; Bank of Jackson Hole and Bank of Jackson Hole Mortgage in Wyoming; and Hillcrest Bank and Hillcrest Bank Mortgage in Texas, Utah, New Mexico and Idaho. Targeting small to medium-sized businesses and consumers, the banks offer traditional deposit products such as health savings accounts, checking and savings accounts, as well as commercial and residential mortgages, business loans, and commercial loans. The bank boasted some $9.6 billion in assets, about $7.2 billion in loans, and about $7.9 billion in deposits.

	Annual Growth	12/19	12/20	12/21	12/22	12/23
Assets ($mil.)	14.0%	5,895.5	6,660.0	7,214.0	9,573.2	9,951.1
Net income ($ mil.)	15.3%	80.4	88.6	93.6	71.3	142.0
Market value ($ mil.)	1.4%	1,330.8	1,237.8	1,660.3	1,589.6	1,405.2
Employees	(0.5%)	1,298	1,224	1,154	1,322	1,274

NATIONAL BANKSHARES INC. (VA)   NAS: NKSH

101 Hubbard Street
Blacksburg, VA 24062-9002
Phone: 540 951-6300
Fax: –
Web: www.nationalbankshares.com

CEO: F B Denardo
CFO: David K Skeens
HR: –
FYE: December 31
Type: Public

National Bankshares is the holding company for National Bank of Blacksburg (National Bank for short), which serves consumers and small business in southwest Virginia through some two dozen branches. The community bank's services include deposit accounts, credit cards, and personal and corporate trust services. Commercial mortgages, including loans secured by college housing and professional office buildings, account for more than half of National Bankshares' loan portfolio; residential mortgages make up more than a quarter. To a lesser extent, the bank also writes business, construction, and consumer loans. Another subsidiary, National Bankshares Financial Services, provides investments and insurance.

	Annual Growth	12/19	12/20	12/21	12/22	12/23
Assets ($mil.)	5.8%	1,321.8	1,519.7	1,702.2	1,677.6	1,655.4
Net income ($ mil.)	(2.6%)	17.5	16.1	20.4	25.9	15.7
Market value ($ mil.)	(7.9%)	264.8	184.5	211.2	237.5	190.7
Employees	(1.7%)	238	229	221	231	222

NATIONAL BASEBALL HALL OF FAME AND MUSEUM, INC.

25 MAIN ST
COOPERSTOWN, NY 133261160
Phone: 607 547-7200
Fax: –
Web: www.baseballhall.org

CEO: –
CFO: –
HR: –
FYE: December 31
Type: Private

The National Baseball Hall of Fame and Museum is most associated with its enshrinement of baseball's elite figures, mainly players but also managers, executives, and umpires. In addition, the organization collects and houses artifacts, recorded video and sound clips, and documents related to the national pastime. The collections are accessible through the A. Bartlett Giamatti Research Center and the Hall of Fame Library and are placed on exhibit in its museum. The National Baseball Hall of Fame and Museum opened in 1939.

	Annual Growth	12/17	12/18	12/19	12/21	12/22
Sales ($mil.)	(0.7%)	–	17.1	14.2	23.1	16.6
Net income ($ mil.)	(12.3%)	–	4.0	1.1	9.4	2.4
Market value ($ mil.)	–	–	–	–	–	–
Employees	–	–	–	–	–	55

NATIONAL BEEF PACKING CO. LLC/NB FINANCE CORP.

12200 North Ambassador Drive
Kansas City, MO 64163
Phone: 800 449-2333
Fax: –
Web: www.nationalbeef.com

CEO: Timothy M Klein
CFO: Simon McGee
HR: Joe Castagno
FYE: August 27
Type: Public

Beef, it's what's for dinner thanks to National Beef Packing Co. (NBPC). One of the biggest US beef processors, it produces name brand boxed, case-ready, portion-controlled, and other fresh and frozen beef products for 900-plus domestic and export markets. The company offers Naturewell Natural Beef and NatureSource brand beef, marketed as US-raised, corn and pasture grass-fed Angus cattle, free of antibiotics or added hormones. National Carriers, a 1,200-unit refrigerated trucking subsidiary, transports the meaty lineup within the US. Brazilian beef giant Marfrig Global Foods bought 51% of NBPC in 2018; holding company Leucadia also owns a stake.

	Annual Growth	08/07	08/08	08/09	08/10	08/11
Sales ($mil.)	5.3%	5,578.5	5,847.3	5,449.3	5,807.9	6,849.5
Net income ($ mil.)	89.6%	20.0	124.5	142.9	247.1	258.5
Market value ($ mil.)	–	–	–	–	–	–
Employees	–	–	–	8,900	9,100	9,100

NATIONAL BEVERAGE CORP.   NMS: FIZZ

8100 SW Tenth Street, Suite 4000
Fort Lauderdale, FL 33324
Phone: 954 581-0922
Fax: –
Web: www.nationalbeverage.com

CEO: Nick A Caporella
CFO: –
HR: –
FYE: April 29
Type: Public

National Beverage makes and distributes the popular LaCroix sparkling water brand, including a variety of flavors. National Beverage also makes the Shasta and Faygo brands of flavored soft drinks (both of which were launched more than a century ago), the Clear Fruit flavored waters, Everfresh and Mr. Pure juice and juice-added drinks, Rip It energy drink, and lemonades and teas. Its creative product designs, innovative packaging, and imaginative flavors, along with its corporate culture and philosophy, make National Beverage unique as a stand-alone entity in the beverage industry. Customers include gas stations, national and regional grocers, convenience stores, and food service distributors. National Beverage operates a dozen facilities located in ten US states. The company is founded in 1985, and is still run by chairman and CEO Nick Caporella.

	Annual Growth	04/19*	05/20	05/21*	04/22	04/23
Sales ($mil.)	3.7%	1,014.1	1,000.4	1,072.2	1,138.0	1,172.9
Net income ($ mil.)	0.2%	140.9	130.0	174.1	158.5	142.2
Market value ($ mil.)	(3.6%)	5,367.8	4,674.2	4,536.0	4,115.0	4,639.7
Employees	–	1,640	1,550	1,550	1,580	

*Fiscal year change

NATIONAL CABLE SATELLITE CORP

400 N CAPITOL ST NW STE 650
WASHINGTON, DC 200011550
Phone: 202 737-3220
Fax: –
Web: www.c-span.org

CEO: Robert Kennedy
CFO: –
HR: –
FYE: March 31
Type: Private

National Cable Satellite Corporation is a political junkie. The company (better known as C-SPAN, which stands for Cable Satellite Public Affairs Network) is a not-for-profit created in 1979 by the cable industry as a public service to provide live coverage of the US House of Representatives. The corporation's C-SPAN, C-SPAN2, and C-SPAN3 air public proceedings such as congressional sessions, White House press briefings and speeches, British House of Commons sessions, and other political and public affairs programs. C-SPAN also runs a radio network with content similar to its TV broadcasts, and publishes more than 15 Web sites. The company gets its funds from license fees paid by cable and satellite systems.

	Annual Growth	03/16	03/17	03/20	03/21	03/22
Sales ($mil.)	(4.4%)	–	67.4	63.8	63.7	53.8
Net income ($ mil.)	–	–	13.0	0.4	5.9	(3.4)
Market value ($ mil.)	–	–	–	–	–	–
Employees	–	–	–	–	–	260

NATIONAL CEMETERY ADMINISTRATION

810 VERMONT AVE NW STE 427
WASHINGTON, DC 204200001
Phone: 800 827-1000
Fax: –
Web: cem.va.gov

CEO: –
CFO: –
HR: –
FYE: December 31
Type: Private

The National Cemetery Administration (NCA) provides US veterans and their families with burial spaces in national shrines. The NCA maintains national cemeteries, supplies government-furnished headstones or markers to families, provides presidential memorial certificates in recognition of service, and administers grants for setting up or expanding state veterans cemeteries. The department traces its roots back to 1862 and is a division of the Department of Veterans Affairs. More than 24 million veterans, reservists, and National Guard members have qualified for burial in a national cemetery.

NATIONAL CENTER FOR STATE COURTS

300 NEWPORT AVE
WILLIAMSBURG, VA 231854147
Phone: 757 253-2000
Fax: –
Web: www.ncsc.org

CEO: –
CFO: Gwen Williams
HR: Deborah Mason
FYE: December 31
Type: Private

Swift Justice isn't the name of a bad legal thriller; it's what the National Center for State Courts is after. The not-for-profit center was founded in 1971 to reduce backlogs and delays in state courts by providing a network to transmit innovations and improvements from one court to another. Today the center acts primarily as an education, training, and advocacy center for judges, administrators, and state court constituents. The organization publishes topical reports with titles such as Trends in the State Courts and Survey of Judicial Salaries, as well as its periodical Justice System Journal.

	Annual Growth	12/12	12/13	12/14	12/15	12/17
Sales ($mil.)	10.8%	–	41.5	53.7	55.0	62.5
Net income ($ mil.)	–	–	2.2	0.6	0.0	(0.5)
Market value ($ mil.)	–	–	–	–	–	–
Employees	–	–	–	–	–	400

NATIONAL CENTER FOR VICTIMS OF CRIME, INC.

8181 PROFESSIONAL PL
HYATTSVILLE, MD 207852264
Phone: 202 467-8700
Fax: –
Web: www.victimsofcrime.org

CEO: –
CFO: –
HR: –
FYE: December 31
Type: Private

Founded in 1985, the National Center for Victims of Crime helps people and communities harmed by crime. The non-profit organization is focused on victim services, public policy, civil justice, and training and technical assistance. It also works to increase public awareness of crimes, including stalking, that in the past have not been recognized as such. Since its founding the group has worked with more than 10,000 grassroots organizations and criminal justice agencies serving millions of crime victims.

	Annual Growth	12/16	12/17	12/18	12/19	12/21
Sales ($mil.)	(7.4%)	–	5.9	6.2	6.4	4.4
Net income ($ mil.)	–	–	0.7	(0.2)	0.4	(0.1)
Market value ($ mil.)	–	–	–	–	–	–
Employees	–	–	–	–	–	20

NATIONAL CINEMEDIA INC

NMS: NCMI

6300 S. Syracuse Way, Suite 300
Centennial, CO 80111
Phone: 303 792-3600
Fax: –
Web: www.ncm.com

CEO: Thomas F Lesinski
CFO: Ronnie Y Ng
HR: Eric S Wohl
FYE: December 28
Type: Public

National CineMedia (NCM) is North America's largest cinema advertising network. NCM's cinema advertising network offers broad reach and unparalleled audience engagement with over 20,000 screens in over 1,500 theaters in some 195 Designated Market Areas. The company also produces and distributes Noovie show is presented exclusively in some 45 leading national and regional theater circuits including AMC, Cinemark, Regal, and almost 45 network affiliate theaters. Additionally, the company provides advertising to theater lobbies on its Lobby Entertainment Network (LEN). Major NCM stockholders include theater operators Cinemark Holdings, Regal Entertainment, and Standard General.

	Annual Growth	12/19	12/20	12/21	12/22	12/23
Sales ($mil.)	(21.9%)	444.8	90.4	114.6	249.2	165.2
Net income ($ mil.)	110.2%	36.1	(65.4)	(48.7)	(28.7)	705.2
Market value ($ mil.)	(12.0%)	699.2	360.2	266.3	23.0	418.3
Employees	(13.9%)	531	419	346	297	292

NATIONAL COLLEGIATE ATHLETIC ASSOCIATION

700 W WASHINGTON ST
INDIANAPOLIS, IN 462042710
Phone: 317 917-6222
Fax: –
Web: www.ncaa.org

CEO: –
CFO: –
HR: –
FYE: August 31
Type: Private

The National Collegiate Athletic Association (NCAA) supports the intercollegiate sports activities of around 1,000 member colleges and universities. A not-for-profit organization, the NCAA administers scholarship and grant programs, enforces conduct and eligibility rules, and works to support and promote the needs of student athletes. The association is known for its lucrative branding and television deals, such as those surrounding the popular "March Madness" tournament for Division I men's basketball. Seeking reform of athletics rules and regulations, officials from 13 schools formed the Intercollegiate Athletic Association of the United States in 1906. The organization took its current name in 1910.

	Annual Growth	08/16	08/17	08/18	08/21	08/22
Sales ($mil.)	2.9%	–	1,061.4	1,064.4	1,108.5	1,224.3
Net income ($ mil.)	(21.2%)	–	104.8	27.1	78.3	32.0
Market value ($ mil.)	–	–	–	–	–	–
Employees	–	–	–	–	–	508

NATIONAL CONSTITUTION CENTER

525 ARCH ST
PHILADELPHIA, PA 191061595
Phone: 215 409-6600
Fax: –
Web: www.constitutioncenter.org

CEO: Jeffrey Rosen
CFO: –
HR: Denzel Cook
FYE: September 30
Type: Private

We the People can learn much from the National Constitution Center. The not-for-profit organization works to increase the understanding and appreciation of the US Constitution, its history, and its relevance to Americans today. Through its facility on Independence Mall, the group houses a museum featuring more than 100 interactive multimedia exhibits, photographs, writings, films, sculptures, and artifacts. It also accommodates the Annenberg Center for Education and Outreach, which is dedicated to national constitutional education. The National Constitution Center was founded in 1988 by the Constitution Heritage Act.

	Annual Growth	09/14	09/15	09/19	09/20	09/22
Sales ($mil.)	8.0%	–	13.5	21.5	18.5	23.0
Net income ($ mil.)	–	–	(4.9)	3.2	2.1	5.3
Market value ($ mil.)	–	–	–	–	–	–
Employees	–	–	–	–	–	160

NATIONAL COOPERATIVE REFINERY ASSOCIATION

2000 South Main Street, P.O. Box 1404
McPherson, KS 67460
Phone: 620 241-2340
Fax: 620 241-5531
Web: www.ncra.coop

CEO: –
CFO: Timothy Skidmore
HR: –
FYE: August 31
Type: Public

Cooperation is a refined art and refining a cooperative art for the National Cooperative Refinery Association (NCRA), which provides its member owners, farm supply cooperatives CHS, GROWMARK, and MFA Oil, with gasoline and diesel fuel through its oil refinery in McPherson, Kansas. The refinery's production rate is 85,000 barrels per day. Fuel from the refinery is allocated to member/owners on the basis of ownership percentages. In addition to the refinery, NCRA owns Jayhawk Pipeline, stakes in two other pipeline companies, and an underground oil storage facility.

	Annual Growth	08/05	08/06	08/07	08/08	08/09
Sales ($mil.)	3.6%	2,047.4	2,379.3	2,694.3	3,641.4	2,355.1
Net income ($ mil.)	10.7%	152.3	364.7	566.1	273.0	228.8
Market value ($ mil.)	–	–	–	–	–	–
Employees	–	–	–	–	–	–

NATIONAL COUNCIL OF YOUNG MEN'S CHRISTIAN ASSOCIATIONS OF THE UNITED STATES OF AMERICA

101 N WACKER DR STE 1600
CHICAGO, IL 606067310
Phone: 312 419-8456
Fax: –
Web: www.ymca.org

CEO: Kevin Washington
CFO: –
HR: –
FYE: December 31
Type: Private

A venerable not-for-profit community service organization, YMCA of the USA (Y-USA) assists the more than 2,700 individual YMCAs across the country and represents them on both national and international levels. Although YMCA stands for Young Men's Christian Association, the organization's programs are open to all. Local YMCAs are leading providers of child care in the US. The facilities also offer programs in aquatics, arts and humanities, education of new immigrants, health and fitness, and teen leadership. Overall, YMCAs serve about 21 million people in some 10,000 neighborhoods across the US, which includes about 9 million children under the age of 17.

	Annual Growth	12/13	12/14	12/15	12/19	12/21
Sales ($mil.)	4.5%	–	114.2	155.9	137.4	155.5
Net income ($ mil.)	51.5%	–	3.1	4.5	(2.1)	55.9
Market value ($ mil.)	–	–	–	–	–	–
Employees						190

NATIONAL COUNCIL ON AGING, INC.

251 18TH ST S STE 500
ARLINGTON, VA 222023410
Phone: 202 479-1200
Fax: –
Web: www.ncoa.org

CEO: James Firman
CFO: Donna Whitt
HR: –
FYE: June 30
Type: Private

The National Council on the Aging (NCOA) can help us all grow old gracefully. The nonprofit is an advocate for the elderly. Its members include adult day service centers, employment services, senior housing facilities, and faith-based organizations. NCOA monitors public policies, business practices, and attitudes concerning older Americans. The group operates a Web site called BenefitsCheckUp, which allows users to search federal, state, and private benefit and prescription savings programs for which they might be eligible. Other programs include matching volunteers with at-risk children and families as well as providing training and employment opportunities to those older than 55. NCOA was formed in 1950.

	Annual Growth	06/14	06/15	06/16	06/20	06/21
Sales ($mil.)	3.0%	–	45.4	48.7	59.8	54.3
Net income ($ mil.)	–	–	1.4	3.0	0.6	(4.9)
Market value ($ mil.)	–	–	–	–	–	–
Employees						80

NATIONAL COUNCIL ON ALCOHOLISM AND DRUG DEPENDENCE INC.

217 BROADWAY RM 712
NEW YORK, NY 100072912
Phone: 212 269-7797
Fax: –
Web: www.recovered.org

CEO: Robert J Lindsey
CFO: –
HR: –
FYE: December 31
Type: Private

Plenty of groups exist to fight alcoholism and drug abuse; this group also fights the stigma associated with alcoholism and drug addiction. The National Council on Alcoholism and Drug Dependence (NCADD) provides advocacy, education, and support for the public with concerns about alcoholism and dependence on drugs. Its programs include awareness-raising events and press releases, prevention and treatment programs, and its Registry of Addiction Recovery, or ROAR, for recovering addicts who aren't afraid to go public and help fight the stigma. The organization also runs a Web site providing medical and scientific information for parents and others concerned about drinking and drug use. NCADD was founded in 1944.

	Annual Growth	12/12	12/13	12/14	12/15	12/16
Sales ($mil.)	(17.9%)	–	1.0	0.9	0.4	0.5
Net income ($ mil.)	–	–	(0.0)	(0.0)	(0.2)	(0.1)
Market value ($ mil.)	–	–	–	–	–	–
Employees						82

NATIONAL DISTRIBUTING COMPANY, INC.

1 NATIONAL DR SW
ATLANTA, GA 303361631
Phone: 404 696-1681
Fax: –
Web: www.rndc-usa.com

CEO: Jay Davis
CFO: John A Carlos
HR: –
FYE: December 31
Type: Private

Residents of Georgia and New Mexico with a thirst for beer, or other alcoholic beverages, may be fortunate to live in a state that National Distributing Company (NDC) serves. The wine, spirits, and beer wholesaler supplies the Peach Tree State and Land of Enchantment and, through NDC affiliate Republic National Distributing Company (RNDC), has a foothold in about 20 other states and Washington, DC. Its suppliers include distillers Diageo and Pernod Ricard, winemaker E & J Gallo, and beer producer United Breweries, along with several other specialty alcoholic beverage makers. Started in 1942 as the Dixie Wine Company, NDC continues under the leadership and ownership of the founding Carlos and Davis families.

NATIONAL EDUCATION ASSOCIATION OF THE UNITED STATES

1201 16TH ST NW STE 410
WASHINGTON, DC 200363290
Phone: 202 833-4000
Fax: –
Web: www.nea.org

CEO: –
CFO: –
HR: Donna Healy
FYE: December 31
Type: Private

The National Education Association (NEA) is dedicated to promoting the cause of public education and the teaching profession. The organization boasts a membership of 3 million elementary and secondary teachers, support professionals, administrators, higher education faculty, and student teachers. It operates in all US states through affiliates. The group's key issues include the No Child Left Behind Act, professional pay, education funding, minority community outreach, dropout prevention, achievement gaps, and other matters facing America's schools. Founded in 1857, the NEA also hosts Read Across America, a one-day reading event held on Dr. Seuss' birthday.

	Annual Growth	08/18	08/19	08/21	08/22*	12/22
Sales ($mil.)	(63.4%)	–	377.1	396.8	108.3	18.5
Net income ($ mil.)	(28.6%)	–	20.6	16.2	(1.7)	7.5
Market value ($ mil.)	–	–	–	–	–	–
Employees	–	–	–	–	–	735

*Fiscal year change

NATIONAL FOOTBALL LEAGUE

345 PARK AVE BSMT LC1
NEW YORK, NY 101540017
Phone: 212 450-2000
Fax: –
Web: www.nfl.com

CEO: –
CFO: –
HR: –
FYE: March 31
Type: Private

In the world of professional sports, the National Football League blitzes the competition. The organization oversees America's most popular spectator sport, acting as a trade association for 32 franchise owners. Among the league's functions, the NFL governs and promotes the game of football, sets and enforces rules, and regulates team ownership. It generates revenue mostly through marketing sponsorships, licensing merchandise, and by selling national broadcasting rights to the games. The teams operate as separate businesses but share a percentage of the league's overall revenue. Founded in 1920 as the American Professional Football Association, the league has been known as the NFL since 1922.

NATIONAL FOOTBALL LEAGUE PLAYERS ASSOCIATION

1133 20TH ST NW FRNT 1
WASHINGTON, DC 200363449
Phone: 202 756-9100
Fax: –
Web: www.nflpa.com

CEO: –
CFO: –
HR: –
FYE: February 28
Type: Private

The National Football League Players Association (NFLPA) represents the interests of people who go to work in helmets and shoulder pads. The union oversees its members' collective bargaining agreement with the National Football League, negotiates and monitors retirement and insurance benefits, and works to promote the image of the players, through marketing and licensing subsidiary NFL PLAYERS (formerly PLAYERS INC). A member of the AFL-CIO, the NFLPA represents both active and retired players. It is governed by a board of player representatives who are chosen by their teammates. The union was established in 1956, more than 35 years after the NFL was organized.

	Annual Growth	02/11	02/12	02/14	02/15	02/22
Sales ($mil.)	5.3%	–	81.3	65.9	84.8	135.8
Net income ($ mil.)	–	–	(36.2)	26.0	46.0	92.2
Market value ($ mil.)	–	–	–	–	–	–
Employees	–	–	–	–	–	89

NATIONAL FOOTBALL MUSEUM, INC.

2121 GEORGE HALAS DR NW
CANTON, OH 447082630
Phone: 330 456-8207
Fax: –
Web: www.nationalfootballmuseum.com

CEO: –
CFO: Bill Allen
HR: –
FYE: December 31
Type: Private

The Professional Football Hall of Fame in Canton, Ohio, enshrines many gridiron greats including players such as Jim Thorpe and Bart Starr and coaching legends Vince Lombardi and George Allen. Although affiliated with the National Football League, the Hall of Fame is operated as an independent, nonprofit organization. More than 8 million people have visted the Pro Football Hall of Fame since its opening in 1963. In 2008, the on-site museum added two new galleries devoted to Moments, Memories & Mementos, and Pro Football Today. The adjacent Fawcett Stadium hosts the NFL's annual AFC-NFC Hall of Fame Game and serves as a home field for local college and high school teams.

	Annual Growth	12/04	12/05	12/09	12/13	12/19
Sales ($mil.)	(53.1%)	–	1,805.5	12.2	14.9	0.0
Net income ($ mil.)	42.1%	–	0.0	0.6	0.8	0.0
Market value ($ mil.)	–	–	–	–	–	–
Employees	–	–	–	–	–	31

NATIONAL FROZEN FOODS CORPORATION

606 OAKESDALE AVE SW STE 201
RENTON, WA 980575228
Phone: 206 322-8900
Fax: –
Web: www.nffc.com

CEO: –
CFO: Janelle McClory
HR: Deanna Stewart
FYE: August 31
Type: Private

Cool Beans! National Frozen Foods has made a name for itself as one of the nation's largest private-label frozen vegetable producers. The family-owned company's products, which include peas, sweet corn, carrots, squash, and beans (green, Italian, lima, and wax), as well as vegetable blends, organic veggies, and pureed items, are available in grocery stores worldwide. National Frozen Foods also provides bulk and custom-packaging services. The company operates four processing plants in Washington and Oregon that offer a combined cold storage capacity for nearly 200 million pounds of frozen vegetables.

	Annual Growth	04/09	04/10	04/11	04/12*	08/13
Sales ($mil.)	(68.0%)	–	–	178.1	197.2	18.2
Net income ($ mil.)	(3.2%)	–	–	6.2	13.6	5.8
Market value ($ mil.)	–	–	–	–	–	–
Employees	–	–	–	–	–	633

*Fiscal year change

NATIONAL FUEL GAS CO. (NJ)

6363 Main Street
Williamsville, NY 14221
Phone: 716 857-7000
Fax: –
Web: www.nationalfuelgas.com

NYS: NFG
CEO: David P Bauer
CFO: Timothy J Silverstein
HR: –
FYE: September 30
Type: Public

National Fuel Gas is a diversified energy company engaged principally in the production, gathering, transportation and distribution of natural gas. The company operates an integrated business, with assets centered in western New York and Pennsylvania, being used for, and benefiting from, the production and transportation of natural gas from the Appalachian basin. It serves around 754,000 customers in New York and Pennsylvania, and engages in energy marketing, and some timber processing. Its oil and gas subsidiary Seneca Resources has proven reserves of around 4.2 billion cu. ft. of natural gas and 250 million barrels of oil.

	Annual Growth	09/19	09/20	09/21	09/22	09/23
Sales ($mil.)	6.4%	1,693.3	1,546.3	1,742.7	2,186.0	2,173.8
Net income ($ mil.)	11.9%	304.5	(123.8)	363.6	566.0	476.9
Market value ($ mil.)	2.6%	4,308.2	3,726.9	4,822.4	5,651.5	4,766.3
Employees	1.5%	2,107	2,162	2,188	2,132	2,240

NATIONAL GALLERY OF ART

6TH AND CONSTITUTION AVE NW
WASHINGTON, DC 205650001
Phone: 202 737-4215
Fax: –
Web: www.nga.gov

CEO: –
CFO: –
HR: –
FYE: September 30
Type: Private

The National Gallery of Art, one of the world's pre-eminent art museums, owns more than 100,000 works of art dating from the Middle Ages to the present. Its collection of European and American art is comprised of works by some 10,000 artists including Leonardo da Vinci, Claude Monet, and Pablo Picasso. The gallery is located on the National Mall in two buildings and an adjacent sculpture garden; its Web site offers virtual collection tours and in-depth study tours, as well as the ability to search the entire collection by artist, title, or style. The National Gallery of Art was established by Congress as an affiliate of the Smithsonian Institution in 1937; some 6 million people visit each year. The idea of a national art museum was the passion of former secretary of state Andrew Mellon, who began collecting works of art for the project in the 1930s. The National Gallery of Art was established in 1937 and the doors to its original West Building were opened in 1941. Mellon donated his collection and funded the gallery's construction; other benefactors have followed suit with large donations, including Samuel H. Kress, Joseph Widener, and Georgia O'Keeffe. The East Building (a modern interpretation of the West Building designed by architect I. M. Pei) opened to the public in 1978 and houses the gallery's modern and contemporary art collections.

	Annual Growth	09/06	09/07	09/08	09/09	09/15
Sales ($mil.)	(1.2%)	–	–	226.8	138.2	207.7
Net income ($ mil.)	(12.9%)	–	–	60.0	(43.2)	22.8
Market value ($ mil.)	–	–	–	–	–	–
Employees	–	–	–	–	–	1,000

NATIONAL GOLF FOUNDATION, INC.

501 N HIGHWAY A1A
JUPITER, FL 334774577
Phone: 561 744-6006
Fax: –
Web: www.ngf.org

CEO: –
CFO: –
HR: –
FYE: December 31
Type: Private

Golf is more than a game to a lot of people. To those at the National Golf Foundation (also known as NGF), golf is serious business. The foundation provides insight into the golf industry by providing research, marketing, and other consulting services. Customers include golf equipment manufacturers, builders and developers, course architects, facilities and practice ranges, retailers, and turf maintenance suppliers. Not at all concerned about "the game," NGF hosts symposiums that focus on business trends in the golf industry. The foundation was established in 1936.

	Annual Growth	12/15	12/16	12/17	12/21	12/22
Sales ($mil.)	6.8%	–	2.0	2.2	3.4	2.9
Net income ($ mil.)	–	–	(0.0)	(0.0)	0.4	0.0
Market value ($ mil.)	–	–	–	–	–	–
Employees	–	–	–	–	–	35

NATIONAL GRAPE CO-OPERATIVE ASSOCIATION, INC.

71 E MAIN ST STE B
WESTFIELD, NY 147871342
Phone: 716 326-5200
Fax: –
Web: –

CEO: –
CFO: –
HR: –
FYE: August 31
Type: Private

Well, of course grape growers want to hang out in a bunch! The more than 1,090 grower/owner-members of the National Grape Cooperative harvest Concord and Niagara grapes from almost 50,000 acres of vineyards. The plucked produce supplies the coop's wholly owned subsidiary Welch Foods. Welch Foods makes and sells fruit-based juices, jams, jellies, and spreads under the Welch's and Bama brands in the US and nearly 50 other countries. Offerings include fresh eating grapes, distributed by C.H. Robinson Worldwide, as well as dried fruit and frozen juice pops. The grape growers own vineyards in Pennsylvania, Michigan, New York, Ohio, Washington, and Ontario, Canada, which produce some 300,000 tons of grapes annually.

	Annual Growth	08/08	08/09	08/10	08/11	08/12
Sales ($mil.)	(0.7%)	–	–	658.7	640.9	649.5
Net income ($ mil.)	(5.1%)	–	–	82.7	74.2	74.4
Market value ($ mil.)	–	–	–	–	–	–
Employees	–	–	–	–	–	1,325

NATIONAL GRID USA SERVICE COMPANY, INC.

170 DATA DR
WALTHAM, MA 024512222
Phone: 800 260-0054
Fax: –
Web: www.nationalgridus.com

CEO: –
CFO: Kenneth D Daly
HR: Chris Lynch
FYE: December 31
Type: Private

National Grid is an electricity, natural gas, and clean energy delivery company serving more than 20 million people through our networks in New York and Massachusetts. National Grid USA is a subsidiary of UK-based electricity and gas transmission company National Grid.

NATIONAL GROCERS ASSOCIATION

601 PENNSYLVANIA AVE NW
WASHINGTON, DC 200042601
Phone: 703 516-0700
Fax: –
Web: www.nationalgrocers.org

CEO: Greg Ferrara
CFO: –
HR: –
FYE: December 31
Type: Private

It's all in the bag for grocery stores at the National Grocers Association (N.G.A.). The group is a trade association that represents US retail and wholesale grocers and their state associations. N.G.A. offers a variety of services, including seminars, professional development, and industry publications (Express Lane) to its membership. The association also provides them with information on workforce development, government regulations, and technology resources. One of the N.G.A.'s primary goals is to level the playing field for competition between large, national supermarket chains, such as A&P and Kroger, and the smaller, family-owned stores.

	Annual Growth	12/15	12/16	12/19	12/21	12/22
Sales ($mil.)	(4.4%)	–	7.2	5.8	6.1	5.5
Net income ($ mil.)	–	–	0.2	(0.2)	0.2	(0.7)
Market value ($ mil.)	–	–	–	–	–	–
Employees	–	–	–	–	–	20

NATIONAL GUARDIAN LIFE INSURANCE CO. (MADISON, WIS.)

2 East Gilman St.
Madison, WI 53703-1494
Phone: 608 257-5611
Fax: –
Web: www.nationalguardian.com

CEO: John D Larson
CFO: Derek Metcalf
HR: –
FYE: December 31
Type: Public

National Guardian Life Insurance Company (NGL) wants to protect its customers' financial security to the very end. Through NGL Insurance Group, the mutual insurance company specializes in senior life products including pre-need and final expense insurance as well as group dental and vision benefits, and a pharmaceutical discount program. The company is licensed in throughout the US and Washington, DC, with the exception of New York. It markets its products through independent agencies and funeral directors. Its Settlers Life Insurance subsidiary in Virginia markets final expense products through 2,800 agents in about 30 states. National Guardian Life was founded in 1910.

	Annual Growth	12/97	12/98	12/99	12/00	12/01
Assets ($mil.)	(0.7%)	774.0	794.0	781.3	793.6	753.2
Net income ($ mil.)	(14.6%)	8.3	2.2	4.5	4.2	4.4
Market value ($ mil.)	–	–	–	–	–	–
Employees	–	–	–	–	–	–

NATIONAL HEAD START ASSOCIATION

1651 PRINCE ST
ALEXANDRIA, VA 223142818
Phone: 703 739-0875
Fax: –
Web: www.nhsa.org

CEO: –
CFO: –
HR: –
FYE: June 30
Type: Private

These children aren't cheating, they are getting a head start. National Head Start Association (NHSA) is a nonprofit that provides low-income families with education, health, nutrition, and parental support services. The membership organization represents more than 1 million children and 2,600 Head Start programs in the US. In addition, NHSA provides Head Start's more than 200,000 staff with professional development and training. The organization publishes research on early childhood education through the periodicals NHSA Dialog and Children and Families . Formed in the 1970s, NHSA was an advocacy group for the Head Start community in Congress. The Head Start program got its start in 1965.

	Annual Growth	06/18	06/19	06/20	06/21	06/22
Sales ($mil.)	23.3%	–	6.6	6.8	9.0	12.5
Net income ($ mil.)	73.8%	–	0.9	1.3	3.6	5.0
Market value ($ mil.)	–	–	–	–	–	–
Employees	–	–	–	–	–	14

NATIONAL HEALTH INVESTORS, INC.   NYS: NHI

222 Robert Rose Drive
Murfreesboro, TN 37129
Phone: 615 890-9100
Fax: –
Web: www.nhireit.com

CEO: D E Mendelsohn
CFO: John L Spaid
HR: –
FYE: December 31
Type: Public

National Health Investors has a financial investment in the nation's health. The real estate investment trust (REIT) owns or makes mortgage investments in health care properties, primarily long-term care facilities. With about 240 properties in nearly 35 states, its holdings also include residences for people with developmental disabilities, assisted-living complexes, medical office buildings, retirement centers, and an acute care hospital. About 40% of National Health Investors' properties are leased to its largest tenant National HealthCare Corporation; nearly 60% are leased to regional health care providers. A majority of the REIT's facilities are located in Florida, Texas, and Tennessee.

	Annual Growth	12/19	12/20	12/21	12/22	12/23
Sales ($mil.)	0.1%	318.1	332.8	298.7	278.2	319.8
Net income ($ mil.)	(4.1%)	160.5	185.1	111.8	66.4	135.7
Market value ($ mil.)	(9.0%)	3,537.0	3,002.7	2,494.8	2,266.9	2,424.4
Employees	11.2%	17	20	20	27	26

NATIONAL HEALTHCARE CORP.
ASE: NHC

100 E. Vine Street
Murfreesboro, TN 37130
Phone: 615 890-2020
Fax: 615 890-0123
Web: www.nhccare.com

CEO: Stephen F Flatt
CFO: -
HR: -
FYE: December 31
Type: Public

National HealthCare (NHC) manages some 75 skilled nursing homes in ten states, mainly in the southeastern, northeastern, and midwestern part of the US. Its facilities house roughly 9,500 beds. In addition to its nursing homes, NHC manages almost 35 homecare locations and about 30 independent and assisted-living facilities. Its business activities include providing sub?acute and post?acute skilled nursing care, intermediate nursing care, rehabilitative care, memory and Alzheimer's care, senior living services, and home health care services. In 2021, NHC acquired the remaining 25% equity interest in Caris Healthcare for $28.7 million.

	Annual Growth	12/19	12/20	12/21	12/22	12/23
Sales ($mil.)	3.5%	996.4	1,028.2	1,074.3	1,085.7	1,141.5
Net income ($ mil.)	(0.5%)	68.2	41.9	138.6	22.4	66.8
Market value ($ mil.)	1.7%	1,326.8	1,019.4	1,042.9	913.4	1,418.7
Employees	(3.1%)	14,881	13,432	12,965	12,355	13,123

NATIONAL INSTITUTES OF HEALTH

9000 ROCKVILLE PIKE # 1
BETHESDA, MD 208920001
Phone: 301 496-4000
Fax: -
Web: www.nih.gov

CEO: -
CFO: -
HR: -
FYE: August 31
Type: Private

National Institutes of Health (NIH), the nation's medical research agency, includes more than 25 institutes and centers and is a component of the US Department of Health and Human Services. NIH is the primary federal agency conducting and supporting basic, clinical, and translational medical research, and is investigating the causes, treatments, and cures for both common and rare diseases. NIH traces its roots to 1887, when a one-room laboratory was created within the Marine Hospital Service (MHS), predecessor agency to the US Public Health Service (PHS).

NATIONAL ITALIAN AMERICAN FOUNDATION, INC.

1860 19TH ST NW
WASHINGTON, DC 200095501
Phone: 202 387-0600
Fax: -
Web: www.niaf.org

CEO: -
CFO: -
HR: -
FYE: December 31
Type: Private

For those whose last name ends in a vowel, the National Italian American Foundation (NIAF) is there to preserve and protect. The not-for-profit organization seeks to promote the interests of Italian-Americans through the development of educational programs, advocacy of representation in government, monitoring how Italians and Italian-Americans are depicted in the media, and the forging of ties between the US and Italy. It also offers scholarships for outstanding Italian-American students and for students embarking on Italian-based studies or trip to Italy. NIAF was founded in 1975.

	Annual Growth	12/13	12/14	12/17	12/21	12/22
Sales ($mil.)	3.8%	-	3.8	5.4	5.1	5.1
Net income ($ mil.)	-	-	(0.5)	(7.0)	2.0	0.2
Market value ($ mil.)	-	-	-	-	-	-
Employees	-	-	-	-	-	16

NATIONAL LAMPOON INC
NBB: NLMP

8228 Sunset Boulevard
West Hollywood, CA 90046
Phone: 310 474-5252
Fax: -
Web: www.nationallampoon.com

CEO: -
CFO: -
HR: -
FYE: July 31
Type: Public

This company wants to turn big yuks into big bucks. National Lampoon is a diversified media company focused on producing and distributing comedy content. It produces feature films and direct-to-video projects and licenses its name for such films as National Lampoon's Animal House, National Lampoon's Vacation , and National Lampoon's Van Wilder . The company also operates retail clothing and comedy Web sites, publishes books, and distributes TV programming to some 200 television stations that reach more than 2 million college students. A group led by CEO Daniel Laikin owns more than 50% of National Lampoon.

	Annual Growth	07/04	07/05	07/06	07/07	07/08
Sales ($mil.)	40.3%	1.9	3.7	3.7	6.1	7.4
Net income ($ mil.)	-	(5.1)	(8.7)	(6.9)	(2.5)	(1.7)
Market value ($ mil.)	(32.4%)	62.9	37.9	13.2	20.0	13.1
Employees	(5.4%)	30	32	25	26	24

NATIONAL MEDICAL ASSOCIATION, INC. A/K/A NATIONAL MEDICAL ASSOCIATION

8403 COLESVILLE RD STE 820
SILVER SPRING, MD 209106331
Phone: 301 585-3693
Fax: -
Web: www.nmanet.org

CEO: Kweisi Mfume
CFO: -
HR: -
FYE: December 31
Type: Private

The National Medical Association (NMA) represents the interests of African American physicians and other health professionals. The organization's more than 30,000 members benefit from services including professional development, advocacy, and research. NMA also publishes a quarterly journal, The Journal of the National Medical Association. It works to promote healthy lifestyles and equity in healthcare for African Americans and other at risk populations by providing national education campaigns on cancer, heart disease, stroke, AIDS, women's health, asthma, and other health issues. The group was founded in 1895 by doctors that were rejected for membership in the whites only American Medical Association.

	Annual Growth	12/14	12/15	12/16	12/17	12/18
Sales ($mil.)	(2.3%)	-	4.7	5.6	4.8	4.4
Net income ($ mil.)	(8.9%)	-	0.3	0.5	0.0	0.3
Market value ($ mil.)	-	-	-	-	-	-
Employees	-	-	-	-	-	35

NATIONAL MULTIPLE SCLEROSIS SOCIETY

733 3RD AVE FL 3
NEW YORK, NY 100173211
Phone: 212 463-9791
Fax: -
Web: www.nmss.org

CEO: Joyce Nelson
CFO: Tami Caesar
HR: -
FYE: September 30
Type: Private

The National Multiple Sclerosis Society funds research intended to find the cause and cure of MS. For people affected by the disease, it offers counseling, education, and equipment assistance. The Society also works to promote public policies and professional education that serve the estimated 500,000 people in the US who have MS, and more than 2 million worldwide. The Society operates through its national office and a 50-state network of chapters. It generates most of its revenue through fundraising and counts some 16,000 federal MS activists. The Society was founded in 1946 after Sylvia Lawry ran a classified ad in The New York Times looking for anyone who had recovered from the disease her brother was battling.

NATIONAL ORGANIZATION FOR WOMEN, INC

1100 H ST NW STE 300
WASHINGTON, DC 200055488
Phone: 202 628-8669
Fax: –
Web: www.now.org

CEO: –
CFO: –
HR: –
FYE: December 31
Type: Private

What do they want? Equality for women! When do they want it? NOW! The National Organization for Women (NOW) works to promote the social, political, and economic interests of women by eliminating job discrimination and harassment, securing reproductive rights, ending violence against women, and supporting civil rights for all. Its tactics include lobbying lawmakers, conducting demonstrations, filing lawsuits, and engaging in political organizing. NOW has about 500,000 members in 550 chapters in all 50 states and the District of Columbia. It publishes the National NOW Times and hosts a national conference each year. NOW was founded in 1966 by a group of 28 women that included author Betty Friedan.

	Annual Growth	12/14	12/15	12/17	12/18	12/19
Sales ($mil.)	(20.6%)	–	2.9	1.2	0.9	1.2
Net income ($ mil.)	13.2%	–	0.3	0.5	0.3	0.5
Market value ($ mil.)	–	–	–	–	–	–
Employees		–	–	–	–	33

NATIONAL PARK FOUNDATION

1500 K ST NW STE 700
WASHINGTON, DC 200051257
Phone: 202 796-2500
Fax: –
Web: www.nationalparks.org

CEO: –
CFO: –
HR: –
FYE: September 30
Type: Private

Chartered by Congress in 1967, the National Park Foundation is a not-for-profit organization responsible for raising funds, establishing grants, and increasing public awareness of national parks in the US. About 70% of funds raised each year are used for programs which include education, community involvement, and volunteerism. The National Park Foundation works with the National Park Service to educate the public about the parks and recruit volunteers to maintain the parks. Each year, more than 150,000 volunteers contribute to preserving about 400 national parks in the US.

	Annual Growth	09/16	09/17	09/18	09/21	09/22
Sales ($mil.)	10.1%	–	92.0	88.9	99.9	148.5
Net income ($ mil.)	24.2%	–	16.0	25.4	29.2	47.3
Market value ($ mil.)	–	–	–	–	–	–
Employees	–	–	–	–	–	92

NATIONAL PARK TRUST, INC.

401 E JEFFERSON ST STE 207
ROCKVILLE, MD 208502617
Phone: 301 279-7275
Fax: –
Web: www.parktrust.org

CEO: William Brownell
CFO: –
HR: –
FYE: June 30
Type: Private

National Park Trust (NPT) knows we can't completely trust the government to care for the nation's national parks. So the not-for-profit organization strives to protect national parks, wildlife, and historical monuments in the US. It purchases or otherwise acquires land in and adjacent to existing parks or land that is suitable for park creation and donates it to groups such as The National Park Service to manage. Past projects have included protecting Abraham Lincoln's boyhood home in Kentucky, acquiring a 907-acre site within Wrangell St. Elias National Park in Alaska, and establishing a buffer along the Fort Union Trading Post National Historic Site in North Dakota. NPT was founded in 1983.

	Annual Growth	06/18	06/19	06/20	06/21	06/22
Sales ($mil.)	19.1%	–	2.7	2.6	3.0	4.5
Net income ($ mil.)	33.0%	–	0.7	0.6	0.2	1.7
Market value ($ mil.)	–	–	–	–	–	–
Employees	–	–	–	–	–	11

NATIONAL PRESTO INDUSTRIES, INC.

NYS: NPK

3925 North Hastings Way
Eau Claire, WI 54703-3703
Phone: 715 839-2121
Fax: –
Web: www.gopresto.com

CEO: Maryjo Cohen
CFO: –
HR: –
FYE: December 31
Type: Public

National Presto Industries makes and distributes small appliances and housewares, including pressure cookers, deep fryers, air fryers, griddles, coffeemakers, kettles, electric heaters, and pizza ovens. The company pours itself into defense work, too, supplying ammunition; medium caliber cartridge cases; precision mechanical and electro-mechanical assemblies; and Load, Assemble, and Pack (LAP) operations on ordnance-related products. Its major customers include US and foreign government agencies, AMTEC Corporation, and other defense contractors. National Presto's products are sold primarily in the US and Canada directly to retailers and also through independent distributors.

	Annual Growth	12/19	12/20	12/21	12/22	12/23
Sales ($mil.)	2.5%	308.5	352.6	355.8	321.6	340.9
Net income ($ mil.)	(4.9%)	42.2	47.0	25.7	20.7	34.6
Market value ($ mil.)	(2.4%)	626.2	626.5	581.1	485.0	568.7
Employees	2.3%	919	955	895	973	1,007

NATIONAL PUBLIC RADIO, INC.

1111 N CAPITOL ST NE
WASHINGTON, DC 200027502
Phone: 202 513-2000
Fax: –
Web: www.npr.org

CEO: John Lansing
CFO: Debbie Cullen
HR: Carrie D Storer
FYE: September 30
Type: Private

This company helps keep radio listeners informed and entertained without commercial interruptions. National Public Radio (NPR) is a privately supported, not-for-profit organization, that produces and syndicates radio programming to 900 independently operated noncommercial radio stations, including about 750 NPR member stations. Its shows include news programs Morning Edition and All Things Considered , as well as cultural programs (Fresh Air) and entertainment shows (Car Talk; Wait, Wait ... Don't Tell Me!). Founded in 1970, NPR is funded through private donations, member station dues, and grants from organizations such as the Corporation for Public Broadcasting and the National Science Foundation.

	Annual Growth	09/18	09/19	09/20	09/21	09/22
Sales ($mil.)	2.5%	–	283.5	277.6	288.1	305.6
Net income ($ mil.)	–	–	1.1	(14.1)	16.9	(1.4)
Market value ($ mil.)	–	–	–	–	–	–
Employees	–	–	–	–	–	741

NATIONAL RAILROAD PASSENGER CORPORATION

1 MASSACHUSETTS AVE NW
WASHINGTON, DC 200011401
Phone: 202 906-3000
Fax: –
Web: www.amtrak.com

CEO: Richard H Anderson
CFO: –
HR: –
FYE: September 30
Type: Private

National Railroad Passenger Corporation, better known as Amtrak, has been riding the rails for more than 40 years. Amtrak is the US' intercity passenger rail provider and its only high-speed rail operator. More than 30 million passengers travel on Amtrak every year on more than 300 daily trains. It connects 46 states, Washington, DC, and three provinces in Canada. Its network consists of about 21,000 route miles of track, most of which is owned by freight railroads. Amtrak also operates commuter rail systems on behalf of several states and transit agencies. Owned by the US government through the US Department of Transportation, Amtrak depends on subsidies from the federal government to operate.

	Annual Growth	09/17	09/18	09/19	09/20	09/21
Sales ($mil.)	(15.0%)	–	3,386.7	3,503.5	2,430.7	2,081.8
Net income ($ mil.)	–	–	(817.2)	(880.9)	(1,679.0)	(2,007.1)
Market value ($ mil.)	–	–	–	–	–	–
Employees	–	–	–	–	–	18,650

NATIONAL RECREATION AND PARK ASSOCIATION, INCORPORATED

22377 BELMONT RIDGE RD   CEO: Barbara Tulipane
ASHBURN, VA 201484501   CFO: –
Phone: 703 858-0784   HR: –
Fax: –   FYE: June 30
Web: www.nrpa.org   Type: Private

A lot of people are telling you to get outdoors and rec-reate these days but this group has been saying it for years. The National Recreation and Park Association (NRPA) is a not-for-profit organization dedicated to preserving recreation, park, and leisure facilities; promoting wellness; developing and influencing public policy in support of recreation; connecting tourism workers with park information; and developing and disseminating recreation program information. To that end, the organization lobbies local, state, and national government and hosts events like the National Health & Livability Summit. It also partners with other organizations to promote outdoor activities for kids. NRPA was formed in 1907.

	Annual Growth	06/16	06/17	06/20	06/21	06/22
Sales ($mil.)	(0.6%)	–	16.8	20.1	21.3	16.4
Net income ($ mil.)	–	–	(0.3)	2.4	5.3	(2.8)
Market value ($ mil.)	–	–	–	–	–	–
Employees	–	–	–	–	–	62

NATIONAL RESEARCH CORP   NMS: NRC

1245 Q Street   CEO: Michael D Hays
Lincoln, NE 68508   CFO: Kevin R Karas
Phone: 402 475-2525   HR: –
Fax: –   FYE: December 31
Web: www.nrchealth.com   Type: Public

National Research Corporation (NRC) is a leading provider of analytics and insights that facilitate measurement and improvement of the patient and employee experience while also increasing patient engagement and customer loyalty for healthcare organizations. Founded in 1981, NRC's Market solutions provide clients with on-demand tools to measure brand value and build brand equity in their markets, evaluate and optimize advertising efficacy and consumer recall, and tailor research to obtain the real-time voice of customer feedback to support branding and loyalty initiatives. NRC's Market Insights is the largest US healthcare consumer database of its kind, measuring the opinions and behaviors of approximately 300,000 healthcare consumers across the contiguous US annually. Almost all of its sales were generated from the US.

	Annual Growth	12/19	12/20	12/21	12/22	12/23
Sales ($mil.)	3.8%	128.0	133.8	148.0	151.6	148.6
Net income ($ mil.)	(1.1%)	32.4	37.3	37.5	31.8	31.0
Market value ($ mil.)	(12.0%)	1,597.1	1,035.4	1,005.6	903.4	958.1
Employees	(2.4%)	480	485	511	491	435

NATIONAL RETAIL FEDERATION, INC.

1101 NEW YORK AVE NW STE 1200   CEO: Matthew Shay
WASHINGTON, DC 200054348   CFO: –
Phone: 202 626-8155   HR: Sharon Guevara
Fax: –   FYE: February 28
Web: www.nrf.com   Type: Private

The National Retail Federation (NRF) wants everyone to shop 'til they drop. The group is a trade association representing the retail industry that works through four divisions addressing technology in retail, chain restaurants, advertising and marketing, and online retail. It functions as both an advocacy group and an informational network for its members, lobbying government, hosting conferences and seminars, and publishing newsletters and books. The NRF magazine, Stores , is published monthly. NRF includes more than 100 US national, state, and international retail associations and more than 1.6 million US retailers with about 42 million employees.

	Annual Growth	02/16	02/17	02/18	02/19	02/22
Sales ($mil.)	(4.3%)	–	60.8	66.4	62.8	48.7
Net income ($ mil.)	–	–	9.1	1.5	(1.1)	(2.8)
Market value ($ mil.)	–	–	–	–	–	–
Employees	–	–	–	–	–	135

NATIONAL REVIEW, INC.

19 W 44TH ST STE 1701   CEO: –
NEW YORK, NY 100366101   CFO: James Kilbridge
Phone: 212 679-7330   HR: –
Fax: –   FYE: July 31
Web: www.nrinstitute.org   Type: Private

Folks on the Left might find this review of the nation a bit lacking. National Review is a magazine and book publisher focusing on international and political news and opinion from a conservative Republican viewpoint. In addition to its semimonthly National Review and the online version National Review Online (NRO), the company publishes such book titles as The National Review Treasury of Classic Bedtime Stories and American Conservatism: An Encyclopedia . The National Review was founded in 1955 by conservative commentator William F. Buckley, who hosted the weekly PBS TV show Firing Line for more than 20 years. Buckley died in 2008.

	Annual Growth	07/06	07/07	07/08	07/15	07/17
Sales ($mil.)	23.9%	–	–	0.8	3.3	5.7
Net income ($ mil.)	32.9%	–	–	0.0	0.9	0.7
Market value ($ mil.)	–	–	–	–	–	–
Employees	–	–	–	–	–	50

NATIONAL RIFLE ASSOCIATION OF AMERICA

11250 WAPLES MILL RD STE 1   CEO: –
FAIRFAX, VA 220309400   CFO: Wilson H Phillips
Phone: 703 267-1263   HR: –
Fax: –   FYE: December 31
Web: agegateway.nrahq.org   Type: Private

The NRA believes in the right to bear arms. With more than 5 million members, The National Rifle Association (NRA) is the staunch defender of Second Amendment rights. It's a major player in the political arena and stands firm in its resolve to protect the right to keep and bear arms. The NRA offers a variety of educational and gun safety programs and publishes magazines (America's 1st Freedom, American Hunter, Women's Outlook). It also caters to more than one million youth through its shooting sports events and affiliated programs with the likes of 4-H, the Boy Scouts of America, and others. It also sells NRA merchandise. Union army veterans William Church and George Wingate founded the NRA in 1871.

	Annual Growth	12/12	12/13	12/14	12/16	12/21
Sales ($mil.)	(5.2%)	–	348.0	310.5	366.9	227.4
Net income ($ mil.)	(20.1%)	–	57.4	(35.1)	(45.8)	9.6
Market value ($ mil.)	–	–	–	–	–	–
Employees	–	–	–	–	–	500

NATIONAL RURAL ELECTRIC COOPERATIVE ASSOCIATION

4301 WILSON BLVD STE 1   CEO: Glenn L English Jr
ARLINGTON, VA 222031867   CFO: –
Phone: 703 907-5500   HR: –
Fax: –   FYE: December 31
Web: www.electric.coop   Type: Private

Would it shock you to learn that consumer-owned cooperatives provide electricity to more than 42 million people in the US? The National Rural Electric Cooperative Association (NRECA) is the cooperatives' voice in politics and policymaking. It publishes a monthly magazine and a weekly newspaper, sponsors conferences and seminars, and represents about 900 rural electric co-ops (from 47 states) in the US Congress and state legislatures. As the nation embraces investor-owned utilities, NRECA has been lobbying hard for more moderate approaches to deregulation in order to protect consumers from potential monopolies. The association also provides power assistance and technical advice to developing nations.

	Annual Growth	12/11	12/12	12/13	12/21	12/22
Sales ($mil.)	(0.1%)	–	208.7	194.5	194.9	205.7
Net income ($ mil.)	(16.5%)	–	4.5	(8.1)	(2.4)	0.7
Market value ($ mil.)	–	–	–	–	–	–
Employees	–	–	–	–	–	885

NATIONAL RURAL UTILITIES COOPERATIVE FINANCE CORP

20701 Cooperative Way
Dulles, VA 20166
Phone: 703 467-1800
Fax: 703 709-6779
Web: www.nrucfc.coop

CEO: Sheldon C Petersen
CFO: J A Don
HR: Brandon Butler
FYE: May 31
Type: Public

Cooperation may work wonders on Sesame Street, but in the real world it takes money to pay the power bill. The National Rural Utilities Cooperative Finance Corporation provides financing and investment services for rural electrical and telephone projects throughout the US. The group is owned by some 1,500 member electric utility and telecommunications systems. National Rural supplements the government loans that traditionally have fueled rural electric utilities by selling commercial paper, medium-term notes, and collateral trust bonds to fund its loan programs. National Rural was formed in 1969 by the National Rural Electric Cooperative Association, a lobby representing the nation's electric co-ops.

	Annual Growth	05/18	05/19	05/20	05/21	05/22
Sales ($mil.)	5.0%	1,326.7	787.7	384.1	1,641.8	1,614.9
Net income ($ mil.)	15.0%	455.2	(149.2)	(585.2)	811.7	795.8
Market value ($ mil.)	–	–	–	–	–	–
Employees	0.5%	254	257	253	248	259

NATIONAL SAFETY COUNCIL

1121 SPRING LAKE DR
ITASCA, IL 601433200
Phone: 630 285-1121
Fax: –
Web: www.nsc.org

CEO: Lorraine M Martin
CFO: Patrick Phelam
HR: –
FYE: June 30
Type: Private

What are the odds of crashing while driving and talking on a cell phone? This is a question the National Safety Council (NSC) can answer. The NSC is a not-for-profit organization dedicated to educating Americans on safety and health to stop as many of the millions of preventable injuries a year as possible. NSC and its about 60 local chapters comprise members from more than 50,000 business, academic, government, community, and labor organizations, as well as individuals. It provides information and training to its members (and members' employees) on injury statistics and prevention. The group also offers consulting services on safety program development, incident investigation, and hazard recognition.

	Annual Growth	06/16	06/17	06/20	06/21	06/22
Sales ($mil.)	(3.2%)	–	59.2	55.7	62.7	50.2
Net income ($ mil.)	–	–	5.2	1.1	14.2	(7.0)
Market value ($ mil.)	–	–	–	–	–	–
Employees	–	–	–	–	–	350

NATIONAL SPACE SOCIETY

1875 I ST NW STE 500
WASHINGTON, DC 200065425
Phone: 202 424-2899
Fax: –
Web: www.nss.org

CEO: Gary P Barnhard
CFO: –
HR: –
FYE: December 31
Type: Private

The National Space Society (NSS) has stars in its eyes. The 12,000-member organization is dedicated to the advancement of human societies in space as a solution to such global threats as overpopulation, the depletion of natural resources, and comet or asteroid impact. Its more than 50 chapters around the world lobby policymakers and participate in educational activities to rally public support for space-related issues. NSS also publishes Ad Astra, a quarterly member magazine featuring news on international space programs and achievements. The organization was founded in 1974 by pioneer rocket scientist Wernher von Braun.

	Annual Growth	12/97	12/98	12/99	12/00	12/13
Sales ($mil.)	(38.8%)	–	1,092.8	1.4	2.0	0.7
Net income ($ mil.)	5.8%	–	0.0	0.2	0.7	0.0
Market value ($ mil.)	–	–	–	–	–	–
Employees	–	–	–	–	–	12

NATIONAL SPINNING CO., INC.

1481 W 2ND ST STE 103
WASHINGTON, NC 278894294
Phone: 252 975-7111
Fax: –
Web: www.natspin.com

CEO: James Chesnutt
CFO: Linda Fanton
HR: Betty Sikes
FYE: December 31
Type: Private

National Spinning Co., Inc. is a leading US-based supplier of raw white (ecru) and fiber-dyed short staple and long staple spun yarns. Offerings include yarns spun from synthetic fibers, natural fibers (including wool and cotton), and technical fibers. It manufactures and distributes wide variety of yarns. Its spinning systems include short staple ring, open end, and worsted spinning and its raw materials include synthetic and natural fibers. Apart from its yarn business, the company has two other operating divisions: Hampton Art designs, produces, and merchandises consumer craft products and Carolina Nonwovens produces and distributes air-laid thermobonded pads and rolls. In addition to these, National Spinning maintains, manage, and leases commercial space in its Washington, NC facility alongside Kennedy Creek. Customers have included Fox River, Gildan, Glen Raven, Julia Knit, and Renfro. In business since 1921, the company is an employee-owned.

NATIONAL STORAGE AFFILIATES TRUST

8400 East Prentice Avenue, 9th Floor
Greenwood Village, CO 80111
Phone: 720 630-2600
Fax: –
Web: www.nationalstorageaffiliates.com

NYS: NSA
CEO: David Cramer
CFO: Tamara D Fischer
HR: –
FYE: December 31
Type: Public

National Storage Affiliates Trust is a fully integrated, self-administered and self-managed real estate investment trust (REIT) focused on the ownership, operation, and acquisition of self-storage properties in the US top 100 metropolitan areas. It is one of the largest owner and operator of self-storage properties and the largest privately owned operator of self-storage properties in the US based on number of properties, units, and rentable square footage, with a portfolio of roughly 845 self-storage properties located in about 35 states and Puerto Rico, comprising approximately 53.5 million rentable square feet, configured in approximately 413,000 storage units.

	Annual Growth	12/19	12/20	12/21	12/22	12/23
Sales ($mil.)	22.0%	387.9	432.2	585.7	801.6	858.1
Net income ($ mil.)	150.4%	4.0	48.6	105.3	103.7	156.7
Market value ($ mil.)	5.4%	2,766.5	2,964.8	5,694.2	2,972.2	3,412.4
Employees	(8.2%)	1,559	1,684	1,175	1,155	1,108

NATIONAL THOROUGHBRED RACING ASSOCIATION, INC.

2525 HARRODSBURG RD STE 510
LEXINGTON, KY 405043355
Phone: 859 245-6872
Fax: –
Web: www.ntra.com

CEO: –
CFO: –
HR: –
FYE: January 31
Type: Private

This enterprise jockeys for position on the sports scene. The National Thoroughbred Racing Association (NTRA) oversees the Thoroughbred horseracing industry, acting as governing body, promoter, and trade association. It sets rules, regulates membership, and organizes races, and it helps promote the sport through negotiating broadcasting rights and marketing sponsorships. In addition, NTRA lobbies on behalf of pari-mutuel wagering (handicapping), licenses thoroughbred breeders, and sells racing merchandise. Along with sister company Breeders' Cup Limited, it hosts the ten Breeders' Cup races, including the Breeders' Cup Classic. NTRA was formed by a consortium of horseracing bodies in 1998.

	Annual Growth	01/10	01/11	01/12	01/15	01/16
Sales ($mil.)	25.7%	–	–	2.8	7.1	6.9
Net income ($ mil.)	–	–	–	0.4	0.0	(0.1)
Market value ($ mil.)	–	–	–	–	–	–
Employees	–	–	–	–	–	30

NATIONAL TRUST FOR HISTORIC PRESERVATION IN THE UNITED STATES

600 14TH ST NW STE 500
WASHINGTON, DC 200052011
Phone: 202 588-6000
Fax: -
Web: www.savingplaces.org
CEO: -
CFO: Carla Washinko
HR: David Field
FYE: June 30
Type: Private

National Trust for Historic Preservation wants to ensure that historic America is protected against destruction and negligence. The not-for-profit organization was founded in 1949 and educates, advocates, and provides resources for the preservation of historic buildings and land (not to be confused with the National Register of Historical Places, which designates buildings and neighborhoods as historic). The group also operates about 30 historic sites across the US. National Trust, which boasts about 270,000 members, operates out of a Washington, DC, headquarters and nine regional and field offices. It also works with thousands of preservation groups in all 50 states.

	Annual Growth	06/10	06/11	06/12	06/13	06/14
Sales ($mil.)	(38.0%)	-	-	-	81.2	50.3
Net income ($ mil.)	-	-	-	-	31.6	(1.8)
Market value ($ mil.)	-	-	-	-	-	-
Employees	-	-	-	-	-	469

NATIONAL UNIVERSITY

9388 LIGHTWAVE AVE
SAN DIEGO, CA 921231426
Phone: 858 642-8000
Fax: -
Web: www.nu.edu
CEO: -
CFO: -
HR: Margaret Greer
FYE: June 30
Type: Private

National University is the flagship school of the National University System. The institution offers more than 150 undergraduate and graduate degrees and teacher credential and certificate programs. A not-for-profit institution, National University programs range across fields including business, engineering, education, media, and human services. The university enrolls 23,000 students at multiple locations in California and Nevada; it also offers about 70 online degree programs. The school conducts research through the National University Community Research Institute (NUCRI). National University was founded in 1971.

	Annual Growth	06/08	06/09	06/10	06/11	06/15
Sales ($mil.)	8.1%	-	165.0	178.6	203.3	263.8
Net income ($ mil.)	37.7%	-	5.2	18.5	25.2	35.3
Market value ($ mil.)	-	-	-	-	-	-
Employees	-	-	-	-	-	1,954

NATIONAL URBAN LEAGUE, INC.

80 PINE ST RM 910
NEW YORK, NY 100051720
Phone: 212 558-5300
Fax: -
Web: www.nul.org
CEO: Marc H Morial
CFO: Sidney Evans Jr
HR: Clarissa Moses
FYE: December 31
Type: Private

National Urban League doesn't care if you live in the city or the country. If you are African American, it wants to empower you to get into the economic and social mainstream. Through 95 affiliates in 35 states and the District of Columbia, the Urban League offers reading and scholarship programs, job and financial literacy training, health information, voter education and registration, and civil rights programs. A few of the league's five publications include Opportunity Journal, Urban Influence, and The State of Black America, an annual report. It also hosts several conferences and summits throughout the year. Founded in 1910 The Urban League reaches more than 2 million people nationwide.

	Annual Growth	12/12	12/13	12/14	12/18	12/19
Sales ($mil.)	0.8%	-	49.2	51.1	50.0	51.7
Net income ($ mil.)	(1.8%)	-	1.0	1.3	(7.2)	0.9
Market value ($ mil.)	-	-	-	-	-	-
Employees	-	-	-	-	-	100

NATIONAL VAN LINES, INC.

2800 W ROOSEVELT RD
BROADVIEW, IL 601553771
Phone: 708 450-2900
Fax: -
Web: www.nationalvanlines.com
CEO: Timothy P Helenthal
CFO: -
HR: -
FYE: April 30
Type: Private

National Van Lines provides moving services for households and businesses. The company, which operates through a national network of some 400 agents, can arrange international as well as domestic moves. Besides consumers and businesses, National Van Lines has a dedicated unit, National Forwarding Company, to serve customers including government agencies such as the US Department of Defense to move military families. CEO Maureen Beal owns National Van Lines, which was founded in 1929 by her grandfather, F.J. McKee.

	Annual Growth	04/06	04/07	04/08	04/09	04/10
Sales ($mil.)	(3.3%)	-	-	86.3	89.4	80.7
Net income ($ mil.)	(30.6%)	-	-	4.5	3.5	2.2
Market value ($ mil.)	-	-	-	-	-	-
Employees	-	-	-	-	-	72

NATIONAL VISION HOLDINGS INC   NMS: EYE

2435 Commerce Avenue, Building 2200
Duluth, GA 30096
Phone: 770 822-3600
Fax: -
Web: www.nationalvision.com
CEO: L R Fahs
CFO: Patrick R Moore
HR: -
FYE: December 30
Type: Public

National Vision is one of the largest optical retailers in the US and a leader in the attractive value segment of the US optical retail industry. It delivers value and convenience to its customers, with an opening price point that strives to be among the lowest in the industry, enabled by its low-cost operating platform. It reaches its customers through a diverse portfolio of about 1,355 retail stores across five brands and more than 15 consumer websites. More than 65% of its stores use America's Best name and are in high-traffic strip malls and other value-focused retailers. National Vision also operates Eyeglass World superstores, as well as Vista Optical and Vision Center.

	Annual Growth	12/19*	01/21	01/22*	12/22	12/23
Sales ($mil.)	5.4%	1,724.3	1,711.8	2,079.5	2,005.4	2,126.5
Net income ($ mil.)	-	32.8	36.3	128.2	42.1	(65.9)
Market value ($ mil.)	(10.8%)	2,592.1	3,546.7	3,758.1	3,035.3	1,639.0
Employees	4.4%	11,781	12,792	13,735	13,975	13,998

*Fiscal year change

NATIONAL WIC ASSOCIATION, INC.

1099 14TH ST NW
WASHINGTON, DC 200054858
Phone: 202 232-5492
Fax: -
Web: www.nwica.org
CEO: -
CFO: -
HR: -
FYE: December 31
Type: Private

NWA wants kids to drink milk and eat veggies. The National WIC Association (NWA) is the nonprofit support agency for the Special Supplemental Nutrition Program for Women, Infants and Children (WIC). Through some 10,000 clinics nationwide, WIC provides nutrition and breastfeeding education and offers programs that include nutritious foods and health care access for more than 9 million low-income women and children. NWA operates through more than 2,000 local agencies in all 50 states, the District of Columbia, more than 30 American Indian tribal organizations, American Samoa, Guam, and Puerto Rico. It also advocates for services for nutritionally at-risk families. NWA was founded in 1983.

	Annual Growth	12/16	12/17	12/19	12/21	12/22
Sales ($mil.)	5.7%	-	5.9	4.6	4.5	7.9
Net income ($ mil.)	-	-	(0.0)	0.0	(1.6)	1.3
Market value ($ mil.)	-	-	-	-	-	-
Employees	-	-	-	-	-	14

NATIONAL WILDLIFE FEDERATION INC

11100 WILDLIFE CENTER DR　　　　　　　　　　CEO: Larry J Schweiger
RESTON, VA 201905362　　　　　　　　　　　　CFO: -
Phone: 703 438-6000　　　　　　　　　　　　　HR: -
Fax: -　　　　　　　　　　　　　　　　　　　FYE: August 31
Web: www.nwf.org　　　　　　　　　　　　　　Type: Private

The National Wildlife Federation (NWF) is America's largest and most trusted conservation organization, with more than six million members and supporters and over 50 state and territorial affiliates. It works to educate the public about conservation of wildlife and other natural resources. The non-profit organization organizes efforts on an educational and political front. Conservation projects include recovering wildlife populations, grassroots programs, protecting endangered species, and advocating for conservation policy. It also conducts wildlife tours and publishes a number of magazines including National Wildlife, Ranger Rick, Ranger Rick Cub, and Ranger Rick Junior and produces film and television programs on conservation. The NWF was founded in 1936.

	Annual Growth	08/18	08/19	08/20	08/21	08/22
Sales ($mil.)	6.1%	-	94.4	82.5	114.1	112.8
Net income ($ mil.)	(6.3%)	-	4.6	(8.7)	18.6	3.8
Market value ($ mil.)	-	-	-	-	-	-
Employees	-	-	-	-	-	350

NATIONSHEALTH INC   OTC: NHRX

13630 N.W. 8th Street, Suite 210　　　　　　　CEO: Stephen Farrell
Sunrise, FL 33325　　　　　　　　　　　　　　CFO: Timothy Fairbanks
Phone: 954 903-5000　　　　　　　　　　　　　HR: Reggie Holt
Fax: -　　　　　　　　　　　　　　　　　　　FYE: December 31
Web: www.nationshealth.com　　　　　　　　　Type: Public

NationsHealth aims to make it easier for Medicare patients to get their prescription drugs and medical supplies. The company delivers diabetes, respiratory, ostomy, urology, and other medical supplies, including insulin and insulin pumps, to the homes of about 80,000 patients. In addition, NationsHealth has partnered with CIGNA and other health insurers to provide business process outsourcing solutions, marketing, training, enrollment and collections for Medicare services, distribution, billing, communications, and disease and wellness programs. The CIGNA collaborative agreement is part of the CIGNA Medicare Rx Part D plan. NationsHealth is owned by investment firm ComVest.

	Annual Growth	12/04	12/05	12/06	12/07	12/08
Sales ($mil.)	7.8%	74.2	87.6	87.2	77.5	100.4
Net income ($ mil.)	-	(26.4)	(19.8)	(11.3)	(5.9)	(4.6)
Market value ($ mil.)	(73.3%)	197.0	223.0	48.3	13.4	1.0
Employees	12.9%	367	780	619	674	597

NATIONWIDE AGRIBUSINESS INSURANCE CO.

1963 Bell Avenue　　　　　　　　　　　　　　CEO: -
Des Moines, IA 50315-1030　　　　　　　　　　CFO: -
Phone: 515 245-8800　　　　　　　　　　　　　HR: -
Fax: -　　　　　　　　　　　　　　　　　　　FYE: December 31
Web: www.farmlandins.com　　　　　　　　　　Type: Public

Whether you're in high cotton or riding out a 17-year locust outbreak, Nationwide Agribusiness Insurance (and affiliate Farmland Mutual Insurance) have your farm covered. The company is one of the leading providers of insurance for the US commercial agribusiness industry, food processors, and farm operators of all sizes. Products include commercial insurance (CommercialGard and AgriChoice), workers' compensation (ComPlus), cotton farmer and ginner coverage (CottonGard), and other specialized farm policies. Additionally, the company offers commercial auto, umbrella liability, and customized policies, as well as various insurance services. Nationwide Agribusiness is a subsidiary of insurance biggie Nationwide.

	Annual Growth	12/97	12/98	12/99	12/00	12/01
Assets ($mil.)	(18.4%)	105.1	84.8	45.2	43.9	46.7
Net income ($ mil.)	(3.0%)	2.1	3.6	6.4	1.4	1.9
Market value ($ mil.)	-	-	-	-	-	-
Employees	-	-	-	-	-	-

NATIONWIDE CHILDREN'S HOSPITAL

700 CHILDRENS DR　　　　　　　　　　　　　CEO: Steve Allen
COLUMBUS, OH 432052639　　　　　　　　　　CFO: Timothy Robinson
Phone: 614 722-2000　　　　　　　　　　　　　HR: Sue Doud
Fax: -　　　　　　　　　　　　　　　　　　　FYE: September 30
Web: www.nationwidechildrens.org　　　　　　Type: Private

Nationwide Children's Hospital is one of America's largest not-for-profit free-standing pediatric health care systems providing unique expertise in pediatric population health, behavioral health, genomics and health equity. Nationwide Children's has a staff of more than 13,000 that provides state-of-the-art wellness, preventive and rehabilitative care and diagnostic treatment during more than 1.6 million patient visits annually. As home to the Department of Pediatrics of The Ohio State University College of Medicine, Nationwide Children's physicians train the next generation of pediatricians and pediatric specialists. The Abigail Wexner Research Institute at Nationwide Children's Hospital is one of the Top 10 National Institutes of Health-funded free-standing pediatric research facilities.

NATIVE ENVIRONMENTAL, L.L.C.

2435 E UNIVERSITY DR　　　　　　　　　　　CEO: -
PHOENIX, AZ 850346910　　　　　　　　　　　CFO: -
Phone: 602 254-0122　　　　　　　　　　　　　HR: Suzie Ellington
Fax: -　　　　　　　　　　　　　　　　　　　FYE: December 31
Web: www.nativeaz.com　　　　　　　　　　　Type: Private

Removal of mold, lead, and asbestos is not a foreign concept at Native Environmental, L.L.C. The Phoenix-based industrial cleaning and environmental contracting company serves Arizona, New Mexico, and thirty other states. Native Environmental focuses on mold remediation, lead-based paint removal, and removal of asbestos. The company contracts with customers like hospitals, governmental entities, and demolition companies, and has short and long-term contracts that range in size from small commercial projects to large industrial projects. Founded by CEO Jon W. Riggs, Native Environmental has been in business since 2000.

NATURAL ALTERNATIVES INTERNATIONAL, INC.   NMS: NAII

1535 Faraday Ave　　　　　　　　　　　　　　CEO: Mark A Ledoux
Carlsbad, CA 92008　　　　　　　　　　　　　CFO: Michael E Fortin
Phone: 760 736-7700　　　　　　　　　　　　　HR: -
Fax: -　　　　　　　　　　　　　　　　　　　FYE: June 30
Web: www.nai-online.com　　　　　　　　　　Type: Public

Natural Alternatives International (NAI) is a natural alternative for nutritional supplement marketers who want to outsource manufacturing. The company provides private-label manufacturing of vitamins, minerals, herbs, and other customized nutritional supplements. Its main customers are direct sellers such as Mannatech and NSA International, for whom it makes JuicePlus+ chewables, capsules, and powdered products. NAI also makes some branded products for sale in the US: the Pathway to Healing brand of nutritional supplements, promoted by doctor and evangelist Reginald B. Cherry.

	Annual Growth	06/19	06/20	06/21	06/22	06/23
Sales ($mil.)	2.7%	138.3	118.9	178.5	171.0	154.0
Net income ($ mil.)	(21.2%)	6.5	(1.6)	10.8	10.7	2.5
Market value ($ mil.)	(11.4%)	70.8	41.5	102.2	63.4	43.7
Employees	0.7%	312	316	342	396	321

NATURAL FRUIT CORP.

770 W 20TH ST
HIALEAH, FL 330102430
Phone: 305 887-7525
Fax: –
Web: www.nfc-fruti.com

CEO: –
CFO: –
HR: –
FYE: December 31
Type: Private

Au naturale isn't just a catchphrase at Natural Fruit Corp. The company manufactures and markets frozen snacks made from 100% natural fruit -- no artificial anything. Its signature product is the Chunks O' Fruti frozen fruit bar, but the company also makes frozen yogurt bars and Allyson JAYNE brand frozen fruit drink mixes. The company's fruit-filled foods are distributed throughout the US and internationally. The Natural Fruit Corp. was founded in 1984 by Colombian brothers Simon (president) and Jorge Bravo, Sr. (EVP).

	Annual Growth	12/11	12/12	12/13	12/14	12/15
Sales ($mil.)	(8.1%)	–	16.3	14.0	12.4	12.6
Net income ($ mil.)	(29.1%)	–	3.4	1.8	1.9	1.2
Market value ($ mil.)	–	–	–	–	–	–
Employees	–	–	–	–	–	50

NATURAL GAS SERVICES GROUP INC   NYS: NGS

404 Veterans Airpark Ln., Ste 300
Midland, TX 79705
Phone: 432 262-2700
Fax: –
Web: www.ngsgi.com

CEO: Stephen C Taylor
CFO: Micah C Foster
HR: –
FYE: December 31
Type: Public

The pressure is on to enhance oil and gas well production. Natural Gas Services Group (NGS) manufactures, fabricates, rents, sells and maintains natural gas compressors and flare systems for oil and natural gas production and plant facilities. The company also provides flare tip burners, ignition systems, and components used to combust waste gases before entering the atmosphere. It offers products and services to exploration and production companies operating in Colorado, Michigan, New Mexico, Ohio, Oklahoma, Pennsylvania, Texas, West Virginia and Wyoming. The company has about 1,420 natural gas compressors in rental fleet totaling about 300,000 horsepower. NGS has shifted its focus over the last several years to medium to large horsepower applications that apply to natural gas associated with oil-weighted production.

	Annual Growth	12/18	12/19	12/20	12/21	12/22
Sales ($mil.)	6.7%	65.5	78.4	68.1	72.4	84.8
Net income ($ mil.)	–	0.4	(13.9)	1.8	(9.2)	(0.6)
Market value ($ mil.)	(8.6%)	200.7	149.7	115.7	127.8	139.9
Employees	(0.6%)	273	270	229	247	266

NATURAL GROCERS BY VITAMIN COTTAGE INC   NYS: NGVC

12612 West Alameda Parkway
Lakewood, CO 80228
Phone: 303 986-4600
Fax: –
Web: www.naturalgrocers.com

CEO: Kemper Isely
CFO: Todd Dissinger
HR: –
FYE: September 30
Type: Public

Natural Grocers by Vitamin Cottage (Natural Grocer) is an expanding specialty retailer of natural and organic groceries and dietary supplements. The fast-growing company (both in sales and store count) operates about 165 stores in some 20 US states that sell natural and organic food, including fresh produce, meat, frozen food, and non-perishable bulk food; vitamins and dietary supplements; personal care products; pet care products; and books. The company sources from approximately 1,000 suppliers and offer approximately 3,100 brands that range from small independent businesses to multi-national conglomerates. Founded by Margaret and Philip Isely in 1958, Natural Grocers is run by members of the Isely family.

	Annual Growth	09/19	09/20	09/21	09/22	09/23
Sales ($mil.)	6.0%	903.6	1,036.8	1,055.5	1,089.6	1,140.6
Net income ($ mil.)	25.3%	9.4	20.0	20.6	21.4	23.2
Market value ($ mil.)	6.6%	227.2	224.2	255.1	245.4	293.6
Employees	3.2%	3,681	4,272	4,192	4,173	4,173

NATURAL RESOURCE PARTNERS LP   NYS: NRP

1415 Louisiana Street, Suite 3325
Houston, TX 77002
Phone: 713 751-7507
Fax: –
Web: www.nrplp.com

CEO: Corbin J Robertson
CFO: –
HR: –
FYE: December 31
Type: Public

Natural Resource Partners (NRP) makes money from coal without getting its hands dirty. Rather than mining the coal itself, NRP leases properties to coal producers. The company's properties -- mainly in Appalachia but also in the Northern Powder River Basin and the Illinois Basin -- contain proved and probable reserves of about 2.4 billion tons of coal. NRP was formed as a partnership between WPP Group (Western Pocahontas Properties, New Gauley Coal, and Great Northern Properties) and Arch Coal. Arch Coal has sold its stake in NRP but remains one of the company's top lessees, along with Alpha Natural Resources. Chairman and CEO Corbin Robertson controls about 35% of NRP, primarily through WPP Group.

	Annual Growth	12/19	12/20	12/21	12/22	12/23
Sales ($mil.)	8.8%	263.9	140.3	216.4	389.0	370.0
Net income ($ mil.)	–	(24.5)	(84.8)	108.9	268.5	278.4
Market value ($ mil.)	46.5%	254.1	173.7	422.2	686.4	1,169.5
Employees	(0.4%)	56	54	52	54	55

NATURAL RESOURCES DEFENSE COUNCIL INC.

40 W 20TH ST
NEW YORK, NY 100114211
Phone: 212 727-2700
Fax: –
Web: www.nrdc.org

CEO: Gina McCarthy
CFO: –
HR: Joe Haseleu
FYE: June 30
Type: Private

Natural Resource Defense Council (NRDC) may be Mother Nature's strongest advocate. It is a nonprofit environmental action organization comprising 1.4-million members dedicated to preserving wildlife and the wilderness. To that end, the NRDC's mission takes aim at curbing global warming; creating a future fueled by clean energy; restoring the Earth's oceans; saving endangered wildlife and wild places; stemming the tide of pollutants that endanger heath; and accelerating the greening of communities. In addition press releases and blog posts, it publishes Nature's Voice , a bulletin on environmental campaigns; O nEarth , its quarterly magazine; and periodic NRDC Reports on specific issues.

	Annual Growth	06/13	06/14	06/20	06/21	06/22
Sales ($mil.)	5.5%	–	121.6	197.6	273.7	186.2
Net income ($ mil.)	–	–	5.9	12.6	91.7	(25.8)
Market value ($ mil.)	–	–	–	–	–	–
Employees	–	–	–	–	–	500

NATURE'S SUNSHINE PRODUCTS, INC.   NAS: NATR

2901 Bluegrass Boulevard, Suite 100
Lehi, UT 84043
Phone: 801 341-7900
Fax: –
Web: www.natr.com

CEO: –
CFO: –
HR: –
FYE: December 31
Type: Public

Nature's Sunshine Products is a natural health and wellness company primarily engaged in the manufacturing and direct selling of nutritional and personal care products. It makes more than 800 products, including herbal supplements (available in capsule, tablet, and liquid form) and vitamins. It has four business segments: Asia, Europe, North America, and Latin America and Other. Each of the geographic segments operate under the Nature's Sunshine Products and Synergy WorldWide brands. The Latin America and Other segment includes its wholesale business in which its sell products to various locally-managed entities independent of the company that it has granted distribution rights for the relevant market. Around 70% of total revenue accounts outside the US.

	Annual Growth	12/19	12/20	12/21	12/22	12/23
Sales ($mil.)	5.3%	362.2	385.2	444.1	421.9	445.3
Net income ($ mil.)	22.2%	6.8	21.3	28.9	(0.4)	15.1
Market value ($ mil.)	18.0%	168.6	282.2	349.2	157.0	326.3
Employees	(0.6%)	834	837	850	800	814

NATUS MEDICAL INCORPORATED

6701 KOLL CENTER PKWY STE 120　　　　　　CEO: Jonathan Kennedy
PLEASANTON, CA 945668061　　　　　　　　CFO: Drew Davies
Phone: 925 223-6700　　　　　　　　　　　HR: Lisa Evou
Fax: -　　　　　　　　　　　　　　　　　FYE: December 31
Web: www.natus.com　　　　　　　　　　　Type: Private

Natus is a leading provider of medical device solutions focused on the screening, diagnosis and treatment of central nervous and sensory system disorders. Natus delivers innovative and trusted solutions to screen, diagnose, and treat disorders affecting the brain, neural pathways, and eight sensory nervous systems to advance the standard of care and improve patient outcomes and quality of life. With sales in over 100 countries, Natus is a leader in neurodiagnostics, pediatric retinal imaging, and infant hearing screening, as well as a leading company in hearing assessment, hearing instrument fitting, balance, and intracranial pressure monitoring. In 2022, Natus was acquired by an affiliate of ArchiMed (ArchiMed), a leading investment firm focused exclusively on the healthcare industry for approximately $1.2 billion.

NAVARRO RESEARCH AND ENGINEERING, INC.

1020 COMMERCE PARK DR STE 4　　　　　CEO: Susana Navarro-Valenti PHD
OAK RIDGE, TN 378308026　　　　　　　　CFO: -
Phone: 865 220-9650　　　　　　　　　　　HR: Harold Lawrence
Fax: -　　　　　　　　　　　　　　　　　FYE: December 31
Web: www.navarro-inc.com　　　　　　　　Type: Private

It's primary mission is about nuclear fission, and making sure that it does not happen. Navarro Research and Engineering provides environmental remediation and related services throughout the US. Specialties include nuclear safety and environmental safety and health. Navarro Research and Engineering's offices tend to be located near sites overseen by the US Department of Energy where nuclear materials have been stored. The company had employees in 14 offices and 23 project locations across the country. Navarro Research and Engineering works on projects for the US Department of Energy, and the National Nuclear Security Administration, and their primary contractors.

	Annual Growth	12/05	12/06	12/07	12/08	12/09
Sales ($mil.)	11.5%	-	-	48.0	49.6	59.6
Net income ($ mil.)	29.2%	-	-	2.4	2.5	4.0
Market value ($ mil.)	-	-	-	-	-	-
Employees	-	-	-	-	-	327

NAVICENT HEALTH, INC.

777 HEMLOCK ST　　　　　　　　　　　　CEO: -
MACON, GA 312012102　　　　　　　　　　CFO: -
Phone: 478 633-1000　　　　　　　　　　　HR: -
Fax: -　　　　　　　　　　　　　　　　　FYE: December 31
Web: www.navicenthealth.org　　　　　　Type: Private

Central Georgia Health Systems (CGHS) helps shepherd Georgians into the world and works to keep the Peach State residents healthy. Serving Bibb, Crawford, Houston, Monroe, Peach, and Twiggs counties, CGHS's main hospital, The Medical Center of Central Georgia (MCCG), serves a 30-county area and maintains more than 630 beds and a children's hospital. It is the primary teaching hospital for Mercer University School of Medicine. The system also operates outpatient clinics and various community health education programs, while also sponsoring Carlyle Place, an assisted-living retirement center. Tracing its roots back to 1895, CGHS provides specialty care in areas such as cardiology, neurology, and orthopedics.

	Annual Growth	09/13	09/14	09/15	09/16*	12/19
Sales ($mil.)	(28.4%)	-	56.6	61.8	0.8	10.7
Net income ($ mil.)	-	-	6.3	4.8	22.3	(11.0)
Market value ($ mil.)	-	-	-	-	-	-
Employees	-	-	-	-	-	3,900

*Fiscal year change

NAVIDEA BIOPHARMACEUTICALS INC　　　ASE: NAVB

4995 Bradenton Avenue, Suite 240　　　　　CEO: Michael S Rosol
Dublin, OH 43017-3552　　　　　　　　　　CFO: -
Phone: 614 793-7500　　　　　　　　　　　HR: -
Fax: 614 793-7520　　　　　　　　　　　　FYE: December 31
Web: www.navidea.com　　　　　　　　　Type: Public

Navidea Biopharmaceuticals is tracking down cancer with targeting agents. The biopharmaceutical company specializes in diagnostics, therapeutics, and radiopharmaceutical agents. It has several radiopharmaceutical products in development designed to help surgeons detect disease. The firm's targeted products and platforms include Manocept and NAV4694. Its Lymphoseek product, part of the Manocept platform, gained FDA approval in 2013 (and European approval in 2014) and is marketed in the US to detect cancerous tissues. Other candidates aim to detect cancer and neurological conditions including Parkinson's disease and Alzheimer's disease. Customers include diagnostic laboratories, physicians, and patients.

	Annual Growth	12/18	12/19	12/20	12/21	12/22
Sales ($mil.)	(51.3%)	1.2	0.7	0.9	0.5	0.0
Net income ($ mil.)	-	(16.1)	(10.9)	(10.7)	(11.7)	(15.2)
Market value ($ mil.)	19.6%	3.4	41.2	70.3	32.7	6.9
Employees	(5.7%)	19	17	18	15	15

NAVIENT CORP　　　　　　　　　　　　　NMS: NAVI

13865 Sunrise Valley Drive　　　　　　　　CEO: David L Yowan
Herndon, VA 20171　　　　　　　　　　　CFO: Joe Fisher
Phone: 703 810-3000　　　　　　　　　　　HR: Erin Baker
Fax: -　　　　　　　　　　　　　　　　　FYE: December 31
Web: www.navient.com　　　　　　　　　Type: Public

Navient is a leader in technology-enabled education finance and business processing solutions for its clients in the education, healthcare, and government. Through its Earnest and NaviRefi brands, its refinancing loan products enable college graduates and professionals to refinance their student loans at lower interest rates. Its Earnest in-school Private Education Loan product offers consumer-friendly features to college students and their cosigners who need additional funding to pursue higher education. The company also offers a parent loan to help parents, guardians, or sponsors cover the cost of a child's education. Navient originates and owns $62.3 billion of education loans.

	Annual Growth	12/19	12/20	12/21	12/22	12/23
Assets ($mil.)	(10.3%)	94,903	87,412	80,605	70,795	61,375
Net income ($ mil.)	(21.4%)	597.0	412.0	717.0	645.0	228.0
Market value ($ mil.)	8.0%	1,559.5	1,119.5	2,419.1	1,875.3	2,122.7
Employees	(6.1%)	5,800	7,410	6,195	4,000	4,500

NAVY EXCHANGE SERVICE COMMAND

3280 VIRGINIA BEACH BLVD　　　　　　　CEO: Gerald Outar
VIRGINIA BEACH, VA 234525799　　　　　CFO: John Best
Phone: 757 463-6200　　　　　　　　　　　HR: -
Fax: -　　　　　　　　　　　　　　　　　FYE: January 28
Web: www.mynavyexchange.com　　　　　Type: Private

Before Old Navy, there was the Navy Exchange Service Command (NEXCOM). Active-duty military personnel, reservists, retirees, and their family members can shop and gas up at more than 100 Navy Exchange (NEX) retail stores (brand-name and private-label merchandise ranging from apparel to home electronics), more than 150 NEXCOM Ships Stores (basic necessities), and its 100-plus Uniform Support Centers (the sole source of authorized uniforms). NEXCOM also runs about 40 Navy Lodges (motels) in the US and about half a dozen foreign countries. NEXCOM receives tax dollars for its shipboard stores, but it is otherwise self-supporting. Most of the profits fund morale, welfare, and recreational programs (MWR) for sailors.

	Annual Growth	01/09	01/10	01/11	01/16	01/17
Sales ($mil.)	(1.1%)	-	-	2,749.4	2,635.7	2,574.3
Net income ($ mil.)	(6.5%)	-	-	68.8	73.4	45.8
Market value ($ mil.)	-	-	-	-	-	-
Employees	-	-	-	-	-	14,000

NBCUNIVERSAL MEDIA, LLC

30 ROCKEFELLER PLZ
NEW YORK, NY 101120037
Phone: 212 664-4444
Fax: –
Web: www.nbcuniversal.com

CEO: Stephen B Burke
CFO: –
HR: –
FYE: December 31
Type: Private

NBCUniversal Media is one of the world's leading media and entertainment companies in the development, production, and marketing of entertainment, news and information to a global audience. Other broadcasting operations owned by NBCUniversal include Spanish-language network Telemundo and a portfolio of cable TV channels that includes Bravo, E! Entertainment, Syfy, USA Network, Oxygen, and news channel MSNBC. It also owns the Universal theme parks, located in the US, Japan, and China. Comcast, one of the top US cable systems operators, owns NBCUniversal. It was founded in 1912.

NBHX TRIM USA CORPORATION

1020 7 MILE RD NW
COMSTOCK PARK, MI 493219542
Phone: 616 785-9400
Fax: –
Web: www.nbhx-trim.com

CEO: –
CFO: –
HR: –
FYE: December 31
Type: Private

NBHX Trim (formerly Behr Industries) manufactures interior wood trim components for OEM automotive, heavy-duty truck, and marine suppliers across North America. It is the only US-based full-service wood component supplier with a domestic production plant. The Michigan-based facility neighbors the Detroit Big Three production plants. NBHX Trim has captured more than 70% of the US market for center consoles, instrument panels, side door panels, and similar wood components. Its fortunes have been closely tied to those of GM's.

	Annual Growth	12/11	12/12	12/13	12/14	12/15
Sales ($mil.)	24.6%	–	49.6	59.9	64.7	96.1
Net income ($ mil.)	103.1%	–	1.3	2.1	3.9	11.0
Market value ($ mil.)	–	–	–	–	–	–
Employees	–	–	–	–	–	425

NBL PERMIAN LLC

1001 NOBLE ENERGY WAY
HOUSTON, TX 770701435
Phone: 281 872-3100
Fax: –
Web: –

CEO: –
CFO: –
HR: –
FYE: December 31
Type: Private

Former Texas gubernatorial candidate Clayton Williams once devoted his energy to politics. Now he's devoted to the independent oil and gas firm that he founded. Clayton Williams Energy explores for oil and gas deposits primarily in Louisiana, New Mexico, and Texas and exploits those resources. The company has estimated proved reserves of 75.4 million barrels of oil equivalent, located mainly in the Permian Basin and South Texas. It has 951,000 gross undeveloped acres. It also operates gas pipeline and a small natural gas processing infrastructure in Louisiana, Mississippi, New Mexico, and Texas and offers contract drilling services. In 2017 the company was acquired by Noble Energy for $2.7 billion.

	Annual Growth	12/12	12/13	12/14	12/15	12/16
Sales ($mil.)	(12.3%)	–	429.2	468.5	232.4	289.4
Net income ($ mil.)	–	–	(24.9)	43.9	(98.2)	(292.2)
Market value ($ mil.)	–	–	–	–	–	–
Employees	–	–	–	–	–	253

NBT BANCORP. INC.

NMS: NBTB

52 South Broad Street
Norwich, NY 13815
Phone: 607 337-2265
Fax: 607 336-7538
Web: www.nbtbancorp.com

CEO: John H Watt Jr
CFO: Scott A Kingsley
HR: –
FYE: December 31
Type: Public

NBT Bancorp is the holding company for NBT Bank (the bank), which operates about 140 branches mainly in suburban and rural areas of New York, Pennsylvania, Massachusetts, New Hampshire, Maine, Connecticut and Vermont. The bank offers traditional deposit accounts and trust services, and specializes in making business and commercial real estate loans. Through NBT Financial, the company operates EPIC Advisors, Inc. (EPIC), a retirement plan administrator. EPIC offers services including retirement plan consulting and recordkeeping services. Through NBT Holdings, the company operates NBT Insurance Agency, a full-service insurance agency. The company has a total assets of $12.0 billion.

	Annual Growth	12/19	12/20	12/21	12/22	12/23
Assets ($mil.)	8.2%	9,715.9	10,933	12,012	11,739	13,309
Net income ($ mil.)	(0.5%)	121.0	104.4	154.9	152.0	118.8
Market value ($ mil.)	0.8%	1,910.8	1,512.2	1,814.7	2,045.5	1,974.4
Employees	3.3%	1,788	1,812	1,801	1,861	2,034

NCH CORPORATION

2727 CHEMSEARCH BLVD
IRVING, TX 750626454
Phone: 972 438-0211
Fax: –
Web: www.nch.com

CEO: –
CFO: Christopher T Sortwell
HR: Becky Mitchell
FYE: April 30
Type: Private

NCH Corporation is a global leader in industrial, commercial, and institutional maintenance products and services, and one of the largest companies in the world to sell such products through direct marketing. The company makes and sells chemical, maintenance, repair, and supply products, including all kinds of cleaners, for customers in more than 50 countries throughout the world. NCH markets its products through a direct sales force to companies in industrial, commercial, and infrastructure markets. Other products include pet care supplies and plumbing parts. Founded in 1919, leadership of the company remains in the hands of the Levy family, descendants of the founding father, Milton P. Levy, Senior.

	Annual Growth	04/09	04/10	04/11	04/12	04/19
Sales ($mil.)	0.7%	–	–	952.5	1,045.1	1,005.4
Net income ($ mil.)	18.5%	–	–	6.7	6.8	26.2
Market value ($ mil.)	–	–	–	–	–	–
Employees	–	–	–	–	–	8,500

NCH HEALTHCARE SYSTEM, INC.

350 7TH ST N
NAPLES, FL 341025754
Phone: 239 624-5000
Fax: –
Web: www.nchmd.org

CEO: Paul Hiltz
CFO: Rick Wyles
HR: –
FYE: September 30
Type: Private

NCH Healthcare System provides a comprehensive range of health care services for residents in southwest Florida. The not-for-profit system includes two acute care hospitals (NCH Baker Hospital Downtown and NCH North Naples Hospital) with a combined 716-bed capacity and regional institutes which specialize in the treatment of cancer and heart ailments. NCH operates a network of inpatient, outpatient, physician and rehabilitation services ranging from diagnostics and rehabilitative care to surgery and emergency care. NCH has over 700 independent physicians and medical facilities in dozens of locations throughout Collier County and Southwest Florida. NCH is a member of the Mayo Clinic Care Network.

	Annual Growth	09/06	09/07	09/08	09/13	09/21
Sales ($mil.)	(30.1%)	–	1,010.2	456.4	–	6.7
Net income ($ mil.)	96.9%	–	0.0	25.4	–	3.2
Market value ($ mil.)	–	–	–	–	–	–
Employees	–	–	–	–	–	3,500

NCI, INC.

11730 PLAZA AMERICA DR
RESTON, VA 201904764
Phone: 703 707-6900
Fax: –
Web: www.nciinc.com

CEO: Paul A Dillahay
CFO: James D Collier
HR: –
FYE: December 31
Type: Private

NCI is an AI company dedicated to helping US federal agencies, such as Department of Defense, includes Army, Navy, Air Force and Joint Chief Staff, Civilian agencies such as FCC, and Healthcare agencies, solve their toughest challenges. Its mission is to help the government customers deploy the most powerful and secure AI technologies to achieve meaningful transformation. These solutions provide practical, sustainable paths to transformation that are true to who its clients are, what it does, where and how it works, and the resources it has.

NCR VOYIX CORP

NYS: VYX

864 Spring Street N.W.
Atlanta, GA 30308
Phone: 937 445-1936
Fax: –
Web: www.ncr.com

CEO: David Wilkinson
CFO: Brian Webb-Walsh
HR: Sharon Mutnick
FYE: December 31
Type: Public

NCR is a software- and services-led enterprise technology provider that runs stores, restaurants and self-directed banking for its customers, which includes businesses of all sizes. Born in the 1880s as National Cash Register, NCR's portfolio includes digital first software and services offerings for banking, retailers and restaurants, as well as payments processing and networks, multi-vendor connected device services, automated teller machines (ATMs), self-checkout (SCO), point of sale (POS) terminals and other self-service technologies. NCR has facilities in some 60 countries with US customers generating some 55% of its sales.

	Annual Growth	12/19	12/20	12/21	12/22	12/23
Sales ($mil.)	(13.7%)	6,915.0	6,207.0	7,156.0	7,844.0	3,830.0
Net income ($ mil.)	–	564.0	(79.0)	97.0	60.0	(423.0)
Market value ($ mil.)	(16.7%)	5,013.8	5,357.5	5,732.5	3,338.3	2,411.4
Employees	(19.0%)	36,000	36,000	38,000	45,000	15,500

NCS MULTISTAGE HOLDINGS INC

NAS: NCSM

19350 State Highway 249, Suite 600
Houston, TX 77070
Phone: 281 453-2222
Fax: –
Web: www.ncsmultistage.com

CEO: Robert Nipper
CFO: Ryan Hummer
HR: Candace Leggett
FYE: December 31
Type: Public

NCS Multistage looks after the well-being of shale oil producers. Its highly engineered products and services enable energy operators to optimize their oil & gas well completions. It specializes in the lateral drilling used in shale plays in Canada, Texas, Oklahoma, and other areas. Its solutions help producers pinpoint segments of the well that need stimulation to release the trapped oil and gas, injecting water and proppants (a sand-like substance) to loosen impediments. The company began in 2006 and held its initial public offering in 2017.

	Annual Growth	12/19	12/20	12/21	12/22	12/23
Sales ($mil.)	(8.7%)	205.5	107.0	118.5	155.6	142.5
Net income ($ mil.)	–	(32.8)	(57.6)	(4.7)	(1.1)	(3.2)
Market value ($ mil.)	70.7%	5.1	55.0	70.8	61.1	43.6
Employees	(11.4%)	395	210	224	262	243

NCS TECHNOLOGIES, INC.

9601 DISCOVERY BLVD
MANASSAS, VA 201094041
Phone: 703 743-8500
Fax: –
Web: www.ncst.com

CEO: –
CFO: –
HR: –
FYE: December 31
Type: Private

NCS Technologies makes enterprise computing needs personal. The company makes and supplies PC products to clients large and small. NCS Technologies offers personal computers, mobile computing, thin client computing, servers and Internet appliances to clients in the government, educational, and private sectors. Products include desktops, notebooks, rugged tablets, and servers. In addition to providing built-to-order hardware, the company also provides software customizations and installation and technical support services. Founded in 1996, the company's single facility in Washington, DC serves clients from across the world.

	Annual Growth	09/04	09/05	09/06*	12/09	12/10
Sales ($mil.)	35.1%	–	–	35.2	80.0	117.5
Net income ($ mil.)	(12.2%)	–	–	1.1	1.3	0.7
Market value ($ mil.)	–	–	–	–	–	–
Employees	–	–	–	–	–	108

*Fiscal year change

NEARFIELD SYSTEMS INC.

19730 MAGELLAN DR
TORRANCE, CA 905021104
Phone: 310 525-7000
Fax: –
Web: www.nearfield.com

CEO: –
CFO: –
HR: –
FYE: December 31
Type: Private

Nearfield Systems makes test systems used to measure the performance characteristics of microwave antennas. Its products are based on instruments and test equipment made by Agilent Technologies. Nearfield Systems has done work for NASA, the National Radio Astronomy Observatory, and the US Navy, among other clients. While the name of the company is Nearfield Systems, the firm also makes far-field antenna measurement systems. Nearfield Systems was founded in 1988.

NEBRASKA DEPARTMENT OF LABOR

550 S 16TH ST
LINCOLN, NE 685082601
Phone: 402 471-9000
Fax: –
Web: www.nebraska.gov

CEO: –
CFO: –
HR: –
FYE: December 31
Type: Private

The Nebraska Department of Labor (NDOL) not only can help get you a job, but also makes sure your employer treats you right. The agency provides a wide variety of services for workers ranging from career planning and training to unemployment benefits and information about safety and labor laws. NDOL assists employers by offering them support in finding skilled employees, which improves their workforce. The department also keeps track of labor market information. In addition, the agency provides veteran services for employment and education.

NEBRASKA PUBLIC POWER DISTRICT

1414 15TH ST
COLUMBUS, NE 686015226
Phone: 877 275-6773
Fax: –
Web: www.nppd.com

CEO: Thomas Kent
CFO: Traci Bender
HR: –
FYE: December 31
Type: Private

Nebraska Public Power District (NPPD) electrifies the Cornhusker State. The government-owned electric utility, the largest in the state, provides power in 86 of the state's 93 counties. The firm has a generating capacity of about 3,130 MW and operates more than 5,200 miles of transmission lines. NPPD distributes electricity to about 89,000 retail customers in 81 cities and towns; it also provides power to about 1 million customers through wholesale power contracts with more than 50 towns and 25 public power districts. In addition, NPPD purchases electricity from the federally owned Western Area Power Administration and operates a surface water irrigation system.

	Annual Growth	12/18	12/19	12/20	12/21	12/22
Sales ($mil.)	3.7%	–	1,074.5	1,103.1	1,221.8	1,197.0
Net income ($ mil.)	(3.2%)	–	89.2	95.9	133.1	81.0
Market value ($ mil.)	–	–	–	–	–	–
Employees	–	–	–	–	–	1,900

NEFFS BANCORP INC.   NBB: NEFB

5629 PA Route 873, P.O. Box 10
Neffs, PA 18065-0010
Phone: 610 767-3875
Fax: –
Web: www.neffsnatl.com

CEO: John J Remaley
CFO: –
HR: –
FYE: December 31
Type: Public

Eneff with the megabanks already! Neffs Bancorp is the holding company for The Neffs National Bank, an independent bank that has been serving eastern Pennsylvania's Lehigh County since 1923. The bank operates a single office in the village of Neffs, north of Allentown. Targeting consumers and local businesses, it provides a variety of deposit products, including checking and savings accounts, CDs, and IRAs. The bank is mainly a real estate lender, with residential mortgages, home equity loans, and commercial mortgages comprising some 90% of its portfolio. Business, consumer, and construction loans round out its lending activities. The Neffs National Bank also offers tax, estate, and investment planning.

	Annual Growth	12/11	12/12	12/13	12/14	12/15
Assets ($mil.)	3.4%	286.5	294.2	303.8	309.9	327.5
Net income ($ mil.)	3.8%	3.7	4.2	4.2	4.0	4.3
Market value ($ mil.)	2.1%	42.2	42.2	43.2	43.8	45.8
Employees	–	–	–	–	–	–

NEIGHBORHOOD REINVESTMENT CORPORATION

999 N CAPITOL ST NE STE 900
WASHINGTON, DC 200026096
Phone: 202 760-4000
Fax: –
Web: www.neighborworks.org

CEO: –
CFO: –
HR: –
FYE: September 30
Type: Private

Neighborhood Reinvestment Corporation (now dba NeighborWorks America) wants to be your neighbor. The not-for-profit organization supports more than 240 independent local organizations in every state, the District of Columbia and Puerto Rico. Programs include financial health, home ownership, rental home and home and finance tips. The organization also offers training for community leaders and would-be homeowners on community planning, green building, business and financing among others. NeighborWorks America is funded by Congress and grants. The company was founded in 1968.

	Annual Growth	09/13	09/14	09/15	09/19	09/22
Sales ($mil.)	(1.7%)	–	261.3	208.0	172.6	227.3
Net income ($ mil.)	–	–	22.1	(16.2)	(27.0)	(0.8)
Market value ($ mil.)	–	–	–	–	–	–
Employees	–	–	–	–	–	260

NEKTAR THERAPEUTICS   NAS: NKTR

455 Mission Bay Boulevard South
San Francisco, CA 94158
Phone: 415 482-5300
Fax: –
Web: www.nektar.com

CEO: Howard W Robin
CFO: Sandra Gardiner
HR: –
FYE: December 31
Type: Public

Nektar Therapeutics is a research-based biopharmaceutical company focused on discovering and developing innovative medicines in areas of high unmet medical need. Nektar's research and development pipeline of new investigational drugs include innovative medicines in the field of immunotherapy. Its pipeline of clinical-stage immunomodulatory agents targets the treatment of autoimmune diseases (e.g. rezpegaldesleukin) and cancer (e.g. NKTR-255). The company's development partners include Bausch Health, Roche, AstraZeneca, Amgen, Takeda, UCB Pharma, and Pfizer. The company's largest market accounts outside the US.

	Annual Growth	12/19	12/20	12/21	12/22	12/23
Sales ($mil.)	(5.8%)	114.6	152.9	101.9	92.1	90.1
Net income ($ mil.)	–	(440.7)	(444.4)	(523.8)	(368.2)	(276.1)
Market value ($ mil.)	(59.8%)	4,131.0	3,253.5	2,585.6	432.5	108.1
Employees	(34.0%)	723	718	740	216	137

NELNET INC   NYS: NNI

121 South 13th Street, Suite 100
Lincoln, NE 68508
Phone: 402 458-2370
Fax: –
Web: www.nelnet.com

CEO: Jeffrey R Noordhoek
CFO: James D Kruger
HR: Mary Burkett
FYE: December 31
Type: Public

Nelnet is a publicly-traded diversified financial services and technology company focused on offering educational services, technology solutions, professional services, telecommunications and asset management. Nelnet serviced $587.5 billion of loans for 17.6 million borrowers in 2022. Nelnet also makes investments to further diversify both within and outside of its historical core education-related businesses including, but not limited to, investments in early-stage and emerging growth companies, real estate, and renewable energy (solar). Substantially all of its revenue comes from the US customers.

	Annual Growth	12/19	12/20	12/21	12/22	12/23
Assets ($mil.)	(8.3%)	23,709	22,646	21,678	19,374	16,737
Net income ($ mil.)	(10.4%)	141.8	352.4	393.3	407.3	91.5
Market value ($ mil.)	10.9%	2,158.6	2,640.4	3,620.4	3,363.5	3,269.8
Employees	3.4%	6,600	6,199	7,988	8,237	7,550

NEMOURS FOUNDATION

10140 CENTURION PKWY N
JACKSONVILLE, FL 322560532
Phone: 904 697-4100
Fax: –
Web: www.nemours.org

CEO: Brian P Anderson
CFO: –
HR: Christina Lynch
FYE: December 31
Type: Private

Even if their offspring are fanatical about Finding Nemo , parents of sick children may prefer finding Nemours. The Nemours Foundation operates the Nemours/Alfred I. duPont Hospital for Children in Wilmington, Delaware; the Nemours Children's Hospital in Orlando, Florida; and dozens of pediatric clinics in Delaware, Florida, New Jersey, and Pennsylvania that treat acutely and chronically ill children. Specialties include orthopedics, cardiology, neurology, and oncology. Nemours also has extensive research programs, and it operates a clinic in Delaware that serves low-income elderly residents. The not-for-profit foundation was created in 1936 through the will of chemicals pioneer Alfred I. duPont.

NEOGEN CORP   NMS: NEOG

620 Lesher Place | CEO: John E Adent
Lansing, MI 48912 | CFO: David H Naemura
Phone: 517 372-9200 | HR: –
Fax: – | FYE: May 31
Web: www.neogen.com | Type: Public

Neogen develops, manufactures, and markets a diverse line of products and services dedicated to food and animal safety. Its Food Safety segment consists primarily of diagnostic test kits and complementary products sold to food producers and processors to detect dangerous and unintended substances in human food and animal feed, such as foodborne pathogens, spoilage organisms, natural toxins, food allergens, genetic modifications, ruminant by-products, meat speciation, drug residues, pesticide residues and general sanitation concerns. Its diagnostic test kits are generally easier to use and provide greater accuracy and speed than conventional diagnostic methods. More than 50% of its total revenue comes from its domestic operations.

	Annual Growth	05/19	05/20	05/21	05/22	05/23
Sales ($mil.)	18.7%	414.2	418.2	468.5	527.2	822.4
Net income ($ mil.)	–	60.2	59.5	60.9	48.3	(22.9)
Market value ($ mil.)	(25.4%)	12,185	15,401	19,962	5,721.9	3,782.1
Employees	11.9%	1,682	1,764	1,841	2,108	2,640

NEOGENOMICS INC   NAS: NEO

9490 NeoGenomics Way | CEO: Christopher Smith
Fort Myers, FL 33912 | CFO: Kathryn B McKenzie
Phone: 239 768-0600 | HR: Estela Villela
Fax: 239 690-4237 | FYE: December 31
Web: www.neogenomics.com | Type: Public

NeoGenomics is a premier cancer diagnostics and pharma services company serving oncologists, pathologists, pharmaceutical companies, academic centers, and others with innovative diagnostic, prognostic and predictive testing. The company's testing services include cytogenetics, FISH, flow cytometry, IHC, molecular testing and morphologic analysis. Its information platform includes one of the largest cancer testing databases, covering the complete spectrum of oncology testing modalities for over 1.6 million patients and growing. NeoGenomics has a network of CAP-accredited, CLIA-certified facilities in the US, and offers global capabilities with laboratories in the China, UK, Switzerland, and Singapore.

	Annual Growth	12/19	12/20	12/21	12/22	12/23
Sales ($mil.)	9.7%	408.8	444.4	484.3	509.7	591.6
Net income ($ mil.)	–	8.0	4.2	(8.3)	(144.3)	(88.0)
Market value ($ mil.)	(13.8%)	3,725.5	6,857.6	4,345.8	1,176.9	2,060.8
Employees	5.4%	1,700	1,700	2,000	2,100	2,100

NEOMAGIC CORP.   NBB: NMGC

2372-A Qume Drive | CEO: Syed Zaidi
San Jose, CA 95131 | CFO: –
Phone: 408 428-9725 | HR: –
Fax: 408 428-9712 | FYE: January 31
Web: www.neomagic.com | Type: Public

NeoMagic is trying to deliver chip magic for everything from smart phones to electronic toll collection systems. The company develops and markets semiconductors, including a family of system-on-chip (SoC) processors sold under the MiMagic brand, and software for audio, video, imaging, graphics, and television. It also provides design services on system and software development that help OEMs bring their products to market. NeoMagic sells through distributors and representatives in the US, the UK, and Asia. Among the company's customers is California-based startup ViV Systems, a home theater developer and manufacturer.

	Annual Growth	01/06	01/07	01/08	01/09	01/10
Sales ($mil.)	(36.2%)	9.4	0.6	2.1	2.0	1.5
Net income ($ mil.)	–	(9.3)	(16.5)	(16.7)	(7.9)	1.2
Market value ($ mil.)	(71.5%)	287.3	165.1	63.9	0.4	1.9
Employees	(48.9%)	103	91	97	5	7

NEOMEDIA TECHNOLOGIES, INC.   NBB: NEOM

1515 Walnut Street, Suite 100 | CEO: Laura A Marriott
Boulder, CO 80302 | CFO: Barry S Baer
Phone: 303 546-7946 | HR: –
Fax: – | FYE: December 31
Web: www.neom.com | Type: Public

NeoMedia Technologies has a new approach to mobile marketing. The company develops hardware and software that allows camera-enabled mobile phones to read and transmit data from bar codes embedded in advertisements. Marketers use the technology to link phone users to targeted URLs. It also offers mobile ticketing and coupon systems. The company also generates revenue by licensing its technology and from designing and implementing mobile marketing campaigns. NeoMedia has undergone significant restructuring in recent years, including the divestiture of a number of business lines.

	Annual Growth	12/10	12/11	12/12	12/13	12/14
Sales ($mil.)	23.2%	1.5	2.3	2.3	5.0	3.5
Net income ($ mil.)	–	35.1	(0.8)	(19.4)	(214.1)	(2.5)
Market value ($ mil.)	(90.4%)	499.9	47.1	10.8	5.8	0.0
Employees	(14.9%)	21	27	14	18	11

NEOS THERAPEUTICS, INC.

2940 N STATE HIGHWAY 360 | CEO: Vipin Garg
GRAND PRAIRIE, TX 75050 | CFO: Richard Eisenstadt
Phone: 972 408-1300 | HR: Christy Close
Fax: – | FYE: December 31
Web: www.aytubio.com | Type: Private

Neos Therapeutics makes generic drugs take their time. The contract pharmaceutical manufacturer develops and manufactures branded and generic prescription and OTC pharmaceuticals with an emphasis on time-released formulations. Its products include cold and cough remedies and nutritional supplements. Customers are primarily pharmaceutical distributors and other manufacturers. Neos Therapeutics was slapped hard by the FDA in 2007 for manufacturing unapproved drugs. The action prompted a change in ownership and the company was required to re-file its drug applications in order to resume manufacturing.In 2017 PDL BioPharma bid to acquire Neos Therapeutics, which rejected the offer.

NEPHROS INC   NAS: NEPH

380 Lackawanna Place | CEO: Robert Banks
South Orange, NJ 07079 | CFO: Judy Krandel
Phone: 201 343-5202 | HR: –
Fax: – | FYE: December 31
Web: www.nephros.com | Type: Public

Nephros develops and makes medical devices that are used to treat irreversible loss of kidney function associated with End Stage Renal Disease, or ESRD. ESRD is often the result of other health problems such as diabetes and high blood pressure. The company's products are designed to replace a patient's kidney function with the device system. Nephros is positioning its therapeutic devices as an alternative to hemodialysis, the most common form of renal replacement therapy. The company's products use a process called "hemodiafiltration" (HDF) combining hemodialysis with hemofiltration to clean the patient's blood.

	Annual Growth	12/19	12/20	12/21	12/22	12/23
Sales ($mil.)	8.3%	10.3	8.6	10.4	10.0	14.2
Net income ($ mil.)	–	(3.4)	(4.8)	(4.1)	(7.4)	(1.6)
Market value ($ mil.)	(23.2%)	104.9	90.5	62.2	12.2	36.5
Employees	5.5%	25	27	34	27	31

NES RENTALS HOLDINGS, INC.

8420 W BRYN MAWR AVE # 300
CHICAGO, IL 606313436
Phone: 773 695-3999
Fax: –
Web: www.nesrentals.com

CEO: –
CFO: –
HR: –
FYE: December 31
Type: Private

Forklifts and other lifts lift the revenues of NES Rentals, formerly National Equipment Services. The company offers industrial and construction customers a range of aerial rental equipment, from scissor and boom lifts to rough terrain and truck-mounted cranes. It also supplies specialty equipment including bulldozers, trenchers, and skid steers, as well as scaffolding systems. In addition to equipment rentals, and repair and maintenance services for nonresidential construction customers, NES sells new and used pieces by OEMs, including BMC, JLG, SkyJack, Sala, Doosan, and Terex. In mid-2017, NES was acquired by rival United Rentals for $965 million.

	Annual Growth	12/07	12/08	12/09	12/13	12/14
Sales ($mil.)	(2.6%)	–	406.3	300.6	317.0	347.0
Net income ($ mil.)	–	–	(18.3)	(17.6)	(25.8)	(1.7)
Market value ($ mil.)	–	–	–	–	–	–
Employees	–	–	–	–	–	1,100

NEST TECHNOLOGIES CORP.

44901 FALCON PL STE 116
STERLING, VA 201669531
Phone: 703 653-1100
Fax: –
Web: www.nesttech.com

CEO: Javad K Hassan
CFO: Michael D Staples
HR: –
FYE: December 31
Type: Private

NeST Technologies wants to give businesses the technological edge they need to take flight. The company provides IT services, including custom software development, systems design and integration, project management, consulting, training, and business process optimization. It specializes in products from vendors including IBM and Symantec. NeST serves customers in such industries as manufacturing, electronics, and consumer goods. Clients have included Brooks Automation, Jet Airways, and Tokyo Electron. The company has international sales and development facilities in Australia, Canada, France, India, Japan, the United Arab Emirates, and the UK. NeST was founded in 1991 by chairman and CEO Javad Hassan.

	Annual Growth	12/04	12/05	12/06	12/07	12/08
Sales ($mil.)	6.4%	–	–	5.3	6.8	6.1
Net income ($ mil.)	(5.4%)	–	–	0.9	1.4	0.8
Market value ($ mil.)	–	–	–	–	–	–
Employees	–	–	–	–	–	10

NET MEDICAL XPRESS SOLUTIONS INC

NBB: NMXS

8206 Louisiana Blvd. N.E., Suite A
Albuquerque, NM 87113
Phone: 505 255-1999
Fax: –
Web: www.netmedical.com

CEO: Richard F Govatski
CFO: –
HR: –
FYE: December 31
Type: Public

NMXS.com has a clear image of what good document management looks like. The company provides software and services for archiving and retrieving documents and images, primarily to health care and medical providers. Its customers have come from fields including health care, government, and entertainment, as well as not-for-profit organizations. NMSC.com's products are made available under the Software-As-a-Service model.

	Annual Growth	12/18	12/19	12/20	12/21	12/22
Sales ($mil.)	25.5%	2.1	1.6	1.1	1.8	5.2
Net income ($ mil.)	–	(0.0)	(0.3)	(0.5)	0.0	0.9
Market value ($ mil.)	(4.2%)	3.3	2.1	1.6	3.0	2.8
Employees	–	–	–	–	–	–

NETAPP, INC.

NMS: NTAP

3060 Olsen Drive
San Jose, CA 95128
Phone: 408 822-6000
Fax: –
Web: www.netapp.com

CEO: George Kurian
CFO: Michael J Berry
HR: –
FYE: April 28
Type: Public

NetApp is a global cloud-led, data-centric software company that provides organizations the ability to manage and share their data across on-premises, private and public clouds. Its products extend customers' IT infrastructure to the cloud environments of Amazon Web Services, Google and Microsoft. NetApp and its certified services partners offer a comprehensive portfolio of assessment, design, implementation, migration, and proactive support services to help customers optimize the performance and efficiency of their on-premises and hybrid multi-cloud storage environments. The company's portfolio of offerings include keystone its storage-as-a-service (STaaS), strategic consulting, professional, managed, and support services. NetApp's customers are in the energy, financial services, government, health care, life sciences, manufacturing, IT, and other sectors. The Americas generates nearly 55% of company's total revenue.

	Annual Growth	04/19	04/20	04/21	04/22	04/23
Sales ($mil.)	0.9%	6,146.0	5,412.0	5,744.0	6,318.0	6,362.0
Net income ($ mil.)	2.2%	1,169.0	819.0	730.0	937.0	1,274.0
Market value ($ mil.)	(3.3%)	15,243	9,128.7	15,834	15,529	13,333
Employees	3.4%	10,500	10,800	11,000	12,000	12,000

NETFLIX INC

NMS: NFLX

121 Albright Way
Los Gatos, CA 95032
Phone: 408 540-3700
Fax: –
Web: www.netflix.com

CEO: Greg Peters
CFO: Spencer Neumann
HR: –
FYE: December 31
Type: Public

Netflix, Inc. is one of the world's leading entertainment services with approximately 231 million paid memberships in over 190 countries enjoying TV series, films and games across a wide variety of genres and languages. Members can play, pause and resume to watch, as much as they want, anytime, anywhere, and can change their plans at any time. Netflix, Inc. was incorporated on August 29, 1997 and began operations on April 14, 1998. Majority of the company's revenue was derived from its streaming services.

	Annual Growth	12/19	12/20	12/21	12/22	12/23
Sales ($mil.)	13.7%	20,156	24,996	29,698	31,616	33,723
Net income ($ mil.)	30.5%	1,866.9	2,761.4	5,116.2	4,491.9	5,408.0
Market value ($ mil.)	10.8%	140,028	234,006	260,712	127,612	210,702
Employees	10.9%	8,600	9,400	11,300	12,800	13,000

NETGEAR INC

NMS: NTGR

350 East Plumeria Drive
San Jose, CA 95134
Phone: 408 907-8000
Fax: –
Web: www.netgear.com

CEO: –
CFO: –
HR: –
FYE: December 31
Type: Public

NETGEAR is a global company that turns ideas into innovative, high-performance, and premium networking products that connect people, power businesses, and service providers. NETGEAR products are designed to simplify and improve people's lives. It is dedicated to delivering innovative and highly differentiated, connected solutions ranging from easy-to-use premium WiFi solutions, security and support services to protect and enhance home networks, to switching and wireless solutions to augment business networks, and audio and video over Ethernet for Pro AV applications. It sells through distributors, including Ingram Micro, D&H Distributing Company, and TD Synnex, and to retailers such as Amazon.com, Wal-Mart Stores, and Best Buy. The company generates almost 65% of its sales in the US.

	Annual Growth	12/19	12/20	12/21	12/22	12/23
Sales ($mil.)	(7.2%)	998.8	1,255.2	1,168.1	932.5	740.8
Net income ($ mil.)	–	25.8	58.3	49.4	(69.0)	(104.8)
Market value ($ mil.)	(12.2%)	725.9	1,203.3	865.1	536.3	431.8
Employees	(5.9%)	809	818	771	691	635

NETLIST INC   NBB: NLST

111 Academy, Suite 100
Irvine, CA 92617
Phone: 949 435-0025
Fax: –
Web: www.netlist.com

CEO: Chun K Hong
CFO: –
HR: Janet Carter
FYE: December 30
Type: Public

Netlist designs, manufactures, and markets high-performance memory subsystems for the OEM market. Its line of board-level memory products are used in IT infrastructure equipment, such as servers, data centers, and other high-performance computing and communications markets. Netlist designs, manufactures and sells a variety of memory circuits with dynamic random access memory (DRAM) and NAND flash memory as well as a hybrid of both. The company targets applications in which the preservation of data stored in memory is important such as cloud computing, big data, and online banking. Key customers include Dell and IBM.

	Annual Growth	12/19*	01/21	01/22*	12/22	12/23
Sales ($mil.)	27.6%	26.1	47.2	142.4	161.6	69.2
Net income ($ mil.)	–	(12.5)	(7.3)	4.8	(33.4)	(60.4)
Market value ($ mil.)	55.8%	80.8	152.9	1,635.7	291.6	476.8
Employees	4.7%	80	70	120	100	96

*Fiscal year change

NETMOTION SOFTWARE, INC.

1505 WESTLAKE AVE N STE 500
SEATTLE, WA 981093010
Phone: 206 691-5500
Fax: –
Web: www.absolute.com

CEO: Chirstopher Kenessey
CFO: –
HR: Nicole Tong
FYE: December 31
Type: Private

NetMotion Wireless sets workers free. The company's mobile VPN software lets mobile workers maintain data connections as they move in and out of wireless coverage areas. NetMotion targets organizations in the communications, health care, local government, public safety and utility, and transportation sectors. Its customers include Ameren and St. Luke's Episcopal Health System. The company has partnerships with AT&T, Sprint, and Sierra Wireless. NetMotion was acquired by Clearlake Capital, a private equity firm, in 2012.

NETSCOUT SYSTEMS INC   NMS: NTCT

310 Littleton Road
Westford, MA 01886
Phone: 978 614-4000
Fax: –
Web: www.netscout.com

CEO: Anil K Singhal
CFO: Jean Bua
HR: Jeannine McCallister
FYE: March 31
Type: Public

NetScout Systems is an industry leader with over three decades of experience in providing service assurance and cybersecurity solutions that are used by many Fortune 500 companies to protect their digital business services against disruption. Service providers and enterprises, including local, state, and federal government agencies, rely on its solutions to achieve the visibility, and protection necessary to optimize network performance, ensure the delivery of high-quality, mission-critical applications and services, gain timely insight into the end-user experience and protect their networks from attack. NetScout's nGeniusONE analytics and its ISNG real-time information platform provide the necessary insight to optimize network performance, restore service, and understand the quality of the users' experience. Most of the company's revenue is generated from the US.

	Annual Growth	03/19	03/20	03/21	03/22	03/23
Sales ($mil.)	0.1%	909.9	891.8	831.3	855.6	914.5
Net income ($ mil.)	–	(73.3)	(2.8)	19.4	35.9	59.6
Market value ($ mil.)	0.5%	2,000.0	1,686.5	2,006.4	2,285.7	2,041.3
Employees	(2.3%)	2,585	2,502	2,421	2,331	2,355

NETSOL TECHNOLOGIES INC   NAS: NTWK

16000 Ventura Blvd., Suite 770
Encino, CA 91436
Phone: 818 222-9195
Fax: 818 222-9197
Web: www.netsoltech.com

CEO: Najeeb Ghauri
CFO: Roger Almond
HR: –
FYE: June 30
Type: Public

NetSol Technologies is sold on the power of IT. The company provides information technology services and software for the banking, financial services, automotive leasing and financing, and healthcare industries. NetSol's LeaseSoft software for asset-based lending organizations automates such tasks as credit valuation, financial comparisons, wholesale finance management, and services tracking. NetSol also offers a hospital management information product. The company's services include assistance with SAP, information security, business intelligence, project management, maintenance, and testing. NetSol Technologies was founded in 1997.

	Annual Growth	06/19	06/20	06/21	06/22	06/23
Sales ($mil.)	(6.2%)	67.8	56.4	54.9	57.2	52.4
Net income ($ mil.)	–	8.6	0.9	1.8	(0.9)	(5.2)
Market value ($ mil.)	(19.4%)	63.4	30.6	53.4	36.1	26.8
Employees	6.8%	1,360	1,400	1,447	1,781	1,770

NETSUITE, INC.

2955 CAMPUS DR STE 100
SAN MATEO, CA 944032539
Phone: 650 627-1000
Fax: –
Web: www.netsuite.com

CEO: –
CFO: –
HR: –
FYE: December 31
Type: Private

NetSuite is a comprehensive and highly efficient cloud-based Enterprise Resource Planning (ERP) suite that provides organizations with a range of tools to operate their businesses more effectively and accelerate their growth. As the world's first cloud company, the company offers a full ERP suite, which includes financials, inventory management, HR, professional services automation, and omni-channel commerce modules. Its platform is designed to deliver scalability, security, and reliability to meet the evolving needs of modern businesses. NetSuite serves a diverse array of industries, including software and technology, transportation and logistics, financial services, nonprofit, food and beverage, health and beauty, restaurants, and hospitality sectors. NetSuite is a unit of Oracle Corp. The company was founded in 1998.

NETWORK MANAGEMENT RESOURCES, INC.

6767 OLD MADISON PIKE NW STE 210
HUNTSVILLE, AL 358062172
Phone: 703 229-1055
Fax: –
Web: www.nmrconsulting.com

CEO: David Jones
CFO: –
HR: –
FYE: December 31
Type: Private

Network Management Resources believes there's a lot to be said for a clear, descriptive name. The company designs, installs, and maintains information technology (IT) equipment. Services include help desk support, network administration, application development, software engineering, and training. Its customers (which include both public and private sector organizations) come from a range of industries including financial services, manufacturing, and health care.

	Annual Growth	12/18	12/19	12/20	12/21	12/22
Sales ($mil.)	1.4%	–	24.6	36.0	33.4	25.7
Net income ($ mil.)	52.0%	–	0.9	4.0	3.8	3.3
Market value ($ mil.)	–	–	–	–	–	–
Employees	–	–	–	–	–	138

NEUBERGER & BERMAN, LLC

1290 AVENUE OF THE AMERICAS
NEW YORK, NY 101040105
Phone: 212 476-9000
Fax: –
Web: –

CEO: –
CFO: –
HR: –
FYE: November 30
Type: Private

Neuberger Berman is a private, 100% independent, employee-owned investment manager. From offices in some 40 cities worldwide, Neuberger Berman manages a range of equity, fixed income, private equity and hedge fund strategies on behalf of institutions, advisors and individual investors worldwide. With about 720 investment professionals based in around 20 portfolio management centers, the firm offers clients around the world investment solutions across asset classes, capitalizations, styles and geographies in both public and private markets, as well as multi-asset class solutions that bring them all together. The firm boasts $408 billion in assets under management, with 70% of that being managed on behalf of institutional clients. Neuberger Berman was founded in 1939.

NEUEHEALTH INC   NYS: NEUE

8000 Norman Center Drive, Suite 900
Minneapolis, MN 55437
Phone: 612 238-1321
Fax: –
Web: www.brighthealthgroup.com

CEO: G M Mikan
CFO: Jay Matushak
HR: –
FYE: December 31
Type: Public

Bright Health Group is the first technology-enabled, Fully Aligned system of care built for healthcare's consumer retail market. Bright Health Group consists of two reportable segments: NeueHealth and Bright HealthCare. NeueHealth, is developing the next generation, integrated healthcare system while Bright HealthCare, delivers simple, personal, and affordable solutions to integrate the consumer into Bright Health's alignment model. Bright HealthCare offers Commercial and Medicare health plan products to over 1 million consumers across the nation. It was founded in 2015 and went public in 2021.

	Annual Growth	12/18	12/19	12/20	12/21	12/22
Sales ($mil.)	107.3%	130.6	280.7	1,207.3	4,029.4	2,412.0
Net income ($ mil.)	–	(62.6)	(125.3)	(248.4)	(1,184.9)	(1,455.5)
Market value ($ mil.)	–	–	–	–	27.0	5.1
Employees	–	–	–	2,056	3,203	2,840

NEULION, INC.

1600 OLD COUNTRY RD
PLAINVIEW, NY 118035013
Phone: 516 622-8300
Fax: –
Web: www.endeavorstreaming.com

CEO: Roy E Reichbach
CFO: Tim Alavathil
HR: Janet Cooklove
FYE: December 31
Type: Private

NeuLion is poised to pounce on Internet-delivered television. The company offers hosted services that allow customers to deliver streaming video over Internet-enabled devices. It works mostly with sports content providers (60% of revenues) such as ESPN , the NFL , and about 150 NCAA schools, but also pay-TV networks and operators such as DISH , The Independent Film Channel , and Univision , to distribute live and on-demand programming over the Internet, viewed on personal computers, laptops, cell phones, and televisions. NeuLion gets most of its revenues in the US and Canada, but also has offices in London and Shanghai. Chairman Charles Wang and CEO Nancy Li, who are married, together own more than half of the company.

	Annual Growth	12/12	12/13	12/14	12/15	12/16
Sales ($mil.)	34.1%	–	–	55.5	94.0	99.8
Net income ($ mil.)	–	–	–	3.6	25.9	(1.8)
Market value ($ mil.)	–	–	–	–	–	–
Employees	–	–	–	–	–	657

NEUMANN SYSTEMS GROUP, INC.

14230 TIMBEREDGE LN
COLORADO SPRINGS, CO 809212956
Phone: 719 593-7848
Fax: –
Web: www.denergysolutions.com

CEO: Todd Tiahrt
CFO: –
HR: –
FYE: December 31
Type: Private

If you direct a lot of energy to one place, you get a beam. At least that's the plan at Neumann Systems Group, doing business as Directed Energy Solutions (DES). The company makes lasers and other optical devices used in research, remote sensing, communication, medical, and military applications. It also works on chemical and biological decontamination products that could be used to sterilize medical equipment and improve indoor air quality. DES, which operates from its 20,000-sq.-ft. research, production, and development facility in Colorado, counts various agencies and branches of the US government, including the Army and Air Force, and Raytheon as customers. CEO David Neumann formed the company in 1999.

	Annual Growth	12/09	12/10	12/11	12/12	12/13
Sales ($mil.)	0.3%	–	–	22.1	25.7	22.2
Net income ($ mil.)	(5.7%)	–	–	1.9	2.2	1.7
Market value ($ mil.)	–	–	–	–	–	–
Employees	–	–	–	–	–	37

NEUROCRINE BIOSCIENCES, INC.   NMS: NBIX

12780 El Camino Real
San Diego, CA 92130
Phone: 858 617-7600
Fax: –
Web: www.neurocrine.com

CEO: Kevin C Gorman
CFO: Matthew C Abernethy
HR: –
FYE: December 31
Type: Public

For Neurocrine Biosciences, drug development is all about body chemistry. The development-stage biotech develops treatments for neurological and endocrine hormone-related diseases, such as insomnia, depression, and menstrual pain. Lead drug candidate Elagolix is designed to treat endometriosis which causes pain and irregular menstrual bleeding in women. Second in line is NBI-98854, a treatment for movement disorders. Neurocrine Biosciences works in additional therapeutic areas including anxiety, cancer, epilepsy, and diabetes. The company has about a dozen drug candidates in various stages of research and clinical development, through both internal programs and collaborative agreements with partners.

	Annual Growth	12/19	12/20	12/21	12/22	12/23
Sales ($mil.)	24.4%	788.1	1,045.9	1,133.5	1,488.7	1,887.1
Net income ($ mil.)	61.2%	37.0	407.3	89.6	154.5	249.7
Market value ($ mil.)	5.2%	10,609	9,460.4	8,406.3	11,789	13,005
Employees	18.9%	700	845	900	1,200	1,400

NEUROGENE INC   NAS: NLTX

188 East Blaine Street, Suite 450
Seattle, WA 98102
Phone: 866 245-0312
Fax: –
Web: www.neoleukin.com

CEO: –
CFO: –
HR: –
FYE: December 31
Type: Public

Aquinox wants nothing more than to raise money by reducing inflammation. The pharmaceutical company is developing treatments for inflammation and cancer occurring in parts of the body with a high concentration of mucus membranes, including the respiratory, gastrointestinal, and urinary tracts. Its former lead candidate, rositopr, failed in trials as a treatment for chronic obstructive pulmonary disease and bladder pain syndrome in 2018. After that disappointing result, Aquinox cut its staff by 53% and shuttered its California location. It will now evaluate its pipeline and consider its strategic options.

	Annual Growth	12/19	12/20	12/21	12/22	12/23
Sales ($mil.)	–	–	–	–	–	–
Net income ($ mil.)	–	(69.4)	(33.3)	(60.7)	(57.6)	(36.3)
Market value ($ mil.)	12.0%	158.0	180.8	61.8	6.5	248.5
Employees	26.1%	36	70	91	56	91

NEUROMETRIX INC

NAS: NURO

4B Gill Street
Woburn, MA 01801
Phone: 781 890-9989
Fax: 781 890-1556
Web: www.neurometrix.com

CEO: –
CFO: –
HR: –
FYE: December 31
Type: Public

NeuroMetrix makes medical devices and consumables that detect, diagnose, and monitor diabetic neuropathies (DPNs) and neurological conditions affecting the peripheral nerves and spine. The company makes two FDA-approved products: a noninvasive NC-stat DPNCheck system designed for endocrinologists, podiatrists, and primary care doctors, and its ADVANCE system used by specialists. Its systems allow doctors to distinguish between pain caused by nerve root compression and pain caused by less-serious factors. NeuroMetrix's pipeline includes the SENSUS device, designed to treat painful DPNs, and the ADVANCE CTS device for diagnosing and evaluating carpal tunnel syndrome. CEO Shai Gozani founded the company in 1996.

	Annual Growth	12/19	12/20	12/21	12/22	12/23
Sales ($mil.)	(10.7%)	9.3	7.4	8.3	8.3	5.9
Net income ($ mil.)	–	(3.8)	(2.1)	(2.3)	(4.4)	(6.5)
Market value ($ mil.)	(4.3%)	6.6	4.8	7.7	2.3	5.5
Employees	3.1%	23	20	23	27	26

NEUSTAR, INC.

1906 RESTON METRO PLZ STE 500
RESTON, VA 201905241
Phone: 571 434-5400
Fax: –
Web: www.home.neustar

CEO: Charles Gottdiener
CFO: Carolyn Ullerick
HR: Marjorie R Bailey
FYE: December 31
Type: Private

Neustar is an information services and technology company and a leader in identity resolution providing the data and technology that enable trusted connections between companies and people at the moments that matter most. Neustar offers industry-leading solutions in marketing, risk, communications, and security that responsibly connect data on people, devices, and locations, continuously corroborated through billions of transactions. Neustar serves more than 8,000 clients worldwide, including 60 of the Fortune 100. In late 2021, TransUnion and Neustar announced that TransUnion has completed its $3.1 billion acquisition of Neustar from a private investment group led by Golden Gate Capital and with minority participation by GIC.

NEUTRAL POSTURE, INC.

3904 N TEXAS AVE
BRYAN, TX 778030555
Phone: 979 778-0502
Fax: –
Web: www.neutralposture.com

CEO: Rebecca Boenigk
CFO: –
HR: Angie Kruljac
FYE: December 31
Type: Private

Neutral Posture makes workplace comfort the focus of its business. Highly imitated and respected leader in adjustable office and industrial seating products of all kinds, the company designs and makes ergonomic office chairs under the AbChair, Balance, Renate, Embrace, and N-tune brands. It also sells keyboard trays and related workstation accessories under the elemental, Easy Combos, Connexion Arm, Monitor Arm, and StandUp brands. Customers include major corporations and government agencies; US General Services Administration is one of its largest customers. Neutral Posture has operations throughout North America. Founded in 1989, its chairs were designed by Texas A&M professor Jerome Congleton, whose research was derived from NASA data on the body's reaction to weightlessness.

	Annual Growth	12/03	12/04	12/05	12/06	12/08
Sales ($mil.)	(1.6%)	–	–	18.2	21.0	17.4
Net income ($ mil.)	–	–	–	5.9	(0.1)	–
Market value ($ mil.)	–	–	–	–	–	–
Employees	–	–	–	–	–	85

NEVADA CITY HOSPITAL (INC)

800 S ASH ST
NEVADA, MO 647723223
Phone: 417 667-3355
Fax: –
Web: www.nrmchealth.com

CEO: –
CFO: –
HR: –
FYE: June 30
Type: Private

Nevada City Hospital (dba Nevada Regional Medical Center) provides health care services for the residents in western Missouri. The facility offers services such as behavioral health, cardiology, emergency medicine, obstetrics, and occupational therapy. In addition to the more than 50-bed hospital, the medical center also operates a nearly 40-bed Alzheimer's unit, a more than 110-bed nursing home, a home health and hospice facility, and various rural health clinics.

	Annual Growth	06/16	06/17	06/19	06/20	06/22
Sales ($mil.)	3.9%	–	34.7	36.5	35.4	42.0
Net income ($ mil.)	–	–	(6.4)	(1.7)	(0.9)	1.1
Market value ($ mil.)	–	–	–	–	–	–
Employees	–	–	–	–	–	450

NEVADA GOLD & CASINOS, INC.

133 E WARM SPRINGS RD STE 102
LAS VEGAS, NV 891194100
Phone: 702 685-1000
Fax: –
Web: www.nevadagold.com

CEO: –
CFO: –
HR: –
FYE: April 30
Type: Private

Nevada Gold & Casinos owns about 10 small casinos in Washington State. Three of these casinos?the Crazy Moose-Pasco, Crazy Moose-Mountlake Terrace, and Coyote Bob-Kennewick?are in close proximity to Seattle, while the remaining properties are located in western Washington. It also owns AG Trucano, Son & Grandsons, a slot machine route in Deadwood, South Dakota. It acquired AG Trucano, which runs the only authorized commercialized gambling location South Dakota, in 2012 for about $5.2 million, adding some 900 slots and 20 sites to Nevada Gold's portfolio.

NEVADA POWER CO.

6226 West Sahara Avenue
Las Vegas, NV 89146
Phone: 702 402-5000
Fax: –
Web: www.nvenergy.com

CEO: Paul J Caudill
CFO: Jonathan S Halkyard
HR: –
FYE: December 31
Type: Public

Those famous bright city lights of gamblers' paradise (Las Vegas) are lit by Nevada Power, a subsidiary of NV Energy (owned by Berkshire Hathaway Energy). The utility transmits and distributes electricity to 1 million customers in Las Vegas, North Las Vegas, Henderson, Searchlight, and adjoining areas. Nevada Power's nine natural gas and oil generating facilities produce about 4,385 MW facility net capacity; it also buys and sells electricity on the wholesale market with other utilities, energy marketing companies, financial institutions and other market participants to balance and optimize economic benefits of electricity generation, retail customer loads and wholesale transactions.

	Annual Growth	12/19	12/20	12/21	12/22	12/23
Sales ($mil.)	9.5%	2,148.0	1,998.0	2,139.0	2,630.0	3,088.0
Net income ($ mil.)	(0.4%)	264.0	295.0	303.0	298.0	260.0
Market value ($ mil.)	–	–	–	–	–	–
Employees	1.7%	1,400	1,400	1,300	1,400	1,500

NEVADA SYSTEM OF HIGHER EDUCATION

2601 ENTERPRISE RD
RENO, NV 895121666
Phone: 775 784-4901
Fax: –
Web: nshe.nevada.edu

CEO: Daniel Klaich
CFO: –
HR: –
FYE: June 30
Type: Private

You can gamble on a solid academic foundation with The Nevada System of Higher Education (NSHE). The system oversees Nevada's public colleges and institutions. NSHE encompasses eight institutions: the University of Nevada, Las Vegas; the University of Nevada, Reno; Nevada State College; community colleges Truckee Meadows, Great Basin College, College of Southern Nevada, and Western Nevada College; and environmental research arm Desert Research Institute (DRI). The system, which enrolls some 106,000 students, is governed by the Nevada Board of Regents, consisting of 13 members elected for six-year terms.

	Annual Growth	06/15	06/16	06/17	06/18	06/19
Sales ($mil.)	(2.4%)	–	1,055.1	1,116.0	953.8	982.4
Net income ($ mil.)	–	–	49.0	140.3	116.4	(6.4)
Market value ($ mil.)	–	–	–	–	–	–
Employees	–	–	–	–	–	8,000

NEW BEDFORD, CITY OF (INC)

133 WILLIAM ST UNIT 208
NEW BEDFORD, MA 027406113
Phone: 508 979-1400
Fax: –
Web: www.newbedford-ma.gov

CEO: –
CFO: –
HR: –
FYE: June 30
Type: Private

The City of New Bedford is probably most famous for its history as a whaling port and for serving as the initial setting of Herman Melville's novel Moby Dick. With a population of more than 90,000, the city covers approximately 20 square miles in southeastern Massachusetts. Incorporated in 1787, the New Bedford area was originally based around farming and fishing villages. Later a major whaling and foreign trade port, Melville penned his classic tale while working in New Bedford. The whaling industry began declining in the 1850s when petroleum was discovered. More recently, fishing and manufacturing have been the city's main bread and butter. City government consists of its mayor and 11 city council members.

	Annual Growth	06/06	06/07	06/08	06/15	06/16
Sales ($mil.)	6.6%	–	–	239.3	382.7	399.5
Net income ($ mil.)	–	–	–	(24.9)	(13.5)	6.8
Market value ($ mil.)	–	–	–	–	–	–
Employees	–	–	–	–	–	3,657

NEW BRAUNFELS UTILITIES

263 MAIN PLZ
NEW BRAUNFELS, TX 781305135
Phone: 830 608-8867
Fax: –
Web: www.nbutexas.com

CEO: Paula J Difonzo
CFO: –
HR: Janice Jessen
FYE: July 31
Type: Private

New Braunfels Utilities is its namesake city's most powerful entity. The utility provides electric, water, and sewage services to New Braunfels, Texas, and nearby communities. Its electric system serves more than 28,200 customers via 700 miles of overhead and underground distribution lines. New Braunfels Utilities' water and sewer systems serve more than 21,600 water and almost 20,000 wastewater customers. The water system operates six groundwater wells over the Edwards Aquifer, as well as an 8 million gallon per day surface water plant on the Guadalupe River. New Braunfels Utilities' three wastewater treatment plants have a total daily capacity of 8.4 million gallons.

	Annual Growth	07/06	07/07	07/16	07/17	07/18
Sales ($mil.)	4.4%	–	89.9	135.4	132.8	144.3
Net income ($ mil.)	(0.7%)	–	17.3	23.4	26.2	16.1
Market value ($ mil.)	–	–	–	–	–	–
Employees	–	–	–	–	–	210

NEW CONCEPT ENERGY, INC.

ASE: GBR

1603 LBJ Freeway, Suite 800
Dallas, TX 75234
Phone: 972 407-8400
Fax: 972 407-8421
Web: www.newconceptenergy.com

CEO: Gene S Bertcher
CFO: Gene S Bertcher
HR: –
FYE: December 31
Type: Public

New Concept Energy is exploring possibilities in natural resources, while keeping one foot planted in the long-term care industry. The firm owns a residential community for senior citizens in Oregon that provides support services for about 115 independent living units. New Concept Energy also has oil and gas production assets in the midwestern US, including about 100 producing wells and 120 non-producing wells, with a total proved reserves of some 7.6 million cu. ft. of natural gas. The company has gone through a number of industries over the years: it has divested most of its former assisted living communities and all of its cable and retail shopping assets, and it is seeking to grow its energy operations.

	Annual Growth	12/18	12/19	12/20	12/21	12/22
Sales ($mil.)	(25.3%)	0.7	0.6	0.1	0.1	0.2
Net income ($ mil.)	–	(0.5)	(2.4)	1.9	0.0	0.2
Market value ($ mil.)	(6.1%)	7.2	6.3	9.9	12.2	5.6
Employees	(15.9%)	6	5	2	3	3

NEW CREATURE HOLDINGS, INC.

2003 S HORSEBARN RD STE 6
ROGERS, AR 727588140
Phone: 479 273-7377
Fax: –
Web: www.new-creature.com

CEO: –
CFO: Joe March
HR: –
FYE: December 31
Type: Private

"Mommy, Mommy, I want that!" is music to the ears of New Creature Holdings. The company designs retail packaging, point-of-purchase, and merchandising displays for such customers as Coca-Cola, Disney, and Kraft; its displays are set at Wal-Mart and Sam's Club. (New Creature's proximity to Wal-Mart's Arkansas headquarters makes it a key vendor to the retail giant's suppliers.) The company also designs promotional kits and trade show kiosks. Its products are made in the US, China, Europe, and South America, and shipped via a distribution network of more than 80 locations across the US. New Creature Holdings was founded in 1999 by Patrick Ybarra and Brad Jones; its name was taken from a Bible verse.

NEW ENGLAND PATRIOTS LLC

1 PATRIOT PL
FOXBORO, MA 020351388
Phone: 508 543-8200
Fax: –
Web: www.patriots.com

CEO: Myra Kraft
CFO: –
HR: Kathleen Sullivan
FYE: December 31
Type: Private

The New England Patriots do battle in the National Football League. The professional football franchise is one of the more popular teams in the NFL, boasting five Super Bowl championship teams. The Patriots won their most recent title in Super Bowl LI (51) after the 2016 season. The team's success on the field has translated into sell-out crowds at the its 68,756-seat capacity Gillette Stadium in Foxborough, Massachusetts. The franchise was founded in 1959 as the Boston Patriots of the American Football League before moving to Foxborough and changing its name in 1971. Robert Kraft owns the franchise through his family holding company The Kraft Group.

NEW ENGLAND POWER COMPANY   NBB: NEWE N

25 Research Drive
Westborough, MA 01582
Phone: 508 389-2000
Fax: –
Web: www.nees.com

CEO: –
CFO: –
HR: –
FYE: March 31
Type: Public

The leaves may change in the area, but New England Power stays strong. The company holds the New England transmission assets of parent National Grid USA (which is a subsidiary of the UK-based National Grid plc). The utility company provides services to National Grid affiliates Granite State Electric, Massachusetts Electric, Nantucket Electric, and Narragansett Electric, as well as to other regional energy companies. It maintains and operates a 9,000-mile transmission system serving five states New England Power also holds interests in inactive nuclear power plants.

	Annual Growth	03/01	03/02	03/03	03/04	03/05
Sales ($mil.)	(8.6%)	656.3	560.4	514.0	457.8	458.3
Net income ($ mil.)	7.1%	58.3	76.8	77.4	72.5	76.8
Market value ($ mil.)	5.5%	297.7	320.4	331.2	343.9	369.2
Employees	(50.2%)	114	72	7	7	7

NEW ENGLAND REALTY ASSOCIATES L.P.   ASE: NEN

39 Brighton Avenue
Allston, MA 02134
Phone: 617 783-0039
Fax: –
Web: –

CEO: –
CFO: –
HR: –
FYE: December 31
Type: Public

New England Realty Associates invests in, develops, operates, and sells residential and commercial real estate, primarily in the Boston area. The company's portfolio includes more than 2,300 apartment and condominium units and about 85,000 sq. ft. of commercial space that includes a shopping center and mixed-use properties. It also has a 50% stake in a portfolio of about 10 commercial properties. New England Realty Associates is managed by general partner NewReal, which in turn is owned by company officers and brothers Ronald and Harold Brown. Harold Brown also owns The Hamilton Company, which manages the partnership's properties.

	Annual Growth	12/19	12/20	12/21	12/22	12/23
Sales ($mil.)	5.3%	60.5	62.1	62.6	68.3	74.5
Net income ($ mil.)	6.6%	6.5	1.4	(2.7)	3.7	8.5
Market value ($ mil.)	3.0%	7.3	5.9	8.0	8.3	8.2
Employees	–	68	66	52	–	–

NEW ENTERPRISE STONE & LIME CO., INC.

3912 BRUMBAUGH RD
NEW ENTERPRISE, PA 166649137
Phone: 814 766-2211
Fax: –
Web: www.nesl.com

CEO: Paul Detwiler III
CFO: Albert L Stone
HR: Daniel Kramer
FYE: February 28
Type: Private

New Enterprise Stone & Lime supplies aggregates, lime, stone, and concrete products for a variety of applications. The company has dozens of limestone, dolomite, gravel, and sandstone mines; stone and sand quarries; and ready-mix concrete and hot-mix blacktop plants throughout Pennsylvania, western New York, and Delaware. It also performs array of construction services ranging from building bridges and roads to paving residential driveways. J. S. Detwiler and his son, Paul, began New Enterprise Stone & Lime in 1924. The company remains family-owned and is run by third- and fourth-generation Detwilers.

NEW HAMPSHIRE ELECTRIC CO-OP FOUNDATION

579 TENNEY MOUNTAIN HWY
PLYMOUTH, NH 032643147
Phone: 603 536-8824
Fax: –
Web: www.nhec.com

CEO: –
CFO: –
HR: –
FYE: December 31
Type: Private

The granite in the Granite State won't keep the folks in New Hampshire warm in winter, but New Hampshire Electric Cooperative will. The utility provides electricity to about 80,000 residential and business customers (who are also member-owners of the cooperative) in 115 New Hampshire towns and cities. The enterprise operates 5,400 miles of distribution lines, and is seeking to become a complete energy solutions organization, offering energy saving options such as equipment retrofits at local schools and selling energy-efficient compact fluorescent light bulbs. Most of New Hampshire Electric Cooperative's revenues comes from residential customers, and the balance form small businesses.

	Annual Growth	12/17	12/18	12/19	12/21	12/22
Sales ($mil.)	6.3%	–	145.7	142.8	155.1	186.1
Net income ($ mil.)	–	–	–	–	(3.1)	(1.5)
Market value ($ mil.)	–	–	–	–	–	–
Employees	–	–	–	–	–	204

NEW HARBINGER PUBLICATIONS, INC.

5674 SHATTUCK AVE
OAKLAND, CA 946091662
Phone: 510 652-0215
Fax: –
Web: www.newharbinger.com

CEO: –
CFO: –
HR: Rebekah Ayers
FYE: December 31
Type: Private

New Harbinger Publications helps readers usher in a new era. A publisher of self-help books for consumers, the company's psychology and medical books are written by clinical professionals and feature step-by-step models. New Harbinger covers topics such as chronic illness, depression, anger, stress reduction, relationships, and self esteem. Titles include The Depression Workbook, Angry All the Time , and Self Esteem . The company's The Anxiety and Phobia Workbook came out in 1989 and has sold more than 750,000 copies. Psychologist Matthew McKay and writer Patrick Fanning founded New Harbinger in 1973.

	Annual Growth	12/07	12/08	12/09	12/10	12/11
Sales ($mil.)	10.6%	–	–	10.2	11.6	12.4
Net income ($ mil.)	60.9%	–	–	0.3	0.9	0.8
Market value ($ mil.)	–	–	–	–	–	–
Employees	–	–	–	–	–	49

NEW HORIZONS WORLDWIDE, LLC

100 4 FALLS CORPORATE CTR STE 408
CONSHOHOCKEN, PA 194282950
Phone: 888 236-3625
Fax: –
Web: www.newhorizons.com

CEO: Mark A Miller
CFO: –
HR: –
FYE: December 31
Type: Private

New Horizons Worldwide is one of the largest independent IT and career training companies in the world. Its centers offer instructor-led training in technical certification programs, health care information management, business analysis, as well as courses covering thousands of software titles from major publishers. New Horizons is certified as an AWS Training Partner, Citrix Authorized Learning Center, Cisco Partner for Platinum Learning Solutions, CompTIA Authorized Platinum Partner, Microsoft Partner with a Gold Learning competency, RedHat Business Partner, and VMware Authorized Training Center. In addition to courses taught at its learning centers, New Horizons provides on-site and online training services. The company started in 1982.

NEW ISRAEL FUND

1320 19TH ST NW STE 400
WASHINGTON, DC 200361635
Phone: 202 842-0900
Fax: –
Web: www.nif.org

CEO: –
CFO: –
HR: –
FYE: December 31
Type: Private

The New Israel Fund (NIF) works for social change in Israel. The organization is dedicated to promoting freedom, justice, and democracy in the Jewish state. NIF, in cooperation with other groups in the US, Europe, and Israel, has pledged more than $200 million to about 800 organizations. It works by distributing grants and providing technical assistance and coalition building. NIF's core issues include civil rights, social justice, religious tolerance, a sustainable environment, absorbing Russian and Ethiopian Jews into Israeli society, and women's rights. The organization founded Shatil, from the Hebrew word for "seedling," to assist like-minded grass roots groups in setting up shop. NIF was founded in 1979.

	Annual Growth	12/12	12/13	12/14	12/15	12/18
Sales ($mil.)	1.8%	–	28.2	29.5	32.9	30.8
Net income ($ mil.)	–	–	(3.7)	(1.3)	2.1	(0.4)
Market value ($ mil.)	–	–	–	–	–	–
Employees	–	–	–	–	–	35

NEW JERSEY DEVILS LLC

165 MULBERRY ST
NEWARK, NJ 071023607
Phone: 973 757-6100
Fax: –
Web: www.nhl.com

CEO: –
CFO: –
HR: Janelle Vizzi
FYE: December 31
Type: Private

These Devils make trouble for their opponents on the ice. The New Jersey Devils professional hockey team entered the National Hockey League in 1974 as the Kansas City Scouts and relocated to Colorado until it settled in the Garden State in 1982. One last relocation saw the Devils take up residence at the Prudential Center in Newark in 2007 after several years playing host at the Meadowlands in East Rutherford. A regular contender for the playoffs, the hockey franchise boasts three Stanley Cup championships, its last in 2003. An investment group led by Jeffrey Vanderbeek has owned the team since 2004.

NEW JERSEY HOUSING AND MORTGAGE FINANCE AGENCY

637 S CLINTON AVE
TRENTON, NJ 086111811
Phone: 609 278-7400
Fax: –
Web: www.njhousing.gov

CEO: –
CFO: –
HR: –
FYE: December 31
Type: Private

So you're from Jersey? What exit? Regardless of where on the turnpike you live or want to live, New Jersey Housing and Mortgage Finance Agency can help you find, fund, and maintain affordable housing. The agency offers low interest mortgage loans to low- and moderate-income families; construction loans and other programs to assist developers with the production of low-cost rental properties and affordable houses; reverse mortgages for seniors; homeownership counseling; and various programs to promote homeownership among its state's disabled, homeless, and adopting families.

	Annual Growth	12/18	12/19	12/20	12/21	12/22
Assets ($mil.)	47.3%	–	432.9	3,993.1	3,945.7	1,384.4
Net income ($ mil.)	69.1%	–	4.4	24.6	87.0	21.4
Market value ($ mil.)	–	–	–	–	–	–
Employees	–	–	–	–	–	250

NEW JERSEY INSTITUTE OF TECHNOLOGY

323 DR MARTIN LUTHER KING JR BLVD
NEWARK, NJ 071021824
Phone: 973 596-3000
Fax: –
Web: www.njit.edu

CEO: –
CFO: Catherine Brennan
HR: Elisa Ellison
FYE: June 30
Type: Private

A public research university, New Jersey Institute of Technology (NJIT) offers about 100 undergraduate and graduate programs, including about 20 doctoral programs in fields including architecture, engineering, computer science, and liberal arts. The school also offers continuing education and distance courses. With some 500 full-time faculty members, NJIT boasts a student-faulty ratio of 16:1. Its Albert Dorman Honors College provides students with individualized curricula and honors colloquia including travel and featured speakers. About 10,000 students attend the NJIT, which operates a single campus in Newark. NJIT was founded in 1881 as the Newark Technical School.

	Annual Growth	06/18	06/19	06/20	06/21	06/22
Sales ($mil.)	2.6%	–	296.6	294.1	297.0	320.5
Net income ($ mil.)	122.2%	–	3.3	(20.9)	51.4	36.4
Market value ($ mil.)	–	–	–	–	–	–
Employees	–	–	–	–	–	1,047

NEW JERSEY RESOURCES CORP

NYS: NJR

1415 Wyckoff Road
Wall, NJ 07719
Phone: 732 938-1480
Fax: –
Web: www.njresources.com

CEO: Stephen D Westhoven
CFO: Patrick J Migliaccio
HR: –
FYE: September 30
Type: Public

New Jersey Resources (NJR) a diversified energy services holding company whose principal business is the distribution of natural gas through a regulated utility, investing in and operating clean energy projects and natural gas storage and transportation assets, and providing other retail and wholesale energy services to customers. Beyond gas distribution, the company also provides HVAC & solar installation services. NJR serves customers like regulated natural gas distribution companies, industrial companies, electric generators, natural gas/liquids processors, retail aggregators, wholesale marketers and natural gas producers.

	Annual Growth	09/19	09/20	09/21	09/22	09/23
Sales ($mil.)	(6.7%)	2,592.0	1,953.7	2,156.6	2,906.0	1,963.0
Net income ($ mil.)	11.8%	169.5	193.9	117.9	274.9	264.7
Market value ($ mil.)	(2.6%)	4,412.8	2,636.7	3,396.9	3,776.5	3,964.9
Employees	5.1%	1,108	1,156	1,251	1,288	1,350

NEW JERSEY TURNPIKE AUTHORITY INC

1 TURNPIKE PLZ
WOODBRIDGE, NJ 070955195
Phone: 732 750-5300
Fax: –
Web: www.njta.com

CEO: Ronald Gravino
CFO: –
HR: Mary E Garri
FYE: December 31
Type: Private

The New Jersey Turnpike Authority operates two toll-supported highways, the New Jersey Turnpike and the Garden State Parkway. The New Jersey Turnpike runs for 148 miles, from the Delaware River Bridge at the southern end of the state to the George Washington Bridge that connects New Jersey with New York. The turnpike includes about 10 rest stops, or service areas, named for former New Jersey residents such as Alexander Hamilton, Vince Lombardi, and Walt Whitman. The Garden State Parkway runs for 173 miles and spans the length of New Jersey's Atlantic coastline.

	Annual Growth	12/17	12/18	12/19	12/20	12/21
Sales ($mil.)	7.6%	–	1,753.0	1,743.9	1,528.9	2,185.4
Net income ($ mil.)	25.3%	–	209.8	191.0	(50.5)	412.5
Market value ($ mil.)	–	–	–	–	–	–
Employees	–	–	–	–	–	2,400

NEW LEAF BRANDS, INC.

One DeWolf Road, Suite 208
Old Tappan, NJ 07675
Phone: 201 784-2400
Fax: –
Web: www.bywd.com

CEO: David Fuselier
CFO: –
HR: –
FYE: December 31
Type: Public

New Leaf Brands (formerly Baywood International) quit taking vitamins and went on a liquid diet. The company, which previously developed and sold dietary supplements (herbs, minerals, and vitamins), sold off its nutritional products business in 2009 and has devoted itself to the manufacture of ready-to-drink beverages. Its New Leaf brand has a regional toehold in the market and is being built up for national distribution and is now available in 35 US states. Its product line includes fruit-flavored ready-to-drink tea blends sold through grocers and other retailers.

	Annual Growth	12/07	12/08	12/09	12/10	12/11
Sales ($mil.)	(30.2%)	9.5	13.5	3.5	4.3	2.3
Net income ($ mil.)	–	(1.7)	(4.2)	(10.9)	(9.1)	(6.7)
Market value ($ mil.)	(59.6%)	113.1	132.7	102.6	22.6	3.0
Employees	(31.6%)	32	49	32	26	7

NEW MEXICO STATE UNIVERSITY

2850 WEDDELL ST RM 210
LAS CRUCES, NM 880031245
Phone: 575 646-4030
Fax: –
Web: www.nmsu.edu

CEO: Andy Burke
CFO: –
HR: –
FYE: June 30
Type: Private

New Mexico State University (NMSU) aims to spice things up for its 30,000 students. The university provides education services from five main campuses, one satellite learning center, and extension offices in every New Mexico county. The university offers certificate, associate, bachelor's, master's, and doctoral degrees through six academic colleges focused on agriculture, arts and sciences, business administration, education, engineering, and health and social services, as well as an honors college and a graduate school. It also provides distance education services and operates about a dozen research and science centers.

	Annual Growth	06/15	06/16	06/17	06/18	06/19
Sales ($mil.)	(2.7%)	–	–	221.7	207.9	209.8
Net income ($ mil.)	–	–	–	(4.0)	(83.3)	(66.6)
Market value ($ mil.)	–	–	–	–	–	–
Employees	–	–	–	–	–	5,000

NEW MILFORD HOSPITAL, INC.

21 ELM ST
NEW MILFORD, CT 067762993
Phone: 860 355-2611
Fax: –
Web: www.nuvancehealth.org

CEO: John M Murphy
CFO: –
HR: –
FYE: September 30
Type: Private

Residents of New Milford, Connecticut, naturally turn to New Milford Hospital for emergency care. Established in 1921, the acute care hospital has some 85 beds and offers cardiology, cancer care, pediatric, and surgical services. The not-for-profit facility also has family birthing, sleep disorder treatment, and cancer research facilities. Affiliate New Milford Visiting Nurse Association provides home health services. New Milford Hospital exited its membership in the NewYork-Presbyterian Healthcare System in 2010. It then formed a new affiliation with Danbury Hospital, and the two hospitals now operate under the administrative umbrella of Western Connecticut Healthcare (formerly Danbury Health Systems).

	Annual Growth	09/09	09/10	09/11	09/12	09/13
Sales ($mil.)	(13.6%)	–	–	93.4	78.1	69.7
Net income ($ mil.)	–	–	–	(4.3)	(6.5)	(3.2)
Market value ($ mil.)	–	–	–	–	–	–
Employees	–	–	–	–	–	400

NEW PRESS

120 WALL ST FL 31
NEW YORK, NY 100054007
Phone: 212 629-8802
Fax: –
Web: www.thenewpress.com

CEO: –
CFO: –
HR: Veronica Hairston
FYE: December 31
Type: Private

The New Press is a not-for-profit independent publishing company. The publisher's titles include national bestsellers such as Studs Terkel's Race and Peter Irons's May It Please the Court. Other titles include East to America: Korean American Life Stories and Dismantling Desegregation: The Quiet Reversal of Brown v. Board of Education. The company's books are distributed to bookstores through W.W. Norton & Company. The New Press was founded in 1990 and uses foundation support to publish its books.

	Annual Growth	12/14	12/15	12/16	12/17	12/18
Sales ($mil.)	3.1%	–	4.1	5.1	5.2	4.5
Net income ($ mil.)	–	–	(0.2)	0.2	(0.1)	(0.0)
Market value ($ mil.)	–	–	–	–	–	–
Employees	–	–	–	–	–	20

NEW PRIME, INC.

2740 N MAYFAIR AVE
SPRINGFIELD, MO 658035084
Phone: 800 321-4552
Fax: –
Web: www.primeinc.com

CEO: –
CFO: Dean Hoedl
HR: Aaron Ellis
FYE: March 31
Type: Private

Specialized carrier New Prime (which does business simply as Prime) provides refrigerated, flatbed, tanker, and intermodal trucking services throughout North America through over 11,600 remotely monitored, temperature-controlled trailers. Prime has been an innovative regional and Over the Road (OTR) trucking company, paving the way for the rest of the trucking industry. In addition Prime serves as a freight broker and logistics service provider for owner-operators and fleet owners throughout North America. The company was founded in 1970.

	Annual Growth	04/10	04/11*	03/12*	04/16*	03/17
Sales ($mil.)	9.8%	–	941.4	1,022.2	1,598.5	1,653.6
Net income ($ mil.)	16.2%	–	47.4	61.0	133.3	116.5
Market value ($ mil.)	–	–	–	–	–	–
Employees	–	–	–	–	–	6,775

*Fiscal year change

NEW SOURCE ENERGY PARTNERS LP

914 North Broadway, Suite 230
Oklahoma City, OK 73102
Phone: 405 272-3028
Fax: 405 272-3034
Web: www.newsource.com

NBB: NUSP Q
CEO: –
CFO: –
HR: –
FYE: December 31
Type: Public

If at first you don't succeed, try, try again. That's the ethos behind New Source Energy Partners L.P., a company formed in October 2012 in the hopes of becoming a publicly traded entity. A previous incarnation, New Source Energy Corporation, formed in July 2011, filed an IPO, but withdrew it in May 2012. Should New Source Energy Partners successfully go public, it will have working interests across more than 30,000 net acres in the Hunton formation in Oklahoma. Those properties produce about 170 barrels of oil per day, 6 million cu. ft. of natural gas, and almost 2,000 barrels per day of natural gas liquids (NGLs). New Source Energy Partners filed an IPO in January 2013 seeking to raise up to $106 million.

	Annual Growth	10/11	10/12*	12/12	12/13	12/14
Sales ($mil.)	–	–	–	–	50.7	165.6
Net income ($ mil.)	–	–	–	–	26.6	(42.3)
Market value ($ mil.)	–	–	–	–	432.8	133.3
Employees	630.6%	–	8	9	136	427

*Fiscal year change

NEW TANGRAM, LLC

9200 SORENSEN AVE
SANTA FE SPRINGS, CA 906702645
Phone: 562 365-5000
Fax: -
Web: www.tangraminteriors.com

CEO: -
CFO: -
HR: Paul Bawol
FYE: December 31
Type: Private

Tangram Interiors keeps it all on the inside. The company is an office furniture manufacturer and dealer specializing in Steelcase products. Other brands include Brayton, Vecta, Metro, and Lightolier. The company, with two showrooms in southern California, offers asset management, furniture rental, network installation, remanufacturing, and moving and relocation assistance. Tangram sells an "acoustic privacy system" that allows workplace conversations to remain private by broadcasting a signal that scrambles speech patterns into white noise. The company's Tangram Studio provides design services, project management, and custom architectural elements. Tangram is part of Steelcase family of companies.

	Annual Growth	12/08	12/09	12/10	12/11	12/12
Sales ($mil.)	7.7%	-	-	84.9	92.4	98.5
Net income ($ mil.)	(63.1%)	-	-	1.7	1.8	0.2
Market value ($ mil.)	-	-	-	-	-	-
Employees	-	-	-	-	-	177

NEW VISION GROUP, LLC

3525 PIEDMONT RD NE
ATLANTA, GA 303051578
Phone: 404 995-4711
Fax: -
Web: www.paycor.com

CEO: -
CFO: -
HR: -
FYE: December 31
Type: Private

If good TV is in the eye of the beholder, then New Vision Television aims to keep the beholders happy. The company owns and operates about 15 television stations in midsized and large markets, primarily in Ohio, Iowa, Georgia, and Hawaii. Its portfolio includes affiliates of all four major broadcast networks, as well as affiliates of smaller networks MyNetworkTV and The CW. New Vision operates multiple stations in several of its markets, allowing those stations to share certain business functions in order to reduce operating costs. Founded in 1993 by CEO Jason Elkin, the company emerged from Chapter 11 bankruptcy in 2009.

NEW YORK ACADEMY OF MEDICINE

1216 5TH AVE 103RD ST
NEW YORK, NY 100295202
Phone: 212 822-7200
Fax: -
Web: www.nyam.org

CEO: -
CFO: -
HR: -
FYE: December 31
Type: Private

The New York Academy of Medicine schools the world on urban health issues. The not-for-profit institution focuses on epidemiologic, health policy, and public health studies with an emphasis on disadvantaged urban populations. The Academy hosts educational conferences and symposia on issues like HIV/AIDS, asthma, substance abuse, and mental health, as well as offering continuing medical education for professionals. The Academy also supports one of the largest privately-owned medical libraries in the world with 800,000 books, some 400 journal subscriptions, and more than 50,000 rare books and manuscripts. The Academy was founded in 1847 by a group of NYC doctors to reform the medical profession and public health.

	Annual Growth	12/14	12/15	12/19	12/21	12/22
Sales ($mil.)	0.5%	-	11.1	-	11.4	11.4
Net income ($ mil.)	-	-	(7.0)	-	(1.2)	(0.8)
Market value ($ mil.)	-	-	-	-	-	-
Employees	-	-	-	-	-	160

NEW YORK BLOOD CENTER, INC.

310 E 67TH ST
NEW YORK, NY 100656273
Phone: 212 570-3010
Fax: -
Web: www.nybc.org

CEO: Christopher D Hillyer
CFO: Lawrence Hannigan
HR: Diane Donlon
FYE: December 31
Type: Private

New York Blood Center (NYBC) is a nonprofit organization that is one of the largest independent, community-based blood centers in the world. NYBC, along with its operating divisions Community Blood Center of Kansas City, Missouri (CBC), Innovative Blood Resources (IBR), Blood Bank of Delmarva (BBD), and Rhode Island Blood Center (RIBC), collect approximately 4,000 units of blood products each day and serve local communities of more than 75 million people in the Tri-State area, Mid Atlantic area, Missouri and Kansas, Minnesota, Nebraska, Rhode Island, and Southern New England. NYBC and its operating divisions also provide a wide array of transfusion-related medical services to over 500 hospitals nationally, including Comprehensive Cell Solutions, the National Center for Blood Group Genomics, the National Cord Blood Program, and the Lindsley F. Kimball Research Institute, which ? among other milestones ? developed a practical screening method for hepatitis B as well as a safe, effective and affordable vaccine, and a patented solvent detergent plasma process innovating blood-purification technology worldwide.

	Annual Growth	03/13	03/14	03/15	03/21*	12/22
Sales ($mil.)	8.0%	-	-	320.3	554.7	550.4
Net income ($ mil.)	-	-	-	(0.9)	47.6	2.2
Market value ($ mil.)	-	-	-	-	-	-
Employees	-	-	-	-	-	1,800

*Fiscal year change

NEW YORK CITY HEALTH AND HOSPITALS CORPORATION

125 WORTH ST RM 514
NEW YORK, NY 100134006
Phone: 212 788-3321
Fax: -
Web: www.nychealthandhospitals.org

CEO: -
CFO: -
HR: -
FYE: June 30
Type: Private

New York City Health and Hospitals Corporation (NYC Health + Hospitals) is the largest public health care system in the nation serving more than a million New Yorkers annually in more than 70 patient care locations across the city's five boroughs. A robust network of outpatient, neighborhood-based primary and specialty care centers anchors care coordination with the system's trauma centers, nursing homes, post-acute care centers, home care agency, and MetroPlus health plan?all supported by more than 10 essential hospitals. Its health plan, MetroPlus, offers low to no-cost health insurance to eligible people living in Manhattan, Brooklyn, Queens, Staten Island, and the Bronx. NYC Health + Hospitals/Community Care offers comprehensive care management and better access to social support services in patients' homes and communities.

	Annual Growth	06/99	06/00	06/01	06/02	06/17
Sales ($mil.)	5.1%	-	4,083.8	4,288.0	4,285.3	9,550.9
Net income ($ mil.)	-	-	9.3	(71.9)	(118.9)	(193.6)
Market value ($ mil.)	-	-	-	-	-	-
Employees	-	-	-	-	-	35,700

NEW YORK CITY TRANSIT AUTHORITY

2 BROADWAY FL 18
NEW YORK, NY 100043357
Phone: 718 330-1234
Fax: -
Web: new.mta.info

CEO: -
CFO: -
HR: -
FYE: December 31
Type: Private

New York City Transit Authority has your ticket to ride in the Big Apple. Known as MTA New York City Transit, it provides subway and bus transportation throughout New York City's five boroughs. It is the primary agency of the MTA and the largest public transportation system in North America. Its subway system -- which includes more than 6,300 subway cars, 468 stations, and 660 miles of track -- serves more than 5.5 million passengers a day day on 238 local, six select bus service, and 61 express routes in the five boroughs. Its more than 5,700 buses transport some 2.6 million riders each day. The agency also operates the Staten Island Railway system.

	Annual Growth	12/17	12/18	12/19	12/21	12/22
Sales ($mil.)	(8.2%)	-	4,892.7	5,061.0	2,815.3	3,468.8
Net income ($ mil.)	45.9%	-	985.8	1,049.9	2,825.9	4,465.6
Market value ($ mil.)	-	-	-	-	-	-
Employees	-	-	-	-	-	47,956

NEW YORK COMMUNITY BANCORP INC.   NYS: NYCB

102 Duffy Avenue
Hicksville, NY 11801
Phone: 516 683-4100
Fax: –
Web: www.mynycb.com

CEO: Thomas R Cangemi
CFO: John J Pinto
HR: –
FYE: December 31
Type: Public

New York Community Bancorp, based in Hicksville, New York, is the parent of a New York State-chartered bank, New York Community Bank. New York Community Bank is a leading producer of multi-family loans in New York City, with an emphasis on non-luxury residential apartment buildings with rent-regulated units that feature below-market rents. In addition to multi-family loans, which are its principal asset, the company originates CRE loans (primarily in New York City), specialty finance loans and leases and, to a much lesser extent, ADC loans, and C&I loans (typically made to small and mid-size business in Metro New York).

	Annual Growth	12/19	12/20	12/21	12/22	12/23
Assets ($mil.)	20.8%	53,641	56,306	59,527	90,144	114,057
Net income ($ mil.)	–	395.0	511.1	596.0	650.0	(79.0)
Market value ($ mil.)	(4.0%)	8,679.2	7,617.8	8,816.4	6,209.8	7,386.7
Employees	33.2%	2,786	2,948	2,815	7,497	8,766

NEW YORK CONVENTION CENTER OPERATING CORPORATION

655 W 34TH ST
NEW YORK, NY 100011114
Phone: 212 216-2000
Fax: –
Web: www.javitscenter.com

CEO: Alan E Steel
CFO: Melanie McManus
HR: Christine McMahon
FYE: March 31
Type: Private

The New York Convention Center Operating Corporation may be able to claim that it has the whole world in its hand since it's the manager and operator of the "marketplace for the world" (also know as the Jacob K. Javits Convention Center in Manhattan). The center serves as host each year for myriad conventions, fashion shows, association meetings, trade shows, and more. The center features such amenities as restaurants and cocktail lounges, temporary private office rentals, and concierge service. The New York Convention Center Operating Corporation (also known as NYCCOC) was established in 1979 to manage the Javits Center.

	Annual Growth	03/16	03/17	03/18	03/19	03/20
Sales ($mil.)	(2.7%)	–	200.6	206.4	210.0	185.0
Net income ($ mil.)	–	–	6.7	8.9	1.4	(2.9)
Market value ($ mil.)	–	–	–	–	–	–
Employees	–	–	–	–	–	3,500

NEW YORK HEALTH CARE INC   NBB: BBAL

1850 McDonald Avenue
Brooklyn, NY 11223
Phone: 718 375-6700
Fax: 718 375-4007
Web: www.nyhc.com

CEO: Murray Englard
CFO: –
HR: Glen Persaud
FYE: December 31
Type: Public

New York Health Care still practices the forgotten art of house calls. The home health care agency provides nursing and assisted living services to patients in the greater New York City area. Services offered include meal preparation, light housekeeping, and shopping, as well as more standard nursing services such as physical therapy and medication administration. Previously, the company conducted research and development on a friendly strain of E. coli in the hopes of turning it into a biotech drug. However, it scaled back its drug development efforts due to lack of funds, and sold the product development rights.

	Annual Growth	12/03	12/04	12/05	12/06	12/07
Sales ($mil.)	(0.4%)	45.1	48.9	44.7	45.6	44.4
Net income ($ mil.)	–	(22.1)	(6.1)	(6.3)	(3.8)	(1.1)
Market value ($ mil.)	(62.4%)	92.6	17.1	26.2	4.4	1.8
Employees	(8.2%)	2,061	1,927	1,679	1,784	1,462

NEW YORK LIFE INSURANCE CO.

51 Madison Avenue
New York, NY 10010
Phone: 212 576-7000
Fax: –
Web: www.newyorklife.com

CEO: Craig L Desanto
CFO: Eric A Feldstein
HR: –
FYE: December 31
Type: Public

New York Life Insurance Company is the nation's largest mutual life insurance company and one of the largest life insurance companies in the world. New York Life and its subsidiaries provide insurance, investment, and retirement solutions that help people at all stages of life achieve financial security, delivered through financial specialists nationwide. New York Life also provides insurance and investment products to the institutional market and operates one of the world's largest global asset managers through New York Life Investments. New York Life has $710 billion assets under management. The company was founded in 1845.

	Annual Growth	12/06	12/07	12/08	12/09	12/10
Assets ($mil.)	5.9%	182,343	198,383	188,908	208,153	228,965
Net income ($ mil.)	(7.9%)	2,298.0	1,497.0	(1,016.0)	1,327.0	1,655.0
Market value ($ mil.)	–	–	–	–	–	–
Employees	–	–	–	–	–	–

NEW YORK MEDICAL COLLEGE

40 SUNSHINE COTTAGE RD
VALHALLA, NY 105951524
Phone: 914 594-4100
Fax: –
Web: www.nymc.edu

CEO: Edward C Halperin
CFO: Stephen Piccolo Jr
HR: –
FYE: June 30
Type: Private

It doesn't take a brain surgeon to figure out this school's specialty. New York Medical College (NYMC) confers advanced degrees to those preparing for careers in the medical and health professions. The institution's three divisions -- the School of Medicine, the School of Public Health, and the Graduate School of Basic Medical Sciences -- offer programs in more than 20 disciplines. NYMC has an enrollment of more than 1,400 students who practice at nearby Westchester Medical Center and the Manhattan location of Saint Vincent Catholic Medical Centers. Founded in 1860, the medical college has been affiliated with the Archdiocese of New York since 1978. NYMC is part of Touro College.

	Annual Growth	06/13	06/14	06/15	06/21	06/22
Sales ($mil.)	(2.5%)	–	151.1	133.0	121.1	123.6
Net income ($ mil.)	9.7%	–	4.6	(3.8)	0.2	9.6
Market value ($ mil.)	–	–	–	–	–	–
Employees	–	–	–	–	–	1,100

NEW YORK MORTGAGE TRUST INC   NAS: NYMT

90 Park Avenue
New York, NY 10016
Phone: 212 792-0107
Fax: –
Web: www.nymtrust.com

CEO: Steven R Mumma
CFO: Kristine R Nario
HR: –
FYE: December 31
Type: Public

New York Mortgage Trust is a self-advised real estate investment trust (REIT) that invests in mortgage-related real estate assets and some financial assets. It mostly invests in residential mortgage loans, including multi-family commercial mortgage-backed securities (CMBS), distressed residential mortgage loans, and direct financing to multi-family property owners through mezzanine loans and preferred equity investments. More than 75% of its revenue comes from interest on multi-family loans held in securitization trusts, though the REIT's fortunes depend heavily on security gains and losses. New York Mortgage Trust was formed in 2003 and is headquartered in New York City.

	Annual Growth	12/19	12/20	12/21	12/22	12/23
Sales ($mil.)	(16.1%)	789.1	(9.6)	378.6	137.9	391.0
Net income ($ mil.)	–	173.7	(288.5)	193.2	(298.6)	(48.7)
Market value ($ mil.)	8.2%	564.9	334.6	337.3	232.1	773.5
Employees	9.5%	55	56	65	74	79

NEW YORK POWER AUTHORITY

123 MAIN ST
WHITE PLAINS, NY 106013104
Phone: 914 681-6200
Fax: -
Web: www.nypa.gov

CEO: Justin E Driscoll
CFO: Adam Barsky
HR: -
FYE: December 31
Type: Private

The New York Power Authority (NYPA) is America's largest state power organization, with around 15 generating facilities and more than 1,400 circuit-miles of transmission lines. More than 80% of the electricity NYPA produces is clean renewable hydropower. The company generates, transmits, and sells electricity principally at wholesale. State and federal regulations shape NYPA's diverse customer base, which includes large and small businesses, not-for-profit organizations, community-owned electric systems and rural electric cooperatives and government entities. NYPA is owned by the State of New York. Governor Franklin D. Roosevelt established New York's model for public power through legislation signed in 1931.

	Annual Growth	12/16	12/17	12/18	12/19	12/20
Sales ($mil.)	(4.2%)	-	2,573.0	2,689.0	2,370.0	2,265.0
Net income ($ mil.)	-	-	119.0	102.0	26.0	(17.0)
Market value ($ mil.)	-	-	-	-	-	-
Employees	-	-	-	-	-	2,237

NEW YORK PUBLIC RADIO

160 VARICK ST FL 7
NEW YORK, NY 100131270
Phone: 646 829-4400
Fax: -
Web: www.nypublicradio.org

CEO: Laura R Walker
CFO: -
HR: -
FYE: June 30
Type: Private

If you want the NPR in NYC, turn your radio dial to WNYC. With more than one million listeners per week, WNYC is the most popular public radio station in the country. The stations broadcasts on FM and AM and produces and airs original programming including daily news reports, talk shows, and music shows, including The Brian Lehrer Show , Radio Lab , and Studio 360 . It also features shows from affiliate National Public Radio (NPR) stations (including All Things Considered and Morning Edition) and Public Radio International. Listeners can also access WYNC's Web site to read the news, download podcasts and hear recently broadcasted shows. The radio station, one of the oldest in the US, began broadcasting on AM in 1922.

	Annual Growth	06/16	06/17	06/20	06/21	06/22
Sales ($mil.)	(1.8%)	-	90.2	81.9	87.3	82.2
Net income ($ mil.)	-	-	2.0	(9.6)	2.0	(0.7)
Market value ($ mil.)	-	-	-	-	-	-
Employees	-	-	-	-	-	120

NEW YORK SHAKESPEARE FESTIVAL

425 LAFAYETTE ST
NEW YORK, NY 100037021
Phone: 212 539-8500
Fax: -
Web: www.publictheater.org

CEO: -
CFO: -
HR: -
FYE: August 31
Type: Private

O, what sweet sorrow to miss Shakespeare performed live. Fortunately, New Yorkers and visitors don't have to, thanks to The New York Shakespeare Festival, a cultural institution which does business as The Public Theater. The theatrical producer puts on classic plays, such as Hamlet and Romeo and Juliet , as well as new plays and musicals. More than 250,000 people attend Public Theater performances each year. Its six stages include Delacorte Theater in Central Park (the site of free summer performances) and Joe's Pub, a venue for musicians, spoken-word artists, and solo performers. The Public Theater also caters to emerging writers and boasts an acting lab workshop that specializes in Shakespearean performance.

	Annual Growth	08/08	08/09	08/10	08/15	08/16
Sales ($mil.)	5.9%	-	22.3	21.5	40.1	33.4
Net income ($ mil.)	-	-	2.5	0.2	7.4	(2.8)
Market value ($ mil.)	-	-	-	-	-	-
Employees	-	-	-	-	-	100

NEW YORK STATE CATHOLIC HEALTH PLAN, INC.

9525 QUEENS BLVD
REGO PARK, NY 113744510
Phone: 888 343-3547
Fax: -
Web: -

CEO: -
CFO: -
HR: -
FYE: December 31
Type: Private

Fidelis Care hopes for always faithful health plan members. The New York State Catholic Health Plan, which does business as Fidelis Care, serves more than 921,000 residents in some 60 counties across the state, including the New York City area. The church-sponsored plan's provider network includes more than 63,000 physicians, hospitals, and other health care professionals and facilities. Fidelis Care provides managed Medicaid, Medicare, and state-sponsored family and children's Health Plus plans, as well as long-term care and behavioral health coverage.

	Annual Growth	12/07	12/08	12/09	12/10	12/14
Assets ($mil.)	-	-	-	490.9	585.7	2,199.6
Net income ($ mil.)	103.1%	-	3.9	27.9	51.4	271.7
Market value ($ mil.)	-	-	-	-	-	-
Employees	-	-	-	-	-	1,625

NEW YORK STATE ENERGY RESEARCH AND DEVELOPMENT AUTHORITY

17 COLUMBIA CIR
ALBANY, NY 122035156
Phone: 518 862-1090
Fax: -
Web: nyserda.ny.gov

CEO: John B Rhodes
CFO: -
HR: Donna Rabito
FYE: March 31
Type: Private

The New York State Energy Research and Development Authority (NYSERDA) uses technological innovation to solve the state's energy and environmental problems. The public benefit corporation funds energy supply and conservation research and energy-related environmental issues. It also conducts research projects that help state and city groups solve their energy problems. Its Energy Efficiency Services group works helps more than 450 schools, businesses, and municipalities find ways to reduce their energy costs. Investor-owned electric and gas utilities, grants, and contributions from the New York Power Authority and the Long Island Power Authority fund NYSERDA, which was created in 1975.

	Annual Growth	03/15	03/16	03/17	03/19	03/22
Sales ($mil.)	502.1%	-	-	0.2	1,091.6	1,614.7
Net income ($ mil.)	-	-	-	(0.6)	51.2	258.1
Market value ($ mil.)	-	-	-	-	-	-
Employees	-	-	-	-	-	345

NEW YORK TIMES CO.

NYS: NYT

620 Eighth Avenue
New York, NY 10018
Phone: 212 556-1234
Fax: -
Web: www.nytco.com

CEO: Meredith K Levien
CFO: Roland A Caputo
HR: -
FYE: December 31
Type: Public

The New York Times is a global media organization focused on creating, collecting, and distributing high-quality news and information that helps its audience understand and engage with the world, and this mission has contributed to its success. The company also publishes an international edition of its flagship paper, tailored for global audiences. The company's other holdings include The Athletic (our sports media product); Cooking (its recipes product); Games (its puzzle games product) and Audm (its read-aloud audio service); Wirecutter (its review and recommendation product); and other related businesses, such as its licensing operations; its commercial printing operations; its live events business; and other products and services under The Times brand.

	Annual Growth	12/19	12/20	12/21	12/22	12/23
Sales ($mil.)	7.6%	1,812.2	1,783.6	2,074.9	2,308.3	2,426.2
Net income ($ mil.)	13.5%	140.0	100.1	220.0	173.9	232.4
Market value ($ mil.)	11.2%	5,273.6	8,449.2	7,796.0	5,341.0	8,060.9
Employees	7.0%	4,500	4,700	2,000	5,800	5,900

NEW YORK UNIVERSITY

70 WASHINGTON SQ S
NEW YORK, NY 100121019
Phone: 212 998-1212
Fax: –
Web: www.nyu.edu

CEO: –
CFO: Stephanie Pianka
HR: Rick Villarreal
FYE: August 31
Type: Private

The setting and heritage of New York University (NYU) make it one of the nation's most popular educational institutions. With more than 65,000 students attending its nearly 20 schools and colleges, NYU is among the largest private schools in the US. Its Tisch School of the Arts is well regarded, and its law school and Leonard N. Stern School of Business are among the foremost in the country. One of the most prominent and respected research universities in the world, featuring top-ranked academic programs and accepting fewer than one in eight undergraduates, NYU's students come from nearly every state and about 135 countries. NYU was founded in 1831.

	Annual Growth	08/04	08/05	08/06	08/11	08/16
Sales ($mil.)	14.7%	–	–	2,148.1	5,172.2	8,500.2
Net income ($ mil.)	(1.0%)	–	–	195.6	563.7	177.5
Market value ($ mil.)	–	–	–	–	–	–
Employees	–	–	–	–	–	21,000

NEW YORK YANKEES PARTNERSHIP

1 E 161ST ST
BRONX, NY 104512100
Phone: 718 293-4300
Fax: –
Web: www.mlb.com

CEO: –
CFO: –
HR: Allyson A Shatz
FYE: April 30
Type: Private

These Yanks are a big hit with New York baseball fans. New York Yankees Partnership owns and operates the New York Yankees professional baseball team, one of the most storied and popular clubs in Major League Baseball. The franchise boasts a record 27 World Series titles and 40 American League pennants, making it the most successful professional sports team in history. Along with that success, the Yankees organization has been associated with such sports icons as Babe Ruth, Lou Gehrig, Joe DiMaggio, and Mickey Mantle. Once known as the Highlanders, the team has represented New York City since 1903. The Steinbrenner family, led by Hal Steinbrenner, has controlled the Yanks since 1973.

NEWARK BETH ISRAEL MEDICAL CENTER INC.

201 LYONS AVE
NEWARK, NJ 071122027
Phone: 973 926-7000
Fax: –
Web: www.rwjbh.org

CEO: Paul Mertz
CFO: Veronica Zichner
HR: Martin S Everhart
FYE: December 31
Type: Private

Part of the RWJBarnabas network, Newark Beth Israel Medical Center is a 670-bed, acute-care regional referral hospital. The facility serves residents of Newark and surrounding areas in northern New Jersey. The hospital offers services including primary, diagnostic, emergency, surgical, and rehabilitative care. It is home to specialized programs such as kidney transplantation, cancer care, dentistry, sleep disorders, geriatrics, and women's health services. Newark Beth Israel Medical Center also houses the Children's Hospital of New Jersey and the Saint Barnabas Heart Center. The research and teaching hospital has a medical staff of more than 800 physicians.

	Annual Growth	12/17	12/18	12/19	12/20	12/21
Sales ($mil.)	(2.1%)	–	645.5	660.7	522.7	605.3
Net income ($ mil.)	(42.9%)	–	19.9	(33.5)	11.2	3.7
Market value ($ mil.)	–	–	–	–	–	–
Employees	–	–	–	–	–	3,000

NEWARK CORPORATION

300 S RIVERSIDE PLZ STE 2200
CHICAGO, IL 606066765
Phone: 773 784-5100
Fax: –
Web: www.newark.com

CEO: –
CFO: –
HR: –
FYE: February 01
Type: Private

Newark offers all sorts of electronic goods in one place, and in places all across the Americas. The company, doing business as Newark element14, distributes some 4.4 million electronic components and supplies, including semiconductors, passive devices, electrical equipment, connectors, wire and cable, optoelectronics, test and measurement instruments, and tools. It is also a source for companies needing parts compliant with the Restrictions of Hazardous Substances order in the European Union. Customers are electronics design engineers, maintenance technicians, and other electronics buyers. Newark element14 is a subsidiary of Premier Farnell, a top UK electronic and industrial parts supplier.

	Annual Growth	02/11	02/12	02/13	02/14	02/15
Sales ($mil.)	(3.2%)	–	–	580.8	541.1	544.0
Net income ($ mil.)	9.6%	–	–	20.3	23.7	24.4
Market value ($ mil.)	–	–	–	–	–	–
Employees	–	–	–	–	–	834

NEWAYGO COUNTY GENERAL HOSPITAL ASSOCIATION

212 S SULLIVAN AVE
FREMONT, MI 494121548
Phone: 231 924-3300
Fax: –
Web: –

CEO: Randal J Stasik
CFO: John Sella
HR: –
FYE: December 31
Type: Private

Gerber Memorial Health Services (GMHS) provides acute medical services for the rural county of Newaygo County, Michigan. The not-for-profit hospital, operating as Spectrum Health Gerber Memorial, has about 60 licensed beds. Services include cancer care, cardiac rehabilitation, orthopedics, surgery, emergency medicine, and women's health. It also provides general practice and home health services. GMHS was founded in 1918. GMHS was acquired by western Michigan health network Spectrum Health in 2010; GMHS had already been affiliated with Spectrum through its membership in the Spectrum Health Regional Hospital Network.

NEWELL BRANDS INC

6655 Peachtree Dunwoody Road
Atlanta, GA 30328
Phone: 770 418-7000
Fax: –
Web: www.newellbrands.com

NMS: NWL
CEO: Christopher H Peterson
CFO: Mark J Erceg
HR: –
FYE: December 31
Type: Public

Newell Brands is a leading global consumer goods company with a strong portfolio of well-known brands, including Rubbermaid, FoodSaver, Sistema, Calphalon, Coleman, Graco, and Sharpie pens. Newell Brands' customers are mainly mass retailers, such as Walmart, Target, and home and office supply stores, such as Staples. Newell's footprint spans approximately 55 manufacturing facilities and some 70 warehouses and regional distribution centers globally. It also has approximately 270 retail stores (some 260 stores are located in US), primarily related to Yankee Candle. Approximately 65% of Newell Brands' sales comes from the US operation.

	Annual Growth	12/19	12/20	12/21	12/22	12/23
Sales ($mil.)	(4.3%)	9,714.9	9,385.0	10,589	9,459.0	8,133.0
Net income ($ mil.)	–	106.6	(770.0)	572.0	197.0	(388.0)
Market value ($ mil.)	(18.0%)	7,962.8	8,795.6	9,048.3	5,419.0	3,596.1
Employees	(4.8%)	30,000	31,000	32,000	28,000	24,600

NEWESCO, INC.

1201 ARTHUR AVE
ELK GROVE VILLAGE, IL 600075705
Phone: 847 437-7050
Fax: –
Web: www.nelsonwesterberg.com

CEO: John R Westerberg
CFO: Lawrence Cap
HR: Jean Madsen
FYE: December 31
Type: Private

An agent of leading mover Atlas Van Lines (part of Atlas World Group), Nelson Westerberg specializes in handling household moves for employees who are being transferred by their companies. It also offers office and industrial moving services and household moves for individuals. (As an agent, the company handles moves within its assigned geographic territory and cooperates with other agents on interstate moves.) Major corporate clients have included Sara Lee and Walgreen. Founded in 1904 by Swedish immigrants Fred Nelson and Oscar Westerberg, the company started out in Chicago hauling coal, ice, and furniture with a horse-drawn wagon. Company chairman and CEO John Westerberg is Oscar's grandson.

	Annual Growth	12/04	12/05	12/06	12/07	12/08
Sales ($mil.)	0.8%	–	–	54.9	61.9	55.8
Net income ($ mil.)	13.1%	–	–	2.8	5.6	3.6
Market value ($ mil.)	–	–	–	–	–	–
Employees	–	–	–	–	–	400

NEWMARK & COMPANY REAL ESTATE, INC.

125 PARK AVE FL 12
NEW YORK, NY 100175529
Phone: 212 372-2000
Fax: –
Web: www.newmarkrealestate.com

CEO: Barry M Gosin
CFO: Michael J Rispoli
HR: –
FYE: December 31
Type: Private

Newmark & Company Real Estate, Inc. and certain of its affiliates, via the Newmark Knight Frank, NKF and NGKF brands, provides real estate brokerage, appraisal and valuation, portfolio and property management, mortgage brokerage, loan servicing, consultancy, advisory, and facilities and construction management services.

	Annual Growth	12/12	12/13	12/14	12/15	12/16
Assets ($mil.)	91.7%	–	–	234.3	694.6	860.6
Net income ($ mil.)	–	–	–	–	139.4	53.8
Market value ($ mil.)	–	–	–	–	–	–
Employees	–	–	–	–	–	2,250

NEWMARK GROUP INC   NMS: NMRK

125 Park Avenue
New York, NY 10017
Phone: 212 372-2000
Fax: –
Web: www.nmrk.com

CEO: Barry M Gosin
CFO: Michael J Rispoli
HR: –
FYE: December 31
Type: Public

Newmark Group, Inc. is a leading full-service commercial real estate services business. It offers a diverse array of integrated services and products designed to meet the full needs of both real estate investors/owners and occupiers. Investor/owner services and products include capital markets (which includes investment sales, commercial mortgage brokerage, and the placement of debt, equity and structured finance.), agency leasing, government-sponsored enterprise (GSE) and Federal Housing Administration (FHA) multifamily lending and loan servicing, Valuation and Advisory, property management, and commercial real estate due diligence consulting and advisory services. The company was founded in 1929.

	Annual Growth	12/19	12/20	12/21	12/22	12/23
Sales ($mil.)	2.7%	2,218.1	1,905.0	2,906.4	2,705.5	2,470.4
Net income ($ mil.)	(22.4%)	117.3	80.1	750.7	83.3	42.6
Market value ($ mil.)	(5.0%)	2,343.9	1,270.4	3,257.7	1,388.4	1,909.3
Employees	5.7%	5,600	5,800	6,200	6,300	7,000

NEWMARKET CORP   NYS: NEU

330 South Fourth Street
Richmond, VA 23219-4350
Phone: 804 788-5000
Fax: –
Web: www.newmarket.com

CEO: Thomas E Gottwald
CFO: Brian D Paliotti
HR: –
FYE: December 31
Type: Public

NewMarket is the holding entity of the following subsidiaries: Afton Chemical (its primary business), Ethyl Corporation, NewMarket Services Corporation, and NewMarket Development Corporation. Afton manufactures petroleum additives, while Ethyl markets antiknock compounds in North America and performs contracted manufacturing and related services. NewMarket Development manages the real property that it owns in Virginia. NewMarket Services provides various administrative services to NewMarket, Afton, Ethyl, and NewMarket Development. NewMarket Services departmental and other expenses are billed to each subsidiary pursuant to services agreements between the companies. Over 65% of the holding company's sales come from outside of US.

	Annual Growth	12/19	12/20	12/21	12/22	12/23
Sales ($mil.)	5.4%	2,190.3	2,010.9	2,356.1	2,764.8	2,698.4
Net income ($ mil.)	11.2%	254.3	270.6	190.9	279.5	388.9
Market value ($ mil.)	2.9%	4,665.8	3,819.6	3,286.7	2,983.6	5,234.6
Employees	(1.4%)	2,118	2,105	2,104	2,058	2,000

NEWMARKET TECHNOLOGY INC

14860 Montfort Drive, Suite 210
Dallas, TX 75254
Phone: 972 386-3372
Fax: –
Web: www.newmarkettechnology.com

CEO: –
CFO: –
HR: –
FYE: December 31
Type: Public

NewMarket Technology is all about growing into new markets. The holding company invests in development-stage tech firms located in emerging markets outside the US. It has a handful of subsidiaries in its portfolio -- China Crescent Enterprises, RKM Suministros (Venezuela), and UniOne Consulting (Brazil) -- that provide systems integration, software development, and telecommunications hardware. It also has equity stakes in other companies, including mobile payment services company Alternet Systems and wireless broadband operator RedMoon. NewMarket's customers have included international giants such as Siemens, ExxonMobil, Visa, and Bayer; customers in China account for most of the company's sales, however.

	Annual Growth	12/06	12/07	12/08	12/09	12/10
Sales ($mil.)	11.1%	77.6	93.1	95.1	98.2	118.3
Net income ($ mil.)	(10.4%)	4.0	7.3	(30.3)	1.6	2.6
Market value ($ mil.)	(19.4%)	3.7	2.3	0.4	0.7	1.6
Employees	(4.5%)	600	600	600	500	500

NEWMONT CORP   NYS: NEM

6900 E. Layton Ave.
Denver, CO 80237
Phone: 303 863-7414
Fax: 303 837-5837
Web: www.newmont.com

CEO: Thomas R Palmer
CFO: Karyn Ovelman
HR: Louis Adams
FYE: December 31
Type: Public

Newmont is a gold producer with significant operations and/or assets in the US, Canada, Mexico, Dominican Republic, Peru, Suriname, Argentina, Chile, Australia, and Ghana. The company had attributable proven and probable gold reserves of 96.1 million ounces and an aggregate land position of approximately 23,700 square miles. Newmont is also engaged in the production of copper, silver, lead, and zinc. While the company's sales mostly come from refined gold, the end product of their operations is dor bars. The company generates most of its revenue outside the US.

	Annual Growth	12/19	12/20	12/21	12/22	12/23
Sales ($mil.)	4.9%	9,740.0	11,497	12,222	11,915	11,812
Net income ($ mil.)	–	2,805.0	2,829.0	1,166.0	(429.0)	–
Market value ($ mil.)	(1.2%)	50,054	68,993	71,447	54,374	47,681
Employees	(9.0%)	31,600	27,800	14,400	14,600	21,700

NEWPARK RESOURCES, INC.   NYS: NR

9320 Lakeside Boulevard, Suite 100 — CEO: Matthew S Lanigan
The Woodlands, TX 77381 — CFO: Gregg S Piontek
Phone: 281 362-6800 — HR: –
Fax: – — FYE: December 31
Web: www.newpark.com — Type: Public

Newpark Resources, Inc. is a geographically diversified supplier providing environmentally-sensitive products, as well as rentals and services to customers across multiple industries. The company provides drilling fluid and engineering services to oil and gas drillers. Newpark Resources also supplies prefab work platforms and provides DuraBase brand composite mats used to make temporary access roads and provide related wellsite services and equipment (through its Newpark Mats & Integrated Services unit). It offers services to a variety of industries, including power transmission, E&P, pipeline, renewable energy, petrochemical, construction and other industries. Newpark Resources founded in 1932. It generates about 65% of total sales from the US.

	Annual Growth	12/19	12/20	12/21	12/22	12/23
Sales ($mil.)	(2.2%)	820.1	492.6	614.8	815.6	749.6
Net income ($ mil.)	–	(12.9)	(80.7)	(25.5)	(20.8)	14.5
Market value ($ mil.)	1.4%	534.2	163.6	250.5	353.6	565.7
Employees	(8.4%)	2,200	1,560	1,565	1,540	1,550

NEWPORT CORPORATION

1791 DEERE AVE — CEO: –
IRVINE, CA 926064814 — CFO: –
Phone: 949 863-3144 — HR: –
Fax: – — FYE: January 03
Web: go.newport.com — Type: Private

Newport is a leading global supplier of advanced technology products and systems to customers in the scientific research, microelectronics, life and health sciences, industrial manufacturing and defense/security markets. The company delivers innovative products in the areas of lasers, photonics instrumentation, sub-micron positioning systems, vibration isolation, and optical components and subsystems to enhance the capabilities and productivity of its customers' manufacturing, engineering and research applications. In addition, Newport has built a strong history of partnering with OEM customers, delivering solutions from subassemblies to full solutions including design, testing and manufacturing. Established in 1969 as Newport Research Corporation, the company is a wholly-owned subsidiary of MKS Instruments, Inc.

	Annual Growth	12/10	12/11	12/12	12/13*	01/15
Sales ($mil.)	0.5%	–	–	595.3	560.1	605.2
Net income ($ mil.)	–	–	–	(90.0)	15.7	35.2
Market value ($ mil.)	–	–	–	–	–	–
Employees	–	–	–	–	–	2,480

*Fiscal year change

NEWPORT DIGITAL TECHNOLOGIES INC.

620 Newport Center Drive, Suite 570 — CEO: –
Newport Beach, CA 92660 — CFO: –
Phone: 949 219-0530 — HR: –
Fax: – — FYE: June 30
Web: www.newportdt.com — Type: Public

Newport Digital Technologies (formerly International Food Products Group) has changed its focus. Once a food manufacturer and a marketer of childhood diabetes products, among other business lines, the company now markets and sells technology products in the areas of e-learning (including an affordable notebook computer for children called ViewSonic Lite Bird), WiMAX communications in Italy, digital signage based on light-emitting diodes (LEDs), security and surveillance equipment, VoIP telephones, and radio-frequency identification (RFID) system tracking tools.

	Annual Growth	06/07	06/08	06/09	06/10	06/11
Sales ($mil.)	–	–	–	–	–	0.0
Net income ($ mil.)	–	–	(1.3)	(3.8)	(6.6)	(1.7)
Market value ($ mil.)	(50.2%)	–	30.1	69.1	9.0	3.7
Employees	–	–	–	12	5	2

NEWS CORP (NEW)   NMS: NWSA

1211 Avenue of the Americas — CEO: Robert J Thomson
New York, NY 10036 — CFO: Susan Panuccio
Phone: 212 416-3400 — HR: –
Fax: – — FYE: June 30
Web: www.newscorp.com — Type: Public

News Corp is a global diversified media and information services company, publishing well-known mastheads such as The Wall Street Journal and New York Post, Australia's Herald Sun, and The Sun and The Times in the UK. The company owns the Dow Jones and Factiva information services, as well as book publisher HarperCollins. In TV, News Corp has a majority stake in Foxtel in Australia and owns the Australian News Channel. Other properties are the real estate websites REA Group and Move. Australia and other countries generate about 45% of revenue.

	Annual Growth	06/19	06/20	06/21	06/22	06/23
Sales ($mil.)	(0.5%)	10,074	9,008.0	9,358.0	10,385	9,879.0
Net income ($ mil.)	(1.0%)	155.0	(1,269.0)	330.0	623.0	149.0
Market value ($ mil.)	9.6%	7,715.7	6,783.4	14,739	8,911.1	11,153
Employees	(2.8%)	28,000	23,500	24,000	25,500	25,000

NEWS/MEDIA ALLIANCE

4401 FAIRFAX DR STE 300 — CEO: Robert Walden
ARLINGTON, VA 222031622 — CFO: Margaret Vassilikos
Phone: 571 366-1000 — HR: –
Fax: – — FYE: December 31
Web: www.newsmediaalliance.org — Type: Private

The Newspaper Association of America (NAA) is aware of "all the news that's fit to print" and "all the news that fits." NAA is a nonprofit organization that represents more than 2,000 newspapers in the US and Canada. Its membership includes daily newspapers, as well as suppliers, vendors, educators, university papers, press associations, and online product producers. The group works to increase newspaper sales, lobbies government in support of First amendment issues, and provides newspapers with technological assistance. The NAA was formed in 1992 when seven separate newspaper associations merged.

	Annual Growth	12/13	12/14	12/15	12/21	12/22
Sales ($mil.)	4.8%	–	8.5	8.4	7.7	12.5
Net income ($ mil.)	36.1%	–	0.3	0.9	(1.1)	3.6
Market value ($ mil.)	–	–	–	–	–	–
Employees	–	–	–	–	–	135

NEWSMAX MEDIA, INC.

750 PARK OF COMMERCE DR STE 100 — CEO: Christopher Ruddy
BOCA RATON, FL 334873650 — CFO: Darryle Burnham
Phone: 561 686-1165 — HR: –
Fax: – — FYE: December 31
Web: www.newsmax.com — Type: Private

NewsMax Media serves up the news with a conservative slant. The company publishes alternative news and opinion content through its monthly magazine NewsMax and corresponding Web site. Columnists include Reed Irvine (founder of conservative watchdog group Accuracy In Media) and national broadcasting hosts and analysts Bill O'Reilly, Ed Koch, and Dick Morris. The company generates sales from advertising, as well as from politically oriented merchandise (clothing, posters, books) showcasing stars of the Republican Party. Former New York Post reporter Christopher Ruddy, the company's CEO, founded NewsMax Media in 1998.

NEWTEKONE INC

NMS: NEWT

4800 T Rex Avenue, Suite 120
Boca Raton, FL 33431
Phone: 212 356-9500
Fax: –
Web: www.newtekone.com

CEO: Barry Sloane
CFO: M S Price
HR: –
FYE: December 31
Type: Public

Newtek Business Services provides a suite of business and financial services to small to midsized businesses, including electronic merchant payment processing, website hosting, Small Business Administration (SBA) loans, data storage, insurance, accounts receivable financing, and payroll management. The company serves more than 100,000 business accounts throughout the US. Newtek also has investments in certified capital companies (Capcos), which are authorized in eight states and Washington, DC. It has stakes in about a dozen Capcos that traditionally have issued debt and equity securities to insurance firms, then used the funds to mainly invest in small and midsized financial and business services firms.

	Annual Growth	12/18	12/19	12/20	12/21	12/22
Sales ($mil.)	14.9%	49.5	59.3	92.2	108.5	86.2
Net income ($ mil.)	–	(7.5)	(5.6)	32.0	25.7	(6.5)
Market value ($ mil.)	(1.8%)	429.2	557.4	484.6	679.9	399.9
Employees	(12.2%)	175	109	110	104	104

NEWTON MEMORIAL HOSPITAL (INC)

175 HIGH ST
NEWTON, NJ 078601099
Phone: 973 383-2121
Fax: –
Web: www.atlantichealth.org

CEO: –
CFO: –
HR: –
FYE: December 31
Type: Private

The folks at Newton Medical Center want to cure what ails you or help you slip into slumber. With about 150 beds and numerous clinical specialties, Newton Memorial provides medical care to residents at the crux of northwestern New Jersey, southwestern New York, and eastern Pennsylvania. Established in 1932, the acute-care hospital offers specialized services such as emergency care, pediatrics, home health, cardiac care, respiratory care, and aesthetic surgery. The not-for-profit hospital also has a sleep lab and inpatient clinics for orthopedics, stroke care, cancer treatment, and rehabilitation. It is part of Atlantic Health System.

	Annual Growth	12/08	12/09	12/17	12/19	12/21
Sales ($mil.)	2.8%	–	138.0	1.7	2.2	192.2
Net income ($ mil.)	4.0%	–	3.7	(0.0)	0.4	6.0
Market value ($ mil.)	–	–	–	–	–	–
Employees	–	–	–	–	–	805

NEWTON WELLESLEY HOSPITAL CORP

2014 WASHINGTON ST
NEWTON, MA 024621607
Phone: 617 243-6000
Fax: –
Web: www.nwh.org

CEO: –
CFO: –
HR: –
FYE: September 30
Type: Private

Newton-Wellesley Hospital provides the Greater Boston area with a full range of medical, surgical, and diagnostic services. The hospital, which boasts more than 260beds, offers a variety of programs, including a full-service diagnostic imaging department, a multiple sclerosis clinic, cancer center, joint reconstruction surgery, physical and occupational therapy, and inpatient psychiatric care. In addition, the Partners Reproductive Medicine Center offers infertility treatment in collaboration with two other area hospitals. Part of the Partners HealthCare family, Newton-Wellesley is a teaching hospital for Tufts University's School of Medicine and the Massachusetts College of Pharmacy and Health Sciences..

	Annual Growth	09/16	09/17	09/18	09/20	09/21
Sales ($mil.)	7.7%	–	435.6	479.2	480.9	587.1
Net income ($ mil.)	–	–	(1.0)	13.3	(34.6)	(62.8)
Market value ($ mil.)	–	–	–	–	–	–
Employees	–	–	–	–	–	2,500

NEWYORK-PRESBYTERIAN/BROOKLYN METHODIST

506 6TH ST
BROOKLYN, NY 112153609
Phone: 718 780-3000
Fax: –
Web: www.nyp.org

CEO: James Perkins
CFO: –
HR: Aaron Kranich
FYE: December 31
Type: Private

New York Methodist Hospital is a not-for-profit, acute-care teaching hospital serving Brooklyn residents. Established in 1881 as the Methodist Episcopal Hospital, the facility has more than 650 licensed beds. It offers a full range of medical services, including primary and emergency care, as well as specialty services such as women's health, cancer, cardiovascular, pediatric, geriatric, and behavioral health. The hospital also operates satellite clinics in surrounding areas. A member of New York-Presbyterian Healthcare System, New York Methodist is a teaching hospital affiliated with Cornell University's Weill Medical College.

	Annual Growth	12/14	12/15	12/16	12/19	12/21
Sales ($mil.)	2.4%	–	732.9	788.1	962.9	847.0
Net income ($ mil.)	2.6%	–	88.9	145.6	123.7	103.8
Market value ($ mil.)	–	–	–	–	–	–
Employees	–	–	–	–	–	4,929

NEWYORK-PRESBYTERIAN/QUEENS

5645 MAIN ST
FLUSHING, NY 113555045
Phone: 718 670-2000
Fax: –
Web: www.nyp.org

CEO: Stephen S Mills
CFO: Kevin Ward
HR: –
FYE: December 31
Type: Private

The New York Hospital Medical Center of Queens aims to provide care that's fit for royalty. Better known as the New York Hospital Queens, the acute care hospital has about 520 beds and provides both primary and tertiary care. Specialist services include cancer, cardiovascular, pediatric, obstetric, surgical, and dental care. The medical center also operates about a dozen outpatient clinics and care centers that offer such services as family health, kidney dialysis, rehabilitation, and dental care, as well as home health care services. New York Hospital Queens is part of the NewYork-Presbyterian Healthcare System.

	Annual Growth	12/16	12/17	12/19	12/21	12/22
Sales ($mil.)	2.2%	–	846.5	841.3	879.3	944.9
Net income ($ mil.)	–	–	5.1	(2.0)	69.3	(25.3)
Market value ($ mil.)	–	–	–	–	–	–
Employees	–	–	–	–	–	2,380

NEXEO SOLUTIONS HOLDINGS, LLC

3 WATERWAY SQUARE PL STE 1000
THE WOODLANDS, TX 773803488
Phone: 281 297-0700
Fax: –
Web: www.univarsolutions.com

CEO: David A Bradley
CFO: Ross J Crane
HR: Lisa P Britt
FYE: September 30
Type: Private

Nexeo Solutions provides answers for customers with chemicals, plastics, and environmental services challenges. The company distributes chemicals, plastics, and composite raw materials (such as resins and fiberglass) to more than 80 countries. Most of its sales, however, come from North America. Nexeo Solutions sells more than 26,000 products, including chemicals from Dow and Eastman and plastics from BASF and SABIC . It also has an environmental services business that provides transportation and logistics services for waste disposal from seven storage facilities in the US. In 2016 WL Ross Holding Corp acquired Nexeo Solutions for $1.58 billion.

NEXPOINT STORAGE PARTNERS, INC.

300 CRESCENT CT STE 700
DALLAS, TX 752017849
Phone: 901 337-5312
Fax: –
Web: www.nexpointstorage.com

CEO: John A Good
CFO: Kelly P Luttrell
HR: –
FYE: December 31
Type: Private

If you're in the self-storage business, Jernigan Capital can help finance your growth. The commercial real estate finance company provides financing options for the construction, redevelopment, acquisition, refinancing, or recapitalization of new or established self-storage facilities in the US. Classified as a tax-friendly real estate investment trust (REIT), Jernigan Capital typically offers financing to private developers, owners, and operators in the self-storage market, and typically lends between $5 and $15 million under a fixed or floating interest rate. The REIT may also take an equity stake in a self-storage business, particularly ones in development. Jernigan went public in March 2015, and is externally managed by JCap Advisors, LLC.

NEXSTAR MEDIA GROUP INC   NMS: NXST

545 E. John Carpenter Freeway, Suite 700
Irving, TX 75062
Phone: 972 373-8800
Fax: –
Web: www.nexstar.tv

CEO: Perry A Sook
CFO: Lee A Gliha
HR: Ana Guerra
FYE: December 31
Type: Public

Nexstar is a leading diversified media company with television broadcasting, television network, and digital media assets operating in the US. It is focused on the acquisition, development and operation of television stations and interactive community websites and digital media services. The company owns, operates, programs or provides sales and other services to almost 200 full power television stations, including those owned by VIEs, and one AM radio station in more than 115 markets in about 40 states and the District of Columbia. Its portfolio includes affiliates of ABC, CBS, FOX, NBC, The CW, MNTV and other broadcast television network. Nexstar has created duopolies by entering into what they refer to as local service agreements. It was founded by Nexstar Chairman and CEO, Perry A. Sook in 1996.

	Annual Growth	12/19	12/20	12/21	12/22	12/23
Sales ($mil.)	12.9%	3,039.3	4,501.3	4,648.4	5,211.0	4,933.0
Net income ($ mil.)	10.7%	230.3	811.4	834.6	971.1	346.0
Market value ($ mil.)	7.5%	3,939.7	3,668.9	5,073.1	5,881.2	5,266.9
Employees	(4.8%)	16,193	12,412	12,473	12,971	13,294

NEXT, INC.

1295 VERNON ST
WABASH, IN 469923444
Phone: 260 563-2186
Fax: –
Web: –

CEO: –
CFO: –
HR: –
FYE: November 28
Type: Private

NEXT designs and markets licensed, branded, and private line promotional items and sportswear. The company's private line comprises the American Biker, American Wildlife, Campus Traditions USA, Class Threads, Ragtops Sportswear, and Cadre Athletic brands. The company's licensing agreements have included automakers Chevy, Dodge, and Ford, as well as Chuck E. Cheese and GRITS (Girls Raised In The South). NEXT distributes its products through mass merchandisers, warehouse clubs, department stores, sporting goods chains, college bookshops, and automotive dealers. Customers include Wal-Mart, Sears, Dillard's, Sam's Club, and Dollar General. It also sells through its own brands' websites.

NEXTERA ENERGY INC   NYS: NEE

700 Universe Boulevard
Juno Beach, FL 33408
Phone: 561 694-4000
Fax: 561 694-4620
Web: www.nexteraenergy.com

CEO: John W Ketchum
CFO: Rebecca J Kujawa
HR: Carol Johnston
FYE: December 31
Type: Public

NextEra Energy (NEE) is an electric power and energy infrastructure companies in North America. NEE has two principal businesses, Florida Power & Light Company (FPL) and NextEra Energy Capital Holdings, Inc. (NEER). FPL is the largest electric utility in the state of Florida and one of the largest electric utilities in the US. FPL's strategic focus is centered on investing in generation, transmission and distribution facilities to deliver on its value proposition of low customer bills, high reliability, outstanding customer service and clean energy for the benefit of its approximately 5.8 million customer accounts. NEER is the world's largest generator of renewable energy from the wind and sun, as well as a world leader in battery storage.

	Annual Growth	12/19	12/20	12/21	12/22	12/23
Sales ($mil.)	10.0%	19,204	17,997	17,069	20,956	28,114
Net income ($ mil.)	18.0%	3,769.0	2,919.0	3,573.0	4,147.0	7,310.0
Market value ($ mil.)	(29.2%)	496,912	158,312	191,575	171,547	124,638
Employees	3.2%	14,800	14,000	9,700	9,300	16,800

NEXTERA ENERGY PARTNERS LP   NYS: NEP

700 Universe Boulevard
Juno Beach, FL 33408
Phone: 561 694-4000
Fax: –
Web: www.nexteraenergypartners.com

CEO: James L Robo
CFO: –
HR: –
FYE: December 31
Type: Public

Formed by NextEra Energy to own, operate, and acquire contracted clean energy projects, NextEra Energy Partners holds a 17.4% limited partner interest in NEE Operating LP, which own interests in ten wind and solar projects. NextEra Energy Partners' objective is to pay stable and growing cash distributions to the holders of its common units, targeting a three-year annual growth rate in cash available for distribution of 12% to 15% per common unit. The company believes its cash flow profile, geographic and technological diversity, and relationship with NextEra Energy provide it with a significant competitive advantage and enables it to execute its growth strategy. The company went public in July 2014.

	Annual Growth	12/19	12/20	12/21	12/22	12/23
Sales ($mil.)	6.0%	855.0	917.0	982.0	1,211.0	1,078.0
Net income ($ mil.)	–	(71.0)	(50.0)	137.0	477.0	200.0
Market value ($ mil.)	(12.8%)	4,917.5	6,262.5	7,883.0	6,546.4	2,840.3
Employees	–	–	–	–	–	–

NEYENESCH PRINTERS, INC.

2750 KETTNER BLVD
SAN DIEGO, CA 921011295
Phone: 619 297-2281
Fax: –
Web: www.neyenesch.com

CEO: Carl A Bentley
CFO: Kandy Neyenesch
HR: –
FYE: December 31
Type: Private

Founded in 1899 by William Barrend Neyenesch, Neyenesch Printers has transitioned from printing menus to a state of the art commercial printing company. The company offers prepress, digital proofing, printing, finishing and fulfillment services putting ink to paper for jobs of all sizes. The independent printer serves clients in the San Diego area. Neyenesch Printers' clients come from a wide range of fields including financial services, retail, transportation, consumer goods, health care, and manufacturing. The company is still owned and operated by members the Neyenesch family.

	Annual Growth	12/00	12/01	12/02	12/04	12/12
Sales ($mil.)	2.2%	–	–	12.2	12.7	15.1
Net income ($ mil.)	9.6%	–	–	0.3	0.6	0.9
Market value ($ mil.)	–	–	–	–	–	–
Employees	–	–	–	–	–	70

NFA CORP.

50 MARTIN ST
CUMBERLAND, RI 028645335
Phone: 401 753-7800
Fax: –
Web: www.hopeglobal.com

CEO: Lee Casty
CFO: –
HR: –
FYE: December 29
Type: Private

Narrow Fabrics of America Corp. (NFA) does business under the high-minded name Hope Global. the company, an operating subsidiary of NFA, makes woven and knitted products, braided cord (shoelaces and parachute cords), and wire products at manufacturing plants in five countries. The company's products are used by automotive manufacturers (Form-a-Grip trunk and door seals), the military and postal service, shoemakers, for industrial use, and others. Its assembly division combines cords, bungee, and mesh materials in value-added products such as shoulder straps and child car seat waist restraints. Hope Global was founded in 1883 as Hope Webbing.

NFI INDUSTRIES, INC.

TRIAD1828, 2 COOPER ST
CAMDEN, NJ 08102
Phone: 877 634-3777
Fax: –
Web: www.nfiindustries.com

CEO: Sidney Brown
CFO: Kelly Sklodowski
HR: –
FYE: December 29
Type: Private

NFI is a fully-integrated North American supply chain solutions provider. The company offers a full range of logistics, distribution, warehousing, real estate, and supply chain services to a variety of markets including retail, beverage, and food and drug stores. The company maintains a fleet of some 5,000 tractors and 14,300 trailers and has approximately 70 million square feet of warehouse space. Employs over 16,800 associates, NFI owns facilities globally. Established in 1932 by Israel Brown, NFI is a privately held owned and run by members of the founding Brown family.

NFINANSE INC

3923 Coconut Palm Drive, Suite 107
Tampa, FL 33619
Phone: 813 367-4400
Fax: –
Web: www.nfinanse.com

NBB: NFSE
CEO: –
CFO: –
HR: –
FYE: January 1
Type: Public

Through nFinanSe Card, the company provides stored value cards, or SVCs. It offers reloadable, Discover-branded spending cards (for consumers without bank cards or credit cards), gift cards, payroll cards, and corporate reward cards; cards issued by nFinanSe bear a logo in the form of a Discover Financial Services hologram. Customers can purchase, load, and reload cards at more than 70,000 locations that are part of the nFinanSe Network; most load stations are found inside Western Union and MoneyGram locations. Formerly named Morgan Beaumont, the company has agreed to be purchased by AccountNow, provider of general purpose reloadable prepaid cards in the direct-to-consumer sales channel.

	Annual Growth	12/06	12/07*	01/09	01/10	01/11
Sales ($mil.)	186.1%	0.0	0.0	0.0	0.0	1.3
Net income ($ mil.)	–	(0.7)	(9.9)	(14.8)	(13.9)	(9.3)
Market value ($ mil.)	(48.6%)	30.1	111.3	23.6	2.6	2.1
Employees	–	–	50	60	53	71

*Fiscal year change

NFP CORP.

200 PARK AVE
NEW YORK, NY 101663201
Phone: 212 301-4000
Fax: –
Web: www.nfp.com

CEO: –
CFO: –
HR: –
FYE: December 31
Type: Private

NFP is a leading property and casualty broker, benefits consultant, wealth manager, and retirement plan advisor that provides solutions enabling client success through the expertise of over 7,000 global employees, investments in innovative technologies, and enduring relationships with highly rated insurers, vendors and financial institutions. NFP is the 9th best place to work for large employers in insurance, 7th largest privately owned broker, 5th largest benefits broker by global revenue and 13th largest broker of US business.

	Annual Growth	12/07	12/08	12/09	12/10	12/11
Assets ($mil.)	(16.6%)	–	1,543.3	970.4	893.1	894.2
Net income ($ mil.)	35.5%	–	14.8	(493.4)	42.6	36.9
Market value ($ mil.)	–	–	–	–	–	–
Employees	–	–	–	–	–	5,130

NGL ENERGY PARTNERS LP

6120 South Yale Avenue, Suite 805
Tulsa, OK 74136
Phone: 918 481-1119
Fax: –
Web: www.nglenergypartners.com

NYS: NGL
CEO: –
CFO: –
HR: –
FYE: March 31
Type: Public

NGL Energy Partners is a diversified midstream energy partnership that transports, treats, recycles and disposes of produced water generated as part of the energy production process as well as transports, stores, markets and provides other logistics services for crude oil and liquid hydrocarbons. Approximately 32.8 million financial barrels (volume amounts are from both internal and external parties) of crude were transported on the Grand Mesa Pipeline. NGL buys refined petroleum in the Gulf Coast, West Coast, and Midwest regions of the US. The company also has a fleet of nearly 400 owned railcars, about 130 trucks and about 215 trailers, as well as a dozen of towboats and about 25 barges.

	Annual Growth	03/19	03/20	03/21	03/22	03/23
Sales ($mil.)	(22.4%)	24,017	7,584.0	5,227.0	7,947.9	8,694.9
Net income ($ mil.)	(38.5%)	360.0	(397.0)	(639.8)	(184.8)	51.4
Market value ($ mil.)	(32.6%)	1,852.8	343.4	269.4	293.2	383.0
Employees	(16.3%)	1,300	1,400	997	842	638

NHL ENTERPRISES, INC.

1185 AVENUE OF THE AMERICAS FL 22
NEW YORK, NY 100362603
Phone: 212 789-2000
Fax: –
Web: www.nhl.com

CEO: –
CFO: –
HR: –
FYE: June 30
Type: Private

Hockey is more than a cool sport for serious fans. The National Hockey League is one of the four major professional sports associations in North America, boasting 30 professional ice hockey franchises in the US and Canada. The NHL governs the game, sets and enforces rules, regulates team ownership, and collects licensing fees for merchandise. It also negotiates fees for national broadcasting rights. (Each team controls the rights to regional broadcasts.) In addition, five minor and semi-pro hockey leagues also fly under the NHL banner. The league was organized in Canada in 1917.

	Annual Growth	06/04	06/05	06/06	06/09	06/14
Sales ($mil.)	15.1%	–	35.2	17.4	74.4	124.4
Net income ($ mil.)	–	–	(1.8)	4.9	(1.3)	(8.5)
Market value ($ mil.)	–	–	–	–	–	–
Employees	–	–	–	–	–	200

NHW HEALTHCARE, INC.

2131 S 17TH ST
WILMINGTON, NC 284017407
Phone: 910 343-7001
Fax: –
Web: www.novanthealth.org

CEO: Carl S Armato
CFO: –
HR: Karen Curran
FYE: June 30
Type: Private

Those living in the Cape Fear area need not fear when it comes to accessing good medical care. Integrated health system New Hanover Regional Medical Center (NHRMC) serves the Wilmington and Cape Fear area of North Carolina through its flagship 855-bed New Hanover Regional Medical Center, the 130-bed Cape Fear Hospital, and the 85-bed Pender Memorial Hospital. NHRMC also operates a rehabilitation center, a behavioral health facility, and a women's and children's hospital, as well as home health, hospice, EMS transport, physician practice, and outpatient care clinic locations. The not-for-profit health network is affiliated with the UNC-Chapel Hill School of Medicine.

NIBCO INC.

1516 MIDDLEBURY ST
ELKHART, IN 465164740
Phone: 574 295-3000
Fax: –
Web: www.nibco.com

CEO: Steve Malm
CFO: –
HR: –
FYE: December 31
Type: Private

NIBCO is a recognized manufacturer and brand leader of valves, fittings and flow-control products that operates throughout the US, Mexico and Poland. Its products include fittings, industrial plastics and valves, made from bronze, stainless steel, plastic, and other materials. NIBCO brand family (Chemtrol, Flo-Boss, Hydrapure, Sure Seal, and Webstone) includes more than 30,000 flow control products for residential, commercial construction, industrial, and irrigation markets worldwide. Spanning five generations of family leadership and associate ownership, NIBCO remains privately-held and is positioned for growth in a global marketplace. It was founded in 1904.

	Annual Growth	12/05	12/06	12/07	12/08	12/09
Sales ($mil.)	–	–	–	(417.3)	–	436.3
Net income ($ mil.)	34690.2 %	–	–	0.0	–	20.2
Market value ($ mil.)	–	–	–	–	–	–
Employees	–	–	–	–	–	2,420

NICHOLAS FINANCIAL INC (BC)

2454 McMullen Booth Road, Building C
Clearwater, FL 33759
Phone: 727 726-0763
Fax: –
Web: www.nicholasfinancial.com

NMS: NICK
CEO: Michael Rost
CFO: Irina Nashtatik
HR: Susan Burek
FYE: March 31
Type: Public

Nickel-less? No problem. Nicholas Financial can still get you behind the wheel of a car. The company buys new and used car loans from some 2,300 car dealers in the Southeast and Midwest US, and conducts its automobile finance business through more than 65 offices in more than 15 states. In addition to its indirect lending activities, Nicholas Financial offers and finances extended warranties, roadside assistance plans, and credit life, accident, and health insurance to its borrowers. Nicholas also makes some direct consumer loans, primarily to customers whose car loans it has bought and serviced.

	Annual Growth	03/19	03/20	03/21	03/22	03/23
Sales ($mil.)	(11.2%)	71.3	62.1	56.0	49.8	44.3
Net income ($ mil.)	–	(3.6)	3.5	8.4	3.0	(34.1)
Market value ($ mil.)	(9.1%)	65.6	42.6	77.1	74.7	44.8
Employees	–	279	260	261	278	–

NICOLET PLASTICS LLC

16685 STATE RD 32
MOUNTAIN, WI 54149
Phone: 715 276-4200
Fax: –
Web: www.nicoletplastics.com

CEO: Robert Macintosh
CFO: –
HR: –
FYE: December 31
Type: Private

Nicolet Plastics is molding its future business success. The company provides custom injection molding and assembly services to businesses throughout the US. Nicolet's menu of offerings encompasses a wide variety of plastic products, including electrical shields, fuel management components, mouth pieces, wire harnesses, access panel covers, automotive components, and industrial equipment. Nicolet uses 3-D modeling and solid modeling software in designing much of its output. The company also provides additional services such as printing and packaging. Customers have included Brady, Evenflo, Kohler, and Sherwin-Williams.

	Annual Growth	12/07	12/08	12/09	12/10	12/11
Sales ($mil.)	20.5%	–	–	5.1	6.7	7.4
Net income ($ mil.)	–	–	–	(0.1)	0.5	0.2
Market value ($ mil.)	–	–	–	–	–	–
Employees	–	–	–	–	–	70

NICOLON CORPORATION

365 S HOLLAND DR
PENDERGRASS, GA 305674625
Phone: 706 693-2226
Fax: –
Web: www.tencategeo.com

CEO: –
CFO: –
HR: –
FYE: December 31
Type: Private

TenCate Geosynthetics North America (formerly Nicolon Corporation), the commercial division of fabric giant Royal Ten Cate, manufactures and distributes a variety of industrial fabrics and geosynthetic textiles used for infrastructure and civil engineering, agriculture, and recreation applications. The company's branded fabrics include Nicolon (truck covers and tennis windscreens); Permatron (trampoline fabric); Aquagrid (fish farming nets); Geotube (dewatering and shoreline protection); GeoDetect (soil reinforcement monitoring system); Mirafi NT (water storage liner for erosion control); and Miragrid (soil reinforcement). Other products include geogrids, paving products, and drainage composites.

	Annual Growth	12/09	12/10	12/11	12/12	12/13
Sales ($mil.)	(5.6%)	–	–	178.9	150.6	159.4
Net income ($ mil.)	–	–	–	–	–	–
Market value ($ mil.)	–	–	–	–	–	–
Employees	–	–	–	–	–	1,975

NIEMANN FOODS, INC.

923 N 12TH ST
QUINCY, IL 623012129
Phone: 217 221-5600
Fax: –
Web: www.mycountymarket.com

CEO: –
CFO: –
HR: –
FYE: December 31
Type: Private

Niemann knows its midwestern food. Niemann Foods operates more than 100 supermarkets and convenience stores mostly under the Country Market, Pick A Dilly's, Cub Foods, and Save-A-Lot banners in Illinois, Iowa, and Missouri. Its Save-A-Lot stores offer a limited assortment of groceries at discount prices while Cub Foods and Country Market are conventional grocery stores. The regional grocery store operator is battling for market share in the Midwest with Hy-Vee and supercenter operator Wal-Mart Stores. The company also runs six pet stores and several Ace Hardware stores. The employee-owned, family-run firm was founded in 1917 by brothers Ferd and Steve Niemann and is currently run by CEO Rich Niemann.

	Annual Growth	12/12	12/13	12/15	12/21	12/22
Sales ($mil.)	(7.9%)	–	0.4	0.1	0.5	0.2
Net income ($ mil.)	(14.4%)	–	0.2	0.0	0.3	0.0
Market value ($ mil.)	–	–	–	–	–	–
Employees	–	–	–	–	–	5,000

NII HOLDINGS INC.

12110 Sunset Hills Road, Suite 600
Reston, VA 20190
Phone: 703 390-5100
Fax: –
Web: www.nii.com

CEO: –
CFO: –
HR: –
FYE: December 31
Type: Public

NII Holdings brings the Nextel brand to Brazil, where it has about 3.2 million consumer and business users. The company's customers are concentrated in the country's urban areas including Rio de Janeiro and São Paulo. The company offers mobile telephone voice and wireless data services; international voice and data roaming services; application-based radio connection; and streaming capabilities. NII was to wind down its legacy iDEN network in 2018, offering those subscribers access to its WCDMA network. The company is based in Reston, Virginia.

NIKE INC

NYS: NKE

One Bowerman Drive
Beaverton, OR 97005-6453
Phone: 503 671-6453
Fax: –
Web: www.nike.com

CEO: John J Donahoe II
CFO: Matthew Friend
HR: –
FYE: May 31
Type: Public

NIKE is the largest seller of athletic footwear and apparel in the world. Its principal business activity is the design, development, and worldwide marketing and selling of athletic footwear, apparel, equipment, accessories and services. Independent contractors manufacture nearly all of its products. The company, which generates roughly 60% of sales outside North America, sells through about 1,030-owned retail stores worldwide and digital platforms, to retail accounts, and to a mix of independent distributors, licensees, and sales representative. Customers in North America account for about 40% of total revenue.

	Annual Growth	05/19	05/20	05/21	05/22	05/23
Sales ($mil.)	7.0%	39,117	37,403	44,538	46,710	51,217
Net income ($ mil.)	5.9%	4,029.0	2,539.0	5,727.0	6,046.0	5,070.0
Market value ($ mil.)	8.1%	118,178	151,025	209,057	182,078	161,258
Employees	2.2%	76,700	75,400	73,300	79,100	83,700

NIMBLE STORAGE, INC.

900 N MCCARTHY BLVD
MILPITAS, CA 950355132
Phone: 408 432-9600
Fax: –
Web: www.hpe.com

CEO: Suresh Vasudevan
CFO: Anup Singh
HR: Paul Whitney
FYE: January 31
Type: Private

In a mashup of Jack be nimble and Jumpin' Jack Flash, Nimble Storage offers data storage systems that are a hybrid between a hard disk drive and a flash memory device. Its CS200 Series is designed for midsize IT organizations, while its CS400 Series is geared for larger-scale deployments. The company even offers data analytics through its InfoSight service. Nimble Storage counts more than 2,330 customers, including cloud-based service providers, government agencies, and financial services, health care, manufacturing, and technology companies. Nimble was bought by Hewlett Packard Enterprise for about $1.1 billion in April 2017.

	Annual Growth	01/13	01/14	01/15	01/16	01/17
Sales ($mil.)	47.4%	–	125.7	227.7	322.2	402.6
Net income ($ mil.)	–	–	(43.1)	(98.8)	(120.1)	(158.3)
Market value ($ mil.)	–	–	–	–	–	–
Employees	–	–	–	–	–	1,300

NINYO & MOORE GEOTECHNICAL & ENVIRONMENTAL SCIENCES CONSULTANTS CORP

5710 RUFFIN RD
SAN DIEGO, CA 921231013
Phone: 858 576-1000
Fax: –
Web: www.ninyoandmoore.com

CEO: Avram Ninyo
CFO: –
HR: –
FYE: December 31
Type: Private

Need more engineering services than are immediately at your disposal? Ninyo & Moore provides geological and technical engineering and consulting services for public and private projects throughout the western US. Its offerings include earthquake and fault studies, hydrogeologic and geologic hazard evaluations, air quality services, and environmental consultations for site developments. The company serves a variety of clients including school districts, property developers, transportation agencies, and the military. Past projects include the Las Vegas monorail and the Emporium redevelopment project in San Francisco. Ninyo & Moore was founded in 1986 and today operates about a dozen offices.

	Annual Growth	12/08	12/09	12/10	12/11	12/12
Sales ($mil.)	1.4%	–	–	52.7	55.0	54.2
Net income ($ mil.)	4.1%	–	–	2.8	4.0	3.0
Market value ($ mil.)	–	–	–	–	–	–
Employees	–	–	–	–	–	350

NISKA GAS STORAGE PARTNERS LLC

170 N RADNOR CHESTER RD STE 150
RADNOR, PA 190875280
Phone: 484 367-7462
Fax: –
Web: www.niskapartners.com

CEO: –
CFO: –
HR: –
FYE: March 31
Type: Private

Niska Gas Storage Partners provides natural gas storage in North America. The company is a large independent owner and operator of natural gas storage facilities in California, Oklahoma, and Alberta, Canada. It had total gas storage capacity of 204.5 billion cu. ft. in 2011. A small portion of that capacity is contracted from Natural Gas Pipeline Company of America, whose pipeline connects the Gulf Coast to certain midwestern US markets. Customers include natural gas producers and marketers, pipelines, power generators, financial institutions, and municipalities. Niska's revenues come from multi-year long-term and fixed-fee short-term contracts.

	Annual Growth	03/11	03/12	03/13	03/14	03/15
Sales ($mil.)	(16.4%)	–	–	140.7	207.4	98.3
Net income ($ mil.)	–	–	–	(43.6)	(9.0)	(350.7)
Market value ($ mil.)	–	–	–	–	–	–
Employees	–	–	–	–	–	121

NISOURCE INC. (HOLDING CO.)

NYS: NI

801 East 86th Avenue
Merrillville, IN 46410
Phone: 877 647-5990
Fax: –
Web: www.nisource.com

CEO: Lloyd M Yates
CFO: Shawn Anderson
HR: –
FYE: December 31
Type: Public

Organized in 1987 under the name of NIPSCO Industries, Inc. and renamed in 1999, eEnergy holding company NiSource manages rate-regulated natural gas and electric utility companies operating in six US states. It is one of the nation's largest natural gas distributors, serving some 3.37 million customers and operating approximately 54,8600 miles of natural gas pipeline. It owns five distribution subsidiaries that provide natural gas to approximately 2.4 million residential, commercial and industrial customers. It further provides electricity to approximately 483,000 customers via power plants that generate some 2,315 MW of electricity annually. NiSource's primary operating subsidiaries include NiSource Gas Distribution Group and NIPSCO.

	Annual Growth	12/19	12/20	12/21	12/22	12/23
Sales ($mil.)	1.4%	5,208.9	4,681.7	4,899.6	5,850.6	5,505.4
Net income ($ mil.)	16.9%	383.1	(17.6)	584.9	804.1	714.3
Market value ($ mil.)	(1.2%)	12,455	10,263	12,352	12,267	11,878
Employees	(3.0%)	8,363	7,389	7,342	7,162	7,411

NL INDUSTRIES, INC.   NYS: NL

5430 LBJ Freeway, Suite 1700   CEO: Courtney J Riley
Dallas, TX 75240-2620   CFO: Amy A Samford
Phone: 972 233-1700   HR: –
Fax: –   FYE: December 31
Web: –   Type: Public

NL Industries operates through its ownership of 30% of Kronos Worldwide, one of the world's largest suppliers of titanium dioxide (TiO 2) which maximizes the whiteness, opacity, and brightness to a range of customer applications and end-use markets, including coatings, plastics, paper, inks, food, cosmetics and other industrial and consumer. Majority-owned (about 85%) subsidiary CompX International makes components such as security products (locking systems), ball bearing slides, and ergonomic computer support systems. Valhi, which is more than 90%-owned by Contran Corporation, in turn owns about 85% of NL Industries. The company also manufactures mechanical and electrical cabinet locks used in a variety of applications including ignition systems, high security medical cabinetry, electronic circuit panels, and vending and cash containment machines. The US generates majority of the company's total sales.

	Annual Growth	12/19	12/20	12/21	12/22	12/23
Sales ($mil.)	6.7%	124.2	114.5	140.8	166.6	161.3
Net income ($ mil.)	–	25.8	14.7	51.2	33.8	(2.3)
Market value ($ mil.)	9.4%	190.9	233.4	361.4	332.6	274.0
Employees	49.8%	547	2,755	2,818	2,875	2,751

NMI HEALTH INC

50 West Liberty Street, Suite 880   CEO: –
Reno, NV 89501   CFO: –
Phone: 914 760-7857   HR: –
Fax: –   FYE: December 31
Web: www.nmihealth.com   Type: Public

NMI Health, formerly Nano Mask, aims to block out germs. The company develops and markets advanced antimicrobial and filtration materials. Its products include the Nano-Zyme enzymatic detergents used for instrument reprocessing and antimicrobial textiles used in hospital apparel and supplies. Its CPR and environmental masks and filters use a proprietary advanced dual filtration system designed to remove infectious bacteria and viruses from air flow systems. Its products are designed to be used by health care providers and emergency response workers.

	Annual Growth	12/09	12/10	12/11	12/12	12/13
Sales ($mil.)	–	–	–	0.0	0.5	0.2
Net income ($ mil.)	–	(0.6)	(0.8)	(0.6)	(0.8)	(0.4)
Market value ($ mil.)	(46.7%)	1.3	0.3	0.3	0.1	0.1
Employees	(5.4%)	5	5	5	5	4

NMI HOLDINGS INC   NMS: NMIH

2100 Powell Street   CEO: Adam Pollitzer
Emeryville, CA 94608   CFO: Ravi Mallela
Phone: 855 530-6642   HR: –
Fax: –   FYE: December 31
Web: www.nationalmi.com   Type: Public

NMI Holdings provides mortgage insurance through two primary subsidiary: National Mortgage Insurance Corp (NMIC) and National Mortgage Reinsurance Inc. One (Re One). NMIC is its primary insurance subsidiary, approved to write coverage in all 50 states and Washington, DC. Re One provides reinsurance to NMIC on insured loans. The company also provides outsourced loan review services to mortgage loan originators through NMI Services. Mortgage insurance protects lenders and investors from default-related losses. The company has issued master policies with about 1,875 customers, including national and regional mortgage banks, money center banks, credit unions, community banks, builder-owned mortgage lenders, internet-sourced lenders and other non-bank lenders.

	Annual Growth	12/19	12/20	12/21	12/22	12/23
Assets ($mil.)	21.2%	1,364.8	2,166.7	2,450.6	2,516.0	2,940.5
Net income ($ mil.)	17.0%	172.0	171.6	231.1	292.9	322.1
Market value ($ mil.)	(2.7%)	2,683.6	1,832.0	1,767.3	1,690.4	2,400.6
Employees	(7.2%)	321	262	247	242	238

NN, INC   NMS: NNBR

6210 Ardrey Kell Road, Suite 600   CEO: Warren Veltman
Charlotte, NC 28277   CFO: Michael C Felcher
Phone: 980 264-4300   HR: Aaron Venezia
Fax: –   FYE: December 31
Web: www.nninc.com   Type: Public

NN is a diversified industrial company that combines in-depth materials science expertise with advanced engineering and production capabilities to design and manufacture high-precision metal and plastic components and assemblies primarily for the electrical, automotive, general industrial, aerospace and defense, and medical end markets. Its technology platform consists of high-precision machining, progressive stamping, injection molding, laser welding, material science, assembly, and design optimization. NN engineering expertise and deep knowledge of precision manufacturing processes add proprietary value throughout the complete lifecycle of its products. Its customers are typically sophisticated, engineering-driven, mechanical systems manufacturers with long histories of product development and reputations for quality. The US and Puerto Rico account for about 60% of its revenue. NN, Inc. was founded in 1980 by Richard Ennen.

	Annual Growth	12/19	12/20	12/21	12/22	12/23
Sales ($mil.)	(12.8%)	847.5	427.5	477.6	498.7	489.3
Net income ($ mil.)	–	(46.7)	(100.6)	(13.2)	(26.1)	(50.2)
Market value ($ mil.)	(18.9%)	437.2	310.6	193.8	70.9	189.1
Employees	(14.0%)	5,787	3,490	3,419	3,661	3,160

NNN REIT INC   NYS: NNN

450 South Orange Avenue, Suite 900   CEO: Julian E Whitehurst
Orlando, FL 32801   CFO: Kevin B Habicht
Phone: 407 265-7348   HR: –
Fax: 407 423-2894   FYE: December 31
Web: www.nnnreit.com   Type: Public

National Retail Properties (NNN) is a fully integrated real estate investment trust (REIT) which acquires, owns, invests, and develops properties that are leased primarily to retail tenants under long-term net leases and are primarily held for investment. Its portfolio includes about 3,410 properties with some 35.0 million sq. ft. of leasable space in almost 50 states, concentrated in Texas, the South, and the Southeast US. NNN's largest lines of trade concentrations are the restaurant (including full and limited service), convenience store, and automotive service sectors.

	Annual Growth	12/19	12/20	12/21	12/22	12/23
Sales ($mil.)	5.4%	670.5	660.7	726.4	773.1	828.1
Net income ($ mil.)	7.0%	299.2	228.8	290.1	334.6	392.3
Market value ($ mil.)	(5.3%)	9,784.3	7,466.9	8,771.6	8,350.0	7,864.7
Employees	4.0%	70	69	72	77	82

NOBILITY HOMES, INC.   NBB: NOBH

3741 S.W. 7th Street   CEO: Terry E Trexler
Ocala, FL 34474   CFO: Thomas W Trexler
Phone: 352 732-5157   HR: –
Fax: –   FYE: November 5
Web: www.nobilityhomes.com   Type: Public

Florida's prince of prefab, Nobility Homes, is a leading player in the state's competitive manufactured-home market. Nobility has built and sold about 50,000 homes through about 20 retail Prestige Home Centers, Majestic Homes retail sales centers and on a wholesale basis to independent dealers and residential communities. Nobility offers some 100 models that range in price from about $30,000 to more than $100,000 and in sizes from about 700 sq. ft. to 2,650 sq. ft. The company also provides financing, mortgage lending and brokerage, and insurance services. Founder and president Terry Trexler and his family control nearly two-thirds of the company.

	Annual Growth	11/18	11/19*	10/20*	11/21	11/22
Sales ($mil.)	4.7%	42.8	46.3	41.6	45.1	51.5
Net income ($ mil.)	9.9%	5.0	8.8	6.0	5.4	7.2
Market value ($ mil.)	1.1%	77.5	83.4	78.4	114.6	80.9
Employees	(0.7%)	149	139	147	131	145

*Fiscal year change

NOBLE INVESTMENT GROUP, LLC

3424 PEACHTREE RD NE
ATLANTA, GA 303261118
Phone: 404 419-1000
Fax: -
Web: www.nobleinvestment.com

CEO: Mit Shah
CFO: George Dabney
HR: -
FYE: December 31
Type: Private

Noble Investment Group holds its head high when walking through a hotel lobby. The company invests in the lodging and hospitality real estate sector. Since its founding in 1993, Noble has invested more than $2 billion in hotels and resorts in the US through its private equity real estate funds. Noble Investment Group is part of The Noble Organization, which also includes the Noble Management Group and the Noble Development Group. Altogether, Noble owns or manages some 40 upscale hotels under brands such as Hilton, Hyatt, Intercontinental Hotels Group, Marriott, and Starwood. Its portfolio also includes restaurants and convention centers. Noble Investment Group was established by CEO Mitesh (Mit) Shah.

	Annual Growth	12/03	12/04	12/05	12/06	12/08
Assets ($mil.)	(43.3%)	-	-	-	14.1	4.5
Net income ($ mil.)	-	-	-	-	-	1.5
Market value ($ mil.)	-	-	-	-	-	-
Employees	-	-	-	-	-	133

NOBLE ROMAN'S, INC.

6612 E. 75th Street, Suite 450
Indianapolis, IN 46250
Phone: 317 634-3377
Fax: -
Web: www.nobleromans.com

NBB: NROM
CEO: A S Mobley
CFO: Paul W Mobley
HR: -
FYE: December 31
Type: Public

This patrician gives a thumbs-up to quick-service pizza. Noble Roman's operates a chain of about 820 franchised quick-service restaurants located mostly in high-traffic areas, such as shopping malls, college campuses, and military bases. Operating primarily under the names Noble Roman's Pizza, Noble Roman's Express, and Noble Roman's Pizza & Subs, the eateries offer a limited menu of pizzas, pasta, and sandwiches. Noble Roman's also has some restaurants operating under the Tuscano's Italian Style Subs brand, as well as a self-service concept designed for convenience stores. The company's restaurants operate in about 45 states and in Canada, Guam, and Italy.

	Annual Growth	12/18	12/19	12/20	12/21	12/22
Sales ($mil.)	3.8%	12.4	11.7	11.5	13.9	14.5
Net income ($ mil.)	-	(3.1)	(0.4)	(5.4)	0.5	(1.1)
Market value ($ mil.)	(9.6%)	8.9	10.9	8.6	9.3	5.9
Employees	14.4%	121	127	235	207	207

NOBLEWORKS, INC

500 PATERSON PLANK RD
UNION CITY, NJ 070873416
Phone: 201 420-0095
Fax: -
Web: www.nobleworkscards.com

CEO: -
CFO: -
HR: -
FYE: March 31
Type: Private

Nobleworks creates humor greeting cards for holidays and special occasions. The company uses artwork from many published cartoonists; its products range from mainstream funny to outrageous, raunchy, and controversial. Nobleworks markets its cards through retail outlets and through its online store, which also offers e-card services. Christopher Noble started the business in 1980.

	Annual Growth	03/04	03/05	03/06	03/07	03/08
Sales ($mil.)	19.2%	-	1.0	1.4	1.5	1.6
Net income ($ mil.)	145.8%	-	0.0	0.0	0.0	1.1
Market value ($ mil.)	-	-	-	-	-	-
Employees	-	-	-	-	-	19

NOBLIS, INC.

2002 EDMUND HALLEY DR
RESTON, VA 201913436
Phone: 703 610-2000
Fax: -
Web: www.noblis.org

CEO: -
CFO: -
HR: -
FYE: September 30
Type: Private

Noblis has been an innovator within the federal government, committed to enriching lives and making the nation safer while investing in the missions of tomorrow. The not-for-profit company, which pledges to serve the public interest, helps various government entities and other clients evaluate technology options and vendors as well as solve complex technical problems. Its wholly owned subsidiary, Noblis ESI, is a recognized leader in providing high-quality advisory and technical services for systems engineering, advanced technology, program management, and acquisition to the federal government. The company addresses problems in areas such as civil, defense, homeland security, and intelligence and law enforcement. Noblis has a partnership with University of Texas at San Antonio to advance cybersecurity research and solutions.

	Annual Growth	09/18	09/19*	10/20	10/21*	09/22
Sales ($mil.)	16.6%	-	293.2	318.4	362.2	465.0
Net income ($ mil.)	-	-	9.5	8.3	33.8	(4.9)
Market value ($ mil.)	-	-	-	-	-	-
Employees	-	-	-	-	-	1,476

*Fiscal year change

NOCO ENERGY CORP.

2440 SHERIDAN DR
TONAWANDA, NY 141509493
Phone: 716 833-6626
Fax: -
Web: www.noco.com

CEO: James D Newman
CFO: Michael Bradley
HR: Janet Wiltse
FYE: December 31
Type: Private

Family-owned NOCO Energy distributes residential heating oil, renewable energy and clean air solutions, bioproducts, natural gas, electric, propane,, commercial fuels, HVAC, used oil and fluid waste recycling to customers located in US states.. Its NOCO Commercial and Industrial Fuels unit is western New York's largest independent fuel supplier (with a 44-million gallon fuel terminal in Tonawanda). . Through heating and cooling division NOCO Home Services, the company sells, installs, and services air conditioning equipment and oil, natural gas, propane, and electric heaters.

	Annual Growth	12/03	12/04	12/06	12/07	12/13
Sales ($mil.)	-	-	(1,886.6)	-	-	0.2
Net income ($ mil.)	46.2%	-	0.0	3.3	4.4	0.0
Market value ($ mil.)	-	-	-	-	-	-
Employees	-	-	-	-	-	900

NOCOPI TECHNOLOGIES INC MD

480 Shoemaker Road, Suite 104
King of Prussia, PA 19406
Phone: 610 834-9600
Fax: -
Web: www.nocopi.com

NBB: NNUP
CEO: Michael S Liebowitz
CFO: Debra Glickman
HR: -
FYE: December 31
Type: Public

Nocopi Technologies develops and markets specialty reactive inks for applications in the large educational and toy products market. The company also develop and market technologies for document and product authentication. Offerings include Copimark, which allows information to be printed invisibly on certain areas of a document, as well as document security products such as its line of printed forms containing areas that can't be copied legibly. Another Nocopi technology, Rub-it & Color, enables publishers to create children's activity books in which colors appear when a page is rubbed.

	Annual Growth	12/19	12/20	12/21	12/22	12/23
Sales ($mil.)	(4.8%)	2.5	2.7	2.0	4.6	2.1
Net income ($ mil.)	-	0.8	0.5	0.0	1.8	(1.4)
Market value ($ mil.)	161.0%	0.8	1.5	1.6	28.9	36.5
Employees	3.9%	6	-	6	8	7

NOFIRE TECHNOLOGIES INC.

NBB: NFTI

21 Industrial Avenue
Upper Saddle River, NJ 07458
Phone: 201 818-1616
Fax: –
Web: www.nofire.com

CEO: Sam Oolie
CFO: –
HR: –
FYE: August 31
Type: Public

Frankenstein's monster and anyone else with a healthy fear of flames can rest easy now -- NoFire Technologies makes a fire retardant that can be used to coat a wide variety of substances (wood, steel, aluminum, textiles). NoFire's fire retardant is manufactured in various liquid forms, depending on the material to be coated. The company also offers textile products, such as woven fiberglass material, coated with the NoFire liquid. It markets its products to commercial, industrial, maritime, and military customers, as well as to consumers. NoFire has a history of operating losses, however, and the company's auditors have questioned whether it will be able to stay in business.

	Annual Growth	08/05	08/06	08/07	08/08	08/09
Sales ($mil.)	12.7%	0.5	0.4	1.0	0.7	0.9
Net income ($ mil.)	–	(1.7)	(1.8)	(3.8)	(1.7)	(1.6)
Market value ($ mil.)	(16.9%)	8.5	8.1	29.3	12.2	4.1
Employees	–	7	7	9	8	7

NOKIA OF AMERICA CORPORATION

600 MOUNTAIN AVE STE 700
NEW PROVIDENCE, NJ 079742008
Phone: 908 582-3275
Fax: –
Web: www.nokia.com

CEO: –
CFO: –
HR: –
FYE: December 31
Type: Private

Alcatel-Lucent USA, the US subsidiary of France-based Alcatel-Lucent (now owned by Nokia) designs, develops, and builds wireline, wireless, and converged communications networks. It supplies equipment, software, and related services to telecom carriers and network service providers such as 360networks, AT&T, and Verizon, as well as enterprise customers. Government customers are served through DC-based subsidiary LGS Innovations, which works with federal agencies, including the US Army, and major contractors such as Raytheon. Alcatel-Lucent USA accounts for more than 40% of its parent's overall revenues. In 2016 Nokia finalized its $17 billion acquisition of Alcatel-Lucent which includes Alatel-Lucent USA and Bell Labs.

	Annual Growth	09/03	09/04	09/05	09/06*	12/08
Sales ($mil.)	(94.6%)	–	–	–	8,796.0	26.1
Net income ($ mil.)	–	–	–	–	527.0	–
Market value ($ mil.)	–	–	–	–	–	–
Employees	–	–	–	–	–	29,921

*Fiscal year change

NOLAND COMPANY

3110 KETTERING BLVD
MORAINE, OH 454391924
Phone: 937 396-7980
Fax: –
Web: –

CEO: –
CFO: –
HR: –
FYE: December 31
Type: Private

Noland is a plumber's land of plenty. The wholesaler operates about 70 branches in a dozen southeastern states that offer plumbing, heating, air conditioning, electrical, industrial, and drilling supplies. Noland carries products such as cable, circuit breakers, lighting, pipes, and tools, from more than 2,000 vendors. About half its branches also house Bath & Idea Centers that spotlight residential plumbing products from Elkay, Moen, and Trane, among others. Customers range from independent contractors to large manufacturers and also include homeowners, utility companies, and government agencies. Founded by the Noland family, the company is owned by Ohio-based distributor WinWholesale.

NON-INVASIVE MONITORING SYSTEMS INC.

NBB: NIMU

4400 Biscayne Blvd., Suite 180
Miami, FL 33137
Phone: 305 575-4207
Fax: 305 575-4201
Web: www.nims-inc.com

CEO: Jane H Hsiao
CFO: James J Martin
HR: –
FYE: July 31
Type: Public

Non-Invasive Monitoring Systems (NIMS) believes being rocked in a cradle is good for grown-ups, too. The company has developed a moving bed-style device that is intended to improve circulation and joint mobility, and possibly to relieve minor aches and pains. Originally tagged as AT-101, the device was sold in Japan and the US until the FDA required the company to get regulatory approval for it. NIMS halted sales and marketing efforts on AT-101 and is seeking FDA approval for a similar but less costly device known as the Exer-Rest, intended for home and clinic use.

	Annual Growth	07/19	07/20	07/21	07/22	07/23
Sales ($mil.)	–	–	–	–	–	–
Net income ($ mil.)	–	(1.6)	(0.2)	(0.2)	(0.2)	(0.2)
Market value ($ mil.)	(32.3%)	14.7	5.7	5.0	2.8	3.1
Employees	–	–	–	–	–	–

NOODLES & CO

NMS: NDLS

520 Zang Street, Suite D
Broomfield, CO 80021
Phone: 720 214-1900
Fax: –
Web: www.noodles.com

CEO: –
CFO: –
HR: –
FYE: January 2
Type: Public

Noodles & Company is a restaurant concept offering lunch and dinner within the fast-casual segment of the restaurant industry that operates about 450 locations in some 25 states. Its restaurants' globally inspired menu includes a wide variety of high quality, cooked-to-order dishes, including noodles and pasta, soups, salads, and appetizers. Most of Noodles & Company's restaurants are company-owned. Noodles & Company opened its first restaurant in Denver, Colorado in 1995, offering noodle and pasta dishes with the goal of delivering fresh ingredients and flavors from around the world under one roof -from Pad Thai to Mac & Cheese. Most of Noodles & Company's eateries are company-owned.

	Annual Growth	12/19	12/20	12/21*	01/23	01/24
Sales ($mil.)	2.1%	462.4	393.7	475.2	509.5	503.4
Net income ($ mil.)	–	1.6	(23.3)	3.7	(3.3)	(9.9)
Market value ($ mil.)	(13.4%)	249.2	353.2	415.3	248.8	139.9
Employees	(3.9%)	8,900	8,400	8,000	8,100	7,600

*Fiscal year change

NORANDA ALUMINUM HOLDING CORP

NBB: NORN Q

801 Crescent Centre Drive, Suite 600
Franklin, TN 37067
Phone: 615 771-5700
Fax: –
Web: www.norandaaluminum.com

CEO: –
CFO: –
HR: –
FYE: December 31
Type: Public

Noranda Aluminum succeeds by keeping its operations -- and profits -- all under the same corporate roof. The company, a vertically integrated aluminum producer, starts the process by producing bauxite in a Jamaican mining project, refining it into alumina in a Louisiana smelter, and then using the alumina to make primary aluminum metal products at its processing facility in Missouri and aluminum coils at four flat rolling facilities in the Southeast. Noranda's primary aluminum products include aluminum rods, extruded billets, and foundry ingots. The downstream business segment manufactures foil and light sheet metal.

	Annual Growth	12/11	12/12	12/13	12/14	12/15
Sales ($mil.)	(5.8%)	1,559.8	1,394.9	1,343.5	1,355.1	1,228.1
Net income ($ mil.)	–	140.9	49.5	(47.6)	(26.6)	(259.6)
Market value ($ mil.)	(55.6%)	82.5	61.1	32.9	35.2	3.2
Employees	(3.1%)	2,500	2,500	2,350	1,600	2,200

NORCRAFT HOLDINGS, L.P.

950 BLUE GENTIAN RD STE 200
EAGAN, MN 551211543
Phone: 800 297-0661
Fax: –
Web: www.masterbrandcabinets.com

CEO: Kurt Wanninger
CFO: Leigh Ginter
HR: –
FYE: December 31
Type: Private

Norcraft Companies make everything but the kitchen sink. The company makes kitchen and bathroom cabinets under several brands, including Mid Continent Cabinetry, StarMark, UltraCraft, and Urban Effects. Its product line includes stock and semi-custom cabinets made in both framed and full access styles, and more than 884,000 door and finish combinations. Norcroft's cabinets are made in the US at six manufacturing plants (Urban Effects' cabinets are also made in Canada). While its products are primarily sold through cabinet dealers and wholesale retailers, it does maintain five retail showrooms. In 2015 Norcraft was acquired by Fortune Brands Home & Security in a $600 million deal.

NORDICUS PARTNERS CORP NBB: NORD

3651 Lindell Road, Suite D565
Las Vegas, NV 89103
Phone: 424 256-8560
Fax: –
Web: –

CEO: –
CFO: –
HR: –
FYE: March 31
Type: Public

If artificial blood becomes a reality, the manufacturers can hook up with AdvanSource Biomaterials, maker of synthetic blood vessels. The company's products replace or bypass damaged and diseased arteries and provide access for dialysis needles in kidney disease patients undergoing hemodialysis. These man-made blood vessels, also called vascular grafts, are made of ChronoFlex, the company's polyurethane-based biomaterial. Its CardioPass product candidate is a synthetic coronary artery bypass graft. AdvanSource's HydroThane polymer-based biomaterial mimics living tissue and is marketed for use by other medical device makers.

	Annual Growth	03/19	03/20	03/21	03/22	03/23
Sales ($mil.)	–	3.3	–	–	–	–
Net income ($ mil.)	–	0.3	5.5	(0.3)	(0.3)	(8.5)
Market value ($ mil.)	75.3%	0.7	1.2	0.2	10.1	7.1
Employees	–	11	1	1	1	–

NORDSON CORP. NMS: NDSN

28601 Clemens Road
Westlake, OH 44145
Phone: 440 892-1580
Fax: –
Web: www.nordson.com

CEO: Sundaram Nagarajan
CFO: Stephen Shamrock
HR: –
FYE: October 31
Type: Public

Nordson Corporation engineers, makes and markets differentiated products and systems used for precision dispensing, applying and controlling of adhesives, coatings, polymers, sealants, biomaterials, and other fluids, to test and inspect for quality, and to treat and cure surfaces and various medical products such as: catheters, cannulas, medical balloons, and medical tubing. Nordson also caters to a wide variety of consumer non-durable, consumer durable and technology end markets including packaging, electronics, medical, appliances, energy, transportation, building and construction, and general product assembly and finishing. The company generates about 40% of its revenue in the US.

	Annual Growth	10/19	10/20	10/21	10/22	10/23
Sales ($mil.)	4.6%	2,194.2	2,121.1	2,362.2	2,590.3	2,628.6
Net income ($ mil.)	9.7%	337.1	249.5	454.4	513.1	487.5
Market value ($ mil.)	7.9%	8,939.3	11,027	14,492	12,827	12,119
Employees	1.0%	7,579	7,555	6,813	7,331	7,900

NORDSTROM, INC. NYS: JWN

1617 Sixth Avenue
Seattle, WA 98101
Phone: 206 628-2111
Fax: –
Web: www.nordstrom.com

CEO: Erik B Nordstrom
CFO: Michael W Maher
HR: –
FYE: February 3
Type: Public

Nordstrom is one of the nation's largest upscale apparel and shoe retailers. It sells apparel, shoes, beauty, accessories and home goods through about 95 Nordstrom full-line stores and more than 240 off-price outlet stores (Nordstrom Rack) and online. The company also operates six full-line and seven Rack stores in Canada, Trunk Club personal clothing service clubhouses, seven Nordstrom Local hubs, and a couple of Last Chance clearance stores. With its easy-return policy, Nordstrom has earned a reputation for top-notch customer service. Nordstrom family members, who own about 30% of the retailer's stock, closely supervise the chain.

	Annual Growth	02/20*	01/21	01/22	01/23*	02/24
Sales ($mil.)	(1.4%)	15,524	10,715	14,789	15,530	14,693
Net income ($ mil.)	(27.9%)	496.0	(690.0)	178.0	245.0	134.0
Market value ($ mil.)	(16.3%)	5,986.1	5,757.1	3,548.4	2,991.4	2,942.7
Employees	(5.6%)	68,000	62,000	72,000	60,000	54,000

*Fiscal year change

NORFOLK IRON & METAL CO.

3001 N VICTORY RD
NORFOLK, NE 687010833
Phone: 402 371-1810
Fax: –
Web: www.norfolkiron.com

CEO: Richard A Robinson
CFO: Steve C Ball
HR: Callie Lowry
FYE: December 31
Type: Private

Steel service center operator Norfolk Iron & Metal processes and distributes about 5,000 steel products, including angles (bar and structure), beams (I-beams and wide flanges), channels (bar, ship and car, and structural), flats (cold-rolled and hot-rolled), pipe (black, galvanized, and untested), and tubing (rectangular, round, and square). The company serves customers throughout the midwestern and western US. Norfolk Iron & Metal was founded in 1908 by John Robinson, grandfather of company president Richard Robinson.

NORFOLK SOUTHERN CORP NYS: NSC

650 West Peachtree Street N.W.
Atlanta, GA 30308-1925
Phone: 855 667-3655
Fax: –
Web: www.norfolksouthern.com

CEO: Alan H Shaw
CFO: Mark R George
HR: –
FYE: December 31
Type: Public

Norfolk Southern Corporation's main subsidiary, Norfolk Southern Railway, transports freight over a network consisting of about 20,000 route miles in more than 20 states, including the District of Columbia. The company is a major transporter of industrial products, such as agriculture, forest, consumer products, chemicals, metals, and construction materials. The company is able to provide services and operates in the East through its most extensive intermodal network. The rail system is made up of more than 35,000 route miles owned by Norfolk Southern and about 29,000 route miles of trackage rights, which allow the company to use tracks owned by other railroads.

	Annual Growth	12/19	12/20	12/21	12/22	12/23
Sales ($mil.)	1.9%	11,296	9,789.0	11,142	12,745	12,156
Net income ($ mil.)	(9.5%)	2,722.0	2,013.0	3,005.0	3,270.0	1,827.0
Market value ($ mil.)	5.0%	43,812	53,624	67,188	55,612	53,347
Employees	(4.2%)	24,587	20,156	18,500	19,300	20,700

NORFOLK STATE UNIVERSITY

700 PARK AVE
NORFOLK, VA 235048090
Phone: 757 823-8600
Fax: –
Web: www.nsu.edu

CEO: –
CFO: Marry Weaver
HR: –
FYE: June 30
Type: Private

Founded in 1935 during the Great Depression, Norfolk State University (NSU) is one of the nation's largest predominately black institutions of higher education. NSU is a four-year state-supported Virginia university offering undergraduate degrees in about 30 disciplines. The school also offers more than 15 master's and three doctoral degree programs. NSU boasts an enrollment of 7,000-plus students at its main campus and at its satellite centers in nearby Virginia cities Portsmouth and Virginia Beach. Some 6,400 of students are undergraduates; the remainder are pursuing graduate degrees. Most of the degrees conferred by the school are in liberal arts, followed by science and technology, and business.

	Annual Growth	06/16	06/17	06/20	06/21	06/22
Sales ($mil.)	2.6%	–	69.7	80.7	66.4	79.2
Net income ($ mil.)	(20.9%)	–	34.2	1.3	16.7	10.6
Market value ($ mil.)	–	–	–	–	–	–
Employees	–	–	–	–	–	1,095

NORKUS ENTERPRISES, INC.

505 RICHMOND AVE
POINT PLEASANT BEACH, NJ 087422552
Phone: 732 899-8485
Fax: –
Web: www.norkus.com

CEO: –
CFO: –
HR: –
FYE: April 25
Type: Private

They sell pasta shells by the Jersey sea shore. Norkus Enterprises operates grocery stores under the Foodtown and Super Foodtown banners in Monmouth County and Ocean County, New Jersey. The regional grocery chain also offers online shopping and home delivery. It was founded when Francis Norkus opened his first grocery store, called Table Talk, in Freehold, New Jersey, in 1935. Norkus Enterprises is a member of the Foodtown Supermarket cooperative. The company also owns four Max's Beer, Wine & Liquor stores located in New Jersey. In 2011, Norkus sold five of its six Foodtown stores -- located in Freehold Township, Manalapan, Neptune City, Point Pleasant Beach, and Long Branch -- to The Stop & Shop Supermarket Company.

	Annual Growth	04/05	04/06	04/07	04/08	04/09
Sales ($mil.)	2.0%	–	148.6	153.2	157.7	157.6
Net income ($ mil.)	29.4%	–	0.3	0.9	1.1	0.6
Market value ($ mil.)	–	–	–	–	–	–
Employees	–	–	–	–	–	1,000

NORMAN REGIONAL HOSPITAL AUTHORITY

901 N PORTER AVE
NORMAN, OK 730716482
Phone: 405 307-1000
Fax: –
Web: www.normanregional.com

CEO: Richie Splitt
CFO: Ken Hopkins
HR: Sharon Goff
FYE: June 30
Type: Private

NORM! Perhaps that's how locals refer to Norman Regional Health System when they are headed there for health care. The system operates in and around Norman, Oklahoma, through the full service, 325-bed Norman Regional Hospital and affiliated health centers, including Moore Medical Center Services and the HealthPlex, a 136-bed specialty hospital focused on cardiology, orthopedic and spine, and women's and children's services. Moore Medical Center's services include include acute care and surgery, diagnostic, and outpatient health care services. The organization's programs include behavioral medicine, rehabilitation, a women's center, and a sleep disorder clinic. The hospital, which employs more than 350 physicians, was established in 1946.

	Annual Growth	06/13	06/14	06/17	06/20	06/21
Sales ($mil.)	(56.4%)	–	347.2	382.6	1.1	1.0
Net income ($ mil.)	(55.9%)	–	24.8	18.7	(0.0)	0.0
Market value ($ mil.)	–	–	–	–	–	–
Employees	–	–	–	–	–	3,500

NORTECH SYSTEMS INC.

NAS: NSYS

7550 Meridian Circle N., Suite # 150
Maple Grove, MN 55369
Phone: 952 345-2244
Fax: –
Web: www.nortechsys.com

CEO: Jay D Miller
CFO: Andrew Lafrence
HR: –
FYE: December 31
Type: Public

Nortech is an Electronic Manufacturing Services (EMS) company that offers a full range of value-added engineering, technical and manufacturing services and support including project management, designing, testing, prototyping, manufacturing, supply chain management and post-market services to a variety of industries, such as aerospace, automotive, medical, and industrial markets. Its manufacturing and engineering services include wire and cable assemblies, printed circuit board assemblies, complete medical devices, and complex higher-level electromechanical assemblies. One customer accounts for around a fifth of revenue.

	Annual Growth	12/19	12/20	12/21	12/22	12/23
Sales ($mil.)	4.6%	116.3	104.1	115.2	134.1	139.3
Net income ($ mil.)	–	(1.2)	(1.5)	7.2	2.0	6.9
Market value ($ mil.)	17.9%	13.1	19.3	27.8	33.0	25.3
Employees	(0.3%)	784	699	807	832	775

NORTEK, INC.

8000 PHOENIX PKWY
O FALLON, MO 633683827
Phone: 636 561-7300
Fax: –
Web: www.nortek.com

CEO: Michael J Clarke
CFO: –
HR: Derick Meyer
FYE: November 30
Type: Private

Nortek offers a wide range of top-quality products that cater to custom and commercial air solutions for high-performance environments. The company also provides residential and commercial HVAC and fresh air ventilation systems for homes. It has an extensive family of brands that combines over 390 years of experience in providing solutions for various markets, including healthcare, education, data center, pharmaceutical, industrial, residential, office, and clean room. Nortek's technology not only enhances indoor air quality, but also improves energy efficiency, reduces operating costs, maximizes performance, lowers noise pollution, and ensures system reliability.

NORTH AMERICAN ELECTRIC RELIABILITY CORPORATION

3353 PEACHTREE RD NE STE 600
ATLANTA, GA 303261063
Phone: 404 446-2560
Fax: –
Web: www.nerc.com

CEO: –
CFO: –
HR: –
FYE: December 31
Type: Private

Working to keep the lights on, the North American Electric Reliability Corp. (NERC) sets standards for the operation of the continent's power grid. The NERC monitors wholesale activities on the grid and provides assessment, training, tools, and services in coordination with regional councils to ensure reliability. It is a self-regulatory organization overseen by the US Federal Energy Regulatory Commission and the Canadian government. The NERC has worked with the FERC to establish legally enforceable reliability standards for the US bulk power system that took effect in 2007. The NERC was formed in 1968, three years after one of the largest blackouts in American history.

	Annual Growth	12/18	12/19	12/20	12/21	12/22
Sales ($mil.)	10.6%	–	–	–	81.8	90.5
Net income ($ mil.)	–	–	–	–	(0.6)	3.2
Market value ($ mil.)	–	–	–	–	–	–
Employees	–	–	–	–	–	175

NORTH AMERICAN LIGHTING, INC.

2275 S MAIN ST
PARIS, IL 619442963
Phone: 217 465-6600
Fax: –
Web: www.nal.com

CEO: –
CFO: –
HR: Erin Marion
FYE: December 31
Type: Private

North American Lighting offers travelers a beacon of safety through the fog. The company is an independent manufacturer of vehicle lighting products in North America. Operating through four assembly plants and one technology center, the company produces a line-up of headlamps, signal lamps, and fog lamps. Its forward-lighting products include mercury-free, high intensity discharge (HID) headlamps and the Adaptive Front Lighting System (AFS). Among its signal lamps are rear-combo and license plate lamps. Its products are tailored to the designs of large auto makers and local Japanese automakers. Founded in 1983, North American Lighting is a subsidiary of Japan-based KOITO MANUFACTURING.

	Annual Growth	12/08	12/09	12/10	12/11	12/17
Sales ($mil.)	25.6%	–	–	297.4	297.4	1,466.4
Net income ($ mil.)	35.6%	–	–	13.2	13.2	111.3
Market value ($ mil.)	–	–	–	–	–	–
Employees	–	–	–	–	–	6,108

NORTH AMERICAN TECHNOLOGIES GROUP, INC.

429 S MEMORY LN
MARSHALL, TX 756708405
Phone: 972 996-5750
Fax: –
Web: –

CEO: D P Long
CFO: –
HR: –
FYE: September 28
Type: Private

North American Technologies Group (NATK) made ties that bind. Its TieTek Technologies subsidiary produced composite railroad crossties made from 75% recycled materials such as plastics and rubber from old tires. It has sold its products to various transportation agencies and railway companies in the US, Australia, Asia, South America, and India. However, due to the recession, the company closed its plants and ceased production of its ties in 2009. NATK was plagued by losses and mounting debt. The company, including its TieTek subsidiary, filed for Chapter 11 bankruptcy in 2010.

NORTH ATLANTIC TRADING COMPANY, INC.

5201 INTERCHANGE WAY
LOUISVILLE, KY 402292184
Phone: 502 778-4421
Fax: –
Web: www.zigzag.com

CEO: Lawrence S Wexler
CFO: Brian C Harris
HR: –
FYE: December 31
Type: Private

North Atlantic Trading Company is on the straight and narrow, but it prefers its business path to incorporate plenty of Zig-Zags. Its North Atlantic Operating Company (NAOC), best known for its Zig-Zag brand of rolling papers, is a top importer and distributor of cigarette rolling papers in the US. NAOC also sells several styles of tobaccos, rolling machines, and accoutrements. North Atlantic Trading's National Tobacco subsidiary is a leading maker of chewing tobacco in the US on the strength of its best-selling Beech-Nut chaw, as well as Havana Blossom, Trophy, Stoker, and others. Chairman Thomas F. Helms Jr. owns about 49% of North Atlantic Trading.

NORTH BAJA PIPELINE, LLC

1 SW COLUMBIA ST STE 475
PORTLAND, OR 972044015
Phone: 503 222-9955
Fax: –
Web: –

CEO: –
CFO: –
HR: –
FYE: December 31
Type: Private

It's a natural assumption to think that gas has a sweet smell to the folks at North Baja Pipeline. The company operates a 220-mile natural gas pipeline for customers in Oregon, Idaho, Washington, and California (primarily Imperial, Riverside, and San Diego counties), as well as in Baja California, Mexico. Completed in 2002, the pipeline is powered by a 21,000 horsepower compressor station that has a capacity of about 500 million cu. ft. In 2009 TransCanada sold North Baja Pipeline to TC PipeLines, but continued to be its operational manager.

NORTH BROWARD HOSPITAL DISTRICT

1800 NW 49TH ST
FORT LAUDERDALE, FL 333093092
Phone: 954 473-7010
Fax: –
Web: www.browardhealth.org

CEO: Gino Santorio
CFO: Kim B Cole
HR: Deven Silverman
FYE: June 30
Type: Private

North Broward Hospital District, which operates as Broward Health, takes care of shark bites and more. The taxpayer-supported, not-for-profit health system serves the coastal city of Fort Lauderdale and the northern two-thirds of Broward County, Florida, with four acute care hospitals and a host of community-based centers. Flagship hospital Broward General Medical Center has more than 700 beds and features the Chris Evert Children's Hospital; all of the hospitals together have more than 1,500 beds. Broward Health boasts about 30 additional facilities, including family health and surgery centers and home health and hospice programs.

	Annual Growth	06/06	06/07	06/08	06/16	06/17
Sales ($mil.)	(2.9%)	–	–	1,335.1	1,014.6	1,025.3
Net income ($ mil.)	(7.5%)	–	–	67.4	(12.9)	33.5
Market value ($ mil.)	–	–	–	–	–	–
Employees	–	–	–	–	–	7,000

NORTH CAROLINA ELECTRIC MEMBERSHIP CORPORATION

3400 SUMNER BLVD
RALEIGH, NC 276162950
Phone: 919 872-0800
Fax: –
Web: www.ncelectriccooperatives.com

CEO: Joe Brannon
CFO: –
HR: –
FYE: December 31
Type: Private

It's a cooperative effort: North Carolina Electric Membership Corporation (NCEMC) generates and transmits electricity to the state's 26 electric cooperatives (more than 2.5 million people) in 93 of 100 North Carolina counties. The co-op owns more than 600 MW of generating capacity through four primarily natural gas peak load generators, plus a 61.5% stake in Catawba Nuclear Station Unit 1, and a 31% stake in the Catawba Nuclear Station in South Carolina. It also buys power from Progress Energy, American Electric Power, and other for-profit utilities. NCEMC's member cooperatives serve more than 950,000 metered businesses and homes in North Carolina. The wholesale co-op also operates an energy operations center.

	Annual Growth	12/18	12/19	12/20	12/21	12/22
Sales ($mil.)	0.1%	–	1,219.1	1,092.2	1,128.1	1,224.4
Net income ($ mil.)	–	–	30.0	29.3	32.8	30.0
Market value ($ mil.)	–	–	–	–	–	–
Employees	–	–	–	–	–	188

NORTH CAROLINA STATE UNIVERSITY

2601 WOLF VILLAGE WAY
RALEIGH, NC 27607
Phone: 919 515-2011
Fax: –
Web: www.ncsu.edu

CEO: –
CFO: –
HR: –
FYE: June 30
Type: Private

Students at NC State are proud to be part of the Wolfpack. North Carolina State University (NC State) has an enrollment of more than 34,000 students and claims two wolves (Mr. and Ms. Wuf) as its mascots. The university offers about 300 undergraduate and graduate degree programs through about a dozen colleges. It also conducts extensive research programs. Core fields of study include the STEM categories of science, technology, engineering, and mathematics. NC State was founded in 1887 and is part of the University of North Carolina (UNC) system.

NORTH CENTRAL FARMERS ELEVATOR

12 5TH AVE
IPSWICH, SD 574517700
Phone: 605 426-6021
Fax: –
Web: www.ncfe.coop

CEO: –
CFO: –
HR: –
FYE: December 31
Type: Private

North Central Farmers Elevator's mission is to give its members a lift. The full-service member-owned agricultural cooperative located in South Dakota offers farm-support goods and services, including feed, seed and other farm supplies, along with agronomy, energy, and marketing services. In conjunction with LOL Farmland Feeds and South Dakota Wheat Growers, North Central Farmers Elevator owns Dakotaland Feeds, which makes and markets feed to producers. It also has a marketing alliance with South Dakota Oilseed Processors to sell its member/farmer's soybean crops. The coop's 21 locations serve more than 2,500 producer-members in north central South Dakota and south central North Dakota.

	Annual Growth	12/03	12/04	12/05	12/06	12/07
Sales ($mil.)	19.2%	–	–	198.2	135.1	281.5
Net income ($ mil.)	1.1%	–	–	2.7	(1.2)	2.7
Market value ($ mil.)	–	–	–	–	–	–
Employees	–	–	–	–	–	200

NORTH COLORADO MEDICAL CENTER FOUNDATION, INC.

1801 16TH ST
GREELEY, CO 806315154
Phone: 970 356-9020
Fax: –
Web: www.weldlegacy.org

CEO: Gene O'Hara
CFO: –
HR: –
FYE: December 31
Type: Private

North Colorado Medical Center is a not-for-profit, tertiary-care hospital which serves residents of southern Wyoming, western Nebraska, western Kansas, and northeast Colorado. The medical center has about 400 patient beds, a Level II trauma center, a cardiovascular institute, a birthing center, and an emergency transport helicopter service. In addition, the medical center provides services in areas such as orthopedics, neurology, rehabilitation, behavioral medicine, and cancer treatment. North Colorado Medical Center also has affiliated outpatient diagnostic facilities and family health clinics in its service territory. The hospital is part of the Banner Health organization.

NORTH DAKOTA MILL & ELEVATOR ASSOCIATION

1823 MILL RD
GRAND FORKS, ND 582031535
Phone: 701 795-7000
Fax: –
Web: www.ndmill.com

CEO: –
CFO: –
HR: –
FYE: June 30
Type: Private

When bakeries need flour, North Dakota Mill & Elevator rises to the occasion. The mill is a producer of wheat flour used specifically in breads and other baked goods like cookies and crackers. It processes more than 78,000 bushels of wheat a day and ships most of its flour in bulk to wholesalers. It offers semolina flour, as well as specialty products such as wholegrain wheat flour, wheat germ, and corn flour for tortillas. The mill also sells pancake mixes, bread machine mixes, and wholewheat, all-purpose and bread flours under the Dakota Maid brand to consumers through its online store. Owned by the State of North Dakota, it contributes 50% of its profits to the North Dakota State General Fund.

	Annual Growth	06/14	06/15	06/16	06/18	06/19
Sales ($mil.)	(0.2%)	–	247.9	216.1	270.6	245.6
Net income ($ mil.)	(33.1%)	–	12.4	4.4	3.3	2.5
Market value ($ mil.)	–	–	–	–	–	–
Employees	–	–	–	–	–	120

NORTH DAKOTA STATE UNIVERSITY

1340 ADMINISTRATION AVE
FARGO, ND 58102
Phone: 701 231-8011
Fax: –
Web: www.ndsu.edu

CEO: –
CFO: –
HR: –
FYE: June 30
Type: Private

The state's leading research institution, North Dakota State University (NDSU) has an enrollment of more than 14,600 students. The university offers more than 100 undergraduate degree programs, some 60 master's degree programs, and more than 40 doctoral and professional programs. Historically, NDSU's strengths have been agriculture and the applied sciences, but the school also offers courses of study in business, liberal arts, engineering, architecture, mathematics, and education. NDSU is a land-grant college; its extension service offers education and outreach programs throughout North Dakota in agriculture, health and nutrition, and community leadership. NDSU, which was established in 1890, is part of the North Dakota University System.

	Annual Growth	06/16	06/17	06/18	06/19	06/20
Sales ($mil.)	(3.1%)	–	–	260.3	256.1	244.4
Net income ($ mil.)	–	–	–	6.3	15.1	(0.1)
Market value ($ mil.)	–	–	–	–	–	–
Employees	–	–	–	–	–	4,500

NORTH DALLAS BANK & TRUST CO (DALLAS, TX)   NBB: NODB

12900 Preston Road
Dallas, TX 75230
Phone: 972 716-7100
Fax: –
Web: www.ndbt.com

CEO: Mike Shipman
CFO: –
HR: –
FYE: December 31
Type: Public

Like many a native Texan, North Dallas Bank & Trust is proud to profess its heritage. The bank operates more than five branches in Dallas and the surrounding communities of Addison, Frisco, Las Colinas, and Plano. Serving local businesses and consumers, it offers standard deposit services such as checking and savings accounts, CDs, and IRAs, as well as trust and financial management services. Commercial real estate loans and residential mortgages account for most of the bank's lending activities. It also originates various consumer and business loans. North Dallas Bank has been owned by basically the same group of investors since it was founded in 1961.

	Annual Growth	12/17	12/18	12/19	12/20	12/21
Assets ($mil.)	5.8%	1,374.7	1,304.0	1,307.8	1,477.9	1,725.6
Net income ($ mil.)	2.9%	6.4	12.2	9.2	8.6	7.1
Market value ($ mil.)	0.5%	198.8	223.5	204.2	200.4	203.0
Employees	–	–	–	–	–	–

NORTH EUROPEAN OIL ROYALTY TRUST

NYS: NRT

5 North Lincoln Street
Keene, NH 03431
Phone: 732 741-4008
Fax: 732 741-3140
Web: www.neort.com

CEO: -
CFO: -
HR: -
FYE: October 31
Type: Public

North European Oil Royalty Trust isn't owned by the crowned oil barons of Europe. The passive fixed investment trust receives royalties based on its interests in natural gas (97% of revenues), oil, and sulfur producing properties in the former state of Oldenburg and portions of northwest Germany. Royalties are generated by the sale of crude oil, natural gas, distillate, and sulfur mined by Exxon Mobil, Royal Dutch Shell, and their subsidiaries; the trust then distributes the royalties to shareholders on a quarterly basis. As a grantor trust, North European Oil is exempt from paying income taxes; shareholders, however, are not.

	Annual Growth	10/19	10/20	10/21	10/22	10/23
Sales ($mil.)	27.6%	8.4	4.1	4.6	17.8	22.1
Net income ($ mil.)	29.3%	7.6	3.3	4.0	17.1	21.2
Market value ($ mil.)	15.6%	56.2	28.8	96.2	142.8	100.4
Employees	-	2	1	2	2	2

NORTH FLORIDA REGIONAL MEDICAL CENTER, INC.

6500 W NEWBERRY RD
GAINESVILLE, FL 326054309
Phone: 352 333-4100
Fax: -
Web: www.hcafloridahealthcare.com

CEO: -
CFO: -
HR: -
FYE: February 28
Type: Private

North Florida Regional Medical Center (NFRMC), part of the HCA health services network, is a 445-bed acute care community hospital serving Gainesville, Florida, and more than a dozen surrounding counties. The hospital boasts specialty centers for diabetes, senior care, obesity surgery, and sleep disorders. It also provides emergency services, cancer care, heart care, imaging services, orthopedics, neurological care, physical therapy, and wound therapy. NFRMC was founded in 1972 by HCA and a group of physicians. As part of HCA's North Florida Regional Healthcare network, it has affiliates including physician practices and express care clinics.

	Annual Growth	12/95	12/96	12/97*	02/09	02/17
Sales ($mil.)	6.2%	-	-	133.3	331.2	443.9
Net income ($ mil.)	7.4%	-	-	26.7	61.8	110.7
Market value ($ mil.)	-	-	-	-	-	-
Employees	-	-	-	-	-	2,000

*Fiscal year change

NORTH MEMORIAL HEALTH CARE

3300 OAKDALE AVE N
ROBBINSDALE, MN 554222900
Phone: 763 520-5200
Fax: -
Web: www.northmemorial.com

CEO: Loren Taylor
CFO: Patrick Boran
HR: Becky Rauen
FYE: December 31
Type: Private

North Memorial Health Care provides access to high-quality, low-cost care throughout the Twin Cities through its medical transportation services and two hospitals ? North Memorial Health Hospital and Maple Grove Hospital. North Memorial Health Clinics which include primary care, specialty care, and hospice are part of a joint venture with Blue Cross and Blue Shield of Minnesota that is transforming the healthcare experience for consumers. Across the North Memorial Health system, more than 900 doctors and about 5,000 team members are dedicated to delivering a more connected experience for its customers. With more than 350 care providers, North Memorial Health serves over 55,000 customers monthly. North Memorial Health started as a single hospital in 1954 by a doctor that wanted to do things differently ? do things better.

	Annual Growth	12/17	12/18	12/20	12/21	12/22
Sales ($mil.)	2.1%	-	720.9	518.4	565.7	782.4
Net income ($ mil.)	-	-	(16.8)	28.2	78.3	(0.1)
Market value ($ mil.)	-	-	-	-	-	-
Employees	-	-	-	-	-	5,180

NORTH MISSISSIPPI HEALTH SERVICES, INC.

830 S GLOSTER ST
TUPELO, MS 388014934
Phone: 662 377-3000
Fax: -
Web: www.nmhs.net

CEO: John Heer
CFO: Sharon Nobles
HR: Sondra Davis
FYE: September 30
Type: Private

North Mississippi Health Services (NMHS) isn't contained by its name: The health system also provides health care to residents of northwestern Alabama. NMHS includes half a dozen community hospitals, including its flagship North Mississippi Medical Center in Tupelo. North Mississippi Medical Clinics, a regional network of more than 30 primary and specialty clinics; and nursing homes. Combined, the facilities have nearly 1,000 beds, designated for acute, long term, and nursing care. Specialty services include home health and long-term care, inpatient and outpatient behavioral health, and treatment centers for cancer and digestive disorders. NMHS also operates outpatient care and wellness clinics in the region.

	Annual Growth	09/13	09/14	09/15	09/16	09/17
Sales ($mil.)	4.9%	-	779.4	860.0	893.0	898.8
Net income ($ mil.)	-	-	(14.4)	19.2	30.5	26.5
Market value ($ mil.)	-	-	-	-	-	-
Employees	-	-	-	-	-	6,000

NORTH MISSISSIPPI MEDICAL CENTER, INC.

830 S GLOSTER ST
TUPELO, MS 388014934
Phone: 662 377-3000
Fax: -
Web: www.nmhs.net

CEO: -
CFO: -
HR: -
FYE: September 30
Type: Private

At North Mississippi Medical Center you might get some Mississippi Mud ice cream after your tonsils are removed. The full-service, 650-bed regional referral hospital in Tupelo, Mississippi, is part of the North Mississippi Health Services system, an affiliation of hospitals and clinics serving northern Mississippi, northwestern Alabama, and parts of Tennessee. It's the largest, private, not-for-profit hospital in Mississippi and the largest non-metropolitan hospital in America. Specialty services at the medical center include cancer treatment, women's health care, cardiology, and behavioral health care. The hospital also operates a skilled-nursing facility and home health and hospice organizations.

	Annual Growth	12/18	12/19*	09/20	09/21	09/22
Sales ($mil.)	1559.1%	-	0.2	680.7	730.1	817.4
Net income ($ mil.)	679.5%	-	0.0	56.2	58.3	39.3
Market value ($ mil.)	-	-	-	-	-	-
Employees	-	-	-	-	-	6,000

*Fiscal year change

NORTH PACIFIC CANNERS & PACKERS, INC.

3225 25TH ST SE
SALEM, OR 973021133
Phone: 503 399-8019
Fax: -
Web: www.norpac.com

CEO: Shawn Campbell
CFO: Richard Munekiyo
HR: -
FYE: December 31
Type: Private

NORPAC Foods is a farmer-owned cooperative that produces frozen fruits and vegetables. Its products are marketed under FLAV-R-PAC Fruit Favorites, Vegetable Collections, American Harvest, Chef Starters, Fruit Toppings, Grande Classics, and Fruit Collection, among other labels. It grows and harvests non-GMO seed fruits and vegetables of unsurpassed quality in processing plants located in the Pacific Northwest. Primarily serving in foodservice industry, the company offers solutions for a wide range of skill sets and culinary complexities. NORPAC Foods was formed by a group of Oregon farmers in 1924. NORPAC is now part of the OPC family of companies.

NORTH PACIFIC PAPER COMPANY, LLC

3001 INDUSTRIAL WAY
LONGVIEW, WA 986321057
Phone: 360 636-6400
Fax: –
Web: www.norpacpaper.com

CEO: Craig Anneberg
CFO: –
HR: –
FYE: December 31
Type: Private

The old adage "all the news fit to print" might not be possible without North Pacific Paper Corporation (NORPAC). The firm, a joint venture between Weyerhaeuser and Nippon Paper, produces newsprint for newspaper publishers and commercial printers. NORPAC manufactures a variety of paper grades, including standard and lightweight newsprint and super- and ultra-lightweight stocks especially for the Japanese market. It produces more than 250,000 tons of newsprint annually at its manufacturing facility in Longview, Washington. Its products are sent via truck and train to customers in the western US or are shipped by boat to customers in Japan. Weyerhaeuser is selling its stake in NORPAC to One Rock Capital Partners.

	Annual Growth	12/04	12/05	12/06	12/07	12/08
Sales ($mil.)	3.5%	–	–	499.0	474.7	534.4
Net income ($ mil.)	7.4%	–	–	19.3	(3.8)	22.2
Market value ($ mil.)	–	–	–	–	–	–
Employees		–	–	–	–	410

NORTH PARK UNIVERSITY

2543 W CULLOM AVE
CHICAGO, IL 606181501
Phone: 773 244-6200
Fax: –
Web: www.northpark.edu

CEO: –
CFO: –
HR: Kiersten Bixby
FYE: June 30
Type: Private

North Park University is a Christian university that is located on Chicago's north side and enrolls more than 3,200 undergraduate and graduate students. The school specializes in liberal arts, business, the health sciences, and education, and also offers seminary degree programs. North Park offers more than 40 majors and pre-professional programs. Undergraduate classes average less than 20 students. Some 87% of North Park full time faculty hold earned PhD's or the highest degree in their field. Founded in 1891 by the Evangelical Covenant Church, the university also has three satellite campuses in the Chicago metropolitan area.

	Annual Growth	06/14	06/15	06/20	06/21	06/22
Sales ($mil.)	(1.3%)	–	89.8	92.5	94.5	82.0
Net income ($ mil.)	–	–	5.6	(5.1)	1.5	(9.5)
Market value ($ mil.)	–	–	–	–	–	–
Employees		–	–	–	–	375

NORTH PHILADELPHIA HEALTH SYSTEM

801 W GIRARD AVE
PHILADELPHIA, PA 191224212
Phone: 215 787-9001
Fax: –
Web: www.bewellctr.org

CEO: George Walmsley III
CFO: –
HR: –
FYE: June 30
Type: Private

Too many Philly cheesesteaks got you feeling down? The North Philadelphia Health System (NPHS) is there to help. The system is composed of two health care facilities serving some of Philadelphia's poorest neighborhoods. The Girard Medical Center provides long-term care, outpatient mental health services, and general medical and surgical care; while Goldman Clinic treats substance abuse. After losing money for two years, NPHS shut down its St. Joseph's Hospital facility in 2016. At the end of that year, NPHS filed for Chapter 11 bankruptcy protection.

	Annual Growth	06/10	06/11	06/12	06/13	06/15
Sales ($mil.)	2.5%	–	–	–	101.8	107.0
Net income ($ mil.)	–	–	–	–	(1.8)	(0.5)
Market value ($ mil.)	–	–	–	–	–	–
Employees		–	–	–	–	900

NORTH SHORE MEDICAL CENTER, INC.

81 HIGHLAND AVE
SALEM, MA 019702768
Phone: 978 741-1200
Fax: –
Web: salem.massgeneralbrigham.org

CEO: –
CFO: Sally M Boemer
HR: –
FYE: September 30
Type: Private

This health system strives to cast a spell of salubriousness over Salem, Massachusetts. The North Shore Medical Center (NSMC) provides medical care to the residents of several cities north of Boston, including Salem (aka The Witch City), Lynn, and Peabody. The network is home to two acute care hospitals, children's and rehabilitation hospitals, a heart institute, a women's center, and a number of community health centers. It also boasts more than 600 physicians and other health care professionals in its North Shore Physician Group. Its flagship, the NSMC Salem Hospital is a nearly 250-bed teaching hospital providing adult and pediatric services. The not-for-profit system is part of Partners HealthCare System.

	Annual Growth	09/16	09/17	09/18	09/20	09/21
Sales ($mil.)	4.8%	–	407.2	416.0	430.9	490.9
Net income ($ mil.)	–	–	(58.0)	(32.5)	648.8	(130.1)
Market value ($ mil.)	–	–	–	–	–	–
Employees		–	–	–	–	5,000

NORTH SHORE UNIVERSITY HOSPITAL

300 COMMUNITY DR
MANHASSET, NY 110303876
Phone: 516 562-0100
Fax: –
Web: www.northwell.edu

CEO: –
CFO: –
HR: –
FYE: December 31
Type: Private

North Shore University Hospital (NSUH) knows you shouldn't have to leave the island for quality health care. The Long Island hospital has more than 800 beds devoted to adult and pediatric medicine, rehabilitation, stroke care, women's health, orthopedics, urology, wound healing, dentistry, and trauma emergency services, among other areas. The hospital is home to specialist institutes for cancer care and cardiology. It also serves as a campus for the Hofstra Northwell Shool of Medicine. NSUH is part of Northwell Health.

	Annual Growth	12/15	12/16	12/17	12/18	12/22
Sales ($mil.)	11.6%	–	1,795.4	1,826.9	1,883.4	3,476.3
Net income ($ mil.)	(13.1%)	–	171.6	191.0	38.7	73.7
Market value ($ mil.)	–	–	–	–	–	–
Employees		–	–	–	–	5,000

NORTH SONOMA COUNTY HOSPITAL DISTRICT

1375 UNIVERSITY ST
HEALDSBURG, CA 954483382
Phone: 707 431-6500
Fax: –
Web: www.healdsburgdistricthospital.org

CEO: –
CFO: –
HR: –
FYE: December 31
Type: Private

The North Sonoma County Hospital District helps more than just those who have tripped while stomping grapes. The district operates Healdsburg District Hospital, an acute care community hospital in northern California. The hospital offers a full array of health services, including emergency and trauma, surgery and rehabilitation, occupational medicine, and clinical laboratory. It also provides hospice care, a clinical laboratory, and an imaging center. Since taking the hospital over from Columbia Healthcare (now HCA) in 2002, the district has doubled the size of the ER and upgraded equipment.

NORTH TEXAS TOLLWAY AUTHORITY

5900 W PLANO PKWY STE 100
PLANO, TX 750934695
Phone: 214 461-2000
Fax: –
Web: www.ntta.org

CEO: –
CFO: Horatio Porter
HR: Kimberly Shaw
FYE: December 31
Type: Private

The North Texas Tollway Authority (NTTA) operates a toll system consisting of about 90 miles of roadway. Facilities include the Dallas North Tollway, the President George Bush Turnpike, the Addison Airport Toll Tunnel, the Mountain Creek Lake Bridge, and the Sam Rayburn Tollway. The authority serves four counties in the Dallas-Fort Worth area. A predecessor agency, the Texas Turnpike Authority, was created by the Texas Legislature in 1953; the NTTA was created by the Legislature in 1997 to take over for the turnpike authority in Collin, Dallas, Denton, and Tarrant counties.

	Annual Growth	12/15	12/16	12/20	12/21	12/22
Sales ($mil.)	7.7%	–	741.1	785.7	979.6	1,159.1
Net income ($ mil.)	16.7%	–	93.3	(1.4)	190.1	235.2
Market value ($ mil.)	–	–	–	–	–	–
Employees	–	–	–	–	–	733

NORTH WIND, INC.

1425 HIGHAM ST
IDAHO FALLS, ID 834021513
Phone: 208 528-8718
Fax: –
Web: www.northwindgrp.com

CEO: –
CFO: –
HR: Andy Henderson
FYE: December 26
Type: Private

"The North wind doth blow, and we shall have".... clean air and water. North Wind works to keep the air clean, the ground fresh, and the water clear in North America. The environmental consulting firm's services include site assessment, soil and groundwater remediation, geographic information system (GIS) data, hazardous and nonhazardous waste management, and project engineering and construction. North Wind has expanded by buying South Carolina-based Pinnacle Consulting Group, which offers engineering, environmental, and information technology consulting services.

	Annual Growth	12/07	12/08	12/09	12/10	12/14
Sales ($mil.)	(35.0%)	–	–	120.2	85.5	13.9
Net income ($ mil.)	(34.8%)	–	–	6.3	4.3	0.7
Market value ($ mil.)	–	–	–	–	–	–
Employees	–	–	–	–	–	86

NORTHEAST BANK (ME)

NMS: NBN

27 Pearl Street
Portland, ME 04101
Phone: 207 786-3245
Fax: –
Web: www.northeastbank.com

CEO: –
CFO: –
HR: –
FYE: June 30
Type: Public

Northeast Bancorp is the holding company for Northeast Bank, which operates about a dozen branches in western and southern Maine. Founded in 1872, the bank offers standard retail services such as checking and savings accounts, NOW and money market accounts, CDs, and trust services, as well as financial planning and brokerage. Residential mortgages account for about a third of all loans; commercial mortgages and consumer loans each make up about 25%. The bank also writes business and construction loans. Newly created investment entity FHB Formation acquired a 60% stake in Northeast Bancorp in 2010. The deal brought in $16 million in capital. The 2011 sale of insurance agency Varney added another $8.4 million.

	Annual Growth	06/19	06/20	06/21	06/22	06/23
Assets ($mil.)	25.6%	1,153.9	1,257.6	2,174.4	1,582.8	2,869.9
Net income ($ mil.)	33.6%	13.9	22.7	71.5	42.2	44.2
Market value ($ mil.)	10.9%	211.5	134.6	229.1	280.1	319.6
Employees	2.1%	183	182	178	180	199

NORTHEAST COMMUNITY BANCORP INC (MD)

NAS: NECB

325 Hamilton Avenue
White Plains, NY 10601
Phone: 914 684-2500
Fax: –
Web: www.necb.com

CEO: Kenneth A Martinek
CFO: Donald S Hom
HR: –
FYE: December 31
Type: Public

Northeast Community Bancorp is the holding company for Northeast Community Bank, which serves consumers and businesses in the New York metropolitan area and Massachusetts. Through about a half-dozen branches, the thrift offers traditional deposit services like checking and savings accounts, as well as a variety of lending products such as commercial and multi-family real estate loans, home equity, construction, and secured loans. While its deposit services are confined to New York and Massachusetts, it markets its loan products throughout the northeastern US. The bank offers investment and financial planning services through Hayden Wealth Management. Northeast Community Bank's roots date back to 1934.

	Annual Growth	12/18	12/19	12/20	12/21	12/22
Assets ($mil.)	13.1%	870.3	955.2	968.2	1,225.1	1,425.0
Net income ($ mil.)	17.5%	13.0	13.0	12.3	11.9	24.8
Market value ($ mil.)	7.7%	178.1	193.4	221.5	178.6	239.5
Employees	–	–	–	125	133	139

NORTHEAST GEORGIA HEALTH SYSTEM, INC.

743 SPRING ST NE
GAINESVILLE, GA 305013715
Phone: 770 219-9000
Fax: –
Web: www.nghs.com

CEO: Carol Burrell
CFO: Brian Steines
HR: Judy Canaday
FYE: September 30
Type: Private

Northeast Georgia Health System (NGHS) is a not-for-profit health system that serves more than 1 million residents in about 20 counties in Georgia. Its Northeast Georgia Medical Center operates four hospital campuses ? NGMC Gainesville, NGMC Braselton, NGMC Barrow and NGMC Lumpkin ? with a total of about 800 beds and more than 1,200 medical staff members representing more than 50 specialties. Its Northeast Georgia Physicians Group (NGPG) includes more than 500 talented physicians, physician assistants, nurse practitioners, midwives and other clinical staff representing about 40 specialties at more than 110 locations across North Georgia. NGHS was founded in 1951.

	Annual Growth	09/12	09/13	09/14	09/15	09/20
Sales ($mil.)	30.6%	–	33.4	50.4	65.9	216.2
Net income ($ mil.)	–	–	9.9	10.0	0.1	(18.5)
Market value ($ mil.)	–	–	–	–	–	–
Employees	–	–	–	–	–	8,000

NORTHEAST HEALTH SYSTEMS INC.

100 POWERS ST STE 1
BEVERLY, MA 019152748
Phone: 978 922-3000
Fax: –
Web: www.beverlyhospital.org

CEO: Dennis S Conroy
CFO: –
HR: Kathleen Ballou
FYE: September 30
Type: Private

If a particularly beastly Nor'easter wreaks havoc on your immune system, you might want to turn to Northeast Health System (NHS) for a little TLC. The organization provides a continuum of health services to residents of Massachusetts' North Shore communities through its network of hospitals, outpatient care facilities, and behavioral health and senior care centers. NHS' hospitals include Addison Gilbert Hospital, a 60-bed full-service acute care facility; the 60-bed BayRidge Hospital, a mental health and drug rehab facility; and Beverly Hospital, with more than 220 beds. The company is a part of the Lahey Health System.

NORTHEAST INDIANA BANCORP INC

NBB: NIDB

648 North Jefferson Street
Huntington, IN 46750
Phone: 260 356-3311
Fax: 260 358-0035
Web: www.firstfedindiana.com

CEO: –
CFO: –
HR: –
FYE: December 31
Type: Public

Northeast Indiana Bancorp is the holding company for First Federal Savings Bank, which operates three branches in Huntington and another in Warsaw. First Federal offers checking, savings, credit cards, money market accounts, CDs, and health savings accounts. Its subsidiary Innovative Financial Services division offers investments, financial planning, and insurance to individuals and corporate clients can set up retirement plans for employees.

	Annual Growth	12/17	12/18	12/19	12/20	12/21
Assets ($mil.)	7.4%	314.2	334.2	353.9	391.3	417.7
Net income ($ mil.)	20.9%	3.4	4.2	4.7	5.6	7.3
Market value ($ mil.)	7.5%	765.4	805.6	873.1	871.0	1,023.4
Employees	–	–	–	–	–	–

NORTHEAST IOWA COMMUNITY COLLEGE

1625 HIGHWAY 150
CALMAR, IA 521327606
Phone: 844 642-2338
Fax: –
Web: www.nicc.edu

CEO: –
CFO: –
HR: –
FYE: June 30
Type: Private

Northeast Iowa Community College (NICC) is a public community college with campuses in Calmar and Peosta, Iowa. NICC is accredited by the North Central Association of Colleges and Schools and offers more than 70 associate and technical degrees. The school also operates the Northeast Iowa Community-based Dairy Center, a laboratory and education center which promotes value-added agriculture. NICC enrolls more than 5,000 students with about half attending on a part-time basis. NICC has a student-to-faculty ratio of 17:1, with some 60% of its students enrolled in Arts and Sciences programs.

	Annual Growth	06/18	06/19	06/20	06/21	06/22
Sales ($mil.)	19.7%	–	1.4	1.5	1.5	2.4
Net income ($ mil.)	–	–	0.6	0.3	1.4	(0.1)
Market value ($ mil.)	–	–	–	–	–	–
Employees	–	–	–	–	–	1,514

NORTHEASTERN SUPPLY, INC.

8323 PULASKI HWY
BALTIMORE, MD 212372941
Phone: 410 574-0010
Fax: –
Web: www.northeastern.com

CEO: Stephen D Cook
CFO: –
HR: Mike Sanphillipo
FYE: December 31
Type: Private

Northeastern Supply is one of the largest independent plumbing, HVAC, water systems, and hardware distributors in the Mid-Atlantic region. Through roughly 40 locations and one showrooms in Delaware, Maryland, Pennsylvania, Virginia, and West Virginia, the company's services include 24-hour emergency service, distribution center, hot water express, H20 water systems, Moffett truck delivery, and jobsite storage. Major brands include American Standard, Bradford White, Campbell, Delta, Elkay, SAS Safety, Victory Pumps, CSI Water Treatment Systems, 3M, and Moen. The company was founded in 1945.

	Annual Growth	12/06	12/07	12/08	12/09	12/11
Sales ($mil.)	(2.1%)	–	–	113.6	100.9	106.5
Net income ($ mil.)	(20.8%)	–	–	2.2	2.6	1.1
Market value ($ mil.)	–	–	–	–	–	–
Employees	–	–	–	–	–	285

NORTHEASTERN UNIVERSITY

360 HUNTINGTON AVE
BOSTON, MA 021155000
Phone: 617 373-2000
Fax: –
Web: www.northeastern.edu

CEO: –
CFO: –
HR: –
FYE: June 30
Type: Private

Founded in 1898, Northeastern University is one of the largest private urban universities in North America. It is a world leader in experiential education, a learning approach that integrates classroom instruction and professional experience. The university is also a leader in the production of use-inspired research to solve global problems. The graduate programs offer professional doctorates, masters, certificates, and all other programs. Undergraduate education offers accounting, biology, business administration, computer science, engineering and more. The university attracts students from all 50 states within the US and about 150 countries, with campuses in Arlington, Boston, Burlington, Charlotte, Miami, Seattle, Portland, Toronto, Vancouver, and London.

	Annual Growth	06/18	06/19	06/20	06/21	06/22
Sales ($mil.)	8.9%	–	1,405.2	1,523.9	1,551.8	1,812.6
Net income ($ mil.)	47.0%	–	230.0	193.9	53.5	730.7
Market value ($ mil.)	–	–	–	–	–	–
Employees	–	–	–	–	–	4,175

NORTHERN ARIZONA HEALTHCARE CORPORATION

1200 N BEAVER ST
FLAGSTAFF, AZ 860013118
Phone: 928 779-3366
Fax: –
Web: www.nahealth.com

CEO: David Cheney
CFO: Gregory D Kuzma
HR: Eileen Vachonvierra
FYE: June 30
Type: Private

Northern Arizona Healthcare (NAH) is an integrated health care system serving residents of northern Arizona. It features two acute care hospitals - Flagstaff Medical Center (FMC), and Verde Valley Medical Center ? as well as through primary care and specialty physician clinics, outpatient surgical centers Cardiovascular Institute, Cancer Centers of Northern Arizona Healthcare, EntireCare Rehab & Sports Medicine, Children's Health Center, Orthopedic & Spine Institute and Guardian Air and Guardian Medical Transport. NAH also operates several area outpatient clinics that provide emergency and primary care services, as well as physical therapy, cancer treatments, and other services. NAH serves more than 700,000 patients annually and employs some 3,000 physicians.

	Annual Growth	06/08	06/09	06/10	06/11	06/15
Sales ($mil.)	5.6%	–	49.4	50.3	53.7	68.5
Net income ($ mil.)	–	–	(0.6)	(0.6)	(0.8)	(3.8)
Market value ($ mil.)	–	–	–	–	–	–
Employees	–	–	–	–	–	2,500

NORTHERN ARIZONA UNIVERSITY

601 S KNOLES DR ROOM 220
FLAGSTAFF, AZ 860015665
Phone: 928 523-9011
Fax: –
Web: www.nau.edu

CEO: –
CFO: –
HR: –
FYE: June 30
Type: Private

Located a stone's throw from the Grand Canyon, Northern Arizona University (NAU) has been educating students to see forever for more than a century. About 20,000 students attend the school, which is dominated by a mountainous landscape. Founded in 1899, NAU offers roughly 100 baccalaureate, about 50 master's, and a handful of doctoral programs. Undergraduate majors include exercise science, hotel and restaurant management, and visual communication. It's home to the High Altitude Sports Training Complex, a multi-sport training center used by athletes to prepare for different environments and enhance performance. NAU's Extended Campuses provide access to higher education for students in their own communities.

	Annual Growth	06/17	06/18	06/19	06/20	06/21
Sales ($mil.)	(2.5%)	–	359.6	368.0	354.8	333.0
Net income ($ mil.)	118.2%	–	5.4	16.8	(8.7)	56.5
Market value ($ mil.)	–	–	–	–	–	–
Employees	–	–	–	–	–	3,863

NORTHERN CALIFORNIA POWER AGENCY

651 COMMERCE DR
ROSEVILLE, CA 956786411
Phone: 916 781-3636
Fax: –
Web: www.ncpa.com

CEO: –
CFO: –
HR: –
FYE: June 30
Type: Private

From Redding and Plumas in the north to Lompoc in the south, Northern California Power Agency provides generation, purchasing, and transmission services to its 17 member organizations. The not-for-profit operates two geothermal plants producing 110 MW each, five hydroelectric plants that can produce more than 250 MW, and six combustion turbine plants with a total generating capacity of 174 MW. Northern California Power Agency's members and associate members include municipalities, rural electric cooperatives, and irrigation districts. The agency also provides legislative and regulatory representation services and trades wholesale energy on the open market.

NORTHERN INDIANA PUBLIC SERVICE COMPANY LLC

801 E 86TH AVE
MERRILLVILLE, IN 464106271
Phone: 800 464-7726
Fax: –
Web: –

CEO: –
CFO: Pete Disser
HR: –
FYE: December 31
Type: Private

Northern Indiana Public Service Company (NIPSCO) can shine a little light on the topic of Hoosiers. The largest subsidiary of utility holding company NiSource, NIPSCO has more than 457,000 electricity customers and more than 786,000 natural gas customers. The utility has three coal-fired power plants with 2,540 MW of generating capacity. On the power side of the business, NIPSCO generates, transmits, and distributes electricity to the northern part of Indiana, and engages in electric wholesale and transmission transactions. The company operates approximately 13,000 miles of electric transmission and distribution lines and 16,000 miles of gas mains.

	Annual Growth	12/05	12/06	12/15	12/16	12/17
Sales ($mil.)	0.8%	–	2,209.6	–	2,252.0	2,418.2
Net income ($ mil.)	3.3%	–	157.9	–	178.3	226.0
Market value ($ mil.)	–	–	–	–	–	–
Employees	–	–	–	–	–	3,096

NORTHERN INYO HEALTHCARE DISTRICT

150 PIONEER LN
BISHOP, CA 935142556
Phone: 760 873-5811
Fax: –
Web: www.nih.org

CEO: Stephen Delrossi
CFO: –
HR: Georgan Stottlemyre
FYE: June 30
Type: Private

Northern Inyo Hospital provides general medical services for the region north of Los Angeles, California. Its staff of physicians specialize in areas such as emergency medicine, obstetrics, urology, ophthalmology, and pediatrics. The company's Rural Health Clinic offers immunizations, wound care, women's and children's health exams, and sports physicals.

	Annual Growth	06/11	06/12	06/13	06/15	06/16
Sales ($mil.)	6.3%	–	59.8	0.0	73.4	76.3
Net income ($ mil.)	(3.5%)	–	1.1	0.0	0.8	1.0
Market value ($ mil.)	–	–	–	–	–	–
Employees	–	–	–	–	–	402

NORTHERN NATURAL GAS COMPANY

1111 S 103RD ST
OMAHA, NE 681241072
Phone: 402 398-7700
Fax: –
Web: www.northernnaturalgas.com

CEO: –
CFO: –
HR: –
FYE: December 31
Type: Private

Northern Natural Gas is a subsidiary of Berkshire Hathaway Energy and has been in business since 1930. The company owns and operates the largest interstate natural gas pipeline system in the US. Its pipeline system stretches across some 10 states, from the Permian Basin in Texas to Michigan's Upper Peninsula, providing access to five of the major natural gas supply regions in North America. Northern Natural's extensive pipeline system, which is interconnected with many interstate and intrastate pipelines in the national grid system, has access to supplies from multiple major supply basins and provides transportation services to utilities and numerous other customers. The company's system includes three underground natural gas storage facilities and two liquefied natural gas storage facilities, with a total firm service and operational storage capacity of 79 billion cubic feet.

	Annual Growth	12/05	12/06	12/07	12/16	12/17
Sales ($mil.)	0.8%	–	633.6	664.0	636.4	693.4
Net income ($ mil.)	1.7%	–	142.4	161.1	159.4	170.6
Market value ($ mil.)	–	–	–	–	–	–
Employees	–	–	–	–	–	1,055

NORTHERN OIL & GAS INC (MN)   NYS: NOG

4350 Baker Road - Suite 400
Minnetonka, MN 55343
Phone: 952 476-9800
Fax: –
Web: www.northernoil.com

CEO: Nicholas O'Grady
CFO: Chad Allen
HR: –
FYE: December 31
Type: Public

Northern Oil and Gas is the leading non-operated working interest franchise in the premier shale basins across the US. It operates with premier operators, landowners and minerals rights owners. Northern has targeted specific areas in active basins that offer the highest rates of return on oil drilling projects. The company focuses its efforts across the most prolific oil and gas producing basins in North America. It has more than 7,000 gross producing wells. Headquartered in Minnetonka, Minnesota, the company was incorporated in 2006.

	Annual Growth	12/19	12/20	12/21	12/22	12/23
Sales ($mil.)	46.3%	472.4	552.2	496.9	1,570.5	2,166.3
Net income ($ mil.)	–	(76.3)	(906.0)	6.4	773.2	923.0
Market value ($ mil.)	99.5%	235.8	882.7	2,073.7	3,105.5	3,735.2
Employees	12.2%	24	25	25	33	38

NORTHERN PRIDE, INC.

401 CONLEY AVE S
THIEF RIVER FALLS, MN 567013117
Phone: 218 681-1201
Fax: –
Web: www.northernprideinc.com

CEO: Troy Stauffenecker
CFO: –
HR: Diane Retke
FYE: December 31
Type: Private

Northern Pride helps northern US turkey farmers take pride in their efforts. The agricultural cooperative processes some 20,000 turkeys a day (or 40 million live pounds of turkey a year) and sells whole bird, bone-in breast, and turkey parts (drums, wings, necks, gizzards, tails, and thighs) under the Snowland, Northern Pride, Harvest Gold, and Premium Specialty brand names throughout the US and in several foreign countries. It also sells a line of free-range and antibiotic turkeys; and offers private-label services. Northern Pride's customers include food retailers, foodservice operators, and food manufacturers.

	Annual Growth	12/07	12/08	12/09	12/10	12/11
Sales ($mil.)	17.7%	–	–	25.9	30.8	35.9
Net income ($ mil.)	7.2%	–	–	0.0	0.1	0.0
Market value ($ mil.)	–	–	–	–	–	–
Employees	–	–	–	–	–	210

NORTHERN TECHNOLOGIES INTERNATIONAL CORP.   NMS: NTIC

4201 Woodland Road, P.O. Box 69
Circle Pines, MN 55014
Phone: 763 225-6600
Fax: –
Web: www.ntic.com

CEO: G P Lynch
CFO: Matthew C Wolsfeld
HR: –
FYE: August 31
Type: Public

Northern Technologies International (NTIC) develops and markets proprietary, environmentally beneficial products and services in over 65 countries either directly or via a network of subsidiaries, joint ventures, independent distributors, and agents. NTIC's primary business is corrosion prevention products and services, marketed mainly under the ZERUST brand. NTIC sells its ZERUST products and services to the automotive, electronics, electrical, mechanical, military, retail consumer, oil and gas industry. Additionally, NTIC markets and sells a portfolio of proprietary bio-based and certified compostable (fully biodegradable) polymer resin compounds and finished products under the Natur-Tec brand. The company generates more than 65% of its revenue from outside of the US.

	Annual Growth	08/19	08/20	08/21	08/22	08/23
Sales ($mil.)	9.4%	55.8	47.6	56.5	74.2	79.9
Net income ($ mil.)	(13.5%)	5.2	(1.3)	6.3	6.3	2.9
Market value ($ mil.)	4.2%	103.2	78.3	157.1	111.0	121.6
Employees	(11.0%)	137	142	171	201	86

NORTHERN TIER ENERGY LP

1250 W WASHINGTON ST STE 300
TEMPE, AZ 852881697
Phone: 602 302-5450
Fax: –
Web: –

CEO: Dave L Lamp
CFO: Karen B Davis
HR: –
FYE: December 31
Type: Private

Northern Tier Energy refines crude oil in the northern reaches of the US. The company owns an oil refinery in Minnesota and around 285 SuperAmerica gas stations across Minnesota and Wisconsin. Its oil refinery produces more than 100,000 barrels per day of gasoline, diesel, jet fuel, and asphalt. The company also owns storage and transportation assets, including terminals, storage tanks, rail loading and unloading facilities, and a dock on the Mississippi River. In addition, Northern Tier Energy owns a 17% stake in the 300-mile Minnesota Pipeline (Koch Industries owns the rest) that transports crude oil to its refinery. The company is a wholly owned subsidiary of Western Refining.

NORTHERN TRUST CORP   NMS: NTRS

50 South La Salle Street
Chicago, IL 60603
Phone: 312 630-6000
Fax: –
Web: www.northerntrust.com

CEO: Michael G O'Grady
CFO: Jason J Tyler
HR: Arnold Greene
FYE: December 31
Type: Public

Through its flagship subsidiary, The Northern Trust Company, Northern Trust Corporation is a leading provider of wealth management, securities lending, asset servicing and management, and banking solutions to corporations, institutions, affluent families and individuals. Founded in 1889, Northern Trust has a global presence with offices in about 25 US states and Washington DC, and across some 25 locations in Canada, Europe, the Middle East and the Asia-Pacific region. The company has consolidated total assets of $155.0 billion and stockholders' equity of $11.3 billion. About 65% of company's total revenue comes from the US.

	Annual Growth	12/19	12/20	12/21	12/22	12/23
Assets ($mil.)	2.5%	136,828	170,004	183,890	155,037	150,783
Net income ($ mil.)	(7.2%)	1,492.2	1,209.3	1,545.3	1,336.0	1,107.3
Market value ($ mil.)	(5.6%)	21,793	19,105	24,535	18,152	17,309
Employees	3.9%	19,800	20,900	21,100	23,600	23,100

NORTHERN UTAH HEALTHCARE CORPORATION

1200 E 3900 S
SALT LAKE CITY, UT 841241300
Phone: 801 268-7111
Fax: –
Web: www.mountainstar.com

CEO: Mark Robinson
CFO: Brian McKenley
HR: Kelly Brimhall
FYE: June 30
Type: Private

St. Mark's Hospital provides a variety of health care services in Salt Lake City and surrounding areas of northern Utah. The medical center has a capacity of some 320 beds and provides acute care and specialty services including cardiology, orthopedics, oncology, women's services, pain management, general surgery, and emergency care. It also offers family practice and specialist services. Established in 1872, St. Mark's Hospital is part of HCA's MountainStar Healthcare Network, which operates hospitals and other health care facilities in Alaska, Idaho, and Utah.

	Annual Growth	05/99	05/00*	12/05*	06/15	06/16
Sales ($mil.)	5.9%	–	140.3	0.3	341.7	352.5
Net income ($ mil.)	11.8%	–	17.5	0.0	110.5	103.9
Market value ($ mil.)		–	–	–	–	–
Employees		–	–	–	–	1,600

*Fiscal year change

NORTHERN VIRGINIA ELECTRIC COOPERATIVE

10323 LOMOND DR
MANASSAS, VA 201093113
Phone: 703 335-0500
Fax: –
Web: www.novec.com

CEO: David E Schleicher
CFO: Wilbur Rollins
HR: Marlane Parsons
FYE: December 31
Type: Private

NOVEC is no novice when it comes to electricity distribution. Northern Virginia Electric Cooperative (NOVEC) is a member-owned not-for profit utility that serves more than 150,000 residential, commercial, industrial, and government customers in a 651-sq. ml. service area in northern Virginia. NOVEC, which has more than 6,790 miles of power lines, receives its power supply from the PJM Interconnection marketplace. The company also markets natural gas to retail customers in Virginia and Maryland through its NOVEC Energy Solutions unit. Subsidiary NOVEC Solutions sells gas and electric water heaters and other energy appliances and provides optical data networking service for large businesses and government agencies.

	Annual Growth	12/13	12/14	12/15	12/21	12/22
Sales ($mil.)	11.0%	–	433.1	472.0	676.7	998.1
Net income ($ mil.)	(6.7%)	–	20.5	20.3	27.0	11.8
Market value ($ mil.)		–	–	–	–	–
Employees		–	–	–	–	275

NORTHFIELD BANCORP INC (DE)   NMS: NFBK

581 Main Street
Woodbridge, NJ 07095
Phone: 732 499-7200
Fax: –
Web: www.enorthfield.com

CEO: Steven M Klein
CFO: William R Jacobs
HR: –
FYE: December 31
Type: Public

Northfield Bancorp is the holding company for Northfield Bank, which operates around 40 branches in New York (Staten Island and Brooklyn) and New Jersey (Hunterdon, Mercer, Middlesex, and Union counties). Northfield Bank offers checking, savings, and retirement accounts; CDs; mortgage and home equity loans; life insurance; and credit cards. Its commercial offerings include checking and money market accounts, commercial lending, and business credit cards. Multifamily real estate loans make up 55% of the bank's loan portfolio, while other commercial real estate loans make up another 15%. Northfield Bank traces its roots back to 1887.

	Annual Growth	12/19	12/20	12/21	12/22	12/23
Assets ($mil.)	2.6%	5,055.3	5,514.5	5,430.5	5,601.3	5,598.4
Net income ($ mil.)	(1.6%)	40.2	37.0	70.7	61.1	37.7
Market value ($ mil.)	(7.2%)	755.1	549.0	719.5	700.4	560.1
Employees	1.5%	380	385	391	404	404

NORTHRIM BANCORP INC
NMS: NRIM

3111 C Street
Anchorage, AK 99503
Phone: 907 562-0062
Fax: –
Web: www.northrim.com

CEO: –
CFO: Jed W Ballard
HR: –
FYE: December 31
Type: Public

Can you get banking services at the north rim of the world? Of course! Northrim BanCorp, formed in 2001 to be the holding company for Northrim Bank, provides a full range of commercial and retail banking services and products through some 10 banking offices in Alaska's Anchorage, Fairbanks North Star, and Matanuska Susitna counties. Division offices that provide short-term capital to customers also are located in Washington and Oregon. The bank offers standard deposit products including checking, savings, and money market accounts; CDs; and IRAs. It uses funds from deposits to write commercial loans (40% of loan portfolio) and real estate term loans (nearly 35%), as well as construction and consumer loans.

	Annual Growth	12/19	12/20	12/21	12/22	12/23
Assets ($mil.)	14.3%	1,644.0	2,121.8	2,724.7	2,674.3	2,807.5
Net income ($ mil.)	5.3%	20.7	32.9	37.5	30.7	25.4
Market value ($ mil.)	10.6%	211.2	187.2	239.6	300.9	315.4
Employees	2.3%	431	438	451	469	472

NORTHROP GRUMMAN CORP
NYS: NOC

2980 Fairview Park Drve
Falls Church, VA 22042
Phone: 703 280-2900
Fax: –
Web: www.northropgrumman.com

CEO: –
CFO: –
HR: –
FYE: December 31
Type: Public

Northrop Grumman Corporation is a leading global aerospace and defense technology company. The company delivers a broad range of products, services and solutions to US and international customers, and principally to the US Department of Defense (DoD) and intelligence community. Its broad portfolio is aligned to support national security priorities and its solutions equip its customers with capabilities they need to connect, protect and advance humanity. Northrop Grumman generates more than 65% of its total sales from the US. It originally was formed in 1939 in Hawthorne, California as Northrop Aircraft Incorporated.

	Annual Growth	12/19	12/20	12/21	12/22	12/23
Sales ($mil.)	3.8%	33,841	36,799	35,667	36,602	39,290
Net income ($ mil.)	(2.2%)	2,248.0	3,189.0	7,005.0	4,896.0	2,056.0
Market value ($ mil.)	8.0%	51,633	45,741	58,103	81,901	70,272
Employees	2.9%	90,000	97,000	88,000	95,000	101,000

NORTHROP GRUMMAN INNOVATION SYSTEMS, INC.

2980 FAIRVIEW PARK DR
FALLS CHURCH, VA 220424511
Phone: 703 406-5000
Fax: –
Web: www.northropgrumman.com

CEO: Kathy Warden
CFO: Heather Crofford
HR: Bender Emily
FYE: December 31
Type: Private

Through several operating segments, Orbital ATK is a leading manufacturer of mission-critical products, including launch vehicles and related propulsion systems; satellites and associated components and services; composite aerospace structures; tactical missiles, subsystems and defense electronics; and precision weapons, armament systems and ammunition. Its operations are divided across the three segments of Flight Systems, Defense Systems, and Space Systems. In late 2017, Orbital ATK agreed to be bought by Northrop Grumman for about $7.8 billion in cash.

NORTHSIDE HOSPITAL

6000 49TH ST N
SAINT PETERSBURG, FL 337092145
Phone: 727 521-4411
Fax: –
Web: www.hcafloridahealthcare.com

CEO: –
CFO: –
HR: –
FYE: September 30
Type: Private

Hurting hearts aren't the only thing Northside Hospital can treat. The acute care facility, which houses the Tampa Bay Heart Institute, has some 290 beds and provides a gamut of medical services to the residents of Pinellas County, Florida. The Heart Institute offers surgical, diagnostic, and rehabilitation services for cardiac patients. In addition to its cardiovascular expertise, Northside Hospital offers specialized treatment for patients with spine disorders and chronic pain conditions, as well as diagnostic imaging, orthopedics, rehabilitation, urology, outpatient surgery. Northside Hospital is part of the HCA family.

NORTHSIDE HOSPITAL, INC.

1000 JOHNSON FERRY RD
ATLANTA, GA 303421611
Phone: 404 851-8000
Fax: –
Web: www.northside.com

CEO: –
CFO: –
HR: –
FYE: September 30
Type: Private

Northside Hospital is committed to health wellness community and offers all benefits of high-touch quality care close to home and the best in class health care delivery. Northside hospitals has grown over the years, expanding across 25 counties with five acute-care hospitals over 275 outpatient facilities, some 3,700 providers, and 25,000 employees. Northside Hospital Atlanta is system's flagship hospital with about 620 beds. Northside Hospital Cherokee is a 326-bed full-service community hospital. Northside Hospital Duluth is a 122-bed hospital that promotes patient healing while offering the very latest medical care for efficient treatment and quick recovery times. Northside Hospital Gwinnett is a Level II Trauma Center that offers nationally recognized and renowned health care services.

NORTHWAY FINANCIAL, INC.
NBB: NWYF

9 Main Street
Berlin, NH 03570
Phone: 603 326-7377
Fax: –
Web: www.northwaybank.com

CEO: William J Woodward
CFO: Richard P Orsillo
HR: –
FYE: December 31
Type: Public

For managing finances way up north, try Northway Financial. Northway Financial is the holding company for Northway Bank, which operates about 20 branches in New Hampshire. The community-oriented bank serves individuals and local business customers by offering deposit products such as checking and savings accounts, NOW and money market accounts, CDs, and IRAs. Lending activities mainly consist of residential and commercial mortgages, which together account for about three-quarters of the company's loan portfolio; other offerings include construction, business, and consumer loans. The bank offers investments, insurance, and retirement services through an agreement with a third-party provider, Infinex Financial.

	Annual Growth	12/18	12/19	12/20	12/21	12/22
Assets ($mil.)	8.9%	926.9	917.0	1,120.7	1,247.5	1,302.6
Net income ($ mil.)	(2.3%)	2.9	9.3	5.2	9.3	2.7
Market value ($ mil.)	(7.6%)	77.6	92.6	77.1	90.1	56.6
Employees		–	–	–	–	–

NORTHWEST BANCSHARES, INC. (MD)
NMS: NWBI

3 Easton Oval, Suite 500
Columbus, OH 43219
Phone: 814 726-2140
Fax: –
Web: www.northwest.com

CEO: Louis J Torchio
CFO: –
HR: Ashley Walker
FYE: December 31
Type: Public

Northwest Bancshares was incorporated in 2009 and the successor corporation of the Northwest Bancorp, Inc. It operates through the Northwest Bank, a community-oriented financial institution offering personal and business banking solutions, investment management and trust services. Northwest Bank operated 170 community-banking locations throughout its market area in Pennsylvania, western New York, eastern Ohio, and Indiana. Its principal lending activities are the origination of loans secured by first mortgages on owner-occupied, one-to-four-family residences, shorter term consumer loans, and commercial business and commercial real estate loans.

	Annual Growth	12/19	12/20	12/21	12/22	12/23
Assets ($mil.)	8.3%	10,494	13,806	14,502	14,113	14,419
Net income ($ mil.)	5.1%	110.4	74.9	154.3	133.7	135.0
Market value ($ mil.)	(6.9%)	2,113.8	1,619.4	1,799.9	1,777.0	1,586.3
Employees	(1.9%)	2,333	2,523	2,413	2,228	2,165

NORTHWEST BIOTHERAPEUTICS INC
NBB: NWBO

4800 Montgomery Lane, Suite 800
Bethesda, MD 20814
Phone: 240 497-9024
Fax: –
Web: www.nwbio.com

CEO: –
CFO: –
HR: –
FYE: December 31
Type: Public

Northwest Biotherapeutics is a development-stage drug company. Its DCVax vaccine platform uses dendritic cells (a type of white blood cell) obtained from a patient's blood to program that patient's own T cells to kill cancer cells. Northwest Biotherapeutics' two DCVax product candidates are being targeted to treat brain and prostate cancer. Both candidates are in late-stage clinical trials. If successful, the therapies could work in conjunction with more traditional cancer treatments. Toucan Capital holds over 85% of the company's shares. Toucan's Cognate Therapeutics subsidiary manufactures the DCVax products and provides additional services to Northwest Biotherapeutics.

	Annual Growth	12/19	12/20	12/21	12/22	12/23
Sales ($mil.)	(5.4%)	2.4	1.3	1.0	1.7	1.9
Net income ($ mil.)	–	(20.3)	(529.8)	179.1	(105.0)	(62.6)
Market value ($ mil.)	34.4%	252.6	1,792.6	822.9	922.2	824.0
Employees	6.7%	17	19	20	20	22

NORTHWEST COMMUNITY HOSPITAL INC

800 W CENTRAL RD
ARLINGTON HEIGHTS, IL 600052349
Phone: 847 618-1000
Fax: –
Web: www.nch.org

CEO: JP Gallagher
CFO: –
HR: –
FYE: December 31
Type: Private

Northwest Community Healthcare (NCH) founded in 1959, is a not-for-profit healthcare system located in Chicago, Illinois. Northwest Community Hospital is a Level II trauma center, as well as Level III NICU, and a dedicated pediatric emergency department. It also provides a full range of outpatient infusion and injection services that include chemotherapy, blood transfusions, and treatments for blood and immunological disorders. Northwest Community Healthcare had 20,000 inpatient and 350,000 outpatient visits. It has more than 38,000 home care visits and 2,700 newborn deliveries, as well as about 76,000 emergency department visits. NCH also operates Wellness Center, a premier health and fitness center and spa on the NCH campus.

	Annual Growth	09/18	09/19	09/20	09/21*	12/22
Sales ($mil.)	12.9%	–	–	464.9	510.0	592.5
Net income ($ mil.)	52.5%	–	–	9.5	17.3	22.1
Market value ($ mil.)	–	–	–	–	–	–
Employees	–	–	–	–	–	4,711

*Fiscal year change

NORTHWEST DAIRY ASSOCIATION

5601 6TH AVE S STE 300
SEATTLE, WA 981082545
Phone: 206 284-7220
Fax: –
Web: www.darigold.com

CEO: Jim Werkhoven
CFO: Mark Garth
HR: Brad Huffer
FYE: March 31
Type: Private

Northwest Dairy Association (NDA) members milk a lot of cows. The dairy cooperative's 550-plus member/farmers ship 7.2 billion pounds of milk annually, which is processed by the co-op's subsidiary Darigold and packaged and sold under the Darigold label. NDA produces fluid and cultured dairy products, including milk, butter, cottage cheese, sour cream, and yogurt that altogether generate some $2 billion in sales. It also makes bulk butter and cheese, milk powder, and whey products. The co-op caters to several sectors nationwide. Its customers include food retailers and wholesalers, as well as foodservice and food-manufacturing companies. The association's membership spans half a dozen US states.

	Annual Growth	03/02	03/03	03/04	03/07	03/08
Sales ($mil.)	14.1%	–	1,140.2	1,297.3	1,450.2	2,207.3
Net income ($ mil.)	107.0%	–	2.3	(6.4)	12.8	87.4
Market value ($ mil.)	–	–	–	–	–	–
Employees	–	–	–	–	–	1,300

NORTHWEST NATURAL HOLDING CO
NYS: NWN

250 SW Taylor Street
Portland, OR 97204
Phone: 503 226-4211
Fax: –
Web: www.nwnaturalholdings.com

CEO: David H Anderson
CFO: Frank H Burkhartsmeyer
HR: –
FYE: December 31
Type: Public

NW Natural is a local distribution company that currently provides natural gas service to approximately 2.5 million people in more than 140 communities through some 795,000 meters in Oregon and Southwest Washington with one of the most modern pipeline systems in the nation. NW Natural's natural gas pipeline system consists of approximately 14,200 miles of distribution and transmission mains and approximately 10,200 miles of service lines located in its territory in Oregon and southwest Washington. NW Natural owns and operates 21 Bcf of underground gas storage capacity in Oregon. NW Natural is part of Northwest Natural Holding Company, which owns NW Natural, NW Natural Water Company (NW Natural Water), and other business interests.

	Annual Growth	12/19	12/20	12/21	12/22	12/23
Sales ($mil.)	12.5%	746.4	773.7	860.4	1,037.4	1,197.5
Net income ($ mil.)	11.0%	61.7	76.8	78.7	86.3	93.9
Market value ($ mil.)	(14.8%)	2,774.5	1,730.7	1,835.7	1,790.9	1,465.4
Employees	(0.1%)	1,220	1,216	1,237	1,258	1,214

NORTHWEST PIPE CO.
NMS: NWPX

201 NE Park Plaza Drive, Suite 100
Vancouver, WA 98684
Phone: 360 397-6250
Fax: 360 397-6257
Web: www.nwpipe.com

CEO: Scott Montross
CFO: Aaron Wilkins
HR: Megan Kendrick
FYE: December 31
Type: Public

Northwest Pipe is the largest manufacturer of engineered steel water pipeline systems in North America. In addition, the company manufactures high-quality precast and reinforced concrete products; water, wastewater, and storm water equipment; steel casing pipe, bar-wrapped concrete cylinder pipe, and one of the largest offerings of pipeline system joints, fittings, and specialized components. The company provides solution-based products for a wide range of markets under the ParkUSA, Geneva Pipe and Precast, Permalok, and Northwest Pipe Company lines. Northwest Pipe has around 15 manufacturing sites across North America. The US generates some 95% of the company's total revenue.

	Annual Growth	12/19	12/20	12/21	12/22	12/23
Sales ($mil.)	12.3%	279.3	285.9	333.3	457.7	444.4
Net income ($ mil.)	(6.8%)	27.9	19.1	11.5	31.1	21.1
Market value ($ mil.)	(2.4%)	332.6	282.6	317.5	336.5	302.2
Employees	14.7%	765	956	1,256	1,312	1,325

NORTHWEST TEXAS HEALTHCARE SYSTEM, INC.

1501 S COULTER ST
AMARILLO, TX 791061770
Phone: 806 354-1000
Fax: –
Web: www.nwths.com

CEO: –
CFO: –
HR: –
FYE: December 31
Type: Private

Northwest Texas Healthcare has a (pan)handle on the medical problems of the state's northernmost region. Part of the Universal Health Services (UHS) health system, Northwest Texas Healthcare System features the Northwest Texas Hospital and its related facilities and programs, which serve residents in and around the Texas Panhandle city of Amarillo. The hospital is a 490-bed academic medical center features a behavioral health pavilion and provides emergency, trauma, diagnostic, surgery, and general inpatient care, as well as about 50 medical specialties. Northwest Texas Healthcare operates various outpatient treatment and health awareness programs and services.

	Annual Growth	12/12	12/13	12/14	12/15	12/16
Sales ($mil.)	6.1%	–	–	246.5	270.5	277.6
Net income ($ mil.)	–	–	–	12.2	23.4	(4.9)
Market value ($ mil.)	–	–	–	–	–	–
Employees	–	–	–	–	–	1,798

NORTHWESTERN ENERGY GROUP INC

3010 W. 69th Street
Sioux Falls, SD 57108
Phone: 605 978-2900
Fax: –
Web: www.northwesternenergy.com

NMS: NWE
CEO: Robert C Rowe
CFO: Brian B Bird
HR: –
FYE: December 31
Type: Public

NorthWestern Corporation, doing business as NorthWestern Energy, provides essential energy infrastructure and valuable services to approximately 764,200 customers in Montana, South Dakota, Nebraska, and Yellowstone National Park. In Montana, it delivers electricity to approximately 398,200 customers in around 220 communities and surrounding rural areas, and around 10 rural electric cooperatives, and in Wyoming to Yellowstone National Park. NorthWestern delivers gas to approximately 209,100 customers in nearly 120 Montana communities. It also distributes natural gas to some 37,000 customers in three Nebraska communities and approximately 49,200 customers in over 80 South Dakota communities.

	Annual Growth	12/19	12/20	12/21	12/22	12/23
Sales ($mil.)	3.1%	1,257.9	1,198.7	1,372.3	1,477.8	1,422.1
Net income ($ mil.)	(1.0%)	202.1	155.2	186.8	183.0	194.1
Market value ($ mil.)	–	–	–	–	–	–
Employees	0.6%	1,533	1,530	1,483	1,530	1,573

NORTHWESTERN LAKE FOREST HOSPITAL

1000 N WESTMORELAND RD
LAKE FOREST, IL 600451658
Phone: 847 234-0945
Fax: –
Web: www.nm.org

CEO: Dean Harrison
CFO: –
HR: –
FYE: August 31
Type: Private

Northwestern Lake Forest Hospital brings good health to Illinois residents. The hospital is licensed for 117 acute care beds, 40 skilled nursing care beds, and 44 long-term care beds and provides acute, long-term, and other health care services to the residents of northeastern Illinois. It offers specialties as cancer and cardiovascular care, speech therapy, behavioral health, and the Hunter Family Center for Women's Health. The hospital includes Westmoreland Nursing Home (senior and hospice care); it also operates a child care center, a home health organization, and several outpatient clinics. Northwestern Lake Forest Hospital is part of the Northwestern Memorial HealthCare system.

	Annual Growth	08/12	08/13	08/14	08/15	08/16
Sales ($mil.)	7.2%	–	–	–	226.8	243.1
Net income ($ mil.)	67.0%	–	–	–	12.9	21.5
Market value ($ mil.)	–	–	–	–	–	–
Employees	–	–	–	–	–	1,700

NORTHWESTERN MEMORIAL HEALTHCARE

251 E HURON ST STE 3-710
CHICAGO, IL 606112908
Phone: 312 926-7146
Fax: –
Web: www.nm.org

CEO: Howard Chrisman
CFO: John Orsin
HR: –
FYE: August 31
Type: Private

If you get blown over in the Windy City, Northwestern Memorial HealthCare (NMHC) can get you upright again. Its primary facility, Northwestern Memorial Hospital (NMH), is a teaching hospital serving residents of the Chicago area, offering virtually every medical specialty. The hospital has more than 890 beds and is affiliated with Northwestern University's Feinberg School of Medicine. NMHC also operates the 200-bed Northwestern Lake Forest Hospital, ambulatory surgery centers, physicians' practices, community clinics, a home hospice program, and health and wellness centers. Other subsidiaries of the NMHC health system include a philanthropic foundation, an insurance company, and a managed care contracts provider.

	Annual Growth	08/09	08/10	08/11	08/12	08/14
Sales ($mil.)	108.0%	–	22.5	27.1	1,701.5	421.3
Net income ($ mil.)	184.3%	–	0.6	1.9	145.5	37.4
Market value ($ mil.)	–	–	–	–	–	–
Employees	–	–	–	–	–	20,000

NORTHWESTERN MUTUAL LIFE INSURANCE CO. (MILWAUKEE, WI)

720 E. Wisconsin Ave., Milwaukee, WI 53202-4797
Milwaukee, WI 53202
Phone: 414 271-1444
Fax: –
Web: www.northwesternmutual.com

CEO: John E Schlifske
CFO: Michael G Carter
HR: –
FYE: December 31
Type: Public

With more than $558 billion in total assets, nearly $35 billion in revenues, and $2.2 trillion worth of life insurance protection in force, Northwestern Mutual delivers financial security to nearly five million people with life, disability income and long-term care insurance, annuities, and brokerage and advisory services. Through a holistic planning approach, Northwestern Mutual combines the expertise of its financial professionals with a personalized digital sexperience and industry-leading products to help its clients plan for what's most important.

	Annual Growth	12/02	12/03	12/04	12/10	12/11
Sales ($mil.)	4.5%	–	16,545	17,310	23,109	23,595
Net income ($ mil.)	(0.9%)	–	692.0	817.0	756.0	645.0
Market value ($ mil.)	–	–	–	–	–	–
Employees	–	–	–	–	1,100	–

NORTHWESTERN UNIVERSITY

633 CLARK ST
EVANSTON, IL 602080001
Phone: 847 491-3741
Fax: –
Web: www.northwestern.edu

CEO: –
CFO: –
HR: –
FYE: August 31
Type: Private

Northwestern University (NU) is a comprehensive research university that is deeply interdisciplinary across multiple schools and units. It serves over 22,000 students through a dozen schools and colleges such as the Medill School of Journalism and the McCormick School of Engineering and Applied Sciences. Its Chicago campus houses the schools of law and medicine, as well as several hospitals of the McGaw Medical Center. The university has a student-to-teacher ratio of about 6:1. NU is home to several research centers and community outreach programs; it also has a branch in Qatar. It is the only private member of the Big Ten conference; varsity sports include baseball, football, basketball, and fencing. The university was established in 1851.

	Annual Growth	08/14	08/15	08/16	08/17	08/18
Sales ($mil.)	6.7%	–	–	–	2,310.0	2,464.5
Net income ($ mil.)	(16.2%)	–	–	–	669.0	560.5
Market value ($ mil.)	–	–	–	–	–	–
Employees	–	–	–	–	–	5,954

NORTON COMMUNITY HOSPITAL AUXILIARY, INC.

100 15TH ST NW
NORTON, VA 242731616
Phone: 276 679-9600
Fax: –
Web: www.nchosp.org

CEO: –
CFO: –
HR: –
FYE: June 30
Type: Private

Norton Community Hospital provides medical, surgical, and therapeutic services in southwest Virginia and southeast Kentucky. Established in 1949 as a hospital for miners, Norton Community Hospital has grown to an acute care facility with some 130 beds. Specialized services include emergency medicine, diagnostics, pulmonary health, orthopedics, obstetrics, cardiology, psychiatry, and oncology. The hospital, which is an affiliate of the Mountain States Health Alliance, also provides home health services through affiliate Community Home Care, and it operates outpatient and family medicine clinics.

	Annual Growth	09/03	09/04	09/05	09/06*	06/08
Sales ($mil.)	(11.3%)	–	–	–	50.0	39.4
Net income ($ mil.)	52.0%	–	–	–	1.1	2.6
Market value ($ mil.)	–	–	–	–	–	–
Employees	–	–	–	–	–	460

*Fiscal year change

NORTON LAIRD TRUST COMPANY

801 2ND AVE STE 1600
SEATTLE, WA 981041521
Phone: 206 464-5100
Fax: –
Web: –

CEO: Jeffery S Vincent
CFO: –
HR: Sherry Lehmann
FYE: December 31
Type: Private

Need to pass the family jewels down the family tree? Talk to the people who know about wood. Laird Norton Tyee Trust Company (LNTyee) caters to the ultra-wealthy. The company grew out of the private asset management efforts of the Laird and Norton families, northwestern timber-industry pioneers and founders of forest products firms such as General Timber Company and Potlach Lumber. The company (categorized as a multi-family office, or MFO) provides wealth management services, along with such necessities as family governance, financial education, and charitable gift planning. The firm has more than $4 billion in assets under advisement for some 430 clients.

NORWEGIAN CRUISE LINE HOLDINGS LTD   NYS: NCLH

7665 Corporate Center Drive
Miami, FL 33126
Phone: 305 436-4000
Fax: –
Web: www.nclhltd.com

CEO: Frank J Del Rio
CFO: Mark A Kempa
HR: Ileana Fraga
FYE: December 31
Type: Public

Norwegian Cruise Line Holdings is a leading global cruise company that operates the Norwegian Cruise Line, Oceania Cruises and Regent Seven Seas Cruises brands. The company has about 30 ships with approximately 62,000 Berths. The company brands offer itineraries to worldwide destinations, including Europe, Asia, Australia, New Zealand, South America, Africa, and more. Norwegian's US-flagged ship, Pride of America, provides the industry's only entirely inter-island itinerary in Hawaii. All company brands offer an assortment of features, amenities and activities, including a variety of accommodations, multiple dining venues, bars and lounges, spas, casinos and more. North American customers account for approximately 65% of sales.

	Annual Growth	12/19	12/20	12/21	12/22	12/23
Sales ($mil.)	7.2%	6,462.4	1,279.9	648.0	4,843.8	8,549.9
Net income ($ mil.)	(35.0%)	930.2	(4,012.5)	(4,506.6)	(2,269.9)	166.2
Market value ($ mil.)	–	–	–	–	–	–
Employees	3.3%	36,000	34,300	34,700	38,900	41,000

NORWICH UNIVERSITY

158 HARMON DR
NORTHFIELD, VT 056631035
Phone: 802 485-2000
Fax: –
Web: www.norwich.edu

CEO: –
CFO: Richard E Rebmann
HR: –
FYE: May 31
Type: Private

Whether military man or regular old citizen, Norwich University could be the perfect place to learn the ropes. As both a traditional and a military college, Norwich accepts military and civilian students. The coeducational school has an undergraduate enrollment of about 2,300. It offers 30 on-campus bachelor's programs, a teacher lincensure program, and four ROTC programs. Its five colleges include the College of Professional Schools and the College of Science and Mathematics. The university is the birthplace of the nation's Reserve Officers' Training Corps (ROTC) program. The oldest private military college in the US, Norwich was founded in 1819 by Captain Alden Partridge.

	Annual Growth	05/18	05/19	05/20	05/21	05/22
Sales ($mil.)	2.7%	–	109.7	108.0	110.7	118.8
Net income ($ mil.)	–	–	2.3	2.7	123.9	(43.8)
Market value ($ mil.)	–	–	–	–	–	–
Employees	–	–	–	–	–	510

NORWOOD FINANCIAL CORP.   NMS: NWFL

717 Main Street
Honesdale, PA 18431
Phone: 570 253-1455
Fax: –
Web: www.waynebank.com

CEO: –
CFO: –
HR: –
FYE: December 31
Type: Public

Norwood Financial, not Batman, owns Wayne Bank. The bank serves individuals and local businesses through about 30 branches in northeastern Pennsylvania. It offers standard deposit products and services including checking and savings accounts, money market savings accounts, CDs, and IRAs. Mortgages account for about 80% of Wayne Bank's loan portfolio. The bank also runs a trust and wealth management division; subsidiary Norwood Investment provides annuities and mutual funds; Norwood Settlement (70%-owned) offers title and settlement services. Norwood Financial bought Delaware Bancshares and its National Bank of Delaware County subsidiary in mid-2016; the purchase nearly doubled its branch network.

	Annual Growth	12/19	12/20	12/21	12/22	12/23
Assets ($mil.)	15.6%	1,230.6	1,851.9	2,068.5	2,047.1	2,201.1
Net income ($ mil.)	4.2%	14.2	15.1	24.9	29.2	16.8
Market value ($ mil.)	(4.1%)	315.5	212.2	210.8	271.2	266.9
Employees	4.8%	220	265	266	276	265

NOTRE DAME OF MARYLAND UNIVERSITY, INC.

4701 N CHARLES ST
BALTIMORE, MD 212102404
Phone: 410 435-0100
Fax: –
Web: www.ndm.edu

CEO: –
CFO: Deanna McCormick
HR: –
FYE: June 30
Type: Private

No, not that Notre Dame. Notre Dame of Maryland University (formerly College of Notre Dame of Maryland) is a four-year institution comprised of three divisions-Women's College, College of Adult Undergraduate Studies, and College of Graduate Studies. (The later two admit men.) As the first Catholic college for women in the US to award the four-year baccalaureate degree, Notre Dame of Maryland University provides roughly 30 undergraduate majors and 10 Weekend College degrees in fields including nursing, education, pharmacy, and arts and sciences. Notre Dame has nearly 3,000 students (of all faiths) and a student to teacher ratio of about 12:1. It was founded in 1895 by the School Sisters of Notre Dame.

	Annual Growth	06/18	06/19	06/20	06/21	06/22
Sales ($mil.)	13.4%	–	43.1	41.4	41.4	62.8
Net income ($ mil.)	–	–	(1.0)	(1.2)	(1.2)	5.4
Market value ($ mil.)	–	–	–	–	–	–
Employees	–	–	–	–	–	440

NOV INC
NYS: NOV

10353 Richmond Avenue
Houston, TX 77042-4103
Phone: 346 223-3000
Fax: –
Web: www.nov.com

CEO: Clay C Williams
CFO: Jose A Bayardo
HR: –
FYE: December 31
Type: Public

Founded in 1862, NOV provides equipment, technology, and services to the global energy industry. The company makes, distributes, and services oil and gas drilling equipment for land and offshore drilling rigs. Its mechanical components include jacking systems, assembly systems, fluid transfer technologies, pressure control equipment, power transmission systems, and control systems. NOV's extensive proprietary technology portfolio supports the industry's full-field drilling, completion, and production needs. NOV continues to develop and introduce technologies that further enhance the economics and efficiencies of energy production, with a focus on automation, predictive analytics, and condition-based maintenance. The US accounts for about 35% of sales.

	Annual Growth	12/19	12/20	12/21	12/22	12/23
Sales ($mil.)	0.3%	8,479.0	6,090.0	5,524.0	7,237.0	8,583.0
Net income ($ mil.)	–	(6,095.0)	(2,542.0)	(250.0)	155.0	993.0
Market value ($ mil.)	(5.1%)	9,868.3	5,408.9	5,338.0	8,229.5	7,989.2
Employees	(1.3%)	35,479	27,631	27,043	32,307	33,676

NOVA SOUTHEASTERN UNIVERSITY, INC.

3301 COLLEGE AVE
DAVIE, FL 333147796
Phone: 954 262-7300
Fax: –
Web: www.nova.edu

CEO: –
CFO: Alyson Silva
HR: Nora Quinlan
FYE: June 30
Type: Private

A dynamic, private research university, Northeast Southeastern University (NSU) is providing high-quality educational and research programs at the undergraduate, graduate, and professional degree levels. Established in 1964, the university includes some 15 colleges, the "theme park" for start-ups, scale-ups, and entrepreneurs, the Alan B. Levan | NSU Broward Center of Innovation, the 215,000-square-foot Center for Collaborative Research, the private PK1-12 grade University School, the world-class NSU Art Museum Fort Lauderdale, and the Alvin Sherman Library, Research and Information Technology Center, one of Florida's largest public libraries. NSU students learn at its campuses in Fort Lauderdale, Fort Myers, Jacksonville, Miami, Miramar, Orlando, Palm Beach, and Tampa, Florida, as well as San Juan, Puerto Rico, and online globally. With more than 22,945 students, NSU has a student-to-faculty ratio of 17:1.

	Annual Growth	06/14	06/15	06/20	06/21	06/22
Sales ($mil.)	3.8%	–	678.2	777.8	836.8	878.1
Net income ($ mil.)	5.6%	–	45.6	24.2	89.5	67.0
Market value ($ mil.)	–	–	–	–	–	–
Employees	–	–	–	–	–	2,500

NOVABAY PHARMACEUTICALS INC
ASE: NBY

2000 Powell Street, Suite 1150
Emeryville, CA 94608
Phone: 510 899-8800
Fax: –
Web: www.novabay.com

CEO: Justin M Hall
CFO: Tommy Law
HR: –
FYE: December 31
Type: Public

NovaBay Pharmaceuticals aims to keep the "bed bugs" away. The clinical-stage biopharmaceutical company develops antimicrobial compounds (known as Aganocide compounds) for the treatment and prevention of infections in hospital and non-hospital environments. Aganocide compounds destroy bacteria by attacking multiple sites, and aim to treat and prevent bacterial, fungal, and viral infections. The compounds are intended to prevent infections resulting from surgical or other hospital procedures, such as nasal surgery, urinary tract catheterization, and wound care, as well as for use on patients with infections of the eyes, ears, sinuses, or skin.

	Annual Growth	12/19	12/20	12/21	12/22	12/23
Sales ($mil.)	22.2%	6.6	9.9	8.4	14.4	14.7
Net income ($ mil.)	–	(9.7)	(11.0)	(5.8)	(10.6)	(9.6)
Market value ($ mil.)	(24.9%)	7.2	7.8	4.2	21.9	2.3
Employees	(1.8%)	28	25	31	33	26

NOVAGOLD RESOURCES INC.
ASE: NG

201 South Main Street, Suite 400
Salt Lake City, UT 84111
Phone: 801 639-0511
Fax: –
Web: –

CEO: –
CFO: –
HR: –
FYE: November 30
Type: Public

NovaGold Resources explores and develops gold and copper mineral properties in Alaska and Canada. Its main asset is the 50%-owned Donlin Gold project in Alaska with partner Barrick Gold. None of its mining operations are in production. During the first five years of full operation, the company expects Donlin Creek to produce average of 1.46 million ounces of gold annually and an average of 1.13 million ounces of gold per year over its projected mine life when its begins operation.

	Annual Growth	11/19	11/20	11/21	11/22	11/23
Sales ($mil.)	–	–	–	–	–	–
Net income ($ mil.)	–	(27.8)	(33.6)	(40.5)	(53.3)	(46.8)
Market value ($ mil.)	(11.9%)	2,326.4	3,329.1	2,256.2	1,928.6	1,403.8
Employees	–	–	12	13	14	13

NOVANT HEALTH, INC.

2085 FRONTIS PLAZA BLVD
WINSTON SALEM, NC 271035614
Phone: 336 277-1120
Fax: –
Web: www.novanthealth.org

CEO: Carl S Armato
CFO: Fred Hargett
HR: Vaso P Ekstein
FYE: December 31
Type: Private

Novant Health is an integrated system of physician practices, hospitals, outpatient centers, and more. Novant Health is a not-for-profit integrated system of around 15 medical centers and more than 1,800 physicians in more than 800 locations and numerous outpatient surgery centers, medical plazas, rehabilitations programs, diagnostic imaging centers and community health outreach programs. Movant provides medical services related to behavioral health, caner care, orthopedic care, and many more. The company was formed in 1997.

	Annual Growth	12/18	12/19	12/20	12/21	12/22
Sales ($mil.)	11.6%	–	5,434.9	5,682.8	7.4	7,552.1
Net income ($ mil.)	–	–	547.6	383.4	0.8	(214.9)
Market value ($ mil.)	–	–	–	–	–	–
Employees	–	–	–	–	–	13,800

NOVANTA INC
NMS: NOVT

125 Middlesex Turnpike
Bedford, MA 01730
Phone: 781 266-5700
Fax: 781 266-5114
Web: www.novanta.com

CEO: Matthijs Glastra
CFO: Robert J Buckley
HR: Charlene Bozzi
FYE: December 31
Type: Public

Novanta is a leading supplier of core technology solutions that uses its expertise in laser and motion control technologies to design and manufacture sets of products that are geared to the medical and healthcare and advanced industrial markets. Sealed CO2 lasers, ultrafast lasers, and optical light engines are sold primarily to the industrial and scientific markets. Novanta supplies lasers, optics, encoders, and air bearing spindles to the healthcare and medical markets, as well as OEM customers for high-precision cutting, trimming, marking, and measuring. The company changed its name to Novanta from GSI Group in 2016. International customers account for more than 55% of sales.

	Annual Growth	12/19	12/20	12/21	12/22	12/23
Sales ($mil.)	8.9%	626.1	590.6	706.8	860.9	881.7
Net income ($ mil.)	15.6%	40.8	44.5	50.3	74.1	72.9
Market value ($ mil.)	17.5%	3,167.4	4,233.9	6,315.1	4,866.0	6,031.4
Employees	6.1%	2,290	2,200	2,700	3,000	2,900

NOVARTIS PHARMACEUTICALS CORPORATION

1 HEALTH PLZ
EAST HANOVER, NJ 079361016
Phone: 862 778-8300
Fax: –
Web: www.novartis.com

CEO: –
CFO: Gary E Rosenthal
HR: –
FYE: December 31
Type: Private

As part of the Innovative Medicines Division of Swiss drug giant Novartis AG, Novartis Pharmaceuticals Corporation (NPC) helps with the development, manufacturing, marketing, and sales of its parent company's products in the US. Its product lines address a range of ailments including cardiovascular and respiratory diseases, central nervous system disorders, cancers, bone and skin conditions, infectious diseases, and organ transplant complications. NPC's key products include tumor growth inhibitor Gleevec, high blood pressure drug Diovan, and attention deficit disorder therapies Focalin and Ritalin. NPC markets its products through an in-house sales team.

	Annual Growth	12/11	12/12	12/13	12/15	12/16
Sales ($mil.)	(5.6%)	–	–	58,831	49,440	49,436
Net income ($ mil.)	(10.3%)	–	–	9,292.0	17,794	6,698.0
Market value ($ mil.)	–	–	–	–	–	–
Employees	–	–	–	–	–	7,000

NOVATION COMPANIES INC

9229 Ward Parkway, Suite 340
Kansas City, MO 64114
Phone: 816 237-7000
Fax: –
Web: www.novationcompanies.com

NBB: NOVC Q

CEO: –
CFO: –
HR: –
FYE: December 31
Type: Public

NovaStar Financial is forging a new life for itself -- one with as little to do with subprime mortgages as possible. The firm bought, originated, serviced, and securitized subprime mortgages until that sector experienced its own flameout. After exiting the lending business, NovaStar began investing in other businesses to reinvent itself. In 2008 it acquired a majority of StreetLinks National Appraisal, which provides property appraisals to residential mortgage lenders. The next year it bought a majority of Advent Financial Services, a startup firm that provides banking services to low- and moderate-income consumers. NovaStar bought 51% of mortgage banking software provider Corvisa in late 2010.

	Annual Growth	12/16	12/17	12/18	12/19	12/20
Sales ($mil.)	78.5%	5.1	28.0	55.1	63.5	51.4
Net income ($ mil.)	–	5.2	(10.9)	6.1	(10.2)	(9.2)
Market value ($ mil.)	1.3%	5.3	7.8	2.5	6.0	5.6
Employees	310.0%	5	1,999	2,269	1,620	1,413

NOVAVAX, INC.

21 Firstfield Road
Gaithersburg, MD 20878
Phone: 240 268-2000
Fax: –
Web: www.novavax.com

NMS: NVAX

CEO: John C Jacobs
CFO: James P Kelly
HR: –
FYE: December 31
Type: Public

Novavax is a biotechnology company that promotes improved health globally through the discovery, development, and commercialization of innovative vaccines to prevent serious infectious diseases. The company's proprietary recombinant technology platform harnesses the power and speed of genetic engineering to efficiently produce highly immunogenic nanoparticles designed to address urgent global health needs. Its vaccine candidates are genetically engineered nanostructures of conformationally correct recombinant proteins that mimic those found on natural pathogens. Additionally, the company is exploring a number of combination vaccine candidates including a COVID-Influenza combination vaccine currently in a Phase 2 clinical trial. These vaccine candidates incorporate its proprietary saponin-based Matrix-M adjuvant to enhance the immune response, stimulate higher levels of functional antibodies, and induce a cellular immune response.

	Annual Growth	12/19	12/20	12/21	12/22	12/23
Sales ($mil.)	169.4%	18.7	475.6	1,146.3	1,981.9	983.7
Net income ($ mil.)	–	(132.7)	(418.3)	(1,743.8)	(657.9)	(545.1)
Market value ($ mil.)	4.8%	555.2	15,556	19,959	1,434.1	669.6
Employees	–	165	791	1,541	1,992	–

NOVELIS ALR ALUMINUM HOLDINGS CORPORATION

3550 PEACHTREE RD NE
ATLANTA, GA 303261203
Phone: 216 910-3400
Fax: –
Web: www.novelis.com

CEO: –
CFO: –
HR: –
FYE: December 31
Type: Private

Aleris is a global leader in the manufacture of aluminum products. The company's rolled products unit supplies product to manufacturers in most major industries, but particularly the automotive, building and construction, transportation, and consumer durables industries. It has manufacturing sites in North America, Europe, and Asia that turn out almost 863,300 tons of finished product each year. Aleris diversified customer base includes a number of industry-leading companies such as Airbus, Audi, Boeing, Bombardier, Daimler, Embraer, Ford, General Motors and Volvo. More than 55% of Aleris' revenue comes from US. Aleris is majority owned by Oaktree Capital.

NOVELIS INC.

3550 PEACHTREE RD NE
ATLANTA, GA 303261203
Phone: 404 760-4000
Fax: –
Web: www.novelis.com

CEO: –
CFO: –
HR: –
FYE: March 31
Type: Private

Novelis is a global leader in the production of innovative aluminum products and solutions and world's largest recycler of aluminum. With operations and recycling facilities across the North and South Americas, Europe and Asia, the company mainly serves the automotive and beverage cans industry. Novelis' enviable breadth of customers include Ball and Ford. It is owned directly by AV Metals Inc., and indirectly by Hindalco Industries Limited of India. Nearly 40% of the company's sales came from its North America segment, around 40% of which were generated domestically.

NOVELSTEM INTERNATIONAL CORP

2255 Glades Road, Suite 221A
Boca Raton, FL 33431
Phone: 410 598-9024
Fax: –
Web: www.hollywoodmedia.com

NBB: NSTM

CEO: Mitchell Rubenstein
CFO: Tammy Hedge
HR: –
FYE: December 31
Type: Public

This company knows advertising drives the movie biz. Hollywood Media Corp. owns ad sales firm UK Theatres Online, which maintains plasma TVs in cinemas, hotels, theaters, and other venues in the UK and Ireland in exchange for the right to sell ads on the screens. In addition, the company's growing intellectual property division operates through 51%-owned Tekno Books and 50%-owned NetCo Partners. The business owns the rights to concepts by authors such as Tom Clancy and Isaac Asimov, developing them into movies, TV shows, software, and other merchandise. Hollywood Media also owns more than a quarter of MovieTickets.com. In 2010 it sold its theater ticketing division, which accounted for most of its business.

	Annual Growth	12/12	12/19	12/20	12/21	12/22
Sales ($mil.)	(32.6%)	0.6	0.0	0.0	0.0	0.0
Net income ($ mil.)	–	10.4	0.0	0.0	(1.4)	(0.8)
Market value ($ mil.)	(17.9%)	63.3	4.2	9.4	13.1	8.8
Employees	–	15	–	–	–	–

NPC RESTAURANT HOLDINGS, LLC

7300 W 129TH ST
OVERLAND PARK, KS 662132631
Phone: 913 327-5555
Fax: –
Web: www.npcinternational.com

CEO: James K Schwartz
CFO: Troy D Cook
HR: –
FYE: December 27
Type: Private

NPC International is the prince of pepperoni in a pizza empire. The world's largest franchisee of Pizza Hut restaurants, NPC owns and operates more than 1,275 pizza restaurants and delivery kitchens in about 30 states. The quick-service eateries, located mostly in such southern states as Alabama, Florida, Georgia, and Tennessee, serve a variety of pizza styles, as well as such items as buffalo wings and pasta. The pizza parlors are franchised from YUM! Brands, the world's largest fast-food restaurant company. NPC was founded in 1962 by former chairman Gene Bicknell, who was one of the first Pizza Hut franchisees. The company was acquired by private equity group NPC International Holdings in late 2011.

	Annual Growth	12/12	12/13	12/14	12/15	12/16
Sales ($mil.)	4.2%	–	1,094.0	1,179.9	1,223.3	1,236.6
Net income ($ mil.)	(33.5%)	–	29.7	1.7	6.7	8.7
Market value ($ mil.)	–	–	–	–	–	–
Employees	–	–	–	–	–	29,000

NRG ENERGY INC

NYS: NRG

910 Louisiana Street
Houston, TX 77002
Phone: 713 537-3000
Fax: –
Web: www.nrg.com

CEO: Lawrence S Coben
CFO: Bruce Chung
HR: –
FYE: December 31
Type: Public

NRG Energy is a consumer services company built on dynamic retail brands. NRG brings the power of energy to customers by producing and selling energy and related products and services, nation-wide in the US and Canada. NRG sells power, natural gas, and home and power services, and develops innovative, sustainable solutions, predominately under the brand names NRG, Reliant, Direct Energy, Green Mountain Energy, Stream, and XOOM Energy. The company owns and leases a diversified wholesale generation portfolio with approximately 16 GW of fossil fuel, nuclear and renewable generation capacity at 25 plants. Through a joint venture, NRG owns a 37.5% interest in Gladstone, a 1,613 MW coal-fueled power generation facility in Queensland, Australia.

	Annual Growth	12/19	12/20	12/21	12/22	12/23
Sales ($mil.)	30.9%	9,821.0	9,093.0	26,989	31,543	28,823
Net income ($ mil.)	–	4,438.0	510.0	2,187.0	1,221.0	(202.0)
Market value ($ mil.)	6.8%	8,273.2	7,815.3	8,966.3	6,622.7	10,760
Employees	41.1%	4,577	4,104	6,635	6,603	18,131

NRI, INC.

1820 JEFFERSON PL NW
WASHINGTON, DC 200362505
Phone: 202 466-4670
Fax: –
Web: www.nri-staffing.com

CEO: –
CFO: –
HR: –
FYE: September 30
Type: Private

If you're looking for a job in the US capital, give NRI a call. The company works with employers in the Washington, DC, and Baltimore metro areas to fill temporary, contract, temp-to-hire, and permanent positions. It specializes in the areas of accounting and finance; office support, administration, and call center; health care; and legal support. In addition to staffing services, NRI also offers training courses and workshops in hiring, leadership, and interviewing skills. NRI, which was founded by Les Meil in 1967, has about a dozen offices throughout the Washington, DC and Baltimore metro areas.

	Annual Growth	09/13	09/14	09/15	09/16	09/17
Sales ($mil.)	(5.9%)	–	–	9.5	8.8	8.4
Net income ($ mil.)	(80.6%)	–	–	0.3	0.2	0.0
Market value ($ mil.)	–	–	–	–	–	–
Employees	–	–	–	–	–	200

NSTAR ELECTRIC CO

NBB: NSAR O

800 Boylston Street
Boston, MA 02199
Phone: 800 286-5000
Fax: –
Web: www.nstar.com

CEO: Leon J Olivier
CFO: Philip J Lembo
HR: –
FYE: December 31
Type: Public

NSTAR Electric plays a starring role in bringing electric power to Boston. The NSTAR company's electric transmission and distribution utility serves 1.1 million residential, commercial, and industrial customers in Beantown and about 80 surrounding communities (including Cambridge, New Bedford, and Plymouth). NSTAR Electric also sells wholesale power to municipal utilities in the area, and it provides standard offer and default supply services to retail customers who choose not to purchase energy from competitive suppliers in the state's deregulated power market. Subsidiary Harbor Electric Energy distributes power to a Massachusetts Water Resources Authority wastewater treatment facility in Boston.

	Annual Growth	12/19	12/20	12/21	12/22	12/23
Sales ($mil.)	3.7%	3,044.6	2,941.1	3,056.4	3,583.1	3,515.5
Net income ($ mil.)	6.0%	432.0	445.0	476.6	492.4	544.5
Market value ($ mil.)	(6.6%)	0.0	0.0	0.0	0.0	0.0
Employees	(1.2%)	1,604	1,611	1,599	1,648	1,529

NTELOS HOLDINGS CORP.

1160 SHENANDOAH VILLAGE DR
WAYNESBORO, VA 229809253
Phone: 540 946-3500
Fax: –
Web: –

CEO: Christopher French
CFO: Adele Skolits
HR: –
FYE: December 31
Type: Private

NTELOS has provided wireless phone service to more than 300,000 subscribers in Virginia and West Virginia and in portions of Maryland, North Carolina, Ohio, Kentucky, and Pennsylvania. Wireless operations include its FRAWG and nTelos-branded retail business, as well as a wholesale business it operates under a contract with Sprint. In 2015 the company had more than 1,000 cell sites in operation. Its NTELOS-branded retail operations sells products and services via direct and indirect distribution channels, and provides network access to other telecommunications carriers, most notably through an arrangement with Sprint. The company's acquisition by Shenandoah Telecommunications Co. for $640 million is expected to close by June 2016.

NTS REALTY HOLDINGS LIMITED PARTNERSHIP

500 N HURSTBOURNE PKWY
LOUISVILLE, KY 402225399
Phone: 502 426-4800
Fax: –
Web: www.ntsdevelopment.com

CEO: Brian F Lavin
CFO: Gregory A Wells
HR: –
FYE: December 31
Type: Private

NTS Realty Holdings invests in, develops, and manages commercial real estate in the Southeast and Midwest. The company's portfolio includes some 25 properties, including about 15 dozen apartment communities, about a half-dozen office centers, and three retail properties in Kentucky, Florida, Indiana, Tennessee, Virginia, and Georgia. Chairman J.D. Nichols owns about 60% of NTS Realty Holdings; he and president Brian Lavin control the company's managing general partner, NTS Realty Capital. The firm's properties are managed by NTS Development Company, an affiliate of NTS Realty Capital. Established in 2004, NTS Realty Holdings is the result of the merger of several property companies and partnerships.

NU SKIN ENTERPRISES, INC.   NYS: NUS

75 West Center Street
Provo, UT 84601
Phone: 801 345-1000
Fax: –
Web: www.nuskin.com

CEO: –
CFO: –
HR: –
FYE: December 31
Type: Public

Nu Skin Enterprises develops and distributes a comprehensive line of premium-quality beauty and wellness solutions such as ageLOC Spa systems and its ageLOC LumiSpa skin treatment and cleansing device. Most of the company's sales are dominated by its brands, Nu Skin, Pharmanex, and ageLOC. Nu Skin has its foot in the door in about 50 global markets, including China. Its subsidiary, Pharmanex, sells LifePak nutritional supplements. In addition, the company has its ageLOC Youth nutritional supplement and ageLOC Me customized skin care system to its markets. Nu Skin was founded in 1984. The US is one of its largest markets, accounting for about 25% of the company's revenues.

	Annual Growth	12/19	12/20	12/21	12/22	12/23
Sales ($mil.)	(5.0%)	2,420.4	2,581.9	2,695.7	2,225.7	1,969.1
Net income ($ mil.)	(52.8%)	173.6	191.4	147.3	104.8	8.6
Market value ($ mil.)	(17.0%)	2,028.5	2,704.2	2,512.1	2,086.9	961.3
Employees	(6.8%)	4,900	5,000	4,600	3,800	3,700

NUCLEAR FUEL SERVICES, INC.

1205 BANNER HILL RD
ERWIN, TN 376509318
Phone: 423 743-9141
Fax: –
Web: www.bwxt.com

CEO: –
CFO: –
HR: –
FYE: December 31
Type: Private

If you've got some excess nuclear warheads just lying around taking up space, you might want to give Nuclear Fuel Services (NFS) a call. The company has a long history of converting swords into plowshares, or in this case, nuclear weapons into nuclear fuel. It converts weapons-grade highly enriched uranium to low-enriched uranium that can be used as fuel for nuclear power plants. NFS also provides decontamination, decommissioning, and remediation of nuclear sites, as well as packaging and shipping of nuclear materials. The company was acquired by Babcock & Wilcox (renamed BWX Technologies) in 2008 for almost $160 million.

NUCOR CORP.   NYS: NUE

1915 Rexford Road
Charlotte, NC 28211
Phone: 704 366-7000
Fax: 704 362-4208
Web: www.nucor.com

CEO: Leon J Topalian
CFO: Stephen D Laxton
HR: –
FYE: December 31
Type: Public

Nucor Corporation is a leading manufacturer, trader, and seller of steel and steel products in the US. It is also North America's largest recycler of scrap metal and a leading scrap broker. The company produces rolled sheets, bars, and beams used in the energy, automotive, transportation, and heavy equipment industries. Its other steel products, including steel joists, electrical conduits, and metal building systems, are sold to fabricators, distributors, and metal manufacturers. Subsidiary Harris Steel fabricates rebar for highways and bridges and other construction projects. Another unit, the David J. Joseph Company, processes and brokers metals, pig iron, hot briquetted iron, and direct reduced iron (DRI).

	Annual Growth	12/19	12/20	12/21	12/22	12/23
Sales ($mil.)	11.3%	22,589	20,140	36,484	41,512	34,714
Net income ($ mil.)	37.4%	1,271.1	721.5	6,827.5	7,607.3	4,524.8
Market value ($ mil.)	32.6%	13,783	13,026	27,956	32,281	42,623
Employees	4.5%	26,800	26,400	28,800	31,400	32,000

NUESKE'S MEAT PRODUCTS, INC.

203 N GENESEE ST
WITTENBERG, WI 544999154
Phone: 715 253-4000
Fax: –
Web: www.nueskes.com

CEO: –
CFO: Mary White
HR: Kerry Rocole
FYE: December 31
Type: Private

Aaahhhh ... Bacon ... Now that we have your attention, you'll want to know that Nueske's Meat Products slow-smokes pork bellies over applewood for 24 hours to make a bacon that's in hot demand. The company also produces hams, sausage, poultry, and other food products, which it sells to foodservice and retail food customers. Nueske's meats and specialty gift foods are also available directly to consumers through its mail order catalog and website. R.C. Nueske began using his family's Old World recipes to market meats to Wisconsin customers in 1933. The company distributes its products both nationally and internationally.

	Annual Growth	12/03	12/04	12/05	12/06	12/09
Sales ($mil.)	3.1%	–	–	21.7	22.3	24.6
Net income ($ mil.)	23.7%	–	–	0.4	0.4	0.9
Market value ($ mil.)	–	–	–	–	–	–
Employees	–	–	–	–	–	140

NUMEREX CORP.

400 INTERSTATE NORTH PKWY SE STE 1350
ATLANTA, GA 303395017
Phone: 770 693-5950
Fax: –
Web: www.sierrawireless.com

CEO: –
CFO: Kenneth L Gayron
HR: –
FYE: December 31
Type: Private

Numerex provides machine-to-machine (M2M) products and services. M2M consists of using a device (sensor or meter) to capture an event (location or environmental status) relayed through a network (wireless, wireline, or hybrid) to an application that translates the data into actionable information. Through its cloud-based service development platform called Numerex FAST, the company aids companies and government entities with monitoring, measuring, and managing their assets. Numerex's combined network services, hardware, and application development capabilities are targeted at various market segments, including energy, security, financial services, health care, and supply chain. In 2017 the company agreed to be bought by Sierra Wireless for about $107 million.

NUO THERAPEUTICS INC   NBB: AURX

8285 El Rio, Suite 190
Houston, TX 77054
Phone: 346 396-4770
Fax: –
Web: www.nuot.com

CEO: David E Jorden
CFO: David E Jorden
HR: –
FYE: December 31
Type: Public

Here's a concept -- using the body's own faculties to heal wounds. Nuo Therapeutics has developed and markets an autologous platelet therapy, which uses a patient's own blood plasma to promote healing. Its AutoloGel System includes a centrifuge and blood draw kit. The centrifuge is used to separate key blood components, including platelets and growth factors, which are then combined with reagents to make a topical gel. When applied to a wound, the gel spurs the body's own healing process. AutoloGel has received FDA approval to treat chronic exuding wounds such as diabetic ulcers. Other products in Nuo's pipeline include an anti-inflammatory peptide that may help treat such diseases as rheumatoid arthritis.

	Annual Growth	12/18	12/19	12/20	12/21	12/22
Sales ($mil.)	(46.5%)	1.4	0.1	–	–	0.1
Net income ($ mil.)	–	(1.5)	(1.2)	(0.1)	(0.1)	(3.2)
Market value ($ mil.)	147.5%	1.7	5.0	18.8	0.0	62.7
Employees	9.3%	7	–	–	5	10

NURX PHARMACEUTICALS, INC.

c/o Aubade Creative, 501 Santa Monica Boulevard, Suite 600
Santa Monica, CA 90401
Phone: 310 526-3227
Fax: –
Web: www.nurxpharmaceuticals.com

CEO: –
CFO: –
HR: –
FYE: September 30
Type: Public

NuRx Pharmaceuticals is promoting a sleek biotechnology development image. Its research and development programs focus on compounds that target oncology, metabolic, and immune system disorders. Its main product candidates aim to treat acute leukemia and lung, breast, and other cancers. The company is also developing treatments for health conditions associated with chemotherapy. In 2010 the company agreed to be acquired by QuantRx Biomedical, a developer of products for advanced diagnosis of serious disease and health conditions. The two companies made the move to expand their presence in the point-of-care diagnostics market.

NUSTAR ENERGY LP

NYS: NS

19003 IH-10 West
San Antonio, TX 78257
Phone: 210 918-2000
Fax: –
Web: www.nustarenergy.com

CEO: Bradley C Barron
CFO: Thomas R Shoaf
HR: Jessica Alvarado
FYE: December 31
Type: Public

NuStar Energy is one of the largest independent pipeline and liquid terminal operators in the US. NuStar currently has approximately 9,500 miles of pipeline and nearly 65 terminal and storage facilities that store and distribute crude oil, refined products, renewable fuels, ammonia, and specialty liquids. Nustar also purchases petroleum products for resale. Its petroleum products consist of gasoline, bunker fuel, and other petroleum products. Materials and supplies mainly consist of blending and additive chemicals and maintenance materials used in its pipeline and storage segments. Overall, NuStar has approximately 49 million barrels of storage capacity at its terminals. The company, which generates almost all of its revenue in the US, also has operations in Mexico.

	Annual Growth	12/19	12/20	12/21	12/22	12/23
Sales ($mil.)	2.2%	1,498.0	1,481.6	1,618.5	1,683.2	1,634.2
Net income ($ mil.)	–	(105.7)	(199.0)	38.2	222.7	273.7
Market value ($ mil.)	(7.8%)	3,270.5	1,823.1	2,009.1	2,024.3	2,363.3
Employees	(4.8%)	1,441	1,408	1,267	1,167	1,184

NUSTAR GP HOLDINGS, LLC

19003 W INTERSTATE 10
SAN ANTONIO, TX 782579518
Phone: 210 918-2311
Fax: –
Web: www.nustargpholdings.com

CEO: Bradley C Barron
CFO: Thomas R Shoaf
HR: –
FYE: December 31
Type: Private

NuStar GP Holdings owns a 2% general-partner interest and a 17% limited-partner interest in NuStar Energy, which operates terminals and petroleum-liquids pipeline systems, primarily in the US. NuStar Energy has 7,480 miles of refined product and ammonia pipelines, 940 miles of crude oil pipelines, 96 refined product terminal facilities, a crude oil storage facility, and two asphalt refineries. It also has terminals in Canada, Mexico, the Netherlands, Turkey, and the UK. Valero GP Holdings was controlled by Valero Energy. Following Valero GP Holdings' 2006 IPO, Valero Energy sold its interest in both Valero L.P. and Valero GP Holdings. In 2007 Valero GP Holdings changed its name to NuStar GP Holdings, LLC.

NUTANIX INC

NMS: NTNX

1740 Technology Drive, Suite 150
San Jose, CA 95110
Phone: 408 216-8360
Fax: –
Web: www.nutanix.com

CEO: –
CFO: –
HR: –
FYE: July 31
Type: Public

Nutanix's software products provide a hyperconverged infrastructure (HCI) that unifies traditional network servers and storage systems running on a variety of underlying hardware platforms into one integrated platform that can be connected to public cloud services. Its flagship Acropolis product provides network virtualization and storage services including automation of common network operations. Nutanix also offers its Prism network management dashboard and Acropolis Hypervisor (AHV) designed to run all virtualized applications throughout the enterprise. The company was founded in 2009. The US generates about 55% of the company's revenue.

	Annual Growth	07/19	07/20	07/21	07/22	07/23
Sales ($mil.)	10.8%	1,236.1	1,307.7	1,394.4	1,580.8	1,862.9
Net income ($ mil.)	–	(621.2)	(872.9)	(1,034.3)	(797.5)	(254.6)
Market value ($ mil.)	7.4%	5,439.1	5,316.9	8,630.6	3,625.3	7,236.1
Employees	4.8%	5,340	6,170	6,080	6,450	6,450

NUTRA PHARMA CORP

NBB: NPHC

1537 NW 65th Avenue
Plantation, FL 33313
Phone: 954 509-0911
Fax: –
Web: www.nutrapharma.com

CEO: Rik J Deitsch
CFO: –
HR: –
FYE: December 31
Type: Public

Nutra Pharma is a biotechnology holding company active in several areas. The company's ReceptoPharm subsidiary holds a pipeline of drug candidates that may eventually treat HIV/AIDS, rabies, and other viral and neurological diseases as well as pain. Another subsidiary, NanoLogix, develops diagnostic test kits to identify infectious diseases, while its Designer Diagnostics subsidiary markets and sells the test kits. One product in development as a possible therapy for MS was based upon cobra venom. That product was then reformulated and launched commercially as an over-the-counter topical analgesic for chronic pain, under the brand name Cobroxin.

	Annual Growth	12/17	12/18	12/19	12/20	12/21
Sales ($mil.)	(5.2%)	0.1	0.1	0.1	0.0	0.0
Net income ($ mil.)	–	(4.0)	(3.9)	(6.6)	(0.8)	(13.1)
Market value ($ mil.)	30.0%	5.1	2.2	3.7	8.8	14.7
Employees	–	4	4	4	4	4

NUTRACEUTICAL INTERNATIONAL CORPORATION

222 S MAIN ST 16TH FL
SALT LAKE CITY, UT 841012174
Phone: 435 655-6000
Fax: –
Web: www.nutraceutical.com

CEO: Monty Sharma
CFO: Cory J McQueen
HR: –
FYE: September 30
Type: Private

Nutraceutical International delivers the only complete wellness from vitamin-A to Zinc Oxide and owns the entire development process for all of its products from sourcing to distribution. Its branded products include such names as KAL, Herbs for Kids, Nature's Life, Solaray, Sunny Green, and Thompson. The company markets its brands in more than 65 countries worldwide. With a comprehensive portfolio of around 35 brands, Nutraceutical International also publishes natural health books under the Woodland name. The company traces its roots back in 1932.

NUTRISYSTEM, INC.

600 OFFICE CENTER DR
FORT WASHINGTON, PA 190343278
Phone: 215 706-5300
Fax: –
Web: www.nutrisystem.com

CEO: Dawn M Zier
CFO: Michael P Monahan
HR: –
FYE: December 31
Type: Private

Nutrisystem is a leader in the weight loss industry, having helped millions of people lose weight for nearly 50 years. It sells prepared meals and grocery items that are delivered directly to US consumers. With up to more than 150 menu choices, the company offers a variety of breakfasts, lunches, dinners, and snacks made with real, quality ingredients. It also offers individualized calorie plans, one-on-one diet counseling, behavior modification, and exercise education and maintenance plans. Nutrisystem meals and snacks, along with fresh grocery additions, deliver a nutritionally balanced meal plan that provides customers the flexibility to align their diet with the US Healthy Eating Meal Pattern, as recommended by the USDA Dietary Guidelines.

NUTRITION MANAGEMENT SERVICES CO.   NBB: NMSC A

Box 725 Kimberton Road
Kimberton, PA 19442
Phone: 610 935-2050
Fax: –
Web: www.nmsc.com

CEO: –
CFO: –
HR: –
FYE: June 30
Type: Public

Nutrition Management Services is a regional foodservices operator that provides retirement communities, hospitals, and other health care facilities with food management services. It offers supervision of dietary operations through onsite management, cost and quality controls, and dietary staff training. In addition, the company operates a conference center and banquet facility used for training. Chairman and CEO Joseph Roberts controls nearly 75% of Nutrition Management Services.

	Annual Growth	06/05	06/06	06/07	06/08	06/09
Sales ($mil.)	(6.9%)	26.6	23.4	20.9	20.9	20.0
Net income ($ mil.)	(42.4%)	0.8	(0.8)	(0.8)	(0.4)	0.0
Market value ($ mil.)	(43.8%)	1.1	1.2	1.3	0.7	0.1
Employees	(4.9%)	354	250	269	323	289

NUVERA COMMUNICATIONS INC   NBB: NUVR

27 North Minnesota Street
New Ulm, MN 56073
Phone: 507 354-4111
Fax: –
Web: www.nuvera.net

CEO: Glenn Zerbe
CFO: Curtis O Kawlewski
HR: –
FYE: December 31
Type: Public

New Ulm Telecom operates three incumbent local-exchange carriers (ILECs) serving southern Minnesota and northern Iowa: an ILEC serving New Ulm, Minnesota, and surrounding communities; subsidiary Western Telephone, operating in the Springfield, Minnesota, area; and Peoples Telephone, serving portions of Cherokee and Buena Vista counties in Iowa. Operating under the common NU-Telecom brand, they make up New Ulm's Telecom Segment and provide traditional phone services, such as local exchange access and long-distance, as well as cable TV and Internet access. The company's Phonery division provides customer premise equipment (CPE), offers transport services, and resells long distance toll services.

	Annual Growth	12/19	12/20	12/21	12/22	12/23
Sales ($mil.)	0.3%	64.9	64.9	65.8	65.7	65.8
Net income ($ mil.)	–	8.3	9.8	12.3	7.2	(3.2)
Market value ($ mil.)	(14.7%)	97.5	99.1	107.8	89.8	51.6
Employees	–	187	204	213	213	–

NUWARE TECH CORP.

100 WOOD AVE S STE 105
ISELIN, NJ 088302716
Phone: 732 494-0550
Fax: –
Web: www.nuware.com

CEO: –
CFO: –
HR: –
FYE: December 31
Type: Private

Nuware Technology hopes to provide you with a new way of looking at technology. The company provides information technology consulting and software services, including software design and implementation, systems integration, network design, and consulting. Nuware's clients come from a variety of industries and have included Dun & Bradstreet and Merrill Lynch.

	Annual Growth	12/10	12/11	12/12	12/13	12/14
Sales ($mil.)	(2.7%)	–	17.0	16.4	16.4	15.7
Net income ($ mil.)	(26.2%)	–	1.2	0.6	0.9	0.5
Market value ($ mil.)	–	–	–	–	–	–
Employees	–	–	–	–	–	100

NV5 GLOBAL INC   NAS: NVEE

200 South Park Road, Suite 350
Hollywood, FL 33021
Phone: 954 495-2112
Fax: –
Web: www.nv5.com

CEO: Dickerson Wright
CFO: Edward H Codispoti
HR: –
FYE: December 30
Type: Public

NV5 Global is a provider of professional and technical engineering and consulting solutions to public and private sector clients in the infrastructure, utility services, construction, real estate, and environmental markets, operating nationwide and abroad. The company's clients include the US Federal, state and local governments, and the private sector. NV5's projects include Boston Logan Airport, Bronx Zoo Astor Court Reconstruction, Dallas Fort Worth International Airport, Manhattan Waterfront Greenway Improvement and Atrium Health, among others. NV5 originally operated as Nolte Associates, Inc. in California prior to its acquisition in 2010. NV5 went public in 2013.

	Annual Growth	12/19*	01/21	01/22*	12/22	12/23
Sales ($mil.)	14.1%	508.9	659.3	706.7	786.8	861.7
Net income ($ mil.)	17.1%	23.8	21.0	47.1	50.0	44.6
Market value ($ mil.)	23.2%	767.9	1,252.2	2,195.5	2,103.3	1,766.3
Employees	3.2%	3,362	3,197	3,428	3,644	3,813

*Fiscal year change

NVE CORP   NAS: NVEC

11409 Valley View Road
Eden Prairie, MN 55344
Phone: 952 829-9217
Fax: –
Web: www.nve.com

CEO: Daniel A Baker
CFO: Curt A Reynders
HR: –
FYE: March 31
Type: Public

NVE is definitely a spin zone, and one with a certain magnetism. The company develops sensors incorporating spintronic (short for spin-based electronic) materials called giant magnetoresistors (GMR). Spintronics differ from conventional electronics in that they use the spin -- rather than the charge -- of electrons to store and transmit data. The company's sensors are used in consumer electronics, automotive, biosensors, factory automation applications, robotics and mechanisms, and medical devices. In addition to analog and digital GMR sensors, NVE offers couplers, and magnetic random-access memory (MRAM). Customers include Abbott Laboratories and Sonova AG.

	Annual Growth	03/19	03/20	03/21	03/22	03/23
Sales ($mil.)	9.6%	26.5	25.4	21.4	27.0	38.3
Net income ($ mil.)	11.8%	14.5	14.5	11.7	14.5	22.7
Market value ($ mil.)	(4.0%)	472.9	251.3	338.6	263.1	400.9
Employees	3.9%	48	46	44	49	56

NVIDIA CORP

NMS: NVDA

2788 San Tomas Expressway
Santa Clara, CA 95051
Phone: 408 486-2000
Fax: –
Web: www.nvidia.com

CEO: Jen-Hsun Huang
CFO: Colette M Kress
HR: –
FYE: January 28
Type: Public

NVIDIA pioneered accelerated computing to help solve the most challenging computational problems. The company's graphics processing units (GPUs) were initially used to simulate human imagination, enabling the virtual worlds of video games and films. NVIDIA has leveraged its GPU architecture to create platforms for scientific computing, artificial intelligence, data science, autonomous vehicles, robotics, metaverse, and 3D internet applications. NVIDIA's GPU brands are GeForce for games, Quadro/NVIDIA RTX GPUs for enterprise workstation graphics, and virtual GPU, for cloud-based visual and virtual computing. The company generates about 30% of the total revenue from the US.

	Annual Growth	01/20	01/21	01/22	01/23	01/24
Sales ($mil.)	53.7%	10,918	16,675	26,914	26,974	60,922
Net income ($ mil.)	80.6%	2,796.0	4,332.0	9,752.0	4,368.0	29,760
Market value ($ mil.)	24.9%	617,183	1,280,270	562,778	501,794	1,503,804
Employees	21.1%	13,775	18,975	22,473	26,196	29,600

NVR INC.

NYS: NVR

11700 Plaza America Drive, Suite 500
Reston, VA 20190
Phone: 703 956-4000
Fax: –
Web: www.nvrinc.com

CEO: Eugene J Bredow
CFO: Daniel D Malzahn
HR: –
FYE: December 31
Type: Public

NVR builds single-family detached homes, townhomes, and condominiums? mainly for first-time and move-up buyers?primarily in the eastern US. NVR's houses range in size from 1,000 to 10,000 finished square feet and sell for an average price of around $403,900. The company's brands include Ryan Homes, Heartland Homes, and NVHomes. Its largest market is the Washington, DC which accounts for over 20% of sales. Its subsidiary NVR Mortgage Finance offers mortgage and title services. The builder was founded in 1980 as NVHomes.

	Annual Growth	12/19	12/20	12/21	12/22	12/23
Sales ($mil.)	6.9%	7,428.4	7,566.0	8,970.1	10,580	9,687.3
Net income ($ mil.)	16.0%	878.5	901.2	1,236.7	1,725.6	1,591.6
Market value ($ mil.)	16.4%	12,167	13,035	18,878	14,737	22,366
Employees	2.5%	5,700	6,100	6,600	6,550	6,300

NYACK COLLEGE

2 WASHINGTON ST
NEW YORK, NY 100041017
Phone: 845 675-7498
Fax: –
Web: www.allianceu.edu

CEO: –
CFO: David C Jennings
HR: Karen Davie
FYE: June 30
Type: Private

Nyack College is a Christian liberal arts college of the Christian and Missionary Alliance. The college has more than 3,000 undergraduate and graduate students, many of whom are enrolled at its main campus in Nyack, New York. The university has an additional campus in New York City, and it offers theology programs on several campuses of the Alliance Theological Seminary, a fellow affiliate of the Christian and Missionary Alliance. (In 2018 Nyack College announced plans to shutter its Nyack campus and operate primarily from its campus in Manhattan.) Other fields of study include arts, sciences, counseling, music, business, nursing, and adult education. Nyack College was founded in New York City in 1882 as the Missionary Training Institute, the first Bible college in America, by missionary Dr. A.B. Simpson.

	Annual Growth	06/15	06/16	06/17	06/20	06/22
Sales ($mil.)	(3.5%)	–	54.0	52.9	40.0	43.6
Net income ($ mil.)	–	–	(8.3)	(6.1)	(12.2)	(9.7)
Market value ($ mil.)	–	–	–	–	–	–
Employees	–	–	–	–	–	300

O'BRIEN & GERE LIMITED

333 W WASHINGTON ST STE 400
SYRACUSE, NY 132029203
Phone: 315 956-6100
Fax: –
Web: www.obg.com

CEO: James A Fox
CFO: Joseph M McNulty
HR: –
FYE: December 26
Type: Private

O'Brien & Gere provides a range of engineering consulting and project management services throughout the US, including wastewater management and water resources, environmental compliance and remediation, civil and facilities engineering, and utility services. It also provides contract operations and maintenance. Employee-owned O'Brien & Gere serves municipal, environmental, manufacturing, and federal clients. The company, which employs hundreds of scientists, engineers, construction, and other personnel, operates nearly 30 offices in about a dozen states.

	Annual Growth	12/04	12/05	12/06	12/11	12/15
Sales ($mil.)	4.7%	–	–	125.4	188.0	189.2
Net income ($ mil.)	9.7%	–	–	1.4	2.8	3.2
Market value ($ mil.)	–	–	–	–	–	–
Employees	–	–	–	–	–	800

O'NEAL STEEL, LLC

744 41ST ST N
BIRMINGHAM, AL 352221124
Phone: 205 599-8000
Fax: –
Web: www.onealsteel.com

CEO: Stephen Armstrong
CFO: Suzanne Lane
HR: Carol Thornburg
FYE: December 31
Type: Private

O'Neal Steel is one of the US' leading metals service companies. The company sells a full range of metal products ? including angles, bars, beams, coil, pipe, plate, and sheet ? made from aluminum, stainless steel, carbon steel, hot rolled, and cold finished steel. It also offers such metal-processing services as forming, laser cutting, shearing, plasma cutting, metal forming, and sawing. Primarily serving customers in the metal industry, the company is part of the O'Neal Industries. Together, its affiliates ? G&L Tube, Leeco Steel, O'Neal Manufacturing Services, Stainless Tubular Products, Slice of Stainless, TW Metals, and United Performance Metals ? represent the US' largest family-owned network of metals service centers and component and tube manufacturing businesses.

O'NEIL INDUSTRIES, INC.

1245 W WASHINGTON BLVD
CHICAGO, IL 606071929
Phone: 773 755-1611
Fax: –
Web: –

CEO: Brian Ramsay
CFO: –
HR: –
FYE: December 31
Type: Private

A family of construction companies, O'Neil Industries has also built W.E. O'Neil Construction Company. The employee-owned company operates in Arizona, California, Colorado, and Illinois, providing general contracting, construction management, design/build, and structural concrete services for commercial projects in the US and Canada. O'Neil Industries has worked on corporate offices, manufacturing and distribution facilities, and mixed-use centers for clients in the education, gaming, health care, hospitality, and retail industries. The company also serves the residential and senior living sectors. Clients have included Boeing, DePaul University, and The Nature Conservancy.

O'REILLY AUTOMOTIVE, INC.   NMS: ORLY

233 South Patterson Avenue
Springfield, MO 65802
Phone: 417 862-6708
Fax: –
Web: www.oreillyauto.com

CEO: –
CFO: –
HR: –
FYE: December 31
Type: Public

O'Reilly Automotive is one of the largest specialty retailers of automotive aftermarket parts, tools, supplies, equipment, and accessories in the US, selling its products to both do-it-yourself (DIY) and professional service provider customers, its "dual market strategy". It also offers a range of enhanced services and programs, including oil and battery recycling, battery testing, custom hydraulic hoses, loaner tool program, paint mixing, tool rental, drum and rotor resurfacing, electric and module testing, battery, wiper, and bulb replacement, and check engine light code extraction. O'Reilly operates through a fast-growing network of almost 5,930 stores across the US, and some 40 stores in Mexico.

	Annual Growth	12/19	12/20	12/21	12/22	12/23
Sales ($mil.)	11.7%	10,150	11,604	13,328	14,410	15,812
Net income ($ mil.)	14.0%	1,391.0	1,752.3	2,164.7	2,172.7	2,346.6
Market value ($ mil.)	21.3%	25,889	26,735	41,719	49,859	56,124
Employees	2.4%	82,167	77,827	83,636	87,745	90,302

O'REILLY MEDIA, INC.

1005 GRAVENSTEIN HWY N
SEBASTOPOL, CA 954722811
Phone: 707 827-7000
Fax: –
Web: www.oreilly.com

CEO: –
CFO: Maria Manrique
HR: –
FYE: December 31
Type: Private

O'Reilly Media aims to be an advocate for computer professionals. The company publishes technology books (including its iconic "animal books" for software developers, featuring illustrations of animals on the cover), and produces technical conferences, websites, and magazines. It also provides research services and software. Topics covered include UNIX, Java, Windows, Apple and Mac, and a slew of other operating systems and Internet programming languages. O'Reilly Media also has books devoted to topics in business and culture. Its events include the O'Reilly Open Source Convention and the Maker Faire. Owner Tim O'Reilly founded the company as a technical writing firm in 1978.

O-I GLASS INC   NYS: OI

One Michael Owens Way
Perrysburg, OH 43551
Phone: 567 336-5000
Fax: –
Web: www.o-i.com

CEO: –
CFO: –
HR: –
FYE: December 31
Type: Public

O-I Glass, Inc. (O-I Glass), through its subsidiaries, is the successor to a business established in 1903. The Company is a manufacturer of glass containers in the world with over 70 plants in around 20 countries. It competes in the glass container segment of the rigid packaging market and is one of the leading glass container manufacturer in most of the countries where it has manufacturing facilities. In late 2019, the Company implemented the Corporate Modernization pursuant to the Agreement and Plan of Merger, among O-I (Owens-Illinois, Inc.), O-I Glass and Paddock Enterprises, LLC. O-I Glass' revenues are mostly generated domestically.

	Annual Growth	12/18	12/19	12/20	12/21	12/22
Sales ($mil.)	(0.1%)	6,877.0	6,691.0	6,091.0	6,357.0	6,856.0
Net income ($ mil.)	22.8%	257.0	(400.0)	249.0	149.0	584.0
Market value ($ mil.)	(1.0%)	2,666.8	1,845.4	1,840.8	1,860.9	2,563.2
Employees	(2.4%)	26,500	27,500	25,000	24,000	24,000

O. C. TANNER COMPANY

1930 S STATE ST
SALT LAKE CITY, UT 841152311
Phone: 801 486-2430
Fax: –
Web: www.octanner.com

CEO: David Petersen
CFO: Scott Archibald
HR: Denise Page
FYE: December 31
Type: Private

O.C. Tanner recognizes that it's nice to be appreciated. The company designs and helps implement employee recognition programs for customers around the world. Related services, intended to help customers take full advantage of their investment in employee recognition, include communication, consulting, research, leadership training, and social programs. The company, which operates from offices in the US, Canada, and the UK, has shipped awards to clients in about 150 countries. Over the years O.C. Tanner has counted numerous Fortune 100 companies among its clients.

	Annual Growth	12/12	12/13	12/14	12/16	12/17
Sales ($mil.)	(0.2%)	–	–	344.1	351.2	342.0
Net income ($ mil.)	(20.9%)	–	–	19.4	16.8	9.6
Market value ($ mil.)	–	–	–	–	–	–
Employees	–	–	–	–	–	1,700

O.P.E.N. AMERICA, INC.

4742 N 24TH ST STE 450
PHOENIX, AZ 850164856
Phone: 602 224-0440
Fax: –
Web: www.openworksweb.com

CEO: Shahrouz Zayanderoudi
CFO: Howard Sckolnik
HR: –
FYE: December 31
Type: Private

OpenWorks closes the door on dirt. The company specialized in delivering high quality commercial cleaning, disinfection, and integrated facilities services. It has regional support centers throughout the United States. Services include general cleaning, floor care, handyman and maintenance repairs, pest control, and plumbing. OpenWorks now boasts over 660 franchisees and has more than 20 regional offices and a network of more than 1,500 elite service providers. It serves education, financial, healthcare and hospitality industries. The clients are Lockheed Martin and Spear Education. OpenWorks was founded in 1983 by CEO Eric Roudi and is headquartered in Arizona.

	Annual Growth	12/03	12/04	12/05	12/06	12/07
Sales ($mil.)	0.3%	–	23.7	24.0	23.8	23.9
Net income ($ mil.)	53.6%	–	0.3	1.0	0.9	1.0
Market value ($ mil.)	–	–	–	–	–	–
Employees	–	–	–	–	–	300

OAK VALLEY BANCORP (OAKDALE, CA)   NAS: OVLY

125 N. Third Ave.
Oakdale, CA 95361
Phone: 209 848-2265
Fax: –
Web: www.ovcb.com

CEO: Christopher M Courtney
CFO: Jeffrey A Gall
HR: –
FYE: December 31
Type: Public

Oak Valley Bancorp was formed in 2008 to be the holding company for Oak Valley Community Bank, which serves individuals and local businesses through about 10 branches in California's Central Valley. Eastern Sierra Community Bank, a division of Oak Valley, has three locations. The banks provide standard deposit products such as savings, checking, and retirement accounts and CDs. Their lending activities consist of commercial real estate loans (more than half of their combined loan portfolio) and business, real estate construction, agricultural, residential mortgage, and consumer loans. Investment products and services are offered through an agreement with PrimeVest Financial Services.

	Annual Growth	12/18	12/19	12/20	12/21	12/22
Assets ($mil.)	15.8%	1,094.9	1,147.8	1,511.5	1,964.5	1,968.3
Net income ($ mil.)	18.7%	11.5	12.5	13.7	16.3	22.9
Market value ($ mil.)	5.5%	151.1	160.7	137.2	143.7	187.0
Employees	2.7%	186	192	191	216	207

OAKLAND UNIVERSITY

2200 N SQUIRREL RD
ROCHESTER, MI 483094401
Phone: 248 370-2100
Fax: –
Web: www.oakland.edu

CEO: –
CFO: –
HR: Sandra Alber
FYE: June 30
Type: Private

Oakland University is the OU of the North. The Michigan public university serves a student body of more than 20,000, offering about 130 baccalaureate degree programs and more than 100 graduate degree and certificate programs. It boasts a student-to-faculty ratio of 22-to-1. In addition to academic and specialty programs in areas ranging from business and technology to nursing and athletics, its faculty members also coordinate hands-on research projects for graduate students. The main university campus spans some 1,400 acres that house seven academic schools and colleges in Rochester, Michigan. Oakland University also has satellite campuses in Macomb County and a law school in Auburn Hills.

	Annual Growth	06/15	06/16	06/17	06/18	06/19
Sales ($mil.)	1.2%	–	–	263.5	262.2	269.8
Net income ($ mil.)	(8.5%)	–	–	22.2	18.9	18.6
Market value ($ mil.)	–	–	–	–	–	–
Employees	–	–	–	–	–	2,650

OAKRIDGE GLOBAL ENERGY SOLUTIONS INC

3520 Dixie Highway NE
Palm Bay, FL 32905
Phone: 321 610-7959
Fax: –
Web: –

CEO: Stephen J Barber
CFO: –
HR: –
FYE: December 31
Type: Public

Oak Ridge Micro-Energy is hoping to provide macro-power. The development-stage company makes thin-film lithium batteries with consumer, industrial, and military applications. Oak Ridge Micro-Energy licensed the thin-film battery technology from Oak Ridge National Laboratory (ORNL) on a non-exclusive basis. Mark Meriwether, president and CEO, owns 20% of Oak Ridge; John Bates (CTO and former CEO) holds about one-quarter of the company. Dr. Bates worked at ORNL for nearly 30 years, developing the technology that is being commercialized by Oak Ridge Micro-Energy. The company is moving into the third phase of its strategic plan, focusing on commercial licensing and marketing of its technology.

	Annual Growth	12/11	12/12	12/13	12/14	12/15
Sales ($mil.)	–	–	–	–	0.0	0.0
Net income ($ mil.)	–	(0.1)	(0.7)	(5.1)	(8.6)	12.3
Market value ($ mil.)	36.0%	65.3	54.4	81.6	125.1	223.1
Employees	169.8%	1	6	18	14	53

OBERG INDUSTRIES, LLC

2301 SILVERVILLE RD
FREEPORT, PA 162291630
Phone: 724 295-2121
Fax: –
Web: www.oberg.com

CEO: Rich Bartek
CFO: Jeffrey M Mattiuz
HR: –
FYE: December 31
Type: Private

With a product range to die for, Oberg Industries manufactures high precision stamping dies and die components such as progressive dies, primary and secondary scroll dies, punches, and die inserts. The family-owned company pioneered the use of tungsten carbide components in the manufacture of high-speed stamping dies. Oberg also provides insert molding, design support, plastic injection, and custom designed automation equipment. It operates more than 70 stamping presses with capacities from 5 tons to 400 tons, and some 35 machining centers. The company serves such industries as automotive, aerospace, medical device, and consumer products.

OBERLIN COLLEGE

173 W LORAIN ST
OBERLIN, OH 440741073
Phone: 440 775-8121
Fax: –
Web: www.oberlin.edu

CEO: –
CFO: –
HR: Joseph Vitale
FYE: June 30
Type: Private

Founded in 1833, Oberlin College was the first college in the US to enroll women on an equal basis with men. The school has a College of Arts and Sciences (about 2,300 enrollees), but may be best known for its Conservatory of Music (about 600 enrollees), the oldest such institution in the US. The College of Arts and Sciences offers nearly 50 undergraduate majors, the Conservatory about 10. Students can earn bachelor's degrees in either program, but can also earn a five-year double-degree in both. In addition, Oberlin offers master's degrees in opera theater, conducting, performance, historical performance, historical instruments, music teaching, and education. It has two-year certificate programs as well.

	Annual Growth	06/18	06/19	06/20	06/21	06/22
Sales ($mil.)	6.3%	–	189.5	187.7	191.3	227.5
Net income ($ mil.)	–	–	(1.2)	19.1	362.2	(58.2)
Market value ($ mil.)	–	–	–	–	–	–
Employees	–	–	–	–	–	1,140

OBJECT MANAGEMENT GROUP, INC.

42 HATHERLY RD
ROCKLAND, MA 023701604
Phone: 781 444-0404
Fax: –
Web: www.omg.org

CEO: –
CFO: –
HR: –
FYE: March 31
Type: Private

Object Management Group is a not-for-profit consortium that creates computer industry standards and specifications for standardized object software design. It promotes various languages and protocols, including CORBA (Common Object Request Broker Architecture), the UML (Unified Modeling Language), MDA (Model Driven Architecture), and MOF (Meta-Object Facility). The group is an open membership one, so any company can join. It works with a range of industries including health care, manufacturing, and telecommunications. OMG also produces technical meetings, conferences, and workshops. The group was founded in 1989.

	Annual Growth	03/14	03/15	03/16	03/18	03/22
Sales ($mil.)	1.2%	–	6.2	8.4	8.9	6.8
Net income ($ mil.)	–	–	0.6	0.8	(0.6)	(0.8)
Market value ($ mil.)	–	–	–	–	–	–
Employees	–	–	–	–	–	31

OBJECT TECHNOLOGY SOLUTIONS, INC.

6363 COLLEGE BLVD STE 230
LEAWOOD, KS 662111883
Phone: 913 345-9080
Fax: –
Web: www.otsi-global.com

CEO: Narasimha Gondi
CFO: –
HR: –
FYE: December 31
Type: Private

Its the object of Object Technology Solution's business to solve its customers' IT infrastructure and business continuity problems. The company, aka OTSI, offers enterprise resource planning (ERP) implementation, application development, custom software development, systems integration, and maintenance and support for all of the above. With offices in the US and India, it offers onsite, offsite, offshore, and combined delivery choices to its clients in the healthcare, IT, manufacturing, retail, energy, and telecom industries. OTSI also serves public sector clients. Major customers include Blue Cross Blue Shield, HP, Sprint, Target, and the Kansas Department of Transportation. The company was formed in 1999.

	Annual Growth	12/05	12/06	12/07	12/08	12/13
Sales ($mil.)	14.4%	–	–	17.0	18.7	38.2
Net income ($ mil.)	(19.9%)	–	–	1.8	0.3	0.5
Market value ($ mil.)	–	–	–	–	–	–
Employees	–	–	–	–	–	176

OBJECTIVITY, INC.

800 W EL CAMINO REAL STE 180
MOUNTAIN VIEW, CA 94040
Phone: 408 992-7100
Fax: –
Web: www.objectivity.com

CEO: John Jarrell
CFO: Gary Lewis
HR: –
FYE: June 30
Type: Private

Objectivity wants to help you objectively address your data needs, whether they be large or small. The company provides data management software, which can function either as a stand-alone database or part of a larger system. The company markets its products to corporations, as well as government agencies (and the contractors that serve them); clients include General Dynamics, Northrop Grumman, and Siemens. Established in 1988, Objectivity has received venture capital funding from a variety of backers, including Adobe Systems, AVI Management Partners, Institutional Venture Partners, Mayfield Fund, New York Life Insurance Company, and Sevin Rosen Funds.

	Annual Growth	06/98	06/99	06/00	06/01	06/08
Sales ($mil.)	(1.2%)	–	–	–	11.8	10.9
Net income ($ mil.)	5.9%	–	–	–	0.2	0.2
Market value ($ mil.)	–	–	–	–	–	–
Employees	–	–	–	–	–	24

OBLONG INC

NAS: OBLG

25587 Conifer Road, Suite 105-231
Conifer, CO 80433
Phone: 303 640-3838
Fax: –
Web: www.oblong.com

CEO: Peter Holst
CFO: David Clark
HR: –
FYE: December 31
Type: Public

Glowpoint adds a little light to virtual meeting rooms, providing hosted and managed video-conferencing services via subscription that allow businesses, government offices, educational institutions, and other customers to engage in two-way video communications over Internet protocol networks. Its cloud-based technology is compatible with any video-conferencing equipment (e.g. Cisco, LifeSize, Polycom, and Avaya) across any IP network. Glowpoint also offers Webcasting services, streaming live and recorded video by standard video-conferencing systems. In addition, the company offers wholesale private labeling of its services to third-party companies. Glowpoint serves some 500 customers across the US and abroad.

	Annual Growth	12/19	12/20	12/21	12/22	12/23
Sales ($mil.)	(26.2%)	12.8	15.3	7.7	5.5	3.8
Net income ($ mil.)	–	(7.8)	(7.4)	(9.1)	(21.9)	(4.4)
Market value ($ mil.)	(38.6%)	23.2	85.8	17.2	2.0	3.3
Employees	(35.6%)	99	42	49	22	17

OBOCON INC

NBB: OBCN

4902 Finchem Court
Fairfax, VA 22030
Phone: 703 310-7334
Fax: –
Web: www.clancysystems.com

CEO: Stanley J Wolfson
CFO: Lizabeth Wolfson
HR: –
FYE: September 30
Type: Public

Clancy Systems designs, develops, and manufactures automated parking enforcement and management systems, including a wireless ticket-writing and printing system. Municipalities, universities, and institutions are among its customers. Clancy Systems also offers online transaction services for processing payments for tickets and registrations. In addition, the company offers software for making double-sided identification badges, a virtual parking permit platform, and a rust-proof vehicle immobilization system called The Denver Boot. CEO Stanley Wolfson and his wife, Lizabeth Wolfson, the company's CFO, together own about 35% of Clancy Systems.

	Annual Growth	09/07	09/08	09/17	09/18	09/19
Sales ($mil.)	–	3.8	4.0	1.4	1.4	–
Net income ($ mil.)	–	0.0	0.7	(0.1)	(0.1)	–
Market value ($ mil.)	15.3%	0.5	0.3	0.0	0.0	2.8
Employees	–	51	51	–	–	–

OCCIDENTAL COLLEGE

1600 CAMPUS RD
LOS ANGELES, CA 900413314
Phone: 323 259-2500
Fax: –
Web: www.oxy.edu

CEO: –
CFO: –
HR: Jamie Murphy
FYE: June 30
Type: Private

It's no accident that Occidental College is a liberal arts school. With more than 2,000 students, an average class size of 19, and a 10:1 student-to-faculty ratio, the school (nicknamed "Oxy") offers a hands-on approach to higher education. Its campus, located in Eagle Rock, is surrounded by the metropolis of Los Angeles. The college has 180 faculty members and offers about 30 majors, including a number of interdisciplinary programs. Occidental students can also take classes at Caltech or the Art Center College of Design and earn joint degrees at Columbia University, Keck Graduate Institute, and Caltech. Occidental students can also participate in service-learning and study abroad programs.

	Annual Growth	06/15	06/16	06/17	06/20	06/22
Sales ($mil.)	(1.9%)	–	162.3	121.9	193.7	145.0
Net income ($ mil.)	–	–	(7.7)	52.0	15.2	7.8
Market value ($ mil.)	–	–	–	–	–	–
Employees	–	–	–	–	–	610

OCCIDENTAL PETROLEUM CORP

NYS: OXY

5 Greenway Plaza, Suite 110
Houston, TX 77046
Phone: 713 215-7000
Fax: –
Web: www.oxy.com

CEO: Vicki Hollub
CFO: Sunil Mathew
HR: –
FYE: December 31
Type: Public

Occidental is an international energy company with assets primarily in the US, the Middle East and North Africa. It is one of the largest oil producers in the US, including a leading producer in the Permian and DJ basins, and offshore Gulf of Mexico. Occidental's midstream and marketing segment supports and enhances its oil and gas and chemical businesses. Its chemical subsidiary OxyChem manufactures the building blocks for life-enhancing products. The company has a legacy of carbon management expertise and investing in other low-carbon technologies intended to reduce emissions of their clients. The US generates around 85% of the company's revenue.

	Annual Growth	12/19	12/20	12/21	12/22	12/23
Sales ($mil.)	8.0%	21,232	16,261	26,314	37,095	28,918
Net income ($ mil.)	–	(667.0)	(14,831.0)	2,322.0	13,304	4,696.0
Market value ($ mil.)	9.7%	36,243	15,224	25,496	55,397	52,513
Employees	(3.3%)	14,400	11,800	11,678	11,973	12,570

OCEAN BEAUTY SEAFOODS LLC

1100 W EWING ST
SEATTLE, WA 981191321
Phone: 206 285-6800
Fax: –
Web: www.oceanbeauty.com

CEO: Mark Palmer
CFO: Tony Ross
HR: –
FYE: December 29
Type: Private

Prefer your piscatory purchase to be fresh, frozen, or canned? Ocean Beauty Seafoods has it covered. Doing no fishing of its own, the company buys seafood from commercial fishermen and then processes, sells, and distributes its seafood products in Alaska and across the continental US. Founded in 1910, the company also exports seafood to Mexico, Europe, Asia, Africa, and the Middle East. Ocean Beauty's specialty products include smoked salmon, smoked salmon spreads, pickled and marinated herring, shrimp cocktail, caviar, and lobster p t . Nonprofit Bristol Bay Economic Development Corporation owns 50% of Ocean Beauty; individual investors own the rest.

	Annual Growth	01/14	01/15	01/16*	12/16	12/18
Sales ($mil.)	0.1%	–	–	437.8	453.9	438.8
Net income ($ mil.)	–	–	–	(4.6)	(27.2)	5.4
Market value ($ mil.)	–	–	–	–	–	–
Employees	–	–	–	–	–	2,500

*Fiscal year change

OCEAN DUKE CORPORATION

21250 HAWTHORNE BLVD STE 500
TORRANCE, CA 905035506
Phone: 310 326-3198
Fax: –
Web: www.oceanduke.com

CEO: –
CFO: Alice Lin
HR: –
FYE: March 31
Type: Private

Ocean Duke maintains a regal demeanor in a fishy environment. The company is a seafood wholesaler offering a variety of frozen raw fish, shrimp, mollusks, and crustaceans. Ocean Duke also sells breaded fish, shrimp, and squid. The company imports its products and serves foodservice, food processing, distribution, and wholesale companies throughout the US.

OCEAN POWER TECHNOLOGIES INC

ASE: OPTT

28 Engelhard Drive, Suite B
Monroe Township, NJ 08831
Phone: 609 730-0400
Fax: –
Web: www.oceanpowertechnologies.com

CEO: Philipp Stratmann
CFO: Robert Powers
HR: –
FYE: April 30
Type: Public

Harnessing the motion of the ocean is what Ocean Power Technologies (OPT) is all about. The company, with offices in the US and UK, uses a proprietary system called PowerBouy to generate electricity using the mechanical energy produced when offshore waves move the anchored buoys up and down. OPT offers a buoy system that connects to power grids as well as an autonomous one that can be used in remote locations and for tsunami monitoring, oceanographic data collection, and offshore aquaculture. Customers include the US Navy, Spanish power producer Iberdrola, and Spanish energy firm TOTAL. It has a contract with Lockheed Martin to build a large power generation system off the west coast of the US.

	Annual Growth	04/19	04/20	04/21	04/22	04/23
Sales ($mil.)	44.2%	0.6	1.7	1.2	1.8	2.7
Net income ($ mil.)	–	(12.2)	(10.4)	(14.8)	(18.9)	(26.3)
Market value ($ mil.)	(34.6%)	156.4	25.1	141.2	59.6	28.6
Employees	16.6%	39	36	46	54	72

OCEAN SPRAY CRANBERRIES, INC.

1 OCEAN SPRAY DR
MIDDLEBORO, MA 023490001
Phone: 508 946-1000
Fax: –
Web: www.oceanspray.com

CEO: Tom Hayes
CFO: Daniel Cunha
HR: Lee Shalita
FYE: August 31
Type: Private

Known for its blue-and-white wave logo, Ocean Spray Cranberries is a top US maker of canned, bottled, and shelf-stable juice drinks. Structured as a cooperative, Ocean Spray is owned by more than 700 cranberry growers in North and South America. It produces juice drinks by blending cranberries with other fruits, typically ranging from apples to blueberries, at its processing facilities. The company's other products include Craisins dried cranberries, sauces, snacks, energy drinks, sparkling, and supplements, along with fresh fruits. Ocean Spray sells its products through food foodservice providers, retailers, distributors, and food makers in over 100 countries worldwide. The vibrant agricultural company was founded in 1930.

	Annual Growth	08/13	08/14	08/15	08/16	08/17
Sales ($mil.)	(1.7%)	–	–	1,719.3	1,706.8	1,661.0
Net income ($ mil.)	(7.4%)	–	–	317.3	334.3	272.2
Market value ($ mil.)	–	–	–	–	–	–
Employees	–	–	–	–	–	2,235

OCEANEERING INTERNATIONAL, INC.

NYS: OII

5875 North Sam Houston Parkway, Suite 400
Houston, TX 77086
Phone: 713 329-4500
Fax: –
Web: www.oceaneering.com

CEO: Roderick A Larson
CFO: Alan R Curtis
HR: –
FYE: December 31
Type: Public

Oceaneering International is one of the world's largest underwater service contract providers. It caters primarily to the oil and gas industry by manufacturing remotely operated vehicles (ROVs) and specialty subsea hardware that are used to control hydrocarbon flow from subsea wellheads. The company also offers services ranging from subsea hardware installation and repair to third-party asset safety inspections. Oceaneering also provides advanced engineering services to US governmental agencies and the commercial theme park industry. It is primarily active in the US but also has operations in Angola, Brazil, United Kingdom, and Australia. The company generates its largest revenue from the US with approximately 45%.

	Annual Growth	12/19	12/20	12/21	12/22	12/23
Sales ($mil.)	4.3%	2,048.1	1,827.9	1,869.3	2,066.1	2,424.7
Net income ($ mil.)	–	(348.4)	(496.8)	(49.3)	25.9	97.4
Market value ($ mil.)	9.3%	1,503.0	801.4	1,140.1	1,763.1	2,145.1
Employees	2.6%	9,100	8,300	8,500	9,200	10,100

OCEANFIRST FINANCIAL CORP

NMS: OCFC

110 West Front Street
Red Bank, NJ 07701
Phone: 732 240-4500
Fax: –
Web: www.oceanfirst.com

CEO: –
CFO: –
HR: –
FYE: December 31
Type: Public

OceanFirst Financial operates as the holding company for OceanFirst Bank, a regional bank operating throughout New Jersey, greater Philadelphia and metropolitan New York. The bank caters to individuals and small to midsized businesses, offering standard products such as checking and savings accounts, CDs, and IRAs. It uses funds from deposits mainly to invest in mortgages, loans, and securities. It has total loans outstanding of $8.62 billion, of which $5.43 billion, or about 65% of total loans, were commercial real estate, multi-family, and land loans.

	Annual Growth	12/19	12/20	12/21	12/22	12/23
Assets ($mil.)	13.2%	8,246.1	11,448	11,740	13,104	13,538
Net income ($ mil.)	4.1%	88.6	63.3	110.1	146.6	104.0
Market value ($ mil.)	(9.2%)	1,518.3	1,107.5	1,319.7	1,263.3	1,032.0
Employees	(0.7%)	924	1,008	937	958	899

OCHOCO LUMBER COMPANY

200 SE COMBS FLAT RD
PRINEVILLE, OR 977542549
Phone: 541 447-6296
Fax: –
Web: www.ochocolumber.com

CEO: –
CFO: –
HR: –
FYE: December 31
Type: Private

Ochoco Lumber produces, markets, and distributes lumber and lumber products. It operates the Malheur Lumber Company sawmill in Oregon and about a half-dozen distribution yards and sales offices in Oregon, Idaho, Washington, and Indiana. The company markets wood products including flooring, panels, mouldings, and hardwood and softwood lumber around the world; it has international operations in Europe, South America, and Asia. Its Lithuanian business purchases lumber from Russia and processes it for international shipping. Ochoco Lumber traces its roots to the 1930s; managing director John Sheik's grandfather was an original investor.

OCI PARTNERS LP

5470 N TWIN CITY HWY
NEDERLAND, TX 776273168
Phone: 409 723-1900
Fax: –
Web: www.oci-global.com

CEO: Ahmed K El-Hoshy
CFO: Beshoy Guirguis
HR: Penny Campbell
FYE: December 31
Type: Private

OCI Partners is bringing methanol production back to the good ol' US of A. The company reopened a methanol and ammonia plant in Beaumont, Texas, in 2012. (It's actually the largest methanol plant in the US; currently, most of the country's methanol is imported from Trinidad.) The plant (shut down by Terra Industries in 2004) has an annual production capacity of 730,000 tons of methanol and 265,000 tons of ammonia. OCI Partners sells the methanol and ammonia to customers such as Koch Industries, Methanex, and Transammonia, who use it to create other chemicals. OCI Partners is affiliated with Egypt-based Orascom Construction Industries (OCI). It went public in 2013.

OCLC, INC.

6565 KILGOUR PL
DUBLIN, OH 430173395
Phone: 614 764-6000
Fax: –
Web: www.oclc.org

CEO: Skip Prichard
CFO: Bill Rozek
HR: –
FYE: June 30
Type: Private

Working to reduce the cost of information, OCLC Online Computer Library Center is a membership cooperative that provides access to the world's information. The group offers services and tools to some 74,000 member libraries in about 170 countries. Services include computer-based cataloging, preservation, and library management. OCLC additionally facilitates interlibrary loan services, administers the Dewey Decimal Classification system, and operates the WorldCat database, an online resource for finding library materials. OCLC was founded in 1967 by presidents of the colleges and universities in Ohio. OCLC, which stands for Ohio College Library Center, opened its first location in Ohio State's main library.

	Annual Growth	06/13	06/14	06/15	06/16	06/17
Sales ($mil.)	(0.8%)	–	213.6	202.8	203.4	208.4
Net income ($ mil.)	(14.0%)	–	21.9	(17.1)	(9.8)	13.9
Market value ($ mil.)	–	–	–	–	–	–
Employees	–	–	–	–	–	1,227

OCONEE REGIONAL HEALTH SYSTEMS, INC.

821 N COBB ST
MILLEDGEVILLE, GA 310612343
Phone: 478 454-3500
Fax: –
Web: –

CEO: –
CFO: –
HR: –
FYE: September 30
Type: Private

Oconee Regional Health Systems (ORHS) helps people return to their natural healthy state, though sometimes using unnatural methods to do so. Oconee Regional Health Systems serves the residents of Baldwin County in central Georgia. Its Oconee Regional Medical Center, founded in 1957, has some 140 beds. Other facilities include Jasper Memorial Hospital (almost 20 beds), Primary Care Center of Monticello, The Retreat Nursing Home, and the ConvenientCare after-hours care center. Specialty services include behavioral medicine, cancer treatment, emergency care, hospice, pediatrics, and physical therapy.

OCULAR THERAPEUTIX INC

NMS: OCUL

24 Crosby Drive
Bedford, MA 01730
Phone: 781 357-4000
Fax: –
Web: www.ocutx.com

CEO: Antony C Mattessich
CFO: Donald Notman
HR: –
FYE: December 31
Type: Public

Ocular Therapeutix develops therapies for eye diseases and conditions. The start-up has several products in development based on its proprietary hydrogel platform technology. Ocular's hydrogel platform technology plans to extend its usage beyond the eye to other areas of the body. The firm's first commercial product, ReSure Sealant, is a hydrogel-based opthalmic wound sealant. The FDA approved Ocular's Dextenza for the treatment of ocular pain following opthalmic surgery. Another candidate, OTX-TP, is being tested for its ability to reduce pressure in patients with glaucoma and ocular hypertension.

	Annual Growth	12/19	12/20	12/21	12/22	12/23
Sales ($mil.)	92.8%	4.2	17.4	43.5	51.5	58.4
Net income ($ mil.)	–	(86.4)	(155.6)	(6.6)	(71.0)	(80.7)
Market value ($ mil.)	3.1%	454.1	2,379.7	801.3	323.0	512.7
Employees	13.5%	161	181	228	274	267

OCUPHIRE PHARMA INC

NAS: OCUP

37000 Grand River Avenue, Suite 120
Farmington Hills, MI 48335
Phone: 248 957-9024
Fax: –
Web: www.rexahn.com

CEO: George Magrath
CFO: –
HR: –
FYE: December 31
Type: Public

Rexahn Pharmaceuticals has its R&D sights set on difficult-to-treat cancers. A biopharmaceutical company, Rexahn has three drug candidates in clinical stages of development: Supinoxin, an orally administered first-in-class small molecule that inhibits the growth of multiple types of human cancer cells; and RX-3117, which inhibits DNA and RNA synthesis and induces apoptotic cell death. It has other compounds in pre-clinical development. The company develops its candidates through its own R&D arm and through partnerships with pharmaceutical and biopharmaceutical companies like Teva Pharmaceutical and TheraTarget.

	Annual Growth	12/19	12/20	12/21	12/22	12/23
Sales ($mil.)	–	–	–	0.6	39.9	19.0
Net income ($ mil.)	–	(8.6)	(24.6)	(56.7)	17.9	(10.0)
Market value ($ mil.)	12.0%	45.8	155.6	89.4	84.6	72.2
Employees	35.8%	5	5	8	9	17

OCWEN FINANCIAL CORP

NYS: OCN

1661 Worthington Road, Suite 100
West Palm Beach, FL 33409
Phone: 561 682-8000
Fax: –
Web: www.ocwen.com

CEO: Glen A Messina
CFO: June C Campbell
HR: Ajay Aurora
FYE: December 31
Type: Public

Ocwen Financial Corporation a leading non-bank mortgage servicer and originator providing solutions through its Eprimary brands, PHH Mortgage and Liberty Reverse Mortgage. PHH Mortgage is one of the largest servicers in the country, focused on delivering a variety of servicing and lending programs. Liberty is one of the nation's largest reverse mortgage lenders dedicated to education and providing loans that help customers meet their personal and financial needs. The company services 1.4 million loans with a total UPB of $289.8.0 billion on behalf of more than 3,900 investors and 115 subservicing clients. Ocwen services all mortgage loan classes, including conventional, government-insured and non-Agency loans. Through its retail, correspondent and wholesale channels, it originate and purchase conventional and government-insured forward and reverse mortgage loans that it sells or securitizes on a servicing retained basis. In addition, it grows its mortgage servicing volume through MSR flow purchase agreements, GSE Cash Window programs, bulk MSR purchase transactions, and subservicing agreements.

	Annual Growth	12/19	12/20	12/21	12/22	12/23
Assets ($mil.)	4.7%	10,406	10,651	12,147	12,399	12,514
Net income ($ mil.)	–	(142.1)	(40.2)	18.1	25.7	(63.7)
Market value ($ mil.)	117.7%	10.5	222.2	307.1	235.0	236.4
Employees	(4.0%)	5,300	5,000	5,700	4,900	4,500

ODOM CORPORATION

11400 SE 8TH ST STE 300
BELLEVUE, WA 980046428
Phone: 425 456-3535
Fax: -
Web: www.odomcorp.com

CEO: Cathi V Sleet
CFO: -
HR: Hillary Judd
FYE: December 31
Type: Private

The Odom Corporation wants you to drink up if you happen to be in the Pacific Northwest. The company distributes beer, wine, and spirits as well as sodas, energy drinks, and bottled waters from more than 500 domestic and foreign suppliers, including Coca-Cola, Diageo, E. & J. Gallo, MillerCoors, and Pernod Ricard. The company serves retail customers throughout the northwestern US, including those in Alaska, Idaho, Oregon, and Washington. It also runs Odom-Southern Holdings, a joint venture with Southern Glazer's Wine and Spirits, the #1 distributor of alcoholic beverages in the US. Milt Odom founded the company in 1933.

	Annual Growth	12/02	12/03	12/04	12/06	12/07
Sales ($mil.)	22.1%	-	151.9	211.0	304.6	337.9
Net income ($ mil.)	4.4%	-	2.5	3.8	1.8	2.9
Market value ($ mil.)	-	-	-	-	-	-
Employees	-	-	-	-	-	1,500

ODP CORP (THE)

6600 North Military Trail
Boca Raton, FL 33496
Phone: 561 438-4800
Fax: 561 265-4406
Web: www.officedepot.com

NMS: ODP
CEO: Gerry Smith
CFO: D A Scaglione
HR: Annie Lau
FYE: December 30
Type: Public

The ODP Corporation, parent company of Office Depot, is a leading provider of business services and supplies, products and digital workplace technology solutions to small, medium and enterprise businesses, through an integrated business-to-business (B2B) distribution platform, which includes world-class supply chain and distribution operations, dedicated sales professionals and technicians, online presence, and about 1,040 stores. Through its banner brands Office Depot, OfficeMax, ODP Business Solutions, Varis, and Grand & Toy, as well as others. In 2020, the company went on reorganization in which the company became the new parent company of Office Depot, Inc.

	Annual Growth	12/19	12/20	12/21	12/22	12/23
Sales ($mil.)	(7.4%)	10,647	9,710.0	8,465.0	8,491.0	7,831.0
Net income ($ mil.)	8.9%	99.0	(319.0)	(208.0)	166.0	139.0
Market value ($ mil.)	115.1%	97.2	1,058.1	1,441.0	1,683.1	2,080.8
Employees	-	40,000	37,000	26,000	25,000	-

ODYSSEY MARINE EXPLORATION, INC.

205 S. Hoover Blvd., Suite 210
Tampa, FL 33609
Phone: 813 876-1776
Fax: -
Web: www.odysseymarine.com

NAS: OMEX
CEO: -
CFO: -
HR: -
FYE: December 31
Type: Public

Gone are the days when one-eyed, peg-legged buccaneers counted their steps to where X marked the spot of lost treasure. Odyssey Marine Exploration, a new breed of treasure hunter, uses sonar, magnetometers, and remotely operated vehicles (ROVs) to locate and excavate shipwrecks, as well as for subsea mineral exploration. The company focuses on deepwater projects where the booty is less susceptible to damage and less likely to have been salvaged. Odyssey Marine Exploration surveys and maps seabeds too; its experience covers more than 10,000 sq. mi. The company sells artifacts (coins, bullion) salvaged from shipwrecks, but also in recent years generates revenue from expedition charter services.

	Annual Growth	12/18	12/19	12/20	12/21	12/22
Sales ($mil.)	(20.1%)	3.3	3.1	2.0	0.9	1.3
Net income ($ mil.)	-	(5.2)	(10.4)	(14.8)	(10.0)	(23.1)
Market value ($ mil.)	3.9%	65.1	62.3	138.7	101.6	75.8
Employees	(4.7%)	17	14	14	13	14

OEWAVES, INC.

465 N HALSTEAD ST STE 140
PASADENA, CA 911073125
Phone: 626 351-4200
Fax: -
Web: www.oewaves.com

CEO: Skip Williams
CFO: Ivan Ivankovich
HR: -
FYE: December 31
Type: Private

OEwaves makes the TIDALwave line of opto-electronic oscillators (OEO) used in military radar, wireless, and fiber-optic communications applications. Founded in 2000, the company licensed the rights to the OEO technology developed at the Jet Propulsion Laboratory which is is run by the California Institute of Technology (Caltech). Investors include Agilent, EnerTech Capital, ITU Ventures, and TL Ventures. The Department of Defense is a major customer.

	Annual Growth	12/02	12/03	12/04	12/06	12/07
Sales ($mil.)	116.8%	-	0.2	2.2	2.9	4.5
Net income ($ mil.)	(50.1%)	-	2.2	(2.5)	(0.1)	0.1
Market value ($ mil.)	-	-	-	-	-	-
Employees	-	-	-	-	-	27

OFFICE MOVERS, INC.

6500 KANE WAY
ELKRIDGE, MD 210756248
Phone: 410 799-3200
Fax: -
Web: -

CEO: -
CFO: -
HR: -
FYE: June 03
Type: Private

Office Movers can't arrange your move into a corner office with windows and a wet bar -- at least not without your manager's approval. But the company will arrange to move your office -- computers, copy machines, desks, and all -- from wherever it's been to wherever it's going in the mid-Atlantic US. Its Library Relocation Services, which moves entire libraries, counts the Library of Congress as one of its customers. Office Movers maintains a fleet of more than 200 vehicles and more than 10 million cu. ft. of climate-controlled warehouse space. A unit of The Kane Company, Office Movers works with affiliates that provide records management services and office furniture installation.

	Annual Growth	12/06	12/07	12/08	12/10*	06/15
Sales ($mil.)	-	-	(976.5)	53.6	36.5	29.9
Net income ($ mil.)	84.1%	-	0.0	2.4	0.8	2.2
Market value ($ mil.)	-	-	-	-	-	-
Employees	-	-	-	-	-	450

*Fiscal year change

OFFICE PROPERTIES INCOME TRUST

Two Newton Place, 255 Washington Street, Suite 300
Newton, MA 02458-1634
Phone: 617 219-1440
Fax: -
Web: www.opireit.com

NMS: OPI
CEO: -
CFO: Mark L Kleifges
HR: -
FYE: December 31
Type: Public

If Office Properties Income Trust had one request of Uncle Sam it would be this: "I want you to lease our properties." As a real estate investment trust (REIT), Office Properties Income Trust invests in properties that are leased to government tenants. It owns about 25.7 million sq. ft. of leasing space across nearly 190 properties across the US. The company's largest tenant is the US Government representing approximately 25% of rental income. It also makes some equity investments.

	Annual Growth	12/19	12/20	12/21	12/22	12/23
Sales ($mil.)	(5.8%)	678.4	587.9	576.5	554.3	533.6
Net income ($ mil.)	-	30.3	6.7	(8.2)	(6.1)	(69.4)
Market value ($ mil.)	(30.9%)	1,567.0	1,107.7	1,211.1	650.9	356.9
Employees	-	-	-	-	-	-

OGE ENERGY CORP
NYS: OGE

321 North Harvey, P.O. Box 321
Oklahoma City, OK 73101-0321
Phone: 405 553-3000
Fax: –
Web: www.oge.com

CEO: –
CFO: –
HR: –
FYE: December 31
Type: Public

OGE Energy is the holding company for the largest electric utility in Oklahoma, with investments in energy and energy services providers offering physical delivery and related services for both electricity and natural gas primarily in the south central US. Its regulated utility, Oklahoma Gas and Electric (OG&E), generates, transmits, and sells electricity in Oklahoma and a slice of western Arkansas. It generates around 7,300 MW of power from natural gas, coal, dual-fuel, wind, and solar generations. OGE Energy also owns roughly 25% of a natural gas gathering, processing, and transport operation, Enable Midstream Partners.

	Annual Growth	12/19	12/20	12/21	12/22	12/23
Sales ($mil.)	4.6%	2,231.6	2,122.3	3,653.7	3,375.7	2,674.3
Net income ($ mil.)	(1.0%)	433.6	(173.7)	737.3	665.7	416.8
Market value ($ mil.)	(5.9%)	8,907.3	6,381.6	7,687.5	7,921.9	6,996.5
Employees	(1.0%)	2,425	2,360	2,185	2,237	2,329

OGLETHORPE POWER CORP

2100 East Exchange Place
Tucker, GA 30084-5336
Phone: 770 270-7600
Fax: –
Web: www.opc.com

CEO: Michael L Smith
CFO: Elizabeth B Higgins
HR: Jami Reusch
FYE: December 31
Type: Public

Not-for-profit Oglethorpe Power Corporation is one of the largest electricity cooperatives in the US, with contracts to supply wholesale power to 38 member/owners (making up most of Georgia's electric distribution cooperatives) until 2050. Oglethorpe's member/owners, which also operate as not-for-profits, serve approximately 2.0 million residential, commercial, and industrial customers (or about 4.4 million people). The company has a generating capacity of around 10,530 MW from fossil-fueled, nuclear, and hydroelectric power plants. Oglethorpe has stakes in more than 30 generating units.

	Annual Growth	12/18	12/19	12/20	12/21	12/22
Sales ($mil.)	9.5%	1,480.1	1,430.3	1,377.6	1,604.9	2,130.1
Net income ($ mil.)	4.8%	51.2	54.5	55.9	57.8	61.7
Market value ($ mil.)	–	–	–	–	–	–
Employees	3.5%	281	299	299	320	323

OHA INVESTMENT CORPORATION

1114 AVENUE OF THE AMERICAS FL 27
NEW YORK, NY 100367703
Phone: 212 852-1900
Fax: –
Web: www.ohainvestmentcorporation.com

CEO: Steven T Wayne
CFO: Cory E Gilbert
HR: –
FYE: December 31
Type: Private

OHA Investment (formerly NGP Capital Resources) capitalizes on investing its resources in small and midsized companies with annual revenues of less than $500 million. Established in 2004, OHA is attracted to exploration and production businesses, as well as midstream companies involved in the processing and transport of oil and gas products. Other investment targets include niche manufacturing, value added distribution, business services, healthcare products and services, and consumer services. Investments range from $10 million to $50 million. In 2013 it closed a $17.5 million loan to partly fund the acquisition of IGI Corp by a portfolio company of Wingate Partners, and a $17.5 million investment in home health provider OCI Holdings.

OHIO ART CO.

P.O. Box 111
Bryan, OH 43506
Phone: 419 636-3141
Fax: 419 636-7614
Web: www.world-of-toys.com

CEO: William C Killgallon
CFO: Thonda James
HR: –
FYE: January 31
Type: Public

Like a kid playing with its best-known product, the Etch A Sketch, The Ohio Art Company tries to draw attention to itself without shaking things up. It's a leader in the metal lithography industry (making metal packaging, serving trays, and metal food containers), but it's best known for its fun fare. Besides Etch A Sketch and other drawing devices, its products include K's Kids musical toys, child-sized sports sets, and the Betty Spaghetty family of dolls. Ohio Art's products are sold to retailers, wholesalers, and catalog companies, and through international licensees. The Killgallon family holds a majority ownership in Ohio Art, which was formed in 1908 and celebrated its 100th anniversary in July 2008.

	Annual Growth	01/00	01/01	01/02	01/03	01/04
Sales ($mil.)	(14.3%)	54.8	46.7	46.9	39.0	29.5
Net income ($ mil.)	–	0.4	(1.4)	3.1	1.2	(0.4)
Market value ($ mil.)	–	–	–	–	–	–
Employees	(11.8%)	309	304	204	191	187

OHIO DEPARTMENT OF TRANSPORTATION

1980 W BROAD ST
COLUMBUS, OH 432231102
Phone: 614 466-7170
Fax: –
Web: transportation.ohio.gov

CEO: –
CFO: –
HR: Carole Dipasquale
FYE: June 30
Type: Private

If you've come to a crossroads in Ohio, the Ohio Department of Transportation has the means to help. The agency, known as ODOT, oversees the road transportation system for the Buckeye State. ODOT is responsible for the design, construction, and maintenance of roads, highways, and bridges. It also helps coordinate other state transportation programs and runs the Ohio Bureau of Motor Vehicles, the Transit Office, and the Office of Aviation as well as managing the storm water program. Among ODOT's priorities is the repaving of the state's portion of the US interstate highway system, an important task since the state's location between the East Coast and Chicago brings it considerable freight traffic.

	Annual Growth	06/16	06/17	06/19	06/20	06/21
Sales ($mil.)	44.4%	–	27.7	24.1	125.6	120.5
Net income ($ mil.)	–	–	(21.3)	99.0	87.2	101.4
Market value ($ mil.)	–	–	–	–	–	–
Employees	–	–	–	–	–	6,500

OHIO EDISON CO

c/o FirstEnergy Corp., 76 South Main Street
Akron, OH 44308
Phone: 800 736-3402
Fax: –
Web: –

CEO: –
CFO: James F Pearson
HR: –
FYE: December 31
Type: Public

Ohio Edison has taken a shine to the folks in the Buckeye state. The company distributes electricity to a population of about 2.3 million (more than 1 million customers) in a 7,000 sq. ml. area of central and northeastern Ohio. Ohio Edison, a unit of FirstEnergy, also has 5,955 MW of generating capacity from interests in primarily fossil-fueled and nuclear generation facilities, and it sells excess power to wholesale customers. The utility's power plants are operated by sister companies FirstEnergy Nuclear and FirstEnergy Generation. Subsidiary Pennsylvania Power Company provides electric service to communities in a 1,100 sq. ml. area of western Pennsylvania, which has a population of approximately 400,000.

	Annual Growth	12/08	12/09	12/10	12/11	12/12
Sales ($mil.)	(11.2%)	2,601.8	2,516.9	1,836.1	1,633.0	1,615.0
Net income ($ mil.)	(16.9%)	211.7	121.9	156.7	128.0	101.0
Market value ($ mil.)	–	–	–	–	–	–
Employees	(2.6%)	1,551	1,391	1,434	1,426	1,397

OHIO LIVING

9200 WORTHINGTON RD STE 300　　　　　　　CEO: Laurence Gumina
WESTERVILLE, OH 430827634　　　　　　　　CFO: Robert Stillman
Phone: 614 888-7800　　　　　　　　　　　　HR: Tiffany Sutton
Fax: –　　　　　　　　　　　　　　　　　　FYE: June 30
Web: www.ohioliving.org　　　　　　　　　　Type: Private

Ohio Presbyterian Retirement Service (OPRS) operates a network of continuing care retirement communities in Ohio. The company offers services through about a dozen senior living communities across the state and serves about 7,000 residents. The centers include skilled nursing, assisted living, and independent living residences. Through its Senior Independence program, the not-for-profit organization also provides independent-living services to about 90,000 seniors in Ohio, including adult day care, home health, hospice, and community health clinics. OPRS was established in 1922.

	Annual Growth	06/18	06/19	06/20	06/21	06/22
Sales ($mil.)	(1.5%)	–	233.3	223.7	218.6	223.1
Net income ($ mil.)	–	–	(0.8)	(3.9)	26.1	(29.2)
Market value ($ mil.)	–	–	–	–	–	–
Employees	–	–	–	–	–	3,100

OHIO POWER COMPANY

1 Riverside Plaza　　　　　　　　　　　　　CEO: Nicholas K Akins
Columbus, OH 43215-2373　　　　　　　　　CFO: Brian X Tierney
Phone: 614 716-1000　　　　　　　　　　　　HR: –
Fax: –　　　　　　　　　　　　　　　　　　FYE: December 31
Web: www.aep.com　　　　　　　　　　　　　Type: Public

To access electricity across the state of Ohio, residents and businesses turn to Ohio Power, which in tandem with Wheeling Power does business as part of AEP Ohio. AEP Ohio serves 1.5 million retail customers. The company, one of American Electric Power's largest utility subsidiaries, operates more than 31,260 miles of transmission and distribution lines. The utility also generates more than 8,500 MW of capacity from primarily hydroelectric and fossil-fueled power plants (the bulk from coal-fired plants), and it sells wholesale electricity to other power companies.

	Annual Growth	12/19	12/20	12/21	12/22	12/23
Sales ($mil.)	8.0%	2,797.6	2,749.1	2,899.1	3,665.1	3,811.4
Net income ($ mil.)	2.5%	297.1	271.4	253.6	287.8	328.2
Market value ($ mil.)	–	–	–	–	–	–
Employees	–	1,681	1,646	1,694	1,713	–

OHIO STATE UNIVERSITY RESEARCH FOUNDATION

1960 KENNY RD　　　　　　　　　　　　　　CEO: –
COLUMBUS, OH 432101016　　　　　　　　　CFO: –
Phone: 614 292-3815　　　　　　　　　　　　HR: –
Fax: –　　　　　　　　　　　　　　　　　　FYE: June 30
Web: research.osu.edu　　　　　　　　　　　Type: Private

The Ohio State University Research Foundation was established in 1936 to function as a central agency for supporting research and development through grants, management, and information technology for Ohio State University, one of the largest public universities in the US. The not-for-profit corporation provides administrative services for research programs, including submitting support requests, managing equipment, and governmental and university compliance oversight. Ohio State University's total awards reached more than $37 million by July 2007, with some 330 awards.

OHIO TURNPIKE AND INFRASTRUCTURE COMMISSION

682 PROSPECT ST　　　　　　　　　　　　　CEO: Randy Cole
BEREA, OH 440172711　　　　　　　　　　　CFO: Martin S Seekely
Phone: 440 234-2081　　　　　　　　　　　　HR: –
Fax: –　　　　　　　　　　　　　　　　　　FYE: December 31
Web: www.ohioturnpike.org　　　　　　　　Type: Private

The Ohio Turnpike Commission operates the 241-mile James W. Shocknessy Ohio Turnpike and its service plazas. The turnpike spans the width of the state. It begins near the Michigan border in the northwest corner of Ohio and passes just south of the Toledo and Cleveland metropolitan areas before terminating east of Youngstown. The turnpike connects with other toll roads in Indiana and Pennsylvania. The Ohio legislature established the turnpike commission in 1949, and the toll road was opened to traffic in 1955. The Ohio Turnpike Commission is governed separately from the state's primary highway agency, the Ohio Department of Transportation.

	Annual Growth	12/18	12/19	12/20	12/21	12/22
Sales ($mil.)	4.2%	–	334.9	303.5	367.8	378.6
Net income ($ mil.)	–	–	(61.2)	(138.3)	(22.2)	53.5
Market value ($ mil.)	–	–	–	–	–	–
Employees	–	–	–	–	–	953

OHIO VALLEY BANC CORP　　　　　　　　NMS: OVBC

420 Third Avenue　　　　　　　　　　　　　CEO: Larry E Miller II
Gallipolis, OH 45631　　　　　　　　　　　　CFO: Scott W Shockey
Phone: 740 446-2631　　　　　　　　　　　　HR: –
Fax: –　　　　　　　　　　　　　　　　　　FYE: December 31
Web: www.ovbc.com　　　　　　　　　　　　Type: Public

Ohio Valley Banc Corp. (OVBC) knows when you go to buy groceries, you'll probably need some cabbage. That's why this holding company likes to operate its Ohio Valley Bank branches inside supermarkets. The bank has some 20 branches in Ohio and West Virginia, about half of which are in Wal-Marts and other stores. The bank accepts deposits in checking, savings, time, and money market accounts, and offers standard banking services, such as safe deposit boxes and wire transfers. Commercial and residential real estate loans combine to make up almost three-quarters of the bank's loan portfolio. Business and consumer loans make up the remainder. Also part of OVBC is life insurance agency Ohio Valley Financial Services.

	Annual Growth	12/19	12/20	12/21	12/22	12/23
Assets ($mil.)	7.5%	1,013.3	1,186.9	1,249.8	1,210.8	1,352.1
Net income ($ mil.)	6.3%	9.9	10.3	11.7	13.3	12.6
Market value ($ mil.)	(12.7%)	189.1	112.6	141.5	126.1	109.8
Employees	(1.3%)	284	270	264	284	270

OHIO VALLEY ELECTRIC CORP.

3932 U.S. Route 23, P.O. Box 468　　　　　　　CEO: –
Piketon, OH 45661　　　　　　　　　　　　　CFO: Justin Cooper
Phone: 740 289-7200　　　　　　　　　　　　HR: Deb Wells
Fax: –　　　　　　　　　　　　　　　　　　FYE: December 31
Web: www.ovec.com　　　　　　　　　　　　Type: Public

Down by the banks of the Ohio, Ohio Valley Electric and its subsidiary, Indiana-Kentucky Electric, generate power for customers across the Ohio River Valley. It operates two coal-fired plants which collectively have about 2,290 MW of generating capacity. Ohio Valley Electric's Kyger Creek Plant (Cheshire, Ohio) and Indiana-Kentucky Electric's Clifty Creek Plant (Madison, Indiana) are linked by 705 miles of transmission lines. Most of Ohio Valley Electric's power goes to its shareholders, (a dozen investor-owned utilities, utility holding entities, led by American Electric Power, and units of generation and transmission rural electric cooperatives). It also supplies energy to the Department of Energy.

	Annual Growth	12/09	12/10	12/11	12/12	12/13
Sales ($mil.)	1.0%	648.6	690.7	716.9	670.8	675.6
Net income ($ mil.)	(6.7%)	2.9	2.2	2.7	2.3	2.2
Market value ($ mil.)	–	–	–	–	–	–
Employees	–	–	–	–	–	–

OHIO VALLEY GENERAL HOSPITAL

25 HECKEL RD
MC KEES ROCKS, PA 151361651
Phone: 412 777-6161
Fax: –
Web: www.heritagevalley.org

CEO: Norman F Mitry
CFO: –
HR: –
FYE: June 30
Type: Private

Ohio Valley General Hospital is a full-service, 140-bed medical center serving western Pennsylvania residents. The not-for-profit community hospital's staff of about 250 doctors (representing about 35 medical specialties) provides emergency, acute, diagnostic, and specialty care, and a variety of inpatient and outpatient care services. Ohio Valley General Hospital's programs include cardiology, occupational medicine, pain treatment, orthopedics, rehabilitation, sleep disorder diagnosis, geriatric psychiatry, and wound care. The hospital also offers assisted living for seniors. Ohio Valley General began serving patients in 1906.

	Annual Growth	06/15	06/16	06/17	06/18	06/20
Sales ($mil.)	(59.6%)	–	67.9	72.1	74.5	1.8
Net income ($ mil.)	–	–	(13.9)	3.1	(5.0)	(2.2)
Market value ($ mil.)	–	–	–	–	–	–
Employees	–	–	–	–	–	570

OHIO VALLEY MEDICAL CENTER INCORPORATED

2000 EOFF ST
WHEELING, WV 260033823
Phone: 304 234-0123
Fax: –
Web: www.ovmc-eorh.com

CEO: –
CFO: –
HR: –
FYE: December 31
Type: Private

Ohio Valley Medical Center (OVMC) is a Wheeling, West Virginia-based medical provider that administers a variety of acute care, primary care, and other health services to patients through a 200-bed hospital. The facility, established in 1890 as City Hospital, specializes in intermediate care, physical rehabilitation, and skilled nursing. Other services include cardiology, cancer care, emergency care, gynecology, neurology, oncology, and psychiatry, as well as home health care. OVMC also operates the Peterson Rehabilitation Center and two-year hospital based education program OVMC School of Radiologic Technology. It partners with nearby East Ohio Regional Hospital to provide 340 total beds.

	Annual Growth	12/06	12/07	12/09	12/14	12/16
Sales ($mil.)	1.5%	–	94.7	106.4	103.2	108.2
Net income ($ mil.)	(16.2%)	–	6.0	(1.8)	4.0	1.2
Market value ($ mil.)	–	–	–	–	–	–
Employees	–	–	–	–	–	1,275

OHIOHEALTH CORPORATION

3430 OHIO HEALTH PKWY 5TH FL
COLUMBUS, OH 43202
Phone: 614 788-8860
Fax: –
Web: www.ohiohealth.com

CEO: David Blom
CFO: Michael W Louge
HR: –
FYE: June 30
Type: Private

OhioHealth is a nationally recognized, not-for-profit, charitable, healthcare outreach of the United Methodist Church. It runs around 15 of hospitals including OhioHealth Riverside Methodist Hospital, OhioHealth Grant Medical Center and OhioHealth Doctors Hospital, among others. All told, OhioHealth has more than 200 ambulatory sites, hospice, home health, medical equipment and other services spanning more than 45 Ohio counties. OhioHealth offers urgent care, physical rehabilitation, diagnostic imaging, and sleep diagnostics services. OhioHealth Physician Group includes 800 primary care physicians and 400 advance practice providers in more than 50 specialties.

	Annual Growth	06/16	06/17	06/18	06/21	06/22
Sales ($mil.)	2.5%	–	3,792.7	4,045.7	3,841.9	4,294.3
Net income ($ mil.)	4.9%	–	631.5	519.0	960.8	801.2
Market value ($ mil.)	–	–	–	–	–	–
Employees	–	–	–	–	–	15,000

OIL STATES INTERNATIONAL, INC.

NYS: OIS

Three Allen Center, 333 Clay Street, Suite 4620
Houston, TX 77002
Phone: 713 652-0582
Fax: –
Web: www.oilstatesintl.com

CEO: Cindy B Taylor
CFO: Lloyd A Hajdik
HR: Shana Oliver
FYE: December 31
Type: Public

Oil States International is an oilfield services company with a leading market position as a manufacturer of products for deepwater production facilities and certain drilling equipment, as well as a provider of completion services and land drilling services to the oil and gas industry, and oil and gas perforation systems and downhole tools. It also offers offshore products, including flex-element technology and deepwater mooring systems. It focuses on supporting explorers in major producing regions throughout the world. Its customers include many national oil and natural gas companies, major and independent oil and natural gas companies. About 75% of its revenue comes from the US.

	Annual Growth	12/19	12/20	12/21	12/22	12/23
Sales ($mil.)	(6.4%)	1,017.4	638.1	573.2	737.7	782.3
Net income ($ mil.)	–	(231.8)	(468.4)	(64.0)	(9.5)	12.9
Market value ($ mil.)	(19.7%)	1,032.9	317.9	314.7	472.4	430.0
Employees	(5.3%)	3,428	2,338	2,373	2,738	2,752

OIL-DRI CORP. OF AMERICA

NYS: ODC

410 North Michigan Avenue, Suite 400
Chicago, IL 60611-4213
Phone: 312 321-1515
Fax: 312 321-9525
Web: www.oildri.com

CEO: Daniel S Jaffee
CFO: Susan M Kreh
HR: Mike Keneda
FYE: July 31
Type: Public

Oil-Dri Corporation (ODC) of America keeps cat lovers' homes from stinking to high heaven. The company produces sorbent products for the consumer, industrial, automotive, agricultural, and fluid-purification markets. It makes and sells traditional coarse and scoopable cat litters under its own Cat's Pride and Jonny Cat brands. ODC manufactures the Fresh Step brand exclusively for Clorox, as well as private label cat litters for others. Its litters are sold by mass merchants (Wal-Mart), supermarkets, pet stores, wholesale clubs, and other retailers. ODC also makes sorbents for oil, grease, and water; bleaching and clarification clays; agricultural and sports fields; and animal health and nutrition products.

	Annual Growth	07/19	07/20	07/21	07/22	07/23
Sales ($mil.)	10.5%	277.0	283.2	305.0	348.6	413.0
Net income ($ mil.)	23.7%	12.6	18.9	11.1	5.7	29.6
Market value ($ mil.)	15.4%	252.9	248.1	253.9	215.1	448.0
Employees	2.5%	801	803	847	869	884

OKEECHOBEE HOSPITAL, INC.

1796 US HIGHWAY 441 N
OKEECHOBEE, FL 349721918
Phone: 863 763-2151
Fax: –
Web: www.hcafloridahealthcare.com

CEO: –
CFO: –
HR: –
FYE: April 30
Type: Private

Raulerson Hospital, part of HCA, is an acute care hospital with some 100 beds. The facility serves the community of Okeechobee and surrounding areas in eastern Florida. The hospital provides a variety of general medical services including diagnostic imaging, laparoscopic surgery, intensive care, neurology, orthopedics, rehabilitation, and physical therapy. Specialty units include a cardiopulmonary department, a sleep disorder lab, a diabetes education unit, and outpatient testing and surgery centers. Raulerson Hospital is part of HCA's East Florida division.

	Annual Growth	04/10	04/11	04/12	04/13	04/15
Sales ($mil.)	2.7%	–	–	–	70.4	74.4
Net income ($ mil.)	7.0%	–	–	–	17.1	19.6
Market value ($ mil.)	–	–	–	–	–	–
Employees	–	–	–	–	–	350

OKLAHOMA STATE UNIVERSITY

401 WHITEHURST HALL
STILLWATER, OK 740781030
Phone: 405 744-5000
Fax: –
Web: agriculture.okstate.edu

CEO: –
CFO: –
HR: Carl Venable
FYE: June 30
Type: Private

Oooooklahoma where the... students come to learn! Oklahoma State University is the flagship campus of its namesake (OSU) system, which also includes OSU-Tulsa, OSU-Oklahoma City, OSU-Okmulgee, the OSU Center for Health Sciences in Tulsa, the OSU College of Veterinary Medicine, and the Oklahoma Agricultural Experiment Station. OSU offers courses in a variety of disciplines and confers undergraduate, graduate, doctoral, and professional degrees in everything from agriculture and the arts to business and engineering. Altogether, the system boasts an enrollment of about 36,000 students across its five campuses; its student-teacher ratio is about 17:1.

	Annual Growth	06/15	06/16	06/17	06/18	06/19
Sales ($mil.)	5.3%	–	–	815.1	802.9	904.1
Net income ($ mil.)	54.2%	–	–	40.3	9.0	96.0
Market value ($ mil.)	–	–	–	–	–	–
Employees	–	–	–	–	–	8,882

OKTA INC

NMS: OKTA

100 First Street, Suite 600
San Francisco, CA 94105
Phone: 888 722-7871
Fax: –
Web: www.okta.com

CEO: Todd McKinnon
CFO: Brett Tighe
HR: Kristina Johnson
FYE: January 31
Type: Public

Okta is one of the leading independent identity management platforms for the enterprise. The Okta Identity Cloud is its category-defining platform that enables its customers to securely connect the right people to the right technologies at the right time. The company claims more than 17,000 corporate customers including more than 3,900 customers with an annual contract value greater than $100,000. Customers include nearly all industry verticals and range from small organizations with fewer than 100 employees to companies in the Fortune 50, some of which use the Okta Identity Cloud to manage millions of their customers' identities. The company generates about 80% of its sales from the US.

	Annual Growth	01/20	01/21	01/22	01/23	01/24
Sales ($mil.)	40.2%	586.1	835.4	1,300.2	1,858.0	2,263.0
Net income ($ mil.)	–	(208.9)	(266.3)	(848.4)	(815.0)	(355.0)
Market value ($ mil.)	(10.4%)	21,400	43,287	33,073	12,302	13,813
Employees	27.3%	2,248	2,806	5,030	6,013	5,908

OLD CLAIMCO, LLC

1707 MARKET PL STE 200
IRVING, TX 750638049
Phone: 972 258-8507
Fax: –
Web: www.chuckecheese.com

CEO: David McKillips
CFO: James A Howell
HR: Nancy Harris
FYE: December 29
Type: Private

Don't let the mouse mascot fool you: This amusement kingdom is founded on the power of pizza. CEC Entertainment operates the Chuck E. Cheese's chain of pizza parlors with more than 610 locations in over 45 states and approximately 15 foreign countries and territories. The restaurants cater mostly to families with children and feature a broad array of entertainment offerings including arcade-style and skill-oriented games, rides, live entertainment shows. Entertainment and merchandise account for some 55% of sales. The menu features pizzas, wings, appetizers, salads, and desserts. CEC Entertainment owns and operates more than 550 of the pizza and fun joints, while the rest are franchised.

	Annual Growth	01/16	01/17*	12/17	12/18	12/19
Sales ($mil.)	(0.6%)	–	923.7	886.8	896.1	912.9
Net income ($ mil.)	–	–	(3.7)	53.1	(20.5)	(28.9)
Market value ($ mil.)	–	–	–	–	–	–
Employees	–	–	–	–	–	17,200

*Fiscal year change

OLD COPPER COMPANY, INC.

6501 LEGACY DR
PLANO, TX 750244161
Phone: 972 431-1000
Fax: –
Web: www.jcpenney.com

CEO: –
CFO: –
HR: –
FYE: February 01
Type: Private

J. C. Penney Company is a holding company for department store operator J. C. Penney Corp. One of the largest department store and e-commerce retailers in the US, J. C. Penney Corp. operates in about 845 JCPenney department stores across the country and in Puerto Rico. Its stores are mostly found in suburban shopping malls, and sell clothing for men, women, and children, as well as footwear and accessories Some stores contain styling salons, optical centers, and portrait studios as well as shop-in-shops such as Sephora cosmetics. J. C. Penney Corp. has been closing stores amid a tough retail environment.

OLD DOMINION ELECTRIC COOPERATIVE

4201 Dominion Boulevard
Glen Allen, VA 23060
Phone: 804 747-0592
Fax: –
Web: www.odec.com

CEO: –
CFO: –
HR: –
FYE: December 31
Type: Public

Ol' Virginny and neighboring states get power from Old Dominion Electric Cooperative, which generates and purchases electricity for its 11 member distribution cooperatives. These in turn serve more than 550,000 customer meters in four northeastern states. The member-owned power utility has more than 2,000 MW of generating capacity from nuclear, hydro, and fossil-fueled power plants and diesel generators; it purchases the remainder of its power from neighboring utilities and power marketers. Old Dominion transmits power to its members through the systems of utilities and transmission operators in the region. It also provides power to TEC Trading, a wholesale company owned by the distribution cooperatives.

	Annual Growth	12/18	12/19	12/20	12/21	12/22
Sales ($mil.)	1.9%	932.6	932.7	807.7	780.6	1,005.9
Net income ($ mil.)	(3.9%)	13.3	17.0	12.2	20.0	11.3
Market value ($ mil.)	–	–	–	–	–	–
Employees	(1.5%)	140	143	137	134	132

OLD DOMINION FREIGHT LINE, INC.

NMS: ODFL

500 Old Dominion Way
Thomasville, NC 27360
Phone: 336 889-5000
Fax: –
Web: www.odfl.com

CEO: David S Congdon
CFO: Adam N Satterfield
HR: Deignan Lomax
FYE: December 31
Type: Public

Old Dominion Freight Line is one of the largest North American less-than-truckload (LTL) motor carriers specializing in less-than-truckload (LTL) shipments (freight from multiple shippers consolidated into a single truckload). It operates a fleet of nearly 11,275 tractors and more than 31,250 linehaul trailers from around 255 service centers. In addition to its core LTL services, Old Dominion offers its customers a range of value-added services including container drayage, truckload brokerage and supply chain consulting. The company traces its historical roots back to 1934.

	Annual Growth	12/19	12/20	12/21	12/22	12/23
Sales ($mil.)	9.3%	4,109.1	4,015.1	5,256.3	6,260.1	5,866.2
Net income ($ mil.)	19.1%	615.5	672.7	1,034.4	1,377.2	1,239.5
Market value ($ mil.)	20.9%	20,679	21,268	39,051	30,922	44,167
Employees	3.3%	20,105	19,779	23,663	23,471	22,902

OLD DOMINION TOBACCO COMPANY INCORPORATED

5400 VIRGINIA BEACH BLVD
VIRGINIA BEACH, VA 234621724
Phone: 757 497-1001
Fax: –
Web: www.atlanticdominiondistributors.com

CEO: –
CFO: –
HR: –
FYE: January 01
Type: Private

Atlantic Dominion has built a business providing convenience to the masses. As part of its distribution arm, the company supplies more than 10,000 products -- including beverages, groceries, snacks, cigars and other tobacco products, and general merchandise -- to retailers along the East Coast. It also services vending machines and provides fixture installation, product ordering, CO gas and dry ice services, and repairs. Customers include drugstores, tobacco merchants, US military bases, and others. Originally a cigar maker, Atlantic Dominion was founded as Old Dominion Tobacco Co. by Leroy Davis in 1875. The company remains family owned and is led by Robin Davis Ray, the founder's great-granddaughter.

OLD NATIONAL BANCORP (EVANSVILLE, IN)   NMS: ONB

One Main Street
Evansville, IN 47708
Phone: 800 731-2265
Fax: –
Web: www.oldnational.com

CEO: James C Ryan III
CFO: Brendon B Falconer
HR: –
FYE: December 31
Type: Public

Old National Bancorp is the financial holding company of Old National Bank, its wholly-owned banking subsidiary. Through its Old National Bank, the company provides a wide range of services, including commercial and consumer loan and depository services, private banking, brokerage, trust, investment advisory, and other traditional banking services. Old National Bank operates nearly 265 banking centers located primarily in Indiana, Iowa, Kentucky, Michigan, Minnesota, and Wisconsin. Old National Bank was founded in 1834 and is the oldest company in Evansville, Indiana. It has consolidated assets of $46.8 billion. In early 2023, Old National and Chicago-based First Midwest Bancorp Inc. have completed their previously-announced $6.5 billion merger, and will operate under the Old National Bancorp and Old National Bank names.

	Annual Growth	12/19	12/20	12/21	12/22	12/23
Assets ($mil.)	24.5%	20,412	22,961	24,454	46,763	49,090
Net income ($ mil.)	25.0%	238.2	226.4	277.5	428.3	582.0
Market value ($ mil.)	(2.0%)	5,352.7	4,846.4	5,302.9	5,261.9	4,942.9
Employees	9.8%	2,709	2,445	2,374	3,967	3,940

OLD POINT FINANCIAL CORP   NAS: OPOF

101 East Queen Street
Hampton, VA 23669
Phone: 757 728-1200
Fax: –
Web: www.oldpoint.com

CEO: Robert F Shuford Jr
CFO: Elizabeth T Beale
HR: –
FYE: December 31
Type: Public

Community banking and wealth management is the point at Old Point Financial. It is the holding company for Old Point National Bank of Phoebus, which has more than 20 branches in the Hampton Roads region of southeastern Virginia. Founded in 1923, the bank serves area businesses and consumers, offering such services as checking and savings accounts, money market accounts, and CDs. With these funds, the bank mainly originates commercial and residential mortgages, which account for a majority of its loans. Subsidiary Old Point Trust & Financial Services provides investment management and tax, estate, and retirement planning services. Old Point National Bank also owns 49% of Old Point Mortgage.

	Annual Growth	12/18	12/19	12/20	12/21	12/22
Assets ($mil.)	6.9%	1,038.2	1,054.5	1,226.2	1,338.2	1,355.3
Net income ($ mil.)	16.7%	4.9	7.9	5.4	8.4	9.1
Market value ($ mil.)	5.5%	109.1	137.4	94.8	116.8	135.0
Employees	(0.4%)	301	297	307	275	296

OLD REPUBLIC INTERNATIONAL CORP.   NYS: ORI

307 North Michigan Avenue
Chicago, IL 60601
Phone: 312 346-8100
Fax: –
Web: www.oldrepublic.com

CEO: Craig R Smiddy
CFO: Frank J Sodaro
HR: –
FYE: December 31
Type: Public

Old Republic International Corporation (Old Republic) is one of the nation's 50 largest shareholder-owned insurance businesses. It is primarily a commercial lines underwriter serving the insurance needs of some organizations, including many of North America's leading industrial and financial services institutions. It conducts its operations through a number of regulated insurance company subsidiaries organized into three major segments: General Insurance (property and liability insurance), Title Insurance, and the Republic Financial Indemnity Group (RFIG) Run-off. The Old Republic traces its roots back to 1923.

	Annual Growth	12/19	12/20	12/21	12/22	12/23
Assets ($mil.)	5.9%	21,076	22,815	24,982	25,159	26,501
Net income ($ mil.)	(13.2%)	1,056.4	558.6	1,534.3	686.4	598.6
Market value ($ mil.)	7.1%	6,227.6	5,487.1	6,842.9	6,723.2	8,184.7
Employees	0.6%	9,000	9,000	9,600	9,500	9,200

OLD SECOND BANCORP., INC. (AURORA, ILL.)   NMS: OSBC

37 South River Street
Aurora, IL 60507
Phone: 630 892-0202
Fax: –
Web: www.oldsecond.com

CEO: James L Eccher
CFO: Bradley S Adams
HR: Chris Lasse
FYE: December 31
Type: Public

Old Second Bancorp is the holding company for Old Second National Bank, which serves the Chicago metropolitan area through some 50 branches in Cook, DeKalb, DuPage, Kane, Kendall, LaSalle and Will counties in Illinois. The bank provides standard services such as checking and savings accounts, credit and debit cards, CDs, mortgages, loans, and trust services to consumers and business clients. Subsidiary River Street Advisors offers investment management and advisory services. Another subsidiary, Old Second Affordable Housing Fund, provides home-buying assistance to lower-income customers. Station I and Melrose Holdings 7, which were formed to hold property acquired by the bank through foreclosure or in the ordinary course of collecting a debt previously contracted with borrowers.

	Annual Growth	12/19	12/20	12/21	12/22	12/23
Assets ($mil.)	21.4%	2,635.5	3,040.8	6,212.2	5,888.3	5,722.8
Net income ($ mil.)	23.5%	39.5	27.8	20.0	67.4	91.7
Market value ($ mil.)	3.5%	602.1	451.4	562.7	717.0	690.1
Employees	11.7%	535	533	891	819	834

OLE' MEXICAN FOODS, INC.

6585 CRESCENT DR
NORCROSS, GA 300712901
Phone: 770 582-9200
Fax: –
Web: www.olemex.com

CEO: Veronica Moreno
CFO: –
HR: –
FYE: December 31
Type: Private

Its a wrap at Ol Mexican Foods. The company makes Mexican-American foods, inducing tortillas and taco shells, under brand names La Banderita, La Centroamericana, Ol , and Verol . The company also produces salsa, sour cream, Mexican cheeses and sausages, tostadas, and tortilla chips, among other items. Its customers include retail food outlets and food service operations. Headquartered in Norcross, Georgia, the company has about a dozen distribution centers across the US. It serves customers across the continental US and Alaska, as well as in Puerto Rico.

	Annual Growth	12/00	12/01	12/02	12/03	12/13
Sales ($mil.)	14.9%	–	–	52.7	65.1	242.7
Net income ($ mil.)	11.9%	–	–	3.6	5.8	12.5
Market value ($ mil.)	–	–	–	–	–	–
Employees	–	–	–	–	–	1,200

OLIN CORP.

NYS: OLN

190 Carondelet Plaza, Suite 1530
Clayton, MO 63105
Phone: 314 480-1400
Fax: –
Web: www.olin.com

CEO: Scott M Sutton
CFO: Todd A Slater
HR: –
FYE: December 31
Type: Public

Olin Corporation manufactures chemicals use to make bleach, water purification and swimming pool chemicals, pulp and paper processing agents, and PVC plastics. Olin also distributes caustic soda, vinyls, epoxies, chlorinated organics, hydrochloric acid, and bleach. Its Chlor Alkali Products and Vinyls segment markets caustic soda. In addition, the company's Winchester develops and manufactures small caliber ammunition for sale to domestic and international retailers, law enforcement agencies and domestic and international militaries. It is the leading US producer of ammunition for recreational shooters, hunters, law enforcement agencies and the US Armed Forces. Roughly 60% of the company's revenue is generated from the US.

	Annual Growth	12/19	12/20	12/21	12/22	12/23
Sales ($mil.)	2.8%	6,110.0	5,758.0	8,910.6	9,376.2	6,833.0
Net income ($ mil.)	–	(11.3)	(969.9)	1,296.7	1,326.9	460.2
Market value ($ mil.)	33.0%	2,073.5	2,952.1	6,913.9	6,363.4	6,484.8
Employees	3.0%	6,500	8,000	7,750	7,780	7,326

OLLIE'S BARGAIN OUTLET HOLDINGS INC

NMS: OLLI

6295 Allentown Boulevard, Suite 1
Harrisburg, PA 17112
Phone: 717 657-2300
Fax: –
Web: www.ollies.us

CEO: John Swygert
CFO: Jay Stasz
HR: –
FYE: January 28
Type: Public

Retailer Ollie's Bargain Outlet has a simple business proposition -- 'Good Stuff Cheap.' The company is a value retailer of brand name merchandise at drastically reduced prices. It offers customers a broad selection of products, including housewares, food, books and stationery, bed and bath, floor coverings, toys and hardware. To give it a marketing edge, Ollie's provides a fun and engaging treasure hunt shopping experience, compelling customer value proposition, and witty, humorous in-store signage and advertising campaigns. These attributes have driven its rapid growth. The company went public in 2015.

	Annual Growth	02/19	02/20*	01/21	01/22	01/23
Sales ($mil.)	10.1%	1,241.4	1,408.2	1,808.8	1,753.0	1,827.0
Net income ($ mil.)	(6.6%)	135.0	141.1	242.7	157.5	102.8
Market value ($ mil.)	(9.2%)	4,920.3	3,288.9	5,874.0	2,786.0	3,346.6
Employees	8.6%	7,700	8,300	9,800	9,900	10,700

*Fiscal year change

OLMSTED MEDICAL CENTER

210 9TH ST SE
ROCHESTER, MN 559046400
Phone: 507 288-3443
Fax: –
Web: www.olmmed.org

CEO: Tim Weir
CFO: –
HR: Kim Kramer
FYE: December 31
Type: Private

Olmsted Medical Center (OMC) provides general medical and surgical care to the Rochester, Minnesota, area. The not-for-profit hospital also partners with regional schools to provide medical, nursing, and technical training, and it engages in clinical research programs. Specialty services include pediatrics, neurology, occupational medicine, and orthopedics. In addition to its hospital, OMC also operates several urgent care, specialty, and general practice clinics in the region. OMC was formed through the merger of Olmsted Community Hospital and Olmsted Medical Group in 1996.

	Annual Growth	12/15	12/16	12/19	12/21	12/22
Sales ($mil.)	3.9%	–	205.3	228.1	259.5	258.7
Net income ($ mil.)	(24.7%)	–	21.5	9.6	15.6	3.9
Market value ($ mil.)	–	–	–	–	–	–
Employees	–	–	–	–	–	1,200

OLYMPIC PIPE LINE COMPANY

2319 LIND AVE SW
RENTON, WA 980573347
Phone: 425 235-7736
Fax: –
Web: –

CEO: –
CFO: –
HR: –
FYE: December 31
Type: Private

Olympic Pipe Line is going for the gold (you know, black gold or Texas tea). The company, owned by Enbridge (65%) and integrated oil giant BP p.l.c. (35%), operates a 400-mile interstate pipeline system used for the transportation of refined petroleum products, including aviation jet fuel, diesel, and gasoline, from Washington to Oregon; through joint ventures the company has operations in 30 US states. Its systems are capable of moving about 285,000 barrels of refined petroleum products per day. In 2006 Enbridge paid BP nearly $100 million for a controlling share in Olympic Pipe Line. BP is the pipeline operator.

	Annual Growth	12/13	12/14	12/15	12/16	12/17
Sales ($mil.)	18.4%	–	–	–	66.1	78.3
Net income ($ mil.)	495.7%	–	–	–	10.1	59.9
Market value ($ mil.)	–	–	–	–	–	–
Employees	–	–	–	–	–	82

OLYMPIC STEEL INC.

NMS: ZEUS

22901 Millcreek Boulevard, Suite 650
Highland Hills, OH 44122
Phone: 216 292-3800
Fax: 216 682-4065
Web: www.olysteel.com

CEO: Richard T Marabito
CFO: Richard A Manson
HR: Brenda Marple
FYE: December 31
Type: Public

Founded in 1954, Olympic Steel is a leading metals service center that provides metals processing and distributions services for a wide range of customers. The company also distributes metal tubing, pipe, bar, valves and fittings, and fabricates parts supplied to various industrial markets. Olympic Steel's services include both traditional service center and higher value-added processes of cutting-to-length, slitting, shearing, blanking, tempering, stretcher-leveling, plate and laser processing, forming and machining, tube processing, finishing, fabrication, and other value-added services pursuant to specific customer orders.

	Annual Growth	12/19	12/20	12/21	12/22	12/23
Sales ($mil.)	8.1%	1,579.0	1,234.1	2,312.3	2,560.0	2,158.2
Net income ($ mil.)	84.3%	3.9	(5.6)	121.1	90.9	44.5
Market value ($ mil.)	38.9%	199.5	148.4	261.6	373.8	742.6
Employees	3.9%	1,860	1,626	1,642	1,668	2,168

OMAGINE INC

NBB: OMAG Q

136 Madison Avenue, 5th Floor
New York, NY 10016
Phone: 212 563-4141
Fax: –
Web: www.omagine.com

CEO: –
CFO: –
HR: –
FYE: December 31
Type: Public

Omagine wants you to imagine investing in beachfront abodes in the Middle East and North Africa (MENA). Formerly Alfa International, Omagine repositioned and rebranded itself in 2007 as it exited the apparel business. The company's Journey of Light subsidiary now intends to tap into the high-margin real estate development and luxury travel markets in MENA. In 2008 Journey of Light was granted initial approval to develop the Omagine Project, a $1.6 billion government-sponsored entertainment, retail, commercial, residential, and hotel real estate development in Oman. Omagine will also provide property management services.

	Annual Growth	12/12	12/13	12/14	12/15	12/16
Sales ($mil.)	–	–	–	–	–	–
Net income ($ mil.)	–	(2.8)	(2.6)	(6.8)	(5.7)	(2.9)
Market value ($ mil.)	(23.0%)	35.8	18.8	52.1	28.6	12.6
Employees	(1.6%)	16	16	16	15	15

OMAHA PUBLIC POWER DISTRICT

444 S 16TH ST
OMAHA, NE 681022608
Phone: 402 636-2000
Fax: –
Web: www.oppd.com

CEO: Gary Gates
CFO: –
HR: James E Gubbels
FYE: December 31
Type: Private

Thirteen's the lucky number for Omaha Public Power District (OPPD). A subdivision of the Nebraska state government, OPPD generates and distributes electricity to residents and businesses in 13 counties in southeastern Nebraska. It operates and maintains its facilities without tax revenues and raises money for major construction through bonds. OPPD serves more than 853,000 customers in an area covering 5,000 sq. mi. The utility has a generating capacity of approximately 2,700 MW, which is powered by primarily nuclear, coal, oil, and natural gas sources. It sells wholesale power to other utilities and offers energy consulting and management services.

	Annual Growth	12/17	12/18	12/19	12/20	12/21
Sales ($mil.)	13.6%	–	–	1,160.7	1,083.9	1,496.9
Net income ($ mil.)	(43.3%)	–	–	86.9	74.0	27.9
Market value ($ mil.)	–	–	–	–	–	–
Employees	–	–	–	–	–	2,300

OMAHA STEAKS INTERNATIONAL, INC.

11030 O ST
OMAHA, NE 681372346
Phone: 402 597-3000
Fax: –
Web: www.omahasteaks.com

CEO: Nate Rempe
CFO: Dave L Hershiser
HR: –
FYE: December 29
Type: Private

Omaha Steaks is one of the leading meat packers and distributors that produce a wide variety of the finest quality USDA-approved, grain-fed beef and other gourmet foods including seafood, pork, poultry, and skillet meals, side dishes, appetizers, and desserts. The fifth-generation, family-owned business sells its products to customers through nearly 50 retail store locations nationwide, as well as through catalogs, mail order, foodservice, and online. Distributing beef to foodservice operators and other retail outlets, Omaha Steaks also serves customers in hotels, restaurants, and institutions. J.J. and B.A Simon founded Omaha Steaks in 1917 as Table Supply Meat Company.

OMEGA FLEX INC

451 Creamery Way
Exton, PA 19341
Phone: 610 524-7272
Fax: 610 524-7282
Web: www.omegaflex.com

NMS: OFLX
CEO: Dean W Rivest
CFO: Matthew F Unger
HR: –
FYE: December 31
Type: Public

Omega Flex makes corrugated metal and flexible tubular and braided metal (stainless steel, bronze) hoses and reinforcements for construction and industrial customers to use in liquid and gas transportation. Its products are designed to deal with high pressure, motion, extreme temperatures, harsh liquids or gases, and abrasion. Other applications include cryogenics and propane and natural gas installations. Other prominent uses include using copper-alloy corrugated piping in medical or health care facilities to carry medical gases (oxygen, nitrogen, vacuum) or pure gases for pharmaceutical applications.

	Annual Growth	12/19	12/20	12/21	12/22	12/23
Sales ($mil.)	–	111.4	105.8	130.0	125.5	111.5
Net income ($ mil.)	4.7%	17.3	19.9	26.2	23.6	20.8
Market value ($ mil.)	(10.0%)	1,083.0	1,473.8	1,281.5	942.0	711.8
Employees	2.7%	151	164	170	177	168

OMEGA HEALTHCARE INVESTORS, INC.

303 International Circle, Suite 200
Hunt Valley, MD 21030
Phone: 410 427-1700
Fax: 410 427-8800
Web: www.omegahealthcare.com

NYS: OHI
CEO: C T Pickett
CFO: Robert O Stephenson
HR: –
FYE: December 31
Type: Public

Omega Healthcare Investors is a triple-net, equity REIT that provides financing and capital to the long-term healthcare industry with a particular focus on skilled nursing facilities (SNFs), assisted living facilities (ALFss), and to a lesser extent, independent living facilities (ILFs), rehabilitation and acute care facilities (specialty facilities), and medical office buildings ("MOBs"). It owns some 925 facilities in about 40 states (US) and in the UK. The company's properties are operated by third-party health care operating companies, including Daybreak and Genesis HealthCare System.

	Annual Growth	12/19	12/20	12/21	12/22	12/23
Sales ($mil.)	0.6%	928.8	892.4	1,062.8	878.2	949.7
Net income ($ mil.)	(8.2%)	341.1	159.3	416.7	426.9	242.2
Market value ($ mil.)	(7.8%)	10,388	8,908.6	7,257.9	6,855.6	7,520.3
Employees	–	49	68	70	52	–

OMEGA INSTITUTE FOR HOLISTIC STUDIES, INC.

150 LAKE DR
RHINEBECK, NY 125723252
Phone: 845 266-4444
Fax: –
Web: www.eomega.org

CEO: –
CFO: –
HR: –
FYE: December 31
Type: Private

The Omega Institute for Holistic Studies wants to be the last word on spiritual healing. The not-for-profit organization offers workshops and retreats designed to improve spirituality and health. Its classes, attended by about 20,000 people each year, include yoga, meditation, and women's empowerment. Omega Institute offers its holistic studies at more than a dozen locations in California, Florida, and New York, as well as in Costa Rica and the Virgin Islands. The organization was started in 1977.

	Annual Growth	12/17	12/18	12/19	12/21	12/22
Sales ($mil.)	(12.4%)	–	24.8	26.8	10.4	14.6
Net income ($ mil.)	–	–	2.0	3.2	(1.4)	(1.7)
Market value ($ mil.)	–	–	–	–	–	–
Employees	–	–	–	–	–	100

OMEGA PROTEIN CORPORATION

610 MENHADEN RD
REEDVILLE, VA 225394126
Phone: 804 453-6262
Fax: –
Web: www.omegaprotein.com

CEO: Bret D Scholtes
CFO: Andrew C Johannesen
HR: Brandy Stargell
FYE: December 31
Type: Private

Omega Protein is the leading, vertically integrated producer in the United States of omega-3-rich fish oil, protein-rich specialty fishmeal and organic fish soluble for livestock and aquaculture feed manufacturers. It has a handful of US processing plants and a fleet of some 30 fishing vessels that harvest menhaden (a fish abundantly found off the coasts of the Gulf of Mexico and the Atlantic Ocean). It provides the food and supplement industry with some of the most trusted, scientifically-recognized, and innovative ingredients in the marketplace. The company is a division of Cooke Inc., a family-owned fishery company based in New Brunswick, Canada.

OMEROS CORP

NMS: OMER

201 Elliott Avenue West
Seattle, WA 98119
Phone: 206 676-5000
Fax: –
Web: www.omeros.com

CEO: –
CFO: –
HR: –
FYE: December 31
Type: Public

Omeros is a clinical-stage biopharmaceutical company committed to discovering, developing and commercializing small-molecule and protein therapeutics for large-market as well as orphan indications targeting immunologic diseases, including complement-mediated diseases and cancers related to dysfunction of the immune system, as well as addictive and compulsive disorders. Other product candidates include treatment for lupus nephritis and other renal diseases (Narsoplimab), for addictions and compulsive disorders, and movement disorders (PDE7), and Atypical Hemolytic Uremic Syndrome (aHUS) (Narsoplimab- Lectin Pathway Disorders). In late 2021, Omeros completed the sale of Omidria to Rayner Surgical for about $126 million.

	Annual Growth	12/18	12/19	12/20	12/21	12/22
Sales ($mil.)	–	29.9	111.8	73.8	–	–
Net income ($ mil.)	–	(126.8)	(84.5)	(138.1)	194.2	47.4
Market value ($ mil.)	(32.9%)	699.9	885.3	897.5	404.0	142.0
Employees	(4.5%)	236	258	277	213	196

OMNI CABLE, LLC

2 HAGERTY BLVD
WEST CHESTER, PA 193827594
Phone: 610 701-0100
Fax: –
Web: www.omnicable.com

CEO: Greg Lampert
CFO: John Cassidy
HR: –
FYE: December 31
Type: Private

Omni Cable is a premier redistributor of wire and cable, electrical products, and value-added services to wholesale customers in the US through nearly 15 distribution centers located in Atlanta, Boston, Chicago, Denver, Houston, Los Angeles, Philadelphia, Seattle, St. Louis, San Francisco, and Tampa. Omni Cable also offers custom paralleling, coloring, striping, lashing, twisting, and imprinting of wires and cables. The company was founded in 1977.

	Annual Growth	12/12	12/13	12/14	12/15	12/16
Sales ($mil.)	(7.4%)	–	–	258.8	234.7	221.9
Net income ($ mil.)	(15.2%)	–	–	15.1	16.2	10.9
Market value ($ mil.)	–	–	–	–	–	–
Employees	–	–	–	–	–	474

OMNI HOTELS CORPORATION

4001 MAPLE AVE STE 500
DALLAS, TX 752193241
Phone: 972 871-5600
Fax: –
Web: www.omnihotels.com

CEO: James D Caldwell
CFO: Mike Garcia
HR: David Ricci
FYE: December 31
Type: Private

Omni Hotels has a portfolio of around 50 hotel properties in the US, Canada, and Mexico. The luxury lodgings are targeted to business travelers and upscale tourists. In addition to comfortable room accommodations, the properties offer business and fitness centers, high-speed and wireless Internet access, and gourmet restaurants. The company's Select Guest is a loyalty program that offers more personalized services for returning members. In total, the company has approximately 23,550 hotel rooms. Texas oil billionaire Robert Rowling owns Omni Hotels through his family's holding company, TRT Holdings. It was founded by the Dunfey family of New England in 1958.

OMNICELL INC

NMS: OMCL

4220 North Freeway
Fort Worth, TX 76137
Phone: 877 415-9990
Fax: –
Web: www.omnicell.com

CEO: Randall A Lipps
CFO: Nchacha E Etta
HR: Jony Ziegler
FYE: December 31
Type: Public

Omnicell a leader in transforming the pharmacy care delivery model, is committed to solving the critical challenges inherent in medication management and elevating the role of clinicians within healthcare as an essential component of care delivery. Through a comprehensive portfolio of automation and advanced services, Omnicell is uniquely positioned to address evolving healthcare challenges, connect settings of care, and streamline the medication management process. Facilities worldwide use its automation and analytics solutions to help increase operational efficiency, reduce medication errors, deliver actionable intelligence, and improve patient safety. Omnicell's medications adherence include its consumables and medication packaging systems designed to improve pharmacy operations and patient adherence to prescriptions and used by retail, community, and outpatient pharmacies, and institutional pharmacies. Around 90% of the company's sales are generated in the US.

	Annual Growth	12/19	12/20	12/21	12/22	12/23
Sales ($mil.)	6.3%	897.0	892.2	1,132.0	1,295.9	1,147.1
Net income ($ mil.)	–	61.3	32.2	77.8	5.6	(20.4)
Market value ($ mil.)	(17.6%)	3,721.4	5,465.6	8,217.1	2,296.1	1,713.6
Employees	7.8%	2,700	2,860	3,800	4,230	3,650

OMNICOM GROUP, INC.

NYS: OMC

280 Park Avenue
New York, NY 10017
Phone: 212 415-3600
Fax: 212 415-3393
Web: www.omnicomgroup.com

CEO: John D Wren
CFO: Philip J Angelastro
HR: Dana Ernst
FYE: December 31
Type: Public

Omnicom Group is a strategic holding company providing advertising, marketing and corporate communications services to clients through its branded networks and agencies around the world. Its portfolio of companies includes global networks, BBDO, DDB, TBWA, Omnicom Media Group, the DAS Group of Companies, and the Communications Consultancy Network. It is a leading global marketing and corporate communications company that provides services to over 5,000 clients across 70-plus countries. Omnicom's branded networks and numerous specialty firms provide advertising, strategic media planning and buying, digital and interactive marketing, direct and promotional marketing, public relations and other specialty communications services. The US accounts for about 60% of sales.

	Annual Growth	12/19	12/20	12/21	12/22	12/23
Sales ($mil.)	(0.4%)	14,954	13,171	14,289	14,289	14,692
Net income ($ mil.)	1.0%	1,339.1	945.4	1,407.8	1,316.5	1,391.4
Market value ($ mil.)	1.7%	16,042	12,349	14,507	16,151	17,129
Employees	2.0%	70,000	64,100	71,700	74,200	75,900

OMNIMAX HOLDINGS, INC.

303 RESEARCH DR STE 400
NORCROSS, GA 300922926
Phone: 770 449-7066
Fax: –
Web: www.omnimax.com

CEO: –
CFO: –
HR: –
FYE: December 31
Type: Private

Euramax Holdings is into metal and vinyl, but it's not involved in the music industry. Operating through Euramax International and other subsidiaries, Euramax produces metal fabricated products used in residential repair and remodeling, commercial construction, and RV markets in North America and Europe. Core lines include preformed drainage systems for roofs, metal roofing and siding, roll-coated aluminum, and aluminum siding for RVs. Most of Euramax's products are fabricated from aluminum, but the company also manufactures materials out of vinyl, steel, and copper. Customers include contractors and home improvement retailers, distributors, and RV OEMs.

OMNIVISION TECHNOLOGIES, INC.

4275 BURTON DR
SANTA CLARA, CA 950541512
Phone: 408 567-3000
Fax: –
Web: www.ovt.com

CEO: –
CFO: –
HR: –
FYE: April 30
Type: Private

OmniVision Technologies develops and delivers advanced imaging, analog, and touch & display solutions to a variety of industrial and consumer markets. Its leading-edge semiconductor solutions produced high-quality still and video images, analog solutions, and touch & display technology from smartphones, surveillance cameras, endoscopes, webcams, automotive cameras, and more. They also enable advanced capabilities such as facial and iris authentication, collision avoidance, gesture recognition, and eye tracking for a host of image-based applications. Its CameraCubeChip integrates image sensors, processor, and lenses in a miniature wafer-level camera module that fits in tiny spaces. The company serves customers in automotive, medical, mobile devices, surveillance, IoT/emerging, and computing industries. The company was founded in 1995.

OMRON ROBOTICS AND SAFETY TECHNOLOGIES, INC.

4225 HACIENDA DR
PLEASANTON, CA 945882720
Phone: 925 245-3400
Fax: –
Web: www.adept.com

CEO: Rob Cain
CFO: Seth Halio
HR: –
FYE: June 30
Type: Private

Within 25-plus years, Adept Technology has evolved from making industrial robots to a lineup of intelligent automation products. Its robots are designed to handle, assemble, test, inspect, and package goods in the electronics, food processing, automotive component, packaging, and pharmaceutical industries. Adept Technology's robots can replicate the movements of human shoulders, elbows, and wrists. The company also makes vision guidance and inspection systems, as well as software that allows operators to control robots from a PC. Adept Technology targets a diverse group of Global 1000 companies, including Procter & Gamble, Johnson & Johnson, Seagate, Boeing, and General Motors.

	Annual Growth	06/10	06/11	06/12	06/13	06/14
Sales ($mil.)	(6.8%)	–	–	66.2	46.8	57.5
Net income ($ mil.)	–	–	–	(3.7)	(10.0)	(0.3)
Market value ($ mil.)	–	–	–	–	–	–
Employees	–	–	–	–	–	170

ON SEMICONDUCTOR CORP

NMS: ON

5701 N. Pima Road
Scottsdale, AZ 85250
Phone: 602 244-6600
Fax: –
Web: www.onsemi.com

CEO: Hassane S El-Khoury
CFO: Thad Trent
HR: –
FYE: December 31
Type: Public

ON Semiconductor (ON) provides industry-leading intelligent power and sensing solutions to help its customers solve the most challenging problems and create cutting-edge products for a better future. Its intelligent power technologies enable the electrification of the automotive industry that allows for lighter and longer-range electric vehicles, empowers efficient fast-charging systems, and propels sustainable energy for the highest efficiency solar strings, industrial power, and storage systems. ON serves a wide range of end-user markets including automotive, communications, computing, and consumer, with a primary focus on automotive and industrial. Most of ON's sales come from outside the US.

	Annual Growth	12/19	12/20	12/21	12/22	12/23
Sales ($mil.)	10.6%	5,517.9	5,255.0	6,739.8	8,326.2	8,253.0
Net income ($ mil.)	79.2%	211.7	234.2	1,009.6	1,902.2	2,183.7
Market value ($ mil.)	36.1%	10,395	13,956	28,960	26,594	35,616
Employees	(3.6%)	34,800	34,500	33,300	31,109	30,100

ON STAGE ENTERTAINMENT INC

4625 W. Nevso Drive
Las Vegas, NV 89103
Phone: 702 253-1333
Fax: –
Web: –

CEO: Timothy Parrott
CFO: John Weil
HR: –
FYE: December 31
Type: Public

Elvis hasn't left the building; he's waiting on stage. On Stage Entertainment produces and markets live theatrical entertainment, including its flagship Legends in Concert tribute shows, which feature impersonators who pay tribute to celebrities of the past and present like Elvis Presley, Cher, Marilyn Monroe, and many others. The show has toured in 15 countries and plays nightly in Las Vegas; Atlantic City, New Jersey; Branson, Missouri; and Myrtle Beach, South Carolina. The company also performs Legends at casinos, state fairs, and amusement parks, as well as traveling productions, cruise ship shows, and corporate entertainment events. On Stage Entertainment was founded in 1983.

	Annual Growth	12/97	12/98	12/99	12/00	12/01
Sales ($mil.)	10.9%	15.7	27.8	28.5	24.1	23.8
Net income ($ mil.)	–	(2.9)	(4.9)	(2.1)	(4.7)	(1.7)
Market value ($ mil.)	(33.4%)	46.6	17.0	4.9	11.4	9.2
Employees	33.5%	169	584	236	402	536

ON-SITE FUEL SERVICE, INC.

1089 OLD FANNIN RD STE A
BRANDON, MS 390479201
Phone: 601 353-4142
Fax: –
Web: www.onsitefuelservice.com

CEO: Kevin T French
CFO: Margaret Wong
HR: Pam Welborn
FYE: December 31
Type: Private

When it comes down to gassing up the fleet, On-Site Fuel Service delivers. The company specializes in dispensing fuel (diesel or regular) to corporate fleets in the most efficient location available. For most customers this means fueling their vehicles once the workday is complete (and eliminating fueling time from the workday). But the company also offers mobile fueling services, allowing vehicles to be refueled in the field or at remote job sites. On-Site Fuel Service dispenses the fuel directly into each vehicle and also provides fueling data and reports for each vehicle (to comply with regulatory requirements when necessary). Its operations extend south from North Carolina to Florida and west to Arizona.

ON-TARGET SUPPLIES & LOGISTICS, LTD.

1133 S MADISON AVE
DALLAS, TX 752086726
Phone: 214 941-4885
Fax: –
Web: www.otsl.com

CEO: –
CFO: –
HR: –
FYE: October 31
Type: Private

Aiming to satisfy its customers, On-Target Supplies & Logistics distributes a variety of office supplies and offers a wide range of logistics services, including transportation management, mail room operations, and warehousing and distribution. The company operates a training and development center and a 160,000 square foot facility, both of which are located in Dallas; it also operates out of offices located in the Houston area and in Tucson, Arizona. On-Target was founded in 1982 by president and CEO Albert Black, Jr. and wife Gwyneith. The Blacks own the company.

ONCOLOGIX TECH INC
NBB: OCLG

370 Amapola Ave., Suite 200-A
Torrance, CA 90501
Phone: 424 358-1046
Fax: –
Web: www.oclgmerger.com

CEO: Roy W Erwin
CFO: Michael A Kramarz
HR: –
FYE: August 31
Type: Public

Oncologix Tech (formerly BestNet Communications) has changed gears. The company, which had developed a system using the Internet and text messaging networks to manage voice communications over public phone networks, merged with JDA Medical Technologies and sold off most of its telephone business assets to Interactive Media Technologies. Oncologix then became a development-stage medical device firm focused on developing microsphere (particle) technology to treat liver and other soft tissue cancers; however, the company licensed out most of its development operations in 2009 to a third party.

	Annual Growth	08/17	08/18	08/19	08/20	08/21
Sales ($mil.)	–	2.9	–	–	–	–
Net income ($ mil.)	–	(2.4)	–	–	–	–
Market value ($ mil.)	125.1%	0.5	0.2	0.2	0.8	11.6
Employees						

ONCOLOGY SERVICES INTERNATIONAL, INC.

102 CHESTNUT RIDGE RD STE 2
MONTVALE, NJ 076451856
Phone: 845 357-6560
Fax: –
Web: www.avantehs.com

CEO: Richard Hall
CFO: –
HR: –
FYE: December 31
Type: Private

Oncology Services International (OSI) sells, installs, and provides radiation therapy equipment and related services, including medical linear accelerators, GE Computed Tomographic Scanners, radiation therapy simulators, and accessories worldwide. The company was formed following the merger between Accelinear and Linac Systems in 2003. OSI has facilities in California, Georgia, New Jersey, Ohio, and Texas.

ONCONOVA THERAPEUTICS INC
NAS: ONTX

12 Penns Trail
Newtown, PA 18940
Phone: 267 759-3680
Fax: –
Web: www.onconova.com

CEO: Steven Fruchtman
CFO: Mark P Guerin
HR: –
FYE: December 31
Type: Public

Onconova Therapeutics is taking a novel approach to oncology. The biopharmaceutical company is developing small molecule drug candidates to treat cancer and protect against certain side effects of radiation. Onconova has three clinical-stage product candidates and six preclinical ones. Its leading drug candidate, rigosertib, is being tested to higher risk myelodysplastic syndromes (MDS), pancreatic cancer, and head and neck cancers. Onconova has revenue-generating collaboration agreements with Baxter in Europe and SymBio in Japan and Korea. The company, which was formed in 1998, went public in mid-2013, raising $78 million in its IPO. It will use the proceeds to further develop its drug candidates.

	Annual Growth	12/18	12/19	12/20	12/21	12/22
Sales ($mil.)	(34.5%)	1.2	2.2	0.2	0.2	0.2
Net income ($ mil.)	–	(20.6)	(21.5)	(25.2)	(16.2)	(19.0)
Market value ($ mil.)	(25.6%)	44.2	8.0	9.7	53.4	13.5
Employees	(9.2%)	25	19	12	15	17

ONCOR ELECTRIC DELIVERY CO LLC

1616 Woodall Rodgers Freeway
Dallas, TX 75202
Phone: 214 486-2000
Fax: –
Web: www.oncor.com

CEO: Allen Nye
CFO: Don J Clevinger
HR: –
FYE: December 31
Type: Public

Oncor Electric Delivery is the largest energy delivery company that provides the essential service of delivering electricity safely, reliably and economically to end-use consumers through its electrical systems, as well as providing transmission grid connections to merchant generation facilities and interconnections to other transmission grids in Texas. It also operates more than 141,000 miles of transmission and distribution lines serving more than 400 incorporated municipalities and more than 120 counties situated in the eastern, north-central, and western portions of the state. The company provides power to more than 3.9 million meters in homes and businesses. Oncor Electric Delivery delivers electricity across a distribution service territory that has a population in approximately 13 million.

	Annual Growth	12/18	12/19	12/20	12/21	12/22
Sales ($mil.)	6.3%	4,101.0	4,347.0	4,511.0	4,764.0	5,243.0
Net income ($ mil.)	13.5%	545.0	651.0	713.0	770.0	905.0
Market value ($ mil.)	–					
Employees	3.2%	4,015	4,165	4,396	4,537	4,561

ONCOTELIC THERAPEUTICS INC
NBB: OTLC

29397 Agoura Road, Suite 107
Agoura Hills, CA 91301
Phone: 650 635-7000
Fax: –
Web: www.mateon.com

CEO: Vuong Trieu
CFO: Amit Shah
HR: –
FYE: December 31
Type: Public

Mateon Therapeutics (formerly OXiGENE) is a biopharmaceutical company focused on vascular targeted therapy in oncology, which starves cancer to death. Its vascular targeted therapy include vascular disrupting agents (VDAs) and anti-angiogenic agents (AAs). VDAs selectively obstruct a tumor's blood supply without obstructing the blood supply to normal tissues, and treatment with our VDAs has been shown to lead to significant central tumor necrosis. Mateon believes that the treatment of cancer is significantly improved if VDAs and AAs are used together. The company's strategy is to identify and license compounds from academic research centers and then shepherd the compounds through clinical trials.

	Annual Growth	12/18	12/19	12/20	12/21	12/22
Sales ($mil.)	–	–	–	1.7	–	–
Net income ($ mil.)	–	(2.7)	(6.6)	(9.5)	(9.4)	5.1
Market value ($ mil.)	(12.6%)	30.2	67.6	84.2	65.8	17.6
Employees	82.1%	2	13	16	16	22

ONCTERNAL THERAPEUTICS INC
NAS: ONCT

12230 El Camino Real, Suite 230
San Diego, CA 92130
Phone: 858 434-1113
Fax: –
Web: www.oncternal.com

CEO: James B Breitmeyer
CFO: Richard G Vincent
HR: –
FYE: December 31
Type: Public

GTx knows hormones are just as important to men as they are to women. The company develops therapies targeting estrogens and androgens for prostate cancer and other diseases. GTx is developing Capesaris, a potential therapy that could cases of metastatic hormone-sensitive prostate cancer and castration resistant prostate cancer with a reduced occurance of side-effects such as osteoporosis and hot flashes. Another candidate, Enobosarm, aims to treat muscle wasting in patients with non-small cell lung cancer and other conditions.

	Annual Growth	12/19	12/20	12/21	12/22	12/23
Sales ($mil.)	(24.6%)	2.4	3.4	4.3	1.5	0.8
Net income ($ mil.)	–	(34.2)	(17.2)	(31.3)	(44.2)	(39.5)
Market value ($ mil.)	(39.3%)	11.6	14.4	6.7	2.9	1.6
Employees	–	14	14	26	32	–

ONE GAS, INC.
NYS: OGS

15 East Fifth Street
Tulsa, OK 74103
Phone: 918 947-7000
Fax: –
Web: www.onegas.com

CEO: Robert S McAnnally
CFO: Caron A Lawhorn
HR: Lehsee Gausi
FYE: December 31
Type: Public

ONE Gas is a 100% regulated natural gas distribution utility and one of the largest publicly traded natural gas utilities in the US. It consists of former ONEOK natural gas utilities: Kansas Gas Service, Oklahoma Natural Gas, and Texas Gas Service. One of the largest publicly traded natural gas utilities in the US, ONE Gas serves approximately 2.3 million customers in about five states. Kansas Gas Service has some 13,200 miles of distribution mains and transmission pipeline; Oklahoma Natural Gas Company has approximately 20,600 miles of distribution mains; while Texas Gas Service has approximately 11,300 miles of distribution mains and transmission pipeline.

	Annual Growth	12/19	12/20	12/21	12/22	12/23
Sales ($mil.)	9.5%	1,652.7	1,530.3	1,808.6	2,578.0	2,372.0
Net income ($ mil.)	5.5%	186.7	196.4	206.4	221.7	231.2
Market value ($ mil.)	(9.2%)	5,291.0	4,341.0	4,387.4	4,281.7	3,603.1
Employees	–	–	3,600	3,700	3,600	3,800

ONE LIBERTY PROPERTIES, INC.
NYS: OLP

60 Cutter Mill Road
Great Neck, NY 11021
Phone: 516 466-3100
Fax: –
Web: www.1liberty.com

CEO: Patrick J Callan Jr
CFO: David W Kalish
HR: –
FYE: December 31
Type: Public

One Liberty Properties may own the space where lovebirds shop for loveseats. Or bird food. The self-managed and self-administered real estate investment trust (REIT) invests in retail, industrial, and office properties throughout the US. It owns or co-owns over 125 properties totaling more than 10.5 million sq. ft. of space; more than half of its portfolio is leased to retailers including Haverty Furniture, PetSmart, and Giant Food Stores. The REIT also owns warehouses, fitness centers, and a movie theater. One Liberty Properties targets net-leased properties, minimizing its responsibilities for taxes, maintenance, and other operating costs. The firm is controlled by the family of its chairman.

	Annual Growth	12/19	12/20	12/21	12/22	12/23
Sales ($mil.)	1.7%	84.7	81.9	82.7	92.2	90.6
Net income ($ mil.)	13.2%	18.0	27.4	38.9	42.2	29.6
Market value ($ mil.)	(5.3%)	552.6	407.9	717.0	451.6	445.3
Employees	2.7%	9	9	9	10	10

ONE PLANET OPS INC.

1820 BONANZA ST STE 200
WALNUT CREEK, CA 945964376
Phone: 925 983-2800
Fax: –
Web: www.oneplanetgroup.com

CEO: Payam Zamani
CFO: –
HR: –
FYE: December 31
Type: Private

Reply! is here to bridge the gap between advertisers and the prospects they seek. The company collects customer prospects and leads from several online sources; its advertising clients purchase "clicks" on a cost-per-lead basis in the form of what it calls an "auction marketplace." In addition to providing their contact information, the prospects also provide user-submitted insight such as where and when they wish to purchase a particular product. Reply! primarily serves locally targeted advertisers residing in the automotive, home improvement, insurance, and real estate sectors. Reply! has generated more than 700,000 leads and serves some 5,000 advertisers. In early 2010, Reply! filed for an IPO with the SEC.

ONE STOP SYSTEMS INC
NAS: OSS

2235 Enterprise Street #110
Escondido, CA 92029
Phone: 760 745-9883
Fax: –
Web: www.onestopsystems.com

CEO: –
CFO: –
HR: –
FYE: December 31
Type: Public

One Stop Systems designs and manufactures industrial computing systems and components, including backplanes, enclosures, filler panels, input/output boards, and power supplies. One Stop's catalog includes a number of products built around the CompactPCI industry standard, an interconnect technology intended for industrial environments that is also being used for military computers and other rugged electronics. The company also makes single-board computers and a variety of custom CPU and I/O boards, enclosures, and systems. One Stop Systems was founded in 1998. CEO Steve Cooper is the majority shareholder of the company. With Cooper, VP Mark Gunn is a co-founder of One Stop Systems.

	Annual Growth	12/19	12/20	12/21	12/22	12/23
Sales ($mil.)	1.1%	58.3	51.9	62.0	72.4	60.9
Net income ($ mil.)	–	(0.9)	(0.0)	2.3	(2.2)	(6.7)
Market value ($ mil.)	1.0%	41.7	82.6	102.3	62.2	43.4
Employees	(2.6%)	118	101	109	112	106

ONE TO ONE INTERACTIVE, INC.

100 FRANKLIN ST STE 407
BOSTON, MA 021101539
Phone: 617 854-8315
Fax: –
Web: –

CEO: Ian Karnell
CFO: Michael McCay
HR: –
FYE: December 31
Type: Private

One to One Interactive specializes in providing Internet marketing services by the numbers. Through several operating units, the company offers marketing, creative, and technology services to companies in such industries as financial services, life sciences, media, telecommunications, and technology. One to One's services include segmentation and predictive modeling, new media planning and buying, e-mail marketing, and search engine optimization. It also provides various creative (visual design, copywriting), advisory, and software development services. Established in 1997, One to One has helped such clients as Nextel and Unisys create their online marketing campaigns.

	Annual Growth	12/04	12/05	12/06	12/07	12/08
Sales ($mil.)	27.7%	–	–	8.2	10.6	13.3
Net income ($ mil.)	–	–	–	1.3	0.4	(0.3)
Market value ($ mil.)	–	–	–	–	–	–
Employees	–	–	–	–	–	145

ONEIDA HEALTH SYSTEMS, INC.

321 GENESEE ST
ONEIDA, NY 134212611
Phone: 315 363-6000
Fax: –
Web: www.oneidahealth.org

CEO: Felissa Koernig
CFO: Jeremiah Sweet
HR: –
FYE: December 31
Type: Private

Oneida is here to make residents in central New York feel alright-a! Oneida Healthcare Center (OHC) is comprised of a more than 100-bed acute care community hospital, a 160-bed skilled nursing facility, and various primary care and specialty health care centers which serve residents from about two dozen communities in north central New York's Madison and western Oneida counties. OHC also operates a maternity and pediatric clinic, as well as a rehabilitation and wellness center. The non-profit healthcare company is governed by Oneida Health Systems, Inc.

	Annual Growth	12/09	12/10	12/11	12/19	12/21
Sales ($mil.)	4.1%	–	–	82.5	10.6	122.9
Net income ($ mil.)	17.3%	–	–	0.8	(8.6)	3.9
Market value ($ mil.)	–	–	–	–	–	–
Employees	–	–	–	–	–	900

ONEMAIN HOLDINGS INC — NYS: OMF

601 Northwest Second Street
Evansville, IN 47708
Phone: 812 424-8031
Fax: -
Web: www.omf.com

CEO: Douglas H Shulman
CFO: Micah R Conrad
HR: -
FYE: December 31
Type: Public

OneMain Holdings, a financial service holding company, and its wholly-owned direct subsidiary, OneMain Finance Corporation (formerly known as Springleaf Finance Corporation ("SFC")). The company offers auto loans and personal loans primarily to non-prime customers who have limited access to credit from banks, credit card companies, and other lenders through approximately 1,400 branches in around 45 states. It also provides credit insurance, non-credit insurance, and related products through subsidiaries AHL, and Triton. The company has around $19.9 billion in personal loan assets due to about 2.5 million customer accounts.

	Annual Growth	12/19	12/20	12/21	12/22	12/23
Assets ($mil.)	1.6%	22,817	22,471	22,079	22,533	24,294
Net income ($ mil.)	(6.9%)	855.0	730.0	1,314.0	878.0	641.0
Market value ($ mil.)	3.9%	5,047.8	5,767.5	5,992.7	3,989.1	5,892.1
Employees	(1.6%)	9,700	8,300	8,800	9,200	9,100

ONEOK INC — NYS: OKE

100 West Fifth Street
Tulsa, OK 74103
Phone: 918 588-7000
Fax: 918 588-7273
Web: www.oneok.com

CEO: Pierce H Norton II
CFO: Walter S Hulse III
HR: Abigail Stein
FYE: December 31
Type: Public

ONEOK is an Oklahoma-based midstream service provider that owns one of the nation's premier NGL systems, connecting NGL supply in the Rocky Mountain, Permian, and Mid-Continent regions with key market centers and an extensive network of natural gas gathering, processing, storage and transportation assets. It serves customers such as petrochemical companies, propane distributors, heating fuel users, ethanol producers, refineries, and exporters. The company has an ownership interest in FERC-regulated NGL gathering and distribution pipelines in Oklahoma, Kansas, Texas, New Mexico, Montana, North Dakota, Wyoming, and Colorado, and terminal and storage facilities in Missouri, Nebraska, Iowa, and Illinois.

	Annual Growth	12/19	12/20	12/21	12/22	12/23
Sales ($mil.)	14.8%	10,164	8,542.2	16,540	22,387	17,677
Net income ($ mil.)	20.1%	1,278.6	612.8	1,499.7	1,722.2	2,659.0
Market value ($ mil.)	(1.9%)	44,123	22,379	34,263	38,309	40,945
Employees	13.5%	2,882	2,886	2,847	2,966	4,775

ONEOK PARTNERS, L.P.

100 W 5TH ST STE LL
TULSA, OK 741034298
Phone: 918 588-7000
Fax: -
Web: www.oneok.com

CEO: Terry K Spencer
CFO: Walter S Hulse III
HR: -
FYE: December 31
Type: Private

For ONEOK Partners it's OK to have three businesses: natural gas pipelines; gas gathering and processing; and natural gas liquids (NGLs). Its pipelines include Midwestern Gas Transmission, Guardian Pipeline, Viking Gas Transmission, and OkTex Pipeline. The ONEOK affiliate operates 17,100 miles of gas-gathering pipeline and 7,600 miles of transportation pipeline, as well as gas processing plants and storage facilities (with 52 billion cu. ft. of capacity). It also owns one of the US's top natural NGL systems (more than 7,200 miles of pipeline). In 2017, 41%-owner ONEOK agreed to buy the stock of ONEOK Partners that it did not already own for $9.3 billion in a stock deal. Operations ONEOK Partners operates in three business segments: natural gas gathering and processing; natural gas pipelines; and natural gas liquids. Geographic Reach The company gathers and processes natural gas in the Mid-Continent region, which includes the NGL-rich Cana-Woodford Shale and Granite Wash formations, the Mississippian Lime formation of Oklahoma and Kansas, and the Hugoton and Central Kansas Uplift Basins of Kansas. The Natural Gas Pipelines segment owns and operates regulated natural gas transmission pipelines, natural gas storage facilities and natural gas gathering systems for nonprocessed gas. It also provide interstate natural gas transportation and storage service. The company's interstate natural gas pipeline assets transport natural gas through pipelines in North Dakota, Minnesota, Wisconsin, Illinois, Indiana, Kentucky, Tennessee, Oklahoma, Texas and New Mexico. Its Natural gas liquids assets provide nondiscretionary services to producers that consist of facilities that gather, fractionate, and treat NGLs and store NGL products primarily in Oklahoma, Kansas and Texas. It also owns or has stakes in natural gas liquids gathering and distribution pipelines in Oklahoma, Kansas, Texas, Wyoming and Colorado, and terminal and storage facilities in Missouri, Nebraska, Iowa and Illinois. In addition it owns natural gas liquids distribution and refined petroleum products pipelines in Kansas, Missouri, Nebraska, Iowa, Illinois and Indiana that connect the company's Mid-Continent assets with Midwest markets, including Chicago.

	Annual Growth	12/12	12/13	12/14	12/15	12/16
Sales ($mil.)	(14.5%)	–	–	12,192	7,761.1	8,918.5
Net income ($ mil.)	8.5%	–	–	911.3	597.9	1,072.3

Market value ($ mil.)	-	-	-	-	-	-	
Employees							2,364

ONESPAN INC
NAS: OSPN

121 West Wacker Drive, Suite 2050
Chicago, IL 60601
Phone: 312 766-4001
Fax: -
Web: www.onespan.com

CEO: Victor Limongelli
CFO: Jorge G Martell
HR: Abby Kehe
FYE: December 31
Type: Public

OneSpan Inc. (formerly VASCO Data Security International, Inc.) designs, develops and markets digital solutions for identity, security, and business productivity that protect and facilitate electronic transactions via mobile and connected devices. The company's products incorporate authentication and has trusted identity platform technologies including Intelligent Adaptive Authentication. EMEA is responsible for about 45% of the sales. OneSpan was founded in 1997.

	Annual Growth	12/19	12/20	12/21	12/22	12/23
Sales ($mil.)	(2.0%)	254.6	215.7	214.5	219.0	235.1
Net income ($ mil.)	-	8.8	(5.5)	(30.6)	(14.4)	(29.8)
Market value ($ mil.)	(11.0%)	642.3	775.9	635.2	419.8	402.2
Employees	(2.4%)	744	870	879	790	676

ONLINE VACATION CENTER HOLDINGS CORP
NBB: ONVC

2307 West Broward Boulevard, Suite 400
Fort Lauderdale, FL 33312
Phone: 954 377-6400
Fax: 954 377-6368
Web: www.onlinevacationcenter.com

CEO: Edward B Rudner
CFO: John Stunson
HR: Denise Barry
FYE: December 31
Type: Public

Online Vacation Center Holdings has quit the cigar business and is spending its future traveling. Previously called Alec Bradley Cigar Corporation, the company was known for importing and selling cigars wholesale. In 2006 the firm completed a reverse merger with Online Vacation Center Holdings. It shuttered its cigar operations and changed its name to reflect its new adventure as an online retailer of vacation packages. The company specializes in cruise deals. Its subsidiaries include Online Vacation Center and Dunhill Vacations. Chairman, CEO, president, and CFO Edward Rudner owns about 60% of Online Vacation Center Holdings.

	Annual Growth	12/17	12/18	12/19	12/21	12/22
Sales ($mil.)	2.1%	16.4	18.2	20.9	7.4	18.2
Net income ($ mil.)	10.1%	0.5	1.3	2.9	1.0	0.8
Market value ($ mil.)	(15.7%)	10.7	12.5	25.8	9.9	4.6
Employees		-	-	-	-	-

ONSTREAM MEDIA CORP

1291 SW 29 Avenue
Pompano Beach, FL 33069
Phone: 954 917-6655
Fax: -
Web: www.onstreammedia.com

CEO: Randy S Selman
CFO: Robert E Tomlinson
HR: -
FYE: September 30
Type: Public

If a picture says a thousand words, then Onstream Media Corporation speaks volumes about corporate communication and digital asset management. The company's Digital Media Services Group provides video and audio Webcasting to corporate clients, and produces Internet-based multimedia streaming promotional videos for hotels and resorts. The group also includes DMSP (Digital Media Services Platform) and UGC (User Generated Content) divisions, which provide encoding, storage, search, retrieval, and reuse of photos, audio files, Web pages, and other digital files. Onstream's Audio & Web Conferencing Services Group includes conferencing provider Infinite, and audio and video networking services provider EDNet.

	Annual Growth	09/11	09/12	09/13	09/14	09/15
Sales ($mil.)	(2.3%)	17.7	18.2	17.2	16.9	16.1
Net income ($ mil.)	-	(5.2)	(2.6)	(7.2)	(1.7)	(8.6)

| Market value ($ mil.) | (26.7%) | 16.6 | 11.0 | 6.2 | 3.7 | 4.8 |
| Employees | (3.1%) | 93 | 102 | 88 | 86 | 82 |

ONTO INNOVATION INC

NYS: ONTO

16 Jonspin Road
Wilmington, MA 01887
Phone: 978 253-6200
Fax: –
Web: www.ontoinnovation.com

CEO: Michael P Plisinski
CFO: Mark R Slicer
HR: –
FYE: December 30
Type: Public

Onto Innovation (formerly Nanometrics) is a worldwide leader in the design, development, manufacture and support of process control tools that perform macro defect inspection and 2D/3D optical metrology, lithography systems, and process control analytical software used by bare silicon wafer manufacturers, semiconductor wafer fabricators, and advanced packaging device manufacturers. Its products are also used in a number of other high technology industries including: light emitting diode (LED); vertical-cavity surface-emitting laser (VCSEL); micro-electromechanical system (MEMS); CMOS image sensor (CIS); power device; RF filter; data storage; and certain industrial and scientific applications. Top customers include Samsung Electronics, Taiwan Semiconductor Manufacturing Company, and SK Hynix. Onto innovation generates most of its sales in Asia. The company, Nanometrics, was founded in 1975.

	Annual Growth	12/19	12/20*	01/22*	12/22	12/23
Sales ($mil.)	27.8%	305.9	556.5	788.9	1,005.2	815.9
Net income ($ mil.)	182.2%	1.9	31.0	142.3	223.3	121.2
Market value ($ mil.)	43.0%	1,793.6	2,357.1	4,969.0	3,342.3	7,505.2
Employees	2.8%	1,340	1,247	1,411	1,636	1,497

*Fiscal year change

ONTRAK INC

NAS: OTRK

333 S. E. 2nd Avenue, Suite 2000
Miami, FL 33131
Phone: 310 444-4300
Fax: –
Web: www.catasys.com

CEO: Brandon Laverne
CFO: –
HR: –
FYE: December 31
Type: Public

Catasys (formerly known as Hythiam) specializes in researching, developing, and licensing medical protocols for the treatment of alcohol and drug addiction. The company's PROMETA treatment programs utilize a combination of medication, nutritional supplements, and counseling to treat drug and alcohol addiction. Catasys' PROMETA Centers are operated through management or licensing agreements with health care providers in the US. PROMETA also provides maintenance support by offering individualized care programs following medically supervised treatment. Namesake program Catasys offers disease management services. The company changed its name in 2011 to reflect its focus on comprehensive behavioral management.

	Annual Growth	12/18	12/19	12/20	12/21	12/22
Sales ($mil.)	(1.1%)	15.2	35.1	82.8	84.1	14.5
Net income ($ mil.)	–	(14.2)	(25.7)	(22.7)	(37.1)	(51.6)
Market value ($ mil.)	(55.5%)	42.4	73.9	279.8	28.5	1.7
Employees	(13.1%)	209	395	726	252	119

ONVIA, INC.

509 OLIVE WAY STE 400
SEATTLE, WA 981011713
Phone: 800 575-1736
Fax: –
Web: www.deltek.com

CEO: Russell Mann
CFO: Cameron S Way
HR: –
FYE: December 31
Type: Private

Onvia aims to help companies win government contracts and government agencies find suppliers by providing a database of business leads. The company identifies purchasing behavior and bid opportunities from some 86,000 federal, state, and local government agencies, as well as more than 400,000 private-sector enterprises, and delivers notices of those opportunities to its subscribers. Its Onvia database includes data on millions of current and historical contracting opportunities in markets such as construction, consulting, and information technology. Subscriptions account for the bulk of the company's sales; It also generates revenues by licensing its content to other companies. Onvia was established in 2000.

OPENDOOR TECHNOLOGIES INC

NMS: OPEN

410 N. Scottsdale Road, Suite 1600
Tempe, AZ 85281
Phone: 480 618-6760
Fax: –
Web: www.opendoor.com

CEO: Carrie Wheeler
CFO: Christina Schwartz
HR: –
FYE: December 31
Type: Public

Founded in 2014, Opendoor Technologies is a leading digital platform for residential real estate. It leverages software, data science, product design and operations, the company has rebuilt the service model for real estate and have made buying and selling possible on a mobile device. The company streamline the process of buying and selling a home into a seamless digital experience that is simple, certain, and fast. Sellers can go to Opendoor.com, receive an offer, and sign and choose their closing date. Buyers can download the Opendoor app, tour and visit both Opendoor and non-Opendoor homes, and make an offer, all with just a mobile device. Opendoor has operations in about 45 markets across the US.

	Annual Growth	12/19	12/20	12/21	12/22	12/23
Sales ($mil.)	–	–	2,583.1	8,021.0	15,567	6,946.0
Net income ($ mil.)	–	(0.0)	(286.8)	(662.0)	(1,353.0)	(275.0)
Market value ($ mil.)	–	–	15,403	9,900.3	786.1	3,035.8
Employees	371.8%	4	1,048	2,816	2,570	1,982

OPENLANE INC.

NYS: KAR

11299 N. Illinois Street
Carmel, IN 46032
Phone: 800 923-3725
Fax: –
Web: www.karauctionservices.com

CEO: Peter J Kelly
CFO: Brad Lakhia
HR: Denise Chudalla
FYE: December 31
Type: Public

KAR Auction Services is a leading provider of used vehicle auctions and related vehicle remarketing services in North America and Europe. Its marketplaces facilitated the sale of approximately 1.3 million used vehicles sold by commercial sellers including vehicle manufacturers, financial institutions, commercial fleet operators and rental car companies, as well as used vehicle dealers, to franchised and independent used vehicle dealers. The company makes money through auction fees extended to vehicle buyers and sellers and by transportation logistics, reconditioning, vehicle inspection and certification, titling, administrative and collateral recovery services and floorplan financing. About 65% of its revenue comes from its US customers. In 2022, the ADESA US physical auction business was sold to Carvana and included all auction sales, operations and staff at ADESA's US vehicle logistics centers and use of the ADESA.com marketplace in the US.

	Annual Growth	12/19	12/20	12/21	12/22	12/23
Sales ($mil.)	(12.3%)	2,781.9	2,187.7	2,251.6	1,519.4	1,645.1
Net income ($ mil.)	–	188.5	0.5	66.5	241.2	(154.1)
Market value ($ mil.)	(9.2%)	2,354.2	2,010.6	1,687.6	1,409.9	1,600.1
Employees	(26.4%)	15,300	10,000	9,600	4,500	4,500

OPENLINK FINANCIAL LLC

800 RXR PLZ FL 8
UNIONDALE, NY 115563818
Phone: 516 227-6600
Fax: –
Web: www.iongroup.com

CEO: Rich Grossi
CFO: –
HR: Debra Mutoli
FYE: December 31
Type: Private

OpenLink Financial develops risk management, trading, portfolio management, and operations processing software for more than 550 clients in the financial services, commodities, and energy industries. Its products, sold worldwide, link and automate front- and back-office applications for banks, corporate treasury departments, energy marketers, and insurance companies. OpenLink also provides professional services (consulting, maintenance, support and training), as well as complementary niche products through subsidiaries such as dbcSMARTsoftware (software for agricultural commodities) and iRM (energy trade processing software). Founded in 1992, the company is owned by Ion Investment Group.

	Annual Growth	12/03	12/04	12/05	12/06	12/08
Sales ($mil.)	35.7%	–	–	73.4	83.6	183.6
Net income ($ mil.)	23.6%	–	–	9.1	0.4	17.2
Market value ($ mil.)	–	–	–	–	–	–
Employees	–	–	–	–	–	1,300

OPENTV CORP.

275 Sacramento Street
San Francisco, CA 94111
Phone: 415 962-5000
Fax: –
Web: www.opentv.com

CEO: –
CFO: –
HR: –
FYE: December 31
Type: Public

OpenTV develops software used by cable and satellite television operators to offer their subscribers enhanced interactive content and services. Its applications allow viewers to use the remote control to not only surf TV channels and control camera angles and instant replays during sporting events, but also access e-mail, download audio and video files from the Internet, and complete shopping and banking transactions. The company also develops the middleware used in set-top boxes as well as software used by network operators to manage advertising. OpenTV is a subsidiary of Swiss digital TV systems and digital security provider Kudelski.

	Annual Growth	12/05	12/06	12/07	12/08	12/09
Sales ($mil.)	8.3%	87.4	101.9	110.0	116.5	120.0
Net income ($ mil.)	–	(8.5)	(10.8)	(5.2)	9.6	6.2
Market value ($ mil.)	(11.7%)	309.6	320.6	182.4	170.0	187.9
Employees	8.0%	433	492	497	521	589

OPERATING ENGINEERS FUNDS INC

100 CORSON ST STE 222
PASADENA, CA 911033892
Phone: 866 400-5200
Fax: –
Web: www.oefi.org

CEO: Mike Roddy
CFO: Chuck Killian
HR: –
FYE: December 31
Type: Private

The Operating Engineers Funds are, in fact, for operating engineers -- not the kind who run trains, but those who operate other large machinery. The company administers employee benefits, including pensions, health, welfare, vacation, and holiday benefit, for more than 35,000 active or retired members of the International Union of Operating Engineers (I.U.O.E.), Local 12, as well as their beneficiaries and dependents. The union consists of individuals in construction-related trades, including heavy equipment operators, soil testers, concrete pumpers, inspectors, and surveyors.

	Annual Growth	06/06	06/07	06/08*	12/08	12/19
Assets ($mil.)	(23.3%)	–	–	28.4	1.7	1.5
Net income ($ mil.)	–	–	–	(1.4)	–	0.2
Market value ($ mil.)	–	–	–	–	–	–
Employees	–	–	–	–	–	170

*Fiscal year change

OPERATION SMILE, INC.

3641 FACULTY BLVD
VIRGINIA BEACH, VA 234538000
Phone: 888 677-6453
Fax: –
Web: www.operationsmile.org

CEO: Magee P William MD
CFO: –
HR: Kim Blackman
FYE: June 30
Type: Private

Operation Smile's mission is simple: Make the children of the world grin. The not-for-profit volunteer group provides reconstructive surgery and health-care services to children and young adults suffering from facial deformities such as cleft lips, cleft palates, burns, and tumors. Operation Smile has assisted more than 120,000 patients in 25 developing countries and the US. The organization also provides educational fellowship programs in craniofacial surgery and runs a physician training program. Operation Smile was founded in 1982 by Dr. William Magee and his wife, Kathleen, a nurse and clinical social worker. A plan to merge with Smile Train in 2011 is being called off due to donor opposition.

	Annual Growth	06/18	06/19	06/20	06/21	06/22
Sales ($mil.)	4.9%	–	79.3	87.8	85.2	91.5
Net income ($ mil.)	5.8%	–	11.7	18.0	20.0	13.8
Market value ($ mil.)	–	–	–	–	–	–
Employees	–	–	–	–	–	128

OPERATIONAL TECHNOLOGIES CORPORATION

4100 NW LOOP 410 STE 230
SAN ANTONIO, TX 782294255
Phone: 210 731-0000
Fax: –
Web: www.otcorp.com

CEO: Ricardo S Sanchez
CFO: William M Henderson
HR: –
FYE: September 30
Type: Private

Operational Technologies Corporation (also known as OpTech) is a diversified company providing a wide range of services to businesses and government agencies. Its supply chain management division offers outsourced fulfillment, purchasing, logistics, and order processing services. The company also resells and installs communications security systems. OpTech also uses government funding to develop chemical and biological warfare sensors. The company also provides human resources consulting and environmental assessment and remediation services. OpTech has offices in San Antonio, Texas, and Dayton, Ohio.

	Annual Growth	09/02	09/03	09/04	09/07	09/09
Sales ($mil.)	–	–	–	(1,469.3)	39.0	65.4
Net income ($ mil.)	1647.6%	–	–	0.0	0.5	3.3
Market value ($ mil.)	–	–	–	–	–	–
Employees	–	–	–	–	–	65

OPKO HEALTH INC

NMS: OPK

4400 Biscayne Blvd.
Miami, FL 33137
Phone: 305 575-4100
Fax: –
Web: www.opko.com

CEO: Phillip Frost
CFO: Adam Logal
HR: Paula M Falero
FYE: December 31
Type: Public

OPKO Health is a multinational biopharmaceutical company that operates clinical laboratories and develops tests and medicines for a range of health indications. The company's BioReference Health is one of the largest clinical lab groups in the US. The subsidiary offers routine and esoteric services including, molecular diagnostics, oncology, women's health, and genetic testing. OPKO's commercial biopharmaceutical offerings include Rayaldee for hyperparathyroidism in kidney disease patients; R&D candidates address endocrine, renal, and metabolic disorders. The US market accounts for most of its revenue.

	Annual Growth	12/19	12/20	12/21	12/22	12/23
Sales ($mil.)	(1.1%)	901.9	1,435.4	1,774.7	1,004.2	863.5
Net income ($ mil.)	–	(314.9)	30.6	(30.1)	(328.4)	(188.9)
Market value ($ mil.)	0.7%	1,136.7	3,054.5	3,719.5	966.6	1,167.7
Employees	(10.4%)	6,096	5,269	5,767	4,196	3,930

OPP LIQUIDATING COMPANY, INC.

4826 HUNT ST
PRYOR, OK 743614512
Phone: 918 825-0616
Fax: –
Web: www.orchidspaper.com

CEO: Jeffrey S Schoen
CFO: Melinda S Bartel
HR: –
FYE: December 31
Type: Private

Orchids Paper Products hopes to leave its end users smelling like a rose. The company makes bulk tissue paper and converts it into bathroom tissue, paper napkins, and paper towels for the consumer market. Most of the company's products are sold as private-label items by discount retailers; Orchids Paper products also are sold under the company's Colortex and Velvet brands. Dollar General is Orchids Paper's largest customer; other big customers include Family Dollar and Wal-Mart. Orchids Paper sells most of its products within a 500-mile radius of its manufacturing plant in northeastern Oklahoma.

	Annual Growth	12/14	12/15	12/16	12/17	12/18
Sales ($mil.)	3.5%	–	168.4	164.5	162.5	186.7
Net income ($ mil.)	–	–	13.6	12.8	6.7	(37.7)
Market value ($ mil.)	–	–	–	–	–	–
Employees	–	–	–	–	–	481

OPPENHEIMER HOLDINGS INC — NYS: OPY

85 Broad Street
New York, NY 10004
Phone: 212 668-8000
Fax: –
Web: www.oppenheimer.com

CEO: –
CFO: –
HR: –
FYE: December 31
Type: Public

Oppenheimer Holdings is a leading middle-market investment bank and full service broker-dealer. Through its subsidiaries, Oppenheimer & Co., Oppenheimer Asset Management and Oppenheimer Trust, it provides a range of financial services including brokerage, investment banking, asset management, lending, and research. The company's Private Client segment, which offers service brokerage, wealth planning, and margin lending to affluent and business clients in the Americas, makes up the bulk of sales. It held client assets under administration of approximately $122.1 billion. Oppenheimer employs more than 150 investment banking professionals in the US, the UK, Germany and Israel. The Americas accounts for about 95% of the company's revenues.

	Annual Growth	12/19	12/20	12/21	12/22	12/23
Sales ($mil.)	4.8%	1,033.4	1,198.7	1,394.0	1,110.9	1,248.8
Net income ($ mil.)	(13.1%)	53.0	123.0	159.0	32.4	30.2
Market value ($ mil.)	10.7%	282.7	323.3	477.0	435.4	425.0
Employees	(0.2%)	2,971	2,908	2,913	2,912	2,942

OPPENHEIMERFUNDS, INC.

225 LIBERTY ST
NEW YORK, NY 102811005
Phone: 212 323-0200
Fax: –
Web: www.invesco.com

CEO: William Glavin Jr
CFO: –
HR: –
FYE: December 31
Type: Private

Oppenheimer Holdings is a leading middle-market investment bank and full service broker-dealer. With roots tracing back to 1881, the company is engaged in a broad range of activities in the financial services industry, including retail securities brokerage, institutional sales and trading, investment banking (both corporate and public finance), equity & fixed income research, market-making, trust services and investment advisory and asset management services. Oppenheimer has some $38.8 billion assets under management. It also provide trust services and products through Oppenheimer Trust Company of Delaware and discount brokerage services through Freedom Investments, Inc. (Freedom). Through OPY Credit Corp., the company offers syndication as well as trading of issued syndicated corporate loans. Vast majority of its revenue comes from Americas region.

	Annual Growth	12/98	12/99	12/00	12/01	12/08
Assets ($mil.)	(53.1%)	–	–	–	1,587.5	8.0
Net income ($ mil.)	–	–	–	–	145.7	–
Market value ($ mil.)	–	–	–	–	–	–
Employees	–	–	–	–	–	1,923

OPTICAL CABLE CORP. — NMS: OCC

5290 Concourse Drive
Roanoke, VA 24019
Phone: 540 265-0690
Fax: –
Web: www.occfiber.com

CEO: Neil D Wilkin Jr
CFO: Tracy G Smith
HR: –
FYE: October 31
Type: Public

Optical Cable Corporation (OCC) is a leading manufacturer of a broad range of fiber optic and copper data communication cabling and connectivity solutions primarily for the enterprise market and various harsh environment and specialty markets (collectively, the non-carrier markets), and also the wireless carrier market, offering integrated suites of high quality products which operate as a system solution or seamlessly integrate with other components. OCC's product offerings include designs for uses ranging from enterprise networks, data centers, residential, campus and Passive Optical LAN (POL) installations to customized products for specialty applications and harsh environments, including military, industrial, mining, petrochemical, renewable energy and broadcast applications, and for the wireless carrier market. The US accounts about 85% of the company's revenue.

	Annual Growth	10/19	10/20	10/21	10/22	10/23
Sales ($mil.)	0.3%	71.3	55.3	59.1	69.1	72.2
Net income ($ mil.)	–	(5.7)	(6.1)	6.6	(0.3)	2.1
Market value ($ mil.)	(2.1%)	23.3	21.1	30.5	28.2	21.4
Employees	(2.8%)	366	317	322	337	327

OPTIMUMBANK HOLDINGS INC — NAS: OPHC

2929 East Commercial Boulevard
Fort Lauderdale, FL 33308
Phone: 954 900-2800
Fax: –
Web: www.optimumbank.com

CEO: Timothy Terry
CFO: Joel Klein
HR: –
FYE: December 31
Type: Public

OptimumBank Holdings is the holding company for OptimumBank, which operates three branches in the communities of Plantation, Fort Lauderdale, and Deerfield Beach in South Florida. The bank is mainly a real estate lender, with commercial mortgages representing the largest portion of its loan portfolio, followed by residential mortgages, land and construction loans, and multifamily residential mortgages. It also offers other standard services such as checking and savings accounts. CDs, credit cards, and personal loans. OptimumBank was founded in 2000 by chairman Albert Finch and president Richard Browdy. As a group, executive officers and directors of OptimumBank Holdings own more than 40% of the company.

	Annual Growth	12/19	12/20	12/21	12/22	12/23
Assets ($mil.)	58.1%	126.7	235.1	351.9	585.2	791.3
Net income ($ mil.)	–	(1.1)	(0.8)	6.3	4.0	6.3
Market value ($ mil.)	10.8%	20.1	24.4	28.5	29.7	30.3
Employees	33.3%	19	27	38	48	60

OPTIMUMCARE CORP.

30011 Ivy Glenn Drive, Suite 219
Laguna Niguel, CA 92677
Phone: 949 495-1100
Fax: 949 495-4316
Web: www.opmc.com

CEO: –
CFO: –
HR: –
FYE: December 31
Type: Public

OptimumCare works under the assumption that to truly be healthy one's body requires a certain amount of attention, but also that one's mind requires optimum care. Established in 1987, OptimumCare is a provider of a variety of behavioral health care services. The company provides contract management of inpatient, partial hospitalization, and outpatient programs for persons suffering from acute mental illness at a network of hospitals, medical centers, and community mental health centers in the southwestern US. It also provides temporary medical staffing services.

	Annual Growth	12/99	12/00	12/01	12/02	12/03
Sales ($mil.)	(11.8%)	10.6	8.1	7.0	5.4	6.4
Net income ($ mil.)	–	0.4	0.4	(0.6)	(0.4)	(0.9)
Market value ($ mil.)	(11.6%)	3.9	4.1	3.1	1.1	2.4
Employees	(3.4%)	117	105	94	129	102

OPTION CARE HEALTH INC — NMS: OPCH

3000 Lakeside Dr., Suite 300N
Bannockburn, IL 60015
Phone: 312 940-2443
Fax: –
Web: www.bioscrip.com

CEO: –
CFO: –
HR: –
FYE: December 31
Type: Public

Option Care Health (formerly BioScrip) is the largest independent provider of home and alternate site infusion services. Option Care Health's nurses administer the medicines to treat hemophilia, cancer, pain management, or even simply hydration. Option Care Health has more than 4,500 clinicians, including pharmacists, pharmacy technicians, nurses, and dietitians, that are able to provide infusion service coverage for nearly all patients across the US needing treatment for complex and chronic medical conditions.

	Annual Growth	12/19	12/20	12/21	12/22	12/23
Sales ($mil.)	16.8%	2,310.4	3,032.6	3,438.6	3,944.7	4,302.3
Net income ($ mil.)	–	(75.9)	(8.1)	139.9	150.6	267.1
Market value ($ mil.)	73.4%	651.2	2,730.4	4,964.9	5,253.0	5,881.4
Employees	7.2%	5,903	5,852	7,238	8,058	7,802

OPTS IDEAS, INC

3026 S BROOKRIDGE WAY
BOISE, ID 837167052
Phone: 415 339-2024
Fax: –
Web: www.optsideas.com

CEO: –
CFO: –
HR: –
FYE: December 31
Type: Private

OPTS Ideas has grandiose ideas for promoting your next big marketing event. The company specializes in conceiving and planning marketing events and outsourcing the production services to its national network of contractors. The company's events have promoted brand awareness for such clients and major brands as Apple, Hallmark, Microsoft, and Washington Mutual. The size of events ranges from gatherings of 100 to 40,000 people. OPTS Ideas operates from offices in California and Idaho.

	Annual Growth	12/07	12/08	12/09	12/10	12/11
Sales ($mil.)	4.1%	–	6.8	3.4	6.7	7.7
Net income ($ mil.)	–	–	0.3	0.2	0.1	(0.4)
Market value ($ mil.)	–	–	–	–	–	–
Employees	–	–	–	–	–	4

ORACLE CORP

2300 Oracle Way
Austin, TX 78741
Phone: 737 867-1000
Fax: –
Web: www.oracle.com

NYS: ORCL
CEO: Safra A Catz
CFO: –
HR: –
FYE: May 31
Type: Public

Oracle provides products and services that address enterprise information technology (IT) environments. The enterprise software company offers a range of cloud-based applications and platforms as well as hardware and services to help companies improve their processes. Oracle's applications center on enterprise resource planning, data management, collaboration, content and experience, business analytics, IT operations management, security, and emerging technologies. In recent years, Oracle has aggressively expanded through acquisitions that have helped build its cloud offerings. The company's mainstay product has been Oracle Database, one of the most popular corporate database offerings. More than half its revenue comes from international customers.

	Annual Growth	05/19	05/20	05/21	05/22	05/23
Sales ($mil.)	6.0%	39,506	39,068	40,479	42,440	49,954
Net income ($ mil.)	(6.4%)	11,083	10,135	13,746	6,717.0	8,503.0
Market value ($ mil.)	20.3%	137,278	145,878	213,622	195,119	287,415
Employees	4.8%	136,000	135,000	132,000	143,000	164,000

ORAGENICS INC

4902 Eisenhower Blvd., Suite 125
Tampa, FL 33634
Phone: 813 286-7900
Fax: 813 286-7904
Web: www.oragenics.com

ASE: OGEN
CEO: Kimberly Murphy
CFO: Janet Huffman
HR: –
FYE: December 31
Type: Public

Oragenics wants to get the beneficial microflora in your mouth to bloom. The biotechnology company is developing an oral topical treatment that could provide life-long protection from most forms of tooth decay. It is also researching an antibiotic that could kill harmful bacteria in the mouth, such as drug-resistant Staphylococcus. It is also developing a weight-loss product. Oragenics aims to turn from product development to commercialization through alliances and partnerships. In 2016 the company sold its Consumer Probiotic Business (including the ProBiora3 and Evora brands to promote oral and periodontal health) to ProBiora Health for $1.7 million.

	Annual Growth	12/18	12/19	12/20	12/21	12/22
Sales ($mil.)	–	–	–	–	0.0	0.1
Net income ($ mil.)	–	(9.9)	(15.6)	(26.4)	(15.7)	(14.3)
Market value ($ mil.)	(40.9%)	1.7	1.1	0.9	0.9	0.2
Employees	–	6	7	7	5	6

ORANGE AND ROCKLAND UTILITIES, INC.

1 BLUE HILL PLZ STE 20
PEARL RIVER, NY 109653100
Phone: 845 352-6000
Fax: –
Web: www.oru.com

CEO: –
CFO: –
HR: –
FYE: December 31
Type: Private

Orange and Rockland Utilities (O&R) operates under the auspices of its big city cousin, holding company Consolidated Edison (Con Edison). O&R's subsidiaries, Rockland Electric and Pike County Power & Light, operate in southeastern New York and adjacent portions of New Jersey and Pennsylvania. The utilities distribute electricity to more than 301,800 customers in about 100 communities in those three states, and deliver natural gas more than to 128,000 customers in New York and Pennsylvania. O&R's transmission and distribution facilities include 5,550 miles of overhead and underground power distribution lines, 560 miles of transmission lines, and more than 1,850 miles of gas pipeline.

	Annual Growth	12/02	12/03	12/04	12/05	12/16
Sales ($mil.)	(0.8%)	–	727.0	703.0	824.0	653.5
Net income ($ mil.)	2.1%	–	45.0	46.0	50.0	59.2
Market value ($ mil.)	–	–	–	–	–	–
Employees	–	–	–	–	–	1,060

ORANGE COAST TITLE COMPANY

1551 N TUSTIN AVE STE 300
SANTA ANA, CA 927058638
Phone: 714 558-2836
Fax: –
Web: www.octitle.com

CEO: –
CFO: –
HR: –
FYE: December 31
Type: Private

Southern California home buyers aren't the only ones who can partake of Orange Coast Title's (OCT) services. OCT and its 10 subsidiaries provide commercial and consumer title insurance and closing services to home buyers and lenders from its offices located across the US. The company also helps subdivision developers complete the necessary filings and maintains a database to match up investors and properties through its Builder Services commercial division. The OCT Lender Services division includes its National Asset Management Group and Integrated Lender Services subsidiaries, which offer foreclosure processing, appraisals, and other services.

ORANGE COUNTY GLOBAL MEDICAL CENTER AUXILIARY

1301 N TUSTIN AVE
SANTA ANA, CA 927058619
Phone: 714 835-3555
Fax: –
Web: www.orangecountyglobalmedicalcenter.com

CEO: Dan Brothman
CFO: –
HR: –
FYE: March 31
Type: Private

Western Medical Center makes sure that The OC keeps health issues out of its drama. Western Medical Center - Santa Ana serves the residents of California's Orange County through an acute care facility that houses some 280 beds. It also boasts doctors who are able to perform heart, lung, liver, and kidney transplants. The hospital is one of three major trauma centers in the county. Tenet sold the facility (as part of a restructuring) to Integrated Healthcare Holdings (based in Costa Mesa, California). After taking over Western Medical Center, IHHI met with some rough financial times and, bleeding capital, faced the possibility of having to sell the center.

ORANGE COUNTY TRANSPORTATION AUTHORITY SCHOLARSHIP FOUNDATION, INC.

550 S MAIN ST
ORANGE, CA 928684506
Phone: 714 636-7433
Fax: –
Web: www.octa.net

CEO: Darrell Johnson
CFO: –
HR: –
FYE: June 30
Type: Private

Public transportation in sunny Orange County, California is overseen by the Orange County Transportation Authority (OCTA). The OCTA is the main provider of bus services in its 800-sq.-mi. territory, which is home to more than 3 million people. In cooperation with the Southern California Regional Rail Authority, the OCTA oversees Metrolink commuter rail service in Orange County. The agency also operates a 10-mile toll road and issues permits to taxi operators. Revenue from a half-cent local sales tax allows the agency to pay for road improvement and mass transit projects.

	Annual Growth	06/17	06/18	06/20	06/21	06/22
Sales ($mil.)	4.7%	–	634.8	708.3	721.8	761.4
Net income ($ mil.)	–	–	(53.2)	(87.7)	(83.1)	184.2
Market value ($ mil.)	–	–	–	–	–	–
Employees	–	–	–	–	–	1,050

ORASURE TECHNOLOGIES INC. NMS: OSUR

220 East First Street
Bethlehem, PA 18015
Phone: 610 882-1820
Fax: –
Web: www.orasure.com

CEO: Carrie E Manner
CFO: Kenneth McGrath
HR: Alexandra Henry
FYE: December 31
Type: Public

OraSure, together with its wholly-owned subsidiaries, DNA Genotek (DNAG), Diversigen, and Novosanis, provides its customers with end-to-end solutions that encompass tools, services and diagnostics. The OraSure family of companies is a leader in the development, manufacture, and distribution of rapid diagnostic tests, sample collection and stabilization devices, and molecular services solutions designed to discover and detect critical medical conditions. OraSure's portfolio of products is sold globally to clinical laboratories, hospitals, physician's offices, clinics, public health and community-based organizations, research institutions, government agencies, pharma, commercial entities and direct to consumers. About 80% of company's revenue comes from domestic operations.

	Annual Growth	12/19	12/20	12/21	12/22	12/23
Sales ($mil.)	27.3%	154.6	171.7	233.7	387.5	405.5
Net income ($ mil.)	34.0%	16.7	(14.9)	(23.0)	(17.9)	53.7
Market value ($ mil.)	0.5%	590.4	778.3	639.0	354.4	602.9
Employees	7.8%	472	570	785	840	638

ORBCOMM INC.

395 W PASSAIC ST STE 325
ROCHELLE PARK, NJ 076623022
Phone: 703 433-6300
Fax: –
Web: www.orbcomm.com

CEO: Sameer Agrawal
CFO: Constantine Milcos
HR: Suzanne Roossien
FYE: December 31
Type: Private

ORBCOMM is a pioneer in IoT technology, empowering customers with insight to make data-driven decisions that help them optimize their operations, maximize profitability and build a more sustainable future. The company deliver smart solutions for a diverse customer base spanning transportation, supply chain, heavy equipment, maritime, natural resources and government. Key clients include Kroger, Costco Wholesale, Volvo, and Swift. ORBCOMM is the global leader in Automatic Identification System (AIS) data services, used by ships and vessel traffic services for identification and location.

ORBIT INTERNATIONAL CORP. NBB: ORBT

80 Cabot Court
Hauppauge, NY 11788
Phone: 631 435-8300
Fax: –
Web: www.orbitintl.com

CEO: Mitchell Binder
CFO: David Goldman
HR: Christine Tracey
FYE: December 31
Type: Public

Orbit International, also known as Orbit, is at home in the world -- on land, in the air, or at sea. The company's core electronics group is comprised of its instrument division, and its Tulip and Q-Vio subsidiary. It specializes in customized display units, intercommunication panels, and keyboards for military programs, as well as power supplies and frequency converters for commercial customers. Orbit's power unit, led by subsidiary Behlman Electronics, makes electrical AC power supplies and frequency converters. Orbit primarily serves the US government and defense contractors. The company generates majority of sales domestically.

	Annual Growth	12/17	12/18	12/19	12/20	12/21
Sales ($mil.)	1.6%	20.9	24.7	26.0	25.9	22.2
Net income ($ mil.)	15.9%	1.8	2.2	0.5	0.6	3.2
Market value ($ mil.)	4.5%	18.8	19.0	20.7	19.5	22.4
Employees	–	–	–	–	–	–

ORBITAL INFRASTRUCTURE GROUP INC NBB: OIGB Q

5444 Westheimer Road, Suite 1650
Houston, TX 77056
Phone: 832 467-1420
Fax: –
Web: www.orbitalenergygroup.com

CEO: James F O'Neil III
CFO: Nicholas M Grindstaff
HR: –
FYE: December 31
Type: Public

Orbital Energy Group, Inc. (OEG), formerly known as CUI Global Inc. is a diversified infrastructure services company serving customers in the electric power, telecommunications, and renewable markets. The company's reportable segments are the Electric Power segment, the Telecommunications segment, and the Renewables segment. In 2021, the company announced the planned divestiture of its previous Integrated Energy Infrastructure Solutions and Services segment. OEG has continuing operations in two countries, including the US and India. The company's largest market is the US with more than 95% of revenue.

	Annual Growth	12/18	12/19	12/20	12/21	12/22
Sales ($mil.)	35.1%	96.8	23.5	38.4	82.9	322.2
Net income ($ mil.)	–	(17.3)	(1.1)	(27.4)	(61.3)	(276.2)
Market value ($ mil.)	(36.7%)	4.8	4.3	8.6	8.6	0.8
Employees	42.9%	357	257	284	1,329	1,490

ORBITZ WORLDWIDE, INC.

500 W MADISON ST STE 700
CHICAGO, IL 606614598
Phone: 312 894-5000
Fax: –
Web: www.homeaway.com

CEO: Barney Harford
CFO: Michael Randolfi
HR: Mike Goldwasser
FYE: December 31
Type: Private

Orbitz is where all travelers are welcome and connects travelers to the world by providing the best planning tools and travel rewards just for going. The Orbitz Reward program allows travelers to instantly earn rewards on flights, hotels and packages that can be instantly redeemed on tens of thousands of hotels worldwide. Orbitz Rewards members can redeem their Orbucks at 385,000-plus hotel properties worldwide, including resorts, brand name hotels, boutiques and hostels. Orbitz is owned by Expedia Group, one of the world's foremost travel companies.

ORCA BAY SEAFOODS, INC.

2729 6TH AVE S STE 200
SEATTLE, WA 981342101
Phone: 425 204-9100
Fax: –
Web: www.orcabayfoods.com

CEO: –
CFO: –
HR: Wendy Kowalski
FYE: February 28
Type: Private

Orca Bay Seafoods is a leading supplier of fresh frozen seafood, sourcing products from oceans all over the world. The company buys flash-frozen fish from suppliers, and keeps it frozen as it cuts individual portions for sale to foodservice companies, supermarkets, club stores, and restaurants across the US. Its products include Ahi tuna, Alaskan cod, Pacific Ocean perch, sockeye salmon, mahi mahi, and tilapia, as well as Mexican white shrimp. Orca Bay was founded by Mike Samsel in 1985; the giant Japanese seafood company Maruha Nichiro owns a minority interest in the company; Japanese conglomerate Tokusui Corporation owns the controlling interest.

	Annual Growth	02/06	02/07	02/08	02/09	02/10
Sales ($mil.)	(10.8%)	–	–	–	157.0	140.0
Net income ($ mil.)	(36.6%)	–	–	–	1.4	0.9
Market value ($ mil.)	–	–	–	–	–	–
Employees	–	–	–	–	–	180

ORCHARD ENTERPRISES NY, INC.

23 E 4TH ST FL 3
NEW YORK, NY 100037023
Phone: 212 201-9280
Fax: –
Web: www.orchard.com

CEO: Bradley Navin
CFO: Nathan Fong
HR: –
FYE: December 31
Type: Private

Music fans looking to pick some tunes online can thank this Orchard. Formerly Digital Music Group, The Orchard Enterprises is a leading digital distributor of audio and video recordings serving both digital downloading services and online retailers. The company boasts a catalog of more than 1.3 million music recordings from independent and major labels, as well as 4,000 titles of video programming. The Orchard supplies digital content to music and video providers such as Apple's iTunes, EMusic.com, and Netflix, and mobile carriers such as Verizon and Vodafone. Dimensional Associates, the private equity arm of JDS Capital Management, controls the company.

ORCHID ISLAND CAPITAL INC

NYS: ORC

3305 Flamingo Drive
Vero Beach, FL 32963
Phone: 772 231-1400
Fax: –
Web: www.orchidislandcapital.com

CEO: Robert E Cauley
CFO: George H Haas IV
HR: –
FYE: December 31
Type: Public

No REIT is an island, unless your name is Orchid Island Capital. The company, which is seeking to become a real estate investment trust, invests in residential mortgage-backed securities (RMBS) that are guaranteed by the US government or federally sponsored entities like Fannie Mae, Freddie Mac, and Ginnie Mae. Its portfolio and principal investment targets consist of pass-through agency RMBS and structured agency RMBS, including fixed-rate mortgages, adjustable-rate mortgages (ARMs), and hybrid ARMs, as well as collateralized mortgage obligations. Formed by mortgage REIT Bimini Capital Management in 2010, Orchid Island Capital filed to go public for the second time in October 2014.

	Annual Growth	12/19	12/20	12/21	12/22	12/23
Assets ($mil.)	2.4%	3,882.1	4,058.1	7,068.7	3,865.7	4,264.9
Net income ($ mil.)	–	24.3	2.1	(64.8)	(258.5)	(39.2)
Market value ($ mil.)	9.6%	302.1	269.5	232.4	542.2	435.3
Employees	–	–	–	–	–	–

ORECUL, INC.

4801 HARDWARE DR NE
ALBUQUERQUE, NM 871092019
Phone: 505 345-5501
Fax: –
Web: www.ccsbts.com

CEO: –
CFO: –
HR: –
FYE: December 31
Type: Private

Sparkle Maintenance provides commercial janitorial and custodial maintenance services on a contract basis. The company has offices in Denver; Albuquerque, Artesia, Espanola, and Las Alamos, New Mexico; and Wichita Falls, Texas. Its contract customers include the federal government, commercial office buildings, high tech facilities, institutions, private and public schools, and industrial facilities in Texas, New Mexico, and Colorado. Sparkle Maintenance was founded in 1964.

OREGON DEPARTMENT OF TRANSPORTATION

355 CAPITOL ST NE MS21
SALEM, OR 973013871
Phone: 503 378-5849
Fax: –
Web: www.oregon.gov

CEO: –
CFO: –
HR: Madilyn Zike
FYE: June 30
Type: Private

The Oregon Department of Transportation (ODOT) helps move people and goods across the state. The agency strives to provide a safe and efficient transportation system -- including highway, rail, and public transit -- for its residents. The department is responsible for construction and maintenance of highways and bridges, improving public transportation services, reducing traffic crashes, and ensuring equal access for low-income and elderly citizens, as well as people with disabilities. Its division of driver and motor vehicles (DMV) provides vehicle registration, driver licenses, and ID cards. The agency also tries to decrease the impact that its transportation system has on air and water quality.

	Annual Growth	06/02	06/03	06/05	06/18	06/19
Sales ($mil.)	10.4%	–	461.6	–	2,017.8	2,260.1
Net income ($ mil.)	–	–	(198.2)	–	23.8	56.2
Market value ($ mil.)	–	–	–	–	–	–
Employees	–	–	–	–	–	4,800

OREGON HEALTH & SCIENCE UNIVERSITY

3181 SW SAM JACKSON PARK RD
PORTLAND, OR 972393011
Phone: 503 494-8311
Fax: –
Web: www.ohsu.edu

CEO: –
CFO: –
HR: –
FYE: June 30
Type: Private

Oregon Health & Science University (OHSU) is Oregon's only academic health center. The University is a system of hospitals and clinics across Oregon and southwest Washington. It is an institution of higher learning, with schools of medicine, nursing, pharmacy, dentistry and public health ? and with a network of campuses and partners throughout Oregon. It is also a national research hub, with thousands of scientists developing lifesaving therapies and deeper understanding. It is a statewide economic engine and Portland's largest employer. OSHU operates OSHU Hospital; OHSU Doernbecher Children's Hospital Hillsboro Medical Center (formerly Tuality Healthcare); Adventist Health Portland; and clinics across Oregon. OHSU traces its roots to 1867, when members of the medical department at Willamette University began the first formal medical students to its Salem campus.

	Annual Growth	06/17	06/18	06/19	06/20	06/22
Sales ($mil.)	6.6%	–	3,050.1	3,178.1	3,313.1	3,942.0
Net income ($ mil.)	–	–	259.7	251.9	(13.9)	(150.3)
Market value ($ mil.)	–	–	–	–	–	–
Employees	–	–	–	–	–	19,500

OREGON PACIFIC BANCORP
NBB: ORPB

1365 Highway 101
Florence, OR 97439
Phone: 541 997-7121
Fax: –
Web: www.opbc.com

CEO: James P Clark
CFO: Joanne A Forsberg
HR: –
FYE: December 31
Type: Public

Clamming is big business along Oregon's coastline, and helping customers manage their clams is big business at Oregon Pacific Bancorp. The holding company owns Oregon Pacific Banking Company, which operates a handful of offices on the state's coastal region west of Eugene. Doing business as Oregon Pacific Bank, it provides standard deposit products including checking, savings, money market accounts, and CDs. The bank primarily uses funds from deposits to originate real estate loans. Oregon Pacific Bank also offers wealth management and corporate trust services.

	Annual Growth	12/17	12/18	12/19	12/20	12/21
Assets ($mil.)	27.6%	261.3	309.5	364.2	537.1	691.7
Net income ($ mil.)	53.0%	1.4	2.6	3.5	4.4	7.8
Market value ($ mil.)	10.8%	34.4	33.5	44.0	36.6	51.8
Employees	–	–	–	–	–	–

OREGON STATE LOTTERY

500 AIRPORT RD SE
SALEM, OR 973015068
Phone: 503 540-1000
Fax: –
Web: www.oregonlottery.org

CEO: –
CFO: –
HR: Janell Simmons
FYE: June 30
Type: Private

The Oregon State Lottery operates the Beaver State's lottery and other state-run games of chance. It offers traditional lotto numbers games and instant-win tickets, and it operates video lottery and video poker machines. Oregon also takes part in the multistate Powerball drawing. About 65% of the lottery's profits are channeled into public education programs, while the rest is used to fund economic development projects, state parks, and other government programs. Oregon created its lottery in 1984.

	Annual Growth	06/17	06/18	06/19	06/20	06/22
Sales ($mil.)	6.5%	–	1,302.9	1,347.7	1,145.3	1,678.7
Net income ($ mil.)	–	–	(14.4)	7.2	(11.5)	59.2
Market value ($ mil.)	–	–	–	–	–	–
Employees	–	–	–	–	–	420

OREGON STATE UNIVERSITY

1500 SW JEFFERSON AVE
CORVALLIS, OR 973318655
Phone: 541 737-1000
Fax: –
Web: www.oregonstate.edu

CEO: –
CFO: –
HR: –
FYE: June 30
Type: Private

Oregon State University (OSU) offers about 200 undergraduate and graduate degree programs at about a dozen colleges and schools, including nationally recognized programs in engineering, environmental sciences, forestry, and pharmacy. Hatfield Marine Science Center is Oregon State University's marine lab serving as a base for distinguished oceanographic research and education, providing academic programs and opportunities for students in secondary and post-secondary education. In addition to its main campus in Corvallis, the university operates OSU-Cascades in Bend, Oregon. OSU has approximately 29,945 undergraduate students and nearly 5,620 graduate students or a total of about 35,240 students. With approximately 4,700 faculty, the university has a student to teacher ratio of 18:1.

ORGANICALLY GROWN COMPANY

1800 PRAIRIE RD STE B
EUGENE, OR 974029722
Phone: 541 689-5320
Fax: –
Web: www.organicgrown.com

CEO: Josh Hinerfeld
CFO: Robbie Vasilinda
HR: Lea Delassus
FYE: December 30
Type: Private

Started by health-conscious Oregon farmers, Organically Grown is exactly what its name says it is. The company grows and sells certified organic fruits, vegetables, and herbs produced by small to medium family-owned farmers located throughout the US's Pacific Northwest. Its line of more than 100 seasonal produce items are sold under the LADYBUG brand to customers including independent retailers, supermarket chains, restaurants, home-delivery services, and wholesalers. Organically Grown, which is owned by its employees and growers, was founded in 1978.

	Annual Growth	12/13	12/14	12/15	12/16	12/17
Sales ($mil.)	(0.1%)	–	163.8	176.4	180.2	163.3
Net income ($ mil.)	(83.1%)	–	2.3	3.1	1.6	0.0
Market value ($ mil.)	–	–	–	–	–	–
Employees	–	–	–	–	–	189

ORGANICS CORPORATION OF AMERICA

55 W END RD
TOTOWA, NJ 075121405
Phone: 973 890-9002
Fax: –
Web: www.ambixlabs.com

CEO: Elkin Serna
CFO: –
HR: –
FYE: June 30
Type: Private

Organics Corporation of America's main division, Ambix Laboratories, is interested in liquid assets. It's a manufacturer of cosmetics and nutritional products for humans and pets. The company supplies private-label personal care products (including prescription and over-the-counter drugs, such as creams, ear drops, nasal sprays, ointments, and syrups) to drugstore chains and wholesale distributors nationwide. It also makes shampoo and nutritional supplements for pets.

ORIGINAL IMPRESSIONS, LLC

2965 W CORPORATE LAKES BLVD
WESTON, FL 333313626
Phone: 305 233-1322
Fax: –
Web: www.originalimpressions.com

CEO: –
CFO: –
HR: Ivan Melcon
FYE: December 31
Type: Private

Original Impressions provides marketing support services, from creative design and production to fulfillment. Catering primarily to the southeastern US, the company operates through four divisions: creative, E-Business, print, and fulfillment. Creative services include graphic design, brand development, and Web design. E-Business consists of Web development for e-commerce applications, document management services, and digital marketing materials management. The company's production services include digital and offset printing of a variety of marketing materials. Established in 1982, Original Impressions also offers database management and fulfillment services.

	Annual Growth	12/07	12/08	12/09	12/10	12/11
Sales ($mil.)	10.2%	–	–	19.7	21.3	24.0
Net income ($ mil.)	36.4%	–	–	1.0	1.3	1.9
Market value ($ mil.)	–	–	–	–	–	–
Employees	–	–	–	–	–	190

ORION ENERGY SYSTEMS INC — NAS: OESX

2210 Woodland Drive
Manitowoc, WI 54220
Phone: 920 892-9340
Fax: –
Web: www.orionlighting.com

CEO: –
CFO: –
HR: –
FYE: March 31
Type: Public

Orion Energy Systems wants customers to see the light ... high intensity fluorescent (HIF) lighting systems, that is. Orion designs, manufactures, and installs energy management systems that include HIF lighting and intelligent lighting controls. Its Apollo Light Pipe product collects and focuses daylight, without consuming electricity. The firm estimates its HIF lineup can help cut customers' lighting-related electricity costs by up to 50%, boost quantity and quality of light, and reduce related carbon-dioxide emissions. In addition, its engineered systems division makes solar photovoltaic products that allow customers to convert sunlight into electricity.

	Annual Growth	03/19	03/20	03/21	03/22	03/23
Sales ($mil.)	4.2%	65.8	150.8	116.8	124.4	77.4
Net income ($ mil.)	–	(6.7)	12.5	26.1	6.1	(34.3)
Market value ($ mil.)	23.0%	28.6	119.5	224.8	90.4	65.6
Employees	(4.7%)	321	181	213	314	265

ORION GROUP HOLDINGS INC — NYS: ORN

12000 Aerospace Avenue, Suite 300
Houston, TX 77034
Phone: 713 852-6500
Fax: –
Web: www.oriongroupholdingsinc.com

CEO: Austin J Shanfelter
CFO: –
HR: Laura Ortiz
FYE: December 31
Type: Public

Orion Group Holdings, Inc., is a leading specialty construction company serving the infrastructure, industrial, and building sectors, providing services both on and off the water in the continental US, Alaska, Canada and the Caribbean Basin through its marine segment and its concrete segment. The company's marine segment provides construction and dredging services relating to marine transportation facility construction, marine pipeline construction, marine environmental structures, dredging of waterways, channels and ports, environmental dredging, design, and specialty services. Its concrete segment provides turnkey concrete construction services including place and finish, site prep, layout, forming, and rebar placement for large commercial, structural and other associated business areas. Orion was founded in 1994 as a marine construction project management business.

	Annual Growth	12/19	12/20	12/21	12/22	12/23
Sales ($mil.)	0.1%	708.4	709.9	601.4	748.3	711.8
Net income ($ mil.)	–	(5.4)	20.2	(14.6)	(12.6)	(17.9)
Market value ($ mil.)	(1.2%)	168.9	161.4	122.7	77.5	160.8
Employees	(8.6%)	2,571	2,297	2,447	2,216	1,796

ORION SEAFOOD INTERNATIONAL, INC.

20 LADD ST STE 300
PORTSMOUTH, NH 038014080
Phone: 603 433-2220
Fax: –
Web: –

CEO: Charles Anastasia
CFO: –
HR: –
FYE: December 31
Type: Private

Orion Seafood International caters to the crab lover; not to mention the lobster lover and the shrimp lover. As a worldwide distributor and marketer, the company serves up such products as snow and king crab meat, lobster claws and tails, scoopable lobster salad, and cooked and raw shrimp. Customers include foodservice providers, supermarket chains, retailers, and cruise lines. Orion's Grill-Cuts brand shrimp for grilling is sold ready-prepped, frozen, and packaged at such grocery stores as Albertsons, Hannaford, and Hy-Vee. Privately held, Orion Seafood International was co-founded by CEO Charles Anastasia in 1988. The company sources its products from North America, South America, Asia, and Russia.

ORLANDO HEALTH, INC.

52 W UNDERWOOD ST
ORLANDO, FL 328061110
Phone: 407 841-5111
Fax: –
Web: www.orlandohealth.com

CEO: –
CFO: –
HR: –
FYE: September 30
Type: Private

Orlando Health is a not-for-profit healthcare organization with $8.1 billion of assets under management that serves the southeastern US. It has about 3,200 beds that includes around two dozen of hospitals and emergency departments. The system also includes nine specialty institutes in aesthetic and reconstructive surgery, cancer, colon and rectal, digestive health, heart and vascular, neuroscience, orthopedics, rehabilitation, weight loss and bariatric surgery. In addition, Orlando Health is home to more than 100 adult and pediatric primary care practices, skilled nursing facilities, an in-patient behavioral health facility under the management of Acadia Healthcare, and more than 60 outpatient facilities that include imaging and laboratory services, wound care centers, home healthcare services in partnership with LHC Group, and urgent care centers in partnership with FastMed Urgent Care. More than 4,000 physicians, representing more than 100 medical specialties and subspecialties have privileges across the Orlando Health system, which employs more than 25,000 team members and more than 1,200 physicians.

	Annual Growth	09/18	09/19	09/20	09/21	09/22
Sales ($mil.)	11.0%	–	2,756.8	2,561.8	2,875.4	3,766.2
Net income ($ mil.)	15.6%	–	509.0	653.0	879.2	787.2
Market value ($ mil.)	–	–	–	–	–	–
Employees	–	–	–	–	–	23,000

ORLANDO UTILITIES COMMISSION (INC)

100 W ANDERSON ST
ORLANDO, FL 328014408
Phone: 407 246-2121
Fax: –
Web: www.ouc.com

CEO: Clint Bullock
CFO: –
HR: Emily Leon
FYE: June 30
Type: Private

Orlando Utilities Commission (OUC) provides electricity and water services to some 275,000 customers in and around Orlando, Florida. OUC is responsible for a portfolio of energy services and solutions including the acquisition, generation, production, transmission and distribution of electric and water services to its customers within Orange and Osceola counties as well as chilled water, and commercial lighting services, back-up generation, electric vehicle charging and solar services and solutions. OUC authorizes an annual average withdrawal rate of some 109.2 million gallons per day. OUC was created in 1923 by a Special Act of the Florida Legislature as a statutory commission of the State of Florida and is governed by a Board consisting of five members including the Mayor of the City of Orlando.

	Annual Growth	09/10	09/11	09/12*	06/14	06/15
Sales ($mil.)	(10.2%)	–	–	854.4	–	619.0
Net income ($ mil.)	7.1%	–	–	34.1	–	42.0
Market value ($ mil.)	–	–	–	–	–	–
Employees	–	–	–	–	–	1,000

*Fiscal year change

ORLEANS HOMEBUILDERS, INC.

3333 STREET RD STE 101
BENSALEM, PA 190202022
Phone: 215 245-7500
Fax: –
Web: www.orleanshomes.com

CEO: Alan E Laing
CFO: Marek Bakun
HR: –
FYE: June 30
Type: Private

Despite its name Orleans Homebuilders (OHB) prefers the City of Brotherly Love to The Big Easy. OHB builds communities of single-family homes, condos, and townhomes for first-time and move-up buyers, luxury homebuyers, empty nesters, and active adult homebuyers. Prices range from $170,000 to about $1.5 million for its dwellings, depending on the region. OHB operates in 10 distinct markets mainly in the Philadelphia metro area, New Jersey, New York, the Carolinas, and Virginia. It is also active in Orlando and Chicago. Hit hard by the US housing downturn, OHB filed for Chapter 11 protection in 2010, seeking to restructure its debts. It emerged early the following year.

ORMAT TECHNOLOGIES INC   NYS: ORA

6140 Plumas Street   CEO: –
Reno, NV 89519-6075   CFO: –
Phone: 775 356-9029   HR: –
Fax: –   FYE: December 31
Web: www.ormat.com   Type: Public

Ormat Technologies is a leading vertically integrated company that is primarily engaged in the geothermal and recovered energy power businesses. The company is also expanding into the solar Photovoltaic (PV) and energy storage and management services business. The company offers its services through its segments: Electricity, Product, and Electricity Storage. Ormat operates power plants in Guatemala, Kenya, Guadeloupe Island, Honduras, Indonesia, New Zealand and the US. The company's largest market is the US, accounting for around 70% of annual revenue. Ormat was established in 1965 by the Bronicki family.

	Annual Growth	12/19	12/20	12/21	12/22	12/23
Sales ($mil.)	2.7%	746.0	705.3	663.1	734.2	829.4
Net income ($ mil.)	9.0%	88.1	85.5	62.1	65.8	124.4
Market value ($ mil.)	0.4%	4,497.9	5,449.2	4,786.5	5,219.8	4,574.6
Employees	2.9%	1,408	1,402	1,385	1,480	1,576

ORRSTOWN FINANCIAL SERVICES, INC.   NAS: ORRF

77 East King Street, P.O. Box 250   CEO: Thomas R Quinn Jr
Shippensburg, PA 17257   CFO: Neelesh Kalani
Phone: 717 532-6114   HR: –
Fax: –   FYE: December 31
Web: www.orrstown.com   Type: Public

Orrstown Financial Services keeps both paddles in the money pool. The institution is the holding company for Orrstown Bank, which operates some 20 branches in Pennsylvania's Cumberland, Perry, and Franklin counties as well as in Maryland's Washington County. In addition to traditional retail deposit offerings, Orrstown also provides investment management services including retirement planning and investment analysis. Real estate mortgages account for about 40% of the bank's lending portfolio, followed by commercial, construction, and consumer loans. Orrstown is growing its mortgage lending capabilities. It launched an online application system in order to increase mortgage origination sales.

	Annual Growth	12/19	12/20	12/21	12/22	12/23
Assets ($mil.)	6.5%	2,383.3	2,750.6	2,834.6	2,922.4	3,064.2
Net income ($ mil.)	20.5%	16.9	26.5	32.9	22.0	35.7
Market value ($ mil.)	6.9%	240.1	175.6	267.4	245.8	313.1
Employees	(2.0%)	460	418	429	419	425

ORYX TECHNOLOGY CORP.

4340 Almaden Expressway, Suite 220   CEO: –
San Jose, CA 95118   CFO: –
Phone: 408 979-2955   HR: –
Fax: 408 979-9276   FYE: February 29
Web: www.oryxtech.com   Type: Public

Oryx Technology has run like a gazelle into restructuring -- but not into black ink. The company shed its power conversion and test equipment segments (in 1998) and its ceramic metallization and materials coating business (in 1999). In 2006, the technology investment and management company sold its SurgX subsidiary, which collects royalties on its over-voltage surge protection technology that is designed to prevent printed circuit boards from being damaged by electrostatic. Oryx Technology's remaining holding, venture capital firm Oryx Ventures, owns approximately 30% of software company S2 Technologies.

	Annual Growth	02/04	02/05	02/06	02/07	02/08
Sales ($mil.)	(21.1%)	0.5	0.3	0.0	0.2	0.2
Net income ($ mil.)	–	(1.0)	(1.2)	2.0	(0.7)	(0.3)
Market value ($ mil.)	(49.2%)	27.2	10.0	3.9	3.2	1.8
Employees	–	2	2	–	–	–

OSBORN & BARR COMMUNICATIONS, INC.

914 SPRUCE ST   CEO: Michael Turley
SAINT LOUIS, MO 631021118   CFO: Rhonda Ries
Phone: 314 726-5511   HR: Shannon Gerli
Fax: –   FYE: December 31
Web: www.obpagency.com   Type: Private

You can take the ad agency out of the country but, well, you know. Osborn & Barr Communications has built its reputation on its work in the agriculture, rural-lifestyle, and outdoors markets, but its portfolio also includes work in government, finance, and leisure industries. The agency offers advertising, public relations, brand management, creative services, social marketing, digital marketing, media services, and strategic marketing for clients across North America. Clients have included Michelin, the USDA, Intervet, and Monsanto. Founded in 1989, Osborn & Barr has offices in St. Louis; Kansas City, Missouri; and Des Moines.

	Annual Growth	12/04	12/05	12/06	12/07	12/08
Sales ($mil.)	2.7%	–	61.2	67.8	56.3	66.3
Net income ($ mil.)	(7.9%)	–	1.7	1.6	1.5	1.3
Market value ($ mil.)	–	–	–	–	–	–
Employees	–	–	–	–	–	117

OSC SPORTS, INC.

5 BRADLEY DR   CEO: Edward P Manganello
WESTBROOK, ME 040922013   CFO: Woodbury Sanders
Phone: 844 511-1721   HR: –
Fax: –   FYE: September 30
Web: www.olympiasport.com   Type: Private

Olympia Sports may not make you an Olympian, but the company carries the gear to help you go for gold. The sporting goods retailer offers sports equipment, fitness gear and apparel, athletic shoes, casual wear, and sports accessories under such brands as Columbia, Louisville Slugger, Bauer, PUMA, Reebok, and Teva. It sells merchandise through its website and via more than 225 banner stores across the Northeast and Mid-Atlantic states. In addition to its retail business, the company oversees the private nonprofit Olympia Sports Foundation, which runs a clothing bank and collaborates on projects with local charities and schools within its retail region. Founder and CEO Ed Manganello owns Olympia.

	Annual Growth	09/05	09/06	09/07	09/08	09/09
Sales ($mil.)	(2.0%)	–	–	172.7	191.0	165.8
Net income ($ mil.)	(70.1%)	–	–	3.1	4.4	0.3
Market value ($ mil.)	–	–	–	–	–	–
Employees	–	–	–	–	–	763

OSCAR DE LA RENTA, LLC

11 W 42ND ST FL 25   CEO: Alexander L Bolen
NEW YORK, NY 100368002   CFO: Giuseppe Celio
Phone: 212 282-0500   HR: Elizabeth Mindel
Fax: –   FYE: December 31
Web: www.oscardelarenta.com   Type: Private

Women navigate toward the Oscar de la Renta style. The late designer's namesake firm designs couture and ready-to-wear apparel for men and women and licenses its name for a number of products, including jewelry, eyewear, lingerie, home furnishings, luggage, swimwear, fragrance, and furs. Other collections made by the company are sold under the OSCAR by Oscar de la Renta and Pink Label brands (the latter licensed to apparel marketer Kellwood). Oscar de la Renta sells its products in upscale department stores and specialty shops worldwide. Its apparel is made in the US and Italy. Dominican Republic-born designer Oscar de la Renta and partner Ben Shaw (both now deceased) founded the company in 1966.

OSCEOLA REGIONAL HOSPITAL, INC.

700 W OAK ST
KISSIMMEE, FL 347414924
Phone: 407 846-2266
Fax: -
Web: www.hcafloridahealthcare.com

CEO: -
CFO: -
HR: -
FYE: December 31
Type: Private

Osceola Regional Medical Center (ORMC) is a general medical and surgical hospital serving the Kissimmee/St. Cloud area of Central Florida. With more than 320 beds with all private rooms, it offers cardiac care through a heart institute and stroke care through a primary stroke center. The medical center's heart institute is one of the few local facilities certified in carotid stenting to increase heart blood flow. ORMC also features a Level II neonatal intensive care unit and specialty services that include pediatrics, oncology, neurology, and psychiatry. The medical center is part of Nashville hospital operator HCA.

	Annual Growth	12/07	12/08	12/09	12/14	12/15
Sales ($mil.)	(13.2%)	-	0.0	0.0	280.6	0.0
Net income ($ mil.)	-	-	-	0.0	47.1	0.0
Market value ($ mil.)	-	-	-	-	-	-
Employees	-	-	-	-	-	1,500

OSF HEALTHCARE SAINT CLARE MEDICAL CENTER

530 PARK AVE E
PRINCETON, IL 613563901
Phone: 815 875-2811
Fax: -
Web: www.osfhealthcare.org

CEO: -
CFO: Alan Nerone
HR: -
FYE: April 30
Type: Private

The Julia Rackley Perry Memorial Hospital offers a variety of specialized services such as emergency medicine, surgery, cardiac rehabilitation, physical therapy, and radiology. Founded in 1916, the nearly 100-bed hospital also provides outreach clinics, a women's health center, an intensive care unit, a skilled nursing center, and classes and support groups.

OSF HEALTHCARE SYSTEM

124 SW ADAMS ST
PEORIA, IL 616021308
Phone: 309 655-2850
Fax: -
Web: www.osfhealthcare.org

CEO: Carol Friesen
CFO: -
HR: Isabella Trevino
FYE: September 30
Type: Private

OSF Healthcare helps patients who are feeling oh-so-frail in northern Illinois and southwestern Michigan. OSF Healthcare system includes 11 acute care hospitals and one long-term care facility that combined are home to more than 1,500 beds and offer a full spectrum of inpatient and outpatient medical and surgical services. The system's primary care physician network consists of about 650 physicians at more than 105 locations throughout its service area. Subsidiary OSF Home Care provides hospice, home visit, and equipment services, and OSF Saint Francis provides ambulance, pharmacy, and health care management services. The not-for-profit system is a subsidiary of the Sisters of The Third Order of St. Francis.

	Annual Growth	09/15	09/16	09/17	09/18	09/19
Sales ($mil.)	2.7%	-	2,422.9	2,561.4	2,826.1	2,622.3
Net income ($ mil.)	52.9%	-	99.2	144.8	155.4	354.5
Market value ($ mil.)	-	-	-	-	-	-
Employees	-	-	-	-	-	4,360

OSHKOSH CORP (NEW)

NYS: OSK

1917 Four Wheel Drive
Oshkosh, WI 54902
Phone: 920 502-3400
Fax: -
Web: www.oshkoshcorp.com

CEO: John C Pfeifer
CFO: Michael E Pack
HR: Britney Diercks
FYE: December 31
Type: Public

Oshkosh makes vehicles that carry troops, lift firefighters, pick up trash, tow cars, and handle an assortment of other heavy vehicle duties. The company's commercial and access lines include products such as McNeilus refuse vehicle bodies, Jerr-Dan tow trucks, and JLG aerial work platforms. Its emergency offerings range of products such as aircraft rescue and firefighting vehicles (Pierce). Oshkosh makes its products in about 30 plants in the US and around the world. North America accounts for most of its sales. Vehicles are sold via dealers to the global airport, institutional, construction, and municipal markets. The company traces its roots back to 1917.

	Annual Growth	09/20	09/21*	12/21	12/22	12/23
Sales ($mil.)	12.1%	6,856.8	7,737.3	1,791.7	8,282.0	9,657.9
Net income ($ mil.)	22.6%	324.5	472.7	6.2	173.9	598.0
Market value ($ mil.)	13.8%	4,812.3	6,702.6	7,379.6	5,774.1	7,098.0
Employees	6.3%	14,400	15,000	-	15,000	17,300

*Fiscal year change

OSI GROUP, LLC

1225 CORP BLVD STE 300
AURORA, IL 60505
Phone: 630 851-6600
Fax: -
Web: www.osigroup.com

CEO: Sheldon Lavin
CFO: -
HR: Areli Cazares
FYE: December 31
Type: Private

OSI Group is a premier global supplier of custom value-added food products to the world's leading foodservice and retail food brands. The group boasts a bulging menu of products that includes a variety of beef, pork, and poultry items ? such as beef patties, hot dogs, sausages, bacon, and chicken nuggets ? as well as entr es, pizza, produce, and soups and beans. As part of its business, OSI also offers other food processors services such as custom food product development and food supply chain management. It has a global food network of more than 65 production facilities in nearly 20 countries. The group was founded in 1909.

	Annual Growth	12/17	12/18	12/19	12/20	12/21
Sales ($mil.)	82.9%	-	-	-	0.2	0.3
Net income ($ mil.)	-	-	-	-	(0.1)	0.0
Market value ($ mil.)	-	-	-	-	-	-
Employees	-	-	-	-	-	9,200

OSI SYSTEMS, INC. (DE)

NMS: OSIS

12525 Chadron Avenue
Hawthorne, CA 90250
Phone: 310 978-0516
Fax: -
Web: www.osi-systems.com

CEO: Deepak Chopra
CFO: Alan Edrick
HR: Heather Zammit
FYE: June 30
Type: Public

OSI Systems is a vertically integrated designer and manufacturer of specialized electronic systems and components for critical applications. The company's security and inspection systems design, manufacture, and market security and inspection systems globally to end users under the Rapiscan Systems, Gatekeeper, and AS&E trade names. Its Spacelabs Healthcare subsidiary makes patient monitoring, cardiac monitoring, and clinical networking systems primarily for hospitals. Under the OSI Optoelectronics, OSI LaserDiode, OSI Laserscan, Semicoa, and Advanced Photonix trade names it makes optoelectronic devices for aerospace/defense electronics, industrial automation, security, medical imaging, and diagnostics, and other applications. It also offers contract electronics manufacturing services (OSI Electronics). The US generates the majority of the company's revenue.

	Annual Growth	06/19	06/20	06/21	06/22	06/23
Sales ($mil.)	2.0%	1,182.1	1,166.0	1,146.9	1,183.2	1,278.4
Net income ($ mil.)	-	-	64.8	75.3	74.0	115.3
Market value ($ mil.)	-	-	-	-	-	-
Employees	-	-	6,667	6,758	6,778	6,298

OTIS WORLDWIDE CORP
NYS: OTIS

One Carrier Place
Farmington, CT 06032
Phone: 860 674-3000
Fax: –
Web: www.otis.com

CEO: Judith F Marks
CFO: Anurag Maheshwari
HR: –
FYE: December 31
Type: Public

Otis Worldwide is the world's leading elevator and escalator manufacturing, installation, and service company. The company serves customers in more than 200 countries and territories worldwide. Otis has global scale and local focus, with over 1,400 branches and offices, and a direct physical presence in approximately 80 countries. Its New Equipment segment develops a range of elevator and escalator solutions. Through its Service segment, the company performs maintenance and repair services, as well as modernization services to upgrade elevators and escalators. The company currently owns approximately 4,200 globally issued patents, and it has approximately 2,300 patent applications pending globally. Most of its revenue originates outside the US.

	Annual Growth	12/19	12/20	12/21	12/22	12/23
Sales ($mil.)	2.0%	13,118	12,756	14,298	13,685	14,209
Net income ($ mil.)	5.9%	1,116.0	906.0	1,246.0	1,253.0	1,406.0
Market value ($ mil.)	–	–	–	27,466	35,403	31,841	36,379
Employees	0.7%	69,000	69,000	70,000	69,000	71,000

OTT HYDROMET CORP

22400 DAVIS DR STE 100
STERLING, VA 201647128
Phone: 703 406-2800
Fax: –
Web: www.otthydromet.com

CEO: –
CFO: Glen E Goold
HR: –
FYE: December 31
Type: Private

Through its Hydromet unit and other segments, Sutron makes equipment that collects and transmits water and weather data. The company also provides related hydrological services. Customers use Sutron products to manage water resources, obtain early warning of potentially disastrous floods or storms, and help hydropower plants operate as efficiently as possible. The company's largest customer is the US government. Other customers include state and local governments, engineering companies, and power companies. In 2012 it acquired meterological firm IPS Meteostar for $4.2 million. Sutron sells its products globally; customers outside the US account for about 40% of sales. CEO Raul McQuivey owns 19% of the company.

OTTER PRODUCTS, LLC

209 S MELDRUM ST
FORT COLLINS, CO 805212603
Phone: 855 688-7269
Fax: –
Web: www.otterbox.com

CEO: JC Richardson
CFO: Gerald Chen
HR: –
FYE: December 31
Type: Private

Otter Products, doing business as OtterBox, is a global innovator of premium protective cases for cell phones, smart phones, tablet computers, and other portable electronics from Apple, LG Corp, Google, Samsung, and other manufacturers. It is focused on breaking ground and leading the way to help people do more and go more places with technology in hand. Brands include OtterBox, LifeProof, OtterCares and Liviri. OtterBox was formed in 1998.

	Annual Growth	12/06	12/07	12/08	12/09	12/10
Sales ($mil.)	309.6%	–	–	10.1	48.6	168.9
Net income ($ mil.)	837.9%	–	–	0.7	15.4	60.4
Market value ($ mil.)	–	–	–	–	–	–
Employees	–	–	–	–	–	1,170

OTTER TAIL CORP.
NMS: OTTR

215 South Cascade Street, P.O. Box 496
Fergus Falls, MN 56538-0496
Phone: 866 410-8780
Fax: –
Web: www.ottertail.com

CEO: Charles S Macfarlane
CFO: Kevin G Moug
HR: Paul Knutson
FYE: December 31
Type: Public

Otter Tail covers a wide portfolio of businesses, from electric services and construction to manufacturing equipment and plastic pipe businesses. The electric utility (Otter Tail Power Company (OTP)) is the company's core business; it keeps the lights on for more than 133,000 customers in more than 400 communities across a predominantly rural and agricultural service territory in Minnesota and the Dakotas. The company also makes PVC pipes (Northern Pipe Products and Vinyltech Corporation), primarily sold in the western half of the US and Canada, and manufactures parts and trays (BTD Manufacturing and T.O. Plastics), primarily sold in the US.

	Annual Growth	12/19	12/20	12/21	12/22	12/23
Sales ($mil.)	10.1%	919.5	890.1	1,196.8	1,460.2	1,349.2
Net income ($ mil.)	35.7%	86.8	95.9	176.8	284.2	294.2
Market value ($ mil.)	13.5%	2,139.3	1,777.3	2,979.0	2,448.8	3,544.1
Employees	4.7%	2,208	2,074	2,487	2,422	2,655

OTTUMWA REGIONAL LEGACY FOUNDATION, INC.

111 E MAIN ST
OTTUMWA, IA 525012915
Phone: 641 455-5260
Fax: –
Web: www.ottumwalegacy.org

CEO: –
CFO: –
HR: –
FYE: December 31
Type: Private

Ottumwa Regional Legacy Foundation is creating a legacy by investing in the wellbeing of Ottumwa, Iowa, residents. The not-for-profit charitable foundation was formed in 2010 with proceeds from the city's sale of the Ottumwa Regional Health Center to the for-profit hospital operator RegionalCare Hospital Partners. The Ottumwa Regional Legacy Foundation plans to use its $60 million endowment to fund community health care and educational programs, as well as other potential development projects. Its philanthropic grants are awarded through a regional application process.

	Annual Growth	12/13	12/14	12/15	12/16	12/22
Sales ($mil.)	(3.8%)	–	2.4	5.9	1.9	1.8
Net income ($ mil.)	–	–	(1.2)	1.8	(4.1)	(2.2)
Market value ($ mil.)	–	–	–	–	–	–
Employees	–	–	–	–	–	850

OUR LADY OF LOURDES HEALTH CARE SERVICES, INC.

1600 HADDON AVE
CAMDEN, NJ 081033101
Phone: 856 757-3500
Fax: –
Web: –

CEO: Alexander J Hatala
CFO: Michael Hammond
HR: –
FYE: June 30
Type: Private

Lourdes Health System is a health care provider to residents of southern New Jersey, with regional hospitals in Camden (Our Lady of Lourdes Medical Center) and Willingboro (Lourdes Medical Center of Burlington County). With more than 650 beds combined, the two medical centers specialize in acute care, cancer, cardiology, diabetes, organ transplantation, and maternity services. The health system also encompasses the Lourdes Wellness Center in Collingswood, which focuses on integrative and holistic medicine. Lourdes Health System is sponsored by the Franciscan Sisters of Alleghany, NY and is a member of Catholic Health East.

	Annual Growth	06/12	06/13	06/14	06/15	06/16
Sales ($mil.)	6.4%	–	–	31.6	35.1	35.7
Net income ($ mil.)	–	–	–	–	–	–
Market value ($ mil.)	–	–	–	–	–	–
Employees	–	–	–	–	–	3,500

OUR LADY OF LOURDES REGIONAL MEDICAL CENTER, INC.

4801 AMBASSADOR CAFFERY PKWY
LAFAYETTE, LA 705086917
Phone: 337 470-2000
Fax: –
Web: www.fmolhs.org

CEO: –
CFO: –
HR: Ashley Callaway
FYE: June 30
Type: Private

Established in 1949 as part of the not-for-profit Franciscan Missionaries of Our Lady Health System, Our Lady of Lourdes Regional Medical Center is a hospital that provides medical care in southern Louisiana. The facility cares for denizens of the bayou with a medical staff of more than 400 physicians representing some 50 specialties including cardiology, neurology, and oncology. The medical center also offers oupatient care and urgent care as well as a general family practice and pediatric care. Our Lady of Lourdes extends its reach outside the facility into the Acadiana regional community by offering primary care physicians' offices, home health care programs, and occupational medicine.

	Annual Growth	06/17	06/18	06/19	06/20	06/21
Sales ($mil.)	19.9%	–	294.8	377.8	450.8	507.9
Net income ($ mil.)	226.9%	–	2.8	12.8	(22.2)	99.3
Market value ($ mil.)	–	–	–	–	–	–
Employees	–	–	–	–	–	1,700

OUR LADY OF THE LAKE HOSPITAL, INC.

5000 HENNESSY BLVD
BATON ROUGE, LA 708084367
Phone: 225 765-6565
Fax: –
Web: www.fmolhs.org

CEO: K S Wester
CFO: Jennifer Clowers
HR: Lori Myles
FYE: June 30
Type: Private

Our Lady of the Lake Regional Medical Center reaches out to Baton Rouge residents with a helping hand. Participating in teaching programs for LSU and Tulane medical schools, the medical center has some 800 inpatient beds and includes trauma emergency, surgery, general medical, and specialty care centers for conditions including heart disease, cancer, orthopedics, and ENT (ear, nose, and throat) disorders. Our Lady of the Lake also includes a Children's Hospital, two nursing homes, and an independent-living facility, and it offers outpatient services at its main campus and at satellite facilities throughout the greater Baton Rouge area.

	Annual Growth	06/17	06/18	06/19	06/21	06/22
Sales ($mil.)	8.9%	–	1,254.6	1,467.4	1,745.4	1,763.4
Net income ($ mil.)	5.7%	–	103.3	33.9	301.2	128.9
Market value ($ mil.)	–	–	–	–	–	–
Employees	–	–	–	–	–	1,800

OUR LADY OF THE LAKE UNIVERSITY OF SAN ANTONIO

411 SW 24TH ST
SAN ANTONIO, TX 782074617
Phone: 210 432-8904
Fax: –
Web: www.ollusa.edu

CEO: –
CFO: –
HR: Patricia Gomez
FYE: May 31
Type: Private

Our Lady of the Lake University was founded in 1895 by the Sisters of the Congregation of Divine Providence, not that lady of the lake. The Catholic college offers undergraduate and graduate education courses at its main campus in San Antonio, Texas, as well as satellite locations in Houston and the Rio Grande Valley. It offers night and weekend classes, as well as online programs. Altogether, its 2,700 students may choose from a variety of liberal arts and science subject areas, including business, information technology, education, social work, and psychology.

	Annual Growth	05/15	05/16	05/17	05/18	05/19
Sales ($mil.)	6.5%	–	73.6	74.9	77.9	88.9
Net income ($ mil.)	57.1%	–	1.8	3.0	1.0	6.8
Market value ($ mil.)	–	–	–	–	–	–
Employees	–	–	–	–	–	504

OUTCOME SCIENCES, INC.

25 THOMSON PL
BOSTON, MA 022101215
Phone: 617 621-1600
Fax: –
Web: –

CEO: Richard Gliklich
CFO: –
HR: –
FYE: December 31
Type: Private

Even after drug developers send their offspring out into the world, they still can't cut the apron-strings altogether. A provider of post-approval data management software, Outcome Sciences keeps the strings intact for pharmaceutical companies once their drugs have received regulatory approval and gone on to market or Phase IV testing. Outcome provides software that follows the drugs into the medical market where they are prescribed. Its Outcome-branded applications enable Web-based data collection about patients reactions to the drugs, as well as online surveys of medical practitioners and study participants. Biopharmaceutical services company Quintiles bought the company in 2011.

	Annual Growth	12/02	12/03	12/04	12/06	12/07
Sales ($mil.)	34.3%	–	–	6.3	–	15.2
Net income ($ mil.)	–	–	–	–	–	1.0
Market value ($ mil.)	–	–	–	–	–	–
Employees	–	–	–	–	–	141

OUTDOOR ADVERTISING ASSOCIATION OF AMERICA, INC.

1850 M ST NW STE 1040
WASHINGTON, DC 200365821
Phone: 202 833-5566
Fax: –
Web: www.oaaa.org

CEO: Anna Bager
CFO: –
HR: –
FYE: December 31
Type: Private

Love them or hate them, the vast number of billboards across the US display the power of the Outdoor Advertising Association of America (OAAA), which works to promote the interests of the outdoor advertising industry. The OAAA focuses its efforts on government relations, marketing communications, membership, and operations. It hosts an annual national convention, as well as conferences dedicated to legal, legislative, and operations issues of interest to members. The association also provides free advertising space for charitable causes and non-profit groups. Founded in 1891, the trade association has about 1,000 member companies.

	Annual Growth	12/98	12/99	12/00*	01/09*	12/14
Sales ($mil.)	–	–	4.7	–	0.2	4.7
Net income ($ mil.)	8.6%	–	0.0	–	0.1	0.2
Market value ($ mil.)	–	–	–	–	–	–
Employees	–	–	–	–	–	14

*Fiscal year change

OUTFRONT MEDIA INC

405 Lexington Avenue, 17th Floor
New York, NY 10174
Phone: 212 297-6400
Fax: –
Web: www.outfrontmedia.com

NYS: OUT
CEO: Jeremy J Male
CFO: Donald R Shassian
HR: Malissa Shiflett
FYE: December 31
Type: Public

This company's business is getting the attention of people on the street. OUTFRONT Media (formerly CBS Outdoor Americas) is one of the world's leading operators of billboards, digital display networks, and other outdoor or "out-of-home advertising" displays. The company maintains about thousands of outdoor media displays throughout North America and South America. In addition to its traditional billboards, OUTFRONT sells advertising space in bus and rail transit systems and in stadiums and malls. OUTFRONT Media's properties include high-visibility locations such as the Bay Bridge in San Francisco, Sunset Boulevard in Los Angeles, and Grand Central Station and Times Square in New York City.

	Annual Growth	12/19	12/20	12/21	12/22	12/23
Sales ($mil.)	0.5%	1,782.2	1,236.3	1,463.9	1,772.1	1,820.6
Net income ($ mil.)	–	140.1	(61.0)	35.6	147.9	(430.4)
Market value ($ mil.)	(15.1%)	4,426.7	3,228.4	4,426.7	2,736.6	2,304.1
Employees	(0.7%)	2,456	2,081	2,195	2,375	2,388

OUTWARD BOUND INC.

1133 ROUTE 55 STE C
LAGRANGEVILLE, NY 125405052
Phone: 720 257-7068
Fax: –
Web: www.outwardbound.com

CEO: Lee Skold
CFO: –
HR: –
FYE: December 31
Type: Private

Outward Bound USA provides adventure and opportunities for personal growth to 60,000 people each year through its four wilderness schools, two urban centers, and school reform program. Programs are designed to challenge, develop self-reliance and leadership skills, and instill integrity in participants. Students participate in outdoor activities such as backpacking, dog sledding, rock climbing, and snowboarding. They learn about natural history, orienteering, cultures, and topography. Courses last from a few days to more than a month, and some colleges and high schools offer academic credit to participants. Outward Bound offers special programs for troubled teens.

	Annual Growth	12/17	12/18	12/19	12/21	12/22
Sales ($mil.)	8.6%	–	5.6	4.8	5.9	7.7
Net income ($ mil.)	–	–	(0.3)	(0.2)	2.0	2.6
Market value ($ mil.)	–	–	–	–	–	–
Employees	–	–	–	–	–	13

OVERLAKE HOSPITAL MEDICAL CENTER

1035 116TH AVE NE
BELLEVUE, WA 980044604
Phone: 425 688-5000
Fax: –
Web: www.overlakehospital.org

CEO: –
CFO: –
HR: Lisa Brock
FYE: June 30
Type: Private

Over the lake and through the sound to Overlake Hospital Medical Center we go! The not-for-profit hospital provides health care services to residents of Bellevue, Washington, in the Puget Sound region. The nearly 350-bed facility provides comprehensive inpatient and outpatient services ranging from cancer care and surgery to specialized senior care. Overlake also operates a number of outpatient clinics providing primary care, urgent care, and specialty care such as weight loss surgery. The organization also provides patients with health and wellness programs, addressing issues like women's and children's health.

	Annual Growth	06/18	06/19	06/20	06/21	06/22
Sales ($mil.)	7.2%	–	570.0	574.7	601.6	702.8
Net income ($ mil.)	–	–	45.7	(3.7)	86.8	(11.2)
Market value ($ mil.)	–	–	–	–	–	–
Employees	–	–	–	–	–	2,450

OVERLAND CONTRACTING INC.

3807 CENTURION DR
GARNER, NC 275298582
Phone: 800 790-2149
Fax: –
Web: www.bv.com

CEO: –
CFO: Jeffrey J Stamm
HR: –
FYE: December 31
Type: Private

With the extent of work the company does, Overland Contracting could be called Overall Contracting. The company, a wholly-owned subsidiary of Black & Veatch, offers engineering, procurement, and construction services on electric utility substations, power plants, water and wastewater facilities, telecommunications sites, and gas, oil, and chemical facilities throughout the US. From testing to laying the foundation, the company is involved in nearly every part of the building process. Headquartered in Georgia, the company also has regional offices in Alabama, Florida, Kansas, Michigan, and North Carolina. Customers have included Florida Power & Light Company and T-Mobile.

	Annual Growth	12/05	12/06	12/07	12/08	12/09
Sales ($mil.)	6.1%	–	318.3	486.1	324.0	380.6
Net income ($ mil.)	–	–	22.8	35.4	11.0	(51.5)
Market value ($ mil.)	–	–	–	–	–	–
Employees	–	–	–	–	–	1,192

OVERSEAS SHIPHOLDING GROUP INC (NEW)

NYS: OSG

302 Knights Run Avenue
Tampa, FL 33602
Phone: 813 209-0600
Fax: –
Web: www.osg.com

CEO: Samuel H Norton
CFO: Richard Trueblood
HR: Deanna Marshall
FYE: December 31
Type: Public

Overseas Shipholding Group (OSG) flies the flags of many nations. The marine transportation company's fleet, made up mainly of crude oil tankers and product carriers, includes vessels registered in the US and in a number of other countries. Through both long-term and spot market contracts, the company charters its fleet to commercial shippers and government agencies. Overall, the OSG fleet consists of about 110 vessels with a capacity of about 11 million deadweight tons (DWT). Transportation of crude oil and refined petroleum products accounts for the bulk of the company's business, but OSG also transports liquefied natural gas (LNG). In late 2012 OSG filed for Chapter 11 bankruptcy. It emerged in 2014.

	Annual Growth	12/19	12/20	12/21	12/22	12/23
Sales ($mil.)	6.2%	355.5	418.7	359.1	466.8	451.9
Net income ($ mil.)	63.8%	8.7	30.0	(46.3)	26.6	62.5
Market value ($ mil.)	23.0%	163.2	151.8	133.4	205.0	373.9
Employees	10.9%	713	931	953	1,023	1,078

OVINTIV EXPLORATION INC.

4 WATERWAY SQUARE PL STE 100
THE WOODLANDS, TX 773802664
Phone: 281 210-5100
Fax: –
Web: www.newfield.com

CEO: Lee K Boothby
CFO: Sherri A Brillon
HR: –
FYE: December 31
Type: Private

Newfield Exploration likes to depend on good old resource plays. The Texas-based energy company explores for crude oil, natural gas, and natural gas liquids, mostly onshore in the US, with some activity offshore China. Its prime asset is the Anadarko and Arkoma plays in Oklahoma, further supported by the Williston in North Dakota and Uinta in Utah. Its estimated proved reserves currently stand at 700 MBoe, with 120 net development wells. In November 2018, the company was bought out by Canada's Encana for US$5.5 billion, in a flurry of mergers in the sector.

OVINTIV INC

NYS: OVV

Suite 1700, 370 17th Street
Denver, CO 80202
Phone: 303 623-2300
Fax: 303 623-2400
Web: www.ovintiv.com

CEO: –
CFO: –
HR: –
FYE: December 31
Type: Public

Canada's Encana Corporation finds, develops, and produces oil, NGL, and natural gas from its North American assets. The company deploys horizontal drilling and other advanced completion methods to maximize yields from its resources plays, i.e. accumulation of hydrocarbons from an expanse of land or thick vertical section. It holds acreages in the Montney in Canada, and the Eagle Ford and the Permian basins in the US, among others. Encana's proven reserves include 375 MMbbls of oil and some 2,500 Bcf of natural gas. Royal Dutch Shell is one of its biggest customers.

	Annual Growth	12/19	12/20	12/21	12/22	12/23
Sales ($mil.)	12.8%	6,726.0	6,087.0	8,658.0	12,464	10,883
Net income ($ mil.)	72.8%	234.0	(6,097.0)	1,416.0	3,637.0	2,085.0
Market value ($ mil.)	74.9%	1,274.3	3,901.6	9,156.3	13,778	11,933
Employees	(9.3%)	2,571	1,916	1,713	1,744	1,743

OVINTIV USA INC.

370 17TH ST STE 1700
DENVER, CO 802025632
Phone: 303 623-2300
Fax: –
Web: www.ovintiv.com

CEO: –
CFO: –
HR: –
FYE: December 31
Type: Private

Encana Oil & Gas (USA) is a south of the border chip off the block of a Canadian energy giant. The exploration and production subsidiary of natural gas giant Encana Corporation explores for and produces hydrocarbons primarily in four key natural gas resource plays (almost 90% of its total US natural gas production) located at Jonah and Piceance in the US Rockies (Wyoming and northwest Colorado) and the Fort Worth and East Texas/Haynesville basins. It also owns stakes in natural gas gathering and processing assets, mainly in Colorado, Texas, Utah, and Wyoming. In 2015 Encana Oil & Gas (USA) had interests in 1.4 million net acres of land, of which 0.9 million net acres were undeveloped.

OWENS & MINOR, INC.   NYS: OMI

9120 Lockwood Boulevard
Mechanicsville, VA 23116
Phone: 804 723-7000
Fax: 804 723-7100
Web: www.owens-minor.com

CEO: Edward A Pesicka
CFO: Alexandar Bruni
HR: –
FYE: December 31
Type: Public

Owens & Minor is a prominent global healthcare solutions company that offers a comprehensive range of products and services to healthcare providers, manufacturers, and patients worldwide. The company's extensive portfolio includes medical products such as surgical drapes and gowns, facial protection, sterilization wrap, protective apparel, and medical exam gloves, as well as custom and minor procedure kits. With facilities in Asia, Australia, Europe, Latin America, and the US, Owens & Minor serves customers in nearly 70 countries, and has some 95% revenue share in the US. In 2022, Owens & Minor made a significant acquisition of Apria for $1.6 billion, further reinforcing its position in the healthcare industry.

	Annual Growth	12/19	12/20	12/21	12/22	12/23
Sales ($mil.)	2.9%	9,210.9	8,480.2	9,785.3	9,955.5	10,334
Net income ($ mil.)	–	(62.4)	29.9	221.6	22.4	(41.3)
Market value ($ mil.)	38.9%	395.7	2,070.6	3,329.8	1,494.9	1,475.0
Employees	(2.9%)	15,400	18,800	17,300	22,500	13,700

OWENS CORNING   NYS: OC

One Owens Corning Parkway
Toledo, OH 43659
Phone: 419 248-8000
Fax: –
Web: www.owenscorning.com

CEO: Brian D Chambers
CFO: Todd W Fister
HR: –
FYE: December 31
Type: Public

Famous for its Pink Panther mascot and its trademarked PINK glass fiber insulation, Owens Corning is one of the top global makers of building and construction materials. The company makes insulation, roofing, fiber-based glass reinforcements, and other materials for the residential, industrial, and commercial markets. Its composite products business makes glass fiber reinforcement materials that can be used in more than 40,000 products for the building and construction, renewable energy, and infrastructure. Its products sold under well-recognized brand names and trademarks such as Owens Corning PINK FIBERGLAS Insulation, FOAMULAR, FOAMGLAS, and Paroc. Owens Corning has operations worldwide, but generates majority of revenue from the US.

	Annual Growth	12/19	12/20	12/21	12/22	12/23
Sales ($mil.)	7.8%	7,160.0	7,055.0	8,498.0	9,761.0	9,677.0
Net income ($ mil.)	31.1%	405.0	(383.0)	995.0	1,241.0	1,196.0
Market value ($ mil.)	22.8%	5,678.5	6,606.3	7,891.6	7,438.2	12,926
Employees	(1.3%)	19,000	19,000	20,000	19,000	18,000

OWENSBORO MUNICIPAL UTILITIES ELECTRIC LIGHT & POWER SYSTEM

2070 TAMARACK RD
OWENSBORO, KY 423016876
Phone: 270 926-3200
Fax: –
Web: www.omu.org

CEO: –
CFO: –
HR: Nicole Murphy
FYE: May 31
Type: Private

Owensboro, Kentucky (named after Abraham Owen, a Shelby County legislator killed in the Battle of Tippecanoe) is served by Owensboro Municipal Utilities, which provides power to almost 26,000 customers and water to 24,500. The city-owned utility operates water treatment facilities and a power plant that uses coal and used tires for fuel. Its operating divisions are Elmer Smith power plant, Engineering & Operations, Water Production, and Customer Service Center. It also offers telecommunications services. Owensboro Municipal Utilities is overseen by the five-member Owensboro Utility Commission, which is appointed by the mayor of Owensboro.

	Annual Growth	05/18	05/19	05/20	05/21	05/22
Sales ($mil.)	(16.3%)	–	155.2	122.6	90.1	91.0
Net income ($ mil.)	(42.1%)	–	7.8	4.7	2.4	1.5
Market value ($ mil.)	–	–	–	–	–	–
Employees	–	–	–	–	–	235

OXBOW CORPORATION

1601 FORUM PL STE 1400
WEST PALM BEACH, FL 334018104
Phone: 561 907-5400
Fax: –
Web: www.oxbow.com

CEO: William I Koch
CFO: William D Parmelee
HR: Kathy Flaherty
FYE: December 31
Type: Private

Oxbow is a worldwide supplier of numerous industrial materials, each critical to the production of a variety of products. The diversified firm's Oxbow Carbon is one of the world's largest recyclers of refinery and natural gas byproducts. The company upgrades, handles, transports, and sells petroleum coke into markets where it can be used to produce aluminum, steel, electric power, cement and other critical products for the world economy. It delivers value to its suppliers and customers through a global network of marketing offices and supply chain assets. The company also trades in products that include gypsum, calcined petroleum coke, and metallurgical coke. Oxbow is controlled by William Koch.

OXFORD INDUSTRIES, INC.   NYS: OXM

999 Peachtree Street, N.E., Suite 688
Atlanta, GA 30309
Phone: 404 659-2424
Fax: –
Web: –

CEO: Thomas C Chubb III
CFO: K S Grassmyer
HR: –
FYE: January 28
Type: Public

Oxford is a leading branded apparel company that designs, sources, markets, and distributes products bearing the trademarks of its Johnny Was, Tommy Bahama, Lilly Pulitzer, Southern Tide, TBBC, and Duck Head lifestyle brands. Its Tommy Bahama unit makes branded men's and women's sportswear and related products and owns more than 155 stores and restaurants in the US. Oxford's customers include national and regional specialty stores, multi-brand e-commerce retailers, and department stores. Purchases its products from approximately 250 suppliers, with a significant concentration of suppliers in Asia, its apparel products generally incorporate fabrics made of cotton, silk, linen, nylon, leather, tencel and other natural and man-made fibers, or blends of two or more of these materials. Virtually all of Oxford's sales comes from the US.

	Annual Growth	02/19	02/20*	01/21	01/22	01/23
Sales ($mil.)	6.3%	1,107.5	1,122.8	748.8	1,142.1	1,411.5
Net income ($ mil.)	25.7%	66.3	68.5	(95.7)	131.3	165.7
Market value ($ mil.)	11.0%	1,218.5	1,094.7	1,029.1	1,276.9	1,849.2
Employees	(0.4%)	6,100	6,100	3,900	4,700	6,000

*Fiscal year change

OZARKS ELECTRIC COOPERATIVE CORPORATION

3641 W WEDINGTON DR
FAYETTEVILLE, AR 727045742
Phone: 479 521-2900
Fax: –
Web: www.ozarksecc.com

CEO: Mitchell Johnson
CFO: –
HR: –
FYE: December 31
Type: Private

Even people living up in the Ozark Mountains need power and Ozarks Electric Cooperative aims to deliver. The member-owned not-for-profit cooperative serves more than 62,000 customers in about a dozen counties spread across northwest Arkansas and northeast Oklahoma. Its 350 miles of line reach industrial, commercial, residential, and agricultural power users. Ozarks Electric provides its customers with energy audits and information on saving energy as well as energy efficient water heaters and surge protectors. It is a member of Touchstone Energy, a national alliance of electric cooperatives in nearly 40 states. The coop was formed in 1938.

	Annual Growth	12/14	12/15	12/16	12/17	12/18
Sales ($mil.)	7.1%	–	123.2	129.7	137.0	151.4
Net income ($ mil.)	9.1%	–	6.3	6.0	7.0	8.2
Market value ($ mil.)	–	–	–	–	–	–
Employees	–	–	–	–	–	190

P AND E, INC.

20643 STEPHENS ST
SAINT CLAIR SHORES, MI 480801047
Phone: 586 771-9880
Fax: –
Web: www.alexanderhornung.com

CEO: –
CFO: –
HR: –
FYE: December 31
Type: Private

You might say this company is trying to be the best of the wurst. Alexander & Hornung is a popular sausage maker that has been serving the Detroit area since 1945. The company makes a variety of bratwursts, knockwursts, and hot dogs, as well as Polish sausages, bologna, and salami. It also offers bacon, ham, and deli meats. In addition it owns Brookside Foods (deli meats), Bosell Foods (deli salads), and Gateway Specialty Foods (meat brokerage). Alexander & Hornung distributes its food products to retail grocers and deli stores throughout the US; it also operates a retail meat store in Detroit. The family-owned business was started by butchers Erich and Willie Alexander and sausage maker Otto Hornung.

	Annual Growth	12/14	12/15	12/16	12/17	12/18
Sales ($mil.)	4.3%	–	34.5	31.9	38.5	39.2
Net income ($ mil.)	(13.0%)	–	3.2	1.8	2.0	2.1
Market value ($ mil.)	–	–	–	–	–	–
Employees	–	–	–	–	–	100

P.A.M. TRANSPORTATION SERVICES, INC.

NMS: PTSI

297 West Henri De Tonti
Tontitown, AR 72770
Phone: 479 361-9111
Fax: –
Web: www.pamtransport.com

CEO: Joseph A Vitiritto
CFO: Allen W West
HR: –
FYE: December 31
Type: Public

Founded in 1980, P.A.M. Transportation Services (P.A.M.) provides nationwide dry-van truckload, expedited truckload, intermodal, and logistics services with a fleet of 2,000 tractors, 6,000 trailers, and 2,400 drivers. The company transports general commodities throughout the continental US, as well as in certain Canadian provinces. It also provides transportation services in Mexico under agreements with Mexican carriers.?The company's freight consists primarily of automotive parts, expedited goods, consumer goods, such as general retail store merchandise, and manufactured goods, such as heating and air conditioning units.

	Annual Growth	12/19	12/20	12/21	12/22	12/23
Sales ($mil.)	12.1%	514.2	486.8	707.1	946.9	810.8
Net income ($ mil.)	23.6%	7.9	17.8	76.5	90.7	18.4
Market value ($ mil.)	(22.5%)	1,270.9	1,079.4	1,563.7	570.4	457.6
Employees	(1.5%)	2,666	2,653	2,510	3,395	2,512

P.J. DICK INCORPORATED

225 N SHORE DR
PITTSBURGH, PA 152125861
Phone: 412 462-9300
Fax: –
Web: www.pjdick.com

CEO: –
CFO: –
HR: –
FYE: December 31
Type: Private

P.J. Dick Incorporated, along with its sister companies, can develop it, build it, and pave it. P.J. Dick is the contracting arm in a family of companies that also includes Trumbull Corporation and Lindy Paving. P.J. Dick builds mostly commercial, industrial, and federal projects such as labs, parking structures, military buildings, and sports facilities. Trumbull Corporation specializes in heavy and highway construction, building roads, dams, bridges, tunnels, and transportation infrastructure. Lindy Paving offers asphalt paving contracting and manufactures asphalt mix at plants in Pennsylvania. Tracing its roots to 1955, P.J. Dick is owned by the families of CEO Clifford Rowe and the late Robert Hecht.

	Annual Growth	12/16	12/17	12/18	12/19	12/20
Sales ($mil.)	23.5%	–	269.6	–	493.5	507.7
Net income ($ mil.)	101.7%	–	1.0	–	7.6	8.3
Market value ($ mil.)	–	–	–	–	–	–
Employees	–	–	–	–	–	400

PAC NORTHWEST ELECTRIC POWER & CONSERVATION PLANNING COUNCIL

851 SW 6TH AVE STE 1100
PORTLAND, OR 972041348
Phone: 503 222-5161
Fax: –
Web: www.nwcouncil.org

CEO: –
CFO: –
HR: –
FYE: September 30
Type: Private

The Northwest Power and Conservation Council focuses on developing a 20-year regional power plan and fish and wildlife program for the Northwest, including Idaho, Montana, Oregon and Washington. It helps protect fish and wildlife in the Columbia River Basin affected by hydropower dams. The Council also makes it a priority to conserve energy and use renewable sources for power such as wind and solar resources. The Northwest Power and Conservation Council, formed under the Northwest Power Act of 1980, has an annual budget appropriation of about $9 million.

	Annual Growth	09/04	09/05	09/06	09/07	09/12
Sales ($mil.)	2.8%	–	10.1	–	9.9	12.2
Net income ($ mil.)	–	–	(0.0)	–	0.2	0.1
Market value ($ mil.)	–	–	–	–	–	–
Employees	–	–	–	–	–	62

PACCAR INC.

NMS: PCAR

777 - 106th Ave. N.E.
Bellevue, WA 98004
Phone: 425 468-7400
Fax: –
Web: www.paccar.com

CEO: R P Feight
CFO: Harrie C Schippers
HR: Jenny Hall
FYE: December 31
Type: Public

Incorporated under the laws of Delaware in 1971, PACCAR one of the world's leading designers and manufacturers of big rig diesel trucks. Its lineup of light-, medium-, and heavy-duty trucks includes the Kenworth, Peterbilt, and DAF nameplates. The company also manufactures and distributes aftermarket truck parts for these brands. PACCAR's other products include Braden, Carco, and Gearmatic industrial winches. PACCAR typically sells its trucks and parts through independent dealers. Its PACCAR Financial Services arm offers vehicle financing and its PacLease subsidiary handles truck leasing. More than 50% of its sales comes from US operations.

	Annual Growth	12/19	12/20	12/21	12/22	12/23
Sales ($mil.)	8.2%	25,600	18,729	23,522	28,820	35,127
Net income ($ mil.)	17.8%	2,387.9	1,298.4	1,852.1	3,011.6	4,600.8
Market value ($ mil.)	5.4%	41,393	45,150	46,186	51,791	51,100
Employees	4.7%	27,000	26,000	28,500	31,100	32,400

PACE UNIVERSITY

1 PACE PLZ
NEW YORK, NY 100381598
Phone: 212 346-1956
Fax: –
Web: www.pace.edu

CEO: Rob Sands
CFO: Robert C Almon
HR: –
FYE: June 30
Type: Private

Students can learn at their own pace at Pace University, which offers certificate programs as well as undergraduate, graduate, and doctoral degrees through half a dozen schools: arts and sciences, business, computer science and information systems, education, law, and nursing. Altogether, the school is home to 100 undergraduate majors offering roughly 30 undergraduate and graduate degrees, 50 master's programs, and four doctoral programs. Nearly 13,000 students attend the university's three New York campuses (Lower Manhattan, Pleasantville-Briarcliff, and White Plains). Pace was founded in 1906 by the brothers Homer and Charles Pace as a co-educational business school called Pace Institute.

	Annual Growth	06/13	06/14	06/16	06/20	06/22
Sales ($mil.)	3.1%	–	493.0	393.7	597.7	627.8
Net income ($ mil.)	5.8%	–	26.6	14.7	14.8	41.7
Market value ($ mil.)	–	–	–	–	–	–
Employees	–	–	–	–	–	1,862

PACERS BASKETBALL, LLC

125 S PENNSYLVANIA ST
INDIANAPOLIS, IN 462043610
Phone: 317 917-2500
Fax: –
Web: www.gainbridgefieldhouse.com

CEO: –
CFO: –
HR: –
FYE: June 30
Type: Private

This team sets the tempo on the basketball court. Pacers Basketball, which does business as Pacers Sports & Entertainment, owns and operates the Indiana Pacers professional basketball franchise of the National Basketball Association along with Indianapolis' Conseco Fieldhouse, the team's home arena. The franchise was formed in 1967 as a charter member of the American Basketball Association by a group of investors that included Richard Tinkman (who also helped found the ABA) and joined the NBA in 1976. Indiana has made just one appearance in the NBA Finals. The sports franchise is owned by shopping-center magnate Herbert Simon, who purchased the Pacers with his brother Melvin in 1983. Melvin Simon died in 2009.

PACIFIC ALLIANCE MEDICAL CENTER, INC.

2525 S DOWNING ST
DENVER, CO 802105817
Phone: 303 778-1955
Fax: –
Web: www.porterhospital.org

CEO: –
CFO: –
HR: –
FYE: June 30
Type: Private

Patients at Porter Adventist Hospital might catch a view of the Rocky Mountains. Part of Centura Health, the 370-bed hospital is a general, acute-care facility that provides a full range of primary care and specialized services in the Denver area. Specialty treatment fields include cardiology, orthopedics, emergency medicine, and cancer treatment. The hospital features a large intensive care unit (ICU), robotic surgery suites, an organ transplant center, and a community education center. Porter Adventist was founded in 1930 by Henry Porter, a businessman from California.

PACIFIC BIOSCIENCES OF CALIFORNIA INC

NMS: PACB

1305 O'Brien Drive
Menlo Park, CA 94025
Phone: 650 521-8000
Fax: –
Web: www.pacb.com

CEO: Christian O Henry
CFO: Susan Kim
HR: Natalie Welch
FYE: December 31
Type: Public

Pacific Biosciences of California (PacBio) is a premier life science technology company that is designing, developing and manufacturing advanced sequencing solutions to help scientists and clinical researchers resolve genetically complex problems. Its products and technology under development stem from two highly differentiated core technologies focused on accuracy, quality and completeness which include its existing HiFi long read sequencing technology and our emerging short read Sequencing by Binding (SBB) technology.. The biotechnology company develops proprietary technology known as SMRT (single molecule, real-time) that performs fast and inexpensive DNA sequencing. The technology performs highly accurate reads of ultra-long sequences with the ability to simultaneously detect epigenetic changes. Some 50% of PacBio's revenue comes from North America.

	Annual Growth	12/19	12/20	12/21	12/22	12/23
Sales ($mil.)	21.9%	90.9	78.9	130.5	128.3	200.5
Net income ($ mil.)	–	(84.1)	29.4	(181.2)	(314.2)	(306.7)
Market value ($ mil.)	17.5%	1,376.2	6,945.3	5,478.0	2,190.1	2,626.6
Employees	18.5%	404	412	728	769	796

PACIFIC BUILDING GROUP

9752 ASPEN CREEK CT STE 100
SAN DIEGO, CA 921261082
Phone: 858 552-0600
Fax: –
Web: www.pacificbuildinggroup.com

CEO: Gregory A Rogers
CFO: Lisa Hitt
HR: Kelly Aziz
FYE: December 31
Type: Private

Pacific Building Group pacifies its clients by taking care of their property construction needs. The general contractor provides services including pre-construction evaluation, facility design/build, tenant improvements, and facilities maintenance. It is known for its work on health care facilities, including laboratories and medical office buildings; the company also provides services for corporate, hospitality, and industrial clients. Pacific Building Group has handled major projects for such customers as IBM, Sharp HealthCare, Sony, and United Airlines. The company operates mainly in Southern California, primarily in San Diego County. CEO and owner Greg Rogers founded the group in 1984.

	Annual Growth	12/09	12/10	12/11	12/12	12/13
Sales ($mil.)	13.8%	–	–	51.1	74.9	66.2
Net income ($ mil.)	70.5%	–	–	0.2	1.9	0.6
Market value ($ mil.)	–	–	–	–	–	–
Employees	–	–	–	–	–	190

PACIFIC CMA INC.

NBB: PACC

153-04 Rockaway Blvd.
Jamaica, NY 11434
Phone: 718 949-9700
Fax: 718 949-9740
Web: –

CEO: –
CFO: –
HR: –
FYE: December 31
Type: Public

This company is banking on the fact that you can't spell "freight forwarding company" without AGI and CMA. Operating primarily through its AGI Logistics (HK) Ltd subsidiary, Pacific CMA offers logistics, supply chain management, and freight forwarding services. Serving mainly the Asia/Pacific region, CMA transports freight by air, ground, rail, river, and sea and offers warehousing services for exporting goods from China to other worldwide destinations. Its customers typically reside in the retail, distribution, and manufacturing and trading sectors. Based in Hong Kong, AGI Logistics also imports and exports cargo for several major cities in China.

	Annual Growth	12/02	12/03	12/04	12/05	12/06
Sales ($mil.)	30.6%	52.9	73.1	99.6	125.0	154.0
Net income ($ mil.)	–	1.1	0.0	0.3	(0.4)	(2.5)
Market value ($ mil.)	(10.4%)	12.9	56.3	24.6	18.8	8.3
Employees	31.7%	92	115	193	238	277

PACIFIC COAST OIL TRUST
NBB: ROYT L

The Bank of New York Mellon Trust Company, N.A., Trustee, 601 Travis Street, 16th Floor
Houston, TX 77002
Phone: 512 236-6555
Fax: –
Web: www.pacificcoastoiltrust.com

CEO: –
CFO: –
HR: –
FYE: December 31
Type: Public

Call it what you will, black gold, Texas tea, or the black blood of the earth, MV Oil Trust is wringing out the value from each drop and distributing it to shareholders. MV Oil Trust receives royalty interests from the mature oil and gas properties of MV Partners located in Kansas and Colorado. The properties have proved reserves of 9.5 million barrels of oil from 922 net wells. The trust receives royalties based on the amount of oil (and gas) produced and sold and then distributes virtually all of the proceeds to shareholders on a regular basis. MV Partners, a private company engaged in the exploration, production, gathering, aggregation, and sale of oil and natural gas, has the rights to 80% of net proceeds.

	Annual Growth	12/14	12/15	12/16	12/17	12/18
Sales ($mil.)	(27.6%)	55.0	11.9	0.8	7.5	15.1
Net income ($ mil.)	(30.5%)	54.1	10.0	0.2	4.4	12.6
Market value ($ mil.)	(24.8%)	197.9	50.9	41.3	74.9	63.3
Employees	–	–	–	–	–	–

PACIFIC COAST PRODUCERS

631 N CLUFF AVE
LODI, CA 952400756
Phone: 209 367-8800
Fax: –
Web: www.pacificcoastproducers.com

CEO: Daniel L Vincent
CFO: Matthew Strong
HR: Christine Cesena
FYE: May 31
Type: Private

Fruits, seafood sauces, and organic tomato puree -- rather than movies -- are the creative output of this particular group of Pacific Coast Producers. The cooperative markets the apricots, grapes, peaches, pears, and tomatoes grown by its approximately 160 California-based members. It turns the produce into private-label canned fruit, sauces, and juices and sells them to the retail and foodservice industries. Pacific Coast Producers typically serves retailers the likes of Albertson's, Aldi, Kroger, Safeway, SUPERVALU, Whole Foods, and Wal-Mart, as well as the US Department of Agriculture. The company, founded in 1971, operates three production sites and one distribution center in California.

	Annual Growth	05/17	05/18	05/19	05/20	05/21
Sales ($mil.)	9.0%	–	668.1	806.2	911.1	864.3
Net income ($ mil.)	27.5%	–	22.8	14.5	27.6	47.1
Market value ($ mil.)	–	–	–	–	–	–
Employees	–	–	–	–	–	1,000

PACIFIC DENTAL SERVICES, LLC

17000 RED HILL AVE
IRVINE, CA 926145626
Phone: 714 845-8500
Fax: –
Web: www.pacificdentalservices.com

CEO: –
CFO: –
HR: –
FYE: December 31
Type: Private

Pacific Dental Services (PDS) provides marketing, accounting and finance, tax, people services, legal, and IT services. The company also provides a wide range of services such as endodontics, oral and maxillofacial surgery, orthodontics, pediatric dentistry, and periodontics. The PDS University ? Institute of Dentistry offers continuing education (CE) in state-of-the-art training facilities, including simulation laboratories. It has strategic partnerships with Dentsply Sirona, Posca Brothers, Ivoclar Vivadent, and Staples Business Advantage. The company also provides legal services such as legal correspondence and complaints, dental board correspondence and inspections, HIPAA and privacy, owner dentist contracts, corporate governance, legal employee matters, and more.

	Annual Growth	12/04	12/05	12/20	12/21	12/22
Sales ($mil.)	(22.5%)	–	134.0	–	1.8	1.8
Net income ($ mil.)	(17.8%)	–	6.7	–	0.5	0.2
Market value ($ mil.)	–	–	–	–	–	–
Employees	–	–	–	–	–	4,500

PACIFIC FINANCIAL CORP.
NBB: PFLC

1216 Skyview Drive
Aberdeen, WA 98520
Phone: 360 533-8870
Fax: –
Web: www.bankofthepacific.com

CEO: Denise J Portmann
CFO: Carla F Tucker
HR: –
FYE: December 31
Type: Public

Pacific Financial Corporation is the holding company for The Bank of the Pacific, which has more than 15 branches in southwestern and northwestern portions of Washington, as well as neighboring parts of Oregon. Serving small to midsized businesses and professionals, the bank offers traditional deposit services, including checking and savings accounts, NOW and money market accounts, CDs, and IRAs. Commercial mortgages dominate the bank's loan portfolio, which also includes business, construction, consumer, residential, farmland, and credit card loans. The bank offers investments and financial planning through an agreement with third-party provider Elliott Cove Capital Management.

	Annual Growth	12/17	12/18	12/19	12/20	12/21
Assets ($mil.)	10.2%	895.0	907.9	929.4	1,167.3	1,320.0
Net income ($ mil.)	16.2%	7.0	11.3	13.8	11.4	12.7
Market value ($ mil.)	2.6%	107.0	116.9	132.9	97.5	118.4
Employees	–	–	–	–	–	–

PACIFIC HIDE & FUR DEPOT

5 RIVER DR S
GREAT FALLS, MT 594051872
Phone: 406 771-7222
Fax: –
Web: www.pacific-steel.com

CEO: –
CFO: Tim Culliton
HR: –
FYE: August 28
Type: Private

Pacific Steel & Recycling was built on a strong foundation, centered on its customers ? reaching out to them, identifying their needs and offering the very best in service and quality. It operates more than 45 recycling centers in the northwestern US and Canada that also handle cardboard and scrap paper in addition to metals. The company's Pacific Steel unit offers new steel sales, a wide variety of processing services for its customers to prepare their steel and agricultural steel products. Pacific Steel's facilities handle items such as bar products and structurals, flat-rolled products, reinforcing bar, and tubing and pipe. The company offers a variety of processing services.

	Annual Growth	08/05	08/06	08/07	08/08	08/10
Sales ($mil.)	–	–	–	301.9	241.4	301.6
Net income ($ mil.)	(16.7%)	–	–	60.3	2.9	34.9
Market value ($ mil.)	–	–	–	–	–	–
Employees	–	–	–	–	–	780

PACIFIC INTERNATIONAL VEGETABLE MARKETING, INC.

1622 MOFFETT ST
SALINAS, CA 939053353
Phone: 831 755-1375
Fax: –
Web: www.pim4u.com

CEO: Dave L Johnson
CFO: –
HR: –
FYE: December 31
Type: Private

Pacific International Vegetable Marketing grows organic and conventional fruits and vegetables for retail and foodservice customers. The company grows, packs, and ships more than 100 different commodities with brand names that include Dynasty Farms, Pacific, Pacific Greens, Green Magic, Rousseau, Contender, Original Spring Mix, and Pure Pacific Organics. It ships more than 20 million packages per year from the Western United States and Mexico. Employee-owned Pacific International Vegetable Marketing was founded in 1989 by president Tom Russell and VP Dave Johnson.

	Annual Growth	12/10	12/11	12/12	12/13	12/14
Sales ($mil.)	69.6%	–	–	11.9	20.4	34.3
Net income ($ mil.)	–	–	–	(0.8)	2.1	0.0
Market value ($ mil.)	–	–	–	–	–	–
Employees	–	–	–	–	–	75

PACIFIC MUTUAL HOLDING CO.

700 Newport Center Drive
Newport Beach, CA 92660-6397
Phone: 949 219-3011
Fax: –
Web: www.pacificmutual.com

CEO: Thomas C Sutton
CFO: –
HR: –
FYE: December 31
Type: Public

Life insurance is "alive and whale" at Pacific Mutual Holding. The company's primary operating subsidiary, Pacific Life Insurance (whose logo is a breaching whale), is a top California-based life insurer. Lines of business include a variety of life insurance products for individuals and businesses; annuities and mutual funds geared to individuals and small businesses; management of stable value funds, fixed income investments, and other investments for institutional clients and pension plans; and real estate investing. Additionally, its Aviation Capital Group subsidiary provides commercial jet aircraft leasing. The company is owned by its Pacific Life shareholders.

	Annual Growth	12/11	12/12	12/13	12/14	12/15
Assets ($mil.)	4.1%	116,811	123,697	129,921	137,048	137,279
Net income ($ mil.)	(0.7%)	679.0	460.0	720.0	540.0	661.0
Market value ($ mil.)	–	–	–	–	–	–
Employees	–	–	–	–	–	–

PACIFIC SANDS INC

4611 Green Bay Road
Kenosha, WI 53144
Phone: 262 925-0123
Fax: –
Web: www.pacificsands.biz

CEO: Michael D Michie
CFO: –
HR: –
FYE: June 30
Type: Public

Not a company that caters to resort-goers but one that cares about clean water, Pacific Sands makes and markets nontoxic liquid and powder cleaning, laundry, and water-treatment products under the Natural Choices (cleaning and laundry products) and ecoone (pool and spa water-management systems) brands. The company, incorporated in 1994, serves the industrial and consumer products industries. It acquired Natural Choices Home Safe Products in early 2008 to further improve its standing as an environmentally friendly products maker. Natural Choices' best known brand is Oxy-Boost cleaning products. Pacific Sands' products are available online and through dealers in the US and internationally.

	Annual Growth	06/11	06/12	06/13	06/14	06/15
Sales ($mil.)	8.5%	1.6	1.9	2.0	2.9	2.2
Net income ($ mil.)	–	0.1	(0.0)	(0.1)	(0.3)	(1.3)
Market value ($ mil.)	(29.1%)	11.7	8.7	4.5	3.6	3.0
Employees	–	11	12	13	–	–

PACIFIC SUNWEAR OF CALIFORNIA, LLC

3450 E MIRALOMA AVE
ANAHEIM, CA 928062101
Phone: 714 414-4000
Fax: –
Web: www.pacsun.com

CEO: Michael Relich
CFO: –
HR: Gary Schoenfeld
FYE: February 01
Type: Private

Pacific Sunwear of California markets apparel via more than 400 stores (down from a peak of 950) in all 50 US states and Puerto Rico under the name PacSun and through an e-commerce site. It courts the young and active consumer by representing brands associated with surfing, skateboarding, and snowboarding, including apparel by Billabong, RVCA, and The North Face, as well as footwear by Vans, Converse, and others. In 2018 private equity firm Golden Gate Capital (Pacific Sunwear's parent company) formed operating company PSEB Group to run both PacSun and Eddie Bauer, another of its retail portfolio companies.

PACIFICA FOUNDATION INC.

3729 CAHUENGA BLVD
STUDIO CITY, CA 916043504
Phone: 510 849-2590
Fax: –
Web: www.pacifica.org

CEO: –
CFO: –
HR: –
FYE: September 30
Type: Private

Pacifica Foundation operates the Pacifica Radio Network, which includes five listener-supported, community oriented radio stations: KPFA 94.1 FM in Berkeley, California; KPFK 90.7 FM in Los Angeles; KPFT 90.1 FM in Houston; WBAI 99.5 FM in New York City; and WPFW 89.3 FM in Washington, DC. Founded in 1949, Pacifica Radio is the nation's first listener-supported, community-based radio network. Pacifica also has more than 100 affiliates in 27 states. The network was founded in 1949 by Lew Hill and blazed the trail for listener-sponsored independent radio.

	Annual Growth	09/08	09/09	09/10	09/15	09/21
Sales ($mil.)	(0.7%)	–	12.3	13.1	12.0	11.3
Net income ($ mil.)	–	–	(2.7)	(2.0)	(0.1)	(0.2)
Market value ($ mil.)	–	–	–	–	–	–
Employees	–	–	–	–	–	179

PACIFICHEALTH LABORATORIES, INC.   NBB: PHLI

100 Matawan Road, Suite 150
Matawan, NJ 07747
Phone: 732 739-2900
Fax: –
Web: www.pacifichealthlabs.com

CEO: –
CFO: –
HR: –
FYE: December 31
Type: Public

PacificHealth Laboratories plans to go the distance with its dietary supplements. The firm develops sports enhancement and weight-loss products, as well as treatments for diabetes, using its proprietary protein-based technologies. It sells sports drinks Endurox and Accelerade to retail outlets including GNC, health clubs, and Internet retailers, and it launched weight-loss drink Satiatrim in 2007. The company is also working on products for oral rehydration, post-surgical muscle recovery, and glucose regulation. PacificHealth sold its Endurox and Accelerade lines to Mott's in 2006, but it continues to sell the products under a royalty-free license. The firm sells its products internationally using distributors.

	Annual Growth	12/07	12/08	12/09	12/10	12/11
Sales ($mil.)	(1.8%)	7.4	7.2	8.0	7.2	6.9
Net income ($ mil.)	–	(1.3)	(2.0)	(1.7)	(0.8)	(0.5)
Market value ($ mil.)	(26.0%)	11.5	2.9	2.9	3.1	3.4
Employees	(12.0%)	15	9	11	10	9

PACIFICORP   NBB: PPWL M

825 Northeast Multnomah Street, Suite 1900
Portland, OR 97232
Phone: 888 221-7070
Fax: –
Web: www.pacificorp.com

CEO: William J Fehrman
CFO: Nikki L Kobliha
HR: Robert Hunter
FYE: December 31
Type: Public

PacifiCorp's core businesses are regulated utilities Pacific Power and Rocky Mountain Power, which together provide electricity to about 2 million customers. The subsidiaries operate some 17,100 miles of transmission lines in ten states, some 65,300 miles of distribution lines, and around 900 substations. PacifiCorp owns or has stakes in more than 35 coal, hydroelectric, natural gas and wind generation facilities that supply its utilities with almost 15,085 MW of net capacity. It also purchases and sells power in wholesale markets to with other utilities, energy marketing companies, financial institutions and other market participants to balance and optimize the economic benefits of electricity generation, retail customer loads and existing wholesale transactions. PacifiCorp, an indirect wholly owned subsidiary of Berkshire Hathaway Energy Company.

	Annual Growth	12/19	12/20	12/21	12/22	12/23
Sales ($mil.)	4.0%	5,068.0	5,341.0	5,296.0	5,679.0	5,936.0
Net income ($ mil.)	–	771.0	739.0	888.0	920.0	(468.0)
Market value ($ mil.)	(6.5%)	55,335	53,961	60,333	47,767	42,251
Employees	–	5,300	5,200	4,800	4,800	–

PACIRA BIOSCIENCES INC — NMS: PCRX

5401 West Kennedy Boulevard, Suite 890
Tampa, FL 33609
Phone: 813 553-6680
Fax: –
Web: www.pacira.com

CEO: David Stack
CFO: Charles A Reinhart III
HR: –
FYE: December 31
Type: Public

Pacira BioSciences is the industry leader in its commitment to non-opioid pain management and providing a non-opioid option to as many patients as possible to redefine the role of opioids as a rescue therapy only. It is advancing a pipeline of unique, safe, best-in-class products across a variety of therapeutic areas that include acute postsurgical pain; acute and chronic osteoarthritis, or OA, pain of the knee; low back and other areas; spasticity and stellate ganglion block of the sympathetic nerves.

	Annual Growth	12/19	12/20	12/21	12/22	12/23
Sales ($mil.)	12.5%	421.0	429.6	541.5	666.8	675.0
Net income ($ mil.)	–	(11.0)	145.5	42.0	15.9	42.0
Market value ($ mil.)	(7.1%)	2,105.6	2,781.4	2,796.8	1,794.6	1,568.3
Employees	4.1%	606	624	697	715	712

PACKAGING CORP OF AMERICA — NYS: PKG

1 North Field Court
Lake Forest, IL 60045
Phone: 847 482-3000
Fax: –
Web: www.packagingcorp.com

CEO: Mark W Kowlzan
CFO: Robert P Mundy
HR: –
FYE: December 31
Type: Public

One of the largest containerboard manufacturers in the US, Packaging Corporation of America (PCA) produces approximately 4.6 million tons of containerboard annually, most of which is converted into corrugated boxes, and ships some 63.4 billion square feet of corrugated products. PCA's mills also churn out linerboard and semi-chemical corrugating medium. The company's corrugated packaging includes shipping containers for manufactured goods, multi-color boxes and displays for retail locations, and honeycomb protective packaging. It also produces packaging materials for food and beverage and other consumer and industrial products. PCA operates approximately 90 manufacturing plants throughout the US.

	Annual Growth	12/19	12/20	12/21	12/22	12/23
Sales ($mil.)	2.9%	6,964.3	6,658.2	7,730.3	8,478.0	7,802.4
Net income ($ mil.)	2.4%	696.4	461.0	841.1	1,029.8	765.2
Market value ($ mil.)	9.8%	10,037	12,360	12,202	11,464	14,601
Employees	(1.0%)	15,500	15,200	15,200	15,100	14,900

PACKAGING MACHINERY MANUFACTURERS INSTITUTE, INCORPORATED

12930 WORLDGATE DR STE 200
HERNDON, VA 201706011
Phone: 703 243-8555
Fax: –
Web: www.pmmi.org

CEO: –
CFO: –
HR: Brianna Dewulf
FYE: December 31
Type: Private

For this group, it's all about thinking inside the box. The Packaging Machinery Manufacturers Institute (PMMI) is a not-for-profit trade association for manufacturers of packaging and related converting machinery in the US, Mexico, and Canada. The organization provides its more than 700 members with industry research and education services and sponsors PACK EXPO, an international packaging show held every two years. It publishes Packaging Machinery Technology magazine, the Packaging Machinery Directory on CD-ROM, a list of colleges and technical schools that offer packaging machinery programs, and several targeted newsletters. The organization was founded in 1933.

	Annual Growth	12/14	12/15	12/16	12/21	12/22
Sales ($mil.)	13.9%	–	36.6	45.4	62.7	90.8
Net income ($ mil.)	–	–	(1.7)	5.2	3.9	10.3
Market value ($ mil.)	–	–	–	–	–	–
Employees	–	–	–	–	–	34

PAGE SOUTHERLAND PAGE, L.L.P.

1100 LOUISIANA ST STE 1
HOUSTON, TX 770025203
Phone: 713 871-8484
Fax: –
Web: www.pagethink.com

CEO: James M Wright
CFO: –
HR: –
FYE: December 31
Type: Private

Page Southerland Page performs pre-design planning, architectural, engineering, historic preservation, interior design, and sustainable design services in Texas and far beyond. Also known as Page since a 2013 rebranding, the company boasts a portfolio of projects that includes corporate, education, healthcare, hospitality, government, sports, and science and technology facilities. Page takes on projects in more than 80 countries worldwide, including the UK, and the Middle East. The construction firm traces its beginnings to a two-person office in Austin, Texas, established by brothers Charles and Louis Page in 1898; Louis Southerland joined the firm during the 1930s.

	Annual Growth	12/07	12/08	12/09	12/11	12/21
Sales ($mil.)	(55.9%)	–	97.4	57.2	61.1	0.0
Net income ($ mil.)	–	–	14.1	6.7	10.0	(0.1)
Market value ($ mil.)	–	–	–	–	–	–
Employees	–	–	–	–	–	150

PAID INC — NBB: PAYD

225 Cedar Hill Street
Marlborough, MA 01752
Phone: 617 861-6050
Fax: –
Web: www.paid.com

CEO: Allan Pratt
CFO: W A Lewis IV
HR: –
FYE: December 31
Type: Public

Paid, Inc. (formerly Sales Online Direct) hopes celebrities and fans will pay it some attention. The company's celebrity services division offers merchandising, brand building, marketing, online ticketing services, and it hosts Web-based fan clubs for clients. Its AuctionInc technology processes and calculates transactions for website owners. The company also auctions collectibles, sports memorabilia, and celebrity-related items through the Internet. Paid, Inc. makes its money on collectibles and through related services (such as appraisals, and its own auction management software).

	Annual Growth	12/18	12/19	12/20	12/21	12/22
Sales ($mil.)	15.7%	9.3	10.5	12.9	14.9	16.6
Net income ($ mil.)	–	(11.5)	0.3	(2.2)	(0.7)	0.7
Market value ($ mil.)	(19.6%)	23.9	22.3	15.9	20.1	10.0
Employees	7.8%	17	17	24	24	23

PAISANO PUBLICATIONS, LLC

28210 DOROTHY DR
AGOURA HILLS, CA 913012693
Phone: 818 889-8740
Fax: –
Web: www.v-twin.com

CEO: John Lagana
CFO: –
HR: –
FYE: December 31
Type: Private

If motorcycles and tattoos are your thing, Paisano Publications can hook you up. The company publishes about a dozen magazines, including motorcycle bible Easyriders, and biker magazines V-Twin and Biker. It also publishes custom truck magazine Tailgate and several tattoo magazines. Its In the Wind publishes photographs reflecting the biker lifestyle, sent in from readers. Paisano Publications also produces events such as Easyriders Bike Shows, Motorcycle Rodeos, and the V-Twin Expo Industry Trade Show, and sells casual clothing, accessories, and novelty items (lighters, ash trays, decals, and shot glasses). The company was originally founded in 1970.

	Annual Growth	12/03	12/04	12/05	12/06	12/07
Sales ($mil.)	(1.5%)	–	–	29.2	30.1	28.4
Net income ($ mil.)	(79.2%)	–	–	8.5	0.8	0.4
Market value ($ mil.)	–	–	–	–	–	–
Employees	–	–	–	–	–	113

PALATIN TECHNOLOGIES INC

ASE: PTN

4B Cedar Brook Drive
Cranbury, NJ 08512
Phone: 609 495-2200
Fax: –
Web: www.palatin.com

CEO: Carl Spana
CFO: Stephen T Wills
HR: –
FYE: June 30
Type: Public

Palatin Technologies fights the perils of poor health with protein and peptide-based therapies. The company researches and develops drugs that target melanocortin (MC) receptors and natriuretic receptors in the brain. Its lead candidate, Vyleesi (bremelanotide), was approved for marketing in the US to treat sexual dysfunction in women in 2019; the drug is licensed to and marketed by AMAG Pharmaceuticals. Other MC-targeted drug candidates aim to treat inflammatory and autoimmune conditions such as dry eye disease and inflammatory bowel disease. Natriuretic (a type of peptide) focused treatments are being studied for the treatment of heart failure, acute asthma, and other cardiovascular diseases.

	Annual Growth	06/19	06/20	06/21	06/22	06/23
Sales ($mil.)	(46.7%)	60.3	0.1	(0.2)	1.5	4.9
Net income ($ mil.)	–	35.8	(22.4)	(33.6)	(36.2)	(27.5)
Market value ($ mil.)	16.0%	13.5	6.0	7.1	3.3	24.5
Employees	–	18	20	26	33	–

PALISADE BIO INC

NAS: PALI

7750 El Camino Real, Suite 2A
Carlsbad, CA 92009
Phone: 858 704-4900
Fax: –
Web: www.palisadebio.com

CEO: JD Finley JD
CFO: –
HR: –
FYE: December 31
Type: Public

Neuralstem is using human neural stem cells to find treatments for central nervous disorders. The company uses a proprietary technology to produce commercial quantities of brain and spinal cord stem cells that are used to develop potential treatments for Lou Gehrig's disease (also known as ALS or amyotrophic lateral sclerosis), Huntington's disease, spinal cord injury, and stroke. Its spinal cord stem cells are part of the first FDA-approved ALS stem cell clinical trial. Neuralstem also has a class of small molecule compounds that it is developing into oral drugs. The first, NSI-189, is undergoing trials to treat major depression. These compounds may also be developed for Alzheimer's disease and schizophrenia.

	Annual Growth	12/19	12/20	12/21	12/22	12/23
Sales ($mil.)	100.7%	0.0	0.0	0.0	0.0	0.3
Net income ($ mil.)	–	(8.4)	(16.3)	(26.6)	(14.3)	(12.3)
Market value ($ mil.)	(12.1%)	9.2	8.2	12.1	48.2	5.5
Employees	15.8%	5	7	13	12	9

PALL CORPORATION

25 HARBOR PARK DR
PORT WASHINGTON, NY 110504664
Phone: 516 484-5400
Fax: –
Web: www.pall.com

CEO: Jennifer Honeycutt
CFO: –
HR: Annette Martinez
FYE: July 31
Type: Private

Pall Corporation is a filtration, separation and purification leader providing solutions to meet the critical fluid management needs of customers across a broad spectrum of industries. Pall works with customers to advance health, safety and environmentally responsible technologies. The company's engineered products enable process and product innovation and minimize emissions and waste. Pall Corporation serves customers worldwide. Pall Corporation is part of Danaher Corporation.

PALMS WEST HOSPITAL LIMITED PARTNERSHIP

13001 SOUTHERN BLVD
LOXAHATCHEE, FL 334709203
Phone: 561 798-3300
Fax: –
Web: www.palmswesthospital.com

CEO: Josh D Tillio
CFO: –
HR: –
FYE: May 31
Type: Private

Palms West Hospital, part of the HCA system of healthcare providers, is a 200-bed acute care hospital that serves western Palm Beach County, Florida. The hospital's specialized care programs include cardiopulmonary services, diabetes education, a birthing center, diagnostics, and rehabilitation. Its pediatric department boasts an emergency clinic and intensive care unit. The medical campus includes physician offices and an outpatient surgery center (Palms West Surgicenter). Palms West Hospital is part of the HCA East Florida division. Affiliate Integrated Regional Laboratories provides medical testing for Palms West and other area facilities.

	Annual Growth	05/12	05/13	05/14	05/15	05/16
Sales ($mil.)	1.9%	–	–	–	167.7	170.9
Net income ($ mil.)	(17.1%)	–	–	–	34.7	28.8
Market value ($ mil.)	–	–	–	–	–	–
Employees	–	–	–	–	–	850

PALO ALTO NETWORKS, INC

NMS: PANW

3000 Tannery Way
Santa Clara, CA 95054
Phone: 408 753-4000
Fax: –
Web: www.paloaltonetworks.com

CEO: Nikesh Arora
CFO: Dipak Golechha
HR: Lauren Lopez
FYE: July 31
Type: Public

Palo Alto Networks is a global cybersecurity provider. It offers enterprise-wide network and cloud security (including security measures for mobile devices) to protect companies from breaches in their corporate networks. The company's hardware and software security products identify network traffic in detail and provide the ability to control access by users. The company provides next-gen cybersecurity to thousands of customers globally, across all sectors. The company's cybersecurity platforms and services aid companies in securing their enterprise users, networks, clouds, and endpoints by delivering comprehensive cybersecurity backed by industry-leading artificial intelligence and automation. It sells products outright as well as through a growing subscription business. The company was incorporated in 2005.

	Annual Growth	07/19	07/20	07/21	07/22	07/23
Sales ($mil.)	24.2%	2,899.6	3,408.4	4,256.1	5,501.5	6,892.7
Net income ($ mil.)	–	(81.9)	(267.0)	(498.9)	(267.0)	439.7
Market value ($ mil.)	2.5%	69,842	78,900	123,027	153,873	77,063
Employees	18.8%	7,014	8,014	10,473	12,561	13,948

PALOMAR COMMUNITY COLLEGE DISTRICT

1140 W MISSION RD
SAN MARCOS, CA 920691415
Phone: 760 744-1150
Fax: –
Web: www.palomar.edu

CEO: –
CFO: –
HR: –
FYE: June 30
Type: Private

Palomar College helps its students reach for the stars in the Golden State. The public two-year community college maintains a student body of approximately 30,000, about a quarter of whom are enrolled full-time. It offers more than 200 associate degree and certificate programs and operates five academic divisions. Palomar College students can also complete the first two years of a bachelor's degree or take not-for-credit personal enrichment classes. In addition to its main campus in San Marcos (30 miles north of San Diego), Palomar College operates an educational center in Escondido and several additional smaller centers throughout San Diego County.

	Annual Growth	06/17	06/18	06/20	06/21	06/22
Sales ($mil.)	5.7%	–	52.3	53.4	54.4	65.4
Net income ($ mil.)	–	–	(25.4)	(18.9)	(2.6)	35.1
Market value ($ mil.)	–	–	–	–	–	–
Employees	–	–	–	–	–	3,323

PALOMAR HEALTH

2125 CITRACADO PKWY # 300
ESCONDIDO, CA 920294159
Phone: 442 281-5000
Fax: –
Web: www.palomarhealth.org

CEO: –
CFO: –
HR: Cindy Paget
FYE: June 30
Type: Private

Palomar Health (formerly Palomar Pomerado Health) has a North County delivery system anchored by two medical center campuses - Palomar Medical Center Escondido and Palomar Medical Center Poway - which provide an array of acute care services, obstetrics, rehabilitation, behavioral health, pediatrics and neonatal intensive care. Its Palomar Health Wound Healing & Hyperbaric Centers uses Hyperbaric Oxygen Therapy, to develop an individualized, aggressive treatment to aid wound closure, new tissue growth and wound tissue regeneration. Palomar Health traces its roots back to 1933. Palomar Health is member of Mayo Clinic Care Network.

PANERA BREAD COMPANY

3630 S GEYER RD STE 400
SAINT LOUIS, MO 631271234
Phone: 314 984-1000
Fax: –
Web: www.panerabread.com

CEO: –
CFO: –
HR: –
FYE: December 31
Type: Private

Panera Bread Company is part of Panera Brands, one of the largest fast casual restaurant platforms in the US. The company operates in about 50 states throughout the US, the District of Columbia and Canada. Its locations, which operate under the banners Panera Bread and Saint Louis Bread Co., offer made-to-order sandwiches using a variety of artisan breads, including Asiago cheese bread, focaccia, and its classic sourdough. The chain's menu also features soups, salads, and gourmet coffees. In addition, Panera sells its bread, bagels, and pastries to go. Privately held German conglomerate JAB Holding Company owns Panera.

PANDORA MEDIA, LLC

2100 FRANKLIN ST STE 700
OAKLAND, CA 946123145
Phone: 510 451-4100
Fax: –
Web: www.pandora.com

CEO: Roger Lynch
CFO: Naveen Chopra
HR: –
FYE: December 31
Type: Private

Pandora is the largest ad-supported audio entertainment streaming service in the US. Pandora provides consumers with a uniquely personalized music and podcast listening experience with its proprietary Music Genome Project and Podcast Genome Project technology. Pandora is also the leading digital audio advertising platform in the US. Through its own Pandora service, its AdsWizz platform, and third-party services, such as SoundCloud, the company connects brands to the largest ad-supported streaming audio marketplace in the country. Pandora is available through its mobile app, on the web at www.pandora.com, and integrations with more than 2,000 connected products. Pandora is a subsidiary of Sirius XM and it generates nearly a quarter of its parent's revenue.

PANGEA, INC.

2604 S JEFFERSON AVE
SAINT LOUIS, MO 631181505
Phone: 314 333-0600
Fax: –
Web: www.pangea-group.com

CEO: Michael Zambrana
CFO: –
HR: –
FYE: December 31
Type: Private

Pangea Group is a titan when it comes to civil and industrial engineering and construction services. The company provides renovation, demolition, and maintenance, as well as technical and environmental services that include waste disposal, remediation, and surveying. Pangea's civil construction team builds concrete foundations and structures, in addition to grading, excavation, and storm sewer work. The firm has completed more than 500 projects over the years for clients such as Ameren and government agencies including the US Army Corps of Engineers, the Department of Energy, and military installations. The Hispanic-owned Pangea Group was founded as a clean-up enterprise for radioactive waste materials in 1994.

PANDUIT CORP.

18900 PANDUIT DR
TINLEY PARK, IL 604873600
Phone: 708 532-1800
Fax: –
Web: www.panduit.com

CEO: Dennis Renaud
CFO: –
HR: –
FYE: December 31
Type: Private

Panduit is a global leader in innovative electrical and network infrastructure solutions. Panduit creates leading-edge physical, electrical, network infrastructure and AV solutions for enterprise-wide environments, from the data center to the telecom room, from the desktop to the plant floor. Products include cabling, connectors, copper wire, fiber-optic components, cabinets and racks, grounding systems, outlets, terminals, and other electrical components. Panduit's products are used in data centers, office buildings, single pair Ethernet, wire harness and other settings. With approximately 2,000 patents, the privately-held company also serves about 90% of the Fortune 100 companies.

	Annual Growth	12/12	12/13	12/14	12/15	12/16
Sales ($mil.)	(1.9%)	–	–	973.7	924.5	937.5
Net income ($ mil.)		–	–	–	–	–
Market value ($ mil.)		–	–	–	–	–
Employees		–	–	–	–	5,110

PANHANDLE EASTERN PIPE LINE COMPANY, LP

8111 WESTCHESTER DR STE 600
DALLAS, TX 752256140
Phone: 214 981-0700
Fax: –
Web: peplmessenger.energytransfer.com

CEO: Kelcy L Warren
CFO: Martin Salinas Jr
HR: –
FYE: December 31
Type: Private

From the oilfield to the burner under a frying pan, Panhandle Eastern Pipe Line can move the gas. The company operates 10,000 miles of interstate pipelines (Panhandle Eastern -- 6,000 miles, Trunkline -- 3,000 miles, and Sea Robin -- 1,000 miles) that can transport 6.4 billion cu. ft. of natural gas a day primarily to markets in the Midwest and Great Lakes regions of the US. It also provides terminalling services through nearly 50 compressor stations and five gas storage fields capable of holding 68.1 billion cu. ft. of natural gas. The company also has liquefied natural gas (LNG) terminalling assets. Panhandle Eastern Pipe Line operates as part of Energy Transfer Equity's Southern Union's Panhandle Energy unit.

PAPA JOHN'S INTERNATIONAL, INC.
NMS: PZZA

2002 Papa John's Boulevard
Louisville, KY 40299-2367
Phone: 502 261-7272
Fax: -
Web: www.papajohns.com

CEO: Robert M Lynch
CFO: Ravi Thanawala
HR: Jason Moore
FYE: December 31
Type: Public

Papa John's International operates and franchises pizza delivery and carryout restaurants and dine-in and delivery restaurants in certain international markets. Also known as Papa John's, the company operates the world's pizza chain with around 5,700 pizzerias across the US and in about 50 international markets. Its restaurants offer several different pizza styles and topping choices, as well as menu innovations that includes Garlic Parmesan Crust, toasted handheld "Papadias" flatbread-style sandwiches, and Jalapeno Popper Rolls, followed by Epic Stuffed Crust Pizza. The company owns and operates about 600 locations, while the rest are franchised. The company generates most of its revenue from its domestic market.

	Annual Growth	12/19	12/20	12/21	12/22	12/23
Sales ($mil.)	7.2%	1,619.2	1,813.2	2,068.4	2,102.1	2,135.7
Net income ($ mil.)	102.7%	4.9	57.9	120.0	67.8	82.1
Market value ($ mil.)	4.3%	2,094.2	2,844.0	4,307.9	2,727.7	2,476.6
Employees	(5.4%)	16,500	16,700	14,000	12,000	13,200

PAPA'S PIZZA TO GO INC

3910 LAKEFIELD DR 200
SUWANEE, GA 300241243
Phone: 770 813-0823
Fax: -
Web: www.papaspizzatogo.com

CEO: -
CFO: -
HR: -
FYE: December 31
Type: Private

Founded in 1986 by president Richard Garland and VP Ken White, Papa's Pizza To-Go offers carry-out pizzas to customers in rural communities (with populations of fewer than 5,000 residents) in the southeastern US. Restaurant menus include pizza, salads, and specialty items like chicken wings and quesadillas. About 80% of the company's more than 100 stores are franchised.

	Annual Growth	12/04	12/05	12/06	12/07	12/08
Sales ($mil.)	(33.1%)	-	10.2	4.9	4.6	3.0
Net income ($ mil.)	(80.0%)	-	4.1	0.3	0.2	0.0
Market value ($ mil.)	-	-	-	-	-	-
Employees	-	-	-	-	-	120

PAPER CONVERTING MACHINE COMPANY

2300 S ASHLAND AVE
GREEN BAY, WI 543045213
Phone: 920 494-5601
Fax: -
Web: www.pcmc.com

CEO: -
CFO: -
HR: Greg Wilson
FYE: September 30
Type: Private

An empire built on paper: The Paper Converting Machine Company (PCMC) does just that -- manufactures machinery for the converting, packaging, printing, and laminating of paper. PCMC makes and sells equipment for tissue converting and packaging; wide-web flexo printing, coating and laminating; coaters; roll engraving; and non-woven converting. Its equipment is used by manufacturers of flexible packaging, non-woven disposable products (wet wipes), and sanitary tissues. PCMC is a division of manufacturing technology supplier Barry-Wehmiller Companies.

	Annual Growth	09/04	09/05	09/06	09/10	09/11
Sales ($mil.)	2.1%	-	-	194.1	196.9	215.7
Net income ($ mil.)	-	-	-	-	-	-
Market value ($ mil.)	-	-	-	-	-	-
Employees	-	-	-	-	-	1,304

PAR PACIFIC HOLDINGS INC
NYS: PARR

825 Town & Country Lane, Suite 1500
Houston, TX 77024
Phone: 281 899-4800
Fax: -
Web: www.parpacific.com

CEO: William C Pate
CFO: -
HR: -
FYE: December 31
Type: Public

Par Pacific owns and operates market-leading energy and infrastructure businesses. The company owns and operates about 155 thousand barrels per day refinery with related logistics and a retail network across the major Hawaiian islands. It owns an equity investment in Laramie Energy which has natural gas production and reserves located in Garfield, Mesa, and Rio Blanco counties, Colorado. In addition, Par Pacific' Wyoming refining business transports refined products through its logistics network to wholesale, bulk, and retail customers primarily in Wyoming and South Dakota.

	Annual Growth	12/19	12/20	12/21	12/22	12/23
Sales ($mil.)	11.1%	5,401.5	3,124.9	4,710.1	7,321.8	8,232.0
Net income ($ mil.)	105.6%	40.8	(409.1)	(81.3)	364.2	728.6
Market value ($ mil.)	11.8%	1,388.7	835.4	985.4	1,389.3	2,173.3
Employees	6.5%	1,408	1,403	1,336	1,397	1,814

PAR TECHNOLOGY CORP.
NYS: PAR

PAR Technology Park, 8383 Seneca Turnpike
New Hartford, NY 13413-4991
Phone: 315 738-0600
Fax: -
Web: www.partech.com

CEO: Savneet Singh
CFO: Bryan Menar
HR: Candice Levy
FYE: December 31
Type: Public

PAR Technology makes point-of-sale (POS) for fast food giants such as McDonald's and Yum! Brands. The company claims the largest integration ecosystem ? over 400 partners across various product solution categories including self-ordering kiosks, kitchen video systems, enterprise reporting, and other solutions, including its cloud-based back-office solution. Through its PAR Government Systems unit, the company designs data processing systems and develops software for advanced radar and other detection systems used by the US Department of Defense (DOD) and other federal and state agencies. The vast majority of sales come from customers in the US.

	Annual Growth	12/19	12/20	12/21	12/22	12/23
Sales ($mil.)	22.1%	187.2	213.8	282.9	355.8	415.8
Net income ($ mil.)	-	(15.6)	(36.6)	(75.8)	(69.3)	(69.8)
Market value ($ mil.)	9.1%	861.6	1,760.0	1,479.1	730.7	1,220.4
Employees	16.5%	1,000	1,053	1,541	1,755	1,841

PARABEL INC

1901 S. Harbor City Blvd., Suite 600
Melbourne, FL 32901
Phone: 321 409-7500
Fax: -
Web: www.parabel.com

CEO: Anthony John Phipps Tia
CFO: Syed Naqvi
HR: -
FYE: December 31
Type: Public

PetroAlgae hopes to help energy and agriculture customers grow greener. Operating through subsidiary PA LLC, the renewable energy company developed a model micro-crop production facility that grows microorganisms into biomass. As a fuel feedstock, the biomass can be converted into end products, such as diesel, jet fuel, ethanol, and butanol, as well as combustible fuel for power generation. These renewable fuels theoretically are made to replace petroleum-based fuels in the refining process. PetroAlgae sells licenses to oil and power companies that want to develop and construct their own bioreactors to produce fuel feedstock. It also offers licenses to agricultural customers that produce proteins for animal feed.

	Annual Growth	12/08	12/09	12/10	12/11	12/12
Sales ($mil.)	-	-	-	-	-	0.7
Net income ($ mil.)	-	(17.1)	(31.5)	(38.0)	(24.9)	(25.4)
Market value ($ mil.)	(38.9%)	668.3	2,458.1	1,165.4	267.3	93.0
Employees	(19.4%)	90	113	109	66	38

PARADIGM MEDICAL INDUSTRIES INC. (DE) NBB: PDMI

4273 South 590 West
Salt Lake City, UT 84123
Phone: 801 977-8970
Fax: 801 977-8973
Web: www.paradigm-medical.com

CEO: –
CFO: –
HR: –
FYE: December 31
Type: Public

Paradigm Medical Industries wants to keep those baby blues seeing clearly with its ophthalmic surgical and diagnostic equipment. Its FDA-approved products include its Blood Flow Analyzer, which measures pressure and blood flow within the eye and is used for early diagnosis of glaucoma, and a line of ultrasound biomicroscopes, which create high-resolution images of the eye that doctors use to diagnose and treat disease. The company has stopped development on its laser cataract removal system (branded Photon) because of lack of funds; it is focusing instead on marketing its diagnostic product line to ophthalmologists and optometrists.

	Annual Growth	12/10	12/11	12/12	12/13	12/14
Sales ($mil.)	–	0.7	0.8	0.3	–	–
Net income ($ mil.)	–	(1.0)	(0.5)	(0.3)	(0.1)	(0.0)
Market value ($ mil.)	18.9%	0.4	0.4	0.4	0.4	0.8
Employees	–	–	6	–	–	–

PARADISE VALLEY HOSPITAL

2400 E 4TH ST
NATIONAL CITY, CA 919502098
Phone: 619 470-4100
Fax: –
Web: www.paradisevalleyhospital.net

CEO: Alan Soderblom
CFO: –
HR: –
FYE: December 31
Type: Private

Paradise Valley Hospital aims to elevate patient care to a divine level. Established in 1904, the medical center serves residents in the San Diego area. This acute-care facility has more than 300 beds, as well as 300 general care and specialty physicians. Paradise Valley Hospital's range of services include health and wellness programs, respiratory therapy, and same-day surgery. Specialty divisions include rehabilitation, behavioral health, cardiac care, and geriatric services. Paradise Valley Hospital is a subsidiary of Prime Healthcare Services, which acquired the hospital from former parent Adventist Health in 2007.

	Annual Growth	12/15	12/16	12/17	12/18	12/21
Sales ($mil.)	(0.4%)	–	143.7	120.4	144.4	140.8
Net income ($ mil.)	–	–	(7.6)	(22.7)	3.5	9.1
Market value ($ mil.)	–	–	–	–	–	–
Employees	–	–	–	–	–	1,200

PARAGON DEVELOPMENT SYSTEMS, INC.

N57W39605 STATE ROAD 16
OCONOMOWOC, WI 530662178
Phone: 262 569-5300
Fax: –
Web: www.pdsit.net

CEO: Craig Schiefelbein
CFO: Thomas Mount
HR: –
FYE: December 31
Type: Private

Paragon Development Systems (PDS) brings Midwestern roots and a nationwide reach to the technology services market. The company offers services ranging from procurement to systems integration, reselling and supporting PCs, networking equipment, printers, servers, software, and storage systems as part of its business. Its supplier list includes Cisco Systems, Fujitsu, Hewlett-Packard, IBM, and Microsoft. Paragon also builds and markets its own PCs under the Infinity, Vector, and Vision brand names. Founded in 1986, PDS partners with US-based medium and large enterprises in a variety of markets, such as healthcare, corporate, government, and education.

	Annual Growth	12/04	12/05	12/06	12/07	12/08
Sales ($mil.)	13.3%	–	94.4	91.1	113.0	137.2
Net income ($ mil.)	144.4%	–	0.5	(0.3)	2.3	6.9
Market value ($ mil.)	–	–	–	–	–	–
Employees	–	–	–	–	–	290

PARAGON SOLUTIONS INC.

25 COMMERCE DR STE 100
CRANFORD, NJ 070163615
Phone: 908 709-6767
Fax: –
Web: www.consultparagon.com

CEO: Daniel J O'Connor
CFO: –
HR: –
FYE: December 31
Type: Private

Paragon Solutions sees itself as a model provider of technical consulting and IT services. The privately-owned company specializes in helping businesses identify enterprise software products that best suit their needs and providing systems integration services to install and support the applications. It also offers such other services as content management, document management, and data archiving. Paragon focuses on the communications, financial services, health care, insurance, and life sciences industries. Customers have included Time Warner Cable, Credit Suisse, and Merck.

	Annual Growth	12/11	12/12	12/13	12/14	12/15
Sales ($mil.)	(9.6%)	–	76.5	64.1	54.7	56.6
Net income ($ mil.)	(12.3%)	–	3.5	0.2	0.7	2.4
Market value ($ mil.)	–	–	–	–	–	–
Employees	–	–	–	–	–	400

PARAGON TECHNOLOGIES INC NBB: PGNT

101 Larry Holmes Drive, Suite 500
Easton, PA 18042
Phone: 610 252-3205
Fax: 610 252-3102
Web: www.pgntgroup.com

CEO: Hesham M Gad
CFO: Deborah Mertz
HR: Diana Maglio
FYE: December 31
Type: Public

Paragon Technologies produces automated order picking systems and other order fulfilling products used by manufacturing, assembly, and order distribution customers. Also known by its major brand name SI Systems, the company supplies customers with horizontal transportation and conveyor systems, related computer software, and other products and services used for improving productivity. Customers are located primarily in the US and have included Caterpillar, engine giant Cummins, General Motors, and contact lens manufacturer Vistakon (a subsidiary of Johnson & Johnson). The company was founded in 1958.

	Annual Growth	12/18	12/19	12/20	12/21	12/22
Sales ($mil.)	12.1%	85.1	112.9	108.0	141.6	134.2
Net income ($ mil.)	49.3%	1.0	1.0	3.6	3.4	4.7
Market value ($ mil.)	63.2%	1.7	3.6	7.9	11.7	12.2
Employees	–	–	–	–	–	–

PARAMOUNT GLOBAL NMS: PARA

1515 Broadway
New York, NY 10036
Phone: 212 258-6000
Fax: –
Web: www.viacbs.com

CEO: Robert M Bakish
CFO: Eric Gray
HR: Ray Kim
FYE: December 31
Type: Public

Paramount is a leading global media and entertainment company that creates content and experiences for audiences worldwide through TV entertainment, cable networks, filmed entertainment and publishing. Paramount owns cable network Showtime, Nickelodeon, MTV, Comedy Central, BET, Paramount+ and Pluto TV. The company produces and distributes TV programming through CBS Television Studios and CBS Television Distribution. In 2022, ViacomCBS has renamed itself Paramount in a nod to the company's historic moviemaking past.

	Annual Growth	12/19	12/20	12/21	12/22	12/23
Sales ($mil.)	1.6%	27,812	25,285	28,586	30,154	29,652
Net income ($ mil.)	–	3,308.0	2,422.0	4,543.0	1,104.0	(608.0)
Market value ($ mil.)	(23.0%)	27,406	24,331	19,708	11,023	9,657.9
Employees	(6.4%)	28,570	26,340	27,265	30,300	21,900

PARAMOUNT GOLD NEVADA CORP
ASE: PZG

665 Anderson Street
Winnemucca, NV 89445
Phone: 775 625-3600
Fax: –
Web: www.paramountnevada.com

CEO: Rachel Goldman
CFO: Carlo Buffone
HR: –
FYE: June 30
Type: Public

Paramount Gold Nevada (formerly Paramount Gold and Silver) is all about the bling. The development-stage company explores for gold, silver, and other metals in Mexico and Nevada gold-producing regions. Through subsidiary Paramount Gold de M xico, the company owns 100% of a 450,000-acre property in Chihuahua that includes seven advanced-stage gold mines. It also owns the Sleeper project in Nevada, a 30-sq.-mi. site that produced gold and silver from 1986 to 1996. The company is conducting exploration drilling and geological surveys but has no proved reserves. Paramount also holds several earlier stage, smaller claims in Nevada, and inactive subsidiaries in Mexico and Peru.

	Annual Growth	06/19	06/20	06/21	06/22	06/23
Sales ($mil.)	–	0.4	0.7	0.3	–	–
Net income ($ mil.)	–	(6.0)	(6.4)	(5.9)	(7.8)	(6.5)
Market value ($ mil.)	(20.3%)	42.8	68.0	53.2	24.1	17.3
Employees	(6.1%)	9	9	8	8	7

PARENTS AS TEACHERS NATIONAL CENTER, INC.

2228 BALL DR
SAINT LOUIS, MO 631468602
Phone: 314 432-4330
Fax: –
Web: www.parentsasteachers.org

CEO: Constance Gully
CFO: –
HR: Randi Halbmaier
FYE: June 30
Type: Private

Parents as Teachers (PAT) has preschool down. The not-for-profit group offers parent education and international support programs for parents to teach their children in the early years before kindergarten. PAT develops curricula, trains early childhood professionals, and certifies parent educators. Its goals are to improve parenting skills, instruct parents to recognize developmental delays, prevent child abuse, and help kids get ready for elementary school. To that end, it advocates at the federal level for legislation to benefit families with young children. PAT has programs in more than 40 US states, and in Canada, Germany, Mexico, the UK, and many other countries. PAT was founded in 1985.

	Annual Growth	06/17	06/18	06/19	06/20	06/22
Sales ($mil.)	9.5%	–	12.6	15.2	13.0	18.2
Net income ($ mil.)	53.3%	–	0.4	2.0	(0.9)	2.2
Market value ($ mil.)	–	–	–	–	–	–
Employees	–	–	–	–	–	123

PARENTS TELEVISION COUNCIL, INC.

707 WILSHIRE BLVD # 2075
LOS ANGELES, CA 900173505
Phone: 213 629-9255
Fax: –
Web: www.parentstv.org

CEO: –
CFO: –
HR: –
FYE: December 31
Type: Private

If the Parents Television Council had been around a little earlier, we may not have ever seen Daisy Duke in those shorts or the shenanigans going on in Jack, Chrissy, and Janet's apartment. The PTC was founded in 1995 to protect children from sex, violence, and profanity on television and in other media. The group, with about 1 million members, advises its members on appropriate actions (letters to sponsors, FCC complaints) and publishes alerts about shows it deems not suitable for children, show and movie reviews, and a parenting column. It also provides TV, Internet, video game, movie, and music ratings guides and lobbies government entities.

	Annual Growth	12/15	12/16	12/17	12/18	12/19
Sales ($mil.)	(8.5%)	–	2.4	2.1	2.2	1.8
Net income ($ mil.)	–	–	0.0	(0.1)	(0.1)	(0.0)
Market value ($ mil.)	–	–	–	–	–	–
Employees	–	–	–	–	–	23

PAREXEL INTERNATIONAL (MA) CORPORATION

275 GROVE ST STE 3101
AUBURNDALE, MA 024662281
Phone: 617 454-9300
Fax: –
Web: www.parexel.com

CEO: Jamie Macdonald
CFO: Greg Rush
HR: –
FYE: June 30
Type: Private

Parexel is a leading global clinical research organization (CRO) focused on development and delivery of innovative new therapies to advance patient health. It provides the clinical development capabilities and integrated consulting expertise it takes to streamline development every step of the way ? faster and more cost-effectively. Parexel has operations in North and South America, Europe, Middle and Africa, and Asia. In 2021, Parexel announced the completion of its acquisition by EQT IX fund (EQT Private Equity) and funds managed by the Private Equity business within Goldman Sachs Asset Management from Pamplona Capital Management LP for $8.5 billion.

	Annual Growth	06/12	06/13	06/14	06/15	06/16
Sales ($mil.)	3.5%	–	–	2,266.3	2,330.3	2,426.3
Net income ($ mil.)	9.5%	–	–	129.1	147.8	154.9
Market value ($ mil.)	–	–	–	–	–	–
Employees	–	–	–	–	–	18,900

PARIC CORPORATION

77 WEST PORT PLZ STE 250
SAINT LOUIS, MO 631463121
Phone: 636 561-9500
Fax: –
Web: www.paric.com

CEO: –
CFO: –
HR: –
FYE: December 31
Type: Private

Paric Corporation pairs design/build services with construction management and general contracting services. The contractor manages commercial, civic, institutional, industrial, and health care construction projects in the Midwest. Its offerings include interior design, construction management, and historic renovation services. Paric specializes in senior living, education, residential, and municipal projects. CEO Joe McKee owns Paric Corporation, which his father Paul McKee, Jr., and Richard Jordan co-founded in 1979.

PARK AEROSPACE CORP
NYS: PKE

1400 Old Country Road
Westbury, NY 11590
Phone: 631 465-3600
Fax: –
Web: www.parkaerospace.com

CEO: Brian E Shore
CFO: P M Farabaugh
HR: –
FYE: February 26
Type: Public

Park Aerospace develops and manufactures advanced composite materials, primary and secondary structures and assemblies and low-volume tooling for the aerospace markets. Park's advanced composite materials include film adhesives and lightning strike protection materials. Park offers an array of composite materials specifically designed for hand lay-up or automated fiber placement (AFP) manufacturing applications. Park's advanced composite materials are used to produce primary and secondary structures for jet engines, large and regional transport aircraft, military aircraft, Unmanned Aerial Vehicles, business jets, general aviation aircraft and rotary wing aircraft. Park also offers specialty ablative materials for rocket motors and nozzles and specially designed materials for radome applications. AEROGLIDE, COREFIX, and EASYCURE are some of the company's brands. Nearly 95% Park's sales come from its domestic customers.

	Annual Growth	03/19	03/20*	02/21	02/22	02/23
Sales ($mil.)	1.4%	51.1	60.0	46.3	53.6	54.1
Net income ($ mil.)	(44.6%)	113.5	9.6	4.9	8.5	10.7
Market value ($ mil.)	(2.0%)	356.2	284.8	284.3	278.8	327.9
Employees	(0.4%)	112	136	106	110	110

*Fiscal year change

PARK CORPORATION

3555 RESERVE COMMONS DR
MEDINA, OH 442565900
Phone: 216 267-4870
Fax: –
Web: www.parkcorp.com

CEO: Raymond P Park
CFO: Tim Geharing
HR: Dory Smodic
FYE: December 31
Type: Private

Park Corporation has a division for all seasons. Areas of involvement for the privately held company span the manufacture of machinery and components for the steel and energy industries; the distribution of metalworking and mining equipment; the sale of integrated steel products; and service of oil refining and power generation operations. Other areas include private aircraft services, convention and trade show services, commercial and industrial real estate development, and fixed-income and private equity investments.

PARK HOTELS & RESORTS INC — NYS: PK

1775 Tysons Boulevard, 7th Floor
Tysons, VA 22102
Phone: 571 302-5757
Fax: –
Web: www.pkhotelsandresorts.com

CEO: Thomas J Baltimore Jr
CFO: Sean M Dell'orto
HR: –
FYE: December 31
Type: Public

Park Hotels & Resorts is the second largest publicly-traded lodging real estate investment trust (REIT) with a diverse portfolio of iconic and market-leading hotels and resorts with significant underlying real estate value. The company's portfolio consists of some 45 premium-branded hotels and resorts with approximately 29,000 rooms, of which some 90% of its rooms are luxury and upper upscale and all of its rooms are located in the US and its territories. The company operates its high-quality hotels in major urban and convention areas including the New York City, Washington, DC, Chicago, San Francisco, Chicago, and others. It operates resorts in leisure areas such as Hawaii, Orlando, Miami Beach and Key West, and operates various hotels and resorts at gateway airports.

	Annual Growth	12/19	12/20	12/21	12/22	12/23
Sales ($mil.)	(1.3%)	2,844.0	852.0	1,362.0	2,501.0	2,698.0
Net income ($ mil.)	(25.0%)	306.0	(1,440.0)	(459.0)	162.0	97.0
Market value ($ mil.)	(12.3%)	5,432.4	3,601.3	3,964.6	2,475.8	3,212.8
Employees	(34.5%)	488	182	80	91	90

PARK NATIONAL CORP (NEWARK, OH) — ASE: PRK

50 North Third Street, P.O. Box 3500
Newark, OH 43058-3500
Phone: 740 349-8451
Fax: –
Web: www.parknationalcorp.com

CEO: David L Trautman
CFO: Brady T Burt
HR: –
FYE: December 31
Type: Public

Park National Corporation is a financial holding company with the principal business of owning and supervising its subsidiaries. The holding company owns Park National Bank, which operates around 100 branches in Ohio, northern Kentucky and the Carolinas. The bank engages in commercial banking and trust business in small and medium population areas such Ohio, North Carolina, and South Carolina. Park National Bank delivers financial services through more than 95 financial services offices and a network of more than 115 automated teller machines. Park's nonbank units include consumer finance outfit Guardian Finance, SE Property Holdings, Scope Leasing, and Vision Bancshares Trust.

	Annual Growth	12/19	12/20	12/21	12/22	12/23
Assets ($mil.)	3.5%	8,558.4	9,279.0	9,560.3	9,855.0	9,836.5
Net income ($ mil.)	5.4%	102.7	127.9	153.9	148.4	126.7
Market value ($ mil.)	6.7%	1,650.0	1,692.4	2,213.0	2,268.4	2,141.2
Employees	(1.7%)	1,907	1,778	1,685	1,794	1,782

PARK NICOLLET HEALTH SERVICES

3800 PARK NICOLLET BLVD
ST LOUIS PARK, MN 554162527
Phone: 952 993-3123
Fax: –
Web: www.parknicollet.com

CEO: David K Wessner
CFO: David J Cooke
HR: Tracy Toulouse
FYE: December 31
Type: Private

Park Nicollet Health Services is part of HealthPartners, the largest consumer-governed, non-profit health care organization in the nation with a mission to improve health and well-being in partnership with members, patients and the community. Park Nicollet is an integrated care system that includes Methodist Hospital, Park Nicollet Clinic and Park Nicollet Foundation. It also runs Park Nicollet Clinic facilities in the Minneapolis/St. Paul metropolitan area that provide primary and specialty care services, including cancer treatment and outpatient surgery.

	Annual Growth	12/18	12/19	12/20	12/21	12/22
Sales ($mil.)	115.6%	–	0.2	0.1	0.9	1.7
Net income ($ mil.)	–	–	–	(0.5)	(0.3)	–
Market value ($ mil.)	–	–	–	–	–	–
Employees	–	–	–	–	–	4,500

PARK NICOLLET METHODIST HOSPITAL

6500 EXCELSIOR BLVD
SAINT LOUIS PARK, MN 554264702
Phone: 952 993-5000
Fax: –
Web: –

CEO: –
CFO: –
HR: –
FYE: December 31
Type: Private

Park Nicollet Methodist Hospital helps keep residents swimmingly healthy in the City of Lakes. Operating as Methodist Hospital, the acute care facility serves the greater Minneapolis area. It has some 430 beds and provides such specialized care programs as cancer treatment, cardiovascular health, emergency care, obstetrics, therapy for eating disorders, and neurological rehabilitation. The facility is home to the Struthers Parkinson's Center, which is devoted to helping patients with Parkinson's disease and their families to cope with the disease. Methodist Hospital is owned by Minnesota-based not-for-profit health care organization HealthPartners.

	Annual Growth	12/00	12/01	12/02*	06/05*	12/14
Sales ($mil.)	(3.1%)	–	734.5	301.7	1.2	490.0
Net income ($ mil.)	150.8%	–	0.0	11.5	0.7	47.1
Market value ($ mil.)	–	–	–	–	–	–
Employees	–	–	–	–	–	2,503

*Fiscal year change

PARK-OHIO HOLDINGS CORP. — NMS: PKOH

6065 Parkland Boulevard
Cleveland, OH 44124
Phone: 440 947-2000
Fax: –
Web: www.pkoh.com

CEO: Matthew Crawford
CFO: Patrick Fogarty
HR: Betty Boris
FYE: December 31
Type: Public

Park-Ohio Holdings (ParkOhio) is a diversified international company providing world-class customers with a supply chain management outsourcing service, capital equipment used on their production lines, and manufactured components used to assemble their products. The company straddles three business segments: Supply Technologies, Assembly Components, and Engineered Products. It markets its products and services in the US, Mexico, Canada, Europe, and Asia. It offers fasteners, valves, hoses, extruded and molded rubber and thermoplastic products, and forging presses, among others, to industries such as automotive, coatings, forgings, agricultural, construction, and marine equipment. Almost 65% of the company's revenue is from the US.

	Annual Growth	12/19	12/20	12/21	12/22	12/23
Sales ($mil.)	0.6%	1,618.3	1,295.2	1,438.0	1,492.9	1,659.7
Net income ($ mil.)	(33.0%)	38.6	(4.5)	(24.8)	(14.2)	7.8
Market value ($ mil.)	(5.4%)	439.8	403.9	276.7	159.9	352.4
Employees	(3.6%)	7,300	6,500	6,900	7,100	6,300

PARKE BANCORP INC

NAS: PKBK

601 Delsea Drive
Washington Township, NJ 08080
Phone: 856 256-2500
Fax: -
Web: www.parkebank.com

CEO: Vito S Pantilione
CFO: Jonathan D Hill
HR: -
FYE: December 31
Type: Public

Community banking is a walk in the park for Parke Bancorp, holding company for Parke Bank, which has three branches in the New Jersey communities of Sewell and Northfield, as well as two loan production offices in the Philadelphia area. The bank provides such traditional products as checking and savings accounts, money market and individual retirement accounts, and certificates of deposit. Parke Bank has a strong focus on business lending -- including operating loans, commercial mortgages, and construction loans -- which accounts for about 90% of the company's loan portfolio. The bank also writes residential real estate and consumer loans.

	Annual Growth	12/19	12/20	12/21	12/22	12/23
Assets ($mil.)	4.7%	1,681.2	2,078.3	2,136.4	1,984.9	2,023.5
Net income ($ mil.)	(1.2%)	29.8	28.4	40.8	41.8	28.5
Market value ($ mil.)	(5.5%)	303.6	186.5	254.4	248.0	242.1
Employees	1.2%	101	97	110	111	106

PARKE-BELL LTD., INC.

709 W 12TH ST
HUNTINGBURG, IN 475428915
Phone: 812 683-3707
Fax: -
Web: www.touchofclass.com

CEO: -
CFO: -
HR: -
FYE: December 31
Type: Private

Backed by its 30-year history and through its Touch of Class catalog, Parke-Bell sells quality bedding, lamps, rugs, wall d cor, and home furnishings. Parke-Bell's vast products portfolio includes a variety of colors, styles, and themes, such as casual, French country, traditional, and Victorian to go with its select-line of products. Customers can get bed linens, towels, and pillows monogrammed using the company's 80 thread-color choices and handful of monogram styles. Parke-Bell also sells framed art, table sculptures, wall tapestries, and wall sculptures in an assortment of themes. The company has been family-owned and -operated since 1978.

PARKER DRILLING CO

NBB: PKDC

5 Greenway Plaza, Suite 100
Houston, TX 77046
Phone: 281 406-2000
Fax: -
Web: -

CEO: Sandy Esslemon
CFO: Michael W Sumruld
HR: Keith Baker
FYE: December 31
Type: Public

Parker Wellbore (formerly Parker Drilling) helps energy companies accomplish their drilling and production goals efficiently, reliably, and safely. It supports oil and gas operators with innovative land and offshore drilling services; premium rental tools and well services; and advanced operations and management support. Founded in 1934, Parker Wellbore helps customers manage their costs and mitigate their risks, to achieve their operational goals in a safe and efficient manner. Parker Wellbore is the new brand name for the integrated companies of Parker Drilling, Quail Tools, and iTS Energy Services.

	Annual Growth	12/16	12/17	12/18*	03/19*	12/19
Sales ($mil.)	3.4%	427.0	442.5	480.8	157.4	472.4
Net income ($ mil.)	-	(230.8)	(118.7)	(165.7)	(90.2)	6.5
Market value ($ mil.)	-	-	-	-	-	338.5
Employees	6.7%	2,199	2,266	2,425	-	2,670

*Fiscal year change

PARKER HANNIFIN CORP

NYS: PH

6035 Parkland Boulevard
Cleveland, OH 44124-4141
Phone: 216 896-3000
Fax: -
Web: www.parker.com

CEO: Jennifer A Parmentier
CFO: Todd M Leombruno
HR: -
FYE: June 30
Type: Public

Parker-Hannifin (Parker) is a worldwide diversified manufacturer of motion and control technologies and systems, providing precision-engineered solutions for a wide variety of mobile, industrial, and aerospace markets. Other business lines include the manufacture of hydraulic, fuel, pneumatic, and electromechanical systems and components for the aerospace/defense industry; and fluid connectors and filtration systems for the heating, ventilation, air conditioning, and refrigeration (HVACR) and transportation industries. Parker owns some 335 manufacturing plants and operates through the two business segments of Diversified Industrial and Aerospace Systems. More than 65% of total revenue is derived from customers in North America. The company traces its historical roots back to 1917.

	Annual Growth	06/19	06/20	06/21	06/22	06/23
Sales ($mil.)	7.4%	14,320	13,696	14,348	15,862	19,065
Net income ($ mil.)	8.3%	1,512.4	1,206.3	1,746.1	1,315.6	2,082.9
Market value ($ mil.)	23.1%	21,835	23,538	39,443	31,601	50,094
Employees	3.1%	55,610	50,520	54,640	55,090	62,730

PARKERVISION INC

NBB: PRKR

4446-1A Hendricks Avenue, Suite 354
Jacksonville, FL 32207
Phone: 904 732-6100
Fax: -
Web: www.parkervision.com

CEO: Jeffrey L Parker
CFO: Cynthia French
HR: -
FYE: December 31
Type: Public

Parkervision is more about sound than sight. The company develops radio frequency integrated circuits (RFICs) for use in wireless networking. The company has produced limited numbers of its chips through contract manufacturers, but it has not recorded a sale in recent years. If it did, the chips could be in mobile handsets, tablets, data cards, femtocells, machine-to-machine communications, embedded applications, even military radios and cable modems. ParkerVision was founded in 1989 by CEO Jeffery Parker. In 2014 it retained advisory firm 3LP Advisors to help execute a licensing strategy and get its business off the ground.

	Annual Growth	12/19	12/20	12/21	12/22	12/23
Sales ($mil.)	328.7%	0.0	-	0.1	0.9	25.0
Net income ($ mil.)	-	(9.5)	(19.6)	(12.3)	(9.8)	9.5
Market value ($ mil.)	0.3%	14.0	42.1	80.7	20.2	14.2
Employees	(9.6%)	12	9	8	8	8

PARKRIDGE MEDICAL CENTER, INC.

2333 MCCALLIE AVE
CHATTANOOGA, TN 374043258
Phone: 423 698-6061
Fax: -
Web: www.parkridgehealth.com

CEO: -
CFO: -
HR: -
FYE: March 31
Type: Private

Parkridge Medical Center provides health care services in southern Tennessee. The hospital also operates two satellite facilities: Parkridge East Hospital, another acute care facility, and Parkridge Valley Hospital, an adult and pediatric behavior health care facility. The hospitals, combined, have some 520 beds. Specialty services include cardiac surgery, orthopedics, and diagnostic imaging. The Sarah Cannon Cancer Center provides oncology therapeutics. Parkridge Medical Center is a subsidiary of HCA and is part of HCA's TriStar Health System.

	Annual Growth	03/06	03/07	03/08	03/09	03/17
Sales ($mil.)	5.1%	-	-	-	216.0	322.4
Net income ($ mil.)	14.9%	-	-	-	24.7	74.7
Market value ($ mil.)	-	-	-	-	-	-
Employees	-	-	-	-	-	1,364

PARKWAY PLASTICS, INC.

561 STELTON RD
PISCATAWAY, NJ 088543868
Phone: 800 881-4996
Fax: –
Web: www.parkwayjars.com

CEO: Ed Rowan
CFO: –
HR: –
FYE: December 31
Type: Private

Parkway Plastics' products line the shelves of convenience stores nationwide, but you'd likely never know it. The company designs, manufactures, and markets more than 150 sizes of stock plastic jars and bottles, from 1/8 ounce to 40 ounces, in customizable colors. In addition to jars, Parkway Plastics makes metal and plastic closures, and dust disk liners (popular in the cosmetics industry), jewelry cleaning baskets, and wax containers (commonly used in the automotive and household products industries). The company boasts more than 8,000 customers across the US. Entrepreneur Edward W. Rowan, Sr. founded Parkway Plastics in 1951; his son, Edward Jr., is chairman and president.

	Annual Growth	12/06	12/07	12/08	12/09	12/10
Sales ($mil.)	–	–	–	(2,045.3)	4.4	5.6
Net income ($ mil.)	1077.3%	–	–	0.0	0.0	0.0
Market value ($ mil.)	–	–	–	–	–	–
Employees	–	–	–	–	–	49

PARKWEST MEDICAL CENTER

9352 PARK WEST BLVD
KNOXVILLE, TN 379234387
Phone: 865 373-1000
Fax: –
Web: www.covenanthealth.com

CEO: –
CFO: Scott Hamilton
HR: Randall Carr
FYE: August 31
Type: Private

Parkwest Medical Center is a wholly-owned subsidiary of Covenant Health and the largest medical center in West Knoxville. Parkwest has more than 285 beds and provides health care services to patients of Knox County, Tennessee. Its various specialties include cardiology, orthopedics, neurology and spine care, women's services, and bariatric surgery. Other services include cardiac rehabilitation, diagnostic services, outpatient surgery, and senior health care. Parkwest's facilities include a 40-bed emergency care center, a 30-bed critical care unit, and a 20-suite childbirth center. The medical center also has a diabetes center and provides dental care.

	Annual Growth	12/04	12/05	12/13*	08/15	08/16
Sales ($mil.)	5.5%	–	172.8	337.2	290.1	311.2
Net income ($ mil.)	21.0%	–	5.4	29.6	35.8	43.9
Market value ($ mil.)	–	–	–	–	–	–
Employees	–	–	–	–	–	1,300

*Fiscal year change

PARLUX HOLDINGS, INC.

11920 MIRAMAR PKWY
MIRAMAR, FL 330257005
Phone: 954 442-5453
Fax: –
Web: www.perfumaniaholdingsinc.com

CEO: Michael W Katz
CFO: Michael Nofi
HR: Sophie Cardone
FYE: January 30
Type: Private

Perfumania Holdings makes dollars with scents. The holding company owns scent-seller Perfumania, which numbers about 230 stores in 40 states (about a third are located in California, Florida, and Texas), Puerto Rico, and the US Virgin Islands, offering some 2,000 fragrance products at discounted prices for men and women. Perfumania also sells cosmetics, skin care, and bath and body products. The company sells perfume online through perfumania.com. Perfumania Holdings, which own fragrance manufacturer Parlux, is also a wholesale supplier of fragrances to other retailers through its Quality King Fragrance unit. In August 2017 Perfumania filed for Chapter 11 bankruptcy relief and planned to close 64 stores.

PARMA COMMUNITY GENERAL HOSPITAL

7007 POWERS BLVD
PARMA, OH 441295437
Phone: 440 743-3000
Fax: –
Web: www.uhhospitals.org

CEO: Patricia A Ruflin
CFO: Barry Franklin
HR: –
FYE: December 31
Type: Private

Parma Community General Hospital, aka University Hospitals Parma Medical Center, cares for residents of Ohio's Cuyahoga County and surrounding areas along the northern Lake Erie shoreline. The 332-bed acute care medical center has a staff of more than 500 physicians representing some 30 medical specialties. It offers a broad range of inpatient care services, including cardiology, oncology, orthopedics, and rehabilitation. Its outpatient and community outreach programs include home health, hospice, senior care, diagnostic labs, and various community health clinics. The hospital was founded in 1961.

	Annual Growth	12/11	12/12	12/13	12/15	12/16
Sales ($mil.)	(0.6%)	–	183.6	180.5	180.9	179.2
Net income ($ mil.)	(4.0%)	–	2.5	(0.2)	3.8	2.1
Market value ($ mil.)	–	–	–	–	–	–
Employees	–	–	–	–	–	2,000

PARRON-HALL CORPORATION

9655 GRANITE RIDGE DR STE 100
SAN DIEGO, CA 92123
Phone: 858 268-1212
Fax: –
Web: www.parronhall.com

CEO: –
CFO: –
HR: –
FYE: December 31
Type: Private

This company can outfit your conference room, waiting area, and hall. Parron-Hall, which does business as Parron Hall Office Interiors, sells office furniture to customers in the San Diego area. The company's inventory includes products manufactured by such companies as Kimball and Knoll, as well as HON, Humanscale, and izzydesign. Parron Hall also offers space planning, installation, warehousing, and maintenance services. Customers include California Highway Patrol, Anheuser-Busch, Garden Fresh Restaurant Corp., and Qualcomm. The company was founded in 1947 but grew out of a business founded in the 1880s by the great great grandfather of company president James Herr.

	Annual Growth	12/12	12/13	12/14	12/16	12/17
Sales ($mil.)	(2.9%)	–	31.0	23.7	36.8	27.5
Net income ($ mil.)	(34.6%)	–	0.3	0.1	0.3	0.0
Market value ($ mil.)	–	–	–	–	–	–
Employees	–	–	–	–	–	68

PARSONS CORP (DE)

5875 Trinity Parkway, #300
Centreville, VA 20120
Phone: 703 988-8500
Fax: –
Web: www.parsons.com

NYS: PSN
CEO: –
CFO: –
HR: –
FYE: December 31
Type: Public

Parsons is a leading disruptive technology provider in the national security and global infrastructure markets, with capabilities across cyber and intelligence, space and missile defense, transportation, environmental remediation, urban development, and critical infrastructure protection. Parsons' unique business model of connecting its Federal Solutions and Critical Infrastructure segments through its One Parsons approach also differentiates the company; helping it become a pioneer in protecting global infrastructure and unlock innovation at the intersection of technology and global infrastructure. Founded in 1944, the company has more than 17,000 employees around the globe delivering integrated, agile solutions for their customer's national security and critical infrastructure requirements.

	Annual Growth	12/19	12/20	12/21	12/22	12/23
Sales ($mil.)	8.3%	3,954.8	3,918.9	3,660.8	4,195.3	5,442.7
Net income ($ mil.)	7.5%	120.5	98.5	64.1	96.7	161.1
Market value ($ mil.)	11.0%	4,369.1	3,853.6	3,561.5	4,895.1	6,637.2
Employees	3.9%	15,879	15,500	15,500	17,000	18,500

PARSONS ENVIRONMENT & INFRASTRUCTURE GROUP INC.

4701 HEDGEMORE DR
CHARLOTTE, NC 282093281
Phone: 704 529-6246
Fax: –
Web: www.parsons.com

CEO: –
CFO: Leslie Bradley
HR: –
FYE: July 29
Type: Private

A unit of Parsons Corporation, Parsons Commercial Technology Group (PARCOMM) provides project management, engineering, construction, design, maintenance, and related services for industrial and commercial projects. The company's clients include firms in the telecommunications, health care, manufacturing, defense, petroleum, and chemical industries. PARCOMM also completes projects for schools, colleges, and government entities. Specialized services include industrial environmental remediation, factory modernization, and developing state vehicle inspection and compliance programs. PARCOMM operates throughout the US and the world.

	Annual Growth	12/09	12/10	12/11	12/12*	07/14
Sales ($mil.)	15.6%	–	–	443.1	684.1	684.1
Net income ($ mil.)	–	–	–	(57.2)	(12.0)	(12.0)
Market value ($ mil.)	–	–	–	–	–	–
Employees	–	–	–	–	–	1,205

*Fiscal year change

PARSONS GOVERNMENT SERVICES INC.

5875 TRINITY PKWY STE 230
CENTREVILLE, VA 201201922
Phone: 703 988-8500
Fax: –
Web: www.parsons.com

CEO: Charles L Harrington
CFO: –
HR: –
FYE: December 31
Type: Private

Parsons Infrastructure & Technology Group is one of the largest members of the Parsons Corporation congregation. The unit provides a range of construction-related services, including project planning, construction management, engineering, and start-up and commissioning operations. Parsons Infrastructure & Technology Group is regularly awarded contracts by local and regional government agencies, as well as the US Army, involving environmental clean-up and chemical neutralization projects across the country. It has also undertaken facilities management work for the US Department of Homeland Security.

PARTECH INTERNATIONAL, INC.

200 CALIFORNIA ST STE 500
SAN FRANCISCO, CA 941114344
Phone: 415 788-2929
Fax: –
Web: www.partechpartners.com

CEO: –
CFO: –
HR: –
FYE: December 31
Type: Private

Partech International places and manages venture capital investments in technology companies, particularly those engaged in software and the Internet, and communications and components. With offices in the US, France, and the Israel, the firm invests in companies at various stages of development that exhibit global market potential. Portfolio companies include storage software provider Bocada and networking software provider Spoke. The firm has some $800 million under active management. Managing partner Vincent Worms co-founded Partech International in 1982.

PARTICIPANT MEDIA, LLC

331 FOOTHILL RD FL 3
BEVERLY HILLS, CA 902103669
Phone: 310 550-5100
Fax: –
Web: www.participant.com

CEO: Jeff Skoll
CFO: Andy Kim
HR: –
FYE: June 30
Type: Private

Participant Media (formerly Participant Productions) produces movies that put human and social issues in the spotlight. Possibly best known for the 2006 Al Gore documentary on global warming An Inconvenient Truth , the media company releases documentaries and feature films and creates social marketing campaigns to coincide with the release of those films. They have included The Kite Runner , Murderball , and Syriana . Participant works with not-for-profit and social sector organizations to create action, discussion, and education programs. It is also involved in television production. The company was founded in 2004 by chairman Jeff Skoll, eBay's founding president.

PARTICLE DRILLING TECHNOLOGIES, INC.

11050 W LITTLE YORK RD BLDG Q
HOUSTON, TX 770415056
Phone: 713 223-3031
Fax: –
Web: www.particledrilling.com

CEO: John D Schiller Jr
CFO: David Elifs
HR: –
FYE: September 30
Type: Private

For oil companies with difficult-to-drill assets, here is some good news. PDTI Holdings (dba Particle Drilling Technologies) is developing an advanced drilling technology it hopes will provide a dramatic increase in penetration rates for drilling oil and gas wells. Its Particle Impact Drilling System advanced drilling technology is designed to drill through deep, hard, and abrasive zones or other difficult-to-drill geologic formations. The Particle Impact Drilling System uses a custom-built drill bit fitted with jetting nozzles and polycrystalline diamond compact cutting structures. Never able to make the technology profitable, the company filed for and emerged from Chapter 11 bankruptcy protection in 2009.

PARTNERSHIP FOR A DRUG-FREE AMERICA, INC.

352 PARK AVE S RM 901
NEW YORK, NY 100101740
Phone: 212 922-1560
Fax: –
Web: www.drugfree.org

CEO: Fred Muench
CFO: Gina Samson
HR: –
FYE: December 31
Type: Private

The Partnership for Drug-Free Kids wants to make sure you know where your kids are and what they're not doing. The group, made up of communication, education, and health professionals, encourages children not to use drugs. The Partnership uses the donated talent, time, and space of its corporate and media partners to create anti-drug advertising and public relations and educational campaigns; themes have included "This is your brain on drugs," "Do you know where your kids are?" and "Above the Influence." It does not accept money from alcohol or tobacco manufacturers. The group has offices throughout the US and in Puerto Rico. The Partnership was founded in 1986.

	Annual Growth	12/14	12/15	12/16	12/17	12/18
Sales ($mil.)	(7.0%)	–	7.0	4.3	7.4	5.6
Net income ($ mil.)	–	–	(0.1)	(2.3)	(0.0)	(1.9)
Market value ($ mil.)	–	–	–	–	–	–
Employees	–	–	–	–	–	44

PARTSBASE, INC.

5401 BROKEN SOUND BLVD NW
BOCA RATON, FL 334873512
Phone: 561 953-0700
Fax: –
Web: www.partsbase.com

CEO: Robert Hammond
CFO: –
HR: –
FYE: June 26
Type: Private

Locator service PartsBase puts aircraft parts online. The company maintains an Internet database of some 50 million new, used, and overhauled parts and products used by companies in the aerospace, aviation, and defense industries. The PartsBase service has more than 4,000 clients, including airlines, fixed-base operators, government contractors, OEMs, parts distributors, and maintenance, repair, and overhaul facilities. Among the companies that use the PartsBase service to buy or sell parts are JetBlue, Honeywell, Lockheed Martin Aeronautics, Raytheon, and all branches of the US Armed Forces. CEO Robert Hammond took the company private in 2003 through a company he set up, Hammond Acquisition Corporation.

	Annual Growth	12/99	12/00	12/01*	06/16	06/17
Sales ($mil.)	1.5%	–	4.1	5.6	–	5.3
Net income ($ mil.)	–	–	(13.5)	(5.6)	–	1.4
Market value ($ mil.)	–	–	–	–	–	–
Employees	–	–	–	–	–	150

*Fiscal year change

PARTY CITY HOLDCO INC

100 Tice Blvd.
Woodcliff Lake, NJ 07677
Phone: 914 345-2020
Fax: –
Web: www.partycity.com

NBB: PRTY Q
CEO: Bradley M Weston
CFO: Jeremy Aguilar
HR: –
FYE: December 31
Type: Public

Party City is a leading party goods company in North America and the largest vertically integrated supplier of decorated party goods globally. A retailer of party supplies in the US and Mexico, Party City operates approximately 830 stores (including franchise stores) under the names of Party City and Halloween City. The shops sell balloons, decorations, tableware, costumes, and more for birthdays, baby showers, anniversaries, weddings, and other special occasions. Party City's stores and e-commerce site (PartyCity.com) are supplied by its manufacturing and wholesale arm Amscan ? which also supplies other party chains, discount and grocery stores, and gift shops around the world. Party City Holdco is a Delaware corporation formed in 2012. Domestic operation accounts for about 95% of total revenue.

	Annual Growth	12/18	12/19	12/20	12/21	12/22
Sales ($mil.)	(2.8%)	2,427.5	2,348.8	1,850.7	2,171.1	2,169.9
Net income ($ mil.)	–	123.3	(532.5)	(528.2)	(6.5)	(942.6)
Market value ($ mil.)	(56.3%)	1,132.8	265.6	698.1	632.2	41.5
Employees	(6.5%)	19,900	18,300	17,298	16,500	15,200

PARTYLITE, INC.

59 ARMSTRONG RD
PLYMOUTH, MA 023607206
Phone: 203 661-1926
Fax: –
Web: www.partylite.com

CEO: –
CFO: –
HR: –
FYE: December 31
Type: Private

Blyth lights up the party with its wicked products. As the largest candle maker in the US, Blyth's PartyLite Worldwide subsidiary sells its scented and unscented candles, flameless products, and reed diffusers all under the PartyLite brand. Blyth's portfolio extends beyond the candle business with ViSalus nutritional supplements, as well as a variety of catalog and online businesses that market household goods and gifts under the Silver Star Brands umbrella. Blyth's products are sold through home parties, online, and by retailers worldwide. The company also supplies institutional customers, such as restaurants and hotels. In 2015 Blyth agreed to be acquired by The Carlyle Group for $98 million.

PASADENA AREA COMMUNITY COLLEGE DISTRICT

1570 E COLORADO BLVD
PASADENA, CA 911062003
Phone: 626 585-7123
Fax: –
Web: www.pasadena.edu

CEO: –
CFO: –
HR: –
FYE: June 30
Type: Private

Pasadena City College (PCC) wants to hand out passes to higher education. PCC is a junior college offering associate's degree and vocational programs to more than 30,000 students a year (including 1,200 international students from more than 90 countries). Among its 60 academic programs are architecture, computer science, journalism, and physics. The college also offers occupational training in 76 areas such as bookkeeping, construction inspection, hospitality, and nursing. PCC also provides community enrichment programs through its Extended Learning Center, which offers non-credit workshops and classes. The college staff includes about 400 faculty, librarians, counselors, and administrators.

	Annual Growth	06/03	06/04	06/05	06/06	06/07
Sales ($mil.)	(55.9%)	–	–	769.9	52.3	149.7
Net income ($ mil.)	72214.0%	–	–	0.0	3.0	89.4
Market value ($ mil.)	–	–	–	–	–	–
Employees	–	–	–	–	–	1,607

PASADENA HOSPITAL ASSOCIATION, LTD.

100 W CALIFORNIA BLVD
PASADENA, CA 911053010
Phone: 626 397-5000
Fax: –
Web: www.huntingtonhealth.org

CEO: Stephen A Ralph
CFO: Steven L Mohr
HR: –
FYE: December 31
Type: Private

No need to hunt for medical care if you're near Huntington Hospital. The not-for-profit Pasadena Hospital Association, which does business as Huntington Hospital, provides health care to residents of the San Gabriel Valley in Southern California. The hospital boasts some 625 beds and offers acute medical and surgical care and community services in a number of specialties, including cardiology, gastroenterology, women's and children's health, orthopedics, and neurology. It engages in clinical cancer research (as well as diagnosis and treatment) through the Huntington Cancer Center. The hospital is also a teaching facility for the University of Southern California (USC) Keck School of Medicine.

	Annual Growth	12/12	12/13	12/14	12/15	12/16
Sales ($mil.)	17.2%	–	–	–	593.6	695.7
Net income ($ mil.)	3283.3%	–	–	–	0.3	8.5
Market value ($ mil.)	–	–	–	–	–	–
Employees	–	–	–	–	–	2,800

PASSUR AEROSPACE, INC.

3452 Lake Lynda Dr, Suite 190
Orlando, FL 32817
Phone: 203 622-4086
Fax: –
Web: www.passur.com

NBB: PSSR
CEO: Brian G Cook
CFO: –
HR: –
FYE: October 31
Type: Public

Anxious to arrive at your destination? PASSUR Aerospace's radar network provides arrival and departure information to airline pilots. Such information is displayed through various data management software used by airports and airlines to track landing and weather conditions. The company's FlightNews Live software displays information to passengers, while FlightPerform gives pilots accurate estimated time of arrival and graphical flight positioning, and OPSnet Airport Communicator incorporates messaging tools. Chairman and former CEO G.S. Beckwith Gilbert owns about 66% of the company.

	Annual Growth	10/17	10/18	10/19	10/20	10/21
Sales ($mil.)	(18.4%)	13.9	14.8	15.0	11.5	6.2
Net income ($ mil.)	–	(3.5)	(5.5)	(3.8)	(12.3)	0.0
Market value ($ mil.)	(32.8%)	20.7	11.2	9.6	2.2	4.2
Employees	(7.7%)	62	56	55	45	45

PATHFINDER CELL THERAPY INC.   NBB: PFND

12 Bow Street   CEO: Richard L Franklin
Cambridge, MA 02138   CFO: John Benson
Phone: 617 245-0289   HR: -
Fax: -   FYE: December 31
Web: -   Type: Public

Pathfinder Cell Therapy (formerly SyntheMed) keeps surgery patients and disease sufferers off the path towards scarring and organ damage. The company develops polymers aimed at preventing or reducing post-operative adhesions (scar tissue) for a variety of surgical procedures. Its REPEL-CV product, used to prevent the formation of scar tissue in open heart surgeries, is marketed internationally and is approved for use in pediatric cardiac surgeries in the US. The firm added development-stage tissue regeneration products for diabetics and others at risk of organ damage through its 2011 merger with biotech firm Pathfinder LLC; its name changed from SyntheMed to Pathfinder Cell Therapy following the merger.

	Annual Growth	12/10	12/11	12/12	12/13	12/14
Sales ($mil.)	-	0.3	0.0	0.1	0.0	-
Net income ($ mil.)	-	(2.1)	(11.3)	(2.2)	(1.7)	(1.4)
Market value ($ mil.)	(74.9%)	133.4	33.4	13.3	9.3	0.5
Employees	18.9%	1	2	2	2	2

PATHFINDER INTERNATIONAL

1015 15TH ST NW STE 1100   CEO: -
WASHINGTON, DC 200052619   CFO: Mike Zeitouny
Phone: 617 924-7200   HR: -
Fax: -   FYE: June 30
Web: www.pathfinder.org   Type: Private

Pathfinder International finds a way to provide reproductive health and family planning information and services to people in developing nations. The organization works in some 25 countries in Africa, Asia, Latin America, and the Caribbean. It partners with local governments and other groups to provide access to sexual health and family planning information, HIV/AIDS prevention and treatment, advocacy for reproductive health policies worldwide, abortion support where it's legal, and post care where it isn't. Pathfinder also publishes newsletters, resource lists, guides, and training information. Founded in 1957, it gets support from the US and European governments, the United Nations, and private sources.

	Annual Growth	06/15	06/16	06/20	06/21	06/22
Sales ($mil.)	0.6%	-	130.2	118.5	143.4	134.9
Net income ($ mil.)	-	-	(2.3)	(2.4)	15.2	4.7
Market value ($ mil.)	-	-	-	-	-	-
Employees	-	-	-	-	-	628

PATHWARD FINANCIAL INC   NMS: CASH

5501 South Broadband Lane   CEO: Brett L Pharr
Sioux Falls, SD 57108   CFO: Gregory A Sigrist
Phone: 877 497-7497   HR: -
Fax: -   FYE: September 30
Web: www.pathwardfinancial.com   Type: Public

Path Financial (formerly known as Meta Financial) is the holding company for Pathward NA (the bank), an industry leading financial empowerment company. The company offers the following innovative solutions: payment, issuing, credit, and tax. Payment solutions accepts and processes payments for all customers' personal and business needs. The bank moves funds daily through high speed banking rails, including ACH, wire transfers, and push to debit. With its Issuing solutions, Pathward is one of the leading debit and prepaid card issuers in the country and holds funds for the programs of its partners in order to provide the consumer protections of a traditional bank account. Its subsidiary Pathward Venture Capital focuses on investing in companies in the financial services industry. First Midwest Financial Capital Trust I and Crestmark Capital Trust I, focus on issuing trust preferred securities.

	Annual Growth	09/19	09/20	09/21	09/22	09/23
Assets ($mil.)	5.1%	6,182.9	6,092.1	6,690.7	6,747.4	7,535.5
Net income ($ mil.)	14.0%	97.0	104.7	141.7	156.4	163.6
Market value ($ mil.)	9.0%	853.8	503.2	1,374.1	863.0	1,206.8
Employees	0.1%	1,186	1,015	1,134	1,154	1,192

PATIENT SATISFACTION PLUS, LLC

1965 EVERGREEN BLVD # 100   CEO: -
DULUTH, GA 300961208   CFO: -
Phone: 770 978-3173   HR: -
Fax: -   FYE: December 31
Web: www.sphanalytics.com   Type: Private

Patient Satisfaction Plus pleases people in the health care industry ... and then some. Conducting business as The Myers Group, the company provides market research and survey services primarily to clients in the health care industry. The company offers data collection services and custom surveys to help clients measure and improve customer satisfaction for managed care organizations, hospital systems and physician group practices, and pharmaceutical firms. The Myers Group has also expanded its expertise beyond the health care sector, serving clients such as federal and state agencies, business and industry coalitions, as well as other market research firms. It was established in 1993.

	Annual Growth	12/03	12/04	12/05	12/06	12/07
Sales ($mil.)	19.6%	-	-	6.0	6.3	8.6
Net income ($ mil.)	101.4%	-	-	2.0	0.3	7.9
Market value ($ mil.)	-	-	-	-	-	-
Employees	-	-	-	-	-	200

PATRIARCH PARTNERS, LLC

1 LIBERTY PLZ RM 3500   CEO: Carlos Mercado
NEW YORK, NY 100061421   CFO: -
Phone: 212 825-0550   HR: Lindsay Maraviglia
Fax: -   FYE: June 30
Web: www.patriarchpartners.com   Type: Private

Patriarch Partners' lofty goal is no less than "rebuilding America, one company at a time, one job at a time." The private equity firm acquires and works to rejuvenate distressed, undervalued, middle-market companies that boast well-established but waning brands and market presence. The firm has investments in about a dozen industries, most prominently manufacturing, consumer goods, business services, media, health care, and textiles. Patriarch Partners, which manages about $8 billion in equity and assets, holds long-term interests in about 75 portfolio companies, more than 50 of them majority-owned. Hardly a patriarchy, the company was founded in 2000 by high-profile, high-style CEO Lynn Tilton.

PATRICK INDUSTRIES INC   NMS: PATK

107 West Franklin Street, P.O. Box 638   CEO: Andy L Nemeth
Elkhart, IN 46515   CFO: Matthew Filer
Phone: 574 294-7511   HR: -
Fax: -   FYE: December 31
Web: www.patrickind.com   Type: Public

Patrick Industries is a leading manufacturer and distributor of building materials and prefinished products, primarily for the manufactured home (MH), recreational vehicle (RV), and marine industries. Patrick Industries manufactures decorative paper and vinyl panels, moldings, countertops, doors, and cabinet and slotwall components. In addition to these, the company distributes roofing, siding, flooring, drywall, ceiling and wall panels, household electronics, electrical and plumbing supplies, and adhesives. Founded in 1959, the company operates approximately 185 manufacturing plants and more than 65 distribution centers and warehouses in about two dozen US states, with a small presence in China, Canada, and Mexico.

	Annual Growth	12/19	12/20	12/21	12/22	12/23
Sales ($mil.)	10.4%	2,337.1	2,486.6	4,078.1	4,881.9	3,468.0
Net income ($ mil.)	12.4%	89.6	97.1	224.9	328.2	142.9
Market value ($ mil.)	17.6%	1,161.9	1,514.7	1,788.1	1,342.9	2,223.8
Employees	7.5%	7,500	8,700	11,000	11,000	10,000

PATRIOT NATIONAL BANCORP INC NMS: PNBK

900 Bedford Street
Stamford, CT 06901
Phone: 203 252-5900
Fax: –
Web: www.bankpatriot.com

CEO: Robert G Russell Jr
CFO: Joseph D Perillo
HR: –
FYE: December 31
Type: Public

What's red, white, blue, and green? Why, Patriot National Bancorp, of course. It's the holding company for Patriot National Bank, which operates about a dozen branches in affluent southwestern Connecticut and a handful more in neighboring New York. Serving consumers, professionals, and small to midsized businesses, the bank offers checking, savings, and money market accounts, as well as CDs, IRAs, and health savings accounts. Real estate loans, including commercial mortgages, residential mortgages, and construction loans dominate its lending activities. To a far lesser extent, the bank also originates business and consumer loans. PNBK Holdings acquired control of Patriot National Bancorp in 2010.

	Annual Growth	12/18	12/19	12/20	12/21	12/22
Assets ($mil.)	2.3%	951.7	979.8	880.7	948.5	1,043.4
Net income ($ mil.)	17.8%	3.2	(2.8)	(3.8)	5.1	6.2
Market value ($ mil.)	(7.1%)	56.5	50.6	39.4	61.7	42.0
Employees	2.5%	118	131	122	128	130

PATTERN ENERGY GROUP INC.

1088 SANSOME ST
SAN FRANCISCO, CA 941111308
Phone: 415 283-4000
Fax: –
Web: www.patternenergy.com

CEO: Michael M Garland
CFO: –
HR: –
FYE: December 31
Type: Private

Pattern Energy is one of the world's leading private renewable energy and transmission companies. It develops, constructs, owns, and operates high-quality wind, solar, transmission, and energy storage projects worldwide. The company has more than 35 utility-scale renewable energy sites, totaling over 6,000 megawatts of installed capacity. It also has some 25GW global development portfolio, more than 500 miles of transmission in operation and in development and over 700 commercial solar projects completed through its affiliate Solect Energy. Its operational portfolio produced over 17,700 GWh of clean electricity, enough to meet the annual needs of more than 4 million people and avoid 18.2 million metric tons of carbon dioxide compared to coal-fired generation.

	Annual Growth	12/14	12/15	12/16	12/17	12/18
Sales ($mil.)	16.8%	–	–	354.1	411.3	483.0
Net income ($ mil.)	–	–	–	(52.3)	(82.4)	(69.0)
Market value ($ mil.)	–	–	–	–	–	–
Employees	–	–	–	–	–	526

PATTERSON BELKNAP WEBB & TYLER LLP

1133 AVENUE OF THE AMERICAS FL 22
NEW YORK, NY 100366710
Phone: 212 336-2000
Fax: –
Web: www.pbwt.com

CEO: –
CFO: –
HR: Constance Chong
FYE: December 31
Type: Private

A full-service law firm, Patterson Belknap Webb & Tyler focuses on representing clients in commercial transactions and litigation. With more than 20 practice areas and more than 200 attorneys, the firm offers up its services to clients ranging from large multinational corporations to not-for-profits to individuals in the entertainment industry. Patterson Belknap Webb & Tyler's practice areas include employment law, intellectual property, mergers and acquisitions, product liability, and white-collar criminal defense. Notable clients have included The Coca-Cola Company and The Associated Press.

PATTERSON COMPANIES INC NMS: PDCO

1031 Mendota Heights Road
St. Paul, MN 55120
Phone: 651 686-1600
Fax: –
Web: www.pattersoncompanies.com

CEO: Don Zurbay
CFO: Kevin Barry
HR: Andrea Cummings
FYE: April 29
Type: Public

Patterson Companies is a value-added specialty distributor serving the US and Canadian dental supply markets and the US, Canadian, and UK animal health supply markets. Patterson operates through its two strategic business units, Patterson Dental and Patterson Animal Health, offering similar products and services to different customer bases. Patterson believes that it has a strong brand identity as a value-added, full-service distributor with broad product and service offerings, having begun distributing dental supplies in 1877. Around 85% of its total revenue comes from the US operations.

	Annual Growth	04/19	04/20	04/21	04/22	04/23
Sales ($mil.)	3.8%	5,574.5	5,490.0	5,912.1	6,499.4	6,471.5
Net income ($ mil.)	25.5%	83.6	(588.4)	156.0	203.2	207.6
Market value ($ mil.)	5.5%	2,110.1	1,474.2	3,223.9	2,964.7	2,612.0
Employees	(0.6%)	7,800	7,800	7,800	7,700	7,600

PATTERSON-UTI ENERGY INC. NMS: PTEN

10713 W. Sam Houston Pkwy. N., Suite 800
Houston, TX 77064
Phone: 281 765-7100
Fax: –
Web: www.patenergy.com

CEO: –
CFO: –
HR: –
FYE: December 31
Type: Public

Patterson-UTI Energy is a Houston, Texas-based oilfield services company that primarily owns and operates one of the largest fleets of land-based drilling rigs in the US and a large fleet of pressure pumping equipment. The company provides onshore contract drilling for oil and natural gas producers and operates over 190 marketed land-based drilling rigs. A drilling rig includes the structure, power source, and machinery necessary to cause a drill bit to penetrate the earth to a depth desired by the customer. Patterson-UTI provides pressure pumping services for oil and natural gas operators. The company has pressure pumping equipment used in providing hydraulic fracturing services as well as cementing and acid pumping services, with a total of approximately 1.2 million horsepower.

	Annual Growth	12/19	12/20	12/21	12/22	12/23
Sales ($mil.)	13.8%	2,470.7	1,124.2	1,357.1	2,647.6	4,146.5
Net income ($ mil.)	–	(425.7)	(803.7)	(654.5)	154.7	246.3
Market value ($ mil.)	0.7%	4,317.6	2,162.9	3,474.6	6,924.5	4,440.9
Employees	–	5,800	3,000	5,000	6,500	–

PATTON WINGS, INC.

5750 NEW KING DR STE 320
TROY, MI 480982634
Phone: 833 374-7282
Fax: –
Web: www.diversifiedrestaurantholdings.com

CEO: T M Ansley
CFO: Toni Werner
HR: –
FYE: December 30
Type: Private

Diversified Restaurant Holdings owns and operates about 65 Buffalo Wild Wings Grill & Bar locations in Florida, Illinois, Indiana, Michigan, and Missouri. Franchised from Buffalo Wild Wings (BWW), the quick-casual eateries are popular for their Buffalo-style chicken wings served with a variety of dipping sauces. The restaurants also serve burgers, sandwiches, and tacos, along with beer and other beverages. Many of the eateries are located near large, suburban shopping and entertainment areas. Diversified Restaurant Holdings also operates its own dining concept, Bagger Dave's Legendary Burgers and Fries, an upscale hamburger joint with two locations in Michigan. In late 2019, private equity firm ICV agreed to acquire the company.

PAUL FREDRICK MENSTYLE, LLC

900 CORPORATE DR
READING, PA 196053340
Phone: 610 944-0909
Fax: –
Web: www.paulfredrick.com

CEO: Neal Black
CFO: David Ullman
HR: Diane Smith
FYE: December 31
Type: Private

Paul Fredrick is an apparel manufacturer and online retailer that does business best by cutting out the middle man. Paul Fredrick MenStyle designs classic men's apparel (dress shirts, pants, neckties, sportcoats, suits, formalwear) and sells direct to the consumer by mail-order catalog and the Internet. The company got its start as part of contract shirt manufacturer Fleetwood Shirt Company (a supplier to high-end department stores for about half a century). An ad in the Wall Street Journal offering dress shirts straight from the manufacturer gave Paul Fredrick its own start in 1986.

PAXTON MEDIA GROUP, LLC

100 TELEVISION LN
PADUCAH, KY 420037905
Phone: 270 575-8630
Fax: –
Web: www.paducahsun.com

CEO: –
CFO: Richard Paxton
HR: –
FYE: December 28
Type: Private

Paxton Media Group owns about 30 daily newspapers in the Midwest and South, including its flagship The Paducah Sun (Kentucky) and The Herald-Sun (Durham, North Carolina). The company also owns several dozen weekly papers and more than 100 free papers, as well as a television station in Paducah, Kentucky. W.F. Paxton launched The Paducah Sun in 1896; his family, led by CEO David Paxton, continues to run the publishing business.

PAYCHEX INC

NMS: PAYX

911 Panorama Trail South
Rochester, NY 14625-2396
Phone: 585 385-6666
Fax: –
Web: www.paychex.com

CEO: –
CFO: –
HR: –
FYE: May 31
Type: Public

Paychex began as a payroll processing firm, but has since expanded to offer a variety of human resources-related services. The company provides payroll services through its SurePayroll online application, while its Paychex Flex platform integrates payroll processing with HR management, employee benefits administration, time tracking, and employee performance management. Paychex processes the payrolls of more than 740,000 clients. The company focuses on small and mid-sized businesses and serves clients throughout the US and Europe.

	Annual Growth	05/19	05/20	05/21	05/22	05/23
Sales ($mil.)	7.3%	3,772.5	4,040.5	4,056.8	4,611.7	5,007.1
Net income ($ mil.)	10.8%	1,034.4	1,098.1	1,097.5	1,392.8	1,557.3
Market value ($ mil.)	5.2%	30,927	26,057	36,461	44,641	37,827
Employees	1.6%	15,600	15,800	15,000	16,000	16,600

PAYLOCITY HOLDING CORP

NMS: PCTY

1400 American Lane
Schaumburg, IL 60173
Phone: 847 463-3200
Fax: –
Web: www.paylocity.com

CEO: Toby J Williams
CFO: Ryan Glenn
HR: –
FYE: June 30
Type: Public

Paylocity a leading cloud-based provider of human capital management, or HCM, and payroll software solutions that deliver a comprehensive platform for the modern workforce. Its HCM and payroll platform offers an intuitive, easy-to-use product suite that helps businesses attract and retain talent, build culture and connection with their employees, and streamline and automate HR and payroll processes. The company provides its software-as-a-service, or SaaS, solutions to approximately 33,300 clients across the US, which on average had over 100 employees. The company's multi-tenants platform highly configurable and includes unified suite of payroll and HCM modules, includes HR, workforce management, talent and benefits. The company was founded in 1997.

	Annual Growth	06/19	06/20	06/21	06/22	06/23
Sales ($mil.)	25.9%	467.6	561.3	635.6	852.7	1,174.6
Net income ($ mil.)	27.2%	53.8	64.5	70.8	90.8	140.8
Market value ($ mil.)	18.4%	5,245.7	8,157.0	10,668	9,752.2	10,317
Employees	18.9%	3,050	3,600	4,150	5,300	6,100

PAYMENTS BUSINESS CORP.

150 S PINE ISLAND RD
PLANTATION, FL 333242669
Phone: 954 510-3750
Fax: –
Web: www.activeworx.com

CEO: Matthew Oakes
CFO: –
HR: –
FYE: December 31
Type: Private

Direct Insite helps give its customers insight into their customers. The company's hosted software and services provide data mining and analysis, reporting, electronic invoice management, and electronic bill presentment and payment functions. Its products are used to manage such functions as customer service workflows, order processing, dispute resolution, and accounts payable and receivable. Direct Insite serves clients in more than 60 countries, with its applications available in 15 languages and all major currencies. IBM is responsible for 51% of the company's sales, while EDS accounts for 46%.

	Annual Growth	12/11	12/12	12/13	12/14	12/15
Sales ($mil.)	(5.6%)	–	–	9.0	8.3	8.0
Net income ($ mil.)	86.1%	–	–	0.2	0.1	0.6
Market value ($ mil.)	–	–	–	–	–	–
Employees	–	–	–	–	–	37

PAYPAL HOLDINGS INC

NMS: PYPL

2211 North First Street
San Jose, CA 95131
Phone: 408 967-1000
Fax: –
Web: www.paypal.com

CEO: Alex Chriss
CFO: Gabrielle Rabinovitch
HR: –
FYE: December 31
Type: Public

PayPal is a leading technology platform and digital payments company that enables individuals and merchants to electronically transfer money via numerous methods, with payments originating from a customer's bank account, credit card, or PayPal account. PayPal has approximately 400 million active accounts and about 35 million merchant accounts across more than 200 markets. It earns fees from payment transactions, foreign exchange, and withdrawals from foreign bank accounts, as well as from interest on customer balances and PayPal-branded credit and debit cards. The company processes approximately 22.3 billion payment transactions a year. The US accounts for about 55% of PayPal's total revenue.

	Annual Growth	12/19	12/20	12/21	12/22	12/23
Sales ($mil.)	13.8%	17,772	21,454	25,371	27,518	29,771
Net income ($ mil.)	14.6%	2,459.0	4,202.0	4,169.0	2,419.0	4,246.0
Market value ($ mil.)	(13.2%)	115,958	251,062	202,158	76,348	65,832
Employees	4.1%	23,200	26,500	30,900	29,900	27,200

PBF ENERGY INC
NYS: PBF

One Sylvan Way, Second Floor
Parsippany, NJ 07054
Phone: 973 455-7500
Fax: –
Web: www.pbfenergy.com

CEO: Matthew C Lucey
CFO: Karen B Davis
HR: –
FYE: December 31
Type: Public

One of the largest independent petroleum refiners, PBF Energy's six oil refineries are located in California, Delaware, Louisiana, New Jersey, and Ohio and have a combined production capacity of about 1 million barrels per day, making the company one of the largest refiners in the US. PBF's refineries produce gasoline, ultra-low-sulfur diesel, heating oil, jet fuel, lubricants, petrochemicals, and asphalt for the Midwestern, Gulf Coast, West Coast, and Northeastern US. The company indirectly owns the general partner and about 50% of the limited partnership interest of PBF Logistics LP. PBF Energy transfers its products to customers through pipelines, the marine terminal, and truck rack.

	Annual Growth	12/19	12/20	12/21	12/22	12/23
Sales ($mil.)	11.8%	24,508	15,116	27,253	46,830	38,325
Net income ($ mil.)	60.9%	319.4	(1,392.4)	231.0	2,876.8	2,140.5
Market value ($ mil.)	8.8%	3,778.2	855.1	1,562.1	4,911.6	5,294.6
Employees	2.3%	3,442	3,729	3,418	3,616	3,776

PBF LOGISTICS LP

1 SYLVAN WAY STE 2
PARSIPPANY, NJ 070543879
Phone: 973 455-7500
Fax: –
Web: www.pbflogistics.com

CEO: Thomas J Nimbley
CFO: C E Young
HR: –
FYE: December 31
Type: Private

Refining giant PBF Energy spun off PBF Logistics in 2014 as a master limited partnership to own or lease, operate, develop, and acquire crude oil and refined petroleum products terminals, pipelines, storage facilities, and related logistics assets. The company handles these assets in support of PBF Energy's three refineries in Toledo, Ohio, Delaware City, Delaware, and Paulsboro, New Jersey. Its initial assets are integral components of the crude oil delivery operations at its parent's refineries. PBF Logistics plans to generate revenues by charging fees for receiving, handling and transferring crude oil via long-term, fee-based commercial agreements with subsidiaries of PBF Energy.

PC CALENDAR 2010, LLC

2501 N HARWOOD ST STE 2600
DALLAS, TX 752011607
Phone: 214 491-5103
Fax: –
Web: –

CEO: –
CFO: –
HR: –
FYE: December 31
Type: Private

Pavestone Company has cobbled together quite a niche. The company manufactures concrete pave stones used to create patios, pathways, driveways, landscape edgers for gardens and flowerbeds, and retaining walls for terraces and larger-scale planters. Pavestone offers its products in a wide range of shapes, colors, and textures. Customers include architects, engineers, and contractors who work on commercial, residential, retail consumer, and industrial projects, as well as do-it-yourself homeowners. Founded in 1980, the company boasts more than 20 regional manufacturing locations throughout the US. Since 2012 it has been owned by packaged concrete company QUIKRETE.

PC CONNECTION, INC.
NMS: CNXN

730 Milford Road
Merrimack, NH 03054
Phone: 603 683-2000
Fax: –
Web: www.connection.com

CEO: Timothy McGrath
CFO: Thomas C Baker
HR: –
FYE: December 31
Type: Public

Doing business as Connection, the company is a national provider of a wide range of information technology, or IT, solutions. It helps its customers design, enable, manage, and service their IT environments. It also provides IT products, including computer systems, data center solutions, software and peripheral equipment, networking communications, and other products and accessories that it purchases from manufacturers, distributors, and other suppliers. It offers more than 460,000 items from manufacturers such as Apple, Cisco Systems, and Microsoft as well as a range of IT services. Through its websites, catalogs, and direct sales force, Connection targets small- and mid-sized businesses, large corporations, government agencies, and educational institutions, as well as individual consumers.

	Annual Growth	12/19	12/20	12/21	12/22	12/23
Sales ($mil.)	0.3%	2,820.0	2,590.3	2,892.6	3,125.0	2,850.6
Net income ($ mil.)	0.4%	82.1	55.8	69.9	89.2	83.3
Market value ($ mil.)	7.9%	1,309.0	1,246.6	1,136.9	1,236.3	1,771.7
Employees	0.9%	2,609	2,598	2,542	2,685	2,703

PC GROUP, INC.
NBB: PCGR

419 Park Avenue South, Suite 500
New York, NY 10016
Phone: 212 687-3260
Fax: 631 667-1203
Web: www.pcgrpinc.com

CEO: –
CFO: –
HR: –
FYE: December 31
Type: Public

PC Group (formerly Langer) wants feet and hands to be soft and comfortable. The firm makes a range of personal care products, including soaps, lotions, and acne creams, as well as gel-based therapeutic products. Its Silipos subsidiary makes gel-based foot and hand care products (such as bandages and wraps) for the consumer market, as well as orthopedic supports and prosthetic liners for medical devices. PC Group's other main operating unit, specialty soap maker Twincraft, creates personal care products for mass marketers and specialty retailers including Bath & Body Works.

	Annual Growth	12/06	12/07	12/08	12/09	12/10
Sales ($mil.)	6.3%	35.2	62.9	45.1	40.9	45.0
Net income ($ mil.)	–	(4.9)	(4.5)	(13.6)	(8.5)	(1.4)
Market value ($ mil.)	(56.8%)	36.0	20.6	5.9	2.5	1.3
Employees	(15.8%)	574	487	261	246	289

PCL CONSTRUCTION ENTERPRISES, INC.

2000 S COLORADO BLVD STE 2-500
DENVER, CO 80222
Phone: 303 365-6500
Fax: –
Web: –

CEO: Dave Filipchuk
CFO: –
HR: Enrico D Borja
FYE: October 31
Type: Private

PCL Construction Enterprises is the contractor to call on for commercial and civil construction concerns. The company serves as the parent to half a dozen US construction companies: PCL Construction Services, PCL Civil Constructors, PCL Construction, PCL Industrial Services, PCL Industrial Construction, and Nordic PCL Construction. The companies serve as the operating entities for PCL, one of Canada's largest general contracting groups. Having completed projects in nearly every US state, PCL Construction Enterprises is active in the commercial, institutional, multi-family residential, heavy industrial, and civil construction sectors. PCL first entered the US construction market in 1975.

	Annual Growth	10/06	10/07	10/08	10/09	10/10
Sales ($mil.)	(16.4%)	–	–	2,315.5	2,182.8	1,616.8
Net income ($ mil.)	(47.2%)	–	–	84.9	52.9	23.6
Market value ($ mil.)	–	–	–	–	–	–
Employees	–	–	–	–	–	3,300

PCS EDVENTURES! INC   NBB: PCSV

11915 W. Executive Dr., Suite 101
Boise, ID 83713
Phone: 208 343-3110
Fax: –
Web: www.edventures.com

CEO: –
CFO: –
HR: –
FYE: March 31
Type: Public

PCS Edventures!.com provides science and engineering-based educational software for elementary and high school children. The company's software offerings include its Academy of Engineering Lab program, which helps students understand simple machines, gear systems, and power transfer systems; Edventures! Lab, which uses Lego materials for online engineering learning; Academy of Robotics Lab, which teaches logic, engineering, and problem-solving skills; and Edventures in Language Arts, which offers literacy learning activities for children.

	Annual Growth	03/18	03/19	03/20	03/21	03/22
Sales ($mil.)	5.4%	3.3	4.9	5.0	2.1	4.1
Net income ($ mil.)	–	(0.9)	0.9	1.0	(0.1)	0.7
Market value ($ mil.)	11.2%	3.3	5.7	5.1	4.0	5.1
Employees	–	–	–	–	–	–

PCTEL INC   NMS: PCTI

471 Brighton Drive
Bloomingdale, IL 60108
Phone: 630 372-6800
Fax: –
Web: www.pctel.com

CEO: –
CFO: –
HR: –
FYE: December 31
Type: Public

PCTEL wants to help its customers find the right connections. The company provides scanning receiver and antenna products to public and private telecom carriers and wireless infrastructure providers. Its products include a broad line of antennas (Bluewave, MAXRAD), scanning receivers (SeeGull), and interference management products (CLARIFY). The company also generates a small portion of revenues from licensing intellectual property related to its discontinued modem business. The company sells directly and through resellers, distributors, and OEM equipment providers. PCTEL serves a variety of markets in addition to telecommunications, such as transportation, public safety, health care, energy, and agriculture.

	Annual Growth	12/18	12/19	12/20	12/21	12/22
Sales ($mil.)	4.6%	83.0	90.6	77.5	87.8	99.4
Net income ($ mil.)	–	(12.9)	3.8	3.4	0.2	2.9
Market value ($ mil.)	0.1%	80.4	158.8	123.2	106.3	80.6
Employees	(17.2%)	454	331	326	304	213

PDB SPORTS, LTD.

13655 BRONCOS PKWY
ENGLEWOOD, CO 801124150
Phone: 303 649-9000
Fax: –
Web: www.denverbroncos.com

CEO: –
CFO: –
HR: Aracely Gomez
FYE: March 31
Type: Private

This company might just take football fans on a wild ride. PDB Sports owns and operates the Denver Broncos professional football team, one of the more successful franchises in the National Football League. The franchise was founded by sports entrepreneur Bob Howsam and first took the field in 1960 as part of the American Football League. Denver joined the NFL when the two leagues merged in 1970. The Broncos made four Super Bowl appearances in the 1970s and 1980s before winning back-to-back championships following the 1997 and 1998 seasons. The team won the AFC Championship and the Super Bowl again after the 2015 season. The Broncos play home games at Denver's INVESCO Field at Mile High.

PDF SOLUTIONS INC.   NMS: PDFS

2858 De La Cruz Blvd.
Santa Clara, CA 95050
Phone: 408 280-7900
Fax: 408 280-7915
Web: www.pdf.com

CEO: John K Kibarian
CFO: Adnan Raza
HR: –
FYE: December 31
Type: Public

PDF Solutions provides comprehensive data solutions designed to empower organizations across the semiconductor ecosystem to improve the yield and quality of their products and operational efficiency for increased profitability. It offers proprietary software, physical intellectual property (or IP) for integrated circuit (or IC) designs, electrical measurement hardware tools, proven methodologies, and professional services. The Exensio data analytics platform (in on-premise or cloud versions) helps customers draw information from manufacturing process data. PDF's largest market is the US which accounts for around 50% of the company's total revenue.

	Annual Growth	12/19	12/20	12/21	12/22	12/23
Sales ($mil.)	18.0%	85.6	88.0	111.1	148.5	165.8
Net income ($ mil.)	–	(5.4)	(40.4)	(21.5)	(3.4)	3.1
Market value ($ mil.)	17.5%	646.7	827.0	1,217.2	1,092.0	1,230.6
Employees	8.7%	353	423	407	458	493

PDG-ENVIRONMENTAL, INC.

1386 Beulah Road, Building 801
Pittsburgh, PA 15235
Phone: 412 243-3200
Fax: 412 243-4900
Web: www.flagshippdg.com

CEO: –
CFO: –
HR: –
FYE: January 31
Type: Public

If you're up to your ankles in asbestos, you can call PDG Environmental. Through its subsidiaries, the company removes and disposes of cancer-causing minerals, encloses asbestos-filled areas, sprays sealants on asbestos-containing materials, and conducts interior demolition projects. PDG Environmental works on commercial buildings, industrial facilities, and government and school buildings. Its services include removing lead-based paint, installing thermal insulation, and providing microbial remediation. The company offers training in mold awareness and remediation through a joint venture. Chairman and CEO John Regan owns 11% of PDG Environmental.

	Annual Growth	01/05	01/06	01/07	01/08	01/09
Sales ($mil.)	8.5%	60.4	78.8	75.0	97.1	83.7
Net income ($ mil.)	–	2.2	0.9	(7.2)	(0.9)	(5.2)
Market value ($ mil.)	(46.0%)	31.9	44.8	14.2	10.4	2.7
Employees	(1.9%)	110	130	123	112	102

PDL BIOPHARMA INC

59 Damonte Ranch Parkway, Suite B-375
Reno, NV 89521
Phone: 775 832-8500
Fax: –
Web: www.pdl.com

CEO: Dominique Monnet
CFO: Edward A Imbrogno
HR: –
FYE: December 31
Type: Public

If your body starts fighting you, PDL BioPharma (PDL) hopes to help you fight back. The company's antibody (protein) humanization technology makes it possible to alter monoclonal antibodies for use in human therapies, such as preventing and treating autoimmune diseases and cancer. The firm has developed the LENSAR, a cataract laser technology used in refractive cataract surgical procedures and it markets and sells to ophthalmic ambulatory surgical centers and specialty ophthalmic hospitals. Other pharmaceutical products consists of branded prescription medicine products sold under Tekturna and Tekturna HCT in the US, Rasilez and Rasilez HCT. Founded in 1986, majority of its revenue accounted outside the US.

	Annual Growth	12/16	12/17	12/18	12/19	12/20
Sales ($mil.)	(50.0%)	244.3	320.1	198.1	54.8	15.3
Net income ($ mil.)	–	63.6	110.7	(68.9)	(70.4)	(77.3)
Market value ($ mil.)	–	241.9	312.7	330.9	370.3	–
Employees	–	11	14	20	75	11

PDS DEFENSE, INC.

300 E JOHN CARPENTER FWY STE 700
IRVING, TX 750622727
Phone: 214 647-9600
Fax: –
Web: www.pdstech.com

CEO: –
CFO: –
HR: –
FYE: December 31
Type: Private

Need an IT pro to assist with your company's computer needs? PDS Tech wants to help. The company provides temporary technical, industrial, and general staffing services through more than 30 offices across the US, with a concentration in Texas and on the East Coast. PDS Tech's specialties include aviation, architecture, engineering, information technology, administration, and maritime staffing. Its PDS Engineering division handles engineering placement for the aerospace, mechanical, and structural engineering industries, while the Information Services division offers technical consulting services in the IT and telecommunication industries. The company was founded in 1977 by aerospace engineer Art Janes.

	Annual Growth	12/13	12/14	12/15	12/16	12/17
Sales ($mil.)	(8.2%)	–	339.6	321.4	287.8	262.5
Net income ($ mil.)	(69.5%)	–	0.4	0.7	0.3	0.0
Market value ($ mil.)	–	–	–	–	–	–
Employees	–	–	–	–	–	4,000

PEABODY ENERGY CORP (NEW)

701 Market Street
St. Louis, MO 63101-1826
Phone: 314 342-3400
Fax: –
Web: www.peabodyenergy.com

NYS: BTU
CEO: –
CFO: –
HR: –
FYE: December 31
Type: Public

Peabody is a leading producer of metallurgical and thermal coal. Peabody supplies some 122.9 million tons of coal to major power and steel customers. With a leading position in the US Powder River and Illinois basins, Peabody sits on an estimated 2.4 billion tons of coal reserves and 2.4 billion tons of coal resources. Major operations (mainly in the US and Australia) include coal trading and brokering, coalbed methane production, transportation-related services, and development of coal-based generating plants. The US customer accounts for more than 35% of Peabody's revenue.

	Annual Growth	12/19	12/20	12/21	12/22	12/23
Sales ($mil.)	1.7%	4,623.4	2,881.1	3,318.3	4,981.9	4,946.7
Net income ($ mil.)	–	(211.3)	(1,870.3)	360.1	1,297.1	759.6
Market value ($ mil.)	27.8%	1,173.7	310.2	1,296.0	3,400.3	3,130.0
Employees	(4.9%)	6,600	4,600	4,900	5,500	5,400

PEACEHEALTH

1115 SE 164TH AVE
VANCOUVER, WA 986839625
Phone: 360 788-6841
Fax: –
Web: www.peacehealth.org

CEO: Charles Prosper
CFO: –
HR: Malisa Glaser
FYE: June 30
Type: Private

PeaceHealth is a not-for-profit Catholic health system that serves residents in Washington, Oregon and Alaska. In all, PeaceHealth has some 16,000 caregivers and a multi-specialty medical group practice with more than 1,100 physicians. It also has ten medical centers in both rural and urban communities throughout the Northwest. Its medical centers include PeaceHealth Ketchikan Medical Center, PeaceHealth St. Joseph Medical Center, PeaceHealth St. John Medical Center, Sacred Heart Medical Center (two campuses), Cottage Grove Community Hospital, Peace Harbor Hospital, PeaceHealth Peace Island Medical Center, and PeaceHealth Southwest Medical Center.

	Annual Growth	06/08	06/09	06/14	06/21	06/22
Sales ($mil.)	7.0%	–	1,372.1	2,249.9	3,054.9	3,291.5
Net income ($ mil.)	–	–	(88.9)	114.5	32.5	(176.9)
Market value ($ mil.)	–	–	–	–	–	–
Employees	–	–	–	–	–	6,690

PEACEHEALTH SOUTHWEST MEDICAL CENTER

400 NE MOTHER JOSEPH PL
VANCOUVER, WA 986643200
Phone: 360 514-2097
Fax: –
Web: www.peacehealth.org

CEO: Tracey Fernandez
CFO: –
HR: –
FYE: June 30
Type: Private

PeaceHealth Southwest Medical Center (PHSW, formerly Southwest Washington Medical Center) represents an original frontier of medicine: It was the first permanent hospital in the Northwest Territories. The 450-bed medical center provides emergency, trauma, diagnostic, and medical services to residents of Vancouver, Washington, and the Portland, Oregon, metropolitan area. Specialty services include cancer, orthopedic, neurology, birthing, heart, and vascular care. It also operates satellite clinics and home health agencies. The not-for-profit organization, founded in 1858, is a top area employer with about 600 physicians. It is part of the Southwest Washington Health System and an affiliate of PeaceHealth.

PEAK METHODS, INC.

1516 S BOSTON AVE STE 211
TULSA, OK 741194058
Phone: 918 252-7753
Fax: –
Web: www.peakuptime.com

CEO: –
CFO: –
HR: –
FYE: September 30
Type: Private

Peak Methods, which does business as Peak UpTime, wants to rid the world, or at least Oklahoma, of computer downtime. The company provides IT services in Oklahoma and surrounding states with a focus on serving small- and midsized companies in the energy, government, educational, medical, and financial services markets. Peak UpTime designs, develops, and integrates software and Web sites; provides remote monitoring and managed access, data centers, and on-site support; and system networking, security applications, telephony, and data storage. The company does business in Texas, Kansas, Louisiana, and Oklahoma from offices it has offices in Oklahoma and Kansas.

PEAPACK-GLADSTONE FINANCIAL CORP.

500 Hills Drive, Suite 300
Bedminster, NJ 07921-0700
Phone: 908 234-0700
Fax: –
Web: www.pgbank.com

NMS: PGC
CEO: Douglas L Kennedy
CFO: Jeffrey J Carfora
HR: –
FYE: December 31
Type: Public

Peapack-Gladstone Financial is the $3.4 billion-asset holding company for the near-century-old Peapack-Gladstone Bank, which operates more than 20 branches in New Jersey's Hunterdon, Morris, Somerset, Middlesex, and Union counties. Founded in 1921, the bank provides traditional deposit accounts, credit cards, and loans to individuals and small businesses, as well as trust and investment management services through its PGB Trust and Investments unit. Multifamily residential mortgages represent nearly 50% of the company's loan portfolio, while commercial mortgages make up around 15%. The bank also originates construction, consumer, and business loans.

	Annual Growth	12/19	12/20	12/21	12/22	12/23
Assets ($mil.)	5.7%	5,182.9	5,890.4	6,078.0	6,353.6	6,476.9
Net income ($ mil.)	0.7%	47.4	26.2	56.6	74.2	48.9
Market value ($ mil.)	(0.9%)	548.2	403.8	628.0	660.3	529.0
Employees	4.0%	446	501	497	498	521

PEBBLEBROOK HOTEL TRUST
NYS: PEB

4747 Bethesda Avenue, Suite 1100
Bethesda, MD 20814
Phone: 240 507-1300
Fax: –
Web: www.pebblebrookhotels.com

CEO: Jon E Bortz
CFO: Raymond D Martz
HR: –
FYE: December 31
Type: Public

Pebblebrook Hotel Trust is a self-managed real estate investment trust (REIT) acquires and manages upscale hotels in the US, targeting mostly full-service and select-service luxury properties that don't need major renovation in major US gateway cities. The REIT owns around 55 hotels with a total of about 13,245 rooms. Nearly 65% of its revenue comes from room fees, while the remainder comes from food and beverage services. Pebblebrook Hotel Trust is the brainchild of CEO Jon Bortz, who also founded LaSalle Hotel Properties.

	Annual Growth	12/19	12/20	12/21	12/22	12/23
Sales ($mil.)	(3.1%)	1,612.2	442.9	733.0	1,391.9	1,419.9
Net income ($ mil.)	–	115.4	(391.7)	(184.9)	(87.2)	(78.0)
Market value ($ mil.)	(12.1%)	3,222.3	2,259.6	2,688.7	1,609.4	1,920.7
Employees	0.9%	58	53	56	58	60

PECO ENERGY COMPANY

2301 MARKET ST
PHILADELPHIA, PA 191031380
Phone: 215 841-4000
Fax: –
Web: www.peco.com

CEO: Craig L Adams
CFO: Phillip S Barnett
HR: Mary Walker
FYE: December 31
Type: Private

PECO Energy propels energy currents in the five-county Philadelphia region. The utility, a subsidiary of Exelon, serves 1.6 million electricity customers and 494,000 natural gas customers. PECO Energy owns 29,000 circuit miles of regulated power transmission and distribution lines; its transmission assets are controlled by regional operator PJM Interconnection. The company also has more than 6,730 miles of underground gas mains. Pennsylvania's largest utility, the company operates some 500 electric substations and almost 30 natural gas gate stations. About 90% of PECO Energy's customers are residential, with the remainder being commercial and industrial.

PEDERNALES ELECTRIC COOPERATIVE, INC.

201 S AVENUE F
JOHNSON CITY, TX 786362072
Phone: 830 868-7155
Fax: –
Web: www.pec.coop

CEO: John Hewa
CFO: –
HR: –
FYE: December 31
Type: Private

Created by Texas ranchers and business owners, Pedernales Electric Cooperative provides electricity services in the Texas Hill Country. The company, the largest electric cooperative in the US, purchases its electricity from wholesale providers, primarily the Lower Colorado River Authority (LCRA), and transmits and distributes it to about 209,350 cooperative members (or more than 247,810 individual customer meters). Pedernales Electric Cooperative operates more than 17,450 miles of power line and maintains 290,000 wooden utility poles in its service area.

	Annual Growth	12/07	12/08	12/09	12/10	12/11
Sales ($mil.)	0.9%	–	–	578.7	550.8	589.1
Net income ($ mil.)	(66.5%)	–	–	57.6	53.7	6.5
Market value ($ mil.)	–	–	–	–	–	–
Employees	–	–	–	–	–	741

PEDEVCO CORP
ASE: PED

575 N. Dairy Ashford, Suite 210
Houston, TX 77079
Phone: 713 221-1768
Fax: –
Web: www.pedevco.com

CEO: Simon Kukes
CFO: –
HR: –
FYE: December 31
Type: Public

Blast Energy Services (formerly Verdisys) is having a blast helping its customers keep pumping out oil from mature fields. Using specially fabricated mobile drilling rigs, the company provides a range of oil and gas services, including lateral drilling and well production enhancement. The company, which emerged from Chapter 11 bankruptcy protection in 2008, acquired $1.2 million of oil and gas properties in Matagorda County, Texas, in 2010, as a way to expand its revenue base and to fund the development of its proprietary Applied Fluid Jetting drilling activity. To raise cash, in 2011 it sold its oilfield satellite telecommunications services unit to GlobaLogix.

	Annual Growth	12/19	12/20	12/21	12/22	12/23
Sales ($mil.)	24.1%	13.0	8.1	15.9	30.0	30.8
Net income ($ mil.)	–	(11.1)	(32.7)	(1.3)	2.8	0.3
Market value ($ mil.)	(17.5%)	144.8	131.7	92.5	96.0	67.2
Employees	(1.6%)	16	15	14	14	15

PEDIATRIX MEDICAL GROUP INC
NYS: MD

1301 Concord Terrace
Sunrise, FL 33323
Phone: 954 384-0175
Fax: –
Web: www.pediatrix.com

CEO: James D Swift
CFO: C M Richards
HR: –
FYE: December 31
Type: Public

Pediatrix Medical Group (formerly Mednax) is a leading provider of physician services including newborn, maternal-fetal, pediatric cardiology, and other pediatric subspecialty care in approximately 35 states. Its national network is comprised of approximately 2,600 affiliated physicians, including approximately 1,330 physicians who provide neonatal clinical care, primarily within hospital-based neonatal intensive care units (NICUs), to babies born prematurely or with medical complications. In addition, Pediatrix provides multiple administrative services to support the practice of medicine by its affiliated physicians including unit management, staffing and scheduling, recruiting, billing, risk, management, and compliance.

	Annual Growth	12/19	12/20	12/21	12/22	12/23
Sales ($mil.)	(13.2%)	3,513.5	1,734.0	1,911.2	1,972.0	1,994.6
Net income ($ mil.)	–	(1,497.7)	(796.5)	131.0	66.3	(60.4)
Market value ($ mil.)	(23.9%)	2,334.9	2,061.8	2,286.1	1,248.5	781.4
Employees	(25.6%)	9,480	7,900	7,400	7,850	2,900

PEEBLES INC.

One Peebles Street
South Hill, VA 23970-5001
Phone: 434 447-5200
Fax: –
Web: –

CEO: Michael L Glazer
CFO: Jason T Curtis
HR: Denise V Conine
FYE: February 2
Type: Public

Burkes Outlets Stores is a privately-held company, rich in tradition, owned by the founding family and its employees. It operates more than 650 retail stores. Customers can find brand name, apparel, and accessories for the entire family at up to 70% off other stores prices daily. Most stores carry shoes, home furnishings, gifts, and toys. Its stores are designed to serve customers of all ages and income levels. The company was founded in 1915. Burkes Outlet and Bealls Outlet will rebrand under the Bealls name by the end of 2023.

	Annual Growth	01/98	01/99	01/00*	02/01	02/02
Sales ($mil.)	9.1%	217.7	265.2	300.8	306.6	308.3
Net income ($ mil.)	24.4%	6.1	6.1	7.0	10.1	14.5
Market value ($ mil.)	–	–	–	–	–	–
Employees	5.8%	2,904	3,780	3,664	3,506	3,640

*Fiscal year change

PEERLESS SYSTEMS CORPORATION

1055 WASHINGTON BLVD FL 8
STAMFORD, CT 069012251
Phone: 203 350-0040
Fax: –
Web: www.peerless.com

CEO: Anthony Bonid
CFO: –
HR: –
FYE: January 31
Type: Private

Peerless Systems lets you peer at digitally produced images more easily. Peerless proffers software-based imaging systems embedded in printers, copiers, scanners, and other digital devices. Its products include designs for application-specific integrated circuits (ASICs), printer drivers, and network interfaces that let digital document companies like Adobe and Ricoh incorporate networking support or multifunction features into equipment. Peerless also offers related engineering services. Top customers include Konica Minolta, Kyocera Mita, Novell, and Seiko Epson, which together account for more than three-quarters of sales. About 90% of the company's revenues comes from customers in Japan.

PEGASYSTEMS INC

One Main Street
Cambridge, MA 02142
Phone: 617 374-9600
Fax: –
Web: www.pega.com

NMS: PEGA
CEO: Alan Trefler
CFO: Kenneth Stillwell
HR: –
FYE: December 31
Type: Public

Pegasystems develops, markets, licenses, hosts, and supports a range of enterprise software applications that help organizations build agility into their business so they can adapt to change. Its powerful low-code platform for workflow automation and artificial intelligence-powered decisioning enables the world's leading brands and government agencies to hyper-personalize customer experiences, streamline customer service, and automate mission-critical business processes and workflows. With Pega, its clients can leverage its intelligent technology and scalable architecture to accelerate their digital transformation. In addition, its client success teams, world-class partners, and clients leverage its Pega Express methodology to design and deploy mission-critical applications quickly and collaboratively. Customers in the US account for about 55% of the company's revenue.

	Annual Growth	12/19	12/20	12/21	12/22	12/23
Sales ($mil.)	12.0%	911.4	1,017.5	1,211.7	1,317.8	1,432.6
Net income ($ mil.)	–	(90.4)	(61.4)	(63.0)	(345.6)	67.8
Market value ($ mil.)	(11.5%)	6,677.9	11,173	9,375.0	2,870.7	4,096.4
Employees	–	5,155	5,576	6,133	6,145	–

PEIRCE COLLEGE

1608 WALNUT ST
PHILADELPHIA, PA 191035443
Phone: 215 545-6400
Fax: –
Web: www.peirce.edu

CEO: Katy Theroux
CFO: –
HR: –
FYE: June 30
Type: Private

Peirce College provides postsecondary career-oriented education to working adult learners. The school offers certificates of proficiency and associate and bachelor degrees in business administration, information technology, and paralegal studies. In addition to traditional classroom-based instruction, Peirce allows students to earn some degrees online or in accelerated night and weekend programs. Its Corporate College offers courses to employees at work or online. Many corporations such as Boeing, UPS, and CIGNA partner with Peirce to offer courses to workers. Thomas Peirce founded the Union Business College in 1865 where veterans could get workplace skills. It took its current name in 1910.

	Annual Growth	06/15	06/16	06/17	06/20	06/22
Sales ($mil.)	(3.4%)	–	27.1	25.5	23.1	22.1
Net income ($ mil.)	–	–	(1.0)	(0.8)	(0.8)	(0.3)
Market value ($ mil.)	–	–	–	–	–	–
Employees	–	–	–	–	–	143

PEIRCE ENTERPRISES, INC.

516 TOWNSHIP LINE RD
BLUE BELL, PA 194222197
Phone: 215 879-7235
Fax: –
Web: www.peirce.com

CEO: Brian G Peirce
CFO: Robert Subranni
HR: Dan Fogarty
FYE: December 31
Type: Private

Peirce-Phelps helps to keep its customers either hot or cold. Through more than 15 locations mostly in Pennsylvania, but also three other eastern states, Peirce-Phelps distributes residential and commercial heating and air-conditioning equipment and supplies. The company primarily caters to HVAC and appliance dealers. It also provides integrated and efficient energy savings through its Building Automation and Energy Management Systems division and offers HVAC training. The company was founded in 1926 by a trio of MIT-trained engineers as a distributor of crystal radio sets. In 2019 Peirce-Phelps agreed to be acquired by HVAC company Watsco.

PELOTON INTERACTIVE INC

441 Ninth Avenue, Sixth Floor
New York, NY 10001
Phone: 929 567-0006
Fax: –
Web: www.onepeloton.com

NMS: PTON
CEO: Barry McCarthy
CFO: Elizabeth F Coddington
HR: –
FYE: June 30
Type: Public

Peloton Interactive is the largest interactive fitness platform in the world with a loyal community of more than 6.5 million members, which it defines as any individual who has a Peloton account through a paid Connected Fitness Subscription or a paid Peloton App membership. The company pioneered connected, technology-enabled fitness, and the streaming of immersive, instructor-led boutique classes to its members. With tens-of-thousands of classes available across 16 fitness modalities, members can access Peloton content via its hardware or the Peloton App, on their phone, tablet, or TV, allowing them to workout when, where, and how they want. Its world-class instructors teach classes across a variety of fitness and wellness disciplines, including indoor cycling, indoor/outdoor running and walking, boot camp, yoga, strength training, stretching, and meditation.

	Annual Growth	06/19	06/20	06/21	06/22	06/23
Sales ($mil.)	32.3%	915.0	1,825.9	4,021.8	3,582.1	2,800.2
Net income ($ mil.)	–	(195.6)	(71.6)	(189.0)	(2,827.7)	(1,261.7)
Market value ($ mil.)	–	–	20,610	44,246	3,275.1	2,743.5
Employees	18.8%	1,800	3,281	6,743	6,195	3,584

PENBAY TECHNOLOGY GROUP LLC

302 WINDING WAY
UNION HALL, VA 241764085
Phone: 540 912-0215
Fax: –
Web: www.penbaytechnologygroup.com

CEO: Robert Santmyer
CFO: –
HR: Lisa Shorey
FYE: December 31
Type: Private

Penobscot Bay Media puts the "multi" in multimedia. The company produces all kinds of media projects, from film and TV to interactive Web sites and distance learning courses. It also offers application development services and specializes in the design of Geographic Information Systems (GIS) applications using ESRI products. Clients include BAE Systems, AstraZeneca, and the US Air Force. Penobscot Bay Media was formed in 1999 after the merger of PBM Associates, Post Office Editorial, and St. George Consulting Group.

PENDLETON WOOLEN MILLS, INC.

220 NW BROADWAY
PORTLAND, OR 972093509
Phone: 503 226-4801
Fax: –
Web: www.pendleton-usa.com

CEO: Mark Korros
CFO: D M Simmonds
HR: –
FYE: December 31
Type: Private

It doesn't raise the sheep, but Pendleton Woolen Mills controls every other step of the production of its men's and women's apparel, blankets, pillows, luggage, furniture, and other items. It buys raw wool; makes fabric and garments at its Nebraska, Oregon, and Washington factories; ships finished goods; and even sells the products in about 70 company-owned Pendleton shops. Founded in 1909 as a blanket maker for Native Americans, it also sells its products through department stores, including Dillard's and Macy's, and in specialty shops, as well as through catalogs and online. Pendleton's goods are sold in the US, Europe, Japan, and Canada. The sixth generation of the Bishop family owns and operates the firm.

PENDRELL CORP

NBB: PCOA

2300 Carillon Point
Kirkland, WA 98033
Phone: 425 278-7100
Fax: –
Web: www.pendrell.com

CEO: Lee E Mikles
CFO: Steven A Ednie
HR: –
FYE: December 31
Type: Public

Pendrell is an asset management company of the intellectual property (IP) kind. It gathers up patents (it holds about 1,200) and licenses them to technology companies thus receiving a cut when a technology is used. Its patent holdings center on technologies for tablets, smart phones, and other consumer electronics devices. Besides licensing IP, Pendrell also develops technologies though none generate revenue yet. Companies that license IP from Pendrell include Casio, Hitachi, LG Electronics, Microsoft, Nokia, Technicolor, and Xerox.

	Annual Growth	12/13	12/14	12/15	12/16	12/17
Sales ($mil.)	34.4%	13.1	42.5	43.5	59.0	42.8
Net income ($ mil.)	–	(55.1)	(51.0)	(109.7)	17.8	19.1
Market value ($ mil.)	311.3%	0.0	0.0	0.0	0.0	0.6
Employees	(36.3%)	73	57	16	14	12

PENGUIN COMPUTING, INC.

45800 NORTHPORT LOOP W
FREMONT, CA 945386413
Phone: 415 954-2800
Fax: –
Web: www.penguinsolutions.com

CEO: –
CFO: –
HR: –
FYE: December 31
Type: Private

Penguin Computing hopes to save the world from the cold clutches of monopolistic operating systems. The company builds and customizes Linux-based workstations, servers, and clustered computing systems. It also offers third-party storage and peripheral equipment. The company's Scyld Software subsidiary, which it acquired in 2003, develops clustered computing software, including its Scyld Beowulf operating system. Penguin's customers have included Brookhaven National Laboratory, CACI International, Caterpillar, Duke University, Genentech, the National Institutes of Health, Northrop Grumman, and Stanford University. Penguin was founded in 1998.

	Annual Growth	12/01	12/02	12/03	12/04	12/17
Sales ($mil.)	–	–	(847.1)	17.9	21.9	166.5
Net income ($ mil.)	104.9%	–	0.0	(0.5)	(2.5)	5.7
Market value ($ mil.)	–	–	–	–	–	–
Employees	–	–	–	–	–	175

PENN ENTERTAINMENT INC

NMS: PENN

825 Berkshire Blvd., Suite 200
Wyomissing, PA 19610
Phone: 610 373-2400
Fax: 610 376-2842
Web: www.pngaming.com

CEO: Jay A Snowden
CFO: Felicia Hendrix
HR: Dajia Conner
FYE: December 31
Type: Public

PENN Entertainment, formerly Penn National Gaming, is a leading regional gaming company that operates or has ownership interests in around 45 casinos, racing facilities, and video gaming terminals across the US. Its holdings feature almost 44,000 gaming machines, about 1,190 table games, and about 7,320 hotel rooms. Many of its properties operate under the Hollywood and Argosy brands. Other facilities include the Tropicana on the Las Vegas Strip; racetracks (horseracing and greyhounds) in New Jersey, and Texas; and dockside casinos mostly in the Midwest and the South. The company also offers online gaming through Penn Interactive Ventures.

	Annual Growth	12/19	12/20	12/21	12/22	12/23
Sales ($mil.)	4.7%	5,301.4	3,578.7	5,905.0	6,401.7	6,362.9
Net income ($ mil.)	–	43.9	(669.5)	420.8	222.1	(490.0)
Market value ($ mil.)	0.4%	3,873.7	13,090	7,858.0	4,501.3	3,943.4
Employees	(4.7%)	28,300	18,321	21,973	21,875	23,333

PENN MUTUAL LIFE INSURANCE CO.

The Penn Mutual Life Insurance Company
Philadelphia, PA 19172
Phone: 215 956-8808
Fax: –
Web: www.pennmutual.com

CEO: Een C McDonnell
CFO: Susan T Deakins
HR: Antonio Juarez
FYE: December 31
Type: Public

Founded in 1847, Penn Mutual Life Insurance offers life insurance, annuities, and investment products and services. Its core product line consists of life insurance every which way, including life insurance products (term life, and permanent life) and a variety of fixed, variable, and immediate annuities. The company supports its financial professionals with retirement and investment services through its subsidiaries to build customized solutions for individuals, families and businesses. Two of its financial services subsidiaries -- broker/dealers Hornor, Townsend & Kent and Janney Montgomery Scott -- also distribute Penn Mutual products.

	Annual Growth	12/97	12/98	12/99	12/00	12/01
Assets ($mil.)	0.5%	7,075.5	7,328.3	7,580.4	7,441.8	7,208.9
Net income ($ mil.)	(1.1%)	63.6	83.7	76.7	122.8	60.9
Market value ($ mil.)	–	–	–	–	–	–
Employees	–	–	–	–	–	–

PENN STATE HEALTH HOLY SPIRIT MEDICAL CENTER

503 N 21ST ST
CAMP HILL, PA 170112204
Phone: 717 763-2100
Fax: –
Web: –

CEO: Steve Massini
CFO: –
HR: –
FYE: June 30
Type: Private

Holy Spirit Health tends to the health of the incarnate. The Holy Spirit Health System (HSHS) provides cardiology, women's health care, pediatric care, and other acute and emergency medical services to the residents of greater Harrisburg in south-central Pennsylvania. The flagship Holy Spirit Hospital has some 310 beds as well as a level III neonatal intensive care unit. The hospital also operates an adjoining cardiac treatment facility, and it has a network of affiliated family practice, urgent care, surgical, and specialty health clinics. HSHS was established in 1963 and is an affiliate of Geisinger Health System.

	Annual Growth	06/07	06/08	06/09	06/10	06/20
Sales ($mil.)	(12.6%)	–	1,650.1	5.6	271.7	326.2
Net income ($ mil.)	–	–	–	–	11.4	30.1
Market value ($ mil.)	–	–	–	–	–	–
Employees	–	–	–	–	–	2,698

PENNICHUCK CORPORATION

25 MANCHESTER ST
MERRIMACK, NH 030544821
Phone: 603 882-5191
Fax: –
Web: www.pennichuck.com

CEO: Duane C Montopoli
CFO: Thomas C Leonard
HR: –
FYE: December 31
Type: Private

How much water would Pennichuck pump if Pennichuck could pump water? Well, Pennichuck does pump water, to about 33,200 customers (about 120,000 people) in New Hampshire and Massachusetts. Its water utility subsidiaries -- Pennichuck Water Works, Pennichuck East Utility, and Pittsfield Aqueduct -- distribute water in more than 30 communities, including the city of Nashua. Most of the company's water comes from a system of ponds. Nonregulated subsidiary The Southwood Corporation develops and sells real estate, and Pennichuck Water Service offers contract maintenance, testing, and billing services. In 2012 the company was acquired by the City of Nashua.

	Annual Growth	12/07	12/08	12/09	12/15	12/16
Sales ($mil.)	(31.9%)	–	923.8	32.8	–	42.7
Net income ($ mil.)	–	–	0.0	2.4	–	(1.2)
Market value ($ mil.)	–	–	–	–	–	–
Employees	–	–	–	–	–	101

PENNONI ASSOCIATES INC.

1900 MARKET ST STE 300
PHILADELPHIA, PA 191033511
Phone: 215 222-3000
Fax: –
Web: www.pennoni.com

CEO: C R Pennoni
CFO: –
HR: –
FYE: December 31
Type: Private

Design consulting and engineering firm Pennoni Associates specializes in the creation of civil infrastructure projects. The company offers construction services, planning, surveys, transportation planning, lab testing, environmental engineering, landscape architecture, site design and other services. Pennoni serves East Coast clients including government entities and private companies. Affiliate Pennoni Engineering and Surveying of New York specializes in heating, ventilation, and air conditioning systems, electrical, plumbing, and fire protection engineering. The employee-owned company was established by chairman Celestino "Chuck" Pennoni in 1966.

	Annual Growth	12/17	12/18	12/20	12/21	12/22
Sales ($mil.)	4.1%	–	191.8	197.1	152.2	225.0
Net income ($ mil.)	12.5%	–	2.4	5.8	3.5	3.8
Market value ($ mil.)	–	–	–	–	–	–
Employees	–	–	–	–	–	900

PENNS WOODS BANCORP, INC. (JERSEY SHORE, PA)   NMS: PWOD

300 Market Street, P.O. Box 967
Williamsport, PA 17703-0967
Phone: 570 322-1111
Fax: –
Web: www.pwod.com

CEO: Richard A Grafmyre
CFO: Brian L Knepp
HR: Kristina Reis
FYE: December 31
Type: Public

Penns Woods Bancorp (PWB) is the holding company for Jersey Shore State Bank (named for the Pennsylvania town, not the coastal vacation spot), which serves north central Pennsylvania through about a dozen branches. The bank accepts deposits from individuals and local businesses, offering checking and savings accounts, money market and NOW accounts, and CDs. Residential real estate loans and commercial mortgages make up the majority of the bank's loan portfolio. The bank's lending activities are rounded out by agricultural, commercial, and consumer loans. PWB also owns Luzerne Bank, which operates eight branch offices providing financial services in Pennsylvania.

	Annual Growth	12/19	12/20	12/21	12/22	12/23
Assets ($mil.)	7.3%	1,665.3	1,834.6	1,940.8	2,000.1	2,204.8
Net income ($ mil.)	1.5%	15.7	15.2	16.0	17.4	16.6
Market value ($ mil.)	(10.8%)	267.0	195.3	177.6	199.9	169.0
Employees	–	–	334	256	247	302

PENNSYLVANIA - AMERICAN WATER COMPANY

852 WESLEY DR
MECHANICSBURG, PA 170554436
Phone: 800 565-7292
Fax: –
Web: www.amwater.com

CEO: –
CFO: –
HR: –
FYE: December 31
Type: Private

Pennsylvania-American Water distributes water and provides wastewater services to a population of more than 2 million people in some 390 communities across Pennsylvania. The company serves 635,000 water customers and 17,500 wastewater customers. It operates about 35 water treatment plants, six wastewater facilities, and 9,800 miles of pipeline. Pennsylvania-American Water's service territory covers some three dozen Pennsylvania counties. The utility, the largest regulated water and wastewater service provider in Pennsylvania, is a subsidiary of New Jersey-based American Water Works.

	Annual Growth	12/12	12/13*	03/14*	06/14*	12/17
Sales ($mil.)	3.7%	–	571.2	584.0	589.8	661.1
Net income ($ mil.)	7.1%	–	122.1	128.2	127.8	160.7
Market value ($ mil.)	–	–	–	–	–	–
Employees	–	–	–	–	–	1,007

*Fiscal year change

PENNSYLVANIA ELECTRIC CO.

c/o FirstEnergy Corp., 76 South Main Street
Akron, OH 44308
Phone: 800 736-3402
Fax: –
Web: www.firstenergycorp.com/content/customer/penelec.htm

CEO: –
CFO: Mark T Clark
HR: –
FYE: December 31
Type: Public

Pennsylvania Electric (Penelec) has elected to provide power to the people of the Keystone State. The company distributes power to a population of 1.6 million in a 17,600-square-mile portion of northern, western, and south-central Pennsylvania. The utility operates more than 20,170 miles of distribution and more than 2,700 transmission lines. The Waverly Electric Light & Power Company, a subsidiary of Penelec, provides electric services to a population of about 8,400 in Waverly, New York. Penelec is an operating subsidiary of regional utility power player FirstEnergy.

	Annual Growth	12/07	12/08	12/09	12/10	12/11
Sales ($mil.)	(6.3%)	1,402.0	1,513.6	1,448.9	1,539.9	1,081.2
Net income ($ mil.)	(9.2%)	92.9	88.2	65.4	59.5	63.1
Market value ($ mil.)	–	–	–	–	–	–
Employees	(1.8%)	964	994	902	899	896

PENNSYLVANIA HIGHER EDUCATION ASSISTANCE AGENCY

1200 N 7TH ST
HARRISBURG, PA 171021419
Phone: 717 720-2700
Fax: –
Web: www.pheaa.org

CEO: James L Preston
CFO: –
HR: Sarah Schultz
FYE: June 30
Type: Private

PHEAA is a national provider of student financial aid services, serving millions of students and thousands of schools through its loan guaranty, loan servicing, financial aid processing, outreach, and other student aid programs. PHEAA conducts its student loan servicing operations nationally as FedLoan Servicing and American Education Services (AES). PHEAA operates its digital technology division as Avereo. PHEAA's earnings are used to support its public service mission and to pay its operating costs, including administration of the PA State Grant and other state-funded student aid programs. Created in 1963 by the Pennsylvania General Assembly, the Pennsylvania Higher Education Assistance Agency (PHEAA) has evolved into one of the nation's leading student aid organizations.

	Annual Growth	03/09	03/10	03/11	03/12*	06/13
Sales ($mil.)	53.8%	–	–	–	436.4	671.2
Net income ($ mil.)	127.6%	–	–	–	68.5	155.8
Market value ($ mil.)	–	–	–	–	–	–
Employees	–	–	–	–	–	2,700

*Fiscal year change

PENNSYLVANIA HOUSING FINANCE AGENCY

211 N FRONT ST
HARRISBURG, PA 171011406
Phone: 717 780-3800
Fax: –
Web: www.phfa.org

CEO: –
CFO: –
HR: Jodi Hall
FYE: June 30
Type: Private

Pennsylvania Housing Finance Agency (PHFA) helps residents of the Keystone State obtain keys to their dream homes. The government-owned agency provides financing for low-income homebuyers, including the elderly and disabled, and participates in rental housing development initiatives. It generates funding from state and federal grants, interest earned on investments and loans, and the sale of its own securities to private investors. The agency is run by a board which includes Pennsylvania's secretary of banking, secretary of community and economic development, secretary of public welfare, and the state treasurer. The PHFA has funded more than 130,000 houses and 54,000 apartment units since its founding in 1972.

	Annual Growth	06/18	06/19	06/20	06/21	06/22
Assets ($mil.)	8.3%	–	4,367.0	4,542.5	4,667.0	5,548.6
Net income ($ mil.)	–	–	22.2	14.8	9.9	(41.5)
Market value ($ mil.)	–	–	–	–	–	–
Employees	–	–	–	–	–	250

PENNSYLVANIA POWER CO.

c/o FirstEnergy Corp., 76 South Main St.
Akron, OH 44308
Phone: 800 736-3402
Fax: –
Web: –

CEO: Anthony J Alexander
CFO: –
HR: –
FYE: December 31
Type: Public

Although this Penn is mighty indeed, powerful is a more apt description. Organized in 1930, Pennsylvania Power (Penn Power), serves 164,000 customers in a 1,100 square mile region of western Pennsylvania. The company's 1,200 MW of power is primarily generated at its fossil-fueled (Bruce Mansfield and W.H. Sammis) and nuclear (Beaver Valley and Perry) power plants. Penn Power maintains nearly 13,540 miles of distribution lines. The company is owned by Ohio Edison Company (which itself is a wholly-owned subsidiary of utility holding company FirstEnergy).

	Annual Growth	12/01	12/02	12/03	12/04	12/05
Sales ($mil.)	2.1%	498.4	506.4	526.9	549.1	540.6
Net income ($ mil.)	12.6%	41.0	47.7	48.5	59.1	65.9
Market value ($ mil.)	–	–	–	–	–	–
Employees	(5.9%)	256	201	201	200	201

PENNSYLVANIA REAL ESTATE INVESTMENT TRUST   NBB: PRET N

One Commerce Square, 2005 Market Street, Suite 1000
Philadelphia, PA 19103
Phone: 215 875-0700
Fax: –
Web: www.preit.com

CEO: –
CFO: Robert F McCadden
HR: –
FYE: December 31
Type: Public

Pennsylvania Real Estate Investment Trust (PREIT) owns, manages, leases, acquires, and renovates shopping malls. It owns more than two dozens of retail properties, including some 20 shopping malls and four other retail properties, as well as several retail properties under development, it has a total of some 19.6 million of sq. ft. and are located in eight states. The largest core mall in its retail portfolio is 1.4 million square feet and contains 175 stores, and the smallest core mall is 0.5 million square feet and contains some 80 stores. The other properties in its retail portfolio range from 377,000 to 778,000 square feet. It counts retailers such as Foot Locker, L Brands, Signet Jewelers, Dick's Sporting Goods, American Eagle Outfitter and Express, among its largest tenants. Founded in 1960, PREIT was one of the first publicly traded REITs in the US.

	Annual Growth	12/18	12/19	12/20	12/21	12/22
Sales ($mil.)	(4.9%)	362.4	336.8	261.8	296.4	296.0
Net income ($ mil.)	–	(110.3)	(10.9)	(259.5)	(132.7)	(148.3)
Market value ($ mil.)	(33.4%)	31.8	28.5	5.4	5.5	6.3
Employees	(13.3%)	274	233	175	158	155

PENNSYLVANIA TURNPIKE COMMISSION

700 S EISENHOWER BLVD
MIDDLETOWN, PA 170575529
Phone: 717 939-9551
Fax: –
Web: www.paturnpike.com

CEO: Mark P Compton
CFO: Nikolaus Grieshaber
HR: Caitlyn Bassett
FYE: May 31
Type: Private

Whether you're headed to Valley Forge or Gettysburg or to Philadelphia or Pittsburgh, a driving trip through Pennsylvania might mean spending time on some of the 545-plus miles of highway operated by the Pennsylvania Turnpike Commission. The toll road's main section runs from the Delaware River to the Pennsylvania-Ohio border, where it connects with the Ohio Turnpike. The Pennsylvania Turnpike also includes northeastern and western extensions. The system includes about 60 toll collection facilities and some 15 service plazas. Opened in 1940, it's known as America's First Superhighway. The Pennsylvania Turnpike Commission consists of five gubernatorial appointees and the state secretary of transportation.

	Annual Growth	05/18	05/19	05/20	05/21	05/22
Sales ($mil.)	22.4%	–	–	–	1,231.5	1,507.5
Net income ($ mil.)	–	–	–	–	(583.8)	(462.8)
Market value ($ mil.)	–	–	–	–	–	–
Employees	–	–	–	–	–	2,200

PENNYMAC FINANCIAL SERVICES INC (NEW)   NYS: PFSI

3043 Townsgate Road
Westlake Village, CA 91361
Phone: 818 224-7442
Fax: –
Web: www.pennymacfinancial.com

CEO: David A Spector
CFO: Daniel S Perotti
HR: –
FYE: December 31
Type: Public

Pennymac Financial Services, Inc. is a specialty financial services firm with a comprehensive mortgage platform and integrated business primarily focused on the production and servicing of US residential mortgage loans (activities which mortgage banking) and the management of investments related to the US mortgage market. It operates through its subsidiaries PennyMac Loan Services, LLC (PLS), and PNMAC Capital Management, LLC (PCM) and conducts its business in three segments: production, servicing (together, production and servicing comprise our mortgage banking activities) and investment management. It was founded in 2008 by members of its executive leadership team and strategic investors, including HC Partners.

	Annual Growth	12/19	12/20	12/21	12/22	12/23
Assets ($mil.)	16.6%	10,204	31,598	18,777	16,823	18,845
Net income ($ mil.)	(22.1%)	393.0	1,646.9	1,003.5	475.5	144.7
Market value ($ mil.)	26.9%	1,708.1	3,292.7	3,501.5	2,843.1	4,434.3
Employees	(1.8%)	4,215	6,000	6,900	4,000	3,914

PENNYMAC MORTGAGE INVESTMENT TRUST   NYS: PMT

3043 Townsgate Road
Westlake Village, CA 91361
Phone: 818 224-7442
Fax: –
Web: www.pennymacmortgageinvestmenttrust.com

CEO: David A Spector
CFO: Anne D McCallion
HR: –
FYE: December 31
Type: Public

PennyMac Mortgage Investment Trust trusts in its ability to acquire distressed US residential mortgage loans. The company seeks to acquire primarily troubled home mortgage loans and mortgage-backed securities, mortgage servicing right and credit risk transfer including CRT agreements and CRT securities. PennyMac is managed by investment adviser PNMAC Capital Management and offers primary and special loan servicing through PennyMac Loan Services. The company is held by Private National Mortgage Acceptance Company (PNMAC).

	Annual Growth	12/19	12/20	12/21	12/22	12/23
Sales ($mil.)	10.3%	786.3	740.1	725.0	714.2	1,165.0
Net income ($ mil.)	(3.1%)	226.4	52.4	56.9	(73.3)	199.7
Market value ($ mil.)	(9.5%)	1,930.8	1,523.7	1,501.2	1,073.3	1,295.0
Employees	62.7%	1	1	1	–	7

PENSKE AUTOMOTIVE GROUP INC — NYS: PAG

2555 Telegraph Road
Bloomfield Hills, MI 48302-0954
Phone: 248 648-2500
Fax: 248 648-2525
Web: www.penskeautomotive.com

CEO: Roger S Penske
CFO: Shelley Hulgrave
HR: Christina Gregory
FYE: December 31
Type: Public

Penske Automotive Group is a diversified international transportation services company that operates automotive and commercial truck dealerships principally in the US, the UK, Canada, Germany, Italy, and Japan and distributes commercial vehicles, diesel engines, gas engines, power systems, and related parts and services principally in Australia and New Zealand. The company has about 340 retail automotive franchises in the US and abroad. It sells more than 35 car brands, including BMW, Audi, Lexus, Mercedes-Benz, Land Rover, and Porsche, generating about 70% of sales. Penske also operates about 20 used vehicle dealerships in the US and the UK, which retail and wholesale used vehicles under a one price, "no-haggle" methodology. Additionally, Penske holds a nearly 30% stake in Penske Truck Leasing (PTL), known for commercial leasing and contract maintenance. The US accounts for approximately 60% of the company's total revenue.

	Annual Growth	12/19	12/20	12/21	12/22	12/23
Sales ($mil.)	6.2%	23,179	20,444	25,555	27,815	29,527
Net income ($ mil.)	24.7%	435.8	543.6	1,187.8	1,380.0	1,053.2
Market value ($ mil.)	33.7%	3,370.3	3,985.7	7,195.7	7,713.1	10,772
Employees	0.9%	27,000	23,000	25,000	26,500	28,000

PENUMBRA INC — NYS: PEN

One Penumbra Place
Alameda, CA 94502
Phone: 510 748-3200
Fax: -
Web: www.penumbrainc.com

CEO: Adam Elsesser
CFO: Maggie Yuen
HR: -
FYE: December 31
Type: Public

Penumbra is hoping that its early successes will foreshadow greater breakthroughs. The global interventional therapies firm designs, develops, makes and markets innovative medical devices for two major markets, neuro and peripheral vascular. The company's products address ischemic stroke and hemorrhagic stroke (blockage or rupture of blood vessels in the brain), and various peripheral vascular conditions that can be treated through thrombectomy and embolization procedures (the removal or treatment of blockages or ruptures of blood vessels). The company's products provide specialist physicians with a means to drive improved clinical outcomes through faster and safer procedures. Penumbra went public in 2015.

	Annual Growth	12/19	12/20	12/21	12/22	12/23
Sales ($mil.)	17.9%	547.4	560.4	747.6	847.1	1,058.5
Net income ($ mil.)	17.0%	48.5	(15.7)	5.3	(2.0)	91.0
Market value ($ mil.)	11.2%	6,354.2	6,769.3	11,114	8,605.1	9,730.0
Employees	11.7%	2,700	3,300	3,800	3,900	4,200

PEOPLE FOR THE ETHICAL TREATMENT OF ANIMALS, INC.

501 FRONT ST
NORFOLK, VA 235101009
Phone: 757 622-7382
Fax: -
Web: www.peta.org

CEO: -
CFO: -
HR: -
FYE: July 31
Type: Private

Talk about a watchdog! People for the Ethical Treatment of Animals (PETA) works to raise public awareness concerning animal rights and issues; its high-profile campaigns promote vegetarianism and veganism, cruelty-free products, and alternatives to animal experimentation. PETA's Domestic Animal Issues & Abuse Department investigates reports of cruelty towards animals; Caring Consumer 101 publishes lists of companies and charities that do and don't perform animal testing, as well as Animal Times and Grrr! (for kids) magazines. the international not-for-profit organization has some 2 million members and affiliates in Europe and Asia. PETA is funded primarily by member contributions.

	Annual Growth	07/15	07/16	07/19	07/20	07/22
Sales ($mil.)	1.5%	-	62.4	48.1	60.6	68.3
Net income ($ mil.)	-	-	16.3	(5.3)	5.9	(0.6)
Market value ($ mil.)	-	-	-	-	-	-
Employees	-	-	-	-	-	14

PEOPLES BANCORP INC (MARIETTA, OH) — NMS: PEBO

138 Putnam Street, P.O. Box 738
Marietta, OH 45750
Phone: 740 373-3155
Fax: -
Web: www.peoplesbancorp.com

CEO: Charles W Sulerzyski
CFO: John Rogers
HR: -
FYE: December 31
Type: Public

Peoples Bancorp Inc. is a financial holding company that offers a full range of financial services and products primarily offered through its some 130 financial service offices and ATMs, including about 115 full-service branches in Ohio, West Virginia, Kentucky, Virginia, Washington, DC, and Maryland, as well as through online resources that are web-based and mobile-based. Peoples' insurance, premium financing and equipment leasing services are offered nationwide. Brokerage services are offered exclusively through an unaffiliated registered broker-dealer located at Peoples Bank's offices. Indirect consumer lending activities are provided through approved dealerships. Peoples Bank's credit card and merchant processing services are provided through joint marketing arrangements with third parties.

	Annual Growth	12/19	12/20	12/21	12/22	12/23
Assets ($mil.)	20.4%	4,354.2	4,760.8	7,063.5	7,207.3	9,157.4
Net income ($ mil.)	20.5%	53.7	34.8	47.6	101.3	113.4
Market value ($ mil.)	(0.7%)	1,220.9	954.2	1,120.5	995.1	1,189.2
Employees	13.2%	900	894	1,188	1,267	1,478

PEOPLES BANCORP OF NORTH CAROLINA INC — NMS: PEBK

518 West C. Street
Newton, NC 28658
Phone: 828 464-5620
Fax: -
Web: www.peoplesbanknc.com

CEO: Lance A Sellers
CFO: Jeffrey Hooper
HR: -
FYE: December 31
Type: Public

Peoples Bancorp of North Carolina owns Peoples Bank, which serves the Catawba Valley region of North Carolina through about 20 locations. It also runs Banco de la Gente ("Peoples Bank" in Spanish), which serves the area's Latino community. The banks offer standard services such as checking and savings accounts; CDs; mortgage, construction, development, and other real estate loans (combined, some 90% of its loan portfolio); and business and consumer loans. Peoples Bank has two subsidiaries: Peoples Investment Services, which provides financial planning and investment products through an agreement with Raymond James Financial, and Real Estate Advisory Services, a real estate brokerage and appraisal services firm.

	Annual Growth	12/19	12/20	12/21	12/22	12/23
Assets ($mil.)	9.1%	1,154.9	1,414.9	1,624.2	1,620.9	1,635.9
Net income ($ mil.)	2.5%	14.1	11.4	15.1	16.1	15.5
Market value ($ mil.)	(1.5%)	181.8	127.4	152.7	180.2	171.2
Employees	(3.5%)	337	317	311	300	292

PEOPLES BANCORP, INC. (MD) — NBB: PEBC

138 Putnam Street,, P.O. Box 738,
Marietta, OH 45750
Phone: 740 373-3155
Fax: 410 778-2089
Web: www.pbkc.com

CEO: -
CFO: -
HR: -
FYE: December 31
Type: Public

People who need Peoples Bancorp may or may not be the luckiest people, but they are Peoples Bancorp customers. The firm is the holding company for Peoples Bank of Kent County, which operates more than five branches in eastern Maryland. Serving local consumers and businesses, the bank provides standard deposit products such as checking and savings accounts, money market accounts, CDs, and IRAs. Commercial real estate loans make up the largest portion of the company's lending portfolio, which also includes residential mortgages and business loans, as well as a lesser amount of construction and consumer loans. Peoples Bancorp also owns insurance agency Fleetwood, Athey, Macbeth & McCown.

	Annual Growth	12/17	12/18	12/19	12/20	12/21
Assets ($mil.)	8.4%	250.3	246.5	249.2	305.2	345.3
Net income ($ mil.)	(0.7%)	1.5	2.1	2.6	2.2	1.5
Market value ($ mil.)	1.8%	20.1	21.5	25.3	18.8	21.6
Employees	-	-	-	-	-	79

PEOPLES EDUCATIONAL HOLDINGS, INC.   NBB: PEDH

299 Market Street
Saddle Brook, NJ 07663
Phone: 201 712-0090
Fax: –
Web: www.peopleseducation.com; www.epathknowledge.com

CEO: Brian T Beckwith
CFO: Michael L Demarco
HR: –
FYE: May 31
Type: Public

Peoples Educational Holdings wants to help make sure your student measures up -- to state standards. Its subsidiary Peoples Education develops and publishes test preparation and supplementary educational materials for students in grades pre-K through 12, focusing on preparation materials for state-specific standardized tests. Its customized Measuring Up products are available in a dozen states. The company also publishes college preparation materials for high school students. Peoples Educational Holdings distributes its own print and electronic publications as well as titles from other publishers. Subjects covered include language arts, mathematics, science, and social studies.

	Annual Growth	05/08	05/09	05/10	05/11	05/12
Sales ($mil.)	(10.5%)	40.0	36.9	34.9	31.3	25.6
Net income ($ mil.)	–	(0.8)	(1.1)	0.3	(0.5)	(9.3)
Market value ($ mil.)	–	31.3	31.3	31.3	31.3	31.3
Employees	(6.2%)	110	82	91	91	85

PEOPLES FINANCIAL CORP (BILOXI, MS)   NBB: PFBX

Lameuse and Howard Avenues
Biloxi, MS 39533
Phone: 228 435-5511
Fax: –
Web: www.thepeoples.com

CEO: Chevis C Swetman
CFO: –
HR: –
FYE: December 31
Type: Public

Peoples Financial helps people with their money. The company owns The Peoples Bank, which operates more than 15 branches along the Mississippi Gulf Coast. The bank offers traditional checking and savings products. Real estate mortgages make up about nearly 65% of its loan portfolio, which also includes business, construction, and personal loans. Other offerings include fixed-rate mortgages, and asset management and trust services. Peoples caters to individuals and middle-market businesses in industries such as seafood, retail, hospitality, gaming, and construction. Chairman and CEO Chevis Swetman owns about 16% of the bank; his family has had an interest in the bank since its inception in 1896.

	Annual Growth	12/19	12/20	12/21	12/22	12/23
Assets ($mil.)	7.6%	594.7	668.0	818.8	861.6	797.7
Net income ($ mil.)	52.9%	1.7	(2.8)	8.6	8.9	9.2
Market value ($ mil.)	11.0%	51.0	62.9	77.6	67.6	77.4
Employees	(2.4%)	154	141	134	135	140

PEOPLES FINANCIAL SERVICES CORP   NMS: PFIS

150 North Washington Avenue
Scranton, PA 18503
Phone: 570 346-7741
Fax: –
Web: –

CEO: Craig W Best
CFO: –
HR: Amy Vieney
FYE: December 31
Type: Public

Power to the Peoples Financial Services. The firm is the holding company for Peoples Security Bank and Trust Company (formerly Peoples National Bank), which operates about 25 branches across northeastern Pennsylvania and neighboring Broome County in New York. Established in 1905, the bank offers standard retail products and services, including checking and savings accounts, CDs, and credit cards to local businesses and individuals. Commercial loans, including mortgages, construction loans, and operating loans, make up the greatest portion (40%) of the company's loan book, followed by residential mortgages (25%), and consumer loans. The company's Peoples Advisors subsidiary provides investment and brokerage services.

	Annual Growth	12/19	12/20	12/21	12/22	12/23
Assets ($mil.)	10.9%	2,475.3	2,883.8	3,369.5	3,553.5	3,742.3
Net income ($ mil.)	1.6%	25.7	29.4	43.5	38.1	27.4
Market value ($ mil.)	(0.8%)	354.5	258.8	371.0	365.0	342.9
Employees	(0.8%)	408	384	396	415	395

PEOPLES NATURAL GAS COMPANY LLC

375 N SHORE DR STE 200
PITTSBURGH, PA 152125866
Phone: 800 764-0111
Fax: –
Web: www.peoples-gas.com

CEO: Morgan O'Brien
CFO: –
HR: Robin Everett
FYE: December 31
Type: Private

Peoples Natural Gas, an Essential Utilities company, provides natural gas service to approximately 750,000 homes and businesses. The company serves approximately 750,000 commercial, industrial, and residential customers in counties throughout North Central West Virginia and Eastern Kentucky. The company has some 12,900 miles of natural gas distribution system, about 150 miles of transmission pipeline and 1,500 miles of gas gathering pipeline.

	Annual Growth	12/14	12/15	12/16	12/17	12/18
Sales ($mil.)	64.5%	–	–	–	0.0	0.0
Net income ($ mil.)	–	–	–	–	(0.1)	0.0
Market value ($ mil.)	–	–	–	–	–	–
Employees	–	–	–	–	–	1,300

PEPCO HOLDINGS LLC

701 9TH ST NW STE 1300
WASHINGTON, DC 200014572
Phone: 202 872-2000
Fax: –
Web: www.exeloncorp.com

CEO: David M Velazquez
CFO: Phillip S Barnett
HR: Samuel Jonjo
FYE: December 31
Type: Private

Pepco Holdings (PHI) delivers safe and reliable energy to customers through its Potomac Electric Power (Pepco), Delmarva Power & Light, and Atlantic City Electric utilities to about 2.4 million customers in the District of Columbia, and Maryland. As a member of the Exelon family of companies, PHI is part of the Mid-Atlantic region's leading electric and gas utility company. The company was first incorporated in 1896.

PEPPER CONSTRUCTION GROUP, LLC

643 N ORLEANS ST
CHICAGO, IL 606543690
Phone: 312 266-4700
Fax: –
Web: www.pepperconstruction.com

CEO: –
CFO: Chris Averill
HR: Julie Kellman
FYE: September 30
Type: Private

Pepper Construction Group spices up the construction business with a little of this and a pinch of that. The company provides general contracting and construction management services for commercial office, education, entertainment, health care, and institutional clients, as well as waterworks projects. (Health care projects account for about 50% of Pepper's revenue.) Its client list includes UBS, Northwestern University, University of Notre Dame, Texas Heart Institute, Loyola University Medical Center, and NASA. Pepper Construction Group has divisions in Illinois, Indiana, Ohio, and Texas. Stanley F. Pepper founded the company in Chicago in 1927. The group is owned by his family and employees of the firm.

	Annual Growth	09/17	09/18	09/19	09/20	09/21
Sales ($mil.)	3.1%	–	–	1,245.2	1,254.9	1,323.6
Net income ($ mil.)	(10.5%)	–	–	23.7	22.6	19.0
Market value ($ mil.)	–	–	–	–	–	–
Employees	–	–	–	–	–	1,100

PEPPERDINE UNIVERSITY

24255 PACIFIC COAST HWY DEPT 5000
MALIBU, CA 902630001
Phone: 310 506-4000
Fax: –
Web: www.pepperdine.edu

CEO: James A Gash
CFO: Paul Lasiter
HR: Lauren Cosentino
FYE: July 31
Type: Private

Pepperdine University is a Christian university committed to the highest standards of academic excellence and Christian values, where students are strengthened for lives of purpose, service, and leadership. The university boasts five colleges and schools: Seaver College of Letters, Arts, and Sciences; the Graziadio Business School; the Caruso School of Law; the School of Public Policy; and the Graduate School of Education and Psychology. Pepperdine, whose 830-acre main campus overlooks the Pacific Ocean in Malibu, California, has three additional campuses in Southern California, as well as international campuses in Argentina, Italy, Germany, Switzerland, Washington, DC, and the UK. The university was founded in 1937 by Christian businessman George Pepperdine, who also founded the Western Auto Supply Company.

	Annual Growth	07/17	07/18	07/19	07/20	07/22
Sales ($mil.)	6.3%	–	383.6	381.0	409.0	488.9
Net income ($ mil.)	–	–	70.6	27.4	(35.8)	(3.4)
Market value ($ mil.)	–	–	–	–	–	–
Employees	–	–	–	–	–	1,500

PEPSI-COLA BOTTLING CO OF CENTRAL VIRGINIA

1150 PEPSI PL
CHARLOTTESVILLE, VA 229012865
Phone: 434 978-2140
Fax: –
Web: www.pepsicva.com

CEO: –
CFO: –
HR: Sena Becton
FYE: December 31
Type: Private

Pepsi-Cola Bottling Co. of Central Virginia (PCBCCV) operates four soda and water bottling plants and distribution centers throughout the state of Virginia. They are located in Charlottesville, Virginia Beach, Warrenton, and Weyer's Cave. In addition to providing some 18 Virginia counties with Pepsi, Gatorade, Tropicana, and other PepsiCo products, the company also distributes Dr Pepper Snapple Group products, such as Snapple, 7UP, and Canada Dry. PCBCCV is the holder of the oldest written franchise (1908) on record with PepsiCo. Founded by Samuel Ambrose Jessup that same year, it is still owned and operated by his descendents.

PEPSICO INC NMS: PEP

700 Anderson Hill Road
Purchase, NY 10577
Phone: 914 253-2000
Fax: –
Web: www.pepsico.com

CEO: Ramon L Laguarta
CFO: James Caulfield
HR: –
FYE: December 30
Type: Public

PepsiCo is a leading global beverage and convenient food company with a complementary portfolio of brands, including Lays, Doritos, Cheetos, Gatorade, Pepsi-Cola, Mountain Dew, Quaker, and SodaStream. The Quaker Foods unit makes Quaker oatmeal, Cap'n Crunch cereal, Life cereal, Quaker rice cakes, Quaker Simply Granola, and Rice-A-Roni side dishes. Through its operations, authorized bottlers, contract manufacturers, and other third parties, PepsiCo makes, markets, distributes, and sells a wide variety of beverages and convenient foods, serving customers and consumers in more than 200 countries and territories. The US accounts for approximately 55% of total sales. In the first quarter of 2022, PepsiCo sold its Tropicana, Naked, and other select juice brands to PAI Partners for approximately $3.5 billion in cash.

	Annual Growth	12/19	12/20	12/21	12/22	12/23
Sales ($mil.)	8.0%	67,161	70,372	79,474	86,392	91,471
Net income ($ mil.)	5.5%	7,314.0	7,120.0	7,618.0	8,910.0	9,074.0
Market value ($ mil.)	5.4%	188,980	199,312	233,278	248,227	233,360
Employees	4.5%	267,000	291,000	309,000	315,000	318,000

PERASO INC NAS: PRSO

2309 Bering Drive
San Jose, CA 95131
Phone: 408 418-7500
Fax: –
Web: www.mosys.com

CEO: Daniel Lewis
CFO: James W Sullivan
HR: –
FYE: December 31
Type: Public

MoSys (formerly Monolithic System Technology) works to keep its licensing mojo workin.' The company knows it can't match the Goliaths of the memory market, so rather than spend a lot of time and money on development, it focuses on licensing the designs of its embedded memory chips for the high-speed networking, communications, storage and computing markets. The fabless semiconductor company licenses its 1T-SRAM technology to manufacturers, which in turn make the chips and embed them in communications and consumer electronics devices. The 1T-SRAM products are sold under the Accelerator Engines brand. Other products are in the company's LineSpeed line integrated circuits. Three-quarter of the company's total revenue comes from the North America.

	Annual Growth	12/18	12/19	12/20	12/21	12/22
Sales ($mil.)	(2.7%)	16.6	10.1	6.8	5.7	14.9
Net income ($ mil.)	–	(11.4)	(2.6)	(3.8)	(10.9)	(32.4)
Market value ($ mil.)	44.7%	0.0	1.0	1.4	2.5	0.4
Employees	36.5%	21	23	24	82	73

PERCEPTRON, INC.

47827 HALYARD DR
PLYMOUTH, MI 481702461
Phone: 734 414-6100
Fax: –
Web: www.perceptron.com

CEO: –
CFO: –
HR: –
FYE: June 30
Type: Private

Perceptron has a multidimensional view of what constitutes quality assurance for carmakers and building tradesmen. The company's proprietary image-processing systems provide 3-D scanning, non-contact measurement, and robot guidance systems for the automotive industry. Automakers use Perceptron's products to detect abnormalities and prevent variations -- such as metal or paint defects -- on formed parts. Perceptron also offers services such as consulting, maintenance, repair work, upgrades, and training. General Motors, VW, BMW, and Snap-on are among its top customers. Roughly half of sales come from the Americas, primarily the US.

PERDOCEO EDUCATION CORP NMS: PRDO

1750 E. Golf Road
Schaumburg, IL 60173
Phone: 847 781-3600
Fax: –
Web: www.perdoceoed.com

CEO: –
CFO: –
HR: –
FYE: December 31
Type: Public

Perdoceo Education Corporation offers a quality postsecondary education primarily online to some 39,200 enrolled students, along with campus-based and blended learning programs. Perdoceo offers certificate and degree programs in areas including information technology, health education, and business studies. The company's two regionally accredited universities include Colorado Technical University (CTU) and American InterContinental University System (AIUS) offers personalized learning technologies like intellipath learning platform and using data analytics and technology to support students and enhance learning.

	Annual Growth	12/19	12/20	12/21	12/22	12/23
Sales ($mil.)	3.1%	627.7	687.3	693.0	695.2	710.0
Net income ($ mil.)	20.5%	70.0	124.3	109.6	95.9	147.7
Market value ($ mil.)	(1.1%)	1,205.4	827.8	770.8	911.1	1,151.0
Employees	2.1%	4,000	4,700	4,300	4,500	4,350

PERERA CONSTRUCTION & DESIGN, INC.

2890 INLAND EMPIRE BLVD STE 102
ONTARIO, CA 917644649
Phone: 909 484-6350
Fax: -
Web: www.pererainc.com

CEO: Henry Perera
CFO: -
HR: -
FYE: June 30
Type: Private

Perera Construction & Design has nailed down a position as one of the largest minority-owned businesses in the US. The company works on commercial and industrial projects in California, Arizona, Utah, Texas, Hawaii and Alaska, and provides construction management, design/build, and general construction services. Its focus is on telecommunications buildings, health care facilities, schools, universities, and design/build projects for such clients as Santa Monica College, Loma Linda University Medical Center, the Richard Nixon Presidential Library and Museum, and the Cedars-Sinai Medical Center.

	Annual Growth	06/15	06/16	06/17	06/18	06/19
Sales ($mil.)	(2.7%)	-	-	37.1	31.9	35.2
Net income ($ mil.)	64.5%	-	-	0.0	0.3	0.3
Market value ($ mil.)	-	-	-	-	-	-
Employees	-	-	-	-	-	35

PEREZ TRADING COMPANY, INC.

3490 NW 125TH ST
MIAMI, FL 331672412
Phone: 305 769-0761
Fax: -
Web: www.pereztrading.com

CEO: -
CFO: -
HR: Alfred Parra
FYE: December 31
Type: Private

Perez Trading is one of the world's leading sources in the graphic arts industry for printing and packaging papers as well as leading edge equipment and technology. Customers include commercial printers, converters, distributors, industrial, and packaging manufacturers. The company partners with global leaders in the fields of manufacturing, logistics, and financing companies such as Condat, Domtar, Mohawk, WestRock, Sonoco, Fujifilm, and Canon. Perez Trading imports and exports to the Caribbean Islands, Latin America, and the US. The company has been family owned and operated since 1947.

	Annual Growth	12/10	12/11	12/12	12/13	12/14
Sales ($mil.)	(5.1%)	-	-	570.5	527.0	514.3
Net income ($ mil.)	(26.3%)	-	-	20.3	16.9	11.0
Market value ($ mil.)	-	-	-	-	-	-
Employees	-	-	-	-	-	250

PERFECTION BAKERIES, INC.

350 PEARL ST
FORT WAYNE, IN 468021508
Phone: 260 424-8245
Fax: -
Web: www.auntmillies.com

CEO: John F Popp
CFO: Jay E Miller
HR: -
FYE: December 31
Type: Private

You might say Perfection Bakeries strives for excellence in baking. A leading producer of baked goods, the company makes such products as bread, hamburger and hotdog buns, and English muffins for the retail market under its flagship Aunt Millie's brand. It also supplies baked goods and mixes to the foodservice industry. Perfection Bakeries has operations in Illinois, Indiana, Kentucky, Michigan, and Ohio, and its products are distributed primarily throughout the Great Lakes region. The family-owned company was founded in 1901 by John Franke as the Wayne Biscuit Company.

PERFICIENT INC

NMS: PRFT

555 Maryville University Drive, Suite 600
Saint Louis, MO 63141
Phone: 314 529-3600
Fax: -
Web: www.perficient.com

CEO: Jeffrey S Davis
CFO: Paul E Martin
HR: -
FYE: December 31
Type: Public

Perficient is a global digital consultancy that provides custom applications, management consulting, analytics, commerce, content management, business integration, portals and collaboration, customer relationship management, business process management, and platform implementations. It has six primary service categories that include strategy and transformation, customer experience and design, innovation and product development, platforms and technology, data and intelligence, and optimized global delivery. Its expertise also encompasses analytics, artificial intelligence and machine learning, big data, business intelligence, and a custom product portfolio. Perficient integrates and supports applications from vendors that include IBM, Oracle, and OneStream-certified training. Virtually all of Perficient's revenue, more than 95% comes from the US.

	Annual Growth	12/19	12/20	12/21	12/22	12/23
Sales ($mil.)	12.5%	565.5	612.1	761.0	905.1	906.5
Net income ($ mil.)	27.8%	37.1	30.2	52.1	104.4	98.9
Market value ($ mil.)	9.3%	1,574.4	1,628.4	4,418.4	2,386.4	2,249.3
Employees	17.3%	3,454	4,277	6,079	6,893	6,547

PERFORMANCE FOOD GROUP CO

NYS: PFGC

12500 West Creek Parkway
Richmond, VA 23238
Phone: 804 484-7700
Fax: -
Web: www.pfgc.com

CEO: George L Holm
CFO: James D Hope
HR: -
FYE: July 1
Type: Public

Performance Food Group (PFG) distributes more than 250,000 national and proprietary-branded food and food-related products from over 140 distribution centers to customers across the US. Its offerings include frozen and canned foods, beverages, fresh produce, dairy products, candy, tobacco, and salty snacks, among others. PFG also sells disposables, cleaning and kitchen supplies, and related products. Its Vistar segment is one of the leading distributors of candy, snacks, and beverages, serving over 75,000 customer locations, including vending and office coffee service distributors, retailers, theaters, and hospitality providers. A leader in its market, the company serves a broad range of customers (more than 300,000) and distributes products to independent and chain restaurants.

	Annual Growth	06/19	06/20*	07/21	07/22	07/23
Sales ($mil.)	30.5%	19,744	25,086	30,399	50,894	57,255
Net income ($ mil.)	24.2%	166.8	(114.1)	40.7	112.5	397.2
Market value ($ mil.)	10.8%	6,184.6	4,307.5	7,414.5	7,314.0	9,307.1
Employees	18.1%	18,000	20,000	23,000	35,000	35,000

*Fiscal year change

PERFORMANT FINANCIAL CORP

NMS: PFMT

333 North Canyons Parkway
Livermore, CA 94551
Phone: 925 960-4800
Fax: -
Web: www.performantcorp.com

CEO: Simeon M Kohl
CFO: Rohit Ramchandani
HR: Katherine Kober
FYE: December 31
Type: Public

Performant Financial Corporation is a top service provider in the US for technology-backed audit, recovery, and analytics services, with a special focus on the healthcare payment integrity services industry. The company works with healthcare payers to identify improper payments through claims auditing and eligibility-based services, also known as coordination-of-benefits (COB). The company assists clients in both government and commercial markets and provides a call center for clients with complex consumer engagement needs. Clients typically operate in highly regulated and intricate environments, and contract with the company for their payment integrity needs to minimize losses on improper healthcare payments. The company was founded in 1976.

	Annual Growth	12/19	12/20	12/21	12/22	12/23
Sales ($mil.)	(6.8%)	150.4	155.9	124.4	109.2	113.7
Net income ($ mil.)	-	(26.8)	(14.0)	(10.3)	(6.5)	(7.5)
Market value ($ mil.)	32.3%	78.5	67.8	185.4	277.7	240.4
Employees	(12.2%)	1,615	1,269	929	1,023	958

PERHAM HOSPITAL DISTRICT

1000 CONEY ST W
PERHAM, MN 565732102
Phone: 218 347-4500
Fax: –
Web: www.perhamhealth.org

CEO: Chuck Hofius
CFO: –
HR: –
FYE: September 30
Type: Private

Perham Memorial Hospital and Home provides acute care health services to residents throughout the Otter Tail County, Minnesota area. Specialty services include cardiac rehabilitation, emergency medicine, general medical and surgical care, labor and delivery, occupational and physical therapy, radiology, and respiratory care. MeritCare Perham, its adjoining facility, houses the offices of nine general providers and a surgeon. Perham Memorial has 25 beds; its skilled "home-like" nursing facility has nearly 100 beds and offers 24-hour nursing assistance.

	Annual Growth	12/14	12/15*	09/16	09/17	09/18
Sales ($mil.)	309.9%	–	0.8	51.0	54.2	55.9
Net income ($ mil.)	–	–	(0.0)	2.4	1.7	3.6
Market value ($ mil.)	–	–	–	–	–	–
Employees	–	–	–	–	–	300

*Fiscal year change

PERICOM SEMICONDUCTOR CORPORATION

1545 BARBER LN
MILPITAS, CA 950357409
Phone: 408 232-9100
Fax: –
Web: www.diodes.com

CEO: Alex C Hui
CFO: Kevin S Bauer
HR: –
FYE: June 27
Type: Private

The scope of Pericom Semiconductor's product line covers analog and mixed-signal integrated circuits that communicate with other devices. The company specializes in chips that control the routing and transfer of data among a system's microprocessor, memory, and peripherals. Targeting the automotive, computer, networking, and telecom markets, Pericom offers various chip product lines: interfaces for data transfer, switches for digital and analog signals, clock management chips, and telecommunications switches and component bridges. Most sales come from customers located outside the US, primarily in the Asia/Pacific region. Pericom was acquired by Diodes in late 2015.

PERKINS & MARIE CALLENDER'S, LLC

6075 POPLAR AVE STE 800
MEMPHIS, TN 381194717
Phone: 901 766-6400
Fax: –
Web: www.perkinsrestaurants.com

CEO: –
CFO: –
HR: –
FYE: December 28
Type: Private

Perkins & Marie Callender's operates and franchises more than 500 full-service restaurants under the banners Perkins Restaurant & Bakery and Marie Callender's Restaurant & Bakery. Its Perkins chain, with about 440 locations, offers standard American fare for breakfast, lunch, and dinner, along with fresh muffins, pies, and cakes. Many locations are open 24 hours a day. Its Marie Callender's chain boasts about 85 locations, offering traditional comfort foods and fresh baked desserts. Some 130 of the restaurants are company-owned.

PERKINS COIE LLP

1201 3RD AVE STE 4900
SEATTLE, WA 981013009
Phone: 206 359-8000
Fax: –
Web: www.perkinscoie.com

CEO: –
CFO: Trevor W Varnes
HR: –
FYE: December 31
Type: Private

Perkins Coie is one of the largest law firms in the Northwest. The firm has more than 1,200 lawyers specializing in such areas as corporate, commercial litigation, regulatory legal advice, and intellectual property. Perkins Coie's clients include individuals, government agencies, and not-for-profit organizations, as well as international companies. The firm serves a diverse array of industries, such as communications, food and beverage, digital media and entertainment, gaming and sports, pharmaceutical, and oil and gas. It has about 20 offices spanning the US and Asia. Perkins Coie traces its historical roots back to 1912.

	Annual Growth	12/05	12/06	12/07	12/08	12/19
Sales ($mil.)	3.6%	–	–	–	1.7	2.5
Net income ($ mil.)	–	–	–	–	–	0.4
Market value ($ mil.)	–	–	–	–	–	–
Employees	–	–	–	–	–	955

PERMA-FIX ENVIRONMENTAL SERVICES, INC.   NAS: PESI

8302 Dunwoody Place, Suite 250
Atlanta, GA 30350
Phone: 770 587-9898
Fax: –
Web: www.perma-fix.com

CEO: Mark Duff
CFO: Ben Naccarato
HR: –
FYE: December 31
Type: Public

Perma-Fix Environmental Services fixes its focus on nuclear waste management and related services. It operates four nuclear waste treatment plants. Its activities include the treatment of radioactive and mixed waste treatment and disposal for customers such as federal agencies, nuclear utilities, and hospitals and research labs. The company's services segment helps customers address regulatory compliance and other environmental concerns, such as permitting and water sampling. Perma-Fix is also involved in researching and developing new ways to process low-level radioactive and mixed waste.

	Annual Growth	12/19	12/20	12/21	12/22	12/23
Sales ($mil.)	5.1%	73.5	105.4	72.2	70.6	89.7
Net income ($ mil.)	(32.3%)	2.3	2.9	0.8	(3.8)	0.5
Market value ($ mil.)	(3.6%)	124.2	81.5	86.4	48.2	107.3
Employees	(2.2%)	325	–	286	296	297

PERMA-PIPE INTERNATIONAL HOLDINGS INC   NMS: PPIH

24900 Pitkin Road, Suite 309
Spring, TX 77386
Phone: 847 966-1000
Fax: –
Web: www.permapipe.com

CEO: David J Mansfield
CFO: Matthew Lewicki
HR: Chuck Heaton
FYE: January 31
Type: Public

MFRI's motto could be: "Pipe down, and take a deep breath." The company makes piping systems, and air filter elements through subsidiaries Perma-Pipe, and Midwesco Filter, respectively. It makes pre-insulated specialty piping systems for oil and gas gathering, district heating and cooling as well as other applications. The company also makes custom-designed industrial filtration products to remove particulates from air and other gas streams. Perma-Pipe's specialty piping systems are used on college campuses, military bases, and other large sites. Midwesco provides products and services for industrial air filtration. Its Filtration Products segment supplies filter elements to more than 4,000 user locations.

	Annual Growth	01/19	01/20	01/21	01/22	01/23
Sales ($mil.)	2.5%	129.0	127.7	84.7	138.6	142.6
Net income ($ mil.)	–	(0.5)	3.6	(7.6)	6.1	5.9
Market value ($ mil.)	3.8%	70.0	72.3	48.7	70.8	81.2
Employees	(1.2%)	701	632	504	184	667

PERMIAN BASIN ROYALTY TRUST — NYS: PBT

Argent Trust Company, 3838 Oak Lawn Avenue, Suite 1720
Dallas, TX 75219
Phone: 855 588-7839
Fax: 214 209-2431
Web: www.pbt-permian.com

CEO: –
CFO: –
HR: –
FYE: December 31
Type: Public

Permian Basin Royalty Trust is a tax-deferred pipeline for Texas oil money. Formed in 1980, the trust derives royalties from the sale of certain oil and gas assets produced by ConocoPhillips in mature oil fields in Texas, including property that's part of the Waddell Ranch. The trust distributes royalties to shareholders monthly based on the amount of oil and gas produced and sold. The company owns royalty interests on proved reserves of 5.5 million barrels of oil and 18.4 billion cu. ft. of natural gas. It also has interests in 1,300 gross wells and more than 76,900 gross acres of land. U.S. Trust, Bank of America Private Wealth Management acts as Trustee.

	Annual Growth	12/19	12/20	12/21	12/22	12/23
Sales ($mil.)	9.1%	20.5	12.0	11.8	54.5	29.1
Net income ($ mil.)	9.6%	19.4	11.0	10.7	53.5	28.0
Market value ($ mil.)	37.9%	179.9	154.3	470.7	1,174.5	650.7
Employees	–	–	–	–	–	–

PERMIANVILLE ROYALTY TRUST — NYS: PVL

The Bank of New York Mellon Trust Company, N.A., Trustee, 601 Travis Street, 16th Floor
Houston, TX 77002
Phone: 512 236-6555
Fax: –
Web: www.permianvilleroyaltytrust.com

CEO: –
CFO: –
HR: –
FYE: December 31
Type: Public

In oil and gas, Enduro trusts. Enduro Royalty Trust is a Delaware trust formed in 2011 that owns royalty interests in oil and gas production properties in Texas, Louisiana, and New Mexico. The trust is entitled to receive 80% of net profits from the sale of oil and natural gas produced by privately held Enduro Sponsor at properties in the Permian Basin and in the East Texas/North Louisiana regions; it then makes monthly distributions to trust unitholders. Enduro Sponsor holds interests in more than 900 net producing wells that are operated by third-party oil and gas companies. Its properties have proved reserves of about 27 million barrels of oil equivalent. Enduro Royalty Trust filed to go public in 2011.

	Annual Growth	12/18	12/19	12/20	12/21	12/22
Sales ($mil.)	(1.3%)	15.9	9.7	5.6	4.4	15.2
Net income ($ mil.)	(1.6%)	14.4	9.5	5.0	3.1	13.5
Market value ($ mil.)	15.5%	62.0	61.1	24.1	69.6	110.6
Employees	–	–	–	–	–	–

PERNIX GROUP INC

151 E. 22nd Street
Lombard, IL 60148
Phone: 630 620-4787
Fax: –
Web: www.pernixgroup.com

CEO: –
CFO: –
HR: –
FYE: December 31
Type: Public

Pernix Group (formerly Telesource International) provides engineering and construction services and operates independent power generation projects in the Pacific region and in the US. The group offers project development and management, specialized construction and engineering, and utility and plant operations. It also brokers goods and services. While its previous focus had been on Fiji and other islands in the Pacific, Pernix Group has shifted its business model to emphasize offering construction services and working on power plant projects in North America.

	Annual Growth	12/11	12/12	12/13	12/14	12/15
Sales ($mil.)	29.3%	69.8	120.0	73.8	85.3	195.5
Net income ($ mil.)	–	–	1.9	0.5	(4.6)	(1.4)	(18.8)
Market value ($ mil.)	151.5%	0.5	23.5	25.3	32.9	18.8
Employees	28.4%	175	105	115	148	475

PERNIX THERAPEUTICS HOLDINGS, INC.

10 N PARK PL STE 201
MORRISTOWN, NJ 079607101
Phone: 862 260-8457
Fax: –
Web: www.curraxpharma.com

CEO: –
CFO: –
HR: –
FYE: December 31
Type: Private

While some consider golf a cure for what ails you, others need actual medicine. Pernix Therapeutics, formerly Golf Trust of America, sells branded and generic drugs for allergies, minor infections, and sleep problems. Its products include Cedax for upper respiratory infections, Silenor for insomnia, Khedezla and Cedax antibiotics for middle ear infections, probiotic Rezyst, and cough and cold treatments Zutripro, Rezira, and Vituz. Recent additions include pain killer Zohydro and migraine medication Treximet. Pernix subsidiaries Cypress and Macoven market generic pharmaceuticals while its own sales force peddles the branded products. The company filed for Ch. 11 bankruptcy protection in February 2018.

PERRY ELLIS INTERNATIONAL INC

3000 NW 107TH AVE
DORAL, FL 331722133
Phone: 305 954-2307
Fax: –
Web: www.pery.com

CEO: –
CFO: Jorge Narino
HR: Ashley Scott
FYE: January 28
Type: Private

Perry Ellis International (PEI) is a leading designer, distributor, and licensor of a broad line of high-quality men's and women's apparel, accessories, and fragrances. Its collection of dresses, casual shirts, golf sportswear, sweaters, casual pants and shorts, jeans, active wear, dresses, and men's and women's swimwear is available through all major levels of retail distribution. The company has a dozen company-owned or licensed brands, including An Original Penguin by Munsingwear, Laundry by Shelli Segal, Rafaella, and namesake Perry Ellis. The company also sells directly to consumers through its own retail stores and e-commerce websites. PEI's customers include some of the nation's largest retailers such as Wal-Mart, Kohl's, Nordstrom, Saks Fifth Avenue, and Macy's. George Feldenkreis founded Perry Ellis International.

PERSPECTIVE THERAPEUTICS INC — ASE: CATX

350 Hills St., Suite 106
Richland, WA 99354
Phone: 509 375-1202
Fax: –
Web: www.isoray.com

CEO: Johan Spoor
CFO: Jonathan Hunt
HR: –
FYE: December 31
Type: Public

IsoRay hopes its medical device is a seed of change for cancer patients. Through subsidiary IsoRay Medical, the company produces and sells FDA-approved Proxcelan Cs-131 brachytherapy seeds, which are mainly used in the treatment of prostate cancer. Brachytherapy is a procedure that implants anywhere from eight to 125 small seed devices containing therapeutic radiation as close as possible to a cancerous tumor. The seeds can be used alone or in combination with external beam radiation, surgery, or other therapies. Proxcelan Cs-131's application is also expanding to other areas of the body, with US approval for use in the treatment of head and neck tumors, as well as eye, lung, colorectal, and chest wall cancers.

	Annual Growth	06/19	06/20	06/21	06/22*	12/22
Sales ($mil.)	(16.5%)	7.3	9.7	10.1	10.8	3.6
Net income ($ mil.)	–	(5.1)	(3.4)	(3.4)	(7.3)	(7.3)
Market value ($ mil.)	(11.9%)	58.3	78.9	113.4	43.9	35.1
Employees	20.6%	43	53	67	66	91

*Fiscal year change

PERVASIP CORP
NBB: PVSP

430 North Street
White Plains, NY 10605
Phone: 914 750-9339
Fax: –
Web: www.canalytix.com

CEO: Paul H Riss
CFO: George Jordan
HR: –
FYE: November 30
Type: Public

As the popularity of computer telephony spreads, Pervasip (formerly eLEC Communications) hopes to cash in on convergence. Through its VoX Communications subsidiary, the company provides wholesale Voice-over-Internet Protocol (VoIP) service to cable network operators, ISPs, competitive local exchange carriers (CLECs), and other resellers. Its customers, in turn, provide private or co-branded VoIP services to the residential and small business markets. VoX's service packages include such features as call return, voicemail, caller ID, and call waiting.

	Annual Growth	11/11	11/12	11/13	11/14	11/15
Sales ($mil.)	(17.3%)	1.3	1.0	0.9	0.5	0.6
Net income ($ mil.)	–	(4.4)	3.2	0.0	(0.5)	0.5
Market value ($ mil.)	(62.0%)	43.8	13.1	8.8	0.4	0.9
Employees	(21.7%)	8	8	4	5	3

PET SUPERMARKET, INC.

1100 INTERNATIONAL PKWY STE 200
SUNRISE, FL 333232886
Phone: 954 351-0834
Fax: –
Web: www.petsupermarket.com

CEO: –
CFO: –
HR: –
FYE: December 31
Type: Private

Pet Supermarket has it all for your furry and feathered friends. The company sells more than 10,000 pet care products, including food, toys, medicine, and clothing, through its website and more than 135 stores in a dozen states, primarily Florida. Stores also offer vaccinations for dogs, cats, and ferrets, and sell a variety of small animals such as hamsters, guinea pigs, rabbits, and tropical fish. In addition, Pet Supermarket works with area organizations to host adoptions and related events for cats and dogs. Like its pet superstore competitors, customers can take their pets shopping with them. Founded in 1973 by Chuck West as Pet Circus, the family-owned company became Pet Supermarket in 1986.

PETCO HEALTH & WELLNESS CO INC
NMS: WOOF

10850 Via Frontera
San Diego, CA 92127
Phone: 858 453-7845
Fax: –
Web: www.petco.com

CEO: Ronald Coughlin Jr
CFO: Brian Larose
HR: –
FYE: January 28
Type: Public

Petco Health and Wellness Company is a category-defining health and wellness company focused on improving the lives of pets, pet parents, and its own partners. Through its integrated ecosystem, the company provides its more than 25 million total active customers with a comprehensive offering of differentiated products and services to fulfill their pets' health and wellness needs through more than 1,500 pet care centers in the US, Mexico, and Puerto Rico, its digital channel, and flexible fulfillment options. The company's service offering includes a broad suite of pet health services, including veterinary care, grooming, and training. In addition, it operates more than 245 full-service veterinary hospitals, and has about 29,000 total Petco partners. The company was founded in 1965.

	Annual Growth	02/19	02/20*	01/21	01/22	01/23
Sales ($mil.)	8.3%	4,392.2	4,434.5	4,920.2	5,807.1	6,036.0
Net income ($ mil.)	–	(413.8)	(95.9)	(26.5)	164.4	90.8
Market value ($ mil.)	–	–	–	7,911.0	5,561.7	3,568.0
Employees	–	–	–	27,081	28,495	29,000

*Fiscal year change

PETER KIEWIT SONS', INC.

3555 FARNAM ST
OMAHA, NE 681313374
Phone: 402 342-2052
Fax: –
Web: www.kiewit.com

CEO: Bruce E Grewcock
CFO: Michael J Piechoski
HR: Caeleb Isabell
FYE: December 29
Type: Private

Kiewit is one of North America's largest construction and engineering companies. The company is active in building, industrial, mining, oil, gas, chemicals, power, transportation, water, and wastewater. It builds everything from roads and dams to high-rise office towers and power plants. Kiewit focuses on projects located throughout the US, Canada, and Mexico. It specializes in mine management, production, infrastructure construction, and maintenance, its mining experience includes constructing infrastructure, performing mine services or contract mining in coal, copper, diamond, gold, nickel, platinum, potash and rare earth mines throughout North America. The company was founded in 1884.

	Annual Growth	12/08	12/09	12/10	12/11	12/12
Sales ($mil.)	6.3%	–	–	9,938.0	10,381	11,220
Net income ($ mil.)	(19.2%)	–	–	789.0	790.0	515.0
Market value ($ mil.)	–	–	–	–	–	–
Employees	–	–	–	–	–	14,700

PETER PAN BUS LINES, INC.

1 PETER PAN WAY # 300
SPRINGFIELD, MA 011031572
Phone: 413 781-2900
Fax: –
Web: www.peterpanbus.com

CEO: Peter A Picknelly
CFO: –
HR: –
FYE: December 31
Type: Private

The Boy Who Wouldn't Grow Up has given up midnight flights to Neverland for the more mundane bus routes of the northeastern and mid-Atlantic US. Peter Pan Bus Lines provides scheduled service to more than 100 cities in about 10 states along the Boston-to-Washington, DC, corridor. It transports packages as well as passengers on its scheduled routes; in addition, the company offers charter and tour bus services in the US and Canada. Overall the company and its subsidiaries, which include Arrow Line and Bonanza Bus Lines, operate a fleet of about 300 buses. Peter Pan Bus Lines was founded in 1933 by Peter C. Picknelly, grandfather of company president Peter A. Picknelly. The Picknelly family owns the company.

	Annual Growth	12/03	12/04	12/05	12/06	12/08
Sales ($mil.)	2.9%	–	51.9	52.6	53.9	58.2
Net income ($ mil.)	(1.5%)	–	2.3	3.2	2.7	2.1
Market value ($ mil.)	–	–	–	–	–	–
Employees	–	–	–	–	–	750

PETMED EXPRESS INC
NMS: PETS

420 South Congress Avenue
Delray Beach, FL 33445
Phone: 561 526-4444
Fax: –
Web: www.petmeds.com

CEO: –
CFO: –
HR: –
FYE: March 31
Type: Public

PetMed Express is a leading nationwide direct-to-consumer pet pharmacy and online provider of prescription and non-prescription medications, food, supplements, supplies, and vet services for dogs, cats, and horses. Through 1-800-PetMeds and 1800petmeds.com, as well as a catalog with hundreds of items, PetMed offers prescription and non-prescription medicines and other pet care supplies for dogs, cats, and horses direct to the consumer. Founded in 1996, the company offers consumers an attractive alternative for obtaining pet medications and supplies in terms of convenience, price, speed of delivery, and valued customer service. Attracts approximately 28 million visits to its website (including its mobile app), PetMed Express makes over 85% of its sales via the company's website. California, Florida, Texas, New York, Pennsylvania, North Carolina, Georgia, and Virginia represent about half of the company's sales.

	Annual Growth	03/19	03/20	03/21	03/22	03/23
Sales ($mil.)	(2.4%)	283.4	284.1	309.2	273.4	256.9
Net income ($ mil.)	(72.0%)	37.7	25.9	30.6	21.1	0.2
Market value ($ mil.)	(8.1%)	480.3	606.8	741.6	544.0	342.4
Employees	11.0%	199	214	219	212	302

PETRO STAR INC.

3900 C ST STE 802
ANCHORAGE, AK 995035963
Phone: 907 339-6600
Fax: –
Web: www.petrostar.com

CEO: –
CFO: –
HR: –
FYE: December 31
Type: Private

Petro Star is an oil refining and fuel marketing shining star that brings heating fuel and energy (heating oil, diesel, and aviation and marine fuels) to the citizens of the communities in the vast, cold, and lonely expanses of the US' largest state, Alaska. It operates refineries at North Pole and Valdez and distributes fuels and lubricants throughout Interior Alaska, Dutch Harbor, Kodiak, and Valdez. Started in 1984 by a group of petroleum industry veterans, the company built its first refinery operations along the Trans-Alaska Pipeline at North Pole, Alaska. Petro Star is a subsidiary of Arctic Slope Regional Corp.

	Annual Growth	12/00	12/01	12/02	12/03	12/08
Sales ($mil.)	19.9%	–	279.2	267.8	291.0	992.1
Net income ($ mil.)	–	–	3.0	1.9	3.6	–
Market value ($ mil.)	–	–	–	–	–	–
Employees	–	–	–	–	–	300

PETROLEUM TRADERS CORPORATION

7120 POINTE INVERNESS WAY
FORT WAYNE, IN 468047928
Phone: 260 432-6622
Fax: –
Web: www.petroleumtraders.com

CEO: Michael Himes
CFO: –
HR: Jen Bynum
FYE: June 30
Type: Private

Petroleum Traders Corporation barters with fuel. The company provides wholesale gasoline, diesel fuel, and heating oil to fuel distributors, government agencies, and other large consumers of fuel such as businesses with vehicle fleets. The largest pure wholesale fuel distributor in the country, Petroleum Traders operates and trades in 44 US states. It supplies #1 and #2 low sulfur diesel fuels, biodiesel, high sulfur heating oil and kerosene, and conventional, ethanol, and reformulated blends of gasoline in regular, midgrade, and premium octane ratings.

	Annual Growth	06/16	06/17	06/18	06/19	06/21
Sales ($mil.)	(6.2%)	–	1,606.4	1,815.8	2,030.7	1,241.1
Net income ($ mil.)	(10.7%)	–	19.0	11.5	39.5	12.1
Market value ($ mil.)	–	–	–	–	–	–
Employees	–	–	–	–	–	142

PETROQUEST ENERGY INC (NEW)

400 E. Kaliste Saloom Road, Suite 6000
Lafayette, LA 70508
Phone: 337 232-7028
Fax: –
Web: www.petroquest.com

CEO: Charles T Goodson
CFO: J B Clement
HR: Gayle George
FYE: December 31
Type: Public

Independent oil and gas exploration and production company PetroQuest Energy once focused its quest for petroleum on the hydrocarbon-rich and high margin Gulf Coast Basin, but in the last decade, in order to diversify its reserve base and allow it more financial flexibility, it has looked to grow its assets in long-lived, lower risk basins onshore. PetroQuest estimates its 2018 production was a little more than 21 billion cubic feet equivalent (bcfe) of gas (about 75% of production), oil (9%), and natural gas liquids (16%). PetroQuest Energy filed for Chapter 11 bankruptcy protection in late 2018 and emerged early the following year.

	Annual Growth	12/14	12/15	12/16	12/17	12/18
Sales ($mil.)	(21.1%)	225.0	116.0	66.7	108.3	87.1
Net income ($ mil.)	–	31.2	(294.8)	(90.9)	(6.6)	(9.5)
Market value ($ mil.)	(81.9%)	95.7	12.8	84.7	48.4	0.1
Employees	(21.3%)	141	119	64	65	54

PETROTAL CORP

TVX: TAL

16200 Park Row, Suite 310
Houston, TX 77084
Phone: 713 609-9101
Fax: –
Web: www.petrotal-corp.com

CEO: –
CFO: –
HR: –
FYE: December 31
Type: Public

Sterling Resources placed its bets on making money by exploiting some of Earth's sterling resources -- oil and gas. The exploration and production independent explores for, develops, and produces crude oil and natural gas, primarily in the UK but also in the Netherlands. In the UK, Sterling Resources has prospects offshore in the North Sea. The company's strategy has been to focus on projects that had the potential for large reserve development. However, difficult market conditions over the past few years has forced the company to sell most of its major assets. In 2017 Sterling Resources agreed to sell its UK unit to Oranje-Nassau Energie for $163 million, following which it planned to dissolve the company.

	Annual Growth	12/18	12/19	12/20	12/21	12/22
Sales ($mil.)	139.2%	10.0	73.6	58.9	150.2	327.1
Net income ($ mil.)	–	(4.6)	20.2	(1.5)	64.0	188.5
Market value ($ mil.)	42.8%	103.5	340.9	170.0	286.3	430.2
Employees	23.0%	52	60	68	89	119

PFENEX INC.

10790 ROSELLE ST
SAN DIEGO, CA 921211508
Phone: 858 352-4400
Fax: –
Web: www.pelicanexpression.com

CEO: Evert B Schimmelpennink
CFO: –
HR: David Pollak
FYE: December 31
Type: Private

Using its patented Pfenex Expression Technology for building complex proteins, Pfenex creates biosimilars or newer versions of existing biologics. The company's lead candidates are PF708, which mimics osteoporosis treatment Eli Lilly's Forteo and novel anthrax vaccine candidates Px563L and RPA563. Pfenex was formed in 2009 as a protein development and production company serving the world's top drug manufacturers; the company believes this history gives it a competitive advantage. More than 85% of its revenue comes from outside of the US. In 2020, Ligand Pharmaceuticals Incorporated and Pfenex Inc. signed an agreement that Ligand will acquire all outstanding shares of Pfenex.

PFG VENTURES, L.P.

8800 E PLEASANT VALLEY RD STE 1
INDEPENDENCE, OH 441315558
Phone: 216 520-8400
Fax: –
Web: www.proforma.com

CEO: Vera Muzzillo
CFO: –
HR: –
FYE: December 31
Type: Private

PFG Ventures takes its customers' businesses forward with Proforma. The company franchises more than 700 Proforma locations across the US and Canada, offering an array of office supplies (such as forms, labels, and stationery), customized promotional products, and printing and e-commerce services. The company has served more than 50,000 clients in a range of industries, including education, finance, food and beverage packaging, health care, manufacturing, and retail. Clients have included Honda, Beck's, the University of Minnesota, and the New York State Nurses Association. After establishing Proforma in 1978, Gregory Muzzillo formed PFG Ventures in 1994 to help franchise the brand.

	Annual Growth	12/03	12/04	12/05	12/06	12/07
Sales ($mil.)	(42.3%)	–	114.0	19.3	21.4	21.9
Net income ($ mil.)	(8.0%)	–	4.2	2.5	3.0	3.3
Market value ($ mil.)	–	–	–	–	–	–
Employees	–	–	–	–	–	103

PFIZER INC

NYS: PFE

66 Hudson Boulevard East
New York, NY 10001 - 2192
Phone: 212 733-2323
Fax: –
Web: www.pfizer.com

CEO: Albert Bourla
CFO: David M Denton
HR: –
FYE: December 31
Type: Public

Pfizer Inc. is one of the world's largest research-based pharmaceutical companies, producing medicines for cardiovascular health, metabolism, oncology, inflammation and immunology, and other areas. The company works across developed and emerging markets to advance wellness, prevention, treatments and cures that challenge the most feared diseases of its time. Pfizer collaborates with healthcare providers, governments and local communities to support and expand access to reliable, affordable healthcare around the world. Pfizer operates around the world and gets more than % of its revenue from its US markets.

	Annual Growth	12/19	12/20	12/21	12/22	12/23
Sales ($mil.)	3.1%	51,750	41,908	81,288	100,330	58,496
Net income ($ mil.)	(39.9%)	16,273	9,616.0	21,980	31,372	2,119.0
Market value ($ mil.)	(7.4%)	221,210	207,829	333,396	289,301	162,548
Employees	(0.1%)	88,300	78,500	79,000	83,000	88,000

PG&E CORP (HOLDING CO)

NYS: PCG

300 Lakeside Drive
Oakland, CA 94612
Phone: 415 973-1000
Fax: 415 267-7265
Web: www.pgecorp.com

CEO: Cheryl F Campbell
CFO: Stephanie N Williams
HR: –
FYE: December 31
Type: Public

Pacific Gas and Electric Company, one of the largest public utility providers in California, supplies electricity and natural gas to residential, commercial, industrial, and agricultural customers in northern and central California. It reaches approximately 5.5 million electric customers via approximately 106,680 miles of electric distribution lines and some 4.5 million gas customers via around 42,140 miles of gas distribution lines. The company sources its electric and natural gas supply from owned generation facilities (some 130 electric plants) and through third-party disposal sites.

	Annual Growth	12/19	12/20	12/21	12/22	12/23
Sales ($mil.)	9.3%	17,129	18,469	20,642	21,680	24,428
Net income ($ mil.)	–	(7,642.0)	(1,304.0)	(88.0)	1,814.0	2,256.0
Market value ($ mil.)	13.5%	23,192	26,585	25,902	34,692	38,469
Employees	(85.6%)	23,000	24,000	26,000	26,000	10

PGA TOUR, INC.

1 PGA TOUR BLVD
PONTE VEDRA BEACH, FL 320822826
Phone: 904 285-3700
Fax: –
Web: www.pgatour.com

CEO: –
CFO: –
HR: Beth Miller
FYE: December 31
Type: Private

The PGA TOUR is the world's premier membership organization for touring professional golfers, co-sanctioning tournaments on the PGA TOUR, PGA TOUR Champions, Korn Ferry Tour, PGA TOUR LatinoamTrica, and PGA TOUR Canada. Each PGA TOUR player has earned a position on the priority-ranking system that is used to select full-field open tournaments. Its major championships are the Masters Tournament, the Open Championship, THE PLAYERS Championship, and PGA Championship, US Open. The company has about 80 active international members from some 25 countries and territories outside the US. The modern-day PGA TOUR was formed in 1968 when a subset of touring professionals broke away from the PGA of America.

	Annual Growth	12/05	12/06	12/13	12/21	12/22
Sales ($mil.)	4.8%	–	894.0	1,075.0	1,586.1	1,897.7
Net income ($ mil.)	15.8%	–	3.1	34.6	33.4	32.0
Market value ($ mil.)	–	–	–	–	–	–
Employees	–	–	–	–	–	3,563

PHARMACY BUYING ASSOCIATION, INC.

6300 ENTERPRISE RD
KANSAS CITY, MO 641201336
Phone: 816 245-5700
Fax: –
Web: www.pbahealth.com

CEO: Nick R Smock
CFO: –
HR: –
FYE: December 31
Type: Private

PBA Health injects the pharmacy industry with the right kind of medicine. Pharmacy Buying Association, operating as PBA Health, is a bit of a "one-stop" provider to pharmacies, including community-based pharmacies, as well as hospitals, clinics, and select pharmaceutical chains. The company provides group purchasing, inventory management, branding, and cost-efficiency services, bringing competitive prices and fair reimbursements to pharmacies on more than 5,500 branded prescription, generic, specialty, and over-the-counter (OTC) drugs. PBA Health also offers its customers in-store operating systems that use proprietary software to track inventory, fill prescriptions, and follow third-party claims.

PHARMACYTE BIOTECH INC

NAS: PMCB

3960 Howard Hughes Parkway, Suite 500
Las Vegas, NV 89169
Phone: 917 595-2850
Fax: –
Web: www.pharmacyte.com

CEO: Joshua N Silverman
CFO: Carlos A Trujillo
HR: –
FYE: April 30
Type: Public

Nuvilex is out to fill niche markets with its products. The company makes and sells a handful of items that can be classified as a couple of parts nutraceutical, a part dermatological, and a little bit environmental. Nuvilex's products are sold worldwide and include nutritional supplements Cinnergen and Cinnechol, tattoo ink Infinitink, and scar cream Talysn. Nuvilex has also developed an environmentally safe germicidal topical spray that kills some of the most frequent bacterial pathogens. The company is also developing a sporicidal to kill anthrax, and has formulated Citroxin, a product designed to knock out avian flu viruses.

	Annual Growth	04/19	04/20	04/21	04/22	04/23
Sales ($mil.)	–	–	–	–	–	–
Net income ($ mil.)	–	(4.1)	(3.8)	(3.6)	(4.2)	(4.3)
Market value ($ mil.)	190.5%	0.7	0.4	0.3	39.1	49.0
Employees	–	12	15	4	27	–

PHARMERICA CORPORATION

805 N WHITTINGTON PKWY
LOUISVILLE, KY 402227101
Phone: 502 627-7000
Fax: –
Web: www.pharmerica.com

CEO: Gregory S Weishar
CFO: Robert E Dries
HR: Kirby N Sullivan
FYE: December 31
Type: Private

PharMerica is a leading provider of institutional, community- and home-based pharmacy services. The company serves the long-term care, senior living, hospital, home infusion, hospice, behavioral, specialty and oncology pharmacy markets. PharMerica operates over 180 long-term care, home infusion, and specialty pharmacies in 50 states. PharMerica is a customer- and patient-focused organization serving health care providers, such as skilled nursing facilities, senior living communities, and hospitals, as well as individuals with behavioral needs, individuals with infusion therapy needs, seniors receiving in-home care, and patients with cancer.

PHASEBIO PHARMACEUTICALS INC
NBB: PHAS Q

1 Great Valley Parkway, Suite 30
Malvern, PA 19355
Phone: 610 981-6500
Fax: –
Web: www.phasebio.com

CEO: Jonathan P Mow
CFO: John P Sharp
HR: Marianne Retif
FYE: December 31
Type: Public

Phase Bioscience is a biotechnology firm that has developed a technology utilizing genetically-engineered biopolymer peptides (ELPs) that changes solubility (from a liquid to a solid and back) based on the temperature and the salt content of the solution. Known as deltaPhase, Phase Bioscience's ELPs are designed to be used by pharmaceutical researchers in drug discovery processes and in life science applications, including recombinant protein purification (isolating a particular protein in a solution) and enzyme biocatalysts (isolating a particular recombinant enzyme in a solution).

	Annual Growth	12/17	12/18	12/19	12/20	12/21
Sales ($mil.)	–	–	0.7	2.4	0.3	10.8
Net income ($ mil.)	–	(10.2)	(23.8)	(39.2)	(98.6)	(131.1)
Market value ($ mil.)	–	–	148.9	294.4	161.9	125.8
Employees	35.1%	18	24	40	50	60

PHELPS DUNBAR, L.L.P.

365 CANAL ST STE 2000
NEW ORLEANS, LA 701306534
Phone: 504 566-1311
Fax: –
Web: www.phelps.com

CEO: –
CFO: –
HR: –
FYE: December 31
Type: Private

A leading regional law firm, Phelps Dunbar has more than 300 attorneys overall. The firm has represented public and private companies, governmental agencies, health care systems, estates, and individuals. Clients have included Renasant Corporation, Enstructure LLC, and Eldorado Resorts. Among Phelps Dunbar's practice areas are admiralty; bankruptcy; commercial litigation; intellectual property; oil and gas; and product liability. Phelps Dunbar is especially focused on clients operating in the oil, gas, and energy industries.

PHELPS MEMORIAL HOSPITAL ASSOCIATION

701 N BROADWAY
SLEEPY HOLLOW, NY 105911096
Phone: 914 366-3000
Fax: –
Web: –

CEO: –
CFO: Vincent Desantis
HR: Luisa Prati
FYE: December 31
Type: Private

If you happen to spot the headless horseman in Sleepy Hollow, it's possible he's on his way to Phelps Memorial Hospital for some medical treatment. The 240-bed hospital provides both physical and mental health care services to residents of Sleepy Hollow and Westchester County, New York. Specialized services include cardiology, emergency care, orthopedics, and psychiatry. It also includes a satellite location of the Memorial Sloan-Kettering Cancer Center, and it provides geriatric health services through a partnership with Mount Sinai Hospital and operates a senior retirement community with Kendal Corporation. Phelps Memorial is one of four hospitals that make up the Stellaris Health Network.

	Annual Growth	12/14	12/15	12/16	12/17	12/21
Sales ($mil.)	7.2%	–	230.0	220.4	240.2	349.2
Net income ($ mil.)	48.1%	–	3.1	21.0	17.8	33.0
Market value ($ mil.)	–	–	–	–	–	–
Employees	–	–	–	–	–	1,200

PHI GROUP INC (DE)
NBB: PHIG

2001 S.E. Evangeline Thruway
Lafayette, LA 70508
Phone: 337 235-2452
Fax: 337 235-1357
Web: www.phihelico.com

CEO: Lance F Bospflug
CFO: Trudy P McConnaughhay
HR: Zonick John
FYE: December 31
Type: Public

One of the world's top commercial helicopter operators, PHI Aviation maintains a fleet of more than 200 aircraft and provides contract transportation services across six continents. Its expansive fleet of light, medium, and heavy lift helicopters includes models from major manufacturers like Bell, Airbus, Leonardo, and Sikorsky. The company's core business consists of offshore operations in the energy basins around the world. The highly skilled staff of pilots and maintenance technicians gives the company great depth in all areas of operation. Its PHI Air Medical is the leading air ambulance provider across the country, providing air medical services and outreach education to local communities and leading healthcare systems. Founded in 1949, Phi has provided safe and reliable helicopter services to customers around the globe.

	Annual Growth	12/14	12/15	12/16	12/17	12/18
Sales ($mil.)	(5.2%)	836.3	804.2	634.1	579.5	674.4
Net income ($ mil.)	–	32.7	26.9	(26.7)	7.5	(141.5)
Market value ($ mil.)	(52.8%)	591.9	259.7	285.2	183.1	29.3
Employees	(5.7%)	2,844	2,694	2,472	2,521	2,246

PHI GROUP INC.
NBB: PHIL

2323 Main Street
Irvine, CA 92614
Phone: 714 793-9227
Fax: –
Web: www.philuxglobal.com

CEO: Henry D Fahman
CFO: Henry D Fahman
HR: –
FYE: June 30
Type: Public

PHI Group rolls a variety of business into one. The holding company focuses its attention on consulting and financial services, real estate investment, and natural resources and energy. At the center of PHI Group's offerings is PHI Vietnam and PHI Capital, which provide assistance to Vietnamese companies that go public in the US. Other PHI Group holdings include PHI Gold Corporation, which invests in gold mines around the world. Real estate arm PHILAND Ranch develops industrial, residential, and hospitality properties in southeast Asia.

	Annual Growth	06/18	06/19	06/20	06/21	06/22
Sales ($mil.)	(63.4%)	1.7	–	0.0	0.0	0.0
Net income ($ mil.)	–	(2.0)	(2.9)	(2.2)	(7.0)	(21.2)
Market value ($ mil.)	(62.3%)	1,084.3	6.3	6.3	292.3	22.0
Employees	–	–	–	–	–	–

PHIBRO ANIMAL HEALTH CORP.
NMS: PAHC

Glenpointe Centre East, 3rd Floor, 300 Frank W. Burr Boulevard, Suite 2
Teaneck, NJ 07666-6712
Phone: 201 329-7300
Fax: –
Web: www.pahc.com

CEO: Jack C Bendheim
CFO: Richard G Johnson
HR: –
FYE: June 30
Type: Public

Phibro Animal Health (Phibro) is a leading global diversified animal health and mineral nutrition company. The company's Animal Health segment develops, manufactures, and markets products such as antibacterials, anticoccidials, nutritional specialty products, and vaccines and vaccine adjuvants that help improve the animal's health and therefore improve performance, food safety, and animal welfare. It markets approximately 770 product lines in more than 80 countries to approximately 4,000 customers, the company develops, manufactures, and markets a broad range of products for food and companion animals including poultry, swine, beef and dairy cattle, aquaculture, and dogs. Phibro sells animal health and mineral nutrition products either directly to integrated poultry, swine, and cattle producers or through animal feed manufacturers, wholesalers, distributors, and veterinarians. Phibro also supplies antimicrobials.

	Annual Growth	06/19	06/20	06/21	06/22	06/23
Sales ($mil.)	4.2%	828.0	800.4	833.4	942.3	977.9
Net income ($ mil.)	(12.1%)	54.7	33.6	54.4	49.2	32.6
Market value ($ mil.)	(19.0%)	1,286.8	1,064.0	1,169.7	774.8	554.9
Employees	4.7%	1,600	1,700	1,725	1,860	1,920

PHILADELPHIA CONSOLIDATED HOLDING CORP.

1 BALA PLZ STE 100
BALA CYNWYD, PA 190041401
Phone: 610 617-7900
Fax: –
Web: www.phly.com

CEO: Robert D O'Leary
CFO: –
HR: Jeanette Fedrick
FYE: December 31
Type: Private

Because each industry has its own unique set of risks, Philadelphia Insurance Companies and its subsidiaries specialize in designing and underwriting commercial property/casualty insurance. Its niche clients include rental car companies (for that insurance they always want to sell you at the counter), not-for-profits, health and fitness centers, and day-care facilities. Its specialty lines include loss-control policies and liability coverage for such professionals as lawyers, doctors, accountants, dog groomers, and even insurance claims adjusters. Philadelphia Insurance Companies is a subsidiary of Tokio Marine Holdings.

	Annual Growth	12/12	12/13	12/14	12/15	12/16
Assets ($mil.)	7.4%	–	–	–	9,047.4	9,719.4
Net income ($ mil.)	7.5%	–	–	–	323.2	347.5
Market value ($ mil.)	–	–	–	–	–	–
Employees	–	–	–	–	–	1,374

PHILADELPHIA UNIVERSITY

4201 HENRY AVE
PHILADELPHIA, PA 191445409
Phone: 215 951-2700
Fax: –
Web: www.philau.edu

CEO: –
CFO: –
HR: Amir Bahr
FYE: June 30
Type: Private

Located in the heart of The City of Brotherly Love , Philadelphia University (PhilaU) offers more than 60 undergraduate and graduate degrees from programs such as architecture, business administration, design and media, engineering and textiles, liberal arts, and science and health. The private school also offers several accelerated degree programs in disciplines such as business and the health sciences aimed primarily at adult learners. It has an enrollment of about 3,200 students. Founded in 1884 as the Philadelphia Textile School, the school changed its name several times before receiving university status in 1999. PhilaU announced plans to merge with Thomas Jefferson University in late 2015.

PHILADELPHIA WORKFORCE DEVELOPMENT CORPORATION

1617 JOHN F KENNEDY BLVD 13TH FL
PHILADELPHIA, PA 191031821
Phone: 215 963-2100
Fax: –
Web: www.philaworks.org

CEO: Mark Edwards
CFO: Dale Porter
HR: John Lasky
FYE: June 30
Type: Private

The Philadelphia Workforce Development Corporation (PWDC) wants Philadelphians to get a job. A tax-exempt not-for-profit, PWDC has served the city's workforce since 1982. For businesses, it offers employee recruitment, development, and retention services; assessment and testing; job fair coordination; wage subsidies; and tax credits. It trains job seekers (including ex-offenders, the homeless, workers with disabilities, and unemployed adults) in areas such as skills development, resume writing, interviewing, and salary negotiations. The agency also funnels state and federal dollars to agencies that provide workforce training. Philadelphia area employers that have partnered with PWDC include ARAMARK and IKEA.

	Annual Growth	06/07	06/08	06/09	06/10	06/11
Sales ($mil.)	4.4%	–	–	110.5	112.8	120.3
Net income ($ mil.)	–	–	–	(0.2)	0.0	(0.2)
Market value ($ mil.)	–	–	–	–	–	–
Employees	–	–	–	–	–	100

PHILIP MORRIS INTERNATIONAL INC   NYS: PM

677 Washington Blvd, Suite 1100
Stamford, CT 06901
Phone: 203 905-2410
Fax: 917 663-5372
Web: www.pmi.com

CEO: Jacek Olczak
CFO: Emmanuel Babeau
HR: –
FYE: December 31
Type: Public

Philip Morris International (PMI) is a leading international tobacco company working to deliver a smoke-free future and evolving its portfolio for the long-term to include products outside of the tobacco and nicotine sector. Despite being US-based, its sales presence is entirely non-US. Its portfolio is led by Marlboro, the world's best-selling international cigarette, which accounts for about 40% of the company's cigarette shipment volume. The company's other leading international cigarette brands are Chesterfield, L&M, and Philip Morris. Top local brands include Fortune, Jackpot, Sampoerna A, and Dji Sam Soe. Most of its revenue originates outside the US.

	Annual Growth	12/19	12/20	12/21	12/22	12/23
Sales ($mil.)	4.2%	29,805	28,694	31,405	31,762	35,174
Net income ($ mil.)	2.1%	7,185.0	8,056.0	9,109.0	9,048.0	7,813.0
Market value ($ mil.)	2.5%	132,096	128,525	147,480	157,121	146,052
Employees	3.0%	73,500	71,000	69,600	79,800	82,700

PHILLIPS 66   NYS: PSX

2331 CityWest Blvd.
Houston, TX 77042
Phone: 832 765-3010
Fax: –
Web: www.phillips66.com

CEO: Mark E Lashier
CFO: Kevin J Mitchell
HR: –
FYE: December 31
Type: Public

Phillips 66 is a diversified energy manufacturing and logistics company with unique businesses in refining, midstream, chemicals, and marketing and specialties. It markets in the US under the Phillips 66, Conoco, and 76 brands and internationally under the JET and Coop brands. It has approximately 7,200 branded outlets in about 50 states and Puerto Rico. One of the largest crude oil refiners, the company processes, transports, and markets natural gas and natural gas liquids, as well as liquefied petroleum gas. It produces olefins and polyolefins and other products through CPChem, a joint venture with Chevron. About 80% of company's revenue comes from US customers.

	Annual Growth	12/19	12/20	12/21	12/22	12/23
Sales ($mil.)	8.2%	109,559	65,494	114,852	175,702	149,890
Net income ($ mil.)	22.9%	3,076.0	(3,975.0)	1,317.0	11,024	7,015.0
Market value ($ mil.)	4.6%	47,958	30,107	31,191	44,803	57,312
Employees	(0.9%)	14,500	14,300	14,000	13,000	14,000

PHILLIPS AND JORDAN, INCORPORATED

10142 PARKSIDE DR STE 500
KNOXVILLE, TN 379221954
Phone: 865 688-8342
Fax: –
Web: www.pandj.com

CEO: William T Phillips Jr
CFO: Bryan McIsaac
HR: –
FYE: December 31
Type: Private

While some like to clear the air, Phillips and Jordan (P&J) prefers to clear the land. Founded in 1952 as a small land clearing firm, P&J is a general and specialty contractor that still provides land clearing services in addition to industrial, commercial, and residential site development and heavy civil construction on dams, highways, bridges, railroads, and waterways. P&J also performs reclamation, landfill, and disaster recovery services. The latter includes handling some of the nation's worst disaster cleanups, including hurricanes, floods, toxic spills, and land and rock slides. P&J operates about a dozen offices in eight states. The Phillips family owns and runs the company.

	Annual Growth	12/11	12/12	12/13	12/14	12/18
Sales ($mil.)	6.9%	–	284.5	215.2	340.9	425.1
Net income ($ mil.)	11.9%	–	11.3	4.5	14.5	22.2
Market value ($ mil.)	–	–	–	–	–	–
Employees	–	–	–	–	–	1,100

PHILLIPS EDISON & COMPANY LLC

11501 NORTHLAKE DR FL 1
CINCINNATI, OH 452491667
Phone: 513 554-1110
Fax: –
Web: www.phillipsedison.com

CEO: Jeffrey S Edison
CFO: Devin I Murphy
HR: Sandy Lambert
FYE: December 31
Type: Private

Phillips Edison & company (PECO) is a real estate investment trust (REIT) that is one of the nation's largest owners and operators of omni-channel grocery-anchored shopping centers. The company owns and manages around 290 properties -- primarily grocery store-anchored shopping centers -- totaling more than 33 million sq. ft. in about 30 states. A majority of its properties are located in the Southwest, Midwest, and West, with concentrations in Florida, Georgia, California and Ohio. Its major tenants include Subway Group, Kroger, Publix and Albertsons-Safeway. PECO was founded in 1991 and went public in 2021.

PHOEBE PUTNEY MEMORIAL HOSPITAL, INC.

417 W 3RD AVE
ALBANY, GA 317011943
Phone: 229 312-1000
Fax: –
Web: www.phoebehealth.com

CEO: Deborah Angerami
CFO: Kerry Loudermilk
HR: Blake Garrett
FYE: July 31
Type: Private

Phoebe Putney Memorial Hospital is a not-for-profit network of more than 4,500 physicians, nurses, professional staff, and volunteers. It delivers compassionate, high quality healthcare to more than 500,000 residents in its 41-county region. The system provides health care services to residents of southwest Georgia. The acute-care hospital provides emergency and inpatient services, as well as cardiology, oncology, psychiatric, women's health, and pediatric specialty care. One of Georgia's largest comprehensive regional medical centers, Phoebe Putney Memorial Hospital is a recognized leader in specialties including cardiovascular medicine, oncology, orthopaedics, and women's health; and it offers patients the most advanced diagnostic and therapeutic treatments available. The health system was founded in 1911.

	Annual Growth	07/14	07/15	07/16	07/21	07/22
Sales ($mil.)	4.6%	–	490.6	498.9	712.3	674.0
Net income ($ mil.)	–	–	32.3	(13.5)	42.8	(71.6)
Market value ($ mil.)	–	–	–	–	–	–
Employees	–	–	–	–	–	3,000

PHOENIX CHILDREN'S HOSPITAL, INC.

1919 E THOMAS RD
PHOENIX, AZ 850167710
Phone: 602 933-1000
Fax: –
Web: www.phoenixchildrens.org

CEO: Robert Meyer
CFO: Craig McKnight
HR: –
FYE: December 31
Type: Private

Founded in 1983, Phoenix Children's Hospital (PCH) one of the largest pediatric healthcare systems in the country provides a comprehensive range of medical services specifically for children and adolescents in the greater Phoenix area. The hospital has about 1,200 specialists who deliver care across more than 75 subspecialties, including emergency care, childhood cancers, hematology, neuroscience, heart disease, trauma, and orthopedics. It also operates a newborn intensive care unit (NICU) at its main campus. PCH has several pediatric outpatient care centers in surrounding Phoenix suburbs.

	Annual Growth	12/10	12/11	12/13	12/14	12/21
Sales ($mil.)	9.8%	–	498.7	655.2	661.6	1,269.7
Net income ($ mil.)	–	–	(5.1)	31.9	26.9	187.2
Market value ($ mil.)	–	–	–	–	–	–
Employees	–	–	–	–	–	3,000

PHOENIX FOOTWEAR GROUP, INC.

NBB: PXFG

2236 Rutherford Road, Suite 113
Carlsbad, CA 92008
Phone: 760 602-9688
Fax: 760 602-9619
Web: www.phoenixfootwear.com

CEO: James R Riedman
CFO: Dennis Nelson
HR: –
FYE: December 31
Type: Public

Phoenix Footwear is a well-shod bird. The company manufactures comfort footwear under the Trotters and SoftWalk names for women and H.S. Trask for men. Trotters products include sandals, boots, and dress and casual footwear. Focused on comfort, the SoftWalk brand boasts clogs, slings, and casual styles. Its Western-inspired footwear, H.S. Trask, comprises boots, oxfords, moccasins, and slippers. Phoenix Footwear's products are manufactured overseas -- primarily in Brazil and China -- and are sold through some 1,155 US retailers, including mass merchants, major department stores, mail order companies, and specialty shoe retailers. Founded in 1882 as Daniel Green Company, the shoemaker changed its name in 2001.

	Annual Growth	12/18	12/19*	01/21	01/22*	12/22
Sales ($mil.)	0.1%	21.6	19.6	12.3	16.2	21.7
Net income ($ mil.)	36.9%	0.4	(0.2)	(0.8)	0.9	1.4
Market value ($ mil.)	(4.3%)	2.2	1.8	0.6	1.1	1.8
Employees	–	–	57	–	–	–

*Fiscal year change

PHOENIX GOLD INTERNATIONAL INC

9300 North Decatur Street
Portland, OR 97203
Phone: 503 286-9300
Fax: 503 978-3380
Web: www.phoenixgold.com

CEO: –
CFO: –
HR: –
FYE: September 30
Type: Public

Products made by Rodin (formerly Phoenix Gold) produce enough throbbing bass to rock your media room and maybe even make your neighbors call the authorities. The company makes high-end audio electronics (amplifiers and equalizers), speakers, and accessories for the home theater market. Its products, originally made in Portland but now overseas, are sold through specialty retailers worldwide under the Phoenix Gold, Carver Professional, and AudioSource brand names. In late 2003 PG Holding (controlled in part by former chairman and CEO Timothy Johnson) purchased a majority stake in the company. Phoenix Gold was acquired, in turn, by a group of investors in 2006 and changed its name in 2007.

	Annual Growth	09/99	09/00	09/01	09/02	09/03
Sales ($mil.)	(2.6%)	27.5	27.3	28.1	29.6	24.8
Net income ($ mil.)	–	0.9	1.0	(0.2)	0.0	(0.8)
Market value ($ mil.)	(13.3%)	7.7	5.6	3.3	5.3	4.4
Employees	(13.3%)	202	190	145	157	114

PHOTRONICS, INC.

NMS: PLAB

15 Secor Road
Brookfield, CT 06804
Phone: 203 775-9000
Fax: –
Web: www.photronics.com

CEO: –
CFO: –
HR: –
FYE: October 31
Type: Public

Photronics is the world's leading manufacturer of photomasks, which are high precision photographic quartz or glass plates containing microscopic images of electronic circuits. Photomasks are a key tool in the process for manufacturing integrated circuits (ICs) and flat-panel displays (FPDs) and are used as masters to transfer circuit patterns onto semiconductor wafers and FPD substrates during the fabrication of ICs, a variety of FPDs and, to a lesser extent, other types of electrical and optical components. About 85% of the company's sales are from customers outside the US. The company was founded in 1969.

	Annual Growth	10/19	10/20	10/21	10/22	10/23
Sales ($mil.)	12.8%	550.7	609.7	663.8	824.5	892.1
Net income ($ mil.)	43.3%	29.8	33.8	55.4	118.8	125.5
Market value ($ mil.)	11.7%	723.5	597.8	796.4	994.4	1,125.7
Employees	1.5%	1,775	1,728	1,728	1,828	1,885

PHX MINERALS INC NYS: PHX

1320 South University Drive, Suite 720
Fort Worth, TX 76107
Phone: 405 948-1560
Fax: 405 948-2038
Web: www.phxmin.com

CEO: –
CFO: –
HR: –
FYE: December 31
Type: Public

PHX Minerals (PHX), formerly Panhandle Oil & Gas, takes pride in owning non-operated oil and natural gas properties in unconventional plays in Arkansas, Oklahoma, North Dakota, New Mexico, and Texas. Assets include mineral acreage, leasehold acreage, and working or royalty interests in producing wells. The company does not operate on its own properties, and engages business partners, mostly well operators, in drilling and production, transportation of oil, and transportation and sales of natural gas. It has proven reserves of over 1.3 million barrels of oil, more than 1.2 million barrels of NGL, and about 42.4 million Mcf of natural gas.

	Annual Growth	09/20	09/21	09/22*	12/22	12/23
Sales ($mil.)	15.4%	29.0	22.0	53.5	18.3	44.5
Net income ($ mil.)	–	(24.0)	(6.2)	20.4	3.3	13.9
Market value ($ mil.)	31.1%	51.5	110.1	116.6	140.0	115.9
Employees	5.6%	17	20	22	–	20

*Fiscal year change

PHYSICIANS FOR HUMAN RIGHTS, INC.

434 MASSACHUSETTS AVE STE 503
BOSTON, MA 02118
Phone: 617 301-4200
Fax: –
Web: www.phr.org

CEO: Donna McKay
CFO: Susan Lowe
HR: –
FYE: June 30
Type: Private

Physicians for Human Rights (PHR) has an broader vision of the Hippocratic Oath. The not-for-profit works to protect human health by protecting human rights around the globe. The group fights to stop torture, disappearances, and political killings and to improve hygiene conditions in prisons. It also defends medical neutrality and the protection of medical personnel during war time. Current projects include the US Campaign to Ban Landmines, Health Action AIDS Campaign, PHR Asylum Network (evaluating asylum seekers), Health and Justice for Youth (monitoring US juvenile detention centers), and Colleagues at Risk (letter-writing campaign to release held medical workers). PHR was founded in 1986.

	Annual Growth	06/07	06/08	06/09	06/10	06/22
Sales ($mil.)	0.5%	–	5.1	4.4	4.7	5.4
Net income ($ mil.)	–	–	0.0	(1.0)	0.4	(2.6)
Market value ($ mil.)	–	–	–	–	–	–
Employees	–	–	–	–	–	28

PICIS CLINICAL SOLUTIONS, INC.

100 QUANNAPOWITT PKWY STE 405
WAKEFIELD, MA 018801319
Phone: 336 397-5336
Fax: –
Web: www.picis.com

CEO: Jeff Bender
CFO: –
HR: –
FYE: December 31
Type: Private

Picis wants ER and OR docs thinking about their patients' health, not about how to manage all the data they generate. The company provides software for automating the most costly and resource-intensive hospital departments: the operating room, the intensive care unit, and the emergency room. Its CareSuite software includes tools for managing preoperative, operating room, and postoperative functions, as well as documenting anesthesia use, tracking surgical patients, and managing critical care charts and clinical documentation. The company's systems are installed in some 2,300 facilities worldwide. Picis is part of health care information provider OptumInsight, a subsidiary of UnitedHealth.

PIEDMONT ATHENS REGIONAL MEDICAL CENTER, INC.

1199 PRINCE AVE
ATHENS, GA 306062797
Phone: 706 475-7000
Fax: –
Web: www.piedmont.org

CEO: Charles Peck
CFO: Wendy J Cook
HR: –
FYE: June 30
Type: Private

Piedmont Athens Regional Medical Center is a full-service health care facility with some 360 beds serving more than 15 counties in Athens and northeastern Georgia. The regional hospital provides general medical, surgical, and diagnostic services, as well as a wide range of specialty care in such areas as oncology, rehabilitation, pediatrics, and radiology. Piedmont Athens Regional is part of the not-for-profit Piedmont Healthcare, which operates about a dozen of hospitals, some 35 urgent care centers, and around 555 physician practice locations across Georgia.

	Annual Growth	06/18	06/19	06/20	06/21	06/22
Sales ($mil.)	10.3%	–	517.1	502.2	586.6	694.3
Net income ($ mil.)	–	–	(21.2)	10.2	65.6	94.8
Market value ($ mil.)	–	–	–	–	–	–
Employees	–	–	–	–	–	3,000

PIEDMONT HOSPITAL, INC.

1968 PEACHTREE RD NW
ATLANTA, GA 303091281
Phone: 404 605-5000
Fax: –
Web: www.piedmont.org

CEO: Leslie A Les Donahue
CFO: Charlie Hall
HR: Amy Stroup
FYE: June 30
Type: Private

Founded in 1905, Piedmont Healthcare is a private, not-for-profit organization that provides a hassle-free, unified experience. Every year, it cares for 3.7 million patients, has over 30 million visits to Piedmont.org, more than 450,000 appointments scheduled online by patients and over 100,000 virtual visits. Piedmont Healthcare is supported by a work force of more than 44,000 across some 1,600 locations and serving communities that comprise 80% of Georgia's population. This includes more than 20 hospitals, including three inpatient rehabilitation hospitals, about 65 Piedmont Urgent Care centers, around 25 QuickCare locations, some 1,875 Piedmont Clinic physician practices and more than 3,075 Piedmont Clinic members. Piedmont Healthcare has provided $1.4 billion in uncompensated care and community benefit programming to the communities it serves over the past five years.

	Annual Growth	06/15	06/16	06/20	06/21	06/22
Sales ($mil.)	6.3%	–	918.1	1,110.0	1,243.4	1,327.0
Net income ($ mil.)	2.7%	–	60.0	128.2	102.4	70.6
Market value ($ mil.)	–	–	–	–	–	–
Employees	–	–	–	–	–	9,589

PIEDMONT MUNICIPAL POWER AGENCY

121 VILLAGE DR
GREER, SC 296511291
Phone: 864 877-9632
Fax: –
Web: www.pmpa.com

CEO: Comer Randall
CFO: Steven Ruark
HR: –
FYE: December 31
Type: Private

Piedmont Municipal Power Agency (Piedmont Power) generates, purchases, and transmits wholesale electricity on behalf of its 10 member municipal utilities, which distribute the power to nearly 95,000 retail customers in northwestern South Carolina. These ten utilities serve the cities of Abbeville, Clinton, Easley, Gaffney, Greer, Laurens, Newberry, Rock Hill, Union, and Westminster. Piedmont Power was created to buy an ownership interest in the Catawba Nuclear Station in York County, South Carolina, in order to secure a reliable source of electric generation for its member utilities. The agency owns a 25% stake in the Catawba plant.

	Annual Growth	12/11	12/12	12/13	12/14	12/15
Sales ($mil.)	6.8%	–	–	219.9	237.5	250.6
Net income ($ mil.)	(29.2%)	–	–	9.4	19.9	4.7
Market value ($ mil.)	–	–	–	–	–	–
Employees	–	–	–	–	–	11

PIEDMONT NATURAL GAS COMPANY, INC.

4720 PIEDMONT ROW DR STE 100
CHARLOTTE, NC 282104294
Phone: 704 364-3120
Fax: –
Web: www.piedmontng.com

CEO: Lynn J Good
CFO: Steven K Young
HR: Tim Ingram
FYE: December 31
Type: Private

Piedmont Natural Gas is a regulated public utility primarily engaged in the distribution of natural gas to more than 1.1 million residential, commercial, industrial and power generation customers (including customers served by municipalities who are wholesale customers) in the Carolinas and Tennessee. Piedmont is a business unit of Duke Energy Corporation.

PIEDMONT OFFICE REALTY TRUST INC

5565 Glenridge Connector Ste. 450
Atlanta, GA 30342
Phone: 770 418-8800
Fax: –
Web: www.piedmontreit.com

NYS: PDM
CEO: C B Smith
CFO: –
HR: –
FYE: December 31
Type: Public

Piedmont Office Realty Trust provides office space for life in the big city. A self-managed and self-administered real estate investment trust (REIT), the company invests in, develops, and manages primarily Class A office buildings in major US markets. One of the nation's largest office REITs, Piedmont owns or partially owns about 75 office and industrial properties, comprising some 21 million sq. ft. of leasable space. Many of its properties are located in Chicago, the New York Metro area, and Washington, DC. Piedmont's holdings include Chicago's Aon Center and the headquarters buildings for US Bancorp and Nestl USA.

	Annual Growth	12/19	12/20	12/21	12/22	12/23
Sales ($mil.)	2.0%	533.2	535.0	528.7	563.8	577.8
Net income ($ mil.)	–	229.3	232.7	(1.2)	146.8	(48.4)
Market value ($ mil.)	(24.8%)	2,751.4	2,007.9	2,273.9	1,134.5	879.6
Employees	2.9%	134	137	134	149	150

PIEDMONT UNIVERSITY, INC.

1021 CENTRAL AVE
DEMOREST, GA 305355252
Phone: 706 778-3000
Fax: –
Web: www.piedmont.edu

CEO: –
CFO: –
HR: –
FYE: June 30
Type: Private

Piedmont College is a private, co-educational, liberal arts college serving a population of more than 2,000 students. It offers nearly 40 undergraduate degree programs, as well as graduate programs in business and education and a doctoral program in education. Piedmont, which has campuses in the Georgia towns of Athens and Demorest, is affiliated with the National Association of Congregational Christian Churches and the United Church of Christ. The college was founded in 1897 under the direction of Methodist minister Reverend Charles C. Spence and the school still strives to instill a sense of moral responsibility to its students.

	Annual Growth	06/13	06/14	06/20	06/21	06/22
Sales ($mil.)	5.0%	–	42.1	59.7	56.8	62.0
Net income ($ mil.)	–	–	1.0	(1.6)	(0.2)	(0.3)
Market value ($ mil.)	–	–	–	–	–	–
Employees	–	–	–	–	–	160

PIH HEALTH GOOD SAMARITAN HOSPITAL

1225 WILSHIRE BLVD
LOS ANGELES, CA 900171901
Phone: 213 977-2121
Fax: –
Web: –

CEO: James West
CFO: Alan Ino
HR: Nancy Clark
FYE: September 30
Type: Private

VIP suites and valet parking are standard fare for hotels in Los Angeles, so why not hospitals too? Good Samaritan Hospital is a 410-bed acute care facility featuring all private rooms, some suites, and, yes, valet parking. Good Samaritan serves patients throughout the greater Los Angeles area. This acute-care facility offers services including cardiac surgery, diagnostic imaging, women's services, ophthalmology, oncology, neurology, respiratory care, and transfusion-free medicine and surgery. Good Samaritan also has centers dedicated to urology, orthopedic care, perinatal medicine, and retinal surgery. The hospital is affiliated with the Episcopalian Church and USC's Keck School of Medicine.

	Annual Growth	08/15	08/16	08/19*	09/21	09/22
Sales ($mil.)	5.3%	–	319.3	6.0	409.9	435.9
Net income ($ mil.)	(53.6%)	–	19.5	(6.3)	(19.8)	0.2
Market value ($ mil.)	–	–	–	–	–	–
Employees	–	–	–	–	–	35,000

*Fiscal year change

PIKEVILLE MEDICAL CENTER, INC.

911 BYPASS RD
PIKEVILLE, KY 415011602
Phone: 606 218-3500
Fax: –
Web: www.pikevillehospital.org

CEO: Walter E May
CFO: Michelle Hagey
HR: Gabriel Stanley
FYE: September 30
Type: Private

Taking a nasty fall while hiking the rugged Appalachians will likely land you at Pikeville Medical Center (PMC). Serving patients in eastern Kentucky, the hospital boasts more than 260 beds and provides a full range of inpatient, outpatient, and surgical services. PMC's centers and departments handle a number of specialties, such as diagnostic imaging, echocardiogram, neurosurgery, cancer care, and bariatric surgery. Employing some 350 physicians, PMC also operates a rehabilitation hospital, a home health agency, and outpatient family practice and specialty clinics, as well as a physician residency program. PMC first opened on Christmas Day in 1924.

	Annual Growth	09/18	09/19	09/20	09/21	09/22
Sales ($mil.)	4.0%	–	547.7	568.1	556.5	616.6
Net income ($ mil.)	–	–	5.8	17.2	29.6	(6.6)
Market value ($ mil.)	–	–	–	–	–	–
Employees	–	–	–	–	–	2,527

PIKSEL, INC.

2100 POWERS FERRY RD SE STE 400
ATLANTA, GA 303395014
Phone: 877 664-6137
Fax: –
Web: www.piksel.com

CEO: Ralf Tillmann
CFO: Fabrice Hamaide
HR: Brittany Williams
FYE: December 31
Type: Private

Piksel provides products and services to help companies capitalize on online video. Its team of experts -- called Televisionaries -- help design, build, and manage online video services, primarily for the media industry and large enterprise brands. Products include the Piksel Video Platform (content management and delivery), Piksel Mosaic (content targeting), EnterpriseTV (digital signage), and Piksel Voyage (trip/travel content). The company serves clients such as AT&T, Sky, Airbus, and Volkswagen from about a dozen offices in the US, as well as across Europe.

PILGRIMS PRIDE CORP.

NMS: PPC

1770 Promontory Circle
Greeley, CO 80634-9038
Phone: 970 506-8000
Fax: –
Web: www.pilgrims.com

CEO: Fabio Sandri
CFO: Matthew Galvanoni
HR: Araceli Burket
FYE: December 31
Type: Public

Pilgrim's Pride is primarily engaged in the production, processing, marketing, and distribution of fresh, frozen and value-added chicken and pork products under a host of brands (Pilgrim's Pride, Gold Kist, and Moy Park among them). Vertically integrated, Pilgrim's Pride has a global network of approximately 4,950 growers, 35 feed mills, more than 45 hatcheries, some 40 processing plants, nearly 35 prepared foods cook plants, some 30 distribution centers, nine rendering facilities, four pet food plants, and three other facilities. The company ? which serves more than 51,100 customers across grocery store chains, wholesale clubs and other retail distributors ? is majority owned by Brazil's JBS. The US accounts for more than 60% of the company's sales.

	Annual Growth	12/19	12/20	12/21	12/22	12/23
Sales ($mil.)	11.1%	11,409	12,092	14,777	17,468	17,362
Net income ($ mil.)	(8.4%)	455.9	94.8	31.0	745.9	321.6
Market value ($ mil.)	(4.3%)	7,807.6	4,581.9	6,523.6	5,635.6	6,549.6
Employees	3.6%	53,100	30,900	59,400	61,500	61,200

PILKINGTON NORTH AMERICA, INC.

811 MADISON AVE FL 3
TOLEDO, OH 436045688
Phone: 419 247-3731
Fax: –
Web: www.pilkington.com

CEO: Richard Altman
CFO: –
HR: Larry Valenti
FYE: March 31
Type: Private

Pilkington North America has a clear view of the US glass market. The company manufactures and markets glass and glazing products primarily for the automotive and building industries. Benefits of its glass include fire protection, noise control, solar heat control, and thermal insulation. A majority of its sales come from automotive glass sold to the original equipment and replacement markets. More than a quarter of sales are made from building glass geared at homeowners and architects. A small but growing part of its business focuses on specialty glass used in solar energy conversion. Pilkington North America is a subsidiary of Pilkington plc, which operates as part of Japanese glass giant Nippon Sheet Glass.

	Annual Growth	03/02	03/03	03/04	03/07	03/08
Sales ($mil.)	1.0%	–	–	931.8	913.4	967.9
Net income ($ mil.)	–	–	–	32.0	(17.2)	(11.4)
Market value ($ mil.)	–	–	–	–	–	–
Employees	–	–	–	–	–	3,981

PILLARSTONE CAPITAL REIT

NBB: PRLE

2600 South Gesssner, Suite 555
Houston, TX 77063
Phone: 832 810-0100
Fax: –
Web: www.pillarstone-capital.com

CEO: Bradford Johnson
CFO: Daniel P Kovacevic
HR: –
FYE: December 31
Type: Public

Ideally, Paragon Real Estate Equity and Investment Trust would be the very model of real estate investing, but it merely is a corporate shell company. The firm is seeking investment opportunities in land development, joint ventures, other real estate companies, and retail, office, industrial, and hospitality properties. In 2008 it began investing in stock of publicly traded real estate investment trusts (REITs). Entities associated with CEO James Mastandrea control more than three-quarters of Paragon, which has expressed doubts about its ability to continue as a going concern and may seek additional investors or sell its corporate shell.

	Annual Growth	12/17	12/18	12/19	12/20	12/21
Sales ($mil.)	–	–	17.2	14.3	9.7	9.3
Net income ($ mil.)	–	(0.0)	1.3	3.1	(0.4)	(0.3)
Market value ($ mil.)	–	–	–	–	–	–
Employees	–	2	3	3	3	2

PILOT CORPORATION

5508 LONAS DR
KNOXVILLE, TN 379093221
Phone: 865 588-7488
Fax: –
Web: www.pilotflyingj.com

CEO: James A Haslam III
CFO: Mitchell D Steenrod
HR: Keonia Reda
FYE: December 31
Type: Private

Pilot offers a salve to those suffering from white-line fever. Its Pilot Flying J, a joint venture between Pilot and CVC Capital Partners, runs more than 650 travel centers that sell fuel and food across North America. Its truck stops feature restaurant chains, such as Subway, Pizza Hut, and Taco Bell, and offer hot showers. Pilot has fuel islands large enough to service several 18-wheelers. Pilot Truck Care Centers provide TLC (tender loving care) for big rigs, while some 45 Pilot Food Marts (all in Tennessee) keep drivers fed. James Haslam II got Pilot off the ground in 1958 as a gas station that sold cigarettes and soft drinks; now his son, CEO James Haslam III, runs the firm. The Haslam family owns the company.

	Annual Growth	12/07	12/08	12/09	12/10	12/11
Sales ($mil.)	(3.2%)	–	–	–	415.1	402.0
Net income ($ mil.)	(2.0%)	–	–	–	373.2	365.7
Market value ($ mil.)	–	–	–	–	–	–
Employees	–	–	–	–	–	51,337

PINE GROVE MANUFACTURED HOMES, INC.

2 PLEASANT VALLEY RD
PINE GROVE, PA 179639563
Phone: 570 345-2011
Fax: –
Web: www.pinegrovehomes.com

CEO: –
CFO: –
HR: –
FYE: October 28
Type: Private

Pine Grove Manufactured Homes designs and builds manufactured homes in the mid-Atlantic and northeastern regions of the US. Its single-section homes range in width from 12 ft. to 16 ft.; its multi-section homes range from 20 ft. to 32 ft. in width and can be built up to 76 ft. in length. Special features offered include gourmet kitchens and spa baths. Sister company Pleasant Valley Modular Homes manufactures ranch, split-level, and two-story residences, as well as log-sided homes and duplexes, in a variety of styles, ranging in size from around 1,000 sq. ft. to 3,000 sq. ft. Pine Grove markets its homes through independent retailers and developers. Privately held, Pine Grove was established in 1982.

	Annual Growth	10/03	10/04	10/05	10/06	10/07
Sales ($mil.)	(15.0%)	–	–	44.1	42.5	31.9
Net income ($ mil.)	(21.5%)	–	–	5.1	5.5	3.1
Market value ($ mil.)	–	–	–	–	–	–
Employees	–	–	–	–	–	100

PINE STATE TRADING CO.

100 ENTERPRISE AVE
GARDINER, ME 043456249
Phone: 207 622-2345
Fax: –
Web: www.supplylogisticssolutions.com

CEO: –
CFO: Garrett Grunewald
HR: Angela Bartlett
FYE: December 31
Type: Private

Pine State Trading distributes tobacco products, food, and beverages to convenient stores throughout New England. Its Pine State Beverage division handles beer and wine sales, and the company also provides paper supplies, foodservice equipment, and general merchandise to more than 5,000 retail customers. The company stocks more than 19,000 products at its five distribution centers (two in Maine and one each in Massachusetts, New Hampshire, and Vermont). In addition, Pine State Trading provides vending services and supplies coffee for corporate break rooms. The family-owned business was founded in 1940 by Charles Canning. Core-Mark Holding Co acquired the company's Pine State Convenience Store division in 2016.

PINEAPPLE ENERGY INC
NAS: PEGY

10900 Red Circle Drive
Minnetonka, MN 55343
Phone: 952 996-1674
Fax: –
Web: www.pineappleenergy.com

CEO: Kyle Udseth
CFO: Eric Ingvaldson
HR: –
FYE: December 31
Type: Public

Pineapple Energy (formerly known as Communications Systems) is focused on growing leading local and regional solar, storage, and energy services companies nationwide. Its portfolio of brands, SUNation Energy, Hawaii Energy Connection, E-Gear, Sungevity and Horizon Solar Power, provide homeowners and small businesses with an end-to-end product offering spanning solar, battery storage, and grid services. Incorporated in 1969 as Communications Systems, Inc., the company changed its name to Pineapple Holdings, Inc. when completing the merger with Pineapple Energy LLC in early 2022. Also in early 2022, the company changed its legal name to Pineapple Energy Inc.

	Annual Growth	12/18	12/19	12/20	12/21	12/22
Sales ($mil.)	(19.6%)	65.8	50.9	42.6	7.0	27.5
Net income ($ mil.)	–	(6.8)	6.5	(0.2)	3.0	(10.4)
Market value ($ mil.)	3.5%	20.1	61.2	45.3	23.8	23.1
Employees	1.4%	241	203	150	39	255

PINEY WOODS HEALTHCARE SYSTEM, L.P.

505 S JOHN REDDITT DR
LUFKIN, TX 759043120
Phone: 936 634-8311
Fax: –
Web: www.woodlandheights.net

CEO: –
CFO: –
HR: –
FYE: December 31
Type: Private

Piney Woods Healthcare does business as Woodland Heights Medical Center and while it's not in the woods and it's not located on a mountain top, it is a full service hospital in Lufkin, Texas. Established in 1918, the medical center has about 150 beds and provides a comprehensive range of inpatient, outpatient, surgical, and emergency services. Specialized treatment programs including cardiac care, maternity care, sports and occupational medicine, physical therapy, and rehabilitation. Woodland Heights also offers community services including its Healthy Woman program, designed to educate the public on women's health issues, and Senior Circle, which offers senior discounts, activities and events, exercise and wellness classes. The company is part of Community Health Systems.

	Annual Growth	12/13	12/14	12/15	12/16	12/17
Sales ($mil.)	(8.3%)	–	122.5	99.7	93.5	94.6
Net income ($ mil.)	(13.2%)	–	10.0	15.5	4.4	6.5
Market value ($ mil.)	–	–	–	–	–	–
Employees	–	–	–	–	–	600

PINNACLE BANCSHARES, INC.
NBB: PCLB

1811 Second Avenue
Jasper, AL 35501
Phone: 205 221-4111
Fax: –
Web: www.pinnaclebancshares.com

CEO: Robert B Nolen Jr
CFO: –
HR: –
FYE: December 31
Type: Public

Pinnacle is on top of Alabama's banking needs. Pinnacle Bancshares is the holding company for Pinnacle Bank, which serves central and northwestern Alabama through more than a half-dozen offices. The bank provides consumer and business banking services, including checking and money market accounts, as well as a variety of consumer and commercial loans. Real estate lending dominates the loan portfolio, with one- to four-family residential mortgages making up the largest percentage, followed by commercial mortgages, business loans, and construction and land development loans. The bank also makes consumer and farm loans.

	Annual Growth	12/13	12/14	12/15	12/16	12/17
Assets ($mil.)	(0.3%)	220.4	219.0	219.5	216.6	217.8
Net income ($ mil.)	4.3%	1.9	2.0	2.2	2.3	2.3
Market value ($ mil.)	11.3%	15.1	17.9	21.1	23.7	23.2
Employees	–	–	–	–	–	–

PINNACLE BANKSHARES CORP
NBB: PPBN

622 Broad Street
Altavista, VA 24517
Phone: 434 369-3000
Fax: –
Web: www.1stnatbk.com

CEO: Aubrey H Hall III
CFO: Bryan M Lemley
HR: –
FYE: December 31
Type: Public

Pinnacle Bankshares is always looking for the high point. The firm is the holding company for the First National Bank, which operates about 10 branches and loan production centers in central Virginia. Serving individuals and businesses in the area, the bank offers standard products and services including checking and savings accounts, IRAs, and merchant bankcard processing. The company uses funds from deposit accounts to originate real estate loans, consumer loans, and business loans. The company, which traces its roots to 1908, also has two real estate subsidiaries, First Properties and FNB Property Corp.

	Annual Growth	12/17	12/18	12/19	12/20	12/21
Assets ($mil.)	23.0%	443.9	470.6	500.5	860.5	1,015.9
Net income ($ mil.)	12.3%	2.7	4.2	4.4	3.1	4.4
Market value ($ mil.)	(4.3%)	64.0	59.6	69.0	49.9	53.6
Employees	–	–	–	–	197	190

PINNACLE FINANCIAL PARTNERS INC
NMS: PNFP

150 Third Avenue South, Suite 900
Nashville, TN 37201
Phone: 615 744-3700
Fax: –
Web: www.pnfp.com

CEO: M T Turner
CFO: Harold R Carpenter Jr
HR: Kelly Morrow
FYE: December 31
Type: Public

Pinnacle Financial Partners is the holding company for Tennessee-based Pinnacle Bank, which has grown to nearly 125 offices in Tennessee, North Carolina, South Carolina, Virginia, Georgia, and Alabama since its founding in 2000. Serving consumers and small- to mid-sized businesses, the $42.0 billion financial institution provides a full range of banking, investment, trust, mortgage, and insurance products and services designed for businesses and their owners and individuals interested in a comprehensive relationship with its financial institution. The company offer its investment and trust services through its Trust & Investment Services department, while its insurance brokerage subsidiary, Miller Loughry Beach and HPB Insurance, specializes in property/casualty policies.

	Annual Growth	12/19	12/20	12/21	12/22	12/23
Assets ($mil.)	14.6%	27,805	34,933	38,469	41,970	47,960
Net income ($ mil.)	8.8%	400.9	312.3	527.3	560.7	562.2
Market value ($ mil.)	8.0%	4,913.1	4,943.8	7,331.2	5,634.7	6,695.6
Employees	7.8%	2,487	2,634	2,841	3,242	3,357

PINNACLE WEST CAPITAL CORP
NYS: PNW

400 North Fifth Street, P.O. Box 53999
Phoenix, AZ 85072-3999
Phone: 602 250-1000
Fax: 602 379-2625
Web: www.pinnaclewest.com

CEO: Jeffrey B Guldner
CFO: Andrew D Cooper
HR: –
FYE: December 31
Type: Public

Pinnacle West Capital is a holding company for the state's largest and longest-serving electric company, Arizona Public Service, which transmits and distributes electricity to approximately 1.3 million residential, commercial, and industrial customers throughout most of the state. The power distribution utility also has about 6,340 MW of regulated generating capacity and has a mix of both long-term and short-term purchased power agreements for additional capacity, including a range of agreements for the purchase of energy from renewable sources. The company's other subsidiaries include El Dorado, BCE and 4CA.

	Annual Growth	12/19	12/20	12/21	12/22	12/23
Sales ($mil.)	7.8%	3,471.2	3,587.0	3,803.8	4,324.4	4,696.0
Net income ($ mil.)	(1.8%)	538.3	550.6	618.7	483.6	501.6
Market value ($ mil.)	(5.5%)	10,200	9,068.3	8,006.6	8,624.8	8,148.4
Employees	(66.2%)	6,210	6,026	5,872	5,861	81

PINTEREST INC
NYS: PINS

651 Brannan Street
San Francisco, CA 94107
Phone: 415 762-7100
Fax: –
Web: www.pinterest.com

CEO: Bill Ready
CFO: Todd Morgenfeld
HR: –
FYE: December 31
Type: Public

Pinterest is a visual discovery engine for finding ideas like recipes, home and style inspiration, and more. The company is where over 450 million people come to discover and bring to life ideas for activities like cooking dinner or deciding what to wear; for major commitments like house remodeling or marathon training; for ongoing passions like gardening or fashion; and milestone events like wedding or dream vacation planning. Pinterest offers a full-funnel marketing solution, creating value for businesses seeking new audiences and sales. Its full funnel advertising solution maps to the consumer buying journey, from building awareness and comprehension at the top of the funnel to supporting consideration and engagement with brands in the middle of the funnel, to driving purchases at the bottom of the funnel.

	Annual Growth	12/19	12/20	12/21	12/22	12/23
Sales ($mil.)	27.9%	1,142.8	1,692.7	2,578.0	2,802.6	3,055.1
Net income ($ mil.)	–	(1,361.4)	(128.3)	316.4	(96.0)	(35.6)
Market value ($ mil.)	18.7%	12,638	44,681	24,646	16,462	25,114
Employees	16.0%	2,217	2,545	3,225	3,987	4,014

PIONEER BANKSHARES INC
NBB: PNBI

263 East Main Street
Stanley, VA 22851
Phone: 540 778-2294
Fax: –
Web: www.pioneerbks.com

CEO: Mark N Reed
CFO: Lori G Hassett
HR: –
FYE: December 31
Type: Public

Although you don't get a coonskin cap when you open an account, Pioneer Bankshares likes to maintain that pioneer spirit. The financial institution is the holding company for Pioneer Bank, which serves northeastern Virginia through about a half dozen branches. It provides standard retail products and services to individuals and small to midsized businesses. Lending activities are focused on real estate loans and mortgages: Loans secured by real estate account for some 80% of its total loan book. The company also offers business and consumer loans. The bank has two subsidiaries, Pioneer Financial Services (insurance and investment products) and Pioneer Special Assets (foreclosures with added liabilities).

	Annual Growth	12/07	12/08	12/09	12/10	12/11
Assets ($mil.)	2.4%	151.8	156.1	159.9	168.2	167.2
Net income ($ mil.)	(1.4%)	1.8	1.1	1.2	1.9	1.7
Market value ($ mil.)	(14.2%)	27.1	18.5	16.1	18.7	14.7
Employees	(5.4%)	65	51	49	50	52

PIONEER DATA SYSTEMS, INC.

33 WOOD AVE S STE 600
ISELIN, NJ 088302717
Phone: 732 603-0001
Fax: –
Web: www.pioneerdata.com

CEO: –
CFO: –
HR: Anisha Mukhi
FYE: December 31
Type: Private

Pioneer Data Systems primarily provides database design, development, and database administration services, with a focus on products developed by Oracle. It also offers such services as consulting, training, support, maintenance, and installation. Pioneer Data Systems, which was founded in 1995, serves customers in such industries as financial services, publishing, and telecommunications. Customers have included Deutsche Bank, Educational Testing Service, and Standard & Poor's.

	Annual Growth	12/13	12/14	12/15	12/16	12/17
Sales ($mil.)	8.0%	–	–	4.5	5.0	5.3
Net income ($ mil.)	3.3%	–	–	0.2	0.3	0.3
Market value ($ mil.)	–	–	–	–	–	–
Employees	–	–	–	–	–	100

PIONEER ENERGY SERVICES CORP.

1250 NE LOOP 410 STE 1000
SAN ANTONIO, TX 782091560
Phone: 855 884-0575
Fax: –
Web: www.patenergy.com

CEO: Matt Porte
CFO: Lorne Phillips
HR: –
FYE: December 31
Type: Private

Pioneer Energy Services Corp. provides land-based drilling services and production services to a diverse group of oil and gas exploration and production companies in the US and internationally in Colombia. In 2020, the company emerged from Chapter 11 bankruptcy and was acquired by Patterson-UTI in mid-2021 for about $278 million. The company was incorporated under the laws of the State of Texas in 1979 as the successor to a business that had been operating since 1968.

PIONEER NATURAL RESOURCES CO
NYS: PXD

777 Hidden Ridge
Irving, TX 75038
Phone: 972 444-9001
Fax: 972 969-3587
Web: www.pxd.com

CEO: Richard P Dealy
CFO: Neal H Shah
HR: Amanda McMahon
FYE: December 31
Type: Public

Pioneer Natural Resources Company explores for, develops and produces oil, NGLs, and gas in the Midland Basin of West Texas. With about 237.2 million barrels of oil equivalent, this independent energy company is one of the biggest energy producers in the Permian Basin. Pioneer's production comes mostly from its Spraberry/Wolfcamp oil field and reports around 8.2 billion net producing wells. Additionally, the company owns interests in about 10 gas-processing plants, including the related gathering systems. Its major customers include Energy Transfer Crude Marketing LLC, Shell Trading US Company, Occidental Energy Marketing Inc., and Plains Marketing Inc.

	Annual Growth	12/19	12/20	12/21	12/22	12/23
Sales ($mil.)	20.1%	9,304.0	6,685.0	14,643	24,294	19,362
Net income ($ mil.)	59.5%	756.0	(200.0)	2,118.0	7,845.0	4,894.0
Market value ($ mil.)	10.4%	35,364	26,607	42,491	53,357	52,537
Employees	(1.2%)	2,323	1,853	1,932	2,076	2,213

PIONEER OIL & GAS
NBB: POGS

1206 West South Jordan Parkway, Unit B
South Jordan, UT 84095-5512
Phone: 801 566-3000
Fax: 801 446-5500
Web: –

CEO: Gregg B Colton
CFO: –
HR: –
FYE: September 30
Type: Public

Pioneering the squeezing of oil and gas profits from mature properties in the Rockies that other oil companies have sold as marginal producers is the work of Pioneer Oil and Gas. The company acquires oil and gas properties from oil explorers, sells producing wells, and acquires new oil and gas leases on properties located in Colorado, Nevada, Utah, and Wyoming. Pioneer Oil and Gas has estimated proved reserves of 1 billion cu. ft. of natural gas and about 30,000 barrels of oil. The oil and gas exploration and production independent was established in 1980. Brothers and top executives Gregg and Don Colton control Pioneer Oil and Gas.

	Annual Growth	09/02	09/03	09/04	09/05	09/06
Sales ($mil.)	37.1%	0.9	1.9	1.9	6.9	3.2
Net income ($ mil.)	–	(0.2)	0.2	0.5	4.1	1.5
Market value ($ mil.)	46.6%	1.9	2.5	6.4	9.7	8.6
Employees	–	–	4	4	4	–	–

PIONEER TELEPHONE COOPERATIVE, INC.

108 E ROBBERTS AVE
KINGFISHER, OK 737502742
Phone: 405 375-4111
Fax: -
Web: www.ptci.com

CEO: -
CFO: -
HR: -
FYE: December 31
Type: Private

It might operate in historical pioneer country, but Pioneer Telephone Cooperative provides really modern telecommunication services to residents of western Oklahoma and southern Kansas. The company has more than 150,000 residential and business subscribers with offerings ranging from landline and cell phone service to online digital TV access. Internet service is available via dial-up, broadband, or wireless, and the company offers almost 160 channels of digital television, including nearly 65 channels in HD. Pioneer Telephone Cooperative also offers security systems, publishes its own Yellow Pages directory, and provides web hosting, e-mail, and networking services. It is owned by the members it serves.

	Annual Growth	12/06	12/07	12/08	12/15	12/19
Sales ($mil.)	(26.8%)	-	119.1	-	1.8	2.8
Net income ($ mil.)	(24.5%)	-	7.8	-	(0.1)	0.3
Market value ($ mil.)	-	-	-	-	-	-
Employees	-	-	-	-	-	550

PIPER SANDLER COMPANIES

NYS: PIPR

800 Nicollet Mall, Suite 900
Minneapolis, MN 55402
Phone: 612 303-6000
Fax: -
Web: www.pipersandler.com

CEO: Chad R Abraham
CFO: Kate Clune
HR: -
FYE: December 31
Type: Public

Investment bank Piper Sandler Companies specializes in supplying clients with mergers and acquisitions advice, financing, and industry research. Founded in 1895, Piper Sandler provides a broad set of products and services, including financial advisory services; equity and debt capital markets products; public finance services; institutional brokerage; fundamental equity and macro research services; fixed income services; and alternative asset management strategies. Piper Sandler targets a variety of clients, including corporations, government entities, not-for-profits, and middle-market companies across the consumer, financial services, healthcare, technology, and industrial sectors. Majority of its revenue comes from US customers.

	Annual Growth	12/19	12/20	12/21	12/22	12/23
Sales ($mil.)	12.3%	846.3	1,252.7	2,041.8	1,435.1	1,348.0
Net income ($ mil.)	(6.5%)	111.7	40.5	278.5	110.7	85.5
Market value ($ mil.)	21.6%	1,215.1	1,533.7	2,713.4	1,978.9	2,658.1
Employees	2.5%	1,565	1,511	1,665	1,790	1,725

PISMO COAST VILLAGE, INC.

165 South Dolliver Street
Pismo Beach, CA 93449
Phone: 805 773-5649
Fax: -
Web: www.pismocoastvillage.com

CEO: -
CFO: -
HR: -
FYE: September 30
Type: Public

Pismo Coast Village will prove that half the fun of owning an RV is parking it. The company runs a full-service recreational vehicle (RV) resort on more than 25 acres in Pismo Beach, California that accommodates up to 400 RVs. Vacationers have access to an onsite general store, heated swimming pool, laundry facilities, mini-golf course, recreation hall, video arcade, wireless Internet, and several playgrounds. Pismo Coast's recreation department aims to keep kids and families busy by renting out sports equipment and planning activities such as arts and crafts, mini-golf tournaments, pet costume contests, and scavenger hunts. The resort also offers an RV repair shop.

	Annual Growth	09/18	09/19	09/20	09/21	09/22
Sales ($mil.)	5.1%	8.5	8.5	7.4	9.8	10.3
Net income ($ mil.)	5.4%	1.6	1.5	0.9	2.4	2.0
Market value ($ mil.)	-	-	-	-	-	-
Employees	3.4%	62	63	62	61	71

PISTON AUTOMOTIVE, L.L.C.

12723 TELEGRAPH RD STE 1
REDFORD, MI 482391489
Phone: 313 541-8674
Fax: -
Web: www.pistonautomotive.com

CEO: Vincent Johnson
CFO: Amit Singhi
HR: Eric Walker
FYE: December 31
Type: Private

Surprisingly, there are no pistons on the workbenches and pallets of Piston Automotive. Less surprisingly, a former Detroit Pistons player, Vinnie "the Microwave" Johnson, leads it as chairman. Piston Automotive specializes in the supply of powertrain systems, front-end and powertrain cooling systems, chassis systems, and interior systems for the automotive industry. The company was formed in 1995 by Johnson to serve major automotive makers and related OEM suppliers in the greater Detroit area. A year later Piston Automotive began suspension module assembly and sequencing operations.

	Annual Growth	12/06	12/07	12/08	12/09	12/10
Sales ($mil.)	41.8%	-	-	162.3	-	326.4
Net income ($ mil.)	1074.5%	-	-	0.0	-	9.7
Market value ($ mil.)	-	-	-	-	-	-
Employees	-	-	-	-	-	7,900

PITNEY BOWES INC

NYS: PBI

3001 Summer Street
Stamford, CT 06926
Phone: 203 356-5000
Fax: 203 351-7336
Web: www.pitneybowes.com

CEO: Jason C Dies
CFO: Ana M Chadwick
HR: -
FYE: December 31
Type: Public

Pitney Bowes Inc. is a global shipping and mailing company that provides technology, logistics, and financial services to small and medium sized businesses, large enterprises, including more than 90% of the Fortune 500, retailers and government clients around the world. Through its wholly owned subsidiary, The Pitney Bowes Bank, it offers a revolving credit solution that enables clients to make meter rental payments and purchase postage, services and supplies and an interest-bearing deposit solution to clients who prefer to prepay postage. It offers financing alternatives for clients to finance or lease other manufacturers' equipment and provide working capital. The US accounts for more than 85% of sales.

	Annual Growth	12/19	12/20	12/21	12/22	12/23
Sales ($mil.)	0.5%	3,205.1	3,554.1	3,673.6	3,538.0	3,266.3
Net income ($ mil.)	-	194.6	(181.5)	(1.4)	36.9	(385.6)
Market value ($ mil.)	2.2%	710.8	1,086.4	1,169.3	670.2	776.0
Employees	(1.2%)	11,000	11,500	11,500	11,000	10,500

PITT COUNTY MEMORIAL HOSPITAL, INCORPORATED

2100 STANTONSBURG RD
GREENVILLE, NC 278342832
Phone: 252 847-4100
Fax: -
Web: www.ecuhealth.org

CEO: Dave McRae
CFO: -
HR: Sonya Peoples
FYE: September 30
Type: Private

Vidant Medical Center is an acute health services facility that serves the vibrant community of Greenville, North Carolina, and surrounding areas. The 909-bed regional referral hospital's specialty divisions include Vidant Children's Hospital, East Carolina Heart Institute, a rehabilitation center, and the outpatient Vidant SurgiCenter. Other services include oncology, transplant, women's health, orthopedic, behavioral care, and home health and hospice care units. The center also serves as a teaching facility for East Carolina University's Brody School of Medicine. Vidant Medical Center (formerly Pitt County Memorial Hospital) is a member of University Health Systems of Eastern Carolina (dba Vidant Health).

	Annual Growth	09/17	09/18	09/20	09/21	09/22
Sales ($mil.)	7.8%	-	1,201.3	1,974.6	1,238.0	1,622.7
Net income ($ mil.)	(5.9%)	-	131.5	58.8	146.0	103.3
Market value ($ mil.)	-	-	-	-	-	-
Employees	-	-	-	-	-	15,000

PITT-OHIO EXPRESS, LLC

15 27TH ST
PITTSBURGH, PA 152224729
Phone: 412 232-3015
Fax: –
Web: www.pittohioexpress.com

CEO: –
CFO: –
HR: –
FYE: December 31
Type: Private

Primarily a regional less-than-truckload (LTL) freight carrier, Pitt Ohio operates a fleet of about 1,000 tractors and 3,100 trailers. (LTL carriers consolidate freight from multiple shippers into a single truckload.) It maintains straight trucks and vans in its fleet. Pitt Ohio additionally provides truckload (TL) transportation through ECM Transport. It operates a network of about 20 terminals, primarily in the Midwest and Mid-Atlantic US. Beyond freight hauling, Pitt Ohio provides specialized logistics services for shippers. The family of Charles Hammel III owns Pitt Ohio, which has grown from a business established by Hammel's grandfather in 1919.

	Annual Growth	12/01	12/02	12/04	12/06	12/07
Sales ($mil.)	5.0%	–	205.6	221.4	243.7	261.8
Net income ($ mil.)	(22.2%)	–	65.9	22.2	24.7	18.8
Market value ($ mil.)	–	–	–	–	–	–
Employees	–	–	–	–	–	3,352

PITTSBURGH ASSOCIATES

115 FEDERAL ST
PITTSBURGH, PA 152125727
Phone: 412 321-2827
Fax: –
Web: www.mlb.com

CEO: Kevin S McClatchy
CFO: James Plake
HR: Kimberlee Matthews
FYE: December 31
Type: Private

These Pirates have been plundering baseball booty for a long time. Pittsburgh Baseball Club owns and operates the Pittsburgh Pirates, one of the oldest and more storied franchises in Major League Baseball. The club joined the National League in 1887 as the Pittsburgh Alleghenies (renamed in 1891) and has won nine NL pennants and five World Series championships, its last in 1979. Pittsburgh's roster has included such stars as Bill Madlock, Willie Stargell, and Kent Tekulve. The team plays host at Pittsburgh's PNC Park. Chairman Bob Nutting bought majority control of the Bucs in 2007.

	Annual Growth	10/96	10/97	10/98	10/99*	12/08
Sales ($mil.)	(50.9%)	–	–	–	62.3	0.1
Net income ($ mil.)	–	–	–	–	(7.7)	–
Market value ($ mil.)	–	–	–	–	–	–
Employees	–	–	–	–	–	300

*Fiscal year change

PITTSBURGH STEELERS SPORTS, INC.

3400 S WATER ST
PITTSBURGH, PA 152032349
Phone: 412 432-7800
Fax: –
Web: www.steelers.com

CEO: –
CFO: –
HR: –
FYE: June 30
Type: Private

Pittsburgh Steelers Sports has forged a championship tradition in Steel Town. The company owns and operates the Pittsburgh Steelers professional football franchise, which has won a record six Super Bowl titles. The team joined the National Football League in 1933 as the Pirates (renamed in 1940) but claimed only eight winning seasons during its first 40 years. However, the Steelers dominated the 1970s when the team won four championships under head coach Chuck Noll with the help of such stars as Terry Bradshaw and Lynn Swann. Pittsburgh won its latest Super Bowl following the 2008 season. Dan Rooney, son of late team founder Art Rooney, and his son Art Rooney II lead a group that owns the Steelers.

	Annual Growth	06/16	06/17	06/18	06/19	06/20
Sales ($mil.)	1.5%	–	–	–	0.6	0.7
Net income ($ mil.)	–	–	–	–	(0.0)	0.0
Market value ($ mil.)	–	–	–	–	–	–
Employees	–	–	–	–	–	60

PITTSBURGH TECHNICAL INSTITUTE, INC.

1111 MCKEE RD
OAKDALE, PA 150713205
Phone: 412 809-5100
Fax: –
Web: www.pti.edu

CEO: –
CFO: –
HR: –
FYE: June 30
Type: Private

Pittsburgh Technical Institute is a two-year school that offers associate degree and certificate programs in business, design, electronics, criminal justice, hospitality, travel and tourism, medical, and computer-related fields. The school is also home to the Center for Certification and Adult Learning division, a program designed specifically for adult career education. Founded in 1946, Pittsburgh Technical Institute has three campuses in western Pennsylvania: downtown Pittsburgh, Oakdale, and Cranberry Township.

	Annual Growth	06/03	06/04	06/05	06/06	06/07
Sales ($mil.)	5.5%	–	26.3	28.7	29.8	30.9
Net income ($ mil.)	43.6%	–	0.7	1.1	1.9	2.0
Market value ($ mil.)	–	–	–	–	–	–
Employees	–	–	–	–	–	326

PIXELWORKS INC

16760 Upper Boones Ferry Rd., Ste. 101
Portland, OR 97224
Phone: 503 601-4545
Fax: –
Web: www.pixelworks.com

NMS: PXLW
CEO: Todd A Debonis
CFO: Linna Liu
HR: Canny Ko
FYE: December 31
Type: Public

Pixelworks' chips put the sizzle in digital displays. The company's display controller integrated circuits (ICs) power visual displays in PCs, TVs, and other electronic devices. Its ImageProcessor system-on-chip ICs combine microprocessor, memory, software, and digital signal processor components onto a single device. Distributor Tokyo Electron Device (TED) accounts for about 44% of sales; distributors are behind more than 60% of Pixelworks' sales. Other customers include SANYO Electric, Seiko Epson, and Hitachi, which each account for 10% of sales. About 90% of the company's sales come from customers in Asia, primarily Japan.

	Annual Growth	12/19	12/20	12/21	12/22	12/23
Sales ($mil.)	(3.5%)	68.8	40.9	55.1	70.1	59.7
Net income ($ mil.)	–	(9.1)	(26.5)	(19.8)	(16.0)	(26.2)
Market value ($ mil.)	(24.0%)	223.9	161.1	251.4	101.1	74.8
Employees	1.1%	229	197	217	222	239

PJM INTERCONNECTION, L.L.C.

2750 MONROE BLVD
NORRISTOWN, PA 194032429
Phone: 610 666-8980
Fax: –
Web: www.pjm.com

CEO: Terry Boston
CFO: Lisa M Drauschak
HR: Kelly Ostertag
FYE: December 31
Type: Private

Interdependence is a given at PJM Interconnection, which oversees a 62,555-mile section of the North American power transmission grid that spans 13 northeastern and midwestern states and the District of Columbia. The regional transmission organization monitors and coordinates the movement of wholesale electricity in its service territory; its 850 members have a combined generating capacity of 185,600 MW. Sanctioned by the Federal Energy Regulatory Commission, PJM is charged with ensuring fair competition among power purchasers, sellers, and traders; it also is responsible for the reliable delivery of distributed electricity to 61 million consumers in its territory.

PJT PARTNERS INC

280 Park Avenue
New York, NY 10017
Phone: 212 364-7810
Fax: –
Web: www.pjtpartners.com

NYS: PJT
CEO: Paul J Taubman
CFO: Helen T Meates
HR: –
FYE: December 31
Type: Public

PJT Partners is a premier global advisory-focused investment bank. The company delivers a range of strategic advisory, capital markets advisory, restructuring and special situations and shareholder advisory services to corporations, financial sponsors, institutional investors and governments around the world. Through PJT Park Hill, a leading global alternative asset advisory and fundraising business, the company provides private fund advisory and fundraising services for a diverse range of investment strategies. Most of its revenue comes from its domestic markets.

	Annual Growth	12/19	12/20	12/21	12/22	12/23
Sales ($mil.)	12.6%	717.6	1,052.3	991.9	1,025.5	1,153.2
Net income ($ mil.)	29.0%	29.6	117.5	106.2	90.5	81.8
Market value ($ mil.)	22.6%	1,091.5	1,820.0	1,791.9	1,782.2	2,463.8
Employees	10.5%	678	749	833	905	1,012

PLACID REFINING COMPANY LLC

2101 CEDAR SPRINGS RD
DALLAS, TX 752011588
Phone: 214 880-8479
Fax: –
Web: www.placidrefining.com

CEO: –
CFO: –
HR: –
FYE: December 31
Type: Private

A calm presence in the volatile oil and gas industry, Placid Refining owns and operates the Port Allen refinery in Louisiana, which converts crude oil into a number of petroleum products, including diesel, ethanol, gasoline, liquid petroleum gas, jet fuel, and fuel oils. Placid Refining's refinery has the capacity to process 80,000 barrels of crude oil per day. The company is one of the largest employers and taxpayers in West Baton Rouge Parish. Placid Refining, which is controlled by Petro-Hunt, distribute fuels across a dozen states in the southeastern US, from Texas to Virginia, and is a major supplier of jet fuel to the US military.

	Annual Growth	12/05	12/06	12/10	12/11	12/13
Sales ($mil.)	7.7%	–	2,925.7	3,686.1	4,699.6	4,929.2
Net income ($ mil.)	(13.1%)	–	128.5	39.3	4.2	47.9
Market value ($ mil.)	–	–	–	–	–	–
Employees	–	–	–	–	–	200

PLAINS ALL AMERICAN PIPELINE LP

333 Clay Street, Suite 1600
Houston, TX 77002
Phone: 713 646-4100
Fax: –
Web: www.plainsallamerican.com

NMS: PAA
CEO: –
CFO: –
HR: –
FYE: December 31
Type: Public

Plains All American Pipeline (PAA) is a publicly traded master limited partnership that owns and operates midstream energy infrastructure and provides logistics services for crude oil and natural gas liquids (NGL). With some 39 million barrels of active above-ground storage capacity, the limited partnership is engaged in the transportation, storage, terminaling, and gathering of crude oil and NGL. Its portfolio includes some 18,075 miles of pipelines and a fleet of about 1,440 trailers, around 720 trucks, and about 2,100 crude oil railcars. Plains All American Pipeline has a presence in the major energy market hubs in US and Canada. Its prominent customers include Marathon Petroleum, ExxonMobil, and BP. Majority of the company's sales were generated in the US.

	Annual Growth	12/19	12/20	12/21	12/22	12/23
Sales ($mil.)	9.7%	33,669	23,290	42,078	57,342	48,712
Net income ($ mil.)	(13.2%)	2,171.0	(2,590.0)	593.0	1,037.0	1,230.0
Market value ($ mil.)	(4.7%)	12,892	5,776.3	6,547.4	8,243.9	10,620
Employees	(4.3%)	5,000	4,400	4,100	4,100	4,200

PLAINS COTTON COOPERATIVE ASSOCIATION

3301 E 50TH ST
LUBBOCK, TX 794044331
Phone: 806 763-8011
Fax: –
Web: www.pcca.com

CEO: Kevin Brinkley
CFO: –
HR: –
FYE: June 30
Type: Private

Plainly speaking, most of the US cotton used by textile mills worldwide starts with the Plains Cotton Cooperative Association (PCCA). The farmer-owned co-op markets millions of bales annually for members in Oklahoma, Kansas, and Texas. To obtain a competitive price for their cotton, PCCA takes advantage of Telmark LP's access to The Seam , an online cotton marketplace that continually updates cotton prices, buyer data, and more. The co-op operates cotton warehouses in Texas, Oklahoma, and Kansas. PCCA sold its textile and apparel operations in 2014 to focus exclusively on cotton marketing and warehousing. Formed in 1953, PCCA's customers include Replay, Urban Outfitters, and Abercrombie & Fitch.

	Annual Growth	06/12	06/13	06/14	06/15	06/16
Sales ($mil.)	(8.6%)	–	–	–	975.5	892.1
Net income ($ mil.)	(7.7%)	–	–	–	25.8	23.8
Market value ($ mil.)	–	–	–	–	–	–
Employees	–	–	–	–	–	170

PLAINSCAPITAL CORP

2323 Victory Avenue, Suite 1400
Dallas, TX 75219
Phone: 214 252-4000
Fax: –
Web: www.plainscapital.com

CEO: Alan B White
CFO: John A Martin
HR: –
FYE: December 31
Type: Public

PlainsCapital isn't just a plain old bank. Founded in 1988, PlainCapital has more than 60 branches in and around the Texas cities of Austin, Dallas, Fort Worth, Lubbock, and San Antonio. The company has tailored solutions for businesses such as small business, agriculture, manufacturing and real estate, among others. It also conducts both commercial and consumer banking. In addition to deposit and loan services, PlainsCapital offers private banking, wealth and investment management, trust services, and correspondent banking. PlainsCapital Bank is a wholly owned subsidiary of Hilltop Holdings.

	Annual Growth	12/07	12/08	12/09	12/10	12/11
Sales ($mil.)	22.9%	305.2	312.5	537.7	650.6	697.2
Net income ($ mil.)	16.8%	28.6	24.1	31.3	32.4	53.2
Market value ($ mil.)	–	–	–	–	–	–
Employees	–	–	–	2,700	3,000	3,400

PLANAR SYSTEMS, INC.

1195 NE COMPTON DR
HILLSBORO, OR 970066959
Phone: 503 748-1100
Fax: –
Web: www.planar.com

CEO: –
CFO: Cindy Bai
HR: Dianne Namgung
FYE: September 27
Type: Private

Planar Systems has no qualms about making a public display. The company makes custom, embedded, and video wall displays used in such applications as vehicle dashboards, instrumentation, security monitoring, and retail systems. Planar also sells desktop monitors and home theater systems. Its products -- marketed under the Planar, Clarity, and Runco brands -- include matrix and mosaic LCD systems, flat-panel displays, rear-project cube displays, touch monitors, and theater front-projection systems. The company serves consumers, as well as clients in the retail, industrial, transportation, and education industries, among others. It generates most of its sales in the US. Planar was bought by Leyard Optoelectronic Co. in late 2015.

PLANET FITNESS INC   NYS: PLNT

4 Liberty Lane West
Hampton, NH 03842
Phone: 603 750-0001
Fax: –
Web: www.planetfitness.com

CEO: –
CFO: –
HR: –
FYE: December 31
Type: Public

Looking to get financially fitter, Planet Fitness, one of the largest and fastest-growing franchisors and operators of fitness centers in the US, went public in 2015. Its judgement-free approach to fitness and exceptional value proposition (it offers a wide choice of equipment and low membership fees) has enabled it to grow revenues to $279.8 million in 2014 and to become an industry leader with $1.2 billion in system-wide sales. That year Planet Fitness had more than 7.1 million members and 976 stores in 47 US states, Puerto Rico, and Canada. In June 2015 it opened its 1,000th store. The company is controlled by investor TGS Funds.

	Annual Growth	12/19	12/20	12/21	12/22	12/23
Sales ($mil.)	11.7%	688.8	406.6	587.0	936.8	1,071.3
Net income ($ mil.)	4.1%	117.7	(15.0)	42.8	99.4	138.3
Market value ($ mil.)	(0.6%)	6,583.6	6,843.6	7,985.3	6,946.8	6,435.5
Employees	23.5%	1,464	1,387	1,770	3,137	3,411

PLANET PAYMENT, INC.

100 W COMMONS BLVD STE 200
NEW CASTLE, DE 197202419
Phone: 516 670-3200
Fax: –
Web: www.planetpayment.com

CEO: –
CFO: –
HR: –
FYE: December 31
Type: Private

Planet Payment may not be able to break language barriers, but its systems can break currency barriers. Through its Pay in Your Currency and other services, Planet Payment provides point-of-sale and e-commerce payment processing services that allow merchants to accept Visa, MasterCard, and American Express credit and debit card payments in multiple currencies. The company's services also help merchants set up pricing in different currencies. It operates at more than 60,000 merchant locations in 20-plus counties in the Asia Pacific region and North America. Customers include hotels, restaurants, and retailers operating in international business and tourist centers. Chairman Philip Beck founded Planet Payment in 1999.

PLANNED PARENTHOOD FEDERATION OF AMERICA, INC.

123 WILLIAM ST FL 10
NEW YORK, NY 100383844
Phone: 212 541-7800
Fax: –
Web: www.plannedparenthood.org

CEO: Alexis McGill
CFO: Wallace D'Sousa
HR: Dannette Hill
FYE: June 30
Type: Private

" He who fails to plan, plans to fail ," could refer to parenting. No fear, the Planned Parenthood Federation Of America provides sexual health information, as well as reproductive healthcare through 800 affiliated health centers to more than 5 million people each year. PPFA also lobbies for reproductive rights and reproductive health issues, and works to extend access to family planning services for all. The not-for-profit organization is supported by private and corporate donations and patient fees, as well as government grants. Founded in 1916 by Margaret Sanger, PPFA has grown to 84 affiliates in all 50 US states and the District of Columbia, and is part of the International Planned Parenthood Federation.

	Annual Growth	06/10	06/11	06/12	06/13	06/14
Sales ($mil.)	5.2%	–	–	159.5	139.4	176.6
Net income ($ mil.)	(8.6%)	–	–	34.0	1.5	28.4
Market value ($ mil.)	–	–	–	–	–	–
Employees	–	–	–	–	–	530

PLANTATION GENERAL HOSPITAL, L.P.

3476 S UNIVERSITY DR
DAVIE, FL 333282000
Phone: 954 587-5010
Fax: –
Web: www.hcafloridahealthcare.com

CEO: Madeline Nava
CFO: David Hughes
HR: Leigh A Sprague
FYE: August 31
Type: Private

Plantation General Hospital cares for patients from the time they are wee seedlings. Plantation General Hospital, an operating subsidiary of the enormous HCA healthcare provider system, is a 264-bed acute care hospital serving Broward County (in Florida's Fort Lauderdale area), and the city of Plantation. The facility offers a full spectrum of health care services, but specializes in maternity, neonatal, and pediatric services. It also offers minimally invasive surgical services and a special care center for high-risk cardiac and pulmonary patients.

PLASTEK INDUSTRIES, INC.

2425 W 23RD ST
ERIE, PA 165062920
Phone: 814 878-4400
Fax: –
Web: www.plastekgroup.com

CEO: Joseph J Prischak
CFO: –
HR: Nichole Freeman
FYE: December 31
Type: Private

When it comes to producing deodorant stick containers, The Plastek Group sticks it to its rivals. It supplies more than 80% of the packaging for oval deodorant sticks manufactured in the US, and was among the first to debut packaging for clear gel anti-perspirants in North America. The Plastek Group designs and manufactures, in fact, a slew of plastics products, including pharmaceutical packaging and personal care containers, for consumer goods makers worldwide. Its portfolio includes flat pack sticks, gel and soft solid sticks, oval and round sticks, and three-piece containers. The company also makes round and straight base jars and jar caps. The Plastek Group operates in the US, the UK, Brazil, and Venezuela.

PLASTIC SUPPLIERS, INC.

2400 MARILYN LN
COLUMBUS, OH 432191721
Phone: 614 471-9100
Fax: –
Web: www.earthfirstfilms.com

CEO: Peter Driscoll
CFO: Steve H Dudley
HR: Brenda Hammond
FYE: October 29
Type: Private

Plastic Suppliers is a world's leader in the manufacturing of compostable, Earthfirst, biopolymer films to a wide range of growing markets. Earthfirst Biopolymer Films by PSI is a global manufacturer of compostable sealant and barrier sealant films within food, beverage, medical, personal care, office, industrial and other CPG segments. Offices in Columbus Ohio and Ghent Belgium serve 50 countries in the Americas, Europe, Asia, Africa and the Middle East. manufactures biopolymer. Its specialty films subsidiary, Sidaplax, is established in Belgium. Plastic Suppliers was founded at Blackwood, New Jersey as a privately held corporation by Joe Tatem.

PLATINUM STUDIOS, INC.

NBB: PDOS

2029 S. Westgate Ave.
Los Angeles, CA 90025
Phone: 310 807-8100
Fax: –
Web: www.platinumstudios.com

CEO: –
CFO: –
HR: –
FYE: December 31
Type: Public

Platinum Studios controls an independent library of comic book characters, which it adapts and produces for film and TV projects. The company owns more than 3,800 characters that have appeared in hundreds of millions of comics in 25 languages and more than 50 countries. Platinum Studios is responsible for the Men in Black comic book; it also co-produced the hit movie-version with Sony Pictures. Platinum Studios was founded in 1997 by Malibu Comics creator Scott Mitchell Rosenberg.

	Annual Growth	12/06	12/07	12/08	12/09	12/10
Sales ($mil.)	88.4%	0.2	2.0	0.8	0.3	2.3
Net income ($ mil.)	–	(4.3)	(5.2)	(11.2)	(3.4)	(9.9)
Market value ($ mil.)	–	–	–	5.9	15.5	19.2
Employees	–	–	26	9	8	7

PLATTE RIVER POWER AUTHORITY (INC)

2000 E HORSETOOTH RD
FORT COLLINS, CO 805252942
Phone: 970 229-5332
Fax: –
Web: www.prpa.org

CEO: –
CFO: David D Smalley
HR: Staci Clemmons
FYE: December 31
Type: Private

Delivering power, not platitudes, Platte River Power Authority supplies wholesale electricity to four municipalities (Estes Park, Fort Collins, Longmont, and Loveland) in northern Colorado, which in turn serve about 146,500 residences and businesses. The utility, which is a political subdivision of the state of Colorado, has interests in fossil-fueled and wind-powered generation facilities; it also operates transmission assets and acts as a wholesale electric utility, acquiring, constructing and operating generation capacity and supplying electric energy on an as needed basis. Platte River Power Authority evolved from the Platte River Municipal Power Association, a consortium of 31 municipalities.

	Annual Growth	12/18	12/19	12/20	12/21	12/22
Sales ($mil.)	5.8%	–	229.2	240.7	265.4	271.8
Net income ($ mil.)	(41.7%)	–	33.5	22.0	35.7	6.7
Market value ($ mil.)	–	–	–	–	–	–
Employees	–	–	–	–	–	172

PLAYBOY ENTERPRISES, INC.

10960 WILSHIRE BLVD FL 22
LOS ANGELES, CA 900243808
Phone: 310 424-1800
Fax: –
Web: www.plbygroup.com

CEO: Ben Kohn
CFO: David Israel
HR: –
FYE: December 31
Type: Private

Playboy keeps printing articles, so someone must be reading them. Playboy Enterprises is an adult entertainment company anchored by its iconic, half-century-old periodical. Playboy, features general-interest and lifestyle articles, interviews, fiction, and, of course, a monthly Playmate centerfold. In addition to publishing operations, Playboy licenses its iconic logo, and operates Playboy.com. The company was founded by Hugh Hefner.

PLAYERS NETWORK (THE)

1771 E. Flamingo Road, #201-A
Las Vegas, NV 89119
Phone: 702 840-3270
Fax: –
Web: –

CEO: Mark Bradley
CFO: –
HR: –
FYE: December 31
Type: Public

Players Network acquires, produces, and distributes video content focused on Las Vegas gaming and nightlife. It has a library of more than 1,000 videos, including instructional programs on gambling and features on Las Vegas casinos and nightspots, as well as videos featuring Vegas entertainers and other personalities. Players Network distributes its programming primarily through cable and satellite video-on-demand (VOD) services and through content partnerships with online video sites, including Google. CEO Mark Bradley and president Michael Berk (who helped create the TV series Baywatch) together own about 30% of the company.

	Annual Growth	12/13	12/14	12/15	12/16	12/17
Sales ($mil.)	173.7%	0.0	0.0	0.0	0.1	0.0
Net income ($ mil.)	–	(1.7)	(3.3)	(2.1)	(1.7)	(14.0)
Market value ($ mil.)	43.0%	18.0	11.6	1.2	8.5	75.2
Employees	82.1%	2	2	1	1	22

PLAYTIKA HOLDING CORP.

2225 VILLAGE WALK DR STE 240
HENDERSON, NV 890527809
Phone: 702 880-4709
Fax: –
Web: www.playtika.com

CEO: –
CFO: –
HR: –
FYE: December 31
Type: Private

Playtika Holding Corp. is a mobile gaming entertainment and technology market leader with a portfolio of multiple game titles. The company has built best-in-class live game operations services and a proprietary technology platform to support its portfolio of games which enable the company to drive strong user engagement and monetization. Its games are free-to-play, and it is experts in providing novel, curated in-game content and offers to its users, at optimal points in their game journeys. Playtika was founded in 2010, when it released its first game, Slotomania, which remains the largest game in its portfolio based on revenue and went public in 2021. The US generates around 70% of Playtika's revenue.

	Annual Growth	12/17	12/18	12/19	12/20	12/22
Sales ($mil.)	5.0%	–	–	–	2,371.5	2,615.5
Net income ($ mil.)	72.9%	–	–	–	92.1	275.3
Market value ($ mil.)	–	–	–	–	–	–
Employees	–	–	–	–	–	319

PLEXUS CORP.

NMS: PLXS

One Plexus Way
Neenah, WI 54957
Phone: 920 969-6000
Fax: 920 751-5395
Web: www.plexus.com

CEO: –
CFO: –
HR: –
FYE: September 30
Type: Public

Plexus is a global leader that specializes in serving customers in industries with highly complex products and demanding regulatory environments. The company develops and manufactures electronic products for companies in the medical, industrial, and defense markets. Plexus typically purchases raw materials, including printed circuit boards (PCBs) and other electronic components. It also purchases non-electronic, typically custom-engineered components such as molded/formed plastics, sheet metal fabrications, aluminum extrusions, robotics, motors, vision sensors, motion/actuation, fluidics, displays, die-castings, and various other hardware and fastener components. It serves approximately 140 customers ranging from large multinational companies to smaller emerging technology companies. Plexus gets most of its revenue from customers outside the US.

	Annual Growth	09/19*	10/20	10/21	10/22*	09/23
Sales ($mil.)	7.4%	3,164.4	3,390.4	3,368.9	3,811.4	4,210.3
Net income ($ mil.)	6.4%	108.6	117.5	138.9	138.2	139.1
Market value ($ mil.)	10.4%	1,718.3	1,948.7	2,501.6	2,404.9	2,553.8
Employees	7.1%	19,000	19,500	19,200	25,000	25,000

*Fiscal year change

PLEXUS INSTALLATIONS, INC.

6400 FRANKFORD AVE STE 17
BALTIMORE, MD 212064970
Phone: 410 777-8233
Fax: –
Web: www.plexus-group.net

CEO: Cristina V Mosby V
CFO: –
HR: –
FYE: December 31
Type: Private

Plexus Installations will do more than just hook up your phone. The company, which does business as Plexus Communications Group, provides services related to the support, design, and implementation of voice and data communications networks for businesses and government agencies. It offers consulting in the area of network security and it provides IT and network engineering services encompassing systems integration and management. Plexus additionally provides network infrastructure services such as cable installation and related network component assembly and construction. Commercial clients come from industries including telecommunications, financial services, and transportation. The company was founded in 1995.

PLUMB SUPPLY COMPANY, LLC

1622 NE 51ST AVE
DES MOINES, IA 503132194
Phone: 515 262-9511
Fax: –
Web: www.plumbsupply.com

CEO: Curt Brighton
CFO: –
HR: –
FYE: December 31
Type: Private

Plumb Supply is plum tickled with the plumbing and HVAC business. Through about 20 locations in Iowa, Plumb Supply distributes plumbing, heating, cooling, and bathroom products to builders and contractors. In addition to air conditioners and heaters, the company sells pipes, valves, fittings, and about 200 other product lines from Bemis Manufacturing, Honeywell, Kohler, Mueller Industries, and Whirlpool. About 10 stores feature Water Concepts Galleries, which showcase kitchen and bathroom fixtures from major brands. The company was founded in 1946 and purchased by Templeton Coal in 1965.

PLUG POWER INC

968 Albany Shaker Road
Latham, NY 12110
Phone: 518 782-7700
Fax: 518 782-9060
Web: www.plugpower.com

NAS: PLUG
CEO: –
CFO: –
HR: –
FYE: December 31
Type: Public

Plug Power is building an end-to-end green hydrogen ecosystem, from green hydrogen production, storage, and delivery to energy generation through mobile or stationary applications, to help its customers meet their business goals and decarbonize the environment. The company is focused on hydrogen and fuel cell systems that are used to power electric motors, primarily in the electric mobility and stationary power markets. It includes electric forklifts and electric industrial vehicles. Plug Power is focused on proton exchange membrane (PEM), fuel cells and fuel processing technologies, fuel cell/battery hybrid technologies, and associated hydrogen, and green hydrogen generation storage, and dispensing infrastructure. The company's GenDrive product is its hydrogen-fueled PEM fuel cell system providing power to material handling electric vehicles, including class 1, 2, 3 and 6 electric forklifts, AGVs, and ground support equipment. North America generates the majority of its revenue.

	Annual Growth	12/19	12/20	12/21	12/22	12/23
Sales ($mil.)	40.3%	230.2	(93.2)	502.3	701.4	891.3
Net income ($ mil.)	–	(85.5)	(596.2)	(460.0)	(724.0)	(1,368.8)
Market value ($ mil.)	9.2%	1,915.4	20,554	17,111	7,497.9	2,727.6
Employees	38.8%	1,041	1,285	2,449	3,353	3,868

PLUS THERAPEUTICS INC

4200 Marathon Blvd., Suite 200
Austin, TX 78756
Phone: 737 255-7194
Fax: –
Web: –

NAS: PSTV
CEO: Marc H Hedrick
CFO: Andrew Sims
HR: –
FYE: December 31
Type: Public

Cytori Therapeutics focuses on the development of regenerative and oncology treatments using its cell therapy and nanoparticle platforms. Its Cytori Cell Therapy treatment has shown evidence of improving blood flow and modulating the body's immune system as well as promoting wound care. The company is investigating its effectiveness in the treatment of a number of diseases, particularly those that have unmet medical needs. Its newest arm, Cytori Nanomedicine, was established in early 2017 when the firm acquired assets of Azaya Therapeutics including a proprietary liposomal nanoparticle that expanded its existing pipeline.

	Annual Growth	12/19	12/20	12/21	12/22	12/23
Sales ($mil.)	–	–	0.3	–	0.2	4.9
Net income ($ mil.)	–	(10.9)	(8.2)	(13.4)	(20.3)	(13.3)
Market value ($ mil.)	(7.6%)	10.7	9.0	4.7	1.4	7.8
Employees	13.6%	12	12	14	17	20

PLUMAS BANCORP INC

5525 Kietzke Lane, Suite 100
Reno, NV 89511
Phone: 775 786-0907
Fax: –
Web: www.plumasbank.com

NAS: PLBC
CEO: Andrew J Ryback
CFO: Richard L Belstock
HR: –
FYE: December 31
Type: Public

Plumas Bancorp is the holding company for Plumas Bank, which serves individuals and businesses in the northeastern corner of California, from Lake Tahoe to the Oregon border. Through more than a dozen branches, the bank offers deposit products such as checking, savings, and retirement accounts and certificates of deposit. Loans secured by real estate account for more than half of Plumas Bank's loan portfolio; combined, commercial and agricultural loans make up about a quarter. The bank writes consumer loans, as well. It also provides access to investment products and services such as financial planning, mutual funds, and annuities.

	Annual Growth	12/19	12/20	12/21	12/22	12/23
Assets ($mil.)	16.8%	865.2	1,111.6	1,614.1	1,621.0	1,610.4
Net income ($ mil.)	17.7%	15.5	14.5	21.0	26.4	29.8
Market value ($ mil.)	11.9%	154.9	138.0	198.4	217.5	242.8
Employees	(1.1%)	183	177	187	193	175

PLX PHARMA INC

9 Fishers Lane, Suite E
Sparta, NJ 07871
Phone: 973 409-6541
Fax: –
Web: www.plxpharma.com

NBB: PLXP
CEO: Natasha Giordano
CFO: Rita O'Connor
HR: –
FYE: December 31
Type: Public

Emerging biotechnology firm Dipexium Pharmaceuticals was formed in 2010 to develop and commercialize Locilex (pexiganan acetate cream 1%), a broad spectrum, small peptide topical antibiotic for the treatment of mild and moderate skin infections in superficial wounds, including mild infections of diabetic foot ulcers. Locilex is also being eyed as a promising product candidate to treat acute bacterial skin and skin structure infections in superficial wounds (including infected burns, decubitus ulcers, and surgical wounds), and to treat methicillin resistant staphylococcus aureus (MRSA) infections in the nose. In late 2016 Dipexium agreed to merge with PLx Pharma, which is developing aspirin product Aspertec.

	Annual Growth	12/17	12/18	12/19	12/20	12/21
Sales ($mil.)	80.2%	0.8	0.8	0.6	0.0	8.2
Net income ($ mil.)	–	(15.3)	0.9	(20.5)	(15.2)	(46.1)
Market value ($ mil.)	3.8%	190.0	42.1	120.3	152.0	220.6
Employees	7.9%	14	15	12	11	19

PLY GEM HOLDINGS, INC.

5020 WESTON PKWY STE 400
CARY, NC 275132322
Phone: 919 677-3900
Fax: –
Web: www.plygem.com

CEO: Gary E Robinette
CFO: Shawn K Poe
HR: Dreama Campbell
FYE: December 31
Type: Private

Ply Gem is a leading exterior home building products manufacturer in North America. Its brands offer a broad selection of quality building products that includes nearly everything on the outside of a house from windows, patio doors and siding to designer accents, stone veneer, and fence and railing. These products lead the industry as the #1 in windows, vinyl siding and metal accessories, with an unmatched portfolio, backed by industry-leading warranties. Every product is rigorously tested to ensure exceptional durability and performance for every region or climate. Limitless color, design and texture options are intended to work together to create custom curb appeal.

	Annual Growth	12/12	12/13	12/14	12/15	12/16
Sales ($mil.)	10.5%	–	–	1,566.6	1,839.7	1,911.8
Net income ($ mil.)	–	–	–	(31.3)	32.3	75.5
Market value ($ mil.)	–	–	–	–	–	–
Employees	–	–	–	–	–	9,000

PMI GROUP, INC.

3003 Oak Road
Walnut Creek, CA 94597
Phone: 925 658-7878
Fax: –
Web: www.pmigroup.com

NBB: PMIR
CEO: L S Smith
CFO: –
HR: –
FYE: December 31
Type: Public

If Barbie couldn't afford a full 20% down payment on her Malibu dream home, her mortgage lender might have brought in The PMI Group. One of the largest US providers of mortgage insurance, PMI protects lenders in case of borrower default. It also insures the bundles of existing loans known as structured finance products. In addition, PMI was the primary investor in the Financial Guaranty Insurance Company, which offered financial guaranty insurance on public bonds. The company's international operations provide mortgage insurance and credit enhancement services in Europe. Despite attempts to survive the real estate-market implosion, the company filed Chapter 11 bankruptcy protection in 2011, emerging in 2013.

	Annual Growth	12/06	12/07	12/08	12/09	12/10
Assets ($mil.)	(5.6%)	5,320.1	5,070.4	4,824.4	4,638.5	4,219.0
Net income ($ mil.)	–	419.7	(915.3)	(928.5)	(659.3)	(773.0)
Market value ($ mil.)	–	–	–	–	–	–
Employees	(8.1%)	1,000	1,084	736	600	712

PNC FINANCIAL SERVICES GROUP (THE)

The Tower at PNC Plaza, 300 Fifth Avenue
Pittsburgh, PA 15222-2401
Phone: 888 762-2265
Fax: –
Web: www.pnc.com

NYS: PNC
CEO: William S Demchak
CFO: Robert Q Reilly
HR: –
FYE: December 31
Type: Public

The PNC Financial Services Group is one of the country's largest providers of diversified financial services with consolidated total assets, total deposits, and total shareholders' equity of approximately $557.2 billion, $457.3 billion, and $55.7 billion, respectively. The firm has businesses engaged in retail banking, including residential mortgage, corporate and institutional banking and asset management, providing many of its products and services nationally. PNC's retail branch network is located coast-to-coast, and it also has strategic international offices in four countries outside the US. Its flagship PNC Bank subsidiary operates branches across the Mid-Atlantic, Midwest, and Southeast. In addition to retail, corporate and institutional banking, which together account for some 90% of total revenue, the firm also offers personal and institutional asset management.

	Annual Growth	12/19	12/20	12/21	12/22	12/23
Assets ($mil.)	8.2%	410,295	466,679	557,191	557,263	561,580
Net income ($ mil.)	1.0%	5,369.0	7,517.0	5,674.0	6,041.0	5,578.0
Market value ($ mil.)	(0.8%)	63,537	59,306	79,813	62,865	61,635
Employees	2.1%	51,918	51,257	59,426	61,545	56,411

PNG BUILDERS

2392 S BATEMAN AVE
DUARTE, CA 910103312
Phone: 626 256-9539
Fax: –
Web: www.pacific-inc.com

CEO: Steven Mathison
CFO: –
HR: –
FYE: December 31
Type: Private

Pacific National Group (PNG) performs general contracting and construction management services in Arizona and Southern California. The company tackles a range of projects, including commercial and industrial complexes, medical buildings, high-tech and aerospace centers, and sports and recreation facilities. The company offers pre-construction through post-construction services as well as site supervision. Its Modulex division manufactures aluminum door frames and glazing systems. PNG's client roster includes Northrop Grumman, Cedars-Sinai Medical Center, Universal Studios, and the Jet Propulsion Laboratory in Pasadena, California. The company was founded in 1959 as Pacific Luminaire.

	Annual Growth	12/17	12/18	12/19	12/20	12/21
Sales ($mil.)	7.2%	–	123.0	163.7	148.2	151.6
Net income ($ mil.)	(20.9%)	–	2.3	3.9	3.8	1.1
Market value ($ mil.)	–	–	–	–	–	–
Employees	–	–	–	–	–	70

PNM RESOURCES INC

414 Silver Ave. S.W.
Albuquerque, NM 87102-3289
Phone: 505 241-2700
Fax: –
Web: www.pnmresources.com

NYS: PNM
CEO: Patricia K Collawn
CFO: Charles N Eldred
HR: Jan Ballard
FYE: December 31
Type: Public

PNM Resources, Inc. and Subsidiaries (PNMR) is an investor-owned holding company with two regulated utilities providing electricity and electric services in New Mexico and Texas. Through its regulated utilities, PNM and TNMP, PNMR serves approximately 815,000 residential, commercial, and industrial customers and end-users of electricity. PNMR serves its customers with a diverse mix of generation and purchased power resources totaling 2.7 gigawatts of capacity. The company's TNMP utilities serve a market of small to medium-sized communities, most of which have populations of less than 50,000. Its PNM utility provides electric generation, transmission, and distribution service to its rate-regulated customers. Most of the company's revenues come from the PNM utilities.

	Annual Growth	12/19	12/20	12/21	12/22	12/23
Sales ($mil.)	7.4%	1,457.6	1,523.0	1,779.9	2,249.6	1,939.2
Net income ($ mil.)	3.2%	77.9	173.3	196.4	170.1	88.3
Market value ($ mil.)	(4.8%)	4,574.1	4,377.4	4,114.0	4,400.9	3,752.3
Employees	(1.0%)	1,668	1,708	1,646	1,500	1,600

POINDEXTER (J.B.) & CO., INC.

600 Travis, Suite 200
Houston, TX 77002
Phone: 713 655-9800
Fax: 713 951-9038
Web: www.jbpoindexter.com

CEO: –
CFO: –
HR: –
FYE: December 31
Type: Public

J.B. Poindexter & Co. (JBPCO) is a privately-held, diversified manufacturing company. The company manages a portfolio of business units engaged in the production of commercial truck bodies, step-vans, service utility truck and van bodies, funeral coaches, limousines, mid-sized buses, vehicle cargo management systems, and pick-up truck bed covers and accessories. JBPCO provides foam molding, fabrication, and cold chain solutions through EFP while servicing oil and gas, aerospace and defense, and industrial and power generation through MIC Group. Established its business units as leaders in their respective markets with excellent operational and financial performance, the company employs about 8,500 team members globally and has manufacturing operations in North America. Among its customers are Verizon, AT&T, Aramark, Schlumberger, Penske, and NOV. The company traces its roots back to 1983.

	Annual Growth	12/07	12/08	12/09	12/10	12/11
Sales ($mil.)	(2.8%)	792.2	706.4	480.6	553.6	708.1
Net income ($ mil.)	–	(0.8)	6.8	(4.9)	(2.0)	14.7
Market value ($ mil.)	–	–	–	–	–	–
Employees	(5.7%)	4,227	3,462	2,890	2,800	3,348

POINT LOMA NAZARENE UNIVERSITY FOUNDATION

3900 LOMALAND DR
SAN DIEGO, CA 921062810
Phone: 619 221-2200
Fax: –
Web: www.pointloma.edu

CEO: Robert Brower
CFO: –
HR: –
FYE: June 30
Type: Private

Point Loma Nazarene University (PLNU) intends to provide a rounded education for Christian students. PLNU offers liberal arts and professional programs in more than 60 areas of study on its main campus in San Diego, and select graduate and professional programs at regional centers in the California towns of Bakersfield, and Mission Valley (San Diego). Areas of study include art, science, business administration, teaching, medicine, and ministry. About 4,600 undergraduate and graduate students are enrolled at the school, which boasts a 14-to-1 faculty-student ratio. PLNU dates back to 1902, when it was established by Dr. Phineas F. Bresee, one of the founders of the Church of the Nazarene.

	Annual Growth	06/16	06/17	06/18	06/20	06/21
Sales ($mil.)	(63.5%)	–	135.8	118.0	151.2	2.4
Net income ($ mil.)	(45.5%)	–	13.6	17.9	6.9	1.2
Market value ($ mil.)	–	–	–	–	–	–
Employees	–	–	–	–	–	688

POINT.360

2701 MEDIA CENTER DR
LOS ANGELES, CA 900651700
Phone: 818 565-1400
Fax: –
Web: www.point360.com

CEO: Haig S Bagerdjian
CFO: Alan R Steel
HR: –
FYE: June 30
Type: Private

Just how do the latest movie trailers make it to a theater near you? The answer is simple: Point.360. The company provides audio, video, and film management and post-production services (including color correction, editing, and animation) for TV programming, feature films, and movie trailers. Clients include film studios, ad agencies, TV networks, and production firms. Point.360 also offers editing, mastering, reformatting, archiving, and electronic distribution services for commercials, press kits, and corporate training. In addition, the company rents and sells DVDs and video games directly to consumers through its MovieQ retail stores. Chairman and CEO Haig Bagerdjian owns more than 50% of Point.360.

POINTS OF LIGHT FOUNDATION

600 MEANS ST NW STE 210
ATLANTA, GA 303185799
Phone: 404 979-2900
Fax: –
Web: www.pointsoflight.org

CEO: Michelle Nun
CFO: Kris Tecce
HR: –
FYE: September 30
Type: Private

Founded in 1990 by former US president George H.W. Bush as the Points of Light Foundation, the group promotes US volunteerism. It became the Points of Light Institute in August 2007 when it merged with the HandsOn Network. It operates through a trio of businesses that include HandsOn Network, MissionFish, and the Civic Incubator. HandsOn tackles projects, such as building wheel chair ramps, through its more than 250 affiliates. MissionFish, which allows sellers on eBay to donate some of their earnings to not-for-profits, has raised more than $125 million to assist some 15,000 nonprofits worldwide. Its Civic Incubator serves up sustainable civic solutions through a network of more than 500,000 AmeriCorps alumni.

	Annual Growth	09/14	09/15	09/19	09/20	09/21
Sales ($mil.)	(4.0%)	–	24.1	18.9	–	18.9
Net income ($ mil.)	–	–	(0.7)	1.1	–	3.7
Market value ($ mil.)	–	–	–	–	–	–
Employees	–	–	–	–	–	207

POLARIS ALPHA, LLC

5450 TECH CENTER DR STE 120
COLORADO SPRINGS, CO 809192339
Phone: 719 452-7000
Fax: –
Web: www.parsons.com

CEO: –
CFO: –
HR: –
FYE: December 31
Type: Private

Intelligent Software Solutions is no dummy when it comes to software development and IT systems analysis. The privately-held company develops and integrates custom software used for such applications as data visualization and analysis, pattern detection, and mission planning for the aerospace, defense, and maritime industries. It also provides on-site product and development support and training. As a government contractor, it serves a range of public sector agencies within the US Department of Defense, US Department of Homeland Security, and US Air Force. Intelligent Software Solutions corporate clients have included Lockheed Martin, Northrop Grumman, and Leidos.

POLARIS INC

NYS: PII

2100 Highway 55
Medina, MN 55340
Phone: 763 542-0500
Fax: –
Web: www.polaris.com

CEO: Michael T Speetzen
CFO: Robert P Mack
HR: –
FYE: December 31
Type: Public

Polaris (formerly known as Polaris Industries Inc.) designs, engineers, and manufactures powersports vehicles which include: off-road vehicles (ORV), all-terrain vehicles (ATVs), side-by-side recreational, snowmobiles, motorcycles, moto-roadsters, quadricicycles, and boats. Its brands include Bennington, Godfrey, and Hurricane, which together provide a full offering of pontoon and deck boats. Offerings include replacement parts, accessories (covers, windshields, backrests), garments, and riding gear (bags and helmets). The company's products are sold online and through dealers and distributors principally located in the US, Canada, Western Europe, Australia, and Mexico. The US accounts for about 80% of the company's total revenue.

	Annual Growth	12/19	12/20	12/21	12/22	12/23
Sales ($mil.)	7.1%	6,782.5	7,027.9	8,198.2	8,589.0	8,934.4
Net income ($ mil.)	11.6%	324.0	124.8	493.9	447.1	502.8
Market value ($ mil.)	(1.7%)	5,746.1	5,383.3	6,209.9	5,706.5	5,354.5
Employees	7.2%	14,000	15,000	16,000	16,200	18,500

POLYCOM, INC.

6001 AMERICA CENTER DR
SAN JOSE, CA 950022562
Phone: 831 426-5858
Fax: –
Web: www.hp.com

CEO: Dave Schull
CFO: –
HR: –
FYE: December 31
Type: Private

Polycom's vision is a world united by video. The company makes video-conferencing and immersive telepresence (which combines digital audio, video, and content sharing) systems that let users collaborate as if they were in the same room. Its products combine camera, microphone, network connection, and external audio and video devices. The company also offers PC-based phones that transmit both voice and video. Polycom's software enables users to manage conferencing locations and connect with them using ISDN and internet protocol connections. It partners with the likes of Microsoft and IBM to develop open standards-based products. Polycom was sold to Siris Capital Group for $1.8 billion in 2016.

POMONA COLLEGE

550 N COLLEGE AVE
CLAREMONT, CA 917114434
Phone: 909 621-8135
Fax: –
Web: www.pomona.edu

CEO: David Oxtoby
CFO: –
HR: –
FYE: June 30
Type: Private

Looking to get an education in sunny California? You might want to consider Pomona College. The school offers about 50 academic programs in areas such as art, humanities, biology, psychology, computer science, and English. It also has research and interdisciplinary study opportunities. The liberal arts college enrolls about 1,600 students. Formed in 1887, Pomona College is the founding member of The Claremont Colleges, an affiliated group of seven independent colleges located on adjoining campuses in Claremont, California. The affiliated campuses are coordinated by one of the member institutions, the Claremont University Consortium.

	Annual Growth	06/15	06/16	06/17	06/19	06/21
Sales ($mil.)	4.0%	–	193.1	193.5	223.2	235.1
Net income ($ mil.)	–	–	(125.3)	211.3	(13.2)	22.1
Market value ($ mil.)	–	–	–	–	–	–
Employees	–	–	–	–	–	500

POMP'S TIRE SERVICE, INC.

1122 CEDAR ST
GREEN BAY, WI 543014704
Phone: 920 435-8301
Fax: –
Web: www.pompstire.com

CEO: –
CFO: –
HR: Donna Gustafson
FYE: December 31
Type: Private

If by circumstance you have a flat tire in the Midwest, limp on over to Pomp's Tire Service. The company sells tires for agricultural, commercial, and industrial vehicles, as well as everyday cars and trucks, from more than 75 locations in eight Midwestern states. (More than half are located in Wisconsin and Illinois.) Its brands include Bridgestone, Goodrich, Goodyear, and Michelin, among others. Pomp's Tire Service also offers 24-hour truck roadside assistance, retread and auto repair services, and has federal contracts with the US Army for vehicle parts. Originally called Pomprowitz Tire Co., the company was founded in 1939 by Andrew "Sparky" Pomprowitz. It is owned by the family of Roger Wochinske, who bought the firm in 1964.

	Annual Growth	12/07	12/08	12/09	12/10	12/11
Sales ($mil.)	18.3%	–	–	284.8	342.4	398.2
Net income ($ mil.)	11.5%	–	–	10.2	11.1	12.7
Market value ($ mil.)	–	–	–	–	–	–
Employees	–	–	–	–	–	2,200

PONIARD PHARMACEUTICALS INC

750 Battery Street, Suite 330
San Francisco, CA 94111
Phone: 650 583-3774
Fax: –
Web: www.poniard.com

CEO: –
CFO: –
HR: –
FYE: December 31
Type: Public

Poniard Pharmaceuticals has been focused on developing better cancer therapies, but wants to take a stab at new therapeutic areas. The firm was focused on the development of picoplatin, an injectable and oral chemotherapy drug that it was investigating as a treatment for solid tumors, including lung, colorectal, and prostate cancers. However, due to financial difficulties, Poniard has laid off most of its workforce and is exploring strategic options, including a possible sale or merger of the company.

	Annual Growth	12/06	12/07	12/08	12/09	12/10
Sales ($mil.)	–	–	–	–	–	–
Net income ($ mil.)	–	(23.3)	(32.8)	(48.6)	(45.7)	(30.1)
Market value ($ mil.)	(43.2%)	6.1	5.4	2.3	2.2	0.6
Employees	(32.3%)	38	55	64	22	8

POOF-SLINKY, LLC

165 GEIGER DR
RIVER VALE, NJ 076755530
Phone: 734 454-9552
Fax: –
Web: www.justplayproducts.com

CEO: –
CFO: –
HR: –
FYE: December 31
Type: Private

What happened when an automotive molding firm took time off to play? Poof! Suddenly, foam was seen in a whole new light. Founded in the 1980s, Poof-Slinky (formerly POOF Products) makes and sells polyurethane foam toys, including planes, rockets, and balls for basketball, football, and other activities. The firm also makes Slinky-brand toys (which originated in 1945 when Slinky inventor Richard James watched a spring fall off a desk) and Slinky Science toys (activity books, puzzles). Its more than 250 toys, made mostly in the US, are sold through retailers nationwide and online. President Ray Dallavecchia and COO Douglas Ferner own Poof-Slinky. In 2010 it acquired the assets of Rapid Displays' Cadaco game unit.

	Annual Growth	12/00	12/01	12/02	12/03	12/08
Sales ($mil.)	4.7%	–	–	20.4	–	26.9
Net income ($ mil.)	–	–	–	–	–	1.4
Market value ($ mil.)	–	–	–	–	–	–
Employees	–	–	–	–	–	130

POOL CORP

NMS: POOL

109 Northpark Boulevard
Covington, LA 70433-5001
Phone: 985 892-5521
Fax: 985 892-2438
Web: www.poolcorp.com

CEO: Peter D Arvan
CFO: Melanie M Hart
HR: –
FYE: December 31
Type: Public

Pool Corporation is the world's largest wholesale distributor of swimming pool supplies, equipment and related leisure products and is one of the leading distributors of irrigation and landscape products in the US. It operates around 420 sales centers throughout the North America, Europe, and Australia, serving roughly 125,000 customers such as pool builders and remodelers, retail pool stores, and pool repair and service companies. Pool Corporation's more than 200,000 products include private-label and name-brand pool maintenance items (chemicals, cleaners), equipment (pumps, filters), accessories (heaters, lights), and packaged pool kits. Founded in 1993 as SCP Holding, Pool Corporation generates most of its sales in the US.

	Annual Growth	12/19	12/20	12/21	12/22	12/23
Sales ($mil.)	14.7%	3,199.5	3,936.6	5,295.6	6,179.7	5,541.6
Net income ($ mil.)	18.9%	261.6	366.7	650.6	748.5	523.2
Market value ($ mil.)	17.1%	8,145.8	14,287	21,709	11,596	15,292
Employees	7.5%	4,500	4,500	5,500	6,000	6,000

POP WARNER LITTLE SCHOLARS INC

586 MIDDLETOWN BLVD C100
LANGHORNE, PA 190471867
Phone: 215 752-2691
Fax: –
Web: www.popwarner.com

CEO: –
CFO: –
HR: –
FYE: March 31
Type: Private

Don't be fooled, Pop Warner isn't all fun and games. Pop Warner Little Scholars (PWLS) is mostly fun and games with incentives for academic achievement. It is a not-for-profit organization that offers football and cheer and dance programs for children ages five to 16. The organization has about 400,000 participants across more than 40 US states and several other countries. In order to participate, little cheerleaders and grid iron wanna-bes are required to maintain academic standards including a minimum 2.0 grade point average. School administrators can petition to have the requirement waived for students they think will benefit from the program.

	Annual Growth	03/16	03/17	03/19	03/20	03/21
Sales ($mil.)	(28.1%)	–	3.5	3.4	1.6	0.9
Net income ($ mil.)	–	–	(0.3)	(0.3)	(0.1)	(0.3)
Market value ($ mil.)	–	–	–	–	–	–
Employees	–	–	–	–	–	7

POPE RESOURCES (A DELAWARE LIMITED PARTNERSHIP)

19950 7TH AVE NE STE 200
POULSBO, WA 983707405
Phone: 360 697-6626
Fax: –
Web: www.orm.com

CEO: Thomas M Ringo
CFO: Daemon P Repp
HR: –
FYE: December 31
Type: Private

More earthly than divine, Pope Resources owns or manages more than 150,000 acres of timberland and development property in Washington. Its holdings include the 70,000-acre Hood Canal and 44,000-acre Columbia tree farms in Washington. It sells its Douglas fir and other timber products mainly in the US, Japan, China, and Korea; Weyerhaeuser and Simpson Investment Company are major customers. Pope Resources also invests in and manages two timberland investment funds and provides investment management and consulting services to third-party timberland owners and managers in Washington, Oregon, and California. Its real estate unit acquires, develops, resells, and rents residential and commercial real estate.

POPEYES LOUISIANA KITCHEN, INC.

5505 BLUE LAGOON DR
MIAMI, FL 331262029
Phone: 404 459-4450
Fax: –
Web: locations.popeyes.com

CEO: –
CFO: –
HR: –
FYE: December 25
Type: Private

A leading fast-food company, Popeyes Louisiana Kitchen operates the Popeyes restaurant chain, the second largest quick service chicken concept as measured by total number of restaurants. The chain boasts some 3,705 locations in the US and around the world. The restaurants feature signature chicken and seafood that is typically served a variety of sides, including Cajun rice, coleslaw, mashed potatoes, or french fries. Popeyes distinguishes itself with a unique New Orleans style menu featuring spicy chicken, chicken tenders, fried shrimp and other regional items. It started in 1972 by Alvin C. Copeland Sr. when he opens the "Chicken on the Run" in the New Orleans suburb of Arabi, serving traditional Southern-fried chicken.

	Annual Growth	12/12	12/13	12/14	12/15	12/16
Sales ($mil.)	9.3%	–	206.0	235.6	259.0	268.9
Net income ($ mil.)	7.9%	–	34.1	38.0	44.1	42.8
Market value ($ mil.)	–	–	–	–	–	–
Employees	–	–	–	–	–	1,000

POPLAR BLUFF REGIONAL MEDICAL CENTER, LLC

3100 OAK GROVE RD
POPLAR BLUFF, MO 639011573
Phone: 573 776-2000
Fax: –
Web: www.pbrmc.com

CEO: Kenneth James
CFO: Kevin Fowler
HR: –
FYE: December 31
Type: Private

Poplar Bluff Regional Medical Center, part of Health Management Associates, serves southeastern Missouri with general and acute care services. The hospital's offerings range from cardiology and pediatrics to home care and maternity services. It also has centers devoted to such areas as cancer care, pain management, and rehabilitation. The two-campus hospital has about 425 beds.

	Annual Growth	12/14	12/15	12/16	12/17	12/18
Sales ($mil.)	(1.4%)	–	215.1	208.8	199.8	206.2
Net income ($ mil.)	(0.3%)	–	28.8	33.9	25.2	28.6
Market value ($ mil.)	–	–	–	–	–	–
Employees	–	–	–	–	–	19

POPULAR INC.

209 Muñoz Rivera Avenue, Hato Rey
San Juan, PR 00918
Phone: 787 765-9800
Fax: –
Web: www.popular.com

NMS: BPOP

CEO: Ignacio Alvarez
CFO: Carlos J Vazquez
HR: Karla Aponte
FYE: December 31
Type: Public

Founded 120 years ago, Popular is a diversified, publicly owned financial holding company for Banco Popular de Puerto Rico, the largest bank in Puerto Rico with over 165 branches and about 585 ATMs. In addition to commercial and retail banking services, Popular owns subsidiaries that offer vehicle financing and leasing (Popular Auto), insurance (Popular Insurance), financial advisory and brokerage services (Popular Securities), and mortgages (Popular Mortgage). Popular serves a mainly Hispanic customer base on the US mainland through its subsidiary Popular Bank, which has branches in New York, New Jersey, and Florida. Additionally, the company has a handful of branches and in the US Virgin Islands.

	Annual Growth	12/19	12/20	12/21	12/22	12/23
Assets ($mil.)	7.9%	52,115	65,926	75,098	67,638	70,758
Net income ($ mil.)	(5.2%)	671.1	506.6	934.9	1,102.6	541.3
Market value ($ mil.)	8.7%	4,239.0	4,063.7	5,919.5	4,785.2	5,921.6
Employees	1.9%	8,560	8,700	8,500	8,900	9,237

POPULATION SERVICES INTERNATIONAL

1120 19TH ST NW STE 600
WASHINGTON, DC 200363605
Phone: 202 785-0072
Fax: –
Web: www.psi.org

CEO: Karl Hofmann
CFO: Kin Schwartz
HR: Bruno Fessy
FYE: December 31
Type: Private

Population Services International (PSI) goes far beyond the scope of its name. Founded in 1970 to promote global family planning, PSI has established social programs that use local networks in low-income regions to distribute such lifelines as insecticide-treated mosquito nets, iodized salt, snake boots, and insect repellent, along with condoms, contraceptives, and pregnancy test kits. The group prides itself on using business principals to confront health issues in more than 65 countries worldwide. It reportedly has averted 4.2 million unintended pregnancies, some 29 million malaria cases, and provided 1.8-plus million clients with of HIV testing and counseling. PSI is also active ensuring safe water supplies.

	Annual Growth	12/99	12/00	12/01	12/21	12/22
Sales ($mil.)	6.1%	–	96.8	121.7	442.5	358.8
Net income ($ mil.)	(8.3%)	–	3.2	(0.8)	9.4	0.5
Market value ($ mil.)	–	–	–	–	–	–
Employees	–	–	–	–	–	438

PORT IMPERIAL FERRY CORP.

4800 AVE AT PORT IMPERIAL BLVD
WEEHAWKEN, NJ 070866938
Phone: 201 902-8700
Fax: –
Web: www.nywaterway.com

CEO: Arthur E Imperatore Sr
CFO: William Maloof
HR: William Reinhold
FYE: December 31
Type: Private

Port Imperial Ferry aims to get passengers coming and going. Doing business as NY Waterway, the company provides commuter ferry services, primarily for New Jersey residents working in New York. It maintains about 10 terminals in New Jersey and about half a dozen in New York, and it provides bus services between its terminals and ground transportation hubs. Along with its commuter-related business, NY Waterway offers sightseeing cruises in New York Harbor and excursions pegged to special events such as Fourth of July and New York Yankees baseball games. CEO Arthur Imperatore founded NY Waterway in 1986.

	Annual Growth	12/99	12/00	12/01	12/02	12/17
Sales ($mil.)	4.8%	–	36.7	46.6	73.8	81.0
Net income ($ mil.)	10.9%	–	2.0	5.8	6.4	11.7
Market value ($ mil.)	–	–	–	–	–	–
Employees	–	–	–	–	–	500

PORT NEWARK CONTAINER TERMINAL LLC

241 CALCUTTA ST
NEWARK, NJ 071143324
Phone: 973 522-2200
Fax: –
Web: www.pnct.net

CEO: Michael Hassing
CFO: Markus Braun
HR: –
FYE: December 31
Type: Private

Port Newark Container Terminal handles boxed freight at one of the busiest ports in the US. In addition to moving containers to and from ships, Port Newark Container Terminal offers a rail terminal to accommodate intermodal freight transportation. The company operates under a long-term lease from the port's owner, The Port Authority of New York and New Jersey. Port Newark Container Terminal is owned by Ports America, Inc., a subsidiary of American International Group (AIG). AIG acquired Port Newark Container Terminal, through PineBridge (formerly AIG Investments) in 2007 as part of its purchase of the US port operations of DP World.

	Annual Growth	12/17	12/18	12/19	12/21	12/22
Sales ($mil.)	20.8%	–	298.0	351.8	595.5	635.6
Net income ($ mil.)	70.9%	–	30.1	33.4	237.4	257.2
Market value ($ mil.)	–	–	–	–	–	–
Employees	–	–	–	–	–	400

PORT OF CORPUS CHRISTI AUTHORITY OF NUECES COUNTY, TEXAS

400 HARBOR DR
CORPUS CHRISTI, TX 784011115
Phone: 361 882-5633
Fax: –
Web: www.portofcc.com

CEO: –
CFO: –
HR: –
FYE: December 31
Type: Private

The Port of Corpus Christi Authority of Nueces County, Texas, owns and operates docks and freight handling facilities at the Port of Corpus Christi, which is on the Gulf of Mexico about 150 miles north of the US-Mexico border. The port has terminals designed to handle general, refrigerated, and liquid and dry bulk cargo. Port facilities are served by rail carriers and highways, as well as by the Gulf Intracoastal Waterway. The agency was created by Nueces County voters in 1922 as Nueces County Navigation District No. 1; it became the Port of Corpus Christi Authority of Nueces County, Texas, by an act of the Texas Legislature in 1981. Commissioners appointed by local government entities oversee the agency.

	Annual Growth	12/16	12/17	12/18	12/19	12/22
Sales ($mil.)	17.7%	–	95.3	105.8	128.2	215.7
Net income ($ mil.)	32.6%	–	35.9	49.3	60.0	147.2
Market value ($ mil.)	–	–	–	–	–	–
Employees	–	–	–	–	–	146

PORT OF HOUSTON AUTHORITY

111 EAST LOOP N
HOUSTON, TX 770294326
Phone: 713 670-2662
Fax: –
Web: www.porthouston.com

CEO: –
CFO: –
HR: Azlina Kabani
FYE: December 31
Type: Private

The company manages the Port of Houston complex, including the Barbours Cut Container Terminal, one of the busiest in the US. Port of Houston facilities are arrayed along the Houston Ship Channel, which is one of the most vital waterways in the country, connecting the nation's largest petrochemical complex to the globe. The company is a complex of nearly 200 private and public industrial terminals. The ship channel was opened in 1914; the Port of Houston Authority was created by the Texas Legislature in 1927.

	Annual Growth	12/16	12/17	12/19	12/20	12/22
Sales ($mil.)	14.4%	–	332.9	391.4	390.7	651.3
Net income ($ mil.)	25.4%	–	103.1	127.6	127.8	320.0
Market value ($ mil.)	–	–	–	–	–	–
Employees	–	–	–	–	–	595

PORT OF NEW ORLEANS

1350 PORT OF NEW ORLEANS PL
NEW ORLEANS, LA 701301805
Phone: 504 522-2551
Fax: –
Web: www.portnola.com

CEO: –
CFO: –
HR: –
FYE: June 30
Type: Private

The Port of New Orleans has played a major part of American history -- after all, the US purchased Louisiana to ensure control of it. By virtue of its location at the mouth of the Mississippi River on the Gulf of Mexico, the port connects the Midwestern US with the world. One of the busiest US ports, the Port of New Orleans handles export cargo such as grain and steel that arrives via the US inland waterway system. The port also is served by six major railroads. Import cargo handled at the port includes coffee, plywood, rubber, and steel. The Port of New Orleans is governed by a seven-member board appointed by the governor of Louisiana; board members represent New Orleans and two neighboring parishes.

	Annual Growth	06/13	06/14	06/15	06/16	06/17
Sales ($mil.)	7.1%	–	–	–	61.0	65.3
Net income ($ mil.)	–	–	–	–	(6.3)	(11.8)
Market value ($ mil.)	–	–	–	–	–	–
Employees	–	–	–	–	–	380

PORT OF SEATTLE

2711 ALASKAN WAY PIER 69
SEATTLE, WA 981211107
Phone: 206 728-3000
Fax: –
Web: www.portseattle.org

CEO: Kurt Beckett
CFO: –
HR: Daniel Breed
FYE: December 31
Type: Private

The Port of Seattle oversees both an airport (Seattle-Tacoma International, also known as Sea-Tac) and a seaport. The agency's aviation division sees more than 35 million passengers a year. During July through October 2021, the Maritime Division successfully and safely hosted over 80 cruise ship calls with 229,000 passengers by complying with national and local healthcare guidelines and working in partnership with the cruise industry, labor, and tourism representatives from Washington State to Alaska. The Port of Seattle is run by a five-member commission elected by King County voters.

	Annual Growth	12/15	12/16	12/17	12/18	12/19
Sales ($mil.)	10.0%	–	–	632.0	689.4	764.2
Net income ($ mil.)	15.6%	–	–	199.8	221.3	267.0
Market value ($ mil.)	–	–	–	–	–	–
Employees	–	–	–	–	–	1,515

PORTLAND GENERAL ELECTRIC CO.

NYS: POR

121 S.W. Salmon Street
Portland, OR 97204
Phone: 503 464-8000
Fax: 503 464-2676
Web: www.portlandgeneral.com

CEO: Maria M Pope
CFO: James Ajello
HR: John Leroux
FYE: December 31
Type: Public

Portland General Electric (PGE) is a vertically-integrated electric utility with about 922,445 retail customers in Oregon. The company generates, transmits, and distributes electricity in around 50 cities in the state, including Portland. The Company operates as a cost-based, regulated electric utility with revenue requirements and customer prices determined based on the forecasted cost to serve retail customers and a reasonable rate of return as determined by the Public Utility Commission of Oregon (OPUC). The company runs a market-leading voluntary renewable energy program for customers.

	Annual Growth	12/19	12/20	12/21	12/22	12/23
Sales ($mil.)	8.3%	2,123.0	2,145.0	2,396.0	2,647.0	2,923.0
Net income ($ mil.)	1.6%	214.0	155.0	244.0	233.0	228.0
Market value ($ mil.)	(6.1%)	5,643.7	4,326.6	5,353.4	4,956.8	4,384.3
Employees	(0.9%)	2,949	3,639	2,839	2,873	2,842

PORTLAND STATE UNIVERSITY

1600 SW 4TH AVE
PORTLAND, OR 972015522
Phone: 503 725-4444
Fax: –
Web: www.pdx.edu

CEO: Pete Nickerson
CFO: –
HR: –
FYE: June 30
Type: Private

Portland State University (PSU) is one of seven institutions of higher learning in the Oregon University System. It offers nearly 100 bachelor's, 90 master's, and 40 doctoral degrees, as well as graduate certificates and continuing education programs. PSU has eight schools and colleges devoted to liberal arts and sciences; engineering and computer science; fine and performing arts; urban and public affairs; business administration; social work; and education. It also has a school dedicated to extended studies, including distance learning, continuing education, and professional development. Student enrollment exceeds 29,000 (80% undergrads), and the student to faculty ratio is 19:1. PSU was established in 1946.

	Annual Growth	06/13	06/14	06/15	06/16	06/17
Sales ($mil.)	0.3%	–	350.0	351.8	357.4	353.1
Net income ($ mil.)	9.2%	–	36.4	181.7	(4.1)	47.4
Market value ($ mil.)	–	–	–	–	–	–
Employees	–	–	–	–	–	4,000

PORTOLA PHARMACEUTICALS, INC.

270 E GRAND AVE
SOUTH SAN FRANCISCO, CA 940804811
Phone: 650 246-7300
Fax: –
Web: www.portola.com

CEO: Scott Garland
CFO: Mardi Dier
HR: –
FYE: December 31
Type: Private

Portola Pharmaceuticals is putting blood, sweat, and tears into developing new medications for blood disorders. The company is a global, commercial-stage biopharmaceutical company focused on the discovery, development and commercialization of novel therapeutics that could significantly advance the fields of thrombosis and other hematologic conditions. The company's first two commercialized products are Andexxa and Bevyxxa (betrixaban). The company is also advancing Cerdulatinib, an investigational SYK/JAK inhibitor being developed for the treatment of hematologic cancers. Founded in 2003, Alexion Pharmaceuticals acquired Portola Pharmaceuticals in a deal worth about $1.41 billion in 2020.

PORTSMOUTH SQUARE, INC.   NBB: PRSI

1516 S. Bundy Dr,, Suite 200
Los Angeles, CA 90025
Phone: 310 889-2500
Fax: 310 899-2525
Web: www.intgla.com

CEO: John V Winfield V
CFO: –
HR: –
FYE: June 30
Type: Public

Investments are a square deal for Portsmouth Square, which owns a 50% partnership interest in Justice Investors, a property investment firm based in San Francisco. Justice Investors owns and operates the Hilton San Francisco Financial District, a hotel property that includes more than 500 individual units, a health and beauty spa, a Chinese cultural center, and an underground parking garage. Portsmouth Square has an investment portfolio valued at some $3 million that includes consumer, financial, material, and communications equities. Through Santa Fe Financial and other entities, CEO John Winfield controls more than 80% of Portsmouth Square.

	Annual Growth	06/18	06/19	06/20	06/21	06/22
Sales ($mil.)	(13.8%)	57.1	59.9	42.8	14.7	31.5
Net income ($ mil.)	–	3.6	2.6	(2.9)	(5.2)	(6.6)
Market value ($ mil.)	(12.2%)	51.4	60.2	26.4	47.0	30.5
Employees	10.7%	2	2	2	3	3

POSITIVEID CORP

1690 South Congress Avenue, Suite 201
Delray Beach, FL 33445
Phone: 561 805-8000
Fax: –
Web: www.positiveidcorp.com

CEO: William J Caragol
CFO: William J Caragol
HR: –
FYE: December 31
Type: Public

Who knew something the size of a grain of rice could protect so much? PositiveID, formerly VeriChip, knows it well. The firm provides implantable radio frequency identification (RFID) microchips for humans and animals. The chip is inserted under the skin and has a unique verification number used to access a subscriber-supplied database providing information when scanned. While its implantable technology has made headlines, most of its business comes from wearable and attachable ID tags, as well as vibration monitoring systems, used to monitor and protect people and assets. In 2009 the company changed its name from VeriChip to PositiveID to reflect a new focus on electronic health records.

	Annual Growth	12/13	12/14	12/15	12/16	12/17
Sales ($mil.)	–	–	0.9	2.9	5.6	5.4
Net income ($ mil.)	–	(4.3)	(7.2)	(11.4)	(13.1)	(8.6)
Market value ($ mil.)	(46.9%)	0.0	0.0	0.0	0.0	0.0
Employees	3.0%	8	9	32	29	9

POSITRON CORP   NBB: POSC

530 Oakmont Lane
Westmont, IL 60559
Phone: 317 576-0183
Fax: –
Web: www.positron.com

CEO: Joseph G Oliverio
CFO: Corey N Conn
HR: –
FYE: December 31
Type: Public

Positron is positive that its imaging systems can figure out what's wrong with you. The firm makes positron emission tomography (PET) scanners under the POSICAM and mPower trade names. The scanners are primarily used to detect coronary artery disease but also have applications in neurology and oncology. Medical centers such as the University of Texas Health Science Center at Houston and the Heart Center of Niagara use the system; the company has an installed base of about 30 systems in the US and abroad. Subsidiary IS2 Medical Systems makes nuclear imaging devices, including the PulseCDC cardiac gamma camera.

	Annual Growth	12/11	12/12	12/13	12/14	12/22
Sales ($mil.)	(18.2%)	6.7	2.8	1.6	1.5	0.7
Net income ($ mil.)	–	(6.1)	(8.0)	(7.1)	(2.6)	(2.3)
Market value ($ mil.)	51.9%	0.2	0.2	0.1	0.0	20.8
Employees	–	32	26	22	19	–

POST HOLDINGS INC   NYS: POST

2503 S. Hanley Road
St. Louis, MO 63144
Phone: 314 644-7600
Fax: –
Web: www.postholdings.com

CEO: Nicolas Catoggio
CFO: Matthew J Mainer
HR: –
FYE: September 30
Type: Public

Post Holdings is a consumer packaged goods holding company with businesses operating in the center-of-the-store, refrigerated, foodservice, and food ingredient categories. The maker of Grape-Nuts, Golden Puffs, Honey Bunches of Oats, Raisin Bran, Shredded Wheat, Pebbles, and Alpha-Bits sells its products through a variety of channels, including grocery, club and drug stores, mass merchandisers, foodservice, food ingredient, and eCommerce. In addition to cereal, the company also makes egg products, potato products, and cheese, pasta, and other dairy-based products. More recently, it has moved beyond the breakfast table by adding snacks, active nutrition products, and pasta through a series of major acquisitions. It also manufactures nut butters and cereals for private labels. The company has warehouses, manufacturing facilities, and distribution facilities located throughout the US and Canada.

	Annual Growth	09/19	09/20	09/21	09/22	09/23
Sales ($mil.)	5.3%	5,681.1	5,698.7	6,226.7	5,851.2	6,991.0
Net income ($ mil.)	24.7%	124.7	0.8	166.7	756.6	301.3
Market value ($ mil.)	(5.1%)	6,392.7	5,194.4	6,653.7	4,947.4	5,178.7
Employees	–	10,100	10,200	10,735	10,420	–

POSTAL INSTANT PRESS INC.

26722 PLAZA
MISSION VIEJO, CA 926918051
Phone: 949 282-3800
Fax: –
Web: www.pip.com

CEO: Dan Lowe
CFO: Dan Conger
HR: –
FYE: December 31
Type: Private

Postal Instant Press boasts about 800 quick-printing franchises that operate under the name PIP Printing and Document Services. The company's PIP stores offer offset and digital printing of business items such as brochures, newsletters, signs, stationery, and direct mail pieces. They also help clients with graphic design, provide photocopying services, and coordinate direct mail campaigns. Postal Instant Press has an online ordering system that allows customers to remotely design and order items like business cards, rubber stamps, and labels. Postal Instant Printing's operations span some 16 countries.

	Annual Growth	12/13	12/14	12/15	12/18	12/19
Sales ($mil.)	(0.6%)	–	2.7	2.5	2.2	2.6
Net income ($ mil.)	14.0%	–	0.3	0.3	0.0	0.6
Market value ($ mil.)	–	–	–	–	–	–
Employees	–	–	–	–	–	75

POSTROCK ENERGY CORP

210 Park Avenue
Oklahoma City, OK 73102
Phone: 405 600-7704
Fax: –
Web: www.pstr.com

NBB: PSTR Q
CEO: –
CFO: –
HR: –
FYE: December 31
Type: Public

PostRock Energy (formerly Quest Resource) is looking to create a rock solid energy company specializing in oil and gas exploration and production and the transportation of natural gas. Its exploration and drilling efforts are focused in the Cherokee Basin of southeastern Kansas and northeastern Oklahoma, and the Appalachian Basin, where it is accumulating leasehold acreage. PostRock Energy has net proved reserves of 192.2 billion cu. ft. of net proved reserves (the bulk of which is coal bed methane gas) and operates more than 2,200 miles of gas gathering pipeline in Kansas and Oklahoma. It also operates more than 1,100 miles of interstate natural gas transmission pipelines in the region.

	Annual Growth	12/10	12/11	12/12	12/13	12/14
Sales ($mil.)	0.3%	82.4	96.3	55.0	72.3	83.5
Net income ($ mil.)	(46.0%)	45.2	20.0	(47.6)	(9.0)	3.9
Market value ($ mil.)	(44.4%)	23.8	17.7	9.1	7.4	2.3
Employees	(9.8%)	300	233	216	209	199

POTBELLY CORP

111 N. Canal Street, Suite 325
Chicago, IL 60606
Phone: 312 951-0600
Fax: –
Web: www.potbelly.com

NMS: PBPB
CEO: Robert Wright
CFO: Steven W Cirulis
HR: –
FYE: December 31
Type: Public

Potbelly is a sandwich concept store that offers sandwiches, signature salads, hand-dipped shakes, freshly-baked cookies and other fresh menu items. The company owns almost 430 quick-service restaurants that specialize in fresh-made sandwiches in more than 30 states and the District of Columbia. Potbelly's franchisees operate some 45 shops. The chain's menu features toasty warm, toasty sandwiches, signature salads, soups, chili, sides, and desserts, and, in its breakfast locations, breakfast sandwiches and steel cut oatmeal. Started in 1977, Potbelly went public in 2013.

	Annual Growth	12/19	12/20	12/21	12/22	12/23
Sales ($mil.)	4.7%	409.7	291.3	380.1	452.0	491.4
Net income ($ mil.)	–	(24.0)	(65.4)	(23.8)	4.3	5.1
Market value ($ mil.)	25.2%	124.5	127.1	154.7	164.1	306.0
Employees	(4.5%)	6,000	5,500	5,500	6,000	5,000

POTLATCHDELTIC CORP

601 West 1st Ave., Suite 1600
Spokane, WA 99201
Phone: 509 835-1500
Fax: –
Web: www.potlatch.com

NMS: PCH
CEO: Eric J Cremers
CFO: Wayne Wasechek
HR: Chelsea Barnhouse
FYE: December 31
Type: Public

PotlatchDeltic Corporation (formerly Potlatch Corporation) is a real estate investment trust (REIT) that harvests timber from some 2.2 million acres of hardwood and softwood forestland in Alabama, Arkansas, Georgia, Idaho, Mississippi, Louisiana, South Carolina, and Minnesota; it claims to be the largest private landowner in Idaho. PotlatchDeltic operates six sawmills and an industrial grade plywood mill, a residential and commercial real estate development business and a rural timberland sales program. Beyond wood product sales, the company generates revenue by leasing its land for hunting, recreation, mineral rights, and carbon sequestration. It also sells real estate through PotlatchDeltic TRS.

	Annual Growth	12/19	12/20	12/21	12/22	12/23
Sales ($mil.)	5.5%	827.1	1,040.9	1,337.4	1,330.8	1,024.1
Net income ($ mil.)	2.8%	55.7	166.8	423.9	333.9	62.1
Market value ($ mil.)	3.2%	3,434.1	3,969.8	4,779.4	3,491.3	3,896.8
Employees	1.4%	1,307	1,316	1,299	1,330	1,384

POTOMAC BANCSHARES, INC.

111 East Washington Street, P.O. Box 906
Charles Town, WV 25414-0906
Phone: 304 725-8431
Fax: 304 725-0059
Web: www.bankatbct.com

NBB: PTBS
CEO: Alice P Frazier
CFO: Dean J Cognetti
HR: –
FYE: December 31
Type: Public

Potomac Bancshares is the holding company for Bank of Charles Town, which serves eastern West Virginia and neighboring parts of Maryland and Virginia. Through about five offices, the bank provides standard deposit products such as checking and savings accounts, CDs, and IRAs, as well as trust services, investments, and financial planning. It uses funds from deposits primarily to write real estate loans. Residential mortgages account for the largest portion of the company's loan portfolio, followed by construction, land development, and commercial real estate loans. Consumer, business, and farm loans round out the bank's lending activities. Bank of Charles Town opened in 1871.

	Annual Growth	12/18	12/19	12/20	12/21	12/22
Assets ($mil.)	11.8%	484.6	515.8	620.9	711.4	756.1
Net income ($ mil.)	21.2%	3.4	3.2	3.8	7.6	7.3
Market value ($ mil.)	3.8%	63.4	63.4	55.3	82.7	73.5
Employees	–	–	–	116	124	125

POTOMAC HOSPITAL CORPORATION OF PRINCE WILLIAM

2300 OPITZ BLVD
WOODBRIDGE, VA 221913399
Phone: 703 523-1000
Fax: –
Web: –

CEO: David L Bernd
CFO: –
HR: –
FYE: December 31
Type: Private

Potomac Hospital Corporation of Prince William -- operating as Sentara Northern Virginia Medical Center -- provides a variety of medical, surgical, and therapeutic services in northern Virginia. The not-for-profit medical center has more than 180 beds and provides emergency medicine, diagnostic imaging, and surgery services, as well as specialized care in fields including cancer treatment, women's health, cardiology, urology, and pediatrics. It also offers health education programs and operates two outpatient care clinics. Sentara Northern Virginia Medical Center is part of the Sentara Healthcare network.

	Annual Growth	12/18	12/19	12/20	12/21	12/22
Sales ($mil.)	4.2%	–	251.0	273.5	277.1	283.9
Net income ($ mil.)	–	–	10.8	27.3	7.0	(16.1)
Market value ($ mil.)	–	–	–	–	–	–
Employees	–	–	–	–	–	1,300

POUDRE VALLEY HEALTH CARE, INC.

12401 E 17TH AVE STE B132
AURORA, CO 800452525
Phone: 970 495-7000
Fax: –
Web: www.uchealth.org

CEO: Rulon Stacey
CFO: –
HR: Gina Draudt
FYE: June 30
Type: Private

Providing health care is what this Poudre Valley is all about. The not-for-profit Poudre Valley Health System (PVHS) cares for residents of Colorado, western Nebraska, and southern Wyoming through the Poudre Valley Hospital and the Medical Center of the Rockies. With a total of about 440 beds, the two hospitals offer general medical and surgical services and trauma care. They also offer treatment centers for specialties including cancer, heart, brain, and spine disorders. PVHS is home to the Mountain Crest Behavioral Healthcare Center, which administers mental health and substance abuse treatment. PVHS is part of the Health District of Northern Larimer County; it is also part of University of Colorado Health.

	Annual Growth	06/14	06/15	06/16	06/19	06/20
Sales ($mil.)	21.4%	–	480.4	523.9	1,412.5	1,266.9
Net income ($ mil.)	16.2%	–	98.8	93.0	340.6	209.5
Market value ($ mil.)	–	–	–	–	–	–
Employees	–	–	–	–	–	2,800

POWELL ELECTRONICS, INC.

200 COMMODORE DR
SWEDESBORO, NJ 080851270
Phone: 856 241-8000
Fax: –
Web: www.powell.com

CEO: Ernest Schilling Jr
CFO: Schawn E Beatty
HR: –
FYE: December 31
Type: Private

Powell Electronics distributes switches, sensors, connectors, relays, and other electronic components. The company stocks more than 100,000 parts from such manufacturers as 3M, Amphenol, AVX, Emerson Network Power, EnerSys, Honeywell, ITT, RF Industries, Winchester Electronics, and TE Connectivity. It also manufactures custom assemblies and offers several services, including bar coding, special packaging, materials management, and wire cutting. Powell Electronics was founded in 1946 by the late Harold Powell, who started selling components from his garage after World War II. His family continues to own the company.

	Annual Growth	03/08	03/09	03/10*	12/10	12/11
Sales ($mil.)	390.4%	–	–	22.4	98.8	109.8
Net income ($ mil.)	651.2%	–	–	0.5	3.7	3.7
Market value ($ mil.)	–	–	–	–	–	–
Employees	–	–	–	–	–	205

*Fiscal year change

POWELL INDUSTRIES, INC. NMS: POWL

8550 Mosley Road
Houston, TX 77075-1180
Phone: 713 944-6900
Fax: –
Web: www.powellind.com

CEO: –
CFO: –
HR: –
FYE: September 30
Type: Public

Founded in 1947, Powell Industries develops, designs, manufactures, and services custom-engineered equipment and systems which distribute, control, and monitor the flow of electrical energy and provide protection to motors, transformers, and other electrically powered equipment. Products include power control room substations, custom-engineered modules, electrical houses, traditional and arc-resistant distribution switchgear and control gear, medium-voltage circuit breakers, monitoring and control communications systems, motor control centers, switches, and bus duct systems. About 75% of the company's sales are generated in the US.

	Annual Growth	09/19	09/20	09/21	09/22	09/23
Sales ($mil.)	7.8%	517.2	518.5	470.6	532.6	699.3
Net income ($ mil.)	53.2%	9.9	16.7	0.6	13.7	54.5
Market value ($ mil.)	20.6%	464.4	286.2	291.4	250.1	983.4
Employees	4.2%	2,312	2,146	2,073	2,171	2,725

POWER CONSTRUCTION COMPANY, LLC

8750 W BRYN MAWR AVE STE 500
CHICAGO, IL 606313546
Phone: 312 596-6960
Fax: –
Web: www.powerconstruction.net

CEO: –
CFO: –
HR: Shahara Byford
FYE: December 31
Type: Private

Power Construction Company, a general contractor operating in the Chicago area for 97 years. The company provides customers with comprehensive preconstruction and construction services and virtual design and construction services. Power Construction also offers MEP planning and coordination services, sustainable construction practices, and more. While the company is a multi-faceted company, having highly specialized teams within the company allows them to better serve its clients. Each group, which includes VIP Group, Workplace Group, Aviation Group, Luxury Residence Group, and United Insulate Structures, has unique expertise, key industry partnerships and proven processes to assure success. The company expands its focus to include construction of K-12 schools and university facilities. Approximately 90% of the firm's business comes from repeat customers. Jerome Goldstein founded the company, which is still owned by family and management, in 1926.

POWER INTEGRATIONS INC. NMS: POWI

5245 Hellyer Avenue
San Jose, CA 95138
Phone: 408 414-9200
Fax: 408 414-9201
Web: www.power.com

CEO: Balu Balakrishnan
CFO: Sandeep Nayyar
HR: –
FYE: December 31
Type: Public

Power Integrations designs, develops, and markets analog and mixed-signal integrated circuits (ICs) and other electronic components and circuitry used in high-voltage power conversion. A large percentage of its products are ICs used in AC-DC power supplies, which convert the high-voltage AC from a wall outlet to the low-voltage DC required by most electronic devices. It also offers high-voltage gate drivers?either standalone ICs or circuit boards containing ICs, electrical isolation components and other circuitry?used to operate high-voltage switches such as insulated-gate bipolar transistors (IGBTs) and silicon-carbide (SiC) MOSFETs. Power Integrations sells its chips to electronics manufacturers and distributors such Avnet. The company makes nearly all of its sales overseas.

	Annual Growth	12/19	12/20	12/21	12/22	12/23
Sales ($mil.)	1.4%	420.7	488.3	703.3	651.1	444.5
Net income ($ mil.)	(26.7%)	193.5	71.2	164.4	170.9	55.7
Market value ($ mil.)	(4.5%)	5,612.0	4,644.6	5,270.4	4,069.2	4,658.8
Employees	4.0%	699	725	773	831	819

POWERFLEET INC NMS: PWFL

123 Tice Boulevard
Woodcliff Lake, NJ 07677
Phone: 201 996-9000
Fax: –
Web: www.powerfleet.com

CEO: Chris Wolfe
CFO: Ned Mavrommatis
HR: –
FYE: December 31
Type: Public

I.D. Systems has taken its tracking business on the road. The company's products track, analyze, and control the movements of objects such as packages and vehicles. Its systems use radio-frequency identification (RFID) technology and tiny computers attached to the object to be monitored, and users can access tracking data via the Internet. The company is focused on vehicle management, rental car, package tracking, and airport ground security applications. Customers include 3M, the FAA, Ford, Hallmark Cards, Target, the US Postal Service (42% of sales), and Wal-Mart Stores (41%).

	Annual Growth	12/18	12/19	12/20	12/21	12/22
Sales ($mil.)	26.3%	53.1	81.9	113.6	126.2	135.2
Net income ($ mil.)	–	(5.8)	(11.0)	(9.0)	(13.3)	(7.0)
Market value ($ mil.)	(16.7%)	202.2	235.5	268.7	171.4	97.3
Employees	54.9%	138	840	772	669	795

POWERLINX, INC.
NBB: PWNX

10901 A Roosevelt Blvd North, Suite 200
St. Petersburg, FL 33716
Phone: 727 866-7440
Fax: 727 866-7480
Web: www.power-linx.com

CEO: –
CFO: –
HR: –
FYE: December 31
Type: Public

Powerlinx designs, manufactures, and distributes products that transmit voice, video, and data over power lines. Through its Security Products segment, the company provides closed-circuit television systems. The company's DC Transportation segment offers view enhancement systems that transmit data through vehicle wiring to allow truck, school bus, and RV drivers to see objects in what otherwise would be blind spots. Through its Marine segment, Powerlinx provides customers with underwater surveillance equipment under the SeaView and SeaMaster brand names. Its Audio Products Division sells audio accessories to the home entertainment market. HSN accounts for 29% of Powerlinx's revenues.

	Annual Growth	12/02	12/03	12/04	12/05	12/06
Sales ($mil.)	25.1%	0.7	1.4	1.4	1.3	1.7
Net income ($ mil.)	–	(4.3)	(4.0)	(5.1)	(5.8)	(3.0)
Market value ($ mil.)	130.8%	0.3	1.7	1.1	0.3	7.3
Employees	11.5%	11	13	24	17	17

POWERSOUTH ENERGY COOPERATIVE

2027 E THREE NOTCH ST
ANDALUSIA, AL 364212427
Phone: 334 427-3000
Fax: –
Web: www.powersouth.com

CEO: Gary Smith
CFO: Rick Kyle
HR: Suzanne Grissett
FYE: December 31
Type: Private

Several hundred thousand Alabamans and Floridians get their electric power courtesy of the work of PowerSouth Energy Cooperative, which provides wholesale power to its member-owners (16 electric cooperatives and four municipal distribution utilities). Its distribution members provide electric services to almost 417,200 customer meters in central and southern Alabama and western Florida. PowerSouth operates a more than 2,200-mile power transmission system and has more than 2,000 MW of generating capacity from interests in six fossil-fueled and hydroelectric power plants.

	Annual Growth	12/18	12/19	12/20	12/21	12/22
Sales ($mil.)	12.0%	–	602.3	547.2	639.8	846.5
Net income ($ mil.)	(2.9%)	–	13.7	12.7	12.5	12.5
Market value ($ mil.)	–	–	–	–	–	–
Employees	–	–	–	–	–	640

PPG INDUSTRIES INC
NYS: PPG

One PPG Place
Pittsburgh, PA 15272
Phone: 412 434-3131
Fax: –
Web: www.ppg.com

CEO: Timothy M Knavish
CFO: Vincent J Morales
HR: –
FYE: December 31
Type: Public

PPG Industries manufactures and distributes a broad range of paints, coatings and specialty materials. The company's Performance and Industrial coatings offerings include paints, stains, adhesives, and sealants for automotive, aerospace, marine, architectural, and industrial applications. Well-known paint brands include Glidden, Olympic, and PPG Pittsburg Paints. Other products include packaging coatings used for the protection and decoration of metal cans, closures, and plastic tubes. PPG's specialty coatings are used in lighting and lens materials and label substrates. The company generates about 40% of sales from the US and Canada.

	Annual Growth	12/19	12/20	12/21	12/22	12/23
Sales ($mil.)	4.8%	15,146	13,834	16,802	17,652	18,246
Net income ($ mil.)	0.5%	1,243.0	1,059.0	1,439.0	1,026.0	1,270.0
Market value ($ mil.)	2.9%	31,398	33,922	40,560	29,575	35,176
Employees	–	27,700	46,900	49,300	52,000	–

PPL CORP
NYS: PPL

Two North Ninth Street
Allentown, PA 18101-1179
Phone: 610 774-5151
Fax: –
Web: www.pplweb.com

CEO: Vincent Sorgi
CFO: Joseph P Bergstein Jr
HR: Cynthia Dubs
FYE: December 31
Type: Public

PPL Corporation is one of the largest utility companies in the world, delivering electricity to more than 1 million customers through its regulated utility subsidiaries in Pennsylvania. The company also has customers in Kentucky and Virginia. Natural gas is offered to customers in Kentucky, and electricity generation for customers in Kentucky. Its subsidiaries LG&E and KU own generating capacities of about 2,760 MW and some 4,755 MW, respectively. Further, PPL Corporation's natural gas storage fields have a working natural gas capacity of about 15 billion cubic feet (BcF).

	Annual Growth	12/19	12/20	12/21	12/22	12/23
Sales ($mil.)	1.7%	7,769.0	7,607.0	5,783.0	7,902.0	8,312.0
Net income ($ mil.)	(19.3%)	1,746.0	1,469.0	(1,480.0)	756.0	740.0
Market value ($ mil.)	(6.8%)	26,448	20,787	22,158	21,539	19,976
Employees	(14.3%)	12,280	12,318	7,351	8,938	6,629

PPL ELECTRIC UTILITIES CORP

Two North Ninth Street
Allentown, PA 18101-1179
Phone: 610 774-5151
Fax: 610 774-4198
Web: –

CEO: –
CFO: –
HR: Amanda Shade
FYE: December 31
Type: Public

PPL Electric Utilities pulls its weight in Pennsylvania's power market. The company, which transmits and distributes electricity to 1.4 million customers in 29 counties in eastern and central portions of the state, is a subsidiary of PPL Corporation. The regulated utility operates more than 48,000 miles of overhead and underground power distribution lines, and it is a member of the PJM Interconnection regional transmission organization (RTO). Under the state's Customer Choice Act, PPL Electric also acts as the Provider of Last Resort for customers who don't choose an alternative supplier.

	Annual Growth	12/19	12/20	12/21	12/22	12/23
Sales ($mil.)	6.3%	2,358.0	2,331.0	2,402.0	3,030.0	3,008.0
Net income ($ mil.)	3.2%	457.0	497.0	445.0	525.0	519.0
Market value ($ mil.)	–	–	–	–	–	–
Employees	–	1,562	1,533	1,596	1,382	–

PRA GROUP INC
NMS: PRAA

120 Corporate Boulevard
Norfolk, VA 23502
Phone: 888 772-7326
Fax: –
Web: www.pragroup.com

CEO: Vikram A Atal
CFO: Peter M Graham
HR: –
FYE: December 31
Type: Public

PRA Group Inc. is a global financial and business services company. Its primary business is the purchase, collection and management of portfolios of nonperforming loans. The accounts it purchases are primarily the unpaid obligations of individuals owed to credit originators, which include banks and other types of consumers, retail and auto finance companies. PRA Group has an 11.7% equity interest in RCB, a servicing platform of nonperforming loans in Brazil. Through its subsidiary, Claims Compensation Bureau (CCB), PRA Group provides fee-based services including class action claims recovery purchasing and servicing. The US accounts for about 55% of total revenue.

	Annual Growth	12/19	12/20	12/21	12/22	12/23
Sales ($mil.)	(5.8%)	1,017.1	1,065.4	1,095.7	966.5	802.6
Net income ($ mil.)	–	86.2	149.3	183.2	117.1	(83.5)
Market value ($ mil.)	(7.8%)	1,424.7	1,556.5	1,970.6	1,325.8	1,028.3
Employees	(8.0%)	4,412	3,820	3,446	3,277	3,155

PRAGMATICS, INC.

1761 BUSINESS CENTER DR STE 110
RESTON, VA 201905333
Phone: 703 890-8500
Fax: –
Web: www.pragmatics.com

CEO: Long Nguyen
CFO: Kimmy Duong
HR: Vibhuti Rana
FYE: September 30
Type: Private

Pragmatics enjoys a practical outlook on technology. The company provides a variety of information technology (IT) services to US military and civilian agencies. Its roster includes such clients as the Defense Information Systems Agency, the Department of Homeland Security, and the Department of the Air Force.the Department of Labor . Pragmatics' corporate clients include contractors for federal IT programs. The company's services include Agile Software Engineeringcustom software development, DevSecOps in the Cloudsystems integration, program IT service management, business intelligence and analytics, cyber security, audiovisual and learning technologies, and IT project managementPragmatic Agility. CEO and owner Long Nguyen founded Pragmatics in 1985. Its industry affiliations are Amazon Partner Network (APN) and Radio Technical Commission for Aeronautics (RTCA).

PRAIRIE FARMS DAIRY, INC.

3744 STAUNTON RD
EDWARDSVILLE, IL 620256936
Phone: 618 659-5700
Fax: –
Web: www.prairiefarms.com

CEO: Ed Mullins
CFO: Jason Geminn
HR: Kayla Samuelson
FYE: September 30
Type: Private

Prairie Farms Dairy is one of the largest and most successful dairy cooperatives in the Midwest and the South. With more than 600 dairy farmer-members, the cooperative offers a full line of retail and food service dairy products. It turns raw milk into fresh, fluid, cultured, and frozen dairy products under the Prairie Farms label. It also makes juices and ice cream novelties. The company's customers include food, drug, and convenience stores, mass merchandisers, schools, restaurants, and other food service operators. Located in Edwardsville, Illinois, it is the managing partner for joint ventures with smaller regional dairies. It makes its products at nearly 50 manufacturing plants and over 100 distribution facilities, which are located throughout the mid-western and southern areas of the US.

	Annual Growth	09/09	09/10	09/11	09/12	09/13
Sales ($mil.)	3.5%	–	–	1,607.2	1,649.9	1,721.3
Net income ($ mil.)	(28.9%)	–	–	28.0	38.8	14.2
Market value ($ mil.)	–	–	–	–	–	–
Employees	–	–	–	–	–	1,965

PRAIRIE VIEW A&M UNIVERSITY

700 UNIVERSITY DR
PRAIRIE VIEW, TX 774456850
Phone: 936 261-3311
Fax: –
Web: www.pvamu.edu

CEO: –
CFO: –
HR: Annette Crutchfield
FYE: August 31
Type: Private

A historically African American institution of higher learning, Prairie View A&M University offers its 8,400 students baccalaureate degrees in about 50 academic majors, nearly 40 graduate degree programs, and four doctoral programs through nine colleges and schools. Its main campus in southeast Texas, home to the university's nine colleges and schools, is about 40 miles outside of Houston; its nursing college maintains a branch in that city's Texas Medical Center. Part of The Texas A&M University System, Prairie View A&M was founded in 1876 and was originally known as Alta Vista Agricultural and Mechanical College of Texas for Colored Youth.

	Annual Growth	08/15	08/16	08/17	08/18	08/19
Sales ($mil.)	6.3%	–	–	91.3	98.8	103.1
Net income ($ mil.)	–	–	–	64.2	44.7	(21.0)
Market value ($ mil.)	–	–	–	–	–	–
Employees	–	–	–	–	–	965

PRATT INDUSTRIES, INC.

1800 SARASOTA PKWY NE STE C
CONYERS, GA 300135775
Phone: 770 918-5678
Fax: –
Web: www.prattindustries.com

CEO: Brian McPheely
CFO: Stephen Ward
HR: Kevin Vickers
FYE: June 30
Type: Private

Pratt Industries (USA) doesn't mill around when it comes to recycling and caring for the environment. The company rivals the world's largest manufacturers of recycled paper and packaging and claims to be the 5th largest box manufacturer in the US and the world's largest, privately-held 100% recycled paper and packaging company. Pratt has a handful of operating divisions: recycling, mills, corrugating, converting, displays, packaging systems, and national accounts. Its products, which include container board and corrugated sheets, are sold to clients such as Rubbermaid and Pringles.

	Annual Growth	06/16	06/17	06/18	06/20	06/21
Sales ($mil.)	7.0%	–	–	2,498.6	2,612.3	3,065.0
Net income ($ mil.)	3.9%	–	–	200.8	200.8	225.2
Market value ($ mil.)	–	–	–	–	–	–
Employees	–	–	–	–	–	8,618

PRECIGEN INC

NMS: PGEN

20374 Seneca Meadows Parkway
Germantown, MD 20876
Phone: 301 556-9900
Fax: –
Web: www.precigen.com

CEO: Helen Sabzevari
CFO: Harry Thomasian Jr
HR: –
FYE: December 31
Type: Public

One man's frankenfood is another man's solution to world hunger. Intrexon is developing technology that uses synthetic biology, or biological engineering, to make advances in everything from pharmaceuticals to genetically modified plants and animals. The company has development agreements with AmpliPhi (antibacterial medication), AquaBounty (genetically modified salmon), BioLife (genetic disease), Eli Lilly (animal medication), Fibrocell (dermatology medication), Genopaver (pharmaceutical ingredients), Oragenics (antibiotics), Soligenix (antibiotics), Synthetic Biologics (antibiotics), and ZIOPHARM (cancer medicine). Intrexon went public in 2013, raising $160 million in its IPO.

	Annual Growth	12/19	12/20	12/21	12/22	12/23
Sales ($mil.)	(48.8%)	90.7	103.2	103.9	26.9	6.2
Net income ($ mil.)	–	(322.3)	(170.5)	(92.2)	28.3	(95.9)
Market value ($ mil.)	(29.7%)	1,364.1	2,539.0	923.5	378.4	333.6
Employees	(30.3%)	857	283	511	209	202

PRECIPIO INC

NAS: PRPO

4 Science Park
New Haven, CT 06511
Phone: 203 787-7888
Fax: –
Web: www.precipiodx.com

CEO: –
CFO: –
HR: –
FYE: December 31
Type: Public

Precipio (formerly Transgenomic) travels the uncharted frontiers of the human genome. Its clinical laboratories arm specializes in molecular diagnostics for cardiology, neurology, mitochondrial disorders, and oncology. Precipio's diagnostic tools arm produces equipment, reagents, and other consumables for clinical and research applications in molecular testing and cytogenetics. The proprietary WAVE System is used for genetic variation detection in molecular genetic research and molecular diagnostics. The company also operates a contract research laboratory that supports all phases of pre-clinical and clinical trials for oncology drugs in development. Transgenomic changed its name when it merged with Precipio Diagnostics in 2017.

	Annual Growth	12/18	12/19	12/20	12/21	12/22
Sales ($mil.)	34.6%	2.9	3.1	6.1	8.8	9.4
Net income ($ mil.)	–	(15.7)	(13.2)	(10.6)	(8.5)	(12.2)
Market value ($ mil.)	37.6%	0.2	2.3	2.4	1.8	0.6
Employees	5.6%	45	51	57	56	56

PRECISION CASTPARTS CORP.

5885 MEADOWS RD STE 620
LAKE OSWEGO, OR 970358647
Phone: 503 946-4800
Fax: –
Web: www.precast.com

CEO: –
CFO: Shawn R Hagel
HR: –
FYE: January 03
Type: Private

Precision Castparts Corp. (PCC) is a market leader in manufacturing large, complex structural investment castings, airfoil castings, forged components, aerostructures and highly engineered, critical fasteners for aerospace applications. In addition, PCC is a leading producer of airfoil castings for the industrial gas turbine. PCC also manufactures extruded seamless pipe, fittings, forgings, and clad products for power generation and oil & gas applications; commercial and military airframe aerostructures; and metal alloys and other materials to the casting and forging industries. The company is a subsidiary of Berkshire Hathaway. PCC was founded in 1947 by Joseph Cox.

	Annual Growth	03/12	03/13	03/14	03/15*	01/16
Sales ($mil.)	(5.8%)	–	8,377.8	9,616.0	10,005	7,002.0
Net income ($ mil.)	(17.0%)	–	1,429.1	1,784.0	1,533.0	817.0
Market value ($ mil.)	–	–	–	–	–	–
Employees	–	–	–	–	–	30,116

*Fiscal year change

PRECISION DATA PRODUCTS, INC.

5036 FALCON VIEW AVE SE
KENTWOOD, MI 495125404
Phone: 616 698-2242
Fax: –
Web: www.precision.com

CEO: –
CFO: –
HR: –
FYE: December 31
Type: Private

Precision Data Products likes to get it right. The company sells electronics such as computers, printers, audiovisual equipment, and accessories directly to customers via telephone and its Web site. Through Precision Data Products' online catalog, customers can view purchasing history, real-time inventory and prices, and product descriptions and white pages on more than 250,000 products. Corporate customers can request custom catalogs with negotiated or contract prices. The company carries brands from manufacturers such as Apple, D-Link, Exabyte, Hewlett-Packard, and Symbol Technologies. It also offers on-site or ship-in repair services for computers and printers.

	Annual Growth	12/10	12/11	12/14	12/15	12/16
Sales ($mil.)	(1.9%)	–	18.5	17.5	16.3	16.7
Net income ($ mil.)	4.1%	–	0.9	1.3	0.9	1.1
Market value ($ mil.)	–	–	–	–	–	–
Employees	–	–	–	–	–	20

PRECISION ENVIRONMENTAL COMPANY

5500 OLD BRECKSVILLE RD
INDEPENDENCE, OH 441311508
Phone: 216 642-6040
Fax: –
Web: www.precision-env.com

CEO: –
CFO: –
HR: –
FYE: December 31
Type: Private

Precision Environmental provides selective demolition, environmental remediation, asbestos and lead abatement, and other services, including indoor air-cleaning services, hazardous waste remediation, and floor and surface preparation services from its offices in Cuyahoga Heights and Independence, Ohio. The company's clients include NASA and the University of Cincinnati. President Tony DiGeronimo and his brothers founded Precision Environmental in 1987.

PRECISION OPTICS CORP INC (MA)

NAS: POCI

22 East Broadway
Gardner, MA 01440-3338
Phone: 978 630-1800
Fax: –
Web: www.poci.com

CEO: Joseph N Forkey
CFO: Wayne Coll
HR: –
FYE: June 30
Type: Public

Precision Optics plays it up close and personal. The company makes specialized video cameras and stereo endoscopes for use in minimally invasive surgery. Its other products include laparoscopes (for abdominal surgery) and arthroscopes (for joint surgery), as well as sterilizable image couplers and beamsplitters that connect endoscopes to video cameras. The US is Precision Optics' biggest market, accounting for almost all sales, although the company has received regulatory approval to sell its products in Europe. In 2019, Precision Optics acquired Ross Optical for $200 million.

	Annual Growth	06/19	06/20	06/21	06/22	06/23
Sales ($mil.)	32.6%	6.8	9.9	10.7	15.7	21.0
Net income ($ mil.)	–	(0.6)	(1.4)	(0.1)	(0.9)	(0.1)
Market value ($ mil.)	52.4%	6.9	8.8	10.2	12.1	37.3
Employees	8.2%	62	60	52	77	85

PRECISION OPTICS INC.

22 East Broadway
Gardner, MA 01440-3338
Phone: 978 630-1800
Fax: –
Web: www.poci.com

CEO: Joseph N Forkey
CFO: Wayne Coll
HR: –
FYE: June 30
Type: Public

Precision Optics plays it up close and personal. The company makes specialized video cameras and stereo endoscopes for use in minimally invasive surgery. Its other products include laparoscopes (for abdominal surgery) and arthroscopes (for joint surgery), as well as sterilizable image couplers and beamsplitters that connect endoscopes to video cameras. The US is Precision Optics' biggest market, accounting for almost all sales, although the company has received regulatory approval to sell its products in Europe. In 2019, Precision Optics acquired Ross Optical for $200 million.

	Annual Growth	06/98	06/99	06/00	06/01	06/02
Sales ($mil.)	(18.7%)	4.1	3.0	3.0	4.2	1.8
Net income ($ mil.)	–	(2.0)	(1.7)	(2.2)	(3.7)	(10.0)
Market value ($ mil.)	(56.0%)	3.3	5.2	3.9	0.3	0.1
Employees	(1.7%)	46	42	53	81	43

PREFERRED APARTMENT COMMUNITIES, LLC

3284 NORTHSIDE PKWY NW STE 150
ATLANTA, GA 303272280
Phone: 770 818-4100
Fax: –
Web: www.pacapts.com

CEO: –
CFO: –
HR: –
FYE: December 31
Type: Private

Preferred Apartment Communities (PAC) is a real estate investment trust engaged primarily in the ownership and operation of Class A multifamily properties, with select investments in grocery-anchored shopping centers. Preferred Apartment Communities' investment objective is to generate attractive, stable returns for stockholders by investing in income-producing properties and acquiring or originating real estate loans. The company owns or invests in nearly 115 properties in roughly 15 states, predominantly in the Southeast region of the US. In mid-2022, Preferred Apartment Communities was acquired by Blackstone Real Estate Income Trust for approximately $5.8 billion.

PREFERRED BANK (LOS ANGELES, CA) — NMS: PFBC

601 S. Figueroa Street, 48th Floor
Los Angeles, CA 90017
Phone: 213 891-1188
Fax: –
Web: www.preferredbank.com

CEO: LI Yu
CFO: Edward J Czajka
HR: Karen Cangey
FYE: December 31
Type: Public

Preferred Bank wants to be the bank of choice of Chinese-Americans in Southern California. Employing a multilingual staff, the bank provides international banking services to companies doing business in the Asia/Pacific region. It targets middle-market businesses, typically manufacturing, service, distribution, and real estate firms, as well as entrepreneurs, professionals, and high-net-worth individuals, through about a dozen branches in Los Angeles, Orange, and San Francisco Counties. Preferred Bank offers standard deposit products such as checking accounts, savings, money market, and NOW accounts. Specialized services include private banking and international trade finance.

	Annual Growth	12/19	12/20	12/21	12/22	12/23
Assets ($mil.)	9.5%	4,628.5	5,143.6	6,046.3	6,425.4	6,659.3
Net income ($ mil.)	17.6%	78.4	69.5	95.2	128.8	150.0
Market value ($ mil.)	5.0%	816.2	685.5	975.1	1,013.6	992.3
Employees	1.8%	279	266	279	299	300

PREFERRED UTILITIES MANUFACTURING CORPORATION

31-35 SOUTH ST
DANBURY, CT 068108147
Phone: 203 743-6741
Fax: –
Web: www.preferred-mfg.com

CEO: David G Bohn
CFO: –
HR: –
FYE: March 31
Type: Private

Preferred Utilities Manufacturing's business is divided into five units: Preferred Instruments makes instrumentation and control systems for combustion applications; Preferred Engineering provides support for nuclear power plant outage activities; Preferred Utilities manufactures fuel oil handling equipment; Preferred Services offers field services related to commissioning new combustion systems and instruments, as well as maintenance and calibration of existing systems; and W.N. Best Combustion makes burners for firing natural gas, fuel oil, and waste liquids. Preferred Utilities Manufacturing was founded in 1920. The company has sales offices in Massachusetts, Oregon, and Texas.

	Annual Growth	03/01	03/02	03/03	03/06	03/16
Sales ($mil.)	5.9%	–	11.3	11.3	11.2	25.3
Net income ($ mil.)	13.3%	–	0.0	5.1	(0.3)	0.3
Market value ($ mil.)	–	–	–	–	–	–
Employees	–	–	–	–	–	80

PREFORMED LINE PRODUCTS CO. — NMS: PLPC

660 Beta Drive
Mayfield Village, OH 44143
Phone: 440 461-5200
Fax: 440 442-8816
Web: www.preformed.com

CEO: Robert G Ruhlman
CFO: Andrew Klaus
HR: Timothy O 'shaughnessy
FYE: December 31
Type: Public

Preformed Line Products (PLP) is an international designer and manufacturer of products and systems employed in the construction and maintenance of overhead, and underground networks for the energy, telecommunication, cable operators, information (data communication) and other similar industries. It provides formed wire products, protective fiber-optic closures, solar hardware systems and mounting hardware for a variety of solar power applications, and data communication cabinets for data communications networks. PLP-USA is responsible for some 60% of the total sales. The company was founded in 1947.

	Annual Growth	12/19	12/20	12/21	12/22	12/23
Sales ($mil.)	10.8%	444.9	466.4	517.4	637.0	669.7
Net income ($ mil.)	28.4%	23.3	29.8	35.7	54.4	63.3
Market value ($ mil.)	22.0%	296.2	335.9	317.6	408.8	657.0
Employees	4.2%	2,983	2,969	2,927	3,261	3,520

PREMIER AG CO-OP, INC.

811 W 2ND ST
SEYMOUR, IN 472742711
Phone: 812 522-4911
Fax: –
Web: www.premierag.com

CEO: Harold Cooper
CFO: –
HR: –
FYE: July 31
Type: Private

Premier AG Co-Op provides the agricultural communities in Bartholomew, Decatur, and Johnson counties of south-central Indiana with farming supplies, services, and marketing assistance. It operates four grain elevators that handle corn, soybeans, and wheat. The co-op operates CountryMark gas stations, as well as one Countrymart store in Greensburg, Indiana. The store sells seed, fertilizer and chemical treatments, lawn and garden products, hardware, apparel, pet food and supplies, animal feed and plants (in season). Premier also owns Premier Energy and Heyob Energy, suppliers of propane and home heating oil.

	Annual Growth	07/11	07/12	07/13	07/14	07/15
Sales ($mil.)	(7.3%)	–	–	141.7	139.8	121.7
Net income ($ mil.)	(12.6%)	–	–	4.5	4.8	3.4
Market value ($ mil.)	–	–	–	–	–	–
Employees	–	–	–	–	–	100

PREMIER ENTERTAINMENT III, LLC

1131 N DUPONT HWY
DOVER, DE 199012008
Phone: 302 674-4600
Fax: –
Web: casinos.ballys.com

CEO: –
CFO: –
HR: –
FYE: December 31
Type: Private

Dover Downs Gaming & Entertainment is betting on being the first stop for gamblers in the First State. The company operates three facilities, all in Dover, Delaware, adjacent to Dover Motorsports' Dover Downs International Speedway. Dover Downs Casino, a 165,000 square-foot facility, has more than 2,700 video slot machines; Dover Downs Hotel and Conference Center is a 500-room luxury hotel featuring ballroom, concert hall, banquet, dining, meeting room, and spa facilities; and Dover Downs Raceway features harness racing and simulcast horse race betting. Dover Downs' video slot operations are operated and administered by the Delaware State Lottery Office. Twin River Worldwide Holdings acquired the company in 2019.

	Annual Growth	12/14	12/15	12/16	12/17	12/18
Sales ($mil.)	(0.6%)	–	182.9	182.3	176.9	179.9
Net income ($ mil.)	(74.8%)	–	1.9	0.8	(1.1)	0.0
Market value ($ mil.)	–	–	–	–	–	–
Employees	–	–	–	–	–	1,388

PREMIER EXHIBITIONS INC — NBB: PRXI Q

3340 Peachtree Road, N.E., Suite 900
Atlanta, GA 30326
Phone: 404 842-2600
Fax: –
Web: www.prxi.com

CEO: Daoping Bao
CFO: Jerome Henshall
HR: –
FYE: February 28
Type: Public

The Titanic was on her maiden trip when an iceberg hit the ship, and Premier Exhibitions is here to tell the tale. The company owns RMS Titanic, which salvages and displays artifacts from the doomed Titanic ocean liner, runs a touring Titanic exhibit, and sells Titanic merchandise. It is considered the salvor-in-possession, or owner, of the wrecked ship. Premier's other exhibits include "Bodies...The Exhibition" and "Bodies Revealed" (preserved bodies and organs) and "Dialog in the Dark" (exploring a world without sight). Premier was created as a holding company in 2004 when it spun off RMS Titanic. The company has announced plans to sell its Titanic holdings to focus on other touring exhibits.

	Annual Growth	02/11	02/12	02/13	02/14	02/15
Sales ($mil.)	(10.0%)	44.8	31.7	39.5	29.3	29.4
Net income ($ mil.)	–	(12.5)	(5.8)	2.0	(0.7)	(10.5)
Market value ($ mil.)	(32.6%)	8.6	12.0	11.3	4.3	1.8
Employees	(5.9%)	222	201	191	196	174

PREMIER FINANCIAL CORP

NMS: PFC

601 Clinton Street
Defiance, OH 43512
Phone: 419 785-8700
Fax: –
Web: www.premierfincorp.com

CEO: –
CFO: –
HR: –
FYE: December 31
Type: Public

Named for its hometown, not its attitude, First Defiance Financial is the holding company for First Federal Bank of the Midwest, which operates more than 30 branches serving northwestern Ohio, western Indiana, and southern Michigan. The thrift offers standard deposit products including checking, savings, and money market accounts and CDs. Commercial real estate loans account for more than half of the bank's loan portfolio; commercial loans make up another quarter of all loans. The company's insurance agency subsidiary, First Insurance Group of the Midwest, which accounts for some 7% of the company's revenues, provides life insurance, property/casualty coverage, and investments. In 2019 First Defiance Financial agreed to merge with Ohio-based United Community Financial (the holding company for Home Savings Bank and HSB Insurance) in a deal valued at $473 million.

	Annual Growth	12/19	12/20	12/21	12/22	12/23
Assets ($mil.)	25.6%	3,469.0	7,211.7	7,481.4	8,455.3	8,625.9
Net income ($ mil.)	22.5%	49.4	63.1	126.1	102.2	111.3
Market value ($ mil.)	(6.5%)	1,125.1	821.8	1,104.4	963.6	861.1
Employees	10.0%	699	1,195	1,180	1,206	1,023

PREMIER HEALTH PARTNERS

110 N MAIN ST STE 450
DAYTON, OH 454023712
Phone: 937 499-9596
Fax: –
Web: www.premierhealth.com

CEO: James R Pancoast
CFO: Thomas M Duncan
HR: Carla Rowe
FYE: December 31
Type: Private

There may not be any red carpets, but this Premier does feature good health. Premier Health Partners is a multi-hospital health system operating in the Dayton, Ohio, area. It includes Miami Valley Hospital and Good Samaritan Hospital, both in Dayton; Atrium Medical Center in nearby Middletown; and Upper Valley Medical Center in Troy. Collectively, the hospitals house about 1,800 inpatient beds. The health system also operates about 65 other facilities including outpatient health centers, a primary care physician group (Premier HealthNet), home health care, psychiatric care, and health outreach programs that provide health screenings, education, and smoking cessation programs.

	Annual Growth	12/16	12/17	12/19	12/21	12/22
Sales ($mil.)	168.5%	–	0.0	2.9	1.8	2.4
Net income ($ mil.)	–	–	(0.6)	(221.4)	(244.6)	(220.7)
Market value ($ mil.)	–	–	–	–	–	–
Employees	–	–	–	–	–	5,336

PREMIERE GLOBAL SERVICES, INC.

2475 NORTHWINDS PKWY STE 200
ALPHARETTA, GA 300094807
Phone: 866 755-4878
Fax: –
Web: www.premiereglobal.com

CEO: Don Joos
CFO: Kevin J McAdams
HR: Francoise Caraguel
FYE: December 31
Type: Private

Premiere Global Services (PGi) provides products and services that include global meet collaboration, global meet webcast, and global operator assisted. The company created GlobalMeet to meet the daily communication needs of business professionals with solutions for web, video, audio, conferencing, webinars and webcasting, project management and productivity. Its conferencing services are provided primarily through GlobalMeet. It includes audio and video conferencing, operator-assisted event conferencing, Hive streaming, and screen sharing. PGi serves more than 60,000 enterprises. It has its presence in North America, Europe and Asia. The company was established in 1991.

PREMIO, INC.

918 RADECKI CT
CITY OF INDUSTRY, CA 917481132
Phone: 626 839-3100
Fax: –
Web: www.premioinc.com

CEO: Crystal Tsao
CFO: –
HR: Lisle Sandoval
FYE: December 31
Type: Private

Premio can sell you one of its computers or build one of your own design. The company provides contract manufacturing services, including the design and assembly, testing, and support of products ranging from computer servers and displays to medical equipment. The company markets its own line of built-to-order desktop and notebooks PCs, servers, workstations, along with third-party peripherals. It sells to customers in the education, medical, government, security, and surveillance markets. Customers have included Sourcefire and Rapiscan Systems. Founded in 1989 by CEO Crystal Wu and Tom Tsao, Premio is owned by its officers.

	Annual Growth	12/10	12/11	12/12	12/13	12/20
Sales ($mil.)	(33.3%)	–	1,592.5	64.5	63.5	41.5
Net income ($ mil.)	178.5%	–	0.0	0.4	0.3	0.3
Market value ($ mil.)	–	–	–	–	–	–
Employees	–	–	–	–	–	140

PREMIUM BEERS OF OKLAHOMA, L.L.C.

9537 N KELLEY AVE STE A
OKLAHOMA CITY, OK 731312438
Phone: 800 889-8418
Fax: –
Web: –

CEO: –
CFO: –
HR: –
FYE: December 31
Type: Private

Premium Beers of Oklahoma is the leading beer distributor in the Sooner State and one of the top Anheuser-Busch distributorships in the country. The company supplies such brands as Budweiser, Michelob, and Busch from distribution facilities in Ardmore, Clinton, and Lawton. It also distributes Mexican beers from Grupo Modelo such as Corona, Corona Light, and Modelo Especial, as well as BACARDI Silver branded malt beverages, Rolling Rock and Stella Artois beers, non-alcoholic O'Doul's beverages, and Monster energy drinks. Premium Beers serves customers primarily in central and south-central Oklahoma. Denny Cresap started the company in 1968 as a one-person, one-route delivery service.

	Annual Growth	12/03	12/04	12/05	12/06	12/07
Sales ($mil.)	5.5%	–	114.8	114.5	121.7	134.7
Net income ($ mil.)	(52.3%)	–	24.3	5.6	4.6	2.6
Market value ($ mil.)	–	–	–	–	–	–
Employees	–	–	–	–	–	300

PREMIUM RETAIL SERVICES, INC.

618 SPIRIT DR STE 200
CHESTERFIELD, MO 630051258
Phone: 636 728-0592
Fax: –
Web: www.premiumretail.com

CEO: Ronald Travers
CFO: –
HR: –
FYE: December 31
Type: Private

Premium Retail Services provides marketing consulting and outsourced merchandising services for a variety of packaged goods manufacturers, as well as retail operators. Premium's solutions offer a comprehensive approach to retail marketing. From market and consumer analysis, to strategy, to program design and implementation. The company's senior leadership represents decades of retail experience in roles with Best Buy, Walmart, Home Depot, and several leading consumer brands. The family-owned Premium Retail Services was founded in 1985 by Ron Travers.

	Annual Growth	12/06	12/07	12/08	12/09	12/12
Sales ($mil.)	16.6%	–	–	–	0.0	0.0
Net income ($ mil.)	–	–	–	–	–	–
Market value ($ mil.)	–	–	–	–	–	–
Employees	–	–	–	–	–	4,000

PRESBYTERIAN HEALTHCARE SERVICES

9521 SAN MATEO BLVD NE
ALBUQUERQUE, NM 871132237
Phone: 505 923-5700
Fax:
Web: www.phs.org

CEO: -
CFO: -
HR: Ashley Sexton
FYE: December 31
Type: Private

Established in the early 1900s as a sanatorium for tuberculosis patients, not-for-profit Presbyterian Healthcare Services (PHS) has morphed over the years into a sprawling network of hospitals and community health centers serving New Mexico. Presbyterian Medical Group has more than 1,100 physicians and advanced practice clinicians in 50 specialties at more than 100 clinics throughout New Mexico. Its regional hospitals provide both acute and preventive care: from surgical, ambulatory and emergency services to health fairs, fun runs, and prevention and screening programs. Its Presbyterian Health Plan offers to Individual and Family Plans through the New Mexico Health Insurance Exchange (also known as beWellnm). In 2023, Presbyterian and UnityPoint Health announced its intent to form new healthcare organization.?

PRESCOTT AEROSPACE, INC.

6600 E 6TH ST
PRESCOTT VALLEY, AZ 863143526
Phone: 928 772-7605
Fax: -
Web: www.prescottaerospace.com

CEO: -
CFO: -
HR: -
FYE: December 31
Type: Private

Prescott Aerospace makes precision parts and hardware. Serving clients in the aerospace and commercial sectors, the company specializes in manufacturing parts to customer blueprints. An OEM manufacturer, the company's major customers deliver military aircraft, ordinance, and NOTAR (no tail rudder) technology for the US government. Prescott Aerospace supports such military aircraft as the Apache AH-64, F15, F18, and C17 programs. The company also manufactures precision parts for commercial aircraft used in law enforcement and as air ambulances. The machine shop was founded in 1983.

	Annual Growth	12/05	12/06	12/07	12/08	12/09
Sales ($mil.)	(1.6%)	-	-	6.8	8.5	6.6
Net income ($ mil.)	(11.0%)	-	-	1.0	1.1	0.8
Market value ($ mil.)	-	-	-	-	-	-
Employees	-	-	-	-	-	57

PRESIDENT & TRUSTEES OF BATES COLLEGE

2 ANDREWS RD
LEWISTON, ME 042406020
Phone: 207 786-6255
Fax: -
Web: www.bates.edu

CEO: -
CFO: -
HR: -
FYE: June 30
Type: Private

Bates College is a selective, private, co-educational liberal arts college granting bachelor of arts and bachelor of science degrees. The institute of higher leatning's more than 1,750 students can choose from 30 majors, the most popular of which include history, environmental studies, political science, English, biology, economics, and psychology. Students enjoy a 10-to-1 student to faculty ratio. Bates' endowment is an estimated $150 million. With tuition and fees hitting almost $59,000, most students receive financial aid. The college has about 220 faculty members.

	Annual Growth	06/18	06/19	06/20	06/21	06/22
Sales ($mil.)	3.9%	-	121.7	127.9	131.5	136.4
Net income ($ mil.)	-	-	20.8	18.9	124.9	(29.5)
Market value ($ mil.)	-	-	-	-	-	-
Employees	-	-	-	-	-	720

PRESIDENT & TRUSTEES OF WILLIAMS COLLEGE

880 MAIN ST FL 1
WILLIAMSTOWN, MA 012672600
Phone: 413 597-4412
Fax: -
Web: www.williams.edu

CEO: Gregory M Avis
CFO: -
HR: Simone Anderson
FYE: June 30
Type: Private

Liberals need apply. Liberal arts majors, that is! Williams College is a private, liberal arts school with an enrollment of more than 2,000 students at its main campus in the Berkshires of northwestern Massachusetts. It also offers programs in England (Williams-Exeter Programme at Oxford), Connecticut (Williams-Mystic Program), and Williams in New York. The majority of its students come from New York, followed by Massachusetts and California. Williams College offers more than 30 undergraduate majors in three academic divisions: humanities, sciences, and social sciences. Founded in 1793 by Colonel Ephraim Williams, the school also confers master's degrees in the history of art and in policy economics.

	Annual Growth	06/07	06/08	06/09	06/10	06/11
Sales ($mil.)	(10.5%)	-	-	187.3	146.9	150.0
Net income ($ mil.)	-	-	-	(419.6)	92.4	245.3
Market value ($ mil.)	-	-	-	-	-	-
Employees	-	-	-	-	-	950

PRESIDENT AND BOARD OF TRUSTEES OF SANTA CLARA COLLEGE

500 EL CAMINO REAL
SANTA CLARA, CA 950504776
Phone: 408 554-4000
Fax: -
Web: www.scu.edu

CEO: -
CFO: -
HR: James S Lai
FYE: June 30
Type: Private

Santa Clara University wants its students to achieve clarity. The Jesuit Catholic school, California's oldest higher-education institution, offers degrees in more than 40 disciplines. Its variety of graduate programs include business, engineering, law, pastoral ministries, counseling, psychology, and education. With more than 8,000 students, Santa Clara University boasts a student/faculty ratio of 12:1 and support from a $760 million endowment. The university occupies a 106-acre campus and has more than 520 full-time and more than 360 part-time faculty members.

	Annual Growth	06/15	06/16	06/17	06/20	06/22
Sales ($mil.)	(0.5%)	-	460.0	363.0	550.7	447.2
Net income ($ mil.)	-	-	16.2	104.8	36.3	(33.5)
Market value ($ mil.)	-	-	-	-	-	-
Employees	-	-	-	-	-	1,431

PRESIDENT AND FELLOWS OF MIDDLEBURY COLLEGE

9 OLD CHAPEL RD
MIDDLEBURY, VT 057536000
Phone: 802 443-5000
Fax: -
Web: www.middlebury.edu

CEO: -
CFO: -
HR: Erin Fierman
FYE: June 30
Type: Private

President and Fellows of Middlebury College operates Middlebury College, a private liberal arts school in Vermont that offers courses of study in the arts, humanities, literature, foreign languages, social sciences, and natural sciences. About 2,450 undergraduates are enrolled at the educational institution. Founded in 1800, it is home to the Bread Loaf School of English, known for its summer graduate courses in literature, as well as instruction in creative writing and theatre. Bread Loaf is located in the Green Mountains a dozen miles east of Middlebury. Every summer Middlebury College also opens the Language Schools, from which the college provides instruction in 10 languages to more than 2,000 students.

	Annual Growth	06/04	06/05	06/06	06/08	06/12
Sales ($mil.)	4.2%	-	-	182.0	278.5	233.4
Net income ($ mil.)	-	-	-	79.8	50.9	(24.7)
Market value ($ mil.)	-	-	-	-	-	-
Employees	-	-	-	-	-	1,000

PRESIDENT AND TRUSTEES OF HAMPDEN-SYDNEY COLLEGE

1 COLLEGE RD
FARMVILLE, VA 239015657
Phone: 434 223-6216
Fax: –
Web: www.hsc.edu

CEO: –
CFO: –
HR: Linda Layne
FYE: June 30
Type: Private

"Hampden-Sydney: Where men are men and women are guests." Hampden-Sydney College is a private four-year liberal arts college for men, with a student population of more than 1,000. The college offers undergraduate degrees in about 30 fields and is affiliated with the Presbyterian Church. Its campus is about 60 miles southwest of Richmond, Virginia. Hampden-Sydney College was founded in 1775, and although the school is not co-educational its location places it in an area with 15 colleges and universities including four women's colleges -- providing ample opportunities to interact with the opposite sex.

	Annual Growth	06/18	06/19	06/20	06/21	06/22
Sales ($mil.)	(21.4%)	–	–	–	102.7	80.7
Net income ($ mil.)	–	–	–	–	25.4	(0.1)
Market value ($ mil.)	–	–	–	–	–	–
Employees	–	–	–	–	–	350

PRESIDENTIAL REALTY CORP.

530 Seventh Avenue, Suite 407
New York, NY 10018
Phone: 914 948-1300
Fax: 914 948-1327
Web: www.presrealty.com

NBB: PDNL B
CEO: Nickolas W Jekogian III
CFO: Alexander Ludwig
HR: –
FYE: December 31
Type: Public

This president may have been elected for a second term. Presidential Realty is a real estate investment trust (REIT) that invests in commercial real estate, loans secured by real estate, and other property-related assets. Its portfolio includes stakes in a handful of properties in Massachusetts and Puerto Rico, including office and industrial properties. Faced with ongoing revenue declines in the turbulent economy, the REIT began liquidating itself in 2011. Later that year it terminated the liquidation, instead coming to an investment agreement with new CEO Nickolas Jekogian through Signature Community Investment Group.

	Annual Growth	12/18	12/19	12/20	12/21	12/22
Sales ($mil.)	3.2%	1.0	1.0	1.0	1.0	1.1
Net income ($ mil.)	–	(4.3)	(0.0)	(0.0)	(0.0)	(0.1)
Market value ($ mil.)	(24.9%)	0.1	0.0	0.1	0.1	0.0
Employees	–	–	–	4	4	4

PRESIDIO, INC.

1 PENN PLZ STE 2832
NEW YORK, NY 101192832
Phone: 212 652-5700
Fax: –
Web: www.presidio.com

CEO: Robert Cagnazzi
CFO: Emmanuel Korakis
HR: –
FYE: June 30
Type: Private

Presidio provides IT services that help its customers build and manage their digital infrastructure, move to and operate in the cloud, and assess and manage security. The company delivers technology expertise through a full life cycle model of professional, managed, and support services including strategy, consulting, implementation and design. It aims for customers in the middle market in financial services, health care, manufacturing, and retail. Serving more than 7,800 customers, the company operates in more than 100 countries. The New York City-based company also works for agencies in the US federal government. Geographically, Presidio focuses on the North American market. The private company was founded in 2003.

PRESONUS AUDIO ELECTRONICS, INC.

18011 GRAND BAY CT
BATON ROUGE, LA 708096769
Phone: 225 216-7887
Fax: –
Web: www.presonus.com

CEO: –
CFO: Chris Elliott
HR: –
FYE: December 31
Type: Private

PreSonus Audio Electronics makes digital audio equipment for amateur musicians and professionals alike. Its product lineup (designed for the purposes of broadcasting, live sound reinforcement, live streaming of audio, and recording) includes items such as preamplifiers, processors, and equalizers. PreSonus sells through more than 800 specialty music retailers (Guitar Center, Hermes) in the US, as well as internationally. The company was founded in 1995.

PRESSURE BIOSCIENCES INC

14 Norfolk Avenue
South Easton, MA 02375
Phone: 508 230-1828
Fax: –
Web: www.pressurebiosciences.com

NBB: PBIO
CEO: Richard T Schumacher
CFO: –
HR: –
FYE: December 31
Type: Public

Pressure BioSciences knows how to strong-arm at the molecular level. Using its pressure cycling technology (PCT), which uses cycles of hydrostatic pressure to control molecular interactions, the company has developed the PCT Sample Preparation System for life science research. The system, which consists of the Barocycler instrument and related consumables, helps researchers extract DNA or other molecules from plant and animal tissues for further study. Pressure BioSciences is working on other applications for PCT, such as protein purification, diagnostics, DNA sequencing, and enzyme reaction control.

	Annual Growth	12/18	12/19	12/20	12/21	12/22
Sales ($mil.)	(8.4%)	2.5	1.8	1.2	2.0	1.7
Net income ($ mil.)	–	(9.7)	(11.7)	(16.0)	(20.2)	(16.1)
Market value ($ mil.)	(12.8%)	30.8	17.1	29.0	31.6	17.8
Employees	(5.9%)	23	14	12	12	18

PRESTIGE CONSUMER HEALTHCARE INC

660 White Plains Road
Tarrytown, NY 10591
Phone: 914 524-6800
Fax: –
Web: www.prestigeconsumerhealthcare.com

NYS: PBH
CEO: Ronald M Lombardi
CFO: Christine Sacco
HR: –
FYE: March 31
Type: Public

Prestige Consumer Health is engaged in the development, manufacturing, marketing, sales, and distribution of well-recognized, brand-name, over-the-counter (OTC) health and personal care products to mass merchandisers, drug, food, dollar, convenience, and club and e-commerce stores in North America, Australia, and certain other international markets. Its portfolio includes Chloraseptic, Clear Eyes, Compound W, Luden's, Monistat, Gaviscon, and many other big-name brands. It develops its existing brands by investing in new product lines, brand extensions, and strong advertising support. The company was formed in 1996 to acquire and revitalize leading but neglected consumer brands divested by major consumer companies. The majority of its revenue is generated in the US.

	Annual Growth	03/19	03/20	03/21	03/22	03/23
Sales ($mil.)	3.7%	975.8	963.0	943.4	1,086.8	1,127.7
Net income ($ mil.)	–	(35.8)	142.3	164.7	205.4	(82.3)
Market value ($ mil.)	20.3%	1,486.3	1,822.7	2,190.4	2,630.7	3,112.2
Employees	1.9%	520	520	505	535	560

PRESTIGE TRAVEL INC

6175 SPRING MOUNTAIN RD STE 2C
LAS VEGAS, NV 891468899
Phone: 702 248-1300
Fax: –
Web: www.prestigecruises.com

CEO: –
CFO: –
HR: –
FYE: December 31
Type: Private

What happens in Vegas may stay in Vegas but if you don't want to stay in Vegas, Prestige Travel can help you out. The company provides leisure and corporate travel services -- serving the US Southwest -- through about 15 Las Vegas-area locations. Prestige Travel's TripRes.com subsidiary allows visitors to book airfare, hotel, car, cruise, and package arrangements, as well as Vegas shows. However, the company's specialty is low-roller rates in high-roller Vegas hotels and casinos. Prestige Travel, an affiliate of American Express, was founded in 1980 by president and CEO Kathy Falkensammer.

	Annual Growth	09/00	09/01	09/02	09/03*	12/09
Sales ($mil.)	1.9%	–	–	68.4	82.3	77.9
Net income ($ mil.)	–	–	–	0.2	(0.1)	(0.5)
Market value ($ mil.)	–	–	–	–	–	–
Employees	–	–	–	–	–	170

*Fiscal year change

PREVENT CANCER FOUNDATION, INC.

1600 DUKE ST STE 500
ALEXANDRIA, VA 223143421
Phone: 703 836-4412
Fax: –
Web: www.preventcancer.org

CEO: Gary R Lytle
CFO: –
HR: –
FYE: December 31
Type: Private

The Prevent Cancer Foundation (formerly The Cancer Research and Prevention Foundation) knows an ounce of prevention can go a long way. The not-for-profit is dedicated to preventing cancer by providing funds for research and public education programs. The foundation concentrates on cancers, such as colorectal, prostate, breast, and skin, that can prevented through lifestyle changes or detection and treatment in their early stages. The group has given funding to more than 300 scientists since its inception. It also works to educate the public on the cancer-fighting benefits of proper diet, exercise, and screenings. Carolyn Aldig founded the organization following her father's death to cancer in 1985.

	Annual Growth	06/18	06/19	06/20*	12/21	12/22
Sales ($mil.)	8.8%	–	6.6	5.9	9.2	8.5
Net income ($ mil.)	–	–	(0.2)	(0.6)	0.9	0.1
Market value ($ mil.)	–	–	–	–	–	–
Employees	–	–	–	–	–	26

*Fiscal year change

PREVENT CHILD ABUSE OF AMERICA

33 N DEARBORN ST
CHICAGO, IL 606023856
Phone: 312 663-3520
Fax: –
Web: www.preventchildabuse.org

CEO: –
CFO: –
HR: –
FYE: December 31
Type: Private

Prevent Child Abuse (PCA) America is a network of more than 45 chapters across the US that works to prevent child abuse by raising awareness and providing education. Its programs at the national level include Healthy Families America for newborns and their parents, National Center on Child Abuse Prevention Research, prevention education, and resource development. The group also lobbies all levels of government, advocating policies to protect children and strengthen families. PCA America publishes comics on topics like preventing bullying and puts out parenting and advocacy newsletters and tip sheets for parents. Local chapters host conferences and do other advocacy and education work.

	Annual Growth	12/16	12/17	12/19	12/21	12/22
Sales ($mil.)	0.9%	–	7.7	7.1	9.3	8.1
Net income ($ mil.)	–	–	3.1	1.4	2.8	(2.5)
Market value ($ mil.)	–	–	–	–	–	–
Employees	–	–	–	–	–	22

PRGX GLOBAL, INC.

200 GALLERIA PKWY SE STE 450
ATLANTA, GA 30339
Phone: 770 779-3900
Fax: –
Web: www.prgx.com

CEO: Ronald E Stewart
CFO: Kurt J Abkemeier
HR: Christine Bonspiel
FYE: December 31
Type: Private

PRGX helps clients get every bit of bang from their buck. The firm provides recovery audit services to organizations with high volumes of payment transactions, including retail and wholesale businesses, manufacturers, health care providers, and government agencies. It uses proprietary tools to mine clients' books and identify erroneous overpayments, which over time can represent a significant loss of money (sometimes to the annual aggregate tune of more than $1 billion). PRGX charges a percentage of the savings realized. The company does business in more than 30 countries around the world; the US accounts for about 60% of its revenue.

PRICESMART INC

9740 Scranton Road
San Diego, CA 92121
Phone: 858 404-8800
Fax: –
Web: www.pricesmart.com

NMS: PSMT

CEO: Robert E Price
CFO: Michael L McCleary
HR: –
FYE: August 31
Type: Public

PriceSmart is the largest operator of membership warehouse clubs that runs about 50 membership stores in a dozen countries in Latin America, the Caribbean, and one US territory. It sells high quality merchandise and services at low prices while charging an annual fee to consumer and business members. Its clubs also provide services at its optical, pharmacy, audiology, and tire departments. PriceSmart stores, ranged at 30,000-60,000 sq. in floor size, are typically smaller than wholesale clubs in the US. Chairman of the Board Robert Price owns around 15% of PriceSmart. Central America generates almost 60% of the company's total sales.

	Annual Growth	08/19	08/20	08/21	08/22	08/23
Sales ($mil.)	8.2%	3,223.9	3,329.2	3,619.9	4,066.1	4,411.8
Net income ($ mil.)	10.5%	73.2	78.1	98.0	104.5	109.2
Market value ($ mil.)	7.1%	1,871.9	2,036.7	2,621.0	1,959.9	2,462.0
Employees	5.1%	9,000	9,500	10,400	10,600	11,000

PRIDGEON & CLAY, INC.

50 COTTAGE GROVE ST SW
GRAND RAPIDS, MI 495071685
Phone: 616 241-5675
Fax: –
Web: www.pridgeonandclay.com

CEO: Robert E Clay
CFO: David Norris
HR: Bruce Penno
FYE: December 31
Type: Private

Pridgeon & Clay (P&C) is one of the largest independent, value-added manufacturers and suppliers of automotive stamped and fine-blanked components in the US. Stamping equipment runs from fine blanking presses to high tonnage and progressive presses. The company provides a wide range of value-added services, including laser welding, robotic and hybrid MIG welding, resistance welding, tapping, grinding, CNC machining, studding and automated assembly, along with a global sales force. The company has more than 100 presses around the globe, ranging from 40 to 1500 tons, to meet customers' needs. It was founded in 1948.

	Annual Growth	12/08	12/09	12/10	12/11	12/12
Sales ($mil.)	15.6%	–	–	220.5	267.6	294.8
Net income ($ mil.)	(66.8%)	–	–	9.7	5.0	1.1
Market value ($ mil.)	–	–	–	–	–	–
Employees	–	–	–	–	–	600

PRIME HEALTHCARE SERVICES - GARDEN CITY, LLC

6245 INKSTER RD
GARDEN CITY, MI 481354001
Phone: 734 458-3300
Fax: -
Web: www.gch.org

CEO: Saju George
CFO: Gina Butcher
HR: -
FYE: December 31
Type: Private

Garden City Hospital provides health care services and medical education in western Wayne County, Michigan. With about 320 licensed beds, the community hospital offers emergency, inpatient, and surgical care in a variety of general and specialist fields including cardiology, women's health, and sports rehabilitation. Some of its more unusual services include clinical hypnotherapy and a massage clinic. Garden City Hospital also provides residency and internship programs through partnerships with universities and medical schools.

	Annual Growth	12/13	12/14	12/15	12/16	12/21
Sales ($mil.)	(3.2%)	-	-	150.7	159.0	124.0
Net income ($ mil.)	0.2%	-	-	17.4	19.8	17.7
Market value ($ mil.)	-	-	-	-	-	-
Employees	-	-	-	-	-	1,200

PRIME HEALTHCARE SERVICES - RENO, LLC

235 W 6TH ST
RENO, NV 895034548
Phone: 775 770-3000
Fax: -
Web: www.saintmarysreno.com

CEO: Helen Lidholm
CFO: Dan Galles
HR: Andrea Garrett
FYE: December 31
Type: Private

Local residents have been betting their health on Saint Mary's for over a century. Reno-based Saint Mary's is a health care system featuring a 380-bed hospital, community health clinics and urgent care clinics, home health care, health plans, and other health care services in northern Nevada. The hospital's services also include hospice and palliative care and women's and children's services. It also operates a sports medicine and primary-care medicine facility at the University of Nevada's Reno campus. The hospital is part of California-based Prime Healthcare Services' network.

	Annual Growth	12/13	12/14	12/15	12/16	12/21
Sales ($mil.)	(0.1%)	-	-	-	294.7	293.9
Net income ($ mil.)	(0.8%)	-	-	-	25.3	24.2
Market value ($ mil.)	-	-	-	-	-	-
Employees	-	-	-	-	-	1,800

PRIME HEALTHCARE SERVICES - SHASTA, LLC

1100 BUTTE ST
REDDING, CA 960010852
Phone: 530 244-5400
Fax: -
Web: www.shastaregional.com

CEO: Cyndy Gordon
CFO: -
HR: Laura V Winkle
FYE: December 31
Type: Private

Shasta Regional Medical Center serves counties in northern California. The medical center offers a variety of services in areas such as surgical and critical care, emergency and trauma, and cardiac care. It has a capacity of about 250 beds. Specialty units include the complex's Chest Pain Center, Vascular Wellness Center, and Cardiovascular Catheterization Laboratory. Other services include diabetes care, neurosciences, orthopedics, radiology, and oncology. Shasta Regional is operated by hospital management firm Prime Healthcare Services.

PRIMECARE SYSTEM, INC.   NBB: PCYS

610 Thimble Shoals Blvd., Ste 402A
Newport News, VA 23606
Phone: 757 591-0323
Fax: -
Web: www.pcare.com

CEO: -
CFO: -
HR: -
FYE: June 30
Type: Public

Software company PrimeCare Systems makes it easy for doctors to collect their patients' information. The company develops electronic patient management software applications for private physician offices and clinics. Both patients and medical staff interact with PrimeCare's software product (which is installed directly on physicians' PCs); patients use in-office PCs to enter personal information and answer medical questions related to their visit, and the medical staff uses the software to manage and monitor patients' medical information. All pertinent and sensitive data is stored remotely at the company's data center. PrimeCare is a former subsidiary of OCG Technology, which spun off the company in 2005.

	Annual Growth	06/06	06/07	06/08	06/09	06/10
Sales ($mil.)	98.3%	-	-	0.0	0.1	0.0
Net income ($ mil.)	-	-	-	(0.3)	(0.4)	(0.3)
Market value ($ mil.)	1.7%	-	-	1.7	1.1	1.7
Employees	-	-	-	-	8	9

PRIMEENERGY RESOURCES CORP   NAS: PNRG

9821 Katy Freeway
Houston, TX 77024
Phone: 713 735-0000
Fax: -
Web: www.primeenergy.com

CEO: Charles E Drimal Jr
CFO: Beverly A Cummings
HR: Virginia Forese
FYE: December 31
Type: Public

PrimeEnergy hopes to keep the pump primed with its oil and gas exploration and production activities, which take place primarily in Colorado, Louisiana, New Mexico, Oklahoma, Texas, West Virginia, and the Gulf of Mexico. The company has proved reserves of 87 billion cu. ft. of natural gas equivalent. It operates 1,500 wells and owns interests in 850 non-operating wells. Its PrimeEnergy Management unit is the managing general partner of 18 oil and gas limited partnerships and two trusts. Subsidiary Southwest Oilfield Construction provides site preparation and construction services for PrimeEnergy and third parties. CEO Charles Drimal owns 32% of the firm.

	Annual Growth	12/18	12/19	12/20	12/21	12/22
Sales ($mil.)	1.4%	118.1	104.8	58.4	79.6	125.1
Net income ($ mil.)	35.3%	14.5	3.5	(2.3)	2.1	48.7
Market value ($ mil.)	5.5%	133.2	287.5	82.1	133.3	165.1
Employees	(7.5%)	156	173	96	113	114

PRIMEMD INC   NBB: PRMD

93 Spyglass Drive
Littleton, CO 80123
Phone: 303 797-6816
Fax: 303 863-0802
Web: -

CEO: -
CFO: -
HR: -
FYE: March 31
Type: Public

Eagle Exploration is digging its talons into some big nests. The company was originally hatched as an oil and gas exploration firm but turned its eye towards real estate in the early 1990s. Eagle Exploration now operates as a property investment and development firm. The company is a member of a consortium that has invested in 320 acres of undeveloped land north of Denver for residential development. Eagle Exploration also owns stakes in some oil and gas properties and related assets (still its sole source of revenue). CEO Raymond Joeckel and his family have a controlling stake in the company.

	Annual Growth	03/04	03/05	03/06	03/07	03/08
Sales ($mil.)	4.0%	0.0	0.0	0.0	0.0	0.0
Net income ($ mil.)	-	(0.1)	(0.2)	(0.2)	0.2	(0.1)
Market value ($ mil.)	(14.7%)	0.5	0.7	0.6	0.7	0.3
Employees	(15.9%)	2	2	2	2	1

PRIMERICA INC

NYS: PRI

1 Primerica Parkway
Duluth, GA 30099
Phone: 770 381-1000
Fax: –
Web: www.primerica.com

CEO: –
CFO: –
HR: –
FYE: December 31
Type: Public

Primerica is a leading provider of financial products to middle-income households in the US and Canada with some 135,200 licensed sales representatives. These independent licensed representatives assist Primerica's clients in meeting their needs for term life insurance, which it underwrites, and mutual funds, annuities, managed investments and other financial products, which it distributes primarily on behalf of third parties. The company insured over 5.7 million lives and had approximately 2.8 million client investment accounts. Primerica went public in 2010. Most of its sales are generated from the US.

	Annual Growth	12/19	12/20	12/21	12/22	12/23
Assets ($mil.)	2.4%	13,689	14,905	16,123	15,349	15,028
Net income ($ mil.)	12.0%	366.4	386.2	373.4	373.0	576.6
Market value ($ mil.)	12.0%	4,569.1	4,687.0	5,363.8	4,963.1	7,200.8
Employees	0.6%	2,803	2,824	3,443	2,646	2,871

PRIMEX INTERNATIONAL TRADING CORPORATION

5777 W CENTURY BLVD STE 1485
LOS ANGELES, CA 900455698
Phone: 310 568-8855
Fax: –
Web: www.primex.us

CEO: Ali Amin
CFO: –
HR: –
FYE: December 31
Type: Private

Primex International Trading is a leading exporter and international trader that specializes in dried fruits and nuts. Through affiliate offices located around the world, the company ships such products as almonds, hazelnuts, and pecans, as well as apricots, figs, and raisins. Primex also has its own pistachio orchards and a processing plant in California. The company was founded in 1989 by Ali Amin, whose family has been involved in producing pistachios for four generations. It first started planting pistachio orchards in 1990. In 2008 the company shipped about 30 million pounds of pistachios and more than 40 million pounds of almonds.

PRIMIS FINANCIAL CORP

NMS: FRST

6830 Old Dominion Drive
McLean, VA 22101
Phone: 703 893-7400
Fax: –
Web: www.sonabank.com

CEO: Dennis J Zember Jr
CFO: Matthew Switzer
HR: –
FYE: December 31
Type: Public

Southern National Bancorp of Virginia is the holding company for Sonabank, which has some 20 locations in central and northern Virginia and southern Maryland. Founded in 2005, the bank serves small and midsized businesses, their owners, and retail consumers. It offers standard deposit products, including checking, savings, and money market accounts, and CDs. The bank's lending is focused on commercial real estate, single-family residential construction, and single-family homes, as well as other types of consumer and commercial loans. In 2009 Southern National Bancorp acquired the failed Greater Atlantic Bank in an FDIC-assisted transaction; in 2012 it acquired the loans and deposits of HarVest Bank of Maryland.

	Annual Growth	12/18	12/19	12/20	12/21	12/22
Assets ($mil.)	7.2%	2,701.3	2,722.2	3,088.7	3,407.4	3,571.5
Net income ($ mil.)	(14.8%)	33.7	33.2	23.3	31.2	17.7
Market value ($ mil.)	(2.7%)	326.3	403.5	298.9	371.2	292.5
Employees	12.9%	348	350	382	418	565

PRIMO WATER CORP (CANADA)

NYS: PRMW

1150 Assembly Dr., Suite 800
Tampa, FL 33607
Phone: 813 544-8515
Fax: –
Web: www.primowatercorp.com

CEO: –
CFO: –
HR: –
FYE: December 30
Type: Public

Cott Corporation is a leading water, coffee, tea and filtration solutions service company with a major presence in the North American and European home and office bottled water delivery industry. The company is a leader in custom coffee roasting, extract solutions, and ice tea blending for the US foodservice industry. It reaches 2.5 million customers and/or delivery points with more than 3,600 direct-to-consumer routes across 20 countries in North America and Europe. Cott's delivered more than 900 million gallons of water annually. About 75% of Cott?s total sales comes from US. Best known by consumers for its soda brands, the company sold its soda beverage business to Refresco in 2018 to focus on its coffee and water activities.

	Annual Growth	12/19*	01/21	01/22*	12/22	12/23
Sales ($mil.)	(7.3%)	2,394.5	1,953.5	2,073.3	2,215.1	1,771.8
Net income ($ mil.)	201.0%	2.9	(131.7)	(3.2)	29.6	238.1
Market value ($ mil.)	2.8%	2,145.0	2,500.7	2,811.6	2,478.3	2,400.2
Employees	(13.8%)	11,580	8,880	9,230	9,240	6,400

*Fiscal year change

PRIMO WATER OPERATIONS LLC

2300 WINDY RIDGE PKWY SE STE 500N
ATLANTA, GA 303398577
Phone: 336 331-4000
Fax: –
Web: www.water.com

CEO: Thomas Harrington
CFO: Mark Castaneda
HR: –
FYE: December 31
Type: Private

Among the amenities of today's home, a water dispenser appears near indispensable. Serving the growing trend of household purified water dispensers, Primo Water provides water dispensers, along with three- and five-gallon purified bottled water, and carbonating beverage appliances. The company's products are sold through US and Canadian retailers, such as Lowe's, Wal-Mart, Kroger, HEB Grocery, and Walgreen. Empty bottles are exchanged at retail locations with Primo Water recycling centers (where consumers receive a discount toward buying a new Primo bottle) or refilled at a self-serve filtered drinking water display. Started in 2005, Primo expanded quickly and went public in both 2010 and 2011.

PRIMORIS SERVICES CORP

NYS: PRIM

2300 N. Field Street, Suite 1900
Dallas, TX 75201
Phone: 214 740-5600
Fax: –
Web: www.prim.com

CEO: Thomas E McCormick
CFO: Ken Dodgen
HR: Brittany Hansen
FYE: December 31
Type: Public

Primoris Services is one of the leading providers of specialty contracting services operating mainly in the US and Canada. The company provides a wide range of specialty construction services, maintenance, replacement, fabrication, and engineering services to a diversified base of customers through its three segments: Utilities, Energy/Renewables and Pipeline Services (Pipeline). Primoris Services' clients are public and private gas and electric utilities, state departments of transportation, pipeline operators, and chemical and energy producers such as Xcel Energy, Pacific Gas & Electric, Southern California Gas, and Oncor Electric, among others. The majority of its revenue is derived from customers in the US. Primoris Services traces its roots back to 1960 as ARB, Inc.

	Annual Growth	12/19	12/20	12/21	12/22	12/23
Sales ($mil.)	16.5%	3,106.3	3,491.5	3,497.6	4,420.6	5,715.3
Net income ($ mil.)	11.3%	82.3	105.0	115.6	133.0	126.1
Market value ($ mil.)	10.5%	1,186.9	1,473.4	1,279.7	1,170.9	1,772.3
Employees	(26.9%)	9,700	10,414	10,810	12,802	2,773

PRIMUS BUILDERS, INC.

8294 HIGHWAY 92 STE 210
WOODSTOCK, GA 301893672
Phone: 770 928-7120
Fax: –
Web: www.primusbuilders.com

CEO: Richard A O'Connell
CFO: –
HR: Chelsea Robinson
FYE: December 31
Type: Private

Primus Builders is proud of leaving its customers in the cold. The design/build firm makes refrigerated, frozen, and ambient storage, processing, and distribution facilities and other industrial buildings. It offers turnkey services as well as planning and design, construction, and construction management a la carte. Primus Builders specializes in restaurants, condominiums, health clubs, office buildings, and retail centers. The company's Primus Properties leases office park space to businesses. Primus Builders shares work and officers with SubZero Constructors but the two do not share any corporate linkage.

PRIMUS SOFTWARE CORPORATION

3061 PEACHTREE INDUSTRIAL BLVD STE 110
DULUTH, GA 300978621
Phone: 770 300-0004
Fax: –
Web: www.primussoft.com

CEO: –
CFO: –
HR: –
FYE: December 31
Type: Private

Primus Software believes that a primary goal should be to tame your technology. The company specializes in custom software development, integration, and programming services, as well as on- and offshore staff augmentation. The company's vendor managed solutions segment supplies Web-enabled software and assistance programs for optimizing the use of temporary labor. Its clients come from a wide range of industries such as financial services, health care, manufacturing, and retail. The company also provides professional services including consulting, support, and training. Primus Software was founded in 1996 and has offices in the US and India.

	Annual Growth	12/10	12/11	12/12	12/13	12/14
Sales ($mil.)	(3.5%)	–	30.9	29.5	24.4	27.7
Net income ($ mil.)	(38.6%)	–	0.7	0.5	0.2	0.2
Market value ($ mil.)	–	–	–	–	–	–
Employees	–	–	–	–	–	150

PRINCETON COMMUNITY HOSPITAL ASSOCIATION, INC.

122 12TH ST
PRINCETON, WV 247402312
Phone: 304 487-7000
Fax: –
Web: www.wvumedicine.org

CEO: Michael Grace
CFO: Frank Sinicrope
HR: –
FYE: June 30
Type: Private

Princeton Community Hospital serves the residents of southern West Virginia. The health care facility provides acute care, home health care services, physical therapy, behavioral medicine, laboratory, and other health care services. Specialty medical divisions include cardiovascular and cancer care, organ transplants, radiology, sleep disorder diagnostics, and women's health. The hospital has about 190 beds and a medical staff of more than 100 physicians. Affiliates include the Athens Family Practice and Mercer Medical Group outpatient clinics and the Princeton Health Care Center nursing home. Princeton Community Hospital was founded in 1970.

	Annual Growth	06/05	06/06	06/15	06/17	06/18
Sales ($mil.)	3.2%	–	93.5	129.1	144.4	135.7
Net income ($ mil.)	–	–	5.4	8.6	9.6	(6.8)
Market value ($ mil.)	–	–	–	–	–	–
Employees	–	–	–	–	–	1,000

PRINCETON HEALTHCARE SYSTEM HOLDING INC.

1 PLAINSBORO RD
PLAINSBORO, NJ 085361913
Phone: 609 497-4190
Fax: –
Web: –

CEO: Barry S Rabner
CFO: –
HR: –
FYE: December 31
Type: Private

Princeton HealthCare System (PHCS) provides acute medical services to Ivy Leaguers (and the rest of us) in central New Jersey. The system is home to the University Medical Center of Princeton, a 310-bed hospital that provides comprehensive medical and surgical services and is a teaching affiliate of the UMDNJ-Robert Wood Johnson Medical School. Other operations include a skilled nursing facility providing transitional and long-term care and the Princeton House Behavioral Health, a 100-bed inpatient psychiatric facility. PHCS also offers acute rehabilitation, home health and hospice care, fitness and wellness programs, and community education. The system plans to join the University of Pennsylvania Health System.

	Annual Growth	12/07	12/08	12/09	12/15	12/17
Assets ($mil.)	(45.5%)	–	–	489.1	2.2	3.8
Net income ($ mil.)	–	–	–	15.7	–	–
Market value ($ mil.)	–	–	–	–	–	–
Employees	–	–	–	–	–	2,000

PRINCETON INSURANCE COMPANY

746 ALEXANDER RD
PRINCETON, NJ 085406305
Phone: 609 452-9404
Fax: –
Web: www.princetoninsurance.com

CEO: –
CFO: –
HR: –
FYE: December 31
Type: Private

Princeton Insurance provides medical professional liability insurance to hospitals and medical professionals in the state of New Jersey, and only New Jersey. It also provides risk management and loss prevention counseling through Princeton Risk Protection; Princeton Advertising & Marketing handles the company's advertising. The firm also offers a bit of property insurance packaged with general liability for doctor's offices to cover fine art and collectibles. Independent agents distribute the company's products. Princeton Insurance was founded in 1976, acquired by New York-based Medical Liability Mutual Insurance Company in 2000, and sold to Berkshire Hathaway's Medical Protective Company in 2012.

PRINCETON LIGHTWAVE, INC.

2555 ROUTE 130 STE 1
CRANBURY, NJ 085123527
Phone: 609 495-2600
Fax: –
Web: www.princetonlightwave.com

CEO: –
CFO: –
HR: –
FYE: December 31
Type: Private

Princeton Lightwave is educated in the ways of wavelengths. The company develops distributed feedback, erbium-doped fiber amplifier, and Raman pump lasers used in optical transmission. Princeton's lines of WavePower and WaveHarp laser components are intended to be incorporated into fiber-optic equipment, such as dense wavelength division multiplexing devices, built by other manufacturers. Its WaveRider amplifier chips are used to boost the power of lasers. Princeton Lightwave was spun off from SRI International subsidiary Sarnoff Corp. in 2000. The company's financial backers include Morgenthaler, U.S. Venture Partners, and Venrock Associates.

PRINCETON NATIONAL BANCORP, INC. NBB: PNBC

606 S. Main St.
Princeton, IL 61356
Phone: 815 875-4444
Fax: 815 875-0250
Web: www.pnbc-inc.com

CEO: Thomas D Ogaard
CFO: –
HR: –
FYE: December 31
Type: Public

Far from the Ivy League institution that shares its name, Princeton National Bancorp is the holding company for Citizens First National Bank in north-central Illinois. Founded in 1865, the bank serves area residents and businesses through more than 20 branches in nearly as many communities. It offers traditional services such as checking and savings accounts, CDs, IRAs, and credit cards. Business loans account for the largest portion of the company's loan portfolio, followed by commercial and residential mortgages. The bank also writes agricultural, construction, and consumer installment loans. Through Citizens Financial Advisors, it offers insurance, investments, farm management, and fiduciary services.

	Annual Growth	12/07	12/08	12/09	12/10	12/11
Assets ($mil.)	(1.6%)	1,080.7	1,163.1	1,260.7	1,096.5	1,014.3
Net income ($ mil.)	–	6.8	7.3	(21.1)	(17.0)	(54.4)
Market value ($ mil.)	(50.0%)	81.0	74.0	36.1	12.2	5.0
Employees	0.1%	351	354	368	363	352

PRINCIPAL FINANCIAL GROUP INC NMS: PFG

711 High Street
Des Moines, IA 50392
Phone: 515 247-5111
Fax: –
Web: www.principal.com

CEO: Daniel J Houston
CFO: Deanna D Strable-Soethou
HR: –
FYE: December 31
Type: Public

Founded in 1879, Principal Financial Group (PFG) is a top global investment management offering businesses, individuals and institutional clients a wide range of financial products and services, including retirement, asset management and insurance through financial services companies. The company offers a range of capabilities, including equity, fixed income, real estate and other alternative investments, as well as fund offerings. PFG has $1.5 billion in assets under administration, including $635.3 billion in assets under management. In addition, PFG is a leading provider of nonqualified plans, defined benefit plans and pension risk transfer services. It is also one of the largest providers of specialty benefits insurance product solutions.

	Annual Growth	12/19	12/20	12/21	12/22	12/23
Assets ($mil.)	2.5%	276,088	296,628	304,657	292,240	305,047
Net income ($ mil.)	(18.2%)	1,394.2	1,395.8	1,710.6	4,811.6	623.2
Market value ($ mil.)	9.4%	13,004	11,730	17,102	19,842	18,601
Employees	3.0%	17,601	17,400	18,600	19,300	19,800

PRINTPACK, INC.

2800 OVERLOOK PKWY NE
ATLANTA, GA 303396240
Phone: 404 460-7000
Fax: –
Web: www.printpack.com

CEO: James E Love III
CFO: Dellmer Seitter
HR: Alex Dedeaux
FYE: July 31
Type: Private

Printpack serves food, non-food, and medicinal markets with its array of packaging products. Its flexible packaging is found on salty snacks, confections, baked goods, and cereal, as well as tissues and paper towels. Other packaging includes plastic film, aluminum foil, metalized films, and paper with specialized coatings, as well as cast and blown monolayer and co-extruded films. The company traces its historical roots back to 1956.

	Annual Growth	06/00	06/01*	07/13	07/14	07/15
Sales ($mil.)	(37.5%)	–	1,026.5	–	0.5	1.4
Net income ($ mil.)	–	–	24.8	–	0.0	–
Market value ($ mil.)	–	–	–	–	–	–
Employees	–	–	–	–	–	3,500

*Fiscal year change

PRISM SOFTWARE CORP. NBB: PSWR

23696 Birtcher
Lake Forest, CA 92630
Phone: 949 855-3100
Fax: –
Web: www.prism-software.com

CEO: –
CFO: –
HR: –
FYE: December 31
Type: Public

Prism Software reflects its business prowess on printing and document management. The company develops print and document management software. Its product include DocRecord, a tool that allows users to capture, categorize, and organize scanned documents. The company's DocForm application creates forms, contracts, and other documents for printing or electronic transfer. Prism also offers tools for managing document workflows processes and digital archiving. The company markets to large and mid-size businesses in a variety of industries. It sells through resellers, systems integrators, and printer manufacturers.

	Annual Growth	12/01	12/02	12/03	12/04	12/05
Sales ($mil.)	30.8%	0.4	0.5	0.5	0.7	1.2
Net income ($ mil.)	–	(2.3)	(2.3)	(5.3)	(1.4)	(1.5)
Market value ($ mil.)	(29.5%)	3.0	1.8	1.4	0.8	0.7
Employees	–	–	15	12	12	14

PRISM TECHNOLOGIES GROUP INC NBB: PRZM

101 Parkshore Drive, Suite 100
Folsom, CA 95630
Phone: 916 932-2860
Fax: –
Web: www.przmgroup.com

CEO: –
CFO: –
HR: –
FYE: December 31
Type: Public

Somehow it seems appropriate to sell the least tangible of products -- insurance distribution -- via a virtual marketplace. InsWeb maintains a portfolio of online insurance distribution patents which it licenses out to others. Previously it operated online portals that allowed consumers to shop for quotes on various property/casualty and life insurance products. The company maintained alliances with about 50 insurance companies and their affiliated agency networks, which paid transaction fees to InsWeb for providing qualified customer leads. Consumers obtained quotes through the company's websites at no charge. InsWeb sold its insurance lead generation assets to Bankrate for $65 million in 2011.

	Annual Growth	12/12	12/13	12/14	12/15	12/16
Sales ($mil.)	–	–	–	–	0.7	–
Net income ($ mil.)	–	(2.7)	(2.7)	(2.6)	(21.6)	(12.8)
Market value ($ mil.)	(46.1%)	35.8	31.4	28.0	10.3	3.0
Employees	27.8%	3	3	3	8	8

PRISMA HEALTH-MIDLANDS

1301 TAYLOR ST STE 9A
COLUMBIA, SC 292012963
Phone: 803 296-2100
Fax: –
Web: www.prismahealth.org

CEO: Charles D Beaman Jr
CFO: Paul Duane
HR: –
FYE: December 31
Type: Private

Palmetto Health (dba Prisma Health-Midlands) provides health care in the Palmetto State. The not-for-profit organization administers a comprehensive range of medical services to residents of Columbia, South Carolina, and surrounding areas through a network of hospitals and other medical providers. The 1,140-bed system includes a 640-bed teaching hospital, Prisma Health Richland, which is affiliated with the University of South Carolina Medical School. Prisma Health-Midlands also operates the 350-bed Prisma Health Baptist hospital and four other hospitals. Palmetto Health merged with Greenville Health System in 2017, creating South Carolina's largest health care system. The combined entity was renamed Prisma Health in early 2019.

	Annual Growth	09/07	09/08	09/18	09/19*	12/20
Sales ($mil.)	(40.2%)	–	1,188.7	–	1,818.2	2.5
Net income ($ mil.)	–	–	–	–	(24.5)	0.7
Market value ($ mil.)	–	–	–	–	–	–
Employees	–	–	–	–	–	10,200

*Fiscal year change

PRISMA HEALTH-UPSTATE

300 E MCBEE AVE STE 302
GREENVILLE, SC 296012899
Phone: 864 455-1120
Fax: –
Web: www.prismahealth.org

CEO: Charles D Beaman Jr
CFO: –
HR: Lee Allen
FYE: September 30
Type: Private

From education and research to primary care and surgery, Upstate Affiliate Organization (dba Prisma Health-Upstate, formerly Greenville Hospital System) is out to keep residents of the "Golden Strip" (the corridor connecting Charlotte, North Carolina, and Atlanta) healthy. Originally founded in 1912, the system encompasses eight inpatient hospitals and more than 100 outpatient facilities. Its flagship facility is Prisma Health Greenville Memorial Hospital, a referral and academic medical center with more than 800 beds; other facilities include several smaller community hospitals, a nursing home, and a long-term acute care hospital. Greenville Hospital System merged with Palmetto Health in 2017; the combined system rebranded as Prisma Health in early 2019.

	Annual Growth	09/02	09/03	09/04	09/05	09/13
Sales ($mil.)	2.9%	–	754.3	789.1	789.1	1,001.1
Net income ($ mil.)	4.4%	–	52.6	21.1	21.1	80.9
Market value ($ mil.)	–	–	–	–	–	–
Employees	–	–	–	–	–	7,200

PRISON REHABILITATIVE INDUSTRIES AND DIVERSIFIED ENTERPRISES, INC.

223 MORRISON RD
BRANDON, FL 335114835
Phone: 813 324-8700
Fax: –
Web: www.pride-enterprises.org

CEO: –
CFO: Peter J Radanovich
HR: Bill Noble
FYE: December 31
Type: Private

Even convicted felons can take PRIDE in their work. Prison Rehabilitative Industries and Diversified Enterprises (PRIDE Enterprises), a not-for-profit corporation, enables inmates in about 20 Florida prisons to learn job skills. PRIDE operates in over 35 job training programs, employing inmates in activities such as furniture making, vehicle renovation, meat processing, and eyewear production. PRIDE is funded exclusively through the net proceeds from sales of products and services manufactured by PRIDE inmate training programs. PRIDE was founded in 1981.

	Annual Growth	12/09	12/10	12/11	12/12	12/15
Sales ($mil.)	4.6%	–	–	63.1	64.4	75.6
Net income ($ mil.)	278.6%	–	–	0.0	4.1	5.2
Market value ($ mil.)	–	–	–	–	–	–
Employees	–	–	–	–	–	250

PRIVATE EXPORT FUNDING CORP.

NBB: PVEX

280 Park Avenue
New York, NY 10017
Phone: 212 916-0300
Fax: 212 286-0304
Web: www.pefco.com

CEO: Rajgopalan Nandkumar
CFO: –
HR: –
FYE: September 30
Type: Public

Private Export Funding Corporation (PEFCO) wants what's "Made in America" to make it outside America. The company, established with the help of the US Department of the Treasury and the Export-Import Bank of the United States, supports the export of US-made goods by purchasing loans in the secondary market from commercial lenders that finance US exports. Lenders sell loans to PEFCO to improve profitability, remove low-yielding assets or loans in high-risk countries from their balance sheets, free up credit capacity for other borrowers, and to reduce the size of their loan portfolios. PEFCO shareowners include major commercial banks involved in US export financing, as well as industrial export companies.

	Annual Growth	09/05	09/06	09/07	09/08	09/09
Sales ($mil.)	(9.5%)	232.1	256.8	271.4	223.6	155.7
Net income ($ mil.)	36.8%	4.2	(1.9)	0.6	6.5	14.5
Market value ($ mil.)	–	–	–	–	–	–
Employees	–	–	–	–	–	–

PRO CONSULTING SERVICES INC.

500 LOVETT BLVD
HOUSTON, TX 770064021
Phone: 713 523-1800
Fax: –
Web: www.proconsrv.com

CEO: Victor Juarez
CFO: –
HR: –
FYE: December 31
Type: Private

PRO Consulting Services is no amateur when it comes to commercial collections. The company, established in 1992, provides accounts receivable management and collections services to clients in the US, Canada, Mexico, and Puerto Rico. The Houston-based firm helps clients manage their receivables portfolios at every stage of delinquency, and also provides professional collections services to mitigate losses and retain customers. Additionally, PRO Consulting Services acts as a third-party billing agent for health care providers, taking on claims preparation and filing.

	Annual Growth	12/07	12/08	12/09	12/10	12/12
Sales ($mil.)	(0.6%)	–	3.3	3.2	4.8	3.2
Net income ($ mil.)	–	–	0.1	0.1	1.1	(0.4)
Market value ($ mil.)	–	–	–	–	–	–
Employees	–	–	–	–	–	19

PRO FARM GROUP, INC.

7780 BRIER CREEK PKWY STE 420
RALEIGH, NC 276177849
Phone: 530 750-2800
Fax: –
Web: www.marronebio.com

CEO: Kevin Helash
CFO: Ladon Johnson
HR: Kathey Dufek
FYE: December 31
Type: Private

Marrone Bio Innovations makes pesticide a little less poisonous. The company's biopesticides are made from eco-friendly ingredients such as plant extracts, bacterium, or fungus. Marrone Bio Innovations has three products on the market and three in development awaiting EPA approval. Its pesticide Grandevo contains bacteria that repels plant-eating insects and kills them if ingested. The company's plant extract-based fungicide Regalia is also used as a seed treatment for corn, cotton, and soybeans, and Zequanox kills mussels found in water pipes. Its products are primarily sold to vegetable growers as alternatives to conventional agricultural chemicals. Marrone Bio Innovations went public in 2013.

PRO-DEX INC. (CO)

NAS: PDEX

2361 McGaw Avenue
Irvine, CA 92614
Phone: 949 769-3200
Fax: –
Web: www.pro-dex.com

CEO: Richard L Van Kirk
CFO: Alisha K Charlton
HR: –
FYE: June 30
Type: Public

Pro-Dex is responsible for that high-pitched whirring sound at the dentist's office. The company designs and manufactures rotary drive systems used in the dental and medical instrument industries. Its motors are used in instruments for arthroscopic, cranial, dental, orthopedic, and spinal surgery. It also markets its own line of dental handpieces under the Micro Motors brand. Pro-Dex also develops motion control systems for industrial manufacturing and scientific research industries under the Oregon Micro Systems brand. In addition to manufacturing, Pro-Dex also offers repair services on its products.

	Annual Growth	06/19	06/20	06/21	06/22	06/23
Sales ($mil.)	14.1%	27.2	34.8	38.0	42.0	46.1
Net income ($ mil.)	14.3%	4.1	6.1	4.5	3.9	7.1
Market value ($ mil.)	10.1%	46.0	63.2	108.3	56.5	67.7
Employees	10.2%	99	122	123	137	146

PRO-FAC COOPERATIVE INC.

590 Willow Brook Office Park
Fairport, NY 14450
Phone: 585 218-4210
Fax: –
Web: www.profaccoop.com

CEO: Stephen R Wright
CFO: Stephen R Wright
HR: –
FYE: June 27
Type: Public

Pro-Fac Cooperative grows big and strong on fruits and veggies. The farm co-op provides marketing and sales services to its approximately 500 member/owners across the US. The agricultural co-op sells its member/farmers' crops to companies in the food-processing industry, including Birds Eye Foods (typically buys more than 40% of crops). Pro-Fac has members primarily in Delaware, Florida, Illinois, Iowa, Michigan, Nebraska, New York, Oregon, Pennsylvania, and Washington. It was formerly a partial owner of Birds Eye, which was sold to Blackstone entity Pinnacle Foods in 2009. Since the sale, Pro-Fac has implemented a liquidation plan and looks to disband in 2012.

	Annual Growth	06/05	06/06	06/07	06/08	06/09
Sales ($mil.)	–	–	0.0	3.6	2.0	2.9
Net income ($ mil.)	–	1.6	(2.2)	3.5	120.8	(1.0)
Market value ($ mil.)	1.8%	34.2	12.5	24.6	38.5	36.6
Employees	7.5%	3	3	4	4	4

PROASSURANCE CORP

100 Brookwood Place
Birmingham, AL 35209
Phone: 205 877-4400
Fax: –
Web: www.proassurance.com

NYS: PRA
CEO: –
CFO: –
HR: –
FYE: December 31
Type: Public

ProAssurance is a specialty property and casualty and workers' compensation insurance carrier. ProAssurance is the holding company for ProAssurance Indemnity, ProAssurance Casualty, and other subsidiaries that sell liability coverage for health care providers, primarily in the South and Midwest. Its wholly-owned insurance subsidiaries provide professional liability insurance, liability insurance for medical technology and life sciences risks, and workers' compensation insurance. The company also provides capital to Syndicate 1729 at Lloyd's of London. Its customers include healthcare professionals and healthcare entities, including hospitals and other healthcare facilities.

	Annual Growth	12/19	12/20	12/21	12/22	12/23
Assets ($mil.)	4.0%	4,805.6	4,654.8	6,191.5	5,700.0	5,631.9
Net income ($ mil.)	–	1.0	(175.7)	144.1	(0.4)	(38.6)
Market value ($ mil.)	(21.4%)	1,842.1	906.8	1,289.5	890.4	702.9
Employees	3.3%	961	827	1,021	1,083	1,094

PROCESSA PHARMACEUTICALS INC

7380 Coca Cola Drive, Suite 106
Hanover, MD 21076
Phone: 443 776-3133
Fax: –
Web: www.processapharmaceuticals.com

NMS: PCSA
CEO: George Ng
CFO: James Stanker
HR: –
FYE: December 31
Type: Public

Heatwurx provides a way to fix cracks and potholes in the roadway not by just laying more asphalt but by repairing them through the use of plenty of heat. The company manufactures machinery that recycles broken asphalt at temperatures above 300 F. with infrared heating equipment that is electrically powered. Heatwurx claims it is an environmentally friendly method by virtue of its reuse of distressed pavement and the lack of need to transport material from asphalt plants. It incorporated in early 2011 and is a development-stage company with negligible sales. In late 2012 Heatwurx filed an IPO initially aiming to raise $7.6 million.

	Annual Growth	12/18	12/19	12/20	12/21	12/22
Sales ($mil.)	–	–	–	–	–	–
Net income ($ mil.)	–	(3.8)	(3.4)	(14.4)	(11.4)	(27.4)
Market value ($ mil.)	(25.7%)	2.9	14.4	5.3	3.9	0.9
Employees	–	15	13	14	15	15

PROCTER & GAMBLE COMPANY (THE)

One Procter & Gamble Plaza
Cincinnati, OH 45202
Phone: 513 983-1100
Fax: –
Web: www.pg.com

NYS: PG
CEO: Jon R Moeller
CFO: Andre Schulten
HR: Daniele Bologna
FYE: June 30
Type: Public

The Procter & Gamble Company (P&G) is a global leader in the fast-moving consumer goods industry, focused on providing branded consumer packaged goods of superior quality and value to its consumers around the world. The company divides its business into five global segments that comprise its vast portfolio of beauty, grooming, health care, fabric and home care, and baby, feminine, and family care product lines. Its around 35 brands include Bounty, Crest, Gillette, Pampers, Pepto-Bismol, Puffs, Old Spice, Swiffer, and Tide. Fabric and home care is P&G's leading product category, accounting for about 35% of its revenue. The company sells products in approximately 180 countries and territories worldwide through numerous channels as well as direct-to-consumer. More than half of the company's sales are generated outside the US.

	Annual Growth	06/19	06/20	06/21	06/22	06/23
Sales ($mil.)	4.9%	67,684	70,950	76,118	80,187	82,006
Net income ($ mil.)	39.3%	3,897.0	13,027	14,306	14,742	14,653
Market value ($ mil.)	8.5%	259,006	282,439	318,721	339,649	358,428
Employees	2.5%	97,000	99,000	101,000	106,000	107,000

PROCYON CORP.

164 Douglas Road
Oldsmar, FL 34677
Phone: 727 447-2998
Fax: –
Web: www.procyoncorp.com

NBB: PCYN
CEO: Justice W Anderson
CFO: James B Anderson
HR: –
FYE: June 30
Type: Public

Procyon sees past people's scars -- though it tries to rid the world of scarring altogether. Through subsidiary Amerx Health Care, Procyon Corporation makes medical products used to treat pressure ulcers, inflammation, dermatitis, and other wounds and skin problems. Amerx makes the AmeriGel wound dressing used by many podiatrists. The company's skin treatment products are sold primarily to distributors, doctors, pharmacies, and end-users. Procyon's Sirius Medical Supply division is a mail-order diabetic medical supply distributor, selling mostly to Medicare customers. The founding Anderson family, including CEO Regina Anderson, owns about 40% of the company.

	Annual Growth	06/19	06/20	06/21	06/22	06/23
Sales ($mil.)	2.8%	4.2	4.3	4.7	4.8	4.7
Net income ($ mil.)	–	0.0	0.1	0.8	(0.2)	(0.1)
Market value ($ mil.)	3.0%	1.8	1.9	3.0	3.8	2.0
Employees	–	18	20	21	19	18

PRODUCERS RICE MILL, INC.

518 E HARRISON ST
STUTTGART, AR 721603700
Phone: 870 673-4444
Fax: –
Web: www.producersrice.com

CEO: Jay Coke
CFO: –
HR: Kris Lindsey
FYE: July 31
Type: Private

These producers aren't just milling about, they're about milling. Producers Rice Mill dries, mills, and markets more than 50 million bushels of rice each year, which it sells both domestically and overseas. The growers' cooperative is one of the largest private-label producers of rice in the US, packaging more than 100 brands for the foodservice, retail, private label, export, and industrial industries. Its brands include ParExcellence, LeGourment, Golden Harvest, Classic Grains, Granada, Mandalay, Bamboo 103, Calrose, and Thai Orchard. It also processes rice for animal feeds, such as Buck Grub deer feed and Equi-Jewel horse feed.

	Annual Growth	07/15	07/16	07/17	07/18	07/19
Sales ($mil.)	2.3%	–	415.0	420.3	436.7	444.0
Net income ($ mil.)	2.9%	–	275.1	276.3	260.3	300.1
Market value ($ mil.)	–	–	–	–	–	–
Employees	–	–	–	–	–	800

PRODUCTS (SE) PIPE LINE CORPORATION

1001 LOUISIANA ST STE 1000
HOUSTON, TX 77002
Phone: 770 751-4000
Fax: –
Web: www.perfectdomain.com

CEO: –
CFO: Park Shaper
HR: –
FYE: December 31
Type: Private

The only green from this company's crop is the cash it gets from its petroleum products transport business. Plantation Pipe Line, one of the largest petroleum products pipeline companies in the US, delivers gasoline, jet fuel, diesel, and heating oils through its 3,100 mile pipeline network which serves oil refiners and fuel wholesalers through connection points in Atlanta, Birmingham, Charlotte, Washington, DC, and other destinations in the Southeast. Plantation Pipe Line delivers more than 600,000 barrels per day to more than 30 delivery points. Kinder Morgan Energy Partners owns a 51% interest in the company, which was founded in 1940. Exxon Mobil owns the rest.

	Annual Growth	12/04	12/05	12/06	12/16	12/17
Sales ($mil.)	4.3%	–	170.5	174.5	273.9	281.7
Net income ($ mil.)	8.8%	–	30.0	15.3	71.7	82.2
Market value ($ mil.)	–	–	–	–	–	–
Employees	–	–	–	–	–	279

PROFESSIONAL DISC GOLF ASSOCIATION

3828 DOGWOOD LN
APPLING, GA 308023012
Phone: 706 309-9017
Fax: –
Web: www.pdga.com

CEO: –
CFO: –
HR: –
FYE: December 31
Type: Private

Some people wouldn't know disc golf from a hole in the ground, but the PDGA does. The Professional Disc Golf Association (PDGA) promotes the sport of disc golf, a game played with specially designed flying discs and baskets, rather than dimpled balls and holes. Founded in 1976, the PDGA sanctions about 550 annual amateur and professional competitions (including championship events) and boasts more than 16,000 members in about 20 countries. The sport has seen rapid growth, from one course in 1975 to more than 2,500 today. The vast majority of disc golf courses are in the US.

	Annual Growth	12/13	12/14	12/15	12/16	12/17
Sales ($mil.)	18.8%	–	2.2	2.6	3.1	3.7
Net income ($ mil.)	–	–	(0.2)	0.0	0.3	0.1
Market value ($ mil.)	–	–	–	–	–	–
Employees	–	–	–	–	–	7

PROFESSIONAL DIVERSITY NETWORK INC   NAS: IPDN

55 E. Monroe Street, Suite 2120
Chicago, IL 60603
Phone: 312 614-0950
Fax: –
Web: www.ipdnusa.com

CEO: Katherine A Butkevich
CFO: Larry S Aichler
HR: –
FYE: December 31
Type: Public

Birds of a feather can build careers together at Professional Diversity Network (PDN). An online professional networking company, PDN operates minority-focused websites that facilitate professional networking within ethnic and social communities. Its websites include iHispano.com, which serves Hispanic-American professionals, and AMightyRiver.com, which caters to African-Americans. The company also operates sites that serve other societal subsets, including women, Asian-Americans, gays and lesbians, and enlisted and veteran military personnel. Together, its websites have 1.8 million members and provide access to job listings, a social network, professional groups, and mentoring. PDN went public in 2013.

	Annual Growth	12/18	12/19	12/20	12/21	12/22
Sales ($mil.)	(0.4%)	8.5	5.0	4.5	6.1	8.3
Net income ($ mil.)	–	(15.1)	(3.8)	(4.4)	(2.8)	(2.6)
Market value ($ mil.)	0.9%	10.4	9.4	26.9	10.1	10.7
Employees	(18.7%)	94	52	39	37	41

PROFESSIONAL GOLFERS ASSOCIATION OF AMERICA INC

100 AVENUE OF CHAMPIONS
PALM BEACH GARDENS, FL 334183653
Phone: 561 624-8400
Fax: –
Web: www.pga.com

CEO: Jim L Awtrey
CFO: –
HR: –
FYE: March 31
Type: Private

The Professional Golfers' Association of America (PGA) is the world's largest professional sports organization with more than 28,000 members. PGA members are primarily club pros, but most touring professionals are also members in addition to holding membership in the separate PGA TOUR organization. The PGA conducts some 40 tournaments and runs four major golf competitions: the Ryder Cup, the PGA Championship, the Senior PGA Championship, and the PGA Grand Slam of Golf. It also operates the PGA Learning Center, a golf instruction school, in Port St. Lucie, Florida. Rodman Wanamaker, a Philadelphia department store tycoon, organized the PGA in 1916.

	Annual Growth	06/13	06/14	06/15*	03/21	03/22
Sales ($mil.)	11.2%	–	82.3	108.2	118.2	192.1
Net income ($ mil.)	–	–	(8.3)	(2.0)	(5.9)	73.7
Market value ($ mil.)	–	–	–	–	–	–
Employees	–	–	–	–	–	270

*Fiscal year change

PROFESSIONAL PLACEMENT RESOURCES LLC

333 1ST ST N STE 200
JACKSONVILLE BEACH, FL 322506939
Phone: 866 581-5038
Fax: –
Web: –

CEO: –
CFO: –
HR: Gina Starr
FYE: December 31
Type: Private

Professional Placement Resources could very well be the ultimate nursing home. The company, doing business as PPR Healthcare Staffing, offers various placement services for nurses, physical therapists, and other health care professionals, particularly those interested in experiencing a variety of locales. Its PPR Travel division recruits and staffs health care personnel, placing them in hospitals nationwide. It also recruits and trains nurses from overseas for placement in the US through PPR International. Serving a client base of more than 700 hospitals, the company was founded in 1996 by fraternity brothers Dwight Cooper and Keith Frein.

	Annual Growth	12/05	12/06	12/07	12/08	12/09
Sales ($mil.)	(25.1%)	–	–	44.4	41.5	24.9
Net income ($ mil.)	–	–	–	(0.3)	0.2	(0.9)
Market value ($ mil.)	–	–	–	–	–	–
Employees	–	–	–	–	–	350

PROFESSIONAL PROJECT SERVICES, INC.

1100 BETHEL VALLEY RD
OAK RIDGE, TN 378308073
Phone: 865 220-4300
Fax: –
Web: www.p2s.com

CEO: –
CFO: –
HR: –
FYE: December 31
Type: Private

Pro2Serve Professional Project Services lives to serve. The contractor provides technical and engineering services that support the security of infrastructures in the US defense, energy, and environmental markets. Pro2Serve designs high-level security systems to protect national laboratories, government facilities, and US nuclear weapons. Its work with the US Department of Energy's National Nuclear Security Administration aims to secure nuclear sites and dangerous radiological materials around the world. The company also offers environmental services, which include facility planning, compliance consulting, remediation, and waste management. Founded by president Barry Goss, Pro2Serve is privately held.

	Annual Growth	12/06	12/07	12/08	12/09	12/10
Sales ($mil.)	15.9%	–	–	43.2	50.5	58.0
Net income ($ mil.)	27.6%	–	–	1.7	1.7	2.8
Market value ($ mil.)	–	–	–	–	–	–
Employees	–	–	–	–	–	340

PROFESSIONALS FOR NON-PROFITS, INC.

515 MADISON AVE RM 1100
NEW YORK, NY 100225497
Phone: 212 546-9091
Fax: –
Web: www.pnpstaffinggroup.com

CEO: –
CFO: –
HR: –
FYE: December 31
Type: Private

Professionals for NonProfits specializes in offering temporary staffing and permanent placement services to more than 800 not-for-profit clients, including social services organizations, universities, foundations, and museums. Founded in 1996, the company provides professionals in areas such as fundraising, public relations, marketing, and information technology. The company serves not-for-profit organizations across the US through offices in New York City and Washington D.C.. Clients include Amnesty International, The Make a Wish Foundation, and the NAACP.

	Annual Growth	12/07	12/08	12/09	12/10	12/11
Sales ($mil.)	(5.7%)	–	–	5.9	6.3	5.3
Net income ($ mil.)	–	–	–	(0.6)	0.2	(0.2)
Market value ($ mil.)	–	–	–	–	–	–
Employees	–	–	–	–	–	25

PROG HOLDINGS INC   NYS: PRG

256 W. Data Drive
Draper, UT 84020-2315
Phone: 385 351-1369
Fax: –
Web: www.progholdings.com

CEO: –
CFO: –
HR: –
FYE: December 31
Type: Public

Aaron's rents and sells furniture, appliances, electronics, computers, and a variety of other products and accessories. The company is one of the leading, technology-enabled, omni-channel provider of lease-to-own (LTO) and purchase solutions generally focused on serving the large, credit-challenged segment of the population. Aaron's has a network of more than 1,300 company-operated and franchised stores. In addition to Ashley, Samsung, GE Appliances, LG, and Sony brands, the company's Woodhaven Furniture bridges together the age-old tradition of handcrafted wood making products that are manufactured using state-of-the-art technology.

	Annual Growth	12/19	12/20	12/21	12/22	12/23
Sales ($mil.)	(11.6%)	3,947.7	2,484.6	2,677.9	2,597.8	2,408.3
Net income ($ mil.)	44.9%	31.5	(61.5)	243.6	98.7	138.8
Market value ($ mil.)	(14.2%)	2,494.2	2,352.7	1,970.1	737.7	1,350.0
Employees	(39.6%)	12,100	1,868	2,023	1,692	1,606

PROGINET CORPORATION

200 GARDEN CY PLZ STE 220
GARDEN CITY, NY 11530
Phone: 516 535-3600
Fax: –
Web: www.tibco.com

CEO: –
CFO: –
HR: –
FYE: July 31
Type: Private

Proginet had a secure grasp on enterprise data. The company provided software that businesses use to create encrypted documents -- including text, graphics, and executable files -- so that they can safely be sent over public networks. The company also offers identity management process automation software, as well as password management tools that eliminate the need for users to remember multiple access codes. Its service portfolio ranges from installation and support to project management, requirements analysis, and security assessments. Proginet was acquired in 2010 by TIBCO Software in an all-cash deal valued at about $20 million.

PROGRESS ENERGY, INC.

410 S WILMINGTON ST
RALEIGH, NC 276011849
Phone: 704 382-3853
Fax: –
Web: www.progress-energy.com

CEO: Lynn J Good
CFO: Steven K Young
HR: –
FYE: December 31
Type: Private

Progress Energy provides electricity to 3.6 million customers. The Duke Energy subsidiary serves customers in North and South Carolina through utility Duke Energy Progress, and in Florida through Duke Energy Florida. The company generates most of its energy from nuclear and fossil-fueled plants and has a total capacity of about 22,950 MW.

PROGRESS INVESTMENT MANAGEMENT COMPANY, LLC

33 NEW MONTGOMERY ST FL 19
SAN FRANCISCO, CA 941054506
Phone: 415 512-3480
Fax: –
Web: –

CEO: –
CFO: –
HR: –
FYE: December 31
Type: Private

Making money is the kind of progress this company strives for. Progress Investment Management specializes in the management of emerging-markets managers, particularly those run by minorities or women; clients include such pension funds as CalPERS, whose manager-development program it manages. Progress Investment Management has approximately $8.4 billion in assets under management. The company has vested with more than 150 emerging managers, representing 39 strategies. Progress Investment Management was founded in 1990 and was under the wings of Bank of America for a time, but is independent after a management buyout.

	Annual Growth	12/14	12/15	12/16	12/17	12/18
Assets ($mil.)	(12.1%)	–	16.5	14.3	12.0	11.2
Net income ($ mil.)	(31.4%)	–	4.8	3.8	2.1	1.6
Market value ($ mil.)	–	–	–	–	–	–
Employees	–	–	–	–	–	35

PROGRESS SOFTWARE CORP   NMS: PRGS

15 Wayside Road, Suite 400
Burlington, MA 01803
Phone: 781 280-4000
Fax: 781 280-4095
Web: www.progress.com

CEO: Yogesh K Gupta
CFO: Anthony Folger
HR: –
FYE: November 30
Type: Public

Progress Software is the trusted provider of the best products to develop, deploy, and manage high-impact business applications. The company's services offerings include application modernization; infrastructure automation; development operations; data management, managed database services; performance enhancements and tuning; and analytics/business intelligence. The company's products are typically sold as perpetual licenses, but certain products makes use of term licensing models and cloud-based offerings use a subscription-based model. More than half of its worldwide license revenue is realized through relationships with indirect channel partners (principally independent software vendors (ISVs)); original equipment manufacturers (OEMs); and value-added resellers (VARs), systems integrators, and distributors.

	Annual Growth	11/19	11/20	11/21	11/22	11/23
Sales ($mil.)	13.9%	413.3	442.2	531.3	602.0	694.4
Net income ($ mil.)	27.7%	26.4	79.7	78.4	95.1	70.2
Market value ($ mil.)	6.4%	1,839.9	1,756.2	2,121.9	2,335.2	2,358.9
Employees	10.4%	1,538	1,796	2,103	2,071	2,284

PROGRESSIVE CORP. (OH) NYS: PGR

6300 Wilson Mills Road
Mayfield Village, OH 44143
Phone: 440 461-5000
Fax: 440 446-7168
Web: www.progressive.com

CEO: Susan P Griffith
CFO: John P Sauerland
HR: –
FYE: December 31
Type: Public

The Progressive Corporation, an insurance holding company, has insurance and non-insurance subsidiaries and affiliates. Its insurance subsidiaries provide personal and commercial auto insurance, personal residential and commercial property insurance, workers' compensation insurance primarily for the transportation industry, business-related general liability insurance, and other specialty property-casualty insurance and related services. Its non-insurance subsidiaries generally support its insurance and investment operations. Progressive operates throughout US.

	Annual Growth	12/19	12/20	12/21	12/22	12/23
Assets ($mil.)	12.7%	54,895	64,098	71,132	75,465	88,691
Net income ($ mil.)	(0.4%)	3,970.3	5,704.6	3,350.9	721.5	3,902.4
Market value ($ mil.)	21.8%	42,370	57,874	60,081	75,919	93,227
Employees	10.2%	41,571	43,326	49,077	55,100	61,400

PROHEALTH CARE, INC.

1111 DELAFIELD ST STE 100
WAUKESHA, WI 531883407
Phone: 262 928-4300
Fax: –
Web: www.regencyseniorcommunities.com

CEO: Donald W Fundingsland
CFO: –
HR: Mary Polaris
FYE: September 30
Type: Private

ProHealth Care has been the health care leader in Waukesha County, Wisconsin, and surrounding areas, providing outstanding care across a full spectrum of services, including internal medicine, pregnancy and birth care, heart and vascular care, dermatology, occupational health, family medicine, home care, hospice care, MRI, behavioral and mental health, breast imaging, and women's health, among others. It provides health care services through a network of four hospitals ? Waukesha Memorial Hospital, Waukesha Memorial Hospital-Mukwonago, Oconomowoc Memorial Hospital, and the Rehabilitation Hospital of Wisconsin. ProHealth was founded in 1914.

	Annual Growth	09/18	09/19	09/20	09/21	09/22
Sales ($mil.)	(40.8%)	–	852.9	865.0	187.4	177.0
Net income ($ mil.)	(25.1%)	–	66.6	21.5	47.8	28.0
Market value ($ mil.)	–	–	–	–	–	–
Employees	–	–	–	–	–	3,000

PROJECT ADVENTURE

719 CABOT ST
BEVERLY, MA 019151027
Phone: 978 524-4555
Fax: –
Web: www.pa.org

CEO: –
CFO: –
HR: –
FYE: December 31
Type: Private

Project Adventure (PA) brings fun to the boardroom, classroom, or breakroom. The not-for-profit organization sells experiential education programs for corporations, schools, and other groups. It also runs several programs for at-risk youth sent to one of its two facilities (in Georgia or California) by the court. PA provides such services as the development of health and physical fitness programs, professional development, college programs, and customized educational workshops. One of the organization's primary activities is designing, installing, and training people to use its ropes challenge courses. PA sells books, kits of props and equipment for facilitators of its exercises, and ropes course supplies.

PROJECT ENHANCEMENT CORP

20300 CENTURY BLVD STE 175
GERMANTOWN, MD 208741189
Phone: 240 686-3059
Fax: –
Web: www.projectenhancement.com

CEO: Ricardo Martinez
CFO: –
HR: –
FYE: September 30
Type: Private

Project Enhancement offers a variety of environmental services, including hazardous waste management, nuclear plant decommissioning, and stabilization and disposition of nuclear materials. The company serves customers throughout the US from offices in Maryland, Tennessee, and Washington state. Clients have included several US Department of Energy nuclear sites, as well a range of industrial manufacturing companies and utilties including Bechtel, British Nuclear Fuels, Commonwealth Edison, Fluor, Lockheed Martin, Morrison Knudsen, and Science Applications International.

	Annual Growth	05/15	05/16	05/17	05/18*	09/19
Sales ($mil.)	38.7%	–	16.5	27.7	35.7	44.1
Net income ($ mil.)	193.6%	–	0.1	0.6	0.8	3.0
Market value ($ mil.)	–	–	–	–	–	–
Employees	–	–	–	–	–	45

*Fiscal year change

PROLOGIS INC NYS: PLD

Pier 1, Bay 1
San Francisco, CA 94111
Phone: 415 394-9000
Fax: 415 394-9001
Web: www.prologis.com

CEO: Hamid R Moghadam
CFO: Timothy D Arndt
HR: –
FYE: December 31
Type: Public

Founded in 1983, Prologis, Inc., is the global leader in logistics real estate with a focus on high-barrier, high-growth markets. Prologis owns, manages and develops well-located, high-quality logistics facilities in about 20 countries across four continents. Prologis acquires and develops facilities for more than 6,600 clients including Amazon, FedEx, Home Depot, Wal-Mart, Geodis, and Keuhne + Nagel. The US accounts for about 85% of total revenue. Prologis is organized as an industrial real estate investment trust (REIT). In 2022, Prologis acquired Duke Realty Corporation, for approximately $23 billion.

	Annual Growth	12/19	12/20	12/21	12/22	12/23
Sales ($mil.)	24.6%	3,330.6	4,438.7	4,759.4	5,973.7	8,023.5
Net income ($ mil.)	18.1%	1,573.0	1,481.8	2,939.7	3,364.9	3,059.2
Market value ($ mil.)	10.6%	82,400	92,125	155,630	104,207	123,221
Employees	10.7%	1,712	1,945	2,053	2,466	2,574

PROMEDICA HEALTH SYSTEM, INC.

100 MADISON AVE
TOLEDO, OH 436041516
Phone: 567 585-9600
Fax: –
Web: www.promedica.org

CEO: Arturo Polizzi
CFO: Terry Metzger
HR: Alania Moody
FYE: December 31
Type: Private

ProMedica Health System is a not-for-profit health care provider offering a full spectrum of medical services to residents of northwestern Ohio and southeastern Michigan. The system is composed of about a dozen hospitals, ambulatory surgery centers, and more than 330 post-acute facilities including senior care, rehabilitation, surgery, physician practice, urgent care, and home health and hospice centers. ProMedica's Paramount unit offers health and dental insurance plans. ProMedica's network of assisted living and skilled nursing facilities expanded to cover nearly 30 states.

	Annual Growth	12/98	12/99	12/00	12/01	12/13
Assets ($mil.)	8.5%	–	–	–	880.3	2,336.3
Net income ($ mil.)	–	–	–	–	–	305.3
Market value ($ mil.)	–	–	–	–	–	–
Employees	–	–	–	–	–	56,000

PROMEGA CORPORATION

2800 WOODS HOLLOW RD
FITCHBURG, WI 537115399
Phone: 608 274-4330
Fax: –
Web: www.promega.com

CEO: –
CFO: –
HR: –
FYE: March 31
Type: Private

Promega is a global biotechnology company that provides innovative solutions and technical support to the life sciences industry. The company sells more than 4,000 products that allow scientists to conduct various experiments in a range of life science work across areas such as cell biology; DNA, RNA, and protein analysis; drug development; human identification; and molecular diagnostics. Promega has branches in over 15 countries around the world. The company sells its products directly and through more than 50 distributors. Promega's products and technology are used by scientists and technicians in labs for academic and government research, forensics, pharmaceuticals, clinical diagnostics, and agricultural and environmental testing. The company was founded in 1978 by Bill Linton.

	Annual Growth	03/16	03/17	03/20	03/21	03/22
Sales ($mil.)	14.0%	–	386.1	487.9	878.4	744.0
Net income ($ mil.)	29.8%	–	55.0	75.5	323.9	202.5
Market value ($ mil.)	–	–	–	–	–	–
Employees	–	–	–	–	–	2,034

PROOF ADVERTISING, LLC

7401 W SLAUGHTER LN PMB 5094
AUSTIN, TX 787391903
Phone: 512 345-6658
Fax: –
Web: www.proof-advertising.com

CEO: Bryan Christian
CFO: –
HR: Abigail Rink
FYE: December 31
Type: Private

Kolar Advertising & Marketing offers full-service advertising services, including strategic planning, market research, direct mail, public relations, and media buying and planning. Kolar Advertising has extensive experience in the business-to-business arena (it was founded as an agency specializing in B2B) but has since expanded its footprint into the consumer domain. The agency's clients include businesses in the high-tech, tourism and hospitality, pharmaceuticals, manufacturing, and retail sectors. The woman-owned agency has conducted advertising and marketing campaigns for such clients as 3M, Baylor University, Dell, Subway, and the US Army. It was established in 1989 by Rhonda Kolar.

	Annual Growth	12/11	12/12	12/13	12/15	12/16
Sales ($mil.)	–	–	(110.4)	26.4	–	33.2
Net income ($ mil.)	734.3%	–	0.0	0.1	–	1.0
Market value ($ mil.)	–	–	–	–	–	–
Employees	–	–	–	–	–	40

PROPELLUS INC

398 Lemon Creek Drive, Suite A
Walnut, CA 91789
Phone: 909 598-0618
Fax: –
Web: –

NBB: PRPS
CEO: –
CFO: –
HR: –
FYE: December 31
Type: Public

Homes and businesses looking to go eco turn to companies like Sunvalley Solar. Sunvalley Solar offers solar power system design, installation, and maintenance services to owners, builders, and architecture firms in the residential, commercial, and government sectors primarily in California. The company also distributes solar equipment, including solar panels, inverters, and related goods from such manufacturers as Canadian Solar and China Electric Equipment Group (CEEG). A portion of Sunvalley Solar's resources are spent on solar technology research and development. Founded in 2007, Sunvalley Solar was the first Chinese-American owned solar installation company in Southern California.

	Annual Growth	12/13	12/14	12/15	12/16	12/17
Sales ($mil.)	8.7%	4.1	3.3	5.8	8.5	5.7
Net income ($ mil.)	–	0.8	(1.3)	0.2	(1.0)	(1.8)
Market value ($ mil.)	21.0%	0.0	0.0	0.0	0.0	0.0
Employees	30.6%	11	11	11	32	32

PROPETRO HOLDING CORP

1706 South Midkiff
Midland, TX 79701
Phone: 432 688-0012
Fax: –
Web: www.propetroservices.com

NYS: PUMP
CEO: Phillip A Gobe
CFO: David Schorlemer
HR: –
FYE: December 31
Type: Public

ProPetro Holding Corp. (ProPetro) is a leading integrated oilfield services company, focused on providing innovative hydraulic fracturing, wireline, and other complementary oilfield completion services to leading upstream oil and gas companies engaged in the exploration and production (E&P) of North American oil and natural gas resources. The company's hydraulic fracturing services own and operate a fleet of mobile hydraulic fracturing units and other auxiliary equipment to perform fracturing services. The company also provides cementing services for the completion of new wells and remedial work on existing wells, as well as wireline and ancillary services such as pump-down on new oil well completions in the Permian Basin. Its operational focus has primarily been on the Permian Basin's Midland sub-basin, where its customers have operated. The company went public in 2017.

	Annual Growth	12/19	12/20	12/21	12/22	12/23
Sales ($mil.)	(5.6%)	2,052.3	789.2	874.5	1,279.7	1,630.4
Net income ($ mil.)	(14.9%)	163.0	(107.0)	(54.2)	2.0	85.6
Market value ($ mil.)	(7.1%)	1,231.7	809.1	886.8	1,135.3	917.5
Employees	(1.5%)	2,200	1,100	1,500	2,000	2,070

PROPHASE LABS INC

711 Stewart Avenue, Suite 200
Garden City, NY 11530
Phone: 215 345-0919
Fax: –
Web: www.prophaselabs.com

NAS: PRPH
CEO: Ted Karkus
CFO: Monica Brady
HR: –
FYE: December 31
Type: Public

ProPhase Labs wants cold sufferers to put away their tissues and tonics and take Cold-EEZE lozenges instead. The firm contends that its Cold-EEZE remedy (a zinc-based nutritional formula available in lozenge, tablet, liquid, and gum forms) lessens the length and severity of the common cold. ProPhase markets its products primarily in the US market. The company's Pharmaloz Manufacturing subsidiary makes Cold-EEZE lozenges and provides contract manufacturing of lozenges for other firms. In early 2017, ProPhase agreed to sell its Cold-EEZE assets to Mylan for some $50 million. It will continue to manufacture the products for Mylan. ProPhase is also conducting research and development programs into potential new OTC medicines.

	Annual Growth	12/18	12/19	12/20	12/21	12/22
Sales ($mil.)	74.8%	13.1	9.9	14.5	79.0	122.6
Net income ($ mil.)	–	(1.7)	(3.1)	(2.1)	6.3	18.5
Market value ($ mil.)	32.2%	51.1	31.9	148.8	116.2	156.1
Employees	26.7%	50	50	95	129	129

PROPPER INTERNATIONAL SALES, INC.

17 RESEARCH PARK DR STE 100
WELDON SPRING, MO 633045620
Phone: 636 685-1000
Fax: –
Web: www.propper.com

CEO: –
CFO: Bob Brinkman
HR: –
FYE: September 30
Type: Private

Propper International Sales is a leading manufacturer of uniforms and specialty apparel for the US Department of Defense. Its products include tactical pants, polo shirts, ems suits, and flight suits in addition to Class A dress uniforms for police, state, and government agencies. Propper's main divisions serve government, law enforcement, and public safety communities. Propper, headquartered in Missouri, operates manufacturing facilities in the US, Haiti, Puerto Rico, and the Dominican Republic, as well as distribution center in Tennessee. The company makes its finished products from its 4,000 sq. ft. design lab and sells it through resellers, and distributors across the US.

PROS HOLDINGS INC

NYS: PRO

3200 Kirby Drive, Suite 600
Houston, TX 77098
Phone: 713 335-5151
Fax: –
Web: www.pros.com

CEO: Andres D Reiner
CFO: Stefan B Schulz
HR: –
FYE: December 31
Type: Public

PROS Holdings provides solutions that optimize shopping and selling experiences. The company's solutions leverage artificial intelligence (AI), self-learning, and automation to ensure that every transactional experience is fast, frictionless and personalized for every shopper, supporting both business-to-business (B2B), and business-to-consumer (B2C) companies across industry verticals. PROS' customers come from the automotive and industrial manufacturing and distribution, consumer goods, transportation and logistics, chemicals and energy, food and consumables, insurance, healthcare, technology and travel industries. In addition, the company also offers selling, pricing, revenue optimization, distribution and retail, and digital offer marketing solutions. It also offers software-related services, including implementation, configuration, consulting, and training services. The US is responsible for around 35% of the total sales.

	Annual Growth	12/19	12/20	12/21	12/22	12/23
Sales ($mil.)	5.0%	250.3	252.4	251.4	276.1	303.7
Net income ($ mil.)	–	(69.1)	(77.0)	(81.2)	(82.2)	(56.4)
Market value ($ mil.)	(10.3%)	2,786.5	2,361.0	1,603.9	1,128.2	1,803.9
Employees	1.3%	1,413	1,403	1,545	1,528	1,486

PROSEGUR SERVICES GROUP, INC.

512 HERNDON PKWY STE A
HERNDON, VA 201705244
Phone: 703 464-4735
Fax: –
Web: www.prosegur.us

CEO: Larry Parrotte
CFO: N P Brost
HR: Kayla Bittle
FYE: March 31
Type: Private

"Somebody's watching me," is a song but also a service, thanks to Command Security. The company provides security guards for commercial, governmental, financial, and industrial clients. About half of Command Security's business comes from its aviation services. Although passenger screening services have been taken over by the US government, Command Security manages support services such as aircraft and baggage-related security duties, and skycap and wheelchair escort services. In addition to general security tasks, the company offers recruiting, hiring, training, and supervisory assistance of operating personnel. Federal Express, the company's most significant customer, accounts for over 20% of total sales.

PROSEK LLC

28 E 28TH ST
NEW YORK, NY 100167939
Phone: 212 279-3115
Fax: –
Web: www.prosek.com

CEO: Wendy Lo
CFO: Mike D Vecchio
HR: Clancy Forte
FYE: December 31
Type: Private

Public relations firm Prosek Partners is positively pleased to provide financial communications and investor relations. It also offers traditional and digital media relations, corporate advisory, editorial, public affairs, and graphic and Web design services. Customers include energy, professional services, financial services, insurance, and technology companies. Prosek Partners serves regional, national, and international clients through offices in London; New York; and Fairfield, Connecticut. Formerly Cubitt Jacobs & Prosek Communications, the public relations agency is a minority- and women-owned business; it changed its name to Prosek Partners in 2012.

PROSPECT WATERBURY, INC.

64 ROBBINS ST
WATERBURY, CT 067082613
Phone: 203 573-6000
Fax: –
Web: www.waterburyhospital.org

CEO: –
CFO: –
HR: Andrew Iava
FYE: December 31
Type: Private

Where do broken hearts go? Waterbury Hospital hopes it's to its cardiologists. The community teaching hospital, serving western Connecticut, has been named one of the top hospitals in the nation for cardiac intervention. Of course, hearts aren't the only body parts Waterbury Hospital treats; the full-service facility has nearly 370 beds and offers services that include behavioral health care, an orthopedic center, and an outpatient surgery center. Waterbury Hospital, founded in 1890, forms the cornerstone of the Greater Waterbury Health Network, which provides a range of outpatient health services, from nursing care to hospice, imaging, and lab services. Prospect Medical Holdings is buying Waterbury Hospital.

	Annual Growth	09/15	09/16*	12/17	12/18	12/21
Sales ($mil.)	4.0%	–	206.9	220.8	228.3	251.4
Net income ($ mil.)	–	–	(3.8)	49.9	(5.1)	15.8
Market value ($ mil.)	–	–	–	–	–	–
Employees	–	–	–	–	–	1,625

*Fiscal year change

PROSPERITY BANCSHARES INC.

NYS: PB

Prosperity Bank Plaza, 4295 San Felipe
Houston, TX 77027
Phone: 281 269-7199
Fax: –
Web: www.prosperitybankusa.com

CEO: David Zalman
CFO: Asylbek Osmonov
HR: –
FYE: December 31
Type: Public

Prosperity Bancshares is the holding company for Prosperity Bank operates about 275 branches across Texas and about 15 in Oklahoma. Serving consumers and small to mid-sized businesses, the bank offers traditional deposit and loan services, in addition to wealth management, retail brokerage, and mortgage banking investment services. Prosperity Bank focuses on real estate lending: Commercial mortgages make up the largest segment of the company's loan portfolio (about 30%), followed by residential mortgages (some 25%). Credit cards, business, auto, consumer, home equity loans round out its lending activities.

	Annual Growth	12/19	12/20	12/21	12/22	12/23
Assets ($mil.)	4.6%	32,186	34,059	37,834	37,690	38,548
Net income ($ mil.)	6.0%	332.6	528.9	519.3	524.5	419.3
Market value ($ mil.)	(1.5%)	6,737.7	6,500.6	6,776.1	6,811.7	6,347.8
Employees	(0.3%)	3,901	3,756	3,704	3,633	3,850

PROSYS INFORMATION SYSTEMS, INC.

6575 THE CORNERS PKWY STE 300
NORCROSS, GA 30092
Phone: 678 268-1300
Fax: –
Web: www.prosysis.com

CEO: Elaine Bellock
CFO: David Ryan
HR: Carolina Retes
FYE: December 31
Type: Private

ProSys Information Systems strives to create sustainable competitive advantages for clients in this fast-paced environment by combining in-depth assessment, IT solution design, planning, complete asset procurement, integration and implementation expertise with the best technology available. The company serves small and midsized companies operating in the financial services, health care, technology, education and government sectors. ProSys operates from nearly 15 offices in the southeastern and mid-Atlantic US. The company was founded in 1997.

PROTAGENIC THERAPEUTICS INC NAS: PTIX

149 Fifth Avenue, Suite 500
New York, NY 10010
Phone: 212 994-8200
Fax: –
Web: www.protagenic.com

CEO: Garo H Armen
CFO: Alexander K Arrow
HR: –
FYE: December 31
Type: Public

Connecting advertisers and music fans online is an intrinsic part of Atrinsic. Through its Atrinsic Interactive brand, the online marketing agency helps companies reach audiences through search marketing, e-mail advertising, subscription-based content, mobile marketing, and traditional display ads. Atrinsic also serves as marketing partner of music downloading service Kazaa (jointly owned by Brilliant Digital Entertainment); it operates Kazaa as a direct-to-consumer subscription business ($9.99 per month) that allows subscribed listeners to stream music, primarily on mobile applications. In addition, the company owns RingTone.com and e-commerce site ShopIt.com. Atrinsic was founded in 2005.

	Annual Growth	12/18	12/19	12/20	12/21	12/22
Sales ($mil.)	–	–	–	–	–	–
Net income ($ mil.)	–	(2.6)	(1.8)	(2.5)	(4.5)	(3.6)
Market value ($ mil.)	(33.1%)	8.6	6.1	4.5	6.0	1.7
Employees	(9.6%)	3	2	2	2	2

PROTALEX INC

131 Columbia Turnpike, Suite 1
Florham Park, NJ 07932
Phone: 215 862-9720
Fax: –
Web: www.protalex.com

CEO: –
CFO: Kirk M Warshaw
HR: –
FYE: May 31
Type: Public

Protalex is developing a technique called bioregulation to make drugs that control a disease instead of treating the symptoms after the disease has wreaked havoc on the body. The company's development programs target autoimmune diseases and inflammatory ailments. Lead drug candidate PRTX-100 is in early stage trials to target rheumatoid arthritis and idiopathic thrombocytopenic purpura (ITP), an autoimmune disorder characterized by excessive bleeding. Other potential disease targets include skin diseases psoriasis and pemphigus, inflammatory bowel condition Crohn's disease, and autoimmune disorders multiple sclerosis and lupus.

	Annual Growth	05/14	05/15	05/16	05/17	05/18
Sales ($mil.)	–	–	–	–	–	–
Net income ($ mil.)	–	(11.9)	(11.6)	(9.4)	(4.6)	(5.0)
Market value ($ mil.)	(54.3%)	389.0	260.3	165.6	33.1	17.0
Employees	(9.6%)	3	3	1	2	2

PROTALIX BIOTHERAPEUTICS INC ASE: PLX

2 University Plaza, Suite 100
Hackensack, NJ 07601
Phone: 201 696-9345
Fax: –
Web: www.protalix.com

CEO: –
CFO: –
HR: –
FYE: December 31
Type: Public

What do you get when you cross a petunia with a person? Protalix BioTherapeutics hopes that whatever it is, it cures or prevents diseases. The biotech firm is splicing human DNA into plant cells and growing active proteins, including monoclonal antibodies and enzymes, that it hopes can turn into drug candidates. The company's lead product, UPLYSO, is an enzyme replacement therapy for Gaucher Disease. Already granted orphan drug status the by FDA, the drug is in late-stage clinical trials. Other product candidates include treatments for specialty diseases including Fabry disease.

	Annual Growth	12/19	12/20	12/21	12/22	12/23
Sales ($mil.)	4.6%	54.7	62.9	38.4	47.6	65.5
Net income ($ mil.)	–	(18.3)	(6.5)	(27.6)	(14.9)	8.3
Market value ($ mil.)	(14.2%)	239.3	264.8	60.7	99.9	129.9
Employees	1.5%	196	207	206	197	208

PROTECTIVE LIFE INSURANCE CO

2801 Highway 280 South
Birmingham, AL 35223
Phone: 205 268-1000
Fax: –
Web: www.protective.com

CEO: Richard J Bielen
CFO: Steven G Walker
HR: –
FYE: December 31
Type: Public

Protective Life & Annuity markets and sells financial security, in the form of term and universal life insurance policies and fixed and variable annuity products. Although the company is based in Alabama and licensed to sell insurance throughout the US, it exclusively serves clients in New York. Sister companies include West Coast Life Insurance (life insurance and annuities), MONY Life Insurance (ditto), and Lyndon Insurance (specialty coverage). Protective Life & Annuity is a unit of Protective Life Insurance, which is part of Dai-Ichi Life Holdings subsidiary Protective Life Corporation.

	Annual Growth	12/17	12/18	12/19	12/20	12/21
Assets ($mil.)	13.6%	79,114	89,383	120,478	126,453	131,572
Net income ($ mil.)	(29.9%)	1,182.4	193.9	553.0	342.4	285.0
Market value ($ mil.)	–	–	–	–	–	–
Employees	6.6%	2,773	2,957	3,096	3,263	3,585

PROTECTIVE LIFE INSURANCE CO. (BIRMINGHAM, ALA.)

2801 Highway 280 South
Birmingham, AL 35223
Phone: 205 268-1000
Fax: –
Web: www.protective.com

CEO: Richard J Bielen
CFO: Steven G Walker
HR: –
FYE: December 31
Type: Public

Protective Life & Annuity markets and sells financial security, in the form of term and universal life insurance policies and fixed and variable annuity products. Although the company is based in Alabama and licensed to sell insurance throughout the US, it exclusively serves clients in New York. Sister companies include West Coast Life Insurance (life insurance and annuities), MONY Life Insurance (ditto), and Lyndon Insurance (specialty coverage). Protective Life & Annuity is a unit of Protective Life Insurance, which is part of Dai-Ichi Life Holdings subsidiary Protective Life Corporation.

	Annual Growth	12/03	12/04	12/05	12/06	12/07
Assets ($mil.)	14.5%	23,971	26,571	28,339	39,158	41,145
Net income ($ mil.)	2.1%	232.0	222.1	235.7	264.9	252.4
Market value ($ mil.)	–	–	–	–	–	–
Employees	4.2%	1,437	1,995	1,612	2,173	1,694

PROTECTIVE LIFE INSURANCE COMPANY

2801 Highway 280 South
Birmingham, AL 35223
Phone: 205 879-9230
Fax: –
Web: –

CEO: Richard J Bielen
CFO: Steven G Walker
HR: –
FYE: December 31
Type: Public

Protective Life & Annuity markets and sells financial security, in the form of term and universal life insurance policies and fixed and variable annuity products. Although the company is based in Alabama and licensed to sell insurance throughout the US, it exclusively serves clients in New York. Sister companies include West Coast Life Insurance (life insurance and annuities), MONY Life Insurance (ditto), and Lyndon Insurance (specialty coverage). Protective Life & Annuity is a unit of Protective Life Insurance, which is part of Dai-Ichi Life Holdings subsidiary Protective Life Corporation.

PROTESTANT MEMORIAL MEDICAL CENTER, INC.

4500 MEMORIAL DR
BELLEVILLE, IL 622265360
Phone: 618 233-7750
Fax: –
Web: www.memhosp.org

CEO: Mark J Turner
CFO: –
HR: Nancy Rader
FYE: December 31
Type: Private

With more than 315 beds, Memorial Hospital has plenty of space to take care of Prairie Staters. The Bellevue, Illinois-based hospital is owned and operated by Protestant Memorial Medical Center, a community-based not-for-profit organization. Memorial Hospital provides general medical, surgical, and emergency care, as well as pediatric, home health, and cardiovascular care. Specialty services include treatment for sleep disorders and women's health. The hospital also operates Memorial Convalescent Center, a nearly 110-bed skilled nursing facility, and the Belleville Health and Sports Center, which provides fitness facilities to promote community health.

	Annual Growth	12/16	12/17	12/18	12/20	12/21
Sales ($mil.)	10.3%	–	237.4	237.3	218.4	351.0
Net income ($ mil.)	–	–	(9.3)	(2.6)	(9.8)	(15.6)
Market value ($ mil.)	–	–	–	–	–	–
Employees	–	–	–	–	–	2,344

PROTEXT MOBILITY INC

NBB: TXTM

One West Las Olas Blvd., Ste 500
Fort Lauderdale, FL 33301
Phone: 779 107-0886
Fax: –
Web: www.protextm.co

CEO: Roger Baylis-Duffield
CFO: –
HR: –
FYE: December 31
Type: Public

Echo Metrix (formerly SearchHelp) makes sure children are always under a watchful eye. The company provides parental control software designed to monitor the activity of children while they surf the Web, send instant messages, or chat online. Its Sentry At Home software alerts parents via e-mail or mobile phone when established usage guidelines are violated. The company's Sentry Remote software allows parents to monitor their children's online activities in real-time and remotely shut down their computers. Echo Metrix also developed an application for tracking registered sex offenders, but it decided to discontinue that line in 2008.

	Annual Growth	12/17	12/18	12/19	12/20	12/21
Sales ($mil.)	–	–	–	–	–	–
Net income ($ mil.)	–	(0.5)	(0.5)	(1.5)	(0.5)	(0.1)
Market value ($ mil.)	1.9%	10.2	2.3	0.8	4.7	11.0
Employees	–	–	–	–	–	–

PROTO LABS INC

NYS: PRLB

5540 Pioneer Creek Drive
Maple Plain, MN 55359
Phone: 763 479-3680
Fax: –
Web: www.protolabs.com

CEO: Robert Bodor
CFO: Daniel Schumacher
HR: –
FYE: December 31
Type: Public

Proto Labs is the world's largest and fastest digital manufacturer of custom prototypes and on-demand production parts. The company targets its products to the millions of product developers and engineers who use three-dimensional computer-aided design (3D CAD) software to design products across a diverse range of end-markets. It manufactures prototype and low volume production parts for companies worldwide, who are under increasing pressure to bring their finished products to market faster than their competition. It utilizes injection molding, computer numerical control (CNC) machining, 3D printing and sheet metal fabrication to manufacture custom parts for its customers. The US accounts for nearly 80% of Proto Labs' sales. The company was founded in 1999 by Larry Lukis.

	Annual Growth	12/19	12/20	12/21	12/22	12/23
Sales ($mil.)	2.4%	458.7	434.4	488.1	488.4	503.9
Net income ($ mil.)	(27.9%)	63.7	50.9	33.4	(103.5)	17.2
Market value ($ mil.)	(21.3%)	2,612.1	3,945.7	1,320.8	656.7	1,002.1
Employees	(1.2%)	2,535	2,408	2,663	2,568	2,415

PROTOSOURCE CORP.

NBB: PSCO

2345 Main Street, Suite C
Hellertown, PA 18055
Phone: 610 332-2893
Fax: –
Web: www.protosource.com

CEO: Peter Wardle
CFO: Peter Wardle
HR: –
FYE: December 31
Type: Public

ProtoSource is a source of change. Through Malaysia-based subsidiary P2i, ProtoSource is engaged in the business of converting print advertisements into Web-based advertising products for newspapers, magazines, and mail-order businesses. Its primary facility is located in Kuala Lumpur where the company receives and processes electronic files sent by its clients (largely from the US). Customers include such publishers as tronc, McClatchy, and Gannett. P2i also serves other content publishers, technology companies, retailers, and government entities. While most of ProtoSource's business is done in the US, it also has customers in the UK, Spain, and Canada.

	Annual Growth	12/04	12/05	12/06	12/07	12/08
Sales ($mil.)	21.2%	1.6	1.9	2.6	3.1	3.5
Net income ($ mil.)	–	(1.2)	(0.5)	(0.3)	(0.9)	(0.6)
Market value ($ mil.)	(3.8%)	0.3	0.4	0.4	0.6	0.3
Employees	21.0%	70	110	141	131	150

PROVECTUS BIOPHARMACEUTICALS INC

NBB: PVCT

800 S Gay Street, Suite 1610
Knoxville, TN 37929
Phone: 866 594-5999
Fax: –
Web: www.provectusbio.com

CEO: Ed Pershing
CFO: Heather Raines
HR: –
FYE: December 31
Type: Public

Provectus prospects the death of cancer. Provectus Pharmaceuticals designs pharmaceuticals for the treatment of cancer and various skin problems. Its Provectus Pharmatech division is developing prescription drugs for the treatment of eczema, psoriasis, and acne, as well as therapeutics targeting breast, liver, and prostate cancers and melanoma. In addition, the company develops laser-based medical devices and anti-cancer vaccines through its Provectus Devicetech and Provectus Biotech divisions, respectively. Provectus also has over-the-counter drug assets through its Pure-ific division.

	Annual Growth	12/19	12/20	12/21	12/22	12/23
Sales ($mil.)	–	–	–	–	1.0	0.6
Net income ($ mil.)	–	(6.9)	(6.7)	(5.5)	(3.6)	(3.1)
Market value ($ mil.)	10.9%	26.6	24.5	23.1	45.4	40.3
Employees	18.9%	2	2	4	4	4

PROVIDENCE AND WORCESTER RAILROAD COMPANY

75 HAMMOND ST STE 1
WORCESTER, MA 016101729
Phone: 508 755-4000
Fax: –
Web: www.pwrr.com

CEO: –
CFO: Daniel T Noreck
HR: –
FYE: December 31
Type: Private

Giving an island its link, Providence and Worcester Railroad (P&W) stands as Rhode Island's sole interstate freight carrier. The regional freight railroad operates over a network of about 545 miles of track in Connecticut, Massachusetts, New York, and Rhode Island. It hauls such goods as chemicals and plastics, construction aggregate, food, and forest and paper products for more than 160 customers. Major customers include Cargill, Dow Chemical, Frito-Lay, International Paper, and GDF SUEZ Energy. P&W interchanges freight traffic with CSX, the New England Central Railroad, the New York and Atlantic Railroad, and Pan Am Railways (formerly Springfield Terminal Railway).

PROVIDENCE COLLEGE

1 CUNNINGHAM SQ
PROVIDENCE, RI 029187001
Phone: 401 865-1000
Fax: –
Web: sites.providence.edu

CEO: –
CFO: –
HR: –
FYE: June 30
Type: Private

Students don't need divine intervention to get into Providence College, they just need good grades and an interest in liberal arts. The Catholic institution of higher education offers undergraduate and graduate degrees at its four schools: Arts and Sciences, Business, Continuing Education, and Professional Studies. It offers degrees in about 50 academic disciplines including biology, business, education, marketing, politics, and psychology. It has a student-to-faculty ratio of 12:1, with students primarily coming from New England and the Midwest and Mid-Atlantic regions. Providence College was founded in 1917 by the Dominican Friars of the Province of St. Joseph and the Diocese of Providence.

	Annual Growth	06/12	06/13	06/15	06/20	06/22
Sales ($mil.)	0.7%	–	237.6	267.4	299.3	252.4
Net income ($ mil.)	–	–	22.4	23.9	4.1	(19.3)
Market value ($ mil.)	–	–	–	–	–	–
Employees	–	–	–	–	–	800

PROVIDENCE HEALTH & SERVICES

1801 LIND AVE SW
RENTON, WA 980573368
Phone: 425 525-3355
Fax: –
Web: www.providence.org

CEO: –
CFO: –
HR: –
FYE: December 31
Type: Private

Providence St. Joseph Health was established in 2016 from the merger of Providence Health & Services and St. Joseph Health System. The not-for-profit operates 50 hospitals and more than 800 clinics in seven states in the western US. Its facilities operate under such brands as Swedish Health Services, Hoag Memorial Hospital Presbyterian, and Covenant Health. It provides health insurance through Providence Health Plans and offers subsidized housing for the low-income elderly and disabled. The young organization has also established the Institute for Mental Health and Wellness to improve access to quality mental health care around the nation.

	Annual Growth	12/06	12/07	12/08	12/12	12/15
Sales ($mil.)	10.8%	–	6,348.0	7,026.1	280.6	14,434
Net income ($ mil.)	(23.8%)	–	434.2	(156.7)	14.9	49.2
Market value ($ mil.)	–	–	–	–	–	–
Employees	–	–	–	–	–	130

PROVIDENCE HEALTH & SERVICES - MONTANA

500 W BROADWAY ST
MISSOULA, MT 598024008
Phone: 406 543-7271
Fax: –
Web: montana.providence.org

CEO: Kirk Bodlovic
CFO: –
HR: Karyn Trainor
FYE: December 31
Type: Private

Feeling a little green? St. Patrick Hospital and Health Sciences Center is there to help. The not-for-profit hospital boasts some 250 beds (acute-care and transitional) and serves nearly 20 counties in and around Missoula, Montana. Its specialty services include cancer treatment, surgery, and occupational health. The center also provides Life Flight air transport to critically ill or injured patients. The hospital provides outpatient primary and specialty care through a host of affiliated physician practices and clinics throughout the area. St. Patrick Hospital and Health Sciences Center is part of Providence Health & Services which has two hospitals and more than 40 clinics across Montana.

	Annual Growth	12/17	12/18	12/20	12/21	12/22
Sales ($mil.)	8.0%	–	352.7	346.0	385.4	480.3
Net income ($ mil.)	–	–	20.0	23.9	32.8	(0.8)
Market value ($ mil.)	–	–	–	–	–	–
Employees	–	–	–	–	–	1,460

PROVIDENCE HOSPITAL

1150 VARNUM ST NE
WASHINGTON, DC 200172104
Phone: 202 269-7000
Fax: –
Web: www.provhosp.org

CEO: Amy Freeman
CFO: –
HR: –
FYE: June 30
Type: Private

Providence Hospital is a pillar in the health care community of Washington, DC. The oldest continuously operating hospital in our nation's capitol, the 410-bed facility provides a full spectrum of services from behavioral health to women's services. It also administers programs for sleep disorders, geriatric care, and palliative care, in addition to its comprehensive medical and surgical services. Providence Hospital's affiliates include the adjacent Carroll Manor Nursing and Rehabilitation Center, a 250-bed facility for long-term and rehabilitative care, as well as several outpatient family, behavioral, and occupational health clinics in the region. Providence Hospital is part of the Ascension Health network.

	Annual Growth	06/08	06/09	06/10	06/15	06/16
Sales ($mil.)	(0.6%)	–	230.6	235.1	212.4	221.2
Net income ($ mil.)	–	–	(13.5)	8.1	16.3	9.3
Market value ($ mil.)	–	–	–	–	–	–
Employees	–	–	–	–	–	2,517

PROVIDENCE ST. JOSEPH HEALTH

1801 LIND AVE SW
RENTON, WA 980573368
Phone: 425 525-3355
Fax: –
Web: www.providence.org

CEO: Kevin Brooks
CFO: Jo A Escasa-Haigh
HR: Susan Marshall
FYE: December 31
Type: Private

Providence St. Joseph Health is a not-for-profit health system that operates more than 50 hospitals and over 1,000 clinics, and many other health and educational services across seven Western US ? Alaska, California, Montana, New Mexico, Oregon, Texas, and Washington. Providence affiliate includes Covenant Health, Facey Medical Group, Kadlec, Pacific Medical Centers, and Swedish Health Services.

PROVIDENT FINANCIAL HOLDINGS, INC. NMS: PROV

3756 Central Avenue
Riverside, CA 92506
Phone: 951 686-6060
Fax: –
Web: www.myprovident.com

CEO: –
CFO: –
HR: –
FYE: June 30
Type: Public

Provident Financial Holdings is the holding company for Provident Savings Bank, which operates more than a dozen branches in Southern California's Riverside and San Bernardino counties. Catering to individuals and small to midsized businesses, the bank offers such standard retail products as checking and savings accounts, money market accounts, and CDs, as well as retirement planning services. Real estate loans including single-family, multifamily, and commercial mortgages and construction loans make up essentially all of the company's loan portfolio. Single-family residential mortgages make up more than half of all loans.

	Annual Growth	06/19	06/20	06/21	06/22	06/23
Assets ($mil.)	5.3%	1,084.9	1,176.8	1,183.6	1,187.0	1,332.9
Net income ($ mil.)	18.1%	4.4	7.7	7.6	9.1	8.6
Market value ($ mil.)	(11.7%)	147.8	94.4	121.6	104.5	89.8
Employees	(3.7%)	187	178	161	179	161

PROVIDENT FINANCIAL SERVICES INC
NYS: PFS

239 Washington Street
Jersey City, NJ 07302
Phone: 732 590-9200
Fax: -
Web: www.provident.bank

CEO: -
CFO: Thomas M Lyons
HR: -
FYE: December 31
Type: Public

Provident Financial Services is the holding company of Provident Bank. The bank is a New Jersey-chartered capital stock savings bank operating full-service branch offices throughout northern and central New Jersey. The bank attracts deposits from the general public and businesses primarily in the areas surrounding its banking offices and uses those funds, together with funds generated from operations and borrowings, to originate commercial real estate loans, commercial business loans, residential mortgage loans, and consumer loans. The bank invests in mortgage-backed securities and other permissible investments. Also, the bank provides fiduciary and wealth management services through its wholly owned subsidiary, Beacon Trust Company and insurance brokerage services through its wholly owned subsidiary, SB One Insurance Agency, Inc. The company's Provident Investment Services subsidiary sells life and health insurance and wealth and asset management.

	Annual Growth	12/19	12/20	12/21	12/22	12/23
Assets ($mil.)	9.7%	9,808.6	12,920	13,781	13,783	14,211
Net income ($ mil.)	3.3%	112.6	97.0	167.9	175.6	128.4
Market value ($ mil.)	(7.5%)	1,862.0	1,356.6	1,829.5	1,613.5	1,361.9
Employees	3.0%	1,015	1,200	1,159	1,153	1,142

PROXIM WIRELESS CORP.
NBB: PRXM

1561 Buckeye Drive
Milpitas, CA 95035
Phone: 408 383-7600
Fax: 408 383-7680
Web: www.proxim.com

CEO: -
CFO: Steve Button
HR: Ginger Macadaeg
FYE: December 31
Type: Public

Proxim Wireless works without a wire when it builds nets. The company provides broadband wireless network equipment, including radios, bridges, and access gear. Communication carriers and service providers, enterprises, government agencies, schools, and health care providers use its products to offer network access, build video surveillance and public safety systems, and provide telecom backhaul connections. Proxim sells its products worldwide through distributors, resellers, systems integrators, and OEMs. Its engineering team works with channel partners and end users.

	Annual Growth	12/05	12/06	12/07	12/08	12/09
Sales ($mil.)	(15.8%)	59.0	75.4	66.3	49.0	29.7
Net income ($ mil.)	-	(11.2)	(23.2)	(19.1)	(10.0)	(7.4)
Market value ($ mil.)	(44.7%)	0.7	0.5	0.2	0.0	0.0
Employees	(8.2%)	258	240	219	203	183

PRUDENTIAL ANNUITIES LIFE ASSURANCE CORP

Ten Exchange Place, Suite 2210
Jersey City, NJ 07302
Phone: 615 981-8801
Fax: -
Web: www.investor.prudential.com

CEO: Alon Neches
CFO: Jeffrey Condit
HR: -
FYE: December 31
Type: Public

Prudential Annuities Life Assurance has a name that fits -- the company is the annuities business unit of life insurance giant Prudential Financial. It offers variable and fixed annuities, and other retirement and long-term investment products and services. Prudential Annuities Life Assurance's products are distributed through independent financial planners, brokers, and banks. It holds the lead position in the US variable annuities market; its variable annuities are distributed by Prudential Annuities Distributors. The company, which is part of Prudential Financial's US Retirement Solutions and Investment Management Division, targets US residents with a household income level of above $100,000.

	Annual Growth	12/17	12/18	12/19	12/20	12/21
Assets ($mil.)	(0.6%)	59,961	54,678	58,835	64,275	58,578
Net income ($ mil.)	-	(83.5)	1,682.7	(989.3)	(3,169.3)	4,965.4
Market value ($ mil.)	-	-	-	-	-	-
Employees	-	-	-	-	-	-

PRUDENTIAL FINANCIAL INC
NYS: PRU

751 Broad Street
Newark, NJ 07102
Phone: 973 802-6000
Fax: -
Web: www.investor.prudential.com

CEO: Charles F Lowrey
CFO: Kenneth Y Tanji
HR: -
FYE: December 31
Type: Public

Prudential Financial is a financial wellness leader and premier global investment manager with around $1.3 trillion of assets under management and operates in the US, Asia, Europe, and Latin America. The company, through its subsidiaries and affiliates, offers financial products and services such as life insurance, annuities, retirement-related products and services, mutual funds and investment management. Prudential Financial offers these products and services to individual and institutional customers through proprietary and third-party distribution networks. The company generates roughly 65% of revenue in the US.

	Annual Growth	12/19	12/20	12/21	12/22	12/23
Assets ($mil.)	(5.3%)	896,552	940,722	937,582	689,917	721,123
Net income ($ mil.)	(12.2%)	4,186.0	(374.0)	7,724.0	(1,438.0)	2,488.0
Market value ($ mil.)	2.6%	33,673	28,044	38,882	35,728	37,254
Employees	(5.7%)	51,511	41,671	40,916	39,854	40,658

PRUDENTIAL OVERALL SUPPLY

1661 ALTON PKWY
IRVINE, CA 926064801
Phone: 949 250-4855
Fax: -
Web: www.prudentialuniforms.com

CEO: -
CFO: -
HR: -
FYE: December 31
Type: Private

Prudential works to outfit every member of your organization. From uniforms to career apparel, Prudential Overall Supply rents, sells, and leases workwear to those in food service, health care, manufacturing, and the government. The company also rents and sells industrial-grade products (entrance and logo mats) and janitorial supplies (dust mops, paper towels, and cleansers). In addition to its products, Prudential offers industrial cleaning and laundering services. The company operates about 30 branches in the US, more than half of which are located in California, and sells its products online and through catalogs. Prudential has been family-owned and -operated since its founding in 1932.

PRWT SERVICES, INC.

1835 MARKET ST STE 800
PHILADELPHIA, PA 191032919
Phone: 215 569-8810
Fax: -
Web: www.prwt.com

CEO: Malik Majeed
CFO: Don Peloso
HR: -
FYE: December 31
Type: Private

Vowels are overrated. PRWT Services provides outsourced customer support services to a variety of industries. Services include payment processing, call center services, document processing, claims administration, mailroom operations, and other technical support services. PRWT also provides toll operations services for Delaware River Authority and fulfillment of stationary, forms, envelopes, business cards, and other business supplies. PRWT's subsidiaries include U.S. Facilities (facilities maintenance and management) and Cherokee Pharmaceuticals (pharmaceutical ingredients manufacturer). PRWT considered forming a subsidiary and merging with KBL Healthcare Acquisition Corp. but the deal fell through in July 2009.

	Annual Growth	12/03	12/04	12/05	12/06	12/10
Sales ($mil.)	5.4%	-	-	68.9	66.5	89.8
Net income ($ mil.)	60.2%	-	-	0.7	0.2	7.7
Market value ($ mil.)	-	-	-	-	-	-
Employees	-	-	-	-	-	1,312

PS BUSINESS PARKS INC
NBB: PSBX P

345 Park Avenue
New York, NY 10154
Phone: 212 583-5000
Fax: –
Web: www.psbusinessparks.com

CEO: Luke Petherbridge
CFO: Matthew L Ostrower
HR: –
FYE: December 31
Type: Public

PS Business Parks is a self-managed real estate investment trust (REIT) that owns, operates, acquires and develops commercial properties, primarily multi-tenant industrial, industrial-flex and low-rise suburban office space. The REIT owns more than 470 business parks in California, Virginia, Maryland, Washington, Florida, and Texas. Its portfolio includes some 20.6 million sq. ft. of multi-tenant industrial and office space, including light manufacturing plants, warehouses, distribution centers, and research and development facilities.

	Annual Growth	12/19	12/20	12/21*	07/22*	12/22
Sales ($mil.)	(26.0%)	429.8	415.6	438.7	246.2	174.2
Net income ($ mil.)	–	175.0	173.5	448.8	130.0	(174.7)
Market value ($ mil.)	(19.8%)	0.0	0.0	0.0	0.0	0.0
Employees	–	155	155	156	–	–

*Fiscal year change

PSCU, LLC

560 CARILLON PKWY
SAINT PETERSBURG, FL 337161294
Phone: 727 572-8822
Fax: –
Web: www.pscu.com

CEO: Chuck Fagan
CFO: –
HR: Darren Williams
FYE: September 30
Type: Private

PSCU (Payment Systems for Credit Unions), the nation's premier payments CUSO, supports the success of 1,900 credit unions representing more than 5.4 billion transactions annually. PSCU's payment processing, risk management, data and analytics, loyalty programs, digital banking, marketing, strategic consulting and mobile platforms help deliver possibilities and seamless member experiences. Comprehensive, 24/7/365 member support is provided by contact centers located throughout the US. Founded in 1977, PSCU was formed by five leading credit union CEOs from GTE Federal Credit Union, Suncoast Schools Federal Credit Union, Pinellas County Teachers Credit Union, Publix Employees Federal Credit Union, and Railroad & Industrial Federal Credit Union.

	Annual Growth	12/10	12/11	12/12*	09/16	09/18
Sales ($mil.)	4.2%	–	–	377.0	458.8	481.7
Net income ($ mil.)	(18.4%)	–	–	38.6	28.1	11.4
Market value ($ mil.)	–	–	–	–	–	–
Employees	–	–	–	–	–	2,100

*Fiscal year change

PSEG POWER LLC

80 Park Plaza
Newark, NJ 07102
Phone: 973 430-7000
Fax: –
Web: www.pseg.com

CEO: Ralph Izzo
CFO: Daniel J Cregg
HR: –
FYE: December 31
Type: Public

Power player PSEG Power does not play with power, it markets it for profit. The company is the independent power production and energy marketing subsidiary of Public Service Enterprise Group (PSEG). The unit owns and/or manages about 25 power stations in Connecticut, New Jersey, New York, and Pennsylvania. It oversees PSEG Nuclear LLC (which operates the Salem and Hope Creek generating stations in New Jersey and owns 50% of the Peach Bottom plant in Pennsylvania) and PSEG Fossil LLC (which has gas, oil, coal, and natural gas power plants). PSEG Power has installed capacity of more than 13,466 MW. Its PSEG Energy Resources and Trade unit buys and sells wholesale power, natural gas, and other energy commodities.

	Annual Growth	12/16	12/17	12/18	12/19	12/20
Sales ($mil.)	(2.5%)	4,023.0	3,930.0	4,146.0	4,385.0	3,634.0
Net income ($ mil.)	139.7%	18.0	479.0	365.0	468.0	594.0
Market value ($ mil.)	–	–	–	–	–	–
Employees	30.1%	2,714	2,367	2,122	2,033	7,786

PSI SERVICES INC.

18000 W 105TH ST
OLATHE, KS 660617543
Phone: 913 895-4600
Fax: –
Web: www.psiexams.com

CEO: Steve Tapp
CFO: Jeff Moxie
HR: –
FYE: December 31
Type: Private

If you think taking tests is hard, try writing them. Founded in 1982 by the National Board for Respiratory Care, Applied Measurement Professionals (AMP) offers test development, assessment, research, and management services to corporations, government agencies, associations, and other organizations. AMP conducts job analysis studies -- collecting and analyzing information about the nature of a given job -- designed to help clients define the characteristics and competencies for particular positions. Based on these analyses, the company develops assessment tests and professional licensing and certification exams, and it helps clients screen job candidates by assessing more than 250,000 candidates each year.

	Annual Growth	12/09	12/10	12/11	12/12	12/13
Sales ($mil.)	6.1%	–	–	24.4	26.5	27.5
Net income ($ mil.)	28.3%	–	–	0.3	0.6	0.6
Market value ($ mil.)	–	–	–	–	–	–
Employees	–	–	–	–	–	170

PSYCHEMEDICS CORP.
NAS: PMD

289 Great Road
Acton, MA 01720
Phone: 978 206-8220
Fax: –
Web: www.psychemedics.com

CEO: Raymond C Kubacki
CFO: –
HR: Hadeel Sarhan
FYE: December 31
Type: Public

Beware of giving a lock of hair as a keepsake -- it could end up at Psychemedics, which provides drug testing services through the analysis of hair samples. Its tests, which it markets under the brand name RIAH (or Radioimmunoassay of Hair), not only reveal that a substance has been consumed, but also detect patterns of use over time; the tests look for cocaine, marijuana, PCP, Ecstasy, and opiates. The company's primary market is employers, who use the service for pre-employment screening, as well as random testing of current employees. Psychemedics also sells its service to hundreds of schools nationwide (and in some foreign countries) and offers a service to parents worried that their kids might be on drugs.

	Annual Growth	12/18	12/19	12/20	12/21	12/22
Sales ($mil.)	(12.3%)	42.7	37.7	21.4	24.9	25.2
Net income ($ mil.)	–	4.6	1.5	(3.9)	(0.7)	(1.1)
Market value ($ mil.)	(25.4%)	90.2	52.0	28.9	39.9	27.9
Employees	(14.6%)	250	204	138	139	133

PTC INC
NMS: PTC

121 Seaport Boulevard
Boston, MA 02210
Phone: 781 370-5000
Fax: –
Web: www.ptc.com

CEO: James Heppelmann
CFO: Kristian Talvitie
HR: –
FYE: September 30
Type: Public

PTC is a global software and services company that serves industrial companies through its offerings in CAD, PLM, the IoT, and AR that help customers digitize operations and collaborate. In computer aided design (CAD), its Creo offering is used to create 3D computer models for products ranging from engines to phones. PTC's Windchill software suite for product lifecycle management (PLM) enables collaborative content and process management over the internet. With ThingWorx, PTC provides a platform for developing applications for the Internet of Things (IoT). The augmented reality (AR) product, Vuforia Studio, overlays digital information such as repair instructions onto the view of physical objects and processes. The Americas account for around 45% of PTC's revenue.

	Annual Growth	09/19	09/20	09/21	09/22	09/23
Sales ($mil.)	13.7%	1,255.6	1,458.4	1,807.2	1,933.3	2,097.1
Net income ($ mil.)	–	(27.5)	130.7	476.9	313.1	245.5
Market value ($ mil.)	20.1%	8,102.9	9,830.9	14,237	12,431	16,838
Employees	4.5%	6,055	6,243	6,709	6,503	7,231

PTC THERAPEUTICS INC

NMS: PTCT

100 Corporate Court
South Plainfield, NJ 07080
Phone: 908 222-7000
Fax: –
Web: www.ptcbio.com

CEO: Stuart W Peltz
CFO: Emily Hill
HR: –
FYE: December 31
Type: Public

PTC Therapeutics is a science-driven global biopharmaceutical company focused on the discovery, development and commercialization of clinically-differentiated medicines that provide benefits to patients with rare disorders. The company has a portfolio pipeline that includes several commercial products and product candidates in various stages of development, including clinical, pre-clinical and research and discovery stages, focused on the development of new treatments for multiple therapeutic areas for rare diseases. It holds the rights for the commercialization of Tegsedi and Waylivra for the treatment of rare diseases in countries in Latin America and the Caribbean pursuant to its collaboration and license agreement with a subsidiary of Ionis Pharmaceuticals, Inc. Its US operations generate the majority of its revenue.

	Annual Growth	12/19	12/20	12/21	12/22	12/23
Sales ($mil.)	32.2%	307.0	380.8	538.6	698.8	937.8
Net income ($ mil.)	–	(251.6)	(438.2)	(523.9)	(559.0)	(626.6)
Market value ($ mil.)	(13.0%)	3,636.3	4,620.5	3,015.5	2,889.8	2,086.5
Employees	6.7%	761	1,089	1,177	1,410	988

PUBCO CORP.

NBB: PUBO

3830 Kelley Avenue
Cleveland, OH 44114
Phone: 216 881-5300
Fax: 216 881-8380
Web: –

CEO: –
CFO: Maria Szubski
HR: –
FYE: December 31
Type: Public

Put on your hard hat. Allied Construction Products offers machinery and other products to companies in the construction and mining industries. It has more than 200 distributors located throughout the US and Canada which provide equipment such as excavators, loader/backhoes, skid-steers and mini-excavator including hydraulic breakers and compactor/drivers. The company also offers reconditioned equipment and support services including product manuals, a certified rebuild program and a technical service group to answer questions. The company was founded in 1942.

	Annual Growth	12/97	12/98	12/99	12/00	12/01
Sales ($mil.)	0.5%	53.9	68.7	67.4	59.3	55.0
Net income ($ mil.)	(34.0%)	10.2	7.3	9.3	3.3	1.9
Market value ($ mil.)	(1.2%)	36.5	31.7	28.2	24.9	34.9
Employees	(6.1%)	335	–	275	–	260

PUBLIC BROADCASTING SERVICE

1225 S CLARK ST
ARLINGTON, VA 222024371
Phone: 703 739-5000
Fax: –
Web: www.pbs.org

CEO: Paula A Kerger
CFO: Barbara L Landes
HR: –
FYE: June 30
Type: Private

PBS is a private, nonprofit corporation, founded in 1969, whose members are America's public TV stations -- noncommercial, educational licensees that operate more than 330 PBS member stations and serve all 50 states, Puerto Rico, US Virgin Islands, Guam, and American Samoa. PBS offers programming that expands the minds of children, documentaries that open up new worlds, non-commercialized news programs that keep citizens informed on world events, and cultures and programs that expose America to the worlds of music, theater, dance and art. It is a multi-platform media organization that serves Americans through television, mobile and connected devices, the web, in the classroom, and more.

	Annual Growth	06/13	06/14	06/15	06/21	06/22
Sales ($mil.)	0.1%	–	539.6	473.3	502.1	543.0
Net income ($ mil.)	(10.7%)	–	89.9	(46.9)	53.4	36.2
Market value ($ mil.)	–	–	–	–	–	–
Employees		–	–	–	–	507

PUBLIC COMMUNICATIONS SERVICES, INC.

11859 WILSHIRE BLVD STE 600
LOS ANGELES, CA 900256616
Phone: 310 231-1000
Fax: –
Web: –

CEO: Paul Jennings
CFO: Dennis Komai
HR: –
FYE: December 31
Type: Private

Public Communications Services (PCS) designs and installs inmate telephone systems for state, federal, and county correctional facilities across the US. Its systems feature collect, pre-paid, and debit calling, as well as automated call processing and security features like blocking of certain phone numbers. Clients can also use the company's proprietary systems management software, called SOPHIA, to run reports on inmate usage and to monitor and record conversations. Customers include the Ventura County, California Sheriff's Department and the Federal Bureau of Prisons.

	Annual Growth	12/02	12/03	12/04	12/07	12/08
Sales ($mil.)	10.1%	–	49.2	34.7	80.5	79.7
Net income ($ mil.)	21.2%	–	1.8	2.8	3.8	4.8
Market value ($ mil.)	–	–	–	–	–	–
Employees		–	–	–	–	150

PUBLIC HEALTH SOLUTIONS

40 WORTH ST FL 5
NEW YORK, NY 100132955
Phone: 646 619-6400
Fax: –
Web: www.healthsolutions.org

CEO: Ellen Rautenberg
CFO: –
HR: –
FYE: December 31
Type: Private

Public Heath Solutions (formerly Medical and Health Research Association of New York City) is here to help. Public Health Solutions (PHS) is a not-for-profit organization that works with the NYC Department of Health to create and administer projects aimed at providing better healthcare to the city's low-income at-risk population. It helps about 200,000 people a year with studies like the Human Papillomavirus Screening Project and others looking at disease awareness and prevention in minority groups. Services include women's and children's health, HIV/AIDS health care, smoking cessation counseling, and access to health care. The organization was founded in 1957 to conduct health research projects.

	Annual Growth	12/12	12/13	12/15	12/19	12/21
Sales ($mil.)	1.9%	–	202.0	207.0	–	234.2
Net income ($ mil.)	(3.3%)	–	2.9	0.4	–	2.2
Market value ($ mil.)	–	–	–	–	–	–
Employees		–	–	–	–	650

PUBLIC LIBRARY OF SCIENCE

1265 BATTERY ST STE 200
SAN FRANCISCO, CA 941116216
Phone: 415 624-1200
Fax: –
Web: www.plos.org

CEO: Alison Mudditt
CFO: –
HR: –
FYE: December 31
Type: Private

What Bill Nye the Science Guy can't answer, perhaps The Public Library of Science (PLoS) can. PLoS is a not-for-profit publishing organization that makes scientific and medical research literature a public resource. While a majority of such literature is accessible only to institutions that can afford to pay for subscriptions, PLoS is using a model known as open access whereby it publishes journals of work from scientists and physicians and makes them available to readers for free online. PLoS ONE is a peer-reviewed journal, while PLoS Biology and PLoS Medicine are editor-selected journals. Others PLoS journals cover specific topics, including computational biology, genetics, pathogens, and tropical diseases.

	Annual Growth	12/14	12/15	12/16	12/21	12/22
Sales ($mil.)	(3.1%)	–	43.5	37.4	38.1	35.0
Net income ($ mil.)	16.2%	–	0.6	(1.7)	5.6	1.6
Market value ($ mil.)	–	–	–	–	–	–
Employees		–	–	–	–	180

PUBLIC RADIO INTERNATIONAL, INC.

15 S 5TH ST STE 1020
MINNEAPOLIS, MN 554021061
Phone: 612 338-5000
Fax: –
Web: www.theworld.org

CEO: Marguerite Hoffman
CFO: –
HR: –
FYE: June 30
Type: Private

Public Radio International (PRI) is an independent not-for-profit producer and distributor of radio programming that serves about 800 affiliate radio stations around the country. Its original programming includes such shows as Studio 360, This American Life, and The Travis Smiley Show. PRI also distributes programming from the BBC World Service (the international radio service of the British Broadcasting Corporation). In addition to serving public radio affiliates, the company distributes programming through satellite radio service Sirius XM Radio and online. PRI is supported by station fees, corporate underwriting, and grants from individuals and foundations. It was founded in 1983. In 2018 the company announced it was merging with content and audio technology provider PRX.

	Annual Growth	06/15	06/16	06/17	06/20	06/21
Sales ($mil.)	(38.7%)	–	22.6	16.1	6.2	2.0
Net income ($ mil.)	–	–	4.2	(2.6)	(8.3)	(2.4)
Market value ($ mil.)	–	–	–	–	–	–
Employees	–	–	–	–	–	45

PUBLIC RELATIONS ADVERTISING COMPANY

2 N NEVADA AVE STE 1400
COLORADO SPRINGS, CO 809031700
Phone: 719 473-0704
Fax: –
Web: www.vladimirjones.com

CEO: Nechie Hall
CFO: Trudy Rowe
HR: Kathy Guetlein
FYE: December 31
Type: Private

Need advertising? Enter Jones, Vladimir Jones. More than just a creative name, the company provides creative ad services in TV, radio, print, outdoor and interactive media as well as public relations services from offices in Denver, and Colorado Springs. Vladimir Jones serves both regional and national accounts, working with such clients as American Heart Association, Colorado PGA, Don King Productions, and the US Golf Association Foundation. The firm was founded in 1970 as Public Relations and Advertising Company (PRACO) by husband and wife team Jim and Nechie Hall. In mid-2008, it rebranded itself under the more provocative name Vladimir Jones. No such person exists with the name.

	Annual Growth	12/09	12/10	12/11	12/12	12/13
Sales ($mil.)	3.3%	–	–	27.7	31.3	29.6
Net income ($ mil.)	98.3%	–	–	0.2	0.7	0.7
Market value ($ mil.)	–	–	–	–	–	–
Employees	–	–	–	–	–	75

PUBLIC SERVICE COMPANY OF NEW HAMPSHIRE

780 NORTH COMMERCIAL ST
MANCHESTER, NH 031011134
Phone: 603 669-4000
Fax: –
Web: –

CEO: Werner J Schweiger
CFO: Philip J Lembo
HR: –
FYE: December 31
Type: Private

The public service that Public Service Company of New Hampshire (PSNH) provides is supplying electricity across the Granite State. The company provides electric utility services to about 500,000 homes and businesses in a 5,630-sq.-mi. area that encompasses more than 210 New Hampshire communities. Although the Eversource Energy subsidiary owns three fossil-fueled and nine hydroelectric power plants that generate about 1,200 MW of capacity for transition and default energy services, it also has contracts to purchase power and buy it on the open market.

PUBLIC SERVICE COMPANY OF OKLAHOMA

NBB: PSOK

1 Riverside Plaza
Columbus, OH 43215-2373
Phone: 614 716-1000
Fax: –
Web: www.aep.com

CEO: Nicholas K Akins
CFO: Brian X Tierney
HR: –
FYE: December 31
Type: Public

Where the wavin' wheat can sure smell sweet, Public Service Company of Oklahoma helps its customers to beat the heat. The utility serves approximately 540,000 homes and businesses in eastern and southwestern Oklahoma. The American Electric Power (AEP) subsidiary operates more than 22,080 miles of electric transmission and distribution lines in eastern and southwestern Oklahoma. The utility also has about 4,230 MW of capacity from interests in fossil-fueled power plants, and it markets wholesale electricity to other utilities and energy companies in the region. it also has wind energy assets.

	Annual Growth	12/19	12/20	12/21	12/22	12/23
Sales ($mil.)	7.5%	1,481.8	1,266.1	1,474.4	1,874.7	1,977.0
Net income ($ mil.)	11.0%	137.6	123.0	141.1	167.6	208.8
Market value ($ mil.)	–	–	–	–	–	–
Employees	–	1,097	1,023	1,018	1,030	–

PUBLIC SERVICE ENTERPRISE GROUP INC

NYS: PEG

80 Park Plaza
Newark, NJ 07102
Phone: 973 430-7000
Fax: –
Web: www.pseg.com

CEO: Ralph Izzo
CFO: Daniel J Cregg
HR: –
FYE: December 31
Type: Public

Public Service Enterprise Group's (PSEG) is an energy company with a diversified business mix. Its operations are located primarily in the Mid-Atlantic US. Regulated subsidiary Public Service Electric and Gas (PSE&G) transmits and distributes electricity to 2.3 million customers and natural gas to 1.9 million customers in New Jersey. Subsidiary PSEG Power operates power generating plants and sells its energy wholesale to PSE&G and others. PSEG Power also owns and operates around 3,765 MW direct current (dc) of PV solar generation facilities. PSEG Power also has a 50% ownership interest in about 210 MW oil-fired generation facility in Hawaii.

	Annual Growth	12/19	12/20	12/21	12/22	12/23
Sales ($mil.)	2.8%	10,076	9,603.0	9,722.0	9,800.0	11,237
Net income ($ mil.)	10.9%	1,693.0	1,905.0	(648.0)	1,031.0	2,563.0
Market value ($ mil.)	0.9%	29,407	29,033	33,232	30,512	30,453
Employees	(0.9%)	12,992	12,788	12,684	12,525	12,543

PUBLIC STORAGE

NYS: PSA

701 Western Avenue
Glendale, CA 91201-2349
Phone: 818 244-8080
Fax: 818 244-0581
Web: www.publicstorage.com

CEO: Joseph D Russell Jr
CFO: H T Boyle
HR: –
FYE: December 31
Type: Public

Public Storage is one of the largest self-storage companies in the US. It operates almost 2,870 storage facilities under the Public Storage brand comprising an aggregate of almost 205 million net rentable sq. ft. of storage space in the US and about 265 facilities in Europe under the Shurgard brand. The REIT's principal business activities include the ownership and operation of self-storage facilities and other related operations including tenant reinsurance and third-party self-storage management. Public Storage also sells supplies such as locks and cardboard boxes.

	Annual Growth	12/19	12/20	12/21	12/22	12/23
Sales ($mil.)	12.2%	2,846.8	2,915.1	3,415.8	4,182.2	4,517.7
Net income ($ mil.)	9.0%	1,520.5	1,357.2	1,953.3	4,349.1	2,148.3
Market value ($ mil.)	9.4%	37,411	40,568	65,799	49,221	53,580
Employees	(2.3%)	5,900	5,400	5,800	5,900	5,380

PUBLIC UTILITIES BOARD OF THE CITY OF BROWNSVILLE, TEXAS

1425 ROBINHOOD ST
BROWNSVILLE, TX 785214230
Phone: 956 983-6100
Fax: –
Web: www.brownsville-pub.com

CEO: Marilyn D Gilbert
CFO: Leandro G Garcia
HR: –
FYE: September 30
Type: Private

This PUB has no beer. Brownsville Public Utilities Board (Brownsville PUB) is a municipally-owned utility company providing electric, water, and wastewater services to residential and commercial customers in Brownsville, Texas. Brownsville PUB serves 46,000 with electric service and 47,000 with water and wastewater service. The utility's two water treatment plants have the capacity to provide 40 million gallons of treated water per day. It gets its water supply from the Rio Grande. The utility's wastewater system has 174 lift stations and two treatment plants.

	Annual Growth	09/18	09/19	09/20	09/21	09/22
Sales ($mil.)	16.2%	–	–	198.5	313.0	268.0
Net income ($ mil.)	83.9%	–	–	10.3	(49.4)	34.9
Market value ($ mil.)	–	–	–	–	–	–
Employees	–	–	–	–	–	604

PUBLIC UTILITY DISTRICT 1 OF CLARK COUNTY

1200 FORT VANCOUVER WAY
VANCOUVER, WA 986633527
Phone: 360 992-3000
Fax: –
Web: www.clarkpublicutilities.com

CEO: Wayne Nelson
CFO: –
HR: –
FYE: December 31
Type: Private

There are no "we're No 1" signs waving at this publicly minded company's head office. Public Utility District No. 1 of Clark County (Clark Public Utilities) provides utility services to residents and businesses in Clark County, Washington. Clark Public Utilities transmits and distributes electricity to more than 184,100 customers; the company operates a 250-MW gas-fired power plant but purchases the bulk of its power from the Bonneville Power Administration. Clark Public Utilities also distributes water to more than 30,640 customers and collects and treats wastewater for the City of La Center, Washington.

	Annual Growth	12/16	12/17	12/18	12/19	12/21
Sales ($mil.)	3.1%	–	502.1	481.7	479.5	566.3
Net income ($ mil.)	2.8%	–	45.7	38.1	28.3	50.9
Market value ($ mil.)	–	–	–	–	–	–
Employees	–	–	–	–	–	325

PUBLIC UTILITY DISTRICT 1 OF SNOHOMISH COUNTY

2320 CALIFORNIA ST
EVERETT, WA 982013750
Phone: 425 257-9288
Fax: –
Web: www.snopud.com

CEO: –
CFO: –
HR: –
FYE: December 31
Type: Private

Keeping its customers' safety is priority No. 1 at Public Utility District No. 1 of Snohomish County, Washington (Snohomish County PUD), which distributes electricity to over 360,000 electric customers in Washington State. The utility, the second largest PUD in the state, with over 2,200 sq. ml. service area, purchases most of its power supply from third parties (Bonneville Power Administration and other producers). It sells surplus power into the wholesale power transactions to balance its supply load. Snohomish County PUD also serves more than 21,000 water utility customers.

PUBLIC UTILITY DISTRICT 2 GRANT COUNTY

30 C ST SW
EPHRATA, WA 988231876
Phone: 509 754-0500
Fax: –
Web: www.grantpud.org

CEO: Kevin Nordt
CFO: –
HR: –
FYE: December 31
Type: Private

Utilitarian sounding Public Utility District No. 2 of Grant County, Washington, probably used up its initial budget before it could hire a team of branding and identity consultants. But its dour name does not stop the power provider (commonly referred to as Grant County PUD) from operating two hydroelectric power plants on the Columbia River (the Priest Rapids and Wanapum dams, with 2,000 MW of generating capacity) and distributing electricity to more than 46,600 retail customers in Washington's Grant County. The district, also sells wholesale power to 23 Pacific Northwest utilities and is developing a wholesale fiber-optic data network (with about 8,290 end-users).

	Annual Growth	11/08	11/09*	12/18	12/19	12/22
Sales ($mil.)	2.7%	–	291.3	–	321.2	409.8
Net income ($ mil.)	11.2%	–	22.9	–	86.3	90.4
Market value ($ mil.)	–	–	–	–	–	–
Employees	–	–	–	–	–	624

*Fiscal year change

PUBLIC UTILITY DISTRICT NO 1 OF COWLITZ COUNTY

961 12TH AVE
LONGVIEW, WA 986322507
Phone: 360 577-7507
Fax: –
Web: www.cowlitzpud.org

CEO: –
CFO: Royce Hagelstein
HR: –
FYE: December 31
Type: Private

Being Number One is old hat for Public Utility District No. 1 of Cowlitz County, Washington (or Cowlitz County Public Utility District), a Depression era institution that provides electric utility services to 47,400 customers (including 42,400 residential customers and 5,200 commercial clients) in its service territory. The municipal utility also serves more than 3,800 Longview-Kelso area water utility customers. Like 27 other PUDs in Washington state, Cowlitz County Public Utility District has the authority to offer electric, water, wastewater, and wholesale telecommunication service.

	Annual Growth	12/09	12/10	12/15	12/16	12/17
Sales ($mil.)	3.5%	–	220.3	138.9	278.7	279.9
Net income ($ mil.)	3.5%	–	2.1	(2.4)	3.8	2.6
Market value ($ mil.)	–	–	–	–	–	–
Employees	–	–	–	–	–	170

PUBLIC UTILITY DISTRICT NO. 1 OF CHELAN COUNTY

203 OLDS STATION RD
WENATCHEE, WA 988015908
Phone: 509 663-8121
Fax: –
Web: www.chelanpud.org

CEO: –
CFO: –
HR: –
FYE: December 31
Type: Private

It's Number One! Public Utility District No. 1 of Chelan County, Washington (Chelan County PUD) provides power and water to residents of the county located in the middle of the Evergreen State. The utility operates three hydroelectric generation facilities on or near the Columbia River that have a combined capacity of 1,988 MW. About 30% of the district's electricity goes to its more than 48,000 residential, commercial, and industrial customers; the rest is sold wholesale to other utilities operating in the northwestern US. Chelan County PUD also provides water and wastewater services to about 5,900 customers. The company's major power purchasers serve 7 million homes and businesses in the Northwest.

	Annual Growth	12/17	12/18	12/19	12/20	12/22
Sales ($mil.)	11.1%	–	386.5	385.2	353.5	589.9
Net income ($ mil.)	17.1%	–	105.3	113.9	76.6	198.2
Market value ($ mil.)	–	–	–	–	–	–
Employees	–	–	–	–	–	841

PUBLISHING OFFICE, US GOVERNMENT

732 N CAPITOL ST NW
WASHINGTON, DC 204010002
Phone: 202 512-0000
Fax: –
Web: www.gpo.gov

CEO: –
CFO: Steven T Shedd
HR: –
FYE: September 30
Type: Private

The US Government Printing Office (GPO) keeps America informed in print and online. The GPO is the Federal government's primary centralized resource for gathering, cataloging, producing, providing, and preserving published information in all its forms. Part of the legislative branch, the GPO offers Congress, the courts, and other government agencies centralized services to enable them to easily produce printed documents according to uniform Federal specifications. The GPO also offers the publications for sale to the public and makes them available at no cost through the Federal Depository Library Program. The GPO is run like a business and requires payment from its government customers for services rendered.

	Annual Growth	09/16	09/17	09/18	09/19	09/20
Sales ($mil.)	1.6%	–	874.3	874.5	937.4	915.9
Net income ($ mil.)	–	–	58.9	52.6	51.7	(14.3)
Market value ($ mil.)	–	–	–	–	–	–
Employees	–	–	–	–	–	1,880

PUBLIX SUPER MARKETS, INC.

3300 PUBLIX CORPORATE PKWY
LAKELAND, FL 338113311
Phone: 863 688-1188
Fax: –
Web: www.publix.com

CEO: Randall T Jones Sr
CFO: David P Phillips
HR: –
FYE: December 31
Type: Private

Publix Super Markets, Inc. is in the business of operating retail food supermarkets in Florida, Georgia, Alabama, South Carolina, Tennessee, North Carolina and Virginia. The company plans to expand its retail operations into Kentucky in 2023. Publix sells a variety of merchandise which includes grocery (including dairy, produce, floral, deli, bakery, meat and seafood), health and beauty care, general merchandise, pharmacy and other products and services. The company had a total of nearly 1,300 supermarkets at the end of 2022. The company was founded in 1930.

PUBLIX SUPER MARKETS, INC.

3300 Publix Corporate Parkway
Lakeland, FL 33811
Phone: 863 688-1188
Fax: –
Web: www.publix.com

CEO: Randall T Jones Sr
CFO: David P Phillips
HR: –
FYE: December 30
Type: Public

Publix Super Markets, Inc. is in the business of operating retail food supermarkets in Florida, Georgia, Alabama, South Carolina, Tennessee, North Carolina and Virginia. The company plans to expand its retail operations into Kentucky in 2023. Publix sells a variety of merchandise which includes grocery (including dairy, produce, floral, deli, bakery, meat and seafood), health and beauty care, general merchandise, pharmacy and other products and services. The company had a total of nearly 1,300 supermarkets at the end of 2022. The company was founded in 1930.

	Annual Growth	12/19	12/20	12/21	12/22	12/23
Sales ($mil.)	10.6%	38,463	45,204	48,394	54,942	57,534
Net income ($ mil.)	9.7%	3,005.4	3,971.8	4,412.2	2,918.0	4,349.0
Market value ($ mil.)	–	–	–	–	–	–
Employees	5.1%	207,000	227,000	232,000	242,000	253,000

PUERTO RICAN FAMILY INSTITUTE, INC.

145 W 15TH ST FL 2
NEW YORK, NY 100116701
Phone: 212 924-6320
Fax: –
Web: www.prfiorg.com

CEO: Maria E Girone
CFO: –
HR: –
FYE: June 30
Type: Private

The Puerto Rican Family Institute (PRFI) wants to keep families intact and healthy. It offers more than 20 social and health care programs to families who live in primarily Latino neighborhoods in New York and New Jersey, as well as Puerto Rico. Services include mental health treatment through clinics in the Bronx, Brooklyn, Jersey City, Manhattan, and Queens; crisis intervention; foster care placement prevention programs; and Head Start programs. PRFI also reaches out to the mentally and developmentally disabled by operating intermediate care and residential alternative facilities. The not-for-profit serves those infected with AIDS through counseling, psychiatric services, and case management.

	Annual Growth	06/14	06/15	06/16	06/20	06/22
Sales ($mil.)	2.6%	–	36.8	34.6	40.0	44.0
Net income ($ mil.)	24.9%	–	0.8	1.6	0.2	3.6
Market value ($ mil.)	–	–	–	–	–	–
Employees	–	–	–	–	–	515

PUGET ENERGY, INC.

355 110TH AVE NE
BELLEVUE, WA 980045862
Phone: 425 454-6363
Fax: –
Web: www.pugetenergy.com

CEO: Kimberly J Harris
CFO: Daniel A Doyle
HR: –
FYE: December 31
Type: Private

Puget Energy is the holding company for one of Washington State's largest utilities, Puget Sound Energy (PSE). The utility provides electricity to some 1.2 million customers and natural gas to over 869,530 customers across Washington. The company's electric power resources have a total capacity of some 6,565 MW. In addition, the utility is one of the nation's largest electric and natural gas utility.

	Annual Growth	12/18	12/19	12/20	12/21	12/22
Sales ($mil.)	7.5%	–	3,401.1	3,326.5	3,805.7	4,221.2
Net income ($ mil.)	31.0%	–	210.7	182.7	260.8	474.0
Market value ($ mil.)	–	–	–	–	–	–
Employees	–	–	–	–	–	2,700

PULMATRIX INC

36 Crosby Drive, Suite 100
Bedford, MA 02421
Phone: 781 357-2333
Fax: –
Web: www.pulmatrix.com

NAS: PULM
CEO: Ted Raad
CFO: William E Duke Jr
HR: –
FYE: December 31
Type: Public

Pulmatrix (formerly Ruthigen) is focused on developing and commercializing inhaled therapeutic products. Its pipeline portfolio is led by PUR0200, a phase II bronchodilator treatment for chronic obstructive pulmonary disease; and PUR1900, an anti-infective for the treatment of cystic fibrosis. Its proprietary dry powder delivery platform, iSPERSE (inhaled small particles easily respirable and emitted), requires no lactose carrier and can deliver very small to large doses. Ruthigen was formed 2013 as a subsidiary of Oculus Innovative Sciences. Oculus spun it off in a 2014 IPO, retaining a 48% stake in the firm. In 2015 Ruthigen acquired Pulmatrix (and its PUR0200/PUR1900 therapies) and took on the Pulmatrix name.

	Annual Growth	12/19	12/20	12/21	12/22	12/23
Sales ($mil.)	(2.0%)	7.9	12.6	5.2	6.1	7.3
Net income ($ mil.)	–	(20.6)	(19.3)	(20.2)	(18.8)	(14.1)
Market value ($ mil.)	21.3%	3.1	4.3	1.6	14.2	6.8
Employees	(1.1%)	23	22	25	29	22

PULSE ELECTRONICS CORPORATION

15255 INNOVATION DR STE 100
SAN DIEGO, CA 921283400
Phone: 858 674-8100
Fax: –
Web: www.pulseelectronics.com

CEO: Mark C Twaalfhoven
CFO: –
HR: Claudia Yeke
FYE: December 26
Type: Private

Pulse Electronics (formerly Technitrol) pulses with the desire to control electronic impulses. The company makes a variety of electronic components used in network, power, and wireless devices. Network products include passive magnetic components, including chokes, filters, transformers, and splitters. Power components include current and voltage sensors, ignition coils, power transformers, and magnetic devices. Its wireless devices are primarily antennas and mounting devices for handsets. Pulse Electronics has manufacturing facilities in China and the US. The company gets around 85% of its sales from outside the US.

PULTEGROUP INC

3350 Peachtree Road N.E., Suite 1500
Atlanta, GA 30326
Phone: 404 978-6400
Fax: –
Web: www.pultegroupinc.com

NYS: PHM

CEO: Ryan R Marshall
CFO: Robert T O'Shaughnessy
HR: Michelle Hairston
FYE: December 31
Type: Public

PulteGroup is one of the largest homebuilders in the US. The company targets a cross-section of home buyers nationwide by buying or optioning land to build single-family houses, duplexes, townhouses, and condominiums. Through its brands, which include Centex, Pulte Homes, Del Webb, DiVosta Homes, John Wieland Homes and Neighborhoods, and American West, PulteGroup offers a wide variety of home designs with varying levels of options and amenities to its major customer groups such as first-time, move-up, and active adult. The company sells its homes in more than 40 markets across roughly 25 states. Its homes go for an average selling price of $542,000. PulteGroup delivers home closing totaling roughly 29,100 homes.

	Annual Growth	12/19	12/20	12/21	12/22	12/23
Sales ($mil.)	12.0%	10,213	11,036	13,927	16,229	16,062
Net income ($ mil.)	26.5%	1,016.7	1,406.8	1,946.3	2,617.3	2,602.4
Market value ($ mil.)	27.7%	8,247.2	9,165.5	12,150	9,677.7	21,940
Employees	5.0%	5,245	5,249	6,182	6,524	6,382

PURADYN FILTER TECHNOLOGIES INC

2017 High Ridge Road
Boynton Beach, FL 33426
Phone: 561 547-9499
Fax: –
Web: www.puradyn.com

NBB: PFTI

CEO: Edward S Vittoria
CFO: –
HR: –
FYE: December 31
Type: Public

Check your oil? Puradyn Filter Technologies would like to. The company has developed a bypass oil filtration system that can be used in internal combustion engines and pieces of hydraulic equipment that rely on lubricating oil. The Puradyn system works in conjunction with a standard oil filter to remove solids as small as a micron (1/39 millionth of an inch), along with liquid and gaseous contaminants. Puradyn markets its filtration systems worldwide; target customers include OEMs, commercial trucking fleets, and operators of construction machinery. Puradyn has not been profitable, however, and the company's auditors have questioned whether it can stay in business.

	Annual Growth	12/15	12/16	12/17	12/18	12/19
Sales ($mil.)	(6.2%)	2.0	1.9	2.3	4.2	1.5
Net income ($ mil.)	–	(1.4)	(1.4)	(1.2)	(0.2)	(1.7)
Market value ($ mil.)	(7.0%)	2.6	5.5	0.9	4.1	2.0
Employees	(11.3%)	21	20	21	20	13

PURE BIOSCIENCE INC

771 Jamacha Rd., #512
El Cajon, CA 92019
Phone: 619 596-8600
Fax: 619 596-8790
Web: www.purebio.com

NBB: PURE

CEO: –
CFO: –
HR: –
FYE: July 31
Type: Public

PURE Bioscience is all about killing what's on the surface. The company makes and markets a patented low-toxicity disinfectant (Axenohl in its concentrated form, Axen, Axen30, or Axen50 in diluted form) approved for use in hospitals, restaurants, and schools, among other commercial and industrial locations. PURE's consumer sanitation products for home use are sold under the PureGreen 24 label. The company is also working to develop consumer products and drug treatments using the disinfectant's base compound, silver dihydrogen citrate, which it also sells as a product ingredient to other manufacturers. PURE Bioscience's products are marketed in countries around the globe.

	Annual Growth	07/19	07/20	07/21	07/22	07/23
Sales ($mil.)	(0.4%)	1.9	6.9	3.9	1.9	1.9
Net income ($ mil.)	–	(6.6)	0.0	(2.3)	(3.5)	(4.0)
Market value ($ mil.)	(28.5%)	36.4	160.0	47.0	22.3	9.5
Employees	2.2%	11	11	11	16	12

PURE CYCLE CORP.

34501 E. Quincy Avenue, Building 65, Suite A
Watkins, CO 80137
Phone: 303 292-3456
Fax: –
Web: www.purecyclewater.com

NAS: PCYO

CEO: Mark W Harding
CFO: Marc S Spezialy
HR: –
FYE: August 31
Type: Public

Struggling to survive in the barren waste without a trace of water is no longer the fate of inhabitants of the Lowry Range, thanks to Pure Cycle. The water utility has the exclusive right to provide water and wastewater services to about 24,000 acres of the Lowry Range, near Denver. Pure Cycle generates revenues from three sources: water and wastewater fees; construction fees; and monthly service fees. In 2009 it served 247 single-family water connections and 157 wastewater connections in the southeastern Denver area. It also has 60,000 acre-feet of water rights in the Arkansas River basin in Southern Colorado. In 2010 Pure Cycle acquired the 931-acre Sky Ranch Property near Denver for $7 million.

	Annual Growth	08/19	08/20	08/21	08/22	08/23
Sales ($mil.)	(8.0%)	20.4	25.9	17.1	23.0	14.6
Net income ($ mil.)	(0.6%)	4.8	6.8	20.1	9.6	4.7
Market value ($ mil.)	0.3%	261.3	235.0	360.0	248.5	264.6
Employees	7.0%	29	31	31	35	38

PURE FISHING, INC.

7 SCIENCE CT
COLUMBIA, SC 292039344
Phone: 803 754-7000
Fax: –
Web: www.purefishing.com

CEO: Harlan Kent
CFO: John K Stipancich
HR: Rachel Walker
FYE: December 31
Type: Private

We're not telling a fish story when we say Pure Fishing is one of the world's largest makers of fishing tackle. It manufactures about 30,000 different types of bait, fishing lures, rods, reels, and lines under brand names including Abu Garcia, All Star, Berkley, Mitchell, Fenwick, SpiderWire, Trilene, and Gulp!, among others. The recreational products company has operations in about 20 countries, from which it provides direct sales, merchandising, and marketing support to more than 15,000 retailers. Pure Fishing is owned by Jarden Corporation and is part of The Coleman Company.

PURE STORAGE INC

NYS: PSTG

2555 Augustine Dr.
Santa Clara, CA 95054
Phone: 800 379-7873
Fax: −
Web: www.purestorage.com

CEO: −
CFO: −
HR: −
FYE: February 5
Type: Public

Pure Storage is a pure play in computer storage, selling an array of solid state storage systems, also called flash storage. The company's products include its solid state drives, Flash Array, the software that operates the drives, and Pure1, which provides cloud-based management and support to customers. It is now offering all of its products and services on a subscription basis, including the company's hardware and software products through Pure as-a-Service and Cloud Data Services. Pure Storage's customers include cloud providers, enterprises and governments. The company works closely with technology partners, some of them include Microsoft, Oracle and SAP. More than 70% Pure Storage's revenue comes from customers in the US.

	Annual Growth	01/19*	02/20*	01/21*	02/22	02/23
Sales ($mil.)	19.3%	1,359.8	1,643.4	1,684.2	2,180.8	2,753.4
Net income ($ mil.)	−	(178.4)	(201.0)	(282.1)	(143.3)	73.1
Market value ($ mil.)	13.7%	5,446.0	5,412.6	7,033.3	8,021.5	9,094.9
Employees	16.2%	2,800	3,400	3,800	4,200	5,100

*Fiscal year change

PURESAFE WATER SYSTEMS INC

850 3rd Ave.
New York, NY 10022
Phone: 516 208-8250
Fax: −
Web: −

CEO: Leslie J Kessler
CFO: −
HR: −
FYE: December 31
Type: Public

PureSafe Water Systems (formerly Water Chef) makes and markets water purification systems under its name brand. The company's PureSafe Water Station, a six-stage system that produces up to 40,000 gallons of water per day, is marketed in the US for government programs, as well as in China. It also makes a line of mobile water decontamination and purification systems, as well as desalination units. PureSafe Water looks to provide its systems to customers in Bangladesh, Peru, Egypt, India, and Honduras. Former chairman, president, and CEO David Conway resigned in 2007, and Leslie J. Kessler took the top spot. The company adopted the PureSafe name in late 2008.

	Annual Growth	12/10	12/11	12/12	12/13	12/14
Sales ($mil.)	−	−	−	0.3	0.5	−
Net income ($ mil.)	−	(6.6)	(3.4)	(2.8)	(3.2)	(4.0)
Market value ($ mil.)	(80.5%)	240.7	101.8	6.8	3.5	0.3
Employees	10.7%	2	10	3	3	3

PURETEK CORPORATION

1145 ARROYO ST STE D
SAN FERNANDO, CA 913401820
Phone: 818 361-3316
Fax: −
Web: www.puretekcorp.com

CEO: Barry Pressman
CFO: −
HR: −
FYE: April 30
Type: Private

PureTek believes in the power of pharmacology, pure and simple. The company, founded in 1991 by CEO Barry Pressman, manufactures a variety of bulk and private label pharmaceutical, nutritional, and personal care products for retail chains and branded drug companies throughout the US. PureTek's nutritional and pharmaceutical products are offered through its Breath Relief, D-Care, PharmaPure, and Pharmaflex brands. Its personal care items are supplied through the Dermectin and Body Essence lines. PureTek has the ability to produce pharmaceutical and nutritional delivery systems encompassing tablets, capsules and liquids, as well as large-batch capacity for personal care liquids, lotions, creams, and oils.

	Annual Growth	04/14	04/15	04/16	04/17	04/18
Sales ($mil.)	(41.3%)	−	−	−	64.7	38.0
Net income ($ mil.)	(62.6%)	−	−	−	4.6	1.7
Market value ($ mil.)	−	−	−	−	−	−
Employees	−	−	−	−	−	164

PURITAN MEDICAL PRODUCTS COMPANY I LP

31 SCHOOL ST
GUILFORD, ME 044436388
Phone: 207 876-3311
Fax: −
Web: www.puritanmedproducts.com

CEO: −
CFO: Scott Wellman
HR: −
FYE: December 31
Type: Private

Hardwood Products Company manufactures woodenware items for applications in the dairy, foodservice, and crafts markets as well as for medical and industrial uses. Its food and craft products include skewers, sticks, spoons, and other items produced under the Gold Bond and Trophy brands. The company markets its single-use swabs, applicators, tongue depressors, and specialty products for medical and diagnostic applications under the Puritan brand. It also offers critical-environment cleaning applicators. Hardwood Products Company was founded in 1919.

	Annual Growth	12/11	12/12	12/13	12/14	12/15
Sales ($mil.)	4.5%	−	−	45.5	46.7	49.8
Net income ($ mil.)	3.9%	−	−	6.1	5.8	6.6
Market value ($ mil.)	−	−	−	−	−	−
Employees	−	−	−	−	−	382

PURITY WHOLESALE GROCERS, INC.

5300 BROKEN SOUND BLVD NW STE 110
BOCA RATON, FL 334873520
Phone: 561 997-8302
Fax: −
Web: www.puritywholesale.com

CEO: Jeffrey A Levitetz
CFO: Alan Rutner
HR: −
FYE: June 30
Type: Private

Purity Wholesale Grocers gets the goods to retailers at a discount. The company, also called PWG, is a leading secondary wholesaler that distributes a broad variety of grocery products, candy, dairy foods, frozen goods, health and beauty care items, and general merchandise to small retailers nationwide. It takes advantage of discounts granted to large wholesalers and retailers (and of the promotional pricing offered in certain regions) and passes those cost savings on to its customers. PWG supplies convenience stores, drugstores, and supermarkets. In addition, the company offers online sourcing services that help retailers to find bargains. PWG was founded in 1982 by owner Jeff Levitetz.

PURPLE COMMUNICATIONS, INC.

13620 RANCH ROAD 620 N BLDG C
AUSTIN, TX 787171145
Phone: 888 900-4780
Fax: −
Web: www.purplevrs.com

CEO: Sherri Turpin
CFO: Michael Flanagan
HR: −
FYE: December 31
Type: Private

Purple Communications (formerly GoAmerica) provides a colorful alternative to traditional phone services for the hearing impaired. It offers telecommunications relay services such as text relay, video relay, and Internet Protocol text relay, whereby hard of hearing subscribers can video chat, send and receive text telephone messages, faxes, and e-mail over computers or wireless devices. Purple Communications maintains 15 call centers in the US to facilitate the calls. The company also offers on-site live interpreting services in a dozen US cities, and via video across the country. Clearlake Capital Group owns nearly all of the company's stock.

	Annual Growth	12/04	12/05	12/06	12/07	12/08
Sales ($mil.)	219.1%	−	−	12.8	18.6	130.1
Net income ($ mil.)	−	−	−	(2.0)	(3.7)	(5.0)
Market value ($ mil.)	−	−	−	−	−	−
Employees	−	−	−	−	−	1,000

PVH CORP

NYS: PVH

285 Madison Avenue
New York, NY 10017
Phone: 212 381-3500
Fax: –
Web: www.pvh.com

CEO: Stefan Larsson
CFO: Zac Coughlin
HR: –
FYE: January 29
Type: Public

A top global apparel player, PVH is the world's largest dress shirt and neckwear company. The company owns three titans of the apparel industry: Calvin Klein, Tommy Hilfiger, and Heritage Brands. Heritage Brands is a luxury apparel wholesaler that owns the brands Van Heusen, IZOD, ARROW, Warner's, Olga, and True & Co. The company generates sales from multiple channels, including approximately 1,500 company-operated free-standing retail stores, and approximately 1,300 shop-in-shop/concession, retail partners, and licensees. It also charges royalty and advertising fees. About a third of sales were generated in the US.

	Annual Growth	02/19	02/20*	01/21	01/22	01/23
Sales ($mil.)	(1.7%)	9,656.8	9,909.0	7,132.6	9,154.7	9,024.2
Net income ($ mil.)	(28.0%)	746.4	417.3	(1,136.1)	952.3	200.4
Market value ($ mil.)	(5.2%)	6,820.3	5,466.4	5,346.6	5,834.5	5,514.7
Employees	(5.0%)	38,000	40,000	33,000	31,000	31,000

*Fiscal year change

PVS TECHNOLOGIES, INC.

10900 HARPER AVE
DETROIT, MI 482133364
Phone: 313 571-1100
Fax: –
Web: www.pvschemicals.com

CEO: James B Nicholson
CFO: Candee Saferian
HR: –
FYE: December 31
Type: Private

When it comes to making chemicals for wastewater treatment and manufacturing, PVS Chemicals is in its element. The company's product list includes sulfuric and hydrochloric acids, liquid caustic soda, ferric chloride, and ammonium thiosulfate. These chemicals are used in applications such as water treatment (wastewater, process, and municipal), electronics manufacture (including semiconductor etching), gold and copper mining, and food and aluminum production. PVS Chemicals' subsidiaries include PVS Technologies (water treatment), Dynecol (transportation, analysis, treatment, and recycling of chemicals), and PVS Nolwood (chemical distribution).

	Annual Growth	12/09	12/10	12/11	12/12	12/15
Sales ($mil.)	8.7%	–	35.2	45.0	48.3	53.5
Net income ($ mil.)	(16.0%)	–	4.7	4.1	2.7	2.0
Market value ($ mil.)	–	–	–	–	–	–
Employees	–	–	–	–	–	60

PYCO INDUSTRIES, INC.

2901 AVENUE A
LUBBOCK, TX 794042231
Phone: 806 747-3434
Fax: –
Web: www.pycoindustries.com

CEO: –
CFO: –
HR: –
FYE: September 30
Type: Private

Ginning up business is the secret to this vegetable oil producer's success. PYCO Industries is said to be the largest cotton seed co-op to serve the southern US. The Texas-based cooperative, comprising more than 60-member gins, processes cottonseed for a broad market through two cottonseed oil mills. Its cottonseed oil is shipped to food manufacturers and other foodservice customers across the country. The co-op also markets whole cottonseed, as well as the by-products of crushing cottonseed, such as cottonseed hulls and cottonseed meal for beef and dairy cattle feed. Cottonseed linters, another byproduct, are used by manufacturers of mattresses and upholstery padding, paper and plastics, and other products.

	Annual Growth	09/14	09/15	09/16	09/17	09/18
Sales ($mil.)	11.3%	–	161.0	201.5	185.6	222.2
Net income ($ mil.)	(7.4%)	–	30.5	23.8	9.8	24.2
Market value ($ mil.)	–	–	–	–	–	–
Employees	–	–	–	–	–	160

PYXUS INTERNATIONAL INC

NBB: PYYX

8001 Aerial Center Parkway
Morrisville, NC 27560
Phone: 919 379-4300
Fax: –
Web: www.pyxus.com

CEO: J P Sikkel
CFO: Flavia B Landsberg
HR: –
FYE: March 31
Type: Public

Pyxus International is a global agricultural company with 150 years of experience delivering value-added products and services to businesses and customers. The company is a trusted provider of responsibly sourced, independently verified, sustainable, and traceable products and ingredients. The company's core business are leaf tobacco, e-liquids, and non-tobacco agriculture products throughout the world. It processes flue-cured, burley, and oriental tobaccos and sells them to large multinational cigarette and cigar manufacturers, including Philip Morris International (PMI), China Tobacco International, Inc. and and British American Tobacco.

	Annual Growth	03/20*	08/20*	03/21	03/22	03/23
Sales ($mil.)	7.8%	1,527.3	447.6	884.3	1,639.9	1,914.9
Net income ($ mil.)	–	(264.7)	19.0	(136.7)	(82.1)	(39.1)
Market value ($ mil.)	–	–	–	107.5	36.3	30.0
Employees	–	3,385	–	2,900	3,000	–

*Fiscal year change

PZENA INVESTMENT MANAGEMENT, INC.

320 PARK AVE FL 8
NEW YORK, NY 100226815
Phone: 212 355-1600
Fax: –
Web: www.pzena.com

CEO: Richard S Pzena
CFO: Jessica R Doran
HR: Katie Hurley
FYE: December 31
Type: Private

Pzena Investment Management is a value-oriented investment management company. The firm serves corporate, institutional, and high-net-worth individual clients in the US and abroad and has about $52.5 billion in assets under management. Pzena also acts as a sub-investment adviser to a variety of SEC-registered mutual funds and non-US funds. The firm is the sole managing member of its operating company, Pzena Investment Management, LLC. The employee-owned firm was founded by chairman and CEO Richard Pzena in 1995.

Q-MATIC CORPORATION

2875 BRECKINRIDGE BLVD STE 100
DULUTH, GA 300964988
Phone: 770 817-4250
Fax: –
Web: –

CEO: Jeffrey Green
CFO: Tobias Martinsson
HR: Margaret Smoot
FYE: August 31
Type: Private

Q-MATIC may help cut down your waiting time. The company (a unit of Sweden-based Q-MATIC Group AB) develops and supports hardware and software systems that banks, government offices, health care companies, retailers, and transportation providers use to manage their flow of customers. Its products include ticket printers, touch screens, LED displays, card readers, and related software. Q-MATIC Group makes sales through regional subsidiaries and relationships with electronics and IT product distributors and has installed 60,000 systems globally. The parent company was founded in Sweden in 1981 and established a US presence in 1987.

Q.E.P. CO., INC.   NBB: QEPC

1001 Broken Sound Parkway NW
Boca Raton, FL 33487
Phone: 561 994-5550
Fax: 561 241-2830
Web: www.qepcorporate.com

CEO: Leonard Gould
CFO: Enos Brown
HR: Marthawayne Fleming
FYE: February 28
Type: Public

Q.E.P. is a leading designer, manufacturer and distributor of a broad range of best-in-class flooring and installation solutions for commercial and home improvement projects worldwide. It manufactures innovative, quality, and value-driven industrial and flooring solutions featuring a comprehensive line of hardwood flooring, flooring installation tools and adhesives, as well as cutting-edge tools for all industrial trades. It sells its products throughout the world to home improvement retail centers, professional specialty distribution outlets, and flooring dealers under brand names QEP, Capitol, ROBERTS, HARRIS, and Vitrex brands, among others. The family-run company was founded by chairman and CEO Lewis Gould in 1979. Vast Majority of its revenue comes from North America region.

	Annual Growth	02/19	02/20	02/21	02/22	02/23
Sales ($mil.)	3.4%	379.4	393.9	387.6	445.5	433.7
Net income ($ mil.)	–	(3.0)	(12.1)	6.9	9.6	(0.1)
Market value ($ mil.)	(14.1%)	81.5	54.3	83.1	65.8	44.5
Employees	–	–	–	–	–	–

QAD INC.

101 INNOVATION PL
SANTA BARBARA, CA 931082268
Phone: 805 566-6000
Fax: –
Web: www.qad.com

CEO: Anton Chilton
CFO: Daniel Lender
HR: Jittiya Klinkosol
FYE: January 31
Type: Private

QAD is a leading provider of next-generation manufacturing and supply chain solutions in the cloud. Thousands of companies have deployed QAD enterprise solutions including enterprise resource planning (ERP), digital commerce (DC), supplier relationship management (SRM), digital supply chain planning (DSCP), global trade and transportation execution (GTTE), enterprise quality management system (EQMS), connected workforce and process intelligence. QAD's customers cluster in the automotive, food and beverage, life sciences, and high-tech industries. The company was founded in 1979.

QC HOLDINGS INC   NBB: QCCO

9401 Indian Creek Parkway, Suite 1500
Overland Park, KS 66210
Phone: 913 234-5000
Fax: –
Web: www.qcholdings.com

CEO: Darrin J Andersen
CFO: Douglas E Nickerson
HR: –
FYE: December 13
Type: Public

Need cash PDQ? Cue QC. QC Holdings runs about 500 payday loan stores operating mostly as Quik Cash or National Quik Cash, but also under about a half-dozen other brands, including California Budget Finance, Express Check Advance of South Carolina, First Payday Loans, Nationwide Budget Finance, and QC Financial Services. Targeting working-class individuals, its stores provide short-term loans ranging from $100 to $500, for a fee typically between 15% to 20% per each $100 of the loan. The company also offers check cashing services, title loans, and Western Union money orders and transfers. It is active in nearly two dozen states; Missouri, California, Illinois, and Kansas are its largest markets.

	Annual Growth	12/14	12/19	12/20	12/21	12/22
Sales ($mil.)	–	153.1	117.3	97.4	90.9	152.8
Net income ($ mil.)	–	5.3	(4.7)	2.9	0.3	(2.8)
Market value ($ mil.)	(12.5%)	28.4	5.5	4.6	12.6	9.7
Employees	–	1,244	–	–	–	–

QCEPT TECHNOLOGIES INC.

1201 PEACHTREE ST NE # 500
ATLANTA, GA 303616342
Phone: 404 685-9434
Fax: –
Web: –

CEO: –
CFO: –
HR: –
FYE: December 31
Type: Private

The devil is in the details, and since the devil went down to Georgia, it's only natural to find a supplier of semiconductor metrology tools in the Peach State. Qcept Technologies markets the Chemetriq Series, which examines silicon wafers for minute details of chemical contamination, micro-scratch detection, and atomic layer deposition process characterization and control, among other functions. The company, founded in 2000, was the first to "graduate" from Georgia Tech's VentureLab program; its offices are close by the Tech campus. Among its investors are Siemens Venture Capital and Pittco Capital Management. Qcept has raised nearly $36 million in private equity funding.

QCR HOLDINGS INC   NMS: QCRH

3551 7th Street
Moline, IL 61265
Phone: 309 736-3580
Fax: –
Web: www.qcrh.com

CEO: Larry J Helling
CFO: Todd A Gipple
HR: –
FYE: December 31
Type: Public

QCR Holdings is the holding company for Quad City Bank & Trust, Cedar Rapids Bank & Trust, Springfield First Community Bank, and Community State Bank. Together, the banks have about 40 offices serving the Quad Cities, Cedar Rapids, Cedar Valley, Des Moines/Ankeny and Springfield communities. The banks provide full-service commercial and consumer banking and trust and wealth management services. Its other operating subsidiaries include m2 which is based in Brookfield, Wisconsin, is engaged in the business of lending and leasing machinery and equipment to C&I businesses under direct financing lease contracts and equipment financing agreements. The company has approximately $7.7 billion in assets, $6.0 billion in loans and $5.9 billion in deposits.

	Annual Growth	12/19	12/20	12/21	12/22	12/23
Assets ($mil.)	14.8%	4,909.1	5,682.8	6,096.1	7,948.8	8,538.9
Net income ($ mil.)	18.6%	57.4	60.6	98.9	99.1	113.6
Market value ($ mil.)	7.4%	734.6	663.1	938.0	831.4	978.0
Employees	10.3%	697	739	756	1,001	1,030

QF LIQUIDATION, INC.

25242 ARCTIC OCEAN DR
LAKE FOREST, CA 926308821
Phone: 949 930-3400
Fax: –
Web: www.qtww.com

CEO: W B Olson
CFO: Bradley J Timon
HR: –
FYE: December 31
Type: Private

If you're ready to make a quantum leap to a new fuel source, then Quantum Fuel Systems Technologies Worldwide is the place to land. Quantum makes fuel storage, delivery devices, and electronic control systems for alternative-fueled vehicles. It serves the military with its branded HyHauler Plus, a transportable hydrogen refueling station that powers battlefield vehicles. Fisker Automotive, a joint venture between Quantum and Fisker Coachbuild, is developing the Karma, an environmentally friendly luxury sports sedan, using Quantum's plug-in-hybrid engine technology. Its customer base also includes aerospace and government entities.

QHG OF SOUTH CAROLINA, INC.

805 PAMPLICO HWY
FLORENCE, SC 295056047
Phone: 843 674-5000
Fax: –
Web: www.muschealth.org

CEO: Darcy Craven
CFO: –
HR: –
FYE: June 30
Type: Private

QHG of South Carolina (dba Carolinas Hospital System), provides acute health care services in the Palmetto State town of Florence. The hospital has some 420 inpatient beds and employs about 300 specialized physicians. In addition to emergency, trauma, general medicine, and surgeries, service specialties at the medical campus include cancer care, diagnostics, women's health, cardiology, pediatrics, urology, orthopedics, rehabilitation, and behavioral health. It also includes affiliated medical emergency clinics, outpatient centers, and doctor's offices. Carolinas Hospital System is a subsidiary of Community Health Systems (CHS).

	Annual Growth	06/12	06/13	06/14	06/15	06/16
Sales ($mil.)	(25.3%)	–	–	–	261.6	195.4
Net income ($ mil.)	(55.1%)	–	–	–	17.9	8.1
Market value ($ mil.)	–	–	–	–	–	–
Employees	–	–	–	–	–	1,500

QLIK TECHNOLOGIES INC.

211 S GULPH RD STE 500
KING OF PRUSSIA, PA 194063101
Phone: 888 828-9768
Fax: –
Web: www.qlik.com

CEO: Mike Capone
CFO: –
HR: –
FYE: December 31
Type: Private

Qlik provides an end-to-end, real-time data integration and analytics cloud platform to close the gaps between data, insights and action. By transforming data into Active Intelligence, businesses can drive better decisions, improve revenue and profitability, and optimize customer relationships. Qlik does business in more than 100 countries and serves over 40,000 customers around the world.

QLOGIC LLC

15485 SAND CANYON AVE
IRVINE, CA 926183154
Phone: 949 389-6000
Fax: –
Web: www.marvell.com

CEO: –
CFO: –
HR: –
FYE: April 03
Type: Private

QLogic keeps its customers on a steady diet of Fibre...Channel. The company designs server and storage system networking products, including switches, adapters, and storage routers. QLogic's products are primarily Fibre Channel and Ethernet-based, but can also operate as Internet Small Computer System Interface (iSCSI) products or as a combination of technologies. The company also provides controllers for embedded applications. QLogic uses contract manufacturers to build its products, which are sold directly to server and workstation manufacturers and through distributors. Customers include Hewlett-Packard (more than a quarter of sales), Dell (17%), and IBM (15%). The company was acquired by Cavium in mid-2016.

	Annual Growth	03/12	03/13	03/14	03/15*	04/16
Sales ($mil.)	(11.8%)	–	–	–	520.2	458.9
Net income ($ mil.)	(8.2%)	–	–	–	50.6	46.5
Market value ($ mil.)	–	–	–	–	–	–
Employees	–	–	–	–	–	782

*Fiscal year change

QNB CORP.

NBB: QNBC

15 North Third Street, P.O. Box 9005
Quakertown, PA 18951-9005
Phone: 215 538-5600
Fax: –
Web: www.qnbbank.com

CEO: David W Freeman
CFO: Janice S McCracken Erke
HR: –
FYE: December 31
Type: Public

QNB Corp. is the holding company for QNB Bank, which provides commercial banking services through 11 branches serving Bucks, Lehigh, and Montgomery counties in southeastern Pennsylvania. QNB offers standard banking services including checking, savings, and money market accounts; IRAs; and CDs. It uses funds from deposits to originate business loans, residential mortgages, and consumer loans. Commercial loans and mortgages account for more than half of its lending portfolio. Unlike many of its peers, QNB Bank does not directly offer trust services or full-service insurance. The company was founded in 1877.

	Annual Growth	12/19	12/20	12/21	12/22	12/23
Assets ($mil.)	8.6%	1,225.0	1,440.2	1,673.3	1,668.5	1,706.3
Net income ($ mil.)	(6.4%)	12.4	12.1	16.5	15.9	9.5
Market value ($ mil.)	(9.4%)	141.2	117.1	131.5	96.2	94.9
Employees	–	203	200	186	271	–

QORVO INC

NMS: QRVO

7628 Thorndike Road
Greensboro, NC 27409-9421
Phone: 336 664-1233
Fax: –
Web: www.qorvo.com

CEO: –
CFO: –
HR: –
FYE: April 1
Type: Public

Qorvo is a global leader in the development and commercialization of technologies and products for wireless, wired, and power markets. Its products are made for mobile devices, cellular infrastructure, aerospace and defense systems, and automotive. It serves major manufacturers such as Apple, Qorvo's largest customer, and Samsung. Qorvo is a leading supplier of RF products and compound semiconductor foundry services to defense primes and other global defense and aerospace customers. It has operations in the US, Costa Rica, China, Taiwan, Europe, and Asia. Qorvo was formed in early 2015 via the merger of RF Micro Devices and TriQuint. The US generates more than 50% of the company's total revenue.

	Annual Growth	03/19	03/20*	04/21	04/22	04/23
Sales ($mil.)	3.7%	3,090.3	3,239.1	4,015.3	4,645.7	3,569.4
Net income ($ mil.)	(6.2%)	133.1	334.3	733.6	1,033.4	103.2
Market value ($ mil.)	9.1%	7,076.1	7,960.0	19,029	11,987	10,020
Employees	1.2%	8,100	7,900	8,400	8,900	8,500

*Fiscal year change

QRS MUSIC TECHNOLOGIES, INC.

269 QUAKER DR
SENECA, PA 163462419
Phone: 814 676-6683
Fax: –
Web: www.qrsmusic.com

CEO: Thomas A Dolan
CFO: Ann A Jones
HR: –
FYE: June 30
Type: Private

Tired ivory ticklers could probably use some Pianomation from QRS Music Technologies. The company manufactures and distributes Story & Clark pianos and Pianomation MIDI systems (digital playback technology for acoustic and digital pianos), which are sold through about 500 independent retailers across the country. It also produces CDs and DVDs that can be synchronized with player pianos, and the company's NetPiano subscription service lets customers download music to their Pianomation systems. QRS Music was founded by Melville Clark in 1900. Chairman Richard Dolan owns about 60% of the company.

QST INDUSTRIES, INC.

1755 PARK ST
NAPERVILLE, IL 605631293
Phone: 312 930-9400
Fax: –
Web: www.qst.com

CEO: Michael Danch
CFO: Jeffrey A Carlevato
HR: –
FYE: December 31
Type: Private

Pockets mean more than pocket change to QST Industries. QST supplies clothing construction components -- including pocketing materials, elastics, linings and interlinings, insulations, and waistbands -- to the apparel industry in more than 130 countries worldwide. Its brands include Q-Loop belt loop tape (guards against belt loop fray on blue jeans), Quick-Stretch clear elastics, and Ban-Rol waistband fabric. QST also supplies home furnishing fabrics and offers custom printing and die and table cutting. Sam Haber founded QST in 1880 when he began selling trimmings to Chicago tailors and sewers.

QUABBIN WIRE & CABLE CO., INC.

10 MAPLE ST
WARE, MA 010821597
Phone: 413 967-6281
Fax: –
Web: www.quabbin.com

CEO: –
CFO: –
HR: –
FYE: October 31
Type: Private

Quabbin Wire & Cable is fighting to protect the future of copper wire makers as the new order of fiber optics is steadily gaining control in the world of connectivity. Quabbin Wire & Cable makes low temperature thermoplastic shielded and unshielded cables used to connect audio and video devices, computers, control and instrumentation systems, LAN systems, point-of-sale equipment, and telecommunication products. The company developed a polyurethane jacketed cable for manufacturing high-strength Industrial Ethernet patch cords. It has been developing other cable jackets that can accommodate various environmental stresses. Quabbin Wire & Cable was founded in 1975 by CEO Paul Engel.

QUAD/GRAPHICS, INC.

N61 W23044 Harry's Way
Sussex, WI 53089-3995
Phone: 414 566-6000
Fax: –
Web: www.qg.com

NYS: QUAD
CEO: J J Quadracci
CFO: Anthony C Staniak
HR: Jim Adams
FYE: December 31
Type: Public

Quad/Graphics is a worldwide marketing solutions partner in the US. The company's services include consumer insights, audience targeting, personalization, media planning and placement, process optimization, campaign planning and creation, pre-media production, videography, photography, digital execution, print execution and logistics. It caters to a wide variety of clients across multiple verticals, including those in industries such as retail, publishing, consumer packaged goods, financial services, healthcare, insurance and direct-to-consumer. With print media in structural decline, the company generates the majority of its revenue domestically. Having nothing to do with the number four, Quad takes its name from Harry Quadracci, who founded the company in 1971.

	Annual Growth	12/19	12/20	12/21	12/22	12/23
Sales ($mil.)	(6.8%)	3,923.4	2,929.6	2,960.4	3,217.0	2,957.7
Net income ($ mil.)	–	(156.3)	(128.3)	37.8	9.3	(55.4)
Market value ($ mil.)	3.8%	238.2	194.8	204.0	208.1	276.4
Employees	(9.5%)	19,600	15,800	15,100	15,300	13,150

QUAKER VALLEY FOODS, INC.

2701 RED LION RD
PHILADELPHIA, PA 191541038
Phone: 215 992-0900
Fax: –
Web: www.quakervalleyfoods.com

CEO: –
CFO: Pat Veasey
HR: –
FYE: January 02
Type: Private

Quaker Valley Foods (QVF) is known by friends high and low for its take-out fresh and frozen staples. The food distributor makes daily deliveries of meat and other provisions to foodservice customers across the Northeast US. QVF, a member of the UNIPRO Foodservice coop, offers beef, pork, poultry, frozen seafood, imported meats (mutton and goat), cheeses, salads, and other items from its Philadelphia warehouse. Customers range from wholesalers and jobbers to independent retail and wholesale groceries, and major supermarket chains. Its vendors include Hormel, Swift, Packerland, Carolina Turkey, Tyson, Alpine Lace, and Land O' Lakes. QVF was started by two brothers-in-law in 1975 and is led by its founders' sons.

	Annual Growth	01/09	01/10	01/11*	12/11*	01/16
Sales ($mil.)	6.9%	–	160.6	177.3	195.5	239.5
Net income ($ mil.)	22.0%	–	0.6	0.4	0.4	2.0
Market value ($ mil.)	–	–	–	–	–	–
Employees	–	–	–	–	–	145

*Fiscal year change

QUALCOMM INC

5775 Morehouse Dr.
San Diego, CA 92121-1714
Phone: 858 587-1121
Fax: –
Web: www.qualcomm.com

NMS: QCOM
CEO: Cristiano R Amon
CFO: Akash Palkhiwala
HR: –
FYE: September 24
Type: Public

QUALCOMM is a leader in the development and commercialization of foundational technologies for the wireless industry. The company has continued to play a leading role in developing system level inventions that serve as foundations for 3G, 4G, and 5G wireless technologies, which include CDMA (Code Division Multiple Access) and ODFMA (Orthogonal Frequency Division Multiple Access) families of technologies, LTE (Long Term Evolution), and 5G NR (New Radio) among others. It also develops and commercializes numerous other key technologies used in mobile and other wireless devices, such as for certain video and audio codecs, Wi-Fi, GPS (Global Positioning System) and Bluetooth. About 95% of the company's sales come from international customers.

	Annual Growth	09/19	09/20	09/21	09/22	09/23
Sales ($mil.)	10.2%	24,273	23,531	33,566	44,200	35,820
Net income ($ mil.)	13.3%	4,386.0	5,198.0	9,043.0	12,936	7,232.0
Market value ($ mil.)	8.9%	85,366	127,553	149,142	135,006	119,956
Employees	7.8%	37,000	41,000	45,000	51,000	50,000

QUALITOR, INC.

127 PUBLIC SQ STE 5300
CLEVELAND, OH 441141219
Phone: 248 204-8600
Fax: –
Web: –

CEO: Gary Cohen
CFO: Scott Gibaratz
HR: –
FYE: December 31
Type: Private

Qualitor keeps the big guys moving. The company makes automotive and heavy-duty truck parts, including brake components and wiper blades. Qualitor consists mainly of Anstro and International Brake Industries (brake manufacturers in the US), Sloan (truck and trailer components in the US), and Pylon (aftermarket wiper blades and replacement pieces in the US). Its switches, sensors, brakes, repair kits, water pumps, and wipers are sold to OEM parts manufacturers, rebuilders, retailers, mass merchants, and auto dealers worldwide; customers include Dana, Wal-Mart, and Standard Motor Parts. Qualitor is majority-owned by Thayer Capital Partners.

QUALITY CONSULTING, INC.

4300 WESTOWN PKWY STE 150
WEST DES MOINES, IA 502661209
Phone: 515 440-4960
Fax: –
Web: www.qci.com

CEO: –
CFO: –
HR: –
FYE: December 31
Type: Private

QCI helps its customers get the most for their technology dollars. The consulting firm helps companies evaluate, buy, build, and manage enterprise infrastructure and software based on business needs. QCI's enterprise infrastructure services assess and optimize systems in such areas as security, business continuity, data management, software deployment, and network design. The company also provides technical staffing services for clients on a temporary, contract-to-hire, or permanent basis. It serves clients in such industries as financial services, health care, and manufacturing. QCI was founded in 1995 and has offices in Iowa, Colorado, and Nebraska.

QUALITY OIL COMPANY, LLC

1540 SILAS CREEK PKWY
WINSTON SALEM, NC 271273705
Phone: 336 722-3441
Fax: –
Web: www.qualityoilnc.com

CEO: –
CFO: –
HR: –
FYE: December 31
Type: Private

With more services than your average oil company, Quality Oil helps its customers get fueled up, cooled off, and well rested. And they can smoke if they want to. The company distributes fuel oil and propane to customers in the Winston-Salem area of North Carolina. Quality Oil provides air conditioning and heating equipment service, operates 47 convenience stores (Quality Marts), and about 20 service stations, and owns hotels in five southern states. In addition, the company operates 60 Quality Plus locations at which drivers can buy cigarettes at discount prices. The company also provides Right-a-Way oil change services at many of its gas stations.

	Annual Growth	12/05	12/06	12/07	12/08	12/09
Sales ($mil.)	5.4%	–	542.2	619.7	806.4	634.8
Net income ($ mil.)	(8.1%)	–	15.2	10.9	27.6	11.8
Market value ($ mil.)	–	–	–	–	–	–
Employees	–	–	–	–	–	1,000

QUALSTAR CORP

NBB: QBAK

15707 Rockfield Boulevard, Suite 105
Irvine, CA 92618
Phone: 805 583-7744
Fax: –
Web: www.qualstar.com

CEO: Steven N Bronson
CFO: Louann L Negrete
HR: –
FYE: December 31
Type: Public

People often refer to 'tape' when speaking about digital video. But Qualstar means it when it talks about tape, especially when storing archival information on tape library systems. The company's products -- tape drives and tape library data storage systems -- house, retrieve, and manage large amounts of data in computer networks. Its other business is power supplies that convert AC voltage to DC. Qualstar's systems are compatible with a variety of operating systems and with storage management software from companies such as Symantec. The company, which incorporates tape drives and media from Quantum and Sony into its libraries, sells mainly to manufacturers and resellers. Two customers account for a combined quarter of revenues.

	Annual Growth	12/18	12/19	12/20	12/21	12/22
Sales ($mil.)	(5.3%)	12.2	13.4	8.1	9.2	9.8
Net income ($ mil.)	(56.1%)	1.5	(0.0)	(1.3)	0.4	0.0
Market value ($ mil.)	(18.6%)	8.5	8.8	4.9	4.1	3.7
Employees	–	20	16	–	–	–

QUALYS, INC.

NMS: QLYS

919 E. Hillsdale Boulevard, 4th Floor
Foster City, CA 94404
Phone: 650 801-6100
Fax: –
Web: www.qualys.com

CEO: Sumedh S Thakar
CFO: Joo M Kim
HR: –
FYE: December 31
Type: Public

Qualys is a pioneer and leading provider of a cloud-based platform delivering information technology (IT), security, and compliance solutions. The Qualys Cloud Platform offers an integrated suite of solutions that automates the lifecycle of asset discovery and management, security assessments, and compliance management for an organization's IT infrastructure and assets, whether such infrastructure and assets reside inside the organization, on their network perimeter, on endpoints or in the cloud. The company counts more than 10,000 customers worldwide, including a majority of each of the Forbes Global 100 and Fortune 100. Qualys reaches many customers through partnerships with managed service providers, consultants, and resellers, including IBM, Fujitsu, Optiv, and Verizon. US accounts for about 60% of the company's total sales.

	Annual Growth	12/19	12/20	12/21	12/22	12/23
Sales ($mil.)	14.6%	321.6	363.0	411.2	489.7	554.5
Net income ($ mil.)	21.6%	69.3	91.6	71.0	108.0	151.6
Market value ($ mil.)	23.9%	3,077.1	4,498.1	5,064.7	4,142.3	7,244.5
Employees	14.1%	1,289	1,498	1,823	2,143	2,188

QUANEX BUILDING PRODUCTS CORP

NYS: NX

945 Bunker Hill Road,, Suite 900
Houston, TX 77024
Phone: 713 961-4600
Fax: –
Web: www.quanex.com

CEO: George L Wilson
CFO: Scott M Zuehlke
HR: Alicia Bendt
FYE: October 31
Type: Public

Quanex Building Products Corp. manufactures components for OEMs of building products. The company believes the primary drivers of its operating results are residential remodeling and replacement activity and new home construction in the markets it serves. The majority of these components can be categorized as window and door (fenestration) components and kitchen and bath cabinet components. It also provide certain other non-fenestration components and products, which include solar panel sealants, trim moldings, vinyl decking, vinyl fencing, water retention barriers, and conservatory roof components. Quanex generates about 75% of its total sales in the US.

	Annual Growth	10/19	10/20	10/21	10/22	10/23
Sales ($mil.)	6.0%	893.8	851.6	1,072.1	1,221.5	1,130.6
Net income ($ mil.)	–	(46.7)	38.5	57.0	88.3	82.5
Market value ($ mil.)	8.6%	636.8	600.8	684.0	731.5	886.5
Employees	1.1%	3,632	3,767	3,860	3,875	3,792

QUANTA SERVICES, INC.

NYS: PWR

2727 North Loop West
Houston, TX 77008
Phone: 713 629-7600
Fax: –
Web: www.quantaservices.com

CEO: Earl C Austin Jr
CFO: Jayshree S Desai
HR: Justin Dunn
FYE: December 31
Type: Public

Quanta Services is a specialty contractor that designs, installs, repairs, and maintains network infrastructure across North America and abroad. The company serves the electric power, pipeline, oil and natural gas, and communication industries. Capabilities include distribution infrastructure, emergency response, and its pipeline and industrial business offers offshore services. Quanta also handles energized installation, electric power infrastructure maintenance and upgrade, installation of smart grid technologies on electric power networks, and building wind and solar power facilities. Quanta gets about 85% of its revenue from customers in the US.

	Annual Growth	12/19	12/20	12/21	12/22	12/23
Sales ($mil.)	14.6%	12,112	11,203	12,980	17,074	20,882
Net income ($ mil.)	16.7%	402.0	445.6	486.0	491.2	744.7
Market value ($ mil.)	51.7%	5,923.7	10,480	16,684	20,735	31,401
Employees	6.8%	40,300	35,800	43,700	47,300	52,500

QUANTUM CORP
NMS: QMCO

224 Airport Parkway, Suite 550
San Jose, CA 95110
Phone: 408 944-4000
Fax: –
Web: www.quantum.com

CEO: James J Lerner
CFO: Kenneth P Gianella
HR: Jamie Girouard
FYE: March 31
Type: Public

Quantum is a data company with a portfolio of products and services for storing, managing, protecting, archiving, and enriching digital data. The company specializes in solutions for video data, images, and other large files because this "unstructured" data represents more than 80% of all data being created, according to leading industry analyst firms. Some of the company's products facilitate the storage and accessing of video and are used by broadcasters, studios, post-production companies, sports franchises, and corporations. Quantum uses distributors, value-added resellers (VARs) and direct market resellers (DMRs) in its sales process. The company generates some 55% of the its revenue from Americas region.

	Annual Growth	03/19	03/20	03/21	03/22	03/23
Sales ($mil.)	0.6%	402.7	402.9	349.6	372.8	412.8
Net income ($ mil.)	–	(42.8)	(5.2)	(35.5)	(32.3)	(37.9)
Market value ($ mil.)	–	–	276.0	779.5	212.4	107.6
Employees	1.5%	800	829	827	905	850

QUANTUM3D, INC.

920 HILLVIEW CT STE 145
MILPITAS, CA 950354558
Phone: 408 600-2500
Fax: –
Web: www.quantum3d.com

CEO: –
CFO: –
HR: –
FYE: December 31
Type: Private

Quantum3D makes open-architecture 3-D visual computer hardware systems, software, and embedded graphics subsystems. The company's products are used for training simulators, 3-D design, and digital media creation. Its embedded graphics subsystems use NVIDIA graphics processors, along with proprietary software, to create realistic graphics. Quantum3D's custom computer systems include high-performance real-time image generators (Independence) and rugged, tactical and vehicle-mounted visual processing systems (Thermite). The company's customers have included Boeing, Ford Motor, Lockheed Martin, Rockwell Collins, and the US Department of Defense. Quantum3D was established in 1997.

	Annual Growth	12/08	12/09	12/10	12/11	12/12
Sales ($mil.)	(11.6%)	–	–	23.8	17.7	18.6
Net income ($ mil.)	–	–	–	0.9	1.8	(4.1)
Market value ($ mil.)	–	–	–	–	–	–
Employees	–	–	–	–	–	22

QUARLES & BRADY LLP

411 E WISCONSIN AVE STE 2350
MILWAUKEE, WI 53202
Phone: 414 277-5000
Fax: –
Web: www.quarles.com

CEO: –
CFO: –
HR: –
FYE: December 31
Type: Private

Quarles & Brady provides legal solutions to a wide range of clients on a national stage. The company is a multidisciplinary Am Law 200 firm with approximately 520 attorneys practicing at the top of the profession in Chicago, Denver, Indianapolis, Madison, Milwaukee, Minneapolis, Naples, Phoenix, San Diego, Tampa, Tucson, and Washington, D.C. The firm's practice areas include bankruptcy, restructuring, and creditor's rights, public finance, data privacy and security, energy and infrastructure, environment and natural resources, estate, trust, and wealth preservation, and tax, among others. They are industry leaders in technology, energy, financial services, health care, insurance, pharmaceuticals, real estate, and manufacturing, to name just a few.

QUEEN OF THE VALLEY MEDICAL CENTER FOUNDATION

1000 TRANCAS ST
NAPA, CA 945582906
Phone: 707 252-4411
Fax: –
Web: www.thequeen.org

CEO: –
CFO: Bob Diehl
HR: –
FYE: June 30
Type: Private

The Queen of the Valley Medical Center reigns over the whole of Napa Valley. The 190-bed hospital provides acute and tertiary care to the residents of California's Napa County. It operates a level III trauma center and provides emergency, surgery, and wound care services, as well as specialty family, work health, nutritional, and rehabilitation services. "The Queen," as it is known colloquially, operates regional cancer, orthopedic, women's, and heart centers, as well as the Napa Valley Imaging Center and the Napa Valley Women's Healthcare Center. Queen of the Valley Medical Center is part of St. Joseph Health.

QUEST DIAGNOSTICS, INC.
NYS: DGX

500 Plaza Drive
Secaucus, NJ 07094
Phone: 973 520-2700
Fax: –
Web: www.questdiagnostics.com

CEO: James E Davis
CFO: Sam A Samad
HR: –
FYE: December 31
Type: Public

Quest Diagnostics is the world's leading provider of diagnostic information services. The company's Diagnostic Information Services develop and deliver diagnostic information services, providing insights that empower and enable a broad range of customers, including patients, clinicians, hospitals, IDNs, health plans, employers, ACOs and DCEs; while the Diagnostic Solutions includes risk assessment services business, which offers solutions for insurers, and healthcare information technology businesses, which offers solutions for healthcare providers. In all, the company serves about one-third of the adult population of the US annually, it also serves about half of the physicians and half of the hospitals in the US per year.

	Annual Growth	12/19	12/20	12/21	12/22	12/23
Sales ($mil.)	4.6%	7,726.0	9,437.0	10,788	9,883.0	9,252.0
Net income ($ mil.)	(0.1%)	858.0	1,431.0	1,995.0	946.0	854.0
Market value ($ mil.)	6.6%	11,854	13,228	19,204	17,365	15,305
Employees	0.5%	47,000	40,000	49,000	49,000	48,000

QUEST MEDIA & SUPPLIES, INC.

9000 FOOTHILLS BLVD STE 100
ROSEVILLE, CA 95747
Phone: 916 338-7070
Fax: –
Web: www.questsys.com

CEO: Timothy Burke
CFO: Francine Walrath
HR: –
FYE: December 31
Type: Private

Quest wants to help guide clients in their technology journeys. Quest Media & Supplies provides a wide range of IT consulting and management services to Fortune 5000 firms, as well as educational institutions, government agencies, and small and midsized companies across the US. Its offerings include cloud hosting, application development, networking, security and disaster recovery, data storage, telecommunications and transport services, and technology staffing. Quest is Gold Certified in the US for Cisco Systems, and also supplies products from Blue Coat, Dell, Hitachi, IBM, Microsoft, Polycom, VMware, and Xerox, among other vendors. The company was founded in 1982 by CEO Tim Burke with his wife, Cindy.

	Annual Growth	12/10	12/11	12/12	12/13	12/14
Sales ($mil.)	19.1%	–	–	118.4	118.3	168.0
Net income ($ mil.)	(24.3%)	–	–	2.1	3.9	1.2
Market value ($ mil.)	–	–	–	–	–	–
Employees	–	–	–	–	–	130

QUESTAR GAS CO.

333 South State Street, P.O. Box 45433
Salt Lake City, UT 84145
Phone: 801 324-5000
Fax: –
Web: www.questar.com

CEO: Ronald W Jibson
CFO: Kevin W Hadlock
HR: Marty Weed
FYE: December 31
Type: Public

Questar Gas's quest is to distribute natural gas to about 1 million customers throughout Utah and in southeastern Idaho and southwestern Wyoming. The regulated utility operates more than 30,000 miles of gas distribution mains and service lines and serves residential, commercial, and industrial retail customers. Part of the Dominion Energy Questar division, Questar Gas is a subsidiary of Dominion Energy and operates as Dominion Energy Utah, Dominion Energy Wyoming, and Dominion Energy Idaho in its respective service territories.

	Annual Growth	12/13	12/14	12/15	12/16	12/17
Sales ($mil.)	(1.0%)	985.8	960.9	917.6	921.3	947.0
Net income ($ mil.)	6.3%	52.8	55.2	64.3	57.2	67.5
Market value ($ mil.)	–	–	–	–	–	–
Employees	(0.5%)	917	1,745	930	900	900

QUICK-MED TECHNOLOGIES INC NBB: QMDT

902 NW 4 Street
Gainesville, FL 32601
Phone: 352 379-0611
Fax: –
Web: www.quickmedtech.com

CEO: –
CFO: –
HR: –
FYE: June 30
Type: Public

Quick-Med Technologies hopes to be floating on a cloud -- but not a cloud of mustard gas. The life sciences development company is working with the US Army to develop a therapy to treat people exposed to mustard gas. The underlying technology for the potential therapy, MultiStat, is also the basis for wound care products and cosmetic ingredient applications. A second technology, NIMBUS (Novel Intrinsically Micro-Bonded Utility Substrate), uses bio-engineered antimicrobial polymers to protect wounds from infection and industrial and consumer goods from harmful microscopic pests.

	Annual Growth	06/09	06/10	06/11	06/12	06/13
Sales ($mil.)	(6.9%)	–	–	–	1.0	0.9
Net income ($ mil.)	–	–	–	–	(1.7)	(0.7)
Market value ($ mil.)	(32.2%)	–	–	–	3.4	2.3
Employees	–	–	–	–	–	7

QUICKLOGIC CORP NAS: QUIK

2220 Lundy Avenue
San Jose, CA 95131-1816
Phone: 408 990-4000
Fax: 408 990-4040
Web: www.quicklogic.com

CEO: Brian C Faith
CFO: Elias Nader
HR: Catriona Meney
FYE: January 1
Type: Public

QuickLogic is quick to get embed. The company designs and sells logic chips that can be programmed by OEMs, as well as low-power customizable chips used to add features to and extend the battery life of mobile, consumer, and business electronics. It also offers related hardware and software, plus custom programming services. The fabless company -- it uses contract manufacturers to produce its chips -- targets smartphone, tablet, and access card manufacturers. Customers for its logic chips come from the aerospace, instrumentation, and military industries, among others. Honeywell (15% of sales) is a top customer.

	Annual Growth	12/18	12/19*	01/21	01/22	01/23
Sales ($mil.)	6.4%	12.6	10.3	8.6	12.7	16.2
Net income ($ mil.)	–	(13.8)	(15.4)	(11.2)	(6.6)	(4.3)
Market value ($ mil.)	61.2%	10.0	60.5	50.0	67.5	67.9
Employees	(13.9%)	82	81	48	48	45

*Fiscal year change

QUICKSILVER RESOURCES INC.

801 CHERRY ST UNIT 19
FORT WORTH, TX 761026833
Phone: 817 665-5000
Fax: –
Web: www.qrinc.com

CEO: Glenn Darden
CFO: Vanessa G Lagatta
HR: –
FYE: December 31
Type: Private

With mercurial speed, Quicksilver Resources' efforts to turn oil and gas finds into profits, have gone. The independent oil and gas company had operated in onshore oil and gas fields in North America. But facing a prolonged oil price slump and heavy debts, in 2016 the company sold its US and Canadian producing properties (in Colorado, Montana, Texas, and Wyoming, as well as Alberta). The company also had oil exploration opportunities in the Midland and Delaware basins in West Texas and Sand Wash basin in northwestern Colorado. Quicksilver Resources filed for Chapter 11 protection in 2015 and subsequently began liquidation procedures in 2016.

QUIDELORTHO CORP NMS: QDEL

9975 Summers Ridge Road
San Diego, CA 92121
Phone: 858 552-1100
Fax: –
Web: www.quidelortho.com

CEO: –
CFO: –
HR: –
FYE: December 31
Type: Public

Quidel Corporation makes rapid diagnostic in vitro test products used at the point-of-care (POC), usually at a doctor's office or other outpatient setting. The diagnostic solutions aid in the detection and diagnosis of many critical diseases and other medical conditions, including infectious diseases, cardiovascular diseases and conditions, women's health, gastrointestinal diseases, autoimmune diseases, bone health and thyroid diseases. Its cardiac immunoassay tests are used in physician offices, hospital laboratories and emergency departments, and other urgent care or alternative site settings. Majority of its revenue comes from its domestic operation.

	Annual Growth	12/19	12/20	12/21*	01/23*	12/23
Sales ($mil.)	53.9%	534.9	1,661.7	1,698.6	3,266.0	2,997.8
Net income ($ mil.)	–	72.9	810.3	704.2	548.7	(10.1)
Market value ($ mil.)	(0.4%)	5,004.5	11,983	9,003.8	5,714.2	4,915.8
Employees	54.4%	1,250	1,370	1,600	7,000	7,100

*Fiscal year change

QUINN EMANUEL URQUHART & SULLIVAN, LLP

865 S FIGUEROA ST FL 10
LOS ANGELES, CA 900175003
Phone: 213 443-3000
Fax: –
Web: www.quinnemanuel.com

CEO: –
CFO: –
HR: Claudia Cuevas
FYE: December 31
Type: Private

Business litigation specialist Quinn Emanuel Urquhart & Sullivan has more than 1,000 lawyers working out of about 35 offices in more than 10 countries across four continents. The firm organizes its trial practices into areas such as antitrust and competition, class actions, construction, health care, intellectual property, real estate, and tax disputes, among others. About 85% of trials and arbitrations that the firm handled won.

QUINNIPIAC UNIVERSITY

275 MOUNT CARMEL AVE
HAMDEN, CT 065181908
Phone: 203 582-8200
Fax: –
Web: www.qu.edu

CEO: –
CFO: –
HR: –
FYE: June 30
Type: Private

At Quinnipiac University the first thing you may have to learn is how to pronounce it (for the record, it's KWIN-uh-pe-ack). The private university offers a variety of liberal arts undergraduate programs, as well as graduate programs in selected professional fields (business, education, health sciences, communications, arts and sciences, nursing, and law) to some 9,000 students with a student-to-faculty ration of 16 to 1. It often appears on lists of top colleges, including those published by U.S. News & World Report. The university, known to political junkies and others for its polling operation, includes eight schools and colleges across three Connecticut campuses (Mount Carmel, York Hill, and North Haven).

	Annual Growth	06/16	06/17	06/20	06/21	06/22
Sales ($mil.)	0.5%	–	343.7	336.6	348.4	351.7
Net income ($ mil.)	–	–	114.2	17.6	242.5	(70.1)
Market value ($ mil.)	–	–	–	–	–	–
Employees	–	–	–	–	–	900

QUINSTREET, INC.

950 Tower Lane, 6th Floor
Foster City, CA 94404
Phone: 650 587-7700
Fax: –
Web: www.quinstreet.com

NMS: QNST

CEO: Douglas Valenti
CFO: Gregory Wong
HR: –
FYE: June 30
Type: Public

QuinStreet is a pioneer in powering decentralized online marketplaces that match searchers and research and compare consumers with brands. It runs these virtual and private-label marketplaces in one of the nation's largest media networks. The company specializes in customer acquisition for clients in high-value, information-intensive markets, or verticals, including financial services and home services. QuinStreet's approach to proprietary performance marketing technologies allows clients to engage high-intent digital media or traffic from a wide range of device types (mobile, desktop, tablet), in multiple formats or types of media (search engines, large and small media properties or websites, email), and a wide range of cost-per-action, or CPA, forms. The company was founded in 1999 and the majority of its operations and revenue are in North America.

	Annual Growth	06/19	06/20	06/21	06/22	06/23
Sales ($mil.)	6.3%	455.2	490.3	578.5	582.1	580.6
Net income ($ mil.)	–	62.5	18.1	23.6	(5.2)	(68.9)
Market value ($ mil.)	(13.6%)	859.0	566.9	1,006.9	545.2	478.5
Employees	10.1%	637	592	614	791	937

QUORUM HEALTH CORPORATION

1573 MALLORY LN STE 100
BRENTWOOD, TN 370272895
Phone: 615 221-1400
Fax: –
Web: www.quorumhealth.com

CEO: Chris Harisson
CFO: Alfred Lumsdaine
HR: –
FYE: December 31
Type: Private

Quorum Health is a leading provider of general acute care hospitals and outpatient services within the US. The company, through its various subsidiaries, owns, leases, or operates a diverse range of about 20 affiliated hospitals located in rural and medium-sized markets across some 15 states, with a combined total of more than 1,815 licensed beds. With a network of associated hospitals, medical practices, and healthcare providers, Quorum Health is committed to driving strategic growth and investment to expand its reach and address the critical healthcare needs of patients in their respective communities.

	Annual Growth	12/16	12/17	12/18	12/21	12/22
Sales ($mil.)	(94.9%)	–	–	1,878.6	–	0.0
Net income ($ mil.)	–	–	–	(198.2)	–	(0.1)
Market value ($ mil.)	–	–	–	–	–	–
Employees	–	–	–	–	–	8,600

QURATE RETAIL INC

12300 Liberty Boulevard
Englewood, CO 80112
Phone: 720 875-5300
Fax: –
Web: www.qurateretail.com

NMS: QRTE A

CEO: David Rawlinson II
CFO: Brian J Wendling
HR: Angela Jaszewski
FYE: December 31
Type: Public

Qurate Retail owns interests in subsidiaries and other companies which are primarily engaged in the video and online commerce industries. Its principal businesses and assets include QVC, HSN, Zulily, Cornerstone, and other cost and equity method investments. The Market-leading home shopping channel, QVC, curates and sells a wide variety of consumer products via highly engaging, video-rich, interactive shopping experiences distributed to approximately 217 million worldwide households each day across the home, apparel, beauty and accessories, jewelry, and electronics categories. In addition, QVC also sells online. The company generates the majority of its revenue in the US.

	Annual Growth	12/19	12/20	12/21	12/22	12/23
Sales ($mil.)	(5.1%)	13,458	14,177	14,044	12,106	10,915
Net income ($ mil.)	–	(456.0)	1,204.0	340.0	(2,594.0)	(145.0)
Market value ($ mil.)	(43.2%)	3,302.4	4,297.5	2,977.3	638.5	343.0
Employees	(5.3%)	25,228	26,424	26,659	24,600	20,300

QURATE RETAIL INC - COM SER A

12300 Liberty Boulevard
Englewood, CO 80112
Phone: 720 875-5300
Fax: –
Web: www.libertymedia.com

NMS: QRTE A

CEO: David Rawlinson II
CFO: Brian J Wendling
HR: Angela Jaszewski
FYE: December 31
Type: Public

Qurate Retail owns interests in subsidiaries and other companies which are primarily engaged in the video and online commerce industries. Its principal businesses and assets include QVC, HSN, Zulily, Cornerstone, and other cost and equity method investments. The Market-leading home shopping channel, QVC, curates and sells a wide variety of consumer products via highly engaging, video-rich, interactive shopping experiences distributed to approximately 217 million worldwide households each day across the home, apparel, beauty and accessories, jewelry, and electronics categories. In addition, QVC also sells online. The company generates the majority of its revenue in the US.

	Annual Growth	12/13	12/14	12/15	12/16	12/17
Sales ($mil.)	0.2%	10,307	10,028	9,169.0	10,219	10,381
Net income ($ mil.)	28.9%	438.0	520.0	640.0	473.0	1,208.0
Market value ($ mil.)	(4.5%)	14,045	14,079	13,074	9,561.2	11,686
Employees	5.2%	23,079	20,078	22,080	21,080	28,255

QURATE RETAIL INC - COM SER B

12300 Liberty Boulevard
Englewood, CO 80112
Phone: 720 875-5400
Fax: –
Web: www.qurateretail.com

NMS: QRTE B

CEO: David Rawlinson II
CFO: Brian J Wendling
HR: Angela Jaszewski
FYE: December 31
Type: Public

Qurate Retail owns interests in subsidiaries and other companies which are primarily engaged in the video and online commerce industries. Its principal businesses and assets include QVC, HSN, Zulily, Cornerstone, and other cost and equity method investments. The Market-leading home shopping channel, QVC, curates and sells a wide variety of consumer products via highly engaging, video-rich, interactive shopping experiences distributed to approximately 217 million worldwide households each day across the home, apparel, beauty and accessories, jewelry, and electronics categories. In addition, QVC also sells online. The company generates the majority of its revenue in the US.

	Annual Growth	12/16	12/17	12/18	12/19	12/20
Sales ($mil.)	8.5%	10,219	10,404	14,070	13,458	14,177
Net income ($ mil.)	26.3%	473.0	2,441.0	916.0	(456.0)	1,204.0
Market value ($ mil.)	(14.4%)	8,333.5	10,103	7,601.0	3,493.9	4,469.2
Employees	5.9%	21,080	–	27,226	25,314	26,508

QVC, INC.

1200 WILSON DR
WEST CHESTER, PA 193804262
Phone: 484 701-1000
Fax: –
Web: www.qvc.com

CEO: David L Rawlinson II
CFO: Bill Wafford
HR: –
FYE: December 31
Type: Private

QVC Inc. is a retailer of a wide range of consumer products, which are marketed and sold primarily by merchandise-focused televised shopping programs, the internet, and mobile applications. QVC is comprised of reportable segments QxH, which programming is available through QVC.com and HSN.com (the company's website), and QVC-International. QVC distributes its programming, via satellite and optical fiber, to cable television, and direct-to-home satellite system operators for retransmission to subscribers in the US, Germany, Japan, the UK, Italy, and neighboring countries. QVC's products are distributed to approximately 217 million worldwide households each day through its broadcast networks. QVC is a subsidiary of the shopping and travel site operator Qurate Retail. The company generates the majority of its revenue in the US.

R & R PRODUCTS, INC.

3334 E MILBER ST
TUCSON, AZ 857142029
Phone: 520 889-3593
Fax: –
Web: www.rrproducts.com

CEO: –
CFO: Brian Larson
HR: Debbie Gilmore
FYE: December 31
Type: Private

If a round or two of golf is your idea of R&R, then you may well have R&R Products to thank. The family-owned and operated company manufactures commercial golf course accessories including ball washers, sand trap rakes, and golf club cleaners. R&R also sells a line of turf products (spray applicators, irrigation gauges, and submersible pumps) and power equipment (generators, mowers, chainsaws, power washers, and leaf blowers) made by other manufacturers including Briggs & Stratton, Kubota, and Husqvarna. Safety equipment, such as chemical distribution cans, storage cabinets, and personnel safety wear, is included in R&R's lineup.

R. B. PAMPLIN CORPORATION

6605 SE LAKE RD
PORTLAND, OR 972222161
Phone: 503 248-1133
Fax: –
Web: www.mvmills.com

CEO: Robert B Pamplin Jr
CFO: –
HR: –
FYE: December 31
Type: Private

Founded by a man of the cloth, Robert B. Pamplin, Pamplin makes denim cloth and a lot more. The family-owned conglomerate has operations ranging from entertainment to retail stores to manufacturing interests (asphalt, concrete, and textiles). The company's Mount Vernon Mills is one of the top denim producers in the US. Pamplin's entertainment concerns include radio broadcasting, and newspapers serving the northwestern US. Other units are as diverse as retail stores and Columbia Empire Farms, which grows berries and grapes used in jams and wine; it also raises cattle.

R. E. MICHEL COMPANY, LLC

ONE R. E. MICHEL DRIVE
GLEN BURNIE, MD 210606408
Phone: 410 760-4000
Fax: –
Web: www.dealerslp.com

CEO: John Michel
CFO: Robert P Michel
HR: Brianna Cannon
FYE: December 31
Type: Private

Blowing hot and cold is good for R.E. Michel. The company is one of the nation's largest wholesale distributors of heating, air-conditioning, and refrigeration (HVAC-R) equipment, parts, and supplies. The family-owned and operated firm offers more than 16,000 items through about 2 sales offices located across the Southern, Mid-Atlantic, and Northeastern regions of the country. R.E. Michel ships more than 20,000 items each day from its 900,000-sq.-ft. distribution center in Maryland. Its Exclusive Supplier Partnership (ESP) program offers customers inventory control, advertising, and marketing support. R.E. Michel was founded in 1935 as a supplier to the home heating oil burner industry.

	Annual Growth	12/16	12/17	12/18	12/19	12/20
Sales ($mil.)	7.5%	–	804.0	898.2	939.4	999.3
Net income ($ mil.)	29.8%	–	26.1	37.1	48.8	57.1
Market value ($ mil.)	–	–	–	–	–	–
Employees	–	–	–	–	–	2,062

R. J. DAUM CONSTRUCTION COMPANY

11581 MONARCH ST
GARDEN GROVE, CA 928411814
Phone: 714 894-4300
Fax: –
Web: www.rjdaum.com

CEO: –
CFO: –
HR: Gretchen Garcia
FYE: June 30
Type: Private

General contractor R. J. Daum Construction specializes in building commercial facilities. The firm's list of projects have included central offices and other facilities for Pacific Bell (now part of SBC), public works (City and County of Los Angeles fire stations), educational facilities, and health care facilities. The company serves Southern California and Nevada from its offices in Garden Grove and San Diego, California. Raymond J. Daum established the company in 1936.

	Annual Growth	06/13	06/14	06/15	06/16	06/21
Sales ($mil.)	(5.1%)	–	32.2	30.9	23.4	22.3
Net income ($ mil.)	–	–	(0.4)	(0.3)	(0.7)	2.8
Market value ($ mil.)	–	–	–	–	–	–
Employees	–	–	–	–	–	25

R. L. JORDAN OIL COMPANY OF NORTH CAROLINA, INC.

1451 FERNWOOD GLENDALE RD STE 1
SPARTANBURG, SC 293073044
Phone: 864 585-2784
Fax: –
Web: www.hotspotcstore.com

CEO: –
CFO: –
HR: –
FYE: September 30
Type: Private

R. L. Jordan Oil Company takes gas from hot spots and sells it -- and lots more -- at Hot Spots. The company operates a chain of more than 50 convenience stores and gas stations under the Hot Spots banner, as well as about 10 fast food restaurants under the Hardee's and Subway names. It operates in the Carolinas. About 75% of the company's stores are located in South Carolina. The family-owned and -operated company was founded by its namesake and former chairman in 1950, the late R. L. Jordan. As part of its operations, the Jordan family also owns a real estate business, Jordan Properties, which operates several hotels and properties in North Carolina.

	Annual Growth	09/03	09/04	09/05	09/06	09/07
Sales ($mil.)	12.3%	–	–	221.0	271.0	278.6
Net income ($ mil.)	–	–	–	(0.9)	(1.7)	(0.3)
Market value ($ mil.)	–	–	–	–	–	–
Employees	–	–	–	–	–	900

R. R. DONNELLEY & SONS COMPANY

35 W WACKER DR
CHICAGO, IL 606011723
Phone: 800 782-4892
Fax: –
Web: www.rrd.com

CEO: Thomas J Quinlan III
CFO: Terry D Peterson
HR: –
FYE: December 31
Type: Private

RR Donnelley & Sons (RRD) is a leading global provider of multichannel business communications services and marketing solutions. The Company offers the industry's most trusted portfolio of creative execution and worldwide business process consulting, with services designed to lower environmental impact. With 22,000 clients, including 93% of the Fortune 100 and, and has operations across 28 countries, RRD brings the expertise, execution, and scale designed to transform customer touchpoints into meaningful moments of impact. In early 2022, R.R. Donnelley & Sons Company was acquired by a leading private investment firm Chatham Asset Management, LLC ("Chatham"), with a total enterprise value estimated to be approximately $2.5 billion.

	Annual Growth	12/16	12/17	12/18	12/19	12/20
Sales ($mil.)	(16.3%)	–	–	6,800.2	6,276.2	4,766.3
Net income ($ mil.)	–	–	–	(9.6)	(92.7)	99.0
Market value ($ mil.)	–	–	–	–	–	–
Employees	–	–	–	–	–	32,000

R.C. WILLEY HOME FURNISHINGS

2301 S 300 W
SOUTH SALT LAKE, UT 841152516
Phone: 801 461-3900
Fax: –
Web: www.rcwilley.com

CEO: –
CFO: –
HR: –
FYE: December 31
Type: Private

R.C. Willey Home Furnishings serves customers across the Western US with locations in Utah, Nevada, California, and Idaho. It sells furniture, appliances, electronics, and flooring. The company also sells mattresses. These products are sold under brand names Samsung, GE, Maytag, and LG, among others. R.C. Willey is owned by the investment giant Warren Buffett of Berkshire Hathaway. Adding the buying power of the other home furnishings stores he owns across the nation, its huge buying power guarantees the lowest price on name-brand merchandise. The company was founded back in 1932 when Rufus Call Willey began selling appliances from the back of his red pickup truck.

	Annual Growth	12/12	12/13	12/14	12/16	12/17
Sales ($mil.)	5.0%	–	664.6	713.0	800.9	807.7
Net income ($ mil.)	6.3%	–	15.4	17.4	26.7	19.6
Market value ($ mil.)	–	–	–	–	–	–
Employees	–	–	–	–	–	3,401

R.J. O'BRIEN & ASSOCIATES, LLC

222 S RIVERSIDE PLZ STE 1200
CHICAGO, IL 60606
Phone: 312 373-5000
Fax: –
Web: www.rjobrien.com

CEO: David Mudie
CFO: Jason Manumaleuna
HR: –
FYE: December 31
Type: Private

R.J. O'Brien (RJO) is one of the nation's oldest independent futures brokerage firms and a founding member of the CME's Chicago Mercantile Exchange. RJO provides electronic execution and clearing services for more than 100,000 clients on futures exchanges worldwide. Serving a network of some 400 introducing brokers, as well as corporations and individual traders, the company deals in such commodities as grains, currencies, metals, energy, livestock, and energy. The firm oversees some $3.6 billion in client assets. The company, majority-owned by the O'Brien family, traces its historical roots all the way back to 1914.

R.S. HUGHES COMPANY, INC.

1162 SONORA CT
SUNNYVALE, CA 940865378
Phone: 408 739-3211
Fax: –
Web: www.rshughes.com

CEO: Peter Biocini
CFO: Thomas Smith
HR: –
FYE: October 02
Type: Private

R.S. Hughes distributes the stuff that holds the world together -- duct tape, that is -- plus, a lot more. Established in 1954, the employee-owned company maintains some 45 warehouse locations in the US and Mexico. It supplies adhesives (epoxies, aerosols, hot glues, silicones), electrical specialties (tubing, terminals, films, tape, and barriers), safety products (glasses, ear plugs, masks), tapes (masking, foam, vinyl, cloth, foil, duct, joining), and abrasives (roll, disc, brush, wheel, belt, and air tools). R.S. Hughes also distributes labels and signs (printable labels and tags, safety signs) and aerosols and coatings (WD-40, paints, lubricants, oils, cleaners).

	Annual Growth	09/18	09/19	09/20*	10/21	10/22
Sales ($mil.)	4.9%	–	429.8	426.5	466.0	495.8
Net income ($ mil.)	7.9%	–	24.5	25.7	34.2	30.8
Market value ($ mil.)	–	–	–	–	–	–
Employees	–	–	–	–	–	592

*Fiscal year change

R1 RCM INC NEW

433 W. Ascension Way, Suite 200
Murray, UT 84123
Phone: 312 324-7820
Fax: –
Web: www.r1rcm.com

NMS: RCM
CEO: Joseph Flanagan
CFO: Jennifer Williams
HR: –
FYE: December 31
Type: Public

R1 RCM (formerly known as Accretive Health) is a leading provider of technology-driven solutions that transform the patient experience and financial performance of healthcare providers. It handles patient registration, benefits verification, medical treatment documentation and coding, billing, and other tasks for clients. The company specializes in enhancing efficiencies and quality while reducing costs. It provides technology solutions and process workflows. Typical customers are not-for-profit and for-profit hospital systems, such as Ascension Health and Intermountain Health, as well as independent medical centers, physician groups, and EMS organizations. The company operates about 15 offices in the US and six offices overseas. In mid-2022, R1 RCM acquired Cloudmed for approximately $4.1 billion.

	Annual Growth	12/19	12/20	12/21	12/22	12/23
Sales ($mil.)	17.4%	1,186.1	1,270.8	1,474.6	1,806.4	2,254.2
Net income ($ mil.)	(27.6%)	12.0	117.1	97.2	(57.6)	3.3
Market value ($ mil.)	(5.0%)	5,454.2	10,093	10,711	4,601.2	4,441.5
Employees	7.4%	22,500	20,200	22,000	27,800	29,900

RAANI CORPORATION

5202 W 70TH PL
BEDFORD PARK, IL 606386320
Phone: 708 496-1035
Fax: –
Web: –

CEO: Rashid A Chaudary
CFO: –
HR: –
FYE: December 31
Type: Private

Raani is a private-label manufacturer and contract packaging firm that offers blending and filling services, research and development, and regulatory guidance to the personal care product industry. The company offers hair care products (especially for the ethnic hair care niche), over-the-counter pharmaceuticals, skin care products, toiletries, cosmetics, and household cleaners. Its client list has included Kmart, Coty, Johnson Publishing, and the Army and Air Force Exchange Service. CEO and president Rashid Chaudary started the business out of a garage in 1983.

	Annual Growth	12/00	12/01	12/02	12/03	12/10
Sales ($mil.)	(45.1%)	–	–	2,076.7	16.7	17.1
Net income ($ mil.)	173.1%	–	–	0.0	1.5	0.7
Market value ($ mil.)	–	–	–	–	–	–
Employees	–	–	–	–	–	150

RACETRAC, INC.

200 GALLERIA PKWY SE STE 900
ATLANTA, GA 303395945
Phone: 770 850-3491
Fax: –
Web: www.racetrac.com

CEO: Natalie Morhous
CFO: Kimberly Turner
HR: Courtney Napier
FYE: December 31
Type: Private

RaceTrac Petroleum is one of the largest privately held companies in the US operating more than 800 retail locations in about a dozen states in the southeast. It is constantly growing throughout the South to deliver on its mission of making people's lives simpler and more enjoyable. RaceTrac stores offer guests an affordable one-stop-shop featuring a wide selection of food and beverage favorites, as well as Swirl World frozen desserts, freshly ground, freshly brewed coffee, and competitively-priced fuel. In addition, it also offers sandwich, salad, and snack options to its customers. Carl Bolch Sr. founded the family-owned company in 1934.

RACKSPACE TECHNOLOGY GLOBAL, INC.

1 FANATICAL PL
SAN ANTONIO, TX 782182179
Phone: 210 728-4549
Fax: –
Web: www.rackspace.com

CEO: Amar Maletira
CFO: Karl Pichler
HR: Aimee Hoyt
FYE: December 31
Type: Private

Rackspace Technology is a leading end-to-end multicloud technology services company. It designs, builds, and operates its customers' cloud environments across all major technology platforms, irrespective of technology stack or deployment model. The company provides expertise that helps companies set up in the cloud in computing through Amazon Web Services, Microsoft Azure, and other cloud environments, whether public, private or hybrid. Rackspace also partners with Google, OpenStack, Oracle, SAP, and VMware. It operates data centers placed around the world and has customers in about 120 countries. Among its clients are Everest Insurance, Teva Pharmaceuticals, Flextech, Walmart, and Nike. Rackspace generates approximately 75% of sales in the Americas.

RACKSPACE TECHNOLOGY INC

NMS: RXT

1 Fanatical Place, City of Windcrest
San Antonio, TX 78218
Phone: 800 961-4454
Fax: –
Web: www.rackspace.com

CEO: Amar Maletira
CFO: Karl Pichler
HR: Aimee Hoyt
FYE: December 31
Type: Public

Rackspace Technology is a leading end-to-end multicloud technology services company. It designs, builds, and operates its customers' cloud environments across all major technology platforms, irrespective of technology stack or deployment model. The company provides expertise that helps companies set up in the cloud in computing through Amazon Web Services, Microsoft Azure, and other cloud environments, whether public, private or hybrid. Rackspace also partners with Google, OpenStack, Oracle, SAP, and VMware. It operates data centers placed around the world and has customers in about 120 countries. Among its clients are Everest Insurance, Teva Pharmaceuticals, Flextech, Walmart, and Nike. Rackspace generates approximately 75% of sales in the Americas.

	Annual Growth	12/19	12/20	12/21	12/22	12/23
Sales ($mil.)	4.9%	2,438.1	2,707.1	3,009.5	3,122.3	2,957.1
Net income ($ mil.)	–	(102.3)	(245.8)	(218.3)	(804.8)	(837.8)
Market value ($ mil.)	–	–	4,143.6	2,928.4	641.3	434.8
Employees	(3.9%)	6,800	7,200	6,600	6,800	5,800

RADIAN GROUP, INC.

NYS: RDN

550 East Swedesford Road, Suite 350
Wayne, PA 19087
Phone: 215 231-1000
Fax: –
Web: www.radian.com

CEO: Richard G Thornberry
CFO: Robert J Quigley
HR: Nakazzi Ramashala
FYE: December 31
Type: Public

Radian Group is a diversified mortgage and real estate services business, providing both credit-related mortgage insurance coverage and an array of other mortgage, risk, title, real estate and technology products and services. Through subsidiaries Radian Guaranty, Radian Mortgage Assurance, and Radian Insurance, Radian provides traditional private mortgage insurance coverage to protect lenders from defaults by borrowers who put down a deposit of less than 20% when buying a home. Radian's customers include mortgage bankers, commercial banks, and savings institutions. The company establishes itself in the mortgage insurance industry as Commonwealth Mortgage Assurance Company (CMAC) in 1977.

	Annual Growth	12/19	12/20	12/21	12/22	12/23
Assets ($mil.)	2.8%	6,808.3	7,948.0	7,839.2	7,063.7	7,593.9
Net income ($ mil.)	(2.7%)	672.3	393.6	600.7	742.9	603.1
Market value ($ mil.)	3.2%	3,854.0	3,101.9	3,236.7	2,921.1	4,373.3
Employees	(13.9%)	2,000	1,600	1,800	1,400	1,100

RADIANT LOGISTICS, INC.

ASE: RLGT

Triton Tower Two, 700 S Renton Village Place, Seventh Floor
Renton, WA 98057
Phone: 425 462-1094
Fax: 425 462-0768
Web: www.radiantdelivers.com

CEO: Bohn H Crain
CFO: Todd E Macomber
HR: –
FYE: June 30
Type: Public

Radiant Logistics operates as a third-party logistics company, providing multi-modal transportation and logistics services primarily to customers based in the US and Canada. The company services a large and diversified account base, which it supports from an extensive network of locations across North America as well as an integrated international service partner network located in other key markets around the globe. Radiant Logistics provides these services through a multi-brand network, which includes over 100 locations operated exclusively on its behalf by independent agents, as well as approximately 25 company-owned offices. The US accounts for about 90% of the company's revenue.

	Annual Growth	06/19	06/20	06/21	06/22	06/23
Sales ($mil.)	5.1%	890.5	855.2	889.1	1,459.4	1,085.5
Net income ($ mil.)	5.9%	16.3	10.5	22.9	44.5	20.6
Market value ($ mil.)	2.3%	290.4	185.9	327.8	350.9	317.8
Employees	6.2%	708	603	685	836	899

RADIANT POWER IDC, LLC

7135 16TH ST E STE 101
SARASOTA, FL 342436818
Phone: 760 945-0230
Fax: –
Web: –

CEO: William J Lang
CFO: Matthew K Thomas
HR: –
FYE: December 31
Type: Private

Like the screens of your laptop computer, cell phone, and PDA, the products of Interface Displays & Controls are designed to display information whenever and wherever it's needed -- but in environments considerably harsher than the typical airport lounge. Interface Displays & Controls makes display devices and controls for use in aviation (including military aircraft), land transportation, and marine environments. The company makes its products, which are ruggedized and designed to withstand extreme temperatures, out of its 25,000 sq. ft. facility in southern California.

	Annual Growth	12/00	12/01	12/02	12/03	12/09
Sales ($mil.)	(27.2%)	–	–	76.1	7.6	8.3
Net income ($ mil.)	(17.5%)	–	–	4.3	1.6	1.1
Market value ($ mil.)	–	–	–	–	–	–
Employees	–	–	–	–	–	50

RADIENT PHARMACEUTICALS CORP

2492 Walnut Avenue, Suite 100
Tustin, CA 92780-7039
Phone: 714 505-4460
Fax: –
Web: www.radient-pharma.com

CEO: –
CFO: –
HR: –
FYE: December 31
Type: Public

Radient Pharmaceuticals (formerly AMDL) is ready to hunt down cancer and some day might even be able to do something about it. The company has developed and manufactures an in vitro blood test to detect over a dozen forms of cancer. Marketed as Onko-Sure, the test kits are approved for use in Europe and Asia; in the US the kits are approved for monitoring colorectal cancer, while in Canada it is used to detect lung cancer. Drug manufacturing facilities in China previously accounted for the bulk of the company's income, but it has chosen to focus its efforts on its Onko-Sure products. Other products in its pipeline include a technology with the potential to develop cancer vaccines.

	Annual Growth	12/07	12/08	12/09	12/10	12/11
Sales ($mil.)	(62.0%)	15.0	28.3	8.6	0.2	0.3
Net income ($ mil.)	–	(2.4)	1.2	(16.6)	(85.7)	(86.2)
Market value ($ mil.)	–	–	–	–	–	–
Employees	(56.8%)	315	500	7	10	11

RADISSON HOTELS INTERNATIONAL, INC.

701 CARLSON PKWY
MINNETONKA, MN 553055237
Phone: 763 212-5000
Fax: –
Web: www.radissonhotelgroup.com

CEO: Curtis C Nelson
CFO: Trudy Rautio
HR: –
FYE: December 31
Type: Private

This hotel caters to explorers traveling in style. Radisson Hotels & Resorts is a leading upscale hotel brand, with about 425 franchised locations in some 70 countries. The chain offers a full complement of amenities for both business and leisure travelers, including fine dining, fitness centers, and meeting rooms. Its resort locations typically boast such niceties as beachfront locations, golf courses, or skiing. Radisson Hotels takes its name from the French explorer Pierre Esprit Radisson, who visited many parts of the Upper Midwest and Canada during the 17th century. The company is the flagship luxury brand of Carlson Hotels Worldwide, part of the hospitality and business services giant Carlson Companies.

RADISYS CORPORATION

8900 NE WALKER RD STE 130
HILLSBORO, OR 970067032
Phone: 503 615-1100
Fax: –
Web: www.radisys.com

CEO: Arun Bhikshesvaran
CFO: Don Crosby
HR: Janella Bennett
FYE: December 31
Type: Private

RadiSys makes hardware and software that help its customers run their networks more efficiently. Its products help route video and audio traffic to systems that will process it most effectively, in terms of quality and cost. Radisys' offerings include application-specific systems, board-level modules, and chip-level components. The company also offers system integration, software, training, and repair services. RadiSys sells its products to companies that make telecommunications products, automated manufacturing devices, gaming machines, cars, medical instruments, and test and measurement tools. Customers range from Aastra and AT&T to Verint Systems and West Corp.

RADIUS RECYCLING INC

299 SW Clay Street, Suite 400
Portland, OR 97201
Phone: 503 224-9900
Fax: –
Web: www.schnitzersteel.com

NMS: RDUS
CEO: –
CFO: –
HR: –
FYE: August 31
Type: Public

Schnitzer Steel Industries is one of North America's largest recyclers of ferrous and nonferrous metal, including end-of-life vehicles, and a manufacturer of finished steel products. The company scrap to steelmakers primarily in the Western US and Western Canada. Schnitzer offers a range of products and services to meet global demand through its network that includes approximately 50 retail self-service auto parts stores, about 55 metals recycling facilities and an electric arc furnace (EAF) steel mill. Its Pick-n-Pull unit procures the significant majority of the company's salvaged vehicles and sell serviceable used auto parts from these vehicles. The US accounts for approximately 45% of the total sales.

	Annual Growth	08/19	08/20	08/21	08/22	08/23
Sales ($mil.)	7.8%	2,132.8	1,712.3	2,758.6	3,485.8	2,882.2
Net income ($ mil.)	–	56.3	(4.1)	165.1	168.8	(25.8)
Market value ($ mil.)	10.7%	609.1	543.1	1,301.6	909.0	913.4
Employees	(0.1%)	3,363	3,032	3,167	3,471	3,353

RADNET INC

1510 Cotner Avenue
Los Angeles, CA 90025
Phone: 310 478-7808
Fax: –
Web: www.radnet.com

NMS: RDNT
CEO: Howard G Berger
CFO: Mark D Stolper
HR: –
FYE: December 31
Type: Public

RadNet is a leading national provider of freestanding, fixed-site outpatient diagnostic imaging services in the US based on number of locations and annual imaging revenue. RadNet owns and/or manages more than 355 centers that offer a variety of diagnostic imaging services, including magnetic resonance imaging (MRI), computed tomography (CT), PET scanning, X-ray, ultrasound, and mammography. The vast majority of its centers offer multi-modality imaging services. Integral to the imaging center business is its software arm headed by eRAD, Inc., which sells computerized systems that distribute, display, store and retrieve digital images. RadNet was founded in 1984.

	Annual Growth	12/19	12/20	12/21	12/22	12/23
Sales ($mil.)	8.8%	1,154.2	1,098.1	1,324.2	1,430.1	1,616.6
Net income ($ mil.)	(32.6%)	14.8	(14.8)	24.7	10.7	3.0
Market value ($ mil.)	14.4%	1,379.5	1,329.9	2,046.2	1,279.6	2,362.8
Employees	(0.2%)	8,498	8,327	8,973	9,067	8,441

RADY CHILDREN'S HOSPITAL-SAN DIEGO

3020 CHILDRENS WAY
SAN DIEGO, CA 921234223
Phone: 858 576-1700
Fax: –
Web: www.rchsd.org

CEO: Donald Kearns
CFO: –
HR: –
FYE: June 30
Type: Private

Rady Children's Hospital-San Diego handles the big injuries of pint-sized patients. Serving as the region's only pediatric trauma center, the nonprofit hospital boasts more than 520 beds. As part of its services, Rady Children's Hospital-San Diego offers comprehensive pediatric care, including surgical services, convalescent care, a neonatal intensive care unit, and orthopedic services. Across its service area the hospital also operates about 25 satellite centers that provide such primary and specialized care services as physical therapy and hearing diagnostics. Rady Children's Hospital, a teaching hospital affiliated with the University of California San Diego Medical School, was founded in 1954.

	Annual Growth	06/14	06/15	06/19	06/20	06/21
Sales ($mil.)	15.7%	–	522.0	1,300.0	1,267.0	1,254.4
Net income ($ mil.)	27.5%	–	104.9	208.6	73.4	449.6
Market value ($ mil.)	–	–	–	–	–	–
Employees	–	–	–	–	–	2,313

RAIT FINANCIAL TRUST

130 W 42ND ST FL 17
NEW YORK, NY 100367904
Phone: 215 243-9000
Fax: -
Web: -

CEO: -
CFO: -
HR: -
FYE: December 31
Type: Private

RAIT Financial Trust is a real estate investment trust (REIT) that specializes in originating commercial real estate loans and acquiring and managing commercial real estate properties. RAIT was formed in 1997 and commenced operations in 1998. RAIT utilizes its in-house commercial real estate asset management platform to manage and service a portfolio of commercial real estate assets totaling more than $1.5 billion. The loan portfolio RAIT manages was previously originated by RAIT and is secured by diverse property types, including apartment, office and light-industrial properties and neighborhood retail centers. In 2020, Bankruptcy court confirms Chapter 11 plan of RAIT Financial Trust.

RALEY'S

500 W CAPITOL AVE
WEST SACRAMENTO, CA 956052696
Phone: 916 373-3333
Fax: -
Web: www.raleys.com

CEO: Michael Teel
CFO: Ken Mueller
HR: -
FYE: June 30
Type: Private

Raley's is a third-generation family business that makes healthier food more accessible to everyone. The largest family-owned company in the greater Sacramento region operates about 130 supermarkets and superstores in northern California and Nevada. In addition to about 80 flagship Raley's Superstores, the company operates about 20 Bel Air Markets (in the Sacramento area), Nob Hill Foods (an upscale Bay Area chain with approximately 20 locations), and five discount warehouse stores under the Food Source banner in Northern California and Nevada. Raley's stores typically offer groceries, natural foods, and liquor, as well as in-store pharmacies. Tom P. Raley opened his first store, Raley's grocery store, in 1935.

RALPH LAUREN CORP

NYS: RL

650 Madison Avenue
New York, NY 10022
Phone: 212 318-7000
Fax: -
Web: www.ralphlauren.com

CEO: Patrice Louvet
CFO: Jane H Nielsen
HR: -
FYE: April 1
Type: Public

Ralph Lauren Corporation is a global leader in the design, marketing, and distribution of premium lifestyle products, including apparel, footwear, accessories, home furnishings, fragrances and hospitality under such brands as Polo by Ralph Lauren, Chaps, RL Restaurant, Club Monaco, and RLX Ralph Lauren. The company sells directly to customers worldwide through its 550 retail stores and 720 concession-based shop-within-shops, as well as through its own digital commerce sites and those of various third-party digital partners. The company generates approximately 50% of revenue from the US.

	Annual Growth	03/19	03/20	03/21*	04/22	04/23
Sales ($mil.)	0.5%	6,313.0	6,159.8	4,400.8	6,218.5	6,443.6
Net income ($ mil.)	4.9%	430.9	384.3	(121.1)	600.1	522.7
Market value ($ mil.)	(2.6%)	8,507.0	4,460.1	8,013.7	7,347.2	7,653.6
Employees	(1.0%)	24,300	24,900	20,300	22,200	23,300

*Fiscal year change

RAMBOLL HOLDINGS, INC.

4245 FAIRFAX DR STE 700
ARLINGTON, VA 222031649
Phone: 703 516-2300
Fax: -
Web: www.ramboll.com

CEO: Stephen T Washburn
CFO: -
HR: -
FYE: December 31
Type: Private

ENVIRON is looking to clean up financially while helping to clean up the environment. An international environmental consulting firm, ENVIRON offers its expertise to companies on how to handle the intersection of science, business, and policy. It specializes in assessing risk factors related to the presence of chemicals in the environment, facilities, and in products such as food, drugs, medical devices, and consumer goods. The consulting firm helps clients comply with changing environmental regulations and policies. The company operates through three practices: environment, facilities, and human health. ENVIRON has completed projects around the world.

	Annual Growth	12/98	12/99	12/00	12/14	12/17
Sales ($mil.)	10.2%	-	55.2	53.7	-	315.0
Net income ($ mil.)	9.0%	-	1.0	1.0	-	4.9
Market value ($ mil.)	-	-	-	-	-	-
Employees	-	-	-	-	-	2,100

RAMBUS INC. (DE)

NMS: RMBS

4453 North First Street, Suite 100
San Jose, CA 95134
Phone: 408 462-8000
Fax: -
Web: www.rambus.com

CEO: Luc Seraphin
CFO: Desmond Lynch
HR: -
FYE: December 31
Type: Public

Rambus makes industry-leading chips and IP that enable critical performance improvements for data center and other growing markets. The ongoing shift to the cloud, along with the widespread advancement of artificial intelligence ("AI") across the data center, edge and Internet of Things (IoT) end points, has led to exponential growth in data usage and tremendous demands on data infrastructure. Rambus' leading licensees include AMD, Fujitsu, NVIDIA, Panasonic, and Broadcom. Rambus products and innovations deliver the increased bandwidth, capacity and security required to meet the customer's data needs and drive ever-greater end-user experiences. The company holds some 2,380 patents and has about 6050 patent applications pending. The US generated majority of its sales.

	Annual Growth	12/19	12/20	12/21	12/22	12/23
Sales ($mil.)	19.8%	224.0	242.7	328.3	454.8	461.1
Net income ($ mil.)	-	(90.4)	(43.6)	18.3	(14.3)	333.9
Market value ($ mil.)	49.2%	1,485.7	1,883.1	3,169.8	3,863.3	7,361.0
Employees	(2.3%)	685	623	690	765	623

RAND LOGISTICS, LLC

333 WASHINGTON ST STE 201
JERSEY CITY, NJ 073023095
Phone: 212 863-9403
Fax: -
Web: www.randlog.com

CEO: Peter Coxon
CFO: Mark S Hiltwein
HR: -
FYE: March 31
Type: Private

Rand Logistics hauls dry bulk cargo across the Great Lakes, calling on ports in the US and Canada. Through subsidiaries Lower Lakes Towing (Canadian ports), Lower Lakes Transportation (US ports), and Grand River Navigation, the company operates a fleet of more than a dozen vessels, consisting mainly of self-unloading bulk carriers. (Self-unloading vessels don't require land-based assistance, so they can arrive at a dock and unload any time.) Conventional bulk carriers and an integrated tug/barge unit make up the rest of Rand Logistics' fleet. Cargo carried by the company includes construction aggregates, coal, grain, iron ore, and salt. Mainly to eliminate about $90 million in outstanding debt, Rand Logistics agreed to be acquired by American Industrial Partners, a New York-based private equity firm, in late 2017.

RANDA ACCESSORIES LEATHER GOODS LLC

5600 N RIVER RD STE 500
ROSEMONT, IL 600185188
Phone: 847 292-8300
Fax: –
Web: www.randa.net

CEO: –
CFO: –
HR: –
FYE: December 31
Type: Private

Randa Accessories Leather Goods, operating as Randa Apparel & Accessories (RAA), is a global powerhouse and one of the world's leading fashion clothing and lifestyle accessories companies. It makes men's, women's, and boys' belts, suspenders, and other personal leather goods, as well as wallets, slippers and seasonal accessories. The company brands include Levi's, Dockers, Dickies, Columbia, Cool Haan, and Arrow brand names, among others. Randa operates a portfolio of over 30 brands across all channels of distribution.

RANGE RESOURCES CORP   NYS: RRC

100 Throckmorton Street, Suite 1200
Fort Worth, TX 76102
Phone: 817 870-2601
Fax: –
Web: www.rangeresources.com

CEO: Dennis L Degner
CFO: Mark S Scucchi
HR: –
FYE: December 31
Type: Public

Range Resources is an independent natural gas, NGLs, and oil company, engaged in the exploration, development, and acquisition of natural gas and oil properties in the US, primarily in the Marcellus Shale of Pennsylvania, and also maintains field offices in its area of operations. The company has 18.1 Tcfe of proved reserves (about 65% of which is natural gas), with an average production of nearly 2.15 per day from some 1,425 net producing wells.

	Annual Growth	12/19	12/20	12/21	12/22	12/23
Sales ($mil.)	4.5%	2,827.6	1,968.7	2,930.2	4,146.8	3,374.4
Net income ($ mil.)	–	(1,716.3)	(711.8)	411.8	1,183.4	871.1
Market value ($ mil.)	58.3%	1,169.0	1,615.0	4,297.7	6,030.8	7,337.3
Employees	(4.4%)	655	533	527	544	548

RANGERS SUB I, LLC

3 BETHESDA METRO CTR STE 1000
BETHESDA, MD 208145330
Phone: 301 280-7777
Fax: –
Web: –

CEO: Ross Bierkan
CFO: –
HR: –
FYE: December 31
Type: Private

FelCor Lodging welcomes weary North American travelers looking for a little luxury. One of the top hotel real estate investment trusts in the US, FelCor owns interests in 60 properties with almost 18,000 rooms in more than 20 US states and one in Toronto, Canada. Most are upscale hotels operating under the Embassy Suites, Holiday Inn, Doubletree, Sheraton, Westin, Renaissance, and Hilton brands. The properties are managed by Hilton Worldwide, InterContinental Hotels, Marriott International, Starwood Hotels & Resorts, and Fairmont. It also has several independent hotels in New York. FelCor's portfolio is concentrated in major metropolitan and resort areas of Florida, California, and Texas. In late-2017 FelCor merger with, and took the name of, RLJ Lodging.

RANKEN TECHNICAL COLLEGE

4431 FINNEY AVE
SAINT LOUIS, MO 631132811
Phone: 314 371-0236
Fax: –
Web: www.ranken.edu

CEO: –
CFO: Peter Murtaugh
HR: –
FYE: June 30
Type: Private

Ranken Technical College offers postsecondary vocational education in a variety of technical and industrial fields. Students can gain certification or associate's degrees in automotive repair, construction, electronics, information technology, and industrial technology. The school is located in the Central West End of St. Louis. Irish-born David Ranken, Jr. fulfilled his dream of founding a school for the teaching of mechanical trades when he established Ranken Technical College (then known as David Ranken, Jr. School of Mechanical Trades) in 1907.

	Annual Growth	06/17	06/18	06/19	06/20	06/22
Sales ($mil.)	9.9%	–	32.3	33.2	40.7	47.1
Net income ($ mil.)	23.2%	–	2.5	(2.9)	(3.8)	5.8
Market value ($ mil.)	–	–	–	–	–	–
Employees	–	–	–	–	–	150

RAPID RESPONSE MONITORING SERVICES INC

400 W DIVISION ST
SYRACUSE, NY 132041552
Phone: 315 424-6794
Fax: –
Web: www.rrms.com

CEO: Russell R Macdonnell
CFO: David Pida
HR: James Runge
FYE: December 31
Type: Private

Rapid Response Monitoring provides wholesale security alarm monitoring services to more than 900 security system dealers. It monitors about 200,000 security systems for customers throughout the US from a central facility in New York state. In addition to security alarm monitoring, Rapid Response also monitors fire alarms and offers GPS tracking and monitoring services. The company is also one of about two dozen firms approved to monitor fire alarms in New York City. Chairman and CEO Russell MacDonnell and president Jeffrey Atkins, owners of Rapid Response Monitoring, founded the company in 1992.

	Annual Growth	12/06	12/07	12/08	12/09	12/10
Sales ($mil.)	12.9%	–	–	18.5	20.4	23.5
Net income ($ mil.)	166.1%	–	–	0.2	(0.2)	1.3
Market value ($ mil.)	–	–	–	–	–	–
Employees	–	–	–	–	–	350

RAPID7 INC   NMS: RPD

120 Causeway Street
Boston, MA 02114
Phone: 617 247-1717
Fax: –
Web: www.rapid7.com

CEO: Corey E Thomas
CFO: Tim Adams
HR: –
FYE: December 31
Type: Public

Cybersecurity attacks threaten companies at a rapid-fire pace. Rapid7 responds in kind. The company's products assess and analyze corporate networks, detect intrusions, and root them out. The company's cloud-based Rapid7 Insight Platform provides customers with a wide view of systems and threats as well as detailed information about users and where vulnerabilities lurk. Rapid7 calls its approach a new model that employs analytics to reduce and manage risks across a system instead of a front-loaded 'block-and-protect' style. Most the company's sales are in the US. Rapid7 was named after a New York City express train that the founders rode to work in the company's early days.

	Annual Growth	12/19	12/20	12/21	12/22	12/23
Sales ($mil.)	24.2%	326.9	411.5	535.4	685.1	777.7
Net income ($ mil.)	–	(53.8)	(98.8)	(146.3)	(124.7)	(149.3)
Market value ($ mil.)	0.5%	3,457.2	5,564.1	7,263.1	2,097.0	3,523.9
Employees	9.6%	1,544	1,847	2,353	2,623	2,228

RAPPAHANNOCK ELECTRIC COOPERATIVE

247 INDUSTRIAL CT
FREDERICKSBURG, VA 224082443
Phone: 540 898-8500
Fax: –
Web: www.myrec.coop

CEO: Kent D Farmer
CFO: –
HR: –
FYE: December 31
Type: Private

Like the river it's named after, the Rappahannock Electric Cooperative (REC) keeps the power running smoothly. The consumer-owned cooperative provides electricity to homes, businesses, and industries in parts of 22 counties from the Blue Ridge Mountains to the mouth of the Rappahannock River in eastern Virginia. REC supplies power to more than 157,000 members over more than 16,000 miles of power line. REC offers surge protection, internet services, and home security plans to entice customers as competition from other suppliers arrives. Once rural in nature, the cooperative's territory has seen large pockets of suburban growth.

	Annual Growth	12/18	12/19	12/20	12/21	12/22
Sales ($mil.)	1.3%	–	461.4	416.4	408.7	479.2
Net income ($ mil.)	(32.1%)	–	18.5	17.8	17.5	5.8
Market value ($ mil.)	–	–	–	–	–	–
Employees	–	–	–	–	–	423

RARITAN BAY MEDICAL CENTER, A NEW JERSEY NONPROFIT CORPORATION

530 NEW BRUNSWICK AVE
PERTH AMBOY, NJ 088613654
Phone: 732 442-3700
Fax: –
Web: www.hackensackmeridianhealth.org

CEO: Mark Danielle
CFO: Thomas Shanahan
HR: Brian McCauley
FYE: December 31
Type: Private

Health care is not rare at Raritan Bay Medical Center (RBMC). The not-for-profit center operates two hospitals in central New Jersey: Its Perth Amboy campus has about 390 beds, and its Old Bridge campus has more than 110 beds. RBMC provides acute care and emergency services, as well as ambulatory care through its outpatient clinics. Its Perth Amboy location provides specialized care in fields including women's and children's health. RBMC is affiliated with the University of Medicine and Dentistry of New Jersey- Robert Wood Johnson Medical School, as well as the Cancer Institute of New Jersey.

	Annual Growth	12/05	12/06	12/08	12/13	12/15
Sales ($mil.)	(0.2%)	–	232.3	228.6	228.2	227.7
Net income ($ mil.)	–	–	3.5	(6.9)	0.2	(9.3)
Market value ($ mil.)	–	–	–	–	–	–
Employees	–	–	–	–	–	1,970

RARITAN VALLEY COMMUNITY COLLEGE

118 LAMINGTON RD
BRANCHBURG, NJ 088763315
Phone: 908 526-1200
Fax: –
Web: www.rvccathletics.com

CEO: –
CFO: –
HR: –
FYE: June 30
Type: Private

Raritan Valley Community College offers more than 90 associate degree and certification programs to residents in central New Jersey's Somerset and Hunterdon counties. The school offers nine academic departments, including Business and Public Service; Communication & Languages; Computer Science; English; Health Science Education; Humanities; Social Science & Education; Mathematics; Science & Engineering; and Visual and Performing Arts. The college, which boasts some 1,400 courses, also provides customized training programs and non-credit courses, as well as job and career counseling services. More than 8,400 students take classes at Raritan Valley Community College, which was founded in 1965.

	Annual Growth	06/15	06/16*	08/19*	06/21	06/22
Sales ($mil.)	(4.9%)	–	1.3	0.0	1.5	1.0
Net income ($ mil.)	–	–	0.4	0.0	0.6	(0.1)
Market value ($ mil.)	–	–	–	–	–	–
Employees	–	–	–	–	–	550

*Fiscal year change

RAVE RESTAURANT GROUP INC

NAS: RAVE

3551 Plano Parkway
The Colony, TX 75056
Phone: 469 384-5000
Fax: –
Web: www.pizzainn.com

CEO: –
CFO: –
HR: –
FYE: June 25
Type: Public

Pizza is the in thing for this company. Pizza Inn operates a chain of franchised quick-service pizza restaurants, with more than 300 locations in the US and the Middle East. The eateries feature a menu of pizzas, pastas, and sandwiches, along with salads and desserts. Most locations offer buffet-style and table service, while other units are strictly delivery and carryout units. The chain also has limited-menu express carryout units in convenience stores and airport terminals, and on college campuses. Pizza Inn's domestic locations are concentrated in more than 15 southern states, with about half located in Texas and North Carolina. Chairman Mark Schwarz owns more than 35% of the company.

	Annual Growth	06/19	06/20	06/21	06/22	06/23
Sales ($mil.)	(0.9%)	12.3	10.0	8.6	10.7	11.9
Net income ($ mil.)	–	(0.8)	(4.2)	1.5	8.0	1.6
Market value ($ mil.)	(11.6%)	43.6	12.7	20.1	15.0	26.6
Employees	(13.7%)	45	22	23	24	25

RAVEN INDUSTRIES, INC

205 E 6TH ST
SIOUX FALLS, SD 571045931
Phone: 605 336-2750
Fax: –
Web: www.ravenind.com

CEO: –
CFO: –
HR: –
FYE: January 31
Type: Private

Quoth the Raven, "Balloons (and more) evermore!" Raven Industries is a diversified technology company that caters to the industrial, agricultural, energy, construction, military, and aerospace sectors. The company's Aerostar division sells high-altitude, research balloons, as well as parachutes and protective wear used by US agencies, while its Engineered Films Division makes reinforced plastic sheeting for various applications. The Applied Technology Division manufactures high-tech agricultural aids, from global positioning system (GPS)-based steering devices and chemical spray equipment to field computers.

RAYBURN COUNTRY ELECTRIC COOPERATIVE, INC.

950 SIDS RD
ROCKWALL, TX 750326512
Phone: 972 771-1336
Fax: –
Web: www.rayburnelectric.com

CEO: –
CFO: David Braun
HR: Staci Bratcher
FYE: December 31
Type: Private

This is indeed Sam Rayburn country. Rayburn Country Electric Cooperative (Rayburn Electric) operates in the old stomping grounds of the legendary Texas politician and former speaker of the US House of Representatives. Rayburn Electric is a power generation and transmission organization that supplies wholesale power to five rural distribution cooperatives operating in 16 counties in north central and northeastern Texas. Five distribution cooperatives (Fannin County Electric Coop, Farmers Electric Coop, Grayson-Collin Electric Coop, Lamar Electric Coop, and Trinity Valley Electric Coop) collectively own the company.

	Annual Growth	12/12	12/13	12/14	12/21	12/22
Sales ($mil.)	7.2%	–	301.3	340.2	1,364.3	563.0
Net income ($ mil.)	37.0%	–	0.0	0.0	0.0	0.0
Market value ($ mil.)	–	–	–	–	–	–
Employees	–	–	–	–	–	27

RAYMOND JAMES & ASSOCIATES INC

880 CARILLON PKWY
SAINT PETERSBURG, FL 337161100
Phone: 727 567-1000
Fax: –
Web: www.raymondjames.com

CEO: Paul Reilly
CFO: Jeffrey P Julien
HR: Mindy Waggener
FYE: September 30
Type: Private

Does everybody love Raymond James & Associates (RJA)? Raymond James Financial hopes so. RJA is that company's primary subsidiary and one of the largest retail brokerages in the US. The unit provides brokerage, financial planning, investments, and related services to consumers. It performs equity and fixed income sales, trading, and research for institutional clients in North America and Europe. Its investment banking group provides corporate and public finance, debt underwriting, and mergers and acquisitions advice. RJA also makes markets for approximately 1,000 stocks, including thinly traded issues. Planning Corporation of America, a wholly-owned subsidiary of RJA, sells insurance and annuities.

	Annual Growth	09/13	09/14	09/15	09/16	09/17
Assets ($mil.)	12.6%	–	6,955.6	7,893.9	10,689	9,917.5
Net income ($ mil.)	2.8%	–	182.7	167.8	145.8	198.5
Market value ($ mil.)	–	–	–	–	–	–
Employees	–	–	–	–	–	10,000

RAYMOND JAMES FINANCIAL, INC.   NYS: RJF

880 Carillon Parkway
St. Petersburg, FL 33716
Phone: 727 567-1000
Fax: –
Web: www.raymondjames.com

CEO: Paul C Reilly
CFO: Paul M Shoukry
HR: –
FYE: September 30
Type: Public

Raymond James Financial, Inc. (RJF) is a leading diversified financial services company providing private client group, capital markets, asset management, banking and other services to individuals, corporations and municipalities. The company is engaged in various financial services activities, including providing investment management services to retail and institutional clients, merger & acquisition and advisory services, the underwriting, distribution, trading and brokerage of equity and debt securities, and the sale of mutual funds and other investment products. It also provides corporate and retail banking services, and trust services. The company primarily earns its revenue from its domestic operations with about 90% of the net revenue.

	Annual Growth	09/19	09/20	09/21	09/22	09/23
Sales ($mil.)	12.8%	8,023.0	8,168.0	9,910.0	11,308	12,992
Net income ($ mil.)	13.9%	1,034.0	818.0	1,403.0	1,509.0	1,739.0
Market value ($ mil.)	5.1%	17,215	15,190	19,265	20,631	20,967
Employees	(17.6%)	18,910	19,635	20,021	22,043	8,712

RAYMOURS FURNITURE COMPANY, INC.

7248 MORGAN RD
LIVERPOOL, NY 130904535
Phone: 888 729-6687
Fax: –
Web: www.raymourflanigan.com

CEO: Neil Goldberg
CFO: James Poole
HR: –
FYE: December 29
Type: Private

Raymours Furniture is heating up the oft-chilly Northeast, doing business as Raymour & Flanigan. The company operates in several states through 94 retail stores, including nearly a dozen clearance centers. It sells furniture for just about every room in the house (bedroom, dining room, home office, living room), offering such pieces as bookcases, entertainment centers, headboards, mattresses, nightstands, recliners, sofas, and tables. Brands such as Broyhill, La-Z-Boy, Natuzzi, and Tempur Sealy are represented. Raymours is run by founding Goldberg family.

	Annual Growth	12/03	12/04	12/05	12/06	12/07
Sales ($mil.)	16.0%	–	–	655.5	780.6	881.8
Net income ($ mil.)	20.2%	–	–	21.0	23.4	30.4
Market value ($ mil.)	–	–	–	–	–	–
Employees	–	–	–	–	–	6,166

RAYONIER ADVANCED MATERIALS INC   NYS: RYAM

1301 Riverplace Boulevard, Suite 2300
Jacksonville, FL 32207
Phone: 904 357-4600
Fax: –
Web: www.ryam.com

CEO: De W Lyle Bloomquis
CFO: Marcus J Moeltner
HR: Duke Hearons
FYE: December 31
Type: Public

Rayonier Advanced Materials (RYAM) is a global leader in specialty cellulose materials with a broad offering of high-purity cellulose specialties, a natural polymer used in the production of a variety of specialty chemical products, including liquid crystal displays, filters, textiles, and performance additives for pharmaceutical, food, and other industrial applications. The company provides some of the highest quality high-purity cellulose pulp products that make up the essential building blocks for its customers' products while providing exceptional service and value. It also produces a unique, lightweight multi-ply paperboard product and a bulky, high-yield pulp product. The company traces its history back to 1926 when the Rainier Pulp & Paper Company began operation in Washington State. The US generates nearly 35% of the company's revenue.

	Annual Growth	12/19	12/20	12/21	12/22	12/23
Sales ($mil.)	(1.9%)	1,775.4	1,738.9	1,407.6	1,717.3	1,643.3
Net income ($ mil.)	–	(22.5)	0.6	66.4	(14.9)	(101.8)
Market value ($ mil.)	1.3%	251.1	426.4	373.4	627.8	264.8
Employees	(8.5%)	4,000	4,000	2,500	2,500	2,800

RAYONIER INC.   NYS: RYN

1 Rayonier Way
Wildlight, FL 32097
Phone: 904 357-9100
Fax: –
Web: www.rayonier.com

CEO: David L Nunes
CFO: Mark D McHugh
HR: Amber Priess
FYE: December 31
Type: Public

Rayonier is a leading timberland real estate investment trust (REIT) with assets located in some of the most productive softwood timber growing regions in the US and New Zealand. The company owns, leases, or manages about 2.8 million acres of timberland and real estate in the US, in addition to some 417,000 acres in New Zealand through a joint venture. In addition, the REIT is engage in the trading of logs to Pacific Rim markets, predominantly from New Zealand and Australia to support its New Zealand export operations. Roughly 65% of total revenue comes from US operations.

	Annual Growth	12/19	12/20	12/21	12/22	12/23
Sales ($mil.)	10.4%	711.6	859.2	1,109.6	909.1	1,056.9
Net income ($ mil.)	30.9%	59.1	37.1	152.6	107.1	173.5
Market value ($ mil.)	0.5%	4,858.3	4,357.0	5,985.4	4,887.9	4,954.7
Employees	5.6%	353	413	406	419	439

RB GLOBAL INC   NYS: RBA

Two Westbrook Corporate Center, Suite 500
Westchester, IL 60154
Phone: 708 492-7000
Fax: –
Web: www.investor.rbglobal.com

CEO: –
CFO: –
HR: –
FYE: December 31
Type: Public

Forget JFK's desk. Ritchie Bros. Auctioneers handles bids for the truck that hauled it. Its "unreserved" auctions (no minimum bids or bids from the seller or auctioneer) include equipment used in the agricultural, construction, forestry, mining, and transportation industries. One of the world's largest industrial auctioneers, it holds more than 350 auctions a year in 110 offices across Asia, Australia, Europe, Central America, the Middle East, and North America. Ritchie Bros., which receives a percentage of the sale price, also offers translation services and arranges for finance companies to be present at its auctions. Established in 1963, the company acquired Houston-based AssetNation.

	Annual Growth	12/19	12/20	12/21	12/22	12/23
Sales ($mil.)	29.2%	1,318.6	1,377.3	1,417.0	1,733.8	3,679.6
Net income ($ mil.)	8.5%	149.0	170.1	151.9	319.7	206.5
Market value ($ mil.)	11.7%	7,853.1	12,717	11,192	10,574	12,230
Employees	41.4%	2,400	2,600	4,300	4,200	9,600

RBC BEARINGS INC

NYS: RBC

One Tribology Center
Oxford, CT 06478
Phone: 203 267-7001
Fax: –
Web: www.rbcbearings.com

CEO: Michael J Hartnett
CFO: Robert M Sullivan
HR: –
FYE: April 1
Type: Public

RBC Bearings is an international manufacturer and marketer of highly engineered precision bearings, components, and essential systems for the industrial, defense, and aerospace industries. Its precision solutions are integral to the manufacture and operation of most machines and mechanical systems, to reduce wear to moving parts, facilitate proper power transmission, reduce damage and energy loss caused by friction, and control pressure and flow. The company's products are used in various industrial applications in the Industrial segment, as well as in commercial aerospace, defense aerospace, and marine ground defense applications in the Aerospace/Defense segment. RBC's top aerospace and defense customers include Airbus, Boeing, Lockheed Martin, Northrop Grumman, and the US Department of Defense. Nearly 90% of sales come from its domestic revenue.

	Annual Growth	03/19	03/20*	04/21	04/22	04/23
Sales ($mil.)	20.3%	702.5	727.5	609.0	942.9	1,469.3
Net income ($ mil.)	12.2%	105.2	126.0	89.6	65.1	166.7
Market value ($ mil.)	16.3%	3,690.9	3,192.6	5,750.7	5,675.6	6,754.7
Employees	(0.6%)	3,764	3,890	3,885	–	–

*Fiscal year change

RBC LIFE SCIENCES INC

NBB: RBCL

2301 Crown Court
Irving, TX 75038
Phone: 972 893-4000
Fax: 972 893-4111
Web: www.rbclifesciences.com

CEO: Clinton H Howard
CFO: Steven E Brown
HR: –
FYE: December 31
Type: Public

RBC Life Sciences offers really big changes to its clients' bodies. RBC markets and distributes more than 75 nutritional, weight loss, and personal care products under the RBC Life brand. The company's leading product, Microhydrin, is touted to increase energy and slow the effects of aging. The company relies on a multi-level marketing network of some 10,000 independent distributors in the US and Canada. It also markets and distributes wound care, pain management, and cancer care products used in clinical settings, and sold under the MPM Medical brand.

	Annual Growth	12/12	12/13	12/14	12/15	12/16
Sales ($mil.)	0.6%	25.2	25.5	28.3	24.4	25.8
Net income ($ mil.)	–	(0.4)	(0.5)	(0.6)	(0.7)	(0.8)
Market value ($ mil.)	31.6%	0.2	3.4	2.9	0.6	0.7
Employees	–	76	76	89	–	–

RBZ LLP

11766 WILSHIRE BLVD FL 9
LOS ANGELES, CA 900256548
Phone: 310 478-4148
Fax: –
Web: www.rbz.com

CEO: –
CFO: –
HR: –
FYE: December 31
Type: Private

The professionals at RBZ are "BZ" making sure their clients' affairs are in order. the Los Angeles-based accounting and consulting firm provides accounting, tax, and management consulting services to clients in the US and abroad (through an affiliation with the International Network of Accountants and Auditors). Founded in 1975, RBZ focuses on business management, international tax, and family wealth services. Its also serves middle market businesses and clients in the real estate industry, as well as law firms, and not-for-profit organizations. Its RBZ Business Management arm serves high net worth individuals and those in the entertainment business. Another division focuses on serving small businesses.

RCI HOSPITALITY HOLDINGS INC

NMS: RICK

10737 Cutten Road
Houston, TX 77066
Phone: 281 397-6730
Fax: –
Web: www.rcihospitality.com

CEO: –
CFO: –
HR: –
FYE: September 30
Type: Public

Far from Casablanca, these night clubs offer topless entertainment as part of the floor show. Rick's Cabaret International operates more than 30 adult night clubs in Arizona, Florida, Minnesota, New York, North Carolina, and Texas. Most of the gentlemen's clubs are run under the Rick's Cabaret name, while others operate under such banners as Club Onyx and XTC. Rick's caters to highbrow patrons with dough to blow: It offers VIP memberships for individual and corporate clients that can cost hundreds of dollars annually. In addition to its night clubs, Rick's operates adult websites and an auction site for adult entertainment products.

	Annual Growth	09/19	09/20	09/21	09/22	09/23
Sales ($mil.)	12.9%	181.1	132.3	195.3	267.6	293.8
Net income ($ mil.)	11.1%	19.2	(6.1)	30.3	46.0	29.2
Market value ($ mil.)	30.9%	194.3	191.7	643.8	614.0	570.1
Employees	14.5%	2,200	2,074	2,529	3,219	3,778

RCM TECHNOLOGIES, INC.

NMS: RCMT

2500 McClellan Avenue, Suite 350
Pennsauken, NJ 08109-4613
Phone: 856 356-4500
Fax: –
Web: www.rcmt.com

CEO: –
CFO: –
HR: –
FYE: December 30
Type: Public

RCM Technologies is a premier provider of business and technology solutions designed to enhance and maximize the operational performance of its customers through the adaptation and deployment of advanced engineering, life sciences, and information technology services. The company is an IT services and engineering firm that performs the design and implementation of technology and software systems, project management, and engineering analysis services. It also provides specialty healthcare staffing for therapists, nurses, and caregivers. The US markets account around 95% of total revenue.

	Annual Growth	12/19*	01/21	01/22*	12/22	12/23
Sales ($mil.)	8.3%	191.1	150.4	203.9	284.7	263.2
Net income ($ mil.)	42.7%	4.1	(8.9)	11.0	20.9	16.8
Market value ($ mil.)	78.4%	22.5	16.2	55.9	96.8	227.8
Employees	0.6%	3,410	2,275	3,630	3,540	3,490

*Fiscal year change

RCS CORPORATION

11605 N COMMUNITY HOUSE RD STE 100
CHARLOTTE, NC 282774797
Phone: 803 507-2842
Fax: –
Web: www.rcs.jobs

CEO: –
CFO: –
HR: –
FYE: December 31
Type: Private

RCS Corporation wants to be your one-stop-shop for hiring engineers, project managers, scientists, and other technical professionals. The company provides professional and technical staffing services for government and commercial clients in the US, Europe, the Middle East, and China. Industries covered include power generation, infrastructure, and petrochemical. In addition to provide direct-hire and contract personnel, the company offers payroll services. RCS Corporation was established by energy industry professionals in 1994.

RDO CONSTRUCTION EQUIPMENT CO.

225 BDWY N
FARGO, ND 581024800
Phone: 701 239-8700
Fax: –
Web: www.rdoequipment.com

CEO: Tim Curoe
CFO: Steven Dewald
HR: –
FYE: April 30
Type: Private

RDO Equipment sells and rents new and used trucks and heavy equipment to customers in the agriculture and construction industries. RDO Equipment operates more than 75 locations across the United States. It offers John Deere agriculture equipment, construction and forestry, and lawn and land, as well as Vermmer, Topcon, and other top brands. RDO also has partnerships in Africa, Australia, Mexico, Russia, and Ukraine, making it a total solutions provider and partner to customers around the globe. Ronald Offutt founded the family-owned and operated company in 1968.

	Annual Growth	04/16	04/17	04/18	04/19	04/20
Sales ($mil.)	2.4%	–	–	2,138.8	2,095.6	2,242.4
Net income ($ mil.)	1.2%	–	–	46.9	52.6	48.1
Market value ($ mil.)	–	–	–	–	–	–
Employees	–	–	–	–	–	1,500

RDR, INC.

14900 CONFERENCE CENTER DR STE 550
CHANTILLY, VA 201513838
Phone: 703 263-0347
Fax: –
Web: www.rdr.com

CEO: Cal Sasai
CFO: –
HR: –
FYE: December 31
Type: Private

RDR provides a variety of information technology (IT) services such as hardware and software systems engineering, network design and implementation, maintenance, and technical support. The company primarily serves government defense and intelligence agencies including the US Navy, and US Department of State. It also develops and maintains custom virtual simulation systems for training military and intelligence personnel. Other areas of specialty include IT project management and security risk assessment. RDR has satellite offices in Florida, North Carolina, and Hawaii. The company was founded in 1986 by chairman Calvin Sasai.

	Annual Growth	12/13	12/14	12/15	12/16	12/17
Sales ($mil.)	1.2%	–	19.6	17.3	18.4	20.3
Net income ($ mil.)	6.6%	–	1.0	1.0	1.2	1.2
Market value ($ mil.)	–	–	–	–	–	–
Employees	–	–	–	–	–	63

RE/MAX, LLC

5075 S SYRACUSE ST
DENVER, CO 802372712
Phone: 303 770-5531
Fax: –
Web: www.remax.com

CEO: –
CFO: –
HR: –
FYE: December 31
Type: Private

RE/MAX is one of the world's leading real estate franchisors. The company operates its real estate brokerage franchise through its RE/MAX and brand and Morro Mortgage Brand. With more than 135,000 real estate agents in a franchise network of independently owned offices in more than 100 countries. RE/MAX was founded and established in 1973, with operations expanding to US and Canada. After 40 years of private ownership, the company went public in 2013. The US is the company's largest market accounting for the majority of its operations.

	Annual Growth	12/96	12/97	12/98	12/99	12/08
Assets ($mil.)	(12.4%)	–	–	13.3	23.2	3.5
Net income ($ mil.)	–	–	–	0.6	0.5	–
Market value ($ mil.)	–	–	–	–	–	–
Employees	–	–	–	–	–	340

REACHLOCAL, INC.

21700 OXNARD ST STE 1600
WOODLAND HILLS, CA 913677586
Phone: 818 274-0260
Fax: –
Web: www.localiq.com

CEO: Sharon T Rowlands
CFO: Ross G Landsbaum
HR: Ron Rudolph
FYE: December 31
Type: Private

When looking to broaden their online presence, local business owners can get a hand from ReachLocal. ReachLocal offers digital marketing products and solutions such as search engine optimization, social media management, listings management, and websites. It is proud to partner with some of the top technology companies on the web like Google, Yahoo!, Bing, Facebook, Yelp, and more. The company serves industries such as automotive, healthcare, legal, education, and more. ReachLocal was founded in 2004 and is now part of USA TODAY NETWORK.

READING HOSPITAL

420 S 5TH AVE
READING, PA 196112143
Phone: 484 628-8000
Fax: –
Web: www.towerhealth.org

CEO: David C Matthews
CFO: Mark Reyngoudt
HR: Lori Fidler
FYE: June 30
Type: Private

No, it's not a square on the game of Monopoly, but The Reading Hospital and Medical Center does treat patients in Berks County, Pennsylvania and the surrounding area. Operating as Reading Health System, the not-for-profit, 735-bed medical center provides acute care and rehabilitation programs, as well as behavioral and occupational health services. Specialty units include cancer, cardiovascular, weight management, diabetes, orthopedic, trauma (level II), and women's health centers. In addition to the main hospital, the Reading Health System includes Reading Health Rehabilitation Hospital and medical centers in nearby communities, as well as laboratory, imaging, and outpatient centers throughout its region.

READING INTERNATIONAL INC

NAS: RDI

189 Second Avenue, Suite 2S
New York, NY 10003
Phone: 213 235-2240
Fax: –
Web: www.readingrdi.com

CEO: Ellen M Cotter
CFO: Gilbert Avanes
HR: –
FYE: December 31
Type: Public

Reading International (Reading) is an internationally diversified company focused on the development, ownership and operation of entertainment and real property assets in Australia, New Zealand, and the US. Cinemas operate under brands such as Reading Cinemas, Angelika Film Centers, Consolidated Theatres, State Cinema, and the unconsolidated joint ventures Rialto Cinemas. Reading also has real estate operations that develop and rent entertainment, commercial, and retail space. Real estate operations have two single-auditorium live theatres in Manhattan (Orpheum, and Minetta Lane). The US accounts for about 50% of total revenue.

	Annual Growth	12/18	12/19	12/20	12/21	12/22
Sales ($mil.)	(10.0%)	309.4	276.8	77.9	139.1	203.1
Net income ($ mil.)	–	14.4	(26.4)	(65.2)	31.9	(36.2)
Market value ($ mil.)	(33.9%)	321.2	247.2	110.9	89.3	61.2
Employees	(8.9%)	2,944	2,988	1,491	2,025	2,025

READING IS FUNDAMENTAL, INC.

750 1ST ST NE STE 920
WASHINGTON, DC 200028005
Phone: 202 536-3400
Fax: –
Web: www.rif.org

CEO: Alicia Levi
CFO: Jeffrey W Galginaitis
HR: –
FYE: September 30
Type: Private

There's nothing more basic (or important) than reading according to RIF. Reading Is Fundamental is a not-for-profit literacy organization that delivers free books and resources focusing on at risk children ages 8 and under. Through its flagship Books for Ownership program, the group gives more than 16 million new free books to some 5 million kids each year. RIF seeks to increase children's interest in reading by providing motivational support, family involvement, and free books the children get to choose. It is supported by the US Department of Education and donations from foundations, companies, and individuals. Margaret McNamara began the program in 1966 with a group of school volunteers in Washington D.C.

	Annual Growth	09/17	09/18	09/19	09/20	09/21
Sales ($mil.)	(3.7%)	–	11.2	11.7	6.7	10.0
Net income ($ mil.)	(11.1%)	–	3.4	2.8	(2.0)	2.4
Market value ($ mil.)	–	–	–	–	–	–
Employees	–	–	–	–	–	95

READY CAPITAL CORP

NYS: RC

1251 Avenue of the Americas, 50th Floor
New York, NY 10020
Phone: 212 257-4600
Fax: –
Web: www.readycapital.com

CEO: Thomas E Capasse
CFO: Frederick C Herbst
HR: Bill Cockrill
FYE: December 31
Type: Public

Ready Capital is a multi-strategy real estate finance company that originates, acquires, finances, and services SBC loans, SBA loans, residential mortgage loans, and to a lesser extent, MBS collateralized primarily by SBC loans, or other real estate-related investments. Its loans range in original principal amounts generally up to approximately $35 million and are used by businesses to purchase real estate used in their operations or by investors seeking to acquire small multi-family, office, retail, mixed use or warehouse properties. In addition to its loan portfolio which concentrates across California, Texas, New York, Florida, and Illinois, the company also invests in countries outside the US.

	Annual Growth	12/19	12/20	12/21	12/22	12/23
Sales ($mil.)	16.0%	352.8	478.9	648.1	926.4	637.8
Net income ($ mil.)	46.9%	73.0	44.9	157.7	194.3	339.5
Market value ($ mil.)	(9.7%)	2,656.5	2,144.8	2,692.7	1,919.2	1,765.8
Employees	–	–	–	–	–	374

REAL FOUNDATION, INC.

5050 QUORUM DR STE 700
DALLAS, TX 752541410
Phone: 214 292-7000
Fax: –
Web: www.realfoundations.net

CEO: Chris Shaida
CFO: –
HR: Justyna Brooks
FYE: December 31
Type: Private

Real Foundation wants to be the palpable substructure to support your consulting needs. Doing business as RealFoundations, the company offers management and technology consulting services focusing on the real estate and construction industries. Its services include business improvement, change management and merger integration, and technology selection and implementation. It has offices in Chicago; Dallas; Denver; New York; and Newport Beach, California. Internationally, it has operations in India, Hong Kong, the UK, and Australia. RealFoundations was established in 2000 when its executives recognized a need for better consultation services in the real estate sector.

	Annual Growth	12/03	12/04	12/05	12/06	12/16
Sales ($mil.)	7.9%	–	17.4	–	43.3	43.1
Net income ($ mil.)	–	–	1.4	–	3.6	(1.1)
Market value ($ mil.)	–	–	–	–	–	–
Employees	–	–	–	–	–	125

REAL GOODS SOLAR INC

110 16th Street, Suite 300
Denver, CO 80202
Phone: 303 222-8300
Fax: –
Web: www.rgsenergy.com

CEO: –
CFO: –
HR: –
FYE: December 31
Type: Public

Real Goods Solar enjoys its time in the sun. The company, which got its start as a small seller of solar panels in 1978, designs and installs solar power systems for homes and small businesses across the US. In addition to design and installation, Real Goods Solar also provides permitting, grid connection, financing referrals and warranty services. The company does not manufacture its own solar panels or equipment, but procures supplies from other companies such as Sharp, SunPower, Sanyo, and Kyocera Solar.

	Annual Growth	12/14	12/15	12/16	12/17	12/18
Sales ($mil.)	(34.9%)	70.8	45.5	17.4	15.2	12.7
Net income ($ mil.)	–	(57.1)	(10.8)	(25.3)	(17.7)	(42.1)
Market value ($ mil.)	2.1%	44.4	57.9	22.1	136.0	48.1
Employees	(27.0%)	246	179	160	140	70

REALD INC.

100 N CRESCENT DR
BEVERLY HILLS, CA 902105403
Phone: 424 702-4327
Fax: –
Web: www.reald.com

CEO: Michael V Lewis V
CFO: Andrew A Skarupa
HR: –
FYE: March 31
Type: Private

RealD is one of the world's largest 3D cinema platforms with more than 2 billion people having experienced a movie in RealD 3D. The pioneer in digital 3D cinema designs and licenses cutting-edge technologies that enable a premium viewing experience in the theater and on mobile and personal devices. As the world's premier visual technology innovator, RealD's network of theaters includes more than 30,000 installed screens in approximately 75 countries with over 1,200 exhibition partners.

REALNETWORKS LLC

1501 1ST AVE S STE 600
SEATTLE, WA 981341470
Phone: 206 674-2700
Fax: –
Web: www.realnetworks.com

CEO: –
CFO: –
HR: –
FYE: December 31
Type: Private

RealNetworks pretty much invented online media streaming with its RealAudio technology way back in 1995, it operates into three business segments: Consumer Media which covers codec technology licensing and PC-based RealPlayer and related products, Mobile Services which includes its SaaS, Kontxt and SAFR services and Games which comprise all-games related businesses, this segment accounts for more than 40% of sales. Its products and services are marketed through direct and indirect channels including social media. Nearly 65% of sales came from its customers from United States.

REALPAGE, INC.

2201 LAKESIDE BLVD
RICHARDSON, TX 750824305
Phone: 972 820-3000
Fax: –
Web: www.realpage.com

CEO: Stephen Winn
CFO: Brian Shelton
HR: –
FYE: December 31
Type: Private

RealPage is a leading global provider of software and data analytics to the real estate industry. The company's on-demand software platform is designed to make the property management process more efficient, enabling owners and managers of single- and multifamily rental properties to oversee their accounting, leasing, marketing, pricing, and screening operations from a single, shared database. It currently serves more than 24 million units around the world from offices in North America, Europe, and Asia. The company was founded in 1998.

	Annual Growth	12/16	12/17	12/18	12/19	12/20
Sales ($mil.)	20.0%	–	671.0	869.5	988.1	1,158.5
Net income ($ mil.)	397.1%	–	0.4	34.7	58.2	46.3
Market value ($ mil.)	–	–	–	–	–	–
Employees	–	–	–	–	–	7,000

REALTY INCOME CORP

NYS: O

11995 El Camino Real
San Diego, CA 92130
Phone: 858 284-5000
Fax: –
Web: www.realtyincome.com

CEO: –
CFO: –
HR: –
FYE: December 31
Type: Public

Realty Income Corporation is an S&P 500 company and member of the S&P 500 Dividend Aristocrats index. The self-administered real estate investment trust (REIT) acquires and manages primarily freestanding commercial properties that generate rental revenue under long-term net lease agreements with its commercial clients. Realty Income owns around 12,235 (mostly retail) properties spanning approximately 236.8 million sq. ft. of leasable space across every US state, though about 30% of the REIT's rental revenue comes from its properties in Texas, Florida, Ohio, Georgia, Illinois, and Tennessee. Realty Income's top five tenants include Walgreens, 7 Eleven, Dollar General, Wynn Resorts, and Dollar Tree/Family Dollar. The US generates about 90% of the company's total revenue.

	Annual Growth	12/19	12/20	12/21	12/22	12/23
Sales ($mil.)	28.6%	1,491.6	1,651.6	2,080.5	3,343.7	4,079.0
Net income ($ mil.)	18.9%	436.5	395.5	359.5	869.4	872.3
Market value ($ mil.)	(6.0%)	55,404	46,780	53,869	47,729	43,206
Employees	21.2%	194	210	371	395	418

RECEPTOS, INC.

3033 SCIENCE PARK RD STE 300
SAN DIEGO, CA 921211168
Phone: 858 652-5700
Fax: –
Web: www.celgene.com

CEO: Faheem Hasnain
CFO: Graham Cooper
HR: –
FYE: December 31
Type: Private

Biopharmaceutical company Receptos hopes its drug candidates are well-received by patients suffering from autoimmune diseases. Receptos' lead candidate, an oral treatment for relapsing multiple sclerosis (RMS), modifies a key white blood cell receptor and effectively aims to temper the immune system's exaggerated response to disease inflammation. The company has other candidates in its pipeline to treat diabetes and eosinophilic esophagitis (food allergy-driven inflammation of the esophagus). Receptos will seek to commercialize its products in the US, Europe, and other markets. Formed in 2008, the company went public in 2013 and was acquired by Celgene for $7.2 billion in 2015.

RECOMMIND, INC.

550 KEARNY ST STE 700
SAN FRANCISCO, CA 941082503
Phone: 415 394-7899
Fax: –
Web: www.recommind.com

CEO: Steve King
CFO: Bernard Huger
HR: –
FYE: December 31
Type: Private

Recommind suggests ways for companies to hone in on the information they really want. Recommind develops software that helps organizations retrieve, categorize, and analyze the information they need from structured and unstructured data sources. The company's patented keyword- and language-agnostic CORE (context optimized relevancy engine) platform powers its product lines: Axcelerate provides e-discovery functions, while Decisiv covers search, access, and governance, and Perceptiv provides contract analysis. Recommind targets customers in the information-reliant legal, life sciences, media and publishing, and federal government markets. Open Text bought Recommind in 2016.

RECON ENVIRONMENTAL, INC.

3111 CAMINO DEL RIO N STE 600
SAN DIEGO, CA 92108
Phone: 619 308-9333
Fax: –
Web: www.recon-us.com

CEO: –
CFO: –
HR: –
FYE: June 30
Type: Private

This firm is on a reconnaissance mission to protect Mother Earth. RECON Environmental provides environmental consulting services for project planning and land development projects, primarily in the western US. Its services include conservation planning, habitat restoration, noise analysis, and air quality assessment. It works with clients in the private sector, the federal government, and state and local agencies. The company, founded in 1972, also provides architectural investigation services used to preserve cultural and biological resources, including historic sites and endangered species.. RECON Environmental has offices in California, Arizona, and Texas.

RECORDING INDUSTRY ASSOCIATION OF AMERICA, INC.

1025 F ST NW STE 1000
WASHINGTON, DC 200041433
Phone: 202 775-0101
Fax: –
Web: www.riaa.com

CEO: Mitch Bainwol
CFO: –
HR: –
FYE: March 31
Type: Private

The RIAA says you better not rip, burn, or copy and, if you're listening, you better have paid. The Recording Industry Association of America (RIAA) represents US record labels in matters of intellectual property rights, First Amendment rights, and piracy. The group has filed lawsuits against Verizon, Aimster, Napster, and MP3 for allowing or encouraging illegal downloads. The RIAA also conducts research on consumer habits and issues certifications for "Gold," "Platinum," "Multi-platinum," and "Diamond" record sales. It has also added Los Premios De Oro y Platino, a Latin music award. The RIAA's members comprise about 90% of the US music industry.

	Annual Growth	03/16	03/17	03/18	03/21	03/22
Sales ($mil.)	4.1%	–	26.7	29.7	26.7	32.6
Net income ($ mil.)	–	–	0.2	0.4	(1.0)	(0.1)
Market value ($ mil.)	–	–	–	–	–	–
Employees	–	–	–	–	–	48

RECTOR & VISITORS OF THE UNIVERSITY OF VIRGINIA

1001 EMMET ST N
CHARLOTTESVILLE, VA 229034833
Phone: 434 924-0311
Fax: –
Web: www.virginia.edu

CEO: –
CFO: –
HR: Alex Joy
FYE: June 30
Type: Private

The nation's third president, Thomas Jefferson founded the University of Virginia in 1819. Named Rector and Visitors of the University of Virginia, the university is known as UVA today. It boasts an enrollment of some 25,300 students throughout the university's more than 10 graduate and undergraduate schools. One of the most prestigious public universities in the US, the school has been noted for its law program, business program, and its student-enforced conduct code (the Honor System). The school also includes the University of Virginia Health System, which trains future doctors and other healthcare workers at its Medical Center hospital.

	Annual Growth	06/06	06/07	06/08	06/10	06/11
Sales ($mil.)	(2.6%)	–	2,121.5	2,181.3	524.6	1,910.0
Net income ($ mil.)	(5.0%)	–	1,114.4	312.9	97.8	909.3
Market value ($ mil.)	–	–	–	–	–	–
Employees	–	–	–	–	–	13,300

RED BLOSSOM SALES, INC.

400 W VENTURA BLVD STE 140
CAMARILLO, CA 930109137
Phone: 805 686-4747
Fax: –
Web: www.redblossom.com

CEO: Craig A Casca
CFO: –
HR: –
FYE: December 31
Type: Private

Red Blossom Sales is berry enthusiastic about its market. The company is one of California's leading strawberry producers with more than 1,200 acres across the cities of Baja, Irvine, Oxnard, Santa Maria, and Salinas/Watsonville. It contracts a hefty chunk of its production to growers in California and Mexico and ships a total of about 8 million cartons of field-packed strawberries throughout the US every year. Red Blossom's products are sold in large retail grocery stores nationwide, including Costco, Safeway, and Vons; it also exports some to Canada and Hong Kong. Established in 2004, the company took on its current moniker when Red Blossom Farms merged with ASG Produce in 2008.

	Annual Growth	12/14	12/15	12/16	12/17	12/18
Sales ($mil.)	6.0%	–	141.5	171.8	154.8	168.4
Net income ($ mil.)	(2.5%)	–	5.5	5.6	0.9	5.0
Market value ($ mil.)	–	–	–	–	–	–
Employees	–	–	–	–	–	1,046

RED JACKET ORCHARDS, INC.

957 STATE ROUTE 5 AND 20
GENEVA, NY 14456
Phone: 315 787-0114
Fax: –
Web: www.redjacketorchards.com

CEO: Brian Nicholson
CFO: –
HR: –
FYE: June 21
Type: Private

Red Jacket Orchards is a leading apple and fruit grower with more than 600 acres of orchards in Upstate New York. The company produces more than 20 different varieties of apples, including Empire, McIntosh, and Red Delicious. Red Jacket also grows apricots, raspberries, and strawberries, along with peaches and plums. The company also produces cider and fruit juices. Red Jacket sells its produce direct to consumers through farmers markets and its own orchard store, as well as through supermarkets and grocery retailers. The company's orchards were originally planted in 1917 and have been operated by the Nicholson family since 1958.

RED LION HOTELS CORPORATION

1550 MARKET ST STE 350
DENVER, CO 802022054
Phone: 509 459-6100
Fax: –
Web: www.redlion.com

CEO: John J Russell Jr
CFO: Gary A Kohn
HR: Jim Baierl
FYE: December 31
Type: Private

Red Lion Hotels family of brands is now a part of Sonesta International Hotels Corporation and offers a complete platform of franchise services, hotel operations and franchise support, featuring industry-leading brands with a wide range of hotel service levels to meet travelers' needs. The company franchises and owns over 1,200 hotels operating under the Red Lion Hotels, Red Lion Inn & Suites, Hotel RL, Signature Inn, Americas Best Value Inn, Canadas Best Value Inn, and other brands. Its properties, which range from economy to upscale hotels, are located primarily in the US, with locations in Canada. The company was established in 1959 in the Pacific Northwest.

RED RIVER COMMODITIES, INC.

501 42ND ST N
FARGO, ND 581023952
Phone: 701 282-2600
Fax: –
Web: www.redriv.com

CEO: –
CFO: Randall C Wigen
HR: Jess Engel
FYE: March 31
Type: Private

Red River Commodities' products may include sunflower seeds, but they're not just for the birds. The company manufactures and markets standard and organic grain and seed products, including oils, to be used for consumption as food for people and as bird food. Its products include in-shell sunflower seeds, sunflower kernels, millet, flax, soybeans, kidney beans, poppy seeds, and caraway seeds. Red River Commodities also makes butter from sunflower seeds. Its bird food products are sold under the Valley Splendor brand. Red River Commodities boasts production facilities in North Dakota, Kansas, Minnesota, and Texas. The seed producer also owns a plant in the Netherlands.

	Annual Growth	03/04	03/05	03/06	03/07	03/08
Sales ($mil.)	–	–	–	(882.0)	92.5	105.7
Net income ($ mil.)	1452.4%	–	–	0.0	11.3	3.9
Market value ($ mil.)	–	–	–	–	–	–
Employees	–	–	–	–	–	250

RED RIVER TECHNOLOGY LLC

21 WATER ST STE 500
CLAREMONT, NH 037432247
Phone: 603 448-8880
Fax: –
Web: www.redriver.com

CEO: –
CFO: –
HR: –
FYE: December 31
Type: Private

Red River Computer helps its customers get data flowing. The company is a computer and communications hardware, software, and peripherals reseller that provides related support services, such as installation, network design, and network engineering. Other areas of specialty include data storage and network security. Red River primarily serves government agencies (GSA, NASA, and NIH) and acts as a subcontractor for major defense contractors. It also counts other commercial enterprises, such as health care companies and universities, among its clients. Founded in 1995, the company is owned by its management team. FusionStorm Global offered to buy Red River for $12.5 million in 2011.

RED ROBIN GOURMET BURGERS INC
NMS: RRGB

10000 E. Geddes Avenue, Suite 500
Englewood, CO 80112
Phone: 303 846-6000
Fax: -
Web: www.redrobin.com

CEO: Gj Hart
CFO: Guy J Constant
HR: Daniel Aron
FYE: December 31
Type: Public

Red Robin Gourmet Burgers, Inc., together with its subsidiaries, primarily operates, franchises, and develops casual dining restaurants in North America famous for serving more than two dozen crave-able, high-quality burgers with Bottomless Steak Fries and sides in a fun environment welcoming to Guests of all ages. Red Robin serves a variety of delicious burgers, salads, entrees, and other favorite items in about 510 of its Red Robin restaurants and franchises across the US and Canada. Its menu features its signature product the Gourmet Burgers, everyday-value line of Red's Tavern Double Burgers, and the Red Robin's Finest line. Red Robin was founded in 1969.

	Annual Growth	12/19	12/20	12/21	12/22	12/23
Sales ($mil.)	(0.2%)	1,315.0	868.7	1,162.1	1,266.6	1,303.0
Net income ($ mil.)	-	(7.9)	(276.1)	(50.0)	(77.8)	(21.2)
Market value ($ mil.)	(20.4%)	481.8	312.1	266.5	88.5	193.6
Employees	(5.8%)	28,586	21,374	22,483	24,335	22,516

RED ROCK RESORTS INC
NMS: RRR

1505 South Pavilion Center Drive
Las Vegas, NV 89135
Phone: 702 495-3000
Fax: -
Web: www.redrockresorts.com

CEO: Frank J Fertitta III
CFO: Stephen L Cootey
HR: Jackie Heese
FYE: December 31
Type: Public

Red Rock Resorts is a leading gaming, development, and management company operating strategically-located casino and entertainment properties. The company's casino properties are located mostly in Las Vegas and provide customers with a wide variety of entertainment and dining options. Its casinos offering visitors a total of around 13,920 slot machines, roughly 235 table games, and some 2,820 hotel rooms. Red Rock Resorts's major properties are master planned for expansion, enabling the company to incrementally expand its facilities as demand dictates. Its also controls six highly desirable gaming-entitled development sites in Las Vegas.

	Annual Growth	12/19	12/20	12/21	12/22	12/23
Sales ($mil.)	(1.8%)	1,856.5	1,182.4	1,617.9	1,663.8	1,724.1
Net income ($ mil.)	-	(3.4)	(150.4)	241.9	205.5	176.0
Market value ($ mil.)	22.2%	2,511.2	2,625.5	5,767.9	4,195.1	5,591.8
Employees	-	14,000	7,600	7,800	7,850	-

REDFIN CORP
NMS: RDFN

1099 Stewart Street, Suite 600
Seattle, WA 98101
Phone: 206 576-8333
Fax: -
Web: www.redfin.com

CEO: Glenn Kelman
CFO: Chris Nielsen
HR: -
FYE: December 31
Type: Public

Redfin adds a fourth item to the three most important things about real estate: location, location, location, and technology. The Seattle-based residential real estate brokerage deploys technology to provide online home listings, make recommendations to prospective buyers, and provide feedback to agents. Information is available on the company's website and through a mobile application. Redfin's proprietary technology includes elements of machine learning, artificial intelligence, and cloud computing. The company operates in more than 80 US markets, where it is represented by real estate agents as well as third-party agents. Redfin raised $138 million in a 2017 initial public offering.

	Annual Growth	12/19	12/20	12/21	12/22	12/23
Sales ($mil.)	5.8%	779.8	886.1	1,922.8	2,284.4	976.7
Net income ($ mil.)	-	(80.8)	(18.5)	(109.6)	(321.1)	(130.0)
Market value ($ mil.)	(16.4%)	2,481.2	8,055.3	4,505.9	497.7	1,211.3
Employees	8.6%	3,377	4,185	6,485	5,572	4,693

REDMOND PARK HOSPITAL, LLC

501 REDMOND RD NW
ROME, GA 301651483
Phone: 706 291-0291
Fax: -
Web: www.adventhealth.com

CEO: -
CFO: Kenneth Metteauer
HR: Patsy Adams
FYE: December 31
Type: Private

Redmond Regional is deeply involved with administering health to those living in the deep South. Serving northwest Georgia and portions of Alabama, Redmond Regional Medical Center houses some 230 beds and employs about 250 physicians in more than 30 areas of specialization. The acute-care facility specializes in cardiology (it's the only dedicated chest pain center in the region), general surgery, orthopedic care, uruology, and vascular care. Redmond Regional Medical Center also provides emergency, oncology, radiology, rehabilitation, and women's health services. It has centers dedicated to diabetes treatment, family care, and sleep disorders. Founded in 1972, the Rome-based hospital is owned by HCA.

REDNER'S MARKETS, INC.

3 QUARRY RD
READING, PA 196059787
Phone: 610 926-3700
Fax: -
Web: www.rednersmarkets.com

CEO: Ryan Redner
CFO: -
HR: Bob McDonough
FYE: October 01
Type: Private

Redner's Markets operates about 45 warehouse club-style supermarkets under the Redner's Warehouse Markets banner and more than a dozen Quick Shoppe convenience stores. Most of the company's stores are located in eastern Pennsylvania, but the regional grocer also operates several locations in Maryland and Delaware, having closed its one New York supermarket. Redner's Warehouse Markets house bakery, deli, meat, produce, and seafood departments, as well as in-store banks. The employee-owned company was founded by namesake Earl Redner in 1970. It is still operated by the Redner family, including chairman and CEO Richard and COO Ryan Redner.

	Annual Growth	09/12	09/13	09/14	09/15*	10/16
Sales ($mil.)	(1.1%)	-	892.5	902.6	884.9	864.2
Net income ($ mil.)	1.8%	-	4.6	1.6	6.1	4.8
Market value ($ mil.)	-	-	-	-	-	-
Employees	-	-	-	-	-	4,800

*Fiscal year change

REDPOINT BIO CORP

5501 Old York Road
Philadelphia, PA 19141
Phone: 215 456-2312
Fax: -
Web: www.redpointbio.com

CEO: Richard P Shanley
CFO: Scott M Horvitz
HR: -
FYE: December 31
Type: Public

Redpoint Bio believes a spoonful of sugar helps the medicine go down. So, the development stage biotechnology company is developing compounds that make foul medicines, foods, and drinks a thing of the bitter past. The company is working on developing bitter blockers, compounds that will prevent taste buds from sensing bitter flavors in pharmaceutical products. It is also developing flavor enhancers which will amplify sweet, savory, and salty taste sensations in foods and beverages, and possibly make processed foods and drinks healthier. Redpoint Bio was founded in 1995 by Robert Margolskee to capitalize on a taste-specific protein he discovered four years earlier.

	Annual Growth	12/07	12/08	12/09	12/10	12/11
Sales ($mil.)	(30.3%)	2.2	4.0	1.9	1.2	0.5
Net income ($ mil.)	-	(10.5)	(9.5)	(8.8)	(5.5)	(0.4)
Market value ($ mil.)	(64.1%)	57.5	11.2	11.2	10.4	1.0
Employees	(56.9%)	29	36	12	10	1

REDWOOD TRUST INC   NYS: RWT

One Belvedere Place, Suite 300   CEO: Christopher J Abate
Mill Valley, CA 94941   CFO: Brooke E Carillo
Phone: 415 389-7373   HR: –
Fax: –   FYE: December 31
Web: www.redwoodtrust.com   Type: Public

Redwood Trust is a real estate investment trust (REIT) that finances, manages, and invests in residential real estate mortgages and securities backed by such loans. It also invests in commercial real estate loans and securities. Redwood acquires assets throughout the US, but has a concentration of business purpose loans in Alabama, California, Texas, New Jersey, Florida, Georgia and Arizona, which hold some of the US' most active real estate markets. The company delivers customized housing credit investments to a diverse mix of investors through its best-in-class securitization platforms, whole-loan distribution activities and its publicly-traded securities. its aggregation, origination and investment activities have evolved to incorporate a diverse mix of residential, business purpose and multifamily assets.

	Annual Growth	12/19	12/20	12/21	12/22	12/23
Assets ($mil.)	(5.2%)	17,995	10,355	14,707	13,031	14,504
Net income ($ mil.)	–	169.2	(581.8)	319.6	(163.5)	(2.3)
Market value ($ mil.)	(18.2%)	2,174.8	1,154.4	1,734.3	888.8	974.3
Employees	(6.1%)	372	247	298	347	289

REEDS INC   NBB: REED

201 Merritt 7   CEO: Norman E Snyder Jr
Norwalk, CT 06851   CFO: Joann Tinnelly
Phone: 800 997-3337   HR: –
Fax: –   FYE: December 31
Web: www.reedsinc.com   Type: Public

Everybody needs a Reed's. The company makes two dozen all-natural soft drinks, such as Original Ginger Brew and Virgil's Root Beer, as well as ginger candy, and three ginger-flavored ice creams. Reed's brews its drinks from roots, herbs, spices, and fruits in a manner similar to how beer is brewed from malt and hops (without alcohol, though -- carbonation is added to Reed's drinks separately). The company also owns the China Cola brand, which contains an herbal mixture designed to help digestion. Reed's products are sold in some 10,500 natural food and traditional supermarkets, as well as specialty stores and restaurants throughout North America. It also makes private-label products for retailers.

	Annual Growth	12/18	12/19	12/20	12/21	12/22
Sales ($mil.)	8.6%	38.1	33.8	41.6	49.6	53.0
Net income ($ mil.)	–	(10.3)	(16.1)	(10.2)	(16.4)	(20.1)
Market value ($ mil.)	(57.1%)	5.2	2.3	1.5	0.9	0.2
Employees	(18.6%)	50	28	34	31	22

REFOCUS GROUP INC   NBB: RFCS

10300 N. Central Expressway #104   CEO: Michael Judy
Dallas, TX 75231   CFO: Zack Thompson
Phone: 214 368-0200   HR: –
Fax: 214 368-0332   FYE: December 31
Web: www.refocus-group.com   Type: Public

Refocus Group is a medical device company that develops surgical treatments for human vision disorders. Therapeutic targets include presbyopia (commonly known as farsightedness), elevated blood pressure in the eye, and a certain form of glaucoma. Its most advanced device is the Scleral Spacing Procedure, which includes an incision handpiece, implants, and related surgical equipment, that could treat the previously mentioned vision disorders. Medcare Investment owns more than half of the firm.

REGAL ENTERTAINMENT GROUP

101 E BLOUNT AVE STE 100   CEO: Nisan Cohen
KNOXVILLE, TN 379201632   CFO: James A Mesterharm
Phone: 865 922-1123   HR: Lisa Beeler
Fax: –   FYE: December 31
Web: www.regmovies.com   Type: Private

Regal Entertainment Group, a subsidiary of the Cineworld Group, operates one of the largest and most geographically diverse theatre circuits in the US, consisting of more than 7,200 screens in almost 550 theatres in more than 45 states along with American Samoa, the District of Columbia, Guam and Saipan. Provides bonus rewards through its Crown Club card, the company partners with Movietickets.com, Variety ? The Children's Charities, NCM ? America's Movie Network, World Travel Services, Will Rogers Institute, Fandango, Elavon and Patricia Neal Rehabilitation Center. The company was founded in 1989.

	Annual Growth	01/14	01/15*	12/15	12/16	12/17
Sales ($mil.)	2.9%	–	2,990.1	3,127.3	3,197.1	3,163.0
Net income ($ mil.)	3.3%	–	105.2	153.2	170.5	112.3
Market value ($ mil.)	–	–	–	–	–	–
Employees	–	–	–	–	–	25,359

*Fiscal year change

REGAL MARKETING, INC.

1600 E 2ND ST   CEO: –
SCOTCH PLAINS, NJ 070761606   CFO: –
Phone: 908 322-3801   HR: –
Fax: –   FYE: November 30
Web: www.regalmarketing.com   Type: Private

Regal Marketing give the royal distribution treatment to fresh fruits and vegetables sourced worldwide. The more than 20-year-old firm is a brokerage for products grown in the US, as well as Asia, Australia, Canada, the Caribbean, Central and South America, Europe, New Zealand, and South Africa. Products shipped include Californian and Mexican grapes, New Zealand Royal Gala apples, and Chilean kiwi fruits.

	Annual Growth	11/05	11/06*	12/13	12/14*	11/15
Sales ($mil.)	4.0%	–	14.6	16.7	–	20.7
Net income ($ mil.)	14.6%	–	0.0	0.2	–	0.0
Market value ($ mil.)	–	–	–	–	–	–
Employees	–	–	–	–	–	8

*Fiscal year change

REGAL REXNORD CORP   NYS: RRX

111 West Michigan Street   CEO: Louis V Pinkham V
Milwaukee, WI 53203   CFO: Robert J Rehard
Phone: 608 364-8800   HR: Cheryl Lewis
Fax: –   FYE: December 31
Web: –   Type: Public

Regal Rexnord Corporation is a global leader in the engineering and manufacturing of industrial powertrain solutions, power transmission components, electric motors and electronic controls, air-moving products, and specialty electrical components and systems, serving customers around the world. The company serves residential, commercial, and industrial original equipment manufacturers (OEMs) customers in a range of industries including HVAC, automotive, aerospace, and oil and gas. It makes electric motors used for heating and air conditioning, generators for prime and standby power, electronic variable speed controls and blowers, and mechanical power transmissions and gear drives. Around 75% of Regal's sales come from North America.

	Annual Growth	12/19*	01/21	01/22*	12/22	12/23
Sales ($mil.)	17.9%	3,238.0	2,907.0	3,810.3	5,217.9	6,250.7
Net income ($ mil.)	–	238.9	189.3	209.9	488.9	(57.4)
Market value ($ mil.)	14.7%	5,663.3	8,142.3	11,283	7,954.7	9,813.7
Employees	13.2%	19,560	23,000	30,000	26,000	32,100

*Fiscal year change

REGAL WARE, INC.

1675 REIGLE DR
KEWASKUM, WI 530408923
Phone: 262 626-2121
Fax: –
Web: www.regalware.com

CEO: Ryan Reigle
CFO: David Kane
HR: Ian Konrath
FYE: December 31
Type: Private

Regal Ware provides the wares for the party fare. The company, a manufacturer of cookware and appliances, sells its products through home parties nationwide. Most of its sales are generated from its stainless-steel and cast iron cookware, and stainless steel bakeware. The company's brand names include Royal Queen, Lifetime, and Marcus, among others. Regal Ware also supplies foodservice operators with commercial coffeemaker urns, drinking water systems, and other beverage accessories. Regal Ware maintains a presence on retail shelves through agreements with the likes of Euromarket Designs' Crate & Barrel and Williams-Sonoma. Regal Ware is owned and run by the Reigle family.

REGEN BIOLOGICS INC

411 Hackensack Avenue, 10th Floor
Hackensack, NJ 07601
Phone: 201 651-5140
Fax: –
Web: www.regenbio.com

CEO: Gerald E Bisbee Jr
CFO: Dennis W O'Dowd
HR: –
FYE: December 31
Type: Public

Injured athletes in need of tissue can dry their eyes thanks to ReGen Biologics. The company makes tissue implants and medical devices that are used to repair damaged or degenerating cartilage. ReGen's product line focuses on the repair and preservation of the meniscus, a piece of cartilage found in the knees. The company makes Menaflex, a collagen matrix product designed to halt deterioration, support natural regrowth of tissue, restore function, and reduce pain; the implant is approved for sale in parts of Europe and Africa. However, its US approval was rescinded following an investigation into the FDA approval process. ReGen filed for bankruptcy protection shortly after the rescission in 2011.

	Annual Growth	12/04	12/05	12/06	12/07	12/08
Sales ($mil.)	28.5%	0.5	0.6	0.6	1.0	1.4
Net income ($ mil.)	–	(6.8)	(11.4)	(12.7)	(10.4)	(10.0)
Market value ($ mil.)	29.1%	8.7	5.5	3.0	0.6	24.1
Employees	2.7%	18	23	24	18	20

REGENCY CENTERS CORP
NMS: REG

One Independent Drive, Suite 114
Jacksonville, FL 32202
Phone: 904 598-7000
Fax: –
Web: www.regencycenters.com

CEO: Lisa Palmer
CFO: Michael J Mas
HR: Jamie Conroy
FYE: December 31
Type: Public

Regency Centers is a fully integrated real estate company and self-administered and self-managed real estate investment trust (REIT) that owns, operates, and develops shopping centers located in suburban trade areas with compelling demographics. Some of its tenants include Publix, Kroger, Albertsons Companies, Amazon, Whole Foods, and TJX. The REIT wholly owns or has interests in about 405 properties measuring over 50 million sq. ft. of leasable space. The REIT focuses on high-growth areas in states including California, Florida, Texas, New York and Georgia, home to the majority of its wholly-owned holdings.

	Annual Growth	12/19	12/20	12/21	12/22	12/23
Sales ($mil.)	3.9%	1,133.1	1,016.2	1,166.2	1,224.0	1,322.5
Net income ($ mil.)	11.1%	239.4	44.9	361.4	482.9	364.6
Market value ($ mil.)	1.5%	11,617	8,394.6	13,874	11,508	12,337
Employees	2.5%	450	431	432	445	497

REGENERON PHARMACEUTICALS, INC.
NMS: REGN

777 Old Saw Mill River Road
Tarrytown, NY 10591-6707
Phone: 914 847-7000
Fax: –
Web: www.regeneron.com

CEO: George D Yancopoulos
CFO: Robert E Landry
HR: –
FYE: December 31
Type: Public

Regeneron Pharmaceuticals is a leading biotechnology company that develops protein-based drugs used to battle a variety of diseases and conditions, including cancer, high cholesterol, inflammatory ailments, cardiovascular and metabolic diseases, infectious disease, rare diseases, and eye diseases. Regeneron is accelerating and improving the traditional drug development process through its proprietary VelociSuite technologies, such as VelocImmune, which uses unique genetically-humanized mice to produce optimized fully-human antibodies and bispecific antibodies, and through ambitious research initiatives such as the Regeneron Genetics Center, which is conducting one of the largest genetics sequencing efforts in the world. In 1988, Regeneron was founded by Leonard S. Schleifer, MD, PhD, a young neurologist and assistant professor at Cornell University Medical College.

	Annual Growth	12/19	12/20	12/21	12/22	12/23
Sales ($mil.)	13.6%	7,863.4	8,497.1	16,072	12,173	13,117
Net income ($ mil.)	16.9%	2,115.8	3,513.2	8,075.3	4,338.4	3,953.6
Market value ($ mil.)	23.7%	41,078	52,852	69,088	78,931	96,085
Employees	13.5%	8,100	9,123	10,368	11,851	13,450

REGENERX BIOPHARMACEUTICALS INC
NBB: RGRX D

15245 Shady Grove Road, Suite 470
Rockville, MD 20850
Phone: 301 208-9191
Fax: –
Web: www.regenerx.com

CEO: J J Finkelstein
CFO: –
HR: –
FYE: December 31
Type: Public

RegeneRx Biopharmaceuticals may not care about the state of your soul, but it does want to help damaged bodily tissue be born again. The firm's main drug candidate, called Thymosin beta 4 ("T 4"), is undergoing clinical trials for use in accelerating wound healing and for treating other medical problems, such as certain kinds of ulcers and ophthalmic conditions. The company operates using an outsourcing business model, contracting most of its research and manufacturing operations to third-parties. It has research and licensing agreements with the National Institutes of Health and George Washington University.

	Annual Growth	12/18	12/19	12/20	12/21	12/22
Sales ($mil.)	2.5%	0.0	0.0	0.0	0.0	0.0
Net income ($ mil.)	–	(2.0)	(1.4)	(1.5)	(1.6)	(1.7)
Market value ($ mil.)	(2.7%)	0.2	0.2	0.6	0.2	0.2
Employees	(9.6%)	3	3	3	3	2

REGENETP INC
NBB: RGTP Q

1960 S. 4250 West
Salt Lake City, UT 84104
Phone: 800 560-3983
Fax: –
Web: www.polarityte.com

CEO: Richard Hague
CFO: Jacob Patterson
HR: –
FYE: December 31
Type: Public

PolarityTE (formerly Majesco Entertainment) has put the games away to focus on regenerative medicine and tissue engineering. Formerly a video game developer, Majesco acquired the intellectual property of PolarityTE in early 2017 and began developing technology that could allow it to regenerate the body's skin, bone, muscle, cartilage, fat, nerves, and blood vessels. Its first product, SkinTE, is in development as the first platform to regenerate skin in the case of burn. If successful, PolarityTE hopes to expand into other markets, including the acute wound, scar, and hair revision markets. Other technologies in development include OsteoTE (bone), AngioTE (vascular tissue), MyoTE (muscle), CartTE (cartilage), NeuralTE (nerves), and AdiposeTE (fat).

	Annual Growth	12/18	12/19	12/20	12/21	12/22
Sales ($mil.)	4.9%	0.7	5.7	10.1	9.4	0.8
Net income ($ mil.)	–	(18.4)	(92.5)	(42.9)	(30.2)	(7.8)
Market value ($ mil.)	(53.1%)	97.9	18.9	4.9	4.3	4.8
Employees	(27.1%)	156	157	85	69	44

REGENTS OF THE UNIVERSITY OF IDAHO

875 PERIMETER DR MS 3151
MOSCOW, ID 838449803
Phone: 208 885-6365
Fax: –
Web: www.uidaho.edu

CEO: Lee Ostrom
CFO: –
HR: –
FYE: June 30
Type: Private

You won't have to learn Russian to attend school in Moscow. The University of Idaho -- located in Moscow, Idaho -- has more than 900 faculty members and an enrollment of more than 12,000 students. It offers undergraduate degree programs in subjects ranging from agriculture and art to natural resources and science. The University of Idaho also offers master's degrees and doctoral degrees in a broad range of subjects, including law. In addition to its main campus, University of Idaho has locations in Boise, Coeur d'Alene, Idaho Falls, and Twin Falls, as well dozens of extension offices statewide. The university was founded in 1889.

	Annual Growth	06/16	06/17	06/18	06/19	06/20
Sales ($mil.)	(0.3%)	–	–	214.0	216.8	212.7
Net income ($ mil.)	–	–	–	(21.1)	(19.3)	0.9
Market value ($ mil.)	–	–	–	–	–	–
Employees	–	–	–	–	–	3,350

REGENTS OF THE UNIVERSITY OF MICHIGAN

500 S STATE ST
ANN ARBOR, MI 481091382
Phone: 734 764-1817
Fax: –
Web: www.umich.edu

CEO: –
CFO: Geoffrey S Chatas
HR: –
FYE: June 30
Type: Private

Ranking among the top US public universities, The University of Michigan boasts roughly 65,000 students in Michigan. Its three campuses in Ann Arbor, Dearborn, and Flint offers more than 250 undergraduate and graduate degree programs in fields including architecture, education, law, medicine, music, and social work. The university has a student to faculty ratio of 15:1. The University of Michigan Health System includes three hospitals and more than 125 health clinics/centers.

	Annual Growth	06/16	06/17	06/18	06/19	06/20
Sales ($mil.)	3.2%	–	–	7,466.9	7,989.9	7,955.6
Net income ($ mil.)	–	–	–	920.4	522.9	(0.3)
Market value ($ mil.)	–	–	–	–	–	–
Employees	–	–	–	–	–	34,624

REGENTS OF THE UNIVERSITY OF MINNESOTA

100 CHURCH ST SE SE202
MINNEAPOLIS, MN 554550149
Phone: 612 626-1616
Fax: –
Web: regents.umn.edu

CEO: –
CFO: –
HR: –
FYE: June 30
Type: Private

One of the most comprehensive in the nation, University of Minnesota (U of M) offers undergraduate and graduate degrees in a wide array of academic fields. It employs a large number of faculty members across five campuses located around the state. The university's flagship Twin Cities campus ranks among the largest in the country in terms of enrollment. U of M's other campuses are located in Crookston, Duluth, Morris, and Rochester. Between the five campuses of the U of M, students can explore nearly 300 different degrees/majors and programs. It also operates research and specialty training programs through extension offices throughout the state.

REGINA MEDICAL CENTER

1175 NININGER RD
HASTINGS, MN 550331098
Phone: 651 480-4100
Fax: –
Web: www.reginamedical.org

CEO: –
CFO: –
HR: –
FYE: December 31
Type: Private

Regina Medical Center is a regional health care provider in southeastern Minnesota. The hospital provides acute and long-term health care services to residents of Dakota County, Minnesota. Founded in 1953, the not-for-profit Regina Medical Center has 60 acute care hospital beds and nearly 200 nursing and assisted living beds. Specialty services include cardiology, obstetrics, pediatrics, urology, and neurology. Regina Medical also operates several community health and surgery centers jointly with Allina Hospitals and Clinics.

	Annual Growth	09/12	09/13*	12/14	12/15	12/16
Sales ($mil.)	1.6%	–	50.2	52.3	52.9	52.6
Net income ($ mil.)	–	–	(10.1)	2.3	1.7	4.7
Market value ($ mil.)	–	–	–	–	–	–
Employees	–	–	–	–	–	520

*Fiscal year change

REGIONAL MANAGEMENT CORP

NYS: RM

979 Batesville Road, Suite B
Greer, SC 29651
Phone: 864 448-7000
Fax: –
Web: www.regionalmanagement.com

CEO: Robert W Beck
CFO: Harpreet Rana
HR: Rene Jennings
FYE: December 31
Type: Public

Regional Management Corp. is a diversified consumer finance company that provides attractive, easy-to-understand installment loan products primarily to customers with limited access to consumer credit from banks, thrifts, credit card companies, and other lenders. Regional Management operates under the name "Regional Finance" in about 350 branch locations in almost 15 states across the US, serving some 460,600 active accounts. Regional sources loans through its multiple channel platform, which includes branches, centrally-managed direct mail campaigns, digital partners, retailers, and its consumer website. The company offers loan products that are structured on a fixed rate, fixed term basis with fully amortizing equal monthly installment payments, repayable at any time without penalty.

	Annual Growth	12/19	12/20	12/21	12/22	12/23
Assets ($mil.)	11.6%	1,158.5	1,103.9	1,459.7	1,725.0	1,794.5
Net income ($ mil.)	(22.7%)	44.7	26.7	88.7	51.2	16.0
Market value ($ mil.)	(4.4%)	293.1	291.4	560.8	274.0	244.8
Employees	6.2%	1,638	1,542	1,691	1,991	2,081

REGIONAL TRANSIT AUTHORITY

2817 CANAL ST
NEW ORLEANS, LA 701196301
Phone: 504 827-8300
Fax: –
Web: www.norta.com

CEO: Justin Augustine
CFO: –
HR: –
FYE: December 31
Type: Private

A streetcar named Desire hasn't run through the Big Easy since 1948, but even Hurricane Katrina couldn't slow down the New Orleans Regional Transit Authority (NORTA). NORTA provides bus and paratransit services and three streetcar lines (including the 175-year-old St. Charles streetcar line) throughout the city of New Orleans. Under a 10-year, $56 million-per-year contract signed in 2009, Veolia Transportation is responsible for all operations, safety, maintenance, customer care, routes, schedules, capital planning, and grant administration for NORTA, whose employees are employees of Veolia. The New Orleans Board of Commissioners retains policy-making authority over NORTA.

	Annual Growth	12/15	12/16	12/18	12/20	12/21
Sales ($mil.)	(14.7%)	–	22.0	22.8	9.5	9.9
Net income ($ mil.)	–	–	(17.7)	(4.1)	28.7	8.0
Market value ($ mil.)	–	–	–	–	–	–
Employees	–	–	–	–	–	560

REGIONS FINANCIAL CORP (NEW)   NYS: RF

1900 Fifth Avenue North
Birmingham, AL 35203
Phone: 800 734-4667
Fax: –
Web: www.regions.com

CEO: –
CFO: –
HR: –
FYE: December 31
Type: Public

The holding company for Alabama-chartered Regions Bank, Regions Financial boasts approximately $162.9 billion in total assets, total consolidated deposits of approximately $155.2 billion, and total consolidated shareholders' equity of approximately $15.9 billion. With more than 1,300 branches and nearly 2,040 ATMs across the South, Midwest, and Texas, Regions offers banking services for large corporations, middle market companies, and commercial real estate developers and investors on top of its main business of standard banking products for retail customers and small businesses. The company's smaller wealth and asset management operations target affluent private individuals, businesses, governmental institutions, and non-profit entities.

	Annual Growth	12/19	12/20	12/21	12/22	12/23
Assets ($mil.)	4.8%	126,240	147,389	162,938	155,220	152,194
Net income ($ mil.)	7.0%	1,582.0	1,094.0	2,521.0	2,245.0	2,074.0
Market value ($ mil.)	3.1%	15,827	14,868	20,107	19,886	17,875
Employees	0.7%	19,564	19,406	19,626	20,073	20,101

REGIONS HOSPITAL FOUNDATION

640 JACKSON ST
SAINT PAUL, MN 551012595
Phone: 651 254-3456
Fax: –
Web: www.regionshospital.com

CEO: –
CFO: Greg Klugherz
HR: –
FYE: December 31
Type: Private

If you live around the Twin Cities, Regions Hospital can help with your medical needs. The not-for-profit hospital has more than 450 beds and provides acute medical and emergency care services, as well as specialty programs in areas including behavioral health, rehabilitation, burn care, cancer, cardiovascular, orthopedic, pediatrics, and women's care. Regions Hospital is one of a handful of level I trauma centers in Minnesota and is also a teaching and residency center for the University of Minnesota Medical School. Regions Hospital is part of HealthPartners, which operates a network of medical centers and a health plan in the Twin Cities area.

	Annual Growth	12/03	12/04	12/05	12/06	12/12
Sales ($mil.)	71.3%	–	7.9	430.7	413.9	582.0
Net income ($ mil.)	320.5%	–	0.0	12.1	4.0	36.6
Market value ($ mil.)	–	–	–	–	–	–
Employees	–	–	–	–	–	3,000

REGIS CORP   NMS: RGS

3701 Wayzata Boulevard
Minneapolis, MN 55416
Phone: 952 947-7777
Fax: –
Web: www.regiscorp.com

CEO: Matthew
CFO: Kersten D Zupfer
HR: Ashley Dittberner
FYE: June 30
Type: Public

Regis is a global leader in beauty salons, with about 4,865 locations worldwide that it owns or franchises. Its salons operate under the trade names of SmartStyle, Supercuts, First Choice Haircutters, Roosters, and Cost Cutters. The company's salons are primarily located in strip center locations and Walmart Supercenters and offer a full range of custom hairstyling, cutting, and coloring services, as well as professional hair care products. The top selling brands within the company's retail assortment include its own Regis DESIGNLINE line, as well as Paul Mitchell, L'Oreal Professional Brands, and Regis Private Label Brand.

	Annual Growth	06/19	06/20	06/21	06/22	06/23
Sales ($mil.)	(31.6%)	1,069.0	669.7	415.1	276.0	233.3
Net income ($ mil.)	–	(14.2)	(171.4)	(113.3)	(85.9)	(7.4)
Market value ($ mil.)	(49.1%)	37.8	18.6	21.3	2.5	2.5
Employees	(61.6%)	20,000	9,000	2,446	630	435

REGULUS THERAPEUTICS INC   NAS: RGLS

4224 Campus Point Court, Suite 210
San Diego, CA 92121
Phone: 858 202-6300
Fax: –
Web: www.regulusrx.com

CEO: –
CFO: –
HR: –
FYE: December 31
Type: Public

At the heart of it, Regulus Therapeutics hopes to fight disease with leonine ferocity. It targets recently discovered microRNA (ribonucleic acid; miRNA), which is important in regulating cellular and biological functions. The company is developing anti-miRNAs that it believes will have the same sort of impact on drug discovery that monoclonal antibodies and biologics have. Through strategic alliances with GlaxoSmithKline, AstraZeneca, and Sanofi, Regulus has three products in development. The candidates target chronic Hepatitis C (RG-101), kidney disease Alport syndrome (RG-012), and non-alcoholic fatty liver disease (NASH) for patients with type 2 diabetes or pre-diabetes (RG-125).

	Annual Growth	12/19	12/20	12/21	12/22	12/23
Sales ($mil.)	–	6.8	10.0	–	–	–
Net income ($ mil.)	–	(18.6)	(15.7)	(27.8)	(28.3)	(30.0)
Market value ($ mil.)	9.5%	18.0	27.3	6.4	27.7	25.9
Employees	9.3%	21	24	26	30	30

REHRIG PACIFIC COMPANY

4010 E 26TH ST
VERNON, CA 900584401
Phone: 323 262-5145
Fax: –
Web: www.rehrigpacific.com

CEO: Michael J Doka
CFO: James L Drew
HR: –
FYE: February 29
Type: Private

Rehrig Pacific is the nation's leading supplier of residential roll out carts and for good reason. It produces specialized products, including reusable plastic containers and pallets, crates, bins, and other storage and transport products to help its clients transport products and goods. It also makes and supplies software products that allow customers to track and manage these products across the supply chain. The company serves such industries as agriculture, bakery, beverage, dairy, ecommerce, food service and retail. Founded in 1913, Rehrig Pacific began as a small Los Angeles manufacturer of reusable wooden crates for the dairy industry.

REI SYSTEMS, INC.

45335 VINTAGE PARK PLZ
STERLING, VA 201666748
Phone: 703 230-0011
Fax: –
Web: www.reisystems.com

CEO: Veer Bhartiya
CFO: –
HR: –
FYE: December 31
Type: Private

No, they don't sell hiking boots or kayaks. REI Systems provides information technology services and develops custom Web-based software used to automate the management of internal business communications, contracts, customer relationships, and grants. Its Electronic Handbooks application is used to manage a variety of data collection and reporting functions; MaintenanceMax is an organizational tool for equipment maintenance providers. The company's IT services include database design, software integration, and network security. REI Systems' clientele is made up largely of US government agencies, such as the Department of Energy and the Department of Defense; commercial clients have included Raytheon.

REINSURANCE GROUP OF AMERICA, INC.   NYS: RGA

16600 Swingley Ridge Road
Chesterfield, MO 63017
Phone: 636 736-7000
Fax: –
Web: www.rgare.com

CEO: Tony Cheng
CFO: Todd C Larson
HR: Jessica Clarke
FYE: December 31
Type: Public

Reinsurance Group of America (RGA) is one of the largest life reinsurers in the US. RGA provides traditional life and health reinsurance and financial solutions. Traditional reinsurance includes individual and group life and health, disability, long-term care, and critical illness coverage, while Financial Solutions includes longevity, capital solutions, stable value, and asset-intensive products. RGA has life reinsurance in force valued at about $3.4 trillion and about $84.7 billion in consolidated assets. RGA has offices in about 50 locations throughout the world and generates almost 55% of RGA's total revenue in the US and Latin American. RGA was founded in 1973, as a reinsurance unit created by General American Life Insurance Company.

	Annual Growth	12/19	12/20	12/21	12/22	12/23
Assets ($mil.)	6.2%	76,731	84,656	92,175	84,706	97,623
Net income ($ mil.)	0.9%	870.0	415.0	617.0	623.0	902.0
Market value ($ mil.)	(0.2%)	10,700	7,605.4	7,184.8	9,324.0	10,616
Employees	5.2%	3,188	3,600	3,500	3,800	3,900

REIS, INC.

1185 AVENUE OF THE AMERICAS FL 30
NEW YORK, NY 100362603
Phone: 212 921-1122
Fax: –
Web: cre.moodysanalytics.com

CEO: Lloyd Lynford
CFO: Mark P Cantaluppi
HR: –
FYE: December 31
Type: Private

Reis knows how to get below the surface of real estate. The company provides commercial real estate market information through online databases containing information on apartment, retail, office, and industrial properties in several US metropolitan markets. Its flagship product, Reis SE, offers trend and forecast analysis, as well as information on rent, vacancy rates, lease terms, sale prices, and new construction listings. Reis also furnishes data to small businesses through its ReisReports product. Its databases are used by real estate investors, lenders, and brokers to make buying, selling, and financing decisions. Customers access Reis' data through subscription or by purchasing reports individually. In 2018, business and financial services company Moody's Corporation announced it was acquiring Reis for $278 million.

RELAX THE BACK CORPORATION

4600 E CONANT ST
LONG BEACH, CA 908081874
Phone: 800 290-2225
Fax: –
Web: www.relaxthebackfranchise.com

CEO: –
CFO: Bryan Cotter
HR: –
FYE: December 31
Type: Private

Relax the Back tries to take the "ERRRGG!" out of ergonomic injuries and chronic back pain. The firm offers muscle-soothing products for the office, home, and gym, including back and neck supports, custom and Tempur Sealy mattresses, desk chairs, educational books and DVDs, exercise and therapy equipment, massage loungers, and recliners. Doctors and therapists advise the company on decisions about products, many of which are supplied by manufacturing unit BackSaver Products. Relax the Back sells through catalogs and the Internet, as well as through more than 100 stores in 30 states in the US and Canada that it owns or franchises. Dominion Ventures owns Relax the Back; it was founded in 1986 by an osteopath.

RELIABILITY FIRST CORPORATION

3 SUMMIT PARK DR STE 600
CLEVELAND, OH 441316900
Phone: 216 503-0600
Fax: –
Web: –

CEO: –
CFO: –
HR: –
FYE: December 31
Type: Private

ReliabilityFirst doesn't want to leave people in the dark. The not-for-profit company supports the delivery of secure and steady electric power in its region. It's one of eight regional reliability councils approved by NERC (North American Electric Reliability Council) to promote cooperation among power producers. The organization works with about 50 electric utilities and independent producers to enforce reliability standards and keep the power flowing in about a dozen northeastern states. It also provides technical and marketing support to members. ReliabilityFirst was formed by the merger of the Mid-American Interconnected Network, the East Central Area Reliability Council, and the Mid-Atlantic Area Council in 2006.

	Annual Growth	12/08	12/09	12/13	12/14	12/15
Sales ($mil.)	13.1%	–	9.2	15.1	15.9	19.2
Net income ($ mil.)	–	–	(1.6)	(2.3)	(2.4)	1.7
Market value ($ mil.)	–	–	–	–	–	–
Employees	–	–	–	–	–	30

RELIABILITY INC   NBB: RLBY

22505 Gateway Center Drive, P.O. Box 71
Clarksburg, MD 20871
Phone: 202 965-1100
Fax: –
Web: www.maslowmedia.com

CEO: –
CFO: Mark Speck
HR: –
FYE: December 31
Type: Public

Reliability wanted integrated circuit (IC) manufacturers to rely on its testing systems, but after a number of moves, it is looking for a new line of business. The company designed, manufactured, and supported testing and conditioning equipment that helped detect defects in ICs. Running low on cash and needing to repay debt in 2006, Reliability sold its headquarters, closed its Singapore burn-in and testing services operations, and sold the assets of its Power Sources division (which made DC-to-DC converters) to Reliability Power, an unaffiliated firm. The company in 2007 acquired Medallion Electric, a Florida-based electrical contractor, but sold it back six months later.

	Annual Growth	12/18	12/19	12/20	12/21	12/22
Sales ($mil.)	–	–	38.4	29.2	26.2	25.7
Net income ($ mil.)	–	(0.0)	0.2	(0.8)	7.9	(0.7)
Market value ($ mil.)	11.2%	8.3	75.0	21.3	10.5	12.6
Employees	64.6%	3	20	22	20	22

RELIABLE WHOLESALE LUMBER, INC.

7600 REDONDO CIR
HUNTINGTON BEACH, CA 926481303
Phone: 714 848-8222
Fax: –
Web: www.rwli.net

CEO: –
CFO: David Higman
HR: –
FYE: December 31
Type: Private

Reliable Wholesale Lumber has room for plenty of board. The company distributes lumber and other forest products to residential contractors, industrial customers, and retail lumberyards, primarily in Southern California, Arizona, and Nevada, as well as panels throughout the US. Through about 10 distribution yards in California, the company is able to ship 600 million board feet of lumber, panels, and engineered wood products per year. Product specialties from Reliable Wholesale Lumber include Durawood Douglas fir decking and oriented strand board. Founded in 1971, Reliable Wholesale Lumber is owned by the Higman family, including president Jerry Higman.

RELIANCE INC
NYS: RS

16100 N. 71st Street, Suite 400
Scottsdale, AZ 85254
Phone: 480 564-5700
Fax: –
Web: www.rsac.com

CEO: Karla R Lewis
CFO: Arthur Ajemyan
HR: Liz Lopez
FYE: December 31
Type: Public

Reliance Steel & Aluminum shows its mettle as North America's largest metals service center company. Operating in about 315 service centers in about 40 US states and a dozen other countries, it processes and distributes more than 100,000 metal products, including alloy, aluminum, brass, copper, carbon steel, stainless steel, titanium and specialty steel products, to more than 125,000 customers in industries, including transportation, aerospace, energy, construction, manufacturing, semiconductor and electronics, agricultural, and mining equipment. The company's trade names include Earle M. Jorgensen, Metals USA, and Precision Strip. The US generates about 95% of total revenue.

	Annual Growth	12/19	12/20	12/21	12/22	12/23
Sales ($mil.)	7.8%	10,974	8,811.9	14,093	17,025	14,806
Net income ($ mil.)	17.5%	701.5	369.1	1,413.0	1,840.1	1,335.9
Market value ($ mil.)	23.6%	6,858.8	6,858.2	9,290.5	11,594	16,018
Employees	(0.5%)	15,300	13,200	14,200	15,000	15,000

RELIV' INTERNATIONAL INC
NBB: RELV

136 Chesterfield Industrial Boulevard
Chesterfield, MO 63005
Phone: 636 537-9715
Fax: 636 537-9753
Web: www.reliv.com

CEO: Ryan A Montgomery
CFO: Steven D Albright
HR: –
FYE: December 31
Type: Public

Reliv' International is offering its customers more than a beverage, it's offering a way of life. Reliv' develops, manufactures, and sells powdered nutritional supplements, weight-management products, sports nutrition drinks, and skin care products. Top seller Reliv' Classic and Reliv NOW are vegetarian beverage powders that contains vitamins, minerals, and soy protein. Other products include Innergize! sports drink and high-fiber supplement FibRestore. The company uses a multi-level marketing system, selling its products through more than 57,000 independent distributors primarily in the US, but also in Canada, Mexico, Europe, and the Pacific Rim.

	Annual Growth	12/17	12/18	12/19	12/20	12/21
Sales ($mil.)	(6.0%)	41.8	36.1	35.1	35.6	32.6
Net income ($ mil.)	–	(0.7)	(1.9)	(0.4)	1.3	(0.4)
Market value ($ mil.)	(2.8%)	5.0	4.5	4.1	3.7	4.5
Employees	–	160	156	91	–	–

RENAISSANCE MARINE GROUP, INC.

908 PORT DR
CLARKSTON, WA 994031845
Phone: 509 758-9189
Fax: –
Web: www.renaissance-marine-group.com

CEO: Daniel Larson
CFO: –
HR: –
FYE: December 31
Type: Private

Duckworth Boat Works thinks there's nothing daffy about aluminum boats -- in fact, they're lightweight and durable. Duckworth builds welded aluminum fishing and sport boats. The company offers inboard, outboard, and specialty models ranging from 18 to 24 feet in length. Duckworth boats are sold through a network of independent dealers in the western US and Canada. In addition to recreational users, customers have included the US Coast Guard, the National Park Service, and the US Fish and Wildlife Service. Duckworth was founded in 1972 and acquired by CEO Dan Larson in 1998.

RENASANT CORP
NYS: RNST

209 Troy Street
Tupelo, MS 38804-4827
Phone: 662 680-1001
Fax: –
Web: www.renasant.com

CEO: E R McGraw
CFO: James C Mabry IV
HR: Atonya Smith
FYE: December 31
Type: Public

Renasant Corporation is the holding company owns Renasant Bank, which serves consumers and local business through about 195 locations in Mississippi, Tennessee, Alabama, Florida, Georgia, North Carolina and South Carolina.. The bank offers standard products such as checking and savings accounts, CDs, credit cards, and loans and mortgages, as well as trust, retail brokerage, and retirement plan services. Its loan portfolio is dominated by residential and commercial real estate loans. The bank also offers agricultural, business, construction, and consumer loans, and lease financing. Subsidiary Renasant Insurance sells personal and business coverage. Renasant has assets of approximately $16.5 billion.

	Annual Growth	12/19	12/20	12/21	12/22	12/23
Assets ($mil.)	6.7%	13,401	14,930	16,810	16,988	17,361
Net income ($ mil.)	(3.6%)	167.6	83.7	175.9	166.1	144.7
Market value ($ mil.)	(1.3%)	1,988.6	1,890.9	2,130.6	2,110.4	1,890.9
Employees	(2.3%)	2,527	2,524	2,409	2,334	2,300

RENESAS ELECTRONICS AMERICA INC.

6024 SILVER CREEK VALLEY RD
SAN JOSE, CA 951381011
Phone: 408 284-8200
Fax: –
Web: www.renesas.com

CEO: Sailesh Chittipeddi
CFO: Aris Bolisay
HR: Elisabeth Dumont
FYE: April 01
Type: Private

Renesas Electronics America is the operating subsidiary of Renesas Electronics Corporation in the North America region. A provider of microcontrollers, analog, power, and SoC products, Renesas provides comprehensive solutions for a broad range of automotive, industrial, home electronics, office automation, and information communication technology applications that help shape a limitless future.

RENESAS ELECTRONICS AMERICA INC.

1001 MURPHY RANCH RD
MILPITAS, CA 950357912
Phone: 408 432-8888
Fax: –
Web: www.intersil.com

CEO: –
CFO: –
HR: –
FYE: January 01
Type: Private

Intersil makes transfer of power an orderly process, at least in electronics. Its line of semiconductor devices for power management include power regulators, converters and controllers, power modules, amplifiers and buffers, proximity and light sensors, data converters, video decoders and interfaces. Its products are components in data centers, computers, smartphones, autos, and a range of other applications. Almost three-quarters of its sales are to customers in Asia. In 2017 Intersil was bought by Renesas Electronics for $3.2 billion.

	Annual Growth	01/12	01/13	01/14	01/15	01/16
Sales ($mil.)	(4.8%)	–	–	575.2	562.6	521.6
Net income ($ mil.)	58.7%	–	–	2.9	54.8	7.2
Market value ($ mil.)	–	–	–	–	–	–
Employees	–	–	–	–	–	1,027

RENESAS ELECTRONICS AMERICA INC.

2801 SCOTT BLVD
SANTA CLARA, CA 950502549
Phone: 408 588-6000
Fax: –
Web: www.am.renesas.com

CEO: –
CFO: –
HR: –
FYE: December 31
Type: Private

Renesas Electronics America was formed in the April 2010 merger of NEC Electronics America and Renesas Technology America. Its Japanese parent, Renesas Electronics, is one of the world's largest manufacturers of semiconductors, and Renesas Electronics America provides more than 7,000 types of application-specific integrated circuits, many kinds of communications chips, microprocessors and microcontrollers, and static random-access memory, flash memory, and mask ROM chips. Its products are used in computers, networking equipment, consumer electronics, and automotive applications. The company also offers contract manufacturing services to other chip makers. The US is one of Renesas Electronics' smaller markets.

RENEWAL FUELS INC

1818 North Farwell Avenue
Milwaukee, WI 53202
Phone: 414 283-2625
Fax: –
Web: www.fuelmeister.com

NBB: RNWF
CEO: Alka Badshah
CFO: –
HR: –
FYE: December 31
Type: Public

Ready to make some biodiesel fuel at home? Don't worry, the "revenooers" won't show up to bust up your still and haul you off to jail for tax evasion. Renewal Fuels' FuelMeister system is a portable biodiesel processor that lets consumers produce their own fuel from used and fresh vegetable oil. The development-stage company has formed a subsidiary, Renewal Plantations, which has two greenhouses in Kansas growing cellulosic feedstock (read: plants, brush, and trees) for turning into biodiesel. Previously an electrical and electronic products maker called Tech Laboratories, the company acquired biofuels processor manufacturer Renewal Fuels in 2007. It then adopted that company's name and changed its focus.

	Annual Growth	12/03	12/04	12/05	12/06	12/07
Sales ($mil.)	30.8%	0.2	0.3	0.0	–	0.7
Net income ($ mil.)	–	(0.8)	(1.4)	(1.6)	(0.7)	(11.1)
Market value ($ mil.)	30.2%	2.3	0.6	0.2	1.0	6.6
Employees	(2.4%)	11	9	–	–	10

RENFRO LLC

661 LINVILLE RD
MOUNT AIRY, NC 270303101
Phone: 336 719-8000
Fax: –
Web: www.renfro.com

CEO: Stanley Jewell
CFO: David Dinkins
HR: Jessica Wilborn
FYE: January 29
Type: Private

Renfro is a leading designer, manufacturer, and marketer of quality socks and legwear products. It stewards globally recognized brands spanning the essentials, fashion, athletics, outdoors, work, and wellness categories. Renfro's products are sold under several brands, including Dr. Scholl's, Copper Defense, Polo/Ralph Lauren, and Sperry, among others. The company also sells its products under its own brands, K. Bell and HotSox. Renfro was founded in 1921.

	Annual Growth	01/06	01/07	01/08	01/10	01/11
Sales ($mil.)	(0.1%)	–	–	391.7	375.6	390.1
Net income ($ mil.)	(29.8%)	–	–	28.0	11.7	9.7
Market value ($ mil.)	–	–	–	–	–	–
Employees	–	–	–	–	–	2,073

RENNOVA HEALTH INC

400 S. Australian Avenue, Suite 800
West Palm Beach, FL 33401
Phone: 561 855-1626
Fax: –
Web: www.rennovahealth.com

NBB: RNVA
CEO: Seamus Lagan
CFO: Seamus Lagan
HR: –
FYE: December 31
Type: Public

Rennova Health (formerly CollabRx) is collaborating between data and health care. The company provides data analytics through its products, including Medytox Diagnostics, HIPAA-compliant tracking software Advantage, lab data management software Clinlab, electronic health record Medical Mime, cancer analytics platform CollabRx, revenue cycle management tool Medical Billing Choices; it also provides access to lending services through Platinum Financial Solutions. Customers include Life Technologies, Inc. and Everyday Health Inc.

	Annual Growth	12/18	12/19	12/20	12/21	12/22
Sales ($mil.)	(2.7%)	14.5	16.0	7.2	3.2	13.0
Net income ($ mil.)	–	(14.0)	(48.0)	(18.3)	5.6	(3.3)
Market value ($ mil.)	(83.3%)	37.8	0.0	381.0	0.0	0.0
Employees	(19.8%)	309	241	93	85	128

RENO CONTRACTING, INC.

7584 METRO DR STE 100
SAN DIEGO, CA 92108
Phone: 619 220-0224
Fax: –
Web: www.renocon.com

CEO: –
CFO: –
HR: –
FYE: October 31
Type: Private

Reno Contracting is building on its commercial state of mind in the southern part of the Golden State. The general contractor specializes in commercial construction projects primarily in its home region of San Diego County, California. Projects include office, retail, and hospitality construction, biotech and industrial facilities, and hospitals. Reno develops properties from the ground up and also performs interior tenant improvements. Clients have included Diversa Corporation , Biosite , and Bridgepoint Education . Reno's green building division, Reno ESP, utilizes energy efficient products and technology in the construction process. The company was founded in 1993 by CEO Matt Reno.

	Annual Growth	10/05	10/06	10/07	10/08	10/10
Sales ($mil.)	(34.7%)	–	–	217.4	213.7	60.5
Net income ($ mil.)	(11.2%)	–	–	1.4	1.4	1.0
Market value ($ mil.)	–	–	–	–	–	–
Employees	–	–	–	–	–	32

RENSSELAER POLYTECHNIC INSTITUTE

110 8TH ST
TROY, NY 121803522
Phone: 518 276-6000
Fax: –
Web: www.rpi.edu

CEO: –
CFO: –
HR: –
FYE: June 30
Type: Private

Rensselaer Polytechnic Institute (RPI) feeds scientific minds. The university offers about 150 bachelor's, master's, and doctoral degree programs, primarily in scientific research and technology fields. With some 7,000 undergraduate and graduate students and a student-to-faculty ratio of 15:1, RPI strives to provide interdisciplinary education programs through its five schools (Architecture; Engineering; Humanities, Arts, and Social Sciences; Management and Technology; and Science). The institute was founded in 1824 and is one of the oldest engineering schools in the country. RPI's main campus is in Troy, New York, but the institute also has a location in Hartford, Connecticut, that caters to working professionals.

	Annual Growth	06/15	06/16	06/17	06/20	06/22
Sales ($mil.)	1.1%	–	–	414.1	653.0	438.4
Net income ($ mil.)	–	–	–	77.7	33.7	(183.1)
Market value ($ mil.)	–	–	–	–	–	–
Employees	–	–	–	–	–	1,500

RENTECH, INC.

10880 WILSHIRE BLVD STE 1101
LOS ANGELES, CA 900244101
Phone: 310 571-9800
Fax: –
Web: www.rentechinc.com

CEO: Keith B Forman
CFO: Paul M Summers
HR: –
FYE: December 31
Type: Private

Rentech owns and operates wood fiber processing and nitrogen fertilizer manufacturing businesses. It also owns the intellectual property including patents, pilot, and demonstration data, and engineering designs for a number of clean energy technologies designed to produce certified synthetic fuels and renewable power when integrated with third-party technologies. Originally a clean energy business that rented (licensed) its alternative energy technology (hence "rent-tech"), the company now gets most of its revenues from its fertilizers and wood fiber processing operations.

REPLACEMENT PARTS, INC.

1901 E ROOSEVELT RD
LITTLE ROCK, AR 722062533
Phone: 501 375-1215
Fax: –
Web: www.btbautoparts.com

CEO: Bill Schlatterer
CFO: –
HR: Jerri Worthington
FYE: December 31
Type: Private

Replacement Parts works Bumper to Bumper. The company's subsidiary Crow-Burlingame operates about 160 stores under the Bumper To Bumper banner in Arkansas, Louisiana, Mississippi, Missouri, Oklahoma, and Texas. Replacement Parts also distributes auto parts through three Parts Warehouses in Arkansas, Louisiana, and Oklahoma. The company was founded in 1919 by grocer J.G. Burlingame and candy salesman William Robert Crow, grandfather of president Fletcher Lord Jr. The duo first entered the auto business by purchasing new cars in St. Louis and driving them around Little Rock to attract buyers. Employees own about 15% of the company through its stock ownership program.

	Annual Growth	12/02	12/03	12/04	12/06	12/07
Sales ($mil.)	47.0%	–	40.1	149.4	179.0	187.3
Net income ($ mil.)	17.7%	–	1.6	2.8	5.1	3.1
Market value ($ mil.)	–	–	–	–	–	–
Employees	–	–	–	–	–	1,200

REPLACEMENTS, LTD.

1089 KNOX RD
MC LEANSVILLE, NC 273019228
Phone: 336 697-3000
Fax: –
Web: www.replacements.com

CEO: Robert L Page
CFO: –
HR: Brian Hicks
FYE: September 30
Type: Private

Face it, the good china is going to get chipped. While throwing it all out is always an option, Replacements offers a cheaper solution. The company offers new and previously-owned china, crystal, flatware, and collectibles from its facilities spanning some 500,000 sq. ft. Its inventory consists of nearly 14 million pieces in more than 340,000 patterns. In addition to its bridal and gift registry, Replacements' website features a dinnerware knowledge base, place-setting guides, pattern identification tools, and showroom tour. Customers can place their orders by mail, phone, fax, e-mail, or in person at the company's store in Greensboro, North Carolina. Replacements was founded by CEO Bob Page in 1981.

	Annual Growth	09/17	09/18	09/19	09/20	09/21
Sales ($mil.)	9.3%	–	83.3	81.5	94.9	108.6
Net income ($ mil.)	26.0%	–	9.8	6.8	14.7	19.7
Market value ($ mil.)	–	–	–	–	–	–
Employees	–	–	–	–	–	400

REPLIGEN CORP.

NMS: RGEN

41 Seyon Street, Bldg. 1, Suite 100
Waltham, MA 02453
Phone: 781 250-0111
Fax: 781 250-0115
Web: www.repligen.com

CEO: Tony J Hunt
CFO: Jon K Snodgres
HR: Kelly Capra
FYE: December 31
Type: Public

Repligen is a global life sciences company that develops and commercializes highly innovated bioprocessing technology and systems that increase efficiencies and flexibility in the process of manufacturing biological drugs. The company's bioprocessing business develops and commercializes proteins and other agents used in the production of biopharmaceuticals. Repligen is a major supplier of Protein A, a recombinant protein used in the production of monoclonal antibodies and other biopharmaceutical manufacturing applications. s. North America accounts for about 45% of the company's total revenue.

	Annual Growth	12/19	12/20	12/21	12/22	12/23
Sales ($mil.)	24.0%	270.2	366.3	670.5	801.5	638.8
Net income ($ mil.)	18.0%	21.4	59.9	128.3	186.0	41.6
Market value ($ mil.)	18.1%	5,158.4	10,686	14,769	9,441.8	10,027
Employees	23.7%	761	1,100	309	2,025	1,783

REPOSITRAK INC

NYS: TRAK

5282 South Commerce Drive, Suite D292
Murray, UT 84107
Phone: 435 645-2000
Fax: –
Web: www.parkcitygroup.com

CEO: –
CFO: –
HR: –
FYE: June 30
Type: Public

Park City Group understands that managing complex retail operations is no picnic. The company supplies retailers with operation management software used to optimize supply chains. Park City sells to supermarkets, convenience stores, and specialty retailers. Its software packages include Fresh Market Manager, ScoreTracker, and ActionManager. Target corporation is a major customer. Park City was founded by chairman and CEO Randy Fields, who also co-founded Mrs. Fields Cookies. Fields controls more than 40% of Park City Group's stock. Almost all of the company's sales came from its domestic customers.

	Annual Growth	06/19	06/20	06/21	06/22	06/23
Sales ($mil.)	(2.5%)	21.2	20.0	21.0	18.0	19.1
Net income ($ mil.)	9.4%	3.9	1.6	4.1	4.0	5.6
Market value ($ mil.)	–	–	–	–	–	–
Employees	(1.7%)	74	81	70	67	69

REPRODUCTIVE FREEDOM FOR ALL

1725 I ST NW STE 900
WASHINGTON, DC 200062420
Phone: 202 973-3000
Fax: –
Web: www.reproductivefreedomforall.org

CEO: Mini Timmaraju
CFO: Steven Kravitz
HR: Anne Diemer
FYE: September 30
Type: Private

NARAL Pro-Choice America believes that you do indeed have to fight for your rights. The group is dedicated to defending reproductive choice for women as well as supporting policies that improve women's health and decrease the need for abortions. It works to help women around the issues of equal access to health and reproductive care, contraception, safe abortions, legal system issues, sex education, and women of color. NARAL Pro-Choice America also lobbies Congress, and publishes reports on its issues and an annual Congressional Record on Choice recording legislators votes on pro-choice issues. The organization was founded in 1969.

	Annual Growth	09/12	09/13	09/14	09/15	09/16
Sales ($mil.)	(2.7%)	–	8.1	8.1	7.2	7.5
Net income ($ mil.)	–	–	(1.2)	0.5	0.0	0.2
Market value ($ mil.)	–	–	–	–	–	–
Employees	–	–	–	–	–	68

REPROS THERAPEUTICS INC.

2408 TIMBERLOCH PL STE B7
THE WOODLANDS, TX 773801021
Phone: 281 719-3400
Fax: -
Web: -
CEO: Larry Dillaha
CFO: Katherine A Anderson
HR: -
FYE: December 31
Type: Private

Repros Therapeutics focuses on reproductive health. The pharmaceutical firm develops small-molecule drugs to treat hormonal and reproductive system disorders. Its lead candidate, Proellex, is a possible therapy for uterine fibroids, endometriosis, and associated anemia. The company is developing an orally delivered version as well as a vaginally delivered one. Repros' second candidate, Androxal, may treat testosterone deficiencies in men, particularly when the deficiency is caused by obesity. The company was formed in 1987 and went public in mid-2013.In late 2017, the company agreed to be acquired by pharmaceutical giant Allergan for $26 million.

REPUBLIC AIRWAYS HOLDINGS INC.

8909 PURDUE RD STE 300
INDIANAPOLIS, IN 462683152
Phone: 317 484-6000
Fax: -
Web: www.shuttleamerica.com
CEO: Bryan K Bedford
CFO: Joseph P Allman
HR: Amy L Springman
FYE: December 31
Type: Private

Republic Airways is one of the largest regional airlines in the US. The company operates about 1,000 flights per day to approximately 100 cities across some 40 US states, as well as Canada, the Caribbean, and Central America. From the world's largest all-Embraer 170/175 fleet of more than 220 aircraft to its new state-of-the-art training facility with simulators that provide its pilots with the best training, Republic operates an innovative and technologically advanced airline with a focus on crew and passenger safety. The company also offers fixed-fee flights with American Airlines, Delta, and United Express. The company was founded in 1974.

REPUBLIC BANCORP, INC. (KY)   NMS: RBCA A

601 West Market Street
Louisville, KY 40202
Phone: 502 584-3600
Fax: -
Web: www.republicbank.com
CEO: Steven E Trager
CFO: Kevin Sipes
HR: -
FYE: December 31
Type: Public

Republic Bancorp is the parent of Republic Bank & Trust, which offers deposit accounts, loans and mortgages, credit cards, private banking, and trust services through about 30 branches in across Kentucky and around 15 in southern Indiana, Nashville, Tennessee, Tampa, Florida, and Cincinnati, Ohio. About one-third of the bank's $4.4 billion-loan portfolio is tied to residential real estate, while another 35% is made up of commercial real estate loans. Warehouse lines of credit, home equity loans, and commercial and industrial loans make up most of the rest. Its subsidiary Captive provides property and casualty insurance coverage to the company and the bank, as well as a group of third-party insurance captives for which insurance may not be available or economically feasible.

	Annual Growth	12/19	12/20	12/21	12/22	12/23
Assets ($mil.)	4.1%	5,620.3	6,168.3	6,093.6	5,835.5	6,594.9
Net income ($ mil.)	(0.4%)	91.7	83.2	86.8	91.1	90.4
Market value ($ mil.)	4.2%	906.0	698.2	984.2	792.1	1,067.8
Employees	(1.5%)	1,092	1,104	1,054	1,012	1,028

REPUBLIC FIRST BANCORP, INC.   NMS: FRBK

50 South 16th Street
Philadelphia, PA 19102
Phone: 215 735-4422
Fax: -
Web: www.myrepublicbank.com
CEO: Thomas X Geisel
CFO: Frank A Cavallaro
HR: -
FYE: December 31
Type: Public

Republic First Bancorp is the holding company for Republic Bank, which serves the Greater Philadelphia area and southern New Jersey from more than 15 branches. Boasting over $1 billion in assets, the bank targets individuals and small to midsized businesses, offering standard deposit products including checking and savings accounts, money market accounts, IRAs, and CDs. Commercial mortgages account for more than 70% of the company's loan portfolio, which also includes consumer loans, business loans, and residential mortgages. Republic has been transitioning from a commercial bank into a major regional retail and commercial bank.

	Annual Growth	12/17	12/18	12/19	12/20	12/21
Assets ($mil.)	24.8%	2,322.3	2,753.3	3,341.3	5,065.7	5,626.7
Net income ($ mil.)	29.7%	8.9	8.6	(3.5)	5.1	25.2
Market value ($ mil.)	(18.5%)	498.1	351.9	246.4	168.0	219.3
Employees	5.5%	448	531	599	499	556

REPUBLIC INDEMNITY CO. OF AMERICA

15821 Ventura Boulevard, Suite 370
Encino, CA 91436
Phone: 818 990-9860
Fax: -
Web: www.dionr@ri-net.com
CEO: Dwayne Marioni
CFO: -
HR: -
FYE: December 31
Type: Public

Republic Indemnity Company of America has tunnel vision when it comes to insurance. The monoline insurer offers one thing to its customers in California and the Western US: workers' compensation insurance. Since 1945, Republic Indemnity has been focused on writing policies through independent agents and brokers for small to midsized businesses. Republic Indemnity tries to differentiate its operations from the rest of the pack by promoting itself as the responsive, readily-accessible insurer offering customizable workers' comp packages. The company is one of a group of subsidiaries operating under Cincinnati-based global property/casualty insurer American Financial Group.

REPUBLIC SERVICES INC   NYS: RSG

18500 North Allied Way
Phoenix, AZ 85054
Phone: 480 627-2700
Fax: -
Web: www.republicservices.com
CEO: Jon V Ark
CFO: Brian Delghiaccio
HR: Carmine Primiano
FYE: December 31
Type: Public

Republic Services is one of the one of the largest providers of environmental services in the US, as measured by revenue. It operates across the US and Canada through about 355 collection operations, 235 transfer stations, 70 recycling centers, 205 active landfills, three treatment, recovery and disposal facilities, 20 treatment, storage and disposal facilities (TSDF), six salt water disposal wells and seven deep injection wells. The company is engaged in about 75 landfill gas-to-energy and other renewable energy projects and had post-closure responsibility for around 130 closed landfills. The company was incorporated in 1996.

	Annual Growth	12/19	12/20	12/21	12/22	12/23
Sales ($mil.)	9.8%	10,299	10,154	11,295	13,511	14,965
Net income ($ mil.)	12.7%	1,073.3	967.2	1,290.4	1,487.6	1,731.0
Market value ($ mil.)	16.5%	28,198	30,296	43,871	40,580	51,881
Employees	3.3%	36,000	35,000	35,000	40,000	41,000

REPUBLICAN GOVERNORS PUBLIC POLICY COMMITTEE

1747 PENNSYLVANIA AVE NW STE 250
WASHINGTON, DC 200064643
Phone: 202 662-4140
Fax: –
Web: www.rgppc.com

CEO: –
CFO: –
HR: –
FYE: December 31
Type: Private

The Republican Governors Association (RGA) wants everyone seeing red. RGA is the national political organization of Republican Governors; it focuses on public policy issues as well as the election and re-election of Republican gubernatorial candidates and therefore strategizing about how to keep "red states" red. The association represents Republican Governors in the US and in Guam and the Commonwealth of the Northern Mariana Islands. Members regularly meet with members of Congress in attempts to influence policy making on tax cuts, welfare, and education among other issues. The organization was founded in 1963.

	Annual Growth	12/12	12/13	12/16	12/21	12/22
Sales ($mil.)	7.7%	–	2.2	1.6	3.9	4.4
Net income ($ mil.)	–	–	1.1	0.5	2.1	(2.2)
Market value ($ mil.)	–	–	–	–	–	–
Employees	–	–	–	–	–	7

RES-CARE, INC.

805 N WHITTINGTON PKWY
LOUISVILLE, KY 402227101
Phone: 502 394-2100
Fax: –
Web: www.rescare.com

CEO: Jon Rousseau
CFO: Jim Mattingly
HR: Anita Lewis
FYE: December 31
Type: Private

BrightSpring Health Services (formerly known ResCare) as is the leading provider of complementary home- and community-based health services for complex populations in need of specialized and/or chronic care. BrightSpring offers comprehensive care services, specialized care and expanding clinical services in all 50 states to over 330,000 patients daily. The company's operations include StepStone Family & Youth Services and All Ways Caring HomeCare (home health for seniors); and ResCare Community Living (community living and daily assistance for disabled clients). Additionally, BrightSpring Health offers neuro rehabilitation, pharmacy, behavioral health, telecare and remote support, hospice, and family and youth care programs.

RESACA EXPLOITATION INC

1331 Lamar, Suite 1450
Houston, TX 77010
Phone: 713 650-1246
Fax: –
Web: www.resacaexploitation.com

CEO: –
CFO: –
HR: –
FYE: June 30
Type: Public

Resaca Exploitation takes its name from the famous Mexican-American War battle of Resaca de la Palma, and hopes it wins the battle to get oil and gas out of the ground. The independent oil and gas company exploits mature oil and gas reserves in the Permian Basin. It reactivates older wells and floods them with water or carbon dioxide to recover previously unreachable deposits. Resaca also gets oil from proven wells by upgrading and improving well facilities. It has proved reserves of about 12 million barrels of oil equivalent (MMBOE). In 2010 the company moved to acquire Texas-based oil company Cano Petroleum, but the deal fell through due to the inability to raise sufficient funds in a depressed market.

	Annual Growth	06/05	06/06	06/07	06/08	06/09
Sales ($mil.)	32.7%	–	–	14.6	6.2	25.7
Net income ($ mil.)	–	–	–	(8.4)	(17.5)	2.7
Market value ($ mil.)	–	–	–	–	–	–
Employees	–	–	–	–	–	80

RESEARCH FRONTIERS INC.

NAS: REFR

240 Crossways Park Drive
Woodbury, NY 11797-2033
Phone: 516 364-1902
Fax: –
Web: www.smartglass.com

CEO: Joseph M Harary
CFO: –
HR: –
FYE: December 31
Type: Public

Research Frontiers is exploring smart light frontiers. The company's suspended-particle device (SPD) technology controls the flow of light. When microscopic particles in a liquid suspension or film are electrically excited, they align. By varying voltage, the amount of light transmitted can be controlled. Applications include "smart windows" that control light transmission, eyewear, auto sunroofs and mirrors, and flat-panel displays for computers and other electronic devices. Research Frontiers licenses its technologies to such manufacturers as Asahi Glass, Dainippon Ink and Chemicals, General Electric, Hitachi Chemical, and Polaroid.

	Annual Growth	12/19	12/20	12/21	12/22	12/23
Sales ($mil.)	(12.7%)	1.6	0.8	1.3	0.5	0.9
Net income ($ mil.)	–	(3.8)	(2.3)	(1.8)	(2.7)	(1.9)
Market value ($ mil.)	(23.9%)	100.9	94.2	57.6	64.0	33.8
Employees	–	8	6	6	6	–

RESEARCH TRIANGLE INSTITUTE INC

3040 CORNWALLIS RD
DURHAM, NC 277090155
Phone: 919 541-6000
Fax: –
Web: www.rti.org

CEO: E W Holden
CFO: Michael H Kaelin Jr
HR: Alisa Bright
FYE: September 30
Type: Private

Founded in 1958, Research Triangle Institute operates mainly under its trade name, RTI International (RTI), is an independent, nonprofit research institute dedicated to improving the human condition. It provides research, development, and technical services to government and commercial clients worldwide. Its experts hold degrees in more than 250 scientific, technical, and professional disciplines across the social and laboratory sciences, engineering, and international development fields. The company conducts research and deliver technical services on behalf of government agencies, universities, foundations, private businesses, and other organizations. It serves clients around the world, with a science-based approach to projects of all sizes?from focused studies and applied R&D to large-scale national and international longitudinal research efforts.

	Annual Growth	09/16	09/17	09/18	09/20	09/21
Sales ($mil.)	2.6%	–	972.3	957.7	912.1	1,077.9
Net income ($ mil.)	27.0%	–	22.9	(1.6)	25.7	59.7
Market value ($ mil.)	–	–	–	–	–	–
Employees	–	–	–	–	–	3,117

RESERVE INDUSTRIES CORP

20 First Plaza, Suite 308
Albuquerque, NM 87102
Phone: 505 247-2384
Fax: –
Web: –

CEO: James J Melfi Jr
CFO: –
HR: –
FYE: November 30
Type: Public

Reserve Industries mines and processes silica sand from its open pit mines outside Seattle, Washington. The company's wet sand products are marketed for construction materials and are used to make sand traps on golf courses. The company's dried silica sand is sold to manufacturers of glass containers. Reserve Industries also operates an all-weather dumpsite near Ravensdale, Washington, that accepts clean fill, paving materials such as concrete and ground asphalt, topsoil with strippings, and items with no petroleum or heavy-metal contaminates. The company sold its Rossborough subsidiary in 2006 to Opta Minerals, a division of SunOpta Inc.

	Annual Growth	11/98	11/99	11/00	11/01	11/02
Sales ($mil.)	60.2%	0.2	0.4	1.8	1.2	1.4
Net income ($ mil.)	–	(2.1)	0.0	(1.2)	(2.0)	(1.8)
Market value ($ mil.)	–	–	–	–	–	–
Employees	(6.1%)	18	16	16	12	14

RESERVE PETROLEUM CO.   NBB: RSRV

6801 Broadway Ext., Suite 300   CEO: Cameron R McLain
Oklahoma City, OK 73116-9037   CFO: Lawrence R Francis
Phone: 405 848-7551   HR: –
Fax: –   FYE: December 31
Web: www.reserve-petro.com   Type: Public

The Reserve Petroleum Company has petroleum reserves of about 266,870 barrels of oil. It also has 1.6 billion cu. ft. of natural gas reserves. In 2008 the oil and gas exploration and production company owned non-producing properties of more than 262,000 gross acres (90,330 net acres), located in nine states. About 64,800 net acres of this land asset are in Oklahoma, South Dakota, and Texas. About 53% of Reserve Petroleum's oil production in 2008 was derived from royalty interests. The company has royalty interests in 33 gross (1.1 net) wells that were drilled and completed as producing wells. President Mason McLain owns about 10% of Reserve Petroleum.

	Annual Growth	12/18	12/19	12/20	12/21	12/22
Sales ($mil.)	18.0%	8.3	6.6	4.1	9.1	16.2
Net income ($ mil.)	14.7%	2.3	(0.3)	(2.0)	1.3	4.0
Market value ($ mil.)	5.0%	30.8	32.4	22.3	27.5	37.5
Employees	(9.6%)	9	7	7	6	6

RESIDEO TECHNOLOGIES INC   NYS: REZI

16100 N. 71st Street, Suite 550   CEO: Jay Geldmacher
Scottsdale, AZ 85254   CFO: Anthony L Trunzo
Phone: 480 573-5340   HR: –
Fax: –   FYE: December 31
Web: www.resideo.com   Type: Public

Resideo Technologies, Inc. is a leading global provider of critical comfort, residential thermal solutions and security solutions primarily in residential environments. The products were installed to over 150 million homes globally. Included in its Products & Solutions segment are traditional products, as well as connected products. Approximately 11 million of its customers are connected via the company's software solutions, providing access to control, monitoring and alerts. Its broad portfolio of innovative products is delivered through a comprehensive network of over 100,000 professional contractors, and over 1,000 original equipment manufacturers (OEMs), as well as major retailers and online merchants. The US generates about 75% of the company's total sales.

	Annual Growth	12/19	12/20	12/21	12/22	12/23
Sales ($mil.)	5.8%	4,988.0	5,071.0	5,846.0	6,370.0	6,242.0
Net income ($ mil.)	55.4%	36.0	37.0	242.0	283.0	210.0
Market value ($ mil.)	12.1%	1,729.9	3,082.7	3,774.4	2,385.3	2,728.9
Employees	1.9%	13,000	14,700	13,300	15,200	14,000

RESIDUAL PUMPKIN ENTITY, LLC

11909 SHELBYVILLE RD   CEO: Jasbir Patel
LOUISVILLE, KY 402431453   CFO: Phillip Milliner
Phone: 919 323-4480   HR: –
Fax: –   FYE: December 31
Web: www.uoshoppes.com   Type: Private

Call it a craft fair that meets Amazon.com. CafePress operates an online service that connects millions of buyers and sellers of print-on-demand products. If you've dreamed up a catchy slogan or an arresting image, the company's flagship website, CafePress.com, will print it for you on a T-shirt, hat, mug, poster, or other product; post it on cafepress.com for sale; and then ship it off and collect payments, keeping a nominal base fee for itself. The company's growing portfolio of websites includes ezprints.com, GreatBigCanvas.com, CanvasOnDemand.com, Imagekind.com, and InvitationBox.com, and boasts more than 19 million members across all of its properties. Founded in 1999, CafePress went public in 2012.

RESMED INC.   NYS: RMD

9001 Spectrum Center Blvd.   CEO: Michael Farrell
San Diego, CA 92123   CFO: Brett Sandercock
Phone: 858 836-5000   HR: –
Fax: –   FYE: June 30
Web: www.resmed.com   Type: Public

ResMed is a global leader in the development, manufacturing, distribution, and marketing of medical devices and cloud-based software applications that diagnoses, treats, and manages respiratory disorders, including SDB, COPD, neuromuscular disease, and other chronic diseases. Its cloud-based digital health applications, along with its devices, are designed to provide connected care to improve patient outcomes and efficiencies for its customers. The company sells its products in more than 140 countries through a combination of wholly owned subsidiaries and independent distributors. ResMed was founded in Australia in 1989 by Dr. Peter Farrell, who remains chairman. The US generates about 65% of total sales.

	Annual Growth	06/19	06/20	06/21	06/22	06/23
Sales ($mil.)	12.8%	2,606.6	2,957.0	3,196.8	3,578.1	4,223.0
Net income ($ mil.)	22.0%	404.6	621.7	474.5	779.4	897.6
Market value ($ mil.)	15.7%	17,946	28,236	36,254	30,829	32,134
Employees	92.4%	740	7,770	7,970	8,160	10,140

RESOLUTE FP US INC.

5020 HIGHWAY 11 S   CEO: Yves Laflamme
CALHOUN, TN 373095248   CFO: Jo-Ann Longworth
Phone: 423 336-2211   HR: Ariel Jones
Fax: –   FYE: December 31
Web: www.resolutefp.com   Type: Private

Resolute FP US is the US subsidiary of Canadian paper and pulp giant Resolute Forest Products. The parent company, which operates some 40 facilities, produces newsprint, specialty papers, market pulp, tissue and wood products. Newsprint and specialty papers together account for more than 45% of sales, while market pulp is responsible for nearly 30%. The US is Resolute Forest Product's largest market, and Resolute FP US accounts for about 70% of the parent company's total revenues. Resolute Forest produce market pulp at five facilities in North America, with total capacity of approximately 1.5 million metric tons, or about 10% of total North American capacity.

RESONATE BLENDS INC   NBB: KOAN

26565 Agoura Road, Suite 200   CEO: Geoffrey Selzer
Calabasas, CA 91302   CFO: Geoffrey Selzer
Phone: 571 888-0009   HR: –
Fax: –   FYE: December 31
Web: www.firstwave.net   Type: Public

Resonate Blends (formerly Textmunication Holdings) is a cannabis holding company centered on value-added holistic wellness and lifestyle brands. The company offers a family of premium cannabis-based products and focuses on finding mutual value between product and consumer by optimizing quality, supply chain resources, and financial performance. To communicate the breadth of wellness products that Resonate is developing, the company created the Resonate System which graphically represents a spectrum of wellness products based on cannabis scaffolding. Because of the unique nature of Resonate's Koan products, Resonate has prioritized a direct-to-consumer method. The company was incorporated in 1984.

	Annual Growth	12/18	12/19	12/20	12/21	12/22
Sales ($mil.)	(53.6%)	1.1	1.1	–	0.0	0.0
Net income ($ mil.)	136.2%	0.0	(3.7)	(1.9)	(4.9)	0.7
Market value ($ mil.)	(52.7%)	49.0	15.0	9.1	25.6	2.5
Employees	(15.9%)	12	11	–	6	6

RESOURCE AMERICA, INC.

1 CRESCENT DR STE 203　　　　　　　　　　　CEO: Jonathan Z Cohen
PHILADELPHIA, PA 191121015　　　　　　　　CFO: Thomas C Elliott
Phone: 215 546-5005　　　　　　　　　　　　　　　　　　　　　HR: –
Fax: –　　　　　　　　　　　　　　　　　　　　　　FYE: December 31
Web: www.c3cp.com　　　　　　　　　　　　　　　　　　　Type: Private

Resource America's resource of choice is real estate investment. The firm manages a series of funds that invest in real estate-related debt, commercial mortgages, and other real estate assets, as well as trust-preferred securities and asset-backed securities. Its financial fund management operations finance, structure, and manage investments in bank loans, securities, bonds, and other instruments. Through its Trapeza Capital Management and Ischus Capital Management divisions and other ventures, the company focuses on financial funds for collateralized debt and loan obligations. Resource America and its affiliates manage some $17.8 billion in assets. C-III Capital Partners acquired Resource America in mid-2016.

RESOURCES CONNECTION INC　　　　　　NMS: RGP

17101 Armstrong Avenue　　　　　　　　　　　CEO: Kate W Duchene
Irvine, CA 92614　　　　　　　　　　　　　　　　CFO: Jennifer Ryu
Phone: 714 430-6400　　　　　　　　　　　　　　HR: Jennifer Stover
Fax: –　　　　　　　　　　　　　　　　　　　　　　　　　　FYE: May 27
Web: www.rgp.com　　　　　　　　　　　　　　　　　　　　Type: Public

Resources Connection, doing business as Resources Global Professional (RGP), is a global consulting firm focused on project execution services that power clients' operational needs and change initiatives utilizing on-demand, experienced, and diverse talent. The firm specializes in the co-delivery of enterprise initiatives typically precipitated by business transformation, strategic transactions, or regulatory change. It primarily conducts business on a project-by-project basis, positioning itself as a flexible alternative to traditional accounting, consulting, and law firms for certain tasks. RGP has approximately 4,100 professionals that serve over 2,000 clients including over 85% of the Fortune 100 from more than 35 cities in about 14 countries across the world. North America generates the majority of its revenue.

	Annual Growth	05/19	05/20	05/21	05/22	05/23
Sales ($mil.)	1.6%	729.0	703.4	629.5	805.0	775.6
Net income ($ mil.)	14.6%	31.5	28.3	25.2	67.2	54.4
Market value ($ mil.)	–	520.9	367.9	488.1	608.6	521.2
Employees	1.0%	3,896	3,433	3,753	4,259	4,062

RESPIRERX PHARMACEUTICALS INC　　　NBB: RSPI

126 Valley Road, Suite C　　　　　　　　　　　　CEO: Arnold S Lippa
Glen Rock, NJ 07452　　　　　　　　　　　　　　CFO: Jeff E Margolis
Phone: 201 444-4947　　　　　　　　　　　　　　　　　　　　HR: –
Fax: –　　　　　　　　　　　　　　　　　　　　　　FYE: December 31
Web: www.respirerx.com　　　　　　　　　　　　　　　　　Type: Public

Cortex Pharmaceuticals develops drugs to treat brain-controlled breathing disorders. It has several compounds designed to prevent or reverse drug-induced respiratory depression and to reduce obstructive sleep apnea in Phase 2 clinical studies. Its leading compounds include CX1739, which targets opiate-induced respiratory depression and central sleep apnea, and dronabinol, a compound being studied in obstructive sleep apnea patients in an National Institutes of Health-funded study. Cortex hopes to obtain orphan drug designation on its compounds, which would give it a relatively quick regulatory pathway and a period of exclusive marketing rights. Cortex merged Pier Pharmaceuticals into its operations in 2012.

	Annual Growth	12/18	12/19	12/20	12/21	12/22
Sales ($mil.)	–	–	–	–	–	–
Net income ($ mil.)	–	(2.6)	(2.1)	(4.3)	(3.1)	(2.1)
Market value ($ mil.)	(75.6%)	81.6	12.6	0.4	1.5	0.3
Employees	7.5%	3	3	5	6	4

RESTAURANT DEVELOPERS CORP.

7002 ENGLE RD STE 100　　　　　　　　　　　　　CEO: Michael Nasr
CLEVELAND, OH 441303403　　　　　　　　　　　　　　　　　CFO: –
Phone: 440 625-3080　　　　　　　　　　　　　　HR: Kathleen Stewart
Fax: –　　　　　　　　　　　　　　　　　　　　　　FYE: December 31
Web: www.mrhero.com　　　　　　　　　　　　　　　　　　Type: Private

Restaurant Developers Corporation (RDC) is a regional franchisor of sandwich shops and coffeehouses. Its flagship Mr. Hero chain serves deli sandwiches, hot hero-style sandwiches, hamburgers, and chicken sandwiches. The eateries also offer sides, salads, and pasta dishes. Its signature Romanburger and Hot Buttered Cheesesteak has made the company a customer favorite from the start. Its Steakery menu features five deliciously unique sandwiches like the Hatta Potatta, Sicilian Parmesan, and Sir Racha Bourbon. In 1965, the first Mr. Hero opened on Cleveland's Westside.

	Annual Growth	12/15	12/16	12/17	12/18	12/20
Sales ($mil.)	0.9%	–	5.2	5.1	5.0	5.4
Net income ($ mil.)	16.8%	–	1.2	1.7	1.8	2.1
Market value ($ mil.)	–	–	–	–	–	–
Employees	–	–	–	–	–	37

RESTAURANT TECHNOLOGIES, INC.

2250 PILOT KNOB RD STE 100　　　　　　　　　CEO: Jeffrey R Kiesel
MENDOTA HEIGHTS, MN 551201127　　　　　　CFO: Robert E Weil
Phone: 888 796-4997　　　　　　　　　　　　　　　　　　　　HR: –
Fax: –　　　　　　　　　　　　　　　　　　　　　　FYE: December 31
Web: www.rti-inc.com　　　　　　　　　　　　　　　　　　Type: Private

Restaurant Technologies, Inc. (RTI) regularly strikes oil. The company provides oil-management equipment and supplies to restaurants and other foodservice operations, specializing in its MaxLife system for handling and disposing of used cooking oil. It also offers oil-disposal services to cart away used frying oil. In turn, it distributes clean cooking oil and other supplies to more than 20,000 customers from facilities in 40-plus metropolitan areas. RTI's Global Tier division markets equipment for monitoring restaurant kitchen equipment, such as walk-in coolers and fryers. In 2011 Swedish investor EQT Infrastructure acquired the company from Parthenon Capital Partners and ABS Capital Partners.

RETAIL INDUSTRY LEADERS ASSOCIATION, INC

99 M ST SE STE 700　　　　　　　　　　　　　　CEO: Gregg Steinhafel
WASHINGTON, DC 200033977　　　　　　　　　　　　　　　　CFO: –
Phone: 703 841-2300　　　　　　　　　　　　　　　　　　　　HR: –
Fax: –　　　　　　　　　　　　　　　　　　　　　　FYE: December 31
Web: www.rila.org　　　　　　　　　　　　　　　　　　　　Type: Private

The Retail Industry Leaders Association (RILA) loves people who shop 'til they drop. The organization is a membership-based alliance of retailers, the manufacturers that supply them, and companies that provide services to the retail industry. It serves as an advocate for the industry before government agencies, does PR for the industry, and fosters networking and relationship-building among its members. RILA, which changed its name from the International Mass Retail Association in 2004, has more than 200 member companies, including giants such as Wal-Mart, Abercrombie & Fitch, and Sears, as well as Coca-Cola and Procter & Gamble. The association was formed in 1969 as the Mass Retailing Institute.

	Annual Growth	12/12	12/13	12/14	12/17	12/18
Sales ($mil.)	0.5%	–	19.4	20.5	22.2	19.8
Net income ($ mil.)	–	–	(0.1)	0.7	0.6	0.6
Market value ($ mil.)	–	–	–	–	–	–
Employees	–	–	–	–	–	23

RETAIL OPPORTUNITY INVESTMENTS CORP — NMS: ROIC

11250 El Camino Real, Suite 200
San Diego, CA 92130
Phone: 858 677-0900
Fax: –
Web: www.roireit.net
CEO: Stuart A Tanz
CFO: Michael B Haines
HR: Diana Storti
FYE: December 31
Type: Public

For this company, opportunity knocking sounds a lot like a neighborhood shopping center. Retail Opportunity Investments (ROIC), true to its name, invests in, owns, leases, and manages shopping centers. It targets densely populated, middle- and upper-class markets and looks for centers anchored by large grocery or drug stores. The self-managed real estate investment trust (REIT), owns nearly 90 shopping centers comprising about 10.1 million sq. ft. in Oregon, Washington, and California. It makes money from rent, management expenses, and mortgage interest. ROIC was formed in 2007 as an acquisition company. It purchased NRDC Capital Management in 2009 and took its current name in 2010.

	Annual Growth	12/19	12/20	12/21	12/22	12/23
Sales ($mil.)	2.7%	295.0	284.1	284.1	312.9	327.7
Net income ($ mil.)	(8.3%)	48.8	32.0	53.5	51.9	34.5
Market value ($ mil.)	(5.6%)	2,241.1	1,699.2	2,487.3	1,907.4	1,780.5
Employees	(0.7%)	73	66	68	70	71

RETAIL PROPERTIES OF AMERICA, INC.

3021 BUTTERFIELD RD
OAK BROOK, IL 605231291
Phone: 630 634-4200
Fax: –
Web: www.kiterealty.com
CEO: Steven P Grimes
CFO: Julie M Swinehart
HR: –
FYE: December 31
Type: Private

You could say Retail Properties of America (formerly Inland Western Retail Real Estate Trust) is a bit of a shopaholic. The self-managed real estate investment trust (REIT) buys, owns, and operates one of the largest retail shopping center portfolios in the US, with more than 225 wholly or partially owned properties that include power centers, community centers, and lifestyle centers. Among its tenants are big-box stores, such as Best Buy, Ross Stores, and TJX Cos. It also has about 20 property management offices to serve its diverse client base with leasing, asset management, and property management services. The company went public in 2012. It was formerly sponsored by an affiliate of The Inland Group.

RETAILMENOT, INC.

301 CONGRESS AVE STE 700
AUSTIN, TX 787012930
Phone: 512 777-2970
Fax: –
Web: –
CEO: –
CFO: –
HR: –
FYE: December 31
Type: Private

Do an Internet search for "coupon code" and you've got this company's formula for success. RetailMeNot is a leading savings destination that influences purchase decisions through the power of savings.. E-tail is big business, and promo codes are incentives that appeal to both retailers and consumers. RetailMeNot has its flagship US website, retailmenot.com features sale items from selected retailers Its international brand portfolio includes VoucherCodes.co.uk in the UK, Ma-Reduc.com and Poulpeo.com in France, and RetailMeNot in Canada. RetailMeNot became a public company in 2013 and in 2017, it came back to private in 2017. In 2020, J2 Global announces agreement to acquire RetailMeNot.

RETIREMENT HOUSING FOUNDATION INC

911 N STUDEBAKER RD STE 100
LONG BEACH, CA 908154980
Phone: 562 257-5100
Fax: –
Web: www.rhf.org
CEO: Laverne R Joseph
CFO: –
HR: Stephanie Butler
FYE: September 30
Type: Private

The Retirement Housing Foundation (RHF) has been giving old folks homes since the mid-1960s. Affiliated with the United Church of Christ, the not-for-profit RHF manages nearly 160 communities -- ranging from a 12-unit home to an apartment complex for more than 1,000 -- in 24 states, Puerto Rico, and the Virgin Islands. RHF's facilities also include skilled nursing homes, respite care, and assisted living homes. Its memory care facilities provide specialized care for people suffering from memory loss. Over its 47 years in operation, RHF has expanded its service line to include people with disabilities and disadvantaged families; today nearly 17,000 people live in RHF housing.

	Annual Growth	09/17	09/18	09/19	09/21	09/22
Assets ($mil.)	(14.7%)	–	374.5	158.3	205.4	198.5
Net income ($ mil.)	(33.4%)	–	100.7	21.5	14.2	19.8
Market value ($ mil.)	–	–	–	–	–	–
Employees	–	–	–	–	–	2,500

RETRACTABLE TECHNOLOGIES INC — ASE: RVP

511 Lobo Lane
Little Elm, TX 75068-5295
Phone: 972 294-1010
Fax: –
Web: www.retractable.com
CEO: Thomas J Shaw
CFO: John W Fort III
HR: Stefanie Perry
FYE: December 31
Type: Public

Retractable Technologies knows you can't be too safe when you work around needles all day. The company develops, makes, and markets safety syringes and other injection technologies for the health care industry. Its flagship VanishPoint syringe retracts after injection, reducing the risk of both syringe reuse and accidental needlesticks (both are means of transmitting HIV and other infectious diseases). Retractable also makes blood collection needles and IV catheters using the VanishPoint technology, which was invented by Thomas Shaw, the company's founder, CEO, and majority owner. The firm sells to hospitals and other care providers in the US and abroad, both directly and through distributors.

	Annual Growth	12/19	12/20	12/21	12/22	12/23
Sales ($mil.)	1.1%	41.8	81.9	188.4	94.8	43.6
Net income ($ mil.)	–	3.1	24.2	56.1	5.1	(7.0)
Market value ($ mil.)	(7.3%)	44.9	321.5	207.5	49.1	33.2
Employees	–	140	182	235	198	–

REUNION INDUSTRIES INC. — NBB: RUNI

11 Stanwix Street, Suite 1400
Pittsburgh, PA 15222
Phone: 412 281-2111
Fax: 412 281-4747
Web: www.reunionindustries.com
CEO: Kimball J Bradley
CFO: John M Froehlich
HR: –
FYE: December 31
Type: Public

Reunion Industries proves its mettle by manufacturing metal products. It makes a slew of machined and fabricated industrial products, from fluid power cylinders to gratings. Its Hanna Cylinders unit builds hydraulic and pneumatic cylinders, actuators, accumulators, and manifolds. The company serves the US defense market as well as the transportation, power generation, chemicals, metals, and electronics industries. Reunion entered Chapter 11 protection from creditors in 2007 and later sought to emerge by selling off its pressure vessels business, CP Industries, to an affiliate of Everest Kanto Cylinder for $66 million. The court confirmed Reunion's plan for reorganization in 2010, closing its bankruptcy case.

	Annual Growth	12/02	12/03	12/04	12/05	12/06
Sales ($mil.)	(4.3%)	70.8	68.5	68.7	49.7	59.5
Net income ($ mil.)	–	(12.9)	2.6	(0.2)	(2.4)	5.4
Market value ($ mil.)	26.8%	2.6	9.9	6.3	5.9	6.8
Employees	(14.4%)	649	545	533	354	349

REV GROUP INC   NYS: REVG

245 South Executive Drive, Suite 100
Brookfield, WI 53005
Phone: 414 290-0190
Fax: –
Web: www.revgroup.com

CEO: –
CFO: –
HR: –
FYE: October 31
Type: Public

REV Group is one of the world's leading designers, manufacturers, and distributors of specialty vehicles and related aftermarket parts and services. The company makes a variety of firetrucks, buses, ambulances, terminal trucks, sweepers, fiberglass body parts, and other accessories. Its products are sold under well-established principal vehicle brands to municipalities, government agencies, private contractors, consumers, and industrial, and commercial end users. REV serves its customers through a manufacturing and service network consisting of about 20 manufacturing facilities and two aftermarket service locations. The company launched an IPO in 2017.

	Annual Growth	10/19	10/20	10/21	10/22	10/23
Sales ($mil.)	2.4%	2,403.7	2,277.6	2,380.8	2,331.6	2,638.0
Net income ($ mil.)	–	(12.3)	(30.5)	44.4	15.2	45.3
Market value ($ mil.)	3.4%	740.3	467.1	899.1	817.6	847.4
Employees	(4.4%)	8,040	7,060	6,800	6,873	6,724

REVA MEDICAL, INC.

5751 Copley Drive
San Diego, CA 92111
Phone: 858 966-3000
Fax: –
Web: www.revamedical.com

CEO: Jeffrey Anderson
CFO: Leigh F Elkolli
HR: –
FYE: December 31
Type: Public

REVA Medical is a medical device company focused on the development of bioreserbable polymers for vascular applications. In its 20-year history, REVA Medical has developed about 20 polymer families. The company's first commercial polymer is Tyrocore which is used to make Fantom Encore, a drug-eluting bioresorbable scaffold for the treatment of coronary disease and is currently available for sale in selected European countries.

	Annual Growth	12/13	12/14	12/15	12/16	12/17
Sales ($mil.)	–	–	–	–	–	0.0
Net income ($ mil.)	–	(27.9)	(51.0)	(82.6)	(54.1)	7.1
Market value ($ mil.)	–	–	–	–	–	–
Employees	(11.7%)	84	46	57	59	51

REVANCE THERAPEUTICS INC   NMS: RVNC

1222 Demonbreun Street, Suite 2000
Nashville, TN 37203
Phone: 615 724-7755
Fax: –
Web: www.revance.com

CEO: Mark J Foley
CFO: Tobin C Schilke
HR: Lindsey Ward
FYE: December 31
Type: Public

Revance is a biotechnology company focused on setting the new standard in healthcare with innovative aesthetic and therapeutic offerings that elevate patient and physician experiences. Revance's aesthetics portfolio of expertly created products and services includes DAXXIFY, the RHA Collection of dermal fillers, and OPUL, the first-of-its-kind relational commerce platform for aesthetic practices, deliver a differentiated and exclusive offering for Revance's elite practice partners and their consumers. It also partnered with Viatris to develop an onabotulinumtoxinA biosimilar, which will compete in the existing short-acting neuromodulator marketplace. Revance's therapeutics pipeline is currently focused on muscle movement disorders including evaluating DAXXIFY in two debilitating conditions, cervical dystonia and upper limb spasticity. Revance was formed in 1999.

	Annual Growth	12/19	12/20	12/21	12/22	12/23
Sales ($mil.)	387.9%	0.4	15.3	77.8	132.6	234.0
Net income ($ mil.)	–	(159.4)	(282.1)	(281.3)	(356.4)	(324.0)
Market value ($ mil.)	(14.2%)	1,427.6	2,492.9	1,435.6	1,623.8	773.2
Employees	32.6%	193	470	495	534	597

REVIEW PUBLISHING LIMITED PARTNERSHIP

1617 JOHN F KENNEDY BLVD STE 1005
PHILADELPHIA, PA 191031825
Phone: 215 563-7400
Fax: –
Web: www.philadelphiaweekly.com

CEO: –
CFO: –
HR: –
FYE: December 31
Type: Private

If you wish to examine the happenings in and around Philadelphia and New Jersey, Review Publishing may have the paper for you. A regional publisher of weekly papers, the company publishes the South Philly Review , a community paper covering news in southern Philadelphia; Philadelphia Weekly , a paper that reports on arts, entertainment, and other events in the city; and Atlantic City Weekly , which covers gambling, dining, entertainment, and nightlife in southern New Jersey. The company's publications reach more than 600,000 readers in Philadelphia County, as well as Cape May and Atlantic counties in New Jersey; it prints more than 200,000 copies each week. Review Publishing was founded in 1986.

REVLON INC   NYS: REV

55 Water Street
New York, NY 10041
Phone: 212 527-4000
Fax: –
Web: www.revloninc.com

CEO: Elizabeth A Smith
CFO: Matt Kvarda
HR: –
FYE: December 31
Type: Public

Revlon is a leading global beauty company with an iconic portfolio of brands. It develops, manufactures, markets, distributes and sells worldwide an extensive array of beauty and personal care products across a variety of distribution channels. Aside from its Almay and Revlon brands of makeup and beauty tools, the company makes Revlon ColorSilk hair color, Mitchum antiperspirants and deodorants, Charlie and Jean Nat fragrances, and Skin Illuminating and Gatineau skincare products. It also owns Elizabeth Arden, a maker of prestige fragrance brands. Revlon's beauty aids are distributed in more than 150 countries, with about half of its revenue generated in North America. Revlon products are primarily sold by mass merchandisers and drugstores such as CVS, Macy's, Target, Walgreens, and Wal-Mart. The company was founded in 1932.

	Annual Growth	12/18	12/19	12/20	12/21	12/22
Sales ($mil.)	(6.3%)	2,564.5	2,419.6	1,904.3	2,078.7	1,980.4
Net income ($ mil.)	–	(294.2)	(157.7)	(619.0)	(206.9)	(673.9)
Market value ($ mil.)	(63.9%)	1,421.4	1,208.6	670.3	639.9	24.3
Employees	(6.4%)	7,300	7,100	6,000	5,800	5,600

REVOLUTION LIGHTING TECHNOLOGIES INC

177 Broad Street, 12th Floor
Stamford, CT 06901
Phone: 203 504-1111
Fax: –
Web: www.rvlti.com

CEO: Robert V Lapenta V
CFO: Joan Nano
HR: –
FYE: December 31
Type: Public

Because you can't have a revolution without light. Revolution Lighting Technologies (formerly Nexxus Lighting) designs, produces, and sells light-emitting diode (LED) replacement light bulbs. Its products, which include multiple-color temperatures and optic/lens options, are marketed for their energy savings, improved lighting and reliability, as well as eco-friendly benefits. It also makes Hyperion R-Lite and Lumeon 360, LED-based signage systems for decorative lighting strips, through subsidiary Lumificient Corp. In late 2012 Nexxus Lighting changed its name to Revolution Lighting Technologies to reflect what it believes is the new change taking place -- LED technology -- in the lighting industry.

	Annual Growth	12/13	12/14	12/15	12/16	12/17
Sales ($mil.)	55.5%	26.1	76.8	129.7	172.1	152.3
Net income ($ mil.)	–	(16.8)	(5.2)	(2.4)	(0.5)	(53.9)
Market value ($ mil.)	(1.0%)	73.1	28.8	17.0	117.4	70.2
Employees	27.2%	103	209	238	300	270

REVVITY INC

940 Winter Street
Waltham, MA 02451
Phone: 781 663-6900
Fax: 781 663-6052
Web: www.perkinelmer.com

NYS: RVTY
CEO: Prahlad R Singh
CFO: Max Krakowiak
HR: –
FYE: December 31
Type: Public

Revvity is a leading provider of products, services, and solutions for the diagnostics, life sciences, and applied markets. It develops and sells equipment such as instruments, tests, and software used by scientists, researchers, and clinicians to address the most critical challenges across science and healthcare. It introduce over 1,500 new antibodies, kits, and reagents for life science research annually, and about 40 million babies screened annually for life-threatening diseases across 110 countries. The company, which distributes its offerings in more than 190 countries, generates most of its sales outside the US.

	Annual Growth	12/19*	01/21	01/22	01/23*	12/23
Sales ($mil.)	(1.2%)	2,883.7	3,782.7	5,067.2	3,311.8	2,750.6
Net income ($ mil.)	32.1%	227.6	727.9	943.2	569.2	693.1
Market value ($ mil.)	3.0%	11,978	17,712	24,816	17,307	13,492
Employees	(3.0%)	13,000	14,000	16,700	16,700	11,500

*Fiscal year change

REX AMERICAN RESOURCES CORP

7720 Paragon Road
Dayton, OH 45459
Phone: 937 276-3931
Fax: –
Web: www.rexamerican.com

NYS: REX
CEO: Zafar Rizvi
CFO: Douglas L Bruggeman
HR: –
FYE: January 31
Type: Public

REX American Resources has interests in six ethanol production facilities, which in aggregate shipped approximately 695 million gallons of ethanol. The company has stakes in three ethanol production entities ? One Earth Energy, LLC (One Earth), NuGen Energy, LLC (NuGen), and Big River Resources, LLC (Big River). Its ethanol operations are highly dependent on commodity prices, especially prices for corn, ethanol, distiller grains, non-food grade corn oil, and natural gas, and availability of corn.

	Annual Growth	01/19	01/20	01/21	01/22	01/23
Sales ($mil.)	15.1%	486.7	418.0	372.8	774.8	855.0
Net income ($ mil.)	(3.3%)	31.6	7.4	3.0	52.4	27.7
Market value ($ mil.)	(18.2%)	1,268.3	1,310.3	1,330.3	1,676.9	569.0
Employees	(1.0%)	127	128	119	124	122

REX CHEMICAL CORPORATION

7575 NW 74TH AVE
MEDLEY, FL 331662422
Phone: 305 634-2471
Fax: –
Web: www.rexchemical.com

CEO: –
CFO: –
HR: –
FYE: December 31
Type: Private

Rex Chemical makes liquid and powdered janitorial chemicals for the food service, housekeeping, laundry, and industrial markets. Among its products are carpet shampoo, degreasers, disinfectants, floor finish and polishes, soaps, stain and mildew removers, and toilet bowl cleaners. It also sells related cleaning equipment, such as aerosols, dishwashers, dispensers, and vacuums. Rex Chemical's main customers include hospitals and schools. Based in South Florida, the company is owned and operated by the Granja family, which founded Rex Chemical in 1965.

	Annual Growth	12/02	12/03	12/06	12/07	12/08
Sales ($mil.)	(2.4%)	–	6.1	5.8	6.2	5.4
Net income ($ mil.)	(13.5%)	–	0.4	0.7	0.6	0.2
Market value ($ mil.)	–	–	–	–	–	–
Employees	–	–	–	–	–	30

REX ENERGY CORP

366 Walker Drive
State College, PA 16801
Phone: 814 278-7267
Fax: –
Web: www.rexenergy.com

NBB: REXX Q
CEO: Thomas C Stabley
CFO: Curtis J Walker
HR: –
FYE: December 31
Type: Public

Though it isn't exactly the T. Rex of the oil and gas industry, Rex Energy is taking a bite out of available hydrocarbon assets. The exploration and production company has estimated proved reserves of In fiscal 2012, the company reported estimated proved reserves of 618.1 billion cu. ft. of natural gas equivalent (42% proved developed), primarily from two regions: the Illinois Basin (in Illinois and Indiana) and the Appalachian Basin (Pennsylvania and West Virginia). The company's Lawrence Field ASP (alkaline-surfactant-polymer) Flood Project uses ASP technology, which washes residual oil from reservoir rock, improving the existing waterflow's ability to sweep the residual oil and increasing oil recoveries.

	Annual Growth	12/13	12/14	12/15	12/16	12/17
Sales ($mil.)	(3.6%)	237.9	298.0	172.0	139.0	205.3
Net income ($ mil.)	–	–	(2.1)	(46.7)	(363.3)	(176.7)	(64.2)
Market value ($ mil.)	(48.6%)	201.9	52.2	10.8	4.8	14.1
Employees	(23.0%)	298	320	274	104	105

REX HEALTHCARE, INC.

4420 LAKE BOONE TRL
RALEIGH, NC 276077505
Phone: 919 784-3100
Fax: –
Web: www.rexhealth.com

CEO: –
CFO: –
HR: –
FYE: June 30
Type: Private

Part of the UNC Health Care, UNC REX Healthcare is a not-for-profit health care provider that serves residents of Raleigh and the rest of Wake County, North Carolina. Founded in 1894, UNC REX Healthcare includes a medical staff of more than 1,100 physicians and 1,700 nurses, as well as primary and specialty care clinics throughout the area. Its facilities include an acute care hospital, five wellness centers and two skilled nursing facilities that provide services such as cancer treatment, same-day surgery, heart and vascular care, pain management, and sleep disorder therapy. UNC HealthCare also includes affiliate UNC Hospitals.

	Annual Growth	06/11	06/12	06/13	06/20	06/22
Sales ($mil.)	7.0%	–	719.9	731.4	1,180.5	1,414.6
Net income ($ mil.)	3.9%	–	34.7	8.9	(2.9)	51.1
Market value ($ mil.)	–	–	–	–	–	–
Employees	–	–	–	–	–	5,500

REXFORD INDUSTRIAL REALTY INC

11620 Wilshire Boulevard, Suite 1000
Los Angeles, CA 90025
Phone: 310 966-1680
Fax: –
Web: www.rexfordindustrial.com

NYS: REXR
CEO: Howard Schwimmer
CFO: Laura Clark
HR: Stephanie Cabrera
FYE: December 31
Type: Public

Rexford Industrial Realty is a self-administered and self-managed full-service REIT focused on owning, operating, and acquiring industrial properties in Southern California infill markets. Rexford Industrial owns and manages a portfolio of around 355 industrial properties, which are all located in Southern California. Its portfolio comprises approximately 42.4 million sq. ft. of warehouse, distribution, and light manufacturing space. In 2022, it executed a total of about 440 new and renewal leases with a combined approximately 5.1 million rentable square feet. It is also acquire or provide mortgage debt secured by industrial property.

	Annual Growth	12/19	12/20	12/21	12/22	12/23
Sales ($mil.)	31.5%	267.2	330.1	452.2	631.2	797.8
Net income ($ mil.)	40.0%	62.0	76.4	128.2	167.6	238.0
Market value ($ mil.)	5.3%	9,697.9	10,428	17,223	11,603	11,913
Employees	18.4%	123	147	186	223	242

REYNOLDS AMERICAN INC.

401 N MAIN ST
WINSTON SALEM, NC 271013804
Phone: 336 741-2000
Fax: –
Web: www.reynoldsamerican.com

CEO: Ricardo Oberlander
CFO: Tony Hayward
HR: –
FYE: December 31
Type: Private

Reynolds American Inc. (RAI) is leading the transformation of the tobacco industry with operating companies that offer a wide range of products to address the evolving preferences of adult tobacco and nicotine consumers. It operates in a broad spectrum of scientific fields including molecular biology, toxicology, and chemistry as it assesses the reduced-risk potential of its products. Its consumer-centric brand portfolio contains product brands Vuse (vapor) and Velo (modern oral). Its non-combustible portfolio also contains Grizzly (traditional oral). Its main combustible brands are Newport, Natural American Spirit, Camel, Pall Mall, and Lucky Strike. RAI is a wholly owned subsidiary of the global BAT Group and the parent company of R.J. Reynolds Tobacco Company, Santa Fe Natural Tobacco Company, Inc., American Snuff Company, LLC, R.J. Reynolds Vapor Company, and Modoral Brands Inc.

RF BINDER PARTNERS INC.

950 3RD AVE FL 8
NEW YORK, NY 100222782
Phone: 212 994-7577
Fax: –
Web: www.rfbinder.com

CEO: Amy Binder
CFO: Jason Buerkle
HR: –
FYE: December 31
Type: Private

RF Binder Partners binds businesses to a better PR strategy. The public relations firm helps clients build corporate reputation; develop communications strategy; reach individuals with sway in capital markets, government, and public opinion; and manage crisis communications. RF Binder Partners serves clients in such industries as financial services, technology, and health care as well as charitable organizations and government agencies. Established in 2001, the company is part of the Ruder Finn Group global public relations and counseling agency. It has US offices in New York City, Boston, Chicago, Washington, D.C., and Los Angeles. It has an international office in Argentina.

RF INDUSTRIES LTD.

NMS: RFIL

16868 Via Del Campo Court, Suite 200
San Diego, CA 92127
Phone: 858 549-6340
Fax: –
Web: www.rfindustries.com

CEO: Robert Dawson
CFO: Peter Yin
HR: –
FYE: October 31
Type: Public

RF Industries (RFI) helps keep the world connected. The company's core business is conducted by its RF Connector division, which makes coaxial connectors used in radio-frequency (RF) communications and computer networking equipment. Its Neulink Division makes wireless digital transmission devices, such as modems and antennas used to link wide-area computer networks and global positioning systems. Through its Bioconnect division, RF Industries also makes cable assemblies, including electric cabling and interconnect products used in medical monitoring applications. Customers in the US account for more than 80% of sales. In 2019, RF Industries bought C Enterprises, a maker of connectivity tools sold to telecommunications and data communications distributors.

	Annual Growth	10/19	10/20	10/21	10/22	10/23
Sales ($mil.)	6.9%	55.3	43.0	57.4	85.3	72.2
Net income ($ mil.)	–	3.5	(0.1)	6.2	1.4	(3.1)
Market value ($ mil.)	(16.0%)	61.4	44.3	78.7	56.0	30.6
Employees	3.4%	281	271	300	344	321

RFD & ASSOCIATES, INC.

3267 BEE CAVES RD STE 107 PMB 61
AUSTIN, TX 78746
Phone: 512 347-9411
Fax: –
Web: www.rfdinc.com

CEO: –
CFO: –
HR: –
FYE: December 31
Type: Private

RFD & Associates hopes you come to associate its name with good service. The company provides a wide range of information technology services such as custom software engineering, systems integration, database conversion, training, testing, technology assessment, and legacy migration. RFD & Associates' clients come from a variety of industries including financial services, health care, retail, and manufacturing. Strategic partners include BEA Systems and Business Objects. RFD & Associates was established in 1986.

	Annual Growth	12/14	12/15	12/16	12/17	12/18
Sales ($mil.)	(6.1%)	–	57.2	34.6	41.3	47.3
Net income ($ mil.)	(63.1%)	–	1.7	(0.3)	0.1	0.0
Market value ($ mil.)	–	–	–	–	–	–
Employees	–	–	–	–	–	40

RGC RESOURCES, INC.

NMS: RGCO

519 Kimball Avenue, N.E.
Roanoke, VA 24016
Phone: 540 777-4427
Fax: 540 777-2636
Web: www.rgcresources.com

CEO: –
CFO: –
HR: –
FYE: September 30
Type: Public

RGC Resources is not only sticking to its knitting (the regulated distribution of natural gas) it is also staying close to home (Roanoke, Virginia). RGC's Roanoke Gas unit distributes natural gas to 56,000 customers in Roanoke. The holding company's Application Resources provides information system services for the utility industry. RGC Resources has taken the proceeds from the sale of its noncore operation to reinvest in its core gas distribution business. In 2008 it installed nine miles of plastic mains and replaced 684 steel main-to-meter service lines with modern plastic service lines (a 40% increase over 2007).

	Annual Growth	09/19	09/20	09/21	09/22	09/23
Sales ($mil.)	9.4%	68.0	63.1	75.2	84.2	97.4
Net income ($ mil.)	6.8%	8.7	10.6	10.1	(31.7)	11.3
Market value ($ mil.)	(12.3%)	292.8	234.9	225.3	210.9	173.3
Employees	(1.7%)	107	101	99	96	100

RH

NYS: RH

15 Koch Road
Corte Madera, CA 94925
Phone: 415 924-1005
Fax: –
Web: www.rh.com

CEO: Gary Friedman
CFO: Jack Preston
HR: –
FYE: January 28
Type: Public

RH is a leading retail and luxury lifestyle brand operating primarily in the home furnishings market. The company sells upscale home and outdoor furnishings, garden products, bathware, lighting, textiles, baby and child, and teen products, and more through around 80 retail and over 35 outlet stores under the Restoration Hardware, RH, and Waterworks names. Furniture accounts for about 70% of total revenue. In addition to stores, RH markets products through its catalogs (called Source Books), e-commerce sites and trade and contracts. The company operate its retail locations throughout the United States, Canada, and the U.K.

	Annual Growth	02/19	02/20*	01/21	01/22	01/23
Sales ($mil.)	9.4%	2,505.7	2,647.4	2,848.6	3,758.8	3,590.5
Net income ($ mil.)	36.9%	150.6	220.4	271.8	688.5	528.5
Market value ($ mil.)	23.5%	2,946.1	4,602.0	10,479	8,640.0	6,848.4
Employees	4.4%	5,200	5,100	5,000	6,500	6,180

*Fiscal year change

RHODE ISLAND HOUSING AND MORTGAGE FINANCE CORPORATION

44 WASHINGTON ST
PROVIDENCE, RI 029031731
Phone: 401 457-1234
Fax: –
Web: www.rihousing.com

CEO: –
CFO: Tom Hogg
HR: Barbara Farrand
FYE: June 30
Type: Private

The State of Rhode Island wants to help you become a homeowner. Rhode Island Housing assists low- to moderate-income Rhode Islanders buy homes by offering low interest mortgages. Income limits are $77,300 for one or two person households and $88,950 for households of three or more. The organization also offers home equity loans, construction loans to real estate developers, reverse mortgages for older homeowners, homebuyer education, and other programs. Rhode Island Housing receives no state funding; instead it sells taxable and tax-exempt bonds on the capital markets to fund its activities. Since its inception in the early 1970s, the organization has helped some 175,000 families fund affordable homes.

	Annual Growth	06/18	06/19	06/20	06/21	06/22
Sales ($mil.)	43.8%	–	126.1	152.7	148.4	374.6
Net income ($ mil.)	–	–	9.2	34.5	22.3	(56.9)
Market value ($ mil.)	–	–	–	–	–	–
Employees	–	–	–	–	–	170

RHODE ISLAND SCHOOL OF DESIGN INC

20 WASHINGTON PL
PROVIDENCE, RI 029031358
Phone: 401 454-6100
Fax: –
Web: www.risd.edu

CEO: –
CFO: –
HR: –
FYE: June 30
Type: Private

The Rhode Island School of Design (RISD, pronounced RIZ-dee) is among the highest-rated fine arts colleges in the US. The private school enrolls about 2,400 undergraduate and graduate students. It offers about 20 fine arts and design programs including art history, apparel design, architecture, jewelry, industrial design, film, printmaking, textiles, and painting. The college also offers continuing education through classes, lectures, workshops, gallery talks, and a six-week pre-college program designed for high schoolers. Notable alumni include David Byrne, Tina Weymouth, and Chris Frantz of the Talking Heads. RISD was founded in 1877.

	Annual Growth	06/14	06/15	06/19	06/20	06/22
Sales ($mil.)	1.7%	–	158.5	221.8	161.2	178.7
Net income ($ mil.)	–	–	2.7	38.2	(4.4)	(57.2)
Market value ($ mil.)	–	–	–	–	–	–
Employees	–	–	–	–	–	1,142

RHODES COLLEGE

2000 N PARKWAY
MEMPHIS, TN 381121624
Phone: 901 843-3000
Fax: –
Web: www.rhodes.edu

CEO: –
CFO: –
HR: Lori V Bokel
FYE: June 30
Type: Private

Rhodes College helps its students get further down the road to edification. A private liberal arts school in historic downtown Memphis, Rhodes College enrolls about 1,700 students in academic majors including biology, English, international studies, and business administration. Rhodes College's students come from about 45 states and 15 countries. It additionally offers a Master's degree in accounting. In total Rhodes College offers more than 30 majors and 35 minors. The school also provides continuing education courses to the community. Founded in 1848, the college is supported by an endowment of more than $230 million. The student-to-faculty ratio is about 10:1 and the average class size is just 13.

	Annual Growth	06/15	06/16	06/20	06/21	06/22
Sales ($mil.)	4.8%	–	82.5	126.6	221.6	109.4
Net income ($ mil.)	–	–	(19.6)	(18.9)	85.1	(47.0)
Market value ($ mil.)	–	–	–	–	–	–
Employees	–	–	–	–	–	1,828

RHYTHM PHARMACEUTICALS INC   NMS: RYTM

222 Berkeley Street, 12th Floor
Boston, MA 02116
Phone: 857 264-4280
Fax: –
Web: www.rhythmtx.com

CEO: David P Meeker
CFO: –
HR: –
FYE: December 31
Type: Public

Rhythm Pharmaceuticals is a biopharmaceutical is developing peptide therapeutics to treat rare genetic deficiencies that lead to metabolic disorders; its sole candidate is IMCIVREE (setmelanotide), which has been approved by the US Food and Drug Administration for chronic weight management in adult and pediatric patients six years of age and older with obesity due to proopiomelanocortin, or POMC, proprotein convertase subtilisin/kexin type 1, or PCSK1, leptin receptor, or LEPR, deficiency confirmed by genetic testing. Setmelanotide works by boosting the activity of a protein that helps regulate extreme appetite. The company serves biotechnology and pharmaceutical industries.

	Annual Growth	12/19	12/20	12/21	12/22	12/23
Sales ($mil.)	–	–	–	3.2	23.6	77.4
Net income ($ mil.)	–	(140.7)	(134.0)	(69.6)	(181.1)	(184.7)
Market value ($ mil.)	19.0%	1,364.4	1,766.8	593.1	1,730.5	2,731.8
Employees	–	70	90	140	177	–

RICEBRAN TECHNOLOGIES   NBB: RIBT

25420 Kuykendahl Rd., Suite B300
Tomball, TX 77375
Phone: 281 675-2421
Fax: –
Web: www.ricebrantech.com

CEO: Eric Tompkins
CFO: William J Keneally
HR: –
FYE: December 31
Type: Public

RiceBran Technologies (formerly NutraCea) hopes that one person's trash really can be another person's treasure. The company uses one of the world's largest wasted food resources, rice bran -- a rice by-product containing oil, protein, carbohydrates, vitamins, minerals, fibers, and antioxidants -- to make and enhance the nutritional value of consumer products such as dietary and food supplements and animal feed. Its products are used by food manufacturers, nutraceutical makers, and petfood and feed manufacturers. Following a strategic change in focus from a multidivisional company to one focused solely on rice bran bio-refining, the company in 2012 changed its name to RiceBran Technologies.

	Annual Growth	12/18	12/19	12/20	12/21	12/22
Sales ($mil.)	29.6%	14.8	23.7	26.2	31.1	41.6
Net income ($ mil.)	–	(8.1)	(14.0)	(11.7)	(8.9)	(7.9)
Market value ($ mil.)	(29.4%)	18.9	9.3	3.8	2.2	4.7
Employees	(2.0%)	102	121	99	101	94

RICELAND FOODS, INC.

2120 S PARK AVE
STUTTGART, AR 721606822
Phone: 870 673-5500
Fax: –
Web: www.riceland.com

CEO: Kevin McGilton
CFO: Sandra Morgan
HR: Cheryl Dunaway
FYE: July 31
Type: Private

Riceland is the world's largest miller and marketer of rice and one of the mid-South's major soybean processors. It handles more than 125 million bushels (approximately 2.5 million metric tons) of grain a year. Each grains are grown in the US and then shipped to its locations in Missouri and Arkansas to be stored and milled. The company sells white and brown rice, plus flavored rice and meal kits under the Riceland and private-label brands. It sells to food retailers, food service, and food manufacturing companies worldwide. Riceland also makes cooking oils and processes soybeans, bran, and lecithin, and offers rice bran and hulls to pet food makers and livestock farmers as feed and bedding.

	Annual Growth	07/15	07/16	07/17	07/21	07/22
Sales ($mil.)	(74.6%)	–	1,007.7	941.1	0.4	0.3
Net income ($ mil.)	(43.4%)	–	5.6	0.2	0.3	0.2
Market value ($ mil.)	–	–	–	–	–	–
Employees	–	–	–	–	–	1,646

RICH PRODUCTS CORPORATION

1 ROBERT RICH WAY
BUFFALO, NY 142131701
Phone: 716 878-8000
Fax: –
Web: www.richs.com

CEO: Richard Ferranti
CFO: David Faturos
HR: Steven Kalicharan
FYE: December 31
Type: Private

Rich Products is a family-owned food company which has grown from a niche maker of soy-based whipped toppings and frozen desserts to a leading global US frozen foods maker. The company has developed other products, such as toppings and icings, and Coffee Rich (non-dairy coffee creamer). It has expanded its product line to include frozen bakery and pizza doughs and ingredients for the food service and in-store bakery markets, plus appetizers, meals and snacks (Farm Rich), baked goods, ice cream cakes (Carvel), seafood (SeaPak), meatballs, and barbecue meat. With more than 4,000 product types, Rich Products has approximately 11,000 associates around the world.

	Annual Growth	12/08	12/09	12/10	12/11	12/12
Sales ($mil.)	7.7%	–	–	2,465.0	2,736.3	2,858.5
Net income ($ mil.)	–	–	–	–	–	–
Market value ($ mil.)	–	–	–	–	–	–
Employees	–	–	–	–	–	12,224

RICHARD J. CARON FOUNDATION

243 N GALEN HALL RD
WERNERSVILLE, PA 195659331
Phone: 610 678-2332
Fax: –
Web: www.caron.org

CEO: Douglas Tieman
CFO: –
HR: –
FYE: June 30
Type: Private

Caron cares -- about addiction to drinking and drugs. The Richard J. Caron Foundation is a not-for-profit organization that runs clinical treatment centers for substance abuse in Pennsylvania, New York, Florida, and Bermuda. It tailors its services gender specifically (under the idea that men and women respond to treatment differently) and serves adolescents, adults, seniors, and families. The foundation offers addiction assessment, as well as residential treatment, extended care, and outpatient counseling. To complement its medical and psychological programs, Caron offers self-development workshops and pastoral services for those wanting to participate in meditation, journal writing, and other exercises.

	Annual Growth	06/18	06/19	06/20	06/21	06/22
Sales ($mil.)	0.4%	–	94.6	91.6	101.6	95.7
Net income ($ mil.)	–	–	8.2	(0.4)	4.3	(2.3)
Market value ($ mil.)	–	–	–	–	–	–
Employees	–	–	–	–	–	500

RICHARDSON COMPANIES, INC.

290 CONSTITUTION BLVD STE C
LAWRENCEVILLE, GA 300465696
Phone: 770 931-4131
Fax: –
Web: –

CEO: –
CFO: –
HR: –
FYE: December 31
Type: Private

Richardson Housing Group is a residential builder and developer serving metropolitan Atlanta's Gwinnet County. The company builds about 200 homes per year, including upscale townhomes and single-family four- and five-bedroom homes. Prices range from about $140,000 to around $250,000. Its portfolio of communities includes Hollowtone, Wynterberry Parke and Castleberry Hills. President Allen Richardson founded the family-owned company in 1973.

	Annual Growth	11/96	11/97	11/98	11/99*	12/19
Sales ($mil.)	1.9%	–	18.9	11.4	16.2	28.8
Net income ($ mil.)	21.7%	–	0.0	–	0.3	4.3
Market value ($ mil.)	–	–	–	–	–	–
Employees	–	–	–	–	–	23

*Fiscal year change

RICHARDSON ELECTRONICS LTD

40W267 Keslinger Road, P.O. Box 393
LaFox, IL 60147-0393
Phone: 630 208-2200
Fax: 630 208-2550
Web: www.rell.com

NMS: RELL
CEO: –
CFO: –
HR: –
FYE: May 27
Type: Public

Richardson Electronics runs the kind of superstore that isn't open to the public. The company distributes electronics products, including electron devices, semiconductor manufacturing equipment, and video display equipment from suppliers that include GE, Thales, TE Connectivity, and Vishay. Richardson also sells its own products under such the National Electronics brand and provides components customized to its customers' specifications. The company primarily sells to the alternative energy, avionics, broadcast and communication, marine, medical, and semiconductor markets. Chairman and CEO Edward Richardson has about 64% voting control of the company.

	Annual Growth	06/19*	05/20	05/21	05/22	05/23
Sales ($mil.)	12.0%	166.7	155.9	176.9	224.6	262.7
Net income ($ mil.)	–	(7.3)	(1.8)	1.7	17.9	22.3
Market value ($ mil.)	36.0%	72.1	59.6	121.3	198.5	246.8
Employees	6.3%	380	394	405	447	485

*Fiscal year change

RICHELIEU FOODS, INC.

222 FORBES RD STE 401
BRAINTREE, MA 021842717
Phone: 781 786-6800
Fax: –
Web: www.richelieufoods.com

CEO: –
CFO: –
HR: Michael McDade
FYE: July 25
Type: Private

Richelieu Foods stocks pantries and freezer shelves with its private-label and contract-packaged foods. The company develops and markets store-branded products, including marinades, salad dressings, flavored dressings, tartar sauce and taco sauces, among others. Richelieu Foods is the nation's top supplier of premium private-label frozen pizza to leading national retailers. The company's Bonne Chere division comes out on top with an extensive line of tasty, on-trend products and proven, flexible solutions for every business, large or small. Catering to health-conscious customers, Richelieu's products can be prepared with organic ingredients. Richelieu Foods, which is a private brand and contract packing food company, is owned by Freiberger USA Inc.

RIECHESBAIRD, INC.

1 WRIGLEY
IRVINE, CA 926182711
Phone: 949 586-1200
Fax: –
Web: www.riechesbaird.com

CEO: Ryan Rieches
CFO: –
HR: –
FYE: June 30
Type: Private

RiechesBaird is an integrated B2B company that believes building brands requires the skill to plan and execute. As such, the company offers an array of services to help chart the course for a business and decide how branding best fits that course. The kicker, as RiechesBaird sees it, is that a business plan and a branding vision are little help without successful marketing and advertising. So RiechesBaird offers that, too. The agency, which was formed in 1994 by Ryan Rieches and Ray Baird, counts Toyota Material Handling, Entergy Corporation, and Cisco Systems among its customers.

RIGEL PHARMACEUTICALS INC   NMS: RIGL

611 Gateway Boulevard, Suite 900
South San Francisco, CA 94080
Phone: 650 624-1100
Fax: 650 624-1101
Web: www.rigel.com

CEO: –
CFO: –
HR: –
FYE: December 31
Type: Public

Rigel Pharmaceuticals is a biotechnology company dedicated to discovering, developing, and providing novel therapy that significantly improves the lives of patients with hematologic disorders and cancer. Its first product approved by the FDA is TAVALISSE (fostamatinib disodium hexahydrate) tablets, the only approved oral spleen tyrosine kinase (SYK) inhibitor, for the treatment of adult patients with chronic immune thrombocytopenia (ITP) who have had an insufficient response to a previous treatment. The product is also commercially available in Europe, the UK, Canada, and Israel for the treatment of chronic ITP in adult patients. It also has an extensive portfolio of investigational agents being developed with our other partners including Axl tyrosine kinase (AXL) and murine double minute 2 (MDM2).

	Annual Growth	12/19	12/20	12/21	12/22	12/23
Sales ($mil.)	18.5%	59.3	108.6	149.2	120.2	116.9
Net income ($ mil.)	–	(66.9)	(29.7)	(17.9)	(58.6)	(25.1)
Market value ($ mil.)	(9.3%)	374.1	611.9	463.3	262.2	253.5
Employees	(2.5%)	163	169	165	155	147

RILEY EXPLORATION PERMIAN INC   ASE: REPX

29 E. Reno Avenue, Suite 500
Oklahoma City, OK 73104
Phone: 405 415-8699
Fax: –
Web: www.tengasco.com

CEO: –
CFO: –
HR: –
FYE: December 31
Type: Public

Tengasco doesn't have the strength of 10 gas companies just yet, but it's getting there. The firm is engaged in exploring for, producing, and transporting oil and natural gas in Kansas (in properties near Hays) and Tennessee (primarily in the Swan Creek Field). Tengasco uses 3-D seismic technology to maximize recovery of its reserves. In 2008 the company reported proved reserves of 900 million cu. ft. of natural gas and 1.3 million barrels of oil. The firm is also involved in natural gas marketing, pipeline construction, and related energy services. Its Tengasco Pipeline unit manages its pipeline operations. Subsidiary Manufactured Methane Corporation operates a landfill gas project in Tennessee.

	Annual Growth	12/19	12/20*	09/21*	12/22	12/23
Sales ($mil.)	195.6%	4.9	3.0	151.0	321.7	375.0
Net income ($ mil.)	–	(0.4)	(3.6)	(65.7)	118.0	111.6
Market value ($ mil.)	173.0%	10.0	25.3	479.1	600.5	555.8
Employees	65.5%	12	12	54	65	90

*Fiscal year change

RINGCENTRAL INC   NYS: RNG

20 Davis Drive
Belmont, CA 94002
Phone: 650 472-4100
Fax: –
Web: www.ringcentral.com

CEO: Vladimir Shmunis
CFO: Mitesh Dhruv
HR: Ashley Madrigal
FYE: December 31
Type: Public

RingCentral is a leading provider of global enterprise cloud communications, video meetings, collaboration, and contact center software-as-a-service (SaaS) solutions. Its innovative, cloud-based communication and customer engagement platform solutions disrupt the large market for business communications and collaboration by providing flexible and cost-effective solutions that support mobile and distributed workforces. Businesses use RingCentral MVP to connect smartphones, tablets, PCs, and desk phones from various locations and allow communication and collaboration across multiple modes, including HD voice, video, SMS, messaging and collaboration, conferencing, online meetings, and fax. The company serves enterprise customers, and businesses from small to medium-sized across a wide range of industries, including financial services, education, healthcare, legal services, real estate, and state and local government, among others. The company generates the majority of its sales from North America.

	Annual Growth	12/19	12/20	12/21	12/22	12/23
Sales ($mil.)	25.0%	902.9	1,183.7	1,594.8	1,988.3	2,202.4
Net income ($ mil.)	–	(53.6)	(83.0)	(376.3)	(879.2)	(165.2)
Market value ($ mil.)	(33.0%)	15,765	35,421	17,511	3,308.7	3,173.2
Employees	14.7%	2,363	3,140	3,919	3,902	4,084

RIO HOLDINGS, INC.

600 CONGRESS AVE STE 200
AUSTIN, TX 787012995
Phone: 512 917-1742
Fax: –
Web: –

CEO: Michael Wilfley
CFO: –
HR: –
FYE: December 31
Type: Private

Grande Communications' big idea is to become a bigger player in Texas telecommunications. Through operating subsidiary Grande Communications Networks, the company provides bundled telephone services, Internet access, and cable television to about 140,000 residential and business customers over its own fiber-optic network. It also offers wholesale communications services to other telecoms and ISPs through its Grande Networks division. While its core Central Texas service area includes Austin, San Marcos, and San Antonio, it also provides service in Corpus Christi, Dallas, Midland, Odessa, and Waco. Grande Communications is controlled by Boston-based private equity firm ABRY Partners.

	Annual Growth	12/04	12/05	12/06	12/07	12/08
Sales ($mil.)	4.0%	–	–	189.9	197.1	205.3
Net income ($ mil.)	–	–	–	(141.6)	(50.5)	(50.4)
Market value ($ mil.)	–	–	–	–	–	–
Employees	–	–	–	–	–	10

RIOT PLATFORMS INC   NAS: RIOT

3855 Ambrosia Street, Suite 301
Castle Rock, CO 80109
Phone: 303 794-2000
Fax: –
Web: www.riotplatforms.com

CEO: Jason Les
CFO: Colin Yee
HR: –
FYE: December 31
Type: Public

Riot Blockchain (formerly Bioptix) has ditched the drug diagnostic machinery business for the digital currency trade. The company invests in cryptocurrency entities, such as Canadian exchange Coinsquare, blockchain accounting and audit technology firm Verady, and payment platform developer Tesspay. It has also launched its own bitcoin mining firm. In 2017, Bioptix changed its course of business (it was developing a platform for the detection of molecular interactions to help determine if a drug will be effective) to focus on the cryptocurrency industry; it sold its biotech-focused patents and intellectual property as part of the change.

	Annual Growth	12/19	12/20	12/21	12/22	12/23
Sales ($mil.)	153.1%	6.8	12.1	213.2	259.2	280.7
Net income ($ mil.)	–	(20.0)	(12.7)	(7.9)	(509.6)	(49.5)
Market value ($ mil.)	92.8%	258.5	3,921.9	5,154.6	782.5	3,571.0
Employees	207.1%	6	8	335	489	534

RIP GRIFFIN TRUCK SERVICE CENTER, INC.

4710 4TH ST
LUBBOCK, TX 794164900
Phone: 806 795-8785
Fax: –
Web: www.ripgriffin.com

CEO: –
CFO: –
HR: –
FYE: December 31
Type: Private

Rip Griffin Truck Service Center tries to make sure you never go hungry again (in Scarlett O'Hara's words), at least when you're driving on the highways of North Texas. Rip Griffin's network of about 10 travel centers offers truckers, tour buses, and other travelers a smorgasbord of features, such as convenience stores, fuel, game rooms, laundry facilities, restaurants, and showers. Locations also offer truck maintenance and repair services. In addition to its travel center business, Rip Griffin sells Freightliner trucks through two Texas dealerships and provides fuel transportation services. In 2004 CEO Rip Griffin sold the company to Ohio-based TravelCenters of America.

	Annual Growth	12/13	12/14	12/15	12/16	12/17
Sales ($mil.)	(8.9%)	–	213.7	145.8	104.3	161.7
Net income ($ mil.)	9.3%	–	3.5	1.5	0.0	4.6
Market value ($ mil.)	–	–	–	–	–	–
Employees	–	–	–	–	–	88

RIPON COLLEGE

300 W SEWARD ST
RIPON, WI 549711477
Phone: 920 748-8108
Fax: –
Web: www.ripon.edu

CEO: –
CFO: –
HR: –
FYE: June 30
Type: Private

Ripon College is a private institution that offers undergraduate degrees in the liberal arts and sciences. It has more than 30 different majors and nearly 45 minor fields of study. The college, which guarantees on-campus housing for students for four years, enrolls approximately 1,000 undergraduates annually and employs more than 75 faculty members. Ripon College was founded in 1851 as a college preparatory school and converted to a four-year college in 1863. It boasts famous alumni such as Al Jarreau, Harrison Ford, and Spencer Tracy.

	Annual Growth	06/18	06/19	06/20	06/21	06/22
Sales ($mil.)	9.1%	–	53.7	50.6	59.1	69.7
Net income ($ mil.)	202.3%	–	0.5	(0.4)	7.4	14.6
Market value ($ mil.)	–	–	–	–	–	–
Employees	–	–	–	–	–	205

RIPTIDE SOFTWARE, INC.

200 EAST PALM VALLEY DR STE 2000
OVIEDO, FL 327654514
Phone: 321 296-7724
Fax: –
Web: www.riptidesoftware.com

CEO: Philip Loeffel
CFO: –
HR: –
FYE: December 31
Type: Private

Riptide doesn't want you getting pulled into the perilous waters of technology without a lifevest. The company primarily offers software development services for commercial and public sector organizations. It customizes and implements enterprise applications primarily from industry leaders Microsoft and Sun Microsystems for such purposes as automating financial systems, managing electronic content, and managing corporate revenue systems. The company also provides such IT services as consulting, systems integration, and legacy migration. Riptide serves the aerospace, military, hospitality, and education markets among others. Clients have included Anteon, Disney, Lockheed Martin, and NASA.

	Annual Growth	12/03	12/04	12/05	12/12	12/16
Sales ($mil.)	15.0%	–	4.1	5.9	22.2	22.0
Net income ($ mil.)	13.6%	–	0.2	0.4	2.0	0.7
Market value ($ mil.)	–	–	–	–	–	–
Employees	–	–	–	–	–	115

RISK GEORGE INDUSTRIES INC

NBB: RSKI A

802 South Elm Street
Kimball, NE 69145
Phone: 308 235-4645
Fax: –
Web: www.grisk.com

CEO: –
CFO: –
HR: –
FYE: April 30
Type: Public

George Risk Industries (GRI) wants customers to be able to manage risks. The company makes burglar alarm components and systems, including panic buttons (for direct access to alarm monitoring centers). In addition to security products, GRI manufactures pool alarms, which are designed to sound alerts when a pool or spa area has been entered. The company also makes thermostats, specialty computer keyboards and keypads, custom-engraved key caps, and push-button switches. Chairman, President, and CEO Stephanie Risk-McElroy, granddaughter of founder George Risk, and daughter of former CEO Ken Risk, controls the company.

	Annual Growth	04/18	04/19	04/20	04/21	04/22
Sales ($mil.)	14.8%	11.9	14.1	14.8	18.5	20.7
Net income ($ mil.)	8.8%	2.5	3.3	2.1	10.8	3.6
Market value ($ mil.)	8.8%	42.2	40.7	41.4	61.7	59.2
Employees	3.4%	175	175	175	195	200

RITE AID CORP

NBB: RADC Q

P.O. Box 3165
Harrisburg, PA 17105
Phone: 717 761-2633
Fax: 717 975-5905
Web: www.riteaid.com

CEO: Elizabeth Burr
CFO: Matthew Schroeder
HR: –
FYE: March 4
Type: Public

Rite Aid is one of the leading providers of health care services and retail products to over one million Americans daily. It nevertheless boasts a formidable presence with approximately 2,300 drugstores in more than 15 states. Rite Aid stores generate approximately 70% of the company's sales from filling prescriptions, while the rest comes from selling health and beauty aids, convenience foods, greeting cards, and more, including Rite Aid brand private-label products. About 60% of all Rite Aid stores are freestanding, drive-through pharmacies provide some 55%, and more than 65% has GNC stores within them.

	Annual Growth	03/19*	02/20	02/21	02/22*	03/23
Sales ($mil.)	2.7%	21,640	21,928	24,043	24,568	24,092
Net income ($ mil.)	–	(422.2)	(452.2)	(90.9)	(538.5)	(749.9)
Market value ($ mil.)	–	–	–	–	–	–
Employees	(3.0%)	53,100	50,000	50,000	53,000	47,000

*Fiscal year change

RITHM CAPITAL CORP

NYS: RITM

799 Broadway
New York, NY 10003
Phone: 212 850-7770
Fax: –
Web: www.rithmcap.com

CEO: Michael Nierenberg
CFO: Nicola Santoro Jr
HR: –
FYE: December 31
Type: Public

Rithm Capital Corp. (formerly known as New Residential Investment Corp.) is an investment manager with a vertically integrated mortgage platform and invests in real estate and related opportunities. It is structured as a real estate investment trust (REIT) for the US federal income tax purposes. Its diversified portfolio includes mortgage servicing rights, mortgage origination and servicing companies (including ancillary mortgage services businesses), residential mortgage-backed securities, single-family rental properties, mortgage loans, consumer loans, and other opportunistic investments. It mortgages origination business operates through the lending divisions of its subsidiaries Newrez and Caliber. Other subsidiaries and affiliates include Shellpoint (mortgage services), Avenue 365 (title insurance), eStreet (appraisal management), Covius (diversified mortgage services), and Guardian Asset Management (field services and property management). Rithm Capital has about $32.5 billion in total assets.

	Annual Growth	12/19	12/20	12/21	12/22	12/23
Sales ($mil.)	(2.6%)	2,585.6	1,013.7	3,521.4	3,498.6	2,325.0
Net income ($ mil.)	2.5%	563.3	(1,410.4)	772.2	954.5	622.3
Market value ($ mil.)	(9.8%)	7,784.8	4,803.3	5,175.4	3,948.0	5,160.9
Employees	18.0%	3,387	5,471	12,296	5,763	6,570

RIVAL TECHNOLOGIES INC

NBB: RVTI

3773 Howard Hughes Pkwy Suite 500
Las Vegas, NV 89169
Phone: 702 751-8846
Fax: –
Web: www.rvti.com

CEO: –
CFO: –
HR: –
FYE: December 31
Type: Public

Rival Technologies is developing two technologies aimed at the oil and gas industry. Its TRU Oiltech subsidiary is developing a thermal reagent that is designed to improve the viscosity of crude oil to better facilitate its transport through pipelines. Its other subsidiary, CWI Technologies, is developing a process for reducing diesel engine emissions and improving fuel efficiency. That technology is slated to be installed on diesel locomotive engines in a deal with Canada-based Neptune Bulk Terminals. Rockridge Capital Corp. owns about 28% of Rival Technologies.

	Annual Growth	12/17	12/18	12/19	12/20	12/21
Sales ($mil.)	–	–	–	–	–	–
Net income ($ mil.)	–	(0.0)	(0.0)	(0.0)	(0.0)	(0.1)
Market value ($ mil.)	(20.5%)	2.4	0.4	0.3	5.0	1.0
Employees	–	–	–	–	–	–

RIVER DISTRICT COMMUNITY HOSPITAL AUTHORITY

4100 RIVER RD
EAST CHINA, MI 480542909
Phone: 810 329-7111
Fax: -
Web: www.stjohns.org

CEO: -
CFO: -
HR: -
FYE: June 30
Type: Private

St. John River District runs deep in the communities it serves. Part of St. John Health, the hospital serves Michigan's St. Clair and Macomb counties (the southern portion of the state's "thumb") with about 70 beds. The acute-care hospital operates five outpatient centers and offers a range of services including cardiology, orthopedics, and vascular diagnostics. St. John River District Hospital also runs a sleep study center and urinary incontinence center. In addition it has a bloodless treatment program for patients whose religious convictions preclude certain treatments. Since its inception in 1965, the hospital undergone seven major renovation programs, including the reconstruction of emergency department.

	Annual Growth	06/15	06/16	06/17	06/18	06/20
Sales ($mil.)	(85.4%)	-	35.1	36.4	0.0	0.0
Net income ($ mil.)	-	-	(4.6)	(3.4)	0.0	(0.0)
Market value ($ mil.)	-	-	-	-	-	-
Employees	-	-	-	-	-	386

RIVERSIDE COMMUNITY COLLEGE DISTRICT FOUNDATION

3801 MARKET ST
RIVERSIDE, CA 925013225
Phone: 951 328-3663
Fax: -
Web: www.rccd.edu

CEO: -
CFO: -
HR: Christi Case
FYE: June 30
Type: Private

Riverside Community College (RCC) offers more than 100 academic programs leading to associate degrees, career certificates, or transfer to a four-year institution. It has campuses in the California communities of Riverside (liberal arts, science, performing arts, nursing, and athletics), Moreno Valley (health, human, and public services), and Norco (technology). RCC also operates the Riverside County Culinary Academy and the Ben Clark Public Safety Training Center. It provides customized consulting and training services to local businesses, as well. RCC has an enrollment of more than 37,000 students and has been in operation since 1916.

	Annual Growth	06/16	06/17	06/18	06/19	06/20
Sales ($mil.)	(56.0%)	-	19.7	88.2	108.2	1.7
Net income ($ mil.)	(80.3%)	-	3.3	(10.8)	(6.9)	0.0
Market value ($ mil.)	-	-	-	-	-	-
Employees	-	-	-	-	-	2,651

RIVERSIDE HEALTHCARE ASSOCIATION, INC.

701 TOWN CENTER DR STE 1000
NEWPORT NEWS, VA 236064283
Phone: 757 534-7000
Fax: -
Web: www.riversideonline.com

CEO: Michael J Dacey
CFO: Walter W Austin Jr
HR: -
FYE: December 31
Type: Private

Extra! Extra! Read all about it! Residents of Newport News (and about a dozen other cities in Eastern Virginia) Turn to Riverside Health for Medical Care. The not-for-profit health care provider administers general, emergency, and specialty medical services from five hospitals, Riverside Regional Medical Center, Riverside Walter Reed Hospital, Riverside Tappahannock Hospital, and Riverside Shore Memorial Hospital, and Riverside Doctors Hospital, as well as a psychiatric hospital, a physical rehabilitation facility, and retirement communities. Riverside also operates physician offices and medical training facilities. Specialty centers provide home and hospice care, cancer treatment, and dialysis.

	Annual Growth	12/11	12/12	12/13	12/14	12/22
Sales ($mil.)	(27.2%)	-	948.0	1,017.5	1,059.2	39.6
Net income ($ mil.)	(23.3%)	-	41.7	102.0	(86.5)	3.0
Market value ($ mil.)	-	-	-	-	-	-
Employees	-	-	-	-	-	8,000

RIVERSIDE HOSPITAL, INC.

500 J CLYDE MORRIS BLVD
NEWPORT NEWS, VA 236011929
Phone: 757 594-2000
Fax: -
Web: www.riversideonline.com

CEO: William B Downey
CFO: -
HR: -
FYE: December 31
Type: Private

Riverside Hospital operates as Riverside Regional Medical Center, a 450-bed acute-care facility that serves the residents of Newport News, Virginia. Founded in 1916, the hospital moved to its current 72-acre campus in 1963, providing more than 30 medical specialties, including cancer treatment, cardiology, birthing, and diagnostic imaging. It specializes in cardiovascular and neurological surgeries and provides radiosurgery (radiation surgery) through a partnership with the University of Virginia Health System. Its emergency department is a 42-room Level II Trauma Center that treats more than 57,000 patients each year. Riverside Hospital is part of the Riverside Health System.

	Annual Growth	12/15	12/16	12/17	12/18	12/21
Sales ($mil.)	6.3%	-	636.7	611.3	618.5	862.6
Net income ($ mil.)	11.6%	-	65.3	57.2	61.7	113.3
Market value ($ mil.)	-	-	-	-	-	-
Employees	-	-	-	-	-	8,000

RIVERVIEW BANCORP, INC.

NMS: RVSB

900 Washington St., Ste. 900
Vancouver, WA 98660
Phone: 360 693-6650
Fax: -
Web: www.riverviewbank.com

CEO: -
CFO: -
HR: -
FYE: March 31
Type: Public

Riverview Bancorp is the holding company for Riverview Community Bank, which operates about 20 branches located primarily in the Columbia River Gorge area of Washington State and Oregon. Serving consumers and local businesses, the bank offers such standard retail banking services as checking and savings accounts, money market accounts, NOW accounts, and CDs. Commercial construction and commercial real estate loans account for nearly 90% of its lending portfolio, which also includes residential mortgages, residential construction loans, and other consumer loans. Trust and investment services are provided through the company's Riverview Asset Management Corp. Riverview Community Bank was founded in 1923.

	Annual Growth	03/19	03/20	03/21	03/22	03/23
Assets ($mil.)	8.3%	1,156.9	1,180.8	1,549.2	1,740.1	1,589.7
Net income ($ mil.)	1.1%	17.3	15.7	10.5	21.8	18.1
Market value ($ mil.)	(7.6%)	155.1	106.3	147.1	160.2	113.3
Employees	(2.2%)	250	252	232	224	229

RIVERVIEW HOSPITAL

395 WESTFIELD RD
NOBLESVILLE, IN 460601434
Phone: 317 773-0760
Fax: -
Web: www.riverview.org

CEO: Dave Hyatt
CFO: -
HR: Jeanne Henry
FYE: December 31
Type: Private

Riverview Hospital (which changed its operating name to Riverside Health in 2014) provides general medical and surgical care to residents in central Indiana. With about 155 beds and 300 physicians representing more than 35 medical specialties, the hospital is a full-service facility that offers specialty care in a number of areas, including heart disease, cancer, women's health, and orthopedics. Besides its main campus, Riverview operates several outpatient facilities, including an occupational health center, a community health clinic, and several rehab and fitness centers.

	Annual Growth	12/15	12/16	12/17	12/18	12/21
Sales ($mil.)	5.3%	-	171.6	179.7	574.6	222.3
Net income ($ mil.)	-	-	1.9	8.6	2.0	(14.0)
Market value ($ mil.)	-	-	-	-	-	-
Employees	-	-	-	-	-	949

RIVERVIEW REALTY PARTNERS LP

401 N MICHIGAN AVE STE 1200
CHICAGO, IL 606114204
Phone: 312 917-1300
Fax: –
Web: www.rrpchicago.com

CEO: Jeffrey A Patterson
CFO: –
HR: –
FYE: December 31
Type: Private

Prime Group holds a prime cut of the Windy City. A self-managed and self-administered real estate investment trust (REIT), the company invests in, develops, renovates, and manages office and industrial space, primarily in the Chicago area. Its portfolio currently includes stakes in four properties containing some 1.4 million sq. ft. of leasable space. Prime Group was acquired by The Lightstone Group for approximately $890 million in 2005. Six years later, Lightstone relinquished its stake in the REIT. Hedge fund Five Mile Capital Partners is acquiring Prime Group Realty Trust.

RLH WRAP-UP, INC.

3101 BEALE AVE
ALTOONA, PA 166011509
Phone: 814 944-6121
Fax: –
Web: –

CEO: T S Lawhead
CFO: Ron Muffie
HR: –
FYE: December 31
Type: Private

Going from a mill supply house to a 20-plus operation takes a bright idea, and The Hite Company has more than a few. It is a wholesale distributor of more than 35,000 lighting products and a slew of electrical supplies. The company's lineup includes data and communications equipment, industrial automation and motor control devices, as well as lamps, and professional video and audio equipment. Hite has represented Sylvania for more than 50 years; it also stocks Square D branded products (Schneider Electric) and others by major OEMs. Hite serves electrical contractors, builders, and residential customers in Pennsylvania, New York, and West Virginia. Founded in 1949, the company is family owned and operated.

	Annual Growth	12/07	12/08	12/09	12/10	12/11
Sales ($mil.)	–	–	–	96.0	96.0	96.0
Net income ($ mil.)	–	–	–	–	–	–
Market value ($ mil.)	–	–	–	–	–	–
Employees	–	–	–	–	–	230

RLI CORP

9025 North Lindbergh Drive
Peoria, IL 61615
Phone: 309 692-1000
Fax: 309 692-1068
Web: www.rlicorp.com

NYS: RLI

CEO: Craig W Kliethermes
CFO: Todd W Bryant
HR: –
FYE: December 31
Type: Public

RLI Corp. underwrites select property and casualty insurance through major subsidiaries collectively known as RLI Insurance Group. Through its subsidiaries, the company mainly offers coverage for US niche markets -- risks that are hard to place in the standard market and are otherwise underserved. It focuses on public and private companies. RLI's commercial property/casualty lines include products liability, property damage, marine cargo, directors and officers liability, medical malpractice, and general liability. It also writes commercial surety bonds and a smattering of specialty personal insurance.

	Annual Growth	12/19	12/20	12/21	12/22	12/23
Assets ($mil.)	9.9%	3,545.7	3,938.5	4,508.3	4,767.1	5,180.2
Net income ($ mil.)	12.3%	191.6	157.1	279.4	583.4	304.6
Market value ($ mil.)	10.3%	4,108.5	4,753.4	5,116.2	5,991.2	6,075.6
Employees	5.0%	905	875	913	1,001	1,099

RM2 INTERNATIONAL INC

810 Flightline Blvd.
Deland, FL 32724
Phone: 386 736-4890
Fax: –
Web: www.rm2.com

NBB: RMTO

CEO: Drew Kelley
CFO: Brian Knaley
HR: Marissa Marten
FYE: June 30
Type: Public

ARC Group puts a modern twist on making old-fashioned parts. The company makes industrial parts for aerospace, automotive, and medical uses with a 3D manufacturing process. The 3D process reduces times to prototype and make a part and helps the customer get its product to market faster. ARC offers more traditional manufacturing processes such as metal injection molding, plastic injection molding, and metal stamping. Those processes are ARC's biggest moneymaker, accounting for more than four-fifths of revenue. The US is, by far, the company's biggest market. It has added to its portfolio of manufacturing processes through a series of acquisitions.

	Annual Growth	06/18	06/19	06/20	06/21	06/22
Sales ($mil.)	(38.3%)	82.4	60.1	48.5	62.2	12.0
Net income ($ mil.)	–	(13.2)	(24.0)	(5.3)	4.6	(16.4)
Market value ($ mil.)	(18.9%)	279.4	51.3	34.1	159.7	120.9
Employees	(54.9%)	530	–	–	–	22

ROADRUNNER TRANSPORTATION SYSTEMS INC

1431 Opus Place, Suite 530
Downers Grove, IL 60515
Phone: 414 615-1500
Fax: –
Web: –

NBB: RRTS

CEO: Curtis W Stoelting
CFO: Patrick J Unzicker
HR: –
FYE: December 31
Type: Public

Roadrunner Transportation Systems (RRTS), doing business as Roadrunner Freight, provides high-quality, scalable LTL services to shippers in major metros across the US. Its LTL services are powered by almost 970 dependable independent contractors who are eager to deliver freight to where it needs to be. Through around 35 brick and mortar service centers, strategic rail partnerships and over 100 pickup and delivery partners, its network enables to ship to all major cities in the US.

	Annual Growth	12/18	12/19	12/20	12/21	12/22
Sales ($mil.)	(34.9%)	2,216.1	1,847.9	443.0	418.7	397.7
Net income ($ mil.)	–	(165.6)	(340.9)	(14.5)	(56.1)	(47.7)
Market value ($ mil.)	31.0%	19.0	352.8	79.3	82.4	55.9
Employees	–	4,600	3,600	–	–	–

ROBERT BOSCH LLC

38000 HILLS TECH DR
FARMINGTON HILLS, MI 483313418
Phone: 248 876-1000
Fax: –
Web: www.bosch.us

CEO: –
CFO: –
HR: Andrea M Cartney
FYE: December 31
Type: Private

Robert Bosch LLC operates across three business sectors Mobility Solutions, At Home, and Industry and Trades. It offers customers a multitude of value-add, cross-sector solutions across a diversity of industry applications. The company provides outstanding products, and it utilizes expertise in sensor technology, systems integration, software and services, as well as its own IoT cloud, to offer each customer connected, cross-domain solutions from a single source. Having established a regional presence in 1906 in North America, the Bosch Group employs about 37,000 associates in more than 100 locations.

	Annual Growth	12/07	12/08	12/09	12/10	12/14
Sales ($mil.)	13.9%	–	–	5,464.0	6,810.0	10,474
Net income ($ mil.)	25.1%	–	–	59.0	326.0	181.0
Market value ($ mil.)	–	–	–	–	–	–
Employees	–	–	–	–	–	1,469

ROBERT HALF INC
NYS: RHI

2884 Sand Hill Road, Suite 200
Menlo Park, CA 94025
Phone: 650 234-6000
Fax: –
Web: www.roberthalf.com

CEO: M K Waddell
CFO: Michael C Buckley
HR: –
FYE: December 31
Type: Public

Robert Half International provides specialized talent solutions and business consulting services through the Robert Half and Protiviti company names. It was originally founded in 1948. Prior to 1986, it was primarily a franchisor, under the names Accountemps and Robert Half, with offices providing contract and permanent professionals in the fields of accounting and finance. Beginning in 1986, it embarked on a strategy of acquiring the franchised locations. also broadened the scope of its services by expanding product offerings to include administrative and customer support, technology, financial project, and consulting and legal talent solutions. The US accounts for about 80% of sales.

	Annual Growth	12/19	12/20	12/21	12/22	12/23
Sales ($mil.)	1.3%	6,074.4	5,109.0	6,461.4	7,238.1	6,392.5
Net income ($ mil.)	(2.5%)	454.4	306.3	598.6	657.9	411.1
Market value ($ mil.)	8.6%	6,643.9	6,573.4	11,733	7,767.6	9,250.0
Employees	(1.6%)	16,000	163,500	191,600	180,500	15,000

ROBERT MORRIS UNIVERSITY

6001 UNIVERSITY BLVD
CORAOPOLIS, PA 151081189
Phone: 412 397-3000
Fax: –
Web: www.rmu.edu

CEO: –
CFO: –
HR: Ellen Wieckowski
FYE: May 31
Type: Private

Robert Morris University is a private, four-year institution located in suburban Pittsburgh. It offers more than 30 undergraduate degree programs and nearly 20 master's and doctoral degree programs, as well as adult and continuing education programs. The school has an enrollment of more than 5,000 students. Named for a Pennsylvanian patriot who helped finance the Revolutionary War and signed the Declaration of Independence, Robert Morris University was founded in 1921. Formerly Robert Morris College, the institution gained university status in 2002.

	Annual Growth	05/18	05/19	05/20	05/21	05/22
Sales ($mil.)	(4.0%)	–	138.4	131.8	119.5	122.6
Net income ($ mil.)	–	–	6.2	7.7	9.4	(4.5)
Market value ($ mil.)	–	–	–	–	–	–
Employees	–	–	–	–	–	500

ROBERT W BAIRD & CO INC

777 E WISCONSIN AVE
MILWAUKEE, WI 532025391
Phone: 414 765-3500
Fax: –
Web: www.rwbaird.com

CEO: Steve Booth
CFO: Terrance Maxwell
HR: Leslie Dixon
FYE: December 31
Type: Private

Employee-owned Robert W. Baird & Co. brings mid-western sensibility to the high-flying world of investment banking. The company offers brokerage, asset management, and investment banking services to middle-market corporations, institutional clients, municipal, and wealthy individuals and families around the world. Its investment banking activities include underwriting and distributing corporate securities, mergers and acquisitions, capital advisory, restructuring advisory, equity capital markets, and institutional sales and trading. The company advises clients on a range of other unique situations, such as fairness opinions, restructurings, takeover defenses and other special situations. Baird is an international financial services firm with more than $375 billion in client assets. The company was founded in 1919.

	Annual Growth	12/05	12/06	12/07	12/08	12/09
Assets ($mil.)	9.8%	–	–	1,712.8	1,080.5	2,063.9
Net income ($ mil.)	(8.6%)	–	–	50.2	36.6	41.9
Market value ($ mil.)	–	–	–	–	–	–
Employees	–	–	–	–	–	2,000

ROBERT W WOODRUFF HEALTH SCIENCES CENTER

1440 CLIFTON ROAD
ATLANTA, GA 303221053
Phone: 404 522-6755
Fax: –
Web: www.woodruff.org

CEO: –
CFO: –
HR: –
FYE: December 31
Type: Private

Charity has historically begun at home for the Robert W. Woodruff Foundation. The foundation, established by former Coca-Cola chairman Robert Woodruff, has provided a lot more than just soda-induced smiles to citizens of the Peach Tree State for more than 60 years. One of the largest foundations in the US (among the W.K. Kellogg Foundation and the Hershey Trust Co.), the Robert W. Woodruff Foundation focuses on awarding grants in conservation, culture, economic development, education, health care, and human services. The foundation gives preference to charities located or operating in Coca-Cola's home state of Georgia. It's helping to fund the expansion of the Georgia Museum of Art in 2009.

	Annual Growth	08/14	08/15	08/16	08/20*	12/22
Sales ($mil.)	17.2%	–	34.0	28.0	98.5	103.0
Net income ($ mil.)	–	–	4.6	(2.0)	(22.1)	(74.0)
Market value ($ mil.)	–	–	–	–	–	–
Employees	–	–	–	–	–	3

*Fiscal year change

ROBERT WOOD JOHNSON UNIVERSITY HOSPITAL AT RAHWAY

865 STONE ST
RAHWAY, NJ 070652742
Phone: 732 381-4200
Fax: –
Web: www.rwjbh.org

CEO: –
CFO: –
HR: –
FYE: December 31
Type: Private

Robert Wood Johnson University Hospital at Rahway (RWJUHR) has the people of Rahway cheering for it. Providing health care services for Rahway and 15 other communities of eastern New Jersey, the hospital has 265 beds. Founded in 1917, RWJUHR offers patients ambulatory, cardiac, geriatric, psychiatric, pulmonary, rehabilitation, and surgical services. The hospital has specialty divisions for wound healing, balance, sleep, and pain care, and it has hospice and long-term stay units. Part of the Robert Wood Johnson Health System and Network since 2003, RWJUH is also affiliated with The University of Medicine and Dentistry of New Jersey's Robert Wood Johnson Medical School.

	Annual Growth	12/16	12/17	12/18	12/19	12/21
Sales ($mil.)	0.8%	–	115.3	115.3	115.5	119.0
Net income ($ mil.)	–	–	23.8	23.8	(5.2)	(0.4)
Market value ($ mil.)	–	–	–	–	–	–
Employees	–	–	–	–	–	700

ROBERT WOOD JOHNSON UNIVERSITY HOSPITAL, INC.

1 ROBERT WOOD JOHNSON PL
NEW BRUNSWICK, NJ 089011928
Phone: 732 828-3000
Fax: –
Web: www.rwjbh.org

CEO: Bill Arnold
CFO: –
HR: Anastasia Jacobs
FYE: December 31
Type: Private

Founded in 1984, Robert Wood Johnson University Hospital (RWJUH) is the flagship facility of the RWJBarnabas Health System and Network. The medical center offers patients acute and tertiary care, including cardiovascular services, organ and tissue transplantation, pediatric care (at The Bristol-Myers Squibb Children's Hospital), Level I trauma care, cancer treatment (at the Cancer Hospital of New Jersey), stroke care, and women's health. RWJUH's other specialties include gastroenterology, orthopedics, pediatrics, plastic and reconstructive surgery, and mental health and behavioral health, among others. As the flagship cancer hospital of Rutgers Cancer Institute of New Jersey and the principal teaching hospital of Rutgers Robert Wood Johnson Medical School in New Brunswick, RWJUH New Brunswick is an innovative leader in advancing state-of-the-art care.

	Annual Growth	12/17	12/18	12/19	12/20	12/21
Sales ($mil.)	(0.7%)	–	1,337.1	1,451.1	1,084.2	1,308.7
Net income ($ mil.)	–	–	(3.0)	(89.8)	22.0	25.8
Market value ($ mil.)	–	–	–	–	–	–
Employees	–	–	–	–	–	4,674

ROBERTS DAIRY COMPANY, LLC

2901 CUMING ST
OMAHA, NE 681312108
Phone: 402 344-4321
Fax: –
Web: www.hilanddairy.com

CEO: –
CFO: –
HR: –
FYE: September 30
Type: Private

Holy cow! Roberts Dairy Foods is a leading producer of fluid, cultured, and frozen dairy products. It offers milk, yogurt, sour cream, cottage cheese, and other dairy products. A division of Hiland Dairy, the firm operates production plants in Omaha and Kansas City and 10 distribution centers located in the Midwest. The company markets its products under the Roberts and Hiland-Dairy brands; it also provides private-label services and school milk. Through a joint venture named Hiland-Roberts, the company makes ice cream products from a facility in Norfolk, Nebraska. Founded as a milk route by J.R. Roberts in 1906, Roberts Dairy Foods serves retail food and food service customers throughout the Midwest.

	Annual Growth	09/04	09/05	09/06	09/07	09/08
Sales ($mil.)	17.7%	–	–	259.5	319.7	359.7
Net income ($ mil.)	(27.8%)	–	–	1.6	2.2	0.9
Market value ($ mil.)	–	–	–	–	–	–
Employees	–	–	–	–	–	320

ROBERTS WESLEYAN COLLEGE

2301 WESTSIDE DR OFC
ROCHESTER, NY 146241997
Phone: 585 594-6000
Fax: –
Web: www.roberts.edu

CEO: –
CFO: –
HR: –
FYE: June 30
Type: Private

At Roberts Wesleyan College getting a degree can be a spiritual experience. The Christian liberal arts college offers more than 50 undergraduate programs, as well as graduate programs in counseling in ministry, education, management, nursing, school counseling, school psychology, and social work. It also offers undergraduate degree-completion programs in nursing and organizational management for working adults. Its Northeastern Seminary offers master's degrees in divinity and theological studies and a doctor of ministry degree. Wesleyan has an enrollment of more than 1,800 students.

	Annual Growth	06/15	06/16	06/19	06/20	06/22
Sales ($mil.)	1.8%	–	54.8	53.6	62.5	61.0
Net income ($ mil.)	–	–	–	(2.6)	5.1	1.9
Market value ($ mil.)	–	–	–	–	–	–
Employees	–	–	–	–	–	500

ROBERTSON GLOBAL HEALTH SOLUTIONS CORP.

3555 Pierce Rd.
Saginaw, MI 48604
Phone: 989 799-8720
Fax: –
Web: www.robertsonhealth.com

CEO: –
CFO: –
HR: –
FYE: September 30
Type: Public

Despite the corporate name, ASI Technology specializes in loaning money for real estate development and for general corporate purposes. The widespread credit crisis has the company lending to less-than-creditworthy borrowers. In 2007 ASI started branching out into specialty finance, making loans to affiliates of Concordia Homes of Nevada, a residential builder in the Las Vegas area, and obtaining a mortgage banking license from the State of Nevada for its ASI Capital subsidiary. ASI Technology also is developing products based on plasma technologies, such as room-temperature ("cold") plasma decontamination and sterilization instruments.

	Annual Growth	09/08	09/09	09/10	09/11	09/12
Sales ($mil.)	–	–	0.8	0.5	–	0.2	–
Net income ($ mil.)	–	–	(2.7)	(0.2)	(3.7)	(2.8)	(1.2)
Market value ($ mil.)	(9.2%)	9.8	3.3	44.3	28.7	6.7
Employees	18.9%	3	3	16	15	6

ROBINS KAPLAN LLP

800 LASALLE AVE STE 2800
MINNEAPOLIS, MN 554022039
Phone: 612 349-8500
Fax: –
Web: www.robinskaplan.com

CEO: –
CFO: –
HR: Cheryl Nelson
FYE: August 31
Type: Private

Robins, Kaplan, Miller & Ciresi earned its litigation stripes in some of the most well-known cases of our age. It won a $6.6-billion settlement against big tobacco for the state of Minnesota, won $38 million for 199 women in Dalkon Shield cases, and represented the government of India in its suit against Union Carbide after the Bhopal chemical disaster. The firm's more than 230 lawyers work out of company offices in half a dozen cities nationwide. Lawyers practice in areas ranging from personal injury and mergers and acquisitions to business litigation and white-collar crime. The late Solly Robins and Julius Davis founded the firm in 1938.

	Annual Growth	08/03	08/04	08/05*	03/09*	08/21
Sales ($mil.)	1.9%	–	–	1.2	–	1.6
Net income ($ mil.)	–	–	–	(0.6)	–	0.7
Market value ($ mil.)	–	–	–	–	–	–
Employees	–	–	–	–	–	600

*Fiscal year change

ROBINSON (C.H.) WORLDWIDE, INC.

NMS: CHRW

14701 Charlson Road
Eden Prairie, MN 55347
Phone: 952 937-8500
Fax: 952 937-6714
Web: www.chrobinson.com

CEO: David P Bozeman
CFO: Michael P Zechmeister
HR: Mariah Hale
FYE: December 31
Type: Public

C.H. Robinson Worldwide is one of the largest global logistics companies in the world. Operating throughout North America, Europe, Asia, Oceania, and South America, the company offers a global suite of services using tailored, market-leading differentiated technology built by and for its global network of supply chain experts working with its customers to drive better outcomes by leveraging its experience, data, technology, and scale. The company handled around 20 million shipments with approximately 100,000 customers and 96,000 contacted transportation companies. It generates the majority of its revenue in the US.

	Annual Growth	12/19	12/20	12/21	12/22	12/23
Sales ($mil.)	3.5%	15,310	16,207	23,102	24,697	17,596
Net income ($ mil.)	(13.4%)	577.0	506.4	844.2	940.5	325.1
Market value ($ mil.)	2.5%	9,131.3	10,961	12,568	10,691	10,088
Employees	(0.3%)	15,427	14,888	16,877	17,399	15,246

ROBINSON HEALTH SYSTEM, INC.

6847 N CHESTNUT ST
RAVENNA, OH 442663929
Phone: 330 297-0811
Fax: –
Web: www.uhhospitals.org

CEO: –
CFO: –
HR: Vanessa Sowell
FYE: December 31
Type: Private

Robinson Health System operates the Portage Medical Center, a 300-bed medical facility serving communities in northeast Ohio. In addition to a Level III trauma center, the hospital offers programs in pediatrics, women's health, home health care, and oncology. It also operates outpatient facilities including urgent care clinics, a freestanding surgery center, an occupational health center, and several physician practices. Robinson Memorial Hospital has nearly 400 physicians representing more than 40 medical specialties. Robinson Health is part of the University Hospitals Health System.

	Annual Growth	12/06	12/07	12/08	12/09	12/14
Sales ($mil.)	1.8%	–	141.4	146.8	6.9	160.6
Net income ($ mil.)	11.8%	–	10.1	10.1	(0.1)	22.0
Market value ($ mil.)	–	–	–	–	–	–
Employees	–	–	–	–	–	26,000

ROBINSON OIL CORPORATION

955 MARTIN AVE
SANTA CLARA, CA 950502608
Phone: 408 327-4300
Fax: –
Web: www.rottenrobbie.com

CEO: –
CFO: Stephen F White
HR: –
FYE: December 31
Type: Private

Like Hamlet's Denmark, something's rotten in the state of Robinson Oil. The company owns and operates Rotten Robbie, a regional brand of independent gas stations that caters to consumer and commercial motorists. The chain consists of some 35 stops in Northern California, mainly around the San Francisco Bay Area. Some stops are kiosks; about half are larger with Mrs. Robbie's Markets, a food store, and several offer commercial fleet fueling services affiliated with Pacific Pride and other cardlock networks. Diesel is available at all locations and, at certain stores, kerosene, propane, and biodiesel. Founded in the 1930s as a private-label fuel retailer, Robinson Oil is a fourth-generation family-owned business.

	Annual Growth	12/07	12/08	12/09	12/12	12/16
Sales ($mil.)	(20.1%)	–	2,048.5	292.4	464.2	339.7
Net income ($ mil.)	352.3%	–	0.0	8.2	10.7	20.9
Market value ($ mil.)	–	–	–	–	–	–
Employees	–	–	–	–	–	250

ROCHESTER GAS & ELECTRIC CORP

89 East Avenue
Rochester, NY 14649
Phone: 585 546-2700
Fax: –
Web: www.rge.com

CEO: –
CFO: –
HR: Dena Paratore
FYE: December 31
Type: Public

Upstate New York residents count on Rochester Gas and Electric (RG&E) to keep the lights turned on. The regulated utility provides electricity to about 370,000 customers and natural gas to 306,000 customers. RG&E operates 22,500 miles of power transmission and distribution lines and has a generating capacity of approximately 400 MW from interests in fossil-fueled and hydroelectric power plants. RG&E and sister utility company New York State Electric & Gas (NYSEG) are subsidiaries of regional power and gas distribution player Avangrid.

	Annual Growth	12/07	12/08	12/09	12/10	12/11
Sales ($mil.)	(5.1%)	1,171.8	1,119.1	1,009.9	982.5	950.4
Net income ($ mil.)	(4.8%)	74.3	4.0	24.6	54.3	61.0
Market value ($ mil.)	–	–	–	–	–	–
Employees	–	–	–	–	–	–

ROCHESTER INSTITUTE OF TECHNOLOGY (INC)

1 LOMB MEMORIAL DR
ROCHESTER, NY 146235698
Phone: 585 475-2411
Fax: –
Web: www.rit.edu

CEO: –
CFO: –
HR: –
FYE: June 30
Type: Private

The Rochester Institute of Technology (RIT) is one of the world's leading technological institutions. RIT is a privately endowed university with eleven colleges focused on providing career-oriented education to some 19,770 students. The university offers approximately 80 bachelor's degree programs in art and design, business, engineering, science, and hospitality. RIT also confers about 70 masters and a dozen of doctorate degrees. The university's National Technical Institute for the Deaf is the first and largest technological college for learners who suffer from hearing loss. RIT traces its roots back to 1829.

	Annual Growth	06/05	06/06	06/12	06/17	06/18
Sales ($mil.)	3.8%	–	370.7	490.3	560.2	579.3
Net income ($ mil.)	13.4%	–	45.1	16.8	74.2	203.8
Market value ($ mil.)	–	–	–	–	–	–
Employees	–	–	–	–	–	3,300

ROCK CREEK PHARMACEUTICALS INC

2040 Whitfield Ave., Suite 300
Sarasota, FL 34243
Phone: 844 727-0727
Fax: –
Web: www.rockcreekpharmaceuticals.com

CEO: –
CFO: –
HR: –
FYE: December 31
Type: Public

Rock Creek Pharmaceuticals (formerly Star Scientific) has a new name and business strategy focused on the development of drugs to treat chronic inflammatory conditions and neurological disorders. The company has adopted the name of its Rock Creek Pharmaceuticals subsidiary (founded in 2007), which makes nutraceuticals using alkaloids found in tobacco and other plants. Its core products are Anatabloc, to reduce inflammation, and CigRx, a tobacco alternative. (Both products are the subject of warning letters from the US Food and Drug Administration.) Formerly a seller of discount cigarettes, the emerging drug development company has since exited the cigarette and dissolvable tobacco businesses.

	Annual Growth	12/11	12/12	12/13	12/14	12/15
Sales ($mil.)	–	1.7	6.2	9.1	–	–
Net income ($ mil.)	–	(38.0)	(22.9)	(32.8)	(38.5)	(6.8)
Market value ($ mil.)	(23.9%)	25.2	31.0	13.4	2.1	8.4
Employees	(37.4%)	39	23	25	11	6

ROCK ENERGY RESOURCES INC

10350 Richmond Avenue, Suite 800
Houston, TX 77042
Phone: 832 301-5968
Fax: –
Web: www.rockenergyresources.com

CEO: –
CFO: –
HR: –
FYE: December 31
Type: Public

Rock Energy Resources is pushing to release oil and gas energy from the rocks in which they are trapped. The former Hanover Gold Company is in the business of natural gas and crude oil production in Texas and California. In 2008, not long after changing its name and its business focus, Rock Energy Resources doubled its ownership interest in the Orcutt project in California. It plans to continue drilling more wells and increase its overall reserve base. In 2010, after a hiatus during which the company sought to obtain more capital, it recommenced work on its Garwood Wilcox properties in Colorado County, Texas.

	Annual Growth	12/07	12/08	12/09	12/10	12/11
Sales ($mil.)	–	–	0.6	–	–	–
Net income ($ mil.)	–	(0.2)	(5.7)	(15.7)	10.5	(1.9)
Market value ($ mil.)	(24.0%)	54.2	144.6	30.7	1.7	18.1
Employees	(20.5%)	5	7	–	–	2

ROCKET SOFTWARE, INC.

77 4TH AVE STE 101
WALTHAM, MA 024577565
Phone: 781 577-4323
Fax: –
Web: www.rocketsoftware.com

CEO: Andy Youniss
CFO: Bruce Bowden
HR: Tracey Leahy
FYE: December 31
Type: Private

Rocket Software develops enterprise infrastructure software for companies looking for a boost in the power of their back office systems. Its products address such needs as data, network, application, and storage management, as well as business intelligence and security; brand names include Mainstar, Seagull Software, Servergraph, and BlueZone. The company partners with information technology product vendors, including IBM, HP, and Microsoft. Rocket was established in 1990 by Andy Youniss and Johan Magnusson Gedda.

	Annual Growth	12/18	12/19	12/20	12/21	12/22
Sales ($mil.)	(57.7%)	–	–	–	1.5	0.7
Net income ($ mil.)	–	–	–	–	0.9	(0.1)
Market value ($ mil.)	–	–	–	–	–	–
Employees	–	–	–	–	–	1,077

ROCKFORD HEALTH SYSTEM

2400 N ROCKTON AVE
ROCKFORD, IL 611033655
Phone: 815 971-5000
Fax: -
Web: -

CEO: -
CFO: -
HR: -
FYE: December 31
Type: Private

Unlike the television detective, this Rockford specializes in solving medical mysteries. Rockford Health System is a leading provider of health services to residents of northern Illinois and southern Wisconsin through a network of hospitals and physicians' practices, as well as a range of community health programs and services. The hub of the system is Rockford Memorial Hospital, a nearly 400-bed tertiary care medical center and a medical staff of more than 440 physicians that administers services ranging from general primary care to surgery. The hospital is home to a children's medical center, a heart and vascular health center, and specialty care facilities for neurosurgery and orthopedics.

ROCKHURST UNIVERSITY

1100 ROCKHURST RD
KANSAS CITY, MO 641102508
Phone: 816 501-4000
Fax: -
Web: www.rockhurst.edu

CEO: -
CFO: Guy Swanson
HR: -
FYE: June 30
Type: Private

Rockhurst University provides education and leadership training in a Catholic, Jesuit institutional environment. The university serves approximately 3,000 students from two campuses in Kansas City, Missouri. The university offers more than 50 undergraduate and graduate programs. Its undergraduate arts and science degrees include business, nursing, information, and engineering programs. On the graduate level, the university offers the Helzberg Executive Fellows MBA program, as well as programs in occupational therapy, physical therapy, speech pathology, and education. Rockhurst was founded by the Jesuits in 1910.

	Annual Growth	06/15	06/16	06/17	06/20	06/22
Sales ($mil.)	17.4%	-	48.3	55.5	98.0	126.6
Net income ($ mil.)	-	-	(3.7)	6.6	6.4	16.4
Market value ($ mil.)	-	-	-	-	-	-
Employees	-	-	-	-	-	250

ROCKVIEW DAIRIES, INC.

7011 STEWART AND GRAY RD
DOWNEY, CA 902414347
Phone: 562 927-5511
Fax: -
Web: www.rockviewfarms.com

CEO: -
CFO: -
HR: -
FYE: March 31
Type: Private

Got organic milk? Rockview Dairies does. Doing business as Rockview Farms, the company produces milk and other dairy products under brand names Rockview Farms and Good Heart Organic Milk. Bucking modern trends, the dairy owns its own farms and cows, which have not been treated with bovine growth hormones. Rockview Dairies processes, packages, and distributes its own milk. It also offers eggs, dressings, fruit drinks, and desserts. The company wholesales its products to food retailers and foodservice operators and, as a bonus, offers home-delivery service. Established in 1927 by Bob Hops, Rockview Dairies serves Southern California. It has been owned and operated by the DeGroot family since 1965.

	Annual Growth	03/04	03/05	03/06	03/07	03/08
Sales ($mil.)	15.3%	-	-	251.2	265.2	333.7
Net income ($ mil.)	21.4%	-	-	5.5	4.0	8.1
Market value ($ mil.)	-	-	-	-	-	-
Employees	-	-	-	-	-	250

ROCKWELL AUTOMATION, INC.

NYS: ROK

1201 South Second Street
Milwaukee, WI 53204
Phone: 414 382-2000
Fax: -
Web: www.rockwellautomation.com

CEO: -
CFO: -
HR: -
FYE: September 30
Type: Public

Rockwell Automation traces its roots back to the Allen Bradley Company founded in the US in 1903, and still sells products under the Allen-Bradley and A-B trademarks, among others. The company makes industrial automation products and digital transformation, including industrial motion control systems, safety components, machine protection modules, and more. Rockwell serves a broad range of global industries, such as automotive, semiconductor, warehousing and logistics, oil and gas, life sciences, and food and beverage. The company operates worldwide but the North America accounts for about 60% of revenue.

	Annual Growth	09/19	09/20	09/21	09/22	09/23
Sales ($mil.)	7.9%	6,694.8	6,329.8	6,997.4	7,760.4	9,058.0
Net income ($ mil.)	18.8%	695.8	1,023.4	1,358.1	932.2	1,387.4
Market value ($ mil.)	14.8%	18,919	25,334	33,756	24,695	32,818
Employees	6.0%	23,000	23,500	24,500	26,000	29,000

ROCKWELL MEDICAL, INC

NAS: RMTI

30142 S. Wixom Road
Wixom, MI 48393
Phone: 248 960-9009
Fax: -
Web: www.rockwellmed.com

CEO: -
CFO: -
HR: -
FYE: December 31
Type: Public

Rockwell Medical is a healthcare company that develops, manufactures, commercializes, and distributes a portfolio of hemodialysis products for dialysis providers worldwide. The company is a revenue-generating business and the second largest supplier of acid and bicarbonate concentrates for dialysis patients in the US. It manufactures hemodialysis concentrates under Current Good Manufacturing Practices (cGMP) regulations at its three facilities in Michigan, Texas, and South Carolina. In addition to its primary focus on hemodialysis concentrates, Rockwell also has a proprietary parenteral iron product, Triferic (ferric pyrophosphate citrate (FPC)), which is indicated to maintain hemoglobin in adult patients with hemodialysis-dependent chronic kidney disease.

	Annual Growth	12/18	12/19	12/20	12/21	12/22
Sales ($mil.)	3.5%	63.4	61.3	62.2	61.9	72.8
Net income ($ mil.)	-	(32.1)	(34.1)	(30.9)	(32.7)	(18.7)
Market value ($ mil.)	(18.1%)	27.5	29.7	12.3	5.0	12.3
Employees	(1.5%)	269	299	300	300	253

ROCKY BRANDS INC

NMS: RCKY

39 East Canal Street
Nelsonville, OH 45764
Phone: 740 753-9100
Fax: -
Web: www.rockybrands.com

CEO: Jason Brooks
CFO: Thomas D Robertson
HR: -
FYE: December 31
Type: Public

Rocky is a sole survivor. Rocky Brands makes and sells men's and women's footwear and apparel. Its footwear brands include Rocky, Georgia Boot, Creative Recreation, Durango, Lehigh, and licensed brand Michelin. The company targets six markets: outdoor, duty, work, military, lifestyle, and western. (Its Rocky brand is sold to the US military.) A wholesaler and retailer, the company's products are sold in the US and Canada through more than 10,000 retail stores, such as sporting goods and outdoor stores (Bass Pro Shops, Cabela's), mass merchandisers, and farm store chains. It also sells Lehigh-brand footwear online and through mobile and outlet stores. Brothers William and F. M. Brooks founded Rocky in 1932.

	Annual Growth	12/19	12/20	12/21	12/22	12/23
Sales ($mil.)	14.3%	270.4	277.3	514.2	615.5	461.8
Net income ($ mil.)	(12.1%)	17.5	21.0	20.6	20.5	10.4
Market value ($ mil.)	0.6%	218.1	208.1	295.0	175.1	223.7
Employees	2.1%	1,929	2,000	2,825	2,500	2,100

ROCKY MOUNTAIN CHOCOLATE FACTORY INC (DE) NMS: RMCF

265 Turner Drive
Durango, CO 81303
Phone: 970 259-0554
Fax: –
Web: www.rmcf.com; www.sweetfranchise.com

CEO: Robert J Sarlls
CFO: A A Arroyo
HR: –
FYE: February 28
Type: Public

Rocky Mountain Chocolate Factory knows that tourists often leave their diets at home. That's why many of its candy stores are intentionally placed in factory outlet malls, regional malls, and tourist areas. The company and its franchisees operate about 300 chocolate stores and another 55 co-branded stores in in 40 US states, Canada, Japan, and the United Arab Emirates. Its majority-owned subsidiary, U-Swirl, operates more than 65 self-serve frozen yogurt stores. The chocolate maker's products are also wholesaled and sold through fundraising programs and a company website. Most of the retailer's sales come from its 300 factory-made premium chocolates and confections; the remainder comes from franchise fees.

	Annual Growth	02/19	02/20	02/21	02/22	02/23
Sales ($mil.)	(3.1%)	34.5	31.8	23.5	32.3	30.4
Net income ($ mil.)	–	2.2	1.0	(0.9)	(0.3)	(5.7)
Market value ($ mil.)	(14.7%)	59.3	47.9	33.1	49.1	31.7
Employees	(9.1%)	231	226	202	217	158

ROEHL TRANSPORT, INC.

1916 E 29TH ST
MARSHFIELD, WI 544495401
Phone: 715 591-3795
Fax: –
Web: www.roehl.jobs

CEO: Richard Roehl
CFO: –
HR: –
FYE: December 31
Type: Private

Roehl Transport hauls a variety of freight with a fleet of some 2,000 power units and approximately 5,000 trailers, and its equipment includes flatbeds, standard dry vans, dry bulk carriers, and trailers designed to carry extra-heavy loads. Roehl also offers refrigerated transportation and logistics services. Headquartered in the Marshfield, Wisconsin, the company has major terminal locations and many other drop yards and offices throughout the country. Everett Roehl founded Roehl Transport in 1962 with a single truck.

ROFIN-SINAR TECHNOLOGIES LLC

40984 CONCEPT DR
PLYMOUTH, MI 481704252
Phone: 734 416-0206
Fax: –
Web: www.coherent.com

CEO: –
CFO: –
HR: –
FYE: September 30
Type: Private

Any way you slice it, ROFIN-SINAR Technologies is one of the world's leading makers of industrial lasers. The company designs, manufactures, and markets lasers primarily used for cutting, welding, and marking a wide range of materials. Its macro (cutting and welding) line is targeted at the machine tool and automotive markets, while its laser marking and micro (fine cutting and welding) product lines are principally geared toward the semiconductor, electronics, and photovoltaic markets. ROFIN sells directly to OEMs, systems integrators, and industrial end users that integrate its lasers into their own systems. Europe (mainly Germany) is its largest market, followed by Asia and North America.

ROGERS CORP. NYS: ROG

2225 W. Chandler Blvd.
Chandler, AZ 85224-6155
Phone: 480 917-6000
Fax: –
Web: www.rogerscorp.com

CEO: R C Gouveia
CFO: Ramakumar Mayampurath
HR: –
FYE: December 31
Type: Public

Rogers Corporation makes and sells specialty materials used for connecting and cushioning as well as managing power in electronic, industrial, and consumer products. The company's connectivity products are circuit materials used in telecommunications infrastructure, automotive applications, and consumer electronics. Its polyurethane and silicone products provide cushioning, sealing, and vibration management in smart phones, automotive and aerospace applications, and venting applications for general industry. Its ceramic substrate materials are used in power-related applications like variable general industrial, aerospace and defense, and renewable energy. International customers generate about 65% of the company's revenue.

	Annual Growth	12/19	12/20	12/21	12/22	12/23
Sales ($mil.)	0.3%	898.3	802.6	932.9	971.2	908.4
Net income ($ mil.)	4.6%	47.3	50.0	108.1	116.6	56.6
Market value ($ mil.)	1.4%	2,320.0	2,888.4	5,077.8	2,219.7	2,456.5
Employees	(2.2%)	3,600	3,350	3,675	3,800	3,300

ROKU INC NMS: ROKU

1173 Coleman Avenue
San Jose, CA 95110
Phone: 408 556-9040
Fax: –
Web: www.roku.com

CEO: Anthony Wood
CFO: Dan Jedda
HR: –
FYE: December 31
Type: Public

Roku is the leading TV streaming platform in the US, Mexico, and Canada by hours streamed. From the Roku home screen, its users can easily find and access TV episodes, shows, news, and movies streamed over the internet from sources that include Netflix, Amazon.com, HBO, YouTube, Hulu, Peacock, TV networks, and thousands of other streaming channels. Roku has approximately 70 million active accounts and they streamed approximately 87.4 billion hours of content. Roku's streaming players are powered the company's operating system, which delivers content and analyzes what users watch. The company makes money from advertising and content distribution services.

	Annual Growth	12/19	12/20	12/21	12/22	12/23
Sales ($mil.)	32.5%	1,128.9	1,778.4	2,764.6	3,126.5	3,484.6
Net income ($ mil.)	–	(59.9)	(17.5)	242.4	(498.0)	(709.6)
Market value ($ mil.)	(9.0%)	19,215	47,646	32,747	5,840.5	13,153
Employees	17.5%	1,650	1,925	3,000	3,600	3,150

ROLAND MACHINERY COMPANY

816 N DIRKSEN PKWY
SPRINGFIELD, IL 627026115
Phone: 217 789-7711
Fax: –
Web: www.rolandmachinery.com

CEO: Raymond E Roland
CFO: Michael Armstrong
HR: Caitlin Graham
FYE: December 31
Type: Private

Midwesterners with some heavy lifting to do can turn to Roland Machinery (RMC). The company sells and rents new and used construction, industrial, and forestry equipment. Its lines are driven through authorized distributors in Illinois, Missouri, Indiana, Wisconsin, and Michigan. RMC represents more than 25 major suppliers, notably Komatsu (backhoe loaders, dozers, crawlers, excavators, graders, and trucks), as well as Kubota (engines, generators), Kolman (conveyors), Atlas Copco (drilling rig equipment), Tiger (boom and rotary mowers) and Metso (mineral crushers). Customers include federal and state agencies, municipalities, and a range of private contractors. The company is owned and led by the Roland family.

ROLLINS COLLEGE

1000 HOLT AVE 2718
WINTER PARK, FL 327894409
Phone: 407 646-2000
Fax: –
Web: www.rollins.edu

CEO: Francis H Barker
CFO: –
HR: Isabelle Meelis
FYE: May 31
Type: Private

Students get rolling at Rollins College. The school is a liberal arts college with an enrollment of some 3,200 undergraduate students seeking associate, bachelor, and master's degrees. Rollins' core arts and sciences and professional studies programs offer about 30 majors. In addition, its Crummer Graduate School of Business offers an MBA program, and its Hamilton Holt School provides undergraduate and graduate evening degree and outreach programs in 10 major fields. The college has 200 faculty members and a student-to-teacher ratio of 10:1. Rollins was founded in 1885 by New England Congregationalists and is the oldest college in Florida. It is named for Chicago businessman and philanthropist Alonzo Rollins.

	Annual Growth	05/16	05/17	05/20	05/21	05/22
Sales ($mil.)	9.1%	–	140.9	139.1	136.6	217.8
Net income ($ mil.)	1.4%	–	20.0	(8.9)	116.9	21.5
Market value ($ mil.)	–	–	–	–	–	–
Employees	–	–	–	–	–	645

ROLLINS, INC.

2170 Piedmont Road, N.E.
Atlanta, GA 30324
Phone: 404 888-2000
Fax: –
Web: www.rollins.com

NYS: ROL
CEO: Jerry E Gahlhoff Jr
CFO: Kenneth D Krause
HR: –
FYE: December 31
Type: Public

Rollins is an international services company that provides provide essential pest and wildlife control services and protection against termite damage, rodents, and insects. Rollins also provides recurring maintenance, monitoring, or inspection services to help protect consumers' property from any future signs of termite activities after the original treatment. The company serves more than 2 million customers in some 70 countries globally. The US operations account for around 95% of sales. Other Rollins brands include HomeTeam Pest Defense Clark Pest Control, Western Pest Services, Critter Control Wildlife, and Northwest Pest Control, among others.

	Annual Growth	12/19	12/20	12/21	12/22	12/23
Sales ($mil.)	11.1%	2,015.5	2,161.2	2,424.3	2,695.8	3,073.3
Net income ($ mil.)	20.9%	203.3	260.8	350.7	368.6	435.0
Market value ($ mil.)	7.1%	16,052	18,913	16,560	17,688	21,140
Employees	6.2%	14,952	15,616	16,482	17,515	19,031

RONALD MCDONALD HOUSE CHARITIES, INC.

110 N CARPENTER ST STE 300
CHICAGO, IL 606074106
Phone: 630 623-7048
Fax: –
Web: www.rmhc.org

CEO: Katie Fitzgerald
CFO: –
HR: –
FYE: December 31
Type: Private

Ronald McDonald House Charities (RMHC) provides temporary housing to families of seriously ill children undergoing treatment. The group's signature Ronald McDonald House program maintains about 295 facilities near hospitals in 30 countries and regions worldwide. RMHC also offers 145 Ronald McDonald Family Rooms, designed to provide places of respite within hospitals. Its 40-vehicle Ronald McDonald Care Mobile program brings routine medical services, including immunizations, to children in underserved communities. RMHC operates through local chapters in about 50 countries and regions worldwide. The first Ronald McDonald House opened in 1974, in memory of McDonald's founder Ray Kroc. RMHC was founded in 1984.

	Annual Growth	12/18	12/19	12/20	12/21	12/22
Sales ($mil.)	9.6%	–	60.5	73.9	90.4	79.6
Net income ($ mil.)	7.4%	–	10.1	20.7	20.3	12.6
Market value ($ mil.)	–	–	–	–	–	–
Employees	–	–	–	–	–	50

RONILE, INC.

701 ORCHARD AVE
ROCKY MOUNT, VA 241511848
Phone: 540 483-0261
Fax: –
Web: www.ronile.com

CEO: Phillip C Essig
CFO: –
HR: –
FYE: June 30
Type: Private

Ronile can spin a yarn -- a textile one, that is. The company manufactures custom-dyed accent yarns, including twisted, space-dyed, air-ply, and heatset yarns. Ronile's slew of finished yarn goods include nylon, polyester, acrylic, and other wool fibers, which are marketed to carpet, rug, home furnishings, craft, and automotive markets. Ronile also operates through subsidiary Bacova Guild, Ltd., a manufacturer and supplier of printed accent rugs, room-size rugs, and bath ensembles to US retail chains, and Gulistan, a division supplying broadloom carpet. Employee-owned, the company is led by its founder's son, Phillip Essig.

	Annual Growth	07/03	07/04	07/05	07/06*	06/07
Sales ($mil.)	1.3%	–	–	226.5	245.5	232.4
Net income ($ mil.)	–	–	–	–	–	–
Market value ($ mil.)	–	–	–	–	–	–
Employees	–	–	–	–	–	1,383

*Fiscal year change

ROOFING WHOLESALE CO., INC.

1918 W GRANT ST
PHOENIX, AZ 850095991
Phone: 602 258-3794
Fax: –
Web: www.rwc.org

CEO: Eric Risser
CFO: Stephen K Rold
HR: –
FYE: December 31
Type: Private

Business at Roofing Wholesale doesn't have to be complicated, but it should be over your head. Roofing Wholesale Company (RWC) distributes residential and commercial roofing, stone flooring, and stucco to contractors, builders, and do-it-yourself home owners through ten locations in Arizona, California, Nevada, and New Mexico. It also operates an online store. Products include asphalt shingles, cedar shakes and shingles, clay tiles, fasteners, marble floors, and slate roofs. John Lisherness, father of current president Harley Lisherness, founded the family-owned company in 1958.

	Annual Growth	12/11	12/12	12/13	12/14	12/15
Sales ($mil.)	4.7%	–	–	106.9	106.9	117.1
Net income ($ mil.)	31.1%	–	–	4.8	7.8	8.2
Market value ($ mil.)	–	–	–	–	–	–
Employees	–	–	–	–	–	225

ROOSEVELT CAPITAL LLC

7601 DURAND AVE
MOUNT PLEASANT, WI 531771905
Phone: 800 992-9307
Fax: –
Web: www.promot.com

CEO: –
CFO: –
HR: –
FYE: December 31
Type: Private

Roosevelt Capital, which does business as Promotions Unlimited, provides advertising and promotional programs for 5,500 retail stores. Its merchandising products include advertising circulars and coupon books, as well as provide online merchandising guides for its clients. Promotions Unlimited also produces "buying shows," allowing retailers to view merchandise, place orders, and attend educational seminars on such topics as advertising, merchandising, and retail management. The family-owned company, founded in 1973 by Ira Greenberg, franchises the Ben Franklin variety and craft stores, providing its merchandising and promotional services to the franchisees.

	Annual Growth	12/09	12/10	12/11	12/12	12/13
Sales ($mil.)	(5.5%)	–	–	40.5	37.3	36.2
Net income ($ mil.)	(12.1%)	–	–	0.3	0.2	0.2
Market value ($ mil.)	–	–	–	–	–	–
Employees	–	–	–	–	–	120

ROOT LLC

5470 MAIN ST STE 100
SYLVANIA, OH 435602164
Phone: 419 874-0077
Fax: –
Web: www.rootinc.com

CEO: Rich Berens
CFO: –
HR: Karen Stigall
FYE: December 31
Type: Private

Root Learning wants to ensure your employees aren't just learning by rote. The company provides teaching tools, facilitator training, and consultative services, including leadership alignment and strategy clarification for businesses. Services help clients create training content, implement learning programs, and measure results. Root also offers software for learning visualization, game-based education, and knowledge management, as well as off-the-shelf courseware that addresses subjects such as workplace diversity, emotional literacy, branding, and business process mapping. Major clients have included Delta and Pepsi. The company was founded in 1993 by former president Randall Root.

	Annual Growth	12/99	12/00	12/01	12/02	12/20
Sales ($mil.)	15.7%	–	18.9	14.6	14.7	346.8
Net income ($ mil.)	–	–	4.1	2.3	2.1	(363.0)
Market value ($ mil.)	–	–	–	–	–	–
Employees	–	–	–	–	–	120

ROOT9B HOLDINGS INC

102 N. Cascade Avenue, Suite 220
Colorado Springs, CO 80903
Phone: 719 358-8735
Fax: –
Web: www.root9bholdings.com

NBB: RTNB
CEO: –
CFO: –
HR: –
FYE: December 31
Type: Public

First and foremost, Premier Alliance Group looks to be a business and technology ally to its customers. Premier Alliance provides technology consulting and professional services to organizations in the education, financial, health care, utility, and other sectors. Core consulting services include systems implementation and architecture, information management, business intelligence, and analysis. It also offers expertise in key professional areas such as risk management, compliance, and finance. Founded in 1995, Premier Alliance has counted Duke Energy, Bank of America, and a handful of other large companies as among its key customers. In 2012 it acquired environmental consulting firm GreenHouse Holdings.

	Annual Growth	12/12	12/13	12/14	12/15	12/16
Sales ($mil.)	(14.8%)	19.5	26.4	20.2	29.4	10.2
Net income ($ mil.)	–	(9.5)	(6.1)	(24.4)	(8.3)	(30.5)
Market value ($ mil.)	97.1%	4.6	3.5	9.5	8.4	70.0
Employees	(1.0%)	160	151	215	224	154

ROPER ST. FRANCIS HEALTHCARE

125 DOUGHTY ST STE 760
CHARLESTON, SC 294035785
Phone: 843 724-2000
Fax: –
Web: www.rsfh.com

CEO: Megan Baker
CFO: –
HR: Deb Obrien
FYE: December 31
Type: Private

CareAlliance Health Services (doing business as Roper St. Francis Healthcare) operates four hospitals -- the 370-bed Roper Hospital, the 200-bed Bon Secours St. Francis Hospital, the 85-bed Mount Pleasant Hospital, and the Roper Rehabilitation Hospital. Besides providing home health services, it also operates outpatient emergency, primary care, and diagnostic facilities. Roper St. Francis Healthcare serves Charleston, South Carolina, and surrounding communities. Its Roper St. Francis Physician Partners is one of the region's largest physician practices.

	Annual Growth	12/07	12/08	12/09	12/14	12/22
Sales ($mil.)	–	–	(1,556.1)	682.8	793.7	108.0
Net income ($ mil.)	104.2%	–	0.0	56.4	(2.5)	11.7
Market value ($ mil.)	–	–	–	–	–	–
Employees	–	–	–	–	–	6,000

ROPER TECHNOLOGIES INC

6496 University Parkway
Sarasota, FL 34240
Phone: 941 556-2601
Fax: –
Web: www.ropertech.com

NMS: ROP
CEO: L N Hunn
CFO: Robert C Crisci
HR: Allison Linares
FYE: December 31
Type: Public

Roper Technologies is a diversified technology and operate businesses that design and develop software (both license and Software-as-a-Services (SaaS)) and engineered products and solutions for a variety of niche end markets. Its business segments include Application Software (CBORD, Aderant, Data Innovations, and Deltek), Network Software (DAT, Foundry, and iPipeline), Technology Enabled Products (CIVCO Medical Solutions, FMI, Inovonics, IPA, Neptune, Northern Digital, rf IDEAS, and Verathon) Roper's businesses serve industries such as healthcare, transportation, government contracting, food markets, water meter technology, and upstream oil and gas end markets. About 85% of total revenue comes from the US.

	Annual Growth	12/19	12/20	12/21	12/22	12/23
Sales ($mil.)	3.6%	5,366.8	5,527.1	5,777.8	5,371.8	6,177.8
Net income ($ mil.)	(5.9%)	1,767.9	949.7	1,152.6	4,544.7	1,384.2
Market value ($ mil.)	11.4%	37,867	46,084	52,580	46,190	58,279
Employees	0.5%	16,460	18,400	19,300	15,800	16,800

ROSE INTERNATIONAL, INC.

16305 SWINGLEY RIDGE RD STE 350
CHESTERFIELD, MO 630171802
Phone: 636 812-4000
Fax: –
Web: www.roseint.com

CEO: Himanshu Bhatia
CFO: –
HR: Dana Schmitz
FYE: December 31
Type: Private

Rose International keep its customers' tech gardens in bloom. The company provides outsourced IT services including database performance optimization, application development, and project management to businesses and government agencies in the US. Other services include vendor management, payroll processing, training, and staffing, and call center operations. Rose -- its name is an acronym for "reliable open systems engineering" -- serves customers in the financial services, energy, technology, telecommunications, and health care industries. Its software development activities in Missouri and India are overseen by subsidiary Rose I.T. Solutions.

	Annual Growth	12/12	12/13	12/14	12/15	12/16
Sales ($mil.)	(10.8%)	–	–	293.5	248.9	233.5
Net income ($ mil.)	(39.5%)	–	–	7.2	5.2	2.6
Market value ($ mil.)	–	–	–	–	–	–
Employees	–	–	–	–	–	6,000

ROSE PAVING, LLC

7300 W 100TH PL
BRIDGEVIEW, IL 604552414
Phone: 708 430-1100
Fax: –
Web: www.rosepaving.com

CEO: Edward Campbell
CFO: Jim Muckerheide
HR: Liz Foley
FYE: December 31
Type: Private

Rose Paving is the largest asphalt and concrete service provider in the US offering the highest quality paving, seal coating and parking lot management services. Its activities include pavement removal, resurfacing, repair, and installation, lot marking, seal coating, crack sealing, storm sewer repair and installation, and installation and repair of concrete curbs, walks, and pads. Clients include commercial and industrial customers in the retail, real estate, hospitality, health care industries, as well as homeowner associations, schools, and religious institutions. Rose Paving started its business in 1974.

ROSE'S SOUTHWEST PAPERS, INC.

1701 2ND ST SW
ALBUQUERQUE, NM 871024505
Phone: 505 842-0134
Fax: –
Web: www.rosessouthwestpapers.com

CEO: Roberto E Espat
CFO: –
HR: –
FYE: December 31
Type: Private

Roses Southwest Papers has bloomed in the desert Southwest by manufacturing napkins, tissue paper, and paper bags used in fast food restaurants and other places of business. The company's tissue products include bathroom tissue, center pull towels, facial tissue, fold towels, kitchen roll towels, jumbo roll tissue, and roll towels. Roses Southwest Papers also provides custom converting and private labeling services. The company counts McDonald's and Burger King among its major clients. Roses Southwest Papers is owned and operated by CEO Roberto Espat and other members of the Espat family.

	Annual Growth	12/03	12/04	12/05	12/06	12/07
Sales ($mil.)	12.0%	–	66.9	76.7	79.9	94.0
Net income ($ mil.)	(2.3%)	–	2.5	1.2	1.2	2.3
Market value ($ mil.)	–	–	–	–	–	–
Employees	–	–	–	–	–	125

ROSEN HOTELS AND RESORTS, INC.

4000 DESTINATION PKWY
ORLANDO, FL 328198106
Phone: 407 996-1706
Fax: –
Web: www.rosenhotels.com

CEO: –
CFO: Frank Santos
HR: Farvy Fils-Aime
FYE: January 31
Type: Private

Rosen Hotels & Resorts is one of the most respected names in the hospitality industry. It owns and operates seven quality properties in Orlando, collectively totaling more than 6,300 rooms and suites. Rosen Hotels & Resorts includes the award-winning convention properties Rosen Shingle Creek, Rosen Plaza, and Rosen Centre in its family, in addition to four leisure properties, Rosen Inn International, Rosen Inn (Closest to Universal), Rosen Inn Pointe Orlando, and Rosen Inn Lake Buena Vista. Its properties have excellent accommodations, facilities, catering, dining, and recreational amenities that represent tremendous value for its guests. In addition, subsidiary Millennium Technology Group manages computer systems for its hotels. The family-owned Rosen Hotels & Resorts was founded by President & COO Harris Rosen in 1974.

	Annual Growth	01/17	01/18	01/19	01/20	01/21
Sales ($mil.)	(39.4%)	–	3.3	–	5.6	0.7
Net income ($ mil.)	–	–	–	–	1.3	–
Market value ($ mil.)	–	–	–	–	–	–
Employees	–	–	–	–	–	3,145

ROSETTA STONE INC.

135 W MARKET ST
HARRISONBURG, VA 228013710
Phone: 877 211-2367
Fax: –
Web: www.rosettastone.com

CEO: A J Hass III
CFO: Thomas Pierno
HR: –
FYE: December 31
Type: Private

Rosetta Stone, a division of IXL Learning, is dedicated to changing people's lives through the power of language education. The company's innovative digital solutions drive positive learning outcomes for the inspired learner at home or in schools and workplaces around the world. Its Rosetta Stone Language Library combines images, text, and audio, without the traditional translation or grammar explanations, to mimic the way children learn their native languages. Rosetta Stone offers software for about some 30 languages. Its products are available through direct sales channels and at selected retailers such as Amazon.com, Best Buy, and Target. The company was founded in 1992. It was acquired by Cambium Learning Group in 2020.

ROSS STORES INC

NMS: ROST

5130 Hacienda Drive
Dublin, CA 94568-7579
Phone: 925 965-4400
Fax: –
Web: www.rossstores.com

CEO: –
CFO: –
HR: –
FYE: January 28
Type: Public

Ross is the largest off-price apparel and home fashion chain in the US, which operates about 1,695 Ross Dress for Less and approximately 320 dd's Discounts stores that sell closeout merchandise, including men's, women's, and children's clothing, at prices well below those of department and specialty stores. While apparel accounts for about half of sales, the company also sells small furniture, home accents, bed and bath, beauty, toys and games, luggage, gourmet food, cookware, jewelry and watches, and pet accessories. Ross' target customers are primarily from middle income households. Ross and dd's stores are predominantly in community and neighborhood shopping centers in approximately 40 states, the District of Columbia, and Guam.

	Annual Growth	02/19	02/20*	01/21	01/22	01/23
Sales ($mil.)	5.7%	14,984	16,039	12,532	18,916	18,696
Net income ($ mil.)	(1.2%)	1,587.5	1,660.9	85.4	1,722.6	1,512.0
Market value ($ mil.)	6.8%	31,441	38,453	38,145	32,825	40,952
Employees	3.5%	88,100	92,500	93,700	100,000	101,000

*Fiscal year change

ROTARY INTERNATIONAL

ONE ROTARY CTR 1560 SHERMAN AVE
EVANSTON, IL 60201
Phone: 847 866-3000
Fax: –
Web: www.rotary.org

CEO: John Hewko
CFO: David Jensen
HR: –
FYE: June 30
Type: Private

The rotary phone may be a thing of the past, but Rotary International (founded in 1905, and now with more than 1.2 million members) is still going strong. The service organization, with a motto of Service Above Self, comprises 34,000-plus clubs in more than 200 countries and territories. Rotary service projects are intended to alleviate problems, such as hunger, illiteracy, poverty, and violence. Grants from the Rotary Foundation support its efforts. Along with its service projects, Rotary aims to promote high ethical standards in the workplace. Membership in Rotary clubs is by invitation. Each club strives to include representatives from major businesses, professions, and institutions in its community.

	Annual Growth	06/11	06/12	06/16	06/21	06/22
Sales ($mil.)	1.4%	–	90.6	356.0	96.4	104.4
Net income ($ mil.)	–	–	(1.0)	(17.8)	10.0	2.5
Market value ($ mil.)	–	–	–	–	–	–
Employees	–	–	–	–	–	800

ROTECH HEALTHCARE INC.

6251 CHANCELLOR DR STE 119
ORLANDO, FL 328095613
Phone: 407 822-4600
Fax: –
Web: www.rotech.com

CEO: Timothy Pigg
CFO: Thomas J Koenig
HR: –
FYE: December 31
Type: Private

Rotech is a leading nationwide provider of respiratory-assistance equipment and durable medical equipment to home-bound patients with breathing disorders and such infirmities as chronic bronchitis, emphysema and obstructive sleep apnea. The company operates through more than 300 locations across the US. Rotech offers home oxygen therapy, sleep apnea therapy and supplies, airway clearance therapy, overnight oximetry services and wound care solutions. The company also offers nebulizer medications and other medical equipment, including hospital beds, walkers and canes and wheelchairs.

ROTH IGA FOODLINER INCORPORATED

4895 INDIAN SCHOOL RD NE
SALEM, OR 973051126
Phone: 503 393-7684
Fax: –
Web: www.roths.com

CEO: –
CFO: –
HR: –
FYE: April 30
Type: Private

Roth's Food Center helps you bring home the bacon; frying it up in a pan is your responsibility. The regional grocery store chain operates about 10 Roth's Fresh Market stores in Oregon's mid-Willamette Valley. The stores sell traditional grocery fare, beer and wine, organic produce, and more. The stores house caterine and floral departments as well. It also sells its groceries online through a partnership with MyWebGrocer.com. In addition the company operates one gasoline station at its store in Silverton, Oregon. The company was founded in 1962 by chairman Orville Roth, father of president Michael Roth.

	Annual Growth	01/01	01/02	01/03	01/04*	04/09
Sales ($mil.)	(68.1%)	–	–	112.1	113.8	0.1
Net income ($ mil.)	(28.2%)	–	–	0.2	0.2	0.0
Market value ($ mil.)	–	–	–	–	–	–
Employees		–	–	–	–	1,005

*Fiscal year change

ROTH PRODUCE CO.

3882 AGLER RD
COLUMBUS, OH 432193607
Phone: 614 337-2825
Fax: –
Web: www.rothproduce.com

CEO: –
CFO: –
HR: –
FYE: December 31
Type: Private

Roth Produce provides fresh produce, herbs, exotic vegetables, dairy products, and frozen breads to foodservice customers in the greater Columbus, Ohio, area. The company distributes to caterers, country clubs, hotels, and other fine dining establishments, as well as to local eateries, pizza parlors, and schools. Roth Produce's gift basket division, Bensoni's Baskets, makes custom gift baskets and fruit baskets.

ROTH STAFFING COMPANIES, L.P.

450 N STATE COLLEGE BLVD
ORANGE, CA 928681708
Phone: 714 939-8600
Fax: –
Web: www.rothstaffing.com

CEO: –
CFO: –
HR: –
FYE: December 31
Type: Private

Roth Staffing offers temporary and temp-to-hire staffing and permanent placement services through its specialized business lines. Ultimate Staffing Services specializes in administrative, customer service, clerical, manufacturing and production positions. Ledgent Finance & Accounting focuses on accounting and finance professionals, while Ledgent Technology builds connections with top tech talent and companies across. Adams & Martin Group builds connections between legal professionals and law firms and legal departments throughout the US. In addition, About Talent provides companies with a highly productive workforce. The company serves clients in around 25 US states and Washington, DC, through more than 100 branches and a number of on-premise locations. The company was founded in 1994.

	Annual Growth	12/09	12/10	12/11	12/12	12/16
Sales ($mil.)	9.3%	–	202.1	244.4	244.4	344.4
Net income ($ mil.)		–	–	–	–	7.1
Market value ($ mil.)		–	–	–	–	–
Employees		–	–	–	–	610

ROUND TABLE PIZZA, INC.

1390 WILLOW PASS RD STE 300
CONCORD, CA 945205200
Phone: 800 866-5866
Fax: –
Web: www.roundtablepizza.com

CEO: Robert McCourt
CFO: Matthew Dowling
HR: –
FYE: December 31
Type: Private

If King Arthur's knights had sat at this Round Table, they would have been eating pizza. Round Table Pizza operates a chain of about 450 family-oriented pizza parlors located primarily in the western US. The pizzerias are known for the colorful names given to menu items, including Guinevere's Garden Delight and Montague's All Meat Marvel. Round Table also serves sandwiches, salads, and appetizers. The eateries offer dine-in seating along with carry-out and delivery services. William Larson opened the first Round Table Pizza in 1959 and began franchising the restaurant concept three years later. The company filed for Chapter 11 bankruptcy protection in 2011 before emerging later that same year.

ROUNDY'S, INC.

875 E WISCONSIN AVE
MILWAUKEE, WI 532025404
Phone: 414 231-5000
Fax: –
Web: www.roundys.com

CEO: –
CFO: –
HR: –
FYE: December 28
Type: Private

Roundy's is a leading grocer in the Midwest. It owns and operates 150 retail grocery stores and over 105 pharmacies under the Pick 'n Save, Metro Market, and Mariano's retail banners in Wisconsin and Illinois. Founded in Milwaukee in 1872, Roundy's is a wholly owned subsidiary of the Kroger Co. The two largest banners are Pick 'n Save, with more than 100 locations throughout the State of Wisconsin, and Mariano's, with over 40 locations throughout the Chicagoland area.

ROWAN REGIONAL MEDICAL CENTER, INC.

612 MOCKSVILLE AVE
SALISBURY, NC 281442799
Phone: 336 277-1120
Fax: –
Web: –

CEO: Carl Armato
CFO: –
HR: –
FYE: December 31
Type: Private

Rowan Regional Medical Center oversees medical care for residents of central North Carolina. The acute care facility has about 270 beds and provides general, emergency, and surgical inpatient services. It also includes a host of centers dedicated to specialty fields such as cancer care, cardiac rehabilitation, behavioral health, pain management, sleep medicine, and women's health. Founded in 1936, Rowan Regional also has specialized physical and respiratory rehabilitation units and home health and hospice organizations. Rowan Regional is part of the Novant Health network.

	Annual Growth	12/13	12/14	12/15	12/16	12/17
Sales ($mil.)	1.1%	–	–	197.0	207.9	201.5
Net income ($ mil.)	(30.2%)	–	–	21.6	22.6	10.5
Market value ($ mil.)	–	–	–	–	–	–
Employees		–	–	–	–	1,196

ROYAL CARIBBEAN GROUP
NYS: RCL

1050 Caribbean Way
Miami, FL 33132
Phone: 305 539-6000
Fax: –
Web: www.rclcorporate.com

CEO: Jason T Liberty
CFO: Naftali Holtz
HR: Barbara Orr
FYE: December 31
Type: Public

Royal Caribbean Cruises is one of the leading cruise companies in the world. It controls and operates three global cruise brands: Royal Caribbean International, Celebrity Cruises and Silversea Cruises. The company also owns a 50% joint venture interest in TUI Cruises GmbH (TUIC) which operates the German brand's TUI Cruises and Hapag-Lloyd Cruises. The company operates a combined total of about 65 ships in the cruise vacation industry with an aggregate capacity of approximately 150,000 berths. The company's ships operate on a selection of worldwide itineraries that call on approximately 1,000 destinations on all seven continents. In addition, Royal Caribbean has offices and a network of international representatives around the world, which primarily focus on sales and market development. Royal Caribbean was founded in 1968 as a partnership. North America generates around 65% of total revenue.

	Annual Growth	12/19	12/20	12/21	12/22	12/23
Sales ($mil.)	6.1%	10,951	2,208.8	1,532.1	8,840.5	13,900
Net income ($ mil.)	(2.5%)	1,878.9	(5,797.5)	(5,260.5)	(2,156.0)	1,697.0
Market value ($ mil.)	–	–	–	–	–	–
Employees	3.6%	85,400	85,000	85,000	102,500	98,200

ROYAL GOLD INC
NMS: RGLD

1144 15th Street, Suite 2500
Denver, CO 80202
Phone: 303 573-1660
Fax: –
Web: www.royalgold.com

CEO: William Heissenbuttel
CFO: Paul Libner
HR: –
FYE: December 31
Type: Public

Royal Gold acquires and manages precious metal streams, royalties, and similar interests. It seeks to acquire existing stream and royalty interests or to finance projects that are in the production, development, or exploration stage in exchange for stream or royalty interests. It does not conduct mining operations on the properties in which it holds stream and royalty interests and is not required to contribute to capital costs, environmental costs, or other operating costs on the properties. The Company owned interests in about 180 properties on five continents, including interests in about 40 producing mines and about 20 development-stage projects. Its operations in Canada account for about 40% of sales.

	Annual Growth	06/20	06/21*	12/21	12/22	12/23
Sales ($mil.)	5.0%	498.8	615.9	343.0	603.2	605.7
Net income ($ mil.)	4.7%	199.3	302.5	138.3	239.0	239.4
Market value ($ mil.)	(0.7%)	8,159.3	7,488.6	6,905.1	7,398.0	7,938.8
Employees	2.7%	27	28	29	31	30

*Fiscal year change

ROYALE ENERGY INC
NBB: ROYL

1530 Hilton Head Road, Suite 205
El Cajon, CA 92021
Phone: 619 383-6600
Fax: –
Web: www.royl.com

CEO: –
CFO: Stephen M Hosmer
HR: Sandy Lafond
FYE: December 31
Type: Public

The geological basins of Northern California are getting the Royale treatment. Using modern computer-aided exploration technologies, Royale Energy concentrates its exploration and production efforts in the Sacramento and San Joaquin basins. The company pursues a strategy of acquiring stakes in oil and gas reserves via private joint ventures. It also owns leasehold interests in Louisiana, Texas, and Utah. Royale Energy has estimated proved reserves of 4 billion cu. ft. of natural gas equivalent. CEO Donald Hosmer, CFO Stephen Hosmer, and their father and company chairman Harry Hosmer together own approximately 36% of Royale Energy. The company made a bid to buy privately held Matrix Oil in 2016.

	Annual Growth	12/18	12/19	12/20	12/21	12/22
Sales ($mil.)	(5.3%)	3.3	3.0	1.6	1.7	2.6
Net income ($ mil.)	–	(23.5)	(0.3)	(8.1)	(3.6)	(0.1)
Market value ($ mil.)	(15.8%)	8.1	7.2	5.3	2.5	4.1
Employees	(2.4%)	11	12	11	11	10

RPC, INC.
NYS: RES

2801 Buford Highway, Suite 300
Atlanta, GA 30329
Phone: 404 321-2140
Fax: –
Web: www.rpc.net

CEO: Richard A Hubbell
CFO: Ben M Palmer
HR: –
FYE: December 31
Type: Public

RPC helps to grease the wheels of oil and gas production through a number of business units. Its Cudd Energy Services division specializes in responding to and controlling oil and gas well emergencies, including blowouts and well fires, domestically and internationally. Patterson Services has the capacity to supply the equipment, expertise and personnel necessary to restore the affected oil and gas wells to production. RPC manages its business as either services offered on the well site with equipment and personnel or services and equipment offered off the well site. Most of the company's revenue comes from the US.

	Annual Growth	12/19	12/20	12/21	12/22	12/23
Sales ($mil.)	7.3%	1,222.4	598.3	864.9	1,601.8	1,617.5
Net income ($ mil.)	–	(87.1)	(212.2)	7.2	218.4	195.1
Market value ($ mil.)	8.6%	1,126.7	677.3	976.2	1,911.6	1,565.4
Employees	(0.1%)	2,700	2,005	2,250	2,732	2,691

RPL INTERNATIONAL INC.

1851 WHITNEY MESA DR
HENDERSON, NV 890142069
Phone: 702 565-7756
Fax: –
Web: www.balticbirch.com

CEO: –
CFO: –
HR: –
FYE: October 31
Type: Private

RPL International, Inc. (RPL) imports a variety of Russian and Polish birch plywood and veneered wood for dieboard and other applications. The company operates a sales and marketing branch in Salem, Massachusetts. RPL sells throughout the US, supplying dealers from warehouses in Baltimore, Maryland; Houston, Texas; Philadelphia, Pennsylvania; and Long Beach and Oakland, California. It's likely RPL stands for the initials of president, founder, and owner Ronald "Ron" P. Liberatori and not Russian, Polish Lumber. But it could. The company's history goes back to 1969, when RPL has been the lead importer and distributor of Russian Birch plywood products in the United States.

	Annual Growth	12/01	12/02	12/03*	10/06	10/07
Sales ($mil.)	8.5%	–	–	16.8	–	23.2
Net income ($ mil.)	48.9%	–	–	0.5	–	2.6
Market value ($ mil.)	–	–	–	–	–	–
Employees	–	–	–	–	–	9

*Fiscal year change

RPM INTERNATIONAL INC (DE)
NYS: RPM

2628 Pearl Road
Medina, OH 44256
Phone: 330 273-5090
Fax: 330 225-8743
Web: www.rpminc.com

CEO: Frank C Sullivan
CFO: Russell L Gordon
HR: –
FYE: May 31
Type: Public

RPM International's products like Rust-Oleum, Zinsser, and DAP are familiar sites on shelves of home improvement stores and consumers' workshops. The company's consumer brands include do-it-yourself caulks and sealants, rust preventatives and general-purpose paints, repair products, personal care items, and hobby paints. Beyond those consumer-related products, RPM offers industrial-grade products for waterproofing, corrosion resistance, floor maintenance, and wall finishing. RPM also offers industrial cleaners, restoration services equipment, and colorants. The company gets nearly 70% of its sales from US customers.

	Annual Growth	05/19	05/20	05/21	05/22	05/23
Sales ($mil.)	6.9%	5,564.6	5,507.0	6,106.3	6,707.7	7,256.4
Net income ($ mil.)	15.8%	266.6	304.4	502.6	491.5	478.7
Market value ($ mil.)	10.5%	6,891.6	9,629.1	12,043	11,344	10,274
Employees	3.7%	14,957	14,621	15,490	16,751	17,274

RPX CORPORATION

4 EMBARCADERO CTR STE 4000
SAN FRANCISCO, CA 941114100
Phone: 866 779-7641
Fax: –
Web: www.rpxcorp.com

CEO: Dan McCurdy
CFO: Robert H Heath
HR: –
FYE: December 31
Type: Private

In our litigious society, RPX Corporation helps keep technology companies out of the courtroom. RPX is one of the largest, most active patent buyers in the patent market and has more than 60,000 patent assets and rights. Its patent portfolio spans nine industries ? automotive, e-commerce, consumer electronics and PCs, financial services, media content and distribution, mobile communications and devices, networking, semiconductors, and software. RPX counts approximately 330 clients, ranging from early-stage firms to Fortune 100 industry leaders. Collectively, the team has completed more than $2.5 billion in patent-related transactions. RPX was founded in 2008.

RS INTEGRATED SUPPLY US INC.

100 W MATSONFORD RD STE 400
RADNOR, PA 190874558
Phone: 610 293-5940
Fax: –
Web: www.rs-integratedsupply.com

CEO: –
CFO: –
HR: –
FYE: December 31
Type: Private

Synovos (formerly Storeroom Solutions) provides onsite management of maintenance, repair, and operating (MRO) supplies for industrial manufacturing facilities. Services include data collection, inventory management, supply chain management consulting, purchasing, and warranty tracking. Synovos serves its clients through more than 140 facilities in more than 30 US states, Canada, Mexico, and Puerto Rico. The company traces its roots back to 1987. It changed its name from Storeroom Solutions to Synovos in 2016.

RS LEGACY CORPORATION

2501 PARKVIEW DR STE 315
FORT WORTH, TX 761025823
Phone: 817 415-3011
Fax: –
Web: www.radioshack.com

CEO: –
CFO: Carlin Adrianopoli
HR: –
FYE: December 31
Type: Private

RadioShack is electronics retailer that offers a variety of products used for home and office such as computers, headphones, TVs, and home theater system. For mobile customers, the company also sells accessories and cables. RadioShack stores also sell a wide range of electronics parts, batteries, and components. In addition, RadioShack sells apparels and personal protective equipment. In the first quarter of 2020, about 400 RadioShack locations opened. The company is owned by Retail Ecommerce Ventures.

RSP PERMIAN, INC.

600 W ILLINOIS AVE
MIDLAND, TX 797014882
Phone: 432 683-7443
Fax: –
Web: –

CEO: Steven Gray
CFO: Scott McNeill
HR: –
FYE: December 31
Type: Private

RSP Permian's presence permeates the sub-basins of the Permian Basin. This independent oil & gas company holds significant contiguous acreage blocks in the core of the Midland Basin and the Delaware Basin. With 142,000 gross (92,000 net) surface acres to its name, RSP Permian engages in the acquisition, exploration, development and production of unconventional oil and associated liquids-rich natural gas reserves in West Texas. It has proved reserves of 376 million boe (70% oil), and an average net daily production of 55,255 boe operated and produced from its nearly 270 horizontal and some 410 vertical wells. Major purchasers include Enterprise, Western Refining, and Shell Trading. In 2018, Concho Resources acquired RSP Permian.

RSR GROUP, INC.

4405 METRIC DR
WINTER PARK, FL 327926904
Phone: 407 677-6114
Fax: –
Web: www.rsrgroup.com

CEO: Joann Weisenford
CFO: John Slogar
HR: Ashley Stuemky
FYE: June 25
Type: Private

RSR Group has its sights fixed on the shooting sports industry. The company distributes firearms, optical accessories, gun cases, cleaning equipment and tools, and related gear to retailers throughout the US. It also offers knives and safety products, such as pepper spray and batons. RSR carries more than 12,000 products from 200 manufacturers, including Remington, Smith & Wesson, Mace Security International, and Pelican. It operates five sales centers across the US and a distribution center in Texas. The company was founded in 1977. In 2005 the RSR family of companies merged into the RSR Group, its parent company.

	Annual Growth	06/06	06/07	06/08	06/09	06/10
Sales ($mil.)	0.4%	–	–	198.5	–	199.9
Net income ($ mil.)	70.7%	–	–	3.2	–	9.2
Market value ($ mil.)	–	–	–	–	–	–
Employees	–	–	–	–	–	220

RTW RETAILWINDS, INC.

330 W 34TH ST FL 9
NEW YORK, NY 100012406
Phone: 212 884-2000
Fax: –
Web: www.nyandcompany.com

CEO: Sheamus Toal
CFO: Sheamus Toal
HR: Douglas Levine
FYE: February 02
Type: Private

RTW Retailwinds (formerly New York & Company) caters to working women ages 25 to 49 looking for moderately priced apparel (jeans, dresses, and coordinates) and accessories (sunglasses, jewelry, and handbags). It offers proprietary branded fashions at more than 385 stores in about three dozen US states and online. The company sells merchandise under the New York & Company and Fashion to Figure names and has collaborations with celebrities such as Eva Mendes, Gabrielle Union, and Kate Hudson. RTW Retailwinds was founded in 1918 and filed for voluntary petitions for relief under Chapter 11 of the Bankruptcy Code in the United States Bankruptcy Court for the District of New Jersey in 2020.

	Annual Growth	01/15	01/16	01/17*	02/18	02/19
Sales ($mil.)	(1.9%)	–	–	929.1	926.9	893.2
Net income ($ mil.)	–	–	–	(17.3)	5.7	4.2
Market value ($ mil.)	–	–	–	–	–	–
Employees	–	–	–	–	–	1,460

*Fiscal year change

RTX CORP

NYS: RTX

1000 Wilson Boulevard
Arlington, VA 22209
Phone: 781 522-3000
Fax: –
Web: www.rtx.com

CEO: Gregory J Hayes
CFO: Neil G Mitchill Jr
HR: –
FYE: December 31
Type: Public

Raytheon Technologies provides high-tech products and services for the aerospace and commercial building industries. It operates through engine aircraft manufacturer Pratt & Whitney; Collins Aerospace Systems, maker of engine controls and flight systems for military and commercial aircraft; Raytheon Intelligence & Space (RIS), developer and provider of integrated sensor and communication systems and Raytheon Missiles & Defense (RMD), designer, developer, integrator producer and sustainer of integrated air and missile defense systems. The company generates the majority of its revenue in the US. The company was incorporated in 1934.

	Annual Growth	12/19	12/20	12/21	12/22	12/23
Sales ($mil.)	(2.7%)	77,046	56,587	64,388	67,074	68,920
Net income ($ mil.)	(12.8%)	5,537.0	(3,519.0)	3,864.0	5,197.0	3,195.0
Market value ($ mil.)	(13.4%)	198,718	94,887	114,194	133,911	111,646
Employees	(6.6%)	243,200	181,000	174,000	182,000	185,000

RUAN TRANSPORTATION MANAGEMENT SYSTEMS, INC.

666 GRAND AVE STE 3100
DES MOINES, IA 503092500
Phone: 515 245-2500
Fax: –
Web: www.ruan.com

CEO: –
CFO: –
HR: –
FYE: June 30
Type: Private

Ruan (pronounced RUE-on) Transportation Management Systems is confident that its trucking customers do not rue the day (just the opposite) they picked Ruan to help them with their trucking activities. Family-owned Ruan provides a variety of trucking-related services including dedicated contract carriage, transportation of liquid and dry bulk cargo, and logistics, such as warehouse management and freight brokerage. For dedicated contract carriage customers, Ruan assigns drivers and equipment to an account long-term. In total, the company operates a fleet of 3,951 tractors, and 7,500 trailers across the US.

RUBICON GENOMICS, INC.

4743 VENTURE DR
ANN ARBOR, MI 481089560
Phone: 734 677-4845
Fax: –
Web: –

CEO: –
CFO: –
HR: –
FYE: December 31
Type: Private

Rubicon Genomics is stoked about its amp technology. The company makes DNA and RNA amplification kits to assist life sciences researchers in their quest to study the human genome. Cancer diagnostics are another focus for the company. Its MethylPlex product tests for diseased tissue linked to the regulation of certain cancer genes. Other products on the market include GenomePlex, which is a research kit used for whole genome amplification and PicoPlex tests for single cell testing. The company also provides contract research services to pharmaceutical companies, academic institutions, and other entities. Takara Holding's Takara Bio USA Holdings unit acquired Rubicon Genomics for some $75 million in early 2017.

	Annual Growth	12/99	12/00	12/01	12/02	12/15
Sales ($mil.)	22.1%	–	–	0.5	0.5	8.3
Net income ($ mil.)	–	–	–	(1.8)	3.7	1.3
Market value ($ mil.)	–	–	–	–	–	–
Employees	–	–	–	–	–	10

RUBICON TECHNOLOGY INC

NBB: RBCN

900 East Green Street
Bensenville, IL 60106
Phone: 847 295-7000
Fax: –
Web: www.rubicontechnology.com

CEO: –
CFO: –
HR: –
FYE: December 31
Type: Public

Sapphires are the jewel in Rubicon Technology's crown. Using proprietary crystal growth technology, Rubicon makes sapphire materials, wafers, and components for a variety of products. In the field of optoelectronics, the vertically integrated company makes sapphire components for light-emitting diodes (LEDs) used in cell phones, video screens, and other items. Rubicon's sapphire materials also are used for compound semiconductor manufacturing and laser imaging. In the telecom sector, the company's silicon materials are in demand for the silicon-on-sapphire (SOS) components of cellular and fiber-optics products. The majority of its sales are to customers in Asia.

	Annual Growth	12/18	12/19	12/20	12/21	12/22
Sales ($mil.)	(1.9%)	3.9	3.5	4.5	4.1	3.6
Net income ($ mil.)	(0.7%)	1.0	(1.1)	(1.1)	(0.7)	0.9
Market value ($ mil.)	(31.5%)	19.5	20.5	22.3	22.1	4.3
Employees	(6.9%)	16	22	18	13	12

RUBY TUESDAY, INC.

216 E CHURCH AVE
MARYVILLE, TN 378045738
Phone: 865 379-5700
Fax: –
Web: www.rubytuesday.com

CEO: Miranda Welch
CFO: Sue Briley
HR: –
FYE: June 06
Type: Private

Founded in 1972, Ruby Tuesday currently owns, operates, and franchises casual dining restaurants across the US, Guam, and in about five foreign countries under the Ruby Tuesday brand. Its menu features signature choices like its Endless Garden Bar with more than 55 fresh ingredients, its delicious ribs with five bold flavors, and its broad selection of premium handcrafted burgers. The full-service eateries offer a menu of American and ethnic foods, including its signature Handcrafted Burgers, create your own fresh garden salad, pasta, and Burrito Bowls. Ruby Tuesday, is dedicated to delighting guests with exceptional casual dining experiences that offer uncompromising quality paired with passionate service every visit.

RUDOLPH AND SLETTEN, INC.

120 CONSTITUTION DR
MENLO PARK, CA 940251107
Phone: 650 216-3600
Fax: –
Web: www.rsconstruction.com

CEO: –
CFO: –
HR: Chris Bloyer
FYE: December 31
Type: Private

Rudolph and Sletten ... the little-known tenth reindeer? More like the elves who built Santa's workshop. The firm is a mainstay of the California construction scene, especially Silicon Valley. It has built corporate campuses for Apple, Microsoft, and Wells Fargo, as well as Lucasfilm's Skywalker Ranch production facility. Rudolph and Sletten is one of the US' largest general building contractors, with site selection, design/build, and construction management capabilities. Key projects also include biotech labs, hospitals, and schools. Onslow "Rudy" Rudolph founded the company in 1959 and was joined by partner Kenneth Sletten in 1962. Rudolph and Sletten is a subsidiary of Tutor Perini Corporation.

	Annual Growth	12/12	12/13	12/14	12/15	12/16
Sales ($mil.)	25.2%	–	666.0	637.1	940.4	1,307.8
Net income ($ mil.)	–	–	(0.0)	3.2	7.0	14.9
Market value ($ mil.)	–	–	–	–	–	–
Employees	–	–	–	–	–	700

RUMSEY ELECTRIC COMPANY

15 COLWELL LN
CONSHOHOCKEN, PA 194281878
Phone: 610 832-9000
Fax: –
Web: www.rumsey.com

CEO: –
CFO: –
HR: –
FYE: December 31
Type: Private

Rumsey Electric distributes electrical construction equipment, utility products and services, and systems for relay and power, and lighting for retailers. Operating through one central distribution facility and a dozen branches, the company also offers training and consulting services which can also include site visit to evaluate current physical and logical design. It is the authorized distributor of Rockwell Automation, a large industrial automation firm. The company operates through its 135,000 sq. ft. central distribution facility and more than 10 branch locations, primarily located in Delaware, Pennsylvania, and New Jersey. Employee-owned, Rumsey Electric has been in business for over 110 years.

	Annual Growth	12/14	12/15	12/16	12/17	12/18
Sales ($mil.)	(0.4%)	–	223.1	218.2	211.8	220.6
Net income ($ mil.)	9.3%	–	8.0	7.2	11.7	10.5
Market value ($ mil.)	–	–	–	–	–	–
Employees	–	–	–	–	–	284

RURAL SCHOOL AND COMMUNITY TRUST

4301 CONN AVE NW STE 100
WASHINGTON, DC 200082304
Phone: 202 822-3919
Fax: –
Web: www.ruraledu.org

CEO: Alan Richard
CFO: –
HR: –
FYE: June 30
Type: Private

The Rural School and Community Trust is dedicated to improving the quality of education in areas without a lot of funding. The nonprofit provides training, technical assistance, and mentoring to teachers and communities in all 50 states. It focuses on communities affected by poverty, racism, major economic changes, and shifts in population. The Rural Trust publishes research and analysis to raise awareness and affect national policy concerning rural education issues. It also works to enhance communities by involving students in civic action and community building. Supporters include Archer Daniels Midland Company, The Ford Foundation, McMaster-Carr Supply, Providence College, and W.K. Kellogg Foundation.

	Annual Growth	06/11	06/12	06/13	06/14	06/15
Sales ($mil.)	(20.0%)	–	1.2	2.4	5.1	0.6
Net income ($ mil.)	–	–	(1.4)	(0.9)	(1.9)	(1.2)
Market value ($ mil.)	–	–	–	–	–	–
Employees	–	–	–	–	–	4

RUSH COPLEY MEDICAL CENTER

2000 OGDEN AVE
AURORA, IL 605045893
Phone: 630 978-6200
Fax: –
Web: www.rush.edu

CEO: John Diederich
CFO: –
HR: Darla Mullner
FYE: June 30
Type: Private

People in a rush to get healthy can find help at Rush-Copley Medical Center. A member of the Rush System for Health family, the medical center serves Illinois' Fox Valley area. The hospital has about 210 beds and provides acute and tertiary medical services, including cardiac care, cancer treatment, neurology, women's services, neonatal care, and health education programs. Its Rush-Copley Surgery Center performs both day surgeries and inpatient procedures while its nearby Rush-Copley Healthcare Center houses doctors' offices and offers outpatient diagnostic imaging services. Other programs include a neuroscience center, a home health care agency, and its Healthplex fitness center.

RUSH ENTERPRISES INC.

NMS: RUSH A

555 I.H. 35 South, Suite 500
New Braunfels, TX 78130
Phone: 830 302-5200
Fax: –
Web: www.rushenterprises.com

CEO: W M Rush
CFO: Steven L Keller
HR: –
FYE: December 31
Type: Public

Rush Enterprises operates a growing network of more than 125 commercial vehicle and service dealerships under the name Rush Truck Centers in nearly 25 states. It is one of the largest Peterbilt truck dealers in the US, but it also sells trucks manufactured by Blue Bird, Ford, Isuzu, Hino, and IC Bus. Additionally, Rush offers aftermarket parts and services, such as body shop repairs, insurance and third-party financing, and rentals and leasing. Founded in 1965, Rush's reach has spread as far as California and Florida. Late chairman W. Marvin Rush's family control the rapidly growing company.

	Annual Growth	12/19	12/20	12/21	12/22	12/23
Sales ($mil.)	8.1%	5,809.8	4,735.9	5,126.1	7,101.7	7,925.0
Net income ($ mil.)	25.1%	141.6	114.9	241.4	391.4	347.1
Market value ($ mil.)	2.0%	3,618.9	3,223.5	4,330.2	4,068.7	3,914.6
Employees	2.1%	7,244	6,307	7,166	7,418	7,860

RUSH SYSTEM FOR HEALTH

1645 W JACKSON BLVD # 501
CHICAGO, IL 606122847
Phone: 312 942-4061
Fax: –
Web: www.rush-health.com

CEO: –
CFO: –
HR: –
FYE: June 30
Type: Private

With its comprehensive health care offerings and multiple facilities, Rush System for Health is in a hurry to get Chicagoans hale and hearty. The health system's cornerstone is the Rush University Medical Center, a more than 670-bed academic medical facility that includes a medical school (Rush University), a children's hospital, and an inpatient rehabilitation and skilled nursing facility (the Johnston R. Bowman Health Center). The Rush System family also includes Rush-Copley Medical Center, Rush North Shore Medical Center, and affiliated community hospitals Rush Oak Park Hospital and Riverside HealthCare.

	Annual Growth	06/06	06/07	06/08	06/12	06/15
Sales ($mil.)	5.5%	–	–	1.2	1.7	1.8
Net income ($ mil.)	–	–	–	(0.0)	(0.1)	(0.0)
Market value ($ mil.)	–	–	–	–	–	–
Employees	–	–	–	–	–	10,700

RUSH TRUCKING CORPORATION

35160 E MICHIGAN AVE
WAYNE, MI 481843698
Phone: 734 641-1711
Fax: –
Web: www.rushtrucking.com

CEO: Andra M Rush
CFO: –
HR: Maynard Borowski
FYE: June 30
Type: Private

In a hurry? Rush Trucking provides truckload transportation services across North America fueled by a fleet of some 1,500 tractors, 3,000 trailers, 100 straight trucks, and 45 flatbeds. Auto OEMs in the US and Canada (Ford, GM, Honda, and Toyota) are among the company's major customers, as well as many Tier 1 auto suppliers. Rush Trucking offers a slate of transportation and logistics services, from short- and long-haul to just-in-time, jointly with affiliates E.D.S. (expedited delivery), RayCan Transport (truckload service in Canada and the US), and Rush Distribution Service (logistics). President and CEO Andra Rush founded Rush Trucking in 1984; it is the largest Native American-owned business in the US.

RUSSELL COUNTY MEDICAL CENTER INC

58 CARROLL ST
LEBANON, VA 24266
Phone: 276 883-8000
Fax: –
Web: www.balladhealth.org

CEO: Eddie Greene
CFO: –
HR: –
FYE: September 30
Type: Private

If you're in the mountains of Virginia and find you need a little first aid, Russell County Medical Center (RCMC) could be the place for you. Part of Mountain States Health Alliance, the 80-bed facility provides a variety of medical, surgical, and therapeutic services through its hospital, outpatient centers, and physical therapy office in southwest Virginia. RCMC also offers home health and hospice care, as well as inpatient psychiatric treatment and emergency medicine. RCMC became a part of MSHA in 2008. The hospital was previously a member of Community Health Systems.

	Annual Growth	09/10	09/11	09/12	09/13	09/15
Sales ($mil.)	(5.4%)	–	–	–	19.4	17.4
Net income ($ mil.)	–	–	–	–	(1.9)	(4.7)
Market value ($ mil.)	–	–	–	–	–	–
Employees	–	–	–	–	–	1

RUSSELL SIGLER, INC.

9702 W TONTO ST
TOLLESON, AZ 853539703
Phone: 623 388-5100
Fax: –
Web: www.siglers.com

CEO: –
CFO: –
HR: Diana Lopez
FYE: December 31
Type: Private

Russell Sigler has built a business providing a rather cool service in a hot region. Through about 30 offices located primarily in California and Arizona (but also in Idaho, Nevada, New Mexico, and Texas), the company provides commercial and residential air conditioning contractors with equipment, parts, supplies, and technical support. Its brands include Carrier, Bryant, and Payne. Russell Sigler has distributed Carrier products for more than 60 years. As part of its business, the company also operates a residential and commercial distribution joint venture with industry giant Carrier. Russell Sigler owns a 60% stake while Carrier holds 40%.

	Annual Growth	12/07	12/08	12/09	12/13	12/14
Sales ($mil.)	19.4%	–	176.9	140.2	488.7	513.4
Net income ($ mil.)	38.4%	–	1.5	(0.5)	6.6	10.2
Market value ($ mil.)	–	–	–	–	–	–
Employees	–	–	–	–	–	912

RUTHERFORD ELECTRIC MEMBERSHIP CORPORATION

186 HUDLOW RD
FOREST CITY, NC 280432575
Phone: 704 245-1621
Fax: –
Web: www.remc.com

CEO: –
CFO: –
HR: –
FYE: December 31
Type: Private

Through a kind of power sharing "brotherhood," Rutherford Electric Membership Corporation provides power to more than 67,000 members located in 10 counties (Burke, Catawba, Caldwell, Cleveland, Gaston, Lincoln, McDowell, Mitchell, Polk and Rutherford) in the Southwestern Piedmont region of North Carolina. The cooperative (which had a membership of only 394 in 1938, but grew rapidly after WWII) owns and maintains about 7,000 miles of power line. Rutherford Electric has total assets of more than $300 million. The cooperative is a member of the Touchstone Energy Cooperatives network.

	Annual Growth	12/15	12/16	12/18	12/21	12/22
Sales ($mil.)	1.9%	–	138.4	141.4	140.3	154.8
Net income ($ mil.)	–	–	0.1	(0.3)	–	–
Market value ($ mil.)	–	–	–	–	–	–
Employees	–	–	–	–	–	178

RWJ BARNABAS HEALTH, INC.

95 OLD SHORT HILLS RD
WEST ORANGE, NJ 070521008
Phone: 973 322-4000
Fax: –
Web: www.rwjbh.org

CEO: Barry Ostrowsky
CFO: Peter Bihuniak
HR: James Rolek
FYE: June 30
Type: Private

RWJ Barnabas Health is the largest and most comprehensive healthcare system in the state of New Jersey. It was formed by the merger of New Jersey health systems Barnabas Health and Robert Wood Johnson. It operates more than 10 acute care hospitals (including Monmouth Medical Center Southern Campus and Newark Beth Israel Medical Center), three acute care children's hospitals, a pediatric rehabilitation hospital with a network of outpatient centers, a freestanding 100-bed behavioral health center, two trauma centers, a satellite emergency department, geriatric centers, and ambulatory care center. RWJ Barnabas employs more than 9,000 physicians statewide and trains approximately 1,000 residents and interns each year. One of the New Jersey's largest private employer, RWJ Barnabas also operates the state's largest behavioral health network.

	Annual Growth	12/17	12/18	12/19	12/20*	06/21
Sales ($mil.)	(15.7%)	–	5,351.3	5,624.9	5,900.6	3,211.0
Net income ($ mil.)	221.2%	–	9.8	602.9	940.6	324.9
Market value ($ mil.)	–	–	–	–	–	–
Employees	–	–	–	–	–	34,000

*Fiscal year change

RYAN BUILDING GROUP, INC.

2700 PATRIOT BLVD STE 430
GLENVIEW, IL 600268078
Phone: 847 995-8700
Fax: –
Web: www.williamryanhomes.com

CEO: –
CFO: John Rushin
HR: –
FYE: December 31
Type: Private

Ryan Building Group understands that there's no place like home, there's no place like home, there's no place like home. Doing business as William Ryan Homes, the company builds and sells single-family homes, townhouses, and duplexes in Arizona, Florida, Illinois, Texas, and Wisconsin. Its homes have from two to five bedrooms and range in size from 1,400 sq. ft. to about 3,500 sq. ft. The company also offers mortgages and insurance through affiliates. CEO William Ryan (part of the building family that also spawned the Ryland Group) founded Ryan Building Group in 1992.

	Annual Growth	12/04	12/05	12/06	12/07	12/08
Sales ($mil.)	(43.0%)	–	–	256.4	214.2	83.4
Net income ($ mil.)	–	–	–	4.0	(0.5)	(19.3)
Market value ($ mil.)	–	–	–	–	–	–
Employees	–	–	–	–	–	85

RYAN, LLC

13155 NOEL RD STE 100
DALLAS, TX 752405050
Phone: 972 934-0022
Fax: –
Web: www.ryan.com

CEO: G B Ryan
CFO: David Oldani
HR: –
FYE: December 31
Type: Private

Ryan is the largest tax services and software provider in the world that is solely focused on business taxes. It provides tax advice, preparation, and planning for major corporations and other businesses. The firm specializes in consulting services such as audit defense, dispute resolution, strategic planning, tax process efficiencies, and tax recovery. Ryan addresses a wide range of industries including blockchain and cryptocurrency, business services, construction, food services, healthcare, manufacturing, utilities, real estate, and retail. With offices strategically located around the world, Ryan represents Global 5000 clients in more than 60 countries.

	Annual Growth	12/09	12/10	12/11	12/12	12/13
Sales ($mil.)	30.3%	–	–	225.3	242.0	382.6
Net income ($ mil.)	25.5%	–	–	25.2	9.9	39.6
Market value ($ mil.)	–	–	–	–	–	–
Employees	–	–	–	–	–	1,598

RYDER SYSTEM, INC.   NYS: R

11690 N.W. 105th Street   CEO: Robert E Sanchez
Miami, FL 33178   CFO: John J Diez
Phone: 305 500-3726   HR: -
Fax: -   FYE: December 31
Web: www.ryder.com   Type: Public

Ryder System is a leading logistics and transportation company. The company's Fleet Management Solutions (FMS) segment provides full-service leasing and leasing with flexible maintenance options, commercial rental, and maintenance services of trucks, tractors and trailers to customers principally in the US and Canada. Similarly, the Supply Chain Solutions (SCS) segment provides integrated logistics solutions, including distribution management, dedicated transportation, transportation management, last mile and professional services in North America. The majority of its revenue comes from the US.

	Annual Growth	12/19	12/20	12/21	12/22	12/23
Sales ($mil.)	7.2%	8,925.8	8,420.1	9,663.0	12,011	11,783
Net income ($ mil.)	-	(24.4)	(122.3)	519.0	867.0	406.0
Market value ($ mil.)	20.6%	2,384.3	2,711.4	3,618.8	3,668.9	5,051.4
Employees	4.5%	39,900	39,000	42,800	48,300	47,500

RYERSON HOLDING CORP   NYS: RYI

227 W. Monroe St., 27th Floor   CEO: Edward J Lehner
Chicago, IL 60606   CFO: James J Claussen
Phone: 312 292-5000   HR: -
Fax: -   FYE: December 31
Web: www.ir.ryerson.com   Type: Public

Aspiring to be the one-stop shop for all your metal needs, Ryerson is a leading industrial metal processor and distributor in North America with some 70,000 products to its name. Ryerson is also well known for providing fabrication services, with nearly 100 locations across the US, Mexico, Canada, and China. Its 40,000 customers include various machinery manufacturers, fabricators, and shops. About 90% of the company's total revenue comes from US.

	Annual Growth	12/19	12/20	12/21	12/22	12/23
Sales ($mil.)	3.2%	4,501.6	3,466.6	5,675.3	6,323.6	5,108.7
Net income ($ mil.)	15.3%	82.4	(65.8)	294.3	391.0	145.7
Market value ($ mil.)	30.8%	402.7	464.3	886.7	1,030.0	1,180.4
Employees	0.6%	4,500	3,900	3,700	4,200	4,600

RYMAN HOSPITALITY PROPERTIES INC   NYS: RHP

One Gaylord Drive   CEO: Colin V Reed V
Nashville, TN 37214   CFO: Mark Fioravanti
Phone: 615 316-6000   HR: Dawn Clark
Fax: -   FYE: December 31
Web: www.rymanhp.com   Type: Public

Ryman Hospitality Properties (formerly Gaylord Entertainment) is a leading lodging and hospitality real estate investment trust that specializes in upscale convention center resorts and country music entertainment experiences. It includes the Gaylord Opryland Resort & Convention Center in Nashville, the Gaylord Palms Resort in Florida (close to Disney World), the Gaylord Texan Resort near Dallas, and the Gaylord National Resort and Convention Center in the Washington, DC, area. Ryman-owned assets include a network of five upscale, meetings-focused resorts totaling over 9,915 rooms that are managed by Marriott under the Gaylord Hotels brand.

	Annual Growth	12/19	12/20	12/21	12/22	12/23
Sales ($mil.)	7.7%	1,604.6	524.5	939.4	1,806.0	2,158.1
Net income ($ mil.)	20.9%	145.8	(417.4)	(177.0)	129.0	311.2
Market value ($ mil.)	6.2%	5,116.6	4,000.8	5,429.7	4,828.6	6,498.4
Employees	5.1%	1,206	995	1,061	1,269	1,471

S & B ENGINEERS AND CONSTRUCTORS, LTD.

7825 PARK PLACE BLVD   CEO: JW Brookshire
HOUSTON, TX 770874697   CFO: Kris Barnhill
Phone: 713 645-4141   HR: -
Fax: -   FYE: December 31
Web: www.sbec.com   Type: Private

S & B Engineers and Constructors (S&B) is one of the leading US-based contractors, providing its clients with true in-house engineering, procurement and direct-hire construction services to multiple industries. It primarily focuses on NGL fractionation, import / export terminals, pipelines, petrochemicals & polymers and refining. S&B is the leading American contractor when it comes to the execution of turnkey engineering, procurement and construction (EPC) of export terminals for ethane, propane and other natural gas liquids, as well as various refined products and petrochemicals. S&B India is an engineering center that is fully owned by the company and is located in New Delhi. Collaborating with their team in India is a standard approach to project execution. S&B India is fully integrated within S&B, using their tools, processes, and procedures to provide even more value to its clients' projects. Founded in 1967, S&B was founded by James G. Slaughter, Sr. and Dr. William A. Brookshire.

	Annual Growth	12/14	12/15	12/16	12/17	12/18
Sales ($mil.)	(15.4%)	-	-	950.2	679.5	679.5
Net income ($ mil.)	-	-	-	-	-	-
Market value ($ mil.)	-	-	-	-	-	-
Employees	-	-	-	-	-	7,700

S & T BANCORP INC (INDIANA, PA)   NMS: STBA

800 Philadelphia Street   CEO: David G Antolik
Indiana, PA 15701   CFO: Mark Kochvar
Phone: 800 325-2265   HR: Susan Nicholson
Fax: -   FYE: December 31
Web: www.stbancorp.com   Type: Public

S&T Bancorp is the bank holding company for S&T Bank, which boasts nearly $9.1 billion in assets and serves customers from almost 75 branch offices in Pennsylvania and Ohio. Targeting individuals, institutions, and local businesses, the bank offers consumer, commercial, and small business banking services, which include accepting time and demand deposits and originating commercial and consumer loans, brokerage services, and trust services including serving as executor and trustee under wills and deeds and as guardian and custodian of employee benefits. Commercial loans make up almost 75% of the company's loan portfolio. The bank also originates residential mortgages, construction loans, and consumer loans. Through subsidiaries, S&T Bank sells life, disability, and commercial property/casualty insurance and provides investment management services. S&T Bank was established in 1902.

	Annual Growth	12/19	12/20	12/21	12/22	12/23
Assets ($mil.)	2.2%	8,764.6	8,967.9	9,488.5	9,110.6	9,551.5
Net income ($ mil.)	10.2%	98.2	21.0	110.3	135.5	144.8
Market value ($ mil.)	(4.6%)	1,540.4	949.7	1,205.1	1,306.8	1,277.7
Employees	0.9%	1,201	1,174	1,160	1,182	1,244

S C & A, INC.

2200 WILSON BLVD STE 300   CEO: Gregory Beronja
ARLINGTON, VA 222015411   CFO: -
Phone: 703 893-6600   HR: -
Fax: -   FYE: September 30
Web: www.scainc.com   Type: Private

Environmental engineering and consulting firm SC&A provides emergency response and homeland security services, environmental management, information and communication, waste remediation, and risk assessment services through its offices in New York, New Jersey, Missouri, and Virginia. The company works mainly for agencies of the US government (including the Department of Defense, the Department of Energy, and the Department of Homeland Security); other clients have included Boeing and General Electric. Company chairman Sanford Cohen is the SC in SC&A; his associates are the A. The company was founded in 1981.

	Annual Growth	09/08	09/09	09/10	09/19	09/20
Sales ($mil.)	2.6%	-	7.8	8.0	12.1	10.4
Net income ($ mil.)	-	-	0.4	0.2	0.6	(0.4)
Market value ($ mil.)	-	-	-	-	-	-
Employees	-	-	-	-	-	67

S&ME, INC.

2724 DISCOVERY DR STE 120
RALEIGH, NC 276161940
Phone: 919 872-2660
Fax: –
Web: www.smeinc.com

CEO: –
CFO: Bruce L Altstaetter
HR: –
FYE: December 31
Type: Private

This is not your S&ME old engineering company. S&ME, which services both public and private entities, focuses on environmental and engineering services. The company's main areas of expertise are: geotechnical engineering; environmental engineering; natural and cultural resource preservation; occupational health and safety; constructional materials engineering and testing; and water resources and solid waste engineering. The employee-owned company, which mainly serves clients in the Southeast, operates from more than 26 offices in nine US states.

	Annual Growth	12/11	12/12	12/13	12/14	12/16
Sales ($mil.)	14.2%	–	–	–	133.6	174.2
Net income ($ mil.)	(3.5%)	–	–	–	2.8	2.6
Market value ($ mil.)	–	–	–	–	–	–
Employees	–	–	–	–	–	1,115

S&P GLOBAL INC

NYS: SPGI

55 Water Street
New York, NY 10041
Phone: 212 438-1000
Fax: –
Web: www.spglobal.com

CEO: Douglas L Peterson
CFO: Ewout L Steenbergen
HR: Carmen Sargent
FYE: December 31
Type: Public

S&P Global is a provider of credit ratings, benchmarks, analytics and workflow solutions in the global capital, commodity, automotive and engineering markets. The capital markets include asset managers, investment banks, commercial banks, insurance companies, exchanges, trading firms and issuers; the commodity markets include producers, traders and intermediaries within energy, petrochemicals, metals & steel and agriculture; the automotive markets include manufacturers, suppliers, dealerships and service shops; and the engineering markets include engineers, builders, and architects. The company serves its global customers through a broad range of products and services available through both third-party and proprietary distribution channels. S&P Global's largest market is the US, which generates about 60% of the company's total sales.

	Annual Growth	12/19	12/20	12/21	12/22	12/23
Sales ($mil.)	16.9%	6,699.0	7,442.0	8,297.0	11,181	12,497
Net income ($ mil.)	5.5%	2,123.0	2,339.0	3,024.0	3,248.0	2,626.0
Market value ($ mil.)	12.7%	87,922	105,851	151,961	107,851	141,847
Employees	15.8%	22,500	23,000	22,850	39,950	40,450

S&W SEED CO.

NAS: SANW

2101 Ken Pratt Blvd., Suite 201
Longmont, CO 80501
Phone: 720 506-9191
Fax: –
Web: www.swseedco.com

CEO: Mark Herrmann
CFO: Elizabeth Horton
HR: –
FYE: June 30
Type: Public

S&W Seed breeds seeds of the alfalfa variety. The agricultural company contracts locally grown alfalfa seeds from farmers in California's San Joaquin Valley, processes them at its production facility, and sells them to agribusinesses and farmers worldwide for use in growing animal feed -- particularly alfalfa hay -- for dairy and beef cattle, horses, and other livestock. About 50% of its certified seeds are sold to customers in the Middle East and Latin America, since the varieties it produces are better suited for warmer climates. S&W Seed also produces wheat on occasion and supplies PureCircle with stevia, a natural no-calorie sweetener. The company went public in May 2010.

	Annual Growth	06/19	06/20	06/21	06/22	06/23
Sales ($mil.)	(9.5%)	109.7	79.6	84.0	71.4	73.5
Net income ($ mil.)	–	(9.3)	(19.7)	(19.2)	(36.4)	14.4
Market value ($ mil.)	(17.6%)	113.5	98.0	156.4	43.0	52.4
Employees	5.0%	126	186	195	180	153

SABEL STEEL SERVICE, INC.

749 N COURT ST
MONTGOMERY, AL 361042301
Phone: 334 265-6771
Fax: –
Web: www.sabelsteel.com

CEO: –
CFO: –
HR: –
FYE: December 31
Type: Private

Sabel Steel processes and distributes steel products through six service centers in Alabama, Georgia, and Lousiana. The company's facilities handle products such as angles, bars, channels, pipe, plate, sheet, structural beams, and tubing. Other Sabel Steel units recycle scrap metal and fabricate reinforcing bar (rebar). The company's Sabel Wholesale Center distributes hardware and plumbing supplies. Sabel Steel, which is owned by the Sabel family, was founded in 1856.

SABINE ROYALTY TRUST

NYS: SBR

Argent Trust Company, 2911 Turtle Creek Boulevard, Suite 850
Dallas, TX 75219
Phone: 855 588-7839
Fax: 214 508-2431
Web: www.sbr-sabine.com

CEO: –
CFO: –
HR: –
FYE: December 31
Type: Public

Sabine Royalty Trust owns royalty interests in oil and gas properties located on about 2.1 million gross acres (216,551 net) in Florida, Louisiana, Mississippi, New Mexico, Oklahoma, and Texas. The trust, which was formed in 1983, receives royalties based on the amount of oil and gas produced and sold and distributes them on a monthly basis to shareholders. Although royalty trusts distribute essentially all royalties received to shareholders (at substantial tax advantage), their profitability depends on the price of oil and gas and the continued productivity of the properties. Sabine Royalty Trust's properties have proved reserves of about 5.3 million barrels of oil and 35.6 billion cu. ft. of natural gas.

	Annual Growth	12/19	12/20	12/21	12/22	12/23
Sales ($mil.)	18.9%	46.9	36.4	60.9	126.0	93.8
Net income ($ mil.)	19.6%	44.0	33.3	57.9	122.7	90.3
Market value ($ mil.)	13.9%	587.5	411.4	607.7	1,245.8	989.4
Employees	–	–	–	–	–	–

SABRA HEALTH CARE REIT INC

NMS: SBRA

18500 Von Karman Avenue, Suite 550
Irvine, CA 92612
Phone: 888 393-8248
Fax: –
Web: www.sabrahealth.com

CEO: –
CFO: –
HR: –
FYE: December 31
Type: Public

Sabra Health Care REIT is a self-administered, self-managed REIT that, through its subsidiaries, owns and invests in real estate serving the healthcare industry. The company invests in income-producing health care facilities in Canada and the US. The REIT's investment portfolio includes about 400 properties, most of which are skilled nursing/transitional care facilities. It also invests in assisted and independent living, memory care and select behavioral health and addiction treatment centers and hospitals. Sabra's facilities house about 39,985 beds in the US and Canada.

	Annual Growth	12/19	12/20	12/21	12/22	12/23
Sales ($mil.)	(0.5%)	661.7	598.6	569.5	624.8	647.5
Net income ($ mil.)	(33.2%)	69.0	138.4	(113.3)	(77.6)	13.8
Market value ($ mil.)	(9.6%)	4,935.2	4,017.1	3,131.3	2,874.6	3,300.2
Employees	9.0%	34	38	42	42	48

SABRE CORP

NMS: SABR

3150 Sabre Drive
Southlake, TX 76092
Phone: 682 605-1000
Fax: –
Web: www.sabre.com

CEO: Sean Menke
CFO: Douglas Barnett
HR: Jodi Rapicano
FYE: December 31
Type: Public

Sabre is a software and technology company that powers the global travel industry. The company connects the world's leading travel suppliers, including airlines, hotels, car rental brands, rail carriers, cruise lines, and tour operators with travel buyers in a comprehensive travel marketplace. In addition, the company also provides software technology products and solutions, through software-as-a-service, and hosted delivery models, to airlines and other travel suppliers. Serving more than 42,000 properties in more than 175 countries, the company generates about 40% of the company's revenue from customers in the US.

	Annual Growth	12/19	12/20	12/21	12/22	12/23
Sales ($mil.)	(7.5%)	3,975.0	1,334.1	1,688.9	2,537.0	2,907.7
Net income ($ mil.)	–	158.6	(1,272.7)	(928.5)	(435.4)	(527.6)
Market value ($ mil.)	(33.5%)	8,517.5	4,562.4	3,260.5	2,345.7	1,670.1
Employees	(9.4%)	9,250	7,531	7,583	7,461	6,232

SACRAMENTO MUNICIPAL UTILITY DISTRICT

6201 S ST
SACRAMENTO, CA 958171818
Phone: 916 452-3211
Fax: –
Web: www.smud.org

CEO: Arlen Orchard
CFO: Jim Tracy
HR: Celine Nguyen
FYE: December 31
Type: Private

The company is one of the largest locally-owned electric utilities in the US, SMUD serves more than 600,000 residential and commercial customer meters (a service area population of approximately 1.5 million) in California's Sacramento and Placer counties. SMUD is responsible for the acquisition, generation, transmission and distribution of electric power to its service area. It began serving Sacramento in 1946.

	Annual Growth	12/18	12/19	12/20	12/21	12/22
Sales ($mil.)	11.3%	–	1,559.2	1,587.9	1,790.6	2,147.3
Net income ($ mil.)	(3.7%)	–	78.9	153.2	339.6	70.5
Market value ($ mil.)	–	–	–	–	–	–
Employees	–	–	–	–	–	2,213

SACRED HEART HEALTH SYSTEM, INC.

5151 N 9TH AVE
PENSACOLA, FL 325048721
Phone: 850 416-1600
Fax: –
Web: healthcare.ascension.org

CEO: –
CFO: Buddy Elmore
HR: –
FYE: June 30
Type: Private

Part of Ascension Health, the Sacred Heart Health System serves residents of Northwestern Florida, primarily through the Sacred Heart Hospital of Pensacola. With more than 560 beds altogether, the acute care medical center boasts the Sacred Heart Children's Hospital, the Sacred Heart Women's Hospital, and the Sacred Heart Regional Heart and Vascular Institute. Sacred Heart Hospital of Pensacola also specializes in trauma care, heart disease, cancer care, weight loss, stroke care, neurology, and orthopedics. It has an educational affiliation with Florida State University College of Medicine. Sacred Heart Health System operates additional acute, long-term, primary, and specialty care centers in the region.

SACRED HEART HOSPITAL OF ALLENTOWN

421 CHEW ST
ALLENTOWN, PA 181023406
Phone: 610 776-4500
Fax: –
Web: www.slhn.org

CEO: –
CFO: Thomas Regner
HR: Vince Sparks
FYE: June 30
Type: Private

Hearts (and all other parts of the body) are sacred to Sacred Heart Hospital of Allentown. The acute care facility has some 230 beds and serves the residents of Pennsylvania's Lehigh Valley. Specialty services include pediatrics, cardiology, obstetrics, weight-loss surgery, orthopedics, behavioral health, and cancer treatment. Sacred Heart Hospital is part of the Sacred Heart Health System, which also operates more than a dozen family practice clinics, as well as specialty clinics, long-term care facilities, and imaging and rehabilitation centers. The hospital was founded by the Missionary Sisters of the Most Sacred Heart (a Catholic religious order) in 1912.

	Annual Growth	06/15	06/16	06/18	06/19	06/20
Sales ($mil.)	(4.8%)	–	106.3	26.2	74.4	87.5
Net income ($ mil.)	–	–	10.7	(2.5)	(1.4)	(12.2)
Market value ($ mil.)	–	–	–	–	–	–
Employees	–	–	–	–	–	1,058

SACRED HEART HOSPITAL OF THE HOSPITAL SISTERS OF THE THIRD ORDER OF ST. FRANCIS

900 W CLAIREMONT AVE
EAU CLAIRE, WI 547016122
Phone: 715 717-3926
Fax: –
Web: www.hshs.org

CEO: Julie Manas
CFO: –
HR: Julia V Loo
FYE: June 30
Type: Private

Sacred Heart Hospital not only cares for hearts that are holey, but also for the rest of what ails residents of western Wisconsin. The more than 300-bed medical center provides specialized services that include cardiology, cancer care, pediatrics, and emergency medicine. The hospital provides community-wide care through affiliations with the Marshfield Clinic (a provider network with more than 700 physicians), Oakleaf Medical Network (an organization of providers and clinics), and Infinity Healthcare and Pathology Services (supplies the hospital with medical x-ray professionals). Founded in 1889 by the Hospital Sisters of the Third Order of St. Francis, the center is part of the Hospital Sisters Health System.

	Annual Growth	06/18	06/19	06/20	06/21	06/22
Sales ($mil.)	2.4%	–	219.5	216.0	252.8	235.9
Net income ($ mil.)	–	–	15.1	(7.4)	23.5	(9.5)
Market value ($ mil.)	–	–	–	–	–	–
Employees	–	–	–	–	–	1,010

SADDLEBACK MEMORIAL MEDICAL CENTER

24451 HEALTH CENTER DR FL 1
LAGUNA HILLS, CA 926533689
Phone: 949 837-4500
Fax: –
Web: www.memorialcare.org

CEO: Steve Geidt
CFO: Aaron Coley
HR: –
FYE: June 30
Type: Private

Saddleback Memorial Medical Center, part of Memorial Health Services (MHS) serves the residents of southern Orange County in California. With some 325 beds, the not-for-profit medical center provides general medical and surgical services, as well as specialty care in areas such as cancer, heart disease, and physical rehabilitation. It operates two campuses, one in Laguna Hills and one in San Clemente. The medical center also features several facilities for women's health, including the Saddleback Women's Hospital and the MemorialCare Breast Center. In addition, Saddleback Memorial provides home health care and hospice services.

SADDLEBROOK RESORTS, INC.

5700 SADDLEBROOK WAY
WESLEY CHAPEL, FL 335434499
Phone: 813 973-1111
Fax: –
Web: www.saddlebrook.com

CEO: –
CFO: –
HR: –
FYE: December 31
Type: Private

Don't expect to see horses saddled up at the creek at Saddlebrook Resorts. Located on approximately 480 Florida acres, the facility contains some 550 condos and hotel rooms, conference facilities, three restaurants, a spa, and retail shops. Recreational opportunities include two 18-hole golf courses, three swimming pools, 45 tennis courts, and a fitness center. The resort is also home to an accredited preparatory school and a tennis training facility. (All students enrolled in Saddlebrook Prep are also enrolled in either the Saddlebrook Tennis Program or the Arnold Palmer Golf Academy.) Chairman and CEO Thomas Dempsey and his family own the company.

SAFECO INSURANCE COMPANY OF AMERICA

SAFECO Plaza
Seattle, WA 98185
Phone: 206 545-5000
Fax: 206 545-5363
Web: www.safeco.com

CEO: –
CFO: –
HR: –
FYE: December 31
Type: Public

While the name doesn't tell you much about the business, Safeco does sound secure, and with insurance that counts for a lot. Safeco Insurance offers personal property/casualty insurance including auto, homeowners, and fire coverage. In addition to its bread and butter standard products, it also offers specialty products including classic car insurance, rental property insurance, and personal umbrella coverage. Its policies are sold and maintained nationally through a network of independent agents and brokers. Safeco is a subsidiary of Liberty Mutual.

	Annual Growth	12/97	12/98	12/99	12/00	12/01
Assets ($mil.)	5.6%	2,731.4	3,121.0	3,246.1	2,999.5	3,394.8
Net income ($ mil.)	–	168.5	168.3	93.6	36.7	(22.1)
Market value ($ mil.)	–	–	–	–	–	–
Employees	–	–	–	–	–	–

SAFEGUARD SCIENTIFICS, INC.

150 N. Radnor Chester Road, Suite F-200
Radnor, PA 19087
Phone: 610 293-0600
Fax: 610 293-0601
Web: www.safeguard.com

NBB: SFES
CEO: Eric C Salzman
CFO: Mark A Herndon
HR: –
FYE: December 31
Type: Public

Safeguard Scientifics' goal is to nurture investments, not protect Poindexters in a lab. The firm invests in growth-stage health care and technology ventures with prospects for growth. It focuses on companies involved in the development of diagnostics, medical devices, specialty pharmaceuticals, new media, and financial services and health care information technology. Safeguard Scientifics has significant minority stakes in about 15 companies; holdings include healthcare AI firm Prognos Health, financial technology firm, Lumesis, and Flashtalking, a data-driven ad management and analytics technology company. Safeguard Scientifics was founded in 1953.

	Annual Growth	12/19	12/20	12/21	12/22	12/23
Sales ($mil.)	–	–	–	–	–	–
Net income ($ mil.)	–	54.6	(37.6)	27.0	(14.3)	(9.8)
Market value ($ mil.)	(48.3%)	182.6	106.1	122.2	51.5	13.0
Employees	–	–	–	–	–	–

SAFEHOLD INC (NEW)

1114 Avenue of the Americas, 39th Floor
New York, NY 10036
Phone: 212 930-9400
Fax: –
Web: www.istar.com

NYS: SAFE
CEO: –
CFO: –
HR: –
FYE: December 31
Type: Public

iStar finances, invests in and develops real estate and real estate related projects as part of its fully-integrated investment platform. The company also manages entities focused on ground lease and net lease investments. The company has invested over $40 billion over the past two decades and is structured as a real estate investment trust (REIT) with a diversified portfolio focused on larger assets located in major metropolitan markets. Its operating properties represent a pool of assets across a broad range of geographies and property types including industrial, hotel, multifamily, retail, condominium, entertainment/leisure and office properties. Office properties make up of some 20% of its secured assets, while land makes up another about 5%.

	Annual Growth	12/19	12/20	12/21	12/22	12/23
Sales ($mil.)	(7.4%)	479.5	530.9	308.6	158.1	352.6
Net income ($ mil.)	–	324.0	(42.4)	132.5	421.3	(55.0)
Market value ($ mil.)	(12.7%)	2,864.4	5,152.4	5,675.5	2,034.2	1,663.2
Employees	(13.7%)	155	143	144	118	86

SAFETY INSURANCE GROUP, INC.

20 Custom House Street
Boston, MA 02110
Phone: 617 951-0600
Fax: 617 603-4837
Web: www.safetyinsurance.com

NMS: SAFT
CEO: George M Murphy
CFO: William J Begley Jr
HR: –
FYE: December 31
Type: Public

Safety Insurance Group, through subsidiaries Safety Insurance, Safety Indemnity, and Safety Property and Casualty, sells property/casualty insurance exclusively in Massachusetts, Maine, and New Hampshire. It is one of the top private passenger automobile and commercial automobile insurers in the region, controlling about 10% of the markets in its home state. Safety Insurance also provides homeowners, dwelling fire, personal umbrella, and business-owner policies; it cross-sells its non-auto property/casualty products to increase its share of the market. The company sells its products through more than 855 independent agents and about 1,090 offices.

	Annual Growth	12/19	12/20	12/21	12/22	12/23
Assets ($mil.)	0.9%	2,022.7	2,054.3	2,117.4	1,972.6	2,094.0
Net income ($ mil.)	(34.0%)	99.6	138.2	130.7	46.6	18.9
Market value ($ mil.)	(4.8%)	1,368.7	1,152.3	1,257.8	1,246.4	1,124.0
Employees	(3.0%)	609	586	552	538	539

SAGA COMMUNICATIONS INC

73 Kercheval Avenue
Grosse Pointe Farms, MI 48236
Phone: 313 886-7070
Fax: 313 886-7150
Web: www.sagacom.com

NMS: SGA
CEO: Edward K Christian
CFO: Samuel D Bush
HR: –
FYE: December 31
Type: Public

Saga Communications is a leading radio broadcaster that focuses on acquiring, developing, and operating broadcast properties. The company has roughly 115 stations serving more than 25 markets offering a variety of formats, including sports, talk, and news, as well as several music formats. Some of these formats include Classic Hits, Adult Hits, Top 40, and Country, among others. Most of the stations serve small and midsize markets. Its stations employ audience promotions to further develop and secure a loyal following. The company was originally a Delaware corporation that was organized in 1986.

	Annual Growth	12/18	12/19	12/20	12/21	12/22
Sales ($mil.)	(2.1%)	124.8	123.1	95.8	108.3	114.9
Net income ($ mil.)	(9.5%)	13.7	13.3	(1.9)	11.2	9.2
Market value ($ mil.)	(8.2%)	203.1	185.8	146.8	147.8	144.3
Employees	(5.9%)	1,031	1,002	828	797	810

SAGARSOFT INC.

200 GLASTONBURY BLVD STE 304
GLASTONBURY, CT 060334418
Phone: 860 633-2025
Fax: –
Web: www.sagarsoft.com

CEO: –
CFO: –
HR: –
FYE: March 31
Type: Private

Sagarsoft hopes to take all of the hard work out of information technology. The company provides information technology (IT) services such as software development, data warehousing, and enterprise application integration. Additional offerings include project management, network design, systems architecture, and support. Sagarsoft's clients have included Pfizer, General Electric, Sprint, and CA. It has partnered with technology products providers including Microsoft, Oracle, Cisco, and others. The company was founded in 1995

	Annual Growth	03/15	03/16	03/17	03/18	03/19
Sales ($mil.)	7.9%	–	16.3	16.3	18.9	20.5
Net income ($ mil.)	28.3%	–	0.2	0.2	0.2	0.3
Market value ($ mil.)	–	–	–	–	–	–
Employees	–	–	–	–	–	95

SAGE HOSPITALITY RESOURCES L.L.C.

1575 WELTON ST STE 300
DENVER, CO 802024218
Phone: 303 595-7200
Fax: –
Web: www.sagehospitalitygroup.com

CEO: Walter Isenberg
CFO: –
HR: Hayley McGettigan
FYE: October 08
Type: Private

Sage Hospitality Resources is wise to the ways of luxurious lodgings. The company is a leading hotel developer and operator. Its portfolio includes full- and limited-service hotels operating under such banners as Marriott, Starwood, and Hilton; it also has independent properties such as Chicago's Essex Inn and The Oxford Hotel in Denver. In addition to its hotels business, the company has restaurant operations devoted to developing restaurants and lounges adjacent to its hotels in major urban locations. CEO Walter Isenberg and his business partner Zack Neumeyer started Sage Hospitality Resources in 1984.

SAGE THERAPEUTICS INC

NMS: SAGE

215 First Street
Cambridge, MA 02142
Phone: 617 299-8380
Fax: 617 299-8379
Web: www.sagerx.com

CEO: –
CFO: –
HR: –
FYE: December 31
Type: Public

Sage Therapeutics is a biopharmaceutical company committed to developing and commercializing novel medicines with the potential to transform the lives of people with debilitating disorders of the brain. Its lead product, Zulresso drug was given FDA approval for the treatment of postpartum depression; it was the first approved therapy for the condition. The company's next most advanced product candidate is Zuranolone (SAGE-217), an oral compound, novel neuroactive steroid that has potential in other indications such as treatment resistant depression, or TRD, bipolar depression and generalized anxiety disorder. It sources all of its clinical and non-clinical material supply through third-party contract manufacturing organizations (CMOs) and market its product across the US.

	Annual Growth	12/19	12/20	12/21	12/22	12/23
Sales ($mil.)	88.4%	6.9	1,114.2	6.3	7.7	86.5
Net income ($ mil.)	–	(680.2)	606.1	(457.9)	(532.8)	(541.5)
Market value ($ mil.)	(26.0%)	4,334.6	5,194.4	2,554.3	2,290.1	1,301.1
Employees	–	675	298	471	689	–

SAGENT PHARMACEUTICALS, INC.

1901 N ROSELLE RD STE 450
SCHAUMBURG, IL 601953181
Phone: 847 908-1600
Fax: –
Web: www.sagentpharma.com

CEO: Peter Kaemmerer
CFO: Jonathon Singer
HR: Carol Dunning
FYE: December 31
Type: Private

Sagent is a customer-focused company, delivering an extensive portfolio of injectable products. Its products -- which include anti-infection drugs and oncology and critical-care treatments used for anesthesia or to stabilize cardiac conditions -- consist of ready-to-use prefilled syringes, single dose vials, and premixed bags, as well as pharmacy bulk package vials. It develops and manufactures such products in its manufacturing facilities that extend across a wide range of therapeutic categories. Japanese generics firm Nichi-Iko Pharmaceutical owns Sagent Pharmaceuticals.

SAIA INC

NMS: SAIA

11465 Johns Creek Parkway, Suite 400
Johns Creek, GA 30097
Phone: 770 232-5067
Fax: –
Web: www.saia.com

CEO: Frederick J Holzgrefe III
CFO: Douglas L Col
HR: –
FYE: December 31
Type: Public

Saia is a holding company for less-than-truckload (LTL) carrier Saia Motor Freight Line, a leading LTL carrier that serves about 45 states and provides LTL services to Canada and Mexico through relationships with third-party interline carriers. Saia Motor Freight specializes in offering its customers a range of LTL services, including time-definite and expedited options. The carrier operates a fleet of some 6,200 tractors and approximately 19,300 trailers from a network of about 175 terminals. Saia's service territory spans throughout the South, Southwest, Midwest, as well as Pacific Northwest, West, and portions of the Northeast US. The company was founded in 1924.

	Annual Growth	12/19	12/20	12/21	12/22	12/23
Sales ($mil.)	12.7%	1,786.7	1,822.4	2,288.7	2,792.1	2,881.4
Net income ($ mil.)	32.9%	113.7	138.3	253.2	357.4	354.9
Market value ($ mil.)	47.3%	2,472.3	4,800.1	8,947.9	5,566.9	11,634
Employees	7.7%	10,400	10,600	11,600	12,300	14,000

SAINT AGNES MEDICAL CENTER

1303 E HERNDON AVE
FRESNO, CA 937203309
Phone: 559 450-3000
Fax: –
Web: www.samc.com

CEO: Nancy R Hollingsworth
CFO: –
HR: Alison Millhollen
FYE: June 30
Type: Private

Protecting and caring for the vulnerable, Saint Agnes continues to ward off death for the patients at Saint Agnes Medical Center. The medical center provides health care to Valley residents of Fresno, California, through a 436-bed acute care hospital. Along with general surgery, the hospital offers a variety of services including asthma management, bariatric surgery (for which it has scored state-wide accolades), cardiac rehabilitation, hospice care, and home care. The facility also runs an internal medicine physician residency and a nurses' residency program. Saint Agnes is part of Trinity Health, one of the largest Catholic health care systems in the US.

	Annual Growth	06/17	06/18	06/20	06/21	06/22
Sales ($mil.)	5.4%	–	513.9	530.9	602.0	635.3
Net income ($ mil.)	–	–	35.6	4.5	67.2	(11.3)
Market value ($ mil.)	–	–	–	–	–	–
Employees	–	–	–	–	–	2,400

SAINT ALPHONSUS REGIONAL MEDICAL CENTER, INC.

1055 N CURTIS RD
BOISE, ID 837061309
Phone: 208 367-2121
Fax: –
Web: www.saintalphonsus.org

CEO: –
CFO: Kenneth Fry
HR: Sandra Bruce
FYE: June 30
Type: Private

Saint Alphonsus Regional Medical Center makes medical care its primary mission. The 384-bed hospital provides Boise, Idaho, and the surrounding region (including eastern Oregon and northern Nevada) with general, acute, and specialized health care services. Its facilities and operations include a level II trauma center, an orthopedic spinal care unit, an air transport service, and a home health and hospice division. Saint Alphonsus Regional Medical Center is part of Trinity Health's four-hospital Saint Alphonsus Health System, which serves Boise and Nampa in Idaho and Ontario and Baker City in Oregon. The Sisters of the Holy Cross founded the hospital in 1894.

	Annual Growth	06/12	06/13	06/14	06/21	06/22
Sales ($mil.)	4.3%	–	545.1	572.4	796.1	796.1
Net income ($ mil.)	–	–	43.1	46.0	88.1	(6.5)
Market value ($ mil.)	–	–	–	–	–	–
Employees	–	–	–	–	–	3,500

SAINT ANSELM COLLEGE

100 SAINT ANSELM DR
MANCHESTER, NH 031021310
Phone: 603 641-7000
Fax: –
Web: www.anselm.edu

CEO: –
CFO: –
HR: Dina Frutosbencze
FYE: June 30
Type: Private

It may be named after a philosopher and theologian, but students of all types are welcome at Saint Anselm College. The Benedictine Catholic liberal arts college offers degrees in more than 40 majors as well as over 20 certificate programs. With an enrollment of some 2,000 and a full-time faculty of around 150 (90% of which hold a doctorate or other terminal degree), the school's student-teacher enrollment is 11:1 with an average class size of 18. Saint Anselm College's core curriculum includes classes in English, humanities, philosophy, foreign language, science, and theology. Located on a hill overlooking Manchester, New Hampshire, Saint Anselm College was founded in 1889 by monks of the Benedictine order.

	Annual Growth	06/14	06/15	06/20	06/21	06/22
Sales ($mil.)	3.1%	–	111.2	136.9	81.2	137.7
Net income ($ mil.)	(12.0%)	–	7.6	6.3	62.8	3.1
Market value ($ mil.)	–	–	–	–	–	–
Employees	–	–	–	–	–	700

SAINT EDWARD'S UNIVERSITY, INC.

3001 S CONGRESS AVE
AUSTIN, TX 787046489
Phone: 512 448-8400
Fax: –
Web: www.stedwards.edu

CEO: –
CFO: Kimberly Kvaal
HR: –
FYE: June 30
Type: Private

St. Edward's University is a private Catholic liberal arts university in Austin, Texas. With an enrollment of about 3,975 students and a student-to-faculty ratio of 15:1, the university offers undergraduate degrees in more than 50 areas of study at schools of behavioral and social sciences, management and business, animation, acting, and Environmental Chemistry. St. Edward's also has about ten master's degree programs in fields including accounting, business administration, information systems, and counseling. It offers numerous study abroad programs in Europe, Latin America, and Asia, as well as continuing education programs through its New College.

	Annual Growth	06/17	06/18	06/20	06/21	06/22
Sales ($mil.)	12.5%	–	122.0	208.8	177.1	195.2
Net income ($ mil.)	(1.2%)	–	2.8	20.6	1.8	2.6
Market value ($ mil.)	–	–	–	–	–	–
Employees	–	–	–	–	–	964

SAINT ELIZABETH MEDICAL CENTER, INC.

1 MEDICAL VILLAGE DR
EDGEWOOD, KY 410173403
Phone: 859 301-2000
Fax: –
Web: www.stelizabeth.com

CEO: –
CFO: Marc Hoffman
HR: Cindy Williams
FYE: December 31
Type: Private

St. Elizabeth's Medical Center, a Boston University Teaching Hospital, provides patients and families access to some of Boston's most respected physicians and advanced treatments offering specialized care, including Advanced Center for Cardiac Surgery; da Vinci Robotic surgery program; Mako Robotic-Arm Assisted Surgery; Level III Neonatal Intensive Care Unit (NICU), and Dana-Farber Cancer Institute at St. Elizabeth's Medical Center. The medical center provides emergency care, bariatrics, orthopedics, maternity, and neurosurgery/stroke services. It treats patients in its community practices in neighborhoods, including Allston, Boston, Brighton, Brookline, Newton, Watertown, and Weston. St. Elizabeth's Medical Center was founded in 1868 by five laywomen members of the third order of St. Francis to care for women from Boston's South End.

	Annual Growth	12/13	12/14	12/19	12/21	12/22
Sales ($mil.)	13.7%	–	633.6	1,293.6	1,815.8	1,768.6
Net income ($ mil.)	8.8%	–	45.3	130.0	265.7	88.8
Market value ($ mil.)	–	–	–	–	–	–
Employees	–	–	–	–	–	6,227

SAINT ELIZABETH REGIONAL MEDICAL CENTER

555 S 70TH ST
LINCOLN, NE 685102462
Phone: 402 219-5200
Fax: –
Web: www.chihealth.com

CEO: –
CFO: –
HR: –
FYE: June 30
Type: Private

Saint Elizabeth Regional Medical Center, a Catholic Health Initiatives (CHI) affiliate, is a 260-bed acute care hospital that serves the Lincoln, Nebraska, area. The not-for-profit hospital, also known as CHI Health St. Elizabeth, provides a variety of services, such as obstetrics, bariatrics, cancer care, burn and wound care, and cardiac and pulmonary care. Some 430 physicians are affiliated with the facility. The hospital also operates community health clinics, urgent care centers, and physical therapy clinics, as well as home health and hospice organizations. CHI Health St. Elizabeth was originally founded as a simple frontier hospital in 1889 by the Sisters of St. Francis of Perpetual Adoration.

	Annual Growth	06/14	06/15	06/19	06/21	06/22
Sales ($mil.)	(2.5%)	–	212.5	191.1	186.7	177.4
Net income ($ mil.)	–	–	(9.3)	10.6	10.5	(3.6)
Market value ($ mil.)	–	–	–	–	–	–
Employees	–	–	–	–	–	1,825

SAINT FRANCIS HEALTH SYSTEM, INC.

6161 S YALE AVE
TULSA, OK 741361902
Phone: 918 494-2200
Fax: –
Web: www.saintfrancis.com

CEO: Jake Henry Jr
CFO: Eric Schick
HR: Allen Hood
FYE: June 30
Type: Private

If you have an ulcer in Tulsa, or a broken arm in Broken Arrow, you'll likely be visiting a Saint Francis Health System facility. The not-for-profit system serves Tulsa and northeastern Oklahoma through its hospitals, clinics, and home health services. Its largest facility is Saint Francis Hospital with about 920 beds and more than 700 doctors. Other facilities include Saint Francis Hospital at Broken Arrow, The Children's Hospital at Saint Francis, the Laureate Psychiatric Clinic and Hospital, and the Saint Francis Heart Hospital. Its Warren Clinic consists of physicians offices in about a dozen cities providing primary and specialty health care.

	Annual Growth	06/09	06/10	06/11	06/15	06/16
Sales ($mil.)	(19.3%)	–	0.4	0.4	1,167.9	0.1
Net income ($ mil.)	–	–	(6.3)	(4.1)	148.1	(5.9)
Market value ($ mil.)	–	–	–	–	–	–
Employees	–	–	–	–	–	8,200

SAINT FRANCIS HOSPITAL AND MEDICAL CENTER FOUNDATION, INC.

114 WOODLAND ST 7TH FL
HARTFORD, CT 061051208
Phone: 860 714-4000
Fax: –
Web: www.trinityhealthofne.org

CEO: –
CFO: Steven H Rosenberg
HR: Jason Kaverud
FYE: September 30
Type: Private

Saint Francis takes care of the hearts of Hartford, Connecticut. The Saint Francis Hospital and Medical Center is a not-for-profit, regional medical center with some 620 beds and 65 bassinets. The hospital specializes in cardiology, oncology, neurology, orthopedics, and women's and children's health services. It also offers behavioral health, weight management, trauma care, and injury rehabilitation programs. Saint Francis serves as a teaching hospital affiliated with the University of Connecticut Schools of Medicine and Dentistry. It also operates laboratories, a home health and hospice agency, and other entities. Saint Francis is part of Catholic health care system Trinity Health.

	Annual Growth	09/17	09/18	09/19	09/21	09/22
Sales ($mil.)	(74.2%)	–	871.5	6.1	3.0	3.9
Net income ($ mil.)	–	–	90.3	3.5	(0.5)	(0.7)
Market value ($ mil.)	–	–	–	–	–	–
Employees	–	–	–	–	–	3,270

SAINT FRANCIS UNIVERSITY

169 LAKEVIEW DR
LORETTO, PA 159409705
Phone: 814 472-3261
Fax: –
Web: www.francis.edu

CEO: –
CFO: –
HR: –
FYE: June 30
Type: Private

Saint Francis University is a Catholic liberal arts college with more than 2,500 full- and part-time students. The university offers undergraduate and graduate degree programs in areas such as business administration, education, medical science, nursing, and computer science. It also has doctorate programs in fields such as education and physical therapy. Its four schools cover arts and letters, health sciences, business, and sciences. Saint Francis University was established when six Franciscan Friars from Ireland founded a boys' academy in the mountain hamlet of Loretto, Pennsylvania in 1847. Now, more than 60% of the student body is made up of women. The former St. Francis College gained university status in 2001.

	Annual Growth	06/14	06/15	06/20	06/21	06/22
Sales ($mil.)	2.8%	–	93.1	95.9	103.7	112.8
Net income ($ mil.)	14.1%	–	2.7	2.3	7.0	6.7
Market value ($ mil.)	–	–	–	–	–	–
Employees	–	–	–	–	–	475

SAINT JOSEPH HOSPITAL, INC

1375 E 19TH AVE
DENVER, CO 802181114
Phone: 303 812-2000
Fax: –
Web: www.saintjosephdenver.org

CEO: William Jessee
CFO: –
HR: –
FYE: December 31
Type: Private

The goal of Saint Joseph Hospital (formerly Exempla Saint Joseph Hospital) is to give residents of the Mile High City exemplary care. The Denver acute care facility has nearly 400 licensed beds and specializes in areas including cardiovascular disease, cancer, orthopedics, pediatrics, neurology, diagnostics, and high-risk labor and delivery. The Catholic not-for-profit hospital sees about 50,000 emergency department visits annually and employs more than 1,300 physicians. The hospital also offers residency programs in family practice, internal medicine, obstetrics and gynecology, and general surgery. Catholic-sponsored Saint Joseph is part of SCL Health - Front Range.

	Annual Growth	12/12	12/13	12/14	12/19	12/21
Sales ($mil.)	3.2%	–	490.0	465.8	614.8	629.8
Net income ($ mil.)	1.7%	–	51.6	25.7	48.4	59.2
Market value ($ mil.)	–	–	–	–	–	–
Employees	–	–	–	–	–	2,300

SAINT JOSEPH'S HOSPITAL INC

300 WERNER ST
HOT SPRINGS, AR 719136448
Phone: 501 622-1000
Fax: –
Web: –

CEO: Tim Johnson
CFO: –
HR: –
FYE: June 30
Type: Private

St. Joseph's has been caring mercifully for residents in the Hot Springs environs for well over a century. St. Joseph's Mercy Health Center, the second-oldest hospital in Arkansas, has more than 300 beds and provides acute and tertiary care, as well as home health care. The hospital is a not-for-profit health facility and is part of the Sisters of Mercy Health System. It has specialty units focused on cancer, cardiovascular, women, and senior care. Established in 1888, in 2010 St. Joseph's Mercy announced it would acquire local rival HealthPark Hospital as well as HealthFirst Physicians Group and Hot Springs Village Clinic. All of the acquired medical providers will operate under the St. Joseph Mercy moniker.

SAINT JOSEPH'S UNIVERSITY

5600 CITY AVE
PHILADELPHIA, PA 191311376
Phone: 610 660-1000
Fax: –
Web: www.sju.edu

CEO: Robert D Falese Jr
CFO: Edward W Moneypenny
HR: Charles Kelly
FYE: May 31
Type: Private

Saint Joseph's University (SJU) has been educating Joes and Janes for more than 150 years. The Catholic Jesuit university provides higher education for about 8,000 students a year from its campus on the outskirts of Philadelphia. It has more than 300 full-time faculty members and offers 50 undergraduate majors and 40 graduate and professional study areas, including an Ed.D. in Educational Leadership. About 650 undergraduates attend its College of Professional and Liberal Studies; the remainder attend the College of Arts and Sciences and the Haub School of Business. SJU also conducts study abroad, honors, service and faith learning, and other special study programs. It was founded in 1851 by the Society of Jesus.

	Annual Growth	05/18	05/19	05/20	05/21	05/22
Sales ($mil.)	13.2%	–	222.3	–	347.1	322.1
Net income ($ mil.)	19.3%	–	8.5	–	61.3	14.5
Market value ($ mil.)	–	–	–	–	–	–
Employees	–	–	–	–	–	1,138

SAINT LOUIS UNIVERSITY

1 N GRAND BLVD
SAINT LOUIS, MO 63103
Phone: 314 977-2500
Fax: –
Web: www.slu.edu

CEO: –
CFO: Robert Woodruff
HR: Bobbi Kysar
FYE: June 30
Type: Private

Saint Louis University (SLU) is one of the nation's oldest and most prestigious Catholic universities. The Jesuit, Catholic school offers more than 95 bachelor's degree programs and about 125 master's and doctoral degree programs through about a dozen schools and colleges, including a school of medicine and a campus in Madrid, Spain. Most programs require core classes in philosophy and theology. SLU has an enrollment of nearly 13,545 students. Its student-teacher ratio is 9:1. Saint Louis University was founded in 1818 by Reverend Louis William Du Bourg, Catholic Bishop of Louisiana.

SAINT LUKE'S HEALTH SYSTEM, INC.

901 E 104TH ST
KANSAS CITY, MO 641314517
Phone: 816 932-2000
Fax: –
Web: www.saintlukeskc.org

CEO: Cliff A Robertson
CFO: Charles Robb
HR: Amy Howell
FYE: December 31
Type: Private

Saint Luke's Health System is a faith-based, not-for-profit organization with about 15 hospitals and campuses and more than 200 primary care and specialty clinics, treating patients in about 65 specialty services across over 65 counties in Missouri and Kansas. The health systems is the region's longest continuously-operating, adult heart transplant program, and one of the nation's top 25 cardiology and heart surgery programs, at Saint Luke's Mid America Heart Institute. It is also the region's only treatment center for advanced breast cancer, the Koontz Center for Advanced Breast Cancer at Saint Luke's Cancer Institute. It has four Neonatal Intensive Care Units, including a Level IIIb unit at Saint Luke's Hospital of Kansas City.

	Annual Growth	12/18	12/19	12/20	12/21	12/22
Sales ($mil.)	3.9%	–	2,100.0	2,153.0	2,367.1	2,354.0
Net income ($ mil.)	–	–	131.7	156.4	278.7	(113.6)
Market value ($ mil.)	–	–	–	–	–	–
Employees	–	–	–	–	–	5,111

SAINT LUKE'S QUAKERTOWN HOSPITAL

1021 PARK AVE
QUAKERTOWN, PA 189510130
Phone: 215 538-4500
Fax: –
Web: www.slhn.org

CEO: –
CFO: –
HR: –
FYE: December 31
Type: Private

St. Luke's Quakertown Hospital provides health care services to the upper portion of Pennsylvania's Bucks County (north of Philadelphia). St. Luke's Quakertown Hospital is an acute-care facility with some 60 beds and offers services including general medical, emergency, surgical, and intensive care. The hospital has about 275 affiliated physicians with 40 specialties such as cardiovascular services and cancer care. St. Luke's Quakertown also operates the adjacent St. Luke's Professional Center, which includes general and specialty physician offices. Founded in 1926, the hospital is part of regional hospital operator St. Luke's Hospital & Health Network.

	Annual Growth	06/17	06/18	06/19	06/21*	12/21
Sales ($mil.)	(75.0%)	–	83.9	86.1	111.0	1.3
Net income ($ mil.)	(52.6%)	–	0.7	12.9	12.5	0.0
Market value ($ mil.)	–	–	–	–	–	–
Employees	–	–	–	–	–	74

*Fiscal year change

SAINT MARY'S UNIVERSITY OF MINNESOTA

700 TERRACE HTS # 8
WINONA, MN 559871320
Phone: 507 457-1436
Fax: –
Web: www.smumn.edu

CEO: –
CFO: –
HR: Paul J Wildenborg
FYE: May 31
Type: Private

Saint Mary's University of Minnesota is a private, Roman Catholic institution that enrolls about 6,000 students. About 20% of students are traditional undergraduates, while the majority are adult learners in the Schools of Graduate and Professional Programs. The school, which was founded in 1912 by Bishop Patrick R. Heffron, has been administered by the Christian Brothers organization (under the De La Salle order) since 1933. It offers instruction in about 55 major, minor, and professional fields including arts, science, education, and psychology.

	Annual Growth	05/18	05/19	05/20	05/21	05/22
Sales ($mil.)	14.8%	–	71.5	–	109.2	108.1
Net income ($ mil.)	–	–	(6.2)	–	12.6	4.8
Market value ($ mil.)	–	–	–	–	–	–
Employees	–	–	–	–	–	1,000

SAINT PETER'S UNIVERSITY HOSPITAL, INC.

254 EASTON AVE
NEW BRUNSWICK, NJ 089011766
Phone: 732 745-8600
Fax: –
Web: –

CEO: Ronald Rak
CFO: Garrick Stoldt
HR: –
FYE: December 31
Type: Private

Saint Peter's University Hospital has about 480 beds. The facility is sponsored by the Roman Catholic Diocese of Metuchen, New Jersey, and provides patients with a staff of more than 3,600 healthcare professionals and support personnel, and more than 1,000 doctors and dentists. Saint Peter's also offers one of the country's largest Neonatal Intensive Care Units, minimally invasive surgical (MIS) procedures, and specialized cancer, diabetes, and geriatric care. In affiliation with the Children's Hospital of Philadelphia, Saint Peter's provides cardiac care for infants and children. Treats over 23,000 inpatients and more than 245,000 outpatients yearly, the first Saint Peter's Hospital opened in New Brunswick in 1872.

	Annual Growth	12/18	12/19	12/20	12/21	12/22
Sales ($mil.)	1908.6%	–	0.0	430.5	492.0	582.1
Net income ($ mil.)	–	–	(0.0)	0.6	105.2	49.2
Market value ($ mil.)	–	–	–	–	–	–
Employees	–	–	–	–	–	3,000

SAINT THOMAS RUTHERFORD HOSPITAL

1700 MEDICAL CENTER PKWY
MURFREESBORO, TN 371292245
Phone: 615 849-4100
Fax: –
Web: healthcare.ascension.org

CEO: Gordon B Ferguson
CFO: Scott Furniss
HR: –
FYE: June 30
Type: Private

Saint Thomas Rutherford Hospital (formerly Middle Tennessee Medical Center) is a 285-bed acute care hospital serving central Tennessee. In addition to general medical, diagnostic, and surgical services, the not-for-profit hospital offers 30 medical specialties including centers devoted to cancer care, pediatrics, cardiology, orthopedics, neurology, diabetes, and women's health. Saint Thomas Rutherford, established in 1927, is part of Saint Thomas Health, which includes four additional area hospitals and is in turn is a member of Ascension Health.

	Annual Growth	06/14	06/15	06/19	06/21	06/22
Sales ($mil.)	7.6%	–	279.5	359.1	420.9	465.9
Net income ($ mil.)	(10.3%)	–	48.0	77.1	71.1	22.5
Market value ($ mil.)	–	–	–	–	–	–
Employees	–	–	–	–	–	1,100

SAINT VINCENT HEALTH SYSTEM

232 W 25TH ST
ERIE, PA 165440002
Phone: 814 452-5000
Fax: –
Web: www.saintvincenthealth.com

CEO: Christopher Clark
CFO: Al Mansfield
HR: –
FYE: December 31
Type: Private

Saint Vincent Health System provides various health care services to northwestern Pennsylvania residents. The health care network includes Saint Vincent Health Center, a regional tertiary care hospital with nearly 370 beds, and Westfield Memorial Hospital, a community hospital with about 25 beds. Other operations include the Saint Vincent Medical Group (a physician's general practice group) and specialty outpatient facilities and surgery centers. The health system offers specialized services such as emergency care, orthopedics, cardiology, rehabilitation, home health, and sports medicine.

SAKAR INTERNATIONAL, INC.

195 CARTER DR
EDISON, NJ 088172068
Phone: 732 248-1306
Fax: –
Web: www.sakar.com

CEO: –
CFO: –
HR: –
FYE: March 31
Type: Private

Ever wonder where Fry's, Best Buy, and RadioShack get all those gizmos and gadgets? Sakar International knows. The company makes consumer electronics, including cameras, handheld games, audio components, MP3 players, and USB hubs along with video game, VoIP, computer, TV, and camera accessories. It also produces computer cables, keyboards, flashlights, and surge protectors. Sakar brands include Crystal Optics, Digital Concepts, Vivitar, and iConcepts and it makes products bearing the Crayola, For Dummies, Hello Kitty, Jeep, Iron Man, and Major League Baseball names under license. CEO Charles Saka founded the company, which distributes worldwide, in 1978.

SALEM HEALTH

890 OAK ST SE
SALEM, OR 973013905
Phone: 503 561-5200
Fax: –
Web: www.salemhealth.org

CEO: Cheryl N Wolfe
CFO: James Parr
HR: Laurie Hickman
FYE: June 30
Type: Private

Salem Hospital serves the healthcare needs of residents in and around Oregon's Willamette Valley. The acute care hospital boasts about 455 beds and a medical staff of 440-plus physicians that represents some 45 specialty areas, such as oncology, joint replacement, obstetrics, diabetes, weight loss, and mental health, among others. The not-for-profit hospital offers a range of services from emergency and critical care to rehabilitation and community wellness programs. Its Center for Outpatient Medicine provides cancer care, outpatient surgery, and imaging services and has a sleep disorders center. Salem Hospital is part of Salem Health, which also includes West Valley Hospital and Willamette Health Partners.

	Annual Growth	06/18	06/19	06/20	06/21	06/22
Sales ($mil.)	7.4%	–	820.1	864.5	953.4	1,017.1
Net income ($ mil.)	–	–	86.2	75.1	241.7	(127.5)
Market value ($ mil.)	–	–	–	–	–	–
Employees	–	–	–	–	–	3,400

SALEM MEDIA GROUP, INC.

NBB: SALM

6400 North Belt Line Road
Irving, TX 75063
Phone: 469 586-0080
Fax: –
Web: www.salemmedia.com

CEO: Edward G Atsinger III
CFO: Evan D Masyr
HR: Kim Lane
FYE: December 31
Type: Public

His eye may be on the sparrow, but Salem Media Group (formerly Salem Communications) hopes His ear is tuned to the radio. The leading Christian radio company operates about 100 stations serving more than 35 markets. Its stations offer Christian-themed talk shows, Christian music, country music, and traditional talk radio. The company also produces and syndicates religious programming through the Salem Radio Network, which boasts about 2,000 affiliates. In addition, Salem Media publishes books and magazines, operates a radio advertising sales firm, and operates the Salem Web Network, a provider of online Christian content. Chairman Stuart Epperson, CEO Edward Atsinger, and other family members control about 85% of the company.

	Annual Growth	12/18	12/19	12/20	12/21	12/22
Sales ($mil.)	0.4%	262.8	253.9	236.2	258.2	267.0
Net income ($ mil.)	–	(3.2)	(27.8)	(54.1)	41.5	(3.2)
Market value ($ mil.)	(15.8%)	56.9	39.2	28.3	83.3	28.6
Employees	(1.9%)	1,552	1,487	1,338	1,336	1,436

SALESFORCE INC

NYS: CRM

Salesforce Tower, 415 Mission Street, 3rd Floor
San Francisco, CA 94105
Phone: 415 901-7000
Fax: –
Web: www.salesforce.com

CEO: Marc Benioff
CFO: Amy Weaver
HR: –
FYE: January 31
Type: Public

Salesforce.com Inc. is a global leader in customer relationship management (CRM) technology that brings companies and their customers together. It delivers a single source of truth, connecting customer data across systems, apps and devices to help companies sell, service, market and conduct commerce from anywhere through its Customer 360. Other products offer e-Commerce, analytics, collaboration, integration and workforce management. Salesforce's customers come from a variety of industries, including financial services, telecommunications, healthcare, and the public sector. The company was founded in 1999. It generates most of its revenue in the Americas.

	Annual Growth	01/20	01/21	01/22	01/23	01/24
Sales ($mil.)	19.5%	17,098	21,252	26,492	31,352	34,857
Net income ($ mil.)	139.4%	126.0	4,072.0	1,444.0	208.0	4,136.0
Market value ($ mil.)	11.4%	177,023	219,094	225,884	163,099	272,938
Employees	10.4%	49,000	56,606	73,541	79,390	72,682

SALINAS VALLEY HEALTH

450 E ROMIE LN
SALINAS, CA 939014029
Phone: 831 757-4333
Fax: –
Web: www.salinasvalleyhealth.com

CEO: Allen Radner
CFO: Julie Jezowski
HR: –
FYE: December 31
Type: Private

The primary facility of the Salinas Valley Memorial Healthcare System (a public hospital district) is Salinas Valley Memorial Hospital, which opened in 1953 and has some 270 acute-care beds. The medical center includes a comprehensive cancer center, joint replacement clinic, regional heart and spine centers, a level III neonatal intensive care unit, and a women's and children's unit. Salinas Valley Memorial Healthcare System also operates the Summerville Harden Ranch, an 80-bed assisted-living facility, and a network of outpatient care clinics. The system has collaborative relationships with other area care providers, as well as a partnership with NASA that allows earthbound physicians to assist astronauts with medical emergencies in space.

	Annual Growth	06/04	06/05	06/15	06/16*	12/21
Sales ($mil.)	(39.9%)	–	874.4	344.2	366.3	0.3
Net income ($ mil.)	–	–	0.0	37.7	44.1	(0.1)
Market value ($ mil.)	–	–	–	–	–	–
Employees	–	–	–	–	–	1,800

*Fiscal year change

SALINE MEMORIAL HOSPITAL AUXILIARY

1 MEDICAL PARK DR
BENTON, AR 720153353
Phone: 501 922-2619
Fax: –
Web: www.salinememorial.org

CEO: –
CFO: –
HR: –
FYE: June 30
Type: Private

Saline Memorial Hospital (SMH) is a not-for-profit medical facility serving the western region of Arkansas. The full-service hospital has about 167 beds and provides inpatient and outpatient care in the areas of cardiology, neurology, otolaryngology (ear, nose, and throat), ophthalmology, pediatrics, psychiatry, and wound care, among others. The hospital's campus also includes a sleep disorder laboratory, two separate medical office buildings, and a home health and hospice services center. In addition, SMH operates two primary care clinics in nearby Bryant.

	Annual Growth	06/15	06/16	06/17	06/18	06/20
Sales ($mil.)	(10.0%)	–	0.0	0.0	0.0	0.0
Net income ($ mil.)	–	–	(0.0)	0.0	(0.0)	0.0
Market value ($ mil.)	–	–	–	–	–	–
Employees	–	–	–	–	–	950

SALISBURY BANCORP, INC.

5 BISSELL ST
LAKEVILLE, CT 060391212
Phone: 860 435-9801
Fax: –
Web: www.nbtbank.com

CEO: –
CFO: –
HR: –
FYE: December 31
Type: Private

Salisbury Bancorp has a stake in New England's financial market. The holding company owns the Salisbury Bank and Trust Company, which operates seven branches in northwestern Connecticut, southwestern Massachusetts, and southeastern New York. With roots dating to 1848, the bank offers a variety of financial products and services, including checking, savings, and money market accounts, CDs, credit cards, and trust services. Residential real estate mortgages make up the largest portion of the bank's loan portfolio by far; commercial real estate, construction, land development, business, financial, agricultural, and consumer loans round out its lending activities.

	Annual Growth	12/18	12/19	12/20	12/21	12/22
Sales ($mil.)	8.3%	–	–	52.7	53.7	61.7
Net income ($ mil.)	21.6%	–	–	11.1	11.9	16.5
Market value ($ mil.)	–	–	–	–	–	–
Employees	–	–	–	–	–	194

SALLY BEAUTY HOLDINGS INC

NYS: SBH

3001 Colorado Boulevard
Denton, TX 76210
Phone: 940 898-7500
Fax: –
Web: www.sallybeautyholdings.com

CEO: Denise Paulonis
CFO: Marlo Cormier
HR: –
FYE: September 30
Type: Public

Sally Beauty Holdings (SBH) is one of the largest retailers and distributors of professional beauty supplies in the US and Europe. The company's segments, Sally Beauty Supply stores and Beauty Systems Group, sell approximately 18,500 hair, skin, and nail products in about 4,795 stores, including franchised locations. Sally Beauty Supply's customers are consumers, salons, and salon professionals while the Beauty Systems Group focuses on salons and professionals. The latter segment operates Armstrong McCall, a beauty supply distributor which sells through franchised stores. While the US accounts for most of its sales, the company also has stores in Canada, Europe, and South America.

	Annual Growth	09/19	09/20	09/21	09/22	09/23
Sales ($mil.)	(1.0%)	3,876.4	3,514.3	3,875.0	3,815.6	3,728.1
Net income ($ mil.)	(9.2%)	271.6	113.2	239.9	183.6	184.6
Market value ($ mil.)	(13.4%)	1,582.3	923.5	1,790.6	1,339.0	890.5
Employees	(3.0%)	30,500	30,000	29,000	29,000	27,000

SALON CITY INC

NBB: SALN

909 N. Palm Ave., Suite 311
West Hollywood, CA 90069
Phone: 310 358-9017
Fax: –
Web: –

CEO: –
CFO: –
HR: –
FYE: December 31
Type: Public

Salon City aims to take on the "big wigs" of the fashion magazine industry. The company publishes the Salon City Magazine and its related Web site, Salon City Online, both of which are marketed to fashionistas who want to keep up with beauty, style, and Hollywood glamour. The magazine was formerly known as Salon City Star, a trade publication for the beauty, spa, and hair care industry; in 2007 the publication changed its name and re-focused on the consumer market. Salon City Magazine is published eight times a year. It is distributed in the US and Canada by Time Warner's Time/Warner Retail, and internationally in about 30 countries by Kable News' Kable Distribution Services.

	Annual Growth	12/03	12/04	12/05	12/06	12/07
Sales ($mil.)	15.5%	–	–	–	0.4	0.5
Net income ($ mil.)	–	–	–	–	(2.5)	(0.8)
Market value ($ mil.)	(61.5%)	–	–	–	0.3	0.0
Employees	–	–	–	–	–	42

SALON MEDIA GROUP INC.

NBB: SLNM

870 Market Street
San Francisco, CA 94102
Phone: 415 870-7566
Fax: –
Web: www.salon.com

CEO: Richard Macwilliams
CFO: Trevor Calhoun
HR: –
FYE: March 31
Type: Public

Salon Media Group (formerly Salon.com) hopes to satisfy sophisticated Web surfers weary of run-of-the-mill Internet schlock. The company that garnered attention for essays by the likes of Camille Paglia and Allen Barra has expanded from its original online magazine format. Salon.com's content includes news, features, interviews, columns, and blogs covering topics such as politics, business, technology, books, sports, and arts and entertainment. Revenues come from advertising and subscription fees. Salon.com and its online communities (Table Talk and The Well) attract more than six million unique visitors a month.

	Annual Growth	03/15	03/16	03/17	03/18	03/19
Sales ($mil.)	–	4.9	7.0	4.6	4.5	–
Net income ($ mil.)	–	(3.9)	(2.0)	(9.6)	(3.1)	(2.7)
Market value ($ mil.)	(42.1%)	24.2	15.1	22.7	9.4	2.7
Employees	(15.5%)	49	53	44	36	25

SALT LAKE COMMUNITY COLLEGE

4600 S REDWOOD RD
SALT LAKE CITY, UT 841233145
Phone: 801 957-4111
Fax: –
Web: www.slcc.edu

CEO: –
CFO: –
HR: –
FYE: June 30
Type: Private

Salt Lake Community College (SLCC) provides day, night, and weekend courses for early risers and night owls alike. SLCC serves more than 60,000 students and has a student-to-teacher ratio of 23:1. The two-year school has more than a dozen campuses and outreach centers in Salt Lake City, Utah, as well as online courses available to reach both traditional and non-traditional students. In addition to being a top US source of associate degrees in arts, science, applied science, and pre-engineering, the community college also has career and technical programs. SLCC was founded in 1948 to provide skilled workforce training for Utah residents.

	Annual Growth	06/12	06/13	06/14	06/15	06/16
Sales ($mil.)	(3.6%)	–	94.1	92.6	85.4	84.4
Net income ($ mil.)	28.3%	–	3.9	55.2	11.2	8.2
Market value ($ mil.)	–	–	–	–	–	–
Employees	–	–	–	–	–	3,200

SALT RIVER PROJECT AGRICULTURAL IMPROVEMENT AND POWER DISTRICT

1500 N MILL AVE
TEMPE, AZ 852881252
Phone: 602 236-5900
Fax: –
Web: www.srpnet.com

CEO: –
CFO: –
HR: –
FYE: April 30
Type: Private

Salt River Project (SRP) is a community-based, not-for-profit organization providing affordable water and power to more than 1.1 million people in greater Phoenix metropolitan area. It is an agricultural improvement district under the laws of the State of Arizona. It operates the Salt River Project (the Project), a federal reclamation project. It also owns and operates an electric system that generates, purchases, transmits and distributes electric power and energy, and provides electric service to residential, commercial, industrial and agricultural power users in a 2,900-square-mile service territory in parts of Maricopa, Gila and Pinal counties, plus mine loads in an adjacent 2,400-square-mile area in Gila and Pinal counties. It was founded in 1903.

	Annual Growth	04/04	04/05*	01/10*	04/20	04/21
Sales ($mil.)	2.7%	–	2,251.7	2,217.5	3,121.4	3,475.5
Net income ($ mil.)	2.9%	–	362.5	517.4	126.5	577.1
Market value ($ mil.)	–	–	–	–	–	–
Employees	–	–	–	–	–	4,336

*Fiscal year change

SALVE REGINA UNIVERSITY

100 OCHRE POINT AVE
NEWPORT, RI 028404149
Phone: 401 847-6650
Fax: –
Web: www.salve.edu

CEO: Janet L Robinson
CFO: –
HR: –
FYE: June 30
Type: Private

"Salve Regina" isn't just an anthem that Catholics sing near Christmas. It's also a college they attend in Rhode Island. Salve Regina (meaning Hail, Holy Queen) is a Catholic university serving more than 2,500 undergraduate and graduate students. The university offers degrees in more than 45 disciplines, including accounting, anthropology, biology, economics, education, and religious studies. Salve Regina offers associate, baccalaureate, and master's degrees, a Certificate of Advanced Graduate Study, and a Ph.D. in humanities. Salve Regina was founded by the Sisters of Mercy in 1934; it opened its doors in 1947.

	Annual Growth	06/15	06/16	06/20	06/21	06/22
Sales ($mil.)	13.2%	–	67.9	118.7	125.9	142.5
Net income ($ mil.)	9.6%	–	8.4	4.2	6.3	14.5
Market value ($ mil.)	–	–	–	–	–	–
Employees	–	–	–	–	–	450

SAM HOUSTON STATE UNIVERSITY

1806 AVE J
HUNTSVILLE, TX 77340
Phone: 936 294-1111
Fax: –
Web: www.shsu.edu

CEO: –
CFO: –
HR: –
FYE: August 31
Type: Private

Part of the Texas State University System, Sam Houston University has an enrollment of nearly 18,500 students. It consists of six schools: Business Administration, Criminal Justice, Education, Fine Arts and Mass Communications, Humanities and Social Sciences, and Sciences. The university offers some 130 undergraduate and master programs, as well as doctoral programs in counselor education, criminal justice, educational leadership, reading, and clinical psychology. It offers more than 20 undergraduate and graduate degrees entirely online. Sam Houston State was founded as Sam Houston Normal Institute in 1879 and is named after Texas hero General Sam Houston.

SAM LEVIN INC.

2301 E EVESHAM RD
VOORHEES, NJ 080434501
Phone: 724 872-2055
Fax: –
Web: www.levinfurniture.com

CEO: –
CFO: –
HR: –
FYE: December 31
Type: Private

Founded in 1920 as a furniture and hardware store by the husband-and-wife team Sam and Jessie Levin, Sam Levin (dba Levin Furniture) sells a wide variety of dining room, bedroom, living room, and office furniture, as well as mattresses, at about a dozen retail locations in northeastern Ohio and southwestern Pennsylvania. It also operates a Sleep Center bedding store in Pennsylvania and a clearance outlet in Ohio. The family-owned-and-run-company offers self-service kiosks in its showrooms and creative exhibits that include sports- and Wizard of Oz-themed displays. Robert Levin, Sam and Jessie's grandson, is president of the company.

	Annual Growth	12/11	12/12	12/13	12/14	12/15
Sales ($mil.)	3.8%	–	–	188.0	188.8	202.7
Net income ($ mil.)	50.5%	–	–	7.2	12.2	16.2
Market value ($ mil.)	–	–	–	–	–	–
Employees	–	–	–	–	–	400

SAM SWOPE AUTO GROUP, LLC

10 SWOPE AUTOCENTER DR
LOUISVILLE, KY 402991806
Phone: 502 499-5000
Fax: –
Web: www.swope.com

CEO: –
CFO: –
HR: –
FYE: December 31
Type: Private

Sam Swope Auto Group has plenty of new cars for old Kentucky. The company owns about two dozen automobile dealerships in the Blue Grass State. Located in Louisville, Lexington, Radcliff, and Elizabethtown, Swope dealerships sell General Motors cars, including Buicks, Cadillacs, GMC trucks, and Saturns. Other company dealerships sell BMW , Honda , Lexus , Toyota , and Volvo models. Sam Swope Auto Group also sells used cars and offers parts and service. In 1952 founder Sam Swope parlayed his love of cars into his first dealership, which sold Plymouth and Dodge cars, in Elizabethtown, Kentucky. The company is still owned and managed by the Swope family.

	Annual Growth	12/03	12/04	12/05	12/06	12/07
Sales ($mil.)	4.6%	–	–	406.8	434.3	444.9
Net income ($ mil.)	183.0%	–	–	7.5	57.2	59.8
Market value ($ mil.)	–	–	–	–	–	–
Employees	–	–	–	–	–	900

SAMARITAN PHARMACEUTICALS

2877 Paradise Road, Suite 801
Las Vegas, NV 89109
Phone: 702 735-7001
Fax: 702 737-7016
Web: www.samaritanpharma.com

CEO: –
CFO: –
HR: –
FYE: December 31
Type: Public

Samaritan Pharmaceuticals is looking to lend a hand to people suffering from disease. The company is developing therapies as well as diagnostics. Disease targets include cancer, cardiovascular disease, infectious disease, and central nervous system (CNS) conditions. Products under development include treatments for HIV, Alzheimer's, coronary disease, and hepatitis C. Samaritan's diagnostic candidates may help doctors pinpoint breast cancer and Alzheimer's faster. The company also has marketing agreements with selected companies to sell approved drugs in certain European markets.

	Annual Growth	12/04	12/05	12/06	12/07	12/08
Sales ($mil.)	–	–	0.3	0.0	4.7	4.2
Net income ($ mil.)	–	(4.9)	(5.6)	(7.6)	(3.0)	(6.3)
Market value ($ mil.)	(48.3%)	35.5	14.5	7.6	11.9	2.5
Employees	–	8	10	16	20	8

SAMARITAN REGIONAL HEALTH SYSTEM

1025 CENTER ST
ASHLAND, OH 448054097
Phone: 419 289-0491
Fax: –
Web: www.uhhospitals.org

CEO: Danny L Boggs
CFO: Mary Griest
HR: –
FYE: December 31
Type: Private

Samaritan Regional Health System (SRHS) provides a wide range of inpatient and outpatient services to the residents of north central Ohio. Among its specialty services are emergency medicine, orthopedics, obstetrics, rehabilitation, cardiology, gastrointestinal disease, pediatrics, and home health care. Its flagship facility, Samaritan Hospital, has about 110 licensed beds and is located in Ashland, Ohio, which is located between the Cleveland and Columbus metropolitan areas. The not-for-profit health system also includes outpatient general care, diagnostic, and specialty clinics. SRHS was founded in 1912 by philanthropists J.L. and Mary Clark.

	Annual Growth	12/12	12/13	12/14	12/15	12/16
Sales ($mil.)	–	–	–	78.6	70.9	74.7
Net income ($ mil.)	62.7%	–	2.0	5.5	4.3	8.6
Market value ($ mil.)	–	–	–	–	–	–
Employees	–	–	–	–	–	650

SAMMONS ENTERPRISES, INC.

5949 SHERRY LN STE 1900　　　　　　　　　　　　　CEO: Heather Kreager
DALLAS, TX 752258015　　　　　　　　　　　　　　　CFO: Pam Doeppe
Phone: 214 210-5000　　　　　　　　　　　　　　　　HR: –
Fax: –　　　　　　　　　　　　　　　　　　　　　　FYE: December 31
Web: www.sammonsenterprises.com　　　　　　　　　Type: Private

Sammons Enterprises is one of the largest privately-held companies in the US. The diversified global holding company's operations include the Sammons Financial Group (life insurance and financial services) and Sammons Industrial (industrial equipment). It also includes Sammons Equity Alliance and Sammons Infrastructure. The company's list of partially-owned holdings runs the range from real estate investments to industrial sector. Sammons Enterprises has assets worth more than $120 billion. It is owned by its employees and prefers to invest in companies with strong employee-ownership programs. Sammons Enterprises was founded by Charles A. Sammons in 1938.

SAMSUNG C&T AMERICA, INC.

105 CHALLENGER RD FL 3　　　　　　　　　　　　　CEO: Hochan Park
RIDGEFIELD PARK, NJ 076602100　　　　　　　　　　CFO: Know-Kook Park
Phone: 201 229-4000　　　　　　　　　　　　　　　　HR: Scott Eivens
Fax: –　　　　　　　　　　　　　　　　　　　　　　FYE: December 31
Web: www.samsungcnt.com　　　　　　　　　　　　　Type: Private

It is Samsung, but instead of just making the stuff you see at the electronics store, it buys and sells a wide range of consumer and industrial goods. Samsung C&T America (SCTA, the C&T stands for construction and trading) is the US arm of the Korean commodities trading, marketing and distribution, and investment company Samsung C&T (a part of the Samsung& chaebol, or industrial group). As a commodities trader, SCTA deals in chemicals, steel, metals, textiles, and natural resources. The company's marketing and distribution efforts include consumer products ranging from health care products to FUBU clothing and US Polo Association footwear.

SAN ANTONIO SPURS, L.L.C.

1 AT AND T CENTER PKWY　　　　　　　　　　　　　CEO: –
SAN ANTONIO, TX 782193604　　　　　　　　　　　　CFO: –
Phone: 210 444-5000　　　　　　　　　　　　　　　　HR: –
Fax: –　　　　　　　　　　　　　　　　　　　　　　FYE: June 30
Web: www.spurs.com　　　　　　　　　　　　　　　　Type: Private

South Central Texas basketball fans hardly need to be prodded to root for this team. The San Antonio Spurs professional basketball franchise was formed by Bob Folsom in 1967 as the Dallas Chaparrals of the American Basketball Association. The team moved to San Antonio in 1973 and joined the National Basketball Association when the leagues merged in 1976. The Spurs franchise boasts five NBA championship titles, its latest in 2014. Peter Holt, whose family owns statewide Caterpillar dealership Holt CAT, has controlled the team since 1996. He also owns the San Antonio Silver Stars of the WNBA.

SAN ANTONIO WATER SYSTEM

2800 US HIGHWAY 281 N　　　　　　　　　　　　　　CEO: Robert R Puente
SAN ANTONIO, TX 782123106　　　　　　　　　　　　CFO: Doug Evanson
Phone: 210 233-3246　　　　　　　　　　　　　　　　HR: Michel McGervey
Fax: –　　　　　　　　　　　　　　　　　　　　　　FYE: December 31
Web: www.saws.org　　　　　　　　　　　　　　　　Type: Private

Wasting water is a sore point in drought-prone South Texas, and San Antonio Water System (SAWS) seeks to husband this precious resource the best it can. The company serves about 511,300 water customers and some 457,600 wastewater customers, or about 2 million people, in the San Antonio metropolitan area (including most of the city of San Antonio, Medina, Anatascosa counties, and adjacent parts of Bexar County). In addition to serving its own retail customers, SAWS provides wholesale water supplies to several smaller utility systems in its service area. The utility is owned by the City of San Antonio.

SAN ANTONIO ZOOLOGICAL SOCIETY

950 E HILDEBRAND AVE　　　　　　　　　　　　　　CEO: Tim Morrow
SAN ANTONIO, TX 782122538　　　　　　　　　　　　CFO: –
Phone: 210 734-7184　　　　　　　　　　　　　　　　HR: Jo L Medlin
Fax: –　　　　　　　　　　　　　　　　　　　　　　FYE: December 31
Web: www.sazoo.org　　　　　　　　　　　　　　　　Type: Private

This society has built a business catering to its animals. The San Antonio Zoological Society, a not-for-profit, operates the San Antonio Zoo, as well as the zoo's wide variety of exhibits. Its exhibits range from an African watering hole with multiple animal species to the Hixon Bird House to Prairie Chickens, Prairie Dogs, and TOADally. The zoo extends throughout a 56-acre site in San Antonio's centrally located Brackenridge Park. The San Antonio Zoo is home to some 3,500 animals, representing about 750 species. The zoo was established in 1914. Several years later, in 1929, the governing zoological society was incorporated as a business entity.

	Annual Growth	09/15	09/16*	12/19	12/20	12/22
Sales ($mil.)	11.1%	–	22.5	28.5	25.1	42.4
Net income ($ mil.)		–	(1.1)	(0.4)	(2.5)	5.0
Market value ($ mil.)		–	–	–	–	–
Employees		–	–	–	–	275

*Fiscal year change

SAN DIEGO CHRISTIAN COLLEGE INC

200 RIVERVIEW PKWY STE 101　　　　　　　　　　　CEO: Paul Ague
SANTEE, CA 92071　　　　　　　　　　　　　　　　 CFO: –
Phone: 619 201-8700　　　　　　　　　　　　　　　　HR: –
Fax: –　　　　　　　　　　　　　　　　　　　　　　FYE: June 30
Web: www.sdcc.edu　　　　　　　　　　　　　　　　Type: Private

San Diego Christian College (formerly Christian Heritage College) is a four-year, private liberal arts college emphasizing religious education. The college has nearly 600 students and offers 15 degree programs. San Diego Christian College is affiliated with the Southern Baptists. It was founded in 1970 by Dr. Tim LaHaye, Dr. Art Peters, and Dr. Henry Morris.

	Annual Growth	06/15	06/16	06/20	06/21	06/22
Sales ($mil.)	(2.2%)	–	21.6	20.3	20.4	18.9
Net income ($ mil.)	(0.5%)	–	0.9	1.1	0.0	0.9
Market value ($ mil.)		–	–	–	–	–
Employees		–	–	–	–	131

SAN DIEGO COUNTY OFFICE OF EDUCATION

6401 LINDA VISTA RD
SAN DIEGO, CA 921117319
Phone: 858 292-3500
Fax: –
Web: www.sdcoe.net

CEO: –
CFO: –
HR: –
FYE: June 30
Type: Private

San Diego County Office of Education (SDCOE) oversees about 45 public school districts and 500,000 students in San Diego County. SDCOE develops and implements programs and strategies to help improve the quality, efficiency, and cost-effectiveness of school districts, with a special emphasis placed on small districts and low-performing schools. SDCOE organizes training sessions for districts, it also oversees special education programs. Other responsibilities include budget auditing, teacher registration, background checks, and attendance record certification.

	Annual Growth	06/02	06/03	06/04	06/05	06/20
Sales ($mil.)	(43.3%)	–	323.9	335.9	376.0	0.0
Net income ($ mil.)	–	–	4.2	1.9	0.6	(0.0)
Market value ($ mil.)	–	–	–	–	–	–
Employees	–	–	–	–	–	1,441

SAN DIEGO COUNTY WATER AUTHORITY

4677 OVERLAND AVE
SAN DIEGO, CA 921231233
Phone: 858 522-6600
Fax: –
Web: www.sdcwa.org

CEO: –
CFO: –
HR: –
FYE: June 30
Type: Private

When you are a big urban area located between the salty sea and a blazing hot desert, making sure that all your 3.1 million citizens have access to safe, reliable drinking water is no easy task. But that is the job of the San Diego County Water Authority (SDCWA), which is in charge of supplying about 95% of San Diego County's potable water supply (80% of which comes directly and indirectly from the Colorado River). The authority provides water to its 24 member agencies (primarily cities and municipal districts), which in turn distribute the water to residents and businesses in the county. SDCWA also has hydroelectric power generation operations.

	Annual Growth	06/12	06/13	06/14	06/15	06/16
Sales ($mil.)	(57.5%)	–	526.0	597.6	588.7	40.4
Net income ($ mil.)	(12.7%)	–	60.9	81.0	86.1	40.5
Market value ($ mil.)	–	–	–	–	–	–
Employees	–	–	–	–	–	280

SAN DIEGO GAS & ELECTRIC COMPANY

8330 CENTURY PARK CT
SAN DIEGO, CA 921231530
Phone: 619 696-2000
Fax: –
Web: www.sdge.com

CEO: Caroline A Winn
CFO: Bruce A Folkmann
HR: Karen S Tyler
FYE: December 31
Type: Private

San Diego Gas & Electric (SDG&E) digs doling out energy in sunny Southern California. The Sempra Energy company is a regulated utility that serves 1.4 million electricity customer meters and 855,000 natural gas customer meters in San Diego County and a portion of southern Orange County. The electric utility owns 22,360 miles of power distribution lines, which serve about 25 communities; its 1,920 miles of transmission lines are managed by the California Independent System Operator. SDG&E also has limited power generation operations (it owns or contracts 4,520 MW of generating capacity). The gas utility operates almost 170 miles of transmission pipelines and about 8,460 miles of distribution mains.

SAN DIEGO STATE UNIVERSITY FOUNDATION

5250 CAMPANILE DR MC1947
SAN DIEGO, CA 921821901
Phone: 619 594-1900
Fax: –
Web: www.sdsu.edu

CEO: –
CFO: Leslie Levinson
HR: Cedric Josafat
FYE: June 30
Type: Private

San Diego State University (SDSU), with an enrollment of more than 31,000, is one of the largest universities in California. It offers some 75 academic programs leading to about 90 bachelor's, 80 master's, and 22 joint-doctoral degrees. Its Imperial Valley campus on the Mexican border provides upper-division courses and exchange programs with Mexican universities in Baja California. More than one-fifth of SDSU's student population is Hispanic. It is part of the California State University System.

	Annual Growth	06/12	06/13	06/15	06/20	06/22
Sales ($mil.)	–	–	175.2	161.3	178.5	174.5
Net income ($ mil.)	–	–	5.3	(1.0)	17.1	(14.2)
Market value ($ mil.)	–	–	–	–	–	–
Employees	–	–	–	–	–	2,500

SAN DIEGO UNIFIED PORT DISTRICT

3165 PACIFIC HWY
SAN DIEGO, CA 921011128
Phone: 619 686-6200
Fax: –
Web: www.portofsandiego.org

CEO: John Bolduc
CFO: Robert Deangelis
HR: Anita Reichert
FYE: June 30
Type: Private

The San Diego Unified Port District (better known as the Port of San Diego) brings in cash from land and sea. The agency manages two marine cargo facilities, as well as a terminal used by cruise ships. Its real estate operations include leasing and managing land around the port, including almost 20 bayfront parks and commercial property. In addition, the Port of San Diego is charged with protecting San Diego Bay and adjoining tidelands from pollution. The agency, which was created in 1962, is governed by a seven-member board appointed by the city councils of San Diego and four neighboring cities.

	Annual Growth	06/18	06/19	06/20	06/21	06/22
Sales ($mil.)	(3.1%)	–	183.8	162.5	143.6	167.0
Net income ($ mil.)	41.2%	–	25.4	(22.0)	(36.4)	71.4
Market value ($ mil.)	–	–	–	–	–	–
Employees	–	–	–	–	–	604

SAN FRANCISCO BAY AREA RAPID TRANSIT DISTRICT

2150 WEBSTER ST
OAKLAND, CA 946123012
Phone: 510 464-6000
Fax: –
Web: www.bart.gov

CEO: –
CFO: –
HR: –
FYE: June 30
Type: Private

If you're going to San Francisco -- from Oakland, Berkeley, or another Bay Area community -- San Francisco Bay Area Rapid Transit District (BART) can take you there. BART's trains carry about 365,000 daily weekday riders from more than 45 stations over more than 100 miles of track, including the 3.6 mile Transbay Tube under the San Francisco Bay that links the City by the Bay with Oakland and other East Bay communities. Directors elected from nine districts in Alameda, Contra Costa, and San Francisco counties oversee BART, which operates with an annual budget of about $480 million. Construction on the rail system began in 1964, and BART carried its first passengers in 1972.

	Annual Growth	06/18	06/19	06/20	06/21	06/22
Sales ($mil.)	(33.1%)	–	554.7	394.9	90.5	166.1
Net income ($ mil.)	13.3%	–	218.3	259.7	323.8	317.7
Market value ($ mil.)	–	–	–	–	–	–
Employees	–	–	–	–	–	3,347

SAN FRANCISCO FORTY NINERS

4949 MARIE P DEBARTOLO WAY
SANTA CLARA, CA 950541156
Phone: 408 562-4949
Fax: –
Web: www.49ers.com

CEO: Peter Harris
CFO: Larry Macneil
HR: Cathy Chau
FYE: March 31
Type: Private

It took some digging, but these 49ers finally struck the mother lode of championship gold. San Francisco Forty Niners owns and operates the San Francisco 49ers professional football team, which boasts five Super Bowl championships (a mark it shares with the Dallas Cowboys). The franchise was started in 1946 as part of the All-American Football Conference (AAFC) and joined the National Football League in 1950. Its burst of championship glory came in the 1980s and 1990s with the help of such stars as Joe Montana and Steve Young. The team was started by brothers Anthony and Victor Morabito; it is owned by Denise DeBartolo York through her family's DeBartolo Corporation.

SAN FRANCISCO OPERA ASSOCIATION

301 VAN NESS AVE
SAN FRANCISCO, CA 941024509
Phone: 415 861-4008
Fax: –
Web: www.sfopera.com

CEO: David Gockley
CFO: Michael Simpson
HR: Gregory Thomas
FYE: July 31
Type: Private

The San Francisco Opera has mighty big lungs. The company is the nation's second largest and its Western Opera Theater is the only national opera touring group. In addition to presenting new and classic works at War Memorial Opera House, it offers the annual free Opera in the Park as well as education and apprenticeship programs for children and young professionals. Considered an innovator, the company pioneered the US use of "supertitles" (an English translation projected over the stage) and has commissioned operas based on plays (A Streetcar Named Desire), people (slain San Francisco city supervisor Harvey Milk), and books (Dead Man Walking, Dangerous Liaisons). It was founded in 1923 by Gaetano Merola.

	Annual Growth	07/15	07/16	07/17	07/18	07/19
Sales ($mil.)	(6.0%)	–	–	39.5	33.2	34.9
Net income ($ mil.)	(67.0%)	–	–	33.8	12.9	3.7
Market value ($ mil.)	–	–	–	–	–	–
Employees	–	–	–	–	–	1,050

SAN FRANCISCO STATE UNIVERSITY

1600 HOLLOWAY AVE
SAN FRANCISCO, CA 941321740
Phone: 415 338-1111
Fax: –
Web: www.sfsu.edu

CEO: –
CFO: –
HR: Jihad Totah
FYE: June 30
Type: Private

San Francisco State University (SFSU) has an enrollment of about 26,000 undergraduate and more than 4,000 graduate students in seven colleges. Its faculty numbers approximately 1,700. SFSU offers 75 bachelor's, more than 70 master's, and four doctorate degree programs with 110 concentrations. It also offers almost 20 credential and some 35 certificate programs. SFSU is part of the California State University System. Notable SFSU alumni include former San Francisco Mayor Willie Brown Jr., former Congressman Ronald Dellums, and author Ernest Gaines.

	Annual Growth	06/13	06/14	06/15	06/21	06/22
Sales ($mil.)	11.3%	–	8.7	14.7	22.5	20.4
Net income ($ mil.)	(33.3%)	–	4.8	0.4	9.9	0.2
Market value ($ mil.)	–	–	–	–	–	–
Employees	–	–	–	–	–	3,500

SAN JOSE WATER COMPANY

110 W TAYLOR ST
SAN JOSE, CA 951102131
Phone: 408 288-5314
Fax: –
Web: www.sjwater.com

CEO: W R Roth
CFO: Angela Yip
HR: –
FYE: December 31
Type: Private

Tapping into a number of water sources, San Jose Water, the primary subsidiary of SJW, provides water utility services to approximately 225,000 customers (about 1 million people) in California's Santa Clara County. To obtain its water supply, San Jose Water taps wells and surface sources and buys water from the Santa Clara Valley Water District. It also collects local mountain surface water from the watershed in the Santa Cruz Mountains, which is then treated at San Jose Water's two treatment plants. This local surface water accounts for about 7% of the water utility's total supply. Purchased water accounts for more than 40%.

	Annual Growth	12/98	12/99	12/00	12/16	12/17
Sales ($mil.)	6.6%	–	115.7	–	318.1	366.9
Net income ($ mil.)	5.7%	–	16.7	12.8	44.0	45.5
Market value ($ mil.)	–	–	–	–	–	–
Employees	–	–	–	–	–	300

SAN JUAN BASIN ROYALTY TRUST

NYS: SJT

PNC Bank, National Association, PNC Asset Management Group, 2200 Post Oak Boulevard, Floor 18
Houston, TX 77056
Phone: 866 809-4553
Fax: –
Web: www.sjbrt.com

CEO: –
CFO: –
HR: –
FYE: December 31
Type: Public

Trusting in the power of rising oil prices to keep investors happy has been a good strategy for San Juan Basin Royalty Trust. The trust owns working and royalty interests in oil and gas properties in the San Juan Basin of northwestern New Mexico. Carved from interests owned by Southland Royalty (now controlled by ConocoPhillips), San Juan Basin Royalty Trust's holdings consist of a 75% stake in about 151,900 gross (119,000 net) productive acres in San Juan, Rio Arriba, and Sandoval counties. The property contains 3,823 gross producing wells with estimated proved reserves of 249,000 barrels of oil and more than 156.3 billion cu. ft. of natural gas.

	Annual Growth	12/18	12/19	12/20	12/21	12/22
Sales ($mil.)	42.0%	19.5	9.9	8.9	37.6	79.1
Net income ($ mil.)	44.1%	18.0	8.1	7.4	36.0	77.6
Market value ($ mil.)	24.2%	223.7	118.4	124.4	283.8	532.3
Employees	–	–	–	–	–	–

SANDERSON FARMS, LLC

127 FLYNT RD
LAUREL, MS 394439062
Phone: 601 649-4030
Fax: –
Web: www.sandersonfarms.com

CEO: –
CFO: –
HR: –
FYE: October 31
Type: Private

Sanderson Farms is the third largest poultry producer in the US. The company is a Fortune 1000 company engaged in the production, processing, marketing, and distribution of fresh and frozen chicken and other prepared food items. Sanderson Farms' locations are strategically located throughout the southeast, processing more than 16 million chickens per week. In mid-2022, Sanderson Farms was acquired by Cargill and Continental Grain for $203 per share in cash, representing a total equity value for Sanderson Farms of approximately $4.53 billion. The Sanderson family founded the company in 1947.

SANDLER, O'NEILL & PARTNERS, L.P.

1251 AVE OF AMERICAS 6T
NEW YORK, NY 10020
Phone: 212 466-7800
Fax: –
Web: www.sandleroneill.com

CEO: –
CFO: –
HR: –
FYE: December 31
Type: Private

Sandler O'Neill + Partners is where banks can go to do their banking. The boutique investment bank focuses on the financial services sector, offering a wide range of services, such as mergers and acquisitions advisory, IPO underwriting, balance sheet management, consulting, and capital raising. The company also handles the demutualization process for insurance companies and thrifts. Sandler O'Neill provides its clients with research, trading, and sales services for bonds and securities of financial services firms. The management-owned firm was founded in 1988.

	Annual Growth	12/05	12/06	12/07	12/08	12/09
Assets ($mil.)	13.9%	–	154.1	175.6	156.8	227.7
Net income ($ mil.)	–	–	–	–	–	–
Market value ($ mil.)	–	–	–	–	–	–
Employees	–	–	–	–	–	262

SANDLER, TRAVIS & ROSENBERG, P.A.

5835 BLUE LAGOON DR # 200
MIAMI, FL 331262061
Phone: 305 267-9200
Fax: –
Web: www.strtrade.com

CEO: –
CFO: –
HR: –
FYE: August 31
Type: Private

Law firm Sandler, Travis & Rosenberg specializes in international trade and customs; its practice areas include border security, international trade, intellectual property, and commercial litigation. The firm's nearly 55 attorneys practice from offices in Chicago, Detroit, Miami, New York, San Francisco, and Washington, DC. Sandler, Travis & Rosenberg also operates international offices in Argentina, Beijing, Brazil, Canada, Hong Kong, and Mexico. The firm's subsidiary, Sandler & Travis Trade Advisory Services, provides trade and customs consulting services.

SANDRIDGE ENERGY INC

1 E. Sheridan Ave, Suite 500
Oklahoma City, OK 73104
Phone: 405 429-5500
Fax: –
Web: www.sandridgeenergy.com

NYS: SD
CEO: Grayson Pranin
CFO: Brandon L Brown Sr
HR: –
FYE: December 31
Type: Public

SandRidge Energy is an independent oil and natural gas company with a principal focus on acquisition, development, and production activities in the US Mid-Continent. With an interest in approximately 1,470 gross producing wells, the company has a total estimated proved reserves of some 74.3 MMBoe, of which 100% were proved developed. SandRidge Energy sells its oil, natural gas and NGLs to a variety of customers, including oil and natural gas companies and trading and energy marketing companies. In addition, the company's primary operations are the development and acquisition of hydrocarbon resources.

	Annual Growth	12/19	12/20	12/21	12/22	12/23
Sales ($mil.)	(13.6%)	266.8	115.0	168.9	254.3	148.6
Net income ($ mil.)	–	(449.3)	(277.4)	116.7	242.2	60.9
Market value ($ mil.)	34.0%	157.3	115.0	388.0	631.7	507.0
Employees	(21.6%)	270	114	101	102	102

SANDSTON CORP

1496 Business Park Drive, Suite A
Traverse City, MI 49868
Phone: 231 943-2221
Fax: –
Web: www.nematron.com

NBB: SDON
CEO: Daniel J Dorman
CFO: Daniel J Dorman
HR: –
FYE: December 31
Type: Public

Sandston had control issues. The company, formerly known as Nematron, is a public shell that is pursuing investment opportunities. In 2004 it sold the assets of its control systems business to a group of private investors and changed its name to Sandston. (The private investors continue to provide industrial workstations used to control factory equipment under the Nematron name.) Dorman Industries, a company controlled by CEO Daniel Dorman, owns about 49% of Sandston; Patricia Dorman, his wife, owns another 5%.

	Annual Growth	12/18	12/19	12/20	12/21	12/22
Sales ($mil.)	–	–	–	–	–	–
Net income ($ mil.)	–	(0.0)	(0.0)	(0.0)	(0.0)	(0.0)
Market value ($ mil.)	31.6%	0.9	1.3	1.4	2.7	2.7
Employees	–	–	–	–	–	–

SANDUSKY INTERNATIONAL INC.

510 W WATER ST
SANDUSKY, OH 44870
Phone: 419 626-5340
Fax: –
Web: www.metaltek.com

CEO: Edward R Ryan
CFO: Richard A Hargrave
HR: –
FYE: June 30
Type: Private

Sandusky International designs, manufactures, and sells paper-making machinery to paper mills. The company supplies such items as stainless steel and bronze suction roll shells, polycast shells, flexible and rigid pipe rolls, and related accessories. Sandusky also offers maintenance and rebuilding services, as well as self-maintenance training. A sister business provides ingot and toll melting services to the stainless steel market. The company operate several foundries and service centers in the US and UK. It was founded in 1904 by William Millspaugh who patented the centrifugal casting process still used. In 2010 the company was acquired by MetalTek International.

SANDY SPRING BANCORP INC

17801 Georgia Avenue
Olney, MD 20832
Phone: 301 774-6400
Fax: –
Web: www.sandyspringbank.com

NMS: SASR
CEO: Daniel J Schrider
CFO: Philip J Mantua
HR: Diana Matthews
FYE: December 31
Type: Public

Sandy Spring Bancorp is the holding company for Sandy Spring Bank, which operates around 50 branches in the Baltimore and Washington, DC, metropolitan areas. Founded in 1868, the bank is one of the largest and oldest headquartered in Maryland. It provides standard deposit services, including checking and savings accounts, money market accounts, and CDs. Commercial and residential real estate loans account for nearly 80% of the company's loan portfolio; the remainder is a mix of consumer loans, business loans, and equipment leases. The company also offers personal investing services, wealth management, trust services, insurance, and retirement planning.

	Annual Growth	12/19	12/20	12/21	12/22	12/23
Assets ($mil.)	12.9%	8,629.0	12,798	12,591	13,833	14,028
Net income ($ mil.)	1.3%	116.4	97.0	235.1	166.3	122.8
Market value ($ mil.)	(7.9%)	1,701.3	1,445.8	2,159.4	1,582.3	1,223.4
Employees	4.5%	932	1,152	1,116	1,169	1,112

SANFILIPPO (JOHN B) & SON INC
NMS: JBSS

1703 North Randall Road
Elgin, IL 60123-7820
Phone: 847 289-1800
Fax: –
Web: www.jbssinc.com

CEO: –
CFO: –
HR: –
FYE: June 29
Type: Public

John B. Sanfilippo & Son (JBSS) is one of the largest processors of peanuts, almonds, pecans, walnuts, cashews, and other nuts in the US. It markets the nuts as snacks and baking ingredients under a number of private labels as well as its own name brands, including Fisher, Orchard Valley Harvest, Squirrel, Southern Style Nuts and Sunshine Country. The company also produces and distributes other foods and snacks, such as peanut butter, dried fruit and trail mixes, corn snacks, sesame sticks and candy. JBSS's products are sold worldwide to consumers and, less so, to commercial ingredient channels (food service and industrial markets) and contract packagers.

	Annual Growth	06/19	06/20	06/21	06/22	06/23
Sales ($mil.)	3.4%	876.2	880.1	858.5	955.9	999.7
Net income ($ mil.)	12.3%	39.5	54.1	59.7	61.8	62.9
Market value ($ mil.)	10.7%	917.5	954.7	1,021.5	837.7	1,379.3
Employees	(1.2%)	1,470	1,370	1,300	1,300	1,400

SANFORD

801 BROADWAY N
FARGO, ND 581023641
Phone: 701 234-6000
Fax: –
Web: www.sanfordhealth.org

CEO: –
CFO: Joann Kunkel
HR: Lori Hisel
FYE: June 30
Type: Private

Sanford (operating as Sanford Health) is one of the largest not-for-profit integrated health care systems in the US. It primarily serves rural areas through its network of about 45 regional and community hospitals in nine states including the Dakotas, Iowa, Minnesota, and Nebraska. The organization also operates about 300 local clinics and specialty outpatient practices. Specialist service include cancer, cardiology, vascular health, neurology, orthopedics, pediatrics, virology, and women's health. Sanford Health added more than 200 senior care locations in 24 states by acquiring Good Samaritan Society in 2019.

	Annual Growth	06/12	06/13	06/14	06/16	06/17
Sales ($mil.)	939.2%	–	–	3.9	4,231.4	4,411.0
Net income ($ mil.)	–	–	–	(11.9)	108.1	175.4
Market value ($ mil.)	–	–	–	–	–	–
Employees	–	–	–	–	–	50,000

SANFORD AIRPORT AUTHORITY

1200 RED CLEVELAND BLVD
SANFORD, FL 327734202
Phone: 407 585-4000
Fax: –
Web: www.flysfb.com

CEO: Nicole Guillet
CFO: Jason Watkins
HR: Danette Maybin
FYE: September 30
Type: Private

The Sanford Airport Authority manages Orlando Sanford International Airport in a partnership with UK-based airport operator TBI. Orlando Sanford International isn't the largest airport in the home region of Walt Disney World and the NBA's Orlando Magic-- that distinction belongs to Orlando International Airport, which is overseen by the Greater Orlando Aviation Authority. The Sanford Airport Authority is run by a nine-member board appointed by the Sanford City Commission.

	Annual Growth	09/14	09/15	09/16	09/19	09/20
Sales ($mil.)	1.4%	–	11.1	11.9	14.4	11.9
Net income ($ mil.)	(5.5%)	–	6.2	10.6	5.8	4.7
Market value ($ mil.)	–	–	–	–	–	–
Employees	–	–	–	–	–	84

SANFORD BURNHAM PREBYS MEDICAL DISCOVERY INSTITUTE

10901 N TORREY PINES RD
LA JOLLA, CA 920371005
Phone: 858 795-5000
Fax: –
Web: www.sbpdiscovery.org

CEO: C R Mills
CFO: Gary Chessum
HR: –
FYE: June 30
Type: Private

Founded in 1976 as the La Jolla Cancer Research Foundation, the Sanford Burnham Prebys Medical Discovery Institute (formerly Sanford-Burnham Medical Research Institute) is a nonprofit organization that performs biomedical research in areas such as cancer, neuroscience, immunology and rare children's diseases. Known for its stem cell research and drug discovery technologies, Sanford-Burnham boasts a handful of research centers, including its NCI-designated Cancer Center, which is one of only seven National Cancer Institute-designated Basic Laboratory Cancer Centers in the nation. Sanford-Burnham's other centers include the Sanford Children's Health Research Center, the Conrad Prebys, Infectious and Inflammatory, Neuroscience and Aging, and Stem Cell Research Center.

	Annual Growth	06/17	06/18	06/19	06/20	06/22
Sales ($mil.)	(5.5%)	–	123.7	117.8	111.6	98.6
Net income ($ mil.)	–	–	(25.5)	(66.1)	(1.5)	(41.1)
Market value ($ mil.)	–	–	–	–	–	–
Employees	–	–	–	–	–	1,000

SANGAMO THERAPEUTICS INC
NMS: SGMO

7000 Marina Blvd.
Brisbane, CA 94005
Phone: 510 970-6000
Fax: –
Web: www.sangamo.com

CEO: –
CFO: –
HR: –
FYE: December 31
Type: Public

Sangamo Therapeutics (formerly Sangamo BioSciences) hopes zinc fingers have the Midas touch when it comes to regulating gene expression. The company's zinc finger DNA-binding proteins (ZFPs) control gene expression (activation) and cell function; the firm aims to develop gene-correcting therapeutics for a variety of indications, including human genetic disorders as well as genetic modifications in plants and animals. Sangamo Therapeutics has candidates in clinical trials and research stages for conditions such as hemophilia, HIV/AIDS, sickle cell disease, blood disorders, and Alzheimer's disease. Other ZFP development programs include research in the areas of lysosomal storage disorders.

	Annual Growth	12/19	12/20	12/21	12/22	12/23
Sales ($mil.)	14.5%	102.4	118.2	110.7	111.3	176.2
Net income ($ mil.)	–	(95.2)	(121.0)	(178.3)	(192.3)	(257.8)
Market value ($ mil.)	(49.5%)	1,491.0	2,779.8	1,336.0	559.3	96.8
Employees	3.4%	354	413	431	478	405

SANMINA CORP
NMS: SANM

2700 N. First St.
San Jose, CA 95134
Phone: 408 964-3500
Fax: –
Web: www.sanmina.com

CEO: Jure Sola
CFO: Jonathan Faust
HR: –
FYE: September 30
Type: Public

Sanmina a leading global provider of integrated manufacturing solutions, components, products and repair, logistics and after-market services. Some of the company's services include manufacturing solutions, components, products and repair, logistics and after-market services. It designs and makes printed circuit boards and board assemblies, backplanes and backplane assemblies, enclosures, cable assemblies, optical components and modules, and memory modules. In addition, the company increasingly provides more value-added services such as design and engineering, materials management, order fulfillment, and in-circuit testing. It serves OEMs in the health care, defense, medical, aerospace, telecommunications, and technology industries, among others. Sanmina puts significant focus with manufacturing facilities close to its customers in lower-cost regions. About 35% of its sales come from the US.

	Annual Growth	09/19*	10/20	10/21	10/22*	09/23
Sales ($mil.)	2.1%	8,233.9	6,960.4	6,756.6	7,890.5	8,935.0
Net income ($ mil.)	21.7%	141.5	139.7	269.0	256.1	310.0
Market value ($ mil.)	14.0%	1,825.4	1,508.9	2,226.7	2,618.8	3,084.8
Employees	(5.7%)	43,000	37,000	35,000	34,000	34,000

*Fiscal year change

SANTA CRUZ SEASIDE COMPANY INC

400 BEACH ST
SANTA CRUZ, CA 950605416
Phone: 831 423-5590
Fax: –
Web: www.scseaside.com

CEO: –
CFO: –
HR: Sabra Reyes
FYE: December 31
Type: Private

Santa Cruz Seaside Company has been making people scream, laugh, and spend money for more than a century. The company operates the Santa Cruz Boardwalk amusement park in California, which has been touted the "Coney Island of the West". The park features about 35 rides, 30 restaurants, 15 retail shops, arcades, miniature golf, bowling, and conference and banquet facilities. The property is a State Historic Landmark, while its Looff Carousel (1911) and Giant Dipper roller coaster (1924) are both National Historic Landmarks. In addition, some arcade games date back to 1910. The Canfield family, including chairman and president Charles own the company. The Boardwalk celebrated its 100th anniversary in 2007.

	Annual Growth	12/08	12/09	12/10	12/11	12/12
Sales ($mil.)	7.2%	–	–	45.2	47.5	51.9
Net income ($ mil.)	31.8%	–	–	3.5	3.8	6.1
Market value ($ mil.)	–	–	–	–	–	–
Employees	–	–	–	–	–	1,000

SANTA FE GOLD CORP

2325 San Pedro NE, Suite 2-J5
Albuquerque, NM 87110
Phone: 505 255-4852
Fax: –
Web: www.santafegoldcorp.com

CEO: Brian Adair
CFO: Stephen J Antol
HR: –
FYE: June 30
Type: Public

Santa Fe Gold hopes it has the Midas touch. The company controls the Summit silver and gold mining project and the Lordsburg mill in southwestern New Mexico. It has also been developing the Ortiz gold property, in north-central New Mexico, and holds the Black Canyon mica deposit and processing equipment near Phoenix. With an increased emphasis on those projects, Santa Fe Gold has transformed itself into a precious metals miner. The company focuses on acquiring and developing gold, silver, copper and industrial mineral assets. Although it dropped its bid to acquire Columbus Silver in 2012, the company plans to buy some of that company's mineral properties.

	Annual Growth	06/17	06/18	06/19	06/21	06/22
Sales ($mil.)	–	–	–	–	–	–
Net income ($ mil.)	–	2.4	(2.6)	8.5	(2.1)	(2.3)
Market value ($ mil.)	–	41.4	40.2	39.7	–	–
Employees	8.4%	2	–	2	–	3

SANTA MONICA COMMUNITY COLLEGE DISTRICT

1900 PICO BLVD
SANTA MONICA, CA 904051628
Phone: 310 434-4000
Fax: –
Web: www.smc.edu

CEO: –
CFO: –
HR: –
FYE: June 30
Type: Private

Talk about a (class)room with a view. Santa Monica Community College is a two-year school with about 34,000 students. The beach-side college offers programs in more than 80 fields of study and leads California's junior colleges in transferring students to the University of California and University of Southern California. Its unique Academy of Entertainment and Technology offers courses in entertainment technology (animation, game development, editing, visual effects), graphic design, and interior architectural design. The school also provides career training in such fields as accounting, automotive technology, computer science, fine arts, and nursing. Santa Monica Community College was founded in 1929.

	Annual Growth	06/18	06/19	06/20	06/21	06/22
Sales ($mil.)	(6.0%)	–	102.8	97.4	105.4	85.2
Net income ($ mil.)	–	–	(8.8)	(32.8)	(6.4)	0.7
Market value ($ mil.)	–	–	–	–	–	–
Employees	–	–	–	–	–	1,300

SANTANDER HOLDINGS USA INC.

75 State Street
Boston, MA 02109
Phone: 800 493-8219
Fax: –
Web: www.santanderus.com/us/investorshareholderrelations

CEO: Timothy H Wennes
CFO: Juan Carlos De Soto
HR: –
FYE: December 31
Type: Public

Santander Holdings USA is the parent company of Sovereign Bank, which reigns in the Northeast with more than 700 branch locations. The bank caters to individuals and small to midsized businesses, offering deposits, credit cards, insurance, and investments, as well as commercial loans and mortgages (which together account for nearly half of its total portfolio) and residential mortgages and home equity loans (more than a quarter). Santander Holdings also owns a majority of Santander Consumer USA, which purchases and services subprime car loans made by auto dealerships and other companies. Spain-based banking giant Banco Santander acquired the rest of Sovereign Bancorp it didn't already own in 2009.

	Annual Growth	12/19	12/20	12/21	12/22	12/23
Sales ($mil.)	6.3%	12,379	11,970	11,745	12,150	15,820
Net income ($ mil.)	5.5%	753.2	(840.4)	2,982.4	1,405.0	932.9
Market value ($ mil.)	–	–	–	–	–	–
Employees	(8.6%)	16,900	15,698	14,600	13,700	11,800

SAPP BROS. PETROLEUM, INC.

9915 S 148TH ST STE 2
OMAHA, NE 681383822
Phone: 402 895-2202
Fax: –
Web: www.sappbros.net

CEO: Allen Marsh
CFO: Tyler A Marsh
HR: –
FYE: March 31
Type: Private

There have been few poor saps in this family since the Sapp brothers made a go of their petroleum products business. Sapp Bros Petroleum distributes petroleum products such as fuels, lubricants, propane, antifreeze, absorbents, additives, and equipment through more than 10 locations in Nebraska and western Iowa. It has a sideline, selling used computer parts such as modems, processors, and keyboards. The regional fuel distributor was founded by the four Sapp brothers in 1980 and is run by CEO Bill Sapp, who also runs sister company Sapp Bros Truck Stops.

	Annual Growth	10/07	10/08	10/09*	03/14	03/22
Sales ($mil.)	(27.6%)	–	922.3	564.0	5.8	10.1
Net income ($ mil.)	(4.3%)	–	3.2	5.6	0.3	1.7
Market value ($ mil.)	–	–	–	–	–	–
Employees	–	–	–	–	–	285

*Fiscal year change

SAPP BROS., INC.

9915 S 148TH ST
OMAHA, NE 681383876
Phone: 402 895-7038
Fax: –
Web: www.sappbros.net

CEO: Andrew Richard
CFO: –
HR: Katie Schrad
FYE: September 30
Type: Private

Need air in those 18 wheels? Sapp Bros Travel Centers (formerly Sapp Bros Truck Stops) has the usual air, gas, food, but also offers human conveniences such as laundry rooms, mailbox rentals, private showers, and TV lounges. The company operates a chain of some 15 truck stops -- readily identifiable by the giant red-and-white coffeepot logo -- along interstate highways from Utah to Pennsylvania; with a concentration in Nebraska. Half of the locations also operate service centers, offering oil changes, new tires, and safety checks. Its sister company, Sapp Bros Petroleum, distributes fuels and lubricants to more than 200 retailers. The firm is run by CEO Bill Sapp, one of the four founding Sapp brothers.

	Annual Growth	09/17	09/18	09/19	09/20	09/21
Sales ($mil.)	(3.6%)	–	1,259.1	1,194.8	920.2	1,128.7
Net income ($ mil.)	21.7%	–	11.7	4.5	17.0	21.1
Market value ($ mil.)	–	–	–	–	–	–
Employees	–	–	–	–	–	1,700

SARA ENTERPRISES, INC.

1999 BROADWAY STE 3550
DENVER, CO 802025750
Phone: 818 553-3200
Fax: –
Web: –

CEO: Joseph McClure
CFO: Julie McClure
HR: –
FYE: December 31
Type: Private

Montrose Travel is going places. The fast-growing company operates through more than 10 divisions including business, leisure, romantic, and group/meetings. It also uses a network of about 170 independent contractors and partner companies. Montrose's business division manages the corporate travel for more than 400 firms. It also specializes in honeymoons and anniversary trips. Joe McClure, Sr. and his wife, Leora, bought the business in 1956. It's still a family affair -- in 1990 the McClure's son, Joe, Jr. (CEO), his wife, Julie (president), and their daughter, Andi (CFO) bought Montrose Travel.

	Annual Growth	12/03	12/04	12/05	12/06	12/07
Sales ($mil.)	7.2%	–	7.6	7.9	–	9.3
Net income ($ mil.)	23.6%	–	0.6	0.7	–	1.1
Market value ($ mil.)	–	–	–	–	–	–
Employees	–	–	–	–	–	160

SARAH BUSH LINCOLN HEALTH CENTER

1000 HEALTH CENTER DR
MATTOON, IL 619389253
Phone: 217 258-2525
Fax: –
Web: www.sarahbush.org

CEO: Jerry Esker
CFO: –
HR: Debbie Saddoris
FYE: June 30
Type: Private

With the moniker of the Illinois' favorite son's stepmother (Sarah Bush Lincoln), who wouldn't want to go to this health center? And apparently the locals agree, since Sarah Bush Lincoln Health Center (SBLHC) has a market share of about 44% in its seven-county service area in east-central Illinois and an inpatient market share for Coles County of nearly 80%. SBLHC has 128 beds and provides a wide range of health care services including emergency medicine, behavioral health care, surgical services, and cancer treatment. Its network also includes about 30 clinics, doctors' offices, and hospice centers. The hospital also offers support groups and continuing education classes.

	Annual Growth	06/18	06/19	06/20	06/21	06/22
Sales ($mil.)	13.1%	–	355.1	379.7	488.5	514.1
Net income ($ mil.)	22.8%	–	29.4	28.3	87.4	54.4
Market value ($ mil.)	–	–	–	–	–	–
Employees	–	–	–	–	–	2,577

SARAH LAWRENCE COLLEGE

1 MEAD WAY
BRONXVILLE, NY 107085999
Phone: 914 337-0700
Fax: –
Web: www.sarahlawrence.edu

CEO: –
CFO: –
HR: Lois Booth
FYE: May 31
Type: Private

Sarah Lawrence College (SLC) was founded in 1926 as an institution of higher education for young women. The private liberal arts school, located on a 44-acre campus in suburban New York, has been coeducational since 1968 and has an annual enrollment of some 1,300 undergraduate and about 350 graduate students. Most of its courses are seminars limited to 14 students; the school has a student-to-faculty ratio of approximately 10-to-1, one of the lowest at any US university. SLC offers a wide range of academic concentrations, including performing arts, natural science, history, teaching, and literature. It was founded by William Lawrence, who named the school after his wife Sarah, a supporter of women's suffrage.

	Annual Growth	05/17	05/18	05/20	05/21	05/22
Sales ($mil.)	2.2%	–	76.4	77.5	65.8	83.3
Net income ($ mil.)	37.2%	–	6.4	(2.8)	28.4	22.5
Market value ($ mil.)	–	–	–	–	–	–
Employees	–	–	–	–	–	450

SARASOTA COUNTY PUBLIC HOSPITAL DISTRICT

1700 S TAMIAMI TRL
SARASOTA, FL 342393509
Phone: 941 917-9000
Fax: –
Web: www.smh.com

CEO: David Verinder
CFO: Jeff Limbocker
HR: Alyssa Griner
FYE: September 30
Type: Private

Sarasota County Public Hospital District, which does business as the Sarasota Memorial Health Care System, is a publicly owned hospital system serving residents in and around Sarasota on Florida's western coast. It is a full-service public health system, with two hospitals offering specialized expertise in heart, vascular, cancer, orthopedic and neuroscience services, as well as a state-of-the-art cancer care center and a network of outpatient centers, urgent care centers, laboratories, diagnostic imaging and physician practices, skilled nursing and rehabilitation among its many programs.

	Annual Growth	09/13	09/14	09/15	09/16	09/20
Sales ($mil.)	10.8%	–	–	590.8	12.5	986.2
Net income ($ mil.)	3.3%	–	–	131.7	0.5	155.0
Market value ($ mil.)	–	–	–	–	–	–
Employees	–	–	–	–	–	7,000

SARATOGA RESOURCES INC

1304 Alta Vista
Austin, TX 78704
Phone: 512 940-1948
Fax: –
Web: www.saratogaresourcesinc.com

CEO: Thomas F Cooke
CFO: –
HR: –
FYE: December 31
Type: Public

Saratoga Resources (SRI) hopes to find more than springs underground. The independent oil and gas company explores for and produces oil and natural gas along the coast of Louisiana. The company's 13 oil fields are spread across more than 52,000 acres with about 90 wells and have proved and probable reserves of about 342 million barrels of oil equivalent, 46% of which is natural gas. SRI produces about 803,400 barrels of oil equivalent per year, about 75% of it oil. The company owns associated infrastructure assets on its oilfields including 100 miles of pipeline, about 90 wellbores, and 10 saltwater disposal wells. SRI entered Chapter 11 bankruptcy protection in 2015 and emerged from it in 2016.

	Annual Growth	12/12	12/13	12/14	12/20	12/21
Sales ($mil.)	–	84.0	67.4	54.4	–	–
Net income ($ mil.)	–	(3.7)	(26.4)	(143.9)	(0.4)	(0.5)
Market value ($ mil.)	–	129.9	41.8	8.0	–	–
Employees	(31.7%)	31	34	32	–	1

SARCOM, INC.

6299 STATE ROUTE 9N
HADLEY, NY 128352406
Phone: 518 696-9970
Fax: –
Web: www.aepcolloids.com

CEO: –
CFO: –
HR: –
FYE: December 31
Type: Private

Petroleum may be necessary, but Sarcom's oils are downright essential. The company distributes essential oils and fine and specialty chemicals for the flavors and fragrance industry; typical products include aromatic chemicals, terpenes, menthol crystals, psyllium seed husk, water-soluble gums, and vanilla beans. In addition to its New York headquarters, Sarcom has offices in Florida and in China, and it has distribution deals with companies in France, China, and the US. It has a joint venture that produces essential oils in China, and its AEP Colloids division imports and distributes food ingredients. The company was founded in 1982.

	Annual Growth	12/14	12/15	12/16	12/17	12/18
Sales ($mil.)	4.6%	–	11.2	9.9	10.5	12.8
Net income ($ mil.)	(17.3%)	–	0.6	0.3	0.1	0.4
Market value ($ mil.)	–	–	–	–	–	–
Employees	–	–	–	–	–	9

SAREPTA THERAPEUTICS INC

NMS: SRPT

215 First Street, Suite 415
Cambridge, MA 02142
Phone: 617 274-4000
Fax: –
Web: www.sarepta.com

CEO: Douglas S Ingram
CFO: Ian M Estepan
HR: –
FYE: December 31
Type: Public

Sarepta Therapeutics is a commercial-stage biopharmaceutical company focused on helping patients through the discovery and development of unique RNA-targeted therapeutics, gene therapy and other genetic therapeutic modalities for the treatment of rare diseases. Applying its proprietary, highly-differentiated and innovative technologies, and through collaborations with its strategic partners, it is developing potential therapeutic candidates for a broad range of diseases and disorders, including Duchenne muscular dystrophy (DMD), Limb-girdle muscular dystrophies (LGMDs) and other neuromuscular and central nervous system (CNS) related disorders.

	Annual Growth	12/19	12/20	12/21	12/22	12/23
Sales ($mil.)	34.4%	380.8	540.1	701.9	933.0	1,243.3
Net income ($ mil.)	–	(715.1)	(554.1)	(418.8)	(703.5)	(536.0)
Market value ($ mil.)	(7.0%)	12,095	15,980	8,440.6	12,146	9,038.6
Employees	15.3%	743	866	840	1,162	1,314

SARGENT ELECTRIC COMPANY

2740 SMALLMAN ST STE 400
PITTSBURGH, PA 152224744
Phone: 412 391-0588
Fax: –
Web: www.sargentelectric.com

CEO: Stephan H Dake
CFO: Elizabeth Lawrence
HR: –
FYE: December 31
Type: Private

Sargent Electric Company has earned its stripes providing electrical services for its customers. Founded in 1907 to serve Pittsburgh's steel industry, the electrical contractor performs construction work for utilities, foundries, oil refineries, chemical processing firms, and steelmakers. Clients have included Allegheny Energy, Duquesne Light, General Electric, and United States Steel. The company also provides electric service and maintenance services to residential, commercial, and government customers. Its service area encompasses about 20 states in the eastern half of the US. Sargent Electric is owned and managed by the Sargent family.

	Annual Growth	12/09	12/10	12/11	12/13	12/14
Sales ($mil.)	(0.1%)	–	–	89.1	187.7	88.9
Net income ($ mil.)	72.2%	–	–	0.3	10.2	1.7
Market value ($ mil.)	–	–	–	–	–	–
Employees	–	–	–	–	–	400

SARGENTO FOODS INC.

1 PERSNICKETY PL
PLYMOUTH, WI 530733544
Phone: 920 893-8484
Fax: –
Web: www.sargento.com

CEO: Louis P Gentine
CFO: Jeremy Behler
HR: Chad Fritz
FYE: January 01
Type: Private

Sargento Foods is one of the largest cheese manufacturers in the US, offering a variety of block cheese and such value-added products as shredded cheese blends and sliced cheeses for sandwiches. The company markets its products through supermarkets and other retail grocery stores nationwide. In addition, the company is also a leading supplier of custom cheese products to restaurants and other food service operators; its food service and ingredients division makes cheese items for other food manufacturers. The company makes its products in its five Wisconsin facilities. The family-owned business was started in 1953 by Leonard Gentine Sr. and his business partner Joseph Sartori.

	Annual Growth	01/10	01/11	01/12*	12/12*	01/17
Sales ($mil.)	10.8%	–	981.0	981.0	–	1,820.0
Net income ($ mil.)	–	–	–	–	–	–
Market value ($ mil.)	–	–	–	–	–	–
Employees	–	–	–	–	–	2,100

*Fiscal year change

SARTORI COMPANY

107 N PLEASANT VIEW RD
PLYMOUTH, WI 530734948
Phone: 920 893-6061
Fax: –
Web: www.sartoricheese.com

CEO: Bert Sartori
CFO: Mark Schwechel
HR: –
FYE: June 30
Type: Private

Sartori makes Italian (parmesan, and asiago), and other aged specialty cheeses. Brands include Sartori, and Bellavitano, and Montamore. The company sells its products through dozens of retailers, such as Whole Foods, Kroger, Publix, Safeway, Wegmans, and more. Sartori was founded in 1939 as S&R Cheese by Italian immigrant Paolo Sartori and Louis Rossini and is still owned and operated by the fourth generation of the Sartori family, including former CEO Jim Sartori.

SAS INSTITUTE INC.

100 SAS CAMPUS DR
CARY, NC 275138617
Phone: 919 677-8000
Fax: –
Web: www.sas.com

CEO: –
CFO: –
HR: –
FYE: December 31
Type: Private

SAS, founded in 1976, delivers leading data management and analytics solutions across the entire analytics life cycle. It offers data access, data preparation, data quality and information cataloging, advanced flow steps and information governance, visualization and reporting, conversational AI and chatbots, statistics, machine learning and deep learning, optimization, econometrics, and model deployment and monitoring. SAS technology solutions help meet the needs of organizations in practically every industry, regardless of size. Its biggest market is the Americas, accounting for almost half of sales.

SATTERFIELD AND PONTIKES CONSTRUCTION, INC.

11750 KATY FWY STE 500
HOUSTON, TX 770791219
Phone: 713 996-1300
Fax: –
Web: www.satpon.com

CEO: George A Pontikes Jr
CFO: Angela Salinas
HR: Jason Kreuiter
FYE: December 31
Type: Private

Satterfield & Pontikes Construction (S&P) provides general contracting, consultation, and construction management services, primarily in the Gulf Coast region of Texas and Louisiana. The company often works on buildings for the commercial, retail, industrial, educational, entertainment, and recreational sectors. High profile projects include the Texas A&M University Health Science Center and the expansion of the World War II Museum in New Orleans. S&P specializes in concrete work and early-stage site work, as well as 3-D modeling and virtual design. The company was founded in 1989 and is headed by majority owner and CEO George Pontikes.

SAUL CENTERS INC
NYS: BFS

7501 Wisconsin Avenue
Bethesda, MD 20814
Phone: 301 986-6200
Fax: –
Web: www.saulcenters.com

CEO: B F Saul II
CFO: Carlos L Heard
HR: –
FYE: December 31
Type: Public

This company might say that with shopping properties, it's "Saul" good. A self-managed and self-administered real estate investment trust (REIT), Saul Centers acquires, develops, and manages commercial real estate, primarily in the Washington, DC, metropolitan area. The REIT owns about 60 strip malls and shopping centers anchored by big-box retailers and supermarkets, along with more than half a dozen mixed-use properties. Altogether its properties comprise some 9.9 million sq. ft. of leasable space. Its major tenants include the likes of Giant Food, Safeway, Capital One Bank, and the US government.

	Annual Growth	12/19	12/20	12/21	12/22	12/23
Sales ($mil.)	2.7%	231.5	225.2	239.2	245.9	257.2
Net income ($ mil.)	0.5%	51.7	40.4	48.4	50.2	52.7
Market value ($ mil.)	(7.1%)	1,271.1	762.9	1,276.9	979.7	945.7
Employees	(11.5%)	116	60	65	70	71

SAVAGE COMPANIES

901 W LEGACY CENTER WAY
MIDVALE, UT 840475765
Phone: 801 944-6600
Fax: –
Web: www.savageco.com

CEO: Kirk Aubry
CFO: Jeff Roberts
HR: –
FYE: December 31
Type: Private

Through a collection of subsidiaries led by Savage Services Corporation, Savage Companies provides a broad portfolio of services to move and manage critical materials with a professional team the customers can trust, innovative solutions to solve their toughest challenges, and consistent results they can count on. Freight handled by the company includes dry bulk and liquid bulk products, including hazardous and non-hazardous materials, petroleum products, food-grade products, chemicals and petrochemicals, and industrial and construction materials. Savage began operations in 1946.

SAVANNAH HEALTH SERVICES, LLC

4700 WATERS AVE
SAVANNAH, GA 314046220
Phone: 912 350-8000
Fax: –
Web: www.memorialhealth.com

CEO: Shayne George
CFO: –
HR: –
FYE: December 31
Type: Private

Memorial Health University Medical Center wants to provide memorable health care to residents of Savannah, Georgia, and surrounding areas. An affiliate of Mercer University School of Medicine, the tertiary care facility provides such services as cardiac and trauma care and rehabilitation. Also known as Memorial University Medical Center (MUMC), the hospital has some 620 beds and includes the MUMC Children's Hospital. It also operates specialty cancer care and women's health centers, as well as research programs. Founded in 1955, MUMC is the flagship facility in a broader system of entities known as Memorial Health, which includes affiliated primary and specialty care clinics in the region.

	Annual Growth	12/07	12/08	12/13	12/14	12/15
Sales ($mil.)	0.4%	–	453.3	547.2	469.4	466.2
Net income ($ mil.)		–	–	(29.3)	38.6	32.3	9.6
Market value ($ mil.)		–	–	–	–	–
Employees		–	–	–	–	4,700

SAVARA INC
NMS: SVRA

1717 Langhorne Newtown Road, Suite 300
Langhorne, PA 19047
Phone: 512 614-1848
Fax: –
Web: www.savarapharma.com

CEO: –
CFO: –
HR: –
FYE: December 31
Type: Public

Mast Therapeutics steers its R&D ship towards investigational drug treatments for genetic disease and cancer. The company is focused on developing a late-stage treatment for sickle-cell disease patients. The drug aims to reduce tissue and organ damage by repairing microvascular function, and is being explored as a treatment for other inflammatory and circulatory disorders. The company also has some candidates in development to treat cancer. The firm's name reflects its focus on its MAST (molecular adhesion and sealant technology) platform. In 2017, Mast agreed to merge with Savara, which specializes in treatments for rare respiratory diseases. The combined firm, to be named Savara, will be headquartered in Austin, Texas.

	Annual Growth	12/19	12/20	12/21	12/22	12/23
Sales ($mil.)	–	–	0.3	–	–	–
Net income ($ mil.)	–	(78.2)	(49.6)	(43.0)	(38.2)	(54.7)
Market value ($ mil.)	1.2%	618.9	158.9	171.3	214.1	649.3
Employees	–	40	27	22	28	–

SAVE MART SUPERMARKETS LLC

1800 STANDIFORD AVE
MODESTO, CA 953500180
Phone: 209 577-1600
Fax: –
Web: www.thesavemartcompanies.com

CEO: Chris McGarry
CFO: Ali Sadiq
HR: Eric Pifer
FYE: December 31
Type: Private

Save Mart Supermarkets is a big wheel in the California grocery business with approximately 200 stores in Northern California, and Nevada. Its major sponsorships include Toyota/Save Mart 350, California State Fair, Farm to Fork Sacramento, Gallo Center for the Arts, Modesto Nuts ? Minor League Baseball, and Fresno Grizzlies ? Minor League Baseball. Its supermarkets and warehouse stores operate under the Save Mart, Lucky, Lucky California, Maxx Value, and FoodMaxx names. Save Mart also operates Smart Refrigerated Transport and is a partner in Super Store Industries. The company was founded in 1952 by Mike Piccinini and Nick Tocco.

SAVE THE CHILDREN FEDERATION, INC.

501 KINGS HWY E STE 400
FAIRFIELD, CT 068254861
Phone: 203 221-4000
Fax: –
Web: www.savethechildren.org

CEO: Carolyn Miles
CFO: –
HR: Carrie Watson
FYE: December 31
Type: Private

Save the Children helps poor and malnourished children in some 15 US states and nearly 120 countries, focusing on such areas as health and nutrition, economic development, education, child protection, and HIV/AIDS. The humanitarian organization also participates in international disaster relief efforts, focusing on children and their families. Save the Children spends about 90% of its budget on program services, with the rest allocated to administration and fundraising. The group was founded in 1932, inspired by the international children's rights movement begun in the UK in 1919 by Eglantyne Jebb, founder of the British Save the Children Fund. It is a member of the International Save the Children Alliance.

	Annual Growth	12/12	12/13	12/14	12/15	12/16
Sales ($mil.)	(3.9%)	–	–	–	678.3	652.0
Net income ($ mil.)	–	–	–	–	(10.1)	(7.5)
Market value ($ mil.)	–	–	–	–	–	–
Employees	–	–	–	–	–	1,300

SAWNEE ELECTRIC MEMBERSHIP CORPORATION

543 ATLANTA RD
CUMMING, GA 300402701
Phone: 770 887-2363
Fax: –
Web: www.sawnee.com

CEO: Michael A Goodroe
CFO: Ginny J Ellis
HR: –
FYE: December 31
Type: Private

Sawnee Electric Membership Corporation (Sawnee EMC) wasn't around on the night the lights went out in Georgia, but it plans to make sure they stay on. The electric distribution cooperative serves about 152,000 residential, commercial and industrial meters in a seven-county area of northern Georgia comprised of Cherokee, Dawson, Forsyth, Fulton, Gwinnett, Hall, and Lumpkin counties. Residential customers in the area (which includes the sprawling Atlanta suburbs) account for two-thirds of electricity usage. While small and medium users must get their electricity from Sawnee, potential customers with loads exceeding 900 kilowatts can shop around. Sawnee EMC distributes electricity over 9,970 miles of power line.

	Annual Growth	12/18	12/19	12/20	12/21	12/22
Sales ($mil.)	7.8%	–	361.1	375.1	399.6	452.3
Net income ($ mil.)	13.2%	–	20.8	17.8	29.2	30.2
Market value ($ mil.)	–	–	–	–	–	–
Employees	–	–	–	–	–	300

SAYERS40, INC

825 CORPORATE WOODS PKWY
VERNON HILLS, IL 600613158
Phone: 800 323-5357
Fax: –
Web: –

CEO: Gale Sayers
CFO: John Altergott
HR: –
FYE: December 31
Type: Private

The game has changed from football to technology products, but NFL Hall of Famer Gale Sayers is still trying to leave his competition in the dust. The former Chicago Bear's eponymous company, Sayers, sells computer hardware and software. It offers services ranging from computer installation to consulting services, such as operating system migration and network design. Other services include technical training, voice and data cabling, and financing. The company offers products from leading manufacturers such as Cisco Systems, Hewlett-Packard, and Sun Microsystems. Chairman and CEO Sayers is the majority owner of the company, which he founded in 1982.

SB FINANCIAL GROUP INC

NAS: SBFG

401 Clinton Street
Defiance, OH 43512
Phone: 419 783-8950
Fax: –
Web: www.yoursbfinancial.com

CEO: Mark A Klein
CFO: Anthony V Cosentino V
HR: –
FYE: December 31
Type: Public

SB Financial Group (formerly Rurban Financial) is the holding company The State Bank and Trust Company (dba State Bank), which has more than 20 branches in northwestern Ohio and another in northeastern Indiana. The banks offer products, including checking and savings accounts, money market accounts, credit cards, IRAs, and CDs. Commercial and agricultural loans account for approximately two-thirds of the company's loan portfolio; the bank also writes mortgage and consumer loans. State Bank Wealth Management (formerly Reliance Financial Services), a unit of State Bank, offers trust and investment management services, as well as brokerage services through an alliance with Raymond James.

	Annual Growth	12/19	12/20	12/21	12/22	12/23
Assets ($mil.)	6.6%	1,038.6	1,257.8	1,330.9	1,335.6	1,343.2
Net income ($ mil.)	0.3%	12.0	14.9	18.3	12.5	12.1
Market value ($ mil.)	(6.0%)	133.3	123.7	133.1	114.7	103.9
Employees	(0.1%)	252	244	269	268	251

SBA COMMUNICATIONS CORP (NEW)

NMS: SBAC

8051 Congress Avenue
Boca Raton, FL 33487
Phone: 561 995-7670
Fax: –
Web: www.sbasite.com

CEO: Jeffrey A Stoops
CFO: Brendan T Cavanagh
HR: –
FYE: December 31
Type: Public

SBA Communications is a leading independent owner and operator of wireless communications infrastructure, including tower structures, rooftops, and other structures that support antennas used for wireless communication. It leases antenna space to wireless service providers and provides site development services, including network design, zoning and permit assistance, and tower construction. SBA owns and operates over 39,310 towers in Central and South America, Canada, and South Africa. It built most of the towers it operates, often through build-to-suit arrangements with carriers. AT&T, Verizon Wireless, and T-Mobile are its three largest customers.

	Annual Growth	12/19	12/20	12/21	12/22	12/23
Sales ($mil.)	7.7%	2,014.6	2,083.1	2,308.8	2,633.5	2,711.6
Net income ($ mil.)	35.9%	147.0	24.1	237.6	461.4	501.8
Market value ($ mil.)	1.3%	26,039	30,484	42,034	30,287	27,411
Employees	5.2%	1,457	1,483	1,596	1,834	1,787

SCAI HOLDINGS, LLC

510 LAKE COOK RD STE 400
DEERFIELD, IL 600155031
Phone: 847 236-0921
Fax: –
Web: www.sca.health

CEO: –
CFO: –
HR: –
FYE: December 31
Type: Private

SCAI Holdings (dba SCA, or Surgical Care Affiliates) can stitch 'em up and move 'em out. The company operates one of the largest networks of outpatient surgery centers in the US. (Also known as ambulatory surgical centers, or ASCs, these facilities charge less than hospitals to perform routine surgeries.) SCA operates more than 200 surgery centers and surgical hospitals in about 35 states. The centers offer non-emergency day surgeries in orthopedics, ophthalmology, gastroenterology, pain management, otolaryngology (ear, nose and throat), urology, and gynecology. The company went public in 2013, but was acquired by insurance giant UnitedHealth in 2017 for some $2.3 billion.

	Annual Growth	12/12	12/13	12/14	12/15	12/16
Sales ($mil.)	16.9%	–	802.0	864.7	1,051.5	1,281.4
Net income ($ mil.)	62.5%	–	52.7	157.1	273.6	226.3
Market value ($ mil.)	–	–	–	–	–	–
Employees	–	–	–	–	–	5,248

SCAN-OPTICS, INC.

169 Progress Drive
Manchester, CT 06040-2294
Phone: 860 645-7878
Fax: 860 645-7995
Web: www.scanoptics.com

CEO: –
CFO: –
HR: –
FYE: December 31
Type: Public

Scan-Optics gives documents more than a cursory glance. Health care organizations, government agencies, financial institutions, and other businesses use the company's data processing and image scanning systems to manage documents and process a variety of forms, such as health care claims, tax returns, and invoices. Scan-Optics' software applications include tools for test scoring, image capture, and tax processing; it also offers third-party applications. Its professional services include consulting and systems integration, business process outsourcing, and installation and support. The company markets directly and through distributors worldwide.

	Annual Growth	12/00	12/01	12/02	12/03	12/04
Sales ($mil.)	(6.9%)	38.3	30.7	29.3	32.1	28.7
Net income ($ mil.)	–	(17.8)	(6.3)	0.8	1.0	(3.8)
Market value ($ mil.)	12.5%	6.5	9.9	11.2	19.1	10.4
Employees	(7.2%)	247	221	192	187	183

SCANNER TECHNOLOGIES CORP

14505 21st Avenue North, Suite 220
Minneapolis, MN 55447
Phone: 763 476-8271
Fax: 763 476-0364
Web: www.scannertech.com

CEO: –
CFO: –
HR: –
FYE: December 31
Type: Public

Scanner Technologies' technology scans integrated circuits (ICs) for accuracy. The company makes machine vision equipment used during semiconductor manufacturing. Its UltraVim and UltraVim Plus modules are used for 2-D and 3-D inspection of leaded and ball grid array ICs, and its UltraMark device checks the accuracy of markings on printed or etched ICs. Singapore-based chip equipment supplier Manufacturing Integration Technology accounts for more than half of Scanner's sales. Former chairman and CEO Elwin Beaty and his wife, Elaine, own about half of Scanner Technologies.

	Annual Growth	12/03	12/04	12/05	12/06	12/07
Sales ($mil.)	(16.7%)	2.8	5.8	1.6	2.5	1.4
Net income ($ mil.)	–	(0.5)	1.1	(1.9)	(1.1)	(5.8)
Market value ($ mil.)	(52.9%)	13.7	33.6	4.5	5.5	0.7
Employees	(18.7%)	16	6	14	10	7

SCANSOURCE, INC.

NMS: SCSC

6 Logue Court
Greenville, SC 29615
Phone: 864 288-2432
Fax: –
Web: www.scansource.com

CEO: Michael L Baur
CFO: Stephen T Jones
HR: –
FYE: June 30
Type: Public

ScanSource is a leading hybrid distributor connecting devices to the cloud and accelerating growth for partners across hardware, Software as a Service (SaaS), connectivity, and cloud. It offers distributors of automatic identification and data capture (AIDC) products, such as bar code scanners, label printers, and portable data collection terminals. It also provides point-of-sale (POS) products, including PC-based terminals, tablets, monitors, payment processing solutions, receipt printers, pole displays, cash drawers, keyboards, peripheral equipment, and fully integrated processing units. In addition, ScanSource distributes voice, data, access, cable collaboration, wireless, and cloud, as well as video surveillance and intrusion-related products and networking infrastructure products. The company's offerings are available in cloud, hybrid, and on-premise versions. ScanSource sells more than 65,000 products from approximately 500 hardware, software, and service suppliers to approximately 30,000 customers.

	Annual Growth	06/19	06/20	06/21	06/22	06/23
Sales ($mil.)	(0.6%)	3,873.1	3,047.7	3,150.8	3,529.9	3,787.7
Net income ($ mil.)	11.7%	57.6	(192.7)	10.8	88.8	89.8
Market value ($ mil.)	(2.4%)	808.9	598.5	698.9	773.6	734.4
Employees	(3.9%)	2,700	2,600	2,200	2,700	2,300

SCHEELS ALL SPORTS, INC.

1707 GOLD DR S
FARGO, ND 581036413
Phone: 701 232-3665
Fax: –
Web: www.scheels.com

CEO: Steve D Scheel
CFO: –
HR: Kristina Horn
FYE: December 31
Type: Private

Scheels All Sports is appropriately-named. The company sells sporting goods and apparel through two dozen stores in more than 10 western and Midwestern states, as well as online. Products include bicycles, fitness equipment, hunting and fishing gear, and seasonal sporting goods (for camping, baseball, golf, soccer, and skateboarding). Scheels offers bike and exercise machine repairs, racquet stringing, and ski equipment maintenance. It has specialists in warranty repair for shotguns, rifles, and handguns, and it offers new and used firearms from Browning, Colt, and Winchester. Employee-owned and run by the founder's great-grandson, Scheels began in 1902 as a hardware and general merchandise store.

SCHEID VINEYARDS INC.

NBB: SVIN

305 Hilltown Road
Salinas, CA 93908
Phone: 831 455-9990
Fax: –
Web: www.scheidvineyards.com

CEO: Scott D Scheid
CFO: Michael S Thomsen
HR: –
FYE: February 28
Type: Public

Scheid Vineyards hasn't shied away from the expensive and timely task of growing grapes for wine. The company works about 5,300 acres of vineyards, mainly located in Monterey County, California. It has the capacity to process approximately 30,000 tons of grapes every harvest. Its main business is producing bulk wine, which it sells to other winemakers for blending. Scheid also makes its own wines under the Scheid Vineyards label; they are available in the Monterey area and through the company's Web site. The Scheid family, including founder and chairman, Alfred Scheid, control a majority of the company.

	Annual Growth	02/18	02/19	02/20	02/21	02/22
Sales ($mil.)	3.3%	57.3	58.5	51.0	62.7	65.1
Net income ($ mil.)	55.4%	2.4	(7.9)	(12.9)	(4.7)	14.2
Market value ($ mil.)	(35.1%)	80.7	73.0	26.4	14.3	14.3
Employees	–	–	–	–	–	–

SCHEIN (HENRY) INC

NMS: HSIC

135 Duryea Road
Melville, NY 11747
Phone: 631 843-5500
Fax: –
Web: www.henryschein.com

CEO: Stanley M Bergman
CFO: –
HR: –
FYE: December 30
Type: Public

Henry Schein is a leading global distributor of healthcare products and services primarily to office-based dental and medical practitioners. It provides everything from infection-control products, hand-pieces, preventatives, impression materials, composites, anesthetics, and dental implants to vaccines, surgical products, diagnostic tests, infection-control products, and X-ray products. Other offerings include practice management software, repair services, and financing. The company offers a comprehensive selection of more than 300,000 branded products and Henry Schein corporate brand products through its distribution centers. Its infrastructure, including over 3.8 million square feet of space in about 30 strategically located distribution and around 20 manufacturing facilities around the world. The US accounts for about 75% of its total revenue. Founded in 1932 by Henry and Esther Schein as a storefront pharmacy, Henry Schein became a public company in 1995.

	Annual Growth	12/19	12/20	12/21	12/22	12/23
Sales ($mil.)	5.4%	9,985.8	10,119	12,401	12,647	12,339
Net income ($ mil.)	(12.0%)	694.7	403.8	631.2	538.0	416.0
Market value ($ mil.)	3.3%	8,605.3	8,508.4	9,684.5	10,323	9,785.3
Employees	7.1%	19,000	19,000	21,600	22,000	25,000

SCHENECTADY COUNTY COMMUNITY COLLEGE

78 WASHINGTON AVE
SCHENECTADY, NY 123052215
Phone: 518 381-1200
Fax: –
Web: www.sunysccc.edu

CEO: –
CFO: –
HR: –
FYE: August 31
Type: Private

Schenectady County Community College (SCCC) offers associates degrees in arts, science, applied science, and occupational studies. A two-year school, it offers more than 25 fields of study, as well as about a dozen career-oriented certificate programs. Its Associate in Arts and Associate in Science degrees can be transferred to a four-year college or university. Once exclusively a commuter school, SCCC plans to open its first student housing facilities in 2010. It was founded in 1967 as part of the State University of New York system and has an enrollment of more than 5,200 students.

SCHENKER, INC.

1305 EXECUTIVE BLVD STE 200
CHESAPEAKE, VA 233203676
Phone: 757 821-3400
Fax: –
Web: www.dbschenker.com

CEO: Jeffery Barrie
CFO: Brent Blake
HR: –
FYE: December 31
Type: Private

Schenker, Inc., doing business as DB Schenker USA, serves as the US-based arm of Germany's DB Schenker Logistics, the logistics business unit of Deutsch Bahn. DB Schenker USA provides land transport, air freight, and ocean freight forwarding, as well as contract logistics and supply chain management services, to industrial and trade customers. The company maintains US regional and international hubs for air and ground freight in Atlanta, Dallas, New York, Los Angeles, Miami, Chicago, San Francisco and its ocean gateways include weekly express service from all major USA points and ports to over 150 global destinations. DB Schenker USA was established in 1947.

SCHEWEL FURNITURE COMPANY INCORPORATED

1031 MAIN ST
LYNCHBURG, VA 245041800
Phone: 434 522-0200
Fax: –
Web: www.schewelshome.com

CEO: Marc A Schewel
CFO: –
HR: –
FYE: March 31
Type: Private

Schewel Furniture Company operates about 50 retail furniture and bedding stores in Virginia, West Virginia, and North Carolina. In addition to home furnishings, the chain sells appliances, electronics, carpeting, and related accessories. Typical store units average 18,000 sq. ft. and primarily target the lower- and middle-income markets. Newer stores are larger, in the 40,000-55,000 square foot range. Customers can also browse furniture collections and other items available at Schewel stores through the company's Web site. The family-run company, now in its fourth generation of management, got its start in 1897 when Elias Schewel began selling small furniture pieces out of his horse-drawn wagon.

	Annual Growth	03/12	03/13	03/14	03/15	03/16
Sales ($mil.)	(1.8%)	–	–	122.0	118.5	117.5
Net income ($ mil.)	(4.2%)	–	–	4.5	4.1	4.1
Market value ($ mil.)	–	–	–	–	–	–
Employees	–	–	–	–	–	668

SCHIFF HARDIN LLP

233 S WACKER DR STE 7100
CHICAGO, IL 606066307
Phone: 312 258-5500
Fax: –
Web: www.schiffhardin.com

CEO: –
CFO: –
HR: –
FYE: November 30
Type: Private

Maintaining some 35 practice areas, ArentFox Schiff (formerly known as Schiff Hardin) specializes in representing clients on matters related to intellectual property, life sciences, and real estate. It serves the fashion, food, drug, medical and cosmetic, government, health care, life sciences, media and entertainment, real estate, and sports industries. The firm's roughly 690 attorneys include its chairman Anthony Lupo, which practices primarily in the entertainment, fashion, and technology industries. ArentFox Schiff was founded in 1942.

	Annual Growth	12/95	12/96	12/97	12/98*	11/19
Sales ($mil.)	(24.5%)	–	–	75.5	–	0.2
Net income ($ mil.)	–	–	–	12.6	–	(0.0)
Market value ($ mil.)	–	–	–	–	–	–
Employees	–	–	–	–	–	630

*Fiscal year change

SCHMITT INDUSTRIES INC (OR)

NBB: SMIT

2765 N.W. Nicolai Street
Portland, OR 97210
Phone: 503 227-7908
Fax: 503 223-1258
Web: www.schmittindustries.com

CEO: Michael R Zapata
CFO: Philip Bosco
HR: –
FYE: May 31
Type: Public

What can we tell you about Schmitt? Schmitt Industries takes a balanced approach; most of its sales comes from its computerized balancing equipment, which machine tool builders and grinding machine operators use to improve the efficiency of rotating devices. Customers incorporate the company's flagship Schmitt Dynamic Balance System into grinding machines. Subsidiary Schmitt Measurement Systems makes laser-based precision-measurement instruments for computer disk drive manufacturing and for military and industrial applications. Schmitt Industries has operations in the UK and the US. Customers in North America account for more than half of the company's sales.

	Annual Growth	05/18	05/19	05/20	05/21	05/22
Sales ($mil.)	(8.1%)	13.9	13.8	4.2	7.9	9.9
Net income ($ mil.)	–	0.2	(1.2)	3.9	(8.1)	(3.3)
Market value ($ mil.)	18.0%	8.8	8.6	10.4	20.7	17.0
Employees	29.4%	56	50	18	138	157

SCHNEIDER NATIONAL INC (WI)

NYS: SNDR

3101 South Packerland Drive
Green Bay, WI 54313
Phone: 920 592-2000
Fax: –
Web: www.schneider.com

CEO: –
CFO: –
HR: –
FYE: December 31
Type: Public

Schneider National is one of the largest truckload carriers in the US. It provides truckload service throughout North America, including truckload, intermodal, and logistics services through its fleet of about 30,000 trucks and about 45,000 trailers. The company's intermodal service transports freight by multiple methods, such as road and rail, Its Logistics segment offers warehousing, brokerage services and supply chain management services while its Schneider Finance subsidiary provides equipment leasing to third parties. Founded by A.J. "Al" Schneider in 1935, Schneider National went public in 2017.

	Annual Growth	12/19	12/20	12/21	12/22	12/23
Sales ($mil.)	3.7%	4,747.0	4,552.8	5,608.7	6,604.4	5,498.9
Net income ($ mil.)	12.9%	147.0	211.7	405.4	457.8	238.5
Market value ($ mil.)	3.9%	3,839.5	3,642.4	4,735.1	4,117.5	4,478.2
Employees	2.5%	15,650	15,225	16,050	17,050	17,300

SCHOLASTIC CORP

NMS: SCHL

557 Broadway
New York, NY 10012
Phone: 212 343-6100
Fax: –
Web: www.scholastic.com

CEO: Peter Warwick
CFO: Kenneth J Cleary
HR: –
FYE: May 31
Type: Public

Scholastic Corporation is one of the world's largest children's book publishers and distributor of children's books, and a leading provider of print and digital instructional materials for grades pre-kindergarten (pre-K) to grade 12 and a producer of educational and entertaining children's media. The Company creates quality books and ebooks, print and technology-based learning materials and programs, classroom magazines, and other products to support children's learning and reading both at school and at home. Scholastic owns the rights to properties such as Goosebumps and The Baby-Sitters Club and is the US distributor of the Harry Potter books, the best-selling children's series of all time. Scholastic is currently in 115,000 schools, reaching 3.8 million educators, 54 million students, and 78 million parents/caregivers domestically. The publisher was founded in 1920.

	Annual Growth	05/19	05/20	05/21	05/22	05/23
Sales ($mil.)	0.7%	1,653.9	1,487.1	1,300.3	1,642.9	1,704.0
Net income ($ mil.)	53.4%	15.6	(43.8)	(11.0)	80.9	86.3
Market value ($ mil.)	–	–	–	–	–	–
Employees	–	8,900	8,300	6,800	6,880	–

SCHONFELD SECURITIES, LLC

2 JERICHO PLZ
JERICHO, NY 117531658
Phone: 212 832-0900
Fax: –
Web: –

CEO: Steven Schonfeld
CFO: Joseph Avantario
HR: Carolina Manser
FYE: December 31
Type: Private

Schonfeld Group wouldn't trade its customers for anything. It performs institutional brokerage services and provides retail trading services for day traders. Its majority-owned Lightspeed Trading platform, which caters to day traders and financial institutions, records approximately 1 million daily average revenue trades. Trillium Trading is a trading firm whose infrastructure supports algorithmic and black-box trading. Another unit, Schonfeld Capital Group, makes strategic investments in alternative assets such as hedge funds, private equity, and real estate. CEO Steve Schonfeld founded Schonfeld Group in 1988.

	Annual Growth	03/99	03/00	03/02	03/03*	12/08
Assets ($mil.)	(65.9%)	–	2,470.7	715.6	427.4	0.5
Net income ($ mil.)	–	–	148.2	97.0	(25.4)	–
Market value ($ mil.)	–	–	–	–	–	–
Employees	–	–	–	–	–	867

*Fiscal year change

SCHOOL ADMINISTRATORS ASSOCIATION OF NYS (INC)

8 AIRPORT PARK BLVD STE 1
LATHAM, NY 121106414
Phone: 518 782-0600
Fax: –
Web: www.saanys.org

CEO: –
CFO: –
HR: –
FYE: August 31
Type: Private

This group sticks with its principals. The School Administrators Association of New York State is a union representing some 6,500 school administrators, coordinators, and supervisors throughout the Empire State. School Administrators Association of New York provides legal advice and assistance, labor relations services, education, and other services to its members.

	Annual Growth	08/16	08/17	08/18	08/21	08/22
Sales ($mil.)	1.2%	–	4.0	3.8	4.3	4.3
Net income ($ mil.)	1.4%	–	0.5	0.2	1.1	0.5
Market value ($ mil.)	–	–	–	–	–	–
Employees	–	–	–	–	–	20

SCHOTTENSTEIN STORES CORPORATION

4300 E 5TH AVE
COLUMBUS, OH 432191816
Phone: 614 221-9200
Fax: –
Web: www.valuecityfurniture.com

CEO: Jay Schottenstein
CFO: Jeffrey Swanson
HR: Daren Revels
FYE: January 31
Type: Private

Schottenstein Stores is where the Schottenstein family stores its retail holdings. The investment firm owns interests in Value City Furniture (more than 125 superstores located primarily in the Eastern US), about 15% of casual clothing chain American Eagle Outfitters (some 1,000 mall stores in the US and Canada), and global retail consultant and liquidator SB Capital Group. It also counts some 50 shopping centers among its holdings. Crystal maker Steuben Glass is also part of its portfolio alongside luxe handbag maker Judith Leiber and Italian fashion brand Shir in the Schottenstein Luxury Group. Schottenstein Stores is part of a consortium of investors led by Cerberus Capital Management.

	Annual Growth	07/05	07/06*	12/08*	01/09	01/22
Sales ($mil.)	(26.2%)	–	4,071.4	–	27.8	31.5
Net income ($ mil.)	(26.6%)	–	112.8	–	–	0.8
Market value ($ mil.)	–	–	–	–	–	–
Employees	–	–	–	–	–	30,050

*Fiscal year change

SCHULZE AND BURCH BISCUIT CO.

1133 W 35TH ST
CHICAGO, IL 606091404
Phone: 773 927-6622
Fax: –
Web: www.schulzeburch.co

CEO: –
CFO: –
HR: Pat Rusthoven
FYE: December 31
Type: Private

Schulze and Burch Biscuit Company's almost 100-year history is a rich one filled with innovation, historic accomplishments and wholesome snacks. The company offers the Flavor Kist name which was born after World War II, when Schulze & Burch shifted their focus back to quality consumer products from Army contracting work. It also features premier quality snack foods available in grocery, drug and convenience stores. Additionally, it makes and markets toaster pastries under its Toast'em Pop-ups brand, as well as for private- and branded-label customers. The privately-held company, Schulze & Burch, has been manufacturing quality baked goods since 1923.

SCHUMACHER ELECTRIC CORPORATION

14200 FAA BLVD
FORT WORTH, TX 761552513
Phone: 847 385-1600
Fax: –
Web: www.schumacherelectric.com

CEO: –
CFO: Daniel Frano
HR: –
FYE: December 31
Type: Private

Schumacher Electric is a global leader of power conversion products. It designs and produces a full complement of power converting products including battery chargers, testers, maintainers, jump starters, portable power, lithium and electric vehicle charging as well as custom transformers for the electronics industry. The company was founded in 1947.

SCHURZ COMMUNICATIONS, INC.

1301 E DOUGLAS RD STE 200
MISHAWAKA, IN 465451732
Phone: 574 247-7237
Fax: –
Web: www.schurz.com

CEO: Todd Schurz
CFO: Gary Hoipkemier
HR: Phr Lock
FYE: December 31
Type: Private

Schurz Communications is a regional media company with publishing and broadcasting operations in about 15 states. Its publishing unit is anchored by about a dozen daily newspapers that serve mostly small communities. The company also publishes a number of weekly papers and shoppers. On the air, Schurz Communications owns about ten television stations and more than a dozen radio stations mostly serving Indiana and South Dakota listeners. Other operations include two cable companies, about 25 websites, a phone directory, and a printing firm. The family-owned company traces its roots to 1872 when Alfred B. Miller and Elmer Crockett started the South Bend Tribune in Indiana.

SCHWAB (CHARLES) CORP (THE)　　　　　　　　　NYS: SCHW

3000 Schwab Way　　　　　　　　　　　　　　CEO: Charles R Schwab
Westlake, TX 76262　　　　　　　　　　　　　　CFO: Peter B Crawford
Phone: 817 859-5000　　　　　　　　　　　　　　HR: –
Fax: –　　　　　　　　　　　　　　　　　FYE: December 31
Web: www.aboutschwab.com　　　　　　　　　　　　Type: Public

The Charles Schwab Corporation is a savings and loan holding company. Charles Schwab engages, through its subsidiaries, in wealth management, securities brokerage, banking, asset management, custody, and financial advisory services. Charles Schwab manages about $7.05 trillion in client assets, 33.8 million active brokerage accounts, 2.4 million corporate retirement plan participants, and 1.7 million banking accounts. Its subsidiaries include Charles Schwab & Co., Inc. (CS&Co), a securities broker-dealer; TD Ameritrade, Inc.; TD Ameritrade Clearing, Inc. (TDAC); Charles Schwab Bank, SSB (CSB), Charles Schwab principal banking entity; and Charles Schwab Investment Management, Inc. (CSIM), the investment advisor for Schwab's proprietary mutual funds (Schwab Funds) and for Schwab's exchange-traded funds (Schwab ETFs).

	Annual Growth	12/19	12/20	12/21	12/22	12/23
Sales ($mil.)	21.3%	11,785	12,109	18,996	22,307	25,521
Net income ($ mil.)	8.1%	3,704.0	3,299.0	5,855.0	7,183.0	5,067.0
Market value ($ mil.)	9.7%	86,726	96,719	153,357	151,825	125,458
Employees	13.8%	19,700	32,000	33,400	35,300	33,000

SCHWEBEL BAKING COMPANY

965 E MIDLOTHIAN BLVD　　　　　　　　　　　　　CEO: –
YOUNGSTOWN, OH 445022869　　　　　　　　　　　　CFO: –
Phone: 330 783-2860　　　　　　　　　　　　　　HR: –
Fax: –　　　　　　　　　　　　　　　　　FYE: December 31
Web: www.schwebels.com　　　　　　　　　　　　Type: Private

Schwebel Baking produces a noseful of wonderful aromas. As one of the fastest-growing independent wholesale bakers in America, it bakes bagels, bread, buns, rolls, pita bread, and tortillas for the consumer food industry. The company's brands include Schwebel's, Sun-Maid, Roman Meal, Country Hearth, Milton's, Vogel's, and Aladdin's. Its products are available in Ohio, Pennsylvania, and New York at retail food stores, restaurants, and more than 30 company-owned bakery outlet stores. It also licenses its brands to other producers, and customers can have bread shipped directly to their homes. Schwebel Baking was founded in 1906 by Joseph and Dora Schwebel and remains a family-owned and -operated company.

SCICLONE PHARMACEUTICALS, INC.

950 TOWER LN STE 900　　　　　　　　　　　　　CEO: –
FOSTER CITY, CA 944042125　　　　　　　　　　　　CFO: –
Phone: 650 358-3456　　　　　　　　　　　　　　HR: –
Fax: –　　　　　　　　　　　　　　　　　FYE: December 31
Web: www.sciclone.com　　　　　　　　　　　　Type: Private

SciClone hopes its drug sales create a whirlwind in China. The drug firm's flagship product Zadaxin is approved for use in more than 30 countries, including China, its primary market. Zadaxin treats hepatitis B, as a vaccine adjuvant (to boost a vaccine's effectiveness), as well as certain cancers. The company also partners with other drug makers, including Baxter International and Pfizer, to market those companies' products in China. SciClone maintains a pipeline of products that it is shepherding through the approval process in China; therapeutic areas of focus include oncology, infectious disease, and cardiovascular disorders. In October 2017, SciClone was taken private by a consortium of Chinese investors led by GL Capital for some $605 million.

SCIENCE APPLICATIONS INTERNATIONAL CORP (NEW)　　　NMS: SAIC

12010 Sunset Hills Road　　　　　　　　　　　　CEO: Toni Townes-Whitley
Reston, VA 20190　　　　　　　　　　　　　　CFO: Prabu Natarajan
Phone: 703 676-4300　　　　　　　　　　　　　　HR: –
Fax: –　　　　　　　　　　　　　　　　　FYE: February 2
Web: www.saic.com　　　　　　　　　　　　　Type: Public

Science Applications International Corporation (SAIC) is a leading provider of technical, engineering and enterprise information technology (IT) services primarily to the US government. The company provides engineering and integration services for large, complex projects and offers a range of services with a targeted emphasis on differentiated technology services. Its end-to-end enterprise IT offerings span the entire spectrum of its customers' IT infrastructure. SAIC works with the Department of Defense, National Aeronautics and Space Administration (NASA), US Department of State, Department of Justice and several sensitive intelligence community agencies. Substantially all of the company's revenues were generated by entities located in the US.

	Annual Growth	01/20	01/21	01/22*	02/23	02/24
Sales ($mil.)	3.9%	6,379.0	7,056.0	7,394.0	7,704.0	7,444.0
Net income ($ mil.)	20.5%	226.0	209.0	277.0	300.0	477.0
Market value ($ mil.)	10.1%	4,564.0	4,993.6	4,228.6	5,412.2	6,708.5
Employees	–	24,000	26,000	26,000	25,000	24,000

*Fiscal year change

SCIENTIFIC INDUSTRIES INC　　　　　　　　　　　　NBB: SCND

80 Orville Drive, Suite 102　　　　　　　　　　　CEO: Helena R Santos
Bohemia, NY 11716　　　　　　　　　　　　　　CFO: Reginald Averilla
Phone: 631 567-4700　　　　　　　　　　　　　　HR: –
Fax: –　　　　　　　　　　　　　　　　　FYE: December 31
Web: www.scientificindustries.com　　　　　　　　Type: Public

There's a whole lotta shakin' goin' on at Scientific Industries. The company manufactures research laboratory equipment, featuring the Genie line of mixers, particularly the Vortex-Genie mixer, as well as orbital, magnetic, and microplate mixers and refrigerated and shaking incubators. The company's products are generally used by clinics, hospitals, and universities, among other customers. In business for more than five decades, Scientific Industries has distributors worldwide. The company also carries spinner flasks made by Bellco Biotechnology. Scientific Industries gets more than half of its sales outside the US.

	Annual Growth	06/19	06/20	06/21	06/22*	12/22
Sales ($mil.)	(15.3%)	10.2	8.6	9.8	11.4	5.2
Net income ($ mil.)	–	0.6	(0.7)	(3.7)	(5.6)	(4.1)
Market value ($ mil.)	5.1%	31.5	58.8	75.1	36.4	38.5
Employees	21.1%	39	44	59	77	84

*Fiscal year change

SCIENTIFIC RESEARCH CORP

2300 WINDY RIDGE PKWY SE STE 400S　　　　　　　CEO: Michael L Watt
ATLANTA, GA 303398431　　　　　　　　　　　　CFO: –
Phone: 770 859-9161　　　　　　　　　　　　　HR: Stephanie Carter
Fax: –　　　　　　　　　　　　　　　　　FYE: December 31
Web: www.scires.com　　　　　　　　　　　　Type: Private

Founded in 1988, Scientific Research Corporation (SRC) is an advanced engineering company providing state-of-the-art solutions in defense, federal, global, and cyber and intelligence markets. SRC's business activities are focused on a broad range of information, communications, intelligence, electronic warfare, simulation, training, and instrumentation systems. SRC is dedicated to a full range of engineering, integration, testing, support, and research and development activities.

	Annual Growth	12/13	12/14	12/15	12/16	12/17
Sales ($mil.)	(4.3%)	–	318.7	293.8	281.9	279.3
Net income ($ mil.)	(2.1%)	–	20.8	19.5	19.5	19.5
Market value ($ mil.)	–	–	–	–	–	–
Employees	–	–	–	–	–	1,006

SCL HEALTH - FRONT RANGE, INC.

2420 W 26TH AVE
DENVER, CO 802115301
Phone: 303 813-5000
Fax: –
Web: www.sclhealth.org

CEO: Lydia Jumonville
CFO: –
HR: –
FYE: December 31
Type: Private

Exempla aims to provide exemplary health care to residents in the Denver area. The Exempla medical network, operating as Exempla Healthcare, includes three hospitals: Exempla Saint Joseph Hospital (570 beds), Exempla Lutheran Medical Center (400 beds), and Good Samaritan Medical Center (more than 230 beds). It also operates the Exempla Physician Network, a chain of primary care clinics. The company employs more than 2,100 physicians. Among its specialties are cardiovascular services and surgeries, rehabilitation, cancer care, orthopedics, and women's and children's services. Exempla Healthcare is sponsored by the Catholic faith-based Sisters of Charity of Leavenworth Health System (SCL Health System).

SCOLR PHARMA INC

19204 North Creek Parkway, Suite 100
Bothell, WA 98011
Phone: 425 368-1050
Fax: –
Web: www.scolr.com

CEO: –
CFO: –
HR: –
FYE: December 31
Type: Public

SCOLR Pharma is a control freak. The company is developing its Controlled Delivery Technology (CDT) to improve the rate of release of a drug into the body. The CDT platform is designed for use with oral solid doses and regulates the drug's release for periods of up to 24 hours. SCOLR's CDT technology is used in private-label nutritional supplements through its partnership with Perrigo. The company is also researching CDT's usefulness for cough and cold remedies, analgesics, cardiovascular treatments, and other medications. SCOLR is seeking additional collaborative partnerships to utilize the CDT system; it has established relationships with BioCryst and Dr. Reddy's.

	Annual Growth	12/06	12/07	12/08	12/09	12/10
Sales ($mil.)	(27.8%)	2.3	2.0	1.0	0.9	0.6
Net income ($ mil.)	–	(10.7)	(10.6)	(6.1)	(6.7)	(3.2)
Market value ($ mil.)	–	152.9	152.9	152.9	152.9	152.9
Employees	(30.0%)	25	24	17	9	6

SCOTT AND WHITE HEALTH PLAN

1206 WEST CAMPUS DR
TEMPLE, TX 765027124
Phone: 254 298-3000
Fax: –
Web: www.bswhealthplan.com

CEO: Jeff Ingrum
CFO: Stephen Bush
HR: –
FYE: December 31
Type: Private

The Scott & White Health Plan (SWHP) works to keep its members Safe & Well. The not-for-profit company provides health insurance plans and related services to more than 200,000 members across some 50 counties in and around Central Texas. Owned by the Scott & White network of hospitals and clinics, SWHP has employer-sponsored plans (including HMO, PPO, and consumer choice options) as well as several choices for individuals and families. It also offers COBRA, state-administered continuation plans, the Young Texan Health Plan for children, Medicare, and dental and vision benefits. The company began offering its services in 1982. Owner Scott & White is exploring a merger with Baylor Health Care System.

	Annual Growth	12/07	12/08	12/09	12/21	12/22
Sales ($mil.)	3.4%	–	621.2	660.1	819.7	990.8
Net income ($ mil.)	–	–	(4.0)	13.3	15.3	(4.1)
Market value ($ mil.)	–	–	–	–	–	–
Employees	–	–	–	–	–	426

SCOTT EQUIPMENT COMPANY, L.L.C.

1000 MARTIN LUTHER KING JR DR
MONROE, LA 712035543
Phone: 318 387-4160
Fax: –
Web: www.scottcompanies.com

CEO: –
CFO: –
HR: Bobby Williams
FYE: December 31
Type: Private

Scott Equipment Company sells and rents construction and farm equipment through some 25 locations located in the South and Midwest. The company also offers parts and service, financing, and insurance. Scott Equipment is part of the Scott family of companies, which also includes Scott Toyota Lift (material handling), Scott Irrigation (pivot irrigation systems), and Scott Truck (sales, leasing, and service). The company's beginnings date back to 1939, when Tom Scott founded Scott Truck & Tractor. It is operated by descendants of the founder. Scott Equipment has shut down several agricultural stores (Scott Tractor) to focus on its Construction Equipment division.

	Annual Growth	12/04	12/05	12/06	12/07	12/08
Sales ($mil.)	6.1%	–	266.0	299.3	323.4	317.6
Net income ($ mil.)	56.8%	–	3.3	6.2	17.7	12.9
Market value ($ mil.)	–	–	–	–	–	–
Employees	–	–	–	–	–	350

SCOTT PET PRODUCTS, INC.

1543 N US HIGHWAY 41
ROCKVILLE, IN 478727146
Phone: 765 569-4636
Fax: –
Web: www.scottpet.com

CEO: Hal Harlan
CFO: –
HR: Tracey Lyons
FYE: December 31
Type: Private

Scott Pet Products wants it Pork Chomps to be the chew of choice for pets over rawhides. The company manufactures products for pets, including collars, feeding bowls, kennels and pet crates, sleeping mats, and baked pork skin chews named Pork Chomps. Scott Pet Products makes and markets birdseed, as well, that accounts for about a quarter of the company sales. The family-owned firm was established to make sporting dog collars in 1975. Its founder, T. E. Scott, has since passed the reins on to his son-in-law and daughter, Mike (CEO) and Kathy (marketing director) Bassett, who run the company today.

	Annual Growth	07/15	07/16	07/17*	12/18	12/19
Sales ($mil.)	20.7%	–	–	42.8	55.6	62.4
Net income ($ mil.)	5.4%	–	–	1.2	1.8	1.4
Market value ($ mil.)	–	–	–	–	–	–
Employees	–	–	–	–	–	170

*Fiscal year change

SCOTT'S LIQUID GOLD, INC.

NBB: SLGD

8400 E. Crescent Parkway, Suite 450
Greenwood Village, CO 80111
Phone: 303 373-4860
Fax: –
Web: www.slginc.com

CEO: Tisha Pedrazzini
CFO: David M Arndt
HR: –
FYE: December 31
Type: Public

Known for its wood furniture cleaner, Scott's Liquid Gold is banking on striking gold in skin care and cosmetics products. While the company generates 46% of its sales from its namesake cleaning product, a growing portion of its business is from its Neoteric Cosmetics subsidiary, which sells skin care products under the Alpha Hydrox and Diabetic Skin Care brand names. Scott's Liquid Gold also makes household items, such as Touch of Scent air fresheners. The company sells its products through retailers in the US, Canada, and abroad; it also distributes Montagne Jeunesse sachets. The children of the late founder Jerome Goldstein (including president and CEO Mark Goldstein) own about a quarter of the company.

	Annual Growth	12/18	12/19	12/20	12/21	12/22
Sales ($mil.)	(18.2%)	37.1	28.5	30.3	33.1	16.6
Net income ($ mil.)	–	2.2	(0.7)	(1.6)	(11.1)	(8.9)
Market value ($ mil.)	(45.7%)	32.6	23.5	23.5	20.3	2.8
Employees	(26.2%)	74	66	36	27	22

SCOTTISH RITE CATHEDRAL OF SAN DIEGO

1895 CAMINO DEL RIO S
SAN DIEGO, CA 921083601
Phone: 619 297-0397
Fax: –
Web: www.sdeventscenter.com

CEO: –
CFO: –
HR: –
FYE: December 31
Type: Private

Those looking for meeting space in San Diego can't go wrong with Scottish Rite. The Scottish Rite Center is the gathering place for Masons in the San Diego area. It also houses more than 15 configurable meeting rooms that range from a capacity of 10 people to 1,000. Rooms are used for board meetings, parties, seminars, and receptions. Its 5,300 square foot Golden Eagle Auditorium is also available for theater performances and presentations. The not-for-profit center also houses a therapy center for childhood language disorders. Scottish Rite is a branch of the international fraternal organization Masons; members are joined by moral and metaphysical ideals.

	Annual Growth	12/13	12/14	12/15	12/17	12/18
Sales ($mil.)	18.7%	–	0.0	–	0.0	0.1
Net income ($ mil.)	–	–	–	–	–	–
Market value ($ mil.)	–	–	–	–	–	–
Employees	–	–	–	–	–	19

SCOTTS MIRACLE-GRO CO (THE)

NYS: SMG

14111 Scottslawn Road
Marysville, OH 43041
Phone: 937 644-0011
Fax: 937 644-7614
Web: www.scotts.com

CEO: James Hagedorn
CFO: Matthew E Garth
HR: –
FYE: September 30
Type: Public

The Scotts Miracle-Gro is the world's largest marketer of branded consumer products for lawn and garden care. The company's Scotts, Miracle-Gro, and Ortho brands are market-leading in their categories. The company's wholly-owned subsidiary, The Hawthorne Gardening Company, is a leading provider of nutrients, lighting, and other materials used in the indoor and hydroponic growing segment. The company is the exclusive agent of the Monsanto Company, a subsidiary of Bayer AG (Monsanto), for the marketing and distribution of certain of Monsanto's consumer Roundup branded products within the US and certain other specified countries. In addition, it has an equity interest in Bonnie Plants, LLC, a joint venture with Alabama Farmers Cooperative, Inc. (AFC), focused on planting, growing, developing, distributing, marketing, and selling live plants. It generates about 90% of its revenue in the US. Scotts Miracle-Gro traces its heritage to a company founded by O.M. Scott in Marysville, Ohio in 1868.

	Annual Growth	09/19	09/20	09/21	09/22	09/23
Sales ($mil.)	3.0%	3,156.0	4,131.6	4,925.0	3,924.1	3,551.3
Net income ($ mil.)	–	460.7	387.4	512.5	(437.5)	(380.1)
Market value ($ mil.)	(15.6%)	5,752.8	8,639.4	8,269.3	2,415.4	2,919.9
Employees	(18.3%)	5,600	5,932	7,300	6,100	2,500

SCRIPPS (EW) COMPANY (THE)

NMS: SSP

312 Walnut Street
Cincinnati, OH 45202
Phone: 513 977-3000
Fax: –
Web: www.scripps.com

CEO: Adam P Symson
CFO: Jason Combs
HR: –
FYE: December 31
Type: Public

The E. W. Scripps Company (Scripps) is a diverse media enterprise, serving audiences and businesses through a portfolio of local television stations and national media brands, including next-generation national news network Newsy; and five national multicast networks ? Bounce, Grit, Laff, Court TV and Court TV Mystery. Scripps also owns about 60 local TV stations in around 40 markets that reach about 25% of US television households. The company has affiliations with all of the "Big Four" television networks as well as the CW network. The company was founded in 1878 by entrepreneurial journalist E.W. Scripps.

	Annual Growth	12/19	12/20	12/21	12/22	12/23
Sales ($mil.)	12.7%	1,423.8	1,857.5	2,283.5	2,453.2	2,292.9
Net income ($ mil.)	–	(18.4)	269.3	122.7	195.9	(947.8)
Market value ($ mil.)	(15.6%)	1,331.8	1,296.2	1,640.4	1,118.2	677.4
Employees	(3.1%)	5,900	5,400	5,600	5,700	5,200

SCRIPPS COLLEGE

1030 COLUMBIA AVE
CLAREMONT, CA 917113948
Phone: 909 621-8000
Fax: –
Web: www.scrippscollege.edu

CEO: –
CFO: –
HR: Jennifer Berklas
FYE: June 30
Type: Private

Scripps helps empower women through academic knowledge. Part of the Claremont University Consortium, the all-women liberal arts college maintains an enrollment of fewer than 1,000 students to encourage active participation in academic and campus life. Students participate in the Core Curriculum for their first three semesters at Scripps; the Core consists of lectures, team teaching, and seminar classes. The college also offers a wide range of courses from art to mathematics to psychology. Notable alumni include late best-selling author Molly Ivins and former White House chief counsel Beth Nolan. The college was founded in 1926 by Ellen Browning Scripps, a newspaper publisher and philanthropist.

	Annual Growth	06/18	06/19	06/20	06/21	06/22
Sales ($mil.)	4.1%	–	105.0	98.6	90.3	118.4
Net income ($ mil.)	(23.1%)	–	11.8	0.3	12.5	5.4
Market value ($ mil.)	–	–	–	–	–	–
Employees	–	–	–	–	–	180

SCRIPPS HEALTH

10140 CAMPUS POINT DR
SAN DIEGO, CA 921211520
Phone: 800 727-4777
Fax: –
Web: www.scripps.org

CEO: Chris D Van Gorder
CFO: Brett Tande
HR: Diana Glanz
FYE: September 30
Type: Private

Scripps Health is a $2.9 billion not-for-profit health system that serves San Diego area through four acute-care hospitals. Altogether, the health system treats more than 700,000 patients annually through more than 3,000 physicians. Its hospitals, along with several outpatient Scripps Clinic and Scripps Coastal Medical Center locations, is a network of integrated facilities with specialists from more than 60 medical and surgical specialists at some 30 outpatient centers and clinics. Scripps Health was founded in 1924 by philanthropist Ellen Browning Scripps.

	Annual Growth	09/13	09/14	09/15	09/21	09/22
Sales ($mil.)	4.7%	–	–	2,943.6	3,760.9	4,062.4
Net income ($ mil.)	(6.5%)	–	–	371.3	245.2	231.2
Market value ($ mil.)	–	–	–	–	–	–
Employees	–	–	–	–	–	5,445

SCRIPPS NETWORKS INTERACTIVE, INC.

9721 SHERRILL BLVD
KNOXVILLE, TN 379323330
Phone: 865 694-2700
Fax: –
Web: www.scrippsnetworksinteractive.com

CEO: –
CFO: –
HR: –
FYE: December 31
Type: Private

Lifestyle TV is a livelihood for this company. Scripps Networks Interactive operates six lifestyle cable networks including Home & Garden Television (home building and decoration), the Food Network (culinary programs), DIY - Do It Yourself Network (home repair and improvement), the Cooking Channel (culinary how-to programming), and the Travel Channel (travel and tourism). The company additionally owns music channel Great American Country, and has minority interests in Asian Food Channel and regional sports network FOX Sports Net South. It also owns a 50% stake in UKTV. Trusts for the Scripps family own majority control of the company. In 2017 Discovery Communications agreed to buy Scripps Networks in a $14.6 billion deal.

	Annual Growth	12/13	12/14	12/15	12/16	12/17
Sales ($mil.)	10.1%	–	2,665.5	3,018.2	3,401.4	3,561.8
Net income ($ mil.)	3.9%	–	726.8	778.5	847.4	814.4
Market value ($ mil.)	–	–	–	–	–	–
Employees	–	–	–	–	–	3,500

SCRYPT INC

NBB: SYPT

9050 N Capital of Texas Highway, Suite III-250
Austin, TX 78759
Phone: 512 493-6228
Fax: –
Web: www.scrypt.com

CEO: Aleksander Szymanski
CFO: Neil Burley
HR: –
FYE: December 31
Type: Public

SecureCARE Technologies (formerly eClickMD) is looking to secure more paying customers for the health of its business. The company provides Internet-based document exchange applications for doctors, clinics, home health care agencies, hospice organizations, and medical equipment providers. Its applications, including its flagship Sfax, enable health care providers to send, receive, and manage patient care documents via the Internet. As eClickMD, the company filed for bankruptcy in 2003 and emerged later that year. It changed its name to SecureCARE Technologies in 2004.

	Annual Growth	12/12	12/13	12/14	12/15	12/16
Sales ($mil.)	61.9%	1.6	2.6	3.7	8.3	11.1
Net income ($ mil.)	–	(0.6)	(0.6)	–	–	–
Market value ($ mil.)	128.4%	1.0	1.0	1.0	12.1	26.7
Employees	–	–	–	–	–	–

SCULPTZ, INC.

340 E MAPLE AVE STE 205
LANGHORNE, PA 190472848
Phone: 215 494-2900
Fax: –
Web: www.silkies.com

CEO: –
CFO: –
HR: –
FYE: December 31
Type: Private

Bursting at the seams? Sculptz is likely to have the right fit. The company makes and sells hosiery under the Silkies brand in more than a dozen styles and nearly as many colors. It also manufactures and sells knee-highs, socks, and tights under the Sculptz Shapewear and Legwear labels, Silkies Enriche anti-aging skincare products, and PainVanish, a pain-relieving cream. Founded in 1974, Sculptz claims to be the largest direct marketer of pantyhose, counting 1.5 million-plus member customers (mainly women) worldwide. Made in the US, the hosiery is sold through a direct mail and online continuity program, whereby additional pairs continue to be sent. Formerly HCI Direct, the company changed its name in 2010.

SCYNEXIS, INC.

NMS: SCYX

1 Evertrust Plaza, 13th Floor
Jersey City, NJ 07302-6548
Phone: 201 884-5485
Fax: –
Web: www.scynexis.com

CEO: David Angulo
CFO: Ivor Macleod
HR: –
FYE: December 31
Type: Public

At the intersection of science and "you don't want to know" you'll find SCYNEXIS. The pharmaceutical company is developing an oral and IV treatment for life-threatening, invasive fungal infections. Increased global use of chemotherapy and other immunosuppressant drugs has lead to an increase in these infections while anti-fungals have begun to produce drug-resistant strains. The company's lead candidate uses a new chemical approach and has been effective against drug-resistant strains of the fungi. SCYNEXIS is also working on anti-virals and it provides contract animal health R&D to third parties. The company was formed in 2000 when it spun off from Aventis as an animal health firm. It went public in 2014.

	Annual Growth	12/18	12/19	12/20	12/21	12/22
Sales ($mil.)	111.0%	0.3	0.1	–	13.2	5.1
Net income ($ mil.)	–	(12.5)	(53.7)	(55.2)	(32.9)	(62.8)
Market value ($ mil.)	34.1%	15.7	29.7	250.0	199.4	51.0
Employees	10.7%	24	27	38	56	36

SDB TRADE INTERNATIONAL, LLC

11200 RICHMOND AVE STE 180
HOUSTON, TX 770822637
Phone: 713 475-0048
Fax: –
Web: www.thesdbgroup.com

CEO: –
CFO: Wesley Sherer
HR: –
FYE: December 31
Type: Private

For SDB Trade International the product pipeline more than a buzzword. An international metals trading company, SDB Trade International deals in steel pipe, ferrous and non-ferrous scrap, coils, and beams. SBD Trade provide import and export services for its products, sourcing its materials primarily from mills in India and China. Specializing in metal pipes for the Oil and Gas delivery and transmission industry -- the company products include seamless tubing and casing, electric resistance welded steel pipes, seamless steel pipes, and large diameter pipes. SDB Trade serves clients located around the world and provides shipping, trucking, storage, repair and inspection services upon request.

	Annual Growth	12/08	12/09	12/11	12/12	12/17
Sales ($mil.)	15.4%	–	29.2	4.0	51.5	91.8
Net income ($ mil.)	17.0%	–	1.7	2.0	1.1	5.9
Market value ($ mil.)	–	–	–	–	–	–
Employees	–	–	–	–	–	16

SDI TECHNOLOGIES INC.

1299 MAIN ST
RAHWAY, NJ 070655224
Phone: 732 574-9000
Fax: –
Web: www.sditechnologies.com

CEO: Ezra S Ashkenazi
CFO: Chabetaye Chraime
HR: Geralyn Zamorski
FYE: December 31
Type: Private

SDI Technologies designs, manufactures, and distributes a broad range of consumer electronics that are both innovative and high in quality. The company, founded in 1956 as Realite and later Soundesign, is licensed to make alarm clocks, clock radios, iPod accessories, and home and portable speaker systems under several well-known brands, including ekids, iHome and Timex. Soundesign, its cornerstone brand, featured the industry's first telephone clock radio, and its iHome division manufactures audio accessories for iPod electronics and expand its product lines to include portable speakers and home audio systems. Affiliate KIDdesigns sells Barbie, Marvel, Star Wars, Transformers, and My Little Pony. The company's iHome brand is now sold in virtually every key retailer in over 60 countries.

SEABOARD CORP.

ASE: SEB

9000 West 67th Street
Merriam, KS 66202
Phone: 913 676-8928
Fax: –
Web: www.seaboardcorp.com

CEO: Robert L Steer
CFO: David H Rankin
HR: Darlene Mann
FYE: December 31
Type: Public

Seaboard is primarily engaged in hog production and pork processing in the US; commodity trading and grain processing in Africa and South America; cargo shipping services in the US, Caribbean, and Central and South America; sugar and alcohol production in Argentina; and electric power generation in the Dominican Republic. Seaboard also has an equity method investment in Butterball, a producer and processor of turkey products. The company sells pork in the US and abroad. Overseas it trades grain (wheat, soybeans), operates power plants and feed and flour mills, and grows and refines sugar cane. The company generates most of its revenue outside the US.

	Annual Growth	12/19	12/20	12/21	12/22	12/23
Sales ($mil.)	8.7%	6,840.0	7,126.0	9,229.0	11,243	9,562.0
Net income ($ mil.)	(5.5%)	283.0	283.0	570.0	580.0	226.0
Market value ($ mil.)	(4.3%)	4,127.5	2,943.3	3,821.1	3,665.9	3,466.8
Employees	(0.2%)	13,100	13,100	13,200	13,000	13,000

SEABROOK BROTHERS & SONS, INC.

85 FINLEY RD
BRIDGETON, NJ 083026078
Phone: 856 455-8080
Fax: –
Web: –

CEO: –
CFO: –
HR: –
FYE: May 28
Type: Private

Seabrook Brothers and Sons almost has an alphabet of products. From asparagus to water chestnuts, the company grows, processes, and freezes a harvest of vegetables. In addition to producing items for retail sale under its Seabrook Farms label, the company supplies vegetables to customers in the industrial ingredients, foodservice, and private-label retail sectors. It serves customers throughout the US, as well as in internationally in Canada, Chile, Israel, Puerto Rico, Mexico, and Saudi Arabia. Seabrook also makes such value-added products as frozen skillet meals, creamed spinach, and butter and cheese sauces. In business since 1978, the company is still run by the founding Seabrook family.

SEACHANGE INTERNATIONAL INC.

177 Huntington Ave, Ste 1703 PMB 73480
Boston, MA 02115
Phone: 978 897-0100
Fax: –
Web: www.seachange.com

CEO: Peter D Aquino
CFO: Kathleen Mosher
HR: Maria Madigan
FYE: January 31
Type: Public

SeaChange International is an industry leader in the delivery of multiscreen, advertising and premium over-the-top (OTT) video management solutions. The company's software products and services facilitate the aggregation, licensing, management and distribution of video and advertising content for service providers, telecommunications companies, satellite operators, broadcasters and other content providers. The company enables service providers to offer other interactive television services that allow subscribers to receive personalized services and interact with their video devices, thereby enhancing their viewing experience. Further, the company's products provide customers an opportunity to insert advertising into broadcast and VOD content. About 60% of revenue comes from customers in North America.

	Annual Growth	01/19	01/20	01/21	01/22	01/23
Sales ($mil.)	(15.1%)	62.4	67.2	22.0	27.3	32.5
Net income ($ mil.)	–	(38.0)	(8.9)	(21.8)	(7.4)	(11.4)
Market value ($ mil.)	(25.1%)	4.0	11.1	3.0	3.1	1.3
Employees	(18.7%)	249	182	153	107	109

SEACOAST BANKING CORP. OF FLORIDA   NMS: SBCF

815 Colorado Avenue
Stuart, FL 34994
Phone: 772 287-4000
Fax: –
Web: www.seacoastbanking.com

CEO: Charles M Shaffer
CFO: –
HR: Charles Olsson
FYE: December 31
Type: Public

Seacoast Banking Corporation is the holding company for Seacoast National Bank, a wholly-owned national banking association (Seacoast Bank), which has about 55 branches in Florida, with a concentration on the state's southeastern coast. Serving individuals and areas businesses, the bank offers a range of financial products and services, including deposit accounts, credit cards, trust services, and private banking. Commercial and residential real estate loans account for most of the bank's lending activities; to a lesser extent, it also originates business and consumer loans. The bank also provides financial planning services, as well as mutual funds and other investments. Seacoast has total consolidated assets of $9.7 billion and total deposits of $8.1 billion.

	Annual Growth	12/19	12/20	12/21	12/22	12/23
Assets ($mil.)	19.7%	7,108.5	8,342.4	9,681.4	12,146	14,580
Net income ($ mil.)	1.3%	98.7	77.8	124.4	106.5	104.0
Market value ($ mil.)	(1.8%)	2,594.2	2,499.2	3,003.2	2,646.8	2,415.2
Employees	15.5%	867	965	989	1,400	1,541

SEACOR HOLDINGS INC.

2200 ELLER DR
FORT LAUDERDALE, FL 333163069
Phone: 954 523-2200
Fax: –
Web: www.seacorholdings.com

CEO: Eric Fabrikant
CFO: Bruce Weins
HR: Adam Faucheaux
FYE: December 31
Type: Private

SEACOR Holdings provides transportation and logistics services to support a wide range of business sectors. SEACOR has interests in domestic and international transportation and logistics. The company also has interests in crisis and emergency management services and clean fuel and power solutions. SEACOR acquired the capacity and operational expertise to tailor logistics solutions and deliver wherever its customers need them. Through well timed investments in diverse assets, technology and people, it has strengthened its business and enlarged its footprint. The company was founded in 1989. In 2021, SEACOR was acquired by American Industrial Partners (AIP) for $41.50 per share in cash.

	Annual Growth	12/15	12/16	12/17	12/18	12/19
Sales ($mil.)	17.7%	–	–	577.9	835.8	800.0
Net income ($ mil.)	(35.5%)	–	–	81.7	83.2	34.0
Market value ($ mil.)	–	–	–	–	–	–
Employees	–	–	–	–	–	2,195

SEAGATE CLOUD SYSTEMS, INC.

389 DISC DR
LONGMONT, CO 805039364
Phone: 303 845-3200
Fax: –
Web: www.seagate.com

CEO: Dave Mosley
CFO: –
HR: Debbie Weaver
FYE: December 31
Type: Private

Dot Hill Systems designs and markets RAID (redundant array of independent disks) storage devices that are used in corporate data centers and other network environments by enterprises in data-intensive industries such as financial services and telecommunications. It also makes entry-level and mid-range storage area network (SANs) and fibre channel systems, and provides storage system and data management software. Dot Hill's products are sold under the Assured brand. Most of the company's sales are made to manufacturing partners, including Hewlett-Packard, which accounts for nearly three-quarters of sales. Dot Hill has international offices in Germany, Israel, Japan, and the UK. Seagate Technology bought Dot Hill in late 2015.

SEAKR ENGINEERING, LLC

6221 S RACINE CIR
CENTENNIAL, CO 801116427
Phone: 303 790-8499
Fax: –
Web: www.seakr.com

CEO: –
CFO: Richard Halvas
HR: –
FYE: December 31
Type: Private

SEAKR Engineering seeks to find more space in space. The company makes data storage and processing systems, primarily for spacecraft and aircraft. Its products include solid-state recorders, on-board processors, command and data handling systems, single-board computers, power supplies, and other components designed for aerospace, military, and other rugged applications. The company counts NASA and the US Department of Defense among its customers. SEAKR also provides electronics manufacturing services to commercial satellite systems developers.

SEALASKA CORPORATION

1 SEALASKA PLZ STE 400
JUNEAU, AK 998011276
Phone: 907 586-1512
Fax: –
Web: www.sealaska.com

CEO: Anthony Mallott
CFO: Doug Morris
HR: Kaylin Anderson
FYE: December 31
Type: Private

Sealaska Corporation is a for-profit Alaska Native Corporation owned by more than 24,000 Tlingit, Haida, and Tsimshian people with more than 10,000 years of ancestral ties to the oceans, forests and communities of Southeast Alaska. Sealaska is pursuant to the Alaska Native Claims Settlement Act (ANCSA), the largest land settlement in US history and addressed the aboriginal claim to the land by Alaska Native people by mandating the formation of for-profit corporations representing different regions of the state. Through ANCSA, approximately 44 million acres of traditional homelands were returned to Alaska Natives in the form of about regional, for-profit corporations.

	Annual Growth	12/15	12/16	12/17	12/18	12/19
Sales ($mil.)	54.4%	–	–	293.4	429.3	699.6
Net income ($ mil.)	37.1%	–	–	45.8	69.1	86.0
Market value ($ mil.)	–	–	–	–	–	–
Employees	–	–	–	–	–	1,400

SEALED AIR CORP

2415 Cascade Pointe Boulevard
Charlotte, NC 28208
Phone: 980 221-3235
Fax: 201 703-4205
Web: www.sealedair.com

NYS: SEE
CEO: Dustin Semach
CFO: Dustin Semach
HR: –
FYE: December 31
Type: Public

Sealed Air is a leading global provider of packaging solutions integrating high-performance materials, automation, equipment and services, offering brands that include Bubble Wrap, Cryovac, Sealed Air, and Autobag. The company's products are used for a variety of purposes, from protecting meat, poultry, and other foods to packaging for medical devices and pharmaceuticals to packaging for e-commerce shipments. Sealed Air has customers in about 115 countries, but roughly 65% of its revenue comes from customers in the Americas. Among its customers are food processors, e-commerce/fulfillment companies, and industrial manufacturers.

	Annual Growth	12/19	12/20	12/21	12/22	12/23
Sales ($mil.)	3.5%	4,791.1	4,903.2	5,533.8	5,641.9	5,488.9
Net income ($ mil.)	6.8%	263.0	502.9	506.8	491.6	341.6
Market value ($ mil.)	(2.1%)	5,754.1	6,615.2	9,747.2	7,206.0	5,276.0
Employees	0.7%	16,500	16,500	16,500	16,300	17,000

SEARS HOLDINGS CORP

3333 Beverly Road
Hoffman Estates, IL 60179
Phone: 847 286-2500
Fax: –
Web: www.sears.com

NBB: SHLD Q
CEO: Edward Lampert
CFO: Robert A Riecker
HR: Robin Batka
FYE: February 3
Type: Public

Sears is a leading integrated retailer providing merchandise and related services. It offers its wide range of home merchandise, apparel, and automotive products and services through Sears-branded and affiliated full-line and specialty retail stores in the US. Sears also offers a variety of merchandise and services through sears.com, landsend.com, and specialty catalogs. It offers consumers leading proprietary brands including Kenmore and DieHard ? among the most trusted and preferred brands in the US. The company is the nation's largest provider of home services, with more than 14 million service and installation calls made annually. Sears has a rich, long history to tell dating back to 1886 when Richard Sears sold the first batch of watches.

	Annual Growth	02/14*	01/15	01/16	01/17*	02/18
Sales ($mil.)	(17.6%)	36,188	31,198	25,146	22,138	16,702
Net income ($ mil.)	–	(1,365.0)	(1,682.0)	(1,129.0)	(2,221.0)	(383.0)
Market value ($ mil.)	(49.6%)	3,928.0	3,438.7	1,830.6	801.4	253.8
Employees	(22.7%)	249,000	196,000	178,000	140,000	89,000

*Fiscal year change

SEARS HOMETOWN STORES, INC.

5500 TRILLIUM BLVD # 501
HOFFMAN ESTATES, IL 601923400
Phone: 847 286-2500
Fax: –
Web: www.shos.com

CEO: –
CFO: –
HR: –
FYE: February 03
Type: Private

Sears Hometown and Outlet (SHO) Stores is a locally owned and operated appliance store that offers great deals on refrigerators & freezers, cooking appliances, washers & dryers, dishwashers, tools, hardware, and lawn mowers under rand name appliances like Kenmore, Samsung, LG, Whirlpool and GE. It has a store count of 900 stores located in smaller communities across the country and serving many areas. It is also the local destination for all your home appliance and mattress needs as well as a great selection of lawn and garden products.

SEATTLE CHILDREN'S HOSPITAL

4800 SAND POINT WAY NE
SEATTLE, WA 981053901
Phone: 206 987-2000
Fax: –
Web: www.seattlechildrens.org

CEO: Jeff Sperring
CFO: Kelly Wallace
HR: Devnee Gadbois
FYE: September 30
Type: Private

Seattle Children's Hospital, which has about 365 beds, serves children and infants of all ages. Its specialty units include psychiatry and behavioral care, neonatal intensive care, and rehabilitation for children disabled by injuries, illness, or congenital complications. In addition to its primary campus, Seattle Children's Hospital operates clinics in Puget Sound, Wenatchee, Federal Way and Bellevue, among others. The company delivers superior patient care, advance new discoveries and treatments through pediatric research and serve as the pediatric and adolescent academic medical center for Washington, Alaska, Montana and Idaho. It was founded in 1907.

SEATTLE UNIVERSITY

901 12TH AVE
SEATTLE, WA 981224411
Phone: 206 296-6150
Fax: –
Web: www.seattleu.edu

CEO: –
CFO: –
HR: Mary Dawson
FYE: June 30
Type: Private

Seattle University isn't very big, but as one of 28 Jesuit universities in the US it is part of a Roman Catholic teaching legacy that spans the country and the world. With an enrollment of about 7,500 students, the school offers 64 undergraduate, more than 35 graduate degree programs and 28 certificate programs through its eight schools (College of Arts and Sciences, Albers School of Business and Economics, College of Education, School of Law, Matteo Ricci College, College of Nursing, College of Science and Engineering, and School of Theology and Ministry).

	Annual Growth	06/18	06/19	06/20	06/21	06/22
Sales ($mil.)	0.7%	–	226.2	223.0	221.7	231.0
Net income ($ mil.)	–	–	24.5	18.4	122.9	(23.5)
Market value ($ mil.)	–	–	–	–	–	–
Employees	–	–	–	–	–	1,100

SECUREWORKS CORP
NMS: SCWX

One Concourse Parkway N.E., Suite 500
Atlanta, GA 30328
Phone: 404 327-6339
Fax: –
Web: www.secureworks.com

CEO: Wendy Thomas
CFO: Paul M Parrish
HR: –
FYE: February 2
Type: Public

SecureWorks endeavors to keep corporate networks free from intrusion and harm. The company, a subsidiary of Dell, offers a suite of data security services, as well as 24x7 monitoring and management by IT analysts in its operations centers, designed to protect its clients' computer networks from hackers, viruses, and other digital threats. Its services include intrusion prevention systems, Internet firewalls, and e-mail filtering and encryption. SecureWorks also provides services such as consulting and testing related to threat assessment and regulatory compliance. Customers are typically in financial services, government, health care, and retail. SecureWorks became publicly traded with an April 2016 IPO.

	Annual Growth	01/20	01/21	01/22*	02/23	02/24
Sales ($mil.)	(9.8%)	552.8	561.0	535.2	463.5	365.9
Net income ($ mil.)	–	(31.7)	(21.9)	(39.8)	(114.5)	(86.0)
Market value ($ mil.)	(16.5%)	1,359.0	1,195.7	1,215.5	735.6	660.9
Employees	(13.1%)	2,663	2,696	2,351	2,149	1,516

*Fiscal year change

SECURIAN FINANCIAL GROUP INC

400 Robert Street North
St. Paul, MN 55101-2098
Phone: 651 665-3500
Fax: –
Web: www.securian.com

CEO: Christopher Hilger
CFO: Warren Zaccaro
HR: –
FYE: December 31
Type: Public

Securian Financial Group provides life and disability insurance, retirement products, asset management, and other financial services in the US and Canada. The company primarily operates through subsidiary Minnesota Life, which offers individual and group life and disability insurance and annuities, as well as retirement services. Other subsidiaries include brokerage network Securian Financial Services and Allied Solutions, which distributes Securian products. Its Securian Asset Management unit provides asset management and investment advisory services.

SECURITIES INVESTOR PROTECTION CORPORATION

1667 K ST NW STE 1000
WASHINGTON, DC 200061620
Phone: 202 371-8300
Fax: –
Web: www.sipc.org

CEO: Josephine Wang
CFO: –
HR: –
FYE: December 31
Type: Private

Securities Investor Protection Corporation (SIPC) is an industry-financed insurance plan that protects clients of most broker-dealers registered with the US Securities and Exchange Commission (SEC). SIPC insures customers' securities (up to $500,000 per account) against losses due to the financial failure of brokerage firms. Losses caused by fluctuations in market value are not protected. The not-for-profit membership corporation was mandated by the Securities Investor Protection Act and has more than 6,000 members. Its board is appointed by the US president, the treasury secretary, and the Federal Reserve Board. Assessments from members and investments in government securities provide money for the SIPC Fund.

	Annual Growth	12/14	12/15	12/16	12/21	12/22
Assets ($mil.)	6.9%	–	2,652.9	2,944.6	4,382.7	4,237.8
Net income ($ mil.)	10.2%	–	169.0	362.2	261.0	333.5
Market value ($ mil.)	–	–	–	–	–	–
Employees	–	–	–	–	–	39

SECURITY FEDERAL CORP (SC)
NBB: SFDL

238 Richland Avenue Northwest
Aiken, SC 29801
Phone: 803 641-3000
Fax: –
Web: www.securityfederalbank.com

CEO: J C Verenes
CFO: Darrell Rains
HR: –
FYE: December 31
Type: Public

Security Federal is the holding company for Security Federal Bank, which has about a dozen offices in southwestern South Carolina's Aiken and Lexington counties. It expanded into Columbia, South Carolina and eastern Georgia in 2007. The bank offers checking and savings accounts, credit cards, CDs, IRAs, and other retail products and services. Commercial business and mortgage loans make up more than 60% of the company's lending portfolio, which also includes residential mortgages (about 25%), and consumer loans. Security Federal also offers trust services, investments, and life, home, and auto insurance.

	Annual Growth	12/19	12/20	12/21	12/22	12/23
Assets ($mil.)	12.6%	963.2	1,171.7	1,301.2	1,381.4	1,549.7
Net income ($ mil.)	6.9%	7.8	7.1	12.8	10.2	10.2
Market value ($ mil.)	(10.0%)	113.0	83.1	103.3	82.2	74.3
Employees	0.8%	250	–	248	258	258

SECURITY FINANCE CORPORATION OF SPARTANBURG

181 SECURITY PL
SPARTANBURG, SC 293075450
Phone: 864 582-8193
Fax: –
Web: www.securityfinance.com

CEO: –
CFO: –
HR: –
FYE: December 31
Type: Private

Folks looking for a little financial security just might turn to Security Finance Corporation of Spartanburg. Founded in 1955, the consumer loan company provides personal loans typically ranging from $100 to $600 (some states, however, allow loan amounts as high as $3,000). Customers can also turn to Security Finance for credit reports and tax preparation services. The company operates approximately 900 offices in more than 15 states that are marketed under the Security Finance, Sunbelt Credit, and PFS banner names. A subsidiary of Security Group, the financial institution also has locations operating as Security Financial Services in North Carolina and Longhorn Finance in Texas.

	Annual Growth	12/12	12/13	12/14	12/15	12/16
Assets ($mil.)	0.5%	–	616.7	648.9	651.5	625.1
Net income ($ mil.)	4.1%	–	62.7	83.1	78.8	70.7
Market value ($ mil.)	–	–	–	–	–	–
Employees	–	–	–	–	–	2,500

SECURITY HEALTH PLAN OF WISCONSIN, INC.

1515 N SAINT JOSEPH AVE
MARSHFIELD, WI 544491343
Phone: 715 221-9555
Fax: –
Web: www.securityhealth.org

CEO: Julie Brussow
CFO: –
HR: –
FYE: December 31
Type: Private

Security Health Plan of Wisconsin provides health insurance coverage and related services to some 200,000 members in more than 35 Wisconsin counties. Its managed network of providers includes more than 4,000 physicians, 40 hospitals, and health care facilities, as well as 55,000 pharmacies across the US. Security Health Plan provides policies for groups and individuals. Its products include HMO coverage plans and supplemental Medicare plans, as well as prescription drug and equipment coverage, disease management programs, and administration services for self-funded plans. Established in 1986, the company is the managed healthcare arm of Marshfield Clinic, which operates medical practices across the state.

	Annual Growth	12/08	12/09	12/17	12/21	12/22
Sales ($mil.)	3.7%	–	814.8	1,234.4	1,232.2	1,309.6
Net income ($ mil.)	(5.2%)	–	27.7	9.8	11.8	13.8
Market value ($ mil.)	–	–	–	–	–	–
Employees	–	–	–	–	–	1,006

SECURITY INDUSTRY ASSOCIATION

8455 COLESVILLE RD STE 1200
SILVER SPRING, MD 209106469
Phone: 301 804-4700
Fax: -
Web: www.securityindustry.org

CEO: -
CFO: -
HR: -
FYE: December 31
Type: Private

If it were up to this group, members would need access cards, security checks, and retina scans before sitting at the roundtable. Security Industry Association (SIA) acts as a watchdog and liaison between the security industry and the government. The membership association promotes international trade, expansion and growth, and industry trend reporting for members that operate within the information technology and physical security markets. SIA also acts as a collective voice for its members wishing to participate in the development of new governmental regulations and standards. More than 300 companies are members of SAI, which was formed in 1969.

	Annual Growth	12/15	12/16	12/17	12/21	12/22
Sales ($mil.)	(0.8%)	–	6.9	7.4	5.3	6.5
Net income ($ mil.)	–	–	1.2	1.7	(0.2)	(0.1)
Market value ($ mil.)	–	–	–	–	–	–
Employees	–	–	–	–	–	16

SECURITY INNOVATION, INC.

187 BALLARDVALE ST
WILMINGTON, MA 018871082
Phone: 978 694-1008
Fax: -
Web: www.securityinnovation.com

CEO: Edward Adams
CFO: -
HR: Kimberly Boroyan
FYE: December 31
Type: Private

Security Innovation studies the bugs that make software vulnerable. The company offers vulnerability assessment, training, and risk management tools designed to protect mid-size and large companies from security risks. Its products and services help development teams build more secure testing processes and applications. With offices in the US and China, Security Innovation supports government clients and numerous top-tier corporations in the financial services, health care, IT, and retail industries, including Northrop Grumman, Visa, Microsoft, Symantec, and Coca-Cola. The privately held company has received investment funding from Brook Venture Partners.

SECURITY LAND & DEVELOPMENT CORP.

NBB: SLDV

2816 Washington Road, #103
Augusta, GA 30909
Phone: 706 736-6334
Fax: -
Web: -

CEO: W S Flanagin
CFO: -
HR: -
FYE: September 30
Type: Public

The management of Security Land and Development could very well equate security with real estate. Security Land and Development invests in and develops land and property for sale or lease. Its primary asset is National Plaza, a 69,000-sq. ft. strip shopping center anchored by a Publix Super Markets grocery store in Augusta, Georgia; it also owns a smattering of additional properties in the area (land, office space, and a single-family residence). Chairman Stewart Flanagin, CEO Greenlee Flanagin, and other members of their family own 44% of Security Land and Development.

	Annual Growth	09/14	09/15	09/16	09/17	09/18
Sales ($mil.)	4.4%	1.5	1.5	1.7	1.7	1.8
Net income ($ mil.)	25.6%	0.3	1.5	0.3	0.3	0.8
Market value ($ mil.)	–	–	–	–	–	–
Employees	5.7%	4	4	4	4	5

SECURITY NATIONAL FINANCIAL CORP

NMS: SNFC A

433 West Ascension Way, 6th Floor
Salt Lake City, UT 84123
Phone: 801 264-1060
Fax: 801 265-9882
Web: www.securitynational.com

CEO: Scott M Quist
CFO: Garrett S Sill
HR: -
FYE: December 31
Type: Public

There are three certainties -- life, death, and mortgage payments -- and Security National Financial has you covered on all fronts. Its largest unit, SecurityNational Mortgage, makes residential and commercial mortgage loans through some 70 offices in more than a dozen states. Its Security National Life, Memorial Insurance Company, and Southern Security Life subsidiaries sell life and diving or related sports accident insurance, annuities, and funeral plans in about 40 states. Security National Financial also owns about 15 mortuaries and cemeteries in Utah, Arizona, and California. The family of chairman and CEO George Quist controls more than half of Security National Financial.

	Annual Growth	12/18	12/19	12/20	12/21	12/22
Assets ($mil.)	8.6%	1,050.8	1,334.4	1,548.9	1,547.6	1,461.1
Net income ($ mil.)	4.3%	21.7	10.9	55.6	39.5	25.7
Market value ($ mil.)	9.1%	113.8	129.1	184.2	203.0	161.1
Employees	3.2%	1,433	1,293	1,708	1,733	1,624

SED INTERNATIONAL HOLDINGS, INC.

NBB: SEDN

2150 Cedars Road, Suite 200
Lawrenceville, GA 30043
Phone: 770 243-1200
Fax: -
Web: www.sedonline.com

CEO: Hesham M Gad
CFO: Juan O Bravo
HR: -
FYE: June 30
Type: Public

SED International keeps North and South America computing. The company distributes PCs, tablet and notebook computers, components, televisions, small appliances, and more to resellers and retailers throughout the US and Latin America. Its computer hardware products, traditionally the company's primary business line, include components, storage devices, networking equipment, peripherals, and systems from about 170 vendors, such as Acer, Dell, Lenovo, and Microsoft. SED also offers customized supply chain management services to its e-commerce, business-to-business, and business-to-consumer clients. Founded in 1980 as Southern Electronics Distributors, SED International is restructuring its operations in the US.

	Annual Growth	06/10	06/11	06/12	06/13	06/14
Sales ($mil.)	(19.1%)	541.7	607.0	577.3	517.4	232.5
Net income ($ mil.)	–	0.3	3.1	1.4	(15.7)	(18.4)
Market value ($ mil.)	(51.0%)	13.5	27.3	27.3	27.3	0.8
Employees	–	388	402	425	327	–

SEDONA CORP

1003 West 9th Avenue, Second Floor
King of Prussia, PA 19406
Phone: 610 337-8400
Fax: -
Web: www.sedonacorp.com

CEO: David R Vey
CFO: -
HR: -
FYE: December 31
Type: Public

SEDONA's software bridges the canyon between financial institutions and their customers. The company provides Web-based customer relationship management software that analyzes customer data, manages marketing campaigns, and generates leads for small and midsized financial institutions. Its Intarsia software also generates customer profiles that include demographic, behavioral, and preference information provided by third parties. Customers include community banks, credit unions, brokerage firms, and insurance agencies.

	Annual Growth	12/11	12/12	12/13	12/14	12/15
Sales ($mil.)	9.7%	1.3	1.5	1.6	1.6	1.9
Net income ($ mil.)	–	(0.7)	(0.6)	(0.7)	(0.7)	(0.5)
Market value ($ mil.)	–	7.1	1.9	2.6	1.5	–
Employees	–	–	–	–	–	–

SEELOS THERAPEUTICS INC
NAS: SEEL

300 Park Avenue, 2nd Floor
New York, NY 10022
Phone: 646 293-2100
Fax: –
Web: www.seelostherapeutics.com

CEO: –
CFO: –
HR: –
FYE: December 31
Type: Public

Seelos Therapeutics (formerly Apricus Biosciences) is focused on finding treatments for central nervous system disorders and rare diseases. It has a portfolio of about a half-dozen candidates, about half of which are in clinical trials. Its pipeline targets such ailments as Parkinson's Disease, Sanfilippo Syndrome, post-operative pain, and suicidality in post-traumatic stress disorder and major depressive disorder. Apricus Biosciences, which was developing topical formulations with improved absorption rates, changed course when it merged with private biotech Seelos Therapeutics in early 2019.

	Annual Growth	12/19	12/20	12/21	12/22	12/23
Sales ($mil.)	55.7%	0.4	–	–	–	2.2
Net income ($ mil.)	–	(51.3)	(19.1)	(66.0)	(73.5)	(37.9)
Market value ($ mil.)	0.9%	13.1	15.5	16.0	6.7	13.6
Employees	(36.1%)	6	10	16	16	1

SEFTON RESOURCES INC

2000 S FAIRPLAY ST
AURORA, CO 800144526
Phone: 303 759-2700
Fax: –
Web: –

CEO: Jim Ellerton
CFO: –
HR: –
FYE: December 31
Type: Private

Looking to strike it rich by sifting through a number of hydrocarbon resource assets, Sefton Resources explores for and produces oil and gas primarily in California and Kansas. Its core area of exploration and production is the East Ventura Basin in California, where Sefton Resources owns two oil fields (Tapia Canyon and Eureka Canyon). In addition, the company owns more than 40,000 acres in the Forest City Basin of Eastern Kansas, which has coalbed methane and conventional oil and gas deposits. The company has proved reserves of 7.6 million barrels of oil equivalent. Its operating subsidiaries are TEG Oil & Gas USA and TEG Oil & Gas MidContinent.

	Annual Growth	12/06	12/07	12/08	12/09	12/10
Sales ($mil.)	9.0%	–	3.0	4.7	2.7	3.9
Net income ($ mil.)	25.4%	–	0.2	0.3	(0.3)	0.4
Market value ($ mil.)	–	–	–	–	–	–
Employees	–	–	–	–	–	10

SEI INVESTMENTS CO
NMS: SEIC

1 Freedom Valley Drive
Oaks, PA 19456-1100
Phone: 610 676-1000
Fax: –
Web: www.seic.com

CEO: Alfred P West Jr
CFO: Dennis J McGonigle
HR: –
FYE: December 31
Type: Public

SEI Investments provides outsourced investment and fund processing for clients, including banks, trust companies, investment advisors and managers, and institutional investors and ultra-high-net-worth families in the US, Canada, the UK, Europe, and other locations throughout the world. Services include securities and investment processing, trust accounting, portfolio analysis, treasury and cash management, and performance measurement reporting. Its investment operations serves managers and distributors of mutual funds, hedge funds, and alternative investments. The company administers or manages approximately $1.2 trillion in hedge, private equity, mutual fund and pooled or separately managed assets, including approximately $399.4 billion in assets under management and $814.6 billion in client assets under administration. The US generates more than 80% of the company's revenue.

	Annual Growth	12/19	12/20	12/21	12/22	12/23
Sales ($mil.)	3.9%	1,649.9	1,684.1	1,918.3	1,991.0	1,919.8
Net income ($ mil.)	(2.0%)	501.4	447.3	546.6	475.5	462.3
Market value ($ mil.)	(0.7%)	8,589.5	7,538.8	7,994.0	7,647.6	8,336.3
Employees	–	3,756	3,988	4,406	4,837	–

SEIBELS BRUCE GROUP, INC. (THE)
NBB: SBBG

1501 Lady Street, P.O. Box 1
Columbia, SC 29201
Phone: 803 748-2000
Fax: 803 748-2839
Web: www.seibels.com

CEO: –
CFO: –
HR: –
FYE: December 31
Type: Public

Seibels Bruce concerns itself with driving disasters and natural disasters. The company writes and sells auto, homeowners, and other property/casualty insurance products and services. Subsidiary Universal Insurance provides standard and nonstandard auto coverage in six Southeastern states. Commercial lines include business owners' policies, commercial auto and umbrella, and commercial package policies. Seibels Bruce, which was taken private in 2004, traces its history back to 1869 and the beginnings of the insurance industry.

	Annual Growth	12/98	12/99	12/00	12/01	12/02
Assets ($mil.)	(18.0%)	295.6	254.8	170.7	150.6	133.7
Net income ($ mil.)	–	(2.9)	(7.5)	(15.4)	4.4	6.1
Market value ($ mil.)	(22.8%)	0.0	0.0	0.0	0.0	0.0
Employees	(16.5%)	544	516	329	296	264

SEITEL INC

10811 S WESTVIEW CIRCLE DR STE 100
HOUSTON, TX 770432748
Phone: 713 881-8900
Fax: –
Web: www.seitel.com

CEO: –
CFO: –
HR: –
FYE: December 31
Type: Private

There aren't any "Quiet" signs in Seitel's library, which consists of more than 43,000 sq. miles of 3-D and about 1.1 million linear miles of 2-D seismic data. The data, which is used to locate oil and gas, primarily covers the Gulf of Mexico, the US Gulf Coast, and western Canada. The company contracts with third-party seismic crews to gather data but handles the processing itself through its Olympic Seismic, Seitel Data, Seitel Matrix, Seitel Solutions business units. The bulk of Seitel's total revenues comes from the acquisition and licensing of seismic data. The balance is primarily generated by its Seitel Solutions subsidiary, which gives customers access to the company's seismic database.

SELECT MEDICAL HOLDINGS CORP
NYS: SEM

4714 Gettysburg Road, P.O. Box 2034
Mechanicsburg, PA 17055
Phone: 717 972-1100
Fax: –
Web: www.selectmedicalholdings.com

CEO: David S Chernow
CFO: Martin F Jackson
HR: Jennie Patkowa
FYE: December 31
Type: Public

Select Medical Holdings Corporation is one of the operators of critical illness recovery hospitals, rehabilitation hospitals, outpatient rehabilitation clinics, and occupational health centers in the US based on a number of facilities. It operates almost 105 critical illness recovery hospitals in roughly 30 states, some 30 rehabilitation hospitals in more than 10 states, and about 1,930 outpatient rehabilitation clinics in nearly 40 states and the District of Columbia. Concentra operated about 540 occupational health centers in around 40 states. Concentra also provides contract services at employer worksites. Select Medical began its operations in 1997.

	Annual Growth	12/19	12/20	12/21	12/22	12/23
Sales ($mil.)	5.1%	5,453.9	5,531.7	6,204.5	6,333.5	6,664.1
Net income ($ mil.)	13.2%	148.4	259.0	402.2	159.0	243.5
Market value ($ mil.)	0.2%	2,996.1	3,550.7	3,774.1	3,187.4	3,016.7
Employees	2.3%	49,900	49,600	50,500	53,800	54,600

SELECT WATER SOLUTIONS INC
NYS: WTTR

1233 W. Loop South, Suite 1400
Houston, TX 77027
Phone: 713 235-9500
Fax: –
Web: www.selectenergy.com

CEO: John D Schmitz
CFO: Nick L Swyka
HR: –
FYE: December 31
Type: Public

Select Water Solutions (formerly Select Energy Services) is a leading provider of sustainable full lifecycle water and chemical solutions to the oil and gas industry in the US. Through its patented WaterONE automation services and its proprietary AquaView software platform, its Water Services segment provides extensive technology solutions that enable 24/7 monitoring and visibility for its customers into all of their water-related operations, including hydrographic mapping, water volume and quality monitoring, remote pit and tank monitoring, among others. Additionally, through its FluidMatch solutions, Select provides comprehensive testing and analysis of its customers' application conditions, product chemistry and key performance requirements for oil and gas well completion fluid-system design.

	Annual Growth	12/19	12/20	12/21	12/22	12/23
Sales ($mil.)	5.3%	1,291.6	605.1	764.6	1,387.4	1,585.4
Net income ($ mil.)	127.4%	2.8	(338.7)	(42.2)	48.3	74.4
Market value ($ mil.)	(4.9%)	1,098.7	485.4	737.6	1,094.0	898.6
Employees	1.9%	3,900	2,000	3,000	4,000	4,200

SELECT WATER SOLUTIONS, LLC

1233 WEST LOOP S STE 1400
HOUSTON, TX 770279122
Phone: 940 668-1818
Fax: –
Web: www.selectwater.com

CEO: John D Schmitz
CFO: –
HR: J B Crouch
FYE: December 31
Type: Private

Pick a service, any service, and Select Energy Services probably provides it to oil and gas producers. The company helps oil and gas producers with the sourcing of water at jobsites. Select Energy Services also provides workforce accommodations and surface rental equipment supporting drilling, completion, and production operations for the onshore oil and gas industry. Its wellsite completion and construction services segment handles crane and logistics services, wellsite and pipeline construction, and field services. Select Energy Services went public in 2017.

	Annual Growth	12/06	12/07	12/08	12/09	12/10
Sales ($mil.)	336.8%	–	–	–	115.1	502.6
Net income ($ mil.)	364.4%	–	–	–	11.9	55.3
Market value ($ mil.)	–	–	–	–	–	–
Employees	–	–	–	–	–	1,600

SELECTIS HEALTH INC
NBB: GBCS

8480 E Orchard Rd, Ste 4900
Greenwood Village, CO 80111
Phone: 720 680-0808
Fax: –
Web: –

CEO: Lance Baller
CFO: Jim Creamer
HR: –
FYE: December 31
Type: Public

Global Casinos owns and operates two casinos in Colorado. Its Bull Durham Saloon & Casino in Black Hawk, Colorado, boasts more than 180 slot machines and offers limited food services along with other customer amenities. Its customer base consists primarily of day visitors from Denver. The company also owns a second property, the Doc Holliday Casino, in Central City, Colorado, with about 200 slot machines. Both casinos offer charter services to bring groups of patrons from Denver. In 2012 the company announced plans to divest of all of its gaming interests and acquire a real estate investment trust (REIT) focused on the healthcare industry. Clifford Neuman owns nearly 10% of Global Casinos.

	Annual Growth	12/17	12/18	12/19	12/20	12/21
Sales ($mil.)	74.9%	3.1	3.6	6.9	20.9	29.3
Net income ($ mil.)	–	(3.0)	(2.0)	(0.9)	3.0	(2.3)
Market value ($ mil.)	89.7%	1.6	0.9	0.7	1.6	21.0
Employees	373.6%	1	2	166	287	503

SELECTIVE INSURANCE GROUP INC
NMS: SIGI

40 Wantage Avenue
Branchville, NJ 07890
Phone: 973 948-3000
Fax: 973 948-0282
Web: www.selective.com

CEO: –
CFO: –
HR: –
FYE: December 31
Type: Public

Property/casualty insurance holding company Selective Insurance Group's reach primarily covers the US. Various state departments of insurance license nine of its subsidiaries as admitted carriers to write specific lines of property and casualty insurance in the standard marketplace and authorize the tenth subsidiary as a non-admitted carrier to write property and casualty insurance in the excess and surplus (E&S) lines market. Commercial policies include workers' compensation and commercial automobile, property, and liability insurance. Personal lines include homeowners and automobile insurance. The Selective Insurance Group operates through four reportable segments: Standard Commercial Lines, Standard Personal Lines, E&S Lines, and Investments.

	Annual Growth	12/19	12/20	12/21	12/22	12/23
Assets ($mil.)	7.6%	8,797.2	9,687.9	10,461	10,802	11,803
Net income ($ mil.)	7.7%	271.6	246.4	403.8	224.9	365.2
Market value ($ mil.)	11.1%	3,952.9	4,061.4	4,968.5	5,373.0	6,032.1
Employees	2.5%	2,400	2,400	2,440	2,520	2,650

SELLAS LIFE SCIENCES GROUP INC
NAS: SLS

7 Times Square, Suite 2503
New York, NY 10036
Phone: 646 200-5278
Fax: –
Web: www.sellaslifesciences.com

CEO: Angelos M Stergiou
CFO: –
HR: –
FYE: December 31
Type: Public

SELLAS Life Sciences (formerly Galena Biopharma) is a biopharmaceutical with a focus on developing novel cancer immunotherapies to treat a number of cancers. Its lead candidate is galinpepimut-S, which is in several trials aimed at treating cancers including leukemia, multiple myeloma, and ovarian cancer. SELLAS licenses galinpepimut-S from Memorial Sloan Kettering Cancer Center, which also owns a stake in the company. Another candidate is Nelipepimut-S or NPS, which is a cancer immunotherapy targeting the human epidermal growth factor receptor 2, or HER2, expressing cancers. The company is headquartered in New York, New York.

	Annual Growth	12/18	12/19	12/20	12/21	12/22
Sales ($mil.)	–	–	–	1.9	7.6	1.0
Net income ($ mil.)	–	(27.7)	(19.3)	(16.8)	(20.7)	(41.3)
Market value ($ mil.)	17.7%	25.8	90.3	122.0	116.2	49.6
Employees	20.7%	8	5	7	11	17

SEMATECH, INC.

257 FULLER RD STE 2200
ALBANY, NY 122033613
Phone: 518 437-8686
Fax: –
Web: www.sematech.org

CEO: Ronald Goldblatt
CFO: Randall Barfield
HR: –
FYE: December 31
Type: Private

SEMATECH (from "semiconductor manufacturing technology") is more than semantics. The not-for-profit research consortium pursues advances in chip manufacturing including design, lithography, metrology, and interconnect processes. It also provides custom wafer processing services and publishes technical reports for its members. The group is funded by member dues. Employees from member companies -- Advanced Micro Devices, Hewlett-Packard, IBM, Infineon, Intel, National Semiconductor, and Texas Instruments, among others -- carry out research at SEMATECH facilities.

SEMCO ENERGY, INC.

1411 3RD ST STE A
PORT HURON, MI 480605480
Phone: 810 987-2200
Fax: –
Web: www.semcoenergy.com

CEO: –
CFO: –
HR: –
FYE: December 31
Type: Private

Alaska and Michigan have more in common than a cold climate. SEMCO ENERGY serves approximately 423,000 natural gas consumers in both states. The company's main subsidiary is utility SEMCO ENERGY Gas, which distributes gas to more than 290,000 customers in 24 Michigan counties. SEMCO's ENSTAR Natural Gas unit distributes gas to more than 133,000 customers in and around Anchorage, Alaska. The company's unregulated operations include propane distribution in Michigan and Wisconsin; pipeline and storage facility operation; and information technology outsourcing. In 2012 SEMCO ENERGY was acquired by AltaGas.

	Annual Growth	12/11	12/12	12/13	12/14	12/16
Sales ($mil.)	(0.3%)	–	582.3	608.1	674.0	576.0
Net income ($ mil.)	5.5%	–	41.6	48.7	51.2	51.6
Market value ($ mil.)	–	–	–	–	–	–
Employees	–	–	–	–	–	500

SEMI

673 S MILPITAS BLVD
MILPITAS, CA 950355473
Phone: 408 943-6900
Fax: –
Web: www.semi.org

CEO: Ajit Manocha
CFO: Richard Salsman
HR: Tin Tran
FYE: December 31
Type: Private

Semiconductor Equipment and Materials International (SEMI) is a global organization comprising, naturally enough, suppliers of semiconductor production equipment and the materials that go into making microchips. The group holds trade exhibitions and industry forums around the world. Its annual SEMICON shows are staged in China, Germany, Japan, Singapore, South Korea, Taiwan, and the US. SEMI advocates for industry interests in Washington, DC, and sponsors industry standards efforts, bringing together competing vendors to agree on common specifications for manufacturing hardware, software, and materials. SEMI was established in 1970.

	Annual Growth	12/11	12/12	12/13	12/21	12/22
Sales ($mil.)	3.1%	–	46.4	41.7	57.6	62.7
Net income ($ mil.)	(0.7%)	–	6.1	3.2	0.0	5.7
Market value ($ mil.)	–	–	–	–	–	–
Employees	–	–	–	–	–	160

SEMINOLE ELECTRIC COOPERATIVE, INC.

16313 North Dale Mabry Highway
Tampa, FL 33688-2000
Phone: 813 963-0994
Fax: 813 264-7906
Web: www.seminole-electric.com

CEO: Lisa Johnson
CFO: Jo Fuller
HR: Tip English
FYE: December 31
Type: Public

This Seminole is not only a native Floridian, but it has also provided electricity in the state since 1948. Seminole Electric Cooperative generates and transmits electricity for 10 member distribution cooperatives that serve 1.4 million residential and business customers in 42 Florida counties. Seminole Electric has more than 3,350 MW of primarily coal-fired generating capacity. The cooperative also buys electricity from other utilities and independent power producers, and it owns 350 miles of transmission lines. Some 90% of its power load uses the transmission systems of other utilities through long-term contracts.

	Annual Growth	12/11	12/12	12/13	12/14	12/15
Sales ($mil.)	(4.0%)	1,291.8	1,222.6	1,213.2	1,129.8	1,098.8
Net income ($ mil.)	0.9%	27.1	11.9	17.7	27.3	28.0
Market value ($ mil.)	–	–	–	–	–	–
Employees	(0.9%)	521	517	515	527	503

SEMLER SCIENTIFIC INC

2340-2348 Walsh Avenue, Suite 2344
Santa Clara, CA 95051
Phone: 877 774-4211
Fax: –
Web: www.semlerscientific.com

NAS: SMLR
CEO: –
CFO: –
HR: –
FYE: December 31
Type: Public

Semler Scientific is an emerging medical device maker with a single product. The company markets the FloChec, a medical device that measures arterial blood flow to the extremities (fingers and toes) quickly and easily in the doctor's office, to diagnose peripheral artery disease. FloChec received FDA clearance in early 2010 and the company began commercially leasing the product in 2011. Founded in 2007 by Dr. Herbert Semler, who invented the technology used in FloChec, the Portland-based company went public in 2014 with an offering valued at $10 million.

	Annual Growth	12/19	12/20	12/21	12/22	12/23
Sales ($mil.)	20.1%	32.8	38.6	53.0	56.7	68.2
Net income ($ mil.)	8.1%	15.1	14.0	17.2	14.3	20.6
Market value ($ mil.)	(2.0%)	330.5	647.2	631.0	227.2	304.9
Employees	8.3%	67	86	124	127	92

SEMPRA

488 8th Avenue
San Diego, CA 92101
Phone: 619 696-2000
Fax: –
Web: www.sempra.com

NYS: SRE
CEO: Jeffrey W Martin
CFO: Karen L Sedgwick
HR: –
FYE: December 31
Type: Public

Sempra Energy is a California-based holding company with energy infrastructure investments in North America. The company invests in, develops, and operates energy infrastructure, and provide electric and gas services to its customers. SoCalGas is the nation's largest gas distribution company and operates more than 50,000 miles of distribution pipelines and more than 3,000 miles of transmission pipelines. SDG&E operates over 25,000 miles of electric transmission and distribution lines. Oncor is a regulated electricity transmission and distribution utility that operates in the north-central, eastern, western and panhandle regions of Texas.

	Annual Growth	12/19	12/20	12/21	12/22	12/23
Sales ($mil.)	11.5%	10,829	11,370	12,857	14,439	16,720
Net income ($ mil.)	8.8%	2,198.0	3,933.0	1,318.0	2,139.0	3,075.0
Market value ($ mil.)	(16.2%)	95,649	80,451	83,526	97,581	47,187
Employees	4.8%	13,969	14,706	15,390	15,785	16,835

SEMTECH CORP.

200 Flynn Road
Camarillo, CA 93012-8790
Phone: 805 498-2111
Fax: –
Web: www.semtech.com

NMS: SMTC
CEO: Paul H Pickle
CFO: Mark Lin
HR: –
FYE: January 29
Type: Public

Semtech is a high-performance semiconductor, IoT systems, and Cloud connectivity service provider. It design, develop, manufacture, and market high-performance analog and mixed-signal semiconductors and advanced algorithms as well as wireless semiconductors, connectivity modules, gateways, routers, and connected services for IoT. The company's products are sold into the infrastructure, high-end consumer, and industrial end markets, and use in a variety of devices, including smartphones and base stations, notebooks, and desktops, passive optical networks, among others. Semtech's LoRa technology for low-power wide-area networks generates a growing amount of revenue for the company. More than 70% of the company's revenue are generated in the Asia/Pacific region.

	Annual Growth	01/19	01/20	01/21	01/22	01/23
Sales ($mil.)	4.8%	627.2	547.5	595.1	740.9	756.5
Net income ($ mil.)	(0.7%)	63.1	31.9	59.9	125.7	61.4
Market value ($ mil.)	(9.7%)	3,178.8	3,354.5	4,531.6	4,332.3	2,117.3
Employees	13.9%	1,335	1,388	1,394	1,439	2,248

SENDEC CORP.

345 POMROYS DR
WINDBER, PA 159632425
Phone: 585 425-3390
Fax: –
Web: –

CEO: –
CFO: –
HR: –
FYE: July 31
Type: Private

SenDEC is a manufacturer's manufacturer. The company, whose name stands for Sen sing D igital E lectronic C ontrols, provides electronics design/prototyping, production, and sub-assembly services on a contract basis to such bigwig manufacturers as Eastman Kodak and Xerox. Those services are offered through its Contract Electronics Manufacturing business unit. A second business unit, SenDEC's Products group, makes and sells digital display and control devices, such as battery discharge indicators, engine monitors, fuel gauges, and volt meters. In 2011 the company was bought by API Technologies, which is looking to boost its defense electronics manufacturing business.

SENOMYX, INC.

4767 NEXUS CENTER DR
SAN DIEGO, CA 921213051
Phone: 858 646-8300
Fax: –
Web: www.senomyx.com

CEO: John Poyhonen
CFO: David Humphrey
HR: –
FYE: December 31
Type: Private

Senomyx nose a good thing when it smells it. The company has identified human receptor genes related to the detection of smells and tastes, and, using this genetic research, the company is developing sweet, salty, and savory flavor enhancers and bitter taste modulators. Potential products include agents that can block bitter tastes in coffee and make low-sodium snacks taste salty. Senomyx collaborates with the likes of PepsiCo, Nestlé, and Firmenich. The company also works with Japan's largest flavors company, Ajinomoto, which has opened up the Asian market for Senomyx. In October 2018, Senomyx was acquired by Switzerland's Firmenich.

SENECA FOODS CORP.

NMS: SENE A

350 WillowBrook Office Park
Fairport, NY 14450
Phone: 585 495-4100
Fax: –
Web: www.senecafoods.com

CEO: Paul L Palmby
CFO: Michael Wolcott
HR: –
FYE: March 31
Type: Public

Seneca Foods is one of the nation's largest manufacturers and suppliers of canned vegetables. Its canned (as well as frozen and bottled) produce lineup is sold under numerous private labels, and national and regional brands, such as Aunt Nellie's, Libby's, Seneca, READ, CherryMan and Green Valley, that the company owns or licenses. Customers are primarily big grocery chains and some export markets and food service operators and food processors. Seneca also supplies frozen fruit and vegetables to private-label retail and food service customers. A short list of fruit and snack chip products is sold to retailers and food processors. The US accounts for the majority of the company's sales.

	Annual Growth	03/19	03/20	03/21	03/22	03/23
Sales ($mil.)	5.9%	1,199.6	1,335.8	1,467.6	1,385.3	1,509.4
Net income ($ mil.)	55.0%	5.7	52.3	126.1	51.0	33.1
Market value ($ mil.)	20.7%	187.8	303.7	359.6	393.5	399.1
Employees	14.7%	3,700	3,200	3,000	3,000	6,409

SENSE TECHNOLOGIES INC

NBB: SNSG F

2535 N. Carleton Avenue
Grand Island, NE 68803
Phone: 308 381-1355
Fax: 308 381-6557
Web: www.sensetech.com

CEO: Bruce E Schreiner
CFO: Bruce E Schreiner
HR: –
FYE: February 29
Type: Public

Objects in your rearview mirror may be LOUDER than they appear with Sense Technologies' Guardian Alert backup warning system. The Guardian Alert uses microwave radar technology to alert drivers of obstacles behind their vehicles. The systems can be attached to car bumpers or license plates. When an obstacle is detected, the system emits an audio and visual warning inside the vehicle. Sense Technologies outsources both the manufacturing and distribution of its Guardian Alert products. The company also markets ScopeOut, a mirror system designed to expand drivers' side and rear views. Sense Technologies' target customers include car dealers, fleet operators, and automotive aftermarket retailers.

	Annual Growth	02/12	02/13	02/14	02/15	02/16
Sales ($mil.)	17.2%	0.2	0.3	0.6	0.1	0.3
Net income ($ mil.)	–	(0.9)	(0.6)	(0.8)	(0.7)	(0.6)
Market value ($ mil.)	(9.1%)	0.3	0.3	0.2	0.1	0.2
Employees	–	–	–	–	–	–

SENIOR SLR INVESTMENT CORP

500 PARK AVE
NEW YORK, NY 100221606
Phone: 212 993-1670
Fax: –
Web: www.slrinvestmentcorp.com

CEO: Michael S Gross
CFO: Richard L Peteka
HR: –
FYE: December 31
Type: Private

Solar Senior Capital won't invest in every company under the sun, but its preferences do span a variety of industries. A closed-end, externally managed investment company, Solar Senior Capital takes minority stakes in leveraged, middle-market companies from the beverage, food, health care, education, aerospace and defense, business services, and other industries. Its investments typically take the form of senior secured loans, including first lien, unitranche, and second lien debt instruments. Formed in 2010, the company went public in 2011. It's classified as a business development company. As such, it distributes 90% of its profits to shareholders. The company is advised by affiliate Solar Capital Ltd.

	Annual Growth	12/17	12/18	12/19	12/20	12/21
Assets ($mil.)	7.6%	–	459.3	578.0	648.0	572.9
Net income ($ mil.)	(14.1%)	–	22.6	22.9	13.9	14.3
Market value ($ mil.)	–	–	–	–	–	–
Employees	–	–	–	–	–	79

SENSEI BIO SUBSIDIARY, INC.

1405 RESEARCH BLVD STE 125
ROCKVILLE, MD 20850
Phone: 240 243-8000
Fax: –
Web: www.panaceapharma.com

CEO: John K Celebi
CFO: –
HR: –
FYE: December 31
Type: Private

If there is a cure-all for cancer, Sensei Biotherapeutics (formerly Panacea Pharmaceuticals) is out to find it. The biotech focuses on next-generation immunotherapies and diagnostics for cancer. Its proprietary SPIRIT drug development platform was designed to help the body's immune system detect and fight cancer. (Cancers are notorious for tricking the immune system and prevent attack.) Sensei's lead drug candidate, SNS-301, is a cancer vaccine in early-stage trials. Founded in 1999, the company performs in-house research and development at its facility in Gaithersburg, Maryland.

	Annual Growth	12/03	12/04	12/05	12/06	12/07
Sales ($mil.)	48.1%	–	–	0.3	0.4	0.6
Net income ($ mil.)	–	–	–	(2.8)	(4.3)	(7.1)
Market value ($ mil.)	–	–	–	–	–	–
Employees	–	–	–	–	–	19

SENSIENT TECHNOLOGIES CORP.

NYS: SXT

777 East Wisconsin Avenue
Milwaukee, WI 53202-5304
Phone: 414 271-6755
Fax: 414 347-4795
Web: www.sensient.com

CEO: Paul Manning
CFO: Stephen J Rolfs
HR: Amy S Jones
FYE: December 31
Type: Public

Incorporated in 1882, Sensient Technologies makes flavors, aromas, and colors that are added to food, beverages, pharmaceuticals, cosmetics, and household products. It also manufactures inks for inkjet printers and specialty chemicals such as industrial dyes for the manufacture of writing instruments, personal care, and household cleaners. Flavors and food and beverage colors together account for about a third of Sensient's sales. It uses advanced technologies and robust global supply chain capabilities to develop specialized solutions. The company, which has facilities worldwide, generates most of its revenue in North America. Its customers include global manufacturers representing many of the world's leading brands.

	Annual Growth	12/19	12/20	12/21	12/22	12/23
Sales ($mil.)	2.4%	1,322.9	1,332.0	1,380.3	1,437.0	1,456.5
Net income ($ mil.)	3.3%	82.0	109.5	118.7	140.9	93.4
Market value ($ mil.)	–	2,780.4	3,103.5	4,209.5	3,067.7	2,776.6
Employees	(0.6%)	4,058	3,948	3,844	4,094	3,956

SENTARA HEALTH

6015 POPLAR HALL DR STE 308
NORFOLK, VA 23502
Phone: 800 736-8272
Fax: –
Web: www.sentara.com

CEO: Howard Kern
CFO: Robert A Broermann
HR: –
FYE: December 31
Type: Private

Sentara is an integrated, not-for-profit system with about a dozen of hospitals in Virginia and Northeastern North Carolina, including Sentara Albemarle Medical Center (with 182 beds), Sentara CarePlex Hospital (224 beds), Sentara Virginia Beach General Hospital (273 beds) and Sentara RMH Medical Center (238 beds), among others. Sentara Health Plans is the health insurance division of Sentara Healthcare, offering health plans through its subsidiaries, Optima Health and Virginia Premier. Collectively, Optima Health and Virginia Premier provide health insurance coverage to over 900,000 members through a full suite of commercial products including consumer-driven, employee-owned and employer-sponsored plans, individual and family health plans, employee assistance plans and plans serving Medicare and Medicaid enrollees. Sentara traces its roots back to 1888 when it was first established as the 25-bed Retreat for the Sick in Norfolk, Virginia.

	Annual Growth	12/14	12/15	12/16	12/17	12/19
Sales ($mil.)	9.9%	–	–	5,083.4	5,297.9	6,753.5
Net income ($ mil.)	28.8%	–	–	329.5	580.3	703.6
Market value ($ mil.)	–	–	–	–	–	–
Employees	–	–	–	–	–	28,500

SENTARA RMH MEDICAL CENTER

235 CANTRELL AVE
HARRISONBURG, VA 228013248
Phone: 540 433-4100
Fax: –
Web: www.sentara.com

CEO: –
CFO: –
HR: –
FYE: December 31
Type: Private

Sentara RMH Medical Center (RMH), formerly known as Rockingham Memorial Hospital, serves residents in Virginia's Shenandoah Valley, offering some 240 beds. In addition to emergency services and general surgeries and care procedures, RMH offers specialized services including cardiovascular care, cancer treatment, sleep disorder diagnosis, behavioral health care, medical imaging, orthopedic procedures, obstetrics, and rehabilitation, as well as home health, hospice, and wellness services. Founded in 1912, RMH is part of the Sentara Healthcare system.

	Annual Growth	12/16	12/17	12/20	12/21	12/22
Sales ($mil.)	3.2%	–	431.4	482.4	458.0	504.3
Net income ($ mil.)	(53.7%)	–	39.8	38.7	27.1	0.8
Market value ($ mil.)	–	–	–	–	–	–
Employees	–	–	–	–	–	1,892

SENTARA WILLIAMSBURG REGIONAL MEDICAL CENTER

100 SENTARA CIR
WILLIAMSBURG, VA 231885713
Phone: 757 984-6000
Fax: –
Web: www.sentara.com

CEO: –
CFO: –
HR: –
FYE: December 31
Type: Private

History buffs flock to Colonial Williamsbug, but if they get sick or injured, they'd rather take a tour of Sentara Williamsburg Regional Medical Center. Part of Sentara Healthcare, the center includes a 145-bed hospital that provides medical, surgical, and home-care services to the residents of (and visitors to) eastern Virginia. Specialized services include cardiac care, pediatrics, emergency medicine, orthopedics, pulmonary diagnostics, and community health education. Additional facilities include centers for outpatient surgery and rehabilitation, senior behaviorial health, sleep wellness, and cancer treatment. The center was founded as a 60-bed hospital in 1961.

	Annual Growth	12/16	12/17	12/19	12/20	12/21
Sales ($mil.)	3.9%	–	162.9	191.5	171.1	189.5
Net income ($ mil.)	57.4%	–	9.4	14.1	(0.3)	57.4
Market value ($ mil.)	–	–	–	–	–	–
Employees	–	–	–	–	–	1,150

SENTRY INSURANCE-A MUTUAL CO. (STEVENS POINT, WISC.)

1800 North Point Drive
Stevens Point, WI 54481-8020
Phone: 715 346-6000
Fax: 715 346-7842
Web: www.sentry.com

CEO: Pete McPartland
CFO: Todd Schroeder
HR: Jason Kirk
FYE: December 31
Type: Public

Sentry Insurance Company (formerly Sentry Insurance a Mutual Company) is built on a foundation of service to its policyholders. The company's commercial offerings include auto, liability, workers' compensation, and business owners' coverage, as well as life policies and annuities. Sentry provides specialized insurance to businesses of all sizes, including manufacturers, distributors, and dealerships who are interested in a high-value product and risk management. The products are sold through direct writers who build strong relationships and leverage their market expertise. The company also offers employee benefit, and retirement options for group accounts, and it provides personal auto and life insurance products. The company was founded in 1904.

	Annual Growth	12/01	12/05	12/06	12/07	12/08
Assets ($mil.)	14.6%	3,757.3	9,354.7	10,024	10,541	9,733.5
Net income ($ mil.)	(10.4%)	22.8	247.5	261.9	305.5	10.6
Market value ($ mil.)	–	–	–	–	–	–
Employees	–	–	–	–	–	–

SENTRY TECHNOLOGY CORP.

NBB: SKVY

1881 Lakeland Avenue
Ronkonkoma, NY 11779
Phone: 631 739-2000
Fax: –
Web: www.sentrytechnology.com

CEO: –
CFO: –
HR: –
FYE: December 31
Type: Public

Always on guard against pilferage, Sentry Technology's surveillance products keep watch over stores and distribution centers. The company manufactures and installs electronic article surveillance (EAS), radio frequency (RF), and closed-circuit television (CCTV) systems. Its traveling SentryVision SmartTrack CCTV system is designed to pan, tilt, and zoom in order to provide unobstructed views. Clients include retailers wanting to deter theft, and institutions wanting to protect assets and people. In addition, Sentry Technology's electro-magnetic (EM) and RF identification (RFID) based Library Management systems are used by libraries to secure inventory and improve operating efficiency.

	Annual Growth	12/09	12/10	12/11	12/12	12/13
Sales ($mil.)	(9.2%)	9.7	9.9	8.6	7.2	6.6
Net income ($ mil.)	–	(1.9)	(1.5)	(2.0)	1.5	(0.7)
Market value ($ mil.)	(41.5%)	14.7	5.9	2.7	0.3	1.7
Employees	–	–	–	–	–	–

SEQUACHEE VALLEY ELECTRIC CO-OPERATIVE INC

512 S CEDAR AVE
SOUTH PITTSBURG, TN 373801310
Phone: 423 837-8605
Fax: –
Web: www.svalleyec.com

CEO: –
CFO: Floyd Hatfield
HR: –
FYE: June 30
Type: Private

Sequachee Valley Electric Cooperative squeezes the most efficiency out of the power distribution cooperative it manages. One of 23 rural electric cooperatives in Tennessee, Sequachee Valley Electric Cooperative distributes power to more than 33,000 residential, commercial, and industrial members in part or all of Bledsoe, Coffee, Grundy, Hamilton, Marion, Rhea, Sequatchie, and Van Buren counties. It buys wholesale power from the Tennessee Valley Authority. Sequachee Valley Electric is governed by an 11-person board of directors, directly elected by its membership.

	Annual Growth	06/12	06/13	06/16	06/19	06/22
Sales ($Mil.)	2.9%	–	81.5	84.2	92.7	105.7
Net income ($ mil.)	13.7%	–	2.8	2.2	3.2	9.0
Market value ($ mil.)	–	–	–	–	–	–
Employees	–	–	–	–	–	74

SEQUENOM, INC.

3595 JOHN HOPKINS CT
SAN DIEGO, CA 921211121
Phone: 858 202-9000
Fax: –
Web: womenshealth.labcorp.com

CEO: –
CFO: –
HR: –
FYE: December 31
Type: Private

Sequenom develops and manufactures tests for the molecular diagnostics market. Its lab-developed tests are primarily focused on prenatal and ophthalmological diseases and conditions. Tests include MaterniT21 Plus (screen for fetal chromosomal abnormalities), HerediT CF (screen for cystic fibrosis genetic mutations), and SensiGene RHD (screen for fetal Rhesus D factor), as well as RetnaGene AMD (predictive test for age-related macular degeneration). The firm formerly offered technology and tools (principally based on its MassARRAY sequencing system) used by researchers, but sold that business in 2014. Sequenom generates about a quarter of sales outside the US. LabCorp acquired Sequenom for $371 million in mid-2016.

SERENA SOFTWARE, INC.

2345 NE OVERLOOK DR STE 200
BEAVERTON, OR 970066972
Phone: 650 481-3400
Fax: –
Web: www.microfocus.com

CEO: Greg Hughes
CFO: Robert Pender Jr
HR: –
FYE: October 31
Type: Private

SERENA Software isn't afraid of capitalizing on change. The firm's application lifecycle management software controls potentially disruptive changes during software installation, migration, and upgrades across multiple platforms, including mainframe, client/server, and Web-based environments. Applications are designed to help information technology staff manage upgrades, improve productivity, and reduce development costs. Its 2,500 customers come from a variety of industries, from aerospace and defense to financial services, retail, and health care. Conducting much of its business in North America, SERENA Software operates from offices in more than a dozen countries. Investment firm HGGC bought the company in 2014.

	Annual Growth	01/10	01/11	01/12*	10/12	10/13
Sales ($Mil.)	(38.5%)	–	–	219.5	–	135.0
Net income ($ mil.)	–	–	–	8.9	–	(3.7)
Market value ($ mil.)	–	–	–	–	–	–
Employees	–	–	–	–	–	400

*Fiscal year change

SERES THERAPEUTICS INC

NMS: MCRB

200 Sidney Street - 4th Floor
Cambridge, MA 02139
Phone: 617 945-9626
Fax: –
Web: www.serestherapeutics.com

CEO: Eric D Shaff
CFO: David Arkowitz
HR: –
FYE: December 31
Type: Public

Seres is serious about balancing bacteria populations in the human body. Seres Therapeutics specializes in microbiome therapeutics, which help restore health to persons whose have an unhealthy (or dysbiotic) microbiome ecology of microorganisms. It is developing biologic drugs to treat metabolic, inflammatory, and infectious diseases, primarily in the colon; its lead drug candidates are SER-109 for the treatment of large-intestine inflammation and SER-262, to prevent recurrence of inflammation. In 2019 the company realigned its pipeline to focus on its highest-priority clinical-stage candidates.

	Annual Growth	12/19	12/20	12/21	12/22	12/23
Sales ($mil.)	38.3%	34.5	33.2	144.9	7.1	126.3
Net income ($ mil.)	–	(70.3)	(89.1)	(65.6)	(250.2)	(113.7)
Market value ($ mil.)	(20.2%)	465.9	3,308.5	1,124.9	756.2	189.1
Employees	21.2%	108	155	333	431	233

SERIOUS FUN CHILDREN'S NETWORK, INC.

228 SAUGATUCK AVE STE 4
WESTPORT, CT 068806444
Phone: 203 562-1203
Fax: –
Web: www.seriousfun.org

CEO: Raymond Empson
CFO: –
HR: –
FYE: December 31
Type: Private

The SeriousFun Children's Network (formerly the Association of Hole in the Wall Gang Camps) helps build and maintain summer camps for children with chronic and life-threatening diseases. During the off-season, the camps offer children and their families support and education programs. The 30 camps under the network operate independently, and span California, Connecticut, Florida, New York, and North Carolina. They're also located in Africa, England, France, Ireland, and Israel. Founded in 1988 by an investment group led by the late actor and philanthropist Paul Newman, the organization changed its name to SeriousFun Children's Network in 2012.

	Annual Growth	12/15	12/16	12/18	12/19	12/22
Sales ($mil.)	(0.2%)	–	14.8	14.0	14.8	14.6
Net income ($ mil.)	–	–	(0.1)	1.5	0.8	0.5
Market value ($ mil.)	–	–	–	–	–	–
Employees	–	–	–	–	–	12

SERVATRON, INC.

12825 E MIRABEAU PKWY STE 104
SPOKANE VALLEY, WA 992161617
Phone: 509 321-9500
Fax: –
Web: www.servatron.com

CEO: –
CFO: –
HR: –
FYE: December 31
Type: Private

At your service! Servatron offers a slate of contract electronics manufacturing. Design, prototyping, testing, supply chain management, and logistics services are among its competencies. Products include printed circuit boards, systems, radio-frequency (RF) components, medical diagnostics, and wireless military defense devices. These are driven through direct sales and sales representatives to small to midsized customers in the US. Servatron was founded in 2000 by four former Itron employees. The business was spurred by Itron's decision discontinue the lineup, and the founders' anticipation of a growing market for electronic manufacturing services. UK-based Volex bought Servatron in 2019.

SERVCO PACIFIC INC.

2850 PUKOLOA ST STE 300
HONOLULU, HI 968194475
Phone: 808 564-1300
Fax: –
Web: www.servco.com

CEO: Mark H Fukunaga
CFO: –
HR: Amber Bundalian
FYE: December 31
Type: Private

Servco Pacific's business flows through an ocean's worth of enterprises. The company sells passenger vehicles (including Toyota, Subaru, Suzuki, and Chevrolet models) and commercial trucks through dealerships in Hawaii and Australia. In addition, Servco Home & Appliance wholesales kitchen and bath products to building professionals throughout the South Pacific; Servco Raynor Overhead Doors installs residential and commercial garage doors; Servco Insurance Services offers insurance coverage for businesses and individuals; and Servco School & Office Furniture outfits educational institutions and government agencies with desks, seating, and other furnishings. Servco Pacific was founded by Peter Fukunaga in 1919.

	Annual Growth	12/11	12/12	12/16	12/17	12/18
Sales ($mil.)	11.8%	–	923.0	1,435.5	1,629.1	1,802.5
Net income ($ mil.)	27.1%	–	15.9	29.6	26.1	66.9
Market value ($ mil.)	–	–	–	–	–	–
Employees	–	–	–	–	–	3,787

SERVICE CORP. INTERNATIONAL NYS: SCI

1929 Allen Parkway
Houston, TX 77019
Phone: 713 522-5141
Fax: –
Web: www.sci-corp.com

CEO: Thomas L Ryan
CFO: Eric D Tanzberger
HR: –
FYE: December 31
Type: Public

Service Corporation International (SCI) is the largest funeral and cemetery services company in North America, operating approximately 1,475 funeral homes and over 490 cemeteries in about 45 US states, eight Canadian provinces, the DC, and Puerto Rico. Its primary services include funeral service/cemetery combination locations, and crematoria. It provides funerals and cremations, including the use of funeral home facilities, arranging and directing services, removal, preparation, embalming, cremations, memorialization, and catering. In addition, SCI also sells traditional funeral necessities, including prearranged funeral services, caskets, burial vaults, cremation receptacles, and flowers. SCI operates under the Dignity Memorial and other brands. The US is the company's largest market.

	Annual Growth	12/19	12/20	12/21	12/22	12/23
Sales ($mil.)	6.1%	3,230.8	3,511.5	4,143.1	4,108.7	4,099.8
Net income ($ mil.)	9.8%	369.6	515.9	802.9	565.3	537.3
Market value ($ mil.)	10.4%	6,735.3	7,184.5	10,387	10,117	10,016
Employees	0.3%	24,594	24,135	24,658	25,139	24,922

SERVICE PROPERTIES TRUST NMS: SVC

Two Newton Place, 255 Washington Street, Suite 300
Newton, MA 02458-1634
Phone: 617 964-8389
Fax: –
Web: www.svcreit.com

CEO: –
CFO: –
HR: –
FYE: December 31
Type: Public

Real estate investment trust (REIT) Service Properties Trust owns some 305 hotels with more than 48,345 rooms or suites in about 40 US states, Washington DC, Canada, and Puerto Rico and around 780 service-oriented retail properties with 13.5 million sq. ft. SPT's properties are managed by or leased to companies including Marriott International, Sonesta, IHG Radisson Hospitality, and Hyatt Hotels. Its hotel properties are typically located in urban or high density suburban locations in the vicinity of major demand generators such as large suburban office parks, urban centers, airports, medical or educational facilities or major tourist attractions.

	Annual Growth	12/19	12/20	12/21	12/22	12/23
Sales ($mil.)	(5.2%)	2,316.1	1,265.3	1,495.6	1,863.0	1,873.9
Net income ($ mil.)	–	259.8	(311.4)	(544.6)	(132.4)	(32.8)
Market value ($ mil.)	(23.0%)	4,033.2	1,904.7	1,457.1	1,208.5	1,415.7
Employees	–	–	–	–	–	–

SERVICENOW INC NYS: NOW

2225 Lawson Lane
Santa Clara, CA 95054
Phone: 408 501-8550
Fax: –
Web: www.servicenow.com

CEO: William R McDermott
CFO: Gina Mastantuono
HR: –
FYE: December 31
Type: Public

ServiceNow seamlessly connects workflows across siloed organizations and systems in a way to unlock productivity and improve experiences for both employees and customers on a single platform called the Now Platform. The Now Platform enables its customers' digital transformation from non-integrated enterprise technology solutions to integrated enterprise technology solutions with automation and connected processes and activities. Its cloud-based platform and solutions help digitize and unify organizations so that they can find smarter, faster, better ways to make workflow. The company has approximately 7,700 enterprise customers that operate in a wide variety of industries, including government, financial services, healthcare, manufacturing, IT services, technology, oil and gas, telecommunications, education, and consumer products. North America accounts for about 65% of total revenue.

	Annual Growth	12/19	12/20	12/21	12/22	12/23
Sales ($mil.)	26.9%	3,460.4	4,519.5	5,896.0	7,245.0	8,971.0
Net income ($ mil.)	28.9%	626.7	118.5	230.0	325.0	1,731.0
Market value ($ mil.)	25.8%	57,798	112,686	132,888	79,488	144,635
Employees	21.6%	10,371	13,096	16,881	20,433	22,668

SERVICESOURCE INTERNATIONAL, INC.

621 MAINSTREAM DR
NASHVILLE, TN 372281210
Phone: 720 889-8500
Fax: –
Web: www.concentrix.com

CEO: Gary B Moore
CFO: Chad W Lyne
HR: –
FYE: December 31
Type: Private

ServiceSource is a leading provider of BPaaS solutions that enable the transformation of go-to-market organizations and functions for global technology clients. It designs, deploys, and operates a suite of innovative solutions and complex processes that support and augment clients' B2B customer acquisition, engagement, expansion, and retention activities. The ServiceSource CJX solution suite has been built on three primary solution pillars, encompassing digital sales, customer success, and channel management, all underpinned by enabling competencies centered around highly trained people, proprietary processes, and best-in-class technologies. The NALA (North America and Latin America) accounts for more than 55% of the company's sales.

SERVISFIRST BANCSHARES INC NYS: SFBS

2500 Woodcrest Place
Birmingham, AL 35209
Phone: 205 949-0302
Fax: –
Web: www.servisfirstbank.com

CEO: Rex D McKinney
CFO: William M Foshee
HR: Margaret Johnson
FYE: December 31
Type: Public

ServisFirst Bancshares is a bank holding company for ServisFirst Bank, a regional commercial bank with about a dozen branches located in Alabama and the Florida panhandle. The bank also has a loan office in Nashville. ServisFirst Bank targets privately-held businesses with $2 million to $250 million in annual sales, as well as professionals and affluent customers. The bank focuses on traditional commercial banking services, including loan origination, deposits, and electronic banking services, such as online and mobile banking. Founded in 2005 by its chairman and CEO Thomas Broughton III, the bank went public in 2014 with an offering valued at nearly $57 million.

	Annual Growth	12/19	12/20	12/21	12/22	12/23
Assets ($mil.)	15.9%	8,947.7	11,933	15,449	14,596	16,130
Net income ($ mil.)	8.5%	149.2	169.6	207.7	251.5	206.9
Market value ($ mil.)	15.3%	2,052.1	2,194.3	4,626.0	3,752.9	3,628.8
Employees	4.0%	505	493	502	571	591

SERVOTRONICS, INC.

1110 Maple Street
Elma, NY 14059
Phone: 716 655-5990
Fax: –
Web: www.servotronics.com

ASE: SVT
CEO: William Farrell Jr
CFO: Robert Fraass
HR: –
FYE: December 31
Type: Public

Servotronics designs, manufactures and market advanced technology products consisting primarily of control components and consumer products consisting of knives and various types of cutlery and other edged products. Its advanced technology products include servo-control components (torque motors, electromagnetic actuators, and hydraulic and pneumatic valves), which it sells mainly to clients in the aerospace industry. These include the US government, related agencies, and allied foreign governments. Servotronics' consumer products makes a broad range of products from machetes and bayonets to kitchen knives and putty knives. The company was founded in 1959.

	Annual Growth	12/19	12/20	12/21	12/22	12/23
Sales ($mil.)	(5.7%)	55.3	49.8	40.6	43.8	43.6
Net income ($ mil.)	–	2.1	0.1	4.1	(2.1)	(10.8)
Market value ($ mil.)	5.6%	25.6	21.6	32.2	26.8	31.8
Employees	(9.2%)	375	318	272	309	255

SERVPRO INTELLECTUAL PROPERTY, INC.

801 INDUSTRIAL BLVD
GALLATIN, TN 370663742
Phone: 615 451-0200
Fax: –
Web: www.servpro.com

CEO: Sue I Steen
CFO: Rick Forster
HR: –
FYE: December 31
Type: Private

If you're dealing with fire or water damage, Servpro hopes you'll let the pros come to your rescue. Servpro Industries provides emergency mitigation services for water-, fire-, and smoke-damaged properties, as well as mold and mildew situations. It operates through more than 1,500 franchised locations throughout the US. Mitigation services include cleaning of carpets, upholstery, air ducts, drapes, ceilings, and walls. The company also offers instruction and training on water- and fire-damage restoration. Originally established as a painting business, the family-owned Servpro Industries was founded in 1967 by Ted and Doris Isaacson.

SETON ASCENSION

1345 PHILOMENA ST
AUSTIN, TX 787233643
Phone: 512 324-5910
Fax: –
Web: www.seton.net

CEO: –
CFO: Scott Herndon
HR: –
FYE: June 30
Type: Private

For those who work hard to Keep Austin Weird, there's Ascension Seton. Formerly named Seton Healthcare Family, the not-for-profit health care system operates nearly a dozen urban and rural acute care hospitals in Central Texas. It also offers psychiatric and children's hospitals and a network of community clinics. With a capacity of some 1,500 beds, Seton's facilities offer a range of services including trauma, heart transplant, neurological, and neonatal intensive care, as well as primary and specialty care services. Seton in Austin was formed in 1902 by the Daughters of Charity of St. Vincent de Paul. Today, it is part of Catholic health system Ascension.

SETON HALL UNIVERSITY

400 S ORANGE AVE
SOUTH ORANGE, NJ 070792697
Phone: 973 761-9000
Fax: –
Web: www.shu.edu

CEO: –
CFO: –
HR: –
FYE: June 30
Type: Private

Seton Hall University is one of the country's leading Catholic universities. The Catholic institution has an enrollment of about 10,000 students (about 6,070 undergraduates and 3,820 graduate students) who hail from nearly 50 countries. The university offers more than 90 majors and programs at around ten colleges and schools, including the College of Arts and Sciences, College of Communication and The Arts, College of Education and Human Services, School of Health and Medical Sciences, Seton Hall Law, College of Nursing, Stillman School of Business, School of Diplomacy and International Relations, and Immaculate Conception Seminary School of Theology. Seton Hall also offers degree and certificate programs online and study abroad opportunities. With over 17,000 internship opportunities, the university has a student-to-faculty ratio of 14:1. Seton Hall is the US's oldest diocesan university and is under the purview of the Archdiocese of Newark.

	Annual Growth	06/17	06/18	06/19	06/21	06/22
Sales ($mil.)	3.2%	–	293.2	308.3	296.8	333.2
Net income ($ mil.)	–	–	9.0	(17.8)	67.5	(25.8)
Market value ($ mil.)	–	–	–	–	–	–
Employees	–	–	–	–	–	2,700

SETTON'S INTERNATIONAL FOODS, INC.

85 AUSTIN BLVD
COMMACK, NY 117255701
Phone: 631 543-8090
Fax: –
Web: www.settonfarms.com

CEO: Joshua Setton
CFO: –
HR: –
FYE: December 31
Type: Private

You might say this company is nuts about pistachios. A leading producer of nuts, edible seeds, and other snacks, Setton International Foods is one of the largest pistachio processors in the US, with more than 5,000 acres of orchards it either owns or farms. The company sells pistachios and more than 1,000 other snack products (candies, chocolate-covered nuts and fruits, dried fruits) to retail customers under the Setton Farms brand; it also supplies goods to customers in the food manufacturing industry. Joshua and Morris Setton founded the family-owned business in 1971.

SEVEN SEAS TECHNOLOGIES INC.

720 SPIRIT 40 PARK DR
CHESTERFIELD, MO 630051122
Phone: 636 778-0705
Fax: –
Web: www.s2tech.com

CEO: Dayakar Veerlapati
CFO: –
HR: Vikram Yellamelli
FYE: December 31
Type: Private

Seven Seas Technologies, which does business as S2 Tech, provides IT services such as custom software development, database administration, and networking. Founded in 1997, the company specializes in managing Medicaid systems and HIPAA compliance, with clients that have included CACI, MasterCard, and Sallie Mae. S2 Tech has locations in the US and India.

	Annual Growth	12/13	12/14	12/16	12/17	12/18
Sales ($mil.)	(10.2%)	–	13.9	19.1	13.0	9.1
Net income ($ mil.)	21.6%	–	0.3	0.5	0.5	0.6
Market value ($ mil.)	–	–	–	–	–	–
Employees	–	–	–	–	–	120

SEVENSON ENVIRONMENTAL SERVICES, INC.

2749 LOCKPORT RD
NIAGARA FALLS, NY 143052229
Phone: 716 284-0431
Fax: –
Web: www.sevenson.com

CEO: –
CFO: –
HR: –
FYE: December 31
Type: Private

Sevenson Environmental Services performs dialysis on Mother Earth by pumping contaminated water out, treating it, and then pumping it back into the ground. The company also cleans soil and contaminated buildings, focusing on the dirty work of hazardous waste remediation. Since working on the Love Canal cleanup in 1979, Sevenson has provided remediation services for more than 1,200 projects. It also decontaminates, demolishes, and closes facilities. Customers have included government entities such as the US Army Corps of Engineers and the Environmental Protection Agency, along with manufacturers in a variety of industries. The Elia family controls the company.

SEVENTY SEVEN ENERGY LLC

777 NW 63RD ST
OKLAHOMA CITY, OK 731167601
Phone: 405 608-7777
Fax: –
Web: www.patenergy.com

CEO: Andy Hendricks
CFO: Cary Baetz
HR: Steve Berry
FYE: December 31
Type: Private

Seventy Seven Energy (formerly Chesapeake Oilfield Services) is a company that was spun off from Chesapeake Energy, one of the top onshore energy companies in the US. Chesapeake Energy reorganized six of its oilfield services subsidiaries into then Chesapeake Oilfield Services to create a new, publicly traded entity that offers drilling, hydraulic fracturing, and trucking services, as well as renting tools and manufacturing natural gas compressor equipment. It operates in onshore plays in the US. The company filed for Chapter 11 bankruptcy protection in 2016. In 2017 the company was bought by Patterson-UTI in a $1.76 billion stock deal, including debt.

	Annual Growth	12/11	12/12	12/13	12/14	12/15
Sales ($mil.)	(45.6%)	–	–	–	2,080.9	1,131.2
Net income ($ mil.)	–	–	–	–	(8.0)	(221.4)
Market value ($ mil.)	–	–	–	–	–	–
Employees	–	–	–	–	–	1,700

SEYFARTH SHAW LLP

233 S WACKER DR STE 8000
CHICAGO, IL 606066448
Phone: 312 460-5000
Fax: –
Web: www.seyfarth.com

CEO: –
CFO: –
HR: –
FYE: December 31
Type: Private

Seyfarth Shaw divides its numerous practices into three main areas: advisory, transactions, and litigation. Overall, Seyfarth Shaw has more than 900 attorneys in over 15 offices ? more than ten spread throughout the US, plus five international outposts. Seyfarth Shaw draws clients from industries such as financial services, hospitality and leisure, life sciences, manufacturing, retail, wholesale and distribution, and real estate. Nationally and locally recognized with rankings in Chambers USA, The Legal 500, U.S. News: Best Lawyers and Best Law Firms, and Law360 in various areas, the firm was founded by distinguished labor attorneys who were both practical and visionary.

	Annual Growth	12/04	12/05	12/06	12/07	12/08
Sales ($mil.)	11.7%	–	332.2	385.6	431.8	463.0
Net income ($ mil.)	5.8%	–	124.1	136.3	141.9	147.0
Market value ($ mil.)	–	–	–	–	–	–
Employees	–	–	–	–	–	1,608

SGPA PLANNING AND ARCHITECTURE SAN DIEGO

3111 CAMINO DEL RIO N STE 500
SAN DIEGO, CA 92108
Phone: 619 297-0131
Fax: –
Web: www.sgpa.com

CEO: –
CFO: –
HR: –
FYE: January 31
Type: Private

SGPA Planning and Architecture (SGPA) offers design, engineering, and planning services for retail shopping and mixed-use centers, senior housing facilities, municipal projects, and such specialty projects as laboratory improvements. The designing company serves clients throughout California through its offices in San Diego and San Francisco. SGPA was established in 1970.

SGT, LLC

7701 GREENBELT RD STE 400
GREENBELT, MD 207706521
Phone: 301 614-8600
Fax: –
Web: www.kbr.com

CEO: –
CFO: –
HR: –
FYE: September 30
Type: Private

Like its acronym name suggests, SGT (aka Stinger Ghaffarian Technologies) is used to taking military orders; in this case very specific, technical ones. An engineering services firm, SGT provides aerospace engineering, project management, IT systems development, and related services to NASA, the US Navy, the US Air Force, and other primarily military-related government entities through contracts. The company also offers science-related services such as earth, climate, and planetary modeling and analysis. SGT's facilities are located near airfields and other military facilities.

	Annual Growth	09/07	09/08	09/12	09/13	09/15
Sales ($mil.)	10.0%	–	293.0	374.7	416.5	570.8
Net income ($ mil.)	16.3%	–	8.3	9.0	15.5	23.9
Market value ($ mil.)	–	–	–	–	–	–
Employees	–	–	–	–	–	2,300

SHAKE SHACK INC

225 Varick Street, Suite 301
New York, NY 10014
Phone: 646 747-7200
Fax: –
Web: www.shakeshack.com

NYS: SHAK
CEO: Randy Garutti
CFO: Katherine Fogertey
HR: Cathy Fendelman
FYE: December 27
Type: Public

Shake Shack serves up burgers, chicken, crinkle cut fries, hot dogs, shakes and frozen custard, beer, wine, and beverages. With its fine dining roots and a commitment to crafting uplifting experiences, Shake Shack has become a cult-brand and created a new category, fine-casual. Its purpose is to Stand For Something Good, from thoughtful ingredient sourcing and employee development to inspiring designs and deep community investment. From humble beginnings as a hot dog cart in New York City, Shake Shack has grown to almost 150 locations in other countries and some 285 locations in about 30 US states. The US generates about 95% of the company's total revenue.

	Annual Growth	12/19	12/20	12/21	12/22	12/23
Sales ($mil.)	16.3%	594.5	522.9	739.9	900.5	1,087.5
Net income ($ mil.)	0.5%	19.8	(42.2)	(8.7)	(24.1)	20.3
Market value ($ mil.)	6.1%	2,536.4	3,590.3	2,966.3	1,800.2	3,212.9
Employees	12.5%	7,603	7,429	9,695	11,704	12,196

SHAKLEE CORPORATION

6920 KOLL CENTER PKWY STE 211
PLEASANTON, CA 945663156
Phone: 925 924-2000
Fax: –
Web: us.shaklee.com

CEO: Roger Barnett
CFO: Mike Batesole
HR: –
FYE: March 31
Type: Private

Shaklee manufactures and sells its vitamins, beauty, sports, and nutrition products, as well as environmentally friendly household cleaners directly to customers. Its products are marketed under Life Shake, Enfuselle, Get Clean, Shaklee, and Vita-Lea brands, among others. In addition, Shaklee also offers personalized supplements called Meology. Its products are backed by more than 100 patents and patents pending and published over 100 scientific papers. The company's products are sold through its website and distributors in the US, Canada, China, Japan, Malaysia, and Taiwan. Shaklee was founded in 1956 by Dr. Shaklee.

	Annual Growth	03/17	03/18	03/19	03/20	03/21
Sales ($mil.)	(7.7%)	–	–	–	0.3	0.2
Net income ($ mil.)	–	–	–	–	(0.2)	0.0
Market value ($ mil.)	–	–	–	–	–	–
Employees	–	–	–	–	–	500

SHAMROCK FOODS COMPANY

3900 E CAMELBACK RD STE 300
PHOENIX, AZ 850182615
Phone: 602 233-6400
Fax: –
Web: www.shamrockfoods.com

CEO: W K McClelland
CFO: Chris Miller
HR: Ashley Amery
FYE: September 30
Type: Private

Shamrock Foods Company is one of the nation's leading foodservice distributors with a strong presence in the western US. It primarily serves restaurants, healthcare facilities, military installations, catering companies, food banks, and hospitality customers by providing everyday staples such as meats, produce, dry goods, beverages, and supplies, as well as ethnic foods and artisanal, gourmet, and other specialty foods. Proprietary brands include Gold Canyon, Four Leaf Roasters, Markon, Jensen Foods, Pier 22 Seafood, and Rideglme. Through Shamrock Farms, the company is also one of the largest family-owned and -operated dairies in the country. Founded in 1922, Shamrock Foods is still owned and operated by the founding McClelland family.

	Annual Growth	09/18	09/19	09/20	09/21	09/22
Sales ($mil.)	23.9%	–	–	–	4,602.9	5,702.4
Net income ($ mil.)	–	–	–	–	–	–
Market value ($ mil.)	–	–	–	–	–	–
Employees	–	–	–	–	–	5,320

SHANDS JACKSONVILLE MEDICAL CENTER, INC.

655 W 8TH ST
JACKSONVILLE, FL 322096511
Phone: 904 244-0411
Fax: –
Web: www.ufhealthjax.org

CEO: David S Guzick
CFO: William J Ryan
HR: –
FYE: June 30
Type: Private

Close to the shifting sands of the northern Florida coast, Shands Jacksonville Medical Center (doing business as UF Health Jacksonville) offers a range of services to the 19 counties it serves in Florida and southern Georgia. The 695-bed hospital includes a cardiovascular center, Level III neonatal intensive care unit, and a Level I trauma center. It also operates primary and specialty clinics in the Jacksonville area. The medical center is affiliated with the University of Florida and is the largest of seven hospitals in the Shands HealthCare family.

	Annual Growth	06/14	06/15	06/16	06/21	06/22
Sales ($mil.)	9.9%	–	480.6	663.3	894.4	929.7
Net income ($ mil.)	(15.3%)	–	10.3	23.6	70.1	3.2
Market value ($ mil.)	–	–	–	–	–	–
Employees	–	–	–	–	–	3,000

SHANDS TEACHING HOSPITAL AND CLINICS, INC.

1600 SW ARCHER RD
GAINESVILLE, FL 326103003
Phone: 352 265-0111
Fax: –
Web: www.ufhealth.org

CEO: Marvin Dewar
CFO: Michael Gleason
HR: –
FYE: June 30
Type: Private

Shands Teaching Hospital and Clinics, known as UF Health Shands, is affiliated with the University of Florida, provides health care services to patients in north-central and northeast Florida. The UF Health network of hospitals and physician practices manages more than 3 million inpatient and outpatient visits each year and serves patients from more than 65 Florida counties, from around the nation and from more than 40 countries. Specialty services include oncology, pediatrics, cardiovascular, transplants, and neurological care. It also includes primary care and specialty practices throughout North Central and Northeast Florida, as well as Southeast Georgia.

	Annual Growth	06/13	06/14	06/19	06/20	06/21
Sales ($mil.)	8.7%	–	1,244.0	1,651.6	1,660.5	2,235.3
Net income ($ mil.)	19.6%	–	66.1	66.7	52.8	231.0
Market value ($ mil.)	–	–	–	–	–	–
Employees	–	–	–	–	–	3,000

SHARI'S MANAGEMENT CORPORATION

4350 ALPHA RD
DALLAS, TX 752444525
Phone: 503 605-4299
Fax: –
Web: www.sharis.com

CEO: –
CFO: –
HR: –
FYE: January 02
Type: Private

This Shari keeps the kitchen open all day and all night. Shari's Management Corporation owns and operates more than 100 Shari's family restaurants in six states (primarily in the Northwest) that serve breakfast, lunch, and dinner 24 hours a day. The chain of eateries offers standard American fare, such as pancakes and eggs, sandwiches and burgers, and beef, chicken, and pasta dishes, as well as a selection of appetizers and desserts through a menu of about 120 items. The company is owned by a group of private investors led by Circle Peak Management. Ron and Sharon (Shari) Berquist opened the first Shari's in Hermiston, Oregon, in 1978.

	Annual Growth	01/04	01/05	01/06	01/07	01/08
Sales ($mil.)	320.4%	–	–	–	40.5	170.3
Net income ($ mil.)	(99.9%)	–	–	–	1,073.7	1.5
Market value ($ mil.)	–	–	–	–	–	–
Employees	–	–	–	–	–	4,000

SHARP HEALTHCARE

8695 SPECTRUM CENTER BLVD
SAN DIEGO, CA 921231489
Phone: 858 499-4000
Fax: –
Web: www.sharp.com

CEO: –
CFO: Ann Pumpian
HR: Carlisle C Lewis III
FYE: September 30
Type: Private

Sharp HealthCare is San Diego's leading health care provider. It is a not-for-profit health network with dedication in delivering the highest quality patient-centered care and the latest medical technology and superior service. The network includes four acute-care hospitals (Sharp Chula Vista Medical Center, Sharp Coronado Hospital, Sharp Grossmont Hospital, and Sharp Memorial Hospital). With approximately 2,700 affiliated physicians and some 19,000 employees, Sharp HealthCare offers cancer treatment and heart and vascular care, endoscopy, mental health, orthopedics, and pregnancy and childbirth, plastic and reconstructive surgery, and hospice care.

	Annual Growth	09/12	09/13	09/14	09/21	09/22
Sales ($mil.)	8.3%	–	1,158.6	1,234.4	1,723.7	2,370.9
Net income ($ mil.)	–	–	(11.4)	(12.1)	(156.0)	436.7
Market value ($ mil.)	–	–	–	–	–	–
Employees	–	–	–	–	–	14,000

SHARP MEMORIAL HOSPITAL

7901 FROST ST
SAN DIEGO, CA 921232701
Phone: 858 939-3636
Fax: –
Web: www.sharp.com

CEO: Tim Smith
CFO: –
HR: –
FYE: September 30
Type: Private

The docs and the scalpels are sharp at Sharp Memorial Hospital. The flagship facility of Sharp HealthCare, the not-for-profit hospital has roughly 675 beds and is a designated trauma center for San Diego County. Specialties include cardiac care, women's health, multi-organ transplantation, and cancer treatment. It also provides skilled nursing, home health, and hospice services. Sharp Memorial Hospital first opened in 1955. Sharp HealthCare completed reconstruction efforts on the Sharp Memorial facility in 2009; the new hospital has improved inpatient, surgery, emergency, trauma, and intensive care facilities.

	Annual Growth	09/17	09/18	09/20	09/21	09/22
Sales ($mil.)	2.4%	–	1,306.7	1,278.1	1,368.3	1,438.9
Net income ($ mil.)	(7.8%)	–	247.8	299.0	386.6	179.0
Market value ($ mil.)	–	–	–	–	–	–
Employees	–	–	–	–	–	3,500

SHARPE RESOURCES CORP.

3258 Mob Neck Road
Heathsville, VA 22473
Phone: 804 580-8107
Fax: 804 580-4132
Web: www.sharperesourcescorporation.com

NBB: SHGP
CEO: –
CFO: –
HR: –
FYE: December 31
Type: Public

Sharpe Resources keeps a sharp eye out for natural resource opportunities in the US. Through subsidiary Standard Energy Company, it focuses on developing coal bed methane (CBM), coal, and shale projects in West Virginia. Coal bed methane is natural gas trapped in coal beds; the CBM is more easily drilled and utilized than other sources of natural gas. Sharpe leases and holds options on about 17,000 acres in West Virginia that it hopes to tap for CBM and coal. It is also exploring the option of creating relatively clean coal energy from underground coal gasification, which allows for the coal to be used in the generation of electricity without the coal having to be mined first.

	Annual Growth	12/08	12/09*	01/10*	12/10	12/11
Sales ($mil.)	45.8%	0.0	0.0	–	0.0	0.1
Net income ($ mil.)	–	(0.3)	(0.1)	–	(0.4)	(0.1)
Market value ($ mil.)	(14.8%)	5.1	1.9	1.9	1.5	3.1
Employees	–	–	–	–	–	–

*Fiscal year change

SHARPLINK GAMING INC

333 Washington Avenue North, Suite 104
Minneapolis, MN 55401
Phone: 347 913-3316
Fax: –
Web: www.sharplink.com

NAS: SBET
CEO: –
CFO: –
HR: –
FYE: December 31
Type: Public

Telecom companies use MER Telemanagement Solutions' (MTS) products to keep tabs on crafty callers. The company develops, sells, and services software designed to track communications costs, recover charges payable by third parties, and detect and prevent phone system abuse. The company distributes its products directly through subsidiaries in Brazil, Hong Kong, the Netherlands, and the US, and through OEM partnerships with Siemens, Phillips, and other vendors. Its products are used by more than 60,000 customers in 60 countries. Chairman Chaim Mer controls about 40% of MTS.

	Annual Growth	12/18	12/19	12/20	12/21	12/22
Sales ($mil.)	5.6%	5.9	5.2	4.0	4.2	7.3
Net income ($ mil.)	–	(1.2)	(0.1)	(1.8)	(55.6)	(15.2)
Market value ($ mil.)	–	–	–	–	–	–
Employees	12.3%	39	34	34	53	62

SHAWMUT WOODWORKING & SUPPLY, INC.

560 HARRISON AVE
BOSTON, MA 021182632
Phone: 617 622-7000
Fax: –
Web: www.shawmut.com

CEO: Lester Hiscoe
CFO: Roger C Tougas
HR: –
FYE: November 30
Type: Private

Shawmut Woodworking & Supply, which does business as Shawmut Design and Construction, provides beginning-to-end construction services, from preconstruction planning to post-construction quality assurance checks. The $1.3 billion national construction management firm has experience building retail, hotel, gaming, spa, sports, restaurant, education, banking, healthcare, and life science facilities. It also handles corporate interiors and high-end residential construction and boasts expertise in cultural and historical preservation projects. The employee-owned company serves clients nationwide from offices in a handful of US states.

	Annual Growth	12/04	12/05*	11/09	11/11	11/14
Sales ($mil.)	9.0%	–	440.7	618.3	662.8	957.6
Net income ($ mil.)	9.9%	–	3.1	(21.6)	3.7	7.2
Market value ($ mil.)	–	–	–	–	–	–
Employees	–	–	–	–	–	1,476

*Fiscal year change

SHAWNEE MISSION MEDICAL CENTER, INC.

9100 W 74TH ST
SHAWNEE MISSION, KS 662044004
Phone: 913 676-2000
Fax: –
Web: www.adventhealth.com

CEO: Ken Bacon
CFO: Jack Wagnar
HR: Julie Jenks
FYE: December 31
Type: Private

Shawnee Mission Medical Center (SMMC) cares for Kansas City residents, primarily on the Kansas-side. The health care facility, located in the city's southwest suburbs, has some 500 inpatient beds. It also offers outpatient surgery and other health services in areas such as pediatrics, rehabilitation, oncology, and radiology. The medical center's emergency department receives some 50,000 visits each year. SMMC also operates satellite facilities, including the Shawnee Mission Outpatient Pavilion in nearby Lenexa, which offers emergency and outpatient diagnostic, general practice, and surgical care. SMMC is part of Adventist Health System.

	Annual Growth	12/15	12/16	12/17	12/19	12/21
Sales ($mil.)	5.1%	–	454.8	491.2	546.8	583.7
Net income ($ mil.)	11.0%	–	54.4	55.5	66.8	91.7
Market value ($ mil.)	–	–	–	–	–	–
Employees	–	–	–	–	–	1,850

SHEARMAN & STERLING LLP

599 LEXINGTON AVE FL 16
NEW YORK, NY 100226069
Phone: 212 848-4000
Fax: –
Web: www.shearman.com

CEO: –
CFO: –
HR: Kellie Parise
FYE: June 30
Type: Private

Shearman & Sterling is a global law firm representing the world's leading corporations and major financial institutions, as well as emerging growth companies, governments, and state-owned enterprises. Long known for representing major US financial institutions, Shearman & Sterling has more than 700 lawyers worldwide speaking over 65 languages and practicing the US, English, French, German, Italian, Hong Kong, OHADA, and Saudi law. About half of the firm's lawyers practice outside the US. Its practice areas include antitrust, bankruptcy, capital markets, intellectual property, litigation, mergers and acquisitions, project development and finance, and tax. Shearman & Sterling collaborates with diversity-related bar associations, committees, and organizations around the world. In mid-2023, Shearman & Sterling and Allen & Overy announced a planned merger to create a unique global law firm named Allen Overy Shearman Sterling ? A&O Shearman for short.

SHEERVISION INC

NBB: SVSO

4030 Palos Verdes Drive North, Suite 104
Rolling Hills Estates, CA 90274
Phone: 310 265-8918
Fax: –
Web: www.sheervision.com

CEO: Suzanne Lewsadder
CFO: Patrick Adams
HR: –
FYE: August 31
Type: Public

SheerVision has a clear vision of a future in the medical instruments industry. The company, formerly Clean Water Technologies, makes surgical loupes and light systems used by dentists, doctors, and vets. Through a reverse merger, Clean Water Technologies acquired SheerVision in 2006; the SheerVision operations became the company's only business after the deal. Prior to the SheerVision combination, the company had no products or services, although it held the license to a technology related to removing arsenic from water. (The license was sold to the former company officers in the reverse merger.) SheerVision distributes its products in the Americas, Asia, Australia, Europe, and the Middle East.

	Annual Growth	06/05*	08/06	08/07	08/08	08/09
Sales ($Mil.)	–	–	3.0	4.4	4.4	3.5
Net income ($ mil.)	–	(0.1)	(2.3)	(0.9)	(0.2)	(0.1)
Market value ($ mil.)	(26.0%)	0.9	14.0	5.1	2.3	0.3
Employees	62.7%	2	24	17	14	14

*Fiscal year change

SHEETZ, INC.

5700 6TH AVE
ALTOONA, PA 166021111
Phone: 814 946-3611
Fax: –
Web: www.sheetz.com

CEO: Travis Sheetz
CFO: –
HR: Charles Sheetz
FYE: December 31
Type: Private

Sheetz is a family owned convenience store chain that operates more than 650 convenience stores throughout Pennsylvania, West Virginia, Virginia, Maryland, Ohio, and North Carolina. The company sells groceries, fountain drinks, baked goods, and made-to-order specialty coffees, sandwiches and salads; it also offers self-service car washes and discount gas, as well as cigarettes under Marlboro, Copenhagen, Skoal, Black and Mild, Camel, Pall Mall, Grizzly, American Spirit, New Port, Vuse, Kool, and Winston brands. Founded in 1952 by Bob Sheetz, the company is owned and run by the Sheetz family.

SHELCO, LLC

2359 PERIMETER POINTE PKWY STE 600
CHARLOTTE, NC 282086833
Phone: 704 367-5600
Fax: –
Web: www.shelcollc.com

CEO: –
CFO: –
HR: –
FYE: December 31
Type: Private

Shelco is trying to see that the South will rise again -- the southeast, that is. One of the largest contractors in the southeastern US, Shelco specializes in the construction of warehouse and distribution facilities; educational, manufacturing, retail, and health care facilities; and office buildings. Repeat customers account for nearly three-quarters of Shelco's business. Not content to stay in its home state of North Carolina, the company is also active in South Carolina, Georgia, and Virgina. The company was founded in 1978 in Winston-Salem, North Carolina by Charles and Edwin Shelton. The Sheltons owned the company until 2003, when they sold Shelco to six senior managers.

SHENANDOAH TELECOMMUNICATIONS CO

NMS: SHEN

500 Shentel Way
Edinburg, VA 22824
Phone: 540 984-4141
Fax: –
Web: www.shentel.com

CEO: Christopher E French
CFO: James J Volk
HR: –
FYE: December 31
Type: Public

Shenandoah Telecommunications Company provides broadband services through its high speed, state-of-the-art cable, fiber-optic and fixed wireless networks to customers in the Mid-Atlantic United States. The company's services include broadband internet, video, and voice; fiber-optic Ethernet, wavelength and leasing; and tower colocation leasing. The company owns an extensive regional network with over 7,400 route miles of fiber and over 220 macro cellular towers.

	Annual Growth	12/19	12/20	12/21	12/22	12/23
Sales ($mil.)	(17.9%)	633.9	220.8	245.2	267.4	287.4
Net income ($ mil.)	(38.2%)	54.9	126.7	998.8	(8.4)	(0.1)
Market value ($ mil.)	(15.1%)	2,091.8	2,174.3	1,281.9	798.3	1,086.9
Employees	(7.0%)	1,130	1,139	860	842	845

SHEPHERD CENTER, INC.

2020 PEACHTREE RD NW
ATLANTA, GA 303091465
Phone: 404 352-2020
Fax: –
Web: www.shepherd.org

CEO: Gary R Ulicny
CFO: Stephen B Holleman
HR: DOT Robinson
FYE: March 31
Type: Private

Shepherd Center is a private, not-for-profit hospital that specializes in medical treatment, research, and rehabilitation for people with multiple sclerosis, spinal cord and brain injuries, as well as patients with neuromuscular disorders, and spine and chronic pain. It also aims to develop, refine, and evaluate new treatments, drugs, surgical techniques, diagnostic tools, and therapeutic interventions. Shepherd Center boasts around 150 beds and a 10-bed intensive care unit. Founded in 1975, Shepherd Center treats about 875 inpatients, some 280-day program patients and more than 7,100 outpatients annually.

SHEPHERD ELECTRIC COMPANY, LLC

7401 PULASKI HWY
BALTIMORE, MD 212372529
Phone: 301 595-9000
Fax: –
Web: www.shepherdelec.com

CEO: Charles C Vogel III
CFO: –
HR: Chris Robinson
FYE: December 31
Type: Private

For well over a hundred years, Shepherd Electric has steered customers through a range of electrical needs. The company supplies a variety of electrical products to wholesale and retail customers primarily to the commercial construction market, but it also serves government entities, industrial firms, and OEMs. Shepherd Electric carries products from major manufacturers such as 3M, Brady, Eaton, Hadco, Fluke, General Electric, and Thomas & Betts, among many others. The company was founded in 1892 by Ernest Fluharty and Henry Shepherd. Shepherd Electric is owned by the Vogel family, which has had a controlling interest in the company since 1931.

	Annual Growth	12/09	12/10	12/11	12/12	12/13
Sales ($Mil.)	7.5%	–	–	163.2	183.9	188.4
Net income ($ mil.)	3.5%	–	–	2.9	5.5	3.1
Market value ($ mil.)	–	–	–	–	–	–
Employees	–	–	–	–	–	185

SHEPPARD, MULLIN, RICHTER & HAMPTON, LLP

333 S HOPE ST FL 43
LOS ANGELES, CA 900711422
Phone: 213 620-1780
Fax: –
Web: www.sheppardmullin.com

CEO: Guy N Halgren
CFO: –
HR: Robin Stoller
FYE: December 31
Type: Private

Sheppard, Mullin, Richter & Hampton is a full service Global 100 firm handling corporate and technology matters, high stakes litigation and complex financial transactions. The firm maintains a wide range of practice areas. It has been recognized for work related to corporate transactions, entertainment, labor and employment, and real estate. The firm has about 1,000 lawyers working from some 15 domestic and international offices. Sheppard Mullin was founded in Los Angeles in 1927.

SHERIDAN COMMUNITY HOSPITAL (OSTEOPATHIC)

301 N MAIN ST
SHERIDAN, MI 488849235
Phone: 989 291-3261
Fax: –
Web: www.sheridanhospital.com

CEO: Bobbi McColley
CFO: Mindy Buffman
HR: –
FYE: March 31
Type: Private

Sheridan Community Hospital certainly lives up to its "community" moniker. Local volunteers are considered a mainstay of the hospital, logging more than 4,000 hours of service every year. The facility offers residents of Montcalm, Michigan and surrounding counties emergency services, occupational health, cardiology, orthopedics, and general surgery. The hospital has begun testing the waters of 21st century technology by investing in digital imaging and high-tech scanning systems. Sheridan Community Hospital has also opened Edmore Care-West, its second family practice location in Edmore.

	Annual Growth	03/11	03/12	03/14	03/20	03/21
Sales ($mil.)	(0.9%)	–	16.2	16.0	9.7	15.0
Net income ($ mil.)	18.8%	–	0.6	(0.6)	(3.0)	2.7
Market value ($ mil.)	–	–	–	–	–	–
Employees	–	–	–	–	–	153

SHERRILL FURNITURE COMPANY INC

2405 HIGHLAND AVE NE
HICKORY, NC 286018164
Phone: 828 322-2640
Fax: –
Web: www.sherrillfurniture.com

CEO: –
CFO: Walter Bost
HR: Dana Pope
FYE: June 02
Type: Private

Sherrill Furniture Company is one of the furniture industry leaders in producing quality home furnishings. Sherrill Furniture Company and its divisions have supplied custom home furniture to major furniture stores and major department stores throughout the US and Canada. The company's living room collections includes sofas, chaises, loveseats, settees, sectionals, chairs, ottomans, and benches. Sherrill's divisions include Whittemore-Sherrill, CTH-Sherrill Occasional, MotionCraft, Precedent Furniture, Lillian August, Mr. & Mrs. Howard, and Hickory White. All the company's factories are in the Hickory, North Carolina. Sherrill got its start in 1945.

SHERRY MATTHEWS, INC.

4200 MARATHON BLVD STE 300
AUSTIN, TX 787563434
Phone: 512 478-4397
Fax: –
Web: www.sherrymatthews.com

CEO: –
CFO: Wardaleen Belvin
HR: –
FYE: October 31
Type: Private

Sherry Matthews provides advocacy marketing and advertising services. It works primarily for not-for-profit and government agencies in Texas, focusing on such areas as the environment, education, drug and alcohol abuse, and teen pregnancy. The agency provides services such as advertising, public relations, research, fund raising, Web development, and media placement. Sherry Matthews also features a Hispanic division. Clients have included the Texas Department of Transportation, Whole Foods Market, and Capital Metropolitan Transportation Authority. Founded in 1983, the agency shifted its primary focus to advocacy marketing in 1990.

SHERWIN-WILLIAMS CO (THE)   NYS: SHW

101 West Prospect Avenue
Cleveland, OH 44115-1075
Phone: 216 566-2000
Fax: 216 566-3310
Web: www.sherwin.com

CEO: Heidi Petz
CFO: Allen J Mistysyn
HR: –
FYE: December 31
Type: Public

For roughly 150 years, Sherwin-Williams has maintained its position as one of the world's top paint manufacturers. Sherwin-Williams' products include a variety of paints, finishes, coatings, applicators, and varnishes sold under brands such as Dutch Boy, Krylon, Sherwin-Williams, and Valspar. The company operates mostly in the US, Canada, Latin America, and the Caribbean through about 4,900 paint stores and sells automotive finishing and refinishing products through wholesale branches. Its other outlets include home centers, independent dealers, and automotive retailers.

	Annual Growth	12/19	12/20	12/21	12/22	12/23
Sales ($mil.)	6.5%	17,901	18,362	19,945	22,149	23,052
Net income ($ mil.)	11.6%	1,541.3	2,030.4	1,864.4	2,020.1	2,388.8
Market value ($ mil.)	(14.5%)	148,536	187,066	89,640	60,411	79,392
Employees	1.2%	61,111	61,031	61,626	64,366	64,088

SHI INTERNATIONAL CORP.

290 DAVIDSON AVE
SOMERSET, NJ 088734145
Phone: 732 764-8888
Fax: –
Web: www.shi.com

CEO: –
CFO: –
HR: –
FYE: December 31
Type: Private

SHI International is one of the world's largest transformational technology solutions providers. The company distributes scores of computer hardware and software products from suppliers such as Adobe, Cisco, Microsoft, VMware, Symantec, and Lenovo. It resells PCs, networking products, data storage systems, printers, software, and keyboards, among other items. SHI offers a range of professional services, including software licensing, asset management, managed desktop services, systems integration, and vocational training. The company serves more than 15,000 academic organizations, corporate, enterprise, government, and healthcare customers from about 40 offices across Australia, Canada, France, Hong Kong, Ireland, Singapore, the US, and the UK. SHI was founded in 1989 by Chairman Koguan Leo.

	Annual Growth	12/15	12/16	12/17	12/18	12/19
Sales ($mil.)	12.6%	–	7,268.9	8,243.6	9,767.0	10,372
Net income ($ mil.)	34.3%	–	104.6	197.7	245.7	253.5
Market value ($ mil.)	–	–	–	–	–	–
Employees	–	–	–	–	–	5,000

SHL LIQUIDATION INDUSTRIES INC.

880 STEEL DR
VALLEY CITY, OH 442809736
Phone: 248 299-7500
Fax: –
Web: www.durashiloh.com

CEO: Mike Putz
CFO: –
HR: –
FYE: October 31
Type: Private

Shiloh Industries is a global innovative solutions provider focusing on lightweighting technologies that provide environmental and safety benefits to the mobility market. The company designs and manufactures products within body structure, chassis and propulsion systems. Shiloh provides multi-component, multi-material solutions, along with a proprietary line of noise and vibration reducing ShilohCore acoustic laminate products. Brands include BlankLight, and StampLight. The company traces its roots back to 1950 when founded as Shiloh Tool & Die Manufacturing.

SHOALS PROVISION, INC.

4144 PARKWAY DR
FLORENCE, AL 356306348
Phone: 256 764-1851
Fax: –
Web: www.shoalsprovision.com

CEO: –
CFO: –
HR: –
FYE: September 30
Type: Private

Shoals Provision delivers a rich haul of meat, fish, and poultry products to restaurants, grocery stores, and other institutions in north Alabama, northeast Mississippi, and south central Tennessee. Its deliverables include chicken and turkey products, beef, pork, deli and smoked meat, catfish, French fries, vegetables and paper supplies. The company was founded in 1972.

	Annual Growth	09/05	09/06	09/09	09/10	09/11
Sales ($mil.)	(1.5%)	–	16.4	19.1	16.5	15.2
Net income ($ mil.)	(4.9%)	–	0.0	0.0	0.0	0.0
Market value ($ mil.)	–	–	–	–	–	–
Employees	–	–	–	–	–	24

SHOE CARNIVAL, INC.
NMS: SCVL

7500 East Columbia Street
Evansville, IN 47715
Phone: 812 867-4034
Fax: –
Web: www.shoecarnival.com

CEO: –
CFO: –
HR: –
FYE: February 3
Type: Public

Shoe Carnival is one of the nation's largest family footwear retailers. The company operates about 395 family footwear stores across approximately 35 US states, including Puerto Rico and offered online shopping at www.shoecarnival.com. The company sell broadly across the family footwear channel, with balanced distribution among type of customer (men, women and children), product (athletics and non-athletics) and age (senior citizens to infants) with no singular reliance on any particular segment. The company offers a mix of footwear necessities for sport, work, daily activities and special events. Its Shoe Carnival stores carry approximately 30,800 pairs of shoes per location, and its Shoe Station physical stores carry 44,100 pairs of shoes per location. The family of Chairman J. Wayne Weaver owns about 30% of Shoe Carnival's shares.

	Annual Growth	02/20*	01/21	01/22	01/23*	02/24
Sales ($mil.)	3.2%	1,036.6	976.8	1,330.4	1,262.2	1,175.9
Net income ($ mil.)	14.3%	42.9	16.0	154.9	110.1	73.3
Market value ($ mil.)	(7.5%)	972.9	1,274.8	896.4	747.7	713.0
Employees	1.0%	5,100	4,700	5,800	5,500	5,300

*Fiscal year change

SHOESTRING VALLEY HOLDINGS INC.

6712 N CUTTER CIR
PORTLAND, OR 972173933
Phone: 503 283-6712
Fax: –
Web: –

CEO: David L Andersen
CFO: Bill Eckhardt
HR: –
FYE: December 31
Type: Private

Andersen Construction Company focuses on commercial and industrial construction in the Western US. The group, which introduced concrete tilt-up construction to the Pacific Northwest, builds everything from parking structures to medical facilities, manufacturing plants, and industrial complexes. It also works on institutional projects for the government and education markets. Other projects include tenant improvements, seismic upgrades, and remediation construction. The company provides construction management (which accounts for 80% of its work), as well as general contracting and design/build delivery. It also offers startup and commissioning services. Chairman and CEO Andy Andersen founded the company in 1950.

	Annual Growth	12/15	12/16	12/17	12/21	12/22
Sales ($mil.)	9.3%	–	–	644.3	735.4	1,005.6
Net income ($ mil.)	47.5%	–	–	1.5	7.8	10.2
Market value ($ mil.)	–	–	–	–	–	–
Employees	–	–	–	–	–	150

SHORE BANCSHARES INC.
NMS: SHBI

18 E. Dover Street
Easton, MD 21601
Phone: 410 763-7800
Fax: –
Web: www.shorebancshares.com

CEO: Lloyd L Beatty Jr
CFO: Edward C Allen
HR: –
FYE: December 31
Type: Public

Shore Bancshares sits on the edge of the banking ocean. The institution is the holding company for Shore United Bank, which operates about 20 branches serving individuals and businesses in the Maryland counties of Caroline, Dorchester, Kent, Queen Anne, and Talbot, as well as in Kent County, Delaware. Shore Bancshares sells insurance through subsidiary The Avon-Dixon Agency (with specialty lines Elliott Wilson Insurance, trucking coverage; and Jack Martin & Associates, marine products). Another subsidiary, Wye Financial & Trust, offers trust and wealth management services. In 2016 the company merged its former two banks, Centreville National Bank and Talbot bank, into the single Shore United Bank.

	Annual Growth	12/19	12/20	12/21	12/22	12/23
Assets ($mil.)	40.1%	1,559.2	1,933.3	3,460.1	3,477.3	6,010.9
Net income ($ mil.)	(8.8%)	16.2	15.7	15.4	31.2	11.2
Market value ($ mil.)	(4.8%)	575.7	484.2	691.4	578.0	472.6
Employees	20.5%	294	295	446	481	620

SHORE MEMORIAL HOSPITAL

100 MEDICAL CENTER WAY
SOMERS POINT, NJ 082442389
Phone: 609 653-3500
Fax: –
Web: www.shoremedicalcenter.org

CEO: –
CFO: –
HR: William Dejesus
FYE: December 31
Type: Private

You might be able to get a room with a view of the ocean at Shore Memorial Hospital. Operating as Shore Medical Center, the facility is a not-for-profit community hospital with some 300 beds. It offers acute care services and more than 35 specialized care programs including oncology, cardiology, neurology, obstetrics, and orthopedic care. Shore Medical Center is affiliated with The University of Pennsylvania Health System and The Children's Hospital of Philadelphia. In addition to the hospital, Shore Medical Center operates community-based health and fitness centers.

	Annual Growth	12/13	12/14	12/15	12/17	12/18
Sales ($mil.)	0.9%	–	187.9	183.3	190.8	194.5
Net income ($ mil.)	–	–	(0.7)	2.0	–	23.6
Market value ($ mil.)	–	–	–	–	–	–
Employees	–	–	–	–	–	1,600

SHOREPOWER TECHNOLOGIES INC
NBB: SPEV

5291 NE Elam Young Pkwy, Suite 160
Hillsboro, OR 97124
Phone: 503 892-7345
Fax: -
Web: -

CEO: Saeb Jannoun
CFO: -
HR: -
FYE: February 28
Type: Public

Basketball fans have more hardwood action to enjoy thanks to this enterprise. The United States Basketball League (USBL) operates an association of professional basketball teams that play a 30-game schedule from April through June. The league encompasses a half dozen teams, including the Brooklyn Kings, the Dodge City Legend, and the Kansas Cagerz, which compete with 11 players each. The USBL generates revenue mostly through franchise fees and marketing sponsorships. It is intended to be a development league for recent college graduates and international players to showcase their skills for scouts from National Basketball Association teams. The founding Meisenheimer family controls about 90% of the USBL.

	Annual Growth	02/19	02/20	02/21	02/22	02/23
Sales ($mil.)	-	-	-	-	0.0	-
Net income ($ mil.)	-	(0.1)	(0.0)	(0.0)	(2.1)	(0.6)
Market value ($ mil.)	33.5%	7.2	3.1	5.7	21.3	22.7
Employees	-	1	1	1	-	-

SHRINERS HOSPITALS FOR CHILDREN

12502 USF PINE DR
TAMPA, FL 336129499
Phone: 813 972-2250
Fax: -
Web: www.shrinerschildrens.org

CEO: -
CFO: -
HR: -
FYE: December 31
Type: Private

Shriners Hospitals For Children is a world-renowned and beloved healthcare system with hospitals, outpatient clinics, ambulatory care centers and outreach locations across the globe. It operates nearly two dozen hospitals throughout North America. The majority of its hospitals specialize in orthopedic conditions while others specialize in treating serious burn injuries, spinal cord injuries, and cleft lips and palates. Shriners Hospitals was founded by fellowship Shriners International, the hospitals are supported by a multitude of fundraising events that are arranged by the organization's members. As a result, Shriners Hospitals is able to treat children regardless of their families' ability to pay.

	Annual Growth	12/08	12/09	12/13	12/14	12/16
Sales ($mil.)	(13.8%)	-	285.1	-	120.0	100.4
Net income ($ mil.)	-	-	(300.9)	45.6	58.4	38.0
Market value ($ mil.)	-	-	-	-	-	-
Employees	-	-	-	-	-	6,100

SHUTTERFLY, LLC

2800 BRIDGE PKWY STE 100
REDWOOD CITY, CA 940651192
Phone: 650 610-5200
Fax: -
Web: www.shutterflyinc.com

CEO: Hilary Schneider
CFO: Mike Eklund
HR: Dionne Hubbard
FYE: December 31
Type: Private

Shutterfly is the leading digital retail and manufacturing platform for personalized products. It provides digital photo products and services offers customers the ability to upload, share, store, and edit digital photos, as well as order prints, via its cloud photos service on Shutterfly.com. It also offers personalized items including cards, stationary, mugs, photo books, gifts and home decor; owns the Lifetouch school and portrait photography service; and has a unit devoted to providing direct marketing and printing services for business customers. Shutterfly is majority-owned by certain investment funds managed directly or indirectly by Apollo Global Management.

SHUTTERSTOCK INC
NYS: SSTK

350 Fifth Avenue, 20th Floor
New York, NY 10118
Phone: 646 710-3417
Fax: -
Web: www.shutterstock.com

CEO: Jonathan Oringer
CFO: Jarrod Yahes
HR: Marilee Gamboa
FYE: December 31
Type: Public

Shutterstock helps creative professionals from all backgrounds and businesses of all sizes produce their best work with incredible content and innovative tools, all on one platform. It is a global creative platform for transformative brands and media companies. The company's platform brings together users and contributors of content by providing readily-searchable content that its customers pay to license and by compensating contributors as their content is licensed. The company's primary customers include marketing professionals and organization, media and broadcast companies, and small- and medium-sizes businesses. The company has over 2.3 million customers in more than 150 countries. North America generates roughly 45% of the company's total sales.

	Annual Growth	12/19	12/20	12/21	12/22	12/23
Sales ($mil.)	7.7%	650.5	666.7	773.4	827.8	874.6
Net income ($ mil.)	53.0%	20.1	71.8	91.9	76.1	110.3
Market value ($ mil.)	3.0%	1,525.3	2,550.4	3,944.1	1,875.3	1,717.4
Employees	3.4%	1,116	967	1,148	1,328	1,274

SHYFT GROUP INC (THE)
NMS: SHYF

41280 Bridge Street
Novi, MI 48375
Phone: 517 543-6400
Fax: -
Web: www.theshyftgroup.com

CEO: John Dunn
CFO: Jonathan C Douyard
HR: -
FYE: December 31
Type: Public

The Shyft Group, Inc. (formerly Spartan Motors) is a niche market leader in specialty vehicle manufacturing and assembly for the commercial vehicle (including last-mile delivery, specialty service, and vocation-specific upfit segments) and recreational vehicle industries. Its products include walk-in vans, truck bodies, and cargo van and pick-up truck upfits used in e-commerce/parcel delivery, upfit equipment used in the mobile retail and utility trades, luxury Class A diesel motor home chassis and contract manufacturing and assembly services. Almost all of its sales were generated from the US.

	Annual Growth	12/19	12/20	12/21	12/22	12/23
Sales ($mil.)	3.6%	756.5	676.0	991.8	1,027.2	872.2
Net income ($ mil.)	-	(12.6)	32.8	68.9	36.6	6.5
Market value ($ mil.)	(9.3%)	620.2	973.5	1,685.3	852.8	419.2
Employees	2.4%	2,724	3,000	3,800	4,200	3,000

SID HARVEY INDUSTRIES, INC.

605 LOCUST ST
GARDEN CITY, NY 115306531
Phone: 516 745-9200
Fax: -
Web: www.sidharvey.com

CEO: Sidney W Harvey
CFO: Russell Tumsuden
HR: -
FYE: March 31
Type: Private

Whether you're too chilly in Colorado or roasting in Rhode Island, Sid Harvey Industries might have the answer. The company makes and wholesales heating, ventilation, air-conditioning, and refrigeration parts and equipment through some 75 locations in about a dozen states. Sid Harvey's also exports worldwide. The company reconditions more than 1,700 used parts and manufactures more than 750 new products at its plants in South Carolina. Its Web site offers a database connecting HVAC professionals and companies looking for qualified job candidates. Sid Harvey Industries was founded in 1931 as an oil industry parts supplier by the grandfather of president and CEO Sid Harvey.

SIDLEY AUSTIN LLP

1 S DEARBORN ST
CHICAGO, IL 606032323
Phone: 312 853-7000
Fax: –
Web: www.sidley.com

CEO: –
CFO: –
HR: Carole Conway
FYE: December 31
Type: Private

Sidley Austin's 2,100 lawyers practice in a wide range of areas from approximately 20 offices around the world. Sidley Austin focuses on business transactions and litigation. Its customers reside in the agribusiness, energy, financial services, insurance, investment fund, life sciences, and technology sectors. Sidley Austin's lawyers and staff devote more than 125,000 hours annually to pro bono work. The law firm traces its historical roots back to when Chicago-based Sidley & Austin was established in 1866.

SIEBERT FINANCIAL CORP   NAS: SIEB

535 Fifth Avenue, 4th Floor
New York, NY 10017
Phone: 212 644-2400
Fax: –
Web: www.siebert.com

CEO: John J Gebbia
CFO: –
HR: Dina Gonzalez
FYE: December 31
Type: Public

Siebert Financial, through subsidiary Muriel Siebert & Co., provides discount securities brokerage and institutional financial services. Its retail division offers equity trading, mutual fund access, and retirement accounts to self-directed individual investors. Customers can access their accounts and trade by phone, Internet, wireless device, or in person at seven retail branches in California, Florida, New Jersey, and New York. Siebert Financial provides securities trading and underwriting and other services to corporations and government entities. Nevada firm Kennedy Cabot Acquisition is buying the 90% of Siebert that is owned by the estate of its founder, Muriel "Mickie" Siebert.

	Annual Growth	12/18	12/19	12/20	12/21	12/22
Sales ($mil.)	13.6%	30.0	28.6	54.9	67.5	50.1
Net income ($ mil.)	–	12.0	3.6	3.0	5.1	(2.0)
Market value ($ mil.)	(44.6%)	470.0	281.2	136.5	75.4	44.2
Employees	11.4%	76	132	125	125	117

SIERRA BANCORP   NMS: BSRR

86 North Main Street
Porterville, CA 93257
Phone: 559 782-4900
Fax: –
Web: www.bankofthesierra.com

CEO: Kevin J McPhaill
CFO: Christopher G Treece
HR: –
FYE: December 31
Type: Public

Sierra Bancorp is the holding company for the nearly $2 billion-asset Bank of the Sierra, which operates approximately 30 branches in Central California's San Joaquin Valley between (and including) Bakersfield and Fresno. The bank offers traditional deposit products and loans to individuals and small and mid-size businesses. About 70% of its loan portfolio is made up of real estate loans, while another 15% is made up of mortgage warehouse loans and a further 10% is tied to commercial and industrial loans (including SBA loans and direct finance leases). The bank also issues agricultural loans, and consumer loans.

	Annual Growth	12/19	12/20	12/21	12/22	12/23
Assets ($mil.)	9.5%	2,593.8	3,220.7	3,371.0	3,608.6	3,729.8
Net income ($ mil.)	(0.8%)	36.0	35.4	43.0	33.7	34.8
Market value ($ mil.)	(6.2%)	430.8	353.9	401.7	314.2	333.6
Employees	0.9%	513	512	492	488	532

SIERRA CLUB

2101 WEBSTER ST STE 1300
OAKLAND, CA 946123011
Phone: 415 977-5500
Fax: –
Web: www.sierraclub.org

CEO: –
CFO: –
HR: –
FYE: December 31
Type: Private

Wanna take a hike with the Sierra Club? The growing grassroots organization promotes outdoor activities and environmental activism on both the local and national levels through political lobbies, education, outings, litigation, and publications. The club's more than 2.4 million members are organized into state and regional chapters throughout the US and Canada. Founded in 1892 by naturalist John Muir, Sierra Club publishes books, calendars, SIERRA magazine, and activist newsletter Currents . Some of Sierra Club's current issues include smart energy solutions, clean water, stopping commercial logging in national forests, ending sprawl, and protecting wetlands.

	Annual Growth	12/07	12/08	12/09	12/13	12/17
Sales ($mil.)	5.5%	–	87.4	97.3	98.2	141.4
Net income ($ mil.)	–	–	(14.4)	6.0	0.3	13.0
Market value ($ mil.)	–	–	–	–	–	–
Employees	–	–	–	–	–	600

SIERRA NEVADA CORPORATION

444 SALOMON CIR
SPARKS, NV 894349651
Phone: 775 331-0222
Fax: –
Web: www.sncorp.com

CEO: –
CFO: –
HR: –
FYE: December 31
Type: Private

Sierra Nevada Corporation (SNC) is a trusted leader in innovative, advanced technology solutions and open architecture integrations in aerospace and national security. Best known for its unique mission applications, SNC creates customized solutions for the world's most pressing technology challenges in the fields of aviation, national security space, electronic warfare, command and control, mission systems and inline cybersecurity. SNC is owned by Chairwoman and President Eren Ozmen and CEO Fatih Ozmen. SNC's subsidiaries and affiliates include Straight Flight, 3S, Deutsche Aircraft, Kutta Technologies Inc. & Kutta Radios Inc., SNC Mission Systems UK, and Sierra Space. The privately held company was founded in 1963.

	Annual Growth	12/10	12/11	12/12	12/13	12/14
Sales ($mil.)	2.9%	–	–	1,400.1	1,623.0	1,481.0
Net income ($ mil.)	–	–	–	–	–	–
Market value ($ mil.)	–	–	–	–	–	–
Employees	–	–	–	–	–	5,464

SIERRA PACIFIC POWER CO.

6100 Neil Road
Reno, NV 89511
Phone: 775 834-4011
Fax: –
Web: www.nvenergy.com

CEO: Paul J Caudill
CFO: E K Bethel
HR: –
FYE: December 31
Type: Public

Sierra Pacific Power mitigates the effects of hot Sierra winds and moist Pacific breezes. The company is a natural gas and electricity distribution utility serving customers in towns and cities across Nevada. Sierra Pacific Power, a subsidiary of NV Energy IncInc., does business as NV Energy . The company serves about 323,000400,000 retail electric power customers and some 200,000153,000 transportation and natural gas customers. Sierra Pacific Power also owns more than 15 fossil-fueled and hydroelectric power plantsfive generating facilities with about 1,6351,510 MW of generating capacity , and it sells excess energy to wholesale customers.

	Annual Growth	12/19	12/20	12/21	12/22	12/23
Sales ($mil.)	12.6%	889.0	854.0	965.0	1,193.0	1,431.0
Net income ($ mil.)	3.2%	103.0	111.0	124.0	118.0	117.0
Market value ($ mil.)	–	–	–	–	–	–
Employees	–	1,000	1,000	900	1,000	1,000

SIERRA VIEW DISTRICT HOSPITAL LEAGUE, INC.

465 W PUTNAM AVE
PORTERVILLE, CA 932573320
Phone: 559 784-1110
Fax: –
Web: www.sierra-view.com

CEO: Donna Hefner
CFO: Douglas Dickson
HR: –
FYE: December 31
Type: Private

Patients at Sierra View District Hospital (SVDH) are likely to have a bedside view of central California's San Joaquin Valley. The not-for-profit acute-care medical center offers a comprehensive range of primary, specialty, and emergency services, serving Porterville, California, and surrounding areas. Divisions at the hospital's nearly 170-bed facility include oncology, pediatrics, diagnostics, women's care, and rehabilitation. SVDH, which boasts a 32-station outpatient dialysis center and the Roger S. Good Cancer Treatment Center, also offers laboratory, wellness, and counseling services. Founded in 1948, the hospital serves more than 40,000 patients in its emergency room each year.

	Annual Growth	06/14	06/15	06/16	06/18*	12/20
Sales ($mil.)	(76.4%)	–	–	138.3	148.0	0.4
Net income ($ mil.)	–	–	–	–	1.1	–
Market value ($ mil.)	–	–	–	–	–	–
Employees	–	–	–	–	–	600

*Fiscal year change

SIERRA-CEDAR, LLC

1255 ALDERMAN DR
ALPHARETTA, GA 300054156
Phone: 678 385-7540
Fax: –
Web: www.sierra-cedar.com

CEO: –
CFO: –
HR: –
FYE: December 31
Type: Private

Sierra-Cedar provides IT services related primarily to the implementation and customization of enterprise software developed by software companies such as Oracle, Peoplesoft, and cloud computing provider Amazon Web Services as well as Hosting and Managed Services. It delivers the best in class services that the clients demand through organic growth, mergers, and acquisitions, major technology shifts, and recessions. It also identifies, embraces, and implements transformative technologies using innovative approaches that empower organizations to modernize and transform with confidence. The company is headquartered in Georgia and has a delivery center in India. Sierra-Cedar serves customers across the US in a broad range of industries, including public sector, commercial, higher education, and healthcare. The company is founded in 1995.

	Annual Growth	03/07	03/08	03/09*	12/12	12/13
Sales ($mil.)	–	–	(479.5)	149.6	–	5.3
Net income ($ mil.)	343.3%	–	0.0	6.7	–	0.4
Market value ($ mil.)	–	–	–	–	–	–
Employees	–	–	–	–	–	660

*Fiscal year change

SIFCO INDUSTRIES INC.

ASE: SIF

970 East 64th Street
Cleveland, OH 44103
Phone: 216 881-8600
Fax: –
Web: www.sifco.com

CEO: Peter W Knapper
CFO: Thomas R Kubera
HR: –
FYE: September 30
Type: Public

Airplanes need parts, and SIFCO coats, machines, and produces jet engine and aerospace components. It forges parts and offers forging, heat-treating, and precision component machining services. Products include components for aircraft and industrial gas turbine engines, structural airframe components, aircraft landing gear components, brakes, and wheels. Aerospace components for both fixed wing aircraft and rotorcraft account for nearly 80% of its total sales. SIFCO caters to original equipment manufacturers (OEMs) for both commercial and defense aerospace applications. It also serves the energy market.

	Annual Growth	09/19	09/20	09/21	09/22	09/23
Sales ($mil.)	(6.2%)	112.5	113.6	99.6	83.9	87.0
Net income ($ mil.)	–	(7.5)	9.2	(0.7)	(9.6)	(8.7)
Market value ($ mil.)	7.9%	16.5	22.5	52.5	18.7	22.4
Employees	(5.4%)	434	446	378	348	348

SIGA TECHNOLOGIES INC

NMS: SIGA

31 East 62nd Street
New York, NY 10065
Phone: 212 672-9100
Fax: –
Web: www.siga.com

CEO: –
CFO: –
HR: –
FYE: December 31
Type: Public

SIGA Technologies is trying to put itself on the front lines of US biodefense efforts. The drug company has a number of development programs for vaccines, antivirals, and antibiotics for drug resistant infections; however, its main focus is on vaccines for bio-defense. Its lead product TPOXX (aka tecovirimat) was the first treatment to be approved for the treatment of smallpox in case of a bioterrorist attack; it was given approval in mid-2018. SIGA is also developing vaccines for use against hemorrhagic fevers and other infectious diseases and biothreats. Much of its work is done through funding from the NIH and the HHS. SIGA emerged from a short stint under Chapter 11 bankruptcy protection in 2016.

	Annual Growth	12/19	12/20	12/21	12/22	12/23
Sales ($mil.)	51.2%	26.7	125.0	133.7	110.8	139.9
Net income ($ mil.)	–	(7.2)	56.3	69.5	33.9	68.1
Market value ($ mil.)	4.1%	339.1	516.8	534.6	523.2	398.1
Employees	–	41	42	39	39	–

SIGMANET, INC.

4290 E BRICKELL ST
ONTARIO, CA 917611524
Phone: 909 230-7500
Fax: –
Web: www.convergeone.com

CEO: –
CFO: –
HR: –
FYE: December 31
Type: Private

SIGMAnet hopes the net result of its services is improved technology in your enterprise. The company offers cloud, analytics, mobility, security, data center, and IT products and services to mid-sized and large corporate clients mostly in California. It also provides networking, systems integration, consulting, and other technical services, as well as procurement services. The company was founded in 1986 and serves customers in a variety of industries such as manufacturing, transportation, energy and utilities, retail, consumer goods, financial services, and technology. The company was acquired by ConvergeOne in late 2015. SIGMAnet adds expertise in Cisco and EMC platforms and expanded geographic reach to ConvergeOne.

SIGMATRON INTERNATIONAL INC.

NAS: SGMA

2201 Landmeier Road
Elk Grove Village, IL 60007
Phone: 847 956-8000
Fax: –
Web: www.sigmatronintl.com

CEO: Gary R Fairhead
CFO: James J Reiman
HR: –
FYE: April 30
Type: Public

An assembly at SigmaTron International doesn't mean fraternizing over a keg. The company produces electronic components, printed circuit board assemblies, and box-build (completely assembled) electronic products on a contract basis for customers in the appliance, automotive, consumer electronics, fitness equipment, industrial electronics, and telecommunications industries. SigmaTron also offers design, testing, shipping, and storage services. Major customers include electronic controls manufacturer Spitfire Controls and fitness equipment maker Life Fitness, together accounting for nearly half of sales. Besides its US manufacturing facilities, the company boasts plants in China, Mexico, and Taiwan.

	Annual Growth	04/19	04/20	04/21	04/22	04/23
Sales ($mil.)	9.3%	290.6	281.0	277.7	378.9	414.4
Net income ($ mil.)	–	(0.9)	0.4	1.5	9.9	(20.6)
Market value ($ mil.)	(4.1%)	16.7	18.0	31.1	40.6	14.1
Employees	(1.3%)	3,106	3,065	3,200	3,100	2,950

SIGNATURE BANK (NEW YORK, NY) — NBB: SBNY P

565 Fifth Avenue
New York, NY 10017
Phone: 646 822-1500
Fax: –
Web: www.signatureny.com

CEO: –
CFO: –
HR: –
FYE: December 31
Type: Public

Signature Bank is a full-service commercial bank that provides customized banking and financial services to smaller private businesses, their owners, and their top executives through some 35 branches across the New York metropolitan area, including those in Connecticut, as well as in California and North Carolina. The bank's lending activities mainly entail real estate and business loans. Subsidiary Signature Securities offers wealth management, brokerage services, asset management, and insurance, while its Signature Financial subsidiary offers equipment financing and leasing. Founded in 2001, the bank now boasts assets of approximately $118.45 billion.

	Annual Growth	12/18	12/19	12/20	12/21	12/22
Assets ($mil.)	23.5%	47,365	50,616	73,888	118,445	110,364
Net income ($ mil.)	27.5%	505.3	588.9	528.4	918.4	1,337.0
Market value ($ mil.)	2.9%	6,469.7	8,596.7	8,513.6	20,356	7,250.7
Employees	12.6%	1,393	1,472	1,652	1,854	2,243

SIGNATURE EYEWEAR INC. — NBB: SEYE

498 North Oak Street
Inglewood, CA 90302
Phone: 310 330-2700
Fax: 310 330-2748
Web: www.signatureeyewear.com

CEO: –
CFO: –
HR: –
FYE: October 31
Type: Public

Signature Eyewear views prescription eyeglasses and sunglasses as the ultimate fashion statement and an integral part of its business. Laura Ashley, Nicole Miller, and bebe licensed eyewear accounts for about three-fourths of the firm's sales. Signature Eyewear also licenses frames by Michael Stars, Dakota Smith, and Hart Schaffner Marx. Its own Signature line of frames is produced by contract manufacturers in Hong Kong, China, Japan, and Italy, and markets them to optical retailers in more than 20 countries. The company markets footwear and accessories through its Signature Fashion Group division, which was formed in 2010.

	Annual Growth	10/06	10/07	10/08	10/09	10/10
Sales ($mil.)	(2.6%)	23.2	25.0	24.5	23.3	20.8
Net income ($ mil.)	(9.3%)	0.7	2.7	0.6	0.7	0.5
Market value ($ mil.)	(17.9%)	3.1	4.3	2.4	2.2	1.4
Employees	0.7%	102	98	98	110	105

SIKA CORPORATION

201 POLITO AVE
LYNDHURST, NJ 070713601
Phone: 201 933-8800
Fax: –
Web: usa.sika.com

CEO: Richard Montani
CFO: Gregory May
HR: Leigh A Paull
FYE: December 31
Type: Private

Sika Corporation is a specialty chemicals company with a leading position in the development and production of systems and solutions for bonding, sealing, damping, reinforcing, and protecting the construction, residential & home improvement, oil and gas pipeline and the transportation, marine, and automotive manufacturing industries. Sika's unique product technologies include concrete admixtures and fibers, mortars, epoxies, urethanes, structural strengthening systems, industrial flooring, PVC and liquid applied membrane roofing systems, thermal insulation, plaster, and stucco, below-grade waterproofing, and acoustical and reinforcing materials. Sika is the US unit of global chemicals company Sika AG.

	Annual Growth	12/13	12/14	12/15	12/16	12/17
Sales ($mil.)	8.6%	–	842.6	915.9	–	1,079.8
Net income ($ mil.)	25.7%	–	42.6	63.7	–	84.6
Market value ($ mil.)	–	–	–	–	–	–
Employees	–	–	–	–	–	1,357

SILGAN HOLDINGS INC — NYS: SLGN

4 Landmark Square
Stamford, CT 06901
Phone: 203 975-7110
Fax: –
Web: www.silganholdings.com

CEO: Adam J Greenlee
CFO: Robert B Lewis
HR: Trish Parker
FYE: December 31
Type: Public

Silgan Holdings is a leading manufacturer of sustainable rigid packaging solutions for consumer goods products. It is the largest manufacturer of metal food containers in North America. Customers such as Campbell's Soup, Del Monte, and Nestl to package soups, vegetables, meat, seafood, and pet food use its containers. Through its Silgan Dispensing Systems business, the company supplies highly engineered pumps, sprayers, foam, and dispensing closure solutions for health care, garden, home, and beauty and food products. Silgan also makes plastic containers used by personal care, food, health care, pharmaceutical, household and industrial chemical, pet food and care, agricultural, automotive and marine chemical products. More than 75% of its revenue comes from North America.

	Annual Growth	12/19	12/20	12/21	12/22	12/23
Sales ($mil.)	7.5%	4,489.9	4,921.9	5,677.1	6,411.5	5,988.2
Net income ($ mil.)	13.9%	193.8	308.7	359.1	340.8	326.0
Market value ($ mil.)	9.8%	3,310.0	3,949.0	4,562.5	5,521.0	4,819.1
Employees	35.5%	3,200	3,500	3,800	3,800	10,800

SILICON GRAPHICS INTERNATIONAL CORP.

940 N MCCARTHY BLVD
MILPITAS, CA 950355128
Phone: 669 900-8000
Fax: –
Web: www.hpe.com

CEO: Jorge L Titinger
CFO: Mack Asrat
HR: –
FYE: June 24
Type: Private

Silicon Graphics International (SGI) handles computing on a large scale. The company provides high-performance computer servers that are based on the Linux operating system and designed for large-scale data center deployments. SGI also offers data storage servers, as well as modular data center systems sold under the ICE brand. Its equipment is tailored to quickly access, analyze, process, manage, visualize, and store large amounts of data. SGI targets the IT, Internet, financial services, government, and electronics sectors, as well as scientific community. Clients have included Amazon.com (18% of sales in 2014), Microsoft, Yahoo!, and Deutsche Bank. In November 2016 SGI was acquired by Hewlett-Packard Enterprise.

	Annual Growth	06/12	06/13	06/14	06/15	06/16
Sales ($mil.)	(11.4%)	–	767.2	529.9	521.3	532.9
Net income ($ mil.)	–	–	(2.8)	(52.8)	(39.1)	(11.2)
Market value ($ mil.)	–	–	–	–	–	–
Employees	–	–	–	–	–	1,100

SILICON LABORATORIES INC — NMS: SLAB

400 West Cesar Chavez
Austin, TX 78701
Phone: 512 416-8500
Fax: –
Web: www.silabs.com

CEO: –
CFO: –
HR: –
FYE: December 30
Type: Public

Silicon Laboratories (also known as Silicon Labs) is a leader in secure, intelligent wireless technology for a more connected world. Its integrated hardware and software platform, intuitive development tools, industry-leading ecosystem, and robust support help customers build advanced industrial, commercial, home, and life applications. The company provide analog-intensive, mixed-signal solutions for use in a variety of electronic products in a broad range of applications for the IoT including connected home and security, industrial automation and control, smart metering, smart lighting, commercial building automation, consumer electronics, asset tracking, and medical instrumentation. Almost 85% of the company's sales come from customers outside the US.

	Annual Growth	12/19*	01/21	01/22*	12/22	12/23
Sales ($mil.)	(1.7%)	837.6	886.7	720.9	1,024.1	782.3
Net income ($ mil.)	–	–	19.3	12.5	2,117.4	91.4	(34.5)
Market value ($ mil.)	3.2%	3,716.6	4,061.8	6,584.2	4,327.5	4,219.0
Employees	4.8%	1,545	1,838	1,667	1,964	1,864

*Fiscal year change

SILICUS TECHNOLOGIES, LLC

2700 POST OAK BLVD STE 1625
HOUSTON, TX 770565838
Phone: 713 353-7400
Fax: –
Web: www.silicus.com

CEO: Sumant Ahuja
CFO: –
HR: –
FYE: December 31
Type: Private

Silicus Technologies has gone soft. The company provides oursourced product development services specializing in software solutions. The company offers expertise in system management, storage platforms, security and compliance, e-mail and messaging, and business productivity solutions using Microsoft, Unix, or mobile platforms. Founded in 2000, the company is headquartered in the US, with its development center located in India. Clients have included HP, Halliburton, and ExxonMobil; the company also has alliances with Microsoft, IBM, and Oracle.

	Annual Growth	12/07	12/08	12/09	12/10	12/11
Sales ($mil.)	–	–	–	(1,043.7)	1.8	3.2
Net income ($ mil.)	2266.1%	–	–	0.0	0.0	0.0
Market value ($ mil.)	–	–	–	–	–	–
Employees	–	–	–	–	–	26

SILVER BAY REALTY TRUST CORP.

3300 FERNBROOK LN N
PLYMOUTH, MN 554475338
Phone: 952 358-4400
Fax: –
Web: www.silverbayrealtytrustcorp.com

CEO: –
CFO: –
HR: –
FYE: December 31
Type: Private

Silver Bay makes green on rentals in sunny locales. The real estate investment trust (REIT) is externally managed by PRCM Real Estate Advisers. It focuses on buying single-family homes in urban markets with an oversupply of housing. Silver Bay acquires properties via foreclosures, auctions, sales listings, and bulk purchases and uses its manager's rental property experience to achieve economies of scale for property management and maintenance. The company has a portfolio of about 2,250 income-generating single-family homes that it leases in Arizona, California, Florida, Georgia, Nevada, North Carolina, and Texas. Real estate investor Two Harbors formed Silver Bay in 2012 and it went public later that year.

	Annual Growth	12/12	12/13	12/14	12/15	12/16
Assets ($mil.)	12.9%	–	846.1	1,002.4	1,224.4	1,218.6
Net income ($ mil.)	–	–	(24.6)	(56.7)	(10.0)	(2.6)
Market value ($ mil.)	–	–	–	–	–	–
Employees	–	–	–	–	–	5

SILVER CROSS HOSPITAL AND MEDICAL CENTERS

1900 SILVER CROSS BLVD
NEW LENOX, IL 604519509
Phone: 815 300-1100
Fax: –
Web: –

CEO: Paul Pawlak
CFO: William Brownlow
HR: –
FYE: September 30
Type: Private

Silver Cross Hospital and Medical Centers serve the Illinois counties of Will, Grundy, and Cook through its 290-bed main hospital campus and nine satellite facilities throughout the area. Services provided by the medical facility include cardiovascular care, women's health, rehabilitation, and behavioral health care. Its outpatient facilities provide primary and specialty care services, such as medical imaging and dialysis. The Silver Cross Hospital and Medical Centers name comes from the emblem (the Maltese Cross) of the Christian organization that founded the not-for-profit hospital, the International Order of The King's Daughters and Sons.

	Annual Growth	09/18	09/19	09/20	09/21	09/22
Sales ($mil.)	4.5%	–	420.0	452.5	477.3	478.7
Net income ($ mil.)	–	–	33.6	53.3	95.2	(47.9)
Market value ($ mil.)	–	–	–	–	–	–
Employees	–	–	–	–	–	1,600

SILVERBOW RESOURCES INC

NYS: SBOW

920 Memorial City Way, Suite 850
Houston, TX 77024
Phone: 281 874-2700
Fax: –
Web: www.sbow.com

CEO: Sean C Woolverton
CFO: Christopher M Abundis
HR: Joe Bisacca
FYE: December 31
Type: Public

No laggard, oil and gas exploration and production company Swift Energy was swift to see the potential of a handful of oil and gas fields in Louisiana and Texas. The company's core exploration areas are the South Bearhead Creek Field and Burr Ferry Field in Louisiana and the Eagle Ford Play in Texas. Swift Energy aims to increase reserves and production by adjusting the balance between drilling and acquisition activities in response to market conditions. Facing a slumping oil market, in late 2015 the company filed for Chapter 11 bankruptcy protection, from which it emerged in April, 2016. That year, it sold its Lake Washington field in Louisiana for $40 million.

	Annual Growth	12/19	12/20	12/21	12/22	12/23
Sales ($mil.)	22.6%	288.6	177.4	407.2	753.4	652.4
Net income ($ mil.)	26.9%	114.7	(309.4)	86.8	340.4	297.7
Market value ($ mil.)	30.9%	251.8	135.0	553.6	719.1	739.5
Employees	11.7%	86	64	62	82	134

SIMMONS FIRST NATIONAL CORP

NMS: SFNC

501 Main Street
Pine Bluff, AR 71601
Phone: 870 541-1000
Fax: –
Web: www.simmonsbank.com

CEO: Robert A Fehlman
CFO: Daniel Hobbs
HR: Gough Greg
FYE: December 31
Type: Public

Simmons First National is a financial holding company of Simmons Bank, an Arkansas state-chartered bank that has been operating since 1903. Simmons Bank provides banking and other financial products and services to individuals and businesses using a network of about 230 financial centers in Arkansas, Kansas, Missouri, Oklahoma, Tennessee, and Texas. The company offers commercial banking products and services to businesses and other corporate customers; it extends loans for a broad range of corporate purposes, including financing commercial real estate, construction of particular properties, commercial and industrial uses, acquisition and equipment financings, and other general corporate needs. The company has a total asset of $27.5 billion.

	Annual Growth	12/19	12/20	12/21	12/22	12/23
Assets ($mil.)	6.5%	21,259	22,360	24,725	27,461	27,346
Net income ($ mil.)	(7.4%)	238.2	254.9	271.2	256.4	175.1
Market value ($ mil.)	(7.2%)	3,353.7	2,702.7	3,702.9	2,701.5	2,483.7
Employees	(2.1%)	3,270	2,923	2,877	3,202	3,007

SIMON PROPERTY GROUP, INC.

NYS: SPG

225 West Washington Street
Indianapolis, IN 46204
Phone: 317 636-1600
Fax: 317 685-7336
Web: www.simon.com

CEO: David Simon
CFO: Brian J McDade
HR: –
FYE: December 31
Type: Public

Simon Property Group is the largest shopping mall and retail center owner in the US. The self-managed, self-administered real estate investment trust (REIT) owns, develops, and manages regional shopping malls, outlet malls (under the Premium Outlet and The Mills brands), boutique malls, and shopping centers. Its real estate portfolio is composed of some 195 retail properties totaling approximately 172.6 million sq. ft. of leasable space. Its portfolio covers more than 35 states and Puerto Rico, about 35 Premium Outlets and Designer Outlet properties primarily located in Asia, Europe, and Canada.

	Annual Growth	12/19	12/20	12/21	12/22	12/23
Sales ($mil.)	(0.4%)	5,755.2	4,607.5	5,116.8	5,291.4	5,658.8
Net income ($ mil.)	2.1%	2,101.6	1,112.6	2,249.6	2,139.5	2,283.1
Market value ($ mil.)	(1.1%)	48,549	27,795	52,072	38,289	46,489
Employees	(15.9%)	6,000	3,300	3,300	3,300	3,000

SIMON WORLDWIDE INC.

NBB: SWWI

18952 MacArthur Boulevard
Irvine, CA 92612
Phone: 949 251-4660
Fax: -
Web: www.cyrk.com

CEO: -
CFO: -
HR: -
FYE: December 31
Type: Public

Here is a true business tragedy, a successful company brought low by the machinations of a lone employee. Simon Worldwide once offered an array of promotional marketing services, but the firm was dealt a severe blow in 2001 when a Simon employee rigged McDonald's Monopoly game promotion by hoarding winning game pieces. (The employee pleaded guilty to embezzlement.) McDonald's, a 25-year client that accounted for the bulk of Simon's sales, stopped doing business with the company, as did Simon's second-largest client, Philip Morris. The company then shut down its promotional marketing business to focus on resolving legal issues arising from the scandal; it has no operations.As it works to settle the remaining claims, contractual obligations, and litigation caused by the 2001 events, Simon is evaluating potential combinations with operating businesses. Since 2001 the company has reduced its workforce from 136 employees to fewer than five, and its auditors have questioned whether Simon will be able to stay in business.

	Annual Growth	12/10	12/11	12/12	12/13	12/14
Sales ($mil.)	-	-	-	-	-	-
Net income ($ mil.)	-	(2.3)	(2.0)	(1.5)	(3.6)	(7.0)
Market value ($ mil.)	(52.0%)	18.3	8.9	7.5	3.7	1.0
Employees			4	4	4	-

SIMPLY INC

NBB: SIMP Q

10801 NW 97th Street, Suite 09
Miami, FL 33178
Phone: 786 254-6709
Fax: -
Web: www.simplyinc.com

CEO: Reinier Voigt
CFO: -
HR: -
FYE: January 29
Type: Public

InfoSonics answers the call for phone fulfillment. The company distributes a wide variety of cell phone models and accessories from electronics manufacturers such as LG Electronics and Novatel Wireless. It supplies and supports retailers, wireless carriers, and distributors in South and Central America, India, and China from facilities centers in San Diego, Miami, and Beijing. InfoSonics' services include inspection, testing, programming, software loading, and light assembly. Its logistics business includes outsourced supply chain services, such as inventory management and customized packaging. InfoSonics also sells its own line of phones under the verykool brand.

	Annual Growth	12/18	12/19*	02/20*	01/21	01/22
Sales ($mil.)	48.5%	24.2	30.4	5.3	68.0	79.1
Net income ($ mil.)	-	(27.3)	(21.0)	(2.1)	4.3	(11.1)
Market value ($ mil.)	6.1%	25.0	1.0	0.8	54.1	29.9
Employees	25.5%	178	528	-	293	352

*Fiscal year change

SIMPSON MANUFACTURING CO., INC. (DE)

NYS: SSD

5956 W. Las Positas Blvd.
Pleasanton, CA 94588
Phone: 925 560-9000
Fax: 925 833-1496
Web: www.simpsonmfg.com

CEO: Michael Olosky
CFO: Brian J Magstadt
HR: -
FYE: December 31
Type: Public

Through its subsidiaries, Simpson Manufacturing including, Simpson Strong-Tie Company Inc. (SST), designs, engineers, and is a leading manufacturer of high quality wood and concrete building construction products designed to make structures safer and more secure, and that perform at high levels. Its concrete construction products are used in concrete, masonry and steel construction and include adhesives, chemicals, mechanical anchors, carbide drill bits, powder actuated tools, fiber reinforced materials and other repair products used for protection and strengthening. The company's products are sold primarily in Canada, Europe, the US, and Pacific Rim. About 75% of sales were generated from the US.

	Annual Growth	12/19	12/20	12/21	12/22	12/23
Sales ($mil.)	18.1%	1,136.5	1,267.9	1,573.2	2,116.1	2,213.8
Net income ($ mil.)	27.5%	134.0	187.0	266.4	334.0	354.0
Market value ($ mil.)	25.3%	3,395.5	3,955.0	5,885.7	3,752.3	8,378.9
Employees	13.3%	3,337	3,562	3,971	5,158	5,497

SIMPSON THACHER & BARTLETT LLP

425 LEXINGTON AVE
NEW YORK, NY 100173903
Phone: 212 455-2000
Fax: -
Web: www.stblaw.com

CEO: -
CFO: Adrienne E Boa
HR: -
FYE: December 31
Type: Private

Simpson Thacher & Bartlett's specialties include litigation, and it has built a substantial mergers and acquisitions practice over the years. Other practice areas include capital markets, government and internal investigations, intellectual property, real estate, and tax. Simpson Thacher's more than 1,000 lawyers practice from around eleven offices in the US and from international offices in Beijing, Hong Kong, London, Tokyo, and S o Paulo. Simpson Thacher was founded in 1884.

SIMTROL INC

NBB: SMRL

520 Guthridge Ct., Suite 250
Norcross, GA 30092
Phone: 770 242-7566
Fax: -
Web: www.simtrol.com

CEO: -
CFO: -
HR: -
FYE: December 31
Type: Public

Lights! Camera! Simtrol! The company's Device Manager software lets users control lighting equipment, sound systems, projectors, computers, temperature controls, VCRs, and other electronic gear with a PC. Simtrol's software provides device management and monitoring capabilities through a Web browser. It also offers a document management and videoconferencing system (Arraigner) designed to make it unnecessary to transport prisoners to courtrooms for arraignment. Simtrol sells its products through resellers, distributors, and systems integrators.

	Annual Growth	12/05	12/06	12/07	12/08	12/09
Sales ($mil.)	47.5%	0.1	0.2	0.2	0.3	0.6
Net income ($ mil.)	-	(1.4)	(1.5)	(4.9)	(4.9)	(2.7)
Market value ($ mil.)	-	27.5	27.5	27.5	27.5	27.5
Employees	(2.2%)	12	9	19	20	11

SIMULATIONS PLUS INC

NMS: SLP

42505 Tenth Street West
Lancaster, CA 93534-7059
Phone: 661 723-7723
Fax: 661 723-5524
Web: www.simulations-plus.com

CEO: -
CFO: -
HR: -
FYE: August 31
Type: Public

Molecular modeling software plus applications to help individuals with disabilities equals Simulations Plus. The company is a leading provider of applications used by pharmaceutical researchers to model absorption rates for orally dosed drug compounds. Its Words+ subsidiary provides augmentative communication software and input devices that help people with disabilities use computers. Simulations Plus also provides educational software targeted to high school and college students through its FutureLab unit. Pharmaceutical giants GlaxoSmithKline and Roche are among its clients. CEO Walter Woltosz and his wife, Virginia (a director), together own about 40% of the company.

	Annual Growth	08/19	08/20	08/21	08/22	08/23
Sales ($mil.)	15.1%	34.0	41.6	46.5	53.9	59.6
Net income ($ mil.)	3.8%	8.6	9.3	9.8	12.5	10.0
Market value ($ mil.)	5.4%	720.0	1,187.9	883.3	1,197.3	887.0
Employees	15.4%	111	137	146	163	197

SINAI HEALTH SYSTEM

1500 S FAIRFIELD AVE
CHICAGO, IL 606081782
Phone: 773 542-2000
Fax: –
Web: www.sinaichicago.org

CEO: –
CFO: Charles Weiss
HR: Jason Spigner
FYE: June 30
Type: Private

You don't have to scale any mountains to reach this Sinai. Sinai Health System provides medical care for the residents of West Side of Chicago. The system is comprised of its flagship Mount Sinai Hospital, Holy Cross Hospital, Schwab Rehabilitation Hospital, and the Sinai Children's Hospital. The health system's Sinai Medical Group provides primary and specialty care through a range of clinics in the area. The Sinai Community Institute offers health, wellness, and educational programs for all ages, and the Sinai Urban Health Institute conducts research and disease outreach programs. Altogether, the system has some 700 inpatient beds and 800 physicians.

	Annual Growth	06/03	06/04	06/05	06/06	06/08
Sales ($mil.)	(77.4%)	–	–	1,764.4	15.3	20.3
Net income ($ mil.)	–	–	–	0.0	–	–
Market value ($ mil.)	–	–	–	–	–	–
Employees	–	–	–	–	–	6,000

SINAI HOSPITAL OF BALTIMORE, INC.

2401 W BELVEDERE AVE
BALTIMORE, MD 212155270
Phone: 410 601-5678
Fax: –
Web: www.lifebridgehealth.org

CEO: Neil Meltzer
CFO: –
HR: –
FYE: June 30
Type: Private

Sinai Hospital of Baltimore, part of the LifeBridge Health network, provides medical care in northwestern Baltimore. The 470-bed hospital is a not-for-profit medical center that includes such facilities as a heart center, a children's hospital, a cancer institute, and a rehab center. Other specialties include orthopedics, neurology, and women's care. Medical students from Johns Hopkins University and the University of Maryland do some of their training at the hospital. Sinai Hospital of Baltimore was founded in 1866 as the Hebrew Hospital and Asylum and became a subsidiary of LifeBridge when it merged with other area providers in 1998.

	Annual Growth	06/18	06/19	06/20	06/21	06/22
Sales ($mil.)	7.7%	–	803.9	853.4	936.8	1,004.5
Net income ($ mil.)	30.6%	–	41.2	59.8	82.1	91.7
Market value ($ mil.)	–	–	–	–	–	–
Employees	–	–	–	–	–	4,497

SINCLAIR INC

NMS: SBGI

10706 Beaver Dam Road
Hunt Valley, MD 21030
Phone: 410 568-1500
Fax: 410 568-1533
Web: www.sbgi.net

CEO: Christopher S Ripley
CFO: Lucy A Rutishauser
HR: Dena Bedri
FYE: December 31
Type: Public

Sinclair Broadcast Group is the largest operator of local TV stations in the US with around 185 TV stations broadcasting and more than 635 channels. The company serves more than 85 markets throughout the US and has a national reach of approximately 40% of the country. Its portfolio includes affiliates of all the major broadcast networks (FOX, ABC, CBS, and NBC) as well as The CW Network and MyNetworkTV. Other assets include science fiction network Comet, action network CHARGE!, the Tennis Channel, and Marquee Sports, a joint venture with the Chicago Cubs that is the exclusive broadcaster of Cubs games. The family of founder Julian Sinclair Smith controls the company.

	Annual Growth	12/19	12/20	12/21	12/22	12/23
Sales ($mil.)	(7.3%)	4,240.0	5,943.0	6,134.0	3,928.0	3,134.0
Net income ($ mil.)	–	47.0	(2,414.0)	(414.0)	2,652.0	(291.0)
Market value ($ mil.)	(20.9%)	2,117.5	2,022.9	1,678.6	985.1	827.6
Employees	(11.3%)	11,800	11,600	11,500	7,900	7,300

SINCLAIR TELEVISION OF CAPITAL DISTRICT, INC.

1000 WILSON BLVD STE 2700
ARLINGTON, VA 222093921
Phone: 703 647-8700
Fax: –
Web: www.allbritton.com

CEO: Robert L Allbritton
CFO: Stephen P Gibson
HR: –
FYE: September 30
Type: Private

Allbritton Communications knows the ABC's of television broadcasting. The company is a leading TV station operator and a top affiliate of Walt Disney's ABC broadcast network. Primarily broadcasting in the Washington, DC market (through its WJLA station), it has a portfolio of about 10 stations that serve markets in Alabama, Arkansas, Oklahoma, Pennsylvania, South Carolina, and Virginia. The company also owns and operates a 24-hour cable news channel (NewsChannel 8) that serves the nation's capitol, and it is affiliated with Politico.com, a site offering political news and opinions. Founded in 1975 by Joe Allbritton, the company is owned by Perpetual Corporation, an entity owned by the Allbritton family.

SINGING MACHINE CO., INC.

NBB: SMDM D

6301 N.W. 5th Way, Suite 2900
Fort Lauderdale, FL 33309
Phone: 954 596-1000
Fax: –
Web: www.singingmachine.com

CEO: Gary Atkinson
CFO: Lionel Marquis
HR: –
FYE: March 31
Type: Public

The Singing Machine Company strives to give everyone their 15 minutes of fame. It sells more than 50 different models of karaoke audio equipment, from basic players to semi-professional machines. The karaoke machines, primarily made in China, are sold through electronics retailers and mass merchants, such as Best Buy, Costco, and RadioShack. About a third of its sales come from outside the US. The Singing Machine Company also produces CDs and audio tapes for use in its karaoke equipment and offers a catalog of more than 2,500 songs. To clear its books of liabilities, The Singing Machine Company sold its Hong Kong unit in late 2006 and consolidated its Hong Kong office into Starlight International Holdings Ltd.

	Annual Growth	03/19	03/20	03/21	03/22	03/23
Sales ($mil.)	(4.1%)	46.5	41.4	45.8	47.5	39.3
Net income ($ mil.)	–	0.6	(2.9)	2.2	0.2	(4.6)
Market value ($ mil.)	–	–	–	–	–	4.9
Employees	0.7%	36	32	33	32	37

SINGULARITY FUTURE TECHNOLOGY LTD

NAS: SGLY

98 Cutter Mill Road, Suite 322
Great Neck, NY 11021
Phone: 718 888-1814
Fax: –
Web: www.singularity.us

CEO: Ziyuan Liu
CFO: Ying Cao
HR: –
FYE: June 30
Type: Public

Sino-Global Shipping America assists foreign companies in navigating the murky regulatory waters of China's marine shipping industry. Through subsidiaries Trans Pacific and Sino-China, the company is a shipping agent for US, Australian, and Hong Kong companies transporting iron ore to China. (Currently, freight forwarding company Beijing Shou Rong is Sino-Global's largest customer, representing more than half of the company's revenues.) Trans Pacific has operations at six ports in China; however, each of the country's 76 ports have different rules. CEO Cao Lei owns more than 70% of Sino-Global Shipping America and Sino-China. Sino-Global Shipping America was founded in 2001.

	Annual Growth	06/19	06/20	06/21	06/22	06/23
Sales ($mil.)	(42.6%)	41.8	6.5	5.2	4.0	4.5
Net income ($ mil.)	–	(6.5)	(16.5)	(6.8)	(28.3)	(23.0)
Market value ($ mil.)	(8.7%)	1.3	1.1	5.7	5.4	0.9
Employees	0.9%	27	20	43	39	28

SINTX TECHNOLOGIES INC   NAS: SINT
1885 West 2100 South   CEO: –
Salt Lake City, UT 84119   CFO: –
Phone: 801 839-3500   HR: –
Fax: –   FYE: December 31
Web: www.sintx.com   Type: Public

You can spin a disc, or burn a disc, but when you blow a disc (in your back) the fun stops, and Amedica steps in. It develops, manufactures, and commercializes joint and spine implants made of silicon nitride ceramic, a more durable, resistant, and patient-compatible alternative to traditional implant materials. Amedica's lead product candidates are its Valeo spinal implants which are intended to restore and maintain vertebrae alignment in the neck and lower back. Valeo spinal spacer implants have received FDA and EU approval for use as vertebra replacements. Amedica's other candidates include ceramic hip and knee implants with material that mimic the porous structure of natural bone. It went public in 2014.

	Annual Growth	12/18	12/19	12/20	12/21	12/22
Sales ($mil.)	101.3%	0.0	0.7	0.6	0.6	1.6
Net income ($ mil.)	–	(8.7)	(4.8)	(7.0)	(8.8)	(12.0)
Market value ($ mil.)	170.8%	0.0	0.8	0.9	0.3	5.2
Employees	21.2%	19	28	32	36	41

SIR SPEEDY, INC.
26722 PLAZA   CEO: Don Lowe
MISSION VIEJO, CA 926916390   CFO: Dan Conger
Phone: 949 348-5000   HR: Justine Lewis
Fax: –   FYE: December 31
Web: www.sirspeedy.com   Type: Private

Gallant knights of printing, Sir Speedy rounds your table with more than 800 franchise locations in more than 15 countries, including more than 400 Sir Speedy franchises in about 40 US states and the District of Columbia. The shops offer printing, copying, mailing, graphic design, and finishing (collating, assembly, binding) services, primarily to corporate and business clients. Its MyDocs document management system allows customers to place and update orders, track progress, review proofs, and manage costs online. Founded in 1968, Sir Speedy is a subsidiary of holding company Franchise Services.

	Annual Growth	12/14	12/15	12/17	12/18	12/19
Assets ($mil.)	(0.1%)	–	7.4	7.1	7.6	7.3
Net income ($ mil.)	13.9%	–	1.5	1.8	2.0	2.6
Market value ($ mil.)	–	–	–	–	–	–
Employees	–	–	–	–	–	60

SIRIUS FEDERAL, LLC
2151 PRIEST BRIDGE DR STE 7   CEO: Mike Greaney
CROFTON, MD 211142451   CFO: Steve Scribner
Phone: 301 261-0204   HR: Tina Werner
Fax: –   FYE: December 31
Web: www.cdwg.com   Type: Private

Sirius Federal (formerly Force 3) provides technology solutions for the nation's most critical infrastructure. As the federal government continues to push for IT modernization, agencies continue to push for mission success without compromising productivity, security, and control of current workloads in a way that is feasible and cost effective. In an ever-changing IT landscape, Sirius Federal offers a comprehensive range of solutions backed by an expert team of engineers and the highest levels of partnership with leading manufacturers. From design to deployment, support, and maintenance, its technology solutions and services are designed with a constant focus on supporting its clients' missions.

	Annual Growth	12/05	12/06	12/07	12/08	12/09
Sales ($mil.)	(5.6%)	–	–	288.8	325.5	257.2
Net income ($ mil.)	52.8%	–	–	3.0	5.7	7.0
Market value ($ mil.)	–	–	–	–	–	–
Employees	–	–	–	–	–	175

SIRIUS XM HOLDINGS INC   NMS: SIRI
1221 Avenue of the Americas, 35th Floor   CEO: –
New York, NY 10020   CFO: –
Phone: 212 584-5100   HR: –
Fax: –   FYE: December 31
Web: www.siriusxm.com   Type: Public

Sirius XM Holdings is the leading audio entertainment company in North America with a portfolio of audio businesses including its flagship subscription entertainment service, Sirius XM; the ad-supported and premium music streaming services of Pandora; a podcast network; an advertising sales group, SXM Media; and a suite of advertising technology solutions. SiriusXM's platforms collectively reach more than 150 million listeners across all categories of digital audio ? music, sports, talk, and podcasts ? the largest reach of any digital audio provider in North America. SiriusXM, through Sirius XM Canada Holdings, Inc., also offers satellite radio and audio entertainment in Canada. In addition to its audio entertainment businesses, SiriusXM offers connected vehicle services to automakers through SiriusXM Connected Vehicle Services. SiriusXM is also a minority investor in SoundCloud, the world's largest open audio platform.

	Annual Growth	12/19	12/20	12/21	12/22	12/23
Sales ($mil.)	3.5%	7,794.0	8,040.0	8,696.0	9,003.0	8,953.0
Net income ($ mil.)	8.3%	914.0	131.0	1,314.0	1,213.0	1,258.0
Market value ($ mil.)	(6.5%)	27,477	24,480	24,403	22,443	21,021
Employees	5.8%	4,534	5,726	5,590	5,869	5,680

SIRVA INC
700 Oakmont Lane   CEO: Tom Oberdorf
Westmont, IL 60559   CFO: Douglas V Gathany V
Phone: 630 570-3000   HR: –
Fax: –   FYE: December 31
Web: www.sirva.com   Type: Public

SIRVA is the global leader in moving and relocation services, offering solutions for mobility programs to companies of every size. With more than 75 SIRVA locations and about 800 franchised and agent locations in about 190 countries, the company offers unmatched global breadth supported by localized attention and innovative technology that strikes the right balance of self-service and human support. From relocation to household goods and commercial moving and storage, its portfolio of brands (SIRVA, Allied, northAmerican, SMARTBOX, SIRVA Mortgage, and Alliance) provides the only integrated moving/relocation solution in the industry. Its technologies are globally consistent to ensure comprehensive end-to-end program management and reporting.

	Annual Growth	12/03	12/04	12/05	12/06	12/07
Sales ($mil.)	14.0%	2,349.9	3,470.3	3,681.2	3,865.3	3,969.9
Net income ($ mil.)	–	19.0	(68.2)	(265.4)	(54.6)	(412.7)
Market value ($ mil.)	–	–	–	–	–	7.6
Employees	(16.4%)	7,772	7,580	5,930	4,630	3,800

SISTERS OF CHARITY OF LEAVENWORTH HEALTH SYSTEM, INC.
500 ELDORADO BLVD STE 6300   CEO: –
BROOMFIELD, CO 800213408   CFO: –
Phone: 303 813-5000   HR: –
Fax: –   FYE: December 31
Web: www.sclhealth.org   Type: Private

SCL Health is a faith-based, nonprofit healthcare organization dedicated to improving the health of the people and communities it serves, especially those who are poor and vulnerable. Founded by the Sisters of Charity of Leavenworth in 1864, its $2.8 billion health network provides comprehensive, coordinated care through eight hospitals, more than 150 physician clinics, and home health, hospice, mental health and safety-net services primarily in Colorado and Montana.

	Annual Growth	12/18	12/19	12/20	12/21	12/22
Sales ($mil.)	(32.9%)	–	2,844.8	2,880.1	3,159.4	861.2
Net income ($ mil.)	–	–	390.0	402.0	278.1	(73.4)
Market value ($ mil.)	–	–	–	–	–	–
Employees	–	–	–	–	–	15,046

SITE CENTERS CORP
NYS: SITC

3300 Enterprise Parkway
Beachwood, OH 44122
Phone: 216 755-5500
Fax: 216 755-1500
Web: www.sitecenters.com

CEO: David R Lukes
CFO: Matthew L Ostrower
HR: –
FYE: December 31
Type: Public

SITE Centers Corp is a self-administered and self-manages real estate investment trust (REIT) that acquires, develops, renovates, leases, and manages shopping centers. Its portfolio includes some 135 shopping centers (including more than 45 centers owned through joint ventures) in more than 20 US states. Altogether, SITE Center owns approximately 42.2 million total square feet of gross leasable area. SITE Centers' largest tenants include Bed Bath & Beyond, PetSmart, TJX, Michaels Companies and Dick's Sporting.

	Annual Growth	12/19	12/20	12/21	12/22	12/23
Sales ($mil.)	1.8%	508.0	460.3	532.9	552.4	546.3
Net income ($ mil.)	27.5%	100.7	35.7	124.9	168.7	265.7
Market value ($ mil.)	(0.7%)	2,930.6	2,115.4	3,309.0	2,855.4	2,849.1
Employees	(11.6%)	361	323	293	267	220

SITEONE LANDSCAPE SUPPLY INC
NYS: SITE

300 Colonial Center Parkway, Suite 600
Roswell, GA 30076
Phone: 470 277-7000
Fax: –
Web: www.siteone.com

CEO: Doug Black
CFO: John T Guthrie
HR: –
FYE: December 31
Type: Public

SiteOne Landscape Supply (SiteOne) is the largest and sole national wholesale distributor of landscape supplies in the US and has a growing presence in Canada. With a comprehensive selection of more than 155,000 stock-keeping units (SKUs), it sells irrigation supplies, nursery products, ice melt products, fertilizer, o lighting, and hardscape materials (pavers, stones, and blocks). SiteOne operates through more than 630 locations in about 45 states and six Canadian provinces. Its customers include commercial and residential landscaping professionals and businesses, as well as golf courses. In addition to its broad product portfolio, convenient branch locations, and a nationwide fleet of more than 2,200 delivery vehicles, the company sources its products from approximately 5,000 suppliers. All of the company's revenue comes from the US operations.

	Annual Growth	12/19*	01/21	01/22	01/23*	12/23
Sales ($mil.)	16.2%	2,357.5	2,704.5	3,475.7	4,014.5	4,301.2
Net income ($ mil.)	22.2%	77.7	121.3	238.4	245.4	173.4
Market value ($ mil.)	15.8%	4,078.1	7,151.4	10,922	5,289.0	7,325.8
Employees	14.1%	4,600	4,900	5,700	7,000	7,800

*Fiscal year change

SIX FLAGS ENTERTAINMENT CORP
NYS: SIX

1000 Ballpark Way, Suite 400
Arlington, TX 76011
Phone: 972 595-5000
Fax: –
Web: www.sixflags.com

CEO: Selim Bassoul
CFO: Gary Mick
HR: –
FYE: December 31
Type: Public

Six Flags are the largest regional theme park operator in the world and the largest operator of water parks in North America based on the number of parks the company operate. Of its over 25 regional theme parks and water parks, almost all are in the US, two are in Mexico, and one is in Canada. Its diversified portfolio of North American parks serves an aggregate population of approximately 145 million people visitors. Most parks operate under the Six Flags banner (including Six Flags Fiesta Texas and Six Flags Magic Mountain) offering state-of-the-art and traditional thrill rides, water attractions, themed areas, concerts and shows, restaurants, game venues and retail outlets. Six Flags licenses characters from Warner Bros. and DC Entertainment such as Looney Tunes and Batman.

	Annual Growth	12/19	12/20*	01/22	01/23*	12/23
Sales ($mil.)	(1.1%)	1,487.6	356.6	1,496.9	1,358.2	1,425.9
Net income ($ mil.)	(31.7%)	179.1	(423.4)	129.9	108.9	39.0
Market value ($ mil.)	(13.6%)	3,794.8	2,868.6	3,582.0	1,955.9	2,109.8
Employees	(59.6%)	50,450	30,950	44,970	41,450	1,350

*Fiscal year change

SIZMEK INC.

2500 BEE CAVES RD STE 1
AUSTIN, TX 787465888
Phone: 512 469-5900
Fax: –
Web: www.sizmek.com

CEO: –
CFO: –
HR: –
FYE: December 31
Type: Private

Sizmek lets advertisers truly size up the impact of their messages. The company's multiscreen services offer agencies and advertisers a variety of solutions to navigate the complexities of cross-platform advertising. Sizmek provides advertisers with start-to-finish creative services, ad delivery, marketing campaign management, and accurate analytics across various channels such as mobile, rich media, video, social, and search. It works to optimize an ad in the first place, optimize the context in which an ad appears, and build out an effective creative message. The goal for all Sizmek ads is for the right audience to see the ad at exactly the right time and place. The company was acquired by affiliates of Vector Capital in late 2016. In 2019 Sizmek filed for Chapter 11 bankruptcy.

SJW GROUP
NYS: SJW

110 West Taylor Street
San Jose, CA 95110
Phone: 408 279-7800
Fax: –
Web: www.sjwgroup.com

CEO: Eric W Thornburg
CFO: James P Lynch
HR: –
FYE: December 31
Type: Public

It is hard to water down SJW Group's contribution in quenching America's thirst. A holding company, it owns public utility services that engage in the production, storage, purification, distribution, and retail sale of water. Its two main subsidiaries, the San Jose Water Company and Canyon Lake Water Service Company (CLWSC), serves nearly 1.5 million residents in California and Texas through nearly 250,000 water connections. The SJW Land Company is a holder of some undeveloped land in Tennessee. In October 2019, the SJW Group announced the close of their merger with the public utility Connecticut Water Service.

	Annual Growth	12/19	12/20	12/21	12/22	12/23
Sales ($mil.)	12.4%	420.5	564.5	573.7	620.7	670.4
Net income ($ mil.)	38.0%	23.4	61.5	60.5	73.8	85.0
Market value ($ mil.)	(2.1%)	2,275.6	2,221.1	2,344.1	2,599.9	2,092.7
Employees	2.5%	732	748	751	757	808

SKADDEN, ARPS, SLATE, MEAGHER & FLOM LLP

ONE MANHATTAN WEST 395 9TH AVE STE 28
NEW YORK, NY 100018600
Phone: 212 735-3000
Fax: –
Web: www.skadden.com

CEO: –
CFO: Kristen Kennedy
HR: Herbert Weldon
FYE: December 31
Type: Private

Skadden, Arps, Slate, Meagher & Flom provides legal services to the business, financial and governmental communities around the world in a wide range of high-profile transactions, regulatory matters, and litigation and controversy issues. A major US law firm and one of the largest in the world, Skadden, Arps, Slate, Meagher & Flom employs over 1,700 attorneys in more than 50 different practice areas. It operates about 20 offices around the globe. The firm's clients range from a variety of small, entrepreneurial companies to a substantial number of the 500 largest US corporations and many of the leading global companies.. Skadden, Arps, Slate, Meagher & Flom was founded in 1948.

SKANSKA USA BUILDING INC.

389 INTERPACE PKWY STE 5
PARSIPPANY, NJ 070541132
Phone: 973 753-3500
Fax: –
Web: usa.skanska.com

CEO: Paul Hewins
CFO: Leo Sinicin
HR: Jamie Diamante
FYE: December 31
Type: Private

One of a handful of US-based units of the Swedish construction giant Skanska AB, Skanska USA Building is one of the largest, most financially sound construction and development companies, with expertise in construction, civil infrastructure, public-private partnerships and commercial development initiatives in select US markets. The company is an industry-leading innovator in both safety and project execution, and offers competitive solutions for both traditional and complex assignments to help build a more sustainable future for its customers and communities. Its client base have included transportation, sports, power, industrial, water/wastewater, education, and health care projects, among others. Headquartered in New York, it has some 30 offices in nearly 30 cities in the US which represents Skanska's single largest market. Skanska AB entered the US in 1971.

SKANSKA USA CIVIL INC.

7520 ASTORIA BLVD STE 200
EAST ELMHURST, NY 113701135
Phone: 718 340-0777
Fax: –
Web: usa.skanska.com

CEO: Salvatore Mancini
CFO: –
HR: Patricia Palmer
FYE: December 31
Type: Private

Skanska USA Civil builds some of the world's largest cable-stayed bridges. Part of the US operations of Swedish engineering and construction giant Skanska, Skanska USA Civil focuses on infrastructure projects throughout the country. Along with sister firm Skanska USA Building, it is a market leader in the New York area, where it has worked on the Brooklyn Bridge, the AirTrain light-rail system, and the Roosevelt Island Bridge. It builds roads, tunnels, and rail systems, in addition to bridges and industrial and marine facilities, such as power and water filtration plants, gas-treatment plants, and dry docks.

	Annual Growth	12/04	12/05	12/06	12/07	12/08
Sales ($mil.)	8.8%	–	–	–	1,611.5	1,753.5
Net income ($ mil.)	5.2%	–	–	–	52.0	54.7
Market value ($ mil.)	–	–	–	–	–	–
Employees	–	–	–	–	–	5,200

SKECHERS USA INC

228 Manhattan Beach Blvd.
Manhattan Beach, CA 90266
Phone: 310 318-3100
Fax: –
Web: www.skechers.com

NYS: SKX
CEO: Robert Greenberg
CFO: John Vandemore
HR: –
FYE: December 31
Type: Public

Skechers USA designs and sells Skechers-branded lifestyle and athletic footwear for men, women, and children. Its products include casual, casual athletic, sport athletic, trail, sandals, boots, and fashion, and also include the well-known Skechers Uno, Skechers Arch Fit, Skechers Hands Free Slip-ins. In addition to many versions of its namesake brand (Skechers Sport, Skechers Performance, BOBS from Skechers, Skechers Kids), the company offers trademarks to be among its most valuable assets including Mark Nason, Max Cushioning, Massage Fit, and D'Lites. Its shoes are sold through roughly 3,095 distributor, licensee and franchise stores in more than 180 countries, as well as outlet stores, wholesale customers, and ecommerce businesses. Skechers generates about 50% its sales from the Americas.

	Annual Growth	12/19	12/20	12/21	12/22	12/23
Sales ($mil.)	11.1%	5,242.5	4,613.4	6,310.2	7,444.6	8,000.3
Net income ($ mil.)	12.0%	346.6	98.6	741.5	373.0	545.8
Market value ($ mil.)	9.6%	6,608.9	5,499.5	6,641.0	6,419.1	9,539.2
Employees	–	–	13,100	11,700	11,700	15,100

SKF USA INC.

890 FORTY FOOT RD
LANSDALE, PA 194464303
Phone: 267 436-6000
Fax: –
Web: www.skf.com

CEO: –
CFO: Drew Cross
HR: Kristina Sarlvik
FYE: December 31
Type: Private

SKF USA is a subsidiary of Swedish ball bearing giant AB SKF and a world leader in rolling bearings and related technologies including sealing solutions, lubrication systems and services. It also specializes in related services, from repair and rebuilding to asset management services. With manufacturing, sales, and authorized distribution locations across the US, SKF USA's offerings are geared at a wide range of industries, including aerospace, automotive, construction, machine tooling, and alternative energy. Brand names include Alemite, Cooper, Kaydon, Lincoln, and Mityvac.

	Annual Growth	12/10	12/11	12/12	12/13	12/14
Sales ($mil.)	14.4%	–	–	2,397.8	2,554.4	3,138.7
Net income ($ mil.)	6.0%	–	–	138.7	95.6	155.9
Market value ($ mil.)	–	–	–	–	–	–
Employees	–	–	–	–	–	4,000

SKIDMORE COLLEGE

815 N BROADWAY
SARATOGA SPRINGS, NY 128661698
Phone: 518 580-5000
Fax: –
Web: www.skidmore.edu

CEO: –
CFO: –
HR: Anita Miczek
FYE: May 31
Type: Private

Skidmore College offers more than 40 degree programs, including majors in both traditional liberal arts disciplines and pre-professional areas. The private college grants bachelor's and master's degrees in the sciences, humanities, social sciences, business, education, social work, and the arts. Skidmore enrolls about 2,400 students from the US and some 40 other countries and boasts a student-faculty ratio of about 9 to 1. It was founded by Lucy Skidmore Scribner in 1903 as the Young Women's Industrial Club of Saratoga.

	Annual Growth	05/17	05/18	05/19	05/20	05/22
Sales ($mil.)	16.1%	–	–	171.7	241.5	268.7
Net income ($ mil.)	55.5%	–	–	10.5	27.0	39.5
Market value ($ mil.)	–	–	–	–	–	–
Employees	–	–	–	–	–	720

SKIDMORE, OWINGS & MERRILL LLP

224 S MICHIGAN AVE # 1000
CHICAGO, IL 606042501
Phone: 312 554-9090
Fax: –
Web: www.som.com

CEO: –
CFO: –
HR: –
FYE: August 31
Type: Private

Skidmore Owings & Merrill prefers a skyline view. One of the world's largest architectural and engineering firms, Skidmore Owings & Merrill (or SOM) has earned its fame with innovative modernist designs and such high-profile projects as the John Hancock Building and Willis Tower (formerly the Sears Tower). Its services include graphics, interior design, and urban design and planning. Transportation planning, infrastructure planning, environmental engineering, and geotechnical engineering are part of its structural and civil engineering offerings. The firm, which has completed more than 10,000 projects in more than 50 countries, has offices in several major metropolitan US cities and in Europe and Asia.

	Annual Growth	08/06	08/07	08/08	08/09	08/22
Sales ($mil.)	3.9%	–	–	–	0.1	0.2
Net income ($ mil.)	–	–	–	–	(0.0)	(0.0)
Market value ($ mil.)	–	–	–	–	–	–
Employees	–	–	–	–	–	724

SKILLSOFT (US) LLC

300 INNOVATIVE WAY STE 201
NASHUA, NH 030625746
Phone: 603 324-3000
Fax: –
Web: www.skillsoft.com

CEO: –
CFO: –
HR: –
FYE: January 31
Type: Private

Skillsoft is a global leader in corporate digital learning, serving more than 75% of the Fortune 1000, customers in over 160 countries, and a community of learners of more than 90 million globally. Skillsoft's primary learning solutions include Percipio, an intelligent and immersive digital learning platform; Global Knowledge, a global provider of authorized information technology & development training and professional skills; Codecademy, an online learning platform for technical skills that uses an innovative, scalable approach to online coding education; Pluma, which offers individualized coaching through a digital platform that provides executive-quality coaching that is personal yet scalable; and SumTotal, a SaaS-based Human Capital Management (HCM) solution with a leading Talent Development platform. About 65% of Skillsoft's revenue comes from the US.

	Annual Growth	01/05	01/06	01/07	01/08	01/09
Sales ($mil.)	20.8%	–	–	225.2	281.2	328.5
Net income ($ mil.)	45.0%	–	–	24.2	60.0	50.8
Market value ($ mil.)	–	–	–	–	–	–
Employees	–	–	–	–	–	2,133

SKINVISIBLE INC

NBB: SKVI

6320 South Sandhill Road, Suite 10
Las Vegas, NV 89120
Phone: 702 433-7154
Fax: –
Web: –

CEO: Terry H Howlett
CFO: Terry H Howlett
HR: –
FYE: December 31
Type: Public

Skinvisible keeps invisible substances like lotion and sunscreen from washing off your skin. The company develops topical drug delivery systems for dermatology and healthcare products including products to treat acne, eczema, fungal infections, and inflammation, as well as sunscreens, anti-aging products, pre-surgical preparations, and various other medical treatments using its Invisicare technology. Licensing its delivery technology is the goal of the firm; its clients include dermatological and other drugmakers, cosmetics companies, and manufacturers of personal care items in Asia, Europe, and the US. Licensees include DRJ Group, J.D. Nelson & Associates, and Embil Pharmaceutical.

	Annual Growth	12/18	12/19	12/20	12/21	12/22
Sales ($mil.)	41.7%	0.0	0.0	0.0	0.7	0.3
Net income ($ mil.)	–	0.2	(1.7)	(1.4)	(1.1)	(1.2)
Market value ($ mil.)	63.9%	0.0	0.4	0.3	1.1	0.5
Employees	(15.9%)	4	3	2	2	2

SKLAR CORP.

889 South Matlack Street
West Chester, PA 19382
Phone: 610 430-3200
Fax: –
Web: –

CEO: –
CFO: –
HR: –
FYE: March 31
Type: Public

If you're going under the knife anytime soon, you might find yourself operated on with some of the products sold by Sklar. The company distributes more than 19,000 handheld surgical and medical instruments, as well as dental and veterinary instruments, to clients around the globe. Sklar also provides hospitals, clinics, and physicians with instrument care and cleaning products, sterilizing kits, and medical sponges. Its instruments and equipment are used in such fields as cardiology, dermatology, obstetrics/gynecology, dentistry, and orthopedics. Sklar Corporation, doing business as Sklar Instruments, traces its roots back to 1892.

	Annual Growth	03/97	03/98	03/99	03/00	03/01
Sales ($mil.)	(3.4%)	14.3	13.8	13.2	12.8	12.5
Net income ($ mil.)	–	0.2	0.3	0.3	0.3	(0.0)
Market value ($ mil.)	–	–	–	–	–	–
Employees	4.5%	63	60	70	75	75

SKULLCANDY, INC.

6301 N LANDMARK DR
PARK CITY, UT 840986439
Phone: 435 940-1545
Fax: –
Web: www.skullcandy.com

CEO: Brian Garofalow
CFO: –
HR: Christianna Donnell
FYE: December 31
Type: Private

Skullcandy is the original lifestyle audio brand and the #1 selling brand in stereo headphones and true wireless earbuds under $100. It was born on a chairlift in Park City, Utah by Rick Alden, and started a company that would not only make a better headphone but also make a snowboarding lifestyle. The company produces earbuds including true wireless brands such as Dime, Rail ANC, Grind Fuel, Sesh ANC True, Jib True 2, and Ink'd+ earbuds with microphone; wireless headphones under such brands as Crushers Evo Sensory Bass Headphones, Riff Wireless 2 On-Ear Headphones, Burton Crusher Evo sensory bass headphones, and Hesh Evo Wireless Headphones, among others; and accessories such as Fat Stash 2 Wireless Battery Pack, Line+ cable, Plyr transmitter, and Fuelbase Max 2.

SKYLINE CHAMPION CORP

NYS: SKY

755 West Big Beaver Road, Suite 1000
Troy, MI 48084
Phone: 248 614-8211
Fax: –
Web: www.skylinechampion.com

CEO: Mark Yost
CFO: Laurie Hough
HR: –
FYE: April 1
Type: Public

Skyline's idea of a beautiful skyline would probably include several rows of double-wides. The company and its subsidiaries design and make manufactured homes. It distributes them to independent dealers and manufactured housing communities throughout the US and Canada. About half of Skyline's revenues come from selling HUD-code manufactured homes (products built according to US Housing and Urban Development standards); the rest of its typically two- to four-bedroom homes are modular in design.

	Annual Growth	03/19	03/20*	04/21	04/22	04/23
Sales ($mil.)	17.7%	1,360.0	1,369.7	1,420.9	2,207.2	2,606.6
Net income ($ mil.)	–	(58.2)	58.2	84.9	248.0	401.8
Market value ($ mil.)	41.1%	1,085.1	880.6	2,708.1	3,171.2	4,296.2
Employees	2.4%	7,000	6,600	7,700	8,400	7,700

*Fiscal year change

SKYLINE MULTIMEDIA ENTERTAINMENT INC

350 Fifth Avenue
New York, NY 10118
Phone: 212 564-2224
Fax: 212 564-0652
Web: –

CEO: Fredrick Schulman
CFO: Michael Leeb
HR: –
FYE: June 30
Type: Public

Skyline Multimedia Entertainment operates the NY SKYRIDE, a simulated "aerial tour" of New York City, located on the second floor of one of the city's most popular tourist sites, the Empire State Building. The flight simulator ride includes a 12-minute bird's-eye view of landmarks and sites through the city's skyline, including a "ride" on the Coney Island Cyclone, a sweep over the Statue of Liberty, and an experience with New York City traffic in Times Square. The attraction is open all year, including holidays, and generates revenue from ticket sales and the sale of souvenirs and concessions. NY SKYRIDE began operations in 1994.The company was hit hard by the September 11, 2001, terrorist attacks on New York City which caused revenue to plummet. The company compensated through increased sponsorship and advertising deals, and its ticket sales have returned to pre-September 11 levels.

	Annual Growth	06/00	06/01	06/02	06/03	06/04
Sales ($mil.)	(7.0%)	10.2	8.0	7.3	6.4	7.6
Net income ($ mil.)	–	0.2	(0.6)	(0.6)	(1.6)	(0.6)
Market value ($ mil.)	(28.9%)	0.7	0.2	0.0	0.0	0.2
Employees	(17.1%)	129	71	59	72	61

SKYWEST INC.

444 South River Road
St. George, UT 84790
Phone: 435 634-3000
Fax: –
Web: www.skywest.com

NMS: SKYW
CEO: Russell A Childs
CFO: –
HR: –
FYE: December 31
Type: Public

SkyWest, Inc. is the holding company for SkyWest Airlines and SkyWest Leasing. SkyWest has destinations in the US, Canada, and Mexico, supporting approximately 1,620 daily departures. When combined, SkyWest's carriers operate a fleet of some 625 aircraft consisting of Canadair regional jets (CRJs, made by Bombardier) and Embraer aircraft. SkyWest also operates through code-sharing agreements with United Airlines (operating as United Express), Delta Air Lines (Delta Connection), American Airlines (American Eagle), and Alaska Airlines. (Code-sharing allows airlines to sell tickets on one another's flights.) SkyWest Airlines was founded in 1972 when Ralph Atkin bought Dixie Airlines.

	Annual Growth	12/19	12/20	12/21	12/22	12/23
Sales ($mil.)	(0.3%)	2,972.0	2,127.1	2,713.5	3,004.9	2,935.4
Net income ($ mil.)	(43.6%)	340.1	(8.5)	111.9	73.0	34.3
Market value ($ mil.)	(5.2%)	2,599.7	1,621.5	1,580.8	664.1	2,099.7
Employees	(1.1%)	13,700	12,502	15,205	13,582	13,121

SKYWORKS SOLUTIONS INC

5260 California Avenue
Irvine, CA 92617
Phone: 949 231-3000
Fax: –
Web: www.skyworksinc.com

NMS: SWKS
CEO: Liam K Griffin
CFO: Kris Sennesael
HR: –
FYE: September 29
Type: Public

Skyworks Solutions manufacture highly innovative analog semiconductors connecting people, places, and things; and the forefront of developing empowering wireless networks, such as 5G and Internet of Things (IoT). Its flagship handset products handle amplification, filtering, tuning, power management, and audio processing in phones used by Apple Inc., Samsung Electronics, Huawei, HTC, ZTE, and many more. Other products include attenuators, diodes, couplers, phase shifters, receivers, and switches used in a broad array of industries. The company serve customers in the aerospace, automotive, broadband, cellular infrastructure, connected home, entertainment and gaming, industrial, medical, military, smartphone, tablet, and wearable markets. About 65% of the company's sales comes from US customers.

	Annual Growth	09/19*	10/20	10/21*	09/22	09/23
Sales ($mil.)	9.0%	3,376.8	3,355.7	5,109.1	5,485.5	4,772.4
Net income ($ mil.)	3.6%	853.6	814.8	1,498.3	1,275.2	982.8
Market value ($ mil.)	6.2%	12,356	23,419	26,145	13,601	15,725
Employees	2.0%	9,000	10,000	11,000	11,150	9,750

*Fiscal year change

SL GREEN REALTY CORP

One Vanderbilt Avenue
New York, NY 10017
Phone: 212 594-2700
Fax: –
Web: www.slgreen.com

NYS: SLG
CEO: Marc Holliday
CFO: Matthew J Diliberto
HR: –
FYE: December 31
Type: Public

SL Green Realty is a self-managed real estate investment trust (REIT), engaged in the acquisition, development, repositioning, ownership, management and operation of commercial and residential real estate properties, principally office properties, located in the New York metropolitan area, principally in Manhattan, a borough of New York City. The firm has interests in about 50 consolidated and unconsolidated properties in Manhattan buildings totaling more than 29.7 million square feet. SL Green's largest tenants by rentable square feet are Paramount Global, Credit Suisse Securities (USA), Inc., and Sony Corporation. The REIT also provides well-collateralized debt and preferred equity investments.

	Annual Growth	12/19	12/20	12/21	12/22	12/23
Sales ($mil.)	(7.3%)	1,239.0	1,052.7	844.0	826.7	913.7
Net income ($ mil.)	–	270.4	371.1	449.8	(78.1)	(564.6)
Market value ($ mil.)	(16.3%)	5,947.0	3,856.4	4,640.9	2,182.6	2,923.7
Employees	3.6%	1,033	794	931	1,137	1,188

SL INDUSTRIES, INC.

590 MADISON AVE FL 32
NEW YORK, NY 100222524
Phone: 212 520-2300
Fax: –
Web: www.slindustries.com

CEO: –
CFO: –
HR: –
FYE: December 31
Type: Private

SL Industries has the power to protect. Operating through four business segments, SL Industries makes and markets custom and standard AC/DC and DC/DC power supplies, surge suppressors, conditioning and distribution units, motion-control systems, and power protection equipment. Products are typically married to larger systems to improve their operating performance and safety. SL sells its power electronics and systems and related products to OEMs in the aerospace, computer, medical, wireless and wireline communications infrastructure, and transportation industries, as well as to US military contractors and municipal utilities.

SL LIQUIDATION LLC

405 WHITE ST
JACKSONVILLE, NC 285466731
Phone: 860 525-0821
Fax: –
Web: www.stanadyne.com

CEO: John A Pinson
CFO: Costas Loukellis
HR: Regina Parnell
FYE: December 31
Type: Private

Stanadyne is a global automotive technology leader in engine-based fuel and air management systems. The company specializes in pioneering technologies in gasoline and diesel fuel injection systems for the engines. It offers superior quality and a competitive edge, delivering power, performance, and efficiency, and enabling its customers to stay ahead of rapidly evolving emissions and consumer demand. The company dates back to 1876 as the Hartford Machine Screw Company.

	Annual Growth	12/07	12/08	12/09	12/11	12/12
Sales ($mil.)	10.6%	–	–	185.8	245.8	251.5
Net income ($ mil.)	–	–	–	(15.2)	(4.6)	(11.5)
Market value ($ mil.)	–	–	–	–	–	–
Employees	–	–	–	–	–	1,316

SLALOM, INC.

255 S KING ST STE 1800
SEATTLE, WA 981043320
Phone: 206 438-5700
Fax: –
Web: www.slalom.com

CEO: –
CFO: Michael Heffernan
HR: –
FYE: July 14
Type: Private

Slalom is a global consulting company focused on strategy, technology, and business transformation. The company provides consulting services in the areas of technology management, development, design, project, artificial intelligence and machine learning. The transformation centers on business changes, cloud solutions, and automation. Slalom clients include more than half the Fortune 100 and a third of the Fortune 500 ? along with startups, not-for-profits, and innovative organizations of all kinds. It serves a wide range of industries such as automotive, food and beverage, hospitality and recreation, media and entertainment, and not-for-profit sectors.

SLEEP NUMBER CORP

NMS: SNBR

1001 Third Avenue South
Minneapolis, MN 55404
Phone: 763 551-7000
Fax: –
Web: www.sleepnumber.com

CEO: Shelly R Ibach
CFO: Francis K Lee
HR: –
FYE: December 30
Type: Public

Sleep Number Corporation (formerly Select Comfort Corporation) is at the forefront of delivering this life-changing benefit with its revolutionary Sleep Number 360 smart beds and SleepIQ technology, which improved nearly 14 million lives. A leading bedding retailer in the US, the company operates approximately 670 company-owned stores in the US. The air-bed maker also sells through a company-operated call center, its own website, phone, and chat. Sleep Number was founded in 1987 and has grown to become one of the nation's leading bed makers and retailers.

	Annual Growth	12/19*	01/21	01/22*	12/22	12/23
Sales ($mil.)	2.7%	1,698.4	1,856.6	2,184.9	2,114.3	1,887.5
Net income ($ mil.)	–	81.8	139.2	153.7	36.6	(15.3)
Market value ($ mil.)	(26.1%)	1,102.6	1,820.2	1,703.2	577.7	329.7
Employees	(2.0%)	4,476	4,679	5,515	5,115	4,131

*Fiscal year change

SLEEPMED INCORPORATED

200 CORPORATE PL STE 5
PEABODY, MA 019603840
Phone: 978 536-7400
Fax: –
Web: –

CEO: Sean Heyniger
CFO: Jack Fiedor
HR: –
FYE: December 31
Type: Private

SleepMed tracks your vital signs while you count sheep. The company provides diagnostic tests and treatments for patients with sleep disorders through more than 160 sleep centers located in hospitals, medical clinics, and freestanding clinics nationwide. SleepMed also partners with epilepsy centers to provide brain monitoring services to patients suffering from seizures or unexplained neurologic episodes. Patients who don't want to travel for treatment can make use of SleepMed's in-home diagnostic services. The company designs and produces neurological testing equipment under the DigiTrace brand. SleepMed was formed by the 1999 merger of DigiTrace Care Services and Sleep Disorder Centers of America.

	Annual Growth	12/06	12/07	12/08	12/09	12/10
Sales ($mil.)	(54.2%)	–	–	437.3	96.0	91.9
Net income ($ mil.)	5680.4%	–	–	0.0	2.3	1.7
Market value ($ mil.)	–	–	–	–	–	–
Employees	–	–	–	–	–	945

SLM CORP.

NMS: SLM

300 Continental Drive
Newark, DE 19713
Phone: 302 451-0200
Fax: –
Web: www.salliemae.com

CEO: Jonathan W Witter
CFO: Steven J McGarry
HR: Kareliz Brown
FYE: December 31
Type: Public

SLM Corporation, more commonly known as Sallie Mae, holds some $19.0 billion in private education loans and originates some $6.0 billion of loans. Its Private Education Loans include important protections for the family, including loan forgiveness in case of death or permanent disability of the student borrower, a free, quarterly FICO score benefit to students and cosigners and, for borrowers with a Smart Option Student Loan, on-line tutoring services to help students succeed in school. SLM's main subsidiary Sallie Mae Bank is one of the nation's largest education loan providers, and specializes in originating, acquiring, financing, and servicing private student loans, which are not guaranteed by the government.

	Annual Growth	12/19	12/20	12/21	12/22	12/23
Assets ($mil.)	(2.8%)	32,686	30,770	29,222	28,811	29,169
Net income ($ mil.)	0.1%	578.3	880.7	1,160.5	469.0	581.4
Market value ($ mil.)	21.0%	1,963.3	2,730.1	4,334.2	3,657.7	4,213.0
Employees	(2.2%)	1,900	1,600	1,450	1,700	1,740

SLOAN IMPLEMENT COMPANY, INC.

120 N BUSINESS 51
ASSUMPTION, IL 625101120
Phone: 217 226-4411
Fax: –
Web: www.sloans.com

CEO: Larry Sloan
CFO: –
HR: Sara McRae
FYE: December 31
Type: Private

There's no slowin' down at Sloan Implement. The company provides the tools of trade for farmers in Illinois. Headquartered in Assumption, Illinois, Sloan is an authorized dealer of John Deere equipment and new and used parts. Founded in 1931, the company sells and services new and used Deere equipment, including combines, tractors, manure spreaders, tillers, earth moving and lawn machinery, and grain-handling equipment at five locations in Wisconsin and at 11 locations in Illinois; it also ships products nationwide and to international customers.

	Annual Growth	12/03	12/04	12/05	12/06	12/07
Sales ($mil.)	10.8%	–	159.4	150.5	146.2	217.2
Net income ($ mil.)	27.2%	–	4.6	5.2	4.3	9.4
Market value ($ mil.)	–	–	–	–	–	–
Employees	–	–	–	–	–	350

SLUMBERLAND, INC.

3505 HIGHPOINT DR N BLDG 2
OAKDALE, MN 551287577
Phone: 651 482-7500
Fax: –
Web: www.slumberland.com

CEO: Kenneth Larson
CFO: –
HR: Erik Larsen
FYE: December 31
Type: Private

Does the Sandman need some help finding you? Slumberland has some reclining, bedding, and sofa solutions. Primarily situated in the upper Midwest region of the US, the company operates more than 125 Slumberland Furniture stores in a dozen states. It first opened its doors as a mattress and La-Z-Boy specialty shop in 1967, but today Slumberland has extended its reach into furniture for the bedroom, dining room, and living room. The company is a leading retailer of La-Z-Boy upholstery and also sells Natuzzi leather pieces and both Sealy and Simmons' Beautyrest mattresses. Founded in 1967 by Ken Larson, Slumberland is a family-owned business.

SM ENERGY CO.

NYS: SM

1700 Lincoln Street, Suite 3200
Denver, CO 80203
Phone: 303 861-8140
Fax: 303 861-0934
Web: www.sm-energy.com

CEO: Herbert S Vogel
CFO: A W Pursell
HR: –
FYE: December 31
Type: Public

Founded in 1908, SM Energy is an independent energy company engaged in the acquisition, exploration, development, and production of oil, gas, and NGLs in Texas, specifically in the Permian Basin in West Texas and the Eagle Ford shale and Maverick Basin Austin Chalk in South Texas. The company has working interests in almost 860 gross (approximately 765 net) productive oil wells and nearly 500 gross (about 465 net) productive gas wells. Productive wells are wells producing in commercial quantities or wells capable of commercial production that are temporarily shut-in. The company generates about 65% revenues from Midland Basin.

	Annual Growth	12/19	12/20	12/21	12/22	12/23
Sales ($mil.)	10.5%	1,590.1	1,126.7	2,622.9	3,358.6	2,373.9
Net income ($ mil.)	–	(187.0)	(764.6)	36.2	1,112.0	817.9
Market value ($ mil.)	36.2%	1,301.0	708.4	3,412.2	4,031.4	4,481.7
Employees	0.7%	530	503	506	539	544

SMALL PARTS MANUFACTURING CO., INC.

4401 NE M L KING BLVD
PORTLAND, OR 972113394
Phone: 503 287-1181
Fax: –
Web: www.machiningcompany.com

CEO: –
CFO: –
HR: –
FYE: September 30
Type: Private

Small parts are big business for Small Parts Manufacturing (SPM). The machine shop pro provides fast turnaround for services including CNC milling and turning, automatic screw machining, grinding, honing, milling, and finishing to customers in aerospace, construction, telecommunications, and trucking. Its parts, prototype to 500 unit orders, are machined from aluminum, brass, and low carbon, alloy, or stainless steels, as well as exotic metals and plastics. Through machinery subcontractors, it also offers plating, heat treating, painting, bending, anodizing, and specialty services. The company inspects its work using an array of meters, gages, and optical comparators. Merton Rockney founded the company in 1946.

SMALLBIZPROS, INC

160 HAWTHORNE PARK
ATHENS, GA 306062147
Phone: 706 548-1040
Fax: –
Web: www.padgettadvisors.com

CEO: Steven Rafsky
CFO: –
HR: –
FYE: December 31
Type: Private

SmallBizPros knows the pros and cons of small businesses. Through Padgett Business Services, the company and its franchisees provide business advice, tax consulting and preparation, government compliance and financial reporting, and payroll services to small businesses throughout the US and Canada. As suggested by its name, SmallBizPros targets owner-operated companies with fewer than 20 employees. There are more than 400 owner-operated offices in the company's network. SmallBizPros was founded as an accounting firm in 1965 and began franchising in 1975.

SMART MOVE INC

5990 Greenwood Plaza Blvd, #2 Suite 390
Greenwood Village, CO 80111
Phone: 720 488-0204
Fax: –
Web: www.gosmartmove.com

CEO: Chris Sapyta
CFO: L E Johnson
HR: –
FYE: December 31
Type: Public

The brains behind Smart Move hope customers will see genius in its approach to moving household possessions. The Smart Move system centers on the SmartVault, a hard plastic container with 262 cu. ft. of space. Smart Move brings empty SmartVaults to your old house, lets you pack them, and then transports the containers to your new house. The actual hauling of the SmartVault is handled through parent company and transportation services firm Atlas World Group, which acquired Smart Move in June 2009. Smart Move offers its services from more than 60 major metropolitan areas in the US. The SmartVaults -- equipped with GPS units so they can be tracked -- are designed to fit into trailers along with other freight.

SMART SAND INC   NMS: SND

28420 Hardy Toll Road, Suite 130
Spring, TX 77373
Phone: 281 231-2660
Fax: –
Web: www.smartsand.com

CEO: Charles E Young
CFO: Lee E Beckelman
HR: –
FYE: December 31
Type: Public

Smart Sand is a fully integrated frac sand supply and services company, offering complete mine to wellsite proppant supply and logistics solutions to its customers. The company is low-cost producer of high-quality Northern White sand, which is a premium sand used as proppant used to enhance hydrocarbon recovery rates in the hydraulic fracturing of oil and natural gas wells and for a variety of industrial applications. Smart Sand sells its product to oil and natural gas exploration and production companies, oilfield service companies and industrial manufacturers. It owns and operates a raw frac sand mine (and related processing facility) near Oakdale, Wisconsin, which had approximately 245 million tons of proven and probable recoverable reserves. A second property in Utica & Peru, Illinois, reported roughly 130 million tons of proven recoverable sand reserves.

	Annual Growth	12/19	12/20	12/21	12/22	12/23
Sales ($mil.)	6.2%	233.1	122.3	126.6	255.7	296.0
Net income ($ mil.)	(38.1%)	31.6	38.0	(50.7)	(0.7)	4.6
Market value ($ mil.)	(6.5%)	97.0	66.2	68.5	68.9	74.3
Employees	7.3%	285	228	239	328	378

SMART STORES OPERATIONS LLC

600 CITADEL DR
COMMERCE, CA 900401562
Phone: 323 869-7500
Fax: –
Web: –

CEO: David G Hirz
CFO: Richard N Phegley
HR: –
FYE: December 31
Type: Private

Smart & Final is one of the longest continuously operating food retailers in the US. It has about 255 grocery and foodservice stores that stock more than 3,000 club-sized items and an assortment of quality, value-priced products, including farm-fresh produce, dairy, deli, meat, and seafood, as well as grocery and household essentials. The stores operate under Smart & Final and Smart & Final Extra! banners in urban and suburban areas in Arizona, California, and Nevada, as well as stores in northern Mexico. In 2021, Smart & Final was acquired by Bodega Latina for approximately $620 million.

SMARTFINANCIAL INC   NYS: SMBK

5401 Kingston Pike, Suite 600
Knoxville, TN 37919
Phone: 865 437-5700
Fax: –
Web: www.smartbank.com

CEO: –
CFO: –
HR: –
FYE: December 31
Type: Public

Cornerstone Bancshares is the holding company for Cornerstone Community Bank, which operates about five locations in Chattanooga, Tennessee, and surrounding communities, in addition to two loan production offices in Knoxville, Tennessee, and Dalton, Georgia. The bank offers standard retail and commercial services, including checking and savings accounts, money market accounts, and CDs. Its lending activities primarily consist of commercial real estate loans, residential mortgages, real estate construction loans, and business and agricultural loans. Another subsidiary of Cornerstone Bancshares, Eagle Financial, purchases accounts receivable and acts as a conduit lender.

	Annual Growth	12/19	12/20	12/21	12/22	12/23
Assets ($mil.)	18.5%	2,449.1	3,304.9	4,611.6	4,637.5	4,829.4
Net income ($ mil.)	1.9%	26.5	24.3	34.8	43.0	28.6
Market value ($ mil.)	0.9%	401.8	308.2	464.8	467.2	416.1
Employees	10.0%	399	475	551	596	585

SMARTRONIX, LLC

44150 SMARTRONIX WAY STE 200   CEO: –
HOLLYWOOD, MD 206363172   CFO: –
Phone: 301 373-6000   HR: –
Fax: –   FYE: December 31
Web: www.smartronix.com   Type: Private

Smartronix works an intelligent approach to electronics. Serving the US Department of Defense and other federal agencies, its IT products and services include cyber security, cloud computing, enterprise software, health IT, network operations, and mission-focused engineering. The company specializes in application development, business management, network management, and systems engineering. Founded in 1995, Smartronix offers ruggedized computing and communications equipment and network diagnostic tools. The company counts the US Air Force, Marine Corps, and Navy among its regular clients, as well as the Department of Homeland Security and the Transportation Security Administration.

	Annual Growth	10/03	10/04	10/05	10/06*	12/07
Sales ($mil.)	–	–	–	–	78.5	78.5
Net income ($ mil.)	–	–	–	–	4.1	4.1
Market value ($ mil.)	–	–	–	–	–	–
Employees	–	–	–	–	–	838

*Fiscal year change

SMC NETWORKS, INC.

20 MASON   CEO: Alex Kim
IRVINE, CA 926182706   CFO: Lane Ruoff
Phone: 949 679-8029   HR: –
Fax: –   FYE: April 19
Web: www.smc.com   Type: Private

SMC Networks serves up networking equipment, with or without wires. The company makes wireless local area network (LAN) devices designed for use in homes and businesses. Its key products are modems, network gateways, and wireless routers. SMC also sells a line of Ethernet products, including adapters and switches, for small and midsized businesses. Other products include Voice-over-Internet Protocol (VoIP) network gateways and physical security system components such as wireless cameras, keypads, motion sensors, and sensors for detecting broken glass. The company sells though resellers, distributors, and retailers. It has partnerships with electronics vendors including Intel, Texas Instruments, and Vitesse.

SMC SYSTEMS, INC.

9570 RGNCY SQ BLVD # 410   CEO: Christopher H Uhland
JACKSONVILLE, FL 322259104   CFO: –
Phone: 904 482-4260   HR: –
Fax: –   FYE: December 31
Web: –   Type: Private

Looking for mold in all the wrong places? SMC Systems, Inc. (also known as SkyeTec) wants to find it for you. Specializing in inspection and diagnosis of mold and mold-related problems, SkyeTec is a third-party indoor environment consultant company that serves property owners, insurance companies, and builders. The company, which does not offer its own mold remediation services, serves both the residential and commercial markets, and also responds to areas affected by catastrophic events like hurricanes and tornadoes. Based in Jacksonville, Florida, the company serves mainly southeastern US and Gulf Coast states. SkyeTec was founded in 1999 by CEO Chris Uhland and Ted Nelson.

SMG INDUSTRIES INC   NBB: SMGI

20475 State Hwy 249, Suite 450   CEO: Matthew C Flemming
Houston, TX 77070   CFO: –
Phone: 713 955-3497   HR: –
Fax: –   FYE: December 31
Web: www.smgindustries.com   Type: Public

SMG Indium Resources has a simple plan. The company has amassed a stockpile of indium (42.5 metric tons) in a vault and plans to sit on it for a few years and ride the appreciation all the way to the bank. The group may lease, lend, or sell portions (or even all) of its stockpile based on market conditions, but does not have any plans to actively speculate on the short-term fluctuations in the price of the metal. Number 49 on the Periodic Table, indium has a number of industrial applications, and its use in the manufacture of flat panel displays has created significant demand for the metal. Indium is also used in solar energy technology. SMG Indium filed an IPO in 2011 and made its first sale in 2012.

	Annual Growth	12/18	12/19	12/20	12/21	12/22
Sales ($mil.)	100.2%	4.4	6.5	26.7	52.1	71.0
Net income ($ mil.)	–	(1.1)	(4.0)	(15.9)	(11.1)	(11.6)
Market value ($ mil.)	(31.4%)	18.4	9.4	3.9	10.2	4.1
Employees	50.1%	53	52	199	258	269

SMITH & WESSON BRANDS INC   NMS: SWBI

2100 Roosevelt Avenue   CEO: Mark P Smith
Springfield, MA 01104   CFO: Deana L McPherson
Phone: 800 331-0852   HR: –
Fax: –   FYE: April 30
Web: www.smith-wesson.com   Type: Public

Smith & Wesson Brands is one of the world's leading manufacturers and designers of firearms. It manufactures a wide array of handguns (including revolvers and pistols), long guns (including modern sporting rifles), handcuffs, firearm suppressors, and other firearm-related products. The company has a wide variety of customers, including firearm enthusiasts, collectors, hunters, sportsmen, competitive shooters, individuals desiring home and personal protection, law enforcement and security agencies and officers, and military agencies in the US and throughout the world. Founded in 1852, the company was renamed from Smith & Wesson Holding Corp to American Outdoor Brands, and later changed its name to Smith & Wesson Brands, Inc. Europe accounts for roughly 35% of the company's international sales.

	Annual Growth	04/19	04/20	04/21	04/22	04/23
Sales ($mil.)	(6.9%)	638.3	678.4	1,059.2	864.1	479.2
Net income ($ mil.)	19.0%	18.4	(61.2)	252.0	194.5	36.9
Market value ($ mil.)	5.1%	453.0	435.3	800.2	631.4	552.8
Employees	(4.0%)	1,988	1,970	2,240	1,723	1,690

SMITH (A O) CORP   NYS: AOS

11270 West Park Place   CEO: Kevin J Wheeler
Milwaukee, WI 53224-9508   CFO: Charles T Lauber
Phone: 414 359-4000   HR: –
Fax: 414 359-4115   FYE: December 31
Web: www.aosmith.com   Type: Public

A.O. Smith is one of the world's leading manufacturers of residential and commercial water heating equipment and boilers, as well as a manufacturer of water treatment products. Its products include home gas, heat pump and electric water heaters, boilers, tanks, and water treatment systems. The company's Lochinvar brand is one of the leading residential and commercial boiler brands in the US. Some of A.O. Smith's most prominent brands include Aquasana, Atlantic Filter, Hague, Water-Right, and Master Water. A.O. Smith sells its products in North America as well as China, Europe, and India. The company sells its products through a network of more than 1,000 wholesale distributors, as well as large hardware and home center retail chains, such as Lowe's. It generates the majority of its revenue in the US.

	Annual Growth	12/19	12/20	12/21	12/22	12/23
Sales ($mil.)	6.5%	2,992.7	2,895.3	3,538.9	3,753.9	3,852.8
Net income ($ mil.)	10.7%	370.0	344.9	487.1	235.7	556.6
Market value ($ mil.)	14.7%	7,028.2	8,087.4	12,665	8,444.5	12,162
Employees	(5.6%)	15,100	13,900	13,700	12,000	12,000

SMITH MICRO SOFTWARE INC NAS: SMSI

5800 Corporate Drive
Pittsburgh, PA 15237
Phone: 412 837-5300
Fax: –
Web: www.smithmicro.com

CEO: William W Smith Jr
CFO: James M Kempton
HR: –
FYE: December 31
Type: Public

Smith Micro Software provides wireless connectivity software designed to enhance the mobile experience for users and optimize network operations for enterprises and wireless service providers. Its primary product families include QuickLink (mobile internet connection), NetWise (data traffic management), and CommSuite (voice, messaging, and video). The company, which operates primarily in the Americas, counts wireless carriers such as Sprint and Verizon Wireless among its leading customers. In addition to wireless connectivity software, Smith Micro develops productivity and graphics software for artists, educators, and other consumers.

	Annual Growth	12/19	12/20	12/21	12/22	12/23
Sales ($mil.)	(1.5%)	43.3	51.3	58.4	48.5	40.9
Net income ($ mil.)	–	10.7	4.2	(31.0)	(29.3)	(24.4)
Market value ($ mil.)	(32.5%)	297.6	405.3	367.9	157.0	61.8
Employees	3.9%	198	255	373	315	231

SMITH-MIDLAND CORP. NAS: SMID

5119 Catlett Road, P.O. Box 300
Midland, VA 22728
Phone: 540 439-3266
Fax: 540 439-1232
Web: www.smithmidland.com

CEO: –
CFO: –
HR: –
FYE: December 31
Type: Public

Smith-Midland has cemented its reputation with stone and concrete products. The company sells its patented precast concrete products to contractors and federal, state, and local transportation authorities in the mid-Atlantic, midwestern, and northeastern US. Products include lightweight concrete and steel exterior wall systems (Slenderwall), precast concrete safety and sound barriers (J-J Hooks), roadside sound barriers (Sierra Wall), portable concrete buildings, and farm products, primarily cattleguards and water and feed troughs. Smith-Midland licenses its products to precast concrete makers in Australia, Belgium, New Zealand, North America, and Spain.

	Annual Growth	12/18	12/19	12/20	12/21	12/22
Sales ($mil.)	5.7%	40.2	46.7	43.9	50.6	50.1
Net income ($ mil.)	(17.0%)	1.7	2.0	2.7	7.6	0.8
Market value ($ mil.)	28.7%	39.3	31.5	49.7	247.1	107.8
Employees	(14.4%)	432	232	200	200	232

SMITHFIELD FOODS, INC.

200 COMMERCE ST
SMITHFIELD, VA 234301204
Phone: 757 365-3000
Fax: –
Web: www.smithfieldfoods.com

CEO: Shane Smith
CFO: Glenn T Nunziata
HR: Bradley Thornton
FYE: December 28
Type: Private

Smithfield Foods is one of the world's largest hog producers and pork processors. Smithfield boasts a portfolio of high-quality iconic brands of fresh pork and value-added pork products, including deli meats and prepared foods. Armour, Cook's, Eckrich, John Morrell, Gwaltney, Healthy Ones, and Margherita are among its brands. The American food company has farms, facilities, and offices in the US, Europe, and Mexico. Smithfield traces its history back to 1936, when Joseph W. Luter Sr. and his son, Joseph W. Luter Jr., opened the Smithfield Packing Company in Smithfield, Virginia.

SMITHGROUP COMPANIES, INC.

500 GRISWOLD ST FL 1700
DETROIT, MI 482268011
Phone: 313 442-8351
Fax: –
Web: www.smithgroup.com

CEO: –
CFO: –
HR: –
FYE: December 31
Type: Private

SmithGroupJJR (formerly SmithGroup) is the oldest continuously practicing architectural and engineering firm in the US. Founded in 1853 in Detroit by architect Sheldon Smith, the firm partnered with engineers in 1907 to become one of the first multidisciplinary firms in the country. SmithGroupJJR influenced the skyline of Detroit with structures like the Guardian, Penobscot, and Buhl buildings. These days the group offers architecture engineering, interiors planning, and consulting services and has about a dozen offices across the US. It targets the office, research, education, health care, technologies, and cities and communities markets.

SMITHSONIAN INSTITUTION

1000 JEFFERSON DR SW
WASHINGTON, DC 205600009
Phone: 202 633-1000
Fax: –
Web: www.si.edu

CEO: Gary M Beer
CFO: Albert Horvath
HR: Maria Wennersten
FYE: September 30
Type: Private

The Smithsonian Institution is the world's largest museum, education, and research complex. It houses some 155 million objects in more than 20 museums, about 20 libraries, many research centers, and National Zoo; and more than the exhibitions at its physical locations. Admission to all but one of the Smithsonian's facilities is free. Some of its museums are Anacostia Community Museum, Air and Space Museum, African Art Museum, American History Museum, Postal Museum, American Art Museum, Renwick Gallery, Sackler Gallery, Portrait Gallery, Smithsonian Gardens, and Smithsonian Castle.

	Annual Growth	09/17	09/18	09/19	09/20	09/22
Sales ($mil.)	4.4%	–	1,563.5	1,375.7	1,389.1	1,856.0
Net income ($ mil.)	20.1%	–	177.0	180.0	302.8	368.3
Market value ($ mil.)	–	–	–	–	–	–
Employees	–	–	–	–	–	6,100

SMS ALTERNATIVES INC NBB: CICN D

8000 Regency Parkway, Suite 542
Cary, NC 27518
Phone: 919 380-5000
Fax: –
Web: www.ciceroinc.com

CEO: John Broderick
CFO: John Broderick
HR: –
FYE: December 31
Type: Public

Cicero takes a philosophical approach to integrating computer applications. The company provides application integration software used to link a variety of enterprise applications (including mainframe, client/server, and Web-based environments), primarily for financial service firms' contact centers. It also provides consulting, project management, and training services, which account for more than a third of revenue. Customers include Affiliated Computer Services, Deutsche Bank, and Merrill Lynch. Cicero's roster of strategic partners includes resellers such as BluePhoenix, MphasiS, and Tata Consultancy. The company gets all of its sales in the US.

	Annual Growth	12/15	12/16	12/17	12/18	12/19
Sales ($mil.)	(5.7%)	1.9	1.3	1.3	0.8	1.5
Net income ($ mil.)	–	(2.8)	(3.9)	(2.1)	(2.1)	(1.6)
Market value ($ mil.)	–	–	–	–	–	–
Employees	(12.6%)	24	16	15	15	14

SMUCKER (J.M.) CO.   NYS: SJM

One Strawberry Lane
Orrville, OH 44667-0280
Phone: 330 682-3000
Fax: –
Web: www.jmsmucker.com

CEO: Mark T Smucker
CFO: Tucker H Marshall
HR: Mallorie Wright
FYE: April 30
Type: Public

The J. M. Smucker Company operates principally in one industry, the manufacturing and marketing of branded food and beverage products on a worldwide basis, although the majority of the sales are in the US. The company's principal products include coffee, cat food, pet snacks, dog food, frozen handheld products, peanut butter, fruit spreads, portion control products, as well as baking mixes and ingredients. Folgers coffee, Jif, and Milk-Bone, plus new favorites like Cafe Bustelo, Smucker's, Uncrustables, and Dunkin, are among its market-leading brands that are sold to consumers through retail outlets in North America. It generates the most revenue from coffee, followed by cat food, pet snacks, and dog food.

	Annual Growth	04/19	04/20	04/21	04/22	04/23
Sales ($mil.)	2.1%	7,838.0	7,801.0	8,002.7	7,998.9	8,529.2
Net income ($ mil.)	–	514.4	779.5	876.3	631.7	(91.3)
Market value ($ mil.)	5.9%	12,802	11,996	13,675	14,295	16,120
Employees	(5.9%)	7,400	7,300	7,100	6,700	5,800

SNAP INC   NYS: SNAP

3000 31st Street
Santa Monica, CA 90405
Phone: 310 399-3339
Fax: –
Web: www.snap.com

CEO: Evan Spiegel
CFO: Derek Andersen
HR: –
FYE: December 31
Type: Public

Snap owns and operates the Snapchat smartphone app, which lets social media users take photos and videos, attach messages, and send them to other users. The company's products include a camera, chat, discover, snap map, memories, and spectacles. Snap serves two constituencies: its users, who average of approximately 375 million a day, and the advertisers who pay Snap to reach those users. Almost all of Snap's revenue comes from advertisers. The company has offices in the US, Europe, Asia, and Australia. Founded in 2010, the company's largest market is North America which accounts for about 70% of total sales.

	Annual Growth	12/19	12/20	12/21	12/22	12/23
Sales ($mil.)	28.0%	1,715.5	2,506.6	4,117.0	4,601.8	4,606.1
Net income ($ mil.)	–	(1,033.7)	(944.8)	(488.0)	(1,429.7)	(1,322.5)
Market value ($ mil.)	0.9%	26,871	82,390	77,388	14,727	27,858
Employees	13.4%	3,195	3,863	5,661	5,288	5,289

SNAP-ON, INC.   NYS: SNA

2801 80th Street
Kenosha, WI 53143
Phone: 262 656-5200
Fax: 262 656-5577
Web: www.snapon.com

CEO: Nicholas T Pinchuk
CFO: Aldo J Pagliari
HR: –
FYE: December 30
Type: Public

Snap-on is a leading global innovator, manufacturer, and marketer of tools, equipment, diagnostics, repair information and systems solutions for professional users performing critical tasks. Other products ? with brand names such as Snap-on, Blackhawk, Hofmann, Car-O-Liner, Lindstr m, John Bean, and Sun ? include collision repair equipment, roll cabinets, tool chests, wheel balancers, and wrenches. Snap-on and its subsidiaries held approximately 870 active and pending patents in the US and approximately 2,780 active and pending patents outside of the US. Founded in 1920, Snap-on originated the mobile-van tool distribution channel in the automotive repair market. Approximately 75% of Snap-on's total revenue comes from North America.

	Annual Growth	12/19*	01/21	01/22*	12/22	12/23
Sales ($mil.)	5.9%	4,067.7	3,942.2	4,601.7	4,842.5	5,108.3
Net income ($ mil.)	9.9%	693.5	627.0	820.5	911.7	1,011.1
Market value ($ mil.)	14.3%	8,915.8	9,018.1	11,349	12,040	15,220
Employees	0.8%	12,800	12,300	12,800	12,900	13,200

*Fiscal year change

SNAPPING SHOALS ELECTRIC TRUST, INC.

14750 BROWN BRIDGE RD
COVINGTON, GA 300164113
Phone: 770 786-3484
Fax: –
Web: www.ssemc.com

CEO: Bradley K Thomas
CFO: Carl Smith
HR: –
FYE: December 31
Type: Private

Named after a geographic area that sounds like an angler's dream, Snapping Shoals Electric Membership Corporation (Snapping Shoals EMC) distributes electricity to 95,000 residential, commercial, and industrial customers in an 8-county region in the southeastern portion of the Atlanta metropolitan area. The member-owned cooperative also provides competitive retail natural gas supply services to customers through Snapping Shoals Energy Management Company, a partnership with SCANA. Snapping Shoals EMC also offers security systems, surge protection services, and security lighting options.

	Annual Growth	12/18	12/19	12/20	12/21	12/22
Sales ($mil.)	765.9%	–	0.4	189.2	210.1	261.5
Net income ($ mil.)	1312.5%	–	0.0	4.4	4.8	4.0
Market value ($ mil.)	–	–	–	–	–	–
Employees	–	–	–	–	–	270

SNAPPY POPCORN COMPANY

610 MAIN ST
BREDA, IA 514368719
Phone: 712 673-2347
Fax: –
Web: www.snappypopcorn.com

CEO: –
CFO: –
HR: –
FYE: August 31
Type: Private

Snap your fingers and, pop!, this company will supply it. Snappy Popcorn Company grows, processes, sells, and distributes popcorn, along with popcorn supplies (oils, seasonings, bag) under the Snappy and Marly's Gourmet labels. The company also offers popcorn popping machines, and other snack-food-concession equipment, including cotton-candy, slush, shaved ice, corn-dog, nacho, funnel-cake and caramel-apple makers. Its customers includes movie theaters and other foodservice outlets, as well as schools, communities, and fundraising groups. The company offers also private-label products and services. In addition to processing and packaging, the company grows its own popcorn variety corn.

	Annual Growth	08/02	08/03	08/06	08/07	08/08
Sales ($mil.)	(42.1%)	–	5.0	7.9	0.6	0.3
Net income ($ mil.)	15.2%	–	0.2	–	0.5	0.3
Market value ($ mil.)	–	–	–	–	–	–
Employees	–	–	–	–	–	40

SNAVELY FOREST PRODUCTS INC

600 DELWAR RD
PITTSBURGH, PA 152361351
Phone: 412 885-4005
Fax: –
Web: www.snavelyforestproducts.com

CEO: Stephen V Snavely V
CFO: Kellie Radzik
HR: –
FYE: December 31
Type: Private

Snavely Forest Products hopes it's never out of the woods. The company wholesales appearance-grade lumber and other wood products through sales and distribution centers. Among the inspired brands Snavely Forest Products distributes and partners with include Anthony Forest Products, Georgia Pacific EWP, Trex, Typar, and Versatex. Snavely Forest Products' operations span Colorado, Maryland, North Carolina, Pennsylvania, and Texas. Its products include doors, engineered wood, deck and railing, boards, lumber and panels, and exterior cladding. The company sources much of its product from sustainable-yield forests. Snavely Forest Products was founded in 1902.

	Annual Growth	12/12	12/13	12/14	12/15	12/16
Sales ($mil.)	8.5%	–	126.7	139.4	146.0	161.6
Net income ($ mil.)	23.0%	–	1.5	2.2	1.7	2.8
Market value ($ mil.)	–	–	–	–	–	–
Employees	–	–	–	–	–	105

SNELL & WILMER L.L.P.

1 E WASHINGTON ST STE 2700
PHOENIX, AZ 850040908
Phone: 602 382-6000
Fax: –
Web: www.swlaw.com

CEO: –
CFO: David Boden
HR: Laura Miller
FYE: December 31
Type: Private

Snell & Wilmer employs about 400 attorneys and is one of the largest full-service law firms in the western US. Its legal expertise covers such practice areas as antitrust and trade regulation, bankruptcy, health care litigation, immigration, and employment law. Snell & Wilmer also offers practices that are important to the region it serves, such as gaming, water law, and American Indian law. Clients have included such notable names as Bank of America, Ford Motor Company, General Motors, and Prudential. The firm was founded in Phoenix in 1938 and has grown to nine offices in about half a dozen US states and Mexico.

SNYDER LANGSTON HOLDINGS, LLC

17962 COWAN
IRVINE, CA 926146026
Phone: 949 863-9200
Fax: –
Web: www.snyderlangston.com

CEO: John Rochford
CFO: Gary Campanaro
HR: Linda Swainger
FYE: December 31
Type: Private

No Snyder Langston isn't the name of a "wacky neighbor" sitcom character, but it might have built the property next door. Snyder Langston develops and builds commercial, industrial, and multifamily residential properties. Serving business clients ranging from start-ups to Fortune 500 firms, the company provides a range of services such as planning, design, financing, government relations, general contracting, and construction management. Properties that Snyder Langston has developed include business parks, retail centers, office buildings, manufacturing facilities, parking garages, car dealerships, condominiums, churches, schools, and hotels. The firm was founded in 1959 by Donald Snyder and William Langston.

	Annual Growth	12/05	12/06	12/07	12/09	12/10
Sales ($mil.)	(45.3%)	–	–	342.1	78.9	56.0
Net income ($ mil.)	–	–	–	5.2	(1.5)	(1.7)
Market value ($ mil.)	–	–	–	–	–	–
Employees	–	–	–	–	–	175

SNYDER'S-LANCE, INC.

13515 BALLANTYNE CORPORATE PL
CHARLOTTE, NC 282772706
Phone: 704 554-1421
Fax: –
Web: www.campbellsoupcompany.com

CEO: –
CFO: –
HR: –
FYE: December 30
Type: Private

Snyder's-Lance manufactures and markets snack foods throughout the US and internationally. Snyder's-Lance's products include pretzels, sandwich crackers, pretzel crackers, potato chips, cookies, tortilla chips, restaurant style crackers, popcorn, nuts, and other snacks. Products are sold under the Snyder's of Hanover, Lance, Kettle Brand, KETTLE Chips, Cape Cod, Snack Factory, Pretzel Crisps, Pop Secret, Emerald, Late July, Krunchers!, Tom's, Archway, Jays, Stella D'oro, Eatsmart Snacks, O-Ke-Doke, Metcalfe's skinny, and other brand names along with a number of third party brands. Products are distributed nationally through grocery and mass merchandisers, convenience stores, club stores, food service outlets and other channels. Snyder's-Lance currently offers plant tours in its Hanover, Pennsylvania bakery and its Cape Cod Potato Chip factory in Hyannis, Massachusetts.

	Annual Growth	12/12	12/13*	01/15*	12/16	12/17
Sales ($mil.)	6.0%	–	1,761.0	1,620.9	2,109.2	2,226.8
Net income ($ mil.)	17.2%	–	79.1	192.5	14.7	149.3
Market value ($ mil.)	–	–	–	–	–	–
Employees	–	–	–	–	–	6,100

*Fiscal year change

SOCIETAL CDMO INC

NAS: SCTL

1 E. Uwchlan Ave, Suite 112
Exton, PA 19341
Phone: 770 534-8239
Fax: –
Web: www.recrocdmo.com

CEO: David Enloe
CFO: Ryan D Lake
HR: Sandra Mathis
FYE: December 31
Type: Public

Recro Pharma is in the business of providing non-opioid treatments for serious pain. The clinical stage specialty pharmaceutical firm is developing pain medications, for use initially in the post-operative setting. By focusing on non-opioid based drugs, Recro expects its products will avoid side effects associated with opioids, including addiction, constipation, and respiratory distress. Its lead product is an injectable form of meloxicam; that medication has had challenges moving through the regulatory process. The company's pipeline also includes Dex-IN, an intranasal formulation of dexmedetomidine.

	Annual Growth	12/19	12/20	12/21	12/22	12/23
Sales ($mil.)	(1.2%)	99.2	66.5	75.4	90.2	94.6
Net income ($ mil.)	–	(18.6)	(27.5)	(11.4)	(19.9)	(13.3)
Market value ($ mil.)	(62.8%)	1,922.0	298.8	179.3	156.2	36.8
Employees	4.7%	215	185	258	275	258

SOCIETY OF MANUFACTURING ENGINEERS

1000 TOWN CTR STE 1910
SOUTHFIELD, MI 480751236
Phone: 313 425-3000
Fax: –
Web: www.sme.org

CEO: Jeff Krause
CFO: –
HR: Julie Krapohl
FYE: December 31
Type: Private

The Society of Manufacturing Engineer (SME) has members in other countries. SME is a nonprofit association of professionals, educators and students committed to promoting and supporting the manufacturing industry. It also organizes expositions and other industry-related events and publishes the monthly magazine Manufacturing Engineering, along with a number of peer-reviewed journals and research publications. SME was founded by some 35 tool engineers in 1932 as The Society of Tool Engineers. It adopted its current name in 1969. Along with its headquarters in Southfield, Michigan, SME also has an office in Cleveland and Toronto.

	Annual Growth	12/17	12/18	12/19	12/21	12/22
Sales ($mil.)	(2.2%)	–	56.5	75.6	66.2	51.6
Net income ($ mil.)	–	–	(1.4)	7.9	9.4	(8.3)
Market value ($ mil.)	–	–	–	–	–	–
Employees	–	–	–	–	–	200

SOCKET HOLDINGS CORPORATION

2703 CLARK LN
COLUMBIA, MO 652022432
Phone: 573 817-0000
Fax: –
Web: www.lakemail.com

CEO: –
CFO: –
HR: –
FYE: December 31
Type: Private

Socket Holdings helps customers in Missouri plug in to the Internet. Socket provides residential and business Internet access, data networking, and Web hosting services, as well as local and long-distance phone service for businesses. The company, formed in 1994 by CEO George Pfeneger and CTO John Dupuy, serves more than 20,000 customers in 400 cities in Missouri.

SOCKET MOBILE INC   NAS: SCKT

40675 Encyclopedia
Fremont, CA 94538
Phone: 510 933-3000
Fax: –
Web: www.socketmobile.com

CEO: Kevin J Mills
CFO: Lynn Zhao
HR: –
FYE: December 31
Type: Public

Socket Mobile plugs expansion devices. The company provides PC and CompactFlash cards for handheld and notebook computers. Its products include peripheral connection and Ethernet cards. It also offers handheld computers, bar code scanners and scanner cards, and cards for digital phones, as well as embedded products, including Bluetooth modules and interface chips. Socket Mobile's largest sales segment, mobile peripheral products, accounts for about half of its revenues. The segment encompasses bar code scanners, data collection plug-in cards, and serial interface products. The company sells worldwide through original equipment manufacturers (OEMs), resellers, and distributors, including Ingram Micro and Tech Data.

	Annual Growth	12/19	12/20	12/21	12/22	12/23
Sales ($mil.)	(3.0%)	19.3	15.7	23.2	21.2	17.0
Net income ($ mil.)	–	0.3	(3.3)	4.5	0.0	(1.9)
Market value ($ mil.)	(7.9%)	11.8	17.5	29.9	14.2	8.5
Employees	2.2%	56	48	53	56	61

SOFT COMPUTER CONSULTANTS INC.

5400 TECH DATA DR
CLEARWATER, FL 337603116
Phone: 727 789-0100
Fax: –
Web: www.softcomputer.com

CEO: Gilbert Hakim
CFO: –
HR: Allison Fink
FYE: December 31
Type: Private

Soft Computer Consultants, Inc. (which does business as SCC Soft Computer) develops laboratory information systems (LIS) and clinical information systems for medical laboratories, radiology departments, genetics laboratories, pharmacies, and blood banks. Its software links labs to other departments in order to enable quick distribution of data and test results. The company also offers clinical accounts receivable and billing software for finance departments and consulting services to help customers improve their workflow processes. SCC was founded in 1979 by the Hakim brothers, Gilbert (CEO) and Jean (President).

	Annual Growth	08/08	08/09	08/10*	12/19	12/21
Sales ($mil.)	4.3%	–	97.7	107.8	151.3	162.0
Net income ($ mil.)	13.4%	–	13.7	23.4	29.4	62.0
Market value ($ mil.)	–	–	–	–	–	–
Employees	–	–	–	–	–	900

*Fiscal year change

SOFTECH, INC   NBB: SOFT

650 Suffolk Street, Suite 415
Lowell, MA 01854
Phone: 978 513-2700
Fax: 978 458-4096
Web: www.softech.com

CEO: Joseph P Mullaney
CFO: –
HR: –
FYE: May 31
Type: Public

SofTech has designs on product manufacturers with its product lifecycle management (PLM) products. SofTech's ProductCenter suite allows users to consolidate product information, automate processes such as review cycles and change orders, facilitate collaboration, and ensure regulatory compliance. The company also provides consulting, maintenance, and training services. Clients include GE, Honeywell, Sikorsky Aircraft, Siemens, and the US Army.

	Annual Growth	05/12	05/13	05/14	05/15	05/16
Sales ($mil.)	(10.2%)	6.4	6.4	5.0	3.9	4.2
Net income ($ mil.)	–	0.4	0.4	(0.7)	(1.3)	(0.7)
Market value ($ mil.)	(2.3%)	1.1	1.5	1.5	1.0	1.0
Employees	(9.9%)	41	40	31	27	27

SOFTHEON, INC.

1500 STONY BROOK RD
STONY BROOK, NY 117944600
Phone: 800 236-7941
Fax: –
Web: www.softheon.com

CEO: –
CFO: –
HR: –
FYE: December 31
Type: Private

Softheon helps health care payers tackle all sorts of hard tasks. The company provides content management and business process management software primarily to health care companies that use the software to manage information across multiple enterprise databases and the Internet, handle claims and grievances, and manage enrollment processes. The company's software allows companies to search, route, audit and monitor documents in various formats and can be customized to meet particular requirements. Softheon also offers consulting, technical support, and training services. The company was founded in 1994.

	Annual Growth	12/01	12/02	12/03	12/04	12/18
Sales ($mil.)	24.2%	–	1.9	5.2	3.3	61.3
Net income ($ mil.)	0.9%	–	3.2	1.0	(1.3)	3.7
Market value ($ mil.)	–	–	–	–	–	–
Employees	–	–	–	–	–	95

SOFTWARE PUBLISHERS ASSOC (INC)

1090 VERMONT AVE NW STE 600
WASHINGTON, DC 200054905
Phone: 202 289-7442
Fax: –
Web: www.siia.net

CEO: –
CFO: –
HR: –
FYE: June 30
Type: Private

The SIIA keeps tabs on Congressional representatives and pirates, alike. The Software & Information Industry Association (SIIA) is an international trade organization for the software and digital content industries. Its more than 500 corporate members include Bank of America, Bloomberg, Dow Jones, and Sun Microsystems. SIIA offers market research, access to industry information, lobbying, awards, and conferences. It also investigates and prosecutes companies accused of using software or content illegally. SIIA was formed in 1999 by the merger of the Software Publishers Association and the Information Industry Association. The Specialized Information Publishers Association is becoming a division of SIIA.

	Annual Growth	06/16	06/17	06/18	06/21	06/22
Sales ($mil.)	(4.0%)	–	9.4	11.0	7.3	7.7
Net income ($ mil.)	–	–	(1.5)	(0.3)	0.6	0.4
Market value ($ mil.)	–	–	–	–	–	–
Employees	–	–	–	–	–	50

SOFTWARE QUALITY ASSOCIATES LLC

3 DAVOL SQ STE B200
PROVIDENCE, RI 029034762
Phone: 888 299-7638
Fax: –
Web: www.sqagroup.com

CEO: –
CFO: –
HR: Shauna Tierney
FYE: December 31
Type: Private

Its no mystery what Software Quality Associates has on its mind. The company, which does business as SQA, provides a range of software QA services such as organizational strategy, design and test automation, staffing support, and outsourced testing. SQA also offers software and systems validation services to assist health care companies in complying with FDA regulations. The company serves clients in such industries as financial services, information technology, health care, manufacturing, and retail. SQA has partnerships with software developers including Borland, Compuware, and RadView.

SOLARCRAFT SERVICES, INC.

8 DIGITAL DR STE 101
NOVATO, CA 949495759
Phone: 415 382-7717
Fax: –
Web: www.solarcraft.com
CEO: Galen Torneby
CFO: Bruce King
HR: –
FYE: December 31
Type: Private

SolarCraft Services designs and installs solar energy systems that capitalize on California's sunshine. The company has installed more than 4,300 solar energy systems for residential and commercial customers in Northern California, including numerous vineyards and wineries. Its largest project was a 1.1 MW system at Paramount Farms, the world's largest grower and processor of pistachios and almonds. SolarCraft Services uses solar panels made by Mitsubishi, Sharp and SunPower, panels for swimming pools made by FAFCO, and components by SatCon. The company was founded in 1984.

	Annual Growth	12/03	12/04	12/05	12/06	12/07
Sales ($mil.)	46.3%	–	3.7	7.4	12.4	11.6
Net income ($ mil.)	19.2%	–	0.0	1.2	0.0	0.1
Market value ($ mil.)	–	–	–	–	–	–
Employees	–	–	–	–	–	44

SOLAREDGE TECHNOLOGIES, INC.

700 TASMAN DR
MILPITAS, CA 950357456
Phone: 510 498-3200
Fax: –
Web: www.solaredge.com
CEO: Zvi Lando
CFO: Ronen Faier
HR: Renee Lach
FYE: December 31
Type: Private

SolarEdge is a leading provider of an optimized inverter solution that changed the way power is harvested and managed in photovoltaic (also known as PV) systems. Its direct current (DC) optimized inverter system maximizes power generation and lowers the cost of energy produced by the system. Its system consists of power optimizers, inverters, and a cloud-based monitoring platform. The product serves a wide variety of solar market segments, from residential solar installations to commercial and small utility-scale solar installations. SolarEdge's products have been installed in solar PV systems in about 135 countries. It has shipped approximately 83.9 million optimizers and some 3.5 million inverters. The company was founded in 2006 and launched an IPO in early 2015. The US generates approximately 40% of the company's revenue.

SOLARIS OILFIELD INFRASTRUCTURE INC   NYS: SOI

9811 Katy Freeway, Suite 700
Houston, TX 77024
Phone: 281 501-3070
Fax: –
Web: www.solarisoilfield.com
CEO: William A Zartler
CFO: Kyle S Ramachandran
HR: Sadia Smith
FYE: December 31
Type: Public

Solaris Oilfield Infrastructure designs, manufactures specialized equipment, which combined with technician support, last mile logistics services and its software solutions, this enables the company to provide a service offering that helps oil and natural gas operators and their suppliers to drive efficiencies and reduce costs during the completion phase of well development in US. The company specializes in developing all-electric equipment that automates the low pressure section of oil and gas well completion sites. The company offers turnkey last mile logistics management services, its proprietary top fill equipment to enable quick unloading from bottom drop trucks, its AutoBlend integrated electric blender, its fluid management systems and its proprietary Solaris Lens software.

	Annual Growth	12/19	12/20	12/21	12/22	12/23
Sales ($mil.)	4.9%	241.7	103.0	159.2	320.0	292.9
Net income ($ mil.)	(17.3%)	52.0	(29.3)	(0.9)	21.2	24.3
Market value ($ mil.)	(13.2%)	597.0	347.1	279.3	423.4	339.4
Employees	8.4%	245	125	179	344	338

SOLARWINDS NORTH AMERICA, INC.

7171 SOUTHWEST PKWY BLDG 400
AUSTIN, TX 787356139
Phone: 512 682-9300
Fax: –
Web: www.solarwinds.com
CEO: –
CFO: –
HR: –
FYE: December 31
Type: Private

SolarWinds provides software for managing information technology (IT) infrastructure such as networks, systems, databases, security, and help desks operating in on-premise, cloud, or hybrid environments. Rather than go through purchasing departments, the company sells directly to the administrators and developers who manage IT systems on a daily basis. While it counts some 275,000 customers in 190 countries, more than 60% of sales are to US customers. The company was taken private in 2016 by private equity firms Thoma Bravo and Silver Lake before making a public stock offering in October 2018.

SOLCO PLUMBING SUPPLY, INC.

413 LIBERTY AVE
BROOKLYN, NY 112073004
Phone: 718 345-1900
Fax: –
Web: www.solco.com
CEO: Stuart Baker
CFO: –
HR: –
FYE: December 31
Type: Private

Solco Plumbing Supply has been solving plumbing problems in the Big Apple for years. The company operates a half-dozen locations including showrooms and offices in Brooklyn, the Bronx, and Manhattan. Solco Plumbing sells wholesale heating, plumbing, ventilation, and air conditioning equipment to contractors, commercial clients, and plumbers in the metropolitan area. The company was founded in 1960 by Sol Shapiro. It is owned by current executives Stanford Weiner and Stuart Baker.

	Annual Growth	12/03	12/04	12/05	12/06	12/07
Sales ($mil.)	10.7%	–	42.0	46.8	–	57.1
Net income ($ mil.)	(24.3%)	–	0.2	0.4	–	0.0
Market value ($ mil.)	–	–	–	–	–	–
Employees	–	–	–	–	–	100

SOLERA HOLDINGS, LLC

1500 SOLANA BLVD STE 6300
WESTLAKE, TX 762621713
Phone: 817 961-2100
Fax: –
Web: www.solera.com
CEO: Jeff Tarr
CFO: Renato Giger
HR: –
FYE: June 30
Type: Private

Solera Holdings is the leading global provider of integrated vehicle lifecycle and fleet management software-as-a-service, data, and services. Through four lines of business ? vehicle claims, vehicle repairs, vehicle solutions and fleet solutions ? Solera is home to many leading brands in the vehicle lifecycle ecosystem, including Identifix, Audatex, DealerSocket, Omnitracs, eDriving/Mentor, Explore, CAP HPI, Autodata, and others. Solera empowers its customers to succeed in the digital age by providing them with a "one-stop shop" solution that streamlines operations, offers data-driven analytics, and enhances customer engagement. The company serves over 300,000 global customers and partners in over 100 countries. Solera was acquired by private equity firm Vista Equity Partners in 2016.

SOLERITY, INC.

2010 CORPORATE RDG STE 450
MC LEAN, VA 22102
Phone: 703 663-2777
Fax: −
Web: www.solerity.com

CEO: Babs Doherty
CFO: Dan Muse
HR: Patricia Williamson
FYE: December 31
Type: Private

Preferred Systems Solutions (PSS) would rather that you not call anyone else for help with your information technology (IT) systems. The company provides a variety of services such as technical call center support, custom software development, database administration, and networking to military and civilian government agencies and commercial organizations. PSS also offers environmental, network, and systems engineering services, as well as program management and consulting. The company's clients have included the Food and Drug Administration, Computer Sciences Corporation, and the US Army.

	Annual Growth	12/95	12/96	12/97	12/98	12/09
Sales ($mil.)	80.4%	−	−	−	0.0	47.5
Net income ($ mil.)	10.6%	−	−	−	0.8	2.4
Market value ($ mil.)	−	−	−	−	−	−
Employees	−	−	−	−	−	375

SOLIGENIX INC

NAS: SNGX

29 Emmons Drive, Suite B-10
Princeton, NJ 08540
Phone: 609 538-8200
Fax: −
Web: www.soligenix.com

CEO: Christopher J Schaber
CFO: Jonathan Guarino
HR: −
FYE: December 31
Type: Public

Soligenix (formerly DOR BioPharma) is opening the door to more effective biodefense. The company's BioDefense unit is focusing on the development of nasally administered vaccines for such bioterror threats as ricin and botulinum toxins. Ricin vaccine candidate RiVax is in early-stage clinical trials. Through its BioTherapeutics division, Soligenix is developing lead candidate orBec, an orally administered drug using the same active ingredient as GlaxoSmithKline's allergy and asthma drug Beconase; orBec is a potential therapy for intestinal graft-versus-host disease, a life-threatening complication of bone marrow transplantation.

	Annual Growth	12/19	12/20	12/21	12/22	12/23
Sales ($mil.)	(34.7%)	4.6	2.4	0.8	0.9	0.8
Net income ($ mil.)	−	(9.4)	(17.7)	(12.6)	(13.8)	(6.1)
Market value ($ mil.)	(15.0%)	15.0	13.3	6.9	4.7	7.9
Employees	(1.6%)	16	18	15	15	15

SOLITARIO RESOURCES CORP

ASE: XPL

4251 Kipling St., Suite 390
Wheat Ridge, CO 80033
Phone: 303 534-1030
Fax: −
Web: www.solitarioxr.com

CEO: −
CFO: −
HR: −
FYE: December 31
Type: Public

Solitude can be a precious resource, but Solitario Exploration & Royalty is more interested in finding precious minerals. The company explores and develops gold, silver, platinum, and zinc properties in Brazil, Mexico, and Peru. Solitario has formed alliances to help finance its exploration work with industry giants like Newmont Mining and Anglo Platinum. None of its properties are in development. The company changed its name from Solitario Resources in 2008. The following year it agreed to buy Metallic Ventures Gold, which has properties in Nevada. Not long after, International Minerals came in with its own offer for Metallic Ventures.

	Annual Growth	12/19	12/20	12/21	12/22	12/23
Sales ($mil.)	−	0.4	−	−	−	−
Net income ($ mil.)	−	(3.3)	(0.9)	(2.4)	(3.9)	(3.8)
Market value ($ mil.)	16.9%	23.9	44.8	39.8	49.4	44.6
Employees	18.9%	3	3	10	6	6

SOLITRON DEVICES, INC.

NBB: SODI

901 Sansburys Way
West Palm Beach, FL 33411
Phone: 561 848-4311
Fax: 561 863-5846
Web: www.solitrondevices.com

CEO: Tim Eriksen
CFO: Tim Eriksen
HR: −
FYE: February 28
Type: Public

Solitron Devices' tiny devices have taken some big trips -- to Jupiter on the Galileo spacecraft and to Mars on the Sojourner. Used primarily in military and aerospace applications, the company's solid-state semiconductor components include thin-film resistors, field-effect and power transistors, and hybrid circuits. Nearly all of Solitron's sales come from US government contractors, including Raytheon and Lockheed Martin and the US government itself. Solitron has faced ongoing financial challenges (plus attention from the EPA in relation to some of the company's former manufacturing sites).

	Annual Growth	02/19	02/20	02/21	02/22	02/23
Sales ($mil.)	(9.1%)	9.4	9.2	10.5	12.3	6.4
Net income ($ mil.)	−	(1.4)	(0.6)	1.4	3.5	0.8
Market value ($ mil.)	43.9%	4.9	5.8	14.0	20.8	21.0
Employees	−	−	74	69	58	47

SOLUNA HOLDINGS INC

NAS: SLNH

325 Washington Avenue Extension
Albany, NY 12205
Phone: 516 216-9257
Fax: −
Web: www.solunacomputing.com

CEO: Michael Toporek
CFO: David Michaels
HR: −
FYE: December 31
Type: Public

Mechanical Technology Inc. (MTI) is warming up to the alternative energy market. The company's MTI Instruments, Inc. subsidiary (MTII) specializes in the design, manufacture and service of non-contact precision test and measurement equipment and makes computer-based aircraft engine balancing systems, capacitance measuring systems, and non-contact sensing instrumentation. MTII Instruments serves customers in the aerospace, automotive, bioengineering, computer, and semiconductor industries. MTI has diversified its offerings by investing in the alternative energy market. MTI was founded by two entrepreneurs in 1961.

	Annual Growth	12/18	12/19	12/20	12/21	12/22
Sales ($mil.)	37.2%	8.1	6.6	9.6	14.3	28.5
Net income ($ mil.)	−	1.9	0.3	1.9	(5.3)	(98.7)
Market value ($ mil.)	(25.1%)	0.6	0.6	0.6	8.0	0.2
Employees	−	−	−	33	62	32

SOMALOGIC OPERATING CO., INC.

2945 WILDERNESS PL
BOULDER, CO 803012255
Phone: 303 625-9000
Fax: −
Web: www.somalogic.com

CEO: −
CFO: Matthew Norkunas
HR: Alexandra Storm
FYE: December 31
Type: Private

SomaLogic is shaking down proteins to find out what they know and how it might be helpful. Its aptamer arrays bind to multiple proteins simultaneously and uses them as biomarkers to reveal a disease's signature. Data gathered from its technology platform and products may eventually be used to develop screenings, diagnostics, and new drugs for a variety of diseases. SomaLogic helps fund its work by entering into research collaboration with larger firms, including Otsuka and Quest Diagnostics.

SOMERSET TIRE SERVICE, INC.

358 SAW MILL RIVER RD
MILLWOOD, NY 105461014
Phone: 732 356-8500
Fax: –
Web: www.mavis.com

CEO: William Caulin
CFO: Anthony Losardo
HR: –
FYE: December 31
Type: Private

Somerset Tire Service (STS) operates about 145 tire and auto centers throughout New Jersey, New York, and Pennsylvania. The company primarily sells tires, auto parts, batteries, and accessories under such top brand names as Bridgestone, Firestone, Michelin, Toyo, Pirelli, Goodyear, Yokohama, and Continental. Operating under the banner STS Tire & Auto Centers, the company's locations feature a window between the store and service bays, so customers can watch the work being done on their cars. STS has grown by acquiring other regional tire and service centers with hopes of saturating the Northeast before moving outside its home region. Founded in 1958, the company is employee-owned.

	Annual Growth	12/09	12/10	12/11	12/12	12/13
Sales ($mil.)	4.4%	–	189.2	201.4	203.6	214.9
Net income ($ mil.)	(2.3%)	–	10.6	8.7	7.7	9.9
Market value ($ mil.)	–	–	–	–	–	–
Employees	–	–	–	–	–	1,000

SONESTA INTERNATIONAL HOTELS CORPORATION

400 CENTRE ST STE 100
NEWTON, MA 024582076
Phone: 770 923-1775
Fax: –
Web: www.sonesta.com

CEO: Carlos Flores
CFO: –
HR: Jennifer Rausch
FYE: December 31
Type: Private

Siesta whenever you want at Sonesta International Hotels. The company operates several hotels in the US (Boston, Miami, New Orleans, and Orlando) and Egypt, while its name is licensed to additional hotels in Chile, Columbia, Egypt, St. Maarten, Brazil, and Peru. The luxury properties cater to upscale business and leisure travelers, and are designed to showcase the history and culture of their locales. Sonesta also operates three cruise ships on the Nile. The firm was founded by "Sonny" Sonnabend in the 1940s. Members of the Sonnabend family (including executive chairman Peter and CEO Stephanie) continue to run the business. "Sonesta" is a combination of the names of Sonny and his wife Esther.

SONIC AUTOMOTIVE, INC.
NYS: SAH

4401 Colwick Road
Charlotte, NC 28211
Phone: 704 566-2400
Fax: 704 536-5116
Web: www.sonicautomotive.com

CEO: –
CFO: –
HR: –
FYE: December 31
Type: Public

Sonic Automotive is one of the leading US auto dealers, with approximately 110 stores in its Franchised Dealerships more than 50 stores in EchoPark segment, and eight stores in the Powersports Segment. Sonic operates more than 140 new vehicle franchises and more than 15 collision repair centers in major markets in about 20 states. The company sells nearly 30 brands of cars and light trucks. In addition, a majority of the company's franchised dealerships are either luxury or mid-line import brands, including BMW, Mercedes, Audi, Honda, Toyota, and some other leading brands. Chairman and Chief Executive Officer, David Bruton Smith, also serves as a director of Speedway Motorsports.

	Annual Growth	12/19	12/20	12/21	12/22	12/23
Sales ($mil.)	8.3%	10,454	9,767.0	12,396	14,001	14,372
Net income ($ mil.)	5.4%	144.1	(51.4)	348.9	88.5	178.2
Market value ($ mil.)	16.0%	1,052.8	1,309.9	1,679.4	1,673.3	1,909.0
Employees	3.1%	9,300	8,100	10,200	10,300	10,500

SONIC FOUNDRY, INC.
NBB: SOFO

222 West Washington Ave
Madison, WI 53703
Phone: 608 443-1600
Fax: –
Web: www.sonicfoundry.com

CEO: –
CFO: –
HR: –
FYE: September 30
Type: Public

It's about more than just sound at Sonic Foundry. The company's Mediasite recorders and software enable educational institutions (more than half of sales), corporations, and government agencies to capture, stream, and archive online multimedia presentations. Its products are used for corporate meetings, media analysis, distance learning, and content publishing. Sonic Foundry also provides webcasting services, and it offers managed communications services -- including content hosting and delivery. It markets through resellers, its own sales team, and system integrator partnerships. The company's customers have included Thermo Fisher Scientific, BAE Systems, and Georgetown University.

	Annual Growth	09/19	09/20	09/21	09/22	09/23
Sales ($mil.)	(10.7%)	34.8	34.8	35.2	27.5	22.1
Net income ($ mil.)	–	(3.6)	(0.2)	3.1	(7.1)	(19.3)
Market value ($ mil.)	(12.5%)	13.6	41.3	46.1	14.9	8.0
Employees	(4.4%)	183	177	180	193	153

SONIC LLC

300 JOHNNY BENCH DR
OKLAHOMA CITY, OK 731042471
Phone: 405 225-5000
Fax: –
Web: online.sonicdrivein.com

CEO: J C Hudson
CFO: –
HR: –
FYE: August 31
Type: Private

SONIC, founded in 1953, is the largest drive-in restaurant brand in the United States with more than 3,500 restaurants in about 45 states. Served by SONIC's iconic Carhops, the restaurant's expansive, award-winning menu offers unique, breakfast, lunch, dinner, snack, and drink options for the whole family. SONIC is part of the Inspire Brands family of restaurants.

	Annual Growth	08/13	08/14	08/15	08/16	08/17
Sales ($mil.)	(11.3%)	–	–	606.1	606.3	477.3
Net income ($ mil.)	(0.6%)	–	–	64.5	64.1	63.7
Market value ($ mil.)	–	–	–	–	–	–
Employees	–	–	–	–	–	6,173

SONIDA SENIOR LIVING INC
NYS: SNDA

16301 Quorum Drive, Suite 160A
Addison, TX 75001
Phone: 972 770-5600
Fax: 972 770-5666
Web: www.capitalsenior.com

CEO: Kimberly S Lody
CFO: Tabitha Obenour
HR: –
FYE: December 31
Type: Public

Sonida Senior Living, Inc. (formerly Capital Senior Living) is one of the leading owner-operators of senior housing communities in the US in terms of resident capacity. It provides independent living, assisted living, and memory care services which may be bridged by home care through independent home care agencies. It owns or manages some 70 senior housing communities with a total of approximately 8,000 residents in roughly 20 states, including around 60 senior housing communities that the Company owned and about 10 communities that the Company third-party managed. Specialized care units for treatment of Alzheimer's patients are available. Private pay sources bring in about 90% of the company's revenue.

	Annual Growth	12/19	12/20	12/21	12/22	12/23
Sales ($mil.)	(13.1%)	447.1	383.9	234.7	238.4	255.3
Net income ($ mil.)	–	(36.0)	(295.4)	125.6	(54.4)	(21.1)
Market value ($ mil.)	33.0%	25.3	100.9	233.0	102.2	79.0
Employees	(12.0%)	6,600	3,416	3,509	3,497	3,955

SONIM TECHNOLOGIES INC
NAS: SONM

4445 Eastgate Mall, Suite 200
San Diego, CA 92121
Phone: 650 378-8100
Fax: –
Web: www.sonimtech.com

CEO: Peter H Liu
CFO: Clay Crolius
HR: –
FYE: December 31
Type: Public

Sonim Technologies makes products that make mobile voice-over-IP communications better. The company manufactures servers and software that allows mobile wireless carriers to provide features like push-to-talk (walkie-talkie) and direct voice messaging. The company has also produced a rugged GSM mobile phone designed for use in harsh environments. Its solutions fall into three main categories: ultra-rugged mobile devices, industrial-grade accessories and cloud-based software and application services. In 2019, it sold approximately 39,000 mobile phones in Canada and 300,000 in the US (which markets include rugged feature phones, smart consumer rugged phones, smart ultra-rugged phones and life-proofed smart phones). Nearly 80% of Somin's revenue comes from US. Founded in 1999, the company goes public in 2019.

	Annual Growth	12/19	12/20	12/21	12/22	12/23
Sales ($mil.)	(5.3%)	116.3	64.0	54.6	69.8	93.6
Net income ($ mil.)	–	(25.8)	(29.9)	(38.6)	(14.1)	(0.1)
Market value ($ mil.)	(32.9%)	156.4	31.2	39.7	18.3	31.7
Employees	(36.1%)	403	317	102	77	67

SONO-TEK CORP.
NAS: SOTK

2012 Route 9W
Milton, NY 12547
Phone: 845 795-2020
Fax: –
Web: www.sono-tek.com

CEO: R S Harshbarger
CFO: Stephen J Bagley
HR: –
FYE: February 28
Type: Public

Sono-Tek wants to spray it, not say it. The company makes ultrasonic liquid atomizing nozzles that can apply fluids such as flux (used with solder on electronic circuit boards), molten metals, and polymeric coatings. Its SonoFlux 2000F spray fluxer product is designed for high-volume operations. SonoFlux XL applies solder flux to electronic printed circuit boards that vary from two inches up to 24 inches in width. Sono-Tek's MediCoat product is used for stent coating, applying thin layers of expensive polymer and drug coating to arterial stents.

	Annual Growth	02/19	02/20	02/21	02/22	02/23
Sales ($mil.)	6.7%	11.6	15.4	14.8	17.1	15.1
Net income ($ mil.)	40.8%	0.2	1.1	1.1	2.5	0.6
Market value ($ mil.)	21.0%	39.7	35.7	66.9	81.1	85.0
Employees	5.4%	68	76	69	81	84

SONOCO PRODUCTS CO.
NYS: SON

1 N. Second St. Hartsville
Hartsville, SC 29550
Phone: 843 383-7000
Fax: 843 383-7008
Web: www.sonoco.com

CEO: R H Coker
CFO: Robert R Dillard
HR: –
FYE: December 31
Type: Public

Sonoco Products is a manufacturer of industrial, consumer protective, and healthcare packaging products. The company has approximately 300 locations in more than 30 countries, serving some of the world's best-known brands in some 85 nations. The company makes composite cans for things like snack foods, powdered beverages, and pet foods and produces flexible and rigid packaging (paper and plastic) for food, personal care items, and chemicals. Sonoco also manufactures thermoformed rigid plastics trays and devices, custom-engineered, molded foam protective packaging and components; temperature-assured packaging; retail security packaging. More than 70% of Sonoco's revenues are generated in the US.

	Annual Growth	12/19	12/20	12/21	12/22	12/23
Sales ($mil.)	6.0%	5,374.2	5,237.4	5,590.4	7,250.6	6,781.3
Net income ($ mil.)	13.0%	291.8	207.5	(85.5)	466.4	475.0
Market value ($ mil.)	(2.5%)	6,045.9	5,804.0	5,670.7	5,947.0	5,472.9
Employees	–	23,000	20,000	20,500	22,000	23,000

SONOMA PHARMACEUTICALS INC
NAS: SNOA

5445 Conestoga Court, Suite 150
Boulder, CO 80301
Phone: 800 759-9305
Fax: –
Web: www.sonomapharma.com

CEO: –
CFO: –
HR: –
FYE: March 31
Type: Public

Sonoma Pharmaceuticals (formerly Oculus) uses super-agents in its fight against the evil super-bug MRSA. The company works with proprietary platform technology Microcyn, a super-oxidized water-based solution designed to safely (i.e., without any known side effects) eliminate a wide range of annoying pathogens (including MRSA) attempting to infect patients with open wounds. Aside from use in wound care, the solution has potential applications for use in disinfectants and sterilization, as well as respiratory, dermatology, veterinary, and dental markets. Oculus' products are primarily sold through partnerships with distributors.

	Annual Growth	03/19	03/20	03/21	03/22	03/23
Sales ($mil.)	(8.5%)	19.0	18.9	18.6	12.6	13.3
Net income ($ mil.)	–	(11.8)	(2.9)	(4.0)	(5.1)	(5.2)
Market value ($ mil.)	0.9%	4.6	24.2	36.7	19.8	4.8
Employees	28.4%	63	300	200	177	171

SONOMA STATE UNIVERSITY

1801 E COTATI AVE
ROHNERT PARK, CA 949283609
Phone: 707 664-2880
Fax: –
Web: www.sonoma.edu

CEO: –
CFO: –
HR: –
FYE: June 30
Type: Private

Sonoma State University (SSU) was founded in 1960 as a center for teacher education; its roots are in a Santa Rosa-based teaching center established in 1956 by San Francisco State College (now San Francisco State University, or SFSU). The wine-country university is one of the smaller institutions in the California State University system. The university, which has about 9,000 students, offers about 60 bachelor's and master's degree at its 269-acre campus. It is divided into six schools: arts and humanities, business and economics, education, extended education, social sciences, and science and technology. SSU also offers joint graduate programs with SFSU, Sacramento State, and UC Davis.

	Annual Growth	06/14	06/15	06/18	06/20	06/22
Sales ($mil.)	8.8%	–	6.6	4.5	5.1	11.9
Net income ($ mil.)	19.6%	–	2.3	0.4	0.9	7.9
Market value ($ mil.)	–	–	–	–	–	–
Employees	–	–	–	–	–	100

SONOMAWEST HOLDINGS, INC.

2064 HWY 116 N
SEBASTOPOL, CA 95472
Phone: 707 824-2534
Fax: –
Web: www.sonomawestholdings.com

CEO: Craig R Stapleton
CFO: Craig R Stapleton
HR: –
FYE: June 30
Type: Private

Formerly Vacu-dry, SonomaWest sold its dehydrated fruit business in 2000 and 2001 in search of a candy apple future in real estate. The company now owns two former agricultural production properties (totaling some 90 acres) left over from its fruity past. The properties are located in Northern California's Sonoma County and are leased to multiple tenants for commercial use; Benziger Family Winery is one of its largest tenants. SonomaWest also holds an investment in telecommunications firm MetroPCS Communications. The Stapleton family, including CEO Craig Stapleton, acquired SonomaWest and took it private in 2011.

SOROS FUND MANAGEMENT LLC

250 W 55TH ST FL 27
NEW YORK, NY 100199710
Phone: 212 872-1054
Fax: –
Web: www.pdsoros.org

CEO: –
CFO: Abbas E Zuaiter
HR: –
FYE: December 31
Type: Private

George Soros makes headlines, but not nearly as well as he makes money. His Soros Fund Management's generally successful hedge funds, including its flagship Quantum Fund, often invest according to macroeconomic trends. The company oversees some $25 billion, which it uses to buy large stakes in the energy, transportation, financial, retail, and other industries. It owns stakes in oil exploration firm Hess Corporation and Ford Motor Company. Other investments include containership owner Global Ship Lease, retail site Bluefly, and Lattice Semiconductor. In 2011 Soros Fund Management closed itself to outside investors and now focuses solely on managing the money of Soros and his family.

	Annual Growth	12/05	12/06	12/07	12/08	12/22
Assets ($mil.)	(6.1%)	–	–	–	157.1	64.7
Net income ($ mil.)	–	–	–	–	–	(0.2)
Market value ($ mil.)	–	–	–	–	–	–
Employees	–	–	–	–	–	160

SOTHEBY'S

1334 YORK AVE
NEW YORK, NY 100214806
Phone: 212 606-7000
Fax: –
Web: www.sothebys.com

CEO: Charles F Stewart
CFO: Michael Goss
HR: Elizabeth Holmes
FYE: December 31
Type: Private

Established in 1744, Sotheby's is the world's largest, most trusted and dynamic marketplace for art and luxury. The company empowers its international community of collectors and connoisseurs to discover, acquire finance and consign fine arts and rare objects. In addition, the company also offers advisory, private sales, fiduciary client group, global partnership, financial services/lending, fine art storage, and more. It has a global network of specialists spanning some 40 countries and almost 45 departments, which include Contemporary Art, Modern and Impressionist Art, Old Masters, Chinese Works of Art, jewelry, watches, wine and spirits, and interiors, among many others.

SOTHERLY HOTELS INC   NMS: SOHO

306 South Henry Street, Suite 100
Williamsburg, VA 23185
Phone: 757 229-5648
Fax: –
Web: www.sotherlyhotels.com

CEO: David R Folsom
CFO: Anthony E Domalski
HR: –
FYE: December 31
Type: Public

MHI Hospitality owns seven full-service hotels operating under the Hilton, Holiday Inn, Sheraton, and Crowne Plaza brands in the mid-Atlantic and southeastern US. The company also holds a minority stake in another hotel, has two under development, and owns leasehold interests in common areas of the Shell Island Resort in Wilmington, North Carolina. MHI Hotel Services, which spun off MHI Hospitality in 2004, manages the REIT's properties. Executive officers and board members of MHI Hospitality collectively own more than a quarter of the company.

	Annual Growth	12/19	12/20	12/21	12/22	12/23
Sales ($mil.)	(1.6%)	185.8	71.5	127.6	166.1	173.8
Net income ($ mil.)	19.9%	1.9	(49.2)	(26.2)	32.5	3.9
Market value ($ mil.)	(31.5%)	133.5	49.2	41.2	35.7	29.3
Employees	(8.8%)	13	10	10	9	9

SOTHYS U.S.A., INC.

1500 NW 94TH AVE
DORAL, FL 331722846
Phone: 305 594-4222
Fax: –
Web: www.sothys.fr

CEO: Yann Pacreau
CFO: –
HR: –
FYE: December 31
Type: Private

Sothys U.S.A. wants women to be able to wash away the stress of the day so that they can keep their girlish glow alive and well. The company offers high-end personal care and beauty products, including cleansers, masks, moisturizers, sun block, and make-up. It also features skin care products for men through its Sothys Homme line. In the company's licensed salons, trained estheticians provide spa treatments and create custom skin care programs for individual clients. Sothys U.S.A. is a subsidiary of Sothys Paris and has had a US presence for more than two decades.

	Annual Growth	12/06	12/07	12/08	12/12	12/13
Sales ($mil.)	(4.4%)	–	9.0	8.3	7.5	6.9
Net income ($ mil.)	–	–	(0.1)	(0.2)	0.0	0.0
Market value ($ mil.)	–	–	–	–	–	–
Employees	–	–	–	–	–	47

SOUND FINANCIAL BANCORP INC   NAS: SFBC

2400 3rd Avenue, Suite 150
Seattle, WA 98121
Phone: 206 448-0884
Fax: –
Web: www.soundcb.com

CEO: Laurie Stewart
CFO: Matthew Deines
HR: –
FYE: December 31
Type: Public

Sounds heard by Sound Financial's banks could include that of crisp $100 bills and the foghorns of passing ships. Located in the Puget Sound region surrounding Seattle, Sound Financial is a bank holding company operating principally through Sound Community Bank and its five area locations. The bank offers traditional savings and checking accounts to retail and business customers, as well as residential mortgages, home equity loans, and various secured and unsecured consumer loans. It also provides construction, land, commercial business, and multifamily housing loans, but to a lesser extent. Sound Community Bank traces it roots back to 1953, when it was founded as a credit union.

	Annual Growth	12/19	12/20	12/21	12/22	12/23
Assets ($mil.)	8.4%	719.9	861.4	919.7	976.4	995.2
Net income ($ mil.)	2.7%	6.7	8.9	9.2	8.8	7.4
Market value ($ mil.)	2.0%	91.8	80.9	112.2	100.1	99.4
Employees	2.6%	132	120	136	140	146

SOUND HEALTH SOLUTIONS INC

2101 Faraday Avenue
Carlsbad, CA 92008
Phone: 760 603-9120
Fax: 760 603-9170
Web: www.ivow.com

CEO: –
CFO: –
HR: –
FYE: December 31
Type: Public

Sound Health Solutions will cut you down to size. The company manages weight loss programs for the employees of large corporations and members of union organizations. Its doctor-supervised programs incorporate exercise, nutrition education, and counseling to help participants control their weight. Sound Health has several clinics in Washington State and one in New York City. It has also developed a Web-based version of its weight-loss program, called eSoundHealth, which works with Microsoft's electronic personal health record product, HealthVault, and makes Sound Health Solutions available to the general public.

	Annual Growth	12/01	12/02	12/03	12/04	12/05
Sales ($mil.)	(39.0%)	9.3	11.1	8.7	1.7	1.3
Net income ($ mil.)	–	(3.2)	(1.1)	(2.0)	(3.6)	(2.7)
Market value ($ mil.)	19.9%	5.7	6.0	2.7	2.4	11.7
Employees	(10.3%)	37	35	35	20	24

SOURCECORP, INCORPORATED

2701 E GRAUWYLER RD
IRVING, TX 750613414
Phone: 866 321-5854
Fax: –
Web: www.exelatech.com

CEO: –
CFO: –
HR: –
FYE: December 31
Type: Private

If your company's business process needs a boost, turn to SourceHOV. Formerly SOURCECORP, the company is a business process outsourcing and consulting firm that provides information management, tax services, and legal consulting to clients from a range of industries. It also has expertise in class action settlement administration, consulting related to employment matters, and consulting for healthcare providers. In 2011, the company (then called SOURCECORP) was acquired by India-based HOV Services Limited and rebranded under the SourceHOV name.

SOUTH BEND MEDICAL FOUNDATION INC

3355 DOUGLAS RD
SOUTH BEND, IN 466351779
Phone: 574 234-4176
Fax: –
Web: www.sbmf.org

CEO: –
CFO: –
HR: Jim Frain
FYE: December 31
Type: Private

South Bend Medical Foundation provides clinical testing and blood bank services for communities in Illinois, Indiana, Kentucky, Michigan, and Ohio. The foundation works together with local hospitals, clinics, and doctors' offices to provide diagnostic laboratory services for patients. It operates about a dozen lab facilities at medical facilities and independent locations. The company's forensic toxicology department conducts employee and athletic drug testing. South Bend Medical Foundation also provides public health screenings for diseases such as sickle cell anemia and prostrate cancer. The foundation was formed in 1912 by a group of physicians.

	Annual Growth	12/14	12/15	12/17	12/19	12/21
Sales ($mil.)	(21.7%)	–	91.8	85.5	129.3	21.2
Net income ($ mil.)	–	–	(0.1)	3.2	64.2	(4.7)
Market value ($ mil.)	–	–	–	–	–	–
Employees	–	–	–	–	–	800

SOUTH BROWARD HOSPITAL DISTRICT

3501 JOHNSON ST
HOLLYWOOD, FL 330215421
Phone: 954 987-2000
Fax: –
Web: www.jdch.com

CEO: K S Wester
CFO: –
HR: –
FYE: April 30
Type: Private

South Broward Hospital District (dba Memorial Healthcare System) is an independent special tax district with hospitals across southern Broward County and has more than 1,700 physicians and APPs providing high-quality health services to residents of South Florida. The system's major hospitals include Memorial Regional Hospital, Memorial Hospital Pembroke, Memorial Hospital West, and Memorial Hospital Miramar. The hospitals have a combined capacity of about 2,045 licensed beds and provide services including diagnostic, emergency, surgical, and rehabilitative care, among others. Memorial also operates a pediatric hospital, cardiac and vascular medicine institute, a cancer treatment center, and a center for women's health, as well as nursing home facilities (120 beds) and community clinics.

	Annual Growth	04/17	04/18	04/19	04/20	04/21
Sales ($mil.)	5.1%	–	2,014.9	2,148.0	2,159.7	2,339.5
Net income ($ mil.)	63.7%	–	64.6	165.5	156.6	283.8
Market value ($ mil.)	–	–	–	–	–	–
Employees	–	–	–	–	–	9,200

SOUTH CAROLINA DEPARTMENT OF EDUCATION

1429 SENATE ST
COLUMBIA, SC 292013730
Phone: 803 734-8500
Fax: –
Web: www.sc.gov

CEO: –
CFO: –
HR: –
FYE: June 30
Type: Private

The South Carolina Department of Education (SDE) still has hope in the public school system. The agency is dedicated to improving the quality of education in the state's some 1,100 public schools in 85 districts through its five divisions. SDE provides services in areas such as curriculum and assessment, quality of leadership, maintenance of school facilities, and food and nutrition. The department also helps enforce state and federal education laws, as well as regulations endorsed by the State Board of Education. The department has an annual budget of nearly $7 billion.

SOUTH CAROLINA PUBLIC SERVICE AUTHORITY (INC)

1 RIVERWOOD DR
MONCKS CORNER, SC 294612998
Phone: 843 761-4121
Fax: –
Web: www.santeecooper.com

CEO: Jimmy Staton
CFO: Jeff Armfield
HR: Edwina Roseborobarnes
FYE: December 31
Type: Private

This company turns the lights on in South Carolina. South Carolina Public Service Authority, known as Santee Cooper (after two interconnected river systems), provides wholesale electricity to 20 cooperatives and two municipalities that serve more than 2 million customers in South Carolina. It directly retails electricity to more than 174,000 customers. One of the largest US state-owned utilities, Santee Cooper operates in all 46 counties in South Carolina and has stakes in power plants (fossil-fueled, nuclear, hydro, and renewable) that give it more than 5,180 MW of generating capacity. Its Santee Cooper Regional Water System also distributes water to customers in its service area.

	Annual Growth	12/18	12/19	12/20	12/21	12/22
Sales ($mil.)	10.4%	–	–	–	1,765.8	1,949.1
Net income ($ mil.)	–	–	–	–	39.1	(4.9)
Market value ($ mil.)	–	–	–	–	–	–
Employees	–	–	–	–	–	1,748

SOUTH CAROLINA STATE PORTS AUTHORITY

200 PORTS AUTHORITY DR
MOUNT PLEASANT, SC 294647998
Phone: 843 723-8651
Fax: –
Web: www.scspa.com

CEO: –
CFO: –
HR: –
FYE: June 30
Type: Private

Offering gateways for trade in the Palmetto State, The South Carolina State Ports Authority (SCSPA) operates marine terminals at the ports in Charleston and Georgetown. The agency maintains its own container terminals at each port and provides container handling services; in addition, space at the ports is leased to other terminal operators. The Port of Charleston provides services for cruise ships as well as for freight-carrying vessels, including freight rail service. SCSPA is overseen by a nine-member board appointed by the governor along with the Secretaries of Transportation and Commerce. The agency, which was founded in 1942, does not receive state money and is funded primarily by its operations.

	Annual Growth	06/18	06/19	06/20	06/21	06/22
Sales ($mil.)	14.6%	–	294.3	292.3	312.8	443.1
Net income ($ mil.)	(2.4%)	–	42.1	(112.5)	(28.5)	39.1
Market value ($ mil.)	–	–	–	–	–	–
Employees	–	–	–	–	–	493

SOUTH CENTRAL COMMUNICATIONS CORPORATION

20 NW 3RD ST STE 1400
EVANSVILLE, IN 477081253
Phone: 812 463-7950
Fax: –
Web: www.southcentralinc.com

CEO: J P Engelbrecht
CFO: Randy Champion
HR: –
FYE: December 31
Type: Private

South Central Communications enjoys making waves in the central US radio market. The company owns and operates more than a dozen radio stations serving midsized and large markets in Tennessee and Indiana with a range of mostly music programming. In addition, the company operates Muzak franchises (subscriber-based radio and voice services targeted to businesses) in seven states. Other operations include Dish Network installation services, restaurant drive-thru intercoms, and office paging systems. Its also owns Knoxville independent digital television station, WMAK. The family-owned company was started in 1946 by John A. Engelbrecht.

	Annual Growth	12/07	12/08	12/09	12/10	12/11
Sales ($mil.)	5.8%	–	–	–	38.6	40.8
Net income ($ mil.)	28.8%	–	–	–	3.2	4.1
Market value ($ mil.)	–	–	–	–	–	–
Employees	–	–	–	–	–	298

SOUTH CENTRAL POWER COMPANY INC

720 MILL PARK DR
LANCASTER, OH 431307933
Phone: 740 653-4422
Fax: –
Web: www.southcentralpower.com

CEO: Rick Lemonds
CFO: Rebecca Witt
HR: –
FYE: December 31
Type: Private

Although South Central Power Company may sound like a power plant in Watts, Los Angeles, it is in fact a member-owned cooperative that provides electricity to consumers and businesses in southern Ohio. An affiliate of the nationwide Touchstone Energy Cooperative network, the electric cooperative provides power to more than 115,570 customers over 11,000 miles of power lines. In addition to distributing electricity, South Central Power also provides outdoor lighting, surge suppression products, security systems, water heater switches, and other energy-related services.

	Annual Growth	12/15	12/16	12/18	12/21	12/22
Sales ($mil.)	4.6%	–	282.1	338.8	353.0	369.5
Net income ($ mil.)	–	–	14.4	–	–	–
Market value ($ mil.)	–	–	–	–	–	–
Employees	–	–	–	–	–	235

SOUTH DAKOTA SCHOOL OF MINES AND TECHNOLOGY FOUNDATION

501 E SAINT JOSEPH ST
RAPID CITY, SD 577013901
Phone: 605 394-2511
Fax: –
Web: www.sdsmt.edu

CEO: –
CFO: –
HR: –
FYE: June 30
Type: Private

The South Dakota School of Mines and Technology, also known as South Dakota Tech, was founded in 1885. About 2,000 Tech students pursue undergraduate and graduate degrees, primarily in science and engineering fields. The school offers instruction through more than a dozen departments in a handful of colleges, which include the College of Earth Systems, the College of Interdisciplinary Studies, the College of Material Sciences and Engineering, and the College of Systems Engineering.

	Annual Growth	06/08	06/09	06/10	06/11	06/21
Sales ($mil.)	49.4%	–	0.2	6.4	0.2	24.6
Net income ($ mil.)	–	–	(0.1)	0.7	(0.0)	17.4
Market value ($ mil.)	–	–	–	–	–	–
Employees	–	–	–	–	–	350

SOUTH DAKOTA SOYBEAN PROCESSORS LLC   NBB: SDSY A

100 Caspian Avenue, P.O. Box 500
Volga, SD 57071
Phone: 605 627-9240
Fax: –
Web: www.sdsbp.com

CEO: –
CFO: –
HR: –
FYE: December 31
Type: Public

Things are "soy-good" at South Dakota Soybean Processors. The agricultural cooperative turns the more than 145 million bushels per year of soybeans from its 2,200 farmer/members into soybean oil, soybean hulls, and soybean meal. Its soybean meal is mainly sold to livestock feed companies and independent livestock producers. Most of South Dakota Soybean's crude soybean oil is sold to manufacturers of various consumer items (plastics and biodiesel manufacturers, for example), who further process it for use in their products. The US generates roughly 80% of the company's revenue.

	Annual Growth	12/18	12/19	12/20	12/21	12/22
Sales ($mil.)	16.5%	391.4	371.3	415.0	590.2	721.5
Net income ($ mil.)	27.1%	25.9	11.0	15.6	28.0	67.5
Market value ($ mil.)	–	–	97.6	110.4	94.3	146.9
Employees	(0.6%)	123	121	118	121	120

SOUTH DAKOTA STATE MEDICAL HOLDING COMPANY, INC.

2600 W 49TH ST STE 200
SIOUX FALLS, SD 571056569
Phone: 605 334-4000
Fax: –
Web: www.sdsma.org

CEO: Kirk Zimmer
CFO: –
HR: Greg Jasmer
FYE: December 31
Type: Private

South Dakota State Medical Holding Company, operating under the name DAKOTACARE, is a statewide HMO plan. Product offerings include comprehensive group and individual medical plans, flexible spending and COBRA plans, Medicare Advantage coverage, and dental, life, and disability policies. All hospitals and nearly all physicians in South Dakota contract with the firm. In addition to serving some 100,000 customers in its home state, third-party administration (TPA) subsidiary DAKOTACARE Administrative Services is active in over a dozen neighboring states. Founded in 1986, DAKOTACARE is the managed care affiliate of the South Dakota State Medical Association.

SOUTH DAKOTA STATE UNIVERSITY

2201 ADMINISTRATION LN
BROOKINGS, SD 570070001
Phone: 605 688-6101
Fax: –
Web: www.sdstate.edu

CEO: –
CFO: –
HR: –
FYE: June 30
Type: Private

South Dakota State University (SDSU) is big on education in the Mount Rushmore State. The college offers undergraduate, graduate, and pre-professional programs to some 13,000 students. Academic offerings include agriculture, engineering, and pharmacy courses. Its SDSU Sioux Falls Program targets non-traditional students (such as students with jobs and families) by providing evening and weekend classes. Notable SDSU alumni include former US Senator Tom Daschle and professional football players Adam Timmerman and Adam Vinatieri. SDSU, a public school governed by the South Dakota Board of Regents, was founded as a land grant college in 1881.

	Annual Growth	06/15	06/16	06/17	06/18	06/19
Sales ($mil.)	0.2%	–	209.8	213.6	213.3	211.3
Net income ($ mil.)	–	–	44.3	31.6	44.3	(86.4)
Market value ($ mil.)	–	–	–	–	–	–
Employees	–	–	–	–	–	2,000

SOUTH JERSEY GAS CO.

1 South Jersey Plaza
Folsom, NJ 08037
Phone: 609 561-9000
Fax: –
Web: www.sjindustries.com

CEO: Jeffrey E Dubois
CFO: Stephen H Clark
HR: –
FYE: December 31
Type: Public

Atlantic City gamblers don't have to gamble on getting hot showers, thanks to South Jersey Gas, which transmits and distributes natural gas to more than 343,560 customers in its regulated service territory in seven southern New Jersey counties. The utility, a subsidiary of South Jersey Industries, also provides gas transportation services and sells wholesale gas to power plant operators and other energy marketing companies. South Jersey Gas's service territory of 2,500 sq. miles includes 112 towns and cities throughout Atlantic, Cape May, Cumberland, and Salem Counties, and in portions of Burlington, Camden, and Gloucester Counties, with an estimated total population of 1.2 million. In 2017 South Jersey Gas agreed to purchase for $1.7 billion Elizabethtown Gas and Elkton Gas from a subsidiary of The Southern Company, adding nearly 300,000 new gas customers.

	Annual Growth	12/17	12/18	12/19	12/20	12/21
Sales ($mil.)	4.6%	517.3	548.0	569.2	571.8	618.4
Net income ($ mil.)	15.2%	72.6	82.9	87.4	108.1	127.6
Market value ($ mil.)	–	–	–	–	–	–
Employees	(5.0%)	530	550	450	441	432

SOUTH JERSEY INDUSTRIES, INC.

1 S JERSEY PLZ
HAMMONTON, NJ 080379109
Phone: 609 561-9000
Fax: –
Web: www.sjindustries.com

CEO: Michael J Renna
CFO: Steven R Cocchi
HR: Karen Phillips
FYE: December 31
Type: Private

South Jersey Industries (SJI) is Atlantic City's answer to cold casino nights. Its main subsidiary, South Jersey Gas (SJG), provided natural gas to nearly 411,300 residential, commercial and industrial customers in southern New Jersey, including Atlantic City. The utility has more than 6,800 miles of transmission and distribution mains; it also sells and transports wholesale gas. The company was founded in 1969. In 2022, South Jersey Industries Inc. agreed to be purchased by Infrastructure Investment Fund, a private vehicle focused on investing critical infrastructure assets, for $ 8.1 billion.

SOUTH MIAMI HOSPITAL, INC.

6200 SW 73RD ST
SOUTH MIAMI, FL 331434679
Phone: 786 662-4000
Fax: –
Web: www.baptisthealth.net

CEO: Lincoln S Mendez
CFO: –
HR: –
FYE: September 30
Type: Private

South Miami Hospital offers primary and tertiary health care services to the residents living near the University of Miami. The hospital has about 470 beds and is one of the largest members of Baptist Health South Florida, a top regional health system. Specialty services include emergency care, cardiovascular services, oncology, neurology, women's health, metabolic care, and rehabilitation. It operates an addiction treatment residential facility, provides home health care, and provides child development diagnostic and early intervention services. South Miami Hospital was founded in 1960.

	Annual Growth	09/18	09/19	09/20	09/21	09/22
Sales ($mil.)	6.6%	–	674.3	506.9	619.6	816.1
Net income ($ mil.)	(1.3%)	–	93.9	50.2	102.1	90.3
Market value ($ mil.)	–	–	–	–	–	–
Employees	–	–	–	–	–	2,205

SOUTH PENINSULA HOSPITAL, INC.

4300 BARTLETT ST
HOMER, AK 996037005
Phone: 907 235-0369
Fax: –
Web: www.sphosp.org

CEO: –
CFO: Lori Meyer
HR: –
FYE: June 30
Type: Private

South Peninsula Hospital provides a variety of medical services, including home health care, emergency medicine, surgery, orthopedics, and ophthalmology, for the residents of the Kenai Peninsula and surrounding areas in Alaska. The hospital also provides a 25-bed long-term facility that offers physical and occupational therapy services. In addition, South Peninsula Hospital provides community and staff education classes.

	Annual Growth	06/18	06/19	06/20	06/21	06/22
Sales ($mil.)	8.6%	–	86.7	87.3	101.4	111.1
Net income ($ mil.)	(24.3%)	–	11.5	10.1	12.9	5.0
Market value ($ mil.)	–	–	–	–	–	–
Employees	–	–	–	–	–	300

SOUTH SHORE HEALTH SYSTEM, INC.

55 FOGG RD
SOUTH WEYMOUTH, MA 021902432
Phone: 781 340-8000
Fax: –
Web: www.southshorehealth.org

CEO: Allen Smith
CFO: Stephen Jenney
HR: Ramona Barros
FYE: September 30
Type: Private

Operating a namesake hospital, South Shore Health and Educational Corporation is a charitable not-for-profit organization governed by a volunteer board of directors. The nearly 380-bed regional facility provides acute, outpatient, home health, emergency, and hospice care for residents of southeastern Massachusetts. Founded in 1922 as Weymouth Hospital, the hospital boasts a medical staff of about 900 physicians and other health care providers; altogether, it employs about 3,800 people. Specialized services include cancer care, emergency medicine, and pediatrics. Its home health care division comprises South Shore Visiting Nurse Association, Hospice of the South Shore, and Home & Health Resources. South Shore is merging with Partners HealthCare System.

	Annual Growth	09/15	09/16	09/19	09/21	09/22
Sales ($mil.)	(8.4%)	–	1.2	3.3	1.2	0.7
Net income ($ mil.)	(10.0%)	–	0.9	2.0	1.2	0.5
Market value ($ mil.)	–	–	–	–	–	–
Employees	–	–	–	–	–	3,000

SOUTH SHORE UNIVERSITY HOSPITAL

301 E MAIN ST
BAY SHORE, NY 117068408
Phone: 631 968-3000
Fax: –
Web: www.southsidehospital.org

CEO: –
CFO: –
HR: –
FYE: December 31
Type: Private

One of Long Island's oldest and largest community hospitals, Southside Hospital offers acute care and other services through its more than 340-bed facility. Established in 1913, Southside Hospital operates as part of North Shore-Long Island Jewish Health System (North Shore-LIJ Health System). Its facilities include a Vascular Institute, the Frank Gulden Radiation Oncology Center, Regional Center for Brain Injury Rehabilitation, Southside Hospital Institute of Neurosciences, and a Center for Wound Healing. As part of its operations, Southside Hospital also provides patients with pain management, cardiology, outpatient surgery, orthopedics, and women's services.

	Annual Growth	12/16	12/17	12/18	12/21	12/22
Sales ($mil.)	16.9%	–	447.0	464.8	672.6	975.3
Net income ($ mil.)	–	–	(20.9)	(20.2)	(0.1)	13.1
Market value ($ mil.)	–	–	–	–	–	–
Employees	–	–	–	–	–	1,900

SOUTHCO DISTRIBUTING COMPANY

2201 S JOHN ST
GOLDSBORO, NC 275307163
Phone: 919 735-8012
Fax: –
Web: www.southcodistributing.com

CEO: –
CFO: –
HR: –
FYE: December 28
Type: Private

This company makes sure you can get subs on the go from the convenience store. Southco Distributing is a leading convenience food supplier that distributes prepackaged sandwiches and other products to retail stores in seven states in the Southeast and Midwest. In addition to prepackaged foods, Southco provides branded quick-service kiosks and equipment that allow convenience stores and other retailers to offer food on the go. Its foodservice programs are branded under the names AutoFry, Pizza Primo, Sub Express, and Squawkers.

	Annual Growth	12/99	12/00	12/05	12/06	12/12
Sales ($mil.)	5.7%	–	203.8	–	253.9	397.2
Net income ($ mil.)	–	–	2.6	–	1.1	2.6
Market value ($ mil.)	–	–	–	–	–	–
Employees	–	–	–	–	–	225

SOUTHCOAST HEALTH SYSTEM, INC.

101 PAGE ST
NEW BEDFORD, MA 027403464
Phone: 508 997-1515
Fax: –
Web: www.southcoast.org

CEO: Keith Hovan
CFO: –
HR: Cheryl Oliveira
FYE: September 30
Type: Private

If you happen to get sick while vacationing on Cape Cod, the Southcoast Health System can help you get well again. The organization operates three Massachusetts hospitals (through its Southcoast Hospitals Group subsidiary) and about 40 other ancillary facilities serving Massachusetts and Rhode Island. The not-for-profit Southcoast Health has about 900 licensed beds total. It also owns assisted-living and other long-term facilities, home health care and hospice, and outpatient medical services. About half of its patients are covered by Medicare. In late 2016 Southcoast dropped its plans to merge with Rhode Island-based Care New England.

	Annual Growth	09/18	09/19	09/20	09/21	09/22
Sales ($mil.)	30.5%	–	20.7	36.1	39.1	46.1
Net income ($ mil.)	35.3%	–	11.2	18.3	25.2	27.8
Market value ($ mil.)	–	–	–	–	–	–
Employees	–	–	–	–	–	6,000

SOUTHCOAST HOSPITALS GROUP, INC.

363 HIGHLAND AVE
FALL RIVER, MA 027203703
Phone: 508 679-3131
Fax: –
Web: www.southcoast.org

CEO: –
CFO: –
HR: –
FYE: September 30
Type: Private

When you feel more than a little physically washed up, get to one of the Southcoast Hospitals Group facilities. The not-for-profit company provides medical services in the southeastern corner of Massachusetts and in Rhode Island. Its primary facilities in Massachusetts are the Charlton Memorial Hospital (with about 330 beds) in Fall River, St. Luke's Hospital (420 beds) in New Bedford, and Tobey Hospital (65 beds) in Wareham, which provide acute medical care and specialty services including cardiology, neurology, orthopedics, and women's care. Southcoast Hospitals Group also operates about 20 ancillary facilities, including nursing and assisted-living facilities and home health and hospice agencies.

	Annual Growth	09/03	09/04	09/06	09/12	09/13
Sales ($mil.)	4.9%	–	445.7	506.5	704.4	687.7
Net income ($ mil.)	5.4%	–	13.9	14.0	49.3	22.4
Market value ($ mil.)	–	–	–	–	–	–
Employees	–	–	–	–	–	3,853

SOUTHCROSS ENERGY PARTNERS LLC

2103 CITYWEST BLVD STE 900
HOUSTON, TX 770422835
Phone: 214 979-3700
Fax: –
Web: www.southcrossenergy.com

CEO: Patrick Giroir
CFO: James Lee
HR: Laura Ball
FYE: December 31
Type: Private

Southcross Energy Partners transports natural gas and natural gas liquids (NGLs) across the southern US. The company operates about 2,500 miles of intrastate pipeline in Alabama, Mississippi, and South Texas. More than half of its pipeline mileage is located in Texas, where it also has two gas processing plants that can process 185 million cu. ft. per day, two treating plants, and one fractionator. Top customers Formosa Hydrocarbons (a subsidiary of Formosa Plastics) and Sherwin Alumina together account for about 35% of sales. Southcross Energy formed in 2009 after it bought the Alabama, Mississippi, and Texas pipeline from Crosstex for $220 million. The company filed Chapter 11 in 2019.

SOUTHEAST MISSOURI STATE UNIVERSITY

1 UNIVERSITY PLZ
CAPE GIRARDEAU, MO 637014710
Phone: 573 651-2000
Fax: –
Web: www.semo.edu

CEO: –
CFO: –
HR: James Cook
FYE: June 30
Type: Private

Guess where this university is located. Southeast Missouri State University -- located in Cape Girardeau, Missouri (two hours south of St. Louis and three hours north of Memphis) -- offers some 200 areas of undergraduate study through five colleges, as well as graduate degrees in biology, business administration, history, mathematics, public administration, and a multitude of other fields. Nearly 12,000 students are enrolled at the school, which has a student-to-faculty ratio of 22-to-1. Southeast Missouri State University was founded in 1873 as a teacher's college.

	Annual Growth	06/18	06/19	06/20	06/21	06/22
Sales ($mil.)	(1.7%)	–	105.5	99.8	95.7	100.2
Net income ($ mil.)	–	–	(10.2)	(13.9)	3.2	3.9
Market value ($ mil.)	–	–	–	–	–	–
Employees	–	–	–	–	–	941

SOUTHEAST TEXAS INDUSTRIES, INC.

35911 US HIGHWAY 96 S
BUNA, TX 776124031
Phone: 409 994-3570
Fax: –
Web: www.setxind.com

CEO: –
CFO: James Parsley
HR: –
FYE: December 31
Type: Private

Southeast Texas Industries (aka STI Group) is a down home manufacturer that likes staying local, but it also keeps an eye open for international opportunities. The company specializes in the fabrication of pipe, plate, pressure vessel, sheet metal, heavy structural steel, and drilling rig products. Southeast Texas Industries also provides project management, construction, and maintenance services. Customers include companies in the oil and gas, power generation, pulp and paper, and petrochemical industries, along with engineering firms that work on industrial projects. Southeast Texas Industries was founded in 1978.

	Annual Growth	12/06	12/07	12/19	12/21	12/22
Sales ($mil.)	(39.3%)	–	126.7	0.0	0.0	0.0
Net income ($ mil.)	(28.1%)	–	5.3	(0.1)	0.0	0.0
Market value ($ mil.)	–	–	–	–	–	–
Employees	–	–	–	–	–	850

SOUTHEASTERN BANKING CORP. (DARIEN, GA)   NBB: SEBC

1010 North Way
Darien, GA 31305
Phone: 912 437-4141
Fax: –
Web: www.southeasternbank.com

CEO: –
CFO: –
HR: –
FYE: December 31
Type: Public

Southeastern Banking Corporation knows which direction the financial winds blow. The institution is the holding company for Southeastern Bank, which provides banking and financial services to individuals and businesses through more than 15 branches in coastal Georgia and northeastern Florida. Traditional offerings include savings, checking, money market, and NOW accounts; IRAs; and CDs. The bank originates commercial and agricultural loans, construction loans, residential mortgages, and consumer loans. It also offers insurance and investment products through an affiliation with Raymond James Financial Services.

	Annual Growth	12/18	12/19	12/20	12/21	12/22
Assets ($mil.)	12.5%	419.6	460.3	543.0	642.1	672.0
Net income ($ mil.)	7.3%	6.8	6.7	5.7	7.5	9.1
Market value ($ mil.)	5.8%	55.1	66.2	56.7	71.5	69.2
Employees	–	–	–	–	–	–

SOUTHEASTERN FREIGHT LINES, INC.

420 DAVEGA DR
LEXINGTON, SC 290737485
Phone: 803 794-7300
Fax: –
Web: www.sefl.com

CEO: –
CFO: –
HR: Lisa Arrington
FYE: December 31
Type: Private

Southeastern Freight Lines is a privately-owned regional less-than-truckload transportation services provider that specializes in next-day service in the Southeast and Southwest United States. Southeastern operates service centers in about 15 states and Puerto Rico. Clients have included Emser Tile, Commissary Express, Inc., Plastics Distributors Co, Inc., Allredi, and Doodad. Southeastern provides service throughout the US, Mexico, and Canada. The company was founded in 1950.

	Annual Growth	12/18	12/19	12/20	12/21	12/22
Sales ($mil.)	18.0%	–	–	–	1,476.0	1,741.1
Net income ($ mil.)	50.5%	–	–	–	240.6	362.1
Market value ($ mil.)	–	–	–	–	–	–
Employees	–	–	–	–	–	8,000

SOUTHEASTERN PENNSYLVANIA TRANSPORTATION AUTHORITY

1234 MARKET ST FL 4
PHILADELPHIA, PA 191073701
Phone: 215 580-7800
Fax: –
Web: www.septa.org

CEO: –
CFO: Richard Burnfield
HR: Susan Rein
FYE: June 30
Type: Private

The Southeastern Pennsylvania Transportation Authority, known as SEPTA, provides passenger transportation services in the Philadelphia area. The agency's operations include buses, subways, trolleys, and commuter rail. Altogether, SEPTA maintains approximately 300 stations chiefly in around five Pennsylvania counties (Bucks, Chester, Delaware, Montgomery, and Philadelphia) and in the neighboring states of Delaware and New Jersey. Its territory spans some 2,200 sq. mi. The Pennsylvania legislature established SEPTA in 1964.

	Annual Growth	06/18	06/19	06/20	06/21	06/22
Sales ($mil.)	(19.2%)	–	518.7	404.6	198.4	273.3
Net income ($ mil.)	(33.2%)	–	311.7	136.1	26.6	93.0
Market value ($ mil.)	–	–	–	–	–	–
Employees	–	–	–	–	–	9,000

SOUTHEASTERN UNIVERSITIES RESEARCH ASSOCIATION, INC.

1201 NEW YORK AVE NW STE 430
WASHINGTON, DC 200053917
Phone: 202 408-7872
Fax: –
Web: www.sura.org

CEO: Scott Hartranft
CFO: Peter Bjonerud
HR: Carl Patton
FYE: September 30
Type: Private

Southeastern Universities Research Association (SURA) is sure about science. The not-for-profit association is a consortium of more than 60 universities and colleges in the southern and eastern US that helps to coordinate and sponsor research projects in engineering, biology, physical sciences, and natural sciences. Its main areas of interest are nuclear physics, information technology, and coastal research. To qualify for SURA sponsorship, a project must be conducted by more than one institution. SURA also operates the Thomas Jefferson National Accelerator Laboratory, a lab dedicated to studying the structure of atoms. SURA was founded in 1980 and SURAnet became the first regional IT network in the mid-1980s.

	Annual Growth	09/15	09/16	09/17	09/18	09/22
Sales ($mil.)	79.0%	–	5.8	11.2	12.0	191.8
Net income ($ mil.)	–	–	(2.2)	3.1	1.5	4.3
Market value ($ mil.)	–	–	–	–	–	–
Employees	–	–	–	–	–	700

SOUTHERN BANC CO., INC.   NBB: SRNN

221 South 6th Street
Gadsden, AL 35901
Phone: 256 543-3860
Fax: 256 543-3864
Web: –

CEO: Gates Little
CFO: –
HR: –
FYE: June 30
Type: Public

The Southern Banc Company is the holding company for The Southern Bank, which operates about five branches in Etowah, Cherokee, and Marshall counties in northeastern Alabama. Serving both local businesses and consumers, the bank offers standard deposit products, including checking and savings accounts, certificates of deposit, and individual retirement accounts. Its loan portfolio is dominated by one-to-four family residential mortgages, business loans, and consumer loans, but Southern Bank also writes nonresidential real estate mortgages and loans secured by savings accounts. The bank also offers "factoring" services for its business-to-business clients, which conducts account receivables management.

	Annual Growth	06/19	06/20	06/21	06/22	06/23
Assets ($mil.)	2.7%	97.7	103.3	112.4	115.3	108.6
Net income ($ mil.)	51.9%	0.5	0.3	0.5	1.7	2.5
Market value ($ mil.)	11.0%	6.7	5.7	7.0	8.9	10.2
Employees	–	–	–	–	–	–

SOUTHERN BANCSHARES (NC), INC.   NBB: SBNC

116 East Main Street
Mount Olive, NC 28365
Phone: 919 658-7000
Fax: –
Web: –

CEO: J G Morgan
CFO: Dan R Ellis Jr
HR: –
FYE: December 31
Type: Public

Southern BancShares (N.C.) is the holding company for Southern Bank & Trust, which operates more than 70 branches throughout eastern and central North Carolina and Virginia. The bank offers standard deposit products, including checking and savings accounts, IRAs, and CDs. It primarily uses funds from deposits to originate residential and commercial mortgages, which represent about half of the company's loan portfolio. The bank also offers business loans, construction loans, consumer loans, and lease financing. The Holding family, which also owns significant stakes in another North Carolina bank, First Citizens BancShares, and in South Carolina's First Citizens Bancorporation, controls Southern BancShares.

	Annual Growth	12/00	12/01	12/02	12/03	12/04
Assets ($mil.)	7.1%	803.4	855.2	920.6	1,016.0	1,057.5
Net income ($ mil.)	11.6%	3.7	8.2	9.1	8.1	5.8
Market value ($ mil.)	–	–	–	–	27.5	30.3
Employees	3.7%	381	387	397	437	440

SOUTHERN CALIFORNIA EDISON CO.

2244 Walnut Grove Avenue, P.O. Box 800
Rosemead, CA 91770
Phone: 626 302-1212
Fax: –
Web: www.edisoninvestor.com

CEO: Kevin M Payne
CFO: William M Petmecky III
HR: –
FYE: December 31
Type: Public

Southern California Edison (SCE) distributes power to more than 5.2 million customers in central, coastal, and southern California (excluding Los Angeles and some other cities). The utility's system consists of supplies and delivers electricity through its electrical infrastructure to an approximately 50,000 square-mile area of Southern California. SCE has about 7,000 MW of generating capacity from stakes in nuclear, hydroelectric, fossil-fueled, and solar power plants. The utility also has power purchase agreements and sells excess power to wholesale customers. SCE is a unit of utility and competitive power holding company Edison International.

	Annual Growth	12/19	12/20	12/21	12/22	12/23
Sales ($mil.)	7.2%	12,306	13,546	14,874	17,172	16,275
Net income ($ mil.)	1.1%	1,530.0	942.0	935.0	954.0	1,597.0
Market value ($ mil.)	–	–	–	–	–	–
Employees	3.0%	12,720	13,067	12,715	12,831	14,316

SOUTHERN CALIFORNIA GAS CO.   NBB: SOCG P

555 West Fifth Street
Los Angeles, CA 90013
Phone: 213 244-1200
Fax: –
Web: www.socalgas.com

CEO: Scott D Drury
CFO: –
HR: –
FYE: December 31
Type: Public

Southern California Gas (SoCalGas) is the nation's largest gas distribution utility in the US. The utility, an indirect subsidiary of Sempra Energy, distributes natural gas to 5.9 million residential, commercial, and industrial meters (21.1 million customers) in more than 500 communities throughout Central and Southern California, from Visalia to the Mexican border. SoCalGas' natural gas facilities include over 3,045 miles of transmission and storage pipelines, about 51,020 miles of distribution pipelines and roughly 48,920 miles of service pipelines. It also includes nine transmission compressor stations and four major interstate pipeline systems: El Paso Natural Gas, Transwestern Pipeline, Kern River Pipeline Company, and Mojave Pipeline Company.

	Annual Growth	12/19	12/20	12/21	12/22	12/23
Sales ($mil.)	16.3%	4,525.0	4,748.0	5,515.0	6,840.0	8,289.0
Net income ($ mil.)	6.0%	642.0	505.0	(426.0)	600.0	812.0
Market value ($ mil.)	(4.3%)	2,734.9	3,423.8	3,126.1	2,300.8	2,291.6
Employees	4.3%	7,596	7,851	8,178	8,460	8,976

SOUTHERN CALIFORNIA REGIONAL RAIL AUTHORITY

900 WILSHIRE BLVD STE 1500
LOS ANGELES, CA 900173402
Phone: 213 452-0200
Fax: –
Web: www.metrolinktrains.com

CEO: Darren M Kettle
CFO: Ronnie Campbell
HR: Belinda Varela
FYE: June 30
Type: Private

The Southern California Regional Rail Authority (SCRRA) operates Metrolink, a regional rail system that offers transportation for commuters and other passengers. Metrolink trains serve more than 55 stations in the greater Los Angeles area on several regional lines, including Antelope Valley, Orange County, Riverside, San Bernardino, and Ventura County. Overall, Metrolink operates over a network of about 510 miles of track, including lines controlled by other entities. The SCRRA was established in 1991; operations began the next year.

	Annual Growth	06/06	06/07	06/08	06/09	06/10
Sales ($mil.)	5.7%	–	96.9	108.9	113.4	114.3
Net income ($ mil.)	29.4%	–	55.5	46.0	71.6	120.4
Market value ($ mil.)	–	–	–	–	–	–
Employees	–	–	–	–	–	275

SOUTHERN COMMUNITY NEWSPAPERS, INC.

725A OLD NORCROSS RD
LAWRENCEVILLE, GA 300464317
Phone: 770 338-7351
Fax: –
Web: www.southerncommunitynewspapers.com

CEO: Robert S Prather Jr
CFO: Mark G Meikle
HR: –
FYE: June 30
Type: Private

You might say this company races to cover the news. Triple Crown Media is a daily newspaper publisher with about a dozen papers serving smaller markets in the suburban Atlanta market. The company's portfolio is anchored by its flagship Gwinnett Daily Post. Its other newspapers include The Albany Herald, the Rockdale Citizen, The Clayton News Daily, The Henry Daily Herald, and The Jackson Progress-Argus. Triple Crown Media's papers boast a total daily circulation of more than 90,000. Spun off from TV station operator Gray Television in late 2005, Triple Crown Media is controlled by investment firms led by GoldenTree Asset Management.

SOUTHERN COMPANY (THE)   NYS: SO

30 Ivan Allen Jr. Boulevard, N.W.
Atlanta, GA 30308
Phone: 404 506-5000
Fax: 404 506-0455
Web: www.southerncompany.com

CEO: Christopher Cummiskey
CFO: Elliott L Spencer
HR: Martin Ingels
FYE: December 31
Type: Public

Southern Power provides power for the burgeoning population in the South. The company owns, builds, acquires and markets energy in the competitive wholesale supply business. It develops and operates independent power plants in the southeastern US. The company, which is part of Southern Company's generation and energy marketing operations, has more than 10,500 MW of primarily fossil-fueled facilities generating capacity operating or under construction in Alabama, California, Florida, Georgia, Nevada, North Carolina, Texas, and New Mexico. Southern Power's electricity output is marketed to wholesale customers in the region. It is growing by acquiring and developing solar power facilities.

	Annual Growth	12/19	12/20	12/21	12/22	12/23
Sales ($mil.)	4.2%	21,419	20,375	23,113	29,279	25,253
Net income ($ mil.)	(4.4%)	4,754.0	3,134.0	2,408.0	3,535.0	3,976.0
Market value ($ mil.)	2.4%	69,497	67,020	74,821	77,908	76,501
Employees	0.1%	27,943	27,700	27,300	27,700	28,100

SOUTHERN COMPANY GAS

10 PEACHTREE PL NE
ATLANTA, GA 303094497
Phone: 404 584-4000
Fax: –
Web: www.southerncompanygas.com

CEO: –
CFO: –
HR: –
FYE: December 31
Type: Private

Southern Company Gas is an energy services holding company whose primary business is the distribution of natural gas in four states ? Illinois, Georgia, Virginia, and Tennessee ? through the natural gas distribution utilities. The company is also involved in several other businesses that are complementary to the distribution of natural gas, including gas pipeline investments and gas marketing services. Its Nicor Gas has around 2.3 million customers in Illinois; Atlanta Gas Light has some 1.7 million natural gas customers in Georgia; Virginia has about 312,000 customers in Virginia; and Chattanooga Gas has around 71,000 customer in Tennessee. The company also distributes natural gas to almost 4.4 million customers in four US states.

SOUTHERN COUNTIES OIL CO.

1800 W KATELLA AVE STE 210　　　　　　　　　　CEO: Shameek Konar
ORANGE, CA 928673417　　　　　　　　　　　　CFO: Mimi Taylor
Phone: 714 744-7140　　　　　　　　　　　　HR: Barbara J Francis
Fax: –　　　　　　　　　　　　　　　　　FYE: December 31
Web: www.scfuels.com　　　　　　　　　　　　Type: Private

Southern Counties Oil Company (SC Fuels) is one of the largest family-owned petroleum distributors in the US. It delivers unbranded and branded gasoline, diesel fuel, alternative fuel, and other petroleum products throughout the US. With more than 11,000 industrial and commercial customers, the company serves small businesses and big energy clients alike. SC Fuels also boasts an in-house fleet card service with a fueling network of around 230,000 cardlock sites, truck stop, and retail stations nationwide. The company is a leading national distributor of popular branded fuels and lubricants like Shell, Valero, 76, and Sinclair.

SOUTHERN FIRST BANCSHARES, INC.　　　　　　NMS: SFST

6 Verdae Boulevard　　　　　　　　　　　CEO: R A Seaver Jr
Greenville, SC 29607　　　　　　　　　　CFO: Andy Borrmann
Phone: 864 679-9000　　　　　　　　　　　HR: Silvia King
Fax: –　　　　　　　　　　　　　　　FYE: December 31
Web: www.southernfirst.com　　　　　　　　Type: Public

Southern First Bancshares operates in two markets: Greenville, South Carolina, where it operates under the Greenville First Bank moniker, and in Columbia, South Carolina as Southern First Bank. Selling itself as a local alternative to larger institutions, the company, which has more than five bank branches, targets individuals and small to midsized businesses. It offers traditional deposit services and products, including checking accounts, savings accounts, and CDs. The banks use funds from deposits mainly to write commercial mortgages, residential mortgages, and commercial business loans.

	Annual Growth	12/19	12/20	12/21	12/22	12/23
Assets ($mil.)	15.7%	2,267.2	2,482.6	2,925.5	3,692.0	4,055.8
Net income ($ mil.)	(16.7%)	27.9	18.3	46.7	29.1	13.4
Market value ($ mil.)	(3.3%)	343.7	285.9	505.4	370.0	300.1
Employees	5.2%	242	254	278	293	296

SOUTHERN ILLINOIS HEALTHCARE ENTERPRISES, INC.

1239 E MAIN ST STE C　　　　　　　　　　CEO: Rex Budde
CARBONDALE, IL 629013176　　　　　　　　CFO: Mike Kasser
Phone: 618 457-5200　　　　　　　　　　　HR: Melissa Tiberend
Fax: –　　　　　　　　　　　　　　　FYE: March 31
Web: www.sih.net　　　　　　　　　　　Type: Private

Southern Illinois Healthcare, a nonprofit health care system, operates the flagship 145-bed tertiary-care Memorial Hospital of Carbondale, as well as Herrin Hospital (with 114 beds) and St. Joseph Memorial Hospital (with 25 beds). The hospitals serve residents of across southern Illinois. The nearly 280-bed system provides services such as birthing, cardiac, cancer, and emergency care, as well as surgery and rehabilitation. Its cardiac care is offered through an affiliation with the Prairie Heart Institute at St. John's Hospital in Springfield, Illinois. The medical school at Southern Illinois University conducts its Family Practice Residency Program at Memorial Hospital of Carbondale.

	Annual Growth	03/18	03/19	03/20	03/21	03/22
Sales ($mil.)	5.1%	–	685.3	696.4	707.7	794.5
Net income ($ mil.)	–	–	–	22.2	(45.9)	123.0	(33.0)
Market value ($ mil.)	–	–	–	–	–	–
Employees	–	–	–	–	–	3,493

SOUTHERN ILLINOIS UNIVERSITY INC

1400 DOUGLAS DR　　　　　　　　　　　CEO: –
CARBONDALE, IL 629014332　　　　　　　　CFO: –
Phone: 618 536-3475　　　　　　　　　　HR: –
Fax: –　　　　　　　　　　　　　　　FYE: June 30
Web: www.siu.edu　　　　　　　　　　　Type: Private

Southern Illinois University (SIU) helps to train future doctors, dentists, and other other professionals. The university enrolls some 32,000 students at its two institutions -- Southern Illinois University at Carbondale (SIUC, which includes medical and law schools) and Southern Illinois University at Edwardsville (SIUE, which houses education, dental, and nursing schools) -- as well as smaller satellite centers. SIU offers associate, baccalaureate, master's, doctoral, and professional degrees. It also boasts a number of study abroad partnerships with international universities. Tracing its roots back to 1869, SIU is known for its extensive research programs.

	Annual Growth	06/18	06/19	06/20	06/21	06/22
Sales ($mil.)	2.8%	–	581.5	578.7	568.9	631.0
Net income ($ mil.)	1.5%	–	28.7	25.7	(8.0)	30.1
Market value ($ mil.)	–	–	–	–	–	–
Employees	–	–	–	–	–	9,576

SOUTHERN MAINE HEALTH CARE

1 MEDICAL CENTER DR　　　　　　　　　　CEO: –
BIDDEFORD, ME 040059422　　　　　　　　CFO: Norm Belair
Phone: 207 283-7000　　　　　　　　　　HR: Lisa Drew
Fax: –　　　　　　　　　　　　　　　FYE: September 30
Web: www.mainehealth.org　　　　　　　　Type: Private

Southern Maine Medical Center (SMMC) provides health care services to the residents of York County, Maine. The central facility of the not-for-profit medical organization is its 150-bed, full-service hospital. Founded in 1906, the medical center also operates a home health care service and outpatient diagnostic and therapy centers. Specialty services include pediatrics, cardiology, oncology, and emergency care. The medical center has a staff of about 200 physicians. SMMC is a member of MaineHealth, a network of area hospitals and health clinics.

	Annual Growth	09/17	09/18	09/19	09/20	09/21
Sales ($mil.)	3.5%	–	293.0	308.7	289.1	325.0
Net income ($ mil.)	–	–	(5.5)	(43.6)	(13.0)	28.0
Market value ($ mil.)	–	–	–	–	–	–
Employees	–	–	–	–	–	1,000

SOUTHERN MANAGEMENT COMPANIES LLC

7950 JONES BRANCH DR　　　　　　　　　CEO: –
MC LEAN, VA 221023268　　　　　　　　　CFO: –
Phone: 703 902-2000　　　　　　　　　　HR: –
Fax: –　　　　　　　　　　　　　　　FYE: December 31
Web: www.southernmanagement.com　　　　Type: Private

Southern Management can show you a little bit of southern hospitality. The privately-owned company invests in, develops, renovates, and manages residential and commercial real estate in the Mid-Atlantic. Its portfolio includes more than 70 apartment communities (about 25,000 individual units) and six office buildings in Maryland and Virginia. It specializes in renovating historic properties, several of which are located in downtown Baltimore. The company also offers discounts for students and military families, and provides temporary corporate suites for partner employers. Its Southern Management University division offers employee training. CEO David Hillman founded Southern Management in 1965.

	Annual Growth	12/05	12/06	12/07	12/08	12/14
Assets ($mil.)	9.6%	–	–	–	2.1	3.6
Net income ($ mil.)	–	–	–	–	–	(0.5)
Market value ($ mil.)	–	–	–	–	–	–
Employees	–	–	–	–	–	1,200

SOUTHERN METHODIST UNIVERSITY INC

6425 BOAZ LANE
DALLAS, TX 752051902
Phone: 214 768-2000
Fax: –
Web: www.smu.edu

CEO: –
CFO: –
HR: Brian Foster
FYE: May 31
Type: Private

Founded by the Methodist Episcopal Church, South, Southern Methodist University (SMU) is a nonsectarian private institution offering undergraduate, graduate, and professional degrees in arts, business, engineering, humanities, law, science, and theology through eight schools. It's one of a handful of schools nationwide to offer an academic major in human rights. SMU provides professional certificates and noncredit offerings through the Continuing and Professional Education program. About 12,055 students attend the university, which has a student-faculty ratio of 11:1. About 85% of full-time faculty hold the doctorate or highest degree in their fields.

	Annual Growth	05/12	05/13	05/17	05/18	05/20
Sales ($mil.)	7.6%	–	563.3	580.6	652.2	940.7
Net income ($ mil.)	(2.0%)	–	115.6	56.9	96.1	100.5
Market value ($ mil.)	–	–	–	–	–	–
Employees	–	–	–	–	–	2,200

SOUTHERN MICHIGAN BANCORP INC   NBB: SOMC

51 West Pearl Street
Coldwater, MI 49036
Phone: 517 279-5500
Fax: 517 279-5578
Web: www.smb-t.com

CEO: John H Castle
CFO: Danice L Chartrand
HR: –
FYE: December 31
Type: Public

Southern Michigan Bancorp is the holding company for Southern Michigan Bank & Trust, which operates about 20 branches in a primarily rural area near Michigan's border with Indiana and Ohio. The bank provides standard deposit services, such as checking and savings accounts, money market and heath savings accounts, CDs, and IRAs. It originates commercial, financial, agricultural, consumer, and mortgage loans. The banks also offers trust and investment services. Southern Michigan Bank & Trust got its start in the room of a hotel named Southern Michigan Hotel in 1872.

	Annual Growth	12/18	12/19	12/20	12/21	12/22
Assets ($mil.)	14.6%	738.8	809.7	997.6	1,161.2	1,276.5
Net income ($ mil.)	13.5%	8.1	8.6	7.4	11.8	13.5
Market value ($ mil.)	(15.7%)	172.2	169.9	153.7	91.3	87.0
Employees	–	–	208	–	212	–

SOUTHERN MINNESOTA BEET SUGAR COOPERATIVE

83550 COUNTY ROAD 21
RENVILLE, MN 562842319
Phone: 320 329-8305
Fax: –
Web: www.smbsc.com

CEO: Kelvin Thompsen
CFO: –
HR: Carol Maurice
FYE: August 31
Type: Private

Southern Minnesota Beet Sugar Cooperative (SMBSC) offers a sweet deal to its approximately 585 member/farmers. The co-op slices about 3 million tons of Minnesota-grown sugar beets annually. Converted products include baker's sugar and fruit sugar, as well as molasses, beet pulp pellets and shreds, and raffinate (liquid from desugaring molasses). The co-op also provides member services, such as seed, agronomy research, farm support products, and workers' compensation insurance. SMBSC's refined and liquid sugars are marketed through Cargill Sweeteners; the by-products (dried beet pulp and beet molasses for use in cattle feed) are marketed by Midwest Agri-Commodities in North American and Europe.

	Annual Growth	08/13	08/14	08/15	08/16	08/17
Sales ($mil.)	–	–	–	350.0	465.2	418.1
Net income ($ mil.)	(7.0%)	–	123.1	101.2	176.5	99.1
Market value ($ mil.)	–	–	–	–	–	–
Employees	–	–	–	–	–	610

SOUTHERN MINNESOTA MUNICIPAL POWER AGENCY

500 1ST AVE SW
ROCHESTER, MN 559023303
Phone: 507 285-0478
Fax: –
Web: www.smmpa.com

CEO: –
CFO: –
HR: –
FYE: December 31
Type: Private

Lake Wobegon may well get its power from the Southern Minnesota Municipal Power Agency. The power provider supplies wholesale electricity to its 18 member municipal distribution utilities, which in turn distribute power to more than 109,000 retail customers. The agency's main power source is the 900 MW Sherco 3-power plant generating unit near Becker, Minnesota. Southern Minnesota Municipal Power Agency owns 41% of the low-sulfur Western coal fueled plant in partnership Northern States Power Company, the unit's operator. It also relies on a range of intermediate and peaking units owned by the agency's members.

SOUTHERN MISSOURI BANCORP, INC.   NMS: SMBC

2991 Oak Grove Road
Poplar Bluff, MO 63901
Phone: 573 778-1800
Fax: –
Web: www.bankwithsouthern.com

CEO: Greg A Steffens
CFO: Stefan Chkautovich
HR: –
FYE: June 30
Type: Public

Southern Missouri Bancorp is the holding company for Southern Bank (formerly Southern Missouri Bank and Trust), which serves local residents and businesses in southeastern Missouri and northeastern Arkansas through more than 10 branches. Residential mortgages account for the largest percentage of the bank's loan portfolio, followed by commercial mortgages and business loans. Construction and consumer loans round out its lending activities. Deposit products include checking, savings and money market accounts, CDs, and IRAs. The bank also offers financial planning and investment services. Originally chartered in 1887, Southern Bank acquired Arkansas-based Southern Bank of Commerce in 2009.

	Annual Growth	06/19	06/20	06/21	06/22	06/23
Assets ($mil.)	18.5%	2,214.4	2,542.2	2,700.5	3,214.8	4,360.2
Net income ($ mil.)	7.9%	28.9	27.5	47.2	47.2	39.2
Market value ($ mil.)	2.5%	394.6	275.3	509.4	512.8	435.7
Employees	10.6%	470	492	488	544	703

SOUTHERN NATURAL GAS CO

El Paso Building, 1001 Louisiana Street
Houston, TX 77002
Phone: 713 420-2600
Fax: –
Web: –

CEO: Norman G Holmes
CFO: John R Sult
HR: –
FYE: December 31
Type: Public

Now here's a company that pipes in the goods that keep the South fueled, naturally. Southern Natural Gas operates an 7,600-mile long natural gas pipeline (SNG System), which serves major markets across the southeastern US. This system transports more than 3 billion cu. ft. of natural gas per day. The SNG pipeline system has about 60 billion cu. ft. of underground working natural gas storage capacity. Major customers include Atlanta Gas Light Company, Alabama Gas, Southern Company, and SCANA . Southern Natural Gas is a unit of El Paso Pipeline Partners.

	Annual Growth	12/09	12/10	12/11	12/12	12/13
Sales ($mil.)	4.0%	510.0	548.0	563.0	584.0	596.0
Net income ($ mil.)	6.0%	208.0	267.0	260.0	274.0	263.0
Market value ($ mil.)	–	–	–	–	–	–
Employees	–	–	–	–	–	–

SOUTHERN NATURAL GAS COMPANY, L.L.C.

1001 LOUISIANA ST
HOUSTON, TX 770025089
Phone: 713 420-2600
Fax: -
Web: www.kindermorgan.com

CEO: Norman G Holmes
CFO: John R Sult
HR: -
FYE: December 31
Type: Private

Now here's a company that pipes in the goods that keep the South fueled, naturally. Southern Natural Gas operates an 7,600-mile long natural gas pipeline (SNG System), which serves major markets across the southeastern US. This system transports more than 3 billion cu. ft. of natural gas per day. The SNG pipeline system has about 60 billion cu. ft. of underground working natural gas storage capacity. Major customers include Atlanta Gas Light Company, Alabama Gas, Southern Company, and SCANA . Southern Natural Gas is a unit of El Paso Pipeline Partners.

	Annual Growth	12/13	12/14	12/15	12/16	12/17
Sales ($mil.)	(0.6%)	-	-	-	609.6	606.1
Net income ($ mil.)	(15.2%)	-	-	-	169.6	143.8
Market value ($ mil.)	-	-	-	-	-	-
Employees	-	-	-	-	-	3

SOUTHERN NEW HAMPSHIRE MEDICAL CENTER

8 PROSPECT ST
NASHUA, NH 030603925
Phone: 603 577-2000
Fax: -
Web: www.snhhealth.org

CEO: -
CFO: -
HR: Alton Jones
FYE: June 30
Type: Private

Southern New Hampshire Medical Center (SNHMC) provides medical care for the residents of the Nashua, New Hampshire area and surrounding region through Southern New Hampshire Medical Center and Foundation Medical Partners. The two-campus hospital, which has about 190 beds and is part of the Southern New Hampshire Health System, offers centers for cancer treatment, diabetes education, fertility and childbirth, obesity, sleep disorders, trauma, and other programs. Outpatient and rehabilitation services are offered through several clinic locations. SNHMC is also affiliated with physician practice organization Foundation Medical Partners, and it is a teaching facility for the Dartmouth Medical School.

	Annual Growth	09/16	09/17	09/18*	06/20	06/22
Sales ($mil.)	5.4%	-	241.2	256.5	262.4	313.8
Net income ($ mil.)	5.1%	-	40.4	27.1	39.6	51.7
Market value ($ mil.)	-	-	-	-	-	-
Employees	-	-	-	-	-	1,200

*Fiscal year change

SOUTHERN NUCLEAR OPERATING COMPANY, INC.

42 INVERNESS CENTER PKWY
HOOVER, AL 352424809
Phone: 205 992-5000
Fax: -
Web: www.southerncompany.com

CEO: -
CFO: -
HR: -
FYE: December 31
Type: Private

The night the lights went out in Georgia, they should have called Southern Nuclear Operating Company. The company, a subsidiary of Southern Company since 1990, operates six nuclear power units at three plant locations, which combined, provide about 20% of the electricity used in Alabama and Georgia. Southern Nuclear's Joseph M. Farley Nuclear Plant began commercial operation in 1977. The Edwin I. Hatch Nuclear Plant and the Alvin W. Vogtle Electric Generating Plant are jointly owned by Southern Company's Georgia Power (50%), Oglethorpe Power (30%), the Municipal Electrical Authority of Georgia (18%), and the city of Dalton.

	Annual Growth	12/01	12/02	12/03	12/04	12/16
Sales ($mil.)	5.2%	-	455.5	441.9	479.8	922.5
Net income ($ mil.)	-	-	-	-	-	0.3
Market value ($ mil.)	-	-	-	-	-	-
Employees	-	-	-	-	-	2,960

SOUTHERN PINE ELECTRIC COOPERATIVE

13491 HWY 28 W
TAYLORSVILLE, MS 39168
Phone: 601 785-6511
Fax: -
Web: www.southernpine.coop

CEO: Donald Jordan
CFO: -
HR: Charlie Ware
FYE: December 31
Type: Private

People pine for electricity and Southern Pine Electric Power Association (Southern Pine EPA) delivers. The consumer-owned utility cooperative that serves about 65,000 members in south central Mississippi. The cooperative provides power over more than 10,000 miles of line to some 60,400 residential meters and 4,600 commercial meters. A board of directors, elected by Southern Pine EPA membership, sets the policies and establishes the business structure of the organization, which is led on a day-to-day operational basis by a general manager. Southern Pine EPA established four district offices in 1994 to enable the cooperative to better serve its large service area.

	Annual Growth	12/14	12/15	12/16	12/21	12/22
Sales ($mil.)	(0.2%)	-	223.2	-	209.7	220.2
Net income ($ mil.)	-	-	-	-	-	-
Market value ($ mil.)	-	-	-	-	-	-
Employees	-	-	-	-	-	260

SOUTHERN PIPE & SUPPLY COMPANY, INC.

4330 HIGHWAY 39 N
MERIDIAN, MS 393011082
Phone: 601 693-2911
Fax: -
Web: www.southernpipe.com

CEO: Martin D Davidson
CFO: Marc Ransier
HR: Felecia Drew
FYE: December 31
Type: Private

Southern Pipe and Supply Co. sells pipes and anything that connects to them. Serving everyone from contractors and homeowners to commercial real estate property owners, Southern Pipe sells plumbing, heating, and air-conditioning supplies through more than 90 stores located throughout seven southeastern states. The company operates a central distribution center and a handful of Southern Bath & Kitchen showrooms that feature various products for homeowners. Southern Pipe's vendors include dozens of supply companies and manufacturers, such as MOEN, Kohler, and Amana Heating and Air Conditioning. Southern Pipe and Supply Co. was founded in 1938.

	Annual Growth	12/12	12/13	12/14	12/15	12/16
Sales ($mil.)	3.6%	-	-	-	436.1	451.8
Net income ($ mil.)	(4.5%)	-	-	-	19.9	19.0
Market value ($ mil.)	-	-	-	-	-	-
Employees	-	-	-	-	-	767

SOUTHERN POLYTECHNIC STATE UNIVERSITY FOUNDATION, INC

1100 S MARIETTA PKWY SE
MARIETTA, GA 300602855
Phone: 678 915-7778
Fax: -
Web: www.spsu.edu

CEO: -
CFO: -
HR: -
FYE: June 30
Type: Private

Southern Polytechnic State University offers a range of science and technology-related degrees such as architecture, civil engineering, and computer engineering. From its main campus, located about 20 minutes from downtown Atlanta, the university offers both graduate and undergraduate programs. More than 6,000 students attend the university, which is part of the University System of Georgia. Southern Polytechnic State was founded in 1948 as a two-year division of Georgia Institute of Technology; it separated ties with Georgia Tech in 1970.

	Annual Growth	06/06	06/07	06/08	06/09	06/10
Sales ($mil.)	54.3%	-	-	2.0	1.9	4.8
Net income ($ mil.)	31.1%	-	-	0.5	-	0.8
Market value ($ mil.)	-	-	-	-	-	-
Employees	-	-	-	-	-	1,100

SOUTHERN POWER CO

30 Ivan Allen Jr., Boulevard N.W.
Atlanta, GA 30308
Phone: 404 506-5000
Fax: –
Web: www.southerncompany.com

CEO: Christopher Cummiskey
CFO: Elliott L Spencer
HR: Martin Ingels
FYE: December 31
Type: Public

Southern Power provides power for the burgeoning population in the South. The company owns, builds, acquires and markets energy in the competitive wholesale supply business. It develops and operates independent power plants in the southeastern US. The company, which is part of Southern Company's generation and energy marketing operations, has more than 10,500 MW of primarily fossil-fueled facilities generating capacity operating or under construction in Alabama, California, Florida, Georgia, Nevada, North Carolina, Texas, and New Mexico. Southern Power's electricity output is marketed to wholesale customers in the region. It is growing by acquiring and developing solar power facilities.

	Annual Growth	12/18	12/19	12/20	12/21	12/22
Sales ($mil.)	11.2%	2,205.0	1,938.0	1,733.0	2,216.0	3,369.0
Net income ($ mil.)	17.3%	187.0	339.0	238.0	266.0	354.0
Market value ($ mil.)	–	–	–	–	–	–
Employees	0.5%	491	460	400	500	500

SOUTHERN RESEARCH INSTITUTE

2000 9TH AVE S
BIRMINGHAM, AL 352052708
Phone: 205 581-2000
Fax: –
Web: www.southernresearch.org

CEO: AME Johnsey
CFO: David A Rutledge
HR: Sheryl Burrage
FYE: December 31
Type: Private

Southern Research Institute performs contract research in areas such as drug development and discovery, engineering, and environmental and energy issues. The not-for-profit organization launched a life science R&D consulting firm, BioSafety Solutions, in 2008. The institute's clients have included large government agencies such as the National Institutes of Health, the US Department of Defense, and NASA as well as corporate clients Mercedes-Benz and Southern Company. The organization tests anti-influenza and anti-HIV drugs for NanoViricides Inc.

	Annual Growth	12/15	12/16	12/17	12/18	12/21
Sales ($mil.)	3.3%	–	72.8	66.3	66.3	85.7
Net income ($ mil.)	–	–	(4.3)	(8.4)	(8.4)	8.5
Market value ($ mil.)	–	–	–	–	–	–
Employees	–	–	–	–	–	535

SOUTHERN STATES COOPERATIVE INC.

NBB: SOCP

6606 West Broad Street, P.O. Box 23264
Richmond, VA 23260
Phone: 804 281-1000
Fax: 804 281-1141
Web: www.southernstates.com

CEO: Steven Becraft
CFO: Leslie T Newton
HR: –
FYE: June 30
Type: Public

Southern States Cooperative is a retail agricultural cooperative serving the agronomy, energy and farm supply needs of its members and customers across eight states in the Southeastern US. The Richmond, VA-based cooperative serves a wide range of farm inputs, including fertilizer, seed, livestock feed, pet food, animal health supplies, and petroleum products, as well as other items for the farm and home. It operates more than 1,200 retail outlets across around 20 states. Southern States Cooperative was founded in 1923 as Virginia Seed Service (VSS) when Virginia farmers were unable to buy seed guaranteed to grow in the Commonwealth and soon expanded to include feed, agronomy inputs, energy and farm supplies.

	Annual Growth	06/99	06/00	06/01	06/02	06/03
Sales ($mil.)	(1.0%)	1,366.4	1,547.1	1,739.0	1,462.5	1,310.5
Net income ($ mil.)	–	(2.1)	5.0	(14.8)	(68.2)	(55.4)
Market value ($ mil.)	–	–	–	–	–	–
Employees	–	–	–	–	–	3,200

SOUTHERN UNION GAS COMPANY, INC.

1300 MAIN ST
HOUSTON, TX 770026803
Phone: 713 989-7153
Fax: –
Web: www.southernunionco.com

CEO: Kelcy Warren
CFO: Richard Marshall
HR: –
FYE: December 31
Type: Private

Diversified natural gas player Southern Union (a subsidiary of Energy Transfer Equity) is looking to form a more perfect union of natural gas transportation, storage, gathering, processing, and distribution assets. Its major utilities, Missouri Gas Energy and New England Gas, distribute natural gas to more than 550,000 customers. Southern Union has gas storage facilities and more than 15,000 miles of interstate natural gas pipeline across the US (primarily through Panhandle Energy and its 50% ownership of Florida Gas). In 2014 the company was merged into Energy Transfer Equity's Panhandle Eastern Pipe Line unit.

SOUTHLAND INDUSTRIES

12131 WESTERN AVE
GARDEN GROVE, CA 928412914
Phone: 800 613-6240
Fax: –
Web: www.southlandind.com

CEO: Theodore Lynch
CFO: Kevin J Coghlan
HR: –
FYE: September 30
Type: Private

Southland Industries designs, builds, and maintains a variety of mechanical systems for facilities around North America. The mechanical engineering firm provides design, construction, fabrication, and maintenance of plumbing, process piping, fire protection, HVAC, and controls and automation systems. Southland Industries' clients are in the health care, life sciences, hospitality, industrial, education, data center, and government sectors. Projects include Doylestown Hospital, Peirce College, Imvax Clinical Manufacturing Facility, The Pennsylvania State University Innovation Hub, and Comcast Technology Center. Southland Industries was founded in 1949.

SOUTHSIDE BANCSHARES, INC.

NMS: SBSI

1201 S. Beckham Avenue
Tyler, TX 75701
Phone: 903 531-7111
Fax: –
Web: www.southside.com

CEO: Lee R Gibson
CFO: Julie N Shamburger
HR: –
FYE: December 31
Type: Public

Southside Bancshares is the holding company for Southside Bank, which boasts nearly 65 branches across East, North, and Central Texas, with many around the cities of Tyler and Longview. About one-third of its branches are located in supermarkets (including Albertsons and Brookshire stores), and 40% are motor bank facilities. The bank provides traditional services such as savings, money market, and checking accounts, CDs, and other deposit products, as well as trust and wealth management services. Real estate loans, primarily residential mortgages, make up about half of the company's loan portfolio, which also includes business, consumer, and municipal loans. The bank has total assets exceeding $4.8 billion.

	Annual Growth	12/19	12/20	12/21	12/22	12/23
Assets ($mil.)	5.3%	6,748.9	7,008.2	7,259.6	7,558.6	8,284.9
Net income ($ mil.)	3.8%	74.6	82.2	113.4	105.0	86.7
Market value ($ mil.)	(4.2%)	1,123.5	938.6	1,265.0	1,088.7	947.4
Employees	(0.9%)	845	832	809	813	815

SOUTHSTAR BANK, S.S.B.

100 S MAIN ST
MOULTON, TX 779754598
Phone: 361 596-4611
Fax: –
Web: www.southstarbank.com

CEO: –
CFO: –
HR: –
FYE: December 31
Type: Private

Lone Star Bank provides banking services, naturally, in the Lone Star State. The bank (not to be confused with the Houston-based financial institution with the same name) operates through branches in Moulton, Shiner, Brazoria, and Gonzales, Texas, and two loan production offices in Austin, Texas. Lone Star Bank, which dates back to 1920, offers checking and savings accounts, investment planning, and loans. Other products include certificates of deposit, IRAs, money market accounts, fixed annuities, and checking accounts for small businesses. The bank also offers life, health, disability, and long-term care insurance.

	Annual Growth	12/12	12/13	12/14	12/21	12/22
Assets ($mil.)	16.3%	–	283.6	316.0	1,160.4	1,106.1
Net income ($ mil.)	18.8%	–	3.3	2.6	15.2	15.8
Market value ($ mil.)	–	–	–	–	–	–
Employees	–	–	–	–	–	20

SOUTHSTATE CORP

1101 First Street South, Suite 202
Winter Haven, FL 33880
Phone: 863 293-4710
Fax: –
Web: www.southstatebank.com

NYS: SSB

CEO: John C Corbett
CFO: –
HR: –
FYE: December 31
Type: Public

South State Corporation is the holding company for South State Bank (the bank). The bank operates through correspondent banking and capital markets service division for over 1,060 small and medium-sized community banks through US. The bank has 280 network branches located in Florida, South Carolina, Alabama, Georgia, North Carolina and Virginia. The company provides commercial real estate, residential real estate loans, commercial and industrial loans and consumer loans, the banks provide deposit accounts, loans, and mortgages, as well as trust and investment planning services. The bank also operates SouthState Advisory, Inc., a wholly owned registered investment advisor, which offers support to the Bank's Wealth line of business. In early 2021, the company completed its acquisition of Duncan-Williams, Inc., a full-service broker dealer that is being integrated into its correspondent division due to the complementary nature of its capital markets business (DWI).

	Annual Growth	12/19	12/20	12/21	12/22	12/23
Assets ($mil.)	29.6%	15,921	37,790	41,960	43,919	44,902
Net income ($ mil.)	27.6%	186.5	120.6	475.5	496.0	494.3
Market value ($ mil.)	(0.7%)	6,594.9	5,496.4	6,090.1	5,805.0	6,420.1
Employees	20.0%	2,547	5,311	5,130	5,126	5,284

SOUTHWEST AIRLINES CO

P.O. Box 36611
Dallas, TX 75235-1611
Phone: 214 792-4000
Fax: 214 792-5015
Web: www.southwest.com

NYS: LUV

CEO: Robert E Jordan
CFO: Tammy Romo
HR: –
FYE: December 31
Type: Public

Southwest Airlines operates Southwest Airlines, a major passenger airline that provides scheduled air transportation in the United States and near-international markets. The airline employs a single aircraft type ? the Boeing 737. Sticking with what has worked, the company has a total of nearly 730 Boeing 737 aircraft in its fleet and around 120 destinations in more than 40 states, the DC, the Commonwealth of Puerto Rico, and ten near-international countries: Mexico, Jamaica, The Bahamas, Aruba, Dominican Republic, Costa Rica, Belize, Cuba, the Cayman Islands, and Turks and Caicos. The airlines was incorporated in 1967.

	Annual Growth	12/19	12/20	12/21	12/22	12/23
Sales ($mil.)	3.9%	22,428	9,048.0	15,790	23,814	26,091
Net income ($ mil.)	(32.9%)	2,300.0	(3,074.0)	977.0	539.0	465.0
Market value ($ mil.)	(14.5%)	32,200	27,803	25,555	20,085	17,227
Employees	5.3%	60,800	56,500	55,100	66,656	74,806

SOUTHWEST GAS HOLDINGS, INC.

8360 S. Durango Drive, Post Office Box 98510
Las Vegas, NV 89193-8510
Phone: 702 876-7237
Fax: 702 873-3820
Web: www.swgasholdings.com

NYS: SWX

CEO: –
CFO: Roy R Centrella
HR: Nonya Krausnick
FYE: December 31
Type: Public

The sunny southwestern US is where Southwest Gas does its business. The largest gas supplier in Arizona and Nevada, it provides natural gas to 1.96 million customers in the two states, as well as in portions of California. Southwest Gas acquires its natural gas from 46 suppliers and pumps it through distribution mains. It also owns a transmission pipeline that supplies the Las Vegas area, and affiliate Paiute Pipeline transports gas from the Idaho-Nevada border to Reno and Lake Tahoe. Another Southwest Gas unit, NPL Construction, is an underground piping contractor that serves gas distributors. Its construction holding company Centuri, led by NPL Construction, serves more than 100 major customers a year.

	Annual Growth	12/19	12/20	12/21	12/22	12/23
Sales ($mil.)	14.9%	3,119.9	3,298.9	3,680.5	4,960.0	5,434.0
Net income ($ mil.)	(8.4%)	213.9	232.3	200.8	(203.3)	150.9
Market value ($ mil.)	(4.4%)	5,436.7	4,347.5	5,013.0	4,428.4	4,533.6
Employees	(22.7%)	6,649	11,149	12,973	13,614	2,371

SOUTHWEST LOUISIANA ELECTRIC MEMBERSHIP CORPORATION

2727 SE EVANGELINE TRWY
LAFAYETTE, LA 705082205
Phone: 337 896-5384
Fax: –
Web: www.slemco.com

CEO: Glenn A Tamporello
CFO: Katherine Domingue
HR: –
FYE: December 31
Type: Private

Southwest Louisiana Electric Membership Corporation (SLEMCO) is no slowpoke when it comes to serving more than 93,400 power customers in eight Louisiana parishes. SLEMCO provides regulated power transmission and distribution services via 9,000 miles of power lines to its residential, commercial, and industrial members. It also provides energy conservation and street and security lighting services. SLEMCO extended assistance to help repair the badly damaged infrastructure in parishes from New Orleans to the Mississippi border following the devastation caused by Hurricane Katrina.

	Annual Growth	12/13	12/14	12/15	12/16	12/18
Sales ($mil.)	3.3%	–	–	211.9	225.4	233.4
Net income ($ mil.)	72.2%	–	–	2.5	(0.5)	12.8
Market value ($ mil.)	–	–	–	–	–	–
Employees	–	–	–	–	–	269

SOUTHWEST MISSISSIPPI REGIONAL MEDICAL CENTER

215 MARION AVE
MCCOMB, MS 396482705
Phone: 601 249-5500
Fax: –
Web: www.smrmc.com

CEO: Norman Price
CFO: Reece Nunnery
HR: –
FYE: September 30
Type: Private

In M-I-S-S-I-S-S-I-P-P-I, health care is spelled S-M-R-M-C. Southwest Mississippi Regional Medical Center (SMRMC) provides health care services to southwestern Mississippi counties and nearby portions of Louisiana. The medical center campus, established in 1969, includes a 165-bed inpatient hospital, as well as cancer and cardiovascular institutes, a geriatric/psychiatric unit, and a home health agency. SMRMC also owns and operates a number of clinics providing family medicine services, as well as outpatient rehabilitation and surgery centers. The medical center, founded in 1969, has about 70 physicians on staff. Its emergency room serves as a regional level III trauma center.

	Annual Growth	09/18	09/19	09/20	09/21	09/22
Sales ($mil.)	7.1%	–	129.4	125.8	141.1	158.9
Net income ($ mil.)	–	–	(6.0)	6.6	2.4	(3.3)
Market value ($ mil.)	–	–	–	–	–	–
Employees	–	–	–	–	–	1,100

SOUTHWEST RESEARCH INSTITUTE INC

6220 CULEBRA RD
SAN ANTONIO, TX 782385100
Phone: 210 684-5111
Fax: –
Web: www.swri.org

CEO: Adam Hamilton
CFO: Beth A Rafferty
HR: Deborah Mathis
FYE: September 24
Type: Private

Founded in 1947 by oilman and rancher Thomas Slick Jr., Southwest Research Institute (SwRI) is one of the oldest and largest independent, nonprofit, applied research and development organizations in the US. The company offers more than 2 million square feet of laboratories, offices, and test facilities at a more than 1,500 acres campus in San Antonio, Texas. It supports work on nearly 4,000 client projects at any given time through a wide range of technical competencies with more than 3,000 staff members in about a dozen of technical divisions.

	Annual Growth	09/16	09/17	09/18	09/19	09/21
Sales ($mil.)	9.9%	–	498.1	583.7	685.5	725.9
Net income ($ mil.)	46.5%	–	11.4	38.4	41.1	52.5
Market value ($ mil.)	–	–	–	–	–	–
Employees	–	–	–	–	–	2,820

SOUTHWESTERN COMMUNITY COLLEGE DISTRICT (INC)

900 OTAY LAKES RD
CHULA VISTA, CA 919107223
Phone: 619 482-6408
Fax: –
Web: www.swccd.edu

CEO: –
CFO: –
HR: Angela Riggs
FYE: June 30
Type: Private

Southwestern College is a community college serving southern San Diego County. The school has an enrollment of about 20,000 students. It offers associate degrees, transferable courses, and vocational certificates in more than 320 fields, as well as noncredit personal and professional development courses through a continuing education department. Academic areas include English, math, arts, social sciences, physical and biological sciences, and foreign languages. The college is composed of a main campus in Chula Vista, the Education Center at San Ysidro, and the Higher Education Center at National City. Southwestern College was established in 1961.

	Annual Growth	06/17	06/18	06/19	06/20	06/22
Sales ($mil.)	34.2%	–	24.4	27.6	34.5	79.3
Net income ($ mil.)	–	–	9.7	2.7	(9.3)	(2.4)
Market value ($ mil.)	–	–	–	–	–	–
Employees	–	–	–	–	–	658

SOUTHWESTERN ELECTRIC POWER CO.

1 Riverside Plaza
Columbus, OH 43215-2373
Phone: 614 716-1000
Fax: –
Web: www.aep.com

CEO: Nicholas K Akins
CFO: Brian Tierney
HR: –
FYE: December 31
Type: Public

Southwestern Electric Power cuts a wide, welcome swath through the southwestern US to help beat the sweltering heat. The utility, founded in 1912, serves some 520,400 electricity customers in portions of Arkansas, Louisiana, and Texas. Southwestern Electric Power operates 20,450 miles of transmission and distribution lines. Southwestern Electric Power also has interests in fossil-fueled power plants (including 73% of the $1.7 billion Turk plant in Arkansas) that give it a generating capacity of 4,850 MW, and it sells power to wholesale customers. The utility is a subsidiary of American Electric Power Company (AEP).

	Annual Growth	12/19	12/20	12/21	12/22	12/23
Sales ($mil.)	5.7%	1,750.9	1,738.5	2,131.8	2,284.4	2,182.8
Net income ($ mil.)	8.6%	158.6	180.8	239.0	290.1	220.3
Market value ($ mil.)	–	–	–	–	–	–
Employees	–	1,469	1,440	1,369	1,372	–

SOUTHWESTERN ENERGY COMPANY

NYS: SWN

10000 Energy Drive
Spring, TX 77389
Phone: 832 796-1000
Fax: –
Web: www.swn.com

CEO: William J Way
CFO: Carl Giesler
HR: Carina Gillenwater
FYE: December 31
Type: Public

Southwestern Energy is an independent energy company engaged in natural gas, oil and NGLs exploration, development, and production. It is also focused on creating and capturing additional value through its marketing business. Its operations in West Virginia, Pennsylvania, and Ohio focus on Marcellus Shale, the Utica, and the Upper Devonian unconventional natural gas and liquids reservoirs, while operations in Louisiana are active on the Haynesville and Bossier natural gas reservoirs. In all, Southwestern boasts estimated proved reserves of about 21,625 BCF of natural gas equivalent. The company conducts most of its businesses through subsidiaries, and currently operates exclusively in the Appalachian and Haynesville natural gas basins in the lower 48 United States.

	Annual Growth	12/19	12/20	12/21	12/22	12/23
Sales ($mil.)	21.0%	3,038.0	2,308.0	6,667.0	15,002	6,522.0
Net income ($ mil.)	15.0%	891.0	(3,112.0)	(25.0)	1,849.0	1,557.0
Market value ($ mil.)	28.3%	2,665.5	3,282.4	5,132.8	6,443.6	7,214.6
Employees	6.0%	923	900	938	1,118	1,165

SOUTHWESTERN UNIVERSITY

1001 E UNIVERSITY AVE
GEORGETOWN, TX 786266107
Phone: 512 863-6511
Fax: –
Web: www.southwestern.edu

CEO: –
CFO: –
HR: –
FYE: June 30
Type: Private

The first institution of higher learning in Texas, Southwestern University was chartered by the Republic of Texas in 1840. The liberal arts university consists of The Brown College of Arts and Sciences and The Sarofim School of Fine Arts. It offers more than two-dozen undergraduate majors, as well as pre-professional and certification programs, and confers bachelor's degrees in arts, music, fine arts, and science. Affiliated with The United Methodist Church, Southwestern University has an enrollment of more than 1,500 students. More than 80% of students live in residence halls on campus, which is located on the edge of the Texas Hill Country in Georgetown, Texas, just north of Austin.

	Annual Growth	06/18	06/19	06/20	06/21	06/22
Sales ($mil.)	4.9%	–	56.5	58.1	61.7	65.2
Net income ($ mil.)	1.2%	–	17.2	(9.5)	80.2	17.8
Market value ($ mil.)	–	–	–	–	–	–
Employees	–	–	–	–	–	357

SOUTHWESTERN VERMONT HEALTH CARE CORPORATION

100 HOSPITAL DR
BENNINGTON, VT 052015004
Phone: 802 442-6361
Fax: –
Web: www.svhealthcare.org

CEO: Thomas A Dee
CFO: Robert Lab
HR: Angie Hatfield
FYE: September 30
Type: Private

From its roots as a small community hospital, Southwestern Vermont Health Care (SVHC) has grown into a full-blown health system serving more than 55,000 people in a three state area (southwestern Vermont and adjacent portions of New York and Massachusetts). The not-for-profit health system's flagship facility is Southwestern Vermont Medical Center, which has about 100 beds and a regional cancer center. The system also includes two community primary care clinics, a 150-bed nursing home, and a home health and hospice organization. SVHC provides health care services for residents of Bennington County and surrounding regions.

	Annual Growth	09/15	09/16	09/19	09/20	09/21
Sales ($mil.)	122.9%	–	2.6	3.6	127.0	145.3
Net income ($ mil.)	106.0%	–	0.3	1.6	8.1	10.3
Market value ($ mil.)	–	–	–	–	–	–
Employees	–	–	–	–	–	1,200

SP PLUS CORP

NMS: SP

200 E. Randolph Street, Suite 7700
Chicago, IL 60601-7702
Phone: 312 274-2000
Fax: –
Web: www.spplus.com

CEO: G M Baumann
CFO: Kristopher H Roy
HR: –
FYE: December 31
Type: Public

SP Plus, which operates through its subsidiaries, blends industry-leading technology and best-in-class operations to deliver mobility solutions that enable the efficient movement of people, vehicles, and personal belongings. It is a leading provider of technology-driven mobility solutions for aviation, commercial, hospitality, and institutional clients. The company serves the industries including commercial real estate, residential communities, hotels and resorts, airports, airlines, cruise lines, healthcare facilities, municipalities and government facilities, retail operations, large event venues, colleges, and universities. SP Plus's clients include but not limited to the US Department of Transportation, Federal Aviation Administration, and Department of Homeland Security.

	Annual Growth	12/19	12/20	12/21	12/22	12/23
Sales ($mil.)	1.7%	1,663.7	1,086.9	1,177.2	1,553.5	1,782.3
Net income ($ mil.)	(10.7%)	48.8	(172.8)	31.7	45.2	31.1
Market value ($ mil.)	4.8%	840.1	570.8	558.7	687.4	1,014.7
Employees	(4.5%)	23,900	12,200	16,600	19,000	19,900

SPACE COAST HEALTH FOUNDATION, INC.

1100 ROCKLEDGE BLVD STE 100
ROCKLEDGE, FL 329552818
Phone: 321 241-6600
Fax: –
Web: www.wuesthoff.com

CEO: –
CFO: –
HR: –
FYE: September 30
Type: Private

When your space capsule crash-lands on Cocoa Beach, at least you know you'll have access to health care. Through its network of hospitals and clinics, Wuesthoff Health System provides a broad range of health services to residents of Brevard County and visitors to Florida's "Space Coast" region. The system is comprised of two hospitals (300-bed Wuesthoff Medical Center-Rockledge and 115-bed Wuesthoff Medical Center-Melbourne) and other facilities that provide diagnostic, behavioral health, nursing and assisted living, urgent care, and primary and specialist care services. The system includes hospice, community health, and home health programs. Wuesthoff Health System is part of Health Management Associates (HMA).

SPACE MICRO INC.

15378 AVENUE OF SCIENCE STE 200
SAN DIEGO, CA 921283451
Phone: 858 332-0700
Fax: –
Web: www.spacemicro.com

CEO: David Czajkowski
CFO: –
HR: –
FYE: June 30
Type: Private

Space Micro makes electronics that can withstand the rigors of space. The high technology firm adapts technologies from the commercial sector for space, aerospace, and military applications. The employee-owned company provides research and development, as well as production services. Products include advanced electronic systems and microelectronics designed to resist damage caused by electromagnetic radiation; other products include sensors, computers, and microelectromechanical systems (MEMS). The company operates through three divisions: Space Electronics, Microwave and RF, and Advanced Materials. Clients include NASA, the Missile Defense Agency, and the US Air Force. The company was founded in 2002.

SPACEQUEST, LTD.

3554 CHAIN BRIDGE RD # 4
FAIRFAX, VA 220302709
Phone: 703 424-7801
Fax: –
Web: www.aac-clyde.space

CEO: –
CFO: –
HR: –
FYE: December 31
Type: Private

For SpaceQuest, the trip usually ends in low Earth orbit. The company develops advanced satellite technology for government, university, and commercial use. SpaceQuest specializes in the design, development, testing, and manufacturing of spacecraft and the components necessary for operation of low-Earth orbiting satellites. SpaceQuest produces such communication components as antenna systems, radios and modems, in addition to power systems, command and data handling systems, attitude determination and control, and software. The company has built micro-satellites and provided components for such clients as Aprize Satellite, Bigelow Aerospace, and NASA. The company was founded in 1994.

SPAHN & ROSE LUMBER CO.

1100 ROCKDALE RD
DUBUQUE, IA 520037875
Phone: 563 582-3606
Fax: –
Web: www.spahnandrose.com

CEO: J P Hannan
CFO: –
HR: –
FYE: June 30
Type: Private

Spahn & Rose Lumber Co. is a retail lumber company with about 25 locations throughout Iowa and, to a lesser extent, in Illinois and Wisconsin. The company, which was organized in 1904, produces roof and floor truss systems and sells a variety of building supply products from such suppliers as Andersen (windows), Georgia-Pacific (lumber), CertainTeed (building materials), DuPont (plastics and flooring), MidContinent Cabinetry, (cabinets), Stanley Black & Decker (hand tools) and more. Spahn & Rose is promoting a range of green products, including recycled goods, solar reflective windows, and arsenic-free lumber.

SPAN-AMERICA MEDICAL SYSTEMS, INC.

70 COMMERCE CTR
GREENVILLE, SC 296155814
Phone: 864 288-8877
Fax: –
Web: www.spanamerica.com

CEO: James D Ferguson
CFO: Richard C Coggins
HR: –
FYE: October 01
Type: Private

With its mattresses and cushioning products, Span-America Medical Systems offers more comfort to the sick and wounded than Grandma's chicken soup. The company's medical products division makes therapeutic mattresses and mattress overlays (under the Geo-Matt and PressureGuard brand names), as well as Span-Aid patient positioners (used to elevate and support body parts) and Isch-Dish pressure-relief seat cushions to aid wound healing. Span-America also markets skin care creams for wound management, and consumer bedding and industrial foam products. It sells its wares through sales staff and distributors to hospitals, home health care dealers, and extended-care facilities in the US and Canada.

SPANG & COMPANY

110 DELTA DR
PITTSBURGH, PA 152382806
Phone: 412 963-9363
Fax: –
Web: www.spang.com

CEO: Frank E Rath Jr
CFO: –
HR: –
FYE: December 31
Type: Private

Spang & Company design, produce and supply precision soft magnetic components and materials to the electronics industry and custom engineered solutions to the power industry by operating three manufacturing divisions. Its magnetics segment makes precision soft magnetic components and materials to the electronics industry. Spang Power Electronics makes dry transformers and power control systems. Spang Engineered Solutions specializes in the design and manufacture of high power switching frequency inductors and transformers.. With headquarters in Pennsylvania, Spang & Company provides products and services on a worldwide scale, with sales offices and manufacturing facilities around the globe. The company was established in 1894 by George Spang.

SPARK NETWORKS, INC.

3400 N ASHTON BLVD STE 175
LEHI, UT 840435310
Phone: 801 377-6411
Fax: –
Web: www.spark.net

CEO: Daniel M Rosenthal
CFO: Robert W O'Hare
HR: Gabby Correa
FYE: December 31
Type: Private

Find yourself humming "Matchmaker, Matchmaker, make me a match" just a little too often? Spark Networks (formerly MatchNet) can help. The company owns and operates a variety of online personal sites, including dating sites JDate.com (for Jewish singles), BlackSingles.com, and ChristianMingle.com. Spark Networks also operates websites in English, Hebrew, and French. Most revenue comes from subscriptions -- members pay a monthly fee to communicate with other users. (Customers are offered discounts for longer-term subscriptions.) In addition, the company offers offline events and opportunities for travel (such as cruises, dinners, speed dating, and mixers) designed to encourage live social interaction.

SPANISH BROADCASTING SYSTEM INC

NBB: SBSA A

7007 NW 77th Ave.
Miami, FL 33166
Phone: 305 441-6901
Fax: –
Web: www.spanishbroadcasting.com

CEO: Raul Alarcon
CFO: Jose I Molina
HR: –
FYE: December 31
Type: Public

You might say this company is turning up the volume on Spanish radio. Spanish Broadcasting System (SBS) is one of the largest Spanish-language radio broadcasters in the US (along with Univision Radio and Entravision) with 20 stations in the US and Puerto Rico. Its radio stations serve such large markets as Chicago, Los Angeles, New York City, and Miami, reaching about half the US Hispanic population with music formats ranging from regional Mexican to Spanish tropical. In addition, the company operates website LaMusica.com, and several TV stations that offer original and syndicated Spanish-language programming under the Mega TV brand. Chairman and CEO Raúl Alarcón Jr. controls about 80% of SBS.

SPARROW EATON HOSPITAL

321 E HARRIS ST
CHARLOTTE, MI 488131629
Phone: 517 543-1050
Fax: –
Web: www.sparrow.org

CEO: Matthew Rush
CFO: Kim Capp
HR: –
FYE: December 31
Type: Private

Hayes Green Beach Memorial Hospital (HGB) provides a variety of medical services for the residents of central Michigan. Specialized services include cardiology, emergency medicine, home care, radiology, pain management, and rehabilitation. The 25-bed hospital also offers wellness programs, a family birthing center, and community education services, and it operates several community clinics. The hospital was founded in 1933 and is governed by the Eaton County Board of Commissioners.

	Annual Growth	12/18	12/19	12/20	12/21	12/22
Sales ($mil.)	4.2%	142.4	156.7	121.9	145.8	168.0
Net income ($ mil.)	–	16.5	(0.9)	(25.1)	1.7	(4.8)
Market value ($ mil.)	38.5%	1.4	2.4	1.7	36.9	5.2
Employees	–	442	451	434	–	–

	Annual Growth	03/14	03/15	03/16*	12/21	12/22
Sales ($mil.)	7.5%	–	49.3	50.9	67.5	81.6
Net income ($ mil.)	–	–	(0.6)	(0.2)	12.3	15.3
Market value ($ mil.)	–	–	–	–	–	–
Employees	–	–	–	–	–	290

*Fiscal year change

SPAR GROUP, INC.

NAS: SGRP

1910 Opdyke Court
Auburn Hills, MI 48326
Phone: 248 364-7727
Fax: –
Web: www.sparinc.com

CEO: Michael R Matacunas
CFO: Antonio C Pato
HR: –
FYE: December 31
Type: Public

SPAR Group knows how to fight for shelf space. Founded in 1967, the company provides an array of marketing and merchandising services to manufacturers and retailers. Clients include drugstore chains, grocery stores, and convenience stores. SPAR Group offers services such as in-store product demonstration and sampling, shelf maintenance, mystery shopping, database marketing, teleservices, and market research. The company has an international presence through operations and joint ventures located in about 10 countries, including Australia, Canada, India, Japan, New Zealand, Romania, South Africa, and China.

SPARROW HEALTH SYSTEM

1215 E MICHIGAN AVE
LANSING, MI 489121811
Phone: 517 364-5000
Fax: –
Web: www.sparrow.org

CEO: Dennis A Swan
CFO: –
HR: Scott Johnson
FYE: December 31
Type: Private

Sparrow Health System is Mid-Michigan's premier health care organization that includes hospitals in Lansing, Charlotte, St. Johns, Ionia and Carson City as well as Physicians Health Plan, Sparrow Care Network, Sparrow Medical Group, the Michigan Athletic Club, and AL!VE. Sparrow is affiliated with Michigan Medicine through the Sparrow Children's Center and with Michigan State University's three human health colleges. Sparrow's Heart and Vascular program provides a broad range of services across Mid-Michigan to patients needing open heart, vascular, and thoracic surgeries. The Sparrow Heart and Vascular Center, a 40,000 square foot state-of-the-art facility with dedicated inpatient units, is the first facility in Mid-Michigan to offer the Angiovac - a special device used to remove clots and mass matter from a patient's heart.

	Annual Growth	12/18	12/19	12/20	12/21	12/22
Sales ($mil.)	3.3%	229.2	252.9	230.5	255.7	261.3
Net income ($ mil.)	–	(1.6)	2.4	3.4	(1.8)	(0.7)
Market value ($ mil.)	24.8%	12.2	29.7	26.3	28.1	29.7
Employees	5.9%	19,900	22,000	20,000	25,000	25,000

	Annual Growth	12/18	12/19	12/20	12/21	12/22
Sales ($mil.)	3.1%	–	1,340.6	1,402.9	1,505.8	1,470.3
Net income ($ mil.)	–	–	99.7	41.5	147.2	(164.5)
Market value ($ mil.)	–	–	–	–	–	–
Employees	–	–	–	–	–	3,400

SPARTANBURG REGIONAL HEALTH SERVICES DISTRICT, INC.

101 E WOOD ST
SPARTANBURG, SC 293033040
Phone: 864 560-6000
Fax: −
Web: www.spartanburgregional.com

CEO: Ingo Angermeier
CFO: Larry Barnette
HR: Kara Peeler
FYE: September 30
Type: Private

Spartanburg Regional Health Services District (dba Spartanburg Regional Healthcare System or SRHS) provides a wide range of care options to northeast South Carolina. It operates Spartanburg Medical Center, Cherokee Medical Center, Pelham Medical Center, Spartanburg Hospital for Restorative Care, Ellen Sagar Nursing Center, Medical Group of the Carolinas, and Union Medical Center. The 745-bed Spartanburg Medical offers services including emergency, surgical, maternity, cancer, a Heart Center and inpatient rehabilitation. It houses the Gibbs Cancer Center & Research Institute, as well as centers specializing in heart, vascular, women's health, and outpatient care. SRHS also operates clinics, specialty outpatient centers, and long-term care, home health, rehabilitation, and hospice facilities. With approximately 700 physicians on staff, SRHS handles some 25,000 surgical procedures, delivers around 4,000 babies and has approximately 200,000 emergency center visits.

	Annual Growth	09/17	09/18	09/19	09/20	09/21
Sales ($mil.)	(0.9%)	−	1,147.6	1,365.4	1,468.0	1,117.1
Net income ($ mil.)	69.6%	−	28.8	42.4	18.8	140.2
Market value ($ mil.)	−	−	−	−	−	−
Employees	−	−	−	−	−	5,000

SPARTANNASH CO

NMS: SPTN

850 76th Street, S.W., P.O. Box 8700
Grand Rapids, MI 49518
Phone: 616 878-2000
Fax: −
Web: www.spartannash.com

CEO: Tony B Sarsam
CFO: Jason Monaco
HR: Derek Tufts
FYE: December 30
Type: Public

Grocery wholesaler and retailer SpartanNash distributes approximately 85,500 stock-keeping units (SKUs) of nationally-branded and private-label products across all 50 US states through some 20 distribution centers. It operates a fleet of approximately 570 over-the-road tractors, about 255 dry vans, and approximately 1,130 refrigerated trailers. In addition, the company distributes goods to approximately 160 US military commissaries and more than 400 exchanges in the US and several other countries. On the retail side, SpartanNash operates more than 145 supermarkets under the Family Fare, D&W Fresh Market, VG's Grocery, Martin's Super Markets, and Sun Mart Foods, among others. Spartan Stores began in 1917.

	Annual Growth	12/19*	01/21	01/22*	12/22	12/23
Sales ($mil.)	3.3%	8,536.1	9,348.5	8,931.0	9,643.1	9,729.2
Net income ($ mil.)	73.7%	5.7	75.9	73.8	34.5	52.2
Market value ($ mil.)	12.9%	488.7	602.6	891.6	1,046.6	794.3
Employees	(0.3%)	17,200	18,000	16,500	17,500	17,000

*Fiscal year change

SPARTON CORPORATION

5612 JOHNSON LAKE RD
DE LEON SPRINGS, FL 321303657
Phone: 847 762-5800
Fax: −
Web: www.sparton.com

CEO: −
CFO: Joseph McCormack
HR: Annette Hooker
FYE: July 02
Type: Private

Sparton is a world leader in the design, development, testing and production of complex maritime electronic systems, including sonobuoys in support of Anti-Submarine Warfare, submarine deployed products supporting Undersea Warfare, and depth-rated encapsulated systems to support Subsea and Seabed Warfare. Sparton's advanced technology expertise is focused on rapid development of custom solutions for use in harsh, maritime environments deployed from a range of undersea, surface and air platforms. Sparton, which tracks its roots back to 1900, was acquired by Elbit Systems of America in 2021.

SPAULDING REHABILITATION HOSPITAL (SRH) VOLUNTEER SERVICES,

300 1ST AVE
CHARLESTOWN, MA 021293109
Phone: 617 952-5000
Fax: −
Web: www.spauldingrehab.org

CEO: Diana Barett
CFO: Kathleen Murphy
HR: −
FYE: September 30
Type: Private

Spaulding Rehabilitation Hospital Network, which includes a nearly 200-bed main hospital and nine outpatient centers throughout Massachusetts, provides a variety of rehabilitation services for persons with disabilities or who are recovering from surgery, illness, or injury. Its inpatient programs include rehabilitation for vascular disease, brain injury, spinal cord injury, and stroke; the network also provides outpatient rehabilitation in such areas as sports injury, physical and occupational therapy, sleep diagnostics, and arthritis management. Spaulding Rehabilitation Hospital is a teaching hospital for Harvard Medical School and is a member of the Partners HealthCare System.

SPAW GLASS HOLDING, LLC

9331 CORPORATE DR
SELMA, TX 781541250
Phone: 210 651-9000
Fax: −
Web: www.spawglass.com

CEO: Joel Stone
CFO: Bobby Friedel
HR: −
FYE: December 31
Type: Private

Deep in the heart of Texas, SpawGlass Holding is busy providing general building and construction management services for commercial and institutional projects through its SpawGlass Construction and SpawGlass Contractors subsidiaries. The group also offers design/build delivery and tenant finish-out services. Among its landmark projects is the interior restoration of the Texas State Capitol. It also worked on the NASA Shuttle Flight Training Facility near Houston and the University of Texas Health Science Center at San Antonio. Louis Spaw and Frank Glass formed SpawGlass in 1953. The company, now employee-owned, has offices in Austin, Houston, San Antonio, and the Rio Grande Valley in Texas.

	Annual Growth	12/04	12/05	12/06	12/07	12/09
Sales ($mil.)	(37.4%)	−	−	1,879.2	336.5	461.0
Net income ($ mil.)	−	−	−	−	5.9	8.7
Market value ($ mil.)	−	−	−	−	−	−
Employees	−	−	−	−	−	650

SPECIAL OLYMPICS, INC.

2600 VIRGINIA AVE NW STE 104
WASHINGTON, DC 20037
Phone: 202 628-3630
Fax: −
Web: www.specialolympics.org

CEO: Mary Davis
CFO: Michael Meenan
HR: Faith Gazdzicki
FYE: December 31
Type: Private

Special Olympics gives special attention to the differently abled. The group is a global movement that unleashes the human spirit every day around the world through the transformative power and joy of sport. Through programming in sports, health, education and community building, Special Olympics is tackling the inactivity, stigma, isolation, and injustice that people with intellectual disabilities (ID) face. More than 6.5 million athletes in more than 170 countries take part in the group's programs. Special Olympics deliver, high- quality training and competition in an inclusive culture through Unified Sports. The group's support comes mainly from contributions made in response to direct-mail campaigns and from individual and corporate sponsorships and donations. The late Eunice Kennedy Shriver organized the First International Special Olympic Games in 1968.

	Annual Growth	12/15	12/16	12/19	12/21	12/22
Sales ($mil.)	4.8%	−	104.6	135.6	148.3	138.3
Net income ($ mil.)	−	−	0.7	7.5	22.3	(4.0)
Market value ($ mil.)	−	−	−	−	−	−
Employees	−	−	−	−	−	160

SPECIALIZED MARKETING SERVICES, INC.

3421 W SEGERSTROM AVE
SANTA ANA, CA 927046404
Phone: 949 553-0890
Fax: –
Web: www.33-degrees.com

CEO: –
CFO: –
HR: –
FYE: December 31
Type: Private

Specialized Marketing Services is an independent direct response marketing firm that offers direct mail and other types of response marketing services for clients in many different industries. It provides marketing campaign development and planning, creative services, and data collection and analysis. In addition to direct mailings, Specialized Marketing Services offers expertise in interactive marketing, direct response print and radio campaigns, and viral marketing efforts. Clients have included Heinz, Samsung, and Walt Disney. CEO Gloria Robbins started the agency in 1988.

SPECIALTY RICE, INC.

1000 W 1ST ST
BRINKLEY, AR 720219000
Phone: 870 734-1233
Fax: –
Web: www.dellarice.com

CEO: –
CFO: –
HR: –
FYE: December 31
Type: Private

Specialty Rice goes beyond the mainstream in the rice industry. The company grows, processes, packages, and sells white and brown basmati, arborio (for making risotto), jasmine, and koshihikari (sushi) rice. Its products are sold under the Della Gourmet Rice brand name in the US and under the Delrose label in Canada. Specialty Rice operates 6,000 acres of farmland in Arkansas. To promote the use of its exotic rice products, the company is offering cooking courses at select supermarkets throughout the US. Specialty Rice is owned and operated by the Ajmera family.

	Annual Growth	12/11	12/12	12/13	12/15	12/16
Sales ($mil.)	3.1%	–	–	24.5	27.3	26.9
Net income ($ mil.)	71.0%	–	–	0.3	0.9	1.3
Market value ($ mil.)	–	–	–	–	–	–
Employees	–	–	–	–	–	52

SPECTRA ENERGY, LLC

5400 WESTHEIMER CT
HOUSTON, TX 770565353
Phone: 713 627-5400
Fax: –
Web: www.spectraenergy.com

CEO: Gregory L Ebel
CFO: John P Reddy
HR: –
FYE: December 31
Type: Private

Spectra Energy covers the spectrum of natural gas activities -- gathering, processing, transmission, storage, and distribution. The company, now part of Enbridge, operates more than 15,400 miles of transmission pipeline and has 305 billion cu. ft. of storage capacity in the US and Canada. Units include U.S. Gas Transmission, Texas Eastern Transmission, Natural Gas Liquids Division, and Market Hub Partners. It also has stakes in DCP Midstream, Maritimes & Northeast Pipeline, Gulfstream Natural Gas System, Spectra Energy Income Fund, and 75% of Spectra Energy Partners. Its Union Gas unit distributes gas to 1.5 million Ontario customers. In 2017, Spectra merged with Enbridge, creating the largest energy infrastructure company in North America.

	Annual Growth	12/12	12/13	12/14	12/15	12/16
Sales ($mil.)	(6.1%)	–	–	–	5,234.0	4,916.0
Net income ($ mil.)	121.7%	–	–	–	460.0	1,020.0
Market value ($ mil.)	–	–	–	–	–	–
Employees	–	–	–	–	–	8,700

SPECTRA SYSTEMS CORP

NBB: SCTQ

40 Westmister Street, 2nd Floor
Providence, RI 02903
Phone: 401 274-4700
Fax: –
Web: www.spsy.com

CEO: –
CFO: –
HR: –
FYE: December 31
Type: Public

Spectra Systems' products aren't always visible to the naked eye. The company makes materials that help to insure the authenticity of documents and products. Its particles, inks, and coatings (which are detected using optical reading devices) mark currency, passports, textiles, and other products. It also develops related hardware and software. Spectra Systems, through partnerships with currency printers including De La Rue, primarily serves the banking industry. The company also resells data reading devices from Zebra Technologies. The company was founded in 1996.

	Annual Growth	12/17	12/18	12/19	12/20	12/21
Sales ($mil.)	8.1%	12.2	12.5	13.2	14.7	16.6
Net income ($ mil.)	12.0%	3.3	4.1	4.3	5.1	5.2
Market value ($ mil.)	–	–	–	–	–	–
Employees	–	28	28	–	–	–

SPECTRANETICS LLC

9965 FEDERAL DR STE 100
COLORADO SPRINGS, CO 809213823
Phone: 719 447-2000
Fax: –
Web: www.spectranetics.com

CEO: Scott Drake
CFO: Stacy McMahan
HR: –
FYE: December 31
Type: Private

Spectranetics, a part of Philips, is helping patients return to the activities they love. It manages every lead, modify all plaque, eradicate restenosis and amputation. It provides solutions for lead management and extraction procedures offered by Philips image guided therapy, which also offers the Vascular suite that is designed to support diverse peripheral, aortic, visceral, arterial, and venous procedures. It also offers Coronary suitr where advances clinical and workflow applications, therapeutic and disgnostic devices, and leading services, all work intelligently together.

SPECTRUM BRANDS HOLDINGS INC (NEW)

NYS: SPB

3001 Deming Way
Middelton, WI 53562
Phone: 608 275-3340
Fax: –
Web: www.spectrumbrands.com

CEO: David M Maura
CFO: Jeremy W Smeltser
HR: –
FYE: September 30
Type: Public

Spectrum Brands Holdings (formerly HRG Group) is a global branded consumer products company. It manufactures, markets and distributes brands including Kwikset, Weiser, Baldwin, National Hardware, Pfister, Remington, George Foreman, Russell Hobbs, Black+Decker, Tetra, Marineland, GloFish, Nature's Miracle, Dingo, 8-in-1, FURminator, and IAMS. The company primarily serves large retailers, pet superstores, online retailers, warehouse clubs, hardware stores, and other specialty retail outlets. Spectrum Brands generates the majority of sales from the US.

	Annual Growth	09/19	09/20	09/21	09/22	09/23
Sales ($mil.)	(6.4%)	3,802.1	3,964.2	2,998.1	3,132.5	2,918.8
Net income ($ mil.)	39.8%	471.9	97.8	189.6	71.6	1,801.5
Market value ($ mil.)	10.4%	1,861.0	2,017.7	3,377.2	1,377.8	2,765.8
Employees	(30.1%)	13,000	12,100	–	11,000	3,100

SPECTRUM BRANDS LEGACY, INC.

3001 DEMING WAY
MIDDLETON, WI 535621431
Phone: 608 275-3340
Fax: –
Web: investor.spectrumbrands.com

CEO: –
CFO: –
HR: –
FYE: September 30
Type: Private

Spectrum Brands is a diversified global branded consumer products and home essentials company. The company manufactures, markets and distributes its products globally in the North America, Europe, Middle East & Africa Latin America, and Asia-Pacific regions through a variety of trade channels, including retailers, wholesalers and distributors. Some of its trusted brands are Kwikset, Baldwin, FURminoator, DreamBone, Russell Hobbs, National Hardware, Pfister, Tetra, GloFish, Remington, Cutter, and Spectracide. Roughly 60% of its revenue were from US customers.

SPECTRUM GROUP INTERNATIONAL INC NBB: SPGZ

1063 McGaw, Suite 250
Irvine, CA 92614
Phone: 949 748-4800
Fax: –
Web: www.spectrumgi.com

CEO: Gregory N Roberts
CFO: Paul Soth
HR: –
FYE: June 30
Type: Public

From gold bullion to fine wine, one auction house spans the spectrum of global collectibles. Spectrum Group International (SGI) operates primarily in the area of collectibles. It conducts traditional live auctions (focused on coins and rare and vintage wines), as well as online and telephone auctions. Its primary auction business is Stack's Bowers Galleries, a California-based auction house that specializes in US and global coins and currency. In 2014 SGI spun off its trading business, A-Mark Precious Metals, which sells coins and other precious metals on a wholesale basis; that business generates most of SGI's revenue. The company was founded by Greg Manning, who started collecting stamps at age 7, and opened an office to market stamps in 1971 at the age of 25.

	Annual Growth	06/09	06/10	06/11	06/12	06/13
Sales ($mil.)	14.6%	4,293.3	6,012.4	7,202.2	7,974.8	7,406.0
Net income ($ mil.)	(17.1%)	7.1	(1.1)	3.8	4.1	3.4
Market value ($ mil.)	–	–	–	–	–	–
Employees	1.2%	142	143	177	190	149

SPEED COMMERCE INC NBB: SPDC

1303 E. Arapaho Road, Suite 200
Richardson, TX 75081
Phone: 866 377-3331
Fax: –
Web: www.speedcommerce.com

CEO: –
CFO: –
HR: –
FYE: March 31
Type: Public

Before there was streaming, there was Speed Commerce. Speed Commerce (formerly Navarre Corporation) distributes home entertainment and multimedia software products and provides logistics for major retail chains (Best Buy, Wal-Mart) and Internet-based retail channels (Amazon, iTunes) throughout North America. Its smaller publishing segment is run through its Encore Software subsidiary, which provides print, education, and family entertainment under such titles as The Print Shop , Mavis Beacon Teaches Typing , Hoyle PC Gaming and Punch Home Design. Founded in 1983 as an entertainment distributor, Speed Commerce has diversified into a licenser and publisher of entertainment.

	Annual Growth	03/11	03/12	03/13	03/14	03/15
Sales ($mil.)	(29.7%)	490.9	480.8	485.3	107.1	120.0
Net income ($ mil.)	–	11.2	(34.3)	(11.8)	(26.6)	(56.0)
Market value ($ mil.)	(23.9%)	7.8	7.3	9.4	15.0	2.6
Employees	40.5%	413	279	819	1,123	1,609

SPEEDUS CORP NBB: SPDE

1 Dag Hammarskjold Blvd.
Freehold, NJ 07728
Phone: 888 773-3669
Fax: –
Web: www.speedus.com

CEO: –
CFO: –
HR: –
FYE: December 31
Type: Public

Speedus is a holding company with investments in two technology companies: medical software firm Zargis Medical Corp. and data storage maker Density Dynamics, Inc. Zargis makes Cardioscan, a software application that can help diagnose heart problems, which is marketed with 3M's Littman brand products. (Speedus owns 90% of Zargis; Siemens holds the remainder of the joint venture.) In 2009 the FDA cleared Zargis to market its Signal X6 device, which records heart and lung sounds through adhesive acoustic sensors. Zargis holds several contracts with the US Army to develop prototype telemedicine systems for use in cardiology. Density Dynamics, 75%-owned, develops solid-state storage devices used in data centers.

	Annual Growth	12/05	12/06	12/07	12/08	12/09
Sales ($mil.)	(18.4%)	1.0	0.8	0.7	0.2	0.5
Net income ($ mil.)	–	(5.5)	(5.6)	(4.4)	(9.2)	(2.8)
Market value ($ mil.)	22.4%	4.7	4.8	7.1	1.6	10.5
Employees	–	–	29	22	20	20

SPEEDWAY MOTORSPORTS, LLC

5555 CONCORD PKWY S
CONCORD, NC 280274600
Phone: 704 532-3320
Fax: –
Web: www.speedwaymotorsports.com

CEO: –
CFO: –
HR: –
FYE: December 31
Type: Private

Speedway Motorsports is a leading marketer, promoter and sponsor of motorsports entertainment in the US. The company, through its subsidiaries, owns and operates a premier facilities, including Atlanta Motor Speedway, Bristol Motor Speedway, Charlotte Motor Speedway, Dover Motor Speedway, Kentucky Speedway, and Texas Motor Speedway, among others. The company provides souvenir merchandising services through its SMI Properties subsidiaries; manufactures and distributes smaller-scale, modified racing cars and parts through its US. Legend Cars International subsidiary; and produces and broadcasts syndicated motorsports programming to radio stations nationwide though its Performance Racing Network subsidiary. The company traces its roots back to 1959 when Executive Chairman O. Bruton Smith began construction of Charlotte Motor Speedway.

SPELMAN COLLEGE

350 SPELMAN LN SW 589
ATLANTA, GA 303144399
Phone: 404 681-3643
Fax: –
Web: www.spelman.edu

CEO: –
CFO: Dawn Alston
HR: Joyce Thompkins
FYE: June 30
Type: Private

Spelman College is a private, historically African American college for women. The college enrolls more than 2,100 students from more than 40 states in the US and 15 countries. It offers majors in areas such as English, economics, mathematics, music, psychology, art, and religion. Tuition (for 12-20 credit hours) costs about $10,650, and the student-faculty ratio is 12-to-1. Its alumnae include Sam's Club CEO Rosalind Brewer; former acting Surgeon General and Spelman's first alumna President Audrey Forbes Manley; author Pearl Cleage; and actress LaTanya Richardson Jackson. Spelman boasts a graduation rate of more than 80%.

	Annual Growth	06/18	06/19	06/20	06/21	06/22
Sales ($mil.)	22.3%	–	111.7	152.0	183.0	204.4
Net income ($ mil.)	60.7%	–	14.2	48.7	65.9	58.8
Market value ($ mil.)	–	–	–	–	–	–
Employees	–	–	–	–	–	550

SPF ENERGY, INC.

100 27TH ST NE BLDG A
MINOT, ND 587035164
Phone: 701 852-1194
Fax: –
Web: –

CEO: –
CFO: –
HR: –
FYE: December 31
Type: Private

Super-jobber SPF Energy is also a super-pumper of petroleum. The company's Superpumper subsidiary runs a chain of about 15 convenience stores and gas stations in Minnesota, Montana, and North Dakota under the Cenex, Conoco, Exxon, Sinclair, Tesoro and Shell banners. Its Farstad Oil subsidiary offers bulk transportation of petroleum products, including the annual distribution of about 250 million gallons of gas, 20 million gallons of propane, and 2.5 million gallons of lubricants. The Farstad fleet serves businesses and government agencies from Montana to eastern Minnesota and from northern Wyoming to the Canadian border. SPF Energy is owned by North American fuel wholesaler Parkland Fuel Corporation.

	Annual Growth	12/11	12/12	12/13	12/14	12/16
Sales ($mil.)	(19.7%)	–	1,062.7	1,012.9	1,026.9	442.7
Net income ($ mil.)	7.7%	–	5.3	8.9	16.4	7.1
Market value ($ mil.)	–	–	–	–	–	–
Employees	–	–	–	–	–	300

SPHEROTECH, INC.

27845 IRMA LEE CIR STE 101
LAKE FOREST, IL 600455100
Phone: 847 680-8922
Fax: –
Web: www.spherotech.com

CEO: Andrew Wang
CFO: –
HR: –
FYE: December 31
Type: Private

Spherotech is very particular about its business. The company manufactures microparticles for the drug and medical device industries. Its product offerings include ferromagnetic, fluorescent, latex, paramagnetic, and various colored microparticles. Spherotech's products are used in applications such as fluorescence and enzyme immunoassay. The company was founded in 1992.

	Annual Growth	12/99	12/00	12/01	12/02	12/20
Sales ($mil.)	16.8%	–	0.6	0.8	1.0	13.4
Net income ($ mil.)	21.6%	–	0.2	0.0	0.0	7.7
Market value ($ mil.)	–	–	–	–	–	–
Employees	–	–	–	–	–	40

SPINDLETOP OIL & GAS CO (TEX)

NBB: SPND

12850 Spurling Road, Suite 200
Dallas, TX 75230
Phone: 972 644-2581
Fax: –
Web: www.spindletopoil.com

CEO: Chris G Mazzini
CFO: –
HR: –
FYE: December 31
Type: Public

In 1901 the discovery of oil at Spindletop marked the beginning of the modern petroleum industry. Today, Spindletop Oil & Gas is keeping that tradition alive in its exploration for and production of oil and natural gas. The company has major operations throughout Texas, as well as interests in oil and gas properties in more than a dozen other states. Spindletop Oil & Gas has proved reserves of more than 323,000 barrels of oil and 12.5 billion cu. ft. of natural gas. The company also operates more than 26 miles of gas pipelines and an oilfield equipment rental business. It manages subsidiaries Prairie Pipeline and Spindletop Drilling. Chairman and president Chris Mazzini and his wife own 77% of the company.

	Annual Growth	12/18	12/19	12/20	12/21	12/22
Sales ($mil.)	5.5%	6.7	5.6	4.2	6.6	8.4
Net income ($ mil.)	26.2%	0.3	(0.6)	(0.9)	1.0	0.7
Market value ($ mil.)	0.7%	25.3	15.7	16.4	23.6	26.1
Employees	(6.4%)	56	47	42	37	43

SPIRE ALABAMA INC.

605 RICHARD ARRINGTON JR BLVD N
BIRMINGHAM, AL 352032707
Phone: 205 326-8100
Fax: –
Web: –

CEO: Steven L Lindsey
CFO: Adam W Woodard
HR: –
FYE: September 30
Type: Private

With all the gas a customer could possibly need, Alagasco is THE gas co. in Alabama. A unit of Spire (formerly The Laclede Group), in 2015 utility Alabama Gas Corporation (Alagasco) distributed natural gas to 425,000 commercial and industrial customers in about half of the counties in the state. The utility also provides gas transportation services to large end users who purchase wholesale gas from suppliers. Alagasco has seven operating districts: Anniston, Birmingham, Gadsden, Montgomery, Opelika, Selma, and Tuscaloosa. The Alagasco distribution system includes 11,230 miles of mains and more than 12,000 miles of service lines.

	Annual Growth	09/14	09/15	09/16	09/17	09/18
Sales ($mil.)	1.5%	–	479.2	368.5	400.5	500.7
Net income ($ mil.)	(70.0%)	–	48.0	53.2	58.1	1.3
Market value ($ mil.)	–	–	–	–	–	–
Employees	–	–	–	–	–	947

SPIRE CORP.

One Patriots Park
Bedford, MA 01730-2396
Phone: 781 275-6000
Fax: –
Web: www.spirecorp.com

CEO: Rodger W Lafavre
CFO: Robert S Lieberman
HR: –
FYE: December 31
Type: Public

Success in solar is more than an aspiration for Spire. Factories worldwide use Spire's photovoltaic solar cell manufacturing equipment, including cell testers and assemblers, to produce modules that convert sunlight into electricity. Its solar systems unit also uses the equipment to make solar energy modules for buildings and homes. Though Spire's roots are in solar energy, the company also has a biomedical unit that provides coating services to orthopedic and other medical device makers. Its products are manufactured at its US headquarters, and Spire gets almost half of its sales domestic customers. Key customers include First Solar and Stryker Orthopedics.

	Annual Growth	12/09	12/10	12/11	12/12	12/13
Sales ($mil.)	(32.4%)	69.9	79.8	61.6	22.1	14.6
Net income ($ mil.)	–	(5.3)	(0.4)	(1.5)	(1.9)	(8.5)
Market value ($ mil.)	(43.7%)	49.4	48.0	5.8	4.6	5.0
Employees	(20.1%)	211	194	173	118	86

SPIRE INC

NYS: SR

700 Market Street
St. Louis, MO 63101
Phone: 314 342-0500
Fax: –
Web: www.spireenergy.com

CEO: Steven L Lindsey
CFO: Steven P Rasche
HR: –
FYE: September 30
Type: Public

Spire Inc. is the holding company for Spire Missouri Inc., Spire Alabama Inc., other gas utilities, and gas-related businesses. Spire is committed to transforming its business and pursuing growth through growing organically, investing in infrastructure, and advancing through innovation. It has two key business segments: Gas Utility and Gas Marketing. Spire Missouri is the largest natural gas distribution utility system in Missouri, serving approximately 1.2 million residential, commercial and industrial customers in Kansas City, and other areas in Missouri.

	Annual Growth	09/19	09/20	09/21	09/22	09/23
Sales ($mil.)	8.1%	1,952.4	1,855.4	2,235.5	2,198.5	2,666.3
Net income ($ mil.)	4.2%	184.6	88.6	271.7	220.8	217.5
Market value ($ mil.)	(10.3%)	4,641.2	2,830.2	3,254.8	3,316.0	3,010.1
Employees	0.4%	3,536	3,583	3,710	3,584	3,589

SPIRIT AEROSYSTEMS HOLDINGS INC   NYS: SPR

3801 South Oliver
Wichita, KS 67210
Phone: 316 526-9000
Fax: –
Web: www.spiritaero.com

CEO: Patrick M Shanahan
CFO: Mark Suchinski
HR: –
FYE: December 31
Type: Public

Spirit AeroSystems Holdings is one of the largest independent non-OEM makers of commercial and military airplane components, such as fuselages, propulsion systems, wings, and wing components. It designs and builds aerostructures for every Boeing aircraft currently in production (including the majority of aerostructures for Boeing's 737) as well as for Boeing's chief rival, Airbus. It is a key supplier of wing parts for Airbus' A320 aircraft. Sales from Boeing and Airbus represent about 80% of the company's business. Spirit AeroSystems also provides maintenance, repair, and overhaul (MRO) services. The company maintains operations in the US, the UK, and Asia; however, the US is its largest market, accounting for about 75% of total revenue.

	Annual Growth	12/19	12/20	12/21	12/22	12/23
Sales ($mil.)	(6.4%)	7,863.1	3,404.8	3,953.0	5,029.6	6,047.9
Net income ($ mil.)	–	530.1	(870.3)	(540.8)	(545.7)	(616.2)
Market value ($ mil.)	(18.7%)	8,458.0	4,536.6	5,000.8	3,435.2	3,688.2
Employees	3.2%	18,200	14,500	16,100	18,235	20,655

SPIRIT AIRLINES INC   NYS: SAVE

2800 Executive Way
Miramar, FL 33025
Phone: 954 447-7920
Fax: –
Web: www.spirit.com

CEO: Edward M Christie III
CFO: Scott Haralson
HR: Carol Hernandez
FYE: December 31
Type: Public

Spirit Airlines offers affordable travel to value-conscious customers. Its all-Airbus fleet is one of the youngest and most fuel efficient in the United States. It operates flights between major US cities and popular vacation spots in the Caribbean, and Latin America, serving around 90 destinations in around 15 countries. The airline operates an all-Airbus fleet of about 195 single-aisle aircraft in the A320 family. Spirit Airlines capitalizes on an ancillary service model, charging separately for baggage, advanced seat selection, and other travel-related upgrades. In addition to scheduled service, the company partners with third-party vendors to offer a slate of vacation packages via its website. Domestic markets account for the majority of the company's sales. The company was founded in 1964 as Clippert Trucking Company.

	Annual Growth	12/19	12/20	12/21	12/22	12/23
Sales ($mil.)	8.8%	3,830.5	1,810.0	3,230.8	5,068.4	5,362.5
Net income ($ mil.)	–	335.3	(428.7)	(472.6)	(554.2)	(447.5)
Market value ($ mil.)	(20.1%)	4,404.4	2,671.5	2,387.4	2,128.4	1,790.8
Employees	10.2%	8,938	8,756	9,823	12,025	13,167

SPITZER MANAGEMENT, INC.

150 E BRIDGE ST
ELYRIA, OH 440355219
Phone: 440 323-4671
Fax: –
Web: www.spitzer.com

CEO: Alan Spitzer
CFO: –
HR: –
FYE: December 31
Type: Private

Pick a car, any car. Spitzer Management, which sells almost every kind of car from A to V (Acura, Buick, Chevy, Dodge, Ford, GMC, Jeep, Kia, Mitsubishi, Scion, Toyota, and Volkswagen), primarily operates through its Spitzer Autoworld unit. The division boasts more than 20 dealerships and some 30 franchises in Ohio, Pennsylvania, and Florida. Spitzer dealerships sell both new and used cars and offer parts, service, and collision-repair departments. The company, founded in 1904 by George G. Spitzer, also has interests in a hotel and marinas in Lorain, Ohio. Additionally, Spitzer manages a golf course in La Grange, Ohio. Spitzer Management is still owned by the Spitzer family.

SPOK HOLDINGS INC   NMS: SPOK

5911 Kingstowne Village Pkwy, 6th Floor
Alexandria, VA 22315
Phone: 800 611-8488
Fax: –
Web: www.spok.com

CEO: Vincent D Kelly
CFO: Calvin C Rice
HR: –
FYE: December 31
Type: Public

Spok Holdings is a leader in healthcare communication. The company's customers rely on Spok for workflow improvement, secure texting, paging services, contact center optimization, and public safety response. Spok develops, sells, and supports enterprise-wide systems primarily for healthcare and other organizations needing to automate, centralize, and standardize their approach to clinical communications. Its solutions can be found in prominent hospitals, large government agencies, leading public safety institutions, colleges and universities; large hotels, resorts and casinos; and well-known manufacturers in the US, Europe, Canada, Australia, Asia, and the Middle East. The majority of the company's revenue comes from the US.

	Annual Growth	12/19	12/20	12/21	12/22	12/23
Sales ($mil.)	(3.5%)	160.3	148.2	142.2	134.5	139.0
Net income ($ mil.)	–	(10.8)	(44.2)	(22.2)	21.9	15.7
Market value ($ mil.)	6.1%	244.5	222.5	186.5	163.7	309.5
Employees	(11.9%)	638	602	563	376	384

SPORTSMAN'S WAREHOUSE HOLDINGS INC   NMS: SPWH

1475 West 9000 South, Suite A
West Jordan, UT 84088
Phone: 801 566-6681
Fax: 801 304-4388
Web: www.sportsmans.com

CEO: Joseph P Schneider
CFO: Jeff White
HR: Shelley Swain
FYE: January 28
Type: Public

Sportsman's Warehouse Holdings makes outdoor pursuits a reality by supplying customers with the proper attire and the right equipment. Sportsman's Warehouse is an outdoor sporting goods retailer focused on meeting the needs of the seasoned outdoor veteran as well as women, and children at over 130 Sportsman's Warehouse stores in about 30 states mostly Washington, California, and Utah. It also sells apparel and gear online. The company also sells gear for camping, fishing, hunting, and other recreational activities. Its vast products portfolio includes such brand names as Carhartt, Columbia Sportswear, Winchester, Johnson Outdoors, Coleman, and Browning, among others. Sportsman's Warehouse was founded in 1986.

	Annual Growth	02/19	02/20*	01/21	01/22	01/23
Sales ($mil.)	13.3%	849.1	886.4	1,451.8	1,506.1	1,399.5
Net income ($ mil.)	14.3%	23.8	20.2	91.4	108.5	40.5
Market value ($ mil.)	16.3%	192.2	243.3	657.7	399.4	352.1
Employees	7.1%	5,100	5,400	7,000	7,700	6,700

*Fiscal year change

SPORTSQUEST INC   NBB: SPQS

500 S Australian Ave, Suite #600
West Palm Beach, FL 33401
Phone: 561 631-9221
Fax: –
Web: www.sports-quest.co

CEO: –
CFO: –
HR: –
FYE: May 31
Type: Public

SportsQuest is on a mission to succeed in the sports and entertainment marketing business. Its primary business consists of developing and managing the U.S. Pro Golf Tour, one of a number of "mini" tours operating in the shadow of the PGA TOUR, the overseer of professional golf's showcase events. The U.S. Pro Golf Tour is owned by Greens Worldwide, which like SportsQuest is controlled and overseen by Thomas Kidd, CEO of both companies. SportsQuest was known as Air Brook Airport Express before Kidd in 2007 bought a controlling stake in the company, which then exited the airport transportation business and changed its name.

	Annual Growth	10/04	10/05	10/06	10/07*	05/08
Sales ($mil.)	(28.9%)	0.0	0.0	0.0	0.0	0.0
Net income ($ mil.)	–	0.0	0.0	0.0	(0.7)	(1.4)
Market value ($ mil.)	(13.1%)	0.9	0.9	1.9	5.6	0.5
Employees	–	–	–	–	1	1

*Fiscal year change

SPOTLIGHT CAPITAL HOLDINGS INC   NBB: SLCH

3723 San Gabriel River Parkway Suite A   CEO: -
Pico Rivera, CA 90660   CFO: -
Phone: -   HR: -
Fax: -   FYE: December 31
Web: www.spotlightcapitalholdings.com   Type: Public

AvStar Aviation Group is making the switch from searching for oil and gas to investing in the aviation sector. Once known as Pangea Petroleum, the company formerly specialized in oil and natural gas exploration and production in the US Gulf Coast region. In 2009, however, Pangea Petroleum was acquired by AvStar Aviation Services, which redirected the company's focus as a service provider to the general aviation industry. Now known as AvStar Aviation Group, the company plans to acquire fixed base operations (FBOs) at airports. Its San Diego Airmotive subsidiary provides maintenance, repair, and overhaul services for aircraft.

	Annual Growth	12/17	12/18	12/19	12/20	12/21
Sales ($mil.)	-	-	-	-	-	-
Net income ($ mil.)	-	(0.0)	(0.0)	(0.0)	(0.0)	(0.1)
Market value ($ mil.)	25.4%	0.3	0.2	0.1	0.2	0.6
Employees	-	-	-	-	-	-

SPRAGUE RESOURCES LP

185 INTERNATIONAL DR   CEO: -
PORTSMOUTH, NH 038016836   CFO: -
Phone: 800 225-1560   HR: -
Fax: -   FYE: December 31
Web: www.spragueenergy.com   Type: Private

Sprague Resources, founded in 1870 as a coal and oil supplier, has grown into one of the largest fuel suppliers in the northeast US. Sprague Resources' products include diesel, gasoline, home heating oil, jet fuel, and residual fuels. The company distributes more than 55 mmbtus of natural gas, about 1.5 billion gallons of refined products, and about 2 million tons of bulk materials each year. It also owns or operates storage tanks in both northeast US and Canada terminals that can hold more than 14.3 million barrels of refined products. The US generated majority of its sales. In 2022, Sprague Resources received an unsolicited non-binding proposal to which Hartree would acquire all of the outstanding common units of Sprague for $16.50 in cash per Common Unit.

SPRENGER ENTERPRISES, INC.

3905 OBERLIN AVE STE 1   CEO: Nicole Sprenger
LORAIN, OH 440532853   CFO: -
Phone: 630 529-0700   HR: -
Fax: -   FYE: December 31
Web: -   Type: Private

Sprenger Enterprises (dba Sprenger Health Care Centers) provides senior Buckeye Staters with a range of housing and care options that include nursing, assisted living, and independent living homes. Scattered throughout northeastern Ohio, Sprenger Health Care operates more than a dozen centers providing services that include physical, occupational, and speech therapy, as well as psychiatric support, respite and hospice care. The centers also administer specialized treatment for patients suffering from Alzheimer's disease and dementia. Founded in 1959 by Grace Sprenger, Sprenger Health Care is owned and operated by members of the Sprenger family.

	Annual Growth	06/02	06/03	06/04	06/05*	12/07
Sales ($mil.)	(3.4%)	-	-	55.0	57.2	49.6
Net income ($ mil.)	(64.9%)	-	-	49.1	53.0	2.1
Market value ($ mil.)	-	-	-	-	-	-
Employees	-	-	-	-	-	1,320

*Fiscal year change

SPRING ARBOR UNIVERSITY

106 E MAIN ST   CEO: -
SPRING ARBOR, MI 492839701   CFO: -
Phone: 517 750-1200   HR: Julie Morse
Fax: -   FYE: May 31
Web: www.arbor.edu   Type: Private

Spring Arbor University is an evangelical Christian university affiliated with the Free Methodist Church. The liberal arts institution offers more than 70 undergraduate and 10 graduate degrees, as well as professional programs. It has an enrollment of more than 4,000 students, most of which hail from Michigan. The school's main 100-acre campus in Spring Arbor, Michigan, is supplemented by about 20 satellite locations in Michigan and Ohio. Academic fields include business, nursing, and spiritual leadership. Spring Arbor University was founded as an elementary and secondary school in 1873.

	Annual Growth	05/17	05/18	05/19	05/20	05/22
Sales ($mil.)	2.1%	-	-	-	68.0	70.9
Net income ($ mil.)	72.9%	-	-	-	3.4	10.2
Market value ($ mil.)	-	-	-	-	-	-
Employees	-	-	-	-	-	340

SPRING HILL COLLEGE

4000 DAUPHIN ST   CEO: -
MOBILE, AL 366081791   CFO: Rhonda Shirazi
Phone: 251 380-3030   HR: Patricia Davis
Fax: -   FYE: June 30
Web: www.shc.edu   Type: Private

Spring Hill College is a private Catholic university with about 1,500 students. The college offers degree programs in such subjects as commercial arts, nursing, philosophy, political science, and education. In order to keep up with a growing student population Spring Hill is expanding its campus by building a new library, a welcome center and student center. Students of all religions are accepted for enrollment by Spring Hill College. The school offers adult programs in theology and ministry not only on its Mobile campus, but also in Jackson, Mississippi; Birmingham; and Atlanta. Spring Hill College was founded in 1830 by Michael Portier, the first bishop of Mobile, Alabama.

	Annual Growth	06/17	06/18	06/20	06/21	06/22
Sales ($mil.)	1.1%	-	40.6	37.8	45.9	42.4
Net income ($ mil.)	-	-	(3.8)	(1.5)	5.9	(5.9)
Market value ($ mil.)	-	-	-	-	-	-
Employees	-	-	-	-	-	297

SPRING, O'BRIEN & COMPANY, INC.

333 W 86TH ST APT 1803   CEO: -
NEW YORK, NY 100243151   CFO: -
Phone: 212 620-7100   HR: -
Fax: -   FYE: December 31
Web: www.spring-obrien.com   Type: Private

Spring, O'Brien & Company is poised and ready to provide seasoned marketing communications. The agency offers integrated advertising and PR services such as media buying, direct marketing, media relations, event planning, and creative development and Web design. Spring, O'Brien & Company specializes in serving clients in the business-to-business and travel and tourism markets. Clients have included American Express, the Bank of New York, and Emirates airlines. The firm was founded in 1982 by President Chris Spring.

SPRINGFIELD ELECTRIC SUPPLY COMPANY, LLC

700 N 9TH ST
SPRINGFIELD, IL 627026307
Phone: 217 788-2100
Fax: –
Web: www.springfieldelectric.com

CEO: –
CFO: Greg Lutchka
HR: –
FYE: December 31
Type: Private

Springfield Electric Supply distributes electrical products and supplies, lighting equipment, motor controls, and communications cable and wiring to customers through 11 branch locations in Illinois. Four locations have lighting showrooms. The company carries 250 product lines and stocks 20,000 products. The firm also provides value-added services such as material management, lighting and fuse audits, and inventory management services. CEO and owner William Schnirring's father acquired the company in 1929.

SPRINGFIELD HOSPITAL INC.

25 RIDGEWOOD RD
SPRINGFIELD, VT 051563057
Phone: 802 885-2151
Fax: –
Web: www.springfieldhospital.org

CEO: Crystal Morey
CFO: Andrew J Majka
HR: –
FYE: September 30
Type: Private

Bart Simpson might wind up in Springfield Hospital after cruising down the town's hilly roads on his skateboard. The 70-bed facility located in Springfield, Vermont (also known as the Home of the Simpsons), serves 16 communities in southeastern Vermont and southwestern New Hampshire. Specialized services include adult day care, emergency medicine, physical therapy, rehabilitation, and surgery. Founded in 1913, the hospital also offers a childbirth center, breast care center, and inpatient and outpatient units for psychiatry, neurology, oncology, and cardiac care. Springfield Hospital is part of the Springfield Medical Care Systems.

	Annual Growth	09/18	09/19	09/20	09/21	09/22
Sales ($mil.)	7.0%	–	50.2	33.7	46.8	61.4
Net income ($ mil.)	–	–	(13.9)	(5.3)	19.9	3.4
Market value ($ mil.)	–	–	–	–	–	–
Employees	–	–	–	–	–	500

SPROUTS FARMERS MARKET INC NMS: SFM

5455 East High Street, Suite 111
Phoenix, AZ 85054
Phone: 480 814-8016
Fax: –
Web: www.sprouts.com

CEO: Jack L Sinclair
CFO: Denise A Paulonis
HR: Gwynn Simpson
FYE: December 31
Type: Public

Sprouts Farmers Market offers a unique grocery experience featuring an open layout with fresh produce at the heart of the store. The company continue to bring the latest in wholesome, innovative products made with lifestyle-friendly ingredients such as organic, plant-based, and gluten-free. It operates about 385 stores in almost two dozen US states, including California, Texas, Arizona, Colorado, and Florida. The stores (average approximately 28,000 sq. ft.) sell fresh, natural, and organic foods including meat, seafood, deli, bakery, dairy, frozen foods, and vitamins and supplements. Roughly 35% of the company's stores are located in California.

	Annual Growth	12/19*	01/21	01/22	01/23*	12/23
Sales ($mil.)	5.0%	5,634.8	6,468.8	6,099.9	6,404.2	6,837.4
Net income ($ mil.)	14.7%	149.6	287.5	244.2	261.2	258.9
Market value ($ mil.)	25.3%	1,974.6	2,034.8	3,004.0	3,276.2	4,869.3
Employees	1.6%	30,000	33,000	31,000	31,000	32,000

*Fiscal year change

SPS COMMERCE, INC. NMS: SPSC

333 South Seventh Street, Suite 1000
Minneapolis, MN 55402
Phone: 612 435-9400
Fax: –
Web: www.spscommerce.com

CEO: Archie C Black
CFO: Kimberly K Nelson
HR: Kim Scott
FYE: December 31
Type: Public

Founded in 1987 as St. Paul Software, SPS Commerce is a leading provider of cloud-based supply chain management services that make it easier for suppliers, retailers, distributors, and logistics companies to orchestrate the management of item data, order fulfillment, inventory control, and sales analytics across all channels. The services offered by SPS Commerce include traditional on-premise software, cloud-based managed services, and cloud-based full-service products. Its business model fundamentally changes how organizations use electronic communication to manage their omnichannel, supply chain, and other business requirements by replacing the collection of traditional, custom-built, point-to-point integrations with a model that facilitates a single automated connection to the entire SPS Commerce network of trading partners. The company has approximately 115,000 customers across approximately 80 countries.

	Annual Growth	12/19	12/20	12/21	12/22	12/23
Sales ($mil.)	17.8%	279.1	312.6	385.3	450.9	536.9
Net income ($ mil.)	18.2%	33.7	45.6	44.6	55.1	65.8
Market value ($ mil.)	36.8%	2,040.6	3,998.3	5,241.3	4,728.8	7,137.2
Employees	16.2%	1,363	1,572	1,901	2,215	2,489

SPX FLOW, INC.

13320 BALLANTYNE CORPORATE PL
CHARLOTTE, NC 282773607
Phone: 704 752-4400
Fax: –
Web: www.spxflow.com

CEO: Marcus G Michael
CFO: Jaime M Easley
HR: Lezlie Lecher
FYE: December 31
Type: Private

SPX Flow is a leading provider of process solutions for the nutrition, health, and industrial markets. The company's products include pumps, valves, mixers, filters, air dryers, hydraulic tools, homogenizers, separators, and heat exchangers. It serves a wide range of end markets including food and beverage, chemical processing, oil and gas, pharmaceutical, waste and water treatment, and mining. A short list of its brands include Bran + Luebbe, Lightnin, Johnson Pump, and Stone. SPX Flow has been a standalone company since 2015, with a heritage that dates back to the establishment of the Piston Ring Company in Michigan in 1912. In early 2022, SPX FLOW was acquired by Lone Star in an all-cash transaction valued at approximately $3.8 billion.

	Annual Growth	12/17	12/18	12/19	12/20	12/21
Sales ($mil.)	(9.9%)	–	2,090.1	1,506.6	1,350.6	1,529.0
Net income ($ mil.)	14.5%	–	44.7	(93.1)	6.5	67.1
Market value ($ mil.)	–	–	–	–	–	–
Employees	–	–	–	–	–	5,000

SPX TECHNOLOGIES INC NYS: SPXC

6325 Ardrey Kell Road, Suite 400
Charlotte, NC 28277
Phone: 980 474-3700
Fax: 704 752-4505
Web: www.spx.com

CEO: Eugene J Lowe III
CFO: Mark A Carano
HR: –
FYE: December 31
Type: Public

SPX supplies infrastructure equipment for heating, ventilation, and air conditioning (HVAC), detection and measurement, and power transmission and generation. It makes and sells cooling towers and boilers, underground pipe and cable locators, power transformers, and heat exchangers. SPX's brands include Berko, Qmark, Fahrenheat, Radiodetection, Pearpoint, Dielectric, and Schonstedt. The company operates in 15 countries with a sales presence in 100 countries. Most of its sales are to customers in the US. SPX was founded in 1912 as Piston Ring Company and went public in 1972.

	Annual Growth	12/19	12/20	12/21	12/22	12/23
Sales ($mil.)	3.4%	1,525.4	1,559.5	1,219.5	1,460.9	1,741.2
Net income ($ mil.)	8.3%	65.3	97.2	425.4	0.2	89.9
Market value ($ mil.)	18.7%	2,323.9	2,491.1	2,725.9	2,998.5	4,613.6
Employees	(2.3%)	4,500	4,500	3,100	3,300	4,100

SPY INC.

1896 RUTHERFORD RD
CARLSBAD, CA 920087326
Phone: 760 804-8420
Fax: -
Web: www.spyoptic.com

CEO: -
CFO: -
HR: -
FYE: December 31
Type: Private

SPY Inc., formerly known as Orange 21, has its sights set on the colorful Gen Y. The company designs and distributes high-end sunglasses and goggles under the Spy, Spy Optic, Margaritaville, and O'Neill brands. SPY markets its upscale eyewear to the club kid scene for use in surfing, skateboarding, snowboarding, and other extreme action sports. The line is available at about 3,000 outlets in the US and Canada, including Sunglass Hut, Sport Chalet, and Zumiez, and internationally through around 3,000 retailers. SPY also markets some apparel and accessories. In late 2010 the company refocused and sold its LEM subsidiary, which made up most of SPY's eyewear and provided manufacturing services for other companies.

SPYR INC

6700 Woodlands Parkway, Suite 230, #331
The Woodlands, TX 77382
Phone: 303 991-8000
Fax: -
Web: www.pocketstarships.com

NBB: SPYR
CEO: James R Thompson
CFO: Trang Nguyen
HR: -
FYE: December 31
Type: Public

Eat At Joe's operates a themed casual-dining restaurant at the Philadelphia airport that offers breakfast, lunch, and dinner. The concept features such interior appointments as 1950s-era Harley-Davidsons, booths resembling 1957 Chevy interiors, and tabletop jukeboxes. Patrons can choose from such menu items as hot dogs, burgers, and meatloaf. CEO Joseph Fiore owns more than 60% of Eat at Joe's.

	Annual Growth	12/17	12/18	12/19	12/20	12/21
Sales ($mil.)	(64.6%)	0.1	0.4	0.4	0.2	0.0
Net income ($ mil.)	-	(16.1)	(7.1)	(2.0)	(3.1)	(5.5)
Market value ($ mil.)	-	-	-	-	-	-
Employees	-	6	4	3	6	-

SQUAB PRODUCERS OF CALIF, INC.

409 PRIMO WAY
MODESTO, CA 953585721
Phone: 209 537-4744
Fax: -
Web: www.squab.com

CEO: -
CFO: -
HR: -
FYE: June 30
Type: Private

Squab Producers of California never squabbles over its birds. The company is an agricultural cooperative that processes and packages fresh and frozen specialty breeds of poultry raised in California's Central Valley. In addition to squab (a young pigeon), it distributes quail, poussin (an unfledged chicken), silkie chicken (an all-black-meat chicken used in Chinese cuisine), and the exclusively bred California Poulet Bleu chicken. With more than 75 member/farmers, the business is the largest squab cooperative in the US. It poultry products are sold to food retailers and foodservice operators throughout the US, as well as internationally. Squab Producers of California was founded in 1943.

SQUAR, MILNER, PETERSON, MIRANDA & WILLIAMSON, CERTIFIED PUBLIC ACCOUNTANTS, LLP

18500 VON KARMAN AVE # 10
IRVINE, CA 926120504
Phone: 949 222-2999
Fax: -
Web: -

CEO: -
CFO: -
HR: -
FYE: December 31
Type: Private

Squar, Milner, Peterson, Miranda & Williamson provides accounting and auditing services, business consulting, and tax planning, preparation, and review services to middle-market companies. The firm serves clients in industries such as technology, real estate and construction, financial services, real estate, retail, and manufacturing. Squar Milner also serves not-for-profit organizations, pension funds, and service companies. Services outside of the US are offered through Squar Milner's affiliation with BKR International. Squar Milner was founded in 1951 and has offices in Los Angeles, New Port Beach, San Diego, and the Cayman Islands.

SRI INTERNATIONAL

333 RAVENSWOOD AVE
MENLO PARK, CA 940253493
Phone: 650 859-2000
Fax: -
Web: www.sri.com

CEO: William Jeffrey
CFO: Jim Doyle
HR: -
FYE: December 29
Type: Private

SRI is an independent nonprofit research institute with a rich history of supporting government and industry. It is a global leader in research and development. The company creates and delivers world-changing solutions for a safer, healthier, and more sustainable future. The company collaborates across technical and scientific disciplines to discover and develop groundbreaking products and technologies and bring innovations and ideas to the marketplace. The Menlo Park, California-based research center was behind many innovations that people benefit from daily, including the network (ARPANET) that led to today's internet, the computer mouse, telerobotic surgery, and voice assistant Siri. SRI works primarily in advanced technology and systems, biosciences, computing and education.

	Annual Growth	12/14	12/15	12/16	12/17	12/18
Sales ($mil.)	(3.5%)	-	513.5	504.0	405.8	461.4
Net income ($ mil.)	(3.6%)	-	2.7	6.8	1.3	2.4
Market value ($ mil.)	-	-	-	-	-	-
Employees	-	-	-	-	-	2,437

SRT COMMUNICATIONS, INC.

3615 N BROADWAY
MINOT, ND 587030408
Phone: 701 858-1200
Fax: -
Web: www.srt.com

CEO: Steve D Lysne
CFO: Perry G Erdmann
HR: -
FYE: December 31
Type: Private

SRT Communications provides local-exchange access and long-distance telephone service to residents of north central North Dakota and Montana. The cooperative serves about 48,000 access lines and operates 25 telephone exchanges, including those in the towns of Minot, Burlington, and Surrey, as well as the Minot Air Force Base. In addition to voice service, the company sells Internet services (including broadband access and Web hosting), as well as PCS wireless service. SRT Communications also distributes business phone systems made by Avaya, Mitel, and 3Com and offers cable television to subscribers in nearly 20 cities and towns.

	Annual Growth	12/13	12/14	12/15	12/16	12/22
Sales ($mil.)	1.7%	-	46.7	46.2	47.4	53.5
Net income ($ mil.)	10.5%	-	3.7	5.1	3.7	8.2
Market value ($ mil.)	-	-	-	-	-	-
Employees	-	-	-	-	-	221

SS&C TECHNOLOGIES HOLDINGS INC
NMS: SSNC

80 Lamberton Road
Windsor, CT 06095
Phone: 860 298-4500
Fax: –
Web: www.ssctech.com

CEO: William C Stone
CFO: Brian Schell
HR: –
FYE: December 31
Type: Public

SS&C Technologies is the world's largest hedge fund and private equity administrator and the largest mutual fund transfer agent. The company has about 20,000 clients spanning the health and financial service industries. The company also provides software-enabled outsourcing services and subscription-based on-demand cloud solutions that are managed and hosted by its facilities and specialized products deployed to clients. SS&C also sells software to the healthcare industry for applying modern technology to medical and pharmacy claims processing, data analytics, and simplifying and improving client users and members. With about 120 offices worldwide, the company generates about 70% of its revenue in the US.

	Annual Growth	12/19	12/20	12/21	12/22	12/23
Sales ($mil.)	4.4%	4,632.9	4,667.9	5,051.0	5,283.0	5,502.8
Net income ($ mil.)	8.5%	438.5	625.2	800.0	650.2	607.1
Market value ($ mil.)	(0.1%)	15,141	17,940	20,216	12,838	15,070
Employees	3.9%	22,800	24,600	7,300	27,600	26,600

SSHT S&T GROUP LTD
NBB: SSHT

2233 Roosevelt Road, Suite #5
St Cloud, MN 56301
Phone: 320 203-7477
Fax: –
Web: –

CEO: –
CFO: –
HR: –
FYE: September 30
Type: Public

Wireless Data Solutions, which operates through subsidiary Distributed Networks (Dinet), makes wireless data terminals used by vehicle fleet operators. The company's FleetVantage software keeps track of where trucks and other vehicles are, using Global Positioning Satellite (GPS) technology. Wireless Data/Dinet has agreed to merge with privately held IDA Corporation, which markets a global tracking data center software system called TRAKIT. The merger is contingent on the loss-ridden Wireless Data's ability to raise capital. Wireless Data has offices in California and Minnesota.

	Annual Growth	09/97	09/98	09/99	09/00	09/01
Sales ($mil.)	(14.7%)	2.4	1.5	1.5	2.0	1.3
Net income ($ mil.)	–	0.0	(0.3)	(0.3)	0.0	(0.6)
Market value ($ mil.)	(37.9%)	0.0	0.0	0.0	0.0	0.0
Employees	–	–	–	–	–	13

SSM HEALTH CARE CORPORATION

12800 CORPORATE HILL DR
SAINT LOUIS, MO 631311845
Phone: 314 994-7800
Fax: –
Web: www.ssmhealth.com

CEO: Bill Thompson
CFO: Kevin Smith
HR: Abby Lorenz
FYE: December 31
Type: Private

The mission of SSM Health began with five nuns who fled religious persecution in Germany in 1872 only to arrive in St. Louis in the midst of a smallpox epidemic. They formed their first hospital there in 1877. Today, the Midwest-based not-for-profit system, sponsored by the Franciscan Sisters of Mary, owns some 25 acute care hospitals more than 290 physician offices and other outpatient and virtual care services, ten post-acute facilities, comprehensive home care and hospice services, a pharmacy benefit company, a health insurance company and an accountable care organization. SSM Health's hospital operations are located primarily in Missouri, Wisconsin, Oklahoma and Illinois and its related businesses provide health related services in about 50 states.

	Annual Growth	12/18	12/19	12/20	12/21	12/22
Sales ($mil.)	(11.9%)	–	–	–	1,122.4	988.6
Net income ($ mil.)	–	–	–	–	69.8	(20.0)
Market value ($ mil.)	–	–	–	–	–	–
Employees	–	–	–	–	–	24,230

SSR MINING INC
NMS: SSRM

Suite 1300 - 6900, E. Layton Ave
Denver, CO 80237
Phone: 303 292-1299
Fax: –
Web: www.ssrmining.com

CEO: –
CFO: –
HR: –
FYE: December 31
Type: Public

SSR Mining (formerly Silver Standard Resources) is a precious metals mining company with four producing assets located in the US, Turkey, Canada and Argentina. The company is primarily engaged in the operation, acquisition, exploration and development of precious metal resource properties located in Turkey and the Americas. The company produces gold dores as well as copper, silver, lead and zinc concentrates. Its four operating assets produced about 795 thousand gold equivalent ounces. The company owns and operates the Pirquitas mine in Jujuy, Argentina, which is one of the largest primary silver mines in the world. Majority of its sales were generated from Turkey.

	Annual Growth	12/19	12/20	12/21	12/22	12/23
Sales ($mil.)	23.8%	606.9	853.1	1,474.2	1,148.0	1,426.9
Net income ($ mil.)	–	57.3	133.5	368.1	194.1	(98.0)
Market value ($ mil.)	(13.5%)	3,908.9	4,081.4	3,592.3	3,180.3	2,183.8
Employees	29.4%	1,926	–	4,037	4,550	5,400

ST BARNABAS MEDICAL CENTER (INC)

94 OLD SHORT HILLS RD STE 1
LIVINGSTON, NJ 070395668
Phone: 973 322-5000
Fax: –
Web: www.rwjbh.org

CEO: Richard Davis
CFO: Patrick Aheran
HR: –
FYE: December 31
Type: Private

Part of the RWJBarnabas Health system, Saint Barnabas Medical Center is a 600-bed, acute-care hospital that provides a full range of health services to residents of Livingston, New Jersey, and surrounding areas. The not-for-profit medical center provides general inpatient and outpatient care programs, as well as burn and perinatal care. It also houses units specializing in organ transplant, stroke care, cardiac surgery, and comprehensive cancer treatment. Its Institute for Reproductive Medicine and Science provides assisted reproductive technology services.

	Annual Growth	12/15	12/16	12/17	12/18	12/20
Sales ($mil.)	3.1%	–	760.4	818.2	818.2	859.0
Net income ($ mil.)	(9.7%)	–	84.2	113.4	113.4	55.9
Market value ($ mil.)	–	–	–	–	–	–
Employees	–	–	–	–	–	4,000

ST BONAVENTURE UNIVERSITY

3261 W STATE RD
SAINT BONAVENTURE, NY 147789800
Phone: 716 375-2000
Fax: –
Web: www.sbu.edu

CEO: –
CFO: –
HR: –
FYE: May 31
Type: Private

St. Bonaventure University is a private Catholic liberal arts institution in southwestern New York. With some 2,700 students, the liberal arts school offers both undergraduate majors and graduate programs in areas including education, psychology, and journalism. A group of Franciscan friars live on the campus, and the university is the home of the School of Franciscan Studies and the Franciscan Institute, which conduct research and education on the history, spirituality, and intellectual life of the Franciscan movement. St. Bonaventure University was founded in 1858 by the Franciscan Friars of the Holy Name Province.

	Annual Growth	05/18	05/19	05/20	05/21	05/22
Sales ($mil.)	6.2%	–	59.9	64.5	65.4	71.9
Net income ($ mil.)	–	–	7.1	7.1	29.3	(1.1)
Market value ($ mil.)	–	–	–	–	–	–
Employees	–	–	–	–	–	540

ST DAVID'S SOUTH AUSTIN MEDICAL CENTER

901 W BEN WHITE BLVD
AUSTIN, TX 787046903
Phone: 512 447-2211
Fax: –
Web: www.stdavids.com

CEO: Charles Laird
CFO: Seth Herrick
HR: –
FYE: October 31
Type: Private

South Austin, baby! St. David's South Austin Medical Center provides health services in the hippest part of the "Live Music Capital of the World." Established in 1982, the acute-care hospital has more than 250 beds. St. David's South Austin Medical Center (formerly known as South Austin Hospital) has a cardiovascular center, an emergency department, an obstetrics unit, and an outpatient surgery center, along with services in diabetes education, diagnostics, oncology, and rehabilitation, among other offerings. It also operates outpatient facilities in the nearby communities. Founded in 1982, the medical center is part of St. David's Health Care System in partnership with nationwide hospital operator HCA.

	Annual Growth	12/13	12/14*	10/15	10/16	10/17
Sales ($mil.)	1392.8%	–	0.0	260.5	289.6	328.1
Net income ($ mil.)	1717.1%	–	0.0	53.8	50.3	55.3
Market value ($ mil.)	–	–	–	–	–	–
Employees	–	–	–	–	–	1,400

*Fiscal year change

ST DAVIDS HEALTHCARE PARTNERSHIP LLP

2400 ROUND ROCK AVE
ROUND ROCK, TX 786814004
Phone: 512 341-1000
Fax: –
Web: www.stdavids.com

CEO: Deborah Ryl
CFO: –
HR: AMI Noak
FYE: February 28
Type: Private

St. David's Round Rock Medical Center serves the growing Williamson County community located in Central Texas. The facility includes an acute care hospital with approximately 175 beds, a heart center, a women's center, and an outpatient surgery center. Other services include respiratory therapy, vascular lab work, orthopedics, and intermediate care. The medical center is part of St. David's HealthCare Partnership, a joint venture between St. David's Health Care System and HCA. The hospital's size was almost doubled through expansion construction in 2006.

	Annual Growth	12/02	12/03	12/04	12/05*	02/17
Sales ($mil.)	13.9%	–	–	–	40.0	190.4
Net income ($ mil.)	(0.3%)	–	–	–	36.1	34.9
Market value ($ mil.)	–	–	–	–	–	–
Employees	–	–	–	–	–	610

*Fiscal year change

ST JAMES HEALTHCARE, INC

400 S CLARK ST
BUTTE, MT 597012328
Phone: 406 723-2484
Fax: –
Web: www.stjameshealthcare.org

CEO: Chuck Wright
CFO: Jay Doyle
HR: Gina Tesoriero
FYE: December 31
Type: Private

St. James Healthcare provides general medical and surgical services as well as specialized care to Southwestern Montana. St. James Healthcare's specialized services include oncology, women's and children's health care, neurology, and cardiac care. The hospital is a member of the Sisters of Charity of Leavenworth Health System. St. James Healthcare was established in 1881.

ST JOHN FISHER COLLEGE

3690 EAST AVE OFC
ROCHESTER, NY 146183597
Phone: 585 385-8000
Fax: –
Web: www.sjf.edu

CEO: –
CFO: –
HR: Elizabeth Skrainar
FYE: May 31
Type: Private

St. John Fisher College is a Catholic liberal arts institution. The independent school offers 35 academic majors in the business, education, humanities, natural sciences, and nursing, as well as about a dozen pre-professional programs, 10 master's programs, and three doctoral programs. Its enrollment includes more than 2,700 full-time undergraduate students, as well as 200 part time students. The student-faculty ratio is 13:1. The college is guided by the educational philosophy of the Congregation of St. Basil. St. John Fisher College was founded in 1948 as a Catholic college for men; it did not become coeducational until 1971. The college was formed by the Congregation of St. Basil.

	Annual Growth	05/18	05/19	05/20	05/21	05/22
Sales ($mil.)	12.0%	–	114.9	–	148.3	161.3
Net income ($ mil.)	(12.7%)	–	16.5	–	9.1	11.0
Market value ($ mil.)	–	–	–	–	–	–
Employees	–	–	–	–	–	574

ST JOHN'S UNIVERSITY, NEW YORK

8000 UTOPIA PKWY
JAMAICA, NY 114399000
Phone: 718 990-6161
Fax: –
Web: www.stjohns.edu

CEO: –
CFO: Sharon H Watkins
HR: –
FYE: May 31
Type: Private

No university is an island, but one of St. John's campuses is on Manhattan Island. A private, co-educational Roman Catholic school, St. John's University offers undergraduate and graduate programs in more than 100 majors through five colleges, a law school, and a distance learning program. St. John's has more than 20,000 students at five campuses (Queens, Staten Island and Manhattan in New York City, one in Oakdale, New York, and one graduate center in Rome). The school has a 17-to-1 student-faculty ratio. More than 80% of its graduates reside in the New York region, including notable alumni such as former New York governors Hugh Carey and Mario Cuomo. The school was founded in 1870 by the Vincentian Community.

	Annual Growth	12/14	12/15	12/16*	05/20	05/22
Sales ($mil.)	467.1%	–	–	0.0	810.7	798.5
Net income ($ mil.)	–	–	–	(0.0)	55.2	55.1
Market value ($ mil.)	–	–	–	–	–	–
Employees	–	–	–	–	–	3,310

*Fiscal year change

ST JOSEPH'S COLLEGE NEW YORK

245 CLINTON AVE
BROOKLYN, NY 112053688
Phone: 718 940-5300
Fax: –
Web: www.sjny.edu

CEO: –
CFO: George A Kelly
HR: –
FYE: June 30
Type: Private

St. Joseph's College is a liberal arts college with two locations in the metropolitan New York City area -- one in Brooklyn and one in Long Island. St. Joseph's offers more than 20 undergraduate majors, pre-professional, and certificate programs, and graduate degrees in management, business, and infant/toddler early childhood special education to over 5,000 students. Its School of Adult and Professional Education provides adult students with certificate and degree programs in fields such as management, computer information systems, and health. Its Brooklyn campus also houses the Dillon Child Study Center, a working preschool where child-study majors gain hands-on experience. St. Joseph's was founded in 1916.

	Annual Growth	06/15	06/16	06/20	06/21	06/22
Sales ($mil.)	5.7%	–	104.2	137.7	139.4	145.1
Net income ($ mil.)	–	–	(4.1)	5.7	6.3	3.0
Market value ($ mil.)	–	–	–	–	–	–
Employees	–	–	–	–	–	800

ST LAWRENCE UNIVERSITY (INC)

23 ROMODA DR 209
CANTON, NY 136171501
Phone: 315 229-5011
Fax: –
Web: www.stlawu.edu

CEO: –
CFO: –
HR: Colleen Manley
FYE: June 30
Type: Private

St. Lawrence University is a four-year liberal arts college that also offers graduate degrees in education. The university has an enrollment of more than 2,500 students, as well as 200 faculty members and a student-to-teacher ratio of 12:1. Major fields of study include biology, computer science, economics, history, psychology, foreign language, and religious studies. Actors Kirk Douglas and Viggo Mortensen and US Senator Susan Collins are among the school's alumni. Founded in 1856 by members of the Universalist Church (now Unitarian Universalist), St. Lawrence is the oldest continuously coeducational institution of higher learning in New York State.

	Annual Growth	06/17	06/18	06/20	06/21	06/22
Sales ($mil.)	10.6%	–	138.2	116.3	118.7	207.0
Net income ($ mil.)	–	–	18.8	2.4	92.6	(9.3)
Market value ($ mil.)	–	–	–	–	–	–
Employees	–	–	–	–	–	700

ST MARY'S REGIONAL HEALTH CENTER

1027 WASHINGTON AVE
DETROIT LAKES, MN 565013409
Phone: 218 847-5611
Fax: –
Web: –

CEO: –
CFO: Ryan Hill
HR: –
FYE: June 30
Type: Private

St. Mary's Innovis Health (formerly St. Mary's Regional Health Center) provides acute and long-term health care services to central Minnesota, including general medical and surgical care, cardiac rehabilitation, and skilled nursing services for the elderly. The health care company's hospital has nearly 90 beds, and its nursing center has about 100 beds. The organization also includes two senior housing facilities, community clinics, surgery centers, home health providers, and an affiliated physician network. St. Mary's is an affiliate of Innovis Health, which operates a network of health care facilities in North Dakota and Minnesota.

	Annual Growth	06/18	06/19	06/20	06/21	06/22
Sales ($mil.)	6.0%	–	146.7	143.4	160.3	174.8
Net income ($ mil.)	14.7%	–	14.8	12.8	18.5	22.3
Market value ($ mil.)	–	–	–	–	–	–
Employees	–	–	–	–	–	400

ST TAMMANY PARISH HOSPITAL SERVICE DISTRICT NO 1

1202 S TYLER ST
COVINGTON, LA 704332330
Phone: 985 898-4000
Fax: –
Web: www.sttammany.health

CEO: Joan Coffman
CFO: Sandra Dipietrio
HR: Maria Hastak
FYE: December 31
Type: Private

St. Tammany Parish Hospital serves communities in St. Tammany Parish and Washington Parish along the northern shores of Lake Ponchartrain in eastern Louisiana. The not-for-profit hospital has about 240 beds and offers acute care, diagnostic, rehabilitation, and community wellness services. It also includes centers and clinics specializing in surgery, breast care, cardiology, and sleep disorders. In addition, St. Tammany Parish Hospital operates a home health and hospice agency, an outpatient services center, and a primary care physicians' office. The company's facilities are served by doctors in St. Tammany Physicians Network.

	Annual Growth	12/18	12/19	12/20	12/21	12/22
Sales ($mil.)	10.1%	–	–	371.6	411.9	450.8
Net income ($ mil.)	(23.5%)	–	–	49.0	34.0	28.7
Market value ($ mil.)	–	–	–	–	–	–
Employees	–	–	–	–	–	1,520

ST THOMAS AQUINAS COLLEGE

125 ROUTE 340
SPARKILL, NY 109761041
Phone: 845 398-4000
Fax: –
Web: www.stac.edu

CEO: –
CFO: –
HR: –
FYE: June 30
Type: Private

St. Thomas Aquinas College seeks to live up to its namesake by offering a wide range of liberal arts-based academic programs. The college's 2,700 full and part-time students can choose from almost 100 different majors, minors, specializations, and dual degree programs. St. Thomas Aquinas College confers both undergraduate and graduate degrees in the humanities, business administration, social sciences, natural sciences and mathematics, and teacher education. The school has a student-teacher ratio of 18:1. It was founded in 1952 in New York's Hudson River Valley by the Dominican Order.

	Annual Growth	06/14	06/15	06/17	06/21	06/22
Sales ($mil.)	1.3%	–	29.6	31.7	32.5	32.3
Net income ($ mil.)	–	–	(1.3)	0.4	(4.2)	(7.3)
Market value ($ mil.)	–	–	–	–	–	–
Employees	–	–	–	–	–	280

ST. AGNES CONTINUING CARE CENTER

3805 WEST CHESTER PIKE STE 100
NEWTOWN SQUARE, PA 190732329
Phone: 267 570-5200
Fax: –
Web: –

CEO: –
CFO: Teresa Gresko
HR: –
FYE: June 30
Type: Private

Triumph Hospital Philadelphia (THP) gives seniors in the city of Brotherly Love a little extra TLC. Offerings at the long-term acute care hospital (formerly known as St. Agnes Continuing Care Center) include residential and home care, kidney dialysis, and other outpatient health and social services, including transitional care. The 60-bed facility was converted from an acute care hospital through an agreement between its former parent, Mercy Health System, and local rival Thomas Jefferson University Hospital, part of Jefferson Health System. THP was then acquired from Mercy by RehabCare in late 2009, which subsequently handed over its management to subsidiary and LTAC operator, Triumph Healthcare.

	Annual Growth	06/17	06/18	06/20	06/21	06/22
Sales ($mil.)	5.7%	–	70.6	90.2	92.6	88.3
Net income ($ mil.)	37.5%	–	5.0	8.2	9.2	17.8
Market value ($ mil.)	–	–	–	–	–	–
Employees	–	–	–	–	–	426

ST. AGNES HEALTHCARE, INC.

900 S CATON AVE
BALTIMORE, MD 212295201
Phone: 667 234-6000
Fax: –
Web: healthcare.ascension.org

CEO: Keith V Kolk
CFO: Rhonda Anderson
HR: –
FYE: June 30
Type: Private

If you're in agony in Charm City, St. Agnes HealthCare is here to help. The Catholic health system provides a spectrum of medical services to the residents of southwest Baltimore. Its flagship facility, St. Agnes Hospital, has 276 beds and offers a comprehensive range of medical and surgical services, including treatment in areas such as oncology, cardiovascular disease, bariatric medicine, women's health, plastic surgery, and orthopedics. The system also includes a multispecialty physicians group (Seton Medical Group) and a diagnostic imaging center. St. Agnes HealthCare is a member of Ascension Health. The health system traces its roots to 1862 when the Daughters of Charity set up a local infirmary in 1862.

	Annual Growth	06/15	06/16	06/20	06/21	06/22
Sales ($mil.)	2.1%	–	447.4	452.0	488.2	506.3
Net income ($ mil.)	6.8%	–	7.7	7.1	41.3	11.4
Market value ($ mil.)	–	–	–	–	–	–
Employees	–	–	–	–	–	2,506

ST. ALEXIUS MEDICAL CENTER

900 E BROADWAY AVE
BISMARCK, ND 585014520
Phone: 701 530-7000
Fax: –
Web: www.chistalexiushealth.org

CEO: Gary P Miller
CFO: Terri Donovan
HR: –
FYE: June 30
Type: Private

Established in 1885, CHI St. Alexius Health (formerly St. Alexius Medical Center) has been serving the health care needs of those who reside in the Dakotas and Montana longer than any other area hospital. The medical facility, with more than 300 beds, caters to central and western North Dakota and parts of South Dakota and Montana. Specialty services include cancer care, trauma care, geriatrics, orthopedics, and rehabilitation. As part of its operations, the longtime hospital also owns and manages a handful of smaller regional hospitals and community clinics. In 2014, St. Alexius joined the Catholic Health Initiatives health care system.

	Annual Growth	06/14	06/15	06/16	06/21	06/22
Sales ($mil.)	(0.7%)	–	289.3	323.2	257.8	274.5
Net income ($ mil.)	–	–	148.1	(10.1)	(93.7)	(45.8)
Market value ($ mil.)	–	–	–	–	–	–
Employees	–	–	–	–	–	1,947

ST. ANTHONY'S HOSPITAL, INC.

1200 7TH AVE N
SAINT PETERSBURG, FL 337051388
Phone: 727 825-1100
Fax: –
Web: www.stanthonysfoundation.org

CEO: –
CFO: Carl Tremonti
HR: –
FYE: December 31
Type: Private

Saint or not, for those needing medical care in St. Petersburg, Florida, St. Anthony's Hospital has you covered. The facility offers a full array of health care services, including emergency medicine, surgery, cancer treatment, and heart care, as well as services in fields including neurology, orthopedics, and metabolic care. The 400-bed hospital also provides outpatient services through a host of ambulatory surgery, rehabilitation, and imaging centers. St. Anthony's Hospital is a member of the BayCare Health System, and as such, provides home health and occupational health services through agencies affiliated with that system.

	Annual Growth	12/15	12/16	12/19	12/21	12/22
Sales ($mil.)	5.9%	–	331.0	419.4	436.9	466.7
Net income ($ mil.)	(7.9%)	–	51.5	30.2	24.7	31.5
Market value ($ mil.)	–	–	–	–	–	–
Employees	–	–	–	–	–	1,076

ST. BERNARD HOSPITAL

326 W 64TH ST
CHICAGO, IL 606213146
Phone: 773 962-3900
Fax: –
Web: www.stbh.org

CEO: –
CFO: –
HR: Donna Dertz
FYE: December 31
Type: Private

Like a giant dog trudging through blinding snow to rescue a traveler in need, St. Bernard Hospital is a powerhouse of betterment for the people it serves. St. Bernard Hospital and Health Care Center serves the residents of Chicago's south side neighborhood of Englewood. The facility has about 200 beds, and its specialties include pediatrics, psychiatry, neurology, orthopedics, and cardiology services. The hospital also offers inpatient detoxification services for patients dependent on opiates or alcohol. St. Bernard has a separate nonprofit unit that takes care of south side residents' residences: Bernard Place Housing Development is a 90-unit affordable homes initiative in the Englewood neighborhood.

	Annual Growth	12/14	12/15	12/17	12/21	12/22
Sales ($mil.)	3.2%	–	94.2	88.8	87.6	117.2
Net income ($ mil.)	–	–	(7.5)	(15.2)	(5.2)	(19.1)
Market value ($ mil.)	–	–	–	–	–	–
Employees	–	–	–	–	–	875

ST. CLAIR HEALTH CORPORATION

1000 BOWER HILL RD
PITTSBURGH, PA 152431873
Phone: 412 561-4900
Fax: –
Web: www.stclair.org

CEO: James Collins
CFO: –
HR: Andrea L Kalina
FYE: June 30
Type: Private

St. Clair Health operates St. Clair Hospital, an acute care hospital with about than 330 beds serving residents in Pittsburgh and southwestern Pennsylvania. The health care provider offers inpatient and outpatient services including specialized units for cancer treatment, behavioral and mental health, cardiovascular therapy, physical rehabilitation, pulmonary therapy, women and children's health, and other niche services. St. Clair Hospital was established in 1954 by members of the Pittsburgh community. St. Clair Health also operates two outpatient centers, a surgical center, an imaging unit, and an occupational medicine division.

	Annual Growth	06/17	06/18	06/20	06/21	06/22
Sales ($mil.)	6.8%	–	344.0	357.2	396.8	447.0
Net income ($ mil.)	–	–	58.1	16.9	110.6	(48.6)
Market value ($ mil.)	–	–	–	–	–	–
Employees	–	–	–	–	–	1,504

ST. FRANCIS HEALTH SERVICES OF MORRIS, INC.

801 NEVADA AVE
MORRIS, MN 562671865
Phone: 320 589-2004
Fax: –
Web: www.sfhs.org

CEO: Luverne Hoffman
CFO: –
HR: Cheri Brouse
FYE: September 30
Type: Private

Whether the care you need is developmental and mental or you are a senior who needs just a little extra help with your day-to-day chores, St. Francis Health Services of Morris is there. The not-for-profit provider operates through two primary divisions: Senior Services and Behavioral Services (which operates under the name Prairie Community Services). St. Francis Health Services of Morris' Senior Services operates about a dozen long term care, assisted living, and home health care locations for seniors and those who need rehabilitation services from traumatic injuries. Prairie Community Services provides adult daycare and other similar services for adults with mental or developmental problems.

ST. FRANCIS HOSPITAL, ROSLYN, NEW YORK

100 PORT WASHINGTON BLVD
ROSLYN, NY 115761347
Phone: 516 562-2000
Fax: –
Web: www.catholichealthli.org

CEO: Charles Lucore
CFO: William C Arms
HR: Betty Anson
FYE: December 31
Type: Private

Sure, St. Francis Hospital can handle your gall bladder and sinus difficulties, but it's really on top of your heart problems. The hospital's Heart Center -- New York State's only specially designated cardiac center -- provides surgical, diagnostic, and treatment services. The 365-bed St. Francis Hospital also has centers for ENT (ear, nose, and throat), orthopedic, vascular, prostate, cancer, gastrointestinal, and general surgery services. As part of Catholic Health Services of Long Island, St. Francis opened its doors in 1954 to children and adults. It was originally established as St. Francis Hospital and Sanatorium for Cardiac Children in 1936.

	Annual Growth	12/01	12/02	12/04	12/08	12/15
Sales ($mil.)	–	–	(828.9)	366.7	385.1	614.2
Net income ($ mil.)	152.0%	–	0.0	47.4	28.5	37.9
Market value ($ mil.)	–	–	–	–	–	–
Employees	–	–	–	–	–	2,184

ST. JOE CO. (THE) NYS: JOE

130 Richard Jackson Boulevard, Suite 200
Panama City Beach, FL 32407
Phone: 850 231-6400
Fax: –
Web: www.joe.com

CEO: Jorge L Gonzalez
CFO: Marek Bakun
HR: Rhea Goff
FYE: December 31
Type: Public

Wanna buy some swampland in Florida? Perhaps something a bit more upscale? St. Joe has it, along with timberland and beaches. Formerly operating in paper, sugar, timber, telephone systems, and railroads, St. Joe is a Florida real estate developer and one of the state's largest private landowners. It holds some 175,000 acres of land, entitled for future development located mostly in northwest Florida. Approximately 90% of its land holdings are within 15 miles of the Gulf of Mexico, including beach frontage and other waterfront properties. The company is primarily engaged in developing residential resorts and towns, commerce parks, and rural property sales. St. Joe also operates a forestry segment, which grows, harvests, and sells timber and wood fiber.

	Annual Growth	12/19	12/20	12/21	12/22	12/23
Sales ($mil.)	32.3%	127.1	160.6	267.0	252.3	389.3
Net income ($ mil.)	30.5%	26.8	45.2	74.6	70.9	77.7
Market value ($ mil.)	32.0%	1,157.5	2,477.9	3,038.3	2,256.1	3,512.8
Employees	32.2%	55	48	662	769	168

ST. JOHN HEALTH SYSTEM, INC.

1923 S UTICA AVE
TULSA, OK 741046520
Phone: 918 744-2180
Fax: –
Web: www.stjohnhealthsystem.com

CEO: Robert Lafortune
CFO: –
HR: Jamie Shklar
FYE: June 30
Type: Private

St. John Health System aims to bring health into the lives of the ill. The not-for-profit system provides health care services to residents of Tulsa and surrounding areas in northeastern Oklahoma and southern Kansas. In addition to flagship facility St. John Medical Center, it owns or manages eight other community hospitals, as well as urgent care and long-term care facilities. St. John Health System provides primary and specialty medical care through OMNI Medical Group, and offers health insurance through CommunityCare health plan. Established in 1926 by the Sisters of the Sorrowful Mother, the health system is part of Marian Health.

	Annual Growth	09/09	09/10	09/11	09/12*	06/14
Sales ($mil.)	5.7%	–	–	895.5	977.4	1,057.0
Net income ($ mil.)	64.9%	–	–	17.7	74.8	79.3
Market value ($ mil.)	–	–	–	–	–	–
Employees	–	–	–	–	–	4,011

*Fiscal year change

ST. JOHN HOSPITAL AND MEDICAL CENTER

28000 DEQUINDRE RD
WARREN, MI 480922468
Phone: 313 343-4000
Fax: –
Web: –

CEO: Mark Taylor
CFO: –
HR: –
FYE: June 30
Type: Private

St. John Hospital & Medical Center is part of the larger Detroit area-based St. John Health regional health care system. Besides providing acute and trauma care, the 770-bed teaching hospital operates specialized cancer and pediatric centers, a hip and knee center, an inpatient mental health unit, and a Parkinson's Disease clinic. It also operates the only emergency trauma center on Detroit's East Side. The hospital was established in 1952 and has grown to include a 200-physician medical team that specializes in more than 50 medical and surgical fields. It boasts 34,000 admissions; 14,500 surgical visits; and more than 126,500 emergency center visits each year.

	Annual Growth	06/02	06/03	06/05	06/09	06/15
Sales ($mil.)	(6.3%)	–	1,642.9	–	638.3	753.3
Net income ($ mil.)	12.0%	–	9.2	–	2.0	36.1
Market value ($ mil.)	–	–	–	–	–	–
Employees	–	–	–	–	–	5,000

ST. JOHN PROVIDENCE

28000 DEQUINDRE RD
WARREN, MI 480922468
Phone: 586 753-0500
Fax: –
Web: www.ascension.org

CEO: –
CFO: –
HR: Erin KummerIdechambe
FYE: June 30
Type: Private

St. John Providence Health System is out to keep southeastern Michigan's denizens healthy. A subsidiary of not-for-profit group Ascension Health, St. John Providence is a regional health care system founded in 1844 that consists of six hospitals with more than 2,000 beds. It has more than 125 additional medical facilities including urgent care clinics, outpatient centers, and doctors' offices. The health system also runs St. John Home Services, a home health care agency providing infusion services, rehabilitative services, and hospice care. Flagship hospital St. John Hospital and Medical Center is a regional referral hospital with more than 800 beds, providing care in numerous medical and surgical specialties.

	Annual Growth	06/07	06/08	06/09	06/13	06/14
Sales ($mil.)	(33.9%)	–	–	2,023.9	257.5	255.0
Net income ($ mil.)	–	–	–	(84.9)	7.8	(8.4)
Market value ($ mil.)	–	–	–	–	–	–
Employees	–	–	–	–	–	17,806

ST. JOHN'S COLLEGE

60 COLLEGE AVE
ANNAPOLIS, MD 214011655
Phone: 410 263-2371
Fax: –
Web: www.sjc.edu

CEO: –
CFO: Bronte Jones
HR: –
FYE: June 30
Type: Private

St. John's College believes in the "Great Books," even as the canon is under attack elsewhere in academia. Students at the college study the classics in literature, math, philosophy, and science. The curriculum starts with Aeschylus, Aristotle, Euclid, and Plato, taught freshman year; students work their way through the millennia of higher learning, finishing with the works of contemporary thinkers and writers, which are taught to seniors. St. John's (not to be confused with the university in New York City) is the third-oldest institution of higher learning in the US (after Harvard and William & Mary); it was founded in Maryland in 1696 and opened a Santa Fe campus in 1964. Each campus has about 450 students.

	Annual Growth	06/14	06/15	06/16	06/18	06/19
Sales ($mil.)	(20.1%)	–	78.8	55.6	26.1	32.2
Net income ($ mil.)	–	–	(2.2)	(18.7)	1.6	15.0
Market value ($ mil.)	–	–	–	–	–	–
Employees	–	–	–	–	–	250

ST. JOHN'S HOSPITAL OF THE HOSPITAL SISTERS OF THE THIRD ORDER OF ST. FRANCIS

800 E CARPENTER ST
SPRINGFIELD, IL 627691000
Phone: 217 544-6464
Fax: –
Web: www.hshs.org

CEO: Charles Lucore
CFO: Larry Ragel
HR: Clay England
FYE: June 30
Type: Private

Truck-struck Homer Simpson might use his last gasp trying to blurt out "St. John's Hospital of the Hospital Sisters of the Third Order of St. Francis-Springfield" to his ambulance driver, but he might be better off using the hospital's more common name, St. John's. D'oh! The 440-bed St. John's Hospital serves residents of central and southern Illinois with general and specialized health care services. The teaching hospital, affiliated with Southern Illinois University's School of Medicine, has centers devoted to women and children's health, trauma, cardiac care, cancer, orthopedics, and neurology. It also operates area health clinics. Founded in 1875, St. John's is part of the Hospital Sisters Health System.

	Annual Growth	06/15	06/16	06/20	06/21	06/22
Sales ($mil.)	3.9%	–	494.4	574.3	602.8	622.6
Net income ($ mil.)	(3.8%)	–	3.4	(11.4)	34.0	2.7
Market value ($ mil.)	–	–	–	–	–	–
Employees	–	–	–	–	–	3,000

ST. JOSEPH HEALTH SYSTEM

3345 MICHELSON DR STE 100
IRVINE, CA 926120693
Phone: 949 381-4000
Fax: –
Web: www.stjhs.org

CEO: Richard Afable
CFO: Jo A Escasa-Halgh
HR: Janet Okimoto
FYE: June 30
Type: Private

St. Joseph Health System has earned a medal for decades by caring for patients on the West Coast and, more recently, the South Plains. The health care network includes 16 acute care hospitals, home health agencies, hospice care, outpatient services, skilled nursing facilities, community clinics, and physician organizations throughout California and in eastern New Mexico and West Texas. In its primary market of California, the health system has some 2,900 beds at 10 hospitals. Its Covenant Health System unit operates in Texas and New Mexico with about 1,200 beds in its network of some 50 primary care facilities. St. Joseph is merging with fellow not-for-profit Providence Health & Services.

	Annual Growth	06/07	06/08	06/09	06/10	06/13
Sales ($mil.)	5.1%	–	–	–	4,268.6	4,955.7
Net income ($ mil.)	98.1%	–	–	–	268.0	2,082.8
Market value ($ mil.)	–	–	–	–	–	–
Employees	–	–	–	–	–	5,400

ST. JOSEPH HEALTHCARE FOUNDATION

360 BROADWAY
BANGOR, ME 044013979
Phone: 207 907-1000
Fax: –
Web: www.stjosephbangor.org

CEO: Mary Prybylo
CFO: –
HR: –
FYE: December 31
Type: Private

If you have a little accident climbing trees in the Pine Tree State, St. Joseph Healthcare can fix you right up. The hospital cares for the people of central Maine through St. Joseph Hospital, a more than 110-bed acute care community hospital. The organization, which is affiliated with Covenant Health System, also operates several specialty outpatient clinics. Services include cardiology, home health, oncology outreach, osteoporosis research, and pain management. St. Joseph physician practices include specialties such as endocrinology and gastroenterology. St. Joseph Healthcare was founded in 1947 by the Felician Sisters of Enfield Connecticut.

	Annual Growth	12/14	12/15	12/20	12/21	12/22
Sales ($mil.)	6.9%	–	120.1	158.5	164.5	191.0
Net income ($ mil.)	–	–	1.8	1.2	1.2	(9.9)
Market value ($ mil.)	–	–	–	–	–	–
Employees	–	–	–	–	–	900

ST. JOSEPH HOSPITAL OF ORANGE

1100 W STEWART DR
ORANGE, CA 928683891
Phone: 714 633-9111
Fax: –
Web: www.sjo.org

CEO: Larry K Ainsworth
CFO: Tina Nycroft
HR: Connie Martin
FYE: June 30
Type: Private

If you're feeling green or blue in Orange County, St. Joseph Hospital of Orange is there to help get back to feeling pink and rosy. The California hospital provides general medical and surgical services, as well as specialty care such as women's health, mental health services, oncology, cardiology, and physical rehabilitation. Part of the St. Joseph Health System, the hospital provides primary care and specialty outpatient services through a network of affiliated physician practices. It also operates low-income and mobile clinics. The hospital has about 468 beds and a medical staff of some 1,000.

	Annual Growth	06/14	06/15	06/16	06/17	06/18
Sales ($mil.)	3.4%	–	567.4	599.1	655.1	627.3
Net income ($ mil.)	144.6%	–	2.8	11.8	29.7	40.5
Market value ($ mil.)	–	–	–	–	–	–
Employees	–	–	–	–	–	3,300

ST. JOSEPH'S HEALTH PARTNERS LLC

703 MAIN ST
PATERSON, NJ 075032621
Phone: 973 569-6006
Fax: –
Web: www.stjosephshealth.org

CEO: –
CFO: Caswell Samms III
HR: –
FYE: December 31
Type: Private

St. Joseph's Healthcare System takes care of northern New Jersey. The system includes St. Joseph's Regional Medical Center, a tertiary teaching hospital with about 650 beds that includes the 120-bed St. Joseph's Children's Hospital. The regional hospital boasts a state-designated trauma center and provides such specialty services as cardiology, oncology, obstetrics, behavioral health, and neurology. The system also operates St. Joseph's Wayne Hospital, a community medical center with about 230 beds. Other operations include St. Vincent's Nursing Home, a home health agency, and a community clinic network. St. Joseph's Healthcare System is sponsored by the Sisters of Charity of Saint Elizabeth.

	Annual Growth	12/14	12/15	12/16	12/17	12/18
Sales ($mil.)	0.8%	–	–	796.1	–	808.6
Net income ($ mil.)	–	–	–	(13.0)	–	(22.6)
Market value ($ mil.)	–	–	–	–	–	–
Employees	–	–	–	–	–	9,746

ST. JOSEPH'S HOSPITAL HEALTH CENTER

301 PROSPECT AVE
SYRACUSE, NY 132031899
Phone: 315 448-5882
Fax: –
Web: www.sjhsyr.org

CEO: Leslie P Luke
CFO: Meredith Price
HR: –
FYE: June 30
Type: Private

With about 450 inpatient beds, St. Joseph's Hospital Health Center serves the residents of 16 central New York counties. The not-for-profit hospital system provides general, emergency, and surgical care, as well as specialty services in areas such as obstetrics, cardiology, dialysis, and wound care. In addition to its inpatient facilities, the organization operates a home health agency, a nursing school, medical and dental residency programs, and several outpatient care centers. Its Franciscan Companies affiliate offers some ancillary services, including the provision of medical supplies, home health equipment, and senior services. St. Joseph's Hospital Health Center was founded in 1869 and became part of Trinity Health in 2015.

	Annual Growth	12/08	12/09	12/14	12/15*	06/21
Sales ($mil.)	3.1%	–	436.3	523.6	542.2	632.2
Net income ($ mil.)	14.9%	–	5.4	0.5	(2.7)	28.5
Market value ($ mil.)	–	–	–	–	–	–
Employees	–	–	–	–	–	3,300

*Fiscal year change

ST. JOSEPH'S HOSPITAL, BREESE, OF THE HOSPITAL SISTERS OF THE THIRD ORDER OF ST. FRANCIS

9515 HOLY CROSS LN
BREESE, IL 622303618
Phone: 618 526-4511
Fax: –
Web: www.hshs.org

CEO: Mark Kloserman
CFO: –
HR: Jed Driemeyer
FYE: June 30
Type: Private

St. Joseph's Hospital of the Hospital Sisters of the Third Order of St. Francis (Breese)is an 85-bed hospital sponsored by the Hospital Sisters of the Third Order of St. Francis. Founded in 1918, this acute-care institution provides a wide range of health care services such as emergency medicine, pediatrics, physical therapy, and surgery. The hospital also operates a women and children's cneter, as well as provides community education. Its full-time medical staff includes about 20 primary physicians.

	Annual Growth	06/15	06/16	06/20	06/21	06/22
Sales ($mil.)	6.1%	–	55.9	62.3	68.6	79.6
Net income ($ mil.)	41.1%	–	2.8	3.3	16.9	22.3
Market value ($ mil.)	–	–	–	–	–	–
Employees	–	–	–	–	–	300

ST. JOSEPH'S WAYNE HOSPITAL, INC.

224 HAMBURG TPKE
WAYNE, NJ 074702124
Phone: 973 942-6900
Fax: –
Web: www.stjosephshealth.org

CEO: Peter J Karl
CFO: –
HR: John Bruno
FYE: December 31
Type: Private

St. Joseph's Wayne Hospital (SJWH) helps its patients get back into a healthy realm. The acute care facility serves the residents of northern New Jersey. With some 230 beds and more than 400 physicians on staff, SJWH offers services including cancer care, neurology, radiology, surgery, rehabilitation, and senior care. It also includes an ambulatory center that offers minor surgery, infusions, and other outpatient procedures, as well as a sleep diagnostics center and affiliated home health and hospice agencies. Established in 1871, the Catholic hospital is part of the St. Joseph's Healthcare System, which is sponsored by the Sisters of Charity of Saint Elizabeth.

	Annual Growth	12/01	12/02	12/03*	06/05*	12/08
Sales ($mil.)	3.3%	–	66.3	73.3	73.3	80.7
Net income ($ mil.)	19.8%	–	1.1	(7.9)	–	3.3
Market value ($ mil.)	–	–	–	–	–	–
Employees	–	–	–	–	–	925

*Fiscal year change

ST. JOSEPH'S/CANDLER HEALTH SYSTEM, INC.

5353 REYNOLDS ST STE 101
SAVANNAH, GA 314056089
Phone: 912 819-6000
Fax: –
Web: –

CEO: Paul P Hinchey
CFO: Gregory J Schaack
HR: –
FYE: June 30
Type: Private

St. Joseph's/Candler Health System (SJ/C) provides health care services in the Savannah, Georgia area. The largest health system in the region, SJ/C is anchored by two main hospitals, St. Joseph's Hospital (approximately 330 beds) and Candler Hospital (about 385 beds). In addition to emergency, critical, diagnostic, and surgical services, the facilities provide a spectrum of specialties that include cardiac and cancer care, orthopedics, digestive health, and robotic surgery. The two hospitals also administer home health care and operate a number of outpatient care centers as well as a wide variety of community outreach and education efforts throughout the region.

	Annual Growth	06/08	06/09	06/10	06/11	06/14
Sales ($mil.)	8.5%	–	–	13.3	–	18.5
Net income ($ mil.)	–	–	–	–	–	–
Market value ($ mil.)	–	–	–	–	–	–
Employees	–	–	–	–	–	3,684

ST. JUDE CHILDREN'S RESEARCH HOSPITAL, INC.

262 DANNY THOMAS PL
MEMPHIS, TN 381053678
Phone: 901 595-3300
Fax: –
Web: www.stjude.org

CEO: James Downing
CFO: Abed Abdoas
HR: Kim Rainey
FYE: June 30
Type: Private

St. Jude Children's Research Hospital is leading the way the world understands, treats and defeats childhood cancer and other lifethreatening disease. It treats children from all 50 states and from around the world. About 8,600 patients are seen at St. Jude annually, most of whom are treated on a continuing outpatient basis and are part of ongoing research programs. The hospital has 77 beds for patients requiring hospitalization during treatment. In addition, St. Jude also treats patients at its eight affiliate clinics. St. Jude Children's Research Hospital was founded in 1962 by Danny Thomas.

	Annual Growth	06/18	06/19	06/20	06/21	06/22
Sales ($mil.)	(50.6%)	–	–	1,238.2	276.4	302.3
Net income ($ mil.)	50.0%	–	–	134.2	2,409.3	302.1
Market value ($ mil.)	–	–	–	–	–	–
Employees	–	–	–	–	–	5,300

ST. JUDE HOSPITAL

101 E VALENCIA MESA DR
FULLERTON, CA 928353875
Phone: 714 871-3280
Fax: –
Web: www.stjudemedicalcenter.org

CEO: Robert Fraschetti
CFO: Lee Penrose
HR: –
FYE: December 31
Type: Private

St. Jude Medical Center gets sickly Southern Californians on their feet again. The faith-based, not-for-profit acute care facility, with some 385 beds, serves the residents of Orange County. The medical center provides an onsite cancer center (the Virginia K. Crosson Cancer Center) and a heart institute that offers cardiac surgeries and rehabilitation programs. It also provides inpatient and outpatient physical rehabilitation services and a variety of community outreach programs. Established by the Sisters of St. Joseph of Orange religious order in the 1950s, St. Jude Medical Center is part of the St. Joseph Health System.

	Annual Growth	12/18	12/19	12/20	12/21	12/22
Sales ($mil.)	4.1%	–	–	–	791.4	824.0
Net income ($ mil.)	(4.2%)	–	–	–	39.7	38.1
Market value ($ mil.)	–	–	–	–	–	–
Employees	–	–	–	–	–	2,600

ST. JUDE MEDICAL, LLC

1 SAINT JUDE MEDICAL DR
SAINT PAUL, MN 551171789
Phone: 651 756-2000
Fax: –
Web: www.cardiovascular.abbott

CEO: Daniel Starks
CFO: Donald J Zurbay
HR: –
FYE: January 03
Type: Private

ST. LUCIE MEDICAL CENTER AUXILIARY, INC.

1800 SE TIFFANY AVE
PORT SAINT LUCIE, FL 349527521
Phone: 772 335-4000
Fax: –
Web: www.hcafloridahealthcare.com

CEO: –
CFO: –
HR: Andy Hooper
FYE: December 31
Type: Private

St. Lucie Medical Center, part of the HCA network of health care providers, is an acute-care hospital serving the Port St. Lucie community in Florida's Treasure Coast region. The hospital has about 200 beds and 250 physicians on staff. Specialty programs and services include cancer care, women's care, orthopedics, physical rehabilitation, and outpatient surgery services. St. Lucie Medical Center, founded in 1983, is part of the HCA East Florida division. Affiliate Integrated Regional Laboratories provides medical testing services for St. Lucie and other area hospitals.

ST. LUKE'S EPISCOPAL HOSPITAL PHYSICIAN HOSPITAL ORGANIZATION, INC.

6720 BERTNER AVE
HOUSTON, TX 770302604
Phone: 832 355-1000
Fax: –
Web: www.stlukeshealth.org

CEO: –
CFO: Alan F Koval
HR: –
FYE: June 30
Type: Private

St. Luke's Episcopal Hospital is deep in the hearts of Texans. Opened in 1954 by the Episcopal Diocese of Texas, the Houston-area hospital is home to the Texas Heart Institute, a leader in cardiovascular research and patient care. The institute is best-known as the location of the world's first artificial heart implantation, as well as the first successful heart transplant in the US. In addition, St. Luke's Episcopal Hospital provides general and advanced medical-surgical care across some 40 medical specialties. With more than 850 beds, the hospital is the flagship facility of St. Luke's Episcopal Health System, which was acquired by Catholic Health Initiatives in 2013.

	Annual Growth	06/16	06/17	06/18	06/19	06/20
Sales ($mil.)	(9.9%)	–	184.5	138.1	124.4	134.9
Net income ($ mil.)	–	–	(12.6)	(31.8)	(44.5)	(30.2)
Market value ($ mil.)	–	–	–	–	–	–
Employees	–	–	–	–	–	4,500

ST. LUKE'S EPISCOPAL-PRESBYTERIAN HOSPITALS

232 S WOODS MILL RD
CHESTERFIELD, MO 630173406
Phone: 314 434-1500
Fax: –
Web: www.stlukes-stl.com

CEO: Christine Candio
CFO: –
HR: –
FYE: June 30
Type: Private

St. Luke's Episcopal-Presbyterian Hospital, doing business as St. Luke's Hospital, provides health care services to St. Louis residents and surrounding areas of eastern Missouri. The medical center houses more than 490 beds and offers general medical and surgical care, as well as specialty services in areas such as heart disease, cancer, neuroscience, orthopedics, pediatrics, and women's health. St. Luke's also operates half a dozen urgent care clinics in St. Louis and St. Charles counties, providing treatment for minor emergencies such as cuts and animal bites, as well as a skilled-nursing facility, rehabilitation hospital, and several diagnostic imaging centers. The not-for-profit hospital was founded in 1866.

	Annual Growth	06/18	06/19	06/20	06/21	06/22
Sales ($mil.)	4.9%	–	520.8	526.2	652.1	601.1
Net income ($ mil.)	13.0%	–	39.2	35.4	150.1	56.5
Market value ($ mil.)	–	–	–	–	–	–
Employees	–	–	–	–	–	3,000

ST. LUKE'S HEALTH NETWORK, INC.

801 OSTRUM ST
BETHLEHEM, PA 180151000
Phone: 610 954-4000
Fax: –
Web: www.slhn.org

CEO: –
CFO: –
HR: –
FYE: June 30
Type: Private

St. Luke's University Hospital (formerly St. Luke's Hospital - Bethlehem Campus) serves residents of Pennsylvania's Lehigh Valley with primary, specialty, and emergency care services. The not-for-profit teaching hospital has about 480 acute-care beds. Its medical specialties include trauma, oncology, cardiology, orthopedics, neurology, open-heart surgery, radiology, and robotic surgery. The medical center also operates outpatient surgery centers and general physician care clinics, and it operates home health and community wellness programs. St. Luke's University Hospital was founded in 1872 and is part of the St. Luke's University Health Network.

	Annual Growth	06/16	06/17	06/18	06/19	06/22
Sales ($mil.)	14.3%	–	1,521.7	1,844.7	2,116.6	2,969.1
Net income ($ mil.)	–	–	121.5	159.0	59.9	(49.7)
Market value ($ mil.)	–	–	–	–	–	–
Employees	–	–	–	–	–	2,958

ST. LUKE'S HEALTH SYSTEM, LTD.

190 E BANNOCK ST
BOISE, ID 837126241
Phone: 208 381-2222
Fax: –
Web: www.stlukesonline.org

CEO: Darren Bass
CFO: –
HR: –
FYE: September 30
Type: Private

Founded in 1902, St. Luke's Health System is a not-for-profit health system and offers an emergency department, advanced inpatient and outpatient surgery, mother-baby services, diagnostics form x-ray to MRI, state of the art cancer treatment, critical care, a chest pain center and more. Its flagship facility, St. Luke's Boise Medical Center, offers an emergency department, advanced inpatient and outpatient surgery, mother-baby services, diagnostics from x-ray to MRI, state-of-the-art cancer treatment, critical care, and more. The campus also includes a wide range of primary and specialty physician clinics and St. Luke's Children's Hospital, the only children's hospital in Idaho.

	Annual Growth	09/18	09/19	09/20	09/21	09/22
Sales ($mil.)	8.3%	–	2,894.8	3,059.7	3,347.3	3,675.5
Net income ($ mil.)	(69.7%)	–	91.8	171.1	337.3	2.5
Market value ($ mil.)	–	–	–	–	–	–
Employees	–	–	–	–	–	7,891

ST. LUKE'S HOSPITAL OF DULUTH

915 E 1ST ST
DULUTH, MN 558052193
Phone: 218 726-5555
Fax: –
Web: www.slhduluth.com

CEO: John Strange
CFO: James Wuellner
HR: –
FYE: December 31
Type: Private

St. Luke's cares for colds, cancers, and other conditions in the chilly northern US. St. Luke's Hospital provides a variety of health care services to patients in northeastern Minnesota, northwestern Wisconsin, and parts of Michigan. The medical center has some 270 beds and a staff of about 370 physicians. Services include cardiology, emergency medicine, pediatrics, oncology, rehabilitation, and vascular surgery. In addition to acute care services, the organization offers primary and specialty health care services through a network of outpatient clinics.

	Annual Growth	12/15	12/16	12/17	12/21	12/22
Sales ($mil.)	4.0%	–	434.4	471.9	488.6	548.8
Net income ($ mil.)	(7.1%)	–	9.1	22.0	15.0	5.8
Market value ($ mil.)	–	–	–	–	–	–
Employees	–	–	–	–	–	2,200

ST. MARY'S HEALTH, INC.

3700 WASHINGTON AVE
EVANSVILLE, IN 477140541
Phone: 812 485-4000
Fax: –
Web: –

CEO: –
CFO: –
HR: Suzanne Fant
FYE: June 30
Type: Private

St. Mary's Medical Center of Evansville is a 433-bed hospital serving Indiana's River City. It is the primary facility in regional St. Mary's Health System, which is in turn part of Ascension Health. The Evansville hospital provides emergency, trauma, diagnostic, surgical, and rehabilitative services, as well as specialized cancer, cardiac, orthopedic, and neurological services. With a total of some 750 physicians, St. Mary's Health System also includes St. Mary's Hospital for Women & Children (100 beds, adjacent to the main hospital) and St. Mary's Warrick (a 25-bed hospital in Boonville, Indiana), as well as specialty outpatient, surgical, cancer, and home health units in surrounding areas of southern Indiana.

ST. MARY'S HOSPITAL, INC.

1230 BAXTER ST
ATHENS, GA 306063791
Phone: 706 389-3000
Fax: –
Web: www.stmaryshealthcaresystem.org

CEO: Don McKenna
CFO: –
HR: Karen Foutz
FYE: June 30
Type: Private

St. Mary's Health Care System cares for the residents of northeast Georgia. Its St. Mary's Hospital has almost 200 acute-care beds. From health and wellness programs to women's and children's services, the hospital also has centers dedicated to outpatient rehabilitation, home health, and long-term care. Specialty services include neurology, cardiovascular care, orthopedics, and gastroenterology. It also operates the 25-bed St. Mary's Good Samaritan Hospital and a retirement village. The organization is sponsored by the Sisters of Mercy of the Americas, St. Mary's Health Care System is a member of CHE Trinity Health (formed in 2013 through the consolidation of Catholic Health East and Trinity Health).

	Annual Growth	06/17	06/18	06/20	06/21	06/22
Sales ($mil.)	(0.9%)	–	285.4	243.4	262.1	274.8
Net income ($ mil.)	(19.3%)	–	9.5	16.4	27.7	4.0
Market value ($ mil.)	–	–	–	–	–	–
Employees	–	–	–	–	–	1,350

ST. MARY'S MEDICAL CENTER, INC.

2900 1ST AVE
HUNTINGTON, WV 257021241
Phone: 304 526-1234
Fax: –
Web: www.st-marys.org

CEO: Michael G Sellards
CFO: –
HR: David Gentry
FYE: September 30
Type: Private

Nobody wants to get sick, but if you're ailing in West Virginia, St. Mary's Medical Center wants you to know you are in good hands. The not-for-profit 395-bed medical facility serves patients in areas such as cardiac, emergency, neuroscience, and cancer treatment. The largest health care facility in the tri-state region, St. Mary's Medical Center is also a teaching facility affiliated with Joan C. Edwards Marshall University School of Medicine. St. Mary's Home Health Services administers care for patients in a six county area in Ohio and West Virginia. Services include IV therapy and occupational and physical therapies. St. Mary's Medical Center was founded in 1924.It now plans to merge with Cabell Huntington Hospital.

	Annual Growth	09/18	09/19	09/20	09/21	09/22
Sales ($mil.)	10.1%	–	450.4	388.9	572.9	600.9
Net income ($ mil.)	–	–	7.6	19.8	(5.5)	(18.4)
Market value ($ mil.)	–	–	–	–	–	–
Employees	–	–	–	–	–	2,000

ST. NORBERT COLLEGE, INC.

100 GRANT ST
DE PERE, WI 541152099
Phone: 920 337-3181
Fax: –
Web: www.snc.edu

CEO: Thomas Kunkel
CFO: –
HR: Michael Ott
FYE: May 31
Type: Private

St. Norbert College is a private, Catholic, liberal arts institution offering undergraduate and graduate programs to approximately 2,200 students. The school offers more than 40 undergraduate programs of study in the natural sciences, social sciences, and humanities and fine arts. It also confers Master's degrees in Science in Education and Theological Studies. The college is one of only a handful of institutions in the US that offer a Peace Corps Preparatory Program. St. Norbert College was founded in 1898 by Abbot Bernard Pennings, a Dutch immigrant priest, as a school to ready men for the priesthood. It became coeducational in 1952.

	Annual Growth	05/18	05/19	05/20	05/21	05/22
Sales ($mil.)	0.1%	–	76.3	70.4	75.1	76.6
Net income ($ mil.)	–	–	0.8	0.3	42.4	(12.8)
Market value ($ mil.)	–	–	–	–	–	–
Employees	–	–	–	–	–	490

ST. OLAF COLLEGE CORP

1520 SAINT OLAF AVE
NORTHFIELD, MN 550571574
Phone: 507 786-2222
Fax: –
Web: wp.stolaf.edu

CEO: –
CFO: Janet Hanson
HR: –
FYE: May 31
Type: Private

The hills of Northfield, Minnesota, are alive with the sounds of St. Olaf College. The private liberal arts university offers undergraduate and pre-professional education to more than 3,000 students, offering degrees in about 45 academic focus areas. The school has a faculty of more than 250 teachers and is recognized for its choral and orchestral music programs, as well as its mathematics department. Other popular majors include English, psychology, biology, economics, social services, theology, language, medical science, and chemistry. St. Olaf College was founded in 1874 by Norwegian immigrants and is affiliated with the Evangelical Lutheran Church of America.

	Annual Growth	05/15	05/16	05/20	05/21	05/22
Sales ($mil.)	(6.6%)	–	198.5	211.8	128.7	131.9
Net income ($ mil.)	–	–	11.9	(5.9)	195.5	(7.5)
Market value ($ mil.)	–	–	–	–	–	–
Employees	–	–	–	–	–	800

ST. PETER'S HEALTH PARTNERS

315 S MANNING BLVD
ALBANY, NY 122081707
Phone: 518 525-1550
Fax: –
Web: www.sphp.com

CEO: Steven Hanks
CFO: Thomas Schuhle
HR: Melanie Lewis
FYE: June 30
Type: Private

St. Peter's Health Partners (formerly St. Peter's Health Care Services) is a not-for-profit health care system that serves northeastern New York. It includes health networks Seton Health and Northeast Health. Its primary facility, St. Peter's Hospital, has more than 440 acute-care beds and a medical staff of more than 600 physicians. Specialty services include emergency medicine, cancer and cardiovascular care, and women's health. St. Peter's also operates community health clinics, long-term care facilities, mental health centers, and home health and hospice agencies. Founded by the Religious Sisters of Mercy in 1869, St. Peter's operates from more than 125 locations and is a subsidiary of Catholic Health East.

	Annual Growth	06/16	06/17	06/18	06/20	06/22
Sales ($mil.)	(14.5%)	–	–	1,337.6	1,446.3	713.2
Net income ($ mil.)	–	–	–	6.1	(10.8)	(1.6)
Market value ($ mil.)	–	–	–	–	–	–
Employees	–	–	–	–	–	617

ST. VINCENT HEALTH SERVICES, INC.

2 SAINT VINCENT CIR
LITTLE ROCK, AR 722055423
Phone: 501 552-2620
Fax: –
Web: www.chistvincent.com

CEO: Ken D Haynes
CFO: Pam Stoyanoff
HR: Ann Hatches
FYE: June 30
Type: Private

If you're sick or in pain, don't be a martyr! Head to CHI St. Vincent Health System to find absolution from what ails you. A member of Catholic Health Initiatives, CHI St. Vincent provides a comprehensive range of health services to residents of central Arkansas through a network of facilities. The hub of the system is the 615-bed St. Vincent Infirmary Medical Center, a full-service acute care hospital in Little Rock that provides services including heart care, orthopedic medicine, wound treatment, stroke recovery, and senior care. CHI St. Vincent also operates two community hospitals; rehabilitation hospitals; primary, urgent, and specialty care clinics; and home health care agencies.

	Annual Growth	06/01	06/02	06/05	06/08	06/22
Sales ($mil.)	4.0%	–	235.9	287.4	17.8	517.0
Net income ($ mil.)	–	–	(22.3)	–	(4.2)	(60.5)
Market value ($ mil.)	–	–	–	–	–	–
Employees	–	–	–	–	–	3,640

ST. VINCENT'S HEALTH SERVICES CORPORATION

2800 MAIN ST
BRIDGEPORT, CT 066064201
Phone: 203 576-6000
Fax: –
Web: www.stvincents.org

CEO: Josephe Maloney
CFO: –
HR: –
FYE: September 30
Type: Private

St. Vincent's Health Services constitutes good health and wellness in the Constitution State. A member of Ascension Health, the full-service health care organization serves southwestern Connecticut and Westchester County, New York. The system includes St. Vincent's Medical Center, a general hospital with about 475 beds, as well as primary and urgent care facilities, a behavioral health care program, and other specialty services. It specializes in open-heart surgery, cancer care, orthopedic services, and bariatric surgery. St. Vincent's Medical Center also renders psychiatric care through a 75-bed inpatient psychiatric facility. Its senior services include geriatric referrals, diagnostic, and therapeutic services.

ST. VINCENT'S HEALTH SYSTEM, INC.

1 SHIRCLIFF WAY
JACKSONVILLE, FL 322044748
Phone: 904 308-7300
Fax: –
Web: healthcare.ascension.org

CEO: Donnie Romine
CFO: –
HR: –
FYE: June 30
Type: Private

As a part of Ascension Health, St. Vincent Health System specifically serves the Jacksonville, Florida, region. Also known by area residents as St. Vincent's HealthCare, the is not-for-profit healthcare system consists of flagship St. Vincent's Medical Center Riverside and two smaller satellite hospitals. Besides its medical center and hospital, other St. Vincent's Health System operations include nursing care and hospice facility St. Catherine Labour Manor, as well as two dozen primary care centers, specialty care centers, laboratory, pharmacy, transportation, and home health care services.

	Annual Growth	06/01	06/02	06/03	06/08	06/21
Sales ($mil.)	2.7%	–	308.4	309.8	9.9	510.6
Net income ($ mil.)	2.5%	–	15.8	5.1	(34.7)	25.5
Market value ($ mil.)	–	–	–	–	–	–
Employees	–	–	–	–	–	4,075

STAAR SURGICAL CO.

25651 Atlantic Ocean Drive
Lake Forest, CA 92630
Phone: 626 303-7902
Fax: –
Web: www.staar.com

NMS: STAA
CEO: Thomas G Frinzi
CFO: Patrick Williams
HR: Phuong Nguyen
FYE: December 29
Type: Public

STAAR Surgical Company designs, develops, manufactures, and sells implantable lenses for the eye companion and delivery systems used to deliver the lenses into the eye. STAAR is the leading manufacturer of lenses used worldwide in corrective or "refractive" surgery. The company also makes lenses for use in surgery that treats cataracts. Its primary products include Visian-branded implantable lenses (ICLs) for correcting such refractive conditions as near- and far-sightedness and astigmatism. All the lenses the company makes are foldable, which allows the surgeon to insert them into the eye through a small incision during minimally invasive surgery. The company sells its products in more than 75 countries. China is STAAR's largest single market.

	Annual Growth	01/20	01/21*	12/21	12/22	12/23
Sales ($mil.)	21.0%	150.2	163.5	230.5	284.4	322.4
Net income ($ mil.)	11.0%	14.0	5.9	24.5	38.8	21.3
Market value ($ mil.)	(2.4%)	1,679.1	3,869.0	4,459.0	2,370.6	1,524.3
Employees	17.7%	550	575	806	964	1,057

*Fiscal year change

STABILLIS SOLUTIONS INC

11750 Katy Freeway, Suite 900
Houston, TX 77079
Phone: 832 456-6500
Fax: –
Web: www.stabilis-solutions.com

NAS: SLNG
CEO: Westervelt T Ballard Jr
CFO: Andrew Puhala
HR: –
FYE: December 31
Type: Public

American Electric Technologies (AETI) tames wild and woolly wiring. Its technical products and services segment makes low- and medium-voltage switchgears for land- and offshore-based oil and gas drilling, as well as refineries and municipal power companies. The electrical and instrumentation construction unit makes electric power delivery and control products and provides technical field services and electrical and instrumentation construction services. American Access Technologies makes zone-cabling cabinets for telephone lines, data networking, and security systems.

	Annual Growth	12/19	12/20	12/21	12/22	12/23
Sales ($mil.)	11.6%	47.1	41.6	77.2	98.8	73.1
Net income ($ mil.)	–	(5.7)	(6.8)	(7.8)	(3.2)	0.1
Market value ($ mil.)	(9.7%)	115.7	115.7	78.6	98.7	77.1
Employees	(10.5%)	162	268	293	100	104

STABLER COMPANIES INC.

635 LUCKNOW RD
HARRISBURG, PA 171101630
Phone: 717 236-9307
Fax: –
Web: www.nesl.com

CEO: –
CFO: Thomas M Minori
HR: –
FYE: February 29
Type: Private

The Stabler Companies' various subsidiaries keep drivers on the go and men at work. Its Eastern Industries quarries aggregates and constructs and rehabilitates roads. ASTI Transportation Systems, Protection Services Inc., Work Area Protection Corporation, and Precision Solar Controls make work-zone and traffic-management devices such as safety signs, barricades, and roadway detection devices. Stabler Land developed the corporate, retail, and residential community Stabler Center in Pennsylvania. Donald Stabler began operations in 1940 that would become the Stabler Companies. The company was purchased in 2008 by Pennsylvania construction firm New Enterprise Stone & Lime Co.

STAFF FORCE, INC.

419 MASON PARK BLVD
KATY, TX 774506187
Phone: 281 492-6044
Fax: –
Web: www.staff-force.com

CEO: –
CFO: Glenn T Van Dusen
HR: –
FYE: December 31
Type: Private

Companies in need of interviewing, hiring, or payroll expertise trust in this Force. Staff Force -- which does business as Staff Force Personnel Services -- provides temporary, temp-to-hire, and direct hire staffing and payroll services in areas such as technology, light industrial, and hospitality. The company also provides employee handbooks (available in both English and Spanish), employee benefits, and criminal background and reference checks. Customers come from industries such as health care, manufacturing, transportation, and consumer goods. Founded in 1989, the company has locations throughout Texas.

	Annual Growth	12/10	12/11	12/12	12/13	12/14
Sales ($mil.)	4.1%	–	–	91.6	94.2	99.2
Net income ($ mil.)	(8.3%)	–	–	0.7	0.7	0.6
Market value ($ mil.)	–	–	–	–	–	–
Employees	–	–	–	–	–	20,000

STAFF ONE, INC.

8605 FREEPORT PKWY STE 100
IRVING, TX 75063
Phone: 214 461-1140
Fax: –
Web: www.staffone.com

CEO: Robert Befidi Jr
CFO: –
HR: –
FYE: December 31
Type: Private

Staff One wants to be #1 in clients' minds when it comes to human resources. The professional employer organization (PEO) provides businesses with outsourced human resource services in areas such as HR management, payroll, benefits, compliance management, tax administration, and workers' compensation. Its customers come from fields including financial services, health care, manufacturing, consumer goods, and retail. The PEO owns about 10 locations across Arkansas, Georgia, Missouri, Oklahoma, and Tennessee. Investment firm Gordian Capital owns Staff One, which was founded in 1988.

STAG INDUSTRIAL INC

One Federal Street, 23rd Floor
Boston, MA 02110
Phone: 617 574-4777
Fax: 617 574-0052
Web: www.stagindustrial.com

NYS: STAG
CEO: –
CFO: –
HR: –
FYE: December 31
Type: Public

If STAG Industrial were to show up alone at a party, it would likely be on the hunt for single tenants looking to lease industrial space. The self-managed and self-administered real estate investment trust (REIT) has built a business acquiring and managing single-tenant industrial properties located across more than 35 states. The company's portfolio consists primarily of about 91.4 million sq. ft. of leasable warehouse, distribution, manufacturing, and office space located in secondary markets. STAG conducts most of its business through its operating partner, STAG Industrial Operating Partnership. Pennsylvania accounts for the highest annual base rental revenue.

	Annual Growth	12/19	12/20	12/21	12/22	12/23
Sales ($mil.)	14.9%	406.0	483.4	562.2	657.3	707.8
Net income ($ mil.)	40.6%	49.3	202.1	192.3	178.3	192.8
Market value ($ mil.)	5.6%	5,736.0	5,690.6	8,713.9	5,870.4	7,133.2
Employees	7.2%	72	78	86	93	95

STAGE STORES, INC.

2425 WEST LOOP S
HOUSTON, TX 770274300
Phone: 713 667-5601
Fax: –
Web: www.burkesoutlet.com

CEO: Michael L Glazer
CFO: Jason T Curtis
HR: Denise V Conine
FYE: February 02
Type: Private

Burkes Outlets Stores is a privately-held company, rich in tradition, owned by the founding family and its employees. It operates more than 650 retail stores. Customers can find brand name, apparel, and accessories for the entire family at up to 70% off other stores prices daily. Most stores carry shoes, home furnishings, gifts, and toys. Its stores are designed to serve customers of all ages and income levels. The company was founded in 1915. Burkes Outlet and Bealls Outlet will rebrand under the Bealls name by the end of 2023.

STAGWELL INC

One World Trade Center, Floor 65
New York, NY 10007
Phone: 646 429-1800
Fax: 212 937-4365
Web: www.stagwellglobal.com

NMS: STGW
CEO: –
CFO: –
HR: –
FYE: December 31
Type: Public

MDC Partners is a leading global marketing and communications network, providing marketing and business solutions that realize the potential of combining data and creativity. Advertising, branding, direct marketing, public relations, and sales promotion are provided through firms such as Allison & Partners, Crispin Porter + Bogusky, Colle & McVoy, Sloane & Company, and Veritas. In addition, the company also delivers data analytics and insights, mobile and technology experiences, media buying, planning and optimization, business consulting, corporate communication, and database customer relationship management, among others. Majority of the company's sales were generated from the U.S.

	Annual Growth	12/19	12/20	12/21	12/22	12/23
Sales ($mil.)	15.6%	1,415.8	1,199.0	1,469.4	2,687.8	2,527.2
Net income ($ mil.)	–	(4.7)	(229.0)	21.0	27.3	0.1
Market value ($ mil.)	24.3%	750.9	678.0	2,341.9	1,677.4	1,790.9
Employees	16.1%	5,647	4,866	10,200	12,150	10,250

STAMFORD HEALTH, INC.

30 SHELBURNE RD
STAMFORD, CT 069023602
Phone: 203 325-7000
Fax: –
Web: www.shccu.org

CEO: –
CFO: –
HR: –
FYE: September 30
Type: Private

It sounds like one of the most famous universities in the country, but it's actually a comprehensive medical center located on the opposite coast. Stamford Health System provides health services to residents of Stamford, Connecticut and surrounding areas through a not-for-profit, 300-bed community medical center called Stamford Hospital. The hospital administers acute and specialty services that include oncology, cardiology, orthopedics, and women's health services. It is a teaching facility for the Columbia University College of Physicians and Surgeons and a member of the New York Presbyterian Health System.

	Annual Growth	09/10	09/11	09/12	09/13	09/15
Sales ($mil.)	28.4%	–	2.9	2.1	6.6	8.0
Net income ($ mil.)	–	–	(1.7)	110.5	2.5	4.4
Market value ($ mil.)	–	–	–	–	–	–
Employees	–	–	–	–	–	1,978

STAMPIN' UP INC.

12907 S 3600 W
RIVERTON, UT 840656972
Phone: 801 257-5400
Fax: –
Web: www.stampinup.com

CEO: Shelli Gardner
CFO: J S Nielsen
HR: Leslie Bosen
FYE: December 31
Type: Private

Stampin' Up! has given the rubber stamp to direct sales. Through a network of more than 40,000 independent sales representatives in North America and internationally, Stampin' Up! markets exclusive wood-mounted rubber stamps and accessories for use in arts and crafts, scrapbooking, greeting card design, and home decoration. California, Michigan, Minnesota, Washington, and Wisconsin are among the states with a large number of distributors. The company, which also boasts representatives in Australia, Canada, France, Germany, New Zealand, and the UK, boasts an 80,000-sq.-ft. manufacturing plant in Utah. CEO Shelli Gardner and her sister (who later left the company) founded the company in 1988.

STAMPS.COM INC.

1990 E GRAND AVE
EL SEGUNDO, CA 902455013
Phone: 310 482-5800
Fax: –
Web: www.auctane.com

CEO: Nathan Jones
CFO: Jeff Carberry
HR: –
FYE: December 31
Type: Private

Stamps.com is the leading provider of Internet-based postage solutions. It was the first company to be approved by the US Postal Service to offer a software-only postage service that lets customers buy and print postage online. Stamps.com is integrated with the shipping industry's leading order management and e-commerce solutions including Auctane, Etsy, Rakuten, Trueship's ReadyShipper, Shopify, and more. Its software solutions allow customers to print mailing and shipping labels for multiple carriers around the world through downloadable software, web-based user interfaces (UIs) and application programming interfaces (APIs). In addition, customers can buy mailing labels, scales, and dedicated postage printers from Stamps.com.

STAND ENERGY CORPORATION

1077 CELESTIAL ST STE 110
CINCINNATI, OH 452021629
Phone: 513 621-1113
Fax: –
Web: www.stand-energy.com

CEO: Judith Phillips
CFO: –
HR: –
FYE: December 31
Type: Private

Stand Energy Corporation (SEC) took a stand in the 1980s when the US government deregulated the natural gas industry. SEC also constructs bypass pipelines for its customers (allowing companies to bypass the local utility) and designs and builds propane backup systems to take advantage of reduced gas rates. Its customer base has broadened to include industrial facilities of all sizes, commercial and government entities, hospitals, and other large energy users. SEC was founded in 1984 by Chairman Matth Toebben and CEO Judith Phillips.

STANDARD AVB FINANCIAL CORP.

2640 MONROEVILLE BLVD
MONROEVILLE, PA 151462314
Phone: 412 856-0363
Fax: –
Web: www.standardbankpa.com

CEO: –
CFO: –
HR: –
FYE: September 30
Type: Private

Standard Financial provides standard banking services and a little bit more. Standard Financial is the holding company of Standard Bank, which offers traditional personal and business checking and savings accounts, as well as loan products. It operates 10 branches serving southwestern Pennsylvania and northern Maryland. Its loan portfolio includes residential and mortgages, home equity loans, and commercial loans; to a lesser extent, it provides consumer and construction loans. Brokerage services, retirement planning, and other investment services are offered through PrimeVest Financial. Standard Financial is combining with Allegheny Valley Bancorp in a $56.5 million merger of equals.

	Annual Growth	09/09	09/10	09/11	09/12	09/13
Assets ($mil.)	0.3%	–	–	434.6	443.4	436.9
Net income ($ mil.)	9.0%	–	–	2.4	3.0	2.9
Market value ($ mil.)	–	–	–	–	–	–
Employees	–	–	–	–	–	158

STANDARD BIOTOOLS INC

NMS: LAB

2 Tower Place, Suite 2000
South San Francisco, CA 94080
Phone: 650 266-6000
Fax: –
Web: www.standardbio.com

CEO: Michael Egholm
CFO: Jeffrey Black
HR: Annie Butler
FYE: December 31
Type: Public

Standard BioTools, Inc. creates, manufactures, and markets a range of products and services, including instruments, consumables, reagents and software that are used by researchers and clinical labs worldwide. It also develops integrated fluidic circuits (IFCs), which incorporate several different types of technology that together enable us to use MSL technology to rapidly design and deploy new microfluidic applications. Fluidigm's BioMark HD and EP1 systems enable genetic analyses including genotyping and high-throughput gene expression. Its Access Array system enables automated sample preparation for DNA sequencing. Most of company's revenue comes from the America.

	Annual Growth	12/19	12/20	12/21	12/22	12/23
Sales ($mil.)	(2.4%)	117.2	138.1	130.6	97.9	106.3
Net income ($ mil.)	–	(64.8)	(53.0)	(59.2)	(190.1)	(74.7)
Market value ($ mil.)	(10.7%)	279.2	481.4	314.5	93.9	177.3
Employees	(1.4%)	566	627	615	523	534

STANDARD ELECTRIC COMPANY

2650 TRAUTNER DR
SAGINAW, MI 486049599
Phone: 989 497-2100
Fax: –
Web: www.standardelectricco.com

CEO: –
CFO: Benjamin F Rosenthal
HR: –
FYE: February 28
Type: Private

Standard Electric and its affiliates distribute electrical and electronic products and supplies to customers through about 30 locations in Michigan. The company was founded in 1929 by Samuel Cohen and brothers Morris and Max Blumberg. The Blumberg brothers earlier established another Michigan-based electrical distributor, Madison Electric, an affiliate of Standard Electric with 10 Michigan locations. Another affiliated firm, U.P. Electric/Wittock Supply Co., is a distributor of electrical and mechanical products with four locations on the upper Michigan peninsula. The company is owned by its directors and their families.

	Annual Growth	02/13	02/14	02/15	02/16	02/17
Sales ($mil.)	5.4%	–	–	173.0	176.1	192.3
Net income ($ mil.)	(2.0%)	–	–	2.2	0.3	2.1
Market value ($ mil.)	–	–	–	–	–	–
Employees	–	–	–	–	–	250

STANDARD ENERGY CORP.

NBB: STDE

447 Bearcat Drive
Salt Lake City, UT 84115-2517
Phone: 801 364-9000
Fax: 801 467-6766
Web: –

CEO: –
CFO: –
HR: –
FYE: March 31
Type: Public

The standard energy sources that Standard Energy taps into are oil and natural gas. The company acquires unproven oil and gas leaseholds (often owned by the US government) and resells them to third parties. The company holds 2,698 net acres of oil and gas leaseholds in Utah, and 1,243 net acres of leasehold properties in Wyoming. Through its subsidiary Petroleum Investment Company, Standard Energy also provides a range of geologic lease evaluation services. The company is also working in the biofuels technology field to commercially recover inorganic materials from the recycling of municipal waste. CEO Dean Rowell owns 65% of the oil and gas independent.

	Annual Growth	03/05	03/06	03/07	03/08	03/09
Sales ($mil.)	(2.7%)	0.0	0.0	0.0	0.0	0.0
Net income ($ mil.)	–	(0.1)	(0.0)	(0.1)	(0.3)	(0.1)
Market value ($ mil.)	(24.0%)	5.6	3.4	9.4	5.6	1.9
Employees	–	3	3	3	3	3

STANDARD MOTOR PRODUCTS, INC. NYS: SMP

37-18 Northern Blvd.
Long Island City, NY 11101
Phone: 718 392-0200
Fax: 718 472-0122
Web: www.smpcorp.com

CEO: Eric P Sills
CFO: Nathan R Iles
HR: –
FYE: December 31
Type: Public

Standard Motor Products (SMP) is a manufacturer and distributor of premium replacement parts utilized in the maintenance, repair, and service of vehicles in the automotive aftermarket industry. The company is organized into two major operating segments. Its largest segment, Engine Management, makes ignition and emission parts, ignition wires, battery cables, fuel system parts, and sensors for vehicle systems. Its Temperature Control segment manufactures and remanufactures air conditioning compressors, heating parts, engine cooling system parts, power window accessories, and windshield washer parts. Customers include warehouse distributors such as Genuine Parts Co., Automotive Distribution Network LLC, and National Automotive Parts Association (NAPA), and retail chains such as O'Reilly Automotive, Inc., Canadian Tire Corporation, and AutoZone. The US is SMP's core market generating most of its revenues.

	Annual Growth	12/19	12/20	12/21	12/22	12/23
Sales ($mil.)	4.5%	1,137.9	1,128.6	1,298.8	1,371.8	1,358.3
Net income ($ mil.)	(12.4%)	57.9	57.4	90.9	55.4	34.1
Market value ($ mil.)	(7.0%)	1,166.4	886.8	1,148.2	762.7	872.5
Employees	5.5%	4,200	4,300	5,000	4,900	5,200

STANDEX INTERNATIONAL CORP. NYS: SXI

23 Keewaydin Drive
Salem, NH 03079
Phone: 603 893-9701
Fax: 603 893-7324
Web: www.standex.com

CEO: David Dunbar
CFO: Ademir Sarcevic
HR: –
FYE: June 30
Type: Public

Standex International Corporation is a diversified industrial manufacturer with leading positions in a variety of products and services that are used in diverse commercial and industrial markets. It has six operating segments aggregated into five reportable segments Electronics, Engraving, Scientific, Engineering Technologies, and Specialty Solutions. It develops and designs new products to meet customer needs, to offer enhanced products or to provide customized solutions for customers. The company's businesses work in close partnership with its customers to deliver custom solutions or engineered components that solve their unique and specific needs. Generating over 60% of revenue from the US, the company has international operations in Europe, Canada, China, Japan, India, Singapore, Korea, Mexico, Turkey, Malaysia, and South Africa. Standex traces its historical roots back to 1955.

	Annual Growth	06/19	06/20	06/21	06/22	06/23
Sales ($mil.)	(1.6%)	791.6	604.5	656.2	735.3	741.0
Net income ($ mil.)	19.6%	67.9	20.2	36.5	61.4	139.0
Market value ($ mil.)	17.9%	859.0	675.9	1,114.7	995.7	1,661.6
Employees	(6.6%)	5,000	3,800	3,900	3,800	3,800

STANFORD HEALTH CARE

300 PASTEUR DR
STANFORD, CA 943052200
Phone: 650 723-4000
Fax: –
Web: www.stanfordhealthcare.org

CEO: David Entwistle
CFO: Lynda Hoff
HR: Cindy Johnson
FYE: August 31
Type: Private

Stanford Health Care, along with Stanford Health Care Tri-Valley and Stanford Medicine Partners, is part of the adult health care delivery system of Stanford Medicine. As Stanford University's primary medical teaching facility, the 604-bed Stanford Hospital specializes in such areas as cardiac care, cancer treatment, neurology, surgery, urology, orthopaedics, and organ transplant. Recognized as No. 1 in the country for ear, nose and throat, and it earned top-10 rankings for cardiology and heart surgery as well as obstetrics and gynecology, Stanford Health Care provides compassionate, coordinated care personalized for the unique needs of every patient.

	Annual Growth	08/18	08/19	08/20	08/21	08/22
Sales ($mil.)	15.4%	–	–	5,567.6	6,772.2	7,412.5
Net income ($ mil.)	61.5%	–	–	104.8	1,517.0	273.4
Market value ($ mil.)	–	–	–	–	–	–
Employees	–	–	–	–	–	14,100

STANION WHOLESALE ELECTRIC CO., INC.

812 S MAIN ST
PRATT, KS 671242600
Phone: 620 672-5678
Fax: –
Web: www.stanion.com

CEO: –
CFO: –
HR: –
FYE: December 31
Type: Private

Stanion Wholesale Electric distributes electrical products and supplies to customers through nearly 20 branch locations in Kansas and Missouri. The company specializes in products for factory automation, lighting, telecommunications, and utilities, carrying items from such manufacturers as Cooper Industries, General Electric, Rockwell Automation, and Thomas & Betts. Stanion Wholesale Electric makes all of its product catalog available over its corporate Web site, along with other e-commerce functions. The family-owned company was founded in 1961 by chairman Jud Stanion and his wife, Bobbe. Stanion Wholesale Electric is owned by Bill Keller (president and CEO) and his wife, Cindy Stanion Keller.

	Annual Growth	12/13	12/14	12/15	12/21	12/22
Sales ($mil.)	–	–	–	84.1	3.2	4.7
Net income ($ mil.)	(40.8%)	–	3.0	(2.8)	(0.1)	0.0
Market value ($ mil.)	–	–	–	–	–	–
Employees	–	–	–	–	–	229

STANLEY BLACK & DECKER INC NYS: SWK

1000 Stanley Drive
New Britain, CT 06053
Phone: 860 225-5111
Fax: 860 827-3895
Web: www.stanleyblackanddecker.com

CEO: Donald Allan Jr
CFO: Corbin B Walburger
HR: –
FYE: December 30
Type: Public

Stanley Black & Decker is a diversified global provider of power tools and equipment (electric power tools, pneumatic tools, and lawn and garden products), hand tools, power tool accessories, and storage products. In addition to its well-known namesake brands, it sells other top brands such as Bostitch, Mac Tools, DEWALT, and Craftsman directly to consumers, as well as through distributors, home centers, and mass-merchant distributors. Stanley Black & Decker also sells engineered fastening and infrastructure products to customers in the automotive, manufacturing, and oil and gas industries, among others, and designs and installs electronic security systems and automatic doors to commercial customers. It generates about 65% of its sales in the US. Frederick T. Stanley founded the company in 1843.

	Annual Growth	12/19*	01/21	01/22*	12/22	12/23
Sales ($mil.)	2.2%	14,442	14,535	15,617	16,947	15,781
Net income ($ mil.)	–	955.8	1,233.8	1,689.2	1,062.5	(310.5)
Market value ($ mil.)	(12.3%)	25,486	27,430	28,976	11,540	15,070
Employees	(4.0%)	59,438	63,600	81,700	59,900	50,500

*Fiscal year change

STANLEY STEEMER INTERNATIONAL, INC.

5800 INNOVATION DR
DUBLIN, OH 430163271
Phone: 614 764-2007
Fax: –
Web: www.stanleysteemer.com

CEO: Wesley C Bates
CFO: –
HR: Eric M Smith
FYE: December 31
Type: Private

Stanley Steemer International provides residential and commercial carpet and upholstery cleaning through nearly 300 franchise and corporate locations in nearly 50 states. In addition to cleaning carpets, the company provides cleaning services for tile and grout, and air ducts, as well as cars, boats, and RVs. The company, which is known for its fleet of yellow vans, sells its own brand of cleaning products through an online store. Founded by Jack Bates in 1947 when he established his own one-man carpet cleaning business, Stanley Steemer is owned by his descendants, including CEO Wesley Bates and President Justin Bates.

	Annual Growth	12/15	12/16	12/17	12/18	12/21
Sales ($mil.)	1.7%	–	242.0	240.0	227.3	263.7
Net income ($ mil.)	9.7%	–	14.7	15.6	11.3	23.3
Market value ($ mil.)	–	–	–	–	–	–
Employees	–	–	–	–	–	2,000

STANLY REGIONAL MEDICAL CENTER

301 YADKIN ST
ALBEMARLE, NC 280013441
Phone: 704 982-3888
Fax: –
Web: www.carolinashealthcare.org/locations/carolinas-healthcare-system-stanly
CEO: –
CFO: –
HR: –
FYE: September 30
Type: Private

Nope, it's not a typo. It really is Stanly without an "e." Stanly Regional Medical Center (SRMC) provides a wide range of general medical services to residents in and around Stanly County in North Carolina. Formed in 1950, the hospital has 120 beds and is under the management of Carolinas HealthCare, which owns or manages about two dozen regional hospitals. The two organizations agreed to the management contract in 2009 to provide SRMC with more access to resources, such as group purchasing, help with physician recruitment, and supply-chain management. SRMC is affiliated with a number of other organizations including about a dozen clinics, a home health agency, a medical equipment company, and a nursing home.

STAPLE COTTON COOPERATIVE ASSOCIATION

214 W MARKET ST
GREENWOOD, MS 389304329
Phone: 662 453-6231
Fax: –
Web: www.staplcotn.com
CEO: Hank Reichle
CFO: Mike Moffatt
HR: Tunya Wells
FYE: August 31
Type: Private

Referred to as Staplcotn, the Staple Cotton Cooperative has been a staple of its member-producers' business lives since 1921. One of the oldest and largest cotton marketing co-ops in the US, it provides domestic and export marketing, cotton warehousing, and agricultural financing to some 9,730 members in 47 states. As of 2011, the co-op handles nearly 14,000 farm accounts in 10 states. Staplcotn's inventory is consigned by member-producers and averages from 2.5 million to 3 million bales of cotton a year. The co-op operates though 15 warehouses serving the mid-south and southeastern US, to supply more than 25% of the cotton consumed by the US textile industry, as well as the needs of textile mills overseas.

	Annual Growth	08/09	08/10	08/11	08/12	08/13
Sales ($mil.)	8.7%	–	–	963.4	1,236.4	1,138.3
Net income ($ mil.)	(91.7%)	–	–	875.1	8.2	6.0
Market value ($ mil.)	–	–	–	–	–	–
Employees	–	–	–	–	–	277

STAPLES CONSTRUCTION COMPANY, INC.

1501 EASTMAN AVE
VENTURA, CA 930036488
Phone: 805 658-8786
Fax: –
Web: www.staplesconstruction.com
CEO: –
CFO: –
HR: –
FYE: December 31
Type: Private

Staples Construction Company uses sturdier material than staples to build with. The company specializes in commercial, industrial, and multi-family residential construction projects such as office buildings, biotech campuses, and public facilities. It built the $22 million corporate offices for A&R Distribution (a division of A&R Transport) in Morris, Illinois; a $14 million renovation project for San Jose State University; and the $16 million Nexus University City Sciences Center in San Jose, California. Staples Construction Company was founded in 1995 by President David Staples. It has regional offices in San Jose and San Diego, California, and Chicago, Illinois.

	Annual Growth	12/09	12/10	12/11	12/13	12/14
Sales ($mil.)	–	–	–	34.9	36.6	–
Net income ($ mil.)	2.5%	–	–	0.4	0.7	0.5
Market value ($ mil.)	–	–	–	–	–	–
Employees	–	–	–	–	–	65

STAR BUFFET, INC.

2501 N. Hayden Road, Suite 103
Scottsdale, AZ 85257
Phone: 480 425-0454
Fax: –
Web: www.starbuffet.com
CEO: Robert E Wheaton
CFO: –
HR: –
FYE: January 28
Type: Public

Star Buffet is a leading operator of buffet-style restaurants with more than 40 dining locations in about 15 states. The eateries, located primarily in the southeastern and western US, offer a wide array of menu items for breakfast, lunch, and dinner. In addition to its buffet-style units, Star Buffet operates a small number of family-style restaurants under the 4B's banner, as well as a couple of WesterN SizzliN steak-buffet restaurants (franchised from Western Sizzlin). CEO Robert Wheaton owns more than 40% of the company. Star Buffet filed for bankruptcy in late 2011.

	Annual Growth	01/15	01/16	01/17	01/18	01/19
Sales ($mil.)	2.6%	23.5	24.5	26.1	26.5	26.0
Net income ($ mil.)	–	2.6	0.8	(0.2)	0.1	(0.5)
Market value ($ mil.)	(7.8%)	2.9	3.2	4.6	2.9	2.1
Employees	(1.4%)	862	793	820	815	815

STAR EQUITY HOLDINGS INC

NMS: STRR

53 Forest Ave., Suite 101
Old Greenwich, CT 06870
Phone: 203 489-9500
Fax: –
Web: www.starequity.com
CEO: Richard K Coleman Jr
CFO: David J Noble
HR: –
FYE: December 31
Type: Public

Digirad makes and sells nuclear imaging equipment and provides mobile imaging services. Nuclear imaging uses low-level radioactive drugs introduced into a patient's bloodstream to detect heart disease, cancer, and neurological disorders. The company leases its equipment and provides staffing through the Diagnostic Services unit. Its Mobile Healthcare unit provides contract imaging services. Digirad sells solid state cameras through its Diagnostic Imaging segment. The company agreed to acquire ATRM Holdings, a maker of modular housing units and structural materials, in 2019 to transition into a diversified holding company structure.

	Annual Growth	12/19	12/20	12/21	12/22	12/23
Sales ($mil.)	(20.4%)	114.2	78.2	106.6	112.2	45.8
Net income ($ mil.)	–	(4.6)	(6.5)	(3.0)	(5.3)	25.1
Market value ($ mil.)	(20.4%)	41.1	56.8	40.4	13.5	16.5
Employees	(27.5%)	618	636	458	413	171

STAR GROUP LP

NYS: SGU

9 West Broad Street
Stamford, CT 06902
Phone: 203 328-7310
Fax: –
Web: www.stargrouplp.com
CEO: –
CFO: –
HR: –
FYE: September 30
Type: Public

Those who wish for heat and power can wish upon a star -- Star Gas Partners. The company is the nation's largest retail distributor of home heating oil. Its Petro Holdings subsidiary provides heating oil and propane to 416,000 customers in the US Northeast and Mid-Atlantic. The company sells home heating oil, gasoline, and diesel fuel to 48,000 customers on a delivery only basis, and provides HVAC and ancillary home services, including home security and plumbing, to 11,500 customers. Investment firm Kestrel Energy Partners controls the general partner of Star Gas Partners.

	Annual Growth	09/19	09/20	09/21	09/22	09/23
Sales ($mil.)	2.7%	1,753.9	1,467.5	1,497.1	2,006.6	1,952.9
Net income ($ mil.)	16.0%	17.6	55.9	87.7	35.3	31.9
Market value ($ mil.)	6.2%	340.2	350.3	366.1	292.1	432.2
Employees	(3.0%)	3,446	3,157	3,121	3,194	3,052

STAR OF THE WEST MILLING COMPANY

121 E TUSCOLA ST
FRANKENMUTH, MI 487341731
Phone: 989 652-9971
Fax: –
Web: www.starofthewest.com

CEO: William A Zehnder III
CFO: –
HR: –
FYE: December 31
Type: Private

All hands are on the mill floor at Star of the West Milling. The company operates five flour mills in four US states an about 10 storage elevators. The mills and elevators store and process wheat, corn, and soybeans. Its flour milling capacity is about 20,000 lbs. per day. North Star Bean, a division of Star of the West, processes beans such as navy, pinto, kidney, and black beans into dry commodity products. The company also owns Eastern Michigan Grain, an elevator that offers grain handling and marketing services. Star of the West Milling sells its flour and beans worldwide to canning and packaging customers the likes of Kellogg, General Mills, Nabisco, and Pepperidge Farm.

	Annual Growth	12/11	12/12	12/13	12/14	12/15
Sales ($mil.)	(2.4%)	–	–	416.9	–	396.8
Net income ($ mil.)	(15.1%)	–	–	15.6	12.9	11.2
Market value ($ mil.)	–	–	–	–	–	–
Employees	–	–	–	–	–	239

STARBUCKS CORP.

NMS: SBUX

2401 Utah Avenue South
Seattle, WA 98134
Phone: 206 447-1575
Fax: –
Web: www.starbucks.com

CEO: Laxman Narasimhan
CFO: Rachel Ruggeri
HR: –
FYE: October 1
Type: Public

Starbucks is a premier roaster, marketer and retailer of specialty coffee globally, operating in more than 80 markets. The company's operating store offers coffee drinks and food items, as well as roasted beans, coffee accessories, and teas. Aside from its flagship stores, the company also sells goods and services under Teavana, Seattle's Best Coffee, Evolution Fresh, Ethos, Starbucks Reserve and Princi. Starbucks operates about 17,000 of its own shops, which are located mostly in the US, while licensees and franchisees operate roughly 17,000 units worldwide. In addition, Starbucks markets its coffee through grocery stores, warehouse clubs, specialty retailers, convenience stores and foodservice accounts. The US accounts for the majority of Starbucks' revenue.

	Annual Growth	09/19	09/20*	10/21	10/22	10/23
Sales ($mil.)	7.9%	26,509	23,518	29,061	32,250	35,976
Net income ($ mil.)	3.5%	3,599.2	928.3	4,199.3	3,281.6	4,124.5
Market value ($ mil.)	0.8%	100,972	96,321	129,022	96,275	104,285
Employees	2.4%	346,000	349,000	383,000	402,000	381,000

*Fiscal year change

STARK HOLDINGS INC.

1705 S TEXAS HWY
AUSTIN, TX 78746
Phone: 512 329-8100
Fax: –
Web: www.starktalent.com

CEO: –
CFO: Wolfgang Metzner
HR: –
FYE: December 31
Type: Private

STARK Holdings (formerly EuroSoft) is a full-service staffing company providing information technology and other personnel to companies in Central Texas. The agency offers contract staffing (for individuals or project teams) and permanent placement for IT positions, as well as office support, call center, accounting, and light industrial staff. Clients have included EDS, the Texas General Land Office, 3M, and Computer Sciences. STARK has branch offices in Austin; Dallas; Irving; and San Antonio, Texas. The company was founded in 1991 as EuroSoft.

	Annual Growth	12/03	12/04	12/05	12/06	12/19
Sales ($mil.)	(39.9%)	–	6.6	8.8	11.6	0.0
Net income ($ mil.)	(20.9%)	–	0.0	0.0	0.2	0.0
Market value ($ mil.)	–	–	–	–	–	–
Employees	–	–	–	–	–	600

STARLIGHT CHILDREN'S FOUNDATION

2049 CENTURY PARK E STE 4320
LOS ANGELES, CA 900673255
Phone: 310 479-1235
Fax: –
Web: www.starlight.org

CEO: Jacqueline Hart-Ibrahim
CFO: –
HR: –
FYE: December 31
Type: Private

Starlight Children's Foundation (formerly Starlight Starbright Children's Foundation) designs educational projects that combine technology, healthcare, and entertainment for some 180,000 seriously and terminally ill children and teens each month. The foundation was formed through the 2004 merger of The Starlight Children's Foundation and The STARBRIGHT Foundation. The group's projects include online communities, the asthma and diabetes CD-ROM games, and video programs, among other projects. Celebrated film director Steven Spielberg serves as chairman emeritus, and Corbin Bleu is the foundation's national spokesperson.

	Annual Growth	12/12	12/13	12/14	12/15	12/16
Sales ($mil.)	4.5%	–	5.3	5.4	6.7	6.0
Net income ($ mil.)	(36.6%)	–	0.6	0.5	0.3	0.2
Market value ($ mil.)	–	–	–	–	–	–
Employees	–	–	–	–	–	40

STARRETT (LS) CO (THE)

NYS: SCX

121 Crescent Street
Athol, MA 01331
Phone: 978 249-3551
Fax: –
Web: www.starrett.com

CEO: Douglas A Starrett
CFO: John C Tripp
HR: –
FYE: June 30
Type: Public

The L.S. Starrett is engaged in the business of manufacturing more than 5,000 products, including hand measuring tools (electronic gages, dial indicators, steel rules, combination squares and micrometers) and precision instruments (vernier calipers and height and depth gauges). The company also makes levels, lubricants, saw blades, chalk products and squares. Starrett caters to machinists in the metalworking industry but also serves the automotive, aerospace, construction, and equipment industries. Starrett sells its products throughout North America and in more than 100 countries, but the majority of its sales were generated in the US. The company was founded in 1880 in Massachusetts by Laroy S. Starrett.

	Annual Growth	06/19	06/20	06/21	06/22	06/23
Sales ($mil.)	3.0%	228.0	201.5	219.6	253.7	256.2
Net income ($ mil.)	39.6%	6.1	(21.8)	15.5	14.9	23.1
Market value ($ mil.)	12.1%	49.2	25.2	69.4	52.2	77.6
Employees	(1.2%)	1,603	1,485	1,436	1,493	1,529

STARWOOD PROPERTY TRUST INC.

NYS: STWD

591 West Putnam Avenue
Greenwich, CT 06830
Phone: 203 422-7700
Fax: –
Web: www.starwoodpropertytrust.com

CEO: Barry S Sternlicht
CFO: Rina Paniry
HR: –
FYE: December 31
Type: Public

Starwood Property Trust hopes to shine brightly in the world of mortgages. A real estate investment trust (REIT), the company originates, finances, and manages US commercial and residential mortgage loans, commercial mortgage-backed securities, and other commercial real estate debt investments. It acquires discounted loans from failed banks and financial institutions, some through the FDIC, which typically auctions off large pools of loan portfolios. Starwood Property Trust is externally managed by SPT Management, LLC, an affiliate of Starwood Capital Group. As a REIT, the trust is exempt from paying federal income tax so long as it distributes quarterly dividends to shareholders.

	Annual Growth	12/19	12/20	12/21	12/22	12/23
Assets ($mil.)	(2.9%)	78,042	80,874	83,850	79,043	69,504
Net income ($ mil.)	(9.7%)	509.7	331.7	447.7	871.5	339.2
Market value ($ mil.)	(4.1%)	7,790.3	6,048.0	7,614.8	5,744.0	6,587.0
Employees	(0.3%)	296	282	277	290	293

STARZ ACQUISITION LLC

8900 LIBERTY CIR
ENGLEWOOD, CO 801127057
Phone: 855 247-9175
Fax: –
Web: –

CEO: Christopher P Albrecht
CFO: Scott D Macdonald
HR: –
FYE: December 31
Type: Private

Starz (formerly Liberty Media Corporation) has a galaxy of premium cable properties, including the Starz, Encore, and MoviePlex networks. The company's 17 channels across those three networks -- Starz Comedy, Encore Black, Encore Espanol, Indieplex, and Retroplex, among them -- serve nearly 60 million subscribers. Starz also distributes content digitally and through DVDs in the US and internationally through its Anchor Bay Entertainment subsidiary and produces animated content via Film Roman. In 2013 the company spun off its other operations (the Atlanta Braves, a majority stake in SIRIUS XM, and other holdings) into the new Liberty Media Corporation; it then took the Starz name.

STATE OF NEW YORK MORTGAGE AGENCY

641 LEXINGTON AVE FL 4
NEW YORK, NY 100224503
Phone: 212 688-4000
Fax: –
Web: hcr.ny.gov

CEO: –
CFO: Sheila Robinson
HR: –
FYE: October 31
Type: Private

The State of New York Mortgage Agency (SONYMA, pronounced "Sony Mae") is a public benefit corporation of the State of New York that makes homebuying more affordable for low- and moderate-income residents of the state. SONYMA has two program divisions: Its single-family programs and financing division provides low-interest rate mortgages to first-time homebuyers with low and moderate incomes through the issuance of mortgage revenue bonds, while its mortgage insurance fund provides mortgage insurance and credit support for multi-family affordable residential projects and special care facilities throughout the state.

	Annual Growth	10/15	10/16	10/17	10/18	10/19
Assets ($mil.)	4.6%	–	5,187.2	5,229.0	5,324.0	5,936.2
Net income ($ mil.)	83.2%	–	63.9	34.8	148.0	392.9
Market value ($ mil.)	–	–	–	–	–	–
Employees	–	–	–	–	–	221

STATE STREET CORP.

NYS: STT

One Congress Street
Boston, MA 02114
Phone: 617 786-3000
Fax: –
Web: www.statestreet.com

CEO: Ronald P O'Hanley
CFO: Eric W Aboaf
HR: –
FYE: December 31
Type: Public

State Street Corporation is one of the world's largest providers of financial services to institutional investors. Through its flagship State Street Bank and other subsidiaries, State Street provides investment servicing (including clearing, settlement, payment, brokerage and trading, and risk and compliance analytics) and investment management services (which include core and enhanced indexing, multi-asset strategies, environment and social investing, and ETFs) to asset managers and owners, insurance companies, official institutions, and central banks. With operations in more than 100 geographic markets, State Street has some $36.74 trillion in assets under custody and administration and roughly $3.48 trillion in assets under management. Most of the company's revenue comes from the US.

	Annual Growth	12/19	12/20	12/21	12/22	12/23
Assets ($mil.)	4.9%	245,610	314,706	314,624	301,450	297,258
Net income ($ mil.)	(3.5%)	2,242.0	2,420.0	2,693.0	2,774.0	1,944.0
Market value ($ mil.)	(0.5%)	23,884	21,975	28,081	23,422	23,389
Employees	4.4%	39,103	39,439	38,784	42,226	46,451

STATE UNIVERSITY OF IOWA FOUNDATION

1 W PARK RD
IOWA CITY, IA 522422000
Phone: 319 335-3305
Fax: –
Web: www.foriowa.org

CEO: –
CFO: –
HR: –
FYE: June 30
Type: Private

If you ever find yourself shouting "Fight! Fight! Fight! for IOWA", most likely you're a current, former, or honorary Hawkeye. Since 1956, The University of Iowa Foundation has been organizing University of Iowa fund-raising campaigns to get private contributions for equipment, facilities, fellowships, professorships, research, and scholarships. Its endowment, which is almost entirely restricted to donor-specified uses, is valued at more than $690 million. Though independent of the school, the not-for-profit organization is the university's preferred channel for contributions.

STATE UNIVERSITY OF NEW YORK

353 BDWY
ALBANY, NY 122462915
Phone: 518 320-1100
Fax: –
Web: www.suny.edu

CEO: Merryl H Tisch
CFO: Kimberly R Cline
HR: Robert McLaine
FYE: June 30
Type: Private

SUNY days are ahead for many New Yorkers seeking higher education. With an enrollment of more than 460,000 students, The State University of New York (SUNY) is vying with California State University System for the title of largest university system in the US. Most students are residents of New York State. Students come from all 50 states as well as 160 countries. SUNY maintains 64 campuses around the state, including four university centers, about two dozen university colleges, 30 community colleges, and a handful of technical colleges, as well as medical centers. The system has a student-teacher ratio of about 16:1.

STATE UNIVERSITY OF NEW YORK COLLEGE AT BROCKPORT

350 NEW CAMPUS DR
BROCKPORT, NY 144202997
Phone: 585 395-2211
Fax: –
Web: www.gobrockport.com

CEO: –
CFO: –
HR: –
FYE: December 31
Type: Private

The State University of New York College at Brockport (SUNY Brockport) is one of about a dozen university colleges in The State University of New York (SUNY) system. It has its origins in the state normal (or teachers) schools, dating back to its founding in 1835. A member of the SUNY System since 1942, the university enrolls approximately 7,000 undergraduates and more than 1,000 graduate students each year. It offers about 50 undergraduate programs and about 45 graduate programs of study, as well as nearly two dozen areas of teacher certification. SUNY Brockport confers bachelor's and master's degrees, as well as certificates of advanced study and accelerated master's degrees with other institutions.

	Annual Growth	06/05	06/06	06/07	06/08*	12/22
Sales ($mil.)	(15.5%)	–	–	–	1.6	0.2
Net income ($ mil.)	–	–	–	–	0.5	(0.0)
Market value ($ mil.)	–	–	–	–	–	–
Employees	–	–	–	–	–	600

*Fiscal year change

STATE WATER RESOURCES CONTROL BOARD

1001 I ST
SACRAMENTO, CA 958142828
Phone: 916 341-5250
Fax: –
Web: waterboards.ca.gov

CEO: –
CFO: –
HR: –
FYE: June 30
Type: Private

California's State Water Resources Control Board (State Water Board) is dedicated to protecting and allocating water from the state's lakes, rivers, streams, and coastal waters. The State Water Board, which consists of five members, was established by the legislature in 1967. An additional nine Regional Water Quality Control Boards develop plans to ensure water quality in the state's different regions. The board also provides a variety of public outreach and educational programs. The governor appoints all board members, which are later approved by the Senate. The State Water Board has an annual budget of about $632 million.

STATEHOUSE HOLDINGS INC   NBB: STHZ F

2100 Embarcadero, Suite 202
Oakland, CA 94606
Phone: 800 892-4209
Fax: –
Web: www.investharborside.com

CEO: –
CFO: –
HR: –
FYE: December 31
Type: Public

Grasslands Entertainment was a leading producer of television programming for the Canadian and US broadcasting markets. Its programs included food and wine show The Thirsty Traveler and The Wine Thief , a spin-off from The Thirsty Traveler offering everything you wanted to know about wine. Other shows included equestrian-themed Complete Rider and the documentary Ocean Wanderer . In 2009 Grasslands Entertainment agreed to a reverse takeover by a subsidiary of Foundation Financial Holdings; it plans to become a merchant bank focused on the energy and mining industries.

STATEN ISLAND UNIVERSITY HOSPITAL

475 SEAVIEW AVE
STATEN ISLAND, NY 103053436
Phone: 718 226-9000
Fax: –
Web: www.northwell.edu

CEO: –
CFO: –
HR: –
FYE: December 31
Type: Private

Staten Island University Hospital (SIUH) ferries health care services to residents of New York City's fastest growing borough and surrounding areas at its two medical campuses. Established in 1861, SIUH maintains about 715 beds and is a teaching affiliate of the State University of New York's Brooklyn Health Science Center. Its larger north campus includes units specializing in cardiology, pathology, cancer, blood-related diseases, burn treatment, trauma, and women's health. The south campus site offers specialty programs such as sleep medicine, geriatric psychiatry, and substance abuse services. A member of Northwell Health, SIUH employs approximately 1,200 physicians.

	Annual Growth	12/16	12/17	12/18	12/21	12/22
Sales ($mil.)	9.0%	–	891.5	934.8	1,134.9	1,369.6
Net income ($ mil.)	(11.6%)	–	69.1	(33.2)	45.3	37.3
Market value ($ mil.)	–	–	–	–	–	–
Employees	–	–	–	–	–	5,700

STATER BROS. HOLDINGS INC.

301 S. Tippecanoe Avenue
San Bernardino, CA 92408
Phone: 909 733-5000
Fax: –
Web: www.staterbros.com

CEO: Van Helden
CFO: –
HR: –
FYE: September 29
Type: Public

Stater Bros. has no shortage of major-league rivals, operating in the same crowded Southern California markets as Kroger-owned Ralphs and Safeway-owned Vons. Stater Bros. Holdings operates more than 165 full-service Stater Bros. Markets in six counties, primarily in the Riverside and San Bernardino areas. Most of the grocery chain's stores have deli department, about 45% house bakeries, while another 25 host Super Rx Pharmacies. The Southern California grocery operator builds and remodels its own stores through its Stater Bros. Development subsidiary. Founded in 1936 by twin brothers Leo and Cleo Stater, Stater Bros. is owned by chairman and CEO Jack Brown through La Cadena Investments.

	Annual Growth	09/09	09/10	09/11	09/12	09/13
Sales ($mil.)	0.6%	3,766.0	3,606.8	3,693.3	3,873.2	3,859.8
Net income ($ mil.)	(3.3%)	34.8	24.6	26.3	37.7	30.4
Market value ($ mil.)	–	–	–	–	–	–
Employees	(2.1%)	17,500	16,300	16,500	16,500	16,100

STATERA BIOPHARMA INC   NBB: STAB

4333 Corbett Drive, Suite 1082
Fort Collins, CO 80525
Phone: 888 613-8802
Fax: –
Web: www.staterabiopharma.com

CEO: Michael K Handley
CFO: Peter Aronstam
HR: –
FYE: December 31
Type: Public

Cleveland BioLabs' scientists are working hard to develop drugs that help healthy cells stay that way, as well as drugs that promote cell death in cancerous tumors. The company has based its research on the suppression and stimulation of the process known as apoptosis, a form of cell-death that occurs after exposure to radiation, toxic chemicals, or internal stresses. In development are two product lines: protectans (suppressing apoptosis in healthy cells after radiation exposure) and curaxins (stimulating apoptosis in some forms of cancer). Protectans have applications in reducing side effects from cancer treatment and terrorist or nuclear events, while curaxins are being developed as anticancer therapies.

	Annual Growth	12/17	12/18	12/19	12/20	12/21
Sales ($mil.)	(6.5%)	1.9	1.1	1.1	0.3	1.5
Net income ($ mil.)	–	(9.7)	(3.6)	(2.6)	(2.4)	(101.9)
Market value ($ mil.)	(13.0%)	142.3	35.8	21.4	122.4	81.6
Employees	24.7%	19	16	12	6	46

STATESVILLE HMA, LLC

218 OLD MOCKSVILLE RD
STATESVILLE, NC 286251930
Phone: 704 873-0281
Fax: –
Web: www.davisregional.com

CEO: –
CFO: –
HR: –
FYE: September 30
Type: Private

Davis Regional Medical Center (DRMC) is a 145-bed acute care hospital that serves Iredell County, North Carolina, and surrounding counties. The medical center has a staff of more than 200 independent physicians representing 40 specialties. DRMC offers a range of emergency, general health, and specialty medical services for adults, children, and the elderly. It is home to centers for rehabilitation, wound treatment, orthopedics, diabetes care, pain management, birthing, surgery, and psychiatric care. Established in 1920, Davis Regional Medical Center is part of the Health Management Associates family of hospitals.

STEADFAST INCOME REIT, INC.

18100 VON KARMAN AVE STE 500
IRVINE, CA 926120169
Phone: 949 852-0700
Fax: –
Web: www.steadfastcompanies.com

CEO: –
CFO: –
HR: –
FYE: December 31
Type: Private

Steadfast Income REIT knows the need for affordable housing is one constant in real estate. The company, operating as an umbrella partnership real estate investment trust (UPREIT), was formed to invest in multifamily residential properties with a focus on the middle-income, senior, and government-assisted housing across the US. The REIT is also open to buying industrial warehouses and other real estate. Steadfast Secure Income REIT is externally advised by Steadfast Income Advisor; both are part of the Steadfast Companies real estate group. Steadfast Income REIT went public in 2013.

STEEL CONNECT INC

590 Madison Avenue
New York, NY 10022
Phone: 914 461-1276
Fax: –
Web: www.steelconnectinc.com

NAS: STCN
CEO: Warren G Lichtenstein
CFO: Ryan O'Herrin
HR: –
FYE: July 31
Type: Public

Steel Connect, Inc., formerly ModusLink Global Solutions, Inc., operates through its wholly-owned subsidiary, ModusLink Corporation, an end-to-end global supply chain solutions and e-commerce provider serving clients in markets such as consumer electronics, communications, computing, medical devices, software and retail. Its IWCO Direct subsidiary was disposed in 2022. ModusLink provides digital and physical supply chain solutions to many of the world's leading brands across a diverse range of industries, including consumer electronics, telecommunications, computing and storage, software and content, consumer packaged goods, medical devices, retail and luxury and connected devices. Steel Connect generates some 75% of its revenue from outside the US.

	Annual Growth	07/19	07/20	07/21	07/22	07/23
Sales ($mil.)	(30.7%)	819.8	782.8	613.8	203.3	189.1
Net income ($ mil.)	–	(66.7)	(5.3)	(44.4)	(11.0)	15.6
Market value ($ mil.)	53.1%	11.1	3.3	11.9	8.4	61.1
Employees	(28.2%)	3,760	3,481	3,120	1,100	1,000

STEEL DYNAMICS INC.

7575 West Jefferson Blvd.
Fort Wayne, IN 46804
Phone: 260 969-3500
Fax: –
Web: www.steeldynamics.com

NMS: STLD
CEO: Mark D Millett
CFO: Theresa E Wagler
HR: –
FYE: December 31
Type: Public

Steel Dynamics is one of the largest domestic steel producers and metal recyclers in the US, based on estimated steelmaking and coating capacity of approximately 16 million tons and actual metals recycling volumes yearly. Its subsidiary OmniSource processes, transports, markets, and brokers ferrous and nonferrous scrap metal. Additionally, its metals recycling operation offers consulting services, as well as provides customized scrap management services. The company sells to companies in the automotive, construction, and manufacturing industries, as well as to steel processors and service centers. Steel Dynamics was founded in 1993 and went public in 1996.

	Annual Growth	12/19	12/20	12/21	12/22	12/23
Sales ($mil.)	15.8%	10,465	9,601.5	18,409	22,261	18,795
Net income ($ mil.)	38.2%	671.1	550.8	3,214.1	3,862.7	2,450.9
Market value ($ mil.)	36.5%	5,447.0	5,899.9	9,932.3	15,634	18,898
Employees	10.7%	8,385	9,625	10,640	12,060	12,600

STEEL OF WEST VIRGINIA, INC.

17TH ST & 2ND AVE
HUNTINGTON, WV 25703
Phone: 304 696-8200
Fax: –
Web: www.swvainc.com

CEO: Timothy R Duke
CFO: –
HR: –
FYE: December 31
Type: Private

Steel of West Virginia (SWV), a subsidiary of Steel Dynamics, owns and operates a steel minimill and steel fabrication facilities in West Virginia and Tennessee. The company custom-designs and manufactures finished steel products, including structural beams, channels, and special shape sections, using electric furnace steel. SWV's products are used as structural elements of trucks, trailers, heavy machinery, and manufactured housing, as well as in guardrail posts, mining applications, and light-rail systems. SWV's custom-finished products are intended to go directly into its customers' assembly lines. Its Tennessee-based subsidiary Marshall Steel fabricates steel cross members. SWV got its start in 1909.

	Annual Growth	12/13	12/14	12/15	12/16	12/17
Sales ($mil.)	(4.6%)	–	357.6	341.5	319.3	310.5
Net income ($ mil.)	–	–	–	–	–	–
Market value ($ mil.)	–	–	–	–	–	–
Employees	–	–	–	–	–	84

STEEL PARTNERS HOLDINGS LP

590 Madison Avenue, 32nd Floor
New York, NY 10022
Phone: 212 520-2300
Fax: –
Web: www.steelpartners.com

NYS: SPLP PRA
CEO: Warren G Lichtenstein
CFO: Douglas B Woodworth
HR: Antwan Ross
FYE: December 31
Type: Public

Steel Partners Holdings is a hedge fund that rules with an iron fist. The activist fund invests in a variety of businesses, from banks to hot dog restaurants. It often takes positions on those companies' boards and is not bashful about making sweeping changes within those enterprises. The firm also likes to hold on to its portfolio assets for the long term. Among its holdings is Utah-based WebBank, which offers commercial, consumer, and mortgage loans, as well as federally guaranteed USDA and SBA loans. With some $4 billion in assets under management, Steel Partners also owns portions of Unisys, Aerojet Rocketdyne, Selectica, SL Industries, and Nathan's Famous. Activist investor Warren Lichtenstein heads the firm.

	Annual Growth	12/19	12/20	12/21	12/22	12/23
Sales ($mil.)	5.1%	1,561.8	1,310.6	1,524.9	1,695.4	1,905.5
Net income ($ mil.)	148.6%	4.0	72.7	131.4	206.0	150.8
Market value ($ mil.)	(0.5%)	496.8	421.7	520.5	489.2	487.7
Employees	0.5%	5,000	4,300	4,500	4,100	5,100

STEEL TECHNOLOGIES LLC

700 N HURSTBOURNE PKWY STE 400
LOUISVILLE, KY 402225396
Phone: 502 245-2110
Fax: –
Web: www.steeltechnologies.com

CEO: Thad Solomon
CFO: –
HR: Marina Monteiro
FYE: December 31
Type: Private

If you need sheets for a bed, try a white sale; if you need sheets to make a car, try Steel Technologies. Founded in 1971 Steel Technologies' lineup includes close-tolerance cold- and hot-rolled strip and sheet, high-carbon, hot-rolled pickle strip and sheet, and alloy strip and sheet metal. The company purchases steel coils from steel mills and produces flat-rolled steel used by the agricultural, appliance, automotive, HVAC, lawn and garden, machinery, and office equipment industries. Automotive customers represent about half of Steel Technologies' sales. In 2010 the company's ownership changed to a 50/50 joint venture between Nucor and former parent Mitsui & Co. (U.S.A.), a subsidiary of Japan's Mitsui.

STEEL VENTURES, L.L.C.

1000 BURLINGTON ST
KANSAS CITY, MO 641164123
Phone: 816 474-5210
Fax: –
Web: –

CEO: –
CFO: –
HR: –
FYE: May 01
Type: Private

Steel Ventures, doing business as Ex-L-Tube, aims to excel in manufacturing mechanical and structural steel tubing. The company's cold-formed tubing products range from 1 inch to 6 inches in diameter and come in a variety of gauges. Ex-L-Tube supplies the lineup to general construction companies for applications in fencing, and light construction of window guards and frames, as well as manufacturers of such products as metal furniture, exercise equipment, and store shelves. Founded in 1981, Ex-L-Tube operates as unit of Manhattan, Kansas-based service center operator Steel & Pipe Supply.

STEELCASE, INC.

NYS: SCS

901 44th Street S.E.
Grand Rapids, MI 49508
Phone: 616 247-2710
Fax: –
Web: www.steelcase.com

CEO: Sara E Armbruster
CFO: David C Sylvester
HR: –
FYE: February 24
Type: Public

Steelcase is a global design and thought leader in the world of work. Its brands provide a comprehensive portfolio of furniture and architectural products for individual and collaborative work across a range of price points. The company's furniture portfolio includes furniture systems, seating, storage, fixed and height-adjustable desks, benches and tables, and complementary products such as work accessories, lighting, mobile power, and screens. The company's major brands include Coalesse, Designtex, AMQ, Steelcase, Smith System, Orangebox, and Viccarbe. Steelcase has operations in the Americas, Europe, and the Asia Pacific, although the US accounts for most of its sales.

	Annual Growth	02/19	02/20	02/21	02/22	02/23
Sales ($mil.)	(1.6%)	3,443.2	3,723.7	2,596.2	2,772.7	3,232.6
Net income ($ mil.)	(27.2%)	126.0	199.7	26.1	4.0	35.3
Market value ($ mil.)	(18.2%)	1,983.0	1,832.7	1,575.1	1,399.9	887.0
Employees	(1.6%)	12,700	14,000	11,900	11,800	11,900

STEELCLOUD INC

20110 Ashbrook Place, Suite 130
Ashburn, VA 20147
Phone: 703 674-5500
Fax: –
Web: www.steelcloud.com

CEO: –
CFO: –
HR: –
FYE: October 31
Type: Public

Federal agencies, defense contractors, and businesses looking for custom systems may have a SteelCloud on their horizon. The company builds network appliances and servers, including ruggedized hardware, that customers sell under their own brand names. SteelCloud integrates the customers' software or software from third-party providers. The company primarily targets systems integrators serving the federal government and independent software vendors (ISVs). SteelCloud also offers an appliance specifically designed to run the BlackBerry Enterprise Server in commercial and defense agency settings.

	Annual Growth	10/05	10/06	10/07	10/08	10/09
Sales ($mil.)	(54.8%)	36.5	24.2	23.3	19.0	1.5
Net income ($ mil.)	–	(0.1)	(10.0)	(1.9)	(2.8)	(3.7)
Market value ($ mil.)	(40.8%)	33.1	10.3	19.5	9.2	4.1
Employees	(35.9%)	89	66	56	48	15

STEIN MART, INC.

1200 RIVERPLACE BLVD STE 1000
JACKSONVILLE, FL 322071809
Phone: 904 346-1500
Fax: –
Web: www.steinmart.com

CEO: Alex Mehr
CFO: –
HR: –
FYE: February 02
Type: Private

Stein Mart is a national online retailer selling discounted branded fashion, home d cor (garden, home, linens, rugs, bed & bath products), and accessories. Stein Mart offers women's dresses, tops (knit tops and woven tops), bottoms (skirts & skorts denim pants shorts & capris leggings), activewear, jackets, sweaters (cardigans and pullovers), loungewear, and plus-sized apparels. It works with trusted brands such as Roz & Ali, Peck & Peck, Cocomo, Westport, Inner Beauty, and Needle & Cloth. Its target customers are mature women with have above-average and a taste for bargains. Customers can easily shop with more convenience than ever online at steinmart.com. Stein Mart is part of the Retail Ecommerce Ventures.

STEINER ELECTRIC COMPANY

1250 TOUHY AVE
ELK GROVE VILLAGE, IL 600075302
Phone: 847 228-0400
Fax: –
Web: www.steinerelectric.com

CEO: –
CFO: Bernie Dost
HR: Janice Hoye
FYE: December 31
Type: Private

Steiner Electric electrifies Chicago by distributing electrical products and providing related supplies and services through locations in southern Wisconsin, northern Illinois, and northwest Indiana. Besides such standard electrical supplies as ballasts and fasteners, the company's products include industrial supplies, automation products, motors and drives, lighting products, generators, and bar code devices. Services include energy audits, turnkey project management, motor repair, and electric vehicle charging. Customers purchase Steiner Electric's products for commercial, construction, residential, and industrial applications. The founding Steiner family owns the firm.

	Annual Growth	12/09	12/10	12/11	12/12	12/13
Sales ($mil.)	12.7%	–	–	181.0	230.0	230.0
Net income ($ mil.)	–	–	–	–	–	–
Market value ($ mil.)	–	–	–	–	–	–
Employees	–	–	–	–	–	480

STELLAR GROUP, INCORPORATED

2900 HARTLEY RD
JACKSONVILLE, FL 322578221
Phone: 904 260-2900
Fax: –
Web: www.stellar.net

CEO: Ronald Foster Jr
CFO: Scott V Witt V
HR: Angela Pesina
FYE: December 31
Type: Private

Stellar Group Incorporated has risen to astral levels in the design world. The firm, founded in 1985, offers architectural, engineering, and mechanical services via design/build, general contracting, and construction management delivery. It targets a cosmos of markets, from education, food, and health care to manufacturing, retail, and utility, among many others. Stellar's performance in designing and constructing perishable food processing and distribution facilities has elevated the company to the top tiers of its industry both domestically and internationally. Stellar has locations throughout the US, in addition to offices in Mexico, Puerto Rico, and Brazil.

STEMLINE THERAPEUTICS, INC.

750 LEXINGTON AVE FL 4
NEW YORK, NY 100229817
Phone: 646 502-2311
Fax: –
Web: www.menarini.com

CEO: Ivan Bergstein
CFO: –
HR: –
FYE: December 31
Type: Private

Stemline Therapeutics is working on ways to eradicate cancer stem cells (CSC) and tumors. The development-stage biopharmaceutical company's pipeline includes three lead clinical-stage candidates (Elzonris, SL-701, and SL-801) for leukemia and brain cancer in children and adults. Its drugs work by targeting CSCs, which are believed to be the seeds of tumors that often survive traditional cancer treatment. Once its candidates are approved, the company intends to file and prosecute patent applications for US, Europe, Canada, Japan, and Australia. The company was acquired by Menarini Group in 2020.

STEN CORP.

10275 Wayzata Blvd S, Suite 310
Minnetonka, MN 55305
Phone: 952 545-2776
Fax: –
Web: www.stencorporation.com

CEO: –
CFO: –
HR: –
FYE: September 28
Type: Public

STEN Corporation is a diversified holding company with operations in automobile financing and contract manufacturing. Its STEN Financial subsidiary operates subprime auto lender and dealership inventory financing business STEN Credit Corporation and the Arizona-based EasyDrive Cars and Credit used car lots. STEN also owns Stencor, which manufactures products including surgical sterilization containers and filters (for STERIS Corporation, its largest customer), air filtration systems, and pest-control systems. CEO Kenneth Brimmer owns about a quarter of the company, as does former director Gary Copperud, who controls former subsidiary Burger Time.

	Annual Growth	09/04	09/05*	10/06*	09/07	09/08
Sales ($mil.)	6.9%	12.1	8.4	8.9	4.6	15.9
Net income ($ mil.)	–	0.2	0.3	(0.6)	(2.2)	(8.0)
Market value ($ mil.)	(35.1%)	13.7	10.2	10.1	8.5	2.4
Employees	(6.9%)	80	194	198	64	60

*Fiscal year change

STEPAN CO. NYS: SCL

1101 Skokie Boulevard, Suite 500
Northbrook, IL 60062
Phone: 847 446-7500
Fax: –
Web: www.stepan.com

CEO: Scott R Behrens
CFO: Luis E Rojo
HR: –
FYE: December 31
Type: Public

Stepan Company makes basic and intermediate chemicals, including surfactants, specialty products, phthalic anhydride, and polyurethane polyols. Surfactants, the company's largest business, are used in cleaning agents and consumer products like detergents, toothpaste, and cosmetics. Stepan's surfactants also have commercial and industrial applications ranging from emulsifiers for agricultural insecticides to agents used in oil recovery. The company also makes phthalic anhydride and other polymers for food and pharmaceutical uses. The US is Stepan's biggest market, accounting for more than 55% of the company's sales.

	Annual Growth	12/19	12/20	12/21	12/22	12/23
Sales ($mil.)	5.8%	1,858.7	1,869.8	2,346.0	2,773.3	2,325.8
Net income ($ mil.)	(21.0%)	103.1	126.8	137.8	147.2	40.2
Market value ($ mil.)	(2.0%)	2,292.4	2,670.1	2,781.3	2,382.3	2,115.8
Employees	1.1%	2,284	2,293	2,439	2,453	2,389

STEPHAN CO (THE) NBB: SPCO

2211 Reach Road, Suite B4
Williamsport, PA 33610
Phone: 800 545-5300
Fax: –
Web: www.thestephanco.com

CEO: Frank F Ferola
CFO: Robert C Spindler
HR: –
FYE: December 31
Type: Public

From hair cream to stretch mark cream, The Stephan Company manages a vast portfolio of products as a maker of branded and private-label personal care items. The company's brands include Cashmere Bouquet, Quinsana Medicated, Balm Barr, Stretch Mark Cr me, Protein 29, Stiff Stuff, Wildroot, and Frances Denney. It sells them worldwide by mail order and in retail stores and salons through its subsidiaries, including Morris Flamingo-Stephan, Old 97, American Manicure, Lee Stafford Beauty Group, Williamsport Barber and Beauty Corp., and Scientific Research Products, among others. Chairman, president, and CEO Frank Ferola owns about 21% of the firm, which bought Bowman Beauty and Barber Supply Company in August 2008.

	Annual Growth	12/18	12/19	12/20	12/21	12/22
Sales ($mil.)	3.9%	9.0	8.8	9.0	9.2	10.4
Net income ($ mil.)	(42.7%)	0.6	0.2	0.8	0.6	0.0
Market value ($ mil.)	2.3%	7.2	7.0	10.8	10.2	7.9
Employees	–	29	21	–	–	–

STEPHEN GOULD CORPORATION

5 GIRALDA FARMS
MADISON, NJ 079401027
Phone: 973 428-1500
Fax: –
Web: www.stephengould.com

CEO: Michael Golden
CFO: Paul Dicicco
HR: –
FYE: December 31
Type: Private

Others can worry about what's inside -- Stephen Gould Corporation concentrates on the package. The company provides a full range of packaging-related design and printing services for customers worldwide. Its products include gift packaging, point-of-purchase displays, product merchandising, and retail and industrial packaging. Stephen Gould Corporation also provides graphic design and package-engineering services, as well as assembly and fulfillment. The company was originally founded in 1939 by Stephen Gould, David Golden, and Leonard Beckerman.

	Annual Growth	12/18	12/19	12/20	12/21	12/22
Sales ($mil.)	12.6%	–	757.7	782.7	951.9	1,080.5
Net income ($ mil.)	60.6%	–	5.9	11.1	18.4	24.6
Market value ($ mil.)	–	–	–	–	–	–
Employees	–	–	–	–	–	512

STEPHENS INC.

111 CENTER ST
LITTLE ROCK, AR 722014402
Phone: 501 377-2000
Fax: –
Web: www.stephens.com

CEO: Warren A Stephens
CFO: –
HR: –
FYE: December 31
Type: Private

Stephens is one of the largest investment banking company. Founded in 1933, the privately-held financial company from Arkansas provides investment banking research, wealth management, public finance, and insurance brokerage services through its roughly 30 offices located mostly in Southern and Eastern US. It also has business lines related to institutional sales and trading, fixed income sales and trading, private wealth management, and capital management. Beyond its service offerings, the company's private equity arm Stephens Capital Partners holds a portfolio with some 45 companies.

	Annual Growth	12/09	12/10	12/11	12/12	12/13
Assets ($mil.)	(8.6%)	–	–	–	436.4	399.0
Net income ($ mil.)	58.5%	–	–	–	87.8	139.2
Market value ($ mil.)	–	–	–	–	–	–
Employees	–	–	–	–	–	475

STEPHENSON WHOLESALE COMPANY, INC.

230 S 22ND AVE
DURANT, OK 747015646
Phone: 580 920-0125
Fax: –
Web: www.inwsupply.com

CEO: –
CFO: –
HR: –
FYE: December 31
Type: Private

Buying a candy bar and a box of nails is made easier thanks to Stephenson Wholesale. Operating through subsidiaries Indian National Wholesale Company and GLC Marketing, the company is a leading supplier of food and non-food goods to convenience stores and other retail outlets in Oklahoma and Texas. It also distributes goods to snack bars, concessions operators, and tribal smoke shops. The family-owned company was founded in 1953 by Ralphen Cross.

	Annual Growth	12/14	12/15	12/16	12/17	12/18
Sales ($mil.)	(2.2%)	–	316.1	297.7	295.3	295.9
Net income ($ mil.)	48.7%	–	0.8	(0.5)	(5.3)	2.7
Market value ($ mil.)	–	–	–	–	–	–
Employees	–	–	–	–	–	305

STEREOTAXIS INC

710 North Tucker Boulevard, Suite 110
St. Louis, MO 63101
Phone: 314 678-6100
Fax: 314 678-6110
Web: www.stereotaxis.com

ASE: STXS
CEO: –
CFO: –
HR: –
FYE: December 31
Type: Public

Stereotaxis can drive in the fast lane through your veins because it has the road map to your heart. The company's systems are used to treat abnormal heart rhythms known as arrhythmias, as well as coronary artery disease. Via digital remote control, doctors steer catheters, guidewires, and stent delivery devices through blood vessels all the way to the chambers of the heart (and all the way back out, if necessary) in a procedure that is less invasive than traditional heart surgeries. Stereotaxis markets the cardiology instrument control system to interventional surgery labs (or "cath labs"), research hospitals, and large commercial medical centers worldwide.

	Annual Growth	12/19	12/20	12/21	12/22	12/23
Sales ($mil.)	(1.9%)	28.9	26.6	35.0	28.1	26.8
Net income ($ mil.)	–	(4.6)	(6.6)	(10.7)	(18.3)	(20.7)
Market value ($ mil.)	(24.2%)	428.2	412.0	501.9	167.6	141.7
Employees	0.8%	118	120	130	130	122

STERICYCLE INC.

2355 Waukegan Road
Bannockburn, IL 60015
Phone: 847 367-5910
Fax: –
Web: www.stericycle.com

NMS: SRCL
CEO: Cindy J Miller
CFO: Janet H Zelenka
HR: –
FYE: December 31
Type: Public

Stericycle is a global business-to-business services company and a leading provider of compliance-based solutions that protects people, promotes health and safeguards the environment. The majority of its customers are healthcare businesses. It has grown from a small start-up in medical waste management into a leader across a range of increasingly complex and highly regulated arenas, serving healthcare organizations and commercial businesses of every size through Regulated Waste and Compliance Services and Secure Information Destruction Services. Founded in 1989, Stericycle serves customers in the US and about 15 other countries worldwide, generating 75% of its revenue in the US.

	Annual Growth	12/19	12/20	12/21	12/22	12/23
Sales ($mil.)	(5.3%)	3,308.9	2,675.5	2,646.9	2,704.7	2,659.3
Net income ($ mil.)	–	(346.8)	(57.3)	(27.8)	56.0	(21.4)
Market value ($ mil.)	(6.1%)	5,908.8	6,420.0	5,522.7	4,619.8	4,589.3
Employees	(8.8%)	19,500	15,000	15,000	15,000	13,500

STERIS INSTRUMENT MANAGEMENT SERVICES, INC.

3316 2ND AVE N
BIRMINGHAM, AL 352221214
Phone: 800 783-9251
Fax: –
Web: www.steris-ims.com

CEO: Gene Robinson
CFO: David Strevy
HR: –
FYE: December 31
Type: Private

STERIS Instrument Management Services (STERIS IMS) repairs, sterilizes, and maintains medical and surgical equipment for health care providers. The company specializes in surgical device, instrument, and scope repair, as well as outsourced management of sterilization departments. It also provides consulting to help hospitals and surgery centers improve their sterile processing procedures. In addition, STERIS IMS sells products such as instrument cabinets and cleaning devices, as well as certified pre-owned surgical equipment. The company is a subsidiary of sterilization equipment maker STERIS.

	Annual Growth	12/05	12/06	12/07	12/08	12/12
Sales ($mil.)	10.5%	–	–	–	79.0	117.9
Net income ($ mil.)	26.7%	–	–	–	1.8	4.6
Market value ($ mil.)	–	–	–	–	–	–
Employees	–	–	–	–	–	1,155

STERLING INFRASTRUCTURE INC

1800 Hughes Landing Blvd.
The Woodlands, TX 77380
Phone: 281 214-0777
Fax: –
Web: www.strlco.com

NMS: STRL
CEO: Joseph A Cutillo
CFO: Ronald A Ballschmiede
HR: –
FYE: December 31
Type: Public

Sterling Construction company specializes in the building, reconstruction, and repair of transportation and water infrastructure. It also works on specialty projects such as excavation, shoring, and drilling. The heavy civil construction company and its subsidiaries (Texas Sterling Construction, Ralph L. Wadsworth Contractors, RDI Foundation Drilling, Myers and Sons, Banicki Construction, and Road and Highway Builders) primarily serve public sector clients throughout the Southwest and West. Transportation projects include excavation and asphalt paving, as well as construction of bridges and rail systems. Water projects include work on sewers and storm drainage systems.

	Annual Growth	12/19	12/20	12/21	12/22	12/23
Sales ($mil.)	15.0%	1,126.3	1,427.4	1,581.8	1,769.4	1,972.2
Net income ($ mil.)	36.5%	39.9	42.3	62.6	106.5	138.7
Market value ($ mil.)	58.1%	435.4	575.5	813.4	1,014.4	2,719.3
Employees	1.7%	2,800	2,600	2,900	3,200	3,000

STERLING SUGARS, INC.

611 IRISH BEND RD
FRANKLIN, LA 705383345
Phone: 337 828-0620
Fax: –
Web: www.sterlingsugars.com

CEO: Craig P Caillier
CFO: –
HR: –
FYE: July 31
Type: Private

Sterling Sugars creates splendid sweetness. The company processes sugarcane to make raw sugar, cane syrup, and blackstrap molasses for sale to sugar refiners and candy and other food manufacturers. Sterling Sugars owns cane cropland, which supplies 35% of the company's raw material. the other 65% is purchased from other growers. It processes about 1.2 million tons of cane per year at its mill in Franklin, Louisiana. Sterling also leases land for oil and natural gas exploration. The company is a subsidiary of M A Patout & Son; it was taken private by shareholders in 2005. Sterling Sugars was founded in 1807.

	Annual Growth	07/13	07/14	07/15	07/16	07/19
Sales ($mil.)	2.2%	–	–	64.2	79.9	70.1
Net income ($ mil.)	(5.2%)	–	–	4.5	3.4	3.6
Market value ($ mil.)	–	–	–	–	–	–
Employees	–	–	–	–	–	188

STETSON UNIVERSITY, INC.

421 N WOODLAND BLVD
DELAND, FL 327238300
Phone: 386 822-7000
Fax: –
Web: www.stetson.edu

CEO: –
CFO: –
HR: –
FYE: June 30
Type: Private

Not everyone at Stetson University wears a cowboy hat but there is a connection (it was named after hat maker and benefactor, John B. Stetson). The school offers Stetson offers 73 academic programs with undergraduate and graduate studies offered through its College of Arts and Sciences, School of Business Administration, School of Music, and College of Law. The university enrolls about 2,200 undergraduate students. Stetson has four campuses located in DeLand (main), Celebration (graduate degrees and continuing education), Tampa (law), and St. Petersburg/Gulfport (law). The university enrolls about 3,900 students a year, of which 2,500 are undergraduate students and about 1,400 graduate students, from 43 states, the District of Columbia and 47 other nations.

	Annual Growth	06/18	06/19	06/20	06/21	06/22
Sales ($mil.)	8.8%	–	–	246.6	288.5	291.6
Net income ($ mil.)	179.7%	–	–	5.2	41.9	40.8
Market value ($ mil.)	–	–	–	–	–	–
Employees	–	–	–	–	–	1,033

STEVENS COMMUNITY MEDICAL CENTER, INC

400 E 1ST ST
MORRIS, MN 562671408
Phone: 320 589-1313
Fax: –
Web: www.scmcinc.org

CEO: Jason Breuer
CFO: –
HR: Becky Anderson
FYE: December 31
Type: Private

Stevens Community Medical Center (SCMC) provides general medical and surgical care to residents in the Morris, Minnesota area. Specialized programs provided by SCMC include kidney dialysis, chemical dependency treatment, and outpatient cardiac rehabilitation. The medical center also offers maternity care, emergency medicine, and home and hospice care. SCMC was established in 1951.

	Annual Growth	12/17	12/18	12/19	12/21	12/22
Sales ($mil.)	6.8%	–	38.7	38.5	47.3	50.3
Net income ($ mil.)	–	–	(0.1)	1.3	7.2	5.5
Market value ($ mil.)	–	–	–	–	–	–
Employees	–	–	–	–	–	300

STEVENS TRANSPORT, INC.

9757 MILITARY PKWY
DALLAS, TX 752274805
Phone: 972 216-9000
Fax: –
Web: www.stevenstransport.com

CEO: –
CFO: –
HR: John Brandt
FYE: December 31
Type: Private

Staying cool is a must for Stevens Transport. An irregular-route, refrigerated truckload carrier (or reefer), Stevens hauls temperature-controlled cargo throughout the US, covering the 48 contiguous states. Through alliances Stevens also covers every province in Canada and every state in Mexico. The company operates a fleet of about 2,000 Kenworth and Peterbuilt tractors and 3,500 Thermo King refrigerated trailers from a network of more than a dozen service centers. Partnerships with railroads allow Stevens to arrange intermodal transport of temperature-controlled cargo. The company also provides third-party logistics services. Stevens Transport was founded in 1980.

	Annual Growth	12/07	12/08	12/11	12/12	12/15
Sales ($mil.)	2.8%	–	550.0	566.9	607.4	668.7
Net income ($ mil.)	505.7%	–	0.0	76.5	85.3	87.0
Market value ($ mil.)	–	–	–	–	–	–
Employees	–	–	–	–	–	2,100

STEVENSON UNIVERSITY INC.

1525 GREENSPRING VALLEY RD
STEVENSON, MD 211530641
Phone: 410 486-7000
Fax: –
Web: www.stevenson.edu

CEO: Henry D Felton IV
CFO: –
HR: –
FYE: June 30
Type: Private

Stevenson University is a career-focused liberal arts college with about 4,300 undergraduate and graduate students. It has more than 500 faculty members and a student-to-teacher ratio of 15:1. The school has two locations in Stevenson and Owings Mills, Maryland, near Baltimore. Stevenson University offers more than 20 bachelor's degree programs, as well as a handful of master's degree programs, at six schools in areas including business and leadership, education, design, humanities, information technologies, and forensic studies. About 83% of the student body are Maryland residents.

	Annual Growth	06/13	06/14	06/15	06/16	06/20
Sales ($mil.)	(8.0%)	–	141.4	143.7	99.5	86.0
Net income ($ mil.)	(0.3%)	–	8.2	5.4	(4.0)	8.0
Market value ($ mil.)	–	–	–	–	–	–
Employees	–	–	–	–	–	550

STEWARD HEALTH CARE SYSTEM LLC

1900 N PEARL ST STE 2400
DALLAS, TX 752012470
Phone: 469 341-8800
Fax: –
Web: www.steward.org

CEO: –
CFO: –
HR: Susan Pacheco
FYE: September 30
Type: Private

Steward Health Care System is the largest private, tax-paying hospital operator in the country. With a total of more than 7,900 beds, Steward Health operates about 35 hospitals in nine states, including Holy Family Hospital, Norwood Hospital, St. Elizabeth's Medical Center, St. Joseph's Medical Center, and Wadley Regional Medical Center. Steward Health serves its patients through a closely integrated network of hospitals, multispecialty medical groups, urgent care centers, skilled nursing facilities and behavioral health centers.

	Annual Growth	09/03	09/04	09/05	09/06	09/07
Sales ($mil.)	572.6%	–	–	27.4	1,220.5	1,240.7
Net income ($ mil.)	272.9%	–	–	2.2	47.6	30.5
Market value ($ mil.)	–	–	–	–	–	–
Employees	–	–	–	–	–	37,000

STEWARD SHARON REGIONAL HEALTH SYSTEM, INC.

740 E STATE ST
SHARON, PA 161463328
Phone: 724 983-3911
Fax: –
Web: www.sharonregionalmedical.org

CEO: –
CFO: Rachel Jones
HR: –
FYE: June 30
Type: Private

Ready to show some mercy to the ill in Mercer County is Sharon Regional Health System (SRHS) serving residents throughout northwestern Pennsylvania and northeastern Ohio. The not-for-profit hospital has some 240 beds and operates a network of nearly 20 outpatient clinics. Specialty services include behavioral health care, cancer treatment, home health and hospice care, women's health services, rehabilitation, and speech and occupational therapy. As one of the region's primary health care providers, SRHS has had to work to keep up with patient demand by opening a new $2 million diagnostic and imaging clinic, expanding existing facilities, and adding new care programs such as its Cancer Genetics Program.

STEWART & STEVENSON INC.

1000 Louisiana St., Suite 5900
Houston, TX 77002
Phone: 713 751-2700
Fax: –
Web: –

CEO: –
CFO: Jack L Pieper
HR: Jonathan Mulder
FYE: January 31
Type: Public

Stewart & Stevenson is a manufacturer and distributor of premier equipment, parts, services, and rental products. Stewart & Stevenson operates two segments: Parts and Services. It offers a broad product line from world-class manufacturers, along with aftermarket parts and services, training, and rental solutions. It serves domestic and global markets through a strategic network of sales and service centers in national and international locations. Its technicians are factory-certified, cross-trained on multiple systems, and fully capable of servicing and repairing equipment and components provided by many different manufacturers. Its turnkey power solutions rental service includes industrial power generator systems, air compressors, lift trucks, and railcar movers. In 1902, the company began as a blacksmith and carriage shop in Houston, Texas.

	Annual Growth	01/08	01/09	01/10	01/11	01/12
Sales ($mil.)	(0.2%)	1,335.4	1,217.1	688.7	861.2	1,324.0
Net income ($ mil.)	1.6%	91.8	50.6	(23.9)	(10.0)	97.9
Market value ($ mil.)	–	–	–	–	–	–
Employees	(3.7%)	3,374	2,852	2,276	2,300	2,900

STEWART BUILDERS, INC.

23000 NW LAKE DR
HOUSTON, TX 770955344
Phone: 713 983-8002
Fax: –
Web: www.keystoneconcrete.com

CEO: –
CFO: –
HR: –
FYE: December 31
Type: Private

Concrete is the key to Stewart Builders' success in the construction industry. Stewart Builders, through main subsidiaries Keystone Concrete Placement and Keystone Structural Concrete, provides concrete construction services for commercial, industrial, and institutional facilities, as well as for residential markets, primarily serving working on projects in the Lone Star State. Other subsidiaries do site work and construct basements. President Don Stewart and his sons founded the firm in 1993. The company has operations in Austin, Georgetown, Houston, and San Antonio, Texas.

	Annual Growth	12/08	12/09	12/10	12/12	12/13
Sales ($mil.)	18.1%	–	–	144.0	206.6	237.0
Net income ($ mil.)	–	–	–	–	5.1	10.2
Market value ($ mil.)	–	–	–	–	–	–
Employees	–	–	–	–	–	1,400

STEWART INFORMATION SERVICES CORP

NYS: STC

1360 Post Oak Blvd., Suite 100
Houston, TX 77056
Phone: 713 625-8100
Fax: 713 629-2244
Web: www.stewart.com

CEO: Frederick H Eppinger Jr
CFO: David C Hisey
HR: –
FYE: December 31
Type: Public

Real estate services company Stewart Information Services distributes residential and commercial title insurance policies and conducts closing and settlement through offices and independent agencies in the US and abroad network of regional offices in Canada, the UK, Australia, Europe, the Caribbean and Mexico. It provides appraisal management services; search and valuation services; online notarization and closing services, loan origination, home and personal insurance services; tax-deferred exchanges; and technology to streamline the real estate process. Stewart was established in 1893 and is headquartered in Houston, Texas. Around 95% of the company's sales were generated in the US.

	Annual Growth	12/19	12/20	12/21	12/22	12/23
Assets ($mil.)	14.1%	1,592.8	1,978.6	2,813.4	2,737.9	2,702.9
Net income ($ mil.)	(21.1%)	78.6	154.9	323.2	162.3	30.4
Market value ($ mil.)	9.6%	1,116.4	1,323.6	2,182.2	1,169.5	1,608.0
Employees	6.4%	5,300	5,800	7,300	7,100	6,800

STEWART'S SHOPS CORP.

2907 STATE ROUTE 9
BALLSTON SPA, NY 120204201
Phone: 518 581-1201
Fax: –
Web: www.stewartsshops.com

CEO: –
CFO: –
HR: Taylor Rozell
FYE: January 02
Type: Private

I scream, you scream, we all scream for Stewart's ice cream -- especially if we live in upstate New York or Vermont, home to some 330 Stewart's Shops. The chain of convenience stores sells more than 3,000 products across 30-plus counties. They include dairy items, groceries, food to go (soup, sandwiches, hot entrees), beer, coffee, gasoline, and, of course, ice cream. In addition to its retail business, the company owns about 100 rental properties, including banks, hair salons, and apartments, near its stores. Stewart's Shops, formerly known as Stewart's Ice Cream Company, was established in 1945. The founding Dake family owns about two-thirds of the company; employee compensation plans own the rest.

	Annual Growth	12/16	12/17	12/19*	01/21	01/22
Sales ($mil.)	7.0%	–	1,542.7	1,699.5	1,667.1	2,164.1
Net income ($ mil.)	12.1%	–	93.0	124.5	166.5	164.4
Market value ($ mil.)	–	–	–	–	–	–
Employees	–	–	–	–	–	5,500

*Fiscal year change

STG LLC

2650 PARK TOWER DR STE 300B
VIENNA, VA 22180
Phone: 703 691-2480
Fax: –
Web: www.stg.com

CEO: –
CFO: –
HR: Colleen Miller
FYE: December 31
Type: Private

STG provides technical TLC to government agencies. Serving the US Defense Department and about 50 other federal agencies, the company provides information technology services such as project management, application development, network implementation, security systems support, and IT systems integration. It also offers mission-critical technology, cyber, and data solutions to its customers worldwide. The company gathers and analyzes data from multiple sources to provide high quality actionable intelligence. STG is a wholly-owned subsidiary of SOS International LLC (SOSi).

	Annual Growth	12/10	12/11	12/12	12/13	12/14
Assets ($mil.)	(3.6%)	–	80.5	91.4	83.0	72.1
Net income ($ mil.)	(40.2%)	–	20.2	5.9	3.8	4.3
Market value ($ mil.)	–	–	–	–	–	–
Employees	–	–	–	–	–	800

STIFEL FINANCIAL CORP

NYS: SF

501 North Broadway
St. Louis, MO 63102-2188
Phone: 314 342-2000
Fax: –
Web: www.stifel.com

CEO: Ronald J Kruszewski
CFO: James M Marischen
HR: –
FYE: December 31
Type: Public

Financial holding company Stifel Financial, through its wholly owned subsidiaries, is principally engaged in retail brokerage; securities trading; investment banking; investment advisory; retail, consumer, and commercial banking; and related financial services. Some of its subsidiaries include Stifel Independent Advisors (SIA), an independent contractor broker-dealer firm; Keefe, Bruyette & Woods, Inc. (KBW), Miller Buckfire & Co, and Vining Sparks IBG, broker-dealer firms; and 1919 Investment Counsel, LLC, an asset management firm. The company's major geographic area of concentration is throughout the US (about 95% of total revenue), with a growing presence in the UK, Europe, and Canada.

	Annual Growth	12/19	12/20	12/21	12/22	12/23
Assets ($mil.)	11.3%	24,610	26,604	34,050	37,196	37,727
Net income ($ mil.)	3.9%	448.4	503.5	824.9	662.2	522.5
Market value ($ mil.)	3.3%	6,129.4	5,099.6	7,116.8	5,899.0	6,988.4
Employees	2.0%	8,300	8,500	8,600	9,000	9,000

STILES CORPORATION

201 E LAS OLAS BLVD STE 1200
FORT LAUDERDALE, FL 333014434
Phone: 954 627-9150
Fax: –
Web: www.stiles.com

CEO: Kenneth Stiles
CFO: Robert Esposito
HR: George Bou
FYE: December 31
Type: Private

Stiles Corporation is a full-service commercial real estate development and investment firm. It provides architectural design and construction, realty services, and property management. The firm operates primarily throughout the southeastern US, with a special interest in Florida. The company's Capital Group unit offers asset management and arranges financing for development projects. Since 1951, when the company was founded, Stiles has built more than 37 million sq. ft. of office, industrial, retail, and mixed use properties. The firm's completed projects include Fort Lauderdale's Las Olas City Centre and Trump International Tower, as well as the PGA Financial Plaza at MacArthur Center in Palm Beach Gardens.

	Annual Growth	12/13	12/14	12/15	12/18	12/19
Sales ($mil.)	11.6%	–	228.3	218.9	262.6	394.5
Net income ($ mil.)	102.7%	–	0.1	4.8	1.7	4.9
Market value ($ mil.)	–	–	–	–	–	–
Employees	–	–	–	–	–	284

STILLWATER MINING COMPANY

536 E PIKE AVE
COLUMBUS, MT 590197616
Phone: 406 373-8700
Fax: –
Web: www.sibanyestillwater.com

CEO: Michael J McMullen
CFO: Christopher M Bateman
HR: Grover Wallace
FYE: December 31
Type: Private

Stillwater Mining has staked a claim to one of the few significant sources of platinum and palladium outside South Africa and Russia. The company extracts, processes, and refines platinum group metals (PGMs) -- platinum, palladium, and associated minerals -- at mines and a smelter in Montana. PGMs are used in catalytic converters for automobiles, as well as in jewelry and other applications. Stillwater Mining also owns exploratory properties of PGM and copper in Canada and copper and gold in Argentina. It produces about 404,000 ounces of palladium and 120,000 ounces of platinum annually. By-products include copper, gold, nickel, and silver. In 2016 Sibanye Gold bid $2.2 billion to buy the company.

	Annual Growth	12/11	12/12	12/13	12/14	12/15
Sales ($mil.)	(16.4%)	–	–	1,039.5	943.6	726.3
Net income ($ mil.)	–	–	–	(302.1)	68.9	(23.7)
Market value ($ mil.)	–	–	–	–	–	–
Employees	–	–	–	–	–	1,432

STOCK YARDS BANCORP INC

1040 East Main Street
Louisville, KY 40206
Phone: 502 582-2571
Fax: –
Web: www.syb.com

NMS: SYBT
CEO: James A Hillebrand
CFO: Nancy B Davis
HR: –
FYE: December 31
Type: Public

Stock Yards Bancorp is the holding company of Stock Yards Bank & Trust, which operates about 35 branches mostly in Louisville, Kentucky, but also in Indianapolis and Cincinnati. Founded in 1904, the $3 billion-asset bank targets individuals and regional business customers, offering standard retail services, such as checking and savings accounts, credit cards, certificates of deposit, and IRAs. It also provides trust services, while brokerage and credit card services are offered through agreements with other banks. Commercial real estate mortgages make up 40% of the bank's loan portfolio, which also includes commercial and industrial loans (30%), residential mortgages (15%), construction loans, and consumer loans.

	Annual Growth	12/19	12/20	12/21	12/22	12/23
Assets ($mil.)	21.7%	3,724.2	4,608.6	6,646.0	7,496.3	8,170.1
Net income ($ mil.)	13.0%	66.1	58.9	74.6	93.0	107.7
Market value ($ mil.)	5.8%	1,204.2	1,187.2	1,873.5	1,905.8	1,510.2
Employees	15.0%	615	641	820	1,040	1,075

STOCKADE COMPANIES, LLC

2908 N PLUM ST STE A
HUTCHINSON, KS 675028419
Phone: 620 669-9372
Fax: –
Web: www.montanamikes.com

CEO: –
CFO: –
HR: –
FYE: September 30
Type: Private

Stockade Companies operates and franchises more than 80 steak-buffet casual dining restaurants. Its flagship concept, Sirloin Stockade, offers a variety of beef, chicken, and pork entrees along with a buffet-style salad bar. The company also operates restaurants under the names Coyote Canyon and Montana Mike's Steakhouse. Stockade Companies has locations in Kansas, Texas, and about a dozen other states, and in Mexico. Founded in 1984 by a group of Sirloin Stockade franchisees, the company is owned by a management group led by CEO and franchisee Tom Ford.

	Annual Growth	09/03	09/04	09/05	09/06	09/07
Assets ($mil.)	(12.9%)	–	–	–	12.9	11.2
Net income ($ mil.)	28.0%	–	–	–	1.3	1.7
Market value ($ mil.)	–	–	–	–	–	–
Employees	–	–	–	–	–	100

STONEMOR PARTNERS L.P.

3331 STREET RD STE 200
BENSALEM, PA 190202042
Phone: 215 826-2800
Fax: –
Web: www.stonemor.com

CEO: Joseph M Redling
CFO: Jeffrey Digiovanni
HR: Gina Mack
FYE: December 31
Type: Private

StoneMor Partners can show you some of the best locations for an extended stay, locations where you may even want to reside permanently. The company operates more than 275 cemeteries and about 90 funeral homes in more than 25 states, primarily along the East Coast but also in Puerto Rico. It also owns most of its properties. StoneMor sells burial lots, lawn and mausoleum crypts, cremation niches, and perpetual care. It offers burial vaults, caskets, grave markers and bases, and memorials. The company has grown since its formation in 2004, when it took over more than 120 properties previously owned by CFSI (then named Cornerstone Family Services), a significant shareholder.

STONERIDGE INC.

39675 MacKenzie Drive, Suite 400
Novi, MI 48377
Phone: 248 489-9300
Fax: –
Web: www.stoneridge.com

NYS: SRI
CEO: Jim Zizelman
CFO: Matthew R Horvath
HR: Charles D Staulo
FYE: December 31
Type: Public

Stoneridge is a global designer and manufacturer of highly engineered electrical and electronic components and modules for automotive, commercial, off-highway, and agricultural vehicle markets. Its custom-engineered products and systems are used to activate equipment and accessories, monitor and display vehicle performance and control, distribute electrical power and signals, and provide vehicle safety, security, and convenience. Its products and systems are critical elements in the management of systems to improve overall vehicle performance, convenience, and monitoring in areas such as safety and security, intelligence, efficiency, and emissions. The company's top five customers include PACCAR, Volvo, VW Group, Ford Motor Company, and Daimler AG. North America accounts for nearly 50% of sales. It has over 20 locations in more than 10 countries worldwide. The company was founded in 1965.

	Annual Growth	12/19	12/20	12/21	12/22	12/23
Sales ($mil.)	4.0%	834.3	648.0	770.5	899.9	975.8
Net income ($ mil.)	–	60.3	(8.0)	3.4	(14.1)	(5.2)
Market value ($ mil.)	(9.6%)	807.7	832.8	543.8	594.0	539.1
Employees	0.8%	4,700	4,800	5,000	5,250	4,850

STONEX GROUP INC
NMS: SNEX

230 Park Ave., 10th Floor
New York, NY 10169
Phone: 212 485-3500
Fax: –
Web: www.stonex.com

CEO: Sean M O'Connor
CFO: William J Dunaway
HR: –
FYE: September 30
Type: Public

StoneX (formerly known as INTL FCStone) operates a global financial services network that connects companies, organizations, traders and investors to the global markets ecosystem through a unique blend of digital platforms, end-to-end clearing and execution services, high-touch service and deep expertise. It serves more than 54,000 commercial, institutional, and global payment clients, and over 400,000 retail accounts to some 40 derivatives exchanges, some 85 foreign exchange markets, most global securities exchanges and over 18,000 over-the-counter markets. It is also one of the leading market makers in foreign securities, making markets in approximately 16,000 different foreign securities. Serving to more than 185 countries, StoneX generates over 85% of its revenue in Middle East and Asia.

	Annual Growth	09/19	09/20	09/21	09/22	09/23
Sales ($mil.)	16.3%	32,742	54,036	42,443	65,856	59,996
Net income ($ mil.)	29.4%	85.1	169.6	116.3	207.1	238.5
Market value ($ mil.)	24.0%	853.9	1,064.0	1,370.5	1,724.9	2,015.6
Employees	19.7%	2,012	2,950	3,242	3,615	4,137

STONY BROOK UNIVERSITY

100 NICOLLS RD
STONY BROOK, NY 117940001
Phone: 631 632-6000
Fax: –
Web: www.stonybrook.edu

CEO: Carol A Gomes
CFO: –
HR: Germaine Hoynos
FYE: June 30
Type: Private

Stony Brook University, New York's flagship university and No. 1 public university, was established in 1957 as a college for the preparation of secondary school teachers of mathematics and science. Stony Brook is part of the State University of New York (SUNY) system, a center of academic excellence and an internationally recognized research institution that offers all students a world-class education. It has an enrollment of approximately 25,710 students, including some 8,200 graduate students. SBU offers more than 200 undergraduate programs, as well as more than 100 master's degrees, more than 50 doctoral programs, and graduate certificates at about a dozen colleges and schools. Most popular undergraduate majors are biology, health science, business management, biochemistry, computer science, economics, applied mathematics and statistics, mathematics, and political science.

STORR OFFICE ENVIRONMENTS INC

10800 WORLD TRADE BLVD
RALEIGH, NC 276174200
Phone: 919 313-3700
Fax: –
Web: www.storr.com

CEO: Tom Vandeguchte
CFO: Terry McGuire
HR: –
FYE: December 31
Type: Private

Change the way you store your employees with the help of Storr Office Environments. The firm is an office furniture supplier to companies in the southeastern US, carrying more than 200 products under brands such as Peter Pepper and Steelcase. It offers the usual desks and seating, as well as interior architecture, floor coverings, and office technology. Storr also provides professional space planning, facility management, and installation services for its clients. The company operates a warehouse, showroom, and distribution center in North Carolina and has offices in Florida. Storr was founded in 1914.

	Annual Growth	12/03	12/04	12/05	12/06	12/07
Sales ($mil.)	19.6%	–	29.7	34.9	42.5	50.9
Net income ($ mil.)	28.4%	–	1.3	1.5	2.1	2.8
Market value ($ mil.)	–	–	–	–	–	–
Employees	–	–	–	–	–	200

STOUGHTON HOSPITAL ASSOCIATION

900 RIDGE ST
STOUGHTON, WI 535891864
Phone: 608 873-2270
Fax: –
Web: www.stoughtonhealth.com

CEO: Terrence J Brenny
CFO: –
HR: Christopher Schmitz
FYE: September 30
Type: Private

Stoughton Hospital is a 69-bed acute care hospital that serves the residents of south-central Wisconson. Specialty services include cardiac rehabilitation, emergency medicine, surgery, and home health care. It also provides a sleep disorders center, as well as community education programs. The hospital was established by Dr. Michael Iverson in 1904.

	Annual Growth	09/18	09/19	09/20	09/21	09/22
Sales ($mil.)	5.6%	–	50.7	41.9	46.8	59.7
Net income ($ mil.)	28.6%	–	4.3	1.6	13.4	9.1
Market value ($ mil.)	–	–	–	–	–	–
Employees	–	–	–	–	–	450

STOWERS INSTITUTE FOR MEDICAL RESEARCH

1000 E 50TH ST
KANSAS CITY, MO 641102262
Phone: 816 926-4000
Fax: –
Web: www.stowers.org

CEO: David Chao
CFO: –
HR: –
FYE: December 31
Type: Private

The Stowers Institute for Medical Research is into mutant life forms. It conducts basic biomedical research on genes and proteins to study the cellular and molecular changes involved in diseases such as cancer, cardiovascular disease, diabetes, and dementia. It carries out its research by causing mutations in mice, chicken embryos, zebra fish, fruit flies, sea urchins, and yeast and by studying the results to see how normal genes function. Cancer survivors Virginia and Jim Stowers founded the organization in 1994 after deciding it was a better legacy to leave their children than a thriving mutual fund. The Stowers Institute planned to open a facility for stem cell research in 2010 but that has been delayed.

	Annual Growth	12/15	12/16	12/19	12/21	12/22
Sales ($mil.)	(5.1%)	–	66.7	73.4	116.4	48.7
Net income ($ mil.)	–	–	(14.1)	(18.3)	27.0	(42.2)
Market value ($ mil.)	–	–	–	–	–	–
Employees	–	–	–	–	–	335

STR HOLDINGS INC.
NBB: STRI

10 Water Street
Enfield, CT 06082
Phone: 860 272-4235
Fax: –
Web: www.strsolar.com

CEO: Robert S Yorgensen
CFO: Thomas D Vitro
HR: –
FYE: December 31
Type: Public

Think of it as plastic wrap for solar cells. STR Holdings operates primarily through subsidiary Specialized Technology Resources, which manufactures solar encapsulants -- polymer films that hold solar modules (panels) together and protect semiconductors from exposure to the elements. The company pioneered the development of ethylene vinyl acetate- (EVA-) based encapsulants for the US Department of Energy in the 1970s. Its PhotoCap- brand encapsulants are sold worldwide to photovoltaic (PV) module makers.The company has production plants in Malaysia and Spain, each with an annual production capacity of 3,000 MW.

	Annual Growth	12/14	12/15	12/16	12/17	12/18
Sales ($mil.)	(27.5%)	39.3	29.8	20.1	13.5	10.9
Net income ($ mil.)	–	(23.6)	(9.5)	(15.9)	(5.1)	(5.8)
Market value ($ mil.)	(31.6%)	27.6	7.4	3.0	4.6	6.0
Employees	(26.8%)	220	165	135	90	63

STRACK AND VAN TIL SUPER MARKET INC.

2244 45TH ST
HIGHLAND, IN 463222629
Phone: 219 924-7588
Fax: –
Web: www.strackandvantil.com

CEO: –
CFO: –
HR: –
FYE: August 01
Type: Private

One of Chicagoland's leading grocery chains, Strack & Van Til operates more than 35 supermarkets in and around Chicago and northern Indiana. Stores operate under the banners of Strack & Van Til, Town & Country Food Market, and Ultra Foods. The regional grocery chain offers fresh and packaged foods and has delicatessen and bakery divisions in each of its stores. Its websites offer weekly circulars and coupons, as well as feature recipes, cooking videos, meal planners, and food-related articles. The company is owned by Chicago-based grocery distributor Central Grocers, which also operates supermarkets under the Berkot's and Key Market banners.In 2017 Central Grocers filed for Chapter 11 bankruptcy protection and put Strack & Van Til up for sale as part of the filing.

	Annual Growth	08/06	08/07	08/08	08/09	08/10
Sales ($mil.)	(3.4%)	–	–	–	995.1	961.6
Net income ($ mil.)	16.1%	–	–	–	13.8	16.0
Market value ($ mil.)	–	–	–	–	–	–
Employees	–	–	–	–	–	2,000

STRAFFORD TECHNOLOGY, INC.

1C COMMONS DR D
LONDONDERRY, NH 030533441
Phone: 603 434-2550
Fax: –
Web: www.strafford.com

CEO: –
CFO: –
HR: –
FYE: December 31
Type: Private

Strafford Technology hopes to help you operate your business in an intelligent fashion. The company provides consulting services for customers looking to implement business intelligence software from vendors such as Cognos, Business Objects, and SAP. Strafford Technology's offerings include implementation, systems integration, training, support, and maintenance. Its clients come from a wide range of industries such as financial services, retail, manufacturing, telecommunications, and health care. The company was founded in 1995.

	Annual Growth	12/99	12/00	12/01	12/12	12/13
Sales ($mil.)	9.5%	–	3.8	3.2	–	12.2
Net income ($ mil.)	–	–	0.0	(0.1)	–	–
Market value ($ mil.)	–	–	–	–	–	–
Employees	–	–	–	–	–	60

STRATA SKIN SCIENCES INC   NAS: SSKN

5 Walnut Grove Drive, Suite 140
Horsham, PA 19044
Phone: 215 619-3200
Fax: –
Web: www.strataskinsciences.com

CEO: Dolev Rafaeli
CFO: Chris Lesovitz
HR: Lisa Phillips
FYE: December 31
Type: Public

Strata Skin Sciences (formerly MELA Sciences) can detect whether that mole is a sign of a more serious medical condition -- melanoma. The company's lead product is a hand-held imaging device called MelaFind, which captures images of suspicious skin lesions, compares them to other malignant and benign lesions stored in a database, and provides information about whether they should be biopsied. Strata Skin Sciences markets the point-of-care product to primary care physicians, dermatologists, and plastic surgeons in the US. Other products include XTRAC (which produces ultraviolet light to treat psoriasis and vitiligo) and VTRAC (a system utilizing a precise wavelength excimer lamp to treat vitiligo patches).

	Annual Growth	12/18	12/19	12/20	12/21	12/22
Sales ($mil.)	4.9%	29.9	31.6	23.1	30.0	36.2
Net income ($ mil.)	–	(4.0)	(3.8)	(4.4)	(2.7)	(5.5)
Market value ($ mil.)	(25.8%)	90.3	72.2	52.1	50.9	27.4
Employees	2.1%	105	115	109	115	114

STRATEGIC EDUCATION INC   NMS: STRA

2303 Dulles Station Boulevard
Herndon, VA 20171
Phone: 703 561-1600
Fax: –
Web: www.strategiceducation.com

CEO: Karl McDonnell
CFO: Daniel W Jackson
HR: Christa Hokenson
FYE: December 31
Type: Public

Strategic Education is an education services company that provides access to high-quality education through campus-based and online post-secondary education offerings, as well as through programs to develop job-ready skills for high-demand markets. It operates primarily through its wholly-owned subsidiaries Strayer University and Capella University, both accredited post-secondary institutions of higher education located in the US, as well as Torrens University, an accredited post-secondary institution of higher education located in Australia. Its operations emphasize relationships through its Education Technology Services segment with employers to build employee education benefits programs that provide employees with access to affordable and industry relevant training, certificate, and degree programs.

	Annual Growth	12/19	12/20	12/21	12/22	12/23
Sales ($mil.)	3.2%	997.1	1,027.7	1,131.7	1,065.5	1,132.9
Net income ($ mil.)	(3.7%)	81.1	86.3	55.1	46.7	69.8
Market value ($ mil.)	(12.7%)	3,878.2	2,326.7	1,411.7	1,911.5	2,254.5
Employees	4.0%	3,229	3,679	3,742	3,907	3,774

STRATTEC SECURITY CORP.   NMS: STRT

3333 West Good Hope Road
Milwaukee, WI 53209
Phone: 414 247-3333
Fax: 414 247-3329
Web: www.strattec.com

CEO: –
CFO: –
HR: –
FYE: July 2
Type: Public

STRATTEC SECURITY designs, develops, manufactures, and markets automotive access control products including mechanical locks and keys, electronically enhanced locks and keys, passive entry passive start systems (PEPS), steering column and instrument panel ignition lock housings, latches, power sliding side door systems, power tailgate systems, power lift gate systems, power deck lid systems, door handles, and related products for primarily North American automotive customers. It also supplies global automotive manufacturers through a strategic relationship with WITTE Automotive (WITTE) of Velbert, Germany and ADAC Automotive (ADAC) of Grand Rapids, Michigan. Under this relationship, STRATTEC, WITTE and ADAC market the products of each company to global customers under the "VAST Automotive Group" brand name.

	Annual Growth	06/19	06/20	06/21*	07/22	07/23
Sales ($mil.)	0.3%	487.0	385.3	485.3	452.3	492.9
Net income ($ mil.)	–	(17.0)	(7.6)	22.5	7.0	(6.7)
Market value ($ mil.)	(6.9%)	94.7	64.4	173.3	129.7	71.3
Employees	(5.5%)	4,209	3,831	3,752	3,373	3,361

*Fiscal year change

STRATUS PROPERTIES INC.   NMS: STRS

212 Lavaca Street, Suite 300
Austin, TX 78701
Phone: 512 478-5788
Fax: –
Web: www.stratusproperties.com

CEO: –
CFO: –
HR: –
FYE: December 31
Type: Public

Stratus Properties is on cloud nine over real estate investments. The company develops, owns, and manages commercial, residential, and mixed-use properties, primarily in Texas, primarily in the Austin area, where it has some 2,500 acres of developed and undeveloped land. The firm's principal developments include Austin's Barton Creek subdivision and portions of the metro area's Circle C Ranch. In partnership with other developers, Stratus is developing two high-profile, mixed-use projects in the city. It also owns a couple of undeveloped acres in San Antonio and has completed the development and sale of a project in Plano.

	Annual Growth	12/18	12/19	12/20	12/21	12/22
Sales ($mil.)	(19.1%)	87.6	30.0	61.0	28.2	37.5
Net income ($ mil.)	–	(4.0)	(2.5)	(22.8)	57.4	90.4
Market value ($ mil.)	(5.3%)	191.6	247.6	203.8	292.2	154.1
Employees	(31.4%)	140	73	73	67	31

STREAMLINE HEALTH SOLUTIONS INC

NAS: STRM

2400 Old Milton Pkwy., Box 1353
Alpharetta, GA 30009
Phone: 888 997-8732
Fax: –
Web: www.streamlinehealth.net

CEO: Wyche T Green III
CFO: Thomas J Gibson
HR: –
FYE: January 31
Type: Public

Streamline Health Solutions (formerly LanVision Systems) helps health care providers streamline business processes. The software developer and service provider offers medical records workflow and document management software that consolidates information from existing media (paper, disk, X-ray film, photographs, video, and audio) into a single database. Products include accessANYware, which captures and manages medical documents; a multimedia system for accessing patient records; and hosted medical records management tools. The company also offers application hosting, project management, and disaster recovery services.

	Annual Growth	01/19	01/20	01/21	01/22	01/23
Sales ($mil.)	2.7%	22.4	20.7	11.3	17.4	24.9
Net income ($ mil.)	–	(5.9)	(2.9)	0.3	(6.5)	(11.4)
Market value ($ mil.)	14.9%	71.4	63.3	106.5	78.9	124.3
Employees	1.4%	106	80	67	134	112

STRECK, INC.

7002 S 109TH ST
LA VISTA, NE 681285729
Phone: 402 333-1982
Fax: –
Web: www.streck.com

CEO: Connie Ryan
CFO: Curtis Akey
HR: Deann M Grovijoh
FYE: December 31
Type: Private

When a vial of your blood goes to the lab, a Streck product might very well be there to meet it. Streck makes more than 30 hematology, chemistry, and immunology products for use in clinical laboratories. The company specializes in hematology control products, which are used to diagnose blood-related problems. Products include cell stabilization kits, urinalysis control tools, blood collection tubes, and molecular diagnostic tests. The company also provides thermometers to monitor refrigerators, freezers, and incubators/room temperatures. Streck sells its products worldwide under its own name, under private labels, and through licenses. Dr. Wayne Ryan founded Streck in 1971.

STRIDE INC

NYS: LRN

11720 Plaza America 9th Floor
Reston, VA 20190
Phone: 703 483-7000
Fax: –
Web: www.stridelearning.com

CEO: James J Rhyu
CFO: Donna Blackman
HR: Valerie Maddy
FYE: June 30
Type: Public

Stride, formerly known as K12, is an education services company providing virtual and blended company. The company's technology-based products and services enable its clients to attract, enroll, educate, track progress, and support students. These products and services, spanning curriculum, systems, instruction, and support services are designed to help learners of all ages reach their full potential through inspired teaching and personalized learning. The company's clients are primarily public and private schools, school districts, and charter boards. Additionally, it offers solutions to employers, government agencies, and consumers. More than three million students have attended schools powered by Stride curriculum and services since 2000.

	Annual Growth	06/19	06/20	06/21	06/22	06/23
Sales ($mil.)	16.0%	1,015.8	1,040.8	1,536.8	1,686.7	1,837.4
Net income ($ mil.)	35.9%	37.2	24.5	71.5	107.1	126.9
Market value ($ mil.)	5.2%	1,307.8	1,171.4	1,381.7	1,754.1	1,601.1
Employees	14.4%	4,550	4,950	7,100	7,500	7,800

STRIKE OPERATING COMPANY LLC

1800 HUGHES LANDING BLVD # 500
THE WOODLANDS, TX 773801684
Phone: 713 389-2400
Fax: –
Web: www.strikeusa.com

CEO: –
CFO: –
HR: –
FYE: December 31
Type: Private

Strike Construction aims to strike it rich by constructing, installing, and testing pipelines for the oil and gas industry. The family-owned contracting firm builds and repairs onshore pipelines and meter stations for customers the likes of Kinder Morgan, SandRidge Energy, and TransCanada. It also performs state-mandated integrity tests to ensure pipeline safety and offers remediation services in case a pipe should require repairs. Subsidiary Pickett Systems designs and installs flow measurement systems for onshore and offshore use; it also offers fabrication services. Strike Construction is licensed to work in about 30 states, but the bulk of its business is concentrated in oil-rich Texas and along the Gulf Coast.

	Annual Growth	12/05	12/06	12/07	12/08	12/10
Sales ($mil.)	–	–	–	(870.6)	114.2	192.4
Net income ($ mil.)	2547.0%	–	–	0.0	7.7	7.9
Market value ($ mil.)	–	–	–	–	–	–
Employees	–	–	–	–	–	1,200

STROBEL CONSTRUCTION UNLIMITED, INC.

106 S GREEN ST
CLARKS, NE 686282755
Phone: 308 548-2264
Fax: –
Web: www.strobelconstruction.net

CEO: –
CFO: –
HR: –
FYE: December 31
Type: Private

As far as Strobel Construction Unlimited is concerned, its construction projects hold water. The company offers construction services to water, wastewater, fertilizer, and fuel-related facilities located throughout the midwestern US. It also provides general contracting services for other facility types. Strobel Construction's capabilities include concrete, excavation, tank construction, mechanical systems, and building and steel structure construction. The company has completed a variety of projects ranging from a concrete "lazy river" at a water amusement park to wastewater facilities. Strobel Construction is a family-owned business with roots that go back to 1969.

	Annual Growth	12/04	12/05	12/06	12/07	12/09
Sales ($mil.)	(10.5%)	–	–	18.6	20.7	13.4
Net income ($ mil.)	(41.7%)	–	–	1.0	0.3	0.2
Market value ($ mil.)	–	–	–	–	–	–
Employees	–	–	–	–	–	56

STRONGWELL CORPORATION

400 COMMONWEALTH AVE
BRISTOL, VA 242013800
Phone: 276 645-8000
Fax: –
Web: www.strongwell.com

CEO: G D Oakley Jr
CFO: Angela C Barr
HR: Susan Barker
FYE: December 31
Type: Private

Strong wells and a myriad of other products can be made by Strongwell, a top pultruder of fiber-reinforced polymer composites. The company's primary division is its pultrusion manufacturing operation (comprised of 65 pultrusion machines) which makes structural shapes, fabricates fiberglass structures and systems, and builds pultrusion equipment and tooling. It primarily has expertise in making grating, panels, fencing products, and stair treads. It serves such markets as energy, automotive, construction, marine, and leisure. Strongwell has three pultrusion manufacturing facilities in Virginia and Minnesota. Through these locations, the company maintains about 647,000 sq. ft. of total manufacturing space.

	Annual Growth	12/07	12/08	12/09	12/10	12/11
Sales ($mil.)	6.7%	–	–	84.7	70.5	96.4
Net income ($ mil.)	0.6%	–	–	2.6	1.0	2.6
Market value ($ mil.)	–	–	–	–	–	–
Employees	–	–	–	–	–	400

STRUCTURAL GROUP, INC.

10150 OLD COLUMBIA RD
COLUMBIA, MD 210461274
Phone: 410 850-7000
Fax: –
Web: www.structuralgroup.com

CEO: –
CFO: –
HR: –
FYE: September 30
Type: Private

Structural Group (STRUCTURAL) has overseen more facelifts than a plastic surgeon. It comprises five companies that serve industrial, commercial, and public sectors. Specialty contractors Structural Preservation Systems and SPS Infrastructure offer structural repair, strengthening, waterproofing, and geotechnical construction on everything from bridges to historic buildings. VSL provides heavy lifting and post-tensioning services (a method of reinforcing concrete with high-strength steel bars). STRUCTURAL's Pullman Power arm repairs chimneys, stacks, and silos. UK-based Electro Tech offers corrosion control and water intrusion services worldwide. The group was founded in 1976 by owner and CEO Peter Emmons.

STRYKER CORP

2825 Airview Boulevard
Kalamazoo, MI 49002
Phone: 269 385-2600
Fax: 269 385-1062
Web: www.stryker.com

NYS: SYK
CEO: Kevin A Lobo
CFO: Glenn S Boehnlein
HR: –
FYE: December 31
Type: Public

Stryker Corporation is one of the world's leading medical technology companies. Stryker offers innovative products and services in Medical and Surgical, Neurotechnology, Orthopaedics and Spine that help improve patient and hospital outcomes. Products include surgical equipment and surgical navigation systems; endoscopic and communications systems; patient handling, emergency medical equipment and intensive care disposable products; neurosurgical and neurovascular devices; implants used in joint replacement and trauma surgeries; Mako Robotic-Arm Assisted technology; spinal devices; as well as other products used in a variety of medical specialties. Stryker's products are marketed globally to doctors, hospitals, and other health care facilities via direct sales personnel and distributors. The US generates around 75% of total revenue.

	Annual Growth	12/19	12/20	12/21	12/22	12/23
Sales ($mil.)	8.3%	14,884	14,351	17,108	18,449	20,498
Net income ($ mil.)	11.0%	2,083.0	1,599.0	1,994.0	2,358.0	3,165.0
Market value ($ mil.)	9.3%	79,798	93,140	101,646	92,931	113,825
Employees	6.8%	40,000	43,000	46,000	51,000	52,000

STUART-DEAN CO. INC.

4350 10TH ST
LONG ISLAND CITY, NY 111016910
Phone: 800 322-3180
Fax: –
Web: www.stuartdean.com

CEO: Mark Parrish
CFO: –
HR: –
FYE: December 31
Type: Private

The Stuart Dean Company provides restoration, refinishing, conservation, and maintenance services for architectural metal, stone, and woodwork in residential, institutional, and commercial buildings. Projects include curtain wall restorations, bronze statue preservation, church pew refinishing, and marble restorations. The company serves a variety of customers including homeowners, corporations, and building industry professionals such as property managers and maintenance engineers. Its diverse group of clients have included AT&T, Hyatt Hotels and Resorts, The Kennedy Center, and Stanford University.

	Annual Growth	12/11	12/12	12/13	12/14	12/15
Sales ($mil.)	(1.4%)	–	–	63.0	61.3	61.3
Net income ($ mil.)	–	–	–	0.3	(1.0)	(1.0)
Market value ($ mil.)	–	–	–	–	–	–
Employees	–	–	–	–	–	450

STUPP BROS., INC.

3800 WEBER RD
SAINT LOUIS, MO 631251160
Phone: 314 544-7555
Fax: –
Web: www.stupp.com

CEO: John P Stupp Jr
CFO: Samuel W Duggan II
HR: Ed Stolle
FYE: December 31
Type: Private

Stupendous may be too strong a term, but Stupp Bros. has set a high standard as a structural steel fabricator. Founded all the way back in 1856, holding company Stupp Bros. owns Stupp Bridge (fabricator of plate girder bridges), Hammerts Iron Works (maker of structural steel used in commercial, institutional, medical, and specialized buildings), Stupp Corporation (produces electric resistance welded pipe for oil and gas transmission), and Bayou Coating (coating for steel line pipe). The company also owns a majority of community bank Midwest BankCentre. The Stupp family controls Stupp Bros.

STURDY MEMORIAL HOSPITAL, INC.

211 PARK ST
ATTLEBORO, MA 027033137
Phone: 508 222-5200
Fax: –
Web: www.sturdymemorial.org

CEO: –
CFO: Amy Posesser
HR: Cheryl Barrows
FYE: September 30
Type: Private

Sturdy Memorial Hospital has been a stalwart provider of health care to southeast Massachusetts and Rhode Island since 1913. In addition to comprehensive medical, surgical, and emergency care, the hospital offers cardiac and pulmonary rehabilitation, women's health services, diagnostic imaging, and a center devoted to treating multiple sclerosis patients. It also operates pain management, cancer, and wound care centers. In 2014, Sturdy Memorial admitted some 7,000 patients, facilitated around 700 births, and had some 51,000 emergency department visits. The not-for-profit hospital employs more than 150 physicians.

	Annual Growth	09/18	09/19	09/20	09/21	09/22
Sales ($mil.)	6.2%	–	232.7	198.1	153.2	278.6
Net income ($ mil.)	(9.2%)	–	18.6	17.0	(49.9)	13.9
Market value ($ mil.)	–	–	–	–	–	–
Employees	–	–	–	–	–	1,300

STURGIS BANCORP INC

113-125 East Chicago Road
Sturgis, MI 49091
Phone: 269 651-9345
Fax: –
Web: www.sturgisbank.com

NBB: STBI
CEO: Eric L Eishen
CFO: Brian Hoggatt
HR: Emily Frohriep
FYE: December 31
Type: Public

Sturgis Bancorp is the holding company for Sturgis Bank & Trust, which has about 10 branches in south-central Michigan. Founded in 1905, the bank offers checking and savings accounts, CDs, trust services, and other standard banking fare. Real estate loans comprise the bulk of its lending activities: one- to four-family residential mortgages make up more than half of the company's loan portfolio. Subsidiary Oak Leaf Financial Services provides insurance and investment products and services from third-party provider Linsco/Private Ledger.

	Annual Growth	12/17	12/18	12/19	12/20	12/21
Assets ($mil.)	16.1%	414.4	431.6	473.4	643.6	751.7
Net income ($ mil.)	19.0%	3.2	4.4	4.9	6.0	6.3
Market value ($ mil.)	0.3%	40.1	42.2	45.8	39.3	40.5
Employees	–	–	–	–	–	–

STURM, RUGER & CO., INC.

One Lacey Place
Southport, CT 06890
Phone: 203 259-7843
Fax: 203 256-3367
Web: www.ruger.com

NYS: RGR
CEO: Christopher J Killoy
CFO: Thomas A Dineen
HR: –
FYE: December 31
Type: Public

Sturm, Ruger & Company is principally engaged in the design, manufacture, and sale of firearms to domestic customers. Models include single shot, autoloading, bolt-action, modern sporting rifles, single- and double-action revolvers, and rimfire and centerfire autoloading pistols. Most firearms are available in several models based on caliber, finish, barrel length, and other features. Its guns are primarily marketed through a network of federally licensed, independent wholesale distributors who purchase the products directly from the company. Ruger also makes investment castings made from steel alloys and metal injection molding (MIM) parts for internal use in firearms.

	Annual Growth	12/19	12/20	12/21	12/22	12/23
Sales ($mil.)	7.3%	410.5	568.9	730.7	595.8	543.8
Net income ($ mil.)	10.5%	32.3	90.4	155.9	88.3	48.2
Market value ($ mil.)	(0.9%)	821.1	1,136.0	1,187.5	883.8	793.5
Employees	–	1,580	1,870	1,912	1,880	–

STUSSY, INC.

17426 DAIMLER ST
IRVINE, CA 926145514
Phone: 949 474-9255
Fax: –
Web: www.stussy.com

CEO: Frank Sinatra
CFO: –
HR: –
FYE: December 31
Type: Private

What do you get when you mix fashion, sports, music, and art? The inspiration behind the St ssy brand. St ssy designs, makes, and markets urban streetwear sold in skate, surf, and snowboard shops, as well as department and specialty stores. Its products include men's and women's apparel (T-shirts, jeans, jackets, and sweats), as well as accessories including hats, backpacks, and sunglasses. St ssy licenses its name for nearly 50 stores in locations such as the UK, Germany, Japan, the US (San Francisco and Los Angeles). President Frank Sinatra (not to be confused with "The Chairman of the Board") owns St ssy. He founded the company with Shawn St ssy in 1980 and then bought out St ssy in 1996.

	Annual Growth	12/09	12/10	12/11	12/12	12/13
Sales ($mil.)	22.0%	–	–	26.0	28.4	38.7
Net income ($ mil.)	13.6%	–	–	1.4	1.0	1.8
Market value ($ mil.)	–	–	–	–	–	–
Employees	–	–	–	–	–	90

STV GROUP, INCORPORATED

205 W WELSH DR
DOUGLASSVILLE, PA 195188713
Phone: 610 385-8200
Fax: –
Web: www.stvinc.com

CEO: Milo E Riverso
CFO: Thomas Butcher
HR: Edward White
FYE: September 30
Type: Private

STV Group helps create the systems through which SUVs, LRVs, and 747s can travel. Its subsidiaries and partnerships provide architectural, engineering, environmental, construction management, interior design, and planning services for infrastructure projects that include airports, light-rail systems, ports, and railroads. STV Group's security division conducts threat assessments and mitigates safety strategies for facilities. Its STV Canada Consulting joint venture is developing the Ottawa Light Rail Transit Project. The group serves public and private clients worldwide, but primarily in the US. The employee-owned STV Group was founded in 1912 and taken private in 2001.

	Annual Growth	09/01	09/02	09/03	09/16	09/17
Sales ($mil.)	2.8%	–	213.9	138.3	301.1	322.3
Net income ($ mil.)	1.8%	–	6.8	4.2	7.0	8.9
Market value ($ mil.)	–	–	–	–	–	–
Employees	–	–	–	–	–	1,700

STV HOLDINGS, INC.

7176 STATE ROUTE 88
RAVENNA, OH 442669189
Phone: 800 824-1868
Fax: –
Web: www.sirnaandsonsproduce.com

CEO: –
CFO: –
HR: –
FYE: December 31
Type: Private

Sirna & Sons Produce cycles produce from grower to marketer to consumer. The company is a fruit and vegetable supplier for the foodservice industry in Indiana, Ohio, Kentucky, Pennsylvania, and West Virginia. It delivers products from two warehouse facilities to customers that include restaurants, country clubs, schools, markets, and other institutions via its fleet of distribution trucks. In addition to fruits and vegetables, Sirna & Sons deals in herbs, specialty and value-added produce, as well as salad dressings and dairy products. It also operates a retail facility, Sirna's Market & Deli, in Aurora, Ohio. The family-owned firm traces its roots to a grocery store business in Chicago in 1939.

	Annual Growth	02/05	02/06	02/07*	12/07	12/08
Assets ($mil.)	79.2%	–	–	6.9	–	12.4
Net income ($ mil.)	260.7%	–	–	0.2	–	0.8
Market value ($ mil.)	–	–	–	–	–	–
Employees	–	–	–	–	–	150

*Fiscal year change

SUBJEX CORP

3240 Aldrich Ave. S, Suite 301
Minneapolis, MN 55408
Phone: 612 382-5566
Fax: –
Web: www.subjex.com

CEO: Andrew D Hyder
CFO: –
HR: –
FYE: December 31
Type: Public

Subjex is more than happy to change the subject, even when it comes to business. The company was originally formed in 1999 as PageLab Network to develop Internet search engine technology but changed direction when it came up with an artificial intelligence-based program that can function as a virtual customer service representative, "talking" with customers through a website interface. Subjex has since focused its efforts on developing software for individual investors that forecasts a variety of financial indexes, such as the Dow Jones Industrial Average.

	Annual Growth	12/06	12/07	12/08	12/09	12/10
Sales ($mil.)	(88.3%)	–	–	0.0	0.0	0.0
Net income ($ mil.)	–	–	–	(0.3)	(0.2)	(0.1)
Market value ($ mil.)	(80.9%)	–	–	4.2	1.1	0.2
Employees	–	–	–	1	1	1

SUBURBAN HOSPITAL, INC.

8600 OLD GEORGETOWN RD
BETHESDA, MD 208141497
Phone: 301 896-3100
Fax: –
Web: www.hopkinsmedicine.org

CEO: Brian A Gragnolati
CFO: –
HR: –
FYE: June 30
Type: Private

Don't let the name fool you, this hospital isn't just for big city expatriates. Suburban Hospital, a member of the Johns Hopkins Medicine network, is an acute-care, medical-surgical hospital with about 235 beds that provides all major medical services, except obstetrics, to the residents of Montgomery County in Maryland. Specialized services include behavioral health, cardiology, cancer care, home care, and pediatrics. Founded in 1943, Suburban Hospital serves as the regional trauma center for the county and is equipped with a helipad. Other services include a center for sleep disorders, 24-hour stroke team, diagnostic pathology and radiology departments, and a range of inpatient and outpatient programs.

	Annual Growth	06/18	06/19	06/20	06/21	06/22
Sales ($mil.)	6.5%	–	–	312.7	349.1	354.8
Net income ($ mil.)	–	–	–	6.7	95.6	(41.6)
Market value ($ mil.)	–	–	–	–	–	–
Employees	–	–	–	–	–	1,550

SUBURBAN PROPANE PARTNERS LP NYS: SPH

240 Route 10 West
Whippany, NJ 07981
Phone: 973 887-5300
Fax: –
Web: www.suburbanpropane.com

CEO: –
CFO: –
HR: –
FYE: September 30
Type: Public

Suburban Propane Partners, one of the top US retail propane marketers, distributes propane, fuel oil and other refined fuels to one million residential, commercial, industrial and agricultural customers through approximately 700 locations in about 40 states with operations principally concentrated in the east and west coast regions of the US, as well as portions of the Midwest region of the US and Alaska. Suburban Propane sold approximately 419.8 million gallons of propane and 24.0 million gallons of fuel oil and refined fuels to retail customers. The company also markets natural gas and electricity in deregulated markets. Other activities specialize in selling, installing, and servicing home comfort equipment, mainly heating and ventilation.

	Annual Growth	09/19	09/20	09/21	09/22	09/23
Sales ($mil.)	3.0%	1,267.7	1,107.9	1,288.8	1,501.5	1,429.2
Net income ($ mil.)	15.9%	68.6	60.8	122.8	139.7	123.8
Market value ($ mil.)	(9.4%)	1,509.9	940.7	964.2	1,006.8	1,019.5
Employees	(1.1%)	3,494	3,274	3,226	3,269	3,345

SUBZERO CONSTRUCTORS, INC.

30055 COMERCIO
RCHO STA MARG, CA 926882106
Phone: 949 216-9500
Fax: –
Web: www.subzeroconstructors.com

CEO: Dean Soll
CFO: –
HR: –
FYE: August 31
Type: Private

This company may leave you feeling cold, but if they didn't you wouldn't be satisfied. SubZero Constructors provides specialty contracting services for the refrigerated storage industry. The company operates through two divisions that have specialty areas of operation in thermal construction and industrial refrigeration. The company's thermal construction division specializes in building cold storage distribution and food processing facilities, while its industrial refrigeration division builds cooling systems. SubZero Constructors provides services nationally and has offices in Lake Forest, California (near Los Angeles) and Woodstock, Georgia (near Atlanta). President Dean Soll founded SubZero in 1997.

SUCAMPO PHARMACEUTICALS, INC.

805 KING FARM BLVD # 550
ROCKVILLE, MD 208506162
Phone: 301 961-3400
Fax: –
Web: www.sucampo.com

CEO: –
CFO: –
HR: Max Donley
FYE: December 31
Type: Private

Sucampo Pharmaceuticals is a biopharmaceutical company with a focus on unmet medical needs around the world. Sucampo works with a group of compounds derived from fatty acids called prostones; it uses prostones in the development of therapies for the treatment of age-related gastrointestinal, respiratory, vascular, and central nervous system disorders. It has two FDA-approved products: AMITIZA, which treats chronic constipation in adults and irritable bowel syndrome in adult women, and Rescula for the treatment of glaucoma and ocular hypertension. Sucampo's pipeline has other candidates in pre-clinical and early stage clinical development to treat a range of conditions. UK-based pharmaceutical Mallinckrodt bought Sucampo for $1.2 billion in early 2018.

SUFFOLK CONSTRUCTION COMPANY, INC.

65 ALLERTON ST
BOSTON, MA 021192923
Phone: 617 445-3500
Fax: –
Web: www.suffolk.com

CEO: John Fish
CFO: Michael Azarela
HR: –
FYE: August 31
Type: Private

Suffolk Construction Company is a national enterprise that invests, innovates, and builds. Suffolk is an end-to-end business that provides value throughout the entire project lifecycle by leveraging its core construction management services with vertical service lines that include real estate capital investment, design, self-perform construction services, technology start-up investment (Suffolk Technologies) and innovation research/development. Suffolk serves clients in every major industry sector, including healthcare, science and technology, education, gaming, transportation/aviation, and commercial. Founded in 1982, the privately-held firm is owned by president and CEO John Fish, whose family has been in construction for four generations.

	Annual Growth	08/11	08/12	08/13	08/14	08/15
Sales ($mil.)	17.0%	–	–	1,825.0	1,761.1	2,500.0
Net income ($ mil.)	–	–	–	–	–	–
Market value ($ mil.)	–	–	–	–	–	–
Employees	–	–	–	–	–	2,536

SUFFOLK COUNTY WATER AUTHORITY INC

4060 SUNRISE HWY
OAKDALE, NY 117691005
Phone: 631 563-0255
Fax: –
Web: www.scwa.com

CEO: Carmen Miller
CFO: Douglas Celiberti
HR: Chas Finello
FYE: May 31
Type: Private

Sufficient to say, Suffolk County Water Authority makes sure that there is potable water across Long Island in addition to the seawater that surrounds it. The utility provides water services to about 1.2 million people in New York's Suffolk County, on the eastern end of Long Island. The water authority's system (the largest water system in the nation operating entirely with groundwater) includes more than 5,500 miles of mains. The authority also runs the largest groundwater testing facility in the US. Suffolk County Water Authority is a public benefit corporation of the state of New York.

	Annual Growth	05/04	05/05	05/06	05/07	05/08
Sales ($mil.)	2.7%	–	–	132.6	130.2	140.0
Net income ($ mil.)	(4.1%)	–	–	16.5	9.7	15.2
Market value ($ mil.)	–	–	–	–	–	–
Employees	–	–	–	–	–	570

SUFFOLK UNIVERSITY

73 TREMONT ST STE 200
BOSTON, MA 021083901
Phone: 617 573-8000
Fax: –
Web: www.suffolk.edu

CEO: –
CFO: –
HR: Elisa Cheng
FYE: June 30
Type: Private

Suffolk University is a private, coeducational, nonsectarian university located in Boston. It provides a well-rounded education from its main campus in Boston and its satellite and branch campuses across Massachusetts. The university offers bachelor's, master's, and doctoral degree programs in its College of Arts and Sciences, Sawyer Business School, and Suffolk University Law School. It also operates the Suffolk University Madrid Campus in Spain, where students can study abroad or earn an entire degree in international relations. With 1:14 faculty-to-student ratio (undergraduate) and 1:10 faculty-to-student ratio (Law School), Suffolk University has an enrollment of about 14,480 students. The university was founded in 1906 as the Suffolk School of Law.

	Annual Growth	06/18	06/19	06/20	06/21	06/22
Sales ($mil.)	0.6%	–	230.5	330.5	225.0	234.7
Net income ($ mil.)	–	–	(2.6)	(8.7)	55.1	(52.3)
Market value ($ mil.)	–	–	–	–	–	–
Employees	–	–	–	–	–	800

SUKUT CONSTRUCTION, INC.

4010 W CHANDLER AVE
SANTA ANA, CA 927045202
Phone: 714 540-5351
Fax: –
Web: www.sukut.com

CEO: –
CFO: Paul Kuliev
HR: Cecilia Rangel
FYE: December 31
Type: Private

Sukut Construction is best at smoothing things over. The site preparation contractor provides mass grading, excavation, and clearing services for commercial developments, residential communities, and California public works projects, including landfills and storm water systems. Its other services include slope repairs, compacting, and environmental cleanup. The firm moves from 1 million to 100 million cubic yards of earth per project, making it California's largest mass excavation contractor. Affiliate Sukut Equipment leases earthmoving equipment; other affiliates are active in real estate development and investment. Chairman Myron Sukut co-founded the employee-owned company in 1968.

SUMMER INFANT, INC.

1275 PARK EAST DR
WOONSOCKET, RI 028956185
Phone: 401 671-6550
Fax: –
Web: www.kids2.com

CEO: Stuart Noyes
CFO: –
HR: –
FYE: January 01
Type: Private

Summer Infant makes products for infants and children that can be used in any season. Through its operating subsidiaries, Summer Infant develops and markets health and safety, and wellness products for children from birth to 3 years old mostly under the Summer Infant and Born Free brand names. Some of its products include booster seats, audio and video monitors, bed rails, safety gates, bedding, and durable bath items. Most of its products are manufactured in Asia (primarily China) and Israel. The company earns the majority of its revenue from the North American market, selling through retailers such as Toys "R" Us, Target, Wal-Mart, and Amazon.com. In Europe customers include Tesco, Argos, and Mothercare.

SULLIVAN & CROMWELL LLP

125 BROAD ST FL 35
NEW YORK, NY 100042498
Phone: 212 558-4000
Fax: –
Web: www.sullcrom.com

CEO: –
CFO: Robert Howard
HR: Claire Howarth
FYE: December 31
Type: Private

Sullivan & Cromwell is a leader in each of its core practice areas and in each of its geographic markets. Founded in 1879 by Algernon Sullivan and William Cromwell, the firm was on hand for the foundation of both Edison General Electric in 1882 and United States Steel in 1901. Sullivan & Cromwell has more than 875 lawyers in nearly 15 offices located in leading financial centers in Asia, Australia, Europe, and the US. The global law firm advises on major domestic and cross-border M&A, finance, corporate and real estate transactions, significant litigation and corporate investigations, and complex restructuring, regulatory, tax and estate planning matters. Sullivan & Cromwell's clients include industrial and commercial companies, financial services firms, private funds, governments, educational and charitable institutions, and individuals, estates, and trusts.

SUMMERLIN HOSPITAL MEDICAL CENTER, LLC

657 N TOWN CENTER DR
LAS VEGAS, NV 891446367
Phone: 702 233-7000
Fax: –
Web: www.summerlinhospital.com

CEO: Robert Freymuller
CFO: Bonny Sorensen
HR: Cynthia Crespo
FYE: December 31
Type: Private

Vegas can take its toll (and not just on your pocketbook). For those who have perhaps overindulged in all the city has to offer, there is Summerlin Hospital Medical Center. The subsidiary of Universal Health Service is a 450-bed acute care hospital on a 40-acre campus in the master-planned community of Summerlin in Las Vegas. The hospital's nearly 300 physicians offer care in roughly 30 specialties including cardiology, cancer, OB-GYN, and wound care. Summerlin Hospital has undergone a series of expansions in recent years that have added a Pediatric Intensive Care Unit and a six-story tower housing about 175 rooms.

SUMMA HEALTH SYSTEM

1077 GORGE BLVD
AKRON, OH 443102408
Phone: 330 375-3000
Fax: –
Web: www.summahealth.org

CEO: Cliff Deveny
CFO: Brian Derrick
HR: –
FYE: December 31
Type: Private

Summa Health is one of the largest integrated healthcare delivery systems in the state. Formed in 1989 with the merger of Akron City and St. Thomas Hospitals, Summa Health now encompasses a network of hospitals, community-based health centers, a health plan, a multi-specialty group practice, an accountable care organization, research and medical education, and Summa Health Foundation. Summa serves more than one million patients each year in comprehensive acute, critical, emergency, outpatient and long-term/home care settings. Outpatient care is extended throughout Summit, Portage and Medina counties in multiple community health centers.

	Annual Growth	12/08	12/09	12/20	12/21	12/22
Sales ($mil.)	19.9%	–	168.6	1,462.5	1,668.7	1,783.8
Net income ($ mil.)	–	–	6.5	(208.1)	163.8	(167.0)
Market value ($ mil.)	–	–	–	–	–	–
Employees	–	–	–	–	–	7,431

SUMMIT BANCSHARES, INC. (CA)

NBB: SMAL

2969 Broadway
Oakland, CA 94611
Phone: 510 839-8800
Fax: 510 839-8853
Web: www.summitbanking.com

CEO: Shirley W Nelson
CFO: Mani Ganesamurthy
HR: –
FYE: December 31
Type: Public

Summit Bancshares wants your business to operate at peak performance. Holding company Summit Bancshares does business through its primary subsidiary Summit Bank, which operates four branch offices in the East Bay communities of Emeryville, Oakland, and Walnut Creek, California. The bank targets professionals, entrepreneurs, and executives and their businesses, offering them standard business and personal checking and savings accounts as well as commercial loans and online banking. It also offers courier service for its busy business-owner customers. Summit Bancshares was formed in 1981.

	Annual Growth	12/02	12/18	12/19	12/20	12/21
Assets ($mil.)	4.9%	147.2	–	258.0	306.9	368.5
Net income ($ mil.)	1.6%	1.7	3.1	4.5	2.8	2.3
Market value ($ mil.)	4.6%	18.2	64.7	46.6	34.0	42.5
Employees	–	44	–	–	–	–

SUMMIT ELECTRIC SUPPLY CO., INC.

2900 STANFORD DR NE
ALBUQUERQUE, NM 871071814
Phone: 505 346-2900
Fax: –
Web: www.summit.com

CEO: –
CFO: –
HR: –
FYE: December 31
Type: Private

Summit is committed to remaining on the leading edge of technology, offering the newest electrical products and services available. Summit Electric Supply distributes goods from manufacturers such as Milwaukee Electric Tool, Eaton, Fluke, Klein Tools, Square D and Panduit. Products include cable, conduits, control and automation, lamps, wire connectors, lugs and terminations, and safety and protective gears. The company provides wholesale electrical equipment, supplies and solutions for electrical professionals in diverse industries such as construction, oil and gas exploration, mining, petrochemical, retail, schools, hospitals and utilities. It has nearly 25 branches located in the US and a service center in Dubai. It was founded in 1977.

	Annual Growth	12/08	12/09	12/10	12/11	12/12
Sales ($mil.)	12.9%	–	–	301.6	358.5	384.7
Net income ($ mil.)	12.8%	–	–	7.9	7.5	10.1
Market value ($ mil.)	–	–	–	–	–	–
Employees	–	–	–	–	–	675

SUMMIT FINANCIAL GROUP INC

NMS: SMMF

300 North Main Street
Moorefield, WV 26836
Phone: 304 530-1000
Fax: –
Web: www.summitfgi.com

CEO: H C Maddy III
CFO: Robert S Tissue
HR: –
FYE: December 31
Type: Public

Summit Financial Group is at the peak of community banking in West Virginia and northern Virginia. The company owns Summit Community Bank, which operates about 20 branches that offer standard retail banking fare such as deposit accounts, loans, and cash management services. Commercial real estate loans, including land development and construction loans, account for about 40% of Summit Financial Group's loan portfolio, which also includes residential mortgages and a smaller percentage of business and consumer loans. The bank's Summit Insurance Services unit sells both commercial and personal coverage.

	Annual Growth	12/19	12/20	12/21	12/22	12/23
Assets ($mil.)	17.8%	2,403.5	3,106.4	3,576.7	3,916.7	4,634.3
Net income ($ mil.)	14.7%	31.9	31.3	45.7	53.2	55.2
Market value ($ mil.)	3.2%	397.8	324.2	403.1	365.5	450.6
Employees	6.7%	383	415	439	432	496

SUMMIT HOTEL PROPERTIES INC

NYS: INN

13215 Bee Cave Parkway, Suite B-300
Austin, TX 78738
Phone: 512 538-2300
Fax: –
Web: www.shpreit.com

CEO: –
CFO: –
HR: –
FYE: December 31
Type: Public

Summit Hotel is a self-managed lodging property investment company that holds a portfolio of roughly 105 lodging properties with almost 15,335 guestrooms located in nearly 25 states. Approximately 85% of its guestrooms were located in the top 50 metropolitan statistical areas (MSAs), about 90% were located within the top 100 MSAs and all of its hotel guestrooms operated under premium franchise brands owned by Marriott, Hilton, Hyatt, and IHG. Its hotels are typically located in markets with multiple demand generators such as corporate offices and headquarters, retail centers, airports, state capitols, convention centers, universities, and leisure attractions. Summit Hotel was organized in 2010 and went public in 2011.

	Annual Growth	12/19	12/20	12/21	12/22	12/23
Sales ($mil.)	7.6%	549.3	234.5	361.9	675.7	736.1
Net income ($ mil.)	–	82.6	(143.3)	(65.6)	1.5	(9.5)
Market value ($ mil.)	(14.1%)	1,327.7	969.4	1,050.1	776.8	723.0
Employees	–	–	59	46	63	74

SUMMIT MATERIALS INC

NYS: SUM

1801 California Street, Suite 3500
Denver, CO 80202
Phone: 303 893-0012
Fax: –
Web: www.summit-materials.com

CEO: Anne P Noonan
CFO: Scott Anderson
HR: –
FYE: December 30
Type: Public

Summit Materials offers customers a single-source provider for construction materials and related downstream products through its vertical integration. The company produces aggregates (a mix of sand, gravel, crushed stone, and other materials), which it sells to customers and uses internally to produce its own cement, ready-mixed concrete, and asphalt paving mix. Summit sells aggregates to customers across the US and British Columbia, Canada. It supplies cement to US states along the Mississippi River, from Minnesota to Louisiana. Primary end uses for Summit's products and services include public infrastructure projects and private residential and nonresidential construction projects. Summit primarily grows through acquisitions.

	Annual Growth	12/19*	01/21	01/22*	12/22	12/23
Sales ($mil.)	4.2%	2,222.1	2,332.5	2,409.7	2,412.5	2,619.5
Net income ($ mil.)	47.1%	61.1	138.0	152.2	275.9	285.9
Market value ($ mil.)	12.7%	2,849.6	2,400.2	4,797.9	3,393.4	4,597.1
Employees	(3.1%)	6,000	6,000	5,500	4,800	5,300

*Fiscal year change

SUMMIT PARTNERS, L.P.

222 BERKELEY ST FL 18
BOSTON, MA 021163755
Phone: 617 824-1000
Fax: –
Web: www.summitpartners.com

CEO: –
CFO: –
HR: –
FYE: July 31
Type: Private

Summit Partners' dough rises a little later rather than earlier. The firm funds later-stage companies, preferring those that are profitable and growing. It invests in a range of industries, including business and financial services, energy, education, health care, communications, media, industrial and consumer products, software, and semiconductors. Summit Partners' private equity investments range from $30 million to more than $500 million per transaction; venture capital investments usually are between $5 million and $30 million. The company also provides mezzanine debt financing. Founded in 1984, its current portfolio includes stakes in more than 70 firms in North America, Europe, and Asia.

	Annual Growth	12/00	12/01	12/02	12/03*	07/19
Assets ($mil.)	(15.8%)	–	21.5	19.5	23.4	1.0
Net income ($ mil.)	(18.5%)	–	32.6	33.3	30.1	0.8
Market value ($ mil.)	–	–	–	–	–	–
Employees	–	–	–	–	–	1,806

*Fiscal year change

SUMMIT STATE BANK (SANTA ROSA, CA)

NMS: SSBI

500 Bicentennial Way
Santa Rosa, CA 95403
Phone: 707 568-6000
Fax: –
Web: www.summitstatebank.com

CEO: Thomas Duryea
CFO: –
HR: Ashley Remini
FYE: December 31
Type: Public

Contrary to its name, Summit State Bank does business in both the hills and the valleys of Sonoma County in western California. Serving consumers and small to midsized businesses, the bank offers standard deposit services like checking, savings, and retirement accounts, as well as lending services such as real estate and commercial loans. Commercial real estate loans account for about 40% of the bank's loan portfolio, while commercial and agriculture loans make up about 20%. Its other lending products include single-family and multifamily mortgages, construction loans, and consumer loans. Summit State Bank operates about half a dozen branches in Petaluma, Rohnert Park, Santa Rosa, and Windsor.

	Annual Growth	12/18	12/19	12/20	12/21	12/22
Assets ($mil.)	15.7%	622.1	696.0	865.9	958.1	1,115.3
Net income ($ mil.)	30.6%	5.8	6.5	10.5	14.7	17.0
Market value ($ mil.)	7.6%	79.2	87.3	90.8	104.3	106.4
Employees	6.2%	89	93	99	107	113

SUMTER COATINGS, INC.

2410 HWY 15 S
SUMTER, SC 291509662
Phone: 803 481-3400
Fax: –
Web: www.sumtercoatings.com

CEO: –
CFO: –
HR: –
FYE: December 31
Type: Private

Sumter Coatings will not render asunder its mission to coat and protect surfaces. The company makes coatings, primers, and sealers for industrial and specialty applications. Its products include metal primers, bake enamel systems, and coatings for metal. Sumter Coatings also provides laboratory and warehousing services, as well as customized coatings. Formed in 1996, the company develops products for structural steel companies, propane tanks, and the ornamental iron industry, among others.

	Annual Growth	12/04	12/05	12/06	12/07	12/08
Sales ($mil.)	–	–	–	(446.8)	11.6	12.2
Net income ($ mil.)	2332.5%	–	–	0.0	0.4	0.3
Market value ($ mil.)	–	–	–	–	–	–
Employees	–	–	–	–	–	60

SUMTER ELECTRIC COOPERATIVE, INC.

330 S US 301
SUMTERVILLE, FL 335854903
Phone: 352 793-3801
Fax: –
Web: www.secoenergy.com

CEO: James P Duncan
CFO: –
HR: –
FYE: December 31
Type: Private

One of the largest of the more than 900 US electric cooperatives, Sumter Electric Cooperative helps lights to shine across the Sunshine State when the sun does not shine. Known as SECO, the customer-owned utility distributes electricity to more than 200,000 homes and businesses across rural Central Florida (Citrus, Hernando, Lake, Levy, Marion, Pasco, and Sumter counties). The co-op operates approximately 12,000 miles of power lines. The co-op is a member of, and receives generation and transmission services from, Seminole Electric Cooperative.

	Annual Growth	12/05	12/06	12/07	12/13	12/22
Sales ($mil.)	–	–	(1,607.7)	274.2	–	535.7
Net income ($ mil.)	88.3%	–	0.0	7.7	10.0	25.0
Market value ($ mil.)	–	–	–	–	–	–
Employees	–	–	–	–	–	390

SUN COAST RESOURCES, LLC

6405 CAVALCADE ST BLDG 1
HOUSTON, TX 770264315
Phone: 713 844-9600
Fax: –
Web: www.suncoastresources.com

CEO: Kathy E Lehne
CFO: Bill Gardiner
HR: –
FYE: December 31
Type: Private

Sun Coast Resources, Inc. is one of the largest wholesale petroleum marketers in the nation. Licensed in nearly 50 states with about 20 facilities located in Texas, Louisiana, New Mexico, Oklahoma, and South Carolina, it offer a vast array of products and services including fuels, lubricants, water, propane, chemical, oil transportation, emergency response, fuel services, and much more. The company has an extensive truck fleet (more than 1,000 vehicles) and delivers gasoline and diesel fuels, marine and aviation fuels, and lubricants. It also provides oilfield transportation and services, onsite and fleet fueling, petroleum tanks, and generator fueling services. Sun Coast was founded in 1985. In 2023, Sun Coast was acquired by RelaDyne, the nation's largest lubricant distributor and market leader in fuel, diesel exhaust fluid (DEF), and industrial reliability services.

	Annual Growth	12/03	12/04	12/05	12/06	12/07
Sales ($mil.)	15.1%	–	697.8	867.9	864.2	1,064.1
Net income ($ mil.)	(2.7%)	–	3.0	13.9	7.2	2.8
Market value ($ mil.)	–	–	–	–	–	–
Employees	–	–	–	–	–	2,226

SUN COMMUNITIES INC

NYS: SUI

27777 Franklin Rd., Suite 300
Southfield, MI 48034
Phone: 248 208-2500
Fax: –
Web: www.suncommunities.com

CEO: Gary A Shiffman
CFO: Fernando Castro-Caratini
HR: Marissa Enciso
FYE: December 31
Type: Public

Sun Communities is a self-managed real estate investment trust (REIT) that owns, develops, and operates manufactured housing (MH) and recreational vehicle (RV) communities and marinas in the US, the UK, and Canada. Its portfolio includes around 670 properties with around 227,540 developed sites comprised of about 118,205 developed MH sites, almost 30,335 annual RV sites (inclusive of both annual and seasonal usage rights), some 31,180 transient RV sites, and about 47,825 wet slips and dry storage spaces. Additionally, the company owns or controls land to support developing and expanding nearly 16,200 additional MH and RV sites suitable for development. Through its taxable REIT subsidiary, Sun Home Services, the company is engaged in the marketing, selling, and leasing of new and pre-owned homes to current and future residents in its communities. The company has been in the business of acquiring, operating, developing, and expanding manufactured home and RV communities since 1975.

	Annual Growth	12/19	12/20	12/21	12/22	12/23
Sales ($mil.)	26.4%	1,264.0	1,398.3	2,272.6	2,969.7	3,224.6
Net income ($ mil.)	–	167.6	138.5	392.2	253.0	(201.0)
Market value ($ mil.)	(2.9%)	18,678	18,908	26,128	17,794	16,631
Employees	21.2%	3,146	4,872	5,961	7,594	6,780

SUN EAGLE CORPORATION

461 N DEAN AVE
CHANDLER, AZ 852262745
Phone: 480 961-0004
Fax: –
Web: www.suneaglecorporation.com

CEO: –
CFO: –
HR: –
FYE: November 30
Type: Private

Sun Eagle has soared by working on construction projects in the US Southwest, primarily in the Phoenix metropolitan area. The minority-owned general contractor and construction management company works on commercial, institutional, and industrial contracts and builds schools, churches, fire stations, libraries, and offices in Arizona, California, Nevada, and New Mexico. Sun Eagle has completed more than 300 projects for clients such as the US Air Force and the Department of the Interior. Many of its projects include educational facilities ranging from colleges, elementary schools, and high schools to charter schools and technical institutes. Sun Eagle was established by the Alvarez family in 1978.

	Annual Growth	11/98	11/99	11/00	11/01	11/07
Sales ($mil.)	5.5%	–	25.1	27.0	33.1	38.4
Net income ($ mil.)	24.7%	–	0.0	0.0	0.2	0.5
Market value ($ mil.)	–	–	–	–	–	–
Employees	–	–	–	–	–	19

SUN ORCHARD FRUIT COMPANY, INC.

2087 TRANSIT RD
BURT, NY 140289797
Phone: 716 778-8544
Fax: –
Web: www.sunorchardapples.com

CEO: –
CFO: –
HR: –
FYE: August 31
Type: Private

Sun Orchard Fruit doesn't grow any fruit. Instead, it gets fruit where it needs to go. The company stores, packages, and delivers apples grown by New York farmers. It fresh-packs some 500,000 cartons of apples harvested by 60 growers in central and western New York and ships them to food wholesalers and retailers around the globe. The company handles 17 of the the most popular Eastern varieties of eating apples including Gala, Honeycrisp, Jonagold, and Empire. Founded in 1952, Sun Orchard Fruit is owned and operated by the Riessen family.

	Annual Growth	08/15	08/16	08/17	08/18	08/19
Sales ($mil.)	(1.7%)	–	15.6	14.4	15.0	14.8
Net income ($ mil.)	(50.6%)	–	0.2	0.4	0.0	0.0
Market value ($ mil.)	–	–	–	–	–	–
Employees	–	–	–	–	–	54

SUN-MAID GROWERS OF CALIFORNIA

6795 N PALM AVE STE 200
FRESNO, CA 937041082
Phone: 559 896-8000
Fax: –
Web: www.sunmaid.com

CEO: Harry J Overly
CFO: Braden Bender
HR: –
FYE: July 31
Type: Private

Sun-Maid Growers is the producer of Sun-Maid Raisins. Packaged in the familiar red boxes with the smiling, red sun-bonneted maid Lorraine Collett Petersen offering her basket laden with grapes, the brand is seen in just about every food store in the US. Sun-Maid raisins and dried fruits provide naturally healthy and surprisingly versatile snack options, perfect for any school, office, or restaurant. The company's other dried fruits include pitted prunes, currants, apricots, cranberries, figs, dates, dried fruit, and raisin. Founded in 1912, the coop is owned by 750 family farmers.

	Annual Growth	07/13	07/14	07/15	07/16	07/17
Sales ($mil.)	(50.1%)	–	–	1,450.2	383.0	360.8
Net income ($ mil.)	84736.0 %	–	–	0.0	15.1	20.2
Market value ($ mil.)	–	–	–	–	–	–
Employees	–	–	–	–	–	800

SUNCAST CORPORATION

701 N KIRK RD
BATAVIA, IL 605101433
Phone: 630 879-2050
Fax: –
Web: www.suncast.com

CEO: –
CFO: –
HR: John Baunach
FYE: December 31
Type: Private

Suncast won't let disorganization cast a shadow over your home, garden, or garage. The company manufactures and markets outdoor storage products made from injection-molded and blow-molded plastics. Outdoor items include gardening stations, fencing, hose reels, rain barrels, sheds, deck boxes, and snow shovels. Suncast's home storage products include resin storage systems, slat wall systems, storage bins, and golf and ceiling storage. It also offers pet products (dog houses, pet carriers, storages, pet feeders, and cat care items). Through its HomePlace Collection unit, Suncast also sells Amish-crafted wooden playhouses, cabins, garden buildings, garages, gazebos, and pergolas.

SUNCLIFF INC

711 Court A, Suite# 204
Tacoma, WA 98402
Phone: 833 761-0007
Fax: –
Web: www.greenlinkholdings.com

NBB: SCLF
CEO: –
CFO: –
HR: –
FYE: December 31
Type: Public

Westsphere Asset Corporation is a holding company that focuses on privately owned banking services in Canada. Saddled with debt and mounting losses, the company restructured in 2009, and combined most of its businesses under its Westsphere Systems subsidiary. Westsphere Systems absorbed Vencash Capital that year and took over its management of more than 800 mostly privately owned, so-called "white label" automated teller machines (ATMs) and point of sale (POS) payment processing machines. Another subsidiary, E-Debit International, which provided pre-paid debit cards, was also consolidated under Westsphere Systems. Its Kan-Can Resorts time-share resort subsidiary was dissolved.

	Annual Growth	12/12	12/18	12/19	12/20	12/21
Sales ($mil.)	(15.6%)	2.3	0.3	0.4	0.5	0.5
Net income ($ mil.)	–	(0.8)	(2.9)	(0.3)	(0.5)	(5.7)
Market value ($ mil.)	27.7%	4.8	22.8	11.3	33.8	43.2
Employees	–	18	–	–	–	–

SUNCOAST POST-TENSION, LTD.

16825 NORTHCHASE DR STE 1100
HOUSTON, TX 770606006
Phone: 281 445-8886
Fax: –
Web: www.suncoast-pt.com

CEO: William Larkin
CFO: –
HR: –
FYE: December 31
Type: Private

Suncoast Post-Tension makes buildings stronger. Operating from 9 locations nationwide, the company specializes in post-tensioning, which reinforces concrete or other materials with high-strength steel bars. Suncoast uses the post-tension technique on commercial, industrial, and residential projects, including parking structures, factory floors, and high-rise buildings. Projects include the Enclave Apartments in San Jose; Foxwood Casino in Connecticut; and Isle of Capri Casino in Mississippi. Established in 1983, Suncoast is a subsidiary of Keller Group plc and often partners with sister company Hayward Baker, which prepares soil foundations.

SUNCOKE ENERGY INC

1011 Warrenville Road, Suite 600
Lisle, IL 60532
Phone: 630 824-1000
Fax: 630 824-1001
Web: www.suncoke.com

NYS: SXC
CEO: Michael G Rippey
CFO: Mark W Marinko
HR: –
FYE: December 31
Type: Public

SunCoke Energy is the largest independent producer of high-quality Coke in the Americas. SunCoke supplies high-quality Coke to domestic and international customers. Its coke is used in the blast furnace production of steel as well as the foundry production of casted iron, with the majority of sales under long-term, take-or-pay contracts. Its owned and operated plants ? located in Virginia, Ohio, Illinois, and Indiana in the US, and Vit ria, Brazil (operated only) ? operates approximately 1,150 coke ovens and can produce an aggregate of more than 5.9 million tons of coke per year. Major customers include US Steel, and Cliff Steel. In addition, the company also owns and operates a logistics business that provides handling and/or mixing services to steel, coke, electric utility, coal producing, and other manufacturing-based customers.

	Annual Growth	12/19	12/20	12/21	12/22	12/23
Sales ($mil.)	6.6%	1,600.3	1,333.0	1,456.0	1,972.5	2,063.2
Net income ($ mil.)	–	(152.3)	3.7	43.4	100.7	57.5
Market value ($ mil.)	14.6%	521.8	364.3	552.0	722.8	899.5
Employees	(0.4%)	1,171	841	848	887	1,151

SUNDANCE INSTITUTE

1500 KEARNS BLVD STE B110
PARK CITY, UT 840607301
Phone: 435 328-3456
Fax: –
Web: www.sundance.org

CEO: Joana Vicente
CFO: Betsy Wallace
HR: Isabel Figueroa
FYE: August 31
Type: Private

What do the films Man on Wire and Hoop Dreams have in common? Both premiered at the Sundance Film Festival -- an annual winter event in Utah sponsored by the Sundance Institute. Founded in 1981 by actor Robert Redford, the non-profit organization provides a curriculum for emerging, independent filmmakers in areas such as documentary and feature film, screenwriting, and film music. It also offers programs for Native American artists and high school students. The Sundance Institute preserves a collection of independent films at UCLA and holds an annual conference for producers focusing on the business aspects of filmmaking. The institute's Sundance Theatre Laboratory assists emerging actors and playwrights.

	Annual Growth	08/18	08/19	08/20	08/21	08/22
Sales ($mil.)	(2.3%)	–	62.8	56.0	34.0	58.6
Net income ($ mil.)	16.1%	–	8.6	6.7	(5.5)	13.4
Market value ($ mil.)	–	–	–	–	–	–
Employees	–	–	–	–	–	180

SUNEDISON SEMICONDUCTOR LTD

501 PEARL DR
SAINT PETERS, MO 633761071
Phone: 636 474-5000
Fax: –
Web: –

CEO: –
CFO: –
HR: –
FYE: December 31
Type: Private

SunEdison Semiconductor (SSI) hopes to be a bright spot for its parent, SunEdison. The company makes a variety of silicon wafers, a key component in semiconductors, which are the basis of electronics including computers, mobile phones, and even appliances as well as solar cells, LEDs, and other modern technology. The 50-year-old company has pioneered many aspects of wafer production. SSI has about a dozen plants, mostly in Asia to be near its customers, but also in the US and Europe. It sells its wafers to semiconductor manufacturers and wafer customization companies. In 2013, after years of declining semiconductor sales, SunEdison spun off its wafer fabrication unit to focus on its high-margin solar farm business.

SUNEDISON, INC.

13736 RIVERPORT DR
MARYLAND HEIGHTS, MO 630434834
Phone: 314 770-7300
Fax: –
Web: www.sunedison.com

CEO: –
CFO: –
HR: –
FYE: December 31
Type: Private

SunEdison (formerly MEMC Electronic Materials) turns sun into power. The company not only makes solar modules, polysilicon, and silicon wafers used in solar panels, it also designs, makes, installs, and maintains solar installations for individuals and corporate customers. The company has 2.4 gigawatts of electricity-producing panels installed and a pipeline of 5.1 gigawatts. It has also begun generating electricity from solar power and selling that electricity to utility customers. The sale of silicon wafers and solar panels are becoming less of the company's business as it focuses on solar power. In 2016 the company filed for Chapter 11 bankruptcy to reorganize.

SUNFLOWER ELECTRIC POWER CORP

301 West 13th Street
Hays, KS 67601
Phone: 785 628-2845
Fax: –
Web: www.sunflower.net

CEO: Steve Epperson
CFO: H D Rooney
HR: Lisa Baker
FYE: December 31
Type: Public

Rural Kansans bloom under the light provided by Sunflower Electric Power, an electricity generation and transmission cooperative. The utility has interests in six fossil-fueled generation facilities (600 MW of capacity) and operates a more-than-1,150-mile transmission system with 76 substations. Sunflower Electric Power provides electricity to its owners, six member distribution cooperatives which collectively have more than 51,000 customers in western Kansas; it also indirectly serves a further 10,000 meters as wholesale power suppliers to regional cities and towns.

	Annual Growth	12/11	12/12	12/13	12/14	12/15
Sales ($mil.)	(14.0%)	–	–	–	250.9	215.8
Net income ($ mil.)	(60.4%)	–	–	–	38.0	15.0
Market value ($ mil.)	–	–	–	–	–	–
Employees	–	–	–	–	–	–

SUNKIST GROWERS, INC.

27770 ENTERTAINMENT DR
VALENCIA, CA 913551091
Phone: 661 290-8900
Fax: –
Web: www.sunkist.com

CEO: Russell Hanlin II
CFO: Richard G French
HR: Diane P Johnson
FYE: October 31
Type: Private

Sunkist Growers is one business that is least susceptible to an outbreak of scurvy among its employees. America's oldest continually operating citrus cooperative, the company is owned by California and Arizona citrus growers who farm some 300,000 acres of citrus trees. Sunkist offers traditional and organic fresh oranges, lemons, limes, grapefruit, and tangerines worldwide. The co-op, which operates some 20 packing facilities, also makes juice and cut fruit packaged in jars. Fruit that doesn't meet fresh market standards is turned into oils and peels for use in food products made by other manufacturers. Sunkist's customers include food retailers and manufacturers and foodservice providers worldwide.

	Annual Growth	10/14	10/15	10/16	10/17	10/18
Sales ($mil.)	6.1%	–	–	1,207.9	1,299.2	1,359.8
Net income ($ mil.)	(37.6%)	–	–	7.0	9.0	2.7
Market value ($ mil.)	–	–	–	–	–	–
Employees	–	–	–	–	–	500

SUNLINK HEALTH SYSTEMS INC

ASE: SSY

900 Circle 75 Parkway, Suite 690
Atlanta, GA 30339
Phone: 770 933-7000
Fax: –
Web: www.sunlinkhealth.com

CEO: Robert M Thornton Jr
CFO: Mark J Stockslager
HR: –
FYE: June 30
Type: Public

SunLink Health Systems is hoping to shine brightly in the health care business through the management of community hospitals. Through its subsidiaries, the firm owns and operates an about 85-bed community hospital and around 65-bed nursing home in Mississippi, and an IT service company based in Georgia. Each hospital is the only acute care facility in its service area. . SunLink also operates a home health agency and SunLink ScriptsRx, a specialty pharmacy business.

	Annual Growth	06/19	06/20	06/21	06/22	06/23
Sales ($mil.)	1.3%	45.6	47.8	40.7	41.3	47.9
Net income ($ mil.)	–	(1.8)	(1.1)	6.9	(2.0)	(1.8)
Market value ($ mil.)	(11.3%)	10.3	6.3	24.0	7.0	6.4
Employees	–	–	–	–	–	–

SUNOCO LP

NYS: SUN

8111 Westchester Drive, Suite 400
Dallas, TX 75225
Phone: 214 981-0700
Fax: –
Web: www.sunocolp.com

CEO: Joseph Kim
CFO: Dylan A Bramhall
HR: Theresa Reyes
FYE: December 31
Type: Public

Sunoco LP (formerly Susser Petroleum Partners) pairs with its parent to proffer petroleum. It operates about 900 convenience stores and retail fuel sites and distributes motor fuel to convenience stores, independent dealers, commercial customers and distributors in more than 30 US states at 6,800 sites, both directly and through its 32% stake in in Sunoco, LLC, owned in partnership with Energy Transfer Partners (ETP). Energy Transfer Equity owns 's general partner and incentive distribution rights. ETP owns a 38.4% limited partner interest in the company. In 2016 Sunoco LP bought the fuels business of Emerge Energy Services LP for $167.7 million.In 2017 Japan-based Seven & i Holdings agreed to buy 1,100 convenience stores and gas stations from Sunoco LP for about $3.3 billion.

	Annual Growth	12/19	12/20	12/21	12/22	12/23
Sales ($mil.)	8.6%	16,596	10,710	17,596	25,729	23,068
Net income ($ mil.)	5.9%	313.0	212.0	524.0	475.0	394.0
Market value ($ mil.)	18.3%	3,085.1	2,901.6	4,116.3	4,345.3	6,042.1
Employees	(4.8%)	2,909	2,282	2,225	2,302	2,389

SUNOPTA INC
NMS: STKL

7078 Shady Oak Road
Eden Prairie, MN 55344
Phone: 952 820-2518
Fax: –
Web: www.sunopta.com

CEO: –
CFO: –
HR: –
FYE: December 30
Type: Public

SunOpta seeks to shine in several industries. The company, through SunOpta Foods Group, sources, processes, and packages natural and organic food products. The group accounts for more than 90% of sales and has grown through some 30 acquisitions since 1999. The company also owns two-thirds of Opta Minerals, which recycles industrial waste, and makes abrasives and bentonite clays for foundries, and those granules that are on roof shingles. However, the company announced plans in 2016 to sell this unit in order to focus on its core food businesses. In 2015 Sun Opta acquired California-based Sunrise Growers for $444 million.

	Annual Growth	12/19*	01/21	01/22*	12/22	12/23
Sales ($mil.)	(14.7%)	1,190.0	789.2	812.6	934.7	630.3
Net income ($ mil.)	–	(0.8)	77.5	(4.1)	(4.8)	(175.0)
Market value ($ mil.)	21.7%	288.7	1,353.2	805.9	978.6	634.3
Employees	(11.3%)	1,900	1,881	2,028	1,946	1,174

*Fiscal year change

SUNPOWER CORP
NMS: SPWR

1414 Harbour Way South, Suite 1901
Richmond, CA 94804
Phone: 408 240-5500
Fax: –
Web: www.sunpower.com

CEO: Peter Faricy
CFO: Elizabeth EBY
HR: –
FYE: January 1
Type: Public

SunPower is a leading solar energy company that delivers complete solar solutions to customers primarily in US and Canada through an array of hardware, software, and financing options, and Smart Energy solutions. Its Smart Energy initiative is designed to add layers of intelligent control to homes, buildings, and grids?all personalized through easy-to-use customer interfaces. Its SunPower Financial offers a complete range of financing products and an increased set of financing options for its customers. Its sales channels include a strong network of both installing and non-installing dealers and resellers that operate in both residential and commercial markets as well as a group of talented and driven in-house sales teams within each segment engaged in direct sales to end customers. SunPower was founded in 1985.

	Annual Growth	12/18	12/19*	01/21	01/22	01/23
Sales ($mil.)	0.2%	1,726.1	1,864.2	1,124.8	1,323.5	1,741.1
Net income ($ mil.)	–	(811.1)	22.2	475.0	(37.4)	56.0
Market value ($ mil.)	37.4%	881.8	1,388.9	4,468.3	3,637.0	3,142.1
Employees	(8.1%)	6,600	8,400	2,200	3,660	4,710

*Fiscal year change

SUNRISE HOSPITAL AND MEDICAL CENTER, LLC

3186 S MARYLAND PKWY
LAS VEGAS, NV 891092317
Phone: 702 731-8080
Fax: –
Web: www.sunrisehospital.com

CEO: Todd Sklamberg
CFO: –
HR: Bob Eisen
FYE: January 31
Type: Private

Sometimes visitors to Las Vegas stay up to watch the sun rise, and sometimes they wind up in Sunrise. Sunrise Hospital and Medical Center is one of the largest hospitals in Las Vegas. The facility has more than 640 beds and employs about 1,500 doctors. Its campus includes the Sunrise Children's Hospital, as well as a level II trauma unit, a chest pain center, a neuroscience institute, a cancer center, a sleep disorder clinic, and diagnostic imaging facilities. Other services include rehabilitation, breast care, orthopedics, pulmonary care, surgery, and wound treatment. Sunrise Hospital and Medical Center is part of the Sunrise Health division of HCA, a leading hospital operator in the US.

SUNRUN INC
NMS: RUN

225 Bush Street, Suite 1400
San Francisco, CA 94104
Phone: 415 580-6900
Fax: –
Web: www.sunrun.com

CEO: Mary Powell
CFO: Danny Abajian
HR: –
FYE: December 31
Type: Public

Sunrun provides homeowners with clean, affordable solar energy by removing the high initial cost and complexity that is used to define the residential solar industry. Its scalable operating platform provides the company with a number of operational advantages. It can drive distribution by marketing solar service offerings through multiple channels, including its diverse partner network and direct-to-consumer operations allowing it to achieve capital-efficient growth. In addition, the company claims that it has superior customer service operations. Sunrun generates revenue from operating leases and incentives and from solar energy systems and product sales.

	Annual Growth	12/19	12/20	12/21	12/22	12/23
Sales ($mil.)	27.4%	858.6	922.2	1,610.0	2,321.4	2,259.8
Net income ($ mil.)	–	26.3	(173.4)	(79.4)	173.4	(1,604.5)
Market value ($ mil.)	9.2%	3,029.8	15,221	7,525.1	5,269.8	4,306.7
Employees	22.6%	4,800	8,500	11,383	12,408	10,833

SUNRUN INSTALLATION SERVICES INC.

225 BUSH ST STE 1400
SAN FRANCISCO, CA 941044249
Phone: 415 580-6900
Fax: –
Web: www.sunrun.com

CEO: Mary Powell
CFO: Robert Komin Jr
HR: Julianne Mart
FYE: December 31
Type: Private

Sunrun Installation Services (formerly REC Solar) helps its customers bid farewell to fossil fuel-burning power dependence. The company designs and installs solar electric systems for more than 11,000 residential customers in seven US states, including Arizona, California, Colorado, Hawaii, and New Jersey. The company primarily makes rooftop panel displays for residential customers. REC Solar uses solar panels manufactured by Kyocera, Mitsubishi, Sanyo, and Sharp, and components by Satcon, SMA Solar Technology, and Xantrex. In 2014 Sunrun acquired REC Solar's residential division and renamed the company.

	Annual Growth	04/03	04/04	04/05	04/06*	12/08
Sales ($mil.)	420.8%	–	–	–	5.7	155.8
Net income ($ mil.)	–	–	–	–	1.4	(3.4)
Market value ($ mil.)	–	–	–	–	–	–
Employees	–	–	–	–	–	4

*Fiscal year change

SUNS LEGACY PARTNERS, L.L.C.

201 E JEFFERSON ST
PHOENIX, AZ 850042412
Phone: 602 379-7900
Fax: –
Web: www.suns.com

CEO: Justin Ishbia
CFO: –
HR: –
FYE: June 30
Type: Private

These Suns give life to desert basketball fans. Suns Legacy Partners owns and operates the Phoenix Suns professional basketball team, which plays host at US Airways Center. The National Basketball Association franchise was awarded to businessman Richard Bloch in 1968 and fronted by investors such as Tony Curtis and Henry Mancini. Phoenix has reached the NBA Finals twice (the last time in 1993) but has yet to win a championship title. An investment group led by real estate executive Robert Sarver owns the team; former owner Jerry Colangelo remains as the team's chairman.

SUNSET DEVELOPMENT COMPANY INC

2600 CAMINO RAMON STE 201
SAN RAMON, CA 945835000
Phone: 925 277-1700
Fax: –
Web: www.bishopranch.com

CEO: Alexander Mehran Jr
CFO: –
HR: –
FYE: December 31
Type: Private

Sunset Development Company is the developer, owner, and manager of Bishop Ranch Business Park, a large office complex in California's San Ramon Valley. Bishop Ranch consists of about a dozen buildings with approximately 10 million sq. ft. of leasable office, hospitality, health care, and retail space. Opened in 1979, the development houses more than 500 tenants, including such corporate giants as AT&T, Toyota, IBM, and Wells Fargo. Sunset Development is working with the city of San Ramon to develop a downtown hub for the sprawling Bay Area community. The mixed-use project is slated to include a city hall, a library, and residential and commercial space.

SUNSWEET GROWERS INC.

901 N WALTON AVE
YUBA CITY, CA 959939370
Phone: 800 417-2253
Fax: –
Web: www.sunsweet.com

CEO: Dane Lance
CFO: –
HR: Cristina Keach
FYE: July 31
Type: Private

Being all dried up is a good thing at Sunsweet Growers. The more than 400 member/grower-owned cooperative processes and markets dried fruit. Sunsweet produces one-third of the world's prunes (it processes more than 50,000 tons of prunes each year). Its other fruit products include prune and other juices, as well as dried apples, apricots, dates, cranberries, blueberries, mangoes, peaches, pears, pineapples, and more. Sunsweet, which has gotten into dietary supplement beverages, supplies its products to retail food and foodservice outlets worldwide. Sunsweet produces some 40,000 cases of dried fruit products every day. The co-op was founded in 1917 as the California Prune and Apricot Growers Association.

	Annual Growth	07/12	07/13	07/14	07/15	07/16
Sales ($mil.)	7.4%	–	–	261.8	277.8	301.8
Net income ($ mil.)	17.2%	–	–	81.9	103.3	112.5
Market value ($ mil.)	–	–	–	–	–	–
Employees	–	–	–	–	–	700

SUNTORY INTERNATIONAL

4141 PARKLAKE AVE STE 600
RALEIGH, NC 276122380
Phone: 917 756-2747
Fax: –
Web: www.beamsuntory.com

CEO: –
CFO: Tsutomu Santoki
HR: –
FYE: December 31
Type: Private

Suntory USA, established in the 1960s on the other side of the globe from its parent, Japanese trading giant Suntory Holdings Limited, imports Suntory products to the US market from its New York headquarters. Well-known offerings include wine, beer, and distilled spirits, such as Yamazaki Single Malt Whisky and Zen Green Tea and Midori Melon liqueurs. Other operations handled by Suntory USA include a soft drink bottling business (Pepsi Bottling Ventures), a winery, various restaurants, and its parent's bottled water division, Suntory Water Group, once the second-largest bottled water producer in the US. Altogether, Suntory USA comprises 17 companies, contributing 4% of its parent's 2013 revenue.

	Annual Growth	12/06	12/07	12/08	12/09	12/10
Sales ($mil.)	5928.4%	–	–	–	13.1	790.4
Net income ($ mil.)	1002.2%	–	–	–	5.5	60.7
Market value ($ mil.)	–	–	–	–	–	–
Employees	–	–	–	–	–	2,199

SUNY AT BINGHAMTON

4400 VESTAL PKWY E
BINGHAMTON, NY 139024400
Phone: 607 777-2000
Fax: –
Web: www.binghamton.edu

CEO: –
CFO: –
HR: Wendy Holmes
FYE: June 30
Type: Private

Binghamton University is one of the four university centers that belong to the State University of New York (SUNY) system. It offers graduate, undergraduate, and professional programs in arts and sciences, communications and public affairs, nursing, education, business, and engineering. The university enrolls some 17,000 students, including more than 13,000 undergraduate students. There are some 550 faculty members, who conduct 130 undergraduate and 90 graduate (master's and doctoral) programs. The school also offers combined degree and study abroad programs, as well as continuing education and non-degree courses.

SUNY AT OLD WESTBURY

223 STORE HILL RD UNIT A
OLD WESTBURY, NY 115681700
Phone: 516 876-3000
Fax: –
Web: www.oldwestbury.edu

CEO: –
CFO: –
HR: –
FYE: June 30
Type: Private

The college may be in Old Westbury, but its primary mission is to educate young Long Islanders and other New Yorkers. Founded in 1965 by the SUNY trustees, The College at Old Westbury began operations in 1968 at the Planting Fields Arboretum in nearby Oyster Bay, then moved to the 604-acre North Shore estate of F.Ambrose Clark in 1971. From 571 students in the early 1970s, Old Westbury's enrollment has risen to around 3,300 students today. The college offers 45 undergraduate degrees in the arts, business, and science, and confers a master's degrees in accounting.

	Annual Growth	06/06	06/07	06/08	06/09	06/19
Sales ($mil.)	4.0%	–	–	–	0.6	0.8
Net income ($ mil.)	(9.1%)	–	–	–	0.1	0.0
Market value ($ mil.)	–	–	–	–	–	–
Employees	–	–	–	–	–	600

SUNY COBLESKILL COLLEGE OF AGRICULTURE AND TECHNOLOGY

STATE RTE 7
COBLESKILL, NY 12043
Phone: 518 255-5700
Fax: –
Web: www.cobleskill.edu

CEO: –
CFO: –
HR: Lynn Berger
FYE: June 30
Type: Private

The State University of New York at Cobleskill (or SUNY Cobleskill) is one of eight technical colleges in the State University of New York system. The Cobleskill campus, which has an annual enrollment of more than 2,500 students, has schools of agriculture and natural resources, business, and liberal arts. It offers more than 30 two-year associate degree programs in applied sciences, art, occupational studies, and science, and about 20 bachelor's degree programs in business administration, science, and technology. SUNY Cobleskill was chartered by the state legislature in 1911.

	Annual Growth	06/05	06/06	06/07	06/08	06/09
Sales ($mil.)	(50.1%)	–	–	–	0.8	0.4
Net income ($ mil.)	–	–	–	–	0.3	(0.1)
Market value ($ mil.)	–	–	–	–	–	–
Employees	–	–	–	–	–	450

SUNY DOWNSTATE MEDICAL CENTER

450 CLARKSON AVE　　　　　　　　　　　　　　　CEO: –
BROOKLYN, NY 112032012　　　　　　　　　　　　CFO: –
Phone: 718 270-1000　　　　　　　　　　　　　　HR: –
Fax: –　　　　　　　　　　　　　　　　　　　　FYE: May 31
Web: www.downstate.edu　　　　　　　　　　　　Type: Private

SUNY Downstate Medical Center brings a healthy dose of education, research, and patient care to Brooklyn. SUNY Downstate is the borough's only academic medical center. It comprises colleges of medicine, nursing, graduate studies, and health; research laboratories; and the University Hospital of Brooklyn (UHB) medical centers. The main UHB facility in Brooklyn is a 380-bed teaching hospital; the Bay Ridge urgent care and surgery center in Brooklyn, and a number of satellite health centers. SUNY Downstate is part of the State University of New York (SUNY) system. Its sister campus, SUNY Upstate, is located in Syracuse, New York. SUNY Downstate Medical Center was founded in 1860.

SUPER MICRO COMPUTER INC　　　　　　　　　　NMS: SMCI

980 Rock Avenue　　　　　　　　　　　　　　　CEO: Charles Liang
San Jose, CA 95131　　　　　　　　　　　　　　CFO: David Weigand
Phone: 408 503-8000　　　　　　　　　　　　　　HR: –
Fax: –　　　　　　　　　　　　　　　　　　　　FYE: June 30
Web: www.supermicro.com　　　　　　　　　　　Type: Public

Super Micro Computer is a provider of accelerated computing platforms that are application-optimized high-performance and high-efficiency server and storage systems for various markets, including enterprise data centers, cloud computing, artificial intelligence, 5G, and edge computing. In addition to its complete server and storage systems business, the company offers a large array of modular server subsystems and accessories, such as server boards, chassis, power supplies, and other accessories. Its open industry-standard remote system management solutions, such as its server management suite is designed to help manage large-scale heterogeneous data center environments. Super Micro markets its products, sold directly and through distributors and resellers, to customers in over 100 countries; Almost 70% of its revenue are generated in the US.

	Annual Growth	06/19	06/20	06/21	06/22	06/23
Sales ($mil.)	19.4%	3,500.4	3,339.3	3,557.4	5,196.1	7,123.5
Net income ($ mil.)	72.7%	71.9	84.3	111.9	285.2	640.0
Market value ($ mil.)	89.4%	1,023.6	1,501.9	1,861.1	2,134.6	13,186
Employees	8.7%	3,670	3,987	4,155	4,607	5,126

SUPERIOR DRILLING PRODUCTS INC　　　　　　　ASE: SDPI

1583 South 1700 East　　　　　　　　　　　　　CEO: G T Meier
Vernal, UT 84078　　　　　　　　　　　　　　　CFO: Christopher D Cashion
Phone: 435 789-0594　　　　　　　　　　　　　　HR: –
Fax: –　　　　　　　　　　　　　　　　　　　　FYE: December 31
Web: www.sdpi.com　　　　　　　　　　　　　　Type: Public

Superior Drilling Products (SDP) believes that it offers just that. The company is a remanufacturer of polycrystalline diamond compact (PDC) drill bits, and a designer and maker of new drill bit and horizontal drill string enhancement tools for the oil, natural gas, and mining services industry. Its business lines include the PDC drill bit remanufacturing service (exclusively for Baker Hughes); a Drill N Ream tool division which will be merged with Hard Rock Solutions and serve as SDP's drilling tool marketing and distribution arm; an emerging technologies business which makes drill bits and custom drill tool products; and a new product development business. SDP went public in 2014.

	Annual Growth	12/19	12/20	12/21	12/22	12/23
Sales ($mil.)	2.5%	19.0	10.5	13.3	19.1	21.0
Net income ($ mil.)	–	(0.9)	(3.4)	(0.5)	1.1	7.4
Market value ($ mil.)	(3.4%)	24.9	18.4	22.2	27.9	21.7
Employees	4.5%	63	41	58	86	75

SUPERIOR ENERGY SERVICES, INC.

1001 Louisiana Street, Suite 2900　　　　　　　　CEO: –
Houston, TX 77002　　　　　　　　　　　　　　CFO: –
Phone: 713 654-2200　　　　　　　　　　　　　　HR: –
Fax: –　　　　　　　　　　　　　　　　　　　　FYE: December 31
Web: www.superiorenergy.com　　　　　　　　　Type: Public

SESI Holdings, formerly known as Superior Energy Services, Inc., provides drilling, completion, and production-related services to major national and independent oil and natural gas companies operating in the Gulf of Mexico, on the US mainland, and internationally. Its international operations extend into the Middle East, Asia/Pacific, and Africa. Superior develops specialized tools and technologies for drilling such as drill pipe strings, landing strings, completion tubulars, associated accessories, non-magnetic drill collars, and hole openers. Less than half of the company's total sales come from the US.

	Annual Growth	12/19	12/20	02/21*	12/21	12/22
Sales ($mil.)	(14.7%)	1,425.4	851.3	45.9	648.8	884.0
Net income ($ mil.)	–	(255.7)	(396.2)	268.8	(162.2)	286.5
Market value ($ mil.)	–	–	–	–	–	–
Employees	(24.9%)	5,200	3,300	–	2,300	2,200

*Fiscal year change

SUPERIOR GRAPHITE CO.

550 W VAN BUREN ST STE 300　　　　　　　　　CEO: Edward O Carney
CHICAGO, IL 606073862　　　　　　　　　　　　CFO: –
Phone: 800 325-0337　　　　　　　　　　　　　　HR: –
Fax: –　　　　　　　　　　　　　　　　　　　　FYE: December 31
Web: www.superiorgraphite.com　　　　　　　　Type: Private

The writing on this company's wall is graphite, not graffiti. Superior Graphite's products include graphite powders for battery makers; silicon carbide for the ceramics industry; and graphites used in lubricants, coatings, and rubber compounds. The company has about 20 brands with a variety of applications, such as railway lubrication, batteries and fuel cells, technical ceramics, heated pavement systems, and toner for printers. Founded in 1917, Superior Graphite provides graphite internationally, and the company maintains its US headquarters in Chicago and its Europe headquarters in Sundsvall, Sweden.

SUPERIOR GROUP OF COMPANIES INC　　　　　　NMS: SGC

200 Central Avenue,, Suite 2000　　　　　　　　CEO: Michael Benstock
St. Petersburg, FL 33701　　　　　　　　　　　CFO: Michael W Koempel
Phone: 727 397-9611　　　　　　　　　　　　　　HR: –
Fax: –　　　　　　　　　　　　　　　　　　　　FYE: December 31
Web: www.superiorgroupofcompanies.com　　　　Type: Public

Superior Group of Companies (formerly Superior Uniform Group) manufactures (through third parties or its own facilities) and sells a wide range of merchandising solutions, promotional products, and branded uniform programs for the retail, hotel, food service, entertainment, technology, transportation, and other industries. It also makes healthcare apparel, such as scrubs, lab coats, protective apparel, and patient gowns, and provides nearshore business process outsourcing, contact, and call-center support services. The company also makes and distributes specialty labels, such as HPI, BAMKO, and CID Resources.

	Annual Growth	12/19	12/20	12/21	12/22	12/23
Sales ($mil.)	9.6%	376.7	526.7	537.0	578.8	543.3
Net income ($ mil.)	(7.7%)	12.1	41.0	29.4	(32.0)	8.8
Market value ($ mil.)	(0.1%)	224.3	385.0	363.4	166.6	223.6
Employees	19.4%	3,400	4,600	6,000	6,800	6,900

SUPERIOR INDUSTRIAL SOLUTIONS, INC.

1411 ROOSEVELT AVE STE 250
INDIANAPOLIS, IN 462011006
Phone: 317 781-4400
Fax: –
Web: www.relyonsuperior.com

CEO: Robert W Andersen
CFO: Douglas P Stewart
HR: Natalie Anderson Phr Sh
FYE: December 31
Type: Private

Despite the name, Superior Oil actually distributes industrial products and provides chemical and recycling and waste management services. Superior Oil's solvents and chemicals division supplies manufacturers of paints and coatings, pharmaceuticals, fabricated metal products, and adhesives. Products under composites and fiberglass materials include fiberglass reinforcements, resins, gel coats, catalysts, fillers, pigments, and much more. Superior Oil also provides blending, solvent reclamation, and hazardous waste removal services. Headquartered in Indianapolis, the company has nine stocking facilities and transportation fleet. The company is owned by members of its management team.

	Annual Growth	12/18	12/19	12/20	12/21	12/22
Sales ($mil.)	20.4%	–	200.0	209.4	290.0	349.1
Net income ($ mil.)	20.0%	–	7.9	8.0	15.8	13.7
Market value ($ mil.)	–	–	–	–	–	–
Employees	–	–	–	–	–	300

SUPERIOR INDUSTRIES INTERNATIONAL, INC.   NYS: SUP

26600 Telegraph Road, Suite 400
Southfield, MI 48033
Phone: 248 352-7300
Fax: 818 780-3500
Web: www.supind.com

CEO: Majdi B Abulaban
CFO: C T Trenary
HR: –
FYE: December 31
Type: Public

Superior Industries International is one of the largest aluminum wheel suppliers to global OEMs and one of the leading European aluminum wheel aftermarket manufacturers and suppliers. The company has nearly ten manufacturing facilities in North America and Europe. Its OEM aluminum wheels accounted for nearly 95 percent of its sales and are primarily sold for factory installation. Globally, the company ships approximately 15.6 million wheel units. It also sells aluminum wheels to the European aftermarket under the brands ATS, RIAL, ALUTEC, and ANZIO. North America represents nearly 60% of sales. Founded in 1957, Superior Industries has grown to become one of the largest light vehicle aluminum wheel suppliers in the world.

	Annual Growth	12/19	12/20	12/21	12/22	12/23
Sales ($mil.)	0.2%	1,372.5	1,100.8	1,384.8	1,639.9	1,385.3
Net income ($ mil.)	–	(96.5)	(243.6)	3.8	37.0	(92.9)
Market value ($ mil.)	(3.5%)	103.7	114.9	125.8	118.5	89.9
Employees	(5.9%)	8,400	9,000	7,800	7,700	6,600

SUPERNUS PHARMACEUTICALS INC   NMS: SUPN

9715 Key West Avenue
Rockville, MD 20850
Phone: 301 838-2500
Fax: –
Web: www.supernus.com

CEO: Jack A Khattar
CFO: Timothy C Dec
HR: Ashley Gomez
FYE: December 31
Type: Public

Supernus Pharmaceuticals is a biopharmaceutical company focused on developing and commercializing products for the treatment of central nervous system (CNS) diseases. Its diverse neuroscience portfolio includes approved treatments for epilepsy, migraine, attention-deficit hyperactivity disorder (ADHD), hypomobility in Parkinson's Disease (PD), cervical dystonia, chronic sialorrhea, dyskinesia in PD patients receiving levodopa-based therapy, and drug induced extrapyramidal reactions in adult patients. The Company is developing a broad range of novel CNS product candidates including new potential treatments for hypomobility in PD, epilepsy, depression, and other CNS disorders.. The company utilizes third-party commercial manufacturing organizations (CMOs) for all of its manufacturing. Its products are sold through pharmacies, hospitals, as well as federal and state entities.

	Annual Growth	12/19	12/20	12/21	12/22	12/23
Sales ($mil.)	11.5%	392.8	520.4	579.8	667.2	607.5
Net income ($ mil.)	(67.2%)	113.1	127.0	53.4	60.7	1.3
Market value ($ mil.)	5.1%	1,298.0	1,376.8	1,595.7	1,952.0	1,583.7
Employees	8.9%	464	563	575	612	652

SUPERSHUTTLE INTERNATIONAL, INC.

14500 N NORTHSIGHT BLVD STE 329
SCOTTSDALE, AZ 852603641
Phone: 800 258-3826
Fax: –
Web: www.supershuttle.com

CEO: R B Wier
CFO: –
HR: –
FYE: December 31
Type: Private

This shuttle leaves the airport without leaving the ground. SuperShuttle International provides door-to-door airport shuttle services in some 50 US metropolitan areas, including Los Angeles, New York, and Washington, DC, with a fleet of about 1,200 blue-and-yellow vans. Customers are grouped by neighborhood through a central reservation system for the shared-ride service. The company also offers charter services for groups and provides executive sedan services through its ExecuCar subsidiary. Overall, SuperShuttle International carries about 8 million passengers a year. The company is a subsidiary of bus system operator Veolia Transportation, which in turn is part of Paris-based Veolia Environnement.

SUPPLY CHAIN CONSULTANTS INC

5460 FAIRMONT DR
WILMINGTON, DE 198083432
Phone: 302 738-9215
Fax: –
Web: www.arkieva.com

CEO: –
CFO: –
HR: –
FYE: December 31
Type: Private

Supply Chain Consultants (SCC) has a realistic self-image. The company provides collaborative supply chain and inventory management software and related services. Its flagship product line is its Zemeter suite of applications, which is used by companies to control inventory by estimating future product sales. SCC serves such industries as chemicals, food manufacturing, and electronics. Customers have included Corning, Sunsweet Growers, and Terra Industries. The company also offers supply chain consulting and technology support services. In addition to its US operations, SCC has an international division in Belgium. The company was founded in 1993 by president Dr. Bibi Singh and CEO Dr. Harpal Singh.

SUPPORT.COM, INC.

1521 CONCORD PIKE STE 301
WILMINGTON, DE 198033644
Phone: 650 556-9440
Fax: –
Web: www.support.com

CEO: Lance Rosenzweig
CFO: Caroline Rook
HR: –
FYE: December 31
Type: Private

Support.com wants to be a pillar of tech support. The company's cloud-based Nexus platform proactively identifies and repairs hardware and software problems, reducing the need for technical support staffing. It also specializes in phone and Web support for a wide variety of technology issues related to computer security, data recovery, networking, file management, and software installation. Support.com serves consumers and small businesses, with its offerings available through its website and through partners such as retailers, broadband providers, and anti-virus software providers. Nearly all sales come from customers in the Americas.

SUPREME GEAR CO.

17430 MALYN BLVD
FRASER, MI 48026
Phone: 586 775-6325
Fax: –
Web: www.supremegear.com

CEO: –
CFO: –
HR: –
FYE: December 31
Type: Private

The Diez Group is a fan of heavy metal. One of the largest minority-owned firms involved in the steel industry, the group owns Supreme Gear, which makes machined parts such as gears, sprockets, and pumps for the aerospace, automotive, and marine industries, and Supreme Drive, which makes USB flash memory storage devices. The Diez Group also owns Promotional Biz, which designs advertising and promotional products. A nosedive in the auto industry forced The Diez Group to close its Lapeer Metal Stamping business in 2008. Four factories that supplied parts to the automotive industry were shuttered. The Diez Group was founded in 1973 by Gerald Diez.

	Annual Growth	09/03	09/04	09/05*	12/06	12/09
Sales ($mil.)	18.1%	–	–	3.1	6.3	6.0
Net income ($ mil.)	21.7%	–	–	0.3	0.4	0.7
Market value ($ mil.)	–	–	–	–	–	–
Employees	–	–	–	–	–	45

*Fiscal year change

SUPREME INDUSTRIES, INC.

2581 KERCHER RD
GOSHEN, IN 465287556
Phone: 574 642-3070
Fax: –
Web: www.onewabash.com

CEO: Brent L Yeagy
CFO: –
HR: Brad Karch
FYE: December 31
Type: Private

Supreme Industries builds and distributes specialized commercial truck bodies and buses, such as armored trucks, dry-freight and insulated cargo vans, service vans, shuttle buses, and trolleys. Its custom-made options include cargo-handling devices, lift gates, refrigeration equipment, and special doors and bumpers. Supreme Industries sells its lineup under the Kold King, Iner-City, Spartan, StarTrans, and other brand names. In addition to vehicle bodies, which represent most sales, the company makes Fuel Shark branded fiberglass wind deflectors. Supreme Industries' customers are truck distributors, commercial dealers, and end-users mainly in the US. In mid-2017, trailer maker Wabash National Corporation agreed to acquire Supreme Industries.

SURFRIDER FOUNDATION, INC

942 CALLE NEGOCIO STE 150
SAN CLEMENTE, CA 926746271
Phone: 949 492-8170
Fax: –
Web: www.surfrider.org

CEO: Chad Nelsen
CFO: –
HR: –
FYE: December 31
Type: Private

The Surfrider Foundation wants to keep the waves clean and the beaches pristine. The group is dedicated to protecting oceans and beaches in the US and abroad. The organization has more than 50,000 members in the US (many of whom are surfers, swimmers, and other beach enthusiasts) and 90 local chapters located along the East, West, Gulf, Puerto Rican, and Hawaiian coasts. It also has branches in Australia, Brazil, France, Japan, and Spain. The Surfrider Foundation works through educational programs such as "Respect the Beach" to reduce pollution, improve water quality, conserve wetlands, and improve surfing access. The group was founded in 1984 in Malibu, California.

	Annual Growth	12/13	12/14	12/15	12/17	12/22
Sales ($mil.)	10.0%	–	5.7	6.3	7.0	12.3
Net income ($ mil.)	–	–	(0.4)	0.1	0.0	1.4
Market value ($ mil.)	–	–	–	–	–	–
Employees	–	–	–	–	–	19

SURGALIGN HOLDINGS INC

NBB: SRGA Q

520 Lake Cook Road, Suite 315
Deerfield, IL 60015
Phone: 224 303-4651
Fax: –
Web: www.rtix.com

CEO: Camille I Farhat
CFO: Bryan Cornwall
HR: –
FYE: December 31
Type: Public

Surgalign Holdings (formerly known as RTI Surgical (RTI)) is a global medical technology company focused on advancing the science of spine care by delivering innovative solutions, including the application of digital technologies. The company has a broad portfolio of spinal hardware implants, including solutions for fusion procedures in the lumbar, thoracic, and cervical spine, motion preservation solutions for the lumbar spine, and a minimally invasive surgical implant system for fusion of the sacroiliac joint. Surgalign sells its allografts implants (made from human tissue) in the US and more than 50 countries around the globe. The company generates about 85% of sales in the US.

	Annual Growth	12/18	12/19	12/20	12/21	12/22
Sales ($mil.)	(26.5%)	280.9	308.4	101.7	90.5	82.0
Net income ($ mil.)	–	(1.3)	(211.6)	(33.8)	(84.7)	(54.6)
Market value ($ mil.)	(14.4%)	29.1	21.5	17.2	5.6	15.6
Employees	(26.3%)	891	935	197	231	263

SURGE COMPONENTS INC

NBB: SPRS

95 East Jefryn Boulevard
Deer Park, NY 11729
Phone: 631 595-1818
Fax: –
Web: –

CEO: Ira Levy
CFO: Ira Levy
HR: –
FYE: November 30
Type: Public

Surge Components is a leading supplier of electronic component products. The company distributes capacitors, which are electrical energy storage devices, and discrete components, such as semiconductor rectifiers, transistors and diodes, which are single function low power semiconductor products that are packaged alone as compared to integrated circuits such as microprocessors. Most of its clients are manufacturers. The company's Challenge/Surge subsidiary (also known as Challenge Electronics) is engaged in the sale of electronic component products and sounding devices from established brand manufacturers to customers located principally throughout North America. Surge represents Lelon Electronics, a Taiwanese manufacturer of aluminum electrolytic capacitors, in North America. Surge Components was established in 1981.

	Annual Growth	11/19	11/20	11/21	11/22	11/23
Sales ($mil.)	2.8%	32.5	31.7	39.8	51.9	36.3
Net income ($ mil.)	(16.9%)	2.0	1.5	2.5	3.7	1.0
Market value ($ mil.)	(3.1%)	16.2	12.4	20.3	17.8	14.3
Employees	2.4%	40	38	43	46	44

SURGE GLOBAL ENERGY INC

75-153 Merle Drive, Suite B
Palm Desert, CA 92211
Phone: 800 284-3898
Fax: 786 923-0963
Web: www.surgeglobalenergy.com

CEO: Clark Morton
CFO: E J Schloss
HR: –
FYE: December 31
Type: Public

Surge Global Energy has the urge to acquire crude oil and natural gas properties in the US and Canada. The company's portfolio includes a well in Wyoming, which it is drilling for commercial production of oil and gas, and the Green Springs Prospect in Nevada, which it plans to tap. Surge also invests in businesses engaged in alternative fuel technologies, such as biodiesel developer 11 Good Energy. Other investments include minority stakes in two Alberta-based companies, Andora Energy and North Peace Energy. Surge divested its interest in an Argentina project in 2008 to focus on its core North American operations and investments. Officers and board members as a group own about one-third of the company.

	Annual Growth	12/10	12/11	12/12	12/13	12/14
Sales ($mil.)	–	–	–	–	0.0	0.0
Net income ($ mil.)	–	–	–	(1.7)	(0.9)	(0.9)
Market value ($ mil.)	253.6%	–	–	0.1	1.2	1.5
Employees	–	–	–	–	5	4

SURGERY PARTNERS INC
NMS: SGRY

340 Seven Springs Way, Suite 600
Brentwood, TN 37027
Phone: 615 234-5900
Fax: –
Web: www.surgerypartners.com

CEO: J E Evans
CFO: David T Doherty
HR: –
FYE: December 31
Type: Public

Surgery Partners is a leading healthcare services company with a differentiated outpatient delivery model focused on providing high-quality, cost-effective solutions for surgical and related ancillary care in support of both patients and physicians. The company owns or operates (primarily in partnership with physicians) a portfolio of over 145 surgical facilities in the US comprised of more than 125 ambulatory surgical centers (ASCs) and about 20 surgical hospitals in about 30 states, including a majority interest in roughly 95 of the surgical facilities. Surgery Partners team is comprised of more than 12,000 employees and some 4,600 affiliated physicians, serving more than 600,000 patients annually. Founded in 2004, the company is one of the largest and fastest-growing surgical services businesses in the US.

	Annual Growth	12/19	12/20	12/21	12/22	12/23
Sales ($mil.)	10.6%	1,831.4	1,860.1	2,225.1	2,539.3	2,743.3
Net income ($ mil.)	–	(74.8)	(116.1)	(70.9)	(54.6)	(11.9)
Market value ($ mil.)	19.6%	1,981.8	3,672.5	6,761.4	3,526.9	4,049.7
Employees	8.9%	9,600	10,800	10,900	12,200	13,500

SURGLINE INTERNATIONAL INC.
NBB: SGLN

319 Clematis Street, Suite 400
West Palm Beach, FL 33401
Phone: 561 514-9042
Fax: –
Web: www.chinanuvosolar.com

CEO: –
CFO: –
HR: –
FYE: July 31
Type: Public

Holding company SurgLine International owns SurgLine and Nuvo Solar Energy. SurgLine distributes medical and surgical products at a discount. It recently expanded that business with the 2012 acquisition of Eden Surgical Technologies, which distributes trauma products, and the creation of subsidiary SurgLine MDC Holdings, which has been tasked with forming joint ventures with orthopedic surgeons to lower the costs of surgical implants. The company's other holding, Nuvo Solar Energy, is a development-stage company with patent pending solar and photovoltaic related technology. The company changed its name from China Nuvo Solar Energy to SurgLine International in 2012.

	Annual Growth	07/08	07/09	07/10	07/11	07/12
Sales ($mil.)	–	–	0.0	–	–	0.1
Net income ($ mil.)	–	(1.1)	(0.8)	(0.8)	(0.3)	(2.7)
Market value ($ mil.)	(60.7%)	115.1	43.8	14.2	12.6	2.7
Employees	–	–	–	–	–	–

SURMODICS INC
NMS: SRDX

9924 West, 74th Street
Eden Prairie, MN 55344
Phone: 952 500-7000
Fax: –
Web: www.surmodics.com

CEO: –
CFO: –
HR: –
FYE: September 30
Type: Public

Surmodics is a leading provider of surface modification technologies for intravascular medical devices and chemical components for in vitro diagnostic (IVD) immunoassay tests and microarrays. Surmodics develops and commercializes highly differentiated vascular intervention medical devices that are designed to address unmet clinical needs and engineered to the most demanding requirements. The company makes vascular intervention medical devices, including drug-coated balloons, mechanical thrombectomy devices, and radial access balloon catheters and guide sheaths. SurModics' accounts for about 75% of total sales.

	Annual Growth	09/19	09/20	09/21	09/22	09/23
Sales ($mil.)	7.3%	100.1	94.9	105.1	100.0	132.6
Net income ($ mil.)	–	7.6	1.1	4.2	(27.3)	(1.5)
Market value ($ mil.)	(8.5%)	647.4	550.8	787.0	430.3	454.2
Employees	0.5%	369	370	389	447	376

SURREY BANCORP (NC)
NBB: SRYB

145 North Renfro Street, P.O. Box 1227
Mount Airy, NC 27030
Phone: 336 783-3900
Fax: –
Web: –

CEO: –
CFO: –
HR: –
FYE: December 31
Type: Public

This surrey doesn't have fringe on top, but it does have funds inside. Surrey Bancorp is the holding company for Surrey Bank & Trust, which serves northwestern North Carolina's Surry County and neighboring portions of Virginia through about five offices and a lending center. The bank offers standard retail services, including checking and savings accounts, CDs, IRAs, and credit and debit cards. Surrey Bank & Trust writes mostly commercial and industrial loans (more than two-thirds of its portfolio), followed by residential mortgages (about 20%). Subsidiary SB&T Insurance sells property/casualty coverage. The bank offers investment services through a third-party provider, UVEST, which is part of LPL Financial.

	Annual Growth	12/17	12/18	12/19	12/20	12/21
Assets ($mil.)	12.5%	300.5	309.2	329.5	431.1	480.5
Net income ($ mil.)	14.0%	3.0	5.1	4.9	4.6	5.1
Market value ($ mil.)	2.9%	55.9	58.7	63.0	48.5	62.6
Employees	–	–	–	–	–	–

SUSQUEHANNA RIVER BASIN COMMISSION

4423 N FRONT ST
HARRISBURG, PA 171101788
Phone: 717 238-0423
Fax: –
Web: www.srbc.gov

CEO: –
CFO: –
HR: –
FYE: June 30
Type: Private

The Susquehanna River Basin Commission (SRBC) protects the 444-mile Susquehanna River Basin, which runs from Otsego Lake near Cooperstown, New York, into the Chesapeake Bay. Established by compact in 1970, SRBC works to reduce flood damage (the basin is one of the most flood-prone areas in the nation); provide surface and ground water for municipal, agricultural, recreational, and other uses; protect fisheries, wetlands, and aquatic habitat; preserve water quality; and ensure future flows into the Atlantic Ocean. The federal-interstate compact commission is comprised of members representing the states of New York, Pennsylvania, and Maryland.

	Annual Growth	06/01	06/02	06/07	06/08	06/09
Sales ($mil.)	(0.8%)	–	7.5	5.0	4.7	7.1
Net income ($ mil.)	26.1%	–	0.2	0.3	0.0	1.1
Market value ($ mil.)	–	–	–	–	–	–
Employees	–	–	–	–	–	35

SUTTER BAY HOSPITALS

475 BRANNAN ST STE 220
SAN FRANCISCO, CA 941075498
Phone: 415 600-1600
Fax: –
Web: www.sutterhealth.org

CEO: Jeff Gerard
CFO: –
HR: –
FYE: December 31
Type: Private

Sutter West Bay Hospitals (doing business as California Pacific Medical Center, or CPMC) is a health care complex located in the heart of hospital-heavy San Francisco. The private, not-for-profit center's four area campuses (California, Davies, Pacific, and St. Luke's) offer acute and specialty care, including obstetrics and gynecology, cardiovascular services, pediatrics, neurosciences, orthopedics, and organ transplantation. With more than 1,300 beds between its campuses, the center also conducts professional education and biomedical, clinical, and behavioral research. CPMC is part of the West Bay Region division of the Sutter Health hospital system.

	Annual Growth	12/06	12/07	12/08	12/09	12/11
Sales ($mil.)	24.9%	–	–	830.0	1,245.9	1,616.0
Net income ($ mil.)	(26.5%)	–	–	168.9	159.1	67.0
Market value ($ mil.)	–	–	–	–	–	–
Employees	–	–	–	–	–	3,597

SUTTER BAY MEDICAL FOUNDATION

795 EL CAMINO REAL
PALO ALTO, CA 943012302
Phone: 650 321-4121
Fax: –
Web: www.pamf.org

CEO: Jeff Gerard
CFO: –
HR: Marcia Vandervinne
FYE: December 31
Type: Private

The Palo Alto Medical Foundation (PAMF) is a not-for-profit, multi-specialty physician group providing medical and outpatient care mostly in the San Francisco Bay Area. It operates through five divisions serving distinct geographical areas: The Palo Alto Medical Clinic and the Camino Medical Group serve Silicon Valley and the East Bay; the Dublin Center and Fremont Center serve Alameda County; the Santa Cruz Medical Foundation; and the Mills-Peninsula Division. An affiliate of Sutter Health, PAMF's more than 1,200 doctors cover dozens of medical specialties; its facilities also provide outpatient surgery, diagnostic imaging, and women's services. Additionally, PAMF houses a Research Institute for medical research.

	Annual Growth	10/99	10/00*	12/01	12/21	12/22
Sales ($mil.)	13.5%	–	198.3	322.0	3,061.0	3,233.0
Net income ($ mil.)	–	–	23.5	5.0	(12.0)	(20.0)
Market value ($ mil.)	–	–	–	–	–	–
Employees	–	–	–	–	–	1,168

*Fiscal year change

SUTTER CENTRAL VALLEY HOSPITALS

1700 COFFEE RD
MODESTO, CA 953552803
Phone: 209 526-4500
Fax: –
Web: www.sutterhealth.org

CEO: David P Benn
CFO: Eric Dalton
HR: –
FYE: December 31
Type: Private

If you've stumbled from tasting too many fruits from the vines at nearby wineries, keep your fingers crossed that someone will help you get to Memorial Medical Center. Not-for-profit Memorial Hospital Association runs the Memorial Medical Center, which provides health care to the residents of Modesto, California, and the surrounding Stanislaus County. Specialized services include surgery, pediatrics, diagnostics, cancer treatment, home health, and emergency medicine. Memorial Hospital Association also operates an air ambulance service. Founded in 1970, the Memorial Medical Center has more than 420 beds. It is a subsidiary of West Coast hospital giant Sutter Health.

SUTTER HEALTH

2200 RIVER PLAZA DR
SACRAMENTO, CA 958334134
Phone: 916 733-8800
Fax: –
Web: www.sutterhealth.org

CEO: Patrick Fry
CFO: –
HR: Julie Fralick
FYE: December 31
Type: Private

Sutter Health provides coordinated care to more than 3 million Californians and its integrated network invests heavily in research and pilot programs that fuel advancement in patient's care and medical research across the country. Sutter Health is one of the region's largest not-for-profit, community-based home care providers, with about 4,175 acute care beds. After being formed through the merger of Sutter Health and California Healthcare System, Sutter Health now caters to residents of more than 100 communities in San Francisco Bay Area, Central Valley, Greater Sacramento Valley, Marin County, Sierra foothills, and Santa Cruz.

	Annual Growth	12/18	12/19	12/20	12/21	12/22
Sales ($mil.)	3.6%	–	13,304	13,220	14,225	14,773
Net income ($ mil.)	21.5%	–	189.0	82.0	1,958.0	339.0
Market value ($ mil.)	–	–	–	–	–	–
Employees	–	–	–	–	–	48,000

SV LABS CORPORATION

480 AIRPORT BLVD
WATSONVILLE, CA 950762002
Phone: 831 722-9526
Fax: –
Web: www.svnaturally.com

CEO: Graham Orriss
CFO: –
HR: Karen R Madrigal
FYE: June 30
Type: Private

The company helps to put "Ahh" in spa. Smith & Vandiver makes and markets foot care and spa items containing natural ingredients, such as shea butter, tea tree oil, and peppermint oil, as well as bath products, soaps, lip balms, and fragrances. The company's product lines are sold through more than 6,000 locations including specialty and gift retailers, as well as department stores. Smith & Vandiver started out as a lotion retailer in Santa Cruz, California, in 1970.

	Annual Growth	06/10	06/11	06/12	06/13	06/14
Sales ($mil.)	4.3%	–	6.5	7.4	7.1	7.4
Net income ($ mil.)	(9.5%)	–	0.3	0.4	0.2	0.2
Market value ($ mil.)	–	–	–	–	–	–
Employees	–	–	–	–	–	175

SVB FINANCIAL GROUP

NBB: SIVB Q

3003 Tasman Drive
Santa Clara, CA 95054-1191
Phone: 408 654-7400
Fax: –
Web: www.svb.com

CEO: Greg W Becker
CFO: Daniel J Beck
HR: Chris Edmondswaters
FYE: December 31
Type: Public

SVB Financial Group is the holding company for Silicon Valley Bank, which serves emerging and established companies involved in technology, life sciences/healthcare industries, and private equity/venture capital firms, and provides customized financing to entrepreneurs and clients of all sizes in those industries. It also lends to individual investors, executives, entrepreneurs or other influencers in the innovation economy, primarily through SVB Private. It also offers deposit account products and services, including checking, money market, certificates of deposit accounts, online banking, credit cards and other personalized banking services. SVB also provides asset management services private wealth management and other investment services. SVB has $211.8 billion in assets and holds $173.1 billion in deposits.

	Annual Growth	12/18	12/19	12/20	12/21	12/22
Assets ($mil.)	38.9%	56,928	71,005	115,511	211,478	211,793
Net income ($ mil.)	14.5%	973.8	1,136.9	1,208.4	1,833.0	1,672.0
Market value ($ mil.)	4.9%	11,238	14,855	22,949	40,133	13,618
Employees	31.0%	2,900	3,564	4,461	6,567	8,553

SWARTHMORE COLLEGE

500 COLLEGE AVE
SWARTHMORE, PA 190811390
Phone: 610 328-8000
Fax: –
Web: www.swarthmore.edu

CEO: –
CFO: –
HR: –
FYE: June 30
Type: Private

The Borough of Swarthmore, Pennsylvania, was established nearly three decades after its namesake Swarthmore College, Founded in 1864 by the Quakers, it is a private liberal arts and engineering college 11 miles southwest of Philadelphia. With a student-teacher ratio of 8:1, the college offers more than 50 academic programs and bachelor's degrees in the arts and sciences. Swarthmore enrolls about 1,550 students, or nearly 25% of the town's population. Notable alumni include Pulitzer Prize-winning author James Michener and former governor of Massachusetts Michael Dukakis.

	Annual Growth	06/18	06/19	06/20	06/21	06/22
Sales ($mil.)	31.6%	–	183.2	183.3	364.5	417.2
Net income ($ mil.)	36.2%	–	64.4	0.4	139.5	162.8
Market value ($ mil.)	–	–	–	–	–	–
Employees	–	–	–	–	–	700

SWAT.FAME, INC.

16425 GALE AVE
CITY OF INDUSTRY, CA 917451722
Phone: 626 961-7928
Fax: –
Web: www.swatfame.com

CEO: –
CFO: –
HR: –
FYE: February 28
Type: Private

When customers see the outcome of this SWAT team, they see trendy clothing rather than smoke bombs, sirens, and tear gas. With offices in Los Angeles and New York, Swat Fame designs and manufactures denim, sportswear, and dresses for juniors, girls, missy, and women's contemporary markets. Speechless is its top brand, alongside other sellers Bu from Malibu, Corey P, Kut from the Kloth, See Thru Soul, and Underground Soul. Swat Fame's collections are sold through US department stores, including Bloomingdale's, Dillard's, Von Maur, Buckle, Windsors, Arden B., Macy's, Nordstrom, J. C. Penney, and Kohl's, as well as through specialty retailers such as Charlotte Russe.

SWEDISH HEALTH SERVICES

747 BROADWAY
SEATTLE, WA 981224379
Phone: 206 386-6000
Fax: –
Web: www.swedish.org

CEO: Guy Hudson
CFO: Mary B Formby
HR: –
FYE: December 31
Type: Private

Swedish Health Services is the largest not-for-profit health provider in the greater Seattle area with five hospital campuses: First Hill, Cherry Hill, Ballard, Edmonds and Issaquah. It also has ambulatory care centers in Redmond and Mill Creek, and a network of more than 100 primary and specialty clinics throughout the greater Puget Sound area. Swedish Medical is affiliated with Providence Health & Services, a Catholic, not-for-profit organization with about 35 hospitals in five states. Swedish's perform procedures such as robotic-assisted surgery and personalized treatment in cardiovascular care, cancer care, neuroscience, orthopedics, high-risk obstetrics, pediatric specialties, organ transplantation and clinical research.

SWEDISHAMERICAN HEALTH SYSTEM CORPORATION

1401 E STATE ST
ROCKFORD, IL 611042315
Phone: 779 696-4400
Fax: –
Web: www.swedishamerican.org

CEO: Travis Andersen
CFO: Patti Dewane
HR: –
FYE: June 30
Type: Private

Swedish, American, or other, SwedishAmerican Health System wants to make you better. The not-for-profit medical provider renders care to residents of northern Illinois and southern Wisconsin through its flagship facility, SwedishAmerican Hospital, as well as a medical center, a network of about 15 primary care and specialty clinics, the region's largest home health care agency, and a full spectrum of outpatient wellness and education programs. The 400-bed SwedishAmerican teaching hospital is affiliated with the University of Illinois College of Medicine and provides patients with a variety of services, including cancer, heart, primary, and surgical care. At the helm of the organization -- founded in 1911 -- is CEO Bill Gorski.

	Annual Growth	06/17	06/18	06/19	06/20	06/21
Sales ($mil.)	34.7%	–	–	–	0.0	0.0
Net income ($ mil.)		–	–	–	(0.9)	(1.1)
Market value ($ mil.)		–	–	–	–	–
Employees		–	–	–	–	2,011

SWIMWEAR ANYWHERE, INC.

85 SHERWOOD AVE
FARMINGDALE, NY 117351717
Phone: 631 420-1400
Fax: –
Web: www.swimwearanywhere.com

CEO: –
CFO: –
HR: –
FYE: December 31
Type: Private

Life would certainly be more interesting if consumers took heed and sported their swimwear anywhere and everywhere. Swimwear Anywhere is a major North American swimwear manufacturer that makes and markets swimwear and beachwear lines under its own private labels and through licensing agreements for brands including DKNY, Juicy Couture, and Carmen Marc Valvo. The company's subsidiary, TYR Sport (named after mythical Norse god of warriors and athletes), makes swimwear and gear designed primarily for professional athletes. Spokespeople have included Olympic swimming medalist Amanda Weir. Swimwear Anywhere was founded in 1993 by its owners Joseph and Rosemarie DiLorenzo.

	Annual Growth	06/99	06/00	06/03	06/04*	12/12
Sales ($mil.)	–	–	53.7	47.1	46.0	53.8
Net income ($ mil.)	(2.6%)	–	0.9	17.2	0.9	0.7
Market value ($ mil.)	–	–	–	–	–	–
Employees	–	–	–	–	–	150

*Fiscal year change

SWINERTON BUILDERS

2001 CLAYTON RD STE 700
CONCORD, CA 945202792
Phone: 925 602-6400
Fax: –
Web: www.swinerton.com

CEO: Eric M Foster
CFO: Bradley K Peterson
HR: Prisma Gonzalez
FYE: December 31
Type: Private

Swinerton Builders, a subsidiary of Swinerton, focuses on commercial and sustainable construction and renovation projects. Operating primarily in the western US, its interiors group offers interior tenant finishes and remodeling, working on such projects as high-tech and lab renovations, hospitals, retail facilities, and seismic upgrades. The employee-owned company's building group focuses on new construction and retrofitting for such projects as the San Francisco Museum of Modern Art, a Lockheed Martin launch vehicle assembly plant in Colorado, and the Bay Bridge toll operations building in San Francisco. Swinerton Builders operates from offices in California, Colorado, Hawaii, Texas, New Mexico, and Washington.

	Annual Growth	12/15	12/16	12/17	12/18	12/19
Sales ($mil.)	5.2%	–	3,664.9	3,306.4	3,542.0	4,272.2
Net income ($ mil.)	(4.8%)	–	53.9	40.0	38.0	46.5
Market value ($ mil.)	–	–	–	–	–	–
Employees	–	–	–	–	–	76

SWINERTON INCORPORATED

2001 CLAYTON RD FL 7
SAN FRANCISCO, CA 94107
Phone: 415 421-2980
Fax: –
Web: www.swinerton.com

CEO: Eric M Foster
CFO: Linda G Showalter
HR: Donald Hill
FYE: December 31
Type: Private

Swinerton is building up the West just as it helped rebuild San Francisco after the 1906 earthquake. One of the largest contractors in California, the construction group builds commercial, industrial, and government facilities, including resorts, subsidized housing, public schools, soundstages, hospitals, and airport terminals. Through its subsidiaries (including Swinerton Builders), Swinerton offers general contracting and design/build services, as well as construction and program management. The firm also provides property management for conventional, subsidized, and assisted living residences, and is active in the renewable energy sector. The 100% employee-owned company traces its roots to 1888.

SWISHER HYGIENE INC.

350 E LAS OLAS BLVD STE 1600
FORT LAUDERDALE, FL 333014211
Phone: 203 682-8331
Fax: –
Web: www.swshinvestors.com

CEO: –
CFO: –
HR: –
FYE: December 31
Type: Private

Swisher Hygiene sweeps away the competition in the corporate world. The company provides commercial cleaning services, equipment, and supplies to more than 50,000 businesses in North America and abroad. Recognized for its restroom cleaning and disinfection services, Swisher also sells soap, cleaning chemicals, and paper products, and it rents facility service items (such as floor mats and mops). The company sells, rents, and maintains commercial dishwashers and other cleaning equipment. Swisher has expertise in serving customers in the foodservice, hospitality, health care, industrial, and retail industries. It boasts a global network of about 80 company-owned operations, 10 franchises, and 10 master licensees.

SWITCH, INC.

7135 S DECATUR BLVD
LAS VEGAS, NV 891184376
Phone: 702 444-4111
Fax: –
Web: www.switch.com

CEO: Rob Roy
CFO: –
HR: –
FYE: December 31
Type: Private

Switch is the independent leader in exascale data center ecosystems, edge data center designs, industry-leading telecommunications solutions, and next-generation technology innovation. Its advanced data centers reside at the center of its platform and provide power densities that exceed industry averages with efficient cooling, while being powered by 100% renewable energy. The company builds its data centers using its Switch Modularly Optimized Designs (Switch MODs) that let it quickly deploy or replace equipment to meet customers' needs. Its technologies were all designed and invented by its founder, Rob Roy, and are protected by over 700 issued and pending patent claims. In 2022, Switch was acquired by DigitalBridge Group (a leading digital infrastructure firm) and IFM Investors (a global investment management firm and one of the largest infrastructure investors in the world), for approximately $11 billion.

SYLVANIA FRANCISCAN HEALTH

1715 INDIAN WOOD CIR # 200
MAUMEE, OH 435374055
Phone: 419 882-8373
Fax: –
Web: –

CEO: –
CFO: –
HR: –
FYE: June 30
Type: Private

Sylvania Franciscan Health (formerly Franciscan Services Corporation) is a Catholic health care system sponsored by the Sisters of St. Francis of Sylvania, Ohio. The health system operates hospitals, long-term care centers, and nursing homes in Kentucky, Ohio, and Texas. Its facilities are organized into regional provider groups including Trinity Health System (Ohio), St. Joseph Health System (Texas), Trinity Health Services Corporation (Texas), and Franciscan Living Communities (Kentucky and Ohio). Sylvania Franciscan Health operates a total of about 950 hospital beds and 1,700 senior living units. It also manages counseling centers and a shelter for domestic violence victims.

	Annual Growth	12/04	12/05	12/06	12/14*	06/15
Sales ($mil.)	(30.7%)	–	490.7	529.9	11.4	12.5
Net income ($ mil.)	(7.3%)	–	20.4	36.7	(3.2)	9.6
Market value ($ mil.)	–	–	–	–	–	–
Employees	–	–	–	–	–	4,800

*Fiscal year change

SYMBION, INC.

340 SEVEN SPRINGS WAY
BRENTWOOD, TN 370275696
Phone: 615 234-5900
Fax: –
Web: www.surgerypartners.com

CEO: Richard E Francis Jr
CFO: Teresa F Sparks
HR: Marisa Kronmueller
FYE: December 31
Type: Private

The speedier the surgery, the better, says Symbion. The company owns and manages 55 outpatient surgery centers in more than two dozen states, mainly in the eastern, midwestern, and southern regions of the US. Physicians at the centers perform a variety of non-emergency procedures in such fields as gastrointestinal medicine, orthopedics, pain management, ophthalmology, and plastic surgery. Surgery Partners operates the centers through partnerships with local doctors or hospitals; it owns a majority interest in most of its practices. In late 2014 Symbion was acquired by Surgery Partners, which is owned by H.I.G. Capital.

SYMBOLIC LOGIC INC

9800 Pyramid Court, Suite 400
Englewood, CO 80112
Phone: 303 802-1000
Fax: –
Web: www.symbl.com

NBB: EVOL
CEO: Matthew Stecker
CFO: –
HR: –
FYE: December 31
Type: Public

Evolving Systems offers software for the ever-evolving telecommunications industry. The company provides applications used by telecom companies to automate and manage parts of their network operations, including tools applications that allow users to route calls and messages to various devices. The company also provides local number portability software that allows telephone customers to keep the same phone number when changing to a new carrier. Evolving Systems has expanded its international operations in Africa, Asia, and Central America and added products for managing SIM cards. The company agreed to sell its number management and monitoring assets to NeuStar in 2011 for $39 million.

	Annual Growth	12/17	12/18	12/19	12/20	12/21
Sales ($mil.)	–	28.8	30.6	25.8	26.4	–
Net income ($ mil.)	62.3%	2.5	(14.8)	(9.7)	0.6	17.4
Market value ($ mil.)	(16.9%)	57.6	14.5	11.0	24.1	27.5
Employees	(60.0%)	314	280	261	277	8

SYMBOLLON PHARMACEUTICALS INC.

99 West Street, Suite J
Medfield, MA 02052
Phone: 508 242-7500
Fax: –
Web: www.symbollon.com

CEO: Paul C Desjourdy
CFO: –
HR: –
FYE: December 31
Type: Public

Symbollon Pharmaceuticals is udderly obsessive-compulsive. It develops iodine-based pharmaceuticals and antimicrobials. The firm's patented technology minimizes staining and is effective against a range of microbes. The company has two products that are commercially available. The first is IodoZyme, a bovine teat sanitizer marketed by WestAgro. Second is IoGen, originally designed to be an orally administered treatment for fibrocystic breast disease, but eventually marketed as a nutritional supplement and now sold through a company web site. Symbollon is developing products to treat conditions including urinary tract infection and various skin diseases. CEO Paul Desjourdy owns about 12% of the company.

	Annual Growth	12/06	12/07	12/08	12/09	12/10
Sales ($mil.)	(12.7%)	0.0	–	0.0	0.0	0.0
Net income ($ mil.)	–	(3.0)	(3.7)	(1.8)	(0.7)	(0.4)
Market value ($ mil.)	(61.4%)	38.4	27.5	0.3	7.2	0.9
Employees	(24.0%)	3	2	1	1	1

SYMMS FRUIT RANCH, INC.

14068 SUNNYSLOPE RD
CALDWELL, ID 836079358
Phone: 208 459-4821
Fax: –
Web: www.symmsfruit.com

CEO: –
CFO: –
HR: –
FYE: September 30
Type: Private

There's more than potatoes in Idaho as Symms Fruit Ranch (which produces a variety of fresh fruit and vegetables) more than adequately demonstrates. The company offers both produce and fruit in season, specializing in apples, apricots, asparagus, cherries, nectarines, peaches, plums, prunes, and raspberries. Symms Fruit Ranch's apple varieties include Fuji, Gala, Golden Delicious, Granny Smith, Jonagold, Jonathan, Pink Lady, Red Delicious, and Rome.

SYMVIONICS, INC.

488 E SANTA CLARA ST STE 201
ARCADIA, CA 910067229
Phone: 626 305-1400
Fax: –
Web: www.symvionics.com

CEO: –
CFO: –
HR: –
FYE: December 31
Type: Private

Symvionics -- melodious, no? -- combines engineering, science, technical, and management expertise to help bring harmony to today's cacophonous business and technology landscape. The company works for the US Department of Defense as a prime contractor and as a subcontractor. Its offerings fall into two main buckets: engineering, scientific, and technical services (systems and software engineering, modeling and simulation, training and weapons systems development, information technology design and services); and management and operations support services (building and grounds maintenance, logistics support, management consulting).

	Annual Growth	12/03	12/04	12/05	12/08	12/09
Sales ($mil.)	(7.4%)	–	–	30.4	25.2	22.3
Net income ($ mil.)	(22.1%)	–	–	2.2	0.6	0.8
Market value ($ mil.)	–	–	–	–	–	–
Employees	–	–	–	–	–	65

SYNACOR, INC.

505 ELLICOTT ST STE 39
BUFFALO, NY 142031547
Phone: 716 853-1362
Fax: –
Web: www.synacor.com

CEO: Himesh Bhise
CFO: Timothy Heasley
HR: –
FYE: December 31
Type: Private

When it comes to digital entertainment, Synacor is at your service. The firm provides a technology platform to broadband service providers, cable TV operators, and other telecom companies that lets end-users receive digital entertainment, services, and apps. It builds the private label portals customers see when they log onto their telecom provider's website, and makes money by selling ads on these sites. Synacor also offers premium online content, e-mail, and security services. It has relationships with content and service providers including CinemaNow, CNN, and MediaNet Digital. Synacor went public in 2011.

	Annual Growth	12/15	12/16	12/17	12/18	12/19
Sales ($mil.)	(6.7%)	–	–	140.0	143.9	121.8
Net income ($ mil.)	–	–	–	(9.8)	(7.6)	(9.0)
Market value ($ mil.)	–	–	–	–	–	–
Employees	–	–	–	–	–	273

SYNAPTICS INC

NMS: SYNA

1109 McKay Drive
San Jose, CA 95131
Phone: 408 904-1100
Fax: –
Web: www.synaptics.com

CEO: Michael Hurlston
CFO: Dean Butler
HR: –
FYE: June 24
Type: Public

Synaptics is a leading worldwide developer and fabless supplier of premium mixed signal semiconductor solutions. Its original equipment manufacturer, or OEM, customers include many of the world's largest OEMs for smart home devices, automotive solutions, notebook computers and peripherals, smartphones and tablets, and many large OEMs for audio and video products. Its TouchPad product can be used for screen navigation and cursor movement; ClickPad, an alternative to conventional input and navigation devices; and ClearPad provides touchscreen control for various mobile devices. Synaptics supply its products through its contract manufacturers, supply chain, or distributors. Majority of sales come from outside the US, about 35% in China.

	Annual Growth	06/19	06/20	06/21	06/22	06/23
Sales ($mil.)	(2.1%)	1,472.2	1,333.9	1,339.6	1,739.7	1,355.1
Net income ($ mil.)	–	(22.9)	79.6	257.5	73.6	
Market value ($ mil.)	29.2%	1,124.0	2,170.0	5,692.3	4,967.2	3,130.4
Employees	0.4%	1,861	1,387	1,463	1,775	1,891

SYNARC INC.

777 MARINERS ISLAND BLVD STE 550
SAN MATEO, CA 944041562
Phone: 415 817-8900
Fax: –
Web: –

CEO: Claus Christiansen
CFO: –
HR: –
FYE: December 31
Type: Private

You put up the compounds, Synarc puts up the trials. The biomedical testing and contract research organization provides medical imaging, patient recruitment, and biomechanical marker services for clinical trials conducted by drug development companies around the globe. Synarc operates clinical research centers in North America, Europe, and Asia. The company has a main focus on neurological research, including Alzheimer's disease studies; other clinical areas include oncology, cardiovascular disease, orthopedics, infectious disease, arthritis, and osteoporosis. Synarc also conducts studies on medical devices.

	Annual Growth	09/97	09/98	09/99	09/00*	12/07
Sales ($mil.)	36.3%	–	–	8.6	12.2	102.2
Net income ($ mil.)	–	–	–	(1.8)	(3.0)	(3.1)
Market value ($ mil.)	–	–	–	–	–	–
Employees	–	–	–	–	–	400

*Fiscal year change

SYNCHRONOSS TECHNOLOGIES INC

NAS: SNCR

200 Crossing Boulevard, 8th Floor
Bridgewater, NJ 08807
Phone: 866 620-3940
Fax: –
Web: www.synchronoss.com

CEO: Jeffrey Miller
CFO: Louis W Ferraro Jr
HR: –
FYE: December 31
Type: Public

Synchronoss is a leading provider of white label cloud, messaging, digital and network management solutions that enable its customers to keep subscribers, systems, networks and content in sync. The company help its customers to connect, engage and monetize subscribers in more meaningful ways by providing trusted platforms through which end users can sync and store content and connect with one another and the brands they love. Synchronoss focus on delivering carrier-grade solutions to three markets globally: communications service providers/multi-service operators (such as cable and mobile network operators), mobile insurance providers, and retailers. Company's platforms were Synchronoss Experience (syncX), EngageX, and Synchronoss Personal Cloud.

	Annual Growth	12/19	12/20	12/21	12/22	12/23
Sales ($mil.)	(14.6%)	308.7	291.7	280.6	252.6	164.2
Net income ($ mil.)	–	(104.6)	(10.7)	(22.9)	(7.9)	(54.5)
Market value ($ mil.)	6.9%	49.0	48.5	25.2	6.4	64.0
Employees	(5.5%)	1,659	1,598	1,536	1,391	1,321

SYNCHRONY FINANCIAL   NYS: SYF

777 Long Ridge Road
Stamford, CT 06902
Phone: 203 585-2400
Fax: –
Web: www.synchrony.com

CEO: Alberto Casellas
CFO: Brian J Wenzel Sr
HR: –
FYE: December 31
Type: Public

Synchrony Financial is a premier consumer financial services company in the US. The company works with a wide range of partners, including national and regional retailers, local merchants, manufacturers, buying groups, industry associations, and healthcare service providers. It utilizes a broad set of distribution channels, including mobile apps and websites, as well as online marketplaces and business management solutions like Point-of-Sale platforms. Its offerings include private label, dual, co-brand and general-purpose credit cards, as well as short- and long-term installment loans and consumer banking products. It processes some $180.2 billion of loan receivables and 70.8 million active accounts. The company also offers retail banking services through Synchrony Bank.

	Annual Growth	12/19	12/20	12/21	12/22	12/23
Assets ($mil.)	2.9%	104,826	95,948	95,748	104,564	117,479
Net income ($ mil.)	(12.1%)	3,747.0	1,385.0	4,221.0	3,016.0	2,238.0
Market value ($ mil.)	1.5%	14,652	14,123	18,875	13,370	15,539
Employees	4.9%	16,500	16,500	18,000	18,500	20,000

SYNCORA HOLDINGS LTD   NBB: SYCR F

555 Madison Avenue, 11th Floor
New York, NY 10022
Phone: –
Fax: –
Web: www.syncora.com

CEO: –
CFO: –
HR: –
FYE: December 31
Type: Public

Syncora Holdings Ltd. used to be a place to get loans insured, but for now new customers will have to look elsewhere. Syncora is a financial guaranty insurer -- the kind of insurance which covers bonds and other investments from the risk of default. Syncora operates in the US through its subsidiary Syncora Guarantee Inc. The company has also provided reinsurance on financial guarantee insurance policies. Both lines of business were closely tied to mortgage-backed securities, leaving Syncora vulnerable to increased default rates. The company is currently not writing new business.

	Annual Growth	12/14	12/15	12/16	12/17	12/18
Assets ($mil.)	(12.6%)	2,895.8	2,625.7	2,394.4	2,385.5	1,690.4
Net income ($ mil.)	–	(102.9)	216.7	32.7	133.5	(31.3)
Market value ($ mil.)	–	–	–	–	–	–
Employees	–	–	–	–	–	–

SYNERGETICS USA, INC.

3845 CORPORATE CENTRE DR
O FALLON, MO 633688678
Phone: 636 939-5100
Fax: –
Web: www.bauschsurgical.com

CEO: –
CFO: –
HR: –
FYE: July 31
Type: Private

Synergetics USA is in sync with surgeons' needs. The firm makes microsurgical instruments and electrosurgery systems used in minimally invasive surgeries, primarily in the fields of ophthalmology and neurology. Among its products are forceps, retractors, scissors, and illuminators used in vitreoretinal surgeries, as well as precision neurosurgery instruments. It also makes bipolar electrosurgical generators, which use electrical currents to cut tissue and seal blood vessels. Synergetics USA sells to hospitals, physicians, and clinics directly and through distributors; it also sells certain items through partnerships with original equipment manufacturers. Valeant acquired Synergetics USA in 2015.

	Annual Growth	07/11	07/12	07/13	07/14	07/15
Sales ($mil.)	7.7%	–	60.0	62.8	64.8	75.0
Net income ($ mil.)	(7.1%)	–	5.6	2.6	3.1	4.5
Market value ($ mil.)	–	–	–	–	–	–
Employees	–	–	–	–	–	418

SYNERGY HEALTH NORTH AMERICA, INC.

5960 HEISLEY RD
MENTOR, OH 440601834
Phone: 813 891-9550
Fax: –
Web: www.synergyhealthplc.com

CEO: –
CFO: –
HR: –
FYE: December 31
Type: Private

Synergy Health has doctors and patients covered, even when the gown opens to the back. The company provides hospital and surgical centers with such reusable surgical products such as gowns and towels. It also provides reprocessed surgical instruments, basins, and surgical accessories that it sorts and sterilizes. The company offers pick-up and delivery service as an alternative to in-house recovery programs. Synergy Health forms multi-year or short-term agreements with such customers as Kaiser Permanente and Novation . Synergy Health was acquired by Steris in 2015.

SYNERGY IT SOLUTIONS OF NYS, INC.

3500 WINTON PL STE 4
ROCHESTER, NY 146232860
Phone: 585 758-7100
Fax: –
Web: www.synergyits.com

CEO: –
CFO: –
HR: Barbara Duffy
FYE: December 31
Type: Private

Synergy Global Solutions has a cooperative view of solving IT problems. The company provides a variety of information technology services and distributes computer hardware and software for businesses in New York state. It installs IT systems from vendors such as Cisco and Symantec that enable computer networking and telephony, data security, and data storage. Synergy also provides consulting and network systems design services. The health care, education, and financial industries are key sectors for the company; it also serves the public sector and law firms. Synergy was founded in 1971 by CEO Ray Hutch. It operates from offices in Amherst, Aurora, and Syracuse, New York, in addition to its headquarters in Victor.

	Annual Growth	12/08	12/09	12/10	12/11	12/12
Sales ($mil.)	(18.6%)	–	–	64.2	51.3	42.5
Net income ($ mil.)	(72.3%)	–	–	2.7	3.9	0.2
Market value ($ mil.)	–	–	–	–	–	–
Employees	–	–	–	–	–	145

SYNIVERSE HOLDINGS, INC.

8125 HIGHWOODS PALM WAY
TAMPA, FL 336471776
Phone: 813 637-5000
Fax: –
Web: www.syniverse.com

CEO: Stephen Gray
CFO: Bob Reich
HR: –
FYE: December 31
Type: Private

Syniverse Holdings opens up new worlds of communication for its clients. The company, which operates as Syniverse Technologies, provides business and network engineering services and software for managing and interconnecting voice and data network systems. It also offers clearing and settlement services, voice and data roaming facilitation, fraud management software, and customer data analysis services to mobile operators, fixed-line carriers, and other telecommunications service providers worldwide. Customers have included Verizon Wireless and Vodafone Group. Syniverse is owned by Carlyle Group affiliate Buccaneer Holdings.

SYNOPSYS INC

NMS: SNPS

675 Almanor Avenue
Sunnyvale, CA 94085
Phone: 650 584-5000
Fax: –
Web: www.synopsys.com

CEO: Sassine Ghazi
CFO: Shelagh Glaser
HR: –
FYE: October 31
Type: Public

Synopsys provides electronic design automation (EDA) software and services used in the making of integrated circuits. Engineers creating advanced semiconductors, product teams developing advanced electronic systems, and software developers use products to develop, simulate, and test the physical design of ICs before production, and then to test finished products for bugs and security vulnerabilities. It provides intellectual property (IP) products, or pre-designed circuits used as part of larger chips. Synopsys added software testing to its portfolio. Customers come from a variety of industries particularly semiconductor and electronics manufacturing as well as automotive and energy. About 45% of company's revenue comes from the US customers.

	Annual Growth	10/19	10/20	10/21	10/22	10/23
Sales ($mil.)	14.8%	3,360.7	3,685.3	4,204.2	5,081.5	5,842.6
Net income ($ mil.)	23.3%	532.4	664.3	757.5	984.6	1,229.9
Market value ($ mil.)	36.4%	20,641	32,518	50,661	44,483	71,380
Employees	9.9%	13,896	15,036	16,361	19,000	20,300

SYNOVUS FINANCIAL CORP

NYS: SNV

1111 Bay Avenue, Suite 500
Columbus, GA 31901
Phone: 706 641-6500
Fax: –
Web: www.synovus.com

CEO: Kevin S Blair
CFO: Andrew J Gregory Jr
HR: –
FYE: December 31
Type: Public

Synovus Financial Corp. is a financial services company and a registered bank holding company that provides commercial and consumer banking, as well as private banking, treasury management, wealth management, mortgage services, premium finance, asset-based lending, structured lending, and international banking to its clients through Synovus Bank. The company operates more than 245 branches and about 365 ATMs throughout Alabama, Florida, Georgia, South Carolina, and Tennessee. It also provides other financial services through direct and indirect wholly-owned non-bank subsidiaries such as Synovus Securities and Synovus Trust, which offer professional portfolio management for fixed-income securities, investment banking, asset management, and financial planning services, among others. The company was incorporated in 1972 and has a total consolidated assets of $59.73 billion and total consolidated deposits of $48.87 billion.

	Annual Growth	12/19	12/20	12/21	12/22	12/23
Assets ($mil.)	5.5%	48,203	54,394	57,317	59,731	59,810
Net income ($ mil.)	(0.9%)	563.8	373.7	760.5	757.9	543.7
Market value ($ mil.)	(1.0%)	5,750.8	4,748.9	7,022.8	5,508.8	5,523.5
Employees	(2.9%)	5,389	5,247	4,988	5,114	4,798

SYNTHESIS ENERGY SYSTEMS INC

NBB: SYNE

One Riverway, Suite 1700
Houston, TX 77056
Phone: 713 579-0600
Fax: 713 579-0610
Web: www.synthesisenergy.com

CEO: Robert Rigdon
CFO: Robert Rigdon
HR: –
FYE: June 30
Type: Public

Synthesis Energy Systems (SES) prefers it when a little waste is produced posthaste. The company owns a coal gasification plant in China that began production in 2008. (Coal gasification converts low-rank coal and coal waste into fuels such as synthetic natural gas, methanol, ammonia, and dimethyl ether, which are used to make gasoline). SES leases the technology behind the plant from the Gas Technology Institute. The company has four more coal gasification plants under development -- two in China with AEI, and two in the US with North American Coal Corporation and CONSOL Energy.

	Annual Growth	06/15	06/16	06/17	06/18	06/19
Sales ($mil.)	–	15.5	6.0	0.2	1.5	–
Net income ($ mil.)	–	(37.9)	(23.1)	(26.2)	(9.6)	(10.7)
Market value ($ mil.)	(31.8%)	2.0	1.5	0.9	4.6	0.4
Employees	(54.7%)	142	135	22	13	6

SYNUTRA INTERNATIONAL, INC.

2275 RESEARCH BLVD STE 500
ROCKVILLE, MD 20850
Phone: 301 840-3888
Fax: –
Web: www.synutraingredients.com

CEO: Liang Zhang
CFO: Ning Cai
HR: –
FYE: March 31
Type: Private

Synutra International is a leading manufacturer and provider of ingredients for dietary supplements, specializing in nutrients for healthy joints. The company owns and operates numerous operating companies overseas through its subsidiary Synutra, Inc., an Illinois corporation, to manufacture, market, and sell infant formulas and other pediatric and adult nutritional products in the growing market of China. In the North America market, the company's formulated and made into dietary supplement products are for sale as branded products or in private label and store brands to distributors and retailers.

SYPRIS SOLUTIONS, INC.

NMS: SYPR

101 Bullitt Lane, Suite 450
Louisville, KY 40222
Phone: 502 329-2000
Fax: –
Web: www.sypris.com

CEO: Jeffrey T Gill
CFO: Anthony C Allen
HR: –
FYE: December 31
Type: Public

Sypris Solutions provides its customers with simple solutions for their manufacturing chores. The company's Industrial Group makes heavy-duty truck components, including axle shafts, gear sets, differential cases, trailer axle beams, and other components. Its Electronics Group provides circuit board and box build manufacturing services, primarily for the aerospace and defense industries, as well as secure communications and data storage products for government clients. Sypris' top customers have traditionally included Dana Holding, ArvinMeritor, Raytheon, Honeywell, Lockheed Martin, and the US Defense Department.

	Annual Growth	12/18	12/19	12/20	12/21	12/22
Sales ($mil.)	5.8%	88.0	87.9	82.3	97.4	110.1
Net income ($ mil.)	–	(3.5)	(3.9)	1.7	2.9	(2.5)
Market value ($ mil.)	27.3%	17.3	17.3	33.7	54.6	45.4
Employees	0.1%	716	630	664	684	719

SYRACUSE UNIVERSITY

900 S CROUSE AVE
SYRACUSE, NY 132444407
Phone: 315 443-1870
Fax: –
Web: www.syracuse.edu

CEO: –
CFO: –
HR: –
FYE: July 31
Type: Private

Syracuse University is a serious school with a silly mascot. While it wasn't until 1995 that Otto the Orange was officially adopted as the school's mascot, Syracuse's tradition of quality higher education dates back to 1870. The school enrolls more than 21,000 undergraduate and graduate students and has some 1,000 full-time faculty members on its campus in central New York State. It offers about 500 degree programs in areas such as communications, computer science, engineering, psychology, art, mathematics, music, and information. Notable alumni include Dick Clark, Ted Koppel, Joyce Carol Oats, Joe Biden, and Aaron Sorkin.

	Annual Growth	06/14	06/15	06/16	06/17*	07/21
Sales ($mil.)	(85.3%)	–	–	–	994.8	0.5
Net income ($ mil.)	(84.0%)	–	–	–	197.6	0.1
Market value ($ mil.)	–	–	–	–	–	–
Employees	–	–	–	–	–	4,350

*Fiscal year change

SYSCO CORP
NYS: SYY

1390 Enclave Parkway
Houston, TX 77077-2099
Phone: 281 584-1390
Fax: 281 584-2880
Web: www.sysco.com

CEO: Kevin P Hourican
CFO: Anita A Zielinski
HR: –
FYE: July 1
Type: Public

Sysco is the largest global distributor of food and related products primarily to the food service or food-away-from-home industry. The company serves approximately 725,000 customer locations in the US and internationally in the restaurant (standalone and chain), healthcare, education, and hotel industries, among others. Its nearly 335 distribution centers and approximately 17,000 delivery vehicles deliver branded and private-label food including among others fresh, frozen, and canned foods, dairy, beverages, seafood, and specialty and meat products as well as non-food items such as silverware, glassware, paper products, cookware, restaurant and kitchen equipment and supplies, and cleaning supplies. The US accounts for more than 80% of sales. The company was founded in 1969.

	Annual Growth	06/19	06/20*	07/21	07/22	07/23
Sales ($mil.)	6.2%	60,114	52,893	51,298	68,636	76,325
Net income ($ mil.)	1.4%	1,674.3	215.5	524.2	1,358.8	1,770.1
Market value ($ mil.)	1.2%	35,722	26,417	38,687	43,601	37,479
Employees	1.1%	69,000	57,000	58,000	71,000	72,000

*Fiscal year change

SYSTEMS ENGINEERING TECHNOLOGIES CORPORATION

6121 LINCOLNIA RD STE 200
ALEXANDRIA, VA 223122707
Phone: 703 941-7887
Fax: –
Web: www.sytechcorp.com

CEO: –
CFO: –
HR: –
FYE: December 31
Type: Private

Systems Engineering Technologies, which does business as SyTech Corporation, makes analog and digital equipment used by law enforcement agencies for wiretap surveillance. Its systems can collect and record data from telephones and radio signals, and it makes equipment for intercepting pager signals and Internet data. In addition to surveillance equipment, SyTech makes radio communications gear used to connect radios and telephones, as well as software for managing radio communications networks. The company sells equipment primarily to state and federal law enforcement agencies and the US military. The company was founded in 1991.

	Annual Growth	12/04	12/05	12/06	12/12	12/13
Sales ($mil.)	–	–	8.2	16.7	8.9	8.2
Net income ($ mil.)	(18.1%)	–	4.7	2.2	1.2	1.0
Market value ($ mil.)	–	–	–	–	–	–
Employees	–	–	–	–	–	50

SYSTRAND MANUFACTURING CORP

19050 ALLEN RD
BROWNSTOWN TWP, MI 481831002
Phone: 734 479-8100
Fax: –
Web: www.systrand.com

CEO: Sharon A Cannarsa
CFO: –
HR: –
FYE: December 31
Type: Private

Move over Rosie the Riveter, a new woman is doing her part to keep American manufacturing humming. Led by Sharon Cannarsa, Systrand is a maker of machined, forged, cast, and powdered-metal automotive components. Operations include high-volume production of engine and transmission parts such as axle shafts, cylinder heads, differential cases, engine blocks, gear housings, hubs and input shafts, manifolds, planetary gears, and power steering housings. With production-run capabilities ranging from a few prototypes to hundreds of thousands of parts, Systrand can supply components ranging in size from under a pound to several hundred pounds. Customers have included Chrysler, General Motors, Ford, and Volkswagen.

	Annual Growth	12/06	12/07	12/08	12/09	12/10
Sales ($mil.)	5.5%	–	–	35.5	17.9	39.5
Net income ($ mil.)	161.4%	–	–	0.1	(5.4)	1.0
Market value ($ mil.)	–	–	–	–	–	–
Employees	–	–	–	–	–	160

SYZYGY TECHNOLOGIES, INC.

12526 HIGH BLUFF DR
SAN DIEGO, CA 921302064
Phone: 619 297-0970
Fax: –
Web: –

CEO: –
CFO: –
HR: –
FYE: December 31
Type: Private

Syzygy Technologies hopes to provide your information systems with all sorts of synergies. The company is an employee-owned information technology services company. It specializes in software development for the defense industry. Syzygy Technologies also provides testing, systems integration, network design, network administration, thin client integration, project management, network engineering, and quality assurance services. The company was founded in 1996.

	Annual Growth	12/03	12/04	12/05	12/06	12/13
Sales ($mil.)	(11.2%)	–	6.8	7.2	7.6	2.3
Net income ($ mil.)	–	–	2.9	0.2	1.0	(0.0)
Market value ($ mil.)	–	–	–	–	–	–
Employees	–	–	–	–	–	60

T & G CORPORATION

8623 COMMODITY CIR
ORLANDO, FL 328199003
Phone: 305 592-0552
Fax: –
Web: www.t-and-g.com

CEO: Rickardo Gonzalez
CFO: Michael Wright
HR: Suzy Grieder
FYE: December 31
Type: Private

T&G Constructors provides design-build commercial construction services for Fortune 500, government, and institutional clients. Services include program management, facility operation, and maintenance support services as well as general construction and renovation services. It specializes in aviation, education, office and retail, churches and other projects. T&G holds contracts with Disney World, Sprint, and Marriott, as well as with public agencies such as the University of Central Florida, the City of Orlando, and the US Navy. President Ricardo Gonzalez owns the company, which was established in 1987.

	Annual Growth	12/10	12/11	12/12	12/13	12/14
Sales ($mil.)	45.7%	–	–	21.7	36.5	46.0
Net income ($ mil.)	100.7%	–	–	0.8	2.1	3.3
Market value ($ mil.)	–	–	–	–	–	–
Employees	–	–	–	–	–	60

T ROWE PRICE GROUP INC.
NMS: TROW

100 East Pratt Street
Baltimore, MD 21202
Phone: 410 345-2000
Fax: 410 752-3477
Web: www.troweprice.com

CEO: Robert W Sharps
CFO: Jennifer B Dardis
HR: –
FYE: December 31
Type: Public

T. Rowe Price Group is a financial services holding company that provides global investment management services through its subsidiaries to investors worldwide. The company provides an array of US mutual funds, sub-advised funds, separately-managed accounts, collective investment trusts, and other T. Rowe Price products. Other services include asset management advisory services (including retirement plan advice for individuals), corporate retirement plan management, separately-managed accounts, variable annuity life insurance plans, discount brokerage, and transfer agency and shareholder services. Founded in 1937, T. Rowe Price has about $1.3 trillion in assets under management.

	Annual Growth	12/19	12/20	12/21	12/22	12/23
Sales ($mil.)	3.6%	5,617.9	6,206.7	7,671.9	6,488.4	6,460.5
Net income ($ mil.)	(4.3%)	2,131.3	2,372.7	3,082.9	1,557.9	1,788.7
Market value ($ mil.)	(3.0%)	27,285	33,902	44,035	24,423	24,116
Employees	1.8%	7,365	7,678	7,529	7,868	7,906

T-MOBILE US INC

NMS: TMUS

12920 SE 38th Street
Bellevue, WA 98006-1350
Phone: 425 378-4000
Fax: –
Web: www.t-mobile.com

CEO: G M Sievert
CFO: Peter Osvaldik
HR: Dalene Heydon
FYE: December 31
Type: Public

T-Mobile US is one of the largest providers of wireless communications services in the US to about 113.6 million postpaid and prepaid customers. The company provides a full range of devices and accessories to its brands, T-Mobile and Metro by T-Mobile. Postpaid phone customers dominate the company's customer base, followed by its prepaid customers. The company sell devices to dealers and other third-party distributors for resale through independent retail outlets as well as a variety of third-party websites. Its primary service plan is Magenta max, which allows customers to subscribe for wireless communications services separately from the purchase of a device. It also offers specific rate plans for qualifying customers such as Military and Veterans, First Responder, Business, and Unlimited 55+.

	Annual Growth	12/19	12/20	12/21	12/22	12/23
Sales ($mil.)	14.9%	44,998	68,397	80,118	79,571	78,558
Net income ($ mil.)	24.4%	3,468.0	3,064.0	3,024.0	2,590.0	8,317.0
Market value ($ mil.)	19.6%	93,775	161,255	138,690	167,413	191,724
Employees	6.0%	53,000	75,000	75,000	71,000	67,000

T. D. WILLIAMSON, INC.

6120 S YALE AVE STE 1700
TULSA, OK 741364235
Phone: 918 493-9494
Fax: –
Web: www.tdwilliamson.com

CEO: Robert D McGrew
CFO: –
HR: Caroline Anberree
FYE: December 31
Type: Private

Keeping onshore and offshore pipelines operating safely flowing freely is what T. D. Williamson is all about. A leading global pipeline equipment and services provider, the company designs, manufactures, and maintains oil field machinery and systems including pipeline pigging (scraping), gas leak detection, pipeline inspection, plugging, tapping, valve and clamp, and cathodic protection equipment. The company also offers general pipeline, training, turnkey, and repair services. T. D. Williamson operates a global network of sales offices and representatives.

	Annual Growth	12/99	12/00	12/01	12/02	12/15
Sales ($mil.)	12.6%	–	91.5	107.0	116.5	539.5
Net income ($ mil.)	–	–	2.3	2.6	1.7	–
Market value ($ mil.)	–	–	–	–	–	–
Employees	–	–	–	–	–	1,425

T.J.T., INC.

NBB: AXLE

843 North Washington Avenue
Emmett, ID 83617
Phone: 208 472-2500
Fax: 208 472-2525
Web: www.tjtusa.com

CEO: Larry E Kling
CFO: Nicole L Glisson
HR: –
FYE: September 30
Type: Public

The next time you pass a house being carted down the road, bet that it will be riding on some of T.J.T.'s tires. T.J.T. buys used axles and tires from manufactured housing dealers, inspects and reconditions them, and then sells them to manufactured home builders. The company also distributes vinyl siding and skirting to manufactured housing dealers and sells vinyl siding to the site-built and manufactured housing markets. It has expanded its line of products and aftermarket accessories for these markets to include skylights, adhesives and sealants, foundation, and other set-up materials. T.J.T. operates primarily in the western US. CEO Terrence Sheldon controls a 30% stake in the company.

	Annual Growth	09/11	09/12	09/13	09/14	09/15
Sales ($mil.)	1.0%	6.0	4.0	4.0	6.2	6.3
Net income ($ mil.)	–	(1.1)	(1.1)	(0.3)	0.8	0.2
Market value ($ mil.)	(10.6%)	2.3	0.7	1.5	1.9	1.5
Employees	–	35	23	24	27	–

TABLEMAX CORP

8025 Black Horse Pike, Suite 470
West Atlantic City, NJ 08232
Phone: 609 484-8866
Fax: –
Web: www.casinocenter.com

CEO: Glenn Fine
CFO: Richard Baldwin
HR: –
FYE: December 31
Type: Public

TableMAX lets casinos take video blackjack to the MAX. The company (formerly CJPG) manufactures multi-player video gaming machines that allow up to five people to play games of blackjack and different variations of poker. A single monitor and optional side bets encourage players to interact and make the games feel more like a live table game. Its gaming software allows the machines to be networked within and across casinos for large progressive jackpots. TableMAX sells directly and through distributors. The company acquired CJPG, previously known as Casino Journal Publishing Group, through a reverse merger in 2008.

	Annual Growth	12/98	12/99	12/00	12/01	12/02
Sales ($mil.)	(6.4%)	9.1	13.4	13.0	10.3	7.0
Net income ($ mil.)	–	(0.2)	(1.7)	(0.0)	0.2	(2.0)
Market value ($ mil.)	(40.9%)	1.1	0.7	0.4	0.3	0.1
Employees	(4.2%)	44	51	51	45	37

TACO JOHN'S INTERNATIONAL, INC.

808 W 20TH ST
CHEYENNE, WY 820013404
Phone: 800 854-0819
Fax: –
Web: www.tacojohns.com

CEO: Barry Sims
CFO: Kelly Hopper
HR: –
FYE: December 31
Type: Private

Taco John's International operates and franchises more than 420 Mexican fast-food restaurants in about 25 states. The eateries feature burritos and tacos, along with quesadillas, nachos, and a selection of breakfast items. Found mostly in smaller markets of the Midwest and West, more than 97% of the locations are run by franchisees. John Turner started the business when he opened his Taco House in Cheyenne, Wyoming; partners James Woodson and Harold Holmes later purchased the franchise rights and changed the name to Taco John's.

	Annual Growth	12/08	12/09	12/10	12/12	12/13
Assets ($mil.)	9.6%	–	–	13.9	17.5	18.4
Net income ($ mil.)	2.9%	–	–	2.7	3.1	2.9
Market value ($ mil.)	–	–	–	–	–	–
Employees	–	–	–	–	–	300

TACOMA PUBLIC UTILITIES

3628 S 35TH ST
TACOMA, WA 984093192
Phone: 253 502-8600
Fax: –
Web: www.mytpu.org

CEO: –
CFO: –
HR: –
FYE: December 31
Type: Private

City of Tacoma Department of Public Utilities (Tacoma Public Utilities) is fated to fulfill the electric and water desires of the City of Destiny's dwellers. The municipal utility's Tacoma Power unit generates, transmits, and distributes electricity to 160,000 homes and businesses in Tacoma, Washington. Tacoma Water serves more than 300,000 customers; the division's water supply comes from wells and the Green River Watershed. Tacoma Public Utilities also oversees Tacoma Rail, a freight-switching railroad with 75 customers and more than 200 miles of track, and the Click! Network, a high-speed data network that serves 23,790 cable TV customers via more than 1,460 miles of fiber-optic and coaxial cable.

	Annual Growth	12/12	12/13	12/15	12/19	12/22
Sales ($mil.)	1.7%	–	414.5	410.6	461.4	480.5
Net income ($ mil.)	–	–	19.9	(1.6)	(31.4)	(0.9)
Market value ($ mil.)	–	–	–	–	–	–
Employees	–	–	–	–	–	1,407

TACONIC BIOSCIENCES, INC.

5 UNIVERSITY PL RM 202
RENSSELAER, NY 121443425
Phone: 609 860-0806
Fax: –
Web: www.taconic.com

CEO: Nancy J Sandy
CFO: Michael Jensen
HR: Ann Ohanlon
FYE: December 31
Type: Private

Yes, they are cute, but Taconic Biosciences prefers that you don't pet its animals. The family-owned company provides research rodents and related products and services to pharmaceutical and biomedical companies, government agencies, and academic institutions in Asia, Europe, and North America through its facilities in Denmark, Germany, and the US. Taconic specially breeds rats and mice, the workhorses of the biomedical industry, to be disease-free or genetically modified to exhibit certain traits to help researchers develop new therapies for human disease. Other company units offer drug- and animal-safety testing and monoclonal antibody production. Private equity firm H.I.G. Capital, in partnership with company management, acquired Taconic Biosciences in 2019.

	Annual Growth	12/07	12/08	12/09	12/10	12/11
Sales ($mil.)	0.8%	–	–	142.6	151.7	144.9
Net income ($ mil.)	–	–	–	5.6	1.2	(23.0)
Market value ($ mil.)	–	–	–	–	–	–
Employees	–	–	–	–	–	850

TACONY CORPORATION

1760 GILSINN LN
FENTON, MO 630262004
Phone: 636 349-3000
Fax: –
Web: www.tacony.com

CEO: –
CFO: –
HR: –
FYE: December 31
Type: Private

Tacony caters to customers one stitch at a time and from ceiling to floor. The largest American-owned distributor of sewing machines, the company makes and distributes products for sewing, home floor care, commercial floor care, and ceiling fans and lighting through about 10 distribution centers nationwide. Its products bear such brands as Baby Lock (sergers and sewing machines), Koala Studios (sewing and craft furniture), Powr-Flite (janitorial equipment), Regency (ceiling fans and lighting), Riccar (vacuum cleaners), and Simplicity (vacuum cleaners). It also runs Missouri's Vacuum Cleaner Museum and Factory Outlet. The family-owned business, founded in 1946, is run by Ken Tacony, son of founder Nick Tacony.

TAILORED BRANDS, INC.

6380 ROGERDALE RD
HOUSTON, TX 770721624
Phone: 281 776-7000
Fax: –
Web: www.tailoredbrands.com

CEO: Bob Hull
CFO: –
HR: Alana Solorzano
FYE: February 01
Type: Private

Tailored Brands is a leading omnichannel retailer delivering personalized products and services through its convenient network of stores and ecommerce sites. The company's brands include leading menswear retailers Men's Wearhouse, Jos. A. Bank, Moores clothing for men, and family retailer K&G Fashion Superstore. It operates in the US and Canada, and ships to more than 150 countries worldwide through the company's brand websites, and Tailored Brands products are manufactured in almost 15 countries across four continents. The company delivers a convenient and modern shopping experience by combining multiple omnichannel options such as hands-free fit technology, BOPIS (Buy Online, Pick Up In-Store), curbside pickup, appointment booking, and contactless payment with its incomparable in-store service and expertise.

TAITRON COMPONENTS INC.

NAS: TAIT

28040 West Harrison Parkway
Valencia, CA 91355-4162
Phone: 661 257-6060
Fax: –
Web: www.taitroncomponents.com

CEO: Stewart Wang
CFO: David Vanderhorst
HR: –
FYE: December 31
Type: Public

Taitron Components is primarily a supplier of original designed and manufactured (ODM) products that include value-added engineering and turn-key solutions. The company also discrete semiconductors, commodity Integrated Circuits (ICs), optoelectronic devices and passive components to other electronic distributors, CEMs and OEMs, who incorporate them in their products. It also distributes brand name electronic components with a vast inventory available on hand. Taitron distributes more than 12,000 different products from about 100 suppliers, including Princeton Technology. The company gets the bulk of its sales in the US.

	Annual Growth	12/18	12/19	12/20	12/21	12/22
Sales ($mil.)	0.6%	8.2	6.8	6.7	8.6	8.4
Net income ($ mil.)	23.5%	1.4	0.8	1.4	2.0	3.2
Market value ($ mil.)	19.1%	10.4	17.0	19.5	24.2	20.9
Employees	(3.1%)	17	18	16	14	15

TAKE-TWO INTERACTIVE SOFTWARE, INC.

NMS: TTWO

110 West 44th Street
New York, NY 10036
Phone: 646 536-2842
Fax: –
Web: www.take2games.com

CEO: Strauss Zelnick
CFO: Lainie Goldstein
HR: –
FYE: March 31
Type: Public

Take-Two is a leading developer, publisher and marketer of interactive entertainment for consumers around the globe. The company's popular mature-rated Grand Theft Auto series and other games are developed by subsidiary Rockstar Games. Its 2K Games subsidiary publishes franchises such as BioShock, Borderlands, and Sid Meier's Civilization; the 2K Sports unit carries titles such as Major League Baseball 2K and NBA 2K. Take-Two's games are played on Microsoft, Sony, and Nintendo game consoles, but also on PCs and handheld devices. Its products are sold through outlets including retail chains, such as GameStop and Steam, and as digital downloads. Approximately 60% of its sales comes from the US.

	Annual Growth	03/19	03/20	03/21	03/22	03/23
Sales ($mil.)	19.0%	2,668.4	3,089.0	3,372.8	3,504.8	5,349.9
Net income ($ mil.)	–	333.8	404.5	588.9	418.0	(1,124.7)
Market value ($ mil.)	6.0%	15,939	20,033	29,845	25,967	20,150
Employees	16.1%	4,896	5,800	6,495	6,042	8,894

TAL INTERNATIONAL GROUP, INC.

100 MANHATTANVILLE RD STE 13
PURCHASE, NY 105772134
Phone: 914 251-9000
Fax: –
Web: –

CEO: Brian M Sondey
CFO: John Burns
HR: –
FYE: December 31
Type: Private

Triton International is a world's largest lessor of large, standardized steel boxes intermodal containers such as dry, tank, refrigerated containers, flat racks, open tops and palletwide containers used to transport freight by ship, rail or truck internationally. Its equipment leasing operations include acquisition, leasing, re-leasing and sale of multiple types of intermodal transportation equipment. It has over 6.0 million twenty-foot equivalents ("TEU") fleet of containers. Through its global network of nearly 20 offices and 3 independent agencies in more than 15 countries, Triton offers its customers access to its containers through approximately 430 third-party owned container depot facilities across above 45 countries. The company also offers equipment like Chassis, Generators sets and Rolltrailers. Its customers include CMA CGM, Hapag-Lloyd, MSC, Cosco Shipping, HMM, Ocean Network Express, Evergreen Marine Corp, Maersk and Yang Ming.

TALENT TECHNICAL SERVICES, INC.

1769 LEXINGTON AVE N
SAINT PAUL, MN 551136522
Phone: 952 417-3600
Fax: –
Web: www.talentstaffingservices.com

CEO: –
CFO: –
HR: Jatin Sati
FYE: December 31
Type: Private

Talent Software Services has a knack for software and services. The company provides information technology consulting; it specializes in enterprise data management, enterprise application services, and security and infrastructure services. Talent serves customers in industries such as financial services, manufacturing, and health care; clients have included Best Buy, Thermo King, Allina Health Systems, United Health Group, Honeywell, Blue Cross Blue Shield, and Carlson Companies. The company primarily operates in the Twin Cities region of Minnesota.

	Annual Growth	12/96	12/97	12/10	12/11	12/12
Sales ($mil.)	1.1%	–	14.4	18.7	18.3	17.0
Net income ($ mil.)	(5.1%)	–	1.6	1.1	1.0	0.7
Market value ($ mil.)	–	–	–	–	–	–
Employees	–	–	–	–	–	49

TALLAHASSEE MEMORIAL HEALTHCARE, INC.

1300 MICCOSUKEE RD
TALLAHASSEE, FL 323085054
Phone: 850 431-1155
Fax: –
Web: www.tmh.org

CEO: –
CFO: William Giudice
HR: Easter Davenport
FYE: September 30
Type: Private

Founded in 1948, Tallahassee Memorial HealthCare (TMH) is a private, not-for-profit community healthcare system committed to transforming care, advancing health, and improving lives with an ultimate vision to elevate the standards of healthcare practice, quality and innovation in the region. Serving a 21-county area in North Florida, South Georgia and South Alabama, TMH is comprised of a 772-bed acute care hospital, a surgery and adult ICU center, a psychiatric hospital, multiple specialty care centers, three residency programs, about 40 affiliated physician practices and partnerships with Alliant Management Services, Apalachee Center, Calhoun Liberty Hospital, Capital Health Plan, Doctors' Memorial Hospital, Florida State University College of Medicine, Radiology Associates, University of Florida Health, Weems Memorial Hospital and Wolfson Children's Hospital.

	Annual Growth	09/17	09/18	09/19	09/21	09/22
Sales ($mil.)	5.9%	–	–	705.3	783.9	837.5
Net income ($ mil.)	–	–	–	6.6	17.9	(5.4)
Market value ($ mil.)	–	–	–	–	–	–
Employees	–	–	–	–	–	6,430

TALLAHASSEE, CITY OF (INC)

300 S ADAMS ST
TALLAHASSEE, FL 323011731
Phone: 850 891-8280
Fax: –
Web: www.talgov.com

CEO: –
CFO: –
HR: Jessica Matson
FYE: September 30
Type: Private

Tallahassee, named for the "old fields" which once inhabited the area, got its moniker from some of its earliest settlers, the Apalachee Indians, around the 16th century. Today, the capital of Florida has a population of about 180,000 people and thrives particularly in the arts and sciences and high tech fields thanks in part to several major educational and research institutes, including Florida State University and Florida A&M University. An elected mayor and four-person city commission serve as the governing body and oversee an annual budget of more than $700 million. Three-fourths of the Tallahassee's revenue comes from fees for city services.

	Annual Growth	09/15	09/16	09/18	09/21	09/22
Sales ($mil.)	2.4%	–	141.2	138.1	163.4	163.1
Net income ($ mil.)	–	–	1.4	14.7	9.6	(13.3)
Market value ($ mil.)	–	–	–	–	–	–
Employees	–	–	–	–	–	3,000

TALLGRASS ENERGY PARTNERS, LP

4200 W 115TH ST STE 350
LEAWOOD, KS 662112733
Phone: 913 928-6060
Fax: –
Web: www.tallgrass.com

CEO: David G Dehaemers Jr
CFO: Gary J Brauchle
HR: Jana Johnston
FYE: December 31
Type: Private

This company hopes there's plenty of green out there in the tall grass. Tallgrass Energy Partners (TEP) provides transportation and storage of natural gas in the Rocky Mountains and Midwest. It also provides natural gas processing and treating at its three facilities in Wyoming. TEP's natural gas transportation systems are located in Colorado, Kansas, Missouri, Nebraska, and Wyoming. TEP also maintains a pipeline from the Colorado and Wyoming border to Beatrice, Nebraska, and it provides water business to customers in Colorado and Texas. TEP was formed in early 2013 to hold the midstream assets of its parent, Tallgrass Development. It became a public company a few months later.

TALLGRASS ENERGY, LP

4200 W 115TH ST STE 350
LEAWOOD, KS 662112733
Phone: 913 928-6060
Fax: –
Web: www.tallgrass.com

CEO: William R Moler
CFO: –
HR: –
FYE: December 31
Type: Private

Tallgrass Energy holds 22.5% of (and manages) Tallgrass Equity, which itself owns (through Tallgrass MLP GP, LLC) all of Tallgrass Energy Partners' (TEP) incentive distribution rights, and a 1.4% general partner interest in TEP. Tallgrass Equity owns a 32.75% limited partner interest in TEP. TEP's business consists of the Tallgrass Interstate Gas Transmission (TIGT) system (in Colorado, Kansas, Missouri, Nebraska, and Wyoming); the Trailblazer Pipeline (Colorado, Wyoming, and Nebraska); a 66.7% membership interest in Tallgrass Pony Express Pipeline; the Casper and Douglas natural gas processing plants; and the West Frenchie Draw natural gas treating facility. It went public in 2015.

	Annual Growth	12/14	12/15	12/16	12/17	12/18
Sales ($mil.)	14.5%	–	–	605.1	655.9	793.3
Net income ($ mil.)	38.7%	–	–	243.0	224.0	467.7
Market value ($ mil.)	–	–	–	–	–	–
Employees	–	–	–	–	–	800

TALON INTERNATIONAL, INC.

21900 Burbank Boulevard, Suite 101
Woodland Hills, CA 91367
Phone: 818 444-4100
Fax: –
Web: www.taloninternational.com

NBB: TALN
CEO: Larry Dyne
CFO: Larry Dyne
HR: –
FYE: December 31
Type: Public

Talon has clawed its way to the top, with some thread, trim, and hang tags. Formerly Tag It Pacific, it develops brand-identity programs for manufacturers of fashion apparel and accessories and for specialty retailers and mass merchants. Talon's "trim packages" include items such as thread, zippers, labels, buttons, and hangers, as well as printed marketing materials (hang tags, bar-coded tags, pocket flashers, size stickers) designed to promote and sell the items. It also distributes its Talon-brand metal and synthetic zippers and other apparel components, such as waistbands, under its TEKFIT name. Its more than 800 customers include Abercrombie & Fitch, Express, PVH, and Victoria's Secret.

	Annual Growth	12/13	12/14	12/15	12/16	12/22
Sales ($mil.)	(3.6%)	52.4	49.3	48.4	48.3	37.5
Net income ($ mil.)	(17.5%)	9.7	0.6	0.5	1.0	1.7
Market value ($ mil.)	(6.2%)	23.1	16.6	15.7	12.0	12.9
Employees	–	–	215	212	195	201

TALOS PETROLEUM LLC

625 E KALISTE SALOOM RD
LAFAYETTE, LA 705082540
Phone: 337 237-0410
Fax: -
Web: -

CEO: -
CFO: -
HR: -
FYE: December 31
Type: Private

You can't squeeze blood from a stone, but as Stone Energy knows, you can squeeze energy. Stone Energy acquires and exploits mature oil and natural gas properties that have high potential. The company, which for 2015 reported estimated proved reserves of 342 billion cu. ft. of natural gas equivalent, has producing properties in the Gulf of Mexico. It has sold the bulk of its Rocky Mountain oil and gas properties in order to focus its energy on targeting reserves and production in the deep shelf and deep water areas of the Gulf of Mexico. In 2015 it had 1.2 million of gross acres of undeveloped properties. The company filed for Chapter 11 bankruptcy protection in late 2016 and emerged from it in early 2017.

TALPHERA INC

NMS: TLPH

1850 Gateway Drive, Suite 175
San Mateo, CA 94404
Phone: 650 216-3500
Fax: -
Web: www.acelrx.com

CEO: Vincent J Angotti
CFO: Raffi Asadorian
HR: -
FYE: December 31
Type: Public

For patients with acute pain, a slip of the tongue could be a useful thing. AcelRx is developing the Sufentanil NanoTab PCA System, which administers pain medication sublingually, or under the tongue. Designed for patients with post-operative pain, the system administers measured doses of the opioid sufentanil in the form of tiny tablets, which quickly dissolve and are absorbed into the body through the lining under the tongue. Currently in late-stage of development, its NanoTab system is also being developed to treat cancer-related pain or provide sedation and pain relief to patients having procedures at doctors' offices. Founded in 2005, AcelRx went public in 2011 through a $40 million IPO.

	Annual Growth	12/19	12/20	12/21	12/22	12/23
Sales ($mil.)	(27.0%)	2.3	5.4	2.8	1.8	0.7
Net income ($ mil.)	-	(53.2)	(40.4)	(35.1)	47.8	(18.4)
Market value ($ mil.)	(23.2%)	35.8	21.0	9.5	38.3	12.5
Employees	(37.6%)	99	54	43	19	15

TAMPA ELECTRIC COMPANY

702 N FRANKLIN ST
TAMPA, FL 336024429
Phone: 813 228-1111
Fax: -
Web: www.tampaelectric.com

CEO: Nancy Tower
CFO: Gregory W Blunden
HR: Lori Clark
FYE: December 31
Type: Private

Tampa Electric Company (TEC) is a public utility operating within the State of Florida. Its electric division, referred to as Tampa Electric, transmits, purchases, and distributes electricity in approximately 2,000-square mile service territory in West Central Florida (including Hillsborough County and parts of Polk, Pasco and Pinellas Counties). The company provides electric service to about 826,700 customers and has a generating capacity of 6,500 MW. It also serves some 468,000 gas customers through its gas operations referred to as PGS. Tampa Electric is a subsidiary of TECO Energy, which is itself a unit of Canada's Emera.

TANDEM DIABETES CARE INC

NMS: TNDM

12400 High Bluff Drive
San Diego, CA 92130
Phone: 858 366-6900
Fax: -
Web: www.tandemdiabetes.com

CEO: John F Sheridan
CFO: Leigh A Vosseller
HR: -
FYE: December 31
Type: Public

Tandem Diabetes Care is a medical device company that manufactures, sells and supports insulin pump products. The company's primary focus is its flagship insulin pump, the t:slim X2 Insulin. Tandem manufactures and sells the t:slim X2 insulin pump with Control-IQ technology. The t:slim X2 pump is capable of remote feature updates using a personal computer. The company shipped about 290,000 pumps to US customers and some 130,000were shipped to international markets. The t:slim is the first and only system cleared by the United States Food and Drug Administration (FDA) to deliver automatic correction boluses in addition to adjusting insulin to help prevent high and low blood sugar. While its products are sold to about 25 countries, the company generates about 75% of revenue from its domestic customers.

	Annual Growth	12/19	12/20	12/21	12/22	12/23
Sales ($mil.)	19.9%	362.3	498.8	702.8	801.2	747.7
Net income ($ mil.)	-	(24.8)	(34.4)	15.6	(94.6)	(222.6)
Market value ($ mil.)	(16.1%)	3,907.6	6,272.0	9,866.9	2,946.6	1,939.0
Employees	23.2%	1,043	1,500	2,000	2,600	2,400

TANDY LEATHER FACTORY INC

NMS: TLF

1900 Southeast Loop 820
Fort Worth, TX 76140
Phone: 817 872-3200
Fax: -
Web: www.tandyleather.com

CEO: Janet Carr
CFO: Michael Galvan
HR: Sherry Longshore
FYE: December 31
Type: Public

Tandy Leather Factory (aka TLF) has built a business turning hides into a cash cow. The company makes, distributes, and sells leather goods and related products, such as leatherworking tools, buckles and belt supplies, leather dyes, saddle and tack hardware, do-it-yourself craft kits, suede lace, and fringe. Its Retail Leathercraft unit, which generates more than 50% of sales, operates about 75 retail leathercraft stores under the Tandy Leather banner that cater to leatherworking hobbyists in the US and Canada. It also sells merchandise online. The company also operates some 30 wholesale stores across in North America. Tandy Leather Factory was founded in 1980 as Midas Leathercraft Tool Co.

	Annual Growth	12/19	12/20	12/21	12/22	12/23
Sales ($mil.)	0.4%	74.9	64.1	82.7	80.3	76.2
Net income ($ mil.)	-	(1.9)	(4.9)	1.4	1.2	3.8
Market value ($ mil.)	(7.1%)	48.0	25.2	25.2	35.7	35.8
Employees	(9.4%)	578	496	593	605	389

TANGER INC

NYS: SKT

3200 Northline Avenue, Suite 360
Greensboro, NC 27408
Phone: 336 292-3010
Fax: 336 297-0931
Web: www.tangeroutlet.com

CEO: -
CFO: -
HR: -
FYE: December 31
Type: Public

One of the top outlet mall developers, Tanger is a real estate investment trust (REIT) that develops, owns, and manages over 30 retail outlet centers, with a total gross leasable area of approximately 11.5 million square feet, which were more than 95% occupied and contained over 2,200 stores representing approximately 500 store brands, including American Eagle Outfitters, Banana Republic Factory Store, Calvin Klein, Coach, Gap Outlet, Hugo Boss Factory Store, and Kate Spade New York. It also had partial ownership interests in six unconsolidated outlet centers totaling approximately 2.1 million square feet, including two outlet centers in Canada.

	Annual Growth	12/19	12/20	12/21	12/22	12/23
Sales ($mil.)	(0.7%)	478.3	390.0	426.5	442.6	464.4
Net income ($ mil.)	3.1%	87.9	(36.3)	9.1	82.1	99.2
Market value ($ mil.)	17.1%	1,602.5	1,083.6	2,097.5	1,951.8	3,015.7
Employees	(10.6%)	636	527	573	603	407

TANGOE US, INC.

8888 KEYSTONE XING STE 1300
INDIANAPOLIS, IN 462404600
Phone: 973 257-0300
Fax: –
Web: www.tangoe.com

CEO: Bob Irwin
CFO: Arun Shivdasani
HR: –
FYE: December 31
Type: Private

Tangoe is the leading global provider of technology expense and asset management solutions. The company, fueled by an innovative automation framework and unified customer experience, seamlessly integrates with hundreds of providers globally to deliver the reporting and insights needed by enterprises of all sizes and scales. It also optimizes spend and resources across telecom, mobile, cloud, and IoT. Nearly half of the Fortune 500 relies on Tangoe to work smarter, save money, and be confident in their decisions. Tangoe also offers such services as Advisory services, Bill Pay, Unified Endpoint Management, and Help Desk.

TANNER INDUSTRIES, INC.

735 DAVISVILLE RD
SOUTHAMPTON, PA 189663282
Phone: 215 322-1238
Fax: –
Web: www.tannerind.com

CEO: –
CFO: Eric R Hindawi
HR: –
FYE: December 31
Type: Private

Tanner plies the trade of chemical shipping and warehousing. The company distributes anhydrous ammonia and ammonium hydroxide by tank truck, railcar, drum, and cylinder to US customers from nearly 15 facilities. It makes more than 20,000 deliveries per year, and operates over 200 tractors and trailers. The company also provides custom blending, contract packaging, and safety training services. Tanner sells its products in cylinders, drums, totes, l.t.l bulk, full of truckloads and rail cars. The company, which was founded in 1954 by Lawrence Tanner, is run by a third generation of Tanner family members.

	Annual Growth	12/03	12/04	12/05	12/06	12/07
Sales ($mil.)	96.2%	–	10.6	64.7	74.1	80.2
Net income ($ mil.)	41.2%	–	1.4	3.5	6.8	4.1
Market value ($ mil.)	–	–	–	–	–	–
Employees	–	–	–	–	–	130

TAOS HEALTH SYSTEMS, INC.

1397 WEIMER RD
TAOS, NM 875716253
Phone: 575 758-8883
Fax: –
Web: www.hcmctaos.com

CEO: Bill Patten
CFO: Ken Verdon
HR: Ann Coppersmith
FYE: May 31
Type: Private

Whether you're skiing in the winter or hiking in the summer, Taos visitors and residents can turn to Holy Cross Hospital for medical care. The medical center provides inpatient and outpatient health care services for Taos and surrounding counties in northern New Mexico. The hospital opened its doors in 1937 and has expanded its facilities to include about 50 licensed beds. Among its specialty services are emergency medicine, general surgery, obstetrics, orthopedics, cardiology, urology, and women's health care. Holy Cross Hospital is part of the Taos Health Systems network, which includes area general care, rehabilitation, surgical, and specialist clinics.

	Annual Growth	05/17	05/18	05/19	05/20	05/22
Sales ($mil.)	12.4%	–	57.3	62.7	63.7	91.5
Net income ($ mil.)	–	–	(5.1)	0.3	(0.3)	6.0
Market value ($ mil.)	–	–	–	–	–	–
Employees	–	–	–	–	–	412

TAOS MOUNTAIN, LLC

1307 S EAGLE FLIGHT WAY
BOISE, ID 837091559
Phone: 408 324-2800
Fax: –
Web: www.ibm.com

CEO: Hamilton Yu
CFO: –
HR: –
FYE: December 31
Type: Private

The San Francisco Bay Area has a lot of technical talent on hand, but not all IT superstars are in the right place at the right time. Taos Mountain provides a variety of IT services, including the evaluation of technical staff and network administration. The company offers interim IT staffing, management consulting, and project delivery services, along with managed services for outsourcing the service desk and other IT functions. Clients include Adobe Systems, Cisco Systems, Clorox, Google, Hewlett-Packard, Intel, Microsoft, Oracle, and Wells Fargo. Co-founders Alexis Tatarsky and CEO Ric Urrutia are the majority shareholders.

TAP ENTERPRISES, INC.

650 N LINCOLN ST
SPRING HILL, KS 660838356
Phone: 913 592-2120
Fax: –
Web: www.tapent.com

CEO: –
CFO: –
HR: –
FYE: December 31
Type: Private

All types of tools are on tap from Tap Enterprises. The company distributes hand tools, power tools, air tools, and air compressors throughout the US. Brands that it peddles include Campbell Hausfeld, Coleman, DeWALT, Makita, Ridgid, and Ryobi, among others. It sells discounted and reconditioned tools through its ToolsNow.com Web site and operates about 10 retail tool stores under the Worldwide Liquidators banner in the Kansas City and St. Louis metropolitan areas, as well as in Illinois. Additionally, the company sells products via traveling tool shows conducted throughout the continental US. Formerly named Cummins Tools, Tap Enterprises was founded by president Bob Cummins in 1977.

TAPESTRY INC

10 Hudson Yards
New York, NY 10001
Phone: 212 946-8400
Fax: –
Web: www.tapestry.com

NYS: TPR
CEO: Joanne Crevoiserat
CFO: Scott Roe
HR: –
FYE: July 1
Type: Public

Tapestry, previously Coach, is one of the leading designers and makers (mostly through third parties) of high-end leather goods and accessories, including handbags, wallets, and luggage under the Coach brand. It also licenses the Coach name for watches, eyewear, and fragrances. In addition, through acquisitions, Tapestry owns the Stuart Weitzman (luxury women's shoes) and Kate Spade (women's apparel and accessories) brands. The company sells its wares through department and outlet stores (in the US and globally) and websites. More than 60% of total revenue comes from the US

	Annual Growth	06/19	06/20*	07/21	07/22	07/23
Sales ($mil.)	2.5%	6,027.1	4,961.4	5,746.3	6,684.5	6,660.9
Net income ($ mil.)	9.8%	643.4	(652.1)	834.2	856.3	936.0
Market value ($ mil.)	7.8%	7,215.4	2,853.9	9,700.9	7,008.5	9,732.7
Employees	(3.1%)	21,000	17,300	16,400	18,100	18,500

*Fiscal year change

TARGA RESOURCES CORP

NYS: TRGP

811 Louisiana Street, Suite 2100
Houston, TX 77002
Phone: 713 584-1000
Fax: 713 584-1100
Web: www.targaresources.com

CEO: Matthew J Meloy
CFO: Jennifer R Kneale
HR: –
FYE: December 31
Type: Public

Targa Resources Corp. is one of the leading providers of midstream services and is one of the largest independent midstream infrastructure companies in North America. The company is primarily engaged in gathering, compressing, treating, processing, transporting and purchasing, selling natural gas, gathering, storing, terminaling and purchasing and selling crude oil as well as purchasing and selling NGLs and NGL products, including services to LPG exporters. Targa owns or operates approximately 30,900 miles of natural gas pipelines and includes more than 50 owned and operated processing plants. It has a presence in many shale basins including the Permian, Eagle Ford, Barnett, Anadarko, Arkoma, and Williston. In 2022, Targa acquired Lucid Energy Delaware, LLC (Lucid) for $3.55 billion. This acquisition extends and further strengthens Targa's position in the core of the Delaware Basin.

	Annual Growth	12/19	12/20	12/21	12/22	12/23
Sales ($mil.)	16.7%	8,671.1	8,260.3	16,950	20,930	16,060
Net income ($ mil.)	–	(209.2)	(1,553.9)	71.2	1,195.5	1,345.9
Market value ($ mil.)	20.8%	9,089.2	5,872.5	11,629	16,362	19,338
Employees	4.4%	2,680	2,372	2,430	2,850	3,182

TARGET CORP

NYS: TGT

1000 Nicollet Mall
Minneapolis, MN 55403
Phone: 612 304-6073
Fax: –
Web: www.target.com

CEO: Brian C Cornell
CFO: Michael Fiddelke
HR: –
FYE: February 3
Type: Public

Target sells a wide assortment of general merchandise and food, including perishables, dry grocery, dairy, and frozen items. The fashion-forward discounter operates about 1,950 Target stores across the US, as well as an online business at Target.com. It sells a broad range of household goods, food and pet supplies, apparel and accessories, electronics, decor, and other items under national brands as well as owned and exclusive brands. Target also sells merchandise through periodic exclusive design and creative partnerships and generate revenue from in-store amenities such as Target Caf and leased or licensed departments such as Target Optical, Starbucks, and other food service offerings. The company also offers pharmacy and clinic services in its stores through an operating agreement with CVS Pharmacy.

	Annual Growth	02/20*	01/21	01/22	01/23*	02/24
Sales ($mil.)	8.3%	78,112	93,561	106,005	109,120	107,412
Net income ($ mil.)	6.0%	3,281.0	4,368.0	6,946.0	2,780.0	4,138.0
Market value ($ mil.)	7.1%	51,126	83,642	100,493	77,797	67,169
Employees	3.1%	368,000	409,000	450,000	440,000	415,000

*Fiscal year change

TARGETED MEDICAL PHARMA, INC.

NBB: TRGM

2980 Beverly Glen Cirlce
Los Angeles, CA 90077
Phone: 310 474-9809
Fax: –
Web: –

CEO: Marcus Charuvastra
CFO: William B Horne
HR: –
FYE: December 31
Type: Public

Targeted Medical Pharma makes medical foods that can be combined with drugs to help manage certain disorders. The company manufactures and markets a line of medical foods -- a class of FDA regulated products that help meet certain nutritional or metabolic deficiencies (think amino acids) -- for patients who suffer from the likes of hypertension, obesity, pain, sleep disorders, and viral infections. Its #1 product, theramine, accounts for more than half of sales. Targeted Medical Pharma also repackages and distributes other pharma maker's drugs with its own medical food products so that physicians can prescribe and dispense them together supposedly for better efficacy. The company withdrew its IPO in 2012.

	Annual Growth	12/11	12/12	12/13	12/14	12/15
Sales ($mil.)	(25.8%)	–	–	9.6	7.1	5.3
Net income ($ mil.)	–	–	–	(9.3)	(3.9)	(3.0)
Market value ($ mil.)	(85.6%)	–	–	20.8	5.6	0.4
Employees	–	–	–	–	45	30

TARLETON STATE UNIVERSITY

1333 W WASHINGTON ST
STEPHENVILLE, TX 764014168
Phone: 254 968-9000
Fax: –
Web: www.tarleton.edu

CEO: –
CFO: –
HR: –
FYE: August 31
Type: Private

Tarleton State University, a member of The Texas A&M University System, has an enrollment of more than 9,500 students on four campuses Central and North Texas. The university confers degrees in undergraduate programs and graduate programs. It also offers a doctorate in educational administration. Tarleton State has approximately 450 full- and part-time faculty providing instruction at six colleges (agriculture and human sciences, business administration, education, liberal and fine arts, science and technology, and graduate studies). It ranks as one of the most affordable four-year universities in Texas.

	Annual Growth	08/16	08/17	08/18	08/19	08/20
Sales ($mil.)	2.3%	–	111.5	116.4	119.4	119.3
Net income ($ mil.)	149.1%	–	16.2	14.9	68.9	251.1
Market value ($ mil.)	–	–	–	–	–	–
Employees	–	–	–	–	–	822

TARRANT COUNTY HOSPITAL DISTRICT

1500 S MAIN ST
FORT WORTH, TX 761044917
Phone: 817 921-3431
Fax: –
Web: www.jpshealthnet.org

CEO: Robert Earley
CFO: Randy Rogers
HR: –
FYE: September 30
Type: Private

If Fort Worth residents are searching for health care, they need look no further than Tarrant County Hospital District (dba JPS Health Network). Founded in 1906 in Fort Worth, Texas, the network's flagship facility, John Peter Smith Hospital, has approximately 540 beds and provides specialty services including orthopedics, cardiology, and women's health. JPS Health Network also includes behavioral health treatment center Trinity Springs Pavilion and the JPS Diagnostic & Surgery Hospital of Arlington. The company provides family medical, dental, and specialty care through dozens of health care centers in northern Texas.

	Annual Growth	09/18	09/19	09/20	09/21	09/22
Sales ($mil.)	13.2%	–	673.0	868.6	982.4	976.3
Net income ($ mil.)	51.0%	–	32.7	198.9	327.1	112.6
Market value ($ mil.)	–	–	–	–	–	–
Employees	–	–	–	–	–	3,000

TAS-CHFH

70 EAST ST
METHUEN, MA 018444597
Phone: 978 687-0156
Fax: –
Web: www.caritasholyfamily.org

CEO: –
CFO: –
HR: –
FYE: September 30
Type: Private

Caritas Holy Family Hospital is part of a large family of hospitals. The acute care medical facility is a more than 260-bed hospital that serves the residents of some 20 communities in northern Massachusetts and southern New Hampshire. Holy Family Hospital offers specialized services in areas including surgery, diagnostics, pediatrics, obstetrics, oncology, cardiology, and psychiatric care. The hospital, founded in 1985, also operates an outpatient surgery center and provides community outreach services. It is a member of Steward Health Care System (formerly Caritas Christi), one of the largest health care systems in New England.

	Annual Growth	09/01	09/02	09/03	09/08	09/09
Sales ($mil.)	2.6%	–	122.0	122.7	149.2	145.7
Net income ($ mil.)	–	–	(4.4)	(1.0)	2.0	6.0
Market value ($ mil.)	–	–	–	–	–	–
Employees	–	–	–	–	–	1,700

TAS-CNH, INC.

800 WASHINGTON ST STE 1   CEO: –
NORWOOD, MA 020623487   CFO: –
Phone: 781 769-4000   HR: –
Fax: –   FYE: September 30
Web: –   Type: Private

Caritas Norwood Hospital cares for hearts (and other body parts) of people in the greater Boston area. Operating as Norwood Hospital, the facility is a community hospital with some 265 beds that serves patients in Norwood, Massachusetts, and surrounding towns. Founded in 1902, the acute care hospital has a medical staff of more than 460 that provides area residents with emergency and general health care and medical transport services. Norwood Hospital is also home to specialized programs including behavioral health services, cancer treatment, cardiology, obstetrics/gynecology, orthopedic medicine, pediatrics, rehabilitation, sleep disorder treatment, and surgery. Norwood Hospital is part of the Steward Health Care System.

	Annual Growth	09/04	09/05	09/06	09/08	09/09
Sales ($mil.)	1.6%	–	150.0	153.4	151.5	159.6
Net income ($ mil.)	(1.1%)	–	4.5	15.1	(3.7)	4.3
Market value ($ mil.)	–	–	–	–	–	–
Employees	–	–	–	–	–	1,800

TATA AMERICA INTERNATIONAL CORPORATION

101 PARK AVE FL 26   CEO: Surya Kant
NEW YORK, NY 101782604   CFO: –
Phone: 212 557-8038   HR: Divya Bindiganavale
Fax: –   FYE: March 31
Web: www.tata.com   Type: Private

Tata America International is the North American holding company for Indian conglomerate Tata Group. In the US the company has about a dozen subsidiaries, including offices for Tata Communications, IT services firm Tata Consultancy Services (with more than 20 locations), and engineering consultancy Tata Technologies. In the industrial sector, Tata America owns steel manufacturing plants in Ohio and Pennsylvania and General Chemical Industrial Products, a soda ash plant in Wyoming. Other holdings include hotels (The Pierre in New York, the Taj Boston and the Taj Campton Place in San Francisco) and sales offices for its beverage brands, Eight O'Clock Coffee, Good Earth, and Tetley.

	Annual Growth	03/16	03/17	03/18	03/19	03/20
Sales ($mil.)	(75.5%)	–	–	8,197.5	538.8	493.8
Net income ($ mil.)	(7.4%)	–	–	121.8	269.6	104.5
Market value ($ mil.)	–	–	–	–	–	–
Employees	–	–	–	–	–	1,700

TATUNG COMPANY OF AMERICA, INC.

2157 MOUNT SHASTA DR   CEO: Huei-Jihn Jih
SAN PEDRO, CA 907321334   CFO: Danny Huang
Phone: 310 637-2105   HR: Albert Perez
Fax: –   FYE: December 31
Web: www.tatungusa.com   Type: Private

Tongue tied by the alphabet soup of electronics? Tatung Company of America untangles the LCDs (liquid crystal displays) from the LEDs (light-emitting diodes). It offers an array of high-tech goods and manufacturing services for PC and electronics OEMs. Its digital line ranges from signage and security surveillance tools, like cameras and monitors, to computer monitors for PCs, point-of-sale terminals, and touch screens. The company also sells home appliances, such as air purifiers and rice cookers, as well as hospitality conveniences, like microwaves and coffee makers. The company is the US arm of Taiwan's Tatung Company.

	Annual Growth	12/03	12/04	12/05	12/07	12/08
Sales ($mil.)	(15.1%)	–	246.9	265.4	138.3	128.5
Net income ($ mil.)	(38.8%)	–	4.3	3.0	1.3	0.6
Market value ($ mil.)	–	–	–	–	–	–
Employees	–	–	–	–	–	105

TAUBER OIL COMPANY

55 WAUGH DR STE 700   CEO: –
HOUSTON, TX 770075837   CFO: –
Phone: 713 869-8700   HR: –
Fax: –   FYE: December 31
Web: www.tauberoil.com   Type: Private

Tauber Oil is a family-owned company that markets refined products, carbon black feedstocks, natural gas liquids, crude oil, chemical feeds, gasoline blending, and emissions and carbon. The company is one of the leading suppliers of Carbon Black Feedstock. Tauber Oil Company's Business Development group explores strategic opportunities to serve new and existing clients requiring petroleum-based products and logistics services. Tauber Petrochemical Co. is a wholly-owned subsidiary of Tauber Oil Company. The Houston-based company serves major and independent oil companies, major petrochemical producers and consumers, and small- to medium-sized end-users. Tauber Oil owned by David and Richard Tauber.

	Annual Growth	12/10	12/11	12/12	12/13	12/14
Sales ($mil.)	(2.6%)	–	–	5,088.2	4,769.4	4,831.2
Net income ($ mil.)	(29.0%)	–	–	21.2	16.3	10.7
Market value ($ mil.)	–	–	–	–	–	–
Employees	–	–	–	–	–	135

TAWA SUPERMARKET, INC.

6281 REGIO AVE   CEO: Chang K Hua Chen
BUENA PARK, CA 906201023   CFO: –
Phone: 714 521-8899   HR: Harry Sun
Fax: –   FYE: December 31
Web: www.168markets.com   Type: Private

TAWA Supermarket works to make ethnic food mainstream with more than 35 Asian-American grocery stores. The company operates its grocery network under the 99 Ranch Market banner. The fast-growing chain is primarily found in California, but also boasts locations in Texas, Nevada, and Washington. Besides groceries, fresh seafood, bakery items, liquor, and produce, 99 Ranch Market supermarkets sell everything from Chinese DVDs to ginseng. The company was founded in 1984 by Taiwanese expatriate Roger Chen to serve immigrants who craved the food products of their homeland. 99 Ranch Market has grown to become the largest Asian supermarket chain in the US.

TAYLOR (CALVIN B.) BANKSHARES, INC. (MD)   NBB: TYCB

24 N. Main Street   CEO: Raymond M Thompson
Berlin, MD 21811   CFO: –
Phone: 410 641-1700   HR: –
Fax: 410 641-0543   FYE: December 31
Web: www.taylorbank.com   Type: Public

Calvin B. Taylor Bankshares be the holding company for Calvin B. Taylor Banking Company (aka Taylor Bank), which has about 10 branches in southeastern Maryland and another in Delaware. The bank offers standard commercial and retail services including checking and savings accounts, money market accounts, and credit cards. It also offers discount securities brokerage through an affiliation with correspondent bank M&T Securities. Real estate loans account for some 90% of the bank's lending portfolio, including residential and commercial mortgages. The bank is named after its founder, who opened a predecessor to Calvin B. Taylor Banking Company in 1890.

	Annual Growth	12/18	12/19	12/20	12/21	12/22
Assets ($mil.)	14.2%	531.9	548.0	711.8	904.5	905.9
Net income ($ mil.)	12.3%	7.4	8.3	7.3	9.5	11.8
Market value ($ mil.)	5.7%	92.8	99.6	97.3	102.1	116.0
Employees	–	–	–	–	–	–

TAYLOR CORPORATION

1725 ROE CREST DR
NORTH MANKATO, MN 560031807
Phone: 507 625-2828
Fax: –
Web: www.taylor.com

CEO: Glen Taylor
CFO: Mike Rozaro
HR: Aaron Lerwill
FYE: December 31
Type: Private

Taylor Corporation is among the top ten graphic communications companies in North America. It engineers print solutions that build businesses. Taylor's combination of printed products, digital services, and integrated technology is the largest in the communications industry. Taylor provide greeting cards and stationery, certificates, envelopes, folders, forms and labels, ID badges, stamps, graphics communications products, and promotional items. It serves manufacturing companies, financial institutions, home improvement retailers, retail banks, credit unions, and wireless providers. It has production and distribution facilities servicing the US and Mexico from coast to coast.

TAYLOR DEVICES INC   NAS: TAYD

90 Taylor Drive
North Tonawanda, NY 14120
Phone: 716 694-0800
Fax: 716 695-6015
Web: www.taylordevices.com

CEO: Timothy J Sopko
CFO: Mark V McDonough V
HR: –
FYE: May 31
Type: Public

Taylor Devices helps buffer buildings and other structures from the forces of earthquakes, high winds, and even roaring crowds. The company makes seismic dampers and other equipment used to absorb shock, control vibration, and store energy. Along with giant dampers used in multi-story buildings -- including Safeco Field, home of the Seattle Mariners baseball team -- Taylor Devices produces a variety of shock absorbers, liquid die springs, and vibration dampers used in equipment and machinery. Taylor Devices primarily sells its products in the US and Canada.

	Annual Growth	05/19	05/20	05/21	05/22	05/23
Sales ($mil.)	4.6%	33.6	28.4	22.5	30.9	40.2
Net income ($ mil.)	25.4%	2.5	3.0	1.1	2.2	6.3
Market value ($ mil.)	13.7%	39.0	38.7	41.7	32.7	65.3
Employees	1.2%	119	115	115	123	125

TAYLOR MORRISON HOME CORP (HOLDING CO)   NYS: TMHC

4900 N. Scottsdale Road, Suite 2000
Scottsdale, AZ 85251
Phone: 480 840-8100
Fax: –
Web: www.taylormorrison.com

CEO: Sheryl D Palmer
CFO: C D Cone
HR: –
FYE: December 31
Type: Public

Taylor Morrison Home designs, builds, and sells single- and multi-family detached and attached homes in the US under the Taylor Morrison and Darling Homes brands. The company targets a wide demographic range of entry level, move-up, and active adult buyers. Its homes has an average selling price of about $436,000 in East; $473,000 in Central; and $541,000 in West. Taylor Morrison's sales are divided across those three geographic segments; the Midwest and eastern states provide its greatest revenue stream. The company also offers financial services, title insurance and closing settlement, and homeowner's insurance policies.

	Annual Growth	12/19	12/20	12/21	12/22	12/23
Sales ($mil.)	11.7%	4,762.1	6,129.3	7,501.3	8,224.9	7,417.8
Net income ($ mil.)	31.8%	254.7	243.4	663.0	1,052.8	768.9
Market value ($ mil.)	25.0%	2,337.2	2,742.4	3,737.8	3,245.0	5,704.1
Employees	5.0%	2,300	2,700	3,000	3,000	2,800

TAYLOR MORRISON HOME CORPORATION

4900 N SCOTTSDALE RD STE 2000
SCOTTSDALE, AZ 852517652
Phone: 480 840-8100
Fax: –
Web: www.taylormorrison.com

CEO: Sheryl D Palmer
CFO: C D Cone
HR: Caroline Noel
FYE: December 31
Type: Private

Taylor Morrison Home Corp (Taylor Morrison) is one of the largest public homebuilders in the US. It designs, builds, and sells single and multi-family detached and attached homes; and develops lifestyle and master-planned communities. It provides financial services to customers through its wholly owned mortgage subsidiary, and title insurance and closing settlement services through its title company. Taylor Morrison operates under the Taylor Morrison, Darling Homes, and Esplanade brand names. As of 2022, Taylor Morrison owned and controlled approximately 74,900 lots.

TAYLOR PRODUCTS INC

66 KINGSBORO AVE
GLOVERSVILLE, NY 120783415
Phone: 518 773-9312
Fax: –
Web: www.taylormadeproducts.com

CEO: James W Taylor
CFO: –
HR: –
FYE: December 31
Type: Private

Taylor Made Group has it made in the marine market. The company (no relation to golf club maker TaylorMade) operates through business units: Taylor Made Systems (includes Taylor Made Glass Systems) makes tempered safety glass products for marine, agricultural, and industrial use, glazing systems, and acrylic boat windshields; Taylor Made Products makes boat covers, flags/pennants, electric winches, rubber dock products, and buoys, as well as outdoor furniture and tarps; Taylor Made Technologies/ Taylorbrite makes marine and industrial lighting systems; Taylor Made Custom Products makes custom fabric awnings and sports vehicle covers. The family of founder Nelson Taylor owns the company.

TBC, INC.

3601 ODONNELL ST STE 100THE
BALTIMORE, MD 212245563
Phone: 410 347-7500
Fax: –
Web: www.tbc.us

CEO: –
CFO: –
HR: –
FYE: December 31
Type: Private

Trahan, Burden & Charles (TBC) is a full-service advertising agency offering creative ad development and campaign management services for a broad range of corporate clients. In addition to traditional creative services for print and broadcasting, TBC provides direct marketing, media planning, and interactive services, as well as public relations. Chairman Allan Charles founded the agency with partners Edward Trahan and Tom Burden in 1974.

	Annual Growth	12/10	12/11	12/12	12/13	12/14
Sales ($mil.)	(5.3%)	–	–	11.5	10.7	10.3
Net income ($ mil.)	9.2%	–	–	0.2	0.2	0.2
Market value ($ mil.)	–	–	–	–	–	–
Employees	–	–	–	–	–	100

TCG FAMILY BUSINESS LLC

200 NW 62ND ST STE 400
FORT LAUDERDALE, FL 333092174
Phone: 954 677-1020
Fax: –
Web: www.dexian.com

CEO: –
CFO: –
HR: –
FYE: December 31
Type: Private

Signature Consultants wants your John Hancock when it comes to signing up for its staffing services. The company provides information technology staffing services to clients from a variety of industries. Signature places IT professionals with expertise in areas like project management, web application development, database administration, storage, and network security. The firm has experience placing IT professionals across such industries as banking and financial services, energy, healthcare, technology, and consumer goods. Signature Consultants was established in 1997.

	Annual Growth	12/12	12/13	12/14	12/15	12/16
Sales ($mil.)	15.8%	–	202.2	235.2	253.2	314.1
Net income ($ mil.)	14.1%	–	3.7	4.3	1.3	5.6
Market value ($ mil.)		–	–	–	–	–
Employees		–	–	–	–	70

TCG, INC.

7348 GEORGIA AVE NW
WASHINGTON, DC 200121720
Phone: 202 986-5533
Fax: –
Web: www.tcg.com

CEO: –
CFO: –
HR: –
FYE: December 31
Type: Private

Turner Consulting Group (TCG) provides Web development and e-commerce services to federal government agencies, corporations, and not-for-profit organizations. It also provides systems integration and other information technology services. The firm was founded by president Daniel Turner in 1994. Its clients include the National Institutes of Health, Sprint Nextel, and the American Red Cross. TCG has offices in 10 states and the District of Columbia.

TD AMERITRADE HOLDING CORPORATION

200 S 108TH AVE
OMAHA, NE 681542631
Phone: 800 669-3900
Fax: –
Web: www.aboutschwab.com

CEO: Stephen J Boyle
CFO: Jon C Peterson
HR: –
FYE: September 30
Type: Private

TD Ameritrade Holding provides investing services and education to self-directed investors and registered investment advisors. A leader in US retail trading, it leverages the latest in cutting edge technologies and one-on-one client care to help its clients stay on top of market trends. A wholly-owned subsidiary of The Charles Schwab Corporation, it traces its roots back in 1975.

TD AMERITRADE, INC.

12800 CORPORATE HILL DR
SAINT LOUIS, MO 631311845
Phone: 314 965-1555
Fax: –
Web: www.tdameritrade.com

CEO: Rodger O Riney
CFO: Drew Dennison
HR: Jaime Berry
FYE: September 30
Type: Private

TD Ameritrade provides investing and trading services for 11 million client accounts that total more than $1 trillion in assets, and custodial services for more than 6,000 independent registered investment advisors. With clients placing, on average, approximately 500,000 trades each day, it maintains the leadership position it assumed when founder Joe Ricketts opened his doors in Omaha, Nebraska in 1975. The company helps to get access to stocks, bonds & CDs, options, mutual funds, futures, forex, commission-free ETFs, and more to stay diversified and ready to take advantage of a wider range of opportunities.

	Annual Growth	09/07	09/08	09/09	09/10	09/11
Assets ($mil.)	(22.7%)	–	–	–	8,566.4	6,619.6
Net income ($ mil.)		–	–	–	–	–
Market value ($ mil.)		–	–	–	–	–
Employees		–	–	–	–	1,600

TD SYNNEX CORP

NYS: SNX

44201 Nobel Drive
Fremont, CA 94538
Phone: 510 656-3333
Fax: –
Web: www.synnex.com

CEO: Richard T Hume
CFO: Marshall Witt
HR: –
FYE: November 30
Type: Public

TD SYNNEX (formerly SYNNEX) is a leading global provider of a comprehensive range of products for the technology industry and design and integrate data center equipment. It distributes more than 200,000 technology products, including IT hardware, software, and systems including personal computing devices and peripherals, mobile phones and accessories, printers, server and datacenter infrastructure, hybrid cloud, security, networking, communications and storage solutions, and system components from 1,500 original equipment manufacturers. It generates about 55% of its revenues from the US.

	Annual Growth	11/19	11/20	11/21	11/22	11/23
Sales ($mil.)	24.8%	23,757	24,676	31,614	62,344	57,555
Net income ($ mil.)	5.8%	500.7	529.2	395.1	651.3	626.9
Market value ($ mil.)	(5.3%)	10,889	14,215	9,173.7	9,070.8	8,746.3
Employees	(44.4%)	240,900	277,900	27,000	28,500	23,000

TEAM AIR EXPRESS, INC.

629 W BROADWAY ST
WINNSBORO, TX 754942059
Phone: 903 342-3516
Fax: –
Web: www.teamww.com

CEO: Jason G Brunson
CFO: –
HR: Cara King
FYE: April 28
Type: Private

This team wants to play in the big leagues of freight transportation. Team Worldwide provides domestic and international freight forwarding and logistics services from a network of about 60 offices in the US and more than 175 offices maintained by partners in other countries. The company specializes in airfreight forwarding; it also arranges surface transportation in the US and provides warehousing and distribution services. It operates through subsidiaries Team Air Express, Team International, and Team Transportation. Chairman Joe E. Brunson and his son, CEO Bobby J. Brunson, founded Team Worldwide in 1979.

TEAM HEALTH HOLDINGS, INC.

265 BROOKVIEW CENTRE WAY STE 400
KNOXVILLE, TN 37919
Phone: 865 693-1000
Fax: –
Web: www.teamhealth.com

CEO: Leif Murphy
CFO: David P Jones
HR: Becky Hillkern
FYE: December 31
Type: Private

Team Health is a physician-led, patient-focused company and one of the largest integrated care providers in the country. The company offers the highest quality staffing, administrative support and management across the full continuum of care, from hospital-based practices to post-acute care and ambulatory centers. It started in emergency medicine, expanded to additional hospital-based practices and also serves post-acute care and ambulatory centers. In addition to the company's network of some 15,000 clinicians, Team Health is proud to be the leading physician practice in the US, driven by its commitment to quality and safety and supported by its world-class operating team.

TEAM INC

13131 Dairy Ashford, Suite 600
Sugar Land, TX 77478
Phone: 281 331-6154
Fax: –
Web: www.teaminc.com

NYS: TISI
CEO: Keith Tucker
CFO: Nelson M Haight
HR: –
FYE: December 31
Type: Public

Team is a global, leading provider of specialty industrial services offering clients access to a full suite of conventional, specialized, and proprietary mechanical, heat-treating, and inspection services. Team integrated solutions involving: inspection to assess condition; engineering assessment to determine fitness for purpose in the context of industry standards and regulatory codes; and mechanical services to repair, rerate or replace based upon the client's election. Mainly serving companies in heavy industries such as the petrochemical, refining, power, pulp and paper, pipeline, and steel industries. The company operates from approximately 150 locations worldwide, but its largest market is the US.

	Annual Growth	12/19	12/20	12/21	12/22	12/23
Sales ($mil.)	(7.2%)	1,163.3	852.5	874.6	840.2	862.6
Net income ($ mil.)	–	(32.4)	(237.2)	(186.0)	70.1	(75.7)
Market value ($ mil.)	(19.8%)	70.5	48.1	4.8	23.2	29.1
Employees	(5.6%)	6,800	5,400	5,200	5,200	5,400

TEAM INDUSTRIES HOLDING CORPORATION

105 PARK AVE NW
BAGLEY, MN 566219558
Phone: 218 694-3550
Fax: –
Web: www.team-ind.com

CEO: David Ricke
CFO: Steve Kast
HR: Julie Bitzer
FYE: September 29
Type: Private

It takes a team, TEAM Industries, to make the drivetrains that and other vehicles parts. The Ricke family owned company designs, tests, manufacturers, and assembles powertrain, transmissions, drivetrains, gear sets, and chassis components for snowmobile, all-terrain vehicle, lawn mowers, and other vehicles through partnerships with CNH, Ford, Honda, Ingersoll-Rand, Kawasaki, Textron, Yamaha, and other OEMs. TEAM maintains half a dozen facilities throughout Minnesota and North Carolina; its manufacturing capabilities run from ductile iron and shaft machining to aluminum die-casting and gear/spline making. The company also offers engineering, R&D, and testing services.

	Annual Growth	09/11	09/12	09/16	09/17	09/18
Sales ($mil.)	2.2%	–	288.4	279.8	286.7	327.8
Net income ($ mil.)	0.9%	–	25.4	19.2	22.4	26.8
Market value ($ mil.)	–	–	–	–	–	–
Employees	–	–	–	–	–	1,100

TEAMQUEST CORPORATION

1 TEAMQUEST WAY
CLEAR LAKE, IA 504282296
Phone: 641 357-2700
Fax: –
Web: www.teamquest.com

CEO: –
CFO: –
HR: –
FYE: December 31
Type: Private

TeamQuest is more than happy collaborate with companies that seek to improve their IT systems. The company offers software products and related services that help organizations manage information technology (IT) performance and capacity planning. Its core product, TeamQuest Performance Software, is a software suite designed to analyze system performance, foresee potential problems with system updates and changes, and monitor data center activities, among other functions. The company's customers have included Hewlett-Packard , the IRS , Air France , and OfficeMax . An employee-owned and operated company, TeamQuest was founded in 1991 by CEO Jerry Ruble and former CEO Bob Krieger, who passed away in 2004.

	Annual Growth	12/10	12/11	12/12	12/13	12/14
Sales ($mil.)	2.6%	–	28.9	29.4	30.6	31.2
Net income ($ mil.)	–	–	–	–	–	–
Market value ($ mil.)	–	–	–	–	–	–
Employees	–	–	–	–	–	110

TECH DATA CORPORATION

5350 TECH DATA DR
CLEARWATER, FL 337603122
Phone: 727 539-7429
Fax: –
Web: www.techdata.com

CEO: –
CFO: –
HR: –
FYE: January 31
Type: Private

Tech Data Corporation is one of the world's largest technology distributors that provides thousands of items to more than 125,000 resellers in 100-plus countries. With catalog of products that includes computer components, networking equipment, peripherals, systems, and software, the company sold more than 150,000 IT products worldwide and caters over 50,000 daily transactions. Tech Data also offer products and services geared to data centers that include storage, networking, servers, and cloud infrastructure. The company, currently wholly owned by funds managed by affiliates of Apollo Global Management, entered into a definitive merger agreement under which SYNNEX and Tech Data will combine in a transaction valued at approximately $7.2 billion.

TECHNICA CORPORATION

22970 INDIAN CREEK DR STE 500
STERLING, VA 201666740
Phone: 703 662-2000
Fax: –
Web: www.technicacorp.com

CEO: –
CFO: Mark Cabrey
HR: Nelly Quintanilla
FYE: June 30
Type: Private

Founded in 1991, Technica provides information technology (IT) consulting services, hardware, and related software, including offerings in voice and data network design, installation, and performance testing. Technica supplies support for technologies and platforms such as storage area networks and metro optical, as well as large systems integration and network security services. The company also offers on-site support and customized training for managers, engineers, and technicians. Its customers include telecommunications providers, government and military agencies, health care and educational clients, and financial markets.

	Annual Growth	12/04	12/05	12/06	12/08*	06/09
Sales ($mil.)	(59.3%)	–	–	411.8	65.1	27.9
Net income ($ mil.)	3320.2%	–	–	0.0	2.2	1.7
Market value ($ mil.)	–	–	–	–	–	–
Employees	–	–	–	–	–	190

*Fiscal year change

TECHNICAL COMMUNICATIONS CORP
NBB: TCCO

100 Domino Drive
Concord, MA 01742-2892
Phone: 978 287-5100
Fax: –
Web: www.tccsecure.com

CEO: Carl H Guild Jr
CFO: –
HR: –
FYE: September 24
Type: Public

Technical Communications Corporation, also known as TCC, helps its customers keep their secrets to themselves. The company makes secure communications equiment that enables users to digitally encrypt and transmit information. It also makes receivers used to decipher the data. TCC's products protect transmissions sent by radios, telephones, fax machines, computer networks, the Internet, fiber-optic cables, and satellite links. The company subcontracts much of its manufacturing and caters largely to government agencies, but it also serves financial institutions and other corporations. It derives the bulk of its sales from a very small number of customers, including the US Army.

	Annual Growth	09/18	09/19	09/20	09/21	09/22
Sales ($mil.)	(22.9%)	3.7	7.0	4.1	1.9	1.3
Net income ($ mil.)	–	(1.5)	0.6	(0.9)	(1.1)	(2.3)
Market value ($ mil.)	(32.4%)	8.4	4.6	5.9	5.5	1.8
Employees	(4.3%)	25	24	23	20	21

TECHNIPFMC PLC
NYS: FTI

One Subsea Lane
Houston, TX 77044
Phone: 281 591-4000
Fax: –
Web: –

CEO: –
CFO: –
HR: –
FYE: December 31
Type: Public

London-based TechnipFMC is a global leader in the energy industry; delivering projects, products, technologies, and services. With proprietary technologies and production systems, integrated expertise, and comprehensive solutions, it transforms project economics. Through innovative technologies and improved efficiencies, its offering unlocks new possibilities for its customers in developing their energy resources and in their positioning to meet the energy transition challenge. It provides front-end engineering and design (FEED), subsea production systems (SPS), subsea flexible pipe, and subsea umbilicals, risers, and flowlines (SURF) and subsea robotics. It also has the capability to install products and related subsea infrastructure with its fleet of highly specialized vessels. The company started its operations in 2015 through a joint venture and has continued to be a leader in the energy industry.

	Annual Growth	12/19	12/20	12/21	12/22	12/23
Sales ($mil.)	(12.6%)	13,409	13,051	6,403.5	6,700.4	7,824.2
Net income ($ mil.)	–	(2,415.2)	(3,287.6)	13.3	(107.2)	56.2
Market value ($ mil.)	–	–	–	–	–	–
Employees	(11.4%)	37,000	35,000	20,000	20,000	22,762

TECHNISCAN INC.
NBB: TSNI

3216 South Highland Drive, Suite 200
Salt Lake City, UT 84106
Phone: 801 521-0444
Fax: –
Web: www.techniscanmedicalsystems.com

CEO: –
CFO: Steven K Passey
HR: –
FYE: December 31
Type: Public

TechniScan (formerly TechniScan Medical Systems) is developing a gentler means of mammography. Its Svara ultrasound imaging system uses a water bath and ultrasound reflective tomography technology to produce scans of the entire breast in about 10 minutes. TechniScan's images are intended to be used when further testing is needed following a conventional mammogram screening. The development stage company was founded in 1984. TechniScan shortened its name when it completed a reverse merger with shell company Castillo Inc. to become a public entity in 2009.

TECHNOLOGY CONCEPTS & DESIGN, INC.

4508 WEYBRIDGE LN
GREENSBORO, NC 274077876
Phone: 336 232-5800
Fax: –
Web: www.tcdi.com

CEO: William D Johnson
CFO: Lisa K Cain
HR: –
FYE: December 31
Type: Private

Founded in 1988, Technology Concepts & Design (TCDI) provides litigation management and online document management software for law firms, corporate counsels, and government agencies. Its TCDI Litigation Technology segment offers tools for managing cases, electronic documents, and discovery processes in law firms and legal departments. TCDI's Federal Systems segment provides knowledge management, systems engineering, programming, information technology operations, and information assurance software and services for the US federal government.

	Annual Growth	12/10	12/11	12/12	12/13	12/14
Sales ($mil.)	7.1%	–	–	16.2	16.2	18.6
Net income ($ mil.)	102.2%	–	–	0.2	0.7	0.9
Market value ($ mil.)	–	–	–	–	–	–
Employees	–	–	–	–	–	84

TECHNOLOGY SERVICE CORPORATION

251 18TH ST S STE 705
ARLINGTON, VA 222023541
Phone: 703 251-6400
Fax: –
Web: www.tsc.com

CEO: Brandon Wolfson
CFO: –
HR: –
FYE: September 30
Type: Private

Radar sensor expert Technology Service Corporation (TSC) provides engineering consulting services and specialized products primarily for US government agencies, such as the Federal Aviation Administration, the Navy, and the Department of Defense, but also for international civil aviation agencies and major radar system suppliers. Its services encompass research and advanced concept development through integrated logistics support. TSC's products include software for radar siting, geographic information services, and sensor simulation. Dr. Peter Swerling founded the employee-owned company in 1966.

	Annual Growth	09/05	09/06	09/07	09/08	09/10
Sales ($mil.)	10.0%	–	–	62.6	75.4	83.3
Net income ($ mil.)	10.5%	–	–	5.1	6.2	6.9
Market value ($ mil.)	–	–	–	–	–	–
Employees	–	–	–	–	–	526

TECHSMITH CORPORATION

14 CRESCENT RD
EAST LANSING, MI 488235708
Phone: 517 381-2300
Fax: –
Web: www.techsmith.com

CEO: Wendy Hamilton
CFO: –
HR: –
FYE: December 31
Type: Private

TechSmith is a master craftsman when it comes to the screen shot. The company provides screen capture and screen recording software for the office and classroom. TechSmith's flagship SnagIt software is a screen capture and editing tool that captures images -- including animation, graphics, text, and video -- then enhances them with special effects and multimedia features. Other products include Camtasia Studio, used to produce videos for the Internet and mobile devices; and Morae, a market research software. The company sells its software worldwide to corporations, educational institutions, government agencies, and small businesses. TechSmith was founded in 1987 by president William Hamilton and other investors.

	Annual Growth	12/10	12/11	12/12	12/13	12/14
Sales ($mil.)	1.6%	–	–	51.4	49.1	53.1
Net income ($ mil.)	(48.2%)	–	–	5.4	1.1	1.4
Market value ($ mil.)	–	–	–	–	–	–
Employees	–	–	–	–	–	175

TECHTARGET INC

NMS: TTGT

275 Grove Street
Newton, MA 02466
Phone: 617 431-9200
Fax: –
Web: www.techtarget.com

CEO: Michael Cotoia
CFO: Daniel T Noreck
HR: –
FYE: December 31
Type: Public

TechTarget is a global data, software, and analytics leader for purchase intent-driven marketing and sales data which delivers business impact for business-to-business (B2B) companies. The company operates a network of about 150 websites and approximately 1,100 webinars and virtual event channels, which each focus on a specific IT sector such as storage, security, or networking. TechTarget has approximately 30.2 million and 29.1 million registered members and users. The company generates substantially all of its revenues from the sale of targeted marketing and advertising campaigns, which the company delivers via its network of websites, event channels, and data analytics solution. Almost 65% of the company's revenue comes from North America.

	Annual Growth	12/19	12/20	12/21	12/22	12/23
Sales ($mil.)	14.5%	134.0	148.4	263.4	297.5	230.0
Net income ($ mil.)	(28.3%)	16.9	17.1	0.9	41.6	4.5
Market value ($ mil.)	7.5%	741.6	1,679.6	2,718.2	1,252.0	990.6
Employees	10.3%	649	940	1,000	1,000	960

TECO ENERGY, INC.

702 N FRANKLIN ST
TAMPA, FL 336024429
Phone: 813 228-1111
Fax: –
Web: www.tecoenergy.com

CEO: John B Ramil
CFO: Sandra W Callahan
HR: Bruce Napier
FYE: December 31
Type: Private

TECO is proud to be a subsidiary of?Emera Inc., a geographically diverse energy and services company headquartered in Halifax, Nova Scotia, Canada. The company invests in electricity generation, transmission and distribution, as well as gas transmission and utility energy services with a strategic focus on transformation from high carbon to low carbon energy sources. The company operates through Tampa Electric and Peoples Gas.

TECO-WESTINGHOUSE MOTOR COMPANY

5100 N INTERSTATE 35 STE A
ROUND ROCK, TX 786812461
Phone: 512 218-7448
Fax: –
Web: www.tecowestinghouse.com

CEO: –
CFO: Emily KAO
HR: –
FYE: December 31
Type: Private

TECO-Westinghouse Motor Company (TWMC) is on a power trip. The subsidiary of TECO Electric & Machinery makes induction, synchronous, and DC electric motors (in sizes from one-quarter horsepower to 100,000 hp), as well as generators and other electrical power products. TWMC also offers motor drives and controls, large-motor repair and testing, replacement parts, and engineering services. The company serves customers in the air conditioning, electrical utility, marine, mining and metal, petrochemical, pulp and paper, and water/wastewater treatment industries.

	Annual Growth	12/01	12/02	12/11	12/12	12/13
Sales ($mil.)	10.6%	–	96.5	226.2	283.7	293.5
Net income ($ mil.)	18.9%	–	3.6	17.1	20.5	23.8
Market value ($ mil.)	–	–	–	–	–	–
Employees	–	–	–	–	–	298

TECOGEN INC

NBB: TGEN

45 First Avenue
Waltham, MA 02451
Phone: 781 466-6402
Fax: –
Web: www.tecogen.com

CEO: Benjamin M Locke
CFO: Abinand Rangesh
HR: Kate Alfieri
FYE: December 31
Type: Public

Tecogen designs and makes natural gas-fueled commercial and industrial cooling and cogeneration systems such as chillers, water heaters, and other types of cooling, refrigeration, and co-generation systems. Its product lines include TECOCHILL 25 to 400 ton engine-driven chillers, Ilios high-efficiency water heaters, and Tecogen co-generation equipment. Tecogen has shipped more than 2,000 units throughout the US. The company was founded in the early 1960s and was spun off from Thermo Electron Corp. (a predecessor to Thermo Fisher Scientific) in 1987. Tecogen went public in 2014 after withdrawing a previous offering in 2013. In 2016 Tecogen agreed to acquire American DG Energy.

	Annual Growth	12/19	12/20	12/21	12/22	12/23
Sales ($mil.)	(6.9%)	33.4	28.3	24.4	25.0	25.1
Net income ($ mil.)	–	(4.7)	(6.2)	3.7	(2.4)	(4.6)
Market value ($ mil.)	(21.4%)	52.7	30.3	29.8	31.1	20.1
Employees	–	93	81	79	86	93

TECPLOT, INC.

3535 FACTORIA BLVD SE STE 550
BELLEVUE, WA 980061213
Phone: 425 653-1200
Fax: –
Web: www.tecplot.com

CEO: –
CFO: –
HR: Laurie Gunn
FYE: December 31
Type: Private

Tecplot can help you chart a path into engineering and scientific data. The company develops software that engineers and scientists use for data visualization and analysis, including applications for 2D and 3D plotting. Tecplot also offers a variety of services such as support, training, and consulting, as well as software development kits that let developers incorporate its plotting and data visualization technology into their own applications. The company was founded in 1981 as Amtec Engineering, changing its name to Tecplot in 2003, after its flagship software package.

	Annual Growth	12/04	12/05	12/06	12/07	12/08
Sales ($mil.)	11.6%	–	–	5.3	6.0	6.6
Net income ($ mil.)	25.6%	–	–	0.6	0.7	0.9
Market value ($ mil.)	–	–	–	–	–	–
Employees	–	–	–	–	–	43

TECUMSEH PRODUCTS COMPANY LLC

5683 HINES DR
ANN ARBOR, MI 481087901
Phone: 734 585-9500
Fax: –
Web: www.tecumseh.com

CEO: Jay Pittas
CFO: Phyllis Knight
HR: Don Tygett
FYE: December 31
Type: Private

Named for the legendary Shawnee chief, Tecumseh Products makes a line of hermetically sealed compressors and heat pumps for residential and commercial refrigerators and freezers, water coolers, air conditioners, dehumidifiers, and vending machines. The company's line of scroll compressor models are suited for demanding commercial refrigeration applications and consist primarily of reciprocating and rotary designs. Tecumseh sells its products to OEMs and aftermarket distributors in more than 100 countries worldwide, with more than 80% of its sales generated outside of the US. In mid-2015, Tecumseh agreed to be acquired by affiliates of Mueller Industries and Atlas Holdings for $123 million.

	Annual Growth	12/10	12/11	12/12	12/13	12/14
Sales ($mil.)	(7.9%)	–	–	854.7	823.6	724.4
Net income ($ mil.)	–	–	–	22.6	(37.5)	(32.7)
Market value ($ mil.)	–	–	–	–	–	–
Employees	–	–	–	–	–	4,800

TEGNA INC

NYS: TGNA

8350 Broad Street, Suite 2000
Tysons, VA 22102-5151
Phone: 703 873-6600
Fax: –
Web: www.tegna.com

CEO: David T Lougee
CFO: Victoria D Harker
HR: –
FYE: December 31
Type: Public

With around 65 television stations and two radio stations in more than 50 markets, TEGNA reaches around 40% of US television households giving it one of the nation's largest portfolios of television stations. It owns affiliates of the four major broadcast networks in the country's top 25 markets. Besides broadcast TV, the company also has a robust digital presence across online, mobile and social platforms, reaching consumers on all devices and platforms they use to consume news content. TEGNA sells advertising, as well as the rights to carry its stations' signals to Pay-TV systems. The firm is made up of the television broadcasting operations formerly owned by Gannett. In 2022, TEGNA and an affiliate of Standard General have entered into a definitive agreement under which TEGNA will be acquired by the Standard General affiliate for $24.00 per share in cash.

	Annual Growth	12/19	12/20	12/21	12/22	12/23
Sales ($mil.)	6.1%	2,299.5	2,937.8	2,991.1	3,279.2	2,910.9
Net income ($ mil.)	13.6%	286.2	482.8	477.0	630.5	476.7
Market value ($ mil.)	(2.2%)	3,002.8	2,509.8	3,339.2	3,812.4	2,752.7
Employees	(2.6%)	6,883	6,430	6,200	6,300	6,200

TEJAS OFFICE PRODUCTS, INC.

1225 W 20TH ST
HOUSTON, TX 770083315
Phone: 713 864-6604
Fax: –
Web: www.tejasoffice.com

CEO: –
CFO: –
HR: –
FYE: September 30
Type: Private

Houston-based Tejas Office Products distributes office products throughout the US. The company offers a huge portfolio of products from such manufacturers as 3M, Crayola (formerly Binney & Smith), Imation, Fellowes, Hewlett Packard, and Nu-Kote International. Tejas Office Products sells more than 10,000 items including furniture, paper products, desk supplies, computer accessories, and office electronics. The company distributes its goods from a 25,999-sq.-ft. warehouse located in the downtown area. Tejas Office Products, founded in 1962, is owned by the Fraga family.

TEJON RANCH CO

NYS: TRC

P.O. Box 1000
Tejon Ranch, CA 93243
Phone: 661 248-3000
Fax: –
Web: www.tejonranch.com

CEO: Gregory S Bielli
CFO: Brett A Brown
HR: –
FYE: December 31
Type: Public

Tejon Ranch is a diversified real estate development and agribusiness company committed to responsibly using its land and resources to meet the housing, employment, and lifestyle needs of Californians and create value for its shareholders. Its current operations consist of land planning and entitlement, land development, commercial land sales, and leasing, leasing of land for mineral royalties, water asset management and sales, grazing leases, farming, and ranch operations. Its prime asset is approximately 270,000 acres of contiguous, largely undeveloped land that, at its most southerly border, 60 miles north of Los Angeles and, at its most northerly border, is 15 miles east of Bakersfield. The company was established in 1843.

	Annual Growth	12/19	12/20	12/21	12/22	12/23
Sales ($mil.)	(2.5%)	49.5	37.8	55.6	79.2	44.7
Net income ($ mil.)	(25.5%)	10.6	(0.7)	5.3	15.8	3.3
Market value ($ mil.)	1.9%	427.8	386.8	510.8	504.4	460.5
Employees	(4.8%)	106	85	90	78	87

TEKNOR APEX COMPANY

505 CENTRAL AVE
PAWTUCKET, RI 028611900
Phone: 401 725-8000
Fax: –
Web: www.teknorapex.com

CEO: Donald Wiseman
CFO: Paul Morrisroe
HR: Denise Pagacik
FYE: July 31
Type: Private

Teknor Apex offers a wide-ranging portfolio of chemicals and synthetic polymers. The company's six business divisions provide colorants (through its Teknor Color unit), vinyl compounds, thermoplastic elastomers, engineering thermoplastics, chemicals for the polyvinyl chloride (PVC) plasticizer market, and garden hoses. The company's compounds are used for building and construction, consumer products, industrial manufacturing, electrical and electronic devices, medical tools, packaging, and vehicular components. Founded in 1924 by Alfred A. Fain and his son-in-law Albert Pilavin, Teknor invented the first plasticized (flexible) PVC.

TEKSYSTEMS, INC.

7437 RACE RD
HANOVER, MD 210761112
Phone: 410 540-7700
Fax: –
Web: www.teksystems.com

CEO: –
CFO: –
HR: –
FYE: December 31
Type: Private

TEKsystems, a subsidiary of staffing giant Allegis, provides IT consulting and staffing services from locations in North America, Europe, and Asia. Considered one of the nation's largest IT staffing firms, the company places more than 80,000 technical professionals each year who work in a variety of fields including telecommunications, construction and engineering. TEKsystems has more than 100 locations serving about 6,000 clients. TEKsystems is an Allegis Group company.

	Annual Growth	12/18	12/19	12/20	12/21	12/22
Sales ($mil.)	13.8%	–	–	4,815.3	–	6,231.6
Net income ($ mil.)	–	–	–	–	–	–
Market value ($ mil.)	–	–	–	–	–	–
Employees	–	–	–	–	–	2,900

TEL INSTRUMENT ELECTRONICS CORP.

NBB: TIKK

One Branca Road
East Rutherford, NJ 07073
Phone: 201 933-1600
Fax: –
Web: www.telinstrument.com

CEO: Jeffrey C O'Hara
CFO: –
HR: –
FYE: March 31
Type: Public

Before airplanes go off into the wild blue yonder, attention must be paid to their avionics. Tel-Instrument Electronics manufactures avionics test equipment for the US Army, the US Navy, and other military and commercial customers. Tel's instruments are used to test navigation and communications equipment installed in aircraft, both on the flight line (known as ramp testers) and in the maintenance shop (bench testers). The US government and military avionics customers (such as Boeing) account for more than two-thirds of sales.

	Annual Growth	03/19	03/20	03/21	03/22	03/23
Sales ($mil.)	(8.1%)	12.1	15.8	11.6	12.9	8.6
Net income ($ mil.)	–	0.2	4.7	0.6	1.3	(0.4)
Market value ($ mil.)	(4.9%)	9.0	10.9	11.4	10.1	7.3
Employees	–	41	45	47	44	–

TELECOMMUNICATION SYSTEMS, INC.

275 WEST ST
ANNAPOLIS, MD 214013400
Phone: 410 263-7616
Fax: –
Web: www.comtech.com

CEO: –
CFO: –
HR: –
FYE: December 31
Type: Private

TeleCommunication Systems (TCS) keeps businesses and government agencies connected. The company develops software and provides services for wireless telecommunications carriers, Internet telephony providers, and branches of the US military, among other clients. Its hosted applications enable phone companies, mainly in the US, to deliver 9-1-1 service, text messaging, location information, and other Internet content to wireless phones. The company provides the Defense Department (DoD) with communications systems integration and IT services through its growing government division, which represented more than half of the company's revenues in 2013.

TELEFLEX INCORPORATED   NYS: TFX

550 East Swedesford Road, Suite 400
Wayne, PA 19087
Phone: 610 225-6800
Fax: –
Web: www.teleflex.com

CEO: Liam J Kelly
CFO: Thomas E Powell
HR: Bianca Atilano
FYE: December 31
Type: Public

Teleflex is a global provider of medical technology products that enhance clinical benefits, improve patient and provider safety and reduce total procedural costs. The company designs, develops, manufactures and supplies single-use medical devices used by hospitals and healthcare providers for common diagnostic and therapeutic procedures in critical care and surgical applications. Its brands include Arrow, Deknatel, LMA, Pilling, QuikClot, Rusch, UroLift System, and Weck. Although the company primarily distributes its products to hospitals and healthcare providers worldwide, the US accounts for roughly 65% of revenue. Teleflex was founded in 1943 as a manufacturer of precision mechanical push/pull controls for military aircraft.

	Annual Growth	12/19	12/20	12/21	12/22	12/23
Sales ($mil.)	3.5%	2,595.4	2,537.2	2,809.6	2,791.0	2,974.5
Net income ($ mil.)	(6.3%)	461.5	335.3	485.4	363.1	356.3
Market value ($ mil.)	(9.8%)	17,708	19,360	15,452	11,743	11,729
Employees	0.2%	14,400	14,000	14,000	15,500	14,500

TELEDYNE LECROY, INC.

700 CHESTNUT RIDGE RD
CHESTNUT RIDGE, NY 109776435
Phone: 845 425-2000
Fax: –
Web: www.teledynelecroy.com

CEO: Sean B O'Connor
CFO: –
HR: Carmine Napolitano
FYE: December 31
Type: Private

Teledyne LeCroy is a leading provider of oscilloscopes, protocol analyzers and related test and measurement solutions that enable companies across a wide range of industries to design and test electronic devices of all types. Teledyne LeCroy offers a comprehensive range of electronic test equipment solutions to complement its well known family of oscilloscopes and analyzers. The company offer these tools under both the Teledyne LeCroy and Teledyne Test Tools brand names. The Teledyne Test Tools family of products was created in collaboration with leading OEM technology partners. The company was founded in 1964.

TELENAV, INC.

2540 MISSION COLLEGE BLVD STE 100
SANTA CLARA, CA 950541215
Phone: 408 245-3800
Fax: –
Web: www.telenav.com

CEO: HP Jin
CFO: Adeel Manzoor
HR: –
FYE: June 30
Type: Private

TeleNav offers a platform and suite of applications that provide mobile navigation and location-based services (LBS) to 34 million users, primarily in the US. Telenav counts among its customers three of the top five automotive OEMs by revenue and sales Ford, GM and Toyota. Navigation and LBS are the primary applications for in-vehicle infotainment (IVI) systems and the company are using its strengths and core competencies to address the growing demand for overall connected car services. In addition to navigation and LBS, TeleNav' connected car platform, VIVID, enables it to deliver in-vehicle infotainment, or IVI, software solutions and services that are growing in importance as consumers increasingly include digital technologies as a factor in their automobile purchase decision.

TELEDYNE TECHNOLOGIES INC   NYS: TDY

1049 Camino Dos Rios
Thousand Oaks, CA 91360-2362
Phone: 805 373-4545
Fax: –
Web: www.teledyne.com

CEO: Aldo Pichelli
CFO: Susan L Main
HR: –
FYE: December 31
Type: Public

Teledyne Technologies provides enabling technologies for industrial growth markets that require advanced technology and high reliability. The company's products include digital imaging sensors, cameras and systems within the visible, infrared and X-ray spectra, monitoring and control instrumentation for marine and environmental applications, harsh environment interconnects, electronic test and measurement equipment, aircraft applications, general aviation batteries, data acquisition, and satellite communications. It also supplies engineered systems for defense, space, environmental and energy applications. Teledyne gets most of its sales from customers in the US.

	Annual Growth	12/19*	01/21	01/22	01/23*	12/23
Sales ($mil.)	15.5%	3,163.6	3,086.2	4,614.3	5,458.6	5,635.5
Net income ($ mil.)	21.8%	402.3	401.9	445.3	788.6	885.7
Market value ($ mil.)	6.4%	16,463	18,553	20,679	18,928	21,124
Employees	6.0%	11,790	10,670	14,500	14,700	14,900

*Fiscal year change

TELEPHONE & DATA SYSTEMS INC   NYS: TDS

30 North LaSalle Street, Suite 4000
Chicago, IL 60602
Phone: 312 630-1900
Fax: 312 630-1908
Web: www.tdsinc.com

CEO: –
CFO: Peter L Sereda
HR: Cynthia Prest
FYE: December 31
Type: Public

Telephone and Data Systems (TDS) provides high-quality communications services to customers with some 4.7 million wireless connections and approximately 1.2 million wireline and cable connections. The company's core business unit, UScellular, serves some 4.7 million customers in around 20 states with key markets in the US. The company also offers fixed-line and broadband internet services in a mix of rural and suburban communities throughout the US through its TDS Telecom subsidiary, which provides local service to some 1.2 million access lines through incumbent local exchange carriers (ILEC).

	Annual Growth	12/19	12/20	12/21	12/22	12/23
Sales ($mil.)	(0.1%)	5,176.0	5,225.0	5,329.0	5,413.0	5,160.0
Net income ($ mil.)	–	121.0	226.0	156.0	62.0	(500.0)
Market value ($ mil.)	(7.8%)	2,873.6	2,098.4	2,277.0	1,185.4	2,073.6
Employees	(1.6%)	9,400	9,200	8,800	9,300	8,800

TELEPHONE ELECTRONICS CORPORATION

236 E CAPITOL ST STE 400
JACKSON, MS 392012416
Phone: 601 354-9070
Fax: –
Web: www.tec.com

CEO: –
CFO: –
HR: –
FYE: December 31
Type: Private

Telephone Electronics Corporation, or TEC, provides communications services for customers in the South. The privately-owned telecommunications carrier provides wired phone, cable TV, and Internet services for residential and business customers through subsidiaries such as CommuniGroup. TEC's rural local-exchange service reach include areas of Alabama, Louisiana, Mississippi, and Tennessee. The company also provides long-distance interexchange services. TEC was founded in 1923 with the purchase of local phone company Bay Springs Telephone Company, which had about 100 customers tied to its switchboard.

	Annual Growth	12/05	12/06	12/07	12/08	12/09
Sales ($mil.)	(9.5%)	–	–	–	38.8	35.1
Net income ($ mil.)	11.1%	–	–	–	2.0	2.3
Market value ($ mil.)	–	–	–	–	–	–
Employees	–	–	–	–	–	250

TELEPHONICS CORPORATION

815 BROADHOLLOW RD
FARMINGDALE, NY 117353937
Phone: 631 755-7000
Fax: –
Web: www.telephonics.com

CEO: –
CFO: –
HR: –
FYE: September 30
Type: Private

Telephonics is an advanced-technology leader in highly sophisticated surveillance, communications, analysis and integration solutions. Its systems are deployed across a wide range of land, sea and air applications, providing its aerospace, defense and commercial customers with a distinct tactical advantage - even in the most unpredictable environments. A maker of communications equipment for military and civilian customers, the company is widely recognized for highly sophisticated surveillance, communications, analysis, and integration solutions. The company traces its roots back in 1933. In mid-2022, TTM Technologies has completed the previously announced acquisition of Telephonics Corporation from Griffon Corporation for approximately $330 million in cash.

	Annual Growth	09/09	09/10	09/11	09/17	09/18
Sales ($mil.)	(3.5%)	–	434.5	455.4	–	326.3
Net income ($ mil.)	(2.9%)	–	24.2	22.6	–	19.1
Market value ($ mil.)	–	–	–	–	–	–
Employees	–	–	–	–	–	1,087

TELEX COMMUNICATIONS, INC.

12000 Portland Avenue South
Burnsville, MN 55337
Phone: 952 884-4051
Fax: 952 884-0043
Web: www.telex.com

CEO: –
CFO: –
HR: –
FYE: December 31
Type: Public

Bosch Communications Systems (formerly Telex Communications) makes sure its customers' voices are heard. The company makes audio and communications equipment for commercial, professional, and industrial use. Its sound systems can be heard in venues from the Metropolitan Opera to Wrigley Field. A large portion of commercial airline pilots use Telex headsets. Other brand names include Electro-Voice, Dynacord, Klark Teknik, Midas, and RTS. Telex Communications was founded in 1936 as a hearing aid manufacturer; Robert Bosch GmbH acquired the company in 2006 and renamed it Bosch Communications Systems.

	Annual Growth	12/02*	11/03*	12/03	12/04	12/05
Sales ($mil.)	4.9%	266.5	243.1	25.4	296.8	307.7
Net income ($ mil.)	–	(30.1)	(6.1)	(0.5)	5.4	13.1
Market value ($ mil.)	–	–	–	–	–	–
Employees	(3.2%)	1,983	–	–	1,838	1,800

*Fiscal year change

TELIGENT INC (NEW)

NBB: TLGT Q

105 Lincoln Ave.
Buena, NJ 08310
Phone: 856 697-1441
Fax: –
Web: www.teligent.com

CEO: John Celentano
CFO: Alyssa Lozynski
HR: –
FYE: December 31
Type: Public

Teligent (formerly IGI) manufactures generic topical, branded generic and generic injectable pharmaceutical products in the US and Canada. In the US, it markets nearly 40 generic topical pharmaceutical products and some 2 branded injectable pharmaceutical products. In Canada, it has about 25 generic, some 3 generic topical, and around 3 generic ophthalmic products. It also provides contract manufacturing services to the pharmaceutical, over-the-counter, (OTC), and cosmetic markets. Its three large wholesale drug distributors have included ABC, Cardinal, and McKesson. Founded in 1977, Teligent became public in 2015.

	Annual Growth	12/16	12/17	12/18	12/19	12/20
Sales ($mil.)	(9.3%)	66.9	67.3	65.9	65.9	45.3
Net income ($ mil.)	–	(12.0)	(15.2)	(36.3)	(25.1)	(122.0)
Market value ($ mil.)	(42.0%)	143.8	79.0	29.8	9.3	16.3
Employees	(1.8%)	153	183	189	252	142

TELKONET INC.

NBB: TKOI

20800 Swenson Drive, Suite 175
Waukesha, WI 53186
Phone: 414 302-2299
Fax: –
Web: –

CEO: Jason L Tienor
CFO: Richard E Mushrush
HR: –
FYE: December 31
Type: Public

Telkonet runs its own Internet of things, but its things are thermostats and other energy controls for hotels, campuses, and other properties. The company's SmartEnergy and EcoSmart line of energy efficiency-related systems are used to manage and monitor HVAC consumption. It also provides high-speed Internet access without the high-cost network upgrades through its EthoStream product line, which enables computer network and Internet access over electrical lines rather than communications cables. In addition to equipment sales, it recognizes recurring support revenue from the 2,300 hotels that use its EthoStream broadband Internet systems. All of its product are marketed primarily to the hospitality industry. Customers include InterContinental, Marriott, and Wyndham.

	Annual Growth	12/18	12/19	12/20	12/21	12/22
Sales ($mil.)	–	8.4	12.0	6.5	6.3	8.4
Net income ($ mil.)	–	(3.0)	(1.9)	(3.1)	(0.4)	(1.3)
Market value ($ mil.)	(26.0%)	33.7	19.4	8.1	5.6	10.1
Employees	(12.4%)	51	38	35	31	30

TELLURIAN INC

ASE: TELL

1201 Louisiana Street, Suite 3100
Houston, TX 77002
Phone: 832 962-4000
Fax: –
Web: www.magellanpetroleum.com

CEO: Octavio Simoes
CFO: Antoine J Lafargue
HR: Lisa Aimone
FYE: December 31
Type: Public

Magellan Petroleum has gone around the world to explore for oil and gas. The independent oil and gas exploration and production company is focused on the development of CO2-enhanced oil recovery projects in the Rocky Mountain region. Historically active internationally, Magellan also owns significant exploration acreage in the Weald Basin, onshore UK, and an exploration block (NT/P82) in the Bonaparte Basin, offshore Northern Territory, Australia. Magellan Petroleum reports proved and probable reserves of approximately 5.7 million barrels of oil equivalent. It sold some of its Weald Basin assets in 2016.

	Annual Growth	12/19	12/20	12/21	12/22	12/23
Sales ($mil.)	55.0%	28.8	37.4	71.3	391.9	166.1
Net income ($ mil.)	–	(151.8)	(210.7)	(114.7)	(49.8)	(166.2)
Market value ($ mil.)	(43.2%)	5,123.2	900.8	2,167.5	1,182.3	531.7
Employees	(1.2%)	176	102	107	171	168

TELOS CORP. (MD)   NMS: TLS

19886 Ashburn Road
Ashburn, VA 20147-2358
Phone: 703 724-3800
Fax: –
Web: www.telos.com

CEO: John B Wood
CFO: G M Bendza
HR: –
FYE: December 31
Type: Public

Telos provides technologically advanced, solutions that empower and protect the world's most security-conscious organizations against rapidly evolving, sophisticated, and pervasive threats, primarily to the US Department of Defense and other federal government agencies. Its commercial customers include leading enterprises such as Amazon, Zscaler, Microsoft, and Salesforce.com. The company's portfolio of security products, services, and expertise empowers its customers with the capabilities to reach new markets, serve their stakeholders more effectively, and successfully defend the nation or their enterprise. Telos protect its customers' people, information, and digital assets, enabling them to pursue their corporate goals and conduct their global missions with confidence in their security and privacy. Most of the company's sales come from the US customers. The company was founded in 1971 and went public in late 2020.

	Annual Growth	12/19	12/20	12/21	12/22	12/23
Sales ($mil.)	(2.2%)	159.2	179.9	242.4	216.9	145.4
Net income ($ mil.)	–	(6.4)	1.7	(43.1)	(53.4)	(34.4)
Market value ($ mil.)	–	–	2,316.5	1,083.1	357.5	256.4
Employees	(4.0%)	730	785	849	738	619

TEMPACO, INC.

1984 W NEW HAMPSHIRE ST
ORLANDO, FL 328046008
Phone: 407 898-3456
Fax: –
Web: www.tempaco.com

CEO: Maria Robinson
CFO: –
HR: –
FYE: March 31
Type: Private

Tempaco wholesales industrial and commercial parts and supplies for heating, cooling, and industrial control systems. It carries some 6,000 products from such manufacturers as A. O. Smith, Automatic Switch, Dormont, Eaton, Fisher Controls International, Honeywell, Johnson Controls, Metal-Fab, Parker Hannifin, and Uniweld Products. The employee-owned company has locations throughout Florida. Tempaco was established in 1954 as Jobber Service and changed its name in 1960. The company belongs to Controls Group North America, a buying consortium of HVAC, control systems, and refrigeration distributors.

TEMPLE UNIVERSITY HEALTH SYSTEM, INC.

2450 W HUNTING PARK AVE
PHILADELPHIA, PA 191291302
Phone: 215 707-2000
Fax: –
Web: www.templehealth.org

CEO: Michael Young
CFO: Michael Difranco
HR: –
FYE: June 30
Type: Private

Temple University Health System (TUHS) is a network of academic and community hospitals associated with the Temple University School of Medicine. It provides primary, secondary, and tertiary care to residents in the Philadelphia County (Pennsylvania) area. The system includes 722-bed Temple University Hospital (a Level 1 trauma center) and a pair of community-based hospitals that provide acute and emergency care as well as the Jeanes Hospital and TUH-Episcopal Campus (home to a 120-bed behavioral health unit). TUHS supports programs in cardiology, organ transplantation, and oncology. In late 2019 the health system agreed to sell the Fox Chase Cancer Center to Philadelphia-based Thomas Jefferson University.

	Annual Growth	06/07	06/08	06/09	06/11	06/12
Sales ($mil.)	1819.9%	–	–	0.1	994.2	1,004.9
Net income ($ mil.)	–	–	–	(0.1)	45.4	(48.8)
Market value ($ mil.)	–	–	–	–	–	–
Employees	–	–	–	–	–	7,573

TEMPLE UNIVERSITY-OF THE COMMONWEALTH SYSTEM OF HIGHER EDUCATION

1801 N BROAD ST
PHILADELPHIA, PA 191226003
Phone: 215 204-1380
Fax: –
Web: www.temple.edu

CEO: –
CFO: Ken Kaiser
HR: –
FYE: June 30
Type: Private

Temple University provides education and training services to approximately 40,000 undergraduate, graduate and professional students are enrolled in its more than 600 academic programs across the Philadelphia university's over 15 schools. Its Health Sciences Center includes Temple University Hospital and schools that teach medicine and dentistry. Part of Pennsylvania's Commonwealth System of Higher Education, Temple has eight different campuses in the Philadelphia area, as well campuses in Tokyo and Rome and offers study abroad programs in various locations. Dr. Russell Conwell founded the university in 1884; it was incorporated as Temple University in 1907.

	Annual Growth	06/12	06/13	06/20	06/21	06/22
Sales ($mil.)	4.6%	–	2,635.5	3,628.8	3,722.1	3,943.9
Net income ($ mil.)	0.3%	–	192.1	154.6	553.7	197.9
Market value ($ mil.)	–	–	–	–	–	–
Employees	–	–	–	–	–	9,061

TEMPUR SEALY INTERNATIONAL, INC.   NYS: TPX

1000 Tempur Way
Lexington, KY 40511
Phone: 800 878-8889
Fax: –
Web: www.tempursealy.com

CEO: Scott L Thompson
CFO: Bhaskar RAO
HR: –
FYE: December 31
Type: Public

Tempur Sealy International is a leading designer, manufacturer, distributor, and retailer of bedding products comprised of traditional innerspring mattresses and non-innerspring mattresses, which include viscoelastic and foam mattresses, innerspring/foam hybrid mattresses, airbeds, and latex mattresses. Its Tempur, Tempur-Pedic, Sealy, Sealy Posturpedic, and Stearns & Foster brands are sold in more than 100 countries through third-party retailers, the company's more than 700 company-owned stores, and its e-commerce platforms. The US accounts for about 75% of Tempur Sealy's revenue.

	Annual Growth	12/19	12/20	12/21	12/22	12/23
Sales ($mil.)	12.2%	3,106.0	3,676.9	4,930.8	4,921.2	4,925.4
Net income ($ mil.)	18.1%	189.5	348.8	624.5	455.7	368.1
Market value ($ mil.)	(12.5%)	15,000	4,652.1	8,103.3	5,915.1	8,782.1
Employees	12.8%	7,400	9,000	12,000	12,000	12,000

TEN PUBCO, INC.

27200 RIVERVIEW CENTER BLVD STE 200
BONITA SPRINGS, FL 341344317
Phone: 239 949-4450
Fax: –
Web: –

CEO: Scott Dickey
CFO: Bill Sutman
HR: –
FYE: January 31
Type: Private

The Enthusiast Network (TEN) revs up its audience with magazines, videos, programming, events, and digital content about cars, surfing, skateboarding, snowboarding, and other fast-paced outdoor activities. MotorTrend Group is the largest automotive media company in the world, bringing the fast growing MotorTrend TV, formerly Velocity, and a vast automotive digital, direct to consumer, social, and live event portfolio, including Automobile, Motor Trend, Road Kill, and 20 more other industry leading brands. The company encompasses television's #1 network for automotive superfans and YouTube channels. In addition, MoterTrend App the only subscription video-on-demand service.

TENAX THERAPEUTICS INC
NAS: TENX

101 Glen Lennox Drive, Suite 300
Chapel Hill, NC 27517
Phone: 919 855-2100
Fax: 919 855-2133
Web: www.tenaxthera.com

CEO: Christopher T Giordano
CFO: Eliot M Lurier
HR: –
FYE: December 31
Type: Public

Oxygen Biotherapeutics prescribes some good ol' O 2 for whatever ails you. The development stage biotechnology company develops products that help deliver oxygen to tissues. Its Dermacyte topical cosmetic line is designed to improve the appearance of skin. A concentrate is currently available and the company is developing Dermacyte formulas specifically for acne, rosacea, sunscreen, and other applications. Pipeline products include Oxycyte, an IV emulsion created to speed surgical and other healing being tested in Israel and Switzerland and Wundecyte gel and bandages in pre-clinical trials. Oxygen Biotherapeutics was formed through a reverse merger with Synthetic Blood International in 2008.

	Annual Growth	12/18	12/19	12/20	12/21	12/22
Sales ($mil.)	–	–	–	–	–	–
Net income ($ mil.)	–	(14.1)	(8.4)	(9.9)	(32.5)	(11.0)
Market value ($ mil.)	(44.9%)	0.0	0.0	0.0	0.0	0.0
Employees	(5.4%)	10	10	10	9	8

TENENBAUM RECYCLING GROUP, LLC

4500 W BETHANY RD
NORTH LITTLE ROCK, AR 721173401
Phone: 501 945-0881
Fax: –
Web: www.trg.net

CEO: Randy Zook
CFO: –
HR: –
FYE: December 31
Type: Private

"Waste not, want not" goes for scrap metal too at A. Tenenbaum Company. Doing business as Tenenbaum Recycling Group (TRG), the company is the oldest scrap metal processor in Arkansas. Established in 1890, TRG's half a dozen scrap metal recycling yards and service centers purchase and process ferrous metals (iron and steel) and nonferrous metals (aluminum, brass, copper, nickel, and stainless steel) to sell to large steel mills, brokers, and exporters across the US. It recycles more than 350,000 tons of steel and 10 million pounds of cans per year. TRG also offers scrap management programs to help both large and small companies assess and improve their disposal methods.

TENERITY, INC.

6 HIGH RIDGE PARK
STAMFORD, CT 069051327
Phone: 203 956-1000
Fax: –
Web: www.tenerity.com

CEO: Greg Miller
CFO: Kanuj Malhotra
HR: Heather Foisset
FYE: December 31
Type: Private

Through its partners and affiliations, Affinion Group aims to make fans of its customers' customers. The company operates membership and loyalty programs on behalf of corporate clients seeking to strengthen their ties to consumers. It specializes in launching a variety of media services -- through direct mail and the Internet -- and packaging these benefits to its clients' customers. Programs overseen include AutoVantage, Buyers Advantage, and Travelers Advantage. Overall, the group offers its programs to some 65 million members worldwide through more than 5,700 partners.

	Annual Growth	12/14	12/15	12/16	12/17	12/18
Sales ($mil.)	(15.0%)	–	–	969.4	953.1	699.8
Net income ($ mil.)	331.4%	–	–	16.3	(24.4)	303.3
Market value ($ mil.)	–	–	–	–	–	–
Employees	–	–	–	–	–	3,860

TENET HEALTHCARE CORP.
NYS: THC

14201 Dallas Parkway
Dallas, TX 75254
Phone: 469 893-2200
Fax: –
Web: www.tenethealth.com

CEO: Saumya Sutaria
CFO: Sun Park
HR: –
FYE: December 31
Type: Public

Tenet Healthcare is a diversified healthcare services company. Its operations include about 60 hospitals and some 575 other healthcare facilities, including ambulatory surgery centers, urgent care centers, imaging centers, surgical hospitals, off-campus emergency departments and micro-hospitals. Its United Surgical Partners International (USPI) operates ambulatory surgery centers, urgent care centers, imaging centers and surgical hospitals. Tenet's Conifer provides comprehensive end to end and focused point business process services, including hospital and physician revenue cycle management, patient communications and engagement support, and value based care solutions. Overall, Tenet's hospitals handle more than 135,150 admissions and 583,455 emergency department visits each year.

	Annual Growth	12/19	12/20	12/21	12/22	12/23
Sales ($mil.)	2.7%	18,479	17,640	19,485	19,174	20,548
Net income ($ mil.)	–	(232.0)	399.0	914.0	411.0	611.0
Market value ($ mil.)	18.7%	3,801.1	3,991.0	8,164.9	4,876.6	7,553.2
Employees	(1.8%)	113,600	110,000	101,100	102,400	105,600

TENFOLD CORPORATION

530 FASHION AVE UPPR 1
NEW YORK, NY 100184906
Phone: 415 599-1170
Fax: –
Web: www.tenfold.com

CEO: –
CFO: –
HR: –
FYE: December 31
Type: Private

TenFold helps those who help themselves. The company has expanded from providing information technology services to selling its proprietary development platform that customers use to build their own applications. TenFold continues to provide application development services, as well as support, implementation, and training offerings including Service Oriented Architecture-compliant applications. The company is targeting customers in the fields of financial services, health care, and insurance; clients have included Allstate, J.P. Morgan Chase & Co., and Abbey National Bank. The company was acquired by Versata in 2008.

TENNANT CO.
NYS: TNC

10400 Clean Street
Eden Prairie, MN 55344
Phone: 763 540-1200
Fax: –
Web: www.tennantco.com

CEO: David W Huml
CFO: Fay West
HR: Amber Caudill
FYE: December 31
Type: Public

Tennant is a world leader in designing, manufacturing and marketing solutions that empower customers to achieve quality cleaning performance, reduce environmental impact and help create a cleaner, safer, healthier world. The Company is committed to creating and commercializing breakthrough, sustainable cleaning innovations to enhance its broad suite of products, including floor maintenance and cleaning equipment, detergent-free and other sustainable cleaning technologies, aftermarket parts and consumables, equipment maintenance and repair service, and asset management solutions. Brand names include Alfa, Tennant, Nobles, and Iris among others. Customers include contract cleaners to whom organizations outsource facilities maintenance as well as businesses that perform facilities maintenance themselves. The Americas account for about 65% of revenue. The company was founded in 1870. In 2021, the company has completed the sales of its coatings business.

	Annual Growth	12/19	12/20	12/21	12/22	12/23
Sales ($mil.)	2.3%	1,137.6	1,001.0	1,090.8	1,092.2	1,243.6
Net income ($ mil.)	24.3%	45.8	33.7	64.9	66.3	109.5
Market value ($ mil.)	4.4%	1,451.8	1,307.4	1,509.9	1,147.1	1,726.9
Employees	0.3%	4,400	4,259	4,263	4,299	4,457

TENNECO INC.

7450 MCCORMICK BLVD
SKOKIE, IL 600764046
Phone: 847 482-5000
Fax: –
Web: www.tenneco.com

CEO: Jim Voss
CFO: –
HR: Katie Rogotzke
FYE: December 31
Type: Private

Tenneco is one of the world's leading designers, manufacturers and marketers of automotive products for original equipment and aftermarket customers, working at more than 260 sites worldwide. Through its four business groups, Motorparts, Performance Solutions, Clean Air and Powertrain, Tenneco is driving advancements in global mobility by delivering technology solutions for diversified global markets, including light vehicle, commercial truck, off-highway, industrial, motorsport and the aftermarket. Tenneco's history as a stand-alone entity began in 1999, when the current company emerged from a conglomerate formerly consisting of six businesses -- shipbuilding, packaging, farm and construction equipment, gas transmission, automotive and chemicals. In late 2022, the company was acquired by Apollo Funds, a high-growth, global alternative asset manager.

TENNESSEE GAS PIPELINE CO.

El Paso Building, 1001 Louisiana Street
Houston, TX 77002
Phone: 713 420-2600
Fax: –
Web: www.elpaso.com

CEO: Richard D Kinder
CFO: –
HR: –
FYE: December 31
Type: Public

Tennessee Gas Pipeline transports natural gas across the US. The company, a subsidiary of diversified energy giant Kinder Morgan, is part of an integrated coast-to-coast pipeline system. Tennessee Gas operates 11,840 miles of interstate natural gas transmission pipeline stretching from Canada to Mexico. The company's system begins in the natural gas-producing regions of the Gulf Coast and extends to the northeast US, including the large urban centers of New York City and Boston. Its South Texas pipeline allows the company to tap into the burgeoning power generation market in northern Mexico.

	Annual Growth	12/10	12/11*	05/12*	12/12	12/13
Sales ($mil.)	7.8%	845.0	976.0	602.0	414.0	1,058.0
Net income ($ mil.)	65.3%	103.0	203.0	182.0	(9.0)	465.0
Market value ($ mil.)	–	–	–	–	–	–
Employees	–	–	1,675	–	–	–

*Fiscal year change

TENNESSEE STATE UNIVERSITY

3500 JOHN A MERRITT BLVD
NASHVILLE, TN 372091561
Phone: 615 963-5000
Fax: –
Web: www.tnstate.edu

CEO: –
CFO: –
HR: –
FYE: June 30
Type: Private

Tennessee State University (TSU) covers its bases in higher learning fields including science and learning. Home to some 9,000 students, TSU is known for its programs in education, nursing, biology, physical therapy, computer engineering, agriculture, public administration, and psychology. The university offers about 45 undergraduate programs and 25 graduate programs through its eight colleges and schools. It also offers doctoral degrees in education, philosophy, and physical therapy. It has 450 full-time faculty members and a student-to-teacher ratio of 16:1.

	Annual Growth	06/03	06/04	06/05	06/08	06/11
Sales ($mil.)	75.0%	–	–	3.7	1.6	105.6
Net income ($ mil.)	39.1%	–	–	2.5	0.4	18.4
Market value ($ mil.)	–	–	–	–	–	–
Employees	–	–	–	–	–	1,234

TENNESSEE TECHNOLOGICAL UNIVERSITY

1 WILLIAM L JONES DR
COOKEVILLE, TN 385050001
Phone: 931 372-3101
Fax: –
Web: www.tntech.edu

CEO: –
CFO: –
HR: –
FYE: June 30
Type: Private

Tennessee Technological University (TTU, or Tennessee Tech) takes on the task of providing academic education and career training services in the Volunteer State. The public university has six college divisions providing more than 60 undergraduate and graduate degrees in the areas of Agriculture and Human Sciences, Arts and Sciences, Business, Education, Engineering, and Interdisciplinary Studies. it aslo offers The university has some 11,500 students enrolled and a faculty of about 400 staff members and has a student-to-faculty ratio of about 22:1.

	Annual Growth	06/09	06/10	06/11	06/12	06/13
Sales ($mil.)	9.7%	–	65.1	65.1	76.8	86.0
Net income ($ mil.)	(6.9%)	–	23.3	23.3	5.6	18.8
Market value ($ mil.)	–	–	–	–	–	–
Employees	–	–	–	–	–	1,096

TENNESSEE VALLEY AUTHORITY

NYS: TVC

400 W. Summit Hill Drive
Knoxville, TN 37902
Phone: 865 632-2101
Fax: –
Web: www.tva.com

CEO: Jeffrey J Lyash
CFO: –
HR: –
FYE: September 30
Type: Public

Tennessee Valley Authority (TVA) is a US government-owned corporation and the largest public power producer in the country. It is primarily a wholesaler of power, selling power to LPCs that then resell power to their customers at retail rates, which serve nearly 10 million people in Tennessee and parts of Alabama, Georgia, Kentucky, Mississippi, North Carolina, and Virginia. It also sells power directly to more than 55 large industrial customers and federal agencies. In addition, TVA provides flood control for the Tennessee River system and assists utilities and state and local governments with economic development.

	Annual Growth	09/19	09/20	09/21	09/22	09/23
Sales ($mil.)	1.6%	11,318	10,249	10,503	12,540	12,054
Net income ($ mil.)	(22.9%)	1,417.0	1,352.0	1,512.0	1,108.0	500.0
Market value ($ mil.)	–	–	–	–	–	–
Employees	2.2%	10,009	9,989	10,192	10,390	10,901

TENSION ENVELOPE CORPORATION

819 E 19TH ST
KANSAS CITY, MO 641081781
Phone: 816 471-3800
Fax: –
Web: www.tension.com

CEO: William S Berkley
CFO: –
HR: –
FYE: September 30
Type: Private

Tension Envelope has an ambition to seal up its market. The family-owned and operated company makes more than 12 billion envelopes each year, selling its product directly to companies in such industries as direct advertising, financial services, publishing, and health care. The company makes standard envelopes as well as producing custom envelopes that include sleeves and wallets, medical sleeves, photo envelopes, and reply envelopes. Other products include financial statement envelopes and photo finishing packaging. Tension Envelope also provides flexographic design guides and art and design service (for more eye-catching envelopes).

TER HOLDINGS I, INC

1000 BOARDWALK VIRGINIA AVE
ATLANTIC CITY, NJ 084017415
Phone: 609 449-5534
Fax: –
Web: www.trumpcasinos.com

CEO: –
CFO: –
HR: –
FYE: December 31
Type: Private

Trump Entertainment Resorts owned and managed the Trump Taj Mahal Casino Resort in Atlantic City, New Jersey. The property houses hotel rooms, gaming tables, and slot machines. Trump Entertainment Resorts' revenues were negatively affected by weak tourism in Atlantic City as well as competition from neighboring Pennsylvania casinos. Donald Trump does not run or control Trump Entertainment Resorts. Billionaire Carl Icahn bought the Taj Mahal and other Trump properties out of bankruptcy in 2014. Icahn's holding company, Icahn Enterprises closed the Taj Mahal in 2016.

TERADATA CORP (DE)

17095 Via Del Campo
San Diego, CA 92127
Phone: 866 548-8348
Fax: –
Web: www.teradata.com

NYS: TDC

CEO: Stephen McMillan
CFO: Claire Bramley
HR: Camille Gaylor
FYE: December 31
Type: Public

Teradata is a multi-cloud enterprise data warehouse platform provider focused on helping companies leverage all their data across an enterprise to uncover real-time intelligence, at scale. Products include its Vantage analytics platform, database software, hardware components, and applications. It also offers consulting, support, and training services. Teradata's software can be used in public, private, and hybrid cloud and on-premise environments. The company's customers are in data-intensive industries such as financial services, communications, government, healthcare, retail, manufacturing, and travel/transportation. The US customers supply about 60% of Teradata's revenue.

	Annual Growth	12/19	12/20	12/21	12/22	12/23
Sales ($mil.)	(0.9%)	1,899.0	1,836.0	1,917.0	1,795.0	1,833.0
Net income ($ mil.)	–	(20.0)	129.0	147.0	33.0	62.0
Market value ($ mil.)	12.9%	2,620.8	2,199.8	4,157.8	3,295.3	4,259.6
Employees	(6.6%)	8,535	7,543	7,200	7,000	6,500

TERADYNE, INC.

600 Riverpark Drive
North Reading, MA 01864
Phone: 978 370-2700
Fax: –
Web: www.teradyne.com

NMS: TER

CEO: Gregory S Smith
CFO: Sanjay Mehta
HR: –
FYE: December 31
Type: Public

Founded in 1960, Teradyne designs, develops, manufactures and sells automated test equipment and robotics solutions. Its automatic test systems are used to test semiconductors, wireless products, data storage and complex electronics systems in many industries, including consumer electronics, wireless, automotive, industrial, computing, communications, and aerospace and defense industries. Teradyne's customers are integrated device manufacturers, fables, foundries, and semiconductor assembly and test providers (OSAT). The company has operations in Asia, Europe, and the Americas, but it generates most of its sales from customers in Asia.

	Annual Growth	12/19	12/20	12/21	12/22	12/23
Sales ($mil.)	3.9%	2,295.0	3,121.5	3,702.9	3,155.0	2,676.3
Net income ($ mil.)	(1.0%)	467.5	784.1	1,014.6	715.5	448.8
Market value ($ mil.)	12.3%	10,412	18,307	24,971	13,338	16,571
Employees	4.7%	5,400	5,500	5,900	6,500	6,500

TERAWULF INC.

9 Federal Street
Easton, MD 21601
Phone: 410 770-9500
Fax: –
Web: www.ikonics.com

NAS: WULF

CEO: Paul Prager
CFO: Jon Gerlach
HR: –
FYE: December 31
Type: Public

IKONICS makes light-sensitive coatings (emulsions) and films, used primarily by the screen printing and abrasive etching markets (to create stencil images for the one and to create architectural glass and art pieces for the other). The company also makes photoresist films and metal etching materials for sign making and ink jet receptive films for creating photopositives and photonegatives. Custom etching services and digital imaging technologies for niche industrial markets is of increasing importance to the company. IKONICS sells its products through about 200 distributors worldwide, although the US accounts for more than two-thirds of sales.

	Annual Growth	12/18	12/19	12/20	12/21	12/22
Sales ($mil.)	(4.7%)	18.2	17.6	13.4	–	15.0
Net income ($ mil.)	–	0.1	(0.8)	(0.4)	(94.0)	(90.8)
Market value ($ mil.)	(47.0%)	1,226.8	778.4	1,450.5	2,189.7	96.8
Employees	(44.1%)	82	82	58	6	8

TEREX CORP.

45 Glover Ave., 4th Floor Norwalk
Westport, CT 06850
Phone: 203 222-7170
Fax: 203 222-7976
Web: www.terex.com

NYS: TEX

CEO: John L Garrison Jr
CFO: Julie Beck
HR: Bronagh McAteer
FYE: December 31
Type: Public

Terex Corporation makes a variety of materials processing machinery and aerial work platforms. The company makes platform equipment, utility equipment, and telehandlers such as material lifts, trailer-mounted articulating booms, and telescopic booms. It also makes all sorts of cranes and specialty equipment such as wood processing, biomass, and recycling equipment. Terex products are sold in more than 100 countries around the globe in the construction, maintenance, manufacturing, energy, and minerals industry under brand names, including the Terex, Genie, and Powerscreen, among others. About 55% of Terex's sales come from North America.

	Annual Growth	12/19	12/20	12/21	12/22	12/23
Sales ($mil.)	4.3%	4,353.1	3,076.4	3,886.8	4,417.7	5,151.5
Net income ($ mil.)	75.7%	54.4	(10.6)	220.9	300.0	518.0
Market value ($ mil.)	17.9%	1,968.5	2,306.2	2,905.1	2,823.8	3,798.1
Employees	1.8%	9,500	8,200	8,600	9,300	10,200

TERRA NITROGEN COMPANY, L.P.

4 PARKWAY NORTH BLVD STE 400
DEERFIELD, IL 600152502
Phone: 847 405-2400
Fax: –
Web: www.cfindustries.com

CEO: W A Will
CFO: Dennis P Kelleher
HR: John Hammond
FYE: December 31
Type: Private

Making the earth's soil produce more crops is the long term mission of Terra Nitrogen, which manufactures nitrogen fertilizer products. The company operates a plant in Oklahoma that produces ammonia and urea ammonium nitrate (UAN) solutions. Farmers use the company's products to improve both the quantity and the quality of crops. It sells its products to parent company, agrochemical giant CF Industries, which in turn sells nitrogen products wholesale to dealers, distributors, and national farm retail chain outlets, primarily in the central and Southern Plains and Corn Belt regions of the US. CF Industries has indirect ownership of Terra Nitrogen's general partner and controls the company.

	Annual Growth	12/13	12/14	12/15	12/16	12/17
Sales ($mil.)	(15.1%)	–	648.3	581.7	418.3	397.2
Net income ($ mil.)	(25.4%)	–	370.0	306.9	209.3	153.9
Market value ($ mil.)	–	–	–	–	–	–
Employees	–	–	–	–	–	250

TERRACON CONSULTANTS, INC.

10841 S RIDGEVIEW RD
OLATHE, KS 660616456
Phone: 913 599-6886
Fax: –
Web: www.terracon.com

CEO: Gayle Packer
CFO: –
HR: –
FYE: December 31
Type: Private

Employee-owned Terracon Consultants (Terracon) provides geotechnical, environmental, construction material evaluation, pavement engineering and construction management, and facilities engineering services. One of the nation's top design firms, the company serves the agriculture, oil & gas, telecommunications, commercial development, and transportation sectors, as well as government clients. It helps its customers comply with new building codes and environmental regulations, assess environmental hazards, and tackle the problem of aging structures.

	Annual Growth	12/18	12/19	12/20	12/21	12/22
Sales ($mil.)	11.4%	–	–	818.1	907.8	1,015.3
Net income ($ mil.)	9.3%	–	–	23.7	29.4	28.3
Market value ($ mil.)	–	–	–	–	–	–
Employees	–	–	–	–	–	6,065

TERRACYCLE, INC.

121 NEW YORK AVE
TRENTON, NJ 086385201
Phone: 609 656-5100
Fax: –
Web: www.terracycle.com

CEO: Tom Szaky
CFO: Javier Daly
HR: –
FYE: December 31
Type: Private

Dumpster diving has never looked so good. TerraCycle makes upcycled products out of previously non-recyclable trash. The company offers tote bags, backpacks, and kites made from snack food wrappers; pencils made out of newspaper; and picture frames made from bicycle chains and circuit boards, among other products. More than 28 million people around the world collect waste for TerraCycle and ship it to the company free of charge. (Companies such as Kraft and Solo Cup that make packaging and wrappers foot the bill for waste collection.) TerraCycle also offers a line of eco-friendly cleaning products; all of its goods are sold at major retailers such as Target, Wal-Mart, and Whole Foods.

TERRAFORM POWER, INC.

200 LIBERTY ST FL 14
NEW YORK, NY 102811117
Phone: 646 992-2400
Fax: –
Web: www.terraform.com

CEO: John Stinebaugh
CFO: Matthew Berger
HR: –
FYE: December 31
Type: Private

TerraForm Power uses green (power) to generate green (money). The company owns and operates 230 solar power generations projects in 15 US states and Puerto Rico, as well as in the UK, Canada, and Chile with total capacity of more than 800 megawatts (MW). It invests in assets already contracted to supply power to utilities, businesses, and homes through long-term agreements. TerraForm plans to branch out into other forms of clean energy. Most of its solar assets were purchased from SunEdison, which has about 900 solar generation facilities in a dozen countries. SunEdison formed TerraForm and took it public in 2014. In 2017 Brookfield Asset Management offered to buy the company for about $1.3 billion.

TERRANEXT, LLC

1660 S ALBION ST STE 900
DENVER, CO 802224046
Phone: 303 399-6145
Fax: –
Web: www.terranext.net

CEO: –
CFO: –
HR: –
FYE: March 31
Type: Private

Terranext focuses its earthbound geotechnical engineering expertise on the next project, as well as the one it is currently working on. An affiliate of engineering group BE&K, Terranext provides environmental engineering and consulting services to industrial, commercial, and government customers through half a dozen offices (in Alabama, Arizona, Colorado, Georgia, Kansas, and New Jersey). The company's services include air quality management, cultural, and natural resource conservation, energy reduction engineering, pollution prevention, water management, and site investigation and remediation. Since 1985 the woman-owned business has conducted more than 3,000 environmental projects.

TERRENO REALTY CORP

NYS: TRNO

10500 N.E. 8th Street, Suite 1910
Bellevue, WA 98004
Phone: 415 655-4580
Fax: –
Web: www.terreno.com

CEO: W B Baird
CFO: Jaime J Cannon
HR: –
FYE: December 31
Type: Public

Terreno Realty has its eyes set on acquiring industrial real estate. The real estate investment trust (REIT) invests in and operates industrial properties in major US coastal markets, including Los Angeles, San Francisco Bay Area, Seattle, Miami, Northern New Jersey/New York City, and Washington, DC. The REIT typically invests in warehouse and distribution facilities, flex buildings for light manufacturing and research and development, and transshipment and improved land. The company owns about 220 buildings spanning about 13.3 million square feet and about 20 improved land parcels totaling about 77.6 acres.

	Annual Growth	12/19	12/20	12/21	12/22	12/23
Sales ($mil.)	17.3%	171.0	186.9	221.9	276.2	323.6
Net income ($ mil.)	28.5%	55.5	79.8	87.3	198.0	151.5
Market value ($ mil.)	3.7%	4,736.6	5,118.9	7,461.8	4,975.4	5,482.8
Employees	–	24	26	34	40	–

TERRITORIAL BANCORP INC

NMS: TBNK

1003 Bishop Street, Pauahi Tower, Suite 500
Honolulu, HI 96813
Phone: 808 946-1400
Fax: –
Web: www.territorialsavings.net

CEO: Allan S Kitagawa
CFO: –
HR: Patti See
FYE: December 31
Type: Public

Territorial Bancorp serves its customers island-style. It is the financial holding company for Territorial Savings Bank, which provides standard products and services such as checking and savings accounts, money market accounts, CDs, IRAs, and loans from its nearly 30 branch locations across Hawaii. Its Territorial Financial Services subsidiary sells insurance, while LPL Financial offers Mutual funds and annuities. Territorial Savings Bank targets the territorial nature of its customers -- one- to four-family residential mortgages account for 95% of its loan portfolio. Multifamily and commercial mortgages and construction and home equity loans round out its lending activities.

	Annual Growth	12/19	12/20	12/21	12/22	12/23
Assets ($mil.)	1.8%	2,086.3	2,110.8	2,130.6	2,169.6	2,236.7
Net income ($ mil.)	(30.9%)	22.0	18.6	17.4	16.2	5.0
Market value ($ mil.)	(22.5%)	273.1	212.1	222.9	211.9	98.4
Employees	(3.9%)	281	281	271	261	240

TESLA ENERGY OPERATIONS, INC.

3055 CLEARVIEW WAY
SAN MATEO, CA 944023709
Phone: 888 765-2489
Fax: –
Web: www.solarcity.com

CEO: Elon Musk
CFO: –
HR: –
FYE: December 31
Type: Private

Ready to get off the grid? SolarCity can help. The company sells, installs, finances, and monitors turnkey solar energy systems that convert sunlight into electricity. Its systems, either mounted on a building's roof or the ground, are used by residential, commercial, and government customers such as eBay, Intel, Wal-Mart, and Homeland Security. SolarCity doesn't manufacture its systems but uses solar panels from Trina Solar, Yingli Green Energy, and Kyocera Solar, and inverters from Power-One, SMA Solar Technology, and Schneider Electric. In late 2016, SolarCity was acquired by Tesla Motors in a deal worth $2.6 billion.

	Annual Growth	12/12	12/13	12/14	12/15	12/16
Sales ($mil.)	64.6%	–	163.8	255.0	399.6	730.3
Net income ($ mil.)	–	–	(151.8)	(375.2)	(768.8)	(820.3)
Market value ($ mil.)	–	–	–	–	–	–
Employees	–	–	–	–	–	12,000

TESLA INC
NMS: TSLA

1 Tesla Road
Austin, TX 78725
Phone: 512 516-8177
Fax: –
Web: www.teslamotors.com

CEO: Elon Musk
CFO: Vaibhav Taneja
HR: –
FYE: December 31
Type: Public

Founded in 2003, Tesla Motors designs, develops, manufactures, and markets high-performance, technologically advanced electric cars and solar energy generation and energy storage products. Tesla sells more than five fully electric cars, among others, the Model X and Y SUVs, as well as the Model S sedan and Model 3 sedan. It has a growing global network of Tesla Superchargers, which are industrial grade, high-speed vehicle chargers, typically placed along well-traveled routes to allow Tesla-owners quick and reliable charging. Tesla offers certain advanced driver assist systems under its Autopilot and Full Self-Driving options. The US customers generate about half of Tesla's sales.

	Annual Growth	12/19	12/20	12/21	12/22	12/23
Sales ($mil.)	40.9%	24,578	31,536	53,823	81,462	96,773
Net income ($ mil.)	–	(862.0)	721.0	5,519.0	12,556	14,999
Market value ($ mil.)	(12.2%)	1,332,381	2,247,559	3,365,844	392,328	791,409
Employees	30.8%	48,016	70,757	99,290	127,855	140,473

TESSERA TECHNOLOGIES, INC.

3025 ORCHARD PKWY
SAN JOSE, CA 951342017
Phone: 408 321-6000
Fax: –
Web: www.adeia.com

CEO: Tom Lacey
CFO: Robert Andersen
HR: Kris M Graves
FYE: December 31
Type: Private

Tessera Technologies licenses its portfolio of patented technologies for semiconductor packaging, interconnects, and imaging in exchange for royalty payments. More than 100 companies, such as Intel , Sony , LG Electronics , and Samsung , use its designs to produce high-performance packages for mobile computing and communications, memory and data storage, and 3D integrated circuit technologies. Tessera has more than 4,000 US and foreign patents and patents applications. The US is Tessera's biggest geographic market.

TETON ENERGY CORPORATION

600 17TH ST STE 1600N
DENVER, CO 802025403
Phone: 303 565-4600
Fax: –
Web: www.caerusoilandgas.com

CEO: James J Woodcock
CFO: Jonathan Bloomfield
HR: –
FYE: December 31
Type: Private

Caerus Oil and Gas (formerly Teton Energy) is looking for energy assets in the Rocky Mountains. The exploration and production company has leasehold interests in the Central Kansas Uplift, the Eastern Denver-Julesburg Basin in Nebraska, and the Big Horn Basin in Wyoming. Teton Energy has spent several years shifting its focus from oil exploration in Russia toward natural gas exploration in the Rocky Mountain region. Running into financial trouble the company filed for Chapter 11 bankruptcy protection in late 2009 and was acquired by Caerus Oil and Gas.

TETRA TECH INC
NMS: TTEK

3475 East Foothill Boulevard
Pasadena, CA 91107
Phone: 626 351-4664
Fax: –
Web: www.tetratech.com

CEO: Dan L Batrack
CFO: Steven M Burdick
HR: –
FYE: October 1
Type: Public

Tetra Tech is a global leader in providing consulting and engineering services in the fields of water, environment, infrastructure, energy, and international development. Its solutions span the entire life cycle of consulting and engineering projects and include applied science, data analytics, research, engineering, design, construction management, and operations and maintenance. The US government is one of Tetra's biggest clients, along with development agencies and commercial clients in aerospace, industrial, manufacturing, energy utilities, and resource management. The company likes to do business under time-and-materials, fixed-price, and cost-plus contracts. About 70% of its revenue comes from the US customers.

	Annual Growth	09/19	09/20*	10/21	10/22	10/23
Sales ($mil.)	11.9%	2,389.6	2,348.6	2,552.2	2,835.6	3,751.1
Net income ($ mil.)	14.6%	158.7	173.9	232.8	263.1	273.4
Market value ($ mil.)	15.7%	4,522.9	4,859.4	8,086.2	6,844.0	8,095.3
Employees	7.8%	20,000	20,000	21,000	21,000	27,000

*Fiscal year change

TETRA TECHNOLOGIES, INC.
NYS: TTI

24955 Interstate 45 North
The Woodlands, TX 77380
Phone: 281 367-1983
Fax: –
Web: www.tetratec.com

CEO: –
CFO: –
HR: –
FYE: December 31
Type: Public

TETRA Technologies is a leading energy services and solutions company operating on six continents, focused on bromine-based completion fluids, calcium chloride, water management solutions, frac flow back, and production well testing services. The company is composed of two divisions: Completion Fluids & Products division manufactures and markets clear brine fluids (CBFs), additives, and associated products and services to the oil and gas industry for use in well drilling, completion, and workover operations; and the Water & Flowback Services division provides a wide variety of water management services that support hydraulic fracturing in unconventional well completions for domestic onshore oil and gas operators. The US generates over 70% of company's revenue. TETRA is a Delaware corporation, incorporated in 1981.

	Annual Growth	12/19	12/20	12/21	12/22	12/23
Sales ($mil.)	(11.9%)	1,037.9	377.7	388.3	553.2	626.3
Net income ($ mil.)	–	(147.4)	(51.1)	103.3	7.8	25.8
Market value ($ mil.)	23.2%	255.0	112.1	369.4	450.1	588.0
Employees	(12.8%)	2,600	1,800	1,100	1,300	1,500

TETRALOGIC PHARMACEUTICALS CORP NBB: TLOG

343 Phoenixville Pike
Malvern, PA 19355
Phone: 610 889-9900
Fax: –
Web: www.tetralogicpharma.com

CEO: J K Buchi
CFO: Pete A Meyers
HR: –
FYE: December 31
Type: Public

TetraLogic would like to stop cancer in its tracks. The biopharmaceutical company has been developing a new type of intravenous drug that would cause cancerous cells that are resistant to the body's immune system to self-destruct. Its product candidate, birinapant, is being tested for efficacy against colorectal, ovarian, and various blood cancers, including myelodysplastic syndromes (MDS). Birinapant is also in pre-clinical development for Hepatitis B. In 2016, the company agreed to sell its birinapant program to Medivir for $12 million plus milestone payments of up to $153 million. It will then terminate all remaining employees. TetraLogic was founded in 2001 as Apop Corp.

TETRAPHASE PHARMACEUTICALS, INC.

35 GATEHOUSE DR
WALTHAM, MA 024511215
Phone: 617 715-3600
Fax: –
Web: www.lajollapharmaceutical.com

CEO: Pavel Raifeld
CFO: –
HR: –
FYE: December 31
Type: Private

Tetraphase Pharmaceuticals knows you have to jump through more than one hoop to have a medication approved for use in the US. The company has developed a powerful antibiotic to treat life-threatening bacterial infections that are resistant to all other antibiotics currently on the market. Xerava (eravacycline) is a synthetic fluorocycline derivative that can be taken orally or intravenously to combat multi-drug resistant bacterial infections, which are considered growing threats to public health. Xerava is available on the market in the US by using a small, targeted commercial and medical affairs groups to build and promote access to Xerava. In 2020, La Jolla Pharmaceutical Company acquired Tetraphase for $43.0 million in upfront cash plus potential future cash payments of up to $16.0 million pursuant to contingent value rights (CVRs).

TEXANS FOR LAWSUIT REFORM FOUNDATION

1701 BRUN ST STE 200
HOUSTON, TX 770195770
Phone: 713 963-9363
Fax: –
Web: www.tortreform.com

CEO: –
CFO: –
HR: –
FYE: December 31
Type: Private

If the magnitude of jury awards in the state of Texas bothers you, you might want to join this group. Texans for Lawsuit Reform (TLR) is a non-partisan political coalition that seeks limits on civil lawsuits; in 2003 the group was successful in passing legislation that sets damage caps on lawsuits brought in Texas. The group's more than 16,000 members seek to change Texas' legal system through political action, research, and grassroots movements. It has individual supporters in 857 towns and cities across Texas, representing some 1,266 different trades, businesses, and professions.

	Annual Growth	12/13	12/14	12/15	12/16	12/22
Sales ($mil.)	(40.8%)	–	3.3	1.1	0.0	0.0
Net income ($ mil.)	–	–	0.9	1.0	(0.1)	(0.1)
Market value ($ mil.)	–	–	–	–	–	–
Employees	–	–	–	–	–	3

TEXAS A & M RESEARCH FOUNDATION INC

400 HARVEY MITCHELL PKWY S STE 300
COLLEGE STATION, TX 778454321
Phone: 979 862-6777
Fax: –
Web: rf.tamu.edu

CEO: –
CFO: Linda Woodman
HR: –
FYE: August 31
Type: Private

Established in 1944, the Texas A&M Research Foundation provides administrative services and support for scientific and technical research, primarily within The Texas A&M University System. Its Program Development Department helps university faculty locate and approach potential sponsors and funding opportunities. The organization also provides accounting and financing support as well as grant and contract negotiations. The foundation supports a number of projects and initiatives, from the Center for Advancement and Study of Early Texas Art to vaccine research at the university system's college of medicine. It is a private, not-for-profit organization.

	Annual Growth	08/18	08/19	08/20	08/21	08/22
Sales ($mil.)	3.2%	–	64.9	62.7	64.7	71.4
Net income ($ mil.)	–	–	(2.1)	(0.4)	0.6	(2.3)
Market value ($ mil.)	–	–	–	–	–	–
Employees	–	–	–	–	–	483

TEXAS CAPITAL BANCSHARES INC NMS: TCBI

2000 McKinney Avenue, Suite 700
Dallas, TX 75201
Phone: 214 932-6600
Fax: –
Web: www.texascapitalbank.com

CEO: Robert C Holmes
CFO: Julie L Anderson
HR: –
FYE: December 31
Type: Public

Texas Capital Bancshares is the parent company of Texas Capital Bank, a full-service financial services firm that delivers customized solutions to businesses, entrepreneurs, and individual customers. The company operates banking offices in the five largest metropolitan areas of Texas, namely, Austin, Dallas, Fort Worth, Houston, and San Antonio. The bank's loan portfolio includes Commercial, Real Estate, Mortgage finance, and Energy. Striving for personalized services for its clients, the bank offers, among other things, commercial loans, real estate term, and construction loans, personal wealth management and trust services, and online and mobile banking. Its Bask Bank division provides online banking services. Founded in 1998, Texas Capital Bancshares has about $28.5 billion in assets.

	Annual Growth	12/19	12/20	12/21	12/22	12/23
Assets ($mil.)	(3.4%)	32,548	37,726	34,732	28,415	28,356
Net income ($ mil.)	(12.5%)	322.9	66.3	253.9	332.5	189.1
Market value ($ mil.)	3.3%	2,681.7	2,810.7	2,846.1	2,848.9	3,053.0
Employees	3.4%	1,738	1,619	1,751	2,198	1,987

TEXAS CHILDREN'S HOSPITAL

6621 FANNIN ST
HOUSTON, TX 770302399
Phone: 832 824-1000
Fax: –
Web: www.texaschildrens.org

CEO: Mark Wallace
CFO: –
HR: Bella Belleza-Bascon
FYE: September 30
Type: Private

Texas Children's Hospital (TCH) is one of the nation's best, largest, and most comprehensive specialty pediatric hospitals, with more than 4.3 million patient encounters annually. Founded in 1954, the not-for-profit hospital provides full-service medical care for children, conducts extensive research, and trains pediatric medical professionals. Part of the Texas Medical Center complex, it has clinical facilities for every ailment ranging from psychological troubles to surgery and physical rehabilitation, as well as specialized heart, cancer, and neurological care. TCH is the primary pediatric training facility for Baylor College of Medicine.

	Annual Growth	09/18	09/19	09/20	09/21	09/22
Sales ($mil.)	44.6%	–	–	–	2,170.9	3,138.2
Net income ($ mil.)	–	–	–	–	45.1	(109.1)
Market value ($ mil.)	–	–	–	–	–	–
Employees	–	–	–	–	–	6,000

TEXAS CHRISTIAN UNIVERSITY INC

2800 S UNIVERSITY DR
FORT WORTH, TX 761290001
Phone: 817 257-7000
Fax: –
Web: www.tcu.edu

CEO: –
CFO: –
HR: –
FYE: May 31
Type: Private

Texas Christian University (TCU) offers customizable paths to promising outcomes with its around 115 undergraduate, some 65 master's level and about 40 doctoral programs. About 12,275 undergraduate and graduate students attend the university's ten colleges and schools the cover fields of study ranging from liberal arts to engineering to business. TCU has nearly 700 full-time faculty members and a student-to-faculty ratio of 13:1. It also has one of the NCAA's top football programs. TCU is affiliated with the Disciples of Christ, a Protestant denomination.

	Annual Growth	05/18	05/19	05/20	05/21	05/22
Sales ($mil.)	7.0%	–	558.4	562.5	545.2	684.3
Net income ($ mil.)	135.4%	–	26.5	(47.9)	443.4	346.3
Market value ($ mil.)	–	–	–	–	–	–
Employees	–	–	–	–	–	3,400

TEXAS DEPARTMENT OF TRANSPORTATION

150 E RIVERSIDE DR
AUSTIN, TX 787041202
Phone: 512 463-8588
Fax: –
Web: www.txdot.gov

CEO: –
CFO: –
HR: –
FYE: August 31
Type: Private

Bob Wills saw Miles and Miles of Texas, and the Texas Department of Transportation (TxDOT) makes sure that we do too. TxDOT builds and maintains interstate, US, and state highways, as well as farm-to-market roads throughout the state. It also oversees public transportation systems in the state. The aviation division helps local governments manage funds for airport development. In 2009 the agency transferred some its responsibilities, including issuing license plates and vehicle titles, to the newly created Texas Department of Motor Vehicles. The governor-appointed, five-member Texas Transportation Commission oversees TxDOT's work. The agency dates back to the Texas Highway Department, created in 1917.

	Annual Growth	08/18	08/19	08/20	08/21	08/22
Sales ($mil.)	(96.8%)	–	12,070	12.9	12,965	0.4
Net income ($ mil.)	(96.0%)	–	1,107.9	(0.1)	734.2	0.0
Market value ($ mil.)	–	–	–	–	–	–
Employees	–	–	–	–	–	14,720

TEXAS GAS TRANSMISSION LLC

3800 Frederica Street
Owensboro, KY 42301
Phone: 270 926-8686
Fax: –
Web: –

CEO: –
CFO: –
HR: –
FYE: December 31
Type: Public

Texas Gas Transmission transmits natural gas from Texas to states in the South and Midwest through the 5,900-mile natural gas pipeline system it owns and operates. The pipeline has the capacity to deliver 3.8 billion cu. ft. of gas a day to customers in eight states; major customers include Anadarko Petroleum, Louisville Gas and Electric, and Memphis Light, Gas and Water. Texas Gas uses third-part pipelines to supply gas to off-system markets in the Northeast. The company also owns nine underground gas storage fields in Indiana and Kentucky, with a storage capacity of 180 billion cu. ft. of gas. Texas Gas is a subsidiary of Boardwalk Pipeline Partners, LP.

	Annual Growth	12/02*	05/03*	12/03	12/04	12/05
Sales ($mil.)	(0.9%)	266.7	113.4	142.9	261.5	259.2
Net income ($ mil.)	(3.1%)	56.1	34.5	26.8	57.6	51.0
Market value ($ mil.)	–	–	–	–	–	–
Employees	1.4%	651	–	692	683	678

*Fiscal year change

TEXAS GUARANTEED STUDENT LOAN CORPORATION

301 SUNDANCE PKWY
ROUND ROCK, TX 786818004
Phone: 512 219-5700
Fax: –
Web: www.trelliscompany.org

CEO: Scott Giles
CFO: –
HR: Linda Hackleman
FYE: September 30
Type: Private

"TG" may sound like a college fraternity, but it's more about tuition and books than togas and beer. Texas Guaranteed Student Loan Corporation, commonly known as TG, was formed by the Texas legislature in 1979 to administer the Federal Family Education Loan Program (FFELP) in the Lone Star State. However, the FFELP was eliminated in 2010 and private borrowers can no longer originate government-sponsored student loans, which are now provided exclusively through the US Department of Education. TG continues to service and provide support for the approximately $26 billion worth of loans in its existing portfolio. TG is a public not-for-profit corporation that receives no state funding.

	Annual Growth	09/12	09/13	09/15	09/17	09/18
Assets ($mil.)	7.9%	–	551.2	632.6	745.7	807.0
Net income ($ mil.)	–	–	(210.8)	84.1	62.5	56.2
Market value ($ mil.)	–	–	–	–	–	–
Employees	–	–	–	–	–	413

TEXAS HEALTH HARRIS METHODIST HOSPITAL FORT WORTH

1301 PENNSYLVANIA AVE
FORT WORTH, TX 761042122
Phone: 817 250-2000
Fax: –
Web: www.texashealth.org

CEO: –
CFO: –
HR: –
FYE: December 31
Type: Private

Harris Methodist Fort Worth Hospital is the largest and busiest hospital in Fort Worth. It is a private, not-for-profit, almost 730-bed tertiary care hospital serving the residents of Tarrant County and nearby communities in Texas. Harris Methodist provides both inpatient and outpatient care through its main medical center and on-site health clinics. Specialized services include emergency medicine, trauma care, orthopedics, occupational health, women's health, oncology, and rehabilitation. Its Harris Methodist Heart Center has about 100 beds. The hospital is the flagship facility of the Texas Health Resources hospitals system.

	Annual Growth	09/19	09/20	09/21*	12/21	12/22
Sales ($mil.)	16.0%	–	787.5	909.9	986.1	1,060.3
Net income ($ mil.)	(12.0%)	–	49.8	110.4	97.8	38.6
Market value ($ mil.)	–	–	–	–	–	–
Employees	–	–	–	–	–	3,500

*Fiscal year change

TEXAS HEALTH PRESBYTERIAN HOSPITAL DALLAS

8200 WALNUT HILL LN
DALLAS, TX 752314402
Phone: 214 345-6789
Fax: –
Web: www.texashealth.org

CEO: –
CFO: Bryan Craft
HR: –
FYE: December 31
Type: Private

Who cares who shot J.R. -- at which hospital was the bullet removed? Perhaps it was at Presbyterian Hospital of Dallas (operating as Texas Health Presbyterian Hospital Dallas), which serves "Big D" and the surrounding area. The medical facility has some 900 beds and is part of Texas Health Resources, which operates hospitals and care centers in North Texas and the Dallas/Fort Worth area. Texas Health Dallas' specialty services include digestive disorders, neuroscience, oncology, orthopedics, and cardiovascular care. The medical center also includes a bariatric surgery center, a fertility center, and rehabilitation facilities, as well as research institutes. Its staff includes more than 1,000 physicians.

	Annual Growth	12/18	12/19	12/20	12/21	12/22
Sales ($mil.)	3.3%	–	–	–	734.4	758.5
Net income ($ mil.)	(60.6%)	–	–	–	90.4	35.6
Market value ($ mil.)	–	–	–	–	–	–
Employees	–	–	–	–	–	3,200

TEXAS HEALTH RESOURCES

612 E LAMAR BLVD STE 400
ARLINGTON, TX 760114125
Phone: 877 847-9355
Fax: –
Web: www.texashealth.org

CEO: Barclay Berdan
CFO: Ronald R Long
HR: Brandy Royal
FYE: December 31
Type: Private

Texas Health Resources (THR) is a faith-based, nonprofit health system that cares for more patients in North Texas than any other provider. THR serves North Texas through primary care and specialty physician practices, hospitals, outpatient facilities, urgent care centers, home health and preventive and fitness services. It has about 30 acute care and short-stay hospitals, including owned, managed, and joint venture facilities. THR also operates outpatient and surgical centers and physicians' offices, and it maintains affiliations with imaging, diagnostic, rehabilitation facilities, and home health agencies. THR's network includes more than 6,400 doctors and more than 4,100 licensed beds.

	Annual Growth	12/12	12/13	12/17	12/21	12/22
Sales ($mil.)	4.9%	–	718.3	4,688.6	1,385.6	1,108.1
Net income ($ mil.)	(1.5%)	–	285.7	869.8	585.3	250.4
Market value ($ mil.)	–	–	–	–	–	–
Employees	–	–	–	–	–	21,277

TEXAS HOSPITAL ASSOCIATION

1108 LAVACA ST STE 700
AUSTIN, TX 787012180
Phone: 512 465-1000
Fax: –
Web: www.tha.org

CEO: John Hawkins
CFO: Ignacio O Zamarron
HR: Paulina Heaney
FYE: December 31
Type: Private

The Texas Hospital Association (THA) is like life support to a vital group of institutions. The not-for-profit organization supports more than 460 hospitals and health systems in Texas primarily through lobbying -- on both state and federal levels. THA also offers it members education and training, and through affiliations with other providers, THA offers insurance, consulting, and software. The association publishes the bi-monthly Texas Hospitals, which updates members on issues and trends in the hospital industry; Rural Route, a bi-monthly for rural and small hospitals; and HOSPAC Notes on the group's Political Action Committee's activities. THA was founded in 1930 by a group of hospital administrators.

	Annual Growth	08/15	08/16	08/17*	12/21	12/22
Sales ($mil.)	(2.8%)	–	14.5	14.6	12.3	12.3
Net income ($ mil.)	26.0%	–	0.3	(0.3)	0.3	1.3
Market value ($ mil.)	–	–	–	–	–	–
Employees	–	–	–	–	–	163

*Fiscal year change

TEXAS INSTRUMENTS INC.   NMS: TXN

12500 TI Boulevard
Dallas, TX 75243
Phone: 214 479-3773
Fax: –
Web: www.ti.com

CEO: Richard K Templeton
CFO: Rafael R Lizardi
HR: –
FYE: December 31
Type: Public

Texas Instruments (TI) produces analog and embedded processors, the workhorses of the industry. The company designs and makes semiconductors that it sells to electronics designers and manufacturers all over the world. Its analog chips provide the power to run devices and the critical interfaces with human beings, the real world and other electronic devices. TI's customers, which number about 100,000, use the company's chips for applications that include autos, industrial machinery, consumer electronics, communications devices, and calculators. The company also sticks to basics in production, operating its own manufacturing facilities in North America, Asia, Japan and Europe. International customers generate about 90% of revenue.

	Annual Growth	12/19	12/20	12/21	12/22	12/23
Sales ($mil.)	5.1%	14,383	14,461	18,344	20,028	17,519
Net income ($ mil.)	6.7%	5,017.0	5,595.0	7,769.0	8,749.0	6,510.0
Market value ($ mil.)	7.4%	116,616	149,194	171,319	150,185	154,948
Employees	3.4%	29,768	30,000	31,000	33,000	34,000

TEXAS LUTHERAN UNIVERSITY

1000 W COURT ST
SEGUIN, TX 781555978
Phone: 830 372-8000
Fax: –
Web: www.tlu.edu

CEO: Robin Melvin
CFO: –
HR: Andy Vasquez
FYE: May 31
Type: Private

Texas Lutheran University (TLU), formerly Texas Lutheran College, is a private, four-year undergraduate university of liberal arts, sciences, and professional studies. The coeducational school annually enrolls about 1,400 students from approximately 23 US states and 8 foreign countries. About two-thirds of its student body resides on campus. TLU offers about 27 majors and more than a dozen pre-professional programs, as well as study abroad programs. The institution has 77 full-time faculty members; its student-faculty ratio is 14:1. The college is affiliated with the Evangelical Lutheran Church in America.

	Annual Growth	05/15	05/16	05/19	05/20	05/22
Sales ($mil.)	4.5%	–	55.0	59.6	60.3	71.5
Net income ($ mil.)	–	–	(1.3)	(3.9)	(2.4)	3.7
Market value ($ mil.)	–	–	–	–	–	–
Employees	–	–	–	–	–	275

TEXAS MEDICAL ASSOCIATION LIBRARY

401 W 15TH ST STE 100
AUSTIN, TX 787011624
Phone: 512 370-1300
Fax: –
Web: –

CEO: –
CFO: John E Dorman
HR: –
FYE: December 31
Type: Private

If you need help in Texas and you're a doctor, you could turn to the Texas Medical Association (TMA). The medical society, which is the largest in the nation, has grown from 35 physicians in 1853 to more than 43,000 doctors and medical students. Members are eligible to receive benefits, such as financial and investment planning, loans, and subscription services. The TMA also publishes articles, newsletters, and a magazine about hot topics in the medical field. Its political arm, the Texas Medical Association Political Action Committee (TEXPAC), acts as an advocate for its members' interests on issues that arise in the state and national legislature.

	Annual Growth	12/14	12/15	12/16	12/21	12/22
Sales ($mil.)	(5.3%)	–	0.2	0.3	0.2	0.1
Net income ($ mil.)	–	–	0.0	0.1	0.0	(0.0)
Market value ($ mil.)	–	–	–	–	–	–
Employees	–	–	–	–	–	30

TEXAS MUNICIPAL POWER AGENCY

12824 FM 244 RD
ANDERSON, TX 778305642
Phone: 936 873-1100
Fax: –
Web: www.texasmpa.org

CEO: –
CFO: –
HR: Susie Johnson
FYE: September 30
Type: Private

Power and Texas come together at the Texas Municipal Power Agency, which provides electricity generation and transmission services to four municipal utilities (Bryan, Denton, Garland, and Greenville). The joint powers agency, which was created in 1975 by its member cities, owns and operates the 462-MW Gibbons Creek power plant and related transmission assets. In the wake of the oil embargo the early 1970s, the Texas Legislature created joint powers agencies that could perform all the duties of utilities except sell power to non-members. Bryan, Denton, Garland, and Greenville then formed the Texas Municipal Power Agency and harnessed locally available lignite to fuel a power generation plant.

	Annual Growth	09/18	09/19	09/20	09/21	09/22
Sales ($mil.)	(13.7%)	–	53.3	54.2	40.1	34.3
Net income ($ mil.)	–	–	(29.7)	3.3	4.8	(74.6)
Market value ($ mil.)	–	–	–	–	–	–
Employees	–	–	–	–	–	137

TEXAS PACIFIC LAND CORP

NYS: TPL

1700 Pacific Avenue, Suite 2900
Dallas, TX 75201
Phone: 214 969-5530
Fax: 214 871-7139
Web: www.texaspacific.com

CEO: David M Peterson
CFO: Robert J Packer
HR: –
FYE: December 31
Type: Public

Texas Pacific Land Trust was created to sell the Texas & Pacific Railway's land after its 1888 bankruptcy, and yup, they're still workin' on it. The trust began with the railroad of about 3.5 million acres; today it is one of the largest private landowners in Texas, with more than 901,000 acres in about 20 counties. Texas Pacific Land Trust's sales come from oil and gas royalties (about 85% of sales), easements, and land sales. It has a perpetual oil and gas royalty interest under some 900,000 acres in West Texas.

	Annual Growth	12/19	12/20	12/21	12/22	12/23
Sales ($mil.)	6.5%	490.5	302.6	451.0	667.4	631.6
Net income ($ mil.)	6.2%	318.7	176.0	270.0	446.4	405.6
Market value ($ mil.)	19.1%	5,991.4	5,575.5	9,577.9	17,978	12,059
Employees	1.6%	94	102	92	99	100

TEXAS RANGERS BASEBALL FOUNDATION

1000 BALLPARK WAY STE 400
ARLINGTON, TX 760115170
Phone: 817 273-5222
Fax: –
Web: www.mlb.com

CEO: –
CFO: –
HR: –
FYE: December 31
Type: Private

You might say these Rangers are guided by the Law of the American League West. Texas Rangers Baseball Club is a professional baseball team that represents the Dallas area in Major League Baseball. Founded in 1961 as the second incarnation of the Washington Senators, the franchise moved to Texas in 1972. Playing host at Rangers Ballpark in Arlington, the Rangers won their first American League pennant in 2010 and their second pennant in 2011. Texas businessman Tom Hicks, who had owned the team since 1998 through his Hicks Sports Group Holdings company, sold the Rangers in 2010 to a group led by sports lawyer Chuck Greenberg and current team CEO and Hall of Fame pitcher Nolan Ryan.

	Annual Growth	12/08	12/09	12/13	12/14	12/15
Sales ($mil.)	9.5%	–	1.1	2.3	2.1	1.9
Net income ($ mil.)	11.5%	–	0.2	0.7	0.4	0.3
Market value ($ mil.)	–	–	–	–	–	–
Employees	–	–	–	–	–	436

TEXAS ROADHOUSE INC

NMS: TXRH

6040 Dutchmans Lane, Suite 200
Louisville, KY 40205
Phone: 502 426-9984
Fax: –
Web: –

CEO: Gerald L Morgan
CFO: Tonya R Robinson
HR: –
FYE: December 26
Type: Public

Texas Roadhouse operates a leading full-service casual dining restaurant chain with approximately 700 company-owned and franchised locations in nearly 50 US states and some 10 countries. The Southwest-themed eatery serves a variety of steaks, ribs, chicken, pork chops, and seafood entrees, along with sandwiches, and a selection of side dishes. The company also operates a few restaurants under the name Bubba's 33 that specializes in burgers, pizza and wings. Despite its name, Texas Roadhouse was founded in Clarksville, Indiana in 1993.

	Annual Growth	12/19	12/20	12/21	12/22	12/23
Sales ($mil.)	13.9%	2,756.2	2,398.1	3,463.9	4,014.9	4,631.7
Net income ($ mil.)	15.0%	174.5	31.3	245.2	269.8	304.9
Market value ($ mil.)	21.6%	3,761.6	5,273.7	5,985.7	6,289.6	8,225.8
Employees	7.6%	67,900	61,600	73,300	82,000	91,000

TEXAS SOUTHERN UNIVERSITY

3100 CLEBURNE ST
HOUSTON, TX 770044598
Phone: 713 313-7011
Fax: –
Web: www.tsu.edu

CEO: –
CFO: –
HR: Carolina Velasco
FYE: August 31
Type: Private

Texas Southern University (TSU) is a historically black public institution. The university, located on a 150-acre campus in downtown Houston, offers about 40 bachelor's degree programs and more than 30 master's and doctoral degree programs. Its 11 colleges and schools include the Thurgood Marshall School of Law and the Barbara Jordan Mickey Leland School of Public Affairs. (Jordan and Leland are both former US representatives and graduates of TSU.) The university has an enrollment of more than 9,500 students and a staff of about 1,000 faculty members and support personnel.

	Annual Growth	08/18	08/19	08/20	08/21	08/22
Sales ($mil.)	(5.1%)	–	124.7	110.5	97.0	106.5
Net income ($ mil.)	–	–	0.2	(22.7)	103.3	(6.2)
Market value ($ mil.)	–	–	–	–	–	–
Employees	–	–	–	–	–	1,000

TEXAS STATE HISTORY MUSEUM FOUNDATION, INC

1800 CONGRESS AVE
AUSTIN, TX 787011342
Phone: 512 320-8204
Fax: –
Web: www.thestoryoftexas.com

CEO: –
CFO: –
HR: –
FYE: August 31
Type: Private

The Bob Bullock Texas State History Museum opened in 2001 and quickly became one of Austin's prime attractions for visitors and locals alike. The museum is named for the former lieutenant governor of Texas, who died in 1999, just months after leaving office. On the wall behind a statue of Bullock is the politician's famous catchphrase, "God bless Texas." The foundation runs the museum, which is governed by the State Preservation Board. The museum covers the history of Texas from prehistoric times, through its independence as the Republic of Texas, and up to the present era. Many artifacts are on loan from other Texas museums. The museum features a 400-seat IMAX theater, a cafe, and a store.

	Annual Growth	08/13	08/14	08/15	08/16	08/17
Sales ($mil.)	(1.9%)	–	1.4	2.7	1.5	1.3
Net income ($ mil.)	–	–	(0.3)	0.4	0.7	0.4
Market value ($ mil.)	–	–	–	–	–	–
Employees	–	–	–	–	–	1

TEXAS STATE UNIVERSITY

601 UNIVERSITY DR
SAN MARCOS, TX 786664684
Phone: 512 245-2111
Fax: –
Web: www.txst.edu

CEO: –
CFO: –
HR: John McBride
FYE: August 31
Type: Private

Texas State University has more than 38,000 students pursuing degrees in more than 200 bachelor's, master's and doctoral programs. Comprising ten colleges and a graduate school, Texas State University is the largest school in the Texas State University System, which includes Lamar University, Sam Houston State University, and Sul Ross State University. In addition to its main campus in San Marcos, Texas, it offers bachelor's and graduate-level courses at a satellite campus in Round Rock. Fields of study include arts, business, education, communication, health, and engineering.

	Annual Growth	08/16	08/17	08/18*	12/19*	08/20
Sales ($mil.)	(0.1%)	–	–	459.6	459.4	458.9
Net income ($ mil.)	52.0%	–	–	27.2	18.3	62.9
Market value ($ mil.)	–	–	–	–	–	–
Employees	–	–	–	–	–	3,156

*Fiscal year change

TEXAS TECH UNIVERSITY SYSTEM

2500 BROADWAY
LUBBOCK, TX 79409
Phone: 806 742-2011
Fax: –
Web: www.texastech.edu

CEO: –
CFO: –
HR: Steven Gates
FYE: August 31
Type: Private

Texas Tech is steadily building its Raiderland empire. The University System comprises the seven campuses of Texas Tech University (TTU), the six campuses belonging to Texas Tech University Health Sciences Center, and Angelo State University. Texas Tech University, home to the Red Raiders, has enjoyed a growth spurt in recent years, with an enrollment at more than 32,000 students. The school's goal is to reach 40,000 students by 2020. It offers doctoral degrees, law degrees, master's degrees, and bachelor's degrees in areas such as engineering, art, psychology, English, communications, biology, and governmental relations. TTU was established in 1923 as Texas Technical College.

	Annual Growth	08/01	08/02	08/03	08/05	08/22
Sales ($mil.)	6.1%	–	–	516.0	595.2	1,585.7
Net income ($ mil.)	6.8%	–	–	51.0	138.1	178.1
Market value ($ mil.)	–	–	–	–	–	–
Employees	–	–	–	–	–	6,635

TEXAS VANGUARD OIL COMPANY

9811 ANDERSON MILL RD
AUSTIN, TX 787502262
Phone: 512 331-6781
Fax: –
Web: www.icij.org

CEO: –
CFO: –
HR: –
FYE: December 31
Type: Private

In the vanguard of companies squeezing oil out of old fields, Texas Vanguard Oil explores and develops oil-producing properties in Nebraska, New Mexico, Oklahoma, Texas, and Wyoming. The company's growth strategy is to acquire working interests in producing oil and natural gas properties already being operated by other oil and gas firms and to then further develop these assets. In 2008 Texas Vanguard Oil reported proved reserves of 358,119 barrels of oil and 2.3 billion cu. ft. of natural gas. A pure exploration and production business, the company does not refine or market its own oil and gas. It also engages independent contractors to drill its wells. Chair Linda Watson owns 74% of Texas Vanguard Oil.

TEXAS WORKFORCE COMMISSION

101 E 15TH ST STE 122
AUSTIN, TX 787780001
Phone: 512 463-2222
Fax: –
Web: www.texasworkforce.org

CEO: –
CFO: –
HR: –
FYE: August 31
Type: Private

The Texas Workforce Commission (TWC) supports economic development in the Lone Star State by developing its workforce. The state government agency with 28 regional workforce boards offers a number of services benefiting employers (recruiting, retention, and outplacement services) and workers (training and job-search resources). The agency also provides support services such as child care for targeted groups, employment and training services for veterans, publishes labor law and labor market information, and administers the state's unemployment insurance program. Texans receive most of TWC's services for free; the agency is funded primarily by the federal government.

	Annual Growth	08/16	08/17	08/18	08/19	08/20
Sales ($mil.)	11.8%	–	–	1,822.8	1,898.5	2,276.5
Net income ($ mil.)	92.3%	–	–	134.1	46.5	495.6
Market value ($ mil.)	–	–	–	–	–	–
Employees	–	–	–	–	–	4,600

TEXAS-NEW MEXICO POWER COMPANY

577 N GARDEN RIDGE BLVD
LEWISVILLE, TX 750672691
Phone: 972 420-4189
Fax: –
Web: www.tnmp.com

CEO: Patricia K Collawn
CFO: –
HR: –
FYE: December 31
Type: Private

The name is a bit misleading. While Texas-New Mexico Power (TNMP) has a heritage of providing energy services in the Lone Star State as well as its neighbor to the West, the Land of Enchantment, it is currently a provider to Texas residents only. The utility, a subsidiary of PNM Resources, an energy company based Albuquerque, New Mexico, provides regulated electric transmission and distribution services to more than 231,000 customers in 76 cities in Texas. The company serves small-to-medium sized communities in Texas on behalf of 65 retail electric providers. (In 2007 PNM Resources assigned the New Mexico regulated electric distribution operations to another business unit.)

TEXTRON FINANCIAL CORP

40 Westminster Street
Providence, RI 02903
Phone: 401 621-4200
Fax: 401 621-5045
Web: www.textronfinancial.com

CEO: Warren R Lyons
CFO: Thomas J Cullen
HR: –
FYE: January 1
Type: Public

Textron Financial isn't something you put in your tank; it's something you take to the bank. The commercial financing company provides customer financing programs for golf carts and aircrafts manufactured by its parent, Textron. It mainly offers loans, finance leases, and operating leases for the purchase of new Cessna airplanes, Bell helicopters, and E-Z-GO and Jacobsen golf equipment. Due to poor market conditions in 2008 the company stopped offering asset-based lending, distribution finance, golf course mortgages, resort financing, and structured capital. However, Textron Financial still manages a portfolio of receivables from that business.

	Annual Growth	12/06	12/07*	01/09	01/10	01/11
Sales ($mil.)	(28.6%)	798.0	875.0	723.0	360.0	207.0
Net income ($ mil.)	–	152.0	145.0	(461.0)	(203.0)	(230.0)
Market value ($ mil.)	–	–	–	–	–	–
Employees	–	–	1,237	1,209	1,024	467

*Fiscal year change

TEXTRON INC

NYS: TXT

40 Westminster Street
Providence, RI 02903
Phone: 401 421-2800
Fax: –
Web: www.textron.com

CEO: Scott C Donnelly
CFO: Frank T Connor
HR: –
FYE: December 30
Type: Public

Textron Inc. is a multi-industry company that leverages its global network of aircraft, defense, industrial and finance businesses to provide customers with innovative products and services around the world. Textron, which generates about 80% of revenue from the US, serves government, industrial, and commercial clients. Textron started as a small textile company in 1923, when 27-year-old Royal Little founded the Special Yarns Corporation in Boston.

	Annual Growth	01/20	01/21	01/22*	12/22	12/23
Sales ($mil.)	0.1%	13,630	11,651	12,382	12,869	13,683
Net income ($ mil.)	3.1%	815.0	309.0	746.0	861.0	921.0
Market value ($ mil.)	15.8%	8,630.3	9,322.8	14,892	13,657	15,513
Employees	–	35,000	33,000	33,000	34,000	35,000

*Fiscal year change

TEXTURA CORPORATION

1405 LAKE COOK RD
DEERFIELD, IL 600155213
Phone: 866 839-8872
Fax: –
Web: www.oracle.com

CEO: Patrick Allin
CFO: –
HR: –
FYE: December 31
Type: Private

Textura brings tech solutions to one of the most concrete industries -- construction. The company's Software-as-a-Service (SaaS) includes tools to facilitate connection and collaboration among commercial construction owners, developers, general contractors, and subcontractors. Its on-demand software covers everything from the bidding process and vendor risk assessment to routing invoices and project documents to billing and documenting subcontractor default. A majority of Textura's revenue comes from customers using its invoicing, document-tracking, and environmental certification products and monthly subscription fees (collectively "activity-driven revenue"). Formed in 2004, the company went public in 2013 and was acquired by Oracle in 2016.

TFS FINANCIAL CORP

NMS: TFSL

7007 Broadway Avenue
Cleveland, OH 44105
Phone: 216 441-6000
Fax: –
Web: www.thirdfederal.com

CEO: Marc A Stefanski
CFO: Timothy W Mulhern
HR: –
FYE: September 30
Type: Public

TFS Financial is the holding company for Third Federal Savings and Loan, a thrift with some 45 branches and loan production offices in Ohio and southern Florida. The bank offers such deposit products as checking, savings, and retirement accounts and CDs. It uses funds from deposits to originate a variety of consumer loans, primarily residential mortgages. Third Federal also offers IRAs, annuities, and mutual funds, as well as retirement and college savings plans. TFS subsidiary Third Capital owns stakes in commercial real estate, private equity funds, and other investments. Mutual holding company Third Federal Savings and Loan Association of Cleveland owns nearly three-quarters of TFS Financial.

	Annual Growth	09/19	09/20	09/21	09/22	09/23
Assets ($mil.)	3.9%	14,542	14,642	14,057	15,790	16,918
Net income ($ mil.)	(1.6%)	80.2	83.3	81.0	74.6	75.3
Market value ($ mil.)	(10.0%)	5,052.1	4,118.5	5,343.6	3,644.7	3,313.8
Employees	–	–	–	1,005	1,025	995

TG THERAPEUTICS INC

NAS: TGTX

3020 Carrington Mill Blvd, Suite 475
Morrisville, NC 27560
Phone: 212 554-4484
Fax: 212 554-4531
Web: www.tgtherapeutics.com

CEO: Michael S Weiss
CFO: Sean A Power
HR: –
FYE: December 31
Type: Public

TG Therapeutics is a drug development and commercializing firm that can change hats quickly when necessary. It delivering medicines for patients with B-cell mediated diseases, including Chronic Lymphocytic Leukemia (CLL), non-Hodgkin Lymphoma (NHL), and Multiple Sclerosis (MS). It has developed a robust B-cell directed research and development (R&D) platform for the identification of key B-cell pathways of interest and rapid clinical testing. It has five B-cell targeted drug candidates in clinical development, with the lead two therapies, ublituximab (TG-1101) and umbralisib (TGR-1202), in pivotal trials for CLL, NHL, and MS. It also actively evaluate complementary products, technologies and companies for in-licensing, partnership, acquisition and/or investment opportunities.

	Annual Growth	12/19	12/20	12/21	12/22	12/23
Sales ($mil.)	526.2%	0.2	0.2	6.7	2.8	233.7
Net income ($ mil.)	–	(172.9)	(279.4)	(348.1)	(198.3)	12.7
Market value ($ mil.)	11.4%	1,680.8	7,877.1	2,877.1	1,791.3	2,586.3
Employees	–	134	272	286	226	–

THANKSGIVING COFFEE COMPANY, INC.

19100 S HARBOR DR
FORT BRAGG, CA 954375718
Phone: 707 964-0118
Fax: –
Web: www.thanksgivingcoffee.com

CEO: Sam Kraynek
CFO: Janet L Aguilar
HR: –
FYE: December 31
Type: Private

Thanksgiving Coffee Company roasts and sells fair trade coffee beans -- roasted, whole, or ground -- to java lovers in Northern California. Fair trade coffee is purchased from small farmers who are paid a price that can sustain their small-scale coffee bean production. The company purchases coffee beans from more than 20 countries and sells some 100 different coffee brands and varieties. In addition, it sells tea under the Royal Gardens banner. Thanksgiving Coffee also owns and operates a bakery in Mendocino, California. The company was founded in 1972 by Paul (CEO) and Joan (president) Katzeff. The Katzeffs own 78% of the company.

THE A C HOUSTON LUMBER COMPANY

320 N LEWIS DR
KETCHUM, ID 83340
Phone: 208 726-5616
Fax: –
Web: www.doitbest.com

CEO: Robert A Houston
CFO: Gordon Barclay
HR: –
FYE: December 31
Type: Private

A.C. Houston Lumber works out west, where it's never heard a discouraging wood. As its name implies, the company specializes in providing a full range of lumber products to the professional builder and do-it-yourselfer. It operates through about 5 locations in California, Idaho, and Nevada. Products include plywood, composition board, dimensional lumber, and specialty woods. Among the brands distributed are BlueLinx, Hampton Lumber Sales, and Weyerhaeuser. Founded in 1884 by A.C. Houston, the company is still owned by the Houston family, including CEO Robert Houston.

THE ADT SECURITY CORPORATION

1501 W YAMATO RD
BOCA RATON, FL 334314438
Phone: 561 988-3600
Fax: –
Web: www.adt.com

CEO: James D Devries
CFO: Jeff Likosar
HR: –
FYE: September 26
Type: Private

ADT wants you to be armed and calm with its alarms. The company provides products and services used for fire protection, access control, alarm monitoring, medical alert system monitoring, video surveillance, and intrusion detection. It divides its security operations across four disciplines: Residential Security (provides burglar, fire, carbon dioxide alarms), Small Business (intruder detection and cameras), ADT Pulse (allows users to access and control security systems remotely), and Home Health (emergency response in the case of medical emergencies). In 2018 the company went public, raising about $1.5 billion. Apollo Global Management, which acquired the company for $6.9 billion in 2016, still owns controlling interest.

THE ADVERTISING COUNCIL INC

815 2ND AVE FL 9
NEW YORK, NY 100174500
Phone: 212 922-1500
Fax: –
Web: www.adcouncil.org

CEO: Dave Senay
CFO: Kenneth Kroll
HR: –
FYE: June 30
Type: Private

The birthplace of Rosie the Riveter and Smokey Bear, The Advertising Council carries out pro bono ad campaigns on behalf of both government and private organizations. Using public service announcements, the not-for-profit organization conducts about 50 campaigns each year aimed at areas such as children's issues, health, community, the environment, and family. The Advertising Council relies on volunteer efforts from advertising firms and receives more than $1.6 billion in donated ad time and space annually. Founded in 1942 as the War Advertising Council, the organization's success in promoting war bonds led President Franklin Roosevelt to ask it to continue applying its efforts to social issues.

	Annual Growth	06/08	06/09	06/10	06/14	06/22
Sales ($mil.)	3.9%	–	40.4	40.0	44.6	66.4
Net income ($ mil.)	–	–	1.0	2.8	2.0	(17.2)
Market value ($ mil.)	–	–	–	–	–	–
Employees	–	–	–	–	–	110

THE ADVISORY BOARD COMPANY

655 NEW YORK AVE NW
WASHINGTON, DC 200014593
Phone: 202 266-5600
Fax: –
Web: www.advisory.com

CEO: Robert W Musslewhite
CFO: –
HR: –
FYE: December 31
Type: Private

The Advisory Board Company provides healthcare consulting and research services to more than 4,500 member organizations, including hospitals, health systems, and medical groups. Offerings include expert consultations, research studies, forecasting and benchmarking tools, and customized reports. Its research operations help provide clarity on current issues in health care as well as strategies for addressing them. The Advisory Board Company operates from two offices in the US and UK. David Bradley founded the firm in 1979 as the Research Council of Washington. The Advisory Board Company is a subsidiary of Optum.

THE AEROSPACE CORPORATION

2310 E EL SEGUNDO BLVD
EL SEGUNDO, CA 902454609
Phone: 310 336-5000
Fax: –
Web: www.aero.org

CEO: –
CFO: –
HR: –
FYE: September 30
Type: Private

The Aerospace Corporation is a national nonprofit corporation that operates a federally funded research and development center and has more than 4,600 employees. With major locations in El Segundo, California; Albuquerque, New Mexico; Colorado Springs, Colorado; and the Washington, DC region, Aerospace addresses complex problems across the space enterprise and other areas of national and international significance through agility, innovation, and objective technical leadership. The Aerospace Corporation was established in 1960 and operates in around 20 locations across about a dozen states.

	Annual Growth	09/12	09/13	09/14	09/15	09/19
Sales ($mil.)	4.2%	–	868.6	881.9	916.7	1,111.6
Net income ($ mil.)	149.2%	–	0.2	5.4	(15.2)	57.0
Market value ($ mil.)	–	–	–	–	–	–
Employees	–	–	–	–	–	3,920

THE AFRICA-AMERICA INSTITUTE

121 FRANKLIN DR
VOORHEES, NJ 080432117
Phone: 212 949-5666
Fax: –
Web: www.aaionline.org

CEO: Amini Kajunju
CFO: –
HR: –
FYE: December 31
Type: Private

The Africa-America Institute (AAI) is a non-profit group that promotes cooperation and understanding between US and African leaders through African higher education and training. The group works with more than 200 colleges and universities in the US to offer degree programs, seminars, conferences, and symposia to Africans in nearly every nation on the continent. AAI receives its funding from private foundations, corporate donors, and the US government. The organization was founded in 1953 just as many African nations were beginning to gain their independence.

	Annual Growth	09/14	09/15	09/16*	12/17	12/18
Sales ($mil.)	36.1%	–	1.0	1.0	4.8	2.6
Net income ($ mil.)	–	–	(0.5)	(0.8)	1.8	(0.8)
Market value ($ mil.)	–	–	–	–	–	–
Employees	–	–	–	–	–	10

*Fiscal year change

THE AMERICAN FARMLAND TRUST

1150 CONNECTICUT AVE NW STE 600
WASHINGTON, DC 200364132
Phone: 202 331-7300
Fax: –
Web: www.farmland.org

CEO: –
CFO: –
HR: –
FYE: September 30
Type: Private

Old McDonald was probably a member of AFT. The not-for-profit American Farmland Trust seeks to protect US farmland by working with farmers, environmentalists, and government agencies to promote sound farming practices, encourage agriculturally-minded community planning, and secure public funds for conservation. Its Farmland Information Center produces analyses and studies while its Center for Agriculture in the Environment looks for environmentally friendly farming practices. The organization also offers consulting services and awards a $10,000 Steward of the Land prize yearly to one of its 50,000 members. AFT was founded in 1980 by farmers and conservationists worried about the loss of farmland to developers.

	Annual Growth	09/10	09/11	09/14	09/15	09/16
Sales ($mil.)	2.5%	–	8.8	11.0	9.2	9.9
Net income ($ mil.)	10.7%	–	0.2	0.9	(2.3)	0.3
Market value ($ mil.)	–	–	–	–	–	–
Employees	–	–	–	–	–	60

THE AMERICAN KENNEL CLUB

101 PARK AVE FL 5
NEW YORK, NY 101780300
Phone: 212 696-8200
Fax: –
Web: www.akc.org

CEO: Dennis B Sprung
CFO: –
HR: Lb Dean
FYE: December 31
Type: Private

The AKC is all about D.O.G.s. The American Kennel Club (AKC) maintains a registry of purebred canines from about 175 breeds. In addition, the group stages dog shows and publishes magazines (AKC Gazette , AKC Family Dog) and newsletters (AKC Breeder, AKC Jr. News) on dog ownership. It sponsors the Canine Health Foundation, Companion Animal Recovery (microchip-implanted dog recovery), the Museum of the Dog, and a pet insurance program. The AKC's Compliance division inspects dog kennels and breeders to ensure the animals receive proper care. About 620 member clubs make up the AKC, which recognizes another 4,500 clubs. The organization was founded in 1884 by a group of men who ran sporting dog clubs.

	Annual Growth	12/16	12/17	12/18	12/19	12/21
Sales ($mil.)	252.9%	–	–	–	9.4	116.8
Net income ($ mil.)	449.8%	–	–	–	1.3	38.6
Market value ($ mil.)	–	–	–	–	–	–
Employees	–	–	–	–	–	278

THE AMERICAN MUSEUM OF NATURAL HISTORY

200 CENTRAL PARK W
NEW YORK, NY 100245102
Phone: 212 769-5000
Fax: –
Web: www.amnh.org

CEO: –
CFO: –
HR: Caitlin Cammarosano
FYE: June 30
Type: Private

The American Museum of Natural History is one of the world's foremost scientific museums. Its landmark building on New York's Central Park West showcases parts of its immense collections of anthropological and zoological specimens, along with meteorites, gemstones, dinosaur fossils, and a butterfly conservatory. The American Museum of Natural History is part of the University of the State of New York. The museum was chartered by the New York legislature in 1869.

	Annual Growth	06/18	06/19	06/20	06/21	06/22
Sales ($mil.)	(7.7%)	–	192.8	175.0	3.2	151.8
Net income ($ mil.)	–	–	(23.6)	(46.6)	118.5	(144.3)
Market value ($ mil.)	–	–	–	–	–	–
Employees	–	–	–	–	–	1,262

THE AMERICAN SOCIETY FOR THE PREVENTION OF CRUELTY TO ANIMALS

424 E 92ND ST
NEW YORK, NY 101286804
Phone: 212 876-7700
Fax: –
Web: www.aspca.org

CEO: Frederick Tanne
CFO: Julia Nelson
HR: Jason Lewis
FYE: December 31
Type: Private

This group watches out for Fidos, Fluffies, and other furry friends all across the country. The ASPCA (American Society for the Prevention of Cruelty to Animals) is a nonprofit organization dedicated to promoting the humane treatment of non-humans. The society's aim is to save the lives of homeless pets and help victims of animal cruelty. It engages in education, public awareness, and government advocacy efforts. It provides medical services and animal placement from facilities in New York City. The privately funded organization was established in 1866 by Henry Bergh.

	Annual Growth	12/13	12/14	12/15	12/16	12/19
Sales ($mil.)	9.0%	–	–	197.5	217.4	279.0
Net income ($ mil.)	39.8%	–	–	7.4	9.0	28.4
Market value ($ mil.)	–	–	–	–	–	–
Employees	–	–	–	–	–	350

THE AMERICAN SOCIETY OF CIVIL ENGINEERS

1801 ALEXANDER BELL DR STE 100
RESTON, VA 201915467
Phone: 703 295-6000
Fax: –
Web: www.asce.org

CEO: –
CFO: Pete Shavalay
HR: –
FYE: September 30
Type: Private

American Society of Civil Engineers (ASCE) represents more than 140,000 members of the civil engineering profession worldwide. The organization operates under the mission of developing leadership, advancing technology, advocating lifelong learning, and promoting the profession. ASCE publications include books, manuals, journals, and magazines, as well as online research databases. It also provides its members with continuing education opportunities. Other ASCE activities include issuing annual report cards on the state of our nation's infrastructure. ASCE was founded in 1852 and is America's oldest national engineering society.

	Annual Growth	09/17	09/18	09/19	09/21	09/22
Sales ($mil.)	3.1%	–	56.5	60.2	62.7	63.8
Net income ($ mil.)	47.6%	–	2.0	(1.6)	15.9	9.6
Market value ($ mil.)	–	–	–	–	–	–
Employees	–	–	–	–	–	260

THE AMERICAN-SCANDINAVIAN FOUNDATION

58 PARK AVE
NEW YORK, NY 100163007
Phone: 212 779-3587
Fax: –
Web: www.amscan.org

CEO: –
CFO: –
HR: –
FYE: June 30
Type: Private

Working to spread the love of all things Nordic, the American-Scandinavian Foundation (AFS) advocates understanding between the US and Scandinavian countries. The group coordinates exchange programs, sending more than 26,000 students back and forth each year, and offers fellowships, grants, and job placement. AFS also publishes Scandinavian Review magazine three times a year and the quarterly Scan newsletter for its 7,000 members. Scandinavia House is the group's US headquarters where it hosts cultural activities and runs a cafe, library, and gift shop.

	Annual Growth	06/16	06/17	06/18	06/20	06/21
Sales ($mil.)	(0.5%)	–	3.6	4.1	5.7	3.6
Net income ($ mil.)	–	–	(1.2)	(0.9)	0.7	(0.2)
Market value ($ mil.)	–	–	–	–	–	–
Employees	–	–	–	–	–	2

THE ANDREW W MELLON FOUNDATION

140 E 62ND ST
NEW YORK, NY 100658124
Phone: 212 838-8400
Fax: –
Web: www.mellon.org

CEO: –
CFO: –
HR: Mark Almozara
FYE: December 31
Type: Private

Recipients of funds from The Andrew W. Mellon Foundation don't take the organization for granted. One of the leading charitable foundations in the US, the organization provides about $280 million annually in grants, including awards in five core areas: including higher education and scholarship, performing arts, and museums and art conservation. Recent grant recipients include the Detroit Symphony Orchestra, Oberlin College, and the Metropolitan Museum of Art. The foundation was created in 1969 when Paul Mellon and Ailsa Mellon Bruce, the son and daughter of banking titan Andrew W. Mellon, merged their charitable foundations (Old Dominion Foundation and Avalon Foundation).

THE ANSCHUTZ CORPORATION

555 17TH ST STE 2400
DENVER, CO 802023987
Phone: 303 298-1000
Fax: –
Web: www.anschutz-exploration.com

CEO: Phillip Anschutz
CFO: Brian D Fleming
HR: –
FYE: November 30
Type: Private

Beyond being known as a leader in the natural resources industry, Anschutz Exploration Corporation (AEC) is a private, independent oil and gas company with current projects located in Wyoming, Colorado and Utah. AEC and its predecessors have participated in significant discoveries and development of oil and gas resources worldwide. The company is currently focused on projects within the US Rockies, which leverages its company history and technical experience. AEC manages its portfolio including existing projects, searching for new areas of interest of divesting areas which no longer fits with company's objectives.

	Annual Growth	12/05	12/06	12/07	12/08*	11/22
Assets ($mil.)	69.9%	–	–	–	0.9	1,477.4
Net income ($ mil.)	–	–	–	–	–	(35.4)
Market value ($ mil.)	–	–	–	–	–	–
Employees	–	–	–	–	–	35,000

*Fiscal year change

THE ARC OF WESTMORELAND

5129 STATE ROUTE 30
GREENSBURG, PA 156016692
Phone: 412 995-5000
Fax: –
Web: –

CEO: Marsha Blanco
CFO: –
HR: –
FYE: June 30
Type: Private

The Arc of Westmoreland serves as a bridge connecting people with disabilities to the community of Westmoreland County in southwest Pennsylvania. A private, not-for-profit organization, The Arc of Westmoreland provides support, programs, services, and opportunities for people with disabilities. Westmoreland Arc Foundation is the fund-raising arm of the group, while Westmoreland Arc ProServ provides vocational training, therapy, and assisted living services for people of all ages. The Arc also offers educational outreach programs regarding mental disabilities. A member of the state and national ARCs (Association for Retarded Citizens), the organization was founded in 1954.

	Annual Growth	06/08	06/09	06/10	06/15	06/16
Sales ($mil.)	44.0%	–	0.7	0.7	9.3	9.4
Net income ($ mil.)	–	–	(0.3)	(0.3)	(0.4)	(0.4)
Market value ($ mil.)	–	–	–	–	–	–
Employees	–	–	–	–	–	175

THE ART BROAD FOUNDATION

221 S GRAND AVE
LOS ANGELES, CA 900123020
Phone: 310 399-4004
Fax: –
Web: www.broadartfoundation.org

CEO: –
CFO: –
HR: –
FYE: December 31
Type: Private

The Elis and Edythe L. Broad Foundation (The Broad Foundations) wants urban K-12 public school students to have broader opportunities. The group consists of The Broad Education Foundation, The Broad Art Foundation, and Scientific and Medical Research Initiatives. The Broad Foundations provide grants to school districts and education union leaders, among others, to improve competition, governance, management, and labor relations. Primary initiatives include The $1 million Broad Prize for Urban Education, The Broad Institute for School Boards, and The Broad Center for the Management of School Systems. Founded by Eli and Edythe Broad in 1999, the foundation has $500 million in assets.

	Annual Growth	12/13	12/14	12/15	12/20	12/21
Sales ($mil.)	21.9%	–	34.4	29.3	–	137.5
Net income ($ mil.)	–	–	(108.3)	13.4	–	132.7
Market value ($ mil.)	–	–	–	–	–	–
Employees	–	–	–	–	–	8

THE ARTERY GROUP LLC

7201 WISCONSIN AVE
BETHESDA, MD 208144843
Phone: 301 961-8000
Fax: –
Web: www.arterycapital.com

CEO: –
CFO: –
HR: –
FYE: December 31
Type: Private

The life blood of The Artery Group is real estate. The company acquires, develops, and invests in commercial and residential properties throughout metropolitan Washington, DC. The company's Artery Development division partners with builders such as Ryland Homes and Beazer to develop residential communities, commercial centers, and mixed-use properties. The Artery Group's portfolio includes single-family homes, rental apartments, office buildings, retail space, and hotels. The company manages more than $1 billion in real estate assets. Chairman and CEO Henry Goldberg founded The Artery Group in 1959.

THE ARTHRITIS FOUNDATION, INC.

1355 PEACHTREE ST NE STE 600
ATLANTA, GA 303093234
Phone: 404 872-7100
Fax: –
Web: www.arthritis.org

CEO: Ann M Palmer
CFO: –
HR: Cathy Hood
FYE: December 31
Type: Private

Arthritis Foundation (AF) wants the country's aches and pains to go away. The not-for-profit organization funds research, advocacy, and support services for various kinds of arthritis and related diseases. The foundation has about 45 chapters in 33 US states and offers programs and services including aquatic programs, information about treatment breakthroughs, exercise tips for people with the disease, and pain management information. AF raises money through The Arthritis Walk, Jingle Bell Walk/Run, and Joints in Motion, a program that trains participants to run a marathon or hike a tough trail and take part in a fund raising event.

	Annual Growth	12/12	12/13	12/14	12/15	12/19
Sales ($mil.)	6.9%	–	49.1	54.5	63.8	73.1
Net income ($ mil.)	–	–	1.4	7.5	2.4	(9.5)
Market value ($ mil.)	–	–	–	–	–	–
Employees	–	–	–	–	–	150

THE ASPEN INSTITUTE INC

2300 N ST NW STE 700
WASHINGTON, DC 200371122
Phone: 202 736-5800
Fax: –
Web: www.aspeninstitute.org

CEO: Dan Porterfield
CFO: Dolores Gorgone
HR: Tiersa Winder
FYE: December 31
Type: Private

If you're attending one of many seminars at the Aspen Institute you really should have your thinking cap on. The Aspen Institute is an international think tank providing a place to exchange ideas about leadership and contemporary issues. The not-for-profit organization holds seminars, programs, and conferences emphasizing a nonpartisan and non-ideological setting. Equity in public education, ethical leadership practices, and global security are among the issues the institute has addressed. It is primarily funded by corporate, individual, and foundation donations. The Aspen Institute was founded in 1950 by Chicago businessman and philanthropist Walter Paepcke.

	Annual Growth	12/17	12/18	12/19	12/21	12/22
Sales ($mil.)	7.7%	–	–	152.1	171.2	189.8
Net income ($ mil.)	–	–	–	6.2	27.5	(3.2)
Market value ($ mil.)	–	–	–	–	–	–
Employees	–	–	–	–	–	300

THE ASSOCIATED PRESS

1 WORLD FINANCIAL CTR FL 19
NEW YORK, NY 102811105
Phone: 212 621-1500
Fax: –
Web: www.ap.org

CEO: Gary Pruitt
CFO: Kenneth Dale
HR: –
FYE: December 31
Type: Private

The Associated Press (AP) is an independent global news organization dedicated to factual reporting. AP is the most trusted source of fast, accurate, unbiased news in all formats and the essential provider of the technology and services vital to the news business, with news bureaus in some 250 locations. It provides some 2,000 stories per day, as well as 70,000 videos and 1 million photos per year. It works with organizations of all sizes across a broad spectrum of industries. A group of New York newspapers founded the AP in 1846 in order to chronicle the US-Mexican War more efficiently.

	Annual Growth	12/12	12/13	12/14	12/15	12/16
Sales ($mil.)	(4.0%)	–	–	604.0	568.0	556.3
Net income ($ mil.)	(89.4%)	–	–	140.8	183.6	1.6
Market value ($ mil.)	–	–	–	–	–	–
Employees	–	–	–	–	–	3,533

THE ASSOCIATION OF JUNIOR LEAGUES INTERNATIONAL INC

80 MAIDEN LN RM 1504
NEW YORK, NY 100384889
Phone: 212 951-8300
Fax: –
Web: www.ajli.org

CEO: Patsy S Doerr
CFO: –
HR: –
FYE: June 30
Type: Private

There's nothing minor about Junior Leagues. The Association of Junior Leagues International (AJLI) is an all female not-for-profit membership organization that boasts more than 170,000 members and operates about 290 Junior Leagues in the US, Canada, Mexico, and the UK. The organization's primary goals are to encourage volunteerism, help women realize their potential, and enhance communities. To achieve these goals, AJLI provides training for its members in the subjects of organizational development, community needs assessment, strategic planning, and fundraising. It also participates in volunteer programs including childhood immunization, family literacy, and leadership development.

	Annual Growth	06/08	06/09	06/12	06/16	06/22
Sales ($mil.)	(1.5%)	–	7.5	6.7	7.5	6.2
Net income ($ mil.)	–	–	–	0.1	(1.6)	0.2	(1.7)
Market value ($ mil.)	–	–	–	–	–	–
Employees	–	–	–	–	–	30

THE BANCORP INC

NMS: TBBK

409 Silverside Road
Wilmington, DE 19809
Phone: 302 385-5000
Fax: –
Web: www.thebancorp.com

CEO: Damian M Kozlowski
CFO: Paul Frenkiel
HR: –
FYE: December 31
Type: Public

The Bancorp, Inc. is a financial holding company of The Bancorp Bank, its primary subsidiary. The company supports the payments and banking needs of nonbank companies, ranging from entrepreneurial startups to those on the Fortune 500. They have four primary lines of specialty lending: securities-backed lines of credit (SBLOC) and insurance policy cash value-backed lines of credit (IBLOC), vehicle fleet and other equipment leasing (direct lease financing), small business administration (SBA) and loans and non-SBA commercial real estate (CRE) loans. The company offers deposit products and services through its payments business line, lending activities through specialty finance, as well as affinity group banking products and services.

	Annual Growth	12/19	12/20	12/21	12/22	12/23
Assets ($mil.)	8.0%	5,657.0	6,276.8	6,843.2	7,903.0	7,705.7
Net income ($ mil.)	39.0%	51.6	80.1	110.7	130.2	192.3
Market value ($ mil.)	31.3%	690.0	726.2	1,346.6	1,509.9	2,051.5
Employees	5.5%	612	635	650	717	757

THE BEHLER-YOUNG COMPANY

4900 CLYDE PARK AVE SW
WYOMING, MI 495095118
Phone: 616 531-3400
Fax: –
Web: www.behler-young.com

CEO: Douglas R Young
CFO: –
HR: Christine Gornik
FYE: December 31
Type: Private

The Behler-Young Company has built its business by warming up to HVAC professionals. Through about 15 branches in Michigan and one in Ohio, the company distributes commercial and residential heating, air conditioning, hydronic, and ventilation equipment to contractors. It carries such brands as Bryant, Johns Manville, Hart & Cooley, Mitsubishi, Payne, and Reznor. Behler-Young was founded in 1926 by John Behler and Wayne Young with a focus on the distribution of sheet metal products. It sold its sheet metal manufacturing plant in 1989 and shifted its focus to HVAC equipment distribution.

THE BELTING COMPANY OF CINCINNATI

5500 RIDGE AVE
CINCINNATI, OH 452132516
Phone: 513 621-9050
Fax: –
Web: www.cbtcompany.com

CEO: –
CFO: –
HR: Melissa Benhase
FYE: December 31
Type: Private

Its belts don't hold up pants, but The Belting Company of Cincinnati does keep businesses moving. Better known as Cincinnati Belting and Transmission (CBT), the company distributes belting and conveyor components, power transmission, pneumatics, and electrical supplies. Products are used on bottling equipment, bakery conveyors, printing presses, and washing systems. CBT has joined the going green effort by supplying energy assessments and upgrades. Besides energy services, CBT provides such client services as asset and lifecycle management, condition monitoring, repair, security, and training. Founded in 1921, president and owner James Stahl Jr. bought CBT in 1975.

	Annual Growth	12/18	12/19	12/20	12/21	12/22
Sales ($mil.)	11.0%	–	–	214.5	270.0	264.4
Net income ($ mil.)	–	–	–	–	–	–
Market value ($ mil.)	–	–	–	–	–	–
Employees	–	–	–	–	–	276

THE BENECON GROUP INC

201 E OREGON RD STE 100
LITITZ, PA 175437440
Phone: 717 723-4600
Fax: –
Web: www.benecon.com

CEO: Samuel Lombardo
CFO: David Digiacomo
HR: –
FYE: December 31
Type: Private

The Benecon Group helps employers create, implement, and manage benefits programs. Benecon operates through four divisions: Consulting and Actuarial services, Broker Services, Municipal Insurance, and Compliance Services. The Consulting and Actuarial services division helps larger corporate clients design and implement benefits programs, while the Municipal Insurance division helps municipalities in central Pennsylvania gain leverage in the benefits markets by creating health insurance cooperatives. Benecon acts as a broker for hundreds of clients, including Capital Blue Cross, Highmark Blue Shield, and UnitedHealth; the Compliance division provides advice on regulations and laws related to benefits packages.

	Annual Growth	12/03	12/04	12/05	12/06	12/08
Sales ($mil.)	15.3%	–	9.7	10.1	12.5	17.1
Net income ($ mil.)	(22.7%)	–	1.0	0.0	0.0	0.4
Market value ($ mil.)	–	–	–	–	–	–
Employees	–	–	–	–	–	70

THE BERND GROUP INC

1251 PINEHURST RD STE 101
DUNEDIN, FL 346985428
Phone: 727 733-0122
Fax: –
Web: www.berndgroup.com

CEO: –
CFO: –
HR: –
FYE: December 31
Type: Private

The Bernd Group gets paid to shop for other companies. The supply chain management company distributes computer hardware, software, and a wide range of industrial and commercial equipment and supplies to companies in the aerospace, construction, manufacturing, and transportation sectors. Customers include Johnson Controls, Lockheed Martin, Pratt & Whitney, Tampa Electric, United Technologies, and other maintenance, repair, and operations (MRO) organizations and original equipment manufacturers (OEM). The Bernd Group draws upon a network of more than 18,000 vendors, and is able to rely on government-based contracts for women-owned companies. President Pilar Ricaurte-Bernd owns the company, which she founded in 1989.

	Annual Growth	12/15	12/16	12/17	12/18	12/19
Sales ($mil.)	5.4%	–	61.8	57.6	70.3	72.5
Net income ($ mil.)	(11.7%)	–	0.7	0.8	0.7	0.5
Market value ($ mil.)	–	–	–	–	–	–
Employees	–	–	–	–	–	90

THE BESSEMER GROUP INCORPORATED

100 WOODBRIDGE CENTER DR
WOODBRIDGE, NJ 070951162
Phone: 732 694-5500
Fax: –
Web: www.bessemertrust.com

CEO: Marc D Stern
CFO: –
HR: –
FYE: December 31
Type: Private

Wealth is personal for Bessemer Group. The privately-owned firm manages $95 billion in assets for wealthy individuals and families who have at least $10 million to invest. Main subsidiary Bessemer Trust administers portfolios with holdings in domestic and international equities and bonds, as well as such alternative assets as hedge funds, real estate, and private equity funds of funds. The group also provides trust, custody, tax, and estate planning; strategic philanthropy; and financial advisory services. It also counsels family businesses. Bessemer handles the assets of more than 2,200 clients.

	Annual Growth	12/06	12/07	12/20	12/21	12/22
Assets ($mil.)	5.5%	–	381.8	828.2	1,485.6	856.0
Net income ($ mil.)	(4.9%)	–	67.0	33.6	37.7	31.7
Market value ($ mil.)	–	–	–	–	–	–
Employees	–	–	–	–	–	657

THE BETTY FORD CENTER

39000 BOB HOPE DR
RANCHO MIRAGE, CA 922703297
Phone: 760 773-4100
Fax: –
Web: www.hazeldenbettyford.org

CEO: Mark Mishek
CFO: James Blaha
HR: –
FYE: June 30
Type: Private

Quite possibly the most famous of California's addiction treatment facilities, The Betty Ford Center provides a variety of drug and alcohol rehabilitation services for all members of a family affected by addiction. Services include a children's program, outpatient and inpatient treatment programs, and clinical diagnostic evaluation. The not-for-profit organization also offers professional education programs to keep its medical providers up-to-date on the latest treatment options. Its primary facility is on the grounds of the Eisenhower Medical Center; it also has children's centers in Colorado and Texas. Betty Ford, the wife of the late President Gerald Ford, along with Leonard Firestone, started the center in 1982. It is part of the Hazelden Betty Ford Foundation.

	Annual Growth	06/08	06/09	06/10	06/11	06/12
Sales ($mil.)	10.4%	–	–	33.0	38.6	40.2
Net income ($ mil.)	–	–	–	(1.4)	1.2	1.1
Market value ($ mil.)	–	–	–	–	–	–
Employees	–	–	–	–	–	260

THE BIDWELL FAMILY CORPORATION

400 E STATE ST
TRENTON, OH 450671549
Phone: 513 988-6351
Fax: –
Web: www.shapecorp.com

CEO: Arthur W Bidwell
CFO: –
HR: Kathleen Gramke
FYE: December 31
Type: Private

For over half a century, the Bidwell family's "bidness" has been aluminum extrusion. Operating through Magnode Corporation, the company is a full-service aluminum extruder, offering engineering, casting, extrusion, forming, fabrication, and finishing services, as well as trucking of finished work. Magnode supplies extruded aluminum products to a range of industries, including automotive, building and construction, consumer electronics, and defense. Magnode operates one of the largest extrusion presses in the US. The 4,500-ton press can extrude up to 17 inches in circle size and up to 23 pounds per foot. Magnode owns manufacturing facilities in America's heartland, and is led by its founder's third generation.

THE BILTMORE COMPANY LLC

1 N PACK SQ STE 400
ASHEVILLE, NC 288013409
Phone: 828 225-6776
Fax: –
Web: www.biltmore.com

CEO: Bill Cecil
CFO: Stephen Watson
HR: Matthew Anders
FYE: December 31
Type: Private

The Baltimore Company oversees the Biltmore Estate, which includes the 250-room home (the largest privately owned in the US), as well as hotels, a winery, restaurants, and licensing rights for a line of home decor products. (Guests don't stay at the Biltmore House, but at the Inn on Biltmore Estate.) The house sits on 8,000 acres of land and encompasses four acres of floor space. It has around 35 bedrooms, about 45 bathrooms, some 65 fireplaces, and three kitchens. The Biltmore is family-owned by descendants of the Vanderbilts, and is one of the few National Historic Landmarks that is entirely privately funded.

	Annual Growth	12/02	12/03	12/04	12/06	12/07
Sales ($mil.)	8.0%	–	57.0	56.8	70.6	77.6
Net income ($ mil.)	(15.0%)	–	4.4	3.0	2.5	2.3
Market value ($ mil.)	–	–	–	–	–	–
Employees	–	–	–	–	–	2,500

THE BMS ENTERPRISES INC

5718 AIRPORT FWY
HALTOM CITY, TX 761176005
Phone: 877 730-1948
Fax: –
Web: www.bmscat.com

CEO: Kirk Blackmon
CFO: Robert D Smith
HR: –
FYE: December 31
Type: Private

The BMS Enterprises (doing business as Blackmon Mooring) doesn't fly in the face of disaster. The company offers disaster recovery services such as fire, water, and smoke damage restoration, as well as mold remediation. For those who haven't experienced flooding, fire, hurricanes, or earthquakes, BMS Enterprises will also clean your carpets, tile floors, furniture, drapes, and air ducts. Its BMS CAT (Catastrophe) unit provides commercial restoration services. The family-owned BMS Enterprises was founded in 1948 by Scott Mooring Jr. and Bill Blackmon, Jr. as a furniture and dye shop.

	Annual Growth	12/02	12/03	12/04	12/05	12/14
Sales ($mil.)	(5.7%)	–	–	–	262.6	155.3
Net income ($ mil.)	(7.0%)	–	–	–	12.8	6.7
Market value ($ mil.)	–	–	–	–	–	–
Employees	–	–	–	–	–	900

THE BRADFORD EXCHANGE LTD

9333 N MILWAUKEE AVE
NILES, IL 607141392
Phone: 847 581-8508
Fax: –
Web: www.bradfordexchange.com

CEO: Richard W Tinberg
CFO: James D Liggett
HR: Diane Quinn
FYE: December 31
Type: Private

The Bradford Exchange is one of the world's largest trading centers for collectibles. The company also sells products such as jewelries, watches, music boxes and collectibles, apparel, bags, shoes, villages and trains, dolls, coins, collections, personal checks and stationery, and others. The Bradford Exchange and its affiliated companies' official affiliate program, represents three longstanding and valued brands: The Bradford Exchange, The Hamilton Collection, and The Ashton-Drake Galleries. It also markets Elvis memorabilia, Disney collectibles and keepsakes to sports collectibles and memorabilia, holiday treasures to Queen Elizabeth II collectibles, and PEANUTS collectibles.

THE BRANCH GROUP INC

442 RUTHERFORD AVE NE
ROANOKE, VA 240162116
Phone: 540 982-1678
Fax: –
Web: www.branchgroup.com

CEO: –
CFO: –
HR: –
FYE: December 31
Type: Private

It's not going out on a limb to say that The Branch Group has paved a lot of roads and built a lot of structures up and down the Atlantic Seaboard. The company, through its subsidiaries, provides heavy/highway construction (Branch Highways and E.V. Williams), building construction (Branch & Associates and R.E. Daffan), and mechanical/electrical construction services (G.J. Hopkins). The group has paved roads for highway departments, built hospitals, schools, factories and infrastructure projects. The employee-owned company began in 1963 as Branch & Associates, Inc., but traces its roots to 1955, when Billy Branch and C. W. McAlister paired up to provide road and site construction services.

	Annual Growth	12/16	12/17	12/18	12/19	12/20
Sales ($mil.)	9.1%	–	363.3	382.1	523.1	471.2
Net income ($ mil.)	–	–	–	–	–	–
Market value ($ mil.)	–	–	–	–	–	–
Employees	–	–	–	–	–	800

THE BRIGHAM AND WOMEN'S HOSPITAL INC

75 FRANCIS ST
BOSTON, MA 021156106
Phone: 617 732-5500
Fax: –
Web: www.brighamandwomens.org

CEO: –
CFO: –
HR: –
FYE: September 30
Type: Private

It took three of Boston's oldest and most prestigious hospitals to form the health care behemoth that is Brigham and Women's Hospital. The Harvard-affiliated facility has nearly 800 beds and includes the Dana-Farber/Brigham and Women's Cancer Center, a partnership between the hospital and the Dana Farber Cancer Institute. Other specialty units focus on cardiology, neurology, transplants, and obstetrics. In addition to being a teaching hospital for Harvard Medical School, Brigham and Women's Hospital conducts research and clinical trials to help advance medical care. It's a top recipient of research grants from the National Institutes of Health and is a founding member of the Partners HealthCare System.

	Annual Growth	09/15	09/16	09/17	09/20	09/21
Sales ($mil.)	6.9%	–	1,938.3	2,128.5	2,282.6	2,707.5
Net income ($ mil.)	27.2%	–	94.4	55.9	(208.6)	314.8
Market value ($ mil.)	–	–	–	–	–	–
Employees	–	–	–	–	–	8,376

THE BROOKDALE HOSPITAL MEDICAL CENTER

1 BROOKDALE PLZ
BROOKLYN, NY 112123198
Phone: 718 240-5000
Fax: –
Web: www.onebrooklynhealth.org

CEO: James Porter
CFO: Mounirf Doss
HR: Gaitre Lorick
FYE: December 31
Type: Private

Serving residents in Brooklyn and south Queens, New York, The Brookdale University Hospital and Medical Center (BUHMC) is a not-for-profit teaching hospital with about 530 beds that offers primary and acute care, as well as specialty services. In addition, the medical center operates about 50 outpatient care centers, including ambulatory surgery, dental, and mental health clinics. It also runs the Schulman and Schachne Institute for Nursing and Rehabilitation (with some 450 beds) and the Arlene and David Schlang Pavilion, an assisted and independent living center with nearly 90 beds. The Brookdale University Hospital and Medical Center was founded in 1921.

THE BROOKINGS INSTITUTION

1775 MASSACHUSETTS AVE NW
WASHINGTON, DC 200362103
Phone: 202 797-6000
Fax: –
Web: www.brookings.edu

CEO: –
CFO: –
HR: –
FYE: June 30
Type: Private

The Brookings Institution is a non-partisan public policy organization. The institute is comprised of more than 300 leading experts in government and academia from all over the world who provide the highest quality research, policy recommendations, and analysis on a full range of public policy issues. The non-profit organization is financed by gifts and grants. Founded in 1916, it is the first private organization devoted to analyzing national public policy issues.

	Annual Growth	06/14	06/15	06/20	06/21	06/22
Sales ($mil.)	1.7%	–	106.4	79.4	67.9	119.3
Net income ($ mil.)	–	–	(1.5)	(15.5)	(17.8)	31.5
Market value ($ mil.)	–	–	–	–	–	–
Employees	–	–	–	–	–	400

THE BROTHER'S BROTHER FOUNDATION

1200 GALVESTON AVE
PITTSBURGH, PA 152331604
Phone: 412 321-3160
Fax: –
Web: www.brothersbrother.org

CEO: –
CFO: –
HR: –
FYE: December 31
Type: Private

He ain't heavy, he's my brother's brother . The lyrics aren't quite right but the sentiment is the same. The not-for-profit Brother's Brother Foundation (BBF) provides emergency and nonemergency medical supplies, textbooks, food, shoes, and other humanitarian supplies to people in some 120 countries using a combination of gifts from the general public, corporations, and the US government. BBF is a gift-in-kind charity, meaning the bulk of the donations are goods, rather than money. The organization was established in 1958 by the renowned anesthesiologist Robert Hingson as Brother's Keeper, but later changed its name. Hingson invented the jet inoculation gun used to provide 1,000 inoculations per hour.

	Annual Growth	12/15	12/16	12/17	12/18	12/19
Sales ($mil.)	(36.4%)	–	217.0	95.3	95.6	55.8
Net income ($ mil.)	–	–	23.8	(24.4)	(8.6)	(10.0)
Market value ($ mil.)	–	–	–	–	–	–
Employees	–	–	–	–	–	12

THE BURTON CORPORATION

180 QUEEN CITY PARK RD
BURLINGTON, VT 054015935
Phone: 800 881-3138
Fax: –
Web: www.burton.com

CEO: John Lacy
CFO: –
HR: Momoko Omiya
FYE: April 30
Type: Private

The Burton Corporation, doing business as Burton Snowboards, is one of the largest snowboard manufacturer around the world. It also makes a growing lineup of men's, women's, and youth snowboarding apparel, eyewear, boots, bindings, and packs under its namesake, as well as the AK, Anon, BOA, Step On, and RED brands. The company operates through a network of retail shops and factory outlets in the US, Italy, Austria, and Japan. It also sells gear through sporting goods stores and online retailers. The company was founded in 1977 by Jake Burton.

THE CADMUS GROUP LLC

410 TOTTEN POND RD FL 4
WALTHAM, MA 024512004
Phone: 617 673-7000
Fax: –
Web: www.cadmusgroup.com

CEO: –
CFO: Cindy Shephard
HR: Joel Demasi
FYE: April 30
Type: Private

Drinking water protection is one of the areas of sage advice offered by The Cadmus Group. The environmental consulting firm (named after Cadmus, the Phoenician prince and renowned wise man who founded the city of Thebes) provides research, analytical, and technical support services, primarily to government agencies. Over time it has established itself as a lead contractor of the US Environmental Protection Agency). Other specialties include air quality, energy conservation, environmental risk assessment, and regulatory support, as well as marketing and public education related to environmental programs. Cadmus operates from 10 offices throughout the US.

	Annual Growth	04/13	04/14	04/15	04/16	04/17
Sales ($mil.)	14.8%	–	68.8	66.9	80.1	104.1
Net income ($ mil.)	–	–	0.8	(1.1)	(0.7)	(0.5)
Market value ($ mil.)	–	–	–	–	–	–
Employees	–	–	–	–	–	500

THE CALIFORNIA ENDOWMENT

1000 N ALAMEDA ST
LOS ANGELES, CA 900121804
Phone: 213 928-8800
Fax: –
Web: www.calendow.org

CEO: –
CFO: –
HR: –
FYE: March 31
Type: Private

The California Endowment awards grants to health care providers in the Golden State. Funding is directed to not-for-profit organizations, particularly those that work with the state's poor and underserved communities, as well as studies of the state's health care industry. Its advocacy interests include health care access, culturally competent health systems, and elimination of health disparities. A private foundation, The California Endowment has awarded more than $1.5 billion in grants since it was established in 1996. It has regional offices in Fresno, Los Angeles, Sacramento, San Diego, and San Francisco.

	Annual Growth	03/13	03/14	03/15	03/16	03/22
Sales ($mil.)	14.9%	–	–	–	201.1	461.7
Net income ($ mil.)	–	–	–	–	(40.4)	248.9
Market value ($ mil.)	–	–	–	–	–	–
Employees	–	–	–	–	–	110

THE CARTER-JONES LUMBER COMPANY

601 TALLMADGE RD
KENT, OH 442407331
Phone: 330 673-6100
Fax: –
Web: www.carterlumber.com

CEO: Neil Sackett
CFO: Jeffrey S Donley
HR: –
FYE: December 31
Type: Private

Carter Lumber has the answer when new home construction has you hollering "timber!" The company owns and operates about 145 lumber and home improvement stores in a dozen states from Michigan to South Carolina. The company caters to both contractors and do-it-yourselfers, supplying them with lumber, plywood, roofing, windows, doors, plumbing and electrical products, heating equipment, tools, siding, and other products. The home improvement retailer also owns Carter-Jones Lumber, which runs a 17-acre lumberyard and custom millwork facilities in Ohio. The company was founded by Warren E. Carter in 1932, and it continues to be a family-owned business.

	Annual Growth	12/06	12/07	12/08	12/09	12/10
Sales ($mil.)	(11.2%)	–	–	424.2	314.4	334.4
Net income ($ mil.)	–	–	–	(1.5)	(4.7)	(4.6)
Market value ($ mil.)	–	–	–	–	–	–
Employees	–	–	–	–	–	1,575

THE CATHOLIC UNIVERSITY OF AMERICA

620 MICHIGAN AVE NE
WASHINGTON, DC 200640002
Phone: 202 319-5300
Fax: –
Web: www.catholic.edu

CEO: –
CFO: –
HR: –
FYE: April 30
Type: Private

The Catholic University of America (CUA), established in 1887 by US bishops, has an enrollment of more than 7,000 students from all 50 states and nearly 100 countries. With graduate and undergraduate programs in 13 colleges, CUA offers degrees in such fields as architecture and planning, arts and sciences, engineering, music, and nursing; it's expanding into business and economics. CUA is the only US university with ecclesiastical faculties granting canonical degrees in canon law, philosophy, and theology. Some 80% of undergraduates and nearly 60% of graduate students are Catholic. The University's Theological College prepares men for the priesthood serving dioceses nationwide.

	Annual Growth	04/18	04/19	04/20	04/21	04/22
Sales ($mil.)	(0.5%)	–	238.3	253.7	227.8	234.8
Net income ($ mil.)	(20.2%)	–	18.9	20.6	97.9	9.6
Market value ($ mil.)	–	–	–	–	–	–
Employees	–	–	–	–	–	4,239

THE CENTECH GROUP INC

4437 BROOKFIELD CORPORATE DR STE 207
CHANTILLY, VA 20151
Phone: 703 525-4444
Fax: –
Web: www.centechgroup.com

CEO: Fernando Galaviz
CFO: –
HR: Lawyer Martin
FYE: December 31
Type: Private

The CENTECH GROUP offers a wide range of information technology services primarily to agencies of the US federal government. The company's areas of expertise include systems engineering, security, business operations support, network services, and software development. Among its clients are the Department of Defense, the Department of Transportation, and the State Department. CENTECH also serves customers in fields that include financial services, manufacturing, retail, and health care. The company's core presence is in Virginia, but it operates from offices in four states and serves clients in more than 20 states across the US. CENTECH was founded in 1988 by CEO Fernando Galaviz.

	Annual Growth	12/07	12/08	12/09	12/10	12/11
Sales ($mil.)	(39.5%)	–	–	–	152.7	92.4
Net income ($ mil.)	(54.3%)	–	–	–	7.2	3.3
Market value ($ mil.)	–	–	–	–	–	–
Employees	–	–	–	–	–	165

THE CHAIR KING INC

5405 W SAM HOUSTON PKWY N
HOUSTON, TX 770415135
Phone: 713 690-1919
Fax: –
Web: www.chairking.com

CEO: –
CFO: –
HR: –
FYE: December 31
Type: Private

Set atop its throne for the past half century, The Chair King has established itself as a leading casual furniture retailer in the state of Texas. The family-run company, with about 20 stores in Houston, Dallas, Austin, and San Antonio, Texas, sells midpriced to high-end indoor (wicker, rattan, and leather) and outdoor furniture (aluminum, cast aluminum, wrought iron, resin, teak, wicker) and related accessories. Furniture and bedding account for the majority of company sales. The Chair King, founded in 1950, sells well known brands including Garden Classics, Berkline, and Solaris Designs.

THE CHAMPAIGN TELEPHONE COMPANY

126 SCIOTO ST
URBANA, OH 430782199
Phone: 937 653-4000
Fax: –
Web: www.ctcomm.net

CEO: –
CFO: –
HR: –
FYE: December 31
Type: Private

The Champaign Telephone Company and its subsidiary CT Communications provide telecommunications services to residential and business customers in Champaign County, Ohio, and in the Village of West Liberty in Logan County, Ohio. Services provided by the company include landline telephone, wired and wireless Internet access, and cable television. It also offers Web hosting, as well as managed data storage services for businesses. The company's CT Wireless Service Division provides cellular phone service through a partnership with Telispire which resells wireless service provided over the Sprint Nextel network.

	Annual Growth	12/05	12/06	12/07	12/08	12/09
Sales ($mil.)	–	–	–	(203.4)	10.8	10.9
Net income ($ mil.)	7177.7%	–	–	0.0	0.3	0.8
Market value ($ mil.)	–	–	–	–	–	–
Employees	–	–	–	–	–	46

THE CHARLES STARK DRAPER LABORATORY INC

555 TECHNOLOGY SQ
CAMBRIDGE, MA 021393539
Phone: 617 258-1000
Fax: –
Web: www.draper.com

CEO: William A Laplante
CFO: Christine Albertelli
HR: Pamela Kennedy
FYE: June 25
Type: Private

The Charles Stark Draper Laboratory (also known as Draper Lab) is a nonprofit engineering innovation company that serves the nation's interests and security needs; advances technologies at the intersection of government, academia, and industry; cultivates the next generation of innovators; and solves the most complex challenges. Multidisciplinary teams drawn from a broad and deep talent pool of 1,300 engineers. Biosurveillance is the company's nation's first line of defense against emerging, endemic and engineered pathogens and genetically modified organisms (GMOs). Draper delivers breakthrough technologies that can drive results in the field, enhancing situational awareness.

THE CHARLOTTE-MECKLENBURG HOSPITAL AUTHORITY

1000 BLYTHE BLVD
CHARLOTTE, NC 282035812
Phone: 704 863-6000
Fax: –
Web: www.atriumhealth.org

CEO: Eugene Woods
CFO: Anthony Defurio
HR: Aaron Harper
FYE: December 31
Type: Private

The medical facilities under the watchful eye of the Charlotte-Mecklenburg Hospital Authority care for the injured and infirmed. As the largest health care system in the Carolinas, the organization, operating as Carolinas HealthCare System (CHS), owns or manages more than 30 affiliated hospitals. It also operates long-term care facilities, research centers, rehabilitation facilities, surgery centers, home health agencies, radiation therapy facilities, and other health care operations. Collectively, CHS facilities have more than 6,400 beds, and affiliated physician practices employ more than 1,700 doctors. The network's flagship facility is the 875-bed Carolinas Medical Center in Charlotte, North Carolina.

	Annual Growth	12/16	12/17	12/18	12/19	12/22
Sales ($mil.)	10.4%	–	–	6,228.2	7,510.7	9,266.0
Net income ($ mil.)	–	–	–	(69.7)	1,223.0	(1,142.5)
Market value ($ mil.)	–	–	–	–	–	–
Employees	–	–	–	–	–	62,000

THE CHILCOTE COMPANY

4600 TIEDEMAN RD
CLEVELAND, OH 441442332
Phone: 216 781-6000
Fax: –
Web: www.oliverinc.com

CEO: Jay A Hyland
CFO: –
HR: Nada Alempijevic
FYE: December 31
Type: Private

The Chilcote Company is in the preservation business. The firm makes and markets presentation and promotional products targeted to professional photographers, scrapbookers, and the hospitality industry. It operates Crown Photo Products, D. Davis Kenny Company (custom presentation and packaging products, Topflight-brand wedding albums), Wooden Nickel Albums (professional photo albums), and Winthrop-Atkins (promotional products). Other units include A La Carte (custom presentations for the hospitality industry), Complements (scrapbooks), Flora Albums (professional photo albums), Graphic Imaginations (promotional advertising, custom products, packaging), and Taprell Loomis (professional photo packaging).

THE CHILDREN'S HEALTH FUND

475 RIVERSIDE DR
NEW YORK, NY 101150002
Phone: 212 535-9400
Fax: –
Web: www.childrenshealthfund.org

CEO: –
CFO: –
HR: –
FYE: December 31
Type: Private

The Children's Health Fund offers health care to homeless and other children in need in rural and urban communities throughout the US. The organization also serves as an advocate for children's medical programs and an educator for health professionals. It supports a network of medical programs and affiliates in about 15 states and Washington, DC, and operates some 40 mobile clinics in poor urban and rural areas. Other programs provide mental treatment, nutrition education, dental care, and developmental screening. Singer and songwriter Paul Simon and doctor Irwin Redlener founded the Children's Health Fund in 1987.

	Annual Growth	12/17	12/18	12/19	12/21	12/22
Sales ($mil.)	(16.3%)	–	11.6	11.4	9.4	5.7
Net income ($ mil.)	–	–	(0.2)	(0.7)	(0.6)	(2.6)
Market value ($ mil.)	–	–	–	–	–	–
Employees	–	–	–	–	–	30

THE CHILDREN'S HOSPITAL CORPORATION

300 LONGWOOD AVE
BOSTON, MA 021155737
Phone: 617 355-6000
Fax: –
Web: www.childrenshospital.org

CEO: James Mandell
CFO: –
HR: –
FYE: September 30
Type: Private

The Children's Hospital Corporation, dba Boston Children's Hospital, is dedicated to improving and advancing the health and well-being of children around the world through its life-changing work in clinical care, biomedical research, medical education and community engagement. The medical center is Harvard Medical School's main teaching hospital for children's health care, and it is the world's largest pediatric research center. Its nursing department partners with more than 25 schools of nursing throughout Massachusetts and New England. It maintains relationships with Brigham and Women's Hospital, Massachusetts General Hospital and many other hospitals in caring for its patients. It has more than 3,000 scientists for its research community.

	Annual Growth	09/18	09/19	09/20	09/21	09/22
Sales ($mil.)	6.8%	–	2,046.7	1,267.8	2,013.3	2,493.0
Net income ($ mil.)	(22.2%)	–	136.7	(38.2)	75.1	64.4
Market value ($ mil.)	–	–	–	–	–	–
Employees	–	–	–	–	–	8,000

THE CHILDREN'S HOSPITAL OF PHILADELPHIA

3401 CIVIC CENTER BLVD
PHILADELPHIA, PA 191044319
Phone: 215 590-1000
Fax: –
Web: www.chop.edu

CEO: Steven M Altschuler
CFO: Sophia G Holder
HR: Patrick Evans
FYE: June 30
Type: Private

The Children's Hospital of Philadelphia (CHOP) is the nation's first hospital devoted exclusively to the care of children. CHOP Primary Care practices, located throughout southeastern Pennsylvania and Southern New Jersey, provide convenient access to primary health and wellness services for children close to home. Children's Hospital Home Care offers a multidisciplinary team of doctors, nurses, pharmacists, respiratory therapists, social workers, dieticians and delivery technicians and others who coordinate home visits, infusion therapy and medical equipment for thousands of area children. CHOP had more than 29,280 inpatient admissions, 1.4 million outpatient visits and more than $645 million in research grants. CHOP was founded in 1855 by Francis West Lewis, MD.

	Annual Growth	06/09	06/10	06/19	06/20	06/21
Sales ($mil.)	(32.1%)	–	1,425.5	3,057.1	2,624.5	20.2
Net income ($ mil.)	–	–	135.7	469.8	163.5	(0.4)
Market value ($ mil.)	–	–	–	–	–	–
Employees	–	–	–	–	–	13,519

THE CHILDRENS HOSPITAL LOS ANGELES

4650 W SUNSET BLVD
LOS ANGELES, CA 900276062
Phone: 323 660-2450
Fax: –
Web: www.chla.org

CEO: Richard Cordova
CFO: Lannie Tonnu
HR: –
FYE: June 30
Type: Private

Childrens Hospital Los Angeles (CHLA) is dedicated to treating the youngest critical care patients in the region. The about 570-bed hospital specializes in treating seriously ill and injured children, from its neonatal intensive care unit to its pediatric organ transplant center. CHLA's pediatric specialists also provide care at its ambulatory care center in Arcadia and through about 40 off-site practice sites. The hospital's pediatric specialties include cancer, kidney failure, and cystic fibrosis care. CHLA serves more than 107,000 children every year. It is one of only 12 children's hospitals in the nation (and the only one in California) ranked in all 10 pediatric specialties by U.S. News & World Report.

	Annual Growth	06/17	06/18	06/19	06/20	06/22
Sales ($mil.)	(0.2%)	–	1,393.4	1,485.5	1,325.7	1,384.5
Net income ($ mil.)	–	–	247.6	216.9	47.6	(116.9)
Market value ($ mil.)	–	–	–	–	–	–
Employees	–	–	–	–	–	3,000

THE CHIMES INC

4815 SETON DR
BALTIMORE, MD 212153234
Phone: 410 358-6400
Fax: –
Web: www.chimes.org

CEO: Martin S Lampner
CFO: Shawna M Gottlieb
HR: Lee A Bussone
FYE: June 30
Type: Private

The sound of bells can induce a message of hope. The Chimes is a private agency serving the needs of about 10,000 people of all ages with mental and physical disabilities. The organization offers a wide range of health, education, job training and placement, housing, and social services in the mid-Atlantic states of the US and in Tel Aviv, Israel. The Chimes offers similar services through two subsidiaries, Developmental Services of New Jersey and Holcomb Behavioral Health Systems. The agency was established in 1947 when a group of Baltimore parents used space in a church to found a school for their mentally disabled children.

	Annual Growth	06/09	06/10	06/14	06/15	06/20
Sales ($mil.)	(4.3%)	–	42.3	50.8	53.5	27.4
Net income ($ mil.)	2.1%	–	1.1	0.2	(0.6)	1.4
Market value ($ mil.)	–	–	–	–	–	–
Employees	–	–	–	–	–	581

THE CHRIST HOSPITAL

2139 AUBURN AVE
CINCINNATI, OH 452192989
Phone: 513 585-2000
Fax: –
Web: www.thechristhospital.com

CEO: Deborah Hayes
CFO: Chris Bergman
HR: Fred Lucas
FYE: June 30
Type: Private

The Christ Hospital oversees the health of ailing residents throughout Greater Cincinnati. Along with the flagship 555-bed hospital, the organization operates in more than 100 locations throughout the area. An extensive network of approximately 1,200 physicians and 600 volunteers, the Christ Hospital offers specialized care in a variety of fields, including cardiac care, cancer treatment, kidney transplantation, spine treatment, and orthopedics. The not-for-profit hospital also provides an internal medicine residency program, a family medicine residency program, and a school of nursing. The Christ Hospital conducts research through its Lindner Research Center.

	Annual Growth	06/15	06/16	06/17	06/18	06/20
Sales ($mil.)	11.4%	–	681.4	929.7	742.8	1,050.4
Net income ($ mil.)	(44.4%)	–	90.1	14.4	95.6	8.6
Market value ($ mil.)	–	–	–	–	–	–
Employees	–	–	–	–	–	4,000

THE CHRISTIAN BROADCASTING NETWORK INC

977 CENTERVILLE TPKE
VIRGINIA BEACH, VA 234631001
Phone: 757 226-3030
Fax: –
Web: www.cbn.com

CEO: Gordon Robertson
CFO: –
HR: –
FYE: March 31
Type: Private

Standards & Practices probably won't find much wrong with these TV programs. The Christian Broadcasting Network (CBN) is one of the leading producers of religious television programming in the country, offering news and entertainment shows with a spiritual message. Its centerpiece is The 700 Club, a daily show featuring a mix of news and commentary, interviews, feature stories, and Christian ministry co-hosted by CBN founder Pat Robertson. The company's programs are syndicated to broadcast and cable TV outlets that reach audiences around the world. CBN generates most of its revenue through ministry donations.

	Annual Growth	03/14	03/15	03/16	03/20	03/22
Sales ($mil.)	1.1%	–	293.8	307.6	289.7	317.9
Net income ($ mil.)	–	–	(8.9)	(7.2)	(12.2)	35.2
Market value ($ mil.)	–	–	–	–	–	–
Employees	–	–	–	–	–	941

THE CHRISTIAN COALITION

499 S CAPITOL ST SW 615
WASHINGTON, DC 200034013
Phone: 202 479-6900
Fax: –
Web: –

CEO: –
CFO: –
HR: –
FYE: December 31
Type: Private

Founded in 1989 by Pat Robertson, the Christian Coalition of America advances its conservative political agenda by lobbying Congress, local councils, school boards, and state legislatures; distributing literature; organizing and training community activists; and hosting major religious events in Washington. The group's grassroots network includes more than 2 million members and 1,500 local chapters, some on college campuses, in all 50 US states. The group supports what it says is a pro-family, non-partisan agenda while educating "people of faith" to influence all levels of government. Issues include ending abortion rights, opposing online gambling, and supporting the nomination of conservative judges.

THE CIGNA GROUP

NYS: CI

900 Cottage Grove Road
Bloomfield, CT 06002
Phone: 860 226-6000
Fax: 860 226-6741
Web: www.cigna.com

CEO: David M Cordani
CFO: Brian C Evanko
HR: –
FYE: December 31
Type: Public

Cigna Corp (Cigna) is a global health services company committed to improving health and vitality. Its global workforce of more than 70,000 colleagues work through Cigna Healthcare and Evernorth Health Services to fulfill its mission to improve the health and vitality of the more than 190 million customer relationships it serves in more than 30 countries and jurisdictions. Its major services include commercial medical health plans, government health plans, and specialty products and services in the areas of medical, behavioral, pharmacy management, dental and vision. Cigna offers these products to employers, organizations, individuals and other groups. A group of prominent citizens form the Insurance Company of North America (INA) started Cigna in 1792.

	Annual Growth	12/19	12/20	12/21	12/22	12/23
Assets ($mil.)	(0.5%)	155,774	155,451	154,889	143,932	152,761
Net income ($ mil.)	0.3%	5,104.0	8,458.0	5,365.0	6,668.0	5,164.0
Market value ($ mil.)	10.0%	59,814	60,893	67,168	96,918	87,590
Employees	(0.4%)	73,700	73,700	73,700	71,300	72,500

THE CITADEL

171 MOULTRIE ST
CHARLESTON, SC 294090002
Phone: 843 953-5110
Fax: –
Web: www.citadel.edu

CEO: –
CFO: –
HR: –
FYE: December 31
Type: Private

A state-supported military college, The Citadel traces its roots back to the 1842 founding of the South Carolina Military Academy. Today's Citadel enrolls about 2,000 undergraduate cadets who reside on the campus barracks. Cadets are given military and academic instruction in addition to physical training and a strict disciplinary regime; about a third of all graduates continue on to military careers. The Citadel enrolls another 1,250 civilian graduate and undergraduate students who attend evening classes. With a student-to-faculty ratio of 13:1, the institution has schools in business, education, engineering, the humanities and social sciences, and science and mathematics.

	Annual Growth	06/11	06/12	06/13	06/14*	12/22
Sales ($mil.)	–	–	(134.7)	81.5	91.9	31.6
Net income ($ mil.)	179.9%	–	0.0	8.7	17.7	7.1
Market value ($ mil.)	–	–	–	–	–	–
Employees	–	–	–	–	–	637

*Fiscal year change

THE CITY OF HUNTSVILLE

308 FOUNTAIN CIR SW FL 8
HUNTSVILLE, AL 358014240
Phone: 256 427-5080
Fax: –
Web: www.huntsvilleal.gov

CEO: –
CFO: –
HR: –
FYE: September 30
Type: Private

Starting out as a single cabin back in 1805, the City of Huntsville has come a long way. Situated in northern Alabama, it has a population of more than 180,100 and covers roughly 174 square miles. The city's economy is heavily dependent on the aerospace and military technology sectors and is home to NASA's Marshall Space Flight Center, US army post Redstone Arsenal, and Cummings Research Park (the second largest research park in the US). It also hosts many technology companies including network access company ADTRAN, computer graphics firm Intergraph, and software switch manufacturer Avocent. Huntsville's city government consists of its mayor and five city council members.

	Annual Growth	09/16	09/17	09/18	09/20	09/22
Sales ($mil.)	8.3%	–	375.1	419.7	454.8	558.6
Net income ($ mil.)	39.5%	–	16.7	56.1	(58.7)	88.1
Market value ($ mil.)	–	–	–	–	–	–
Employees	–	–	–	–	–	2,400

THE CITY OF SEATTLE-CITY LIGHT DEPARTMENT

700 5TH AVE STE 3200
SEATTLE, WA 981045065
Phone: 206 684-3200
Fax: –
Web: www.seattle.gov

CEO: Jorge Carrasco
CFO: Brian Brunfield
HR: –
FYE: December 31
Type: Private

City of Seattle - City Light Department (Seattle City Light) keeps guitars humming and coffee grinders running in the Seattle metropolitan area. The US's 10th largest municipally owned power company, Seattle City Light transmits and distributes electricity to almost 1 million residential, commercial, industrial, and government customers and owns hydroelectric power plants with more than 1,800 MW of generation capacity. The utility also purchases power from the Bonneville Power Administration and other generators, and it sells power to wholesale customers.

	Annual Growth	12/16	12/17	12/18	12/21	12/22
Sales ($mil.)	4.6%	–	989.7	991.6	1,109.0	1,238.7
Net income ($ mil.)	17.3%	–	120.4	162.2	198.4	267.3
Market value ($ mil.)	–	–	–	–	–	–
Employees	–	–	–	–	–	1,600

THE CLAREMONT COLLEGES INC

101 S MILLS AVE
CLAREMONT, CA 917115053
Phone: 909 621-8000
Fax: –
Web: www.claremont.edu

CEO: M L Dinkel
CFO: Ken Pifer
HR: –
FYE: June 30
Type: Private

Claremont University Consortium (CUC) provides administrative and support services to The Claremont Colleges, a group of independent colleges located on adjoining campuses in Claremont, California. The colleges collectively serve some 6,300 students and include Claremont McKenna (public affairs), Harvey Mudd (science, engineering, and math), Pitzer (social science), Pomona and Claremont Graduate University (liberal arts), Scripps (women's college), and Keck Graduate Institute (applied life sciences). The consortium operates the campus facilities including the bookstore, libraries, labs, and health centers. CUC was founded in 1925 and modeled after the University of Oxford.

	Annual Growth	06/18	06/19	06/20	06/21	06/22
Sales ($mil.)	(0.3%)	–	46.0	47.6	40.2	45.6
Net income ($ mil.)	–	–	11.4	8.6	17.9	(26.7)
Market value ($ mil.)	–	–	–	–	–	–
Employees	–	–	–	–	–	500

THE CLEVELAND CLINIC FOUNDATION

9500 EUCLID AVE
CLEVELAND, OH 441950002
Phone: 216 636-8335
Fax: –
Web: www.clevelandclinic.org

CEO: Brian Donley
CFO: Dennis Laraway
HR: –
FYE: December 31
Type: Private

The not-for-profit Cleveland Clinic Foundation operates about 20 hospitals in Ohio, Florida, Nevada, Abu Dhabi, Toronto, and London. Combined, the foundation's hospitals have about 6,665 beds. Its flagship location is its namesake Cleveland Clinic Health System, an academic medical center in Cleveland, Ohio. The system specializes in cardiac care, digestive disease treatment, and urological and kidney care, along with education and research opportunities. It has an international care center, a children'ss hospital, and an outpatient center; it also contains research and educational institutes covering clinical drug research, ophthalmic studies, and cancer research, as well as physician and scientist training programs.

	Annual Growth	12/18	12/19	12/20	12/21	12/22
Sales ($mil.)	7.2%	–	10,560	10,628	12,441	13,003
Net income ($ mil.)	–	–	2,239.2	1,482.7	2,420.7	(1,004.5)
Market value ($ mil.)	–	–	–	–	–	–
Employees	–	–	–	–	–	44,000

THE COAST DISTRIBUTION SYSTEM INC

44 TUNKHANNOCK AVE
EXETER, PA 186431221
Phone: 408 782-6686
Fax: –
Web: www.ntpstag.com

CEO: –
CFO: –
HR: –
FYE: December 31
Type: Private

Be it on wheels or on the water, there's no place like home with accessories from The Coast. The Coast Distribution System wholesales accessories, replacement parts, and supplies for recreational vehicles (RVs). Tapping outdoor recreational markets with much in common, the company also distributes boating and marine accessories and parts. Its lineup includes close to 11,000 products, many of them Coast branded, from various appliances to awnings, boat covers, life jackets, and trailer hitches. Products are channeled from 17 distribution centers in the US and Canada to more than 15,000 customers, primarily RV and boat dealerships, supply stores, and service centers.

THE COLLEGE NETWORK INC

3815 RIVER CROSSING PKWY STE 260
INDIANAPOLIS, IN 462407758
Phone: 800 395-3276
Fax: –
Web: www.collegenetwork.com

CEO: –
CFO: –
HR: –
FYE: December 31
Type: Private

The College Network is for students who want all the advantages of a college degree without all of that sitting in classrooms and listening to lectures. The company publishes educational materials that help its customers -- typically working adults -- gain college credit, certificates, or degrees from its university partners without attending physical class. Students use the company's online study modules to prepare for college equivalency tests, earning up to 82 credit hours. They then enroll in online degree programs through the company's partner schools. Participating schools include Boston University, University of Southern California, and Angelo State University. The College Network was founded in 1992.

	Annual Growth	12/04	12/05	12/06	12/07	12/08
Sales ($mil.)	13.4%	–	–	72.1	102.9	92.8
Net income ($ mil.)		–	–	1.0	5.2	(0.1)
Market value ($ mil.)		–	–	–	–	–
Employees		–	–	–	–	100

THE COLLEGE OF CHARLESTON

66 GEORGE ST
CHARLESTON, SC 294240001
Phone: 843 953-5570
Fax: –
Web: www.charleston.edu

CEO: –
CFO: –
HR: –
FYE: June 30
Type: Private

The College of Charleston (CofC), one of the oldest universities in the nation, is a state-supported institution emphasizing areas of study in the arts and sciences, education, and business. The liberal arts school enrolls more than 11,000 undergraduate and graduate students who study in some 60 major fields and some 20 master's degree programs. CofC boasts a student-faculty ratio of about 16:1 with an average class size of 26. Some two-thirds of students are from South Carolina. The school was founded in 1770 by a group that included three future signers of the Declaration of Independence.

	Annual Growth	06/18	06/19	06/20	06/21	06/22
Sales ($mil.)	2.3%	–	234.6	225.7	214.4	251.1
Net income ($ mil.)	317.6%	–	0.5	(1.2)	(2.5)	37.8
Market value ($ mil.)	–	–	–	–	–	–
Employees	–	–	–	–	–	1,500

THE COLLEGE OF WILLIAM & MARY

261 RICHMOND RD
WILLIAMSBURG, VA 231853534
Phone: 757 221-3966
Fax: –
Web: www.wm.edu

CEO: –
CFO: –
HR: –
FYE: June 30
Type: Private

Not every Tom, Dick, and Harry gets into The College of William & Mary. The median SAT score for incoming freshmen is about 1,345 (out of 1,600). The second-oldest college in the US (Harvard is the oldest), William & Mary (W&M) is a "public ivy" university with an enrollment of 8,300 undergraduate and graduate students. W&M offers more than 30 undergraduate and 10 graduate programs at schools of arts and sciences, business, education, law, and marine sciences. It also conducts research programs. Among its notable alumni are The Daily Show 's Jon Stewart and three US presidents: Thomas Jefferson, James Monroe, and John Tyler.

	Annual Growth	06/15	06/16	06/17	06/18	06/22
Sales ($mil.)	(18.8%)	–	350.3	329.8	315.4	100.7
Net income ($ mil.)	6.2%	–	40.8	38.2	18.6	58.4
Market value ($ mil.)	–	–	–	–	–	–
Employees	–	–	–	–	–	3,500

THE COLLEGE OF WOOSTER

1101 N BEVER ST
WOOSTER, OH 44691
Phone: 330 263-2018
Fax: –
Web: www.wooster.edu

CEO: –
CFO: –
HR: Anthony Boughner
FYE: June 30
Type: Private

The College of Wooster is a private college providing undergraduate education in the liberal arts and sciences. It grants Bachelor of Arts (BA), Bachelor of Music (BM), and Bachelor of Music Education (BME) degrees. It offers about 50 majors including English, geology, film, theater dance, history, biology, math, neuroscience, psychology, and computer science, as well as pre-law, pre-engineering and pre-health programs. The school's unique curriculum includes an independent study requirement, in which seniors produce original work in the form of a research project. The College of Wooster enrolls about 2,000 students. The school was founded in 1866 by a group of Ohio Presbyterians.

	Annual Growth	06/16	06/17	06/20	06/21	06/22
Sales ($mil.)	11.5%	–	102.6	158.6	184.9	176.6
Net income ($ mil.)	(31.2%)	–	33.5	(2.5)	26.1	5.2
Market value ($ mil.)	–	–	–	–	–	–
Employees	–	–	–	–	–	610

THE COLLEGIATE SCHOOL

103 N MOORELAND RD
RICHMOND, VA 232297170
Phone: 804 740-7077
Fax: –
Web: www.collegiate-va.org

CEO: –
CFO: –
HR: Jill Aveson
FYE: June 30
Type: Private

This school may sound "college like," but it's really meant for Kindergartners through 12th graders. Collegiate School has some 1,500 students enrolled in its lower school (grades K through 4th), middle school (grades 5th through 8th), and upper school (grades 9th through 12th). The private school's offerings include multiple foreign languages, individual music instruction, and community service and travel opportunities. Collegiate was founded in 1915 as Collegiate School for Girls in downtown Richmond, Virginia, by Helen Baker with help from Mary Carter Anderson. Just 13 years after its founding, boys were admitted, but just to the Kindergarten. The first group of boys actually graduated in 1963.

	Annual Growth	06/18	06/19	06/20	06/21	06/22
Sales ($mil.)	0.8%	–	47.6	47.2	56.3	48.8
Net income ($ mil.)		–	(1.9)	(0.7)	22.5	(7.2)
Market value ($ mil.)		–	–	–	–	–
Employees		–	–	–	–	300

THE COLONIAL WILLIAMSBURG FOUNDATION

427 FRANKLIN ST RM 212
WILLIAMSBURG, VA 231854304
Phone: 757 229-1000
Fax: –
Web: www.colonialwilliamsburg.org

CEO: –
CFO: –
HR: Davelin B Forrest
FYE: December 31
Type: Private

The Colonial Williamsburg Foundation is a private, not-for-profit educational institution and the largest US history museum in the world. The organization restored Williamsburg, Virginia to 18th-century appearance. Williamsburg served as the colony's capital from 1699 to 1780. The organization has about 300-acre city to explore, almost 90 original buildings to see, and more than 20 historic trades to discover. Preservation efforts at Williamsburg were launched by the Rev. Dr. W. A. R. Goodwin and John D. Rockefeller, Jr., in 1926.

	Annual Growth	12/05	12/06	12/13	12/21	12/22
Sales ($mil.)	(4.4%)	–	235.0	139.0	164.1	115.3
Net income ($ mil.)	(23.6%)	–	93.9	7.3	52.9	1.3
Market value ($ mil.)	–	–	–	–	–	–
Employees	–	–	–	–	–	3,100

THE COMMUNITY HOSPITAL GROUP INC

98 JAMES ST STE 400
EDISON, NJ 088203902
Phone: 732 321-7000
Fax: –
Web: –

CEO: John P McGee
CFO: –
HR: –
FYE: December 31
Type: Private

JFK Medical Center plays a central role in health care in central New Jersey. The medical center is an acute care facility with some 500 beds and 950 physicians providing emergency, surgical, trauma, and other inpatient services. The hospital includes the JFK New Jersey Neuroscience Institute, which treats stroke and other neurological conditions, and the JFK Johnson Rehabilitation Institute, which treats traumatic injuries. JFK Medical Center also offers diagnostic imaging, cancer care, senior and hospice care, and family practice services. It is also a teaching hospital, affiliated with several area universities. The hospital is part of the JFK Health System.

	Annual Growth	12/09	12/10	12/14	12/16	12/17
Sales ($mil.)	3.7%	–	427.1	467.9	532.1	551.6
Net income ($ mil.)	–	–	(17.5)	(3.2)	28.2	(13.3)
Market value ($ mil.)	–	–	–	–	–	–
Employees	–	–	–	–	–	3,000

THE COMPUTER MERCHANT LTD

95 LONGWATER CIR
NORWELL, MA 020611635
Phone: 781 878-1070
Fax: –
Web: www.itstaffing.com

CEO: John R Danieli
CFO: –
HR: –
FYE: December 31
Type: Private

The Computer Merchant (TCM) provide customers with information technology assets with a pulse. The company provides IT services, such as staffing and consulting, primarily to Fortune 1000 companies. It places more than 10,000 consultants each year. TCM provides application development, infrastructure management, help desk and business support, and technology deployments. The IT placement firm's clients have included ePresence, Unisys, and Premier, among others. It primarily serves IT service providers, large corporations, and public sector clients. A preferred vendor for many government contractors, TCM was founded in 1980 by CEO and former US Marine John Danieli.

	Annual Growth	12/15	12/16	12/17	12/18	12/19
Sales ($mil.)	(11.4%)	–	61.1	44.5	45.9	42.5
Net income ($ mil.)	(12.0%)	–	1.0	(0.3)	0.4	0.7
Market value ($ mil.)	–	–	–	–	–	–
Employees	–	–	–	–	–	1,500

THE COMPUTING TECHNOLOGY INDUSTRY ASSOCIATION INC

3500 LACEY RD STE 100
DOWNERS GROVE, IL 605155439
Phone: 630 678-8300
Fax: –
Web: www.comptia.org

CEO: Todd Thibodeaux
CFO: Brian Laffey
HR: –
FYE: December 31
Type: Private

Welcome to the IT club. The Computing Technology Industry Association (CompTIA) is a not-for-profit trade organization that provides research, training, networking, and partnering services to its 2,000-plus members. It serves more than 100 countries with offices in Australia, Canada, China, Germany, Hong Kong, India, Japan, South Africa, South Korea, Taiwan, and the UK. CompTIA also helps companies implement best practices and administers vendor-neutral IT certification exams in about a dozen areas including cloud essentials, green IT, security, Linux, and storage. Like the industry it serves, CompTIA has grown dramatically since it was founded in 1982 by representatives of five computer dealerships.

	Annual Growth	12/18	12/19	12/20	12/21	12/22
Sales ($mil.)	17.8%	–	–	–	122.9	144.8
Net income ($ mil.)	187.6%	–	–	–	2.6	7.6
Market value ($ mil.)	–	–	–	–	–	–
Employees	–	–	–	–	–	280

THE CONFERENCE BOARD INC

845 3RD AVE
NEW YORK, NY 100226600
Phone: 212 759-0900
Fax: –
Web: www.conference-board.org

CEO: Jonathan Spector
CFO: –
HR: Alana Trimmier
FYE: December 31
Type: Private

The Conference Board is as serious as it sounds. The not-for-profit membership organization focuses on increasing the effectiveness of businesses through its 100-plus member councils. The global entity does research on corporate citizenship and governance, human resource issues, and strategic planning and sponsors conferences, makes forecasts, and publishes economic reports and other products. In addition to research and executive action reports, it publishes The Conference Board Review, a magazine for senior executives, and newsletters for US, European, and Asian members.

	Annual Growth	06/11	06/12	06/13	06/14*	12/19
Sales ($mil.)	4.3%	–	53.8	57.2	57.0	72.1
Net income ($ mil.)	–	–	(13.7)	3.6	(0.1)	4.1
Market value ($ mil.)	–	–	–	–	–	–
Employees	–	–	–	–	–	283

*Fiscal year change

THE CONNELL COMPANY

300 CONNELL DR STE 4000
BERKELEY HEIGHTS, NJ 079222899
Phone: 908 673-3700
Fax: –
Web: www.connellco.com

CEO: –
CFO: Terry Connell
HR: –
FYE: December 31
Type: Private

Add rice and stir -- it's just one of the ingredients that go into The Connell Company. Through a number of subsidiaries, the diversified firm is involved in wholesale food ingredient distribution, international industrial equipment supply and leasing, real estate development and leasing, and business services. Its Connell Rice & Sugar subsidiary is a leading exporter and distributor of domestic rice, mainly serving markets in Japan, Taiwan, Korea, and the Middle East. Connell International exports industrial equipment to customers worldwide. Other units include Connell Real Estate & Development, Connell Finance, Connell Equipment Leasing, and Connell Mining. The family-owned business was started in 1926.

	Annual Growth	12/18	12/19	12/20	12/21	12/22
Assets ($mil.)	7.9%	–	–	680.6	648.3	791.9
Net income ($ mil.)	–	–	–	–	–	–
Market value ($ mil.)	–	–	–	–	–	–
Employees	–	–	–	–	–	620

THE CONSERVATION FUND A NONPROFIT CORPORATION

1655 FORT MYER DR STE 1300
ARLINGTON, VA 222093113
Phone: 703 525-6300
Fax: –
Web: www.conservationfund.org

CEO: –
CFO: –
HR: Joyce Ferrell
FYE: December 31
Type: Private

The Conservation Fund was green before green was cool. The nonprofit organization is well known for negotiating deals to protect environmentally sensitive lands. It will typically purchase property, financed through a revolving land fund, federal and state grants, and contributions from various sources, and sell it back to local groups to manage. It also invests in small businesses that show a sustainable use of natural resources, as well as works with communities and other not-for-profits to plan for growth and conservation. Since its founding in 1985, the Fund and its partners have protected more than 7 million acres of wildlife habitat and watersheds, working landscapes, and open-spaces in all 50 US states.

	Annual Growth	12/13	12/14	12/16	12/19	12/22
Sales ($mil.)	2.8%	–	242.6	215.5	221.5	302.3
Net income ($ mil.)	–	–	39.5	(2.3)	2.9	(2.3)
Market value ($ mil.)	–	–	–	–	–	–
Employees	–	–	–	–	–	95

THE COOPER HEALTH SYSTEM A NEW JERSEY NON-PROFIT CORPORATION

1 COOPER PLZ
CAMDEN, NJ 081031461
Phone: 856 342-2000
Fax: –
Web: www.cooperhealth.org

CEO: Anthony J Mazzarelli
CFO: Brian M Reilly
HR: –
FYE: December 31
Type: Private

Cooper Health System, also known as Cooper University Health Care, is the leading academic health system in South Jersey and provides access to primary, specialty, tertiary, and urgent care, all within one complete health system. Cooper includes South Jersey's only Level I trauma center (Cooper University Hospital), which is the busiest trauma center in the Philadelphia region. Cooper is also home to a leading cancer center (MD Anderson Cancer Center at Cooper), the only Level II pediatric trauma center in the Delaware Valley (Children's Regional Hospital at Cooper), three urgent care centers, and more than 100 outpatient offices from Southeastern Pennsylvania to the Jersey Shore, including large regional hubs in Camden, Cherry Hill, Voorhees, Willingboro, and Sewell. Cooper University Health Care receives more than 1.9 million patient visits annually, and treats patients from all 50 states and 35 countries.

	Annual Growth	12/18	12/19	12/20	12/21	12/22
Sales ($mil.)	12.4%	–	1,439.4	1,545.6	1,304.9	2,041.4
Net income ($ mil.)	22.4%	–	105.4	73.1	200.9	193.2
Market value ($ mil.)	–	–	–	–	–	–
Employees	–	–	–	–	–	4,900

THE COOPER UNION FOR THE ADVANCEMENT OF SCIENCE AND ART

30 COOPER SQ FL 7
NEW YORK, NY 100037120
Phone: 212 353-4150
Fax: –
Web: www.cooper.edu

CEO: –
CFO: –
HR: Ann Gong
FYE: June 30
Type: Private

The Cooper Union for the Advancement of Science and Art was founded in 1859 by inventor and industrialist Peter Cooper, who created the US's first steam train engine and rose from poverty to build a fortune. Cooper's endowment, along with subsequent gifts, allowed the school to fund a full-tuition scholarship for each of its undergraduate students until Fall 2014 when it implemented a sliding scale tuition. Cooper Union, which serves about 1,000 students, is located in the East Village in downtown New York City. It offers degree programs in art, architecture, and engineering, as well as a wide variety of lectures and continuing education courses for the public.

	Annual Growth	06/13	06/14	06/15	06/20	06/22
Sales ($mil.)	14.7%	–	–	57.4	120.5	150.2
Net income ($ mil.)	–	–	–	(18.8)	11.6	33.5
Market value ($ mil.)	–	–	–	–	–	–
Employees	–	–	–	–	–	650

THE CORPORATION OF HAVERFORD COLLEGE

370 W LANCASTER AVE
HAVERFORD, PA 190411336
Phone: 610 896-1000
Fax: –
Web: www.haverford.edu

CEO: –
CFO: –
HR: –
FYE: June 30
Type: Private

Haverford College is one of the nation's top 10 liberal arts colleges, according to US News & World Report 's 2007 annual ranking. The college is a private school located 10 miles away from Philadelphia that serves about 1,200 students. Among its staff are more than 135 full-time faculty members. Haverford College has a student-faculty ratio of 9:1. The college offers more than 30 departmental majors. The school boasts such notable alumni as former Time Warner CEO Gerald Levin, Time editor-in-chief Norman Pearlstine, and humorist Dave Barry. Haverford College was established by Quakers in 1833 as a college of higher learning.

	Annual Growth	06/14	06/15	06/20	06/21	06/22
Sales ($mil.)	4.0%	–	131.5	138.8	139.7	172.7
Net income ($ mil.)	11.5%	–	9.8	(1.8)	4.2	21.1
Market value ($ mil.)	–	–	–	–	–	–
Employees	–	–	–	–	–	600

THE CORPORATION OF MERCER UNIVERSITY

1501 MERCER UNIVERSITY DR
MACON, GA 312071515
Phone: 478 301-2700
Fax: –
Web: www.mercer.edu

CEO: David Hudson
CFO: –
HR: –
FYE: June 30
Type: Private

Mercer University covers a lot of Georgia, with one campus in Macon, another in Atlanta, and a third in Savannah. The main campus in Macon includes the Walter F. George School of Law (one of the nation's oldest law schools), while The Cecil B. Day Graduate and Professional campus in Atlanta includes schools of theology, pharmacy, and nursing. Savannah is home to a new four-year M.D. program at the Mercer School of Medicine at Memorial University Medical Center. The university, which has a total enrollment of more than 8,300 students, also has educational centers in Douglas County, Henry County, and Eastman. Mercer was founded in 1833 by Jesse Mercer, a prominent Georgia Baptist.

	Annual Growth	06/17	06/18	06/20	06/21	06/22
Sales ($mil.)	12.4%	–	277.6	406.5	444.0	443.0
Net income ($ mil.)	(9.8%)	–	39.3	28.1	54.8	26.0
Market value ($ mil.)	–	–	–	–	–	–
Employees	–	–	–	–	–	1,658

THE COUNCIL POPULATION INC

1 DAG HAMMARSKJOLD PLZ FL 3
NEW YORK, NY 100172251
Phone: 212 339-0500
Fax: –
Web: www.popcouncil.org

CEO: –
CFO: –
HR: –
FYE: December 31
Type: Private

The Population Council is a not-for-profit organization that performs biomedical, public health, and social science research. The organization focuses on areas such as HIV and AIDS; poverty, gender, and youth; and reproductive health. Specifically, it conducts research on sociological topics like gender inequality, population trends, and sexuality education; it also assists international governments with policy and program development as they pertain to these issues. The Population Council is typically funded by governments, foundations, individuals, and other organizations.

	Annual Growth	12/16	12/17	12/19	12/21	12/22
Sales ($mil.)	(2.2%)	–	91.4	82.6	58.2	81.6
Net income ($ mil.)	35.0%	–	4.7	11.6	(2.7)	21.1
Market value ($ mil.)	–	–	–	–	–	–
Employees	–	–	–	–	–	603

THE CULINARY INSTITUTE OF AMERICA

1946 CAMPUS DR
HYDE PARK, NY 125381430
Phone: 845 452-9600
Fax: –
Web: www.ciachef.edu

CEO: –
CFO: –
HR: –
FYE: May 31
Type: Private

At this CIA they work on countertops, not counterterrorism. The Culinary Institute of America (CIA) offers bachelor's and associate degrees in Culinary Arts, Culinary Science, and Baking and Pastry Arts fields of study. It also offers continuing education programs, conferences, travel programs, and e-learning. The independent, not-for-profit educational organization enrolls some 2,800 students and employs more than 125 chef-instructors and other faculty members at campuses in the US and overseas. Notable graduates include media personalities Anthony Bourdain and Rocco DiSpirito and Steven Ellis, founder of Chipotle Mexican Grill.

	Annual Growth	05/10	05/11	05/12	05/13	05/14
Sales ($mil.)	1.3%	–	–	141.4	147.3	145.3
Net income ($ mil.)	38.4%	–	–	11.1	28.7	21.2
Market value ($ mil.)	–	–	–	–	–	–
Employees	–	–	–	–	–	750

THE DASTON CORPORATION

19 E MARKET ST STE 101
LEESBURG, VA 201763001
Phone: 703 288-3200
Fax: –
Web: www.daston.com

CEO: –
CFO: –
HR: –
FYE: December 31
Type: Private

Daston hopes to be a bastion of support amidst trying technological times. The company provides a variety of information technology, financial management, and management consulting services. It offers such services as application development, project management, network design, systems integration, training, staffing, and desktop and network support. Daston serves both the public sector, including state and local government agencies, and commercial clients. Customers come from such industries as financial services, health care, transportation, electronics, retail, and manufacturing. The company was founded in 1992 by CEO Muriel Sarmadi.

	Annual Growth	12/11	12/12	12/13	12/14	12/15
Sales ($mil.)	(16.5%)	–	–	9.6	6.3	6.7
Net income ($ mil.)	(13.3%)	–	–	1.1	0.7	0.9
Market value ($ mil.)	–	–	–	–	–	–
Employees	–	–	–	–	–	25

THE DAVID AND LUCILE PACKARD FOUNDATION

343 2ND ST
LOS ALTOS, CA 940223639
Phone: 650 917-7167
Fax: –
Web: www.packard.org

CEO: Carol S Larson
CFO: –
HR: Lisa Clark
FYE: December 31
Type: Private

One of the wealthiest philanthropic organizations in the US, The David and Lucile Packard Foundation primarily provides grants to not-for-profit entities. The foundation focuses on operating in three areas: conservation and science; children, families, and communities; and population. The David and Lucile Packard Foundation boasts approximately $4.6 billion in assets. In 2009, the organization committed $100 million for the expansion of the Lucile Packard Children's Hospital at Stanford. The late David Packard (co-founder of Hewlett-Packard) and his wife, the late Lucile Salter Packard, created the foundation in 1964. Their children run the organization.

	Annual Growth	12/04	12/05	12/06	12/09	12/10
Sales ($mil.)	302.5%	–	0.7	809.5	398.2	701.2
Net income ($ mil.)	289.2%	–	0.5	587.9	74.8	412.6
Market value ($ mil.)	–	–	–	–	–	–
Employees	–	–	–	–	–	85

THE DCH HEALTH CARE AUTHORITY

809 UNIVERSITY BLVD E
TUSCALOOSA, AL 354012029
Phone: 205 759-7111
Fax: –
Web: www.dchsystem.com

CEO: Bryan Kindred
CFO: Bob Tracz
HR: –
FYE: September 30
Type: Private

The DCH Healthcare Authority, which does business as DCH Health System, provides health services to residents of Tuscaloosa and several other communities in Western Alabama. Its flagship facility is the roughly 585-bed DCH Regional Medical Center, offers a variety of specialty units and advanced services, including cancer, cardiology, robotic and minimally invasive surgery, and the region's advanced trauma center. DCH Health System also includes the Northport, and Fayette medical centers, which together houses some 265 acute-care beds. The hospitals offer a full range of inpatient and outpatient services, including primary, diagnostic, emergency, surgical, rehabilitative, and home health care.

	Annual Growth	09/17	09/18	09/19	09/20	09/21
Sales ($mil.)	2.9%	–	520.6	547.5	534.4	566.8
Net income ($ mil.)	–	–	6.9	26.2	18.3	(9.9)
Market value ($ mil.)	–	–	–	–	–	–
Employees	–	–	–	–	–	4,683

THE DEACONESS ASSOCIATIONS INC

615 ELSINORE PL STE 900
CINCINNATI, OH 452021459
Phone: 513 559-2100
Fax: –
Web: www.deaconess-healthcare.com

CEO: E A Woods
CFO: Dave M Adams
HR: –
FYE: December 31
Type: Private

Much like its Greek origins imply (diakonos means helper), Deaconess Associations Incorporated (DAI) is out to make life a little easier for the sick and disabled. The company operates an acute-care hospital; about two dozen long-term care facilities (nursing homes, retirement centers and assisted living facilities); as well as home care operations (including adult Medicare and pediatric nursing, infusion and respiratory therapy, and home medical equipment services). The company's facilities can be found in Ohio, Kansas, and Missouri, with the biggest concentration in Missouri. DAI traces its origins to Deaconess Hospital, its acute care facility founded in 1888 in Cincinnati.

	Annual Growth	12/99	12/00	12/05	12/19	12/22
Sales ($mil.)	(10.9%)	–	243.9	0.0	26.1	19.3
Net income ($ mil.)	(1.2%)	–	15.1	0.0	17.6	11.5
Market value ($ mil.)	–	–	–	–	–	–
Employees	–	–	–	–	–	500

THE DEPOSITORY TRUST & CLEARING CORPORATION

570 WASHINGTON BLVD
JERSEY CITY, NJ 073101617
Phone: 212 855-1000
Fax: –
Web: www.dtcc.com

CEO: Michael C Bodson
CFO: Susan Cosgrove
HR: Elena Lagrimas
FYE: December 31
Type: Private

The Depository Trust & Clearing Corporation (DTCC) is the premier post-trade market infrastructure in the industry, advancing the automation, centralization, standardization and streamlining of processes critical to the markets' safety and soundness. Through its subsidiaries, the company simplifies the complexities of clearance, settlement, global data management and information services for equities, corporate and municipal bonds, government and mortgage-backed securities, derivatives, money market instruments, syndicated loans, mutual funds, alternative investment products and insurance transactions. DTCC's subsidiaries processed securities transactions valued at some $2.5 quadrillion. Its depository provides custody and asset servicing for securities issues from more than 150 countries and territories were valued at some $72 trillion. Annually, DTCC's Global Trade Repository service processes more than 17.5 billion messages.

THE DONOHOE COMPANIES INC

7101 WISCONSIN AVE STE 700
BETHESDA, MD 208144871
Phone: 202 333-0880
Fax: –
Web: www.donohoe.com

CEO: –
CFO: Gerard M Goeke
HR: –
FYE: December 31
Type: Private

The Donohoe Companies have more than 125 years of experience with real estate in Washington, DC. Founded in 1884, Donohoe operates through its five business subsidiaries. Its Donohoe Hospitality arm owns nearly a dozen Marriott, Hilton, and InterContinental Hotels properties in the DC area. Another subsidiary, Donohoe Real Estate Services, manages and leases more than 6 million sq. ft. of space for institutional and private investors. Donohoe Construction builds commercial, residential, and government projects. Often acting in concert with its construction counterpart, Donohoe Development works on residential and commercial properties. Complete Building Services (CBS) focuses on building maintenance.

THE DOW CHEMICAL COMPANY

2211 H H DOW WAY
MIDLAND, MI 486424815
Phone: 989 636-1000
Fax: –
Web: www.dow.com

CEO: James R Fitterling
CFO: Howard Ungerleider
HR: –
FYE: December 31
Type: Private

The Dow Chemical Company (TDCC) is a leading producer of plastics, chemicals, and hydrocarbons. One of the largest material and chemical companies in the US and the world. It uses hydrocarbon-based raw materials to make some 6,100 finished chemical products at nearly 110 sites in more than 30 countries. The company's products are used in industries such as automotive, transportation, consumer goods, industrial equipment, building and construction, and energy. Its largest market is the US and Canada. After the separation of DowDuPont in early 2019, Dow Inc. became the direct parent company of TDCC and its subsidiaries.

THE DREES COMPANY

515 S CAPITAL OF TEXAS HWY
WEST LAKE HILLS, TX 787464314
Phone: 859 578-4200
Fax: –
Web: www.dreeshomes.com

CEO: Ralph Drees
CFO: –
HR: –
FYE: March 31
Type: Private

The Drees Company is a big homebuilder in Cincinnati and one of the nation's top private builders. Drees targets first-time and move-up buyers with homes that are priced from about $100,000 to more than $1 million. Drees also builds condominiums, townhomes, and patio homes. Its homes portfolio ranges from its former Zaring Premier Homes luxury division to the company's more financially accessible and modest Marquis Homes division. Drees is active in Florida, Indiana, Kentucky, Maryland, North Carolina, Ohio, Tennessee, Texas, Virginia, and Washington, DC. The family-owned firm was founded in 1928.

	Annual Growth	03/12	03/13	03/14	03/15	03/16
Sales ($mil.)	7.3%	–	585.0	683.8	669.3	722.7
Net income ($ mil.)	17.6%	–	19.1	35.9	36.3	31.1
Market value ($ mil.)	–	–	–	–	–	–
Employees		–	–	–	–	549

THE DUN & BRADSTREET CORPORATION

5335 GATE PKWY
JACKSONVILLE, FL 322563071
Phone: 904 648-6350
Fax: –
Web: www.dnb.com

CEO: –
CFO: –
HR: –
FYE: December 31
Type: Private

The Dun & Bradstreet Corporation is one of the world's leading suppliers of business information with a global database (The Dun & Bradstreet Data Cloud) covering some 315 million companies. It mines data to help customers manage risk, accelerate sales, and lower costs through Data-as-a-Service (DaaS) integrations, software and subscriptions, and files and reports. The company's product areas include credit and risk, sales and marketing, master data, supply chain management, and compliance. Dun & Bradstreet, the publisher of this profile, in early 2019 was acquired by an investor group led by CC Capital, Bilcar, Cannae Holdings, Black Knight, and funds affiliated with Thomas H. Lee Partners.

THE DYSON-KISSNER-MORAN CORPORATION

2515 SOUTH RD STE 5
POUGHKEEPSIE, NY 126015474
Phone: 212 661-4600
Fax: –
Web: www.dkmcorp.com

CEO: Robert R Dyson
CFO: –
HR: –
FYE: December 31
Type: Private

Size matters to some, but not as much to Dyson-Kissner-Moran (DKM). Experienced in buying family-owned businesses, the private investment firm normally seeks majority stakes in companies that earn more than $50 million in annual revenues and have experienced management teams. DKM mainly uses its own capital, supplemented by bank debt, to fund acquisitions and keeps its investments long term; typical transactions range from $50 million to $150 million. Its portfolio includes aluminum products manufacturers Hapco and Tri-City Extrusion, as well as the Recreational Vehicle Group (RV appliances and supplies) and the Plaid Creative Group (do-it-yourself craft products).

THE EARST FOUNDATION INC

300 W 57TH ST FL 26
NEW YORK, NY 100193741
Phone: 212 586-5404
Fax: –
Web: –

CEO: –
CFO: –
HR: –
FYE: December 31
Type: Private

The Hearst Foundation is a sister organization of The William Randolph Hearst Foundation, both founded by William Randolph Hearst in the 1940s. The two foundations share goals, a headquarters, and management (Robert Frehse Jr., is an executive director of both), but are divided only by geography: The William Randolph Hearst Foundation grants funding to organizations west of the Mississippi River and The Hearst Foundation focuses on the eastern US. The foundation's four major charitable interests are culture, education, health, and social service.

THE ELECTRONIC RETAILING ASSOCIATION

7918 JONES BRANCH DR # 300
MC LEAN, VA 221023337
Phone: 703 841-1751
Fax: –
Web: www.retailing.org

CEO: –
CFO: –
HR: –
FYE: June 30
Type: Private

This ERA is about equal rights for businesses that peddle their wares through electronic media. The Electronic Retailing Association (ERA) promotes the interests of more than 450 Internet, television, and radio retailers, and major retailers with online operations, worldwide. Members include eBay, Google, HSN, and QVC. The association also lobbies regulators and lawmakers on behalf of its members. Members' benefits include discounted trade shows and meetings, subscriptions to Electronic Retailer (the association's official magazine), access to government tracking services, and other related services. The group began in 1991 as the National Infomercial Marketing Association.

	Annual Growth	06/13	06/14	06/15	06/16	06/17
Sales ($mil.)	(14.2%)	–	5.5	5.2	4.5	3.5
Net income ($ mil.)	–	–	0.4	0.2	(0.1)	(1.1)
Market value ($ mil.)	–	–	–	–	–	–
Employees	–	–	–	–	–	8

THE EMPIRE DISTRICT ELECTRIC COMPANY

602 S JOPLIN AVE
JOPLIN, MO 648012337
Phone: 417 625-5100
Fax: –
Web: www.empiredistrict.com

CEO: Bradley P Beecher
CFO: Laurie Delano
HR: –
FYE: December 31
Type: Private

Empire District Electric (EDE) light ups the middle of the US. The utility transmits and distributes electricity to a population base of more than 450,000 (about 217,000 customers in southwestern Missouri and adjacent areas of Arkansas, Kansas, and Oklahoma. It also supplies water to three Missouri towns and natural gas throughout most of the state. EDE's interests in fossil-fueled and hydroelectric power plants give it a generating capacity of 1,377 MW; it also wholesales power. The company also provides fiber-optic services. In early 2017 the company was bought by an Algonquin Power & Utilities unit in a C$3.2 billion (US$2.3 billion) deal.

	Annual Growth	12/13	12/14	12/15	12/16	12/17
Sales ($mil.)	(3.6%)	–	652.3	605.6	568.8	584.8
Net income ($ mil.)	(18.2%)	–	67.1	56.6	64.0	36.7
Market value ($ mil.)	–	–	–	–	–	–
Employees	–	–	–	–	–	749

THE EVANGELICAL LUTHERAN GOOD SAMARITAN SOCIETY

4800 W 57TH ST
SIOUX FALLS, SD 571082239
Phone: 866 928-1635
Fax: –
Web: www.good-sam.com

CEO: –
CFO: Raye N Nylander
HR: Cheyenne Trososki
FYE: December 31
Type: Private

The Evangelical Lutheran Good Samaritan Society strives to be a good neighbor to all, particularly to the elderly people in need of housing and health care. The not-for-profit organization owns or leases some 200 senior living facilities, including nursing homes, assisted living facilities, and affordable housing projects for seniors. Through its facilities, it also provides home health care services, outpatient rehabilitation, adult day care, and a variety of other services, such as specialized units for people with Alzheimer's disease and related dementias. Good Samaritan Society merged with hospital system Sanford Health in early 2019.

	Annual Growth	12/05	12/06	12/07	12/13	12/15
Sales ($mil.)	2.1%	–	836.5	841.8	979.8	1,011.8
Net income ($ mil.)	–	–	44.2	18.0	0.3	(33.8)
Market value ($ mil.)	–	–	–	–	–	–
Employees	–	–	–	–	–	24,000

THE F DOHMEN CO

2007 N DR MARTIN LUTHER KING JR DR
MILWAUKEE, WI 532123152
Phone: 866 336-1336
Fax: –
Web: www.dohmencompanyfoundation.org

CEO: Cynthia A Laconte
CFO: –
HR: Chandra Knight
FYE: December 31
Type: Private

The company is a philanthropic enterprise. Dohmen Company and The Dohmen Company Foundation are creating an enduring financial and ecological model, using food, innovation and anchor employment to revitalize the health of individuals and communities. In 2019, the Dohmen Company was first in the nation to transition from a family-owned S-corporation to a company wholly-owned by a private foundation.

THE FINISH LINE INC

3308 N MITTHOEFER RD
INDIANAPOLIS, IN 462352332
Phone: 317 899-1022
Fax: –
Web: www.finishline.com

CEO: Samuel M Sato
CFO: Edward W Wilhelm
HR: Jennifer Pund
FYE: February 25
Type: Private

The Finish Line sells performance and casual footwear and apparel through more than 900 Finish Line retail locations in about 45 states and Puerto Rico. Its core Finish Line stores are bigger than those of competitors and offer a wider array of clothing, accessories, and other merchandise, including jackets, backpacks, socks, hats, beanies, gloves, and underwear. Finish Line offers big brand names (such as adidas, NIKE, and Timberland). The company also sells athletic shoes and apparel online. It is a subsidiary of European sports retailer JD Sports Fashion.

	Annual Growth	02/13	02/14	02/15	02/16	02/17
Sales ($mil.)	0.7%	–	–	1,820.6	1,888.9	1,844.4
Net income ($ mil.)	–	–	–	79.7	21.8	(18.2)
Market value ($ mil.)	–	–	–	–	–	–
Employees	–	–	–	–	–	13,500

THE FISHEL COMPANY

1366 DUBLIN RD
COLUMBUS, OH 432151093
Phone: 614 274-8100
Fax: –
Web: www.teamfishel.com

CEO: John Phillips
CFO: Paul Riewe
HR: Fernando Rocha
FYE: December 31
Type: Private

The Fishel Company reels in revenues by laying out lines. The company (also known as Team Fishel) provides engineering, construction, management, and maintenance services for electric and gas utility and communications infrastructure projects. The aerial and underground utility contractor designs and builds distribution networks for telecommunications, cable and broadband television, gas transmission and distribution, and electric utilities throughout the US. It also counts municipalities, state and federal agencies, universities, commercial building owners, financial services companies, health care providers, manufacturers and residential real estate developers among its clients.

	Annual Growth	12/18	12/19	12/20	12/21	12/22
Sales ($mil.)	19.1%	–	–	–	636.4	758.3
Net income ($ mil.)	26.4%	–	–	–	60.8	76.8
Market value ($ mil.)	–	–	–	–	–	–
Employees	–	–	–	–	–	2,512

THE FLOATING HOSPITAL INCORPORATED

2101 41ST AVE
LONG ISLAND CITY, NY 111014801
Phone: 718 784-2240
Fax: –
Web: www.thefloatinghospital.org

CEO: Sean Granahan
CFO: S Nyerere
HR: –
FYE: December 31
Type: Private

New York City's Floating Hospital has its origins in a ferryboat ride for newsboys organized by The New York Times in 1866. The newspaper appealed to the public to provide funds for excursions each summer to help the young ragamuffins escape the sweltering streets for a few hours. Management of the program was turned over to a charity, St. John's Guild, in 1873, and the group soon began to put doctors on the ferryboats to provide health services for the newsboys and other city children. The organization provided ship-based until 2001, when it could no longer afford dock space. Today The Floating Hospital provides health care services to indigent New Yorkers via a network of clinics located throughout the city.

	Annual Growth	12/17	12/18	12/19	12/21	12/22
Sales ($mil.)	9.5%	–	21.0	21.5	29.3	30.3
Net income ($ mil.)	(40.8%)	–	1.1	(0.0)	1.5	0.1
Market value ($ mil.)	–	–	–	–	–	–
Employees	–	–	–	–	–	151

THE FORD FOUNDATION

320 E 43RD ST FL 4
NEW YORK, NY 100174890
Phone: 212 573-5370
Fax: –
Web: www.fordfoundation.org

CEO: –
CFO: –
HR: Chance Mullen
FYE: December 31
Type: Private

As one of the nation's largest philanthropic organizations, the Ford Foundation can afford to be generous. The foundation offers grants to individuals and institutions worldwide that work to meet its goals of strengthening democratic values, reducing poverty and injustice, promoting international cooperation, and advancing human achievement. The Ford Foundation's charitable giving has run the gamut from A (Association for Asian Studies) to Z (Zanzibar International Film Festival). The foundation has an endowment of about $10 billion. Established in 1936 by Edsel Ford, whose father founded the Ford Motor Company, the foundation no longer owns stock in the automaker or has ties to the founding family.

	Annual Growth	09/08	09/09	09/11*	12/14	12/15
Assets ($mil.)	2.8%	–	10,235	10,345	12,400	12,114
Net income ($ mil.)	–	–	–	(5.3)	(7.5)	(270.2)
Market value ($ mil.)	–	–	–	–	–	–
Employees	–	–	–	–	–	556

*Fiscal year change

THE FOUNDATION FOR AIDS RESEARCH

120 WALL ST FL 13
NEW YORK, NY 100053908
Phone: 212 806-1600
Fax: –
Web: www.amfar.org

CEO: Kevin R Frost
CFO: Bradley Jensen
HR: –
FYE: September 30
Type: Private

The Foundation for AIDS Research, more commonly known as amfAR, offers grants and fundraising activities to support research on the acquired immunodeficiency virus. The organization also supports efforts to raise awareness and educate the public on AIDS and AIDS prevention. It lobbies for appropriate AIDS-related public policy and legislation and publishes newsletters and briefs on topics like Gender-Based Violence and HIV Among Women and Efficacy of Abstinence. Funding comes from individuals, companies, and foundations; amfAR has invested close to $400 million in its programs and has awarded more than 3,300 grants to research teams worldwide since its inception in 1985.

	Annual Growth	09/16	09/17	09/18	09/19	09/22
Sales ($mil.)	(5.4%)	–	41.6	32.3	31.3	31.4
Net income ($ mil.)	–	–	(1.9)	(6.7)	(3.6)	3.4
Market value ($ mil.)	–	–	–	–	–	–
Employees	–	–	–	–	–	85

THE FOX CHASE CANCER CENTER FOUNDATION

333 COTTMAN AVE
PHILADELPHIA, PA 191112434
Phone: 215 728-6900
Fax: –
Web: www.foxchase.org

CEO: Robert Uzzo
CFO: –
HR: –
FYE: June 30
Type: Private

Fox Chase Cancer Center looks at cancer from all angles. The 100-bed, not-for-profit medical center specializes in cancer research, detection, and treatment. Founded as one of the few US institutions dedicated exclusively to cancer, Fox Chase Cancer Center provides diagnostic, radiation oncology, pathology, robotic and laser surgery, and other cancer-centric medical services. Its research center supports clinical trials of possible new treatments as well as standard care for cancer patients. Much of its work is focused on cancer prevention and identifying risk levels in populations. Fox Chase Cancer Center is part of the Temple University Health System.

	Annual Growth	06/10	06/11	06/20	06/21	06/22
Sales ($mil.)	(17.7%)	–	44.1	5.2	6.3	5.2
Net income ($ mil.)	–	–	(9.5)	3.4	2.9	2.1
Market value ($ mil.)	–	–	–	–	–	–
Employees	–	–	–	–	–	1,900

THE FREDERICK GUNN SCHOOL INCORPORATED

99 GREEN HILL RD
WASHINGTON, CT 067931200
Phone: 860 868-7334
Fax: –
Web: www.frederickgunn.org

CEO: –
CFO: –
HR: –
FYE: June 30
Type: Private

The Gunnery arms students with the ammunition needed to become productive adults. The 220-acre, co-ed college preparatory day and boarding school is tucked into the foothills of Connecticut's Berkshire Mountains in the small town of Washington. The Gunnery teaches about 300 students (grades 9 through 12) from many different states and countries. Some 70% of those enrolled are boarders; about 15% are international students. Small class sizes (average 14 students) and excellent student to teacher ratio (7-to-1) come at a price: Yearly tuition ranges from $26,000 to $35,200. The Gunnery was founded in 1850 by educator, abolitionist, and outdoorsman Frederick William Gunn and his wife Abigail Brinsmade Gunn.

	Annual Growth	06/16	06/17	06/20	06/21	06/22
Sales ($mil.)	10.0%	–	21.4	23.8	33.1	34.4
Net income ($ mil.)	–	–	(0.1)	(0.2)	8.1	7.1
Market value ($ mil.)	–	–	–	–	–	–
Employees	–	–	–	–	–	50

THE FRESH MARKET INC

300 N GREENE ST STE 1100
GREENSBORO, NC 274012171
Phone: 336 272-1338
Fax: –
Web: www.thefreshmarket.com

CEO: –
CFO: –
HR: –
FYE: January 31
Type: Private

The Fresh Market is a specialty grocery retailer that operates about 160 full-service upscale specialty grocery stores in over 20 US states, from Florida to New York. As the name suggests, the chain specializes in perishable goods, including fruits and vegetables, meat, and seafood. The initial 14,000-square-foot store differentiated itself from conventional supermarkets with a farmer's market atmosphere. It is a destination for those looking to discover the best including convenient, restaurant-quality meals, hand-picked produce, premium baked goods, fresh-cut flowers, custom-cut meats and carefully curated offerings. The company was founded by husband-and-wife team Ray and Beverly Berry, who opened their first store in 1982.

	Annual Growth	01/12	01/13	01/14	01/15	01/16
Sales ($mil.)	11.8%	–	1,329.1	1,511.7	1,753.2	1,857.0
Net income ($ mil.)	0.7%	–	64.1	50.8	63.0	65.5
Market value ($ mil.)	–	–	–	–	–	–
Employees	–	–	–	–	–	12,600

THE FULTON DEKALB HOSPITAL AUTHORITY

191 PEACHTREE ST NE STE 820
ATLANTA, GA 303031740
Phone: 404 489-1234
Fax: –
Web: www.gradyhealth.org

CEO: John Haupert
CFO: –
HR: –
FYE: December 31
Type: Private

The Fulton-DeKalb Hospital Authority (FDHA) is a volunteer board that governs the Grady Health System in Atlanta. The Grady Health System operates the Grady Memorial Hospital (an acute-care, 950-bed medical facility), primary and specialty care centers, and a network of community health centers in the Atlanta metro area. The Grady Memorial Hospital is the teaching hospital for the medical schools of Emory University and Morehouse College. The Fulton and DeKalb county commissioner boards appoint the FDHA board members. Not-for-profit Grady Memorial Hospital Corporation (GMHC) manages the daily activities of the Grady Health System.

THE G W VAN KEPPEL COMPANY

5800 E BANNISTER RD
KANSAS CITY, MO 641341192
Phone: 913 281-4800
Fax: –
Web: www.vankeppel.com

CEO: –
CFO: –
HR: Reneta Blanks
FYE: November 30
Type: Private

If you ask The G. W. Van Keppel Co., being stuck in the middle isn't half bad. The company touts its role as a middle man, matching original equipment manufacturers with operators of their heavy duty workhorses. Founded in 1926, it has grown to distribute a slew of construction, aggregate, and material handling equipment under blue chip brands, including Volvo, Hyster, and Champion Motor Graders. The company also offers repair and maintenance services, rental equipment, and aftermarket parts for its equipment. G. W. Van Keppel is led by its founder's third generation, chairman and president Bill Walker.

	Annual Growth	11/01	11/02	11/04	11/05	11/07
Sales ($mil.)	9.0%	–	106.2	115.7	139.3	163.3
Net income ($ mil.)	(41.4%)	–	19.8	2.4	20.6	1.4
Market value ($ mil.)	–	–	–	–	–	–
Employees	–	–	–	–	–	200

THE GAP INC

Two Folsom Street
San Francisco, CA 94105
Phone: 415 427-0100
Fax: –
Web: www.gapinc.com

NYS: GPS
CEO: Mark Breitbard
CFO: Katrina O'Connell
HR: –
FYE: February 3
Type: Public

The Gap is a collection of purpose-led, lifestyle brands offering apparel, accessories, and personal care products for women, men, and children. The company operates about 3,715 owned and franchised stores worldwide. Over the years, it has extended its namesake brand to include Gap Body, GapKids, Gap Maternity, Gap Teen, Yeezy Gap, and babyGap, among others, and added brands such as the urban chic Banana Republic, family budgeteer Old Navy, and women's activewear chain Athleta. The company generates approximately 85% of its revenue from the US.

	Annual Growth	02/20*	01/21	01/22	01/23*	02/24
Sales ($mil.)	(2.4%)	16,383	13,800	16,670	15,616	14,889
Net income ($ mil.)	9.4%	351.0	(665.0)	256.0	(202.0)	502.0
Market value ($ mil.)	3.3%	6,476.5	7,533.0	6,610.4	4,910.4	7,369.3
Employees	(9.9%)	129,000	117,000	97,000	95,000	85,000

*Fiscal year change

THE GENERATION COMPANIES LLC

4242 SIX FORKS RD STE 1550
RALEIGH, NC 276096084
Phone: 919 361-9000
Fax: –
Web: www.generationcompanies.com

CEO: –
CFO: David Cook
HR: –
FYE: December 31
Type: Private

Generation puts out the welcome mat, fluffs the pillows, and generally invites you to stay. The company develops, owns, and manages more than six extended-stay hotels. Brands in the firm's portfolio include Suburban Extended Homewood Suites by Hilton, Candlewood Suites, MainStay Suites, and Staybridge Suites; its properties are located in seven states in the US: Florida, North Carolina, Tennessee, Texas, and Virginia. The company is also active in real estate development, with some $300 million in real estate assets under management. Generation was founded in 1996 by CEO Mark Daley. His father, Hugh M. Daley, was one of the original Holiday Inn franchisees in 1959.

	Annual Growth	12/07	12/08	12/09	12/11	12/12
Assets ($mil.)	(5.7%)	–	–	207.9	4.5	174.6
Net income ($ mil.)	–	–	–	(4.0)	1.5	0.6
Market value ($ mil.)	–	–	–	–	–	–
Employees	–	–	–	–	–	350

THE GEORGE J FALTER COMPANY

3501 BENSON AVE
HALETHORPE, MD 212271098
Phone: 410 644-6414
Fax: –
Web: www.georgejfalter.com

CEO: Frank H Falter Jr
CFO: –
HR: –
FYE: December 31
Type: Private

The George J. Falter Company is a leading independent wholesale distributor of food and merchandise serving grocery stores, convienience stores, and other retailers throughout Maryland. It supplies customers with such goods as beverages, dry goods, and frozen foods, as well as health and beauty items, tobacco products, and other merchandise. In addition, George J. Falter distributes candy for fund raising activities. The company has delivery operations as well as a cash & carry outlet in Baltimore. The family-owned business was founded in 1878 as a candy distributor.

	Annual Growth	06/05	06/06	06/07*	12/08	12/09
Sales ($mil.)	4.8%	–	–	171.7	181.2	188.4
Net income ($ mil.)	222.4%	–	–	0.0	0.7	0.6
Market value ($ mil.)	–	–	–	–	–	–
Employees	–	–	–	–	–	130

*Fiscal year change

THE GEORGE LUCAS EDUCATIONAL FOUNDATION

5858 LUCAS VALLEY RD
NICASIO, CA 949469703
Phone: 415 623-1000
Fax: –
Web: www.edutopia.org

CEO: –
CFO: –
HR: –
FYE: December 31
Type: Private

Yoda's teaching methods must seem old-fashioned to The George Lucas Educational Foundation (GLEF). The group has documents and disseminates information about successful K-12 schools to help spread their practices nationwide. It focuses on issues such as technology integration, real-world applications, project-based learning, community involvement, and development of emotional intelligence. The organization also documents new ways of evaluating student achievement and educating teachers. GLEF provides information about innovative learning methods through books, DVDs, its Edutopia magazine, e-newsletters, and the foundation's Web site. Filmmaker George Lucas started the foundation in 1991.

THE GEORGE WASHINGTON UNIVERSITY

1918 F ST NW
WASHINGTON, DC 200520042
Phone: 202 994-6600
Fax: –
Web: www.gwu.edu

CEO: –
CFO: Mark Diaz
HR: Daniel Warwick
FYE: June 30
Type: Private

The George Washington University (the University or GWU) is a private, not-for-profit institution of higher education based in Washington, DC. The University provides education and training services, primarily for students at the undergraduate, graduate, and postdoctoral levels, and performs research, training, and other services under grants, contracts, and similar agreements with sponsoring organizations, primarily departments and agencies of the US Government. The University's more than 26,000 undergraduate graduate students are scattered across its primary campus at Foggy Bottom as well as its campuses in Mount Vernon and Ashburn, Virginia.

	Annual Growth	06/03	06/04	06/05	06/06	06/13
Sales ($mil.)	4.4%	–	–	832.9	921.5	1,178.0
Net income ($ mil.)	(7.9%)	–	–	115.2	146.1	59.4
Market value ($ mil.)	–	–	–	–	–	–
Employees	–	–	–	–	–	5,000

THE GEORGETOWN UNIVERSITY

37TH AND O ST NW
WASHINGTON, DC 200570001
Phone: 202 687-0100
Fax: –
Web: www.georgetown.edu

CEO: –
CFO: –
HR: Deborah Bassard
FYE: June 30
Type: Private

Georgetown University is one of the world's leading academic and research institutions. The university is a major international research university, which includes four undergraduate schools; a school for continuing studies; graduate schools in the arts and sciences, nursing and health studies, business, foreign services, and public policy; and professional schools in law and medicine. In addition to providing educational services, the university performs research, training, and other services under grants, contracts, and similar agreements with sponsoring organization primarily to departments and agencies of the US Government. Founded in 1789 by John Carroll, Georgetown is the nation's oldest Catholic and Jesuit university.

	Annual Growth	06/18	06/19	06/20	06/21	06/22
Sales ($mil.)	6.2%	–	1,330.0	1,341.5	1,274.3	1,591.1
Net income ($ mil.)	–	–	(77.6)	(128.9)	756.8	(34.6)
Market value ($ mil.)	–	–	–	–	–	–
Employees	–	–	–	–	–	9,700

THE GETTYSBURG HOSPITAL

147 GETTYS ST
GETTYSBURG, PA 173252536
Phone: 717 334-2121
Fax: –
Web: www.wellspan.org

CEO: –
CFO: –
HR: –
FYE: June 30
Type: Private

Gettysburg Hospital serves the here-and-now sick and wounded residents of historic Gettysburg, Pennsylvania, Adams County, and parts of northern Maryland. Specialized services include a maternity center, emergency medicine, and home health care. The facility is affiliated with nearby York Hospital through the regional WellSpan Health organization. In 2008, Gettysburg Hospital began work on an expansive project to increase ER capacity, add new patient floors, and build a new maternity center.

THE GLIK COMPANY

25 ABC PKWY
COLLINSVILLE, IL 622347431
Phone: 618 876-6717
Fax: –
Web: www.gliks.com

CEO: –
CFO: –
HR: –
FYE: January 03
Type: Private

Glik's is watching the urban fashion scene closely and working to cater to the crowds. The Glik Company operates about 55 Glik's apparel, accessories, and shoe stores in small towns in eight Midwestern states (primarily in Illinois, Michigan, and Minnesota). The stores offer men's and women's products with a hip-hop and sporty flair under national brands, such as Roxy, DC Shoes, Hurley, Billabong, Burton, The North Face, Volcom, and Silver Jeans. Glik's Grand, the company's largest store format, features motocross and action sportswear for surfing, skating, and water sports. Founded in 1897 by Joseph Glik, today the family-owned firm is run by president and CEO Jeff Glik, his great-grandson.

	Annual Growth	12/11	12/12	12/13	12/14*	01/16
Sales ($mil.)	5.7%	–	–	36.2	17.2	42.8
Net income ($ mil.)	30.3%	–	–	0.9	1.3	2.0
Market value ($ mil.)	–	–	–	–	–	–
Employees	–	–	–	–	–	500

*Fiscal year change

THE GLOBAL FUND FOR WOMEN INC

505 MONTGOMERY ST
SAN FRANCISCO, CA 941112585
Phone: 415 248-4800
Fax: –
Web: www.globalfundforwomen.org

CEO: Latanya M Frett
CFO: Jennifer Quinn
HR: Anil Awasti
FYE: June 30
Type: Private

The Global Fund for Women believes every woman has a right to equality and social justice and the group has the money to back it up. The not-for-profit offers grants to women's groups worldwide (some 120 countries outside the US) that are working on stopping gender-based violence, ensuring economic and environmental justice, advancing health and reproductive rights, increasing political participation, and improving access to education. One of the group's biggest causes is trying to end trafficking in women and girls. The Global Fund gives small grants of money to local women's groups that report back on progress and problems. Some $7.7 million in 2006 was granted to support the fund's programs.

	Annual Growth	06/14	06/15	06/16	06/17	06/20
Sales ($mil.)	17.8%	–	14.2	16.0	16.1	32.1
Net income ($ mil.)	–	–	(0.7)	2.3	(0.7)	12.8
Market value ($ mil.)	–	–	–	–	–	–
Employees	–	–	–	–	–	44

THE GOLDFIELD CORPORATION DEL

1688 W HIBISCUS BLVD
MELBOURNE, FL 329013082
Phone: 321 724-1700
Fax: –
Web: www.gridtekus.com

CEO: Jason M Spivey
CFO: Stephen R Wherry
HR: –
FYE: December 31
Type: Private

The Goldfield Corporation earns more laying cable now than it used to digging for mother lodes. Through subsidiary Southeast Power, Goldfield builds and maintains electrical facilities in the Southeast, West, and Mid-Atlantic regions for utilities and industrial customers, including Florida Power & Light Company and Duke Energy. The unit also installs transmission lines and fiber-optic cable. Goldfield's Bayswater Development subsidiary maintains real estate operations in Florida, specializing in developing waterfront condominiums for retirees. The company, which had been in the mining industry since 1906, divested those operations in 2002 after deciding that it had become economically unfeasible.

	Annual Growth	12/15	12/16	12/17	12/18	12/19
Sales ($mil.)	25.9%	–	–	114.0	138.1	180.6
Net income ($ mil.)	(10.0%)	–	–	8.3	5.0	6.7
Market value ($ mil.)	–	–	–	–	–	–
Employees	–	–	–	–	–	536

THE GOLUB CORPORATION

461 NOTT ST
SCHENECTADY, NY 123081812
Phone: 518 355-5000
Fax: -
Web: www.pricechopper.com

CEO: Blaine R Bringhurst
CFO: Jim Peterson
HR: Shelley Florence
FYE: April 24
Type: Private

The Golub Corporation operates supermarkets under the Price Chopper, Market 32, and Market Bistro banners. The company offers a wide range of fresh and high-quality meat, poultry, seafood, vegetables, and fruit products, as well as, frozen goods including frozen veggies, breakfasts, and pizzas. It also sells baby care, personal care, health care, pet care, and various other grocery products. Additionally, the company also offers catering services offering a wide selection of best-in-fresh deli platters, specialty cheeses, snack-size apps, prepared meals, seafood, breads, desserts, fruit baskets, floral arrangements, and more. The company operates about 130 stores located in New York (its largest market), Connecticut, Massachusetts, Vermont, Pennsylvania, and New Hampshire.

	Annual Growth	04/12	04/13	04/14	04/15	04/16
Sales ($mil.)	(0.7%)	-	-	3,472.5	3,476.9	3,427.1
Net income ($ mil.)	(32.3%)	-	-	18.3	21.2	8.4
Market value ($ mil.)	-	-	-	-	-	-
Employees	-	-	-	-	-	19,500

THE GOOD SAMARITAN HOSPITAL OF MD INC

5601 LOCH RAVEN BLVD
BALTIMORE, MD 212392945
Phone: 443 444-8000
Fax: -
Web: www.medstarhealth.org

CEO: Jeffrey A Matton
CFO: Deana Stout
HR: -
FYE: June 30
Type: Private

Good Samaritan Hospital of Maryland provides emergency care and promotes good health in the Baltimore area. The 300-bed hospital, operating as MedStar Good Samaritan, provides acute medical and specialty services including rehabilitation (50-bed ward), transitional care (30-bed sub-acute ward), orthopedics, cancer care, cardiology, dialysis, and women's health, as well as serving as a community teaching facility. The hospital, founded in 1968, also operates nursing and assisted-living facilities for the elderly, and it provides educational seminars, diagnostic screening, and preventative medical care through its Good Health Center. MedStar Good Samaritan of Maryland is part of the MedStar Health system.

	Annual Growth	06/14	06/15	06/16	06/20	06/22
Sales ($mil.)	(2.5%)	-	325.0	315.4	266.5	271.9
Net income ($ mil.)	-	-	16.9	7.9	1.5	(12.9)
Market value ($ mil.)	-	-	-	-	-	-
Employees	-	-	-	-	-	2,146

THE GOOD SHEPHERD HOSPITAL INC

700 E MARSHALL AVE
LONGVIEW, TX 756015572
Phone: 903 315-2000
Fax: -
Web: www.christushealth.org

CEO: -
CFO: -
HR: -
FYE: September 30
Type: Private

Leading its citizens toward good health, Good Shepherd Health System provides medical and surgical care to patients throughout the Piney Woods region of northeastern Texas. Its flagship facility is Good Shepherd Medical Center in Longview, a more than 425-bed regional referral hospital providing specialty care in areas such as trauma, cardiology, neurology, and pulmonology. Good Shepherd also has small inpatient facilities, as well as a freestanding outpatient surgery center and several primary care Family Health Centers located throughout its service area. The hospital was established in 1935 as the 50-bed Gregg Memorial Hospital. Duke LifePoint Healthcare is buying Good Shepherd Health System.

	Annual Growth	09/12	09/13	09/14	09/15	09/16
Sales ($mil.)	(3.0%)	-	270.0	244.6	279.6	246.7
Net income ($ mil.)	-	-	2.3	(7.3)	0.8	(17.0)
Market value ($ mil.)	-	-	-	-	-	-
Employees	-	-	-	-	-	2,200

THE GREAT ATLANTIC & PACIFIC TEA CO INC

2 PARAGON DR
MONTVALE, NJ 076451718
Phone: 201 573-9700
Fax: -
Web: www.aptea.com

CEO: -
CFO: -
HR: -
FYE: February 26
Type: Private

Once one of the biggest baggers of groceries in the US, The Great Atlantic & Pacific Tea Company (A&P) has been reduced to a shrinking portfolio of regional grocery chains. It now runs about 300 supermarkets in New Jersey, New York, and four other eastern states. In addition to its mainstay A&P chain, the company operates five banners: Pathmark, Waldbaum's, Superfresh, Food Emporium, and Food Basics. A&P acquired its longtime rival in the Northeast, Pathmark Stores, for about $1.4 billion, but the purchase failed to reverse A&P's lagging fortunes. A&P was exploring a potential sale of the company after emerging from bankruptcy in 2012 when it filed for protection again in 2015.

THE GRIFFIN HOSPITAL

130 DIVISION ST
DERBY, CT 064181326
Phone: 203 735-7421
Fax: -
Web: www.griffinhealth.org

CEO: Patrick Charmel
CFO: Mark O'Neill
HR: Steve Mordecai
FYE: September 30
Type: Private

Griffin Hospital is a not-for-profit community hospital and subsidiary of Griffin Health Services Corporation. The 160-bed acute-care hospital serves residents in and around Derby, Connecticut. Its specialties include cardiac and physical rehabilitation, psychiatry and mental health, surgical services, and centers for childbirth and bladder and bowel control. The hospital is a teaching center affiliated with Yale University's School of Medicine. Griffin Hospital is the flagship hospital of consumer health care organization Planetree, which implements a model of patient-centered care that encourages patients to actively participate in their treatment processes.

	Annual Growth	09/18	09/19	09/20	09/21	09/22
Sales ($mil.)	9.7%	-	203.6	169.0	203.1	269.0
Net income ($ mil.)	22.3%	-	9.6	13.1	27.1	17.5
Market value ($ mil.)	-	-	-	-	-	-
Employees	-	-	-	-	-	1,100

THE H T HACKNEY CO

502 S GAY ST STE 300
KNOXVILLE, TN 379023607
Phone: 865 546-1291
Fax: -
Web: www.hthackney.com

CEO: William B Sansom
CFO: Michael D Morton
HR: -
FYE: June 30
Type: Private

The H. T. Hackney Company is one of the nation's largest wholesale distributors of food products and other retail items in the US. It offers a complete lineup of best-in-class foodservice equipment solutions, everything from fryers and ovens to refrigerators and beverage systems. In addition, Hackney hosted shows educating and offering retailers tools for expanding or starting their foodservice offerings, as well as events bringing vendors and retailers together for cross-promotional growth potential, innovation, as well as excellent deals each spring. It also participates in national, regional, and state trade shows maintaining a strong presence in the market. H. T. Hackney was founded in 1891.

	Annual Growth	06/11	06/12	06/13	06/19	06/22
Sales ($mil.)	1.5%	-	-	21.1	21.6	24.1
Net income ($ mil.)	-	-	-	-	(1.6)	(0.6)
Market value ($ mil.)	-	-	-	-	-	-
Employees	-	-	-	-	-	3,600

THE HEALTH CARE AUTHORITY OF THE CITY OF HUNTSVILLE

101 SIVLEY RD SW
HUNTSVILLE, AL 358014421
Phone: 256 265-1000
Fax: –
Web: www.huntsvillehospital.org

CEO: –
CFO: Kelly Towers
HR: –
FYE: June 30
Type: Private

Health Care Authority of the City of Huntsville ensures that residents get the medical attention they need. The volunteer board consists of nine members that governs the more than 880-bed Huntsville Hospital, one of the largest medical centers in Alabama with a staff of more than 650 physicians, as well as other medical facilities. Huntsville Hospital is also a teaching facility for the University of Alabama-Birmingham. The Health Care Authority of the City of Huntsville provides a list of nominees for board members to the City Council, which decides who is appointed to the board.

	Annual Growth	06/06	06/07	06/17	06/18	06/19
Sales ($mil.)	9.2%	–	591.3	1,407.5	1,524.4	1,700.2
Net income ($ mil.)	13.3%	–	49.1	46.3	53.8	218.8
Market value ($ mil.)	–	–	–	–	–	–
Employees	–	–	–	–	–	14,000

THE HENRY FRANCIS DUPONT WINTERTHUR MUSEUM INC

5105 KENNETT PIKE
WINTERTHUR, DE 197351819
Phone: 302 888-4852
Fax: –
Web: www.winterthur.org

CEO: –
CFO: –
HR: –
FYE: June 30
Type: Private

The Henry Francis du Pont Winterthur Museum offers collections of antiques and Americana, a 60-acre naturalistic garden, and an 87,000-volume library specializing in American culture. Into 2012, the museum showcases The John and Carolyn Grossman Collection of printed paper from the Victorian and Edwardian periods. It also promotes its Enchanted Woods fairy-tale garden, aimed at the young and young-at-heart, containing sites such as a faerie cottage and a troll bridge. The 979-acre estate is the former home of Henry Francis du Pont, a director of chemical maker DuPont from 1915 to 1958. The Winterthur country estate was converted into a museum and opened to the public in 1951.

	Annual Growth	06/13	06/14	06/20	06/21	06/22
Sales ($mil.)	0.2%	–	25.5	–	27.7	25.9
Net income ($ mil.)	–	–	(2.3)	–	1.1	(3.6)
Market value ($ mil.)	–	–	–	–	–	–
Employees	–	–	–	–	–	160

THE HERITAGE FOUNDATION

214 MASSACHUSETTS AVE NE
WASHINGTON, DC 200024999
Phone: 202 546-4400
Fax: –
Web: www.heritage.org

CEO: –
CFO: –
HR: –
FYE: December 31
Type: Private

A conservative public policy think tank, The Heritage Foundation offers research and advocacy on topics ranging from agriculture and labor to missile defense, religion, crime, and education. The Heritage Foundation promotes a conservative agenda based on the tenets of free enterprise, limited government, individual freedom, traditional American values, and a strong national defense. The foundation is supported mainly by individuals, as well as by other foundations and by corporations. Its donors number 410,000 and its expense budget has reached $61 million. The late beer magnate Joseph Coors provided seed money for The Heritage Foundation, which was founded in 1973.

	Annual Growth	12/15	12/16	12/19	12/21	12/22
Sales ($mil.)	4.4%	–	82.2	122.9	101.8	106.3
Net income ($ mil.)	66.8%	–	0.6	44.9	16.0	12.7
Market value ($ mil.)	–	–	–	–	–	–
Employees	–	–	–	–	–	270

THE HERSHEY SALTY SNACKS SALES COMPANY

19 E CHOCOLATE AVE
HERSHEY, PA 170331314
Phone: 717 534-4200
Fax: –
Web: www.amplifysnackbrands.com

CEO: Thomas C Ennis
CFO: Brian Goldberg
HR: –
FYE: December 31
Type: Private

Amplifying its bottom line without amplifying its customers' waistlines is what Amplify Snack Brands is all about. The high-growth snack food company is focused on developing and marketing products that appeal to consumers' growing preference for healthier snacks. Its anchor brand, SkinnyPop, is a rapidly growing, highly profitable, and market leading healthy popcorn brand. SkinnyPop has amassed a loyal and growing customer base across a wide range of food distribution channels in the US. To increase its global marketing reach, Amplify Snack Brands was acquired by chocolate-making giant The Hershey Company for $1.6 billion in early 2018.

THE HIBBERT COMPANY

400 PENNINGTON AVE
TRENTON, NJ 086183105
Phone: 609 392-0478
Fax: –
Web: www.hibbert.com

CEO: Timothy J Moonan
CFO: –
HR: Bonnie Yahner
FYE: December 31
Type: Private

The Hibbert Company, doing business as The Hibbert Group, offers marketing support services. Its flagship services consist of the fulfillment; professional services; and database and omnichannelmcm marketing. The company serves clients in industries such as pharmaceutical, telecommunications, finance, technology, electronics, and advertising and marketing. Hibbert has around ten locations in Delaware, Colorado, and New Jersey. In 1881, William Hibbert, a newspaper typesetter in Trenton, started Hibbert Printing Company. Tim and Tom Moonan and their family have owned the company since 1936.

	Annual Growth	12/04	12/05	12/06	12/08	12/09
Sales ($mil.)	–	–	–	78.8	78.8	78.8
Net income ($ mil.)	–	–	–	3.5	3.5	3.5
Market value ($ mil.)	–	–	–	–	–	–
Employees	–	–	–	–	–	446

THE HILLMAN COMPANIES INC

10590 HAMILTON AVE
CINCINNATI, OH 452311764
Phone: 513 851-4900
Fax: –
Web: www.hillmangroup.com

CEO: Douglas J Cahill
CFO: Robert O Kraft
HR: Ann Holmes
FYE: December 26
Type: Private

Operating primarily through wholly owned subsidiary The Hillman Group, Inc., the company is a leading North American provider of complete hardware solutions, delivered with industry best customer service to over 26,000 customers. Product lines include thousands of small parts such as fasteners and related hardware items; threaded rod and metal shapes; keys, key duplication systems, and accessories; builder's hardware; personal protective equipment, such as gloves and eye-wear; and identification items, such as tags and letters, numbers, and signs. Max W. Hillman Sr. started the fastener company serving independently-owned hardware stores in 1964.

THE HOME CITY ICE COMPANY

6045 BRIDGETOWN RD STE 1
CINCINNATI, OH 452483047
Phone: 513 574-1800
Fax: –
Web: www.homecityice.com

CEO: –
CFO: –
HR: Inaiara Galle
FYE: December 31
Type: Private

Home City Ice (HCI) has its business down cold. The company manufactures some 5,700 tons of ice per day in its three dozen ice-manufacturing plants. It operates a distribution network made up of about 55 centers and a fleet of more than 725 vehicles. HCI stocks up on ice in 88 freezers across the region and the network delivers the company's frozen product to individual customers and company-owned ice merchandising machines located in more than a dozen US states, primarily in the Midwest. The company dates back to 1896 and is owned by the Sedler family, which began its association with the company in the 1920s.

THE HOPKINS JOHNS UNIVERSITY

3400 N CHARLES ST
BALTIMORE, MD 212182680
Phone: 410 516-8000
Fax: –
Web: www.jhu.edu

CEO: –
CFO: –
HR: Denise Lannon
FYE: June 30
Type: Private

Founded in 1876, The Johns Hopkins University is a premier, privately-endowed institution that provides education and related services to students and others, research and related services to sponsoring organizations, and professional medical services to patients. While renowned for its School of Medicine, the private university offers more than 400 academic programs spanning fields of study including arts and sciences, business, engineering, and international studies. The university enrolls more than 32,000 full- and part-time students throughout nine academic divisions. Johns Hopkins is based in Baltimore, but its 10 divisions are spread out across 10 campuses on three continents. The student-teacher ratio is 7:1. Jhpiego, a nonprofit health organization is affiliated with the university.

	Annual Growth	06/17	06/18	06/19	06/20	06/21
Sales ($mil.)	1.9%	–	–	6,410.1	6,470.6	6,659.0
Net income ($ mil.)	30.3%	–	–	2,017.6	903.8	3,427.4
Market value ($ mil.)	–	–	–	–	–	–
Employees	–	–	–	–	–	37,600

THE HOSPITAL FOR SICK CHILDREN PEDIATRIC CENTER

1731 BUNKER HILL RD NE
WASHINGTON, DC 200173096
Phone: 202 832-4400
Fax: –
Web: www.childrensnational.org

CEO: –
CFO: –
HR: Giselle Jones
FYE: December 31
Type: Private

The HSC Pediatric Center (formerly The Hospital for Sick Children) provides medical and rehabilitative care for infants, children, adolescents, and young adults. The organization provides specialized care for young people in the transition from acute care to home care. Clinical experts at the center include doctors and nurses, as well as physical therapists, speech therapists, dieticians, and case managers. The organization's origins date back to 1883, when young women of St. John's Episcopal Church in Washington, DC, opened the "Children's Country Home," at what was then the outskirts of the district, as a place for kids to escape from the city during the summertime.

	Annual Growth	12/05	12/06	12/09	12/13	12/14
Sales ($mil.)	(0.5%)	–	33.0	39.1	47.9	31.6
Net income ($ mil.)	–	–	–	(0.8)	7.4	(7.9)
Market value ($ mil.)	–	–	–	–	–	–
Employees	–	–	–	–	–	350

THE HOWARD UNIVERSITY

2400 6TH ST NW
WASHINGTON, DC 200590002
Phone: 202 806-6100
Fax: –
Web: www.howard.edu

CEO: –
CFO: –
HR: –
FYE: June 30
Type: Private

Howard University is a predominantly African-American university enrolling some 11,000 students in Washington, DC. The university offers undergraduate, graduate, and professional degrees in 120 areas including engineering, education, divinity, dentistry, law, medicine, history, political science, music, and social work through its 12 schools and colleges. It has about 1,000 full-time faculty members and has a low student-to-teacher ratio of about 8:1. Established in 1867, the school was named after one of its founders, General Oliver O. Howard, a Civil War hero who was commissioner of the Freedman's Bureau.

THE HUMANE SOCIETY OF THE UNITED STATES

1255 23RD ST NW STE 450
WASHINGTON, DC 200371168
Phone: 202 452-1100
Fax: –
Web: www.humanesociety.org

CEO: Kitty Block
CFO: G T Waite III
HR: –
FYE: December 31
Type: Private

The Humane Society of the United States (HSUS) is a watchdog for dogs and all sorts of other domestic animals and wildlife. Founded in 1954, HSUS is the country's largest animal protection organization with 11 million members and constituents. The organization supports the work of local humane societies and implements a variety of investigative, educational, advocacy, and legislative programs to promote animal welfare. Its campaigns have addressed such issues as animal fighting, factory farming, animal testing, the fur trade, and hunting practices. Most of HSUS's revenue comes from contributions and grants. An affiliate, Humane Society International, takes the cause to other countries.

THE INGALLS MEMORIAL HOSPITAL

1 INGALLS DR
HARVEY, IL 604263558
Phone: 708 333-2300
Fax: –
Web: www.uchicagomedicine.org

CEO: Kurt Johnson
CFO: Vince Pryor
HR: Aletha Ross
FYE: June 30
Type: Private

Ingalls Memorial Hospital serves Chicago's south suburbs. With more than 560 beds, the main hospital offers a variety of acute and tertiary health care services, including cancer treatment, cardiovascular care, orthopedic surgery, rehabilitation services, neurosurgery, women's health, and other clinical services. It also includes specialty centers in areas such as sleep therapy and addiction treatment. Ingalls Memorial Hospital also acts as a health system, operating outpatient offices and clinics and providing home health and hospice services in the area.

	Annual Growth	09/14	09/15*	06/20	06/21	06/22
Sales ($mil.)	3.0%	–	285.4	304.0	340.8	350.3
Net income ($ mil.)	–	–	7.3	(22.5)	(1.0)	(8.5)
Market value ($ mil.)	–	–	–	–	–	–
Employees	–	–	–	–	–	2,296

*Fiscal year change

THE INSTITUTE OF ELECTRICAL AND ELECTRONICS ENGINEERS INCORPORATED

445 HOES LN
PISCATAWAY, NJ 088544141
Phone: 212 419-7900
Fax: –
Web: ieeeshutpages.s3-website-us-west-2.amazonaws.com
CEO: Karen Barleston
CFO: Thomas Siegert
HR: –
FYE: December 31
Type: Private

The Institute of Electrical and Electronics Engineers (IEEE) has over 427,000 members, including nearly about 145,000 students in over 190 countries. The IEEE is the world's largest technical professional organization dedicated to advancing technology for the benefit of humanity. IEEE and its members inspire a global community through its highly cited publications, conferences, technology standards, and professional and educational activities. It sponsors some 2,000 annual conferences and publishes nearly a third of the world's technical literature, including journals, magazines, and conference proceedings. The IEEE was formed in 1963 in a combination of the American Institute of Electrical Engineers (founded in 1884) and the Institute of Radio Engineers (founded in 19Annual Majority of its members were in the US.

	Annual Growth	12/16	12/17	12/19	12/21	12/22
Sales ($mil.)	2.8%	–	494.4	563.3	524.8	566.4
Net income ($ mil.)	22.6%	–	34.1	80.3	142.6	94.2
Market value ($ mil.)	–	–	–	–	–	–
Employees	–	–	–	–	–	1,068

THE INSTITUTE OF INTERNATIONAL FINANCE INC

1333 H ST NW STE 800E
WASHINGTON, DC 200054770
Phone: 202 857-3600
Fax: –
Web: www.iif.com
CEO: Timothy D Adams
CFO: –
HR: Jennifer Grant
FYE: December 31
Type: Private

This group gives all-new meaning to the phrase "show me the money." Member rolls of the International Institute of Finance (IIF) are virtually a who's who of the global financial world and include more than 375 commercial and investment banks, insurance companies, investment management firms, and financial institutions from some 70 countries. About half of the IFF's members are based in Europe. The organization serves as a forum and collaborative vehicle for its members; it also provides them with risk management information regarding emerging markets. Founded in 1983, the IFF began in response to the international debt crisis.

	Annual Growth	12/17	12/18	12/19	12/21	12/22
Sales ($mil.)	(1.7%)	–	34.5	33.6	36.1	32.3
Net income ($ mil.)	–	–	(0.7)	0.1	1.7	(0.4)
Market value ($ mil.)	–	–	–	–	–	–
Employees	–	–	–	–	–	60

THE INTERFAITH ALLIANCE INC

1212 NEW YORK AVE NW FL 7
WASHINGTON, DC 200053905
Phone: 202 639-6370
Fax: –
Web: www.interfaithalliance.org
CEO: –
CFO: –
HR: –
FYE: December 31
Type: Private

The Interfaith Alliance (TIA) cuts across all religions to find common ground for the common good. The not-for-profit fosters democratic values and tolerance for different religious beliefs. The organization has more than 185,000 members in the US from some 75 different faiths. They work to promote civic participation, freedom of religion, civility in public discourse, and political involvement through town hall meetings, publications, teach-ins, vigils, and lobbying. TIA also airs State of Belief, a weekly radio show that explores religious issues and conflicts. The group was founded in 1994 by a group of religious leaders of different denominations.

	Annual Growth	12/05	12/06	12/13	12/14	12/15
Sales ($mil.)	(18.1%)	–	4.2	1.1	0.8	0.7
Net income ($ mil.)	–	–	0.2	0.2	0.0	(0.1)
Market value ($ mil.)	–	–	–	–	–	–
Employees	–	–	–	–	–	12

THE INTERNATIONAL ASSOCIATION OF LIONS CLUBS INCORPORATED

300 W 22ND ST
OAK BROOK, IL 605238815
Phone: 630 571-5466
Fax: –
Web: www.lionsclubs.org
CEO: –
CFO: –
HR: –
FYE: June 30
Type: Private

With a growl of great compassion, The International Association of Lions Clubs offers people the opportunity to volunteer in their local areas and global community. Its more than 1 million members are involved in a range of projects, from neighborhood initiatives to far-reaching international campaigns. Lions clubs conduct vision and hearing screenings, sponsor youth camps, build homes for the disabled, provide disaster relief, and develop international relations. It also promotes educational programs for diabetes and drug awareness. The group has about 45,000 branches in more than 200 countries. It was founded in 1917 as a way for business organizations to better their communities and the world.

THE INTERNATIONAL CITY MANAGEMENT ASSOCIATION RETIREMENT CORPORATION

777 N CAPITOL ST NE STE 600
WASHINGTON, DC 200024239
Phone: 202 962-4600
Fax: –
Web: www.icmarc.org
CEO: –
CFO: Michael Guarasci
HR: Edwina Brooks
FYE: December 31
Type: Private

Because public servants need financial security, too. ICMA Retirement Corporation (ICMA-RC) offers retirement planning and advisory services exclusively for public-sector employees. A not-for-profit organization, it offers 401(a), 401(k), and 457 plans, individual retirement accounts, certificates of deposit, retirement health savings plans, brokerage accounts, and access to long-term care insurance. The company also manages the VantageTrustfamily of funds. ICMA-RC serves some 1.2 million employees of state and local governments from more than 9,000 public sector plans. Founded in 1972 by public-sector employees, ICMA-RC has approximately $57 billion in plan assets under management.

	Annual Growth	12/06	12/07	12/08	12/09	12/14
Assets ($mil.)	11.4%	–	–	–	287.7	493.9
Net income ($ mil.)	–	–	–	–	(4.8)	42.9
Market value ($ mil.)	–	–	–	–	–	–
Employees	–	–	–	–	–	850

THE JACKSON LABORATORY

600 MAIN ST
BAR HARBOR, ME 046091500
Phone: 207 288-6000
Fax: –
Web: www.jax.org
CEO: Edison T Liu
CFO: Linda Jensen
HR: Bonnie Lyons
FYE: December 31
Type: Private

The Jackson Laboratory (JAX) is a world leader in mammalian genetics and human genomics research. Founded in 1929, JAX an independent, non-profit research institution with locations in Maine, Connecticut, California, Japan and China. Much of its research into mammalian genetics is focused on mice, which share a similar genetic makeup to humans. In addition to its own research in areas such as Alzheimer's, cancer, immunology, and diabetes, the organization maintains colonies of mice and supplies them under the brand name JAX to other laboratories around the globe. Additionally, JAX offers educational programs ? including online learning and mini-courses, workshops, and postdoctoral programs ? for both current and future scientists.

	Annual Growth	12/17	12/18	12/19	12/21	12/22
Sales ($mil.)	8.8%	–	394.8	440.8	572.9	553.5
Net income ($ mil.)	(6.5%)	–	27.0	95.4	63.4	20.7
Market value ($ mil.)	–	–	–	–	–	–
Employees	–	–	–	–	–	2,100

THE JAMAICA HOSPITAL

8900 VAN WYCK EXPY FL 4N
JAMAICA, NY 114182897
Phone: 718 206-6290
Fax: –
Web: www.jamaicahospital.org

CEO: Neil F Phillips
CFO: –
HR: Matilda Miceli
FYE: December 31
Type: Private

Jamaica Hospital Medical Center has been operating in the Queens Borough of New York since before the nation of Jamaica even was born. The hospital serves Queens and eastern Brooklyn with general medical, pediatric, psychiatric, and ambulatory care services. The facility has about 430 beds. Its specialty services include a coma recovery unit, a dialysis center, a psychiatric emergency department, a rehabilitation center, as well as a traumatic brain injury recovery unit. The hospital also operates a nursing home with more than 220 beds, as well as family practice, ambulance, and home health services. Jamaica Hospital Medical Center is a subsidiary of MediSys Health Network.

	Annual Growth	12/18	12/19	12/20	12/21	12/22
Sales ($mil.)	15.3%	–	623.2	845.5	896.0	954.9
Net income ($ mil.)	–	–	11.4	35.9	18.0	(1.5)
Market value ($ mil.)	–	–	–	–	–	–
Employees	–	–	–	–	–	1,311

THE JANE GOODALL INSTITUTE FOR WILDLIFE RESEARCH EDUCATION AND CONSERVATION

1120 20TH ST NW STE 520S
WASHINGTON, DC 200363407
Phone: 703 682-9220
Fax: –
Web: www.janegoodall.org

CEO: –
CFO: –
HR: –
FYE: December 31
Type: Private

The Jane Goodall Institute (JGI) knows it's not all good in the monkey world. The not-for-profit organization is dedicated to supporting the welfare of chimpanzees and other primates through education and public awareness. The group's main goals are to conserve primate habitat; promote an understanding of the interrelatedness of humans, animals, and the environment; increase non-invasive research on chimps and other primates; and improve the general welfare of chimpanzees and other animals. JGI has about 40 offices in Africa, Asia, Europe, and North America, including about 10 for child and teen program Roots & Shoots. The institute was founded in 1977 by Dr. Jane Goodall and Princess Genevieve di San Faustino.

	Annual Growth	12/15	12/16	12/17	12/21	12/22
Sales ($mil.)	13.4%	–	12.5	20.4	22.8	26.5
Net income ($ mil.)	–	–	(1.6)	3.6	2.3	4.3
Market value ($ mil.)	–	–	–	–	–	–
Employees	–	–	–	–	–	60

THE JAY GROUP INC

700 INDIAN SPRINGS DR
LANCASTER, PA 176017800
Phone: 717 285-6200
Fax: –
Web: www.jaygroup.com

CEO: J F Chryst
CFO: Craig Robinson
HR: –
FYE: December 31
Type: Private

The Jay Group provides outsourced marketing and fulfillment services to clients such as Reebok, iRobot, and Pfizer. The company's roster of services includes product fulfillment, call center services, procurement, and packaging services. The Jay Group's fulfillment programs serve business-to-business and business-to-consumer clients providing literature, product, and catalog fulfillment, as well as rebate processing, incentive program management, and sweepstakes management for sales promotions. The company's contact center services include order processing, customer service, and help desk support. It was established by J. Freeland Chryst in 1965; his daughter, Dana Chryst, leads the company as CEO.

	Annual Growth	12/04	12/05	12/06	12/07	12/08
Sales ($mil.)	2.5%	–	47.5	51.1	47.3	51.2
Net income ($ mil.)	(26.4%)	–	3.5	2.2	2.2	1.4
Market value ($ mil.)	–	–	–	–	–	–
Employees	–	–	–	–	–	273

THE JEWISH FEDERATIONS OF NORTH AMERICA INC

25 BDWY FL 17 STE 1700
NEW YORK, NY 100041015
Phone: 212 284-6500
Fax: –
Web: www.jewishfederations.org

CEO: Eric D Fingerhut
CFO: –
HR: Fran Vago
FYE: June 30
Type: Private

From supporting food banks in the US to helping migr s fleeing Ethiopia for Israel, The Jewish Federations of North America (formerly the United Jewish Communities) works to better Jewish life across the globe. One of North America's leading not-for-profit organizations, the JFNA represents more than 150 Jewish federations and about 400 independent Jewish communities across the continent. The federation raises and distributes more than $3.5 billion annually for social welfare, social services, and educational needs in its effort to support Israel and Jews worldwide. The organization changed its name from United Jewish Communities to The Jewish Federations of North America in 2009.

	Annual Growth	06/14	06/15	06/17	06/21	06/22
Sales ($mil.)	1.1%	–	338.1	261.2	264.9	364.9
Net income ($ mil.)	29.1%	–	13.4	(0.3)	9.9	79.8
Market value ($ mil.)	–	–	–	–	–	–
Employees	–	–	–	–	–	150

THE JOCKEY CLUB

250 PARK AVE
NEW YORK, NY 101772021
Phone: 212 371-5970
Fax: –
Web: www.jockeyclub.com

CEO: –
CFO: Laura Barillaro
HR: Lynn Scholler
FYE: December 31
Type: Private

The Jockey Club can locate any thoroughbred horse and owner in the US, Canada, and Puerto Rico. The company's The American Stud Book is an annual directory of horses listing pedigrees and owners, which is also available online. Other offerings include a history of the thoroughbred breed, an online fact book about thoroughbred breeding and racing, and an information guide to the industry. Through subsidiaries and partnerships, The Jockey Club also operates the Equibase Company (racing information database), equineline.com (online marketplace), and InCompass (software applications and systems for racetracks and simulcast outlets). The company was founded in 1894 by several thoroughbred owners and breeders.

	Annual Growth	12/14	12/15	12/16	12/21	12/22
Sales ($mil.)	(0.3%)	–	15.4	10.7	14.1	15.1
Net income ($ mil.)	–	–	1.1	(1.8)	(2.1)	(2.7)
Market value ($ mil.)	–	–	–	–	–	–
Employees	–	–	–	–	–	250

THE JOHN AND MARY R MARKLE FOUNDATION

10 ROCKEFELLER PLZ FL 16
NEW YORK, NY 100201903
Phone: 212 713-7600
Fax: –
Web: www.markle.org

CEO: –
CFO: Susan Roberson
HR: –
FYE: June 30
Type: Private

Focusing on the effects of technology on society, the Markle Foundation has funded research into such topics as universal e-mail access and the role of information technology in health care. The foundation was formed in 1927 to "promote the advancement and diffusion of knowledge ... and the general good of mankind." Named after philanthropy-friendly businessman John Markle and his wife Mary, the foundation's previous areas of concentrations include social welfare and academic medicine. The foundation's current focus is on the use of technology to address health and national security issues.

	Annual Growth	06/15	06/16	06/17	06/18	06/22
Sales ($mil.)	7.4%	–	14.8	15.3	16.5	22.7
Net income ($ mil.)	–	–	(21.6)	21.2	(6.1)	5.9
Market value ($ mil.)	–	–	–	–	–	–
Employees	–	–	–	–	–	20

THE JOHN GORE ORGANIZATION INC

1619 BROADWAY FL 9
NEW YORK, NY 100197412
Phone: 917 421-5400
Fax: –
Web: www.johngore.com

CEO: John Gore
CFO: Paul Dietz
HR: Jennifer Granvil
FYE: June 30
Type: Private

Key Brand Entertainment (KBE) brings a theatrical touch to the business world. The entertainment company produces and distributes live theater across the US, Canada, Japan, and the UK. It has invested in the production of Broadway hits Hairspray, Chicago, Wicked, and Avenue Q , among others . KBE owns six theaters in Boston, Minneapolis, and Baltimore as well as touring company Broadway Across America, which takes hits to more than 40 North American markets. Subsidiary Broadway.com operates a website and phone service for purchasing tickets to all Broadway shows and most off-Broadway and West End (London) shows. The site also offers tour packages, show reviews, and related information. KBE was formed in 2004.

THE JOHNS HOPKINS HEALTH SYSTEM CORPORATION

600 N WOLFE ST
BALTIMORE, MD 212870005
Phone: 410 955-5000
Fax: –
Web: www.hopkinsmedicine.org

CEO: C M Amstrong
CFO: Ronald J Werthman
HR: Denise Lannon
FYE: June 30
Type: Private

Named after philanthropist Johns Hopkins, the Johns Hopkins Health System (JHHS) gifts Baltimore residents with an array of health care services. The health system is an affiliate of world-renowned Johns Hopkins Medicine and oversees six hospitals: All Children's Hospital, Johns Hopkins Hospital, Bayview Medical Center, Howard County General Hospital, Sibley Memorial Hospital, and Suburban Hospital. The not-for-profit teaching hospitals offer inpatient and outpatient health services that include general medicine, emergency/trauma care, pediatrics, maternity care, senior care, and numerous specialized areas of medicine. JHHS also operates community health and satellite care facilities.

	Annual Growth	06/18	06/19	06/20	06/21	06/22
Sales ($mil.)	6.1%	–	6,826.9	7,110.5	7,807.8	8,155.7
Net income ($ mil.)	–	–	(59.3)	(306.9)	1,434.3	(0.7)
Market value ($ mil.)	–	–	–	–	–	–
Employees	–	–	–	–	–	13,000

THE JUDGE GROUP INC

151 S WARNER RD STE 100
WAYNE, PA 190872127
Phone: 610 667-7700
Fax: –
Web: www.judge.com

CEO: Martin Judge III
CFO: Robert Alessandrini
HR: –
FYE: September 30
Type: Private

The Judge Group is an international leader in business technology consulting, managed service and talent solutions, and learning and development. With over 30 locations across the United States, Canada, and India, Judge is proud to partner with the best and brightest companies in business today, including over 60 of the Fortune 100. The company offers IT consulting services, learning solutions, and talent staffing and executive search services. It provides workforce training and learning solutions, talent and executive search, and technology solutions to organizations in banking, financial services, insurance, healthcare, life sciences, government, manufacturing, and technology and telecommunications. Armed with an exciting business idea and a $2,000 loan, Martin E. Judge, Jr. founded The Judge Group in 1970 to help organizations find qualified engineering and management professionals.

	Annual Growth	09/17	09/18	09/19	09/20	09/22
Sales ($mil.)	13.6%	–	437.7	427.7	428.5	729.1
Net income ($ mil.)	30.4%	–	6.5	6.0	8.9	18.8
Market value ($ mil.)	–	–	–	–	–	–
Employees	–	–	–	–	–	7,000

THE JUILLIARD SCHOOL INC

60 LINCOLN CENTER PLZ
NEW YORK, NY 100236588
Phone: 212 799-5000
Fax: –
Web: www.juilliard.edu

CEO: –
CFO: –
HR: –
FYE: June 30
Type: Private

The Juilliard School educates some of the top performers from around the world. Students can earn undergraduate and graduate degrees in dance, drama, and music. The school also has an Evening Division that is geared toward working adults as well as a Pre-College Division that meets on Saturdays between September and May. Primarily a performing arts conservatory, the school also enriches the community through outreach and other special programs. Juilliard was founded in 1905 in Greenwich Village and took up residence at Lincoln Center in 1969. Famed alumni include William Hurt, Val Kilmer, Kevin Kline, Laura Linney, Winton Marsalis, Christopher Reeve, Ving Rhames, Nadja Salerno-Sonnenberg, and Robin Williams.

	Annual Growth	06/17	06/18	06/20	06/21	06/22
Sales ($mil.)	2.5%	–	108.5	140.6	127.7	119.6
Net income ($ mil.)	–	–	69.7	(3.7)	359.1	(33.8)
Market value ($ mil.)	–	–	–	–	–	–
Employees	–	–	–	–	–	550

THE KANE COMPANY

6500 KANE WAY
ELKRIDGE, MD 210756000
Phone: 410 799-3200
Fax: –
Web: –

CEO: –
CFO: –
HR: –
FYE: June 03
Type: Private

Many people do business in offices, but offices are business for The Kane Company. Through its subsidiaries, Kane moves office contents (Office Movers), stores office records (Office Archives), shreds offices records (Office Shredding) and installs office furniture (Office Installers). Another Kane unit offers third-party logistics services, including supply chain management and warehousing and distribution; an affiliate provides printing services. Kane, which operates from offices in Delaware, Maryland, New Jersey, and Virginia, has long relied on federal government agencies in the area as a major source of business. The company was founded in 1969.

	Annual Growth	12/06	12/07	12/08	12/10*	06/15
Sales ($mil.)	(34.0%)	–	1,627.5	81.8	56.2	58.2
Net income ($ mil.)	286.2%	–	0.0	1.7	1.1	2.0
Market value ($ mil.)	–	–	–	–	–	–
Employees	–	–	–	–	–	1,500

*Fiscal year change

THE KENNETH T AND EILEEN L NORRIS FOUNDATION

11 GOLDEN SHORE STE 450
LONG BEACH, CA 908024274
Phone: 562 435-8444
Fax: –
Web: www.norrisfoundation.org

CEO: –
CFO: –
HR: –
FYE: November 30
Type: Private

The Norris Foundation awards grants in five categories: community, culture and the arts, education and science, medicine, and youth. The organization provides funding primarily for organizations in Southern California; it was the largest benefactor for the development of the USC/Norris Comprehensive Cancer Center. Other grant recipients include Midnight Mission (fighting homelessness), the Museum of the American West, and TreePeople (sponsoring its campus forestry and education program). Kenneth and Eileen Norris -- founders of manufacturing firm Norris Industries -- established the foundation in 1963.

	Annual Growth	11/11	11/12	11/13	11/14	11/15
Sales ($mil.)	3.5%	–	–	5.4	9.2	5.8
Net income ($ mil.)	–	–	–	(3.1)	(0.0)	(4.0)
Market value ($ mil.)	–	–	–	–	–	–
Employees	–	–	–	–	–	5

THE KEYW HOLDING CORPORATION

7740 MILESTONE PKWY STE 400
HANOVER, MD 210762289
Phone: 443 733-1600
Fax: -
Web: www.keywcorp.com

CEO: -
CFO: -
HR: -
FYE: December 31
Type: Private

KeyW is a key player in US cybersecurity with its eyes focused on the intelligence community. Operating through contractor KeyW Corp. and its subsidiaries including Sotera Defense, the company is an IT contractor to the federal government. Its capabilities include cyber operations and training; geospatial intelligence; cloud and data analytics; engineering; and intelligence analysis and operations. Customers include US government intelligence and defense agencies like the National Security Agency and the FBI and agencies in US Department of Defense. Some 95% of the company's revenue comes from the US government. KeyW agreed to an $815 million acquisition offer from Jacobs Engineering Group in 2019.

THE KLEINFELDER GROUP INC

770 1ST AVE STE 400
SAN DIEGO, CA 921016171
Phone: 619 831-4600
Fax: -
Web: www.kleinfelder.com

CEO: Louis Armstrong
CFO: Erik Soderquist
HR: -
FYE: March 31
Type: Private

The Kleinfelder Group is one of the leading engineering, design, construction management, construction materials inspection and testing, and environmental professional services groups in the US. Kleinfelder's operating subsidiaries offer construction materials engineering and testing, geotechnical engineering, construction management, design and environmental services. With over 100 domestic offices and locations in Australia and Canada, the group targets the energy, transportation, water, facilities, and government markets, including marine ports and harbor, solar power, institutional, industrial water and wastewater, National Guard, U.S. Air Force, U.S. Army Corps of Engineers and the US Navy. Jim Kleinfelder founded the Kleinfelder Group in 1961.

THE KRYSTAL COMPANY

1455 LINCOLN PKWY E # 600
DUNWOODY, GA 303462209
Phone: 770 351-4500
Fax: -
Web: www.krystal.com

CEO: -
CFO: Carl Jakaitis
HR: -
FYE: June 30
Type: Private

The Krystal Company is a fast-food gem of the South. The company's chain of more than 360 restaurants are known for their petite, square hamburgers (what Northerners might call a slider). In addition, Krystal's menu features a larger-sized hamburger, chicken wings and sandwiches, chili dogs, and breakfast items. The company also sells its frozen burgers through grocery stores. The chain got its start in 1932 when R.B. Davenport Jr. and J. Glenn Sherrill opened up shop in Chattanooga, Tennessee. Private investment firm Argonne Capital Group acquired the chain in 2012.

THE LANCASTER GENERAL HOSPITAL

555 N DUKE ST
LANCASTER, PA 176022207
Phone: 717 544-5511
Fax: -
Web: www.lancastergeneralhealth.org

CEO: Jan L Bergen
CFO: -
HR: Kristina Lucia
FYE: June 30
Type: Private

Lancaster General Health (LGH), a flagship facility for Penn Medicine Lancaster General Health, is a 525-bed not-for-profit health system with a comprehensive network of care. LGH is the only accredited Level 1 Trauma Center in Lancaster County. In addition to a trauma surgeon onsite 24 hours a day and a dedicated operating room, Level 1 trauma centers offer access to a full spectrum of advanced medical and surgical specialists, as well as trauma research and physician residency programs. Its membership in Penn Medicine brings together the strengths of a world-renowned, not-for-profit academic medical center and a nationally recognized, not-for-profit community health care system.

	Annual Growth	06/14	06/15	06/16	06/21	06/22
Sales ($mil.)	6.4%	-	920.3	958.7	1,359.5	1,418.1
Net income ($ mil.)	2.0%	-	111.0	122.3	173.8	127.6
Market value ($ mil.)		-	-	-	-	-
Employees		-	-	-	-	7,000

THE LANE CONSTRUCTION CORPORATION

90 FIELDSTONE CT
CHESHIRE, CT 064101212
Phone: 203 235-3351
Fax: -
Web: www.laneconstruct.com

CEO: Ignacio Botella
CFO: -
HR: Alexa Matic
FYE: December 31
Type: Private

Lane likes people to be in the fast lane. For more than a century, the heavy civil contractor and its affiliates have been widening, paving, and constructing lanes for highways, bridges, runways, railroads, dams, and mass transit systems in the eastern and southern US. The group also produces bituminous and precast concrete and mines aggregates at plants and quarries in the northeastern, mid-Atlantic, and southern US. Additionally, it sells and leases construction equipment. Founded in 1902, Lane Construction has offices in more than 20 states and is owned by descendants of Lane and employees.

	Annual Growth	12/14	12/15	12/16	12/17	12/18
Sales ($mil.)	(8.7%)	-	1,115.4	1,196.8	1,476.3	847.9
Net income ($ mil.)		-	-	(16.1)	39.7	19.0	76.1
Market value ($ mil.)		-	-	-	-	-
Employees		-	-	-	-	3,500

THE LAYTON COMPANIES INC

9090 S SANDY PKWY
SANDY, UT 840706409
Phone: 801 568-9090
Fax: -
Web: www.laytonconstruction.com

CEO: David S Layton
CFO: Dallis Christensen
HR: Utah-Gerald Biesinger
FYE: December 31
Type: Private

The Layton Companies likes to keep its hand in a lot of construction pots. The holding company for Interior Construction Specialists and Layton Construction Company provides engineering and construction services for just about any kind of structure, from retail stores to hazardous waste incineration facilities. Founded in 1953, it has completed projects in some 25 states, although its primary focus is the West. Interior Construction Specialists provides interior build-outs and remodeling, while Layton Construction Company is dedicated to commercial construction. The company sold subsidiary CEntry Constructors & Engineers to Danish firm FLSmidth & Co. in 2008.

	Annual Growth	12/03	12/04	12/05	12/06	12/12
Sales ($mil.)	(74.9%)	-	-	648.3	577.1	0.0
Net income ($ mil.)	116.1%	-	-	0.0	-	0.0
Market value ($ mil.)		-	-	-	-	-
Employees		-	-	-	-	650

THE LEGAL AID SOCIETY INC

199 WATER ST FRNT 3
NEW YORK, NY 100383526
Phone: 212 577-3346
Fax: –
Web: www.legalaidnyc.org

CEO: Richard J Davis
CFO: –
HR: Joe Alexandre
FYE: June 30
Type: Private

Serving as a law firm for many of New York City's less fortunate residents, The Legal Aid Society represents people who could not otherwise afford a lawyer in civil, criminal, and juvenile rights cases. It also draws upon the work of investigators, social workers, and paralegals. The company advocates for the financial rights of New Yorkers, it also defend LGBTQ+ members from abuse and discrimination, and defend clients in trial. The Legal Aid Society was founded in 1876.

	Annual Growth	06/12	06/13	06/14	06/20	06/21
Sales ($mil.)	5.2%	–	217.8	224.7	330.8	327.4
Net income ($ mil.)	–	–	8.6	0.7	8.6	(6.9)
Market value ($ mil.)	–	–	–	–	–	–
Employees	–	–	–	–	–	1,600

THE LIFE IS GOOD COMPANY

51 MELCHER ST STE 901
BOSTON, MA 022101500
Phone: 617 867-8900
Fax: –
Web: www.lifeisgood.com

CEO: Albert A Jacobs
CFO: –
HR: –
FYE: December 31
Type: Private

Life certainly sounds good for brothers Bert and John Jacobs, who went from living in their van and subsisting on peanut butter and jelly sandwiches to running a $100-million-plus firm in just a few years. The Life is good co-founders sold T-shirts to college students up and down the East Coast before creating the firm's stick-figure mascot, Jake. Life is good got its official start in 1994 and, today, the unconventional company sells casual apparel (T-shirts, lounge pants, boxers) and accessories, caps, backpacks, jewelry, pet gear, and home goods through a handful of company-owned stores, its website, and through more than 4,500 specialty and sporting goods stores in the US, Canada, and 30 other countries.

	Annual Growth	12/05	12/06	12/07	12/08	12/19
Sales ($mil.)	6.2%	–	–	–	1.3	2.6
Net income ($ mil.)	–	–	–	–	–	0.5
Market value ($ mil.)	–	–	–	–	–	–
Employees	–	–	–	–	–	340

THE LIGHTSTONE GROUP LLC

460 PARK AVE RM 1300
NEW YORK, NY 100221861
Phone: 212 616-9969
Fax: –
Web: www.lightstonegroup.com

CEO: David Lichtenstein
CFO: Donna Brandin
HR: Marie McGarr
FYE: December 31
Type: Private

Like a beacon in the night, Lightstone will lead you to lodging, food, work, and more. The company invests in income-producing multifamily and commercial, mostly retail, real estate in the US. Lightstone owns more than 10,000 individual apartment units and some 20 million sq. ft. of commercial space, primarily in the Northeast, Southeast, and South. Subsidiary Beacon Management operates a portfolio of around 30 apartment communities. Chairman David Lichtenstein (German for "lightstone") founded The Lightstone Group in 1988.

THE LINUX FOUNDATION

548 MARKET ST PMB 57274
SAN FRANCISCO, CA 941045401
Phone: 415 723-9709
Fax: –
Web: www.linuxfoundation.org

CEO: Jim Zemlin
CFO: Lisbeth McNabb
HR: Teri Brooks
FYE: December 31
Type: Private

The Linux Foundation is dedicated to promoting the use of the Linux computer operating system in academia, the corporate world, and government. The company was formed in 2007 by the merger of Open Source Development Labs with the Free Standards Group. The Linux Foundation promotes and standardizes the Linux operating system by providing resources and services needed for open source development, including offering intellectual property protection for developers. The foundation operates the Linux.com Web site to provide information on Linux. Linux serves as an alternative to Microsoft's Windows operating system, on which most of the PCs in the world are based, and is derived from the UNIX operating system.

	Annual Growth	12/14	12/15	12/16	12/21	12/22
Sales ($mil.)	24.0%	–	39.3	61.1	140.0	177.1
Net income ($ mil.)	24.3%	–	3.7	9.4	26.2	17.0
Market value ($ mil.)	–	–	–	–	–	–
Employees	–	–	–	–	–	230

THE LONG & FOSTER COMPANIES INC

3975 FAIR RIDGE DR
FAIRFAX, VA 220332911
Phone: 703 653-8500
Fax: –
Web: www.longandfoster.com

CEO: Patrick Bain
CFO: Gregory J Cross
HR: Helina Dancer
FYE: December 31
Type: Private

As the nation's No. 1 independent real estate brand, Long & Foster has guided people home since 1968. The company offers brokerage firms, residential and commercial real estate, mortgage, settlement, insurance, property management, corporate relocation and vacation rental services. The company's flagship subsidiary, Long & Foster Real Estate, is one of the largest privately-owned real estate companies in the mid-Atlantic and Northeast regions, with more than 200 offices, primarily in the Washington, DC/Baltimore area. The real estate brokerage has more than 8,000 sales agents. Chairman P. Wesley Foster founded the company.

THE LOS ANGELES KINGS HOCKEY CLUB L P

800 W OLYMPIC BLVD
LOS ANGELES, CA 900151360
Phone: 888 546-4752
Fax: –
Web: www.nhl.com

CEO: –
CFO: –
HR: –
FYE: June 30
Type: Private

The Los Angeles Kings Hockey Club professional hockey team entered the National Hockey League in 1967. The franchise plays host at the Staples Center, which it shares with the title-laden Los Angeles Lakers basketball team. The Kings have made three appearances in the Stanley Cup Finals. The team won its first ever Stanley Cup in 2012 and then followed that up two years later by winning the Stanley Cup again in 2014. Denver billionaire Philip Anschutz and Los Angeles developer Edward Roski have owned the Kings since 1995. The partners also own the Staples Center and a minority stake in the Lakers.

THE MAIDS INTERNATIONAL LLC

9394 W DODGE RD STE 140
OMAHA, NE 681143326
Phone: 402 558-5555
Fax: –
Web: www.maids.com

CEO: –
CFO: –
HR: –
FYE: September 30
Type: Private

The Maids International franchises The Maids Home Services, a residential cleaning service. It serves more than 800 locations through some 160 franchise partners in the US and Canada. It promotes its 22-step Healthy Touch deep cleaning system, which lists the services the workers perform in every room -- from removing cobwebs, window-washing, and carpet cleaning, to disinfecting floors, changing furnace filters, and cleaning showers and tubs. In addition, its Web site provides articles on advice and tips for cleaning. CEO Daniel Bishop founded the company in 1979 and began franchising in 1980.

	Annual Growth	09/11	09/12	09/16	09/20	09/21
Sales ($mil.)	3.2%	–	12.5	16.2	–	16.6
Net income ($ mil.)	–	–	0.2	0.7	–	(0.7)
Market value ($ mil.)	–	–	–	–	–	–
Employees	–	–	–	–	–	350

THE MARCUS & MILLICHAP COMPANY

777 CALIFORNIA AVE
PALO ALTO, CA 943041179
Phone: 650 494-1400
Fax: –
Web: www.mmcrealestate.com

CEO: –
CFO: Alex Yamolinski
HR: –
FYE: December 31
Type: Private

If you've got several million burning a hole in your pocket, or you're looking to unload that old skyscraper, Marcus & Millichap can help. One of the largest commercial real estate brokers in the US (with about 75 offices), the firm focuses on investment brokerage and provides financing, research, and advisory services to both buyers and sellers. The company is organized into groups by property type, including shopping centers, apartments, office and industrial buildings, and distressed properties. Marcus & Millichap was one of the earliest brokerages to maintain a centralized database to link potential buyers and sellers. In 2013 the company went public, raising $72 million, which it will use for general corporate purposes.

THE MARINE MAMMAL CENTER

2000 BUNKER RD
SAUSALITO, CA 949652697
Phone: 415 339-0430
Fax: –
Web: www.marinemammalcenter.org

CEO: Jeffrey R Boehm
CFO: Marci Davis
HR: Teri Padilla
FYE: September 30
Type: Private

The Marine Mammal Center thinks we ought to help otters and work for whales. The not-for-profit group works from five locations to protect marine mammals and their environment along the northern California coast. Its programs include rescuing and treating about 1,000 injured, ill, or orphaned marine mammals annually and returning all healthy animals to their habitat. The center also works with scientists in Europe and South America in conducting research to better understand marine mammals and their environment. The center's educational programs reach more than 100,000 people each year and it publishes Release , a member newsletter. About 90% of funds go to programs. The Marine Mammal Center was founded in 1975.

	Annual Growth	09/14	09/15	09/16	09/19	09/22
Sales ($mil.)	13.7%	–	9.2	12.4	15.3	22.6
Net income ($ mil.)	58.9%	–	0.2	2.5	1.1	5.3
Market value ($ mil.)	–	–	–	–	–	–
Employees	–	–	–	–	–	50

THE MASSACHUSETTS GENERAL HOSPITAL

55 FRUIT ST
BOSTON, MA 021142696
Phone: 617 726-2000
Fax: –
Web: www.massgeneral.org

CEO: –
CFO: Laura Wysk
HR: –
FYE: September 30
Type: Private

Founded in 1811, Massachusetts General Hospital (Mass General), is the original and largest teaching hospital of Harvard Medical School. Mass General provides comprehensive primary care and medical specialty services to some 200,000 adult and pediatric patients in about 15 locations throughout Greater Boston. Its specialized medical departments include cancer, cardiology and heart surgery; neurology and neurosurgery; and diabetes and endocrinology. As a leading research facility, Mass General hosts a number of clinical drug and device trials and has an annual research budget of more than $1 billion.

	Annual Growth	09/12	09/13	09/14	09/20	09/21
Sales ($mil.)	5.1%	–	2,274.6	2,201.9	2,954.6	3,376.5
Net income ($ mil.)	49.2%	–	148.3	186.8	51.7	3,644.6
Market value ($ mil.)	–	–	–	–	–	–
Employees	–	–	–	–	–	10,156

THE MAUREEN AND MIKE MANSFIELD FOUNDATION

MANSFIELD LIBRARY
MISSOULA, MT 598120001
Phone: 406 243-2215
Fax: –
Web: www.mansfieldfdn.org

CEO: –
CFO: Elizabeth Oleson
HR: –
FYE: June 30
Type: Private

The Maureen and Mike Mansfield Foundation was established by its namesakes in 1983 to advance cooperation among the countries of Asia and the US through fellowships, publications, and other programs. Based in Washington, DC, the foundation also has offices in Japan and in Montana (during his career in public service Mike Mansfield was both an ambassador to Japan and a senator from Montana), where it also provides support to the Maureen and Mike Mansfield Center at the University of Montana. The foundation doesn't provide grants; rather, it receives support from individuals, corporations and charitable organizations.

	Annual Growth	06/17	06/18	06/19	06/20	06/22
Sales ($mil.)	(3.7%)	–	3.3	2.8	3.8	2.8
Net income ($ mil.)	–	–	(0.2)	(0.2)	0.7	(0.4)
Market value ($ mil.)	–	–	–	–	–	–
Employees	–	–	–	–	–	11

THE MCLEAN HOSPITAL CORPORATION

115 MILL ST
BELMONT, MA 024781048
Phone: 617 855-2000
Fax: –
Web: www.mcleanhospital.org

CEO: –
CFO: David A Lagasse
HR: –
FYE: September 30
Type: Private

The researchers and teachers at McLean Hospital are into heady topics. McLean Hospital, a major teaching facility of Harvard Medical School, provides mental and behavioral health services to the Boston, Massachusetts, area and surrounding communities. McLean is home to specialized programs for the research and treatment of psychiatric and neurological illnesses, including depression, bipolar and psychotic disorders, mood and anxiety disorders, substance abuse, eating disorders, geriatric mental illnesses, and child and adolescent psychiatric disorders. The hospital offers inpatient and residential care and a range of outpatient services. McLean is an affiliate of Partners HealthCare System.

	Annual Growth	09/13	09/14	09/15	09/20	09/21
Sales ($mil.)	8.4%	–	–	116.5	165.3	188.7
Net income ($ mil.)	–	–	–	3.0	(63.0)	(0.2)
Market value ($ mil.)	–	–	–	–	–	–
Employees	–	–	–	–	–	1,213

THE MEDICAL UNIVERSITY OF SOUTH CAROLINA

171 ASHLEY AVE
CHARLESTON, SC 294258908
Phone: 843 792-2123
Fax: -
Web: www.musc.edu

CEO: Stuart G Ames
CFO: Patrick Wamsley
HR: -
FYE: June 30
Type: Private

Established in 1824, the Medical University of South Carolina (MUSC) provides Charleston with a wide range of health-related services including medical care, training, and research. MUSC has more than 3,200 full- and part-time students and over 900 residents each year through its six schools, which cover dental medicine, graduate studies, health professions, medicine, nursing, and pharmacy. The MUSC Health organization includes the MUSC Medical Center in Charleston, which has some 2,700 beds and four additional hospital locations in development. For the 9th consecutive year, U.S. News & World Report named MUSC Health University Medical Center in Charleston the No. 1 hospital in South Carolina.

	Annual Growth	06/08	06/09	06/13	06/17	06/18
Sales ($mil.)	1.9%	-	836.5	780.9	914.1	992.5
Net income ($ mil.)	1.8%	-	3.5	26.0	9.1	4.1
Market value ($ mil.)	-	-	-	-	-	-
Employees	-	-	-	-	-	5,500

THE MEDICINES COMPANY

8 SYLVAN WAY
PARSIPPANY, NJ 070543801
Phone: 973 290-6000
Fax: -
Web: www.novartis.com

CEO: Mark Timney
CFO: Christopher J Visioli
HR: -
FYE: December 31
Type: Private

The Medicines Company will meet you at the hospital. The drug developer focuses on treatments used in acute care settings, including the ER, the surgical suite, and the cardiac catheterization lab. It aims to be a leader in the areas of acute cardiovascular care and surgery and perioperative care. Its marketed products include Angiomax, an anticoagulant used during coronary angioplasties; it also sells Brilinta. The Medicines Company has other compounds in various stages of development including cangrelor, an antiplatelet agent with possible use during cardiac catheterization, and antibiotic oritavancin.

THE MEMORIAL HOSPITAL

455 TOLL GATE RD
WARWICK, RI 028862759
Phone: 401 729-2000
Fax: -
Web: www.carenewengland.org

CEO: -
CFO: -
HR: -
FYE: September 30
Type: Private

The Memorial Hospital, known as Memorial Hospital of Rhode Island (MHRI), brings a reminder of good health to the residents of the Blackstone Valley, which encompasses parts of southern Massachusetts and northern Rhode Island. Founded in 1901, the not-for-profit hospital has some 300 beds and offers general medical and surgical care, as well as specialty services in oncology, cardiovascular care, orthopedics, and hernia treatment. It is also a teaching institution for Brown University's Warren Alpert Medical School. Through a handful of satellite clinics located throughout its service area, MHRI provides primary and preventive care. The hospital is part of Care of New England Health System.

	Annual Growth	09/10	09/11	09/12	09/13	09/15
Sales ($mil.)	(3.1%)	-	-	-	142.2	133.6
Net income ($ mil.)	-	-	-	-	(35.9)	(27.1)
Market value ($ mil.)	-	-	-	-	-	-
Employees	-	-	-	-	-	1,400

THE MEMORIAL HOSPITAL

750 HOSPITAL LOOP
CRAIG, CO 816258750
Phone: 970 824-9411
Fax: -
Web: www.memorialregionalhealth.com

CEO: John Rossfeld
CFO: Bryan Chalmers
HR: -
FYE: December 31
Type: Private

If you fall down while skiing near the town of Craig, Colorado, you might end up at The Memorial Hospital. The community medical center, which has 25 beds, provides acute health care services to the residents of Colorado's Moffat and Routt counties. Specialty services at The Memorial Hospital include emergency care, cardiac rehabilitation, physical therapy, nuclear medicine, diagnostic imaging, and women's health. Founded in 1949, the hospital was rebuilt in 2009.

	Annual Growth	12/09	12/10	12/14	12/20	12/21
Sales ($mil.)	6.9%	-	30.2	33.8	58.0	63.0
Net income ($ mil.)	110.9%	-	0.0	0.2	2.4	4.8
Market value ($ mil.)	-	-	-	-	-	-
Employees	-	-	-	-	-	200

THE MERCHANTS COMPANY LLC

1100 EDWARDS ST
HATTIESBURG, MS 394015511
Phone: 800 844-3663
Fax: -
Web: www.performancefoodservice.com

CEO: Andrew B Mercier
CFO: Jarrod Gray
HR: -
FYE: September 30
Type: Private

The Merchants Company, which does business as Merchants Foodservice, is a leading foodservice supplier that serves more than 6,000 customers in more than 10 states. From a handful of distribution warehouses in Alabama, Mississippi, and South Carolina, the company supplies a wide range of food and non-food items to restaurants, hospitals, retirement centers, and nursing homes. The company was founded in 1904 as Fain Grocery Company a wholesale grocery distributor, and changed its name to Merchants Company in 1927. It began focusing on foodservice distribution in 1982 and was acquired by family owned holding company Tatum Development in 1988.

	Annual Growth	09/06	09/07	09/08	09/10	09/11
Sales ($mil.)	18.5%	-	-	294.3	441.5	489.1
Net income ($ mil.)	24.2%	-	-	1.3	5.2	2.4
Market value ($ mil.)	-	-	-	-	-	-
Employees	-	-	-	-	-	500

THE METHODIST HOSPITAL

6565 FANNIN ST
HOUSTON, TX 770302892
Phone: 713 441-2340
Fax: -
Web: www.houstonmethodist.org

CEO: -
CFO: Kevin Burns
HR: Elizabeth Acevedo
FYE: December 31
Type: Private

Houston Methodist (formerly The Methodist Hospital) owns and operates eight Houston-area medical centers, including the flagship hospital, Houston Methodist Hospital, which has roughly 900 operating beds and is known for innovations in urology and neurosurgery, among other specialties. Other hospitals include Houston Methodist Baytown, Houston Methodist Clear Lake, Houston Methodist Sugar Land, Houston Methodist The Woodlands, Houston Methodist West, Houston Methodist Willowbrook, and Houston Methodist Continuing Care. The Houston Methodist Institute for Technology, Innovation and Education (MITIE), Houston Methodist Hospital's 35,000-square-foot surgical training center and virtual hospital, provides ongoing physician education and surgical training in the latest techniques and technologies.

	Annual Growth	12/16	12/17	12/18	12/21	12/22
Sales ($mil.)	(5.7%)	-	3,887.3	4,496.7	2,451.7	2,895.5
Net income ($ mil.)	(17.0%)	-	531.5	291.3	249.1	208.8
Market value ($ mil.)	-	-	-	-	-	-
Employees	-	-	-	-	-	15,000

THE METHODIST HOSPITALS, INC.

600 GRANT ST
GARY, IN 464026001
Phone: 219 886-4000
Fax: –
Web: www.methodisthospitals.org

CEO: Ian E McFadden
CFO: John C Diehl
HR: Kurt Meyer
FYE: December 31
Type: Private

The Methodist Hospitals, Inc., is a not-for-profit, community-based health care system that provides medical care to Indiana residents. More than 580 physicians representing some 60 specialties serve its two campus hospitals which have a combined total of about 640 beds. The system provides care for a range of specialized areas from neurology and neurosurgery, oncology, and home health and hospice to rehabilitation and orthopedics. The emergency department treats more than 59,000 patients a year. The system also provides screenings, charitable care, and community education programs. The Methodist Hospitals, established in 1923, reinvests all of its profits to improve patient care.

THE METROHEALTH SYSTEM

2500 METROHEALTH DR
CLEVELAND, OH 441091900
Phone: 216 398-6000
Fax: –
Web: www.metrohealth.org

CEO: –
CFO: –
HR: –
FYE: December 31
Type: Private

Founded in 1837, MetroHealth System is redefining health care by going beyond medical treatment to improve the foundations of community health and well-being: affordable housing, a cleaner environment, economic opportunity and access to fresh food, convenient transportation, legal help and other services. MetroHealth has an academic medical center to research and for teaching and caregivers. Each active physicians holds an appointment at Case Western Reserve University Schools of Medicine. Its main campus hospital houses the Cleveland Metropolitan School District's Lincoln-West School of Science & Health, the only high school in America located inside a hospital.

	Annual Growth	12/07	12/08	12/09	12/13	12/15
Sales ($mil.)	4.7%	–	–	673.5	813.1	888.4
Net income ($ mil.)	(7.1%)	–	–	58.3	41.8	37.4
Market value ($ mil.)	–	–	–	–	–	–
Employees	–	–	–	–	–	7,700

THE METROPOLITAN MUSEUM OF ART

1000 5TH AVE
NEW YORK, NY 100280198
Phone: 212 535-7710
Fax: –
Web: www.metmuseum.org

CEO: James R Houghton
CFO: –
HR: –
FYE: June 30
Type: Private

You won't find too much about a certain New York baseball team at this Met. One of the world's premier cultural institutions, The Metropolitan Museum of Art (also known as "the Met") acquires and exhibits artwork from around the world. Its collection of more than 2 million pieces ranges from the prehistoric era to the present day. In addition to hosting exhibits, the Met loans artwork to other museums, publishes books and catalogs, and develops educational programs. It also displays art online. The City of New York owns the museum's 2 million-sq.-ft. complex, which is located on the east side of Central Park; the museum itself owns its art collection. The Met was founded in 1870.

	Annual Growth	06/16	06/17	06/18	06/19	06/20
Sales ($mil.)	(8.1%)	–	–	369.3	370.4	311.7
Net income ($ mil.)	–	–	–	237.7	63.1	(57.1)
Market value ($ mil.)	–	–	–	–	–	–
Employees	–	–	–	–	–	2,547

THE MICHAELS COMPANIES INC

3939 W JOHN CARPENTER FWY
IRVING, TX 750632909
Phone: 972 409-1300
Fax: –
Web: www.michaels.com

CEO: Ashley Buchanan
CFO: Michael Diamond
HR: Connie Tippett
FYE: February 01
Type: Private

The Michaels Companies is one of North America's leading arts and crafts retailers with approximately 1,275 Michaels stores across the country and in Canada. In addition to its retail outlets, the company also owns multiple brands that allow it to collectively provide arts, crafts, framing, floral, home d cor, and seasonal merchandise to hobbyists and do-it-yourself home decorators. It serves customers through digital platforms including Michaels.com and Michaels.ca. The company was founded in 1973.

	Annual Growth	02/17	02/18	02/19*	12/19*	02/20
Sales ($mil.)	(3.8%)	–	–	5,271.9	5,072.0	5,072.0
Net income ($ mil.)	(14.7%)	–	–	319.5	272.6	272.6
Market value ($ mil.)	–	–	–	–	–	–
Employees	–	–	–	–	–	45,000

*Fiscal year change

THE MIDDLE TENNESSEE ELECTRIC MEMBERSHIP CORPORATION

555 NEW SALEM HWY
MURFREESBORO, TN 371293390
Phone: 615 890-9762
Fax: –
Web: www.mte.com

CEO: –
CFO: Bernie Steen
HR: Angela F Jordan
FYE: December 31
Type: Private

Middle Tennessee Electric Membership Corporation's service territory is smack dab in the middle of Tennessee. The utility cooperative distributes electricity to 190,750 residential and business customers (member/owners) in four counties (Cannon, Rutherford, Williamson, and Wilson), via more than 10,470 miles of power lines connected to 34 electric distribution substations. Middle Tennessee Electric purchases its power supply from the Tennessee Valley Authority. The corporation is Tennessee's largest electric cooperative and the sixth largest in the US.

	Annual Growth	06/15	06/16*	12/19	12/21	12/22
Sales ($mil.)	9.9%	–	542.2	618.6	816.2	956.6
Net income ($ mil.)	–	–	10.1	–	–	–
Market value ($ mil.)	–	–	–	–	–	–
Employees	–	–	–	–	–	410

*Fiscal year change

THE MILL STEEL CO

2905 LUCERNE DR SE STE 100
GRAND RAPIDS, MI 495467160
Phone: 800 247-6455
Fax: –
Web: www.millsteel.com

CEO: Pam Heglund
CFO: Marc Rabitoy
HR: Debby Schaefer
FYE: December 31
Type: Private

Steel comes not only from steel mills, but also from Mill Steel. Service center operator Mill Steel processes and distributes flat-rolled carbon steel products to customers in North America through two locations in Michigan, Alabama, Texas, and Indiana. The company offers hot-rolled, cold-rolled, coil, aluminized, and galvanized products. Processing services include slitting, pickling, round edge conditioning, metallurgical service and coil testing, and leveling and inspection. Mill Steel serves customers in the agriculture, appliance, automotive, construction, HVAC, and office furniture industries. Mill Steel was founded in 1959.

THE MITRE CORPORATION

202 BURLINGTON RD
BEDFORD, MA 017301420
Phone: 781 271-2000
Fax: –
Web: www.mitre.org

CEO: Alfred Grasso
CFO: Wilson Wang
HR: Julie Gravallese
FYE: October 05
Type: Private

A private, not-for-profit organization, the MITRE Corporation provides consulting, engineering, and technical research services primarily for agencies of the federal government. In addition to its two primary research facilities in Massachusetts and Virginia, MITRE also has additional sites across the country and around the world. It also manages several federally funded research and development centers serving organizations such as the Department of Defense, the Federal Aviation Administration, the Internal Revenue Service, and the Department of Veterans Affairs. MITRE was founded in 1958 by former MIT researchers.

	Annual Growth	10/04	10/05	10/06	10/07	10/08
Sales ($mil.)	10.9%	–	–	–	1,113.7	1,234.7
Net income ($ mil.)	(4.6%)	–	–	–	23.4	22.3
Market value ($ mil.)	–	–	–	–	–	–
Employees	–	–	–	–	–	7,000

THE MONARCH BEVERAGE COMPANY INC

2299 PERIMETER PARK DR STE 240
ATLANTA, GA 303411320
Phone: 404 262-4040
Fax: –
Web: www.monarchbeverages.com

CEO: Jacques Bombal
CFO: –
HR: –
FYE: December 31
Type: Private

The bubbly stuff just flies out of their factory. The Monarch Beverage Company makes the sports and energy beverages, including All Sport, which the company acquired from PepsiCo. Other brands sold by the company include Rush! Energy, Acute Fruit, CoMotion and NTrinsic. The company sold its Dad's Root Beer brand to Hedinger Brands and its Moxie brand to Cornucopia in 2007. Monarch Beverage's drinks are available worldwide, including in the countires of Brazil, Canada, China, France, the Ivory Coast, Mexico, Peru, South Africa, and the US. The company was founded in Atlanta in 1965.

THE MOORE COMPANY

36 BEACH ST
WESTERLY, RI 028912771
Phone: 401 596-2816
Fax: –
Web: www.themooreco.com

CEO: Dana Barlow
CFO: –
HR: Monica Coughlin
FYE: December 31
Type: Private

"The more the merrier" has proven to be a flexible business formula for rubber materials and elastic textiles manufacturer The Moore Company. The company's five manufacturing divisions stretch into a diversity of goods including tricot and satin wrap-knit elastic fabrics and narrow elastic for active wear to intimate apparel, plastic components used in boat manufacturing, separators for making batteries, and thin gauge rubber calendered elastics (elastic tape, thread, and rubber sheeting). The Moore Company operates through Darlington Fabrics, Fulflex, George C. Moore Company, Amer-Sil, and Moeller Marine Products. The family-owned company sold its ZED Instruments division to Swiss-based Luscher in 2004.

THE MORGANTI GROUP INC

100 RESERVE RD
DANBURY, CT 068105267
Phone: 203 743-2675
Fax: –
Web: www.morganti.com

CEO: Thamer Rushaidat
CFO: –
HR: –
FYE: December 31
Type: Private

Morganti is giganti when it comes to construction. The Morganti Group specializes in design/build construction services and project management, tackling such big projects as offices and other commercial buildings, schools, hospitals, airports, and wastewater treatment facilities. A few of its projects include the Key West International Airport, the Broward County Convention Center, and a distribution center for the US Postal Service. The company, which was founded in 1920, is a subsidiary of Athens-based construction conglomerate Consolidated Contractors Company (CCC). The Morganti Group operates primarily in the US from offices in Connecticut, Texas, North Carolina, New York, and Florida.

THE MOSES H CONE MEMORIAL HOSPITAL OPERATING CORPORATION

1200 N ELM ST
GREENSBORO, NC 274011004
Phone: 336 832-7000
Fax: –
Web: –

CEO: –
CFO: –
HR: Debbie Shelton
FYE: December 31
Type: Private

Cone Health (formerly Moses Cone Health System) serves patients in central North Carolina through five acute and specialty care hospitals with a total of more than 1,000 beds. Its facilities include Moses H. Cone Memorial Hospital, Wesley Long Community Hospital, Annie Penn Hospital, Moses Cone Behavioral Health Center, and the Women's Hospital of Greensboro. Specialty services include rehabilitation, cancer treatment, neurology, and heart and vascular care. The health care provider also operates outpatient clinics and nursing homes. Founded in 1911; its flagship hospital was named after textile giant Cone Denim's founder, Moses Cone (it was started in Cone's honor by his wife, Bertha Cone).

THE NATIONAL ALLIANCE TO END HOMELESSNESS INCORPORATED

1518 K ST NW FL 2
WASHINGTON, DC 200051269
Phone: 202 638-1526
Fax: –
Web: www.endhomelessness.org

CEO: Ann M Oliva
CFO: –
HR: –
FYE: December 31
Type: Private

This group wants to put roofs over the heads of the estimated 675,000 people who are homeless in America each night. The National Alliance to End Homelessness is dedicated to solving the problem of homelessness in every community. The organization works with around 5,000 public, private, and not-for-profit sectors in its plan to end homelessness in 10 years (or by 2010). The Alliance lobbies government, supports local assistance groups, and educates the public about the causes, effects, and solutions to homelessness. It also promotes best practices by sharing the programs that are working in communities. The Alliance was founded in 1983 as homelessness began to be a problem in the US.

	Annual Growth	12/17	12/18	12/19	12/21	12/22
Sales ($mil.)	21.2%	–	4.2	5.8	7.7	9.0
Net income ($ mil.)	–	–	(0.0)	1.4	3.3	3.7
Market value ($ mil.)	–	–	–	–	–	–
Employees	–	–	–	–	–	27

THE NATIONAL ASSOCIATION FOR THE EXCHANGE OF INDUSTRIAL RESOURCES INC

560 MCCLURE ST
GALESBURG, IL 614014286
Phone: 309 343-0704
Fax: –
Web: www.naeir.org

CEO: –
CFO: –
HR: –
FYE: June 30
Type: Private

The National Association for the Exchange of Industrial Resources (NAEIR) is like a modern day Robin Hood, without the stealing or tights. The non-profit organization collects excess inventory from corporations and distributes the merchandise to its members: schools, churches, and charities. Members pay a fee to join and shipping costs for the items, but the goods are free. Donations include office supplies, computer software, clothing, books, classroom materials, toys, and personal care products from donors including Microsoft, Kid Brands, and General Electric. NAEIR has 18,650 members and receives donations from several thousand corporations. Manufacturing executive Norbert Smith founded NAEIR in 1977.

	Annual Growth	06/13	06/14	06/15	06/19	06/20
Sales ($mil.)	6.5%	–	56.1	78.3	108.8	81.7
Net income ($ mil.)	–	–	(12.1)	(28.3)	8.6	(28.1)
Market value ($ mil.)	–	–	–	–	–	–
Employees	–	–	–	–	–	80

THE NATIONAL ASSOCIATION OF PROFESSIONAL BASEBALL LEAGUES INC

1641 COMMERCE AVE N
SAINT PETERSBURG, FL 337164205
Phone: 727 822-6937
Fax: –
Web: www.minorleaguebaseball.com

CEO: –
CFO: –
HR: –
FYE: December 31
Type: Private

National Association of Professional Baseball Leagues (NAPBL), better known as Minor League Baseball, steps up to the plate as the governing body for nearly 20 leagues and about 250 teams, ranging from the Hickory Crawdads to the Durham Bulls to the Savannah Sand Gnats. Each team in the minor leagues (generally classified as either Rookie, Class A, Class Double-A, or Class Triple-A) is affiliated with a team in Major League Baseball and is part of a farm system to develop players hoping to make it to "The Show." Minor League Baseball also helps rehab major league players who've been sent down to work out any kinks and get back in game shape.

	Annual Growth	12/07	12/08	12/12	12/13	12/15
Sales ($mil.)	64.9%	–	0.1	4.5	5.2	4.8
Net income ($ mil.)	78.8%	–	0.0	1.2	1.5	1.2
Market value ($ mil.)	–	–	–	–	–	–
Employees	–	–	–	–	–	50

THE NATIONAL FOOTBALL FOUNDATION AND COLLEGE HALL OF FAME INC

433 LAS COLINAS BLVD E STE 1130
IRVING, TX 750395581
Phone: 972 556-1000
Fax: –
Web: www.footballfoundation.org

CEO: Steve Hatchell
CFO: –
HR: –
FYE: December 31
Type: Private

The National Football Foundation & College Hall of Fame (NFF) is a member organization dedicated to promoting and developing the sport of amateur football. The foundation runs the College Football Hall of Fame in South Bend, Indiana, a museum celebrating elite college football players and coaches. It also tabulates and disseminates the weekly standings for college football's Bowl Championship Series; awards over $1 million in athletic scholarships annually; and, through its Play It Smart program, organizes mentoring for more than 10,000 at-risk youth and high school student athletes. Founded in 1947, the NFF has some 120 chapters and more than 12,000 members throughout the US.

	Annual Growth	12/16	12/17	12/18	12/19	12/22
Sales ($mil.)	(1.6%)	–	4.7	5.4	3.9	4.3
Net income ($ mil.)	–	–	1.7	2.0	(0.0)	(1.1)
Market value ($ mil.)	–	–	–	–	–	–
Employees	–	–	–	–	–	22

THE NATIONAL PARKS & CONSERVATION ASSOCIATION

777 6TH ST NW STE 700
WASHINGTON, DC 200013723
Phone: 202 223-6722
Fax: –
Web: www.npca.org

CEO: –
CFO: –
HR: Sasha Johnson
FYE: June 30
Type: Private

Purple mountain majesties and amber waves of grain -- that's the stuff the National Parks Conservation Association (NPCA) aims to protect. A private association that is both a partner and critic of the federal National Park Service and National Park Foundation, the NPCA is a nonpartisan, public advocacy organization whose mission is to educate the public about the parks, protect park resources, improve park funding, and ensure the high quality of visitors' experiences. The organization publishes National Parks magazine quarterly. Founded in 1919, the NPCA claims 300,000 members and 20-plus regional and field offices across the US.

	Annual Growth	06/18	06/19	06/20	06/21	06/22
Sales ($mil.)	1.0%	–	47.0	40.1	41.7	48.5
Net income ($ mil.)	(24.5%)	–	11.0	1.7	3.4	4.7
Market value ($ mil.)	–	–	–	–	–	–
Employees	–	–	–	–	–	102

THE NATORI COMPANY INCORPORATED

180 MADISON AVE FL 18
NEW YORK, NY 100165267
Phone: 424 275-6478
Fax: –
Web: www.natori.com

CEO: –
CFO: –
HR: –
FYE: December 31
Type: Private

Natori is a risk taker, intimate apparel maker, and, after more than 30 years in the lingerie business, still a ground-breaker. The company makes four branded collections: Josie Natori Collection, Josie, Cruz, and Josie Natori Couture. Its Natori lines are sophisticated, using silks and fine fabrics. Its Josie brand is playful, while Cruz is more relaxed; both are more loung-erie than lingerie. Natori's accessories include handbags and scarves. It distributes its under-wares across the US through major high-end department stores, such as Saks, Neiman Marcus, Bergdorf Goodman, Nordstrom, and Macy's. Former child prodigy pianist Josie Natori and her husband, Ken, own and operate the company.

THE NATURE CONSERVANCY

4245 FAIRFAX DR STE 100
ARLINGTON, VA 222031650
Phone: 703 841-5300
Fax: –
Web: www.nature.org

CEO: –
CFO: Stephen Howell
HR: Brian Martin
FYE: June 30
Type: Private

The Nature Conservancy is a global environmental nonprofit working to create a world where people and nature can thrive. The Conservancy conducts its activities throughout the US, Canada, Latin America, the Caribbean, Europe, Africa, Asia, and the Pacific. It preserves the diversity of Earth's wildlife by saving more than 125 million acres of land and over 100 marine areas in every US state and over 70 countries worldwide. The Nature Conservancy has grown to become one of the most effective and wide-reaching environmental organizations worldwide. The Nature Conservancy was founded in 1951.

	Annual Growth	06/12	06/13	06/14	06/16	06/19
Sales ($mil.)	2.4%	–	859.1	950.0	804.0	992.1
Net income ($ mil.)	1.7%	–	106.9	201.3	(8.7)	118.2
Market value ($ mil.)	–	–	–	–	–	–
Employees	–	–	–	–	–	3,400

THE NATURE'S BOUNTY CO

2100 SMITHTOWN AVE
RONKONKOMA, NY 117797347
Phone: 631 200-2000
Fax: –
Web: www.naturesbounty.com

CEO: –
CFO: –
HR: –
FYE: September 30
Type: Private

The Bountiful Company, a Nestl Health Science Company, is a pure play branded leader in global nutrition, living at the intersection of science and nature. As a manufacturer, marketer and seller of vitamins, minerals, herbal and other specialty supplements, and active nutrition products, the company is focused on enhancing the health and wellness of people's lives. Brands include Ester-C, Nature's Bounty, Balance, Solgar, Osteo Bi-Flex, and Sundown Naturals. Formerly The Nature's Bounty Co., The Bountiful Company was founded in 1971.

THE NAVSYS CORPORATION

14960 WOODCARVER RD
COLORADO SPRINGS, CO 809212370
Phone: 719 481-4877
Fax: –
Web: www.navsys.com

CEO: –
CFO: –
HR: –
FYE: September 24
Type: Private

From its home at the base of Colorado Rockies, NAVSYS helps you figure out where on earth you are. The company develops Global Positioning System (GPS) products for commercial and military applications, such as GPS receivers. It also produces inertial navigation systems and communications systems. The company works closely with the University of Colorado at Colorado Springs to develop and test products. NAVSYS uses field-programmable gate arrays, configurable chips that can be changed on the fly by engineers, made by Xilinx. The company was founded in 1986 by CEO and top shareholder Dr. Alison Brown.

	Annual Growth	09/03	09/04	09/05	09/09	09/10
Sales ($mil.)	(1.7%)	–	–	7.4	5.9	6.8
Net income ($ mil.)				(1.4)	1.0	0.5
Market value ($ mil.)	–	–	–	–	–	–
Employees	–	–	–	–	–	30

THE NEAD ORGANIZATION

187 E UNION AVE
EAST RUTHERFORD, NJ 070732123
Phone: 201 460-5200
Fax: –
Web: www.neadorganization.com

CEO: –
CFO: –
HR: –
FYE: December 31
Type: Private

Clients who "nead" electrical and communications contracting and engineering services in the Northeast might turn to The Nead Organization. The company provides electrical and engineering services through its Nead Electric New York/New Jersey subsidiary. Voice, data, and imaging system telecommunications services are offered through the subsidiary's Nead Technologies unit. Projects have included office, commercial, and industrial work mainly in the New York/New Jersey area. The Nead Organization operates office and warehousing facilities in Carlstadt, New Jersey; it also has an office in New York City.

THE NEBRASKA MEDICAL CENTER

987400 NEBRASKA MEDICAL CTR
OMAHA, NE 681980001
Phone: 402 552-2000
Fax: –
Web: www.nebraskamed.com

CEO: William S Dinsmoor
CFO: –
HR: –
FYE: June 30
Type: Private

Cornhuskers take note: If health care is what you seek, The Nebraska Medical Center aims to please. The not-for-profit health system provides tertiary care at two campuses in Omaha, University Hospital and Clarkson Hospital, that collectively house about 680 licensed beds. The medical center, the largest health care facility in Nebraska, is the primary teaching facility of the University of Nebraska Medical Center (UNMC). It also serves as a designated trauma facility for eastern Nebraska and western Iowa, and provides highly specialized care, including organ transplantation. Its Clarkson West Medical Center campus houses outpatient surgery facilities, an emergency room, and doctors' offices.

	Annual Growth	06/15	06/16	06/17	06/21	06/22
Sales ($mil.)	8.8%	–	1,119.2	1,389.4	1,852.7	1,855.9
Net income ($ mil.)	(7.0%)	–	60.9	74.4	173.3	39.3
Market value ($ mil.)	–	–	–	–	–	–
Employees	–	–	–	–	–	4,100

THE NEW HOME COMPANY INC

8501 N SCOTTSDALE RD STE 280
PARADISE VALLEY, AZ 852532759
Phone: 949 382-7800
Fax: –
Web: www.newhomeco.com

CEO: Matthew R Zaist
CFO: –
HR: –
FYE: December 31
Type: Private

The New Home Company (TNHC) is the top 2 of overall homebuyer satisfaction, as well as America's top builder company. The New Home Company is a new generation homebuilder focused on the design, construction and sale of innovative and consumer-driven homes in major metropolitan areas within select growth markets in California, Arizona and Colorado, including coastal Southern California, the San Francisco Bay area, metro Sacramento, Phoenix, and Denver.

THE NEW JERSEY TRANSIT CORPORATION

1 PENN PLZ E
NEWARK, NJ 071052245
Phone: 973 491-7000
Fax: –
Web: www.njtransit.com

CEO: –
CFO: William Viqueira
HR: Daniel Isiwele
FYE: June 30
Type: Private

Government-owned New Jersey Transit (NJ TRANSIT) is the nation's third largest provider of bus, rail, and light rail passenger transportation services. Its systems connect major points in New Jersey and provide links to the neighboring New York City and Philadelphia metropolitan areas. Overall, the NJ TRANSIT service area spans about 5,325 sq. miles. One of the largest transportation companies of its kind in the US, NJ TRANSIT operates a fleet of around 2,220 buses, approximately 1,230 trains, and about 95 light rail vehicles. Collectively, the agency's passengers make nearly 270 million trips a year. NJ TRANSIT also administers several publicly funded transit programs for people with disabilities, senior citizens and people living in the state's rural areas who have no other means of transportation.

	Annual Growth	06/01	06/02	06/03	06/04	06/18
Sales ($mil.)	4.2%	–	–	569.1	583.3	1,056.3
Net income ($ mil.)	–	–	–	482.1	256.9	(67.6)
Market value ($ mil.)	–	–	–	–	–	–
Employees	–	–	–	–	–	1,000

THE NEW LIBERTY HOSPITAL DISTRICT OF CLAY COUNTY MISSOURI

2525 GLENN HENDREN DR
LIBERTY, MO 640689625
Phone: 816 781-7200
Fax: –
Web: www.libertyhospital.org

CEO: Raghu Adiga
CFO: –
HR: Julie McAnally
FYE: June 30
Type: Private

New Liberty Hospital District, which operates as Liberty Hospital, hopes to liberate health care patients in northwestern Missouri. The facility is a 250-bed acute care hospital that serves communities located north of Kansas City. Founded in 1974, Liberty Hospital offers general and specialty health care services including trauma care, obstetrics, cancer care, diagnostics, surgical services, vascular and cardiac medicine (including open-heart surgery), rehabilitation, and pediatrics. The not-for-profit medical facility has more than 300 physicians on staff and also operates a skilled nursing facility and offers home health and hospice services.

	Annual Growth	06/15	06/16	06/17	06/18	06/19
Sales ($mil.)	7.7%	–	179.7	185.5	196.3	224.4
Net income ($ mil.)	–	–	2.1	(1.8)	(5.9)	(15.3)
Market value ($ mil.)	–	–	–	–	–	–
Employees	–	–	–	–	–	1,700

THE NEW SCHOOL

66 W 12TH ST
NEW YORK, NY 100118603
Phone: 212 229-5600
Fax: –
Web: www.newschool.edu

CEO: –
CFO: –
HR: Annaka Olsen
FYE: June 30
Type: Private

When James Lipton asks you what your favorite swear word is, you know you've made it. The New School's drama department (formerly called The Actor's Studio) was made famous by the cable show Inside the Actors Studio, which features Lipton interviewing movie and television stars. The school offers degrees in theater for playwriting, directing, and acting, and has taught "Method" acting to grads such as Marlon Brando and Robert De Niro. It is also home to Parsons The New School for Design and has schools devoted to general studies, liberal arts, social research, management and urban policy, and music. More than 10,500 traditional students and 5,600 continuing education students are enrolled at The New School.

	Annual Growth	06/18	06/19	06/20	06/21	06/22
Sales ($mil.)	47.8%	–	–	–	319.1	471.5
Net income ($ mil.)	–	–	–	–	29.6	(35.7)
Market value ($ mil.)	–	–	–	–	–	–
Employees	–	–	–	–	–	855

THE NEW YORK AND PRESBYTERIAN HOSPITAL

525 E 68TH ST
NEW YORK, NY 100654870
Phone: 212 746-5454
Fax: –
Web: www.nyp.org

CEO: Herbert Pardes
CFO: Phyllis R Lantos
HR: –
FYE: December 31
Type: Private

The New York and Presbyterian Hospital is one of the most comprehensive, integrated academic health care delivery systems, and affiliated with two renowned medical schools, Weill Cornell Medicine and Columbia University of Vagelos College of Physician and Surgeons, New Presbyterian is consistently recognized as leader of medical education, groundbreaking research, and innovative, patient-centered clinical care. New York and Presbyterian Hospital have 2,600 beds, 6,500 affiliated physicians, and four major division: New York and Presbyterian Hospital, NewYork-Presbyterian Regional Hospital Network, NewYork-Presbyterian Physician Services, and NewYork-Presbyterian Community and Population Health. Formed in 1998 by the merger of The New York Hospital and The Presbyterian Hospital.

	Annual Growth	12/17	12/18	12/20	12/21	12/22
Sales ($mil.)	6.0%	–	8,483.9	9,115.1	9,859.5	10,728
Net income ($ mil.)	–	–	526.7	(382.6)	1,578.2	(39.1)
Market value ($ mil.)	–	–	–	–	–	–
Employees	–	–	–	–	–	23,709

THE NEW YORK INDEPENDENT SYSTEM OPERATOR INC

10 KREY BLVD
RENSSELAER, NY 121449681
Phone: 518 356-6000
Fax: –
Web: www.nyiso.com

CEO: –
CFO: –
HR: –
FYE: December 31
Type: Private

The New York Independent System Operator (New York ISO). The company, which replaced the New York Power Pool, manages and monitors wholesale activities on the state's transmission grid, which consists of more than 11,000 miles of high-voltage lines. The New York ISO is charged with providing fair access to the state's competitive wholesale power market while ensuring the reliable, efficient, and safe delivery of power to New York's 20.2 million residents. The not-for-profit company is governed by board of directors, as well as a committee structure consisting of market participant representatives.

THE NEW YORK PUBLIC LIBRARY

5TH AVE & 42ND ST
NEW YORK, NY 10018
Phone: 212 592-7400
Fax: –
Web: shop.nypl.org

CEO: Anthony Marx
CFO: –
HR: –
FYE: June 30
Type: Private

Q: Where can you learn the names of the marble lions outside New York Public Library's main branch? A: Inside the library, where Patience and Fortitude (their names), along with much more information, can be found. The library's four research centers and about 90 branches in metropolitan New York contain more material than any other library in the US -- about 50 million items. Each year more than 18 million people visit the library's branches, which house such treasures as a Gutenberg Bible and a hand-engraved Songs of Innocence. The library was formed by the 1895 consolidation of the Astor Library, the Lenox Library, and the Tilden Trust and by a merger with the New York Free Circulating Library in 1901.

	Annual Growth	06/07	06/08	06/09	06/16	06/17
Sales ($mil.)	(0.8%)	–	–	362.9	300.5	341.0
Net income ($ mil.)	–	–	–	(166.3)	(93.1)	25.0
Market value ($ mil.)	–	–	–	–	–	–
Employees	–	–	–	–	–	3,645

THE NEWTRON GROUP L L C

8183 W EL CAJON DR
BATON ROUGE, LA 708158093
Phone: 225 927-8921
Fax: –
Web: www.thenewtrongroup.com

CEO: Newton B Thomas
CFO: Tami H Misuraca
HR: –
FYE: June 30
Type: Private

The Newtron Group is one of the largest privately-owned Specialty Electrical Construction companies in the US and is among the nation's leading Industrial Electrical and Instrumentation providers. Through subsidiaries, The Newtron Group offers a suite of innovative and customized Analytical, Automation, Heat Trace, Integration and Design solutions for a wide range of industries. Subsidiaries include Triad Electric & Controls and Triad Control Systems. Founded in 1973, The Newtron Group serves the US from offices in California, Louisiana, Nevada, and Texas.

	Annual Growth	06/16	06/17	06/18	06/19	06/20
Sales ($mil.)	1.3%	–	450.0	489.9	622.9	468.1
Net income ($ mil.)	–	–	–	–	–	–
Market value ($ mil.)	–	–	–	–	–	–
Employees	–	–	–	–	–	3,500

THE NORTH HIGHLAND COMPANY LLC

3333 PIEDMONT RD NE STE 1000
ATLANTA, GA 303051843
Phone: 404 233-1015
Fax: –
Web: www.northhighland.com

CEO: –
CFO: Beth Schiavo
HR: –
FYE: December 31
Type: Private

The North Highland Company makes change happen, helping businesses transform, with people at the heart of every decision. The employee-owned company provides management and technology consulting services through more than 5,000 consultants working out of over 65 offices around the globe. Its services include data & analytics, change management, process & business analysis, and program & project management, among others. North Highland is a member of Cordence Worldwide, a global management consulting alliance.

	Annual Growth	12/02	12/03	12/04	12/05	12/08
Sales ($mil.)	30.2%	–	–	59.5	87.3	170.9
Net income ($ mil.)	(38.8%)	–	–	57.4	2.3	8.0
Market value ($ mil.)	–	–	–	–	–	–
Employees	–	–	–	–	–	2,300

THE NORTHERN ILLINOIS UNIVERSITY

1425 W LINCOLN HWY
DEKALB, IL 601152825
Phone: 815 753-9500
Fax: –
Web: www.niu.edu

CEO: –
CFO: –
HR: Laurie Johnson
FYE: June 30
Type: Private

From its roots as a normal school, Northern Illinois University (NIU) has branched out to offer higher education on a wide breadth of subjects. The university has an enrollment of about 15,505 students. It offers more than 100 undergraduate majors and more than 80 graduate programs in fields ranging from education and business to engineering and law. Courses are offered at NIU's more than 40 schools and departments within seven colleges. The university has about 1,040 international students from nearly 75 different countries. Founded in 1895, the university has more than 1,230 faculty members and boasts a student-to-faculty ratio of 15:1.

	Annual Growth	06/17	06/18	06/19	06/20	06/21
Sales ($mil.)	(9.7%)	–	–	–	241.2	217.8
Net income ($ mil.)	–	–	–	–	(38.0)	(10.6)
Market value ($ mil.)	–	–	–	–	–	–
Employees	–	–	–	–	–	8,500

THE OCEAN CONSERVANCY INC

1300 19TH ST NW STE 800
WASHINGTON, DC 200361653
Phone: 202 429-5609
Fax: –
Web: www.oceanconservancy.org

CEO: –
CFO: –
HR: –
FYE: June 30
Type: Private

The Ocean Conservancy prefers its fish wild, thanks. The not-for-profit organization strives to protect the oceans and its wildlife. The group's some 500,000 members work toward the goal of "wild, healthy oceans" by targeting artificial reef building, cruise ships, marine protected areas, overfishing, runoff pollution, and whaling. The Ocean Conservancy also publishes the quarterly Blue Planet magazine and hosts activities like the International Coastal Cleanup, Adopt-A-Reef, the Marine Debris Study, and Storm Drain Sentries. It has also lead the campaign to restore the Gulf of Mexico after the 2010 BP Deepwater Horizon oil spill. The Ocean Conservancy was founded in 1972 to protest commercial whaling.

	Annual Growth	06/16	06/17	06/18	06/20	06/22
Sales ($mil.)	15.0%	–	24.7	37.4	33.8	49.7
Net income ($ mil.)	63.8%	–	0.7	11.4	1.7	8.8
Market value ($ mil.)	–	–	–	–	–	–
Employees	–	–	–	–	–	95

THE OGDEN NEWSPAPERS INC

1500 MAIN ST
WHEELING, WV 260032826
Phone: 304 233-0100
Fax: –
Web: www.ogdennews.com

CEO: Robert M Nutting
CFO: –
HR: –
FYE: December 31
Type: Private

Despite its name, newspapers aren't the only game for this company. Ogden Newspapers is a leading publisher with more than 40 daily papers serving mostly small markets in about 15 states. Its portfolio includes The Messenger (Fort Dodge, Iowa), The News-Sentinel (Fort Wayne, Indiana), and the Wheeling News-Register (West Virginia). Ogden Newspapers also publishes several weeklies and a magazine division H.C. Ogden founded the Wheeling News in 1890. His descendents, the Nutting family, continue to control the business.

THE OLTMANS CONSTRUCTION CO

10005 MISSION MILL RD
WHITTIER, CA 906011739
Phone: 562 948-4242
Fax: –
Web: www.oltmans.com

CEO: Joseph O Oltmans II
CFO: Dan Schlothan
HR: Chris Goelz
FYE: December 31
Type: Private

With projects ranging from the California Speedway to a distribution/warehouse building for TV retail giant HSN, Oltmans Construction has done it all. The group offers preconstruction, general contracting and design/build project delivery, construction management, tenant improvements, and seismic retrofits among its services for commercial and industrial buildings throughout California, Nevada, and Arizona. The company also completes its own concrete work. Oltmans is one of the top general contractors in its home state, as well as one of the top builders of distribution facilities in the US. The company was founded in 1932 and has been led by three generations of the Oltmans family.

	Annual Growth	03/05	03/06	03/07	03/08*	12/21
Sales ($mil.)	(39.9%)	–	317.3	315.5	326.3	0.2
Net income ($ mil.)	–	–	3.5	4.2	5.1	(0.4)
Market value ($ mil.)	–	–	–	–	–	–
Employees	–	–	–	–	–	535

*Fiscal year change

THE OPTIONS CLEARING CORPORATION

125 S FRANKLIN ST STE 1200
CHICAGO, IL 606064601
Phone: 312 322-6200
Fax: –
Web: www.optionseducation.org

CEO: Wayne P Luthringshausen
CFO: Frank J Larocca
HR: –
FYE: December 31
Type: Private

The Options Clearing Corporation (OCC) is the world's largest equity derivatives clearinghouse. The corporation clears transactions for call and put options on equities, stock indices, foreign currencies, and interest rate products. It also performs clearing and settlement services on futures, options on futures, and securities lending transactions. The OCC serves about 120 members, including broker-dealers, US futures commission merchants, and foreign securities firms. It handles some 4.5 billion transactions annually. Participating exchanges include Chicago Board Options Exchange, Nasdaq OMX, Nasdaq OMX PHLX, and NYSE Amex.

THE PARADIES SHOPS LLC

2849 PACES FERRY RD SE STE 400
ATLANTA, GA 303396201
Phone: 404 344-7905
Fax: –
Web: www.paradieslagardere.com

CEO: –
CFO: –
HR: –
FYE: June 30
Type: Private

Paradies Lagard re (formerly The Paradies Shops), the nation's leading travel retailer and restaurateur, brings experience and best practices in delivering engaging traveler experiences. It operates approximately 1,020 stores and restaurants in more than 100 airports. The company works closely with airports to tailor their program and brings popular brands that elevate their retail offerings in the categories of fashion, luxury, electronics, convenience, sports, luggage, jewelry, souvenirs, and duty free. Paradies is also an exclusive licensee of Brooks Brothers, NBC's Today, TripAdvisors, P.F. Chang's, and Chick-fil-A. It also partners with celebrity chefs such as Cat Cora and Michael Symon. The company was founded by the Paradies family in 1960.

	Annual Growth	06/00	06/01	06/02	06/03	06/07
Sales ($mil.)	10.8%	–	–	223.1	248.0	372.7
Net income ($ mil.)	–	–	–	–	–	13.7
Market value ($ mil.)	–	–	–	–	–	–
Employees	–	–	–	–	–	4,000

THE PARTNERSHIP FOR NEW YORK CITY INC

1 BATTERY PARK PLZ FL 5
NEW YORK, NY 100041464
Phone: 212 493-7400
Fax: –
Web: www.pfnyc.org

CEO: Rich Parsons
CFO: Alice Gleason
HR: –
FYE: December 31
Type: Private

The Partnership for New York City is a group of business leaders pledged to work for the economic and cultural betterment of all five boroughs. To achieve its goal of maintaining New York City's position as the global center of commerce, culture, and innovation, it conducts research, participates in policy making, lobbies government, and invests in economic development efforts. Its many partners include American Express, Con Edison, Macys, Tiffany & Co. The group was formed in 2002 from a combination of two already-affiliated organizations with complementary missions: the New York City Partnership, founded by David Rockefeller in 1979, and the New York Chamber of Commerce and Industry, which was formed in 1768.

THE PENNSYLVANIA HOSPITAL OF THE UNIVERSITY OF PENNSYLVANIA HEALTH SYSTEM

800 SPRUCE ST
PHILADELPHIA, PA 191076130
Phone: 215 829-3000
Fax: –
Web: www.pennmedicine.org

CEO: –
CFO: –
HR: Jana Romano
FYE: June 30
Type: Private

Early to bed, early to rise may have made Ben Franklin healthy, wealthy, and wise. But for those not so healthy, he (along with Dr. Thomas Bond) found it wise to establish Pennsylvania Hospital, the nation's first such medical institution. The hospital is now a part of the University of Pennsylvania Health System (UPHS) and offers a comprehensive range of medical, surgical, and diagnostic services to the Philadelphia County area. Housing some 520 beds, Pennsylvania Hospital offers specialized care in areas such as orthopedics, vascular surgery, neurosurgery, and obstetrics; it is also a leading teaching hospital and a center for clinical research.

	Annual Growth	06/09	06/10	06/14	06/15	06/20
Sales ($mil.)	3.4%	–	485.5	534.4	579.8	678.1
Net income ($ mil.)	(20.8%)	–	27.5	(2.3)	21.7	2.7
Market value ($ mil.)	–	–	–	–	–	–
Employees	–	–	–	–	–	2,200

THE PENNSYLVANIA STATE UNIVERSITY

201 OLD MAIN
UNIVERSITY PARK, PA 168021503
Phone: 814 865-4700
Fax: –
Web: www.psu.edu

CEO: –
CFO: –
HR: Carol Eicher
FYE: June 30
Type: Private

The Pennsylvania State University (Penn State) is one of the top of the world universities. Penn State has an enrollment of about 88,100 students. It offers more than 275 undergraduate programs at some 25 campuses. It operates two law schools ? Dickinson Law (in Carlisle, Pennsylvania) and Penn State Law (on the University Park campus). The university's oldest and largest campus, with about half of the system's undergraduate students, is at University Park in central Pennsylvania. Other sites include the Penn State College of Medicine in Hershey, Pennsylvania, and the Dickinson School of Law in Carlisle, Pennsylvania.

	Annual Growth	06/18	06/19	06/20	06/21	06/22
Sales ($mil.)	6.2%	–	6,576.5	6,795.9	7,275.6	7,867.4
Net income ($ mil.)	–	–	583.9	(712.6)	2,444.9	(14.1)
Market value ($ mil.)	–	–	–	–	–	–
Employees	–	–	–	–	–	44,000

THE PENROD COMPANY

272 BENDIX RD STE 550
VIRGINIA BEACH, VA 234521393
Phone: 757 498-0186
Fax: –
Web: www.thepenrodcompany.com

CEO: Edward Heidt Jr
CFO: –
HR: –
FYE: December 31
Type: Private

Diversified distribution firm The Penrod Company imports and exports forest products for use in the hardwood plywood, flooring, and furniture industries worldwide. The company also distributes PVC products and metal door hinges and fasteners for use in the residential and commercial construction industries. Penrod operates through offices in the US, Canada, China, Brazil, and Africa. Around since 1888, Penrod has supplied materials for some iconic products such as Wurlitzer organs, Zenith television cabinets, and mahogany interiors for 1965 Cadillac and Buicks.

THE PEP BOYS - MANNY MOE & JACK

1 PRESIDENTIAL BLVD STE 400
BALA CYNWYD, PA 190041016
Phone: 215 430-9000
Fax: –
Web: www.pepboys.com

CEO: William Inhken
CFO: –
HR: –
FYE: February 01
Type: Private

The Pep Boys - Manny, Moe & Jack is one of the nation's leading automotive aftermarket chains. The company sells brand name and private label auto parts, and provides select services through more than 1,000 locations in the US and Puerto Rico. The Pep Boys operates some 9,000 service bays for automotive maintenance and repairs, inspections, and parts installations. It also offers quick service, towing program, and fleet management software solutions. Founded in 1921 by Philadelphians Manny, Moe, and Jack, Pep Boys is owned by billionaire investor Carl Icahn's Icahn Enterprises.

THE PEW CHARITABLE TRUSTS

2005 MARKET ST FL 28　　　　　　　　　　CEO: Susan Urahn
PHILADELPHIA, PA 191037019　　　　　　　CFO: –
Phone: 215 575-9050　　　　　　　　　　　HR: –
Fax: –　　　　　　　　　　　　　　　　　FYE: June 30
Web: www.pewtrusts.org　　　　　　　　　Type: Private

Green is the grease The Pew Charitable Trusts uses to help not-for-profits run smoothly. Among the nation's largest private foundations, it was established in 1948 in memory of Sun Oil founder Joseph Pew and his wife Mary by four of their children. Seven trusts were created between 1948 and 1979 to promote public health and welfare and to strengthen communities. With more than $5 billion in assets, it distributes more than $100 million in grants annually to charitable organizations in culture, education, environment, health and human services, public policy, and religion. The Pew Trusts has strong ties to Philadelphia and allocates a portion of its grants to programs in that area.

	Annual Growth	06/15	06/16	06/17	06/19	06/21
Sales ($mil.)	(2.9%)	–	397.1	708.5	373.9	343.5
Net income ($ mil.)	–	–	77.5	407.8	(23.7)	(4.3)
Market value ($ mil.)	–	–	–	–	–	–
Employees	–	–	–	–	–	1,100

THE PHARMACY AT CMC

300 SINGLETON RIDGE RD　　　　　　　　CEO: Philip A Clayton
CONWAY, SC 295269142　　　　　　　　　CFO: Bret Barr
Phone: 843 347-7111　　　　　　　　　　　HR: –
Fax: –　　　　　　　　　　　　　　　　　FYE: September 30
Web: www.conwaymedicalcenter.com　　　Type: Private

Conway Medical Center (CMC) finds a way to provide a wide range of health care services to residents of eastern South Carolina. The private, not-for-profit, 210-bed hospital (served by a medical staff of 200) provides services including primary, diagnostic, emergency, surgical, maternal and pediatric, and rehabilitative care. CMC specializes in heart health, hospice care, and occupational health. Additionally, CMC operates the Kingston Nursing Center, an about 90-bed long-term nursing and rehabilitative care facility and the Conway Physicians Group, which is home to about 10 physician practices offering a range of specialties.

	Annual Growth	09/13	09/14	09/19	09/20	09/21
Sales ($mil.)	3.3%	–	179.2	5.3	178.1	224.6
Net income ($ mil.)	0.8%	–	28.2	(1.6)	7.2	29.8
Market value ($ mil.)	–	–	–	–	–	–
Employees	–	–	–	–	–	1,200

THE PHILADELPHIA PARKING AUTHORITY

701 MARKET ST STE 5400　　　　　　　　CEO: Vincent J Fenerty Jr
PHILADELPHIA, PA 191062895　　　　　　CFO: Barry Kavtsty
Phone: 215 222-0224　　　　　　　　　　HR: Antonina Miller
Fax: –　　　　　　　　　　　　　　　　　FYE: March 31
Web: www.philapark.org　　　　　　　　　Type: Private

If you're driving into the City of Brotherly Love, steer clear of getting a parking ticket, because then you'll have to face the Philadelphia Parking Authority. The agency oversees 14,500 on-street metered parking spaces and 17,000 off-street facilities such as lots and garages throughout the city, including parking spaces at Philadelphia International Airport. In addition to collecting revenue, the agency enforces parking regulations by issuing tickets, and when necessary, disabling or towing and impounding vehicles. It also regulates taxi and limousine services and the 10 red light cameras operating within the city. The Philadelphia Parking Authority was created in 1950.

	Annual Growth	12/07	12/08*	03/10	03/17	03/19
Sales ($mil.)	3.0%	–	201.6	213.0	259.5	280.5
Net income ($ mil.)	7.2%	–	13.8	10.3	8.4	29.8
Market value ($ mil.)	–	–	–	–	–	–
Employees	–	–	–	–	–	1,100

*Fiscal year change

THE PHILHARMONIC-SYMPHONY SOCIETY OF NEW YORK INC

10 LINCOLN CENTER PLZ　　　　　　　　CEO: Zarin Mehta
NEW YORK, NY 100236912　　　　　　　　CFO: –
Phone: 212 875-5656　　　　　　　　　　HR: Kristen McKniff
Fax: –　　　　　　　　　　　　　　　　　FYE: August 31
Web: www.nyphil.org　　　　　　　　　　Type: Private

The New York Philharmonic fills up music halls with musical harmony. In addition to the music of Beethoven and Tchaikovsky, over the years the orchestra has performed the works of numerous other classical composers, along with specially commissioned new music. It presents some 180 concerts annually. The New York Philharmonic's musical director, Alan Gilbert, is the son of two of the orchestra's violinists and the second-youngest person to hold the position in its history. The New York Philharmonic was founded in 1842 and is the oldest orchestra in the US.

THE PLAZA GROUP, INC

1177 WEST LOOP S STE 1450　　　　　　　CEO: –
HOUSTON, TX 770279020　　　　　　　　CFO: –
Phone: 713 266-0707　　　　　　　　　　HR: –
Fax: –　　　　　　　　　　　　　　　　　FYE: September 25
Web: www.theplazagrp.com　　　　　　　Type: Private

The Plaza Group (TPG) is an international distributor of petrochemical solvents and chemical intermediates. Established in 1994, TPG is the exclusive marketer of some products from companies such as Shell Oil and Frontier Oil. The company markets to FORTUNE 500 companies, major international enterprises, direct consumers, and chemical distributors. Its products are used in the production of resins, coatings, and adhesives. TPG partners with global suppliers (like SABIC Innovative Plastics, Total Petrochemicals, and Alon) in Asia, Australia, Europe, and the Americas. The company is owned by president Randy Velarde.

THE PORT AUTHORITY OF NEW YORK & NEW JERSEY

4 WORLD TRADE CENTER 150 GREENWICH ST FL 23　　CEO: –
NEW YORK, NY 100070042　　　　　　　　CFO: Elizabeth McCarthy
Phone: 212 435-7000　　　　　　　　　　HR: –
Fax: –　　　　　　　　　　　　　　　　　FYE: December 31
Web: www.panynj.gov　　　　　　　　　　Type: Private

The Port Authority of New York and New Jersey builds, operates, and maintains many of the most important transportation and trade infrastructure assets in the country, through air, land, rail, and sea. The bi-state agency operates and maintains airports, tunnels, bridges, a commuter rail system, shipping terminals, and other facilities within the 1,500-sq.-mi. Port District surrounding New York Harbor, including the World Trade Center site in Lower Manhattan. Aviation operations account for the majority of its revenue. The two governors each appoint six of the 12 members of the agency's board and review its decisions.

THE POYNTER INSTITUTE FOR MEDIA STUDIES INC

801 3RD ST S
SAINT PETERSBURG, FL 337014920
Phone: 727 821-9494
Fax: -
Web: www.poynter.org

CEO: -
CFO: Jana Jones
HR: -
FYE: December 31
Type: Private

Reporters have to hold their questions and instead give the answers at The Poynter Institute, which provides seminars, workshops, and interactive courses for broadcast, print, and online journalists, as well as educators and students. In addition to reporting-focused courses, Poynter offers programs on ethics, design, photo and visual journalism, and leadership. The institute maintains a variety of resources, including a research library. Poynter owns the Times Publishing Company, which publishes the Florida-based St. Petersburg Times and its Washington affiliate, Congressional Quarterly. The institute was founded in 1975 by newspaper publisher Nelson Poynter.

	Annual Growth	12/15	12/16	12/19	12/21	12/22
Sales ($mil.)	16.6%	-	5.9	14.9	13.2	15.0
Net income ($ mil.)	(0.8%)	-	0.6	5.8	2.6	0.6
Market value ($ mil.)	-	-	-	-	-	-
Employees	-	-	-	-	-	3,260

THE PRESIDENT AND TRUSTEES OF COLBY COLLEGE

4120 MAYFLOWER HL
WATERVILLE, ME 049018841
Phone: 207 859-4000
Fax: -
Web: www.colby.edu

CEO: James B Crawford
CFO: -
HR: Danielle Cossio
FYE: June 30
Type: Private

Colby College is one of the nation's oldest liberal arts colleges. The school was founded in 1813 as the Maine Literary and Theological Institution, and in 1871 it became the first previously all-male college in New England to admit women. Colby College offers 500 courses, 55 majors, 30-plus minors, and independent major options. Its two dozen academic departments and nearly 10 interdisciplinary programs serve an enrollment of approximately 1,800 students. Popular majors are biology, economics, English, government, history, and international studies. Besides being one of the nation's oldest, Colby College is one of the most pricey: Annual tuition, room and board, and fees total more than $46,000.

	Annual Growth	06/18	06/19	06/20	06/21	06/22
Sales ($mil.)	5.5%	-	165.2	292.4	172.1	194.2
Net income ($ mil.)	-	-	83.2	80.1	389.7	(91.5)
Market value ($ mil.)	-	-	-	-	-	-
Employees	-	-	-	-	-	844

THE PUBLIC HEALTH TRUST OF MIAMI-DADE COUNTY

1611 NW 12TH AVE
MIAMI, FL 331361005
Phone: 305 585-1111
Fax: -
Web: www.jacksonhealth.org

CEO: Carlos A Migoya
CFO: Tony Gomez
HR: Rosa Ruiz
FYE: September 30
Type: Private

Jackson Memorial Hospital is the flagship facility of the Jackson Health System (JHS). It has roughly 1,150 beds and offers a wide variety of services, including burn treatment, trauma, pediatrics, rehabilitation, obstetrics, and transplants. The system also includes two neighborhood community hospitals? Jackson South, Jackson North, and Jackson West?along with Holtz Children's Hospital, Jackson Behavioral Health Hospital, the Christine E. Lynn Rehabilitation Center for The Miami Project to Cure Paralysis at UHealth/Jackson Memorial, two nursing homes and a network of UHealth/Jackson Urgent Care centers, physician practices, and clinics. Jackson Memorial Hospital and JHS are overseen by The Public Health Trust of Miami-Dade County.

THE RALPH M PARSONS FOUNDATION

888 W 6TH ST STE 700
LOS ANGELES, CA 900172733
Phone: 213 362-7600
Fax: -
Web: www.rmpf.org

CEO: Jennifer Price-Letscher
CFO: -
HR: -
FYE: December 31
Type: Private

After a life well lived, Ralph M. Parsons left Southern California just a little bit better off and ready to give back. With a focus on civic and cultural programs, health and higher education, and social impact programs, the foundation he established supports not-for-profit groups in Los Angeles County. The organization typically grants awards ranging from $25,000 to $50,000. Past recipients have included the National Audubon Society, Children's Hospital of Los Angeles, Southwestern University School of Law, and Echo Park Boys & Girls Club. Ralph Parsons, founder of engineering and construction firm Parsons, established the foundation in 1961, but the foundation has been independent of Parsons since 1976.

	Annual Growth	12/11	12/12	12/15	12/16	12/17
Sales ($mil.)	11.2%	-	16.9	23.6	-	28.8
Net income ($ mil.)	-	-	(7.5)	(0.7)	-	(0.3)
Market value ($ mil.)	-	-	-	-	-	-
Employees	-	-	-	-	-	8

THE RDW GROUP INC

225 DYER ST
PROVIDENCE, RI 029033927
Phone: 401 521-2700
Fax: -
Web: www.rdwgroup.com

CEO: James Malachowski
CFO: -
HR: -
FYE: December 31
Type: Private

The RDW Group is a communications services agency that offers creative advertising, public relations, and direct marketing services to clients mostly in New England. In addition to traditional advertising and market services, the firm provides digital communications services, website design, and media planning services. RDW operates through offices in Boston; Providence, Rhode Island; and Worcester, Massachusetts. The firm was started as Doyle and Walsh in 1986, changing its name to Rivers, Doyle, Walsh, and Co. a decade later.

THE REED INSTITUTE

3203 SE WOODSTOCK BLVD
PORTLAND, OR 972028138
Phone: 503 771-1112
Fax: -
Web: www.reed.edu

CEO: -
CFO: -
HR: Diane Gumz
FYE: June 30
Type: Private

Reed College offers bachelor's degrees in nearly 30 fields and a master of arts degree in liberal studies. Its special master's degree allows students to study both liberal arts and the sciences. Each year, the school enrolls more than 1,400 students who become known as "Reedies." Additionally, it boasts an average of 17 students in its conference-style classes and a student-to-faculty ratio of 10 to 1. Reed College, which has produced more than 30 Rhodes Scholars, also houses a nuclear reactor that is operated primarily by undergraduates. Founded in 1908, Reed College is named for Oregon pioneers Simeon and Amanda Reed.

	Annual Growth	06/18	06/19	06/20	06/21	06/22
Sales ($mil.)	10.2%	-	138.0	130.1	135.5	184.8
Net income ($ mil.)	81.9%	-	6.4	(5.6)	5.9	38.5
Market value ($ mil.)	-	-	-	-	-	-
Employees	-	-	-	-	-	400

THE REGENTS OF THE UNIVERSITY OF COLORADO

3100 MARINE ST STE 481572　　　　　　　　　　　　　　CEO: -
BOULDER, CO 803090001　　　　　　　　　　　CFO: Chad Marturano
Phone: 303 735-6624　　　　　　　　　　　　HR: Karen Dempsey
Fax: -　　　　　　　　　　　　　　　　　　　　　FYE: June 30
Web: www.colorado.edu　　　　　　　　　　　　　　Type: Private

The University of Colorado System spans four campuses and some 60,000 students. The Boulder campus, home to about 30,000 students, provides more than 2,500 courses in 150-plus fields through nine colleges and schools. The University of Colorado at Denver has an enrollment of more than 14,000 and has 120 study programs at a dozen schools, and its nearby Anschutz Medical Campus serves more than 500,000 patients annually. The smallest campus, University of Colorado at Colorado Springs, has six colleges with about 10,000 students and offers nearly 60 undergraduate, graduate, and doctoral degree programs. The system, which began in Boulder as the University of Colorado in 1876, boasts more than 4,000 faculty members.

	Annual Growth	06/17	06/18	06/20	06/21	06/22
Sales ($mil.)	5.0%	-	3,833.9	4,239.6	4,139.5	4,658.9
Net income ($ mil.)	-	-	(197.3)	584.9	1,170.0	(205.2)
Market value ($ mil.)	-	-	-	-	-	-
Employees	-	-	-	-	-	12,980

THE RESEARCH FOUNDATION FOR THE STATE UNIVERSITY OF NEW YORK

35 STATE ST　　　　　　　　　　　　　　　　CEO: Jeffrey Chee
ALBANY, NY 122072826　　　　　　　　　　　　　　　CFO: -
Phone: 518 434-7000　　　　　　　　　　　　HR: Lu A Augustine
Fax: -　　　　　　　　　　　　　　　　　　　　　FYE: June 30
Web: www.rfsuny.org　　　　　　　　　　　　　　　Type: Private

The Research Foundation of State University of New York (The Research Foundation) collects and administers research and education grants from state and federal governments, corporations, and foundations on behalf of the 24-campus State University of New York, known as SUNY. The foundation has formed several affiliated divisions -- including Long Island High Technology Incubator and NanoTech Resources -- to operate research facilities, encourage scientific collaboration, and otherwise facilitate research for the university. It facilitates research for studies such as engineering and nanotechnology; physical sciences and medicine; life sciences and medicine; social sciences; and computer and information sciences.

	Annual Growth	06/18	06/19	06/20	06/21	06/22
Sales ($mil.)	(15.6%)	-	-	1,572.9	1,300.7	1,119.8
Net income ($ mil.)	(56.0%)	-	-	422.0	52.3	81.7
Market value ($ mil.)	-	-	-	-	-	-
Employees	-	-	-	-	-	15,000

THE ROCK AND ROLL HALL OF FAME AND MUSEUM INC

1100 ROCK AND ROLL BLVD　　　　　　　　　　　　CEO: Greg Harris
CLEVELAND, OH 441141023　　　　　　　　　　　　　　CFO: -
Phone: 216 781-7625　　　　　　　　　　　　　HR: Holly Kosalko
Fax: -　　　　　　　　　　　　　　　　　　　　FYE: December 31
Web: www.rockhall.com　　　　　　　　　　　　　　Type: Private

This museum wants you to rock until you drop. The Rock and Roll Hall of Fame and Museum pays homage to the great American art form of rock and roll music. The organization honors the legends of the genre, from early 20th century artists like blues man Robert Johnson and country singer Jimmie Rodgers, to still performing artists such as piano man Billy Joel and guitarist Eric Clapton. The Rock and Roll Hall of Fame and Museum is a nonprofit organization that is supported through memberships, planned giving, endowments, and events such as its It's Only Rock and Roll "party of the year." The venue also can be rented for private museum viewing or sit-down dinners for more than 300 people.

	Annual Growth	12/14	12/15	12/16	12/19	12/20
Sales ($mil.)	(5.6%)	-	24.0	36.4	36.8	18.0
Net income ($ mil.)	-	-	(3.2)	13.8	8.0	(4.9)
Market value ($ mil.)	-	-	-	-	-	-
Employees	-	-	-	-	-	100

THE ROCKEFELLER FOUNDATION

420 5TH AVE　　　　　　　　　　　　　　　　　　　　CEO: -
NEW YORK, NY 100182711　　　　　　　　　　　　　　CFO: -
Phone: 212 869-8500　　　　　　　　　　　　　HR: Claire Raynes
Fax: -　　　　　　　　　　　　　　　　　　　　FYE: December 31
Web: www.rockefellerfoundation.org　　　　　　　　Type: Private

The Rockefeller Foundation, established in 1913, is one of the oldest private charitable organizations in the US. It supports grants, fellowships, and conferences for programs that concentrate on identifying and alleviating need and suffering worldwide. These programs (or themes) include initiatives to foster fair implementation of health care, job opportunities for America's urban poor, creative expression through the humanities and arts, and agricultural policies that ensure food distribution to people in developing countries. An additional theme -- global inclusion -- serves as a connection between the foundation's other programs and as a way to ensure that poor people benefit from global trade increases.

	Annual Growth	12/04	12/05	12/09	12/14	12/16
Sales ($mil.)	(12.8%)	-	343.8	34.0	401.8	75.8
Net income ($ mil.)	-	-	188.7	(150.5)	223.6	(164.9)
Market value ($ mil.)	-	-	-	-	-	-
Employees	-	-	-	-	-	150

THE ROCKEFELLER UNIVERSITY FACULTY AND STUDENTS CLUB INC

1230 YORK AVE　　　　　　　　　　　　　　　　　　　CEO: -
NEW YORK, NY 100656307　　　　　　　　　　　CFO: James H Lapple
Phone: 212 327-8078　　　　　　　　　　　　HR: Antonia Martinez
Fax: -　　　　　　　　　　　　　　　　　　　　　FYE: June 30
Web: www.rockefeller.edu　　　　　　　　　　　　　Type: Private

Rockefeller University sniffs out solid scientific evidence. The university is a leading US research institution and scientific graduate school, providing training in biomedical and physical science fields such as biochemistry, structural biology, immunology, neuroscience, and human genetics. The university is centered around 76 research laboratories and a hospital, and it runs M.D.-Ph.D. programs in conjunction with the Memorial Sloan-Kettering Cancer Center and the Weill Medical College at Cornell University. Rockefeller University's research is funded by entities such as the National Institutes of Health and the Howard Hughes Medical Institute, as well as private gifts and endowments.

THE RUDOLPH/LIBBE COMPANIES INC

6494 LATCHA RD　　　　　　　　　　　　　　　　　　CEO: -
WALBRIDGE, OH 434659788　　　　　　　　　　CFO: Robert Pruger
Phone: 419 241-5000　　　　　　　　　　　　　　　　HR: -
Fax: -　　　　　　　　　　　　　　　　　　　　FYE: December 31
Web: www.rlgbuilds.com　　　　　　　　　　　　　Type: Private

The corporate model of a conglomerate composed of independent, unrelated businesses is not for The Rudolph/Libbe Companies. The group of companies can build or oversee real estate projects (general contractor Rudolph/Libbe Inc.); perform mechanical, electrical, and structural work (GEM Industrial); and then represent those properties in the market (RLWest Properties). Operating in the Ohio/Michigan corridor, the group provides site selection, design/build, and construction management. Its portfolio includes industrial, retail, municipal, residential, educational, health care, and mixed-use projects. Fritz and Phil Rudolph and their cousin Allan Libbe founded flagship subsidiary Rudolph/Libbe Inc. in 1955.

	Annual Growth	12/14	12/15	12/16	12/17	12/18
Sales ($mil.)	10.5%	-	425.4	502.7	567.8	573.4
Net income ($ mil.)	(0.2%)	-	16.2	24.0	20.1	16.2
Market value ($ mil.)	-	-	-	-	-	-
Employees	-	-	-	-	-	600

THE RUTLAND HOSPITAL INC

160 ALLEN ST
RUTLAND, VT 057014595
Phone: 802 775-7111
Fax: –
Web: rrmccareers.hctsportals.com

CEO: Judy Fox
CFO: Edward Ogorzalek
HR: –
FYE: September 30
Type: Private

For those seeking health care in the New England region, Rutland Regional Medical Center (RRMC) just might be the destination for you. Part of Rutland Regional Health Services, it runs a hospital that boasts more than 120 beds and serves patients in Vermont and eastern New York. RRMC offers about 40 medical specialties including cancer care, diabetes treatment, and total joint replacement. The acute-care facility also has centers dedicated to cardiac rehabilitation and women's health. To meet growing community medical needs, RRMC also operates a prostate care unit and a 30-bed psychiatric unit. Along with a range of specialty care options, RRMC administers primary care and emergency medical transport.

	Annual Growth	09/17	09/18	09/20	09/21	09/22
Sales ($mil.)	7.2%	–	254.2	225.5	257.5	336.3
Net income ($ mil.)	–	–	1.3	13.3	35.3	(7.7)
Market value ($ mil.)	–	–	–	–	–	–
Employees	–	–	–	–	–	1,350

THE SALVATION ARMY

16941 KEEGAN AVE
CARSON, CA 907461307
Phone: 562 491-8496
Fax: –
Web: www.salvationarmy.org

CEO: James M Knaggs
CFO: –
HR: Iona Manigault-Hardw
FYE: September 30
Type: Private

The Salvation Army USA Western Territory is one of four regional commands carrying out the social services mission of The Salvation Army in the US. The faith-based group seeks to address a wide variety of human needs through programs and facilities such as adult rehabilitation centers, domestic violence shelters, and transitional and permanent housing. Its territory spans 13 western states, including Alaska and Hawaii, as well as The Territory of Guam, the Commonwealth of the Northern Mariana Islands, the Federated States of Micronesia, and the Republic of the Marshall Islands. The Salvation Army's international headquarters is in London where the group was founded in 1865. It began operating in the US in 1880.

	Annual Growth	09/07	09/08*	12/09*	09/19	09/20
Sales ($mil.)	(18.7%)	–	6.2	–	0.3	0.5
Net income ($ mil.)	(16.9%)	–	0.4	–	(0.1)	0.0
Market value ($ mil.)	–	–	–	–	–	–
Employees	–	–	–	–	–	320

*Fiscal year change

THE SALVATION ARMY NATIONAL CORPORATION

615 SLATERS LN
ALEXANDRIA, VA 223141112
Phone: 703 684-5500
Fax: –
Web: www.salvationarmyusa.org

CEO: –
CFO: –
HR: Cynthia Cunningham
FYE: September 30
Type: Private

The Salvation Army is one of the world's largest faith-based charities with approximately 1.45 million members consisting of officers, soldiers, and adherents. Its Christian faith-based programs include homeless shelters, spiritual healing, job training, summer camps, and services for the ages among others. Serving approximately 30 million Americans yearly, the organization also provides disaster-relief services. The Salvation Army also manages ministries for women, prisoners, and people who want to play music. The US organization is a unit of the London-based Salvation Army, which oversees activities in about 130 countries. The company was founded in 1865 by William Booth.

	Annual Growth	09/07	09/08	09/09	09/10	09/12
Sales ($mil.)	4.6%	–	–	36.8	3.7	42.1
Net income ($ mil.)	–	–	–	(10.1)	0.4	2.4
Market value ($ mil.)	–	–	–	–	–	–
Employees	–	–	–	–	–	16,170

THE SAVANNAH COLLEGE OF ART AND DESIGN INC

126 E GASTON ST
SAVANNAH, GA 314015604
Phone: 912 525-5000
Fax: –
Web: www.scad.edu

CEO: –
CFO: –
HR: –
FYE: June 30
Type: Private

With more than 12,000 students, Savannah College of Art and Design (SCAD) in Georgia is a private, nonprofit, accredited university with students from across the US and more than 100 countries. It has undergraduate degrees in arts and fine arts as well as master's degrees in a range of subjects. The institution offers courses of study in 40-plus majors including fields such as architecture, interior and graphic design, fashion, film and television, painting, dance, and art history. The school also offers certificates in digital publishing, digital publishing management, historic preservation, interactive design, and typeface design and more than 60 other minors.

	Annual Growth	06/08	06/09	06/10	06/21	06/22
Sales ($mil.)	6.2%	–	283.0	314.1	558.1	622.4
Net income ($ mil.)	13.0%	–	21.8	10.0	144.3	106.8
Market value ($ mil.)	–	–	–	–	–	–
Employees	–	–	–	–	–	1,200

THE SCOTIA GROUP INC

411 N SAM HOUSTON PKWY E STE 400
HOUSTON, TX 770603545
Phone: 281 448-6188
Fax: –
Web: –

CEO: –
CFO: Maryann Moss
HR: –
FYE: December 31
Type: Private

The nova that RPS Scotia (formerly The Scotia Group) hopes to produce is new oil and gas finds. The oil and gas services consultancy specializes in technical and economic analysis, and strategic advice related to exploration and reserves. Clients have included major and independent oil companies (BP, Chevron, Shell), financial institutions (Goldman Sachs & Company, J.P. Morgan), and legal entities (US Department of Justice, Haynes and Boone). The company has offices in Dallas and Houston, and in Reynosa, Mexico. About 60% of the company's work is conducted internationally, and 45% of its clients are independent oil and gas companies. In 2007 The Scotia Group was acquired by the RPS Group's RPS Energy unit.

	Annual Growth	12/03	12/04	12/05	12/06	12/08
Sales ($mil.)	30.1%	–	4.6	5.9	6.7	13.1
Net income ($ mil.)	32.4%	–	0.9	1.5	1.9	2.7
Market value ($ mil.)	–	–	–	–	–	–
Employees	–	–	–	–	–	21

THE SCOTT FETZER COMPANY

28800 CLEMENS RD
WESTLAKE, OH 441451197
Phone: 440 892-3000
Fax: –
Web: www.scottfetzer.com

CEO: Kenneth J Semelsberger
CFO: –
HR: –
FYE: December 31
Type: Private

The Scott Fetzer Company is a leading manufacturer of high-quality products for the home, family and industries, including advancements in healthcare technologies. The diversified manufacturer of consumer, commercial, and industrial products is a holding company for a group of around 25 businesses. Among its best-known activities are Adalet (electronic enclosure system), Kingston (timers, range locks, and asynchronous motor), and World Book (encyclopedias and reference materials). Other holdings include Powerex (air systems), Northland (electric motors), Stahl (commercial truck and crane equipment), Arbortech (forestry bodies and chip bodies) and Western Enterprises (gas fittings).

THE SCOULAR COMPANY

13660 CALIFORNIA ST
OMAHA, NE 681545233
Phone: 402 342-3500
Fax: –
Web: www.scoular.com

CEO: Paul Maass
CFO: Andrew Kenny
HR: Amy Bauman
FYE: May 31
Type: Private

The Scoular Company buys, sells, stores, handles, processes, and transports agricultural products (mainly grains) worldwide. It gets the mainstays of farming ? corn, feed grains, rye, peas and lentils, soybeans, and wheat ? where they need to go. The company transports these products via rail, truck, and barge shipping partners. Scoular's other divisions offer fishmeal products for farm-animal, pet, and aquaculture feeds; ingredients for food manufacturers; and renewable fuels, as well as a host of risk management, logistics, and product-related services. Scoular has more than 100 locations locally and internationally.

	Annual Growth	05/17	05/18	05/19	05/20	05/21
Sales ($mil.)	30.2%	–	–	–	4,612.9	6,004.0
Net income ($ mil.)	65.8%	–	–	–	32.5	53.8
Market value ($ mil.)	–	–	–	–	–	–
Employees	–	–	–	–	–	730

THE SCRIPPS RESEARCH INSTITUTE

10550 N TORREY PINES RD
LA JOLLA, CA 920371000
Phone: 858 784-1000
Fax: –
Web: www.scripps.edu

CEO: Peter G Schultz
CFO: Cary E Thomas
HR: Paige Gearhart
FYE: September 30
Type: Private

The Scripps Research Institute (TSRI) is a not-for profit organization that performs basic biomedical research in molecular and cellular biology, chemistry, immunology, neuroscience, disease, and vaccine development. TSRI receives the majority of its funding from federal agencies such as the National Institutes of Health. TRSI opened a second facility in Florida in 2009. Its staff includes more than 2,900 scientists and lab technicians, and the organization traces its history back to 1924, when philanthropist Ellen Browning Scripps founded Scripps Metabolic Clinic.

	Annual Growth	09/08	09/09	09/16	09/19	09/22
Sales ($mil.)	4.3%	–	375.5	348.6	412.2	652.0
Net income ($ mil.)	–	–	(18.8)	(16.1)	(20.4)	(273.2)
Market value ($ mil.)	–	–	–	–	–	–
Employees	–	–	–	–	–	209

THE SEGERDAHL CORP

1351 WHEELING RD
WHEELING, IL 600905997
Phone: 847 541-1080
Fax: –
Web: www.sg360.com

CEO: Jim Andersen
CFO: Gary Gardner
HR: –
FYE: December 31
Type: Private

Segerdahl Corp doing business as SG360, is a printing company specializes in digital pre-press, printing, finishing, and shipping services for advertising and marketing projects. SG360 offers web printing and sheet fed printing. A member of the Segerdahl Company, the company produces brochures, folders, envelopes, cards, foil stamping, mailers, and other materials for a variety of national clients. SG360 serves various industries such as automotive, consumer packaged goods, financial services, healthcare and telecommunications.

THE SHAMROCK COMPANIES INC

24090 DETROIT RD
WESTLAKE, OH 441451513
Phone: 440 899-9510
Fax: –
Web: www.shamrockcompanies.net

CEO: Tim Connor
CFO: Gary A Lesjak
HR: –
FYE: December 31
Type: Private

The Shamrock Companies is a full-service, integrated marketing solutions company with offices throughout the US. It provides business fulfillment, technology, warehousing, photography, marketing and creative services, packaging, print, and promotional products. It works with clients such as Verizon, FedEx, Stryker, SummaCare, Komatsu, Vitamix, and American Heart Association, among others. The full-service, integrated marketing solutions company is currently led by CEO Robert Troop. The Shamrock Companies has many representatives spread out throughout the US, and it also has a number of physical locations including its headquarters in Ohio.

	Annual Growth	12/00	12/01	12/02	12/03	12/07
Sales ($mil.)	8.2%	–	42.7	43.9	51.8	68.4
Net income ($ mil.)	5.4%	–	3.1	2.5	1.6	4.2
Market value ($ mil.)	–	–	–	–	–	–
Employees	–	–	–	–	–	140

THE SHERIDAN GROUP INC

450 FAME AVE
HANOVER, PA 173311585
Phone: 717 632-3535
Fax: –
Web: www.sheridangroupinc.com

CEO: John A Saxton
CFO: Robert M Jakobe
HR: –
FYE: December 31
Type: Private

According to The Sheridan Group, commercial printing (through both traditional and digital printing) still can hold its own in a rapidly changing business environment. Through its five specialized printing businesses, The Sheridan Group prints books, catalogs, journals, and magazines. Its Sheridan Press and Dartmouth Journal Services units print short- and medium-run scholarly and technical journals. The Dingley Press prints catalogs, while Sheridan Books manufactures and distributes custom books, and Dartmouth Printing specializes in magazine, journal, and catalog printing.

THE SHUBERT FOUNDATION INC

234 W 44TH ST FL 6
NEW YORK, NY 100363909
Phone: 212 944-3777
Fax: –
Web: www.shubertfoundation.org

CEO: –
CFO: –
HR: Cathy Cozens
FYE: May 31
Type: Private

The Shubert Foundation is a non-profit organization that is the parent company of major Broadway theater owner The Shubert Organization. The organization, which is the oldest professional theater company in the nation, owns and operates more than 20 theaters -- 17 of which are on Broadway. The balance of its theaters are either off-Broadway (The Little Shubert) or in Boston, Philadelphia, or Washington, D.C. In addition The Shubert Foundation, which was founded in 1945 by Lee and J.J. Shubert in honor of their brother Sam, distributes grants (from $5,000 to $275,000) to some 200 non-profit theater and dance companies annually.

	Annual Growth	05/13	05/14	05/15	05/16	05/22
Sales ($mil.)	1.9%	–	49.4	–	–	57.7
Net income ($ mil.)	(4.4%)	–	19.8	–	–	13.8
Market value ($ mil.)	–	–	–	–	–	–
Employees	–	–	–	–	–	1,700

THE SIMON KONOVER COMPANY

342 N MAIN ST STE 200
WEST HARTFORD, CT 061172507
Phone: 860 570-2000
Fax: –
Web: www.simonkonover.com

CEO: Jane K Coppa
CFO: Mark P Consoli
HR: –
FYE: December 31
Type: Private

Konover Properties acquires, develops, and manages real estate in the eastern and midwestern US. The firm's portfolio includes hotels, residential complexes, retail and mixed-use properties, and office buildings. Konover Residential manages about 4,000 apartment units in some 20 communities; Konover Office and Commercial manages more than 1 million sq. ft. of office and retail space. SIKON Construction Services (formerly Construction Oversight Services) provides construction management for commercial and residential properties; it has overseen many of the developments in Konover Properties' portfolio. CEO and philanthropist Simon Konover founded Konover Properties in the early 1950s.

THE STEP2 COMPANY LLC

10010 AURORA HUDSON RD
STREETSBORO, OH 442411619
Phone: 866 429-5200
Fax: –
Web: www.step2.com

CEO: Christopher P Quinn
CFO: –
HR: Kellie Kerr
FYE: December 31
Type: Private

The Step2 Company is the largest manufacturer of preschool and toddler toys in America and the largest rotational molder of plastics in the world. It sells a variety of plastic toys for toddlers and preschoolers, as well as outdoor furniture and pet beds. The company also initiates the "Learn to Play. Play to Learn" which promotes a deeper understanding of how Step2 toys can nurture children's minds through fun, imaginative play. This program will also focus on educating parents on the clinical research behind play-based learning. Step2 operates retail stores in Ohio and also sells its offerings online and through retailers in the US, Canada, and more than 70 other countries. Step2 began its operations in 1991.

THE SOLOMON-PAGE GROUP LLC

260 MADISON AVE FL 4
NEW YORK, NY 100162422
Phone: 212 403-6100
Fax: –
Web: www.solomonpage.com

CEO: –
CFO: –
HR: Christine Martinez
FYE: September 30
Type: Private

Are your worker bees buzzing off? Solomon-Page Group (SPG) knows where to find more. The company offers temporary staffing and permanent recruitment services to clients ranging from startups to FORTUNE 500 companies. Its temporary staffing division provides personnel for positions in information technology, accounting, human resources, and legal fields. SPG also provides executive search and permanent recruitment services for businesses in publishing, health care, banking, fashion services, and other industries. The company was founded in 1990.

THE SUNDT COMPANIES INC

2620 S 55TH ST
TEMPE, AZ 852821903
Phone: 480 293-3000
Fax: –
Web: www.sundt.com

CEO: Michael Hoover
CFO: Keenan E Driscoll
HR: –
FYE: September 30
Type: Private

Sundt has put its stamp on the Southwest. Through Sundt Construction and other subsidiaries, The Sundt Companies offers preconstruction, construction management, general contracting, and design/build services for commercial, government, and industrial clients. Projects include commercial buildings, military bases, light rails, airports, and schools. It builds mostly in Arizona, Nevada, California, New Mexico, and Texas. Sundt has overseen some notable projects including the development of the top-secret town of Los Alamos, New Mexico (where the first atomic bomb was built) and the relocation of the London Bridge to Arizona. Sundt Companies was formed in 1998 as a holding company for various company interests.

	Annual Growth	09/08	09/09	09/10	09/11	09/13
Sales ($mil.)	13.2%	–	94.1	110.8	124.7	154.4
Net income ($ mil.)	–	–	(2.5)	1.5	0.7	1.5
Market value ($ mil.)	–	–	–	–	–	–
Employees	–	–	–	–	–	300

THE SOUTHERN POVERTY LAW CENTER INC

400 WASHINGTON AVE
MONTGOMERY, AL 361044344
Phone: 334 956-8200
Fax: –
Web: www.splcenter.org

CEO: Margaret Huang
CFO: –
HR: –
FYE: October 31
Type: Private

Founded in 1971 as a small civil rights law firm, the Southern Poverty Law Center (SPLC) is a non-profit organization dedicated to increasing tolerance through education and, when or if that fails, litigation. The center provides legal services to minorities and the poor while its Intelligence Project monitors hate groups in the US. SPLC's quarterly Intelligence Report is distributed to more than 60,000 law enforcement officials. The organization also operates Tolerance.org, a collection of online resources for those fighting bigotry in their own communities. SPLC is credited with weakening the financial structure of white supremacist groups the likes of the Ku Klux Klan and Aryan Nation.

THE SUSAN G KOMEN BREAST CANCER FOUNDATION INC

13770 NOEL RD UNIT 801889
DALLAS, TX 753800147
Phone: 972 855-1600
Fax: –
Web: www.komen.org

CEO: Judith A Salerno
CFO: Bob Green
HR: Catherine Olivieri
FYE: March 31
Type: Private

Susan G. Komen For the Cure is dedicated to fighting breast cancer through education, research, screening, and treatment programs. One of its well known fundraisers is an annual 5-K foot race called the Komen Race for the Cure which is conducted in numerous locations across the US and in other countries. The organization also operates a national help line and a website. Since its founding, Komen for the Cure has invested more than $1.7 billion on screening, education, treatment and psychosocial support programs, including more than $800 million to medical research, as part of a broad campaign to combat breast cancer.

	Annual Growth	10/18	10/19	10/20	10/21	10/22
Sales ($mil.)	(2.5%)	–	117.0	145.6	290.0	108.3
Net income ($ mil.)	–	–	28.6	45.6	182.3	(1.9)
Market value ($ mil.)	–	–	–	–	–	–
Employees	–	–	–	–	–	225

	Annual Growth	03/14	03/15	03/16	03/20	03/22
Sales ($mil.)	(0.9%)	–	118.4	258.4	74.8	111.3
Net income ($ mil.)	–	–	(2.0)	21.2	5.9	10.6
Market value ($ mil.)	–	–	–	–	–	–
Employees	–	–	–	–	–	260

THE SYNERGOS INSTITUTE INC

1 E 53RD ST FL 7
NEW YORK, NY 100224235
Phone: 646 590-4794
Fax: -
Web: www.synergos.org

CEO: -
CFO: -
HR: -
FYE: December 31
Type: Private

The Synergos Institute is a nonprofit organization that focuses on reducing poverty in the developing world by providing technical assistance to grantmaking groups primarily in Africa, Asia, and Latin America. Each year Synergos helps nearly 200 organizations that work directly with community development, tailors giving programs for wealthy families and individuals to channel their funds into poverty-ending work, and trains local leaders to help people work together to solve conflict. Synergos was founded in 1987 by Peggy Dulany, daughter of bank president David Rockefeller and heir to the Rockefeller Standard Oil fortune.

THE TECH INTERACTIVE

201 S MARKET ST
SAN JOSE, CA 951132008
Phone: 408 795-6116
Fax: -
Web: www.thetech.org

CEO: Peter Friess
CFO: Naresh Kapahi
HR: Judy Sanders
FYE: June 30
Type: Private

If the words "tech" and "Trek" are not part of your vernacular, this museum experience may open your eyes to a whole new world. The Tech Museum of Innovation (known as The Tech), is a science museum focused on high technology. Boasting about 250 exhibits and the only IMAX theater in Northern California, The Tech showcases the latest gizmos and gadgets, as well as interactive exhibits and speakers' series. It also has two signature programs: The Tech Museum Awards: Technology Benefiting Humanity; and Tech Challenge, an annual design challenge for youth in grades 5-12. The museum is visited by 400,000 visitors per year. Members of Silicon Valley's high-tech community founded The Tech Museum.

	Annual Growth	06/14	06/15	06/16	06/20	06/22
Sales ($mil.)	(0.8%)	-	17.9	19.9	24.7	17.0
Net income ($ mil.)	-	-	2.0	1.7	2.6	(1.1)
Market value ($ mil.)	-	-	-	-	-	-
Employees	-	-	-	-	-	164

THE TECHNOLOGY ASSOCIATION OF AMERICA

601 PENNSYLVANIA AVE NW
WASHINGTON, DC 200042601
Phone: 202 682-9110
Fax: -
Web: -

CEO: Phillip Bond
CFO: -
HR: -
FYE: December 31
Type: Private

What do you get when you combine the nation's largest technology trade association with the leading information technology and electronics industry association? The answer is The Technology Association of America (aka TechAmerica), created by the 2009 merger of the American Electronics Association (AeA) with the Information Technology Association of America (ITAA), in a bid to form a more powerful federal lobbying organization. The newly-formed organization represents about 1,500 member companies, advocates on technology issues, and provides networking and other business services to its constituents.

	Annual Growth	12/96	12/97	12/98	12/99	12/12
Sales ($mil.)	6.9%	-	3.8	5.3	-	10.5
Net income ($ mil.)	-	-	0.0	0.1	-	(1.2)
Market value ($ mil.)	-	-	-	-	-	-
Employees	-	-	-	-	-	35

THE TEXAS A&M UNIVERSITY SYSTEM

301 TARROW ST FL 3
COLLEGE STATION, TX 778407896
Phone: 979 458-7700
Fax: -
Web: www.tamus.edu

CEO: -
CFO: Barry Nelson
HR: -
FYE: August 31
Type: Private

Everything is bigger in Texas, even its universities. With more than 120,000 students at 11 institutions, The Texas A&M University System ranks among the largest in the US. Its flagship Texas A&M University at College Station is well known not only for its programs in engineering and agriculture, but also for its long-held traditions and school spirit. Other system institutions include Tarleton State University and Prairie View A&M, seven state agencies, and a health sciences center. Texas A&M was founded as the Agricultural and Mechanical College of Texas in 1876. The system, which was formed in 1948, is funded, in part, by a state endowment that is shared with the University of Texas.

THE TRADE EVENT RESOURCE MANAGEMENT GROUP LLC

222 WILLIAM ST
BENSENVILLE, IL 601063325
Phone: 630 766-8376
Fax: -
Web: -

CEO: -
CFO: -
HR: -
FYE: December 31
Type: Private

If they build it, trade show attendees will come. The TERM Group ("term" stands for Trade Event Resource Management) provides labor to corporate clients staging booths at conventions or trade shows. TERM's employees help to set up and dismantle the client's displays or booths, manage computer or audiovisual equipment, and perform other logistical services. The company serves clients across the US with offices in California, Florida, Georgia, Illinois, Nevada, Oregon, Texas, and Washington. The TERM Group was formed in 1998, when it merged with Metro Exhibitors Service.

THE TRUMP ORGANIZATION INC

725 5TH AVE BSMT A
NEW YORK, NY 100222516
Phone: 212 832-2000
Fax: -
Web: www.trump.com

CEO: Eric Trump
CFO: -
HR: Rhona Graff
FYE: December 31
Type: Private

Founded by current US President Donald Trump, the Manhattan-based Trump Organization owns high-end, high-rise real estate in the Big Apple and other areas. Properties include Trump International Hotel & Tower, Trump Tower, and 40 Wall Street. It also owns and operates hotels, resorts, residential towers, and 18 golf resorts in major US markets and abroad. Trump holds a stake in Trump Entertainment Resorts, the owner and operator of the Trump Taj Mahal and Trump Plaza casinos in New Jersey's Atlantic City. In 2016 the company sold the Miss USA, Miss Teen USA, and Miss Universe beauty pageants to WME Entertainment. Donald Trump's sons, Donald Jr. and Eric, manage the company.

	Annual Growth	12/18	12/19	12/20	12/21	12/22
Assets ($mil.)	(40.4%)	-	-	-	0.6	0.3
Net income ($ mil.)	-	-	-	-	0.2	(0.3)
Market value ($ mil.)	-	-	-	-	-	-
Employees	-	-	-	-	-	4,000

THE TRUSTEES OF DAVIDSON COLLEGE

209 RIDGE RD
DAVIDSON, NC 280360407
Phone: 704 894-2000
Fax: –
Web: www.davidson.edu

CEO: –
CFO: –
HR: –
FYE: June 30
Type: Private

The 1,850 students at Davidson College account for about a fifth of the population in the small North Carolina town with the same name. Located just north of Charlotte, the liberal arts school offers more than 25 majors and 17 minors in areas such as anthropology, art, economics, history, and philosophy. It also offers pre-professional programs in medicine, law, business, ministerial, and management. Students are bound by a strict honor code that allows self-scheduled, unproctored exams and prohibits students from cheating and stealing.

	Annual Growth	06/08	06/09	06/10	06/21	06/22
Sales ($mil.)	10.5%	–	97.0	100.3	194.8	353.4
Net income ($ mil.)	–	–	(137.1)	71.7	14.2	179.7
Market value ($ mil.)	–	–	–	–	–	–
Employees	–	–	–	–	–	800

THE TRUSTEES OF GRINNELL COLLEGE

733 BROAD ST
GRINNELL, IA 501122227
Phone: 641 269-3500
Fax: –
Web: www.grinnell.edu

CEO: –
CFO: –
HR: –
FYE: June 30
Type: Private

Ear to ear might be pushing it, but the students at Grinnell College have reason to be happy. On its 120-acre campus in rural Grinnell, Iowa, more than 1,600 students choose from courses in some 25 major fields. Programs are centered on social studies, science, and the humanities at this private, four-year liberal arts school. The college has an open curriculum, allowing students to design their own academic programs. It also offers general literary studies and has a student-to-teacher ratio of 9:1. The college, which was founded in 1846, is named after abolitionist minister Josiah Bushnell Grinnell.

	Annual Growth	06/15	06/16	06/17	06/18	06/20
Sales ($mil.)	3.2%	–	126.9	139.6	137.2	143.8
Net income ($ mil.)	–	–	(134.3)	236.0	137.9	24.2
Market value ($ mil.)	–	–	–	–	–	–
Employees	–	–	–	–	–	535

THE TRUSTEES OF MOUNT HOLYOKE COLLEGE

50 COLLEGE ST
SOUTH HADLEY, MA 010751448
Phone: 413 538-2000
Fax: –
Web: www.mtholyoke.edu

CEO: –
CFO: –
HR: Lauren Turner
FYE: June 30
Type: Private

Mount Holyoke College was the first of the Seven Sisters -- the female equivalent of the predominantly male Ivy League. The nation's oldest continuing institution of higher learning for women, Mount Holyoke offers nearly 50 departmental and interdisciplinary majors to about 2,300 female students. Mount Holyoke is part of the Five College Consortium, which also includes Amherst, Hampshire, Smith, and the University of Massachusetts. (Mount Holyoke students can take classes at any of these schools.) Notable alumnae include poet Emily Dickinson and Tony- and Pulitzer Prize-winning playwright Wendy Wasserstein.

	Annual Growth	06/18	06/19	06/20	06/21	06/22
Sales ($mil.)	12.5%	–	151.5	203.2	296.4	216.0
Net income ($ mil.)	–	–	17.9	(3.2)	116.1	(8.0)
Market value ($ mil.)	–	–	–	–	–	–
Employees	–	–	–	–	–	1,000

THE TRUSTEES OF PRINCETON UNIVERSITY

1 NASSAU HALL
PRINCETON, NJ 085442001
Phone: 609 258-3000
Fax: –
Web: www.princeton.edu

CEO: –
CFO: –
HR: Stacey Burd
FYE: June 30
Type: Private

Princeton University is a vibrant community of scholarship and learning that stands in the nation's service and the service of humanity. As one of the eight elite Ivy League schools in the Northeastern US, Princeton is a research university that offers students degrees across around 35 departments and nearly 65 undergraduate minors and interdisciplinary certificate programs. Princeton also offers about 45 doctoral departments and programs, about 25 interdisciplinary/interdepartmental doctoral programs, and some 10 master's degree programs. With more than 8,800 students and over 1,265 faculty, Princeton has a student-to-faculty ratio of 5:1. Nobel Prize winners associated with Princeton include Woodrow Wilson, writer Toni Morrison, and physicist Richard Feynman. One of the nation's wealthiest universities, Princeton has an endowment of more than $35.8 billion.

	Annual Growth	06/18	06/19	06/20	06/21	06/22
Sales ($mil.)	3.2%	–	2,146.2	2,173.1	2,162.5	2,357.1
Net income ($ mil.)	–	–	677.4	383.6	10,984	(1,275.6)
Market value ($ mil.)	–	–	–	–	–	–
Employees	–	–	–	–	–	6,000

THE TRUSTEES OF PURDUE UNIVERSITY

2550 NORTHWESTERN AVE STE 1100
WEST LAFAYETTE, IN 47906
Phone: 765 494-8000
Fax: –
Web: www.purdue.edu

CEO: –
CFO: –
HR: –
FYE: June 30
Type: Private

Purdue University enrolls some 50,885 undergraduate, graduate, and continuing education students at its flagship West Lafayette campus, Fort Wayne, Indianapolis, Northwest, and the Purdue Polytechnic Institute Statewide Locations. The university offers undergraduate and graduate programs from about a dozen colleges, including agriculture, education, veterinary medicine, and health and human sciences, among others. Purdue also offers about 400 study abroad programs in more than 50 countries. It employs more than 2,000 faculty and staff and has a student-faculty ratio of 13:1. Operating more than 400 research laboratories and 100 discipline-specific centers and institutes, Purdue University is a world-renowned, public research university that advances discoveries in science, technology, engineering and math. It was founded in 1869.

THE TRUSTEES OF THE SMITH COLLEGE

10 ELM ST
NORTHAMPTON, MA 010630001
Phone: 413 585-2550
Fax: –
Web: www.smith.edu

CEO: –
CFO: –
HR: –
FYE: June 30
Type: Private

Girl Power abounds at Smith. The nation's largest liberal arts college for women, Smith College provides 1,000 courses in some 50 academic areas including the arts, humanities, languages, sciences, and social sciences. It enrolls nearly 2,900 undergraduate students and employs about 300 professors. Annually, nearly half of Smith juniors study abroad. Founded in 1871 by Sophia Smith (who left funds in her will to create a women's college) and her minister John Greene, the school also offers graduate degrees in areas such as education, social work, and fine arts. Smith's notable alumna include chef Julia Child, author and political commentator Molly Ivins, and feminist icon Gloria Steinem.

	Annual Growth	12/06	12/07	12/08*	06/11	06/12
Sales ($mil.)	326.6%	–	–	0.7	206.7	218.3
Net income ($ mil.)	–	–	–	–	221.9	(37.6)
Market value ($ mil.)	–	–	–	–	–	–
Employees	–	–	–	–	–	1,300

*Fiscal year change

THE TRUSTEES OF THE STEVENS INSTITUTE OF TECHNOLOGY

1 CASTLE POINT TER
HOBOKEN, NJ 070305906
Phone: 201 216-5000
Fax: –
Web: www.stevens.edu

CEO: –
CFO: Randy L Greene
HR: –
FYE: June 30
Type: Private

Stevens Institute of Technology was educating students in science, technology, and engineering. Founded in 1870 through an endowment from engineer Edwin Stevens, the university offers undergraduate, master's, and doctoral degrees in engineering, science, humanities, computer science, and technology management. The school enrolls some 4,070 undergraduates and roughly 5,245 graduate students. Stevens Institute teams up with corporate and military institutions to provide students with hands-on research experience; technology drives every program at Stevens, from medical device design to cybersecurity to music and arts coursework.

	Annual Growth	06/18	06/19	06/20	06/21	06/22
Sales ($mil.)	20.6%	–	265.8	277.3	267.4	466.4
Net income ($ mil.)	20.6%	–	29.1	25.7	71.8	51.0
Market value ($ mil.)	–	–	–	–	–	–
Employees	–	–	–	–	–	500

THE TRUSTEES OF THE UNIVERSITY OF PENNSYLVANIA

3451 WALNUT ST RM 440A
PHILADELPHIA, PA 191046205
Phone: 215 898-5000
Fax: –
Web: www.upenn.edu

CEO: –
CFO: –
HR: Gina Delaurentiis
FYE: June 30
Type: Private

The University of Pennsylvania was founded by Benjamin Franklin when he had a little down time between establishing a country and experimenting with lightning. Since opening its doors to students in 1751, the Ivy League university has accumulated a notable list of accomplishments, including the creation of one of the first medical schools in the US. The university currently has a total of nearly 28,200 students who pursue their studies in four undergraduate schools and a dozen graduate and professional schools, including the renowned Wharton School and the Annenberg School for Communications. Its student-teacher ratio is a very low 6:1.

	Annual Growth	06/14	06/15	06/16	06/17	06/20
Sales ($mil.)	(83.1%)	–	–	–	9,194.2	44.5
Net income ($ mil.)	(79.5%)	–	–	–	1,734.8	15.0
Market value ($ mil.)	–	–	–	–	–	–
Employees	–	–	–	–	–	20,433

THE TRUSTEES OF WHEATON COLLEGE

501 COLLEGE AVE
WHEATON, IL 601875501
Phone: 630 752-5000
Fax: –
Web: www.wheaton.edu

CEO: –
CFO: –
HR: –
FYE: June 30
Type: Private

Wheaton College located in Wheaton, Illinois -- not to be confused with a school of the same name in Massachusetts -- is a interdenominational Christian college. The private school offers dozens of liberal arts programs of study, including a Ph.D. in Biblical and Theological Studies, to its undergraduate and graduate students. Liberal arts programs include literature, music, fine arts, biology, economics, and psychology. Wheaton College has about 3,000 students and a 12:1 student-teacher ratio. Wheaton College was founded in 1860 and is named after Warren L. Wheaton, who donated land to the school.

	Annual Growth	06/18	06/19	06/20	06/21	06/22
Sales ($mil.)	0.4%	–	128.7	127.2	280.8	130.4
Net income ($ mil.)	–	–	4.5	(4.8)	117.2	(111.8)
Market value ($ mil.)	–	–	–	–	–	–
Employees	–	–	–	–	–	820

THE TURNER CORPORATION

66 HUDSON BLVD E FL 36
NEW YORK, NY 100012196
Phone: 212 229-6000
Fax: –
Web: www.turnerconstruction.com

CEO: Peter J Davoren
CFO: Karen Gould
HR: Serena Roman
FYE: December 31
Type: Private

The Turner Corporation, a subsidiary of German construction giant HOCHTIEF, is the leading general building and construction management firm in the US (as ranked by Engineering News-Record), ahead of rivals Bechtel and Fluor. The firm operates primarily through subsidiary Turner Construction, and has worked on notable projects such as Madison Square Garden, the UN headquarters, Yankee Stadium, the Taipei 101 Tower, and the 68,000-seat open-air stadium for the San Francisco 49ers. Known for its large projects, also offers services for midsized and smaller projects and provides interior construction and renovation services.

	Annual Growth	12/11	12/12	12/13	12/14	12/15
Sales ($mil.)	7.1%	–	8,575.9	9,522.4	10,560	10,524
Net income ($ mil.)	12.9%	–	74.8	80.5	96.0	107.7
Market value ($ mil.)	–	–	–	–	–	–
Employees	–	–	–	–	–	5,000

THE UCLA FOUNDATION

10889 WILSHIRE BLVD STE 1100
LOS ANGELES, CA 900244200
Phone: 310 794-3193
Fax: –
Web: www.uclafoundation.org

CEO: –
CFO: –
HR: –
FYE: June 30
Type: Private

Helping to make La-La Land a little more erudite, The UCLA Foundation raises, manages, and disperses funds to help support the tripartite education, research, and service mission of UCLA. With more than $1 billion in assets, the organization funds the aforementioned purposes, as well as campus improvements and special programs. About half of the foundation's gifts received are provided by foundations; corporations and alumni each account for some 15% of gifts. The UCLA Progress Fund, predecessor of the foundation, was established in 1945 by the school's alumni association.

	Annual Growth	06/14	06/15	06/16	06/17	06/18
Assets ($mil.)	16.0%	–	–	–	3,050.8	3,539.4
Net income ($ mil.)	(3.1%)	–	–	–	346.9	336.4
Market value ($ mil.)	–	–	–	–	–	–
Employees	–	–	–	–	–	317

THE UNION MEMORIAL HOSPITAL

201 E UNIVERSITY PKWY
BALTIMORE, MD 212182891
Phone: 410 554-2865
Fax: –
Web: www.medstarhealth.org

CEO: –
CFO: –
HR: Holly P Adams
FYE: June 30
Type: Private

Not quite for time immemorial, but MedStar Union Memorial Hospital (formerly Union Memorial Hospital) has been caring for patients for more than 160 years. The Baltimore-area facility is a specialty acute-care hospital with about 250 beds and more than 620 physicians. Areas of clinical research and expertise include cardiac care, orthopedics and sports medicine. In addition, it offers a range of inpatient and outpatient services including diabetes and endocrine center, eye surgery center, general surgery, oncology, and thoracic and vascular surgery. MedStar Union Memorial offers post-graduate programs, orthopedic surgery residencies, and hand surgery fellowships. The company is a part of MedStar Health.

	Annual Growth	06/18	06/19	06/20	06/21	06/22
Sales ($mil.)	(2.0%)	–	440.2	446.1	463.7	413.9
Net income ($ mil.)	–	–	(8.2)	15.5	(6.2)	(20.5)
Market value ($ mil.)	–	–	–	–	–	–
Employees	–	–	–	–	–	2,400

THE UNITED METHODIST PUBLISHING HOUSE

2222 ROSA L PARKS BLVD
NASHVILLE, TN 372281306
Phone: 615 749-6000
Fax: –
Web: www.abingdonpress.com

CEO: –
CFO: –
HR: –
FYE: July 31
Type: Private

The United Methodist Publishing House (UMPH) keeps Christian clergy from running out of reading material. Operated by a board of directors selected by the United Methodist Church's jurisdictional conferences and Council of Bishops, the company publishes and distributes content for Christian clergy and laity. It develops, produces, and sells official denominational church school curriculum materials, books, bibles, and multimedia resources for homes, churches and offices. Founded in 1789, UMPH is the oldest and largest general agency of the United Methodist Church.

	Annual Growth	07/09	07/10	07/11	07/12	07/13
Sales ($mil.)	(19.7%)	–	88.6	84.3	51.8	45.9
Net income ($ mil.)	–	–	(0.9)	6.5	(19.1)	(6.5)
Market value ($ mil.)	–	–	–	–	–	–
Employees	–	–	–	–	–	1,000

THE UNIVERSITY OF AKRON

302 BUCHTEL MALL
AKRON, OH 443250002
Phone: 330 972-7111
Fax: –
Web: www.uakron.edu

CEO: –
CFO: Dallas A Grundy
HR: –
FYE: June 30
Type: Private

"Zip it!" may be an insult some places, but not at The University of Akron. The school, which has an enrollment of more than 28,000 students, plays collegiate sports as the Zips (Zippy the Kangaroo is its mascot). It offers more than 200 undergraduate majors and 100 master's degree programs, as well as certificate and associate degree programs, through a handful of schools and colleges. The University operates one branch campus, Wayne College in Orrville, Ohio, and four educational centers in Ohio: the Medina County University Center in Medina, the Holmes County Higher Education Center in Millersburg, UA Lakewood in Lakewood, and the Midpoint Campus Center in Brunswick.

	Annual Growth	06/03	06/04	06/05	06/06	06/10
Sales ($mil.)	5.5%	–	–	231.0	237.7	302.1
Net income ($ mil.)	19.4%	–	–	20.3	463.9	49.3
Market value ($ mil.)	–	–	–	–	–	–
Employees	–	–	–	–	–	5,445

THE UNIVERSITY OF ALABAMA SYSTEM

500 UNIVERSITY BLVD E
TUSCALOOSA, AL 354012181
Phone: 205 348-5861
Fax: –
Web: www.uasystem.edu

CEO: –
CFO: –
HR: Jessica Harrison
FYE: September 30
Type: Private

Students in the Heart of Dixie can choose from among three campuses overseen by The University of Alabama system. The flagship Tuscaloosa campus, created in 1936, offers more than 200 degree programs to more than 25,000 students. The University of Alabama at Birmingham offers nearly 140 degree programs and has an enrollment of more than 16,000 students; it is also home to the university's school of medicine and a 900-bed hospital. The system's Huntsville campus has about 7,000 students enrolled in its five colleges and graduate school. Each campus offers bachelor's, master's, and doctoral degree programs. The University of Alabama was founded in Tuscaloosa in 1831 as the state's first public university.

THE UNIVERSITY OF ARIZONA FOUNDATION

1111 N CHERRY AVE
TUCSON, AZ 857210111
Phone: 520 621-5494
Fax: –
Web: www.uafoundation.org

CEO: –
CFO: –
HR: –
FYE: June 30
Type: Private

The University of Arizona Foundation keeps Wildcat funds flowing. The not-for-profit organization raises funds and manages assets for the University of Arizona. Its eight-year Campaign Arizona fund-raising program, begun in 1998, garnered $1.2 billion for the school. That money went to endowing faculty positions, increasing scholarships, promoting research, and improving facilities and technology. The Foundation's asset management duties include protecting the value of stocks, bonds, real estate, and other university investments. It also funds and develops educational programs, provides construction assistance, and gives grants to faculty, students, and researchers. The organization was founded in 1958.

	Annual Growth	06/17	06/18	06/19	06/20	06/22
Sales ($mil.)	7.5%	–	209.0	207.0	161.2	279.1
Net income ($ mil.)	4.4%	–	109.6	89.1	43.8	130.2
Market value ($ mil.)	–	–	–	–	–	–
Employees	–	–	–	–	–	2

THE UNIVERSITY OF CENTRAL FLORIDA BOARD OF TRUSTEES

4000 CENTRAL FLORIDA BLVD
ORLANDO, FL 328168005
Phone: 407 823-2000
Fax: –
Web: www.ucf.edu

CEO: Beverly Seay
CFO: William F Merck II
HR: –
FYE: June 30
Type: Private

The University of Central Florida (UCF, whose mascot is a stylized knight) is part of the State University System of Florida. Boasting an enrollment of more than 68,440 students, UCF offers more than 240 degree programs through a dozen colleges. Areas of study include psychology, health sciences, biomedical sciences, nursing, computer science, mechanical engineering, biology, integrated business, finance, and hospitality management. From the main campus in east Orlando to UCF Downtown and Rosen College of Hospitality Management to the Academic Health Sciences Campus, UCF also has multiple regional locations and fully online programs ? including online bachelor's degrees, online graduate degrees, and online certificate.

	Annual Growth	06/06	06/07	06/08	06/21	06/22
Sales ($mil.)	2.7%	–	382.1	374.7	570.3	569.4
Net income ($ mil.)	–	–	152.7	108.3	(23.8)	(8.4)
Market value ($ mil.)	–	–	–	–	–	–
Employees	–	–	–	–	–	6,500

THE UNIVERSITY OF CHICAGO

5801 S ELLIS AVE
CHICAGO, IL 606375418
Phone: 773 702-1234
Fax: –
Web: www.uchicago.edu

CEO: Joseph Neubauer
CFO: Brett Padgett
HR: –
FYE: June 30
Type: Private

The University of Chicago ranks among the world's most esteemed major universities. The private institution has an enrollment of some 7,010 undergraduate and about 10,460 graduate students. The undergraduate branch offers a core liberal arts curriculum and majors in about 55 majors and over 45 minor areas. Graduate programs include the University of Chicago Law School and Booth School of Business, both of which consistently rank in the top 10 according to US News & World Report. The school also operates the University of Chicago Medicine, an academic health system, and has extensive research operations.

THE UNIVERSITY OF CHICAGO MEDICAL CENTER

5841 S MARYLAND AVE STE MC6051
CHICAGO, IL 606371443
Phone: 773 702-1000
Fax: –
Web: www.uchicagomedicine.org

CEO: James L Maderd
CFO: James M Watson
HR: Carolyn Burton
FYE: June 30
Type: Private

The University of Chicago Medical Center (UCMC) is a not-for-profit academic medical health system based on the campus of the University of Chicago in Hyde Park, and with hospitals, outpatient clinics and physician practices throughout Chicago and its suburbs. UCMC include the acute care Bernard A. Mitchell Hospital, the Comer Children's Hospital, a women's health and maternity facility, and an outpatient care center. UChicago Medicine unites five organizations to fulfill its tripartite mission of medical education, research and patient care: Pritzker School of Medicine, Biological Sciences Division, Medical Center, Community Health and Hospital Division, and UChicago Medicine Physicians. UCMC houses around 810 beds.

	Annual Growth	06/18	06/19	06/20	06/21	06/22
Sales ($mil.)	7.7%	–	2,387.5	2,547.7	2,789.2	2,985.4
Net income ($ mil.)	–	–	27.6	(53.7)	519.5	(90.6)
Market value ($ mil.)	–	–	–	–	–	–
Employees	–	–	–	–	–	9,346

THE UNIVERSITY OF DAYTON

300 COLLEGE PARK AVE
DAYTON, OH 454690002
Phone: 937 229-2919
Fax: –
Web: www.udayton.edu

CEO: Daniel J Curran Dr
CFO: –
HR: –
FYE: June 30
Type: Private

Approximately 11,770 students make the University of Dayton one of the nation's largest Catholic universities and the largest private university in Ohio. The institution offers more than 80 undergraduate and 50 graduate and doctoral programs. Students are recruited on a national basis and from foreign countries. The student population is about 8,445 undergraduate and more than 3,325 graduate students. It has a student-to-faculty ratio of 15:1. Well-known alumni include the late author and columnist Erma Bombeck.

	Annual Growth	06/18	06/19	06/20	06/21	06/22
Sales ($mil.)	5.6%	–	774.9	747.9	827.0	911.4
Net income ($ mil.)	34.4%	–	30.9	29.6	63.9	75.1
Market value ($ mil.)	–	–	–	–	–	–
Employees	–	–	–	–	–	4,500

THE UNIVERSITY OF HARTFORD

200 BLOOMFIELD AVE
WEST HARTFORD, CT 061171599
Phone: 860 768-4100
Fax: –
Web: www.hartford.edu

CEO: –
CFO: –
HR: –
FYE: June 30
Type: Private

While its roots date back to 1877, The University of Hartford wasn't officially chartered until 1957 with the merger of the Hartford Art School, the Hartt School of Music, and Hillyer College. The modern-day university still has a strong arts and music programs, and its Museum of American Political Life is home to what has been called the country's largest private collection of political memorabilia. University of Hartford, which operates three campuses in West Hartford, has about 7,000 students enrolled in more than 80 undergraduate and 30 graduate programs including business, nursing, and engineering.

	Annual Growth	06/17	06/18	06/19	06/20	06/22
Sales ($mil.)	(1.2%)	–	176.1	180.3	278.7	167.8
Net income ($ mil.)	–	–	12.8	(1.7)	(1.0)	(58.3)
Market value ($ mil.)	–	–	–	–	–	–
Employees	–	–	–	–	–	950

THE UNIVERSITY OF IOWA

125 N MADISON ST
IOWA CITY, IA 52242
Phone: 319 335-3500
Fax: –
Web: www.uiowa.edu

CEO: Lynette Marshall
CFO: Terry Johnson
HR: Brenda Dodge
FYE: June 30
Type: Private

The University of Iowa is one of America's premier public research universities. Founded in 1847, the University of Iowa has over 31,450 students (and a student-faculty ratio of approximately 15:1) at its Iowa City campus. It is home to a dozen colleges spanning more than 200 areas of study, including distinguished programs in applied physics, astronomy, speech and hearing sciences, nursing, and creative writing. It also offers more than 100 graduate, doctoral, and professional programs. Its Writers' Workshop was the nation's first creative writing advanced degree program. It also includes programs in law, engineering, teaching, and medicine, as well as the affiliated University of Iowa Hospitals and Clinics health care organization.

	Annual Growth	06/09	06/10	06/11	06/16	06/22
Sales ($mil.)	7.0%	–	–	2,067.9	2,859.6	4,357.2
Net income ($ mil.)	0.4%	–	–	253.8	253.9	265.1
Market value ($ mil.)	–	–	–	–	–	–
Employees	–	–	–	–	–	17,000

THE UNIVERSITY OF NORTH CAROLINA

910 RALEIGH RD
CHAPEL HILL, NC 275143916
Phone: 919 962-2211
Fax: –
Web: www.northcarolina.edu

CEO: L L Isley
CFO: Charles Perusse
HR: Ann Pittard
FYE: June 30
Type: Private

Tar heels can sink their feet into academia and athletics at The University of North Carolina. The system of 17 universities, including the flagship University of North Carolina at Chapel Hill campus, counts more than 220,000 undergraduate and graduate students across its campuses. It offers degrees in more than 200 disciplines. The university system, chartered in 1789, is home to medical schools, a teaching hospital, law schools, a veterinary school at NC State, a school of pharmacy, nursing programs, schools of education, schools of engineering, and a school for the arts. In addition, the system also operates the NC School of Science and Mathematics, a public residential high school for gifted students.

	Annual Growth	06/04	06/05	06/06	06/12	06/13
Sales ($mil.)	79.3%	–	–	30.9	0.2	1,838.7
Net income ($ mil.)	–	–	–	(9.5)	(0.6)	267.8
Market value ($ mil.)	–	–	–	–	–	–
Employees	–	–	–	–	–	55,000

THE UNIVERSITY OF NORTH CAROLINA AT CHARLOTTE

9201 UNIVERSITY CITY BLVD
CHARLOTTE, NC 282230001
Phone: 704 687-5727
Fax: –
Web: www.charlotte.edu

CEO: –
CFO: –
HR: –
FYE: June 30
Type: Private

The University of North Carolina at Charlotte is the second-largest of 17 institution members of the University of North Carolina system. Known as UNC Charlotte, the university offers about 170 undergraduate and graduate programs, including education, architecture, business, and engineering. The university spans 1,000 acres across four Charlotte campuses, including a research campus with programs in manufacturing, opto-electronics, and information technology. More than 1,000 full-time faculty members serve more than 27,000 students -- representing 22,000 undergraduates and 5,000 post-graduates. UNC Charlotte, founded in 1946 to serve returning WWII veterans, became a member of the UNC System in 1965.

	Annual Growth	06/16	06/17	06/18	06/19	06/21
Sales ($mil.)	(76.5%)	–	331.4	346.8	359.8	1.0
Net income ($ mil.)	(71.9%)	–	59.0	60.0	87.9	0.4
Market value ($ mil.)	–	–	–	–	–	–
Employees	–	–	–	–	–	3,030

THE UNIVERSITY OF NORTH CAROLINA HEALTH SYSTEM

101 MANNING DR
CHAPEL HILL, NC 275144423
Phone: 919 966-5111
Fax: –
Web: med.unc.edu

CEO: –
CFO: Chris Ellington
HR: Scott Doak
FYE: June 30
Type: Private

University of North Carolina Hospitals (UNCH) is at the heart of the UNC Health Care System (UNC HCS). The medical center provides acute care to the Tar Heel State through North Carolina Memorial Hospital, North Carolina Children's Hospital, North Carolina Neurosciences Hospital, and North Carolina Women's Hospital. Combined, the facilities have more than 800 beds. Specialties include cancer treatment at the North Carolina Cancer Hospital, organ transplantation, cardiac care, orthopedics, wound management, and rehabilitation. Not-for-profit UNC HCS is owned by the state of North Carolina and is affiliated with the UNC-Chapel Hill School of Medicine.

	Annual Growth	06/13	06/14	06/15	06/16	06/21
Sales ($mil.)	9.6%	–	–	1,385.6	1,551.3	2,397.8
Net income ($ mil.)	29.2%	–	–	110.9	87.6	516.6
Market value ($ mil.)	–	–	–	–	–	–
Employees		–	–	–	–	6,000

THE UNIVERSITY OF NORTH FLORIDA

1 UNF DR
JACKSONVILLE, FL 32224
Phone: 904 620-1000
Fax: –
Web: www.unf.edu

CEO: –
CFO: –
HR: Cheryl S Gonzalez
FYE: June 30
Type: Private

The University of North Florida, home of the fighting Ospreys, contains a handful of colleges in core fields of liberal arts and sciences. The public university provides about 50 undergraduate and 25 graduate degrees, including doctoral programs in health care and education. Florida residents traditionally make up about half of the university's student body of more than 16,250. It has about 13,540 undergraduate students, more than 1,730 graduate students, and more than 980 post-baccalaureate and non-degree students. About 56% of its students are female.

	Annual Growth	06/18	06/19	06/20	06/21	06/22
Sales ($mil.)	4.1%	–	126.7	124.3	139.5	142.8
Net income ($ mil.)	–	–	(0.3)	(4.4)	3.0	21.9
Market value ($ mil.)	–	–	–	–	–	–
Employees		–	–	–	–	1,400

THE UNIVERSITY OF SOUTHERN MISSISSIPPI

118 COLLEGE DR
HATTIESBURG, MS 394060002
Phone: 601 266-1000
Fax: –
Web: www.usm.edu

CEO: –
CFO: –
HR: –
FYE: June 30
Type: Private

You don't have to be a belle to attend Southern Miss, but it never hurts. The University of Southern Mississippi (USM or Southern Miss for short) was established by the state legislature in 1910 to educate Mississippi's teachers. The school has grown to boast an enrollment of more than 15,000 students with a student-teacher ratio of 17:1. USM offers bachelor's, master's, doctoral, and post-master's degrees through five colleges: College of Arts and Letters, College of Business, College of Education and Psychology, College of Health, and College of Science and Technology. Southern Miss also runs an Honors College and engages in extensive research in a range of disciplines including health and technology.

THE UNIVERSITY OF THE SOUTH

735 UNIVERSITY AVE
SEWANEE, TN 373831000
Phone: 931 598-1000
Fax: –
Web: www.sewanee.edu

CEO: –
CFO: –
HR: –
FYE: June 30
Type: Private

With more than two dozen Rhodes Scholars among its alumni, The University of the South, known as Sewanee, is ranked among America's top private liberal arts colleges. Sewanee, which serves about 1,600 students and boasts a student to faculty ratio of 10:1, offers more than 35 majors including computer science, mathematics, theology, and history. It is also home to a seminary of the Episcopal Church and a School of Letters summer Master's Degree program in English and creative writing. It holds the copyrights to Tennessee Williams' body of work, which was left to the school by the playwright. Sewanee traces its roots back to 1857 when Episcopal leaders from 10 southern states met to discuss the formation of the school.

	Annual Growth	06/17	06/18	06/19	06/20	06/22
Sales ($mil.)	1.3%	–	112.6	122.9	110.7	118.6
Net income ($ mil.)	–	–	23.3	18.1	10.7	(83.8)
Market value ($ mil.)	–	–	–	–	–	–
Employees		–	–	–	–	550

THE UNIVERSITY OF TOLEDO

2801 W BANCROFT ST
TOLEDO, OH 436063390
Phone: 419 530-4636
Fax: –
Web: www.utoledo.edu

CEO: –
CFO: –
HR: Bonnie Harrell
FYE: June 30
Type: Private

The University of Toledo is one of just 27 public research universities in the country to offer such a comprehensive menu of academic options of more than 300 undergraduate and graduate degree programs across the arts, business, education, engineering, law, medicine, natural sciences, nursing, and pharmacy both on-campus and online. Serving more than 14,600 students, the university has a student-to-faculty ratio of 18:1. UT's about 15 colleges focus on subjects ranging from arts and letters to business and innovation, as well as education, engineering, law, medicine, nursing, pharmacy, natural sciences, mathematics, chemistry, and health and human services. The school also operates the University of Toledo Medical Center.

	Annual Growth	06/16	06/17	06/18	06/21	06/22
Sales ($mil.)	2.8%	–	728.1	716.8	754.8	835.6
Net income ($ mil.)	–	–	(62.5)	55.7	274.3	79.3
Market value ($ mil.)	–	–	–	–	–	–
Employees		–	–	–	–	7,000

THE UNIVERSITY OF TULSA

800 S TUCKER DR
TULSA, OK 741049700
Phone: 918 631-2000
Fax: –
Web: www.utulsa.edu

CEO: –
CFO: –
HR: –
FYE: June 30
Type: Private

If you're "Living on Tulsa Time" and looking for an education, then the home of the Golden Hurricanes is the place to be. The University of Tulsa is a private university affiliated with the Presbyterian Church (USA) with an enrollment of about 5,000 students. The school offers more than 60 undergraduate and about 35 graduate programs, including a dozen doctoral degree programs, at colleges of arts and sciences, business, and engineering and natural sciences. The University of Tulsa was founded in Muskogee in 1882 as the Presbyterian School for Indian Girls and was chartered as Henry Kendall College in 1894. The school moved to Tulsa in 1907 and became The University of Tulsa in 1920.

	Annual Growth	06/14	06/15	06/20	06/21	06/22
Sales ($mil.)	7.7%	–	206.1	292.1	321.4	346.9
Net income ($ mil.)	10.1%	–	30.7	(13.1)	47.2	60.0
Market value ($ mil.)	–	–	–	–	–	–
Employees		–	–	–	–	1,033

THE UNIVERSITY OF UTAH

201 PRESIDENTS CIR
SALT LAKE CITY, UT 841129049
Phone: 801 581-7200
Fax: –
Web: www.utah.edu

CEO: –
CFO: –
HR: Mary A Berzins
FYE: June 30
Type: Private

The University of Utah (U of U) is the state's oldest and most comprehensive institution of higher education and is the flagship institution of the state system of higher education. Founded in 1850 as the University of Deseret, the U of U has a total enrollment of more than 34,700 undergraduate and graduate students, with a student-to-faculty ratio of some 18:1. It offers over 100 major subjects at the undergraduate and graduate level at about 20 colleges and schools; its business, science, humanities, and engineering departments are the university's largest. It also offers medical, nursing, and pharmacy programs, as well as health and social science research programs. U of U confers about 8,700 baccalaureate, masters, and doctoral degrees annually.

	Annual Growth	06/06	06/07	06/08*	12/08*	06/13
Sales ($mil.)	164.4%	–	–	22.5	0.6	2,907.6
Net income ($ mil.)	–	–	–	(10.8)	–	186.7
Market value ($ mil.)	–	–	–	–	–	–
Employees	–	–	–	–	–	18,000

*Fiscal year change

THE UNIVERSITY OF VERMONT MEDICAL CENTER INC

111 COLCHESTER AVE
BURLINGTON, VT 054011473
Phone: 802 847-0000
Fax: –
Web: www.uvmhealth.org

CEO: John R Brumssted
CFO: Todd Keating
HR: –
FYE: September 30
Type: Private

The University of Vermont Medical Center (formerly Fletcher Allen Health Care) provides medical care in the Green Mountain State. It operates an academic medical center in alliance with the University of Vermont College of Medicine. The not-for-profit health system serves residents of Vermont and northern New York through three primary hospital campuses in Chittenden County, Vermont, over 65 outpatient practices and more than 100 clinics, programs, and services. The UVM Medical Center is Vermont's only Level 1 Trauma Center, with the state's sole Neonatal Intensive Care Unit. The University of Vermont Medical Center, its three founding organizations and the Larner College of Medicine at UVM, share a rich history dating back to the 1800s.

	Annual Growth	09/15	09/16	09/17	09/18	09/20
Sales ($mil.)	(3.3%)	–	1,181.7	1,246.9	1,363.5	1,033.4
Net income ($ mil.)	(19.6%)	–	85.1	129.4	68.9	35.5
Market value ($ mil.)	–	–	–	–	–	–
Employees	–	–	–	–	–	7,000

THE UNLV RESEARCH FOUNDATION

4505 S MARYLAND PKWY
LAS VEGAS, NV 891549900
Phone: 702 405-9100
Fax: –
Web: www.epscorspo.nevada.edu

CEO: Jeremy Aguero
CFO: –
HR: Kelly Scherado
FYE: June 30
Type: Private

Sometimes what happens in Vegas doesn't stay there -- especially if you attended school there. The UNLV Foundation raises and manages funds for the University of Nevada, Las Vegas (UNLV); it uses donations and gifts to support the school with school programs, equipment, endowments, scholarships, and facilities management. Among the not-for-profit's money-raising activities are the Rebel Ringers Phonathon (student outreach to school alumni and friends) and the Academic Corporate Council (the members of which donate more than $5,000 of unrestricted gifts annually).

	Annual Growth	06/15	06/16	06/18	06/19	06/21
Sales ($mil.)	36.4%	–	0.1	0.4	0.7	0.5
Net income ($ mil.)	–	–	(0.6)	(0.3)	0.0	0.2
Market value ($ mil.)	–	–	–	–	–	–
Employees	–	–	–	–	–	9

THE URBAN INSTITUTE

500 LENFANT PLZ SW FL 2
WASHINGTON, DC 200242274
Phone: 202 833-7200
Fax: –
Web: www.urban.org

CEO: –
CFO: –
HR: Gabriela Basma
FYE: December 31
Type: Private

The Urban Institute is a not-for-profit economic and social policy research organization that oversees research projects in such areas as education, health policy, employment, income and benefits, housing and communities, population studies, poverty, and judicial issues. Its Urban Institute Press publishes books and reports addressing social and economic issues from tax policy to prison reform. About three-fourths of the institution's funding comes from the federal government; most of the rest comes from foundations including The Aspen Institute and the California Endowment. The Urban Institute was established as a non-partisan research facility in 1968 by the Johnson Administration.

	Annual Growth	12/10	12/11	12/12	12/13	12/17
Sales ($mil.)	3.1%	–	71.8	82.5	77.0	86.1
Net income ($ mil.)	–	–	(2.8)	17.6	(0.5)	(7.1)
Market value ($ mil.)	–	–	–	–	–	–
Employees	–	–	–	–	–	400

THE VALLEY HOSPITAL INC

223 N VAN DIEN AVE
RIDGEWOOD, NJ 074502736
Phone: 201 447-8000
Fax: –
Web: www.valleyhealth.com

CEO: –
CFO: –
HR: Jose Balderrama
FYE: December 31
Type: Private

The Valley Hospital is second to none when it comes to its Same-Day Service program. More than one-third of the company's annual patients experience its longstanding continuum of one-day service; fully half the surgeries performed are same-day. The not-for-profit hospital is a 450-bed facility providing general and emergency services to residents of New Jersey's Bergen County. The hospital belongs to the Valley Health System, which also includes subsidiaries Valley Home Care and Valley Health Medical Group, and is an affiliate member of NewYork-Presbyterian Healthcare. The Valley Hospital, New Jersey's second busiest, has more than 800 physicians on its medical staff.

	Annual Growth	12/17	12/18	12/19	12/20	12/21
Sales ($mil.)	7.8%	–	695.1	860.1	739.6	869.7
Net income ($ mil.)	7.0%	–	128.1	113.3	161.5	157.0
Market value ($ mil.)	–	–	–	–	–	–
Employees	–	–	–	–	–	2,900

THE VANDERBILT UNIVERSITY

2301 VANDERBILT PL
NASHVILLE, TN 372350002
Phone: 615 322-7311
Fax: –
Web: www.vanderbilt.edu

CEO: Mark Dalton
CFO: Brett Sweet
HR: –
FYE: June 30
Type: Private

The Vanderbilt University was founded in 1873 with a $1 million grant from industrialist Cornelius Vanderbilt. Since then, the university's endowment has grown to approximately $6.9 billion, making the Nashville school a haven for its more than 12,300 students and nearly 4,360 full-time faculty members. Boasting a 7:1 student-faculty ratio, Vanderbilt offers undergraduate and graduate programs in areas such as education and human development, divinity, engineering, and the arts and sciences. The university operates some 10 schools and colleges. Vanderbilt's Owen Graduate School of Management and its medical school regularly rank near the top in national surveys.

	Annual Growth	06/13	06/14	06/15	06/16	06/17
Sales ($mil.)	(43.6%)	–	–	4,121.8	1,270.8	1,311.5
Net income ($ mil.)	68.9%	–	–	131.3	(569.3)	374.6
Market value ($ mil.)	–	–	–	–	–	–
Employees	–	–	–	–	–	21,000

THE VANGUARD GROUP INC

100 VANGUARD BLVD
MALVERN, PA 193552331
Phone: 877 662-7447
Fax: –
Web: www.vanguardag.com

CEO: Mortimer Buckley
CFO: –
HR: –
FYE: December 31
Type: Private

The Vanguard Group is one of the world's most respected investment management companies, offering a broad selection of investments, advice, retirement services, and insights to individual investors, institutions, and financial professionals. Boasting more than $7.6 trillion of assets under management, Vanguard is one of the largest investment companies. Vanguard offers about 205 US funds and more than 225 funds outside the US to its more than 50 million investors. Known for its low-cost mutual funds, Vanguard was founded in 1975.

	Annual Growth	12/03	12/04	12/05	12/06	12/21
Assets ($mil.)	(22.6%)	–	–	1,582.6	1,830.1	26.3
Net income ($ mil.)	–	–	–	116.5	151.8	(2.5)
Market value ($ mil.)	–	–	–	–	–	–
Employees	–	–	–	–	–	22,507

THE VISCARDI CENTER INC

201 I U WILLETS RD
ALBERTSON, NY 115071516
Phone: 516 747-5400
Fax: –
Web: www.viscardicenter.org

CEO: Chris Rosa
CFO: –
HR: –
FYE: June 30
Type: Private

Abilities! helps people find theirs. The not-for-profit organization works to support people with disabilities through education and training programs, research, public policy, and advocacy. Its Kornreich Technology Center provides demonstrations and training on assistive technology while the Smeal Learning Center offers audiovisual production tools and conference space. Its Henry Viscardi School educates disabled students in and around New York City from pre-K through 12th grades. Dr. Henry Viscardi founded Abilities, Inc., in 1952 to help disabled people (primarily WWII veterans) find employment. Known as the National Center for Disability Services since 1991, the group changed its name again in 2004.

	Annual Growth	06/09	06/10	06/11	06/15	06/22
Sales ($mil.)	2.9%	–	3.7	2.7	8.6	5.2
Net income ($ mil.)	–	–	(1.8)	(4.5)	3.8	0.0
Market value ($ mil.)	–	–	–	–	–	–
Employees	–	–	–	–	–	72

THE WACHTELL LIPTON ROSEN & KATZ FOUNDATION

51 W 52ND ST
NEW YORK, NY 100196119
Phone: 212 403-1000
Fax: –
Web: www.wlrk.com

CEO: –
CFO: –
HR: Elizabeth Acierno
FYE: September 30
Type: Private

Wachtell, Lipton, Rosen & Katz specializes in representing companies involved in mergers and acquisitions and corporate securities transactions. Its practice is comprised of a dedicated core of attorneys with deep experience with high-stakes issues confronting financial institutions ? mergers, acquisitions, restructurings, financings, joint ventures, enforcement actions, internal investigations, executive succession, and crisis management. Represented the NYSE in connection with the Exchange's listing standards and corporate governance initiatives for listed companies, the firm also represented a number of major corporations in connection with corporate governance and related matters. It also advised special committees of boards of directors, including the boards of Novartis, Publicis and National Australia Bank, in connection with corporate governance investigations and related matters. The firm was founded on a handshake in 1965 as a small group of lawyers dedicated to providing advice and expertise at the highest levels.

THE WALDINGER CORPORATION

6200 SCOUT TRL
DES MOINES, IA 503211189
Phone: 515 284-1911
Fax: –
Web: www.waldinger.com

CEO: Thomas K Koehn
CFO: –
HR: Juanita McCarthy
FYE: December 31
Type: Private

The Waldinger Corporation may actually do most of its work before the walls are even up. The company is an electrical, mechanical, and sheet metal contractor that primarily serves US customers across the Midwest and Southeast. Through its work in more than 40 states, Waldinger designs, fabricates, installs, and maintains HVAC, refrigeration, electrical, plumbing, and piping for commercial, institutional, and industrial clients. Waldinger also operates a division devoted to the food service industry. The company has offices in Iowa, Kansas, Missouri, and Nebraska. Austrian tinsmith Harry Waldinger founded the company as Capital City Tin Shop in 1906.

THE WALMAN OPTICAL COMPANY

801 12TH AVE N STE 1
MINNEAPOLIS, MN 554114502
Phone: 612 520-6000
Fax: –
Web: www.walman.com

CEO: Martin Bassett
CFO: Dustin J Lavalley
HR: Nancy Klaers
FYE: November 30
Type: Private

Walman Optical brings it all into focus. The wholesaler processes ophthalmic components, providing finished lenses and frames to ophthalmologists, optometrists, and opticians. Walman Optical has more than 40 offices in nearly 20 US states. Half of those locations are prescription lens-finishing labs, while the rest offer optical instruments, contacts, designer lines, and a discount buying club for ophthalmologists, optometrists, and opticians. The company also runs Walman University, a traveling accredited school for eyecare professionals, and supplies safety eyewear to companies such as AT&T, Medtronic, Thermo-King, and the Norfolk Naval Shipyard. The company was founded in 1915 by optican J.A.L. Walman.

THE WALSH GROUP LTD

929 W ADAMS ST
CHICAGO, IL 606073021
Phone: 312 563-5400
Fax: –
Web: www.walshgroup.com

CEO: Matthew M Walsh
CFO: –
HR: –
FYE: December 31
Type: Private

Operating through subsidiaries Walsh Construction, Walsh Canada, and Archer Western Contractors, The Walsh Group provides design/build, general contracting, and construction services for industrial, public, and commercial projects. The family-owned company offers complete project management services, from demolition and planning to general contracting and finance. The company is involved in the construction of highways, water treatment facilities, airports, hotels, convention centers, correctional facilities, and commercial, industrial, and residential buildings. Walsh operates out of roughly 20 offices in North America. The company was founded in 1898 by Matthew Myles Walsh.

	Annual Growth	12/06	12/07	12/08	12/09	12/10
Sales ($mil.)	(1.0%)	–	–	3,534.7	3,316.0	3,462.3
Net income ($ mil.)	(4.4%)	–	–	203.6	191.9	186.2
Market value ($ mil.)	–	–	–	–	–	–
Employees	–	–	–	–	–	5,000

THE WARRIOR GROUP INC

1624 FALCON DR STE 100
DESOTO, TX 751152543
Phone: 972 228-9955
Fax: –
Web: facebook.com/warrior-group-154809827874149/

CEO: –
CFO: –
HR: –
FYE: December 31
Type: Private

The Warrior Group has its work cut out for it, literally. A modular construction and construction management services company, Warrior Group builds permanent modular buildings -- including military dormitories, student housing, and office buildings -- from prefabricated wood and metal components. Its construction management offerings include planning, design, purchasing, engineering, and post-construction services. In recent years, the company has worked on projects for the Veterans Administration in Marion, Illinois; built barracks at Fort Bliss and other military installations; and managed a construction project at the University of North Texas. Warrior Group was founded in 1997 by CEO Gail Warrior-Lawrence.

	Annual Growth	12/05	12/06	12/07	12/08	12/09
Sales ($mil.)	72.5%	–	–	41.7	0.3	124.0
Net income ($ mil.)	167.2%	–	–	1.4	0.0	9.7
Market value ($ mil.)	–	–	–	–	–	–
Employees	–	–	–	–	–	36

THE WASHINGTON AND LEE UNIVERSITY

204 W WASHINGTON ST
LEXINGTON, VA 244502554
Phone: 540 458-8400
Fax: –
Web: www.wlu.edu

CEO: –
CFO: –
HR: –
FYE: June 30
Type: Private

One of the oldest colleges in the country, Washington and Lee University (W&L) was founded in 1749 and is named after George Washington (who bequeathed the school its first major endowment) and Confederate general Robert E. Lee (a former president of the institution). The highly ranked liberal arts school in Lexington, Virginia is attended by more than 2,300 students who take courses in about 40 major areas including public policy, politics, international studies, physics, and biochemistry. The university has more than 200 faculty and a student-to-faculty ratio of 9:1. Former US Supreme Court Justice and W&L alumni Lewis F. Powell donated his personal and professional papers to the university's prestigious law school.

	Annual Growth	06/13	06/14	06/20	06/21	06/22
Sales ($mil.)	3.2%	–	194.0	186.2	178.4	248.8
Net income ($ mil.)	–	–	0.7	(55.0)	474.3	(6.1)
Market value ($ mil.)	–	–	–	–	–	–
Employees	–	–	–	–	–	700

THE WASHINGTON UNIVERSITY

1 BROOKINGS DR
SAINT LOUIS, MO 631304899
Phone: 314 935-5000
Fax: –
Web: www.wustl.edu

CEO: –
CFO: –
HR: –
FYE: June 30
Type: Private

Washington University in St. Louis is among the world's leaders in teaching, research, patient care, and service to society. It is an institution of higher education that, in furtherance of its role as a charitable and educational institution, engages in various activities, including instruction, research and provision of medical care. Founded in 1853 by William Green Leaf Eliot Jr., the independent university offers more than 300 academic programs such as accounting, biology, chemistry, dance, economics, French and more. With a student to faculty ratio of 7:1, it has about 4,320 faculty members. The university has more than 17,045 undergraduates and graduate and professional students from more than 100 countries and all 50 states, the District of Columbia, Guam, Puerto Rico, and the Northern Mariana Islands. It has about 380 undergraduate student groups and more than 150 graduate student groups. The affiliated Washington University Medical Center is an acute-care hospital that also provides educational training and research services.

	Annual Growth	06/18	06/19	06/20	06/21	06/22
Sales ($mil.)	7.8%	–	3,544.5	3,749.7	3,837.7	4,435.6
Net income ($ mil.)	–	–	555.0	719.4	5,981.8	(1,705.7)
Market value ($ mil.)	–	–	–	–	–	–
Employees	–	–	–	–	–	9,600

THE WATER WORKS BOARD OF THE CITY OF BIRMINGHAM

3600 1ST AVE N
BIRMINGHAM, AL 352221210
Phone: 205 244-4000
Fax: –
Web: www.bwwb.org

CEO: –
CFO: –
HR: Latasia Sanford
FYE: December 31
Type: Private

Water works like magic in the Magic City. The Birmingham Water Works Board distributes water in and around the city of Birmingham, Alabama. The company serves more than 600,000 customers in a five-county area. It draws water from surface sources in the Black Warrior and Cahaba river basins and maintains a system of more than 3,900 miles of transmission lines. Birmingham Water Works also runs two sewage treatment facilities, but most of the wastewater service in the company's territory is provided by other companies. Founded in 1951, Birmingham Water Works is an independent agency run by a board appointed by the Birmingham city government.

	Annual Growth	12/07	12/08	12/16	12/18	12/22
Sales ($mil.)	4.2%	–	120.2	173.0	184.3	213.1
Net income ($ mil.)	–	–	(7.2)	16.2	26.2	32.0
Market value ($ mil.)	–	–	–	–	–	–
Employees	–	–	–	–	–	460

THE WATSON INSTITUTE

301 CAMPMEETING RD
SEWICKLEY, PA 151438773
Phone: 412 741-1800
Fax: –
Web: www.thewatsoninstitute.org

CEO: Barry W Bohn
CFO: –
HR: Linda Campbell
FYE: June 30
Type: Private

There's nothing elementary, my dear, about this Watson. The Watson Institute provides special education and related programs for children with special needs ranging in age from 3 to 21. It operates preschool and summer camp programs, and provides child assessment and therapy for children with autism, cerebral palsy, brain injuries, neurological impairments, and other developmental and emotional disabilities. The institute also helps families through its in-home CareBreak program, support groups, and day and overnight respite camps. The Watson Institute was founded by Pittsburgh business leader David Thompson Watson and his wife Maria Morgan Watson.

	Annual Growth	06/17	06/18	06/19	06/20	06/22
Sales ($mil.)	22.0%	–	5.8	6.8	19.4	12.9
Net income ($ mil.)	(8.0%)	–	7.9	5.1	12.7	5.6
Market value ($ mil.)	–	–	–	–	–	–
Employees	–	–	–	–	–	262

THE WESTERN & SOUTHERN LIFE INSURANCE COMPANY

400 BROADWAY ST STOP G
CINCINNATI, OH 452023341
Phone: 513 629-1800
Fax: –
Web: www.westernsouthern.com

CEO: John F Barrett
CFO: –
HR: Beth Brozzart
FYE: December 31
Type: Private

The Western and Southern Life Insurance Company, and its wholly-owned subsidiary, Western-Southern Life Assurance Company (both known as Western & Southern Life), offer fixed annuities, limited health insurance products and life insurance products for individuals, families and businesses. The Western and Southern Life Insurance Company, established in 1888, conducts business in the District of Columbia and all states except Alaska, Maine, Massachusetts and New York. Western-Southern Life Assurance Company, established in 1981, conducts business in the District of Columbia and all states except New York. Both are based in Cincinnati, Ohio and are member companies of Western & Southern Financial Group.

	Annual Growth	12/04	12/05	12/09	12/21	12/22
Assets ($mil.)	(32.5%)	–	8,308.1	8.0	9.8	10.3
Net income ($ mil.)	–	–	–	(2.0)	(1.0)	2.7
Market value ($ mil.)	–	–	–	–	–	–
Employees	–	–	–	–	–	4,000

THE WHITING-TURNER CONTRACTING COMPANY

300 E JOPPA RD
BALTIMORE, MD 212863047
Phone: 410 821-1100
Fax: –
Web: www.whiting-turner.com

CEO: Timothy J Regan
CFO: –
HR: Shawna Apodaca
FYE: December 31
Type: Private

The Whiting-Turner Contracting provides construction management, general contracting, and design/build, and integrated services, primarily for large commercial, institutional, and infrastructure projects conducted across the US. A key player in retail construction, the employee-owned company also undertakes such projects as biotech cleanrooms, theme parks, historical restorations, senior living residences, educational facilities, stadiums, and corporate headquarters. Its clients include the US Marine, FedEx Ground, IBM, Costco, Las Vegas City Hall, Yale University, Stanford University, and NASA Langley Research Center Headquarters Building, among others. Operates from more than 50 locations across the US, Whiting-Turner Contracting was founded by G.W.C. Whiting and LeBaron Turner in 1909.

	Annual Growth	12/12	12/13	12/14	12/15	12/16
Sales ($mil.)	(6.7%)	–	–	6,347.1	5,729.8	5,522.3
Net income ($ mil.)	9.8%	–	–	75.3	80.0	90.9
Market value ($ mil.)	–	–	–	–	–	–
Employees						4,560

THE WILL-BURT COMPANY

401 COLLINS BLVD
ORRVILLE, OH 446679752
Phone: 330 682-7015
Fax: –
Web: www.willburt.com

CEO: Jeffrey Evans
CFO: –
HR: Courtney Abel
FYE: November 13
Type: Private

It's a Roger WILCO for Will-Burt Company, a manufacturer of roof- and vertical-mounted masts for use in fire and rescue, police and security, weather, military, broadcast, and cellular applications. The pneumatic and mechanical telescoping masts and accessories elevate lights, communication (antennae) and surveillance equipment, and cameras. Military masts include vehicle mounted and portable field masts. Will-Burt also designs and develops lighting systems, mobile command centers, and printed circuit boards. Customers include large companies in the US, as well as government and military clients worldwide. Will-Burt, an employee-owned company, has offices in the US, the UK, Germany, and Singapore.

THE WILLAMETTE VALLEY COMPANY LLC

990 OWEN LOOP N
EUGENE, OR 974029173
Phone: 541 484-9621
Fax: –
Web: www.wilvaco.com

CEO: John Murray
CFO: Jason Cunningham
HR: –
FYE: December 31
Type: Private

Willamette Valley makes a wide landscape of synthetic paints, primers, sealers, and adhesives for the wood products industry. It also provides metering, dispensing, and application equipment. The company's divisions include Canadian Willamette, Tapel Willamette (a Chilean coatings subsidiary), Idaho Milling and Grain, and Eclectic Products (adhesives, spackle, and so forth). Willamette Valley has manufacturing operations and subsidiaries throughout the US as well as in Canada and Chile; it also provides services to European and Asian customers.

THE WILLS GROUP INC

6355 CRAIN HWY
LA PLATA, MD 206464267
Phone: 301 932-3600
Fax: –
Web: www.willsgroup.com

CEO: Julian B Wills
CFO: –
HR: Steve Niven
FYE: September 30
Type: Private

The Wills Group willingly delivers petroleum products and related products and services to its customer base in southern Maryland and adjacent areas. The family-owned company operates four business subsidiaries: Dash-In Convenience Stores (with 35 locations, including 18 franchises); DMO (provider of propane, heating oil, and HVAC equipment); and Southern Maryland Oil (SMO) and SMO Motor Fuels (distribution of diesel, gasoline, and kerosene products). More than 90% of SMO's gasoline products are Shell-branded fuels. The Wills Group supplies more than 300 dealer-operated gas stations in Delaware, southern Maryland, and Washington, DC.

THE WINE GROUP INC

17000 E STATE HIGHWAY 120
RIPON, CA 953669412
Phone: 209 599-4111
Fax: –
Web: www.thewinegroup.com

CEO: Arthur Ciocca
CFO: –
HR: Melissa Moore
FYE: December 31
Type: Private

One of the largest wine producers in the world, The Wine Group (TWG) offers bargain and premium table wines (bottled and boxed). The company takes pride in producing award-winning, quality wine for all occasions. It has over 60 brand names that include Concannon, Ava Grace, Franzia, Glen Ellen, Almaden, Foxhorn, and Fish Eye, among others. The company has multiple facilities located across California, in addition to Westfield, New York and Loxton, Australia. Once part of Coca-Cola in 1970, TWG is a partnership formed in 1981 to buy Franzia Brothers Winery, Mogen David, and Tribuno.

THE WISTAR INSTITUTE OF ANATOMY AND BIOLOGY

3601 SPRUCE ST
PHILADELPHIA, PA 191044265
Phone: 215 898-1570
Fax: –
Web: www.wistar.org

CEO: Russel E Kaufman
CFO: –
HR: –
FYE: December 31
Type: Private

When the ailing wish upon a star, Wistar might be able to find them a cure. Founded in 1892, The Wistar Institute is a not-for-profit biomedical research institution concentrating on major diseases such as cancer, immune-system disorders, heart ailments, and infectious diseases. The institute operates from about 30 laboratories with research programs targeting genetic, molecular, and cellular discoveries. The company's research has been used in the development of vaccines, pharmaceuticals, and biotechnology drugs. Wistar collaborates with educational and governmental partners.

THE WORKERS COMPENSATION RESEARCH INSTITUTE

955 MASSACHUSETTS AVE STE 600
CAMBRIDGE, MA 02139
Phone: 617 661-9274
Fax: –
Web: www.wcrinet.org

CEO: –
CFO: –
HR: –
FYE: June 30
Type: Private

The Workers Compensation Research Institute (WCRI) provides independent research on the performance of workers' comp systems. So it can focus on unbiased studies and information gathering, the not-for-profit organization doesn't take positions on public policy issues. Among the topics on which WCRI conducts research are the performance of different workers' comp systems, system costs, and effects of regulatory changes. Members of WCRI, who support the institute's work and receive its reports, include insurers, government entities, and large employers. WCRI was founded in 1983.

	Annual Growth	06/17	06/18	06/19	06/20	06/22
Sales ($mil.)	0.8%	–	7.9	8.6	8.1	8.1
Net income ($ mil.)	–	–	(0.2)	(0.1)	(0.5)	(0.1)
Market value ($ mil.)	–	–	–	–	–	–
Employees	–	–	–	–	–	20

THE YATES COMPANIES INC

1 GULLY AVE
PHILADELPHIA, MS 39350
Phone: 601 656-5411
Fax: –
Web: www.yatescompanies.com

CEO: –
CFO: Brandon Dunn
HR: –
FYE: November 21
Type: Private

The Yates Companies operates an extended family of construction firms, comprising W.G. Yates & Sons Construction, Yates Electrical Division, Mississippi-based JESCO, and Tennessee-based Blaine Construction. The group provides a broad range of construction-related services, including engineering, electrical and mechanical construction, millwrighting, and steel fabrication. It operates mostly in the Southeast and along the East Coast through nearly 20 offices. Completed projects include casinos, sports facilities, schools, and military facilities. William Yates, Jr., co-founded the family-owned company in 1964 with his father, the late William Gully Yates. The Yates family still leads the company.

THEDACARE REGIONAL MEDICAL CENTER - APPLETON, INC.

1818 N MEADE ST
APPLETON, WI 549113454
Phone: 920 731-4101
Fax: –
Web: www.thedacare.org

CEO: Dean Gruner
CFO: Tim Olson
HR: –
FYE: December 31
Type: Private

If an apple a day doesn't keep the doctor away, residents of northeastern Wisconsin can always turn to Appleton Medical Center. Along with general and specialized health services, the medical center's specialties include cardiac, cancer, and orthopedic care. Appleton Medical Center is operated by ThedaCare. Established in 1958, the non-sectarian not-for-profit hospital started the first fertility program in the region.

	Annual Growth	12/00	12/01	12/02	12/05	12/19
Sales ($mil.)	–	–	(1,467.5)	–	429.8	0.0
Net income ($ mil.)	22.6%	–	0.0	–	11.4	0.0
Market value ($ mil.)	–	–	–	–	–	–
Employees	–	–	–	–	–	1,230

THEDACARE, INC.

3 NEENAH CTR
NEENAH, WI 549563070
Phone: 920 454-4156
Fax: –
Web: www.thedacare.org

CEO: Imran Andrabi
CFO: Tim Olson
HR: –
FYE: December 31
Type: Private

ThedaCare is one of the leading nonprofit providers in northeast and central Wisconsin. It consists of seven hospitals, including Appleton Medical Center, Theda Clark Medical Center, New London Family Medical Center, Shawano Medical Center, and ThedaCare Medical Center in Waupaca; three dozen physician clinics; and community health and wellness programs. The hospitals provide pain management, neurology and stroke, behavioral health, orthopedics and cardiovascular services. ThedaCare also operates long-term care and assisted living facilities and provides occupational health and emergency transport services.

	Annual Growth	12/16	12/17	12/18	12/19	12/22
Sales ($mil.)	4.7%	–	–	995.2	1,057.4	1,197.0
Net income ($ mil.)	–	–	–	(1.7)	126.6	(95.7)
Market value ($ mil.)	–	–	–	–	–	–
Employees	–	–	–	–	–	7,000

THERAPEUTICSMD INC

NMS: TXMD

951 Yamato Road, Suite 220
Boca Raton, FL 33431
Phone: 561 961-1900
Fax: –
Web: www.therapeuticsmd.com

CEO: Hugh O'Dowd
CFO: James C D'Arecca
HR: Daniel Escobar
FYE: December 31
Type: Public

TherapeuticsMD is a women's healthcare company with a mission of creating and commercializing innovative products to support the lifespan of women from pregnancy prevention through menopause. The company makes prescription prenatal vitamins under the brand vitaMedMD and authorized generic formulations of its prescription prenatal vitamin products under the brand BocaGreenMD. Its products are made by Lang Pharma Nutrition. Its solutions range from a patient-controlled, long-lasting contraceptive to advanced hormone therapy pharmaceutical products. In addition, TherapeuticsMD is developing products for the treatment of moderate-to-severe dyspareunia (vaginal pain associated with sexual activity), a symptom of vulvar and vaginal atrophy due to menopause.

	Annual Growth	12/18	12/19	12/20	12/21	12/22
Sales ($mil.)	44.4%	16.1	49.6	64.9	87.0	70.0
Net income ($ mil.)	–	(132.6)	(176.1)	(183.5)	(172.4)	112.0
Market value ($ mil.)	10.1%	36.2	23.0	11.5	3.4	53.1
Employees	(74.6%)	241	348	400	416	1

THERIVA BIOLOGICS INC

ASE: TOVX

9605 Medical Center Drive, Suite 270
Rockville, MD 20850
Phone: 301 417-4364
Fax: –
Web: www.therivabio.com

CEO: Steven A Shallcross
CFO: Steven A Shallcross
HR: –
FYE: December 31
Type: Public

Synthetic Biologics is developing drugs for the treatment of serious central nervous system disorders. In its pipeline are a prescription medical food -- specifically an oral tablet of zinc and an amino acid called cysteine -- for Alzheimer's disease and drugs for age-related macular degeneration (loss of vision), fibromyalgia (arthritis-related muscle pain), multiple sclerosis, and rheumatoid arthritis. The company generally prefers to in-license product candidates that have already shown certain clinical efficacy and then either develop them to commercialization or attract development partners, such as it did with Meda, which holds rights to complete development of Synthetic's fibromyalgia drug Effirma.

	Annual Growth	12/19	12/20	12/21	12/22	12/23
Sales ($mil.)	–	–	–	–	–	–
Net income ($ mil.)	–	(15.3)	(10.0)	(14.3)	(19.7)	(18.3)
Market value ($ mil.)	(4.0%)	8.7	6.6	4.7	7.8	7.4
Employees	–	11	10	16	21	–

THERMO FISHER SCIENTIFIC INC   NYS: TMO

168 Third Avenue
Waltham, MA 02451
Phone: 781 622-1000
Fax: 781 933-4476
Web: www.thermofisher.com

CEO: Marc N Casper
CFO: Stephen Williamson
HR: –
FYE: December 31
Type: Public

Thermo Fisher Scientific is considered as one of the world's leaders in serving science. The company makes and distributes analytical instruments, scientific equipment, consumables, and other laboratory supplies. Products range from chromatographs and spectrometers to bulk-elemental analysis instruments, among others. Moving into other areas, it offers testing and manufacturing of drugs, including biologicals. Thermo Fisher also provides specialty diagnostic testing products, as well as clinical analytical tools. The company tallies customers located worldwide in Its key markets the includes pharmaceutical and biotech, diagnostics and health care, academic and government, and industrial and applied research. About 55% of the company's sales were generated in North America.

	Annual Growth	12/19	12/20	12/21	12/22	12/23
Sales ($mil.)	13.8%	25,542	32,218	39,211	44,915	42,857
Net income ($ mil.)	12.9%	3,696.0	6,375.0	7,725.0	6,950.0	5,995.0
Market value ($ mil.)	13.1%	125,610	180,093	257,987	212,923	205,229
Employees	12.9%	75,000	80,000	130,000	130,000	122,000

THERMODYNETICS INC. (NV)   NBB: TDYT

651 Day Hill Road
Windsor, CT 06095
Phone: 860 683-2005
Fax: –
Web: –

CEO: –
CFO: –
HR: –
FYE: March 31
Type: Public

Thermodynetics is not a hotter version of L. Ron Hubbard's Dianetics. More practically, the company engages in the work of making products that can handle temperature changes. The specialty manufacturer offers tubing products supporting a wide array of heat transfer needs, including coaxial condensers, evaporators, and heat recovery systems. Thermodynetics, which operates through subsidiaries Turbotec Products PLC, Turbotec Products Inc., and National Energy Systems, makes products used in such industries as food processing, heating and air conditioning, and medical equipment. The company sells products across the US, and in Asia, Australia, Canada, and Europe.

	Annual Growth	03/07	03/08	03/09	03/10	03/11
Sales ($mil.)	(60.9%)	23.5	28.0	27.0	0.5	0.6
Net income ($ mil.)	(23.4%)	2.5	0.4	(0.2)	(5.5)	0.9
Market value ($ mil.)	(25.2%)	14.8	11.1	3.1	4.9	4.6
Employees	(62.2%)	98	105	96	3	2

THERMOENERGY CORP   NBB: TMEN

10 New Bond Street
Worcester, MA 01606
Phone: 508 854-1628
Fax: –
Web: www.thermoenergy.com

CEO: –
CFO: –
HR: –
FYE: December 31
Type: Public

You want clean air and clean water? Then ThermoEnergy Corporation's your guy. The company develops and markets wastewater treatment and clean energy technologies from its base in Little Rock, Arkansas. ThermoEnergy licenses three clean water process technologies that serve different purposes along the water treatment assembly line. The company also is the owner of a clean energy technology that converts fossil fuels into electricity without producing air emissions; this process also captures CO_2 in liquid form for alternative uses. ThermoEnergy is contracted to build and operate a 500,000 gallon water treatment ammonia recovery plant to serve New York City.

	Annual Growth	12/09	12/10	12/11	12/12	12/13
Sales ($mil.)	(8.5%)	4.0	2.9	5.6	7.0	2.8
Net income ($ mil.)	–	(13.0)	(9.9)	(17.3)	(7.4)	(1.6)
Market value ($ mil.)	(43.3%)	38.0	35.3	25.1	12.1	3.9
Employees	1.1%	23	25	29	26	24

THERMOGENESIS HOLDINGS INC   NAS: THMO

2711 Citrus Road
Rancho Cordova, CA 95742
Phone: 916 858-5100
Fax: –
Web: www.thermogenesis.com

CEO: Xiaochun Xu
CFO: Jeff Cauble
HR: –
FYE: December 31
Type: Public

ThermoGenesis makes blood run cold...really cold. The firm makes equipment that harvests, freezes, and thaws stem cells and other blood components taken from adult sources like umbilical cord blood, placentas, and bone marrow. Its core products include the AutoXpress System (AXP), a medical device that retrieves stem cells from cord blood; and the BioArchive System, which freezes and stores stem cells harvested from such blood. Other products include Res-Q, which processes stems cells from bone marrow. Founded in 1986, the company sells its products to cord blood banks, stem cell researchers, and clinical laboratories around the world.

	Annual Growth	12/18	12/19	12/20	12/21	12/22
Sales ($mil.)	2.0%	9.7	13.0	9.7	9.3	10.5
Net income ($ mil.)	–	(39.7)	(9.5)	(16.4)	(11.4)	(11.3)
Market value ($ mil.)	86.1%	0.3	4.6	2.2	1.0	3.3
Employees	(6.2%)	53	50	41	40	41

THERMON GROUP HOLDINGS INC   NYS: THR

7171 Southwest Parkway, Building 300, Suite 200
Austin, TX 78735
Phone: 512 690-0600
Fax: –
Web: www.thermon.com

CEO: –
CFO: –
HR: –
FYE: March 31
Type: Public

Thermon Group is one of the largest providers of highly engineered industrial process heating solutions for process industries. Through its subsidiaries, Thermon offers a full suite of products (heating units, heating cables, tubing bundles, heated blankets, and temporary power solutions), services (engineering, installation, and maintenance services), and software (design optimization and wireless and network control systems) required to deliver comprehensive solutions to some of the world's largest and most complex projects. Its core customers include chemical and petrochemical, oil, gas, power generation, commercial, rail and transit, and others that use Thermon's products to maintain temperatures of materials transported or stored in pipes and vessels, as well as for freeze protection in harsh environments. The majority of the company's sales were generated in the US and Latin America.

	Annual Growth	03/19	03/20	03/21	03/22	03/23
Sales ($mil.)	1.7%	412.6	383.5	276.2	355.7	440.6
Net income ($ mil.)	10.3%	22.8	11.9	1.2	20.1	33.7
Market value ($ mil.)	0.4%	821.3	505.0	653.1	542.8	835.0
Employees	(4.6%)	1,693	1,536	1,083	1,227	1,405

THERMWOOD CORP.   NBB: TOOD

Old Buffaloville Road, P.O. Box 436
Dale, IN 47523
Phone: 812 937-4476
Fax: –
Web: www.thermwood.com

CEO: Kenneth Susnjara
CFO: –
HR: Connie Gates
FYE: July 31
Type: Public

Shaping wood is all to the good at Thermwood. The company makes computer numerical control (CNC) systems known as CNC routers that handle complex tasks to cut, trim, and shape wood and other materials, such as aluminum, foam, and plastic. Thermwood sells its routers and corresponding software mainly to small and midsized manufacturers in the aerospace, furniture, plastics, and woodworking industries who use them to build airplane interiors, Space Shuttle parts, and movie sets. The company has operations in the US and UK and sales offices in another dozen countries. It was founded in 1969 as a plastic molder of wood-grained parts for the furniture industry and moved into the CNC router business in the 1970s.

	Annual Growth	07/97	07/98	07/99	07/00	07/01
Sales ($mil.)	5.9%	17.8	21.8	21.7	25.7	22.4
Net income ($ mil.)	–	1.2	1.3	0.6	0.4	(0.9)
Market value ($ mil.)	9.2%	2.2	8.2	5.9	5.2	3.2
Employees	5.7%	120	145	152	160	150

THESTREET, INC.
200 VESEY ST FL 24
NEW YORK, NY 102815509
Phone: 212 321-5000
Fax: –
Web: www.thestreet.com

CEO: –
CFO: –
HR: –
FYE: December 31
Type: Private

If you're looking for investment advice, you might want to check the word on the street. TheStreet offers financial news, tools, and analysis, as well as community features such as online chats and message boards, on both its advertising supported flagship website TheStreet.com and on its subscription-based site RealMoney.com, which also features commentary from market experts. Its MainStreet.com site features content related to personal finance topics. Sales come from advertising and subscriber fees. The company also distributes content through syndication deals with sites such as Yahoo! Finance, MSN Money, and CNN Money, and provides equity research and brokerage services to institutional clients.

THIRD COAST MIDSTREAM, LLC
1501 MCKINNEY ST
HOUSTON, TX 770104010
Phone: 346 241-3400
Fax: –
Web: www.third-coast.com

CEO: Matthew W Rowland
CFO: –
HR: –
FYE: December 31
Type: Private

Serving oil and gas end-use markets, Third Coast Midstream (formerly American Midstream) gathers, treats, processes, and transports natural gas, crude oil, and natural gas liquids (NGLs). Its assets include 5,100 miles of pipelines, gas processing plants, fractionation facilities, and a semi-submersible floating production system. In 2019, American Midstream merged with ArcLight Energy Partners Fund V, LP. and subsequently changed its name to Third Coast Midstream. Later that year the company agreed to sell its natural gas transmission business to Basalt Infrastructure Partners II GP Limited. The deal includes seven natural gas pipelines supplying customers in Alabama, Louisiana, Mississippi, Tennessee, and Arkansas.

THIRDERA, LLC
215 DEPOT CT SE STE 213
LEESBURG, VA 201753017
Phone: 571 262-0977
Fax: –
Web: www.thirdera.com

CEO: –
CFO: –
HR: –
FYE: December 31
Type: Private

Evergreen Systems wants to keep your enterprise running smoothly, like a clear mountain stream. The company provides a variety of IT consulting services, including network and security administration, technical asset management, and IT infrastructure library (ITIL) consulting. Evergreen serves customers in such industries as financial services, insurance, health care, and retail; clients have included Farmers Insurance, IDEC Pharmaceuticals, and Southern California Edison, as well as such public sector agencies as the SEC. The company was founded in 1997 by CEO Donald Casson, president Clay Flory, and EVP Sean Dougherty. In 2008 Evergreen merged with net.works, another reseller of Hewlett-Packard software.

	Annual Growth	12/05	12/06	12/07	12/09	12/10
Sales ($mil.)	26.4%	–	–	6.9	12.4	13.9
Net income ($ mil.)		–	–	(0.1)	0.2	0.8
Market value ($ mil.)		–	–	–	–	–
Employees		–	–	–	–	65

THIRTEEN PRODUCTIONS LLC
825 8TH AVE FL 14
NEW YORK, NY 100197435
Phone: 212 560-2000
Fax: –
Web: www.thirteen.org

CEO: –
CFO: Robert Clauser
HR: –
FYE: June 30
Type: Private

You might say this broadcaster has some public appeal for New Yorkers. Educational Broadcasting Corporation (EBC) operates two public broadcasting stations serving the New York City area. Its flagship Thirteen/WNET, the highest-rated public TV station in the US, offers a wealth of locally produced content focused on the Big Apple, as well as programming supplied by the Public Broadcasting Service (PBS). Thirteen/WNET is also a major producer of shows for PBS that are distributed to other public TV stations. Thirteen/WNET began broadcasting in 1962.

	Annual Growth	06/07	06/08	06/09	06/10	06/11
Sales ($mil.)	(15.0%)	–	–	146.1	127.3	105.7
Net income ($ mil.)		–	–	(39.7)	10.0	12.2
Market value ($ mil.)		–	–	–	–	–
Employees		–	–	–	–	120

THOMAS GRAPHICS, INC.
9501 N INTERSTATE 35
AUSTIN, TX 787533821
Phone: 512 719-3535
Fax: –
Web: www.thomasgraphicsinc.com

CEO: –
CFO: –
HR: –
FYE: December 31
Type: Private

Thomas Graphics provides graphics and commercial printing services in Central Texas. The company offers digital pre-press, printing, binding, labeling, mailing, and list management services. In offset printing it can print in one-, two-, three-, and full-color on a variety of paper sizes and stocks, including cardstock and all sizes of envelopes. It also provides digital printing services and mailing servicesOn the promotional marketing side Thomas Graphics prints business cards, envelopes, annual reports, and other collateral marketing materials. President and CEO, Bob Thomas founded the company in Austin, Texas, in 1982.

	Annual Growth	12/04	12/05	12/06	12/08	12/09
Sales ($mil.)	(21.3%)	–	–	11.7	–	5.7
Net income ($ mil.)		–	–	–	–	(0.1)
Market value ($ mil.)		–	–	–	–	–
Employees		–	–	–	–	53

THOMAS JEFFERSON SCHOOL OF LAW
701 B ST STE 100
SAN DIEGO, CA 921014604
Phone: 619 297-9700
Fax: –
Web: www.tjsl.edu

CEO: –
CFO: –
HR: –
FYE: June 30
Type: Private

If Thomas Jefferson ever wanted to sunbathe between bouts of shaping our nation, this would have been the place. Thomas Jefferson School of Law (TJSL) offers a traditional program of legal education leading to the award of master's degrees and Juris Doctor degrees. The private school offers a three year full-time or a four year part-time program. Its campus is located in the historic Old Town section of San Diego. Thomas Jefferson School of Law has about 800 students and was founded in 1969 as the the Western State University College of Law. It achieved independence and accreditation with the American Bar Association in 1996. The school is building a new $40 million downtown campus.

	Annual Growth	06/14	06/15	06/20	06/21	06/22
Sales ($mil.)	(16.8%)	–	38.2	12.0	10.9	10.6
Net income ($ mil.)	(6.4%)	–	1.3	(0.6)	1.5	0.8
Market value ($ mil.)		–	–	–	–	–
Employees		–	–	–	–	120

THOMAS JEFFERSON UNIVERSITY

1101 MARKET ST FL 21
PHILADELPHIA, PA 191072900
Phone: 215 955-6000
Fax: –
Web: www.jefferson.edu

CEO: H R Haverstick Jr
CFO: –
HR: –
FYE: June 30
Type: Private

Thomas Jefferson University, founded in 1824 as the Jefferson Medical College, is today a national doctoral research university and a pioneer in transdisciplinary, professional education. Home of the Sidney Kimmel Medical College and the Kanbar College of Design, Engineering and Commerce, Jefferson is a preeminent academic institution delivering high-impact education in over 200 undergraduate and graduate programs to 8,400 students across ten colleges. The university's academic offerings now include architecture, business, design, engineering, fashion, health, medicine, science, social science and textiles. Student-athletes compete as the Jefferson Rams in the NCAA Division II Central Atlantic Collegiate Conference.

	Annual Growth	06/18	06/19	06/20	06/21	06/22
Sales ($mil.)	(2.2%)	–	–	–	1,370.6	1,341.0
Net income ($ mil.)	(78.0%)	–	–	–	49.0	10.8
Market value ($ mil.)	–	–	–	–	–	–
Employees	–	–	–	–	–	10,625

THOMAS JEFFERSON UNIVERSITY HOSPITALS, INC.

111 S 11TH ST
PHILADELPHIA, PA 191074824
Phone: 215 955-5600
Fax: –
Web: www.jeffersonhealth.org

CEO: –
CFO: –
HR: –
FYE: June 30
Type: Private

Named after the "Man of the People," Thomas Jefferson University Hospitals (dba Jefferson Health) serves the people of the Keystone State with a medical staff of more than 1,200 and some 1,550 beds. The system provides acute, tertiary, and specialty medical care from a dozen hospitals, nearly 20 outpatient centers, and about 10 urgent care centers. The hospital also administers cardiac care at the Jefferson Heart Institute, which provides everything from minimally invasive surgical procedures to heart transplants. Additionally, Jefferson Health operates as the teaching hospital for Thomas Jefferson University.

	Annual Growth	06/09	06/10	06/14	06/15	06/16
Sales ($mil.)	3.0%	–	1,250.4	1,510.0	1,456.3	1,495.4
Net income ($ mil.)	7.7%	–	49.4	51.0	42.8	76.9
Market value ($ mil.)	–	–	–	–	–	–
Employees	–	–	–	–	–	4,701

THOMAS SAINT MIDTOWN HOSPITAL

2000 CHURCH ST
NASHVILLE, TN 372360002
Phone: 615 284-5555
Fax: –
Web: –

CEO: Bernie Sherry
CFO: Ken Venuto
HR: –
FYE: June 30
Type: Private

Titans and tots can find care at Saint Thomas Midtown Hospital (formerly Baptist Hospital) in Nashville, Tennessee. With more than 680 beds, Saint Thomas is one of the largest not-for-profit hospitals in the area. It provides general medical and surgical care, along with specialty care in areas such as cardiovascular disease, cancer, orthopedics, and pulmonary disease. Among other things, the hospital also features a neurosciences institute, a weight loss surgery center, and a sports medicine division that serves the Tennessee Titans. Founded in 1919 as Protestant Hospital and later renamed Baptist Hospital, it is now owned by Saint Thomas Health Services, a Catholic health care system that is a member of Ascension Health.

THOMASVILLE BANCSHARES, INC.   NBB: THVB

301 North Broad Street
Thomasville, GA 31792
Phone: 229 226-3300
Fax: –
Web: www.tnbank.com

CEO: –
CFO: –
HR: –
FYE: December 31
Type: Public

This Thomasville is more about the money under your bed than the bed itself. Thomasville Bancshares is the holding company for Thomasville National Bank, which serves area consumers and businesses from two offices in Thomasville, Georgia. Established in 1995, the bank offers standard services such as deposit accounts and credit cards. Real estate mortgages comprise most of the company's loan portfolio, followed by commercial, financial, and agricultural loans. The company provides trust, asset management, and brokerage services through its TNB Financial Services unit. Executive officers and directors of Thomasville Bancshares collectively own more than a quarter of the company.

	Annual Growth	12/17	12/18	12/19	12/20	12/21
Assets ($mil.)	16.1%	806.5	880.5	956.7	1,227.5	1,463.1
Net income ($ mil.)	17.7%	12.0	16.9	18.8	19.4	23.1
Market value ($ mil.)	12.7%	241.4	247.4	277.6	307.8	389.3
Employees	–	–	–	–	–	–

THOMPSON CREEK METALS COMPANY USA

10 LANGELOTH PLANT DR
LANGELOTH, PA 150541148
Phone: 303 761-8801
Fax: –
Web: –

CEO: Jacques Perron
CFO: Pamela L Saxton
HR: –
FYE: December 31
Type: Private

Thompson Creek Metals has branched out from only mining molybdenum at its Thompson Creek site in Idaho to holding a diversified North American portfolio that also includes copper, gold, and silver assets. The company still obtains most of its sales (97%) from producing molybdenum, a metal used to strengthen steel and make it corrosion-resistant. It operates the Thompson Creek mine and mill in Idaho and owns 75% of the Endako mine in British Columbia (Japan's Sojitz owns 25%). Thompson Creek has a metallurgical facility in Pennsylvania and holds exploration assets in British Columbia and in the Yukon and Nunavut territories. It controls about 449 million pounds of molybdenum proved and probable reserves.

	Annual Growth	12/10	12/11	12/12	12/13	12/14
Sales ($mil.)	41.8%	–	–	401.4	434.4	806.7
Net income ($ mil.)	–	–	–	(546.3)	(215.0)	(124.2)
Market value ($ mil.)	–	–	–	–	–	–
Employees	–	–	–	–	–	1,700

THOMPSON HOSPITALITY CORPORATION

1741 BUSINESS CENTER DR STE 200
RESTON, VA 20190
Phone: 703 757-5500
Fax: –
Web: www.thompsonhospitality.com

CEO: –
CFO: –
HR: –
FYE: December 25
Type: Private

A side of diversity, please: One of the largest minority-owned companies in the US, Thompson Hospitality is a contract foodservice provider to businesses, government agencies, and educational institutions. The foodservice operator's clients include a number of historically black colleges and universities, notably Delaware State and Norfolk State, as well as institutions around Washington, DC, such as Walter Reed Army Hospital. Thompson Hospitality also owns a handful of chain restaurants, including Austin Grill. Formed through an alliance with major food provider Compass Group, Thompson Hospitality has a presence in more than 45 states and four foreign countries. The two companies still partner on contracts.

	Annual Growth	12/07	12/08	12/09	12/10	12/11
Sales ($mil.)	6.1%	–	–	97.2	101.3	109.5
Net income ($ mil.)	25.0%	–	–	2.9	10.0	4.6
Market value ($ mil.)	–	–	–	–	–	–
Employees	–	–	–	–	–	3,000

THOMPSON STEEL COMPANY, INC.

120 ROYALL ST STE 2
CANTON, MA 020211096
Phone: 781 828-8800
Fax: –
Web: www.thompsonsteelco.com

CEO: –
CFO: –
HR: –
FYE: December 30
Type: Private

Through its three subsidiaries, Thompson Steel offers a wide range of steel products and services. Thompson Dayton Steel Service operates five strip steel facilities that offer cold-rolled, hot rolled, pickled, oiled, electro-galvanized, and aluminized steel. Its steel products go toward making can openers, connectors, door hinges, gears, hand and rasp saws, and springs. Arrow Thompson Metals cuts all grade and types of stainless steel blanks. Optimal Steel Service serves up steel products including stainless, hot- and cold rolled, pickled, hardened, and oiled steel, as well as coated steels and cold rolled strip steel.

THOR INDUSTRIES, INC.

601 East Beardsley Ave.
Elkhart, IN 46514-3305
Phone: 574 970-7460
Fax: –
Web: www.thorindustries.com

NYS: THO
CEO: Robert W Martin
CFO: Colleen Zuhl
HR: Erin Kent
FYE: July 31
Type: Public

Thor Industries was founded in 1980 and has grown to become the largest manufacturer of recreational vehicles (RVs) in the world. It is also the largest manufacturer of RVs in North America, and one of the largest manufacturers of RVs in Europe. The company manufactures a wide variety of RVs in the US and Europe, and sells those vehicles, as well as related parts and accessories, primarily to approximately 2,400 independent, non-franchise dealers throughout the US, Canada and Europe. Its principal subsidiaries include Airstream, Heartland, DRV, Keystone, Thor Motor Coach, Tiffin Group, and Jayco. The US is its largest market, accounting for more than 65% of total revenue.

	Annual Growth	07/19	07/20	07/21	07/22	07/23
Sales ($mil.)	9.0%	7,864.8	8,167.9	12,317	16,313	11,122
Net income ($ mil.)	29.5%	133.3	223.0	659.9	1,137.8	374.3
Market value ($ mil.)	18.0%	3,177.5	6,077.3	6,310.3	4,496.0	6,157.3
Employees	3.4%	21,750	22,250	31,000	32,000	24,900

THORATEC LLC

6035 STONERIDGE DR
PLEASANTON, CA 945883270
Phone: 925 847-8600
Fax: –
Web: –

CEO: –
CFO: Taylor C Harris
HR: Jessica Hupman
FYE: December 28
Type: Private

Suffering from a broken heart? Thoratec's there for the rebound. The company, a world leader in mechanical circulatory support, makes ventricular assist devices (VAD) for patients suffering late-stage heart failure, including those awaiting a heart transplant. Thoratec offers external and implantable products that provide circulatory support for both acute and long-term needs. Its products are sold under the HeartMate, CentriMag, and Thoratec brands. The company works closely with hospitals and cardiac surgery centers primarily in the US and Europe. St. Jude Medical bought Thoratec for $3.4 billion in late 2015.

THOS. S. BYRNE, INC.

551 E BERRY ST
FORT WORTH, TX 761104329
Phone: 817 335-3394
Fax: –
Web: www.tsbyrne.com

CEO: John Avila Jr
CFO: –
HR: –
FYE: June 30
Type: Private

That they build it big in Texas is good news for Thos. S. Byrne. Doing business as Byrne Construction Services, the general contractor performs new construction and renovation for commercial, industrial, cultural, and municipal projects, mostly in the Dallas-Fort Worth area. Byrne-associated projects include Fort Worth's acclaimed Amon Carter and Kimball Art museums, the ballpark home of the Texas Rangers, facilities for Miller Brewing (now part of MillerCoors), and renovations at DFW Airport. Byrne has offices in Austin, Dallas, Fort Worth, and San Antonio. Thomas Sneed Byrne founded Byrne Construction Services in 1923; the company is now owned by CEO John Avila, Jr.

THRUSTMASTER OF TEXAS, INC.

6900 THRUSTMASTER DR
HOUSTON, TX 770412682
Phone: 713 937-6295
Fax: –
Web: www.thrustmaster.net

CEO: –
CFO: –
HR: –
FYE: December 31
Type: Private

Thrustmaster of Texas trades on power, but it does not lack finesse. The company manufactures heavy-duty commercial marine propulsion equipment including deck-mounted propulsion units, thru-hull azimuthing thrusters, retractable thrusters, tunnel thrusters, and portable dynamic positioning systems. The company's thrusters vary in size, power, and design with applications that include main propulsion, slow-speed maneuvering, and dynamic positioning. Thrusters range in power from 35hp to more than 3,000hp and find uses in barges, cruise ships, tugs, military vessels, offshore platforms, and other floating structures. Thrustmaster of Texas serves a global clientele through an international sales network.

	Annual Growth	12/08	12/09	12/10	12/11	12/12
Sales ($mil.)	18.3%	–	–	62.9	84.6	87.9
Net income ($ mil.)	60.0%	–	–	6.6	7.4	17.0
Market value ($ mil.)	–	–	–	–	–	–
Employees	–	–	–	–	–	275

THRUWAY AUTHORITY OF NEW YORK STATE

200 SOUTHERN BLVD
ALBANY, NY 122092018
Phone: 518 436-2700
Fax: –
Web: thruway.ny.gov

CEO: Joanne M Mahoney
CFO: –
HR: –
FYE: December 31
Type: Private

Leaving Manhattan or Brooklyn to shuffle off to Buffalo? The New York State Thruway Authority oversees a 641-mile toll road system and a 524-mile canal system. The authority's toll road system, known as the Governor Thomas E. Dewey Thruway, is the largest in the US. It crosses the state from New York City to Buffalo, and more than 80% of the population of New York State lives along the corridor formed by the Thruway's 426-mile main line. Other arms of the Thruway connect with toll roads and other highways in neighboring states. The New York State Canal Corporation oversees the state's canal system of five lakes and four canals, which connect bodies of water such as the Hudson River with Lake Champlain.

	Annual Growth	12/06	12/07	12/08	12/09	12/10
Sales ($mil.)	6.1%	–	–	598.8	640.6	674.3
Net income ($ mil.)	–	–	–	(129.9)	(129.3)	(127.3)
Market value ($ mil.)	–	–	–	–	–	–
Employees	–	–	–	–	–	2,840

THRYV HOLDINGS INC
NAS: THRY

2200 West Airfield Drive, P.O. Box 619810 D/FW
Airport, TX 75261
Phone: 972 453-7000
Fax: –
Web: www.corporate.thryv.com

CEO: Joseph A Walsh
CFO: Paul D Rouse
HR: –
FYE: December 31
Type: Public

Thryv (formerly DexYP) is dedicated to supporting local, independent service-based businesses and emerging franchises by providing innovative marketing solutions and cloud-based tools to the entrepreneurs who run them. It is one of the largest domestic providers of print and digital marketing solutions to SMBs and SaaS end-to-end customer experience tools. The company enables SMBs to craft a comprehensive marketing strategy with its full portfolio of marketing solutions including PYP, IYP, SEM, online display and social advertising, online presence, and video, and SEO tools. Its solutions enable its SMB clients to generate new business leads, manage SMB customer relationships, and run their day-to-day operations, and serves approximately 390,000 SMB clients.

	Annual Growth	12/19	12/20	12/21	12/22	12/23
Sales ($mil.)	(10.4%)	1,421.4	1,109.4	1,113.4	1,202.4	917.0
Net income ($ mil.)	–	–	35.5	149.2	101.6	54.3	(259.3)
Market value ($ mil.)	17.5%	376.9	476.6	1,452.0	670.8	718.4
Employees	–	–	2,313	2,630	2,955	3,049

THUNDER MOUNTAIN GOLD, INC.
TVX: THM

11770 W. President Dr. Ste. F.
Boise, ID 83713-8986
Phone: 208 658-1037
Fax: –
Web: www.thundermountaingold.com

CEO: Eric T Jones
CFO: Larry Thackery
HR: –
FYE: December 31
Type: Public

Mining company Thunder Mountain Gold is looking for its next project. In 2005 the company sold its real property and mining claims in the Thunder Mountain District of Valley County, Idaho, to the Trust For Public Land, an environmental group that buys land for conservation. No minerals had been produced on Thunder Mountain Gold's Idaho properties since the early 1990s. Currently the company operates no producing mines and owns no mining properties; it is firmly in the exploration stage. In 2007 Thunder Mountain Gold acquired South Mountain Mines. Two years later it agreed to buy Kenai Resources, combining to form a new company called Thunder Mountain Resources.

	Annual Growth	12/19	12/20	12/21	12/22	12/23
Sales ($mil.)	–	2.0	0.6	0.8	0.3	–
Net income ($ mil.)	–	1.1	1.2	(0.6)	(1.2)	(0.8)
Market value ($ mil.)	(14.1%)	4.7	9.7	8.8	5.0	2.6
Employees	–	3	3	3	3	3

TI GOTHAM INC.

225 LIBERTY ST
NEW YORK, NY 102811048
Phone: 212 522-8282
Fax: –
Web: www.dotdashmeredith.com

CEO: Joseph Ceryanec
CFO: –
HR: –
FYE: December 31
Type: Private

TI Gotham (formerly Time Inc.) is now part of Meredith Corporation, a leading consumer magazine publisher with more than 25 US magazines and corresponding websites. Its titles include Entertainment Weekly, Food & Wine, People, and Travel + Leisure. IPC Group Limited is the UK's top magazine publisher (Now, Look). TI Gotham is a subsidiary of Meredith Corporation. Meredith purchased Time Inc. in 2018, then sold off TIME, Sports Illustrated, and Fortune magazines to third parties.

TIDEWATER INC (NEW)
NYS: TDW

842 West Sam Houston Parkway North, Suite 400
Houston, TX 77024
Phone: 713 470-5300
Fax: –
Web: www.tdw.com

CEO: Quintin V Kneen V
CFO: Sam R Rubio
HR: –
FYE: December 31
Type: Public

Tidewater provides offshore support vessels and offshore marine support services to the global offshore energy industry through the operation of a diversified fleet of marine service vessels. The company's fleet of nearly 185 vessels provides oil and gas exploration, field development, and production, as well as wind farm development and maintenance. Services encompass transporting crews and supplies to offshore platforms, towing of and anchor handling for mobile rigs, and aiding in offshore construction and seismic and subsea support, geotechnical survey support for wind farm construction; and a variety of specialized services such as pipe and cable laying. More than 75% of Tidewater's revenues are generated in international waters. The company was incorporated in 1956.

	Annual Growth	12/19	12/20	12/21	12/22	12/23
Sales ($mil.)	20.0%	486.5	397.0	371.0	647.7	1,010.0
Net income ($ mil.)	–	(141.7)	(196.2)	(129.0)	(21.7)	97.2
Market value ($ mil.)	39.1%	1,007.6	451.5	559.7	1,925.8	3,768.4
Employees	8.3%	5,300	5,400	4,400	6,300	7,300

TIFFIN MOTOR HOMES, INC.

105 2ND ST NW
RED BAY, AL 355823859
Phone: 256 356-8661
Fax: –
Web: www.tiffinmotorhomes.com

CEO: –
CFO: –
HR: Bobby White
FYE: February 28
Type: Private

At Tiffin Motorhomes, the family that stays together makes recreational vehicles together. The family-owned manufacturer builds a line of luxury recreational vehicles (RVs) including the Allegro, Allegro Bus, Phaeton, and Zephyr models. RVs span 35 to 44 feet in length and offer amenities from washers and dryers, to garden tubs, to side-by-side refrigerators. Construction features are thick glass windows, added storage, and reinforced steel crossbracing. Tiffin's vehicles are sold by dealers across the US and Canada, as well as in Australia and New Zealand. Spotlighting its nameplates, the company owns the Tiffin Allegro Club, an organization of more than 7,500 Tiffin owners that promotes race car rallies and RV events. Robert Tiffin founded the company in 1972.

	Annual Growth	02/02	02/03	02/04	02/05	02/07
Sales ($mil.)	26.6%	–	–	207.0	286.0	419.6
Net income ($ mil.)	104.8%	–	–	2.9	(0.5)	24.6
Market value ($ mil.)	–	–	–	–	–	–
Employees	–	–	–	–	–	545

TIFT REGIONAL MEDICAL CENTER FOUNDATION, INC.

2301 N ASHLEY ST
VALDOSTA, GA 316022620
Phone: 229 382-7120
Fax: –
Web: www.mysouthwell.com

CEO: –
CFO: –
HR: –
FYE: September 30
Type: Private

Tift Regional Medical Center (TRMC) helps keep people healthy in the Peach State. The medical center, with more than 125 physicians on staff representing some 30 specialties, serves residents across a dozen counties in south central Georgia. TRMC offers its patients a wide range of services including cancer treatment, cardiology, neurology, occupational and physical therapy, obstetrics, and surgical care. The not-for-profit medical center has a capacity of about 190 beds. It also operates an outpatient services clinic, Cook Medical Center, and Cook Senior Living Center. Tift County Hospital Authority owns and operates TRMC. The hospital is also affiliated with the Emory Healthcare network.

	Annual Growth	09/08	09/09	09/14	09/15	09/16
Sales ($mil.)	(53.6%)	–	216.2	1.0	288.5	1.0
Net income ($ mil.)	(42.3%)	–	30.5	0.7	(0.6)	0.6
Market value ($ mil.)	–	–	–	–	–	–
Employees	–	–	–	–	–	252

TIGERLOGIC CORPORATION

4030 CANAL WOODS CT
LAKE OSWEGO, OR 970347221
Phone: 503 765-8046
Fax: –
Web: www.omnis.net

CEO: Bradley N Timchuk
CFO: Roger Rowe
HR: –
FYE: March 31
Type: Private

TigerLogic (formerly Raining Data) can help you catch data by the tail. The company's ChunkIt! browser-based application enhances and personalizes searches of popular search engines or Web pages. TigerLogic also provides applications that software developers use to construct a variety of software programs and build databases. Its software lets users create, compile, test, and run programs. Customers use TigerLogic's rapid application development software to build programs that can easily be updated. The company also provides maintenance, implementation, technical support, and training services. Through investment firm Astoria Capital Partners, former CEO Carlton Baab owns about 60% of the company.

TIGRENT INC   NBB: TIGE

1612 East Cape Coral Parkway
Cape Coral, FL 33904
Phone: 239 542-0643
Fax: –
Web: www.tigrent.com

CEO: Steven C Barre
CFO: Charles F Kuehne
HR: Cindy Prout
FYE: December 31
Type: Public

Tigrent (formerly Whitney Information Network) wants to help show you the money. The company sells educational materials and provides training courses that teach students strategies for success in real estate investments and financial markets. It offers about 150 educational courses and training programs per month covering dozens of subjects. Its 51%-owned Rich Dad Education subsidiary offers real estate and finance courses based on the writings of Robert Kiyosaki, author of the popular Rich Dad Poor Dad series of books. Its other course brand names include Tigrent Learning (formerly Wealth Intelligence Academy), Building Wealth, and Teach Me To Trade.

	Annual Growth	12/06	12/07	12/08	12/09	12/10
Sales ($mil.)	(17.8%)	224.7	207.6	171.7	170.9	102.6
Net income ($ mil.)	–	1.8	(6.6)	0.6	10.1	(0.9)
Market value ($ mil.)	(67.5%)	70.0	38.0	8.5	8.5	0.8
Employees	(22.6%)	744	457	340	347	267

TIMBERCON, INC.

20245 SW 95TH AVE
TUALATIN, OR 970627541
Phone: 503 827-8141
Fax: –
Web: www.timbercon.com

CEO: –
CFO: –
HR: –
FYE: December 31
Type: Private

Timbercon has nothing to do with falling trees and everything to do with fiber optics. The company develops and manufactures fiber-optic cables and other products for the aerospace/defense, industrial, medical, and telecommunications industries. Its cables, loopbacks, couplers, splitters, and attenuators are used in harsh environments, such as scientific research and development, military testing and measurement, and broadband networking. In addition to its products, Timbercon offers services that include consulting, contract manufacturing, product design, and repair, testing, and analysis on fiber-optic products. Founded in 1997, Timbercon is privately owned by its employees.

	Annual Growth	12/04	12/05	12/06	12/07	12/08
Sales ($mil.)	–	–	–	(2,003.6)	8.4	10.7
Net income ($ mil.)	5206.2%	–	–	0.0	0.6	0.5
Market value ($ mil.)	–	–	–	–	–	–
Employees	–	–	–	–	–	64

TIMBERLAND BANCORP, INC.   NMS: TSBK

624 Simpson Avenue
Hoquiam, WA 98550
Phone: 360 533-4747
Fax: –
Web: www.timberlandbank.com

CEO: –
CFO: –
HR: –
FYE: September 30
Type: Public

Located among the tall trees of the Pacific Northwest, Timberland Bancorp is the holding company for Timberland Savings Bank, which operates more than 20 branches in western Washington. The bank targets individuals and regional businesses, offering checking, savings, and money market accounts, and CDs. Timberland Savings Bank, concentrates on real estate lending, including commercial and residential mortgages, multifamily residential loans, and land develoment loans; it also writes business loans and other types of loans. Timberland Savings Bank was founded in 1915 as a savings and loan.

	Annual Growth	09/19	09/20	09/21	09/22	09/23
Assets ($mil.)	10.2%	1,247.1	1,566.0	1,792.2	1,860.5	1,839.9
Net income ($ mil.)	3.1%	24.0	24.3	27.6	23.6	27.1
Market value ($ mil.)	(0.4%)	222.9	145.9	234.2	224.1	219.7
Employees	(45.7%)	298	286	288	295	26

TIMBERLINE RESOURCES CORP   TVX: TBR

101 East Lakeside Avenue
Coeur D'Alene, ID 83814
Phone: 208 664-4859
Fax: –
Web: www.timberline-resources.com

CEO: Patrick Highsmith
CFO: Ted R Sharp
HR: –
FYE: September 30
Type: Public

Timberline Resources is hoping that all (or at least some) of what glitters deep in its underground mines is gold. An exploration and development company, Timberline Resources conducts underground gold mining operations on two core precious metal properties in Nevada collectively known as South Eureka Property, located in the state's Battle Mountain-Eureka gold-producing area. The company also conducts gold mining operations through its Montana-based Butte Highlands Joint Venture, in which it owns a 50% interest and is acquiring the rest. In addition to mining, Timberline provides contract underground diamond drilling services to third-party mining companies through its Timberline Drilling subsidiary.

	Annual Growth	09/19	09/20	09/21	09/22	09/23
Sales ($mil.)	–	–	–	–	–	–
Net income ($ mil.)	–	(1.7)	(3.4)	(4.7)	(6.0)	(2.2)
Market value ($ mil.)	(8.3%)	13.6	40.8	24.4	19.0	9.6
Employees	31.6%	1	2	2	3	3

TIME WARNER ENTERTAINMENT CO., L.P.

75 Rockefeller Plaza
New York, NY 10019
Phone: 212 484-8000
Fax: –
Web: –

CEO: Richard D Parsons
CFO: Wayne H Pace
HR: –
FYE: December 31
Type: Public

Spectrum is a suite of advanced broadband services offered by Charter Communications, Inc. Spectrum provides a full range of services, including Spectrum TV, Spectrum Internet, Spectrum Voice and Spectrum Mobile. Spectrum covers more ground that it used to. Spectrum has operations in more than 40 states across the US, serving about 32 million customers with video, high-speed data, and voice offerings, as well as security and home management. In addition to video, voice, and data, other business services include networking and transport, outsourced IT, and cloud computing. The cable TV provider is the Charter Communications-engineered combination of Charter's own cable operations and Time Warner Cable and Bright House Networks, which Charter acquired in 2016.

	Annual Growth	12/98	12/99	12/00	12/01	12/02
Sales ($mil.)	7.6%	12,246	13,164	13,982	15,302	16,425
Net income ($ mil.)	–	326.0	2,759.0	229.0	(1,032.0)	(21,219.0)
Market value ($ mil.)	–	–	–	–	–	–
Employees	1.5%	29,400	30,000	–	35,300	31,200

TIMIOS NATIONAL CORPORATION

5716 CORSA AVE STE 102
WESTLAKE VILLAGE, CA 913627354
Phone: 818 706-6400
Fax: –
Web: www.timiosinc.com

CEO: Trevor Stoffer
CFO: Michael T Brigante
HR: –
FYE: December 31
Type: Private

Homeland Security Capital stakes its financial security on the nation's security. The investment firm acquires, operates, and develops companies that offer homeland security services and products. It hopes to capitalize on the highly fragmented nature of the young industry, which brings potential customers in the government and private sectors. The company owns Polimnatrix, which provides radiation dectection and protection services. Homeland Security Capital entered the mortgage and settlement services industry when it acquired Timios, a provider of paperless insurance and escrow services.

TIMKEN CO. (THE)   NYS: TKR

4500 Mount Pleasant Street NW
North Canton, OH 44720-5450
Phone: 234 262-3000
Fax: –
Web: www.timken.com

CEO: Richard G Kyle
CFO: Philip D Fracassa
HR: Dinesh Singh
FYE: December 31
Type: Public

Founded in 1899, The Timken Company designs and manages a portfolio of engineered bearings and power transmission products and related services. Timken also makes helicopter transmission systems, rotor-head assemblies, turbine engine components, gears, and housings for civil and military aircraft. Its customers include manufacturers of cars, light, medium, and heavy-duty trucks, railcars and locomotives, and heavy-duty industrial vehicles. Process industry customers include metals, oil and gas, pulp and paper, and food and beverage. The Company's growing portfolio features many strong brands, including Timken , Philadelphia Gear , GGB , Drives , Cone Drive , Rollon , Lovejoy , Diamond , BEKA , Groeneveld and Spinea . The US accounts for nearly 45% of sales.

	Annual Growth	12/19	12/20	12/21	12/22	12/23
Sales ($mil.)	5.9%	3,789.9	3,513.2	4,132.9	4,496.7	4,769.0
Net income ($ mil.)	2.1%	362.1	284.5	369.1	407.4	394.1
Market value ($ mil.)	9.2%	3,948.8	5,425.0	4,859.1	4,955.9	5,620.7
Employees	2.2%	18,000	17,430	18,000	19,000	19,602

TIPTREE INC   NAS: TIPT

660 Steamboat Road, 2nd Floor
Greenwich, CT 06830
Phone: 212 446-1400
Fax: –
Web: www.tiptreeinc.com

CEO: Jonathan Ilany
CFO: Sandra Bell
HR: –
FYE: December 31
Type: Public

Tiptree is a holding company that allocates capital across a broad spectrum of businesses, assets and other investments. Tiptree's principal operating subsidiary, The Fortegra Group, LLC and its subsidiaries (Fortegra), is a leading provider of specialty insurance, service contract products and related service solutions. As a global specialty insurer, the company is focused on program business, specifically niche commercial and personal lines. It underwrites a comprehensive and diverse set of admitted and surplus insurance products. In addition to insurance, Tiptree has various unregulated products and services such as captive administration, program administration and premium financing. In Europe, Tiptree offers a variety of programs, including auto extended warranties, wireless device protection and consumer products accidental damage.

	Annual Growth	12/19	12/20	12/21	12/22	12/23
Sales ($mil.)	20.9%	772.7	810.3	1,200.5	1,397.8	1,649.0
Net income ($ mil.)	(6.6%)	18.4	(29.2)	38.1	(8.3)	14.0
Market value ($ mil.)	23.5%	299.2	184.5	508.3	508.7	696.9
Employees	10.5%	1,009	1,372	231	47	1,504

TIS MORTGAGE INVESTMENT CO.

655 Montgomery St, Suite 800
San Francisco, CA 94111
Phone: 415 393-8000
Fax: 415 981-2017
Web: –

CEO: –
CFO: –
HR: –
FYE: December 31
Type: Public

No matter how you serve it up, TIS Mortgage Investment Company is hungry for real estate. Previously engaged in retail and multifamily property developments, the self-managed real estate investment trust (REIT) has sold most of its real property assets to concentrate on mortgage banking and servicing. TIS Mortgage Investment Company established subsidiary TiServ in 2002 to own mortgage servicing rights.

	Annual Growth	12/99	12/00	12/01	12/02	12/03
Sales ($mil.)	(62.7%)	4.4	3.7	1.9	1.1	0.0
Net income ($ mil.)	–	(3.9)	(3.0)	(2.0)	(0.0)	(1.0)
Market value ($ mil.)	–	–	1.7	1.8	1.8	6.2
Employees	(9.6%)	3	2	2	–	2

TITAN INTERNATIONAL INC   NYS: TWI

1525 Kautz Road, Suite 600
West Chicago, IL 60185
Phone: 630 377-0486
Fax: –
Web: www.titan-intl.com

CEO: Paul G Reitz
CFO: David A Martin
HR: Dolly Gobble
FYE: December 31
Type: Public

Titan International is a global wheel, tire, and undercarriage industrial manufacturer and supplier that services customers across the globe. As a leading manufacturer in the off-highway industry, Titan produces a broad range of products to meet the specifications of original equipment manufacturers (OEMs) and aftermarket customers in the agricultural, earthmoving/construction, and consumer markets. It manufactures and sells certain tires under the Goodyear Farm Tire, Titan Tire, and Voltyre-Prom Tire brands and has complete research and development facilities to validate tire and wheel designs. Its products are available for use on various agricultural equipment and various types of OTR earthmoving, mining, military, construction, and forestry equipment. In terms of geographic sales, the US was responsible for about 50% of its totality.

	Annual Growth	12/19	12/20	12/21	12/22	12/23
Sales ($mil.)	5.9%	1,448.7	1,259.3	1,780.2	2,169.4	1,821.8
Net income ($ mil.)	–	(48.4)	(60.4)	49.6	176.3	78.8
Market value ($ mil.)	42.4%	219.8	295.1	665.4	930.2	903.5
Employees	2.7%	6,200	6,800	7,500	7,500	6,900

TITAN MACHINERY, INC.   NMS: TITN

644 East Beaton Drive
West Fargo, ND 58078-2648
Phone: 701 356-0130
Fax: –
Web: www.titanmachinery.com

CEO: David Meyer
CFO: Mark Kalvoda
HR: –
FYE: January 31
Type: Public

Titan Machinery owns and operates a network of full-service agricultural and construction equipment stores in the US and Europe. The company runs over 120 agricultural and construction equipment stores that sell and rent new and used machinery, attachments, and parts, as well as service equipment. It represents equipment by CNH's Case IH, New Holland Agriculture, Case Construction, and New Holland Construction. Titan Machinery's customers include small, single-machine owners to large farming operations to large commercial application operations, construction contractors, public utilities, forestry, energy companies, farmers, municipalities, and maintenance contractors. Other products include machinery used for heavy construction and light industrial jobs, in commercial or residential building, roadwork, and forestry. Titan Machinery was founded in 1980.

	Annual Growth	01/19	01/20	01/21	01/22	01/23
Sales ($mil.)	15.0%	1,261.5	1,305.2	1,411.2	1,711.9	2,209.3
Net income ($ mil.)	70.1%	12.2	14.0	19.4	66.0	101.9
Market value ($ mil.)	23.7%	425.4	277.1	483.5	699.1	997.3
Employees	14.8%	1,661	1,730	2,383	2,436	2,886

TITAN PHARMACEUTICALS INC (DE) NAS: TTNP

400 Oyster Point Blvd., Suite 505
South San Francisco, CA 94080
Phone: 650 244-4990
Fax: –
Web: www.titanpharm.com

CEO: David Lazar
CFO: –
HR: –
FYE: December 31
Type: Public

Titan Pharmaceuticals thinks big. The development-stage firm is working on drug treatments for large pharmaceutical markets, including central nervous system disorders like chronic pain, Parkinson's disease, and schizophrenia. On its own, the company is developing Probuphine, which may treat opioid addiction; Probuphine combines an already-approved chemical compound with Titan's continuous-release drug delivery technology called ProNeura. Titan is working with Vanda Pharmaceuticals on late-stage compound Iloperidone, a possible treatment for schizophrenia.

	Annual Growth	12/18	12/19	12/20	12/21	12/22
Sales ($mil.)	(46.1%)	6.6	3.6	4.8	1.5	0.6
Net income ($ mil.)	–	(9.0)	(16.5)	(18.2)	(8.8)	(10.2)
Market value ($ mil.)	36.9%	0.2	0.1	2.5	0.8	0.6
Employees	(35.4%)	23	21	12	11	4

TITUSVILLE AREA HOSPITAL

406 W OAK ST
TITUSVILLE, PA 163541499
Phone: 814 827-1851
Fax: –
Web: www.titusvillehospital.org

CEO: Anthony Nasralla
CFO: –
HR: –
FYE: June 30
Type: Private

Titusville Area Hospital, an acute care health facility, provides diagnostic, primary treatment, and emergency health services to more than 30,000 residents in the Crawford County, Pennsylvania region. Specific services at Titusville include birthing, home health care, lithotripsy, and pain management. Titusville Area Hospital opened its doors in 1901.

	Annual Growth	06/17	06/18	06/20	06/21	06/22
Sales ($mil.)	18.0%	–	30.2	43.9	54.1	58.5
Net income ($ mil.)	44.4%	–	1.4	(1.5)	5.0	6.1
Market value ($ mil.)	–	–	–	–	–	–
Employees	–	–	–	–	–	300

TIVITY HEALTH, INC.

4031 ASPEN GROVE DR STE 250
FRANKLIN, TN 370672949
Phone: 800 869-5311
Fax: –
Web: www.tivityhealth.com

CEO: Richard M Ashworth
CFO: Adam C Holland
HR: Jamie Logel
FYE: December 31
Type: Private

Tivity Health is a leading provider of healthy life-changing solutions, including SilverSneakers, Prime Fitness, Burnalong, and WholeHealth Living. SilverSneakers by Tivity Health is the nation's leading community fitness program available to more than 18 million eligible Medicare seniors. SilverSneakers empowers members and drives sustainable behavior change through convenient access to its nationwide fitness network, a variety of programming options and activities that incorporate physical well-being and social interaction. In mid-2022, Tivity Health was acquired by Stone Point Capital for $32.50 in cash per share, representing a total transaction value of $2.0 billion.

TIVO CORPORATION

2160 GOLD ST
SAN JOSE, CA 950023700
Phone: 408 519-9100
Fax: –
Web: www.tivo.com

CEO: David Shull
CFO: Peter Halt
HR: –
FYE: December 31
Type: Private

TiVo lets people watch entertainment they want to watch exactly when they want to watch it. The company is responsible for making several entertainment technology breakthroughs from the creation of the interactive TV program guide to the DVR. The company serves up the best movies, shows, sports and videos from across live TV, on demand, streaming services and countless apps. Its highly engaging, visually-rich user experience is designed to drive customer satisfaction and reduce churn. TiVo's technology-agnostic solutions, flexible APIs and toolsets adapt existing infrastructure and speed time to market. With its high-quality set-top-box data, it fuels, measures and optimizes advertising and marketing initiatives.

TIVO SOLUTIONS INC.

2160 GOLD ST
ALVISO, CA 950023700
Phone: 408 519-9100
Fax: –
Web: –

CEO: –
CFO: –
HR: –
FYE: January 31
Type: Private

TiVo serves up the best movies, shows, sports, and videos from across live TV, on demand, streaming services and countless apps. The company delivers passionate audiences and creates new revenue streams everywhere people watch. From studios and networks to pay-TV operators, advertisers and more, its clients and partners benefit from the company's versatile platform and audience analytics that deepen engagement, drive viewership, and reduce churn. Serving content creators, pay-TV and streaming providers, device manufacturers, data companies, retailers, and consumers, millions of households and the world's top media and entertainment brands choose TiVo.

TIX CORP NBB: TIXC

731-A Pilot Road
Las Vegas, NV 89119
Phone: 818 761-1002
Fax: 818 761-1072
Web: www.tixcorp.com

CEO: –
CFO: –
HR: –
FYE: December 31
Type: Public

Tix Corporation has got a ticket to ride. Through its Tix4Tonight subsidiary, the company sells discounted same-day tickets to Las Vegas shows from about a dozen locations in Las Vegas. Tix4Tonight also includes Tix4Dinner (discounted dinners on the Vegas strip) and Tix4Golf (discounted golf reservations in the Las Vegas area). The company's Exhibit Merchandising sells branded merchandise (souvenir posters, memorabilia) related to museum exhibits and theatrical productions. Sales are made in temporary specialty stores set up in conjunction with the touring event.

	Annual Growth	12/16	12/17	12/18	12/19	12/20
Sales ($mil.)	(45.0%)	21.4	17.4	13.0	12.7	2.0
Net income ($ mil.)	–	1.9	(4.7)	(7.6)	(3.0)	(4.7)
Market value ($ mil.)	(46.4%)	27.3	6.3	3.7	8.6	2.3
Employees	–	–	–	94	98	–

TJX COMPANIES, INC. NYS: TJX

770 Cochituate Road
Framingham, MA 01701
Phone: 508 390-1000
Fax: 508 390-2091
Web: www.tjx.com

CEO: Ernie L Herrman
CFO: John Klinger
HR: –
FYE: January 28
Type: Public

The TJX Companies is one of the leading off-price apparel and home fashions retailer in the US and worldwide. It operates more than 4,800 stores worldwide and five distinctive branded e-commerce sites, including the two largest off-price clothing retailers in the US: T.J. Maxx and Marshalls, which operate more than 2,482 stores nationwide. T.J. Maxx sells brand-name family apparel, accessories, shoes, domestics, giftware, and jewelry at discount prices, while Marshalls offers similar items plus a broader selection of shoes and menswear through about 1,185 stores worldwide. Its HomeGoods chain of approximately 940 US stores focuses exclusively on home furnishings. It trades as T.K. Maxx in Europe with about 620 stores in the UK, Ireland, Austria, Germany, Poland, and the Netherlands. TJX keeps prices low by scooping up excess stock from manufacturers and department stores. The US generates the largest revenue amounting nearly 80%.

	Annual Growth	02/19	02/20*	01/21	01/22	01/23
Sales ($mil.)	6.4%	38,973	41,717	32,137	48,550	49,936
Net income ($ mil.)	3.4%	3,059.8	3,272.2	90.5	3,282.8	3,498.0
Market value ($ mil.)	13.8%	56,501	68,217	73,994	82,475	94,619
Employees	5.1%	270,000	286,000	320,000	340,000	329,000

*Fiscal year change

TLIC WORLDWIDE, INC

400 SOUTH COUNTY TRL STE A208
EXETER, RI 02822
Phone: 401 295-2244
Fax: –
Web: www.tlic.com

CEO: –
CFO: –
HR: –
FYE: December 31
Type: Private

TLIC Worldwide hopes to provide your network with some secure, tender loving care. The company is a provider of integrated information technology solutions in the US partnering with the leading vendors' and offers IT solutions. The company sells products from vendors such as McAfee, Microsoft, and Kaspersky, and offers volume licensing. TLIC Worldwide also offers professional services that include implementing and managing various security offerings such as anti-virus protection, and security technologies. The company's customers come from a variety of fields including education, health care, and government. The company was founded in 1998.

TMA SYSTEMS, L.L.C.

1876 UTICA SQ FL 3
TULSA, OK 741141429
Phone: 918 858-6600
Fax: –
Web: www.tmasystems.com

CEO: Mark Simner
CFO: –
HR: –
FYE: December 31
Type: Private

TMA Systems won't actually perform the work, but its software will make maintenance and asset management less of a chore. The company's products help clients burdened with extensive facilities management requirements manage and maintain their assets. Clients include universities, government entities, health care organizations, and large corporations. The company's software, available as a desktop application or as a Web-based solution, provides work order management, materials and inventory management, contract management, fleet management, custodial management, and room inspection functions. TMA also provides training, implementation, and consulting services related to its software.

	Annual Growth	12/14	12/15	12/16	12/17	12/18
Sales ($mil.)	1.1%	–	14.8	15.3	15.3	15.3
Net income ($ mil.)	5.6%	–	6.2	6.9	7.1	7.3
Market value ($ mil.)	–	–	–	–	–	–
Employees	–	–	–	–	–	75

TNEMEC COMPANY, INC.

123 W 23RD AVE
KANSAS CITY, MO 641163013
Phone: 816 483-3400
Fax: –
Web: www.tnemec.com

CEO: Albert C Bean IV
CFO: –
HR: Tracy Wakeman
FYE: December 31
Type: Private

Tnemec (pronouced tah-KNEE-mick, it is cement spelled backwards) makes more than 100 different paints and coatings that can be used as primers on concrete, masonry, steel, and flooring materials. It also provides waterproofing, corrosion prevention (for wastewater facilities), and exterior finishing products. Tnemec serves customers in different markets including architectural, industrial, manufacturing, oilfield services, water and wastewater, and water storage tanks. Its Chemprobe line specializes in masonry products, while the company's StrataShield line focuses on floor and wall coatings.

	Annual Growth	12/13	12/14	12/15	12/16	12/17
Sales ($mil.)	1.5%	–	–	120.5	118.3	124.2
Net income ($ mil.)	16.2%	–	–	2.5	3.3	3.4
Market value ($ mil.)	–	–	–	–	–	–
Employees	–	–	–	–	–	272

TOASTMASTERS INTERNATIONAL

9127 S JAMAICA ST STE 400
ENGLEWOOD, CO 801126339
Phone: 949 858-8255
Fax: –
Web: www.toastmasters.org

CEO: –
CFO: –
HR: –
FYE: December 31
Type: Private

Toastmasters International has an idea for people terrified of public speaking -- speak up! The organization's program is designed to improve public speaking and leadership skills through having its members run meetings and give prepared and impromptu speeches. The nonprofit group boasts about 250,000 members in some 12,500 clubs across the US and in 100 other countries worldwide. Toastmasters counts actor Tim Allen, Reagan press secretary James Brady, tennis star Billie Jean King, former US astronaut James Lovell, and many elected officials among its membership. Toastmasters International was established in 1924 by Ralph Smedley.

	Annual Growth	12/14	12/15	12/19	12/21	12/22
Sales ($mil.)	(4.0%)	–	34.9	39.8	29.2	26.2
Net income ($ mil.)		–	0.7	1.0	6.0	(2.6)
Market value ($ mil.)		–	–	–	–	–
Employees		–	–	–	–	165

TOBIRA THERAPEUTICS, INC.

701 GATEWAY BLVD STE 300
SOUTH SAN FRANCISCO, CA 940807412
Phone: 650 741-6625
Fax: –
Web: –

CEO: Laurent Fischer
CFO: Christopher Peetz
HR: –
FYE: December 31
Type: Private

Tobira Therapeutics (formerly Regado Biosciences)is a clinical-stage biopharmaceutical with an eye on treating non-alcoholic steatohepatitis (NASH) and other liver diseases. Its lead candidates are cenicriviroc, which is being studied for the treatment of NASH and as an adjunctive therapy for the treatment of HIV, and Evogliptin, which controls blood glucose levels and is approved in South Korea for the the treatment of type 2 diabetes mellitus. In addition to liver diseases, the company targets inflammation, fibrosis, and HIV. Tobira Therapeutics went public in 2013 and was acquired by Allergan in 2016.

TOFUTTI BRANDS INC

NBB: TOFB

50 Jackson Drive
Cranford, NJ 07016
Phone: 908 272-2400
Fax: –
Web: www.tofutti.com

CEO: Steven Kass
CFO: Steven Kass
HR: –
FYE: December 31
Type: Public

Tofutti Brands makes Tofutti Cuties and Marry Me Bars and while the company may get silly with its brand names, don't let that fool you. Its soy-based foods are aimed at lactose-intolerant, kosher, and health-conscious consumers. Its flagship product, Tofutti frozen dessert, is sold by the pint and in novelty forms. The company also offers nondairy cheeses and sour cream. Tofutti's products are developed by the company at its own labs but they do no manufacturing of their own. Instead, the company contracts with co-packers to furnish its products. Chairman and CEO David Mintz owns about 50% of the firm; the Financial & Investment Management Group owns almost 8%.

	Annual Growth	12/18	12/19*	01/21	01/22*	12/22
Sales ($mil.)	(0.5%)	13.1	13.1	13.8	12.6	12.8
Net income ($ mil.)	–	0.5	0.0	0.6	0.1	(0.5)
Market value ($ mil.)	(10.1%)	9.4	9.5	9.4	13.6	6.1
Employees	(13.7%)	9	8	4	5	5

*Fiscal year change

TOLEDO EDISON CO

c/o FirstEnergy Corp., 76 South Main Street
Akron, OH 44308
Phone: 800 736-3402
Fax: –
Web: –

CEO: C E Jones
CFO: Mark Clark
HR: –
FYE: December 31
Type: Public

Holy Toledo... this utility can sure crank out some power! Toledo Edison, a subsidiary of FirstEnergy, distributes electricity to more than 303,000 residential, commercial, and industrial customers in about 2,300 square miles in northwestern Ohio. The company has about 2,280 MW of generating capacity. Toledo Edison also markets excess power to wholesale customers. The company owns interests in both Ohio Valley Electric Corporation and Indiana-Kentucky Electric Corporation. Overall, First Energy's utilities provide electricity to 4.5 million customers in Ohio, Pennsylvania, and New Jersey.

	Annual Growth	12/07	12/08	12/09	12/10	12/11
Sales ($mil.)	(16.1%)	963.9	895.5	833.9	516.7	477.0
Net income ($ mil.)	(21.5%)	91.2	74.9	24.0	33.0	34.7
Market value ($ mil.)	–	–	–	–	–	–
Employees	(3.2%)	445	445	396	394	390

TOLEDO PROMEDICA HOSPITAL

2142 N COVE BLVD
TOLEDO, OH 436063895
Phone: 419 291-4000
Fax: –
Web: www.promedica.org

CEO: Alan Brass
CFO: Cathy Hanley
HR: Jeff Moss
FYE: December 31
Type: Private

One of the region's largest acute-care facilities, The Toledo Hospital provides medical care to the residents of northwestern Ohio and southeastern Michigan. Boasting nearly 800 beds, the facility offers several specialties and services, including the Jobst Vascular Center, which provides cardiac and vascular services in conjunction with The University of Michigan. The Toledo Hospital, which shares a medical complex with the Toledo Children's Hospital, also operates trauma, emergency, outpatient, arthritis, sleep disorder, and women's health centers. The Toledo Hospital is a member of Toledo-based ProMedica Health System, a mission-based, not-for-profit healthcare organization formed in 1986.

	Annual Growth	12/08	12/09	12/14	12/17	12/21
Sales ($mil.)	6.0%	–	635.7	745.4	854.4	1,282.0
Net income ($ mil.)	–	–	19.2	21.0	(115.8)	(154.8)
Market value ($ mil.)	–	–	–	–	–	–
Employees	–	–	–	–	–	5,586

TOLL BROTHERS INC.

NYS: TOL

1140 Virginia Drive
Fort Washington, PA 19034
Phone: 215 938-8000
Fax: 215 938-8023
Web: www.tollbrothers.com

CEO: Douglas C Yearley Jr
CFO: Martin P Connor
HR: –
FYE: October 31
Type: Public

Toll Brothers builds luxury homes caters to move-up, empty nester, and second-home buyers in the US, as well as urban and suburban renters under the brand names Toll Brothers Apartment Living and Toll Brothers Campus Living. The company also develops communities for active adults and operates country club communities. Toll Brothers delivers some 45,370 homes from some 905 communities, including roughly 10,515 homes from more than 490 communities. It has some 980 communities in various stages of planning, development or operations containing approximately 76,000 home sites that it owned or controlled through options. It also designs, builds, markets, and sells high-density, high-rise urban luxury condominiums with third-party joint venture partners through Toll Brothers City Living (City Living). The company operates in about 25 states and in the District of Columbia.

	Annual Growth	10/19	10/20	10/21	10/22	10/23
Sales ($mil.)	8.5%	7,224.0	7,077.7	8,790.4	10,276	9,994.9
Net income ($ mil.)	23.5%	590.0	446.6	833.6	1,286.5	1,372.1
Market value ($ mil.)	15.5%	4,127.8	4,388.3	6,245.1	4,471.3	7,339.1
Employees	(1.5%)	5,100	4,500	5,100	5,200	4,800

TOM JAMES COMPANY

263 SEABOARD LN
FRANKLIN, TN 370674877
Phone: 615 771-1122
Fax: –
Web: www.tomjames.com

CEO: Sergio Casalena
CFO: James P Williams
HR: Byron Wooten
FYE: June 30
Type: Private

Tom James wants to fit you for your next business suit in the comfort of your own home or office. With more than 100 locations worldwide, Tom James is a leading manufacturer and retailer of bespoke men's and women's clothing. It primarily sells suits and executive apparel. The company sells most of its clothing to customers through its direct marketing efforts. In addition to custom suits, Tom James also sells sportswear, custom shirts, outerwear, shoes, and accessories. Founded in 1966 by Nashville businessman and multimillionaire Spencer Hays, Tom James is the largest of multiple businesses run by Hays, who is also Tom James' majority shareholder.

TOM LANGE COMPANY, INC.

500 N BROADWAY STE 1320
SAINT LOUIS, MO 631022100
Phone: 314 934-2800
Fax: –
Web: www.tomlange.com

CEO: Rock Gumpert
CFO: –
HR: –
FYE: August 31
Type: Private

Tom Lange Company wants you to eat your veggies. One of the largest purchasers and distributors of fresh fruits and vegetables in the US, Tom Lange supplies its comestibles to clients in the retail, wholesale, and food service trades. The company also provides third party logistics services specializing in truckload freight movement. The company was founded in 1960 as a three-man operation in St. Louis, Missouri, Tom Lange has grown to encompass 35 offices in the US and Canada. Produce subsidiaries include Seven Seas, M&M Marketing, and Seven Seas Fruit.

	Annual Growth	08/18	08/19	08/20	08/21	08/22
Sales ($mil.)	7.3%	–	–	578.4	609.1	665.7
Net income ($ mil.)	74.1%	–	–	6.2	11.5	18.7
Market value ($ mil.)	–	–	–	–	–	–
Employees	–	–	–	–	–	160

TOMAH MEMORIAL HOSPITAL, INC.

501 GOPHER DR
TOMAH, WI 546604513
Phone: 608 372-2181
Fax: -
Web: www.tomahhealth.org

CEO: Phil Stuart
CFO: -
HR: Brenda Reinert
FYE: September 30
Type: Private

Tomah Memorial Hospital provides a wide range of medical services for the residents of western Wisconsin and southern Minnesota. The hospital's staff of about 100 health care professionals includes specialists in cardiology, internal medicine, oncology, general and orthopedic surgery, and emergency medicine. In 2005 the hospital completed a nearly $10 million construction and renovation project, which included a new 20,000 sq. ft. facility on its premises. With help and donations from many community residents, Tomah Memorial opened its doors in 1952 with 29 beds.

	Annual Growth	09/17	09/18	09/20	09/21	09/22
Sales ($mil.)	8.4%	-	55.7	65.6	71.4	76.8
Net income ($ mil.)	15.8%	-	2.1	(1.1)	13.5	3.9
Market value ($ mil.)	-	-	-	-	-	-
Employees	-	-	-	-	-	215

TOMBALL HOSPITAL AUTHORITY

605 HOLDERRIETH BLVD
TOMBALL, TX 773756445
Phone: 281 351-1623
Fax: -
Web: www.tomballregionalmedicalcenter.com

CEO: -
CFO: -
HR: -
FYE: June 30
Type: Private

When it comes to keeping Lone Star Staters healthy, these physicians are on the ball. Tomball Regional Hospital, operating as Tomball Regional Medical Center, provides health care services to residents of Tomball, Texas and the surrounding areas, including Northwest Houston. The 360-bed Tomball Regional Medical Center provides specialized services in emergency and cardiac care, sports medicine, cancer treatment, and outpatient surgery. The medical center also provides diagnostic imaging, home health, and rehabilitation services, and operates outpatient facilities including an emergency clinic, a women's health center, and a retirement community. The hospital was acquired by Community Health Systems in late 2011.

TOMPKINS CORTLAND COMMUNITY COLLEGE ALUMNI ASSOCIATION, INC.

170 NORTH ST
DRYDEN, NY 130538504
Phone: 607 844-8211
Fax: -
Web: www.tompkinscortland.edu

CEO: -
CFO: -
HR: -
FYE: August 31
Type: Private

Tompkins Cortland Community College is one of about 30 community colleges in the State University of New York (SUNY) system. It offers nearly 40 academic programs in areas including liberal arts, business administration, technology, health and human services, visual media, and hospitality. Informally known as TC3, the college has approximately 6,000 students in either credit programs, non-credit workshops, or customized training programs; about half of them transfer as juniors to colleges offering bachelor's degree programs. The school also offers athletics, international programs, and on-campus housing. TC3 was founded in 1968.

TOMPKINS FINANCIAL CORP

ASE: TMP

P.O. Box 460
Ithaca, NY 14851
Phone: 888 503-5753
Fax: -
Web: www.tompkinsfinancial.com

CEO: Stephen S Romaine
CFO: Matthew Tomazin
HR: -
FYE: December 31
Type: Public

Tompkins Financial is a $7.8 billion in assets financial services holding company. The company is a locally oriented, community-based financial services organization that offers a full array of products and services, including commercial and consumer banking, leasing, trust and investment management, financial planning and wealth management, and insurance. Banking services consist primarily of attracting deposits from the areas served by the company's some 65 banking offices, and using those deposits to originate a variety of commercial loans, agricultural loans, consumer loans, real estate loans, and leases in those same areas. The company has a wholly-owned insurance agency subsidiary, Tompkins Insurance. Tompkins Community Bank provides a full array of trust and investment services under the Tompkins Financial Advisors brand, including investment management, trust and estate, financial and tax planning as well as life, disability and long-term care insurance services.

	Annual Growth	12/19	12/20	12/21	12/22	12/23
Assets ($mil.)	3.8%	6,725.6	7,622.2	7,820.0	7,670.7	7,819.7
Net income ($ mil.)	(41.6%)	81.7	77.6	89.3	85.0	9.5
Market value ($ mil.)	(9.9%)	1,309.3	1,010.3	1,196.0	1,110.1	861.9
Employees	(0.4%)	1,048	1,084	1,074	1,072	1,032

TOOTSIE ROLL INDUSTRIES INC

NYS: TR

7401 South Cicero Avenue
Chicago, IL 60629
Phone: 773 838-3400
Fax: 773 838-3534
Web: www.tootsie.com

CEO: Ellen R Gordon
CFO: G H Ember Jr
HR: Diana White
FYE: December 31
Type: Public

Tootsie Roll Industries is one of the country's largest candy companies. It makes and sells the vaguely chocolate-flavored Tootsie Roll, which has been produced with the same formula and name for more than a century. The company also makes such well-known candies as Sugar Babies, Junior Mints, Charleston Chew, and Sugar Daddy. Tootsie Roll Industries sells its candy directly and through food and grocery brokers to thousands of retail customers across the US (although Wal-mart and Dollar Tree together account for around 35%). The company's principal markets are in the US, Canada and Mexico.

	Annual Growth	12/19	12/20	12/21	12/22	12/23
Sales ($mil.)	9.9%	527.1	471.1	570.8	687.0	769.4
Net income ($ mil.)	9.1%	64.9	59.0	65.3	75.9	91.9
Market value ($ mil.)	(0.7%)	2,438.4	2,121.2	2,587.6	3,040.4	2,374.1
Employees	3.6%	2,000	2,000	2,000	2,300	2,300

TOP DOWN SYSTEMS CORPORATION

9210 CORPORATE BLVD STE 401
ROCKVILLE, MD 20850
Phone: 800 361-1211
Fax: -
Web: www.topdownsystems.com

CEO: -
CFO: -
HR: -
FYE: December 31
Type: Private

Top Down Systems can help you manage your enterprise from the top down. The company makes enterprise software including its two main products: Client Letter, which links clients to server systems and INTOUCH, a 100% cloud, microservices-based, containerized SaaS application built upon the Amazon Web Services (AWS) public cloud platform. Top Down's customers come from a variety of industries including financial services, health care, utilities and telecom providers, and the government. The company was founded in 1981.

	Annual Growth	12/13	12/14	12/15	12/18	12/19
Sales ($mil.)	1.1%	-	-	5.7	4.8	5.9
Net income ($ mil.)	-	-	-	(0.1)	(0.0)	(0.0)
Market value ($ mil.)	-	-	-	-	-	-
Employees	-	-	-	-	-	25

TOPBUILD CORP   NYS: BLD

475 North Williamson Boulevard
Daytona Beach, FL 32114
Phone: 386 304-2200
Fax: –
Web: www.topbuild.com

CEO: Robert M Buck
CFO: Robert M Kuhns
HR: –
FYE: December 31
Type: Public

TopBuild is a leading installer and distributor of insulation products to the US construction industry. Beyond insulation products, TopBuild also installs or ships other building products like rain gutters, fireplaces, shower enclosures, roofing materials, closet shelving, and garage doors. The company provides insulation installation services nationwide through its contractor services which has about 230 branches located across the US. TopBuild serves a thousand of insulation contractors of all sizes serving a wide variety of commercial and industrial industries and other contractors, dealers, metal building erectors and modular home builds through its over 160 distribution centers across the US and over 15 branches in Canada.

	Annual Growth	12/19	12/20	12/21	12/22	12/23
Sales ($mil.)	18.6%	2,624.1	2,718.0	3,486.2	5,008.7	5,194.7
Net income ($ mil.)	33.9%	191.0	247.0	324.0	556.0	614.3
Market value ($ mil.)	38.0%	3,275.5	5,849.3	8,767.3	4,972.6	11,893
Employees	7.7%	10,400	10,540	13,006	13,119	14,012

TOPGOLF CALLAWAY BRANDS CORP   NYS: MODG

2180 Rutherford Road
Carlsbad, CA 92008
Phone: 760 931-1771
Fax: –
Web: www.topgolfcallawaybrands.com

CEO: Oliver G Brewer III
CFO: Brian P Lynch
HR: –
FYE: December 31
Type: Public

Topgolf Callaway Brands Corp (formerly Callaway Golf Company) is a technology-enabled modern golf company delivering leading golf equipment, apparel, and entertainment with a portfolio of global brands. The company's other drivers, as well as its fairway woods, irons, wedges, packaged sets, and hybrids, are sold under the Callaway, and putters are sold under the Odyssey brand, including Toulon Design by Odyssey. It also makes golf balls, golf bags, and golf apparel among others. In addition, the company offers high-quality soft goods products under the Callaway, OGIO, TravisMathew, and Jack Wolfskin brands. Its products are sold through its websites and in more than 120 countries by golf pro shops, sporting goods retailers, online, and mass merchants. The US accounts for about 70% of the company's revenue.

	Annual Growth	12/19	12/20	12/21	12/22	12/23
Sales ($mil.)	26.0%	1,701.1	1,589.5	3,133.4	3,995.7	4,284.8
Net income ($ mil.)	4.6%	79.4	(126.9)	322.0	157.9	95.0
Market value ($ mil.)	(9.3%)	3,894.4	4,410.6	5,040.7	3,628.1	2,634.3
Employees	48.4%	6,600	4,200	29,000	32,000	32,000

TOR MINERALS INTERNATIONAL INC   NBB: TORM

615 N. Upper Broadway, Suite 410
Corpus Christi, TX 78401
Phone: 361 883-5591
Fax: –
Web: www.torminerals.com

CEO: –
CFO: –
HR: –
FYE: December 31
Type: Public

It doesn't make winter outerwear, but TOR Minerals International is concerned about good, durable coats. The company makes pigments and pigment extenders that are used in paints, industrial coatings, and plastics. HITOX, TOR's primary product, is a beige titanium dioxide pigment used to add opacity and durability to paints. Other TOR products include pigment extenders that add strength and weight to end products, and pigment fillers with flame-retardant and smoke-suppressant properties. The company's customers include paint and plastics manufacturers. TOR has production facilities in Corpus Christi, Texas; the Netherlands; and Malaysia. Chairman Bernard Paulson owns 34% of the company.

	Annual Growth	12/18	12/19	12/20	12/21	12/22
Sales ($mil.)	(6.7%)	39.4	35.3	30.9	29.2	29.9
Net income ($ mil.)	–	(0.8)	(2.2)	(2.3)	(1.2)	(1.3)
Market value ($ mil.)	(1.6%)	9.0	5.4	4.4	7.7	8.5
Employees	–	–	–	–	–	–

TORCH ENERGY ROYALTY TRUST   NBB: TRRU

Rodney Square North, 1100 North Market Street
Wilmington, DE 19890
Phone: 302 636-6435
Fax: –
Web: www.torchroyalty.com

CEO: –
CFO: –
HR: –
FYE: December 31
Type: Public

Investors in Torch Energy Royalty Trust probably won't light an eternal flame in remembrance when the gas is all gone. The trust distributes to shareholders the royalties from natural gas properties and oil wells in which it owns stakes. The trust's gas fields are in Texas, Alabama, and Louisiana. As a grantor trust, Torch Energy does not pay federal income tax; instead, the shareholders who receive quarterly royalties are taxed directly, but receive tax credits on gas extracted from some of the trust's hard-to-drill properties. Torch Energy Royalty Trust's investors have voted to wind up and liquidate the trust.

	Annual Growth	12/08	12/09	12/10	12/11	12/12
Sales ($mil.)	(61.5%)	6.4	2.6	3.2	2.7	0.1
Net income ($ mil.)	–	3.2	1.2	2.1	1.3	(1.1)
Market value ($ mil.)	(17.3%)	12.4	40.9	31.2	18.1	5.8
Employees	–	–	–	–	–	–

TORO COMPANY (THE)   NYS: TTC

8111 Lyndale Avenue South
Bloomington, MN 55420-1196
Phone: 952 888-8801
Fax: –
Web: www.thetorocompany.com

CEO: Richard M Olson
CFO: Angela C Drake
HR: –
FYE: October 31
Type: Public

The Toro Company is a worldwide provider of turf maintenance equipment and precision irrigation systems. It manufactures lawn mowers, snow throwers, and other such tools for professional and residential landscaping. Its lineup of products helps create, illuminate, and irrigate lawns and landscapes; install, repair and replace underground utilities; and manage ice and snow. Marketed and sold worldwide through a network of distributors, dealers, mass retailers, hardware retailers, equipment rental centers, home centers, as well as online under the primary trademarks of American Augers, BOSS, Ditch Witch, eXmark, Spartan, Toro, and Ventrac. Toro's products are typically used in golf courses, sports fields, municipal, residential, and commercial properties. About 80% of its revenue derives from the US customers. Toro traces its roots back to 1914 as The Toro Motor Company.

	Annual Growth	10/19	10/20	10/21	10/22	10/23
Sales ($mil.)	9.8%	3,138.1	3,378.8	3,959.6	4,514.7	4,553.2
Net income ($ mil.)	4.7%	274.0	329.7	409.9	443.3	329.7
Market value ($ mil.)	1.2%	8,009.4	8,525.6	9,913.9	10,948	8,394.7
Employees	3.5%	9,329	10,385	10,982	11,287	10,706

TORRANCE MEMORIAL MEDICAL CENTER

3330 LOMITA BLVD
TORRANCE, CA 905055002
Phone: 310 325-9110
Fax: –
Web: www.torrancememorial.org

CEO: Keith Hobbs
CFO: –
HR: Latasha Poydras
FYE: June 30
Type: Private

Founded in 1925 by Jared Sidney and Helena Childs Torrance, Torrance Memorial Medical Center is a 443-bed, nonprofit medical center established to provide quality health care services predominantly to the residents of the South Bay, Peninsula and Harbor communities. Torrance Memorial seeks to offer the most current and effective medical technologies rendered in a compassionate, caring manner. It includes an extensive integrated system of physicians and comprehensive medical services to provide coordinated communication and continuum of care. Torrance Memorial is affiliated with Cedars-Sinai under the umbrella of Cedars-Sinai Health System.

	Annual Growth	03/19	03/20*	06/20	06/21	06/22
Sales ($mil.)	29.0%	–	503.8	695.2	724.6	838.1
Net income ($ mil.)	110.4%	–	15.6	23.4	76.7	69.0
Market value ($ mil.)	–	–	–	–	–	–
Employees	–	–	–	–	–	3,500

*Fiscal year change

TOTAL HEALTH CARE, INC.

1231 E BELTLINE AVE NE
GRAND RAPIDS, MI 495254501
Phone: 313 871-2000
Fax: -
Web: www.thcmi.com

CEO: -
CFO: -
HR: -
FYE: December 31
Type: Private

Total Health Care provides health care coverage and related services to members in southeast Michigan (the greater Detroit area) and surrounding counties. Groups and individuals can choose Total Health Care for their health insurance. The HMO serves more than 80,000 members through individual and group health plan policies. Total Health Care also has a contract with the State of Michigan to serve patients with coverage through Medicaid and the State's MI Child program. Pharmacy services are provided through a contracted network of pharmacy providers.

	Annual Growth	12/13	12/14	12/15	12/18	12/21
Sales ($mil.)	(7.9%)	-	272.3	322.5	183.5	152.6
Net income ($ mil.)	-	-	5.0	5.9	10.6	(0.3)
Market value ($ mil.)	-	-	-	-	-	-
Employees						100

TOTE MARITIME PUERTO RICO, LLC

10401 DEERWOOD PARK BLVD BLDG 1
JACKSONVILLE, FL 322565007
Phone: 904 855-1260
Fax: -
Web: www.totemaritime.com

CEO: Tim Nolan
CFO: Hugh Simpson
HR: Stephanie Montieth
FYE: December 31
Type: Private

Marine transportation company Sea Star Line carries cargo between the US and Puerto Rico, the Dominican Republic, the US Virgin Islands, and the Caribbean on three combination roll-on/roll-off/lift-on/lift-off vessels. (The vessels are so named because shipping containers, cars, and heavy equipment can be rolled onto them on chassis or lifted on by cranes.) Saltchuk Resources, owner of Totem Ocean Trailer Express, owns 90% of Sea Star Lines; Puerto Rico-based Taino Star owns 10%. Sea Star is subject to the Jones Act, a federal law that allows only vessels controlled and operated by US companies to transport cargo between US ports.

	Annual Growth	12/03	12/04	12/05	12/06	12/07
Sales ($mil.)	5.3%	-	186.8	-	-	218.1
Net income ($ mil.)	-	-	-	-	-	17.3
Market value ($ mil.)	-	-	-	-	-	-
Employees	-	-	-	-	-	265

TOUCHSTONE BANKSHARES INC

4300 Crossings Boulevard
Prince George, VA 23875
Phone: 888 478-4434
Fax: -
Web: www.touchstone.bank

NBB: TSBA

CEO: -
CFO: -
HR: -
FYE: December 31
Type: Public

This company can help you make the most of your McKenney penny or your Dinwiddie dollar. The Bank of McKenney is a community thrift serving central Virginia's Dinwiddie and Chesterfield counties, the independent city of Colonial Heights, and surrounding areas. The bank's six branches offer traditional deposit products including savings and checking accounts, NOW accounts, money markets, and CDs. Commercial real estate loans make up about half of the company's lending portfolio; residential mortgages and trusts make up about 35%. Subsidiary McKenney Group provides investment services, insurance products, and business management services.

	Annual Growth	12/15	12/16	12/19	12/20	12/21
Assets ($mil.)	17.7%	218.3	222.8	468.2	532.7	581.1
Net income ($ mil.)	17.2%	1.7	1.7	3.3	2.3	4.4
Market value ($ mil.)	2.8%	33.1	34.3	44.3	30.7	39.2
Employees						

TOUCHSTONE ENERGY COOPERATIVE, INC.

4301 WILSON BLVD
ARLINGTON, VA 222034419
Phone: 703 907-5500
Fax: -
Web: www.touchstoneenergy.com

CEO: -
CFO: -
HR: -
FYE: December 31
Type: Private

Touchstone Energy keeps in touch with the energy of its members. The organization is a national alliance of local, consumer-owned electric utility cooperatives providing service to more than 30 million customers through more than 660 affiliated cooperatives in 46 states. Touchstone Energy champions the cause of electric cooperatives nationwide through organizing branding events, media projects, and other public relations activities. The alliance runs television ads on various channels, including CNN, ESPN, TNT, The Weather Channel, TBS, and The Learning Channel. It also places print ads in national magazines and newspapers, including Reader's Digest and other major publications.

TOURO COLLEGE

50 W 47TH ST FL 12
NEW YORK, NY 100368687
Phone: 646 565-6026
Fax: -
Web: gst.touro.edu

CEO: Bernard J Luskin
CFO: -
HR: Kathy Lowe
FYE: June 30
Type: Private

Touro College is a Jewish university (the largest private Jewish-based educational institution in the US) and has sister institutions in France, Germany, Israel, and Russia, and branches in California, Florida, and Nevada. Some 19,000 (Jewish and non-Jewish) students are enrolled in its 32 schools on 25 campuses, which offer associate, bachelor's, and master's degrees in business, education, and law, as well as professional degrees in osteopathic medicine, pharmacy, law, and other fields. Touro also oversees the operations of New York Medical College. The institution claims some 75,000 alumni.

	Annual Growth	06/08	06/09	06/10	06/19	06/20
Sales ($mil.)	(7.4%)	-	145.5	277.4	308.7	62.2
Net income ($ mil.)	-	-	-	15.8	(1.1)	6.7
Market value ($ mil.)	-	-	-	-	-	-
Employees	-	-	-	-	-	4,600

TOWER INTERNATIONAL, INC.

17672 N LAUREL PARK DR STE 400E
LIVONIA, MI 481523984
Phone: 248 675-6000
Fax: -
Web: www.autokiniton.com

CEO: -
CFO: -
HR: Gustavo Bello
FYE: December 31
Type: Private

Tower International is a manufacturer of automotive structural metal components and assemblies primarily serving original equipment manufacturers. Its supplies body-structure stampings, frame and structural designs, and complex welded assemblies for small and large cars, crossovers, pickups, and sport utility vehicles. The company is now part of Autokiniton, a leading North American supplier of propulsion-agnostic, structural automotive components and assemblies.

TOWER TECH, INC.

5400 NW 5TH ST
OKLAHOMA CITY, OK 731275810
Phone: 405 290-7788
Fax: –
Web: www.towertechinc.com

CEO: –
CFO: –
HR: –
FYE: January 31
Type: Private

Tower Tech makes factory-assembled fiberglass cooling towers for a variety of facilities including power generation, manufacturing, commercial, health care, and public facilities. The company also offers temporary cooling towers that are available for rapid installation in case of emergency and/or supplementary need, for temporary usage, and lease-to-own. Additionally, Tower Tech offers accessories including electrical control panels, pumps, and variable frequency drives. Inventor Harold Curtis founded Tower Tech in 1985. The company is not related to wind energy components maker Tower Tech Holdings.

TOWERSTREAM CORP   NBB: TWER

76 Hammarlund Way
Middletown, RI 02842
Phone: 401 848-5848
Fax: –
Web: www.towerstream.com

CEO: Ernest Ortega
CFO: John Macdonald
HR: –
FYE: December 31
Type: Public

TowerStream maintains a commanding view of the wireless landscape. The company provides wireless broadband network services to businesses over its network of rooftop and tower-mounted antennas. Its networks can be accessed by customers within a 10-mile radius. The company has about 3,600 business customers, including retailers, educational institutions, and banks. Charging a monthly subscription fee, TowerStream provides service in a more than a dozen US markets: Boston, Chicago, Dallas, Houston, Las Vegas/Reno, Los Angeles, Miami, Nashville, New York City, Philadelphia, San Francisco, and Seattle, as well Providence, Rhode Island.

	Annual Growth	12/14	12/15	12/16	12/17	12/18
Sales ($mil.)	(7.1%)	33.0	27.9	26.9	26.2	24.6
Net income ($ mil.)	–	(27.6)	(40.5)	(20.4)	(12.5)	(10.2)
Market value ($ mil.)	3.2%	0.7	0.1	0.0	1.2	0.8
Employees	(23.5%)	140	154	88	83	48

TOWN SPORTS INTERNATIONAL HOLDINGS INC   NBB: CLUB Q

1001 US North Highway 1, Suite 201
Jupiter, FL 33477
Phone: 914 347-4009
Fax: –
Web: www.townsportsinternational.com

CEO: Patrick Walsh
CFO: Carolyn Spatafora
HR: –
FYE: December 31
Type: Public

Town Sports International wants to be the apple a day that keeps the doctor away in NYC. The company owns and operates some 160 full-service health clubs, about two-thirds of which are in the New York City area under the New York Sports Club banner. The company also has clubs in Boston, Philadelphia, and Washington, D.C., and claims about 510,000 members. It offers various membership plans that cater to its members' usage needs. Members designate a specific "home" club they can use at any time and retain an option to upgrade and gain access to multiple clubs within a single region, or pay even more to gain access to all clubs in all four regions. Town Sports also has three clubs in Switzerland.

	Annual Growth	12/15	12/16	12/17	12/18	12/19
Sales ($mil.)	2.4%	424.3	396.9	403.0	443.1	466.8
Net income ($ mil.)	–	21.2	8.0	4.4	0.0	(18.6)
Market value ($ mil.)	9.5%	35.0	73.6	163.3	188.3	50.3
Employees	5.2%	7,500	7,600	5,900	7,700	9,200

TOWNSHIP HIGH SCHOOL DISTRICT 211 FOUNDATION

1750 S ROSELLE RD
PALATINE, IL 600677302
Phone: 708 359-3300
Fax: –
Web: adc.d211.org

CEO: –
CFO: –
HR: –
FYE: June 30
Type: Private

Township High School District 211 is the largest high school district in Illinois with some 12,500 students attending its five high schools (grades 9 to 12) -- James B. Conant, William Fremd, Hoffman Estates, Palatine, and Schaumburg -- and two special education academies. The district's student-teacher ratio is nearly 14-to-1 and serves several suburban communities 25 miles northwest of Chicago. The school district started as one school (Palatine High School) in the Palatine-Schaumburg Township area in 1875 with the first graduating class in 1877.

	Annual Growth	06/14	06/15	06/16	06/17	06/18
Sales ($mil.)	3.9%	–	296.9	304.9	331.1	333.2
Net income ($ mil.)	–	–	(17.2)	(10.4)	(15.1)	(10.4)
Market value ($ mil.)	–	–	–	–	–	–
Employees	–	–	–	–	–	1,909

TOWNSQUARE MEDIA INC   NYS: TSQ

One Manhattanville Road, Suite 202
Purchase, NY 10577
Phone: 203 861-0900
Fax: –
Web: www.townsquaremedia.com

CEO: Bill Wilson
CFO: Stuart Rosenstein
HR: –
FYE: December 31
Type: Public

Townsquare Media is a community-focused digital media, digital marketing solutions, and radio company focused outside the Top 50 markets in the US. The company owns and operates around 355 radio stations and more than 400 local news and entertainment websites in almost 75 US markets. Its assets include digital marketing services subscription business (Townsquare Interactive) providing website design, creation and hosting, search engine optimization, social platforms, and online reputation management for approximately 30,650 small to medium sized businesses. It also include a robust digital advertising division (Townsquare Ignite), a proprietary digital programmatic advertising technology stack with an in-house demand and data management platform.

	Annual Growth	12/19	12/20	12/21	12/22	12/23
Sales ($mil.)	1.3%	431.4	371.3	418.0	463.1	454.2
Net income ($ mil.)	–	(67.8)	(82.5)	16.7	12.3	(45.0)
Market value ($ mil.)	1.4%	167.5	111.9	223.9	121.8	177.4
Employees	(6.6%)	2,836	2,257	2,340	2,442	2,159

TOYOTA MOTOR CREDIT CORP.

6565 Headquarters Drive
Plano, TX 75024
Phone: 469 486-9300
Fax: –
Web: www.toyotafinancial.com

CEO: Mark S Templin
CFO: Scott Cooke
HR: –
FYE: March 31
Type: Public

Toyota Motor Credit (TMCC) is the US financing arm of Toyota Financial Services, which is a subsidiary of Toyota Motor Corporation, the world's largest carmaker. TMCC provides a variety of finance and voluntary vehicle and payment protection products and services to authorized Toyota and Lexus dealers and their customers for the purchase of new and used cars and trucks. TMCC, which underwrites and services the finance contracts, operates three regional experience centers and dealer sales and service branches across the US and Puerto Rico. Its regional experience centers support customer account servicing functions such as collections, lease terminations, and administration of both retail and lease contract customer accounts. TMCC is marketed under the brands of Toyota Financial Services, Lexus Financial Services, and Mazda Financial Services.

	Annual Growth	03/18	03/19	03/20	03/21	03/22
Sales ($mil.)	2.2%	11,856	12,836	13,284	13,165	12,909
Net income ($ mil.)	(7.1%)	3,410.0	795.0	913.0	2,017.0	2,535.0
Market value ($ mil.)	–	–	–	–	–	–
Employees	2.9%	3,300	3,200	3,300	3,600	3,700

TOYOTA MOTOR SALES USA INC

6565 HEADQUARTERS DR APT W1-3C
PLANO, TX 75024
Phone: –
Fax: –
Web: www.toyota.com

CEO: –
CFO: Tracey Doi
HR: Jermaine Richardson
FYE: December 31
Type: Private

Toyota Motor Sales, U.S.A. (TMS) is the US sales, distribution, and marketing unit for Toyota Motor's Toyota, and Lexus brands. Other models include the Avalon, Camry, Highlander, Sequoia, Sienna, Tacoma, Tundra, and Venza. Sales are conducted through about 1,800 dealerships throughout North America. The company's TRD (Toyota Racing Development) USA division designs and assembles engines and develops chassis and other technology for Toyota-sponsored race cars. The company traces its roots back to 1957.

TOYS "R" US, INC.

1 GEOFFREY WAY
WAYNE, NJ 074702035
Phone: 973 617-3500
Fax: –
Web: www.toysrusinc.com

CEO: –
CFO: –
HR: –
FYE: January 28
Type: Private

Geoffrey the Giraffe may be going extinct. After filing for Chapter 11 bankruptcy protection in late 2017, the company in 2018 began liquidating and closing all its US stores. Once one of the world's largest toy retailers, the company had been grappling for years with how to grow its business amid a weak selling environment for specialty retailers. It was competing with Wal-Mart Stores and Target, which both lure shoppers with groceries and other basics. Furthermore, its breadth of selection was being challenged by online giant Amazon.com. The company is searching for buyers (or other options) for its Canadian and other international operations.

TPG RE FINANCE TRUST INC   NYS: TRTX

888 Seventh Avenue, 35th Floor
New York, NY 10106
Phone: 212 601-4700
Fax: –
Web: www.tpgrefinance.com

CEO: AVI Banyasz
CFO: Obert Foley
HR: –
FYE: December 31
Type: Public

TPG RE Finance Trust (operating as TPG Real Estate Finance Trust) originates, buys, and manages real estate-related debt instruments including commercial mortgages, mezzanine loans, and commercial mortgage-backed securities (CMBS). A real estate investment trust (REIT), it targets loans secured by properties that are being renovated, re-tenanted, or otherwise transitioning toward having a higher asset value. The company is poised to take advantage of the reduction in supply of commercial real estate debt capital, as well as the shrinking new issuance market for CMBS. TPG Real Estate Finance Trust, which went public in July 2017, is sponsored by alternative investment firm TPG.

	Annual Growth	12/19	12/20	12/21	12/22	12/23
Sales ($mil.)	3.4%	341.6	284.2	240.7	305.7	390.3
Net income ($ mil.)	–	126.3	(136.8)	138.6	(60.1)	(116.7)
Market value ($ mil.)	(24.7%)	1,578.4	827.0	959.3	528.7	506.1
Employees	–	–	–	–	–	–

TPI ACQUISITION, INC.

2300 S WATNEY WAY STE F
FAIRFIELD, CA 945336737
Phone: 925 277-9014
Fax: –
Web: –

CEO: –
CFO: –
HR: –
FYE: December 31
Type: Private

TPI Acquisition, which operates through its Telpro Technologies subsidiary, provides engineering services to the telecommunications industry. It provides site surveys, specification engineering, drafting, installation, maintenance, and training. Projects include new system installations, system upgrades, loop enhancements, and equipment removal. The company has offices in California and also maintains contractors licenses in Arizona, Nevada, and Oregon. Through TPI Acquisition, founder and CEO Larry Jordan reacquired Telpro Technologies in 2004 from Linc.net (following Linc.net's Chapter 11 bankruptcy filing). Jordan originally founded the company in 1990, and sold it to Linc.net in 2000.

TPI COMPOSITES INC   NMS: TPIC

9200 E. Pima Center Parkway, Suite 250
Scottsdale, AZ 85258
Phone: 480 305-8910
Fax: –
Web: www.tpicomposites.com

CEO: William E Siwek
CFO: Ryan Miller
HR: Libby Lipinski
FYE: December 31
Type: Public

TPI Composites is an independent manufacturer of composite wind blades for the wind energy market with a global manufacturing footprint. It enables many of the industry's leading wind turbine original equipment manufacturers (OEM) to outsource the manufacturing of some of their wind blades through its global footprint of advanced manufacturing facilities. The company is a key supplier to its OEM customers in the manufacture of wind blades and related precision molding and assembly systems. Major customers include GE Renewable Energy, Vestas, Nordex, and ENERCON. The company operates through domestic and international facilities in Denmark, Germany, Mexico, Spain, Turkey, and India. Most of its revenue originates outside the US. TPI traces its founding back to 1968.

	Annual Growth	12/19	12/20	12/21	12/22	12/23
Sales ($mil.)	0.3%	1,436.5	1,670.1	1,732.6	1,522.7	1,455.2
Net income ($ mil.)	–	(15.7)	(19.0)	(159.5)	(124.2)	(177.6)
Market value ($ mil.)	(31.2%)	860.2	2,452.7	695.2	471.2	192.4
Employees	(1.9%)	13,300	14,900	14,000	13,500	12,300

TRACK DATA CORP.   NBB: TRAC

95 Rockwell Place
Brooklyn, NY 11217
Phone: 718 522-7373
Fax: –
Web: www.trackdata.com

CEO: Martin Kaye
CFO: Martin Kaye
HR: –
FYE: December 31
Type: Public

Track Data Corporation (TDC) won't tell you if your train is on time, but it might tell you that your ship has come in. The firm offers real-time financial and market data and trading through its proTrack Online Trading system for the institutional trader. Its FastTrack provides real-time quotes and market data, news, and historical information to professional investors. TDC also operates Track ECN, an electronic communications network that enables traders to display and match limit orders for stocks. The company offers services to non-professional individual investors through its myTrack and myTrack Edge products.

	Annual Growth	12/04	12/05	12/06	12/07	12/08
Sales ($mil.)	(6.5%)	40.1	36.1	42.0	34.1	30.7
Net income ($ mil.)	(28.7%)	5.2	(0.0)	1.5	(0.1)	1.3
Market value ($ mil.)	(3.9%)	0.0	0.3	0.3	0.2	0.0
Employees	(9.3%)	170	150	135	130	115

TRACK GROUP INC

NBB: TRCK

200 E. 5th Avenue, Suite 100
Naperville, IL 60563
Phone: 877 260-2010
Fax: –
Web: www.trackgrp.com

CEO: Derek Cassell
CFO: Peter K Poli
HR: –
FYE: September 30
Type: Public

Thanks in part to SecureAlert, you can run, but you can not hide. The company (formerly RemoteMDx) develops, markets, and sells wireless monitoring equipment and services to law enforcement and bail bond agencies. Its primary product is TrackerPAL -- tracking devices worn on the ankle to monitor the whereabouts of criminals on parole or probation. Using global positioning system and cellular technology, the device features two-way voice communications, alarms, and Web-based location tracking in real time. The company's SecureAlert Monitoring subsidiary provides monitoring services. The company electronically monitors some 12,700 offenders.

	Annual Growth	09/19	09/20	09/21	09/22	09/23
Sales ($mil.)	0.3%	34.0	33.9	39.7	37.0	34.5
Net income ($ mil.)	–	(2.6)	(0.1)	3.4	(7.4)	(3.4)
Market value ($ mil.)	(1.0%)	6.1	4.4	35.6	6.1	5.8
Employees	0.2%	166	151	159	161	167

TRACTOR & EQUIPMENT COMPANY INC

5336 AIRPORT HWY
BIRMINGHAM, AL 352121599
Phone: 205 591-2131
Fax: –
Web: www.tec1943.com

CEO: Dan Stracener
CFO: Jamie Steele
HR: –
FYE: December 31
Type: Private

The Tractor & Equipment Company (TEC) probably knows the words to "Sweet Home Alabama." Considering how many Komatsu products it sells, it might even know them in Japanese. Founded in Birmingham, Alabama in 1943, TEC sells and leases new and used equipment and parts for the construction, mining, and forestry industries. It offers equipment made under a broad range of brands; besides Komatsu, it offers products from manufacturers including Dressta, Gradall, CMI Thrashmasters, and Moxy. TEC operates through more than 20 locations in Alabama, Georgia, and northwestern Florida.

TRACTOR SUPPLY CO.

NMS: TSCO

5401 Virginia Way
Brentwood, TN 37027
Phone: 615 440-4000
Fax: –
Web: www.tractorsupply.com

CEO: Harry A Lawton III
CFO: Kurt D Barton
HR: –
FYE: December 30
Type: Public

Tractor Supply Company (TSC) is the largest rural lifestyle retailer in the US. Besides providing agricultural machine parts, TSC offers animal products, fencing, tool products, clothing, seasonal products, and pet supplies as well as footwear, and maintenance products for agricultural and rural use. It has nationwide scope, operating about 2,335 stores across the US under the Tractor Supply Company, Orscheln Farm and Home, and Petsense banners. Stores are located primarily in towns outlying major metropolitan markets and in rural communities to cater to recreational farmers, ranchers, and all those who enjoy living the rural lifestyle. TSC also sells online. The first Tractor Supply store opened in 1938 in Minot, North Dakota.

	Annual Growth	12/19	12/20	12/21	12/22	12/23
Sales ($mil.)	14.9%	8,351.9	10,620	12,731	14,205	14,556
Net income ($ mil.)	18.5%	562.4	749.0	997.1	1,088.7	1,107.2
Market value ($ mil.)	23.5%	9,966.2	15,860	24,648	24,291	23,218
Employees	11.8%	32,000	41,000	46,000	49,000	50,000

TRADEWEB MARKETS INC

NMS: TW

1177 Avenue of the Americas
New York, NY 10036
Phone: 646 430-6000
Fax: –
Web: www.tradeweb.com

CEO: –
CFO: Robert Warshaw
HR: Gabrielle D'annunzio
FYE: December 31
Type: Public

Tradeweb Markets is an electronic security trading network, providing clients with solutions across the trade lifecycle including pre-trade data and analytics, intelligent trade execution, straight-through processing and post-trade data, analytics and reporting. Its network is comprised of clients across the institutional, wholesale and retail client sectors, including many of the largest global asset managers, hedge funds, insurance companies, central banks, banks and dealers, proprietary trading firms and retail brokerage and financial advisory firms, as well as regional dealers. The company's electronic marketplace matches more than 65 countries with offices in North America, Europe, and Asia. Established in 1996, Tradeweb handles an average of some 7.9 trillion worth of trading volume per day. Majority of its revenue comes from the US.

	Annual Growth	12/19	12/20	12/21	12/22	12/23
Sales ($mil.)	14.6%	775.6	892.7	1,076.4	1,188.8	1,338.2
Net income ($ mil.)	44.5%	83.8	166.3	226.8	309.3	364.9
Market value ($ mil.)	18.3%	10,897	14,682	23,543	15,265	21,366
Employees	6.4%	919	961	1,046	1,091	1,179

TRADITIONAL MEDICINALS, INC.

4515 ROSS RD
SEBASTOPOL, CA 954722225
Phone: 707 823-8911
Fax: –
Web: www.traditionalmedicinals.com

CEO: –
CFO: –
HR: –
FYE: September 30
Type: Private

Bloated, wired, queasy, or snuffly? Traditional Medicinals has a cup of tea to address whatever your ailment. The company produces organic herbal teas, syrups, and capsules under such names as Nighty Night (calming), Smooth Move (laxative), Throat Coat (sore throat) and Breathe Easy (decongestant). Traditional Medicinals' teas have received approval as over-the-counter medicines in Canada and the US where they are sold at natural food, drug, and grocery retailers. In the UK the company's teas are sold without specific medicinal claims due to that country's regulations. Traditional Medicinals sells its products worldwide and has operations in Canada, the US, the UK, and the Benelux countries.

TRAIL BLAZERS INC.

1 N CENTER COURT ST STE 200
PORTLAND, OR 972272103
Phone: 503 234-9291
Fax: –
Web: www.trailblazers.com

CEO: Paul Allen
CFO: –
HR: Bindhu Newell
FYE: June 30
Type: Private

This enterprise has opened a path for basketball fans in the Beaver State. Trail Blazers, Inc., owns and operates the Portland Trail Blazers professional basketball franchise, which plays host at Portland's Rose Garden Arena. The team boasts three NBA Finals appearances (its last in 1992), winning one championship in 1977. The Blazers joined the National Basketball Association in 1970 as an expansion franchise awarded to Harry Glickman, a local journalist turned sports promoter. Microsoft co-founder Paul Allen, who also owns the Seattle Seahawks, has controlled the team since 1988.

	Annual Growth	06/17	06/18	06/19	06/20	06/21
Sales ($mil.)	(11.5%)	–	–	0.9	0.9	0.7
Net income ($ mil.)	(53.0%)	–	–	0.3	(0.3)	0.0
Market value ($ mil.)	–	–	–	–	–	–
Employees	–	–	–	–	–	200

TRAILER BRIDGE, INC.

10405 NEW BERLIN RD E
JACKSONVILLE, FL 322262291
Phone: 904 751-7100
Fax: –
Web: www.trailerbridge.com

CEO: Mitch Luchiano
CFO: –
HR: Alison Brannon
FYE: December 31
Type: Private

Traversing land and sea, Trailer Bridge connects the continental US, Puerto Rico, and the Dominican Republic. The company's oceangoing barges, designed to carry shipping containers, sail between Jacksonville, Florida, and the two islands. Southbound shipments, which represent about 75% of the freight transported, include raw materials, consumer goods, furniture, and vehicles. Trailer Bridge's land-based assets move freight within the US and abroad. Its fleet comprises some 140 tractors, 500 dry van trailers and car carriers, 3,960 high-cube containers, and 3,150 chassis including two roll-on/roll-off (ro/ro) multiuse barges and two container barges. Trailer Bridge emerged from Chapter 11 proceedings in 2012.

	Annual Growth	12/07	12/08	12/09	12/17	12/18
Sales ($mil.)	2.7%	–	133.0	114.3	–	173.5
Net income ($ mil.)	–	–	(3.2)	2.6	–	16.5
Market value ($ mil.)	–	–	–	–	–	–
Employees	–	–	–	–	–	133

TRAMMO, INC.

8 W 40TH ST FL 12
NEW YORK, NY 100182307
Phone: 212 223-3200
Fax: –
Web: www.trammo.com

CEO: Edward G Weiner
CFO: William E Markstein
HR: Lois Mattaboni
FYE: December 31
Type: Private

Trammo, Inc. is a leading global commodity merchandiser engaged in the marketing, trading, distribution, and transportation of a wide variety of commodity products, including being a market leader in anhydrous ammonia, sulfur, sulfuric acid, nitric acid, and petroleum coke. Trammo was founded by Ronald P. Stanton in 1965 with the intention of specializing in the international trade of ammonia. Trammo remains privately held and manages its operations through its headquarters in New York City and offices worldwide.

	Annual Growth	12/18	12/19	12/20	12/21	12/22
Sales ($mil.)	88.7%	–	–	1,786.2	4,161.3	6,361.6
Net income ($ mil.)	195.8%	–	–	21.2	82.1	185.8
Market value ($ mil.)	–	–	–	–	–	–
Employees	–	–	–	–	–	184

TRANDES CORP.

5200 GLEN ARM RD STE A
GLEN ARM, MD 210579475
Phone: 301 459-0200
Fax: –
Web: www.trandes.com

CEO: –
CFO: Dennis H O'Brien
HR: –
FYE: December 31
Type: Private

Trandes is right there in the trenches with the US government. The contractor provides engineering services for the Department of Defense (primarily the US Navy) and other federal agencies. Its offerings range from the repair of advanced communications equipment and systems engineering to acquisitions support and field services. Trandes also provides IT services including systems design, technical support, and training. The company has about a half-dozen offices strategically located near military locations in Florida, California, and near Washington, DC. CEO James Brusse founded Trandes in 1972 to provide the public transportation sector with software design and support services.

	Annual Growth	12/08	12/09	12/10	12/11	12/12
Sales ($mil.)	(1.7%)	–	–	21.1	25.3	20.3
Net income ($ mil.)	(10.4%)	–	–	0.9	0.9	0.7
Market value ($ mil.)	–	–	–	–	–	–
Employees	–	–	–	–	–	50

TRANS WORLD CORPORATION

545 5TH AVE RM 940
NEW YORK, NY 100173638
Phone: 212 983-3355
Fax: –
Web: www.transwc.com

CEO: Rami S Ramadan
CFO: Hung D Le
HR: –
FYE: December 31
Type: Private

American-style gambling is a global bread winner for Trans World. The company, which focuses on small and midsized casinos and gaming parlors, owns and operates four niche casinos that feature slot machines and gaming tables in the Czech Republic. The casinos operate under the name American Chance Casinos and feature themes from different eras of US history (Chicago in the Roaring 1920s, Miami Beach in the 1950s, New Orleans in the 1920s, and the Pacific South Seas). The company also operates a casino in Croatia near a resort city on the coast of the Adriatic Sea. Trans World is in the process of adding hotels to its operations. An investment group led by director Timothy Ewing owns nearly 40% of the company.

	Annual Growth	12/13	12/14	12/15	12/16	12/17
Sales ($mil.)	12.0%	–	38.5	42.4	53.2	54.1
Net income ($ mil.)	(10.6%)	–	2.6	3.9	6.3	1.9
Market value ($ mil.)	–	–	–	–	–	–
Employees	–	–	–	–	–	629

TRANS-SYSTEM, INC.

7405 S HAYFORD RD
CHENEY, WA 990049633
Phone: 509 623-4001
Fax: –
Web: www.trans-system.com

CEO: James C Williams
CFO: Gary R King
HR: Nicole Hansen
FYE: March 31
Type: Private

Freight hauler Trans-System is the parent company for the three companies: System Transport (flatbed); TW Transport (refrigerated and dry van); and James J. Williams (bulk commodities). The Trans-System trucking companies operate from ten terminals in the western US. Overall, the company's fleet consists of about 1,000 tractors. The company was founded in 1972.

	Annual Growth	03/12	03/13	03/14	03/15	03/16
Sales ($mil.)	6.2%	–	197.7	210.0	228.1	236.9
Net income ($ mil.)	(14.7%)	–	8.1	6.6	15.0	5.0
Market value ($ mil.)	–	–	–	–	–	–
Employees	–	–	–	–	–	650

TRANSACT TECHNOLOGIES INC.

NMS: TACT

One Hamden Center, 2319 Whitney Avenue, Suite 3B
Hamden, CT 06518
Phone: 203 859-6800
Fax: –
Web: www.transact-tech.com

CEO: –
CFO: –
HR: –
FYE: December 31
Type: Public

TransAct Technologies knows how to ink the deal. The company makes thermal, inkjet, and impact printers under the Epic, EPICENTRAL, and other brands, that record transaction information for point-of-sale (POS), casino and gaming, lottery, banking, food safety, and e-commerce transactions. TransAct's printers and terminals produce receipts, coupons, lottery tickets, and other printed records. TransAct also makes document transport mechanisms for ATMs and kiosks and manufactures custom printers for electronics manufacturers and oil and gas exploration companies. TransAct sells its products to OEMs, VARs, and other distributors, as well as directly to end-users. About 75% of sales comes from customers in the US.

	Annual Growth	12/19	12/20	12/21	12/22	12/23
Sales ($mil.)	12.3%	45.7	30.6	39.4	58.1	72.6
Net income ($ mil.)	74.2%	0.5	(5.6)	(4.1)	(5.9)	4.7
Market value ($ mil.)	(10.7%)	109.2	70.7	108.6	62.9	69.5
Employees	(3.3%)	134	112	118	128	117

TRANSATLANTIC PETROLEUM LTD.

16803 DALLAS PKWY
ADDISON, TX 750015212
Phone: 214 220-4323
Fax: –
Web: www.transatlanticpetroleum.com

CEO: –
CFO: –
HR: –
FYE: December 31
Type: Private

TransAtlantic Petroleum crossed the Atlantic in its search for profitable oil and gas assets. The crude oil and natural gas exploration, development, and production company, which was formed in 1985, has operations in Bulgaria, Romania, and Turkey. It has producing rigs at Turkey's Selmo oil field and Thrace Basin (natural gas) through its Viking International subsidiary as well as more than 7 million undeveloped acres in Turkey. Its exploration operations include acreage in Romania (shale gas) and Bulgaria (natural gas). In 2012 the company sold its drilling services business to a company owned by TransAtlantic Petroleum's CEO for $167 million.

TRANSCAT INC   NMS: TRNS

35 Vantage Point Drive
Rochester, NY 14624
Phone: 585 352-7777
Fax: 800 395-0543
Web: www.transcat.com

CEO: Lee D Rudow
CFO: Thomas L Barbato
HR: Angela Spaulding
FYE: March 25
Type: Public

Transcat is a leading provider of accredited calibration services, enterprise asset management services, and value-added distributors of professional-grade handheld test, measurement, and control instrumentation. The company is focused on providing services and products to highly regulated industries, particularly the life science industry, which includes pharmaceutical, biotechnology, medical device, and other FDA-regulated businesses. Additional industries served include FAA-regulated businesses, including aerospace and defense industrial manufacturing; energy and utilities, including oil and gas and alternative energy; and other industries that require accuracy in their processes, confirmation of the capabilities of their equipment, and for which the risk of failure is very costly. Majority of its sales were generated in the US. It was founded in 1964.

	Annual Growth	03/19	03/20	03/21	03/22	03/23
Sales ($mil.)	9.4%	160.9	173.1	173.3	205.0	230.6
Net income ($ mil.)	10.6%	7.1	8.1	7.8	11.4	10.7
Market value ($ mil.)	39.4%	173.8	191.8	402.1	561.2	656.4
Employees	10.7%	685	772	765	918	1,030

TRANSCHEMICAL INCORPORATED

419 E DE SOTO AVE
SAINT LOUIS, MO 631473113
Phone: 314 231-6905
Fax: –
Web: www.transchemical.com

CEO: –
CFO: Gary Collins
HR: –
FYE: December 31
Type: Private

With a strong belief that good chemical products translates into good profits, Transchemical distributes chemicals including alcohols, esters, ketones, solvents, and surfactants. The distributor also provides solvent reclamation and blending services. Transchemical supplies customers in the biofuels, cosmetics and personal care, food and beverage, paints and coatings, and plastic and rubber industries. The company, based in Missouri, operates throughout the Midwest. TransChemical was founded as an independent distributor of chemicals and solvents in 1974. Some of the brand names the company uses to distribute are: Caltran, Drakeol, Hydrocal Naphthenic Base Oils, Sundex, and Sunpar.

	Annual Growth	12/04	12/05	12/06	12/07	12/08
Sales ($mil.)	4.0%	–	40.3	41.1	42.0	45.4
Net income ($ mil.)	10.5%	–	0.3	0.5	0.9	0.5
Market value ($ mil.)	–	–	–	–	–	–
Employees		–	–	–	–	31

TRANSCONTINENTAL GAS PIPE LINE COMPANY, LLC

2800 POST OAK BLVD
HOUSTON, TX 770566100
Phone: 713 215-2000
Fax: –
Web: www.gardencenter-durham.com

CEO: –
CFO: –
HR: –
FYE: December 31
Type: Private

As coast to coast as it name implies, Transcontinental Gas Pipe Line Corporation (commonly known as Transco) is an interstate natural gas transmission company. Transco operates about 9,800 miles of natural gas pipeline extending from the Gulf of Mexico to New York. The company also operates 45 gas compressor stations, four underground storage fields, and a liquefied natural gas (LNG) storage facility. In 2011 Transco had access to 200 billion cu. ft. of natural gas. Its customers include natural gas distributors such as Public Service Enterprise Group, National Grid USA, and Piedmont Natural Gas Company. Transco is a subsidiary of Williams Partners, itself a subsidiary of The Williams Companies.

TRANSCONTINENTAL REALTY INVESTORS, INC.   NYS: TCI

1603 Lyndon B.Johnson Freeway, Suite 800
Dallas, TX 75234
Phone: 469 522-4200
Fax: –
Web: www.transconrealty-invest.com

CEO: Bradley J Muth
CFO: Erik L Johnson
HR: –
FYE: December 31
Type: Public

Transcontinental Realty likes to find diamonds in the rough. The company acquires, develops, and owns income-producing commercial and residential real estate, particularly properties that it believes are undervalued. Its portfolio consists nearly 40 apartment complexes with more than 6,000 units in the southern US, in addition to about 7.7 million sq.ft. of rentable commercial space, including nearly 8 commercial properties. Texas is its largest market by far. Additionally, the company has investments in apartment projects under development and more than 4,000 acres of undeveloped and partially developed land, most of it also in Texas.

	Annual Growth	12/19	12/20	12/21	12/22	12/23
Sales ($mil.)	1.0%	48.0	57.0	40.8	36.7	49.9
Net income ($ mil.)	–	(26.9)	6.7	9.4	468.3	5.9
Market value ($ mil.)	(3.5%)	344.5	208.3	337.8	381.7	298.6
Employees		–	–	–	–	–

TRANSDEV NORTH AMERICA, INC.

720 E BUTTERFIELD RD STE 300
LOMBARD, IL 60148
Phone: 630 571-7070
Fax: –
Web: www.transdevna.com

CEO: Yann Leriche
CFO: Jacques Laherre
HR: Shulonda Chaffee
FYE: December 31
Type: Private

Veolia Transportation helps commuters make the connection between home and work. The private operator offers public bus transportation in about a dozen states in the US and a handful of cities in Canada. In addition to fixed-route bus networks, it provides shuttle buses for companies and universities, and paratransit services (on-call rides for people with disabilities) in several states. Its SuperShuttle van unit transports travelers on demand to and from airports in 30 US cities. Veolia also contracts to operate commuter rail systems in Boston, Los Angeles, Miami, and San Diego. The company is a unit of Veolia Transport, a provider of bus and train services in Europe, and a subsidiary of Veolia Environnement.

TRANSDIGM GROUP INC

NYS: TDG

1301 East 9th Street, Suite 3000
Cleveland, OH 44114
Phone: 216 706-2960
Fax: –
Web: www.transdigm.com

CEO: Kevin Stein
CFO: Sarah Wynne
HR: –
FYE: September 30
Type: Public

TransDigm Group is a leading global designer, producer and supplier of highly engineered aircraft components, including audio systems, pumps and valves, and power conditioning devices, among others. Operating through a plethora of subsidiaries, TransDigm makes and distributes systems and components for commercial and military aircraft. Its products are found in several Boeing (formerly Aviall) and Satair A/S (a subsidiary of Airbus) airplanes. About two-thirds of the company's total revenue comes from US.

	Annual Growth	09/19	09/20	09/21	09/22	09/23
Sales ($mil.)	6.0%	5,223.2	5,103.0	4,798.0	5,429.0	6,585.0
Net income ($ mil.)	9.9%	889.8	699.0	680.0	866.0	1,298.0
Market value ($ mil.)	12.8%	28,797	26,277	34,543	29,026	46,631
Employees	(4.1%)	18,300	14,200	13,300	14,600	15,500

TRANSITCENTER, INC.

1 WHITEHALL ST 17TH FL
NEW YORK, NY 100042147
Phone: 646 395-9555
Fax: –
Web: www.transitcenter.org

CEO: –
CFO: –
HR: –
FYE: December 31
Type: Private

TransitCenter's mission is to get commuters out of their cars and onto a bus, ferry, train, van, or cable car. The not-for-profit company is charged with encouraging greater use of public and private transit services to improve mobility, reduce traffic, help the environment, and support the economy. Its website provides transit guides for a dozen US cities, including Atlanta and Washington, D.C. TransitCenter sold its TransitChek program, developed to encourage businesses and their employees to use public transportation through incentives that reduce payroll taxes for employers and allow commuters to pay for daily travel using pretax dollars. It continues to advocate for public transportation.

	Annual Growth	12/08	12/09	12/13	12/14	12/22
Sales ($mil.)	(19.3%)	–	22.1	1.6	3.5	1.4
Net income ($ mil.)	–	–	2.7	0.5	1.4	(4.4)
Market value ($ mil.)	–	–	–	–	–	–
Employees	–	–	–	–	–	74

TRANSMONTAIGNE PARTNERS LLC

1670 BROADWAY STE 3100
DENVER, CO 802024815
Phone: 303 626-8200
Fax: –
Web: www.transmontaignepartners.com

CEO: Randal Maffett
CFO: Robert T Fuller
HR: –
FYE: December 31
Type: Private

TransMontaigne Partners, an affiliate of TransMontaigne Inc., provides integrated terminaling, storage, and pipeline services for companies that market and distribute refined products and crude oil. TransMontaigne Partners handles light refined products (gasolines, heating oils, and jet and diesel fuels), heavy refined products (asphalt and residual fuel oils), and crude oil. It operates about 50 terminals (with a storage of capacity of 23.7 million barrels of oil and gas) and other facilities along the Gulf Coast and major rivers in the South and Midwest; it also operates pipelines. Customers include Marathon and a marketing and supply unit of Valero.

	Annual Growth	12/18	12/19	12/20	12/21	12/22
Sales ($mil.)	36.3%	–	263.0	277.1	520.7	666.4
Net income ($ mil.)	(3.0%)	–	45.9	61.3	38.3	41.9
Market value ($ mil.)	–	–	–	–	–	–
Employees	–	–	–	–	–	57

TRANSNET CORPORATION

45 COLUMBIA RD STE A
BRANCHBURG, NJ 088763576
Phone: 646 221-6725
Fax: –
Web: www.transnet.com

CEO: John J Wilk
CFO: John J Wilk
HR: –
FYE: June 30
Type: Private

TransNet sells and supports computers, networking equipment, peripherals, and software. It provides PCs from Hewlett-Packard, IBM, and Apple. TransNet also supplies peripherals, networking products, software, and telephony equipment from such manufacturers as Nortel Networks, Microsoft, 3Com, Novell, and Cisco. The company's services include network support, maintenance, systems integration, installation, and training. Its clients are located primarily in the New York City/New Jersey and Eastern Pennsylvania regions. TransNet's customers have included pharmaceutical giant Schering-Plough.

TRANSPERFECT TRANSLATIONS INTERNATIONAL INC.

1250 BDWY FL 7
NEW YORK, NY 100013749
Phone: 212 689-5555
Fax: –
Web: www.transperfect.com

CEO: Philip R Shawe
CFO: –
HR: Bella Meziani
FYE: December 31
Type: Private

TransPerfect Translations International is the world's largest language services provider that offers document translation, multicultural marketing, multilingual staffing, and interpretation. Its network of more than 10,000 certified linguists and subject-area specialists handle more than 170 languages through offices located in over 100 cities spanning six continents. Works with many of the world's most recognizable enterprises, its global group of companies completes over 300,000 projects annually. With more than 10,000 clients, TransPerfect serves a wide array of industries, including advertising, energy and mining, financial services, legal, life science, technology, digital marketing and advertising, and travel. TransPerfect was founded in 1992 by Liz Elting and Phil Shawe.

	Annual Growth	12/03	12/04	12/05	12/06	12/07
Sales ($mil.)	45.7%	–	–	73.7	79.6	156.5
Net income ($ mil.)	58.5%	–	–	11.5	11.8	29.0
Market value ($ mil.)	–	–	–	–	–	–
Employees	–	–	–	–	–	3,612

TRANSPORTATION INSIGHT, LLC

310 MAIN AVENUE WAY SE
HICKORY, NC 286023513
Phone: 828 485-5000
Fax: –
Web: www.transportationinsight.com

CEO: Ken Beyer
CFO: Mark Vale
HR: Christina Sherrill
FYE: December 31
Type: Private

Transportation Insight is the combination of industry-leading logistics providers, Transportation Insight (TI) and Nolan Transportation Group (NTG). TI brings over two decades of multimodal expertise and technology to the logistics industry and ranks amongst North America's top logistics companies. It services more than 14,000 shippers and over 80,000 carriers through its proprietary Beon Digital Logistics Platform, a single point of access to TI's mode-agnostic network and services from port to porch. It also offers best-in-class technology solutions including Insight TMS and Insight Fusion.

TRANSTECH INDUSTRIES, INC.   NBB: TRTI

200 Centennial Avenue, Suite 202   CEO: -
Piscataway, NJ 08854   CFO: -
Phone: 732 564-3122   HR: Donna Woodward
Fax: 732 981-1856   FYE: December 31
Web: www.transtechindustries.com   Type: Public

Through its subsidiaries, Transtech Industries supervises and performs landfill monitoring, closure and post-closure procedures, and it oversees methane gas recovery operations. The company also generates electricity from methane gas produced at a company-owned landfill site; this business accounts for all of Transtech's revenue from external customers. Transtech's environmental services unit is engaged in closure and remediation of landfill sites formerly operated by other Transtech units. Transtech previously has provided environmental services for third parties, and the company hopes to do so again. Members of the family of former company executive Marvin Mahan are the largest shareholders of Transtech.

	Annual Growth	12/05	12/06	12/07	12/08	12/09
Sales ($mil.)	(2.2%)	0.5	0.4	0.5	0.7	0.4
Net income ($ mil.)	-	2.0	0.6	(0.8)	(0.9)	(0.7)
Market value ($ mil.)	(45.9%)	1.0	0.7	0.6	0.3	0.0
Employees	-	11	13	12	11	11

TRANSUNION   NYS: TRU

555 West Adams   CEO: Pamela A Joseph
Chicago, IL 60661   CFO: Todd M Cello
Phone: 312 985-2000   HR: -
Fax: -   FYE: December 31
Web: www.transunion.com   Type: Public

TransUnion provides consumer reports, actionable insights and analytics such as credit and other scores, and technology solutions to businesses. Businesses embed its solutions into their process workflows to acquire new customers, assess consumer ability to pay for services, identify cross-selling opportunities, measure and manage debt portfolio risk, collect a debt, verify consumer identities and investigate potential fraud. TransUnion has a deep domain expertise across a number of attractive industries, which it also refers to as verticals, including financial services, insurance, and other markets it serves. TransUnion has a global presence in over 30 countries and territories across North America, Latin America, Europe, Africa, India, and Asia Pacific. Substantially all of the company's revenue comes from the US.

	Annual Growth	12/19	12/20	12/21	12/22	12/23
Sales ($mil.)	9.6%	2,656.1	2,716.6	2,960.2	3,709.9	3,831.2
Net income ($ mil.)	-	346.9	343.2	1,387.1	269.5	(206.2)
Market value ($ mil.)	(5.3%)	16,591	19,229	22,981	10,998	13,316
Employees	13.3%	8,000	8,200	10,200	12,200	13,200

TRAVEL + LEISURE CO   NYS: TNL

6277 Sea Harbor Drive   CEO: Michael D Brown
Orlando, FL 32821   CFO: Michael A Hug
Phone: 407 626-5200   HR: Barbara Thomas
Fax: -   FYE: December 31
Web: www.travelandleisureco.com   Type: Public

Travel + Leisure Co. is the world's leading membership and leisure travel company. The company provides vacation experiences and travel inspiration to millions of owners, members, and subscribers through its products and services. With nearly 20 travel brands across its resort, travel club, and lifestyle portfolio, the company provides outstanding vacation experiences and travel inspiration to millions of owners, members, and subscribers every year through its products and services: Wyndham Destinations, the largest vacation ownership company with more than 245 vacation club resort locations across the globe; Panorama, the world's foremost membership travel business that includes the largest vacation exchange company and subscription travel brands; and Travel + Leisure Group, featuring top travel content and travel services including the brand's eponymous travel club. Travel + Leisure gets almost 90% of its revenue from the US.

	Annual Growth	12/19	12/20	12/21	12/22	12/23
Sales ($mil.)	(1.9%)	4,043.0	2,160.0	3,134.0	3,567.0	3,750.0
Net income ($ mil.)	(6.0%)	507.0	(255.0)	308.0	357.0	396.0
Market value ($ mil.)	(6.7%)	3,692.3	3,204.4	3,948.0	2,600.1	2,792.2
Employees	(4.1%)	22,500	15,500	16,800	18,200	19,000

TRAVEL STORE

11601 WILSHIRE BLVD STE 300   CEO: Wido Schaefer
LOS ANGELES, CA 900250509   CFO: Osvaldo Ramos
Phone: 310 575-5540   HR: Mel Bautistasabino
Fax: -   FYE: December 31
Web: www.travelstore.com   Type: Private

Travel Store wants you to pack your bags. The company operates a chain of full-service travel agencies in California under the Travel Store name. Travel Store offers travelers vacations, cruises, and other travel arrangements, as well as package deals, an online reservation system (travelstore.com), and a deferred payment option. Operating since 1975, the company also provides corporate travel services, including a 24-hour, worldwide, toll-free service and group travel options. President and CEO Wido Schaefer, a former Lufthansa executive, founded the company, which became employee-owned in 2005.

	Annual Growth	12/06	12/07	12/08	12/09	12/10
Sales ($mil.)	(5.7%)	-	-	20.4	14.9	18.2
Net income ($ mil.)	(27.5%)	-	-	3.7	0.6	2.0
Market value ($ mil.)	-	-	-	-	-	-
Employees	-	-	-	-	-	290

TRAVELERS COMPANIES INC (THE)   NYS: TRV

485 Lexington Avenue   CEO: Alan D Schnitzer
New York, NY 10017   CFO: Daniel S Frey
Phone: 917 778-6000   HR: -
Fax: -   FYE: December 31
Web: www.travelers.com   Type: Public

Through its subsidiaries, the Travelers Companies (Travelers) is a holding company engaged in providing various commercial and personal property and casualty insurance products and services to businesses, government units, associations, and individuals. Travelers is one of the largest commercial insurance carrier in the US, providing commercial auto, property, workers' compensation, and general liability coverage to companies. Personal insurance offerings include auto and homeowners policies. The company also offers surety and fidelity bonds as well as professional and management liability coverage. The US accounts for a majority of sales, though the company has international operations. Travelers is one of the oldest insurance organizations in the US, dating back to 1853.

	Annual Growth	12/19	12/20	12/21	12/22	12/23
Assets ($mil.)	3.4%	110,122	116,764	120,466	115,717	125,978
Net income ($ mil.)	3.3%	2,622.0	2,697.0	3,662.0	2,842.0	2,991.0
Market value ($ mil.)	8.6%	31,252	32,032	35,697	42,785	43,470
Employees	2.0%	30,800	30,600	30,800	32,500	33,300

TRAVELZOO   NMS: TZOO

590 Madison Avenue, 35th Floor   CEO: Holger Bartel
New York, NY 10022   CFO: -
Phone: 212 516-1300   HR: Lynne Bosnack
Fax: -   FYE: December 31
Web: www.travelzoo.com   Type: Public

Travelzoo provides its approximately 30 million members insider deals and one-of-a-kind experiences personally reviewed by one of the company's deal experts worldwide. More than 5,000 travel companies use Travelzoo's services. Airlines, cruise lines, hotels, vacation packagers, entertainment, local businesses, and travel agencies pay Travelzoo for a fast, flexible, and cost-effective way to reach millions of internet users, through its newsletters, and across its e-mail alert service. The company also connects with its customers through social media platforms. Ralph Bartel founded Travelzoo in 1998.

	Annual Growth	12/19	12/20	12/21	12/22	12/23
Sales ($mil.)	(6.7%)	111.4	53.6	62.7	70.6	84.5
Net income ($ mil.)	31.3%	4.2	(13.4)	0.9	6.6	12.4
Market value ($ mil.)	(2.9%)	145.3	128.1	127.9	60.4	129.4
Employees	(14.5%)	418	236	214	237	223

TRAYLOR BROS., INC.

835 N CONGRESS AVE
EVANSVILLE, IN 477152484
Phone: 812 477-1542
Fax: –
Web: www.traylor.com

CEO: Christopher S Traylor
CFO: –
HR: Kathy Gray
FYE: December 31
Type: Private

Traylor Bros Inc. (TBI) is a family-owned heavy/civil construction company mostly builds suspension and segmental bridges, dams and ports, sewers, and transit terminals. Its Underground division works on tunneling projects, while it's Traylor Mining, LLC subsidiary works on mine development and management. It also offers mechanical excavation in hard rock and soft ground, including sequential mining. TBI projects include Howard Frankland Bridge, Airport Guideway and Stations Design-Build Contract, and Stan Musial Veterans Memorial Bridge. Civil engineer William Traylor founded TBI in Indiana in 1946.

TRC COMPANIES, INC.

21 GRIFFIN RD N
WINDSOR, CT 060951590
Phone: 860 298-9692
Fax: –
Web: www.trccompanies.com

CEO: Christopher Vincze
CFO: Thomas Bennet
HR: Rosana Flores
FYE: June 30
Type: Private

TRC Companies is a leading global consulting, engineering and construction company that provides environmentally focused and digitally powered solutions. The company provides engineering, construction, and remediation services for power and utilities, industrial, transportation, real estate, water and government. Services include operation and consulting, filed services and inspection, engineering, and procurement and construction, among others. The company was incorporated in Connecticut in 1969, and a subsidiary of New Mountain Capital.

	Annual Growth	06/18	06/19	06/20	06/21	06/22
Sales ($mil.)	(17.7%)	–	–	711.8	738.9	482.4
Net income ($ mil.)		–	–	(58.7)	(16.2)	2.0
Market value ($ mil.)		–	–	–	–	–
Employees		–	–	–	–	4,865

TREATY ENERGY CORP.

317 Exchange Place
New Orleans, LA 70130
Phone: 504 301-4475
Fax: –
Web: www.treatyenergy.com

CEO: David W Shutte
CFO: –
HR: –
FYE: December 31
Type: Public

Treaty Energy (formerly Alternate Energy) sought to provide alternative methods of fuel and power production, but the power of petroleum won out. The company had been involved in hydrogen production and fuel cell development. In 2008 it completed a reverse merger with Treaty Petroleum and changed its focus to oil and gas development. The company focuses on the Permian Basin of West Texas, and has more than 2 million barrels of proved reserves. In 2010 it was eyeing exploration prospects in Belize. It also bought Town Oil Company in 2011 to give it about 7,800 acres of oil and gas leases in Kansas. In 2011 the company also acquired C&C Petroleum Management, with oil and gas properties in Texas.

	Annual Growth	12/08	12/09	12/10	12/11	12/12
Sales ($mil.)	50.4%	0.0	0.0	0.0	0.1	0.2
Net income ($ mil.)		(0.2)	(1.2)	(0.8)	(7.1)	(12.2)
Market value ($ mil.)	25.3%	7.1	14.7	9.5	38.8	17.5
Employees		–	–	–	–	–

TRECORA LLC

1650 HIGHWAY 6 STE 190
SUGAR LAND, TX 774784926
Phone: 281 980-5522
Fax: –
Web: www.trecora.com

CEO: Patrick D Quarles
CFO: Connie Cook
HR: –
FYE: December 31
Type: Private

Trecora Resources manufactures various specialty petrochemicals products and specialty waxes and provides custom processing services. Through South Hampton Resources (SHR), Trecora produces high purity hydrocarbons and other petroleum based products including isopentane, normal pentane, isohexane and hexane. Its Trecora Chemical produces specialty polyethylene and poly alpha olefin waxes and provides custom processing services. Trecora owns approximately 100 storage tanks with total capacity approaching 294,000 barrels, and 127 acres of land at the plant site, 107 acres of which are developed. It also owns a truck and railroad loading terminal consisting of storage tanks, nine rail spurs, and truck and tank car loading facilities Trecora traces its roots back to 1967 as Arabian Shield Development Company.

	Annual Growth	12/16	12/17	12/18	12/19	12/20
Sales ($mil.)	(14.9%)	–	–	287.9	259.0	208.6
Net income ($ mil.)		–	–	(2.3)	(12.9)	31.2
Market value ($ mil.)		–	–	–	–	–
Employees		–	–	–	–	270

TREDEGAR CORP.

NYS: TG

1100 Boulders Parkway
Richmond, VA 23225
Phone: 804 330-1000
Fax: –
Web: www.tredegar.com

CEO: John M Steitz
CFO: D A Edwards
HR: Melinda Higgs
FYE: December 31
Type: Public

Tredegar Corporation is engaged, through its subsidiaries, in the manufacture of aluminum extrusions, polyethylene (PE) plastic films, and polyester (PET) films. Aluminum Extrusions, also referred to as Bonnell Aluminum, are used mainly in building and construction, automotive and transportation, consumer durables goods, machinery and equipment, electrical and renewable energy, and distribution markets. Its primary raw materials of aluminum ingot, aluminum scrap, and various alloys, which are purchased from domestic and foreign producers in open-market purchases and under annual contracts. It also manufactures surface protection films for high-technology applications in the global electronics industry through its PE Films segment; and specialized polyester films primarily for the Latin American flexible packaging market through its Flexible Packaging Films segment. More than 75% of company's sales is generated from the US.

	Annual Growth	12/19	12/20	12/21	12/22	12/23
Sales ($mil.)	(8.6%)	1,007.2	688.0	846.8	939.5	702.7
Net income ($ mil.)		48.3	(75.4)	57.8	28.5	(105.9)
Market value ($ mil.)	(29.9%)	769.0	574.6	406.7	351.7	186.2
Employees	(10.8%)	3,000	2,400	2,400	2,300	1,900

TREE TOP, INC.

220 E 2ND AVE
SELAH, WA 989421408
Phone: 509 697-7251
Fax: –
Web: www.treetop.com

CEO: Tom Hurson
CFO: –
HR: Erika Belmontes
FYE: July 31
Type: Private

Tree Top is one of the leading processors of dried, frozen, pureed, and concentrated fruits, providing food ingredient to more than 20 of the world's top 25 companies. The company produces the Tree Top brand of apple and blended fruit juices and apple sauce, among many offerings, for consumers and food service vendors. It also processes dehydrated and frozen fruit products for food makers worldwide through its ingredients unit. Tree Top's wholly-owned subsidiary, Northwest Naturals, is a leader in the production of specialty blended, all natural, fruit juice concentrates, WONF juice blends, and turnkey liquid fruit solutions. The Tree Top cooperative was formed in 1960.

	Annual Growth	07/06	07/07	07/08	07/09	07/10
Sales ($mil.)	2.0%	–	–	350.7	359.0	365.0
Net income ($ mil.)	27535.3%	–	–	0.0	37.2	27.0
Market value ($ mil.)		–	–	–	–	–
Employees		–	–	–	–	1,100

TREECON RESOURCES INC

6004 South U.S. Highway 59
Lufkin, TX 75901
Phone: 936 634-3365
Fax: –
Web: –

NBB: TCOR
CEO: James Rudis
CFO: John W Langford
HR: –
FYE: September 30
Type: Public

TreeCon is trying to turn over a new leaf. Previously known as Overhill Corporation (and Polyphase before that), the company was created when Overhill spun off its Overhill Farms frozen food subsidiary in October 2002. TreeCon's Texas Timberjack subsidiary makes logging machines that cut timber (shears), stack logs onto trucks (loaders), and transport logs out of the forest and onto loaders (skidders). The company primarily serves East Texas and western Louisiana. It is also involved in sawmill operations and the sale of lumber products. In addition, its Texas Timberjack subsidiary also leases and finances industrial farming equipment. Aptly named Polyphase has been through many phases, from FORTUNE magazine's fastest-growing company one year to a heavy loss and a period of halted trading the next. The Addison, Texas-based company operates through three subsidiaries: Food processing group Overhill Farms (about 65% of sales) produces frozen entrees and other foods for the airline, food service, health care, and retail industries; its forestry group, Texas Timberjack, distributes, leases, and finances timber and logging equipment; and Polyphase Instrument, its transformer segment, makes power and communications transformers. Harold Estes, president of Texas Timberjack, owns about 25% of Polyphase.

	Annual Growth	09/99	09/00	09/01	09/02	09/03
Sales ($mil.)	(28.5%)	158.3	189.1	43.3	38.7	41.3
Net income ($ mil.)	–	(1.6)	3.8	(1.1)	(5.0)	(2.9)
Market value ($ mil.)	(71.5%)	141.9	141.9	141.9	141.9	0.9
Employees	(36.9%)	912	1,200	1,201	137	145

TREEHOUSE FOODS INC

2021 Spring Road, Suite 600
Oak Brook, IL 60523
Phone: 708 483-1300
Fax: –
Web: www.treehousefoods.com

NYS: THS
CEO: Steven Oakland
CFO: Patrick O'Donnell
HR: Anne Holland
FYE: December 31
Type: Public

TreeHouse Foods is a leading manufacturer and distributor of private label and branded packaged foods and beverages in North America. The company makes shelf stable, refrigerated, frozen and fresh products, including snacking offerings (crackers, pretzels, in-store bakery items, frozen griddle items, cookies, snack bars, and unique candy offerings), beverage and drink mix offerings (non-dairy creamer, single serve beverages, broths/stocks, powdered beverages, and other blends, tea, and ready-to-drink-beverages), and grocery offerings (pickles, refrigerated dough, hot cereal, and cheese and pudding). TreeHouse makes private-label products for foodservice distributors and restaurant chains, as well as for supermarkets and mass merchandisers. The company also works with co-pack business and industrial customers. The US generates most of the company's sales. In late 2022, the company completed the sale of a significant portion of its Meal Preparation business to Investindustrial for approximately $950 million.

	Annual Growth	12/19	12/20	12/21	12/22	12/23
Sales ($mil.)	(5.4%)	4,288.9	4,349.7	4,327.6	3,454.0	3,431.6
Net income ($ mil.)	–	(361.0)	13.8	(12.5)	(146.3)	53.1
Market value ($ mil.)	(3.9%)	2,623.9	2,298.7	2,192.7	2,671.5	2,242.4
Employees	(9.0%)	10,800	10,900	10,000	7,500	7,400

TRELLIS EARTH PRODUCTS, INC.

11010 NE EVERETT ST
PORTLAND, OR 972203221
Phone: 503 582-1300
Fax: –
Web: www.trellisbioplastics.com

CEO: Michael Senzaki
CFO: –
HR: –
FYE: December 31
Type: Private

Sure, you can recycle that disposable plastic cup, but you'll earn double points with Mother Nature if it's made from bioplastic. Trellis Earth Products' disposable cups, bowls, plates, trays, cutlery, and bags are made from bioplastic, a material derived from renewable sources such as soybeans, corn starch, wheat chaff, rice hulls, or sugarcane. Bioplastic is less expensive and more sustainable than petroleum-based plastic. Its products are sold to more than 500 foodservice customers, primarily on the West Coast, including Bunzl Distribution USA, Costco, Food Services of America, Kroger, Sysco, and West Coast Paper. Trellis Earth Products filed a $22 million initial public offering in September 2011.

TREVENA INC

955 Chesterbrook Boulevard, Suite 110
Chesterbrook, PA 19087
Phone: 610 354-8840
Fax: –
Web: www.trevena.com

NAS: TRVN
CEO: Carrie L Bourdow
CFO: Barry Shin
HR: –
FYE: December 31
Type: Public

Trevena hopes to make tremendous strides in medicine. The biopharmaceutical firm focused on the development and commercialization of novel medicines for patients affected by central nervous system (CNS) disorders. Its product includes Oliceridine injection, a G-protein biased mu-opioid receptor, or MOR, ligand, for the management of moderate-to-severe acute pain in hospitals or other controlled clinical settings where intravenous, or IV, administration of opioids is warranted. Its product candidate also includes TRV250 for the treatment of acute migraine. TRV250 also may have utility in a range of other CNS indications. Trevena was founded in 2007.

	Annual Growth	12/18	12/19	12/20	12/21	12/22
Sales ($mil.)	–	5.7	0.0	3.1	0.6	(0.4)
Net income ($ mil.)	–	(30.8)	(24.9)	(29.4)	(51.6)	(53.7)
Market value ($ mil.)	35.0%	3.3	6.5	16.6	4.5	11.1
Employees	4.8%	29	24	25	43	35

TREX CO INC

2500 Trex Way
Winchester, VA 22601
Phone: 540 542-6300
Fax: –
Web: www.trex.com

NYS: TREX
CEO: –
CFO: –
HR: –
FYE: December 31
Type: Public

Trex Company is one of the world's largest makers of wood-alternative decking and railing products, which are used in the construction of residential and commercial decks and rails. Marketed under the Trex name, products resemble wood and have the workability of wood, but require less long-term maintenance. The Trex Residential composite is made of waste wood fibers and reclaimed plastic. Trex serves professional installation contractors and do-it-yourselfers through the company's more than 50 distributors and two national merchandisers, which in turn sell to retailers including Home Depot and Lowe's. Trex products are available in more than 40 countries worldwide.

	Annual Growth	12/19	12/20	12/21	12/22	12/23
Sales ($mil.)	10.1%	745.3	880.8	1,197.0	1,106.0	1,094.8
Net income ($ mil.)	9.1%	144.7	175.6	208.7	184.6	205.4
Market value ($ mil.)	(2.0%)	9,762.0	9,093.0	14,666	4,597.5	8,991.9
Employees	10.8%	1,173	1,719	2,074	1,636	1,765

TRG PRODUCTS, INC.

2859 104TH ST
DES MOINES, IA 503223814
Phone: 515 252-7522
Fax: –
Web: www.handera.com

CEO: –
CFO: –
HR: –
FYE: July 31
Type: Private

HandEra provides contract engineering and design services to companies that make electronics for the consumer, medical, automotive, and industrial markets. It develops electronics hardware and technology for devices running Windows, Linux, and Android operating systems. The company got its start in mobile device by making handheld devices running the the Palm operating system. It offers turnkey design and manufacturing services. HandEra also developed embedded software products ranging from WiFi modules to AC power supplies. The company operates its design and manufacturing facility in Des Moines, Iowa. Customers have included Samsung, Epson, AT&T, Honeywell, and IBM. The company was established in 1992 and is owned by its officers and outside investors.

TRI HARBOR HOLDINGS CORPORATION

4 TRI HARBOR CT
PORT WASHINGTON, NY 110504661
Phone: 516 627-6000
Fax: -
Web: www.actylis.com

CEO: William Kennally
CFO: Rebecca Roof
HR: Samuel Stoddard
FYE: June 30
Type: Private

Aceto sources and distributes more than 1,100 chemical compounds used as ingredients or finished products by customers in the pharmaceutical, nutraceutical, agricultural, coatings, and industrial chemical industries. It generates more than half its sales from finished dosages of generic drugs and nutraceutical products sold to wholesalers, drug stores, distributors, and mass merchandisers. The company also provides active pharmaceutical ingredients and pharmaceutical intermediates to drugmakers; specialty chemicals for use in plastics, coatings, textiles, and lubricants; and crop protection products such as herbicides and insecticides. Aceto sources about 65% of its products from Asia and generates most of its sales in the US.

TRI-CITY ELECTRICAL CONTRACTORS, INC.

430 WEST DR
ALTAMONTE SPRINGS, FL 327143378
Phone: 407 788-3500
Fax: -
Web: www.tcelectric.com

CEO: -
CFO: Michael A Germana
HR: Marissa Williams
FYE: December 31
Type: Private

Plugged in to the electrical contracting scene, Tri-City Electrical Contractors targets Florida's commercial, government, industrial, residential, and communications markets. The company designs, installs and services electrical systems in apartment buildings, courthouses, convention centers, sports arenas, resorts, condos, single- and multi-family dwellings, and more. Once part of now-bankrupt Encompass Services, Tri-City Electrical Contractors was repurchased by founder and chairman Buddy Eidel in 2003. Tri-City Electrical Contractors, which traces its roots to 1958, operates from its Central Florida headquarters and two divisional offices throughout the Sunshine State.

	Annual Growth	12/11	12/12	12/13	12/17	12/18
Sales ($mil.)	21.2%	-	87.6	126.8	-	277.9
Net income ($ mil.)	-	-	(1.2)	2.7	-	23.5
Market value ($ mil.)	-	-	-	-	-	-
Employees	-	-	-	-	-	947

TRI-CITY HOSPITAL DISTRICT (INC)

4002 VISTA WAY
OCEANSIDE, CA 920564506
Phone: 760 724-8411
Fax: -
Web: www.tricitymed.org

CEO: Steve Dietlin
CFO: Ray Rivas
HR: -
FYE: June 30
Type: Private

For those in southern California's North County, the Tri-City Healthcare District is there to take care of your medical needs. The organization provides primary and acute health care services primarily through Tri-City Medical Center. The hospital, which has more than 500 physicians representing 60 specialties, boasts about 400 beds. In addition to the medical center, Tri-City Healthcare District operates the Beatrice Riggs French Women's Center, an outpatient facility that offers services to women and newborns. One of the hospital's specialties is diagnosing and treating behavioral and developmental difficulties in children. In addition, Tri-City Healthcare District offers home and hospice care.

	Annual Growth	06/06	06/07	06/08	06/10	06/15
Sales ($mil.)	2.7%	-	-	267.7	279.5	321.9
Net income ($ mil.)	(21.6%)	-	-	9.3	(11.2)	1.7
Market value ($ mil.)	-	-	-	-	-	-
Employees	-	-	-	-	-	2,121

TRI-COR INDUSTRIES, INC.

1818 LIBRARY ST STE 500
RESTON, VA 201906274
Phone: 571 458-3824
Fax: -
Web: www.tricorind.com

CEO: -
CFO: -
HR: -
FYE: September 30
Type: Private

Need help getting your computer systems up to snuff? Let TRI-COR Industries take a shot at it. The company provides information technology services for government and commercial customers. Some of its client are United States Transportation Command and United States Air Force Air Mobility Command (AMC). It has partnerships with Red Hat and ViON. Areas of expertise include digital services, application, data and infrastructure services, cyber security, professional and customer support services. The company also offers full stack coverage of hardware and operating systems. TRI-COR was founded in 1983 by CEO and owner Louis Gonzalez. It has satellite locations in Colorado, Missouri and Virginia.

	Annual Growth	09/05	09/06	09/07	09/08	09/13
Sales ($mil.)	(0.7%)	-	-	21.9	17.5	21.0
Net income ($ mil.)	(18.4%)	-	-	5.7	3.6	1.7
Market value ($ mil.)	-	-	-	-	-	-
Employees	-	-	-	-	-	200

TRI-S SECURITY CORP

11675 Great Oaks Way, Suite 120
Alpharetta, GA 30022
Phone: 678 808-1540
Fax: -
Web: www.trissecurity.com

CEO: -
CFO: -
HR: -
FYE: December 31
Type: Public

Keeping others fully guarded keeps Tri-S Security in business. Through its Paragon Systems subsidiary, the company provides contract security guard services to US government agencies. Its guards are used for activities such as access control, crowd control, perimeter security, personal protection, and surveillance. In 2009 Tri-S Security sold its Cornwall Group subsidiary, a provider of security and investigative services such as armed and unarmed uniformed guards and alarm monitoring throughout the Miami-Dade, Broward, and Palm Beach counties of Florida. Chairman, president, and CEO Ronald Farrell controls nearly 40% of Tri-S Security.

	Annual Growth	12/04	12/05	12/06	12/07	12/08
Sales ($mil.)	53.5%	25.4	42.0	75.7	88.9	141.3
Net income ($ mil.)	-	(1.6)	(2.3)	(3.8)	(4.3)	(15.8)
Market value ($ mil.)	-	-	18.5	9.3	6.5	2.3
Employees	41.0%	760	2,500	2,400	2,600	3,000

TRI-WEST, LTD.

12005 PIKE ST
SANTA FE SPRINGS, CA 906706100
Phone: 562 692-9166
Fax: -
Web: www.triwestltd.com

CEO: -
CFO: Randy Sims
HR: Jo Taylor
FYE: December 31
Type: Private

Tri-West tends to floor both residential and commercial customers with its broad selection of floor coverings. Founded in 1981, the company distributes floor coverings through more than 10 warehouse facilities located in the western US and the Hawaiian Islands. Tri-West offers major manufacturers' products, including carpets, resilient sheet, specialty tile, hardwood flooring, laminate and wall coverings.

	Annual Growth	12/09	12/10	12/11	12/12	12/13
Sales ($mil.)	17.4%	-	-	117.7	141.9	162.3
Net income ($ mil.)	41.0%	-	-	7.1	10.2	14.2
Market value ($ mil.)	-	-	-	-	-	-
Employees	-	-	-	-	-	304

TRIBUNE PUBLISHING COMPANY

560 W GRAND AVE
CHICAGO, IL 606544592
Phone: 312 222-9100
Fax: –
Web: www.tribpub.com

CEO: Terry Jimenez
CFO: Michael N Lavey
HR: –
FYE: December 31
Type: Private

Tribune Publishing is a media company rooted in award-winning journalism. The company, formerly known as Tronco, operates local media businesses in eight key markets including the Chicago Tribune, the Baltimore Sun, Orlando Sentinel, South Florida's Sun Sentinel, Virginia's Daily Press, and The Virginian-Pilot, The Morning Call of Lehigh Valley, Pennsylvania and the Hartford Courant. In addition to award-winning local media businesses, Tribune Publishing operates national and international brands such as Tribune Content Agency. Its trusted brands play a critical role in informing, inspiring, and engaging the countless communities it serves. It takes pride in the legacy of its brands and draws on its vast experiences as it continues to share its content as a digitally-focused, premium content company.

TRILOGY COMMUNICATIONS, INC.

2910 HIGHWAY 80 E
PEARL, MS 392083495
Phone: 601 932-4461
Fax: –
Web: www.trilogyrf.com

CEO: Sidney S Lee
CFO: –
HR: –
FYE: September 30
Type: Private

Trilogy Communications plans to keep it up in the air. A technological leader in the telecommunications industry, Trilogy Communications' high-performance wireless products include AirCell Transline Cable (used for Tower and Rooftop Applications), AirCell Radiating Cable (used in RF Confined areas, such as Subways and Metros), and AirCell Plenum and Plenum Radiating Cable (distributed Antenna Systems). AirCell products can be found in such big name spots as London's Heathrow Airport and the US. Customers are from various industries, namely, healthcare, education and enterprise. The company is was founded in 1985.

TRICO BANCSHARES (CHICO, CA)   NMS: TCBK

63 Constitution Drive
Chico, CA 95973
Phone: 530 898-0300
Fax: –
Web: www.tcbk.com

CEO: Richard P Smith
CFO: Peter G Wiese
HR: –
FYE: December 31
Type: Public

People looking for a community bank in California's Sacramento Valley can try TriCo. TriCo Bancshares is the holding company for Tri Counties Bank, which serves customers through some 65 traditional and in-store branches in 23 counties in Northern and Central California. Founded in 1974, Tri Counties Bank provides a variety of deposit services, including checking and savings accounts, money market accounts, and CDs. Most patrons are retail customers and small to midsized businesses. The bank primarily originates real estate mortgages, which account for about 65% of its loan portfolio; consumer loans contribute about 25%. TriCo has agreed to acquire rival North Valley Bancorp.

	Annual Growth	12/19	12/20	12/21	12/22	12/23
Assets ($mil.)	11.2%	6,471.2	7,639.5	8,614.8	9,931.0	9,910.1
Net income ($ mil.)	6.3%	92.1	64.8	117.7	125.4	117.4
Market value ($ mil.)	1.3%	1,357.7	1,173.7	1,429.2	1,696.3	1,429.5
Employees	0.5%	1,184	1,068	1,094	1,231	1,207

TRIM-LOK INC.

6855 HERMOSA CIR
BUENA PARK, CA 906201151
Phone: 714 562-0500
Fax: –
Web: www.trimlok.com

CEO: Gary Whitener
CFO: –
HR: –
FYE: November 30
Type: Private

Trim-Lok locks in profits by making high quality, competitively priced vinyl and rubber trims and seals. Its divisions, which include Industrial Extrusions (Mylar wrapped trim, 3M adhesive attachments), Rubber Trim Products (rubber, neoprene, and silicone extrusion), and GripTek (molded grips for fitness and gardening equipment), make standard and customized products -- decorative trim and flap seals, instant adhesive, locking gaskets, rubber guards, regular and upholstery trims, cutting tools and accessories -- for aerospace, automotive, furniture, boating, and RV applications. Trim-Lok distributes more than 200 different aftermarket offerings through 30 domestic and almost 10 international stock locations.

	Annual Growth	11/08	11/09	11/10	11/11	11/12
Sales ($mil.)	19.2%	–	–	23.2	28.2	32.9
Net income ($ mil.)	(1.8%)	–	–	4.0	5.6	3.8
Market value ($ mil.)	–	–	–	–	–	–
Employees	–	–	–	–	–	180

TRIHEALTH, INC.

625 EDEN PARK DR
CINCINNATI, OH 452026005
Phone: 513 569-5400
Fax: –
Web: www.trihealth.com

CEO: Mark Clement
CFO: Andrew Devoe
HR: Brittany Walpole
FYE: June 30
Type: Private

Established in 1995, TriHealth is the integrated health care system that formed as a partnership between Good Samaritan Hospital and Bethesda Hospital, Inc. TriHealth is a full-service, not-for-profit health system that provides a wide range of clinical, educational, preventive and social programs. TriHealth operates five acute care and surgery hospitals, including Bethesda North Hospital, which has approximately 420 beds and provides trauma, birthing, and heart care services; the 590-bed Good Samaritan Hospital; and Bethesda Butler Hospital surgical hospital. TriHealth also operates a vast network of outpatient care centers and conducts medical education and research programs. TriHealth is affiliated with Xavier University.

	Annual Growth	06/18	06/19	06/20	06/21	06/22
Sales ($mil.)	(4.8%)	–	–	552.9	553.8	501.2
Net income ($ mil.)	–	–	–	(185.3)	(158.6)	(165.5)
Market value ($ mil.)	–	–	–	–	–	–
Employees	–	–	–	–	–	13,000

TRIMAS CORP (NEW)   NMS: TRS

38505 Woodward Avenue, Suite 200
Bloomfield Hills, MI 48304
Phone: 248 631-5450
Fax: –
Web: www.trimascorp.com

CEO: Thomas A Amato
CFO: Corey Coosaia
HR: –
FYE: December 31
Type: Public

TriMas is designs, develops and manufactures a diverse set of products primarily for the consumer products, aerospace and industrial markets through its TriMas Packaging, TriMas Aerospace and Specialty Products groups. The company's primary brands are Rieke, Taplast, Affaba & Ferrari, Monogram Aerospace Fasteners, Martinic Engineering, and Norris Cylinder among others. TriMas also designs and manufactures a diverse range of products, including highly-engineered fasteners, collars, blind bolts, and rivets among others. It also has specialty products comprised of Norris Cylinder, and Arrow Engine businesses. It has over 40 manufacturing and support locations in nearly 15 countries but generates majority of sales in its home country, the US.

	Annual Growth	12/19	12/20	12/21	12/22	12/23
Sales ($mil.)	5.4%	723.5	770.0	857.1	883.8	893.6
Net income ($ mil.)	(20.0%)	98.6	(79.8)	57.3	66.2	40.4
Market value ($ mil.)	(5.2%)	1,294.2	1,304.9	1,524.5	1,142.9	1,043.6
Employees	(0.7%)	3,500	3,200	3,500	3,500	3,400

TRIMBLE INC
NMS: TRMB

10368 Westmoor Drive
Westminster, CO 80021
Phone: 720 887-6100
Fax: –
Web: www.trimble.com

CEO: –
CFO: –
HR: –
FYE: December 29
Type: Public

Trimble Inc. is a leading provider of technology solutions that enable professionals and field mobile workers to improve or transform their work processes. The company makes GPS, Global Navigation Satellite System, laser, and optical technologies, inertial, or other technologies to establish real-time position. The company's products target areas such as agriculture, architecture, civil engineering, survey, construction, geospatial, government, natural resources, transportation, and utilities. Trimble sells to end users, such as government entities, farmers, engineering and construction firms as well as equipment manufacturers. Around 55% of the company's revenue comes from North America.

	Annual Growth	01/20	01/21*	12/21	12/22	12/23
Sales ($mil.)	3.9%	3,264.3	3,147.7	3,659.1	3,676.3	3,798.7
Net income ($ mil.)	(11.8%)	514.3	389.9	492.7	449.7	311.3
Market value ($ mil.)	6.4%	10,232	16,459	21,492	12,463	13,114
Employees	2.5%	11,484	11,402	11,931	11,825	12,700

*Fiscal year change

TRIMEDYNE INC
NBB: TMED

5 Holland #223
Irvine, CA 92618
Phone: 949 951-3800
Fax: 949 855-8206
Web: www.trimedyne.com

CEO: –
CFO: –
HR: Mary Isun
FYE: September 30
Type: Public

Trimedyne doesn't play tag with lasers, but it does use them to help surgeons do their jobs. The company's cold-pulsed lasers and fiber-optic laser energy delivery devices (including needles and fibers) are used in gastrointestinal, orthopedic, urologic, and general surgeries, as well as gynecology, arthroscopy, and ear, nose, and throat (ENT) procedures. Trimedyne markets its products to hospitals and surgery centers in the US via direct sales and internationally through distributors. The company's Mobile Surgical Technologies unit rents lasers and provides related services to health care facilities on a "fee per use" basis.

	Annual Growth	09/11	09/12	09/13	09/14	09/15
Sales ($mil.)	(5.4%)	6.7	6.1	6.0	5.5	5.3
Net income ($ mil.)	–	(1.5)	(0.8)	0.3	(0.4)	(0.6)
Market value ($ mil.)	(19.0%)	0.0	0.0	0.0	0.0	0.0
Employees	(7.2%)	62	55	42	52	46

TRIMEGA PURCHASING ASSOCIATION

5600 N RIVER RD STE 700
ROSEMONT, IL 600185165
Phone: 847 699-3330
Fax: –
Web: www.trimega.org

CEO: –
CFO: –
HR: –
FYE: December 31
Type: Private

Smart office products dealers pledge to buya lotta TriMega. The TriMega Purchasing Association is a product and services buying group made up of 590 independently owned office-supply dealers. TriMega, in turn, is a member of the larger Business Products Group International (BPGI), which gives TriMega's member dealers even more buying power and helps them compete with nationwide chains such as OfficeMax and Staples . TriMega also supplies its own Value Plus brand of office products. The not-for-profit cooperative was founded in 1987 and serves company's large and small from across the US.

	Annual Growth	03/07	03/08	03/09*	06/11*	12/11
Sales ($mil.)	107.6%	–	–	90.0	280.1	387.9
Net income ($ mil.)	87.1%	–	–	10.4	26.1	36.4
Market value ($ mil.)	–	–	–	–	–	–
Employees	–	–	–	–	–	27

*Fiscal year change

TRIMOL GROUP, INC.
NBB: TMOL

45 Rockefeller Plaza, Suite 2000
New York, NY 10111
Phone: 212 554-4394
Fax: –
Web: –

CEO: –
CFO: –
HR: –
FYE: December 31
Type: Public

Trimol Group has a license for a mechanically rechargeable aluminum-air fuel cell for use in portable consumer electronics, but the company isn't actively developing the technology. Its Intercomsoft subsidiary provides technology and consumables for producing secure government identification documents. The technology was developed by Supercom of Israel, which broke off its supply agreement with Intercomsoft in early 2005. Intercomsoft continued to provide support services to the Republic of Moldova (traditionally its only customer), but the Republic of Moldova has indicated that it does not intend to renew its supply agreement. Chairman Boris Birshtein owns more than three-quarters of Trimol Group.

	Annual Growth	12/10	12/11	12/12	12/13	12/14
Sales ($mil.)	–	–	–	–	–	–
Net income ($ mil.)	–	(1.0)	(0.8)	(0.6)	(0.2)	(0.2)
Market value ($ mil.)	30.0%	0.2	0.6	0.2	0.7	0.6
Employees	–	–	2	2	2	2

TRINET GROUP INC.
NYS: TNET

One Park Place, Suite 600
Dublin, CA 94568
Phone: 510 352-5000
Fax: –
Web: www.trinet.com

CEO: Burton M Goldfield
CFO: Kelly Tuminelli
HR: –
FYE: December 31
Type: Public

TriNet Group is a leading provider of human resources expertise, payroll services, employee benefits and employment risk mitigation services for small- and medium-size business. Clients primarily come from the financial, technology, hospitality, and nonprofit industries. TriNet offers talent management, retention and terminations, benefits enrollment, immigration and visas, payroll tax credits, labor law and regulatory developments and many other industry-specific and general HR topics. Founded in 1988, TriNet processed approximately $75 billion in payroll and payroll taxes for its clients and ended the year with approximately 22,000 clients and 348,700 WSEs, primarily in the US.

	Annual Growth	12/19	12/20	12/21	12/22	12/23
Sales ($mil.)	6.3%	3,856.0	4,034.0	4,540.0	4,885.0	4,922.0
Net income ($ mil.)	15.3%	212.0	272.0	338.0	355.0	375.0
Market value ($ mil.)	20.4%	2,868.1	4,083.6	4,826.3	3,435.1	6,025.5
Employees	5.6%	2,900	2,700	2,800	3,600	3,600

TRINITAS REGIONAL MEDICAL CENTER

225 WILLIAMSON ST
ELIZABETH, NJ 072023625
Phone: 908 351-0714
Fax: –
Web: www.rwjbh.org

CEO: –
CFO: –
HR: Curry Bucu
FYE: December 31
Type: Private

Trinitas Regional Medical Center (formerly Trinitas Hospital) serves eastern and central Union County in New Jersey. The Catholic teaching hospital has more than 530 beds and offers acute, tertiary, and long-term health care services on its two campuses. It has special centers for cancer care, sleep disorders, cardiovascular conditions, diabetes care, pediatrics, and women's health. The hospital also offers inpatient behavioral health care, operates a local clinic, and provides educational services to students of Seton Hall University's School of Health and Medical Sciences. Trinitas Regional Medical Center is co-sponsored by the Sisters of Charity of Saint Elizabeth and the Elizabethtown Healthcare Foundation.

	Annual Growth	12/17	12/18	12/19	12/20	12/21
Sales ($mil.)	4.9%	–	299.7	302.6	313.5	346.0
Net income ($ mil.)	124.2%	–	1.8	24.6	13.0	20.4
Market value ($ mil.)	–	–	–	–	–	–
Employees	–	–	–	–	–	2,700

TRINITY CHRISTIAN CENTER OF SANTA ANA, INC.

13600 HERITAGE PKWY
FORT WORTH, TX 761774324
Phone: 714 665-3619
Fax: –
Web: www.tbn.org

CEO: –
CFO: –
HR: Alayna York
FYE: December 31
Type: Private

TBN doesn't stand for The Bible Network, but much of its source material comes from the good book. Trinity Broadcasting Network (TBN) operates the world's largest Christian TV network, reaching nearly 100 million US households through some 7,500 cable and more than 400 broadcast affiliates, mostly low-powered stations. The network offers mostly original faith programming, including its flagship Praise the Lord . It reaches international audiences via approximately 65 satellites. TBN was founded in 1973 by Paul and Jan Crouch, who started the network in partnership with Jim and Tammy Faye Bakker, broadcasting from a single TV station in Santa Ana, California.

TRINITY HEALTH CORPORATION

20555 VICTOR PKWY
LIVONIA, MI 481527096
Phone: 734 343-1000
Fax: –
Web: www.trinity-health.org

CEO: Michael Slubowski
CFO: Cynthia Clemence
HR: Karen Evans
FYE: June 30
Type: Private

One of the largest not-for-profit, Catholic health care systems in the US, Trinity Health runs roughly 90 acute care hospitals and approximately 135 continuing care facilities in more than 25 US states. It operates a comprehensive integrated network of health services, including inpatient and outpatient services, physician services, managed care coverage, home health care, long-term care, assisted living care and rehabilitation services. It offers a Clinically Integrated Network (CIN) of physicians and primary care services as well as Medical Groups and Clinic-Based Urgent Care. The company employs approximately 8,300 physicians and clinicians.

	Annual Growth	06/14	06/15	06/19	06/21	06/22
Sales ($mil.)	8.9%	–	1,375.5	2,046.3	3,007.1	2,491.0
Net income ($ mil.)	(3.2%)	–	19.1	38.1	407.8	15.3
Market value ($ mil.)	–	–	–	–	–	–
Employees	–	–	–	–	–	51,220

TRINITY HEALTH SYSTEM

380 SUMMIT AVE
STEUBENVILLE, OH 439522667
Phone: 740 283-7000
Fax: –
Web: www.trinityhealth.com

CEO: –
CFO: –
HR: –
FYE: June 30
Type: Private

Despite its name Trinity Health System serves eastern Ohio through a mere two facilities -- Trinity Medical Center East and Trinity Medical Center West. Combined, they have some 470 beds and offer patients emergency and general medical, diagnostic, and surgical services, as well as specialty care in fields including rehabilitation, skilled nursing, and women's health services. Hospital specialty units also include the Tony Teramana Cancer Center, a sleep center, and a heart center. Trinity Health's outpatient facilities include an imaging center, a school of nursing, and community health clinics. The not-for-profit health system is sponsored by Tri-State Health Services and Franciscan Services organizations.

	Annual Growth	12/14	12/15*	06/20	06/21	06/22
Sales ($mil.)	1.1%	–	256.1	236.4	276.0	277.1
Net income ($ mil.)	(18.7%)	–	12.8	0.9	20.2	3.0
Market value ($ mil.)	–	–	–	–	–	–
Employees	–	–	–	–	–	1,640

*Fiscal year change

TRINITY INDUSTRIES, INC.
NYS: TRN

14221 N. Dallas Parkway, Suite 1100
Dallas, TX 75254-2957
Phone: 214 631-4420
Fax: 214 589-8501
Web: www.trin.net

CEO: E J Savage
CFO: Eric R Marchetto
HR: Claudia Varela
FYE: December 31
Type: Public

Trinity Industries, Inc. and its subsidiaries own businesses that are leading providers of railcar products and services in North America. Its rail-related businesses market their railcar products and services under the trade name TrinityRail. Under the TrinityRail platform, the company leases and manages railcar fleets. Its customers include railroads, leasing companies, and industrial shippers of products in various markets, such as agriculture, construction and metals, consumer products, energy, and refined products and chemicals. Trinity also owns a transportation company that provides support services to Trinity as well as other industrial manufacturers.

	Annual Growth	12/19	12/20	12/21	12/22	12/23
Sales ($mil.)	(0.2%)	3,005.1	1,999.4	1,516.0	1,977.3	2,983.3
Net income ($ mil.)	(6.3%)	137.6	(147.3)	182.0	60.1	106.0
Market value ($ mil.)	4.7%	1,811.9	2,158.7	2,470.4	2,418.8	2,175.1
Employees	(5.5%)	11,875	6,375	5,845	9,215	9,480

TRINITY UNIVERSITY

1 TRINITY PL
SAN ANTONIO, TX 782124674
Phone: 210 999-7011
Fax: –
Web: www.trinity.edu

CEO: –
CFO: –
HR: –
FYE: May 31
Type: Private

Trinity University offers about 50 undergraduate degree programs in the arts, sciences, and music, along with more than 60 minor study programs. The university also offers master's degree programs in accounting, education, psychology, and health care administration. Trinity University has more than 2,500 undergraduate and graduate students hailing from across the US and more than 55 international countries. The student/faculty ratio is 9:1. The university was founded by Presbyterians in 1869 in Tehuacana, Texas, and moved to San Antonio in 1942.

	Annual Growth	05/17	05/18	05/19	05/20	05/22
Sales ($mil.)	22.6%	–	139.3	150.2	216.2	314.5
Net income ($ mil.)	(2.1%)	–	86.0	(21.7)	0.4	79.1
Market value ($ mil.)	–	–	–	–	–	–
Employees	–	–	–	–	–	700

TRINSEO PLC
NYS: TSE

440 East Swedesford Road, Suite 301
Wayne, PA 19087
Phone: 610 240-3200
Fax: –
Web: www.trinseo.com

CEO: –
CFO: –
HR: –
FYE: December 31
Type: Public

Trinseo is a specialty material solutions provider with a focus on partnering with companies to bring ideas to life in an imaginative, smart, and sustainability-focused manner. Trinseo manufactures plastics, latex binders, polystyrene, and feedstocks, including various advanced specialty products and sustainable solutions. Its products are incorporated into a wide range of its customers' products including products for automotive applications, consumer electronics, appliances, medical devices, packaging, footwear, carpet, paper and board, building and construction, and wellness, among others. The company's operations are located in Europe, North America, and Asia Pacific, supplemented by Americas Styrenics, a styrenics joint venture with Chevron Phillips Chemical Company LP. About 55% of its revenue comes from its customers in Europe.

	Annual Growth	12/18	12/19	12/20	12/21	12/22
Sales ($mil.)	1.8%	4,622.8	3,775.8	3,035.5	4,827.5	4,965.5
Net income ($ mil.)	–	292.5	92.0	7.9	440.0	(430.9)
Market value ($ mil.)	–	–	–	–	–	–
Employees	8.0%	2,500	2,700	2,600	3,100	3,400

TRIPADVISOR INC
NMS: TRIP

400 1st Avenue
Needham, MA 02494
Phone: 781 800-5000
Fax: –
Web: www.tripadvisor.com

CEO: Stephen Kaufer
CFO: Mike Noonan
HR: –
FYE: December 31
Type: Public

TripAdvisor is a leading online travel company. It leverages its brands, technology platforms, and capabilities to connect its large, global audience with partners by offering rich content, travel guidance products and services, and two-sided marketplaces for experiences, accommodations, restaurants, and other travel categories. It features more than 1 billion reviews and opinions on nearly 8 million experiences, accommodations, restaurants, airlines, and cruises. The company partners with top online travel businesses, such as Expedia and Booking. The US is responsible for about 60% of the company's sales.

	Annual Growth	12/19	12/20	12/21	12/22	12/23
Sales ($mil.)	3.5%	1,560.0	604.0	902.0	1,492.0	1,788.0
Net income ($ mil.)	(46.9%)	126.0	(289.0)	(148.0)	20.0	10.0
Market value ($ mil.)	(8.2%)	4,182.8	3,962.5	3,753.2	2,475.5	2,964.3
Employees	(9.2%)	4,194	2,596	2,691	3,100	2,845

TRIPLE "B" CORPORATION

4103 2ND AVE S
SEATTLE, WA 981342305
Phone: 206 625-1412
Fax: –
Web: www.charliesproduce.com

CEO: Charlie Billow
CFO: –
HR: Brandi Gunn
FYE: December 25
Type: Private

This company offers a triple threat in the food distribution business. Triple B Corporation operates Charlie's Produce, a leading wholesale supplier of fresh fruit, vegetables, and floral products serving grocery retailers in Idaho, Montana, Oregon, and Washington. The company also distributes dairy products, frozen foods, and meat products through its subsidiary Rogge. Rogge mainly serves the fishing industry in Seattle and Alaska. In addition, Triple B delivers grocery goods to customers in Alaska through Highliner Foods. The company's distribution operations also serve some customers in the food service industry, as well as other wholesale operators. CEO Charlie Billow founded Triple B in 1978.

TRIPPE MANUFACTURING CO

10000 WOODWARD AVE
WOODRIDGE, IL 605174943
Phone: 773 869-1111
Fax: –
Web: tripplite.eaton.com

CEO: –
CFO: –
HR: –
FYE: December 31
Type: Private

Trippe Manufacturing trips the light fantastic by selling protection from power trips. Doing business as Tripp Lite, the privately owned company makes more than 3,000 products used to protect, power, and connect electronic equipment. Its surge suppressors guard against surges, spikes, and over-voltages that can damage personal computers and other electronic equipment. The company's uninterruptible power supply (UPS) systems provide battery backup power, while its inverters are used to power laptops and other products when other power sources are not available. Tripp Lite products also include power strips, cables and connectors, laptop accessories, and power-management software.

TRIUMPH APPAREL CORP
NBB: TRUA

530 Seventh Avenue
New York, NY 10018
Phone: 212 764-4630
Fax: 212 764-7265
Web: www.danskins.com

CEO: Carol Hockman
CFO: John A Sarto
HR: –
FYE: December 29
Type: Public

Triumph Apparel posts a profit when its customers outfit themselves to bust a move. Formerly known as Danskin, the company designs and manufactures girls' and women's dance and active wear (including tights and leotards), and it also offers women's fitness equipment, such as toning balls and yoga mats. Triumph sells its products to mass merchandisers (Target, Wal-Mart), department stores, sporting goods stores, and other specialty shops, as well as online, under the licensed Danskin name. In early 2009 KSL Ventures acquired 55% of the company.

	Annual Growth	12/97	12/98	12/99	12/00	12/01
Sales ($mil.)	(9.5%)	122.0	108.7	88.0	84.7	81.8
Net income ($ mil.)	–	0.4	(6.9)	(19.9)	(7.9)	(10.0)
Market value ($ mil.)	(50.2%)	44.8	60.3	21.4	11.0	2.8
Employees	(14.6%)	1,551	1,463	1,071	937	825

TRIUMPH GROUP INC.
NYS: TGI

555 E Lancaster Avenue, Suite 400
Radnor, PA 19087
Phone: 610 251-1000
Fax: –
Web: www.triumphgroup.com

CEO: Daniel J Crowley
CFO: James F McCabe Jr
HR: –
FYE: March 31
Type: Public

Triumph Group's companies design, engineer, manufacture, repair, and overhaul a variety of a broad portfolio of aerospace and defense systems, subsystems, components, and structures for customers that include global aviation industry, including original equipment manufacturers (OEMs) and the full spectrum of military and commercial aircraft operators through the aircraft life cycle. Extensive product and service offerings include full post-delivery value chain services that simplify the maintenance, repair and overhaul ("MRO") supply chain. Through its ground support equipment maintenance, component MRO and post-production supply chain activities, Systems & Support is positioned to provide integrated planeside repair solutions globally.

	Annual Growth	03/19	03/20	03/21	03/22	03/23
Sales ($mil.)	(20.0%)	3,364.9	2,900.1	1,869.7	1,459.9	1,379.1
Net income ($ mil.)	–	(321.8)	(28.1)	(450.9)	(42.8)	89.6
Market value ($ mil.)	(11.7%)	1,247.1	442.3	1,202.7	1,654.1	758.4
Employees	(17.7%)	10,776	9,989	6,692	5,340	4,937

TRIVASCULAR TECHNOLOGIES, INC.

2 MUSICK
IRVINE, CA 926181631
Phone: 707 543-8800
Fax: –
Web: www.endologix.com

CEO: Christopher G Chavez
CFO: Michael R Kramer
HR: –
FYE: December 31
Type: Private

TriVascular has a triple-A solution. The firm produces medical devices for minimally invasive treatment of abdominal aortic aneurysms (AAA, a ballooning of the main vessel delivering blood to the abdominal cavity). It uses principles from other industries, including aerospace and automotive, to develop unique solutions for unmet medical needs. Its only current product, the Ovation System, treats AAA through minimally invasive endovascular aortic repair (EVAR); the device can be customized to each individual patient's specific anatomy. TriVascular sells its product in the US, Germany, and the UK. The firm was formed in 1998 and went public in 2014; in early 2016 TriVascular was acquired by Endologix.

TROIKA MEDIA GROUP INC

NBB: TRKA Q

25 West 39th Street, 6th Floor
New York, NY 10018
Phone: 212 213-0111
Fax: -
Web: -

CEO: -
CFO: -
HR: -
FYE: December 31
Type: Public

Roomlinx believes high-speed networking should be a standard hotel amenity. The company provides wireless and wired Internet installation and support services, primarily to customers in the hospitality industry. Roomlinx's services are used to provide access in hotel rooms, convention centers, corporate apartments, and for special events. The company has serviced more than 140 hotels, equipping more than 24,000 rooms. The company is also moving into the in-room entertainment market, offering a system that includes a flat-panel display and a media console for distributing movies, advertising, and other content.

	Annual Growth	12/15*	06/20	06/21	06/22*	12/22
Sales ($mil.)	50.8%	10.6	24.6	16.2	116.4	187.9
Net income ($ mil.)	-	(81.5)	(14.4)	(16.0)	(38.7)	(9.6)
Market value ($ mil.)	-	-	-	15.8	4.2	0.6
Employees	16.7%	33	-	120	208	97

*Fiscal year change

TROY UNIVERSITY

600 UNIVERSITY AVE
TROY, AL 360820001
Phone: 334 670-3179
Fax: -
Web: www.troy.edu

CEO: -
CFO: -
HR: -
FYE: September 30
Type: Private

Troy University is not the topic of a Homeric poem, but you'd probably find a Helen enrolled there. The school is a public institution composed of a network of campuses throughout Alabama and worldwide. The network includes campuses and teaching sites in some seven US states and four other countries. Troy University has a total student enrollment of about 23,000, and offers degrees in arts and sciences, business, communications and fine arts, education, and health and human services. The school also operates the Confucius Institute to promote understanding of Chinese language and culture.

	Annual Growth	09/18	09/19	09/20	09/21	09/22
Sales ($mil.)	(1.7%)	-	171.6	175.1	168.1	163.1
Net income ($ mil.)	(10.2%)	-	8.1	43.4	49.3	5.9
Market value ($ mil.)	-	-	-	-	-	-
Employees	-	-	-	-	-	3,000

TRONOX LLC

263 TRESSER BLVD STE 1100
STAMFORD, CT 069013227
Phone: 203 705-3800
Fax: -
Web: www.tronox.com

CEO: Jean-Franois Turgeon
CFO: Russ Austin
HR: -
FYE: December 31
Type: Private

Tronox is the world's leading vertically integrated manufacturer of titanium dioxide (TiO2) pigments. The company operates titanium-bearing mineral sand mines, and beneficiation and smelting operations in Australia and South Africa to produce feedstock materials that can be processed into TiO2 for pigment, high-purity titanium chemicals, including titanium tetrachloride, and ultrafine TiO2 used in certain specialty applications. Tronox products add brightness and durability to paints, plastics, paper, and other everyday products. The company has an annual production capacity of approximately 832,000 metric tons (MT) of titanium feedstock, which is comprised of 182,000 MT of rutile and leucoxene, 240,000 MT of synthetic rutile and 410,000 MT of titanium slag. About 40% of the company's revenue is generated from the EMEA region.

TRT HOLDINGS, INC

4001 MAPLE AVE
DALLAS, TX 752193241
Phone: 214 283-8500
Fax: -
Web: www.trtholdings.com

CEO: Robert B Rowling
CFO: Terrance Philen
HR: Karina Alvarez
FYE: December 31
Type: Private

TRT Holdings has interests in guest pampering, iron pumping, and oil prospecting. A diversified holding company for Texas billionaire Robert Rowling, TRT owns the luxury Omni Hotels & Resorts chain, Waldo's Dollar Mart in Mexico, and Gold's Gym International, the world's largest full-service fitness center franchiser. In addition, TRT is involved in oil and gas exploration through Tana Exploration Company. Rowling and his father, Reese Rowling, made a fortune in the oil business through Tana Oil & Gas. They formed TRT Holdings in 1989 when they sold most of their energy interests to Texaco (now part of Chevron).

TROUT-BLUE CHELAN-MAGI, LLC

5 HOWSER RD
CHELAN, WA 988169590
Phone: 509 682-2591
Fax: -
Web: www.chelanfruit.com

CEO: Ed Johnson
CFO: Todd Kammers
HR: Alissa Senyitko
FYE: August 31
Type: Private

Trout-Blue Chelan-Magi has a simpler and more apt name by which it does business -- Chelan Fruit. The company is fruit growers' cooperative with some 420 member/growers located in Washington State. The co-op prepares, packs, and sells its members' apples, pears, cherries and other stone fruits, including peaches, apricots, nectarines, and plums. The fruit is shipped both domestically and internationally. Product marketing is conducted through Chelan Fresh Marketing. The co-op was formed through the 1995 merger of two cooperatives, Trout and Blue Chelan; the combined company changed its name again in 2004 with the acquisition of Magi.

	Annual Growth	08/12	08/13	08/14	08/15	08/16
Sales ($mil.)	(5.0%)	-	180.9	156.3	169.6	154.9
Net income ($ mil.)	98.0%	-	5.1	4.1	4.6	39.3
Market value ($ mil.)	-	-	-	-	-	-
Employees	-	-	-	-	-	675

TRUBRIDGE INC

NMS: TBRG

54 St. Emanuel Street
Mobile, AL 36602
Phone: 251 639-8100
Fax: -
Web: www.cpsi.com

CEO: Christopher L Fowler
CFO: Matt J Chambless
HR: Susan Kluver
FYE: December 31
Type: Public

Computer Programs and Systems Inc. (CPSI) is a leading provider of healthcare solutions and services for community hospitals, its clinics, and other healthcare systems. CPSI offers its products and services through six companies - Evident, American HealthTech, TruBridge, iNetXperts, TruCode, and Healthcare Resource Group. These combined companies are focused on improving the health of the communities it serves, connecting communities for a better patient care experience, and improving the financial operations of its clients. In the US, there are approximately 3,800 community hospitals with fewer than 200 acute care beds, with approximately 2,900 of these having fewer than 100 acute care beds. Almost all of the company's sales were generated from its domestic markets.

	Annual Growth	12/19	12/20	12/21	12/22	12/23
Sales ($mil.)	5.4%	274.6	264.5	280.6	326.6	339.4
Net income ($ mil.)	-	20.5	14.2	18.4	15.9	(45.8)
Market value ($ mil.)	(19.3%)	384.1	390.5	426.3	396.0	162.9
Employees	12.6%	2,000	2,000	2,000	2,500	3,219

TRUE VALUE COMPANY, L.L.C.

8600 W BRYN MAWR AVE
CHICAGO, IL 606313579
Phone: 773 695-5000
Fax: –
Web: www.truevalue.com

CEO: Chris Kempa
CFO: Jeff Olson
HR: Gabrielle Gambrell
FYE: January 02
Type: Private

True Value Company is one of the world's leading hardline wholesalers with a globally recognized brand serving independent hardware retailers. Coast to Coast, the independent wholesale hardware distributor serves some 4,500 retail outlets in more than 60 countries. Products offered include home improvement and garden supplies, as well as appliances, housewares, sporting goods, and pet food. In addition to the flagship True Value banner, the company offers dealers support for other brand concepts including Taylor Rental, Grand Rental Station, Home & Garden Showplace, and True Value MRO. True Value traced its roots back to 1948.

TRUEBLUE INC
NYS: TBI

1015 A Street
Tacoma, WA 98402
Phone: 253 383-9101
Fax: 253 383-9311
Web: www.trueblue.com

CEO: A P Beharelle
CFO: Derrek L Gafford
HR: Anamaria Barahona
FYE: December 31
Type: Public

TrueBlue is a leading provider of specialized workforce solutions that help clients achieve business growth and improve productivity. The company offers general labor staffing services from about 600 branches throughout the US, Puerto Rico, and Canada, mostly through its PeopleReady segment. The PeopleManagement segment finds contingent labor and on-site industrial staffing, while the PeopleScout segment provides recruitment process outsourcing. TrueBlue mainly serves companies in the construction, manufacturing and logistics, warehousing and distribution, waste and recycling, energy, transportation, retail, hospitality, and others. Vast majority of its revenue comes from US operations.

	Annual Growth	12/19	12/20	12/21	12/22	12/23
Sales ($mil.)	(5.3%)	2,368.8	1,846.4	2,173.6	2,254.2	1,906.2
Net income ($ mil.)	–	63.1	(141.8)	61.6	62.3	(14.2)
Market value ($ mil.)	(10.2%)	738.0	599.3	863.9	600.5	479.3
Employees	(5.2%)	6,200	5,200	6,400	6,500	5,000

TRUECAR INC
NMS: TRUE

1401 Ocean Ave, Suite 300
Santa Monica, CA 90401
Phone: 800 200-2000
Fax: –
Web: www.truecar.com

CEO: Jantoon Reigersman
CFO: Jantoon E Reigersman
HR: Meghan Nelson
FYE: December 31
Type: Public

TrueCar is a leading automotive digital marketplace that offers car buyers to connect to its network of Certified Dealers. The company has established a diverse software ecosystem on a common technology infrastructure, powered by proprietary data and analytics. Operating in all 50 states and the District of Columbia, its network of TrueCar Certified Dealers consists primarily of new car franchises, representing all major makes of cars, as well as independent dealers selling used vehicles. TrueCar went public in 2014 to increase its financial flexibility.

	Annual Growth	12/19	12/20	12/21	12/22	12/23
Sales ($mil.)	(18.2%)	353.9	278.7	231.7	161.5	158.7
Net income ($ mil.)	–	(54.9)	76.5	(38.3)	(118.7)	(49.8)
Market value ($ mil.)	(7.6%)	432.7	382.6	309.7	228.6	315.2
Employees	(17.7%)	709	435	428	441	325

TRUIST FINANCIAL CORP
NYS: TFC

214 North Tryon Street
Charlotte, NC 28202
Phone: 336 733-2000
Fax: 336 671-2399
Web: www.bbt.com

CEO: William H Rogers Jr
CFO: Michael B Maguire
HR: –
FYE: December 31
Type: Public

BB&T is now Truist. Truist Financial Corporation is a purpose-driven financial services company committed to inspire and build better lives and communities. Formed by the historic merger of equals of BB&T and SunTrust, Truist has leading market share in many high-growth markets in the country. The company offers a wide range of services including retail, small business and commercial banking; asset management; capital markets; commercial real estate; corporate and institutional banking; insurance; mortgage; payments; specialized lending; and wealth management. Truist conducts its business operations primarily through its bank subsidiary, Truist Bank, and other nonbank subsidiaries.

	Annual Growth	12/19	12/20	12/21	12/22	12/23
Assets ($mil.)	3.1%	473,078	509,228	541,241	555,255	535,349
Net income ($ mil.)	–	3,224.0	4,482.0	6,440.0	6,260.0	(1,091.0)
Market value ($ mil.)	(10.0%)	75,116	63,926	78,091	57,391	49,242
Employees	(3.7%)	59,000	54,982	52,641	55,126	50,832

TRUJILLO & SONS, INC.

3325 NW 62ND ST
MIAMI, FL 331477533
Phone: 305 696-8701
Fax: –
Web: www.trujilloandsons.com

CEO: –
CFO: –
HR: –
FYE: December 31
Type: Private

Trujillo and Sons is a leading food distributor that supplies foodservice operators and retail grocery stores with dry goods, canned foods, beverages, and a variety of other goods. Most of its products are sold under the Alberto and Don Lucas brands; the company also provides private label packaging services through affiliated companies Trujillo Oil Plant (vegetable and cooking oils) and American Spice Company. Trujillo and Sons serves customers throughout the US, and in the Caribbean and South America. The family-owned company was founded in 1966 by Lucas Trujillo Sr.

	Annual Growth	12/04	12/05	12/06	12/08	12/09
Sales ($mil.)	(4.3%)	–	–	101.1	93.2	88.5
Net income ($ mil.)	(34.7%)	–	–	4.5	3.7	1.3
Market value ($ mil.)	–	–	–	–	–	–
Employees	–	–	–	–	–	130

TRULIA, INC.

535 MISSION ST STE 700
SAN FRANCISCO, CA 941053223
Phone: 415 648-4358
Fax: –
Web: www.trulia.com

CEO: Peter Flint
CFO: Prashant Aggarwal
HR: –
FYE: December 31
Type: Private

Trulia.com offers a Web-based database of more than 1 million homes and apartments for sale or rent in the US. The site also offers information on local schools, and crime statistics, as well as user-generated content for local insight into communities. It also has "The What Locals Say" feature which lets residents share what they love about living in their neighborhood.

TRUMAN ARNOLD COMPANIES

100 CRESCENT CT STE 1600
DALLAS, TX 752011832
Phone: 903 794-3835
Fax: –
Web: www.thearnoldcos.com

CEO: –
CFO: –
HR: –
FYE: September 30
Type: Private

The Arnold Companies (TAC) is one of the largest independent fuel wholesalers and aviation service providers in the US. The company is one of the leader in aviation industry with the elite services of business aviation ground handling, fueling, aircraft maintenance, charter and commercial support. TACenergy is a Dallas, TX-based independent wholesale fuels distributor of refined petroleum products. TACenergy fine-tunes the optimal combination of pull points, supply, carriers and price.

	Annual Growth	09/13	09/14	09/15	09/16	09/17
Sales ($mil.)	15.2%	–	–	1,595.9	1,525.8	2,119.3
Net income ($ mil.)	2.4%	–	–	17.8	18.6	18.6
Market value ($ mil.)	–	–	–	–	–	–
Employees	–	–	–	–	–	550

TRUMAN MEDICAL CENTER, INCORPORATED

2301 HOLMES ST
KANSAS CITY, MO 641082677
Phone: 816 404-1000
Fax: –
Web: www.universityhealthkc.org

CEO: –
CFO: –
HR: Cedric Cobin
FYE: June 30
Type: Private

Truman Medical Center (also known as Truman Medical Centers/University Health) provides primary and mental health care at two not-for-profit hospitals in the Kansas City (Missouri) area. Its Hospital Hill runs one of the busiest emergency rooms in Kansas City and is known for treatments related to asthma, diabetes, obstetrics, ophthalmology, weight management, and women's health. TMC Lakewood, a 110-bed hospital, is a leading academic medical center providing a range of health care services to the greater Kansas City metropolitan area, including uninsured patients. The Lakewood Family Birthplace delivers more than 1,500 babies annually.

	Annual Growth	06/18	06/19	06/20	06/21	06/22
Sales ($mil.)	6.0%	–	666.6	693.4	736.6	793.5
Net income ($ mil.)	(3.2%)	–	13.1	(21.4)	50.3	11.9
Market value ($ mil.)	–	–	–	–	–	–
Employees	–	–	–	–	–	3,000

TRUSTCO BANK CORP. (N.Y.)

5 Sarnowski Drive
Glenville, NY 12302
Phone: 518 377-3311
Fax: 518 381-3668
Web: www.trustcobank.com

NMS: TRST
CEO: –
CFO: –
HR: –
FYE: December 31
Type: Public

In Banking They Trust. TrustCo Bank Corp is the holding company for Trustco Bank, which boasts more than 140 branches across eastern New York, central and western Florida, and parts of Vermont, Massachusetts, and New Jersey. The bank offers personal and business customers a variety of deposit products, loans and mortgages, and trust and investment services. It primarily originates residential and commercial mortgages, which account for more than three-quarters of its loan portfolio. It also writes business, construction, and installment loans and home equity lines of credit.

	Annual Growth	12/19	12/20	12/21	12/22	12/23
Assets ($mil.)	4.3%	5,221.3	5,901.8	6,196.5	6,000.1	6,168.2
Net income ($ mil.)	0.3%	57.8	52.5	61.5	75.2	58.6
Market value ($ mil.)	37.6%	164.9	126.9	633.7	715.1	590.7
Employees	(2.0%)	814	778	759	750	750

TRUSTEES OF BOSTON COLLEGE

140 COMMONWEALTH AVE
CHESTNUT HILL, MA 024673800
Phone: 617 552-8000
Fax: –
Web: www.bc.edu

CEO: –
CFO: –
HR: Bernard O'Kane
FYE: May 31
Type: Private

Operating in the city of Boston, Boston College (BC) enrolls some 15,075 students. It has a student-teacher ratio of 10:1. BC offers degrees in more than 50 fields of study through its eight schools and colleges on four campuses. Some programs include biology, law, accounting, mathematics, chemistry, economics, geology, philosophy, and theology. The university also has more than 35 research centers, including the Institute for Scientific Research, and the Center for International Higher Education. Founded in 1863, BC is one of the oldest Jesuit Catholic universities in the nation and has the largest Jesuit community in the world.

	Annual Growth	05/17	05/18	05/20	05/21	05/22
Sales ($mil.)	18.3%	–	835.6	865.5	889.8	1,638.2
Net income ($ mil.)	25.1%	–	169.1	(41.4)	1,274.4	414.6
Market value ($ mil.)	–	–	–	–	–	–
Employees	–	–	–	–	–	2,493

TRUSTEES OF CLARK UNIVERSITY

950 MAIN ST
WORCESTER, MA 016101400
Phone: 508 793-7711
Fax: –
Web: www.clarku.edu

CEO: –
CFO: –
HR: GE Gao
FYE: May 31
Type: Private

If you don't want to live in the dark, get an education at Clark! Clark University is a private, co-educational liberal arts university with an enrollment of more than 2,200 undergraduate students and more than 1,000 graduate students. It offers about 30 undergraduate majors (psychology is the most popular) and about two dozen master's degree programs. Clark University has 200 full-time faculty members of which 96% hold doctoral or terminal degrees. It has a student/faculty ratio of 10:1. The university offers 17 Varsity sports (NCAA Division III). Clark University has been a pioneer in the academic study of geography; it has awarded more doctorates in the discipline than any other US school.

	Annual Growth	05/17	05/18	05/19	05/20	05/22
Sales ($mil.)	14.8%	–	114.1	120.2	200.9	198.4
Net income ($ mil.)	–	–	33.5	(14.2)	3.6	(30.4)
Market value ($ mil.)	–	–	–	–	–	–
Employees	–	–	–	–	–	600

TRUSTEES OF DARTMOUTH COLLEGE

545 BOYLSTON ST STE 900
BOSTON, MA 021163674
Phone: 603 646-1110
Fax: –
Web: home.dartmouth.edu

CEO: –
CFO: –
HR: Scot Bemis
FYE: June 30
Type: Private

Part of the esteemed Ivy League, Dartmouth College is a private, four-year liberal arts college with an enrollment of more than 6,000 students. The university has an undergraduate college (offering about 40 programs) and graduate schools of business, engineering, and medicine, plus graduate programs in the arts and sciences. Its student-teacher ratio is about 6:1. It is also home to a number of centers and institutes including Children's Hospital at Dartmouth; Dartmouth Center on Addiction, Recovery, and Education; and Center for Digital Strategies. Notable alumni include Daniel Webster, Robert Frost, Theodore "Dr. Seuss" Geisel, and Nelson Rockefeller.

	Annual Growth	06/16	06/17	06/20	06/21	06/22
Sales ($mil.)	(6.0%)	–	1,370.0	909.1	1,028.6	1,007.4
Net income ($ mil.)	–	–	691.4	411.3	2,858.8	(273.9)
Market value ($ mil.)	–	–	–	–	–	–
Employees	–	–	–	–	–	5,000

TRUSTEES OF INDIANA UNIVERSITY

107 S INDIANA AVE
BLOOMINGTON, IN 474057000
Phone: 812 855-4848
Fax: –
Web: bloomington.iu.edu

CEO: Michael J Mirro
CFO: –
HR: Beth East
FYE: June 30
Type: Private

Founded in 1820, Indiana University is one of the top public research universities in the world. With a population of some 71,000 degree-seeking undergraduate students, more than 19,000 students in graduate program, and 7,200 international students from about 165 countries. The university's flagship institution IU-Bloomington; regional campuses in Fort Wayne, Gary, Kokomo, New Albany, Richmond, and South Bend; and an urban campus in Indianapolis that is operated with Purdue University. The university has more than 21,000 faculty and professional and support staff. It has over 200 museums, research centers, and institutes and offers more than 380 overseas study programs in more than 70 countries.

	Annual Growth	06/12	06/13	06/14	06/15	06/16
Sales ($mil.)	1.7%	–	2,146.7	2,195.2	2,207.6	2,256.2
Net income ($ mil.)	(17.7%)	–	189.3	201.2	138.4	105.7
Market value ($ mil.)	–	–	–	–	–	–
Employees	–	–	–	–	–	16,000

TRUSTEES OF THE COLORADO SCHOOL OF MINES

1500 ILLINOIS ST
GOLDEN, CO 804011887
Phone: 303 273-3000
Fax: –
Web: www.mines.edu

CEO: –
CFO: –
HR: –
FYE: June 30
Type: Private

Colorado School of Mines (CSM) is the oldest public institution of higher education in Colorado. The school offers about 20 undergraduate and 20 graduate academic programs in such fields as applied science and mathematics, engineering, and geoscience and resource engineering. Students can minor in areas related to humanities and social sciences. In addition, graduate students can pursue higher degrees in social and management science. The school claims that its "M" symbol on a nearby mountainside is the nation's largest single-letter, electronically lighted school emblem. Colorado School of Mines, which has an enrollment of about 5,500, was founded in 1874.

	Annual Growth	06/04	06/05	06/06	06/16	06/17
Sales ($mil.)	62.4%	–	0.7	102.3	215.7	222.1
Net income ($ mil.)	–	–	(0.2)	4.6	(2.0)	(76.8)
Market value ($ mil.)	–	–	–	–	–	–
Employees	–	–	–	–	–	1,000

TRUSTEES OF THE ESTATE OF BERNICE PAUAHI BISHOP

567 S KING ST STE 200
HONOLULU, HI 968133002
Phone: 808 523-6200
Fax: –
Web: www.ksbe.edu

CEO: Dee J Mailer
CFO: Michael Loo
HR: Michelle Swan
FYE: June 30
Type: Private

Kamehameha Schools provides an education fit for a king ... or queen. The private charitable trust was founded and endowed by Princess Bernice Pauahi Bishop, great granddaughter and last royal descendant of Kamehameha the Great. One of the largest independent schools in the US, Kamehameha educates more than 5,000 elementary, middle school, and high school students, many of whom board at one of its three Hawaii campuses. In addition, it operates some 30 preschools with a total enrollment of about 1,500. Kamehameha Schools is also the largest private property owner in the state of Hawaii, and uses the proceeds from its real estate operations to support its schools.

	Annual Growth	06/13	06/14	06/15	06/20	06/22
Sales ($mil.)	–	–	915.0	767.2	548.1	917.0
Net income ($ mil.)	(5.0%)	–	482.1	334.0	14.9	320.2
Market value ($ mil.)	–	–	–	–	–	–
Employees	–	–	–	–	–	1,500

TRUSTEES OF TUFTS COLLEGE

169 HOLLAND ST STE 318
SOMERVILLE, MA 021442401
Phone: 617 628-5000
Fax: –
Web: www.tufts.edu

CEO: –
CFO: –
HR: –
FYE: June 30
Type: Private

Tufts University wants to light up the minds of New England scholars. The school offers undergraduate and graduate degrees in areas such as education, engineering, psychology, art, English, music, and medicine. The university enrolls some 11,000 students and has 1,300 faculty members, and it offers classes in 70 fields at three campuses in Massachusetts (Boston, Medford/Somerville, and Grafton). It also has an international campus in Talloires, France. Tufts University's Fletcher School of Law and Diplomacy is the oldest continuous international relations graduate program in the country. The school is also home to New England's only Veterinary School.

	Annual Growth	06/14	06/15	06/20	06/21	06/22
Sales ($mil.)	6.6%	–	914.4	1,118.6	1,033.7	1,433.1
Net income ($ mil.)	–	–	(25.6)	32.0	806.0	180.6
Market value ($ mil.)	–	–	–	–	–	–
Employees	–	–	–	–	–	4,100

TRUSTEES OF UNION COLLEGE IN THE TOWN OF SCHENECTADY IN THE STATE OF NEW YORK

807 UNION ST
SCHENECTADY, NY 123083256
Phone: 518 388-6000
Fax: –
Web: www.union.edu

CEO: –
CFO: –
HR: –
FYE: June 30
Type: Private

Union College brings liberal arts and engineering together. Union College is a private liberal arts school that offers courses in the humanities, the social sciences, the sciences, and engineering. Notable alumni include the father of Franklin D. Roosevelt, the grandfather of Winston Churchill, and former US president Chester A. Arthur (class of 1848). Founded in 1795 with a class of 16, the college is supported by an endowment of more than $270 million.

	Annual Growth	06/14	06/15	06/18	06/21	06/22
Sales ($mil.)	3.9%	–	173.1	143.5	197.8	225.6
Net income ($ mil.)	14.4%	–	8.0	41.5	11.7	20.6
Market value ($ mil.)	–	–	–	–	–	–
Employees	–	–	–	–	–	870

TRUSTMARK CORP

NMS: TRMK

248 East Capitol Street
Jackson, MS 39201
Phone: 601 208-5111
Fax: 601 354-5053
Web: www.trustmark.com

CEO: Duane A Dewey
CFO: –
HR: Tammie McCullough
FYE: December 31
Type: Public

Trustmark Corporation is the holding company for Trustmark National Bank, which has about 170 locations, mainly in Mississippi, but also in the Florida panhandle, Alabama, Texas, and Tennessee. Serving consumer, corporate, small, and middle-market businesses, Trustmark offers a range of financial products and services, such as checking and savings accounts, certificates of deposit, credit cards, insurance, investments, and trust services, as well as mortgage banking services, including construction financing, production of conventional and government insured mortgages, secondary marketing and mortgage servicing. The diversified financial services firm has about $18.013 billion in assets. The bank, which was founded in 1889, has a vast network of ATMs and ITMs throughout the Southeast.

	Annual Growth	12/19	12/20	12/21	12/22	12/23
Assets ($mil.)	8.5%	13,498	16,552	17,596	18,015	18,722
Net income ($ mil.)	2.4%	150.5	160.0	147.4	71.9	165.5
Market value ($ mil.)	(5.2%)	2,107.6	1,667.9	1,982.4	2,132.0	1,702.7
Employees	(0.8%)	2,844	2,797	2,692	2,738	2,757

TRUTH INITIATIVE FOUNDATION

900 G ST NW FL 4
WASHINGTON, DC 200015332
Phone: 202 454-5555
Fax: –
Web: www.truthinitiative.org

CEO: –
CFO: –
HR: Adrienne Neal
FYE: June 30
Type: Private

Truth Initiative, formerly American Legacy Foundation, tells the truth. Its "truth" anti-smoking campaign is the most public face of this not-for-profit group that seeks to reach young smokers with no-nonsense TV and print ads, as well as its Web site, thetruth.com. The foundation's goals are to keep young people from lighting up and smoking, and to make cessation tools accessible to everyone through grants, training, activism, and community outreach. The organization was established in 1999 as a result of the Master Settlement Agreement between the attorneys general of 46 states and the tobacco industry; the settlement is the major source of funding for the Truth Initiative.

	Annual Growth	06/14	06/15	06/17	06/19	06/20
Sales ($mil.)	6.2%	–	42.7	67.5	98.7	57.7
Net income ($ mil.)	–	–	(62.5)	(46.3)	(6.2)	(51.6)
Market value ($ mil.)	–	–	–	–	–	–
Employees	–	–	–	–	–	130

TSI HOLDING COMPANY

182 NW INDUSTRIAL CT
BRIDGETON, MO 630441276
Phone: 314 628-6000
Fax: –
Web: www.registrar-transfers.com

CEO: –
CFO: Annette M Eckerle
HR: –
FYE: December 31
Type: Private

TSI Holding Company is an investment firm with holdings in middle-market manufacturing and distribution companies with annual revenues between $30 million and $150 million. A long-term investor, the firm often leaves incumbent management in place and builds its portfolio companies by making all-cash add-on acquisitions. Its holdings include charter airline Miami Air International, jewelry designers and distributors Sunstone Imports and Roman Company, and pipe distributor Tubular Steel (TSI Holding's predecessor company). TSI traces its roots to 1953 when founder John M. Hauck started off selling steel tubing out of a room in the Railway Exchange Building in St. Louis. His son John C. Hauck continues to run TSI.

TSR INC

400 Oser Avenue, Suite 150
Hauppauge, NY 11788
Phone: 631 231-0333
Fax: –
Web: www.tsrconsulting.com

NAS: TSRI
CEO: Thomas Salerno
CFO: John G Sharkey
HR: –
FYE: May 31
Type: Public

Prowling for programmers? TSR would like to help. The company provides contract computer programmers and other information technology (IT) personnel, mainly to FORTUNE 1000 companies that need to augment their in-house IT staffs. TSR specializes in serving the telecommunications industry; major customers have included purchasing outsourcer ProcureStaff (primarily to fulfill a contract with AT&T) and publishing giant S&P Global. Overall, TSR serves more than 80 clients in the northeastern and mid-Atlantic regions of the US. In addition to providing contract personnel, TSR offers direct staffing (helping clients find people for permanent placement) and project management services.

	Annual Growth	05/19	05/20	05/21	05/22	05/23
Sales ($mil.)	12.5%	63.3	59.1	68.8	97.3	101.4
Net income ($ mil.)	–	(1.3)	(1.1)	(0.6)	6.9	1.7
Market value ($ mil.)	7.4%	10.4	7.2	17.4	16.1	13.8
Employees	2.6%	389	338	606	632	431

TSRC, INC.

14140 WASHINGTON HWY
ASHLAND, VA 230057237
Phone: 804 412-1200
Fax: –
Web: www.thesupplyroom.com

CEO: Patricia Barber
CFO: John Arkesteyn
HR: Teresa Lee
FYE: December 31
Type: Private

TSRC does more than stock the supply room. Operating through seven sales offices across Virginia, the company (formerly named The Supply Room Companies) markets office products, computer accessories, and furniture to both the private sector and government agencies. The company has grown by acquiring other office supply dealers in the state, including Frank Parsons. The company traced its roots in 1951 when Meade Jones founded Meade & Company.

	Annual Growth	12/11	12/12	12/13	12/14	12/16
Sales ($mil.)	1.5%	–	70.8	67.3	66.6	75.1
Net income ($ mil.)	(7.0%)	–	0.2	0.0	0.0	0.1
Market value ($ mil.)	–	–	–	–	–	–
Employees	–	–	–	–	–	200

TSS INC DE

110 E. Old Settlers Blvd
Round Rock, TX 78664
Phone: 512 310-1000
Fax: –
Web: www.totalsitesolutions.com

NBB: TSSI
CEO: Anthony Angelini
CFO: –
HR: –
FYE: December 31
Type: Public

Fortress International Group, Inc. (FIGI) is a bastion of security. FIGI companies design, build, and maintain secure, temperature-controlled data centers and IT storage facilities for private companies and government agencies. FIGI offers its start-to-finish service by operating through subsidiaries that specialize in a certain function, such as IT consulting, design, construction, or engineering. Projects are either built from scratch or upgraded through renovations. While most of its customers are top secret, FIGI has worked with Digital Realty Trust and Internap, and is cleared to work at Department of Defense and US Army Corps of Engineers properties.

	Annual Growth	12/18	12/19	12/20	12/21	12/22
Sales ($mil.)	8.2%	22.3	32.8	45.1	27.4	30.6
Net income ($ mil.)	–	2.4	0.1	0.0	(1.3)	(0.1)
Market value ($ mil.)	(9.7%)	18.1	35.1	15.3	9.7	12.0
Employees	1.1%	67	65	63	67	70

TTEC HOLDINGS INC

6312 South Fiddlers Green Circle,. Suite 100N
Greenwood Village, CO 80111
Phone: 303 397-8100
Fax: –
Web: www.ttec.com

NMS: TTEC
CEO: –
CFO: –
HR: –
FYE: December 31
Type: Public

TTEC Holdings (formerly known as TeleTech Holdings) is leading global customer experience as a service (CXaaS) provider for a number of brands. The company provides a range of business process outsourcing (BPO) services including customer acquisition, customer care, tech support, and order fulfillment services, as well as digitally enabled back office and specialty services. The company delivered its onshore, nearshore and offshore services to about 20 countries on six continents. Customers are mainly major global enterprises such as automotive, communications, financial services, government, health care, logistics, media and entertainment retail, technology and travel and transportation industries. TTEC also offers management consulting services. Most of the company's sales are generated in the US accounting to around 70% of total sales.

	Annual Growth	12/19	12/20	12/21	12/22	12/23
Sales ($mil.)	10.6%	1,643.7	1,949.2	2,273.1	2,443.7	2,462.8
Net income ($ mil.)	(42.5%)	77.2	118.6	141.0	103.2	8.4
Market value ($ mil.)	(14.0%)	1,879.1	3,458.9	4,294.5	2,093.0	1,027.7
Employees	5.0%	49,500	61,000	65,000	69,400	60,055

TTM TECHNOLOGIES INC NMS: TTMI

200 East Sandpointe, Suite 400
Santa Ana, CA 92707
Phone: 714 327-3000
Fax: -
Web: www.ttm.com

CEO: -
CFO: -
HR: -
FYE: January 1
Type: Public

TTM Technologies is a leading global manufacturer of technology solutions, including engineered systems, radio frequency (RF) components and RF microwave/microelectronic assemblies, and printed circuit boards (PCB). TTM operates about 25 specialized facilities in North America and China. It serves a diversified customer base consisting of approximately 1,500 customers in various markets globally, including aerospace and defense, data center computing, automotive, medical, industrial, and instrumentation, as well as networking and telecommunications. Its customers include original equipment manufacturers (OEMs), electronic manufacturing services (EMS) providers, original design manufacturers (ODMs), distributors, and government agencies. TTM customers in the US account for almost 50% of its revenue.

	Annual Growth	12/19	12/20*	01/22	01/23	01/24
Sales ($mil.)	(4.5%)	2,689.3	2,105.3	2,248.7	2,495.0	2,232.6
Net income ($ mil.)	-	41.3	177.5	54.4	94.6	(18.7)
Market value ($ mil.)	1.5%	1,519.4	1,404.0	1,545.9	1,539.8	1,614.3
Employees	(11.5%)	25,700	16,700	16,100	17,800	15,800

*Fiscal year change

TTX CO.

101 North Wacker Dr.
Chicago, IL 60606
Phone: 312 853-3223
Fax: 312 984-3855
Web: www.ttx.com

CEO: -
CFO: -
HR: -
FYE: December 31
Type: Public

TTX Company is a leading provider of railcars and related freight car management services to the North American rail industry. The company serves as a railcar pooling cooperative where other railroads share cars and capacity under a pooling agreement approved by the Surface Transportation Board. Its fleet of about 170,000 railcars serves North America's railroads and the world's freight needs, from the largest Class I railroads to the smaller regional and short-line railroads alike. It comprises flat cars and intermodal wells, boxcars, and gondolas that haul intermodal containers, vehicles, and commodities such as lumber, steel, and farm and construction equipment. Its operations are supported by maintenance and repair shops across the US. Founded as Trailer Train in 1955, TTX is privately owned by multiple North American railroads.

	Annual Growth	12/04	12/05	12/06	12/07	12/08
Sales ($mil.)	2.3%	1,015.0	1,134.1	1,156.3	1,118.1	1,112.3
Net income ($ mil.)	(3.2%)	88.6	115.3	107.8	83.6	77.8
Market value ($ mil.)	-	-	-	-	-	-
Employees	(5.0%)	1,582	1,670	-	1,673	1,289

TUBBY'S SUB SHOPS, INC

30551 EDISON DR
ROSEVILLE, MI 480661571
Phone: 586 293-5099
Fax: -
Web: www.tubbys.com

CEO: -
CFO: -
HR: -
FYE: November 30
Type: Private

With a name like Tubby's, the sandwiches had better be big. Tubby's Sub Shops franchises more than 60 Tubby's submarine sandwich restaurants located primarily in Michigan. Each quick service restaurant serves a variety of made-to-order submarine and pita sandwiches, along with soups, salads, curly fries, and desserts. Many of its restaurants are free-standing units while others are located in shopping malls. The company was co-founded in 1968 by Rick Paganes and his brothers Robert (CEO) and Peter (VP). The Paganes family continues to own the Tubby's chain. The company began franchising its units in 1978 and went public in 1986, but struggled financially. The Paganes family took Tubby's private in 2000 after a failed merger attempt with Popeyes franchisee Interfoods of America.

	Annual Growth	11/14	11/15	11/16*	12/17*	11/18
Sales ($mil.)	4.3%	-	7.8	8.2	8.4	8.9
Net income ($ mil.)	16.9%	-	0.6	0.7	1.0	1.0
Market value ($ mil.)	-	-	-	-	-	-
Employees	-	-	-	-	-	16

*Fiscal year change

TUBEMOGUL, INC.

1250 53RD ST STE 1
EMERYVILLE, CA 946082965
Phone: 510 653-0126
Fax: -
Web: -

CEO: -
CFO: -
HR: -
FYE: December 31
Type: Private

TubeMogul aims to help its customers rule digital video advertising like, well, moguls. The company's software platform is designed to enhance digital branding efforts by giving advertisers greater control of their digital video spending. The video-ad-buying software company's platform allows users to plan, buy, measure, and optimize their digital video advertising spending on their own or with help from the company's Platform Services Group (60% of sales). Seeking to capitalize on the accelerating migration of ad spending from TV to the digital realm, TubeMogul went public in 2014 with an offering that raised nearly $44 million. In 2016, the company agreed to be bought by Adobe Systems for about $540 million.

TUCSON ELECTRIC POWER COMPANY

88 East Broadway Boulevard
Tucson, AZ 85701
Phone: 520 571-4000
Fax: -
Web: www.tep.com/investor-information/

CEO: Susan M Gray
CFO: Frank P Marino
HR: -
FYE: December 31
Type: Public

Tucson Electric Power (TEP) provides electricity to some 438,000 residential, commercial, and industrial retail customers in Tucson and surrounding areas in southeastern Arizona. With about 3,185 MW of net generating capacity (primarily natural gas), TEP is a regulated utility that generates, transmits, and distributes electricity to its customers, and it also sells energy wholesale to utilities and power marketers in the western US. TEP is a wholly-owned subsidiary of UNS Energy, a utility services holding company. UNS Energy is an indirect wholly-owned subsidiary of Fortis which is a leader in the North American electric and gas utility business.

	Annual Growth	12/18	12/19	12/20	12/21	12/22
Sales ($mil.)	6.0%	1,432.6	1,418.3	1,424.7	1,592.6	1,808.1
Net income ($ mil.)	3.7%	188.3	186.5	191.4	201.2	217.4
Market value ($ mil.)	-	-	-	-	-	-
Employees	2.3%	1,528	1,587	1,575	1,719	1,675

TUESDAY MORNING CORP (NEW) NBB: TUEM Q

6250 LBJ Freeway
Dallas, TX 75240
Phone: 972 387-3562
Fax: -
Web: www.tuesdaymorning.com

CEO: Andrew T Berger
CFO: William M Baumann
HR: -
FYE: July 2
Type: Public

Tuesday Morning is a leading destination for unique home and lifestyle goods. The company is an off-price retailer, selling high-quality products at prices generally below those found in boutiques, specialty and department stores, catalogs, and online retailers. Its primary merchandise typically includes upscale home textiles, home furnishings, housewares, gourmet food, toys, and seasonal d cor. Tuesday Morning's more than 485 stores in some 40 states operate seven days a week excluding holidays. Its customers are primarily from middle- and upper-income households. Filed for Chapter 11 in early 2023, the company was acquired by Hilco Merchant Resources for approximately $32 million in a court-approved bankruptcy sale in mid-2023.

	Annual Growth	06/18	06/19	06/20	06/21*	07/22
Sales ($mil.)	(7.1%)	1,006.3	1,007.2	874.9	690.8	749.8
Net income ($ mil.)	-	(21.9)	(12.4)	(166.3)	3.0	(59.0)
Market value ($ mil.)	(42.2%)	8.7	4.8	0.5	12.9	1.0
Employees	(9.6%)	9,062	9,634	7,433	6,299	6,046

*Fiscal year change

TUFCO TECHNOLOGIES, INC.

3161 S RIDGE RD
GREEN BAY, WI 543045626
Phone: 920 336-0054
Fax: –
Web: www.tufco.com

CEO: Larry Grabowy
CFO: –
HR: –
FYE: September 30
Type: Private

Tough stains are no match for Tufco Technologies' cleaning products. Its cleaning wipes are used for industrial, automotive, personal care, home, and institutional applications. To complement the needs of its wipes customers, Tufco also offers custom formulation development and blending as well as microbiological services. Customers are multinational consumer products businesses and, less so, business paper distributors. The company was originally founded in 1974 by converting industry veterans Samuel Bero and Patrick Garland; it was acquired by investment firm Griffin Holdings in 2014.

TUMAC LUMBER CO., INC.

16821 SE MCGILLIVRAY BLVD STE 204
VANCOUVER, WA 986830402
Phone: 503 226-6661
Fax: –
Web: www.tumac.com

CEO: Bradley McMurchie
CFO: James Adcock
HR: –
FYE: October 31
Type: Private

Tumac Lumber is one of the oldest and most successful international and domestic wholesale trading companies in the US. The company and its subsidiaries sell products such as panels, MDF, hardwood, plywood, doors and components, door skins, decking, veneers, lumber, logs, industrial and agricultural, construction mats, and furniture and components. Tumac actively maintains strategic inventories in over 50 locations across North America. The company distributes wood products through its wholly owned subsidiaries, Disdero Lumber (Clackamas, Oregon) and Specialty Wood Products (Aurora, Colorado). Paul McCracken and Bill MacPherson established Tumac Lumber in 1959.

TUNNELL CONSULTING, INC.

900 E 8TH AVE STE 106
KING OF PRUSSIA, PA 194061324
Phone: 610 337-0820
Fax: –
Web: www.tunnellconsulting.com

CEO: Maryann Gallivan
CFO: –
HR: –
FYE: December 31
Type: Private

Tunnel vision can be a good thing in the life sciences. Tunnell Consulting helps clients in the biotech and pharmaceutical manufacturing industries achieve operational excellence. The company focuses on key areas such as regulation, compliance, and quality; technical services; operational improvement; and turnkey solutions. Specifically, the firm can help start up facilities and reduce costs of established businesses. Abbott Labs, IBM, and 3M are among the company's customers. Tunnell Consulting was founded in 1962. It has been employee-owned since 1988.

	Annual Growth	12/10	12/11	12/12	12/13	12/14
Sales ($mil.)	0.4%	–	42.6	43.3	39.7	43.1
Net income ($ mil.)	5.9%	–	0.2	0.7	0.1	0.2
Market value ($ mil.)	–	–	–	–	–	–
Employees	–	–	–	–	–	90

TUPPERWARE BRANDS CORP

NYS: TUP

14901 South Orange Blossom Trail
Orlando, FL 32837
Phone: 407 826-5050
Fax: –
Web: www.tupperwarebrands.com

CEO: –
CFO: –
HR: –
FYE: December 31
Type: Public

Tupperware Brands Corporation (TBC) is a leading global consumer products company that designs innovative, functional, and environmentally responsible products. It offers preparation, storage, and serving containers for kitchen and home uses through its well-known Tupperware brand. This iconic brand has more than 8,500 functional design and utility patents for solution-oriented kitchen and home products. TBC deploys a sales force across about 70 countries to sell its products. The company's signature container created the modern food storage category that revolutionized the way the world stores, serves, and prepares food. Most of its revenue originates outside the US.

	Annual Growth	12/18	12/19	12/20	12/21	12/22
Sales ($mil.)	(10.9%)	2,069.7	1,797.9	1,740.1	1,602.3	1,304.0
Net income ($ mil.)	–	155.9	12.4	112.2	18.6	(232.5)
Market value ($ mil.)	(39.6%)	1,388.1	365.9	1,574.6	677.6	184.3
Employees	(13.9%)	12,000	11,300	10,698	10,000	6,600

TURLOCK IRRIGATION DISTRICT EMPLOYEES ASSOCIATION

333 E CANAL DR
TURLOCK, CA 953803946
Phone: 209 883-8222
Fax: –
Web: www.tid.org

CEO: –
CFO: Joe Malaski
HR: Adam Bolanos
FYE: December 31
Type: Private

Staying true to its more-than-a-century-old watery origins, Turlock Irrigation District (TID) provides irrigation services to more than 5,800 farmers in its service area (149,500 acres of farmland). Its primary water supply comes from the Tuolumne river. The company also provides electric generation, transmission, and distribution services (the main source of its revenues) to more than 98,000 retail customers in and around Turlock, California, and it sells power and natural gas to wholesale customers. TID provides electric service to its customer base in a 662-sq.-ml. service area encompassing portions of Merced, Stanislaus, and Tuolumne counties, over 2,200 miles of distribution line.

	Annual Growth	12/05	12/06	12/07	12/08	12/19
Sales ($mil.)	2.2%	–	257.9	306.8	336.6	343.0
Net income ($ mil.)	1.8%	–	24.0	14.6	12.2	30.1
Market value ($ mil.)	–	–	–	–	–	–
Employees	–	–	–	–	–	250

TURNER CONSTRUCTION COMPANY INC

66 HUDSON BLVD E FL 36
NEW YORK, NY 100012196
Phone: 212 229-6000
Fax: –
Web: www.turnerconstruction.com

CEO: Peter J Davoren
CFO: Karen Gould
HR: Amanda Montan
FYE: December 31
Type: Private

Turner Construction is a North America-based, international construction services company and is a leading builder in diverse market segments. With more than 1,500 dedicated staff, Turner provides construction services and technical expertise for commercial and multifamily buildings, airports, and stadiums, as well as correctional, educational, entertainment, and manufacturing facilities. Turner utilizes the most robust project management control systems, scheduling software, data visualization tools, and 360 photography, and have the capability to provide building information modeling (BIM) services through Turner Technical Services. Henry Turner founded Turner Construction Company in 1902.

	Annual Growth	12/10	12/11	12/12	12/13	12/14
Sales ($mil.)	10.9%	–	–	8,552.1	9,488.5	10,516
Net income ($ mil.)	17.2%	–	–	70.4	76.6	96.7
Market value ($ mil.)	–	–	–	–	–	–
Employees	–	–	–	–	–	5,000

TURTLE & HUGHES, INC

100 WALNUT AVE
CLARK, NJ 070661253
Phone: 732 574-3600
Fax: –
Web: www.turtle.com

CEO: Kathleen Shanahan
CFO: Christopher Rausch
HR: –
FYE: September 30
Type: Private

Turtle & Hughes is one of the nation's largest independent electrical and industrial distributors. The company's products are sold through two divisions: Electrical Distribution, which operates in more than 15 branches and two distribution centers, provides electrical services and solutions backed by a commitment to technical and product expertise, and Turtle & Hughes Integrated Supply (THIS), which provides on-site MRO procurement, cost saving and spend analytics operating across the US, and in Canada, Puerto Rico, and Mexico. Family-owned, the company is founded in 1923.

	Annual Growth	09/16	09/17	09/18	09/19	09/21
Sales ($mil.)	3.1%	–	671.4	754.7	758.1	758.4
Net income ($ mil.)	(10.1%)	–	18.1	20.2	21.0	11.8
Market value ($ mil.)	–	–	–	–	–	–
Employees	–	–	–	–	–	900

TURTLE BEACH CORP   NMS: HEAR

44 South Broadway, 4th Floor
White Plains, NY 10601
Phone: 888 496-8001
Fax: –
Web: www.parametricsound.com

CEO: –
CFO: –
HR: –
FYE: December 31
Type: Public

Using proprietary technology, Turtle Beach (formerly Parametric Sound) makes speakers that offer focused and directional sound for an immersive experience. Its current product is the HS-3000 line of speakers for the commercial market including digital kiosks and slot machines. The company is developing its Hypersonic line for the consumer market where it hopes its thin, two-speaker system will rival traditional multi-speaker setups used for surround sound and be used in computers, video games, and mobile devices. Turtle Beach sells its products in North America, Asia, and Europe to OEMs for inclusion in new and existing products.

	Annual Growth	12/19	12/20	12/21	12/22	12/23
Sales ($mil.)	2.4%	234.7	360.1	366.4	240.2	258.1
Net income ($ mil.)	–	17.9	38.7	17.7	(59.5)	(17.7)
Market value ($ mil.)	3.8%	165.7	377.8	390.3	125.7	192.0
Employees	(2.3%)	245	300	304	269	223

TUTOR PERINI CORP   NYS: TPC

15901 Olden Street
Sylmar, CA 91342-1093
Phone: 818 362-8391
Fax: –
Web: www.tutorperini.com

CEO: Ronald N Tutor
CFO: –
HR: –
FYE: December 31
Type: Public

Construction company Tutor Perini builds projects ranging from casinos and hotels to highways and housing developments. One of the largest builders in the US, the company also builds schools, healthcare facilities, airports, and industrial buildings. It offers general contracting, pre-construction planning and comprehensive project management services, including the planning and scheduling of the manpower, equipment, materials and subcontractors required for a project. The company also offers self-performed construction services including site work; concrete forming and placement; steel erection; electrical; mechanical; plumbing; heating, ventilation and air conditioning (HVAC); and fire protection. Some 90% of the company's total revenue comes from the US.

	Annual Growth	12/19	12/20	12/21	12/22	12/23
Sales ($mil.)	(3.4%)	4,450.8	5,318.8	4,641.8	3,790.8	3,880.2
Net income ($ mil.)	–	(387.7)	108.4	91.9	(210.0)	(171.2)
Market value ($ mil.)	(8.3%)	669.0	673.7	643.6	392.8	473.4
Employees	(2.6%)	9,100	8,700	7,800	8,100	8,200

TUTOR-SALIBA CORPORATION

15901 OLDEN ST
RANCHO CASCADES, CA 913421051
Phone: 818 362-8391
Fax: –
Web: www.tutorperini.com

CEO: –
CFO: –
HR: –
FYE: December 31
Type: Private

Beneath California's glamour, Tutor-Saliba makes tracks. The construction and civil engineering company offers construction management and design/build services for infrastructure projects. A key player in US transportation construction, it was the lead builder of Los Angeles' subway system and San Francisco's BART extension to the airport. Tutor-Saliba is also known for its California public works projects, including the Los Angeles Central Library and the San Francisco Main Post Office. The company has completed more than $15 billion in completed projects since it was founded over 50 years ago. The company merged with Perini Corporation in 2008 to form the Tutor Perini Corporation.

	Annual Growth	12/10	12/11	12/12	12/13	12/14
Sales ($mil.)	(13.6%)	–	–	–	98.2	84.8
Net income ($ mil.)	(50.5%)	–	–	–	5.7	2.8
Market value ($ mil.)	–	–	–	–	–	–
Employees	–	–	–	–	–	1,200

TWILIO INC   NYS: TWLO

101 Spear Street, Fifth Floor
San Francisco, CA 94105
Phone: 415 390-2337
Fax: –
Web: www.twilio.com

CEO: Khozema Shipchandler
CFO: Aidan Viggiano
HR: –
FYE: December 31
Type: Public

Twilio offers a customer engagement platform with software designed to address specific use cases, like account security and contact centers, and a set of Application Programming Interfaces (APIs) that handles the higher-level communication logic needed for nearly every type of customer engagement. These APIs are focused on the business challenges that a developer is looking to address, allowing its customers to more quickly and easily build better ways to engage with their customers throughout their journey. The US generates some 65% of total revenue.

	Annual Growth	12/19	12/20	12/21	12/22	12/23
Sales ($mil.)	38.3%	1,134.5	1,761.8	2,841.8	3,826.3	4,153.9
Net income ($ mil.)	–	(307.1)	(491.0)	(949.9)	(1,256.1)	(1,015.4)
Market value ($ mil.)	(6.3%)	17,882	61,589	47,914	8,908.1	13,804
Employees	19.2%	2,905	4,629	7,867	8,156	5,867

TWIN CITIES PUBLIC TELEVISION, INC.

172 4TH ST E
SAINT PAUL, MN 551011447
Phone: 651 222-1717
Fax: –
Web: www.tpt.org

CEO: Jim Pagliarini
CFO: Jennifer Schmidt
HR: –
FYE: August 31
Type: Private

Twin Cities Public Television (TPT) serves the Minneapolis-Saint Paul (Minnesota) community with national and local public television programming. TPT produces original programming, such as the Emmy-winning documentary The Forgetting: A Portrait of Alzheimer's ; DragonflyTV , a science show for kids; and popular public affairs program Almanac . TPT operates a half dozen digital stations, in addition to analog channels tpt2 and tpt17. Revenues come from viewer support, PBS and CPB grants, as well as gifts from corporations and foundations..

	Annual Growth	08/18	08/19	08/20	08/21	08/22
Sales ($mil.)	11.5%	–	44.7	–	49.6	62.0
Net income ($ mil.)	–	–	(1.7)	–	6.5	21.0
Market value ($ mil.)	–	–	–	–	–	–
Employees	–	–	–	–	–	180

TWIN COUNTY COMMUNITY FOUNDATION

1117 E STUART DR STE 145
GALAX, VA 243332656
Phone: 276 236-8181
Fax: –
Web: www.tcrh.org

CEO: –
CFO: –
HR: Leslie Bowers
FYE: September 30
Type: Private

Twin County Regional Healthcare provides a variety of medical services to residents in Virginia. Its hospital offers specialized services such as emergency medicine, obstetrics, rehabilitation, and cardiac care. The health care center, which has more than 140 beds, also provides home health and hospice services, as well as wellness and behavioral health centers. Its emergency department treats some 16,300 patients each year.

	Annual Growth	09/15	09/16	09/17	09/18	09/21
Sales ($mil.)	260.3%	–	0.0	50.3	48.8	54.8
Net income ($ mil.)	21.2%	–	0.0	(3.3)	(4.4)	0.1
Market value ($ mil.)	–	–	–	–	–	–
Employees	–	–	–	–	–	659

TWIN DISC INCORPORATED

NMS: TWIN

222 East Erie Street, Suite 400
Milwaukee, WI 53202
Phone: 262 638-4000
Fax: 262 638-4481
Web: www.twindisc.com

CEO: John H Batten
CFO: Jeffrey S Knutson
HR: –
FYE: June 30
Type: Public

Twin Disc designs, manufactures, and sells heavy-duty power transmission equipment for the marine and off-highway vehicle markets. Its lineup includes marine transmissions, propellers and boat management systems, power-shift transmissions, hydraulic torque converters, power take-offs, and industrial clutches and control systems. The company sells its products to customers primarily in the pleasure craft, commercial and military marine markets, as well as in the energy and natural resources, government, and industrial markets. Twin Disc markets its products through both a direct sales force and a distributor network. About 35% of the company's sales came from its customer in the US market.

	Annual Growth	06/19	06/20	06/21	06/22	06/23
Sales ($mil.)	(2.2%)	302.7	246.8	218.6	242.9	277.0
Net income ($ mil.)	(0.7%)	10.7	(39.8)	(29.7)	8.1	10.4
Market value ($ mil.)	(7.1%)	208.7	76.6	196.6	125.2	155.6
Employees	(4.1%)	873	806	743	761	739

TWIN VEE POWERCATS INC

NBB: TVPC

3101 S. US-1
Fort Pierce, FL 34982
Phone: 772 429-2525
Fax: –
Web: www.twinvee.com

CEO: –
CFO: –
HR: –
FYE: December 31
Type: Public

The value-add for ValueRich is to create wealth by bringing small-cap companies and investors together. The company's Web-based platform, magazine, and events are designed to help small-cap companies raise capital, go public, and attract shareholders. Its iValueRich.com site allows investors to directly connect with companies that are seeking investors. ValueRich also manages and holds regular tradeshows, where attendees can highlight their prospects for investment bankers and other potential investors. The company's ValueRich quarterly magazine is distributed free to a select group of executives and investment professionals in the small-cap community. ValueRich was founded in 2003.

	Annual Growth	12/17	12/18	12/19	12/20	12/21
Sales ($mil.)	22.0%	7.1	10.6	10.4	11.1	15.8
Net income ($ mil.)	–	0.4	0.7	0.0	1.1	(1.2)
Market value ($ mil.)	(14.5%)	22.2	15.8	9.3	25.0	11.8
Employees	–	–	–	–	–	–

TWITTER, INC.

1355 MARKET ST STE 900
SAN FRANCISCO, CA 941031337
Phone: 415 222-9670
Fax: –
Web: www.twitter.com

CEO: –
CFO: –
HR: –
FYE: December 31
Type: Private

Twitter is a global platform for public self-expression and conversation in real time. Twitter allows people to consume, create, distribute and discover content and has democratized content creation and distribution. The service has become a key real-time communication platform as major events unfold around the world. Twitter is available in more than 30 languages around the world. The US is its largest market, accounting for more than half of the company's revenues. It makes most of its money from advertisers trying to reach those users.

TWO HARBORS INVESTMENT CORP

NYS: TWO

1601 Utica Avenue South, Suite 900
St. Louis Park, MN 55416
Phone: 612 453-4100
Fax: –
Web: www.twoharborsinvestment.com

CEO: William Greenberg
CFO: Mary Riskey
HR: –
FYE: December 31
Type: Public

Two Harbors Investment Corp. is ready to double its money. The real estate investment trust (REIT) is managed and advised by (and was founded by) PRCM Advisers, a subsidiary of Pine River Capital Management. The trust primarily invests in agency residential mortgage-backed securities (RMBS) with fixed or adjustable interest rates that are backed by government-supported enterprises Fannie Mae, Freddie Mac, or Ginnie Mae. About a quarter of its mortgage portfolio is made up of non-agency RMBS, such as subprime mortgages, which carry more risk than federally-backed securities but offer higher yields.

	Annual Growth	12/19	12/20	12/21	12/22	12/23
Assets ($mil.)	(22.2%)	35,922	19,516	12,114	13,466	13,139
Net income ($ mil.)	–	324.0	(1,630.1)	187.2	220.2	(106.4)
Market value ($ mil.)	(1.2%)	1,508.9	657.4	595.5	1,627.6	1,437.7
Employees	–	–	–	105	97	466

TYLER TECHNOLOGIES, INC.

NYS: TYL

5101 Tennyson Parkway
Plano, TX 75024
Phone: 972 713-3700
Fax: –
Web: www.tylertech.com

CEO: H L Moore Jr
CFO: Brian K Miller
HR: Dustin Beazer
FYE: December 31
Type: Public

Tyler Technologies is a major provider of integrated information management solutions and services for the public sector. Tyler's has a broad line of software solutions and services to address the information technology (IT) needs of major areas of operations for cities, counties, schools, and other government entities. Tyler provides professional IT services to its clients, including software and hardware installation, data conversion, training, and, at times, product modifications. It also provides outsourced property appraisal services for taxing jurisdictions. In addition, it also provides electronic document filing (e-filing) solutions, as well as digital government services and payment solutions. Tyler has more than 40,000 successful installations across nearly 13,000 locations, with clients in all 50 states, Canada, the Caribbean, Australia, and other international locations.

	Annual Growth	12/19	12/20	12/21	12/22	12/23
Sales ($mil.)	15.8%	1,086.4	1,116.7	1,592.3	1,850.2	1,951.8
Net income ($ mil.)	3.2%	146.5	194.8	161.5	164.2	165.9
Market value ($ mil.)	8.7%	12,688	18,460	22,750	13,635	17,682
Employees	8.0%	5,368	5,536	6,800	7,200	7,300

TYNDALE HOUSE PUBLISHERS, INC.

351 EXECUTIVE DR
CAROL STREAM, IL 601882420
Phone: 630 668-8300
Fax: -
Web: www.tyndale.com

CEO: -
CFO: -
HR: -
FYE: April 30
Type: Private

Christian-focused publisher Tyndale House Publishers publishes fiction, non-fiction, and children's books, as well as bibles. One of its best-selling titles is the novel Left Behind, a fictional account of the apocalypse written by Jerry B. Jenkins. The titles success inspired the Left Behind series of novels, which has sole some 63 million copies, as well as Left Behind comic books, music, and three movies. Tyndale House was founded in 1962 by Kenneth N. Taylor, who wrote The Living Bible in order to translate the old English in the King James Version of the Bible into a more accessible language for his children. Taylor, who died in 2005, named the company after 16th Century English translator William Tyndale.

	Annual Growth	04/14	04/15	04/16	04/17	04/18
Sales ($mil.)	(4.5%)	-	77.9	73.6	70.2	67.8
Net income ($ mil.)	(28.8%)	-	3.6	2.9	0.3	1.3
Market value ($ mil.)	-	-	-	-	-	-
Employees	-	-	-	-	-	259

TYSON FOODS INC

2200 West Don Tyson Parkway
Springdale, AR 72762-6999
Phone: 479 290-4000
Fax: 479 290-7984
Web: www.tyson.com

NYS: TSN
CEO: Donnie King
CFO: John R Tyson
HR: -
FYE: September 30
Type: Public

Tyson Foods is one of the leading food companies and a recognized leader in protein worldwide. Through its wholly-owned subsidiary, Cobb-Vantress, it is one of the leading poultry breeding stock suppliers in the world. The company also offers value-added processed and pre-cooked meats and refrigerated and frozen prepared foods. Its chicken operations are vertically integrated ? the company hatches the eggs, supplies contract growers with the chicks and feed, and brings them back for processing when ready. Tyson's brands include Tyson, Jimmy Dean, Hillshire Farm, Ball Park, Wright, ibp, Aidells, and State Fair. Its customers include retail, wholesale, and food service companies worldwide, although the US accounts for most sales. The company was founded in 1935 by John W. Tyson and grown under four generations of family leadership.

	Annual Growth	09/19*	10/20	10/21	10/22*	09/23
Sales ($mil.)	5.7%	42,405	43,185	47,049	53,282	52,881
Net income ($ mil.)	-	2,022.0	2,140.0	3,047.0	3,238.0	(648.0)
Market value ($ mil.)	(12.3%)	30,331	21,114	27,878	23,471	17,974
Employees	(0.4%)	141,000	139,000	137,000	142,000	139,000

*Fiscal year change

U-HAUL HOLDING CO

5555 Kietzke Lane, Suite 100
Reno, NV 89511
Phone: 775 688-6300
Fax: 775 688-6338
Web: www.amerco.com

NYS: UHAL B
CEO: Edward J Shoen
CFO: Jason A Berg
HR: -
FYE: March 31
Type: Public

AMERCO is North America's largest "do-it-yourself" moving and storage operator, through nearly 21,100 independent dealers and more than 2,100 company-owned centers across the US and Canada. Operating through its principal subsidiary U-Haul International, the company serves customers through rentals of its ubiquitous orange-and-white trucks, trailers, as well as sales self-storage units. AMERCO owns U-Haul-managed self-storage facilities and provides property and casualty insurance to U-Haul customers through Repwest. Its Oxford Life unit provides annuities, Medicare supplement, and life insurance coverage. Most of its revenue are generated in the US.

	Annual Growth	03/19	03/20	03/21	03/22	03/23
Sales ($mil.)	11.7%	3,768.7	3,978.9	4,542.0	5,739.7	5,864.7
Net income ($ mil.)	25.6%	370.9	442.0	610.9	1,123.3	923.0
Market value ($ mil.)	-	-	-	-	-	10,167
Employees	4.0%	30,000	30,000	29,800	32,200	35,100

U-SWIRL INC.

265 Turner Dr.
Durango, CO 81303
Phone: 702 586-8700
Fax: -
Web: -

NBB: SWRL
CEO: -
CFO: Jeremy M Kinney
HR: -
FYE: February 28
Type: Public

This company hopes to have customers circling its frozen yogurt shops. U-Swirl (formerly Healthy Fast Food) operates and franchises a small number of U-SWIRL Frozen Yogurt outlets. The chain offers non-fat frozen yogurt treats available with more than 60 different toppings. U-SWIRL locations operate primarily in Nevada. In addition to its yogurt franchising business, U-Swirl operates two franchised hamburger outlets under the EVOS banner. Before changing its name to U-Swirl in 2011, Healthy Fast Food acquired the global development rights to the U-SWIRL Frozen Yogurt concept in 2008. U-Swirl plans to build the chain through franchising.

	Annual Growth	12/11	12/12*	02/13	02/14	02/15
Sales ($mil.)	41.7%	2.6	2.8	0.6	5.5	7.5
Net income ($ mil.)	-	(0.7)	(0.5)	(0.4)	(2.1)	(0.3)
Market value ($ mil.)	10.1%	6.5	4.4	8.1	18.5	8.7
Employees	24.9%	40	80	88	117	78

*Fiscal year change

U.G.N., INC.

2650 WARRENVILLE RD STE 300
DOWNERS GROVE, IL 605152075
Phone: 773 437-2400
Fax: -
Web: www.ugn.com

CEO: Peter Anthony
CFO: Steve Hamilton
HR: Jennifer Dove
FYE: December 31
Type: Private

Buying a Japanese car? Sounds good. Especially if the vehicle has acoustic molding and other sound-dampening acoustic automotive trim products made by UGN. The company produces molding from a variety of materials, including cotton fiber and foam, for vehicles assembled in North America by US and Japanese auto makers. UGN also makes automotive interior trim and thermal management parts. Its products are used to reduce interior noise and fine tune acoustical signals. The company's clientele has included such heavy hitters as Honda, Nissan, and Toyota. UGN was established in 1986 and is a joint venture between Autoneum and Nihon Tokushu Toryo (Nittoku).

	Annual Growth	12/04	12/05	12/06	12/07	12/08
Sales ($mil.)	1.7%	-	213.9	223.1	239.0	225.0
Net income ($ mil.)	10.3%	-	8.5	13.1	-	11.4
Market value ($ mil.)	-	-	-	-	-	-
Employees	-	-	-	-	-	1,250

U.S. EQUITIES REALTY, LLC

20 N MICHIGAN AVE STE 400
CHICAGO, IL 606024828
Phone: 312 456-7000
Fax: -
Web: www.cbre.com

CEO: Robert A Wislow
CFO: Michael Brim
HR: -
FYE: December 31
Type: Private

U.S. Equities provides commercial real estate brokerage, development, advisory, financing, and management services to clients in the US and South America. The company has developed more than 12.7 million sq. ft. of property (including the headquarters of MB Financial and Compuware, and multiple projects for the University of Chicago). It also manages and leases the second-tallest building in the US, the Willis Tower (formerly the Sears Tower). In addition to commercial real estate, U.S. Equities also manages high-end apartment buildings, student housing facilities, and public housing. U.S. Equities was founded in 1978 by chairman and CEO Robert Winslow and vice chairman Camille Julmy.

U.S. GENERAL SERVICES ADMINISTRATION

1800 F ST NW RM 6100
WASHINGTON, DC 204050001
Phone: 202 501-0450
Fax: -
Web: www.gsa.gov

CEO: -
CFO: Kathleen M Turco
HR: -
FYE: September 30
Type: Private

The U.S. General Services Administration (GSA) manages the rental of almost 364 million square feet of real estate in US government-owned properties. In addition to acting as the government's landlord in obtaining office space for over a million federal workers, the GSA also manages properties and supplies equipment, telecommunications, and information technology products to its customer agencies. It spends around $87.5 billion annually for goods and services supporting about 8,400 buildings and more than 227,000 vehicles. The GSA was established in 1949 to streamline the administrative work of the federal government.

U.S. GEOTHERMAL INC.

6140 PLUMAS ST STE 200
RENO, NV 895196072
Phone: 208 424-1027
Fax: -
Web: -

CEO: Douglas J Glaspey
CFO: Kerry D Hawkley
HR: -
FYE: December 31
Type: Private

U.S. Geothermal likes things bubbling just under the surface. Operating through its Idaho-based subsidiary Geo-Idaho, the company runs geothermal power plants, which use heat from beneath the Earth's surface to generate electricity. Its Idaho plant generates 8 MW of power for Idaho Power; the operation is a joint venture with Goldman Sachs, which contributed about $34 million to plant construction. The Nevada plant produces about 2.5 MW for Sierra Pacific Power. U.S. Geothermal also has exploration and development-stage properties in Oregon, Nevada, Idaho, and in Guatemala. In addition to power generation, the company produces revenue by selling its green energy credits to other power generators (7% of sales).

	Annual Growth	12/13	12/14	12/15	12/16	12/17
Sales ($mil.)	1.2%	-	31.0	31.2	31.5	32.1
Net income ($ mil.)	-	-	14.9	5.0	3.6	(0.5)
Market value ($ mil.)	-	-	-	-	-	-
Employees	-	-	-	-	-	49

U.S. PHYSICAL THERAPY, INC.   NYS: USPH

1300 West Sam Houston Parkway South, Suite 300
Houston, TX 77042
Phone: 713 297-7000
Fax: -
Web: www.usph.com

CEO: Christopher J Reading
CFO: Carey Hendrickson
HR: Brenda Benitez
FYE: December 31
Type: Public

US Physical Therapy (USPH), is one of the largest publicly-traded, pure-play operators of outpatient physical and occupational therapy clinics, with over 640 Clinics in about 40 States. The company's clinics provide preventative and post-operative care for a variety of orthopedic-related disorders and sports-related injuries, treatment for neurologically-related injuries, and rehabilitation of injured workers. In addition to owning and operating clinics, the company manages some 40 physical therapy facilities for unaffiliated third parties, including hospitals and physician groups. The company also has an industrial injury prevention business that provides onsite services for clients' employees including injury prevention and rehabilitation, performance optimization, post-offer employment testing, functional capacity evaluations, and ergonomic assessments. The company was founded in 1990.

	Annual Growth	12/19	12/20	12/21	12/22	12/23
Sales ($mil.)	5.8%	482.0	423.0	495.0	553.1	604.8
Net income ($ mil.)	(8.4%)	40.0	35.2	40.8	32.2	28.2
Market value ($ mil.)	(5.0%)	1,713.8	1,802.3	1,432.1	1,214.4	1,395.9
Employees	5.6%	5,400	4,630	5,500	6,135	6,720

U.S. SHIPPING CORP

399 THORNALL ST FL 8
EDISON, NJ 088372240
Phone: 732 635-1500
Fax: -
Web: -

CEO: Ronald L O'Kelley
CFO: Dennis J Fiore
HR: -
FYE: December 31
Type: Private

U.S. Shipping Corporation (formerly U.S. Shipping Partners L.P.) hopes smooth sailing is in its future. The company provides long-haul marine transport services to US ports, delivering refined and specialty petroleum and chemical products. Its fleet of about a dozen vessels includes tug-barge units and tankers. U.S. Shipping's main customers, which are large oil and chemical companies, have included BP, SeaRiver Maritime (a unit of Exxon Mobil), and Shell. U.S. Shipping exited Chapter 11 bankruptcy protection in late 2009 after voluntarily filing earlier in the year. It was converted from a partnership to a private corporation after emerging from bankruptcy.

U.S. VENTURE, INC.

425 BETTER WAY
APPLETON, WI 549156192
Phone: 920 739-6101
Fax: -
Web: www.usventure.com

CEO: John Schmidt
CFO: Jay Walters
HR: Jenni Molash
FYE: July 31
Type: Private

Privately-held US Venture, Inc. is an innovative leader in the distribution of renewable and traditional energy products, lubricants, tires, parts, and using data-driven insights to manage energy and information in the global movement of goods. The company delivers creative, sustainable solutions that give their customers a competitive edge, and enable the company to support the communities in which they live, work, and play. Through the values lived by their family of brands, US Energy, US AutoForce, Max Finkelstein, LLC, Breakthrough, US Lubricants, US Petroleum Equipment, and IGEN, the company seeks new ways to drive business success while being steadfast in its commitment to making the world a better place.

	Annual Growth	07/11	07/12	07/13	07/14	07/15
Sales ($mil.)	4.9%	-	-	7,346.1	9,088.9	8,076.1
Net income ($ mil.)	91.7%	-	-	47.2	49.3	173.5
Market value ($ mil.)	-	-	-	-	-	-
Employees	-	-	-	-	-	2,160

UBER TECHNOLOGIES INC   NYS: UBER

1515 3rd Street
San Francisco, CA 94158
Phone: 415 612-8582
Fax: -
Web: www.uber.com

CEO: Dara Khosrowshahi
CFO: Nelson Chai
HR: -
FYE: December 31
Type: Public

Uber Technologies Inc. (Uber) is a technology platform that uses a massive network, leading technology, operational excellence and product expertise to power movement from point A to point B. It develops and operates proprietary technology applications supporting a variety of offerings on its platform. Uber connects riders with drivers or independent ride solution providers. The company offers pick up and drop services at airports across continents. The company, through its technology platform, also provides food, meal and grocery delivery services. The company provides freight and logistics services. Majority of its sales come from the US and Canada.

	Annual Growth	12/19	12/20	12/21	12/22	12/23
Sales ($mil.)	27.4%	14,147	11,139	17,455	31,877	37,281
Net income ($ mil.)	-	(8,506.0)	(6,768.0)	(496.0)	(9,141.0)	1,887.0
Market value ($ mil.)	20.0%	61,596	105,628	86,843	51,219	127,520
Employees	3.1%	26,900	22,800	29,300	32,800	30,400

UC HEALTH, LLC.

3200 BURNET AVE
CINCINNATI, OH 452293019
Phone: 513 585-6000
Fax: –
Web: www.uchealth.com

CEO: –
CFO: –
HR: –
FYE: June 30
Type: Private

From its flagship University of Cincinnati Medical Center to its state-of-the-art West Chester Hospital, UC Health provides cancer care, dental care, surgery, transplant, trauma care and women's health. UC Health includes University of Cincinnati Medical Center, West Chester Hospital, Daniel Drake Center for Post-Acute Care, UC Gardner Neuroscience Institute, Lindner Center of HOPE, Bridgeway Pointe, and University of Cincinnati Physicians. The not-for-profit UC Health was formed in 2010 as collaboration between University of Cincinnati Physicians, University of Cincinnati Medical Center and West Chester Hospital.

	Annual Growth	06/08	06/09	06/10	06/17	06/18
Sales ($mil.)	36.3%	–	102.5	138.5	1,586.1	1,661.9
Net income ($ mil.)	–	–	–	(81.4)	73.9	40.9
Market value ($ mil.)	–	–	–	–	–	–
Employees	–	–	–	–	–	10,000

UCH-MHS

1400 E BOULDER ST
COLORADO SPRINGS, CO 809095533
Phone: 719 365-5000
Fax: –
Web: www.uchealth.org

CEO: Mike Scialdone
CFO: –
HR: Janiece McNichols
FYE: June 30
Type: Private

Memorial Hospital tries to keep good health more than a memory for the patients in its care. The hospital is a 520-bed general hospital which provides a range of children's and adult health-care services and specialties, including cardiac care, cancer treatment, trauma care, women's services, pediatric medicine, and rehabilitation. The hospital has about 700 physicians on its medical staff. Memorial Hospital also includes the 100-bed Memorial Hospital North and Children's Hospital Colorado, as well as outpatient clinics throughout the Colorado Springs area. In 2012 it became an affiliate of University of Colorado Health.

	Annual Growth	06/15	06/16	06/19	06/20	06/21
Sales ($mil.)	10.6%	–	693.8	1,051.0	1,037.3	1,150.7
Net income ($ mil.)	38.1%	–	25.7	97.6	50.0	128.9
Market value ($ mil.)	–	–	–	–	–	–
Employees	–	–	–	–	–	2,438

UCI MEDICAL AFFILIATES, INC.

1818 HENDERSON ST
COLUMBIA, SC 292012619
Phone: 803 782-4278
Fax: –
Web: www.ucimedinc.com

CEO: Michael Stout
CFO: Joseph A Boyle
HR: Farrar Stewart
FYE: September 30
Type: Private

UCI Medical Affiliates seeks out doctors looking to avoid paperwork. The company provides practice management services to about 60 freestanding medical clinics, mostly in South Carolina. (It has one center in Tennessee.) The clinics operate primarily under the Doctors Care and Progressive Physical Therapy names. UCI provides nonmedical management and administrative services, such as planning, accounting, insurance contracting and billing, non-medical staffing, and other office services. Its Doctors Care locations are urgent care clinics that handle minor emergencies and provide primary care services. Blue Cross and Blue Shield of South Carolina is the company's principal stockholder.

UDR INC

1745 Shea Center Drive, Suite 200
Highlands Ranch, CO 80129
Phone: 720 283-6120
Fax: –
Web: www.udr.com

NYS: UDR
CEO: Thomas W Toomey
CFO: Joseph D Fisher
HR: –
FYE: December 31
Type: Public

UDR (formerly United Dominion Realty Trust) is a self-administered real estate investment trust (REIT) that owns, operates, acquires, renovates, develops, redevelops, disposes of, and manages some 165 multi-family apartment communities with about 55,000 units. Its holdings are primarily located in fast-growing urban markets on both US coasts; about 10% of its income comes from Orange County, California; over 15% from Metropolitan D.C., over 10% from Boston, Massachusetts, and over 5% from Seattle, Washington markets. It has ownership interest in some 9,100 completed or to-be-completed apartment homes through unconsolidated joint ventures or partnerships, including over 6,260 apartment homes owned by entities in which it holds preferred equity investments.

	Annual Growth	12/19	12/20	12/21	12/22	12/23
Sales ($mil.)	9.0%	1,152.2	1,241.2	1,290.8	1,517.4	1,627.5
Net income ($ mil.)	24.5%	185.0	64.3	150.0	86.9	444.4
Market value ($ mil.)	(4.8%)	15,365	12,644	19,738	12,743	12,598
Employees	1.1%	1,351	1,271	1,229	1,326	1,410

UFP INDUSTRIES INC

2801 East Beltline N.E.
Grand Rapids, MI 49525
Phone: 616 364-6161
Fax: 616 364-5558
Web: www.ufpi.com

NMS: UFPI
CEO: Matthew J Missad
CFO: Michael R Cole
HR: –
FYE: December 30
Type: Public

UFP Industries is a holding company with subsidiaries throughout North America, Europe, Asia, and Australia that supply products primarily manufactured from wood, wood and non-wood composites, and other materials to three markets: retail, industrial, and construction. UFP is one of the largest domestic buyers of solid sawn softwood lumber in the US. It primarily uses southern yellow pine in its pressure-treating operations and site-built component plants in the Southeastern US. The company has facilities worldwide but generates most of its revenue in the US.

	Annual Growth	12/19	12/20	12/21	12/22	12/23
Sales ($mil.)	13.1%	4,416.0	5,154.0	8,636.1	9,626.7	7,218.4
Net income ($ mil.)	30.1%	179.7	246.8	535.6	692.7	514.3
Market value ($ mil.)	26.7%	3,002.2	3,476.0	5,406.0	4,883.5	7,736.5
Employees	7.1%	12,000	12,000	15,000	15,500	15,800

UFP TECHNOLOGIES INC.

100 Hale Street
Newburyport, MA 01950
Phone: 978 352-2200
Fax: –
Web: www.ufpt.com

NAS: UFPT
CEO: R J Bailly
CFO: Ronald J Lataille
HR: –
FYE: December 31
Type: Public

UFP Technologies is an innovative designer and custom manufacturer of comprehensive solutions for medical devices, sterile packaging, and other highly engineered custom products. UFP is an important link in the medical device supply chain and a valued outsource partner to many of the top medical device manufacturers in the world. The company's manufacturing operations consist primarily of cutting, routing, compression and injection, molding, vacuum-forming, laminating, radio frequency and impulse welding and assembling. UFP's cross-linked foams are fabricated by cutting shapes from blocks of foam, using specialized cutting tools, routers, water jets, and hot wire equipment. In 2022, UFP sells molded fiber business and related real estate in Iowa to CKF, Inc. for approximately $32 million.

	Annual Growth	12/19	12/20	12/21	12/22	12/23
Sales ($mil.)	19.2%	198.4	179.4	206.3	353.8	400.1
Net income ($ mil.)	22.8%	19.8	13.4	15.9	41.8	44.9
Market value ($ mil.)	36.5%	379.0	356.0	536.8	900.7	1,314.3
Employees	–	1,154	1,010	2,015	2,968	–

UGI CORP.   NYS: UGI

500 North Gulph Road
King of Prussia, PA 19406
Phone: 610 337-1000
Fax: –
Web: www.ugicorp.com

CEO: Mario Longhi
CFO: Sean P O'Brien
HR: –
FYE: September 30
Type: Public

UGI Corporation is a leading energy products supplier to residential, commercial, agricultural, motor fuel, and wholesale customers across the US and Europe. The company distributes, stores, transports and markets energy products and related services; it also generates some electricity. In the US, UGI serves nearly 1.3 million customers, thanks to its partnership with AmeriGas Partners and several subsidiaries. Its trade names include AmeriGas, America's Propane Company, Propane That's Pro-You, Driving Every Day, Cynch, and Relationships Matter.

	Annual Growth	09/19	09/20	09/21	09/22	09/23
Sales ($mil.)	5.1%	7,320.4	6,559.0	7,447.0	10,106	8,928.0
Net income ($ mil.)	–	256.2	532.0	1,467.0	1,073.0	(1,502.0)
Market value ($ mil.)	(17.8%)	10,531	6,909.1	8,928.7	6,773.0	4,818.4
Employees	(20.3%)	12,800	11,300	5,800	4,700	5,160

UKG INC.

900 CHELMSFORD ST
LOWELL, MA 018518100
Phone: 978 947-2855
Fax: –
Web: www.ukg.com

CEO: Aron AIN
CFO: John Butler
HR: Jonathan Alphin
FYE: December 31
Type: Private

UKG (formerly known as The Ultimate Software Group or USG) is one of the largest cloud companies in the world. As a leading global provider of HCM, payroll, HR service delivery, and workforce management solutions, the company delivers award-winning Pro, Dimensions, and Ready solutions to help tens of thousands of organizations across geographies and in every industry drive better business outcomes, improve HR effectiveness, streamline the payroll process, and help make work a better, more connected experience for everyone. Aerospace and defense, education, finance, government, healthcare, retail, technology, and transportation are the industries it targets. The company helps more than 70,000 organizations across every industry.

ULINE, INC.

12575 ULINE DR
PLEASANT PRAIRIE, WI 531583686
Phone: 800 295-5510
Fax: –
Web: www.uline.com

CEO: Dick Uihlein
CFO: –
HR: Amanda Russell
FYE: December 31
Type: Private

Uline is the leading distributor of shipping, industrial and packaging materials to businesses throughout North America. The family-owned business' over 800 pages catalog contains more than 40,000 packaging and shipping products (such as bubble wrap, corrugated boxes, envelopes, and tape), warehouse supplies (work tables and dock equipment), janitorial products (brooms and cleansers), and retail supplies (bags, merchandise tags, and pricing devices). Uline's operations are supported by about a dozen of distribution centers strategically located throughout the US (including in California, Georgia, and Texas), as well as facilities in Canada and Mexico. The company also markets its products through its website. Uline is owned and operated by the Uihlein family from which it takes its name.

ULTA BEAUTY INC   NMS: ULTA

1000 Remington Blvd., Suite 120
Bolingbrook, IL 60440
Phone: 630 410-4800
Fax: –
Web: www.ulta.com

CEO: Dave C Kimbell
CFO: Scott M Settersten
HR: Susan Jasinski
FYE: February 3
Type: Public

Ulta Beauty operates more than 1,350 stores across the US, making it the premier beauty destination for cosmetics, fragrance, skin care products, hair care products, and salon services. The company offers the widest selection of beauty categories, including prestige and mass cosmetics, fragrance, haircare, prestige and mass skincare, bath and body products, professional hair products, and salon styling tools. In addition to its brick-and-mortar presence in retail power centers, the company operates an e-commerce site that sells items available in stores plus brands available only online. Ulta Beauty was founded in 1990 by former Osco executives Terry Hanson and Dick George.

	Annual Growth	02/20*	01/21	01/22	01/23*	02/24
Sales ($mil.)	10.9%	7,398.1	6,152.0	8,630.9	10,209	11,207
Net income ($ mil.)	16.3%	705.9	175.8	985.8	1,242.4	1,291.0
Market value ($ mil.)	17.2%	12,946	13,519	17,340	24,436	24,420
Employees	6.2%	44,000	37,000	40,500	53,000	56,000

*Fiscal year change

ULTA SALON, COSMETICS & FRAGRANCE, INC.

1000 REMINGTON BLVD STE 120
BOLINGBROOK, IL 604405114
Phone: 630 410-4800
Fax: –
Web: www.ulta.com

CEO: Charles J Philippin
CFO: Scott M Settersten
HR: –
FYE: February 03
Type: Private

Ulta Salon, Cosmetics & Fragrance operates more than 870 beauty stores nationwide. About a third of its locations are in Illinois, Texas, Florida, and California. Ulta stocks more than 20,000 prestige and mass-market products, including cosmetics, fragrances, skin and hair care products, salon styling tools, and accessories. Stores offer hair salon services, as well as manicures, pedicures, massages, waxing, and other beauty treatments. In addition to its brick-and-mortar presence, the company markets more than 20,000 products and more than 500 brand names through its e-commerce site. Ulta was founded in 1990 by Terry Hanson and Dick George.

ULTRA CLEAN HOLDINGS INC   NMS: UCTT

26462 Corporate Avenue
Hayward, CA 94545
Phone: 510 576-4400
Fax: –
Web: www.uct.com

CEO: James P Scholhamer
CFO: Sheri Savage
HR: –
FYE: December 29
Type: Public

Ultra Clean Holdings (UCT) is a leading developer and supplier of critical subsystems, components, parts, and ultra-high purity cleaning and analytical services primarily for the semiconductor industry. The company designs, engineers, and manufactures production tools, modules and subsystems for the semiconductor and display capital equipment markets. Majority of the company's sales were generated outside the US. UCT was founded as a unit of Mitsubishi Metals in 1991.

	Annual Growth	12/19	12/20	12/21	12/22	12/23
Sales ($mil.)	12.9%	1,066.2	1,398.6	2,101.6	2,374.3	1,734.5
Net income ($ mil.)	–	(9.4)	77.6	119.5	40.4	(31.1)
Market value ($ mil.)	9.9%	1,043.6	1,411.6	2,558.3	1,478.5	1,522.6
Employees	10.9%	4,400	4,996	7,066	7,765	6,657

ULTRAGENYX PHARMACEUTICAL INC
NMS: RARE

60 Leveroni Court
Novato, CA 94949
Phone: 415 483-8800
Fax: –
Web: www.ultragenyx.com

CEO: –
CFO: –
HR: –
FYE: December 31
Type: Public

Ultragenyx Pharmaceuticals is a biopharmaceutical company focused on the identification, acquisition, development, and commercialization of novel products for the treatment of serious rare and ultra-rare genetic diseases. The company targets diseases for which the unmet medical need is high, the biology for treatment is clear, and for which there are typically no approved therapies treating the underlying disease. Ultragenyx divides its candidates into four categories: biologics, gene therapy, small molecules, and nucleic acid products. North America generates about 80% of the company's revenue. Ultragenyx was founded in 2010 by the President and Chief Executive Officer, Emil Kakkis, M.D., Ph.D.

	Annual Growth	12/19	12/20	12/21	12/22	12/23
Sales ($mil.)	43.0%	103.7	271.0	351.4	363.3	434.2
Net income ($ mil.)	–	(402.7)	(186.6)	(454.0)	(707.4)	(606.6)
Market value ($ mil.)	2.9%	3,515.7	11,395	6,921.9	3,813.7	3,936.3
Employees	14.6%	740	893	1,119	1,311	1,276

ULTRALIFE CORP
NMS: ULBI

2000 Technology Parkway
Newark, NY 14513
Phone: 315 332-7100
Fax: –
Web: www.ultralifecorporation.com

CEO: Michael E Manna
CFO: Philip A Fain
HR: –
FYE: December 31
Type: Public

Maybe you could sum up Ultralife's business model as PC, as in power and communications, that is. The company's main business is the design and manufacture of rechargeable and non-rechargeable batteries. Accounting for about a quarter of sales, its Communications Systems Division provides such products as amplified speakers and cable assemblies. Ultralife sells its products around the world to OEMs, distributors, and retailers. The company also sells directly to the US and foreign defense departments. Military sales (both directly and indirectly) account for about 50% of Ultralife's revenues.

	Annual Growth	12/19	12/20	12/21	12/22	12/23
Sales ($mil.)	10.4%	106.8	107.7	98.3	131.8	158.6
Net income ($ mil.)	8.4%	5.2	5.2	(0.2)	(0.1)	7.2
Market value ($ mil.)	(2.0%)	120.8	105.8	98.7	63.1	111.5
Employees	(1.7%)	573	532	560	547	536

ULTRATECH, INC.

3050 ZANKER RD
SAN JOSE, CA 951342126
Phone: 408 321-8835
Fax: –
Web: www.ultratech.com

CEO: –
CFO: –
HR: –
FYE: December 31
Type: Private

Ultratech, Inc. is a full-service, prototype to production volume precision sheet metal fabricator providing customers with turnkey sheet metal brackets, chassis, enclosures, racks, and more. This is accomplished through soft-tool manufacturing utilizing CNC laser cutters, turret punch presses, and press brakes. It also offers engineering, welding, spot welding, PEM hardware insertion, polishing, mechanical assembly, and kitting services. It provides its precision sheet metal fabrication and assembly services to a diverse customer base, including OEMs and Contract Manufacturers, located throughout North America, Europe and Asia. The company traces its roots back in 1995.

ULURU INC
NBB: ULUR

4410 Beltway Drive
Addison, TX 75001
Phone: 214 905-5145
Fax: –
Web: www.uluruinc.com

CEO: Vaidehi Shah
CFO: Terrance K Wallberg
HR: –
FYE: December 31
Type: Public

ULURU, named after a giant monolith in Australia, is also a specialty pharmaceutical company that develops and commercializes wound care products. Based on its Nanoflex drug delivery technology, ULURU has developed marketable products, including Altrazeal powder dressing to treat abrasions, burns, donor sites, and surgical wounds and Aphthasol oral paste for canker sores. Using an FDA-approved muco-adhesive thin film technology called OraDisc, ULURU is also developing a line of OraDisc disc and strip products that can be applied directly to the mucosal tissue to deliver medication or active ingredients for canker sores, oral pain, and teeth whitening. It is working with several licensing partners around the world.

	Annual Growth	12/13	12/14	12/15	12/16	12/17
Sales ($mil.)	17.9%	0.4	0.9	0.9	0.4	0.7
Net income ($ mil.)	–	(3.1)	(1.9)	(2.7)	(4.5)	(1.9)
Market value ($ mil.)	(54.5%)	13.9	16.9	3.6	0.8	0.6
Employees	(26.9%)	7	7	5	2	2

UMB FINANCIAL CORP
NMS: UMBF

1010 Grand Boulevard
Kansas City, MO 64106
Phone: 816 860-7000
Fax: 816 860-7143
Web: www.umb.com

CEO: J M Kemper
CFO: Ram Shankar
HR: –
FYE: December 31
Type: Public

UMB Financial is a financial holding company that provides banking services and asset servicing to its customer in the US and around the globe. The company's national bank, UMB Bank offers a full complement of banking products and other services to commercial, retail, government, and correspondent-bank customers, including a wide range of asset-management, trust, bankcard, and cash-management services. The bank operates about 90 banking centers. Loans represent the company's largest source of interest income, with commercial and industrial loans having the largest percentage of total loans. Beyond its banking business, it offers insurance, brokerage services, leasing, treasury management, and health savings accounts. The company also owns a non-bank subsidiary UMB Fund Services that provides fund accounting, transfer agency, and other services to mutual fund and alternative-investment groups.

	Annual Growth	12/19	12/20	12/21	12/22	12/23
Assets ($mil.)	13.5%	26,561	33,128	42,693	38,512	44,012
Net income ($ mil.)	9.5%	243.6	286.5	353.0	431.7	350.0
Market value ($ mil.)	5.0%	3,332.8	3,349.7	5,152.1	4,055.2	4,056.7
Employees	(0.5%)	3,670	3,591	3,529	3,770	3,599

UMH PROPERTIES INC
NYS: UMH

Juniper Business Plaza,, 3499 Route 9 North, Suite 3-C
Freehold, NJ 07728
Phone: 732 577-9997
Fax: –
Web: www.umh.reit

CEO: Samuel A Landy
CFO: Anna T Chew
HR: –
FYE: December 31
Type: Public

UMH Properties (formerly United Mobile Homes) is a real estate investment trust (REIT) that owns and manages more than 120 manufactured home communities containing approximately 23,100 developed lots in New Jersey, New York, Ohio, Pennsylvania, and several other states. The company leases home sites to private homeowners on a monthly basis and rents a small number of homes to residents. Communities offer such amenities as swimming pools, playgrounds, and municipal water and sewer services. The REIT sells and finances manufactured homes through subsidiary UMH Sales and Finance and owns approximately 1,700 acres of land for development. UMH Properties also invests in other REITs.

	Annual Growth	12/19	12/20	12/21	12/22	12/23
Sales ($mil.)	10.8%	146.6	163.6	186.1	195.8	220.9
Net income ($ mil.)	(26.7%)	27.8	5.1	51.1	(4.9)	8.0
Market value ($ mil.)	(0.7%)	1,069.3	1,006.8	1,857.8	1,094.4	1,041.4
Employees	3.4%	420	440	430	460	480

UNBOUND INC

1 ELMWOOD AVE
KANSAS CITY, KS 661032118
Phone: 913 384-6500
Fax: –
Web: www.unbound.org

CEO: Scott Wasserman
CFO: –
HR: –
FYE: December 31
Type: Private

The Christian Foundation for Children and Aging (CFCA) may seem at cross purposes but it helps the poor on both ends of the age spectrum. The lay Catholic not-for-profit organization works in about two dozen countries in Africa, Asia, The Americas and Caribbean. CFCA provides services for children and the elderly in areas such as education, medical care, clothing, and nutrition. It sets up relationships between more than 270,000 sponsors in the US and about 310,000 who need assistance in countries like Bolivia, El Salvador, Guatemala, India, Tanzania, and Uganda. CFCA was founded in 1981 by a group of missionaries including its president Bob Hentzen.

	Annual Growth	12/14	12/15	12/19	12/21	12/22
Sales ($mil.)	1.7%	–	123.5	139.4	145.4	139.3
Net income ($ mil.)	10.3%	–	1.6	6.2	9.9	3.1
Market value ($ mil.)	–	–	–	–	–	–
Employees	–	–	–	–	–	160

UNDER ARMOUR INC   NYS: UAA

1020 Hull Street
Baltimore, MD 21230
Phone: 410 468-2512
Fax: –
Web: www.underarmour.com

CEO: Stephanie Linnartz
CFO: David E Bergman
HR: –
FYE: March 31
Type: Public

Under Armour develops, markets and distributes branded performance apparel and accessories, baby and youth apparel, team uniforms, socks, water bottles, eyewear and other specific hard goods equipment that feature performance advantages and functionality similar to its other product offerings. The company also makes technology that helps customers track their fitness. It sells its products directly to consumers through the company's global network of Brand and Factory House stores and e-commerce websites. The company leases more than 420 brand and factory house stores located primarily in the US, China, Canada, Australia, Korea, Malaysia, and Mexico. Under Armour operates worldwide but generates most of its revenue in North America.

	Annual Growth	12/19	12/20	12/21*	03/22	03/23
Sales ($mil.)	3.9%	5,267.1	4,474.7	5,683.5	1,300.9	5,903.6
Net income ($ mil.)	61.3%	92.1	(549.2)	360.1	(59.6)	386.8
Market value ($ mil.)	(24.0%)	9,601.2	7,632.1	9,419.0	7,565.4	4,218.3
Employees	(2.9%)	16,400	16,600	17,500	–	15,000

*Fiscal year change

UNDERWOOD JEWELERS CORP.

2044 SAN MARCO BLVD
JACKSONVILLE, FL 322073214
Phone: 904 398-9741
Fax: –
Web: www.underwoodjewelers.com

CEO: –
CFO: –
HR: –
FYE: June 30
Type: Private

Because there can't be enough bling in Florida, there's regional player Underwood Jewelers. The high-end jewelry chain operates three stores in the Jacksonville area of Florida which offer the usual mix of jewelry, watches, and collectables, as well as silver serving platters and china dinnerware. Additionally, Underwood offers a bridal registry, and sells collections of diamond, gold, and silver earrings, and baby gifts online. The company was founded as a diamond and watch store in 1928 by namesake Herbert F. Underwood. Bromberg and Co. purchased Underwood in 1974, and although Bromberg family members remain involved in Underwood, the two companies operate seperately.

UNDERWRITERS LABORATORIES INC.

1603 ORRINGTON AVE STE 2000
EVANSTON, IL 602013841
Phone: 847 272-8800
Fax: –
Web: www.ul.com

CEO: Jennifer Scanlon
CFO: –
HR: –
FYE: December 31
Type: Private

UL Solutions, formerly known as Underwriters Laboratory is a global leader in applied safety science delivering testing, inspection, and certification services, together with software products and advisory offerings that support its customer's product innovation and business growth. It offers advisory, auditing and inspection, certification, digital applications, learning and development, testing, and verification services. The company is active in the healthcare, retail, government, industrial, materials and chemicals, energy, and automotive sectors. In addition, its proprietary library of more than 1,500 courses include over 1,000 EHS course titles and over 400 Life Sciences regulatory course titles (many of which are co-developed with the US FDA). William Henry Merrill, Jr. founded the not-for-profit lab in 1894.

	Annual Growth	12/06	12/07	12/08	12/17	12/22
Sales ($mil.)	(34.3%)	–	895.5	994.1	29.7	1.6
Net income ($ mil.)	–	–	160.5	(23.1)	(5.1)	(57.6)
Market value ($ mil.)	–	–	–	–	–	–
Employees	–	–	–	–	–	10,876

UNFI GROCERS DISTRIBUTION, INC.

2500 S ATLANTIC BLVD
COMMERCE, CA 900402004
Phone: 323 264-5200
Fax: –
Web: www.unfi.com

CEO: Jill E Sutton
CFO: Bruce H Besanko
HR: Steve Bourrne
FYE: October 01
Type: Private

This company's unity of purpose helps put groceries on the shelves. Unified Grocers is the largest wholesale grocery distributor in the western US, serving about 3,000 independent grocers, cash and carry outlets, and major grocery chain stores, including Smart & Final . The cooperative operates about a dozen distribution centers that supply its members and nonmember stores with around 100,000 items, including meat, dairy goods, fresh produce, and general merchandise. It offers many national brands, as well as private labels including Cottage Hearth, Golden Cr me, Natural Directions, Special Value, Springfield, and Western Family. Unified Grocers was formed in 1922 as Certified Grocers of California. In 2017 grocery retailer SUPERVALU agreed to acquire the company in a transaction valued at $375 million.

UNICO AMERICAN CORP.   NBB: UNAM Q

5230 Las Virgenes Road, #100
Calabasas, CA 91302
Phone: 818 591-9800
Fax: –
Web: –

CEO: Steven L Shea
CFO: Jennifer E Ziegler
HR: –
FYE: December 31
Type: Public

Unico American helps protect California businesses from a variety of afflictions. Its Crusader Insurance subsidiary provides commercial multiperil property/casualty insurance, including liability, property, and workers' compensation. Sister company Unifax Insurance services Crusader's policies. Unico American subsidiaries also act as agents for non-affiliated insurers, provide claims-adjusting services and premium financing, and market individual and group medical, dental, life, and accidental death coverage. All of its policies are marketed by independent insurance agencies and brokers.

	Annual Growth	12/17	12/18	12/19	12/20	12/21
Assets ($mil.)	(0.7%)	130.3	125.6	130.3	131.9	126.9
Net income ($ mil.)	–	(8.7)	(3.2)	(3.1)	(21.5)	(5.7)
Market value ($ mil.)	(20.4%)	45.4	33.8	33.4	24.1	18.2
Employees	(16.7%)	79	76	72	76	38

UNIDOSUS

1126 16TH ST NW STE 600
WASHINGTON, DC 200364845
Phone: 202 785-1670
Fax: –
Web: www.unidosus.org

CEO: –
CFO: Holly Blanchard
HR: Sonia Guerrero
FYE: September 30
Type: Private

What the NAACP is for African-Americans, The National Council of La Raza (NCLR) is for Hispanic-Americans. A not-for-profit, nonpartisan organization, NCLR promotes and protects the rights of "la raza" or "the race" to experience equal rights, education, gainful employment, affordable housing, and adequate health care in America. NCLR comprises a network of some 300 community-based organizations that provide services such as after-school programs, charter schools, community health and activities centers, English language classes, homeownership counseling, and job training. Headquartered in Washington, DC, NCLR is a voice on Capitol Hill, helping shape policies that promote economic and social equality.

	Annual Growth	09/15	09/16	09/17	09/19	09/22
Sales ($mil.)	12.9%	–	–	32.5	–	59.8
Net income ($ mil.)	–	–	–	0.9	–	(3.1)
Market value ($ mil.)	–	–	–	–	–	–
Employees	–	–	–	–	–	110

UNIFI, INC.

7201 West Friendly Avenue
Greensboro, NC 27410
Phone: 336 294-4410
Fax: –
Web: www.unifi.com

NYS: UFI
CEO: Edmund M Ingle
CFO: Andrew J Eaker
HR: –
FYE: July 2
Type: Public

UNIFI is a global textile solutions provider and one of the world's leading innovators in manufacturing synthetic and recycled performance fibers. Through REPREVE, one of Unifi's proprietary technologies and the global leader in branded recycled performance fibers, Unifi has transformed more than 35 billion plastic bottles into recycled fiber for new apparel, footwear, home goods, and other consumer products. UNIFI collaborates with many of the world's most influential brands in the sports apparel, fashion, home, automotive, and other industries. Polyester products include partially oriented yarn (POY) and textured, solution and package dyed, twisted, beamed, and draw wound yarns, and each is available in virgin or recycled varieties. Nylon products include virgin or recycled textured, solution-dyed, and spandex-covered yarns. UNIFI was formed in 1969. The US is UNIFI's largest market.

	Annual Growth	06/19	06/20	06/21*	07/22	07/23
Sales ($mil.)	(3.2%)	708.8	606.5	667.6	815.8	623.5
Net income ($ mil.)	–	2.5	(57.2)	29.1	15.2	(46.3)
Market value ($ mil.)	(18.4%)	328.5	211.0	447.5	253.5	145.9
Employees	(2.2%)	3,060	2,760	3,110	3,100	2,800

*Fiscal year change

UNIFIRST CORP

68 Jonspin Road
Wilmington, MA 01887
Phone: 978 658-8888
Fax: –
Web: www.unifirst.com

NYS: UNF
CEO: Steven S Sintros
CFO: Shane O'Connor
HR: –
FYE: August 26
Type: Public

UniFirst is one of the largest providers of workplace uniforms and protective work wear clothing in the US. It designs, manufactures, personalizes, rents, cleans, delivers, and sells a wide range of uniforms and protective clothing, including shirts, pants, jackets, coveralls, lab coats, smocks, aprons, and specialized protective wear, such as flame resistant and high visibility garments. The company also rents and sells industrial wiping products, floor mats, facility service products and other non-garment items, and provides restroom and cleaning supplies and first aid cabinet services and other safety supplies as well as certain safety training. Customers include auto service centers, restaurants, transportation companies, and utilities operating nuclear reactors, among other customers. UniFirst also provides first-aid cabinet services and supplies. The company generates the vast majority of its revenue in the US.

	Annual Growth	08/19	08/20	08/21	08/22	08/23
Sales ($mil.)	5.4%	1,809.4	1,804.2	1,826.2	2,000.8	2,233.0
Net income ($ mil.)	(12.8%)	179.1	135.8	151.1	103.4	103.7
Market value ($ mil.)	(2.9%)	3,662.5	3,683.4	4,277.9	3,423.0	3,251.2
Employees	3.4%	14,000	14,000	14,000	14,000	16,000

UNIFORMED SERVICES UNIVERSITY OF THE HEALTH SCIENCES

4301 JONES BRIDGE RD
BETHESDA, MD 208144712
Phone: 301 295-3013
Fax: –
Web: www.deploymentpsych.org

CEO: –
CFO: –
HR: –
FYE: June 30
Type: Private

The Uniformed Services University of the Health Sciences (USU) teaches future military doctors and nurses to care for those in harm's way. Its education and research focus on military and disaster medicine, tropical and infectious diseases, military medical readiness, and adaptation to extreme conditions. Its F. Edward H bert School of Medicine offers a four-year curriculum of 700 hours (longer than most US medical schools). Doctoral and masters degrees are also awarded. Additionally, USU operates a Graduate School of Nursing. Students receive salary and benefits in exchange for a seven-year service commitment; the DoD pays the tuition. About 75% of active duty military medical officers are USU graduates.

	Annual Growth	06/06	06/07	06/08	06/09	06/15
Sales ($mil.)	4.3%	–	–	–	0.0	0.0
Net income ($ mil.)	–	–	–	–	(0.0)	0.0
Market value ($ mil.)	–	–	–	–	–	–
Employees	–	–	–	–	–	1,124

UNIHEALTH FOUNDATION

800 WILSHIRE BLVD STE 1300
LOS ANGELES, CA 900172665
Phone: 213 630-6500
Fax: –
Web: www.unihealthfoundation.org

CEO: David Carpenter
CFO: –
HR: –
FYE: September 30
Type: Private

UniHealth Foundation has discovered that charity begins at home. UniHealth Foundation is what is left of what was once one of California's fastest-growing health systems. After spending some 10 years trying to build an integrated health care delivery system, the company sold its eight hospitals to Catholic Healthcare West, and its CliniShare home health services and ElderMed senior citizens care services to Trinity Care. UniHealth used those assets to begin its second life in 1998 as a grant-making organization with more than $42 million in assets through its Facey Medical Foundation. The foundation focuses on supporting health care education and care for the indigent.

	Annual Growth	09/11	09/12	09/15	09/17	09/22
Sales ($mil.)	8.9%	–	11.6	22.0	19.0	27.1
Net income ($ mil.)	–	–	(7.1)	2.9	1.0	0.8
Market value ($ mil.)	–	–	–	–	–	–
Employees	–	–	–	–	–	8

UNION BANK AND TRUST COMPANY

3643 S 48TH ST
LINCOLN, NE 685064390
Phone: 402 323-1235
Fax: –
Web: www.ubt.com

CEO: –
CFO: –
HR: –
FYE: December 31
Type: Private

Union Bank & Trust, a subsidiary of financial services holding company Farmers & Merchants Investment, operates more than 35 branches throughout Nebraska and in Kansas. As Nebraska's third-largest privately-owned bank, it offers traditional deposit and trust services, as well as insurance, equipment finance, and investment management services. Consumer loans account for the largest portion of the bank's portfolio, followed by commercial real estate and farmland loans. Union Bank also originates business loans and residential mortgages. Affiliate company Union Investment Advisors manages the Stratus family of mutual funds. Another Farmers & Merchants unit, Nelnet Capital, offers brokerage services.

	Annual Growth	12/14	12/15	12/16	12/17	12/18
Assets ($mil.)	7.4%	–	3,351.9	3,595.6	3,836.5	4,149.7
Net income ($ mil.)	28.7%	–	32.2	40.9	45.8	68.5
Market value ($ mil.)	–	–	–	–	–	–
Employees	–	–	–	–	–	650

UNION BANKSHARES, INC. (MORRISVILLE, VT)   NMS: UNB

P.O. Box 667, 20 Lower Main Street
Morrisville, VT 05661-0667
Phone: 802 888-6600
Fax: –
Web: www.ublocal.com

CEO: David S Silverman
CFO: Karyn J Hale
HR: –
FYE: December 31
Type: Public

Union Bankshares is the holding company for Union Bank, which serves individuals and small to mid-sized businesses in northern Vermont and Northwestern New Hampshire through 17 branches; it opened its first office in New Hampshire in 2006. Founded in 1891, the bank offers standard deposit products such as savings, checking, money market, and NOW accounts, as well as certificates of deposit, retirement savings programs, investment management, and trust services. It uses fund from deposits primarily to originate commercial real estate loans and residential real estate loans. Other loan products include business, consumer, construction, and municipal loans.

	Annual Growth	12/19	12/20	12/21	12/22	12/23
Assets ($mil.)	13.9%	872.9	1,093.6	1,205.4	1,336.5	1,468.9
Net income ($ mil.)	1.4%	10.6	12.8	13.2	12.6	11.3
Market value ($ mil.)	(4.1%)	163.9	116.2	134.8	108.5	138.5
Employees	(0.5%)	201	193	194	188	197

UNION CARBIDE CORPORATION

7501 STATE HWY 185 N
SEADRIFT, TX 77983
Phone: 361 553-2997
Fax: –
Web: www.unioncarbide.com

CEO: Fernando Signorini
CFO: Ignacio Molina
HR: –
FYE: December 31
Type: Private

Union Carbide Corporation makes the legos of the chemicals world. The company, a subsidiary of Dow, turns out building-block chemicals such as ethylene and propylene, which are converted into widely used plastics resins, primarily polyethylene. The chemical company is also a leading producer of ethylene oxide and ethylene glycol used to make polyester fibers and antifreeze, respectively. Union Carbide makes solvents and intermediates (such as oxo aldehydes and esters), vinyl acetate monomer, water-soluble polymers, and polyolefin-based compounds.

UNION HEALTH SERVICE INC

1634 W POLK ST
CHICAGO, IL 606124352
Phone: 312 423-4200
Fax: –
Web: www.unionhealth.org

CEO: –
CFO: –
HR: –
FYE: December 31
Type: Private

Union Health Service brings together doctors and patients in the Chicago area. The company is a not-for-profit health care services provider which supplies health insurance to its members through HMO (health maintenance organization) and medical prepayment plans. Union Health Service also provides primary health care, as well as vision, laboratory, radiology, and pharmacy services, to its members through about 20 group practice clinics in Aurora, Chicago, Norridge, Oak Park, and other area communities. The company was established in 1955.

	Annual Growth	12/16	12/17	12/19	12/21	12/22
Sales ($mil.)	3.3%	–	74.2	85.3	88.9	87.1
Net income ($ mil.)	–	–	(1.0)	(1.6)	1.2	3.0
Market value ($ mil.)	–	–	–	–	–	–
Employees	–	–	–	–	–	279

UNION HOSPITAL, INC.

1606 N 7TH ST
TERRE HAUTE, IN 478042780
Phone: 812 238-7000
Fax: –
Web: www.myunionhealth.org

CEO: Steven M Holman
CFO: Wayne R Hutson
HR: Joanne Davignon
FYE: December 31
Type: Private

Union Hospital is the flagship facility of the Union Hospital Health Group, a health care system that serves communities in western Indiana and eastern Illinois. The not-for-profit hospital has about 320 beds, boasts an equal number of physicians, and provides general medical and surgical care, as well as specialty services in areas such as women's health, newborn intensive care unit (Level II), cancer, cardiovascular disease, and sports medicine. It also offers occupational health and physical rehabilitation, as well as medical training programs. Other facilities that comprise the Union system include Union Hospital Clinton, physician practices, specialty clinics, and a home health agency.

	Annual Growth	12/15	12/16	12/17	12/21	12/22
Sales ($mil.)	7.6%	–	416.3	465.1	528.2	647.0
Net income ($ mil.)	–	–	(11.6)	17.2	67.3	64.6
Market value ($ mil.)	–	–	–	–	–	–
Employees	–	–	–	–	–	2,700

UNION OF CONCERNED SCIENTISTS, INC.

2 BRATTLE SQ STE 6
CAMBRIDGE, MA 021383780
Phone: 617 547-5552
Fax: –
Web: www.ucsusa.org

CEO: –
CFO: –
HR: –
FYE: September 30
Type: Private

This UCS isn't full of sun bathing coeds or surfers. It's packed with scientists. The Union of Concerned Scientists (UCS) is an environmental organization that researches air quality, alternative energy sources, food safety and other public health issues, and the impact of global warming and nuclear war. The not-for-profit alliance includes more than 250,000 scientists and other individuals. The UCS publishes reports as well as Catalyst magazine and the Earthwise newsletter. About half of the organization's funding comes from grants and foundations. Faculty and students of MIT founded UCS in 1969 to redirect scientific research to environmental and social problems.

	Annual Growth	09/18	09/19	09/20	09/21	09/22
Sales ($mil.)	7.0%	–	39.7	45.8	64.0	48.7
Net income ($ mil.)	–	–	(1.0)	4.2	19.4	(6.1)
Market value ($ mil.)	–	–	–	–	–	–
Employees	–	–	–	–	–	210

UNION PACIFIC CORP   NYS: UNP

1400 Douglas Street
Omaha, NE 68179
Phone: 402 544-5000
Fax: –
Web: www.up.com

CEO: Jim Vena
CFO: Jennifer L Hamann
HR: –
FYE: December 31
Type: Public

Union Pacific Corporation has been chugging down the track since 1969. Owned by Union Pacific Corporation (UPC), Union Pacific Railroad Company (UPRR) operates almost 56,380 freight cars and nearly 7,340 locomotives. UPRR transports automobiles, chemicals, energy, and industrial, agricultural, and other bulk freight over a system of nearly 32,535 route miles in roughly 25 states in the western two-thirds of the US. It owns about 26,120 route miles of its rail network and operate on the remainder pursuant to trackage rights or leases. Through all of these, the company is able to serve roughly 10,000 customers.

	Annual Growth	12/19	12/20	12/21	12/22	12/23
Sales ($mil.)	2.7%	21,708	19,533	21,804	24,875	24,119
Net income ($ mil.)	1.9%	5,919.0	5,349.0	6,523.0	6,998.0	6,379.0
Market value ($ mil.)	8.0%	110,228	126,953	153,603	126,251	149,755
Employees	(3.2%)	37,483	30,960	32,124	33,179	32,973

UNION PACIFIC RAILROAD CO

1400 Douglas Street
Omaha, NE 68179
Phone: 402 544-5000
Fax: –
Web: www.up.com

CEO: –
CFO: Robert M Knight Jr
HR: –
FYE: December 31
Type: Public

Union Pacific Railroad is the principal operating subsidiary of Union Pacific and is one of North America's largest railroads, providing freight transportation almost 32,535 route miles of track across the western two-thirds of the US. It serves many of the fastest-growing U.S. population centers, operates from all major West Coast and Gulf Coast ports to Eastern gateways, connects with Canada's rail systems, and is the only railroad serving all six major Mexico gateways. Union Pacific Railroad's diversified business mix includes its Bulk, Industrial and Premium business groups.

	Annual Growth	12/02	12/03	12/04	12/05	12/06
Sales ($mil.)	10.5%	–	11,509	12,180	13,545	15,546
Net income ($ mil.)	3.5%	–	1,414.0	617.0	1,036.0	1,570.0
Market value ($ mil.)	–	–	–	–	–	–
Employees	–	–	–	–	49,330	50,379

UNIPRO FOODSERVICE, INC.

2500 CUMBERLAND PKWY SE STE 600
ATLANTA, GA 303393942
Phone: 770 952-0871
Fax: –
Web: www.uniprofoodservice.com

CEO: –
CFO: –
HR: Timothy Moten
FYE: December 31
Type: Private

UniPro Foodservice knows there's strength in numbers. As the largest US food service cooperative, its members include more than 650 independent member companies that provide food and food-related products to more than 800,000 food service customers, including health care and educational institutions, military installations, and restaurants. UniPro provides training, collective purchasing, and marketing materials to all distributors. Its products -- which include dry groceries and frozen and refrigerated foods -- are sold under the brand names CODE, ComSource, Nifda, and Nugget. Suppliers include Kraft Foods, Reynolds Food Packaging, Solo Cup, Tyson Foods, and Unilever Foodsolutions.

	Annual Growth	12/08	12/09	12/10	12/11	12/12
Sales ($mil.)	22.5%	–	–	657.5	881.2	987.1
Net income ($ mil.)	–	–	–	–	–	(0.2)
Market value ($ mil.)	–	–	–	–	–	–
Employees	–	–	–	–	–	140

UNIROYAL GLOBAL ENGINEERED PRODUCTS INC   NBB: UNIR

1800 2nd Street, Suite 970
Sarasota, FL 34236
Phone: 941 906-8580
Fax: –
Web: www.uniroyalglobal.com

CEO: Howard R Curd
CFO: Edmund C King
HR: Irene Chen
FYE: January 2
Type: Public

Invisa develops and manufactures sensors used to ensure safety and security. The company's SmartGate safety sensors are used in traffic and parking control, fence and gate access, and industrial automation safety applications. The sensors are meant to keep doors and gates from closing on people or objects. Invisa's InvisaShield technology is designed to detect the presence of intruders in a monitored zone, such as the area around a museum exhibit. Customer Magnetic Automation Corp., a manufacturer of barrier gates, accounts for nearly 30% of product sales.

	Annual Growth	12/17	12/18	12/19*	01/21	01/22
Sales ($mil.)	(7.5%)	98.1	99.6	91.1	60.2	71.7
Net income ($ mil.)	–	(0.1)	1.2	1.0	(1.2)	(1.7)
Market value ($ mil.)	3.1%	5.5	5.6	2.8	5.6	6.2
Employees	(7.9%)	408	393	337	302	294

*Fiscal year change

UNISYS CORP   NYS: UIS

801 Lakeview Drive, Suite 100
Blue Bell, PA 19422
Phone: 215 986-4011
Fax: –
Web: www.unisys.com

CEO: Peter A Altabef
CFO: Debra McCann
HR: Ashley Stephens
FYE: December 31
Type: Public

Unisys Corporation is a global information technology (IT) services company that delivers successful outcomes for the most demanding businesses and governments. The company provides services that include digital workplace services, cloud and infrastructure services, and software operating environments for high-intensity enterprise computing. Its technology division develops software operating environments and related applications for high-intensity enterprise computing. Unisys is among the largest government IT contractors, serving local, state, and federal agencies, as well as foreign governments. Other key sectors include financial services and transportation. The US accounts for around 45% of sales.

	Annual Growth	12/19	12/20	12/21	12/22	12/23
Sales ($mil.)	(9.1%)	2,948.7	2,026.3	2,054.4	1,979.9	2,015.4
Net income ($ mil.)	–	(17.2)	750.7	(448.5)	(106.0)	(430.7)
Market value ($ mil.)	(17.0%)	811.2	1,346.1	1,407.0	349.5	384.4
Employees	(5.9%)	21,000	17,200	16,300	16,200	16,500

UNIT CORP.   NBB: UNTC

8200 South Unit Drive
Tulsa, OK 74132
Phone: 918 493-7700
Fax: –
Web: www.unitcorp.com

CEO: Philip B Smith
CFO: Thomas D Sell
HR: Phyllis Dutton
FYE: December 31
Type: Public

Unit Corporation is an oil and natural gas contract drilling company. The company also has operations in exploration and productions as well as investments in mid-stream. Through Unit Drilling, it has a drilling of about 20 rigs. The company owns stakes in roughly 4,200 wells. Unit also has a mid-stream business. Its Superior Pipeline subsidiary buys, sells, gathers, processes, and treats natural gas. The company was founded in 1963.

	Annual Growth	12/19*	08/20*	12/20	12/21	12/22
Sales ($mil.)	(6.8%)	674.6	277.0	133.5	638.7	545.5
Net income ($ mil.)	–	(553.9)	(931.0)	(18.1)	60.6	148.4
Market value ($ mil.)	–	–	–	–	311.0	557.1
Employees	(14.8%)	1,054	–	645	788	653

*Fiscal year change

UNITARIAN UNIVERSALIST ASSOCIATION, INC

24 FARNSWORTH ST
BOSTON, MA 022101264
Phone: 617 742-2100
Fax: –
Web: www.uua.org

CEO: –
CFO: Kaitthy Brennan
HR: Dorothy Labranche
FYE: June 30
Type: Private

The Unitarian Universalist Association (UUA) consults and provides resources to more than 1,000 UU congregations located in the US, Canada, and overseas. Each congregation is associated with one of nearly 20 districts. The organization creates religious curricula, produces religious publications, and supports the settlement of professional religious leaders. Each church is independent and self-governing but pledges to help other members of the association in times of need and put forth a theology of compassion, interdependence, and tolerance. The group was formed in 1961 by the combination of the Universalist Church of America (begun in 1793) and the American Unitarian Association (begun in 1825).

	Annual Growth	06/07	06/08	06/09	06/21	06/22
Sales ($mil.)	7.7%	–	5.6	0.0	13.7	15.7
Net income ($ mil.)	–	–	1.2	0.0	(1.9)	(1.1)
Market value ($ mil.)	–	–	–	–	–	–
Employees	–	–	–	–	–	225

UNITED AIRLINES HOLDINGS INC
NMS: UAL

233 South Wacker Drive
Chicago, IL 60606
Phone: 872 825-4000
Fax: –
Web: www.united.com

CEO: J S Kirby
CFO: Michael D Leskinen
HR: –
FYE: December 31
Type: Public

United Airlines Holdings, Inc. (UAL) is a holding company and its principal, wholly-owned subsidiary is United Airlines, Inc. All of the company's domestic hubs are located in large business and population centers, contributing to a large amount of origin and destination traffic. In addition, UAL is a member of the Star Alliance, a marketing and code-sharing group (the largest in the world) that includes several international airlines. The company transports people and cargo throughout North America and to destinations in Asia, Europe, Africa, the Pacific, the Middle East, and Latin America. Majority of its revenue comes from its domestic markets.

	Annual Growth	12/19	12/20	12/21	12/22	12/23
Sales ($mil.)	5.6%	43,259	15,355	24,634	44,955	53,717
Net income ($ mil.)	(3.4%)	3,009.0	(7,069.0)	(1,964.0)	737.0	2,618.0
Market value ($ mil.)	(17.3%)	28,895	14,187	14,361	12,366	13,534
Employees	1.8%	96,000	74,400	84,100	92,800	103,300

UNITED AIRLINES, INC.

233 S WACKER DR
CHICAGO, IL 606066462
Phone: 872 825-4000
Fax: –
Web: www.unitedgroundexpress.com

CEO: –
CFO: –
HR: –
FYE: December 31
Type: Private

United Airlines is a leading passenger and cargo airline operating more than 4,800 flights a day to more than 350 airports. It serves destinations across five continents from US hubs in Newark, Chicago, Denver, Houston, Los Angeles, San Francisco, Washington, DC, and the US island of Guam. The airline, which also offers regional services via subsidiary United Express, operates a fleet of more than 1,300 aircraft. In addition, United is a member of the Star Alliance, a marketing and code-sharing group (the largest in the world) that includes several international airlines. United is a subsidiary of United Continental Holdings.

UNITED APPLE SALES, LLC

99 WEST AVE
LYNDONVILLE, NY 140989744
Phone: 585 765-2460
Fax: –
Web: www.unitedapplesales.com

CEO: –
CFO: –
HR: –
FYE: June 30
Type: Private

United Apple Sales (UAS) is a leading supplier of fresh fruit in the US. It primarily distributes apples under the America's Fruit label from growers in Michigan, New York, Pennsylvania, Virginia, and Washington to fresh produce buyers throughout the country. Its products include Empire, Red Delicious, Pink Lady, and Macintosh varieties. The company also distributes produce (pears and and other stone fruits) harvested in South America. The company is owned by president Ward Dobbins, who also controls apple packhouse H. H. Dobbins.

	Annual Growth	06/15	06/16	06/17	06/18	06/19
Sales ($mil.)	4.3%	–	21.5	20.3	23.7	24.4
Net income ($ mil.)	5.5%	–	0.6	0.4	0.7	0.7
Market value ($ mil.)	–	–	–	–	–	–
Employees	–	–	–	–	–	4

UNITED BANCORP, INC. (MARTINS FERRY, OH)
NAS: UBCP

201 South Fourth Street
Martins Ferry, OH 43935-0010
Phone: 740 633-0445
Fax: 740 633-1448
Web: www.unitedbancorp.com

CEO: Scott A Everson
CFO: Randall M Greenwood
HR: Seth Abraham
FYE: December 31
Type: Public

United Bancorp is the holding company of Ohio's Citizens Savings Bank, which operates as Citizens Savings Bank and The Community Bank. The bank divisions together operate some 20 branches, offering deposit and lending products including savings and checking accounts, commercial and residential mortgages, and consumer installment loans. Commercial loans and mortgages combined account for about 60% of the company's loan portfolio. In 2008 Citizens Savings Bank acquired the deposits of three failed banking offices from the FDIC.

	Annual Growth	12/19	12/20	12/21	12/22	12/23
Assets ($mil.)	4.6%	685.7	693.4	724.5	757.4	819.4
Net income ($ mil.)	7.1%	6.8	8.0	9.5	8.7	9.0
Market value ($ mil.)	(2.7%)	81.5	75.2	95.0	83.9	73.2
Employees	(1.2%)	132	132	144	142	126

UNITED BANCSHARES INC. (OH)
NBB: UBOH

105 Progressive Drive
Columbus Grove, OH 45830
Phone: 419 659-2141
Fax: –
Web: www.theubank.com

CEO: Brian D Young
CFO: Stacy A Cox
HR: –
FYE: December 31
Type: Public

United Bancshares is a blend of checks and (account) balances. The institution is the holding company for The Union Bank Company, a community bank serving northwestern Ohio through about a dozen branches. The commercial bank offers such retail services and products as checking and savings accounts, NOW and money market accounts, IRAs, and CDs. It uses funds from deposits to write commercial loans (about half of its lending portfolio), residential mortgages, agriculture loans, and consumer loans. The Union Bank Company was originally established in 1904.

	Annual Growth	12/18	12/19	12/20	12/21	12/22
Assets ($mil.)	7.0%	830.3	880.0	978.5	1,076.6	1,087.3
Net income ($ mil.)	8.3%	8.2	10.7	13.8	13.6	11.3
Market value ($ mil.)	(1.7%)	63.1	71.6	80.2	96.3	59.0
Employees	4.2%	179	217	222	211	211

UNITED BANKSHARES INC
NMS: UBSI

300 United Center, 500 Virginia Street, East
Charleston, WV 25301
Phone: 304 424-8716
Fax: –
Web: www.ubsi-inc.com

CEO: Richard M Adams Jr
CFO: W M Tatterson
HR: –
FYE: December 31
Type: Public

United Bankshares is the parent company of its banking subsidiary United Bank, which comprises nearly 250 full-service banking offices in Virginia, West Virginia, Maryland, North Carolina, South Carolina, Ohio, and Pennsylvania, as well as Washington, D.C., where it is the largest community bank in the D.C. Metropolitan region. The bank offers a full range of commercial and retail banking services and products. United also owns nonbank subsidiaries which engage in other community banking services such as asset management, real property title insurance, financial planning, mortgage banking, and brokerage services. The company has about $29.49 billion in total assets.

	Annual Growth	12/19	12/20	12/21	12/22	12/23
Assets ($mil.)	11.1%	19,662	26,184	29,329	29,489	29,926
Net income ($ mil.)	8.9%	260.1	289.0	367.7	379.6	366.3
Market value ($ mil.)	(0.7%)	5,217.1	4,372.3	4,896.0	5,464.1	5,067.3
Employees	4.6%	2,204	3,051	2,966	2,765	2,635

UNITED BRASS WORKS, INC.

714 S MAIN ST
RANDLEMAN, NC 273172100
Phone: 336 498-2661
Fax: –
Web: www.ubw.com

CEO: Michael Berkelhammer
CFO: Anthony Forman
HR: –
FYE: December 31
Type: Private

Bold as brass, United Brass Works manufactures steam valves and components, primarily for steam equipment. The company's main customers are in the dry cleaning and laundry equipment, electrical apparatus, fire protection, and steam boiler markets. United Brass Works' Keystone Foundry manufactures pressure-tight brass sand castings for OEMs across the US, and it offers pattern and tool services for repair, maintenance, and modifications. United Brass Works also provides custom-designed products, as well as in-house engineering, design, and prototyping services. The company was founded in 1910 in New York City.

	Annual Growth	12/05	12/06	12/07	12/08	12/12
Sales ($mil.)	(67.2%)	–	–	19.8	20.9	0.0
Net income ($ mil.)	(68.2%)	–	–	3.3	1.3	0.0
Market value ($ mil.)	–	–	–	–	–	–
Employees	–	–	–	–	–	174

UNITED CEREBRAL PALSY ASSOCIATIONS OF NEW YORK STATE, INC.

40 RECTOR ST FL 15
NEW YORK, NY 100061722
Phone: 212 947-5770
Fax: –
Web: www.cpofnys.org

CEO: Susan Constantino
CFO: Thomas Mandelkow
HR: –
FYE: June 30
Type: Private

Cerebral Palsy Associations of New York State (CP of NYS) provides health care services for people suffering with cerebral palsy and other developmental disabilities. The organization includes 24 associations that provide day treatment programs, community dwelling access, and at-home residential support, as well as early childhood, mental health, and transportation services. Serving more than 100,000 patients throughout the state, it also acts as an advocate for its patients through legislative involvement. CP of NYS was founded in 1946 by parents seeking health and advocacy services for their children. The organization provides services directly to patients.

	Annual Growth	06/14	06/15	06/20	06/21	06/22
Sales ($mil.)	11.5%	–	115.5	210.4	203.4	246.8
Net income ($ mil.)	48.3%	–	0.3	0.0	0.7	4.6
Market value ($ mil.)	–	–	–	–	–	–
Employees	–	–	–	–	–	1,700

UNITED COMMUNITY BANKS INC (BLAIRSVILLE, GA)   NMS: UCBI

125 Highway 515 East
Blairsville, GA 30512
Phone: 706 781-2265
Fax: –
Web: www.ucbi.com

CEO: H L Harton
CFO: Jefferson L Harralson
HR: –
FYE: December 31
Type: Public

United Community Banks is the holding company for United Community Bank (UCB). UCB provides consumer and business banking products and services through some 195 branches across Florida, Georgia, North Carolina, Tennessee, and South Carolina. Approximately 75% of its loan portfolio consisted of commercial loans, including commercial and industrial, equipment financing, commercial construction and commercial real estate mortgage loans. The company also has a mortgage lending division, and provides insurance through its United Community Insurance Services subsidiary. The company has some $24.2 billion in assets.

	Annual Growth	12/19	12/20	12/21	12/22	12/23
Assets ($mil.)	20.6%	12,916	17,794	20,947	24,009	27,297
Net income ($ mil.)	0.2%	185.7	164.1	269.8	277.5	187.5
Market value ($ mil.)	(1.3%)	3,675.0	3,384.7	4,277.2	4,022.5	3,482.2
Employees	7.8%	2,309	2,406	2,921	3,046	3,121

UNITED DAIRY FARMERS, INC

3955 MONTGOMERY RD
CINCINNATI, OH 452123798
Phone: 513 396-8700
Fax: –
Web: www.udfinc.com

CEO: Brad Lindner
CFO: Marilyn Mitchell
HR: –
FYE: December 31
Type: Private

United Dairy Farmers remembers when milk was delivered to the door. Founded by Carl H. Lindner, Sr., United Dairy Farmers (UDF) changed that by launching Cincinnati's first cash-and-carry retail dairy store in 1940. UDF buys milk from area dairy farmers, then processes and packages it for sale. The company has grown into a chain of about 200 convenience stores, located mostly in Ohio, but also in Kentucky and southeast Indiana. It also operates a wholesale ice cream business. Owned and run by the Lindner family, UDF retails its own milk products, Homemade Brand ice cream and frozen desserts, and several other food items. UDF locations also offer in-store ice cream parlors and distribute Mobil-brand gas.

UNITED DAIRYMEN OF ARIZONA

2008 S HARDY DR
TEMPE, AZ 852821211
Phone: 480 966-7211
Fax: –
Web: www.uda.coop

CEO: –
CFO: –
HR: –
FYE: September 30
Type: Private

Its name says it all: United Dairymen of Arizona (UDA) is a group of Arizona-based dairy farmers united together to stabilize and strengthen the market for milk products. Supplied by some 90-member producers, the cooperative's plant has the capacity to process 10 million pounds of milk per day, about 90% of the milk in the state. Products include sweet cream and butter, fluid and condensed skim milk, and non-fat dry milk, among others. Customers include onsite cheese maker Schreiber Foods, fluid milk processors, and supermarket chains throughout The Grand Canyon State. UDA also makes dried lactose powder for food manufacturers. Started in 1960, the co-op was formed through a merger of two dairy associations.

	Annual Growth	09/07	09/08	09/09	09/10	09/11
Sales ($mil.)	0.8%	–	–	812.2	612.6	825.8
Net income ($ mil.)	203.7%	–	–	2.3	12.3	21.3
Market value ($ mil.)	–	–	–	–	–	–
Employees	–	–	–	–	–	190

UNITED ELECTRIC SUPPLY COMPANY, INC.

10 BELLECOR DR
NEW CASTLE, DE 197201763
Phone: 800 322-3374
Fax: –
Web: www.westwayelectricsupply.com

CEO: George Vorwick
CFO: –
HR: Lindsey Cropper
FYE: December 31
Type: Private

United Electric Supply Co. Inc. is a nationally recognized, 100% employee-owned company that is a major supplier of electrical products, and advanced services for the construction and industrial markets. The company offers a full range of electrical products and services with concentrations in industrial automation, building automation, lighting, wire/cable/conduit, distribution and control, data communications, electro-mechanical, and energy solutions. United was founded in 1965 as a general-line distributor of electrical supplies to local industrial, commercial, and construction customers in Delaware.

	Annual Growth	12/17	12/18	12/19	12/20	12/21
Sales ($mil.)	3.4%	–	221.4	223.7	194.3	244.5
Net income ($ mil.)	5.8%	–	5.2	5.7	6.4	6.2
Market value ($ mil.)	–	–	–	–	–	–
Employees	–	–	–	–	–	343

UNITED FARMERS COOPERATIVE

705 E 4TH ST
WINTHROP, MN 553962362
Phone: 507 237-2281
Fax: –
Web: www.ufcmn.com

CEO: Jeff Nielsen
CFO: Lorie Reinarts
HR: Cheri Lebrun
FYE: August 31
Type: Private

United Farmers Cooperative has it all altogether. The agricultural cooperative supplies products and services to its members through 17 locations in eight rural communities across Minnesota. The farmer-owned co-op offers farm supplies such as energy, feed, seed, fertilizer, grain milling and blending, and farm machinery, as well as construction, finance, insurance, and repair services. Originally known as the Cooperative Creamery Association, United Farmers Cooperative (UFC) has been helping farmers in central Minnesota since 1915 (the creamery division was sold to Mid America Dairies in 1969).

	Annual Growth	08/03	08/04	08/05	08/06	08/07
Sales ($mil.)	33.0%	–	–	72.0	93.9	127.4
Net income ($ mil.)	4.5%	–	–	2.2	1.4	2.4
Market value ($ mil.)	–	–	–	–	–	–
Employees	–	–	–	–	–	269

UNITED FIRE GROUP, INC.

NMS: UFCS

118 Second Avenue S.E.
Cedar Rapids, IA 52401
Phone: 319 399-5700
Fax: –
Web: www.ufginsurance.com

CEO: –
CFO: –
HR: –
FYE: December 31
Type: Public

The United Fire Group (UFG) through its subsidiaries and affiliates, is engaged in the business of writing property and casualty insurance through a network of independent agencies. Some of its subsidiaries include United Fire & Casualty Company, an Iowa property and casualty insurer; Addison Insurance Company, an Iowa property and casualty insurer; Lafayette Insurance Company, a Louisiana property and casualty insurer; and Franklin Insurance Company, a Pennsylvania property and casualty insurer. UFG's more than 1,100 workforce delivers exceptional protection and service to its thousands of policyholders in every region of the US. Founded in 1946, UFG is currently licensed as a property and casualty insurer in 50 states, plus the District of Columbia.

	Annual Growth	12/19	12/20	12/21	12/22	12/23
Assets ($mil.)	1.1%	3,013.5	3,069.7	3,012.7	2,882.3	3,144.2
Net income ($ mil.)	–	14.8	(112.7)	80.6	15.0	(29.7)
Market value ($ mil.)	(17.6%)	1,105.1	634.3	586.0	691.4	508.4
Employees	(7.9%)	1,185	1,165	1,086	1,091	852

UNITED GILSONITE LABORATORIES, INC.

1396 JEFFERSON AVE
DUNMORE, PA 185092425
Phone: 570 344-1202
Fax: –
Web: www.ugl.com

CEO: James Tate
CFO: James Hartman
HR: –
FYE: December 31
Type: Private

United Gilsonite Laboratories (UGL) prevents leaky roofs and warped decks. The company manufactures paint and wood and masonry finishing products including cement paints, caulking compounds, wall patching materials, and waterproofing products. Its brand names include DRYLOK and ZAR. Founded in 1932 by Gerald Payne, UGL has four manufacturing centers in Illinois, Mississippi, Nevada, and Pennsylvania. It sells more than 80 products through 15,000 dealers, including hardware stores and home repair centers, paint stores and lumber merchants in the US and internationally.

	Annual Growth	12/11	12/12	12/13	12/14	12/15
Sales ($mil.)	6.9%	–	45.0	47.8	48.8	55.1
Net income ($ mil.)	–	–	(0.1)	1.0	(10.0)	3.4
Market value ($ mil.)	–	–	–	–	–	–
Employees	–	–	–	–	–	149

UNITED HARDWARE DISTRIBUTING CO

5005 NATHAN LN N
PLYMOUTH, MN 554423208
Phone: 763 559-1800
Fax: –
Web: newsite.unitedhardware.com

CEO: Chad Ruth
CFO: –
HR: –
FYE: November 30
Type: Private

United Hardware Distributing is in the business of building relationships. The member-owned distributor delivers hammers, nails, and all the other hardware necessities to dealers in 18 states across the central US. The company is not a franchiser, but it provides retail support, education, buying markets, and consulting services to its members. In addition to providing hardware, United Hardware offers expertise in accounting, store design, pricing, marketing, purchasing, and merchandising. Its client list of about 1,200 member stores include Hardware Hank, Trustworthy Hardware, Golden Rule Lumber, Ranch & Pet Supply, and other independent retailers.

	Annual Growth	11/07	11/08	11/09	11/10	11/11
Sales ($mil.)	2.6%	–	–	180.0	178.9	189.6
Net income ($ mil.)	22.7%	–	–	3.9	4.0	5.9
Market value ($ mil.)	–	–	–	–	–	–
Employees	–	–	–	–	–	330

UNITED HEALTH SERVICES HOSPITALS, INC.

1042 MITCHELL AVE
BINGHAMTON, NY 139031617
Phone: 607 762-2200
Fax: –
Web: www.nyuhs.org

CEO: –
CFO: –
HR: –
FYE: September 30
Type: Private

United Health Services Hospitals (UHS Hospitals) can service injuries from a slip in the snow or a slipped disc to health that's just plain slipping. The organization operates Binghamton General Hospital (about 200 beds), Wilson Medical Center (some 280 beds), and a group of primary and specialty care clinics in upstate New York. Specialty services include cardiology, dialysis, neurology, rehabilitation, pediatrics, and psychiatry. The Wilson Medical Center serves as a teaching hospital offering residency and fellowship programs. UHS Hospitals is a subsidiary of United Health Services, which operates a network of affiliated hospitals, clinics, long-term care centers, and home health agencies in the region.

	Annual Growth	12/18	12/19	12/20	12/21*	09/22
Sales ($mil.)	(4.7%)	–	732.7	753.8	792.2	633.5
Net income ($ mil.)	–	–	32.8	(1.4)	46.0	(13.0)
Market value ($ mil.)	–	–	–	–	–	–
Employees	–	–	–	–	–	5,000

*Fiscal year change

UNITED HEALTH SERVICES, INC.

1042 MITCHELL AVE
BINGHAMTON, NY 139031678
Phone: 607 762-3024
Fax: –
Web: www.nyuhs.org

CEO: Mathew Salanger
CFO: –
HR: –
FYE: December 31
Type: Private

United Health Services (UHS) is a regional health system in upstate New York. The not-for-profit health care network includes seven divisions: Chenango Memorial Hospital, Delaware Valley Hospital, Senior Living at Ideal, UHS Home Care, UHS Primary Care, Binghamton General Hospital, and Wilson Regional Medical Center. The latter three make up the UHS Hospitals subsidiary. All together, the system has almost 920 beds. Among its specialized services are oncology, heart care, neurology, orthopedics, diagnostics, and emergency medicine. Other services include care centers for children and families, home health care providers, and an independent and assisted-living center for senior citizens.

	Annual Growth	12/14	12/15	12/19	12/21	12/22
Sales ($mil.)	1.5%	–	8.7	8.8	10.9	9.6
Net income ($ mil.)	–	–	0.4	(0.9)	0.7	(0.9)
Market value ($ mil.)	–	–	–	–	–	–
Employees	–	–	–	–	–	5,190

UNITED MARITIME GROUP, LLC

1801 SAHLMAN DR STE A
TAMPA, FL 336056002
Phone: 813 209-4200
Fax: –
Web: www.intship.com

CEO: –
CFO: –
HR: –
FYE: December 31
Type: Private

United Maritime joins the forces of three subsidiaries engaged in transporting dry bulk commodities. Operations serve deep-water ports and inland waterways in the US and abroad. The company maintains a dozen ocean-going vessels, and 20 river barges; it also owns a transfer and storage terminal and related logistics services. United Maritime's ocean-going fleet, made up of US-flag vessels, has an overall capacity of some 400,000 deadweight tons (DWT). Handled commodities include coal, grain, petroleum coke, and phosphate. United Maritime, known as TECO Transport prior to December 2007, was sold by its former parent TECO Energy to an investment group led by an affiliate of Miami-based Greenstreet Equity Partners.

UNITED MINE WORKERS OF AMERICA

18354 QUANTICO GATEWAY DR STE 200
TRIANGLE, VA 221721779
Phone: 703 291-2400
Fax: –
Web: www.umwa.org

CEO: –
CFO: –
HR: –
FYE: December 31
Type: Private

The United Mine Workers of America is a bit of misnomer. While the labor union still represents coal miners and clean coal technicians throughout the US and Canada, it also welcomes truck drivers, school board employees, and health care professionals to its 100,000-plus active members and retirees. The group helps members organize for workers' rights, publishes newsletters, lobbies congress, and disseminates information on health, safety, and welfare issues for miners as well as political and economic concerns. The labor union also runs a Career Center in Pennsylvania to train new miners. Founded in 1890, the United Mine Workers of American is affiliated with the AFL-CIO and the Central Labor Council.

	Annual Growth	12/15	12/16	12/17	12/21	12/22
Sales ($mil.)	(7.9%)	–	22.1	31.4	29.3	13.5
Net income ($ mil.)	–	–	(10.4)	5.7	(10.5)	(31.9)
Market value ($ mil.)	–	–	–	–	–	–
Employees	–	–	–	–	–	250

UNITED NATURAL FOODS INC.   NMS: UNFI

313 Iron Horse Way
Providence, RI 02908
Phone: 401 528-8634
Fax: –
Web: www.unfi.com

CEO: –
CFO: –
HR: –
FYE: July 29
Type: Public

United Natural Foods, Inc. (UNFI) is a leading distributor of grocery and non-food products, and support services provider to retailers in the US and Canada. It has about 55 distribution centers and warehouses that supply approximately 250,000 items to more than 30,000 customer locations ranging from some of the largest grocers in the country to smaller independents. It has customers in all 50 states in the US as well as all 10 provinces in Canada. The company offers groceries, supplements, produce, frozen foods, and ethnic and kosher food products. UNFI also markets roasted nuts, dried fruits, trail mixes, granola, natural and organic snack items, and other snack items through subsidiary Woodstock Farms.

	Annual Growth	08/19	08/20*	07/21	07/22	07/23
Sales ($mil.)	9.1%	21,387	26,514	26,950	28,928	30,272
Net income ($ mil.)	–	(285.0)	(274.1)	149.0	248.0	24.0
Market value ($ mil.)	25.2%	492.6	1,161.2	1,937.5	2,486.8	1,212.1
Employees	11.6%	19,000	28,300	28,300	30,300	29,455

*Fiscal year change

UNITED NEGRO COLLEGE FUND, INC.

1805 7TH ST NW STE 100
WASHINGTON, DC 200013187
Phone: 800 331-2244
Fax: –
Web: www.uncf.org

CEO: –
CFO: –
HR: –
FYE: March 31
Type: Private

"A mind is a terrible thing to waste." In this spirit, the United Negro College Fund (UNCF) offers financial assistance to students of color from low- to moderate-income families pursuing a higher education. UNCF, the oldest and largest higher non-profit education assistance program for African-Americans, enables some 60,000 students to attend college each year. About 60% of the students are the first in their families to attend college. UNCF also provides operating funds and IT services to historically black colleges and universities, such as Bethune-Cookman, Morehouse, Xavier, and Voorhees College.

	Annual Growth	03/09	03/10	03/14	03/15	03/17
Sales ($mil.)	(12.2%)	–	197.8	208.5	221.4	79.9
Net income ($ mil.)	–	–	51.3	40.1	50.3	(104.0)
Market value ($ mil.)	–	–	–	–	–	–
Employees	–	–	–	–	–	257

UNITED OF OMAHA LIFE INSURANCE CO.   NBB: UNOM

Mutual of Omaha Plaza
Omaha, NE 68175
Phone: 402 342-7600
Fax: –
Web: www.mutualofomaha.com

CEO: Daniel P Neary
CFO: –
HR: –
FYE: December 31
Type: Public

A subsidiary of mutual insurance giant Mutual of Omaha, United of Omaha Life Insurance tames the wild kingdom of financial uncertainty for its clients. The company offers a range of protection and retirement products to employer groups and individuals, including life insurance, fixed annuities, and related financial products and services in all states but New York (where sister firm Companion Life Insurance Company of New York operates). United of Omaha Life Insurance was founded in 1926 as United Benefit Life Insurance Company.

	Annual Growth	12/97	12/98	12/99	12/00	12/01
Assets ($mil.)	5.6%	9,286.6	10,023	10,748	11,067	11,533
Net income ($ mil.)	(14.7%)	93.4	49.5	55.0	125.9	49.4
Market value ($ mil.)	–	–	–	–	–	–
Employees	–	–	–	–	–	–

UNITED ONLINE, INC.

30870 RUSSELL RANCH RD # 250
WESTLAKE VILLAGE, CA 913627366
Phone: 818 287-3000
Fax: –
Web: www.untd.com

CEO: Jeff Goldstein
CFO: Edward Zinser
HR: –
FYE: December 31
Type: Private

United Online keeps people connected. Through its subsidiaries, the company operates subscription-based social networking websites, including Memory Lane (historic magazines, newsreels, sports highlights, and yearbook moments) and Classmates and StayFriends. It also operates rewards membership program MyPoints and provides Internet access under the NetZero and Juno Online brands and web hosting through MySite. In late 2013 United Online spun off its largest operation, floral retailer FTD. The company was created by the 2001 merger of NetZero and Juno; in subsequent years, it moved to diversify its business in light of a decline in dial-up Internet subscribers. In 2016 B. Riley Financial acquired United Online in a transaction valued at $170 million.

UNITED PARCEL SERVICE INC
NYS: UPS

55 Glenlake Parkway N.E.
Atlanta, GA 30328
Phone: 404 828-6000
Fax: –
Web: www.ups.com

CEO: Carol B Tome
CFO: Brian Newman
HR: –
FYE: December 31
Type: Public

United Parcel Services (UPS) is the world's premier package delivery company and a leading provider of global supply chain management solutions. The company offers a broad range of industry-leading products and services through its extensive global presence. Its services include transportation and delivery, distribution, contract logistics, ocean freight, airfreight, customs brokerage and insurance. UPS operates one of the largest airlines and one of the largest fleets of alternative fuel vehicles under a global UPS brand. The company delivers packages each business day for approximately 1.6 million shipping customers to 11.1 million delivery recipients in over 220 countries and territories. In 2022, UPS delivered an average of 24.3 million packages per day, totaling 6.2 billion packages during the year. The company generates about 80% of its total revenue from the US.

	Annual Growth	12/19	12/20	12/21	12/22	12/23
Sales ($mil.)	5.3%	74,094	84,628	97,287	100,338	90,958
Net income ($ mil.)	10.9%	4,440.0	1,343.0	12,890	11,548	6,708.0
Market value ($ mil.)	7.7%	99,829	143,612	182,789	148,251	134,086
Employees	(1.7%)	495,000	543,000	534,000	536,000	462,000

UNITED PARKS & RESORTS INC
NYS: PRKS

6240 Sea Harbor Drive
Orlando, FL 32821
Phone: 407 226-5011
Fax: –
Web: www.seaworldentertainment.com

CEO: Marc G Swanson
CFO: Jim Forrester
HR: Katie Domes
FYE: December 31
Type: Public

SeaWorld Entertainment is a leading theme park and entertainment company providing experiences that matter and inspiring guests to protect animals and the wild wonders of our world. SeaWorld theme parks offer guests a variety of exhilarating experiences, from animal encounters that invite exploration and appreciation of the natural world, to both thrilling and family-friendly rides, educational presentations and spectacular shows. It also provides guests with special events and concerts, including its Seven Seas Food, Festivals, Sesame Street Kids' Weekends, and Viva La Musica among others. SeaWorld develops a dozen diversified portfolios of theme parks. In addition, the company is also one of the world's foremost zoological organizations and a global leader in animal welfare, training, husbandry, veterinary care and marine animal rescue.

	Annual Growth	12/19	12/20	12/21	12/22	12/23
Sales ($mil.)	5.4%	1,398.2	431.8	1,503.7	1,731.2	1,726.6
Net income ($ mil.)	27.2%	89.5	(312.3)	256.5	291.2	234.2
Market value ($ mil.)	13.6%	2,028.5	2,020.8	4,149.1	3,423.0	3,379.5
Employees	1.9%	15,300	10,500	14,200	15,100	16,700

UNITED PERFORMING ARTS FUND, INC.

301 W WISCONSIN AVE STE 600
MILWAUKEE, WI 53203
Phone: 414 273-8723
Fax: –
Web: www.upaf.org

CEO: Scott Beightol
CFO: –
HR: –
FYE: August 31
Type: Private

The United Performing Arts Fund (UPAF) is a not-for-profit organization that does fund raising work for some 40 performing arts groups in greater Milwaukee and southeastern Wisconsin -- including symphonies and orchestras, ballet and opera companies, theater groups, dance studios, and performing arts schools. Large corporate donations (more than $25,000) make up about a third of UPAF's campaign revenues; other categories of giving include individual donations through company campaigns, private foundations, and special events. The organization was founded in 1966

	Annual Growth	08/18	08/19	08/20	08/21	08/22
Sales ($mil.)	(2.1%)	–	10.3	9.2	9.4	9.7
Net income ($ mil.)	–	–	(0.3)	(1.0)	(0.4)	0.0
Market value ($ mil.)	–	–	–	–	–	–
Employees	–	–	–	–	–	21

UNITED REFINING COMPANY

15 BRADLEY ST
WARREN, PA 163653299
Phone: 814 723-1500
Fax: –
Web: www.urc.com

CEO: John A Catsimatidis
CFO: James E Murphy
HR: –
FYE: August 31
Type: Private

Part of the Red Apple Group family of companies, United Refining Company refines and markets petroleum products in the northeastern US and portions of New York and Ohio. It owns and operates a refinery with which it produces primarily gasoline and distillate fuels, and also various grades of asphalt, kerosene, industrial fuels, LPG, propane, diesel fuel and home heating oil. The company has over 350 retail outlets in Pennsylvania, Ohio, and New York, which include service station/convenience stores, truck stops, restaurants and garages. The locations are branded Kwik Fill / Red Apple Food Marts and Country Fair. United Refining averages approximately 70,000 barrels per day of oil at its facility. The company traces its roots back to 1902.

UNITED REGIONAL HEALTH CARE SYSTEM, INC.

1600 11TH ST
WICHITA FALLS, TX 763014300
Phone: 940 764-3211
Fax: –
Web: www.unitedregional.org

CEO: Phyliss Cowling
CFO: –
HR: –
FYE: December 31
Type: Private

If you take a fall in Wichita Falls, United Regional Health Care System (URHCS) will be there. The health care provider serves the residents of northern Texas through two hospitals that combined have some 500 beds. Specialized services include emergency medicine, cardiac care, diagnostic imaging, surgery, obstetrics, and pediatrics. The health care system also offers cancer treatment, childbirth, wound care, and sleep diagnostic centers. It is the only comprehensive cardiac care facility and only Level II trauma center in the region. URHCS operates a Care Flight Helicopter to get those traumas to care quicker.

	Annual Growth	12/14	12/15	12/16	12/21	12/22
Sales ($mil.)	8.8%	–	299.6	333.3	397.2	539.7
Net income ($ mil.)	17.5%	–	32.6	53.2	89.1	101.0
Market value ($ mil.)	–	–	–	–	–	–
Employees	–	–	–	–	–	1,950

UNITED RENTALS INC
NYS: URI

100 First Stamford Place, Suite 700
Stamford, CT 06902
Phone: 203 622-3131
Fax: –
Web: www.unitedrentals.com

CEO: Matthew J Flannery
CFO: William E Grace
HR: –
FYE: December 31
Type: Public

United Rentals considers itself the largest equipment rental company in the world, operates throughout the US and Canada, and has a limited presence in Europe, Australia and New Zealand. United Rentals deploys $19.61 billion of fleet (original equipment cost) through approximately 1,520 branches, a centralized reservation service and automated online ordering. Its branches are fully integrated through technology, allowing them to collaborate on solving customer needs. Its customer base is a diverse mix of construction and industrial companies, utilities, municipalities, government agencies and others. The US accounts for more than 90% of total sales. The company was founded in 1997.

	Annual Growth	12/19	12/20	12/21	12/22	12/23
Sales ($mil.)	11.3%	9,351.0	8,530.0	9,716.0	11,642	14,332
Net income ($ mil.)	19.9%	1,174.0	890.0	1,386.0	2,105.0	2,424.0
Market value ($ mil.)	36.2%	11,219	15,600	22,353	23,909	38,574
Employees	8.3%	19,100	18,250	20,400	24,600	26,300

UNITED SECURITY BANCSHARES (CA)   NMS: UBFO

2126 Inyo Street
Fresno, CA 93721
Phone: 559 248-4943
Fax: 559 248-5088
Web: www.unitedsecuritybank.com

CEO: Dennis R Woods
CFO: Bhavneet Gill
HR: –
FYE: December 31
Type: Public

United Security Bancshares (unrelated to the Alabama-based corporation of the same name) is the holding company for United Security Bank, which operates about 10 branches, loan offices and financial services offices in central California's San Joaquin Valley. The bank attracts deposits from area businesses and individuals by offering checking and savings accounts, NOW and money market accounts, certificates of deposit, and IRAs. In 2007 United Security Bancshares bought Legacy Bank, which had a single branch in Campbell, California. A year later the company purchased ICG Financial and then formed a wealth management, consulting and insurance division, USB Financial Services.

	Annual Growth	12/19	12/20	12/21	12/22	12/23
Assets ($mil.)	6.1%	956.9	1,092.7	1,330.9	1,299.2	1,211.0
Net income ($ mil.)	6.9%	15.2	9.0	10.1	15.7	19.8
Market value ($ mil.)	(5.9%)	184.2	121.0	139.4	125.5	144.4
Employees	(1.1%)	119	121	119	117	114

UNITED SERVICES AUTOMOBILE ASSOCIATION

9800 Fredericksburg Rd.
San Antonio, TX 78288
Phone: 800 531-8722
Fax: –
Web: www.usaa.com

CEO: Wayne Peacock
CFO: Jeff Wallace
HR: Nydia Rodaniche
FYE: December 31
Type: Public

The United Services Automobile Association (USAA) is a mutual insurance company that serves some 13 million member customers?primarily military personnel, military retirees, cadets or midshipmen, and their families. Its lineup of offerings includes property/casualty and life insurance, banking, discount brokerage, investment management, and real estate services. The company also provides discount shopping (floral, jewelry, and safety items) and travel and delivery services to its members. The company traces its roots back to 1922 when 25 Army officers met in San Antonio and decided to insure each other's vehicles.

	Annual Growth	12/11	12/12	12/13	12/14	12/15
Sales ($mil.)	5.5%	–	20,729	20,971	24,033	24,361
Net income ($ mil.)	(7.1%)	–	2,832.0	2,726.0	3,410.0	2,272.0
Market value ($ mil.)	–	–	–	–	–	–
Employees	–	–	–	–	27,000	28,000

UNITED SPACE ALLIANCE, LLC

3700 BAY AREA BLVD # 100
HOUSTON, TX 770582783
Phone: 281 282-2592
Fax: –
Web: www.unitedspacealliance.com

CEO: –
CFO: –
HR: –
FYE: December 31
Type: Private

United Space Alliance (USA) is a space-race heavyweight; the Houston-based prime contractor has run NASA's 173,000 pound Shuttles -- Discovery, Atlantis, and Endeavour. USA, a joint venture between Lockheed Martin and Boeing, was formed in response to NASA's move to consolidate multiple Space Shuttle contracts under a single entity. It is now wrapping up those contracts. USA has supported mission operations, astronaut and flight controller training, flight software development, Shuttle payload integration, and vehicle processing, launch, and recovery. It also has led training and planning for the International Space Station. USA served the Johnson and Kennedy Space Centers, and Marshall Space Flight Center.

	Annual Growth	12/03	12/04	12/05	12/06	12/07
Sales ($mil.)	(3.2%)	–	–	–	1,920.5	1,859.8
Net income ($ mil.)	14.8%	–	–	–	146.3	168.0
Market value ($ mil.)	–	–	–	–	–	–
Employees	–	–	–	–	–	8,000

UNITED STARS, INC.

1546 HENRY AVE
BELOIT, WI 535113668
Phone: 608 368-4625
Fax: –
Web: www.ustars.com

CEO: Roger W West
CFO: –
HR: –
FYE: December 31
Type: Private

United Stars is the parent company for a group of market leading manufacturers. Founded in 1936, the company and its subsidiaries manufacture a wide variety of precision engineered metal products including stainless steel welded tubing, industrial gears and shafts, electrical copper components, stainless steel and high-alloy castings, and fine-finish precision machined products for a broad-based mix of end markets and industrial applications, including the automotive, food processing, pharmaceutical, chemical/petro-chemical, transportation, electrical equipment, power generation industries. The company is a best-in-class precision metal products manufacturer that maintains an excellent reputation with its customers, which consist of industry leading OEMs and Tier 1 suppliers in diverse end markets.

UNITED STATES ANTIMONY CORP.   ASE: UAMY

P.O. Box 643
Thompson Falls, MT 59873
Phone: 406 827-3523
Fax: –
Web: www.usantimony.com

CEO: John C Gustavsen
CFO: Richard R Isaak
HR: –
FYE: December 31
Type: Public

The products of United States Antimony don't span the alphabet from A to Z, but they do include both antimony and zeolite. The company produces antimony oxide, which is used as a flame retardant in plastics, fiberglass, and textiles and as a color fastener in paint. U.S. Antimony buys most of its raw antimony from China and Canada. The company has begun exploratory mining operations on a property in Mexico. U.S. Antimony also processes zeolite, which is used in animal feed, fertilizer, water filtration, and other applications.

	Annual Growth	12/18	12/19	12/20	12/21	12/22
Sales ($mil.)	5.2%	9.0	8.3	5.2	7.7	11.0
Net income ($ mil.)	(16.3%)	0.9	(3.7)	(3.3)	(0.1)	0.4
Market value ($ mil.)	(4.3%)	61.7	41.0	55.5	53.0	51.8
Employees	(47.3%)	207	177	56	17	16

UNITED STATES BEEF CORPORATION

4923 E 49TH ST
TULSA, OK 741357002
Phone: 918 665-0740
Fax: –
Web: www.ceousbeefcorp.com

CEO: John Davis
CFO: Lori Humphrey
HR: Kim Thompson
FYE: December 31
Type: Private

This company has carved out a sandwich empire in the middle of the country. United States Beef Corporation is the largest franchisee of Arby's fast-food restaurants in the US with more than 365 locations in half a dozen states, mostly in Kansas, Missouri, and Oklahoma. The restaurants, franchised from Arby's Restaurant Group (part of Wendy's/Arby's Group), serve the chain's signature roast beef sandwiches and curly fries, as well as ham, chicken, and turkey subs. Bob Davis and his wife Connie opened their first Arby's in 1969 and founded United States Beef in 1974. United States Beef is now owned by Flynn Restaurant Group.

	Annual Growth	12/11	12/12	12/13	12/15	12/17
Sales ($mil.)	8.7%	–	246.9	256.5	351.1	374.0
Net income ($ mil.)	19.8%	–	7.3	7.9	14.6	18.0
Market value ($ mil.)	–	–	–	–	–	–
Employees	–	–	–	–	–	7,000

UNITED STATES CELLULAR CORP
NYS: USM

8410 West Bryn Mawr
Chicago, IL 60631
Phone: 773 399-8900
Fax: –
Web: www.uscellular.com

CEO: Laurent C Therivel
CFO: Douglas W Chambers
HR: –
FYE: December 31
Type: Public

United States Cellular Corporation (UScellular) provides telecommunications services service to customers with 4.7 million retail connections in portions of more than 20 states. It offers advanced wireless solutions to consumers and business and government customers, including a fast-growing and expansive suite of connected Internet of Things (IoT) solutions and software applications across the categories of monitor and control (sensors and cameras), business automation/operations (e-forms, office solutions), communication (enterprise messaging, back-up router for business continuity services), fleet and asset management, smart water solutions, private cellular networks and custom, and bespoke end-to-end IoT solutions et al. Its offerings also include a comprehensive range of devices such as smartphones and other handsets, tablets, wearables, mobile hotspots, routers, and IoT devices. UScellular's revenue are concentrated in the US.

	Annual Growth	12/19	12/20	12/21	12/22	12/23
Sales ($mil.)	(0.7%)	4,022.0	4,037.0	4,122.0	4,169.0	3,906.0
Net income ($ mil.)	(19.2%)	127.0	229.0	155.0	30.0	54.0
Market value ($ mil.)	3.5%	3,079.6	2,608.7	2,679.2	1,772.3	3,530.9
Employees	(6.0%)	5,500	5,300	4,800	4,900	4,300

UNITED STATES FUND FOR UNICEF

125 MAIDEN LN
NEW YORK, NY 100384999
Phone: 800 367-5437
Fax: –
Web: www.unicefusa.org

CEO: Michael J Nyenhuis
CFO: –
HR: Jevgenija Barone
FYE: June 30
Type: Private

The US Fund for UNICEF is one of about 40 committees in America that raises money for The United Nations Children's Fund (better known as UNICEF, a not-for-profit organization that works for the human rights, protection, and development of children worldwide through education, advocacy, and fundraising. Among its dedicated programs are the five-year, $100 million fundraising campaign for HIV/AIDS prevention and a campaign to protect mothers and newborns from tetanus. The US Fund for UNICEF derives revenue from public support -- through its signature Trick-or-Treat for UNICEF program, gifts, corporate grants, and the sale of greeting cards and educational materials. The organization was founded in 1947.

	Annual Growth	06/15	06/16	06/18	06/19	06/21
Sales ($mil.)	(2.1%)	–	568.3	567.1	539.8	510.7
Net income ($ mil.)	34.8%	–	7.1	19.3	19.0	31.5
Market value ($ mil.)	–	–	–	–	–	–
Employees	–	–	–	–	–	230

UNITED STATES GOLF ASSOCIATION, INC.

77 LIBERTY CORNER RD
FAR HILLS, NJ 079312570
Phone: 908 234-2300
Fax: –
Web: www.usga.org

CEO: –
CFO: –
HR: –
FYE: November 30
Type: Private

Making sure golf stays clear of the rough is par for the course at this organization. The United States Golf Association is the governing body for golf in the US, its territories, and Mexico. The not-for-profit group writes and interprets the rules of the game, provides handicap information, offers turf consulting, and funds equipment and course maintenance research and testing. It also holds several national championship events, including the US Open, the US Women's Open, and the US Senior Open. The group generates most of its revenue from the sale of broadcast rights to championship tournaments and other matches, as well as through membership fees. The USGA was founded in 1894.

	Annual Growth	11/12	11/13	11/14	11/15	11/17
Sales ($mil.)	8.2%	–	156.6	164.7	208.9	215.0
Net income ($ mil.)	17.4%	–	6.8	(5.3)	16.5	12.9
Market value ($ mil.)	–	–	–	–	–	–
Employees	–	–	–	–	–	350

UNITED STATES HOLOCAUST MEMORIAL MUSEUM

100 RAOUL WALLENBERG PL SW
WASHINGTON, DC 200242126
Phone: 202 488-0400
Fax: –
Web: www.ushmm.org

CEO: –
CFO: –
HR: Jerry Pena
FYE: September 30
Type: Private

The United States Holocaust Memorial Museum has a lesson to share. The museum's primary mission is to advance and disseminate knowledge about the Holocaust, to preserve the memory of those who suffered, and to encourage its visitors to reflect on the moral and spiritual questions raised by the tragic events of the Holocaust. The museum broadens the public understanding of the Holocaust through exhibitions; research and publications; collecting and preserving material evidence; distribution of educational materials; and through a number of other programs. Chartered by an Act of Congress in 1980, the United States Holocaust Memorial Museum is a public-private partnership relying on both federal appropriations and private donations.

	Annual Growth	09/17	09/18	09/19	09/21	09/22
Sales ($mil.)	2.1%	–	170.1	164.8	175.4	184.7
Net income ($ mil.)	(4.3%)	–	49.5	37.9	37.9	41.6
Market value ($ mil.)	–	–	–	–	–	–
Employees	–	–	–	–	–	400

UNITED STATES LIME & MINERALS INC.
NMS: USLM

5429 LBJ Freeway, Suite 230
Dallas, TX 75240
Phone: 972 991-8400
Fax: 972 385-1340
Web: www.uslm.com

CEO: Timothy W Byrne
CFO: Michael L Wiedemer
HR: –
FYE: December 31
Type: Public

United States Lime & Minerals through its Lime and Limestone Operations, is a manufacturer of lime and limestone products, supplying primarily the construction, industrial, metals, environmental, roof shingle manufacturers, agricultural, and oil and gas services industries. It extracts high-quality limestone from its open-pit quarries and underground mines and then processes it for sale as pulverized limestone (PLS), aggregate, quicklime, hydrated lime, and lime slurry. The company has approximately 650 customers, primarily in the US. In addition to its lime operations, United States Lime & Minerals also has natural gas interests. The company was incorporated in 1950, and it generates most of its revenue from its Lime and limestone business.

	Annual Growth	12/19	12/20	12/21	12/22	12/23
Sales ($mil.)	15.5%	158.3	160.7	189.3	236.2	281.3
Net income ($ mil.)	30.1%	26.1	28.2	37.0	45.4	74.5
Market value ($ mil.)	26.4%	515.1	650.3	736.0	803.0	1,314.0
Employees	4.2%	282	317	308	338	333

UNITED STATES OLYMPIC COMMITTEE INC

1 OLYMPIC PLZ
COLORADO SPRINGS, CO 80903
Phone: 719 632-5551
Fax: –
Web: www.teamusa.org

CEO: Sarah Hirshland
CFO: Moran Kerek
HR: –
FYE: December 31
Type: Private

The United States Olympic & Paralympic Committee (USOPC), formerly the United States Olympic Committee, is the governing body of the Olympic and Paralympic movement in the US and oversees the organization, selection, and training of the country's Olympic athletes and teams. The not-for-profit organization operates training centers around the country where athletes prepare for the Olympic Games, the Paralympic Games, and the Youth Olympic Games or the Pan American Games. The USOPC is funded by corporate sponsorships, private contributions, and sales of licensed apparel. More than 80% of the USOPC's budget has a direct impact on its mission of supporting athletes via a variety of programs for both athletes and their National Governing Bodies. The organization was founded in 1894.

	Annual Growth	12/13	12/14	12/15	12/16	12/17
Sales ($mil.)	(10.5%)	–	270.3	141.6	336.1	193.9
Net income ($ mil.)	–	–	47.9	(57.7)	78.5	(15.0)
Market value ($ mil.)	–	–	–	–	–	–
Employees	–	–	–	–	–	400

UNITED STATES PARACHUTE ASSOCIATION

5401 SOUTHPOINT CENTRE BLVD
FREDERICKSBURG, VA 224072612
Phone: 540 604-9740
Fax: –
Web: www.uspa.org

CEO: –
CFO: –
HR: –
FYE: December 31
Type: Private

As David Lee Roth sang in his prime with Van Halen, "Jump! Might as well jump. Go ahead, jump. Jump!" If you're jumping from a great height, please use a parachute. The United States Parachute Association (USPA) is a membership organization of 34,000 skydiving enthusiasts. The USPA's activities include promoting skydiving competitions and establishing safety standards and instruction programs. The association was established in 1946.

	Annual Growth	12/16	12/17	12/18	12/21	12/22
Sales ($mil.)	3.5%	–	3.5	4.1	4.1	4.2
Net income ($ mil.)	52.2%	–	0.0	0.3	0.5	0.5
Market value ($ mil.)	–	–	–	–	–	–
Employees	–	–	–	–	–	28

UNITED STATES SOCCER FEDERATION, INC.

303 E WACKER DR STE 1200
CHICAGO, IL 606015278
Phone: 312 808-1300
Fax: –
Web: www.ussoccer.com

CEO: Will Wilson
CFO: –
HR: –
FYE: March 31
Type: Private

The U.S. Soccer Federation knows how its members like to get their kicks. The organization is the governing body for the sport of soccer (known around the world as football) in the United States. It promotes the game and organizes both recreational and professional competition, overseeing such leagues as Major League Soccer, United Soccer Leagues, and Women's Professional Soccer. U.S. Soccer hosts World Cups and Olympic soccer and runs the National Soccer Training Center. The federation is a member of the F d ration Internationale de Football Association (FIFA), the world soccer governing body. The organization was founded in 1914 as the U.S. Football Association.

	Annual Growth	03/17	03/18	03/19	03/20	03/22
Sales ($mil.)	(6.0%)	–	–	–	138.3	122.3
Net income ($ mil.)	–	–	–	–	(26.6)	(22.8)
Market value ($ mil.)	–	–	–	–	–	–
Employees	–	–	–	–	–	92

UNITED STATES SPORTS ACADEMY, INC.

1 ACADEMY DR
DAPHNE, AL 365267055
Phone: 251 626-3303
Fax: –
Web: www.ussa.edu

CEO: –
CFO: –
HR: Jessica Arnold
FYE: August 31
Type: Private

Jocks hit the books at The United States Sports Academy. The not-for-profit school offers bachelor's and graduate programs in sports-related fields. Course offerings include history of sports, public relations, law, and ethics classes. It offers master's degrees in management, sport medicine, coaching, and recreation and fitness management, as well as doctorates in sports management. Many of the school's courses are delivered online. The academy was founded in 1972 after an American study showed a correlation between high school athletic injuries and coaches who were poorly educated in physical education and sports.

	Annual Growth	08/17	08/18	08/19	08/20	08/22
Sales ($mil.)	(5.3%)	–	5.9	4.4	5.5	4.7
Net income ($ mil.)	(51.3%)	–	1.3	(0.3)	0.8	0.0
Market value ($ mil.)	–	–	–	–	–	–
Employees	–	–	–	–	–	48

UNITED STATES STEEL CORP.   NYS: X

600 Grant Street
Pittsburgh, PA 15219-2800
Phone: 412 433-1121
Fax: 412 433-4818
Web: www.ussteel.com

CEO: –
CFO: –
HR: –
FYE: December 31
Type: Public

United States Steel (US Steel) is North America's largest integrated steel producer. The company operates mills throughout the US and in Slovakia. US Steel makes a wide range of flat-rolled and tubular steel products, and its annual production capability is about 22.4 million net tons of raw steel. Its customers are primarily in the automotive, appliance, construction, electrical, industrial equipment, oil and gas, and petrochemical industries. In addition, US Steel mines iron ore and coke, which provides the primary raw materials used in steel making. It is also engaged in real estate operations. North America accounts for about 80% of total revenue.

	Annual Growth	12/19	12/20	12/21	12/22	12/23
Sales ($mil.)	8.7%	12,937	9,741.0	20,275	21,065	18,053
Net income ($ mil.)	–	(630.0)	(1,165.0)	4,174.0	2,524.0	895.0
Market value ($ mil.)	43.7%	2,552.1	3,751.0	5,325.6	5,603.0	10,882
Employees	(5.6%)	27,500	23,350	24,540	22,740	21,803

UNITED STATES SUGAR CORPORATION

1731 S W C OWEN AVE
CLEWISTON, FL 334404902
Phone: 863 983-8121
Fax: –
Web: www.ussugar.com

CEO: Robert H Buker Jr
CFO: –
HR: –
FYE: November 05
Type: Private

U.S. Sugar is tangy and sweet. The company is a top US cane sugar maker and citrus grower. It produces up to 750,000 tons of refined sugar a year, nearly 10% of the nation's supply. U.S. Sugar farms about 180,000 acres of sugarcane in South Florida; it's sold to baked-goods, ice-cream, and other food manufacturers, as well as to food retailers. The company also makes citrus molasses, used by distillers and as a feed supplement for cattle. Its subsidiary Southern Gardens Citrus (SGC) is one of the largest suppliers of not-from-concentrate orange juice in the US. SGC farms 16,500 acres of orange groves, producing more than 100 million gallons of orange juice annually. U.S Sugar was formed in 1931.

UNITED STATES TELEPHONE ASSOCIATION

601 NEW JERSEY AVE NW STE 600
WASHINGTON, DC 200012018
Phone: 202 326-7300
Fax: –
Web: www.ustelecom.org

CEO: Skip Frantz
CFO: –
HR: –
FYE: December 31
Type: Private

Did you ever wonder who telecom service providers call when they need a connection? The United States Telecom Association (USTA) is a trade association that listens to and speaks up for the telecom industry. It represents more than 1,200 local exchange, long distance, wireless, Internet, and cable services companies. The group lobbies Congress for telecommunications-friendly legislation and encourages investment in high-speed Internet access. USTA traces its roots back to 1897, when a group of independent (not part of the Bell System) telephone executives joined forces to advocate for independent companies.

	Annual Growth	12/08	12/09	12/17	12/21	12/22
Sales ($mil.)	45.2%	–	0.1	14.0	14.4	14.3
Net income ($ mil.)	–	–	(0.1)	2.7	2.0	(1.8)
Market value ($ mil.)	–	–	–	–	–	–
Employees	–	–	–	–	–	50

UNITED STATES TENNIS ASSOCIATION INCORPORATED

70 W RED OAK LN FL 1
WHITE PLAINS, NY 106043602
Phone: 914 696-7000
Fax: –
Web: www.usta.com

CEO: –
CFO: –
HR: Dario Otero
FYE: December 31
Type: Private

This sports group makes quite a racquet on the court. The United States Tennis Association (USTA) serves as the governing body for the sport of tennis in the US. It sets the rules of play and develops and promotes the sport at the local and professional levels. USTA also owns and operates the US Open, the annual Grand Slam event held at Arthur Ashe Stadium in Flushing Meadows, New York. In addition, the not-for-profit organization selects players to compete in such tournaments as the Davis Cup, the Fed Cup, and the Olympics. Founded in 1881 as the United States National Lawn Tennis Association, the USTA has grown to more than 700,000 individual members and 8,000 organizational members.

	Annual Growth	12/12	12/13	12/19	12/21	12/22
Sales ($mil.)	10.2%	–	250.2	8.1	334.8	599.1
Net income ($ mil.)	25.8%	–	36.1	0.2	59.9	285.4
Market value ($ mil.)	–	–	–	–	–	–
Employees	–	–	–	–	–	350

UNITED SURGICAL PARTNERS INTERNATIONAL, INC.

14201 DALLAS PKWY
DALLAS, TX 752542916
Phone: 972 713-3500
Fax: –
Web: www.uspi.com

CEO: William H Wilcox
CFO: Owen Morris
HR: –
FYE: December 31
Type: Private

Founded in 1998, United Surgical Partners International (USPI) owns or manages over 475 ambulatory facilities that serve more than 11,000 physicians and over 1.95 million patients annually. USPI acquires and develops its facilities primarily through the formation of joint ventures with physicians and health systems. USPI's subsidiaries hold ownership interests in the facilities directly or indirectly and operate the facilities on a day-to-day basis through management services contracts. USPI is a subsidiary of Tenet Healthcare Corp.

UNITED THERAPEUTICS CORP

NMS: UTHR

1040 Spring Street
Silver Spring, MD 20910
Phone: 301 608-9292
Fax: –
Web: www.unither.com

CEO: –
CFO: –
HR: –
FYE: December 31
Type: Public

United Therapeutics focuses on the strength of a balanced, value-creating biotechnology model. Its injectable drug Remodulin treats pulmonary hypertension, which affects the blood vessels between the heart and lungs; it also treats cancer and viral illnesses. The product is marketed directly and through distributors in North America, Europe, and the Asia/Pacific region. Other hypertension treatments include Adcirca, Tyvaso, and Orenitram. The company's development pipeline includes additional treatments for cardiovascular disease, as well as various cancers, respiratory conditions, and infectious diseases. The US market accounts the largest for about 95% of total revenue.

	Annual Growth	12/19	12/20	12/21	12/22	12/23
Sales ($mil.)	12.6%	1,448.8	1,483.3	1,685.5	1,936.3	2,327.5
Net income ($ mil.)	–	(104.5)	514.8	475.8	727.3	984.8
Market value ($ mil.)	25.7%	4,143.3	7,140.3	10,165	13,082	10,344
Employees	6.1%	920	950	965	985	1,168

UNITED WAY WORLDWIDE

701 N FAIRFAX ST
ALEXANDRIA, VA 223142045
Phone: 703 836-7100
Fax: –
Web: www.unitedway.org

CEO: Brian A Gallagher
CFO: –
HR: Julia McNeely
FYE: December 31
Type: Private

Where there's a will, there's a Way. Working to raise money for charitable causes, United Way Worldwide unites some 1,800 namesake organizations active in about 40 countries and territories. While its specific priorities are set by local entities, the global organization tends to focus on helping children achieve their potential, promoting financial stability, and improving access to health care. Major recipients of its contributions have included the American Cancer Society, Big Brothers/Big Sisters, Catholic Charities, Girl Scouts, Boy Scouts, and The Salvation Army, among other worthy organizations. United Way Worldwide was formed by the merger of United Way of America and United Way International.

	Annual Growth	12/16	12/17	12/19	12/21	12/22
Sales ($mil.)	(10.9%)	–	175.8	248.8	113.4	98.5
Net income ($ mil.)	(12.7%)	–	28.5	(7.9)	4.2	14.4
Market value ($ mil.)	–	–	–	–	–	–
Employees	–	–	–	–	–	204

UNITED WISCONSIN GRAIN PRODUCERS, LLC

W1231 TESSMANN DR
FRIESLAND, WI 539239510
Phone: 920 348-5016
Fax: –
Web: www.uwgp.com

CEO: Jeffrey F Robertson
CFO: Barb J Bontrager
HR: –
FYE: March 31
Type: Private

It's not going against the grain to turn farm crops into motor fuels. Certainly not for United Wisconsin Grain Producers (UWGP), which like many other agribusinesses in the Midwest and Great Plains, is pushing grain-based ethanol as a viable and renewable fuel additive. Ethanol is an alcohol fuel produced by fermenting converted starch from corn with yeast. Most ethanol is blended with unleaded gasoline and other fuel products. In 2005 UWGP completed the construction of and began operating an ethanol facility that manufactures 40 million gallons of ethanol a year. It has since expanded the plant to a capacity of more than 50 million gallons.

UNITED-GUARDIAN, INC.

NMS: UG

230 Marcus Boulevard
Hauppauge, NY 11788
Phone: 631 273-0900
Fax: 631 273-0858
Web: www.u-g.com

CEO: Kenneth H Globus
CFO: –
HR: –
FYE: December 31
Type: Public

Through its Guardian Laboratories division, United-Guardian makes a variety of cosmetic ingredients, personal care products, and pharmaceuticals. Its top-selling Lubrajel line is a moisturizer used in cosmetics and as a lubricant for medical catheters. Other cosmetic products include Klensoft surfactants used in shampoos, and Unitwix, a thickening agent for cosmetic oils and liquids. United-Guardian's main pharmaceutical product is Renacidin Irrigation, a prescription drug used to keep urinary catheters clear. In 2007 the company sold the assets of its Eastern Chemical subsidiary, which distributed organic and research chemicals, dyes, reagents, and other chemicals.

	Annual Growth	12/19	12/20	12/21	12/22	12/23
Sales ($mil.)	(5.4%)	13.6	11.0	13.9	12.7	10.9
Net income ($ mil.)	(14.2%)	4.8	3.3	4.7	2.6	2.6
Market value ($ mil.)	(22.2%)	90.3	66.1	75.6	48.0	33.1
Employees	–	–	28	25	24	24	28

UNITEDHEALTH GROUP INC
NYS: UNH

UnitedHealth Group Center, 9900 Bren Road East
Minnetonka, MN 55343
Phone: 952 936-1300
Fax: –
Web: www.unitedhealthgroup.com

CEO: Andrew P Witty
CFO: John F Rex
HR: Mary Knight
FYE: December 31
Type: Public

UnitedHealth Group is a leading US health insurer offering a variety of plans and services to group and individual customers nationwide. Its UnitedHealthcare health benefits segment manages health maintenance organization (HMO), preferred provider organization (PPO), and point-of-service (POS) plans, as well as Medicare, Medicaid, state-funded, and supplemental vision and dental options. In addition, UnitedHealth's Optum health services units ? OptumHealth, OptumInsight, and OptumRx ? provide wellness and care management programs, financial services, information technology solutions, and pharmacy benefit management (PBM) services to individuals and the health care industry.

	Annual Growth	12/19	12/20	12/21	12/22	12/23
Sales ($mil.)	11.3%	242,155	257,141	287,597	324,162	371,622
Net income ($ mil.)	12.8%	13,839	15,403	17,285	20,120	22,381
Market value ($ mil.)	15.7%	271,638	324,028	463,977	489,886	486,458
Employees	7.9%	325,000	330,000	350,000	400,000	440,000

UNITEK GLOBAL SERVICES, INC.

1817 CRANE RIDGE DR STE 500
JACKSON, MS 392164979
Phone: 267 464-1700
Fax: –
Web: www.unitekglobalservices.com

CEO: –
CFO: –
HR: –
FYE: December 31
Type: Private

UniTek Global Services has a variety of ways to keep the lines of communications companies open. A provider of outsourced infrastructure services, UniTek and its subsidiaries offers technical, engineering and design, repair, construction, and other services to major satellite, cable, and wireless communications companies in the US and Canada. Its services range from residential and commercial installation to design and construction of fiber optic networks. Customers include AT&T, Comcast, and DIRECTV.

UNITI GROUP INC
NMS: UNIT

2101 Riverfront Drive, Suite A
Little Rock, AR 72202
Phone: 501 850-0820
Fax: –
Web: www.uniti.com

CEO: Kenneth A Gunderman
CFO: Paul E Bullington
HR: Amanda Stanisor
FYE: December 31
Type: Public

Uniti Group is an independent, internally managed real estate investment trust (REIT) engaged in the acquisition and construction of mission critical infrastructure in the communications industry. It is principally focused on acquiring and constructing fiber optic, copper and coaxial broadband networks and data centers. Uniti owns over 128,000 fiber network route miles, representing approximately 7.69 million fiber strand miles, approximately 230,000 route miles of copper cable lines, central office land and buildings across some 45 states. The current communications infrastructure industry is marked by the growing demand for and use of bandwidth-intensive devices and applications, such as smart devices, real-time and online streaming video, cloud-based applications, social media and mobile broadband.

	Annual Growth	12/19	12/20	12/21	12/22	12/23
Sales ($mil.)	2.1%	1,057.6	1,067.0	1,100.5	1,128.8	1,149.8
Net income ($ mil.)	–	10.6	(706.3)	123.7	(8.3)	(81.7)
Market value ($ mil.)	(8.4%)	1,942.1	2,774.8	3,314.2	1,308.2	1,367.3
Employees	(2.5%)	899	787	754	784	813

UNITIL CORP
NYS: UTL

6 Liberty Lane West
Hampton, NH 03842-1720
Phone: 603 772-0775
Fax: 603 772-4651
Web: www.unitil.com

CEO: Thomas P Meissner
CFO: –
HR: –
FYE: December 31
Type: Public

New England electric and gas company Unitil serves about 108,100 electric customers and 87,500 natural gas customers. Unitil's principal business is the local distribution of electricity and natural gas to customers throughout its service territories in the states of New Hampshire, Massachusetts, and Maine. Unitil Energy and Fitchburg units provide retail supply services to customers who don't choose to purchase energy from a third-party marketer. In addition, Unitil is the parent company of Granite State, a natural gas transmission pipeline, regulated by the FERC, operating about 85 miles of underground gas transmission pipeline primarily located in Maine and New Hampshire. Granite State provides Northern Utilities with interconnection to three major natural gas pipelines and access to North American pipeline supplies.

	Annual Growth	12/19	12/20	12/21	12/22	12/23
Sales ($mil.)	6.2%	438.2	418.6	473.3	563.2	557.1
Net income ($ mil.)	0.6%	44.2	32.2	36.1	41.4	45.2
Market value ($ mil.)	(4.0%)	996.3	713.5	741.2	827.8	847.3
Employees	0.9%	513	512	508	516	531

UNITY BANCORP, INC.
NMS: UNTY

64 Old Highway 22
Clinton, NJ 08809
Phone: 800 618-2265
Fax: –
Web: www.unitybank.com

CEO: –
CFO: –
HR: –
FYE: December 31
Type: Public

Unity Bancorp wants to keep you and your money united. The institution is the holding company for Unity Bank, a commercial bank that serves small and midsized businesses, as well as individual consumers, through nearly 20 offices in north-central New Jersey and eastern Pennsylvania. Unity Bank's deposit products include checking, savings, money market, and NOW accounts, and CDs. Lending to businesses is the company's life blood: Commercial loans, including Small Business Administration (SBA) and real estate loans, account for about 60% of its loan portfolio, which is rounded out by residential mortgage and consumer loans.

	Annual Growth	12/19	12/20	12/21	12/22	12/23
Assets ($mil.)	10.7%	1,718.9	1,958.9	2,033.7	2,444.9	2,578.5
Net income ($ mil.)	13.8%	23.7	23.6	36.1	38.5	39.7
Market value ($ mil.)	7.0%	227.1	176.6	264.2	275.0	297.8
Employees	3.2%	209	210	214	232	237

UNIVERSAL CORP
NYS: UVV

9201 Forest Hill Avenue
Richmond, VA 23235
Phone: 804 359-9311
Fax: –
Web: www.universalcorp.com

CEO: George C Freeman III
CFO: Johan C Kroner
HR: –
FYE: March 31
Type: Public

Operating mainly through its flagship subsidiaries, Universal Leaf Tobacco Company and Universal Global Ventures, Universal Corporation is a global business-to-business agri-products supplier to consumer product manufacturers, operating in more than 30 countries on five continents. The largest portion of its business involves procuring and processing flue-cured, burley, and dark air-cured leaf tobacco for manufacturers of consumer tobacco products. The company operates in major dark tobacco-producing countries, including the US, the Dominican Republic, Ecuador, Indonesia, Paraguay, the Philippines, and Brazil. Through its plant-based ingredients platform, the company provides a variety of value-added manufacturing processes to produce high-quality, specialty vegetable- and fruit-based ingredients as well as botanical extracts and flavorings. Universal also has a business that recycles waste materials from tobacco production. The US generates more than 20% of the company's total sales.

	Annual Growth	03/19	03/20	03/21	03/22	03/23
Sales ($mil.)	3.6%	2,227.2	1,910.0	1,983.4	2,103.6	2,569.8
Net income ($ mil.)	4.5%	104.1	71.7	87.4	86.6	124.1
Market value ($ mil.)	(2.1%)	1,415.1	1,085.6	1,448.5	1,425.9	1,298.7
Employees	–	28,000	24,000	20,000	25,000	28,000

UNIVERSAL DETECTION TECHNOLOGY

340 North Camden Drive, Suite 302
Beverly Hills, CA 90210
Phone: 310 248-3655
Fax: –
Web: www.udetection.com

CEO: –
CFO: –
HR: –
FYE: December 31
Type: Public

Universal Detection Technology (UDT) has traded in acid rain for bioterrorism. UDT has leveraged its expertise in air pollution monitoring into products to identify airborne biological and chemical hazards in bioterrorism monitoring systems. Its first product -- originally called the Anthrax Smoke Detector and now known as the BSM-2000 -- is intended to continuously check the air in public buildings for anthrax spores. The device is an outgrowth of an agreement with NASA's Jet Propulsion Laboratory (JPL) that called for JPL to develop its bacterial spore detection technology for integration into UDT's aerosol monitoring system.

	Annual Growth	12/11	12/12	12/13	12/14	12/15
Sales ($mil.)	–	0.2	0.0	0.0	0.0	–
Net income ($ mil.)	–	(2.6)	(1.6)	(0.4)	(0.1)	(0.2)
Market value ($ mil.)	354.0%	0.0	0.5	0.1	0.1	0.1
Employees	(29.3%)	4	4	1	1	1

UNIVERSAL DISPLAY CORP

250 Phillips Boulevard
Ewing, NJ 08618
Phone: 609 671-0980
Fax: –
Web: www.oled.com

NMS: OLED
CEO: –
CFO: –
HR: –
FYE: December 31
Type: Public

Universal Display is a leader in the research, development and commercialization of organic light emitting diode (OLED) technologies and materials for use in display and solid-state lighting applications. OLEDs are thin, lightweight and power-efficient solid-state devices that emit light and can be manufactured on both flexible and rigid substrates, making them highly suitable for use in full-color displays and as lighting products. OLED displays are capturing a growing share of the display market, especially in the mobile phone, television, monitor, wearable, tablet, notebook and personal computer, augmented reality (AR), virtual reality (VR) and automotive markets. Although the company is based in the US, it generates most of its revenue in South Korea. Universal Display was founded by Sherwin Seligsohn in 1994.

	Annual Growth	12/19	12/20	12/21	12/22	12/23
Sales ($mil.)	9.2%	405.2	428.9	553.5	616.6	576.4
Net income ($ mil.)	10.1%	138.3	133.4	184.2	210.1	203.0
Market value ($ mil.)	(1.8%)	9,760.6	10,885	7,816.7	5,117.4	9,059.1
Employees	10.0%	311	350	417	445	456

UNIVERSAL ELECTRONICS INC.

15147 N. Scottsdale Road, Suite H300
Scottsdale, AZ 85254-2494
Phone: 480 530-3000
Fax: –
Web: www.uei.com

NMS: UEIC
CEO: Paul D Arling
CFO: Bryan M Hackworth
HR: –
FYE: December 31
Type: Public

Universal Electronics designs, develops, manufactures, ships and supports control and sensor technology solutions and a broad line of universal control systems, audio-video (AV) accessories, and intelligent wireless security and smart home products. The company's One For All remotes and AV accessories are sold to retailers through its international subsidiaries and direct to retailers in key markets, such as in the US, the UK, Germany, France, Spain, and Italy. Universal Electronics' product platform, Nevo Butler, offers a turnkey smart home hub with nevo.ai and QuickSet pre-integrated. The US generates around 35% of the company's revenue.

	Annual Growth	12/19	12/20	12/21	12/22	12/23
Sales ($mil.)	(13.6%)	753.5	614.7	601.6	542.8	420.5
Net income ($ mil.)	–	3.6	38.6	5.3	0.4	(98.2)
Market value ($ mil.)	(34.9%)	673.5	676.0	525.1	268.2	121.0
Employees	(1.0%)	4,347	3,839	3,945	4,658	4,177

UNIVERSAL HEALTH REALTY INCOME TRUST

Universal Corporate Center, 367 South Gulph Road
King of Prussia, PA 19406-0958
Phone: 610 265-0688
Fax: 610 768-3336
Web: www.uhrit.com

NYS: UHT
CEO: Alan B Miller
CFO: Charles F Boyle
HR: –
FYE: December 31
Type: Public

Universal Health Realty Income Trust (UHT) is a real estate investment trust (REIT) that primarily invests in healthcare facilities and human services. The REIT owns more than 70 facilities in about 20 states, including acute care hospitals, behavioral healthcare facilities, rehabilitation hospitals, sub-acute facilities, surgery centers, childcare centers, and medical office buildings. McAllen Medical Center in Texas is UHT's largest facility. Many properties are owned via limited liability companies in which the trust holds an equity interest. UHT's hospitals boast more than 720 beds. Subsidiaries of Universal Health Services lease most of UHT's hospitals and provide their own maintenance and renovation services.

	Annual Growth	12/19	12/20	12/21	12/22	12/23
Sales ($mil.)	5.5%	77.2	78.0	84.2	90.6	95.6
Net income ($ mil.)	(5.1%)	19.0	19.4	109.2	21.1	15.4
Market value ($ mil.)	(22.1%)	1,622.4	888.5	822.1	659.8	597.9
Employees	–	–	–	–	–	–

UNIVERSAL HEALTH SERVICES, INC.

Universal Corporate Center, 367 South Gulph Road
King of Prussia, PA 19406
Phone: 610 768-3300
Fax: –
Web: www.uhsinc.com

NYS: UHS
CEO: –
CFO: –
HR: –
FYE: December 31
Type: Public

Universal Health Services (UHS) is one of the nation's largest for-profit hospital operators. It owns or leases about 25 acute care hospitals with a total of about 6,545 beds, primarily in rural and suburban communities. The system also operates outpatient centers and behavioral health treatment facilities, most located near its acute care hospitals. In addition, UHS' behavioral health division operates approximately 335 inpatient facilities and 15 outpatient facilities with a combined capacity of some 23,740 beds. Its UK-based Cygnet unit operates more than 55 facilities. It acts as the advisor to Universal Health Realty Income Trust, a real estate investment trust. UHS is controlled by founder and CEO Alan Miller.

	Annual Growth	12/19	12/20	12/21	12/22	12/23
Sales ($mil.)	5.8%	11,378	11,559	12,642	13,399	14,282
Net income ($ mil.)	(3.1%)	814.9	944.0	991.6	675.6	717.8
Market value ($ mil.)	1.5%	9,637.9	9,237.5	8,710.8	9,465.2	10,241
Employees	(5.1%)	90,400	89,000	89,400	93,800	73,350

UNIVERSAL INSURANCE HOLDINGS INC

1110 W. Commercial Blvd.
Fort Lauderdale, FL 33309
Phone: 954 958-1200
Fax: –
Web: www.universalinsuranceholdings.com

NYS: UVE
CEO: Stephen J Donaghy
CFO: Frank C Wilcox
HR: Greg Ruth
FYE: December 31
Type: Public

Universal Insurance Holdings is a holding company offering property and casualty insurance and value-added insurance services. The company develops, markets and underwrites insurance products for consumers predominantly in the personal residential homeowners lines of business and perform substantially all other insurance-related services for our primary insurance entities, including risk management, claims management, and distribution. Our primary insurance entities, Universal Property & Casualty Insurance Company (UPCIC) and American Platinum Property and Casualty Insurance Company (APPCIC), offer insurance products through both its appointed independent agent network and its online distribution channels across some 20 states (primarily in Florida), with licenses to write insurance in two additional states. Florida generates some 85% of its total direct premiums written.

	Annual Growth	12/19	12/20	12/21	12/22	12/23
Assets ($mil.)	7.7%	1,719.9	1,758.7	2,056.1	2,890.2	2,316.6
Net income ($ mil.)	9.5%	46.5	19.1	20.4	(22.3)	66.8
Market value ($ mil.)	(13.1%)	810.8	437.7	492.4	306.7	462.9
Employees	11.5%	805	909	1,047	1,223	1,244

UNIVERSAL LOGISTICS HOLDINGS INC
NMS: ULH

12755 E. Nine Mile Road
Warren, MI 48089
Phone: 586 920-0100
Fax: –
Web: www.universallogistics.com

CEO: Tim Phillips
CFO: Jude M Beres
HR: Christina Lang
FYE: December 31
Type: Public

Universal Logistics Holdings (formerly Universal Truckload Services) is a leading asset-light provider of customized transportation and logistics solutions throughout the US, Canada, Mexico, and Colombia. The company operates through a network of union and non-union employee drivers, owner-operators, and contract drivers. It can call upon a fleet of almost 4,055 tractors, nearly 245 yard tractors, some 5,180 trailers, roughly 3,375 chassis, and almost 130 containers; the majority of its tractors and trailers are owned by others. Its operating subsidiaries provide customers a broad array of services across their entire supply chain, including truckload, brokerage, intermodal, dedicated, and value-added services. Vast majority of sales comes from US.

	Annual Growth	12/19	12/20	12/21	12/22	12/23
Sales ($mil.)	2.4%	1,512.0	1,391.1	1,751.0	2,015.5	1,662.1
Net income ($ mil.)	25.4%	37.6	48.1	73.7	168.6	92.9
Market value ($ mil.)	10.3%	498.3	541.2	495.7	878.9	736.5
Employees	9.2%	6,541	6,187	8,004	8,646	9,311

UNIVERSAL MANUFACTURING CO
NBB: UFMG

1128 Lincoln Mall, Suite 301
Lincoln, NE 68508
Phone: 515 295-3557
Fax: 515 295-5537
Web: www.universalmanf.com

CEO: Thomas Hance
CFO: –
HR: –
FYE: July 31
Type: Public

Parts are the best part of Universal Manufacturing. The company is a remanufacturer and distributor of automotive parts, including fuel pumps, engines, and master cylinders. Universal Manufacturing sells its remanufactured products wholesale -- under the brand name ReTech -- to automotive dealers, warehouse distributors, and parts supply stores in the midwestern US. The firm also distributes remanufactured engines. Although specializing in the car and truck industry, it also has facilities for serving the marine, railroad, aircraft, motor sport, and industrial engine markets. Universal Manufacturing was founded in 1946.

	Annual Growth	07/13	07/14	07/15	07/16	07/17
Sales ($mil.)	17.0%	23.1	27.7	23.9	67.3	43.4
Net income ($ mil.)	–	0.8	1.7	(1.5)	0.3	(3.3)
Market value ($ mil.)	18.9%	7.0	11.9	14.3	10.5	14.0
Employees	–	–	3	200	–	–

UNIVERSAL POWER GROUP, INC.

488 S ROYAL LN
COPPELL, TX 750193820
Phone: 469 892-1122
Fax: –
Web: www.upgi.com

CEO: Ian C Edmonds
CFO: –
HR: –
FYE: December 31
Type: Private

Universal Power Group (UPG) gives its customers a charge. The company is a leading distributor of sealed lead-acid batteries to manufacturers and retailers in the US. Other products include lithium and nickel-cadmium batteries, portable battery-powered products including jump starters, solar power generators, and solar panels. UPG also supplies components used in security systems, including alarm panels, perimeter access controls, sirens, speakers, cable, and wire. In addition, UPG provides services such as inventory management, kitting and packaging, and battery recycling. ADT Security Services (16% of sales), Cabelas, Protection One, and RadioShack are among the company's customers.

	Annual Growth	12/09	12/10	12/11	12/14	12/15
Sales ($mil.)	(34.2%)	–	738.8	89.3	–	90.9
Net income ($ mil.)	884.5%	–	0.0	0.2	–	0.6
Market value ($ mil.)	–	–	–	–	–	–
Employees	–	–	–	–	–	158

UNIVERSAL SECURITY INSTRUMENTS, INC.
ASE: UUU

11407 Cronhill Drive, Suite A
Owings Mills, MD 21117
Phone: 410 363-3000
Fax: 410 363-2218
Web: www.universalsecurity.com

CEO: Harvey B Grossblatt
CFO: James B Huff
HR: –
FYE: March 31
Type: Public

Where there's smoke, there's Universal Security Instruments. The company designs and markets (to 30 countries) smoke alarms and carbon monoxide alarms, as well as other safety products such as outdoor floodlights, door chimes, and ground fault circuit interrupter (GFCI) units. Universal Security Instruments has warehouse facilities in Maryland and Illinois. Most of its products are sold through retail stores and are designed to be installed by consumers. Products that require professional installation, such as smoke alarms for the hearing-impaired, are marketed to electrical products distributors by subsidiary USI Electric. The company was founded in 1969.

	Annual Growth	03/19	03/20	03/21	03/22	03/23
Sales ($mil.)	6.0%	17.6	14.8	17.5	19.5	22.2
Net income ($ mil.)	–	(1.3)	(5.8)	0.3	(0.1)	0.7
Market value ($ mil.)	14.7%	3.1	0.9	15.6	9.8	5.4
Employees	(4.1%)	13	13	13	12	11

UNIVERSAL STAINLESS & ALLOY PRODUCTS, INC.
NMS: USAP

600 Mayer Street
Bridgeville, PA 15017
Phone: 412 257-7600
Fax: –
Web: www.univstainless.com

CEO: Dennis M Oates
CFO: Steven V Ditommaso V
HR: –
FYE: December 31
Type: Public

At Universal Stainless & Alloy Products, even if something isn't totally finished, that's OK. The company makes both semi-finished and finished specialty steels, including stainless, tool, and alloyed steels. Universal Stainless' stainless steel products are used in end products made by the automotive, aerospace, power generation, oil and gas, and heavy equipment manufacturing and medical industries; its high-temperature steel is produced mainly for the aerospace industry. Before the products get there, however, Universal Stainless sells them to service centers, rerollers, OEMs, forgers, and wire redrawers.

	Annual Growth	12/18	12/19	12/20	12/21	12/22
Sales ($mil.)	(5.7%)	255.9	243.0	179.7	155.9	202.1
Net income ($ mil.)	–	10.7	4.3	(19.0)	(0.8)	(8.1)
Market value ($ mil.)	(18.4%)	146.7	134.8	67.7	71.9	64.9
Employees	(5.5%)	781	795	566	558	622

UNIVERSAL TECHNICAL INSTITUTE, INC.
NYS: UTI

4225 East Windrose Drive, Suite 200
Phoenix, AZ 85032
Phone: 623 445-9500
Fax: –
Web: www.uti.edu

CEO: Jerome A Grant
CFO: Troy R Anderson
HR: –
FYE: September 30
Type: Public

Universal Technical Institute (UTI) is the leading provider of postsecondary education for students seeking careers as professional automotive, diesel, collision repair, motorcycle and marine technicians as measured by total average full-time enrollment and graduates. It also provides programs for welders and computer numeric control (CNC) machining technicians. UTI offers certificate, diploma or degree programs at some 15 campuses across the US under the banner of several well-known brands, including Universal Technical Institute (UTI), Motorcycle Mechanics Institute and Marine Mechanics Institute (MMI) and NASCAR Technical Institute (NASCAR Tech). Additionally, it offers manufacturer specific advanced training (MSAT) programs, including student-paid electives, at its campuses and manufacturer or dealer sponsored training at certain campuses and dedicated training centers. UTI was founded in 1965.

	Annual Growth	09/19	09/20	09/21	09/22	09/23
Sales ($mil.)	16.3%	331.5	300.8	335.1	418.8	607.4
Net income ($ mil.)	–	(7.9)	8.0	14.6	25.8	12.3
Market value ($ mil.)	11.4%	185.4	173.1	230.3	185.4	285.5
Employees	15.8%	1,670	1,575	1,660	1,950	3,000

UNIVERSAL WILDE, INC.

135 WILL DR UNIT 2
CANTON, MA 020213771
Phone: 781 251-2700
Fax: –
Web: www.universalwilde.com

CEO: William Fitzgerald
CFO: Joe Musanti
HR: –
FYE: December 31
Type: Private

Sometimes the world of direct-mail marketing can seem like a jungle, but W.A. Wilde can serve as your guide. The company provides tools and services for direct marketing campaigns, such as fulfillment, mailing, print management, statement processing, and telemarketing. Its offerings can be purchased as a package or la carte. The company operate through three main units: Wilde Agency, a full-service direct-marketing provider; Wilde Interactive, which specializes in online campaigns; and L.W. Robbins Associates, an agency catering to nonprofit organizations. Family-owned W.A. Wilde traces its roots back to 1868, when William A. Wilde began publishing books.

UNIVERSITIES OF WISCONSIN

1220 LINDEN DR
MADISON, WI 537061525
Phone: 608 262-2321
Fax: –
Web: www.wisconsin.edu

CEO: –
CFO: –
HR: Vicki Kenyon
FYE: June 30
Type: Private

The University of Wisconsin System (UW System) is one of the largest public university systems in the US. With about 15 universities across nearly 25 campuses and a statewide extension, the UW System is home to world-class education, research, and public service. The UW System has approximately 161,000 students and about 35,000 faculty and staff members. Its two main campuses are UW at Madison and UW at Milwaukee, which offer hundreds of undergraduate and graduate programs including doctoral and professional degrees. The university was founded in 1848 by the state of constitution.

	Annual Growth	06/14	06/15	06/16	06/17	06/18
Sales ($mil.)	(2.4%)	–	–	–	3,702.8	3,614.0
Net income ($ mil.)	–	–	–	–	(20.4)	203.5
Market value ($ mil.)	–	–	–	–	–	–
Employees	–	–	–	–	–	21,605

UNIVERSITIES RESEARCH ASSOCIATION INC.

1140 19TH ST NW STE 900
WASHINGTON, DC 200366606
Phone: 202 293-1382
Fax: –
Web: www.ura-hq.org

CEO: –
CFO: Jeffrey Shapiro
HR: –
FYE: September 30
Type: Private

Universities Research Association (URA) is a consortium of 89 research-oriented universities organized in 1965 to oversee and operate selected national research facilities. The URA and the University of Chicago are the prime contractors in charge of the Fermi National Accelerator Laboratory (Fermilab), one of the world's largest high-energy particle accelerators. (The URA was the sole contractor from 1967-2006). The URA also manages the $100 million Pierre Auger Cosmic Ray Observatory Project. URA receives funding primarily from the US Department of Energy, NASA, and the National Science Foundation. Its membership mostly consists of US universities but also includes institutions from Canada, Italy, and Japan.

	Annual Growth	09/17	09/18	09/19	09/21	09/22
Sales ($mil.)	8.2%	–	4.7	5.8	6.0	6.4
Net income ($ mil.)	(4.3%)	–	2.4	2.4	2.1	2.0
Market value ($ mil.)	–	–	–	–	–	–
Employees	–	–	–	–	–	5

UNIVERSITY AT ALBANY

1400 WASHINGTON AVE
ALBANY, NY 122220100
Phone: 518 442-3300
Fax: –
Web: www.albany.edu

CEO: –
CFO: –
HR: Amanda Harrington
FYE: August 31
Type: Private

The University at Albany (UAlbany) was established in 1844 as a teachers college and designated as a State University of New York (SUNY) university center in 1962. The university has three campuses around New York's state capital city. The main campus is the futuristic Uptown Campus, which was built in the 1960s when former Governor Nelson Rockefeller was ambitiously expanding the state university system. UAlbany has more than 17,000 undergraduate and graduate students. The university offers some 120 undergraduate majors and minors and about 140 graduate programs and certificates including art history, biochemistry, business, education, information technology, and public health.

UNIVERSITY BANCORP INC. (MI)

2015 Washtenaw Avenue
Ann Arbor, MI 48104
Phone: 734 741-5858
Fax: 734 741-5859
Web: www.university-bank.com

NBB: UNIB
CEO: Stephen L Ranzini
CFO: Michael M Yeager
HR: –
FYE: December 31
Type: Public

University Bancorp is the holding company for University Bank. From one branch in Ann Arbor (the home of The University of Michigan), the bank offers standard services such as deposit accounts and loans. It mainly originates residential mortgages, with commercial mortgages, business loans, and consumer loans rounding out its lending activities. Shariah-compliant banking services (banking consistent with Islamic law) are offered through University Islamic Financial, which operates within University Bank's office. University Bancorp also owns University Insurance and Investments Services, and a majority of Midwest Loan Services, which provides mortgage origination and subservicing to credit unions.

	Annual Growth	12/18	12/19	12/20	12/21	12/22
Assets ($mil.)	33.9%	247.0	362.0	557.7	500.4	794.2
Net income ($ mil.)	14.2%	2.2	3.6	28.0	25.3	3.8
Market value ($ mil.)	17.1%	44.4	39.7	61.9	111.2	83.5
Employees	–	–	–	–	–	–

UNIVERSITY COMMUNITY HOSPITAL, INC.

3100 E FLETCHER AVE
TAMPA, FL 336134613
Phone: 813 971-6000
Fax: –
Web: www.universitycommunityhospital.com

CEO: –
CFO: –
HR: –
FYE: December 31
Type: Private

University Community Health (doing business as Florida Hospital Tampa Bay Division) is a 1,000-bed regional health care system with four locations spanning the Hillsborough, Pinellas, and Pasco counties of Florida. It oversees a network of eight hospitals in Florida's Tampa Bay area. Its four general hospitals -- three located in Tampa and one in nearby Tarpon Springs -- collectively house some 860 beds and provide emergency, surgical, and acute medical care, as well as provide outpatient services. The system also includes a specialty heart hospital, a women's hospital, and a long-term acute care hospital. Florida Hospital Tampa Bay Division is part of the Adventist Health System.

	Annual Growth	12/15	12/16	12/17	12/19	12/21
Sales ($mil.)	13.6%	–	483.2	688.2	761.9	915.7
Net income ($ mil.)	(6.8%)	–	39.8	66.1	62.3	27.9
Market value ($ mil.)	–	–	–	–	–	–
Employees	–	–	–	–	–	8,000

UNIVERSITY CORPORATION FOR ATMOSPHERIC RESEARCH

3090 CENTER GREEN DR
BOULDER, CO 803012252
Phone: 303 497-1000
Fax: -
Web: www.ucar.edu

CEO: -
CFO: Erica Smith
HR: Konnie Phillips
FYE: September 30
Type: Private

The University Corporation for Atmospheric Research (UCAR) is a not-for-profit corporation founded in 1960 to promote research in atmospheric and related environmental sciences. A consortium of more than 100 universities, UCAR provides real-time weather data to universities, educates weather forecasters, and organizes international experiments through its Office of Programs. The organization also maintains aircraft, and computer models for weather and climate through the National Center for Atmospheric Research (NCAR). UCAR is funded by sponsors such as the National Science Foundation, the National Oceanic and Atmospheric Administration, and NASA.

	Annual Growth	09/18	09/19	09/20	09/21	09/22
Sales ($mil.)	(1.1%)	-	230.4	267.3	266.8	223.2
Net income ($ mil.)	-	-	(8.1)	22.1	36.9	(29.0)
Market value ($ mil.)	-	-	-	-	-	-
Employees	-	-	-	-	-	1,565

UNIVERSITY HEALTH CARE, INC.

312 S 4TH ST STE 700
LOUISVILLE, KY 402023046
Phone: 502 585-7900
Fax: -
Web: -

CEO: -
CFO: -
HR: Leah Inlow
FYE: December 31
Type: Private

University Health Care wants to give patients a passport to good health. The company, which does business as Passport Health Plan, provides managed Medicaid insurance services to about 150,000 members throughout 16 counties in Kentucky. Offerings include HMO, Medicare Advantage, and children's health plans. University Health Care was founded in 1997 by a group of affiliated providers including the University of Louisville Medical Center, Jewish Hospital and St. Mary's HealthCare, and the Louisville/Jefferson County Primary Care Association. The health plan has an administration partnership with the AmeriHealth Mercy organization, a Medicaid managed care joint venture between AmeriHealth and Mercy Health System.

	Annual Growth	12/97	12/98	12/99	12/00	12/14
Sales ($mil.)	3.0%	-	810.0	284.5	330.1	1,299.5
Net income ($ mil.)	-	-	-	5.8	3.8	115.0
Market value ($ mil.)	-	-	-	-	-	-
Employees	-	-	-	-	-	165

UNIVERSITY HEALTH SERVICES, INC.

1350 WALTON WAY
AUGUSTA, GA 309012612
Phone: 706 722-9011
Fax: -
Web: www.piedmont.org

CEO: Atoya Jones
CFO: Dave Belkoski
HR: -
FYE: December 31
Type: Private

University Health Services, doing business as University Health Care System, serves the communities of some 15 counties in Georgia's Central Savannah River Area and neighboring South Carolina. The system includes University Hospital with more than 580 beds, a women's center, a cancer center, and a heart center. It operates two separate nursing care facilities with a total of 249 beds, and maintains a home health care service. University Health Link is a managed care contractor co-owned by University Health Services and a group of 440 physicians serving companies in the region.

UNIVERSITY HEALTH SYSTEM SERVICES OF TEXAS, INC.

4502 MEDICAL DR STOP 85-1
SAN ANTONIO, TX 782294402
Phone: 210 358-4000
Fax: -
Web: www.universityhealth.com

CEO: George B Hernndez Jr
CFO: Peggy Demming
HR: -
FYE: December 31
Type: Private

As the hospital system of the Bexar County Hospital District, University Health System serves residents of San Antonio and the surrounding region. University Hospital is proud to serve as the region's only Level I trauma center for both adults and children. Its network of health care services includes dozens of primary, specialty and walk-in centers, mobile health units, and an academic hospital that has earned its place among the top in the nation and recognized as the most preferred hospital in San Antonio. In addition to its hospital and network of health centers, University Health also includes Community First Health Plans, University Medicine Associates, and University Health Foundation. The company was founded in 1917 with the opening of the Robert B. Green Memorial Hospital.

	Annual Growth	12/18	12/19	12/20	12/21	12/22
Sales ($mil.)	13.1%	-	1,610.8	1,780.9	1,976.9	2,330.0
Net income ($ mil.)	14.9%	-	150.4	249.2	292.7	228.1
Market value ($ mil.)	-	-	-	-	-	-
Employees	-	-	-	-	-	3,998

UNIVERSITY HEALTH SYSTEM, INC.

1924 ALCOA HWY
KNOXVILLE, TN 379201511
Phone: 865 305-9000
Fax: -
Web: www.utmedicalcenter.org

CEO: Joseph R Landsman
CFO: -
HR: Betsy Cunningham
FYE: December 31
Type: Private

University Health System (UHS) is all for one and one for Vols! Affiliated with the University of Tennessee's Graduate School of Medicine, the not-for-profit regional health system oversees the University of Tennessee Medical Center, a 580-bed hospital that serves the eastern Tennessee, southeastern Kentucky, and western North Carolina regions with a full range of medical services covering the brain, heart, lung, spine, and vascular system, as well as cancer, childbirth, and emergency trauma. UHS is also comprised of an independent physicians' association and has partnerships with a clinical laboratory services provider and a group dedicated to helping patients involved in pharmaceutical clinical trials.

	Annual Growth	12/17	12/18	12/19	12/21	12/22
Sales ($mil.)	6.9%	-	-	1,059.0	1,232.9	1,294.1
Net income ($ mil.)	-	-	-	42.4	40.7	(12.3)
Market value ($ mil.)	-	-	-	-	-	-
Employees	-	-	-	-	-	3,200

UNIVERSITY HEALTH SYSTEMS OF EASTERN CAROLINA, INC.

800 WH SMITH BLVD
GREENVILLE, NC 278343763
Phone: 252 847-6690
Fax: -
Web: www.ecuhealth.org

CEO: Michael Waldrum
CFO: -
HR: -
FYE: March 31
Type: Private

University Health Systems of Eastern Carolina is an integrated not-for-profit health system that serves residents of eastern North Carolina. Doing business as Vidant Health, it operates nine hospitals, including eight community hospitals and its tertiary care center, Vidant Medical Center, with 1,400 beds and academic affiliation with the Brody School of Medicine at East Carolina University. Vidant Health also operates centers for surgery, home health, hospice,and wellness and engages in community health programs. Its physician group has more than 350 primary and specialty care providers who operate frommore than 50 locations.

	Annual Growth	09/13	09/14	09/15*	03/18	03/19
Sales ($mil.)	(11.6%)	-	-	1,581.1	-	963.5
Net income ($ mil.)	-	-	-	(6.1)	-	6.5
Market value ($ mil.)	-	-	-	-	-	-
Employees	-	-	-	-	-	15,000

*Fiscal year change

UNIVERSITY HOSPITALS HEALTH SYSTEM, INC.

3605 WARRENSVILLE CENTER RD
SHAKER HEIGHTS, OH 441229100
Phone: 216 767-8900
Fax: –
Web: www.uhhospitals.org

CEO: Thomas S Zenty
CFO: Michael Szubski
HR: –
FYE: December 31
Type: Private

University Hospitals Health System (UHHS) is on a mission to teach, research, and administer good health throughout northeastern Ohio. Its flagship facility University Hospitals of Cleveland (UHC), which operates as University Hospitals Case Medical Center (UHCMC), is a more than 1,000-bed tertiary care center serving Cleveland and other parts of northeastern Ohio. The teaching hospital, which is affiliated with Case Western Reserve University, is also home to Rainbow Babies & Children's Hospital, Seidman Cancer Center, and MacDonald Women's Hospital. the not-for-profit UHHS is also home to community hospitals, outpatient health and surgery centers, mental health facilities, and senior care centers.

	Annual Growth	12/11	12/12	12/17	12/21	12/22
Sales ($mil.)	(9.0%)	–	2,266.3	580.1	960.1	878.2
Net income ($ mil.)	–	–	54.3	33.3	117.7	(25.9)
Market value ($ mil.)	–	–	–	–	–	–
Employees	–	–	–	–	–	30,099

UNIVERSITY MEDICAL CENTER OF SOUTHERN NEVADA

1800 W CHARLESTON BLVD
LAS VEGAS, NV 891022329
Phone: 702 383-2000
Fax: –
Web: www.umcsn.com

CEO: Anson V Houweling
CFO: –
HR: –
FYE: June 30
Type: Private

For those who want to learn while they heal the ill, University Medical Center of Southern Nevada (UMC)-- an affiliate of the University of Nevada School of Medicine might just be the place. The medical center includes a teaching hospital and a network of community and urgent care health centers. Among its specialized services are cancer treatment, heart care, pediatrics, and rehabilitation. It also offers birthing, wound and burn care, neurological disorder, Level II Pediatric Trauma, Lions Burn Care Center, and Level 1 trauma centers. UMC serves southern Nevada along with parts of Arizona, California, and Utah.

UNIVERSITY OF ALASKA SYSTEM

910 YUKON DR
FAIRBANKS, AK 997750001
Phone: 907 450-8079
Fax: –
Web: www.alaska.edu

CEO: –
CFO: –
HR: Gwenna Richardson
FYE: June 30
Type: Private

The University of Alaska System (UA) has this education thing down cold. UA governs three major campuses: the University of Alaska Anchorage, the University of Alaska Fairbanks, and the University of Alaska Southeast, which each anchor part of a regional system of 17 community colleges. UA enrolls about 35,000 students, offering some 500 degrees, certificates, and endorsements. Programs include science, engineering, education, business, journalism and communications, aviation, health occupations, history, English, arts and humanities, and others. An 11-member Board of Regents governs the system. Founded in 1917 as Alaska Agricultural College and School of Mines, it was named University of Alaska in 1935.

UNIVERSITY OF ARIZONA

845 N PARK AVE RM 538
TUCSON, AZ 857194871
Phone: 520 626-6000
Fax: –
Web: www.arizona.edu

CEO: –
CFO: Gregg Goldman
HR: Brian Engstrom
FYE: June 30
Type: Private

The University of Arizona is a public research university that offers more than 100 doctoral programs, over 150 master's programs, and more than 60 graduate certificate programs available through the University of Arizona's Graduate College. Known as UA, the educational institution serves more than 40,405 undergraduate students. It boasts some 20 colleges and schools, and it also offers outreach and extension of hundreds of programs, events, seminars, and classes available to the public across the state. Established in 1885, nearly three decades before Arizona achieved statehood, the school has a student-teacher ratio of approximately 17:1.

UNIVERSITY OF ARKANSAS SYSTEM

2404 N UNIVERSITY AVE
LITTLE ROCK, AR 722073608
Phone: 501 686-2500
Fax: –
Web: www.uasys.edu

CEO: –
CFO: Chaundra Hall
HR: –
FYE: June 30
Type: Private

Calling "Wooo, Pig, Sooie," at anyone in The University of Arkansas System (UA) is not an insult. The system encompasses more than a dozen schools, institutes, and campuses throughout the state, including five universities, a college of medicine, a math and science high school, and the Clinton School of Public Service, started in 2004 by former president Bill Clinton and offering the only Master of Public Service degree in the country. UA, which has an enrollment of more than 60,000, hails the razorback, or hog, as its mascot. "Wooo, Pig, Sooie" or "hog calling" is the school's cheer at sporting events. Its student-teacher ratio is 19:1; it has about 17,000 employees.

	Annual Growth	06/18	06/19	06/20	06/21	06/22
Sales ($mil.)	3.2%	–	2,515.6	2,449.0	2,635.5	2,765.9
Net income ($ mil.)	(13.4%)	–	153.9	85.1	222.9	99.9
Market value ($ mil.)	–	–	–	–	–	–
Employees	–	–	–	–	–	14,025

UNIVERSITY OF CALIFORNIA, DAVIS

1 SHIELDS AVE
DAVIS, CA 956168500
Phone: 530 752-1011
Fax: –
Web: www.ucdavis.edu

CEO: –
CFO: –
HR: –
FYE: June 30
Type: Private

The University of California, Davis (UC Davis) is a top tier public research university. The school, one of 10 University of California campuses, offers a wide variety of agricultural programs; its Viticulture and Enology department provides professional education for aspiring winemakers. Located between Sacramento and San Francisco, UC Davis also has colleges and professional schools in biology, engineering, education, law, business, medicine, and veterinary medicine, and it is recognized for its research programs. Offering over 105 academic majors and some 100 graduate degrees throughout its six schools, UC Davis enrolls more than 38,345 undergraduate, graduate, and professional students, and it has a student-faculty ratio of 21:1.

	Annual Growth	06/06	06/07	06/08*	12/08*	06/11
Sales ($mil.)	474.6%	–	–	14.2	0.5	2,697.4
Net income ($ mil.)	644.1%	–	–	0.9	0.0	360.1
Market value ($ mil.)	–	–	–	–	–	–
Employees	–	–	–	–	–	17,741

*Fiscal year change

UNIVERSITY OF CALIFORNIA, IRVINE

510 ALDRICH HALL
IRVINE, CA 926970001
Phone: 949 824-5011
Fax: –
Web: www.uci.edu

CEO: –
CFO: –
HR: Bea Tran
FYE: June 30
Type: Private

Sun, the beach, Nobel Prize winners, and a Southern California location, what more could you want in a university? The University of California, Irvine (UCI) has about 29,600 students, 1,100 faculty members, and 9,400 staff. With a 19:1 student-to-teacher ratio, it offers about 90 undergraduate degree programs, 60 master's degree programs, and 50 doctoral programs. In addition to training future physicians, the UCI Medical Center offers inpatient and outpatient health care services to the surrounding community. The second-largest employer in Orange County, UCI generates an annual economic impact for the county of $4.3 billion. It is a part of the University of California system.

UNIVERSITY OF CALIFORNIA, LOS ANGELES

405 HILGARD AVE
LOS ANGELES, CA 900959000
Phone: 310 825-4321
Fax: –
Web: www.ucla.edu

CEO: –
CFO: –
HR: Letitia Lynex
FYE: June 30
Type: Private

As a public research university, University of California, Los Angeles (UCLA) boasts an undergraduate and graduate population of approximately 46,430 students. It's also the second-oldest university in the system (after Berkeley), founded in 1919. UCLA's campus extends about 420 acres at the base of the Santa Monica mountains. UCLA offers more than 130 graduate and professional programs, ranging from an extensive selection of business and medical programs to degrees in 40 different languages. UCLA curriculum features more than 3,900 courses, 130 majors, and 90 minors for undergraduates.

	Annual Growth	06/14	06/15	06/16	06/17	06/22
Sales ($mil.)	248.8%	–	–	–	6.5	3,353.9
Net income ($ mil.)	–	–	–	–	0.2	(245.0)
Market value ($ mil.)	–	–	–	–	–	–
Employees	–	–	–	–	–	3,326

UNIVERSITY OF CALIFORNIA, MERCED

5200 N LAKE RD
MERCED, CA 953435001
Phone: 209 228-4400
Fax: –
Web: www.ucmerced.edu

CEO: Josh Becker
CFO: –
HR: –
FYE: June 30
Type: Private

The University of California at Merced is four-year educational institution in the Golden State. Opened in 2005, the tenth campus in the UC system was built on some 7,000 San Joaquin Valley acres donated by the Virginia Smith Trust, funded by a grant of nearly $12 million from The David and Lucile Packard Foundation. The school's inaugural class included about 1,000 students. In 2009 UC Merced had some 3,400 mostly undergraduate students (about 7% are graduate students). Primarily a research school, UC Merced offers degree programs in such areas as engineering, biology, computer science, history, and environmental systems, among others.

	Annual Growth	06/06	06/07	06/08	06/11	06/16
Sales ($mil.)	(12.3%)	–	–	5.4	94.9	1.9
Net income ($ mil.)	(24.7%)	–	–	2.2	5.1	0.2
Market value ($ mil.)	–	–	–	–	–	–
Employees	–	–	–	–	–	238

UNIVERSITY OF CALIFORNIA, RIVERSIDE, ALUMNI ASSOCIATION

900 UNIVERSITY AVE
RIVERSIDE, CA 925219800
Phone: 951 827-1012
Fax: –
Web: alumni.ucr.edu

CEO: –
CFO: –
HR: –
FYE: June 30
Type: Private

The University of California, Riverside is not among the best known of the 10 UC campuses, but it is home to about 17,000 students, including some 2,000 graduate students. The campus covers 1,200 acres and is located 50 miles east of Los Angeles. A branch campus is located in Palm Desert. The school has its origins in a citrus agricultural station established in 1907, where grad students did coursework. A college opened for classes in early 1954, and it was designated a university in 1959. UC Riverside offers bachelor's and master's degrees, as well as Ph.D. programs. Students can choose to study a variety of subjects including engineering, agricultural sciences, business management, or education.

UNIVERSITY OF CALIFORNIA, SAN DIEGO

9500 GILMAN DR
LA JOLLA, CA 920935004
Phone: 858 534-2230
Fax: –
Web: www.ucsd.edu

CEO: –
CFO: –
HR: Nancy Rodriguez
FYE: June 30
Type: Private

The University of California San Diego (UCSD) is one of the leading research universities around the world. Founded in 1960 as a forward-thinking research institution for graduate and undergraduate study, the university is home to the the Scripps Institution of Oceanography, the UC San Diego Health System, and the UC San Diego Medical Center, among other research organizations. Its faculty boasts a number of Nobel laureates, National Medal of Science winners, and MacArthur Fellowship (the genius awards). With an enrollment of about 42,970 students, UCSD has about 10 academic, professional, and graduate schools and eight undergraduate residential colleges. The school is one of the ten campuses in the University of California system.

	Annual Growth	06/09	06/10	06/11*	12/20*	06/22
Sales ($mil.)	0.6%	–	–	2,879.9	0.0	3,061.7
Net income ($ mil.)	–	–	–	621.5	0.0	(135.8)
Market value ($ mil.)	–	–	–	–	–	–
Employees	–	–	–	–	–	25,400

*Fiscal year change

UNIVERSITY OF CALIFORNIA, SAN FRANCISCO

513 PARNASSUS AVE 115F
SAN FRANCISCO, CA 941432205
Phone: 415 476-9000
Fax: –
Web: www.ucsf.edu

CEO: –
CFO: –
HR: –
FYE: June 30
Type: Private

The University of California, San Francisco (UCSF) is part of the 10-campus University of California, the world's premier public research university system, and the only of its campuses dedicated to graduate and professional education. As a professional graduate school, UCSF offers degrees to some 3,200 students in schools of dentistry, medicine, nursing, and pharmacy. In addition to highly recognized medical programs, UCSF Medical Center is also renowned in the health care field. The university operates four campuses in San Francisco, including its main Parnassus Heights campus. As a leading health sciences university, UCSF is actively involved in more than 1,700 clinical trials.

UNIVERSITY OF CINCINNATI

2600 CLIFTON AVE
CINCINNATI, OH 452202872
Phone: 513 556-6000
Fax: –
Web: www.uc.edu

CEO: –
CFO: –
HR: –
FYE: June 30
Type: Private

The University of Cincinnati (UC) is a public research university offering undergraduate, graduate, and professional education from its campuses in Ohio including UC Blue Ash College and UC Clermont College, Graduate School, and College of Law, among others. The university enrolls about 50,920 students and has about 15 colleges. Academic offerings include business, law, medicine, engineering, and applied science, pharmacy, and music. The institution offers about 440 degree programs and more than 210 minors and certificates. UC was founded in 1819 and became a state university in 1977; the school has an endowment of approximately $1.6 billion. Notable alumni include former US president William Howard Taft and architect Michael Graves.

	Annual Growth	06/04	06/05	06/06	06/07	06/11
Sales ($mil.)	16.6%	–	–	557.1	594.3	1,198.3
Net income ($ mil.)	19.2%	–	–	20.3	112.1	48.9
Market value ($ mil.)	–	–	–	–	–	–
Employees	–	–	–	–	–	14,600

UNIVERSITY OF COLORADO FOUNDATION

1800 N GRANT ST STE 725
DENVER, CO 802031114
Phone: 303 813-7935
Fax: –
Web: giving.cu.edu

CEO: Jack Finlaw
CFO: Charlene Laus
HR: Felicity O 'herron
FYE: June 30
Type: Private

Operating independently from the University of Colorado, the University of Colorado Foundation (CU Foundation) engages in not-for-profit fundraising on behalf of the University. It partners with the University to raise, manage, and invest private support for the University's benefit. The foundation manages more than $125 million annually from nearly 50,000 donors; the funds it raises are used to support scholarships, research, athletics, building construction, and faculty and staff at the University. The CU Foundation also manages the University's Creating Futures fundraising campaign, which aims to raise $1.5 billion.

	Annual Growth	06/15	06/16	06/19	06/20	06/22
Sales ($mil.)	19.0%	–	158.5	289.0	259.1	449.4
Net income ($ mil.)	34.1%	–	27.2	76.1	31.3	158.0
Market value ($ mil.)	–	–	–	–	–	–
Employees	–	–	–	–	–	180

UNIVERSITY OF COLORADO HOSPITAL FOUNDATION

4200 E 9TH AVE
DENVER, CO 802023706
Phone: 720 848-0000
Fax: –
Web: www.uchealth.org

CEO: –
CFO: –
HR: –
FYE: June 30
Type: Private

University of Colorado Hospital Authority, doing business as UCHealth, operates the University of Colorado Hospital (UCH) in Aurora, Colorado. The facility is a teaching institution for the University of Colorado. UCH is a community hospital that includes a number of specialty care facilities, including centers specializing in oncology, respiratory care, and endocrinology. The facility also conducts medical training and research programs in partnership with the University of Colorado's Denver School of Medicine. In addition, UCHealth operates primary care clinics in the Denver metropolitan area.

	Annual Growth	06/03	06/04	06/05	06/09	06/10
Sales ($mil.)	11.4%	–	–	464.2	1.0	796.0
Net income ($ mil.)	169.7%	–	–	1.1	–	151.7
Market value ($ mil.)	–	–	–	–	–	–
Employees	–	–	–	–	–	4,200

UNIVERSITY OF DELAWARE

210 S COLLEGE AVE
NEWARK, DE 197165200
Phone: 302 831-2107
Fax: –
Web: www.udel.edu

CEO: –
CFO: –
HR: Chris Clendening
FYE: June 30
Type: Private

Delaware brings up images of many things, our first president, that famous river, and now the private University of Delaware (UD). The school's flagship campus in Newark has an enrollment of roughly 17,000 undergraduate and close to 4,000 graduate students. The school also has four auxiliary campuses around the state. UD offers almost 150 undergraduate degrees, about 120 master's programs, and more than 50 doctoral programs, as well as associate's and dual graduate programs through seven academic schools. Among its instructors are well-known authors, scientists, artists, and Nobel Laureates.

	Annual Growth	06/18	06/19	06/20	06/21	06/22
Sales ($mil.)	14.4%	–	1,069.4	1,312.6	1,380.7	1,599.0
Net income ($ mil.)	51.2%	–	60.5	(19.1)	101.9	209.1
Market value ($ mil.)	–	–	–	–	–	–
Employees	–	–	–	–	–	3,600

UNIVERSITY OF DENVER

2199 S UNIVERSITY BLVD
DENVER, CO 802104711
Phone: 303 871-3014
Fax: –
Web: www.du.edu

CEO: –
CFO: –
HR: –
FYE: June 30
Type: Private

Want a mile-high education? Colorado Seminary, which does business as University of Denver (DU), offers graduate and undergraduate degrees in more than 300 fields of study, including law, political science, humanities, education, engineering, and psychology. About 12,000 undergraduate and graduate students from across the US and more than 80 countries are enrolled at the school. Founded in 1864, the university has a student-to-faculty ratio of 11:1. DU is located on a 125-acre campus. Former Secretary of State Condoleezza Rice, former Interior Secretary Gale Norton, and former Coors Brewing CEO Peter Coors attended DU.

	Annual Growth	06/18	06/19	06/20	06/21	06/22
Sales ($mil.)	17.4%	–	521.2	716.7	784.5	843.0
Net income ($ mil.)	17.6%	–	43.7	(11.2)	77.3	71.2
Market value ($ mil.)	–	–	–	–	–	–
Employees	–	–	–	–	–	1,400

UNIVERSITY OF DETROIT MERCY

4001 W MCNICHOLS RD
DETROIT, MI 482213038
Phone: 313 993-6000
Fax: –
Web: www.udmercy.edu

CEO: –
CFO: –
HR: –
FYE: June 30
Type: Private

Perhaps students taking a really tough test wish for mercy at University of Detroit Mercy (UDM). Michigan's largest and most comprehensive Catholic university is sponsored by the Society of Jesus (Jesuits) and the Religious Sisters of Mercy. UDM has an enrollment of about 5,100 students at its three campuses (two located in residential northwest Detroit and one in downtown Detroit). UDM has a student-faculty ratio of 13:1. It offers 100 academic programs in fields such as architecture and psychology, nursing, teacher education, and engineering through seven schools and colleges.

	Annual Growth	06/17	06/18	06/20	06/21	06/22
Sales ($mil.)	4.5%	–	158.7	175.0	171.8	189.0
Net income ($ mil.)	53.4%	–	3.2	10.6	11.3	17.5
Market value ($ mil.)	–	–	–	–	–	–
Employees	–	–	–	–	–	950

UNIVERSITY OF EVANSVILLE

1800 LINCOLN AVE
EVANSVILLE, IN 477221000
Phone: 812 488-2000
Fax: –
Web: www.evansville.edu

CEO: –
CFO: –
HR: Keith Gehlhausen
FYE: May 31
Type: Private

The University of Evansville, affiliated with the United Methodist Church, offers more than 80 academic areas of study for undergraduate and graduate students. The university consists of three colleges (College of Arts and Sciences, College of Education and Health Sciences, College of Engineering and Computer Science) and one school (Schroeder School of Business). It has an annual enrollment of more than 2,600 students. Recognized for its study-abroad program, the university also has a campus in the UK (Harlaxton College) in addition to its main campus in Indiana's third-largest city. The University of Evansville was founded in 1854 as Moores Hill Male and Female Collegiate Institute.

	Annual Growth	05/18	05/19	05/20	05/21	05/22
Sales ($mil.)	(0.3%)	–	77.0	82.1	76.5	76.4
Net income ($ mil.)	–	–	(1.0)	12.4	48.2	(13.1)
Market value ($ mil.)	–	–	–	–	–	–
Employees	–	–	–	–	–	500

UNIVERSITY OF FLORIDA

300 SW 13TH ST
GAINESVILLE, FL 326110001
Phone: 352 392-3261
Fax: –
Web: www.ufl.edu

CEO: –
CFO: –
HR: –
FYE: June 30
Type: Private

Founded in 1853, the University of Florida (UF) is one of the largest in the country, with about 55,780 students and around 5,415 full-time faculty members. UF is a major land-grant research university encompassing 2,000 acres in Gainesville, Florida. The university's around 15 colleges offer more than 300 undergraduate and graduate degree options, plus a comprehensive array of courses, including education, law, medicine, psychology, and philosophy. It is also a member of the Association of American Universities, a confederation of the top research universities in North America. A founding member of the Southeastern Conference, UF's athletic teams (the Florida Gators) are typically ranked nationally.

	Annual Growth	06/14	06/15	06/20	06/21	06/22
Sales ($mil.)	4.4%	–	1,735.3	2,019.0	2,081.3	2,351.5
Net income ($ mil.)	7.7%	–	262.0	(15.4)	218.8	440.1
Market value ($ mil.)	–	–	–	–	–	–
Employees	–	–	–	–	–	5,106

UNIVERSITY OF GEORGIA

424 E BROAD ST
ATHENS, GA 306021535
Phone: 706 542-2471
Fax: –
Web: www.uga.edu

CEO: –
CFO: –
HR: –
FYE: June 30
Type: Private

Located in the quintessential college town of Athens, The University of Georgia (UGA) offers a wide range of degree programs to nearly 35,000 students. Forest resources, veterinary medicine, and law are a few of the school's academic programs. UGA, which also runs 170-plus study-abroad and exchange programs, administers the prestigious Peabody Awards, which honors media achievements, and boasts one of the nation's largest map collections. Famous alumni include former US Senator Phil Gramm, TV journalist Deborah Norville, and former PBS president Pat Mitchell. The University of Georgia was chartered by the State of Georgia in 1785 and graduated its first class in 1804.

	Annual Growth	06/16	06/17	06/18	06/19	06/20
Sales ($mil.)	3.4%	–	–	997.9	1,094.1	1,067.4
Net income ($ mil.)	–	–	–	111.7	72.9	(22.8)
Market value ($ mil.)	–	–	–	–	–	–
Employees	–	–	–	–	–	17,800

UNIVERSITY OF HAWAII SYSTEM

2444 DOLE ST
HONOLULU, HI 968222399
Phone: 808 956-8111
Fax: –
Web: www.hawaii.edu

CEO: David McClain
CFO: Kalbert Young
HR: –
FYE: June 30
Type: Private

With a reach that extends across half a dozen islands, the University of Hawai'i System consists of three university campuses, seven community college campuses, and several job training and research centers. The public higher education system has an enrollment of more than 60,000 students, about 85% of which are Hawaii residents. It offers more than 600 different doctorate, graduate, undergraduate, and associate degrees, as well as professional certificates, in more than 200 fields of study. The University of Hawai'i was founded in 1907 as the College of Agriculture and Mechanic Arts in Honolulu, incidentally while Hawaii was still a US territory.

	Annual Growth	06/16	06/17	06/18	06/21	06/22
Sales ($mil.)	0.3%	–	771.5	772.1	728.1	783.8
Net income ($ mil.)	43.5%	–	33.1	51.9	(70.9)	201.6
Market value ($ mil.)	–	–	–	–	–	–
Employees	–	–	–	–	–	12,000

UNIVERSITY OF HOUSTON SYSTEM

4302 UNIVERSITY DR
HOUSTON, TX 772042011
Phone: 713 743-0945
Fax: –
Web: www.uhsystem.edu

CEO: –
CFO: –
HR: –
FYE: August 31
Type: Private

The University of Houston System plays an essential role in meeting the higher education needs of the Houston metropolitan area and Texas as the region's largest provider of comprehensive university services. The university system serves more than 73,530 students at four Houston-area universities. Flagship institution the University of Houston was founded in 1927 and offers about 275 undergraduate and graduate academic programs. Also under the system's umbrella are the University of Houston-Clear Lake, the University of Houston-Downtown, and the University of Houston-Victoria. In addition, it also operates six multi-institution instructional sites to meet the educational needs of students in high growth parts of the metropolitan area that don't have easy access to one of the UH System campuses. The system was established in 1977.

	Annual Growth	08/11	08/12	08/13	08/14	08/15
Sales ($mil.)	(4.2%)	–	688.2	1.3	742.5	605.5
Net income ($ mil.)	(31.9%)	–	132.7	81.1	46.4	41.9
Market value ($ mil.)	–	–	–	–	–	–
Employees	–	–	–	–	–	12,608

UNIVERSITY OF KENTUCKY HOSPITAL AUXILIARY INC.

800 ROSE ST
LEXINGTON, KY 405360001
Phone: 859 323-5000
Fax: –
Web: www.uky.edu

CEO: –
CFO: –
HR: –
FYE: June 30
Type: Private

For the times when there's a physical reason to be carried "back to my old Kentucky home," being lugged to University of Kentucky Albert B. Chandler Hospital might be a better option. The 500-bed academic hospital is operated by the University of Kentucky Auxiliary. It is located within the University of Kentucky Medical Center complex, which includes the specialized medical colleges of the University of Kentucky and affiliated clinical treatment facilities (under the UK HealthCare umbrella). UK Chandler Hospital's services include oncology, pediatrics, cardiology, orthopedics, and women's health, and it operates eastern Kentucky's only Level I trauma and Level III neonatal ICU units.

	Annual Growth	06/09	06/10	06/11	06/12	06/13
Sales ($mil.)	(98.1%)	–	–	797.5	912.8	0.3
Net income ($ mil.)	(97.5%)	–	–	41.3	13.1	0.0
Market value ($ mil.)	–	–	–	–	–	–
Employees	–	–	–	–	–	2,879

UNIVERSITY OF LA VERNE

1950 3RD ST
LA VERNE, CA 917504401
Phone: 909 593-3511
Fax: –
Web: www.laverne.edu

CEO: Devorah Liberman
CFO: –
HR: –
FYE: June 30
Type: Private

University of La Verne (ULV) offers 55 undergraduate degree programs through colleges of arts and sciences, business and public management, education and organizational leadership, and law. It also boasts more than 30 masters, four doctoral programs and dozens of certificates and credentials in education, psychology and counseling, business, leadership, public administration, health services, and gerontology. In addition to the central campus in La Verne, California, the university operates eight regional campuses in California. It has an annual enrollment of more than 8,600 undergraduate, masters, law, continuing education, and online students. ULV has a student/faculty ratio of 15:1. The university was founded in 1891 by members of the Church of the Brethren.

	Annual Growth	06/15	06/16	06/20	06/21	06/22
Sales ($mil.)	(1.6%)	–	169.1	161.0	145.4	153.6
Net income ($ mil.)	–	–	18.7	7.0	44.4	(27.7)
Market value ($ mil.)	–	–	–	–	–	–
Employees	–	–	–	–	–	2,200

UNIVERSITY OF LOUISVILLE

2301 S 3RD ST
LOUISVILLE, KY 402922001
Phone: 502 852-5555
Fax: –
Web: www.louisville.edu

CEO: Mary Nixon
CFO: –
HR: –
FYE: June 30
Type: Private

Living up to its mandate to be a leading metropolitan research university, the University of Louisville (U of L) has hit a few out of the park. The U of L completed the first self-contained artificial heart implant and the first successful hand transplant at its University of Louisville Hospital. The health care focused university offers associate, baccalaureate, master's, professional, and doctorate degrees in some 170 fields of study including medicine, dentistry, nursing, and public health, as well as arts and sciences, education, business, law, music, social work, and engineering. It has more than 22,000 students enrolled in about a dozen colleges and schools on three campuses.

	Annual Growth	06/11	06/12	06/18	06/21	06/22
Sales ($mil.)	5.4%	–	559.1	717.3	850.2	947.5
Net income ($ mil.)	–	–	(37.0)	3.1	64.5	53.2
Market value ($ mil.)	–	–	–	–	–	–
Employees	–	–	–	–	–	6,275

UNIVERSITY OF LYNCHBURG

1501 LAKESIDE DR
LYNCHBURG, VA 245013113
Phone: 434 544-8100
Fax: –
Web: www.lynchburg.edu

CEO: –
CFO: –
HR: –
FYE: June 30
Type: Private

In Lynchburg, Tennessee, they make whiskey. In Lynchburg, Virginia, they make graduates. Lynchburg College is an independent residential college with more than 170 full-time faculty members and about 2,300 undergraduate and graduate students across some 40 majors. It consists of six schools: Business and Economics, Communication and the Arts, Education and Human Development, Health Sciences and Human Performance, Humanities and Social Sciences, and Sciences. Tuition is about $14,000 per semester; however, virtually all students receive financial aid. The college was founded in 1903 by Dr. Josephus Hopwood, a Christian Church (Disciples of Christ) minister, and his wife Sarah.

	Annual Growth	06/18	06/19	06/20	06/21	06/22
Sales ($mil.)	(0.9%)	–	77.8	73.6	80.2	75.8
Net income ($ mil.)	–	–	7.6	(3.9)	44.0	(7.9)
Market value ($ mil.)	–	–	–	–	–	–
Employees	–	–	–	–	–	1,077

UNIVERSITY OF MAINE SYSTEMS INC

5703 ALUMNI HALL STE 101
ORONO, ME 044695703
Phone: 207 973-3300
Fax: –
Web: www.maine.edu

CEO: –
CFO: –
HR: –
FYE: June 30
Type: Private

University of Maine System is composed of seven public universities throughout Maine serving some 40,000 students. It also operates eight regional outreach centers as well as distance education programs. The University of Maine System offers nearly 600 majors, minors, and concentrations; its flagship campus in Orono (UMaine) offers nearly 90 bachelor's degree programs, more than 60 master's degree programs, and about two dozen doctoral programs. UMaine was established in 1862 as the Maine College of Agriculture and Mechanic Arts; it adopted its current name in 1897. The University of Maine System was created in 1968 by the state legislature.

	Annual Growth	06/12	06/13	06/17	06/18	06/19
Sales ($mil.)	0.3%	–	460.2	448.2	458.0	469.9
Net income ($ mil.)	(26.1%)	–	27.9	20.7	15.8	4.5
Market value ($ mil.)	–	–	–	–	–	–
Employees	–	–	–	–	–	3,000

UNIVERSITY OF MARYLAND MEDICAL SYSTEM CORPORATION

250 W PRATT ST
BALTIMORE, MD 212012423
Phone: 410 328-8667
Fax: –
Web: www.umms.org

CEO: Mohan Suntha MBA MD
CFO: Henry J Franey
HR: –
FYE: June 30
Type: Private

The University of Maryland Medical System (UMMS) is a private, university-based regional health care system focused on serving the health care needs of Maryland. The UMMS, one of the largest employers in the Baltimore area, has about 2,460 licensed beds and attends to such specialties as trauma care, cancer, cardiac, women's, vascular and neuroscience services, orthopedic rehabilitation, and pediatric care. University of Maryland Medical Center, the system's teaching hub, is one of the oldest academic hospitals in the US. In addition to its hospitals, UMMS also includes community clinics to address mental health, rehabilitation, and primary care.

	Annual Growth	06/18	06/19	06/20	06/21	06/22
Sales ($mil.)	4.9%	–	4,235.3	4,364.1	4,769.8	4,893.1
Net income ($ mil.)	–	–	36.2	70.0	428.8	(82.0)
Market value ($ mil.)	–	–	–	–	–	–
Employees	–	–	–	–	–	12,000

UNIVERSITY OF MARYLAND ST. JOSEPH MEDICAL CENTER, LLC

7601 OSLER DR
TOWSON, MD 212047700
Phone: 410 337-1000
Fax: –
Web: www.umms.org

CEO: –
CFO: –
HR: Katelyn Decarlo
FYE: June 30
Type: Private

University of Maryland St. Joseph Medical Center (UM-St. Joseph) provides acute care services in the Baltimore area. The hospital, with some 260 acute-care beds, features a heart institute, cancer center, orthopedic institute, eating disorder ward, and women's and children's unit, as well as emergency, neurology, radiology, and surgery divisions. The medical center boasts a level III-plus neonatal intensive care unit, which offers care to infants with diseases and infections. A subsidiary of the University of Maryland Medical System, UM-St. Joseph was founded in 1864 by the Sisters of St. Francis of Philadelphia.

	Annual Growth	06/17	06/18	06/19	06/20	06/21
Sales ($mil.)	10.5%	–	364.4	432.4	445.5	492.3
Net income ($ mil.)	(0.2%)	–	27.5	12.8	7.2	27.3
Market value ($ mil.)	–	–	–	–	–	–
Employees	–	–	–	–	–	1,950

UNIVERSITY OF MASSACHUSETTS INCORPORATED

1 BEACON ST
BOSTON, MA 021083107
Phone: 617 287-7000
Fax: –
Web: www.massachusetts.edu
CEO: John Cunningham
CFO: –
HR: –
FYE: June 30
Type: Private

The University of Massachusetts (UMass) is the engine for one of the world's most innovative and energized economies. It has been expanding across the commonwealth since its founding in 1863. About 74,000 students are enrolled each year. The university's flagship campus is in Amherst, with more than 28,000 students and over 200 distinct academic programs including highly ranked programs in business computer science, health care and social science and largest public research university in New England. UMass is the third-largest research university in Massachusetts and the fourth-largest research university in New England, behind only Harvard, MIT, and Yale with a record $813 million in annual research and development.

	Annual Growth	06/16	06/17	06/18	06/20	06/22
Sales ($mil.)	2.2%	–	2,443.0	2,468.8	2,426.0	2,721.3
Net income ($ mil.)	(13.1%)	–	325.2	77.6	(39.6)	160.8
Market value ($ mil.)	–	–	–	–	–	–
Employees	–	–	–	–	–	13,196

UNIVERSITY OF MISSISSIPPI

113 FALKNER
UNIVERSITY, MS 386779704
Phone: 662 915-6538
Fax: –
Web: www.olemiss.edu
CEO: Dodie McElmurray
CFO: –
HR: Andrea Jekabsons
FYE: December 31
Type: Private

They call her "Ole Miss," and she really is old: The University of Mississippi was chartered in 1844 as the first public university in the state and opened in 1848. Starting with 80 students, the school's enrollment has grown to more than 23,000, with most students attending the main Oxford campus. Ole Miss has additional campuses in Southaven (Desoto County) and Tupelo, and it operates the University of Mississippi Medical Center in Jackson. The school is home to more than 30 research centers that specialize in business, engineering, law, and other disciplines. Its academic institutes include the Croft Institute for International Studies and the William Winter Institute for Racial Reconciliation.

	Annual Growth	12/18	12/19*	06/20	06/21*	12/22
Sales ($mil.)	15.9%	–	462.5	442.3	452.9	719.5
Net income ($ mil.)		–	–	34.7	10.3	66.1	(13.9)
Market value ($ mil.)	–	–	–	–	–	–
Employees	–	–	–	–	–	8,700

*Fiscal year change

UNIVERSITY OF MISSOURI SYSTEM

1 HOSPITAL DR
COLUMBIA, MO 652121000
Phone: 573 882-2712
Fax: –
Web: www.umsystem.edu
CEO: –
CFO: –
HR: –
FYE: June 30
Type: Private

The University of Missouri System (UM) is one of the nation's largest higher education institutions. Founded in 1839, UM System educates more than 70,000 students at four campuses and through a statewide extension program with activities in every county of the state. Serving nearly 115 counties, the university's campuses are University of Missouri-Columbia (MU), University of Missouri-Kansas City (UMKC), Missouri University of Science and Technology (S&T), and University of Missouri-St. Louis (UMSL). MU Extension is a partnership of the University of Missouri campuses, Lincoln University, the people of Missouri through county extension councils, and the National Institute for Food and Agriculture of the US Department of Agriculture. Collectively, the UM System is a $3.0 billion enterprise that represents one of the greatest assets of the state of Missouri.

	Annual Growth	06/11	06/12	06/13	06/16	06/18
Sales ($mil.)	3.5%	–	–	2,404.7	2,702.4	2,851.2
Net income ($ mil.)	3.8%	–	–	222.0	108.6	267.6
Market value ($ mil.)	–	–	–	–	–	–
Employees	–	–	–	–	–	30,282

UNIVERSITY OF MOBILE, INC.

5735 COLLEGE PKWY
MOBILE, AL 366132842
Phone: 251 675-5990
Fax: –
Web: www.umobile.edu
CEO: –
CFO: –
HR: –
FYE: June 30
Type: Private

The University of Mobile touts a "distinctively Christian" environment as it offers bachelor's degrees, associate's degrees, and pre-professional programs in more than 40 areas of study across six schools: the College of Arts and Sciences, the School of Business, the School of Education, the School of Leadership Development, the School of Nursing, and the School of Christian Studies. It also offers master's programs in Business Administration, Nursing, Education, and Religious Studies. Affiliated with the Southern Baptist Convention, the university was founded in 1961. It has an enrollment of approximately 2,000 students.

	Annual Growth	06/09	06/10	06/17	06/21	06/22
Sales ($mil.)	3.7%	–	30.2	29.3	35.0	46.7
Net income ($ mil.)	–	–	(1.4)	0.8	5.1	2.5
Market value ($ mil.)	–	–	–	–	–	–
Employees	–	–	–	–	–	251

UNIVERSITY OF MONTANA

32 CAMPUS DR
MISSOULA, MT 598120001
Phone: 406 243-0211
Fax: –
Web: www.umt.edu
CEO: –
CFO: –
HR: Sara Drake
FYE: June 30
Type: Private

Sometimes referred to as the Harvard of the West, The University of Montana's motto is Lux et Veritas (Light and Truth). The Big Sky Country certainly provides plenty of light for the university, which is a leading producer of Rhodes Scholars. The University of Montana (UM) is a member of the Montana University System and offers associate's, bachelor's, master's, first-professional, and doctoral degrees, as well as technical certificates. About 21,000 undergraduate and graduate students enroll at UM's four campuses. Founded in 1893, UM also gets high marks for the physical beauty of its campus and nearby wilderness areas.

	Annual Growth	06/18	06/19	06/20	06/21	06/22
Sales ($mil.)	2.6%	–	277.9	270.8	261.1	300.2
Net income ($ mil.)	2.1%	–	21.2	(11.5)	(3.8)	22.6
Market value ($ mil.)	–	–	–	–	–	–
Employees	–	–	–	–	–	2,450

UNIVERSITY OF NEW HAVEN, INCORPORATED

300 BOSTON POST RD
WEST HAVEN, CT 065161999
Phone: 203 932-7000
Fax: –
Web: www.newhaven.edu
CEO: –
CFO: –
HR: Maurice Cayer
FYE: June 30
Type: Private

The University of New Haven (UNH) offers more than 80 undergraduate and 30 graduate degree programs from its five colleges. Fields of study include arts and sciences, business, criminal justice and forensic science, and engineering. The private university has about 6,500 students and 500 faculty members, with a student-to-teacher ratio of 16:1. The University of New Haven was founded in 1920 as the New Haven YMCA Junior College. It held classes in space rented from Yale University for nearly 40 years before its own building was constructed.

	Annual Growth	06/13	06/14	06/15	06/20	06/22
Sales ($mil.)	(2.5%)	–	–	258.4	189.7	216.8
Net income ($ mil.)	–	–	–	19.3	6.1	(5.4)
Market value ($ mil.)	–	–	–	–	–	–
Employees	–	–	–	–	–	696

UNIVERSITY OF NEW MEXICO

1800 ROMA BLVD NE
ALBUQUERQUE, NM 871310001
Phone: 505 277-0111
Fax: –
Web: gallup.unm.edu

CEO: –
CFO: –
HR: A Barron
FYE: June 30
Type: Private

The University of New Mexico (UNM) is most renowned for its schools of medicine, law, engineering, and education. Students also attend one of the school's four branches located around the northern part of the state at Gallup, Los Alamos, Taos, and Valencia. Through its schools and colleges, the university offers about 95 bachelor's degrees, around 70 master's degrees, more than 35 doctorate degrees, as well as professional practice programs in law, medicine, and pharmacy. Founded in 1889, UNM are recognized as a Carnegie Highest Research Activity Institution and a federally-designated Hispanic Serving Institution. It is also a leading research institution, providing students with opportunities to engage in cutting-edge research projects and gain valuable experience.

	Annual Growth	06/18	06/19	06/20	06/21	06/22
Sales ($mil.)	7.9%	–	1,913.9	2,050.4	2,316.2	2,407.1
Net income ($ mil.)	–	–	(137.9)	629.0	(0.4)	110.6
Market value ($ mil.)	–	–	–	–	–	–
Employees	–	–	–	–	–	18,362

UNIVERSITY OF NEW ORLEANS

2000 LAKESHORE DR
NEW ORLEANS, LA 701483520
Phone: 888 514-4275
Fax: –
Web: www.uno.edu

CEO: –
CFO: –
HR: Ron Boudreaux
FYE: June 30
Type: Private

From its campus on Lake Pontchartrain, the University of New Orleans (UNO) provides graduate and undergraduate study programs to some 11,000 students. The university offers about 100 degree and pre-professional programs at colleges of business, education and human development, engineering, liberal arts, and sciences; graduate programs include applied physics, business administration, and urban studies. Its students conduct extensive research programs at about 20 institutes and centers. UNO has a student-to-teacher ratio of 18:1. The university was founded by an act of the state legislature in 1956; it is part of the Louisiana State University System.

	Annual Growth	06/18	06/19	06/20	06/21	06/22
Sales ($mil.)	(3.8%)	–	120.4	119.2	115.3	107.3
Net income ($ mil.)	72.3%	–	2.1	5.4	(4.0)	10.8
Market value ($ mil.)	–	–	–	–	–	–
Employees	–	–	–	–	–	1,500

UNIVERSITY OF NORTH CAROLINA AT CHAPEL HILL

104 AIRPORT DR
CHAPEL HILL, NC 275995023
Phone: 919 962-1370
Fax: –
Web: www.unc.edu

CEO: Michael A Steinback
CFO: –
HR: Lori Harrell
FYE: June 30
Type: Private

The University of North Carolina at Chapel Hill (UNC-Chapel Hill) has the education market cornered. One of the three original points making up North Carolina's Research Triangle (along with Duke University and North Carolina State University), Carolina is the flagship campus of the University of North Carolina (UNC) system. The institution is consistently among the top-ranked research schools in the US. It enrolls some 29,000 students and offers more than 250 undergraduate, graduate, and professional programs including law and medicine. It has 3,200 full-time faculty members.

	Annual Growth	06/07	06/08	06/11	06/17	06/19
Sales ($mil.)	19.9%	–	281.7	1,704.9	1,773.6	2,073.7
Net income ($ mil.)	3.9%	–	149.7	391.4	95.3	229.1
Market value ($ mil.)	–	–	–	–	–	–
Employees	–	–	–	–	–	12,204

UNIVERSITY OF NORTH CAROLINA AT GREENSBORO

1000 SPRING GARDEN ST
GREENSBORO, NC 274125068
Phone: 336 334-5000
Fax: –
Web: hhs.uncg.edu

CEO: –
CFO: –
HR: –
FYE: June 30
Type: Private

The University of North Carolina at Greensboro (UNCG) has an enrollment of about 19,000 students, including approximately 14,000 undergraduates. The university offers 75 undergraduate degree programs (in 100 subject areas), about 75 master's degrees, and 30 doctoral programs through nearly ten colleges and professional schools. It also has a Division of Continual Learning that caters to non-traditional students. Originally a women's college, UNCG was established in 1891; it became coeducational in 1964, when it also became a part of the University of North Carolina system and adopted its current name.

	Annual Growth	06/09	06/10	06/14	06/16	06/17
Sales ($mil.)	4.8%	–	127.2	18.5	10.1	176.8
Net income ($ mil.)	1.9%	–	42.2	9.3	(1.5)	48.1
Market value ($ mil.)	–	–	–	–	–	–
Employees	–	–	–	–	–	2,400

UNIVERSITY OF NORTH DAKOTA

264 CENTENNIAL DR
GRAND FORKS, ND 582026059
Phone: 701 777-4321
Fax: –
Web: www.und.edu

CEO: –
CFO: –
HR: Misty Brustad
FYE: June 30
Type: Private

Way up in the Upper Midwest is the University of North Dakota (UND), the largest and oldest institution of higher learning in the state, with an enrollment of approximately 15,000 students. It offers undergraduate and graduate programs in close to 225 fields through nine colleges and schools (aerospace sciences, arts and sciences, business and public administration, education and human development, engineering and mines, law, medical and health sciences, nursing, and a graduate school). The university also has nearly 20 doctoral programs, as well as certificate degree programs, distance degree programs, and a continuing education division. UND was founded in 1883, six years before North Dakota achieved statehood.

	Annual Growth	06/17	06/18	06/19	06/20	06/21
Sales ($mil.)	5.2%	–	325.7	329.0	323.8	378.8
Net income ($ mil.)	31.4%	–	12.6	4.5	4.4	28.7
Market value ($ mil.)	–	–	–	–	–	–
Employees	–	–	–	–	–	2,756

UNIVERSITY OF NORTHERN IOWA

1227 W 27TH ST
CEDAR FALLS, IA 506140012
Phone: 319 242-7325
Fax: –
Web: www.uni.edu

CEO: –
CFO: –
HR: –
FYE: June 30
Type: Private

University of Northern Iowa (UNI) offers more than 90 majors for students in a range of fields. It provides undergraduate, graduate, and doctoral degree programs to more than 12,000 students (about 90% of which are Iowa residents). The school is comprised of four undergraduate colleges (business administration, education, humanities and liberal arts, and social and behavioral sciences) and one graduate college. Students are also engaged in research programs. UNI was founded as Iowa State Normal School in 1876; it gained university status in 1967 and has oversight by the state board of regents. Notable alumni include US Senator Charles Grassley and NFL quarterback Kurt Warner.

	Annual Growth	06/18	06/19	06/20	06/21	06/22
Sales ($mil.)	(8.2%)	–	158.6	144.0	118.6	122.7
Net income ($ mil.)	(12.3%)	–	9.3	14.6	27.6	6.3
Market value ($ mil.)	–	–	–	–	–	–
Employees	–	–	–	–	–	3,071

UNIVERSITY OF OKLAHOMA

660 PARRINGTON OVAL
NORMAN, OK 730193003
Phone: 405 325-0000
Fax: –
Web: www.ou.edu

CEO: –
CFO: Joe Castiglione
HR: Jason McPhaul
FYE: June 30
Type: Private

The University of Oklahoma has a primary goal: to better the Sooner. Founded in 1890 and known as OU, the university has 20 colleges that offer some 160 bachelor's degrees, 170 master's degrees, and about 80 doctoral degrees through three campuses in Norman, Oklahoma City, and Tulsa. The Norman campus is where the main academic programs reside, while OU's seven health-related professional colleges are based at the Health Sciences Center in Oklahoma City. OU's enrollment has reached about 31,000 students who are instructed by 1,500 full-time faculty members. The university adopted the Sooner nickname in 1908, deriving the moniker from homesteaders who arrived too soon in Oklahoma's 1889 Land Run.

UNIVERSITY OF OREGON

1585 E 13TH AVE
EUGENE, OR 974031657
Phone: 541 346-1000
Fax: –
Web: www.uoregon.edu

CEO: –
CFO: –
HR: Judy Gates
FYE: June 30
Type: Private

As one of the largest schools in the state, the University of Oregon (UO) has an enrollment of over 23,200 students and more than 1,990 faculty members. It offers its students nine different schools and colleges, plus a graduate college, with fields of study ranging from the arts and journalism to business and law. Founded in 1876, UO is one of the top public universities in the nation offering more than 300 undergraduate programs and more than 120 graduate programs. The University of Oregon is one of just two schools in the Pacific Northwest selected for membership in the prestigious Association of American Universities, a consortium of more than 70 leading public and private research institutions in the US and Canada.

	Annual Growth	06/17	06/18	06/20	06/21	06/22
Sales ($mil.)	4.2%	–	740.1	741.3	692.8	871.9
Net income ($ mil.)	–	–	(8.2)	329.2	(16.8)	158.7
Market value ($ mil.)	–	–	–	–	–	–
Employees	–	–	–	–	–	7,971

UNIVERSITY OF PITTSBURGH-OF THE COMMONWEALTH SYSTEM OF HIGHER EDUCATION

4200 5TH AVE
PITTSBURGH, PA 152600001
Phone: 412 624-4141
Fax: –
Web: www.pitt.edu

CEO: Mark Nordenberg
CFO: –
HR: Laurel R Phillips
FYE: June 30
Type: Private

The University of Pittsburgh (Pitt for short) operates its flagship campus in the Oakland neighborhood of Pittsburgh. More than 35,000 graduate and undergraduate students attend the main campus, as well as four regional campuses. Pitt Panthers pursue degrees in about 400 disciplines, including arts and sciences, business, law, medicine, and engineering. The school has a student-teacher ratio of 14:1. Pitt is also affiliated with the UPMC health system, which operates about 20 hospitals, numerous clinics, and an insurance company. Pitt was founded in 1787, making it one of the oldest universities in the US.

	Annual Growth	06/17	06/18	06/19	06/20	06/21
Sales ($mil.)	3.2%	–	2,276.0	2,353.0	2,353.0	2,502.6
Net income ($ mil.)	59.5%	–	381.7	112.0	(168.1)	1,548.5
Market value ($ mil.)	–	–	–	–	–	–
Employees	–	–	–	–	–	9,607

UNIVERSITY OF PUGET SOUND

1500 N WARNER ST
TACOMA, WA 984160005
Phone: 253 879-3100
Fax: –
Web: www.pugetsound.edu

CEO: –
CFO: –
HR: Erin Ruff
FYE: June 30
Type: Private

The University of Puget Sound is a private liberal arts college located in the Pacific Northwest with an enrollment of some 2,600 students and a student-faculty ratio of 12:1. It boasts more than 50 traditional and interdisciplinary programs and about 1,200 courses. Based south of Seattle in Tacoma, Washington, the school offers a wide range of undergraduate degrees, as well as graduate degrees in education, occupational therapy, and physical therapy. Students come from nearly 50 states and 15 countries. Founded in 1888 by the Methodist Church, The University of Puget Sound divested its affiliation with the church in 1980. Notable alumni include Verio founder Justin Jaschke and Alaska governor Sean Parnell.

	Annual Growth	06/18	06/19	06/20	06/21	06/22
Sales ($mil.)	7.9%	–	123.4	118.1	141.2	155.0
Net income ($ mil.)	–	–	13.1	(4.4)	(14.0)	(10.9)
Market value ($ mil.)	–	–	–	–	–	–
Employees	–	–	–	–	–	1,700

UNIVERSITY OF REDLANDS

1200 E COLTON AVE
REDLANDS, CA 923743720
Phone: 909 793-2121
Fax: –
Web: www.redlands.edu

CEO: –
CFO: –
HR: Cindy Tengler
FYE: June 30
Type: Private

Focused on liberal arts and sciences, private University of Redlands consists of a College of Arts and Sciences and a School of Education both located in Southern California's City of Redlands. Its School of Business is located on campus and in regional centers throughout Southern California. The institution offers more than 40 undergraduate majors, about a dozen master's degree programs, a doctorate in leadership for educational justice, and professional credential and certificate programs. With an enrollment of about 2,400 students, University of Redlands was founded in 1907 on land donated by banker and Baptist layman Karl C. Wells; it maintains an informal relationship with the American Baptist church.

	Annual Growth	06/18	06/19	06/20	06/21	06/22
Sales ($mil.)	(0.9%)	–	129.0	130.7	109.2	125.7
Net income ($ mil.)	–	–	7.4	78.4	42.2	(28.3)
Market value ($ mil.)	–	–	–	–	–	–
Employees	–	–	–	–	–	1,017

UNIVERSITY OF RHODE ISLAND

75 LOWER COLLEGE RD
KINGSTON, RI 028811974
Phone: 401 874-1000
Fax: –
Web: www.uri.edu

CEO: –
CFO: –
HR: Paula Murray
FYE: June 30
Type: Private

The University of Rhode Island (URI) offers more than 80 undergraduate majors, specializing in nursing, psychology, communication studies, kinesiology, and human development. It also offers master's, doctoral, and professional degrees from its nine colleges at four campuses across the state. URI's main campus is located in Kingston, the W. Alton Jones Campus is in West Greenwich, its Graduate School of Oceanography is located on Narragansett Bay, and Providence is home to the university's Alan Shawn Feinstein College of Continuing Education. URI, which has an enrollment of more than 16,500 students, was chartered as the state's agricultural school in 1888.

	Annual Growth	06/16	06/17	06/18	06/19	06/20
Sales ($mil.)	1.6%	–	–	440.0	449.5	454.3
Net income ($ mil.)	(8.4%)	–	–	45.3	85.6	38.0
Market value ($ mil.)	–	–	–	–	–	–
Employees	–	–	–	–	–	2,600

UNIVERSITY OF RICHMOND

110 UR DR
RICHMOND, VA 231730008
Phone: 804 289-8133
Fax: –
Web: www.richmond.edu

CEO: –
CFO: –
HR: –
FYE: June 30
Type: Private

Suffering from arachnophobia? You may want to steer clear of the more than 4,300 Spiders who are enrolled at the University of Richmond (UR). UR consists of five schools: Jepson School of Leadership Studies, Richmond School of Law, Robins School of Business, School of Arts and Sciences, and School of Continuing Studies. The university offers some 60 undergraduate majors, as well as graduate and master's programs in business, accounting, and law. UR also offers some 75 study-abroad programs, in which more than half of its students participate. Founded in 1830 by Virginia Baptists as a seminary for men, the school became Richmond College in 1840.

	Annual Growth	06/17	06/18	06/20	06/21	06/22
Sales ($mil.)	1.8%	–	308.9	312.9	319.5	331.1
Net income ($ mil.)	–	–	157.2	(118.8)	965.8	(206.4)
Market value ($ mil.)	–	–	–	–	–	–
Employees	–	–	–	–	–	1,400

UNIVERSITY OF SAN DIEGO

5998 ALCALA PARK FRNT
SAN DIEGO, CA 921102492
Phone: 619 260-4600
Fax: –
Web: www.sandiego.edu

CEO: –
CFO: –
HR: Amber J Koch
FYE: June 30
Type: Private

The University of San Diego (USD) is a private college located close to southern California's beaches and the Mexican border. The coeducational Roman Catholic university has an enrollment of around 8,815 students. USD offers about 85 bachelor's, master's, and doctoral degrees in areas such as arts and sciences, business administration, education, engineering, law, and nursing. It has a faculty of around 495 full time staff members. The university also home to the Joan B. Kroc School of Peace Studies, established in 2003 by the wife of McDonald's founder Ray Kroc.

	Annual Growth	06/16	06/17	06/18	06/19	06/22
Sales ($mil.)	1.8%	–	350.0	365.2	387.0	382.5
Net income ($ mil.)	–	–	92.6	103.2	64.3	(25.7)
Market value ($ mil.)	–	–	–	–	–	–
Employees	–	–	–	–	–	1,600

UNIVERSITY OF SAN FRANCISCO INC

2130 FULTON ST
SAN FRANCISCO, CA 941171050
Phone: 415 422-5555
Fax: –
Web: www.usfca.edu

CEO: Stephen A Privett
CFO: –
HR: –
FYE: May 31
Type: Private

University of San Francisco (USF) is one Jesuit Catholic colleges and universities in the US. The main USF campus sits on 55 acres near Golden Gate Park in San Francisco. The school, which was formed in 1855 as St. Ignatius Academy, enrolls about 9,690 undergraduate and graduate students combined. USF operates five schools and colleges, including the College of Arts and Sciences, School of Management, and School of Nursing and Health Professions as well as the School of Law and the School of Education (both of which enroll graduate students only). Tuition, fees, and room and board average a total of more than $65,135 per year for a traditional undergraduate student.

	Annual Growth	05/16	05/17	05/20	05/21	05/22
Sales ($mil.)	6.4%	–	417.8	554.8	571.8	568.8
Net income ($ mil.)	(14.7%)	–	50.4	34.6	117.7	22.7
Market value ($ mil.)	–	–	–	–	–	–
Employees	–	–	–	–	–	1,200

UNIVERSITY OF SCRANTON

800 LINDEN ST
SCRANTON, PA 185104501
Phone: 888 727-2686
Fax: –
Web: www.scranton.edu

CEO: –
CFO: –
HR: Denise Gurz
FYE: May 31
Type: Private

The University of Scranton is a Catholic and Jesuit liberal arts university with a student population of more than 5,420, including more than 600 graduate students. Its schools and colleges include the College of Arts & Sciences, Panuska College of Professional Studies, and Kania School of Management. It offers programs in areas such as theology, music, technology, athletics, nursing, and continuing education and has some 300 faculty members. The school offers 66 undergraduate and 29 graduate programs. The University of Scranton, which is overseen by the Society of Jesus (the Jesuits), was founded in 1888 as Saint Thomas College.

	Annual Growth	05/15	05/16	05/20	05/21	05/22
Sales ($mil.)	1.6%	–	231.5	244.3	164.6	255.1
Net income ($ mil.)	(4.7%)	–	8.2	(0.2)	60.4	6.1
Market value ($ mil.)	–	–	–	–	–	–
Employees	–	–	–	–	–	1,050

UNIVERSITY OF SOUTH ALABAMA

307 N UNIVERSITY BLVD
MOBILE, AL 366883053
Phone: 251 460-6101
Fax: –
Web: www.southalabama.edu

CEO: –
CFO: –
HR: Gerald Gattis
FYE: September 30
Type: Private

When you go by the moniker USA and the campus beauty queen wins the Miss USA title year after year (the Pi Kappa Phi Miss USA pageant, that is) you're standing on hallowed ground. In this case it's the ground of the University of South Alabama, situated on the upper Gulf Coast. The school's crown jewel is its College of Medicine and other facilities, including USA Medical Center, USA Knollwood Hospital, and USA Children's and Women's Hospital. USA also offers degrees in Health, Arts and Sciences, Business, Education, Engineering, Nursing, Computer and Information Sciences, Continuing Education and Special Programs, and the Graduate School. More than 14,880 students call the USA home.

	Annual Growth	09/16	09/17	09/18	09/20	09/21
Sales ($mil.)	6.8%	–	662.5	653.1	782.7	860.7
Net income ($ mil.)	27.4%	–	47.8	(0.7)	124.2	126.0
Market value ($ mil.)	–	–	–	–	–	–
Employees	–	–	–	–	–	5,403

UNIVERSITY OF SOUTH CAROLINA

1600 HAMPTON ST STE 414
COLUMBIA, SC 292083403
Phone: 803 777-2001
Fax: –
Web: www.sc.edu

CEO: –
CFO: –
HR: Heidi Thompson
FYE: June 30
Type: Private

The Fighting Gamecocks lead the way at the University of South Carolina (USC). The university, which comprises 14 colleges and schools, offers more than 350 courses of study. Areas of study concentrate on medicine, law, business, education, science and math, liberal arts, and other fields. Nearly 2,200 full-time faculty members teach a student body of some 46,250 across eight campuses, from South Carolina's Aiken to Union. USC's main campus is located on the site of its 1801 founding in the state's capital city of Columbia. Tuition runs about $10,500 a year for residents and $27,500 for out-of-state students. USC has an endowment of some $514 million.

UNIVERSITY OF SOUTH FLORIDA

4202 E FOWLER AVE
TAMPA, FL 336208000
Phone: 813 974-2011
Fax: –
Web: www.usf.edu

CEO: –
CFO: –
HR: Angela Badell
FYE: June 30
Type: Private

The University of South Florida (USF) is the fastest-rising university in America. The university has about 49,765 students at three campuses in Tampa, St. Petersburg, and Sarasota/Manatee. It offers some 180 undergraduate, graduate, specialist, and doctoral degree programs through about 15 colleges, including Arts, Arts and Sciences, Behavioral and Community Sciences, Honors College, Business, Education, Engineering, Marine Science, Pharmacy, and Public Health, among others. USF also offers continuing education programs, graduate certificates, distance and online learning, workforce development, noncredit education, pre-college programs, and the Osher Lifelong Learning Institute, and is one of the top public research universities in the US. USF was founded in 1960; its mascot is the bull.

	Annual Growth	06/18	06/19	06/20	06/21	06/22
Sales ($mil.)	1.7%	–	849.2	821.8	795.4	894.2
Net income ($ mil.)	87.9%	–	4.4	(95.0)	(23.4)	29.4
Market value ($ mil.)	–	–	–	–	–	–
Employees	–	–	–	–	–	16,165

UNIVERSITY OF SOUTHERN CALIFORNIA

3720 S FLOWER ST FL 3
LOS ANGELES, CA 900894304
Phone: 213 740-4542
Fax: –
Web: www.usc.edu

CEO: –
CFO: –
HR: Sonia Perez
FYE: June 30
Type: Private

University of Southern California (USC) is one of the world's leading private research universities. Founded in 1880, the university (with a Trojan mascot) grew up with the city of Los Angeles, and is now one of the city's largest private employers. USC offers programs in fields such as business and entrepreneurship, engineering, dentistry, public policy and law, health and medicine, and science. It also has several associated hospitals and medical centers including Keck Hospital and Norris Cancer Hospital. In addition to its campuses in Los Angeles, USC also has programs and centers around the world. USC has a total of approximately 49,500 undergraduate and graduate students and about 4,625 full-time faculty members.

UNIVERSITY OF ST. THOMAS

2115 SUMMIT AVE
SAINT PAUL, MN 551051096
Phone: 651 962-5000
Fax: –
Web: www.stthomas.edu

CEO: –
CFO: –
HR: –
FYE: June 30
Type: Private

Far from any Bahamian beaches or Caribbean hot spots sits The University of St. Thomas (UST). The school is a Catholic university with campuses in Minneapolis and St. Paul, Minnesota. It offers about 90 undergraduate and 60 graduate programs in seven academic divisions: education and philosophy, arts and sciences, business, engineering, divinity, law, and social work. The school has an enrollment of about 11,000 undergraduate and graduate students with a student-to-teacher ratio of 14:1. UST, along with military prep school St. Thomas Academy, grew out of St. Thomas Aquinas Seminary, which was founded in 1885 by Archbishop John Ireland.

	Annual Growth	06/18	06/19	06/20	06/21	06/22
Sales ($mil.)	4.1%	–	278.2	273.2	287.2	314.0
Net income ($ mil.)	(39.9%)	–	28.8	16.6	227.5	6.2
Market value ($ mil.)	–	–	–	–	–	–
Employees	–	–	–	–	–	1,900

UNIVERSITY OF TENNESSEE

1331 CIR PARK DR
KNOXVILLE, TN 379163801
Phone: 865 974-1000
Fax: –
Web: www.utk.edu

CEO: –
CFO: –
HR: –
FYE: June 30
Type: Private

Whether you want to learn the art of aviation or get ready for a career in public service, the University of Tennessee System (UT) is here to help. The 200-year-old school provides undergraduate, graduate, and professional academic programs to about 50,000 students; programs include business, engineering, law, pharmacy, medicine, and veterinary medicine. It has a student-teacher ratio of about 16:1. Campuses include the flagship Knoxville location, as well as the Health Science Center at Memphis, the Space Institute at Tullahoma, the statewide Institute for Public Service, and the Institute of Agriculture. Other UT System campuses are located in Chattanooga and Martin. UT was founded in 1794 as Blount College.

	Annual Growth	12/06	12/07	12/08*	06/11	06/12
Sales ($mil.)	440.1%	–	–	1.3	1,034.3	1,092.9
Net income ($ mil.)	–	–	–	–	296.5	60.5
Market value ($ mil.)	–	–	–	–	–	–
Employees	–	–	–	–	–	12,000

*Fiscal year change

UNIVERSITY OF TEXAS AT AUSTIN

110 INNER CAMPUS DR
AUSTIN, TX 787121139
Phone: 512 471-3434
Fax: –
Web: www.utexas.edu

CEO: –
CFO: –
HR: –
FYE: August 31
Type: Private

The University of Texas at Austin (UT Austin) is one of the world's leading research universities. With approximately 52,385 students in about 20 colleges and schools, UT Austin consistently ranks on the list of the country's largest student bodies and offers about 155 undergraduate and nearly 140 graduate degree programs. In addition to its 430-acre downtown Austin academic campus, UT Austin maintains extensive research locations including the J.J. Pickle Research Campus and West Pickle Research Building in northwest Austin, the McDonald Observatory in West Texas, Lady Bird Johnson Wildflower Center in southwest Austin, the Marine Science Institute on the Texas coast, and Center for Global Innovation and Entrepreneurship in Nuevo Le n, Mexico. The university was founded in 1883.

UNIVERSITY OF TEXAS AT DALLAS

800 W CAMPBELL RD
RICHARDSON, TX 750803021
Phone: 972 883-2295
Fax: –
Web: sites.utdallas.edu

CEO: –
CFO: –
HR: –
FYE: October 31
Type: Private

As part of The University of Texas System, the University of Texas at Dallas offers more than 140 undergraduate and graduate programs to a student body of more than 29,000. It has a student-to-teacher ratio of about 24:1. Perhaps best known now for its computer science and business administration programs, UT Dallas also operates schools of arts and humanities, economics, political science, criminal justice, technology, engineering, public affairs, and natural sciences and mathematics.

	Annual Growth	08/06	08/07	08/08	08/09*	10/10
Sales ($mil.)	14.4%	–	–	158.5	181.5	207.3
Net income ($ mil.)	42.8%	–	–	59.7	(23.0)	121.9
Market value ($ mil.)	–	–	–	–	–	–
Employees	–	–	–	–	–	1,500

*Fiscal year change

UNIVERSITY OF TEXAS AT EL PASO

500 W UNIVERSITY AVE
EL PASO, TX 799688900
Phone: 915 747-5000
Fax: –
Web: www.utep.edu

CEO: –
CFO: –
HR: –
FYE: August 31
Type: Private

UTEP's Miners dig the importance of higher education. The University of Texas at El Paso (UTEP) was originally founded as a mining school but now offers about 150 bachelor's and master's degrees and some 20 doctoral degrees through six academic colleges. The university's six colleges offer education in business, engineering, education, health sciences, liberal arts, and science. The school draws much of its population -- a majority of which is Mexican-American -- from the US-Mexico border. UTEP enrolls some 23,000 students annually and is part of the Austin-based University of Texas System. It was formed in 1914 as the Texas State School of Mines and Metallurgy.

	Annual Growth	08/03	08/04	08/05	08/08	08/11
Sales ($mil.)	9.3%	–	–	122.9	187.1	209.8
Net income ($ mil.)	–	–	–	–	(0.4)	50.5
Market value ($ mil.)	–	–	–	–	–	–
Employees	–	–	–	–	–	3,700

UNIVERSITY OF TEXAS SYSTEM

210 W 7TH ST
AUSTIN, TX 787012903
Phone: 512 499-4587
Fax: –
Web: www.utsystem.edu

CEO: –
CFO: –
HR: Geisu Lewis
FYE: August 31
Type: Private

The University of Texas System is one of the nation's largest public university systems of higher education. It runs about 15 universities throughout the Lone Star State with a total enrollment of more than 243,000 students at academic and health institutions across the state, as well as an operating budget of $25.2 billion. UT System also runs about half a dozen health institutions, including medical schools. The system also offers undergraduate and graduate degrees in fields including science, technology, engineering, and math. Established in 1876, UT Austin opened in 1883. The UT System was formally organized in 1950.

	Annual Growth	08/18	08/19	08/20	08/21	08/22
Sales ($mil.)	973.4%	–	16.0	16,360	17.8	19,848
Net income ($ mil.)	–	–	0.5	2.8	16.4	(201.9)
Market value ($ mil.)	–	–	–	–	–	–
Employees	–	–	–	–	–	104,000

UNIVERSITY OF THE OZARKS

415 N COLLEGE AVE
CLARKSVILLE, AR 728302880
Phone: 479 979-1000
Fax: –
Web: www.ozarks.edu

CEO: –
CFO: Gloria M Arcia
HR: Karen Schluterman
FYE: June 30
Type: Private

University of the Ozarks is a private liberal arts school located at the foot of the Ozarks in rural Clarksville, Arkansas. It offers undergraduate and graduate programs in more than 25 academic areas, as well as pre-professional programs in engineering and medical, pharmaceutical, and veterinary sciences. With a total enrollment of around 650, the school boasts small classes (averaging 15 students) and a student-to-faculty ration of 12:1. The school is affiliated with the Presbyterian Church and promotes Christian values and service while respecting its students' individual beliefs. Founded in 1834, University of the Ozarks is the oldest institution of higher education in Arkansas.

	Annual Growth	06/16	06/17	06/18	06/20	06/22
Sales ($mil.)	2.3%	–	38.5	33.7	40.9	43.3
Net income ($ mil.)	–	–	7.7	(1.2)	3.5	(0.1)
Market value ($ mil.)	–	–	–	–	–	–
Employees	–	–	–	–	–	215

UNIVERSITY OF THE PACIFIC

3601 PACIFIC AVE
STOCKTON, CA 952110197
Phone: 209 946-2401
Fax: –
Web: www.pacific.edu

CEO: –
CFO: –
HR: Joanne Carvana
FYE: June 30
Type: Private

Situated next to the largest body of water on earth, the University of the Pacific holds a sizable body of knowledge. The school offers more than 80 undergraduate majors and about 20 graduate programs in such fields as art, language, biology, business, computer science, engineering, history, and pharmacy. It offers undergraduate, graduate, and professional degree programs in nine colleges, and enrolls about 7,000 students at its main campus in Stockton, California, the McGeorge School of Law in Sacramento, and the Arthur A. Dugoni School of Dentistry in San Francisco. California's first chartered institution of higher education, University of the Pacific was founded in 1851.

	Annual Growth	06/16	06/17	06/18	06/20	06/22
Sales ($mil.)	0.6%	–	–	341.6	460.4	350.1
Net income ($ mil.)	–	–	–	20.7	43.9	(45.7)
Market value ($ mil.)	–	–	–	–	–	–
Employees	–	–	–	–	–	1,500

UNIVERSITY OF UTAH HEALTH HOSPITALS AND CLINICS

50 N MEDICAL DR
SALT LAKE CITY, UT 841320001
Phone: 801 581-2121
Fax: –
Web: healthcare.utah.edu

CEO: Dan Lundergan
CFO: –
HR: –
FYE: June 30
Type: Private

University of Utah Health is the only academic medical center in the state of Utah and the Mountain West and provides patient care for the people of Utah, Idaho, Wyoming, Montana, western Colorado, and much of Nevada. It also serves as the training ground for the majority of the state's physicians, nurses, pharmacists, therapists, and other health care professionals. Its system is comprised of five hospitals and twelve community health care centers, as well six schools and colleges, including the colleges of Health, Nursing, and Pharmacy, the Eccles Health Sciences Library, and the schools of Dentistry and Medicine. The University Hospital provides care in areas including surgery, emergency care, cardiology, radiology, and organ transplant services; it also houses centers for medical education, training, and research. It is headquartered in Salt Lake City, Utah.

	Annual Growth	06/03	06/04	06/05	06/06	06/14
Sales ($mil.)	126.0%	–	–	0.8	0.8	1,282.5
Net income ($ mil.)	–	–	–	(0.5)	(0.5)	21.0
Market value ($ mil.)	–	–	–	–	–	–
Employees	–	–	–	–	–	4,200

UNIVERSITY OF VERMONT & STATE AGRICULTURAL COLLEGE

85 S PROSPECT ST
BURLINGTON, VT 054050001
Phone: 802 656-3131
Fax: –
Web: www.uvmhealth.org

CEO: –
CFO: –
HR: –
FYE: June 30
Type: Private

The University of Vermont (UVM) boasts scenic views and comprehensive secondary education. the university offers more than 100 majors through its seven undergraduate colleges, as well 46 master's programs and 21 doctoral programs at its Graduate College and College of Medicine. UVM has an enrollment of more than 12,820 students, including undergraduate, graduate, medical, and continuing education program participants. The university also conducts research programs in areas including translational science, cancer care, and transportation. UVM, a public land grant university, has more than 1,360 faculty members.

	Annual Growth	06/18	06/19	06/20	06/21	06/22
Sales ($mil.)	2.1%	–	650.1	661.8	647.0	691.3
Net income ($ mil.)	(49.0%)	–	39.7	24.0	188.7	5.3
Market value ($ mil.)	–	–	–	–	–	–
Employees	–	–	–	–	–	3,710

UNIVERSITY OF WASHINGTON INC

4300 ROOSEVELT WAY NE
SEATTLE, WA 981054718
Phone: 206 543-4444
Fax: –
Web: www.washington.edu

CEO: –
CFO: –
HR: Kira Thomsen-Cheek
FYE: June 30
Type: Private

The University of Washington (UW) is one of the world's preeminent public universities. Founded in 1861 as the Territorial University of Washington, UW has smaller branches in Tacoma and Bothell in addition to its main campus in downtown Seattle. The university offers more than 370 graduate programs across all three UW campuses and online, from master's to doctoral programs for people who are launching or continuing academic, research or professional careers. It also operates University of Washington Medical Center, Harborview Medical Center, Fred Hutchinson Cancer Center, UW Medicine Primary Care, UW Physicians, University of Washington School of Medicine, Airlift Northwest, and Valley Medical Center.

	Annual Growth	06/18	06/19	06/20	06/21	06/22
Sales ($mil.)	6.2%	–	5,485.2	5,511.5	5,841.4	6,570.8
Net income ($ mil.)	(0.6%)	–	481.5	343.2	2,001.7	472.3
Market value ($ mil.)	–	–	–	–	–	–
Employees	–	–	–	–	–	27,228

UNIVERSITY OF WEST GEORGIA

1601 MAPLE ST
CARROLLTON, GA 301180001
Phone: 678 839-4780
Fax: –
Web: www.westga.edu

CEO: –
CFO: –
HR: Thomas Gainey
FYE: June 30
Type: Private

Go West, young men and women, and join more than 13,200 students who attend University of West Georgia (UWG). UWG students major in nearly 90 programs through the university's schools and colleges (Arts and Sciences, Business, Education, and the Graduate School). UWG also allows select high school students to earn both college and high school credits simultaneously. UWG also offers a full program of distance education via the Internet through its eCore program. The school was founded in 1906 as the Fourth District Agricultural and Mechanical School in Carrollton, Georgia. The school became State University of West Georgia in 1996; it dropped "State" from its name in 2005.

	Annual Growth	06/15	06/16	06/19	06/20	06/22
Sales ($mil.)	(1.2%)	–	122.6	132.3	120.7	114.0
Net income ($ mil.)	44.3%	–	4.4	14.8	(25.9)	39.8
Market value ($ mil.)	–	–	–	–	–	–
Employees	–	–	–	–	–	993

UNIVERSITY OF WISCONSIN FOUNDATION

1848 UNIVERSITY AVE
MADISON, WI 537264090
Phone: 608 263-4545
Fax: –
Web: www.supportuw.org

CEO: –
CFO: –
HR: –
FYE: June 30
Type: Private

Because even Badgers need help, the University of Wisconsin Foundation raises funds, receives gifts, and manages assets for The University of Wisconsin-Madison and other donor-designated units of The University of Wisconsin System. (Bucky Badger is the school's mascot.) The foundation supports special programs and projects, including professorships, fellowships, scholarships, research efforts, and building projects. The not-for-profit organization has received more than $2.4 billion in donations since it was founded in 1945.

	Annual Growth	06/18	06/19	06/20	06/21	06/22
Sales ($mil.)	38.1%	–	495.6	528.9	739.0	1,306.1
Net income ($ mil.)	74.0%	–	175.9	214.8	347.4	926.5
Market value ($ mil.)	–	–	–	–	–	–
Employees	–	–	–	–	–	275

UNIVERSITY OF WISCONSIN HOSPITALS AND CLINICS AUTHORITY

600 HIGHLAND AVE
MADISON, WI 537920001
Phone: 608 263-6400
Fax: –
Web: www.uwhealth.org

CEO: Alan Kaplan
CFO: Robert Flannery
HR: Franchesca Beswick
FYE: June 30
Type: Private

The University of Wisconsin Hospital and Clinics Authority (UW Hospital and Clinics) is the integrated health system of the University of Wisconsin-Madison, caring for more than 700,000 patients each year with about 1,850 employed physicians and 21,000 employees at seven hospitals and more than 80 clinic locations. Governed by the UW Hospitals and Clinics Authority in Wisconsin they partner with the UW School of Medicine and Public Health to fulfill its patient care, research, education and community services missions.

	Annual Growth	06/18	06/19	06/20	06/21	06/22
Sales ($mil.)	5.9%	–	3,396.1	2,075.6	2,337.1	4,027.9
Net income ($ mil.)	–	–	231.8	202.5	435.0	(27.5)
Market value ($ mil.)	–	–	–	–	–	–
Employees	–	–	–	–	–	1,350

UNIVERSITY OF WISCONSIN MEDICAL FOUNDATION, INC.

7974 UW HEALTH CT
MIDDLETON, WI 535625531
Phone: 608 821-4223
Fax: –
Web: www.uwhealth.org

CEO: Alan Kaplan
CFO: –
HR: –
FYE: June 30
Type: Private

UW Medical Foundation provides administrative services to faculty physicians at the University of Wisconsin School of Medicine and Public Health. The foundation, a not-for-profit entity, is a physician practice organization that works in cooperation with the UW Hospital and Clinics and other medical offices and clinics throughout the Badger State. The foundation coordinates clinical sites and provides technical and professional staffing services, as well as administrative support for legal, marketing, information technology, and logistics functions.

	Annual Growth	06/17	06/18	06/19	06/20	06/21
Sales ($mil.)	1.7%	–	784.9	796.5	785.7	824.6
Net income ($ mil.)	(5.1%)	–	40.7	2.2	7.5	34.8
Market value ($ mil.)	–	–	–	–	–	–
Employees	–	–	–	–	–	3,200

UNIVERSITY OF WYOMING

1000 E UNIVERSITY AVE
LARAMIE, WY 820712001
Phone: 307 766-5766
Fax: –
Web: www.uwyo.edu

CEO: –
CFO: –
HR: –
FYE: June 30
Type: Private

For folks who live in Wyoming, the University of Wyoming (UW) is it -- the only place offering baccalaureate and graduate degrees, as well as research and outreach services that stretch across the state. The main campus is in Laramie, but the school also has a campus in Casper (offering coordinated education programs with the Casper College), plus regional outreach education centers stationed throughout the state. Founded in 1887, UW has grown to serve more than 13,000 students with about 200 programs of study through seven academic colleges, as well as numerous schools and institutes. The university has a student-to-faculty ratio of 14:1.

	Annual Growth	06/07	06/08	06/09	06/10	06/13
Sales ($mil.)	3.6%	–	–	195.5	195.6	225.3
Net income ($ mil.)	22.0%	–	–	52.9	31.7	117.0
Market value ($ mil.)	–	–	–	–	–	–
Employees	–	–	–	–	–	7,000

UNIVERSITY SYSTEM OF MARYLAND

3300 METZEROTT RD
ADELPHI, MD 207831651
Phone: 301 445-2740
Fax: –
Web: www.usmd.edu

CEO: –
CFO: –
HR: Saijal Khatri
FYE: June 30
Type: Private

The University System of Maryland (USM) operates one of the largest public university systems in the country, serving approximately 162,515 students through a dozen institutions, including Towson University, University of Baltimore, Frostburg State University, University of Maryland Global Campus, and Bowie State University. The USM comprises eleven degree-granting institutions, one research entity and an administrative unit. Its degree-granting institutions provide a full range of undergraduate, graduate, professional, and continuing education opportunities for students. Its research entity conducts basic and applied research, and transfers new technology to constituencies. The administrative unit includes the System Chancellor and staff who support the Board.

	Annual Growth	06/15	06/16	06/17	06/18	06/21
Sales ($mil.)	(0.4%)	–	–	3,515.7	3,601.9	3,454.4
Net income ($ mil.)	(25.2%)	–	–	355.6	338.4	111.1
Market value ($ mil.)	–	–	–	–	–	–
Employees	–	–	–	–	–	28,000

UNIVERSITY SYSTEM OF NEW HAMPSHIRE

5 CHENELL DR STE 301
CONCORD, NH 033018522
Phone: 603 862-1800
Fax: –
Web: www.usnh.edu

CEO: –
CFO: –
HR: –
FYE: June 30
Type: Private

The University of New Hampshire (UNH) is a liberal arts college that serves about 12,600 undergraduate and more than 2,200 graduate students. The institution offers more than 100 majors and academic programs of study at nine colleges and schools. The student-faculty ratio is 20:1. UNH is the flagship institution of the University System of New Hampshire. In 2007 the university graduated its first international class in Seoul under a program run by its Whittemore School of Business and Economics. Founded in 1866 as the New Hampshire College of Agriculture and the Mechanic Arts, UNH is a designated land-grant, sea-grant, and space-grant chartered school.

	Annual Growth	06/18	06/19	06/20	06/21	06/22
Sales ($mil.)	4.9%	–	–	642.8	633.7	707.3
Net income ($ mil.)	–	–	–	(1.2)	161.3	(36.9)
Market value ($ mil.)	–	–	–	–	–	–
Employees	–	–	–	–	–	16,000

UNIVEST FINANCIAL CORP

14 North Main Street
Souderton, PA 18964
Phone: 215 721-2400
Fax: –
Web: www.univest.net

NMS: UVSP
CEO: Jeffrey M Schweitzer
CFO: Brian J Richardson
HR: –
FYE: December 31
Type: Public

Univest Financial, including its wholly-owned subsidiary Univest Bank and Trust, has approximately $7.6 billion in assets and $4.5 billion in assets under management and supervision through its wealth management lines of business. Founded in 1876, Univest and its subsidiaries provide a full-range of financial solutions for individuals, businesses, municipalities, and nonprofit organizations primarily in the Mid-Atlantic Region. The company delivers these services through a network of more than 50 offices and online at www.univest.net. The Bank is the parent company of Girard Investment Services, LLC, a full-service registered introducing broker-dealer and a licensed insurance agency, Girard Advisory Services, LLC, a registered investment advisory firm, and Girard Pension Services, LLC, a registered investment advisor, which provides investment consulting and management services to municipal entities.

	Annual Growth	12/19	12/20	12/21	12/22	12/23
Assets ($mil.)	9.7%	5,380.9	6,336.5	7,122.4	7,222.0	7,780.6
Net income ($ mil.)	2.0%	65.7	46.9	91.8	78.1	71.1
Market value ($ mil.)	(4.8%)	790.3	607.4	883.0	771.1	650.1
Employees	2.9%	873	896	920	973	979

UNIVISION COMMUNICATIONS INC.

8551 NW 30TH TER
DORAL, FL 331221908
Phone: 212 455-5200
Fax: –
Web: www.univision.com

CEO: Raju Narisetti
CFO: Peter H Lori
HR: Santos Beatriz
FYE: December 31
Type: Private

TelevisaUnivision Inc. (formerly Univision Communications) is a leading Spanish-language media and content company. It features the largest library of owned content and industry-leading production capabilities that power its streaming, digital and linear television offerings, as well as its radio platforms. The company's media portfolio includes the top-rated broadcast networks Univision and UniM s in the US and Las Estrellas and Canal 5 in Mexico. TelevisaUnivision is home to around 35 Spanish-language cable networks, including Galavisi n and TUDN, the No. 1 Spanish-language sports network in the US and Mexico.

UNIWORLD GROUP, INC.

1 METROTECH CTR N STE 11
BROOKLYN, NY 112013875
Phone: 212 219-1600
Fax: –
Web: www.uwginc.com

CEO: Monique L Nelson
CFO: –
HR: Alicia Guscott
FYE: December 31
Type: Private

UniWorld Group is doing its part for world unity -- bringing together consumers and the products they think they want. As one of the largest African-American-owned ad firm in the US, UniWorld is a full-service agency that has helped such clients as AT&T, Burger King, Ford Motor Company, and The Home Depot reach minority consumers. The agency targets the "urban" market which it equates with America's trendsetters of the global pop culture. Services include advertising, promotions, event marketing, public relations, and direct marketing. Chairman and CEO Byron Lewis founded UniWorld in 1969. It is a subsidiary of advertising conglomerate WPP Group.

UNMC PHYSICIANS

988101 NEBRASKA MEDICAL CTR
OMAHA, NE 681980001
Phone: 402 559-9700
Fax: –
Web: www.unmc.edu

CEO: –
CFO: Troy Wilhelm
HR: –
FYE: June 30
Type: Private

If you're in Nebraska and your doctor suddenly tells you to, "Go Big Red!" -- don't be shocked, he's probably just a member of the not-for-profit, UNMC Physicians (formerly University Medical Associates). Many of the more than 500 physicians in the UNMC group practice were trained and now teach at the University of Nebraska Medical Center. Additionally, UNMC partners with The Nebraska Medical Center and the Olson Center for Women's Health to share best practices and resources. The physicians, who also operate 10 family health clinics in the area, provide services in about 50 specialties such as obstetrics, cancer care, family medicine, cardiology, and pediatrics.

	Annual Growth	06/13	06/14	06/16	06/21	06/22
Sales ($mil.)	8.9%	–	245.5	199.7	431.5	486.9
Net income ($ mil.)	–	–	11.7	(109.6)	–	–
Market value ($ mil.)	–	–	–	–	–	–
Employees	–	–	–	–	–	1,200

UNUM GROUP
NYS: UNM

1 Fountain Square
Chattanooga, TN 37402
Phone: 423 294-1011
Fax: –
Web: www.unum.com

CEO: –
CFO: –
HR: –
FYE: December 31
Type: Public

Unum Group is a leading provider of financial protection benefits in the US and the UK. The company offers short-term and long-term disability insurance, supplemental health coverage, and life and accidental death and dismemberment insurance to individuals and groups. Its Colonial Life segment offers expanded cancer, critical illness, vision products, and dental insurance. Additional subsidiaries include Unum Life Insurance Company of America, Provident Life and Accident, First Unum Life, Colonial Life & Accident, Paul Revere Life Insurance, Starmount Life Insurance, and Unum Poland. The company operates as Unum Limited in the UK.

	Annual Growth	12/19	12/20	12/21	12/22	12/23
Assets ($mil.)	(1.4%)	67,013	70,626	70,116	61,435	63,255
Net income ($ mil.)	3.9%	1,100.3	793.0	824.2	1,314.2	1,283.8
Market value ($ mil.)	11.6%	5,638.7	4,436.0	4,751.2	7,934.1	8,744.3
Employees	0.6%	10,300	10,700	10,300	10,937	10,553

UPBOUND GROUP INC
NMS: UPBD

5501 Headquarters Drive
Plano, TX 75024
Phone: 972 801-1100
Fax: 972 701-0360
Web: www.rentacenter.com

CEO: Mitchell E Fadel
CFO: Fahmi W Karam
HR: –
FYE: December 31
Type: Public

Upbound, formerly Rent-A-Center (RAC), is one of the leading rent-to-own chain nationwide. The company owns and operates some 1,850 company-owned stores throughout the US, and Puerto Rico under Get It Now, and Home Choice names. It also franchises about 445 stores through subsidiary Rent-A-Center Franchising International, under Rent-A-Center, ColorTyme, and RimTyme names. The stores rent name-brand home electronics, furniture, accessories, tablets, tools, handbags, smartphones, appliances, and computers. While customers have the option to eventually own their rented items. Almost all of the company's sales were generated in the US.

	Annual Growth	12/19	12/20	12/21	12/22	12/23
Sales ($mil.)	10.6%	2,669.9	2,814.2	4,583.5	4,245.4	3,992.4
Net income ($ mil.)	–	173.5	208.1	134.9	12.4	(5.2)
Market value ($ mil.)	4.2%	1,567.6	2,081.2	2,611.2	1,225.7	1,846.4
Employees	(2.7%)	14,500	14,320	14,290	12,690	12,970

UPMC

200 LOTHROP ST
PITTSBURGH, PA 152132536
Phone: 412 647-8762
Fax: –
Web: www.upmc.com

CEO: –
CFO: Robert B Michiei
HR: –
FYE: December 31
Type: Private

UPMC is a world-renowned health care provider and insurer. It is an international health care leader ? pioneering groundbreaking research, treatments, and clinical care. UPMC operates approximately 40 academic, community, and specialty hospitals, some 800 doctors' offices and outpatient sites, employs more than 5,000 physicians, and offers an array of rehabilitation, retirement, and long-term care facilities in western and central Pennsylvania, Maryland, New York, and around the globe. As a leading academic medical center with world-class clinical expertise and a growing, financially sound health insurance company, UPMC offers a seamless experience for patients across a continuously expanding geographic footprint.

	Annual Growth	12/18	12/19	12/20	12/21	12/22
Sales ($mil.)	7.4%	–	20,609	23,093	24,366	25,532
Net income ($ mil.)	–	–	–	462.6	1,113.1	1,857.2	(1,371.5)
Market value ($ mil.)	–	–	–	–	–	–
Employees	–	–	–	–	–	80,000

UPMC ALTOONA

620 HOWARD AVE
ALTOONA, PA 166014804
Phone: 814 889-2011
Fax: –
Web: www.altoonaregional.org

CEO: Jerry Murray
CFO: Charles R Zorger
HR: –
FYE: June 30
Type: Private

UPMC Altoona (formerly Altoona Regional Health System) moves patients upstream towards better health. Operating in Altoona and surrounding areas in central Pennsylvania, the health system's facilities include Altoona Hospital, an acute care center with 380 licensed beds that provides specialized care in areas including cardiovascular ailments, cancer, behavioral health, and neurology, as well as general emergency, trauma, birthing, and surgery services. UPMC Altoona also offers a variety of outpatient care facilities and programs, including home health care, a primary care physicians' group, and laboratory services. The not-for-profit system merged with Pennsylvania hospital operator University of Pittsburgh Medical Center (UPMC) in 2013.

	Annual Growth	06/11	06/12	06/13	06/14	06/15
Sales ($mil.)	0.2%	–	–	–	393.1	394.0
Net income ($ mil.)	70.1%	–	–	–	15.0	25.5
Market value ($ mil.)	–	–	–	–	–	–
Employees	–	–	–	–	–	2,494

UPMC CHILDREN'S HOSPITAL OF PITTSBURGH

4401 PENN AVE
PITTSBURGH, PA 152241334
Phone: 412 692-5437
Fax: –
Web: www.chp.edu

CEO: –
CFO: –
HR: –
FYE: June 30
Type: Private

From polio to poison control, Children's Hospital of Pittsburgh (CHP) has long been at the forefront of children's health care. Jonas Salk developed the polio vaccine there in the 1950s, and the ubiquitous Mr. Yuk poison label also got its start there. Founded in 1890, CHPI cares for thousands of sick kids each year -- both those who stay in one of its 300 inpatient beds and those who visit its outpatient, ambulatory surgery, and primary care centers. CHP doctors handle everything from flu to organ transplantation, and they engage in wide-ranging pediatric medical research as well, much of it funded by grants from the National Institutes of Health. CHP is part of Pittsburgh's gigantic UPMC health care system.

	Annual Growth	06/04	06/05	06/06	06/08	06/22
Sales ($mil.)	8.9%	–	15.2	423.4	45.6	65.1
Net income ($ mil.)	5.0%	–	9.9	32.5	12.5	22.6
Market value ($ mil.)	–	–	–	–	–	–
Employees	–	–	–	–	–	2,500

UPMC PINNACLE

409 S 2ND ST STE 2B
HARRISBURG, PA 171041612
Phone: 717 231-8900
Fax: –
Web: www.upmcpinnacle.com

CEO: –
CFO: –
HR: –
FYE: June 30
Type: Private

UPMC Pinnacle (formerly PinnacleHealth) helps central Pennsylvanians reach the peaks of wellness. The system provides a continuum of care through its eight hospitals that have a combined total of about 1,360 beds. Together, the hospitals provide general and specialty services in areas such as oncology, cardiovascular medicine, neurology, mental health, physical therapy, women's health, and orthopedics. UPMC Pinnacle is also home to a network of community health, diagnostic, ambulatory surgery, and outpatient centers. Additionally, the system administers home care and hospice care programs. UPMC bought PinnacleHealth in 2017.

	Annual Growth	06/06	06/07	06/08	06/09	06/21
Sales ($mil.)	72.1%	–	–	–	0.0	10.6
Net income ($ mil.)	–	–	–	–	(2.6)	(0.2)
Market value ($ mil.)	–	–	–	–	–	–
Employees	–	–	–	–	–	4,837

UPP TECHNOLOGY, INC.

130 S ELM ST
HINSDALE, IL 605214227
Phone: 630 493-7800
Fax: –
Web: www.upp.com

CEO: Scott Upp
CFO: –
HR: –
FYE: December 31
Type: Private

Upp Technology wants to help you ramp up your warehouse management skills to a whole new level. The company designs, develops, and implements warehouse fulfillment and distribution solutions. The company's customers use its products to manage their warehouses and order fulfillment processes. Clients come from a variety of industries including retail, manufacturing, distribution, and logistics; the company serves both public and private sector customers. Upp was formed in early 2009 when Integrated Warehousing Solutions and Upp Business Systems merged their businesses and began operating under the name Upp Technology.

	Annual Growth	12/08	12/09	12/10	12/11	12/12
Sales ($mil.)	(3.0%)	–	–	19.5	21.3	18.3
Net income ($ mil.)	(43.8%)	–	–	1.6	1.4	0.5
Market value ($ mil.)	–	–	–	–	–	–
Employees	–	–	–	–	–	75

UPPER CHESAPEAKE HEALTH FOUNDATION, INC.

520 UPPER CHESAPEAKE DR STE 405
BEL AIR, MD 210144339
Phone: 443 643-3390
Fax: –
Web: www.uchfoundation.org

CEO: Lyle E Sheldon
CFO: Joseph Hoffman
HR: Craig Willig
FYE: June 30
Type: Private

Upper Chesapeake Health (UCH) provides medical care services to the residents of northeastern Maryland. The not-for-profit health care system owns and operates Upper Chesapeake Medical Center and Harford Memorial Hospital. Specialized services include cardiovascular, behavioral health, birthing, pediatric, metabolic, wound care, and orthopedic services. The system also operates an ambulatory care center, medical office buildings, and physician practices. UCH is an affiliate of the University of Maryland Medical System.

	Annual Growth	06/14	06/15	06/19	06/20	06/21
Sales ($mil.)	(3.2%)	–	4.7	–	4.0	3.9
Net income ($ mil.)	–	–	3.5	–	(0.6)	(0.6)
Market value ($ mil.)	–	–	–	–	–	–
Employees	–	–	–	–	–	2,200

UPSON COUNTY HOSPITAL, INC.

801 W GORDON ST
THOMASTON, GA 302863426
Phone: 706 647-8111
Fax: –
Web: www.urmc.org

CEO: David L Castleberry
CFO: John Williams
HR: –
FYE: December 31
Type: Private

Upson Regional Medical Center is a 115-bed hospital that serves the communities in and around Thomaston, Georgia. In addition to general surgery and acute care, the hospital offers specialty services including occupational therapy, rehabilitation, pediatrics, and emergency care. Upson Regional also houses a neonatal special care unit, a sleep disorders center, and a wound healing center. The medical center has expanded its footprint with new medical offices and dining facilities.

	Annual Growth	12/18	12/19	12/20	12/21	12/22
Sales ($mil.)	6.6%	–	100.7	85.9	118.6	122.0
Net income ($ mil.)	(4.6%)	–	7.3	36.3	21.5	6.3
Market value ($ mil.)	–	–	–	–	–	–
Employees	–	–	–	–	–	625

UPSTATE MEDICAL UNIVERSITY

750 E ADAMS ST
SYRACUSE, NY 132101834
Phone: 315 464-7087
Fax: –
Web: www.upstate.edu

CEO: John McCabe
CFO: Sturat Wright
HR: –
FYE: December 31
Type: Private

SUNY Upstate Medical University is on the up-and-up when it comes to medical training and care. Serving Syracuse and surrounding areas, the university's medical campus features the University Hospital, a 700-bed, two-campus teaching and research hospital with numerous specialty departments including Level I trauma, burn, cancer, AIDS, diabetes, and neurosurgery centers, as well as the Golisano Children's Hospital. It also conducts community health outreach programs. As part of the State University of New York (SUNY), the medical complex also comprises four professional colleges (Medicine, Nursing, Health Professions, and Graduate Studies), an extensive Health Sciences Library, and clinical research facilities.

UQM TECHNOLOGIES, INC.

4120 SPECIALTY PL
LONGMONT, CO 805045400
Phone: 303 682-4900
Fax: –
Web: www.danfoss.com

CEO: Joseph R Mitchell
CFO: David I Rosenthal
HR: Sherry Knoll
FYE: December 31
Type: Private

UQM Technologies is revving up for the electric vehicle wars. The company builds permanent magnet electric motors for hybrid and electric vehicles -- and the gears and electronic controls needed to operate them. UQM developed hybrid electric powertrains for GM's Precept concept car and the US Army's Humvee vehicle (made by AM General). UQM has customers in the aerospace, industrial, medical, and telecommunications industries, but views the auto industry as having the greatest potential. Denver's Regional Transportation District accounts for 12% of sales, while Lippert Components is responsible for 17%; US government agencies and their contractors account for 31%.

URATA & SONS CONCRETE, INC.

3430 LUYUNG DR
RANCHO CORDOVA, CA 957426871
Phone: 916 638-5364
Fax: –
Web: www.urataconcrete.com

CEO: –
CFO: –
HR: –
FYE: December 31
Type: Private

Urata & Sons is a solidly established provider of concrete contracting services including slab and curb and gutter work. The firm focuses on large scale tilt-up buildings, parking structures, schools, hospitals, public works projects, multi-family residences, and other commercial ventures, including malls, casinos and resorts, and industrial complexes. Most of its projects are in California and Nevada. Urata & Sons' customers include high-profile contractors DPR Construction, Turner Construction, and The Walsh Group. The company was started in 1974 by Sofio Urata and his sons, Charles and Frank, who began by paving residential patios and driveways.

	Annual Growth	12/01	12/02	12/03	12/04	12/16
Sales ($mil.)	3.1%	–	–	–	49.2	71.1
Net income ($ mil.)	(3.8%)	–	–	–	3.4	2.2
Market value ($ mil.)	–	–	–	–	–	–
Employees	–	–	–	–	–	125

URBAN AFFAIRS COALITION

1650 ARCH ST
PHILADELPHIA, PA 191032000
Phone: 215 851-0110
Fax: –
Web: www.uac.org

CEO: Sharmain Turner
CFO: Cynthia Ray
HR: Sandra Higginbotham
FYE: June 30
Type: Private

The Urban Affairs Coalition is a not-for-profit coalition of more than 55 partners that works with business and community leaders to provide economic development, education, and workforce development for needy neighborhoods in Philadelphia. The group assists other grassroots organizations by providing financial management services, as well as loans and grants; it also operates more than 30 programs of its own, including youth services and literacy programs. The organization is funded through government and foundation grants, corporate contributions, and individual donations. The Urban Affairs Coalition was formed by the 1991 merger of The Urban Affairs Partnership and the Philadelphia Urban Coalition.

	Annual Growth	06/09	06/10	06/13	06/16	06/20
Sales ($mil.)	4.1%	–	30.9	24.3	27.9	46.0
Net income ($ mil.)	–	–	(2.2)	(0.6)	8.7	0.2
Market value ($ mil.)	–	–	–	–	–	–
Employees	–	–	–	–	–	550

URBAN EDGE PROPERTIES NYS: UE

888 Seventh Avenue
New York, NY 10019
Phone: 212 956-2556
Fax: –
Web: www.uedge.com

CEO: Jeffrey S Olson
CFO: Mark J Langer
HR: –
FYE: December 31
Type: Public

Urban Edge Properties is a Maryland REIT that manages, develops, redevelops, and acquires retail real estate, primarily in the Washington, DC to Boston corridor with a concentration on the New York metropolitan area. The real estate investment trust (REIT) owns, leases, and operates almost 70 shopping centers, five malls and two industrial park which spans some 17.2 million square feet. Its tenants include several national retailers such as Home Depot, Walmart, Best Buy, Lowe's, the TJX Companies, Kohl's, Burlington, BJ's Wholesale Club, Ahold Delhaize, and ShopRite.

	Annual Growth	12/19	12/20	12/21	12/22	12/23
Sales ($mil.)	1.8%	387.6	330.1	425.1	397.9	416.9
Net income ($ mil.)	22.7%	109.5	93.6	102.7	46.2	248.5
Market value ($ mil.)	(1.2%)	2,256.6	1,522.4	2,235.4	1,657.7	2,153.0
Employees	(1.8%)	117	106	116	115	109

URBAN ONE INC NAS: UONE

1010 Wayne Avenue, 14th Floor
Silver Spring, MD 20910
Phone: 301 429-3200
Fax: –
Web: www.urban1.com

CEO: Catherine L Hughes
CFO: Peter D Thompson
HR: Rashaad Williams
FYE: December 31
Type: Public

Radio One ranks #1 among African-American audiences. The largest radio broadcaster serving black listeners, the company owns about 55 stations in 15 mostly urban markets. Its radio stations, which mostly operate in market clusters, offer a variety of music formats, as well as news and talk shows. In addition to broadcasting, Radio One has a 80% stake in Reach Media. Radio One operates several websites and the company also owns more than 50% of TV One, a cable television venture with Comcast. Founder and chairperson Catherine Hughes and her son, president and CEO Alfred Liggins, together control more than 90% of the company.

	Annual Growth	12/18	12/19	12/20	12/21	12/22
Sales ($mil.)	2.5%	439.1	436.9	376.3	441.5	484.6
Net income ($ mil.)	(28.3%)	141.0	0.9	(8.1)	38.4	37.3
Market value ($ mil.)	23.6%	77.9	91.9	56.6	164.0	181.9
Employees	(3.2%)	1,466	1,441	1,212	1,155	1,289

URBAN OUTFITTERS, INC. NMS: URBN

5000 South Broad Street
Philadelphia, PA 19112-1495
Phone: 215 454-5500
Fax: –
Web: www.urbn.com

CEO: Richard A Hayne
CFO: Melanie Marein-Efron
HR: Charlene Putt
FYE: January 31
Type: Public

Urban Outfitters is a leading lifestyle products and services company that operates a portfolio of global consumer brands comprised of Anthropologie, Free People, and more. The company's almost 710 namesake stores (mainly in the US, but also in Canada, and Europe) offer highly differentiated collections of fashion apparel, accessories, and home goods, among other things. The retailer's Urban Outfitters brand markets its products through almost 270 stores and targets young adults. Anthropologie brand courts women in the 28-45 demographic and has about 240 shops. Its Free People brand is sold through nearly 190 retail locations. The company also has a Menus & Venues division that operates some ten dining and event locations in the US. The US generates approximately 85% of the company's revenue.

	Annual Growth	01/19	01/20	01/21	01/22	01/23
Sales ($mil.)	5.0%	3,950.6	3,983.8	3,449.7	4,548.8	4,795.2
Net income ($ mil.)	(14.4%)	298.0	168.1	1.2	310.6	159.7
Market value ($ mil.)	(4.0%)	2,977.4	2,359.8	2,528.5	2,647.4	2,524.8
Employees	2.0%	24,000	24,000	19,000	23,000	26,000

UREACH TECHNOLOGIES INC.

2137 STATE ROUTE 35
HOLMDEL, NJ 07733
Phone: 732 335-5400
Fax: –
Web: –

CEO: –
CFO: David J Warnock
HR: –
FYE: December 31
Type: Private

U should know that uReach Technologies enables access to messaging services across fixed-line, mobile, and broadband networks. The company's unified messaging software is used to route calls to alternate destinations in order to reach people on the move, among other things. Its mobile media and Web, visual voicemail, and one-number applications can forward calls to mobile phones and devices, e-mail, and faxes. uReach's converged services framework and messaging platform are geared for telecommunications carriers and large corporations. uReach was founded in 1998 and has been used by such carriers as Verizon and Cox Communications. Outside of New Jersey, it has facilities in Massachusetts and India.

URM STORES, INC.

7511 N FREYA ST
SPOKANE, WA 992178043
Phone: 509 467-2620
Fax: –
Web: www.urmstores.com

CEO: Ray Sprinkle
CFO: Laurie Bigej
HR: Christopher Hayward
FYE: August 02
Type: Private

URM Stores is a leading wholesale food distribution cooperative serving more than 160 grocery stores in the Northwest. Its member-owner stores operate under a variety of banners, including Family Foods, Harvest Foods, Super 1 Foods, Trading Co. Stores, and Yoke's Fresh Market. It also owns the Rosauers Supermarkets chain. In addition to grocery stores, URM supplies 1,500-plus restaurants, hotels, and convenience stores; it also offers such services as merchandising, store development consulting, and technology purchasing. The cooperative was founded in 1921 as United Retail Merchants. The business is privately owned by its members.

	Annual Growth	07/04	07/05	07/06	07/07*	08/08
Sales ($mil.)	8.0%	–	–	799.4	859.9	932.8
Net income ($ mil.)	41.0%	–	–	4.4	7.2	8.8
Market value ($ mil.)	–	–	–	–	–	–
Employees	–	–	–	–	–	2,100

*Fiscal year change

UROLOGIX INC.

14405 21st Avenue North
Minneapolis, MN 55447
Phone: 763 475-1400
Fax: –
Web: www.urologix.com

NBB: ULGX
CEO: Gregory J Fluet
CFO: Scott M Madson
HR: –
FYE: June 30
Type: Public

For men whose prostate has them prostrate, Urologix has the answer. The company's Targis and CoolWave systems are designed to treat benign prostate hyperplasia, or enlargement of the prostate. The systems use Cooled ThermoTherapy, a noninvasive catheter-based therapy that applies microwave heat to the diseased areas of the prostate, while cooling and protecting urethral tissue. The treatment, an alternative to drug therapy, does not require anesthesia or surgery and can be administered on an outpatient basis. Urologix markets its products through a direct sales force in the US, as well as through international distributors.

	Annual Growth	06/10	06/11	06/12	06/13	06/14
Sales ($mil.)	(0.9%)	14.8	12.6	17.0	16.6	14.2
Net income ($ mil.)	–	(2.2)	(3.7)	(4.7)	(4.3)	(7.6)
Market value ($ mil.)	(36.4%)	22.4	19.9	16.1	3.5	3.7
Employees	(10.7%)	96	88	94	95	61

US 1 INDUSTRIES, INC.

336 W US HWY 30 STE 201
VALPARAISO, IN 463855345
Phone: 219 476-1300
Fax: –
Web: www.uslindustries.com

CEO: –
CFO: –
HR: –
FYE: December 31
Type: Private

The US market is the one and only concern for US 1 Industries, which partners with its subsidiaries to provide truckload transportation services in the 48 contiguous states. The company owns no trucks; instead, it does business through a network of independent sales agents, who arrange freight transportation via independent truck owner-operators. About 160 commission-based agents monitor shipments. US 1's contractors transport freight in temperature-controlled trailers and flatbeds, as well as in standard dry vans. One of its specialties is the hauling of intermodal shipping containers, which can be transported by trucks, trains, and ships. In 2011 US 1 agreed to be acquired by Trucking Investment Co.

US BANCORP (DE)

800 Nicollet Mall
Minneapolis, MN 55402
Phone: 651 466-3000
Fax: –
Web: www.usbank.com

NYS: USB
CEO: Andrew Cecere
CFO: Terrance R Dolan
HR: –
FYE: December 31
Type: Public

US Bancorp is a financial services holding company that provides a full range of financial services, including lending and depository services, cash management, capital markets, and trust and investment management services. It also engages in credit cards services as well as merchant and ATM processing, mortgage banking, trust and investment management, brokerage, insurance, and corporate payments. The bank provides banking and investment services through a network of approximately 2,500 banking offices and nearly 4,500 ATMs primarily in the Midwest and West regions of the US. In late 2022, the bank agreed to acquire MUFG Union Bank's core regional banking franchise from Mitsubishi UFJ Financial Group for $5.5 billion in cash and approximately 44 million shares of US Bancorp common stock.

	Annual Growth	12/19	12/20	12/21	12/22	12/23
Assets ($mil.)	7.6%	495,426	553,905	573,284	674,805	663,491
Net income ($ mil.)	(5.9%)	6,914.0	4,959.0	7,963.0	5,825.0	5,429.0
Market value ($ mil.)	(7.6%)	92,373	72,587	87,512	67,944	67,430
Employees	2.0%	69,651	68,108	68,796	78,192	75,465

US CHINA MINING GROUP INC

15310 Amberly Drive, Suite 250
Tampa, FL 33647
Phone: 813 514-2873
Fax: –
Web: www.uschinamining.com

CEO: –
CFO: –
HR: –
FYE: December 31
Type: Public

It's a cold, coal world for U.S. China Mining Group. The company operates three coal mines in Heilongjiang Province, the northeastern-most part of China. Its three mines -- Tong Gong, Hong Yuan, and Sheng Yu -- produce almost 1 million tons of coal a year. The group sells its coal to power plants, cement factories, wholesalers, and individuals for home heating. Three customers account for the majority of sales -- Heilongjiang QiQiHaEr Huadian Power Plants Co., Ltd. accounted for 60% in 2010; Heilongjiang Beihai Logistics Company and Changchun Rail Transportation Co., Ltd. together accounted for another 30%. Chairman Guoqing Yue owns a third of the company's stock.

	Annual Growth	12/09	12/10	12/11	12/12	12/13
Sales ($mil.)	(53.6%)	65.0	69.0	54.0	30.9	3.0
Net income ($ mil.)	–	25.1	13.4	15.2	(31.2)	(7.7)
Market value ($ mil.)	(68.5%)	152.9	119.9	20.7	7.2	1.5
Employees	(38.8%)	655	1,017	1,186	91	92

US DAIRY EXPORT COUNCIL

2107 WILSON BLVD STE 600
ARLINGTON, VA 222013042
Phone: 703 528-3049
Fax: –
Web: www.usdec.org

CEO: Krysta Harden
CFO: –
HR: Omar Syed
FYE: December 31
Type: Private

Got milk? These guys do. Lots of it. The U.S. Dairy Export Council (USDEC) is a not-for-profit organization designed to increase the volume and value of US-based dairy producers' exported products. The independent membership organization represents the interests of US milk producers, dairy cooperatives, export traders, industry suppliers, and proprietary processors. The US dairy industry exports $3.8 billion worth of product each year and USDEC helps its members maintain and hopefully increase that dollar amount through its involvement in global trade issues and building demand for US dairy products. The organization, founded in 1995, has offices in 15 countries worldwide.

	Annual Growth	12/11	12/12	12/13	12/14	12/16
Sales ($mil.)	4.2%	–	23.0	22.0	24.0	27.2
Net income ($ mil.)	–	–	0.4	0.0	(0.3)	(0.4)
Market value ($ mil.)	–	–	–	–	–	–
Employees	–	–	–	–	–	20

US ENERGY CORP

1616 S. Voss Rd., Suite 725
Houston, TX 77057
Phone: 346 509-8734
Fax: –
Web: www.usnrg.com

NAS: USEG
CEO: Ryan L Smith
CFO: Mark Zajac
HR: –
FYE: December 31
Type: Public

U.S. Energy (USE) has put its energy in many places, including oil and gas exploration and production, geothermal energy projects, and molybdenum mining. It operates oil and gas wells on the coast of the Gulf of Mexico and in Texas. The company bought a quarter stake in Standard Steam Trust in 2008, giving USE entry into the geothermal energy market. It also is developing a molybdenum mining project in Colorado. U.S. Energy has an agreement with Thompson Creek Metals to fund development of the project. The company had owned almost half of Sutter Gold Mining but sold most of its stake in the gold miner in 2008.

	Annual Growth	12/18	12/19	12/20	12/21	12/22
Sales ($mil.)	68.4%	5.5	6.6	2.3	6.7	44.6
Net income ($ mil.)	–	(1.0)	(0.6)	(6.4)	(1.8)	(1.0)
Market value ($ mil.)	36.1%	16.8	7.6	92.1	81.8	57.6
Employees	94.6%	3	2	2	25	43

US FOODS HOLDING CORP
NYS: USFD

9399 W. Higgins Road, Suite 100
Rosemont, IL 60018
Phone: 847 720-8000
Fax: –
Web: www.usfoods.com

CEO: David E Flitman
CFO: Dirk J Locascio
HR: –
FYE: December 30
Type: Public

US Foods is one of America's great food companies and leading foodservice distributors. It distributes food and non-food supplies to approximately 250,000 customers. The company's nearly 70 distribution facilities supply more than 400,000 fresh, frozen, and dry food stock-keeping units (SKUs), as well as non-food items, sourced from approximately 6,000 suppliers, to single- and multi-unit restaurants and regional and national restaurant chains as well as hospitals, nursing homes, hotels and motels, country clubs, government and military organizations, colleges and universities, and retail locations. In addition to food items and ingredients, US Foods distributes kitchen and cleaning supplies and restaurant equipment. Some of its brands include its US Foods, Food Fanatics, Chef'Store and Smart Foodservice.

	Annual Growth	12/19*	01/21	01/22*	12/22	12/23
Sales ($mil.)	8.2%	25,939	22,885	29,487	34,057	35,597
Net income ($ mil.)	7.1%	385.0	(226.0)	164.0	265.0	506.0
Market value ($ mil.)	2.1%	10,242	8,167.6	8,540.3	8,341.7	11,135
Employees	1.7%	28,000	26,000	28,000	29,000	30,000

*Fiscal year change

US FOODS, INC.

9399 W HIGGINS RD BLDG 100
ROSEMONT, IL 600186900
Phone: 847 720-8000
Fax: –
Web: www.usfoods.com

CEO: Dave Flitman
CFO: –
HR: –
FYE: January 02
Type: Private

Many restaurant-goers in the US can thank this company for the food on their plates. US Foods (formerly U.S. Foodservice), is the nation's #2 food service supplier (with about half the sales of rival Sysco), distributing food and nonfood supplies to more than 250,000 customers. The company's 75-plus distribution facilities supply over 350,000 products to restaurants, hotels, schools, health care facilities, and institutional food service operators. In addition to food items and ingredients, US Foods distributes kitchen and cleaning supplies and restaurant equipment. Tracing its roots to 1853, private equity firms KKR & Co. and Clayton, Dubilier & Rice own the company. The company filed an IPO in 2016 and raised $1.02 billion in proceeds.

US GLOBAL INVESTORS INC
NAS: GROW

7900 Callaghan Road
San Antonio, TX 78229
Phone: 210 308-1234
Fax: –
Web: www.usfunds.com

CEO: Frank E Holmes
CFO: Lisa C Callicotte
HR: –
FYE: June 30
Type: Public

While it may be a small world, financial investment company U.S. Global Investors wants to make it a little greener, after all. Primarily serving the U.S. Global Investors Funds and the U.S. Global Accolade Funds, the company is a mutual fund manager providing investment advisory, transfer agency, broker-dealer, and mailing services. It offers a family of no-load mutual funds generally geared toward long-term investing. The company also engages in corporate investment activities. U.S. Global Investors had about $724 million in assets under management in 2015.

	Annual Growth	06/19	06/20	06/21	06/22	06/23
Sales ($mil.)	32.3%	4.9	4.5	21.7	24.7	15.1
Net income ($ mil.)	–	(3.4)	(4.7)	32.0	5.5	3.1
Market value ($ mil.)	14.0%	26.4	27.7	90.2	64.4	44.6
Employees	–	24	23	23	22	24

US GOLD CORP (CANADA)
NAS: USAU

1910 East Idaho Street, Suite 102-Box 604
Elko, NV 89801
Phone: 800 557-4550
Fax: –
Web: www.usgoldcorp.gold

CEO: George Bee
CFO: –
HR: –
FYE: April 30
Type: Public

Dataram wants you to remember your DRAMs. The company makes add-in memory boards and modules that expand the capacity of computer servers and workstations running under UNIX and Windows operating systems. Its products, which use DRAM memory chips, are compatible with systems from scores of companies such as HP, IBM, and Dell, and with microprocessors made by AMD and Intel. The company sells its products to OEMs, distributors, value-added resellers, and end-users. The company has a plant in the US & sales offices in the US, Japan, and Europe. Most sales come from customers in the US.

	Annual Growth	04/19	04/20	04/21	04/22	04/23
Sales ($mil.)	–	–	–	–	–	–
Net income ($ mil.)	–	(8.0)	(5.2)	(12.4)	(13.9)	(7.6)
Market value ($ mil.)	38.5%	10.9	47.5	102.3	52.5	40.1
Employees	7.5%	3	3	3	4	4

US PREMIUM BEEF LLC
NBB: USBF U

12200 North Ambassador Drive
Kansas City, MO 64163
Phone: 866 877-2525
Fax: –
Web: –

CEO: Stanley D Linville
CFO: Scott J Miller
HR: –
FYE: December 26
Type: Public

From ranch to plate, U.S. Premium Beef (USPB) is making money. USPB buys cattle from producers' ranches in 36 states, through the feedlots, and sends them off to its subsidiary beef processor National Beef Packing Co. (NBPC). From there, some of the company's better steaks head to the Kansas City Steak Company, a foodservice distributor that it partially owns, which supplies high-end steakhouses and restaurants. The rest of its value-added and branded beef is boxed and sold to food retailers and foodservice distributors throughout the US. Founded in 1997, the company operates a mail-order business for its products. Leucadia National Corporation acquired a 79% stake in NBPC in 2011 and, as a result, USPB.

US SILICA HOLDINGS, INC.
NYS: SLCA

24275 Katy Freeway, Suite 600
Katy, TX 77494
Phone: 281 258-2170
Fax: –
Web: www.ussilica.com

CEO: Bryan A Shinn
CFO: Alex Lavergne
HR: Nicole Schaeffer
FYE: December 31
Type: Public

US Silica is a global performance materials company and a leading producer of commercial silica used in a wide range of industrial applications and in the oil and gas industry. In addition, through its subsidiary EP Minerals (EPM), it is an industry leader in the production of products derived from diatomaceous earth, perlite, engineered clays, and non-activated clays. It controls some 468 million tons of reserves of commercial silica, which can be processed to make 182 million tons of finished products that meet American Petroleum Institute (API) frac sand specifications, and 82 million tons of reserves of diatomaceous earth, perlite, and clays.

	Annual Growth	12/19	12/20	12/21	12/22	12/23
Sales ($mil.)	1.3%	1,474.5	845.9	1,103.9	1,525.1	1,552.0
Net income ($ mil.)	–	(329.1)	(114.1)	(33.8)	78.2	146.9
Market value ($ mil.)	16.5%	474.7	541.9	725.6	964.9	873.0
Employees	(3.7%)	2,177	1,613	1,863	2,013	1,873

US STEM CELL INC

1560 Sawgrass Corporate Pkwy., 4th Floor
Sunrise, FL 33323
Phone: 954 835-1500
Fax: 954 845-9976
Web: www.us-stemcell.com

NBB: USRM
CEO: Mike Tomas
CFO: Mike Tomas
HR: –
FYE: December 31
Type: Public

Broken hearts are no fun, but damaged hearts are worse and Bioheart aims to help. The biotech company is focused on the discovery, development, and commercialization of therapies treating heart damage. Because the heart does not have cells to naturally repair itself, Bioheart is exploring the use of cells derived from the patient's own thigh muscle to improve cardiac function after a heart has been damaged by a heart attack. Its lead candidate, MyoCell, uses precursor muscle cells called myoblasts to strengthen scar tissue with living muscle tissue. The company is also developing a number of proprietary techniques and processes used to obtain and inject MyoCell.

	Annual Growth	12/18	12/19	12/20	12/21	12/22
Sales ($mil.)	(66.7%)	6.7	3.1	0.3	0.2	0.0
Net income ($ mil.)	–	(2.2)	(3.8)	(2.9)	(3.3)	(2.9)
Market value ($ mil.)	(26.0%)	10.2	2.2	7.7	3.8	3.0
Employees	–	11	–	–	–	–

US VENTURE PARTNERS III LLC

1460 EL CAMINO REAL STE 100
MENLO PARK, CA 940254123
Phone: 650 854-9080
Fax: –
Web: www.usvp.com

CEO: –
CFO: –
HR: –
FYE: December 31
Type: Private

If you're a sapling looking for seed money, U.S. Venture Partners (USVP) can give you a little something to help you grow. Usually an early-stage, long-term investor that holds on to companies for five years or more, the firm focuses on technologies for adapting to or mitigating climate change (including clean technologies), information technologies, and life sciences. Since its founding in 1981, USVP has invested $2.4 billion in more than 420 companies and has taken approximately one-fifth of them public. Past successes include Sun Microsystems, Altus Pharmaceuticals, and Mellanox Technologies. USVP's current portfolio consists of about 100 firms, including Redline Communications and Minerva Networks.

USA ENVIRONMENTAL MANAGEMENT, INC.

8436 ENTERPRISE AVE
PHILADELPHIA, PA 191533802
Phone: 215 365-5810
Fax: –
Web: www.usaemi.com

CEO: –
CFO: Tracy L Smith
HR: –
FYE: December 31
Type: Private

USA Environmental Management builds, cleans, and leads projects mostly for the federal government. The company provides environmental engineering and construction services, such as remediation and facility renovation, hazardous materials management, asbestos abatement, air quality monitoring, design/build services, and demolition. USA Environmental Management operates offices in the Northeast, but performs jobs around the country. Clients have included the US Army Corps of Engineers, the National Park Service, and the Philadelphia Housing Authority. The minority-owned company was formed in 1994 to serve the government and private sectors.

USA HOCKEY, INC.

1775 BOB JOHNSON DR
COLORADO SPRINGS, CO 809064090
Phone: 719 527-3360
Fax: –
Web: www.usahockey.com

CEO: –
CFO: –
HR: –
FYE: August 31
Type: Private

Whenever a puck is dropped, boards banged, or empty nets scored on, USA Hockey is there. The group serves as the governing body for amateur hockey and works to promote the sport with more than 585,000 members (ice and in-line hockey players, coaches, and officials). An official representative to the United States Olympic Committee and the International Ice Hockey Federation, the organization supports development of hockey through its affiliation with more than 30 amateur leagues. It trains Olympians and works with the National Hockey League and the National Collegiate Athletic Association as well as publishing American Hockey Magazine . In-line skaters were included in 1994; the group formed in 1936.

	Annual Growth	08/14	08/15	08/16	08/19	08/22
Sales ($mil.)	2.5%	–	42.0	42.2	43.2	49.9
Net income ($ mil.)	–	–	0.7	0.0	(3.3)	(0.8)
Market value ($ mil.)	–	–	–	–	–	–
Employees	–	–	–	–	–	38

USA TRACK & FIELD, INC.

130 E WASHINGTON ST STE 800
INDIANAPOLIS, IN 462044605
Phone: 317 261-0500
Fax: –
Web: www.usatf.org

CEO: Max Siegel
CFO: Sara Reese
HR: –
FYE: December 31
Type: Private

USA Track & Field (USATF) has its membership on the run -- and the discus, shot-put, decathlon, and javelin. The group is the governing body for track and field sports, long distance running, and race walking in the US. It has more than 130,000 members and sanctions more than 8,000 events a year; member groups include the NCAA, Road Runners Club of America, Running USA, and the National Federation of State High School Associations. The organization sets rules, promotes the sport, and selects the US track and field Olympic teams. Its around 55 associations oversee the sport and its more than 3,000 local clubs. USATF traces its heritage to the Amateur Athletic Union, founded in New York City in 1878.

	Annual Growth	12/07	12/08	12/09	12/13	12/21
Sales ($mil.)	35.6%	–	0.6	12.7	17.7	33.7
Net income ($ mil.)	–	–	(0.1)	(1.2)	(0.8)	(0.5)
Market value ($ mil.)	–	–	–	–	–	–
Employees	–	–	–	–	–	65

USA TRUCK, INC.

3200 INDUSTRIAL PARK RD
VAN BUREN, AR 729566110
Phone: 479 471-2500
Fax: –
Web: www.dbschenker.com

CEO: David Buss
CFO: –
HR: –
FYE: December 31
Type: Private

Truckload carrier USA Truck moves freight not only in the US, but also in Canada, and, through partners, into Mexico. USA Truck has a fleet of over 2,155 tractors and nearly 6,550 trailers. The company provides both medium-haul and regional truckload services, along with dedicated contract carriage. USA Truck team members have cultivated a thorough understanding of the needs of shippers in key industries, which the company believes helps with the development of long-term, service-oriented relationships with its customers.

USANA HEALTH SCIENCES INC   NYS: USNA

3838 West Parkway Blvd.   CEO: Kevin G Guest
Salt Lake City, UT 84120   CFO: G D Hekking
Phone: 801 954-7100   HR: −
Fax: −   FYE: December 30
Web: www.usanahealthsciences.com   Type: Public

USANA Health Sciences develops and manufactures high quality, science-based nutritional and personal care and skincare products that are distributed internationally through direct selling. Its customer base is primarily comprised of two types of customers: Associates and Preferred Customers. Its Associates also sell its products to retail customers. Preferred Customers purchase its products strictly for personal use and are not permitted to resell or to distribute the products. USANA has approximately 490,000 active customers worldwide. Chairman and founder Myron Wentz controls 41.6% of USANA. China is its largest market and single largest source of revenue, representing about 45% of net sales and some 45% of active customers.

	Annual Growth	12/19*	01/21	01/22*	12/22	12/23
Sales ($mil.)	(3.5%)	1,060.9	1,134.6	1,186.5	998.6	921.0
Net income ($ mil.)	(10.7%)	100.5	124.7	116.5	69.4	63.8
Market value ($ mil.)	(9.5%)	1,530.4	1,474.9	1,936.0	1,017.7	1,025.4
Employees	−	1,909	1,943	1,978	1,900	−

*Fiscal year change

USC ARCADIA HOSPITAL

300 W HUNTINGTON DR   CEO: Ikenna Mmeje
ARCADIA, CA 910073402   CFO: −
Phone: 626 898-8000   HR: Cassandra Wright
Fax: −   FYE: December 31
Web: www.uscarcadiahospital.org   Type: Private

If you're dehydrated in the Valley, Methodist Hospital of Southern California can help. The hospital provides medical care to the residents of California's central San Gabriel Valley. The healthcare facility boasts some 600 beds and is part of Southern California Healthcare Systems. The not-for-profit hospital provides comprehensive acute care, including surgical, pediatric, and intensive care units. It also offers a wide range of specialty services such as cardiology, oncology, neurology, bariatrics, and orthopedics. The hospital opened its doors in 1903 with five beds.

	Annual Growth	12/15	12/16	12/17	12/19	12/21
Sales ($mil.)	(2.1%)	−	297.4	300.0	299.1	267.5
Net income ($ mil.)	(37.3%)	−	14.0	19.2	19.8	1.4
Market value ($ mil.)	−	−	−	−	−	−
Employees	−	−	−	−	−	2,200

USFALCON, INC.

100 REGENCY FOREST DR STE 150   CEO: Zannie Smith
CARY, NC 275188597   CFO: Leigh Barnhill
Phone: 919 388-3778   HR: −
Fax: −   FYE: September 30
Web: www.usfalcon.com   Type: Private

Government contractor USfalcon has been flying high with the big boys -- Booz Allen Hamilton, CACI, and Lockheed Martin-- ever since it became a preferred contractor under the Army's S3 (Strategic Services Sourcing) program in 2006. USfalcon assists the Defense Department and other federal agencies with information technology (IT) services in the areas of aerospace, national security and intelligence, and defense. The company is also awarded contracts through the Navy's SeaPort and works as a subcontractor for IT giants NCI and Leidos. USfalcon operates from seven offices in the US. The veteran-owned small business was taken over by owner Col. Peter von Jess (Ret.) in 2003.

	Annual Growth	09/07	09/08	09/09	09/10	09/11
Sales ($mil.)	−	−	−	(510.3)	102.6	105.5
Net income ($ mil.)	48891.4%	−	−	0.0	3.7	3.4
Market value ($ mil.)	−	−	−	−	−	−
Employees	−	−	−	−	−	250

USG CORPORATION

550 W ADAMS ST   CEO: Christopher R Griffin
CHICAGO, IL 606613665   CFO: Christopher R Griffin
Phone: 312 436-4000   HR: Carrie Hogland
Fax: −   FYE: December 31
Web: www.usg.com   Type: Private

USG Corporation is a market leader in wallboard and gypsum products in North America. It is a top seller of wallboard, gypsum fiberboard, and construction plaster products that are used for finishing interior walls, ceilings, and floors. The company is also a major North American supplier of building-related performance materials, ceiling grid, and acoustic tiles. Recognized brands include Sheetrock, Durock, Fiberock, and Donn. Its products are used to build some of the world's most iconic structures, such as the Freedom Tower in New York, Burj Khalifa in Dubai, and Lotte Tower in Seoul. In 1902, some 20 independent gypsum rock and plaster manufacturing companies merged to consolidate their resources and form the United States Gypsum Company.

	Annual Growth	12/13	12/14	12/15	12/16	12/17
Sales ($mil.)	6.2%	−	−	−	3,017.0	3,204.5
Net income ($ mil.)	(82.7%)	−	−	−	510.0	88.0
Market value ($ mil.)	−	−	−	−	−	−
Employees	−	−	−	−	−	7,300

USHIO AMERICA, INC.

5440 CERRITOS AVE   CEO: William Mackenzie
CYPRESS, CA 906304567   CFO: Shinji Kameda
Phone: 714 236-8600   HR: −
Fax: −   FYE: January 31
Web: www.ushio.com   Type: Private

USHIO America discharges its duties by designing, manufacturing, and distributing discharge and halogen lighting. A subsidiary of USHIO, the company has an arsenal of over 3,500 general and specialty lighting products. Its main customers are in the biotechnology, electronics, image information processing, medical, and semiconductor industries. Ushio America's sister affiliate production bases include Ushio America-Oregon, USHIO Philippines, BLV Licht-und Vakuumetechnik GmbH, Taiwan USHIO Lighting, and USHIO Hong Kong. The company puts a high premium on the research and development of advanced photon and electron beam technology and their adaptation for use in industrial lighting and processing equipment.

	Annual Growth	03/03	03/04	03/05	03/06*	01/07
Sales ($mil.)	(6.0%)	−	−	79.2	346.2	70.0
Net income ($ mil.)	−	−	−	−	5.3	3.1
Market value ($ mil.)	−	−	−	−	−	−
Employees	−	−	−	−	−	200

*Fiscal year change

USIO INC   NMS: USIO

3611 Paesanos Parkway, Suite 300   CEO: Louis A Hoch
San Antonio, TX 78231   CFO: Tom Jewell
Phone: 210 249-4100   HR: −
Fax: −   FYE: December 31
Web: www.usio.com   Type: Public

Usio, Inc. (formerly Payment Data Systems) offers electronic payment processing services, including automated clearinghouse (ACH) and credit/debit card transaction processing, to merchants and businesses. Usio also operates billx.com, an online payment processing website that allows consumers to pay anyone, anywhere, for a flat monthly fee. Additionally, the company is developing and marketing prepaid gift cards and debit cards issued by Meta Financial Group. Usio operates solely in the US.

	Annual Growth	12/18	12/19	12/20	12/21	12/22
Sales ($mil.)	29.1%	25.0	28.2	32.3	61.9	69.4
Net income ($ mil.)	−	(3.8)	(5.1)	(2.9)	(0.3)	(5.5)
Market value ($ mil.)	(0.2%)	41.7	39.2	67.0	109.4	41.4
Employees	28.4%	43	51	89	108	117

USS-UPI, LLC

900 LOVERIDGE RD
PITTSBURG, CA 945652808
Phone: 800 877-7672
Fax: –
Web: www.ussposco.com

CEO: –
CFO: –
HR: Joann Rowney
FYE: December 31
Type: Private

US and Korean steel manufacturing interests come together in the form of USS-POSCO Industries (UPI), a 50/50 joint venture between United States Steel (US Steel) and POSCO. The company operates a steel plant (formerly owned by US Steel) in Pittsburg, Northern California. It manufactures flat-rolled steel sheets in various forms: cold-rolled steel, galvanized steel, and tinplate. In addition, USS-POSCO churns out iron oxide, which is used to make hard and soft ferrites. UPI sells its products to more than 150 customers in more than dozen states throughout the western US. End products include office furniture, computer cabinets, metal studs, cans, culverts, and metal building materials.

	Annual Growth	12/05	12/06	12/07	12/08	12/15
Sales ($mil.)	(5.1%)	–	1,034.7	998.7	1,198.0	649.0
Net income ($ mil.)	–	–	14.7	(40.1)	11.9	(4.3)
Market value ($ mil.)	–	–	–	–	–	–
Employees	–	–	–	–	–	1,326

UT MEDICAL GROUP, INC.

1407 UNION AVE STE 700
MEMPHIS, TN 381043641
Phone: 901 866-8864
Fax: –
Web: www.universityclinicalhealth.com

CEO: Shannon Tacker
CFO: Mike Jackson
HR: Franswil Boyd
FYE: December 31
Type: Private

UT Medical Group knows that a little practice can go a long way. The organization is the private physician practice affiliated with the University of Tennessee Health Science Center. The not-for-profit physician group consists of more than 100 doctors serving the greater Memphis, Tennessee area. Specialized practices include emergency medicine, pediatrics, surgery, ophthalmology, and cardiology. The company was founded in 1974 as the Faculty Medical Practice Corporation; one decade later its name was changed to reflect its association with University of Tennessee.

UTAH ASSOCIATED MUNICIPAL POWER SYSTEMS

155 N 400 W STE 480
SALT LAKE CITY, UT 841031150
Phone: 801 566-3938
Fax: –
Web: www.uamps.com

CEO: –
CFO: –
HR: –
FYE: March 31
Type: Private

Even the hardiest citizens of the Intermountain West need access to a reliable power supply. Utah Associated Municipal Power Systems supplies power to 52 member municipal utilities primarily in Utah, as well as in Arizona, California, Idaho, Nevada, and New Mexico, Oregon, and Wyoming. These municipal electric utilities and other local government units provide retail electric or other utility services in their respective service areas. The company obtains electricity from interests in generation facilities and through power purchase agreements with other generators; Utah Associated Municipal Power Systems also has interests in traditional power transmission facilities, and in wind power generation plants.

	Annual Growth	03/17	03/18	03/19	03/20	03/21
Sales ($mil.)	2.5%	–	194.8	203.9	187.7	209.7
Net income ($ mil.)	(6.2%)	–	4.4	7.4	5.2	3.6
Market value ($ mil.)	–	–	–	–	–	–
Employees	–	–	–	–	–	27

UTAH MEDICAL PRODUCTS, INC.

NMS: UTMD

7043 South 300 West
Midvale, UT 84047
Phone: 801 566-1200
Fax: 801 566-7305
Web: www.utahmed.com

CEO: –
CFO: –
HR: –
FYE: December 31
Type: Public

Utah Medical Products (UTMD) is in the business of producing high-quality cost-effective medical devices that are predominantly differentiated by safety and improved patient outcomes. The company designs and makes a variety of medical products used in labor and delivery and in neonatal intensive care, as well as products for gynecological and blood pressure monitoring. Products include disposable pressure transducers to monitor blood pressure, intrauterine catheters used to monitor pressure in the womb during high-risk births, and a device that clamps and cuts the umbilical cord and collects a blood sample from the cord. UTMD, which has manufacturing facilities in the US, Ireland, England, Australia, and Canada, sells its products around the world through a domestic sales force and over 200 independent regional distributors. The US market accounts for about 60% of its total revenue.

	Annual Growth	12/19	12/20	12/21	12/22	12/23
Sales ($mil.)	1.7%	46.9	42.2	49.1	52.3	50.2
Net income ($ mil.)	3.1%	14.7	10.8	14.8	16.5	16.6
Market value ($ mil.)	(6.0%)	391.7	306.0	363.0	364.9	305.7
Employees	(1.4%)	201	200	229	254	190

UTAH STATE UNIVERSITY

1000 OLD MAIN HL
LOGAN, UT 843221000
Phone: 435 797-1000
Fax: –
Web: www.usu.edu

CEO: –
CFO: –
HR: Jodi Morgan
FYE: June 30
Type: Private

Utah State University (USU) has more than 40 academic departments at colleges of agriculture, arts, business, education and human services, engineering, science, natural resources, and humanities and social sciences. It offers about 170 bachelor's degree programs and more than 140 graduate degree programs. Biology, elementary education, mechanical and aerospace engineering, and business administration are among the university's most popular majors. About 29,000 students attend its main campus in northern Utah, its three branch campuses, or extension facilities located across the state. USU was established in 1888 as an agricultural college.

	Annual Growth	06/18	06/19	06/20	06/21	06/22
Sales ($mil.)	4.3%	–	537.8	559.2	560.2	610.3
Net income ($ mil.)	(17.3%)	–	94.3	77.5	187.3	53.3
Market value ($ mil.)	–	–	–	–	–	–
Employees	–	–	–	–	–	700

UTG INC

NBB: UTGN

205 North Depot Street
Stanford, KY 40484
Phone: 217 241-6300
Fax: –
Web: www.utgins.com

CEO: Jesse T Correll
CFO: Theodore C Miller
HR: –
FYE: December 31
Type: Public

UTG doesn't feel the need to spell out United Trust Group anymore, but it is still a life insurance holding company. Universal Guaranty Life Insurance, American Capitol Insurance, and other subsidiaries offer individual life insurance as well as third-party administration (TPA) services for other providers. UTG's Roosevelt Equity subsidiary provides investment brokerage services to the company's insurance customers, while other subsidiaries handle UTG's real estate investments. Some 20 general agents represent the company's products and focus on retaining and expanding current customer policies. CEO Jesse Correll owns about two-thirds of the company.

	Annual Growth	12/18	12/19	12/20	12/21	12/22
Assets ($mil.)	3.1%	395.5	418.7	419.1	438.5	447.5
Net income ($ mil.)	28.9%	12.4	16.3	2.1	9.7	34.3
Market value ($ mil.)	(6.3%)	102.9	112.4	83.9	86.1	79.3
Employees	–	–	40	40	35	40	40

UTICA COLLEGE

1600 BURRSTONE RD — CEO: –
UTICA, NY 135024892 — CFO: –
Phone: 315 792-3111 — HR: –
Fax: – — FYE: May 31
Web: www.utica.edu — Type: Private

Utica College is a liberal arts college with an enrollment of approximately 2,500 full- and part-time students. The private school was founded in 1946 by Syracuse University and became an independent institution in 1995. Utica College offers about 30 undergraduate majors and 15 graduate programs. Its students earn Syracuse baccalaureate degrees for undergrads and Utica College master's and doctorate degrees.

	Annual Growth	05/17	05/18	05/19	05/20	05/21
Sales ($mil.)	(1.7%)	–	86.6	88.4	83.4	82.4
Net income ($ mil.)	2.4%	–	11.5	5.2	1.6	12.4
Market value ($ mil.)	–	–	–	–	–	–
Employees	–	–	–	–	–	646

UTILITIES TELECOM COUNCIL

2550 S CLARK ST STE 960 — CEO: Jimmy R Williams
ARLINGTON, VA 222023997 — CFO: –
Phone: 202 833-6817 — HR: –
Fax: – — FYE: December 31
Web: www.utc.org — Type: Private

United Telecom Council (UTC) is telecom for the other guys. The group is a business association representing the telecommunications interests of electric, gas, and water utilities; natural gas pipelines; and critical infrastructure firms. It lobbies Congress and other government bodies to create a favorable regulatory climate, publishes newsletters and bulletins, conducts industry research, and provides consulting on regulatory and legal matters. UTC members can attend several annual conferences and meetings and network with members in the US, Europe, and Canada. UTC was formed in 1948 as the National Committee for Utilities Radio and adopted its current name in 1968.

	Annual Growth	09/14	09/15	09/16*	12/17	12/21
Sales ($mil.)	(3.8%)	–	6.6	6.3	1.0	5.2
Net income ($ mil.)	16.8%	–	0.0	(0.0)	(0.4)	0.2
Market value ($ mil.)	–	–	–	–	–	–
Employees	–	–	–	–	–	19

*Fiscal year change

UVA PRINCE WILLIAM HEALTH SYSTEM

8650 SUDLEY RD STE 411 — CEO: Michael Schwartz
MANASSAS, VA 201104416 — CFO: Robert W Reily
Phone: 703 369-8270 — HR: –
Fax: – — FYE: December 31
Web: – — Type: Private

Whether prince or pauper, Prince William Health System (PWHS) gives ailing northern Virginians the royal treatment. The hospital system provides medical, surgical, and therapeutic services through the not-for-profit Prince William Hospital. PWHS also offers assisted living, rehabilitation, wellness, and home care services. Founded in 1964, the Prince William Hospital has about 170 beds and provides specialty services including emergency room, cancer care, imaging, diagnostics, cardiac rehabilitation, pediatrics, and mental health care. The health system has a strategic partnership with area medical network Novant Health.

	Annual Growth	12/01	12/02	12/03	12/08	12/21
Sales ($mil.)	(4.8%)	–	124.1	133.2	2.7	48.9
Net income ($ mil.)	–	–	3.8	19.4	–	(16.3)
Market value ($ mil.)	–	–	–	–	–	–
Employees	–	–	–	–	–	1,700

UWHARRIE CAPITAL CORP.   NBB: UWHR

132 North First Street — CEO: Roger L Dick
Albemarle, NC 28001 — CFO: Heather H Almond
Phone: 704 983-6181 — HR: –
Fax: – — FYE: December 31
Web: www.uwharrie.com — Type: Public

Uwharrie Capital is the multibank holding company for Anson Bank & Trust, Bank of Stanly, and Cabarrus Bank & Trust, which operate a total of about ten branches in west-central North Carolina. Serving consumers and local business customers, the banks offer a variety of deposit accounts and credit cards, as well as investments, insurance, asset management, and brokerage services offered by other Uwharrie subsidiaries such as insurance agency BOS Agency, securities broker-dealer Strategic Alliance, mortgage brokerage Gateway Mortgage, and Strategic Investment Advisors. The banks mainly write residential and commercial mortgages, but also construction, business, and consumer loans.

	Annual Growth	12/18	12/19	12/20	12/21	12/22
Assets ($mil.)	12.7%	632.3	656.8	827.8	939.7	1,019.5
Net income ($ mil.)	41.7%	1.9	2.5	7.5	9.5	7.7
Market value ($ mil.)	11.1%	37.9	41.4	37.9	64.9	57.7
Employees	0.5%	189	191	315	191	193

UWINK INC. DELAWARE   NBB: UWKI

16106 Hart Street — CEO: Nolan Bushnell
Van Nuys, CA 91406 — CFO: –
Phone: 818 909-6030 — HR: –
Fax: – — FYE: January 1
Web: www.uwink.com — Type: Public

Dining and digital entertainment are on the menu for uWink. The company operates two casual dining restaurants in California featuring its proprietary touchscreen terminals at each table that offer interactive games, movie trailers, and other digital media. The screens are also used by customers to order food from a menu of burgers, pizza, sandwiches, and other American fare. In addition to dining, each location features a bar area where patrons can enjoy drinks and play games. uWink is the brainchild of Chuck E. Cheese founder Nolan Bushnell.

	Annual Growth	12/03	12/04	12/05*	01/07	01/08
Sales ($mil.)	93.1%	–	–	0.7	0.5	2.5
Net income ($ mil.)	–	–	–	(3.2)	(10.4)	(5.3)
Market value ($ mil.)	–	–	–	–	–	–
Employees	–	–	–	–	14	21

*Fiscal year change

VAALCO ENERGY, INC.   NYS: EGY

9800 Richmond Avenue, Suite 700 — CEO: George W Maxwell
Houston, TX 77042 — CFO: Ronald Y Bain
Phone: 713 623-0801 — HR: –
Fax: – — FYE: December 31
Web: www.vaalco.com — Type: Public

VAALCO Energy valiantly pursues energy opportunities. The small independent is engaged in the acquisition, exploration, development, and production of oil and gas. VAALCO Energy holds high-risk exploration assets in Angola and Gabon through participating in oil company consortia, and has exploration assets in Gulf Coast of Texas and Louisiana, and in Montana. VAALCO's near-term production strategy is to focus on developing its reserves in Gabon through the exploitation of the Etame Marin block (the Etame, Avouma, South Tchibala, and Ebouri fields). In 2013 the company reported proved reserves of 7.2 million barrels of crude oil (46% developed); and 1.3 million cu ft. of natural gas located in the US).

	Annual Growth	12/19	12/20	12/21	12/22	12/23
Sales ($mil.)	52.3%	84.5	67.2	199.1	354.3	455.1
Net income ($ mil.)	120.3%	2.6	(48.2)	81.8	51.9	60.4
Market value ($ mil.)	19.3%	231.6	184.7	335.0	475.8	468.5
Employees	14.2%	111	102	117	185	189

VAIL RESORTS INC NYS: MTN

390 Interlocken Crescent
Broomfield, CO 80021
Phone: 303 404-1800
Fax: 303 404-6415
Web: www.vailresorts.com

CEO: Kirsten A Lynch
CFO: Angela Korch
HR: Debra Taylor
FYE: July 31
Type: Public

Vail Resorts is the premier mountain resort company in the world and a leader in luxury, destination-based travel at iconic locations. The company's operations are grouped into three business segments: Mountain, Lodging, and Real Estate. Mountain segment operates about world-class destination mountain resorts and regional ski areas. Additionally, the segment includes ancillary services, primarily including ski school, dining, and retail/rental operations. In the Lodging segment, the company owns and/or manages a collection of luxury hotels and condominiums under RockResorts brand; other strategic lodging properties and a large number of condominiums located in proximity to its North American mountain resorts; National Park Service (NPS) concessioner properties including the Grand Teton Lodge Company (GTLC), which operates destination resorts in Grand Teton National Park; a Colorado resort ground transportation company and mountain resort golf courses. Real Estate segment owns, develops, and sells real estate in and around its resort communities. Vail Resorts generates the majority of its revenue in the US.

	Annual Growth	07/19	07/20	07/21	07/22	07/23
Sales ($mil.)	6.2%	2,271.6	1,963.7	1,909.7	2,525.9	2,889.4
Net income ($ mil.)	(2.9%)	301.2	98.8	127.9	347.9	268.1
Market value ($ mil.)	(1.1%)	9,404.7	7,325.9	11,643	9,046.5	8,983.9
Employees	10.0%	38,500	43,500	46,300	45,000	56,400

VALDOSTA STATE UNIVERSITY

1500 N PATTERSON ST
VALDOSTA, GA 316980001
Phone: 229 333-5800
Fax: –
Web: www.valdosta.edu

CEO: –
CFO: –
HR: –
FYE: June 30
Type: Private

Valdosta State University (VSU) nurtures higher education students as they blossom into professionals. The school, a regional university of the University System of Georgia, is located in the southern Georgia town of Valdosta, which is known for its flower gardens and trails. The school has two campuses, less than a mile apart, that house six colleges and offer about 60 undergraduate and 40 graduate degree programs, as well as doctorates in education and public administration. VSU was founded in 1906 as South Georgia State Normal College. Originally a girls' school, the institution became co-educational in 1950. It has some 650 faculty members and a student body of about 11,200.

	Annual Growth	06/10	06/11*	12/15	12/17*	06/19
Sales ($mil.)	(0.2%)	–	101.5	11.5	9.6	99.8
Net income ($ mil.)	–	–	9.0	7.8	5.4	(0.2)
Market value ($ mil.)	–	–	–	–	–	–
Employees	–	–	–	–	–	1,956

*Fiscal year change

VALENCE TECHNOLOGY, INC.

1807 W BRAKER LN STE C500
AUSTIN, TX 787583618
Phone: 512 527-2900
Fax: –
Web: www.valence.com

CEO: –
CFO: –
HR: –
FYE: March 31
Type: Private

If you charged Valence Technology with battery, you'd be right. The company's rechargeable lithium polymer batteries are designed for use in industrial (forklifts), military (robotics), stationary (generators), and transportation-related (cars and boats) electrical power applications. Valence touts its U-Charge lithium iron magnesium phosphate (LiFeMgPO4) energy storage systems as having a longer life and being safer and more stable under extreme conditions than even lithium-ion batteries that use oxide-based cathode materials.

VALERO ENERGY CORP NYS: VLO

One Valero Way
San Antonio, TX 78249
Phone: 210 345-2000
Fax: 210 246-2646
Web: www.valero.com

CEO: –
CFO: –
HR: –
FYE: December 31
Type: Public

Valero Energy is one of the largest independent petroleum refiners in the world and the world's second largest renewable fuels producer. Valero churns out approximately 3.2 million barrels per day, refining conventional and premium gasoline, diesel, low-cost diesel, ultra-low-sulfur diesel and other refined petroleum products. It operates approximately 15 refineries in the US, Canada, and the UK. It also has more than 10 ethanol plants with a combined production capacity of about 1.6 billion gallons per year. The company sells its gasoline and distillate products through bulk sales channels in the US and international markets. The US accounts for more than 70% of total revenue.

	Annual Growth	12/19	12/20	12/21	12/22	12/23
Sales ($mil.)	7.5%	108,324	64,912	113,977	176,383	144,766
Net income ($ mil.)	38.2%	2,422.0	(1,421.0)	930.0	11,528	8,835.0
Market value ($ mil.)	8.5%	31,214	18,855	25,034	42,283	43,329
Employees	(0.8%)	10,222	9,964	9,813	9,743	9,908

VALHI, INC. NYS: VHI

5430 LBJ Freeway, Suite 1700
Dallas, TX 75240-2620
Phone: 972 233-1700
Fax: 972 448-1445
Web: www.valhi.net

CEO: Loretta J Feehan
CFO: Amy A Samford
HR: –
FYE: December 31
Type: Public

Valhi is primarily a holding company that operates through its wholly-owned and majority-owned subsidiaries. The company's Kronos unit, is a leading maker of titanium dioxide pigment, which is used to whiten and add opacity to fibers, paper, paint, and plastic. Other subsidiaries include CompX (a leading manufacturer of security products), Tremont (titanium metal products for aerospace and other markets), and NL Industries. The company also operates in real estate management and development through BMI and LandWell. BMI provides utility services to certain industrial and municipal customers. North America generates about 45% of the company's revenue.

	Annual Growth	12/19	12/20	12/21	12/22	12/23
Sales ($mil.)	0.5%	1,938.4	1,878.1	2,335.4	2,266.2	1,977.1
Net income ($ mil.)	–	49.2	55.2	127.2	90.2	(12.1)
Market value ($ mil.)	68.8%	53.3	433.2	819.4	627.0	432.9
Employees	–	2,200	2,242	2,248	2,266	2,196

VALLEY HEALTH SYSTEM

220 CAMPUS BLVD
WINCHESTER, VA 226012888
Phone: 540 536-8000
Fax: –
Web: www.valleyhealthlink.com

CEO: Mark H Merrill
CFO: Pete Gallagher
HR: Linda Kirton
FYE: December 31
Type: Private

Valley Health's medical centers can be found in the in the Shenandoah Valley region. The not-for-profit organization operates six hospitals in Virginia and West Virginia that house a combined total of roughly 600 beds and a medical staff of more than 500. The facilities include the flagship Winchester Medical Center, as well as Warren Memorial Hospital, Shenandoah Memorial Hospital, and a handful of smaller community hospitals. Valley Health also operates outpatient surgery, nursing home, rehabilitation, urgent care, and family practice centers, and it offers ambulance and home health care services.

	Annual Growth	09/11	09/12	09/13*	12/21	12/22
Sales ($mil.)	(6.8%)	–	–	351.6	160.8	187.4
Net income ($ mil.)	(14.4%)	–	–	23.8	2.2	5.9
Market value ($ mil.)	–	–	–	–	–	–
Employees	–	–	–	–	–	4,300

*Fiscal year change

VALLEY HEALTH SYSTEM LLC

2075 E FLAMINGO RD
LAS VEGAS, NV 891195188
Phone: 702 369-7612
Fax: -
Web: www.desertspringshospital.com

CEO: Sam Kaufman
CFO: -
HR: -
FYE: December 31
Type: Private

Desert Springs Hospital Medical Center helps patients feel that health care is more calculated risk than wild gamble. Desert Springs Hospital Medical Center, part of Universal Health Service's Valley Health System subsidiary, is a 290-bed acute care hospital located in southeastern Las Vegas. It operates an American Diabetes Association-accredited diabetes treatment center and is a leader in cardiac care, operating several full-service catheterization labs. The medical center also boasts affiliated physician offices and an outpatient surgery facility.

	Annual Growth	12/13	12/14	12/15	12/16	12/17
Sales ($mil.)	1.8%	-	238.2	243.7	249.0	251.2
Net income ($ mil.)	(5.0%)	-	21.3	17.4	21.4	18.3
Market value ($ mil.)	-	-	-	-	-	-
Employees	-	-	-	-	-	12

VALLEY HEALTH SYSTEM LLC

620 SHADOW LN
LAS VEGAS, NV 891064119
Phone: 702 388-4000
Fax: -
Web: www.valleyhospital.net

CEO: Sam Kaufman
CFO: -
HR: -
FYE: December 31
Type: Private

If you hit the Las Vegas Strip a bit too hard, Valley Hospital Medical Center could be a site you weren't planning to see. Part of Universal Health Services' subsidiary The Valley Health System, Valley Hospital has about 400 beds and offers inpatient, outpatient, and emergency care. Founded in 1972, it also operates a Cardiac Center and the HealthPlace for Women and Children's unit (which includes a Level III Neonatal Intensive Care Unit). Valley Medical was the first hospital in the region to receive accreditation as a Primary Stroke Center, a Certified Chest Pain Center, and a Heart Failure Center.

	Annual Growth	12/07	12/08	12/14	12/15	12/16
Sales ($mil.)	(0.9%)	-	305.6	244.2	269.8	283.5
Net income ($ mil.)	(6.8%)	-	26.1	5.6	15.4	14.9
Market value ($ mil.)	-	-	-	-	-	-
Employees	-	-	-	-	-	1,350

VALLEY HEALTH SYSTEM, INC.

223 N VAN DIEN AVE
RIDGEWOOD, NJ 074502726
Phone: 201 447-8000
Fax: -
Web: www.valleyhealthcareers.com

CEO: Audrey Meyers
CFO: Richard D Keenan
HR: Patricia Miller
FYE: December 31
Type: Private

The Valley Health System makes sure that it accounts for the hills and valleys of an individual's healthcare journey for the folks of the Village of Ridgewood, New Jersey. The system includes The Valley Hospital, (a 451-bed, not-for-profit, acute-care hospital); Valley Home Care, a home care and hospice agency; and Valley Health Medical Group (satellite clinics), a multispecialty group practice of doctors and advanced practice professionals representing more than 30 specialties. It employs more than 1,000 physicians in its various facilities. The Valley Health System is governed by a 12-member board and supported by The Valley Hospital Foundation and nearly 4,000 volunteers and auxiliary members.

	Annual Growth	12/14	12/15	12/19	12/21	12/22
Sales ($mil.)	68.9%	-	2.6	82.8	105.9	103.1
Net income ($ mil.)	-	-	-	1.7	(6.6)	(0.3)
Market value ($ mil.)	-	-	-	-	-	-
Employees	-	-	-	-	-	4,000

VALLEY HOME & COMMUNITY HEALTH CARE INC

15 ENJEX RD STE 301
PARAMUS, NJ 07652
Phone: 201 291-6000
Fax: -
Web: -

CEO: -
CFO: -
HR: -
FYE: December 31
Type: Private

Valley Home Care is there when you need care at home in the valley. The company offers specialty health care as well as end-of-life palliative care in patients' homes. Specialist tend to those who need follow up care after a stay at sibling The Valley Hospital or other area hospitals. Valley Home Care's services include maternal and child care, rehabilitation therapy, nutritional counseling, diabetes support, IV therapy, and eldercare. Its hospice program has doctors, nurses, social workers, clergy, and companion volunteers available. Its Butterflies and Journeys programs provide medical care, education, and family support for dying children and their families. Valley Home Care is part of Valley Health System.

	Annual Growth	12/99	12/00	12/01	12/02	12/22
Sales ($mil.)	22.2%	-	0.8	19.7	22.1	66.3
Net income ($ mil.)	105.3%	-	0.0	0.6	0.7	7.5
Market value ($ mil.)	-	-	-	-	-	-
Employees	-	-	-	-	-	400

VALLEY NATIONAL BANCORP (NJ)

NMS: VLY

One Penn Plaza
New York, NY 10119
Phone: 973 305-8800
Fax: -
Web: www.valley.com

CEO: Ira Robbins
CFO: Michael D Hagedorn
HR: -
FYE: December 31
Type: Public

Valley National Bancorp owns Valley National Bank with approximately $50 billion in assets. The company serves customers through more than 230 branches in northern and central New Jersey and the New York City boroughs of Manhattan, Brooklyn, and Queens, as well as on Long Island, Westchester County, New York, Florida, Alabama, California, and Illinois. The company offer a full suite of national and regional banking solutions through various commercial, private banking, retail, insurance and wealth management financial services products. Subsidiaries offer asset management, mortgage and auto loan servicing, title insurance, and property/casualty, life, and health insurance. The company was founded in 1927. In early 2022, Valley acquired Bank Leumi Le-Israel Corporation, the U.S. subsidiary of Bank Leumi Le-Israel B.M., and parent company of Bank Leumi USA for $1.2 billion.

	Annual Growth	12/19	12/20	12/21	12/22	12/23
Assets ($mil.)	13.0%	37,436	40,686	43,446	57,463	60,935
Net income ($ mil.)	12.6%	309.8	390.6	473.8	568.9	498.5
Market value ($ mil.)	(1.3%)	5,813.3	4,950.2	6,981.0	5,742.2	5,513.7
Employees	4.3%	3,174	3,155	3,370	3,826	3,749

VALLEY VIEW COMMUNITY UNIT SCHOOL DISTRICT 365U

801 W NORMANTOWN RD
ROMEOVILLE, IL 604464330
Phone: 815 886-2700
Fax: -
Web: www.vvsd.org

CEO: -
CFO: -
HR: -
FYE: June 30
Type: Private

Located about 35 miles southwest of downtown Chicago, Valley View School District 365U provides education to 18,000 elementary, middle, and high school students -- the district also includes one alternative school and one preschool. The 20 schools included in the district (serving Romeoville and Bolingbrook communities) total approximately 2.4 million square feet. With more than 2,000 full time employees, Valley View School District 365U is one of Will County's largest employers. The seven-member school board (elected for a four-year term) hires and supervises the superintendent of schools and sets district policies.

	Annual Growth	06/18	06/19	06/20	06/21	06/22
Sales ($mil.)	3.2%	-	366.1	384.2	397.9	402.8
Net income ($ mil.)	(15.6%)	-	33.1	(10.9)	7.4	19.9
Market value ($ mil.)	-	-	-	-	-	-
Employees	-	-	-	-	-	3,000

VALMONT INDUSTRIES INC   NYS: VMI

15000 Valmont Plaza   CEO: Avner M Applbaum
Omaha, NE 68154   CFO: Timothy P Francis
Phone: 402 963-1000   HR: –
Fax: 402 963-1198   FYE: December 30
Web: www.valmont.com   Type: Public

Valmont Industries is a diversified manufacturer of products and services for infrastructure and agriculture markets. Its Infrastructure products and services create communities that are safer, cleaner, more efficient, and better connected. Its Agriculture products and services help growers produce greater crop yields with fewer inputs. The company provides its products to industrial customers, municipalities and government entities, contractors, as well as telecommunications and utility companies. Valmont, which generates most of its sales in the US, was established in 1946.

	Annual Growth	12/19	12/20	12/21	12/22	12/23
Sales ($mil.)	10.8%	2,767.0	2,895.4	3,501.6	4,345.3	4,174.6
Net income ($ mil.)	(0.5%)	153.8	140.7	195.6	250.9	150.8
Market value ($ mil.)	11.6%	3,038.8	3,477.1	4,946.9	6,682.4	4,719.0
Employees	3.1%	9,862	10,840	11,041	11,364	11,125

VALUE DRUG COMPANY

195 THEATER DR   CEO: Rowland Tibbott
DUNCANSVILLE, PA 166357144   CFO: Robert E Tyler
Phone: 814 944-9316   HR: –
Fax: –   FYE: March 31
Web: www.valuedrugco.com   Type: Private

Value Drug Company (Value Drug) is committed to providing transparency in its pricing and optimizing manufacturer relationships and purchasing power to improve buying conditions for its members. The company has established partnerships with industry-leading suppliers to offer a sizeable selection of products, including brand, generic, injectable, and specialty pharmaceuticals, an extensive line of regularly stocked home health care items, long-term care supplies, and the latest in innovative and trending health, beauty & wellness. The company works with some of the world's largest pharmaceutical makers. Value Drug was founded in 1934 and incorporated in 1936.

	Annual Growth	12/17	12/18*	03/20	03/21	03/22
Sales ($mil.)	(1.9%)	–	1,034.2	1,156.4	1,010.8	956.0
Net income ($ mil.)	–	–	(0.1)	0.8	1.6	1.4
Market value ($ mil.)	–	–	–	–	–	–
Employees	–	–	–	–	–	200

*Fiscal year change

VALUE LINE INC   NAS: VALU

551 Fifth Avenue   CEO: Howard A Brecher
New York, NY 10176-0001   CFO: Stephen R Anastasio
Phone: 212 907-1500   HR: –
Fax: –   FYE: April 30
Web: www.valueline.com   Type: Public

Value Line's investment-related publications are likely to be found on the bookshelves of the serious investor. Its flagship publication, The Value Line Investment Survey, features stock reports that incorporate objective analysis, financial information, and forecasts of stock performance. Its print and electronic products also include Value Line Fund Advisor, which offers mutual fund evaluations and rankings, and investment analysis software, The Value Line Investment Analyzer. The company's electronic products are available via CD-ROM and via the company's website. All total, Value Line collects data and provides analysis on some 7,000 stocks; 18,000 mutual funds; 200,000 options; and other securities.

	Annual Growth	04/19	04/20	04/21	04/22	04/23
Sales ($mil.)	2.3%	36.3	40.3	40.4	40.5	39.7
Net income ($ mil.)	12.8%	11.2	15.7	23.3	23.8	18.1
Market value ($ mil.)	18.6%	218.4	292.3	288.1	617.7	432.1
Employees	(3.9%)	162	161	166	140	138

VALVOLINE INC   NYS: VVV

100 Valvoline Way, Suite 100   CEO: Lori A Flees
Lexington, KY 40509   CFO: Mary E Meixelsperger
Phone: 859 357-7777   HR: –
Fax: –   FYE: September 30
Web: www.valvoline.com   Type: Public

Valvoline is a leader in preventive maintenance delivering convenient and trusted automotive services in its retail stores throughout the US and Canada. The company operates and franchises approximately 1,700 service center locations and is the #2 and #3 largest chain in the US and Canada, respectively, by number of stores. With sales in more than 140 countries and territories, Valvoline's solutions are available for every engine and drivetrain, including high-mileage and heavy-duty vehicles, and are offered at more than 80,000 locations worldwide. Creating the next generation of advanced automotive solutions, Valvoline has established itself as the world's leading supplier of battery fluids to electric vehicle manufacturers, offering tailored products to help extend vehicle range and efficiency. The company generates the vast majority of its revenue in the US.

	Annual Growth	09/19	09/20	09/21	09/22	09/23
Sales ($mil.)	(11.8%)	2,390.0	2,353.0	2,981.0	1,236.1	1,443.5
Net income ($ mil.)	61.6%	208.0	317.0	420.0	424.3	1,419.7
Market value ($ mil.)	10.0%	2,969.6	2,566.6	4,203.1	3,415.8	4,346.0
Employees	8.4%	7,900	8,800	9,800	8,900	10,900

VAN ATLAS LINES INC

1212 SAINT GEORGE RD   CEO: John P Griffin
EVANSVILLE, IN 477112364   CFO: Donald R Breivogel Jr
Phone: 812 424-4326   HR: –
Fax: –   FYE: December 31
Web: www.atlasvanlines.com   Type: Private

The main subsidiary of Atlas World Group, moving company Atlas Van Lines provides transportation of household goods throughout the US and between the US and Canada. The company is one of the largest movers in the US. Atlas Van Lines also offers specialized transportation services for such cargo as trade show materials, fine art, electronics, pianos, store fixtures, and even individual cars and motorcycles. It operates through a network of some 500 agents in the US and about 150 in Canada -- independent companies that use the Atlas brand in assigned geographic territories and cooperate on interstate moves. Atlas Van Lines was formed in 1948 by a group of 33 small moving companies.

	Annual Growth	12/03	12/04	12/05	12/06	12/08
Sales ($mil.)	127.4%	–	–	59.2	58.1	696.0
Net income ($ mil.)	71.0%	–	–	3.8	2.5	19.2
Market value ($ mil.)	–	–	–	–	–	–
Employees	–	–	–	–	–	606

VAN BUDD LINES INC

24 SCHOOLHOUSE RD   CEO: –
SOMERSET, NJ 088731213   CFO: –
Phone: 732 627-0600   HR: –
Fax: –   FYE: December 31
Web: www.buddvanlines.com   Type: Private

No hothouse flower, Budd Van Lines aims to be a hardy perennial of the corporate relocation business. From coast to coast, the independent van line company moves the household goods of employees who are relocating at the behest of their employers, about 6,500 annually. It offers packing and moving services to all 48 contiguous states from branch offices in New Jersey, California, Wisconsin, Georgia, Ohio, and Texas. Companies that have called upon Budd Van Lines to help employees move include Bristol-Myers Squibb, Merck & Co., and PricewaterhouseCoopers. Budd Van Lines was founded in 1975.

	Annual Growth	12/05	12/06	12/07	12/08	12/10
Sales ($mil.)	(0.1%)	–	–	47.5	47.1	47.2
Net income ($ mil.)	11.1%	–	–	0.8	0.3	1.1
Market value ($ mil.)	–	–	–	–	–	–
Employees	–	–	–	–	–	155

VAN HORN METZ & CO., INC.

201 E ELM ST
CONSHOHOCKEN, PA 194282029
Phone: 610 828-4500
Fax: –
Web: www.vanhornmetz.com

CEO: –
CFO: –
HR: –
FYE: December 31
Type: Private

Van Horn, Metz & Co. (or, Van Horn Metz) distributes chemical ingredients such as pigments, dyes, extenders, additives, resins, lubricants, and base stocks. The company's customers include makers of plastic and rubber products, inks, adhesives and sealants, and paints and coatings. Founded in 1950 by Harold Van Horn and Donald Metz, the company serves customers throughout the eastern half of the US. Van Horn Metz operates 12 warehouses and six sales offices.

	Annual Growth	12/06	12/07	12/08	12/09	12/10
Sales ($mil.)	(7.4%)	–	–	45.9	35.5	39.4
Net income ($ mil.)	–	–	–	–	–	–
Market value ($ mil.)	–	–	–	–	–	–
Employees	–	–	–	–	–	45

VANDA PHARMACEUTICALS INC

2200 Pennsylvania Avenue NW, Suite 300E
Washington, DC 20037
Phone: 202 734-3400
Fax: –
Web: www.vandapharma.com

NMS: VNDA
CEO: Mihael H Polymeropoulos
CFO: Kevin Moran
HR: –
FYE: December 31
Type: Public

Vanda Pharmaceuticals is a leading global biopharmaceutical company focused on the development and commercialization of innovative therapies to address high unmet medical needs and improve the lives of patients. Commercial portfolio is currently comprised of two products, HETLIOZ for the treatment of Non-24-Hour Sleep-Wake Disorder (Non-24) and nighttime sleep disturbances in Smith-Magenis Syndrome (SMS) and Fanapt for the treatment of schizophrenia. Other drug candidates are for the treatments of atopic dermatitis, gastroparesis and motion sickness, as well as a portfolio of Cystic Fibrosis Transmembrane Conductance Regulator (CFTR) activators and inhibitors for the treatment of dry eye and ocular inflammation. Vanda typically licenses development and commercialization rights for its compounds from (and to) companies including Bristol-Myers Squibb, Eli Lilly, and Novartis.

	Annual Growth	12/19	12/20	12/21	12/22	12/23
Sales ($mil.)	(4.0%)	227.2	248.2	268.7	254.4	192.6
Net income ($ mil.)	(61.6%)	115.6	23.3	33.2	6.3	2.5
Market value ($ mil.)	(28.8%)	944.1	756.0	902.7	425.2	242.8
Employees	(8.1%)	284	292	278	290	203

VANDERBILT UNIVERSITY MEDICAL CENTER

1211 MEDICAL CENTER DR
NASHVILLE, TN 372320004
Phone: 615 322-5000
Fax: –
Web: www.vanderbilthealth.com

CEO: –
CFO: –
HR: –
FYE: June 30
Type: Private

Vanderbilt University Medical Center (VUMC) is one of the largest comprehensive research, teaching, and patient care health system in the Mid-South region. VUMC has a total of about 1,710 licensed hospital beds at Vanderbilt University Hospital, Monroe Carell Jr. Children's Hospital at Vanderbilt, Vanderbilt Psychiatric Hospital, Vanderbilt Stallworth Rehabilitation Hospital, Vanderbilt Wilson County Hospital, Vanderbilt Bedford Hospital, and Vanderbilt Tullahoma-Harton Hospital. VUMC is a Level 1 Trauma Center and Burn Center in the region. Its world-leading academic departments and centers make scientific discoveries, advance clinical care, and train the next generation of health care professionals through more than 100 residency and fellowship programs. VUMC was founded in 1874.

	Annual Growth	06/17	06/18	06/20	06/21	06/22
Sales ($mil.)	11.9%	–	4,086.4	4,930.3	5,574.6	6,413.3
Net income ($ mil.)	21.5%	–	98.1	182.8	210.9	214.2
Market value ($ mil.)	–	–	–	–	–	–
Employees	–	–	–	–	–	19,000

VANTAGE DRILLING CO

777 Post Oak Boulevard, Suite 800
Houston, TX 77056
Phone: 281 404-4700
Fax: 281 404-4749
Web: www.vantagedrilling.com

NBB: VTGD F
CEO: Ihab Toma
CFO: Douglas E Stewart
HR: –
FYE: December 31
Type: Public

From its vantage point, Vantage Drilling Company sees nothing but the high seas from atop its drilling rigs. An offshore drilling contractor, Vantage Drilling provides oil and natural gas drilling services to multinational oil and natural gas companies operating in shallow to ultra-deepwater environments. The company owns and operates four jackup rigs (for shallow water drilling) and three ultra-deep drillship (designed for drilling in water depths of 12,000 ft.) Vantage Drilling typically operates in Southeast Asia, West Africa, and other oil-rich offshore regions.

	Annual Growth	12/11	12/12	12/13	12/14	12/15
Sales ($mil.)	12.3%	485.3	471.5	732.1	875.6	772.3
Net income ($ mil.)	–	(80.0)	(145.3)	(81.8)	42.0	17.2
Market value ($ mil.)	–	–	–	–	–	–
Employees	(3.7%)	980	1,056	1,274	1,295	843

VANTAGE DRILLING INTERNATIONAL

c/o Vantage Energy Services, Inc., 777 Post Oak Boulevard, Suite 440
Houston, TX 77056
Phone: 281 404-4700
Fax: –
Web: www.vantagedrilling.com

NBB: VTDR F
CEO: Ihab Toma
CFO: Douglas E Stewart
HR: –
FYE: December 31
Type: Public

From its vantage point, Vantage Drilling Company sees nothing but the high seas from atop its drilling rigs. An offshore drilling contractor, Vantage Drilling provides oil and natural gas drilling services to multinational oil and natural gas companies operating in shallow to ultra-deepwater environments. The company owns and operates four jackup rigs (for shallow water drilling) and three ultra-deep drillship (designed for drilling in water depths of 12,000 ft.) Vantage Drilling typically operates in Southeast Asia, West Africa, and other oil-rich offshore regions.

	Annual Growth	12/18	12/19	12/20	12/21	12/22
Sales ($mil.)	5.4%	225.7	760.8	126.9	158.4	278.7
Net income ($ mil.)	–	(141.5)	455.7	(276.7)	(110.1)	(3.4)
Market value ($ mil.)	–	–	–	–	–	–
Employees	0.2%	894	940	670	1,030	900

VANTAGE GROUP INC

29 N PLAINS INDUSTRIAL RD UNIT 15
WALLINGFORD, CT 064925841
Phone: 203 234-7737
Fax: –
Web: www.mosaicinfo.org

CEO: William Cramer
CFO: –
HR: –
FYE: June 30
Type: Private

Vantage gives an advantage to the disadvantaged. The nonprofit helps about 65 individuals with developmental disabilities living in five Connecticut communities find and keep employment and participate in community-based residential programs. It also sponsors workshops and classes in addition to health care and career counseling for the people it serves. Vantage hosts fund- and awareness-raising dinners as well as talent and art shows for program participants and community members. It is also supported by state funding. The group was established in 1984.

	Annual Growth	06/14	06/15	06/19	06/20	06/21
Sales ($mil.)	6.8%	–	5.4	6.9	7.5	7.9
Net income ($ mil.)	41.0%	–	0.1	0.1	0.2	0.9
Market value ($ mil.)	–	–	–	–	–	–
Employees	–	–	–	–	–	75

VAREX IMAGING CORP

NMS: VREX

1678 S. Pioneer Road
Salt Lake City, UT 84104
Phone: 801 972-5000
Fax: –
Web: www.vareximaging.com

CEO: Sunny S Sanyal
CFO: Shubham Maheshwari
HR: –
FYE: September 29
Type: Public

Varex is a leading innovator, designer and manufacturer of X-ray tubes, digital detectors, linear accelerators and other image software processing solutions, which are critical components in a variety of X-ray-based imaging equipment. Its products include X-ray tubes, flat panel detectors, and imaging software, as well as high-energy inspection accelerators and high-voltage connectors. It produces more than 160,000 X-ray tubes and approximately 170,000 X-ray detectors. Customers include radiology original equipment manufacturers (OEMs), which make systems for medical diagnostic radiology applications, airport baggage inspection systems, manufacturing quality control devices, and other systems. More than 30% of its total revenue comes from the US.

	Annual Growth	09/19*	10/20	10/21*	09/22	09/23
Sales ($mil.)	3.4%	780.6	738.3	818.1	859.4	893.4
Net income ($ mil.)	32.8%	15.5	(57.9)	17.4	30.3	48.2
Market value ($ mil.)	(9.7%)	1,146.2	501.4	1,158.3	856.8	761.6
Employees	4.7%	2,000	2,000	2,100	2,300	2,400

*Fiscal year change

VARIETY CHILDREN'S HOSPITAL

3100 SW 62ND AVE
MIAMI, FL 331553009
Phone: 305 666-6511
Fax: –
Web: www.nicklauschildrens.org

CEO: Narendra M Kini
CFO: –
HR: –
FYE: December 31
Type: Private

Miami Children's Hospital (MCH), a not-for-profit medical center, boasts some 290 beds and offers more than 40 different health care specialties and sub-specialties represented by more than 650 physicians and more than 130 pediatric sub-specialists. Some specialties include pediatric emergency care, cancer treatment, orthopedics, and rehabilitation services. The hospital's neonatal unit treats newborns referred from other hospitals. Miami Children's Hospital operates the region's only free-standing pediatric trauma center. The MCH Research Institute conducts more than 210 clinical research studies in 26 sub-specialties.

	Annual Growth	12/17	12/18	12/19	12/21	12/22
Sales ($mil.)	5.6%	–	656.0	681.0	777.0	816.9
Net income ($ mil.)	–	–	(23.5)	(44.5)	105.5	96.8
Market value ($ mil.)	–	–	–	–	–	–
Employees	–	–	–	–	–	3,700

VARONIS SYSTEMS, INC

NMS: VRNS

1250 Broadway, 28th Floor
New York, NY 10001
Phone: 877 292-8767
Fax: –
Web: www.varonis.com

CEO: Yakov Faitelson
CFO: Guy Melamed
HR: –
FYE: December 31
Type: Public

Varonis Systems is a pioneer in data security and analytics, fighting a different battle than conventional cybersecurity companies. Its software specializes in data protection, threat detection and response, data privacy and compliance. Varonis software enables enterprises of all sizes and industries to protect data stored on-premises and in the cloud, including: sensitive files and emails; confidential personal data belonging to customers, patients and employees; financial records; source code, strategic and product plans; and other intellectual property. The company's proprietary Metadata Framework software platform extracts critical metadata, or data about data, from an enterprise's information technology ("IT") infrastructure. Its Data Security Platform uses this contextual information to map functional relationships among employees, data objects, systems, content and usage. North America accounts for around 75% of total revenue.

	Annual Growth	12/19	12/20	12/21	12/22	12/23
Sales ($mil.)	18.4%	254.2	292.7	390.1	473.6	499.2
Net income ($ mil.)	–	(78.8)	(94.0)	(116.9)	(124.5)	(100.9)
Market value ($ mil.)	(12.6%)	8,478.5	17,850	5,322.1	2,611.9	4,940.2
Employees	9.1%	1,574	1,719	2,065	2,143	2,233

VARTECH SYSTEMS, INC.

NBB: VRTK

11301 Industriplex Boulevard, Suite 4
Baton Rouge, LA 70809
Phone: 225 298-0300
Fax: –
Web: –

CEO: –
CFO: –
HR: –
FYE: July 31
Type: Public

VarTech Systems thinks tough. Its rugged computer monitors and LCD-based displays work in harsh environments and military field conditions, as well as in factories and control rooms. VarTech also produces industrial computers, including panel PCs, intended to save space on the factory floor by packing a fully functional computer into the back of a display. The company manufactures monitors and displays (including CRT-based displays), resells these products from other makers, and offers repair services. Founded in 1988 and going public soon after that, VarTech Systems withdrew its stock listing in 2003.

	Annual Growth	07/99	07/00	07/01	07/02	07/03
Sales ($mil.)	7.8%	5.7	6.6	6.8	6.1	7.7
Net income ($ mil.)	–	(0.2)	0.1	0.1	0.2	0.2
Market value ($ mil.)	(11.1%)	4.2	3.4	0.9	0.8	2.6
Employees	(11.3%)	50	45	40	35	31

VASAMED INC

NBB: VSMD

7615 Golden Triangle Drive, Suite C
Minneapolis, MN 55344-3733
Phone: 952 944-5857
Fax: 952 944-6022
Web: www.opsi.com

CEO: –
CFO: –
HR: –
FYE: December 31
Type: Public

V samed takes all things vascular to heart. The company, formerly operating under the name Optical Sensors, makes products that monitor the health of patients' hearts and blood vessels. Its patented SensiLase system provides wound care analysis, amputation planning, and microvascular assessment. Its AcQtrac ICG product monitors hemodynamic cardiac functions using a proprietary cardiograph technology. V samed sells the FDA-approved SensiLase and AcQtrac equipment through direct sales representatives and distributors the Americas, Europe, and Asia.

	Annual Growth	12/04	12/05	12/06	12/07	12/08
Sales ($mil.)	30.9%	1.1	1.4	2.0	3.1	3.1
Net income ($ mil.)	–	(6.4)	(4.9)	(6.4)	(5.6)	(2.9)
Market value ($ mil.)	(54.4%)	24.0	16.0	6.9	8.0	1.0
Employees	–	27	36	–	–	–

VASO CORP

NBB: VASO

137 Commercial Street, Suite 200
Plainview, NY 11803
Phone: 516 997-4600
Fax: 516 997-2299
Web: www.vasocorporation.com

CEO: Jun MA
CFO: Jonathan P Newton
HR: –
FYE: December 31
Type: Public

Vasomedical's noninvasive treatments for angina and congestive heart failure get patients' blood pumping. The company's main product is the EECP (enhanced external counterpulsation) system, which is also approved to treat coronary artery disease and cardiogenic shock. During the company's Medicare-covered treatments, cuffs attached to the patient's calves and thighs inflate and deflate in sync with the patient's heartbeat, increasing and decreasing aortic blood pressure. After about 35 treatments, patients may experience years of symptomatic relief. Vasomedical sells the system to hospitals, clinics, and other health care providers worldwide through a direct sales force and independent distributors.

	Annual Growth	12/18	12/19	12/20	12/21	12/22
Sales ($mil.)	2.0%	74.0	75.7	69.9	75.6	80.0
Net income ($ mil.)	–	(3.7)	0.0	0.4	6.1	11.9
Market value ($ mil.)	59.6%	4.4	5.2	15.6	9.6	28.9
Employees	(3.8%)	317	294	268	256	272

VASQUEZ & COMPANY LLP

655 N CENTRAL AVE STE 1550
GLENDALE, CA 912031451
Phone: 213 873-1700
Fax: –
Web: vasquez.cpa

CEO: –
CFO: –
HR: Eden Marfori
FYE: December 31
Type: Private

Vasquez & Company performs a variety of accounting and consulting services including auditing, bookkeeping, tax planning and preparation, cash flow and budget analysis, litigation support, and fraud prevention and detection. It also assists clients in buying or selling a business. The company specializes in the health care, manufacturing, technology, and real estate industries. It also serves government agencies, not-for-profit organizations, and individuals. Active primarily in California, Vasquez & Company was founded in 1969 and is a member of the BDO Seidman Alliance network of independent firms.

VASSAR COLLEGE

124 RAYMOND AVE BOX 12
POUGHKEEPSIE, NY 126040001
Phone: 845 437-7000
Fax: –
Web: www.vassar.edu

CEO: –
CFO: –
HR: Alphine Logan
FYE: June 30
Type: Private

A cool nickname and certain heritage aren't enough to assure some students entrance into Vassar College. The highly selective school enrolls some 2,400 students annually, most of whom graduated in the top 20% of their high school class. It has a student-faculty ratio of 8:1 and a list of alumni that includes standouts in areas from business to philanthropy. Because Vassar has no core curriculum, students may concentrate in a single discipline, a multidisciplinary program, or design an independent major. The only universal requirements for graduation are proficiency in a foreign language, a freshman composition class, and a quantitative class. Vassar was founded in 1861 as a women's school; it went coed in 1969.

VAUGHAN FURNITURE COMPANY, INCORPORATED

816 GLENDALE RD
GALAX, VA 243332311
Phone: 276 236-6111
Fax: –
Web: vaughanfurniture.magix.net

CEO: Taylor C Vaughan
CFO: –
HR: –
FYE: November 30
Type: Private

They may not be the singing von Trapp family, but this family of Vaughans has built a lasting empire of its own. Vaughan Furniture, founded in 1923 by brothers Taylor G. Vaughan, Sr., and Bunyan C. Vaughan, makes wood furniture for the bedroom, dining room, and living room. The company's collections are distributed to more than 2,000 dealers internationally. It added the Kathy Ireland label in 2009. Its growing youth line (including its NASCAR Youth Collection) is responsible for a significant portion of Vaughan's revenue. The third generation of the Vaughan family took the company reins in the 1995, when Bill Vaughan was elected president and CEO. Taylor Vaughan became the company's sixth president in 2007.

	Annual Growth	11/09	11/10	11/11	11/12	11/13
Sales ($mil.)	(18.2%)	–	12.5	9.2	8.5	6.8
Net income ($ mil.)	–	–	(1.8)	(1.2)	0.9	(1.9)
Market value ($ mil.)	–	–	–	–	–	–
Employees	–	–	–	–	–	28

VAUGHAN-BASSETT FURNITURE COMPANY, INCORPORATED

300 E GRAYSON ST
GALAX, VA 243332964
Phone: 276 236-6161
Fax: –
Web: www.vaughanbassett.com

CEO: John D Bassett III
CFO: Andrew Williamson
HR: –
FYE: November 27
Type: Private

Vaughan-Bassett Furniture Company, which specializes in making bedroom and dining room furniture, is counted among the leading wood furniture manufacturers in the US. It's one of the few companies that operates furniture factories in America -- in Virginia and North Carolina. Vaughan-Bassett collections are made using wood solids and wood veneers from pine, oak, cherry, maple, ash, beech, poplar, and birch trees. It also operates a One for One tree-planting program to promote sustainability. At the helm is namesake John Bassett III, who comes from a family of furniture entrepreneurs. His grandfather founded industry leader Bassett Furniture Industries in 1902.

	Annual Growth	11/06	11/07	11/08	11/09	11/10
Sales ($mil.)	(10.7%)	–	–	98.1	85.5	78.2
Net income ($ mil.)	7.4%	–	–	1.0	2.0	1.2
Market value ($ mil.)	–	–	–	–	–	–
Employees	–	–	–	–	–	1,564

VAXART INC

170 Harbor Way, Suite 300
South San Francisco, CA 94080
Phone: 650 550-3500
Fax: –
Web: www.aviragentherapeutics.com

NAS: VXRT
CEO: Michael J Finney
CFO: Phillip Lee
HR: –
FYE: December 31
Type: Public

Aviragen Therapeutics (formerly Biota Biopharmaceuticals) would like to wave bye-bye to a host of viral infections plaguing mankind. It has a handful of drugs in active clinical development, including Laninamivir octanoate for the treatment of influenza, vapendavir for the treatment of human rhinovirus (common cold) upper respiratory infections in asthmatics, and BTA585 for the treatment and prevention of condyloma caused by human papillomavirus types 6 and 11. Its Zanamivir flu treatment is marketed by GlaxoSmithKline as Relenza, while another flu treatment, laninamivir octanoate, is marketed by Daiichi Sankyo as Inavir in Japan. Aviragen merged with California-based oral vaccine developer Vaxart in February 2018.

	Annual Growth	12/19	12/20	12/21	12/22	12/23
Sales ($mil.)	(7.0%)	9.9	4.0	0.9	0.1	7.4
Net income ($ mil.)	–	(18.6)	(32.2)	(70.5)	(107.8)	(82.5)
Market value ($ mil.)	13.1%	53.8	876.2	962.1	147.5	87.9
Employees	67.0%	14	28	110	177	109

VBI VACCINES (DELAWARE) INC.

160 2ND ST STE 3
CAMBRIDGE, MA 021421525
Phone: 617 830-3031
Fax: –
Web: www.vbivaccines.com

CEO: Jeff R Baxter
CFO: –
HR: –
FYE: December 31
Type: Private

Paulson Capital is a financial services holding company operating through its sole subsidiary, Paulson Investment Company. A full-service brokerage, Paulson Investment is one of the largest independent brokerage firms in the Pacific Northwest. It acts as an agent for its customers in the purchase and sale of stocks, options, and debt securities. The company also offers market-making and underwriting services for small and emerging companies. Paulson Investment has more than 40 branches in about a dozen states; most are run by independent contractors. The company has agreed to sell its Paulson Investment retail operations to Tampa-based JHS Capital Advisors.

	Annual Growth	12/11	12/12	12/13	12/14	12/15
Sales ($mil.)	(62.9%)	–	7.7	10.8	–	0.4
Net income ($ mil.)	–	–	(0.4)	(1.5)	–	(13.9)
Market value ($ mil.)	–	–	–	–	–	–
Employees	–	–	–	–	–	65

VCA INC.

12401 W OLYMPIC BLVD
LOS ANGELES, CA 900641022
Phone: 310 571-6500
Fax: –
Web: www.vcahospitals.com

CEO: Doug Drew
CFO: –
HR: –
FYE: December 31
Type: Private

A leader in veterinary care, VCA is a family of hometown animal hospitals committed to making a positive impact on pets, people, and communities. The national network of hometown hospitals has a network of more than 35,000 VCA associates. The company operates the nation's largest chain of animal hospitals with more than 1,000 in over 45 US states and five Canadian provinces. It provides a full range of general, surgical, and specialized treatments for pets. Equipped with state-of-the-art diagnostic imaging equipment, on-site digital x-ray, and an ultrasound unit, the company focuses on maintaining the highest standards of pet health care available anywhere. Founded in 1986, VCA joined the Mars family in 2017.

VCOM3D, INC.

13501 INGENUITY DR # 128
ORLANDO, FL 328263018
Phone: 321 710-4342
Fax: –
Web: www.vcom3d.com

CEO: Carol J Wideman
CFO: Jeff Parsons
HR: –
FYE: December 31
Type: Private

Vcom3D develops virtual technology used to create 3D animated characters that communicate through body language (including gesture or sign language), facial expressions, and lip-synched speech. Its technology is used in education and training software for deaf and hard-of-hearing users, as well as in broader marketing and communications contexts. Vcom3D also offers its Sign Smith authoring tool enables users to create education resources, training courses, and Web sites accessible to deaf users. Its clients include schools, law enforcement agencies, and government agencies, as well as corporations and individuals.

	Annual Growth	12/04	12/05	12/06	12/07	12/08
Sales ($mil.)	33.5%	–	–	1.6	2.3	2.9
Net income ($ mil.)	111.7%	–	–	0.0	0.0	0.2
Market value ($ mil.)	–	–	–	–	–	–
Employees	–	–	–	–	–	14

VECELLIO & GROGAN, INC.

2251 ROBERT C BYRD DR
BECKLEY, WV 258018790
Phone: 304 252-6575
Fax: –
Web: www.vecelliogrogan.com

CEO: Leo A Vecellio Jr
CFO: –
HR: –
FYE: December 31
Type: Private

Vecellio & Grogan paves the way for smooth motoring down the Atlantic seaboard and beyond. The company, which has divisions in West Virginia and the Carolinas, builds highways and provides heavy construction services throughout the mid-Atlantic and southeastern regions of the US. Vecellio & Grogan is part of the Vecellio Group, which also participates in site preparation and land reclamation. Other companies in the Vecellio Group include White Rock Quarries (limestone production), Ranger Golf (golf course construction), and Sharpe Bros. (road grading). The company, which was founded in 1938, is owned by Leo Vecellio Jr. and his family.

VECTOR GROUP LTD

4400 Biscayne Boulevard
Miami, FL 33137
Phone: 305 579-8000
Fax: –
Web: www.vectorgroupltd.com

NYS: VGR
CEO: Howard M Lorber
CFO: J B Kirkland III
HR: –
FYE: December 31
Type: Public

Vector Group is principally in tobacco and real estate. It holds a strong position in the US discount tobacco market through its Liggett and Vector Tobacco subsidiaries. The companies manufacture discount cigarettes under brands including Eagle 20's, Pyramid, Montego, Grand Prix, Liggett Select, and Eve. Vector also makes discount cigarettes under partner and private-label brands, including the USA brand. The group manufactures cigarettes in North Carolina and distributes them throughout the US. In addition, New Valley is Vector Group's real estate investment business.

	Annual Growth	12/19	12/20	12/21	12/22	12/23
Sales ($mil.)	(7.0%)	1,903.7	2,002.7	1,441.0	1,424.3	
Net income ($ mil.)	16.1%	101.0	92.9	219.5	158.7	183.5
Market value ($ mil.)	(4.2%)	2,088.5	1,817.1	1,790.6	1,849.9	1,759.4
Employees	(21.0%)	1,418	1,275	500	536	551

VECTOR PIPELINE L.P.

38705 7 MILE RD STE 490
LIVONIA, MI 481523990
Phone: 734 462-0231
Fax: –
Web: www.vector-pipeline.com

CEO: –
CFO: –
HR: –
FYE: December 31
Type: Private

If you were to ask "what's our vector, Victor?" Vector Pipelines would include mainline natural gas transportation in its answer, whereas the cast from Airplane would surely answer differently (so please don't call the company "Shirley"). In service since 2000, Vector Pipelines operates a pipeline nearly 350 miles in length with receipt and delivery points in Illinois, Indiana, Michigan, and Ontario. Approximately 95% of the pipeline is located in the US; Vector Pipeline Limited Partnership is responsible for the 15 miles of pipeline in Canada. Calgary-based Enbridge owns a 60% stake in Vector Pipeline, and Detroit-based DTE Energy Company owns 40%.

VECTRA CO.

425 S WOODS MILL RD STE 250
CHESTERFIELD, MO 630173441
Phone: 314 797-8600
Fax: –
Web: www.vectraco.com

CEO: Joseph Scaminace
CFO: Christopher M Hix
HR: –
FYE: December 31
Type: Private

Vectra (formerly the OM Group) has two specialty technology divisions. Vacuumschelze is a leading global manufacturer of advanced magnetic materials and related products. It serves markets that include battery materials, semiconductors, ceramics, chemical, and defense. It also makes magnetic technologies products for electronic equipment, auto, and alternative energy markets. EaglePicher Technologies makes up its battery technologies segment, which serves the defense, aerospace, and medical markets. The company was acquired by Apollo Global Management in 2015. In 2017 Vectra sold its Borchers specialty chemical additives division to affiliates of The Jordan Company, L.P.

VEECO INSTRUMENTS INC (DE)

NMS: VECO

Terminal Drive
Plainview, NY 11803
Phone: 516 677-0200
Fax: –
Web: www.veeco.com

CEO: William J Miller
CFO: John P Kiernan
HR: –
FYE: December 31
Type: Public

Veeco Instruments is a manufacturer of advanced semiconductor process equipment that solves an array of challenging materials engineering problems for its customers. The company's comprehensive collection of ion beam, laser annealing, metal-organic chemical vapor deposition (MOCVD), advanced packaging lithography, single wafer wet processing, molecular beam epitaxy (MBE), and atomic layer deposition (ALD) technologies play an integral role in the fabrication of key devices. Veeco's products are used in a wide range of markets and applications such as energy, optical, electronics, microelectromechanical (MEMS), nanostructures, and biomedical. Veeco gets about 70% of its sales from outside the US. The company traces its roots back to 1945 as Vacuum Electronic Equipment Co.

	Annual Growth	12/19	12/20	12/21	12/22	12/23
Sales ($mil.)	12.3%	419.3	454.2	583.3	646.1	666.4
Net income ($ mil.)	–	(78.7)	(8.4)	26.0	166.9	(30.4)
Market value ($ mil.)	20.6%	827.7	978.5	1,604.7	1,047.2	1,749.0
Employees	6.2%	954	993	1,091	1,221	1,215

VEEVA SYSTEMS INC

NYS: VEEV

4280 Hacienda Drive
Pleasanton, CA 94588
Phone: 925 452-6500
Fax: 925 452-6504
Web: www.veeva.com

CEO: Peter P Gassner
CFO: Gordon Heneweer
HR: –
FYE: January 31
Type: Public

Veeva Systems is breathing new life into software for the health care industry. Its cloud-based software and mobile apps are used by pharmaceutical and biotechnology companies to manage critical business functions. Veeva Systems' customer relationship management software uses Salesforce's platform to manage sales and marketing functions. Its Veeva Vault provides content management and collaboration software for quality management in clinical trials and regulatory compliance for new drug submissions. Its software is used in 75 countries and available in more than 25 languages, but North America is its largest market. Founded in 2007, Veeva Systems went public in 2013.

	Annual Growth	01/20	01/21	01/22	01/23	01/24
Sales ($mil.)	21.0%	1,104.1	1,465.1	1,850.8	2,155.1	2,363.7
Net income ($ mil.)	14.9%	301.1	380.0	427.4	487.7	525.7
Market value ($ mil.)	9.1%	23,642	44,579	38,144	27,503	33,447
Employees	19.6%	3,501	4,506	5,482	6,744	7,172

VENOCO, LLC

370 17TH ST STE 3900
DENVER, CO 802025610
Phone: 303 626-8300
Fax: –
Web: –

CEO: Mark A Depuy
CFO: Scott M Pinsonnault
HR: Alisa Otten
FYE: December 31
Type: Private

Santa Barbara's pristine beaches and Venoco's oil and gas exploration and production activities make for a volatile mix. Although Venoco has traditionally operated in the environmentally sensitive Santa Barbara Channel, it has been expanding its geographic reach and diversifying its operations. It owns interests in more than 146 active producing wells, primarily in the Monterey shale formation. It even has a drilling location in Beverly Hills. In 2014 Venoco reported proved reserves of 40.3 million barrels of oil equivalent and produced about 6,233 barrels of oil equivalent per day. Hammered by low oil prices, Venoco filed for Chapter 11 bankruptcy protection in 2016.

VENTAS INC

NYS: VTR

353 N. Clark Street, Suite 3300
Chicago, IL 60654
Phone: 877 483-6827
Fax: –
Web: www.ventasreit.com

CEO: Debra A Cafaro
CFO: Robert F Probst
HR: –
FYE: December 31
Type: Public

Ventas is a real estate investment trust (REIT) that holds a highly diversified portfolio of senior housing communities, medical office buildings (MOBs), life science, research and innovation centers, hospitals and other healthcare facilities located throughout the US, Canada, and the UK. Ventas's portfolio of more than 1,300 properties is buoyed by the demographic tailwind of a large and growing aging population. The company has a third-party institutional capital management business, Ventas Investment Management (VIM), which includes its open-ended investment vehicle, the Ventas Life Science & Healthcare Real Estate Fund (the Ventas Fund). The US generates the most revenue with nearly 90% of the company's total revenue.

	Annual Growth	12/19	12/20	12/21	12/22	12/23
Sales ($mil.)	3.8%	3,872.8	3,795.4	3,828.0	4,129.2	4,497.8
Net income ($ mil.)	–	433.0	439.1	49.0	(47.4)	(41.0)
Market value ($ mil.)	(3.6%)	23,217	19,719	20,555	18,115	20,041
Employees	(1.5%)	516	448	434	451	486

VENTERA CORPORATION

1875 CAMPUS COMMONS DR
RESTON, VA 201911533
Phone: 703 760-4600
Fax: –
Web: www.ventera.com

CEO: –
CFO: –
HR: –
FYE: December 31
Type: Private

Ventera, which likens itself to a bulldog in its marketing materials, would like clients to take note of its tenacity as a business rather than looking for a more physical resemblance between its consultants and its mascot. The company provides information technology and management consulting services to clients in both the private and public sectors. It offers application development, network design, systems integration, and project management services among others. Ventera serves the financial services, manufacturing, telecommunications, and retail industries among others. Customers have included the US Department of Agriculture and Sprint. The company was founded in 1996 by CEO Robert Acosta.

	Annual Growth	12/03	12/04	12/05	12/06	12/07
Sales ($mil.)	17.2%	–	–	18.0	30.7	24.8
Net income ($ mil.)	(16.9%)	–	–	2.4	(173.4)	1.7
Market value ($ mil.)	–	–	–	–	–	–
Employees	–	–	–	–	–	100

VENTURE CONSTRUCTION COMPANY INC

5660 PEACHTREE INDUSTRIAL BLVD
NORCROSS, GA 300711496
Phone: 770 441-6555
Fax: –
Web: www.ventureconstruction.com

CEO: –
CFO: –
HR: –
FYE: December 31
Type: Private

Building businesses is the primary business for Venture Construction Company. The company builds and remodels fast food and full-service restaurants, retail stores (including drug stores), and office buildings. The company operates throughout the US and has divisional offices in Tennessee, North Carolina, Virginia, Georgia, and Florida. Its customers include Applebee's, Chick-fil-A, McDonald's, Taco Bell, Rite Aid, Pizza Hut, Walgreen, Winn Dixie, Blockbuster, AutoZone, and many more. Founded in 1969, Venture Construction Company is owned by president E. Ray Morris.

	Annual Growth	12/16	12/17	12/19	12/21	12/22
Sales ($mil.)	3.4%	–	284.5	278.7	303.2	336.6
Net income ($ mil.)	0.9%	–	10.1	10.5	9.5	10.6
Market value ($ mil.)	–	–	–	–	–	–
Employees	–	–	–	–	–	177

VERA BRADLEY INC.   NMS: VRA

12420 Stonebridge Road
Roanoke, IN 46783
Phone: 877 708-8372
Fax: –
Web: www.verabradley.com

CEO: Robert Wallstrom
CFO: John Enwright
HR: Sally Pietzak
FYE: February 3
Type: Public

Vera Bradley is a designer of women's handbags, luggage and travel items, fashion and home accessories, and unique gifts. Its goods are available through approximately 1,700 specialty retail locations throughout the US, as well as select department stores, national accounts and third-party e-commerce sites. It also operates approximately 80 factory outlet shops. It operates two unique lifestyle brands ? Vera Bradley and Pura Vida. Both with multi-generational female customer bases and positioning as "gifting" brands. Founded in 1982 as Vera Bradley Designs by Patricia Miller and Barbara Bradley Baekgaard, the company has floated publicly since 2010.

	Annual Growth	02/20*	01/21	01/22	01/23*	02/24
Sales ($mil.)	(1.3%)	495.2	468.3	540.5	500.0	470.8
Net income ($ mil.)	(16.4%)	16.0	8.7	17.8	(59.7)	7.8
Market value ($ mil.)	(4.9%)	295.2	260.4	243.7	171.0	241.6
Employees	(5.7%)	2,700	2,450	2,490	2,180	2,135

*Fiscal year change

VERACYTE INC   NMS: VCYT

6000 Shoreline Court, Suite 300
South San Francisco, CA 94080
Phone: 650 243-6300
Fax: –
Web: www.veracyte.com

CEO: Marc Stapley
CFO: Beverly J Alley
HR: Geraldine Yamaguchi
FYE: December 31
Type: Public

Veracyte is a global genomic diagnostics company that aims to improve patient care through better diagnosis and treatment decisions for patients with cancer and other diseases. Aside from genomic tests, the company also offers its exclusive nCounter Analysis System, which Veracyte believes is the best-in-class diagnostics platform that enables the company to deliver tests to patients globally and hospitals locally. The company currently offers tests in thyroid cancer (Afirma); prostate cancer (Decipher Prostate); breast cancer (Prosigna); interstitial lung diseases (Envisia); and bladder cancer (Decipher Bladder). Its tests for kidney cancer and lymphoma are in development, the latter as a companion diagnostic. The US accounts for about 90% of the company's total revenue.

	Annual Growth	12/19	12/20	12/21	12/22	12/23
Sales ($mil.)	31.6%	120.4	117.5	219.5	296.5	361.1
Net income ($ mil.)	–	(12.6)	(34.9)	(75.6)	(36.6)	(74.4)
Market value ($ mil.)	(0.4%)	2,045.6	3,585.6	3,018.5	1,738.6	2,015.5
Employees	23.2%	354	320	761	787	815

VERADIGM INC   NBB: MDRX

222 Merchandise Mart Plaza, Suite 2024
Chicago, IL 60654
Phone: 800 334-8534
Fax: –
Web: www.allscripts.com

CEO: Shih-Yin Ho
CFO: Lee Westerfield
HR: Lisa Hammond
FYE: December 31
Type: Public

Allscripts Healthcare Solutions provides information technology (IT) solutions and services to help healthcare organizations around the world achieve optimal clinical, financial and operational results. The company provides electronic health record (EHR), financial management, population health management, and consumer solutions. Built on an open integrated platform, its solutions enable users to streamline workflows, leverage functionality from other software vender and exchange date. The Allscripts Developer Program focuses on nurturing partnerships with other developers to help clients optimize the value of their Allscripts investment. The US accounts for approximately 95% of revenue. The company was founded in 1986.

	Annual Growth	12/17	12/18	12/19	12/20	12/21
Sales ($mil.)	(4.5%)	1,806.3	1,750.0	1,771.7	1,502.7	1,503.0
Net income ($ mil.)	–	(152.6)	412.3	(182.5)	700.4	134.4
Market value ($ mil.)	6.1%	1,689.5	1,119.3	1,139.7	1,676.7	2,142.3
Employees	(2.6%)	8,900	9,500	9,600	8,400	8,000

VERASTEM INC   NAS: VSTM

117 Kendrick Street, Suite 500
Needham, MA 02494
Phone: 781 292-4200
Fax: –
Web: www.verastem.com

CEO: –
CFO: –
HR: –
FYE: December 31
Type: Public

Verastem believes the truth behind recurrent tumors lies in cancer stem cells (CSCs), aggressive tumor cells that survive conventional treatment to cause recurrence. Those CSCs are the target of its biopharmaceutical R&D efforts; the company is working to produce small molecule drugs that target the cells while conventional therapy targets the rest of the tumor. Verastem's work rests on a technology, licensed from MIT's Whitehead Institute, that allows it to create stable CSCs in the lab, something not possible in the past. Its leading drug candidate targets a type of breast cancer with a low survival rate. The company is also developing CSC diagnostics. Formed in 2010, Verastem completed an IPO in 2012.

	Annual Growth	12/19	12/20	12/21	12/22	12/23
Sales ($mil.)	–	17.5	88.5	2.1	2.6	–
Net income ($ mil.)	–	(149.2)	(67.7)	(71.2)	(73.8)	(87.4)
Market value ($ mil.)	57.0%	33.9	53.8	51.8	10.2	205.8
Employees	(13.1%)	135	48	48	57	77

VERICAST CORP.

15955 LA CANTERA PKWY
SAN ANTONIO, TX 782562589
Phone: 210 697-8888
Fax: –
Web: www.vericast.com

CEO: –
CFO: –
HR: –
FYE: December 31
Type: Private

Vericast fuels commerce, drives economic growth and directly accelerates revenue potential for thousands of brands and businesses. The company offers its customers a wide of range of services including data intelligence, marketing services, transaction solutions, campaign management and media delivery. In 2020, Harland Clarke, NCH, QuickPivot, and Valassis were unified under the Vericast brand.

VERICEL CORP   NMS: VCEL

64 Sidney Street
Cambridge, MA 02139
Phone: 617 588-5555
Fax: –
Web: www.vcel.com

CEO: Dominick C Colangelo
CFO: –
HR: –
FYE: December 31
Type: Public

Vericel brings new life to dying tissue. The company's proprietary tissue repair technology uses a patient's own cells (harvested from bone marrow) to manufacture treatments for a number of chronic diseases. The new cells, created through a sterile, automated process, are then used in tissue regeneration therapies for the donor patient. Vericel has two products on the market in the US: MACI, which is used for the repair of knee cartilage; and Epicel, a permanent skin replacement for patients with burns on 30% or more of the body.

	Annual Growth	12/19	12/20	12/21	12/22	12/23
Sales ($mil.)	13.8%	117.9	124.2	156.2	164.4	197.5
Net income ($ mil.)	–	(9.7)	2.9	(7.5)	(16.7)	(3.2)
Market value ($ mil.)	19.6%	832.2	1,477.0	1,879.7	1,259.8	1,703.2
Employees	6.8%	241	273	281	305	314

VERIFONE SYSTEMS, INC.

2744 N UNIVERSITY DR
CORAL SPRINGS, FL 330655111
Phone: 408 232-7800
Fax: –
Web: www.verifone.com

CEO: Mike Pulli
CFO: Marc E Rothman
HR: –
FYE: October 31
Type: Private

Verifone is the payments architect shaping ecosystems for online and in-person commerce experiences, including everything businesses need ? from secure payment devices to eCommerce tools, acquiring services, advanced business insights, and much more. As a global FinTech leader, Verifone powers omni-commerce growth for companies in over 165 countries and is trusted by the world's best-known brands, small businesses and major financial institutions. The Verifone platform is built on a four-decade history of innovation and uncompromised security, annually managing more than 12 billion transactions worth over $500 billion on physical and digital channels.

VERIFYME INC

801 International Parkway, Fifth Floor
Lake Mary, FL 32746
Phone: 585 736-9400
Fax: –
Web: www.verifyme.com

NAS: VRME
CEO: Patrick White
CFO: Margaret Gezerlis
HR: –
FYE: December 31
Type: Public

Willy Wonka could have used LaserLock Technologies to help ensure that each Golden Ticket was the genuine article. A development-stage company, LaserLock plans to license an invisible ink to third parties that can be used to authenticate documents. The company's system is targeted to the gambling industry, where uses could include verification of cashless tickets from slot machines and detection of counterfeit cards, chips, or dice. LaserLock has plans to raise additional capital and/or enter into strategic alliances or partnerships with other companies in order to do business.

	Annual Growth	12/18	12/19	12/20	12/21	12/22
Sales ($mil.)	302.1%	0.0	0.2	0.3	0.9	19.6
Net income ($ mil.)	–	(2.9)	(2.5)	(5.9)	3.6	(14.4)
Market value ($ mil.)	51.6%	2.0	0.6	32.2	28.4	10.4
Employees	102.1%	3	4	4	8	50

VERINT SYSTEMS INC

175 Broadhollow Road
Melville, NY 11747
Phone: 631 962-9600
Fax: –
Web: www.verint.com

NMS: VRNT
CEO: –
CFO: –
HR: –
FYE: January 31
Type: Public

Verint Systems is uniquely positioned to help organizations close the Engagement Capacity Gap with its differentiated Verint Customer Engagement Cloud Platform. Through the Verint Customer Engagement Cloud Platform, Verint offers its customers and partners solutions that are based on artificial intelligence (AI) and are developed specifically for customer engagement. These solutions automate workflows across enterprise silos to optimize workforce expense and at the same time drive an elevated consumer experience. More than 10,000 organizations in 180 countries ? including over 85 of the Fortune 100 companies ? are using the Verint Customer Engagement Platform including financial services, healthcare, utilities, technology, and government to draw on the latest advancements in AI, analytics, and an open cloud architecture to elevate customer experience. It generates about 65% of sales inside the US.

	Annual Growth	01/19	01/20	01/21	01/22	01/23
Sales ($mil.)	(7.4%)	1,229.7	1,303.6	1,273.7	874.5	902.2
Net income ($ mil.)	(31.1%)	66.0	28.7	(7.3)	14.4	14.9
Market value ($ mil.)	(5.9%)	3,163.6	3,793.4	4,828.8	3,357.2	2,483.4
Employees	(8.4%)	6,100	6,500	4,300	4,400	4,300

VERIS RESIDENTIAL INC

Harborside 3, 210 Hudson St., Ste. 400
Jersey City, NJ 07311
Phone: 732 590-1010
Fax: –
Web: www.verisresidential.com

NYS: VRE
CEO: Mahbod Nia
CFO: Anthony Krug
HR: –
FYE: December 31
Type: Public

Veris Residential (formerly known as Mack-Cali Realty) is a self-administered and self-managed real estate investment trust (REIT) that owns, develops, leases, and manages a real estate portfolio comprised predominantly of Class A office and multi-family rental properties located primarily in the New Jersey, New York and Massachusetts. The company owns or has interests in about 35 properties, consisting of more than 20 multifamily rental properties containing about 6,690 apartment units as well as non-core assets comprised of seven office properties, four parking/retail properties, three hotels plus developable land. In 2021, the company changed its name from Mack-Cali Realty to Veris Residential.

	Annual Growth	12/19	12/20	12/21	12/22	12/23
Sales ($mil.)	(5.5%)	350.9	313.6	329.3	355.0	279.9
Net income ($ mil.)	–	111.9	(51.4)	(119.0)	(52.1)	(107.3)
Market value ($ mil.)	(9.2%)	2,133.3	1,149.2	1,695.2	1,469.2	1,450.8
Employees	(8.7%)	283	256	234	215	197

VERISIGN INC

12061 Bluemont Way
Reston, VA 20190
Phone: 703 948-3200
Fax: –
Web: www.verisign.com

NMS: VRSN
CEO: –
CFO: –
HR: –
FYE: December 31
Type: Public

VeriSign is a global provider of domain name registry services and internet infrastructure, enabling internet navigation for many of the world's most recognized domain names. The company enables the security, stability, and resiliency of key internet infrastructure and services, including providing Root Zone Maintainer services, operating two of nearly 15 global internet root servers, and providing registration services and authoritative resolution for the .com and .net top-level domains (TLDs), which support the majority of global e-commerce. It is also the exclusive registry of domain names within certain transliterations of .com and .net in several different native languages and scripts (IDN gTLDs).The company generates more than 65% of sales in the US.

	Annual Growth	12/19	12/20	12/21	12/22	12/23
Sales ($mil.)	4.9%	1,231.7	1,265.1	1,327.6	1,424.9	1,493.1
Net income ($ mil.)	7.5%	612.3	814.9	784.8	673.8	817.6
Market value ($ mil.)	1.7%	19,518	21,921	25,712	20,811	20,864
Employees	1.0%	872	909	904	917	908

VERISK ANALYTICS INC

545 Washington Boulevard
Jersey City, NJ 07310-1686
Phone: 201 469-3000
Fax: –
Web: www.verisk.com

NMS: VRSK
CEO: Lee M Shavel
CFO: Elizabeth D Mann
HR: –
FYE: December 31
Type: Public

Verisk Analytics is a leading strategic data analytics and technology partner to the global insurance industry. It empowers clients to strengthen operating efficiency, improve underwriting and claims outcomes, combat fraud and make informed decisions about global risks, including climate change, extreme events, political topics and ESG issues. Through advanced data analytics, software, scientific research and deep industry knowledge, Verisk helps build global resilience for individuals, communities and businesses. With operations across more than 20 countries, Verisk generates around 85% of its revenue in the US.

	Annual Growth	12/19	12/20	12/21	12/22	12/23
Sales ($mil.)	0.7%	2,607.1	2,784.6	2,998.6	2,497.0	2,681.4
Net income ($ mil.)	8.1%	449.9	712.7	666.2	953.9	614.6
Market value ($ mil.)	12.5%	21,402	29,749	32,779	25,283	34,231
Employees	(5.2%)	9,300	8,960	9,367	7,000	7,500

VERITEQ CORP

6560 W. Rogers Circle, Suite 19
Boca Raton, FL 33487
Phone: 954 574-9720
Fax: –
Web: www.veriteqcorp.com

CEO: Scott R Silverman
CFO: Michael E Krawitz
HR: –
FYE: December 31
Type: Public

Digital Angel puts a British accent on two-way communication equipment. The company develops emergency identification products for use in global positioning systems and other applications and distributes them in the UK. Digital Angel's conventional radio systems provide such services as site monitoring for construction companies and manufacturers while its trunked radio systems serve the security needs of large customers, such as local governments and public utilities. In mid-2012 the company announced a strategic shift toward the development of games and applications for mobile devices. It has several titles in progress.

	Annual Growth	12/11	12/12	12/13	12/14	12/15
Sales ($mil.)	–	3.7	–	0.0	0.2	–
Net income ($ mil.)	–	(10.3)	(6.3)	(15.1)	(3.9)	(11.1)
Market value ($ mil.)	(27.5%)	0.3	0.0	1.7	0.0	0.0
Employees	–	36	15	13	13	–

VERIZON COMMUNICATIONS INC

NYS: VZ

1095 Avenue of the Americas
New York, NY 10036
Phone: 212 395-1000
Fax: –
Web: www.verizon.com

CEO: Hans E Vestberg
CFO: Anthony T Skiadas
HR: –
FYE: December 31
Type: Public

Verizon Communications is one of the world's leading providers of communications, technology, information, and entertainment products and services to consumers, businesses, and government entities. With a presence around the world, Verizon offers data, video, and voice services and solutions on its networks and platforms that are designed to meet customers' demand for mobility, reliable network connectivity, security, and control. The company also sells devices such as smartphones, tablets, laptop computers and netbooks, and other wireless-enabled connected devices, such as smartwatches and other wearables.

	Annual Growth	12/19	12/20	12/21	12/22	12/23
Sales ($mil.)	0.4%	131,868	128,292	133,613	136,835	133,974
Net income ($ mil.)	(11.9%)	19,265	17,801	22,065	21,256	11,614
Market value ($ mil.)	(11.5%)	258,142	247,000	218,453	165,648	158,501
Employees	(6.0%)	135,000	132,200	118,400	117,100	105,400

VERMEER MANUFACTURING COMPANY

1210 E VERMEER RD
PELLA, IA 502197660
Phone: 641 628-3141
Fax: –
Web: www.vermeer.com

CEO: Jason Andringa
CFO: –
HR: Kala Talsma
FYE: December 31
Type: Private

Vermeer is a manufacturer of industrial and agricultural machinery and other heavy equipment. The company's machines are made to equip its customers to do more across a diverse group of important markets including underground construction, infrastructure, surface mining, tree care, environmental and agriculture. The family-owned and-operated company Vermeer was established in 1948 by Gary Vermeer.

VERSANT POWER

BANGOR, ME 04401
Phone: 207 973-2000
Fax: –
Web: www.versantpower.com

CEO: –
CFO: –
HR: Ryan Rudolph
FYE: December 31
Type: Private

Emera Maine provides electric utility services in northern and eastern Maine. The company transmits and distributes power to some 160,000 residential, commercial, and industrial customers. Formerly named Bangor Hydro-Electric (BHE), the company changed its name to Emera Maine after merging with Maine Public Service in 2014. Parent company Emera, which operates utilities in the US and Canada, agreed to sell Emera Maine to Canadian utility Enmax in 2019.

	Annual Growth	12/18	12/19	12/20	12/21	12/22
Sales ($mil.)	9.7%	–	167.0	165.1	194.6	220.7
Net income ($ mil.)	(2.2%)	–	33.4	19.3	34.6	31.3
Market value ($ mil.)	–	–	–	–	–	–
Employees	–	–	–	–	–	250

VERSAR, INC.

1025 VERMONT AVE NW STE 500
WASHINGTON, DC 200053516
Phone: 703 750-3000
Fax: –
Web: www.versar.com

CEO: James Jaska
CFO: Christopher Phelps
HR: Kristen Heymer
FYE: December 31
Type: Private

Environmental engineering company Versar is well-versed in keeping the homeland clean and secure. The company's infrastructure and management services business, which accounts for most of Versar's sales, helps clients with six main tasks: compliance with environmental regulations, conservation of natural resources, construction oversight, engineering and design, pollution prevention, and restoration of contaminated sites. Major customers include the US Department of Defense and the US Environmental Protection Agency. Subsidiary GEOMET Technologies, which constitutes Versar's national defense business segment, makes biohazard suits for agencies involved in emergency response and counterterrorism efforts.

	Annual Growth	06/14	06/15*	07/16*	06/17*	12/18
Sales ($mil.)	(24.2%)	–	159.9	167.9	111.8	69.7
Net income ($ mil.)	(6.5%)	–	1.4	(37.9)	(9.6)	1.1
Market value ($ mil.)	–	–	–	–	–	–
Employees	–	–	–	–	–	1,956

*Fiscal year change

VERST GROUP LOGISTICS, INC.

300 SHORLAND DR
WALTON, KY 410949328
Phone: 859 485-1212
Fax: –
Web: www.verstlogistics.com

CEO: Paul T Verst
CFO: James Stadtmiller
HR: –
FYE: December 31
Type: Private

Verst wants to be first when it comes to storing its customers' items. A warehousing and distribution specialist, Verst Group Logistics maintains over 5 million sq. ft. of warehouse space. The company operates from facilities in the Cincinnati metropolitan area and in northern Kentucky. Verst Group Logistics uses its own trucking fleet to provide freight transportation services through subsidiary Zenith Logistics and a network of carriers to arrange long-distance transportation of customers' freight. It serves customers residing in the food and beverage, retail and consumer products, paper, and automotive industries. William Verst, the father of president and CEO Paul Verst, founded the company in 1968.

	Annual Growth	12/10	12/11	12/12	12/13	12/16
Sales ($mil.)	–	–	(137.2)	148.8	157.7	59.2
Net income ($ mil.)	822.7%	–	0.0	–	–	1.7
Market value ($ mil.)	–	–	–	–	–	–
Employees	–	–	–	–	–	1,300

VERTEX INC

NMS: VERX

2301 Renaissance Blvd
King of Prussia, PA 19406
Phone: 800 355-3500
Fax: -
Web: www.vertexinc.com

CEO: -
CFO: -
HR: -
FYE: December 31
Type: Public

Vertex is a leading provider of enterprise tax technology solutions with more than 4,200 customers, including the majority of the Fortune 500. It provides tax support to its customers in over 130 countries. The company software enables tax determination, compliance, and reporting, tax data management and document management, and analytics and insights with powerful pre-built integrations to core business applications used by most companies. Its software and solutions are built upon a robust set of technology capabilities designed for flexibility, configurability, speed, and scale to handle complex tax scenarios and processing volumes and interoperability across core business applications. Its software is fueled by over 500 million data-driven effective tax rules and supports indirect tax compliance in more than 19,000 jurisdictions worldwide.

	Annual Growth	12/19	12/20	12/21	12/22	12/23
Sales ($mil.)	15.5%	321.5	374.7	425.5	491.6	572.4
Net income ($ mil.)	-	31.1	(78.9)	(1.5)	(12.3)	(13.1)
Market value ($ mil.)	-	-	5,354.7	2,438.4	2,229.5	4,139.3
Employees	8.1%	1,100	1,200	1,300	1,400	1,500

VERTEX PHARMACEUTICALS, INC.

NMS: VRTX

50 Northern Avenue
Boston, MA 02210
Phone: 617 341-6100
Fax: -
Web: www.vrtx.com

CEO: Reshma Kewalramani
CFO: Charles F Wagner Jr
HR: -
FYE: December 31
Type: Public

Vertex Pharmaceuticals is focused on developing treatments for cystic fibrosis (CF) and other life-threatening diseases. The biotechnology company has four commercial drugs -- TRIKAFTA/KAFTRIO, SYMDEKO/SYMKEVI, ORKAMBI and KALYDECO -- used to treat CF. Vertex has other drugs in development including additional CF treatments and medications addressing sickle cell disease, beta thalassemia, alpha-1 antitrypsin deficiency, and pain, among others. While the US generates some 65% of the company's revenue, Vertex's medicines are sold in some part of North America, Europe, and Australia.

	Annual Growth	12/19	12/20	12/21	12/22	12/23
Sales ($mil.)	24.1%	4,162.8	6,205.7	7,574.4	8,930.7	9,869.2
Net income ($ mil.)	32.4%	1,176.8	2,711.6	2,342.1	3,322.0	3,619.6
Market value ($ mil.)	16.8%	56,422	60,904	56,590	74,417	104,854
Employees	15.8%	3,000	3,400	3,900	4,800	5,400

VERTICAL COMMUNICATIONS, INC.

1000 HOLCOMB WOODS PKWY STE 300
ROSWELL, GA 300762585
Phone: 877 837-8422
Fax: -
Web: www.vertical.com

CEO: Richard Anderson
CFO: David Krietzberg
HR: -
FYE: June 30
Type: Private

Vertical Communications hopes that Internet protocol telephony can keep its top line from going horizontal. The company focuses on its software-based phone systems which provide unified communications functions such as call control, message forwarding, e-mail integration, and call routing and screening. Its products also include applications for managing call center operations, including agent monitoring, coaching, and recording. Vertical targets operations with less than 1,000 employees in markets such as retail, financial services, health care, and education. It sells through a global network of 1,800 business partners. Its customers have included CVS Health, Staples, and Apria Healthcare.

	Annual Growth	06/03	06/04	06/05	06/06	06/07
Sales ($mil.)	112.9%	-	-	17.5	55.5	79.1
Net income ($ mil.)	-	-	-	(15.5)	(16.0)	(16.0)
Market value ($ mil.)	-	-	-	-	-	-
Employees	-	-	-	-	-	142

VERTICAL COMPUTER SYSTEMS, INC.

101 West Renner Road, Suite 300
Richardson, TX 75082
Phone: 972 437-5200
Fax: -
Web: www.vcsy.com

CEO: Richard S Wade
CFO: -
HR: -
FYE: December 31
Type: Public

Vertical Computer Systems develops Web services development applications and administrative software. The company's SiteFlash software enables Web content management, e-commerce, and workflow functions. Other Web service-related offerings include ResponseFlash, an emergency communications system, and the Emily XML scripting language. Its administrative software line includes emPath, a Web-based human resources management and payroll application that it offers using the software-as-a-service (SaaS) model. Vertical Computer Systems markets emPath through its NOW Solutions subsidiary.

	Annual Growth	12/13	12/14	12/15	12/16	12/17
Sales ($mil.)	(11.2%)	6.1	7.4	4.3	3.8	3.8
Net income ($ mil.)	-	(2.5)	(1.5)	(2.6)	(5.3)	(3.1)
Market value ($ mil.)	(27.5%)	70.1	13.8	25.2	28.0	19.4
Employees	(1.1%)	24	29	28	27	23

VERTIV HOLDINGS CO

NYS: VRT

505 N. Cleveland Ave.
Westerville, OH 43082
Phone: 614 888-0246
Fax: -
Web: www.vertiv.com

CEO: Giordano Albertazzi
CFO: David J Fallon
HR: -
FYE: December 31
Type: Public

Vertiv is a global leader in the design, manufacturing and servicing of critical digital infrastructure technology that powers, cools, deploys, secures and maintains electronics that process, store and transmit data. The company provides this technology to data centers, communication networks and commercial & industrial environments worldwide. It has a suite of comprehensive offerings, innovative solutions and a leading service organization that supports a diversified group of customers, which the company delivers from engineering, manufacturing, sales and service locations in more than 40 countries across the Americas, Asia Pacific and Europe, the Middle East and Africa (EMEA). Vertiv provides the hardware, software and services to facilitate an increasingly interconnected marketplace of digital systems where large amounts of indispensable data need to be transmitted, analyzed, processed and stored. The US and Canada accounts for about 50% of company's total revenue.

	Annual Growth	12/19	12/20	12/21	12/22	12/23
Sales ($mil.)	368.5%	14.2	4,370.6	4,998.1	5,691.5	6,863.2
Net income ($ mil.)	220.0%	4.4	(183.6)	119.6	76.6	460.2
Market value ($ mil.)	44.5%	4,211.1	7,128.0	9,533.3	5,215.2	18,337
Employees	8.1%	19,800	20,972	24,000	27,000	27,000

VERU INC

NAS: VERU

2916 N. Miami Avenue, Suite 1000
Miami, FL 33127
Phone: 305 509-6897
Fax: -
Web: www.veruhealthcare.com

CEO: Mitchell S Steiner
CFO: -
HR: -
FYE: September 30
Type: Public

Move over, Trojan Man! Business at The Female Health Company (FHC), maker of condoms for women, is gaining momentum. The female condom is the only female contraceptive that is FDA-approved for preventing both pregnancy and sexually transmitted diseases, including HIV/AIDS. The firm's condoms are sold in 140-plus countries worldwide (under the FC2 name), mostly in South Africa, Brazil, and Uganda. Outside the US, many of its products bear the Femidom name, among others. FHC also provides low-cost female condoms in Africa through an agreement with the Joint United Nations Programme on HIV/AIDS (UNAIDS). It sponsors the Female Health Foundation, which provides women with health education.

	Annual Growth	09/19	09/20	09/21	09/22	09/23
Sales ($mil.)	(15.4%)	31.8	42.6	61.3	39.4	16.3
Net income ($ mil.)	-	(12.0)	(19.0)	7.4	(83.8)	(93.1)
Market value ($ mil.)	(24.0%)	198.3	240.5	782.9	1,057.3	66.0
Employees	-	386	339	252	233	-

VESCO OIL CORPORATION

16055 W 12 MILE RD
SOUTHFIELD, MI 480762979
Phone: 800 527-5358
Fax: –
Web: www.vescooil.com

CEO: Lilly E Stotland
CFO: Cheryl R Reitzloff
HR: –
FYE: December 31
Type: Private

Vesco Oil gives motorists a hand in the Upper Hand and elsewhere in the state of Michigan. The company is a wholesale distributor of Valvoline and Exxon Mobil brand lubricants to automotive and industrial customers in Michigan. It also provides environmental services such as bulk and hazardous waste management. Vesco Oil has warehouse and distribution facilities in Detroit, Grand Rapids, Mancelona, and Zilwaukee. It has expanded its warehouse and distribution center in Mancelona to better serve its northern Michigan customers. Vesco Oil is managed by president and CEO Donald Epstein, the great-grandson of the company's founder, Eugene Epstein.

	Annual Growth	12/07	12/08	12/09	12/10	12/18
Sales ($mil.)	4.9%	–	119.2	100.8	108.2	191.6
Net income ($ mil.)	7.0%	–	1.6	(0.3)	3.3	3.2
Market value ($ mil.)	–	–	–	–	–	–
Employees	–	–	–	–	–	210

VESTAR CAPITAL PARTNERS, INC.

245 PARK AVE RM 4100
NEW YORK, NY 101674196
Phone: 212 351-1600
Fax: –
Web: www.vestarcapital.com

CEO: Daniel S O'Connell
CFO: Brendon Spillane
HR: –
FYE: December 31
Type: Private

Vestar Capital Partners is on a quest to invest. Specializing in management buyouts, growth capital investments, and recapitalizations, the firm seeks out established middle-market firms (valued between $250 million and $3 billion) in the consumer products, financial services, media and communications, health care, and manufacturing sectors. It typically invests up to $700 million per transaction. An active, long-term investor that partners with the management of its portfolio companies, the company oversees some $7 billion of committed equity capital on behalf of financial institutions, endowments, foundations, funds of funds, and public and private pension plans. It has five offices in the US and Europe.

VETERANS OF FOREIGN WARS OF THE UNITED STATES

406 W 34TH ST
KANSAS CITY, MO 641112721
Phone: 816 756-3390
Fax: –
Web: www.vfw.org

CEO: Kevin Jones
CFO: Jr H Vander Clute Jr
HR: Craig Rose
FYE: August 31
Type: Private

The Veterans of Foreign Wars of the United States (VFW) serves those who served. The membership organization is an advocacy group for former members of any branch of the US military who have served honorably in conflicts. Services provided by the group include helping veterans secure benefits and entitlements and advocating legislation in support of veterans and their needs. The VFW also provides flag education, citizenship classes, and other mentoring services to young people. The organization, which was chartered by Congress in 1936, serves as a visible reminder of the contributions of all veterans by marching in parades and holding public services on national holidays.

	Annual Growth	08/11	08/12	08/13	08/14	08/19
Sales ($mil.)	(49.5%)	–	529.5	100.5	92.1	4.5
Net income ($ mil.)	–	–	0.0	23.4	5.9	(0.5)
Market value ($ mil.)	–	–	–	–	–	–
Employees	–	–	–	–	–	185

VF CORP.

NYS: VFC

1551 Wewatta Street
Denver, CO 80202
Phone: 720 778-4000
Fax: –
Web: www.vfc.com

CEO: Bracken Darrell
CFO: Matthew H Puckett
HR: –
FYE: April 1
Type: Public

VF Corporation is a leading manufacturer and retailer in the outdoor and action sports apparel industry, owning brands in specialist product categories: Dickies, Timberland and The North Face (outdoor oriented brands), and Vans (skateboard-inspired footwear). The company sells directly to consumers online and through roughly than 1,300 VF-operated retail stores worldwide. It also sells wholesale to department and specialty stores, national chains, independently-operated partnership stores and mass merchants. Founded in 1899, VF obtains its products primarily from about 340 independent contractor manufacturing facilities in about 35 countries. The US accounts for about 50% of the company's revenue.

	Annual Growth	03/19	03/20*	04/21	04/22	04/23
Sales ($mil.)	(4.3%)	13,849	10,489	9,238.8	11,842	11,612
Net income ($ mil.)	(44.6%)	1,259.8	679.4	407.9	1,386.9	118.6
Market value ($ mil.)	(28.3%)	33,779	22,461	30,895	21,975	8,904.3
Employees	(18.6%)	75,000	48,000	40,000	35,000	33,000

*Fiscal year change

VHS ACQUISITION SUBSIDIARY NUMBER 3, INC.

4646 N MARINE DR
CHICAGO, IL 606405759
Phone: 773 878-8700
Fax: –
Web: www.weisshospital.com

CEO: –
CFO: –
HR: –
FYE: May 31
Type: Private

Vanguard Weiss Memorial Hospital serves the residents of Chicago's North Side. The facility has about 240 beds and some 450 physicians covering more than 40 specialties. It conducts medical research and education programs through its affiliation with the University of Chicago Medical Center. Generally known as Weiss Memorial Hospital, the center offers full acute care including orthopedics, cardiology, vascular, rehabilitation, cancer, geriatrics, and women's health care. Specialty divisions provide laboratory, radiology, wound, and hospice care. Tenet Healthcare owns 80% of the hospital (gained through its 2013 acquisition of Vanguard Health Systems) and the University of Chicago Medical Center owns the rest.

	Annual Growth	06/00	06/01	06/02	06/03*	05/15
Sales ($mil.)	0.4%	–	106.0	280.1	110.3	112.1
Net income ($ mil.)	–	–	(7.4)	(10.8)	0.6	(2.8)
Market value ($ mil.)	–	–	–	–	–	–
Employees	–	–	–	–	–	1,100

*Fiscal year change

VHS OF ILLINOIS, INC.

1445 ROSS AVE STE 1400
DALLAS, TX 752022703
Phone: 708 783-9100
Fax: –
Web: –

CEO: Charles Martin Jr
CFO: Emmy Cleary
HR: –
FYE: September 30
Type: Private

University of Illinois medical students wanting to learn family medicine can find their home-away-from-home through the residency program at MacNeal Hospital, a full-service facility serving the suburbs of Chicago. Among its specialty services are behavioral health, occupational health, home and hospice care, and radiology. With some 430 beds, the teaching hospital has about 400 physicians on staff. By offering specialty care services, like open heart surgery, MacNeal is able to hang on to many patients who would otherwise travel from the suburbs into the Windy City itself for care. MacNeal is owned by Tenet Healthcare (gained through Tenet's 2013 purchase of Vanguard Health Systems).

	Annual Growth	09/11	09/12	09/13	09/14	09/15
Sales ($mil.)	4.1%	–	–	–	255.2	265.5
Net income ($ mil.)	98.5%	–	–	–	24.3	48.2
Market value ($ mil.)	–	–	–	–	–	–
Employees	–	–	–	–	–	2,500

VIA RENEWABLES INC
NMS: VIAS P

12140 Wickchester Ln., Suite 100
Houston, TX 77079
Phone: 713 600-2600
Fax: –
Web: www.sparkenergy.com

CEO: W K Maxwell III
CFO: James G Jones II
HR: –
FYE: December 31
Type: Public

Independent retail energy services company Via Renewables, formerly Spark Energy, provides residential and commercial customers in competitive markets across the US with an alternative choice for their natural gas and electricity. It buys natural gas and electricity supply from a variety of wholesale providers and bills customers monthly for the delivery of natural gas and electricity based on their consumption at either a fixed or variable price. Natural gas and electricity are then distributed to customers by local regulated utility companies through their existing infrastructure. The company's largest primary market is the Mid-Atlantic with more than 35% of sales. The company was founded in 1999.

	Annual Growth	12/19	12/20	12/21	12/22	12/23
Sales ($mil.)	(14.5%)	813.7	554.9	393.5	460.5	435.2
Net income ($ mil.)	15.4%	8.5	29.3	5.2	7.6	15.0
Market value ($ mil.)	0.5%	66.8	69.2	82.7	37.0	68.0
Employees	(0.6%)	164	159	169	160	160

VIAD CORP.
NYS: VVI

7000 East 1st Avenue
Scottsdale, AZ 85251-4304
Phone: 602 207-1000
Fax: –
Web: www.viad.com

CEO: –
CFO: –
HR: –
FYE: December 31
Type: Public

Viad (pronounced VEE-ahd) is a leading global provider of extraordinary experiences, including hospitality and leisure activities, experiential marketing, and live events. Its primary business, GES (Global Experience Specialists) Exhibitions is a global exhibition services company that partners with leading exhibition and conference organizers as a full-service provider of strategic and logistics solutions to manage the complexity of their shows. Viad's other business, Pursuit is a collection of inspiring and unforgettable travel experiences that includes recreational attractions, unique hotels and lodges, food and beverage, retail, sightseeing, and ground transportation services. Viad has operations across North America, Europe, Asia Pacific, and Australia, but most of its revenue is generated in the US.

	Annual Growth	12/19	12/20	12/21	12/22	12/23
Sales ($mil.)	(2.5%)	1,371.7	415.4	507.3	1,127.3	1,238.7
Net income ($ mil.)	(7.7%)	22.0	(374.1)	(92.7)	23.2	16.0
Market value ($ mil.)	(14.4%)	1,683.1	901.9	1,067.0	608.2	902.6
Employees	(6.1%)	5,196	1,697	3,512	3,387	4,035

VIASAT INC
NMS: VSAT

6155 El Camino Real
Carlsbad, CA 92009
Phone: 760 476-2200
Fax: –
Web: www.viasat.com

CEO: Mark Dankberg
CFO: Shawn Duffy
HR: –
FYE: March 31
Type: Public

ViaSat is an innovator in communications technologies and services, focused on making connectivity accessible, available, and secure for all. Its end-to-end platform of high-capacity Ka-band satellites, ground infrastructure, and user terminals enables the company to provide cost-effective, high-speed, high-quality broadband solutions to enterprises, consumers, military, and government users around the globe, whether on the ground, in the air, or at sea. For the commercial market, ViaSat produces satellite broadband systems for consumer applications as well as antenna systems, and mobile satellite systems. The company's IFC systems were installed and in service on approximately 2,270 commercial aircraft. ViaSat generates the majority of its sales from the US customers. Viasat founded by Mark Dankberg, Steve Hart, and Mark Miller in 1986.

	Annual Growth	03/19	03/20	03/21	03/22	03/23
Sales ($mil.)	5.4%	2,068.3	2,309.2	2,256.1	2,787.6	2,556.2
Net income ($ mil.)	–	(67.6)	(0.2)	3.7	(15.5)	1,084.8
Market value ($ mil.)	(18.7%)	5,960.7	2,762.7	3,697.2	3,753.3	2,602.7
Employees	5.0%	5,600	6,100	5,800	7,000	6,800

VIAVI SOLUTIONS INC
NMS: VIAV

1445 South Spectrum Blvd, Suite 102
Chandler, AZ 85286
Phone: 408 404-3600
Fax: –
Web: www.viavisolutions.com

CEO: Oleg Khaykin
CFO: Ilan Daskal
HR: –
FYE: July 1
Type: Public

Viavi Solutions is a global provider of network test, monitoring, and assurance solutions that are used to build and improve communications equipment and broadband networks. Viavi's AvComm products are a global leader in test and measurement (T&M) instrumentation for communication and safety in the government, aerospace, and military markets. It also provides test products and services for private enterprise networks. Another Viavi offering is an optical technology, which includes tools for detecting counterfeit currency as well as optical filters for sensor applications. About a third of Viavi's revenue are to customers in the US. Viavi was created in 2015 when JDS Uniphase split into two companies.

	Annual Growth	06/19	06/20*	07/21	07/22	07/23
Sales ($mil.)	(0.5%)	1,130.3	1,136.3	1,198.9	1,292.4	1,106.1
Net income ($ mil.)	47.4%	5.4	28.7	46.1	15.5	25.5
Market value ($ mil.)	(3.9%)	2,950.4	2,775.0	3,878.3	2,906.0	2,515.3
Employees	–	3,600	3,600	3,600	3,600	3,600

*Fiscal year change

VIBRANTZ CORPORATION

6060 PARKLAND BLVD STE 250
MAYFIELD HEIGHTS, OH 441244225
Phone: 216 875-5600
Fax: –
Web: www.vibrantz.com

CEO: Glenn Fish
CFO: Mark Whitney
HR: Andrew Eastham
FYE: December 31
Type: Private

Ferro is a leading producer of specialty materials that are sold to a broad range of manufacturers who, in turn, make products for many end-use markets. With nearly 50 manufacturing plants worldwide, the company make various colorants, including ceramic glazes, pigments, and porcelain enamels. It also produces electronics, and color (such as conductive metals and pastes used in solar cells), and polymer and ceramic engineered materials. Its products are used in construction and by makers of appliances, autos, building and renovation, electronics, sanitary, packaging, consumer products and household furnishings. The company gets more than 65% of its revenue from international customers.

	Annual Growth	12/16	12/17	12/18	12/19	12/20
Sales ($mil.)	(22.9%)	–	–	1,612.4	1,018.4	959.0
Net income ($ mil.)	(26.2%)	–	–	80.9	7.4	44.0
Market value ($ mil.)	–	–	–	–	–	–
Employees	–	–	–	–	–	3,585

VICOR CORP
NMS: VICR

25 Frontage Road
Andover, MA 01810
Phone: 978 470-2900
Fax: –
Web: www.vicorpower.com

CEO: Patrizio Vinciarelli
CFO: James F Schmidt
HR: –
FYE: December 31
Type: Public

Vicor designs, develops, manufactures, and markets modular power components and power systems for converting electrical power. In electrically-powered devices utilizing alternating current (AC) voltage from a primary AC source, a power system converts AC voltage into the stable direct current (DC) voltage necessary to power subsystems and/or individual applications and devices (loads). Customers includes global OEMs and small manufacturers of specialized electronics devices. Vicor power component design methodology offers a comprehensive range of modular building blocks enabling rapid design of a power system. The company also sells a range of electrical and mechanical accessories for use with their products. Vicor derives over 30% of its sales from customers in the US.

	Annual Growth	12/19	12/20	12/21	12/22	12/23
Sales ($mil.)	11.4%	263.0	296.6	359.4	399.1	405.1
Net income ($ mil.)	39.6%	14.1	17.9	56.6	25.4	53.6
Market value ($ mil.)	(1.0%)	2,077.3	4,100.4	5,645.9	2,389.9	1,998.2
Employees	1.2%	1,014	1,049	1,027	1,088	1,063

VICTORIAS SECRET & CO

NYS: VSCO

4 Limited Parkway East
Reynoldsburg, OH 43068
Phone: 614 577-7000
Fax: –
Web: www.victoriassecretandco.com

CEO: Amy Hauk
CFO: –
HR: –
FYE: February 3
Type: Public

Victoria's Secret & Co. is a specialty retailer of women's intimate and other apparel and beauty products marketed under the Victoria's Secret and PINK brand names. The company operates more than 910 Victoria's Secret and PINK stores in the US, Canada, and Greater China as well as online at www.VictoriasSecret.com, www.PINK.com, www.AdoreMe.com, and other online channels worldwide. Additionally, Victoria's Secret and PINK have more than 450 stores in more than 70 countries operating under franchise, license, and wholesale arrangements. The company also includes the Victoria's Secret and PINK merchandise sourcing and production function serving the company and its international partners. It operates as a single segment designed to seamlessly serve customers worldwide through stores and online channels.

	Annual Growth	02/20*	01/21	01/22	01/23*	02/24
Sales ($mil.)	(4.7%)	7,509.0	5,413.0	6,785.0	6,344.0	6,182.0
Net income ($ mil.)	–	(897.0)	(72.0)	646.0	348.0	109.0
Market value ($ mil.)	–	–	–	4,345.4	3,049.8	2,107.6
Employees	–	–	27,900	34,000	31,000	

*Fiscal year change

VICTORY PACKAGING, L.P.

3555 TIMMONS LN STE 1440
HOUSTON, TX 770276435
Phone: 713 961-3299
Fax: –
Web: www.victorypackaging.com

CEO: –
CFO: –
HR: Cari Crawford
FYE: December 31
Type: Private

Victory Packaging is a national distribution company that specializes in solving packaging complexities and optimizing total cost associated with packaging for its clients on a national scale, as well as to oversee local packaging and distribution for regional clients. It manufactures and distributes protective foam, rigid containers, bubble wrap, shrink film, tape, equipment, and other packaging materials. The company operates through a network of warehouse and distribution centers in the US, Canada, and Mexico. Its solutions include packaging, engineering and design, fulfillment, equipment and automation, e-commerce and supply chain solutions. Founded in 1976 by Vic Samuels, Victory Packaging is a division of the WestRock Company, a leader in sustainable, fiber-based packaging solutions.

VICTORY SCREEN PRINTING, INC.

346 N JUSTINE ST STE 504
CHICAGO, IL 606071021
Phone: 312 666-8661
Fax: –
Web: www.victoryrecords.com

CEO: Tony Brummel
CFO: –
HR: –
FYE: June 30
Type: Private

Achieving victory is hard. Victory Records was founded as an independent hardcore punk label, but the company has since branched out into other genres. Its recording artists include main acts such as Atreyu (hard rock), Darkest Hour (heavy metal), and Silverstein (punk). In addition to its label, Victory Records also operates an in-house concert booking division to organize tours for its bands. Its VicTorV is an online video program showcasing artist interviews, live performances, behind the scenes footage, music news, product information, and Victory artists' music videos. Victory Records was founded by CEO Tony Brummel in 1989.

	Annual Growth	12/97	12/98	12/99	12/00*	06/22
Sales ($mil.)	(3.6%)	–	–	–	4.2	1.9
Net income ($ mil.)	–	–	–	–	0.0	(0.6)
Market value ($ mil.)	–	–	–	–	–	–
Employees	–	–	–	–	–	37

*Fiscal year change

VIDEO DISPLAY CORP

NBB: VIDE

5155 King Street
Cocoa, FL 32926
Phone: 800 241-5005
Fax: –
Web: –

CEO: Ronald D Ordway
CFO: Greggory Osborn
HR: –
FYE: February 28
Type: Public

Video may have killed the radio star, but it's been pretty good to Video Display. The company makes and distributes flat-panel, projection, and cathode-ray tube (CRT) display systems. Its products -- both new and reconditioned -- are often customized for specific needs such as space limitations or being ruggedized for adverse environments. They are targeted at niche settings such as military training and simulation displays among other applications. Its data display business (about 10% of sales) focuses on CRTs for uses such as medical monitoring equipment and computer terminals. Its largest customer is the US government, primarily the Department of Defense (more than 40% of sales).

	Annual Growth	02/19	02/20	02/21	02/22	02/23
Sales ($mil.)	(14.3%)	15.0	10.6	12.5	7.0	8.1
Net income ($ mil.)	–	0.0	(1.2)	0.8	(2.6)	(2.0)
Market value ($ mil.)	9.4%	5.9	6.1	15.9	5.3	8.4
Employees	(8.6%)	83	84	73	64	58

VIDEON CENTRAL, INC.

2171 SANDY DR
STATE COLLEGE, PA 168032283
Phone: 814 235-1111
Fax: –
Web: www.videonlabs.com

CEO: Todd Erdley
CFO: Paul Brown
HR: Joan Potter
FYE: June 30
Type: Private

Video Central wants to put high performance video in the center of your world. The consumer electronics maker develops digital audio and video technology components, including Blu-Ray and DVD players and 3D systems, used in in-flight entertainment centers and home theater systems. It also provides engineering, design, development, integration, and testing services to OEMs. Videon's Advanced Technology Group creates Blu-ray Disc and DVD software used for control, navigation, and playback features. The company manufacturers its products at its facility in Pennsylvania. It was established in 1997 and it is owned by its officers.

	Annual Growth	06/02	06/03	06/04	06/06	06/12
Sales ($mil.)	16.1%	–	–	4.3	8.0	14.2
Net income ($ mil.)	10.2%	–	–	0.1	0.3	0.3
Market value ($ mil.)	–	–	–	–	–	–
Employees	–	–	–	–	–	63

VIETNAM VETERANS OF AMERICA, INC.

8719 COLESVILLE RD STE 100
SILVER SPRING, MD 209103919
Phone: 301 585-4000
Fax: –
Web: www.vva.org

CEO: –
CFO: –
HR: –
FYE: February 28
Type: Private

Vietnam Veterans of America (VVA) has a Congressional charter to care. The not-for-profit group provides support for Vietnam veterans and their families and is the only such agency sanctioned by the US government. It promotes Vietnam veterans' issues including homelessness and health care -- Agent Orange exposure is one key issue -- and has about 50,000 members and 635 local chapters throughout the US, Puerto Rico, the Virgin Islands, and Guam. VVA seeks to eliminate discrimination toward Vietnam Veterans. It has programs specifically for women and minorities, scholarships, government benefit assistance, and government advocacy. Founded in 1978, VVA is funded completely by private donations.

	Annual Growth	02/17	02/18	02/20	02/21	02/22
Sales ($mil.)	3.1%	–	9.7	0.1	9.2	10.9
Net income ($ mil.)	(5.1%)	–	1.8	0.0	1.9	1.5
Market value ($ mil.)	–	–	–	–	–	–
Employees	–	–	–	–	–	300

VIEW SYSTEMS, INC.

7833 Walker Drive, Suite 520
Greenbelt, MD 20770
Phone: 410 236-8200
Fax: –
Web: –

CEO: Gunther Than
CFO: –
HR: –
FYE: December 31
Type: Public

View Systems keeps a systematic eye out for potential dangers. The company's ViewMaxx digital video system captures and stores closed-circuit television images on computer disks for efficient monitoring. Its View Scan system offers walk-through weapons detectors under the SecureScan brand name. View Systems' wireless video camera system, Visual First Responder, allows emergency response teams to size up a situation before heading into harm's way. View Systems also offers biometric verification systems that can be integrated with its SecureScan and ViewMaxx products. The company acquired Colorado-based electronics manufacturing company Wytan in 2008.

	Annual Growth	12/16	12/17	12/18	12/19	12/20
Sales ($mil.)	(52.8%)	0.0	0.0	0.0	0.0	0.0
Net income ($ mil.)	–	(0.2)	(0.2)	0.9	(1.2)	(1.1)
Market value ($ mil.)	(24.0%)	8.6	5.9	12.2	2.7	2.9
Employees	(15.9%)	8	8	8	4	4

VIEWCAST.COM INC.

NBB: VCST

3701 W. Plano Parkway, Suite 300
Plano, TX 75075
Phone: 972 488-7200
Fax: –
Web: www.viewcast.com

CEO: –
CFO: –
HR: –
FYE: December 31
Type: Public

ViewCast.com allows its customers to fling their video content to audiences far and wide. The company, which does business as simply ViewCast, provides hardware and software for capturing, managing, and streaming media over the broadband and mobile networks. It offers its video capture cards under the Osprey brand name and streaming systems under the Niagara product line, as well as related software. ViewCast, founded in 1994, sells to customers such as media, finance, security, health care, and cable providers, as well as government agencies and educators. The company sells directly and through distributors and resellers, with two distributors generating about 35% of sales.

	Annual Growth	12/08	12/09	12/10	12/11	12/12
Sales ($mil.)	(8.6%)	17.4	13.9	17.3	14.1	12.1
Net income ($ mil.)	–	0.5	(2.8)	(0.6)	(3.0)	(1.5)
Market value ($ mil.)	(37.4%)	24.3	11.9	16.2	5.1	3.7
Employees	(14.5%)	88	73	84	61	47

VIEWSONIC CORPORATION

10 POINTE DR STE 200
BREA, CA 928217620
Phone: 909 444-8888
Fax: –
Web: www.viewsonic.com

CEO: James Chu
CFO: Sung Yi
HR: Camila Armas
FYE: December 31
Type: Private

ViewSonic makes LCD and LED computer displays, including models for high-end computer-aided design and desktop publishing, and office, home, gaming, internet browsing, and multimedia applications. It is a channel-first company delivering performance, value and world-class support with one of the widest array of visual engagement solutions, best-in-class service and programs to ensure that its partners thrive. ViewSonic also offers a viewboard, digital displays, outlets, accessories, digital displays, and projectors. The company produces a Microsoft Windows-based ViewPad tablet PC and has other versions which use Google's Android operating system. Chairman and CEO James Chu founded the company in 1987.

	Annual Growth	12/03	12/04	12/05	12/14	12/15
Sales ($mil.)	(4.8%)	–	–	690.0	–	423.7
Net income ($ mil.)	–	–	–	–	–	13.8
Market value ($ mil.)	–	–	–	–	–	–
Employees	–	–	–	–	–	786

VIFOR PHARMA, INC.

200 CARDINAL WAY
REDWOOD CITY, CA 940634702
Phone: 650 421-9500
Fax: –
Web: www.viforpharma.com

CEO: Greg Oaks
CFO: –
HR: –
FYE: December 31
Type: Private

Relypsa knows that too much of a good thing can be bad for your health. A pharmaceutical company, Relypsa has developed a drug to treat hyperkalemia, a potentially life-threatening condition defined by high levels of potassium in the blood caused by kidney dysfunction. The company's first commercialized medicine, Veltassa (patiromer), is an orally administered, non-absorbed drug that binds to ingested potassium and reduces its absorption by the body. Relypsa received FDA approval for Veltassa in 2015. The company went public in 2013. Swiss firm Galenica acquired Relypsa for $1.5 billion in mid-2016.

VIKING YACHT COMPANY

ROUTE 9 ON THE BASS RIVER
NEW GRETNA, NJ 08224
Phone: 609 296-6000
Fax: –
Web: www.vikingyachts.com

CEO: Robert T Healey
CFO: Gerard D Straub Sr
HR: –
FYE: July 31
Type: Private

Leif Eriksson's oceangoing Viking explorers could only dream of vessels like those made by the Viking Yacht Company. Viking Yacht can build more than 100 semi-custom fiberglass pleasure boats, primarily used for sport fishing. About 90% of each yacht is made in-house. Its line of yachts vary in length from approximately 42 to 92 feet and include convertible and enclosed-bridge convertible vessels, open sportfish models, and a 52-foot sport yacht. The luxury boats are sold through a network of more than 40 dealers, six of which are based outside the US. Founders and brothers Bob and Bill Healey own Viking Yacht Company.

	Annual Growth	07/11	07/12	07/13	07/14	07/15
Sales ($mil.)	26.3%	–	–	–	194.1	245.1
Net income ($ mil.)	8.1%	–	–	–	16.3	17.6
Market value ($ mil.)	–	–	–	–	–	–
Employees	–	–	–	–	–	775

VILLAGE BANK & TRUST FINANCIAL CORP

NAS: VBFC

13319 Midlothian Turnpike
Midlothian, VA 23113
Phone: 804 897-3900
Fax: –
Web: www.villagebank.com

CEO: James E Hendricks
CFO: Donald M Kaloski Jr
HR: Renee Agan
FYE: December 31
Type: Public

Does it take a village to raise a bank? Village Bank & Trust is the holding company for Village Bank, which has about a dozen branches in the suburbs of Richmond, Virginia. It offers standard services, including deposit accounts, loans, and credit cards. Deposit funds are used to write loans for consumers and businesses in the area; commercial real estate loans, mainly secured by owner-occupied businesses, account for about half of the bank's lending portfolio, which also includes business, construction, residential mortgage, and consumer loans. In 2008 Village Bank & Trust acquired the three-branch River City Bank in a transaction worth more than $20 million.

	Annual Growth	12/19	12/20	12/21	12/22	12/23
Assets ($mil.)	8.1%	540.3	706.2	748.4	723.3	736.6
Net income ($ mil.)	(19.1%)	4.5	8.6	12.5	8.3	1.9
Market value ($ mil.)	1.8%	55.4	51.3	86.4	77.6	59.5
Employees	(0.2%)	146	152	152	148	145

VILLAGE SUPER MARKET, INC.

NMS: VLGE A

733 Mountain Avenue
Springfield, NJ 07081
Phone: 973 467-2200
Fax: –
Web: www.shoprite.com

CEO: Robert P Sumas
CFO: John L Van Orden
HR: –
FYE: July 29
Type: Public

It may take a village to raise a child, but it takes the Sumases to raise and run the Village. Run by the Sumas family since its founding in 1937, Village Super Market operates some 30 ShopRite supermarkets throughout New Jersey, northeastern Pennsylvania, and Maryland. It is a member of Wakefern Food, the largest retailer-owned food cooperative in the US and owner of the ShopRite brand name. The affiliation gives Village Super Market economies of scale in purchasing, distribution, and advertising. Most outlets are superstores measuring more than 60,000 sq. ft. Its Power Alley store format features high-margin fresh and convenience foods, such as baked goods, sushi and salad bars, and take-home hot-meal sections.

	Annual Growth	07/19	07/20	07/21	07/22	07/23
Sales ($mil.)	7.2%	1,643.5	1,804.6	2,030.3	2,061.1	2,166.7
Net income ($ mil.)	18.1%	25.5	24.9	20.0	26.8	49.7
Market value ($ mil.)	(1.7%)	370.8	398.4	335.0	335.3	346.4
Employees	1.0%	6,731	8,713	7,268	7,177	7,000

VILLANOVA UNIVERSITY IN THE STATE OF PENNSYLVANIA

800 E LANCASTER AVE
VILLANOVA, PA 190851603
Phone: 610 519-4500
Fax: –
Web: www.villanova.edu

CEO: –
CFO: –
HR: –
FYE: May 31
Type: Private

Since 1842, Villanova University's Augustinian Catholic intellectual tradition has been the cornerstone of an academic community in which students learn to think critically, act compassionately and succeed while serving others. There are more than 7,000 undergraduates, graduate and law students in the University's six colleges ? the College of Liberal Arts and Sciences, the Villanova School of Business, the College of Engineering, the M. Louise Fitzpatrick College of Nursing, the College of Professional Studies, and the Charles Widger School of Law.

	Annual Growth	05/18	05/19	05/20	05/21	05/22
Sales ($mil.)	20.7%	–	496.0	501.3	516.3	872.3
Net income ($ mil.)	46.4%	–	65.5	78.9	355.2	205.3
Market value ($ mil.)	–	–	–	–	–	–
Employees	–	–	–	–	–	2,022

VINCE HOLDING CORP

NYS: VNCE

500 5th Avenue-20th Floor
New York, NY 10110
Phone: 212 944-2600
Fax: –
Web: www.vince.com

CEO: Brendan Hoffman
CFO: David Stefko
HR: –
FYE: January 28
Type: Public

Upscale apparel company Vince Holding is a global contemporary group, consisting of three brands: Vince (luxury apparel and accessories), Rebecca Taylor (womenswear line lauded for its signature prints, romantic detailing and vintage inspired aesthetic, reimagined for a modern era), and Parker (trend focused). Known for its range of luxury products, Vince offers women's and men's ready-to-wear, footwear and accessories through some 50 full-price retail stores, more than 15 outlet stores, its e-commerce site, vince.com, and through its subscription service Vince Unfold, vinceunfold.com, as well as through premium wholesale channels globally. The company designs its products in the US and source the vast majority of its products from contract manufacturers outside the US, primarily in Asia.

	Annual Growth	02/19	02/20*	01/21	01/22	01/23
Sales ($mil.)	6.4%	279.0	375.2	219.9	322.7	357.4
Net income ($ mil.)	–	–	(2.0)	30.4	(65.6)	(12.7)	(38.3)
Market value ($ mil.)	(10.0%)	145.7	182.2	101.0	104.9	95.5
Employees	–	–	599	768	497	697	599

*Fiscal year change

VINING-SPARKS IBG, LIMITED PARTNERSHIP

775 RIDGE LAKE BLVD STE 200
MEMPHIS, TN 381209459
Phone: 901 766-3000
Fax: –
Web: www.stifelinstitutional.com

CEO: Mark A Medford
CFO: Allen Riggs
HR: Karen Cox
FYE: December 31
Type: Private

Realizing that it only takes a spark to get a fire going, Vining-Sparks IBG wants to help institutional investors kindle an investment blaze. Operating as Vining Sparks, the financial services firm provides broker/dealer services to institutional investors that include financial companies, money managers, funds, insurance firms, and municipalities. Through its alliance with Howe Barnes, the company offers investment banking services the likes of debt and equity offerings and mergers and acquisitions advisory. Chairman James Vining founded the company in 1981 to serve community banks.

VINO.COM, L.L.C.

421 WANDO PARK BLVD STE 200
MOUNT PLEASANT, SC 294647960
Phone: 843 881-0761
Fax: –
Web: www.totalbeveragesolution.com

CEO: –
CFO: –
HR: –
FYE: December 31
Type: Private

If wine, beer, and whisky covers the sum of beverages you desire, then Total Beverage Solution (TBS) is the answer. The company imports and distributes small batch single malt Scotch whisky (three brands); Australian, Canadian, Italian, Californian, and New Zealand wines (10 brands); and Czech, British, German, and US beers (six brands). Its offerings include wine made by the indigenous Maori people of New Zealand, whisky from the site of Scotland's oldest brewery, and beer from the world's oldest brewery, located in Germany. TBS, which looks for well-known brands not snatched up by big companies, sells its wares to wholesale distributors in more than 45 states. CEO Dave Pardus started the business in 2002.

	Annual Growth	12/09	12/10	12/11	12/12	12/13
Sales ($mil.)	11.5%	–	–	36.1	41.5	44.9
Net income ($ mil.)	(14.6%)	–	–	1.6	2.0	1.1
Market value ($ mil.)	–	–	–	–	–	–
Employees	–	–	–	–	–	51

VIPER ENERGY INC

NMS: VNOM

500 West Texas Ave., Suite 100
Midland, TX 79701
Phone: 432 221-7400
Fax: –
Web: www.viperenergy.com

CEO: Travis D Stice
CFO: Teresa L Dick
HR: –
FYE: December 31
Type: Public

Tackling energy challenges with some venom, Viper Energy Partners was formed by Diamondback Energy to own, acquire, and exploit oil and natural gas properties in North America. It plans expansion via organic growth and by pursuing accretive growth opportunities through acquisitions of assets from Diamondback Energy and from third parties. Its initial assets consist of oil and gas holdings in the Permian Basin in West Texas, substantially all of which are leased to working interest owners who bear the costs of operation and development. Diamondback Energy contributed these assets, which it acquired in September 2013 from a third party for cash, to Viper Energy following its 2014 IPO.

	Annual Growth	12/19	12/20	12/21	12/22	12/23
Sales ($mil.)	29.1%	298.3	250.6	504.9	866.5	827.7
Net income ($ mil.)	44.2%	46.3	(192.3)	57.9	151.7	200.1
Market value ($ mil.)	6.2%	4,361.2	2,055.0	3,768.8	5,622.2	5,549.7
Employees	–	–	–	–	–	–

VIRA MANUFACTURING INC

1 BUCKINGHAM AVE
PERTH AMBOY, NJ 088613532
Phone: 732 442-6756
Fax: –
Web: www.viranet.com

CEO: –
CFO: –
HR: –
FYE: December 31
Type: Private

VIRA Insight (formerly Vira Manufacturing) helps stores stay tidy and well-organized. The company manufactures merchandising systems and fixtures for the retail industry, including kiosks, display cases, cabinets, dressing rooms, garment racks, and wall systems. It also offers such services as fixture design, prototyping, installation, and spatial analysis. VIRA's customers have included electronics, fashion, and home goods retailers, as well as banking institutions. Vira Manufacturing, which was founded in 1991, merged with Insight Merchandising in 2015 to form VIRA Insight.

VIRACTA THERAPEUTICS INC   NMS: VIRX

2533 S. Coast Hwy. 101, Suite 210
Cardiff, CA 92007
Phone: 858 400-8470
Fax: –
Web: www.sunesis.com

CEO: Mark Rothera
CFO: Daniel Chevallard
HR: –
FYE: December 31
Type: Public

Sunesis builds drugs in miniature first before it builds them in full scale. The biotech firm's method involves building small drug fragments then examining their protein-binding ability and potential for development. Once a fragment shows potential, Sunesis then builds a larger therapeutic compound based upon its model. Its drug candidates target various forms of cancer. Its lead candidate Vosaroxin (SNS-595) is in clinical trials to evaluate its effect on ovarian cancer and acute myeloid leukemia. Other candidates are being studied for treatment of solid tumors and other forms of cancer, both independently and through partnerships. Milestone payments from those partnerships are Sunesis' only revenue to date.

	Annual Growth	12/19	12/20	12/21	12/22	12/23
Sales ($mil.)	–	2.1	0.1	–	–	–
Net income ($ mil.)	–	(23.3)	(21.6)	(114.8)	(49.2)	(51.1)
Market value ($ mil.)	14.0%	13.2	77.8	142.7	57.1	22.3
Employees	13.6%	24	8	24	32	40

VIRBAC CORPORATION

1301 SOLANA BLVD STE 2400
WESTLAKE, TX 762622305
Phone: 800 338-3659
Fax: –
Web: us.virbac.com

CEO: –
CFO: Karen M Miller
HR: Carol Buys-Michala
FYE: December 31
Type: Private

Hairballs and ticks and worms -- oh my! Virbac Corporation is an animal health care company that makes pharmaceutical products mainly for companion pets (dogs, cats, and horses) in the areas of heartworm, flea and tick, dermatology, hormone disorders, oral hygiene, and antibiotics. It is the North American subsidiary of France's Virbac, one of the largest veterinary drugmakers in the world. Among Virbac Corporation's brands are C.E.T. dental products, Clintabs antibiotic tablets, Epi-Otic ear cleanser, Iverhart heartworm preventive, Ketochlor and Pyoben shampoos, and Preventic tick collars. Products are geared towards veterinarians and pet store retailers in Canada and the US.

VIRCO MANUFACTURING CORP.   NMS: VIRC

2027 Harpers Way
Torrance, CA 90501
Phone: 310 533-0474
Fax: –
Web: www.virco.com

CEO: Robert A Virtue
CFO: Robert E Dose
HR: –
FYE: January 31
Type: Public

Have childhood memories of metal-legged folding tables, upholstered auditorium seats, or molded plastic chairs with attached wooden desks designed mostly for right-handers? Thank Virco Mfg. for the memories. The company makes a broad range of furniture and fixtures for the education market, including student and teacher desks, chairs, tables, computer furniture, mobile pedestals and tables with combined seating for cafeterias, A/V equipment, and filing and storage cabinets. It also offers seating, tables, media units, and other furniture for hotels, government agencies, churches, and convention centers. Founded in 1950, Virco provides delivery and installation services, as well.

	Annual Growth	01/19	01/20	01/21	01/22	01/23
Sales ($mil.)	3.6%	200.7	191.1	152.8	184.8	231.1
Net income ($ mil.)	–	(1.6)	2.4	(2.2)	(15.1)	16.5
Market value ($ mil.)	3.7%	68.7	67.1	44.6	48.1	79.4
Employees	(1.2%)	840	825	775	815	800

VIRGIN AMERICA INC.

555 AIRPORT BLVD
BURLINGAME, CA 940102000
Phone: 877 359-8474
Fax: –
Web: –

CEO: –
CFO: –
HR: –
FYE: December 31
Type: Private

Virgin America provides service to about 25 cities in the US as well as Canada and Mexico with a fleet of 50-plus Airbus A320 jets. It competes as a low-fare carrier, but distinguishes itself from rivals by providing first-class service and an assortment of in-flight entertainment options. In late 2016, the company was acquired by Alaska Air Group for $2.6 billion. Combined the companies offer almost 290 daily flights to 52 destinations from California, including 113 daily nonstop flights to 32 destinations from three Bay Area airports and more than 100 daily nonstop flights to 37 destinations from four Los Angeles area airports.

VIRGINIA COMMONWEALTH UNIVERSITY

912 W FRANKLIN ST
RICHMOND, VA 232849040
Phone: 804 828-0100
Fax: –
Web: www.vcu.edu

CEO: –
CFO: –
HR: –
FYE: June 30
Type: Private

Virginia Commonwealth University (VCU) serves the common interests of its more than 30,000 enrolled students. The university offers more than 200 certificate, undergraduate, graduate, and doctoral programs through its 15 schools. Spread across two campuses in Richmond: Monroe Park and Medical College of Virginia (MCV), which includes the Schools of Allied Health, Dentistry, Medicine, Nursing, Pharmacy, and Public Health. Specialty facilities include the VCU Medical Center and a branch campus of the School of the Arts in Qatar. Founded in 1917 as the Richmond School of Social Work and Public Health, in 1968 the school merged with the Medical College of Virginia to form VCU.

	Annual Growth	06/17	06/18	06/20	06/21	06/22
Sales ($mil.)	1.7%	–	763.2	784.5	775.6	815.4
Net income ($ mil.)	83.5%	–	12.8	49.1	157.7	145.1
Market value ($ mil.)	–	–	–	–	–	–
Employees	–	–	–	–	–	11,000

VIRGINIA ELECTRIC & POWER CO.

120 Tredegar Street
Richmond, VA 23219
Phone: 804 819-2284
Fax: –
Web: www.dominionenergy.com

CEO: Robert M Blue
CFO: James R Chapman
HR: –
FYE: December 31
Type: Public

Virginia Electric and Power Company (Virginia Power) operates under the Dominion Virginia Power and Dominion North Carolina Power brands and provides regulated electric delivery services to about 2.4 million homes and businesses. Power generation is derived by means of coal, gas, oil, hydro, and nuclear plants. The utility's power plants (with 24,300 MW of generating capacity) are managed by the Dominion Generation unit of parent Dominion Energy. Control of Virginia Power's transmission facilities is maintained by PJM Interconnection. Dominion Virginia Power also sells wholesale power to other users.

	Annual Growth	12/19	12/20	12/21	12/22	12/23
Sales ($mil.)	4.2%	8,108.0	7,763.0	7,470.0	9,654.0	9,573.0
Net income ($ mil.)	6.0%	1,149.0	1,021.0	1,712.0	1,215.0	1,452.0
Market value ($ mil.)	–	–	–	–	–	–
Employees	1.6%	6,000	6,000	6,000	6,100	6,400

VIRGINIA HOSPITAL CENTER ARLINGTON HEALTH SYSTEM

1701 N GEORGE MASON DR
ARLINGTON, VA 222053610
Phone: 703 558-5668
Fax: –
Web: –

CEO: James Cole
CFO: –
HR: Lashawn Wilson
FYE: December 31
Type: Private

Virginia Hospital Center-Arlington Health Systems is a general medical-surgical facility providing health care services to residents of northern Virginia. The hospital has about 350 beds and boasts all-private rooms. The acute medical center includes emergency, cardiology, neurology, orthopedics, respiratory, urology, cancer care, and women's health divisions, as well as radiology and diagnostic imaging facilities. In addition, Virginia Hospital Center provides outpatient rehabilitation services and runs an urgent care clinic that furnishes primary care for minor emergencies. The hospital is a teaching facility for the Georgetown University School of Medicine.

	Annual Growth	12/09	12/10	12/17	12/21	12/22
Sales ($mil.)	107.8%	–	0.1	524.9	582.9	718.8
Net income ($ mil.)	–	–	(0.0)	54.3	145.5	22.0
Market value ($ mil.)	–	–	–	–	–	–
Employees	–	–	–	–	–	2,000

VIRGINIA HOUSING DEVELOPMENT AUTHORITY

601 S BELVIDERE ST
RICHMOND, VA 232206504
Phone: 804 780-0789
Fax: –
Web: www.virginiahousing.com

CEO: –
CFO: –
HR: –
FYE: June 30
Type: Private

Though Virginia is famous for its Civil War-era plantations, these historic estates represent a lifestyle out of reach for most. For Virginians seeking a more modest homestead, there's the Virginia Housing Development Authority (VHDA). The not-for-profit quasi-government agency, founded by the Virginia General Assembly in 1972, provides developers of rental properties and low- to moderate-income borrowers with low interest rate loans to renovate or purchase houses and apartments across the state. Its loan products are offered by more than 140 authorized lenders throughout Virginia. The VHDA is self-supporting, issuing bonds to raise capital.

	Annual Growth	06/12	06/13	06/14	06/15	06/16
Assets ($mil.)	0.1%	–	–	8,014.9	8,070.7	8,024.9
Net income ($ mil.)	13.7%	–	–	132.8	176.7	171.7
Market value ($ mil.)	–	–	–	–	–	–
Employees	–	–	–	–	–	300

VIRGINIA INTERNATIONAL TERMINALS, LLC

601 WORLD TRADE CENTER
NORFOLK, VA 23510
Phone: 757 440-7120
Fax: –
Web: www.vit.org

CEO: Joseph P Ruddy
CFO: –
HR: –
FYE: June 30
Type: Private

Virginia International Terminals (VIT) operates marine terminals and an inland port on behalf of the Virginia Port Authority (VPA), a state agency. Established in 1982, VIT's marine terminals handle containerships and other vessels in Newport News, Norfolk, and Portsmouth. The terminals are linked by rail to the Virginia Inland Port in Front Royal, which serves as an intermodal container transfer facility conveying cargo from ships to trucks and vice versa. CenterPoint Properties, investment firm The Carlyle Group, and terminal operator Carrix Inc. bid to create a public-private partnership with VIT. The Transportation Secretary dismissed the bids in late 2010, after cargo activity started improving.

	Annual Growth	06/15	06/16	06/17	06/18	06/19
Sales ($mil.)	7.3%	–	–	478.6	521.1	551.2
Net income ($ mil.)	–	–	–	(7.8)	16.1	(1.2)
Market value ($ mil.)	–	–	–	–	–	–
Employees	–	–	–	–	–	400

VIRGINIA MILITARY INSTITUTE

319 LETCHER AVE
LEXINGTON, VA 244502148
Phone: 540 464-7230
Fax: –
Web: www.vmi.edu

CEO: –
CFO: –
HR: Elizabeth Dunlap
FYE: June 30
Type: Private

The Virginia Military Institute (VMI) is the nation's oldest state military college. VMI offers bachelor's degrees in majors such as engineering, science, and the humanities. It has about 1,500 cadets and 145 faculty members. VMI offers 14 majors offering 18 degrees and 26 minors. All students must take classes in one of the four Reserve Officer Training Corps (ROTC) programs (Army, Navy, Air Force, or Marines). About half of its graduates go on to serve in the military. The institute enrolls cadets from 34 US states and six countries and has a cadet-faculty ratio of 11.3:1.

	Annual Growth	06/18	06/19	06/20	06/21	06/22
Sales ($mil.)	18.0%	–	54.8	52.8	53.9	90.1
Net income ($ mil.)	(47.9%)	–	5.1	39.3	47.7	0.7
Market value ($ mil.)	–	–	–	–	–	–
Employees	–	–	–	–	–	550

VIRGINIA POLYTECHNIC INSTITUTE & STATE UNIVERSITY

300 TURNER ST NW STE 4200
BLACKSBURG, VA 240616100
Phone: 540 231-6000
Fax: –
Web: www.vt.edu

CEO: –
CFO: M D Shelton Jr
HR: Jamie Boggs
FYE: June 30
Type: Private

Virginia Polytechnic Institute and State University, more commonly known as Virginia Tech, is the commonwealth's most comprehensive university and a leading research institution, enrolling some 37,000 undergraduate, graduate, and professional students across the commonwealth and managing a research portfolio of more than $556 million. The university offers some 110 undergraduate degree programs and more than 120 master's and doctoral degree programs through nine colleges and a graduate school. It has a student-teacher ratio of 13 to 1. Some of the school's academic majors include agriculture, business, biology, architecture, chemistry, computer science, economics, geoscience, communications, medicine, mathematics, education, physics, arts, and engineering. Virginia Tech, which was formed in 1872, serves the surrounding community through outreach and education programs.

	Annual Growth	06/18	06/19	06/20	06/21	06/22
Sales ($mil.)	4.2%	–	1,160.4	1,188.8	1,162.3	1,311.6
Net income ($ mil.)	33.3%	–	130.5	121.0	300.2	308.9
Market value ($ mil.)	–	–	–	–	–	–
Employees	–	–	–	–	–	6,866

VIRIDIAN THERAPEUTICS INC   NAS: VRDN

221 Crescent Street, Suite 401
Waltham, MA 02453
Phone: 617 272-4600
Fax: –
Web: www.miragentherapeutics.com
CEO: Stephen Mahoney
CFO: Kristian Humer
HR: Stephanie Hartsel
FYE: December 31
Type: Public

Miragen Therapeutics (formerly Signal Genetics) is a biopharmaceutical firm engaged in the discovery and development of RNA-targeted therapeutics designed to treat diseases with highly unmet medical needs. The company's two primary candidates are MRG-106 for the treatment of certain cancers and MRG-201 for the treatment of pathological fibrosis. It has a number of pre-clinical candidates in development, as well. In early 2017, private biotech Miragen Therapeutics acquired public molecular diagnostic company Signal Genetics in a reverse merger; it then began trading on the NASDAQ.

	Annual Growth	12/19	12/20	12/21	12/22	12/23
Sales ($mil.)	(48.5%)	4.5	1.1	3.0	1.8	0.3
Net income ($ mil.)	–	(41.9)	(110.7)	(79.4)	(129.9)	(237.7)
Market value ($ mil.)	159.6%	25.9	888.1	1,067.3	1,576.9	1,175.8
Employees	19.6%	46	27	50	86	94

VIRNETX HOLDING CORP   NYS: VHC

308 Dorla Court, Suite 206
Zephyr Cove, NV 89448
Phone: 775 548-1785
Fax: –
Web: www.virnetx.com
CEO: Kendall Larsen
CFO: –
HR: –
FYE: December 31
Type: Public

VirnetX is involved in a net of legal battles. The company owns more than 70 US technology patents for establishing secure mobile internet communications over the 4G LTE network, but it claims several major tech firms including Apple and Cisco Systems are giving away its patented internet security software for free. VirnetX bought the core patents from federal IT contractor Leidos in 2006, and has been working to commercialize its mobile communications software, branded as GABRIEL Connection Technology, as well as a secure domain name registry service. Before the company can convince customers to license its software, it must resolve about 10 patent infringement lawsuits against Apple and Cisco.

	Annual Growth	12/19	12/20	12/21	12/22	12/23
Sales ($mil.)	(46.4%)	0.0	302.6	0.0	0.0	0.0
Net income ($ mil.)	–	(19.2)	280.4	(39.6)	(36.3)	(27.9)
Market value ($ mil.)	16.5%	13.8	18.2	9.4	4.7	25.3
Employees	7.8%	20	21	24	25	27

VIRTRA INC   NAS: VTSI

295 E. Corporate Place
Chandler, AZ 85225
Phone: 480 968-1488
Fax: 480 968-1448
Web: www.virtra.com
CEO: Robert D Ferris
CFO: –
HR: Amanda Opiola
FYE: December 31
Type: Public

Forget reality TV -- this company provides onscreen shows that are much closer to the real world for America's next top soldiers and cops . VirTra Systems develops, sells, and supports a line of virtual reality firearm training systems (FATS) used at law enforcement and military organizations around the world. Its two main brands, the IVR 4G military and the IVR HD law enforcement series, include realistic 360-degree scenarios (on multiple screens) to help physically and mentally prepare trainees to survive real-life situations involving gunfire. The company's proprietary Threat-Fire belt even simulates return fire by very briefly stunning the trainee with an electric shock. VirTra Systems was founded in 1993.

	Annual Growth	12/18	12/19	12/20	12/21	12/22
Sales ($mil.)	11.9%	18.1	18.7	19.1	24.4	28.3
Net income ($ mil.)	24.3%	0.8	(0.1)	1.5	2.5	2.0
Market value ($ mil.)	11.1%	33.5	53.2	38.5	76.5	51.1
Employees	11.2%	79	88	92	121	121

VIRTU FINANCIAL INC   NMS: VIRT

1633 Broadway
New York, NY 10019
Phone: 212 418-0100
Fax: –
Web: www.virtu.com
CEO: Douglas A Cifu
CFO: Sean P Galvin
HR: –
FYE: December 31
Type: Public

Virtu Financial is a leading financial firm that leverages cutting edge technology to deliver liquidity to the global markets and innovative, transparent trading solutions to its clients. The company buys or sells a broad range of securities and other financial instruments, and it generates revenue through market making activities, commission and fees on execution service activities. Its integrated, multi-asset analytics platform provides a range of pre- and post-trade services, data products and compliance tools that its clients rely upon to invest, trade and manage risk across global markets.

	Annual Growth	12/19	12/20	12/21	12/22	12/23
Sales ($mil.)	10.6%	1,530.1	3,239.3	2,811.5	2,364.8	2,293.4
Net income ($ mil.)	–	(58.6)	649.2	476.9	265.0	142.0
Market value ($ mil.)	6.1%	1,424.6	2,242.5	2,568.5	1,818.4	1,805.0
Employees	–	1,012	976	973	993	

VIRTUA MEMORIAL HOSPITAL BURLINGTON COUNTY, INC

175 MADISON AVE
MOUNT HOLLY, NJ 080602099
Phone: 609 267-0700
Fax: –
Web: www.virtua.org
CEO: Richard P Miller
CFO: –
HR: –
FYE: December 31
Type: Private

Virtua Memorial Hospital of Burlington County provides acute care to patients in southern New Jersey and the Philadelphia metropolitan area. Part of the Virtua Health network, the hospital has more than 430 beds and is well-known for its women's and children's health services and stroke care. Other specialty programs include a sleep center, cardiac rehabilitation, diabetes treatment, and wound care. Virtua Memorial provides a full range of cancer treatments through its collaboration with Philadelphia's Fox Chase Cancer Center and operates an in-hospital hospice center for terminally ill patients through a partnership with Samaritan Hospice.Strategy

VIRTUA OUR LADY OF LOURDES HOSPITAL, INC.

1600 HADDON AVE
CAMDEN, NJ 081033101
Phone: 856 757-3500
Fax: –
Web: www.lourdesnet.org
CEO: Dennis Pullin
CFO: –
HR: Annmarie Horan
FYE: December 31
Type: Private

Our Lady of Lourdes Medical Center tends to the sick of southern New Jersey. The hospital is a general acute care facility with about 325 inpatient beds. In addition to general medical, emergency, and surgical care, the hospital specializes in organ transplantation, joint replacement, rehabilitation, dialysis treatment, cardiac care, and birthing care. The hospital also offers nursing and other medical training programs, and it operates area clinics and provides community health and outreach services. Our Lady of Lourdes Medical Center, part of Catholic Health East's Lourdes Health System, was purchased by Virtua Health in 2019.

	Annual Growth	12/18	12/19	12/20	12/21	12/22
Sales ($mil.)	11.4%	–	–	–	410.0	456.6
Net income ($ mil.)	(27.3%)	–	–	–	33.8	24.5
Market value ($ mil.)	–	–	–	–	–	–
Employees	–	–	–	–	–	3,000

VIRTUAL ENTERPRISES, INC.

12405 GRANT ST
THORNTON, CO 802412415
Phone: 303 301-3000
Fax: –
Web: –

CEO: –
CFO: –
HR: –
FYE: June 30
Type: Private

Virtual Enterprises tames IT problems in the Wild West and beyond. Doing business as Advanced Systems Group (ASG), the company provides information technology services, including maintenance and support, assessments and audits, training, consulting, financing, and hardware and software implementation primarily in the western US. With a focus on data storage, cloud computing and virtualization, data security, and networking, the company supplies and supports computer and network hardware and software from leading suppliers such as Brocade Communications Systems, Cisco Systems, Hitachi Data Systems, HP, and VMware.

VIRTUSA CORPORATION

132 TURNPIKE RD STE 300
SOUTHBOROUGH, MA 017722173
Phone: 508 389-7300
Fax: –
Web: www.virtusa.com

CEO: Santosh Thomas
CFO: Ranjan Kalia
HR: –
FYE: March 31
Type: Private

Virtusa is a global provider of a variety of offshore-based software development and information technology services, including digitization, cloud computing, software engineering, application development, application outsourcing, maintenance, systems integration, and legacy asset management. The company's customers come from industries such as banking, financial services, independent software vendor, insurance, telecommunications, transportation and logistics, media and entertainment, and healthcare. With offices around the globe, Virtusa has a strong partner ecosystem including a variety of Fintech and Insurtech startup partnerships. In early 2021, Virtusa was acquired by Baring Private Equity Asia for approximately $2.0 billion.

VIRTUALSCOPICS, INC.

500 LINDEN OAKS
ROCHESTER, NY 146252823
Phone: 585 249-6231
Fax: –
Web: www.gobio.com

CEO: Eric Converse
CFO: James Groff
HR: –
FYE: December 31
Type: Private

VirtualScopics makes medical imaging analysis tools that help clinical researchers speed up the drug development process. Its patented algorithms let researchers analyze data from computed tomography, MRI, PET, and ultrasound scans, with the aim of helping pharmaceutical, biotech, and medical device companies determine how an investigational drug is working (or not working). The firm also hopes its products can be used to develop diagnostic tools to help with disease treatment and surgery. VirtualScopics provides services for many large pharmaceutical companies, including GlaxoSmithKline and Johnson & Johnson; its largest customer is Pfizer. In 2016 BioTelemetry paid some $15.5 million to buy VirtualScopics.

VISA INC   NYS: V

P.O. Box 8999
San Francisco, CA 94128-8999
Phone: 650 432-3200
Fax: –
Web: www.corporate.visa.com

CEO: Ryan McInerney
CFO: Chris Suh
HR: –
FYE: September 30
Type: Public

Visa is one of the world's leaders in digital payments (far ahead of rivals MasterCard and American Express) and boasts nearly 3.9 billion credit and other payment cards in circulation across more than 200 countries The company is focused on extending, enhancing and investing in its proprietary network, VisaNet, to offer a single connection point for facilitating payment transactions to multiple endpoints through various form factors. The company also offers debit cards, as well as prepaid cards. It facilitates commerce and money movement among a global set of consumers, merchants, financial institutions and government entities through innovative technologies. The majority of its sales were generated outside the US.

	Annual Growth	09/19	09/20	09/21	09/22	09/23
Sales ($mil.)	9.2%	22,977	21,846	24,105	29,310	32,653
Net income ($ mil.)	9.4%	12,080	10,866	12,311	14,957	17,273
Market value ($ mil.)	7.5%	318,046	369,745	411,865	328,475	425,288
Employees	10.2%	19,500	20,500	21,500	26,500	28,800

VIRTUS INVESTMENT PARTNERS INC   NYS: VRTS

One Financial Plaza
Hartford, CT 06103
Phone: 800 248-7971
Fax: –
Web: www.virtus.com

CEO: George R Aylward
CFO: Michael A Angerthal
HR: Alida Whiteway
FYE: December 31
Type: Public

Virtus Investment Partners provides investment management services to individuals and institutions. Boasting approximately $150 billion in assets under management, it operates through affiliated advisors, including Duff & Phelps, Kayne Anderson Rudnick, and Newfleet Asset Management, as well as outside subadvisors. Virtus markets diverse investment products, such as open- and closed-end funds, and managed account services, to high-net-worth individuals. It also manages institutional accounts for corporations and other investors. The firm was formed in 1995 through a reverse merger with Duff & Phelps.

	Annual Growth	12/19	12/20	12/21	12/22	12/23
Sales ($mil.)	10.7%	563.2	603.9	979.2	886.4	845.3
Net income ($ mil.)	8.1%	95.6	80.0	208.1	117.5	130.6
Market value ($ mil.)	18.7%	862.7	1,538.0	2,105.8	1,356.9	1,713.5
Employees	9.3%	578	581	668	772	824

VISHAY INTERTECHNOLOGY, INC.   NYS: VSH

63 Lancaster Avenue
Malvern, PA 19355-2143
Phone: 610 644-1300
Fax: –
Web: www.vishay.com

CEO: Joel Smejkal
CFO: Lori Lipcaman
HR: –
FYE: December 31
Type: Public

Vishay Intertechnology is a leader in the market for discrete semiconductor components that are used for a wide variety of functions, including power control, power conversion, power management, signal switching, signal routing, signal blocking, signal amplification, two-way data transfer, one-way remote control, and circuit isolation. Vishay is also one of the world's largest portfolios of passive electronic components that are used to restrict current flow, suppress voltage increases, store and discharge energy, control alternating current (AC) and voltage, filter out unwanted electrical signals, and perform other functions. Vishay supports innovative designs in the automotive, industrial, computing, consumer, telecommunications, military, aerospace, and medical markets. Almost 40% of Vishay's revenue comes from Asia.

	Annual Growth	12/19	12/20	12/21	12/22	12/23
Sales ($mil.)	6.3%	2,668.3	2,501.9	3,240.5	3,497.4	3,402.0
Net income ($ mil.)	18.6%	163.9	122.9	298.0	428.8	323.8
Market value ($ mil.)	3.0%	3,093.1	3,008.9	3,177.4	3,133.8	3,482.5
Employees	1.2%	22,400	21,600	22,800	23,900	23,500

VISHAY PRECISION GROUP INC.

NYS: VPG

3 Great Valley Parkway, Suite 150
Malvern, PA 19355
Phone: 484 321-5300
Fax: 484 321-5301
Web: www.vpgsensors.com

CEO: -
CFO: -
HR: -
FYE: December 31
Type: Public

Vishay Precision Group (VPG) is a global, diversified company focused on precision measurement sensing technologies, including specialized sensors, weighing solutions, and measurement systems. VPG's Vishay Intertechnology expanded its sensor and measurement business through acquisitions, extending its business from its initial focus on precision foil resistors and foil strain gages o include an array of load cell-based solutions. The company's products are used in industrial applications, including military, agricultural, aerospace, medical, and construction. US customers account for some 45% of sales.

	Annual Growth	12/19	12/20	12/21	12/22	12/23
Sales ($mil.)	5.7%	284.0	269.8	317.9	362.6	355.0
Net income ($ mil.)	3.7%	22.2	10.8	20.2	36.1	25.7
Market value ($ mil.)	0.1%	456.6	422.7	498.4	519.0	457.5
Employees	(1.1%)	2,400	2,300	2,600	2,700	2,300

VISIONWORKS OF AMERICA, INC.

175 E. HOUSTON ST
SAN ANTONIO, TX 782052299
Phone: 800 669-1183
Fax: -
Web: www.visionworks.com

CEO: -
CFO: Jennifer L Taylor
HR: Mary B Lemley
FYE: December 29
Type: Private

Visionworks of America operates a large national retail eyewear chain. The company owns or manages about 700 optical stores in some 40 states. The stores, which operate under the Visonworks name, sell contact lenses, prescription eyewear, sunglasses, and accessories and offer contacts and eyeglass frames under its own and designer brands. Stores also provide access to one-hour services, on-site processing labs, and independent optometrists. Founded in 1984, Visionworks is majority owned by health insurer Highmark. Vision benefits firm VSP Global agreed to acquire Visionworks in 2019.

VISITING NURSE SERVICE OF NEW YORK

220 E 42ND ST FL 6
NEW YORK, NY 100175831
Phone: 212 609-6100
Fax: -
Web: www.vnshealth.org

CEO: Mary A Christopher
CFO: Polina Kogan
HR: Monica Gall
FYE: December 31
Type: Private

Visiting Nurse Service of New York (VNSNY), now operating as VNS Health after rebranding in 2022, is one of the largest not-for-profit home health care providers in the US. The company provides a wide range of home care services including personal care, nursing, senior care, and more as well as rehabilitation therapy, mental health, hospice, and pediatrics, as well as Medicare/Medicaid programs. VNS Health was founded in 1893 by Lilian Wald. Now, it has a diverse team of nearly 10,000 individuals and expands its services from just home care and community programs to include hospice care, personal care, behavioral health, and care management.

	Annual Growth	12/00	12/01	12/17	12/21	12/22
Sales ($mil.)	(12.5%)	-	725.0	100.4	46.5	43.4
Net income ($ mil.)	-	-	(61.1)	69.0	25.1	17.2
Market value ($ mil.)	-	-	-	-	-	-
Employees	-	-	-	-	-	11,780

VISTA GOLD CORP

ASE: VGZ

8310 S Valley Hwy, Suite 300
Englewood, CO 80112
Phone: 720 981-1185
Fax: 720 981-1186
Web: www.vistagold.com

CEO: -
CFO: -
HR: -
FYE: December 31
Type: Public

When it views its holdings, Vista Gold hopes its prospects for gold are good. Since 2001 the company has acquired five gold projects with the expectation that gold prices would increase. It is developing the Mt. Todd gold project in Australia's Northern Territories and the Los Cardones gold project in Mexico's Baja California Sur. Other holdings by Vista are the Guadelupe de los Reyes gold and silver mining complex in Mexico, the Awak Mas gold mine in Indonesia, and the Long Valley gold project in California. In 2012 Vista reported proved and probable reserves of 7.4 million ounces of gold.

	Annual Growth	12/19	12/20	12/21	12/22	12/23
Sales ($mil.)	-	-	-	-	-	-
Net income ($ mil.)	-	(9.4)	0.4	(15.2)	(4.9)	(6.6)
Market value ($ mil.)	(11.1%)	87.8	130.8	85.9	60.0	54.7
Employees	(5.4%)	15	14	17	14	12

VISTA INTERNATIONAL TECHNOLOGIES INC

4835 Monaco St
Commerce City, CO 80022
Phone: 303 690-8300
Fax: 970 535-4784
Web: www.vvit.us

CEO: -
CFO: -
HR: -
FYE: December 31
Type: Public

Vista International Technologies sees itself as a potential leader in renewable energy technology on a global scale. The company is working to develop and market its Thermal Gasifier Technology and to build and operate small power plants. Colorado-based Vista has operations in waste-to-energy gassification, low-wind-speed generators, alternative fuels, and energy-saving lighting. Its primary operation is a facility in Texas that converts used tires into fuel. The company is looking for partners to build, own, and operate small waste-to-energy plants or utilize the company's technology under license. Investor Richard Strain owns just under 50% of Vista, while board member Timothy Ruddy owns a 10% stake.

	Annual Growth	12/10	12/11	12/12	12/13	12/14
Sales ($mil.)	11.0%	0.6	0.5	0.7	0.8	0.9
Net income ($ mil.)	-	(0.9)	(1.1)	(0.4)	(0.8)	(0.3)
Market value ($ mil.)	7.8%	0.6	0.9	1.5	1.7	0.8
Employees	(19.1%)	7	7	3	3	3

VISTA OUTDOOR INC

NYS: VSTO

1 Vista Way
Anoka, MN 55303
Phone: 763 433-1000
Fax: -
Web: www.vistaoutdoor.com

CEO: Gary L McArthur
CFO: Andrew Keegan
HR: -
FYE: March 31
Type: Public

Vista Outdoor is a leading global designer, manufacturer, and marketer of outdoor recreation and shooting sports products. It markets through a diverse portfolio of almost 40 well-recognized brands. Its products include commercial ammunition, golf rangefinders, bike and hike hydration packs, and biking helmets and accessories. Some of its popular brands include Federal Premium (ammunition) and Bushnell (optics products). Its customers include outdoor enthusiasts, hunters and recreational shooters, athletes, as well as law enforcement and military professionals. Its products are sold through specialty and independent retailers such as Walmart, Cabela's/Bass Pro Shops, Academy, Target, and Sportsman's Warehouse. The US accounts for about 85% of sales.

	Annual Growth	03/19	03/20	03/21	03/22	03/23
Sales ($mil.)	10.6%	2,058.5	1,755.9	2,225.5	3,044.6	3,079.8
Net income ($ mil.)	-	(648.4)	(155.1)	266.0	473.2	(9.7)
Market value ($ mil.)	36.4%	457.3	502.4	1,830.7	2,037.4	1,581.8
Employees	7.7%	5,200	4,400	5,900	6,900	7,000

VISTEON CORP
NMS: VC

One Village Center Drive
Van Buren Township, MI 48111
Phone: 734 710-8349
Fax: –
Web: www.visteon.com

CEO: Sachin S Lawande
CFO: Jerome J Rouquet
HR: –
FYE: December 31
Type: Public

Visteon Corporation is a global automotive supplier that designs, engineers, and manufactures innovative automotive electronics and connected car solutions for the world's major vehicle manufacturers, including BMW, Ford, Geely, General Motors, Honda, Jaguar/Land Rover, Mahindra, Mazda, Mercedes-Benz, Mitsubishi, Nissan, Renault, Stellantis, Tata, Toyota, and Volkswagen. The company is focused on cockpit electronics such as instrument clusters, information displays, infotainment systems, audio systems, battery management systems, and telematics products. Asia-Pacific generates the largest revenue for about 40%.

	Annual Growth	12/19	12/20	12/21	12/22	12/23
Sales ($mil.)	7.6%	2,945.0	2,548.0	2,773.0	3,756.0	3,954.0
Net income ($ mil.)	62.3%	70.0	(56.0)	41.0	124.0	486.0
Market value ($ mil.)	9.6%	2,393.8	3,470.1	3,072.5	3,616.9	3,453.0
Employees	(2.4%)	11,000	10,000	10,000	10,000	10,000

VISTRA CORP
NYS: VST

6555 Sierra Drive
Irving, TX 75039
Phone: 214 812-4600
Fax: –
Web: www.vistracorp.com

CEO: James A Burke
CFO: Kristopher E Moldovan
HR: –
FYE: December 31
Type: Public

Vistra Energy is a holding company operating an integrated retail and electric power generation business primarily in markets throughout the US. Through its subsidiaries, the company is engaged in competitive energy activities including electricity generation, wholesale energy sales and purchases, commodity risk management and retail sales of electricity and natural gas to end users. It serves approximately 3.5 million customers and operates in around 20 states and the District of Columbia. Its generation fleet totals approximately 37,000 MW of generation capacity with a portfolio of natural gas, nuclear, coal, solar and battery energy storage facilities.

	Annual Growth	12/19	12/20	12/21	12/22	12/23
Sales ($mil.)	5.8%	11,809	11,443	12,077	13,728	14,779
Net income ($ mil.)	12.6%	928.0	636.0	(1,274.0)	(1,227.0)	1,493.0
Market value ($ mil.)	13.8%	8,080.0	6,909.6	8,002.7	8,153.8	13,538
Employees	(2.9%)	5,475	1,640	5,060	4,910	4,870

VISTRONIX, LLC

11091 SUNSET HILLS RD STE 700
RESTON, VA 201905380
Phone: 301 837-5377
Fax: –
Web: www.vistronix.net

CEO: John Hassoun
CFO: Alan Stewart
HR: Elizabeth Alston
FYE: December 31
Type: Private

Vistronix keeps on the right side of the information technology (IT) highway. Founded in 1990, the company provides IT consulting services primarily to the government services market in the areas of content management, enterprise solutions, and grants management. Vistronix's service solutions are divided up into three practice areas or groups: eSolutions Consulting, Enterprise Systems Management, and Information Management Solutions. The firm's past clients have included the EPA, the US Department of Defense, and the Bureau of Transportation Statistics.

	Annual Growth	12/06	12/07	12/08	12/09	12/10
Sales ($mil.)	14.3%	–	–	30.9	37.1	40.4
Net income ($ mil.)	19.2%	–	–	1.8	2.1	2.6
Market value ($ mil.)	–	–	–	–	–	–
Employees	–	–	–	–	–	400

VITA FOOD PRODUCTS, INC.

2222 W LAKE ST
CHICAGO, IL 606122281
Phone: 312 738-4500
Fax: –
Web: www.vitafoodproducts.com

CEO: Clifford K Bolen
CFO: R A Nelson
HR: –
FYE: December 31
Type: Private

Vita Food Products won't lead you astray with a red herring -- their herring are properly pickled. Under the Vita and Elf brand names, the company produces refrigerated and frozen kosher salmon products (lox, smoked, cured) and pickled herring in various sauces. It markets salad dressings and specialty condiments (sauces, seasonings, syrups, jellies) under license for Jim Beam, Budweiser, Dr Pepper, 7UP, and Jelly Belly. Vita is also home to Scorned Woman Hot Sauce. The company's products are distributed to US supermarkets, wholesale clubs, and foodservice providers, and they are sold online. Vita Food went private in 2009 when board member and stockholder Howard E. Bedford bought the company.

	Annual Growth	03/10	03/11	03/12*	12/12	12/13
Sales ($mil.)	233.4%	–	–	16.5	56.4	55.0
Net income ($ mil.)	1009.1%	–	–	0.0	0.5	1.1
Market value ($ mil.)	–	–	–	–	–	–
Employees	–	–	–	–	–	130

*Fiscal year change

VITALANT

9305 E VIA DE VENTURA
SCOTTSDALE, AZ 852583597
Phone: 800 288-2199
Fax: –
Web: www.vitalant.org

CEO: David Green
CFO: Susan L Barnes
HR: Penny Barnett
FYE: December 31
Type: Private

Vitalant is one of the nation's leading nonprofit blood and biotherapies healthcare organizations, providing hospitals and patients across the US a safe blood supply, specialized laboratory services, transfusion medicine expertise, and world-renowned research. It provides lifesaving blood and comprehensive transfusion medicine services for about 900 hospitals nationwide. The world-renowned Vitalant Research Institute is engaged in scientific studies ranging from blood donor epidemiology to cellular therapy to virus discovery. Vitalant is also a partner in the operation of Creative Testing Solutions, the largest independent blood donor testing organization in the US. Vitalant offers not only blood products, but also a vast array of transfusion, laboratory, therapeutic, biotherapy, and specialty services. It provides blood, blood components and clinical services across more than two dozen states. Vitalant was founded in 1943.

VITALSMARTS, LC

320 RIVER PARK DR STE SWB
PROVO, UT 846046065
Phone: 801 765-9600
Fax: –
Web: www.cruciallearning.com

CEO: Andrew Shimberg
CFO: Troy Giles
HR: –
FYE: December 31
Type: Private

VitalSmarts puts the life back into corporations that need a little jolt. The firm develops best practices training programs focused on areas such as team-building, creative thinking, leadership development, and accountability. It offers open-enrollment seminars, in-house training programs, and free Webinars among its training products, which include Crucial Conversations and Crucial Confrontations Training. It also provides keynote speakers and consulting services. Clients include Accenture, IBM, AT&T, and Intel in the US and about 20 other countries. Former CEO Al Switzler founded the company in 2001 along with former officers Joseph Grenny, Kerry Patterson, and Ron McMillan.

	Annual Growth	12/05	12/06	12/07	12/09	12/10
Sales ($mil.)	15.0%	–	–	21.2	25.3	32.3
Net income ($ mil.)	24.4%	–	–	6.5	4.3	12.5
Market value ($ mil.)	–	–	–	–	–	–
Employees	–	–	–	–	–	100

VIVEVE MEDICAL INC

NBB: VIVE

345 Inverness Drive South, Building B, Suite 250
Englewood, CO 80112
Phone: 720 696-8100
Fax: –
Web: www.viveve.com

CEO: Scott Durbin
CFO: –
HR: –
FYE: December 31
Type: Public

Viveve Medical (formerly PLC Systems) is a medical technology company that designs, develops, manufactures and markets a platform medical technology. Its proprietary CMRF technology is delivered through a radiofrequency generator, handpiece and treatment tip, which collectively, it refers to as the Viveve System. The Viveve System is currently being marketed internationally for the non-invasive treatment of vaginal introital laxity, sexual function, vaginal rejuvenation, and stress urinary incontinence depending on the relevant country-specific clearance or approval. The company targets a broad number of physician specialties, with a primary focus on OBGYNs, urogynecologists, and urologists. The Asia Pacific region provides about 50% of the company's revenue.

	Annual Growth	12/17	12/18	12/19	12/20	12/21
Sales ($mil.)	(19.5%)	15.3	18.5	6.6	5.5	6.4
Net income ($ mil.)	–	(37.0)	(50.0)	(42.5)	(21.9)	(22.0)
Market value ($ mil.)	(30.8%)	52.8	11.2	13.4	49.9	12.1
Employees	(17.8%)	103	67	55	42	47

VIZIO HOLDING CORP

NYS: VZIO

39 Tesla
Irvine, CA 92618
Phone: 949 428-2525
Fax: –
Web: www.vizio.com

CEO: William Wang
CFO: Adam Townsend
HR: –
FYE: December 31
Type: Public

Vizio is driving the future of televisions through its integrated platform of cutting-edge Smart TVs and a powerful SmartCast operating system. SmartCast delivers a compelling array of content and applications through an elegant and easy-to-use interface. In addition to watching cable TV, viewers can use its platform to stream a movie or show from their favorite OTT service, watch hundreds of free channels through its platform, including on its WatchFree+ offering, enjoy an enhanced immersive experience catered to gaming, or access a variety of other content options. It offers a broad range of high-performance Smart TVs; a portfolio of innovative sound bars; and a proprietary Smart TV operating system, SmartCast.

	Annual Growth	12/19	12/20	12/21	12/22	12/23
Sales ($mil.)	(2.2%)	1,836.8	2,042.5	2,124.0	1,862.8	1,680.0
Net income ($ mil.)	5.1%	23.1	102.5	(39.4)	(0.4)	28.2
Market value ($ mil.)	–	–	–	3,841.3	1,465.0	1,522.3
Employees	–	–	527	800	900	900

VIZIO, INC.

39 TESLA
IRVINE, CA 926184603
Phone: 855 833-3221
Fax: –
Web: www.vizio.com

CEO: William Wang
CFO: Adam Townsend
HR: –
FYE: December 31
Type: Private

VIZIO offers HDTVs and sound bars on its webstore, online across dozens of retailers, and in thousands of brick and mortar stores throughout the US. The company also offers a portfolio of innovative sound bars that deliver consumers an elevated audio experience, as well as Universal SmartCast TV remotes and sound bar display remotes. VIZIO sells many of its low-priced electronics through top discount chains including Amazon, Best Buy, Costco, Sam's Club, Target, and Walmart. Thanks to its low prices, VIZIO ranked as the #1 American-based sound bar brand.

	Annual Growth	12/03	12/04	12/06	12/07	12/08
Sales ($mil.)	155.8%	–	46.9	671.3	1,929.2	2,006.3
Net income ($ mil.)	115.7%	–	0.5	1.3	7.6	10.3
Market value ($ mil.)	–	–	–	–	–	–
Employees	–	–	–	–	–	398

VJS CONSTRUCTION SERVICES, INC.

W233N2847 ROUNDY CIR W
PEWAUKEE, WI 530726285
Phone: 262 542-9000
Fax: –
Web: www.vjscs.com

CEO: –
CFO: –
HR: –
FYE: September 30
Type: Private

VJS Construction Services (formerly Voss Jorgensen Schueler Co.) is one of the Wisconsin's premier general construction firms. The private company, which was founded in 1947, specializes in building education, senior living, retail, apartments and condos, manufacturing, medical, and office facilities. VJS handles a variety of projects including restaurants, schools, churches, hospitals, and hotels from beginning to end by providing cost analysis, construction administration and bidding and scheduling services. The contractor also can provide demolition and concrete and carpentry work for interior build out and renovation projects. Its clients have included US Bank, PNC Bank, St. Augustine Preparatory Academy, and Mount Mary University.

VOLT INFORMATION SCIENCES INC

2401 N GLASSELL ST
ORANGE, CA 928652705
Phone: 714 921-8800
Fax: –
Web: www.volt.com

CEO: Art Knapp
CFO: Herbert M Mueller
HR: Kendra Bellman
FYE: October 31
Type: Private

Volt Information Sciences is a global provider of staffing services. The company provides contingent workers, personnel recruitment services and managed staffing services programs. Volt's programs primarily support administrative and light industrial (commercial) workers, as well as technical, information technology and engineering (professional) positions. It also involves managing the procurement and on-boarding of contingent workers from multiple providers. While Volt has business in approximately 60 locations in Asia Pacific, Europe and Canada, more than 85% of revenues are generated in the US. Brothers William and Jerome Shaw founded the business in 1950.

VOLUNTEER BANCORP, INC.

210 East Main Street
Rogersville, TN 37857
Phone: 423 272-2200
Fax: –
Web: –

CEO: Lyons Price
CFO: –
HR: –
FYE: December 31
Type: Public

Volunteer Bancorp is the holding company for The Citizens Bank of East Tennessee, which has four branches in Hawkins and Hancock counties. The community-oriented bank serves consumers and businesses, offering standard services such as checking and savings accounts, personal and commercial money market accounts, certificates of deposit, individual retirement accounts, and online banking. One- to four-family residential mortgages make up the largest potion of the company's loan portfolio, followed by commercial mortgages and construction and land loans. Other lending products include business, consumer, and farm loans. The Citizens Bank of East Tennessee was founded in 1906.

	Annual Growth	12/07	12/08	12/09	12/10	12/11
Sales ($mil.)	(2.4%)	–	–	–	6.8	6.7
Net income ($ mil.)	–	–	–	–	(3.6)	(1.1)
Market value ($ mil.)	–	–	–	–	–	–
Employees	–	–	–	–	–	42

VOLUNTEER ENERGY COOPERATIVE

18359 STATE HIGHWAY 58 N
DECATUR, TN 373227825
Phone: 423 334-1020
Fax: –
Web: www.vec.org

CEO: Gene Carmichael
CFO: –
HR: –
FYE: June 30
Type: Private

In the strong tradition of volunteering in Tennessee, Volunteer Energy Cooperative is voluntarily cooperating with its members to serve their energy needs. The distribution utility serves more than 109,000 customers (who also own the cooperative) in 17 central and eastern Tennessee counties. It operates more than 9,000 miles of power lines. Volunteer Energy purchases its power supply from the Tennessee Valley Authority. The company also provides metered natural gas and propane service, and offers telecommunications (Internet access and long-distance phone) services. In addition, Volunteer Energy offers its customer surge protection and security equipment.

	Annual Growth	06/15	06/16	06/19	06/20	06/22
Sales ($mil.)	2.5%	–	232.7	252.5	244.7	270.0
Net income ($ mil.)	(0.2%)	–	11.1	11.6	8.7	11.0
Market value ($ mil.)	–	–	–	–	–	–
Employees	–	–	–	–	–	175

VOLUNTEERS OF AMERICA, INC.

1660 DUKE ST STE 100
ALEXANDRIA, VA 223143427
Phone: 703 341-5000
Fax: –
Web: www.voa.org

CEO: Michael King
CFO: Lawrence Mitchell
HR: Leslie Quon
FYE: June 30
Type: Private

Volunteers of America is a national faith-based nonprofit organization that provides community-level human services to approximately 1.5 million people in more than 400 communities a year. Its services include children, youths, and families, adults, older adults, veterans, persons with disabilities, and women. The organization is one of the nation's largest, established comprehensive human services organizations with some 16,000 mission-driven professionals, dedicated to helping those in need rebuild their lives and reach their full potential. Its services are delivered through a partnership of professional staff, volunteers, and other community supporters. Volunteers of America was organized in 1896 by Ballington and Maud Booth.

VON MAUR, INC.

6565 N BRADY ST
DAVENPORT, IA 528062054
Phone: 563 388-2200
Fax: –
Web: www.vonmaur.com

CEO: –
CFO: Robert L Larsen
HR: Andrea Mlot
FYE: February 03
Type: Private

Family-owned and -operated Von Maur runs over 35 upscale department stores, primarily in the Midwest, offering shoppers amenities such as an interest-free credit card, free gift wrapping, online shopping, and free shipping within the US. The stores offer clothing from brands such as adidas, Burberry, Eileen Fisher, Kenneth Cole, Lacoste, O'Neill, Under Armour, and Tommy Bahama, among others. The company steadily expands its locations and the variety of services offered to its customers. Von Maur was founded in 1872.

VONAGE HOLDINGS CORP.

101 CRAWFORDS CORNER RD STE 2416
HOLMDEL, NJ 07733
Phone: 732 528-2600
Fax: –
Web: www.vonage.com

CEO: Rory Read
CFO: Stephen Lasher
HR: –
FYE: December 31
Type: Private

Vonage is a global cloud communications leader, helps businesses accelerate their digital transformation. Vonage's Communications Platform is fully programmable and allows for the integration of Video, Voice, Chat, Messaging, AI and Verification into existing products, workflows and systems. The Vonage conversational commerce application enables businesses to create AI-powered omnichannel experiences that boost sales and increase customer satisfaction. Vonage's fully programmable unified communications, contact center and conversational commerce applications are built from the Vonage platform and enable companies to transform how they communicate and operate from the office or remotely - providing the flexibility required to create meaningful engagements. Vonage is a wholly-owned subsidiary of Ericsson, and a business area within the Ericsson Group called Business Area Global Communications Platform.

VONTIER CORP — NYS: VNT

5438 Wade Park Boulevard, Suite 600
Raleigh, NC 27607
Phone: 984 275-6000
Fax: –
Web: www.vontier.com

CEO: Mark D Morelli
CFO: David H Naemura
HR: –
FYE: December 31
Type: Public

Vontier is a global industrial technology company that focuses on critical technical equipment, components, software, and services for manufacturing, repair, and servicing in the mobility infrastructure industry worldwide. It supplies a wide range of solutions spanning advanced environmental sensors; fueling equipment; field payment hardware; point-of-sale; workflow and monitoring software; vehicle tracking and fleet management; software solutions for traffic light control; and vehicle mechanics' and technicians' equipment. The company markets its products and services to retail and commercial fueling operators, convenience store and in-bay car wash operators, tunnel car wash businesses, commercial vehicle repair businesses, municipal governments, public safety entities, and fleet owners/operators on a global basis. North America generates the majority of the company's revenue.

	Annual Growth	12/19	12/20	12/21	12/22	12/23
Sales ($mil.)	2.8%	2,772.1	2,704.6	2,990.7	3,184.4	3,095.2
Net income ($ mil.)	(3.6%)	436.5	342.0	413.0	401.3	376.9
Market value ($ mil.)	–	–	5,153.6	4,741.6	2,982.6	5,331.1
Employees	(0.9%)	8,300	8,400	8,500	8,100	8,000

VORNADO REALTY L.P.

888 Seventh Avenue
New York, NY 10019
Phone: 212 894-7000
Fax: –
Web: www.vno.com

CEO: Steven Roth
CFO: Michael J Franco
HR: Alyssa Muller
FYE: December 31
Type: Public

Vornado Realty Trust is a real estate investment trust (REIT) with holdings in office, retail, hospitality, and residential space. The company's commercial property holdings total approximately 19.9 million sq. ft. of space, primarily in New York City. It also owns the 3.7 million sq. ft. theMART office building in Chicago, and a controlling stake in San Francisco's 1.8 million sq. ft. office complex 555 California Street. In addition, Vornado owns about a third of New York retail property owner Alexander's. Building Maintenance Services LLC (BMS), a wholly owned subsidiary, which provides cleaning and security services for its buildings and third parties.

	Annual Growth	12/18	12/19	12/20	12/21	12/22
Sales ($mil.)	(4.5%)	2,163.7	1,924.7	1,528.0	1,589.2	1,800.0
Net income ($ mil.)	–	475.6	3,358.8	(322.0)	183.5	(376.9)
Market value ($ mil.)	–	–	–	–	–	–
Employees	(5.4%)	3,928	4,008	2,899	3,224	3,146

VORNADO REALTY TRUST
NYS: VNO

888 Seventh Avenue
New York, NY 10019
Phone: 212 894-7000
Fax: –
Web: www.vno.com

CEO: Steven Roth
CFO: Michael J Franco
HR: Alyssa Muller
FYE: December 31
Type: Public

Vornado Realty Trust is a real estate investment trust (REIT) with holdings in office, retail, hospitality, and residential space. The company's commercial property holdings total approximately 19.9 million sq. ft. of space, primarily in New York City. It also owns the 3.7 million sq. ft. theMART office building in Chicago, and a controlling stake in San Francisco's 1.8 million sq. ft. office complex 555 California Street. In addition, Vornado owns about a third of New York retail property owner Alexander's. Building Maintenance Services LLC (BMS), a wholly owned subsidiary, which provides cleaning and security services for its buildings and third parties.

	Annual Growth	12/19	12/20	12/21	12/22	12/23
Sales ($mil.)	(1.5%)	1,924.7	1,528.0	1,589.2	1,800.0	1,811.2
Net income ($ mil.)	(57.2%)	3,147.9	(297.0)	176.0	(346.5)	105.5
Market value ($ mil.)	(19.3%)	12,661	7,109.2	7,969.8	3,962.0	5,378.5
Employees	(7.5%)	4,008	2,899	3,224	3,146	2,935

VOXWARE, INC.

3705 MERCERVILLE QUAKERBRIDGE RD STE 210
TRENTON, NJ 086191288
Phone: 609 570-6800
Fax: –
Web: www.voxware.com

CEO: –
CFO: –
HR: –
FYE: June 30
Type: Private

Voxware has a hands-free approach to information management. The company makes speech recognition systems that include voice recognition software, a portable computer, and a headset microphone. The systems enables workers to enter data by voice, keeping their hands and eyes free to pick, receive, and sort materials; take inventory; and run inspections. Voxware also offers stationary systems for less mobile applications such as mail and package sorting. The company targets distribution centers and warehouses in such markets as consumer goods, grocery, logistics, and retail. Customers have included retailer 7-Eleven, vehicle glass repair specialist Belron, and U.S. Foodservice.

	Annual Growth	06/05	06/06	06/07	06/08	06/09
Sales ($mil.)	(2.9%)	–	–	15.4	23.4	14.5
Net income ($ mil.)	–	–	–	(1.9)	0.6	(4.8)
Market value ($ mil.)	–	–	–	–	–	–
Employees	–	–	–	–	–	56

VOXX INTERNATIONAL CORP
NMS: VOXX

2351 J. Lawson Boulevard
Orlando, FL 32824
Phone: 800 645-7750
Fax: –
Web: www.voxxintl.com

CEO: Patrick M Lavelle
CFO: Charles M Stoehr
HR: –
FYE: February 28
Type: Public

VOXX International is a leading international manufacturer and distributor in the automotive electronics, consumer electronics, and biometrics industries. With a portfolio of approximately 35 trusted brands, VOXX has built market-leading positions in in-vehicle entertainment, automotive security, reception products, several premium audio market segments, and more. The company counts Acoustic Research, Audiovox, Car Link, Omega, Prestige, Rosen, and Schwaiger, among its brands. VOXX is a global company, with an extensive distribution network that includes power retailers, mass merchandisers, 12-volt specialists, and many of the world's leading automotive manufacturers. Its products include HDTV and WiFi antennas, power cords, universal remotes, infant/nursery products, auto security and remote start systems, and power lift gates among others. The company generates the majority of its revenue in the US.

	Annual Growth	02/19	02/20	02/21	02/22	02/23
Sales ($mil.)	4.6%	446.8	394.9	563.6	635.9	534.0
Net income ($ mil.)	–	(46.1)	(26.4)	26.8	(22.3)	(28.6)
Market value ($ mil.)	23.0%	117.1	86.9	485.7	251.4	267.8
Employees	4.5%	885	912	921	1,082	1,055

VOYAGER DIGITAL LTD
NBB: VYGV Q

33 Irving Plaza
New York, NY 10003
Phone: 212 547-8807
Fax: –
Web: www.ucresources.net

CEO: –
CFO: –
HR: –
FYE: June 30
Type: Public

Voyager Digital is a fast-growing cryptocurrency platform in the US founded in 2018 to bring choice, transparency, and cost efficiency to the marketplace. Voyager offers a secure way to trade more than 100 different crypto assets using its easy-to-use mobile application, and earn rewards up to over 10% annually on more than 40 cryptocurrencies. Through its subsidiary Coinify ApS, Voyager provides crypto payment solutions for both consumers and merchants around the globe. Voyager filed for Chapter 11 bankruptcy protection in mid-2022.

	Annual Growth	06/17	06/18	06/19	06/20	06/21
Sales ($mil.)	–	–	–	0.0	1.1	175.1
Net income ($ mil.)	–	(0.1)	(0.2)	(30.8)	(10.2)	(51.5)
Market value ($ mil.)	229.1%	22.7	0.4	81.9	67.2	2,666.7
Employees	–	–	–	–	24	141

VOYAGER ENTERTAINMENT INTERNATIONAL INC

4483 West Reno Avenue
Las Vegas, NV 89118
Phone: 702 221-8070
Fax: –
Web: www.voyagervegas.com

CEO: –
CFO: –
HR: –
FYE: December 31
Type: Public

Voyager Entertainment International aims to have the world's tallest observation attractions. Modeled after the Ferris wheel, the Voyager attraction will consist of 30 cabs called Orbiters that hold about 20 passengers each and revolve to a height of 600 feet for a view of the surrounding area. Plans are to have Voyager attractions in Las Vegas and Dubai. The company is seeking financing and attempting to acquire proper locations in Las Vegas and Dubai.

	Annual Growth	12/06	12/07	12/08	12/09	12/10
Sales ($mil.)	–	–	–	–	–	–
Net income ($ mil.)	–	(1.9)	(2.5)	(1.2)	(1.5)	(1.1)
Market value ($ mil.)	(30.9%)	12.0	11.2	5.2	1.3	2.8
Employees	–	4	3	–	–	–

VRATSINAS CONSTRUCTION COMPANY

1 INFORMATION WAY STE 300
LITTLE ROCK, AR 722022288
Phone: 501 376-0017
Fax: –
Web: www.vccusa.com

CEO: Sam K Alley
CFO: –
HR: –
FYE: December 31
Type: Private

Malls and more -- office buildings, retail shopping centers, theater complexes, and lodging facilities -- are the focus of commercial builder Vratsinas Construction Company (VCC). The company is registered and licensed in all 50 states in the US and builds and renovates large scale commercial buildings, such as a hotel and mixed use property for Simon Property Group, shopping malls for General Growth Properties, and movie theaters for AMC Entertainment. Engineer News-Record ranks the company as one of the top 100 contractors in the US and it operates through offices in Little Rock; Irvine, California; Atlanta; Phoenix; and Dallas. Chairman and CEO Gus Vratsinas founded the company in 1987.

	Annual Growth	12/11	12/12	12/13	12/14	12/15
Sales ($mil.)	(67.3%)	–	–	2.8	0.3	0.3
Net income ($ mil.)	–	–	–	9.7	–	–
Market value ($ mil.)	–	–	–	–	–	–
Employees	–	–	–	–	–	7

VROOM AUTOMOTIVE FINANCE CORPORATION

1071 CAMELBACK ST STE 100
NEWPORT BEACH, CA 926603046
Phone: 949 224-1226
Fax: –
Web: –

CEO: James Vagim
CFO: –
HR: –
FYE: December 31
Type: Private

United PanAm Financial flies the choppy skies of nonprime lending. Through subsidiary United Auto Credit Corporation (UACC), the specialty finance firm originates, buys, and services auto loan contracts for high-risk customers. The company buys contracts from independent and franchised used car dealers. Most borrowers have less-than-perfect credit histories, which impairs their ability to secure loans. UACC, once heavily localized in California, now has more than 15 offices throughout the country -- a dramatic decrease from what it had only a few years ago. Chairman Guillermo Bron and investment firm Pine Brook Road bought United PanAm and took it private in 2011.

VROOM INC
NMS: VRM

3600 W Sam Houston Pkwy S, Floor 4
Houston, TX 77042
Phone: 518 535-9125
Fax: –
Web: www.vroom.com

CEO: Paul J Hennessy
CFO: Robert R Krakowiak
HR: –
FYE: December 31
Type: Public

Vroom is an innovative, end-to-end e-commerce platform that transforms the used vehicle industry by offering a better way to buy and a better way to sell used vehicles. The leading e-commerce used automotive retailer[1] scalable, data-driven technology brings all phases of the car buying and selling process to consumers wherever they are, and offers an extensive selection of used vehicles, transparent pricing, competitive financing, and at-home pick-up and delivery. Its platform encompasses e-commerce, vehicle operations, data science and experimentation, and vehicle financing. Among its brands are Vroom, Sell Us Your Car, CarStory, Vroom Financial Services, United Auto Credit, and Vast. The holding was incorporated in 2012.

	Annual Growth	12/19	12/20	12/21	12/22	12/23
Sales ($mil.)	(7.0%)	1,191.8	1,357.7	3,184.3	1,948.9	893.2
Net income ($ mil.)	–	(143.0)	(202.8)	(370.9)	(451.9)	(365.5)
Market value ($ mil.)	–	–	–	73.4	19.3	1.8	1.1
Employees	20.3%	800	944	1,807	1,323	1,675

VSE CORP.
NMS: VSEC

6348 Walker Lane
Alexandria, VA 22310
Phone: 703 960-4600
Fax: 703 960-2688
Web: www.vsecorp.com

CEO: John A Cuomo
CFO: Stephen D Griffin
HR: –
FYE: December 31
Type: Public

VSE Corporation is a diversified aftermarket products and services company providing repair services, parts distribution, logistics, supply chain management and consulting services for land, sea and air transportation assets for the US Government, including the US Department of Defense (DoD), and other government agencies on a contract basis. It also provides vehicle and equipment refurbishment, logistics, engineering support, data management and healthcare IT solutions, and clean energy consulting services. VSE generates almost 90% of its revenues from the US.

	Annual Growth	12/19	12/20	12/21	12/22	12/23
Sales ($mil.)	3.4%	752.6	661.7	750.9	949.8	860.5
Net income ($ mil.)	1.4%	37.0	(5.2)	8.0	28.1	39.1
Market value ($ mil.)	14.2%	599.4	606.5	960.2	738.7	1,018.1
Employees	(18.9%)	2,776	1,900	2,500	2,000	1,200

VSOFT CORPORATION

303 PERIMETER CTR N STE 250
ATLANTA, GA 303463402
Phone: 770 840-0097
Fax: –
Web: www.vsoftcorp.com

CEO: Murthy Veeraghanta
CFO: –
HR: Rachel Hoover
FYE: March 31
Type: Private

Turning real checks into virtual checks is money in the bank at VSoft Corporation. Serving primarily financial institutions, the company offers check and payment processing software and imaging technologies used to scan and change paper checks into electronic images; the images effectively replace, and are processed faster than, paper checks. VSoft offers these technologies -- teller/branch capture (for financial institution use) and remote capture products (for merchant and financial institution customer use) -- to more than 1,700 credit unions, banks, and other financial institutions around the world.

	Annual Growth	03/11	03/12	03/14	03/17	03/18
Sales ($mil.)	2.5%	–	16.4	17.6	21.3	19.0
Net income ($ mil.)	14.5%	–	0.5	0.8	0.5	1.1
Market value ($ mil.)	–	–	–	–	–	–
Employees	–	–	–	–	–	85

VTV THERAPEUTICS INC
NAS: VTVT

3980 Premier Dr, Suite 310
High Point, NC 27265
Phone: 336 841-0300
Fax: –
Web: www.vtvtherapeutics.com

CEO: Rich Nelson
CFO: Steven Tuch
HR: –
FYE: December 31
Type: Public

Clinical-stage biopharmaceutical firm vTv Therapeutics (formerly TransTech Pharma) is seeking to improve the quality of life for those suffering from a variety of health issues. Its pipeline of orally administered small molecule drug candidates includes TTP399 and TTP273, both treatments for type 2 diabetes which will soon commence phase 2 trials. Other products under development target such ailments as muscle weakness, inflammatory disorders, and cancer. Former lead drug azeliragon aims to block proteins that potentially play a role in the development of Alzheimer's disease; it failed in phase 3 clinical trials in 2018.

	Annual Growth	12/19	12/20	12/21	12/22	12/23
Sales ($mil.)	–	2.8	6.4	4.0	2.0	–
Net income ($ mil.)	–	(13.0)	(8.5)	(13.0)	(19.2)	(20.3)
Market value ($ mil.)	61.3%	4.5	5.0	2.6	1.8	30.6
Employees	(11.4%)	26	25	9	13	16

VU1 CORP

1001 Camelia Street
Berkeley, CA 94710
Phone: 855 881-2852
Fax: –
Web: www.vu1.com

CEO: –
CFO: Matthew J Devries
HR: –
FYE: December 31
Type: Public

Vu1 Corporation has a bright idea, and it takes the form of a light bulb. Parting ways with existing florescent, LED, and incandescent light bulb technologies, Vu1 (pronounced "view one") is developing a new type of light bulb that it boasts is energy efficient and mercury-free, unlike florescent lights, which contain trace amounts of the element. Its proprietary technology, Electron Stimulated Luminescence, or ESL, uses cathode ray tube (CRT) technologies to produce light. (CRTs were commonly used in older-style TVs). In 2010, Vu1 received UL certification for its first product, a R30 floodlight-style bulb for use in recessed ceiling lighting, and subsequently began selling the bulb in the US.

	Annual Growth	12/10	12/11	12/12	12/13	12/14
Sales ($mil.)	–	–	0.0	–	–	–
Net income ($ mil.)	–	(4.6)	(9.1)	(3.8)	(5.0)	(3.0)
Market value ($ mil.)	16.6%	7.7	61.4	8.4	14.5	14.2
Employees	–	38	75	–	–	–

VULCAN INTERNATIONAL CORP.   NBB: VULC

300 Delaware Ave, Suite 1704
Wilmington, DE 19801
Phone: 302 427-5804
Fax: –
Web: –

CEO: Benjamin Gettler
CFO: –
HR: –
FYE: December 31
Type: Public

It would be logical for Star Trek's Mr. Spock to contact Vulcan International for rubber material. The company operates through four subsidiaries, one of them, Vulcan Corp., manufactures rubber and foam. Its lineup includes rubber sheet stock for US shoemakers (a large customer), flooring for sports centers, backing for car mats, and various high-density foam products. A property management subsidiary oversees the company's commercial property, three office buildings in Cincinnati. Thousands of acres of Michigan timberland are under the watch of Vulcan Timberlands. Vulcan Development manages the company's eclectic asset mix. Chairman Benjamin Gettler and his wife are major corporate stakeholders.

	Annual Growth	12/00	12/01	12/02	12/03	12/04
Sales ($mil.)	(2.7%)	11.2	10.7	11.3	12.6	10.1
Net income ($ mil.)	14.8%	1.8	2.9	2.2	2.5	3.1
Market value ($ mil.)	8.1%	33.9	39.6	34.5	43.0	46.4
Employees	–	–	73	67	66	68

VULCAN MATERIALS CO (HOLDING COMPANY)   NYS: VMC

1200 Urban Center Drive
Birmingham, AL 35242
Phone: 205 298-3000
Fax: 205 298-2963
Web: www.vulcanmaterials.com

CEO: J T Hill
CFO: Suzanne H Wood
HR: Alice Barley
FYE: December 31
Type: Public

Vulcan Materials Company (Vulcan) is one of the largest producers of construction aggregates in the US. Vulcan produces and distributes aggregates (crushed stone, gravel, and sand), asphalt mix, calcium, and ready-mixed concrete from more than 400 active aggregate facilities, some 70 asphalt facilities, and more than 140 concrete facilities in nine states, as well as the U.S. Virgin Islands, and Washington D.C. Its aggregates are primarily used in the construction and maintenance of highways, streets and other public works and in the construction of housing and commercial, industrial and other nonresidential facilities. The company has 15.6 billion tons of proven and probable aggregate reserves. The company generates around 45% of its revenue from its gulf coast markets.

	Annual Growth	12/19	12/20	12/21	12/22	12/23
Sales ($mil.)	12.1%	4,929.1	4,856.8	5,552.2	7,315.2	7,781.9
Net income ($ mil.)	10.9%	617.7	584.5	670.8	575.6	933.2
Market value ($ mil.)	12.1%	19,021	19,592	27,421	23,132	29,988
Employees	–	9,173	8,431	11,437	11,397	–

VUZIX CORP   NAS: VUZI

25 Hendrix Road
West Henrietta, NY 14586
Phone: 585 359-5900
Fax: –
Web: www.vuzix.com

CEO: Paul J Travers
CFO: Grant Russell
HR: –
FYE: December 31
Type: Public

Virtual reality is in the eye of the beholder. Or in Vuzix's case, the eyewear of the beholder. The company designs, manufactures, and sells video eyewear that simulates viewing a large-screen TV or computer monitor. Its products are used to view high-resolution video and digital information from mobile devices, such as cell phones, laptops, and media players. These wearable devices are marketed to consumers (gaming enthusiasts in particular), as well as defense and industrial markets, which account for about half of its revenues. Military products include personal head-mounted displays for night-vision applications. Founded in 1997, Vuzix went public in late 2009.

	Annual Growth	12/18	12/19	12/20	12/21	12/22
Sales ($mil.)	10.0%	8.1	6.7	11.6	13.2	11.8
Net income ($ mil.)	–	(21.9)	(26.5)	(18.0)	(40.4)	(40.8)
Market value ($ mil.)	(6.7%)	304.6	127.3	574.9	549.0	230.5
Employees	7.0%	80	92	101	106	105

VWR CORPORATION

100 W MATSONFORD RD STE 1
RADNOR, PA 190874565
Phone: 610 386-1700
Fax: –
Web: www.avantorsciences.com

CEO: Michael Stubblefield
CFO: Gregory L Cowan
HR: Eric McAllister
FYE: December 31
Type: Private

VWR Corporation, through principal operating subsidiary VWR International, is a global distributor of scientific and technical laboratory supplies, including chemicals, glassware, instruments, protective clothing, and production supplies. The company also provides technical services, on-site storeroom services, lab and furniture design and installation, and supply chain services. With operations in approximately 30 countries, its primary customers are North American and European research labs within pharmaceutical, biotech, and chemical companies; government agencies; and universities and research institutes. VWR operates as a wholly-owned subsidiary of US life sciences company Avantor.

VYANT BIO INC   NAS: VYNT

2 Executive Campus, 2370 State Route 70, Ste 310
Cherry Hill, NJ 08002
Phone: 201 479-1357
Fax: –
Web: www.vyantbio.com

CEO: John A Roberts
CFO: Andrew D Lafrence
HR: –
FYE: December 31
Type: Public

Cancer Genetics, Inc. (CGI) takes a personalized approach to diagnosing leukemia. The company developed a DNA-based genomic test to identify chronic lymphocytic leukemia in patients. Called MatBA-CLL, the microarray test can improve the diagnosis, prognosis, and response to treatment. CGI's lab in New Jersey caters to area hospitals, cancer centers, reference laboratories, and doctors' offices. It also has a pipeline of other genomic tests for hematological, urogenital (kidney, prostate and bladder cancer), and HPV-associated cancers that are complicated to predict. In late 2018 the company dropped its plans to merge with Israeli functional genomics firm NovellusDx; it is now exploring its strategic options including a possible sale. CGI was founded in 1999 by Chairman Dr. Raju Chaganti.

	Annual Growth	12/18	12/19	12/20	12/21	12/22
Sales ($mil.)	(60.5%)	27.5	7.3	5.8	1.1	0.7
Net income ($ mil.)	–	(20.4)	(6.7)	(8.0)	(40.9)	(22.7)
Market value ($ mil.)	30.5%	1.4	35.3	16.4	8.0	4.2
Employees	(53.3%)	168	110	40	72	8

VYDROTECH INC   NBB: VYDR

VydroTech, Inc., 8140 Walnut Hill Lane, Suite 925
Dallas, TX 75231
Phone: 214 593-6919
Fax: –
Web: www.vydrotech.com

CEO: Don Navarro
CFO: –
HR: –
FYE: December 31
Type: Public

VydroTech (formerly Ronn Motor Company) is seeing green when it comes to automotive design and manufacturing. The company manufactures green-oriented hydrogen injection technology for engines used in both transportation and fixed platforms. Its products are installed in large diesel trucks (18-wheelers), barges, tugboats, and large land-based diesel generators. They help clients be compliant with government regulations and reduce diesel fuel costs and the amount of harmful gas emissions. In order to reflect its specific product focus, the former Ronn Motor Company changed its name to VydroTech in 2012. Its new name stems from the first few letters in the phrase "visionary hydrogen technology."

VYSTAR CORP
NBB: VYST

725 Southbridge St
Worcester, MA 01610
Phone: 508 791-9114
Fax: 770 965-0162
Web: www.vytex.com

CEO: Steven Rotman
CFO: Steven Rotman
HR: -
FYE: December 31
Type: Public

Vystar is vying to be a health care star. The company makes Vytex, a natural rubber latex product that retains the positive properties of latex (strength, comfort, availability, good barrier) without producing the allergic reaction that plagues about 20% of health care workers and more than 70% of patients. Vytex is used in health care supplies including surgical and exam gloves, probe covers, catheters, tubing, and adhesives. Other uses include sponges, balloons, condoms, threads, and mattresses. Vystar's goods are made by Revertex Malaysia. In 2012 Vystar entered the sleep disorder market by acquiring Georgia-based SleepHealth. Vystar plans to market its foam bedding products through the company.

	Annual Growth	12/18	12/19	12/20	12/21	12/22
Sales ($mil.)	(23.6%)	0.3	13.7	21.0	27.6	0.1
Net income ($ mil.)	-	(5.4)	(7.7)	(7.6)	(2.7)	(4.0)
Market value ($ mil.)	224.3%	0.0	0.1	0.4	0.1	1.6
Employees	-	1	3	1	1	-

W & T OFFSHORE INC
NYS: WTI

5718 Westheimer Road, Suite 700
Houston, TX 77057-5745
Phone: 713 626-8525
Fax: 713 626-8527
Web: www.wtoffshore.com

CEO: Tracy W Krohn
CFO: Janet Yang
HR: Beth Cornwell
FYE: December 31
Type: Public

W&T Offshore (W&T) is an independent oil and natural gas company engages in acquisition, exploration, development, and production of oil and natural gas properties in the Gulf of Mexico. With more than 456,800 gross acres under company lease, W&T has working interests in more than 45 producing fields in federal and state waters. It reports proved reserves of approximately 110.3 million barrels of oil equivalent. W&T was founded in 1983 by the Chairman and CEO Tracy Krohn.

	Annual Growth	12/19	12/20	12/21	12/22	12/23
Sales ($mil.)	(0.1%)	534.9	346.6	558.0	921.0	532.7
Net income ($ mil.)	(32.3%)	74.1	37.8	(41.5)	231.1	15.6
Market value ($ mil.)	(12.5%)	815.0	318.1	473.5	817.9	477.9
Employees	7.9%	291	303	323	365	395

W WORLD CORP
NBB: WWHC

530 5th Ave, 9th Floor
New York, NY 10036
Phone: 212 999-7909
Fax: -
Web: www.wworldusa.com

CEO: Robert F Johnston
CFO: S C Neill
HR: -
FYE: December 31
Type: Public

Drug developer Pharmos has focused its attention on the central nervous system. Its stable of drug candidates aim to treat conditions such as pain, inflammation, and autoimmune conditions. It gained its lead candidate dextofisopam when it acquired Vela Pharmaceuticals; the compound is a potential treatment for irritable bowel syndrome, a condition associated with the "brain-gut axis," or the connection between the nervous system and the intestines. Pharmos has also discovered several compounds in-house using its expertise in cannabinoid compounds (the kind without psychotropic effects). It is investigating several such compounds as treatments for pain and inflammation.

	Annual Growth	12/10	12/11	12/19	12/20	12/21
Sales ($mil.)	-	-	-	-	-	-
Net income ($ mil.)	-	(1.5)	(2.0)	(0.0)	(2.6)	(0.0)
Market value ($ mil.)	37.5%	9.3	5.0	0.8	200.6	310.9
Employees	-	2	2	-	-	-

W. C. BRADLEY CO.

1017 FRONT AVE
COLUMBUS, GA 319015260
Phone: 706 571-7000
Fax: -
Web: www.wcbradley.com

CEO: -
CFO: -
HR: -
FYE: December 31
Type: Private

Without the airy outdoors, W.C. Bradley would suffocate. The company's Char-Broil division is a leading maker of outdoor barbecue gas and electric grills. In addition, W.C. Bradley makes Thermos-brand grills; Lamplight Farms oil lamps, Tiki torches, and scented candles; and Lew's, Martin, Quantum, Van Staal, and Zebco fishing gear. The company's wares are sold to major retailers worldwide, including Sears, Roebuck, Home Depot, Kmart, and Wal-Mart, and through its own web sites. The company also ran a PGA Tour Stop shop in Florida until 2013. Founded in 1885 by William C. Bradley, the company is run by the family's fourth generation; chairman Steve Butler is the nephew of Bradley's grandson.

W. E. AUBUCHON CO., INC.

95 AUBUCHON DR
WESTMINSTER, MA 014731470
Phone: 978 874-0521
Fax: -
Web: www.acehardware.com

CEO: William E Aubuchon IV
CFO: Jeffrey M Aubuchon
HR: Daniel Aubuchon
FYE: December 31
Type: Private

Old houses in New England get a facelift with assistance from W.E. Aubuchon. The company operates more than 125 hardware stores throughout New England and New York, as well as e-commerce site HardwareStore.com and in-store kiosks. Stores stock about 50,000 products, including appliances, plumbing, camping gear, hardware, housewares, paint, and tools. W.E. Aubuchon carries such name brands as Delta Faucet, Honeywell, Stanley, and Weber. Store services include rug cleaner rentals, propane tank filling, free assembling and delivery, and key cutting, among many other services. Founded in 1908 by William Aubuchon, a French-Canadian immigrant, the company is still owned by the Aubuchon family.

	Annual Growth	12/11	12/12	12/13	12/14	12/15
Sales ($mil.)	4.3%	-	-	146.3	154.4	159.2
Net income ($ mil.)	-	-	-	(3.3)	1.9	2.7
Market value ($ mil.)	-	-	-	-	-	-
Employees	-	-	-	-	-	1,517

W. K. KELLOGG FOUNDATION

1 MICHIGAN AVE E
BATTLE CREEK, MI 490174012
Phone: 269 968-1611
Fax: -
Web: www.wkkf.org

CEO: Sterling K Speirn
CFO: -
HR: -
FYE: August 31
Type: Private

Charitable grants from W.K. Kellogg Foundation are grrrrrrrrreat! Founded in 1930 by cereal industry pioneer Will Keith Kellogg, the foundation provides more than $300 million in grants annually to programs focused on youth and education, health, food systems and rural development, and philanthropy and volunteerism. About two-thirds of its grants go to initiatives in the US (mostly in Michigan, Mississippi, and New Mexico), although it also serves others through grants in Latin America, Mexico, the Caribbean, Brazil, and South Africa. The work of the W.K. Kellogg Foundation is supported by a related trust; together they have assets of more than $9 billion -- mainly in Kellogg Company stock.

	Annual Growth	08/14	08/15	08/16	08/21	08/22
Sales ($mil.)	1.8%	-	350.9	404.3	669.8	396.2
Net income ($ mil.)	-	-	(5.9)	(75.7)	98.1	29.8
Market value ($ mil.)	-	-	-	-	-	-
Employees	-	-	-	-	-	200

W. L. BUTLER CONSTRUCTION, INC.

1629 MAIN ST
REDWOOD CITY, CA 940632121
Phone: 650 361-1270
Fax: –
Web: www.wlbutler.com

CEO: –
CFO: –
HR: –
FYE: December 31
Type: Private

W. L. Butler Construction is building up its reputation in the western region. The general contractor caters to customers needing commercial and light industrial construction services in Arizona, California, Colorado, Idaho, Montana, Nevada, and Washington. W. L. Butler Construction also has the capability to complete electrical and HVAC services. Projects include car dealerships, retail centers, medical offices, industrial warehouses, corporate headquarters, and not-for-profit facilities. Commercial clients include Aetna Life Insurance, Cisco Systems, Home Depot, Target, and Walgreen's. W. L. Butler Construction was founded in 1975 by CEO William Butler as a residential remodeling contracting operation.

W. M. KECK FOUNDATION

515 S FLOWER ST STE 800
LOS ANGELES, CA 900712240
Phone: 213 680-3833
Fax: –
Web: www.wmkeck.org

CEO: –
CFO: –
HR: –
FYE: December 31
Type: Private

The W. M. Keck Foundation offers grants to research, education, and civic institutions, primarily in the areas of medical research, science, and engineering. Established by William Myron Keck (founder of Superior Oil Company) in 1954, the foundation's assets now exceed $1 billion dollars. The foundation has established five broad grant areas: Liberal Arts, Medical Research, Science and Engineering Research, Southern California, and Undergraduate Science and Engineering. The Southern California program offers support in the areas of civic and community services, healthcare, education, and the arts.

	Annual Growth	12/13	12/14	12/15	12/21	12/22
Assets ($mil.)	1.3%	–	1,234.4	1,122.7	1,878.6	1,370.4
Net income ($ mil.)	–	–	8.1	29.3	33.3	(25.6)
Market value ($ mil.)	–	–	–	–	–	–
Employees	–	–	–	–	–	23

W. R. GRACE & CO.

7500 GRACE DR
COLUMBIA, MD 210444029
Phone: 410 531-4000
Fax: –
Web: www.grace.com

CEO: Hudson L Force
CFO: William C Dockman
HR: Deb McIntyre
FYE: December 31
Type: Private

W. R. Grace & Co. (Grace), a Standard Industries company, is a leading global supplier of catalysts, engineered materials, and fine chemicals. The company's two industry-leading business segments?Catalysts Technologies and Materials Technologies?provide innovative products, technologies, and services that enhance the products and processes of its customers around the world. The company serves the world's leading energy, petrochemical, and industrial companies, including some of the most respected Fortune 500 companies. Founded in 1854, Grace sells its products to more than 100 countries.

	Annual Growth	12/18	12/19	12/20	12/21	12/22
Sales ($mil.)	(92.0%)	–	1,958.1	–	1.0	1.0
Net income ($ mil.)	–	–	126.7	–	0.2	(0.2)
Market value ($ mil.)	–	–	–	–	–	–
Employees	–	–	–	–	–	4,000

W. THOMAS CO.

531 CANAL ST STE 201
READING, PA 196022631
Phone: 610 372-9765
Fax: –
Web: www.billskhakis.com

CEO: –
CFO: –
HR: –
FYE: December 31
Type: Private

Talk about retro-fitting: Bills Khakis fit the bill when you're looking for trousers like Grandpa brought back from the war. The company, headquartered in a refurbished Rust Belt factory, makes all of its premium khaki pants, five-pocket jeans, corduroys, seersucker pants, shorts, shirts, headwear, and other apparel in the US. Products are distributed through men's and women's clothing stores, including Nordstrom and specialty shops, as well as the company's Web site. Limited edition products are issued annually while retired items are "archived." CEO Bill Thomas founded the company when he could no longer find the WWII army surplus khakis that he loved.

	Annual Growth	12/06	12/07	12/08	12/09	12/10
Sales ($mil.)	(90.4%)	–	–	976.9	7.7	9.0
Net income ($ mil.)	11526.7%	–	–	0.0	0.0	0.1
Market value ($ mil.)	–	–	–	–	–	–
Employees	–	–	–	–	–	29

W.J. DEUTSCH & SONS LTD.

201 TRESSER BLVD STE 500
STAMFORD, CT 069013435
Phone: 203 965-4100
Fax: –
Web: www.deutschfamily.com

CEO: William J Deutsch
CFO: –
HR: –
FYE: December 31
Type: Private

W.J. Deutsch and Sons distributes wine throughout the US that it imports from privately owned vineyards in Australia, France, Italy, New Zealand, Portugal, and Spain. The company is noted for importing Yellow Tail-brand wine, made by Australia's Casella Estates. The brand is considered to be one of the best-selling labels imported into the US. W.J. Deutsch and Sons is also co-owner and exclusive importer of Spain's Diego Samora wines. As part of its portfolio, the distributor also offers US-made wines, mainly from California. Due to steady growth, the company restructured itself in recent years into two sales zones: eastern and western. Family-owned and -operated, W.J. Deutsch was founded in 1981.

	Annual Growth	12/98	12/99	12/00	12/08	12/12
Sales ($mil.)	(18.3%)	–	34.4	–	–	2.5
Net income ($ mil.)	–	–	–	–	–	2.3
Market value ($ mil.)	–	–	–	–	–	–
Employees	–	–	–	–	–	220

W.M. JORDAN COMPANY, INCORPORATED

11010 JEFFERSON AVE
NEWPORT NEWS, VA 236012717
Phone: 757 596-6341
Fax: –
Web: www.wmjordan.com

CEO: John R Lawson
CFO: –
HR: –
FYE: December 31
Type: Private

W.M. Jordan Company has built a reputation as being a top construction company on the Atlantic Seaboard. The company provides construction management, preconstruction, design/build, and general contracting services in Virginia. The company's projects include new construction, renovations, additions, and expansions to commercial, educational, cultural, health care, municipal, and industrial facilities. W.M Jordan has completed projects for clients such as Gateway, SunTrust, and the US Navy. It operates from its Virginia offices located in Newport News and Richmond. Robert T. Lawson and William M. Jordan founded the company in 1958. The Lawson family still control and manage the company.

W.P. CAREY INC

NYS: WPC

One Manhattan West, 395 9th Avenue, 58th Floor
New York, NY 10001
Phone: 212 492-1100
Fax: –
Web: www.wpcarey.com

CEO: –
CFO: –
HR: –
FYE: December 31
Type: Public

Need help managing your property portfolio? Keep calm and Carey on. W. P. Carey invests in and manages commercial real estate, including office, distribution, retail, and industrial facilities. The company owns more than 1,000 properties mainly in the US and Europe, and manages properties for several non-traded real estate investment trusts (REITs). Its management portfolio totals some $15 billion. W. P. Carey typically acquires properties and then leases them back to the sellers/occupants on a long-term basis. It also provides build-to-suit financing for investors worldwide. W. P. Carey is converting to a REIT, a corporate structure that comes with tax benefits and more flexibilty in investing in real estate.

	Annual Growth	12/19	12/20	12/21	12/22	12/23
Sales ($mil.)	9.0%	1,232.8	1,209.3	1,331.5	1,479.1	1,741.4
Net income ($ mil.)	23.4%	305.2	455.4	410.0	599.1	708.3
Market value ($ mil.)	(5.1%)	17,502	15,434	17,942	17,089	14,172
Employees	(0.9%)	204	188	183	193	197

W.S. BADCOCK LLC

200 NW PHOSPHATE BLVD
MULBERRY, FL 338602328
Phone: 863 425-4921
Fax: –
Web: www.badcock.com

CEO: –
CFO: Thomas Gieseking
HR: Andrea Huggins
FYE: June 30
Type: Private

W.S. Badcock furnishes homes down in Dixie and beyond. As one of the largest privately-owned furniture retailers in the US, the company sells furniture for every room in the house. It sells its furniture and accessories through more than 300 stores that operate under the banner names Badcock Home Furnishing Centers and Badcock &more. Aside from its e-commerce site, Badcock's stores network extends to nearly 10 southeastern states. Stores also carry appliances, lawn equipment, electronics, mattresses, rugs, bedding, lighting, wall art, and other decorative accessories. The company was founded by Henry S. Badcock in 1904 as a general mercantile store. Today it is in its fourth generation of family management.

WABASH COLLEGE

301 W WABASH AVE
CRAWFORDSVILLE, IN 479332484
Phone: 765 361-6100
Fax: –
Web: www.wabash.edu

CEO: –
CFO: Larry Griffith
HR: –
FYE: June 30
Type: Private

Wabash College is a private, all-male liberal arts school that confers Bachelor of Arts degrees in 22 majors. Engineering programs are offered in conjunction with Purdue University, Washington University in St. Louis, and Columbia University. Other programs range from art and biochemistry to Latin and philosophy, as well as economics, music, psychology, and religion. With an enrollment of about 900 students, Wabash College is an independent and non-sectarian college founded in 1832. The school is one of the few remaining all-male colleges in the US.

	Annual Growth	06/14	06/15	06/16	06/21	06/22
Sales ($mil.)	4.0%	–	71.6	58.3	85.4	93.9
Net income ($ mil.)	12.8%	–	2.9	(12.1)	2.7	6.7
Market value ($ mil.)	–	–	–	–	–	–
Employees		–	–	–	–	225

WABASH COUNTY HOSPITAL

710 N EAST ST
WABASH, IN 469921924
Phone: 260 563-3131
Fax: –
Web: www.wchospital.com

CEO: –
CFO: –
HR: –
FYE: December 31
Type: Private

Wabash County Hospital is a small community hospital with 25 beds and offers patients a range of services including cancer treatment; cardiac and pulmonary rehabilitation; critical and acute care; and general, laparoscopic, and orthopedic surgery. The facility also provides hospice and home health care programs, occupational health services, and emergency medicine.

	Annual Growth	12/04	12/05	12/08	12/09	12/12
Sales ($mil.)	1.6%	–	31.4	32.0	32.9	35.1
Net income ($ mil.)	(24.8%)	–	4.0	0.2	(0.1)	0.5
Market value ($ mil.)	–	–	–	–	–	–
Employees	–	–	–	–	–	375

WABASH NATIONAL CORP

NYS: WNC

3900 McCarty Lane
Lafayette, IN 47905
Phone: 765 771-5310
Fax: –
Web: www.wabashnational.com

CEO: Brent L Yeagy
CFO: Mike Pettit
HR: Ron Pitrelli
FYE: December 31
Type: Public

Wabash National makes dry freight and refrigerated vans, flatbed and drop deck trailers, and intermodal equipment. Trailers are marketed under such brands as DuraPlate and ArcticLite through network of factory-direct sales representatives and independent dealers. Customers have included Averitt Express, FedEx, and Swift. The company also makes stainless steel and aluminum tank trailers for liquid transport and engineered stainless steel tanks for use in the food, beverage, pharmaceutical, and chemical industries. Additional products include composite panels used in truck bodies, and containment and isolation systems for the pharmaceutical, chemical, and nuclear industries.

	Annual Growth	12/19	12/20	12/21	12/22	12/23
Sales ($mil.)	2.3%	2,319.1	1,481.9	1,803.3	2,502.1	2,536.5
Net income ($ mil.)	26.8%	89.6	(97.4)	1.2	112.3	231.3
Market value ($ mil.)	14.9%	666.8	782.1	886.1	1,025.9	1,163.0
Employees	(0.7%)	6,900	5,800	6,200	6,900	6,700

WABASH POWER EQUIPMENT CO.

444 CARPENTER AVE
WHEELING, IL 600906014
Phone: 847 541-5600
Fax: –
Web: www.wabashpower.com

CEO: –
CFO: David Goldstein
HR: –
FYE: December 31
Type: Private

The "mighty rush of engine" you hear is not that of the Wabash Cannonball , but the muscle machines of Wabash Power Equipment. The company leases and sells new and reconditioned power generation and boiler equipment for primarily industrial use. Operating from warehouses in the Midwest US, Wabash Power Equipment carries a giant inventory of diesel generators, gas turbine generators, firetub boilers, watertube boilers, pulverizers and mils, and associated parts. It has served domestic and international customers for more than a half a century, from Abbot Laboratories to FMC Corporation, Miller Brewing Company, Mitsubishi Industries, and Union Carbide. The company is led by its founder's son, Richard Caitung.

WABCO HOLDINGS INC.

1220 PACIFIC DR
AUBURN HILLS, MI 483261589
Phone: 248 260-9032
Fax: –
Web: www.zf.com

CEO: Jon Morrison
CFO: Shiva Narayanaswami
HR: Barbara Fischer
FYE: December 31
Type: Private

WABCO is the leading global supplier of braking control systems and other advanced technologies that improve the safety, efficiency and connectivity of commercial vehicles. It is continuously innovating and investing to deliver the key enabling technologies that will fully leverage the 'increasing intelligence' of commercial vehicles, creating a safer environment for all road users and providing ever-more productive fleet applications. In 2020, WABCO was bought by German driveline and chassis company ZF Friedrichshafen for over $7 billion. It will now operate under the ZF brand as its new Commercial Vehicle Control Systems division.

WADA FARMS MARKETING GROUP LLC

2155 PROVIDENCE WAY
IDAHO FALLS, ID 834044951
Phone: 208 542-2898
Fax: –
Web: www.wadafarms.com

CEO: Bryan Wada
CFO: –
HR: –
FYE: December 31
Type: Private

The Wada Farms folk grow, pack, and supply Idaho potatoes all of us meat-and-potatoes folks. And, in addition to everyone's favorite starchy tuber, Wada Farms does the same with sweet potatoes and onions. It also offers value-added items such as Easy-Bakers and Easy-Steamers -- potatoes packaged in special plastic that can be cooked right in their packaging. The company cultivates more than 30,000 acres of farmland and operates a 140,000-sq.-ft. processing facility; its customers include retail, wholesaler, and foodservice companies across the US. Wada Farms was founded in 1943 by Frank Wada, whose family moved inland during WWII to avoid the internment imposed on Japanese-Americans on the West Coast.

	Annual Growth	12/08	12/09	12/10	12/11	12/12
Sales ($mil.)	4.8%	–	–	150.9	201.7	165.8
Net income ($ mil.)	13.4%	–	–	1.5	2.0	1.9
Market value ($ mil.)	–	–	–	–	–	–
Employees	–	–	–	–	–	39

WADLEY REGIONAL MEDICAL CENTER

1000 PINE ST
TEXARKANA, TX 755015100
Phone: 903 798-8000
Fax: –
Web: www.wadleyhealth.org

CEO: Thomas Gilbert
CFO: –
HR: Amanda Bauer
FYE: December 31
Type: Private

Wadley Regional Medical Center is a general hospital serving patients from the Ark-La-Tex region -- that is, Arkansas, Louisiana, and Texas. It also offers in-patient geriatric behavioral health, cancer treatment, cardiac rehabilitation, and surgical services. The center, founded in 1900, has about 370 beds and operates clinics dedicated to areas such as pediatric care and women's health. Citing lower patient counts, the hospital filed for Chapter 11 bankruptcy protection in early 2009 but was quickly purchased by hospital management firm Brim Holdings. In 2010, however, Brim Holdings and Wadley Regional were acquired by hospital operator IASIS Healthcare.

	Annual Growth	12/13	12/14	12/15*	04/21*	12/21
Sales ($mil.)	(4.2%)	–	116.6	129.0	0.0	86.5
Net income ($ mil.)	–	–	(0.2)	10.7	0.0	(4.3)
Market value ($ mil.)	–	–	–	–	–	–
Employees	–	–	–	–	–	1,285

*Fiscal year change

WAFD INC

NMS: WAFD

425 Pike Street
Seattle, WA 98101
Phone: 206 624-7930
Fax: –
Web: www.wafdbank.com

CEO: –
CFO: –
HR: –
FYE: September 30
Type: Public

Washington Federal is the holding company for Washington Federal Bank, which operates about 220 branches in eight western states. The company, which was founded in 1917, engages primarily in providing lending, depository, insurance and other banking services to consumers, mid-sized to large businesses, and owners and developers of commercial real estate. Commercial loans account for more than 60% of its loan portfolio. The bank also writes business, consumer, construction, land, and multifamily residential loans.

	Annual Growth	09/19	09/20	09/21	09/22	09/23
Assets ($mil.)	8.1%	16,475	18,794	19,651	20,772	22,475
Net income ($ mil.)	5.2%	210.3	173.4	183.6	236.3	257.4
Market value ($ mil.)	(8.8%)	2,394.6	1,350.4	2,221.1	1,940.8	1,658.6
Employees	1.8%	1,971	2,080	2,082	2,132	2,120

WAGNER INDUSTRIES, LLC

1201 E 12TH AVE
NORTH KANSAS CITY, MO 641164306
Phone: 816 421-3520
Fax: –
Web: www.wagnerlogistics.com

CEO: Brian Smith
CFO: –
HR: –
FYE: December 31
Type: Private

When freight needs to stop between origin and destination, Wagner Industries can offer the hospitality of its distribution facilities. The company maintains about 4 million sq. ft. of warehouse space, largely in the Kansas City metropolitan area but also in several states in the southeastern and western US. Overall, the company operates a dozen distribution centers. In addition to warehousing and distribution, Wagner Industries offers packaging and transportation management services. Customers include companies from the consumer products, paper, and retail industries. Owned by the Wagner family, including company president John Wagner Jr., Wagner Industries was founded in 1946.

	Annual Growth	12/04	12/05	12/06	12/07	12/08
Sales ($mil.)	(8.3%)	–	58.7	51.4	52.0	45.2
Net income ($ mil.)	–	–	1.0	0.3	40.8	(0.3)
Market value ($ mil.)	–	–	–	–	–	–
Employees	–	–	–	–	–	500

WAHL CLIPPER CORPORATION

2900 LOCUST ST
STERLING, IL 610819500
Phone: 815 625-6525
Fax: –
Web: us.wahl.com

CEO: John Wahl
CFO: Scott Hamilton
HR: –
FYE: December 31
Type: Private

Wahl Clipper Corporation has been the leader in the hair grooming industry. It makes and markets electric hair clippers, massagers, beard trimmers, and other accessories. The grooming products giant also operates four operating divisions: Professional, Home Use, Professional Animal, and Home Pet. Wahl products are available all over the world and sells its products through authorized retailers and wholesalers. With six global manufacturing facilities as well as about 10 sales offices, its products are sold in approximately 165 countries worldwide. The world leader in the manufacture and distribution of professional and consumer clippers, trimmers, shavers, and personal care devices was founded in 1919 by Leo J. Wahl.

WAKE FOREST UNIVERSITY

1834 WAKE FOREST RD # 7326
WINSTON SALEM, NC 271096054
Phone: 336 758-5000
Fax: –
Web: www.wfu.edu

CEO: Eugene A Woods
CFO: Jacqueline Travisano
HR: –
FYE: June 30
Type: Private

Wake Forest University (WFU), home of the Demon Deacon mascot, is a private liberal arts institution that operates through six colleges and schools: law, medicine, arts and sciences, business and accountancy, management, and divinity. WFU provides more than 50 majors and some 60 minors and offers a low student-faculty ratio of 11:1. Its around 8,965 students can also study abroad in France, Spain, Japan, and Cuba, among other countries. The university has over 250 student organizations. WFU was established in 1834 in Wake Forest, North Carolina. It moved to its present location in Winston-Salem in 1956.

WAKE FOREST UNIVERSITY BAPTIST MEDICAL CENTER

MEDICAL CENTER BLVD
WINSTON SALEM, NC 271570001
Phone: 336 716-2011
Fax: –
Web: www.wakehealth.edu

CEO: –
CFO: –
HR: –
FYE: June 30
Type: Private

Wake Forest Baptist Medical Center (formerly Wake Forest University Baptist Medical Center) promotes health in the thick of tobacco country. The not-for-profit system operates Wake Forest University Health Sciences with its School of Medicine, Wake Forest University Physicians, 16 dialysis centers, and Piedmont Triad Research Park. It also operates the North Carolina Baptist Hospital, with facilities devoted to geriatrics, cancer, pediatrics, and more. The system has about 20 subsidiary or affiliate hospitals and operates about 120 regional outreach activities from satellite clinics to health fairs. Wake Forest Baptist offers rehab, skilled nursing, and home health services; it also has a unit that coordinates special services for international patients.

WAKEFERN FOOD CORP.

5000 RIVERSIDE DR
KEASBEY, NJ 088321209
Phone: 908 527-3300
Fax: –
Web: www.wakefern.com

CEO: Joseph Colalillo
CFO: Douglas Wille
HR: Pat Durning
FYE: September 27
Type: Private

Wakefern Food is the largest retailer-owned cooperative in the nation with approximately 50 member companies who independently own and operate more than 360 supermarkets across the northeastern US. The members of the Wakefern cooperative benefit from the company's purchasing power of more than $10 billion and unmatched support services, including private label brand development, advertising support, category management, engineering services, store quality assurance and inspections, health and wellness services, marketing, retail store development, pharmacy support services, and media and public relations. The members' stores operate under the Fairway Market, ShopRite, The Fresh Grocer, Price Rite Marketplace, Gourmet Garage, and Dearborn Market banners. Wakefern was founded by eight independent grocers in 1946.

	Annual Growth	09/10	09/11	09/12	09/13	09/14
Sales ($mil.)	3.8%	–	–	11,010	11,456	11,871
Net income ($ mil.)	–	–	–	5.0	0.0	5.0
Market value ($ mil.)	–	–	–	–	–	–
Employees	–	–	–	–	–	3,500

WAKEMED

3000 NEW BERN AVE STE G100
RALEIGH, NC 276101231
Phone: 919 350-8000
Fax: –
Web: www.wakemed.org

CEO: Donald R Gintzig
CFO: Michael D Vaughn
HR: Lisa Lassiter
FYE: September 30
Type: Private

WakeMed is a not-for-profit health care system founded in 1961. WakeMed's 970-bed system comprises a network of facilities throughout the Triangle area, including three full-service hospitals, emergency departments, a dedicated Children's Hospital and Rehabilitation Hospital, more than 90 physician offices and Wake County's only Level I Trauma Center. It also has three healthplexes with stand-alone, 24/7 emergency departments and a variety of outpatient services throughout the region. Raleigh Campus is WakeMed's flagship facility and leading provider of advanced health care services. Raleigh Campus also features some of the most advanced pathology laboratories, imaging technology, and surgical technology available.

	Annual Growth	09/13	09/14	09/15	09/21	09/22
Sales ($mil.)	8.7%	–	–	1,065.2	1,481.7	1,905.9
Net income ($ mil.)	–	–	–	(33.0)	34.7	(1.8)
Market value ($ mil.)	–	–	–	–	–	–
Employees	–	–	–	–	–	16,933

WALGREENS BOOTS ALLIANCE INC   NMS: WBA

108 Wilmot Road
Deerfield, IL 60015
Phone: 847 315-3700
Fax: –
Web: www.walgreensbootsalliance.com

CEO: Timothy C Wentworth
CFO: Manmohan Mahajan
HR: –
FYE: August 31
Type: Public

Walgreens Boots Alliance is an integrated healthcare, pharmacy and retail leader serving millions of customers and patients every day. The company is one of the world's largest purchasers of prescription drugs and many other health and well-being products. It is the largest retail pharmacy, health and daily living destination across the US and Europe. The company provides customers with convenient, omni-channel access through its portfolio of retail and business brands which includes Walgreens, Boots and Duane Reade as well as increasingly global health and beauty product brands, such as No7, NICE!, Soap & Glory, Finest Nutrition, Liz Earle, Botanics, Sleek MakeUP and YourGoodSkin. The company's global brands portfolio is enhanced by its in-house product research and development capabilities. Additionally, the company has a portfolio of healthcare-focused investments located in several countries, including in the US and China. With approximately 13,000 locations across the US, Europe and Latin America, Walgreens Boots Alliance generates 85% of revenue from the US.

	Annual Growth	08/19	08/20	08/21	08/22	08/23
Sales ($mil.)	0.4%	136,866	139,537	132,509	132,703	139,081
Net income ($ mil.)	–	3,982.0	456.0	2,542.0	4,337.0	(3,080.0)
Market value ($ mil.)	(16.1%)	44,211	32,837	43,831	30,280	21,860
Employees	(0.8%)	342,000	331,000	315,000	325,000	331,000

WALKER & DUNLOP INC   NYS: WD

7272 Wisconsin Avenue, Suite 1300
Bethesda, MD 20814
Phone: 301 215-5500
Fax: –
Web: www.walkerdunlop.com

CEO: –
CFO: –
HR: –
FYE: December 31
Type: Public

Walker & Dunlop is one of the leading commercial real estate services and finance companies in the US, with a primary focus on multifamily lending and property sales, commercial real estate debt brokerage, and affordable housing investment management. It originates and sells its products (e.g. mortgages, supplemental financing, construction loans, and mezzanine loans) primarily through government-sponsored enterprises (GSEs) like Fannie Mae and Freddie Mac, as well as through HUD. To a lesser extent, the company originates loans for insurance companies, banks, and institutional investors.

	Annual Growth	12/19	12/20	12/21	12/22	12/23
Sales ($mil.)	6.6%	817.2	1,083.7	1,259.2	1,258.8	1,054.4
Net income ($ mil.)	(11.3%)	173.4	246.2	265.8	213.8	107.4
Market value ($ mil.)	14.5%	2,126.3	3,025.1	4,960.0	2,580.0	3,649.3
Employees	12.7%	823	988	1,305	1,451	1,326

WALKER DIE CASTING, INC.

1125 HIGGS RD
LEWISBURG, TN 370914408
Phone: 931 359-6206
Fax: –
Web: www.walkerdiecasting.com

CEO: –
CFO: –
HR: –
FYE: December 31
Type: Private

Walker Die Casting doesn't leave things to chance. The company is a producer of high-pressure aluminum castings for industrial applications. Walker Die Casting provides custom die fabrication services to customers in the automotive, appliance, lawn and garden, marine, and power tool industries. Products include parts such as adapter plates, brackets, oil pans, gear cases, and housings for transmissions, engines, axles, and flywheels. Walker Die Casting also offers product design, finishing, testing, machining, and warehousing services. The company was founded in 1958 by Robert Walker.

WALMART INC

702 S.W. 8th Street
Bentonville, AR 72716
Phone: 479 273-4000
Fax: –
Web: www.stock.walmart.com

NYS: WMT
CEO: C D McMillon
CFO: John D Rainey
HR: –
FYE: January 31
Type: Public

Walmart is one of the world's largest companies by revenue and the largest employer with approximately 2.1 million associates. Walmart sells groceries and general merchandise, operating more than 5,315 stores in the US, including over 4,715 international Walmart stores and approximately 600 Sam's Club membership-only warehouse clubs. Walmart's international segment numbers about 4,965 locations; operating through regional subsidiaries, it operates in Canada, Chile, China, Africa, India, as well as Mexico and Central America. Some 240 million customers visit Walmart's stores and websites each week. The US market accounts for some 85% of the company's sales.

	Annual Growth	01/20	01/21	01/22	01/23	01/24
Sales ($mil.)	5.5%	523,964	559,151	572,754	611,289	648,125
Net income ($ mil.)	1.0%	14,881	13,510	13,673	11,680	15,511
Market value ($ mil.)	9.6%	922,102	1,131,506	1,126,030	1,158,729	1,330,924
Employees	(1.2%)	2,200,000	2,300,000	2,300,000	2,100,000	2,100,000

WALSH & ASSOCIATES, INC.

1400 MACKLIND AVE
SAINT LOUIS, MO 631102004
Phone: 314 781-2520
Fax: –
Web: www.walsh-assoc.com

CEO: Ellen Murphy
CFO: –
HR: –
FYE: December 31
Type: Private

Walsh & Associates fills its tote with chemical products and carries it throughout North America. The company distributes chemical ingredients and raw materials (for ink, paints and coatings, plastics, soaps, sealants, food, and personal care products), containers (paint cans, plastic pails, and plastic drums), and equipment (can crushers, filling machines, and mixers). Suppliers include Akzo Nobel, EvonikDegussa, and Rhodia. Walsh & Associates maintains locations in Colorado, Michigan, Missouri, Tennessee, Texas, and Utah. The company was founded in 1968 by Robert Walsh, Arthur Schmidt, and George Claytor.

WALSH BROTHERS, INCORPORATED

210 COMMERCIAL ST
BOSTON, MA 021091381
Phone: 617 878-4800
Fax: –
Web: www.walshbrothers.com

CEO: –
CFO: –
HR: –
FYE: December 31
Type: Private

This pair of Boston brothers has been building Beantown for more than a century. Walsh Brothers Incorporated, a Boston-based construction management and contracting company that specializes in building cultural, educational, medical, and research facilities throughout New England, is known for its work on iconic projects such as Boston's Fenway Park and Morgan Hall. The firm also offers historic renovation services and has refurbished places such as the Boston Symphony Orchestra and New England Conservatory of Music. Its clients have included Harvard University, Dana-Faber Cancer Institute, Amgen, Novartis, and Proctor & Gamble. Founded in 1901 by brothers James and Thomas Walsh, the builder continues to be run by the Walsh family.

	Annual Growth	12/05	12/06	12/07	12/08	12/09
Sales ($mil.)	10.3%	–	–	335.8	545.8	408.4
Net income ($ mil.)	30.2%	–	–	3.7	9.2	6.3
Market value ($ mil.)	–	–	–	–	–	–
Employees	–	–	–	–	–	246

WALTER ENERGY, INC.

3000 Riverchase Galleria, Suite 1700
Birmingham, AL 35244
Phone: 205 745-2000
Fax: –
Web: www.walterenergy.com

CEO: –
CFO: –
HR: –
FYE: December 31
Type: Public

Walter Energy has renewed energy for exploiting natural resources. Its subsidiaries include Jim Walter Resources (coal production) and Walter Coke (foundry and furnace coke). Its primary business is the mining and exporting of hard coking coal for the steel industry through its US Operations segment which accounts for more than 70% of Walter Energy's total sales. The company also develops also produces thermal coal, anthracite, metallurgical coke and coal bed methane gas (found in coal seams). Formerly a diversified company that included water products, homebuilding, and financing units, Walter Energy has divested itself of all but its natural resources and energy businesses. It declared bankruptcy in 2015 and had sold assets as part of the process.

	Annual Growth	12/10	12/11	12/12	12/13	12/14
Sales ($mil.)	(3.0%)	1,587.7	2,571.4	2,399.9	1,860.6	1,407.3
Net income ($ mil.)	–	385.8	349.2	(1,060.4)	(359.0)	(470.6)
Market value ($ mil.)	(67.8%)	9,201.7	4,359.0	2,582.6	1,197.0	99.3
Employees	6.3%	2,100	4,200	4,100	3,600	2,680

WALTERS-DIMMICK PETROLEUM, INC.

1620 S KALAMAZOO AVE
MARSHALL, MI 490689576
Phone: 269 781-4654
Fax: –
Web: www.johnnysmarkets.com

CEO: John P Walters II
CFO: Jeff Newhouse
HR: –
FYE: December 31
Type: Private

Walters-Dimmick Petroleum (WDP) operates about 60 retail gasoline stations in northern Indiana, southwestern Michigan, and northern Ohio that sell Shell brand petroleum products. In addition to gasoline, some WDP locations have convenience stores, fast-food restaurants (such as A&W and Subway sandwich shops), and car washes. Affiliate WDS Ventures -- a partnership between WDP and Shell Oil Products US-- is a wholesale marketer of Shell petroleum products which it markets through dealer operated, Shell branded gas stations in the Grand Rapids, Kalamazoo, and Battle Creek market areas.

WALTON & POST, INC.

9375 NW 117TH AVE
MEDLEY, FL 331781263
Phone: 305 591-1111
Fax: –
Web: www.waltonpost.com

CEO: Jose A Garrido Sr
CFO: –
HR: –
FYE: December 31
Type: Private

Walton & Post is a wholesale distributor of food and related products that serves retail and wholesale customers. The company supplies such products as canned and packaged goods, fresh fruit and produce, and ethnic food items, as well as candies, chocolates, health and beauty products, and paper goods. It primarily serves customers in the southeastern US. Part of Miami-based Garrido Group, Walton & Post is one of several distribution businesses owned by the Garrido family.

	Annual Growth	12/06	12/07	12/08	12/09	12/10
Sales ($mil.)	5.0%	–	–	36.1	38.6	39.8
Net income ($ mil.)	65.4%	–	–	0.4	0.1	1.0
Market value ($ mil.)	–	–	–	–	–	–
Employees	–	–	–	–	–	75

WALTON ELECTRIC MEMBERSHIP CORPORATION

842 HIGHWAY 78
MONROE, GA 306554475
Phone: 770 267-2505
Fax: –
Web: www.waltonemc.com

CEO: Ronnie Lee
CFO: Marsha L Shumate
HR: –
FYE: December 31
Type: Private

Good night John-Boy. This Walton family serves more than 118,400 residential, agricultural, commercial, and industrial customers in northeastern Georgia. The Walton Electric Membership Corporation (Walton EMC) operates 6,840 miles of power lines spanning across all or portions of ten counties (Athens-Clarke, Barrow, DeKalb, Greene, Gwinnett, Morgan, Newton, Oconee, Rockdale, and Walton). Subsidiary Walton EMC Natural Gas competes in the state's deregulated retail gas supply market, and has about 64,000 customers. Other operations include security systems installation and monitoring, appliance sales and rebates, and outdoor lighting services.

	Annual Growth	06/19	06/20	06/21	06/22*	12/22
Sales ($mil.)	(1.5%)	–	380.6	399.1	428.1	369.4
Net income ($ mil.)	–	–	14.5	21.1	7.4	(6.0)
Market value ($ mil.)	–	–	–	–	–	–
Employees	–	–	–	–	–	273

*Fiscal year change

WAR MEMORIAL HOSPITAL, INC.

1 HEALTHY WAY
BERKELEY SPRINGS, WV 254117463
Phone: 304 258-1234
Fax: –
Web: www.valleyhealthlink.com

CEO: –
CFO: –
HR: –
FYE: December 31
Type: Private

Morgan County War Memorial Hospital provides a wide range of inpatient and outpatient medical services, including acute, emergency, and long-term health services for the residents of Morgan County, West Virginia, and surrounding areas. The not-for-profit hospital has about 25 beds, as well as a 16-bed long-term care unit. War Memorial was founded in 1934 as a treatment center for post-paralysis care.

	Annual Growth	12/16	12/17	12/18	12/20	12/21
Sales ($mil.)	4.1%	–	24.4	24.2	23.8	28.7
Net income ($ mil.)	64.9%	–	0.3	(0.3)	3.7	1.8
Market value ($ mil.)	–	–	–	–	–	–
Employees	–	–	–	–	–	172

WARD TRUCKING, LLC

1436 WARD TRUCKING DR
ALTOONA, PA 166027110
Phone: 814 944-0803
Fax: –
Web: www.wardtlc.com

CEO: –
CFO: –
HR: –
FYE: December 31
Type: Private

Less-than-truckload (LTL) carrier Ward Trucking operates primarily in the northeastern and mid-Atlantic US. (LTL carriers consolidate freight from multiple shippers into a single truckload.) In addition to its LTL business, the company offers full truckload and logistics services through the Ward Transport & Logistics brand name. Ward Trucking operates a fleet of about 450 tractors, 60 trucks, and 1,180 trailers from a network of terminals, stretching from New York to Illinois. William W. Ward founded the company in 1931 to haul freight from central Pennsylvania to New York City. Ward Trucking is run by members of the Ward family.

	Annual Growth	12/10	12/11	12/12	12/13	12/14
Sales ($mil.)	1.1%	–	–	149.5	140.0	152.7
Net income ($ mil.)	78.6%	–	–	1.2	2.0	3.8
Market value ($ mil.)	–	–	–	–	–	–
Employees	–	–	–	–	–	1,057

WARNER BROS DISCOVERY INC

NMS: WBD

230 Park Avenue South
New York, NY 10003
Phone: 212 548-5555
Fax: –
Web: www.discoverycommunications.com

CEO: –
CFO: –
HR: –
FYE: December 31
Type: Public

Discovery is a global media company that provides content across multiple distribution platforms, including linear platforms such as pay-television (pay-TV), free-to-air (FTA) and broadcast television, authenticated GO applications, digital distribution arrangements, content licensing arrangements and direct-to-consumer (DTC) subscription products. The company is one of the world's largest pay-TV programmers that provides original and purchased content and live events to some 3.5 billion subscribers and viewers worldwide through networks that it wholly or partially owns. Properties include the Discovery Channel, HGTV, Food Network, TLC, Animal Planet, Investigation Discovery, Travel Channel, Science Channel, and MotorTrend (previously known as Velocity domestically and currently known as Turbo in most international countries). Discovery also operates stream, mobile devices, video on demand ("VOD") and broadband channels. The US accounts for about 65% of revenue.

	Annual Growth	12/19	12/20	12/21	12/22	12/23
Sales ($mil.)	38.8%	11,144	10,671	12,191	33,817	41,321
Net income ($ mil.)	–	2,069.0	1,219.0	1,006.0	(7,371.0)	(3,126.0)
Market value ($ mil.)	(23.2%)	79,853	73,390	57,414	23,122	27,756
Employees	40.0%	9,200	9,800	11,000	37,500	35,300

WARNER MEDIA, LLC

30 HUDSON YARDS
NEW YORK, NY 100012170
Phone: 212 484-8000
Fax: –
Web: www.wbd.com

CEO: Jason Kilar
CFO: –
HR: –
FYE: December 31
Type: Private

Warner Media is a powerful portfolio of iconic entertainment, news, and sports brands. The company runs a portfolio of cable TV networks, including CNN, TBS, and TNT. Time Warner also operates pay-TV channels HBO and Cinemax. Its Warner Bros. Entertainment, meanwhile, includes film studios (Warner Bros. Pictures, New Line Cinema), TV production units (Warner Bros. Television Group), and comic book publisher DC Entertainment. Its premier brands and franchises, along with its industry-leading scale, attract the best talent in media and entertainment, who work with its people to create the highest-quality content. In addition, WarnerMedia is not only a first-in-class media company, but a robust technology organization that brings content to life in exciting new ways.

WARNER MUSIC GROUP CORP
NMS: WMG

1633 Broadway
New York, NY 10019
Phone: 212 275-2000
Fax: –
Web: www.wmg.com

CEO: Robert Kyncl
CFO: Bryan Castellani
HR: –
FYE: September 30
Type: Public

Warner Music Group (WMG) is one of the world's leading recording companies. Its renowned family of iconic record labels, including Atlantic Records, Warner Records, Elektra Records and Parlophone Records, is home to many of the world's most popular and influential recording artists. In addition, Warner Chappell Music, its global music publishing business, boasts an extraordinary catalog that includes timeless standards and contemporary hits, representing works by over 100,000 songwriters and composers, with a global collection of more than one million musical compositions. WMG is owned by diversified business group Access Industries. The majority of sales were generated outside the US.

	Annual Growth	09/19	09/20	09/21	09/22	09/23
Sales ($mil.)	7.8%	4,475.0	4,463.0	5,301.0	5,919.0	6,037.0
Net income ($ mil.)	13.8%	256.0	(475.0)	304.0	551.0	430.0
Market value ($ mil.)	–	–	–	14,830	22,054	11,976	16,202
Employees	2.2%	5,400	5,500	5,900	6,200	5,900

WARREN RESOURCES INC (MD)

5420 LBJ Freeway, Suite 600
Dallas, TX 75240
Phone: 214 393-9688
Fax: –
Web: www.warrenresources.com

CEO: James A Watt
CFO: Frank T Smith
HR: –
FYE: December 31
Type: Public

Warren Resources believes that its heavy investment in oil and gas is warranted. The independent exploration and production company is focused on waterflood oil recovery programs in tar fields in California's Los Angeles Basin and the development of coalbed methane natural gas properties located in the Washakie Basin in the Greater Green River Basin in southwestern Wyoming. Warren Resources also owns oil and gas properties in New Mexico and Texas. In 2012 the company reported proved reserves of 51.2 billion cu. ft. of natural gas ans 24.9 million barrels of oil. In 2016 Warren Resources filed for Chapter 11 bankruptcy protection.

	Annual Growth	12/13	12/14	12/15*	09/16*	12/16
Sales ($mil.)	(48.3%)	128.8	150.7	88.4	42.9	17.8
Net income ($ mil.)	–	30.4	24.0	(620.0)	(150.5)	(167.1)
Market value ($ mil.)	–	–	–	–	–	–
Employees	2.1%	62	87	75	–	66

*Fiscal year change

WARREN RURAL ELECTRIC COOPERATIVE CORPORATION

951 FAIRVIEW AVE
BOWLING GREEN, KY 421014937
Phone: 270 842-6541
Fax: –
Web: www.wrecc.com

CEO: David Anderson
CFO: Roxanne Gray
HR: Greg D Vp of
FYE: June 30
Type: Private

This Warren needs no commission, just a cooperative, in order to deliver electric results to the people. Warren Rural Electric Cooperative Corporation (Warren RECC) provides its member customers with electricity, security systems, and surge suppression equipment, as well as with floodlighting and street lighting. It offers propane through non-affiliated Propane Energy Partners. The co-op serves more than 55,300 customers in an eight-county service area (Barren, Butler, Edmonson, Grayson, Logan, Ohio, Simpson, and Warren counties) in rural south-central Kentucky. Warren RECC is affiliated with the Tennessee Valley Authority and a member of Touchstone Energy, a 600-member alliance of electricity co-ops.

	Annual Growth	12/13	12/14*	06/15	06/19	06/20
Sales ($mil.)	1.1%	–	187.4	182.2	200.9	200.5
Net income ($ mil.)	14.4%	–	5.7	5.4	1.8	12.7
Market value ($ mil.)	–	–	–	–	–	–
Employees	–	–	–	–	–	165

*Fiscal year change

WARRIOR MET COAL INC
NYS: HCC

16243 Highway 216
Brookwood, AL 35444
Phone: 205 554-6150
Fax: –
Web: www.warriormetcoal.com

CEO: Walter J Scheller III
CFO: Dale W Boyles
HR: Alfarzia Sterling
FYE: December 31
Type: Public

Warrior Met Coal is a large-scale, low-cost producer and exporter of premium met coal, operating highly-efficient longwall operations in their underground mines based in Alabama, Mine No. 4 and Mine No. 7. The company entirely mines non-thermal met coal used as a critical component of steel production by metal manufacturers in Europe, South America, and Asia. Its met coal production totaled 5.1 million in 2021. Its natural gas operations remove and sell natural gas from the coal seams owned or leased by reducing natural gas levels in its mines. The met coal is mined using longwall extraction technology with development support from continuous miners.

	Annual Growth	12/19	12/20	12/21	12/22	12/23
Sales ($mil.)	7.2%	1,268.3	782.7	1,059.2	1,738.7	1,676.6
Net income ($ mil.)	12.2%	301.7	(35.8)	150.9	641.3	478.6
Market value ($ mil.)	30.3%	1,099.2	1,109.0	1,337.4	1,801.9	3,171.6
Employees	(5.2%)	1,417	1,401	704	854	1,143

WASHINGTON HOSPITAL CENTER CORPORATION

110 IRVING ST NW
WASHINGTON, DC 200103017
Phone: 202 877-7000
Fax: –
Web: www.medstarhealth.org

CEO: Kent Samet
CFO: –
HR: –
FYE: June 30
Type: Private

Washington Hospital Center (doing business as MedStar Washington Hospital Center) may be the official hospital of the Washington Redskins, but you don't have to be a professional football player to make use of the facility's services. The hospital, at the heart of the MedStar Health system, serves some 500,000 patients living in and around the nation's capital each year. Washington Hospital Center has 912 beds and includes specialized care centers for cancer, cardiovascular conditions, and stroke. Other offerings include organ transplantation, a regional burn treatment center, and emergency air transportation. MedStar Washington also conducts clinical research and offers educational residency and fellowship programs.

	Annual Growth	06/18	06/19	06/20	06/21	06/22
Sales ($mil.)	7.2%	–	–	–	1,591.0	1,704.9
Net income ($ mil.)	(15.5%)	–	–	–	69.8	59.0
Market value ($ mil.)	–	–	–	–	–	–
Employees	–	–	–	–	–	5,637

WASHINGTON LEGAL FOUNDATION

2009 MASSACHUSETTS AVE NW
WASHINGTON, DC 200361011
Phone: 202 588-0302
Fax: –
Web: www.wlf.org

CEO: –
CFO: –
HR: –
FYE: December 31
Type: Private

The Washington Legal Foundation is a public interest law center and legal think tank that operates with an eye toward defending free enterprise in the courts. Its law center brings original lawsuits and participates in other legal proceedings at the federal, state, and agency levels throughout the US. Its Legal Studies Division produces policy papers authored by legislators, judges, and legal scholars; its Civic Communications Program publishes the recurring In All Fairness feature in purchased space on the op-ed page of the New York Times. The Washington Legal Foundation was founded in 1977.

	Annual Growth	12/17	12/18	12/19	12/21	12/22
Sales ($mil.)	0.4%	–	3.7	2.6	3.7	3.8
Net income ($ mil.)	11.6%	–	1.3	0.2	2.0	2.1
Market value ($ mil.)	–	–	–	–	–	–
Employees	–	–	–	–	–	11

WASHINGTON METROPOLITAN AREA TRANSIT AUTHORITY

800 5TH ST NW
WASHINGTON, DC 200012622
Phone: 202 962-1000
Fax: –
Web: www.wmata.com

CEO: Andy Off
CFO: –
HR: –
FYE: June 30
Type: Private

Washington Metropolitan Area Transit Authority (WMATA or the Metro) operates the second largest rail transit system (Metrorail) and one of the largest bus networks (Metrobus) in the US. Transporting roughly a third of federal government employees to work and millions of tourists, its transit service zone covers Washington, DC and neighboring counties and suburbs in Maryland and Virginia. The authority's rail system consists of about 90 stations served by more than 115 miles of track, both underground and aboveground. It operates a fleet of about 1,400 buses. WMATA also offers MetroAccess paratransit service for eligible people with disabilities.

	Annual Growth	06/02	06/03	06/04	06/08	06/16
Sales ($mil.)	(38.2%)	–	451.1	500.0	0.7	0.9
Net income ($ mil.)	(40.1%)	–	239.4	(76.2)	(0.2)	0.3
Market value ($ mil.)	–	–	–	–	–	–
Employees	–	–	–	–	–	11,790

WASHINGTON REGIONAL MEDICAL CENTER

3215 N NORTHHILLS BLVD
FAYETTEVILLE, AR 727034424
Phone: 479 463-1000
Fax: –
Web: www.wregional.com

CEO: Amanze Ugoji
CFO: Dan Eckels
HR: –
FYE: December 31
Type: Private

Washington Regional Medical System (formerly Washington Regional Medical Center) provides acute care services to the people of northwestern Arkansas. The system's main hospital has about 370 beds in Fayetteville, and also includes assisted living facilities, home health and hospice services, and general practice and specialty clinics. Specialty services at the medical center include cardiac and vascular care (Walker Family Heart and Vascular Institute), emergency medicine, kidney dialysis, women's health services (Johnelle Hunt Women's Center), cancer treatment, and rehabilitation.

	Annual Growth	12/14	12/15	12/16	12/21	12/22
Sales ($mil.)	6.3%	–	245.3	300.4	356.9	376.1
Net income ($ mil.)	(19.1%)	–	45.4	58.5	57.0	10.3
Market value ($ mil.)	–	–	–	–	–	–
Employees	–	–	–	–	–	2,000

WASHINGTON SPORTS & ENTERTAINMENT, INC.

601 F ST NW
WASHINGTON, DC 200041605
Phone: 202 661-5000
Fax: –
Web: www.monumentalsports.com

CEO: Ted Leonsis
CFO: –
HR: –
FYE: December 31
Type: Private

Washington Sports & Entertainment is a holding company that controls four sports franchises in Washington, DC, including the Washington Wizards professional basketball team, the Washington Capitals hockey club, the Washington Mystics women's basketball franchise, and an arena football team. The company also owns and operates the city's Verizon Center, an all-purpose venue that serves as home for all three sports teams. In addition, Washington Sports manages the Patriot Center at George Mason University in Fairfax, Virginia. Chairman and majority owner Ted Leonsis formed the company when he acquired the Washington Wizards in 2010.

WASHINGTON SUBURBAN SANITARY COMMISSION (INC)

14501 SWEITZER LN
LAUREL, MD 207075901
Phone: 301 206-8000
Fax: –
Web: www.wsscwater.com

CEO: –
CFO: –
HR: –
FYE: June 30
Type: Private

Washington Suburban Sanitary Commission (WSSC) provides water and wastewater services in Maryland's Montgomery and Prince George's counties, just outside the nation's capital. WSSC serves around 475,000 customers, representing 2 million residents, in an area of about 1,000 square miles. The agency draws water from the Potomac and Patuxtent rivers and maintains three reservoirs. The commission also operates two water filtration plants, six wastewater treatment plants, and some 11,000 miles of sewer and water main lines, including a network of nearly 5,900 miles of fresh water pipeline and over 5,600 miles of sewer pipeline. WSSC was established in 1918.

	Annual Growth	06/18	06/19	06/20	06/21	06/22
Sales ($mil.)	4.1%	–	742.8	749.8	749.6	837.7
Net income ($ mil.)	2.3%	–	139.7	23.7	49.1	149.7
Market value ($ mil.)	–	–	–	–	–	–
Employees	–	–	–	–	–	2,000

WASHINGTON TRUST BANCORP, INC.

NMS: WASH

23 Broad Street
Westerly, RI 02891
Phone: 401 348-1200
Fax: –
Web: www.washtrust.com

CEO: Edward O Handy III
CFO: Ronald S Ohsberg
HR: –
FYE: December 31
Type: Public

Without seeming naive, Washington Trust Bancorp can utter Washington and trust in the same breath. The holding company owns The Washington Trust Company, one of the oldest and largest banks in Rhode Island and one of the oldest banks in the entire US. Chartered in 1800, the bank boasts over $3.5 billion in assets and operates nearly 20 branches in the state, and one in southeastern Connecticut. Washington Trust offers standard services such as deposit accounts, CDs, and credit cards. The company's commercial mortgages and loans account for more than half of its loan portfolio, while residential mortgages and consumer loans make up most of the rest. The bank also offers wealth management services.

	Annual Growth	12/19	12/20	12/21	12/22	12/23
Assets ($mil.)	8.0%	5,292.7	5,713.2	5,851.1	6,660.1	7,202.8
Net income ($ mil.)	(8.6%)	69.1	69.8	76.9	71.7	48.2
Market value ($ mil.)	(11.9%)	916.1	763.0	960.0	803.5	551.5
Employees	1.8%	619	609	623	651	665

WASTE CONNECTIONS US, INC.

3 WATERWAY SQUARE PL STE 110
THE WOODLANDS, TX 773803487
Phone: 832 442-2200
Fax: –
Web: www.wasteconnections.com

CEO: Worthing F Jackman
CFO: –
HR: –
FYE: December 31
Type: Private

Waste Connections is the third largest solid waste services company in North America. It provides non-hazardous waste collection, transfer, and disposal services, along with resource recovery primarily through recycling and renewable fuel generation. The company serves more than eight million residential, commercial, and industrial customers in mostly exclusive and secondary markets in roughly 45 states in the US and over five provinces in Canada. It owns and operates about 360 solid waste collection operations, over 155 transfer stations, roughly 65 MSW landfills, about ten E&P waste landfills, over 15 non-MSW landfills, some 80 recycling facilities, over 20 E&P liquid waste injection wells, nearly 20 E&P waste treatment and oil recovery facilities.

WASTE CONTROL SPECIALISTS LLC

17103 PRESTON RD STE 200
DALLAS, TX 752481499
Phone: 682 503-0030
Fax: -
Web: www.wcstexas.com

CEO: -
CFO: -
HR: -
FYE: December 31
Type: Private

Everything's bigger in Texas, including its capacity to store nuclear waste. Waste Control Specialists (WCS) operates a disposal facility for hazardous, toxic, and low-level radioactive waste in Andrews County in far West Texas, on the border of southeast New Mexico. The 1,300-acre site can store up to 1.8 million cu. ft. of class A, B and C low-level radioactive waste more than 100 feet underground. It is licensed to accept waste from nuclear power plants in Texas and Vermont and for treatment and storage from commercial and federal generators such as the Dept. of Energy. WCS is a subsidiary of Valhi. In 2015 EnergySolutions agreed to buy the company for $270 million.

WASTE MANAGEMENT, INC. (DE)
NYS: WM

800 Capitol Street, Suite 3000
Houston, TX 77002
Phone: 713 512-6200
Fax: -
Web: www.wm.com

CEO: James C Fish Jr
CFO: Devina A Rankin
HR: -
FYE: December 31
Type: Public

Holding company Waste Management is a leading provider of comprehensive waste management environmental services, providing services to millions of residential, industrial, municipal, and commercial customers throughout the US and Canada. Waste Management provides waste collection, transfer, recycling and resource recovery, and disposal services. It also use waste to create energy by using gas naturally as waste decomposes in landfills and in generators to make electricity. Its sites include about 260 owned or operated landfills (the industry's largest network) and more than 335 transfer stations. The US accounts for about 95% of total revenue.

	Annual Growth	12/19	12/20	12/21	12/22	12/23
Sales ($mil.)	7.2%	15,455	15,218	17,931	19,698	20,426
Net income ($ mil.)	8.4%	1,670.0	1,496.0	1,816.0	2,238.0	2,304.0
Market value ($ mil.)	12.0%	45,750	47,344	67,003	62,980	71,901
Employees	1.7%	44,900	48,250	48,500	49,500	48,000

WATERFURNACE RENEWABLE ENERGY INC

9000 CONSERVATION WAY
FORT WAYNE, IN 468099794
Phone: 260 478-5667
Fax: -
Web: www.waterfurnace.com

CEO: -
CFO: -
HR: -
FYE: December 31
Type: Private

WaterFurnace Renewable Energy relies on the heat within the earth to energize its products. The company, also doing business as WaterFurnace International, makes and sells geothermal HVAC systems that utilize heat stored in the ground for residential, commercial, and institutional applications. Its cooling systems work in reverse, extracting heat from indoors. Touting its systems as more efficient, safer, and more environmentally friendly than HVAC systems that use fossil fuels, the company has installed more than 300,000 units. Other operations install geothermal loops that heat and cool homes and businesses by circulating pressurized water through hundreds of feet of looped pipe that is buried on-site.

WATERS CORP.
NYS: WAT

34 Maple Street
Milford, MA 01757
Phone: 508 478-2000
Fax: 508 872-1990
Web: www.waters.com

CEO: Udit Batra
CFO: Amol Chaubal
HR: Patrick Conway
FYE: December 31
Type: Public

Waters Corporation makes high-performance liquid chromatography instruments used to identify and analyze the constituent components of a variety of chemicals and other materials. Waters also makes mass spectrometers that help identify chemical compounds. In addition, the company designs, manufactures, sells and services thermal analysis, rheometry and calorimetry instruments through its TA Instruments (TA) product line. Its products are used in pharmaceutical, clinical, biochemical, industrial, nutritional safety, environmental, academic and governmental customers working in research and development, quality assurance, and other laboratory applications. Operating directly in more than 35 countries, Waters generates most of its revenue outside of the US. In 2023, Waters agreed to acquire Wyatt Technology, a leader in light scattering instrument and software, for $1.36 billion in cash.

	Annual Growth	12/19	12/20	12/21	12/22	12/23
Sales ($mil.)	5.3%	2,406.6	2,365.4	2,785.9	2,972.0	2,956.4
Net income ($ mil.)	2.0%	592.2	521.6	692.8	707.8	642.2
Market value ($ mil.)	9.0%	13,826	14,641	22,049	20,273	19,483
Employees	1.3%	7,500	7,400	7,800	8,200	7,900

WATKINS AND SHEPARD TRUCKING, INC.

3101 PACKERLAND DR
GREEN BAY, WI 543136187
Phone: 406 532-6121
Fax: -
Web: www.wksh.com

CEO: Ray Kuntz
CFO: -
HR: -
FYE: December 31
Type: Private

Watkins & Shepard Trucking offers less-than-truckload (LTL) and truckload freight hauling throughout the US from about 20 terminals, mainly west of the Rockies. (LTL carriers consolidate cargo from multiple shippers into a single trailer.) The company's fleet consists of about 850 tractors and 2,500 trailers. Standard dry vans account for the majority of the company's trailers; Watkins & Shepard also uses flatbed trailers. In addition, the company arranges intermodal transportation, which involves hauling freight by multiple methods, such as road and rail. In the summer of 2016, Watkins & Shepard was acquired by Schneider National.

	Annual Growth	12/98	12/99	12/00	12/12	12/13
Sales ($mil.)	3.8%	-	95.7	102.4	157.9	160.6
Net income ($ mil.)	-	-	2.6	0.9	3.1	2.5
Market value ($ mil.)	-	-	-	-	-	-
Employees	-	-	-	-	-	1,300

WATKINS ASSOCIATED INDUSTRIES, INC.

1958 MONROE DR NE
ATLANTA, GA 303244887
Phone: 404 872-8359
Fax: -
Web: www.watkins.com

CEO: Eric Wahlen
CFO: John Maggard
HR: -
FYE: December 31
Type: Private

Watkins Associated Industries does business over the road, on the ground, and by the sea. Its trucking businesses include Highway Transport Chemical (liquid chemical transport), Highway Transport Petroleum, Highway Transport Logistics, Land Span (general cargo), Sunco Carriers (refrigerated cargo), and Watson Truckload Services (regional general cargo). Another unit, Tampa Maid Foods, sources, processes, and markets seafood such as shrimp, calamari, scallops, oysters, and crab. Its Watkins Retail Group is a shopping center development, leasing, and management company that was founded in 1977. Bill Watkins founded the family-owned company in 1932 with a $300 pickup truck.

WATONWAN FARM SERVICE, INC

233 W CIRO ST
TRUMAN, MN 560882018
Phone: 507 776-1244
Fax: –
Web: www.cfscoop.com

CEO: Ed Bosanko
CFO: –
HR: –
FYE: July 31
Type: Private

Watonwan Farm Service, which does business as WFS, helps out its south central Minnesota and north central Iowa member-farmers with complete farm-management services and products. Offering marketing opportunities, financial services, and farming supplies such as chemicals, fertilizers, livestock feed, petroleum products, and seed, the agricultural cooperative serves more than 4,000 producers from its 22 locations. The primary crops of its members include corn, soybean, and specialty canning crops; most of its livestock farmers raise hogs and cattle. The co-op was called the Consumers Cooperative Oil Company of St. James when it was founded in 1937.

	Annual Growth	07/11	07/12	07/13	07/14	07/15
Sales ($mil.)	(15.4%)	–	592.5	701.2	468.3	358.6
Net income ($ mil.)	(7.9%)	–	6.7	7.7	7.7	5.2
Market value ($ mil.)	–	–	–	–	–	–
Employees	–	–	–	–	–	255

WATSCO INC.

NYS: WSO

2665 South Bayshore Drive, Suite 901
Miami, FL 33133
Phone: 305 714-4100
Fax: –
Web: www.watsco.com

CEO: Albert H Nahmad
CFO: Ana M Menendez
HR: Debra Rose
FYE: December 31
Type: Public

Watsco is one of the Americas' largest distributors of air conditioning, heating, and refrigeration equipment and related parts and supplies (HVAC/R). The company's nearly 670 stores span about 40 states, Puerto Rico, Canada, and Mexico. It also exports to Latin America and the Caribbean. Additionally, the company sells a variety of non-equipment products including parts, ductwork, air movement products, insulation, tools, installation supplies, thermostats, and air quality products. Customers include more than 120,000 contractors and dealers who install and replace HVAC equipment. Watsco generates most of its sales in the US.

	Annual Growth	12/19	12/20	12/21	12/22	12/23
Sales ($mil.)	11.2%	4,770.4	5,054.9	6,280.2	7,274.3	7,283.8
Net income ($ mil.)	21.5%	246.0	269.6	418.9	601.2	536.3
Market value ($ mil.)	24.2%	7,975.0	10,029	13,851	11,041	18,968
Employees	6.1%	5,800	5,800	6,900	7,275	7,350

WATTS WATER TECHNOLOGIES INC

NYS: WTS

815 Chestnut Street
North Andover, MA 01845
Phone: 978 688-1811
Fax: –
Web: www.wattswater.com

CEO: Robert J Pagano Jr
CFO: Shashank Patel
HR: Leah Mix
FYE: December 31
Type: Public

Watts Water Technologies is a leading supplier of products, solutions and systems that manage and conserve the flow of fluids and energy into, through and out of buildings in the commercial and residential markets. It also makes water quality products such as backflow preventers and filtration systems, water pressure regulators, and drainage devices. Watts operates in the Americas, Europe, and the Asia Pacific, Middle East, and Africa (APMEA) region. The majority of the company's sales are generated through plumbing, heating, and mechanical wholesale distributors. The Americas region is its largest geographic market, accounting for about 70% of the company's sales.

	Annual Growth	12/19	12/20	12/21	12/22	12/23
Sales ($mil.)	6.5%	1,600.5	1,508.6	1,809.2	1,979.5	2,056.3
Net income ($ mil.)	18.8%	131.5	114.3	165.7	251.5	262.1
Market value ($ mil.)	20.2%	3,323.1	4,053.9	6,468.0	4,871.1	6,940.0
Employees	1.5%	4,800	4,465	4,597	4,600	5,100

WAUKESHA MEMORIAL HOSPITAL, INC.

725 AMERICAN AVE
WAUKESHA, WI 531885099
Phone: 262 928-1000
Fax: –
Web: www.prohealthcare.org

CEO: –
CFO: Pam Kleba
HR: –
FYE: September 30
Type: Private

Waukesha Memorial Hospital is a 300-bed teaching hospital that provides health care services for Wisconsin's Milwaukee, Waukesha, and Dane counties. With about 670 physicians representing several specialties and 2,700 employees, the hospital operates centers for excellence focused on cardiology, oncology, neurology, women's health, and orthopedics, as well as emergency, neonatal, and family practice services. Additionally, Waukesha Memorial Hospital conducts a physician residency program. Established in 1914, the medical facility is a subsidiary of not-for-profit ProHealth Care, a medical network that serves southeastern Wisconsin with acute care and specialty health services.

	Annual Growth	09/18	09/19	09/20	09/21	09/22
Sales ($mil.)	2.6%	–	543.7	498.2	529.8	586.9
Net income ($ mil.)	49.1%	–	13.5	5.9	96.4	44.7
Market value ($ mil.)	–	–	–	–	–	–
Employees	–	–	–	–	–	2,071

WAUKESHA-PEARCE INDUSTRIES, LLC

12320 MAIN ST
HOUSTON, TX 770356206
Phone: 713 723-1050
Fax: –
Web: www.wpi.com

CEO: Al H Bentley
CFO: –
HR: –
FYE: March 31
Type: Private

Through its Energy Solutions, Waukesha-Pearce Industries (WPI) offers power generation, compression solutions, and drilling solutions. WPI also offers a slate of heavy construction and mining products, including earth movers and demolition equipment made by such OEMs as Komatsu, Takeuchi, Bomag, Sennebogen, and Gradall Industries, through its Construction Solutions. As part of its business, the company sells used equipment and leases heavy earth-moving equipment. Founded in 1924 by Louis M. Pearce, Sr., the company is owned and run by the Pearce family.

	Annual Growth	03/08	03/09	03/10	03/11	03/15
Sales ($mil.)	18.4%	–	–	197.8	248.7	461.1
Net income ($ mil.)	39.5%	–	–	1.7	4.7	8.8
Market value ($ mil.)	–	–	–	–	–	–
Employees	–	–	–	–	–	600

WAUSAU FINANCIAL SYSTEMS, INC.

400 WESTWOOD DR
WAUSAU, WI 544017801
Phone: 715 359-0427
Fax: –
Web: www.wausauwi.gov

CEO: –
CFO: –
HR: –
FYE: May 31
Type: Private

Wausau Financial Systems tracks dollars and cents throughout the enterprise. The Frontenac-owned company provides software (Optima3 IMS) and outsourced information technology services, including systems integration and custom software design, related to payment and transaction processing. It helps customers with check processing, automated clearing house payments, and electronic billing presentment. Customers include financial institutions, government agencies, insurance companies, retailers, and utilities.

WAUSAU PAPER CORP.

2929 ARCH ST STE 2600
PHILADELPHIA, PA 191042863
Phone: 866 722-8675
Fax: -
Web: www.torkusa.com

CEO: -
CFO: -
HR: -
FYE: December 31
Type: Private

With more than 110 years' experience, Wausau Paper has proficiency in selling paper and tissue products. The company produces Bay West branded towel, tissue, soap, and dispensing products for hotels, hospitals, schools, and office buildings. Other paper brands include DublSoft, EcoSoft, OptiCore, Revolution, and Dubl Nature. Its products are primarily sold within the US and Canada. Most of its US customers are regional and national sanitation supply distributors and paper merchants. In early 2016 Wausau Paper was bought by Sweden-based SCA for $500 million.

WAVEDANCER INC

NAS: WAVD

12015 Lee Jackson Memorial Highway, Suite 210
Fairfax, VA 22033
Phone: 703 383-3000
Fax: -
Web: www.infoa.com

CEO: G J Benoit Jr
CFO: Timothy G Hannon
HR: -
FYE: December 31
Type: Public

Obsolete computer programs goto that great big disk drive in the sky thanks to Information Analysis Incorporated (IAI). The company's software and services help government agencies and corporations migrate from older, mainframe-based computer systems to client-server and Web-based applications. IAI offers programming, platform migration, systems analysis, training, and maintenance. The company is a Micro Focus partner and uses its modernization software, as well as applications by Oracle and SAP. The federal government accounts for the majority of sales, but corporate clients include Aleris and Rich Products. IAI was founded in 1979; chairman and CEO Sandor Rosenberg controls 16% of the company's stock.

	Annual Growth	12/18	12/19	12/20	12/21	12/22
Sales ($mil.)	7.7%	8.9	10.2	13.9	15.0	12.0
Net income ($ mil.)	-	(0.1)	(0.7)	0.4	(1.1)	(17.8)
Market value ($ mil.)	33.7%	0.3	0.3	0.3	9.5	0.9
Employees	26.3%	24	24	37	55	61

WAXMAN INDUSTRIES INC.

NBB: WXMN

24460 Aurora Road
Bedford Heights, OH 44146
Phone: 440 439-1830
Fax: 440 439-8678
Web: www.waxmanind.com

CEO: Armond Waxman
CFO: Mark Wester
HR: -
FYE: June 30
Type: Public

Waxman Industries is one of the world's most trusted providers of bathroom and kitchen home hardware and accessories, serving many of the largest retailers in the US. The company is also a leader in the design, development, and distribution of innovative home organization and storage solutions; surface protection and floor care products; and, other home improvement and hardware products, including faucets and showers; and plumbing products and accessories. The remaining operations for Waxman includes Leaksmart, a small smart home solutions company providing complete home water protection systems and a small industrial sales operations that sells products in the US and in abroad. Beyond American borders, Waxman operates internationally through its subsidiaries, TWI International and Waxman Technology China.

	Annual Growth	06/99	06/00	06/01	06/02	06/03
Sales ($mil.)	(9.3%)	99.1	81.4	73.5	70.4	67.1
Net income ($ mil.)	-	(7.5)	(28.8)	100.0	1.6	0.4
Market value ($ mil.)	77.1%	0.5	0.3	1.9	7.6	4.9
Employees	(12.1%)	733	543	370	405	437

WAYFAIR INC

NYS: W

4 Copley Place
Boston, MA 02116
Phone: 617 532-6100
Fax: -
Web: www.wayfair.com

CEO: Steven Conine
CFO: Kate Gulliver
HR: -
FYE: December 31
Type: Public

Wayfair is one of the world's leading online retailers of home furniture, decor, lighting, and more. Through its e-commerce platform, the company offers customers visually inspired browsing, compelling merchandising, easy product discovery and attractive prices for more than 40 million products from over 20,000 suppliers. It has approximately 22.1 million active customers over the last twelve months. In addition to its eponymous brand, Wayfair operates through six other websites under the Wayfair, Joss & Main, AllModern, Perigold, Wayfair Professional, and Birch Lane names. The company generates most of its sales in the US. It was founded in 2002 by co-chairmen Niraj Shah and Steve Conine.

	Annual Growth	12/19	12/20	12/21	12/22	12/23
Sales ($mil.)	7.1%	9,127.1	14,145	13,708	12,218	12,003
Net income ($ mil.)	-	(984.6)	185.0	(131.0)	(1,331.0)	(738.0)
Market value ($ mil.)	(9.1%)	10,677	26,679	22,445	3,885.9	7,289.8
Employees	(4.0%)	16,985	16,122	16,681	15,745	14,400

WAYLAND BAPTIST UNIVERSITY INC

1900 W 7TH ST
PLAINVIEW, TX 790726900
Phone: 806 291-1000
Fax: -
Web: www.wbu.edu

CEO: -
CFO: Lezlie Hukill
HR: -
FYE: June 30
Type: Private

You gotta have faith to attend Wayland Baptist University. The private, co-educational Baptist institution offers more than 40 undergraduate majors, about a dozen pre-professional programs, and graduate programs in fields such as business administration, Christian ministry, counseling, education, management, public administration, religion, and science. It has an enrollment of approximately 7,000 students at some 15 campuses in Alaska, Arizona, Hawaii, New Mexico, Oklahoma, and Texas, as well as Kenya. The university was founded in 1906 by Dr. and Mrs. Henry Wayland and the Staked Plains Baptist Association.

	Annual Growth	06/18	06/19	06/20	06/21	06/22
Sales ($mil.)	8.0%	-	58.5	52.6	76.3	73.8
Net income ($ mil.)	96.9%	-	0.5	(7.0)	7.6	3.7
Market value ($ mil.)	-	-	-	-	-	-
Employees	-	-	-	-	-	281

WAYNE J. GRIFFIN ELECTRIC, INC.

116 HOPPING BROOK RD
HOLLISTON, MA 017461455
Phone: 508 429-8830
Fax: -
Web: www.waynejgriffinelectric.com

CEO: -
CFO: -
HR: Ryan Leary
FYE: December 31
Type: Private

Wayne J. Griffin Electric is one of the leading electrical contractors that brings a certain spark to New England and the Southeast. With offices in Massachusetts, Georgia, North Carolina, and Alabama, the electrical contractor offers construction and installation services on hospitals, hotels, industrial and high-tech buildings, offices, prisons, research laboratories, retirement communities, and schools. The company's service division provides small project management and facility maintenance. Its telecom division collaborates with Corning, Mohawk, Siemon, Panduit, Hubbell, Hitachi, Genaral Cable, and Berk-Tek. Wayne J. Griffin Electric was founded in 1978.

	Annual Growth	12/14	12/15	12/16	12/17	12/18
Sales ($mil.)	7.0%	-	-	333.6	355.5	382.1
Net income ($ mil.)	-	-	-	27.3	29.6	-
Market value ($ mil.)	-	-	-	-	-	-
Employees	-	-	-	-	-	1,100

WAYNE MEMORIAL HEALTH SYSTEM, INC.

601 PARK ST
HONESDALE, PA 184311445
Phone: 570 253-8100
Fax: –
Web: www.wmh.org

CEO: –
CFO: –
HR: –
FYE: June 30
Type: Private

Wayne Memorial Health System provides general medical and surgical health services, primary care and family medicine, long-term and intermediate care, and assisted living services to communities in northeastern Pennsylvania. It also offers home health care, nutritional counseling, and wellness programs. The Wayne Memorial Hospital has about 100 beds.

	Annual Growth	06/11	06/12	06/15	06/16	06/18
Sales ($mil.)	91.1%	–	2.1	2.3	94.0	100.5
Net income ($ mil.)	46.5%	–	0.5	0.5	(3.0)	4.7
Market value ($ mil.)	–	–	–	–	–	–
Employees	–	–	–	–	–	600

WAYNE SAVINGS BANCSHARES INC

151 North Market Street
Wooster, OH 44691
Phone: 800 414-1103
Fax: –
Web: www.waynesavings.com

NBB: WAYN
CEO: –
CFO: –
HR: –
FYE: December 31
Type: Public

Holy bank vaults, Batman! Wayne Savings Bancshares is the holding company for Wayne Savings Community Bank, which serves individuals and local businesses through about a dozen locations in north-central Ohio. Serving Ashland, Holmes, Medina, Stark, and Wayne counties, the bank offers checking and savings accounts, retirement and education savings accounts, certificates of deposit, and debit cards. One- to four-family residential mortgages make up more than half of the company's loan portfolio. To a lesser extent, the bank writes business, commercial mortgage, land, and consumer loans. It offers investments, insurance, and brokerage accounts through a agreement with third-party provider Infinex.

	Annual Growth	12/18	12/19	12/20	12/21	12/22
Assets ($mil.)	11.5%	472.9	492.6	591.6	636.0	729.8
Net income ($ mil.)	15.0%	5.1	6.5	6.7	7.4	9.0
Market value ($ mil.)	9.7%	40.9	51.5	47.3	57.0	59.2
Employees	–	–	–	–	–	–

WAYNE STATE UNIVERSITY

6135 WOODWARD AVE
DETROIT, MI 482023502
Phone: 313 577-1771
Fax: –
Web: www.wayne.edu

CEO: –
CFO: –
HR: Ida Taylor
FYE: September 30
Type: Private

Wayne State University (WSU) is a comprehensive university with about a dozen colleges and schools. It offers more than 370 academic programs, including some 125 bachelor's degree programs, about 140 master's degree programs, some 60 doctoral degree programs, and about 30 certificate, specialist, and professional programs. With approximately 24,000 students and about 3,000 full-time faculty experts, WSU has a student-to-faculty ratio of 16:1. WSU is a partner with Michigan State University and the University of Michigan in the University Research Corridor, one of the nation's top academic research clusters. Located in midtown Detroit, WSU traces its heritage back to 1868 with the founding of the Detroit Medical College, now part of its School of Medicine.

	Annual Growth	09/10	09/11	09/17	09/21	09/22
Sales ($mil.)	1.3%	–	520.9	640.4	0.6	597.9
Net income ($ mil.)	–	–	(15.7)	46.3	0.0	(5.6)
Market value ($ mil.)	–	–	–	–	–	–
Employees	–	–	–	–	–	8,500

WBI ENERGY TRANSMISSION, INC

1250 W CENTURY AVE
BISMARCK, ND 585030911
Phone: 701 530-1601
Fax: –
Web: www.wbienergy.com

CEO: –
CFO: –
HR: –
FYE: December 31
Type: Private

This company likes to keep gas in its pipes. Williston Basin Interstate Pipeline provides customers in the Upper Midwest region of the US with natural gas gathering, transportation, and underground storage services. It operates 3,350 miles of natural gas transmission pipeline, nearly 350 miles of gathering pipeline, and 30 compressor stations capable of holding more than 193 billion cu. ft. of natural gas. Williston Basin Interstate Pipeline's system connects major natural gas suppliers with markets between Canada and the Central region of the US. The company is an indirect subsidiary of MDU Resources.

	Annual Growth	12/95	12/96	12/97	12/16	12/17
Sales ($mil.)	1.3%	–	78.6	–	102.2	102.7
Net income ($ mil.)	9.0%	–	3.4	–	22.1	20.6
Market value ($ mil.)	–	–	–	–	–	–
Employees	–	–	–	–	–	277

WCI COMMUNITIES, INC.

10481 BEN C PRATT/6 MILE CYPRESS PKWY
FORT MYERS, FL 33966
Phone: 239 947-2600
Fax: –
Web: www.lennar.com

CEO: Keith E Bass
CFO: Russell Devendorf
HR: –
FYE: December 31
Type: Private

WCI Communities develops luxury residential communities and homes in Florida. Founded in 1946, it caters primarily to retirement and second-home buyers, offering single-family homes, vacation homes, villas, and high-rise condominiums ranging in price from about $150,000 to $1.3 million. WCI's 14 master-planned communities typically offer such amenities as golf courses, tennis courts, dining and entertainment facilities, and nature trails. The company also offers architectural and design services as well as financing and title services. Its real estate brokerage, Berkshire Hathaway HomeServices, boasts 40-plus locations that serve 18 Florida counties. WCI Communities was acquired by Lennar in 2017 for $643 million.

WD-40 CO

9715 Businesspark Avenue
San Diego, CA 92131
Phone: 619 275-1400
Fax: –
Web: www.wd40company.com

NMS: WDFC
CEO: Steven A Brass
CFO: Peter Williams
HR: –
FYE: August 31
Type: Public

WD-40 Company is a global marketing organization dedicated to creating positive lasting memories by developing and selling products that solve problems in workshops, factories, and homes around the world. The company's WD-40 product, used as a lubricant, rust preventative, moisture displacer, and penetrant, is a staple in many homes. Its 3-IN-ONE Oil brand consists of multi-purpose drip oil, specialty drip oils, and spray lubricant products, as well as other specialty maintenance products. It also makes household cleaning and deodorizing products under the brands X-14, Carpet Fresh, No Vac, 1001, and 2000 Flushes, among others. It currently markets and sells its products in more than 175 countries and territories worldwide. The company generated the majority of its sales outside the US.

	Annual Growth	08/19	08/20	08/21	08/22	08/23
Sales ($mil.)	6.1%	423.4	408.5	488.1	518.8	537.3
Net income ($ mil.)	4.2%	55.9	60.7	70.2	67.3	66.0
Market value ($ mil.)	4.2%	2,472.6	2,772.1	3,250.2	2,565.7	2,914.4
Employees	5.5%	495	522	540	583	613

WEATHERFORD INTERNATIONAL PLC

NMS: WFRD

2000 St. James Place
Houston, TX 77056
Phone: 713 836-4000
Fax: –
Web: www.weatherford.com

CEO: –
CFO: –
HR: –
FYE: December 31
Type: Public

Weatherford International can weather the natural and economic storms that affect the oil and gas market. The company, which is domiciled in Switzerland but operationally based in Houston, supplies a wide range of equipment and services used in the oil and gas drilling industry, and operates in 100 countries. Weatherford provides well installation and completion systems, equipment rental, and fishing services (removing debris from wells). It provides pipeline services and oil recovery and hydraulic lift and electric submersible pumps to the oil and gas industry. The company also offers contract land drilling services.

	Annual Growth	12/19	12/20	12/21	12/22	12/23
Sales ($mil.)	110.6%	261.0	3,685.0	3,645.0	4,331.0	5,135.0
Net income ($ mil.)	–	(26.0)	(1,921.0)	(450.0)	26.0	417.0
Market value ($ mil.)	–	–	–	–	–	–
Employees	(6.3%)	24,000	17,200	17,000	17,700	18,500

WEAVER POPCORN MANUFACTURING, LLC

4485 PERRY WORTH RD
WHITESTOWN, IN 460758804
Phone: 765 934-2101
Fax: –
Web: www.popweaver.com

CEO: Jason Kashman
CFO: –
HR: Ashton Russow
FYE: December 31
Type: Private

There's another company that says Snap, Crackle, and Pop! But at Weaver it's all Pop! Weaver Popcorn makes raw, already popped, and microwave gourmet popcorns. In addition to its Pop Weaver retail products, the company packages popcorn under the Trail's End name for Boy Scout fundraising, and also offers products for private-label and concession customers. Weaver owns and cultivates farmland in the US and Argentina and grows its own specially bred hybrid corn. With popcorn as its only business, the company produces about 30% of the world's popcorn, second only to ConAgra Foods. The family-owned-and-operated company was founded in 1928 by Rev. Ira E. Weaver.

WEB.COM GROUP, INC.

5335 GATE PKWY
JACKSONVILLE, FL 322563071
Phone: 904 680-6600
Fax: –
Web: www.web.com

CEO: David L Brown
CFO: Christina Clohecy
HR: Jennifer Shoemaker
FYE: December 31
Type: Private

Web.com is one of the leading web technology company and one of the nation's largest providers of website builder and online marketing services. With its extensive product offerings and personalized support, the company helps businesses of all sizes succeed online and offers a variety of options and solutions tailored to meet its customers' specific needs. The company is recognized as one of the longest-standing tech companies in the business with products and services that help small businesses around the world get online. It also offers expert services such as Custom Website Design, eCommerce Website Design, WordPress Website Design, Local SEO Services, Search Engine Optimization, and Pay-Per-Click Advertising.

WEBASTO ROOF SYSTEMS INC.

2500 EXECUTIVE HILLS DR
AUBURN HILLS, MI 483262983
Phone: 248 997-5100
Fax: –
Web: www.webasto.com

CEO: Andre Schoenekaes
CFO: Philipp Schramm
HR: –
FYE: December 31
Type: Private

Webasto Roof Systems believes your car is the best place for a little sun and fresh air. The company, founded in 1974, makes and markets convertible roof systems and sunroofs for carmakers across North America, as well as for the automotive aftermarket. Webasto also builds temperature-management systems -- air conditioners and heaters that don't need the engine to run -- for cars, trucks, RVs, emergency vehicles, buses, rail cars, boats, and specialty vehicles. The company sells its products by partnering with nearly every major OEM and through distributors worldwide. Webasto Roof Systems is a unit of family-owned German auto parts maker Webasto AG.

WEBB CHEMICAL SERVICE CORPORATION

2708 JARMAN ST
MUSKEGON, MI 494442225
Phone: 231 733-2181
Fax: –
Web: www.webbchemical.com

CEO: Brad Hilleary
CFO: –
HR: Melisa Baker
FYE: December 31
Type: Private

With its distribution routes spidering across America, Webb Chemical Service will deliver your hydrochloric and sulfuric acid, saving you the trip. The nationwide chemical distributor based in Michigan has a fleet of tankers, trailers, and freight boxes that it uses to transport chemicals to customers. Chemicals transported by Webb include acids (more than a million pounds a week), chlor-alkalis, alcohols, ketones, and acetates. In addition to transportation, the company also provides safety training, inventory management, warehousing, liquid blending, and contract packaging services.

	Annual Growth	12/05	12/06	12/07	12/08	12/09
Sales ($mil.)	44.0%	–	–	17.9	47.8	37.1
Net income ($ mil.)	90.0%	–	–	0.1	(0.0)	0.4
Market value ($ mil.)	–	–	–	–	–	–
Employees	–	–	–	–	–	100

WEBCO INDUSTRIES INC.

NBB: WEBC

9101 West 21st Street
Sand Springs, OK 74063
Phone: 918 241-1094
Fax: –
Web: www.webcotube.com

CEO: Dana S Weber
CFO: Michael P Howard
HR: Amber Sphr
FYE: July 31
Type: Public

Webco is North America's leading manufacturer of precision welded tubing, producing carbon, stainless and specialty steel, nickel, titanium, and other alloy tube products for a variety of applications. The company's primary product types include welded tubing seamless cold-drawn and welded cold-drawn tubing. It also offers alloy/grade tubing such as carbon tubing, nickel alloys, specialty alloys, stainless steel tubing, and titanium tubing, as well as tubing for a variety of applications including air coolers, air heaters, boiler tubes, coiled tubing, steam surface condenser, feed water heater, heat exchanger tubing, and mechanical tube, among others. Webco Industries' customers include customers in the agricultural, automotive, housing, oil and gas, and petrochemical industries, among others. Bill Weber founded Webco Industries in 1969 with a goal of creating a vibrant company for the ages.

	Annual Growth	07/17	07/18	07/19	07/20	07/21
Sales ($mil.)	4.9%	384.9	500.4	548.6	428.8	466.6
Net income ($ mil.)	36.8%	5.6	23.3	25.6	4.2	19.7
Market value ($ mil.)	12.2%	66.7	93.4	106.8	66.7	106.0
Employees	–	–	–	–	–	–

WEBER DISTRIBUTION, LLC

13530 ROSECRANS AVE
SANTA FE SPRINGS, CA 906705087
Phone: 855 469-3237
Fax: –
Web: www.weberlogistics.com

CEO: Bob Lilja
CFO: Maggie Movius
HR: –
FYE: December 31
Type: Private

Third-party logistics (3PL) provider Weber Distribution (dba Weber Logistics) arranges the transportation, storage, and distribution of freight for customers in the chemical, food/beverage, paper, and retail industries, including Wal-Mart, Target, and Spectrum Brands. The company operates about 5 million sq. ft. of warehouse space, including more than 1 million sq. ft. of refrigerated space, at 17 facilities in the Western US. It also operates its own trucking fleet and provides a wide range of logistics services. Chairman Nicholas Weber represents the third generation of his family to own and lead the company, which was founded in 1924.

WEBER STATE UNIVERSITY

1014 DIXON PKWY DEPT 1014
OGDEN, UT 844080001
Phone: 801 626-6606
Fax: –
Web: www.weber.edu

CEO: –
CFO: Steven E Nabor
HR: –
FYE: June 30
Type: Private

There may be more well-known universities in Utah but none with more choices. Weber State University (WSU) boasts more than 250 undergraduate certificate and degree programs, which it claims is the most in the state. It also grants 11 graduate degrees in fields including accounting, athletic training, business administration, criminal justice, education, English, health administration, and nursing. The school also offers online, distance, and evening courses. Some 27,000 students attend the university, which has campuses Ogden and Layton, Utah. It was founded as Weber Stake Academy in 1889 and officially became WSU in 1991.

	Annual Growth	06/07	06/08	06/09	06/10	06/14
Sales ($mil.)	5.8%	–	–	76.8	84.8	101.7
Net income ($ mil.)	9.0%	–	–	15.4	27.4	23.7
Market value ($ mil.)	–	–	–	–	–	–
Employees	–	–	–	–	–	3,500

WEBMD HEALTH CORP.

395 HUDSON ST FL 3
NEW YORK, NY 100147455
Phone: 212 624-3700
Fax: –
Web: www.wbmd.com

CEO: Robert N Brisco
CFO: Blake Desimone
HR: –
FYE: December 31
Type: Private

WebMD Health Corp. provides valuable health information, tools for managing your health, and support to those who seek information. It is a leading provider of health information services to consumers, physicians and other healthcare professionals, employers and health plans through the company's public and private online portals, mobile platforms and health-focused publications. Its WebMD.com portal is the company's primary public portal for consumers and related mobile-optimized sites and mobile apps. WebMD's Medscape is the leading online global destination for physicians and healthcare professionals worldwide, offering the latest medical news and expert perspectives; essential point-of-care drug and disease information; and relevant professional education and CME.

WEBSTER FINANCIAL CORP (WATERBURY, CONN)   NYS: WBS

200 Elm Street
Stamford, CT 06902
Phone: 203 578-2202
Fax: –
Web: www.websterbank.com

CEO: John R Ciulla
CFO: Glenn I Macinnes
HR: Chris Muller
FYE: December 31
Type: Public

Webster Financial Corporation is the holding company for Webster Bank, which operates over 200 branches in Connecticut, New York, Massachusetts, and Rhode Island. Webster Bank, National Association (Webster Bank) and its HSA Bank division deliver a wide range of digital and traditional financial solutions to individuals, families, and businesses. Webster Bank serves consumer and business customers with mortgage lending, financial planning, trust, and investment services through a distribution network consisting of banking centers, ATMs, a customer care center, and a full range of web and mobile-based banking services. It also offers equipment financing, commercial real estate lending, asset-based lending, and treasury and payment solutions primarily in the eastern US. Webster has approximately $64.8 billion in assets.

	Annual Growth	12/19	12/20	12/21	12/22	12/23
Assets ($mil.)	25.3%	30,389	32,591	34,916	71,278	74,945
Net income ($ mil.)	22.7%	382.7	220.6	408.9	644.3	867.8
Market value ($ mil.)	(1.2%)	9,179.1	7,250.7	9,605.7	8,143.5	8,731.8
Employees	6.6%	3,298	3,345	3,245	4,746	4,261

WEBSTER PREFERRED CAPITAL CORP.

145 Bank Street
Waterbury, CT 06702
Phone: 203 578-2202
Fax: –
Web: www.websteronline.com

CEO: –
CFO: Gregory S Madar
HR: –
FYE: December 31
Type: Public

If you're grappling with the proper definition of a REIT, turn to Webster. A real estate investment trust (or REIT), Webster Preferred Capital invests in real estate mortgage assets, primarily Connecticut residential mortgage loans (both conforming and nonconforming) and mortgage-backed securities, typically those guaranteed by the federal government. Webster Preferred Capital is a wholly owned subsidiary of Webster Bank, the banking subsidiary of Webster Financial. The REIT buys all of its residential loans from Webster Bank; the bank also provides advisory and administrative services for Webster Preferred.

	Annual Growth	12/06	12/07	12/08	12/09	12/10
Sales ($mil.)	(30.0%)	27.0	19.4	14.6	8.8	6.5
Net income ($ mil.)	(30.9%)	26.7	19.4	13.8	8.2	6.1
Market value ($ mil.)	(0.5%)	0.0	0.0	0.0	0.0	0.0
Employees	13.6%	3	3	7	7	5

WEBSTER UNIVERSITY

470 E LOCKWOOD AVE
SAINT LOUIS, MO 631193194
Phone: 314 968-6900
Fax: –
Web: www.webster.edu

CEO: –
CFO: Ken Creehan
HR: Lisa Scott
FYE: May 31
Type: Private

They have more than dictionaries at this Webster. Webster University is a private school that serves about 22,000 undergraduate and graduate students through an international network of more than 100 campuses. Its main campus in St. Louis, Missouri, has an enrollment of more than 8,000 students and 700 faculty and staff members. Other locations span the US, and are also present in Europe, Asia, and other regions; many campuses are on military bases. Alumni include former shuttle commander Eileen Collins, actress Marsha Mason, and Indonesia's first democratically elected president, Susilo Bambang Yudhoyono. Webster University was founded as a small Catholic women's college in 1915.

	Annual Growth	05/15	05/16	05/20	05/21	05/22
Sales ($mil.)	(8.8%)	–	212.2	149.0	133.6	122.4
Net income ($ mil.)	–	–	16.0	(17.5)	2.3	(39.7)
Market value ($ mil.)	–	–	–	–	–	–
Employees	–	–	–	–	–	4,500

WEC ENERGY GROUP INC   NYS: WEC

231 West Michigan Street, P.O. Box 1331
Milwaukee, WI 53201
Phone: 414 221-2345
Fax: 414 221-2172
Web: www.wecenergygroup.com

CEO: J K Fletcher
CFO: Xia Liu
HR: John Niehaus
FYE: December 31
Type: Public

WEC Energy Group keeps the lights illuminated and the gas fires burning for approximately 4.6 million customers in Wisconsin, Illinois, Michigan, and Minnesota. The company owns approximately 7,700 MW of generation capacity, and approximately 51,400 miles of natural gas distribution and transmission lines. It also provides Milwaukee with steam for use in processing, space heating, hot water, and humidification. Its generation capacity includes ten coal-fired and about 40 natural gas-fired plants as well as solar, wind, hydro, and biomass plants. WEC is the largest electric utility company in Wisconsin, serving residential customers as well as industries such as paper, metals, manufacturing, health services, and education on a retail or wholesale basis.

	Annual Growth	12/19	12/20	12/21	12/22	12/23
Sales ($mil.)	4.3%	7,523.1	7,241.7	8,316.0	9,597.4	8,893.0
Net income ($ mil.)	4.1%	1,135.2	1,201.1	1,301.5	1,409.3	1,332.9
Market value ($ mil.)	(2.3%)	29,093	29,029	30,619	29,575	26,550
Employees	(1.7%)	7,509	7,273	6,938	7,022	7,000

WEDBUSH SECURITIES INC.

1000 WILSHIRE BLVD STE 900
LOS ANGELES, CA 900171774
Phone: 213 688-8000
Fax: -
Web: www.wedbush.com

CEO: Edward W Wedbush
CFO: Dan Billings
HR: Aline Rosenberg
FYE: June 30
Type: Private

Operating from the famed Wilshire Boulevard in Los Angeles, brokerage firm Wedbush Securities offers investment banking and a range of financial services, including financial planning, sales and trading, and clearing services. The firm targets mid-market growth companies and entrepreneurs in California and the western US. It provides research to institutional clients in the consumer products, retail, health care, and other sectors. Its ClientLink service provides clients access to account information and reports via the Internet. Wedbush Securities is affiliated with investment firm Wedbush Capital Partners; both entities are controlled by holding company Wedbush, Inc.

WEGENER CORP.   NBB: WGNR

11350 Technology Circle
Johns Creek, GA 30097
Phone: 770 814-4015
Fax: 770 623-0698
Web: www.wegener.com

CEO: -
CFO: -
HR: -
FYE: December 31
Type: Public

Wegener doesn't mind broadcasting its business. The company, through its Wegener Communications subsidiary, makes transmission and receiving equipment primarily for the broadcast and data communications markets. Its products include digital and analog compression equipment that increases satellite channel capacity, cue and control products that enable cable networks to insert local commercials, devices that feed data to news and weather services, and equipment that transmits background music to businesses. Customers include MUZAK and Roberts Communications.

	Annual Growth	09/16	09/17*	12/19	12/20	12/21
Sales ($mil.)	(9.0%)	3.5	3.4	3.4	0.9	2.2
Net income ($ mil.)	-	(0.2)	(0.1)	0.0	(1.1)	0.2
Market value ($ mil.)	7.6%	0.3	0.5	0.3	0.3	0.5
Employees	-	21	21	-	-	-

*Fiscal year change

WEGMANS FOOD MARKETS, INC.

1500 BROOKS AVE
ROCHESTER, NY 146243589
Phone: 585 328-2550
Fax: -
Web: www.wegmans.com

CEO: Colleen Wegman
CFO: James J Leo
HR: Cheryl Geer
FYE: December 26
Type: Private

Wegmans is a regional supermarket chain and is one of the largest private companies in the US. The regional grocery chain owns more than 110 stores. Wegmans raves about the open-air market ambiance, the selection of foods, and the award-winning service. It offers a wide variety of delicious, freshly prepared meals and catered favorites for delivery, curbside pickup, or carryout. Founded in 1916, John Wegman opens the Rochester Fruit & Vegetable Company, which marks the beginning of Wegmans Food Markets.

WEEKS MARINE, INC.

4 COMMERCE DR FL 2
CRANFORD, NJ 070163520
Phone: 908 272-4010
Fax: -
Web: www.weeksmarine.com

CEO: Richard S Weeks
CFO: Arthur Smeding
HR: -
FYE: December 31
Type: Private

Weeks Marine is a leader in maritime construction. The company has five specialized divisions ? marine construction, dredging, marine services, tunneling, and aggregates with completed projects throughout North and South America, from inland waterways to off-shore sites in the Pacific and the Atlantic. The company also performs construction and building of docks, wharves, piers, bridges, subaqueous pipelines, and other waterfront structures. Weeks is internationally recognized as a leader in marine construction, working across multiple market sectors including energy, transportation, heavy civil infrastructure, environmental remediation, and coastal resiliency. The company was founded by Francis H. and Richard B. Weeks in 1919 as the Weeks Stevedoring Company. In early 2023, Weeks Marine and its subsidiaries Healy Tibbitts Builders, McNally International. and North American Aggregates was acquired by Kiewit Corporation for an undisclosed amount.

	Annual Growth	12/05	12/06	12/07	12/08	12/10
Sales ($mil.)	4.3%	-	-	472.1	439.7	536.1
Net income ($ mil.)	23.7%	-	-	53.1	61.7	100.4
Market value ($ mil.)	-	-	-	-	-	-
Employees	-	-	-	-	-	1,500

WEIRTON MEDICAL CENTER, INC.

601 COLLIERS WAY
WEIRTON, WV 260625014
Phone: 304 797-6000
Fax: -
Web: www.weirtonmedical.com

CEO: Charles M Obrien Jr
CFO: -
HR: Angela Shughart
FYE: June 30
Type: Private

There's nothing weird about Weirton Medical Center. The 240-bed, not-for-profit hospital provides a wide range of health services to the tri-state region of West Virginia, Ohio, and Pennsylvania. Inpatient services include pediatrics, obstetrics, and other acute care services. Founded in 1953, the hospital also offers clinical and diagnostic care services such as emergency medicine, home health care, rehabilitation, and occupational therapy. Weirton Medical Center has seen a steady decrease in patient volumes in recent years forcing the hospital to enact a number of cost-saving measures including cutting back on some services and laying off employees.

	Annual Growth	06/18	06/19	06/20	06/21	06/22
Sales ($mil.)	3.1%	-	204.3	200.1	205.1	223.7
Net income ($ mil.)	-	-	(5.1)	3.9	1.3	10.1
Market value ($ mil.)	-	-	-	-	-	-
Employees	-	-	-	-	-	1,100

WEIS MARKETS, INC.

1000 S. Second Street, P.O. Box 471
Sunbury, PA 17801-0471
Phone: 570 286-4571
Fax: –
Web: www.weismarkets.com

NYS: WMK
CEO: Jonathan H Weis
CFO: Scott F Frost
HR: Art Bandy
FYE: December 30
Type: Public

Weis (pronounced "Wise") Markets owns around 195 grocery stores, mostly in Pennsylvania. The stores range from 8,000 to 71,000 sq. ft. (with an average size of about 49,000 sq. ft.) and offer a host of traditional grocery items -- dairy products, frozen foods, general merchandise, seafood, deli products -- as well as pharmacy and fuel services. The store product selection includes national, local and private brands including natural, gluten-free and organic varieties. Weis Markets was established in 1912 by Harry and Sigmund Weis in Sunbury, Pennsylvania. The Weis family still controls about 65% of the company's voting power.

	Annual Growth	12/19	12/20	12/21	12/22	12/23
Sales ($mil.)	7.3%	3,543.3	4,112.6	4,224.4	4,695.9	4,697.0
Net income ($ mil.)	11.2%	68.0	118.9	108.8	125.2	103.8
Market value ($ mil.)	12.4%	1,079.2	1,275.8	1,742.2	2,213.5	1,720.4
Employees	–	23,000	24,000	24,000	23,000	23,000

WELBILT, INC.

2227 WELBILT BLVD
TRINITY, FL 346555130
Phone: 727 375-7010
Fax: –
Web: www.welbilt.com

CEO: William C Johnson
CFO: Martin D Agard
HR: –
FYE: December 31
Type: Private

Welbilt, Inc., an Ali Group company, provides the world's top chefs, premier chain operators and growing independents with industry-leading equipment and solutions. Its portfolio of award-winning product brands includes Cleveland, Convotherm, Crem, Delfield, Frymaster, Garland, Kolpak, Lincoln, Merco, Merrychef, and Multiplex. These product brands are supported by three service brands: KitchenCare, its aftermarket parts and service brand, FitKitchen, its fully-integrated kitchen systems brand, and KitchenConnect, its cloud-based digital platform brand. The company sells its products through a global network of over 5,000 distributors, dealers, buying groups and manufacturers' representatives in over 100 countries.

WELCH FOODS INC., A COOPERATIVE

575 VIRGINIA RD
CONCORD, MA 017422761
Phone: 978 371-1000
Fax: –
Web: www.welchs.com

CEO: Trevor Bynum
CFO: Michael Perda
HR: –
FYE: August 31
Type: Private

Welch Foods is a co-op owned by more than 700 American farming families across the country who bring their best to every harvest. The company produces Welch's brand grape and white grape juices. Its beverage line includes sparkling juices and cocktails. Welch also makes and markets fresh grapes and snacks as well as preserved offerings (jellies, jams, and spreads). Its products are made from Concord and Niagara grapes grown at family farms across the US. The company was founded in 1849 by Ephraim Bull when he grew the first Concord grape on his farm in Massachusetts.

	Annual Growth	08/12	08/13	08/14	08/15	08/16
Sales ($mil.)	(0.5%)	–	608.5	609.9	609.1	600.2
Net income ($ mil.)	8.8%	–	65.1	76.9	81.3	83.9
Market value ($ mil.)	–	–	–	–	–	–
Employees	–	–	–	–	–	1,000

WELLESLEY COLLEGE

106 CENTRAL ST
WELLESLEY, MA 024818203
Phone: 781 283-1000
Fax: –
Web: www.wellesley.edu

CEO: –
CFO: –
HR: Eloise McGaw
FYE: June 30
Type: Private

Wellesley College is a liberal arts women's college (one of the famed "Seven Sisters" schools) that offers majors in more than 50 fields of study, including anthropology, computer science, education, physics, and sociology. It has a three-college collaboration with Massachusetts' Babson and Olin Colleges to provide additional opportunities for its students, and also has cross-registration agreements with MIT and Brandeis. Wellesley's Davis Degree program is geared toward women beyond traditional college age. The college has a student enrollment of some 2,500 and a student-faculty ratio of about 7 to 1.

	Annual Growth	06/18	06/19	06/20	06/21	06/22
Sales ($mil.)	1.9%	–	239.3	233.0	221.1	252.9
Net income ($ mil.)	–	–	43.8	109.4	981.9	(366.5)
Market value ($ mil.)	–	–	–	–	–	–
Employees	–	–	–	–	–	2,000

WELLEX CORPORATION

551 BROWN RD
FREMONT, CA 945397003
Phone: 510 743-1818
Fax: –
Web: www.wellex.com

CEO: Chiennan Huang
CFO: –
HR: Gina Chen
FYE: December 31
Type: Private

Wellex provides a welcome break from manufacturing chores. As a contract electronics manufacturer, Wellex makes printed circuit boards (PCBs) for OEMs in the industrial and commercial equipment, medical, networking, security systems, automotive, and solar industries. The company offers surface-mount and pin-through-hole PCB assemblies, along with design, testing, and repair services, to such diverse customers as Eastman Kodak, Ingersoll-Rand, and St. Jude Medical, with plants in China and the US. Wellex was founded in 1983 by Jackson Wang (CEO), Chern Lee (former CEO), and Danny Lee (former chairman).

	Annual Growth	12/03	12/04	12/05	12/06	12/07
Sales ($mil.)	4.7%	–	–	26.2	29.7	28.7
Net income ($ mil.)	(14.5%)	–	–	0.5	0.6	0.4
Market value ($ mil.)	–	–	–	–	–	–
Employees	–	–	–	–	–	150

WELLMONT HEALTH SYSTEM

1905 AMERICAN WAY
KINGSPORT, TN 376605882
Phone: 423 230-8200
Fax: –
Web: www.balladhealth.org

CEO: –
CFO: –
HR: –
FYE: June 30
Type: Private

At Wellmont Health System, wellness is paramount. Wellmont Health System provides general and advanced medical-surgical care to residents of northeastern Tennessee and southwestern Virginia. The health system consists of about a dozen owned and affiliated hospitals that collectively have more than 1,000 licensed beds. One of its facilities is a rehabilitation hospital operated in partnership with HealthSouth. The system's Holston Valley Medical Center features a level I trauma center and a level III neonatal intensive care unit (NICU). Wellmont also operates numerous ancillary facilities, including an assisted living center, a mental health clinic, home health care and hospice agencies, and outpatient centers.

	Annual Growth	06/15	06/16	06/17	06/21	06/22
Sales ($mil.)	(1.4%)	–	–	908.1	807.5	845.5
Net income ($ mil.)	(2.4%)	–	–	53.7	92.0	47.7
Market value ($ mil.)	–	–	–	–	–	–
Employees	–	–	–	–	–	6,114

WELLSKY CORPORATION

11300 SWITZER RD
OVERLAND PARK, KS 662103665
Phone: 913 307-1000
Fax: –
Web: www.wellsky.com

CEO: Bill Miller
CFO: Robert Watkins
HR: –
FYE: June 30
Type: Private

Mediware Information Systems keeps blood banks' computers from becoming a bloody mess. The company offers data management systems for blood banks, hospitals, and pharmacies. Mediware is known for its clinical information systems, which combine third-party and proprietary software to manage hospital departments. Products include the HCLL transfusion management system for tracking blood bank and transfusion facility inventories, the WORx drug therapy management software for pharmacies, and the InSight performance management software suite. Mediware has been owned by private equity firms since 2012.

WELLSTAR HEALTH SYSTEM, INC.

793 SAWYER RD
MARIETTA, GA 300622222
Phone: 770 956-7827
Fax: –
Web: www.wellstar.org

CEO: Jim Budzinksi
CFO: A J Budzinski
HR: Danyale Ziglor
FYE: June 30
Type: Private

The not-for-profit WellStar Health System is Georgia's largest health system, with nine hospitals, five health parks, more than 80 rehabilitation centers, about 20 urgent care locations, and more than 300 medical office locations. WellStar has more than 24,000 team members?including 6,000 nurses and more than 3,000 physicians and advanced practitioners?providing compassionate, high-quality care. It is also the only health system with a network of Level 1, Level 2, and Level 3 trauma centers in metro Atlanta. These centers help WellStar serves the most critical patients with a range of emergency care options.

	Annual Growth	06/14	06/15	06/19	06/20	06/21
Sales ($mil.)	(60.9%)	–	823.9	1.5	1.1	2.9
Net income ($ mil.)	(63.4%)	–	49.8	1.2	0.7	0.1
Market value ($ mil.)	–	–	–	–	–	–
Employees	–	–	–	–	–	11,985

WELLTOWER INC
NYS: WELL

4500 Dorr Street
Toledo, OH 43615
Phone: 419 247-2800
Fax: –
Web: www.welltower.com

CEO: Shankh Mitra
CFO: Timothy G McHugh
HR: –
FYE: December 31
Type: Public

Welltower, a real estate investment trust (REIT), owns interests in properties concentrated in major, high-growth markets in the US, Canada and the UK, consisting of seniors housing, post-acute communities and outpatient medical properties. The company invests with leading seniors housing operators, post-acute providers and health systems to fund the real estate and infrastructure needed to scale innovative care delivery models and improve people's wellness and overall health care experience. Its portfolio includes around 1,500 properties leased to healthcare operators in around 45 states in the US ? its largest market.

	Annual Growth	12/18	12/19	12/20	12/21	12/22
Sales ($mil.)	5.7%	4,700.5	5,121.3	4,606.0	4,742.1	5,860.6
Net income ($ mil.)	(35.3%)	805.0	1,232.4	978.8	336.1	141.2
Market value ($ mil.)	(1.4%)	34,046	40,114	31,697	42,071	32,153
Employees	7.6%	384	443	423	464	514

WENDY'S CO (THE)
NMS: WEN

One Dave Thomas Blvd.
Dublin, OH 43017
Phone: 614 764-3100
Fax: –
Web: www.wendys.com

CEO: Kirk Tanner
CFO: Gunther Plosch
HR: Richard Grossman
FYE: December 31
Type: Public

The Wendy's Company is one of the largest quick-service restaurant companies in the hamburger sandwich segment in the US. The chain consists of about 5,995 Wendy's restaurants in operation in the US, roughly 405 of which are owned and operated by the company; the rest are franchised. In addition, it has about 1,100 Wendy's restaurants in operation in over 30 foreign countries and US territories. Its restaurant offers an extensive menu specializing in hamburger sandwiches and featuring filet of chicken breast sandwiches, it also serves chicken sandwiches, chicken nuggets, baked potatoes, freshly prepared salads, soft drinks, Frosty desserts, and kids' meals. Dave Thomas opened the company's first restaurant in Columbus, Ohio in 1969 and named it after his daughter.

	Annual Growth	12/19*	01/21	01/22	01/23*	12/23
Sales ($mil.)	6.3%	1,709.0	1,733.8	1,897.0	2,095.5	2,181.6
Net income ($ mil.)	10.5%	136.9	117.8	200.4	177.4	204.4
Market value ($ mil.)	(3.2%)	4,551.6	4,502.3	4,898.7	4,648.1	4,001.1
Employees	3.6%	13,300	14,000	14,500	14,500	15,300

*Fiscal year change

WERNER ENTERPRISES, INC.
NMS: WERN

14507 Frontier Road, Post Office Box 45308
Omaha, NE 68145-0308
Phone: 402 895-6640
Fax: –
Web: www.werner.com

CEO: Derek J Leathers
CFO: Christopher D Wikoff
HR: –
FYE: December 31
Type: Public

Founded in 1956, Werner Enterprises is a transportation and logistics company engaged primarily in transporting truckload shipments of general commodities in both interstate and intrastate commerce in and between the US and Canada as well as cross-border services into Mexico. One of the largest truckload carriers in the US, Werner boasts some 8,305 company tractors and about 295 tractors owned by independent contractors, and approximately 29,965 trailers. Its Truckload business offers dry-van and specialized trucking services on a dedicated basis, in addition to one-way trucking services, such as cross-border, time-sensitive, and temperature-controlled. Werner's Logistics business provides complete management of global shipments from origin to destination. The US generates roughly 95% of the company's sales.

	Annual Growth	12/19	12/20	12/21	12/22	12/23
Sales ($mil.)	7.4%	2,463.7	2,372.2	2,734.4	3,290.0	3,283.5
Net income ($ mil.)	(9.4%)	166.9	169.1	259.1	241.3	112.4
Market value ($ mil.)	3.9%	2,308.8	2,488.3	3,023.8	2,554.3	2,688.2
Employees	1.0%	13,276	12,732	13,815	14,595	13,809

WESBANCO INC
NMS: WSBC

1 Bank Plaza
Wheeling, WV 26003
Phone: 304 234-9000
Fax: –
Web: www.wesbanco.com

CEO: Todd F Clossin
CFO: Daniel K Weiss Jr
HR: Rachael Robb
FYE: December 31
Type: Public

Founded in 1870, WesBanco is a diversified and balanced financial services company that delivers large bank capabilities with a community bank feel. It offers a full range of financial services including retail banking, corporate trust services, personal and corporate trust services, brokerage services, mortgage banking, and insurance. WesBanco operates one commercial bank: Wesbanco Bank which has about 205 branches and nearly 205 ATM machines located in West Virginia, Ohio, western Pennsylvania, Kentucky, southern Indiana and Maryland. Wesbanco offers its services through its community banking and trust and investment services segments. Wesbanco's non-banking operations include brokerage firm Wesbanco Securities, real estate company Wesbanco Properties, investment firm Wesbanco Asset Management and multi-line insurance provider Wesbanco Insurance Services.

	Annual Growth	12/19	12/20	12/21	12/22	12/23
Assets ($mil.)	3.0%	15,720	16,426	16,927	16,932	17,712
Net income ($ mil.)	–	158.9	122.0	242.3	192.1	159.0
Market value ($ mil.)	(4.5%)	2,243.8	1,778.9	2,077.6	2,195.7	1,862.6
Employees	(3.8%)	2,705	2,612	2,389	2,426	2,321

WESCO AIRCRAFT HOLDINGS, INC.

2601 MEACHAM BLVD STE 400
FORT WORTH, TX 761374213
Phone: 817 284-4449
Fax: –
Web: www.incora.com

CEO: David Coleal
CFO: Ray Carney
HR: –
FYE: September 30
Type: Private

Incora, formerly Wesco Aircraft and Pattonair, is a leading, independent distributor and global provider of innovative supply chain solutions. Beginning with a strong foundation in aerospace and defense, Incora also utilizes its supply chain expertise to serve automotive, healthcare, energy, electronics, pest control, industrial equipment manufacturing, marine, pharmaceuticals and beyond. Incora incorporates itself into customers' businesses, managing all aspects of supply chain from procurement and inventory management to logistics and on-site customer services. With more than 644,000 SKUs, the company serves more than 8,400 customers globally.

	Annual Growth	09/15	09/16	09/17	09/18	09/19
Sales ($mil.)	4.7%	–	1,477.4	1,429.4	1,570.5	1,696.5
Net income ($ mil.)	(38.4%)	–	91.4	(237.3)	32.7	21.4
Market value ($ mil.)	–	–	–	–	–	–
Employees	–	–	–	–	–	3,070

WESCO INTERNATIONAL, INC.

225 West Station Square Drive, Suite 700
Pittsburgh, PA 15219
Phone: 412 454-2200
Fax: –
Web: www.wesco.com

NYS: WCC
CEO: –
CFO: –
HR: –
FYE: December 31
Type: Public

WESCO is a leading provider of business-to-business distribution, logistics services, and supply chain solutions. The main product categories Wesco sources are electrical distribution and controls, communications and security, wire, cable and conduit, lighting and sustainability, automation and motors, and general supplies across commercial and industrial businesses, contractors, government agencies, institutions, telecommunications providers, and utilities. Its innovative value-added solutions include supply chain management, logistics and transportation, procurement, warehousing and inventory management, kitting and labeling, limited assembly of products and installation enhancement. WESCO offers millions of products from some 50,000 suppliers, with about 150,000 customers worldwide. The company generates almost 75% of its sales in the US.

	Annual Growth	12/19	12/20	12/21	12/22	12/23
Sales ($mil.)	27.9%	8,358.9	12,326	18,218	21,420	22,385
Net income ($ mil.)	36.1%	223.4	100.6	465.4	860.5	765.5
Market value ($ mil.)	30.8%	3,022.8	3,995.4	6,697.6	6,372.3	8,850.0
Employees	20.5%	9,500	18,000	18,000	20,000	20,000

WESLEYAN UNIVERSITY

45 WYLLYS AVE
MIDDLETOWN, CT 064593211
Phone: 860 685-2000
Fax: –
Web: www.wesleyan.edu

CEO: –
CFO: –
HR: –
FYE: June 30
Type: Private

Wesleyan University is a private institution offering liberal arts and sciences education from its 360-acre campus in Middletown, Connecticut. Some 3,500 undergraduate and graduate students attend the university, which has programs in academic areas including American studies, film studies, and psychology. Notable alumni include television producer Joss Whedon and educational writer Ted Fiske. Founded in 1831, Wesleyan was the first of several US colleges and universities to be named after John Wesley, founder of the Methodist church; it ended its formal affiliation with the church in 1937.

	Annual Growth	06/18	06/19	06/20	06/21	06/22
Sales ($mil.)	5.1%	–	231.5	232.3	227.0	268.4
Net income ($ mil.)	–	–	33.2	84.4	606.5	(67.4)
Market value ($ mil.)	–	–	–	–	–	–
Employees	–	–	–	–	–	900

WESSCO INTERNATIONAL LTD., A CALIFORNIA LIMITED PARTNERSHIP

11400 W OLYMPIC BLVD STE 450
LOS ANGELES, CA 900641550
Phone: 310 477-4272
Fax: –
Web: www.wessco.net

CEO: –
CFO: Tyler Shepodd
HR: –
FYE: December 31
Type: Private

Wessco International is a leading supplier and wholesaler of customized amenities and accessories (personal care products, bathroom accessories, and food and beverage serviceware) to the global lodging and cruise line industry. The company's clients have included Ritz Carlton, Four Seasons, Omni, Westin, Adams Mark, Bellagio, the Venetian, Royal Caribbean, Disney, Holland America, and Norwegian. Wessco International also offers customized onboard service products (tableware, hot towels, amenity kits, children's items, and passenger comfort items) to top airlines worldwide, such as American, Continental, British, KLM, AeroMexico, Singapore, and Cathay Pacific.

WEST BANCORPORATION, INC.

1601 22nd Street
West Des Moines, IA 50266
Phone: 515 222-2300
Fax: –
Web: www.westbankstrong.com

NMS: WTBA
CEO: David D Nelson
CFO: Douglas R Gulling
HR: –
FYE: December 31
Type: Public

West Bancorporation is the holding company for West Bank, which serves individuals and small to midsized businesses through about a dozen branches, mainly in the Des Moines and Iowa City, Iowa areas. Founded in 1893, the bank offers checking, savings, and money market accounts, CDs, Visa credit cards, and trust services. The bank's lending activities primarily consist of commercial mortgages; construction, land, and land development loans; and business loans, such as revolving lines of credit, inventory and accounts receivable financing, equipment financing, and capital expenditure loans, to borrowers in Iowa.

	Annual Growth	12/19	12/20	12/21	12/22	12/23
Assets ($mil.)	11.5%	2,473.7	3,185.7	3,500.2	3,613.2	3,825.8
Net income ($ mil.)	(4.2%)	28.7	32.7	49.6	46.4	24.1
Market value ($ mil.)	(4.6%)	428.7	322.8	519.6	427.3	354.6
Employees	2.7%	171	350	362	364	190

WEST CENTRAL COOPERATIVE

406 1ST ST
RALSTON, IA 514597714
Phone: 712 667-3200
Fax: –
Web: www.west-central.com

CEO: –
CFO: –
HR: –
FYE: January 31
Type: Private

Going with the grain, West Central Cooperative serves farmers in west-central Iowa. The full-service, farmer-owned agricultural co-op is made up of some 3,100 farmers in 10 counties. It provides administrative services, agronomy services grain marketing (88 million bushels per year), and feed, seed, fertilizer, and soybean processing to its members. The cooperative also operates facilities, the Renewable Energy Group, which converts soy oil into alternative energy fuels. In 2016 it merged with Farmers Cooperative Company to become Landus Cooperative.

WEST COAST NOVELTY CORPORATION

2401 MONARCH ST
ALAMEDA, CA 945017513
Phone: 510 748-4248
Fax: –
Web: www.thewcngroup.com

CEO: –
CFO: –
HR: –
FYE: August 31
Type: Private

West Coast Novelty Corp., founded in the 1920s, doesn't make concessions as one of the largest suppliers of licensed sports merchandise in the US. The firm has grown from its beginnings as a souvenir and concession operator to a nationwide distributor of licensed items, such as jerseys, T-shirts, and headwear. West Coast Novelty boasts a vast portfolio of team licenses based on its agreements with the NFL, MLB, NBA, WWF, and the Collegiate Licensing Company. To extend its reach into the Eastern and Southern US, the company operates a distribution center in Memphis, Tennessee, to supplement operations at its Alameda, California, facility.

	Annual Growth	08/06	08/07	08/08	08/09	08/10
Sales ($mil.)	(20.9%)	–	–	60.1	45.0	37.6
Net income ($ mil.)	–	–	–	1.2	(0.5)	(0.0)
Market value ($ mil.)	–	–	–	–	–	–
Employees	–	–	–	–	–	80

WEST MARINE, INC.

1 E BROWARD BLVD STE 200
FORT LAUDERDALE, FL 333011872
Phone: 831 728-2700
Fax: –
Web: www.westmarine.com

CEO: Matthew L Hyde
CFO: Cheryl Miller
HR: –
FYE: January 02
Type: Private

West Marine is the premier retailer of boating, fishing, sailing and paddling gear. With more than 240 stores located in about 40 US states and Puerto Rico and an eCommerce website reaching domestic, international and professional customers, the company is recognized as a leading resource for cruisers, sailors, anglers and paddlesports enthusiasts. The company serves customers through its largest store, westmarine.com, which features more than 100,000 products. Randy Repass, West Marine's founder, began selling nylon rope by mail order under the name West Coast Ropes in 1968.

WEST PHARMACEUTICAL SERVICES, INC.
NYS: WST

530 Herman O. West Drive
Exton, PA 19341-0645
Phone: 610 594-2900
Fax: –
Web: www.westpharma.com

CEO: Eric M Green
CFO: Bernard J Birkett
HR: –
FYE: December 31
Type: Public

West Pharmaceutical Services is a leading global manufacturer in the design and production of technologically advanced, high-quality, integrated containment and delivery components for pharmaceutical and health care products. The company's proprietary drug and biologic packaging products include seals and stoppers for injectable medicine, syringe components, and injection systems. It also has vast expertise in product design and development, including in-house mold design, process design and validation and high-speed automated assemblies for pharmaceutical, diagnostic, and medical device customers. The US is West's largest single market, accounting for about 45% of total revenue.

	Annual Growth	12/19	12/20	12/21	12/22	12/23
Sales ($mil.)	12.5%	1,839.9	2,146.9	2,831.6	2,886.9	2,949.8
Net income ($ mil.)	25.2%	241.7	346.2	661.8	585.9	593.4
Market value ($ mil.)	23.7%	11,049	20,823	34,472	17,298	25,881
Employees	6.6%	8,200	9,200	10,065	10,700	10,600

WEST TECHNOLOGY GROUP, LLC

11650 MIRACLE HILLS DR
OMAHA, NE 681544498
Phone: 402 963-1200
Fax: –
Web: www.intrado.com

CEO: –
CFO: –
HR: –
FYE: December 31
Type: Private

West Technology Group, LLC (formerly Intrado Corporation) is an innovative, cloud-based, global technology partner to clients around the world. Its solutions connect people and organizations at the right time and in the right ways, making those mission-critical connections more relevant, engaging, and actionable - turning Information to Insight. Its omnichannel capabilities enable a vast array of essential solutions for a diverse client base that includes Fortune 1000 companies, state, and local governments, along with small and medium enterprises in a variety of vertical industries.

WEST TEXAS GAS, INC.

303 VETERANS AIRPARK LN STE 5100
MIDLAND, TX 797054512
Phone: 432 682-4349
Fax: –
Web: www.westtexasgas.com

CEO: –
CFO: –
HR: Nanc Chandlerdavis
FYE: December 31
Type: Private

With a deep understanding the utility of natural gas, natural gas utility West Texas Gas distributes more than 25 billion cu. ft. of natural gas, propane, and other petroleum products to more than 25,000 residential, commercial, agricultural, and governmental customers in Texas and Oklahoma Panhandle region. The company, the fourth-largest investor-owned public utility in Texas, also operates retail gasoline stations and convenience stores and has gas gathering, production, transmission, and marketing operations. West Texas Gas is 100%-owned by CEO J. L. Davis.

WEST VIRGINIA UNIVERSITY HOSPITALS, INC.

1 MEDICAL CENTER DR
MORGANTOWN, WV 265061200
Phone: 304 598-4000
Fax: –
Web: account.mayoclinic.org

CEO: Albert L Wright Jr
CFO: –
HR: Cheryl Maynard
FYE: December 31
Type: Private

West Virginia University Hospitals (WVUH) has West Virginians covered. The health care system's 530-bed main campus includes the Ruby Memorial Hospital, the WVU Children's Hospital, and the behavioral health Chestnut Ridge Center, as well as outpatient care centers. Other services include centers for eye and dental care, cancer treatment, and family medicine. WVUH's facilities serve as the primary teaching locations for the West Virginia University's health professions schools. Cheat Lake Physicians is the physicians group associated with the health system. WVUH is a member of the West Virginia United Health System.

	Annual Growth	12/17	12/18	12/20	12/21	12/22
Sales ($mil.)	10.8%	–	1,193.9	1,452.7	1,391.4	1,797.7
Net income ($ mil.)	–	–	(39.8)	57.4	175.4	(26.5)
Market value ($ mil.)	–	–	–	–	–	–
Employees	–	–	–	–	–	6,267

WEST VIRGINIA UNITED HEALTH SYSTEM, INC.

1 MEDICAL CENTER DR
MORGANTOWN, WV 265061200
Phone: 304 598-4000
Fax: –
Web: www.wvumedicine.org

CEO: Christophe Colenda MD
CFO: –
HR: –
FYE: December 31
Type: Private

West Virginia United Health System (WVUHS) helps residents in the Mountain State stay on top of their health. The system operates United Hospital Center (in Clarksburg), as well as hospitals in the West Virginia University Hospitals (WVUH) system, including City Hospital (Martinsburg), Jefferson Memorial Hospital (Ranson), and WVUH's home hospital in Morgantown. In addition, WVUHS operates WVUH's Cheat Lake physicians ambulatory center, as well as a network of about a dozen primary care clinics located throughout central and northern West Virginia. Combined, the system's hospitals and clinics have more than 1000 beds and treat approximately 1.4 million patients annually.

	Annual Growth	12/15	12/16	12/17	12/19	12/22
Sales ($mil.)	16.5%	–	–	2,172.7	2,770.2	4,663.9
Net income ($ mil.)	7.8%	–	–	132.6	238.2	192.6
Market value ($ mil.)	–	–	–	–	–	–
Employees	–	–	–	–	–	7,000

WEST VIRGINIA UNIVERSITY

1500 UNIVERSITY AVE
MORGANTOWN, WV 26506
Phone: 304 293-2545
Fax: –
Web: www.wvu.edu

CEO: –
CFO: –
HR: –
FYE: June 30
Type: Private

West Virginia University (WVU) is the intellectual home of more than 29,000 Mountaineers (the school's mascot) and the state's preeminent institution of higher learning. WVU offers more than 180 bachelor's, master's, doctoral, and professional degree programs through some 15 colleges and schools. The university's clinical psychology and forestry programs have been recognized nationally and it boasts 100% post-graduate job placement for its nursing, pharmacy, and mining engineering majors. WVU also runs a two-year, residential school, Potomac State College, in Keyser, West Virginia.

	Annual Growth	06/15	06/16	06/17	06/18	06/22
Sales ($mil.)	1.8%	–	–	783.2	808.1	856.0
Net income ($ mil.)	(45.8%)	–	–	8.4	41.1	0.4
Market value ($ mil.)	–	–	–	–	–	–
Employees	–	–	–	–	–	6,245

WEST VIRGINIA UNIVERSITY FOUNDATION, INCORPORATED

1 WATERFRONT PL FL 7
MORGANTOWN, WV 265015978
Phone: 304 284-4000
Fax: –
Web: www.wvuf.org

CEO: Marshall Miller
CFO: –
HR: Hope Gage
FYE: June 30
Type: Private

The West Virginia University Foundation provides fund raising services and manages the financial assets of West Virginia University. The foundation seeks support for faculty, programs, services, equipment, and facilities that the state of West Virginia might not be able to fund though other fiscal sources. Provided about $75 million, the foundation obtains funds from individuals, corporations and philanthropic foundations in support of West Virginia University and its non-profit affiliates. The university founded the organization in 1954 as an independent, non-profit corporation.

	Annual Growth	06/16	06/17	06/18	06/20	06/22
Assets ($mil.)	9.5%	–	1,690.9	1,783.3	1,952.2	2,666.9
Net income ($ mil.)	22.2%	–	42.9	7.1	49.1	116.8
Market value ($ mil.)	–	–	–	–	–	–
Employees	–	–	–	–	–	115

WESTAMERICA BANCORPORATION

NMS: WABC

1108 Fifth Avenue
San Rafael, CA 94901
Phone: 707 863-6000
Fax: –
Web: www.westamerica.com

CEO: David L Payne
CFO: Robert Thorson
HR: Steve Ensinger
FYE: December 31
Type: Public

Annie get your checkbook? Maybe not as wild as Buffalo Bill's West, but Westamerica Bancorporation still shoots high with its subsidiary Westamerica Bank. The bank operates through 80 branches in Northern and Central California. It offers individuals and businesses such standard fare as checking and savings accounts, as well as online banking, loans and credits, and credit cards. It focuses on the banking needs of small businesses; business loans and commercial mortgages together account for more than three-quarters of the company's loan portfolio. Westamerica Bank was chartered in 1884

	Annual Growth	12/19	12/20	12/21	12/22	12/23
Assets ($mil.)	3.2%	5,619.6	6,747.9	7,461.0	6,950.3	6,364.6
Net income ($ mil.)	19.1%	80.4	80.4	86.5	122.0	161.8
Market value ($ mil.)	(4.5%)	1,807.5	1,474.6	1,539.7	1,573.9	1,504.5
Employees	(3.4%)	737	767	703	664	641

WESTAT, INC.

1600 RESEARCH BLVD
ROCKVILLE, MD 208503129
Phone: 301 251-1500
Fax: –
Web: www.westat.com

CEO: Graham Kalton
CFO: –
HR: –
FYE: December 31
Type: Private

Westat offers innovative professional services to help clients improve outcomes in health, education, social policy, and transportation. Westat offers a range of services including large- and small-scale surveys, program assessments and evaluation, capacity building and training, clinical trials management and operations, epidemiological studies, and communication and dissemination strategies. Westat serves the US Departments of Health and Human Services, Education, Agriculture, Treasury, Justice, Energy, Labor, and many other federal agencies, in addition to state and local governments, associations and foundations. The company was founded in 1963 and is an employee-owned.

	Annual Growth	12/12	12/13	12/14	12/15	12/16
Sales ($mil.)	(4.3%)	–	582.5	517.4	509.9	510.7
Net income ($ mil.)	0.2%	–	23.8	22.4	20.6	24.0
Market value ($ mil.)	–	–	–	–	–	–
Employees	–	–	–	–	–	2,000

WESTBRIDGE RESEARCH GROUP

1260 AVENIDA CHELSEA
VISTA, CA 920818315
Phone: 760 599-8855
Fax: –
Web: www.westbridge.com

CEO: Tina Koenemann
CFO: Christine Koenemann
HR: –
FYE: November 30
Type: Private

Westbridge Research Group wants to survive for another thousand years or so, and its products will make sure the planet will be here as well. The company manufactures environmentally safe agricultural chemicals for agriculture (fruits and vegetables), gardens, lawn, and turf. Its offerings include bioremediation (sewage treatment) products, fertilizers, and plant-growth regulators, all safe for consumers, workers, and the environment. The company's brands include TRIGGRR (plant-growth regulator) and BIOLINK (fertilizer). Westbridge Research also develops formulations for private-labels clients. The company was founded in 1982.

WESTECH CAPITAL CORP

8226 Bee Caves Road
Austin, TX 78746
Phone: 512 306-8222
Fax: –
Web: www.tejassec.com

CEO: –
CFO: –
HR: –
FYE: December 31
Type: Public

Westech Capital Corporation is the holding company for Tejas Securities Group, an investment banking and brokerage firm serving institutional and private clients throughout the US. Products include equities, fixed-income products, mutual funds, and other investment securities. The company's investment research focuses on such industries as telecommunications, technology, health care, and municipal securities; it has expertise in distressed or bankrupt companies and securities. Tejas Securities offers PIPE (private investment in public equity) transactions, securities underwriting, bridge financing, and merger and acquisition advice.

	Annual Growth	12/03	12/04	12/05	12/06	12/07
Assets ($mil.)	31.7%	8.4	22.5	81.0	31.8	25.2
Net income ($ mil.)	–	0.8	7.3	(4.5)	(43.4)	(4.4)
Market value ($ mil.)	(36.1%)	40.4	85.4	29.8	14.4	6.7
Employees	(2.1%)	61	61	73	67	56

WESTELL TECHNOLOGIES INC   NBB: WSTL

750 North Commons Drive
Aurora, IL 60504
Phone: 630 898-2500
Fax: –
Web: www.westell.com

CEO: Timothy L Duitsman
CFO: Jeniffer L Jaynes
HR: –
FYE: March 31
Type: Public

Westell Technologies knows the value of the great outdoors for communication service providers. The company makes outside plant equipment used by telecommunications providers for digital transmission, remote monitoring, power distribution and other functions that link customer locations with central office facilities. Its products include outdoor passively cooled equipment enclosures, mountings, and fuse panels. The company also provides services such as design, assembly, and testing. It generates most of its sales from major US telecommunications service providers.

	Annual Growth	03/19	03/20	03/21	03/22	03/23
Sales ($mil.)	2.1%	43.6	30.0	29.9	38.0	47.3
Net income ($ mil.)	–	(11.4)	(10.1)	(2.7)	3.9	3.8
Market value ($ mil.)	(5.2%)	23.4	8.9	8.9	15.0	18.9
Employees	–	127	102	96	–	–

WESTERN & SOUTHERN FINANCIAL GROUP, INC

400 East Fourth Street
Cincinnati, OH 45202
Phone: –
Fax: 513 629-1220
Web: www.westernsouthern.com

CEO: John F Barrett
CFO: James N Clark
HR: Shawna Kinsel
FYE: December 31
Type: Public

Western & Southern Mutual Holding Company is among the financially strongest life insurance groups in the world. It offers a wide range of insurance, investment, and retirement solutions for individuals, families, businesses, foundations, and nonprofit organizations. It also serves financial professionals and institutions with small business solutions, institutional portfolio management, private equity, real estate development, brokerage, and distribution services. Subsidiaries have included Western & Southern Life, W&S Financial Group Distributors, and Eagle Realty Group, to name a few.

WESTERN ALLIANCE BANCORPORATION   NYS: WAL

One E. Washington Street, Suite 1400
Phoenix, AZ 85004
Phone: 602 389-3500
Fax: –
Web: www.westernalliancebancorporation.com

CEO: Kenneth A Vecchione
CFO: Dale Gibbons
HR: –
FYE: December 31
Type: Public

Western Alliance Bancorporation and its flagship Western Alliance Bank (WAB) has an alliance with several bank brands in the West, operating as the Alliance Bank of Arizona; Bank of Nevada; First Independent Bank, as well as Bridge Bank, and Torrey Pines Bank. The bank provides an array of specialized financial services to business customers across the country, including mortgage banking services through AmeriHome, and has added to its capabilities with the acquisition of DST, which provides digital payment services for the class action legal industry. About 40% of the Western Alliance's loan portfolio is made up of commercial and industrial loans, while over 30% is made up of residential real estate loans. It also makes land development loans and consumer residential mortgages and other lines of credit.

	Annual Growth	12/19	12/20	12/21	12/22	12/23
Assets ($mil.)	27.5%	26,822	36,461	55,983	67,734	70,862
Net income ($ mil.)	9.7%	499.2	506.6	899.2	1,057.3	722.4
Market value ($ mil.)	3.7%	6,239.6	6,562.5	11,784	6,519.8	7,201.8
Employees	15.5%	1,835	1,915	3,139	3,365	3,260

WESTERN CONNECTICUT HEALTH NETWORK, INC.

24 HOSPITAL AVE
DANBURY, CT 068106099
Phone: 203 739-7000
Fax: –
Web: www.nuvancehealth.org

CEO: –
CFO: –
HR: Elissabeth Griffin
FYE: September 30
Type: Private

Nuvance Health is a not-for-profit health system serving New York's Hudson Valley and western Connecticut. The system has about a half-dozen hospitals, including Connecticut's Danbury Hospital and New Milford Hospital and New York's Northern Dutchess Hospital and Putnam Hospital Center. It also includes a network of primary care and specialty practices. Altogether, the system has more than 2,600 aligned physicians. Nuvance Health was established through the 2019 merger of Western Connecticut Health Network and New York-based Health Quest.

	Annual Growth	09/18	09/19	09/20	09/21	09/22
Sales ($mil.)	(70.7%)	–	–	135.5	32.5	11.6
Net income ($ mil.)	–	–	–	(2.8)	(2.7)	0.1
Market value ($ mil.)	–	–	–	–	–	–
Employees	–	–	–	–	–	3,000

WESTERN CONSTRUCTION GROUP, INC.

1637 N WARSON RD
SAINT LOUIS, MO 631321027
Phone: 314 427-1637
Fax: –
Web: www.westernspecialtycontractors.com

CEO: Benjamin Bishop Jr
CFO: Michael E Harmon
HR: Emma Thomure
FYE: December 31
Type: Private

It's more than bricks and mortar for Western Construction Group, a specialty contractor with expertise in masonry and concrete restoration and preventive waterproofing. It also performs specialty services such as installation of commercial and industrial roofing and insulation, architectural metal restoration and fabrication, seismic upgrades, and disaster recovery. The group's eight member companies operate more than 35 offices throughout the US. Western Construction Group was founded as Western Waterproofing Co. in 1915 by George Bishop Sr. and Ben Many. It has been privately held by the Bishop family for three generations.

WESTERN DIGITAL CORP
NMS: WDC

5601 Great Oaks Parkway
San Jose, CA 95119
Phone: 408 717-6000
Fax: –
Web: www.westerndigital.com

CEO: David V Goeckeler V
CFO: Wissam G Jabre
HR: –
FYE: June 30
Type: Public

Western Digital is a leading developer, manufacturer, and provider of data storage devices and solutions that address the evolving needs of information technology (IT) and the infrastructure that enables the proliferation of data in virtually every industry. The company makes hard disk drives (HDDs), which record, store, and recall volumes of data, and fast-growing solid-state drives (SSDs), known as flash drives, used in many mobile devices. HDD accounts for a major portion of Western Digital's revenues, although the company also makes devices used in servers, cloud computing data centers, and home entertainment products such as set-top boxes and video game consoles as well as mobile phones. The company sells to manufacturers, retailers, and distributors and generates around half of its revenue from the Asia/Pacific region.

	Annual Growth	06/19*	07/20	07/21	07/22*	06/23
Sales ($mil.)	(7.1%)	16,569	16,736	16,922	18,793	12,318
Net income ($ mil.)	–	(754.0)	(250.0)	821.0	1,500.0	(1,706.0)
Market value ($ mil.)	(5.5%)	15,311	13,666	22,608	13,981	12,213
Employees	(3.8%)	61,800	63,800	65,600	65,000	53,000

*Fiscal year change

WESTERN FARMERS ELECTRIC COOPERATIVE

701 N.E. 7th
Anadarko, OK 73005
Phone: 405 247-3351
Fax: –
Web: www.wfec.com

CEO: Gary R Roulet
CFO: –
HR: –
FYE: December 31
Type: Public

Power also comes sweeping down the plain in Oklahoma thanks to the Western Farmers Electric Cooperative. Led by its coal- and natural gas-fueled generating plants -- three in Anadarko, one in Mooreland, and one in Hugo (all in Oklahoma) -- the generation and transmission co-op produces more than 1,845 MW of capacity. It pipes power over 3,700 miles of transmission lines to two-thirds of rural Oklahoma, and parts of New Mexico. It also operates 264 substations and 59 switch stations. Western Farmers Electric Cooperative, which is owned by its member distribution cooperatives, supplies 22 distribution co-ops and Altus Air Force base, which serve a total of a half million members.

	Annual Growth	12/11	12/12	12/13	12/14	12/15
Sales ($mil.)	(4.4%)	–	–	–	702.3	671.5
Net income ($ mil.)	(23.9%)	–	–	–	40.9	31.2
Market value ($ mil.)	–	–	–	–	–	–
Employees	–	–	–	–	–	376

WESTERN FUELS ASSOCIATION, INC.

12050 PECOS ST
DENVER, CO 802343695
Phone: 720 697-6956
Fax: –
Web: www.westernfuels.org

CEO: –
CFO: –
HR: –
FYE: December 31
Type: Private

Western Fuels Association knows it can get cold when the wind comes sweepin' down the plain. The organization is a cooperative of coal mining companies as well as more than 20 municipal, independent, and consumer-owned utilities serving the Great Plains, the Rocky Mountains, and the Southwest US. It operates surface coal mines in Wyoming and Colorado and manages a fleet of more than 1600 rail cars through contracts with Burlington Northern Santa Fe (BSNF) and Union Pacific railroads. It also owns the Escalante-Western Railway, which connects its Lee Ranch Mine to the rail line. Western Fuels Association was formed in 1973.

	Annual Growth	12/05	12/06	12/07	12/08	12/09
Sales ($mil.)	(86.2%)	–	–	287.4	5.5	5.5
Net income ($ mil.)	10.8%	–	–	1.8	2.2	2.2
Market value ($ mil.)	–	–	–	–	–	–
Employees	–	–	–	–	–	19

WESTERN ILLINOIS UNIVERSITY INC

1 UNIVERSITY CIR
MACOMB, IL 614551390
Phone: 309 298-1800
Fax: –
Web: www.wiu.edu

CEO: –
CFO: –
HR: Susan Stewart
FYE: June 30
Type: Private

Western Illinois University (WIU) is exactly where you think it is. And it's a public school that has an annual enrollment of some 14,000 students at its main campus in Macomb, a commuter campus in Moline, and at extension sites throughout the state. With a student-to-faculty ratio of 15:1, the university offers about 65 undergraduate majors, 40 graduate degree programs, and about a dozen pre-professional degrees at colleges of arts and sciences, business and technology, education and human services, and fine arts and communication. The bill to establish the university, then called Western Illinois Normal School, was passed in 1899 by the Illinois General Assembly.

	Annual Growth	06/18	06/19	06/20	06/21	06/22
Sales ($mil.)	(3.9%)	–	102.1	86.6	81.9	90.5
Net income ($ mil.)	–	–	(9.7)	(3.8)	(6.9)	1.0
Market value ($ mil.)	–	–	–	–	–	–
Employees	–	–	–	–	–	2,048

WESTERN MAGNESIUM CORP
TVX: WMG H

8180 Greensboro Drive, Suite 720
McLean, VA 22102
Phone: 571 378-0762
Fax: –
Web: www.westernmagnesium.com

CEO: –
CFO: –
HR: –
FYE: October 31
Type: Public

Nevada Clean Magnesium (formerly Molycor Gold) is now turning its focus away from precious metals and on to magnesium. It plans to develop its Tami-Mosi project in Nevada, which has 412 million metric tons of inferred magnesium resources capable of producing 30,000 metric tons per year for 30 years. The junior resources company also prospects for gold, silver, and molybdenum. It has multiple resource properties in British Columbia and Nevada and is involved in joint ventures for several of these exploration projects with sister Canadian mining company Goldrea Resources. None of its projects are in production. In 2012 it optioned a 60% stake in its Griffon gold property in Nevada to Pilot Gold.

	Annual Growth	10/17	10/18	10/19	10/20	10/21
Sales ($mil.)	–	–	–	–	–	–
Net income ($ mil.)	–	(0.7)	(0.9)	(5.0)	(4.7)	(23.5)
Market value ($ mil.)	95.2%	15.7	14.1	44.0	38.1	228.1
Employees	–	–	–	–	–	19

WESTERN MASSACHUSETTS ELECTRIC CO.
NBB: WMAS L

300 Cadwell Drive
Springfield, MA 01104
Phone: 800 286-5000
Fax: –
Web: –

CEO: Werner J Schweiger
CFO: James J Judge
HR: –
FYE: December 31
Type: Public

Western Massachusetts Electric shines a light on the masses in western Mass. The company provides electric power services to more than 200,000 customers in about 60 towns and cities in a 1,490-sq.-mi. service area in Massachusetts. Western Massachusetts Electric purchases its electricity from affiliate Select Energy. It is an operating subsidiary of Eversource Energy, one of the largest utility companies in New England. The company operates 4,200 miles of distribution lines and 415 miles of transmission lines. It also has 45 substations and 35,200 transformer locations.

	Annual Growth	12/12	12/13	12/14	12/15	12/16
Sales ($mil.)	2.4%	441.2	472.7	493.4	518.1	484.2
Net income ($ mil.)	1.6%	54.5	60.4	57.8	56.5	58.1
Market value ($ mil.)	–	–	–	–	–	–
Employees	(3.9%)	348	308	310	291	297

WESTERN MICHIGAN UNIVERSITY

1903 W MICHIGAN AVE
KALAMAZOO, MI 490085200
Phone: 269 387-1000
Fax: –
Web: www.wmich.edu

CEO: –
CFO: Jan Van Der Kley
HR: Denise Richards
FYE: June 30
Type: Private

Western Michigan University (WMU) provides education to approximately 17,835 students at its main campus in Kalamazoo and branch campuses in Battle Creek, Benton Harbor-St. Joseph, Grand Rapids, Holland, Lansing, Muskegon, South Haven, and Traverse City, Michigan. The public university offers more than 150 majors for undergraduate programs as well as over 250 academic programs through ten colleges. WMU's undergraduate programs have included accountancy, aerospace engineering, aviation management, psychology, aviation flight science, biomedical sciences, computer science, finance, marketing, mechanical engineering, and operations. WMU was founded in 1903.

	Annual Growth	06/09	06/10	06/11	06/13	06/22
Sales ($mil.)	(0.5%)	–	–	363.1	385.1	344.6
Net income ($ mil.)	5.1%	–	–	30.2	22.3	52.4
Market value ($ mil.)	–	–	–	–	–	–
Employees	–	–	–	–	–	861

WESTERN MIDSTREAM PARTNERS LP
NYS: WES

9950 Woodloch Forest Drive, Suite 2800
The Woodlands, TX 77380
Phone: 346 786-5000
Fax: –
Web: www.westerngas.com

CEO: Michael P Ure
CFO: Jaime R Casas
HR: –
FYE: December 31
Type: Public

Western Midstream Partners (WES) is a Delaware master limited partnership formed to acquire, own, develop, and operate midstream assets. With midstream assets located in the Rocky Mountains, North-central Pennsylvania, Texas, and New Mexico, WES is engaged in the business of gathering, compressing, treating, processing, and transporting natural gas; gathering, stabilizing, and transporting condensate, NGLs, and crude oil; and gathering and disposing of produced water for its customers. In addition to the company's capacity as a processor of natural gas, WES also buys and sells natural gas, NGLs, and condensate on behalf of itself and as an agent for its customers under certain of its contracts.

	Annual Growth	12/19	12/20	12/21	12/22	12/23
Sales ($mil.)	3.1%	2,746.2	2,772.6	2,877.2	3,251.7	3,106.5
Net income ($ mil.)	10.0%	697.2	527.0	916.3	1,217.1	1,022.2
Market value ($ mil.)	10.4%	7,651.2	5,370.2	8,653.7	10,433	11,370
Employees	191.8%	19	1,045	1,127	1,217	1,377

WESTERN NEW ENGLAND BANCORP INC
NMS: WNEB

141 Elm Street
Westfield, MA 01086
Phone: 413 568-1911
Fax: –
Web: www.westfieldbank.com

CEO: James C Hagan
CFO: Guida R Sajdak
HR: –
FYE: December 31
Type: Public

Westfield Financial is the holding company for Westfield Bank, which serves western Massachusetts' Hampden County and surrounding areas from more than 20 branch locations. Founded in 1853, the bank has traditionally been a community-oriented provider of retail deposit accounts and loans, but it is placing more emphasis on serving commercial and industrial clients. Commercial real estate loans account for approximately 45% of the company's loan portfolio and business loans are more than 25%. The bank also makes a smaller number of consumer and home equity loans. In 2016, Westfield Financial merged with Chicopee Bancorp, the holding company of Chicopee Savings Bank (another bank serving Hampden County).

	Annual Growth	12/19	12/20	12/21	12/22	12/23
Assets ($mil.)	4.1%	2,181.5	2,365.9	2,538.4	2,553.2	2,564.6
Net income ($ mil.)	3.1%	13.3	11.2	23.7	25.9	15.1
Market value ($ mil.)	(1.7%)	208.7	149.3	189.8	205.0	195.0
Employees	0.6%	340	358	355	337	348

WESTERN PENNSYLVANIA HOSPITAL

4800 FRIENDSHIP AVE
PITTSBURGH, PA 152241722
Phone: 412 578-5000
Fax: –
Web: www.ahn.org

CEO: Dtephen M Patz
CFO: –
HR: –
FYE: June 30
Type: Private

When you really feel like the pits, visit The Western Pennsylvania Hospital. Based in Pittsburgh, The Western Pennsylvania Hospital is a part of the West Penn Allegheny Health System. The 512-bed teaching hospital is affiliated with Clarion University, Indiana University of Pennsylvania, Pennsylvania State University, and Temple University. It offers specialized services such as emergency medicine, heart care, breast disease treatment, cancer treatment, orthopedics, and surgery (including microscopic surgery). Special facilities include an area burn center, cancer treatment center, and a hospice facility.

	Annual Growth	06/12	06/13	06/14	06/15	06/16
Sales ($mil.)	18.5%	–	–	–	336.0	398.2
Net income ($ mil.)	107.3%	–	–	–	32.0	66.4
Market value ($ mil.)	–	–	–	–	–	–
Employees	–	–	–	–	–	217

WESTERN REFINING LOGISTICS, LP

212 N CLARK DR
EL PASO, TX 799053106
Phone: 915 534-1400
Fax: –
Web: www.wnrl.com

CEO: –
CFO: –
HR: –
FYE: December 31
Type: Private

Western Refining Logistics holds the midstream assets of Western Refining. The company owns and operates 300 miles of crude oil pipelines and crude oil storage facilities with a capacity of almost 7 million barrels. Its pipeline and storage facilities serve Western Refining's two refineries in Texas and New Mexico. It also provides asphalt terminalling and processing services for Western Refining's asphalt plants in Arizona, New Mexico, and Texas. Western Refining formed Western Refining Logistics in 2013 as a limited partnership, or an investment vehicle that is exempt from paying federal income tax. The company raised $303 million in its IPO, which it will use to pay off Western Refining in exchange for the pipelines and storage facilities.

WESTERN REFINING, INC.

212 N CLARK DR
EL PASO, TX 799053106
Phone: 915 775-3300
Fax: –
Web: www.wnr.com

CEO: Jeff A Stevens
CFO: Karen B Davis
HR: Joe McCormack
FYE: December 31
Type: Private

It's the quality and volumes of its refined products that makes Western Refining a major player in the West. The independent oil refiner operates primarily in the Southwest region of the US. Western Refining's refineries (one in El Paso, one in the Four Corners region of northern New Mexico, and one in Minnesota) have a crude oil refining capacity of 262,000 barrels per day. More than 90% of its refined products are made up of light transportation fuels, including diesel and gasoline. It owns a wholesale division that complements the refining operations. Western Refining also owns about 260 retail outlets in the Southwest. In 2017 Western Refining (except its logistics arm) was acquired by Tesoro in a $6.4 billion deal. The combined Tesoro-Western company is now called Andeavor.

WESTERN SUMMIT CONSTRUCTORS, INC.

4790 REGENT BLVD STE 150
IRVING, TX 750632445
Phone: 303 298-9500
Fax: –
Web: www.westernsummit.com

CEO: –
CFO: –
HR: –
FYE: December 31
Type: Private

Western Summit Constructors' business flows. The company, a subsidiary of TIC Holdings (now owned by Peter Kiewit), designs and builds municipal and industrial water and wastewater systems, as well as water storage facilities in the US. The company operates nationwide from offices in California, Colorado, New Mexico, Georgia, and Texas. Western Summit was founded in 1981 and joined TIC Holdings in 1993. The firm is solely focused on constructing and upgrading water and wastewater projects that typically range from $100,000 to $250 million. Among Western Summit's projects is the expansion of the Miramar Water Treatment plant in San Diego and the Aurora Prairie Waters Purification Facility in Colorado.

	Annual Growth	06/06	06/07	06/08	06/10*	12/13
Sales ($mil.)	(72.0%)	–	–	0.8	1.0	0.0
Net income ($ mil.)	–	–	–	(0.2)	0.3	(0.0)
Market value ($ mil.)	–	–	–	–	–	–
Employees	–	–	–	–	–	400

*Fiscal year change

WESTERN SWITCHES AND CONTROLS INC.

590 W LAMBERT RD
BREA, CA 928213914
Phone: 714 482-4100
Fax: –
Web: www.westernswitches.com

CEO: –
CFO: –
HR: –
FYE: October 31
Type: Private

Western Switches and Controls (WSC) distributes electrical, electronic, and automation components and equipment, such as bar code readers, circuit breakers, sensors, enclosures, light-emitting diodes (LEDs), transformers, solenoids, relays, heaters, and -- of course -- switches. The company principally serves manufacturers, including those in the pool and spa business. WSC offers a radio-frequency identification (RFID) development kit for manufacturers, using RFID products from Precision Dynamics. Co-founder and CEO Leo Alonzo owns part of Western Switches and Controls. Established in 1976, the company has locations in Arizona and California.

	Annual Growth	10/08	10/09	10/10	10/11	10/12
Sales ($mil.)	–	–	–	(1,141.3)	12.8	15.4
Net income ($ mil.)	8438.0%	–	–	0.0	0.0	0.5
Market value ($ mil.)	–	–	–	–	–	–
Employees	–	–	–	–	–	16

WESTERN UNION CO

7001 East Belleview Avenue
Denver, CO 80237
Phone: 866 405-5012
Fax: –
Web: www.westernunion.com

NYS: WU
CEO: Hikmet Ersek
CFO: Matthew Cagwin
HR: Marilia Maya
FYE: December 31
Type: Public

The Western Union Company is globally recognized and represents speed, reliability, trust, and convenience. Its Business Solutions services facilitate payment and foreign exchange solutions, primarily cross-border, cross-currency transactions, for small and medium-sized enterprises and other organizations and individuals. It achieves this with a global network of some 400,000 agent locations in more than 200 countries and territories. Western Union agents work out of kiosks located in a variety of businesses including post offices, banks, retailers, and other established organizations as well as smaller independent retail locations, which typically provide other consumer products and services. About 65% of its total revenue comes from international operations.

	Annual Growth	12/19	12/20	12/21	12/22	12/23
Sales ($mil.)	(4.7%)	5,292.1	4,835.0	5,070.8	4,475.5	4,357.0
Net income ($ mil.)	(12.3%)	1,058.3	744.3	805.8	910.6	626.0
Market value ($ mil.)	(18.3%)	9,386.4	7,690.0	6,252.9	4,826.4	4,178.0
Employees	(5.9%)	11,500	11,000	10,500	8,900	9,000

WESTERN WASHINGTON UNIVERSITY

516 HIGH ST
BELLINGHAM, WA 982255996
Phone: 360 650-3720
Fax: –
Web: www.wwu.edu

CEO: –
CFO: –
HR: –
FYE: June 30
Type: Private

If you're in the West and you're looking for a liberal arts education, look no further than Western Washington University. The university is located in northwest Washington state, and is one of a handful of state-funded, four-year institutions of higher education in Washington. The school has an enrollment of about 15,000 students; roughly 95% of those are undergraduate students. Western Washington University has a student-teacher ratio of roughly 21:1. The university has students from almost every other state and from three dozen other countries. Western, which began as a teachers college accepting its first students in 1899, became a full university in 1977.

	Annual Growth	06/12	06/13	06/14	06/15	06/16
Sales ($mil.)	2.4%	–	196.9	200.6	207.0	211.3
Net income ($ mil.)	39.4%	–	5.5	3.8	1.3	14.8
Market value ($ mil.)	–	–	–	–	–	–
Employees	–	–	–	–	–	466

WESTERN WYOMING COMMUNITY COLLEGE DISTRICT

2500 COLLEGE DR
ROCK SPRINGS, WY 829015802
Phone: 307 382-1600
Fax: –
Web: www.westernwyoming.edu

CEO: –
CFO: –
HR: Joy Adams
FYE: June 30
Type: Private

Western Wyoming Community College (WWCC) provides public-access post-secondary academics and vocational-technical training. The school offers two-year transfer programs for students pursuing a baccalaureate, two-year occupational degrees, and a number of occupational certificate programs. Courses are taught in fields such as the humanities, fine arts, social science, natural science, math, business, technology and industry, and health science. WWCC has more than 2,000 students, about 60% of which are part time. The school offers distance education courses and programs through the Internet.

	Annual Growth	06/15	06/16	06/17	06/18	06/19
Sales ($mil.)	(5.2%)	–	–	8.3	8.3	7.5
Net income ($ mil.)	–	–	–	(1.5)	(5.1)	(2.9)
Market value ($ mil.)	–	–	–	–	–	–
Employees	–	–	–	–	–	445

WESTINGHOUSE LIGHTING CORPORATION

12401 MCNULTY RD
PHILADELPHIA, PA 191541004
Phone: 215 671-2000
Fax: –
Web: www.westinghouselighting.com

CEO: –
CFO: –
HR: –
FYE: December 31
Type: Private

And George Westinghouse said "Let there be light." Following in the great man's footsteps, Westinghouse Lighting Corporation (WLC) makes more than 5,000 electrical and lighting products including light bulbs, lighting fixtures and hardware, door chimes, and wall plates. The Energy Star certified manufacturer also makes ceiling fans for indoor and outdoor use under brands such as Builder and Industrial Plus. Its decorative electrical lineup extends from lighting hardware to glassware. The company's global distribution facilities dot Mexico, Germany, Canada, Panama, and China, catering to residential, commercial, and industrial markets.

WESTLAKE CHLOR-VINYLS CORPORATION

2801 POST OAK BLVD STE 600
HOUSTON, TX 770566136
Phone: 304 455-2200
Fax: –
Web: www.westlake.com

CEO: Albert Chao
CFO: M S Bender
HR: –
FYE: December 31
Type: Private

Axiall's business revolves around the axis of commodity chemicals. The company makes chlorovinyls used by the construction and housing, plastics, pulp and paper, and pharmaceutical industries. Its primary chlorovinyl products are PVC (polyvinyl chloride), caustic soda, and chlorine. The chlorovinyl segment also makes vinyl chloride monomer (VCM), used to make PVC resins, chlorinated ethylene, calcium hypochlorite, and hydrochloric acid. Its building products unit makes extruded vinyl window and door profiles and moldings products. In 2016 Axiall was acquired by rival Westlake Chemical for $3.8 billion.

WESTLAKE CORP
NYS: WLK

2801 Post Oak Boulevard, Suite 600
Houston, TX 77056
Phone: 713 960-9111
Fax: –
Web: www.westlake.com

CEO: Albert Y Chao
CFO: M S Bender
HR: Mark Tice
FYE: December 31
Type: Public

Founded in 1986, Westlake, formerly known as Westlake Chemical, is a vertically integrated global manufacturer and marketer of performance and essential materials and housing and infrastructure products that enhance the lives of people every day. Its products include materials that are fundamental to many diverse consumer and industrial markets, including residential construction, flexible and rigid packaging, automotive products, healthcare products, water treatment, coatings as well as other durable and non-durable goods. Westlake is the second-largest producer of both PVC and chlor-alkali in the world. The US accounts for about 70% of the company's total revenue.

	Annual Growth	12/19	12/20	12/21	12/22	12/23
Sales ($mil.)	11.5%	8,118.0	7,504.0	11,778	15,794	12,548
Net income ($ mil.)	3.3%	421.0	330.0	2,015.0	2,247.0	479.0
Market value ($ mil.)	18.8%	8,994.1	10,462	12,453	13,147	17,945
Employees	13.3%	9,430	9,220	14,550	15,920	15,520

WESTMINSTER MANOR

4100 JACKSON AVE APT 470
AUSTIN, TX 787316083
Phone: 512 454-2140
Fax: –
Web: www.westminsteraustintx.org

CEO: –
CFO: –
HR: –
FYE: December 31
Type: Private

Westminster Manor helps to care for the elderly in the Austin, Texas area. The company is a not-for-profit long-term care facility that provides skilled nursing care and occupational, physical, respiratory, and speech therapy. Westminster Manor also offers individual and group activity programs, as well as specialized diet services. The facility has about 90 beds.

	Annual Growth	12/16	12/17	12/18	12/19	12/20
Sales ($mil.)	89.9%	–	4.7	4.9	36.6	31.9
Net income ($ mil.)	6.3%	–	7.9	(0.5)	6.2	9.5
Market value ($ mil.)	–	–	–	–	–	–
Employees	–	–	–	–	–	175

WESTMINSTER UNIVERSITY

1840 S 1300 E
SALT LAKE CITY, UT 841053617
Phone: 801 484-7651
Fax: –
Web: www.westminsteru.edu

CEO: –
CFO: –
HR: –
FYE: June 30
Type: Private

Westminster College is a private liberal arts school that offers more than 70 academic programs including undergraduate bachelor of arts (BA) and bachelor of science (BS) degrees, as well as select graduate degrees. Its programs are offered through four schools devoted to arts and sciences, business, education, and nursing and health sciences. The school has an enrollment of approximately 2,300 undergraduate students and 800 graduate students and has more than 400 full- and part-time faculty members. Westminster College was founded in 1875 as a preparatory school called the Salt Lake Collegiate Institute. It first offered college classes in 1897 (as Sheldon Jackson College) and adopted its current name in 1902.

	Annual Growth	06/18	06/19	06/20	06/21	06/22
Sales ($mil.)	(9.2%)	–	63.1	56.9	48.3	47.3
Net income ($ mil.)	–	–	(3.8)	(4.6)	21.1	(15.2)
Market value ($ mil.)	–	–	–	–	–	–
Employees	–	–	–	–	–	500

WESTMORELAND RESOURCE PARTNERS LP
NBB: WMLP Q

9540 South Maroon Circle, Suite 300
Englewood, CO 80112
Phone: 855 922-6463
Fax: –
Web: www. westmorelandmlp.com

CEO: Martin Purvis
CFO: –
HR: –
FYE: December 31
Type: Public

Oxford Resource Partners strives to get its customers steamed. An operator and acquirer of surface coal mines, the company produces steam coal used by power plants and other energy producers to fire steam boilers. It owns and operates about 19 surface mines in the Northern Appalachia region and the Illinois Basin. In 2009 the company, which has assets that include more than 91 million tons of proved and probable reserves, produced 5.8 million tons of coal. It serves markets in Illinois, Indiana, Kentucky, Ohio, Pennsylvania, and West Virginia and has counted AEP, Duke Energy, and East Kentucky Power as major customers. Formed in 2008, Oxford Resource Partners filed an initial public offering (IPO) in 2010.

	Annual Growth	12/14	12/15	12/16	12/17	12/18
Sales ($mil.)	–	–	384.7	349.3	315.6	271.0
Net income ($ mil.)	–	(4.4)	(33.7)	(31.6)	(31.8)	(139.2)
Market value ($ mil.)	(41.1%)	22.9	91.5	129.1	63.8	2.7
Employees	(1.1%)	602	658	640	570	576

WESTROCK CO
NYS: WRK

1000 Abernathy Road N.E.
Atlanta, GA 30328
Phone: 770 448-2193
Fax: –
Web: www.westrock.com

CEO: Alexander W Pease
CFO: Ward H Dickson
HR: –
FYE: September 30
Type: Public

WRKCo Inc. is primarily engaged in manufacturing paperboard, including paperboard coated on the paperboard machine, from wood pulp and other fiber pulp; and which may also manufacture converted paperboard products.

	Annual Growth	09/19	09/20	09/21	09/22	09/23
Sales ($mil.)	2.7%	18,289	17,579	18,746	21,257	20,310
Net income ($ mil.)	–	862.9	(690.9)	838.3	944.6	(1,649.0)
Market value ($ mil.)	(0.4%)	9,345.8	8,907.3	12,776	7,920.2	9,179.1
Employees	2.4%	51,100	49,300	49,900	50,500	56,100

WESTROCK COMPANY

1000 ABERNATHY RD
ATLANTA, GA 303285606
Phone: 770 448-2193
Fax: –
Web: www.westrock.com

CEO: David B Sewell
CFO: Alexander W Pease
HR: –
FYE: September 30
Type: Private

WestRock is a multinational provider of sustainable fiber-based paper and packaging solutions. It manufactures and distributes containerboard and paperboard products such as folding cartons, coated paperboard, bleached paperboard, coated recycled paperboard, partitions and protective packaging, and pulp products. WestRock also provides kraft paper and pulp, recycled linerboard, coated white top linerboard, and corrugated containers. The company's products find their applications in various industries such as retail, food, healthcare, beverage, commercial printing, tobacco, home, and garden. Generates more than 80% of revenue in the US, the company's operations are spread across North America, South America, Europe, Asia, and Australia.

WESTROCK PAPER AND PACKAGING, LLC

1000 ABERNATHY RD
ATLANTA, GA 303285606
Phone: 770 448-2193
Fax: –
Web: www.westrock.com

CEO: Steve C Voorhees
CFO: Ward H Dickson
HR: Vicki Lostetter
FYE: December 31
Type: Private

KapStone Paper and Packaging keeps things under wraps. The company manufactures linerboard, a type of paperboard that is converted into laminated tier sheets and wrapping material. It also produces kraft paper (industry-speak for strong wrapping paper) for multiwall bags; saturating kraft (sold under the Durasorb brand) to produce mainly high pressure laminates for furniture, construction materials, and electronics; and unbleached folding carton board (Kraftpak), which is converted into packaging for consumer goods. The US accounts for more than 85% of KapStone's total sales. KapStone was acquired by WestRock in 2018.

WESTSIDE FAMILY HEALTH CENTER

3861 SEPULVEDA BLVD
CULVER CITY, CA 902304605
Phone: 310 450-4773
Fax: –
Web: www.wfhcenter.org

CEO: –
CFO: –
HR: –
FYE: June 30
Type: Private

The Westside Women's Health Center treats more than 7,400 lower-income women, men, and children in the Ocean Park section of Santa Monica. Services include pregnancy testing and prenatal care, mammograms, pediatric services, nutritional counseling, and teen parenting classes, as well as a family practice program with a focus on healthy aging. The center was established by a group of feminists and clinicians as the Women's Health Care Project in 1974. Approximately 90% of its clients do not have health insurance and are living at or below the federal poverty level.

	Annual Growth	06/17	06/18	06/20	06/21	06/22
Sales ($mil.)	17.4%	–	5.6	8.1	9.0	10.6
Net income ($ mil.)	(46.4%)	–	0.3	0.0	0.0	0.0
Market value ($ mil.)	–	–	–	–	–	–
Employees	–	–	–	–	–	34

WESTWATER RESOURCES INC

ASE: WWR

6950 S. Potomac Street, Suite 300
Centennial, CO 80112
Phone: 303 531-0516
Fax: –
Web: www.westwaterresources.net

CEO: –
CFO: –
HR: –
FYE: December 31
Type: Public

Mining company Uranium Resources (URI) glows with anticipation when it thinks about the fuel needs of nuclear power plants. The company has been preparing its main uranium assets in South Texas (the Kingsville Dome and Rosita mines and processing plants) for a restart in production. It also has big plans for its exploration and development interests in New Mexico. URI holds 102.1 million pounds of in-place mineralized uranium material. In 2012 the company acquired Neutron Energy in a $38 million deal. The deal adds significantly to the company's New Mexico assets and positions it as one of the US' largest uranium developers. Neutron will operate as a URI subsidiary.

	Annual Growth	12/19	12/20	12/21	12/22	12/23
Sales ($mil.)	–	–	–	–	–	–
Net income ($ mil.)	–	(10.6)	(23.6)	(16.1)	(11.1)	(7.8)
Market value ($ mil.)	(28.1%)	116.9	273.1	119.1	43.8	31.3
Employees	(3.8%)	28	11	15	34	24

WESTWOOD GROUP INC (THE)

190 V.F.W. Parkway
Revere, MA 02151
Phone: 781 284-2600
Fax: –
Web: –

CEO: Richard P Dalton
CFO: –
HR: –
FYE: December 31
Type: Public

Westwood lets the dogs out. The Westwood Group, Inc. operates Wonderland Greyhound Park, a pari-mutuel greyhound racing park that opened in 1935 in Revere, Massachusetts. The track also offers simulcasts with other racing facilities around the country. Wonderland features a concession stands, a trackside pub, private dining suites, and a clubhouse dining room for large parties. Its non-profit Wonderdogs program places retired greyhounds in new homes. Formerly a publicly traded company, The Westwood Group went private in 2004 under the direction of company chairman Charles Sarkis.

	Annual Growth	12/99	12/00	12/01	12/02	12/03
Sales ($mil.)	(6.8%)	17.5	17.7	17.0	15.8	13.2
Net income ($ mil.)	–	(1.8)	(0.5)	1.4	(1.2)	(2.7)
Market value ($ mil.)	46.6%	0.0	0.0	0.0	0.0	0.0
Employees	–	350	350	350	350	350

WESTWOOD HOLDINGS GROUP, INC.

NYS: WHG

200 Crescent Court, Suite 1200
Dallas, TX 75201
Phone: 214 756-6900
Fax: –
Web: www.westwoodgroup.com

CEO: Brian O Casey
CFO: –
HR: –
FYE: December 31
Type: Public

Westwood Holdings Group manages investment assets and provide services for its clients through its subsidiaries, Westwood Management Corp. and Westwood Advisors, L.L.C. (referred to hereinafter together as Westwood Management" and Westwood Trust. Westwood Trust provides trust, custodial and investment management services through use of commingled funds and individual securities to institutions and high net worth individuals. Westwood Management provides investment advisory services to institutional investors, a family of mutual funds called the Westwood Funds, other mutual funds, individual investors and clients of Westwood Trust. Westwood Holdings Group boasts approximately $14.5 billion in assets under management. The US accounts for over 95% of total revenue.

	Annual Growth	12/19	12/20	12/21	12/22	12/23
Sales ($mil.)	1.7%	84.1	65.1	73.1	68.7	89.8
Net income ($ mil.)	12.7%	5.9	(8.9)	9.8	(4.6)	9.5
Market value ($ mil.)	(19.3%)	270.7	132.5	154.8	101.8	114.9
Employees	(3.2%)	165	136	130	152	145

WEWORK INC

NBB: WEWK Q

12 East 49th Street, 3rd floor
New York, NY 10017
Phone: 646 389-3922
Fax: –
Web: –

CEO: David Tolley
CFO: Kurt Wehner
HR: –
FYE: December 31
Type: Public

WeWork, Inc. is a leading global flexible workspace provider, serving a membership base of businesses large and small through its network of about 780 locations around the world. Its membership offering ranges from a monthly subscription basis to a multi-year membership agreement. WeWork's core business offering provides flexibility across space, time, and cost. It offers business and technical service solutions, including professional employer organization (PEO) and payroll services, remote workforce solutions, human resources benefits, dedicated bandwidth, and IT equipment co-location. WeWork All Access can be purchased by individuals and companies looking for flexible solutions for touch-down space in major urban centers where WeWork has a presence. WeWork's largest market is the US with around 45% of the company's revenue.

	Annual Growth	12/18	12/19	12/20	12/21	12/22
Sales ($mil.)	–	–	–	–	2,570.1	3,245.0
Net income ($ mil.)	–	–	–	(0.1)	(4,439.0)	(2,034.0)
Market value ($ mil.)	(62.7%)	–	–	186.8	156.5	26.0
Employees	–	–	–	–	4,400	4,300

WEX INC

NYS: WEX

1 Hancock Street
Portland, ME 04101
Phone: 207 773-8171
Fax: –
Web: www.wexinc.com

CEO: Melissa Smith
CFO: Jagtar Narula
HR: –
FYE: December 31
Type: Public

WEX is the global commerce platform that simplifies the business of running a business. The company has more than 600,000 fleet customers worldwide and partners with 9 of the top 10 US fuel retailers. WEX simplifies administration of benefits for employers, including consumer directed health accounts in the US both directly and through partners. It serves more than half of the Fortune 1000 companies in the US. WEX is both one of the largest commercial payment companies in the world as well as a trusted technology partner for some of the largest organizations in the world. Around 18 million vehicles use WEX for fleet management. The US accounts for the majority of the company's revenue.

	Annual Growth	12/19	12/20	12/21	12/22	12/23
Sales ($mil.)	10.3%	1,723.7	1,559.9	1,850.5	2,350.5	2,548.0
Net income ($ mil.)	14.3%	156.3	(284.0)	135.3	167.2	266.6
Market value ($ mil.)	(1.8%)	8,776.4	8,527.9	5,882.3	6,856.9	8,151.6
Employees	9.5%	5,000	5,300	5,600	6,100	7,200

WEXFORD HEALTH SOURCES, INC.

501 HOLIDAY DR
PITTSBURGH, PA 15220
Phone: 888 633-6468
Fax: –
Web: www.wexfordhealth.com

CEO: Kevin C Halloran
CFO: –
HR: Mark Blewett
FYE: December 31
Type: Private

Wexford Health Sources provides health care services to inmates doing time in the big house. The company has contracts at more than 100 government-run facilities, including county jails, state and federal prisons, juvenile detention centers, substance abuse treatment centers, psychiatric hospitals, and correctional centers for sex offenders. Wexford Health staffs professionals that perform medical and mental health care, dentistry, pharmacy services, and administration services, and serves about 90,000 inmates and patients through contracts in five states -- Illinois, Mississippi, Ohio, Pennsylvania, and West Virginia. Wexford Health was founded in 1992.

	Annual Growth	12/99	12/00	12/01	12/05	12/08
Sales ($mil.)	4.3%	–	–	119.4	160.6	160.0
Net income ($ mil.)	43.8%	–	–	1.3	6.4	16.6
Market value ($ mil.)	–	–	–	–	–	–
Employees	–	–	–	–	–	1,525

WEYCO GROUP, INC

NMS: WEYS

333 W. Estabrook Boulevard, P.O. Box 1188
Milwaukee, WI 53201
Phone: 414 908-1600
Fax: –
Web: www.weycogroup.com

CEO: Thomas W Florsheim Jr
CFO: Judy Anderson
HR: –
FYE: December 31
Type: Public

Weyco Group is engaged in one line of business: the design and distribution of quality and innovative footwear. The company imports men's footwear, including mid-priced leather dress and casual shoes, sold under the Florsheim, Nunn Bush, and Stacy Adams brands. It also offers casual footwear for women and children under the BOGS, and Rafters labels. Weyco sells its shoes to more than 10,000 shoe, clothing, and department stores in the US and Canada. Most of the company's sales come from the US.

	Annual Growth	12/19	12/20	12/21	12/22	12/23
Sales ($mil.)	1.1%	304.0	195.4	267.6	351.7	318.0
Net income ($ mil.)	9.7%	20.9	(8.5)	20.6	29.5	30.2
Market value ($ mil.)	4.3%	251.2	150.4	227.4	201.0	297.8
Employees	(1.8%)	654	556	608	643	608

WEYERHAEUSER CO

NYS: WY

220 Occidental Avenue South
Seattle, WA 98104-7800
Phone: 206 539-3000
Fax: –
Web: www.weyerhaeuser.com

CEO: Devin W Stockfish
CFO: David M Wold
HR: –
FYE: December 31
Type: Public

Weyerhaeuser Company is one of the largest manufacturers of wood products in North America. The company makes and distributes high-quality wood products, including structural lumber, oriented strand board, engineered wood products and other specialty products to residential, multi-family, industrial, light commercial as well as repair and remodel markets. It is also one of the world's largest private owners of timberland. The company harvests trees for its products from 10.6 million acres of forest that it owns in the US and 14.1 million acres that it manages in Canada. The US generates about 85% of the company's revenue. Incorporated in 1900 as Weyerhaeuser Timber Company in the state of Washington, when Frederick Weyerhaeuser and 15 partners bought 900,000 acres of timberland.

	Annual Growth	12/19	12/20	12/21	12/22	12/23
Sales ($mil.)	4.0%	6,554.0	7,532.0	10,201	10,184	7,674.0
Net income ($ mil.)	–	(76.0)	797.0	2,607.0	1,880.0	839.0
Market value ($ mil.)	3.6%	22,039	24,469	30,051	22,622	25,374
Employees	(0.2%)	9,400	9,372	9,214	9,264	9,318

WGBH EDUCATIONAL FOUNDATION

1 GUEST ST
BOSTON, MA 021352104
Phone: 617 300-2000
Fax: –
Web: www.wgbh.org

CEO: Jonathan C Abbott
CFO: –
HR: Alexa Walker
FYE: June 30
Type: Private

Public broadcasting forms the basis of this organization. WGBH Educational Foundation owns and operates the WGBH public TV and radio stations that serve the Boston area. Its television operations include several digital channels (WGBH Create, WGBH World) as well as an on-demand service. WGBH is also one of the largest producers of programming for the Public Broadcasting Service, including such shows as Antiques Roadshow , Arthur , Curious George , Frontline , Masterpiece , and Nova . The foundation gets funding from corporate grants and individual contributions, as well as from PBS and the Corporation for Public Broadcasting.

	Annual Growth	06/13	06/14	06/20	06/21	06/22
Sales ($mil.)	4.0%	–	195.4	198.4	288.8	268.1
Net income ($ mil.)	–	–	15.8	(23.9)	150.6	(128.8)
Market value ($ mil.)	–	–	–	–	–	–
Employees	–	–	–	–	–	1,100

WGL HOLDINGS, INC.

1000 MAINE AVE SW
WASHINGTON, DC 200243494
Phone: 202 624-6011
Fax: –
Web: www.wgl.com

CEO: Adrian P Chapman
CFO: Vincent L Ammann Jr
HR: –
FYE: September 30
Type: Private

WGL Holdings ?is a leading source for clean, efficient and diverse energy solutions. With activities and assets across the US, WGL provides options for natural gas, electricity, green power and energy services, including generation, storage, transportation, distribution, supply and efficiency. Its customers include homeowner, renter, small business, multinational corporation, state and local or federal agency. Its family of companies? Washington Gas, WGL Energy and Hampshire Gas?are now indirect, wholly-owned subsidiaries of AltaGas Ltd.

	Annual Growth	09/14	09/15	09/16	09/17	09/18
Sales ($mil.)	(4.2%)	–	2,659.8	2,349.6	2,354.7	2,341.8
Net income ($ mil.)	(45.8%)	–	132.6	168.4	177.9	21.1
Market value ($ mil.)	–	–	–	–	–	–
Employees	–	–	–	–	–	1,586

WGNB CORP.

201 Maple Street, P.O. Box 280
Carrollton, GA 30112
Phone: 770 832-3557
Fax: –
Web: www.wgnb.com

CEO: –
CFO: –
HR: –
FYE: December 31
Type: Public

WGNB, not to be confused with the Christian radio station in Michigan with those call letters, is the holding company for First National Bank of Georgia (formerly West Georgia National Bank), which operates about 15 branches in Carroll, Douglas, and Haralson counties. It also runs Banco de Progreso, which serves the area's Spanish-speaking population. The banks offer standard retail products and services, including checking and savings accounts, CDs, and NOW accounts. They use funds from deposits to write primarily real estate loans, including commercial and residential mortgages and loans for real estate acquisition, development, or construction. The banks also make business and consumer loans.

	Annual Growth	12/04	12/05	12/06	12/07	12/08
Assets ($mil.)	19.2%	441.9	523.6	575.3	883.7	892.2
Net income ($ mil.)	–	6.1	7.1	8.3	3.0	(30.8)
Market value ($ mil.)	–	–	–	–	–	–
Employees	14.8%	143	154	182	268	248

WHALLEY COMPUTER ASSOCIATES, INC.

1 WHALLEY WAY
SOUTHWICK, MA 010779222
Phone: 413 569-4200
Fax: –
Web: www.wcaoem.com

CEO: –
CFO: –
HR: –
FYE: December 31
Type: Private

Whalley Computer Associates (WCA) provides information technology products distribution, consulting, and technical support services primarily in Massachusets. The company sells and distributes computer hardware, software, and peripherals from such vendors as Hewlett-Packard, 3Com, and Cisco. Other services include systems integration, maintenance, network design, project management, and remote monitoring. WCA's customers come from a variety of industries including manufacturing, consumer goods, and retail, as well as the public sector. The company was founded in 1979 by president John Whalley.

	Annual Growth	12/03	12/04	12/05	12/06	12/07
Sales ($mil.)	14.9%	–	67.2	73.4	87.8	101.9
Net income ($ mil.)	22.9%	–	2.4	3.0	3.9	4.5
Market value ($ mil.)	–	–	–	–	–	–
Employees	–	–	–	–	–	104

WHEATON COLLEGE

26 E MAIN ST
NORTON, MA 027662322
Phone: 508 286-8200
Fax: –
Web: www.wheatoncollege.edu

CEO: –
CFO: –
HR: –
FYE: June 30
Type: Private

Wheaton College (not to be confused with a school of the same name in Illinois) is a four-year private liberal arts college that enrolls about 1,600 undergraduates for study in more than 40 major fields as well as 60 minors. The college boasts a student-faculty radio of 11:1. The most popular courses of study include biology, economics, English, history, psychology, and sociology. The Wheaton College campus is located 35 miles south of Boston and 15 miles north of Providence. Founded as a seminary for women in 1834, it was chartered as a women's liberal arts college in 1912. Wheaton became coeducational in 1987.

	Annual Growth	06/17	06/18	06/19	06/20	06/22
Sales ($mil.)	2.2%	–	78.5	78.6	74.6	85.7
Net income ($ mil.)	–	–	0.9	(3.9)	(5.2)	(13.7)
Market value ($ mil.)	–	–	–	–	–	–
Employees	–	–	–	–	–	545

WHEATON FRANCISCAN SERVICES, INC.

400 W RIVER WOODS PKWY
GLENDALE, WI 532121060
Phone: 414 465-3000
Fax: –
Web: www.mywheaton.org

CEO: John D Oliverio
CFO: –
HR: –
FYE: June 30
Type: Private

Wheaton Franciscan Services, Inc. (WFSI) is the not-for-profit parent company for more than 100 health care, housing, and social service organizations in Colorado, Illinois, Iowa, and Wisconsin. Also known as Wheaton Franciscan Healthcare, WFSI operates about 15 hospitals including Affinity Health System, Rush Oak Park Hospital, and United Hospital System, with more than 1,600 beds total. WFSI also includes long-term care centers, home health agencies, and physician offices. Its Franciscan Ministries division provides affordable housing units including assisted-living facilities and low-income dwellings. The health system is sponsored by The Franciscan Sisters, Daughters of the Sacred Hearts of Jesus and Mary.

	Annual Growth	06/10	06/11	06/12	06/13	06/14
Sales ($mil.)	0.9%	–	–	1,723.5	1,763.4	1,754.2
Net income ($ mil.)	–	–	–	(112.6)	177.5	128.7
Market value ($ mil.)	–	–	–	–	–	–
Employees	–	–	–	–	–	18,000

WHEATON VAN LINES INC

8010 CASTLETON RD
INDIANAPOLIS, IN 462502005
Phone: 317 849-7900
Fax: –
Web: www.wheatonworldwide.com

CEO: Mark Kirschner
CFO: –
HR: Heather Gustafson
FYE: December 31
Type: Private

Wheaton Van Lines, which operates under the Wheaton World Wide Moving and Bekins Van Lines brands, provides interstate and international transportation and relocation services for individuals, businesses, and government agencies. Wheaton also provides relocation services for US military personnel. The company's specialties include transportation of medical equipment, computers, new furniture, store fixtures, and Steinway pianos. Wheaton Van Lines operates through a network of about 370 agents in the US. The company is owned by its employees.

	Annual Growth	12/05	12/06	12/07	12/08	12/09
Sales ($mil.)	(4.4%)	–	–	104.2	99.3	95.2
Net income ($ mil.)	9.0%	–	–	6.3	7.8	7.5
Market value ($ mil.)	–	–	–	–	–	–
Employees	–	–	–	–	–	725

WHEELER REAL ESTATE INVESTMENT TRUST INC   NAS: WHLR

2529 Virginia Beach Blvd.
Virginia Beach, VA 23452
Phone: 757 627-9088
Fax: –
Web: www.whlr.us

CEO: –
CFO: –
HR: –
FYE: December 31
Type: Public

Wheeler Real Estate Investment Trust develops and manages shopping centers and other real estate properties. The REIT owns eight properties, including five shopping centers, two stand-alone buildings, and one office building. Most are in Virginia, but the company plans to target the Mid-Atlantic, Southeast, and Southwest. It will develop and manage strip centers and free-standing retail properties with a specific focus on revamping properties in secondary and tertiary markets. Wheeler Real Estate Investment Trust will be managed by WHLR Management, a company owned by company founder, chairman, and president Jon Wheeler. The REIT was formed in early 2011 and filed to go public later that year.

	Annual Growth	12/19	12/20	12/21	12/22	12/23
Sales ($mil.)	12.8%	63.2	61.0	61.3	76.6	102.3
Net income ($ mil.)	–	(8.0)	0.2	(9.4)	(12.5)	(4.7)
Market value ($ mil.)	(34.3%)	88.2	148.9	104.3	75.1	16.4
Employees	2.6%	47	35	36	47	52

WHEELING & LAKE ERIE RAILWAY COMPANY

100 EAST FIRST ST
BREWSTER, OH 446131202
Phone: 330 767-3401
Fax: –
Web: www.wlerwy.com

CEO: Larry R Parsons
CFO: Donna L Phillips
HR: –
FYE: June 30
Type: Private

Wheeling & Lake Erie Railway operates over a network of about 950 miles of track between the Ohio River and Lake Erie, passing through parts of Maryland, Ohio, Pennsylvania, and West Virginia. The company's system links the coal fields of West Virginia (Wheeling) with industrial Cleveland and its docks (Lake Erie). In addition to coal, the railroad hauls cargo including aggregates, iron ore, steel products, agricultural products, plastic resins. Wheeling & Lake Erie Railway owns some 575 miles of track; trackage rights over other railroads account for the rest of the company's network. The railroad traces its roots back to 1871 but took its current form in 1990.

	Annual Growth	06/03	06/04	06/05	06/06	06/14
Sales ($mil.)	(25.3%)	–	1,860.8	61.6	73.0	100.7
Net income ($ mil.)	180.2%	–	0.0	6.4	7.7	17.8
Market value ($ mil.)	–	–	–	–	–	–
Employees	–	–	–	–	–	416

WHEELING-NIPPON STEEL, INC.

400 PENN ST
FOLLANSBEE, WV 260371412
Phone: 304 527-2800
Fax: –
Web: www.wheeling-nipponsteel.com

CEO: Kenichi Hoshi
CFO: Noburu Sakai
HR: –
FYE: December 31
Type: Private

Wheeling-Nisshin, a subsidiary of Nisshin Steel, produces a variety of hot-dip coated steels, such as stainless steel. The company's output includes 400,000 tons produced at its aluminizing and galvanizing line facility and 300,000 tons produced at its continuous galvanizing line facility. Both of the facilities are located at the company's headquarters site in West Virginia. Its primary customers are in the automotive, appliance, and construction industries. Wheeling-Nisshin was founded in 1986. It had been a joint venture between Nisshin and US steel producer Wheeling Pitt (now operating as Severstal Wheeling) until the Japanese steel company bought out its partner in early 2008.

	Annual Growth	12/10	12/11	12/12	12/13	12/14
Sales ($mil.)	23.5%	–	–	–	391.2	483.1
Net income ($ mil.)	100.5%	–	–	–	2.9	5.8
Market value ($ mil.)	–	–	–	–	–	–
Employees	–	–	–	–	–	180

WHIRLPOOL CORP   NYS: WHR

2000 North M-63
Benton Harbor, MI 49022-2692
Phone: 269 923-5000
Fax: –
Web: www.whirlpoolcorp.com

CEO: Marc R Bitzer
CFO: James W Peters
HR: Darrell Morrison
FYE: December 31
Type: Public

Whirlpool is a global kitchen and laundry company. Its principal products are laundry appliances, refrigerators and freezers, cooking appliances, and dishwashers, including Whirlpool, Amana, Brastemp, KitchenAid, Maytag, Jenn-Air, and Roper. The company distributes and markets these major home appliances in North America, Latin America, EMEA (Europe, the Middle East, and Africa), and Asia. It has principal manufacturing operations carried on at 35 locations in some 10 countries. Major customer includes retailer Lowe's. Almost 60% of the company's sales come from customers in North America.

	Annual Growth	12/19	12/20	12/21	12/22	12/23
Sales ($mil.)	(1.2%)	20,419	19,456	21,985	19,724	19,455
Net income ($ mil.)	(20.2%)	1,184.0	1,081.0	1,783.0	(1,519.0)	481.0
Market value ($ mil.)	(4.7%)	8,114.2	9,927.0	12,906	7,780.3	6,697.4
Employees	(6.4%)	77,000	78,000	69,000	61,000	59,000

WHITE CASTLE SYSTEM, INC.

555 EDGAR WALDO WAY
COLUMBUS, OH 432153070
Phone: 614 228-5781
Fax: –
Web: www.whitecastle.com

CEO: Edgar W Ingram III
CFO: Russell J Meyer
HR: Ida Fiegelis
FYE: December 28
Type: Private

White Castle System, America's first fast-food hamburger chain, has been making hot and tasty Sliders as a family-owned business for over 100 years. White Castle known for their little square burgers called Sliders owns and operates more than 350 White Castle hamburger joints dedicated to satisfying customers' cravings morning, noon, and night and sells its famous fare in retail stores nationwide. White Castle can be brought across US and Canada through select Canadian grocery stores. The company also sells Sliders through supermarket chains. The first fast food chain in the US, White Castle was founded by Walter Anderson and real estate broker E. W. "Billy" Ingram in 1921. The Ingram family continues to control the company.

WHITE COUNTY MEDICAL CENTER

3214 E RACE AVE
SEARCY, AR 721434810
Phone: 501 268-6121
Fax: –
Web: www.unity-health.org

CEO: Ray Montgomery
CFO: Stuart Hill
HR: Katye Ledbetter
FYE: September 30
Type: Private

If you're sick in Searcy, you may want to visit White County Medical Center (WCMC). The organization provides health care to Central Arkansas' residents. It has about 440 licensed inpatient beds on two hospital campuses (WCMC North and WCMC South), as well as a number of outpatient surgery centers, primary care clinics, and a retirement community called River Oaks Village. The WCMC South campus features an inpatient rehabilitation center that helps patients recover from injury and illness, as well as a long-term acute care hospital for patients needing extended general care. In addition, WCMC provides home health care services and runs a training program for certified nurse assistants. WCMC operates under the Unity Health brand.

	Annual Growth	09/18	09/19	09/20	09/21	09/22
Sales ($mil.)	3.1%	–	285.0	242.5	272.3	312.0
Net income ($ mil.)	–	–	16.0	29.6	52.2	(7.0)
Market value ($ mil.)	–	–	–	–	–	–
Employees	–	–	–	–	–	3,010

WHITE MEMORIAL MEDICAL CENTER INC

1720 E CESAR E CHAVEZ AVE
LOS ANGELES, CA 900332414
Phone: 323 268-5000
Fax: –
Web: www.adventisthealth.org

CEO: Beth D Zachary
CFO: Terri Day
HR: Sergio Vazquez
FYE: December 31
Type: Private

White Memorial Medical Center provides health care services to the colorful Los Angeles community. The faith-based, not-for-profit hospital has more than 350 beds and provides acute health care to residents in and around the "City of Flowers and Sunshine." Services include inpatient psychiatric care, cancer and heart care centers, diabetes programs, orthopedics, pediatrics, women's health, and other acute and specialty programs. Part of Adventist Health, White Memorial is also a teaching hospital and is affiliated with Loma Linda University and the Linda Loma University Medical Center. The White Memorial Medical Center was founded in 1913 by the Seventh-day Adventist Church.

	Annual Growth	12/16	12/17	12/18	12/21	12/22
Sales ($mil.)	(0.6%)	–	–	504.0	412.2	491.6
Net income ($ mil.)	–	–	–	79.0	(7.1)	(48.1)
Market value ($ mil.)	–	–	–	–	–	–
Employees	–	–	–	–	–	2,000

WHITE RIVER HEALTH SYSTEM, INC.

1710 HARRISON ST
BATESVILLE, AR 725017303
Phone: 870 262-1200
Fax: –
Web: www.whiteriverhealth.org

CEO: –
CFO: –
HR: –
FYE: September 30
Type: Private

White River Health System offers health care services to residents of north central Arkansas. The not-for-profit organization operates two hospitals, the flagship White River Medical Center and acute care facility Stone County Medical Center, which provides health care services to rural communities. Combined, the two hospitals have about 225 beds and provide a range of emergency, surgical, medical, and diagnostic services. The system also includes outpatient facilities, primary care and specialty physician offices, long-term care facilities for the elderly and those unable to live independently.

	Annual Growth	09/18	09/19	09/20	09/21	09/22
Sales ($mil.)	3.4%	–	264.1	247.5	295.2	291.7
Net income ($ mil.)	–	–	1.3	3.8	36.5	(3.7)
Market value ($ mil.)	–	–	–	–	–	–
Employees	–	–	–	–	–	1,500

WHITEHEAD INSTITUTE FOR BIOMEDICAL RESEARCH

455 MAIN ST
CAMBRIDGE, MA 021421025
Phone: 617 258-5000
Fax: –
Web: wi.mit.edu

CEO: Susan Whitehead
CFO: –
HR: Jen Fairchild
FYE: June 30
Type: Private

The Whitehead Institute for Biomedical Research blazes new trails in bioscience. The organization, funded by both the public and private sectors, investigates such diseases as Parkinson's and cancer and dives into the depths of biology, genomics, and genetics to gain new understanding about disease and health. The Whitehead Institute contributed to the international effort to map the human genome, and is actively researching stem cells. Other achievements include discovering a system for multiplying adult stem cells and creating the first genetically defined human cancer cell. The enterprise draws researchers from nearby MIT (with which it is affiliated in its teaching activities) and from all over the world.

	Annual Growth	06/17	06/18	06/20	06/21	06/22
Sales ($mil.)	13.0%	–	68.0	72.3	97.6	110.9
Net income ($ mil.)	(58.7%)	–	22.3	(4.8)	0.9	0.6
Market value ($ mil.)	–	–	–	–	–	–
Employees	–	–	–	–	–	550

WHITESTONE REIT

NYS: WSR

2600 South Gessner, Suite 500
Houston, TX 77063
Phone: 713 827-9595
Fax: 713 465-8847
Web: www.whitestonereit.com

CEO: Dave Holeman
CFO: David K Holeman
HR: –
FYE: December 31
Type: Public

Whitestone REIT is out to make a name for itself in real estate. The self-managed real estate investment trust owns, leases, and operates around 60 retail, office, and warehouse properties in Texas (Houston is the company's largest market), Illinois, and Arizona totaling about 5 million sq. ft. Whitestone focuses on what it calls community-centered properties, or high-visibility properties in established or developing culturally diverse neighborhoods It recruits retail, grocery, financial services, and other tenants to its Whitestone branded commercial centers. Some of its top tenants include Safeway, Dollar Tree, Wells Fargo, Walgreens, Frost Bank, and Alamo Drafthouse.

	Annual Growth	12/19	12/20	12/21	12/22	12/23
Sales ($mil.)	5.4%	119.3	117.9	125.4	139.4	147.0
Net income ($ mil.)	(5.1%)	23.7	6.0	12.0	35.3	19.2
Market value ($ mil.)	(2.5%)	675.7	395.4	502.6	478.2	609.7
Employees	(7.5%)	108	88	86	75	79

WHITMAN COLLEGE

345 BOYER AVE
WALLA WALLA, WA 993622083
Phone: 509 527-5111
Fax: –
Web: www.whitman.edu

CEO: –
CFO: –
HR: –
FYE: June 30
Type: Private

Students attending this Walla Walla school hope to get more Bing Bang for their educational buck. Whitman College, located in Walla Walla, Washington, is an independent, co-educational, non-sectarian undergraduate school. It offers bachelor's degrees in more than 40 liberal arts and sciences areas, including education, environmental studies, biology, English, music, mathematics, and religion. Whitman College also offers extensive study abroad programs. It has about 1,500 students and a 9:1 student-to-faculty ratio. About two-thirds of Whitman students live on campus.

	Annual Growth	06/18	06/19	06/20	06/21	06/22
Sales ($mil.)	–	–	90.8	94.8	79.3	90.9
Net income ($ mil.)	–	–	8.8	24.3	272.4	(171.7)
Market value ($ mil.)	–	–	–	–	–	–
Employees	–	–	–	–	–	1,095

WHITNEY MUSEUM OF AMERICAN ART

99 GANSEVOORT ST
NEW YORK, NY 100141404
Phone: 212 570-3600
Fax: –
Web: www.whitney.org

CEO: –
CFO: Alice P Burns
HR: Angie Salerno
FYE: June 30
Type: Private

The Whitney Museum of American Art houses some 12,000 works of 20th- and 21st-century American art, including paintings, sculptures, drawings, photographs, and prints, by about 2,000 artists. It contains the entirety of Edward Hopper's artistic estate, as well as pieces by artists such as Georgia O'Keefe, Kiki Smith, Louise Nevelson, and Andy Warhol. The museum also offers public programs including lectures, seminars, and performances. The museum is housed in a large granite building at the corner of Madison Avenue and 75th Street designed by the Hungarian-born, Bauhaus-trained architect Marcel Breuer. Whitney Museum of American Art was founded in 1930 by sculptor and art patron Gertrude Vanderbilt Whitney.

	Annual Growth	06/18	06/19	06/20	06/21	06/22
Sales ($mil.)	1.8%	–	91.8	91.8	72.8	96.8
Net income ($ mil.)	–	–	2.5	11.4	56.9	(70.6)
Market value ($ mil.)	–	–	–	–	–	–
Employees	–	–	–	–	–	167

WHOLE FOODS MARKET, INC.

550 BOWIE ST
AUSTIN, TX 787034644
Phone: 512 477-4455
Fax: –
Web: www.wholefoodsmarket.com

CEO: –
CFO: –
HR: –
FYE: September 24
Type: Private

Whole Foods Market is the world's #1 natural and organic foods grocery store chain. The company operates more than 535 retail and non-retail stores throughout the US, Canada, and the UK. Its product categories include bakery, beauty and body care, beer, bulk, catering, cheese, floral, grocery, meat, prepared foods, produce, seafood, wellness and supplements, and wine. Most of the food and other items the stores sell are free of pesticides, preservatives, sweeteners, and cruelty. Founded in Austin, Texas in 1980, Whole Foods pioneered the supermarket concept in natural and organic foods retailing.

	Annual Growth	09/13	09/14	09/15	09/16	09/17
Sales ($mil.)	4.1%	–	14,194	15,389	15,724	16,030
Net income ($ mil.)	(24.9%)	–	579.0	536.0	507.0	245.0
Market value ($ mil.)	–	–	–	–	–	–
Employees	–	–	–	–	–	95,000

WHOLESALE SUPPLY GROUP, INC.

885 KEITH ST NW
CLEVELAND, TN 373111802
Phone: 423 716-6722
Fax: –
Web: www.wholesalesupply.us

CEO: –
CFO: –
HR: –
FYE: July 31
Type: Private

Wholesale Supply Group is a wholesale and retail supplier of electrical, HVAC, and plumbing products to customers in Alabama, Georgia, Kentucky, North Carolina, Tennessee, and Virginia. The company carries new and discontinued products under the American Water Heaters, Aqua Glass, Kohler, Delta, Moen, GE Appliances, Progress Lighting, Square D, Lithonia, and Luxaire brands. Its customers include home owners, local contractors, electricians, and plumbers in commercial, residential, and industrial markets. The enterprise, which began as a concrete block-making business founded by Roy Higgins and Gene Davis in 1942, operates from more than 30 branches.

	Annual Growth	07/15	07/16	07/17	07/18	07/19
Sales ($mil.)	5.5%	–	–	–	48.2	50.9
Net income ($ mil.)	(38.1%)	–	–	–	1.3	0.8
Market value ($ mil.)	–	–	–	–	–	–
Employees	–	–	–	–	–	335

WHYY, INC.

100 N INDEPENDENCE MALL W
PHILADELPHIA, PA 191061521
Phone: 215 351-1200
Fax: –
Web: www.whyy.org

CEO: –
CFO: –
HR: –
FYE: June 30
Type: Private

WHYY provides the media landscape with a little Fresh Air . The company operates public radio station WHYY 90.9 FM, which produces the popular NPR talk show with host Terry Gross. It also runs public television stations WHYY-TV and WDPB-TV. All three serve parts of Pennsylvania, Delaware, and New Jersey. Its Learning Lab offers multimedia journalism and video production training to WHYY members, as well as to teens, teachers, and seniors. The company planted its roots in the 1950s, when The Metropolitan Philadelphia Educational Radio and Television Corporation began broadcasting cultural and educational radio programming. About 100,000 members -- along with corporations and government agencies -- fund WHYY.

	Annual Growth	06/14	06/15	06/20	06/21	06/22
Sales ($mil.)	6.7%	–	32.5	39.0	48.8	51.0
Net income ($ mil.)	31.8%	–	2.0	0.9	11.2	13.5
Market value ($ mil.)	–	–	–	–	–	–
Employees	–	–	–	–	–	160

WICHITA STATE UNIVERSITY

1845 FAIRMOUNT ST
WICHITA, KS 672600001
Phone: 316 978-3001
Fax: –
Web: www.wichita.edu

CEO: –
CFO: –
HR: –
FYE: June 30
Type: Private

State-supported Wichita State University (WSU) enrolls over 21,940 students, with the bulk hailing from Kansas. Along with its main campus, WSU also has six satellite locations in the area. The school offers 70 undergraduate degrees in more than 200 subjects. Its Graduate School offers more than 40 master's programs, a dozen doctoral degree programs, an educational specialist program, and a growing number of graduate certificate programs, as well as research opportunities. WSU colleges include business, education, engineering, fine arts, health professions, and liberal arts and sciences. The school was founded in 1895 as a Congregational institution.

	Annual Growth	06/16	06/17	06/18	06/19	06/20
Sales ($mil.)	11.4%	–	189.3	26.4	230.7	261.5
Net income ($ mil.)	8.5%	–	17.5	3.2	6.7	22.4
Market value ($ mil.)	–	–	–	–	–	–
Employees	–	–	–	–	–	3,395

WICHITA, CITY OF (INC)

455 N MAIN ST FL 5
WICHITA, KS 672021620
Phone: 316 268-4351
Fax: –
Web: www.wichita.gov

CEO: –
CFO: –
HR: Chris Bezruki
FYE: December 31
Type: Private

What do Wyatt Earp, Cessna, and the first sub-four minute mile have in common? The City of Wichita. known as Cow Town and the Air Capital of the World, was incorporated in 1870. The city has a population of more than 380,000 occupying a little more than 163 sq. mi. Wichita State and 14 other campuses of higher education provide technical skills for leading employers. Boeing, Learjet, Raytheon, Cargill, and Koch are major companies with operations in the city.

	Annual Growth	12/17	12/18	12/20	12/21	12/22
Sales ($mil.)	0.1%	–	453.1	429.4	453.7	454.9
Net income ($ mil.)	–	–	(3.1)	(71.8)	15.3	7.8
Market value ($ mil.)	–	–	–	–	–	–
Employees	–	–	–	–	–	2,200

WIDENER UNIVERSITY

1 UNIVERSITY PL
CHESTER, PA 190135792
Phone: 610 499-4000
Fax: –
Web: www.widener.edu

CEO: –
CFO: Joseph J Baker
HR: –
FYE: June 30
Type: Private

You probably won't find any narrow-minded students at Widener. A private, co-educational liberal arts college, Widener University offers a curriculum that emphasizes academic excellence, career preparation, and civic engagement. It has an enrollment of more than 6,000 students and a student-to-faculty ratio of 12:1. The university grants undergraduate degrees in about 45 majors and graduate degrees in more than a dozen fields; its programs are divided into eight schools and colleges that cover areas including arts and sciences, business, education, engineering, law, hospitality, human services, and nursing. Widener University has had its current name since 1979, but its roots reach back to 1821, when it was founded as a Quaker school for boys.

	Annual Growth	06/18	06/19	06/20	06/21	06/22
Sales ($mil.)	16.0%	–	162.8	157.2	146.4	254.3
Net income ($ mil.)	–	–	10.7	(8.5)	27.0	(3.1)
Market value ($ mil.)	–	–	–	–	–	–
Employees	–	–	–	–	–	1,021

WIDEOPENWEST INC
NYS: WOW

7887 East Belleview Avenue, Suite 1000
Englewood, CO 80111
Phone: 720 479-3500
Fax: –
Web: www.wowway.com

CEO: Teresa Elder
CFO: John S Rego
HR: –
FYE: December 31
Type: Public

Cable operator WideOpenWest (WOW) is a leading broadband services provider offering high-speed data (HSD), cable television (Video), and digital telephony (Telephony) services to residential customers and offers a full range of products and services to business customers. Operating in half a dozen states in the Midwest and South, WOW's broadband networks passed 1.9 million homes and businesses and served some 530,600 customers. It also builds fiber networks for other companies. WOW raised about $310 million in an IPO in 2017.

	Annual Growth	12/19	12/20	12/21	12/22	12/23
Sales ($mil.)	(12.0%)	1,145.8	1,148.4	725.7	704.9	686.7
Net income ($ mil.)	–	36.4	14.4	770.5	(2.5)	(287.7)
Market value ($ mil.)	(14.0%)	620.0	891.6	1,798.2	761.2	338.3
Employees	(11.3%)	2,200	2,000	1,500	1,390	1,360

WIDEPOINT CORP
ASE: WYY

11250 Waples Mill Road, South Tower 210
Fairfax, VA 22030
Phone: 703 349-2577
Fax: –
Web: www.widepoint.com

CEO: Jin Kang
CFO: Robert J George
HR: Amy Obryan
FYE: December 31
Type: Public

WidePoint stretches to provide a variety of IT services to government and enterprise customers. The company provides wireless telecom management and business process outsourcing (BPO) services. Its cybersecurity segment provides identity management services including identity proofing, credential issuing, and public key infrastructure. The company also provides more traditional IT services such as architecture and planning, integration services, and vulnerability testing. WidePoint focuses its operations toward US federal government clients including the Department of Homeland Security (more than a quarter of sales), the TSA (nearly a quarter), the FBI, Customs and Border Protection, and the Justice department.

	Annual Growth	12/19	12/20	12/21	12/22	12/23
Sales ($mil.)	1.0%	101.7	180.3	87.3	94.1	106.0
Net income ($ mil.)	–	0.2	10.3	0.3	(23.6)	(4.0)
Market value ($ mil.)	55.4%	3.5	89.9	35.0	16.2	20.6
Employees	(3.5%)	249	238	260	238	216

WIKIMEDIA FOUNDATION, INC.

1 MONTGOMERY ST STE 1600
SAN FRANCISCO, CA 941045516
Phone: 415 839-6885
Fax: –
Web: www.wikimediafoundation.org

CEO: Maryana Ishkander
CFO: V R Kessler V
HR: –
FYE: June 30
Type: Private

Want free access to the sum of all human knowledge? Wikimedia Foundation can give it to you. The not-for-profit organization has produced a plethora of free-content wiki projects, including one of the most visited sites on the Internet, online collaborative encyclopedia Wikipedia (the foundation's first project). The term wiki (a Hawaiian word for "fast") describes a collection of Web pages designed to enable anyone with Internet access to contribute or modify content. Wikimedia has a paid staff of about 280, while hundreds of thousands of volunteers contribute content. The Wikimedia Foundation is funded primarily through donations and grants, and was founded by Internet entrepreneur Jimmy Wales and philosopher Lawrence Sanger in 2001.

	Annual Growth	06/16	06/17	06/20	06/21	06/22
Sales ($mil.)	13.3%	–	90.0	124.6	159.0	167.9
Net income ($ mil.)	1.1%	–	20.9	12.5	47.3	22.1
Market value ($ mil.)	–	–	–	–	–	–
Employees	–	–	–	–	–	284

WIKOFF COLOR CORPORATION

1886 MERRITT RD
FORT MILL, SC 297157707
Phone: 803 548-2210
Fax: –
Web: www.wikoff.com

CEO: Mark C Lewis
CFO: Martin Iles
HR: Jon Lucas
FYE: May 31
Type: Private

Wikoff Color makes a rainbow of color products for use by graphic arts companies. The company is dedicated to developing tailor-made inks to maximize printing pressroom efficiencies and providing highly technical, service-oriented approaches to ink making. Wikoff Color makes aqueous coatings and overprint varnishes in addition to its line of inks marketed around the globe. Its products are primarily used by customers in the graphic arts industry for lithography, flexography, letterpress, and gravure printing processes. Wikoff Color also makes functional coatings and specialty items.

WILBUR SMITH ASSOCIATES, INC.

1301 GERVAIS ST STE 1600
COLUMBIA, SC 292013361
Phone: 803 758-4500
Fax: –
Web: www.wilbursmith.com

CEO: –
CFO: –
HR: –
FYE: December 25
Type: Private

For many cities around the world, where there's a Wilbur, there's a roadway. Wilbur Smith Associates provides engineering, design, planning, construction, and economic consulting services for municipal works and infrastructure jobs including highways, bridges, railroads, waterways, airports, and public buildings. Wilbur Smith is active throughout the US, Europe, Central America, the UK, the Middle East, and Asia. Pioneer transportation engineer Wilbur Smith founded the firm in 1952. The company was acquired by Camp Dresser & McKee (CDM) in 2011. The deal helped broaden both firms' service capabilities and geographic reach.

	Annual Growth	12/05	12/06	12/07	12/08	12/09
Sales ($mil.)	–	–	–	(436.9)	183.4	182.4
Net income ($ mil.)	789.0%	–	–	0.0	3.3	1.3
Market value ($ mil.)	–	–	–	–	–	–
Employees	–	–	–	–	–	1,217

WILBUR-ELLIS HOLDINGS II, INC.

345 CALIFORNIA ST FL 27
SAN FRANCISCO, CA 941042644
Phone: 415 772-4000
Fax: –
Web: www.wilburellis.com

CEO: –
CFO: Michael J Hunter
HR: –
FYE: December 31
Type: Private

Wilbur-Ellis is a leading US privately- and family-owned international distribution business with sales over $4 billion. Through its agribusiness division, Wilbur-Ellis sells fertilizer, herbicides, insecticides, seed, and farm machinery in North America. The Cavallo division exports and distributes food ingredients and specialty chemicals throughout the Pacific Rim. Its nutrition division serves international customers in the livestock, pet food, and aquaculture industries. Additionally, Wilbur-Ellis new division, Nachurs Alpine Solutions sells liquid fertilizer into turf, specialty, international, and private label markets. Wilbur-Ellis was founded in 1921 by Brayton Wilbur Sr., Floyd Ellis and Thomas Franck.

	Annual Growth	12/99	12/00	12/09	12/10	12/11
Sales ($mil.)	8.9%	–	1,100.0	–	2,342.5	2,812.0
Net income ($ mil.)	–	–	–	–	–	–
Market value ($ mil.)	–	–	–	–	–	–
Employees	–	–	–	–	–	4,600

WILDLIFE CONSERVATION SOCIETY

2300 SOUTHERN BLVD
BRONX, NY 104601090
Phone: 718 220-5100
Fax: –
Web: www.wcs.org

CEO: Christian Samper
CFO: Laura Stolzenthaler
HR: Emily Ramos
FYE: June 30
Type: Private

From Congo gorillas to humpback whales off the coast of Gabon, all life is worth conserving to the Wildlife Conservation Society (WCS). The group, founded in 1895, works to protect wildlife and lands throughout the world and to instill in humans a concern about nature. The not-for-profit organization operates New York City's Bronx Zoo, New York Aquarium, Central Park Zoo, Prospect Park Zoo, and the Queens Zoo. WCS's environmental education programs are used in US schools, as well as those in other nations. The society has ongoing efforts in more than 60 countries to protect endangered species and ecosystems. About a quarter of the funding for its work comes from visitors at its handful of parks.

	Annual Growth	06/15	06/16	06/20	06/21	06/22
Sales ($mil.)	7.1%	–	260.3	255.6	415.9	393.2
Net income ($ mil.)	–	–	(23.8)	(43.0)	83.3	56.2
Market value ($ mil.)	–	–	–	–	–	–
Employees	–	–	–	–	–	4,000

WILEY (JOHN) & SONS INC.
NYS: WLY

111 River Street
Hoboken, NJ 07030
Phone: 201 748-6000
Fax: –
Web: www.wiley.com

CEO: Matthew S Kissner
CFO: Christina V Tassell
HR: –
FYE: April 30
Type: Public

John Wiley & Sons (Wiley) is a global leader in scientific research and career-connected education, unlocking human potential by enabling discovery, powering education, and shaping workforces. Its online publishing platform Literatum delivers integrated access to more than 10 million articles from approximately 2,100 journals as well as over 27,000 online books and hundreds of multi-volume reference works, laboratory protocols, and databases. Journal subscriptions are primarily licensed through contracts for digital content available via its Wiley Online Library platform. It also engages in co-publishing titles with international publishers and receive licensing revenue from photocopies, reproductions, translations, and digital uses of its content and use of the Knewton adaptive engine. About half of its revenue comes from the US.

	Annual Growth	04/19	04/20	04/21	04/22	04/23
Sales ($mil.)	2.9%	1,800.1	1,831.5	1,941.5	2,082.9	2,019.9
Net income ($ mil.)	(43.4%)	168.3	(74.3)	148.3	148.3	17.2
Market value ($ mil.)	(4.4%)	2,552.6	2,075.5	3,147.3	2,812.9	2,131.9
Employees	11.5%	5,700	6,900	7,400	9,500	8,800

WILHELM CONSTRUCTION, INC.

3914 PROSPECT ST
INDIANAPOLIS, IN 462032344
Phone: 317 359-5411
Fax: –
Web: www.fawilhelm.com

CEO: –
CFO: –
HR: Timika Mitchell
FYE: December 31
Type: Private

General contractor F.A. Wilhelm Construction Company provides construction and construction management in the Midwest, particularly in its home state of Indiana. It focuses on commercial, industrial, and institutional buildings for the corporate, entertainment, food and beverage, healthcare, research, and education sectors, as well as public works projects, including water treatment plants. It also owns fabrication facilities that produce concrete formwork, process piping, sheet metal, and structural steel. F.A. Wilhelm also operates mechanical contractor Freitag-Weinhardt, sheet metal contractor Poynter, a full-service automatic sprinkler contractor RSQ Fire Protection, and electrical and systems contractor Industrial Electric.

WILHELMINA INTERNATIONAL, INC.
NAS: WHLM

5420 Lyndon B Johnson Freeway, Box #25
Dallas, TX 75240
Phone: 214 661-7488
Fax: –
Web: –

CEO: Mark E Schwarz
CFO: James A McCarthy
HR: –
FYE: December 31
Type: Public

Wilhelmina International has a new face. Formerly a billing services and software provider serving the telecommunications industry, New Century Equity Holdings reinvented itself as a holding company and in 2009 acquired Wilhelmina International -- the company responsible for the iconic modeling agency Wilhelmina Models. The $30 million transaction also included affiliates Wilhelmina Miami, Wilhelmina Film & TV, and Wilhelmina Artist Management. Upon the deal's closure, New Century changed its name to Wilhelmina International, reflecting its new primary business focus. The Wilhelmina deal came after more than four years of scouting new investment opportunities.

	Annual Growth	12/19	12/20	12/21	12/22	12/23
Sales ($mil.)	(30.9%)	75.5	41.6	56.8	17.8	17.2
Net income ($ mil.)	–	(4.8)	(4.9)	4.5	3.5	0.4
Market value ($ mil.)	(0.2%)	21.4	23.7	27.1	18.3	21.2
Employees	(6.5%)	114	70	80	85	87

WILKES-BARRE HOSPITAL COMPANY, LLC

575 N RIVER ST
WILKES BARRE, PA 187640999
Phone: 570 829-8111
Fax: –
Web: www.commonwealthhealth.net

CEO: Cor Catena
CFO: Maggie Koehler
HR: –
FYE: June 30
Type: Private

Wyoming Valley Health Care System (WVHCS) cares for the rugged folk in the wilds of Pennsylvania. WVHCS, part of the Community Health Systems network, operates the Wilkes-Barre General Hospital, an acute care facility with some 410 beds that serves northeastern Pennsylvania residents. The hospital includes a women's and children's center, cardiac care unit, and a cancer care center. The WVHCS network also includes a behavioral health hospital, the First Hospital Wyoming Valley (also known as Nesbitt Memorial Medical Center). Other system facilities include primary care physician offices, behavioral health clinics, long-term and hospice care centers, and a home health agency.

WILKINSON-COOPER PRODUCE INC

701 NW 12TH ST
BELLE GLADE, FL 334301739
Phone: 561 996-7959
Fax: –
Web: www.wilkinson-cooper.com

CEO: –
CFO: –
HR: –
FYE: July 31
Type: Private

Wilkinson-Cooper Produce is a fresh vegetable wholesaler. Its products include corn, cucumbers, endives, green beans, parsley, peppers, radishes, squash, watercress, and zucchinis. It ships wholesale mixed vegetables from Florida between November and May, and from Georgia in June and July. The Florida-based company has been shipping vegetables across the continental US, as well as Canada and Europe, since 1965.

	Annual Growth	07/15	07/16	07/17	07/18	07/19
Sales ($mil.)	9.1%	–	–	–	37.2	40.6
Net income ($ mil.)	–	–	–	–	0.0	(0.0)
Market value ($ mil.)	–	–	–	–	–	–
Employees	–	–	–	–	–	15

WILL COUNTY

302 N CHICAGO ST
JOLIET, IL 604324078
Phone: 815 740-4602
Fax: –
Web: www.willcountyillinois.com

CEO: –
CFO: –
HR: Bruce Tidwell
FYE: November 30
Type: Private

Will County is a rapidly growing county in Illinois. The regional government, based in Joliet (about 45 miles southwest of Chicago), provides a multitude of services, including animal control, health programs, highway planning and maintenance, veterans assistance, and workforce training to about 670,000 citizens in about 40 municipalities and 24 townships. The Will County Board consists of elected officials from nine districts who establish policies and the county executive, who oversees day-to-day operations. The county was formed in 1836 and is named after a salt production businessman named Dr. Conrad Will.

	Annual Growth	11/18	11/19	11/20	11/21	11/22
Sales ($mil.)	8.1%	–	348.7	470.5	447.8	440.4
Net income ($ mil.)	–	–	(11.6)	(18.8)	52.0	40.7
Market value ($ mil.)	–	–	–	–	–	–
Employees	–	–	–	–	–	2,000

WILLAMETTE UNIVERSITY

900 STATE ST
SALEM, OR 973013930
Phone: 503 370-6210
Fax: –
Web: www.willamette.edu

CEO: –
CFO: –
HR: –
FYE: June 30
Type: Private

Willamette University's claim to fame is its status as the first university in the West. About 3,000 students are enrolled in the private, co-educational liberal arts school that offers undergraduate and graduate degrees. Undergraduate degrees encompass nearly 50 fields -- politics, biology, English, psychology, and economics are among the most pursued majors -- and graduate degrees in business, law, and education. The university has a student-to-faculty ratio of 10:1. Founded in the early days of the Oregon Territory by missionary Jason Lee as a school for Native American children, Willamette University was established in 1842.

	Annual Growth	05/17	05/18	05/19	05/20*	06/22
Sales ($mil.)	0.6%	–	96.5	91.4	95.1	98.8
Net income ($ mil.)	–	–	14.5	(5.5)	(15.7)	(65.5)
Market value ($ mil.)	–	–	–	–	–	–
Employees	–	–	–	–	–	700

*Fiscal year change

WILLAMETTE VALLEY VINEYARD INC.   NAS: WVVI

8800 Enchanted Way S.E.
Turner, OR 97392
Phone: 503 588-9463
Fax: –
Web: www.wvv.com

CEO: James W Bernau
CFO: John Ferry
HR: Mariah Longfellow
FYE: December 31
Type: Public

Willamette Valley Vineyards is a leading producer of premium varietal wines, including chardonnay, dry riesling, and pinot gris, along with its flagship pinot noir. In addition to Willamette Valley, it also makes wine under the Tualatin Estates and Griffin Creek labels. The winemaker owns, leases, or contracts almost 800 acres of vineyards and produced about 121,000 cases of wine during 2008. Its wines are sold in Oregon through its Bacchus Fine Wines distribution operation and are available elsewhere in the US through other distributors and brokers. Founder and CEO Jim Bernau owns 12% of the company.

	Annual Growth	12/19	12/20	12/21	12/22	12/23
Sales ($mil.)	12.1%	24.7	27.3	31.8	33.9	39.1
Net income ($ mil.)	–	2.5	3.4	2.4	(0.6)	(1.2)
Market value ($ mil.)	(6.2%)	34.4	31.6	43.0	29.6	26.6
Employees	13.8%	206	213	266	362	346

WILLBROS GROUP, INC.

4400 POST OAK PKWY STE 1000
HOUSTON, TX 770273439
Phone: 713 403-8000
Fax: –
Web: www.willbros.com

CEO: David King
CFO: Peter J Moerbeek
HR: –
FYE: December 31
Type: Private

Willbros Group develops infrastructure worldwide, but primarily in North America. A construction and engineering contractor targeting oil, gas, and power industries, the firm specializes in projects in emerging nations. Willbros has completed major pipeline systems, oil and gas production plants, piers, and bridges. Engineering services include design, feasibility studies, and project management. It also offers specialty services such as dredging, and pipeline. Willbros' inventory features a large fleet of company-owned and leased equipment, such as camp equipment, marine vessels, and pipe-laying and transportation equipment. The company also offers utility transmission and distribution services.

WILLDAN GROUP INC   NMS: WLDN

2401 East Katella Avenue, Suite 300
Anaheim, CA 92806
Phone: 800 424-9144
Fax: –
Web: www.willdan.com

CEO: Thomas D Brisbin
CFO: Creighton Early
HR: Scott Dippolito
FYE: December 29
Type: Public

Willdan Group can and will do what it takes to meet its customers' numerous engineering needs. The company has four operating service segments: engineering (Willdan Engineering), energy efficiency (Willdan Energy Solutions), public finance (Willdan Financial Services) and homeland security (Willdan Homeland Solutions). Clients include federal and local governments, school districts, public utilities, and some private industries. Willdan focuses on small- to mid-sized clients that may fall below the radar of larger competitors. The company was founded in 1964.

	Annual Growth	12/19*	01/21*	12/21	12/22	12/23
Sales ($mil.)	3.6%	443.1	391.0	353.8	429.1	510.1
Net income ($ mil.)	22.6%	4.8	(14.5)	(8.4)	(8.4)	10.9
Market value ($ mil.)	(8.9%)	427.0	570.5	481.6	244.2	294.2
Employees	2.7%	1,451	1,353	1,560	1,491	1,616

*Fiscal year change

WILLIAM BEAUMONT HOSPITAL

3601 W 13 MILE RD
ROYAL OAK, MI 480736712
Phone: 947 522-1177
Fax: –
Web: www.beaumont.org

CEO: Gene Michalski
CFO: –
HR: –
FYE: December 31
Type: Private

Beaumont Health System is an eight-hospital regional health system with more than 3,337 beds and more than 5,000 physicians along with numerous community-based medical centers throughout suburban Detroit (in Oakland, Macomb, and Wayne counties). Additional facilities include nursing homes, a home health care agency, a research institute, and primary and specialty care clinics, as well as rehabilitation, cardiology, and cancer centers. Beaumont is the exclusive clinical teaching site for the Oakland University William Beaumont School of Medicine; it also has affiliations with Michigan State University College of Osteopathic Medicine and Wayne State University School of Medicine.

	Annual Growth	12/13	12/14	12/15	12/16	12/17
Sales ($mil.)	6.5%	–	–	1,300.1	1,396.6	1,473.3
Net income ($ mil.)	(29.1%)	–	–	142.2	118.1	71.5
Market value ($ mil.)	–	–	–	–	–	–
Employees	–	–	–	–	–	18,050

WILLIAM BLAIR & COMPANY LLC

150 N RIVERSIDE PLZ # 3500
CHICAGO, IL 606065042
Phone: 312 236-1600
Fax: –
Web: www.williamblair.com

CEO: Brent Gledhill
CFO: Michael Trimberger
HR: Jami Waggoner
FYE: December 31
Type: Private

William Blair & Company is the premier global boutique with expertise in investment banking, investment management, and private wealth management. The firm has strategic partnerships with Allier Capital, BDA Partners, and Poalim Capital Markets. As an independent and employee-owned firm, together with its strategic partners, William Blair & Company operates in more than 20 offices worldwide. The firm's client services include investment banking, asset management, wealth planning, equity research, and institutional sales and trading. William Blair & Company was founded in 1935 by William McCormick Blair and Francis Bonner.

	Annual Growth	12/07	12/08	12/13	12/21	12/22
Assets ($mil.)	(27.6%)	–	569.5	687.1	6.7	6.2
Net income ($ mil.)	–	–	–	–	2.4	(0.5)
Market value ($ mil.)	–	–	–	–	–	–
Employees	–	–	–	–	–	1,980

WILLIAM MARSH RICE UNIVERSITY INC

6100 MAIN ST
HOUSTON, TX 770051827
Phone: 713 348-4055
Fax: –
Web: www.rice.edu

CEO: –
CFO: –
HR: –
FYE: June 30
Type: Private

Boasting a 300-acre tree-lined campus in Houston, Rice University is ranked among the nation's top 20 universities by US News & World Report. Rice has a 6-to-1 undergraduate student-to-faculty ratio, and a residential college system, which supports students intellectually, emotionally, and culturally through social events, intramural sports, student plays, lectures series, courses and student government. Rice offers programs through eight schools in areas such as engineering, humanities, natural science, social sciences, economics, music, and architecture. A growing segment of undergraduate and graduate students at Rice hail from more than 60 countries around the world. The university opened in 1912 with funds from the estate of William Marsh Rice.

	Annual Growth	06/10	06/11	06/12	06/13	06/14
Sales ($mil.)	–	–	551.0	551.0	568.3	–
Net income ($ mil.)	(1.9%)	–	695.4	(34.0)	460.0	657.6
Market value ($ mil.)	–	–	–	–	–	–
Employees	–	–	–	–	–	2,600

WILLIAM PATERSON UNIVERSITY

300 POMPTON RD
WAYNE, NJ 074702103
Phone: 973 720-2000
Fax: –
Web: www.wpunj.edu

CEO: –
CFO: –
HR: Julie O 'neill
FYE: June 30
Type: Private

William Paterson University has evolved into a fully accredited liberal-arts university. William Paterson, which has more than 400 full-time faculty members, enrolls about 11,000 undergraduate and graduate students, and offers more than offers 45 undergraduate, 22 masters, one doctoral, and three post-baccalaureate certificate programs through five colleges. The university has a 370-acre campus with some 40 major buildings and other facilities, including the David and Lorraine Cheng Library, which boasts more than 350,000 bound volumes. William Paterson is accredited by the Middle States Association of Colleges and Secondary Schools. William Paterson was founded in 1855 as a normal school (teacher's college).

	Annual Growth	06/18	06/19	06/20	06/21	06/22
Sales ($mil.)	(2.3%)	–	148.5	144.1	130.5	138.7
Net income ($ mil.)	–	–	(5.4)	(8.5)	9.2	8.6
Market value ($ mil.)	–	–	–	–	–	–
Employees	–	–	–	–	–	1,300

WILLIAMS INDUSTRIAL SERVICES GROUP INC

NBB: WLMS Q

200 Ashford Center North, Suite 425
Atlanta, GA 30338
Phone: 770 879-4400
Fax: –
Web: www.wisgrp.com

CEO: Tracy D Pagliara
CFO: Damien Vassall
HR: –
FYE: December 31
Type: Public

Global Power Equipment Group keeps its customers in power. Through its subsidiaries, the company designs and manufactures power generation equipment for OEMs, engineering, construction, and power generation customers. Its products, sold under its Braden Manufacturing, Consolidated Fabricators, TOG, and Koontz-Wagner brands, include auxiliary parts for steam and gas turbines, electric transmission systems and controls, and custom components. Additionally, subsidiary Williams Industrial Services offers upgrades and maintenance services to industrial and utility companies and nuclear and hydroelectric power plants, while its Hetsco unit provides welding and fabrication services. The company was formed in 1998.

	Annual Growth	12/18	12/19	12/20	12/21	12/22
Sales ($mil.)	6.0%	188.9	245.8	269.1	304.9	238.1
Net income ($ mil.)	–	(25.4)	2.2	1.5	2.7	(13.7)
Market value ($ mil.)	8.1%	62.1	45.7	69.0	84.9	84.9
Employees	2.6%	457	420	460	572	506

WILLIAMS PARTNERS L.P.

1 ONE WILLIAMS CTR BSMT 2
TULSA, OK 741720172
Phone: 918 573-2000
Fax: –
Web: www.williams.com

CEO: Alan S Armstrong
CFO: John D Chandler
HR: Danna Yeargin
FYE: December 31
Type: Private

Williams Partners (formerly Access Midstream Partners) is a midstream gathering company that owns, operates, develops, and acquires natural gas, natural gas liquids (NGLs), and oil gathering assets in the US. It gathers about 3.9 billion cu. ft. of natural gas per day via some 5,800 miles of gathering and transmission lines. The company also has processing facilities that provide services to thousands of wells. Its assets are located in a dozen states, with operations in the Barnett, Eagle Ford, Haynesville, Marcellus, Niobrara, and Utica shales and several unconventional plays in the Mid-Continent region.

WILLIAMS SAUSAGE COMPANY, INC.

5132 OLD TROY HICKMAN RD
UNION CITY, TN 382617702
Phone: 731 885-5841
Fax: –
Web: www.williams-sausage.com

CEO: –
CFO: –
HR: –
FYE: March 31
Type: Private

Union City, Tennessee-headquartered Williams Sausage is a regional meat processor that makes sausage, ham, and bacon products for both retail and wholesale food customers. Its product lines include several varieties of pork sausage, cured hams, and smoked bacon. The company also markets microwavable pork biscuit sandwiches and smoked pork sausages. Most of its meat products are sold under the Williams brand, but it also markets sausage and bacon under the Ole South label. The family-owned company was founded by Harold Williams in 1958.

	Annual Growth	03/03	03/04	03/05	03/06	03/07
Sales ($mil.)	4.5%	–	–	42.7	49.3	46.6
Net income ($ mil.)	(37.5%)	–	–	7.8	6.8	3.1
Market value ($ mil.)	–	–	–	–	–	–
Employees	–	–	–	–	–	490

WILLIAMS SCOTSMAN INC

8211 Town Center Drive
Baltimore, MD 21236
Phone: 410 931-6000
Fax: –
Web: www.willscot.com

CEO: Bradley L Soultz
CFO: Timothy D Boswell
HR: –
FYE: December 31
Type: Public

Williams Scotsman is North America's leading site solution provider. Customers include government agencies, schools, and hospitals. The company maintains a fleet of some 350,000 units for all industry types, ready to roll from over 275 locations across Mexico, UK, and the North America (US and Canada). Started in 1944 as Williams Mobile Offices and formed through the 1990 merger of Williams Mobile Offices and Scotsman Manufacturing, Williams Scotsman merged with Mobile Mini in 2020.

	Annual Growth	12/00	12/01	12/02	12/03	12/04
Sales ($mil.)	3.6%	432.1	492.3	495.2	437.8	497.9
Net income ($ mil.)	–	16.1	22.7	15.2	(11.6)	(3.4)
Market value ($ mil.)	–	–	–	–	–	–
Employees	1.0%	1,200	1,300	1,200	1,150	1,250

WILLIAMS SONOMA INC

NYS: WSM

3250 Van Ness Avenue
San Francisco, CA 94109
Phone: 415 421-7900
Fax: 415 434-0881
Web: www.williams-sonomainc.com

CEO: –
CFO: –
HR: –
FYE: January 28
Type: Public

Williams-Sonoma is one of the leading multichannel retailers of high-end goods for well-appointed kitchens, bedrooms, and baths. Home products include bath and storage, bedding, cookware, furniture, lighting, and tableware. The company's retail chains, including Williams Sonoma (upscale cookware), West Elm (modern housewares), and Pottery Barn and Pottery Barn Kids and Teen (housewares, furniture) as well as Rejuvenation and Mark and Graham (home d cor, women's and men's accessories, seasonal items, personalized gifts), sell wares through approximately 530 stores across the US and in Canada, Australia, the UK, Washington, DC, and Puerto Rico, as well as e-commerce websites in certain locations.

	Annual Growth	02/20*	01/21	01/22	01/23	01/24
Sales ($mil.)	7.1%	5,898.0	6,783.2	8,245.9	8,674.4	7,750.7
Net income ($ mil.)	27.8%	356.1	680.7	1,126.3	1,127.9	949.8
Market value ($ mil.)	31.3%	4,495.7	8,270.3	9,931.2	8,126.0	13,379
Employees	(20.7%)	27,000	21,000	21,000	21,100	10,700

*Fiscal year change

WILLIS LEASE FINANCE CORP.

NMS: WLFC

4700 Lyons Technology Parkway
Coconut Creek, FL 33073
Phone: 561 349-9989
Fax: –
Web: www.willislease.com

CEO: –
CFO: –
HR: –
FYE: December 31
Type: Public

Hey, buddy, got any spare Pratt & Whitneys? Willis Lease Finance buys and sells aircraft engines that it leases to commercial airlines, air cargo carriers, and maintenance/repair/overhaul organizations in some 30 countries. Its portfolio includes about 180 aircraft engines and related equipment made by Pratt & Whitney, Rolls-Royce, CFMI, GE Aviation, and International Aero. The engine models in the company's portfolio are used on popular Airbus and Boeing aircraft. The Willis Lease portfolio also includes four de Havilland DHC-8 commuter aircraft. Customers include Island Air, Alaska Airlines, American Airlines, and Southwest Airlines. Almost 80% of the company's engines are leased and operated outside the US.

	Annual Growth	12/18	12/19	12/20	12/21	12/22
Sales ($mil.)	(2.7%)	348.3	409.2	288.7	274.2	311.9
Net income ($ mil.)	(40.4%)	43.2	66.9	9.7	3.4	5.4
Market value ($ mil.)	14.3%	228.9	389.7	201.5	249.1	390.4
Employees	13.3%	175	232	232	243	288

WILMER CUTLER PICKERING HALE AND DORR LLP

1875 PENNSYLVANIA AVE NW
WASHINGTON, DC 200063642
Phone: 202 663-6000
Fax: –
Web: www.wilmerhale.com

CEO: –
CFO: –
HR: –
FYE: June 30
Type: Private

Wilmer Cutler Pickering Hale and Dorr, known as WilmerHale, has around 1,145 lawyers in about 15 cities in the US, Europe, and Asia. Major practice areas include antitrust and competition; corporate governance and disclosure; bankruptcy and financial restructuring; government regulation; intellectual property; securities enforcement; and labor and employment. WilmerHale was formed in the 2004 merger of Washington, DC-based Wilmer, Cutler, & Pickering and Boston-based Hale and Dorr.

WILSHIRE ENTERPRISES, INC.

100 EAGLE ROCK AVE # 100
EAST HANOVER, NJ 079363155
Phone: 973 585-7770
Fax: –
Web: www.wilshireenterprisesinc.com

CEO: S W Izak
CFO: –
HR: –
FYE: December 31
Type: Private

Wilshire Enterprises invests in and operates commercial real estate and land. It owns a portfolio of more than a dozen multifamily, retail, and office properties and land tracts in Arizona, Florida, New Jersey, and Texas. The company has shed some of its non-core and other properties, and has upgraded other properties. Its land holdings (parcels of land totaling about 20 acres, all located in New Jersey) have either been put up for sale or are under contract for sale already. Wilshire Enterprises is seeking sale or merger opportunities. In 2008 it entered an acquisition deal with property investment and redevelopment firm NWJ Companies, but the agreement was later terminated.

WILSON SONSINI GOODRICH & ROSATI, PROFESSIONAL CORPORATION

650 PAGE MILL RD
PALO ALTO, CA 943041001
Phone: 650 493-9300
Fax: –
Web: www.wsgr.com

CEO: –
CFO: –
HR: –
FYE: December 31
Type: Private

You might say these lawyers can get downright technical. Wilson Sonsini Goodrich & Rosati (WSGR) is one of the largest law firms in the US specializing in representing high-tech corporations. Its client roster has included several big Silicon Valley names such as Google, Cisco, Salesforce.com, Hewlett-Packard, Jive Software, Oracle, and Bazaarvoice. WSGR has advised hundreds of clients on their IPOs and has been involved in more than 500 merger and acquisition transactions (valued at more than $150 billion) in the last five years. WSGR has litigated hundreds of patent lawsuits over the years. The firm was originally founded in 1961.

	Annual Growth	12/06	12/07	12/08	12/21	12/22
Sales ($mil.)	7.6%	–	–	0.7	1.7	2.0
Net income ($ mil.)	–	–	–	–	0.2	0.2
Market value ($ mil.)	–	–	–	–	–	–
Employees	–	–	–	–	–	1,300

WILSON TRUCKING CORPORATION

137 WILSON BLVD
FISHERSVILLE, VA 22939
Phone: 540 949-3200
Fax: –
Web: www.wilsontrucking.com

CEO: –
CFO: –
HR: –
FYE: December 31
Type: Private

A less-than-truckload (LTL) carrier, Wilson Trucking hauls freight from about 45 terminals in the southeastern and mid-Atlantic US. LTL carriers combine freight from multiple shippers into a single truckload; Wilson Trucking tries to haul freight directly from origin terminal to destination terminal, avoiding when possible intermediate stops at terminals to break down and reassemble loads. The company operates a fleet of about 970 tractors and 1,800 trailers. Outside its core region, Wilson Trucking offers service elsewhere in the US and in parts of Canada through partnerships with other carriers. In early 2017, it agreed to be acquired by rival LTL carrier Central Freight Lines.

	Annual Growth	12/09	12/10	12/11	12/14	12/15
Sales ($mil.)	3.2%	–	125.8	136.8	148.3	147.6
Net income ($ mil.)	–	–	(2.9)	(1.5)	(4.6)	(1.9)
Market value ($ mil.)	–	–	–	–	–	–
Employees	–	–	–	–	–	1,400

WINCHESTER HEALTHCARE MANAGEMENT, INC.

41 HIGHLAND AVE
WINCHESTER, MA 018901446
Phone: 781 756-2126
Fax: –
Web: www.winchesterhospital.org

CEO: –
CFO: –
HR: –
FYE: September 30
Type: Private

Winchester Healthcare Management provides a variety of health care services to patients in the Boston area. The not-for-profit company owns and operates Winchester Hospital, a 230-bed acute care medical center. The hospital is a leading area facility for pediatric and women's health services, and it offers specialty services including diagnostics, cardiology, oncology, pulmonary, and orthopedic medical care. Winchester Healthcare also operates about 20 community family health and specialty clinics, as well as a home care agency. The flagship hospital was founded in 1912.

WINCHESTER MEDICAL CENTER AUXILIARY, INC.

1840 AMHERST ST
WINCHESTER, VA 226012808
Phone: 540 536-8000
Fax: –
Web: www.valleyhealthlink.com

CEO: –
CFO: J C Lewis
HR: –
FYE: December 31
Type: Private

Winchester Medical Center is the flagship facility of Valley Health System, a not-for-profit health care organization serving the residents of Virginia's Shenandoah Valley. The full-service general hospital, which has more than 400 inpatient beds, serves as a regional referral center for the system's smaller community hospitals. It provides medical services across a number of specialties (including neuroscience, heart disease, and cancer) and offers surgical, diagnostic, and rehabilitative care. The hospital's campus also features outpatient diagnostic and surgical facilities, an adult psychiatric facility, and doctors' offices. Winchester Medical Center opened its doors in 1903.

	Annual Growth	12/03	12/04	12/05	12/06	12/07
Sales ($mil.)	8.9%	–	–	382.8	413.3	453.7
Net income ($ mil.)	(6.6%)	–	–	55.9	61.7	48.8
Market value ($ mil.)	–	–	–	–	–	–
Employees	–	–	–	–	–	2,046

WINCO FOODS, LLC

650 N ARMSTRONG PL
BOISE, ID 837040825
Phone: 208 377-0110
Fax: –
Web: www.wincofoods.com

CEO: Steven Goddard
CFO: David Butler
HR: –
FYE: December 31
Type: Private

WinCo Foods is one of the largest ESOP companies in the nation. Inside the cavernous stores of this 24-hour, discount supermarket chain, customers shop for food in bulk, pay in cash, and bag their own groceries. The company's nearly 140 stores feature pizza platters, bakeries, health and beauty products, and organic foods. WinCo Foods, formerly known as Waremart Foods, was renamed as a shortened version of "Winning and Company". The name is also an acronym for its early stages of operation, which include Washington, Idaho, Nevada, California, and Oregon. Founded in 1967, employees, past, and present, own the company.

	Annual Growth	04/03	04/04	04/05	04/06*	12/22
Sales ($mil.)	(43.3%)	–	2,148.9	2,388.9	2,650.1	0.0
Net income ($ mil.)	(32.2%)	–	57.5	177.4	191.2	0.0
Market value ($ mil.)	–	–	–	–	–	–
Employees	–	–	–	–	–	12,000

*Fiscal year change

WINDOW TO THE WORLD COMMUNICATIONS, INC.

5400 N SAINT LOUIS AVE
CHICAGO, IL 606254623
Phone: 773 509-1111
Fax: –
Web: www.wttw.com

CEO: Daniel J Schmidt
CFO: –
HR: Kari Hurley
FYE: June 30
Type: Private

Window To The World Communications (WTTW) broadcasts arts, children's, current events, humanities, and science programming via its Chicago television station (WTTW Channel 11, with the nation's largest viewer base) and radio station (98.7 WFMT). The company's programming focuses on events and issues that effect the Chicago metropolitan area, and special emphasis is given to cultural and educational topics. WTTW is a nonprofit governed by about 50 trustees representing the greater Chicago community. It is licensed by the FCC as a public TV station and is funded and governed by the community it serves. The station, started by Inland Steel chairman Edward Ryerson, began broadcasting in 1955.

	Annual Growth	06/14	06/15	06/20	06/21	06/22
Sales ($mil.)	(1.3%)	–	54.0	43.6	58.1	49.2
Net income ($ mil.)	3.2%	–	5.1	0.9	17.2	6.3
Market value ($ mil.)	–	–	–	–	–	–
Employees	–	–	–	–	–	192

WINDSOR DISTRIBUTING, INC.

5495 BRYSON DR STE 411
NAPLES, FL 341090920
Phone: 239 592-9715
Fax: –
Web: www.windsor-dist.com

CEO: Jonathan Karalekas
CFO: –
HR: –
FYE: September 30
Type: Private

Windsor Distributing's domain is the fruit and vegetable shipping and brokering business. The company purchases fresh produce from growers throughout the US, as well as in Canada, and Mexico. Headquartered in Naples, Florida, it partners with fruit and vegetable shipping companies as Ocean Mist, Tanimura & Antle, and A. Duda & Sons to get the ordered products to its foodservice, retail, and wholesale customers. The firm has seven distribution centers spread across the country and offers a wide variety of produce, including asparagus, bell peppers, cabbage, carrots, cucumbers, eggplant, melons, lettuce, and tomatoes. Windsor Distribution was founded in 1995 by CEO and owner John Karalekas.

	Annual Growth	09/07	09/08	09/09	09/10	09/11
Sales ($mil.)	2.2%	–	–	26.1	0.9	27.3
Net income ($ mil.)	(0.1%)	–	–	0.2	(0.0)	0.2
Market value ($ mil.)	–	–	–	–	–	–
Employees	–	–	–	–	–	8

WINDSTREAM BV HOLDINGS, LLC

4001 N RODNEY PARHAM RD
LITTLE ROCK, AR 722122459
Phone: 877 858-3855
Fax: –
Web: www.windstream.com

CEO: –
CFO: –
HR: –
FYE: December 31
Type: Private

Broadview Networks seeks to expand its customers' horizons along with its own. The telecom company provides local and long-distance voice and data communications, hosted VoIP systems, data services, and managed services. The company also provides bundled, hosted IP phone and cloud computing services sold under the OfficeSuite brand. It caters to small, midsized, and large businesses across the country. Most of Broadview's sales are made to retail customers, but about 10% of sales are to wholesalers and other telecom carriers. In 2017, Broadview was acquired by Windstream Holdings for about $230 million.

WINDSTREAM HOLDINGS, INC.

4001 N RODNEY PARHAM RD STE 101
LITTLE ROCK, AR 722122490
Phone: 501 748-7000
Fax: –
Web: www.windstream.com

CEO: Paul H Sunu
CFO: Drew Smith
HR: Penni McClellan
FYE: December 31
Type: Private

Windstream Holdings is a leading provider of advanced network communications and technology solutions for consumers, small businesses, enterprise organizations and carrier partners across the US. Windstream offers bundled services, including broadband, security solutions, voice and digital TV to consumers. The company also provides data, cloud solutions, unified communications and managed services to business and enterprise clients. The company supplies core transport solutions on a local and long-haul fiber-optic network spanning approximately 150,000 miles. The company traces its roots back to 1943.

WINDTREE THERAPEUTICS INC

2600 Kelly Road, Suite 100
Warrington, PA 18976-3622
Phone: 215 488-9300
Fax: –
Web: www.windtreetx.com

NAS: WINT
CEO: Craig E Fraser
CFO: John P Hamill
HR: –
FYE: December 31
Type: Public

If you're waiting to exhale, Windtree Therapeutics may be able to help. Formerly named Discovery Laboratories, the biotechnology company focuses on treatments for respiratory disorders. It bases its therapies on surfactants, which are naturally produced by the lungs and essential for breathing. The firm's only product, Surfaxin, gained FDA approval in 2012 for the prevention of respiratory distress syndrome (RDS) in premature infants. Another candidate, Aerosurf (licensed from Philip Morris), will allow for the delivery of RDS surfactant medicine in aerosol form, and is being developed as an alternative to endotracheal intubation and conventional mechanical ventilation. The firm also makes respiratory drug delivery devices.

	Annual Growth	12/18	12/19	12/20	12/21	12/22
Sales ($mil.)	–	1.8	0.2	–	–	–
Net income ($ mil.)	–	(20.5)	(27.5)	(32.6)	(67.6)	(39.2)
Market value ($ mil.)	(57.1%)	3.9	3.3	4.0	1.2	0.1
Employees	(11.8%)	33	32	31	33	20

WINDWARD CONSULTING GROUP, INC.

2201 COOPERATIVE WAY STE 600
HERNDON, VA 20171
Phone: 703 812-0000
Fax: –
Web: www.windward.com

CEO: Sean McDermott
CFO: –
HR: –
FYE: December 31
Type: Private

Windward IT Solutions (formerly Windward Consulting Group) provides operational management services for businesses with large-scale information technology infrastructures through the design, implementation, and management of computer systems and networks. Specific services include systems integration, consulting, support, training, and application development. Key clients come from such industries as financial services and communications services, as well as agencies of the US federal government including the US Department of the Interior and the US Air Force. Founded in 1997, the company changed its name to Winward IT Solutions in early 2008.

	Annual Growth	12/04	12/05	12/06	12/08	12/09
Sales ($mil.)	(2.6%)	–	–	21.8	25.2	20.1
Net income ($ mil.)	(61.7%)	–	–	6.2	0.4	0.3
Market value ($ mil.)	–	–	–	–	–	–
Employees	–	–	–	–	–	61

WINE & SPIRITS WHOLESALERS OF AMERICA, INC.

805 15TH ST NW STE 430
WASHINGTON, DC 200052273
Phone: 202 371-9792
Fax: –
Web: www.wswa.org

CEO: Craig Wolf
CFO: –
HR: –
FYE: December 31
Type: Private

The Wine & Spirits Wholesalers of America (WSWA) is a trade organization that counts wine and spirits distributors and wholesalers among its 360 member companies in 42 states, Puerto Rico, and the District of Columbia. Members of the organization distribute more than 80% of all wholesale wines and spirits in the US. WSWA represents its members' interests before governmental regulatory bodies, executive agencies, and the courts; it also hosts conferences for members and provides educational and social responsibility information. The WSWA was founded in 1943.

	Annual Growth	12/15	12/16	12/17	12/18	12/21
Sales ($mil.)	(5.8%)	–	–	11.0	13.0	8.6
Net income ($ mil.)	25.9%	–	–	0.3	2.0	0.8
Market value ($ mil.)	–	–	–	–	–	–
Employees	–	–	–	–	–	18

WINLAND HOLDINGS CORP

424 North Riverfront Drive, Suite 200
Mankato, MN 56001
Phone: 507 625-7231
Fax: –
Web: www.winland.com

NBB: WELX
CEO: –
CFO: –
HR: –
FYE: December 31
Type: Public

Winland Electronics has gone from good sleep to loud beeps. Formerly a contract manufacturer of electronics for such products as the Sleep Number bed, Winland sold that division in order to focus on its own line of environmental monitoring products, including sensors and alarms that check for changes in temperature, humidity, water leakage, and power failure. It also makes a driveway warning system that detects when a vehicle enters a driveway or road. Winland Electronics gets almost all of its sales in the US. The company sold its electronics manufacturing services (EMS) business, which made electronic controls and circuit board assemblies, to Nortech in early 2011.

	Annual Growth	12/18	12/19	12/20	12/21	12/22
Sales ($mil.)	6.5%	3.8	3.3	3.7	6.3	4.8
Net income ($ mil.)	–	0.0	(0.2)	0.4	1.5	(1.0)
Market value ($ mil.)	13.7%	5.3	5.4	14.7	20.5	8.9
Employees	–	–	–	–	–	–

WINMARK CORP

NMS: WINA

605 Highway 169 North, Suite 400
Minneapolis, MN 55441
Phone: 763 520-8500
Fax: –
Web: www.winmarkcorporation.com

CEO: Brett D Heffes
CFO: Anthony D Ishaug
HR: –
FYE: December 30
Type: Public

Winmark Corporation is a nationally recognized franchisor of five value-oriented retail concepts that buy, sell and trade gently used merchandise at about 1,295 stores across the US and Canada. Its retail brands buy and sell gently used or new merchandise and accessories brands include Plato's Closet for the teenage and young adult market; Once Upon A Child for children ages infant to 12 years; Play It Again Sports for sporting goods and equipment; Style Encore for women's apparel and accessories; Music Go Round for musical instruments and electronics. Each of its resale brands emphasizes consumer value by offering high-quality used merchandise at substantial savings from the price of new merchandise and by purchasing customers' used goods that have been outgrown or are no longer used.

	Annual Growth	12/19	12/20	12/21	12/22	12/23
Sales ($mil.)	3.2%	73.3	66.1	78.2	81.4	83.2
Net income ($ mil.)	5.7%	32.1	29.8	39.9	39.4	40.2
Market value ($ mil.)	20.8%	686.1	643.5	845.8	824.7	1,460.2
Employees	(4.1%)	98	26	85	83	83

WINNEBAGO INDUSTRIES, INC.

NYS: WGO

13200 Pioneer Trail
Eden Prairie, MN 55347
Phone: 952 829-8600
Fax: 641 585-6966
Web: www.winnebagoind.com

CEO: Michael J Happe
CFO: Bryan L Hughes
HR: –
FYE: August 26
Type: Public

Winnebago Industries is one of the leading North American manufacturers of recreation vehicles (RVs) and marine products with a diversified portfolio used primarily in leisure travel and outdoor recreational activities. Majority of the company's sales come from its motor homes and towables, which are sold via independent dealers throughout the US and Canada under the Winnebago, Grand Design RV, Chris-Craft, Newmar, Barletta, Adventurer, and Micro Minnie brands, among others. In addition, the company produces original equipment manufacturing (OEM) parts for other RV manufacturers and for use in commercial vehicles. The company traces its roots back in 1958. About 95% of the company's sales were generated from the US.

	Annual Growth	08/19	08/20	08/21	08/22	08/23
Sales ($mil.)	15.1%	1,985.7	2,355.5	3,629.8	4,957.7	3,490.7
Net income ($ mil.)	17.9%	111.8	61.4	281.9	390.6	215.9
Market value ($ mil.)	18.7%	954.2	1,740.6	2,178.7	1,824.4	1,896.8
Employees	8.6%	4,500	5,505	6,532	7,445	6,250

WINSTON & STRAWN LLP

35 W WACKER DR STE 4200
CHICAGO, IL 606011695
Phone: 312 558-5600
Fax: –
Web: www.winston.com

CEO: –
CFO: –
HR: Araceli Rocha
FYE: January 31
Type: Private

Winston & Strawn is a global law firm operating through various separate and distinct legal entities. Over the years, Winston & Strawn has developed a reputation for its work in litigation and labor and employment law, but the firm's practices encompass a wide range of specialties, from antitrust to intellectual property to tax. The international law firm has more than 900 attorneys across nearly offices in Brussels, Charlotte, Chicago, Dallas, Hong Kong, Houston, London, Los Angeles, Miami, New York, Paris, San Francisco, Shanghai, S o Paulo, Silicon Valley, and Washington, DC. In addition, the firm has significant resources devoted to clients and matters in Africa, the Middle East, and Latin America. Serving over 950 clients, Winston attorneys devoted more than 60,000 pro bono hours.

WINTER HAVEN HOSPITAL, INC.

200 AVENUE F NE
WINTER HAVEN, FL 338814193
Phone: 863 293-1121
Fax: –
Web: www.baycare.org

CEO: Steve Nierman
CFO: –
HR: –
FYE: December 31
Type: Private

Winter Haven Hospital, serves eastern Polk County in central Florida, with general medical, surgical, and emergency care. The health care facility also offers specialty care in areas such as cancer, heart disease, stroke, and a memory clinic for patients suffering from dementia and other memory disorders. The hospital's Regency Medical Center provides maternity and other health care services for women and newborns. Outpatient care is provided through an ambulatory surgery and diagnostic center and several community clinics. Winter Haven Hospital is owned by Tampa-based BayCare Health System; it was founded in 1926 as a charter hospital.

	Annual Growth	12/18	12/19	12/20	12/21	12/22
Sales ($mil.)	0.5%	–	–	–	436.7	439.1
Net income ($ mil.)	–	–	–	–	16.6	(16.5)
Market value ($ mil.)	–	–	–	–	–	–
Employees	–	–	–	–	–	1,480

WINTER SPORTS INC

P.O. Box 1400
Whitefish, MT 59937-1400
Phone: 406 862-1900
Fax: 406 862-2955
Web: www.bigmtn.com

CEO: –
CFO: –
HR: –
FYE: May 31
Type: Public

Winter Sports wants you to tread some slippery slopes. The company operates the Whitefish Mountain Resort (formerly Big Mountain) near Glacier National Park in Montana, offering outdoor enthusiasts miles of ski slopes and trails. It includes about a dozen ski lifts serving more than 3,000 acres of land, more than 2,500 acres of which are leased from the U.S. Forest Service under a special permit. Whitefish Mountain also features ski rental and retail shops, lodging, and a skiing school. The ski area, open from November to April, offers visitors shopping, snowmobile riding, sleigh rides, and other activities. Summer guests can hike, sightsee, mountain bike, and go horseback riding.

	Annual Growth	05/99	05/00	05/01	05/02	05/03
Sales ($mil.)	(4.9%)	12.6	15.2	12.9	13.0	10.3
Net income ($ mil.)	–	(0.4)	1.5	(0.0)	1.6	(0.6)
Market value ($ mil.)	7.1%	0.0	0.0	0.0	0.0	0.0
Employees	12.5%	50	50	80	80	80

WINTHROP NYU HOSPITAL

259 1ST ST
MINEOLA, NY 115013957
Phone: 516 663-0333
Fax: –
Web: www.nyulangone.org

CEO: John F Collins
CFO: –
HR: –
FYE: December 31
Type: Private

From providing it to teaching it, Winthrop-University Hospital is focused on health care. The medical center boasts some 590 beds and offers a full range of acute and tertiary health care services. Services include pediatric, women's health, and cancer care, as well as home health services. Winthrop-University Hospital is also a leading provider of cardiovascular surgeries in the region. The hospital is a member of Winthrop-South Nassau University Health System along with sister facility South Nassau Communities Hospital. Winthrop-University Hospital serves as a teaching hospital for the SUNY at Stony Brook School of Medicine.

WINTHROP REALTY LIQUIDATING TRUST

2 LIBERTY SQ FL 9
BOSTON, MA 021094884
Phone: 617 570-4614
Fax: –
Web: –

CEO: –
CFO: –
HR: –
FYE: March 31
Type: Private

Winthrop Realty Trust thinks real estate loans can be just as profitable as the real thing. The externally managed real estate investment trust (REIT) invests in property, real estate-related collateralized debt, and other REITs. Its property portfolio consists of more than a dozen office buildings, a handful of retail properties, and seven apartment buildings across 15 states totaling 3.5 million square feet. Top commercial tenants include Spectra Energy's Houston headquarters, grocer Kroger, and e-tailer Football Fanatics' 500,000-sq.-ft. distribution center. Winthrop is liquidating its assets and winding down operations.

WINTRUST FINANCIAL CORP (IL)   NMS: WTFC

9700 W. Higgins Road, Suite 800
Rosemont, IL 60018
Phone: 847 939-9000
Fax: –
Web: www.wintrust.com

CEO: –
CFO: –
HR: –
FYE: December 31
Type: Public

Wintrust Financial is a holding company of about 15 subsidiary banks (mostly named after the individual communities it serves) with branches primarily located in metropolitan Chicago, southern Wisconsin, and northwest Indiana. Boasting assets of more than $52.9 billion, the banks offer personal and commercial banking, wealth management, and specialty finance services, with commercial and commercial real estate loans accounting for over 55% of its loan portfolio, the majority of which is commercial. Wintrust's banks target individuals, small to mid-sized businesses, local governmental units, and institutional clients, among others. The company also operates various non-bank subsidiaries including among others Tricom which provides high-yielding, short-term accounts receivable financing and value-added outsourced administrative services, and Chicago Trust Company which specializes in trust and estate planning.

	Annual Growth	12/19	12/20	12/21	12/22	12/23
Assets ($mil.)	11.3%	36,621	45,081	50,142	52,950	56,260
Net income ($ mil.)	15.0%	355.7	293.0	466.2	509.7	622.6
Market value ($ mil.)	6.9%	4,342.2	3,741.4	5,562.1	5,176.3	5,680.3
Employees	2.2%	5,057	5,364	5,239	5,275	5,521

WIRELESS XCESSORIES GROUP, INC.   NBB: WIRX

1840 County Line Road, Suite 301
Huntingdon Valley, PA 19006
Phone: 215 322-4600
Fax: 215 233-0220
Web: www.wirexgroup.com

CEO: –
CFO: –
HR: –
FYE: December 31
Type: Public

Wireless Xcessories Group dresses up cellular phones. The company markets and distributes about 3,000 accessory products for wireless phones and other portable devices. Decorative carrying cases, hands-free kits, rechargeable batteries, chargers, antennae, and other items are sold primarily in North America through retailers and distributors, and from its e-commerce Web site; a majority of its products are manufactured in China and Taiwan. Wireless Xcessories also offers ancillary products and services such as retail packaging, displays, posters, and marketing. In addition, the company distributes third-party cell phone products made by Motorola Mobility, Nokia, and other cell phone manufacturers.

	Annual Growth	12/03	12/04	12/05	12/06	12/07
Sales ($mil.)	18.4%	11.5	15.3	22.1	22.9	22.5
Net income ($ mil.)	–	–	(0.2)	1.0	2.0	1.2	0.5
Market value ($ mil.)	40.3%	1.8	8.4	22.1	12.9	6.8
Employees	2.4%	71	80	83	85	78

WISCONSIN GAS LLC

231 West Michigan Street, PO Box 2046
Milwaukee, WI 53201
Phone: 414 221-2345
Fax: –
Web: –

CEO: –
CFO: –
HR: –
FYE: December 31
Type: Public

Wisconsin's cold winters would be that much colder without Wisconsin Gas' steady supply of natural gas to residential, commercial, and industrial customers across that state. The company provides natural gas and ancillary services. Wisconsin Gas (in combination with sister companies Wisconsin Electric Power and Edison Sault) serves more than 1 million natural gas customers. The utility operates about 10,800 miles of gas mains. Wisconsin Gas distributes 40% of the natural gas consumed in Wisconsin. Along with Wisconsin Electric Power, it is a subsidiary of regional utility holding company WEC Energy. The two subsidiaries use the trade name We Energies.

	Annual Growth	12/01	12/02	12/03	12/04	12/05
Sales ($mil.)	7.5%	618.5	530.0	714.8	730.9	826.2
Net income ($ mil.)	23.9%	10.9	33.2	36.8	(20.4)	25.7
Market value ($ mil.)	–	–	–	–	–	–
Employees	(5.7%)	783	746	701	674	619

WISCONSIN POWER AND LIGHT CO

4902 N BILTMORE LN STE 1000
MADISON, WI 537182148
Phone: 608 458-3311
Fax: –
Web: www.alliantenergy.com

CEO: John O Larsen
CFO: Robert J Durian
HR: –
FYE: December 31
Type: Private

Wisconsin Power and Light (WPL) illuminates central and southern Wisconsin. The subsidiary of Alliant Energy distributes electricity to 459,000 customers and natural gas to 180,000 customers in Dairyland. WPL has some 1,900 MW of generating capacity from interests in fossil-fueled, nuclear, and hydroelectric power plants; it sells some of its power to wholesale customers. The power and gas utility also owns a 16% stake in American Transmission, which operates the company's former transmission assets, and it provides energy facility management services.

WISETECH GLOBAL (US) INC.

1051 E WOODFIELD RD
SCHAUMBURG, IL 601734706
Phone: 847 364-5600
Fax: –
Web: www.wisetechglobal.com

CEO: Richard White
CFO: Peter Willis
HR: –
FYE: June 30
Type: Private

CargoWise edi develops logistics and warehouse-management software for the freight forwarding and shipping industries. Transportation companies, customs brokers, container terminals, and warehouses in 45 countries use the company's edi Enterprise suite of products to automate their operations. Clients have included Ozburn-Hessey. CargoWise also offers professional services including software customization, training, and technical support. It maintains offices in Europe and the US, as well as in the Asia Pacific region. The company was founded as Eagle Datamation International by CEO Richard White. It became CargoWise edi after merging with Fountainhead International (EDI) in 2006.

	Annual Growth	06/05	06/06	06/07	06/08	06/13
Sales ($mil.)	(8.2%)	–	–	16.5	20.2	9.9
Net income ($ mil.)	(21.2%)	–	–	1.4	1.6	0.3
Market value ($ mil.)	–	–	–	–	–	–
Employees	–	–	–	–	–	56

WITHLACOOCHEE RIVER ELECTRIC COOPERATIVE INC

14651 21ST ST
DADE CITY, FL 335232920
Phone: 352 567-5133
Fax: –
Web: www.wrec.net

CEO: –
CFO: –
HR: Connie Hobbs
FYE: December 31
Type: Private

Withlacoochee River Electric Cooperative keeps the power flowing to the residences and businesses of more than 200,360 member-owners in five counties along the central Florida Gulf Coast. The power distribution utility, which was originally set up in 1941, receives wholesale generation and transmission services from the Seminole Electric Cooperative. Withlacoochee River Electric, a non-profit organization, returns any funds remaining at the end of each year to its membership. The cooperative has returned more than $190 million to its member-owners.

	Annual Growth	12/14	12/15	12/16	12/19	12/22
Sales ($mil.)	2.8%	–	474.1	458.3	484.7	576.5
Net income ($ mil.)	11.4%	–	24.3	26.4	23.1	51.8
Market value ($ mil.)	–	–	–	–	–	–
Employees		–	–	–	–	458

WIXON INC.

1390 E BOLIVAR AVE
MILWAUKEE, WI 532354506
Phone: 414 769-3000
Fax: –
Web: www.wixon.com

CEO: –
CFO: –
HR: –
FYE: December 31
Type: Private

Wixon kicks the flavor of food up a notch. The company, which began as a single spice manufacturer in 1907, produces a range of wet and dry spice blends, seasonings, and flavor modifiers that enhance the taste of everything from meats and snacks to beverages and baked goods. Certain products extend shelf life, reduce sodium, and enhance protein content. As a fully integrated operation, Wixon also offers services, such as product and menu development, packaging design, market research, manufacturing, and warehousing and distribution. It serves the catalog, food service, grocery, health and nutrition, private label, and restaurant industries. Wixon is co-owned by members of its executive management team.

	Annual Growth	12/02	12/03	12/04	12/06	12/07
Sales ($mil.)	4.3%	–	46.7	47.1	–	55.2
Net income ($ mil.)	–	–	–	–	–	–
Market value ($ mil.)	–	–	–	–	–	–
Employees		–	–	–	–	200

WM. WRIGLEY JR. COMPANY

930 W EVERGREEN AVE
CHICAGO, IL 606422437
Phone: 312 280-4710
Fax: –
Web: –

CEO: –
CFO: Reuben Gamoran
HR: –
FYE: December 31
Type: Private

The Wm. Wrigley Jr. Company chews up the competition as the world's #1 maker of chewing gum. The company's products include such popular chewing gums as Big Red, Doublemint, Spearmint, Eclipse, Extra, and Juicy Fruit, as well as novelty gums Hubba Bubba and other kid-friendly gums. Wrigley's non-gum items include breath mints Altoids and Velamints and candies Creme Savers and Life Savers. As part of its business, Wrigley also makes chewing-gum bases for other companies as a supplier to the ingredients sector. Owned by confectionery giant Mars Incorporated , Wrigley boasts operations in more than 50 countries and sells its products in about 180 countries worldwide.

WOC, INC.

700 MAIN ST STE 2
BANGOR, ME 044016800
Phone: 207 942-5501
Fax: –
Web: www.citgo.com

CEO: –
CFO: –
HR: –
FYE: August 31
Type: Private

Webber Oil (doing business as Webber Energy Fuels) warms up homes on cold New England nights. The company provides home heating oil and propane in Maine and New Hampshire. Webber Oil has 18 heating oil and propane supply locations in Maine, and three in New Hampshire. The company, which was founded in 1935 by Alburney Webber, also rents and installs energy efficient space heaters and hot water heaters, and provides other energy-related services. It once owned and operated more than a dozen gas stations and convenience stores in the region, but in late 2008 decided to exit that business.

	Annual Growth	08/07	08/08	08/09	08/10	08/14
Sales ($mil.)	30.7%	–	–	0.0	0.0	0.0
Net income ($ mil.)	–	–	–	(0.0)	(0.0)	(0.0)
Market value ($ mil.)	–	–	–	–	–	–
Employees		–	–	–	–	550

WOLF CREEK NUCLEAR OPERATING CORPORATION

1550 OXEN LN
BURLINGTON, KS 668399127
Phone: 620 364-4141
Fax: –
Web: www.wolfcreeknuclear.com

CEO: Matt Sunseri
CFO: –
HR: –
FYE: December 31
Type: Private

Wolf Creek Nuclear Operating Corporation helps to sate the energy hunger of the US public. The nuclear plant operator is in charge of the Wolf Creek Generating Station in Kansas, which houses a four-loop pressurized water reactor that generates about 1,200 MW of electricity (enough to power some 800,000 homes). Wolf Creek Nuclear Operating Corporation is a joint venture between Westar Energy, which owns a 47% stake, Great Plains Energy (which through subsidiary Kansas City Power & Light owns 47%), and Kansas Electric Power Cooperative, 6%. Its job description is to operate, maintain, repair, and eventually decommission the Wolf Creek Generating Station. In 2017 Westar and Great Plains agreed to merge, a transaction that is expected to complete in the first half of 2018..

WOLF ENERGY SERVICES INC

408 State Hwy 135N
Kilgore, TX 75662
Phone: 903 392-0948
Fax: –
Web: www.evtn.com

NBB: WOEN
CEO: Jimmy Reedy
CFO: –
HR: –
FYE: December 31
Type: Public

Enviro Voraxial Technology has a voracious appetite for developing equipment to separate solids and liquids with different specific gravities. The company's Voraxial Separator can be used for wastewater treatment, grit and sand separation, oil and water separation, marine-oil-spill cleanup, bilge and ballast treatment, stormwater treatment, and food-processing-waste treatment. The separator is capable of processing volumes as low as 3 gallons per minute, as well as volumes of more than 10,000 gallons per minute, with only one moving part. Chairman and CEO Alberto DiBella, officers, and directors control almost 35% of the company.

	Annual Growth	12/17	12/18	12/19	12/20	12/21
Sales ($mil.)	(20.2%)	0.3	1.3	2.8	0.0	0.1
Net income ($ mil.)	–	2.1	(0.5)	0.6	(1.0)	(0.7)
Market value ($ mil.)	18.8%	1.0	0.8	1.0	2.3	2.0
Employees	(8.1%)	7	7	6	5	5

WOLFSPEED INC
NYS: WOLF

4600 Silicon Drive
Durham, NC 27703
Phone: 919 407-5300
Fax: 919 313-5615
Web: www.wolfspeed.com

CEO: Gregg A Lowe
CFO: Neill P Reynolds
HR: –
FYE: June 25
Type: Public

Wolfspeed, Inc. (formerly known as Cree, Inc.) is an innovator of wide bandgap semiconductors, focused on silicon carbide and gallium nitride materials and devices for power and radio-frequency (RF) applications. Its product families include silicon carbide and GaN materials, power devices, and RF devices, and its products are targeted for various applications such as electric vehicles, fast charging, 5G, renewable energy and storage, and aerospace and defense. Wolfspeed's materials products and power devices are used in electric vehicles, motor drives, power supplies, solar, and transportation applications. Its materials products and RF devices are used in military communications, radar, satellite, and telecommunication applications. Europe is responsible for over 30% of its revenue. The company was founded in 1987.

	Annual Growth	06/19	06/20	06/21	06/22	06/23
Sales ($mil.)	(3.9%)	1,080.0	903.9	525.6	746.2	921.9
Net income ($ mil.)	–	(375.1)	(191.7)	(523.9)	(200.9)	(329.9)
Market value ($ mil.)	(3.1%)	7,010.9	7,205.6	12,303	8,910.3	6,171.1
Employees	(2.5%)	5,319	5,130	3,466	4,017	4,802

WOLVERINE PIPE LINE COMPANY

8075 CREEKSIDE DR STE 210
PORTAGE, MI 490246303
Phone: 269 323-2491
Fax: –
Web: www.wolverinepipeline.com

CEO: –
CFO: –
HR: –
FYE: December 31
Type: Private

Named after a powerful weasel (the mascot of the University of Michigan), Wolverine Pipe Line transports a range of refined petroleum products across the US Midwest. It operates more than 630 miles of six-inch to 18-inch diameter pipeline which stretches through Illinois, Indiana, and Michigan. Wolverine Pipe Line's system also includes 12 pumping stations and transports more than 350,000 barrels (or 14.7 million gallons) of refined products a day. The company also supplies about 30% of Michigan's refined petroleum products. Wolverine Pipe Line was incorporated in 1952.

WOLVERINE POWER SUPPLY COOPERATIVE, INC.

10125 W WATERGATE RD
CADILLAC, MI 496018458
Phone: 231 775-5700
Fax: –
Web: www.wolverinepowercooperative.com

CEO: Eric Baker
CFO: Janet Kass
HR: Michelle Denike
FYE: December 31
Type: Private

Named after a voracious carnivore, Wolverine Power Supply Cooperative makes sure that that voracious consumer of electricity -- the American public -- gets the power its needs. The non-profit company is an electric generation and transmission utility that provides services to five member distribution cooperatives in Michigan. Wolverine Power Supply Cooperative monitors and operates 1,600 miles of bulk transmission lines and owns five power plants that generate 200 megawatts of capacity. It also maintains about 130 distribution substations and 36 transmission stations, as well as purchases power (including windpower energy) from other utilities and marketers to distribute to its customers.

	Annual Growth	12/17	12/18	12/19	12/21	12/22
Sales ($mil.)	10.4%	–	476.4	435.8	555.9	706.6
Net income ($ mil.)	(45.0%)	–	19.8	17.2	21.0	1.8
Market value ($ mil.)	–	–	–	–	–	–
Employees		–	–	–	–	110

WOLVERINE WORLD WIDE, INC.
NYS: WWW

9341 Courtland Drive N.E.
Rockford, MI 49351
Phone: 616 866-5500
Fax: –
Web: www.wolverineworldwide.com

CEO: Christopher E Hufnagel
CFO: Michael D Stornant
HR: Lindsay Truesdell
FYE: December 30
Type: Public

Wolverine World Wide is a leading designer, marketer and licensor of a broad range of quality casual footwear and apparel, performance outdoor and athletic footwear and apparel, kids' footwear, industrial work boots and apparel, and uniform shoes and boots. Wolverine also boasts several licenses from Caterpillar (Cat) and Harley-Davidson to make branded footwear. The company licenses its Stride Rite brand under a global license arrangement. Its footwear is sold worldwide through department and specialty stores, national chains, catalog retailers, independent distributors, uniform outlets, Internet retailers, and about 155 retail stores in the US, the UK, and Canada. Wolverine also maintains some 65 consumer-direct e-commerce sites. About 60% of the company's total sales come from the US.

	Annual Growth	12/19*	01/21	01/22*	12/22	12/23
Sales ($mil.)	(0.3%)	2,273.7	1,791.1	2,414.9	2,684.8	2,242.9
Net income ($ mil.)	–	128.5	(136.9)	68.6	(188.3)	(39.6)
Market value ($ mil.)	(28.4%)	2,684.0	2,486.0	2,291.8	869.5	707.2
Employees	0.6%	4,000	3,400	4,400	4,300	4,100

*Fiscal year change

WOMACK PUBLISHING COMPANY, INC.

28 N MAIN ST
CHATHAM, VA 245315557
Phone: 434 432-2791
Fax: –
Web: www.womackpublishing.com

CEO: –
CFO: –
HR: –
FYE: June 30
Type: Private

Womack Publishing isn't whistling Dixie, but it is covering Dixie's news. As an independent publisher of community-oriented newspapers, Womack Publishing operates 14 print newspapers for markets in Virginia and North Carolina, including the Montgomery Herald and News of Orange County in North Carolina and the Star-Tribune (Chatham) and the Brunswick Times-Gazette in Virginia. It also operates Web sites for select newspapers, as well as two state-wide legal notice and public notice Web sites. Founded in 1960, Womack Publishing is owned and managed by chairman Charles "Zan" Womack and family.

WOMAN'S HOSPITAL FOUNDATION INC

100 WOMANS WAY
BATON ROUGE, LA 708175100
Phone: 225 927-1300
Fax: –
Web: www.womans.org

CEO: Robert Burgess
CFO: Nina Dusang
HR: –
FYE: September 30
Type: Private

Woman's Hospital is a 168-bed hospital catering to the needs of women and infants in Louisiana. Founded in 1968, the hospital was one of the nation's first women's specialty hospitals. Services include breast and gynecologic oncology, genetics counseling, colonoscopy, endocrinology, and speech therapy. The not-for-profit hospital performs more than 7,900 surgeries and 42,000 breast procedures, reads more than 56,000 Pap screens, and delivers about 8,100 babies each year. In addition to the main hospital facility, the company operates a child development center, a wellness center, a physician office, a cancer pavilion, and an ambulatory surgery center.

	Annual Growth	09/15	09/16	09/19	09/20	09/21
Sales ($mil.)	(0.5%)	–	288.6	2.6	259.9	282.0
Net income ($ mil.)	12.2%	–	47.0	0.0	28.0	83.5
Market value ($ mil.)		–	–	–	–	–
Employees		–	–	–	–	1,850

WOMEN & CHILDRENS HOSPITAL LLC

4200 NELSON RD
LAKE CHARLES, LA 706054118
Phone: 337 474-1209
Fax: –
Web: –

CEO: Bryan Bateman
CFO: Dawn Hatcher
HR: –
FYE: May 31
Type: Private

If mama and baby overindulge at one of Lake Charles' many food festivals, Women & Children's Hospital of Lake Charles is there to help. The specialty hospital has been serving the ladies and their babies in southwestern Louisiana for more than two decades. The acute care facility provides patients with a range of services including emergency and maternity care, a neonatal intensive care unit, a pediatrics unit, and radiology. The hospital has expedited its admitting process in recent years by allowing patients to pre-register online with their eAdmitting program. It also offers new mommies a "Baby University" to help them unlock the mysteries of parenting. The facility is part of Community Health Systems.

WOODS HOLE, MARTHA'S VINEYARD AND NANTUCKET STEAMSHIP AUTHORITY

1 COWDRY RD
WOODS HOLE, MA 025431039
Phone: 508 548-5011
Fax: –
Web: www.steamshipauthority.com

CEO: Debra Rogers
CFO: –
HR: Robert Davis
FYE: December 31
Type: Private

Woods Hole, Martha's Vineyard and Nantucket Steamship Authority, known to owners of summer homes and year-round residents as the Steamship Authority, provides ferry service from the Massachusetts ports of Woods Hole and Hyannis to the islands of Martha's Vineyard and Nantucket, off the coast of Massachusetts. The company operates a fleet of nine vessels designed to carry passengers, vehicles, and other cargo. In 2014, it ferried 2.5 million passengers, 460,000 automobiles, and 166,500 trucks. The Steamship Authority is a quasi-public agency, created by the Massachusetts legislature, that competes with other private ferries but also oversees and licenses their operations.

	Annual Growth	12/16	12/17	12/18	12/19	12/22
Sales ($mil.)	5.0%	–	102.9	104.8	110.7	131.2
Net income ($ mil.)	11.2%	–	10.3	0.7	2.0	17.6
Market value ($ mil.)	–	–	–	–	–	–
Employees	–	–	–	–	–	750

WOODSTOCK HOLDINGS INC

335 Parkway 575, Suite 210A
Woodstock, GA 30188
Phone: 770 373-3410
Fax: 877 431-5717
Web: www.woodstockholdingsinc.com

NBB: WSFL
CEO: –
CFO: –
HR: –
FYE: December 31
Type: Public

Woodstock Financial Group offers up financial advice, but just don't expect to hear about hippie stock picks. The company, formerly Raike Financial Group, brokers support services for brokers. Founded in 1995, the company provides licensing, clearing, IT support, education, and various administrative services to a network of independent financial planners, insurance agents, and traditional and discount securities brokers. Woodstock handles a range of investment products, including stocks, bonds, mutual funds, annuities, and life insurance. Online trading is offered through its Woodstock Discount Brokerage division. Founder and CEO William Raike owns about 80% of the company.

	Annual Growth	12/17	12/18	12/19	12/20	12/21
Sales ($mil.)	(11.9%)	6.7	6.2	4.7	3.0	4.0
Net income ($ mil.)	–	(0.2)	(0.4)	0.0	(0.3)	0.1
Market value ($ mil.)	(34.5%)	1.0	1.0	0.4	0.2	0.2
Employees	–	9	8	–	–	–

WOODWARD, INC.

1081 Woodward Way
Fort Collins, CO 80524
Phone: 970 482-5811
Fax: –
Web: www.woodward.com

NMS: WWD
CEO: Charles P Blanskenship Jr
CFO: William F Lacey
HR: –
FYE: September 30
Type: Public

Woodward manufactures, designs and services providers of control solutions for the aerospace and industrial markets such as fluid energy, combustion control, electrical energy, and motion control systems flowing through aircraft, vehicles, turbine and piston engines, and electrical power equipment. Its products ? valves, nozzles, actuators, sensors, and more ? go to OEMs and prime contractors around the world for use in commercial airlines, repair facilities, military depots, third party repair shops, and other end users. The company's largest customers include Raytheon Technologies, Boeing and GE. Woodward makes its products primarily in the US, which accounts for some 55% of its sales.

	Annual Growth	09/19	09/20	09/21	09/22	09/23
Sales ($mil.)	0.1%	2,900.2	2,495.7	2,245.8	2,382.8	2,914.6
Net income ($ mil.)	(2.7%)	259.6	240.4	208.6	171.7	232.4
Market value ($ mil.)	3.6%	6,452.0	4,796.4	6,773.3	4,802.4	7,435.1
Employees	(0.6%)	9,000	7,100	7,200	8,300	8,800

WOOLRICH, INC.

33 BOARDMAN DR
WOOLRICH, PA 17779
Phone: 570 769-6464
Fax: –
Web: www.woolrich.com

CEO: –
CFO: –
HR: –
FYE: December 31
Type: Private

Woolrich has branched out beyond woolen textiles. As the US's oldest continuously operating apparel manufacturer and woolen mill, the outdoor apparel maker's products include men's and women's sportswear and outerwear, woolen fabrics, blankets, and home furnishings. Woolrich also licenses its name for the sale of furniture and accessories. Its branded products are marketed domestically and internationally. In addition, Woolrich supplies woolen yard goods to apparel and home furnishings makers. The firm distributes several million catalogs per year and sells via the Internet. The Rich family founded Woolrich in 1830.

	Annual Growth	12/06	12/07*	01/09	01/10*	12/14
Sales ($mil.)	–	–	(1,608.9)	114.4	99.4	0.0
Net income ($ mil.)	99.3%	–	0.0	(1.9)	0.8	0.0
Market value ($ mil.)	–	–	–	–	–	–
Employees	–	–	–	–	–	200

*Fiscal year change

WORKDAY INC

6110 Stoneridge Mall Road
Pleasanton, CA 94588
Phone: 925 951-9000
Fax: –
Web: www.workday.com

NMS: WDAY
CEO: Aneel Bhusri
CFO: Zane Rowe
HR: –
FYE: January 31
Type: Public

Workday is a computer software company that makes cloud-based enterprise applications to manage financial and human capital resources as well as planning and analytics tools. The company offers their products and services to about 10,000 organizations through software-as-a-service solutions that strengthen their workforce and manage its finances. The company has customers from medium-sized businesses to more than half of the Fortune 500. Around 75% of its sales came from its domestic customers. Some of these customers are from financial, healthcare, manufacturing, and retail industries.

	Annual Growth	01/20	01/21	01/22	01/23	01/24
Sales ($mil.)	18.9%	3,627.2	4,318.0	5,138.8	6,215.8	7,259.0
Net income ($ mil.)	–	(480.7)	(282.4)	29.4	(366.7)	1,381.0
Market value ($ mil.)	12.1%	48,717	60,037	66,760	47,872	76,802
Employees	11.4%	12,200	12,500	15,200	17,700	18,800

WORKFORCELOGIC LLC

2365 IRON POINT RD
FOLSOM, CA 956308711
Phone: 877 937-6242
Fax: –
Web: www.magnitglobal.com

CEO: Kevin Akeroyd
CFO: Ben Barstow
HR: Priscilla Molina
FYE: December 31
Type: Private

ZeroChaos offers clients a way to remove some of the uncertainty when dealing with contract employees. Specializing in contract staffing services, ZeroChaos helps clients find and manage their contract labor workforce. Services include payroll and back office processes, risk management, private label sourcing (allowing clients to build their own pools of quality contract workers), as well as vendor management and invoicing. The company provides its services entirely through an automated and Web-enabled delivery platform. The company was a subsidiary of human resources administration and outsourcing company Co-Advantage until early 2005, when CEO Harold Mills and other investors acquired ZeroChaos.

WORKMAN PUBLISHING CO. INC.

1290 AVENUE OF THE AMERICAS
NEW YORK, NY 101040101
Phone: 212 254-5900
Fax: –
Web: www.hachettebookgroup.com

CEO: Dan Reynolds
CFO: –
HR: –
FYE: December 31
Type: Private

Who says publishing is work? Workman Publishing offers titles that are fun (The Official Preppy Handbook and 1,000 Places to See Before You Die); helpful (What to Expect When You're Expecting); and informative (Feathering Your Nest: The Retirement Planner). The company primarily publishes non-fiction books; it also produces calendars, gift cards, journals and children's educational games, such as the Brain Quest quiz card product. Workman imprints include Algonquin Books of Chapel Hill, Artisan, and Timber Press. Products are available online, and through a variety of book stores and other retail outlets. Peter Workman founded the company in 1968 with the publication of the book Yoga 28-Day Exercise Plan .

WORLD ACCEPTANCE CORP.   NMS: WRLD

104 S. Main Street
Greenville, SC 29601
Phone: 864 298-9800
Fax: –
Web: www.loansbyworld.com

CEO: R C Prashad
CFO: John L Calmes Jr
HR: Amy M Hilka
FYE: March 31
Type: Public

World Acceptance Corporation is a consumer finance company that offers short-term and medium-term loans and credit insurance to individuals with limited access to other credit sources. The company offers standardized installment loans generally between $500 and $6,000, with the average loan origination being $2,359 in fiscal 2023. The company generally serves individuals with limited access to other sources of consumer credit such as banks, credit unions, other consumer finance businesses and credit card lenders. The company also offers income tax return preparation services to its loan customers and other individuals. The fast-growing company has about 1,075 branches in more than 15 US states.

	Annual Growth	03/19	03/20	03/21	03/22	03/23
Sales ($mil.)	3.2%	544.5	590.0	525.5	582.4	616.5
Net income ($ mil.)	(13.1%)	37.2	28.2	88.3	53.9	21.2
Market value ($ mil.)	(8.2%)	729.8	340.3	808.5	1,195.4	519.0
Employees	(4.0%)	3,624	3,744	3,175	3,121	3,075

WORLD BUSINESS CHICAGO

180 N LA SALLE ST STE 2505
CHICAGO, IL 606012705
Phone: 312 553-0500
Fax: –
Web: www.worldbusinesschicago.com

CEO: –
CFO: –
HR: –
FYE: December 31
Type: Private

Chicago may be that toddlin' (fast moving) town in the music world, but it wants to be known in the business world as an international toddlin' town. To that end, the City of Chicago and the private sector formed World Business Chicago (WBC) to help market the city to the global business community. The not-for-profit economic development corporation provides data and statistics on the city as well as information about state and local incentives for businesses. It is run by a board of about two dozen area business executives; the board is chaired by Mayor Rahm Emmanuel.

	Annual Growth	12/12	12/13	12/17	12/21	12/22
Sales ($mil.)	10.6%	–	4.6	10.6	9.9	11.3
Net income ($ mil.)	–	–	(9.6)	(1.4)	1.0	(0.4)
Market value ($ mil.)	–	–	–	–	–	–
Employees	–	–	–	–	–	15

WORLD FINER FOODS, LLC

1455 BROAD ST STE 4
BLOOMFIELD, NJ 070033039
Phone: 973 338-0300
Fax: –
Web: www.worldfiner.com

CEO: Frank Muchel
CFO: William Flynn
HR: –
FYE: December 31
Type: Private

Fine food is quite a find for this company and its customers. World Finer Foods distributes more than 900 specialty food items to US supermarkets and gourmet food stores. Its inventory boasts some 40 brands, including Blanchard & Blanchard, La Vie, Mrs. Leeper's Pasta, and Panni. The company also markets its own food products under such names as DaVinci, London Pub, Pritikin, and Reese. Its InterNatural Foods unit represents its natural foods division while its Liberty Richter division distributes domestic and imported gourmet food items. Founded as VIP Foods in 1971, World Finer Foods is a cooperative owned by food distributors Millbrook Distribution (a unit of United Natural Foods) and Kehe Food.

	Annual Growth	12/05	12/06	12/07	12/08	12/10
Sales ($mil.)	13.2%	–	–	–	126.0	161.4
Net income ($ mil.)	(68.7%)	–	–	–	0.7	0.0
Market value ($ mil.)	–	–	–	–	–	–
Employees	–	–	–	–	–	137

WORLD KINECT CORP   NYS: WKC

9800 Northwest 41st Street
Miami, FL 33178
Phone: 305 428-8000
Fax: 305 392-5621
Web: www.wfscorp.com

CEO: Michael J Kasbar
CFO: Ira M Birns
HR: –
FYE: December 31
Type: Public

World Fuel Services is a leading global fuel services company, principally engaged in the distribution of fuel and related products and services in the aviation, land and marine transportation industries. In recent years, the company has expanded its land product and service offerings to include energy advisory services and supply fulfillment for natural gas and power to commercial, industrial and government customers. The company conduct its operations through numerous locations both within the US and throughout various foreign jurisdictions. It gets more than 50% of its revenue from the US. World Fuel sells about 15 billion gallons of fuel a year from its aviation and land segments.

	Annual Growth	12/19	12/20	12/21	12/22	12/23
Sales ($mil.)	6.7%	36,819	20,358	31,337	59,043	47,711
Net income ($ mil.)	(26.3%)	178.9	109.6	73.7	114.1	52.9
Market value ($ mil.)	(14.9%)	2,596.5	1,863.4	1,582.9	1,634.3	1,362.2
Employees	(1.0%)	5,500	4,300	4,414	5,214	5,289

WORLD POINT TERMINALS, LP

8235 FORSYTH BLVD STE 400
SAINT LOUIS, MO 631051621
Phone: 314 889-9660
Fax: –
Web: www.worldpointterminals.com

CEO: –
CFO: –
HR: –
FYE: December 31
Type: Private

World Point Terminals is really more concerned with storing oil just in the continental US. The company formed in April 2013 to own storage terminals for crude oil and other refined petroleum products. It was formed by Apex Oil (the two companies are located in the same office) to take over the terminals owned by Apex Oil subsidiary Center Point Terminal. It owns Center Point's 15 storage facilities in a dozen states along the East Coast, Gulf Coast, and Midwest regions. Organized as a limited partnership (LP), World Point Terminals is exempt from paying federal income tax. World Point Terminals went public in 2013.

WORLD SURVEILLANCE GROUP INC

State Road 405, Building M6-306A, Room 1400, Kennedy Space Center
Merritt Island, FL 32815
Phone: 321 452-3545
Fax: –
Web: www.wsgi.com

CEO: –
CFO: –
HR: –
FYE: December 31
Type: Public

Sanswire isn't known for a down-to-earth approach to product development. The company (formerly known as GlobeTel Communications) is developing airship "stratellites" (essentially blimps equipped with wireless gear that float in the stratosphere) to enable its planned wireless broadband network. Other intended uses for Sanswire's unmanned aerial vehicles include security and surveillance (Skysat) and payload transport and delivery (PADD). The company is developing its products in conjunction with Stuttgart, Germany-based TAO Technologies GmbH.

	Annual Growth	12/09	12/10	12/11	12/12	12/13
Sales ($mil.)	–	–	0.3	0.2	1.1	1.9
Net income ($ mil.)	–	(9.4)	(9.8)	(1.1)	(3.4)	(3.4)
Market value ($ mil.)	(39.8%)	48.8	56.2	25.4	8.9	6.4
Employees	15.0%	4	4	5	5	7

WORLD VISION INTERNATIONAL

800 W CHESTNUT AVE
MONROVIA, CA 910163198
Phone: 626 303-8811
Fax: –
Web: www.wvi.org

CEO: Andrew Morley
CFO: –
HR: –
FYE: September 30
Type: Private

World Vision International sees a world where all children are fed, sheltered, educated, valued, and loved. The Christian relief organization advocates for children and the poor and for the development of families and communities worldwide. Operating in nearly 100 countries from some 40 international offices, the group focuses on education, health care, emergency relief efforts, and economic and agricultural development. Its donors sponsor more than 3 million children. While the organization prohibits proselytizing, 60% of its budget goes to programs that include "domestic ministry." The group receives its contributions mainly from private sources. World Vision was founded in 1950 by the Rev. Bob Pierce.

	Annual Growth	09/02	09/03	09/04	09/05	09/09
Sales ($mil.)	(57.2%)	–	–	962.5	1,245.2	13.9
Net income ($ mil.)	(32.4%)	–	–	43.5	93.8	6.2
Market value ($ mil.)	–	–	–	–	–	–
Employees	–	–	–	–	–	200

WORLD WIDE TECHNOLOGY, LLC

1 WORLD WIDE WAY
SAINT LOUIS, MO 631463002
Phone: 314 569-7000
Fax: –
Web: www.wwt.com

CEO: Jim Kavanaugh
CFO: Thomas W Strunk
HR: –
FYE: December 31
Type: Private

World Wide Technology (WWT) is a global technology solution provider that primarily provides such IT services as network design and installation, systems and application integration, and license consulting. It works with the world's trusted brands such as Cisco, VMware, NetApp, Dell Technologies, Red Hat and several others, but also include emerging tech players like Tanium and Dedrone. WWT serves businesses in the retail, oil and gas, financial services, life sciences, energy and utilities industries, as well as public sectors. With more than 300 labs, the company has over 200 technology partners in the Advanced Technology Center (ATC). WWT was founded in 1990.

	Annual Growth	12/13	12/14	12/15	12/21	12/22
Sales ($mil.)	(60.9%)	–	5,057.3	5,927.7	11.0	2.8
Net income ($ mil.)	–	–	95.0	95.1	5.5	(5.3)
Market value ($ mil.)	–	–	–	–	–	–
Employees	–	–	–	–	–	2,286

WORLD WILDLIFE FUND, INC.

1250 24TH ST NW
WASHINGTON, DC 200371193
Phone: 202 293-4800
Fax: –
Web: www.worldwildlife.org

CEO: Neville Isdell
CFO: –
HR: Lee Zahnow
FYE: June 30
Type: Private

A fuzzy-wuzzy with kung fu strength, the panda embodies mission of the World Wildlife Fund (WWF). The conservation organization has worked on more than 13,000 projects in about 100 countries to save endangered species and natural areas, as well as to address threats such as global warming and the exploitation of forests. By 2020 WWF aims to conserve 15 of the world's more ecologically important regions. Its work crosses Africa, Asia, Latin America, North America, and Eurasia through national affiliates in about 100 countries. The group publishes data on wildlife, wild places, and global environmental challenges. Founded in 1961, WWF is joined by 1.1 million members in the US and some 5 million overseas.

	Annual Growth	06/12	06/13	06/14	06/19	06/22
Sales ($mil.)	5.8%	–	229.2	227.7	249.9	381.6
Net income ($ mil.)	11.0%	–	25.5	6.9	13.7	65.3
Market value ($ mil.)	–	–	–	–	–	–
Employees	–	–	–	–	–	615

WORLD WRESTLING ENTERTAINMENT, LLC

1241 E MAIN ST
STAMFORD, CT 069023520
Phone: 203 352-8600
Fax: –
Web: www.wwe.com

CEO: –
CFO: Frank A Riddick III
HR: –
FYE: December 31
Type: Private

WWE, a publicly traded company, is an integrated media organization and recognized leader in global entertainment. The company consists of a portfolio of businesses that create and deliver original content 52 weeks a year to a global audience. WWE's TV-PG programming can be seen in more than 1 billion homes worldwide in 25 languages through world-class distribution partners including NBCUniversal, FOX, BT Sport, Sony India, and Rogers. The company currently produce seven hours of original weekly domestic television programming, RAW, SmackDown, and NXT. WWE also licenses characters for merchandise, and sells video games, toys, and apparel. WWE's largest market is North America, accounting for around 75% of revenues.

	Annual Growth	12/18	12/19	12/20	12/21	12/22
Sales ($mil.)	10.4%	–	960.4	974.2	1,095.2	1,291.5
Net income ($ mil.)	36.4%	–	77.1	131.8	180.4	195.6
Market value ($ mil.)	–	–	–	–	–	–
Employees	–	–	–	–	–	890

WORLD'S FINEST CHOCOLATE, INC.

4801 S LAWNDALE AVE
CHICAGO, IL 606323065
Phone: 773 847-4600
Fax: –
Web: www.worldsfinestchocolate.com

CEO: Edmond F Opler
CFO: –
HR: Lori Piest
FYE: December 31
Type: Private

World's Finest Chocolate (WFC) has crafted premium chocolate directly from the cocoa bean since 1939. The confectioner is a maker of chocolate candy for fundraisers. WFC manufactures chocolate bars, panned chocolates, and foil-wrapped chocolates. As part of its business, WFC provides custom and personalized labeling services. In addition, it is the #1 product fundraising company in the US, annually raising more than $150 million for charities and communities. WFC works with retailers of both national and regional scales, across all classes of trade (including convenience, dollar, drug, grocery, and mass), to raise money for any charity or non-profit organization of the retailer's choosing. Its retail partners include, but are not limited to, Alta, Dollar General, FredMeyer, HyVee, Schnucks, Rural King, TA Express.

WORTH GROUP, ARCHITECTS, A PROFESSIONAL CORPORATION

900 S BROADWAY STE 150
DENVER, CO 80209
Phone: 303 649-1095
Fax: –
Web: www.worthgroup.com

CEO: Douglas Worth
CFO: –
HR: –
FYE: December 31
Type: Private

WorthGroup designs and builds commercial gaming, entertainment, and hospitality facilities; sports and recreation projects; retail and commercial buildings; public works; health care and wellness structures; educational facilities; and more. The masterbuilder provides pre-construction, general construction, construction and project management, occupancy analyses, scheduling, and other services. Its client roster includes Native Americans, the University of Nevada (Reno), Ironhorse Village Condominiums, Blue Sky Casino and Events Center, Bull Durham Casino, Circus Circus (Reno). WorthGroup operates from offices in Nevada (in Las Vegas and Reno) and Colorado (in Englewood).

WORLDWIDE MEDIA SERVICES GROUP INC.

4 NEW YORK PLZ FL 2
NEW YORK, NY 100042466
Phone: 800 929-8274
Fax: –
Web: www.accelerate360.com

CEO: David Pecker
CFO: Chris Polimeni
HR: –
FYE: March 31
Type: Private

Worldwide Media Services is a publisher of tabloid newspapers and magazines, including National Enquirer and Star. The company also publishes women's health magazine Shape, as well as a number of other magazines including Flex, Men's Fitness, and Natural Health. In addition to publishing its own titles, Worldwide Media also distributes and markets other publishers' periodicals. The company is owned by a group of investment firms including Angelo, Gordon & Co.

	Annual Growth	03/11	03/12	03/13	03/14	03/15
Sales ($mil.)	(28.8%)	–	–	–	344.2	245.2
Net income ($ mil.)	–	–	–	–	(53.3)	(25.9)
Market value ($ mil.)	–	–	–	–	–	–
Employees	–	–	–	–	–	14,615

WORTHINGTON ENTERPRISES INC   NYS: WOR

200 West Old Wilson Bridge Road
Columbus, OH 43085
Phone: 614 438-3210
Fax: 614 438-3256
Web: www.worthingtonindustries.com

CEO: B A Rose
CFO: Joseph B Hayek
HR: Jordan Doone
FYE: May 31
Type: Public

Worthington Industries is one of the largest steel processors in the US, processing flat-rolled steel and related products for industrial customers, including automotive, construction and retail industries. The company also forms flat-rolled steel to exact customer specifications, filling a niche in the steel industry by focusing on products requiring exact specifications. Worthington's subsidiaries make products such as pressure cylinders for liquefied petroleum gas (LPG), compressed natural gas (CNG), oxygen, refrigerant, and other industrial gas storage. Through joint ventures, the company also makes steel products such as complete ceiling grid solutions and laser-welded blanks. The vast majority of its revenue comes from North America.

	Annual Growth	05/19	05/20	05/21	05/22	05/23
Sales ($mil.)	6.9%	3,759.6	3,059.1	3,171.4	5,242.2	4,916.4
Net income ($ mil.)	13.7%	153.5	78.8	723.8	379.4	256.5
Market value ($ mil.)	13.2%	1,661.2	1,455.9	3,229.5	2,269.5	2,731.2
Employees	(9.1%)	12,000	9,000	9,000	8,400	8,200

WORLDWIDE TRAVEL STAFFING LTD

2829 SHERIDAN DR
TONAWANDA, NY 141509420
Phone: 866 633-3700
Fax: –
Web: www.worldwidetravelstaffing.com

CEO: –
CFO: –
HR: –
FYE: December 31
Type: Private

From RNs in Rhode Island to psychiatrists in St. Croix, Worldwide Travel Staffing (WTS) provides nurses, psychiatrists, and other medical personnel to hospitals in the US, the Caribbean, and about a dozen other international locations. Its 30,000 personnel, in 20 different specialties, staff hospitals and clinics for short- and long-term assignments. Traveling nurses typically make more than their stay-at-home counterparts; WTS also pays standard benefits and referral bonuses. In addition to traditional hospital duty, its staff often volunteers for disaster relief in places like post-Katrina Louisiana, and in South America and Africa. The company, which was formed in 1993, is owned by its employees.

	Annual Growth	12/03	12/04	12/05	12/06	12/08
Sales ($mil.)	64.9%	–	3.0	4.1	10.5	22.7
Net income ($ mil.)	19.6%	–	0.2	0.0	0.4	0.3
Market value ($ mil.)	–	–	–	–	–	–
Employees	–	–	–	–	–	327

WQN INC   NBB: WQNI

509 Madison Ave., Suite 1510
New York, NY 10022
Phone: 212 774-3655
Fax: –
Web: www.wqn.com

CEO: Stuart Ehrlich
CFO: –
HR: –
FYE: December 31
Type: Public

Parents can't be in all places at all times, so WQN hopes to be your child's virtual bodyguard. Operating as WebSafety, the company makes applications that help protect children while they surf the Web or use cell phones. Its software blocks dangerous content from reaching young users; its word monitoring program sends email and text alerts to parents when one of more than 8,000 suspicious words are detected. With its GPS cell phone technology, parents can find missing children (and monitor their whereabouts), as well as disable phone features including texting during driving. The company's latest incarnation was established in 2007 through the merger of software firms WebSafety and MyNabyoo.com.

	Annual Growth	12/01	12/02	12/03	12/04	12/05
Sales ($mil.)	–	12.2	11.5	9.9	15.3	–
Net income ($ mil.)	–	(7.2)	(2.9)	(3.3)	(3.2)	0.3
Market value ($ mil.)	(12.6%)	18.9	12.9	22.0	21.2	11.0
Employees	(29.3%)	28	28	25	22	7

WRIGHT INVESTORS' SERVICE HOLDINGS, INC.

NBB: IWSH

118 North Bedford Road, Ste. 100
Mount Kisco, NY 10549
Phone: 914 242-5700
Fax: –
Web: www.corporateinformation.com

CEO: Harvey P Eisen
CFO: Harold D Kahn
HR: –
FYE: December 31
Type: Public

National Patent Development (NPD) is a shell company that holds stakes in plastics molding and precision coatings manufacturer MXL Industries and Endo International, which is developing treatments for pain, overactive bladder, prostate cancer, and the early onset of puberty. The scaled-down NPD also owns real estate in Connecticut. In 2010 the company sold its home improvement products wholesaler Five Star Products, a core unit that had represented 100% of its 2009 sales, to The Merit Group for more than $30 million; NPD netted about $10 million from the deal. Investment management and financial advisory firm The Winthrop Corporation bought NPD in late 2012.

	Annual Growth	12/18	12/19	12/20	12/21	12/22
Sales ($mil.)	–	–	–	–	–	–
Net income ($ mil.)	–	(1.7)	(2.0)	(1.0)	(1.1)	(1.2)
Market value ($ mil.)	(25.4%)	7.7	8.6	5.4	5.9	2.4
Employees	–	2	2	2	2	2

WRIGHT MEDICAL GROUP, INC.

1023 CHERRY RD
MEMPHIS, TN 381175423
Phone: 901 867-9971
Fax: –
Web: www.wright.com

CEO: Robert J Palmisano
CFO: Lance A Berry
HR: Brooke Wood
FYE: December 31
Type: Private

Wright Medical Group Inc. makes replacement parts for humans. The firm makes reconstructive implants for the foot, ankle, hand, elbow, shoulder, and other defective joints. Product lines include the INBONE, CLAW, and ORTHOLOC systems for feet and ankles, MICRONAIL implants to repair wrist fractures. Wright makes an injectable putty for bone defects, as well as bone graft and tissue substitute materials, such as OSTEOSET pellets used to regenerate bone. The company sold its hip and knee implant business, OrthoRecon, in 2014. Wright's products are sold in more than 60 countries, although the US is its largest market. In 2015 the company merged with Netherlands-based Tornier to create Wright Medical Group N.V.

WRIGHT STATE UNIVERSITY

3640 COLONEL GLENN HWY
DAYTON, OH 454350002
Phone: 937 775-3333
Fax: –
Web: www.wright.edu

CEO: –
CFO: –
HR: Aaron Bock
FYE: June 30
Type: Private

Wright State University, named after aviation pioneers the Wright Brothers, has more than 11,000 students and offers approximately 315 undergraduate, graduate, doctoral, and professional degree programs. It consists of six colleges (including Engineering and Computer Science; Health, Education, and Human Services; Liberal Arts; Raj Soin College of Business; Science and Mathematics; Graduate Programs and Honors Studies), one school (Boonshoft School of Medicine), and a single branch campus (Wright State University? Lake Campus). Wright State has a student-to-faculty ratio of 13:1. Originally a branch campus of Ohio State University and Miami University, Wright State became an independent university in 1967.

	Annual Growth	06/14	06/15	06/16	06/17	06/22
Sales ($mil.)	(5.2%)	–	233.5	238.2	230.3	161.1
Net income ($ mil.)	–	–	(22.0)	(37.4)	(47.1)	64.7
Market value ($ mil.)	–	–	–	–	–	–
Employees	–	–	–	–	–	2,748

WRITERS GUILD OF AMERICA WEST, INC.

7000 W 3RD ST
LOS ANGELES, CA 900484321
Phone: 323 951-4000
Fax: –
Web: www.wga.org

CEO: David Young
CFO: –
HR: Christine Sul
FYE: March 31
Type: Private

The Writers Guild of America, west puts the H in Hollywood, the T in TV, and the N in new media. It's the West Coast version of the Writers Guild of America and a labor union that represents more than 7,000 writers in the motion picture, broadcast, cable, and new technologies industries. The union, which began in 1921, backs members in contract negotiations and enforcement, oversees credits for films and TV shows, collects and distributes payments for the reuse of movies and TV shows, and conducts educational events. It does not act as an employment agency for writers or recommend them. The WGAw also maintains a registry that covers some 55,000 written works each year, protecting the authors from plagiarism.

	Annual Growth	03/16	03/17	03/20	03/21	03/22
Sales ($mil.)	3.6%	–	32.4	41.7	36.8	38.7
Net income ($ mil.)	(1.0%)	–	4.9	4.3	1.1	4.6
Market value ($ mil.)	–	–	–	–	–	–
Employees	–	–	–	–	–	160

WSFS FINANCIAL CORP

NMS: WSFS

500 Delaware Avenue
Wilmington, DE 19801
Phone: 302 792-6000
Fax: –
Web: www.wsfsbank.com

CEO: Rodger Levenson
CFO: Arthur J Bacci
HR: –
FYE: December 31
Type: Public

WSFS Financial Corporation (WSFS) is a multi-billion dollar financial services company. Its primary subsidiary, WSFS Bank, is the oldest and largest banks in the US. WSFS has $20.0 billion in assets and $61.4 billion in assets under management and administration. WSFS operates from about 120 offices, more than 90 of which are banking offices, located in Pennsylvania (about 60), Delaware (around 40), New Jersey (over 15), one in Virginia and one in Nevada and provides comprehensive financial services including commercial banking, retail banking, cash management and trust and wealth management. Other subsidiaries or divisions include Arrow Land Transfer, Bryn Mawr Trust, The Bryn Mawr Trust Company of Delaware, Cash Connect, Cypress Capital Management, LLC, NewLane Finance, Powdermill Financial Solutions, West Capital Management, WSFS Institutional Services, WSFS Mortgage, and WSFS Wealth Investments.

	Annual Growth	12/19	12/20	12/21	12/22	12/23
Assets ($mil.)	13.9%	12,256	14,334	15,777	19,915	20,595
Net income ($ mil.)	16.0%	148.8	114.8	271.4	222.4	269.2
Market value ($ mil.)	1.1%	2,663.1	2,716.9	3,034.2	2,744.8	2,780.5
Employees	5.8%	1,782	1,838	1,839	2,160	2,229

WSO2 LLC

3080 OLCOTT ST STE C220
SANTA CLARA, CA 950543281
Phone: 650 745-4499
Fax: –
Web: www.wso2.com

CEO: Sanjiva Weerawarana
CFO: –
HR: –
FYE: December 31
Type: Private

WSO2's middleware acts as a computer network's middleman, linking disparate applications together. Programmers use its open source middleware platform to connect programs running on different operating systems for an integrated experience. WSO2's Carbon platform offers more than a dozen different configurations within a modular framework, and its applications are available as Platform-as-a-Service (PaaS), so developers only pay for what they need. Customers have included Boeing, Deutsche Bank, and eBay. WSO2 has offices in the US, UK, and Sri Lanka. The company, founded in 2005 by CEO Sanjiva Weerawarana and former CTO Paul Fremantle, counts Quest Software and Intel as investors.

	Annual Growth	12/18	12/19	12/20	12/21	12/22
Sales ($mil.)	14.7%	–	39.4	46.7	51.5	59.5
Net income ($ mil.)	–	–	(0.4)	7.3	(20.3)	(26.0)
Market value ($ mil.)	–	–	–	–	–	–
Employees	–	–	–	–	–	500

WSP FLACK + KURTZ, INC.

512 FASHION AVE FL 13
NEW YORK, NY 100180807
Phone: 212 532-9600
Fax: –
Web: www.wsp.com

CEO: –
CFO: –
HR: –
FYE: December 31
Type: Private

WSP Flack + Kurtz is one of the leading building-services engineering firms in the US. A subsidiary of the UK-based WSP Group, the company performs a range of electrical and mechanical engineering services, including the design and installation of lighting, fire protection, plumbing, information technology, and security systems. It is active in many sectors, from residential and commercial to health care and education to airports, museums, and stadiums. Parent company WSP Group is being acquired by Canada-based construction consultancy GENIVAR.

	Annual Growth	12/06	12/07	12/08	12/09	12/10
Sales ($mil.)	(15.6%)	–	–	84.0	64.7	59.9
Net income ($ mil.)	(15.3%)	–	–	3.7	3.1	2.7
Market value ($ mil.)	–	–	–	–	–	–
Employees	–	–	–	–	–	335

WTA TOUR, INC.

100 2ND AVE S STE 1100S
SAINT PETERSBURG, FL 337014208
Phone: 727 895-5000
Fax: –
Web: www.wtatennis.com

CEO: Steve Simon
CFO: –
HR: Alyssa Chmura
FYE: December 31
Type: Private

This organization is aces with fans of women's tennis. The governing body for professional women's tennis, WTA Tour regulates the sport as a member of the International Tennis Federation and it sanctions 55 tennis events each year in more than 30 countries. Boasting more than 2,500 players from more than 95 different countries, the association markets the game and its players and generates revenue through merchandising, sponsorships, and selling broadcasting rights to its events. The WTA Tour was founded in 1973 when a number of top players, including Billie Jean King, decided to take the sport from an amateur level to professional.

	Annual Growth	12/12	12/13	12/14	12/21	12/22
Sales ($mil.)	6.8%	–	63.3	69.7	87.8	114.0
Net income ($ mil.)	3.2%	–	2.8	4.7	(15.2)	3.8
Market value ($ mil.)	–	–	–	–	–	–
Employees	–	–	–	–	–	100

WVS FINANCIAL CORP.

NBB: WVFC

9001 Perry Highway
Pittsburgh, PA 15237
Phone: 412 364-1911
Fax: –
Web: www.wvsbank.com

CEO: David J Bursic
CFO: –
HR: –
FYE: June 30
Type: Public

WVS Financial is the holding company for West View Savings Bank, which serves Pittsburgh's North Hills suburbs from about a half-dozen offices. The bank, which opened in 1908, offers standard deposit products such as checking and savings accounts, CDs, and IRAs. Its lending activities primarily consist of real estate loans, including construction loans and commercial, multifamily, and single-family mortgages. West View Savings Bank also writes consumer (mainly home equity) and business loans. Interest from investments in securities such as US government agency securities, municipal and corporate bonds, and mortgage-backed securities account for about half of WVS Financial's revenue.

	Annual Growth	06/19	06/20	06/21	06/22	06/23
Assets ($mil.)	0.5%	355.8	357.1	346.1	362.8	362.8
Net income ($ mil.)	(11.6%)	2.8	2.5	1.3	1.2	1.7
Market value ($ mil.)	(8.4%)	30.4	22.9	28.4	25.8	21.4
Employees	–	39	32	34	–	–

WW INTERNATIONAL INC

NMS: WW

675 Avenue of the Americas, 6th Floor
New York, NY 10010
Phone: 212 589-2700
Fax: –
Web: www.weightwatchersinternational.com

CEO: Sima Sistani
CFO: Heather Stark
HR: –
FYE: December 30
Type: Public

WW International, formerly known as Weight Watchers International, is a human-centric technology company powered by its proven, science-based, clinically effective weight loss and weight management program, and an award-winning digital subscription platform. WW-branded services and products include digital offerings provided through its apps and websites, workshops, consumer products, and various events. The company has a total of approximately 3.5 million subscribers, of which approximately 2.8 million were Digital subscribers and approximately 0.7 million were Workshops + Digital subscribers. WW also sells a range of consumer products, including bars, snacks, cookbooks, and kitchen tools. The company generates most of its revenue from the US.

	Annual Growth	12/19*	01/21	01/22*	12/22	12/23
Sales ($mil.)	(10.9%)	1,413.3	1,378.1	1,212.5	1,040.9	889.6
Net income ($ mil.)	–	119.6	75.1	66.9	(251.4)	(112.3)
Market value ($ mil.)	(30.6%)	2,979.1	1,932.2	1,277.3	305.7	692.9
Employees	(26.9%)	17,000	10,000	7,700	7,100	4,850

*Fiscal year change

WYCKOFF HEIGHTS MEDICAL CENTER

374 STOCKHOLM ST
BROOKLYN, NY 112374006
Phone: 718 963-7272
Fax: –
Web: www.whmcny.org

CEO: Dominick Gio
CFO: –
HR: Crystal Worrell
FYE: December 31
Type: Private

Wyckoff Heights is taking health care to new levels. Serving the New York boroughs of Brooklyn and Queens, Wyckoff Heights Medical Center maintains some 350 beds and provides a comprehensive range of specialized services, including diagnostics, radiology, cardiology, obstetrics, pediatrics, surgery, and rehabilitative care. The hospital also provides educational services through a partnership with the Weill Medical College of Cornell University, and it offers outpatient services through several family health clinics in the area. The not-for-profit medical center is governed by an independent board of trustees.

	Annual Growth	12/13	12/14	12/17	12/19	12/21
Sales ($mil.)	(0.5%)	–	249.7	7.0	329.4	241.3
Net income ($ mil.)	–	–	2.1	2.2	19.3	(12.6)
Market value ($ mil.)	–	–	–	–	–	–
Employees	–	–	–	–	–	1,900

WYNALDA LITHO, INC.

8221 GRAPHIC DR NE
BELMONT, MI 493068934
Phone: 616 866-1561
Fax: –
Web: www.wynalda.com

CEO: Robert M Wynalda Sr
CFO: –
HR: –
FYE: December 31
Type: Private

Wynalda Packaging produces and prints folding cartons for clients in the food and beverage, computer software, pharmaceutical, beauty, and entertainment industries. The company has two production facilities in Rockford, Michigan, strategically located between Chicago and Detroit. Wynalda Packaging also has regularly scheduled deliveries to most major manufacturing centers across North America. The company's range of services includes package design, manufacturing, and printing. It also offer in-house special enhancements including bindery, embossing, die-cutting, foil stamping, and gluing. Robert Wynalda Sr. founded Wynalda Litho in 1970.

WYNN RESORTS LTD
NMS: WYNN

3131 Las Vegas Boulevard South
Las Vegas, NV 89109
Phone: 702 770-7555
Fax: –
Web: www.wynnresorts.com

CEO: Craig S Billings
CFO: Julie Cameron-Doe
HR: –
FYE: December 31
Type: Public

Wynn Resorts operates a handful of luxury casino resorts, including the Wynn Las Vegas in Las Vegas, and the Wynn Macau and the Wynn Palace in Macau, China, the only place in China where gambling is legal. The company's properties integrate luxury hotel rooms, high-end retail, an array of dining and entertainment options, meeting and convention space, and gaming. Most revenue comes from its Las Vegas operations at around 55% of sales. The firm works to attract international customers through marketing offices in Hong Kong, Singapore, Japan, Taiwan, and Canada. The company was founded in 2002.

	Annual Growth	12/19	12/20	12/21	12/22	12/23
Sales ($mil.)	(0.3%)	6,611.1	2,095.9	3,763.7	3,756.8	6,531.9
Net income ($ mil.)	56.1%	123.0	(2,067.2)	(755.8)	(423.9)	730.0
Market value ($ mil.)	(10.0%)	15,517	12,607	9,502.1	9,215.0	10,180
Employees	(2.0%)	30,200	27,500	26,950	27,000	27,800

WYOMING MEDICAL CENTER, INC.

1233 E 2ND ST
CASPER, WY 826012988
Phone: 307 577-7201
Fax: –
Web: www.bannerhealth.com

CEO: Lance Porter
CFO: Jeanne Ehlebracht
HR: Cassie Barker
FYE: December 31
Type: Private

Wyoming Medical Center is The Cowboy State's largest medical facility. The hospital, founded in 1911, offers those who live in and around Wyoming's Natrona County more than 50 medical specialties thanks to its 150 physicians. The health care services provider boasts nearly 1,300 skilled staff members and more than 190 beds. It offers services such as an emergency air transport system, trauma care, diagnostic services, diabetes care center, nephrology, and surgical care. The facility is a community-owned, not-for-profit hospital.that also operates the Heart Center of Wyoming, the Wyoming Neuroscience and Spine Institute, and a network of about a dozen community clinics throughout Wyoming.

	Annual Growth	06/18	06/19	06/20*	12/21	12/22
Sales ($mil.)	(3.2%)	–	260.9	293.5	267.2	236.8
Net income ($ mil.)	(37.9%)	–	18.5	9.4	19.3	4.4
Market value ($ mil.)	–	–	–	–	–	–
Employees	–	–	–	–	–	1,149

*Fiscal year change

WYSE ADVERTISING, INC.

668 EUCLID AVE STE 100
CLEVELAND, OH 441143024
Phone: 216 696-2424
Fax: –
Web: www.wyseadv.com

CEO: –
CFO: –
HR: –
FYE: December 31
Type: Private

Wyse is wise in the ways of advertising be it television, radio, print, or electronic media. One of the largest and oldest independent agencies in the Mid-West, Wyse Advertising serves regional, national, amd international clientele from its Cleveland, Ohio office. Wyse Advertising has created some memorable slogans in its time, including "Ask Sherwin-Williams" and "With a name like Smucker's, it has to be good." In addition to creative services, the agency offers Web development and interactive marketing, direct marketing, research, and brand planning services. The employee-owned agency boasts such clients as Kelly Services and Wendy's. Wyse Advertising was founded in 1951.

X PRIZE FOUNDATION, INC.

10736 JEFFERSON BLVD PMB 406
CULVER CITY, CA 902304933
Phone: 310 741-4880
Fax: –
Web: www.xprize.org

CEO: –
CFO: –
HR: –
FYE: December 31
Type: Private

X PRIZE's mission is to boldly go where no one has gone before. The foundation set a $10 million prize for the first privately financed team to build a spaceship able to travel 62 miles (100km) into space two consecutive times within a two week period. Mojave Aerospace Ventures won the ANSARI X prize in October 2004 when its SpaceShipOne craft reached 360,000 feet. X PRIZE plans to organize further annual space vehicle competitions with the goal of jump-starting the space tourism industry, much like what the Orteig Prize (which offered a $25,000 prize to the first person to fly non-stop between New York and Paris in the 1920's) did for air transportation. Chairman Peter Diamandis founded X PRIZE in 1995.

	Annual Growth	12/11	12/12	12/13	12/21	12/22
Sales ($mil.)	(2.1%)	–	–	22.3	19.8	18.4
Net income ($ mil.)	–	–	–	(1.7)	(3.7)	(5.8)
Market value ($ mil.)	–	–	–	–	–	–
Employees	–	–	–	–	–	50

XAVIER UNIVERSITY

3800 VICTORY PKWY
CINCINNATI, OH 452071092
Phone: 513 745-3000
Fax: –
Web: www.xavier.edu

CEO: –
CFO: Maribeth Amyot
HR: David Zoogah
FYE: June 30
Type: Private

Xavier University is a not-for-profit Jesuit Catholic institution that operates from a single campus located in Cincinnati, Ohio. The private school, which has recently grown its enrollment numbers to about 7,000 students, offers nearly 90 undergraduate programs and about 20 graduate programs. Xavier University's programs range from arts and sciences to social sciences and business. Boasting small class sizes, the university's student-to-faculty ratio is a noteworthy 12:1. Known among sports circles as having a highly respected men's basketball program, Xavier University also manages to graduate every member of its men's Musketeers group. Xavier University was founded in 1831.

	Annual Growth	06/12	06/13	06/20	06/21	06/22
Sales ($mil.)	7.8%	–	163.5	–	321.9	321.0
Net income ($ mil.)	0.4%	–	14.3	–	19.9	14.9
Market value ($ mil.)	–	–	–	–	–	–
Employees	–	–	–	–	–	940

XCEL ENERGY INC
NMS: XEL

414 Nicollet Mall
Minneapolis, MN 55401
Phone: 612 330-5500
Fax: –
Web: www.xcelenergy.com

CEO: Robert C Frenzel
CFO: Brian J Van Abel
HR: –
FYE: December 31
Type: Public

Xcel Energy is a major U.S. regulated electric and natural gas delivery company distributing electricity to approximately 3.8 million customers and natural gas to about 2.1 million customers in eight states through its four regulated utilities: Northern States Power Minnesota (NSP-Minnesota), Northern States Power Wisconsin (NSP-Wisconsin), the Public Service Company of Colorado (PSCo), and Southwestern Public Service (SPS). It also owns transmission and distribution lines as well as natural gas assets. Along with the utility subsidiaries, the transmission-only subsidiaries, WYCO and WGI comprise the regulated utility operations. The company's nonregulated subsidiaries include Eloigne, Capital Services, Venture Holdings, and Nicollet Project Holdings.

	Annual Growth	12/19	12/20	12/21	12/22	12/23
Sales ($mil.)	5.4%	11,529	11,526	13,431	15,310	14,206
Net income ($ mil.)	6.6%	1,372.0	1,473.0	1,597.0	1,736.0	1,771.0
Market value ($ mil.)	(0.6%)	35,233	36,998	37,570	38,907	34,356
Employees	1.7%	11,317	11,367	11,321	11,982	12,100

XENCOR, INC

NMS: XNCR

465 North Halstead Street, Suite 200
Pasadena, CA 91107
Phone: 626 305-5900
Fax: –
Web: www.xencor.com

CEO: Bassil I Dahiyat
CFO: –
HR: –
FYE: December 31
Type: Public

Xencor is a clinical-stage biopharmaceutical company focused on discovering and developing engineered monoclonal antibodies and cytokine therapeutics to treat patients with cancer and autoimmune diseases who have unmet medical needs. It is advancing a broad portfolio of clinical-stage XmAb drug candidates from its proprietary protein FC technology platforms. It also uses its protein engineering capabilities to increase its understanding of protein structure and interactions and to design new technologies and XmAb development candidates with improved properties. It also licenses its technology to major pharmaceutical companies ? Janssen, Genentech, MorphoSys, Nestl, Zenas BioPharma, and INmune Bio, among others. The company was founded in 1997.

	Annual Growth	12/19	12/20	12/21	12/22	12/23
Sales ($mil.)	1.8%	156.7	122.7	275.1	164.6	168.3
Net income ($ mil.)	–	26.9	(69.3)	82.6	(55.2)	(126.1)
Market value ($ mil.)	(11.4%)	2,097.7	2,661.4	2,447.2	1,588.4	1,295.0
Employees	14.0%	166	202	254	281	280

XENONICS HOLDINGS INC

NBB: XNNH Q

3445 Lawrence Avenue
Oceanside, NY 11572
Phone: 646 768-8417
Fax: –
Web: www.xenonics.com

CEO: Alan P Magerman
CFO: Richard S Kay
HR: –
FYE: September 30
Type: Public

Xenonics Holdings says fiat lux ("Let there be light"). Its NightHunter high-intensity, portable lighting products are used worldwide by American military forces and by law enforcement agencies to illuminate dark areas. The SuperVision high-definition night-vision product is aimed at the commercial market and represents a growing portion of the company's sales. Xenonics' products are also used as part of security systems for facilities. Military customers -- including the US Air Force, US Army, US Marine Corps, US Navy, and military equipment resellers -- account for about 90% of the company's sales.

	Annual Growth	09/14	09/15	09/16	09/17	09/18
Sales ($mil.)	–	0.8	–	–	–	–
Net income ($ mil.)	–	(2.6)	2.1	–	–	–
Market value ($ mil.)	(60.2%)	5.9	3.4	0.0	0.0	0.1
Employees	–	10	–	–	–	–

XENOPORT, INC.

6 CONCOURSE PKWY STE 1800
ATLANTA, GA 303285353
Phone: 408 616-7200
Fax: –
Web: –

CEO: Vincent J Angotti
CFO: William G Harris
HR: –
FYE: December 31
Type: Private

XenoPort sounds like something straight out of science fiction, but there's nothing fictional about XenoPort's job of improving drugs' ability to be absorbed by tissues in the body. The development firm uses genomics to identify transporter proteins. It then designs oral drug molecules to find and ride these transporters through the gastrointestinal tract to their destinations. Its marketed drug in the US is Horizant (gabapentin enacarbil), a treatment for restless leg syndrome and post-herpetic neuralgia. XenoPort and Astellas Pharma jointly market gabapentin enacarbil tablets under the name Regnite in Japan. Arbor Pharmaceuticals is buying XenoPort for $467 million.

XEROX CREDIT CORP.

45 Glover Avenue
Norwalk, CT 06856-4505
Phone: 203 968-3000
Fax: –
Web: –

CEO: Steven J Bandrowczak
CFO: Xavier Heiss
HR: –
FYE: December 31
Type: Public

Xerox is a workplace technology company, building and integrating software and hardware for enterprises large and small. Xerox has long defined the modern work experience and continues to do so with investments in artificial intelligence (AI), augmented reality (AR)-driven service experiences, robotic process automation (RPA) and other technologies that enable Xerox to deliver essential products and services to address productivity challenges of a hybrid workplace and distributed workforce. US customers account for around 55% of sales. The company traces its roots back to 1906.

	Annual Growth	12/05	12/06	12/07	12/08	12/09
Sales ($mil.)	(23.9%)	119.0	103.0	88.0	57.0	40.0
Net income ($ mil.)	(15.9%)	44.0	44.0	42.0	30.0	22.0
Market value ($ mil.)	–	–	–	–	–	–
Employees	–	–	–	–	–	–

XEROX HOLDINGS CORP

NMS: XRX

P.O. Box 4505, 201 Merritt 7
Norwalk, CT 06851-1056
Phone: 203 849-5216
Fax: –
Web: www.xerox.com

CEO: Steven J Bandrowczak
CFO: Xavier Heiss
HR: –
FYE: December 31
Type: Public

Xerox is a workplace technology company, building and integrating software and hardware for enterprises large and small. Xerox has long defined the modern work experience and continues to do so with investments in artificial intelligence (AI), augmented reality (AR)-driven service experiences, robotic process automation (RPA) and other technologies that enable Xerox to deliver essential products and services to address productivity challenges of a hybrid workplace and distributed workforce. US customers account for around 55% of sales. The company traces its roots back to 1906.

	Annual Growth	12/19	12/20	12/21	12/22	12/23
Sales ($mil.)	(6.6%)	9,066.0	7,022.0	7,038.0	7,107.0	6,886.0
Net income ($ mil.)	(83.5%)	1,353.0	192.0	(455.0)	(322.0)	1.0
Market value ($ mil.)	(16.0%)	4,540.3	2,855.7	2,788.0	1,797.9	2,257.2
Employees	(7.1%)	27,000	24,700	23,300	20,500	20,100

XO GROUP INC.

2 WISCONSIN CIR STE 300
CHEVY CHASE, MD 208157014
Phone: 212 219-8555
Fax: –
Web: www.theknotww.com

CEO: Michael Steib
CFO: Gillian Munson
HR: –
FYE: December 31
Type: Private

The Knot (formerly known as XO Group) is an authority on wedding planning and advice, offering a seamless, all-in-one solution?from finding inspiration and local vendors to creating and managing all guest experiences, wedding registries, invitations and more. The trusted brand reaches a majority of engaged couples in the US through its leading wedding planning website TheKnot.com and leading iOS and Android mobile app The Knot Wedding Planner, The Knot national wedding magazine, and The Knot book series. The Knot has presences in North America, Europe, Latin America and Asia.

XO HOLDINGS, INC

13865 SUNRISE VALLEY DR STE 400
HERNDON, VA 201716187
Phone: 703 547-2000
Fax: –
Web: –

CEO: –
CFO: –
HR: –
FYE: December 31
Type: Private

XO Holdings gets down to the Xs and Os of business telecom services. Through its operational subsidiary XO Communications, the company provides telecommunications services to large corporations, small and midsized businesses, government agencies, and other telecom carriers via a network of about 1.6 million miles of metropolitan fiber. XO Communications offers local and long-distance voice, dedicated Internet access, private networking, data transport, and managed services such as Web hosting and bundled voice and data services. The company has customers in about 85 US markets and internationally. Billionaire financier Carl Icahn owns the company through his ACF Industries.

XOMA CORP

NMS: XOMA

2200 Powell Street, Suite 310
Emeryville, CA 94608
Phone: 510 204-7200
Fax: –
Web: www.xoma.com

CEO: Owen Hughes
CFO: Thomas Burns
HR: –
FYE: December 31
Type: Public

XOMA Corporation doesn't want to toil in anonymity. Instead, the company pairs with larger drug firms to develop and market its products, primarily monoclonal antibodies (biotech drugs based on cloned proteins). It's developing lead candidate gevokizumab with Novartis. The firm partners on therapeutics for various clinical development stages, targeting the adenosine pathway with potential applications in solid tumors, non-Hodgkin's lymphoma, asthma/chronic obstructive pulmonary disease, inflammatory bowel disease, idiopathic pulmonary fibrosis, lung cancer, psoriasis and nonalcoholic steatohepatitis and other indications. XOMA has collaborative agreements with pharma companies Takeda Pharmaceutical and Merck; it also has metabolic and oncology candidates. The US generates about 95% of the company's revenue.

	Annual Growth	12/19	12/20	12/21	12/22	12/23
Sales ($mil.)	(28.7%)	18.4	29.4	38.2	6.0	4.8
Net income ($ mil.)	–	(2.0)	13.3	15.8	(17.1)	(40.8)
Market value ($ mil.)	(9.3%)	313.8	507.3	239.7	211.5	212.7
Employees	–	–	10	10	12	13

XORIANT CORPORATION

1248 REAMWOOD AVE
SUNNYVALE, CA 940892225
Phone: 408 743-4400
Fax: –
Web: www.xoriant.com

CEO: Girish Gaitonde
CFO: Mahesh Nalavade
HR: Mahima Kulkarni
FYE: December 31
Type: Private

Xoriant is not exorbitant about offering IT services. The firm provides outsourced application development, engineering, and consulting services to technology start-ups such as software developers, as well as banks, telecommunications companies, and health care providers among other businesses. The company specializes in implementing technology to enable cloud, Web, social networking, payment, embedded, media and mobile applications and services. Other services included testing and technical support. Xoriant's customers have included TIBCO Software.

	Annual Growth	12/12	12/13	12/14	12/16	12/17
Sales ($mil.)	12.5%	–	–	125.2	150.6	178.0
Net income ($ mil.)	(5.9%)	–	–	3.7	6.7	3.1
Market value ($ mil.)	–	–	–	–	–	–
Employees	–	–	–	–	–	3,950

XPLORE TECHNOLOGIES CORP.

8601 RANCH ROAD 2222 BLDG 2
AUSTIN, TX 787302304
Phone: 512 637-1100
Fax: –
Web: –

CEO: –
CFO: –
HR: –
FYE: March 31
Type: Private

Xplore Technologies ensures that you can take your computer with you no matter what difficult terrain you're exploring. The company manufactures and sells ruggedized tablet PCs and handheld computers. The company primarily targets manufacturers, distributors, and systems integrators that supply field service personnel, factory workers, public safety officials, military personnel, and other customers that require durable mobile computers. Its products incorporate wireless networking technology and can be mounted in vehicles such as carts and forklifts. Xplore was founded in 1996. The company agreed to be bought by Zebra Technologies for about $66 million in 2018.

	Annual Growth	03/14	03/15	03/16	03/17	03/18
Sales ($mil.)	26.8%	–	42.6	100.5	77.9	86.9
Net income ($ mil.)	6.4%	–	0.2	(0.4)	(2.6)	0.3
Market value ($ mil.)	–	–	–	–	–	–
Employees	–	–	–	–	–	211

XPO INC

NYS: XPO

Five American Lane
Greenwich, CT 06831
Phone: 855 976-6951
Fax: –
Web: www.xpo.com

CEO: Drew Wilkerson
CFO: Kyle Wismans
HR: Cathy Butler
FYE: December 31
Type: Public

XPO is a leading provider of freight transportation services. It uses proprietary technology to move goods efficiently through its customers' supply chains, primarily by providing less-than-truckload (LTL) and truck brokerage services. Its LTL sales and service professionals and network of drivers, tractors, trailers and terminals serve approximately 27,000 customers in North America. Its customers include companies in retail and e-commerce, food and beverage, consumer packaged goods, and industrial markets. The US is its largest market, generating about 60% of its revenue.

	Annual Growth	12/19	12/20	12/21	12/22	12/23
Sales ($mil.)	(17.4%)	16,648	16,252	12,806	7,718.0	7,744.0
Net income ($ mil.)	(18.0%)	419.0	110.0	336.0	666.0	189.0
Market value ($ mil.)	2.4%	9,251.0	13,836	8,987.5	3,864.1	10,167
Employees	(21.5%)	100,000	102,000	42,000	38,000	38,000

XPONENTIAL, INC.

6400 ATL BLVD STE 190
NORCROSS, GA 30071
Phone: 678 305-7211
Fax: –
Web: –

CEO: –
CFO: –
HR: –
FYE: June 30
Type: Private

Xponential is the holding company for PawnMart, which makes small short-term loans secured by personal property, such as jewelry, electronics, tools, and cars. The shops specialize in lending on heavy equipment, boats, and motorcycles. PawnMart typically makes loans of less than $500, charges annual interest rates of 24%-300%, and sells the property if the customer defaults. To compete with discount retailers, the company operates clean, well-lit stores in suburban areas, and sells no handguns or rifles. PawnMart has about 25 locations in Georgia and North Carolina.

XTANT MEDICAL HOLDINGS INC
ASE: XTNT

664 Cruiser Lane
Belgrade, MT 59714
Phone: 406 388-0480
Fax: 406 388-1354
Web: www.xtantmedical.com

CEO: –
CFO: –
HR: –
FYE: December 31
Type: Public

Xtant Medical Holdings has your back(bone). Formerly named Bacterin International, the company develops, manufactures, and markets biomedical devices, including orthopedic biomaterials used for bone grafts, joint surgery, and other skeletal reconstructive procedures. Its biologics products include OsteoSponge, a bone void filler made of 100% human bone; OsteoLock, a stabilization dowel for spinal procedures; and BacFast, a dowel with demineralization technology to aid in bone grafting. Additionally, the company makes implants and surgical instruments under the Axle, IRIX-C, Calix, Xpress, and Silex brand names. The company was founded in 1998.

	Annual Growth	12/18	12/19	12/20	12/21	12/22
Sales ($mil.)	(5.3%)	72.2	64.7	53.3	55.3	58.0
Net income ($ mil.)	–	(70.1)	(8.2)	(7.0)	(4.8)	(8.5)
Market value ($ mil.)	(20.0%)	175.3	174.2	130.2	61.0	71.9
Employees	(5.0%)	166	141	110	118	135

XTERA COMMUNICATIONS INC
NBB: XCOM Q

500 W. Bethany Drive, Suite 100
Allen, TX 75013
Phone: 972 649-5000
Fax: –
Web: www.xtera.com

CEO: –
CFO: –
HR: –
FYE: September 30
Type: Public

Xtera Communications tries to provide extra performance to network infrastructures. The company makes fiber-optic transmission equipment used in both the terrestrial and undersea sections of telecommunications networks. Its Nu-Wave systems increase the bandwidth capacity of fiber-optic strands, enabling converged communications. Xtera also offers load balancers and traffic management devices for wide area networks. The company serves wholesale telecommunications carriers and other service providers; clients have included Pacnet. Xtera has attracted investments from a wide range of private equity firms, including Accel Partners, ARCH Venture Partners, New Enterprise Associates, and Sevin Rosen.

	Annual Growth	09/11	09/12	09/13	09/14	09/15
Sales ($mil.)	35.6%	–	–	31.9	25.0	58.7
Net income ($ mil.)	–	–	–	(24.6)	(26.1)	(16.6)
Market value ($ mil.)	–	–	–	–	–	–
Employees	–	–	–	–	108	109

XWELL INC
NAS: XWEL

254 West 31st Street, 11th Floor
New York, NY 10001
Phone: 212 750-9595
Fax: –
Web: www.xpressspagroup.com

CEO: Scott R Milford
CFO: Suzanne A Scrabis
HR: –
FYE: December 31
Type: Public

Vringo is brinnggg brinnggg bringing its video ringtones to consumer mobile phones. The upstart company is riding the next wave in mobile ringtone technology beyond just audio clips with video clips that users can upload to their phones. Subscribers of Vringo's service can browse and purchase content from its Web site, which houses a library of more than 4,000 video ringtones, as well as tools to create, customize, and share them through social media networks. The company reaches subscribers through partnerships with certain mobile carriers in Armenia, Malaysia, Turkey, and the United Arab Emirates, with hopes to establish more throughout the world. Vringo filed to go public in January 2010.

	Annual Growth	12/18	12/19	12/20	12/21	12/22
Sales ($mil.)	2.8%	50.1	48.5	8.4	73.7	55.9
Net income ($ mil.)	–	(37.2)	(21.2)	(90.5)	3.3	(32.8)
Market value ($ mil.)	23.5%	0.6	2.8	5.0	8.4	1.5
Employees	(9.0%)	703	728	152	429	483

XYLEM INC
NYS: XYL

301 Water Street SE
Washington, DC 20003
Phone: 202 869-9150
Fax: –
Web: www.xyleminc.com

CEO: –
CFO: –
HR: –
FYE: December 31
Type: Public

Xylem is a leading global water technology company that designs, manufactures and services highly engineered products and solutions across a wide variety of critical applications primarily in the water sector, but also in energy. Its broad portfolio of products, services and solutions addresses customer needs across the water cycle, from the delivery, measurement and use of drinking water, to the collection, testing, analysis and treatment of wastewater, to the return of water to the environment. Xylem's products are sold under about 20 different brands, including Flygt, Goulds, and Pure. About 45% of its revenue comes from the US.

	Annual Growth	12/19	12/20	12/21	12/22	12/23
Sales ($mil.)	8.8%	5,249.0	4,876.0	5,195.0	5,522.0	7,364.0
Net income ($ mil.)	11.0%	401.0	254.0	427.0	355.0	609.0
Market value ($ mil.)	9.8%	19,036	24,592	28,973	26,714	27,629
Employees	9.0%	16,300	16,700	17,300	17,800	23,000

YAHOO INC.

770 BROADWAY FL 9
NEW YORK, NY 100039522
Phone: 212 652-6400
Fax: –
Web: advertising.yahooinc.com

CEO: Jim Lanzone
CFO: –
HR: –
FYE: December 31
Type: Private

Yahoo (formerly known as Verizon Media) is one of the world's premier global technology and media companies. The company reaches nearly 900 million active users around the world. It provides a full-stack platform for businesses to amplify growth and drive more meaningful connections across advertising, search, and media. In late 2021, Apollo completed its approximately $5 billion acquisition of Verizon Media, now known as Yahoo. Yahoo now operates as a standalone company under Apollo Funds. In addition, Verizon has retained a 10% stake in Yahoo.

YAKIMA VALLEY MEMORIAL HOSPITAL ASSOCIATION INC

2811 TIETON DR
YAKIMA, WA 989023761
Phone: 509 249-5129
Fax: –
Web: www.multicare.org

CEO: –
CFO: –
HR: –
FYE: December 31
Type: Private

Whether you're a major yakker or quiet as a mouse, Yakima Valley Memorial Hospital serves the health care needs of patients of all types. The health provider's acute-care hospital, skilled-nursing facilities, and outpatient specialty treatment facilities serve patients in and around Yakima in Washington State. The hospital has about 225 beds and provides a variety of services such as heart care, orthopedics, pediatrics, cancer treatment, women's health, and mental health care. It also offers sleep and wound care and provides home health and hospice services. The organization is a not-for-profit group governed by a board of directors.

	Annual Growth	12/18	12/19	12/20	12/21	12/22
Sales ($mil.)	1.8%	–	500.8	517.9	558.7	528.5
Net income ($ mil.)	–	–	9.8	11.8	10.3	(27.3)
Market value ($ mil.)	–	–	–	–	–	–
Employees	–	–	–	–	–	1,150

YALE NEW HAVEN HEALTH SERVICES CORPORATION

789 HOWARD AVE
NEW HAVEN, CT 065191300
Phone: 203 688-4242
Fax: –
Web: www.ynhh.org

CEO: –
CFO: –
HR: –
FYE: September 30
Type: Private

Yale New Haven Health System is Connecticut's leading healthcare system. The company operates Bridgeport, Greenwich, Lawrence + Memorial, Yale New Haven and Westerly hospitals, and Northeast Medical Group, a physician foundation of primary care and medical specialists. In addition, Yale New Haven Health operates outpatient facilities and provides such managed care services as network contracting, as well as disease management programs. Yale New Haven Health System had 151,850 inpatient visits annually, 5.2 million outpatient encounters, and accumulated total assets of approximately $8.15 billion.

	Annual Growth	09/18	09/19	09/20	09/21	09/22
Sales ($mil.)	11.9%	–	657.9	742.3	836.6	921.3
Net income ($ mil.)	294.1%	–	0.2	(1.4)	(8.6)	15.0
Market value ($ mil.)	–	–	–	–	–	–
Employees		–	–	–	–	52,768

YALE NEW HAVEN HOSPITAL, INC.

20 YORK ST
NEW HAVEN, CT 065103220
Phone: 203 688-4242
Fax: –
Web: www.ynhh.org

CEO: Christopher M Oconnor
CFO: –
HR: –
FYE: September 30
Type: Private

Yale-New Haven Hospital (YNHH) is the flagship member of the Yale New Haven Health System. It provides tertiary care in more than 100 medical specialties to residents of southwestern Connecticut. The not-for-profit hospital has around 1,540 beds. Its main location includes the Yale-New Haven Children's Hospital and the Yale-New Haven Psychiatric Hospital. Its Smilow Cancer Hospital provides the very best cancer care available. YNHH provides cardiac and cancer care, performs organ transplants, and offers a variety of outpatient clinics. Yale New Haven Hospital was founded as the General Hospital Society of Connecticut in 1826.

	Annual Growth	09/18	09/19	09/20	09/21	09/22
Sales ($mil.)	6.1%	–	3,266.2	2,923.0	3,238.5	3,904.3
Net income ($ mil.)	–	–	258.4	49.1	476.5	(64.1)
Market value ($ mil.)	–	–	–	–	–	–
Employees		–	–	–	–	30,278

YALE UNIVERSITY

105 WALL ST
NEW HAVEN, CT 065118917
Phone: 203 432-2550
Fax: –
Web: www.yale.edu

CEO: –
CFO: –
HR: –
FYE: June 30
Type: Private

What do former President George W. Bush and actress Meryl Streep have in common? They are Yalies. Yale University is one of the nation's most prestigious private liberal arts institutions, as well as one of its oldest (founded in 1701). Yale comprises an undergraduate college, a graduate school, and more than a dozen professional schools. Programs of study include architecture, law, medicine, and drama. Its 12 residential colleges (a system borrowed from Oxford) serve as dormitory, dining hall, and social center. The school has around 12,000 students and nearly 4,000 faculty members.

	Annual Growth	06/16	06/17	06/18	06/19	06/22
Sales ($mil.)	15.2%	–	3,647.6	3,848.3	4,105.4	7,410.4
Net income ($ mil.)	(1.3%)	–	2,447.7	3,271.0	(15.4)	2,297.0
Market value ($ mil.)	–	–	–	–	–	–
Employees		–	–	–	–	11,000

YANKEE PUBLISHING INCORPORATED

1121 MAIN ST
DUBLIN, NH 034448246
Phone: 603 563-8111
Fax: –
Web: www.newengland.com

CEO: –
CFO: –
HR: –
FYE: June 30
Type: Private

Poet Emily Dickinson once wrote, "I think New Englandy," and Yankee Publishing tries to abide by her words. The publisher of the monthly Yankee magazine is devoted to what it calls "the New England way of life," with region-specific features such as throwing a classic clambake and finding the best country roads for viewing fall foliage. The company operates a digital version of the title with classified ads and e-commerce options. It also publishes The Old Farmer's Almanac ; America's oldest continuously published periodical, the almanac was first published in 1792 during George Washington's first term as president. Yankee Publishing was founded in 1935 by Robb and Beatrix Sagendorph, and remains family-owned.

YASH TECHNOLOGIES, INC.

605 17TH AVE
EAST MOLINE, IL 612442045
Phone: 309 755-0433
Fax: –
Web: www.yash.com

CEO: –
CFO: –
HR: –
FYE: December 31
Type: Private

YASH Technologies is a leading technology integrator that provides information technology (IT) services such as consulting, systems integration, and enterprise modernization, as well as software development and business process outsourcing. It has expertise in business software from leading providers including IBM, Microsoft, Oracle, AWS, Cisco, and SAP, among others. YASH primarily targets corporations in such fields as life- sciences, mining, agribusiness, aviation, education, financial services, healthcare, government, manufacturing, and retail. The company was founded in 1996.

YATES GROUP, INC.

2015 GALLERIA OAKS DR
TEXARKANA, TX 755034618
Phone: 903 336-6246
Fax: –
Web: www.phillips66.com

CEO: –
CFO: –
HR: –
FYE: December 31
Type: Private

E-Z Mart Stores aims to make filling gas tanks and stomachs EZR for small-town America. The regional convenience store chain operates about 295 stores across four neighboring states, including Arkansas, Louisiana, Oklahoma, and Texas. Rather than build its own stores, the company usually expands through acquisitions. In addition to the standard hot dogs, sodas, coffee, and cigarettes, most E-Z Mart locations also offer Shell, Conoco, Phillips 66, or CITGO gasoline. E-Z Mart was founded in 1970 by Jim Yates in Nashville, Arkansas. Yates died in 1998 when the plane he was piloting crashed, leaving his daughter Sonja Hubbard at the company's helm as CEO.

	Annual Growth	12/12	12/13	12/14	12/15	12/16
Sales ($mil.)	(7.8%)	–	1,003.8	1,026.3	827.8	786.1
Net income ($ mil.)	3.2%	–	15.2	19.3	16.8	16.7
Market value ($ mil.)	–	–	–	–	–	–
Employees		–	–	–	–	2,100

YAVAPAI COUNTY COMMUNITY COLLEGE DISTRICT

1100 E SHELDON ST
PRESCOTT, AZ 863013220
Phone: 928 445-7300
Fax: -
Web: www.yc.edu

CEO: -
CFO: -
HR: -
FYE: June 30
Type: Private

Located in mountains of central Arizona, Yavapai College bills itself as the friendliest college in the West. It offers more than 30 degrees and 60 certificate programs from six campuses and centers, as well as nearly 80 class sites throughout Yavapai County. Its Sedona Center for Arts and Technology offers digital media arts, digital storytelling, web design, filmmaking, and general art classes. The college, which boasts about 12,000 students, also has programs in such fields as accounting, computer systems and applications, early childhood education, nursing, fire science, gunsmithing, and paralegal studies. Yavapai College was established in 1966.

	Annual Growth	06/18	06/19	06/20	06/21	06/22
Sales ($mil.)	(4.0%)	-	11.5	10.7	8.7	10.2
Net income ($ mil.)	3.0%	-	13.5	8.1	8.1	14.8
Market value ($ mil.)	-	-	-	-	-	-
Employees	-	-	-	-	-	1,017

YELLOW CORP (NEW)

501 Commerce Street, Suite 1120
Nashville, TN 37203
Phone: 913 696-6100
Fax: -
Web: www.myyellow.com

NBB: YELL Q

CEO: Darren D Hawkins
CFO: Daniel L Olivier
HR: -
FYE: December 31
Type: Public

Yellow Corporation is one of the largest less-than-truckload (LTL) networks in North America, with local, regional, national, and international capabilities. The company provides higher-margin specialized services, including guaranteed expedited services, time-specific deliveries, cross-border services, exhibit services, product returns, and government material shipments. It also provides logistics solutions for customer-specific needs with custom projects, consolidation and distribution, reverse logistics, and residential white glove service offerings. Yellow Corporation's LTL subsidiaries include Holland, New Penn, Reddaway, YRC Inc., and YRC Freight Canada Company (both doing business as, collectively, YRC Freight). The company offer services through Yellow Logistics, Inc. (Yellow Logistics and f/k/a HNRY Logistics, Inc.), its customer-specific logistics solutions provider, specializing in truckload, residential, and warehouse solutions.

	Annual Growth	12/18	12/19	12/20	12/21	12/22
Sales ($mil.)	0.7%	5,092.0	4,871.2	4,513.7	5,121.8	5,244.7
Net income ($ mil.)	1.9%	20.2	(104.0)	(53.5)	(109.1)	21.8
Market value ($ mil.)	(5.5%)	163.2	132.1	229.5	652.3	130.0
Employees	(0.8%)	31,000	29,000	30,000	32,000	30,000

YELP INC

350 Mission Street, 10th Floor
San Francisco, CA 94105
Phone: 415 908-3801
Fax: -
Web: www.yelp.com

NYS: YELP

CEO: Jeremy Stoppelman
CFO: David Schwarzbach
HR: -
FYE: December 31
Type: Public

Yelp has built one of the best-known internet brands in the US. Its content covers restaurants, beauty and fitness, health, and home and local services, as well as shopping providers. It includes over 240 million consumer reviews. Yelp's advertising products help businesses of all sizes reach a large audience, advertise their products and drive conversion of their services. As a one-stop local platform, Yelp helps consumers easily discover, connect and transact with businesses across a broad range of categories by making it easy to request a quote for a service, book a table at a restaurant, and more. With a presence in cities across North America and Europe, Yelp generates most of its sales from the US. The company was founded in 2004.

	Annual Growth	12/19	12/20	12/21	12/22	12/23
Sales ($mil.)	7.2%	1,014.2	872.9	1,031.8	1,193.5	1,337.1
Net income ($ mil.)	24.8%	40.9	(19.4)	39.7	36.3	99.2
Market value ($ mil.)	8.0%	2,398.5	2,249.8	2,495.6	1,882.7	3,260.0
Employees	(5.7%)	5,950	3,900	4,400	4,900	4,713

YEO & YEO, P.C.

5300 BAY RD
SAGINAW, MI 486042506
Phone: 989 793-9830
Fax: -
Web: www.yeoandyeo.com

CEO: Thomas E Hollerback
CFO: -
HR: -
FYE: December 31
Type: Private

Yeo & Yeo can help make sure all your I's are dotted and your T's are crossed. The firm provides certified public accounting services for individuals, businesses, not-for-profit organizations, and government entities in Michigan. With eight offices throughout the state, the firm has divisions specializing in the health care, manufacturing, and construction industries. Offerings include auditing, estate planning, and tax preparation services as well as medical practice management. The company also has teams dedicated to technology consultation and investment services. James Yeo and his son found Yeo & Yeo in 1923.

	Annual Growth	12/01	12/02	12/03	12/07	12/14
Sales ($mil.)	5.4%	-	-	18.0	-	32.3
Net income ($ mil.)	-	-	-	-	-	1.1
Market value ($ mil.)	-	-	-	-	-	-
Employees	-	-	-	-	-	200

YESHIVA UNIVERSITY

500 W 185TH ST
NEW YORK, NY 100333299
Phone: 212 960-5400
Fax: -
Web: www.yu.edu

CEO: -
CFO: -
HR: Julie Auster
FYE: June 30
Type: Private

Yeshivas are traditional Jewish schools, and Yeshiva University believes strongly in following tradition. The Jewish higher education institution serves more than 7,000 undergraduate and graduate students at four campuses in New York City. Subjects taught include liberal arts, sciences, medicine, law, business, social work, and psychology. It also has extensive Jewish studies and education programs, including study abroad opportunities. Yeshiva University, also known as YU, has an undergraduate student-to-teacher ratio of 6:1. Its graduate programs include medicine, law, psychology, and Jewish education.

	Annual Growth	06/15	06/16	06/20	06/21	06/22
Sales ($mil.)	7.9%	-	244.6	314.0	354.8	385.6
Net income ($ mil.)	-	-	(589.3)	(33.2)	18.1	25.4
Market value ($ mil.)	-	-	-	-	-	-
Employees	-	-	-	-	-	4,500

YETI HOLDINGS INC

7601 Southwest Parkway
Austin, TX 78735
Phone: 512 394-9384
Fax: -
Web: www.yeti.com

NYS: YETI

CEO: Matthew J Reintjes
CFO: Michael McMullen
HR: -
FYE: December 30
Type: Public

YETI is a global designer, retailer, and distributor of innovative outdoor products. The company designs and develops its products to provide superior performance and functionality in a variety of environments. Its product portfolio is comprised of Coolers & Equipment (comprised of hard coolers, soft coolers, cargo, bags, outdoor living, and associated accessories); Drinkware (made with durable, kitchen-grade, 18/8 stainless-steel, and double-wall vacuum insulation and its innovative No Sweat design); and an array of YETI-branded gear, such as hats, shirts, bottle openers, and ice substitutes. The company offers its products in the US, Canada, Australia, New Zealand, Europe, and Japan through a diverse omnichannel strategy. Generates most of its sales in the US, YETI was founded in 2006 by avid outdoorsmen, Roy and Ryan Seiders.

	Annual Growth	12/19*	01/21	01/22*	12/22	12/23
Sales ($mil.)	16.1%	913.7	1,091.7	1,411.0	1,595.2	1,658.7
Net income ($ mil.)	35.5%	50.4	155.8	212.6	89.7	169.9
Market value ($ mil.)	10.3%	3,040.3	5,951.2	7,199.3	3,590.5	4,500.5
Employees	7.4%	790	701	823	922	1,050

*Fiscal year change

YEXT INC

NYS: YEXT

61 Ninth Avenue
New York, NY 10011
Phone: 212 994-3900
Fax: -
Web: www.yext.com

CEO: Michael Walrath
CFO: Darryl Bond
HR: -
FYE: January 31
Type: Public

Yext organizes a business's facts so it can deliver relevant, actionable answers to consumer questions throughout the digital ecosystem. The company's database software platform, the Knowledge Graph, lets businesses sync and store its digital data to approximately 200 service and application providers, which Yext refer to as its Publisher Network providers including Amazon Alexa, Apple Maps, Bing, Cortana, Facebook, Google, Google Assistance, Google Maps, Siri, and Yelp. Its platform powers all of the company's key features, including listings, pages, and search, along with its other features and capabilities. Customers include many leading businesses in a diverse set of industries, such as healthcare, retail, and financial services. Most of its revenue was generated from North America.

	Annual Growth	01/20	01/21	01/22	01/23	01/24
Sales ($mil.)	7.9%	298.8	354.7	390.6	400.9	404.3
Net income ($ mil.)	-	(121.5)	(94.7)	(93.3)	(65.9)	(2.6)
Market value ($ mil.)	(20.6%)	1,865.5	2,106.5	1,011.4	867.8	740.5
Employees	(2.2%)	1,200	1,300	1,400	1,200	1,100

YIELD10 BIOSCIENCE INC

NAS: YTEN

19 Presidential Way
Woburn, MA 01801
Phone: 617 583-1700
Fax: -
Web: www.yield10bio.com

CEO: Joseph Shaulson
CFO: -
HR: -
FYE: December 31
Type: Public

Yield10 Bioscience (formerly Metabolix) is an agricultural bioscience company focused on developing disruptive technologies to improve crop yield for food and feed crops in order to enhance global food security. Yield10 is targeting new agricultural biotechnology approaches to improve fundamental elements of plant metabolism through enhanced photosynthetic efficiency and directed carbon utilization. In particular, Yield10 is working to develop, validate, and commercialize new traits and identify gene editing targets in canola, soybean, corn, and other key crops. Yield10 was launched in 2015. In 2016 Metabolix sold its biopolymer intellectual property (the company's former key asset) for $10 million.

	Annual Growth	12/18	12/19	12/20	12/21	12/22
Sales ($mil.)	(5.2%)	0.6	0.8	0.8	0.6	0.5
Net income ($ mil.)	-	(9.2)	(13.0)	(10.2)	(11.0)	(13.6)
Market value ($ mil.)	19.1%	4.1	0.8	28.6	24.3	8.3
Employees	8.1%	22	25	25	29	30

YOAKUM COMMUNITY HOSPITAL

1200 CARL RAMERT DR
YOAKUM, TX 779954868
Phone: 361 293-2321
Fax: -
Web: www.yoakumhospital.org

CEO: Karen Barber
CFO: -
HR: -
FYE: June 30
Type: Private

No it's not Dwight's hospital, but you can still get some down-home health care at Yoakum Community Hospital. The facility serves rural communities in South Central Texas by offering specialized services such as surgery, emergency medicine, labor and deliver, physical therapy, and radiology. The 25-bed facility, which has a staff of about 10 physicians, was founded in 1922. The hospital was originally owned by the city but has passed through numerous hands over the years including, the Sisters of the Incarnate Word and Blessed Sacrament and Sisters of Charity of the Incarnate word. Houston-based Memorial Hermann Healthcare System now provides the hospital with management services.

	Annual Growth	06/14	06/15	06/16	06/18	06/20
Sales ($mil.)	(61.8%)	-	18.9	19.6	0.5	0.2
Net income ($ mil.)	-	-	1.8	1.2	0.0	(0.0)
Market value ($ mil.)	-	-	-	-	-	-
Employees	-	-	-	-	-	150

YORK HOSPITAL

1001 S GEORGE ST
YORK, PA 174033645
Phone: 717 851-2345
Fax: -
Web: www.wellspan.org

CEO: Donald B Dellinger
CFO: Michael F O'Connor
HR: -
FYE: June 30
Type: Private

York Hospital, operating as WellSpan York Hospital, takes its name from the community whose health it seeks to preserve. Part of WellSpan Health, the medical center has about 570 beds and serves residents of York and surrounding area of south-central Pennsylvania. It is a regional leader in cardiovascular and orthopedic care and has programs in other specialty areas, including oncology, behavioral health, and geriatrics. Additionally, WellSpan York Hospital operates a Level 1 trauma center, offers outpatient surgery, emergency, home health, and diagnostic imaging services. It is also has teaching and research programs. The hospital was founded in 1880.

	Annual Growth	06/14	06/15	06/16	06/18	06/20
Sales ($mil.)	4.7%	-	925.9	990.5	1,063.5	1,163.9
Net income ($ mil.)	(28.3%)	-	82.9	17.9	181.2	15.8
Market value ($ mil.)	-	-	-	-	-	-
Employees	-	-	-	-	-	6,200

YORK PENNSYLVANIA HOSPITAL COMPANY LLC

325 S BELMONT ST
YORK, PA 174032608
Phone: 717 843-8623
Fax: -
Web: www.mhyork.org

CEO: Sally J Dixon
CFO: Brent Smith
HR: -
FYE: June 30
Type: Private

Memorial Hospital serves the York County region of southeastern Pennsylvania, in the midst of Amish country. The hospital offers emergency, critical care, diagnostic, surgery, and rehabilitation services, as well as specialty cardiovascular, orthopedic, and obstetric services. In addition to the 100-bed acute care facility, Memorial Hospital operates Greenbriar Medical Center (a diagnostic imaging and rehabilitation center), the Surgical Center of York (outpatient surgery facility), home health and hospice agencies, and primary and specialist care clinics. Memorial Hospital is part of the Community Health Systems (CHS) network.

	Annual Growth	06/08	06/09	06/10	06/12	06/15
Sales ($mil.)	(0.6%)	-	100.7	100.8	102.0	97.2
Net income ($ mil.)	-	-	-	2.1	(5.9)	(1.7)
Market value ($ mil.)	-	-	-	-	-	-
Employees	-	-	-	-	-	900

YORK WATER CO

NMS: YORW

130 East Market Street
York, PA 17401
Phone: 717 845-3601
Fax: -
Web: www.yorkwater.com

CEO: Jeffrey R Hines
CFO: Matthew E Poff
HR: -
FYE: December 31
Type: Public

The York Water Company goes with the flow, as long as its water flows primarily within York County, Pennsylvania. The regulated water utility distributes approximately 20.1 million gallons of water daily to 39 municipalities in York County, and to nine communities in nearby Adams County. It serves more than 71,400 residential and business customers in a service territory with a population of 201,000. York Water obtains its water primarily from two reservoirs that together hold about 2.2 billion gallons. It gets an additional 12 million gallons of untreated water per day from the Susquehanna River.

	Annual Growth	12/19	12/20	12/21	12/22	12/23
Sales ($mil.)	8.3%	51.6	53.9	55.1	60.1	71.0
Net income ($ mil.)	13.3%	14.4	16.6	17.0	19.6	23.8
Market value ($ mil.)	(4.3%)	660.9	667.9	713.5	644.7	553.5
Employees	5.2%	106	108	110	116	130

YOUNG BROADCASTING, LLC

599 LEXINGTON AVE
NEW YORK, NY 100226030
Phone: 517 372-8282
Fax: –
Web: www.klfy.com

CEO: –
CFO: James A Morgan
HR: –
FYE: December 31
Type: Private

New Young Broadcasting Holding Co. (formerly known as Young Broadcasting) is a television broadcaster that owns 10 TV stations throughout the country. Five of its stations are affiliated with Walt Disney's ABC network and serve small and midsized markets. Three of its stations are affiliated with CBS, and it has one station operating in San Francisco affiliated with News Corporation's MyNetworkTV and an NBC station in Iowa. New Young Broadcasting also operates a national television sales representation firm, Adam Young Inc. In mid-2013 the company agreed to merge with Media General.

	Annual Growth	12/03	12/04	12/05	12/06	12/07
Sales ($mil.)	(30.9%)	–	–	–	225.2	155.7
Net income ($ mil.)	–	–	–	–	(56.6)	(72.7)
Market value ($ mil.)	–	–	–	–	–	–
Employees	–	–	–	–	–	1,097

YOUNG ELECTRIC SIGN COMPANY INC

2401 S FOOTHILL DR
SALT LAKE CITY, UT 841091479
Phone: 801 464-4600
Fax: –
Web: www.yesco.com

CEO: –
CFO: –
HR: Kelli Pachowicz
FYE: December 31
Type: Private

YESCO makes signs shine. Young Electric Sign Company (YESCO) custom designs displays and signs for companies of all sizes and in a variety of industries. Products include neon signs, billboards, custom spectaculars, LED video displays, and electronic message centers. The company also provides maintenance and repair services for its products and retrofit services which reduce energy costs. It boasts more than 2,000 sign installations across the US and around the world. YESCO has locations in about 27 states and one location in Canada. In early 2015, the company was acquired by electronics giant Samsung.

YOUNG LIFE

420 N CASCADE AVE
COLORADO SPRINGS, CO 809033325
Phone: 719 381-1800
Fax: –
Web: www.younglife.org

CEO: –
CFO: –
HR: Ann Shackelton
FYE: September 30
Type: Private

Young Life is focused on promoting Christianity among teenagers in the US and in more than 50 other countries. Founded in 1941, the not-for-profit organization provides activities and support for junior high, middle school, and high school students located in rural and urban communities. Young Life also operates week-long summer camp programs at about 20 locations throughout North America, as well as retreats held throughout the year. The group has grown throughout the years from a single club in Texas to about 600 international Young Life ministries dotting the globe. The organization boasts about 3,000 staffers and more than 27,000 volunteers.

	Annual Growth	09/12	09/13	09/14	09/15	09/16
Sales ($mil.)	7.6%	–	276.1	311.2	331.4	343.5
Net income ($ mil.)	1.4%	–	18.0	31.9	29.9	18.7
Market value ($ mil.)	–	–	–	–	–	–
Employees	–	–	–	–	–	3,100

YOUNGS NURSERIES INCORPORATED

211 DANBURY RD
WILTON, CT 068974005
Phone: 203 762-5511
Fax: –
Web: www.youngsnurseries.com

CEO: –
CFO: –
HR: –
FYE: December 31
Type: Private

Young's Nurseries is actually more than 70 years old. The company, founded in 1930 by brothers John and David Young, operates two nurseries in Wilton and Woodbury, Connecticut. It offers trees, shrubs, flowering and foliage plants, and local favorites along with delivery and installation. Its design center specializes in landscape design and installation, including pools, patios, and water features, for home owners and businesses. The company is owned by its president Scott Denison and vice presidents Thomas Daily, Dave Gindek, and Thomas Kuring.

	Annual Growth	12/04	12/05	12/06	12/07	12/08
Sales ($mil.)	(0.9%)	–	11.2	11.3	10.7	10.9
Net income ($ mil.)	–	–	0.1	0.2	0.4	(0.0)
Market value ($ mil.)	–	–	–	–	–	–
Employees	–	–	–	–	–	52

YOUNGSTOWN STATE UNIVERSITY INC

1 UNIVERSITY PLZ
YOUNGSTOWN, OH 445550002
Phone: 330 941-3000
Fax: –
Web: www.ysu.edu

CEO: –
CFO: –
HR: –
FYE: June 30
Type: Private

Youngstown State University (YSU) offers about 100 undergraduate majors, more than 30 graduate programs, and doctorate programs in education and physical therapy. The university has an enrollment of approximately 14,000 students in its six undergraduate colleges (business administration; education; health and human services; fine and performing arts; liberal arts and social sciences; and science, technology, engineering, and mathematics), as well as a school of graduate studies and research. Its tuition is the lowest among Ohio's major public universities. Its athletic teams are known as the Penguins.

	Annual Growth	06/01	06/02	06/05	06/06	06/17
Sales ($mil.)	(14.1%)	–	1,141.2	92.9	98.5	116.3
Net income ($ mil.)	–	–	0.0	(6.6)	(4.1)	(1.2)
Market value ($ mil.)	–	–	–	–	–	–
Employees	–	–	–	–	–	2,105

YUM CHINA HOLDINGS INC

101 East Park Boulevard, Suite 805
Plano, TX 75074
Phone: 469 980-2898
Fax: –
Web: www.yumchina.com

NYS: YUMC
CEO: Joey Wat
CFO: Andy Yeung
HR: –
FYE: December 31
Type: Public

Yum China Holdings owns and operates about 13,000 fast food restaurants across China, making it the largest western fast food company active in the country. The company operates the popular quick-service restaurant chains Pizza Hut, KFC, and Taco Bell, as well as hot pot restaurant brand Huang Ji Huang, Little Sheep, KFC-style Chinese food quick-service chain East Dawning, and coffee shop chain COFFii & JOY. Yum China owns and operates most of its restaurants, with approximately 15% being franchise locations. KFC is the company's biggest operation with more than 9,000 restaurants.

	Annual Growth	12/19	12/20	12/21	12/22	12/23
Sales ($mil.)	5.8%	8,776.0	8,263.0	9,853.0	9,569.0	10,978
Net income ($ mil.)	3.8%	713.0	784.0	990.0	442.0	827.0
Market value ($ mil.)	(3.0%)	19,540	23,236	20,285	22,243	17,269
Employees	(1.0%)	450,000	406,000	450,000	406,000	432,000

YUM! BRANDS INC   NYS: YUM

1441 Gardiner Lane
Louisville, KY 40213
Phone: 502 874-8300
Fax: –
Web: www.yum.com

CEO: Mark King
CFO: Christopher Turner
HR: –
FYE: December 31
Type: Public

YUM! Brands is the largest fast-food operator in the world in terms of number of locations, with more than 55,000 KFC, Pizza Hut, and Taco Bell outlets in more than 155 countries. The company's flagship chains are #1 chicken fryer KFC (with about 28,000), top pizza joint Pizza Hut (more than 19,000), Habit Burger Grill restaurant (some 350 units) and quick-service Mexican leader Taco Bell (roughly 8,200). Franchisees, affiliates, and licensed operators run about 45% of the company's restaurants. The company was incorporated in 1997.

	Annual Growth	12/19	12/20	12/21	12/22	12/23
Sales ($mil.)	6.0%	5,597.0	5,652.0	6,584.0	6,842.0	7,076.0
Net income ($ mil.)	5.4%	1,294.0	904.0	1,575.0	1,325.0	1,597.0
Market value ($ mil.)	6.7%	28,305	30,505	39,020	35,990	36,715
Employees	(7.4%)	34,000	38,000	36,000	36,000	25,000

YUMA ENERGY INC (NEW)   NBB: YUMA Q

1177 West Loop South, Suite 1825
Houston, TX 77027
Phone: 713 968-7000
Fax: –
Web: www.yumaenergyinc.com

CEO: –
CFO: –
HR: –
FYE: December 31
Type: Public

Not as ancient as Egypt's pyramids, but quite venerable in its own right, Pyramid Oil has been in business for more than a century, focusing on the exploration, development, and production of crude oil and natural gas. The company's major operations and all of its income-producing assets are located in Kern and Santa Barbara counties in Southern California, where it owns and operates about 30 oil and gas leases. Pyramid Oil also holds minority stakes in some oil and gas leases in New York, Texas, and Wyoming. In 2008 Pyramid Oil reported proved reserves of more than 470,000 barrels of oil and 330 million cu. ft. of natural gas. Company chairman Michael Herman owns about 36% of Pyramid Oil.

	Annual Growth	12/14	12/15	12/16	12/17	12/18
Sales ($mil.)	(16.1%)	43.3	23.7	14.8	25.4	21.5
Net income ($ mil.)	–	(20.2)	(11.0)	(41.6)	(5.4)	(15.6)
Market value ($ mil.)	(46.3%)	2.8	0.3	5.3	1.8	0.2
Employees	(13.5%)	41	30	30	31	23

YUMA REGIONAL MEDICAL CENTER INC

2400 S AVENUE A
YUMA, AZ 853647170
Phone: 928 344-2000
Fax: –
Web: www.yumaregional.org

CEO: Pat T Walz
CFO: Tony Struck
HR: Diane Poirot
FYE: September 30
Type: Private

Yuma Regional Medical Center (YRMC) is an acute care hospital that provides medical services for Yuma, Arizona, and its surrounding communities. The not-for-profit hospital, which has more than 400 beds and 400 doctors, provides general medical, surgical, and emergency services. YRMC also operates about 45 additional facilities around Yuma, including a rehabilitation hospital, laboratories, a wound care clinic, primary care clinics, and diagnostic imaging centers.

	Annual Growth	09/18	09/19	09/20	09/21	09/22
Sales ($mil.)	12.1%	–	544.0	512.0	643.1	765.9
Net income ($ mil.)	37.9%	–	28.3	54.0	167.5	74.1
Market value ($ mil.)	–	–	–	–	–	–
Employees	–	–	–	–	–	2,400

YUME, INC.

601 MONTGOMERY ST STE 1600
SAN FRANCISCO, CA 941112602
Phone: 650 591-9400
Fax: –
Web: –

CEO: –
CFO: Ed Reginelli
HR: Stephanie Parks
FYE: December 31
Type: Private

YuMe's technology enables video advertisements to display on personal computers, smartphones, tablets, set-top boxes, game consoles, and Internet-connected TVs. YuMe makes money by selling on a cost-per-click basis, and its technology matches the viewer with the most appropriate ad, so that an ad for acne cream won't appear on a video targeting an older demographic. Advertising agencies such as Omnicom use YuMe to power digital ads on behalf of some 880 customers, including American Express, AT&T, GlaxoSmithKline, Home Depot, and McDonald's. The company was acquired in 2018 by digital media advertising firm, RhythmOne. The combined company operates as YuMe by RhythmOne.

YUNHONG GREEN CTI LTD   NAS: YHGJ

22160 N. Pepper Road
Barrington, IL 60010
Phone: 847 382-1000
Fax: 847 382-1219
Web: www.ctiindustries.com

CEO: –
CFO: –
HR: –
FYE: December 31
Type: Public

CTI Industries is full of hot air, and that's just fine considering its best-selling product is usually filled with helium. The company designs, produces, and distributes foil balloons and latex balloons for parties, fairs, amusement parks, and other entertainment-related venues. In addition to its novelty products, CTI makes flexible containers, primarily zippered bags and pouches for food and household use, and film products, including specialty film for medical applications and laminated, coated, and printed films that are sold to industrial and commercial customers who generally convert them into flexible packaging for liquid food products. CTI's largest market is the US, followed by Mexico and the UK.

	Annual Growth	12/18	12/19	12/20	12/21	12/22
Sales ($mil.)	(24.5%)	55.6	40.5	26.5	24.1	18.0
Net income ($ mil.)	–	(3.6)	(7.1)	(4.4)	(8.3)	(1.5)
Market value ($ mil.)	(23.8%)	49.6	13.5	27.6	19.1	16.7
Employees	(40.3%)	457	380	366	66	58

YWCA OF THE USA, NATIONAL BOARD (INC)

1020 19TH ST NW
WASHINGTON, DC 200366101
Phone: 202 467-0801
Fax: –
Web: www.ywca.org

CEO: Lorraine Cole
CFO: –
HR: –
FYE: August 31
Type: Private

Although it has yet to be immortalized in song like its male counterpart, YWCA of the U.S.A. promotes the empowerment of women and girls through some 300 locations across the US. The not-for-profit organization provides 2.6 million women with services such as sports and physical fitness programs, shelters, child care, employment training and job placement, and youth development programs. It also sponsors racial justice, antiviolence, and women's economic advancement programs. YWCA of the U.S.A. is a founding member of World YWCA, which represents more than 25 million women in about 120 countries. The first YWCA in the US was founded in New York City in 1858. The national organization was created in 1907.

	Annual Growth	08/09	08/10	08/11	08/12	08/17
Sales ($mil.)	24.0%	–	1.3	2.5	2.4	5.7
Net income ($ mil.)	–	–	(2.4)	(1.7)	(2.7)	(1.3)
Market value ($ mil.)	–	–	–	–	–	–
Employees	–	–	–	–	–	53

Z GALLERIE, LLC

1855 W 139TH ST
GARDENA, CA 902493013
Phone: 310 630-1200
Fax: –
Web: www.zgallerie.com

CEO: –
CFO: –
HR: –
FYE: December 31
Type: Private

Cain and Abel they're not! Brothers and executives Joe and Mike Zeiden founded Z Gallerie in 1979, using their parents' garage for a warehouse and production facility. Initially Z Gallerie (later joined by sister Carole Malfatti) sold poster art, but in the 1980s the trio added home furnishings and accessories to the merchandising mix. Today Z Gallerie stores, which span some 10,000 sq. ft. on average, feature bedding and pillows, dinnerware, glassware, rugs, lamps, candleholders, clocks, frames and albums, games, and gifts. The company's eclectic pieces are sold through its website and about 55 US retail locations in nearly 20 states. Z Gallerie is privately owned.

	Annual Growth	03/08	03/09	03/10*	12/11	12/12
Sales ($mil.)	139.4%	–	–	30.8	154.4	176.4
Net income ($ mil.)	176.5%	–	–	3.3	20.6	25.5
Market value ($ mil.)	–	–	–	–	–	–
Employees	–	–	–	–	–	950

*Fiscal year change

Z PIZZA INC

909 CANYON VIEW DR
LAGUNA BEACH, CA 926512612
Phone: 323 377-6464
Fax: –
Web: www.zpizza.com

CEO: –
CFO: –
HR: –
FYE: December 31
Type: Private

Zis company eez zealous about zee healzy pizza piez. Z Pizza operates and franchises a chain of more than 70 zpizza gourmet pizza parlors in California and about a dozen other states. The company serves brick oven pizzas made with such gourmet toppings as pili pili, Shitake mushrooms, truffle oil; natural ingredients include additive-free meats and organic tomato sauce. zpizza also offers sandwiches, calzones, salads, and desserts. Catering to a younger, urban market, the restaurants feature sofas, overstuffed lounge chairs, and ottomans for dine-in service; most locations also offer take-out and delivery, as well as catering services. Chairman Sid Fanarof founded the chain in 1986.

ZACHARY CONFECTIONS, INC.

2130 W STATE ROAD 28
FRANKFORT, IN 460418771
Phone: 765 659-4751
Fax: –
Web: www.zacharyconfections.com

CEO: John J Zachary Jr
CFO: Lance Aukerman
HR: Susan Kuhn
FYE: June 30
Type: Private

Candy corn, chocolate bunnies, bon-bons in a big, red, heart-shaped box -- these are things that make the holidays sweet, and Zachary Confections makes them. The company also makes boxed chocolates, chocolate-covered raisins, mints, caramels, and marshmallow candies, among others. In addition to making candy for the usual holidays, it also offers every-day, private-label and corporate-gift confections. Zachary Confections' manufacturing facility is located in Frankfort, Indiana. The Zachary family owns and runs the company, which was founded in 1950 by J. J. and Helen Zachary.

ZAGG INC

910 W LEGACY CENTER WAY STE 500
MIDVALE, UT 840475845
Phone: 801 263-0699
Fax: –
Web: www.zagg.com

CEO: Chris M Ahern
CFO: Taylor D Smith
HR: –
FYE: December 31
Type: Private

ZAGG is a global leader in accessories and technologies that empower mobile lifestyles. Its award-winning product portfolio includes screen protection, power management solutions, mobile keyboards, cases, and personal audio. Its smart phone and tablet screen protectors and cases are marketed primarily under the InvisibleShield name. The company's other products include power stations and wireless chargers; earbuds, headphones, and speakers; and keyboards, and other accessories. ZAGG mobile accessories are available worldwide and can be found at leading retailers including Verizon, AT&T, T-Mobile, Best Buy, Walmart, Target, Currys, MediaMarkt, JB Hi-Fi, Harvey Norman, and Vodaphone.

ZANETT, INC.

635 MADISON AVE FL 15
NEW YORK, NY 100221009
Phone: 212 201-3500
Fax: –
Web: –

CEO: Claudio M Guazzoni
CFO: Dennis Harkins
HR: –
FYE: December 31
Type: Private

Zanett is in the business of collecting companies. The company selects and acquires IT consulting firms that serve commercial and government clients, including FORTUNE 500 and mid-market businesses and government agencies that operate in the defense and homeland security sectors. Services offered include consulting, systems integration, supply chain management, implementation, support, and network design. Its commercial clients come from a variety of industries such as financial services, health care, and manufacturing. Founder Claudio Guazzoni and his uncle, Bruno Guazzoni, own about 24% and 28% of Zanett respectively.

ZAP

2 West 3rd Street
Santa Rosa, CA 95401
Phone: 707 525-8658
Fax: –
Web: www.zapworld.com

CEO: –
CFO: –
HR: –
FYE: December 31
Type: Public

ZAP is driving the future. An acronym for "zero air pollution," ZAP provides efficient, alternative-energy vehicles and products for corporate and government fleets, security, and environmentally conscious consumers around the globe. Products include the Xebra Sedan and Truck, Zappy 3 and Zapino scooters, ZAP Taxi, electric bicycles. The company has two primary businesses -- ZAP Automotive (alternative energy vehicles) and ZAP Power Systems (personal transporters and ATVs) -- to manufacture products that meet the growing demands of eco-friendly consumers.

	Annual Growth	12/12	12/13	12/14	12/15	12/16
Sales ($mil.)	(32.0%)	50.3	51.5	28.7	29.5	10.8
Net income ($ mil.)	–	(21.8)	(15.0)	(17.6)	(14.1)	(23.5)
Market value ($ mil.)	(36.8%)	47.9	60.6	58.2	37.9	7.6
Employees	(3.7%)	506	405	402	400	435

ZAYO GROUP HOLDINGS, INC.

1821 30TH ST STE A
BOULDER, CO 803011075
Phone: 303 381-4683
Fax: –
Web: www.zayo.com

CEO: Steve Smith
CFO: Matt Steinfort
HR: –
FYE: June 30
Type: Private

Zayo Group Holdings is the leading global communications infrastructure provider, empowering some of the world's largest and most innovative companies to continue changing the world by providing them with the purpose-built network and connectivity solutions needed to drive what's next. The company provides high-speed fiber-based bandwidth and services over their network that exceeds 141,000 route miles. Spanning around 1,400 on-net data centers across North America and Europe, the company penetrates more than 400 markets. Zayo's tailored connectivity and edge solutions enable carriers, cloud providers, data centers, schools, and enterprises to deliver exceptional experiences, from core to cloud to edge.

ZAZA ENERGY CORP.

NBB: ZAZA

1301 McKinney St Suite 2800
Houston, TX 77010
Phone: 713 595-1900
Fax: –
Web: www.zazaenergy.com

CEO: Todd A Brooks
CFO: Paul F Jansen
HR: –
FYE: December 31
Type: Public

Despite the current economic downturn, Toreador Resources is hopeful that a future bull market in oil prices will lift its revenues and its long term prospects. The oil and gas explorer owns royalty and mineral interests in properties located in France (in the Paris Basin Oil Shale), where it has 340,000 net acres of primarily undeveloped land. Toreador, sells its oil and production to France-based oil giant TOTAL, which accounts for 98% of total revenues. Once a global player, the company has shifted all its attention to its France. In 2012 the company merged its operations with US oil and gas explorer ZaZa Energy, LCC. The expanded company was named ZaZa Energy Corporation.

	Annual Growth	12/10	12/11	12/12	12/13	12/14
Sales ($mil.)	2.3%	10.5	17.6	205.2	8.9	11.5
Net income ($ mil.)	–	6.5	(2.9)	(106.2)	(67.6)	(8.2)
Market value ($ mil.)	–	–	–	26.9	12.6	33.1
Employees	–	–	123	70	29	32

ZEBRA TECHNOLOGIES CORP.

NMS: ZBRA

3 Overlook Point
Lincolnshire, IL 60069
Phone: 847 634-6700
Fax: –
Web: www.zebra.com

CEO: William J Burns
CFO: Nathan A Winters
HR: –
FYE: December 31
Type: Public

Zebra Technologies is a global leader providing Enterprise Asset Intelligence solutions in the Automation Identification and Data Capture (AIDC) industry. The company also designs, manufactures, and sells a broad range of products and solutions, including mobile computers, barcode scanners and imagers, RFID readers, specialty printers for barcode labeling and personal identification, real-time location systems (RTLS), related accessories and supplies, such as labels and other consumables, and related software applications. Zebra's customers are in the retail and e-commerce, manufacturing, transportation and logistics, healthcare, public sector, and other industries. About half of the company's revenue were generated in the US.

	Annual Growth	12/19	12/20	12/21	12/22	12/23
Sales ($mil.)	0.5%	4,485.0	4,448.0	5,627.0	5,781.0	4,584.0
Net income ($ mil.)	(14.1%)	544.0	504.0	837.0	463.0	296.0
Market value ($ mil.)	1.7%	13,124	19,746	30,581	13,174	14,043
Employees	4.4%	8,200	8,800	9,800	10,500	9,750

ZEELAND COMMUNITY HOSPITAL

8333 FELCH ST STE 202
ZEELAND, MI 494642609
Phone: 616 772-4644
Fax: –
Web: www.spectrumhealth.org

CEO: –
CFO: –
HR: –
FYE: June 30
Type: Private

Zeeland Community Hospital provides acute medical services for the residents of western Michigan. The hospital has nearly 60 beds and provides emergency, diagnostic, inpatient, and outpatient services. Its specialty services include diabetes care, orthopedics, cardiology, pain management, rehabilitation, and surgery. Zeeland Community Hospital has some 200 physicians on its medical staff, which includes its two affiliated physician groups, Zeeland Physicians and Georgetown Physicians. Zeeland Community Hospital was founded in 1928 as a 10-bed hospital.

	Annual Growth	09/03	09/04	09/05	09/09*	06/12
Sales ($mil.)	5.8%	–	–	36.5	47.8	54.2
Net income ($ mil.)	(7.1%)	–	–	2.8	1.8	1.7
Market value ($ mil.)	–	–	–	–	–	–
Employees	–	–	–	–	–	33

*Fiscal year change

ZELTIQ AESTHETICS, INC.

4410 ROSEWOOD DR
PLEASANTON, CA 945883050
Phone: 925 474-2500
Fax: –
Web: www.coolsculpting.com

CEO: Mark J Foley
CFO: Taylor Harris
HR: –
FYE: December 31
Type: Private

ZELTIQ Aesthetics is winning the battle of the bulge. The company's CoolSculpting device offers a non-invasive alternative to liposuction to knock out fat cells. The treatment uses controlled cooling to reduce the temperature of fat cells and melt fat without causing scar tissue or skin damage. ZELTIQ sells the CoolSculpting device and related consumables in the US for use on targeted areas of the torso and thighs, but it is also used more freely in about 45 other international markets. The CoolSculpting system is sold to dermatologists, plastic surgeons, and aesthetic specialists such as medical spas. The company was incorporated in 2005 as Juniper Medical. Allergan bought ZELTIQ for $2.5 billion in 2017.

	Annual Growth	12/11	12/12	12/13	12/14	12/15
Sales ($mil.)	51.3%	–	–	111.6	174.5	255.4
Net income ($ mil.)	–	–	–	(19.3)	1.5	41.8
Market value ($ mil.)	–	–	–	–	–	–
Employees	–	–	–	–	–	686

ZENDESK, INC.

989 MARKET ST
SAN FRANCISCO, CA 941031708
Phone: 415 418-7506
Fax: –
Web: www.zendesk.com

CEO: –
CFO: –
HR: –
FYE: December 31
Type: Private

Zendesk is a service-first CRM company that builds software designed to improve customer relationships. Its customer service and sales solutions are built to help organizations address the rise in customer expectations and to craft their customer experiences into a competitive differentiator through Zendesk Support, Zendesk Talk, Zendesk Chat, or Zendesk Guide. Zendesk serves customers in over 30 languages and in more than 160 countries. The company has an aggregate of approximately 111,100 logos using its solutions. Zendesk was founded in 2007. The US accounts for about half of the company's total sales.

ZENITH ENERGY LOGISTICS PARTNERS LP

3900 ESSEX LN STE 700
HOUSTON, TX 770275114
Phone: 713 395-6200
Fax: –
Web: –

CEO: Jeffrey R Armstrong
CFO: Carlos Ruiz
HR: –
FYE: December 31
Type: Private

Arc Logistics Partners owns more than a dozen fuel storage terminals in 10 states that can hold almost 5 million barrels of oil, ethanol, and other types of petroleum products. It also owns two rail transloading facilities in Alabama that can move 23,000 barrels per day and a liquefied natural gas storage facility in Mississippi. Customers include oil and gas companies, refineries, marketers, distributors, and other industrial manufacturers. Arc Logistics Partners was formed by Lightfoot Capital Partners (which is majority owned by GE). Organized as a limited partnership, Arc is exempt from paying corporate income tax as long as it distributes quarterly dividends to shareholders. The partnership went public in 2013.

ZERIFY INC

NBB: ZRFY

1090 King Georges Post Road, Suite 603
Edison, NJ 08837
Phone: 732 661-9641
Fax: –
Web: www.strikeforcetech.com

CEO: Mark L Kay
CFO: Philip E Blocker
HR: –
FYE: December 31
Type: Public

StrikeForce Technologies doesn't want your identity getting away from you. The company develops software that guards consumers and businesses against identity theft, encompassing areas such as identity management, remote access, and biometric layering. StrikeForce's products guard against phishing attempts, keylogging, malware, and spyware. StrikeForce also offers professional services such as consulting, implementation, maintenance, and support. Its customers come from a range of industries, including financial services, health care, and manufacturing.

	Annual Growth	12/17	12/18	12/19	12/20	12/21
Sales ($mil.)	(8.4%)	0.3	0.2	0.8	0.2	0.2
Net income ($ mil.)	–	(3.2)	(3.3)	(3.5)	(10.0)	(17.2)
Market value ($ mil.)	58.9%	6.0	13.9	3.1	61.0	38.4
Employees	2.7%	9	9	9	9	10

ZERO MOUNTAIN, INC.

8425 HIGHWAY 45
FORT SMITH, AR 729169383
Phone: 479 434-5478
Fax: –
Web: www.zeromtn.com

CEO: Mark Rumsey
CFO: Toni Bell
HR: –
FYE: June 30
Type: Private

Sometimes being less than zero -- zero degrees that is -- is a good thing. The company operates four temperature-controlled warehouses in Arkansas (Johnson, Fort Smith, Lowell, and Russellville). Combined, the company's facilities include about 30 million cu. ft. of below-zero storage space. In addition to warehousing, Zero Mountain offers freezer storage (0 o to -10 o Fahrenheit), ammonia refrigeration, forced air circulation, and blast freezing. Major Zero Mountain customers have included poultry producers Cargill, ConAgra, Simmons, Tyson Foods, and Wal-Mart. The company exports frozen food products to over 30 countries worldwide, as well as trademarked mugs, apparel, and hats. The company was founded in 1955.

	Annual Growth	06/06	06/07	06/08	06/10	06/18
Sales ($mil.)	6.8%	–	27.4	27.4	20.5	56.8
Net income ($ mil.)	11.3%	–	1.9	1.9	0.9	6.2
Market value ($ mil.)	–	–	–	–	–	–
Employees	–	–	–	–	–	90

ZHEJIANG DASHANG MEDIA CO LTD

NBB: TKVR

1 Van Der Donck Street, Second Floor
Yonkers, NY 10701
Phone: 914 623-0700
Fax: 914 395-3498
Web: www.evcinc.com

CEO: –
CFO: –
HR: –
FYE: December 31
Type: Public

EVCI provides on-campus college education through three institutions: the Interboro Institute, Technical Career Institutes, and Pennsylvania School of Business. Interboro (2,700 students) offers associate degrees to students who have GEDs or did not graduate from high school. Students earn an associate of occupational studies degree in areas such as accounting, medical assistant, executive assistant, paralegal studies, ophthalmic dispensing, and security. Technical Career (3,000 students) degrees include office technology, facilities management technology, and industrial technology. The Pennsylvania School of Business (325 students) offers training in office and medical billing operations, among others.

	Annual Growth	12/02	12/03	12/04	12/05	12/06
Sales ($mil.)	43.5%	15.4	20.2	33.1	50.7	65.4
Net income ($ mil.)	–	(2.0)	3.4	6.3	0.4	(13.5)
Market value ($ mil.)	(8.8%)	2.7	22.8	40.6	6.8	1.9
Employees	31.1%	237	303	531	849	700

ZIEGLER COS., INC. (WI)

NBB: ZGCO

200 South Wacker Drive, Suite 2000
Chicago, IL 60606
Phone: 312 263-0110
Fax: 312 263-5217
Web: www.ziegler.com

CEO: Thomas R Paprocki
CFO: –
HR: –
FYE: December 31
Type: Public

Health and wealth go hand-in-hand for The Ziegler Companies. The firm, operating through several subsidiaries, offers specialty investment banking and asset management services. Catering mainly to not-for-profit institutions such as health care providers, senior living facilities, charter schools, and churches, the company provides financing, advisory services, and securities underwriting, sales, and trading. It also serves renewable energy companies. In addition, Ziegler offers brokerage, financial planning, and asset management services, including its North Track family of mutual funds, to both institutional and individual investors.

	Annual Growth	12/09	12/10	12/11	12/12	12/13
Sales ($mil.)	(4.3%)	88.7	77.6	67.6	92.5	74.5
Net income ($ mil.)	23.6%	0.8	0.9	1.5	3.6	1.8
Market value ($ mil.)	21.1%	15.4	21.6	21.6	29.6	33.0
Employees	(4.0%)	309	279	254	255	262

ZIEGLER INC

901 W 94TH ST
MINNEAPOLIS, MN 554204299
Phone: 952 888-4121
Fax: –
Web: www.zieglercat.com

CEO: Stanley Erickson
CFO: –
HR: –
FYE: December 31
Type: Private

Here's a cat that doesn't have your tongue, but it does have your bulldozer. Caterpillar dealership Ziegler Inc., also known as Ziegler Cat, sells and leases new and used Caterpillar brand equipment for multiple industries including construction, forestry, mining, and waste. With a large rural sales territory, Ziegler also sells Challenger brand tractors and combines built by Agco Corp. (whose engines and components are made by CAT), and other ag equipment makers and brands (LEXION, Ag-Chem, Sunflower, and White Planters), as well as related industrial work tools. Sales are leveraged by stocking over 250,000 parts for Caterpillar and non-CAT equipment.

	Annual Growth	12/04	12/05	12/09	12/20	12/21
Sales ($mil.)	(4.1%)	–	0.2	0.1	0.1	0.0
Net income ($ mil.)	(4.8%)	–	0.0	(0.0)	0.0	0.0
Market value ($ mil.)	–	–	–	–	–	–
Employees	–	–	–	–	–	1,045

ZIFF DAVIS INC

NMS: ZD

114 5th Avenue, 15th Floor
New York, NY 10011
Phone: 212 503-3500
Fax: –
Web: www.j2.com

CEO: Vivek Shah
CFO: –
HR: –
FYE: December 31
Type: Public

Ziff Davis (formerly known as j2 Global) is a vertically-focused digital media and internet company. The company's Digital Media business specializes in the technology, shopping, gaming and entertainment, connectivity, and healthcare markets, offering content, tools and services to consumers and businesses. Its Cybersecurity and Martech business provides cloud-based subscription services to consumers and businesses including cybersecurity, privacy, and marketing technology. The company's portfolio of web properties and apps includes Mashable, PCMag, Humble Bundle, Speedtest, Black Friday, and RetailMeNot. About 85% of sales come from US customers.

	Annual Growth	12/19	12/20	12/21	12/22	12/23
Sales ($mil.)	(0.1%)	1,372.1	1,489.6	1,416.7	1,391.0	1,364.0
Net income ($ mil.)	(34.0%)	218.8	150.7	496.7	63.8	41.5
Market value ($ mil.)	(8.0%)	4,318.0	4,501.4	5,108.3	3,644.8	3,096.0
Employees	8.0%	3,090	4,700	4,900	4,400	4,200

ZIMMER BIOMET HOLDINGS INC

NYS: ZBH

345 East Main Street
Warsaw, IN 46580
Phone: 574 373-3333
Fax: –
Web: www.zimmerbiomet.com

CEO: Ivan Tornos
CFO: Suketu Upadhyay
HR: Jack Heeter
FYE: December 31
Type: Public

Zimmer Biomet is the top global manufacturer of reconstructive implants used in knee or hip replacement surgery. It makes a variety of other orthopedic devices including shoulder implants, bone and tissue grafting materials, sports medicine products, and trauma products for broken bones (such as screws). Additionally, Zimmer Biomet makes medical equipment used in orthopedic surgeries, and related surgical products. In 2022, the company completed the spin-off of its spine and dental businesses into a new public company, ZimVie Inc. (ZimVie). Zimmer Biomet sells its products in more than 100 countries and derives more than 40% of its revenue from outside the US.

	Annual Growth	12/19	12/20	12/21	12/22	12/23
Sales ($mil.)	(1.9%)	7,982.2	7,024.5	7,836.2	6,939.9	7,394.2
Net income ($ mil.)	(2.5%)	1,131.6	(138.9)	401.6	231.4	1,024.0
Market value ($ mil.)	(5.0%)	30,774	31,681	26,119	26,214	25,022
Employees	(2.5%)	19,900	20,000	19,500	18,000	18,000

ZIMMER GUNSUL FRASCA ARCHITECTS LLP

1223 SW WASHINGTON ST STE 200
PORTLAND, OR 972052360
Phone: 503 224-3860
Fax: –
Web: –

CEO: –
CFO: –
HR: –
FYE: December 31
Type: Private

Zimmer Gunsul Frasca may not be a household name, but the firm has created homes for businesses and institutions on both coasts. The company, which is among the nation's top 10 green design firms, provides architectural planning and interior and urban design services for customers through its offices in Los Angeles, Portland, Seattle, New York, and Washington, D.C. Zimmer Gunsul Frasca (ZGF) works on civic, corporate, academic, health care, and research facilities and has designed for such clients as the Environmental Protection Agency, Microsoft, Iowa State University, and The University of Arizona. The firm was established in 1942 by Norman Zimmer.

	Annual Growth	12/05	12/06	12/07	12/08	12/09
Sales ($mil.)	31.0%	–	–	65.8	149.0	112.9
Net income ($ mil.)	4827.8%	–	–	0.0	8.5	39.8
Market value ($ mil.)	–	–	–	–	–	–
Employees	–	–	–	–	–	600

ZINKAN ENTERPRISES, INC.

1919 CASE PKWY
TWINSBURG, OH 440872343
Phone: 330 487-1500
Fax: –
Web: www.getchemready.com

CEO: –
CFO: –
HR: –
FYE: December 31
Type: Private

Zinkan Enterprises is very enterprising when its comes to its special chemical production. The company is a manufacturer of specialty chemicals for use in a range of industries, including coal, utilities, oil and gas, aggregates and concrete, steel, and water treatment. The company's products are used in dust control freeze control, moisture control and material flow, among others. Zinkan has about 10 manufacturing and distribution locations in the US, mostly in the Midwest. It is also an authorized dealer of Liquidow and Matec Machinery Technology products.

	Annual Growth	06/05	06/06	06/07	06/08*	12/09
Sales ($mil.)	8.8%	–	–	21.4	23.2	25.3
Net income ($ mil.)	104.9%	–	–	0.7	0.9	3.1
Market value ($ mil.)	–	–	–	–	–	–
Employees	–	–	–	–	–	42

*Fiscal year change

ZION OIL & GAS INC

NBB: ZNOG

12655 N Central Expressway, Suite 1000
Dallas, TX 75243
Phone: 214 221-4610
Fax: 214 221-6510
Web: www.zionoil.com

CEO: John M Brown
CFO: Michael B Croswell Jr
HR: –
FYE: December 31
Type: Public

Zion Oil and Gas is on a mission in Israel. As an oil and gas exploration company, Zion has exploration operations primarily on two onshore properties that cover about 162,000 acres between Tel-Aviv and Haifa. The company operates through two licenses that were issued by the State of Israel, and it owns 100% of the working interest in both licenses. When it eventually discovers oil and gas, Zion has stated that it will focus its production operations on helping Israel become a more energy-independent country. The company, which was founded in 2000 by chairman John M. Brown, went public in 2007.

	Annual Growth	12/19	12/20	12/21	12/22	12/23
Sales ($mil.)	–	–	–	–	–	–
Net income ($ mil.)	–	(6.7)	(7.0)	(10.7)	(55.1)	(8.0)
Market value ($ mil.)	(18.8%)	110.5	576.0	106.2	36.5	47.9
Employees	(3.1%)	25	26	24	23	22

ZIONS BANCORPORATION, N.A.

NMS: ZION

One South Main
Salt Lake City, UT 84133-1109
Phone: 801 844-8208
Fax: –
Web: www.zionsbancorporation.com

CEO: Harris H Simmons
CFO: Paul E Burdiss
HR: Annette Langheinrich
FYE: December 31
Type: Public

Zions Bancorporation operates about 435 banking branches at year-end 2019, and is currently planning to close 12 branches during 2020. The Bank provides a full range of banking and related services, primarily in Arizona, California, Colorado, Idaho, Nevada, New Mexico, Oregon, Texas, Utah, Washington, and Wyoming. The Bank focuses on providing community banking services by continuously strengthening its core business lines of small- and medium-sized business and corporate banking; commercial and residential development, construction and term lending; retail banking; treasury cash management and related products and services; residential mortgage lending and servicing; trust and wealth management; capital markets activities, including municipal finance advisory and underwriting; and investment activities. It operates primarily through seven geographic regions, each with its own local branding, chief executive officer and management team. Still headquartered in Salt Lake City, Zions Bank was founded in 1873 as Utah's first bank by Mormon leader Brigham Young.

	Annual Growth	12/19	12/20	12/21	12/22	12/23
Assets ($mil.)	6.0%	69,172	81,479	93,200	89,545	87,203
Net income ($ mil.)	(4.5%)	816.0	539.0	1,129.0	907.0	680.0
Market value ($ mil.)	(4.1%)	7,692.1	6,435.8	9,357.3	7,283.2	6,499.5
Employees	(0.5%)	9,873	9,678	9,685	9,989	9,679

ZOETIS INC
NYS: ZTS

10 Sylvan Way
Parsippany, NJ 07054
Phone: 973 822-7000
Fax: –
Web: www.zoetis.com

CEO: Kristin C Peck
CFO: Wetteny Joseph
HR: –
FYE: December 31
Type: Public

Zoetis Inc. is a global leader in the animal health industry, focused on the discovery, development, manufacture and commercialization of medicines, vaccines, diagnostic products and services, biodevices, genetic tests and precision animal health technology. It has a diversified business, commercializing products across eight core species: dogs, cats, horses, cattle, swine, poultry, fish and sheep ? within seven major product categories: vaccines, parasiticides, anti-infectives, dermatology, other pharmaceutical products, medicated feed additives and animal health diagnostics. Zoetis boasts approximately 300 product lines sold in more than 100 countries around the world, making it one of the world's largest animal health businesses. Roughly 55% of the company's total revenue comes from the US.

	Annual Growth	12/19	12/20	12/21	12/22	12/23
Sales ($mil.)	8.1%	6,260.0	6,675.0	7,776.0	8,080.0	8,544.0
Net income ($ mil.)	11.8%	1,500.0	1,638.0	2,037.0	2,114.0	2,344.0
Market value ($ mil.)	10.5%	60,665	75,860	111,855	67,174	90,468
Employees	7.4%	10,600	11,300	12,100	13,800	14,100

ZOOLOGICAL SOCIETY OF SAN DIEGO

2920 ZOO DR
SAN DIEGO, CA 921011646
Phone: 619 231-1515
Fax: –
Web: www.sandiegozoowildlifealliance.org

CEO: Paul Baribault
CFO: David Franco
HR: Aida Rosa
FYE: December 31
Type: Private

San Diego Zoo Wildlife Alliance is a not-for-profit organization that operates the 100-acre San Diego Zoo, which cares for more than 12,000 individual animals representing more than 650 species and subspecies as well as a collection of more than 700,000 exotic plants. The Zoological Society also manages the 1,800-acre San Diego Zoo Safari Park and the center for Conservation and Research. The zoo entertains all with its daily shows, guided tours, and special events. The society also supports conservation science with its dedication to inspiring passion for nature. In 2021, San Diego Zoo Global, the parent organization of the zoo and Safari Park, announced that it is rebranding as the San Diego Zoo Wildlife Alliance.

	Annual Growth	12/12	12/13	12/14	12/15	12/19
Sales ($mil.)	16.2%	–	171.9	295.0	274.6	422.1
Net income ($ mil.)	943.2%	–	0.0	68.7	29.7	118.6
Market value ($ mil.)	–	–	–	–	–	–
Employees	–	–	–	–	–	2,300

ZOOM VIDEO COMMUNICATIONS INC
NMS: ZM

55 Almaden Boulevard, 6th Floor
San Jose, CA 95113
Phone: 888 799-9666
Fax: –
Web: www.zoom.com

CEO: Eric S Yuan
CFO: Kelly Steckelberg
HR: –
FYE: January 31
Type: Public

Zoom Videos Communications, Inc. enables people to connect to others, share ideas, make plans, and build toward a future limited only by their imagination. Zoom's frictionless communications and collaborative platform started with video as its foundation, and the company has set the standard for innovation ever since. That is why Zoom is an intuitive, scalable, and secure choice for large enterprises, small businesses, and individuals alike. Zoom's cloud-native platform delivers reliable, high-quality video and voice solutions that are easy to use, manage, and deploy; provide an attractive return on investment; and is scalable and easily integrates with physical spaces and applications. The company's largest market was the Americas region with about 70% of its revenue.

	Annual Growth	01/20	01/21	01/22	01/23	01/24
Sales ($mil.)	64.2%	622.7	2,651.4	4,099.9	4,393.0	4,527.2
Net income ($ mil.)	124.0%	25.3	672.3	1,375.6	103.7	637.5
Market value ($ mil.)	(4.1%)	23,467	114,433	47,450	23,067	19,871
Employees	30.8%	2,532	4,422	6,787	8,484	7,420

ZOOMAWAY TECHNOLOGIES INC
TVX: ZMA

960 Matley Lane #4
Reno, NV 89502
Phone: 866 848-3427
Fax: –
Web: www.zoomaway.ca

CEO: –
CFO: –
HR: –
FYE: December 31
Type: Public

Multivision Communications Corp. operates a subscription television service in Bolivia through wholly owned subsidiary, Multivision S.A. The company's service, which has more than 60 channels, is available in four main cities in Bolivia (Cochabamba, La Paz, Santa Cruz, and Sucre) and about 30 channels in Tarija. Multivision delivers its service via wireless MMDS technology (Multi-channel Multi-point Distribution System), so it isn't tethered to coaxial cables. The company also provides Wi-Fi Internet access and other data services in a joint-venture arrangement with South American telecom company, Entel. Multivision Communications was formed in 1987.

	Annual Growth	12/16	12/17	12/18	12/19	12/20
Sales ($mil.)	–	0.0	0.3	0.2	0.0	(0.0)
Net income ($ mil.)	–	(3.5)	(1.5)	(0.5)	(0.7)	(1.8)
Market value ($ mil.)	(37.7%)	1.7	0.6	0.2	0.8	0.3
Employees	–	–	–	–	–	–

ZOOMINFO TECHNOLOGIES INC
NMS: ZI

805 Broadway Street, Suite 900
Vancouver, WA 98660
Phone: 800 914-1220
Fax: –
Web: www.zoominfo.com

CEO: Henry Schuck
CFO: Cameron Hyzer
HR: Elaine Manuels
FYE: December 31
Type: Public

ZoomInfo Technologies is a global leader in modern go-to-market software, data, and intelligence for sales, marketing, operations, and recruiting teams for over 30,000 companies. The company delivers high-quality intelligence at scale by leveraging an artificial intelligence (AI) and machine learning (ML) powered engine that gathers data from millions of sources in real time and standardizes, matches to entities, verifies, cleans, and applies the processed data to companies and people at scale. With operations in the US and internationally, ZoomInfo generates roughly 90% of its revenue in the US.

	Annual Growth	12/19	12/20	12/21	12/22	12/23
Sales ($mil.)	43.4%	293.3	476.2	747.2	1,098.0	1,239.5
Net income ($ mil.)	–	(78.0)	(9.1)	116.8	63.2	107.3
Market value ($ mil.)	–	–	18,560	24,706	11,587	7,115.5
Employees	28.6%	1,287	1,747	2,742	3,540	3,516

ZOVIO INC
NBB: ZVOI

1811 E. Northrop Blvd.
Chandler, AZ 85286
Phone: 858 668-2586
Fax: –
Web: www.bridgepointeducation.com

CEO: Randy Hendricks
CFO: Kevin S Royal
HR: Stacey McGonegal
FYE: December 31
Type: Public

Zovio, Inc., formerly known as Bridgepoint Education, is an education technology services company. The company provides student recruitment and enrollment systems, retention strategies, educational tools and curriculums. The technology and academic services primarily relate to the educational infrastructure, including online course delivery and management, assessment, customer relations management and other internal administrative systems. This also includes providing support for curriculum and new program development, support for faculty training and development, technical support.

	Annual Growth	12/17	12/18	12/19	12/20	12/21
Sales ($mil.)	(13.9%)	478.4	443.4	417.8	397.1	263.0
Net income ($ mil.)	–	10.5	4.6	(54.8)	(49.0)	(42.3)
Market value ($ mil.)	(37.5%)	278.4	235.2	69.1	159.0	42.6
Employees	(29.3%)	5,600	4,790	4,420	1,550	1,400

ZUMIEZ INC

4001 204th Street S.W.
Lynnwood, WA 98036
Phone: 425 551-1500
Fax: –
Web: www.zumiez.com

NMS: ZUMZ
CEO: –
CFO: –
HR: –
FYE: February 3
Type: Public

Zumiez is a leading specialty retailer of apparel, footwear, accessories and hardgoods for young men and women who want to express their individuality through the fashion, music, art and culture of action sports, streetwear and other unique lifestyles. The company operates about 740 mall-based stores across North America, Europe and Australia, as well as an online store. It trades under three banners, Zumiez, Blue Tomato, and Fast Times. Zumiez was founded in 1978 by chairman Thomas Campion. The US generates about 85% of the company's total revenue.

	Annual Growth	02/20*	01/21	01/22	01/23*	02/24
Sales ($mil.)	(4.1%)	1,034.1	990.7	1,183.9	958.4	875.5
Net income ($ mil.)	–	66.9	76.2	119.3	21.0	(62.6)
Market value ($ mil.)	(13.2%)	618.2	854.4	857.8	510.7	351.0
Employees	(0.8%)	9,195	8,800	9,500	9,400	8,900

*Fiscal year change

ZURN ELKAY WATER SOLUTIONS CORP

511 W. Freshwater Way
Milwaukee, WI 53204
Phone: 855 480-5050
Fax: –
Web: www.zurn-elkay.com

NYS: ZWS
CEO: Todd A Adams
CFO: Mark W Peterson
HR: Glen Russell
FYE: December 31
Type: Public

Zurn Water Solutions Corporation (formerly known as Rexnord Corporation) is a leading provider of specification-driven water management solutions to the multi-billion-dollar construction market of primarily commercial and institutional buildings and to a lesser extent, to the waterworks and multi-family residential construction markets. Its product portfolio includes professional grade water safety and control, flow systems and hygienic and environmental products for public and private spaces that deliver superior value to building owners, positively impact the environment and human hygiene and reduce product installation time. The company's products are marketed and sold under widely recognized brand names, including Zurn, Wilkins, Green Turtle, World Dryer, StainlessDrains.com, JUST, Hadrian, and Wade. Zurn racks up most of its sales in the US.

	Annual Growth	03/20*	12/20	12/21	12/22	12/23
Sales ($mil.)	(7.3%)	2,068.3	1,433.1	910.9	1,281.8	1,530.5
Net income ($ mil.)	(11.1%)	180.1	118.2	120.9	61.7	112.7
Market value ($ mil.)	6.7%	3,905.2	6,802.6	6,270.3	3,643.3	5,066.2
Employees	(22.9%)	6,800	6,570	1,300	2,700	2,400

*Fiscal year change

ZVELO INC.

295 Interlocken Boulevard, Suite 500
Broomfield, CO 80021
Phone: 303 444-1600
Fax: 303 444-1640
Web: www.esoft.com

NBB: ZVLO
CEO: Jeffrey Finn
CFO: –
HR: –
FYE: December 31
Type: Public

zvelo (formerly eSoft) strives to untangle the World Wide Web. Through its zveloDB URL database, zvelo categorizes content from websites; customers then use the database in web filtering, ad placement, endpoint security, and other applications. The company primarily licenses zveloDB to OEM partners, including wireless and Internet service providers, advertising network providers, content filtering firms, and gateway appliance vendors. In addition to being sold as part of a software development kit, zveloDB is available via the company's cloud-based zveloNET network. In 2010 eSoft sold its Internet security appliance business and changed its name to zvelo as part of a rebranding effort.

	Annual Growth	12/97	12/98	12/99	12/00	12/01
Sales ($mil.)	66.6%	1.2	3.9	9.1	8.8	9.5
Net income ($ mil.)	–	(0.4)	(2.9)	(10.8)	(16.0)	(8.4)
Market value ($ mil.)	–	–	87.0	445.3	14.3	12.4
Employees	34.0%	22	31	99	82	71

ZYLA LIFE SCIENCES, LLC

100 SAUNDERS RD STE 300
LAKE FOREST, IL 600452508
Phone: 224 419-7106
Fax: –
Web: www.assertiotx.com

CEO: –
CFO: Paul Schwichtenberg
HR: –
FYE: December 31
Type: Private

Egalet wants to get the pain while skipping the abuse. The development stage pharmaceutical company is working on specially formulated pain pills designed to be more difficult to crush or dissolve, ineffective in the presence of alcohol, or otherwise abuse-resistant. It uses a hard plastic case that dissolves in stomach acid but becomes a gel when it contacts water. Egalet's two lead candidates are based on morphine and oxycodone but it believes its deterrence technology can be used in other products. It has licensed development of abuse-deterrent hydrocodone products to Shionogi. Once it has an approved product, Egalet intends to hire its own sales force. The company was formed in 2013 and went public in 2014.

Hoover's MasterList
of U.S. Companies

Indexes

COMPANIES LISTED ALPHABETICALLY

1 Source Consulting, Inc. 2
1-800 Flowers.com, Inc. 2
123greetings.com, Inc. 2
1399 Internet Technology Application Group Inc 2
180 Degree Capital Corp 2
1st Colonial Bancorp Inc 2
1st Franklin Financial Corp. 3
1st Source Corp 3
2u Inc 3
374water Inc 3
3d Systems Corp. (de) 3
3m Co 3
5linx Holdings Inc. 4
8point3 Energy Partners Lp 4
8x8 Inc 4
99 Cents Only Stores Llc 4
A & E Stores, Inc. 4
A & K Railroad Materials, Inc. 4
A & T Systems, Inc. 5
A-1 Express Delivery Service, Inc. 5
A-1 Freeman Moving & Storage, L.l.c. 5
A-mark Precious Metals, Inc 5
A-mrazek Moving Systems, Inc. 5
A. Duda & Sons, Inc. 5
A. Duie Pyle Inc. 6
A. Epstein And Sons International, Inc. 6
A. P. Hubbard Wholesale Lumber Corporation 6
A. Stucki Company 6
A.b.c. Home Furnishings, Inc. 6
A.l.l. Masonry Construction Co., Inc. 6
A.v. Thomas Produce, Inc. 7
A10 Networks Inc 7
Aaa Cooper Transportation 7
Aac Group Holding Corp. 7
Aalfs Manufacturing, Inc. 7
Aaon, Inc. 7
Aar Corp 8
Aaron And Company, Inc. 8
Aarp 8
Aatrix Software, Inc. 8
Abatix Corp. 8
Abaxis, Inc. 8
Abbott Laboratories 9
Abbott Northwestern Hospital 9
Abbvie Inc 9
Abdon Callais Offshore, Llc 9
Abeona Therapeutics Inc 9
Abercrombie & Fitch Co 9
Abf Freight System, Inc. 10
Abilene Christian University Inc 10
Abilitypath 10
Abington Memorial Hospital 10
Abl Management, Inc. 10
Abm Industries, Inc. 10
Abs Capital Partners Iii, L.p. 11
Acacia Research Corp 11
Academy Of Motion Picture Arts & Sciences 11
Academy Of Television Arts And Sciences 11
Academy Sports & Outdoors Inc 11
Acadia Healthcare Company Inc. 11
Acadia Pharmaceuticals Inc 12
Acadia Realty Trust 12
Acadian Ambulance Service, Inc. 12
Acas, Llc 12
Accelerate Diagnostics Inc 12
Accelpath Inc 12
Access Business Group Llc 13
Access Capital, Inc. 13
Access Worldwide Communications, Inc. 13
Accesslex Institute 13
Accion International 13
Acco Brands Corp 13
Accucode, Inc. 14
Accuray Inc (ca) 14
Accuride Corporation 14
Ace Hardware Corp. 14
Ace Relocation Systems, Inc. 14
Acentra Health, Llc 14

Ach Food Companies, Inc. 15
Achieve Life Science Inc 15
Achillion Pharmaceuticals Inc 15
Aci Worldwide Inc 15
Ackermann Pr, Inc. 15
Acmat Corp. 15
Acme Communications, Inc. 16
Acme United Corp. 16
Acnb Corp 16
Acolad Inc 16
Acorda Therapeutics Inc 16
Acorn Energy Inc 16
Acre Realty Investors Inc 17
Acres Commercial Realty Corp 17
Act, Inc. 17
Actelis Networks Inc 17
Action For Boston Community Development, Inc. 17
Actionet, Inc. 17
Actiontec Electronics, Inc. 18
Active Media Services, Inc. 18
Actividentity Corporation 18
Acts Retirement-life Communities, Inc. 18
Actua Corp 18
Acturus, Inc. 18
Acuative Corporation 19
Acuity Brands Inc (holding Company) 19
Acura Pharmaceuticals Inc 19
Acushnet Holdings Corp 19
Adac Plastics, Inc. 19
Adams Fairacre Farms, Inc. 19
Adams Resources & Energy, Inc. 20
Adams State University 20
Adams Wood Products, Inc. 20
Adams-columbia Electric Cooperative 20
Adapthealth Corp 20
Adco Electrical Corp. 20
Addus Homecare Corp 21
Addvantage Technologies Group, Inc. 21
Addx Corporation 21
Adeia Inc 21
Adelberg, Rudow, Dorf, Hendler, Llc 21
Adelphi University 21
Adena Health System 22
Adeptus Health Inc. 22
Adhera Therapeutics Inc 22
Adhesives Research, Inc. 22
Adirondack Community College (inc) 22
Adm Tronics Unlimited, Inc. 22
Adobe Inc 23
Adolfson & Peterson Inc 23
Ads Media Group, Inc. 23
Adstar, Inc. 23
Adt Inc (de) 23
Adtalem Global Education Inc 23
Adtran Holdings Inc 24
Advance Auto Parts Inc 24
Advanced Composite Structures, Llc 24
Advanced Disposal Services, Inc. 24
Advanced Drainage Systems Inc 24
Advanced Energy Industries Inc 24
Advanced Lighting Technologies, Llc 25
Advanced Micro Devices Inc 25
Advancepierre Foods, Inc. 25
Advancia Corporation 25
Advansix Inc 25
Advant-e Corporation 25
Advantage Solutions Inc 26
Advantego Corp 26
Advanzeon Solutions Inc 26
Adventist Health System/sunbelt, Inc. 26
Adventist Health System/sunbelt, Inc. 26
Adventist Health System/west, Corporation 26
Adventist Healthcare, Inc. 27
Adverum Biotechnologies Inc 27
Advocate Aurora Health Inc. 27
Advocate Charitable Foundation Inc 27
Advocate Health And Hospitals Corporation 27

Advocate Health Care Network 27
Aecom 28
Aegion Corporation 28
Aegis Aerospace, Inc. 28
Aehr Test Systems 28
Aeolus Pharmaceuticals Inc 28
Aeon Global Health Corp 28
Aep Texas Central Co 29
Aerokool Aviation Corporation 29
Aeronet Worldwide, Inc. 29
Aerotek Affiliated Services, Inc. 29
Aerovironment, Inc. 29
Aes Corp 29
Aetea Information Technology, Inc. 30
Aeterna Zentaris Inc 30
Affiliated Foods Midwest Cooperative, Inc. 30
Affiliated Foods, Inc. 30
Affiliated Managers Group Inc. 30
Affinity Interactive 30
Affinity Solutions, Inc. 31
Affirmative Insurance Holdings Inc 31
Affymax Inc 31
Affymetrix, Inc. 31
Aflac Inc 31
Afp Imaging Corp. 31
Africare 32
After, Inc. 32
Ag Mortgage Investment Trust Inc 32
Ag Processing Inc A Cooperative 32
Ag&e Holdings Inc. 32
Agco Corp. 32
Age Group Ltd. 33
Ageagle Aerial Systems Inc (new) 33
Agent Information Software Inc 33
Agenus Inc 33
Agfirst Farm Credit Bank 33
Agile Therapeutics Inc 33
Agilent Technologies, Inc. 34
Agiliti Health, Inc. 34
Agilysys Inc (de) 34
Agios Pharmaceuticals Inc 34
Agnc Investment Corp 34
Agnes Scott College, Inc. 34
Agree Realty Corp. 35
Agribank, Fcb 35
Agritech Worldwide Inc 35
Agtegra Cooperative 35
Agwest Farm Credit, Flca 35
Agy Holding Corp. 35
Ahmc Anaheim Regional Medical Center Lp 36
Ahs Hillcrest Medical Center, Llc 36
Aiadvertising Inc 36
Aim Immunotech Inc 36
Ainos Inc 36
Air Lease Corp 36
Air Methods Llc 37
Air Products & Chemicals Inc 37
Air Serv International, Inc. 37
Air T Inc 37
Air Transport Services Group, Inc. 37
Airbnb Inc 37
Aircastle Limited 38
Aire-master Of America, Inc. 38
Airgas, Inc. 38
Airnet Systems, Inc. 38
Ajax Metal Processing, Inc. 38
Akal Security, Inc. 38
Akamai Technologies Inc 39
Akela Pharma Inc 39
Akron General Health System 39
Akron General Medical Center Inc 39
Alabama Farmers Cooperative, Inc. 39
Alabama Power Co 39
Alabama State Port Authority 40
Alamance Regional Medical Center, Inc. 40
Alambic, Inc. 40
Alameda Corridor Transportation Authority 40
Alamo Community College District 40

Alamo Group, Inc. 40
Alanco Technologies Inc 41
Alaska Air Group, Inc. 41
Alaska Communications Systems Group, Inc. 41
Alaska Conservation Foundation 41
Alaska Native Tribal Health Consortium 41
Alaska Railroad Corporation 41
Alaskan Copper Companies, Inc. 42
Alaunos Therapeutics Inc 42
Alban Tractor, Llc 42
Albany College Of Pharmacy And Health Sciences 42
Albany International Corp 42
Albany Med Health System 42
Albemarle Corp. 43
Alberici Corporation 43
Albertsons Companies Inc 43
Albion College 43
Albright College 43
Alc Holdings, Inc. 43
Alco Stores, Inc. 44
Alcoa Corporation 44
Alcor Life Extension Foundation 44
Aldeyra Therapeutics Inc 44
Aldridge Electric, Inc. 44
Alegent Creighton Health 44
Alere Inc. 45
Alerislife Inc. 45
Alex Lee, Inc. 45
Alexander & Baldwin Inc (reit) 45
Alexander's Inc 45
Alexandria Extrusion Company 45
Alexandria Inova Hospital 46
Alexandria Real Estate Equities Inc 46
Alexian Brothers Health System 46
Alfa Tech Consulting Engineers, Inc. 46
Alfred Nickles Bakery, Inc. 46
Alfred University 46
Alico, Inc. 47
Alight 47
Align Communications Inc. 47
Align Technology Inc 47
Alimera Sciences Inc 47
Alinabal Holdings Corporation 47
Alithya Usa, Inc. 48
Alj Regional Holdings Inc 48
All American Containers, Inc. 48
All Points Cooperative 48
All Sensors Corporation 48
All Star Glass, Inc. 48
All Star Premium Products, Inc 49
Allan Myers, Inc. 49
Allegheny College 49
Allegheny Energy Supply Company, Llc 49
Allegheny General Hospital Inc 49
Allegiant Travel Company 49
Allegis Group, Inc. 50
Allegro Corporation 50
Allegro Microsystems, Llc 50
Allen & Company Incorporated 50
Allen Communication Learning Services, Inc. 50
Allen Lund Company, Llc 50
Allergy Research Group Llc 51
Allete Inc 51
Alley-cassetty Companies, Inc. 51
Alliance Fiber Optic Products, Inc. 51
Alliance For Audited Media 51
Alliance For Cooperative Energy Services Power Marketing Llc 51
Alliance Healthcare Services, Inc. 52
Alliance Holdings Gp, L.p. 52
Alliance Laundry Holdings Llc 52
Alliance Of Professionals & Consultants, Inc. 52
Alliance Resource Partners Lp 52
Alliance Shippers Inc. 52
Alliancebernstein Holding L.p. 53
Alliancebernstein Holding Lp 53
Alliant Energy Corp 53

Alliant International University, Inc. 53
Allied Beverage Group L.l.c. 53
Allied Healthcare Products Inc 53
Allied International Corporation Of Virginia 54
Allied Resources Inc 54
Allied Security Holdings Llc 54
Allied Universal Electronic Monitoring Us, Inc. 54
Allient Inc 54
Allin Corp 54
Allina Health System 55
Allison Transmission Holdings Inc 55
Allstate Corp 55
Ally Bank 55
Ally Financial Inc 55
Alma College 55
Almost Family, Inc. 56
Alnylam Pharmaceuticals Inc 56
Alon Usa Partners, Lp 56
Alpha Natural Resources, Inc. 56
Alpha-en Corp 56
Alphabet Inc 56
Alphatec Holdings Inc 57
Alpine Air Express, Inc. 57
Alro Steel Corporation 57
Als Therapy Development Foundation Inc 57
Alsco Inc. 57
Alseres Pharmaceuticals Inc 57
Alston & Bird Llp 58
Alston Construction Company, Inc. 58
Alta Mesa Resources, Lp 58
Altaba Inc. 58
Altair Engineering Inc 58
Altair Nanotechnologies Inc 58
Altar Produce, Llc 59
Altarum Institute 59
Altenburg Hardwood Lumber Co Inc 59
Altera Corporation 59
Alterra Mountain Company 59
Alteryx, Inc. 59
Alteva, Inc. 60
Altex Industries, Inc. 60
Altice Usa Inc 60
Alticor Inc. 60
Altigen Communications Inc 60
Altimmune Inc 60
Alto Ingredients Inc 61
Altria Group Inc 61
Altru Health System 61
Altum, Incorporated 61
Alvernia University 61
Alverno College 61
Aly Energy Services Inc (de) 62
Aly Energy Services, Inc. 62
Alyeska Pipeline Service Company 62
Alzheimer's Disease And Related Disorders Association, Inc. 62
Am Opterna Inc 62
Amacore Group Inc 62
Amag Pharmaceuticals, Inc. 63
Amalgamated Financial Corp 63
Amalgated Sugar Company 63
Amanasu Environment Corp 63
Amazon.com Inc 63
Amb Financial Corp 63
Ambac Financial Group, Inc. 64
Ambarella, Inc. 64
Ambassador Programs, Inc. 64
Amber Road, Inc. 64
Amc Entertainment Holdings Inc. 64
Amc Networks Inc 64
Amcon Distributing Company 65
Amdocs Ltd. 65
Amedisys, Inc. 65
Amen Properties Inc 65
Ameramex International Inc 65
Ameren Corp 65
Ameren Illinois Co 66
Ameresco Inc 66

America Chung Nam (group) Holdings Llc 66
America's Car-mart Inc 66
America's Charities 66
America's Home Place, Inc. 66
American Academy Of Pediatrics 67
American Airlines Group Inc 67
American Arbitration Association, Inc. 67
American Assets Trust, Inc. 67
American Association For The Advancement Of Science 67
American Association Of Advertising Agencies, Inc. 67
American Axle & Manufacturing Holdings Inc 68
American Bancorp, Inc (la) 68
American Bank Inc (pa) 68
American Bankers Association Inc 68
American Banknote Corporation 68
American Bar Association 68
American Biltrite Inc. 69
American Bio Medica Corp. 69
American Blue Ribbon Holdings, Llc 69
American Booksellers Association, Inc. 69
American Bureau Of Shipping 69
American Bus Association Inc. 69
American Business Bank (los Angeles, Ca) 70
American Campus Communities Llc 70
American Cannabis Co Inc 70
American Caresource Holdings Inc 70
American Cast Iron Pipe Company 70
American Century Companies, Inc. 70
American Chemical Society 71
American Civil Liberties Union Foundation, Inc. 71
American Coastal Insurance Corp 71
American College Of Healthcare Executives 71
American Commerce Solutions Inc 71
American Community Properties Trust Inc 71
American Council Of The Blind Inc 72
American Crystal Sugar Company 72
American Defense Systems Inc 72
American Dental Association 72
American Dental Association Foundation 72
American Dental Education Association 72
American Dg Energy Inc. 73
American Diabetes Association 73
American Eagle Outfitters, Inc. 73
American Electric Power Co Inc 73
American Equity Investment Life Holding Co 73
American Express Co. 73
American Farms, Llc 74
American Federation Of Labor & Congress Of Industrial Organzation 74
American Federation Of State County & Municipal Employees 74
American Federation Of Teachers Afl-cio Aft Committee On Political 74
American Fiber Green Products Inc 74
American Financial Group Inc 74
American Forests 75
American Fruit & Produce, Corp. 75
American Furniture Warehouse Co. 75
American Future Systems, Inc. 75
American Gaming Association 75
American Greetings Corporation 75
American Healthchoice, Inc. 76
American Hockey League Inc 76
American Homestar Corporation 76
American Honda Finance Corporation 76
American Hospital Association 76
American Indian College Fund, The (inc) 76
American Institute For Foreign Study, Inc. 77
American Institute Of Architects, Inc 77
American Institute Of Baking 77
American Institute Of Certified Public Accountants 77
American Institute Of Physics Incorporated 77
American Institutes For Research In The Behavioral Sciences 77
American Insurance Association Inc. 78

COMPANIES LISTED ALPHABETICALLY

American International Group Inc 78
American International Industries Inc 78
American Jewish World Service, Inc. 78
American Learning Corporation 78
American Library Association 78
American Locker Group, Inc. 79
American Lung Association 79
American Management Association International, Inc. 79
American Marketing Association Inc 79
American Medical Association Inc 79
American Medical Technologies Inc 79
American Millennium Inc 80
American Motorcycle Association 80
American Municipal Power, Inc. 80
American Natural Energy Corp 80
American Noble Gas Inc 80
American Outdoor Products, Inc. 80
American Payroll Institute, Inc. 81
American Pet Products Association, Inc. 81
American Petroleum Institute Inc 81
American Plastic Toys, Inc. 81
American Podiatric Medical Association, Incorporated 81
American Poolplayers Association, Inc. 81
American Power Group Corp 82
American Productivity & Quality Center, Inc. 82
American Psychological Association, Inc. 82
American Public Education Inc 82
American Railcar Industries, Inc. 82
American Realty Investors, Inc. 82
American Red Ball Transit Company, Inc 83
American Science And Engineering, Inc. 83
American Services Technology, Inc. 83
American Shared Hospital Services 83
American Society For Testing And Materials 83
American Software Inc 83
American Soil Technologies Inc 84
American Spectrum Realty, Inc. 84
American Speech-language-hearing Association 84
American Staffing Association 84
American States Water Co 84
American Superconductor Corp. 84
American Systems Corporation 85
American Terrazzo Company, Ltd. 85
American Tire Distributors Holdings, Inc. 85
American Tower Corp (new) 85
American Transmission Company, Llc 85
American Trucking Associations, Inc. 85
American United Mutual Insurance Holding Company 86
American University 86
American Vanguard Corp. 86
American Water Works Co, Inc. 86
American Way Van And Storage, Inc. 86
American Wholesale Marketers Assn, Inc 86
American Woodmark Corp. 87
Americares Foundation, Inc. 87
Americold Realty Trust Inc 87
Americus Mortgage Corporation 87
Ameriprise Financial Inc 87
Ameris Bancorp 87
Amerisafe Inc 88
Ameriserv Financial Inc. 88
Ameristeel Corp. 88
Amerityre Corporation 88
Amery Regional Medical Center, Inc. 88
Ames Construction, Inc. 88
Ames National Corp. 89
Ametek Inc 89
Amexdrug Corp. 89
Amgen Inc 89
Amicus Therapeutics Inc 89
Amkor Technology Inc. 89
Amn Healthcare Services Inc 90
Amneal Pharmaceuticals Inc 90
Ampco Services, L.l.c. 90
Ampco-pittsburgh Corp. 90

Amphastar Pharmaceuticals Inc (de) 90
Amphenol Corp. 90
Ampio Pharmaceuticals Inc 91
Amplify Energy Corp (new) 91
Amplify Energy Holdings Llc 91
Amrep Corp. 91
Amron International, Inc. 91
Amryt Pharmaceuticals Inc. 91
Ams Health Sciences, Inc. 92
Amsted Industries Incorporated 92
Amtech Systems, Inc. 92
Amx International, Inc. 92
Amyris Inc 92
Anacor Pharmaceuticals, Inc. 92
Analog Devices Inc 93
Analogic Corporation 93
Analogix Semiconductor, Inc. 93
Anchin, Block & Anchin Llp 93
Anchorage, Municipality Of (inc) 93
Andalay Solar Inc 93
Andeavor Llc 94
Andersen Corporation 94
Anderson And Dubose, Inc. 94
Andersons Inc 94
Andes Chemical, Llc 94
Andrea Electronics Corp. 94
Angelo Iafrate Construction Company 95
Angelo State University 95
Angels Baseball Lp 95
Angi Inc 95
Angie's List, Inc. 95
Angiodynamics Inc 95
Ani Pharmaceuticals Inc 96
Anika Therapeutics Inc. 96
Anixa Biosciences Inc 96
Anmed Health Services, Inc. 96
Ann & Hope, Inc. 96
Ann & Robert H. Lurie Children's Hospital Of Chicago 96
Annaly Capital Management Inc 97
Annams Systems Corporation 97
Anr Pipeline Company 97
Ansys Inc. 97
Antero Midstream Corp 97
Antero Resources Corp 97
Anthera Pharmaceuticals Inc 98
Anthony Forest Products Company, Llc 98
Anti-defamation League 98
Ants Software Inc. 98
Anywhere Real Estate Group Llc 98
Aoxing Pharmaceutical Co Inc 98
Apa Corp 99
Apache Construction Company, Inc. 99
Apartment Income Reit, L.p. 99
Apartment Investment & Management Co 99
Apex Data Services, Inc. 99
Apex Global Brands Inc. 99
Apex Oil Company, Inc. 100
Api Group Life Safety Usa Llc 100
Api Group, Inc. 100
Api Technologies Corp. 100
Apics, Inc. 100
Apogee 21 Holdings Inc 100
Apogee Enterprises Inc 101
Apogee Technology, Inc. 101
Apollo Commercial Real Estate Finance Inc. 101
Apollo Education Group, Inc. 101
Apollo Global Management Inc (new) 101
Apollo Residential Mortgage, Inc. 101
Apollo Theatre Foundation Inc 102
App Winddown, Llc 102
Appalachian Power Co. 102
Appalachian Regional Commission Inc 102
Appalachian Regional Healthcare, Inc. 102
Appalachian State University Inc 102
Appian Corp 103
Apple American Group Llc 103
Apple Inc 103

Applied Card Systems Inc. 103
Applied Digital Corp 103
Applied Dna Sciences Inc 103
Applied Energetics Inc 104
Applied Industrial Technologies, Inc. 104
Applied Materials, Inc. 104
Applied Micro Circuits Corp 104
Applied Minerals Inc 104
Applied Optoelectronics Inc 104
Applied Research Associates, Inc. 105
Applied Trust Engineering, Inc. 105
Applied Visual Sciences Inc 105
Appliedinfo Partners, Inc. 105
Applovin Corp 105
Approach Resources Inc. 105
Apptech Corp 106
Apptix, Inc. 106
Appvion, Inc. 106
Apria Healthcare Group Llc 106
Aptargroup Inc. 106
Apx, Inc. 106
Apyx Medical Corp 107
Aquis Communications Group, Inc 107
Aradigm Corporation 107
Aramark 107
Aravive Inc 107
Arbitech, Llc 107
Arbor Realty Trust Inc 108
Arbutus Biopharma Corp 108
Arc Document Solutions, Inc. 108
Arca Biopharma Inc 108
Arcadis Inc. 108
Arcbest Corp 108
Arch Resources Inc (de) 109
Arch Venture Corporation 109
Archer Daniels Midland Co. 109
Archon Corp 109
Archrock Inc 109
Archrock Partners, L.p. 109
Arconic Corporation 110
Arctic Cat Inc. 110
Arctic Slope Regional Corporation 110
Arcturus Therapeutics Holdings Inc 110
Ardelyx Inc 110
Arena 3d Holdings, Inc. 110
Arena Group Holdings Inc Del 111
Ares Commercial Real Estate Corp 111
Ares Management Corp 111
Aretec Group, Inc. 111
Argan Inc 111
Argo International Corporation 111
Argos Therapeutics, Inc. 112
Ariad Pharmaceuticals, Inc. 112
Arista Investors Corp. 112
Arista Networks Inc 112
Arizona Professional Baseball Lp 112
Arizona Public Service Co. 112
Arizona State University 113
Ark Restaurants Corp 113
Arkansas Children's Hospital 113
Arkansas Department Of Corrections 113
Arkansas Electric Cooperative Corp. 113
Arkansas Heart Hospital, Llc 113
Arkansas State University 114
Arkansas Tech University 114
Arko Corp 114
Arlington Industries, Inc. 114
Armanino Foods Of Distinction, Inc. 114
Armata Pharmaceuticals Inc 114
Armco Metals Holdings Inc 115
Armed Forces Benefit Association 115
Armour Residential Reit Inc. 115
Armstrong Energy Inc 115
Armstrong World Industries Inc 115
Army & Air Force Exchange Service 115
Arnet Pharmaceutical Corporation 116
Arnold & Porter Kaye Scholer Llp 116
Arnold Machinery Company 116

Aro Liquidation, Inc. 116
Arotech Corporation 116
Arpin Moving, Inc. 116
Arq Inc 117
Arqule, Inc. 117
Array Networks, Inc. 117
Arris Group, Inc. 117
Arrow Electronics, Inc. 117
Arrow Financial Corp. 117
Arrow Resources Development, Inc. 118
Arrowhead Pharmaceuticals Inc 118
Arrowhead Regional Medical Center 118
Art Center College Of Design Inc 118
Art Van Furniture, Llc 118
Artech L.l.c. 118
Artel, Llc 119
Artesian Resources Corp. 119
Artisan Partners Asset Management Inc 119
Artisanal Brands Inc. 119
Artivion Inc 119
Arts Way Manufacturing Co Inc 119
Artsquest 120
Aruba Networks, Inc. 120
Arvin Sango, Inc. 120
Asa Electronics Llc 120
Asa International Ltd. 120
Asap Solutions Group, Llc 120
Asarco Llc 121
Asbury Automotive Group Inc 121
Ascendium Education Group, Inc. 121
Ascension Borgess Hospital 121
Ascension Genesys Hospital 121
Ascension Health 121
Ascension Providence Hospital 122
Ascension Providence Rochester Hospital 122
Ascension Via Christi Health, Inc. 122
Ascent Capital Group, Inc. 122
Ascent Industries Co 122
Ascent Solar Technologies Inc 122
Asg Technologies Group, Inc. 123
Asgn Inc 123
Ash Stevens Llc 123
Ashford Hospitality Trust Inc 123
Ashland Inc (new) 123
Ashland Llc 123
Asi Computer Technologies Inc 124
Asis International, Inc. 124
Aspen Aerogels Inc 124
Aspen Skiing Company, L.l.c. 124
Aspira Womens Health Inc 124
Aspirus, Inc. 124
Aspyra Inc 125
Assembly Biosciences Inc 125
Assertio Holdings Inc 125
Asset Acquisition Authority, Inc. 125
Asset Protection & Security Services, Lp 125
Associated Banc-corp 125
Associated Catholic Charities Inc. 126
Associated Electric Cooperative, Inc. 126
Associated Equipment Distributors 126
Associated Food Stores, Llc 126
Associated Grocers Of New England, Inc. 126
Associated Grocers Of The South, Inc. 126
Associated Grocers, Inc. 127
Associated Materials, Llc 127
Associated Wholesale Grocers, Inc. 127
Association For Creative Industries 127
Association For Financial Professionals, Inc. 127
Association For Intelligent Information
 Management 127
Association Of Universities For Research In
 Astronomy, Inc. 128
Assuranceamerica Corp 128
Assurant Inc 128
Asta Funding, Inc. 128
Astec Industries, Inc. 128
Astellas Institute For Regenerative Medicine 128
Astron Wireless Technologies Inc. 129

Astronautics Corporation Of America 129
Astronics Corp 129
Astronova Inc 129
Astrotech Corp 129
Asura Development Group, Inc 129
Asure Software Inc 130
At&t Inc 130
Atalanta Corporation 130
Atalian Us Northeast, Llc 130
Atc Group Services Llc 130
Atc Venture Group Inc 130
Atco Rubber Products, Inc. 131
Ateeco, Inc. 131
Athena Engineering, Inc. 131
Athenahealth, Inc. 131
Athersys Inc 131
Ati Inc (new) 131
Atkore Inc 132
Atkore International Holdings Inc. 132
Atlanta Clark University Inc 132
Atlanta Hardwood Corporation 132
Atlanta National League Baseball Club, Llc 132
Atlantic American Corp. 132
Atlantic City Electric Co 133
Atlantic Diving Supply, Inc. 133
Atlantic Health System Inc. 133
Atlantic Power Corporation 133
Atlantic Union Bankshares Corp 133
Atlanticare Health System Inc. 133
Atlanticus Holdings Corp 134
Atlas Air Worldwide Holdings, Inc. 134
Atlas Industrial Contractors, L.l.c. 134
Atlas World Group, Inc. 134
Atlassian Corp 134
Atmel Corporation 134
Atmos Energy Corp. 135
Atn International Inc 135
Atos Syntel Inc. 135
Atricure Inc 135
Atrion Corp. 135
Atrion, Inc. 135
Atrius Health, Inc. 136
Atrix International, Inc. 136
Atrm Holdings, Inc. 136
Attorney General, Texas 136
Attronica Computers, Inc. 136
Atwell, Llc 136
Atwood Oceanics, Inc. 137
Au Medical Center, Inc. 137
Auburn National Bancorp, Inc. 137
Auburn University 137
Audacy Inc 137
Audio-technica U.s., Inc. 137
Audubon Metals Llc 138
Augusta University 138
Augustana College 138
Augustana University Association 138
Ault Alliance Inc 138
Aultman Health Foundation 138
Aura Minerals Inc (british Virgin Islands) 139
Aura Systems Inc 139
Auraria Higher Education Center 139
Aurora Flight Sciences Corp 139
Aurora Organic Dairy Corp. 139
Aurora Wholesalers, Llc 139
Austin College 140
Austin Community College 140
Austin Task, Inc. 140
Auto Brakes, Inc. 140
Autodesk Inc 140
Autoliv Asp, Inc. 140
Automatic Data Processing Inc. 141
Automatic Steel , Inc. 141
Automation Alley 141
Automotive Finance Corporation 141
Autonation, Inc. 141
Autoscope Technologies Corp 141
Autotrader.com, Inc. 142

Autoweb, Inc. 142
Autozone, Inc. 142
Auvil Fruit Company, Inc. 142
Av Homes, Inc. 142
Avalon Correctional Services, Inc. 142
Avalon Holdings Corp. 143
Avalonbay Communities, Inc. 143
Avangrid Inc 143
Avanos Medical Inc 143
Avantor Inc 143
Avax Technologies, Inc. 143
Avaya Holdings Corp 144
Avaya Llc 144
Ave Maria University, Inc. 144
Avenue Group Inc 144
Aveo Pharmaceuticals, Inc. 144
Avera Health 144
Avera St. Mary's 145
Averitt Express, Inc. 145
Avery Dennison Corp 145
Avery Design Systems Inc 145
Avi Systems, Inc. 145
Aviat Networks, Inc. 145
Avid Bioservices Inc 146
Avient Corp 146
Avintiv Specialty Materials Inc. 146
Avis Budget Group Inc 146
Avista Corp 146
Avistar Communications Corp 146
Avnet Inc 147
Avon Products, Inc. 147
Aware Inc. (ma) 147
Axcelis Technologies Inc 147
Axel Johnson Inc. 147
Axesstel Inc 147
Axis Construction Corp. 148
Axogen Inc 148
Axon Enterprise Inc 148
Axos Financial Inc 148
Axt Inc 148
Ayro Inc 148
Azek Co Inc (the) 149
Azenta Inc 149
Azure Dynamics Corp. 149
Azure Midstream Partners Lp 149
Azusa Pacific University 149
Azz Inc 149
B & G Food Enterprises, Llc 150
B&g Foods Inc 150
B. L. Harbert International, L.l.c. 150
B/e Aerospace, Inc. 150
Bab Inc 150
Babcock & Jenkins, Inc. 150
Babcock Lumber Company 151
Babson College 151
Badger Meter Inc 151
Baer's Furniture Co., Inc. 151
Bain Capital, Lp 151
Baker & Hostetler Llp 151
Baker Book House Company 152
Baker Hughes Company 152
Baker Hughes Holdings Llc 152
Balchem Corp. 152
Baldwin Technology Company, Inc. 152
Balfour Beatty Construction Group, Inc. 152
Balfour Beatty Infrastructure, Inc. 153
Ball Corp 153
Ball Horticultural Company 153
Ball State University 153
Ballet Makers, Inc. 153
Ballistic Recovery Systems, Inc. 153
Ballston Spa Bancorp Inc 154
Baltimore Gas And Electric Company 154
Baltimore Ravens Limited Partnership 154
Banc Of California Inc 154
Bancfirst Corp. (oklahoma City, Okla) 154
Bancroft Construction Company 154
Bandwidth Inc 155

COMPANIES LISTED ALPHABETICALLY

Bank Of America Corp 155
Bank Of Hawaii Corp 155
Bank Of Marin Bancorp 155
Bank Of New York Mellon Corp 155
Bank Of South Carolina Corp 155
Bank Of The James Financial Group Inc 156
Bank Of The West (san Francisco, Ca) 156
Bank Ozk 156
Bankfinancial Corp 156
Bankunited Inc. 156
Banner Corp. 156
Banner Health 157
Banner-university Medical Center Tucson Campus Llc 157
Bantam Electronics, Inc. 157
Baptist Health 157
Baptist Health Care Corporation 157
Baptist Health South Florida, Inc. 157
Baptist Health System, Inc. 158
Baptist Healthcare System, Inc. 158
Baptist Hospital Of Miami, Inc. 158
Baptist Memorial Health Care System, Inc. 158
Baptist Memorial Hospital 158
Baptist/st. Anthony's Health System 158
Bar Harbor Bankshares 159
Barclays Bank Delaware 159
Bard College 159
Barnes & Noble Education Inc 159
Barnes & Noble, Inc. 159
Barnes Group Inc. 159
Barnwell Industries, Inc. 160
Barracuda Networks, Inc. 160
Barrett Business Services, Inc. 160
Barry University, Inc. 160
Barry-wehmiller Group, Inc. 160
Bartlett Agri Enterprises, Inc. 160
Barton Malow Company 161
Basic Energy Services Inc 161
Basin Electric Power Cooperative 161
Bassett Furniture Industries, Inc 161
Bath & Body Works Inc 161
Baton Rouge General Medical Center 161
Battalion Oil Corp 162
Battelle Memorial Institute Inc 162
Battle Creek Farmers Cooperative, Non-stock 162
Bauer Built, Inc. 162
Baxley & Appling County Hospital Authority 162
Baxter County Regional Hospital, Inc. 162
Baxter International Inc 163
Bay Cities Paving & Grading, Inc. 163
Bay County Health System, Llc 163
Baycare Health System, Inc. 163
Baylor Scott & White Health 163
Baylor University 163
Baylor University Medical Center 164
Bayou City Exploration, Inc. 164
Bayside Fuel Oil Depot Corp 164
Baystate Health Inc. 164
Baystate Health System Health Services, Inc. 164
Bayview Electric Company, Llc 164
Bazaarvoice, Inc. 165
Bbx Capital Corporation 165
Bcb Bancorp Inc 165
Bdp International, Inc. 165
Beachbody Co Inc (the) 165
Beacon Medical Group, Inc. 165
Beacon Roofing Supply Inc 166
Beacon Technologies, Inc 166
Beall's, Inc. 166
Bearing Distributors, Inc. 166
Beasley Broadcast Group Inc 166
Beaufort Memorial Hospital 166
Beaumont Health 167
Beaumont Products Incorporated 167
Beaver Dam Community Hospitals, Inc. 167
Beaver Street Fisheries, Inc. 167
Beazer Homes Usa, Inc. 167
Bebe Stores Inc 167

Bechtel Group, Inc. 168
Beck Suppliers, Inc. 168
Becton, Dickinson & Co 168
Bed, Bath & Beyond, Inc. 168
Beebe Medical Center, Inc. 168
Bel Fuse Inc 168
Belcan Government Solutions, Inc. 169
Belcan, Llc 169
Belden & Blake Corporation 169
Belden Inc 169
Belkin International, Inc. 169
Bell Industries Inc (de) 169
Bell Partners Inc. 170
Belleharvest Sales, Inc. 170
Beloit College 170
Beloit Health System, Inc. 170
Bemis Manufacturing Company Inc 170
Ben E. Keith Company 170
Benchmark Electronics, Inc. 171
Benco Dental Supply Co. 171
Bend The Arc A Jewish Partnership For Justice 171
Benedict College 171
Benedictine College 171
Benedictine Health System 171
Benevolent And Protective Order Of Elks 172
Bennett College 172
Bennington College Corporation 172
Bent Grass Holdings, Inc. 172
Bentley University 172
Berea College 172
Bergelectric Corp. 173
Bergen Community College 173
Bergen Pines County Hospital Inc 173
Bergstrom Inc. 173
Berklee College Of Music, Inc. 173
Berkley (wr) Corp 173
Berkshire Hathaway Energy Company 174
Berkshire Hathaway Inc 174
Berkshire Health Systems, Inc. 174
Berkshire Hills Bancorp Inc 174
Berkshire Income Realty, Inc. 174
Berkshire Production Supply Llc 174
Bermello, Ajamil & Partners, Inc. 175
Bernatello's Pizza, Inc. 175
Berner Food & Beverage, Llc 175
Berry Companies, Inc. 175
Berry Corp (bry) 175
Berry Global Films, Llc 175
Berry Global Group Inc 176
Berry Petroleum Company, Llc 176
Best Buy Inc 176
Best Western International, Inc. 176
Beth Israel Deaconess Medical Center, Inc. 176
Beth Israel Medical Center 176
Bethesda Hospital, Inc. 177
Bethune-cookman University Inc. 177
Bexil Corp 177
Beyond Inc 177
Bg Medicine Inc 177
Bgc Group Inc 177
Bgr Government Affairs, Llc 178
Bh Media, Inc. 178
Bi-rite Restaurant Supply Co., Inc. 178
Biddeford Internet Corp. 178
Big 5 Sporting Goods Corp 178
Big Brothers Big Sisters Of America Corporation 178
Big Buck Brewery & Steakhouse, Inc. 179
Big Heart Pet Brands, Inc. 179
Big Jack Ultimate Holdings Lp 179
Big Lots, Inc. 179
Big Rock Sports, Llc 179
Big West Oil, Llc 179
Big-d Construction Corp. 180
Bill & Melinda Gates Foundation 180
Billing Services Group Ltd. 180
Billings Clinic 180
Bio-key International Inc 180

Bio-rad Laboratories Inc 180
Bio-techne Corp 181
Biocardia Inc 181
Biocept Inc 181
Biocom Institute 181
Biocryst Pharmaceuticals Inc 181
Biogen Inc 181
Biogenex Laboratories 182
Bioject Medical Technologies Inc 182
Biola University, Inc. 182
Biolargo Inc 182
Biolase Inc 182
Biolife Solutions Inc 182
Biomarin Pharmaceutical Inc 183
Biomed Realty Trust, Inc. 183
Biomedical Technology Solutions Holdings, Inc. 183
Biomerica Inc 183
Bion Environmental Technologies Inc 183
Biosynergy, Inc. 183
Bioverativ Inc. 184
Biovest International, Inc. 184
Birds Eye Foods Inc 184
Birmingham-southern College Inc 184
Birner Dental Management Services, Inc. 184
Bit Mining Ltd 184
Bj's Restaurants Inc 185
Bj's Wholesale Club Holdings Inc 185
Bjt, Inc. 185
Bk Technologies Corp 185
Bkf Capital Group Inc 185
Black & Veatch Corporation 185
Black Hills Corporation 186
Black Hills Power Inc. 186
Black Knight, Inc. 186
Black Raven Energy, Inc. 186
Black Stone Minerals Lp 186
Blackbaud, Inc. 186
Blackfoot Telephone Cooperative, Inc. 187
Blackhawk Bancorp Inc 187
Blackline Inc 187
Blackrock Inc 187
Blackstone Inc 187
Blackstone Mortgage Trust Inc 187
Blarney Castle Oil Co. 188
Blessing Hospital 188
Blish-mize Co. 188
Blistex Inc. 188
Block (h & R), Inc. 188
Block Communications, Inc. 188
Block Inc 189
Blonder Tongue Laboratories, Inc. 189
Bloodworks 189
Bloom Energy Corp 189
Bloomin' Brands Inc 189
Blount International, Inc. 189
Blount Memorial Hospital, Incorporated 190
Blubuzzard Inc 190
Blue Beacon, Inc. 190
Blue Bird Corp 190
Blue Buffalo Pet Products, Inc. 190
Blue Cross & Blue Shield Association 190
Blue Cross And Blue Shield Of Arizona, Inc. 191
Blue Cross Blue Shield Of North Dakota 191
Blue Dolphin Energy Co. 191
Blue Nile, Inc. 191
Blue Ridge Energy Members Foundation 191
Blue Ridge Healthcare Hospitals, Inc. 191
Blue Ridge Healthcare System, Inc.. 192
Blue River Bancshares, Inc. 192
Blue Tee Corp. 192
Bluebird Bio Inc 192
Bluebonnet Electric Cooperative, Inc. 192
Bluebonnet Nutrition Corporation 192
Bluelinx Holdings Inc 193
Blueprint Medicines Corp 193
Bluescope Construction, Inc. 193
Blum Capital Partners T, L.p. 193

Blumenthal Distributing, Inc. 193
Bmc Holdings, Inc. 193
Bnccorp Inc 194
Board Of Regents Of The University Of Nebraska 194
Board Of Trustees Of Community College District 508 (inc) 194
Board Of Trustees Of Illinois State University 194
Boardriders, Inc. 194
Bob Evans Farms, Inc. 194
Bob Ross Buick, Inc. 195
Boddie-noell Enterprises, Inc. 195
Boehringer Ingelheim Corporation 195
Boehringer Ingelheim Pharmaceuticals, Inc. 195
Boeing Capital Corp 195
Boeing Co. (the) 195
Boingo Wireless, Inc. 196
Boise Cascade Co. (de) 196
Boise State University Foundation, Inc. 196
Bojangles', Inc. 196
Bok Financial Corp 196
Boker Usa, Inc. 196
Bollore Logistics Usa Inc. 197
Bolner's Fiesta Products, Inc. 197
Bon Secours - Richmond Community Hospital, Incorporated 197
Bon Secours Mercy Health, Inc. 197
Bon-ton Stores Inc 197
Bonitz, Inc. 197
Bonneville Power Administration 198
Booking Holdings Inc 198
Books-a-million, Inc. 198
Boone Hospital Center 198
Booz Allen Hamilton Holding Corp. 198
Borgess Health Alliance, Inc. 198
Borgwarner Inc 199
Borgwarner Massachusetts Inc. 199
Born Free Usa, United With Animal Protection Institute 199
Boss Holdings, Inc. 199
Boston Beer Co Inc (the) 199
Boston Medical Center Corporation 199
Boston Properties Inc 200
Boston Sand & Gravel Co. 200
Boston Scientific Corp. 200
Boston Symphony Orchestra, Inc. 200
Bottomline Technologies, Inc. 200
Boulder Brands, Inc. 200
Bourns, Inc. 201
Bowdoin College 201
Bowen Engineering Corporation 201
Bowflex Inc 201
Bowlin Travel Centers Inc 201
Bowling Green State University 201
Bowman Consulting Group Ltd 202
Bowtie, Inc. 202
Box Inc 202
Boy Scouts Of America 202
Boyd Gaming Corp. 202
Boyd Laconia, Llc 202
Boyds Collection Ltd 203
Boys & Girls Clubs Of America 203
Bozzuto's, Inc. 203
Bpz Resources, Inc. 203
Bradford White Corporation 203
Bradley Company, Llc 203
Bradley University 204
Brady Corp 204
Brainworks Software Development Corporation 204
Brakebush Brothers, Inc. 204
Brammo, Inc. 204
Branch Builds, Inc. 204
Brandeis University 205
Brandywine Communications 205
Brandywine Realty Trust 205
Brasfield & Gorrie, L.l.c. 205
Bravo Group, Inc. 205
Brazos Electric Power Cooperative, Inc. 205

Brazos Higher Education Service Corporation, Inc. 206
Brc Merger Sub, Llc 206
Bread Financial Holdings Inc 206
Bread For The World, Inc. 206
Breaking Ground Housing Development Fund Corporation 206
Breeze-eastern Llc 206
Breg, Inc. 207
Breitburn Energy Partners Lp 207
Bremer Financial Corp. 207
Brendan Technologies Inc 207
Brenden Theatre Corporation 207
Brentwood Industries, Inc. 207
Brescia University 208
Bretford Manufacturing, Inc. 208
Brg Sports, Inc. 208
Bridgeline Digital Inc 208
Bridgeport Hospital & Healthcare Services Inc 208
Bridgford Foods Corp. 208
Briggs & Stratton Corporation 209
Brigham Young University 209
Brightcove Inc 209
Brighthouse Financial Inc 209
Brightland Homes, Ltd. 209
Brightview Holdings Inc 209
Brinker International, Inc. 210
Brinks Co (the) 210
Bristol Hospital Incorporated 210
Bristol Myers Squibb Co. 210
Bristow Group Inc (de) 210
Brixmor Property Group Inc 210
Broadcom Inc (de) 211
Broadridge Financial Solutions Inc 211
Broadsoft, Inc. 211
Broadview Institute, Inc. 211
Broadway Bancshares, Inc. (tx) 211
Broadway Financial Corp. (de) 211
Broadwind Inc 212
Brocade Communications Systems Llc 212
Brockton Hospital, Inc. 212
Broder Bros., Co. 212
Bromberg & Company, Inc. 212
Bronson Battle Creek Hospital 212
Bronson Health Care Group, Inc. 213
Bronson Methodist Hospital Inc 213
Bronxcare Health System 213
Brookdale Senior Living Inc 213
Brookfield Oaktree Holdings Llc 213
Brookline Bancorp Inc (de) 213
Brooklyn Academy Of Music Inc 214
Brooklyn Hospital Center 214
Brooklyn Institute Of Arts And Sciences 214
Brooklyn Navy Yard Development Corporation 214
Brooklyn Nets, Llc 214
Brookmount Explorations Inc 214
Brooks Tropicals Holding, Inc. 215
Brother International Corporation 215
Brothers Produce, Incorporated 215
Brown & Bigelow, Inc. 215
Brown & Brown Inc 215
Brown & Haley 215
Brown Rudnick Llp 216
Brown University 216
Brown-forman Corp 216
Brt Apartments Corp 216
Brtrc Federal Solutions, Inc. 216
Bruce Oakley, Inc. 216
Bruker Corp 217
Brunswick Corp. 217
Bryan Cave Leighton Paisner Llp 217
Bryan Medical Center 217
Bryn Mawr College 217
Bsa Business Software Alliance, Inc 217
Bsd Medical Corporation 218
Btd Manufacturing, Inc. 218
Buchanan Technologies, Inc. 218
Buchbinder Tunick & Company L.l.p 218

Buckeye Partners, L.p. 218
Buckeye Pipe Line Company, L P 218
Buckeye Power, Inc. 219
Buckle, Inc. (the) 219
Bucknell University 219
Buffalo Wild Wings, Inc. 219
Build-a-bear Workshop Inc 219
Builders Firstsource Inc. 219
Building Materials Corp. Of America 220
Bulova Technologies Group, Inc 220
Bunge Global Sa 220
Bunge North America, Inc. 220
Burke Herbert Financial Services Corp 220
Burke Rehabilitation Hospital 220
Burke, Inc. 221
Burkhart Dental Supply Co. 221
Burlington Northern & Santa Fe Railway Co. (the) 221
Burlington Northern Santa Fe, Llc 221
Burlington Stores Inc 221
Burns Motor Freight, Inc. 221
Burton Lumber & Hardware Co. 222
Buschman Corporation 222
Business For Social Responsibility 222
Busken Bakery, Inc. 222
Busy Beaver Building Centers, Inc. 222
Butler Health System, Inc. 222
Butler Manufacturing Company Inc 223
Butler National Corp. 223
Bvsn, Llc 223
Bwmb, Llc 223
Bwx Technologies Inc 223
Bycor General Contractors, Inc. 223
Byline Bancorp Inc 224
C & F Financial Corp. 224
C & K Market, Inc. 224
C&s Wholesale Grocers, Llc 224
C. G. Schmidt, Inc. 224
C. Overaa & Co. 224
C. R. Bard, Inc. 225
C.d. Smith Construction, Inc. 225
C.r. England, Inc. 225
Cable One Inc 225
Cablevision Systems Corporation 225
Cabot Corp. 225
Cabral Roofing & Waterproofing Corporation 226
Cache Valley Electric Company 226
Caci International Inc 226
Caddo International Inc 226
Cadence Design Systems Inc 226
Cadence Mcshane Construction Company Llc 226
Cadiz Inc 227
Caesars Entertainment Inc (new) 227
Cai International, Inc. 227
Cajun Industries Holdings, Llc 227
Cal-maine Foods Inc 227
Calamos Asset Management, Inc. 227
Calamp Corp 228
Calatlantic Group, Inc. 228
Calavo Growers, Inc. 228
Calcot, Ltd. 228
Caleres Inc 228
Calgon Carbon Corporation 228
Calhoun Enterprises, Inc. 229
Caliber Imaging & Diagnostic Inc 229
Calibre Systems, Inc. 229
California Beer And Beverage Distributors 229
California Cedar Products Company 229
California Center For The Arts, Escondido, Foundation 229
California Coastal Communities, Inc. 230
California Community Foundation 230
California Department Of Water Resources 230
California First Leasing Corp 230
California Independent System Operator Corporation 230
California Institute Of Technology 230
California Pharmacists Association 231

COMPANIES LISTED ALPHABETICALLY

California Polytechnic State University 231
California Resources Corp 231
California State Polytechnic University Of Pomona 231
California State University East Bay 231
California State University System 231
California State University, Fresno 232
California State University, Los Angeles 232
California State University, Monterey Bay 232
California State University, Northridge 232
California State University, Sacramento 232
California State University, San Marcos 232
California Steel Industries, Inc. 233
California Water Service Group (de) 233
California Wellness Foundation 233
Calix Inc 233
Call Now Inc. 233
Call2recycle, Inc. 233
Callahan Chemical Company, Llc 234
Callidus Software Inc. 234
Calloway's Nursery, Inc. 234
Callwave Inc 234
Calmare Therapeutics Inc 234
Calnet, Inc. 234
Calpine Corporation 235
Calumet Specialty Product Partners Lp 235
Calvary Hospital, Inc. 235
Calvert Company, Inc. 235
Calverthealth Medical Center, Inc. 235
Calypte Biomedical Corp 235
Camber Energy Inc 236
Cambium Learning Group, Inc. 236
Cambrex Corporation 236
Cambridge Bancorp 236
Cambridge Heart Inc. 236
Cambridge Public Health Commission 236
Camden National Corp. (me) 237
Camden Property Trust 237
Cameron International Corporation 237
Campagna-turano Bakery, Inc. 237
Campbell Lodging, Inc. 237
Campbell Soup Co 237
Camping World Holdings Inc 238
Campus Apartments, Inc. 238
Can-am Consulting Services, Inc 238
Canal Capital Corp. 238
Canam Steel Corporation 238
Canandaigua National Corp. 238
Cancer Care, Inc. 239
Cancer Research Fund Of The Damon Runyon-walter Winchell Foundation 239
Candid 239
Cannabis Global Inc 239
Cannae Holdings Inc 239
Cano Container Corporation 239
Cantaloupe Inc 240
Cantel Medical Llc 240
Canterbury Park Holding Corp (new) 240
Cape Cod Healthcare, Inc. 240
Cape Cod Hospital 240
Cape Environmental Management Inc. 240
Capella Education Company 241
Capillary Brierley Inc 241
Capital City Bank Group, Inc. 241
Capital Directions, Inc. 241
Capital District Physicians' Health Plan, Inc. 241
Capital Health System, Inc. 241
Capital Metropolitan Transportation Authority 242
Capital One Financial Corp 242
Capital Properties, Inc. 242
Capitol Federal Financial Inc 242
Capps Manufacturing, Incorporated 242
Capricor Therapeutics Inc 242
Capstead Mortgage Corporation 243
Capstone Green Energy Corp 243
Capstone Holding Corp 243
Captech Ventures, Inc. 243
Cara Therapeutics Inc 243

Carbo Ceramics Inc. 243
Carbonite, Inc. 244
Cardenas Markets Llc 244
Cardiacassist, Inc. 244
Cardinal Health, Inc. 244
Cardiovascular Biotherapeutics Inc 244
Cardiovascular Systems, Inc. 244
Cardtronics, Inc. 245
Care New England Health System Inc 245
Careadvantage, Inc. 245
Carecloud Inc 245
Caredx Inc 245
Caregroup, Inc. 245
Caretrust Reit Inc 246
Carhartt, Inc. 246
Caribou Coffee Company, Inc. 246
Carilion Clinic 246
Carisma Therapeutics Inc 246
Carl Buddig And Company 246
Carle Foundation Hospital 247
Carleton College 247
Carling Technologies, Inc. 247
Carlisle Companies Inc. 247
Carlyle Group Inc (the) 247
Carma Laboratories, Inc. 247
Carmax Inc. 248
Carmike Cinemas, Llc 248
Carnegie Institution Of Washington 248
Carnegie-mellon University 248
Carnival Corp 248
Carolina Handling, Llc 248
Carolinas Medical Center-lincoln 249
Caromont Health, Inc. 249
Carparts.com Inc (new) 249
Carpenter Contractors Of America, Inc. 249
Carpenter Technology Corp. 249
Carriage Services, Inc. 249
Carrier Alliance Holdings Inc 250
Carrier Global Corp 250
Carrio Cabling Corporation 250
Carrix, Inc. 250
Carrols Restaurant Group Inc 250
Carry Transit, Llc 250
Carson Tahoe Regional Healthcare 251
Carter's Inc 251
Cartesian, Inc. 251
Carvana Co 251
Carver Bancorp Inc. 251
Carvin Corp. 251
Cascade Engineering, Inc. 252
Cascade Forest Corporation 252
Cascadian Therapeutics, Inc. 252
Case Western Reserve University 252
Casella Waste Systems, Inc. 252
Casey Industrial, Inc. 252
Casey's General Stores, Inc. 253
Cash-wa Distributing Co. Of Kearney, Inc. 253
Caspian Services Inc 253
Cass Information Systems Inc. 253
Cassava Sciences Inc 253
Castle (am) & Co 253
Castlight Health, Inc. 254
Catalent Inc 254
Catalyst Direct, Inc. 254
Catalyst Pharmaceuticals Inc 254
Catalyst, Inc. 254
Catamount Constructors, Inc. 254
Catchmark Timber Trust, Inc. 255
Caterpillar Financial Services Corp 255
Caterpillar Inc. 255
Cathay General Bancorp 255
Catholic Charities Usa 255
Catholic Health Care System 255
Catholic Health System Of Long Island, Inc. 256
Catholic Health System, Inc. 256
Catholic Medical Center 256
Cato Corp. 256
Cato Institute, Inc. 256

Cavaliers Operating Company, Llc 256
Cavco Industries Inc (de) 257
Cavium, Llc 257
Cazenovia College 257
Cbiz Inc 257
Cbl & Associates Properties Inc 257
Cboe Bats, Llc 257
Cboe Global Markets Inc 258
Cbre Group Inc 258
Cca Industries, Inc. 258
Ccc Group, Inc. 258
Ccc Intelligent Solutions Holdings Inc 258
Ccur Holdings Inc 258
Cd International Enterprises Inc 259
Cd Warehouse Inc 259
Cdc Small Business Finance Corp. 259
Cdgjl, Inc. 259
Cdi Contractors, Llc 259
Cdi Corp. 259
Cdk Global, Inc. 260
Cdti Advanced Materials Inc 260
Cdw Corp 260
Ceb Inc. 260
Cecil Bancorp Inc 260
Ceco Environmental Corp. 260
Cedar Fair Lp 261
Cedar Realty Trust Inc 261
Cedars-sinai Medical Center 261
Cel-sci Corporation 261
Celadon Group Inc 261
Celanese Corp (de) 261
Cell Tech International, Inc. 262
Celldex Therapeutics, Inc. 262
Celsius Holdings Inc 262
Celtic Investment, Inc. 262
Cemex De Puerto Rico, Inc. 262
Cencora Inc 262
Centauri, Llc 263
Centegra Health System 263
Centene Corp 263
Centennial Specialty Foods Corp 263
Center For Constitutional Rights Inc 263
Center For Creative Leadership 263
Center For Victims Of Torture 264
Centerpoint Energy Houston Electric Llc 264
Centerpoint Energy, Inc 264
Centerspace 264
Centerwell Health Services, Inc. 264
Centimark Corporation 264
Centra Health, Inc. 265
Centracare Health Foundation 265
Central City Opera House Association 265
Central Dupage Hospital Association 265
Central Garden & Pet Co 265
Central Grocers, Inc. 265
Central Illinois Light Co 266
Central Iowa Power Cooperative 266
Central Maine Power Co. 266
Central Michigan University 266
Central Ohio Transit Authority 266
Central Pacific Financial Corp 266
Central Refrigerated Service, Llc 267
Central Steel And Wire Company, Llc 267
Central Suffolk Hospital 267
Centrastate Healthcare Partners Limited Liability Company 267
Centre College Of Kentucky 267
Centric Brands Llc 267
Centrus Energy Corp 268
Century Aluminum Co. 268
Century Casinos Inc. 268
Century Communities Inc 268
Ceres Solutions, Llp 268
Ceres, Inc. 268
Ceridian Corporation 269
Cerritos Community College District 269
Certainteed Gypsum Products, Inc. 269
Certco, Inc. 269

Cerus Corp. 269
Cervomed Inc 269
Ceva Inc 270
Cf Bankshares Inc 270
Cf Industries Holdings Inc 270
Cgb Enterprises, Inc. 270
Ch2m Hill Companies Ltd 270
Cha Hollywood Medical Center Lp 270
Chadron State College 271
Challenger International, Inc. 271
Chamber Of Commerce Of The United States Of America 271
Champion Industries Inc (wv) 271
Champions Oncology Inc 271
Championx Corp 271
Chancelight, Inc. 272
Change Healthcare Holdings, Inc. 272
Channeladvisor Corporation 272
Channell Commercial Corporation 272
Channellock, Inc. 272
Chapman University 272
Chargepoint, Inc. 273
Chargers Football Company, Llc 273
Charles & Colvard Ltd 273
Charles And Helen Schwab Foundation Inc 273
Charles C Parks Co Inc 273
Charles Regional Medical Center Foundation Inc. 273
Charles River Laboratories International Inc. 274
Charleston Area Medical Center, Inc. 274
Charleston Hospital, Inc. 274
Charlies Holdings Inc 274
Charlotte Pipe And Foundry Company 274
Chart Industries Inc 274
Charter Communications Inc (new) 275
Charter Manufacturing Company, Inc. 275
Charter Oak Equity, Lp 275
Charter Solutions, Inc. 275
Chatham Lodging Trust 275
Chatham University 275
Chca Conroe, L.p. 276
Checkpoint Systems, Inc. 276
Cheesecake Factory Inc. (the) 276
Chefs International, Inc. 276
Chefs' Warehouse Inc (the) 276
Chegg Inc 276
Chemed Corp 277
Chemours Co (the) 277
Chemung Financial Corp. 277
Chenega Corporation 277
Cheniere Energy Inc. 277
Cheniere Energy Partners L P 277
Cheniere Energy Partners Lp Holdings, Llc 278
Cherokee Nation Industries, L.l.c. 278
Cherry Bekaert Llp 278
Cherry Central Cooperative, Inc. 278
Cherry Hill Mortgage Investment Corp 278
Chesapeake Energy Corp. 278
Chesapeake Utilities Corp. 279
Chester Bancorp Inc. 279
Chevron Corporation 279
Chevron Phillips Chemical Company Llc 279
Chevron Pipe Line Company 279
Chewy Inc 279
Chicago Bears Football Club, Inc. 280
Chicago Blackhawk Hockey Team, Inc. 280
Chicago Community Trust 280
Chicago Professional Sports Corporation 280
Chicago Review Press Incorporated 280
Chicago Rivet & Machine Co. 280
Chicago Transit Authority (inc) 281
Chicago White Sox, Ltd. 281
Chickasaw Holding Company 281
Chico State Enterprises 281
Chief Consolidated Mining Co. 281
Chief Industries, Inc. 281
Child Welfare League Of America, Inc. 282
Childfund International, Usa 282

Children's Health Care 282
Children's Healthcare Of Atlanta, Inc. 282
Children's Healthcare Of California 282
Children's Hospital & Medical Center 282
Children's Hospital & Research Center At Oakland 283
Children's Hospital And Health System, Inc. 283
Children's Hospital Colorado 283
Children's Hospital Foundation 283
Children's Hospital Medical Center 283
Children's Medical Center Of Dallas 283
Children's Miracle Network 284
Children's National Medical Center 284
Children's Place Inc (the) 284
Children's Specialized Hospital Inc 284
Childrens Health System, Inc. 284
Childrens Hospital Medical Center Of Akron 284
Chilton Hospital 285
Chimera Investment Corp 285
Chimerix Inc. 285
China Huaren Organic Products Inc 285
China North East Petroleum Holdings Limited 285
Chipotle Mexican Grill Inc 285
Chippewa Valley Bean Company, Inc. 286
Chipton-ross, Inc. 286
Choate Construction Company 286
Choice Hotels International, Inc. 286
Choiceone Financial Services, Inc. 286
Chord Energy Corp 286
Christian Hospital Northeast - Northwest 287
Christiana Care Health System, Inc. 287
Christopher & Banks Corp. 287
Christopher Ranch, Llc 287
Christus Health 287
Christus Health Central Louisiana 287
Christus Spohn Health System Corporation 288
Christus-trinity Mother Frances Foundation 288
Christy Sports L.l.c. 288
Chromadex Corp 288
Chs Acquisition Corp. 288
Chs Inc 288
Chugach Alaska Corporation 289
Chugach Electric Association, Inc. 289
Church & Dwight Co Inc 289
Church Loans & Investment Trust 289
Churchill Downs, Inc. 289
Chuy's Holdings Inc 289
Cianbro Corporation 290
Cib Marine Bancshares Inc 290
Cic Group, Inc. 290
Ciee, Inc. 290
Ciena Corp 290
Cifc Corp. 290
Cigital, Inc. 291
Cimarron Mortgage Company 291
Cincinnati Bell Inc. 291
Cincinnati Financial Corp. 291
Cinemark Holdings Inc 291
Cineverse Corp 291
Cintas Corporation 292
Cipherloc Corporation 292
Circus And Eldorado Joint Venture, Llc 292
Cirrus Logic Inc 292
Cirtran Corp 292
Cisco Systems Inc 292
Citadel Enterprise Americas Llc 293
Citation Oil & Gas Corp. 293
Citgo Petroleum Corp. 293
Citi Trends Inc 293
Citigroup Global Markets Holdings Inc 293
Citigroup Global Markets Holdings Inc 293
Citigroup Inc 294
Citizant, Inc. 294
Citizen Schools, Inc. 294
Citizens & Northern Corp 294
Citizens Bancorp (corvallis, Or) 294
Citizens Bancshares Corp. (ga) 294
Citizens Community Bancorp Inc (md) 295

Citizens Energy Group 295
Citizens Financial Corp. (ky) 295
Citizens Financial Corp. (wv) 295
Citizens Financial Group Inc (new) 295
Citizens Financial Services Inc 295
Citizens Holding Co 296
Citizens, Inc. (austin, Tx) 296
Citrin Cooperman & Company, Llp 296
Citrix Systems, Inc. 296
Citrus Community College District 296
Citrus World, Inc. 296
City & County Of Honolulu 297
City & County Of San Francisco 297
City Capital Corp 297
City Harvest, Inc. 297
City Holding Co. 297
City National Bancshares Corp. (newark, N.j.) 297
City Of Akron 298
City Of Albuquerque 298
City Of Alexandria 298
City Of Anaheim 298
City Of Arlington 298
City Of Atlanta 298
City Of Austin 299
City Of Bakersfield 299
City Of Baltimore 299
City Of Baton Rouge 299
City Of Bellevue 299
City Of Berkeley 299
City Of Birmingham 300
City Of Boston 300
City Of Brockton 300
City Of Brownsville 300
City Of Buffalo 300
City Of Cambridge 300
City Of Chandler 301
City Of Charlotte 301
City Of Chesapeake 301
City Of Chicago 301
City Of Chula Vista 301
City Of Cincinnati 301
City Of Cleveland 302
City Of Colorado Springs 302
City Of Columbus 302
City Of Corpus Christi 302
City Of Dallas 302
City Of Dayton 302
City Of Denton 303
City Of El Paso 303
City Of Fontana 303
City Of Fort Wayne 303
City Of Fremont 303
City Of Fresno 303
City Of Garland 304
City Of Glendale 304
City Of Glendale 304
City Of Greensboro 304
City Of Henderson 304
City Of Hialeah 304
City Of Houston 305
City Of Independence 305
City Of Irving 305
City Of Jacksonville 305
City Of Jersey City 305
City Of Laredo 305
City Of Las Vegas 306
City Of Lincoln 306
City Of Long Beach 306
City Of Los Angeles 306
City Of Lubbock 306
City Of Madison 306
City Of Memphis 307
City Of Mesa 307
City Of Miami 307
City Of Minneapolis 307
City Of Modesto 307
City Of Montgomery 307
City Of New Orleans 308

COMPANIES LISTED ALPHABETICALLY

City Of New York 308
City Of Newport News 308
City Of Newton 308
City Of Norfolk 308
City Of Oakland 308
City Of Oklahoma City 309
City Of Omaha 309
City Of Orlando 309
City Of Oxnard 309
City Of Peoria 309
City Of Philadelphia 309
City Of Phoenix 310
City Of Pittsburgh 310
City Of Plano 310
City Of Portland 310
City Of Raleigh 310
City Of Richmond 310
City Of Richmond 311
City Of Riverside 311
City Of Rochester 311
City Of Sacramento 311
City Of Saint Paul 311
City Of Saint Petersburg 311
City Of Salinas 312
City Of San Antonio 312
City Of San Diego 312
City Of San Jose 312
City Of Santa Ana 312
City Of Seattle 312
City Of Shreveport 313
City Of St. Louis 313
City Of Stockton 313
City Of Syracuse 313
City Of Tampa 313
City Of Toledo 313
City Of Trenton 314
City Of Tucson 314
City Of Tulsa 314
City Of Virginia Beach 314
City Of Yonkers 314
City Public Services Of San Antonio 314
City Utilities Of Springfield Mo 315
Cityservicevalcon, Llc 315
Civeo U.s. Holdings Llc 315
Civista Bancshares Inc 315
Civitas Resources Inc 315
Ck Construction Group Inc. 315
Ckhs, Inc. 316
Ckx Lands Inc 316
Claflin University 316
Clarcor Inc. 316
Clare Rose, Inc. 316
Claremont Graduate University 316
Claremont Mckenna College Foundation 317
Clarient, Inc. 317
Clark Construction Group, Llc 317
Clark Dubin & Company Inc 317
Clark Enterprises, Inc. 317
Clark, Schaefer, Hackett & Co. 317
Clarkson University 318
Clarocity Corp 318
Clarus Corp (new) 318
Clay Electric Cooperative, Inc. 318
Clayco, Inc. 318
Clean Energy Fuels Corp 318
Clean Harbors Inc 319
Cleannet U.s.a., Inc. 319
Clear Channel Outdoor Holdings Inc (new) 319
Clearday Inc 319
Clearfield Hospital 319
Clearfield Inc 319
Clearone Inc 320
Clearpoint Neuro Inc 320
Clearsign Technologies Corp 320
Clearwater Paper Corp 320
Clearway Energy Inc 320
Cleary University 320
Cleco Corporate Holdings Llc 321

Cleveland Browns Football Company Llc 321
Cleveland Clinic Mercy Hospital 321
Cleveland Construction, Inc. 321
Cleveland Electric Illuminating Co 321
Cleveland State University 321
Cleveland-cliffs Inc (new) 322
Clicker Inc 322
Client Services, Inc. 322
Clif Bar & Company, Llc 322
Cliftonlarsonallen Llp 322
Climb Global Solutions Inc 322
Clinch Valley Medical Center, Inc. 323
Clorox Co (the) 323
Cloud Peak Energy Inc. 323
Clovis Oncology Inc 323
Clubcorp Holdings, Inc. 323
Cme Group Inc 323
Cms Energy Corp 324
Cmtsu Liquidation Inc 324
Cna Financial Corp 324
Cnb Corp (mi) 324
Cnb Financial Corp. (clearfield, Pa) 324
Cno Financial Group Inc 324
Cnx Resources Corp 325
Co Holdings, Llc 325
Coast Citrus Distributors 325
Coast Electric Power Association 325
Coastal Carolina University Alumni Association, Inc. 325
Coastal Pacific Food Distributors, Inc. 325
Coates International Ltd 326
Cobank Acb 326
Cobb Electric Membership Corporation 326
Coborn's, Incorporated 326
Coca-cola Co (the) 326
Coca-cola Consolidated Inc 326
Codale Electric Supply, Inc. 327
Codexis Inc 327
Codorus Valley Bancorp, Inc. 327
Coe College 327
Coeur Mining Inc 327
Coffee Holding Co Inc 327
Cogent Communications Holdings, Inc. 328
Cogentix Medical, Inc. 328
Cogentrix Energy, Inc. 328
Cognex Corp 328
Cognition Financial Corporation 328
Cognizant Technology Solutions Corp. 328
Cohen & Company Inc (new) 329
Cohen & Steers Inc 329
Coherent Corp 329
Cohesant Inc. 329
Cohu Inc 329
Coinbase Global Inc 329
Coinstar, Llc 330
Colavita Usa L.l.c. 330
Cold Jet, Llc 330
Coleman University 330
Colgate University 330
Colgate-palmolive Co. 330
Collectors Universe, Inc. 331
College Entrance Examination Board 331
College Of Saint Benedict 331
College Of The Holy Cross (inc) 331
Collegium Pharmaceutical Inc 331
Collin County Community College District 331
Colombia Energy Resources Inc. 332
Colonial Metals Co. 332
Colonial Pipeline Company 332
Colony Bankcorp, Inc. 332
Colony Brands, Inc. 332
Colony Capital, Inc. 332
Colony Resorts Lvh Acquisitions, Llc 333
Color Me Mine Enterprises Inc 333
Colorado College 333
Colorado Interstate Gas Co. 333
Colorado Mesa University 333
Colorado Rockies Baseball Club, Ltd. 333

Colorado Springs Utilities 334
Colorado State University 334
Colorado State University-pueblo Foundation 334
Colorado Structures, Inc. 334
Coloredge, Inc. 334
Colquitt Electric Membership Corporation 334
Colsa Corporation 335
Colson & Colson Construction Co 335
Colt Defense Llc 335
Columbia Banking System Inc 335
Columbia College Chicago 335
Columbia Forest Products, Inc. 335
Columbia Gas Of Ohio, Inc. 336
Columbia Gulf Transmission, Llc 336
Columbia Hospital (palm Beaches) Limited Partnership 336
Columbia Ogden Medical Center, Inc. 336
Columbia Pipeline Group, Inc. 336
Columbia Pipeline Partners Lp 336
Columbia Sportswear Co. 337
Columbia Sussex Corporation 337
Columbia Valley Healthcare System, L.p. 337
Columbus Mckinnon Corp. (ny) 337
Columbus Regional Healthcare System, Inc 337
Comarco Inc. 337
Combimatrix Corporation 338
Comcast Corp 338
Comenity Bank 338
Comerica, Inc. 338
Comerton Corp 338
Comfort Systems Usa Inc 338
Commerce Bancshares Inc 339
Commerce Energy Group Inc 339
Commerce Group Corp. 339
Commercial Energy Of Montana Inc. 339
Commercial Metals Co. 339
Commercial National Financial Corp. (pa) 339
Commercial Vehicle Group Inc 340
Commodore Applied Technologies, Inc. 340
Commonspirit Health 340
Commonwealth Edison Company 340
Commonwealth Equity Services, Llc 340
Commonwealth Health Corporation, Inc. 340
Commscope Holding Co Inc 341
Communications Test Design, Inc. 341
Communications Workers Of America, Afl-cio, Clc 341
Community Asphalt Corp. 341
Community Bancorp. (derby, Vt) 341
Community Bank System Inc 341
Community Capital Bancshares Inc 342
Community Choice Financial Inc 342
Community Energy, Inc. 342
Community Health Charities 342
Community Health Group 342
Community Health Network, Inc. 342
Community Health Systems, Inc. 343
Community Healthcare Trust Inc 343
Community Hospital Of Anderson And Madison County, Incorporated 343
Community Hospital Of San Bernardino 343
Community Hospital Of The Monterey Peninsula 343
Community Hospitals Of Central California 343
Community Investors Bancorp, Inc 344
Community Medical Center, Inc. 344
Community Trust Bancorp, Inc. 344
Community West Bancshares 344
Commvault Systems Inc 344
Companion Professional Services Llc 344
Compass Diversified 345
Compass Inc 345
Compass Minerals International Inc 345
Compumed 345
Compunet Clinical Laboratories, Llc 345
Computer Aid, Inc. 345
Computer Enterprises Inc 346
Computer Sciences Corporation 346

Compx International, Inc. 346
Comscore Inc 346
Comstock Holding Companies, Inc 346
Comstock Resources Inc 346
Comtech Telecommunications Corp. 347
Comtex News Network Inc 347
Conagra Brands Inc 347
Concentric Consumer Marketing, Inc. 347
Concho Resources Inc. 347
Concord Hospital, Inc. 347
Concord Litho Group Llc 348
Concordia College - New York Foundation, Inc. 348
Concurrent Technologies Corporation 348
Condor Hospitality Trust Inc 348
Conduent Inc 348
Conemaugh Health Company, Llc 348
Congoleum Corp (new) 349
Conmed Corp 349
Connecticut Children's Medical Center 349
Connecticut College 349
Connecticut Department Of Labor 349
Connecticut Light & Power Co 349
Connecticut State University System 350
Connecton, Inc. 350
Connectone Bancorp Inc (new) 350
Connectria, Llc 350
Connexus Energy 350
Connor Co. 350
Conns Inc 351
Conolog Corp 351
Conrad Industries Inc 351
Conservation International Foundation 351
Consolidated Communications Holdings Inc 351
Consolidated Contracting Services, Inc. 351
Consolidated Edison Co. Of New York, Inc. 352
Consolidated Edison Inc 352
Consolidated Health Systems, Inc. 352
Consolidated Pipe & Supply Company, Inc. 352
Constant Contact, Inc. 352
Constantin Associates, Llp 352
Constellation Brands Inc 353
Consulier Engineering, Inc. 353
Consumer Portfolio Services, Inc. 353
Consumer Product Distributors, Llc 353
Consumer Reports, Inc. 353
Consumer Technology Association 353
Consumers Bancorp, Inc. (minerva, Oh) 354
Consumers Energy Co. 354
Container Store Group, Inc 354
Conti Enterprises Inc. 354
Continental Materials Corp. 354
Continental Resources, Inc. 354
Continental Resources, Inc. 355
Contractors Steel Company 355
Control Chief Holdings, Inc. 355
Control4 Corporation 355
Convaid Products Llc 355
Convergent Outsourcing, Inc. 355
Convergint Technologies Llc 356
Conway Regional Medical Center, Inc. 356
Cook Children's Health Care System 356
Cookeville Regional Medical Center 356
Coolsystems, Inc. 356
Cooper Communities, Inc. 356
Cooper Companies, Inc. (the) 357
Cooper-standard Holdings Inc 357
Cooperative Elevator Co. 357
Cooperative For Assistance And Relief Everywhere, Inc. (care) 357
Cooperative Regions Of Organic Producer Pools 357
Copart Inc 357
Copt Defense Properties 358
Corascloud, Inc. 358
Corcentric, Llc 358
Corcept Therapeutics Inc 358
Core & Main Inc 358
Core Construction, Inc. 358
Core Laboratories Inc 359

Core Molding Technologies Inc 359
Corecard Corp 359
Corecivic Inc 359
Corenergy Infrastructure Trust Inc 359
Corenet Global, Inc. 359
Coresite Realty Corporation 360
Corewell Health 360
Corium, Llc 360
Cormedix Inc 360
Cornell University 360
Cornerstone Agency Inc. 360
Cornerstone Building Brands, Inc. 361
Cornerstone Ondemand, Inc. 361
Corning Inc 361
Corning Natural Gas Corp 361
Corplay Inc 361
Corporate Computer Centers, Inc. 361
Corporate Fitness Works, Inc. 362
Corporate Travel Consultants, Inc. 362
Corporate Travel Management North America, Inc. 362
Corporation For Public Broadcasting 362
Correlate Energy Corp 362
Corvel Corp 362
Cosco Fire Protection, Inc. 363
Cosi, Inc. 363
Costar Group, Inc. 363
Costco Wholesale Corp 363
Coterra Energy Inc 363
Cotiviti Holdings, Inc. 363
Cotton Incorporated 364
Coty, Inc. 364
Council For Economic Education 364
Council Of Better Business Bureaus, Inc. 364
Council On Foreign Relations, Inc. 364
Counterpart International Inc 364
Country Casualty Insurance Co. (bloomington, Il) 365
Country Investors Life Assurance Co. (bloomington, Il) 365
Country Pride Cooperative, Inc. 365
County Of Alameda 365
County Of Los Angeles 365
Cousins Properties Inc 365
Covanta Holding Corporation 366
Covenant Health 366
Covenant Health System 366
Covenant House 366
Covenant Logistics Group Inc 366
Covenant Medical Center, Inc. 366
Cover-all Technologies Inc. 367
Coverall North America, Inc. 367
Covetrus North America, Llc 367
Covisint Corporation 367
Covista Communications Inc. 367
Cowan Systems, Llc 367
Cox Enterprises, Inc. 368
Cozen O'connor 368
Cpi Aerostructures, Inc. 368
Cpi Card Group Inc 368
Cpp International, Llc 368
Cps Technologies Corp 368
Cra International Inc 369
Cracker Barrel Old Country Store Inc 369
Crain Communications, Inc. 369
Crane Nxt Co 369
Crawford & Co. 369
Crawford Memorial Foundation 369
Crawford United Corp 370
Crayola Llc 370
Crazy Woman Creek Bancorp Inc. 370
Creation Technologies New York Inc. 370
Creative Group, Inc. 370
Creative Media & Community Trust Corp 370
Creative Realities Inc 371
Credit Acceptance Corp (mi) 371
Credit Suisse (usa) Inc 371
Creditriskmonitor.com, Inc. 371

Creighton University 371
Crescent Electric Supply Company 371
Crest Operations, Llc 372
Crestwood Midstream Partners Lp 372
Crete Carrier Corporation 372
Crexendo Inc 372
Crider, Inc. 372
Crista Ministries 372
Crocs Inc 373
Croghan Bancshares, Inc. 373
Cross Border Resources Inc. 373
Cross Country Healthcare Inc 373
Cross Technologies, Inc. 373
Cross Timbers Royalty Trust 373
Crossamerica Partners Lp 374
Crossland Construction Company, Inc. 374
Crossroads Impact Corp 374
Crowder Construction Company Inc 374
Crowell & Moring Llp 374
Crowley Maritime Corporation 374
Crown Battery Manufacturing Company 375
Crown Castle Inc 375
Crown Crafts, Inc. 375
Crown Equipment Corporation 375
Crown Holdings Inc 375
Crown Media Holdings, Inc. 375
Crst International, Inc. 376
Cryo-cell International Inc 376
Crystal Flash, Inc. 376
Crystal Rock Holdings, Inc. 376
Csg Systems International Inc. 376
Csi Compressco Lp 376
Csi Leasing, Inc. 377
Csp Inc 377
Csra Inc. 377
Css Industries, Inc. 377
Cssi, Inc. 377
Cst Brands, Llc 377
Csu Fullerton Auxiliary Services Corporation 378
Csx Corp 378
Cto Realty Growth Inc (new) 378
Ctpartners Executive Search Inc 378
Cts Corp 378
Ctsc, Llc 378
Cubesmart, L.p. 379
Cubic Corporation 379
Cuisine Solutions, Inc. 379
Cuivre River Electric Cooperative, Inc. 379
Culinaire International, Inc. 379
Cullen/frost Bankers, Inc. 379
Culp Inc 380
Culver Franchising System, Llc 380
Cumberland County Hospital System, Inc. 380
Cumberland Pharmaceuticals Inc 380
Cummins, Inc. 380
Cumulus Media Inc 380
Curaegis Technologies Inc 381
Curia Global, Inc. 381
Curis Inc 381
Curran Group, Inc. 381
Curtis C. Gunn, Inc. 381
Curtiss-wright Corp. 381
Cuso Financial Services, L.p. 382
Customers Bancorp Inc 382
Customink, Llc 382
Cutco Corporation 382
Cutera Inc 382
Cvb Financial Corp 382
Cvd Equipment Corp. 383
Cvent, Inc. 383
Cvr Energy Inc 383
Cvr Partners Lp 383
Cvs Health Corporation 383
Cxtec Inc. 383
Cyanotech Corp. 384
Cyberthink, Inc. 384
Cyclacel Pharmaceuticals Inc 384
Cymer, Inc. 384

Cynergistek, Inc. 384
Cynosure, Llc 384
Cypress Bioscience, Inc. 385
Cypress Environmental Partners Lp 385
Cyrq Energy, Llc 385
Cys Investments, Inc. 385
Cystic Fibrosis Foundation 385
Cytokinetics Inc 385
D & A Building Services, Inc. 386
D W W Co., Inc. 386
D. C. Taylor Co. 386
D.m. Bowman, Inc. 386
D.r. Systems, Inc. 386
D/l Cooperative Inc. 386
Dac Technologies Group International Inc. 387
Daegis Inc. 387
Daemen University 387
Daily Express, Inc. 387
Daily Journal Corporation 387
Daily News, L.p. 387
Dairy Farmers Of America, Inc. 388
Dairyland Power Cooperative 388
Dais Corp 388
Dakota Electric Association 388
Dakota Gasification Company Inc 388
Dakota State University 388
Dakota Supply Group, Inc. 389
Daktronics Inc. 389
Dallas Basketball Limited 389
Dallas County Hospital District 389
Dallas-fort Worth International Airport Facility Improvement Corporation 389
Dallasnews Corp 389
Dana Inc 390
Dana-farber Cancer Institute, Inc. 390
Danaher Corp 390
Danfoss Power Solutions Inc. 390
Daniel F. Young, Incorporated 390
Daniel J. Edelman, Inc. 390
Danis Building Construction Company 391
Danone Us, Inc. 391
Danville Regional Medical Center, Llc 391
Darden Restaurants, Inc. 391
Dare Bioscience Inc 391
Darkpulse Inc 391
Darling Ingredients Inc 392
Dartmouth-hitchcock Clinic 392
Data I/o Corp. 392
Data Systems Analysts, Inc. 392
Data2logistics, Llc 392
Datacon, Inc. 392
Datalink Corporation 393
Datasite Global Corporation 393
Datatrak International Inc. 393
Dats Trucking, Inc. 393
Daubert Industries, Inc. 393
Davco Restaurants, Inc. 393
Dave & Buster's, Inc. 394
Dave & Busters Entertainment Inc 394
Davenport University 394
Davey Tree Expert Co. (the) 394
David E. Harvey Builders, Inc. 394
David Montoya Construction, Inc. 394
David Yurman Enterprises Llc 395
Davidson Hotel Company Llc 395
Daviess County Hospital 395
Davita Inc 395
Daw Technologies Inc. 395
Dawson Geophysical Co (new) 395
Dawson Metal Company, Inc. 396
Day Kimball Healthcare, Inc. 396
Dayforce Inc 396
Daylight Donut Flour Company Llc 396
Dbm Global Inc 396
Dc Group Inc. 396
Dcp Midstream Lp 397
Deaconess Health System, Inc. 397
Deaconess Hospital Inc 397

Dealers Supply Company, Inc. 397
Dealertrack Technologies, Inc. 397
Dean Foods Company 397
Debartolo, Inc. 398
Debt Resolve Inc 398
Decatur Memorial Hospital 398
Deciphera Pharmaceuticals Inc 398
Decision Diagnostics Corp 398
Decisionpoint Systems Inc (new) 398
Deckers Outdoor Corp. 399
Deep Foods Inc. 399
Deere & Co. 399
Defender Industries, Inc. 399
Defenders Of Wildlife 399
Defoe Corp. 399
Dei Holdings Inc 400
Dekalb Medical Center, Inc. 400
Del Friscos Of Georgia, Llc 400
Del Monaco Foods, Llc 400
Del West Engineering, Inc. 400
Delaware River Basin Commission 400
Delaware River Port Authority 401
Delaware State University 401
Delaware Valley University 401
Delawie 401
Delcath Systems Inc 401
Delek Logistics Partners Lp 401
Delek Us Energy, Inc. 402
Delek Us Holdings Inc (new) 402
Delgado Community College 402
Deli Management, Inc. 402
Dell Inc. 402
Dell Technologies Inc 402
Delmarva Power & Light Co. 403
Delphax Technologies Inc 403
Delta Air Lines Inc (de) 403
Delta Apparel Inc. 403
Delta College Foundation 403
Delta Corporate Services, Inc 403
Delta Dental Plans Association 404
Delta Health System 404
Delta Natural Gas Company, Inc. 404
Delta Tucker Holdings Inc 404
Deluxe Corp 404
Demandware, Llc 404
Democrasoft, Holdings Inc 405
Denison University 405
Denny's Corp 405
Denton County Electric Cooperative, Inc. 405
Dentsply Sirona Inc 405
Denver Board Of Water Commissioners 405
Denver Health And Hospitals Authority Inc 406
Depaul University 406
Depauw University 406
Dept Of Education Alabama 406
Derive Technologies Llc 406
Derma Sciences, Inc. 406
Dermalogica, Llc 407
Desales University 407
Deschutes Brewery, Inc. 407
Deseret Generation And Transmission Co-operative 407
Designer Brands Inc 407
Desktop Service Center, Inc. 407
Destination Maternity Corp 408
Destination Xl Group Inc 408
Determine, Inc. 408
Detroit Pistons Basketball Company 408
Devcon Construction Incorporated 408
Devereux Foundation 408
Devon Energy Corp. 409
Dewey Electronics Corp. 409
Dexcom Inc 409
Dfb Pharmaceuticals, Llc 409
Dgo Corporation 409
Dgt Holdings Corp. 409
Dhi Group Inc 410
Diagnostic Laboratory Services, Inc. 410

Diakon 410
Dialysis Clinic, Inc. 410
Diamond Discoveries International Corp 410
Diamond Hill Investment Group Inc. 410
Diamond Offshore Drilling Inc (new) 411
Diamond Parking Services, Llc 411
Diamondback Energy, Inc. 411
Diamondhead Casino Corp 411
Diamondrock Hospitality Co. 411
Diaspark Inc. 411
Dicerna Pharmaceuticals, Inc. 412
Dick's Sporting Goods, Inc 412
Dickinson College 412
Diebold Nixdorf Inc 412
Digerati Technologies Inc 412
Digi International Inc 412
Digicon Corporation 413
Digimarc Corp 413
Digital Ally Inc (new) 413
Digital Realty Trust Inc 413
Digital Turbine Inc 413
Digitalbridge Group Inc 413
Dignity Health 414
Dillard University 414
Dillard's Inc. 414
Dime Community Bancshares Inc (new) 414
Dimensions Health Corporation 414
Dimeo Construction Company 414
Dine Brands Global Inc 415
Dinewise Inc 415
Diodes, Inc. 415
Direct Marketing Association, Incorporated 415
Direct Relief Foundation 415
Direct Selling Association (inc) 415
Disabled American Veterans 416
Discount Drug Mart, Inc. 416
Discover Financial Services 416
Dish Network Corp 416
Disney (walt) Co. (the) 416
Distribution Solutions Group Inc 416
Ditech Holding Corporation 417
Diversicare Healthcare Services, Inc. 417
Diversified Chemical Technologies, Inc. 417
Diversified Communications 417
Diversified Healthcare Trust 417
Dixie Group Inc. 417
Dixon Ticonderoga Company 418
Djsp Enterprises, Inc. 418
Dla Piper Llp (us) 418
Dlh Holdings Corp 418
Dlh Solutions, Inc 418
Dmc Global Inc 418
Dmh Real Estate Holdings, Inc. 419
Dmk Pharmaceuticals Corp 419
Dnow Inc 419
Do It Best Corp. 419
Doctor's Associates Inc. 419
Doctors Hospital Of Augusta, Llc 419
Document Capture Technologies, Inc. 420
Docusign Inc 420
Dolby Laboratories Inc 420
Dollar General Corp 420
Dollar Tree Inc 420
Domain Associates L.l.c. 420
Dominari Holdings Inc 421
Dominion Energy Inc (new) 421
Dominion Energy Questar Corporation 421
Dominion Energy South Carolina, Inc. 421
Dominion Resources Black Warrior Trust 421
Dominos Pizza Inc. 421
Domtar Corporation 422
Donaldson Co. Inc. 422
Donegal Group Inc. 422
Donnelley Financial Solutions Inc 422
Doordash Inc 422
Dorchester Minerals Lp 422
Dorman Products Inc 423
Dorsey & Whitney Llp 423

Doster Construction Company, Inc. 423
Dougherty's Pharmacy Inc 423
Douglas Dynamics, Inc. 423
Douglas Emmett Inc 423
Dover Corp 424
Dover Motorsports, Inc. 424
Dover Saddlery, Inc. 424
Dow Inc 424
Dowling College 424
Doylestown Hospital Health And Wellness Center, Inc. 424
Dpl Inc. 425
Dpr Construction, Inc. 425
Drake University 425
Draper And Kramer, Incorporated 425
Dress For Success Worldwide 425
Drew University 425
Drexel University 426
Dril-quip Inc 426
Drinks Americas Holdings, Ltd. 426
Drive Shack Inc 426
Drivetime Automotive Group Inc 426
Dropbox Inc 426
Drx, Ltd. 427
Dss Inc 427
Dst Systems, Inc. 427
Dte Electric Company 427
Dte Energy Co 427
Dts, Inc. 427
Ducks Unlimited, Inc. 428
Ducommun Inc. 428
Duke Energy Carolinas Llc 428
Duke Energy Corp 428
Duke Energy Florida Llc 428
Duke Energy Indiana, Inc. 428
Duke Energy Of Kentucky 429
Duke Energy Ohio, Inc. 429
Duke Energy Progress, Llc 429
Duke Realty L.p. 429
Duke Realty Llc 429
Duke University 429
Duke University Health System, Inc. 430
Dun & Bradstreet Holdings Inc 430
Duncan-williams, Inc. 430
Dunham & Associates Investment Counsel, Inc. 430
Dunkin' Brands Group, Inc. 430
Duo-gard Industries, Inc. 430
Dupont De Nemours Inc 431
Dupont Fabros Technology, Inc. 431
Duquesne Light Co 431
Duquesne Light Holdings, Inc. 431
Duquesne University Of The Holy Spirit 431
Dura Automotive Systems Inc 431
Dura Coat Products, Inc. 432
Durect Corp 432
Dvl, Inc. 432
Dwa Holdings, Llc 432
Dxc Technology Co 432
Dxp Enterprises, Inc. 432
Dyadic International Inc 433
Dyax Corp. 433
Dycom Industries, Inc. 433
Dyna Group International, Inc. 433
Dynacq Healthcare Inc 433
Dynamix Group, Inc 433
Dynasil Corp Of America 434
Dynatem Inc 434
Dynatronics Corp. 434
Dynavax Technologies Corp 434
Dynex Capital Inc 434
Dyonyx, L.p. 434
Dzs Inc 435
E -pacific I Inc 435
E Trade Financial Corporation 435
E Z Loader Boat Trailers, Inc. 435
E-lynxx Corporation 435
E. & J. Gallo Winery 435
E. C. Barton & Company 436

E.digital Corp. 436
E.l.f. Beauty Inc 436
E.n.m.r. Telephone Cooperative 436
Ea Engineering, Science, And Technology, Inc., Pbc 436
Eaco Corp 436
Eagle Bancorp Inc (md) 437
Eagle Bancorp Montana, Inc. 437
Eagle Bulk Shipping Inc 437
Eagle Materials Inc 437
Eagle Pharmaceuticals, Inc. 437
Ealixir Inc 437
Earl G. Graves, Ltd. 438
Earl L. Henderson Trucking Company, Llc 438
Earlham College 438
Earnhardt Management Company 438
Earth Search Sciences Inc. 438
Earth Share 438
Earth Sun Moon Trading Company, Inc. 439
East Alabama Health Care Authority 439
East Bay Municipal Utility District, Water System 439
East Of Chicago Pizza Inc 439
East Orange General Hospital (inc) 439
East Tennessee Children's Hospital Association, Inc. 439
East Tennessee State University 440
East Texas Medical Center Regional Healthcare System 440
East West Bancorp, Inc 440
Easter Seals, Inc. 440
Easterly Government Properties Inc 440
Eastern Bag And Paper Company, Incorporated 440
Eastern Co. 441
Eastern Gas Transmission And Storage, Inc. 441
Eastern Kentucky University 441
Eastern Light Capital Inc 441
Eastern Maine Healthcare Systems 441
Eastern Michigan University 441
Eastern Virginia Medical School 442
Eastern Washington University Inc 442
Eastgroup Properties Inc 442
Eastland Memorial Hospital District 442
Eastman Chemical Co 442
Eastman Kodak Co. 442
Easton Bancorp, Inc. 443
Eau Technologies Inc 443
Ebay Inc. 443
Ebix Inc 443
Eby Corporation 443
Eby-brown Company, Llc 443
Ecc Capital Corp 444
Echelon Corporation 444
Echl Inc. 444
Echo Global Logistics, Inc. 444
Echo Therapeutics Inc 444
Echostar Corp 444
Eckerd College, Inc. 445
Eckerd Youth Alternatives, Inc. 445
Eco2 Plastics, Inc. 445
Ecolab Inc 445
Ecology And Environment Inc. 445
Ecovyst Inc 445
Ecs Federal, Llc 446
Edd Helms Group 446
Edelbrock, Llc 446
Edelman Financial Engines, Llc 446
Eden Foods, Inc. 446
Edgewave, Inc 446
Edgewell Personal Care Co 447
Edgio Inc 447
Edi Specialists, Inc. 447
Edible International, Llc 447
Edison International 447
Edisonlearning, Inc. 447
Editas Medicine Inc 448
Edsi 448
Education Management Corp 448

Educational & Institutional Cooperative Service, Inc. 448
Educational Development Corp. 448
Educational Funding Of The South, Inc. 448
Educational Testing Service 449
Edw. C. Levy Co. 449
Edward D. Jones & Co., L.p. 449
Edwards Lifesciences Corp 449
Eei Holding Corporation 449
Egain Corp 449
Eger Health Care And Rehabilitation Center 450
Egpi Firecreek Inc 450
Ehealth Inc 450
Eide Bailly Llp 450
Eidp, Inc. 450
Eiger Biopharmaceuticals Inc 450
Eileen Fisher, Inc. 451
Eisenhower Medical Center 451
Eisneramper Llp 451
El Dorado Furniture Corp 451
El Paso County Hospital District 451
El Paso Electric Company 451
El Pollo Loco Holdings Inc 452
Elah Holdings Inc 452
Elamex, S.a. De C.v. (mexico) 452
Elanco Animal Health Inc 452
Elcom International, Inc. 452
Elderhostel, Inc. 452
Eldorado Artesian Springs Inc 453
Electric & Gas Technology, Inc. 453
Electric Energy, Inc. 453
Electric Power Board Of Chattanooga 453
Electric Power Board Of The Metropolitan Government Of Nashville & Davidson County 453
Electric Power Research Institute, Inc. 453
Electric Reliability Council Of Texas, Inc. 454
Electrical Apparatus Service Association Inc 454
Electrical Geodesics, Inc 454
Electro-matic Ventures, Inc. 454
Electro-sensors, Inc. 454
Electromed, Inc. 454
Electronic Arts, Inc. 455
Electronic Control Security Inc. 455
Electronic Instrumentation And Technology, Llc 455
Electronic Knowledge Interchange Inc 455
Electronic Systems Technology, Inc. 455
Electronic Tele-communications, Inc. 455
Electronics For Imaging, Inc. 456
Elegant Illusions Inc 456
Element Solutions Inc 456
Elevance Health Inc 456
Elevate Textiles, Inc. 456
Elgin Separation Solutions Industrials Llc 456
Elite Pharmaceuticals Inc 457
Elixir Industries 457
Elkhart General Hospital, Inc. 457
Elkins Constructors, Inc. 457
Ellington Financial Inc 457
Ellington Residential Mortgaging Real Estate Investment Trust 457
Elliot Hospital Of The City Of Manchester 458
Ellis Hospital 458
Ellsworth Cooperative Creamery 458
Ellucian Inc. 458
Elma Electronic Inc. 458
Elme Communities 458
Elmhurst Memorial Hospital Inc 459
Eloxx Pharmaceuticals Inc 459
Elwyn Of Pennsylvania And Delaware 459
Emanate Health Medical Group 459
Embree Construction Group, Inc. 459
Embry-riddle Aeronautical University, Inc. 459
Emcor Group, Inc. 460
Emcore Corp. 460
Emerald Dairy Inc 460
Emerald Holding Inc 460
Emerald Oil, Inc. 460

COMPANIES LISTED ALPHABETICALLY

Emerge Energy Services Lp 460
Emergent Biosolutions Inc 461
Emerson College 461
Emerson Electric Co. 461
Emerson Hospital 461
Emerson Radio Corp. 461
Emi Holding, Inc. 461
Emj Corporation 462
Emkay, Inc. 462
Emmet, Marvin & Martin, Llp 462
Emmis Corp 462
Empire Energy Corp International 462
Empire Resorts, Inc. 462
Empire Resources, Inc. 463
Empire Southwest, Llc 463
Empire State Realty Op Lp 463
Empire State Realty Trust Inc 463
Employers Holdings Inc 463
Emporia State University 463
Emulex Corporation 464
Enable Holdings, Inc. 464
Enactus 464
Enanta Pharmaceuticals Inc 464
Encision Inc. 464
Encompass Energy Services Inc 464
Encompass Health Corp 465
Encompass Holdings, Inc. 465
Encore Capital Group Inc 465
Encore Nationwide, Inc. 465
Encore Wire Corp. 465
Endeavor Health Clinical Operations 465
Endi Corp 466
Endologix, Inc. 466
Enel X North America, Inc. 466
Ener1, Inc. 466
Enerfab, Inc. 466
Energizer Holdings Inc (new) 466
Energous Corp 467
Energy & Environmental Services Inc 467
Energy Focus Inc 467
Energy Future Holdings Corp 467
Energy Northwest 467
Energy Recovery Inc 467
Energy Services Of America Corp. 468
Energy Services Providers, Inc. 468
Energy Transfer Lp 468
Energyunited Electric Membership Corporation 468
Enerpac Tool Group Corp 468
Enersys 468
Enerwise Global Technologies, Llc Dba Cpower 469
Engelberth Construction, Inc. 469
Enghouse Networks (us) Inc. 469
Englefield, Inc. 469
Englewood Hospital And Medical Center Foundation Inc. 469
Englobal Corp. 469
Enherent Corp 470
Eniva Usa, Inc. 470
Enlink Midstream Llc 470
Enlink Midstream Partners, Lp 470
Ennis Inc 470
Enova International Inc 470
Enova Systems Inc 471
Enovis Corp 471
Enphase Energy Inc. 471
Enpro Inc 471
Enservco Corp 471
Ensign Group Inc 471
Ensign-bickford Industries, Inc. 472
Ensync Inc 472
Entech Sales And Service, Llc 472
Entech Solar, Inc 472
Entegee, Inc. 472
Entegris Inc 472
Entergy Arkansas Llc 473
Entergy Corp 473
Entergy Gulf States Louisiana, L.l.c. 473

Entergy Louisiana Llc (new) 473
Entergy Mississippi Llc 473
Entergy New Orleans Llc 473
Enterprise Bancorp, Inc. (ma) 474
Enterprise Community Partners, Inc. 474
Enterprise Electric, Llc 474
Enterprise Financial Services Corp 474
Enterprise Financial Services Group Inc 474
Enterprise Florida, Inc. 474
Enterprise Informatics Inc 475
Enterprise Mobility 475
Enterprise Partners Management, Llc 475
Enterprise Products Partners L.p. 475
Entorian Technologies Inc. 475
Entravision Communications Corp. 475
Entrx Corporation 476
Envela Corp 476
Envestnet Inc 476
Enviri Corp 476
Enviromedia, Inc. 476
Environmental Defense Fund, Incorporated 476
Environmental Health & Engineering, Inc. 477
Environmental Tectonics Corp. 477
Envision Healthcare Corporation 477
Enviva Inc 477
Envivio, Inc. 477
Enxnet Inc. 477
Enzo Biochem, Inc. 478
Enzon Pharmaceuticals Inc 478
Eog Resources, Inc. 478
Eom Pharmaceutical Holdings Inc 478
Ep Energy Corp. 478
Epam Systems, Inc. 478
Epi Group, Llc. 479
Epiq Systems, Inc. 479
Epitec, Inc. 479
Eplus Inc 479
Epr Properties 479
Epsilon Systems Solutions, Inc. 479
Eqt Corp 480
Equifax Inc 480
Equinix Inc 480
Equinor Marketing & Trading (us) Inc. 480
Equitable Holdings Inc 480
Equitrans, L.p. 480
Equity Commonwealth 481
Equity Lifestyle Properties Inc 481
Equity One, Inc. 481
Equity Residential 481
Erba Diagnostics 481
Ergon Asphalt Partners, Lp 481
Erhc Energy Inc 482
Erickson Incorporated 482
Erie Indemnity Co. 482
Erin Energy Corp 482
Ernst & Young Llp 482
Eroom System Technologies Inc 482
Eros Media World Plc 483
Ervin Industries, Inc. 483
Escalade, Inc. 483
Escalera Resources Co 483
Escalon Medical Corp 483
Esco Technologies, Inc. 483
Esperion Therapeutics Inc (new) 484
Espey Manufacturing & Electronics Corp. 484
Essa Bancorp Inc 484
Essendant Inc. 484
Essential Utilities Inc 484
Essex Property Trust Inc 484
Essex Rental Corp 485
Essilor Of America, Inc. 485
Essroc Holdings Llc 485
Estes Express Lines 485
Eterna Therapeutics Inc 485
Ethan Allen Interiors, Inc. 485
Etna Distributors, Llc 486
Etp Legacy Lp 486
Etsy Inc 486

Eugene Water & Electric Board 486
Euro Group Of Companies Inc 486
Eurofins Lancaster Laboratories, Inc. 486
Euronav Mi Ii Inc. 487
Euronet Worldwide Inc. 487
Evangelical Community Hospital 487
Evans & Sutherland Computer Corporation 487
Evans Bancorp, Inc. 487
Event Network, Llc 487
Everbank Financial Corp 488
Evercore Inc 488
Everglades Steel Corporation 488
Evergreen Fs, Inc 488
Evergreen State College 488
Evergy Inc 488
Everi Holdings Inc 489
Eversource Energy 489
Eversource Energy Service Company 489
Everspin Technologies Inc 489
Evertec, Inc. 489
Everyday Health, Inc. 489
Evi Industries Inc 490
Evofem, Inc. 490
Evoke Pharma Inc 490
Evolution Petroleum Corp 490
Evolve Transition Infrastructure Lp 490
Evolveware, Inc. 490
Ewing Irrigation Products, Inc. 491
Ex-students Association Of The University Of Texas 491
Exa Corporation 491
Exact Sciences Corp. 491
Exactech, Inc. 491
Exar Corporation 491
Excel Interior Construction Corp. 492
Excel Railcar Corporation 492
Excela Health Holding Company, Inc. 492
Exchange Bank (santa Rosa, Ca) 492
Exco Resources Inc 492
Exelixis Inc 492
Exelon Corp 493
Exelon Generation Co Llc 493
Exeter Health Resources, Inc. 493
Exide Technologies 493
Exlservice Holdings Inc 493
Exp World Holdings Inc 493
Expedia Group Inc 494
Expeditors International Of Washington, Inc. 494
Experian Information Solutions, Inc. 494
Experience Learning Community 494
Experience Works, Inc. 494
Exponent Inc. 494
Export-import Bank Of The United States 495
Express Inc 495
Express Scripts Holding Company 495
Express Services, Inc. 495
Expro Group Holdings Nv 495
Extended Stay America, Inc. 495
Extra Space Storage Inc 496
Extreme Networks Inc 496
Exxon Mobil Corp 496
Exxonmobil Pipeline Company 496
Ezcorp, Inc. 496
F & M Bank Corp. 496
F&s Produce Company, Inc. 497
F5 Inc 497
Fa Finale, Inc. 497
Factset Research Systems Inc. 497
Faegre Drinker Biddle & Reath Llp 497
Fafco, Inc. 497
Fahlgren, Inc. 498
Fair Isaac Corp 498
Fairchild Semiconductor International, Inc. 498
Fairfield Medical Center 498
Fairfield University 498
Fairleigh Dickinson University 498
Fairpoint Communications, Inc. 499
Fairview Health Services 499

Fairway Group Holdings Corp 499
Faith Technologies, Inc. 499
Falcon Northwest Computer Systems, Inc. 499
Falconstor Software Inc 499
Falkenberg Construction Co., Inc. 500
Famc Subsidiary Company 500
Family Express Corporation 500
Family Health International Inc 500
Fannie Mae 500
Fansteel Inc. 500
Far Technologies Holdings, Inc. 501
Fareway Stores, Inc. 501
Farm Aid Inc 501
Farm Credit Bank Of Texas 501
Farm Service Cooperative 501
Farmer Bros. Co. 501
Farmers Co-operative Society, Sioux Center, Iowa 502
Farmers Cooperative Company 502
Farmers National Banc Corp. (canfield,oh) 502
Farmers New World Life Insurance Co. 502
Farmers Pride, Inc. 502
Farmers Telecommunications Cooperative, Inc. 502
Farmers Telephone Cooperative, Inc. 503
Farmington Foods, Inc. 503
Farmland Mutual Insurance Co 503
Farmland Partners Inc 503
Farmvet.com, Inc. 503
Faro Technologies Inc. 503
Farouk Systems, Inc. 504
Farrel Corporation 504
Fashion Institute Of Technology 504
Fastenal Co. 504
Fate Therapeutics Inc 504
Fayette Community Hospital, Inc. 504
Fayetteville Public Works Commission 505
Faygo Beverages, Inc. 505
Fb Financial Corp 505
Federal Agricultural Mortgage Corp 505
Federal Deposit Insurance Corp. 505
Federal Express Corporation 505
Federal Home Loan Bank Boston 506
Federal Home Loan Bank Chicago 506
Federal Home Loan Bank Indianapolis 506
Federal Home Loan Bank New York 506
Federal Home Loan Bank Of Atlanta 506
Federal Home Loan Bank Of Cincinnati 506
Federal Home Loan Bank Of Dallas 507
Federal Home Loan Bank Of Des Moines 507
Federal Home Loan Bank Of Pittsburgh 507
Federal Home Loan Bank Of San Francisco 507
Federal Home Loan Bank Topeka 507
Federal Prison Industries, Inc 507
Federal Realty Investment Trust (new) 508
Federal Reserve Bank Of Atlanta, Dist. No. 6 508
Federal Reserve Bank Of Boston, Dist. No. 1 508
Federal Reserve Bank Of Chicago, Dist. No. 7 508
Federal Reserve Bank Of Cleveland, Dist. No. 4 508
Federal Reserve Bank Of Dallas, Dist. No. 11 508
Federal Reserve Bank Of Kansas City, Dist. No. 10 509
Federal Reserve Bank Of Minneapolis, Dist. No. 9 509
Federal Reserve Bank Of New York, Dist. No. 2 509
Federal Reserve Bank Of Philadelphia, Dist. No. 3 509
Federal Reserve Bank Of Richmond, Dist. No. 5 509
Federal Reserve Bank Of San Francisco, Dist. No. 12 509
Federal Reserve Bank Of St. Louis, Dist. No. 8 510
Federal Reserve System 510
Federal Screw Works 510
Federal Signal Corp. 510
Federated Hermes Inc 510
Federated Mutual Insurance Co. (owatonna, Minn.) 510
Federated Service Insurance Co. (owatonna, Mn) 511

Fedex Corp 511
Fednat Holding Co 511
Feed The Children, Inc. 511
Feminist Majority Foundation 511
Fennec Pharmaceuticals Inc 511
Fentura Financial Inc 512
Fenway Partners, Llc 512
Ferguson Enterprises, Llc 512
Ferrellgas Partners Lp 512
Ferris State University (inc) 512
Fetch Logistics, Inc. 512
Ffd Financial Corp 513
Ffw Corp. 513
Fgi Industries Ltd 513
Fhi Services 513
Fibertower Corporation 513
Fibrocell Science, Inc. 513
Fibrogen Inc 514
Fidelity D&d Bancorp Inc 514
Fidelity Federal Bancorp 514
Fidelity National Financial Inc 514
Fidelity National Information Services Inc 514
Field Museum Of Natural History 514
Fieldale Farms Corporation 515
Fieldpoint Petroleum Corp 515
Fifth Third Bancorp (cincinnati, Oh) 515
Fiji Water Company, Llc 515
Financial Executives International 515
Financial Industry Regulatory Authority, Inc. 515
Financial Institutions Inc. 516
Financialcontent Inc 516
Findex.com, Inc. 516
Finjan Holdings, Inc. 516
Finward Bancorp 516
Fiorano Software, Inc. 516
Firecom, Inc. 517
Fired Up, Inc. 517
Firelands Regional Health System 517
First Acceptance Corp 517
First Advantage Corp (new) 517
First American Financial Corp 517
First Bancorp (nc) 518
First Bancorp Inc (me) 518
First Bancorp Of Indiana Inc 518
First Bancshares Inc (ms) 518
First Bancshares Inc. (mo) 518
First Banks, Inc. (mo) 518
First Busey Corp 519
First Business Financial Services, Inc. 519
First Capital Inc. 519
First Care Medical Services 519
First Citizens Bancshares Inc (de) 519
First Commonwealth Financial Corp (indiana, Pa) 519
First Community Bankshares Inc (va) 520
First Community Corp (sc) 520
First Eagle Private Credit, Llc 520
First Electric Co-operative Corporation 520
First Financial Bancorp (oh) 520
First Financial Bankshares, Inc. 520
First Financial Corp. (in) 521
First Financial Northwest Inc 521
First Hartford Corp 521
First Hawaiian Inc 521
First Horizon Corp 521
First Industrial Realty Trust Inc 521
First Internet Bancorp 522
First Interstate Bancsystem Inc 522
First Keystone Corp 522
First Manhattan Co 522
First Merchants Corp 522
First Mid Bancshares Inc 522
First Mortgage Corp 523
First National Bank Alaska 523
First National Corp. (strasburg, Va) 523
First National Of Nebraska, Inc. 523
First Niles Financial Inc. 523

First Nonprofit Unemployment Administration Company, Llc 523
First Northern Community Bancorp 524
First Of Long Island Corp 524
First Physicians Capital Group Inc 524
First Republic Bank (san Francisco, Ca) 524
First Republic Preferred Capital Corp 524
First Robinson Financial Corp. 524
First Savings Financial Group Inc 525
First Solar Inc 525
First United Corporation (md) 525
First Us Bancshares Inc 525
Firstcash Holdings Inc 525
Firstenergy Corp 525
Firstfleet, Inc. 526
Firsthand Technology Value Fund, Inc. 526
Firsthealth Of The Carolinas, Inc. 526
Fiserv Inc 526
Fisher Pen Company 526
Fisk University 526
Five Below Inc 527
Five Point Holdings Llc 527
Five Star Cooperative 527
Five9, Inc 527
Flagstaff Medical Center, Inc. 527
Flanders Corporation 527
Flanigan's Enterprises, Inc. 528
Flavorx, Inc. 528
Fletcher Music Centers, Inc. 528
Flexera Software Llc 528
Flexiinternational Software, Inc. 528
Flexsteel Industries, Inc. 528
Flint Electric Membership Corporation 529
Floor & Decor Holdings Inc 529
Florida A & M University 529
Florida Atlantic University 529
Florida Department Of Lottery 529
Florida Gas Transmission Company, Llc 529
Florida Health Sciences Center, Inc. 530
Florida Hospital Waterman, Inc. 530
Florida Housing Finance Corp 530
Florida International University 530
Florida Memorial University, Inc. 530
Florida Municipal Power Agency 530
Florida Panthers Hockey Club, Ltd. 531
Florida Power & Light Co. 531
Florida State College At Jacksonville 531
Florida State University 531
Florstar Sales, Inc. 531
Flotek Industries Inc 531
Flowers Foods, Inc. 532
Flowserve Corp 532
Floyd Healthcare Management, Inc. 532
Fluor Corp. 532
Flushing Financial Corp. 532
Flyers Energy, Llc 532
Fmc Corp. 533
Fmc Technologies, Inc. 533
Fnb Corp 533
Fncb Bancorp Inc 533
Fogo De Chao, Inc. 533
Foley Hoag Llp 533
Fonar Corp 534
Fonix Corp. (de) 534
Fonon Corp 534
Food Export U S A North East 534
Food For The Poor, Inc. 534
Foot Locker, Inc. 534
Football Northwest Llc 535
Forbes Energy Services Ltd 535
Ford Motor Co. (de) 535
Ford Motor Credit Company Llc 535
Fordham Preparatory School 535
Fordham University 535
Forescout Technologies, Inc. 536
Forest Besse Products Inc 536
Forest City Enterprises, L.p. 536
Forestar Group Inc (new) 536

Forevergreen Worldwide Corp 536
Forge Industries, Inc. 536
Formfactor Beaverton, Inc. 537
Formfactor Inc 537
Formosa Plastics Corporation, U.s.a. 537
Forms & Supply, Inc. 537
Forrest County General Hospital 537
Forrester Research Inc. 537
Forsyth Medical Center Foundation 538
Fort Hays State University Foundation 538
Forth Smith Hma, Llc 538
Fortinet Inc 538
Fortis Construction, Inc. 538
Fortive Corp 538
Fortovia Therapeutics, Inc. 539
Fortress Investment Group Llc 539
Fortune Brands Innovations Inc 539
Forum Energy Technologies Inc 539
Forward Air Corp 539
Forward Industries, Inc. 539
Fossil Group Inc 540
Foster (l.b.) Co 540
Foundation Building Materials, Inc. 540
Foundation For National Progress 540
Foundation Healthcare, Inc. 540
Foundation Medicine, Inc. 540
Foundation Of Northern New Jersey Inc. 541
Foundever Operating Corporation 541
Fountain Powerboat Industries, Inc. 541
Four B Corp. 541
Fox Bsb Holdco, Inc. 541
Fox Corp 541
Fox Factory Holding Corp 542
Fox Head, Inc. 542
Foxworth-galbraith Lumber Company 542
Fp Acquisition Company 3.5 Llc 542
Fpb Bancorp Inc 542
Franchise Services, Inc. 542
Francis Saint Medical Center 543
Franciscan Alliance, Inc. 543
Franciscan Health System 543
Franciscan University Of Steubenville 543
Frank Consolidated Enterprises, Inc. 543
Franklin And Marshall College 543
Franklin Community Health Network 544
Franklin Covey Co 544
Franklin Credit Holding Corporation 544
Franklin Electric Co., Inc. 544
Franklin Financial Services Corp 544
Franklin Hospital 544
Franklin Resources Inc 545
Franklin Square Hospital Center, Inc. 545
Franklin Street Properties Corp 545
Franklin Wireless Corp 545
Fraser/white, Inc. 545
Frazier Industrial Company 545
Fred Jones Enterprises, L.l.c. 546
Fred Usinger, Inc. 546
Fred's, Inc. 546
Freddie Mac 546
Frederick Health Hospital, Inc. 546
Freedom From Hunger Foundation 546
Freeman Health System 547
Freeport Regional Health Care Foundation 547
Freeport-mcmoran Inc 547
Freese And Nichols, Inc. 547
Freightcar America Inc 547
Fremont Contract Carriers, Inc. 547
Fremont Health 548
Frequency Electronics Inc 548
Fresh Mark, Inc. 548
Fresh Tracks Therapeutics Inc 548
Frick Collection 548
Friedman Industries, Inc. 548
Friendfinder Networks Inc 549
Frisbie Memorial Hospital 549
Froedtert Memorial Lutheran Hospital, Inc. 549
Front Porch, Inc. 549

Frontier Communications Parent Inc 549
Frontier Merger Sub Llc 549
Frozen Food Express Industries, Inc. 550
Frp Holdings Inc 550
Fruit Growers Supply Company Inc 550
Fruth, Inc. 550
Fs Bancorp Inc (washington) 550
Ftai Aviation Ltd 550
Ftd Companies, Inc. 551
Fti Consulting Inc. 551
Fts International, Inc. 551
Fuel Tech Inc 551
Fuelcell Energy Inc 551
Fuelstream, Inc. 551
Full House Resorts, Inc. 552
Fuller (hb) Company 552
Fuller Theological Seminary 552
Fullmer Construction 552
Fullnet Communications Inc 552
Fulton Financial Corp. (pa) 552
Fundamental Global Inc 553
Funrise, Inc. 553
Furman Foods, Inc. 553
Furman University Foundation, Inc. 553
Furmanite, Llc 553
Future Farmers Of America Incorporated 553
Future Tech Enterprise, Inc. 554
Futurefuel Corp 554
Futures Without Violence 554
Fx Energy, Inc. 554
G&p Trucking Company, Inc. 554
G-iii Apparel Group Ltd. 554
G.e.c. Associates, Inc. 555
G.s.e. Construction Company, Inc. 555
G1 Therapeutics Inc 555
G4s Secure Integration Llc 555
G4s Secure Solutions (usa) Inc. 555
Ga Communications, Inc. 555
Ga Telesis, Llc 556
Gadsden Properties Inc 556
Gadsden Regional Medical Center, Llc 556
Gaia Inc (new) 556
Gainesville Regional Utilities 556
Gale's Willoughby Hills Garden Center, Inc. 556
Galectin Therapeutics Inc 557
Gallagher (arthur J.) & Co. 557
Gallaudet University 557
Gallery Model Homes, Inc. 557
Gallup, Inc. 557
Gamco Investors Inc 557
Gamefly Holdings, Llc 558
Gamestop Corp 558
Gaming Commission, New York 558
Gaming Partners International Corporation 558
Gan Ltd 558
Gancedo Lumber Co., Inc. 558
Gannett Co Inc (new) 559
Gannett Fleming, Inc. 559
Gardner Denver Investments, Inc. 559
Garney Holding Company 559
Garrett Motion Inc. 559
Gartner Inc 559
Gary Rabine & Sons, Inc. 560
Gas Transmission Northwest Llc 560
Gasco Energy Inc. 560
Gate 1, Ltd 560
Gates Industrial Corp Plc 560
Gateway Energy Corporation 560
Gatx Corp 561
Gaucho Group Holdings Inc 561
Gc Services Limited Partnership 561
Gcp Applied Technologies Inc. 561
Gct Semiconductor, Inc. 561
Gee Group Inc 561
Geisinger Health 562
Gelber Group, Llc 562
Gemstone Solutions Group, Inc 562
Gen Digital Inc 562

Genasys Inc 562
Genco Shipping & Trading Ltd 562
Gencor Industries Inc 563
Gene Biotherapeutics Inc 563
Geneca, L.l.c. 563
Genelink Inc 563
Generac Holdings Inc 563
General Atlantic Llc 563
General Cable Corporation 564
General Casualty Co. Of Wisconsin (sun Prairie) 564
General Dynamics Corp 564
General Electric Co 564
General Finance Corporation 564
General Hardware And Builders Supply, Inc. 564
General Health System 565
General Insurance Company Of America 565
General Mills Inc 565
General Moly, Inc. 565
General Motors Co 565
General Motors Financial Co Inc 565
General Sports And Entertainment, L.l.c. 566
Generex Biotechnology Corp (de) 566
Genesco Inc. 566
Genesee & Wyoming Inc. 566
Genesee Valley Group Health Association 566
Genesis Corp. 566
Genesis Energy L.p. 567
Genesis Health System 567
Genesis Health, Inc. 567
Genesis Healthcare Inc 567
Genesis Healthcare System 567
Genesiscare Usa, Inc. 567
Genethera, Inc. 568
Genica Corporation 568
Genie Energy Ltd 568
Genmark Diagnostics, Inc. 568
Genocea Biosciences Inc 568
Gentex Corp. 568
Gentherm Inc 569
Genuine Parts Co. 569
Genvec, Inc. 569
Genworth Financial, Inc. (holding Co) 569
Geo Group Inc (the) (new) 569
Geobio Energy Inc 569
Geokinetics Inc. 570
Geopetro Resources Co 570
George E. Warren Llc 570
George Mason University 570
George W. Auch Company 570
Georgetown Memorial Hospital 570
Georgia Farm Bureau Mutual Insurance Company 571
Georgia O'keeffe Museum 571
Georgia Ports Authority 571
Georgia Power Co 571
Georgia Rehabilitation Institute, Inc. 571
Georgia Southern University 571
Georgia Transmission Corporation (an Electric Membership Corporation) 572
Georgian Court University 572
Geos Communications, Inc. 572
Geospace Technologies Corp 572
Geosyntec Consultants, Inc. 572
Gerber Childrenswear Llc 572
German American Bancorp Inc 573
Geron Corp. 573
Gerrity's Super Market, Inc. 573
Getty Images Holdings Inc 573
Getty Realty Corp. 573
Gettysburg College 573
Gevo Inc 574
Gf Health Products, Inc. 574
Giant Eagle, Inc. 574
Gibbs Die Casting Corporation 574
Gibraltar Industries Inc 574
Gibson Overseas, Inc. 574
Gibson, Dunn & Crutcher Llp 575

Giga-tronics Inc 575
Gigamon Inc. 575
Gilbane Building Company 575
Gilbane Development Company 575
Gilbert May, Inc. 575
Gilead Sciences Inc 576
Gillette Children's Specialty Healthcare 576
Girl Scouts Of The United States Of America 576
Girls Incorporated Of New York City 576
Give Something Back, Inc. 576
Glacier Bancorp, Inc. 576
Gladstone Commercial Corp 577
Gladstone Land Corp 577
Glassbridge Enterprises Inc 577
Glatfelter Corp 577
Glen Burnie Bancorp 577
Glen Rose Petroleum Corp 577
Glendale Adventist Medical Center Inc 578
Glendale Community College Dist 578
Glendive Medical Center, Inc. 578
Glenn A. Rick Engineering And Development Co. 578
Glenn O. Hawbaker, Inc. 578
Global Acquisitions Corp 578
Global Brokerage Inc 579
Global Contact Services, Llc 579
Global Diversified Industries, Inc. 579
Global Exchange 579
Global Gear & Machining Llc 579
Global Geophysical Services Inc 579
Global Industrial Company 580
Global Infotek, Inc. 580
Global Market Development Center 580
Global Partners Lp 580
Global Payment Technologies, Inc. 580
Global Payments Inc 580
Globalfluency, Inc. 581
Globalscape, Inc. 581
Globalstar Inc 581
Globalworks Group Llc 581
Globe Life Inc 581
Globecomm Systems Inc. 581
Globeimmune, Inc 582
Globus Medical Inc 582
Glori Energy Inc 582
Glu Mobile Inc. 582
Gly Construction, Inc. 582
Glycomimetics Inc 582
Gms Inc 583
Godaddy Inc 583
Goddard College Corporation 583
Gold Reserve Inc 583
Gold Resource Corp 583
Gold Star Chili, Inc. 583
Gold-eagle Cooperative 584
Golden Enterprises, Inc. 584
Golden Entertainment Inc 584
Golden Gate National Parks Conservancy 584
Golden Grain Energy, Llc 584
Golden Krust Caribbean Bakery Inc. 584
Golden Minerals Co 585
Golden Star Enterprises Ltd 585
Golden State Foods Corp. 585
Golden State Health Centers, Inc. 585
Golden State Warriors, Llc 585
Goldman Sachs Group Inc 585
Goldrich Mining Co 586
Gonzaga University 586
Good Karma Broadcasting Llc 586
Good Samaritan Hospital 586
Good Samaritan Hospital 586
Good Samaritan Hospital Medical Center 586
Good Samaritan Hospital, L.p. 587
Good Times Restaurants Inc. 587
Good360 587
Goodfellow Bros. Llc 587
Goodheart-willcox Co., Inc. 587
Goodman Networks Incorporated 587

Goodrich Petroleum Corporation 588
Goodwill Industries International, Inc. 588
Goodwill Industries Of Central Texas 588
Goodyear Tire & Rubber Co. 588
Gopro Inc 588
Gordon Brothers Group, Llc 588
Gordon College 589
Gordon Food Service, Inc. 589
Gordon Rees Scully Mansukhani, Llp. 589
Gorman-rupp Company (the) 589
Goto Group, Inc. 589
Gottlieb Memorial Hospital 589
Gourmet Specialties, Inc. 590
Gouverneur Bancorp Inc Md 590
Gov New Oppty Reit 590
Government National Mortgage Assn. 590
Government Of District Of Columbia 590
Goya Foods, Inc. 590
Gpm Investments, Llc 591
Graceland Fruit, Inc. 591
Graco Inc 591
Graebel Companies, Inc. 591
Graftech International Ltd 591
Graham Corp. 591
Graham Holdings Co. 592
Grainger (w.w.) Inc. 592
Grand Canyon Education Inc 592
Grand Piano & Furniture Co. 592
Grand River Dam Authority 592
Grand Strand Regional Medical Center, Llc 592
Grand Valley State University 593
Grand View Hospital 593
Grandsouth Bancorporation 593
Grandview Management, Inc. 593
Granite Broadcasting Corp 593
Granite City Food & Brewery Ltd 593
Granite Construction Inc 594
Granite Point Mortgage Trust Inc 594
Granite Telecommunications Llc 594
Graphic Packaging Holding Co 594
Gray Television Inc 594
Graybar Electric Co., Inc. 594
Great American Bancorp Inc 595
Great American Insurance Co. 595
Great Lakes Aviation Ltd. 595
Great Lakes Cheese Co., Inc. 595
Great Lakes Dredge & Dock Corp 595
Great Northern Iron Ore Properties 595
Great Plains Manufacturing Incorporated 596
Great River Energy 596
Great Southern Bancorp, Inc. 596
Great West Life & Annuity Insurance Co - Insurance Products 596
Greatamerica Financial Services Corporation 596
Greater Baltimore Medical Center, Inc. 596
Greater Lafayette Health Services, Inc. 597
Greater Omaha Packing Co., Inc. 597
Greater Orlando Aviation Authority 597
Greater Washington Educational Telecommunications Association, Inc. 597
Green Bay Packers, Inc. 597
Green Brick Partners Inc 597
Green Dot Corp 598
Green Mill Restaurants, Llc 598
Green Mountain Power Corporation 598
Green Plains Inc. 598
Green St. Energy, Inc 598
Greenbrier Companies Inc (the) 598
Greene County Bancorp Inc 599
Greene, Tweed & Co., Inc. 599
Greenleaf Book Group, Llc 599
Greenshift Corp 599
Greenstone Farm Credit Services Aca 599
Greenville Utilities Commission 599
Greenwood Mills, Inc. 600
Greif Inc 600
Grenadier Realty Corp. 600
Greystone Logistics Inc 600

Greystone Power Corporation, An Electric Membership Corporation 600
Griffin Health Services Corporation 600
Griffith Foods Group Inc. 601
Griffon Corp. 601
Grill Concepts, Inc. 601
Grocery Outlet Holding Corp 601
Groen Brothers Aviation Inc 601
Groove Botanicals Inc 601
Grossmont Hospital Corporation 602
Group 1 Automotive, Inc. 602
Group O, Inc. 602
Groupon Inc 602
Growmark, Inc. 602
Gruma Corporation 602
Grunley Construction Co., Inc. 603
Gse Systems Inc 603
Gsi Technology Inc 603
Gsv Inc 603
Gt Advanced Technologies Inc. 603
Gt Biopharma Inc 603
Gtc Systems Inc. 604
Gts Technology Solutions, Inc. 604
Gtt Communications, Inc 604
Guadalupe Valley Telephone Cooperative, Inc. 604
Guarantee Electrical Company 604
Guaranteed Rate, Inc. 604
Guaranty Bancorp Inc (nh) 605
Guaranty Bancshares Inc 605
Guardian Glass Company 605
Guardian Life Insurance Co. Of America (nyc) 605
Guest Services, Inc. 605
Guidance Software, Inc. 605
Guide Dog Foundation For The Blind, Inc. 606
Guided Therapeutics Inc 606
Guidehouse Inc. 606
Guidewire Software Inc 606
Guild Mortgage Company 606
Guildmaster, Inc. 606
Guitar Center Holdings, Inc. 607
Gulf Coast Project Services, Inc. 607
Gulf Island Fabrication, Inc. 607
Gulf Power Co 607
Gulf South Pipeline Company, Llc 607
Gulf United Energy Inc 607
Gulfport Energy Corp. 608
Gulfstream Natural Gas System, L.l.c. 608
Gundersen Lutheran Medical Center, Inc. 608
Gursey, Schneider & Co. Llc 608
Gustavus Adolphus College 608
Guthrie Towanda Memorial Hospital 608
Guthy-renker Llc 609
Gutierrez-palmenberg, Inc. 609
Gwinnett Health System, Inc. 609
Gxo Logistics Inc 609
Gyre Therapeutics Inc 609
H And M Construction Co., Inc. 609
H Group Holding, Inc 610
H Munoz And Company, Inc. 610
H W D Casings, Inc. 610
H&e Equipment Services Inc 610
H. H. Dobbins, Inc. 610
H. J. Russell & Company 610
H. Lee Moffitt Cancer Center And Research Institute Hospital, Inc. 611
H.c. Schmieding Produce Company, Llc 611
Habitat For Humanity International, Inc. 611
Hackett Group Inc 611
Hackley Hospital 611
Haemonetics Corp. 611
Hagerman Construction Corporation 612
Haggen, Inc. 612
Hain Celestial Group Inc 612
Hajoca Corporation 612
Hallador Energy Co 612
Halliburton Company 612
Hallmark Financial Services Inc. 613
Halozyme Therapeutics Inc 613

Hamagami/carroll, Inc. 613
Hamilton Beach Brands Holding Co 613
Hamilton Chattanooga County Hospital Authority 613
Hamilton College 613
Hamilton Lane Inc 614
Hamilton Partners, Inc. 614
Hamot Health Foundation 614
Hampton University 614
Hamrick Mills 614
Hancock Whitney Corp 614
Handy & Harman Ltd. 615
Hanesbrands Inc 615
Hanger, Inc. 615
Hanmi Financial Corp. 615
Hanna Steel Corporation 615
Hannon Armstrong Sustainable Infrastructure Capital Inc 615
Hanover College 616
Hanover Health Corporation, Inc. 616
Hanover Insurance Group Inc 616
Hansen Medical, Inc. 616
Harbor Bankshares Corp. 616
Harbor Hospital Foundation, Inc. 616
Harborquest, Inc. 617
Harbour Contractors, Inc. 617
Hard And Soft Fishing, Llc 617
Hard Rock Heals Foundation, Inc. 617
Hardaway Construction Corp. 617
Hardinge Inc. 617
Hardwood Flooring And Paneling, Inc. 618
Hargrove, Llc 618
Harland M. Braun & Co., Inc. 618
Harley Ellis Devereaux Corp 618
Harley-davidson Inc 618
Harleysville Financial Corp 618
Harmonic, Inc. 619
Harnish Group Inc. 619
Harper's Magazine Foundation 619
Harrington Memorial Hospital, Inc. 619
Harte Hanks Inc 619
Hartford Financial Services Group Inc. 619
Hartford Healthcare Corporation 620
Harvard Bioscience Inc. 620
Harvard Student Agencies Inc 620
Harvest Natural Resources, Inc. 620
Harvest Oil & Gas Corp 620
Harvey Industries, Llc 620
Harvey Mudd College 621
Hasbro, Inc. 621
Haselden Construction, Llc 621
Hastings Entertainment, Inc. 621
Hastings Manufacturing Co 621
Hauppauge Digital, Inc. 621
Haviland Enterprises, Inc. 622
Hawai I Pacific Health 622
Hawai I Pacific University 622
Hawaii Department Of Transportation 622
Hawaiian Electric Industries Inc 622
Hawaiian Holdings Inc 622
Hawaiian Macadamia Nut Orchards Lp 623
Hawaiian Telcom Holdco, Inc. 623
Hawkins Construction Company 623
Hawkins Inc 623
Hawthorne Machinery Co. 623
Hay House, Llc 623
Haynes International, Inc. 624
Hays Medical Center, Inc. 624
Haywood Health Authority 624
Hazen And Sawyer, D.p.c. 624
Hbe Corporation 624
Hca Florida Englewood Hospital 624
Hca Healthcare Inc 625
Hci Group Inc 625
Hdr, Inc. 625
Hea Legacy, Inc. 625
Headwaters Incorporated 625
Health Diagnostics, Llc 625

Health First Shared Services, Inc. 626
Health Industry Distributors Association 626
Health Partners Plans, Inc. 626
Health Research, Inc. 626
Healthcare Distribution Alliance 626
Healthcare Services Group, Inc. 626
Healtheast Diversified Services, Inc. 627
Healtheast St John's Hospital 627
Healthequity Inc 627
Healthfirst, Inc. 627
Healthpeak Properties Inc 627
Healthplan Holdings, Inc. 627
Healthspan Integrated Care 628
Healthstream Inc 628
Healthwarehouse.com, Inc. 628
Healthy Mothers Healthy Babies Inc 628
Hearst, William Randolph Foundation 628
Hearthstone Utilities, Inc. 628
Heartland Co-op 629
Heartland Express, Inc. 629
Heartland Financial Usa, Inc. (dubuque, Ia) 629
Heartland Payment Systems, Llc 629
Heartland Regional Medical Center 629
Heartware International, Inc. 629
Hecla Mining Co 630
Heico Corp 630
Heidrick & Struggles International, Inc. 630
Heifer Project International Inc 630
Helen Keller International 630
Helena Agri-enterprises, Llc 630
Helios & Matheson Analytics Inc 631
Helios Technologies Inc 631
Helix Biomedix Inc 631
Helix Energy Solutions Group Inc 631
Helmerich & Payne, Inc. 631
Helmsman Management Services Llc 631
Hemagen Diagnostics Inc 632
Hendrick Southwestern Health Development Corporation 632
Henricksen & Company, Inc. 632
Henry County Bancshares Inc (stockbridge, Ga) 632
Henry County Memorial Hospital 632
Henry Ford Health System 632
Henry J Kaiser Family Foundation 633
Henry Mayo Newhall Memorial Hospital 633
Henry Modell & Company, Inc. 633
Henry Wurst, Inc. 633
Hensel Phelps Construction Co. 633
Her Interactive, Inc. 633
Herborium Group Inc 634
Herc Holdings Inc 634
Hereuare, Inc. 634
Heritage Commerce Corp 634
Heritage Financial Corp (wa) 634
Heritage Insurance Holdings Inc 634
Heritage University 635
Heritage Valley Health System, Inc. 635
Heroix Llc 635
Heron Therapeutics Inc 635
Herr Foods Incorporated 635
Herschend Entertainment Company, Llc 635
Hersha Hospitality Trust 636
Hershey Company (the) 636
Hershey Entertainment & Resorts Company 636
Hertz Global Holdings Inc (new) 636
Hess Corp 636
Hess Midstream Lp 636
Hewlett Packard Enterprise Co 637
Hewlett, William And Flora Foundation (inc) 637
Hexcel Corp. 637
Hexion Inc 637
Hf Sinclair Corp 637
Hfb Financial Corp. 637
Hg Holdings Inc 638
Hhgregg Inc 638
Hibbett Inc 638
Hickman, Williams & Company 638
High Concrete Group Llc 638

High Country Bancorp, Inc. 638
High Country Fusion Company, Inc. 639
High Hotels, Ltd. 639
High Industries Inc. 639
High Point Regional Health 639
High Point Solutions Inc. 639
High Steel Structures Llc 639
Higher One Holdings, Inc. 640
Highlands Bankshares Inc. 640
Highwoods Properties, Inc. 640
Hii Mission Technologies Corp. 640
Hil Technology, Inc. 640
Hiland Dairy Foods Company., Llc 640
Hiland Holdings Gp, Lp 641
Hilbert College 641
Hilite International, Inc. 641
Hill Country Memorial Hospital 641
Hill International, Inc. 641
Hill Physicians Medical Group, Inc. 641
Hillenbrand Inc 642
Hills Bancorporation 642
Hillsborough County Aviation Authority 642
Hilltop Holdings, Inc. 642
Hilton Grand Vacations Inc 642
Hilton Worldwide Holdings Inc 642
Hines Interests Limited Partnership 643
Hingham Institution For Savings 643
Hinshaw & Culbertson Llp 643
Hirequest Inc 643
Hirotec America Inc. 643
Histogen Inc 643
Hitchiner Manufacturing Co., Inc. 644
Hitt Contracting, Inc. 644
Hkn, Inc. 644
Hks, Inc. 644
Hlss Management Llc 644
Hmg/courtland Properties, Inc. 644
Hmh Hospitals Corporation 645
Hmn Financial Inc. 645
Hms Holdings Llc 645
Hni Corp 645
Ho-chunk, Inc. 645
Hoag Hospital Foundation 645
Hoag Memorial Hospital Presbyterian 646
Hoak Media, Llc 646
Hobart And William Smith Colleges 646
Hobby Lobby Stores, Inc. 646
Hodgson Mill, Inc. 646
Hoffman Corporation 646
Hofmann Industries, Inc. 647
Hofstra University 647
Hohner, Inc. 647
Holder Properties, Inc. 647
Holiday Builders, Inc. 647
Holiday Inn Club Vacations Incorporated 647
Holiday Island Holdings Inc 648
Holiday Wholesale, Inc. 648
Holland Community Hospital Auxiliary, Inc. 648
Holland Southwest International, Incorporated 648
Hollingsworth Oil Company, Inc. 648
Hollins University Corporation 648
Holmes Lumber & Building Center, Inc. 649
Holmes Regional Medical Center, Inc. 649
Holobeam, Inc. 649
Hologic Inc 649
Holy Cross Hospital, Inc. 649
Homasote Co. 649
Home Bancorp Inc 650
Home Bancshares Inc 650
Home Depot Inc 650
Home Energy Savings Corp 650
Home Instead, Inc. 650
Home Loan Financial Corp 650
Home Products International Inc. 651
Homestreet Inc 651
Hometown America, L.l.c. 651
Homevestors Of America, Inc. 651
Honeywell International Inc 651

Honorhealth Ambulatory 651
Honshy Electric Co., Inc. 652
Hooker Furnishings Corp 652
Hoosier Energy Rural Electric Cooperative Inc 652
Hop Energy, Llc 652
Hopto Inc 652
Horace Mann Educators Corp. 652
Horizon Bancorp Inc 653
Horizon Pharma, Inc. 653
Horizon Pharmaceutical Llc 653
Horizon Telcom, Inc. 653
Hormel Foods Corp. 653
Hornblower Yachts, Llc 653
Horne International Inc 654
Horry Telephone Cooperative, Inc. 654
Horton (dr) Inc 654
Hospice Of Michigan, Inc. 654
Hospira, Inc. 654
Hospital Authority Of Valdosta And Lowndes County, Georgia 654
Hospital Of Central Connecticut 655
Hospital Service District 1 Inc 655
Hospital Service District 1 Of East Baton Rouge Parish 655
Hospital Service District No. 1 655
Hospital Sisters Health System 655
Hospital Solutions, Inc. 655
Hoss's Steak & Sea House, Inc. 656
Host Hotels & Resorts Inc 656
Houchens Industries, Inc. 656
Houghton Chemical Corporation 656
Houghton Mifflin Harcourt Company 656
Houlihan Lokey Inc 656
House Of Representatives, United States 657
Housing Finance Agency, California 657
Houston American Energy Corp. 657
Houston Community College, Inc. 657
Houston County Healthcare Authority 657
Houston Grand Opera Association, Inc. 657
Houston Livestock Show And Rodeo Educational Fund 658
Houston Museum Of Natural Science 658
Houston Wire & Cable Company Inc 658
Houston Zoo, Inc. 658
Hovnanian Enterprises, Inc. 658
Howard Building Corporation 658
Howard Community College 659
Howard Hughes Holdings Inc 659
Howard Miller Company 659
Howard Young Health Care, Inc 659
Howmet Aerospace Inc 659
Hp Inc 659
Hr Policy Association 660
Hsbc Usa, Inc. 660
Hsn, Inc. 660
Hub Group, Inc. 660
Hubbell Inc. 660
Hubspot Inc 660
Hudson Global Inc 661
Hudson Pacific Properties Inc 661
Hudson Technologies Inc 661
Hugoton Royalty Trust (tx) 661
Human Pheromone Sciences, Inc. 661
Human Rights Watch, Inc. 661
Humana Inc. 662
Humangood Norcal 662
Humanigen Inc 662
Humanscale Corporation 662
Humax Usa, Inc. 662
Hunt (j.b.) Transport Services, Inc. 662
Hunt Memorial Hospital District 663
Hunterdon Healthcare System 663
Huntington Bancshares Inc 663
Huntington Hospital Dolan Family Health Center, Inc. 663
Huntington Ingalls Industries, Inc. 663
Huntsman Corp 663
Huntsman International Llc 664

Hunzicker Brothers, Inc. 664
Hunzinger Construction Company 664
Hurco Companies Inc 664
Hurlen Corporation 664
Hurley Medical Center 664
Huron Consulting Group Inc 665
Hurricanes Hockey Limited Partnership 665
Hussey Seating Company 665
Husson University 665
Hutchinson & Bloodgood Llp 665
Hutchinson Technology Incorporated 665
Huttig Building Products, Inc. 666
Hy-vee, Inc. 666
Hyatt Hotels Corp 666
Hycroft Mining Corporation 666
Hyde Group, Inc. 666
Hydromer, Inc. 666
Hydron Technologies, Inc. 667
Hynes Industries, Inc. 667
Hyperdynamics Corp 667
Hyspan Precision Products, Inc. 667
Hyster-yale Materials Handling Inc 667
I O Interconnect, Ltd. 667
I-5 Design Build Inc. 668
I/omagic Corporation 668
Iac Inc 668
Iag Corp. 668
Iap Worldwide Services, Inc. 668
Iasis Healthcare Llc 668
Ibasis, Inc. 669
Ibiquity Digital Corporation 669
Ibw Financial Corp 669
Ic Compliance Llc 669
Icad Inc 669
Icahn Enterprises Lp 669
Ice Data Services, Inc. 670
Icf International Inc 670
Icicle Seafoods, Inc. 670
Icims, Inc. 670
Icoa Inc 670
Icon Health & Fitness, Inc. 670
Icon Identity Solutions, Inc. 671
Iconix Brand Group, Inc. 671
Iconma, L.l.c. 671
Icore Networks, Inc. 671
Icu Medical Inc 671
Idacorp Inc 671
Idaho Power Co 672
Idaho State University 672
Idaho Strategic Resources Inc 672
Ideal Shield, L.l.c. 672
Idemia Identity & Security Usa Llc 672
Identiv Inc 672
Idex Corporation 673
Idexx Laboratories, Inc. 673
Idi Logistics, Llc 673
Ids International, Llc 673
Idt Corp 673
Idw Media Holdings Inc 673
Ientertainment Network, Inc. 674
Ies Holdings Inc 674
Ifx Corp 674
Igc Pharma Inc 674
Igene Biotechnology, Inc. 674
Iheartmedia Inc 674
Ihs Inc. 675
Ii-vi Optoelectronic Devices, Inc. 675
Ikano Communications, Inc. 675
Ilc Industries, Llc 675
Ilg, Llc 675
Ilitch Holdings, Inc. 675
Illinois Department Of Employment Security 676
Illinois Environmental Protection Agency 676
Illinois Historic Preservation Agency 676
Illinois Housing Development Authority (inc) 676
Illinois Institute Of Technology 676
Illinois State Board Of Education 676
Illinois State Of Toll Highway Authority 677

Illinois Tool Works, Inc. 677
Illinois Wesleyan University 677
Illinois Wholesale Cash Register, Inc. 677
Illumina Inc 677
Image Api, Llc 677
Image Microsystems Inc 678
Image Software, Inc. 678
Imagetrend, Llc 678
Imageware Systems Inc 678
Imagine Schools, Inc. 678
Imaging Business Machines, L.l.c. 678
Imaging Diagnostic Systems Inc 679
Imh Financial Corporation 679
Immersion Corp 679
Immixgroup, Inc. 679
Immtech Pharmaceuticals, Inc. 679
Immucell Corp. 679
Immucor, Inc. 680
Immune Design Corp. 680
Immune Pharmaceuticals Inc 680
Immunic Inc 680
Impac Mortgage Holdings, Inc. 680
Imperial Distributors, Inc. 680
Imperial Irrigation District 681
Imperial Petroleum Recovery Corp. 681
Imperva, Inc. 681
Impinj Inc 681
Impreso Inc. 681
Imris Inc 681
Imunon Inc 682
In-n-out Burgers 682
In-q-tel, Inc 682
Inc.jet Holding Inc 682
Income Opportunity Realty Investors Inc 682
Incontact, Inc. 682
Incredible Pizza Co., Inc. 683
Incyte Corporation 683
Independent Bank (ionia, Mi) 683
Independent Bank Corp (ma) 683
Independent Bank Corporation (ionia, Mi) 683
Independent Bank Group Inc. 683
Independent Chemical Corp 684
Independent Health Association, Inc. 684
Index Fresh, Inc. 684
Indiana Botanic Gardens Inc 684
Indiana Farm Bureau, Inc. 684
Indiana Harbor Belt Railroad Co 684
Indiana Michigan Power Company 685
Indiana Municipal Power Agency 685
Indiana Symphony Society, Inc. 685
Indiana University Foundation, Inc. 685
Indiana University Health Ball Memorial Hospital, Inc. 685
Indiana University Health Bloomington, Inc. 685
Indiana University Health, Inc. 686
Indiana University Of Pennsylvania 686
Indiana University Research And Technology Corporation 686
Indianapolis Colts, Inc. 686
Indianapolis Motor Speedway Foundation Inc 686
Indiepub Entertainment Inc. 686
Indotronix International Corp 687
Indus Corporation 687
Industrial Scientific Corporation 687
Industrial Supply Association 687
Industrial Turnaround Corporation 687
Indyne, Inc. 687
Infinera Corp 688
Infinite Energy, Llc 688
Infinite Graphics Incorporated 688
Infinite Group, Inc. 688
Infinity Pharmaceuticals Inc 688
Infinity Software Development, Inc. 688
Influence Health, Inc. 689
Infoblox Inc. 689
Infocrossing, Llc 689
Infogain Corporation 689
Infonow Corp. 689

Infor, Inc. 689
Informatica Llc 690
Information Builders, Inc. 690
Information Services Group Inc 690
Ingersoll Machine Tools, Inc. 690
Ingersoll Rand Inc 690
Ingevity Corp 690
Ingles Markets Inc 691
Ingram Micro Inc. 691
Ingredion Inc 691
Inhibitor Therapeutics Inc 691
Innodata Inc 691
Innophos Holdings, Inc. 691
Innosight Consulting, Llc 692
Innospec Inc 692
Innovaro Inc. 692
Innovate Corp 692
Innovative Card Technologies Inc 692
Innovative Software Technologies Inc 692
Innovative Solutions And Support Inc 693
Innoviva Inc 693
Innsuites Hospitality Trust 693
Inogen, Inc 693
Inotiv Inc 693
Inova Health System Foundation 693
Inova Technology Inc 694
Inovalon Holdings, Inc. 694
Inovio Pharmaceuticals Inc. 694
Inphi Corporation 694
Inrad Optics Inc 694
Inroads, Inc. 694
Inseego Wireless, Inc. 695
Insight Enterprises Inc. 695
Insmed Inc 695
Insperity Inc 695
Inspira Health Network, Inc. 695
Installed Building Products Inc 695
Insteel Industries, Inc. 696
Institute For Defense Analyses Inc 696
Institute Of Gas Technology 696
Institute Of The Americas 696
Insulet Corp 696
Integer Holdings Corp 696
Integra Lifesciences Holdings Corp 697
Integral Technologies Inc. 697
Integral Vision Inc. 697
Integrated Biopharma Inc 697
Integrated Business Systems & Services, Inc. 697
Integrated Control Systems, Inc. 697
Integrated Data Corp 698
Integrated Management Services, P.a. 698
Integrated Project Management Company, Inc. 698
Integrated Silicon Solution, Inc. 698
Integris Baptist Medical Center, Inc. 698
Integris Health, Inc. 698
Intel Corp 699
Inteliquent, Inc. 699
Intellabridge Technology Corp 699
Intellect Design Arena Inc. 699
Intellicheck Inc 699
Intellidyne, L.l.c. 699
Intellisys Technology, L.l.c. 700
Inter Parfums, Inc. 700
Inter-american Development Bank 700
Interact Holdings Group Inc 700
Interactive Brokers Group Inc 700
Interactive Intelligence Group, Inc. 700
Interbond Of America, Llc 701
Intercloud Systems Inc 701
Intercontinental Exchange Inc 701
Interdenominational Theological Center, Inc. 701
Interdent, Inc. 701
Interface Inc. 701
Intergroup Corp. (the) 702
Interim Healthcare Inc. 702
Interior Concepts Corporation 702
Interlink Electronics Inc 702
Intermark Industries, Inc. 702

Intermatic Incorporated 702
Intermetro Communications, Inc. (nv) 703
Intermountain Health Care Inc 703
Internap Corp 703
International Association Of Amusement Parks And Attractions 703
International Association Of Machinists And Aerospace Workers 703
International Baler Corp 703
International Bancshares Corp. 704
International Brotherhood Of Electrical Workers 704
International Brotherhood Of Teamsters 704
International Building Technologies Group Inc 704
International Business Machines Corp 704
International Center For Entrepreneurial Development Inc 704
International Center For Research On Women 705
International Dispensing Corp 705
International Falls Memorial Hospital Association 705
International Finance Corp. (world Corporations Gov't) 705
International Flavors & Fragrances Inc. 705
International Fleet Sales, Inc. 705
International Industries, Inc. 706
International Isotopes Inc 706
International Lease Finance Corp. 706
International Management Group (overseas), Llc 706
International Market Brands, Inc. 706
International Monetary Systems Ltd 706
International Paper Co 707
International Shipholding Corporation 707
International Sign Association Inc 707
International Software Systems, Inc. 707
International Speedway Corporation 707
International Union, Untd Autmble, Arspce And Agrcltrl Implmnt Wrkrs Of Amrica 707
International Wire Group, Inc. 708
Internet America Inc 708
Internet Corporation For Assigned Names And Numbers 708
Internetarray Inc 708
Interpace Biosciences Inc 708
Interpublic Group Of Companies Inc. 708
Intersections Inc. 709
Interstate Resources, Inc. 709
Intest Corp. 709
Intevac, Inc. 709
Intrepid Capital Corporation 709
Intrepid Museum Foundation, Inc. 709
Intrepid Potash Inc 710
Intricon Corporation 710
Intrinsix Corp. 710
Intrusion Inc 710
Intrust Financial Corp. 710
Intuit Inc 710
Intuitive Surgical Inc 711
Inuvo Inc 711
Invacare Corp 711
Invenda Corporation 711
Invensense, Inc. 711
Inventergy Global Inc 711
Invesco Ltd 712
Invesco Mortgage Capital Inc 712
Investar Holding Corp 712
Investors Title Co. 712
Invitation Homes Inc 712
Io Integration Inc. 712
Ioco 713
Ion Geophysical Corp 713
Ionis Pharmaceuticals Inc 713
Iowa First Bancshares Corp. 713
Iowa Health System 713
Iowa State University Of Science And Technology 713
Ipalco Enterprises, Inc. 714

Ipayment, Inc. 714
Ipc Healthcare, Inc. 714
Ipco Us Llc 714
Ipg Photonics Corp 714
Iqvia Holdings Inc 714
Irby Construction Company 715
Irc Retail Centers Llc 715
Irell & Manella Llp 715
Irex Corporation 715
Iridex Corp. 715
Iridium Communications Inc 715
Irobot Corp 716
Iron Eagle Group, Inc. 716
Iron Mountain Inc (new) 716
Ironwood Pharmaceuticals Inc 716
Iroquois Memorial Hospital & Resident Home 716
Isco International, Inc. 716
Isg Technology, Llc 717
Isign Solutions Inc 717
Isle Of Capri Casinos Llc 717
Iso New England Inc. 717
Isomet Corp. 717
Ita Group, Inc 717
Itc Holdings Corp. 718
Iteris Inc 718
Itex Corp 718
Itg Cigars Inc. 718
Iti Tropicals Inc. 718
Itis Holdings Inc 718
Itron Inc 719
Itron Networked Solutions, Inc. 719
Itronics Inc. 719
Itt Educational Services Inc 719
Itt Inc 719
Ivci, Llc 719
Iveric Bio, Inc. 720
Ivey Mechanical Company, Llc 720
Iw Group 720
Ixia 720
Ixys, Llc 720
J & D Produce, Inc. 720
J M Smith Corporation 721
J&j Snack Foods Corp. 721
J. Alexander's Holdings, Inc. 721
J. C. Blair Memorial Hospital 721
J. Crew Group, Llc 721
J. D. Streett & Company, Inc. 721
J. F. White Contracting Company 722
J. H. Findorff & Son Inc. 722
J. Lohr Winery Corporation 722
J. Stokes & Assoc., Inc. 722
J.d. Abrams, L.p. 722
J.e. Dunn Construction Company 722
J.e. Dunn Construction Group, Inc. 723
J.j. Gumberg Co. 723
J.jill Inc 723
J.m. Huber Corporation 723
Jabil Inc 723
Jack Henry & Associates, Inc. 723
Jack In The Box, Inc. 724
Jackson County Hospital District 724
Jackson County Memorial Hospital Authority 724
Jackson Electric Membership Corporation 724
Jackson Energy Authority 724
Jackson Healthcare, Llc 724
Jackson Hewitt Tax Service Inc. 725
Jackson Hospital & Clinic, Inc. 725
Jackson State University 725
Jacksonville Electric Authority 725
Jacksonville Jaguars, Llc 725
Jacksonville University 725
Jaco Electronics, Inc. 726
Jaco Oil Company 726
Jacobs Entertainment, Inc. 726
Jacobs Financial Group Inc 726
Jacobs Solutions Inc 726
Jacobs, Malcolm & Burtt 726
Jacobson & Company, Inc 727

Jaffe Associates Incorporated 727
Jaggaer, Llc 727
Jagged Peak, Inc. 727
Jakks Pacific Inc 727
Jamba, Inc. 727
James Madison University 728
James River Coal Company 728
Janel Corp 728
Jani-king International, Inc. 728
Janone Inc 728
Janus Capital Group Inc. 728
Japan Society, Inc. 729
Jarvis Christian University 729
Jauregui, Inc. 729
Javelin Mortgage Investment Corp. 729
Javo Beverage Company, Inc. 729
Jayhawk Pipeline, L.l.c. 729
Jbg Smith Properties 730
Jck Legacy Company 730
Jcm Partners, Llc 730
Jds Uniphase Canada Ltd 730
Jefferies Financial Group Inc 730
Jefferies Group Llc 730
Jefferson County Hma, Llc 731
Jefferson Health - Northeast 731
Jefferson Homebuilders, Inc. 731
Jefferson Hospital Association, Inc. 731
Jeffersonville Bancorp 731
Jeld-wen Holding Inc 731
Jelly Belly Candy Company 732
Jennifer Convertibles, Inc. 732
Jenzabar, Inc. 732
Jer Investors Trust Inc 732
Jerry Biggers Chevrolet, Inc. 732
Jersey Central Power & Light Co. 732
Jersey City Medical Center, Inc. 733
Jesco, Inc. 733
Jetblue Airways Corp 733
Jewett-cameron Trading Co. Ltd. 733
Jfk Health System, Inc. 733
Jg Wentworth Co (the) 733
Jit Manufacturing, Inc. 734
Jive Software, Inc. 734
Jlm Couture Inc. 734
Jmp Group Inc. 734
Joann Inc 734
Job Options, Incorporated 734
Joe Granato, Incorporated 735
John Bean Technologies Corp 735
John Brown University 735
John C. Lincoln Health Network 735
John Carroll University 735
John D And Catherine T Macarthur Foundation 735
John F Kennedy Center For The Performing Arts 736
John F. Kennedy University 736
John Hine Pontiac 736
John Muir Health 736
John T. Mather Memorial Hospital Of Port Jefferson, New York, Inc. 736
Johns Hopkins All Children's Hospital, Inc. 736
Johns Hopkins Bayview Medical Center, Inc. 737
Johnson & Jennings Inc 737
Johnson & Johnson 737
Johnson & Wales University Inc 737
Johnson C. Smith University, Incorporated 737
Johnson City Energy Authority 737
Johnson Contractors, Inc. 738
Johnson Controls Fire Protection Lp 738
Johnson Controls, Inc. 738
Johnson Outdoors Inc 738
Johnson Supply And Equipment Corporation 738
Johnsonville, Llc 738
Johnston Enterprises, Inc. 739
Joint Commission On Accreditation Of Healthcare Organizations 739
Jonathan Sprouts, Inc. 739
Jones Financial Companies Lllp 739

Jones Lang Lasalle Inc 739
Jones Soda Co. 739
Jordan Cf Investments Llp 740
Joseph Drown Foundation 740
Joyce Leslie Inc 740
Jpmorgan Chase & Co 740
Jsd Management, Inc. 740
Jsj Corporation 740
Judlau Contracting, Inc. 741
Juniata College 741
Juniata Valley Financial Corp 741
Junior Achievement Usa 741
Juniper Group Inc. 741
Juniper Networks Inc 741
Juniper Pharmaceuticals, Inc. 742
Jupiter Marine International Holdings, Inc. 742
Jupiter Medical Center, Inc. 742
Just Born, Inc. 742
K-micro, Inc. 742
K-tel International Inc 742
K-va-t Food Stores, Inc. 743
K. V. Mart Co. 743
Kadant Inc 743
Kadlec Regional Medical Center 743
Kaiser Aluminum Corp. 743
Kaiser Foundation Health Plan, Inc. 743
Kaiser Foundation Hospitals Inc 744
Kaiser Group Holdings, Inc. 744
Kaiser-francis Oil Company 744
Kala Bio Inc 744
Kaleida Health 744
Kaman Corp. 744
Kane Upmc 745
Kansas City Board Of Public Utilities 745
Kansas City Life Insurance Co (kansas City, Mo) 745
Kansas Department Of Transportation 745
Kansas Electric Power Cooperative, Inc. 745
Kansas State University 745
Karyopharm Therapeutics Inc 746
Kaspien Holdings Inc 746
Kate Spade Holdings Llc 746
Kayem Foods, Inc. 746
Kb Home 746
Kbr Inc 746
Kbs, Inc. 747
Kearny Financial Corp (md) 747
Keck Graduate Institute Of Applied Life Sciences 747
Keenan, Hopkins, Schmidt And Stowell Contractors, Inc. 747
Kellanova 747
Keller North America, Inc. 747
Kellstrom Aerospace, Llc 748
Kelly Services, Inc. 748
Kelso & Company, L.p. 748
Kelso-burnett Co. 748
Kemper Corp (de) 748
Kenergy Corp. 748
Kennametal Inc. 749
Kennedy Health System, Inc. 749
Kennedy Krieger Institute, Inc. 749
Kennedy-wilson Holdings Inc 749
Kennesaw State University 749
Kennestone Hospital At Windy Hill, Inc. 749
Kenosha Beef International, Ltd. 750
Kensington Publishing Corp. 750
Kent County Memorial Hospital 750
Kent State University 750
Kentucky First Federal Bancorp 750
Kentucky Medical Services Foundation, Inc. 750
Kentucky Neighborhood Bank, Inc. 751
Kentucky Power Company 751
Kentucky Utilities Company Inc 751
Kenyon College 751
Kepner-tregoe, Inc. 751
Kettering Adventist Healthcare 751
Kettering University 752
Keuka College 752

Keurig Dr Pepper Inc 752
Keurig Green Mountain, Inc. 752
Kewaunee Scientific Corporation 752
Key City Furniture Company Inc 752
Key Energy Services Inc (de) 753
Key Food Stores Co-operative, Inc. 753
Key Technology, Inc. 753
Key Tronic Corp 753
Keycorp 753
Keysight Technologies Inc 753
Keystone Consolidated Industries, Inc. 754
Keystone Dedicated Logistics Co Llc 754
Kforce Inc. 754
Kgbo Holdings, Inc. 754
Kid Brands, Inc. 754
Kid Galaxy, Inc. 754
Kilgore Junior College District 755
Killbuck Bancshares, Inc. 755
Kilroy Realty Corp 755
Kimball Electronics Inc 755
Kimball Medical Center Inc. 755
Kimbell Art Foundation 755
Kimberly-clark Corp. 756
Kimco Realty Corp 756
Kinder Morgan Inc. 756
Kinetic Systems, Inc. 756
King Fish Media, Llc 756
King Ranch, Inc. 756
King's College 757
Kingsbrook Jewish Medical Center Inc 757
Kingstone Companies Inc 757
Kingsway Financial Services Inc (de) 757
Kinsale Capital Group Inc 757
Kinseth Hospitality Company, Inc. 757
Kior, Inc. 758
Kirby Corp. 758
Kirby Risk Corporation 758
Kirkland's Inc 758
Kish Bancorp Inc. 758
Kishhealth System 758
Kissimmee Utility Authority (inc) 759
Kitchell Corporation 759
Kite Pharma, Inc. 759
Kite Realty Group Trust 759
Kitz Corporation Of America 759
Kiwanis International, Inc. 759
Kiwibox.com, Inc. 760
Kkr & Co Inc 760
Kkr Financial Holdings Llc 760
Kkr Real Estate Finance Trust Inc 760
Kla Corp 760
Kleinknecht Electric Company, Inc. 760
Knight Transportation, Inc. 761
Knight-swift Transportation Holdings Inc 761
Knights Of Columbus 761
Knouse Foods Cooperative, Inc. 761
Knowles Corp 761
Knox Nursery, Inc. 761
Knoxville Utilities Board 762
Koch Enterprises, Inc. 762
Koch Supply & Trading, Lp 762
Kohl's Corp. 762
Kohler Co. 762
Kohn Pedersen Fox Associates, Pc 762
Kohr Brothers, Inc. 763
Koil Energy Solutions Inc 763
Kokosing Construction Company, Inc. 763
Kolorfusion International Inc 763
Komatsu Mining Corp. 763
Kongsberg Power Products Systems I, Llc 763
Kontoor Brands Inc 764
Kopin Corp. 764
Koppers Holdings Inc 764
Koppers Utility And Industrial Products Inc. 764
Korn Ferry 764
Korte Construction Company 764
Koru Medical Systems Inc 765
Kosciusko 21st Century Foundation, Inc. 765

Kosmos Energy Ltd (de) 765
Koss Corp 765
Kph Healthcare Services, Inc. 765
Kpmg Llp 765
Kprs Construction Services, Inc. 766
Kqed Inc. 766
Kraft Heinz Co (the) 766
Krasdale Foods, Inc. 766
Kraton Corporation 766
Kratos Defense & Security Solutions, Inc. 766
Kraus-anderson, Incorporated 767
Krause Gentle, L.l.c. 767
Kreher Steel Company, Llc 767
Kroenke Sports Holdings Llc 767
Kroger Co (the) 767
Krones, Inc. 767
Kronos Worldwide Inc 768
Krueger International, Inc. 768
Ks Bancorp Inc 768
Kuakini Health System 768
Kurt Manufacturing Company, Inc. 768
Kutak Rock Llp 768
Kvh Industries, Inc. 769
Kwalu Llc 769
Kwik Trip, Inc. 769
Kynect, Ltd. 769
L & L Franchise, Inc. 769
L & M Companies Inc. 769
L & S Electric, Inc. 770
L&l Energy Inc 770
L&m Technologies, Inc. 770
L.d. Mcfarland Company, Limited 770
L3harris Technologies Inc 770
La France Corp. 770
La India Packing Co. 771
La Jolla Pharmaceutical Company 771
La Quinta Holdings Inc. 771
La-z-boy Inc. 771
Laboratory Corporation Of America Holdings 771
Ladder Capital Corp 771
Ladenburg Thalmann Financial Services Inc 772
Ladies Professional Golf Association 772
Ladrx Corp 772
Laemmle Theatres, Llc 772
Lafayette College 772
Lafayette General Medical Center, Inc. 772
Lahey Health System, Inc. 773
Laird & Company 773
Lake Area Corn Processors Co-operative 773
Lake Forest College 773
Lake Hospital System, Inc. 773
Lake Shore Bancorp Inc 773
Lakeland Bancorp, Inc. 774
Lakeland Community Hospital, Watervliet 774
Lakeland Financial Corp 774
Lakeland Industries, Inc. 774
Lakeland Regional Medical Center, Inc. 774
Lakeside Industries, Inc. 774
Lam Research Corp 775
Lamar Advertising Co (new) 775
Lamb Weston Holdings Inc 775
Lancaster Colony Corp 775
Lancesoft, Inc. 775
Land O' Lakes Inc 775
Land O'frost, Inc. 776
Landauer, Inc. 776
Landcar Management, Ltd. 776
Landmark Bancorp Inc 776
Lands' End Inc 776
Landscapes Unlimited, L.l.c. 776
Landstar System, Inc. 777
Lane College 777
Lane Powell Pc 777
Lanier Parking Holdings, Inc. 777
Lannett Co., Inc. 777
Lansing Board Of Water And Light 777
Lantronix Inc. 778
Lapham-hickey Steel Corp. 778

Lapolla Industries, Llc 778
Larimar Therapeutics Inc 778
Larkin Community Hospital, Inc. 778
Larkin Enterprises, Inc. 778
Las Vegas Events, Inc. 779
Las Vegas Sands Corp 779
Las Vegas Valley Water District 779
Lasalle University 779
Laser Master International, Inc 779
Lasersight Inc 779
Latinworks Marketing Llc 780
Lattice Inc 780
Lattice Semiconductor Corp 780
Laureate Education Inc 780
Lauren Engineers & Constructors, Inc. 780
Laurens County Health Care System 780
Lauth Properties, Llc 781
Lawnwood Medical Center, Inc. 781
Lawrence + Memorial Hospital, Inc. 781
Lawrence R. Mccoy & Co., Inc. 781
Layne Christensen Company 781
Layne Marx & Company 781
Lazare Kaplan International Inc. 782
Lcc International Inc 782
Lci Industries 782
Lcnb Corp 782
Ldr Holding Corporation 782
Le Moyne College 782
Leadventure Inc. 783
Leaf Group Ltd. 783
Leaf Software Solutions, Inc. 783
Leanlogistics, Inc. 783
Leapfrog Enterprises, Inc. 783
Lear Corp. 783
Learning Ally, Inc. 784
Learning Express, Inc. 784
Learning Tree International Inc 784
Ledtronics, Inc. 784
Lee County Electric Cooperative, Inc. 784
Lee Enterprises, Inc. 784
Lee Lewis Construction, Inc. 785
Lee Memorial Health System Foundation, Inc. 785
Lee University 785
Leerink Partners Llc 785
Legacy Awc, Inc. 785
Legacy Emanuel Hospital & Health Center 785
Legacy Farmers Cooperative 786
Legacy Health 786
Legacy Imbds Inc 786
Legacy Reserves Lp 786
Legal Services Corporation 786
Legend Oil & Gas Ltd 786
Leggett & Platt, Inc. 787
Lehigh University 787
Lehigh Valley Health Network, Inc. 787
Lehman Brothers Holdings Inc. 787
Lehman Trikes Inc 787
Leidos Holdings Inc 787
Leland Stanford Junior University 788
Lemaitre Vascular Inc 788
Lemieux Group Lp 788
Lemoyne-owen College 788
Lendingtree Inc (new) 788
Lendway Inc 788
Lennar Corp 789
Lennox International Inc 789
Lenox Corporation 789
Leo A. Daly Company 789
Leonard Green & Partners, L.p. 789
Leonardo Drs Inc 789
Leopardo Companies Inc. 790
Leprino Foods Company 790
Lescarden Inc 790
Lester E. Cox Medical Centers 790
Levcor International Inc. 790
Level 3 Parent, Llc 790
Levenger Company 791
Levi Strauss & Co. 791

Levi Strauss & Co. 791
Levindale Hebrew Geriatric Center And Hospital, Inc. 791
Lewis & Clark College 791
Lewis Brothers Bakeries Inc 791
Lexicon Pharmaceuticals, Inc. 792
Lexington Medical Center 792
Lexmark International, Inc. 792
Lgi Homes, Inc. 792
Lgl Group Inc (the) 792
Lhh Corporation 792
Liberty Energy Inc 793
Liberty Homes Inc 793
Liberty Media Corp (de) 793
Liberty Media Corp (de) - Common Series B Braves Group 793
Liberty Media Corp (de) - Formula One Group 793
Liberty Mutual Holding Co., Inc. 793
Liberty Orchards Company, Inc. 794
Liberty Regional Medical Center Inc. 794
Library Of Congress 794
Licking Memorial Health Systems 794
Lict Corp 794
Lidestri Foods, Inc. 794
Life Care Centers Of America, Inc. 795
Lifebridge Health, Inc. 795
Lifecell Corporation 795
Lifecore Biomedical Inc 795
Lifequest World Corp 795
Lifespan Corporation 795
Lifestore Financial Group 796
Lifetime Brands Inc 796
Lifeway Christian Resources Of The Southern Baptist Convention 796
Lifeway Foods, Inc. 796
Ligand Pharmaceuticals Inc 796
Light & Wonder Inc 796
Lightbridge Corp 797
Lighthouse Computer Services, Inc. 797
Lighting Science Group Corp 797
Lightpath Technologies, Inc. 797
Lilly (eli) & Co 797
Limetree Bay Terminals Llc 797
Limoneira Co 798
Lin Holdings Corp. 798
Lincoln Benefit Life Co 798
Lincoln Center For The Performing Arts, Inc. 798
Lincoln Educational Services Corp 798
Lincoln Electric Holdings, Inc. 798
Lincoln Industries, Inc. 799
Lincoln International Llc 799
Lincoln National Corp. 799
Linde Plc (new) 799
Lindsay Corp 799
Lineage Cell Therapeutics Inc 799
Linear Technology Llc 800
Linkage, Inc. 800
Linkedin Corporation 800
Linkmont Technologies, Inc. 800
Lion Copper & Gold Corp 800
Lionbridge Technologies, Llc 800
Lipscomb University 801
Liquid Holdings Group Inc 801
Liquid Investments, Inc. 801
Liquidity Services Inc 801
Liquidmetal Technologies Inc 801
Lisata Therapeutics Inc 801
Litco International, Inc. 802
Litehouse, Inc. 802
Lithia Motors Inc 802
Littelfuse Inc 802
Little League Baseball Inc 802
Little Sioux Corn Processors Llc 802
Littlefield Corp 803
Littler Mendelson, P.c. 803
Livanova Usa, Inc. 803
Live Current Media Inc 803
Live Microsystems Inc 803

Live Nation Entertainment Inc 803
Live Ventures Inc 804
Liveperson Inc 804
Liveramp Holdings Inc 804
Livestyle, Inc. 804
Liveworld, Inc. 804
Livingstone College, Inc. 804
Lkq Corp 805
Ll Flooring Holdings Inc 805
Ll&e Royalty Trust Co. 805
Lloyd Staffing, Inc. 805
Lmi Aerospace, Inc. 805
Local Corp 805
Loeber Motors, Inc. 806
Loeffler Associates, Inc. 806
Loews Corp. 806
Logansport Financial Corp. 806
Logic Devices Inc 806
Logical Ventures, Inc. 806
Logicalis, Inc. 807
Logicquest Technology Inc 807
Logility, Inc. 807
Logistics Plus, Inc. 807
Lojack Corporation 807
Loma Linda University 807
Loma Linda University Medical Center 808
London Fruit, Inc. 808
Long Beach Medical Center 808
Long Island Community Hospital At Nyu Langone Health 808
Long Island Jewish Medical Center 808
Long Island Power Authority 808
Long Island University Westchester & Rockland Alumni Association Ltd. 809
Long Wave Inc. 809
Loop Llc 809
Loos & Co., Inc. 809
Lopito, Ileana & Howie Inc. 809
Loral Space & Communications Inc. 809
Los Angeles Department Of Water And Power 810
Los Angeles Philharmonic Association 810
Loud Technologies Inc 810
Louisiana Tech University 810
Louisiana-pacific Corp 810
Louisville-jefferson County Metro Government 810
Low Temp Industries, Inc. 811
Lowe's Companies Inc 811
Lowell, City Of (inc) 811
Lowenstein Sandler Llp 811
Lower Colorado River Authority 811
Lowry Holding Company, Inc. 811
Loyola Marymount University 812
Loyola University Maryland, Inc. 812
Loyola University Of Chicago Inc 812
Loyola University, New Orleans 812
Lozier Corporation 812
Lpl Financial Holdings Inc. 812
Lri Holdings, Inc. 813
Lrr Energy, L.p. 813
Ls Gallegos & Associates Inc 813
Lsb Industries, Inc. 813
Lsi Industries Inc. 813
Lsref4 Lighthouse Corporate Acquisitions, Llc 813
Ltc Properties, Inc. 814
Lub Liquidating Trust. 814
Luck Stone Corporation 814
Luckey Farmers, Inc. 814
Lucy Webb Hayes National Training School For Deaconesses And Missionaries 814
Lumen Technologies Inc 814
Lumentum Holdings Inc 815
Luminex Corporation 815
Luminis Health Anne Arundel Medical Center, Inc 815
Luminis Health Doctors Community Medical Center Foundation, Inc. 815
Lumos Networks Corp. 815
Lumos Pharma Inc 815

Luna Innovations Inc 816
Lundbeck Seattle Biopharmaceuticals, Inc. 816
Lundy Services, L.l.c. 816
Lupus Research Alliance, Inc. 816
Luster Products, Inc. 816
Luther Burbank Corp 816
Luther College 817
Lutheran Services In America Inc 817
Luxfer Holdings Plc 817
Lxp Industrial Trust 817
Lydall, Inc. 817
Lyft Inc 817
Lyne Laboratories, Inc. 818
Lyntegar Electric Cooperative, Inc. 818
Lyon College 818
Lyondellbasell Advanced Polymers Inc. 818
Lyric Opera Of Chicago 818
Lyris, Inc. 818
M & F Bancorp Inc 819
M & T Bank Corp 819
M V M, Inc. 819
M. A. Mortenson Company 819
M. B. Kahn Construction Co., Inc. 819
M. J. Brunner Inc 819
M.a. Patout & Son Limited, L.l.c. 820
M.c.a. Communications, Inc. 820
M.d.c. Holdings, Inc. 820
M/i Homes Inc 820
Mac Beath Hardwood Company 820
Macalester College 820
Macallister Machinery Co Inc 821
Macatawa Bank Corp. 821
Mace Security International, Inc. 821
Macerich Co (the) 821
Mach 1 Global Services, Inc. 821
Machado/garcia-serra Publicidad, Inc. 821
Macias Gini & O'connell Llp 822
Mack & Associates Ltd. 822
Macom Technology Solutions Holdings Inc 822
Macomb-oakland Regional Center, Inc. 822
Macrogenics, Inc 822
Madden (steven) Ltd. 822
Madison Area Technical College District 823
Madison Electric Company 823
Madison Huntsville County Airport Authority 823
Madix, Inc. 823
Madonna Rehabilitation Hospital 823
Madrigal Pharmaceuticals Inc 823
Magee Rehabilitation Hospital Foundation 824
Magneco/metrel, Inc. 824
Magnetek, Inc. 824
Magnite Inc 824
Magnum Construction Management, Llc 824
Magyar Bancorp Inc 824
Mahwah Bergen Retail Group, Inc. 825
Maimonides Medical Center 825
Main Line Health System 825
Main Line Hospitals, Inc. 825
Maine & Maritimes Corporation 825
Maine Coast Regional Health Facilities Inc 825
Mainegeneral Health 826
Mainehealth 826
Mainehealth Services 826
Major League Baseball Players Association 826
Make-a-wish Foundation Of America 826
Maldonado Nursery & Landscaping Inc. 826
Mammoth Energy Services Inc 827
Management & Training Corporation 827
Manatee Memorial Hospital, L.p. 827
Manhattan Associates, Inc. 827
Manhattan Bridge Capital, Inc. 827
Manhattan College Corp 827
Manhattan School Of Music Inc 828
Manhattanville College 828
Manitex International Inc 828
Manitou America Holding, Inc. 828
Manitowoc Company Inc (the) 828

Mann+hummel Filtration Technology Intermediate Holdings Inc. 828
Mannatech Inc 829
Manning & Napier, Inc. 829
Mannkind Corp 829
Manor Care, Inc. 829
Manpowergroup Inc 829
Mantech International Corporation 829
Manufactured Housing Enterprises, Inc. 830
Maq, Llc 830
Mar-jac Poultry, Inc. 830
Marathon Oil Corp. 830
Marathon Petroleum Corp. 830
Marbridge Foundation, Inc. 830
March Of Dimes Inc. 831
Marchex Inc 831
Marchon Eyewear, Inc. 831
Marco's Franchising, Llc 831
Marcum Llp 831
Marcus Center For The Performing Arts, Inc. 831
Marcus Corp. (the) 832
Margate Medical Staff, Inc. 832
Mariah Media, Inc. 832
Marian University, Inc. 832
Marietta Corporation 832
Marin General Hospital 832
Marin Software Inc 833
Marine Products Corp 833
Marine Toys For Tots Foundation 833
Marinemax Inc 833
Marinus Pharmaceuticals Inc 833
Marion Community Hospital Inc 833
Marist College 834
Maritz Holdings Inc. 834
Mark Master, Inc. 834
Markel Group Inc 834
Marker 29 Produce, Inc. 834
Marker Therapeutics Inc 834
Market & Johnson, Inc. 835
Market America, Inc. 835
Marketaxess Holdings Inc. 835
Marketing Analysts Inc. 835
Marketo, Inc. 835
Markmonitor Inc. 835
Marks Paneth Llp 836
Markwest Energy Partners, L.p. 836
Markwins Beauty Brands, Inc. 836
Marlin Business Services Corp. 836
Marquette Lumber Company, Incorporated 836
Marquette University 836
Marriott International, Inc. 837
Marriott Vacations Worldwide Corp. 837
Marsh & Mclennan Companies Inc. 837
Marshall Marketing & Communications, Inc. 837
Marshall University 837
Marshfield Clinic Health System, Inc. 837
Marshfield Clinic, Inc. 838
Marten Transport Ltd 838
Martha Jefferson Health Services Corporation 838
Martha Stewart Living Omnimedia, Inc. 838
Martin & Bayley, Inc. 838
Martin Marietta Materials, Inc. 838
Martin Midstream Partners Lp 839
Martin Resource Management Corporation 839
Marvell Technology Inc 839
Marvin Engineering Co., Inc. 839
Mary Washington Healthcare 839
Maryland And Virginia Milk Producers Cooperative Association, Incorporated 839
Maryland Department Of Transportation 840
Maryland Southern Electric Cooperative Inc 840
Marymount Manhattan College 840
Maryville Consulting Group, Inc. 840
Masco Corp. 840
Mashantucket Pequot Tribal Nation 840
Masimo Corp. 841
Mass General Brigham Health Plan, Inc. 841
Mass General Brigham Incorporated 841

COMPANIES LISTED ALPHABETICALLY

Massachusetts Department Of Transportation 841
Massachusetts Higher Education Assistance Corporation 841
Massachusetts Institute Of Technology 841
Massachusetts Medical Society Inc 842
Massachusetts Municipal Wholesale Electric Company 842
Massachusetts Mutual Life Insurance Co. (springfield, Ma) 842
Massachusetts Port Authority 842
Mastec Inc. (fl) 842
Mastech Digital Inc 842
Mastercard Inc 843
Mastercraft Boat Holdings Inc 843
Masterspas, Llc 843
Matanuska Telecom Association, Incorporated 843
Materion Corp 843
Mativ Inc 843
Matlen Silver Group, Inc. 844
Matrix Service Co. 844
Matson Inc 844
Mattel Inc 844
Mattersight Corporation 844
Matteson-ridolfi, Inc. 844
Matthews International Corp 845
Mattingly Foods, Inc. 845
Mattress Firm Holding Corp. 845
Mattson Technology, Inc. 845
Maui Land & Pineapple Co., Inc. 845
Mavenir, Inc. 845
Maxcyte Inc 846
Maxim Healthcare Services, Inc. 846
Maximus Inc. 846
Maxitrol Company 846
Maxlinear Inc 846
Maxor National Pharmacy Services Llc 846
Maxus Realty Trust Inc 847
Maxx Sports Tv Inc 847
Mayer Electric Supply Company, Inc. 847
Mayo Clinic Health System - Northwest Wisconsin Region, Inc. 847
Mayo Clinic Health System-franciscan Healthcare, Inc. 847
Mayo Clinic Hospital-rochester 847
Mayo Clinic Jacksonville (a Nonprofit Corporation) 848
Mays (j.w.), Inc. 848
Mayville Engineering Co Inc 848
Mbc Holdings, Inc. 848
Mbi, Inc. 848
Mbia Inc. 848
Mcafee Corp. 849
Mcap Inc (new) 849
Mccarthy Building Companies, Inc. 849
Mccloskey Mechanical Contractors, Inc. 849
Mccormick & Co Inc 849
Mccoy-rockford, Inc. 849
Mcdaniel College, Inc. 850
Mcdonald's Corp 850
Mcdonough County Hospital District 850
Mcg-hjt, Inc. 850
Mcgough Construction Co., Llc 850
Mcgrath Rentcorp 850
Mckee Wallwork & Company, Llc 851
Mckesson Corp 851
Mclane Company, Inc. 851
Mclaren Bay Region 851
Mclaren Health Care Corporation 851
Mclaren Macomb 851
Mcloone Metal Graphics, Inc. 852
Mcmaster-carr Supply Company 852
Mcnaughton-mckay Electric Co. 852
Mcneese State University 852
Mcnichols Company 852
Mcphee Electric, Ltd 852
Mcrae Industries, Inc. 853
Mcshane Construction Company Llc 853
Mcshane Development Company Llc 853
Mdu Resources Group Inc 853
Meals On Wheels America 853
Mechanics' Institute 853
Mecklermedia Corp 854
Medaille College Foundation, Inc. 854
Medaire Inc 854
Medallion Financial Corp 854
Media Sciences International, Inc. 854
Media Storm, Llc 854
Medianews Group, Inc. 855
Medical Information Technology, Inc. 855
Medical Properties Trust Inc 855
Medicinova Inc 855
Medidata Solutions, Inc. 855
Medifast Inc 855
Medisys Health Network Inc. 856
Medivation, Inc. 856
Medler Electric Company 856
Medley Steel And Supply, Inc. 856
Medline Industries, Lp 856
Medlink International Inc 856
Medstar Health, Inc. 857
Medstar-georgetown Medical Center, Inc. 857
Mega Matrix Corp 857
Megatech Corp. 857
Meherrin Agricultural & Chemical Co 857
Meijer, Inc. 857
Melaleuca, Inc. 858
Melinta Therapeutics, Llc 858
Melrosewakefield Healthcare Parent Corporation 858
Memorial Behavioral Health Center In Springfield 858
Memorial Health Services 858
Memorial Health System 858
Memorial Health System Of East Texas 859
Memorial Hermann Healthcare System 859
Memorial Hospital 859
Memorial Hospital Auxiliary, Inc. 859
Memorial Sloan-kettering Cancer Center 859
Mendocino Brewing Co Inc 859
Mendocino Coast District Hospital 860
Menil Foundation, Inc. 860
Menlo College 860
Menno Travel Service, Inc. 860
Mentor Graphics Corporation 860
Mera Pharmaceuticals, Inc. 860
Merakey Usa 861
Mercantile Bank Corp. 861
Merchants Bancorp (indiana) 861
Merck & Co Inc 861
Mercury General Corp. 861
Mercury Systems Inc 861
Mercy Care 862
Mercy Children's Hospital 862
Mercy Corps 862
Mercy Gwynedd University 862
Mercy Health 862
Mercy Health 862
Mercy Health - St. Rita's Medical Center, Llc 863
Mercy Health Foundation Of Southeastern Pennsylvania 863
Mercy Health Network, Inc. 863
Mercy Health North Llc 863
Mercy Hospital 863
Mercy Hospital And Medical Center 863
Mercy Hospital South 864
Mercy Hospital Springfield 864
Mercy Medical Center 864
Mercy Ships International 864
Mercy University 864
Meredith Enterprises Inc 864
Mereo Biopharma 5 Inc 865
Meridian Bioscience, Inc. 865
Meridian Partners, Llc 865
Meridian Technology Group, Inc. 865
Merit Medical Systems, Inc. 865
Meritage Homes Corp 865
Meritage Hospitality Group Inc 866
Meriter Health Services, Inc. 866
Meritus Health, Inc. 866
Merle Norman Cosmetics, Inc. 866
Merriam-webster, Incorporated 866
Merrimack Pharmaceuticals Inc 866
Merriman Holdings Inc. 867
Mesa Air Group Inc 867
Mesa Laboratories, Inc. 867
Mesabi Trust 867
Mesquite Energy, Inc. 867
Messer Construction Co. 867
Messiah University 868
Mestek Inc. 868
Meta Platforms Inc 868
Metaldyne Performance Group Inc. 868
Metalico, Inc. 868
Metallus Inc 868
Metals Recovery Holdings Llc 869
Methes Energies International Ltd 869
Methode Electronics Inc 869
Methodist Hospitals Of Dallas Inc 869
Methodist Le Bonheur Healthcare 869
Metlife Inc 869
Metric & Multistandard Components Corp. 870
Metro Packaging & Imaging Inc 870
Metro-north Commuter Railroad Co Inc 870
Metroplex Adventist Hospital, Inc. 870
Metropolitan Airports Commission 870
Metropolitan Bank Holding Corp 870
Metropolitan College Of New York 871
Metropolitan Edison Company 871
Metropolitan Government Of Nashville & Davidson County 871
Metropolitan Group Property & Casualty Insurance Co. 871
Metropolitan Opera Association, Inc. 871
Metropolitan Property & Casualty Insurance Co. 871
Metropolitan Security Services, Inc. 872
Metropolitan St. Louis Sewer District 872
Metropolitan State University Of Denver 872
Metropolitan Transit Authority Of Harris County 872
Metropolitan Transportation Authority 872
Metropolitan Utilities District Of Omaha 872
Metropolitan Washington Airports Authority 873
Metrostar Systems, Llc 873
Metters Industries, Inc. 873
Mettler-toledo International, Inc. 873
Metwood Inc 873
Mexco Energy Corp. 873
Mexican American Opportunity Foundation 874
Meyer & Wallis, Inc. 874
Mfa Financial, Inc. 874
Mfa Incorporated 874
Mfa Oil Company 874
Mge Energy Inc 874
Mgic Investment Corp. (wi) 875
Mgm Resorts International 875
Mgp Ingredients Inc (new) 875
Mgt Capital Investments Inc 875
Miami Jewish Health Systems, Inc. 875
Miami University 875
Miami Valley Hospital 876
Michael Anthony Jewelers Inc 876
Michael Baker International, Inc. 876
Michael Foods Group, Inc. 876
Michael Merger Sub Llc 876
Michels Corporation 876
Michigan Consolidated Gas Co 877
Michigan Milk Producers Association 877
Michigan State University 877
Michigan Technological University 877
Micro Imaging Technology Inc 877
Microblend, Inc. 877
Microbot Medical Inc 878
Microchip Technology Inc 878

Microfinancial Incorporated 878
Micron Solutions Inc (de) 878
Micron Technology Inc. 878
Micropac Industries, Inc. 878
Microsemi Corporation 879
Microsoft Corporation 879
Microstrategy Inc. 879
Microtechnologies Llc 879
Microvision Inc. 879
Microwave Filter Co., Inc. 879
Microwave Transmission Systems, Inc 880
Mid America Clinical Laboratories Llc 880
Mid Penn Bancorp Inc 880
Mid Ventures Inc. 880
Mid-am Building Supply, Inc. 880
Mid-america Apartment Communities Inc 880
Midas Medici Group Holdings Inc 881
Midcoast Energy Partners, L.p. 881
Midcontinent Independent System Operator, Inc. 881
Midcontinent Media, Inc. 881
Middle Tennessee State University 881
Middleby Corp 881
Middlefield Banc Corp. 882
Middlesex Water Co. 882
Midland Capital Holdings Corp 882
Midland Cogeneration Venture Limited Partnership 882
Midland States Bancorp Inc 882
Midmark Corporation 882
Midnite Express Inc. 883
Midstate Medical Center 883
Midwave Wireless, Inc. 883
Midway Ford Truck Center, Inc. 883
Midwest Air Technologies, Inc. 883
Midwest Energy, Inc. 883
Midwest Game Supply Company 884
Midwestern State University 884
Midwestone Financial Group, Inc. 884
Mikart, Llc 884
Milaeger's, Inc. 884
Milbank Manufacturing Co. 884
Milberg Llp 885
Miles College, Inc. 885
Miles Health Care, Inc 885
Milestone Construction Services, Inc. 885
Milestone Scientific Inc. 885
Milford Regional Medical Center, Inc. 885
Milken Family Foundation 886
Millennial Media, Inc. 886
Millennium Prime Inc 886
Miller & Chevalier Chartered 886
Miller Electric Company 886
Miller Electric Construction, Inc 886
Miller Industries Inc. (tn) 887
Miller Transportation Services, Inc. 887
Miller Waste Mills, Incorporated 887
Miller Zell, Inc. 887
Millerknoll Inc 887
Millinocket Regional Hospital Inc 887
Mills-peninsula Health Services 888
Milton Hershey School 888
Miltope Corporation 888
Milwaukee Area Technical College Foundation, Inc. 888
Milwaukee Bucks, Llc 888
Milwaukee County War Memorial, Inc. 888
Mind Technology Inc 889
Mindbody, Inc. 889
Minerals Technologies, Inc. 889
Miners Incorporated 889
Minerva Neurosciences Inc 889
Mines Management, Inc. 889
Mini-systems, Inc. 890
Minim Inc 890
Ministry Health Care, Inc. 890
Minitab, Llc 890
Minn-dak Farmers Cooperative Inc 890

Minnesota State Colleges And Universities 890
Minnesota Wild Hockey Club, Lp 891
Minnkota Power Cooperative, Inc. 891
Minuteman Press International, Inc. 891
Miracle Software Systems Inc. 891
Miracosta Community College District 891
Miratek Corp. 891
Mirenco Inc 892
Misonix Opco, Inc. 892
Mission Broadcasting, Inc. 892
Mission Hospital, Inc. 892
Mission Pharmacal Company 892
Mississippi County Electric Cooperative, Inc. 892
Mississippi Power Co 893
Mississippi State University 893
Missouri City Of Kansas City 893
Missouri Department Of Transportation 893
Missouri Higher Education Loan Authority 893
Missouri State University 893
Mistras Group Inc 894
Mitchell Silberberg & Knupp Llp 894
Mitek Systems, Inc. 894
Mitel Networks, Inc. 894
Mjb Wood Group, Llc 894
Mks Instruments Inc 894
Mmc Corp 895
Mmc Materials, Inc. 895
Mmr Group, Inc. 895
Mmrglobal Inc 895
Mnp Corporation 895
Mobile Area Networks Inc 895
Mobileiron, Inc. 896
Mobilepro Corp. 896
Mocon, Inc. 896
Mod-pac Corp. 896
Model N, Inc 896
Modern Woodmen Of America 896
Moderna Inc 897
Modesto Irrigation District (inc) 897
Modine Manufacturing Co 897
Modivcare Inc 897
Modivcare Solutions, Llc 897
Mohawk Industries, Inc. 897
Mohegan Tribal Gaming Authority 898
Moistureshield Inc. 898
Molecular Templates Inc 898
Molina Healthcare Inc 898
Moller International Inc 898
Molloy College 898
Monarch Casino & Resort, Inc. 899
Monarch Cement Co. 899
Monarch Services Inc. 899
Mondelez International Inc 899
Mongodb Inc 899
Monitronics International, Inc. 899
Monje, Inc. 900
Monmouth Medical Center Inc. 900
Monmouth University Inc 900
Monmouth-ocean Hospital Service Corporation 900
Monogram Food Solutions, Llc 900
Monolithic Power Systems Inc 900
Monongahela Power Co 901
Monotype Imaging Holdings Inc. 901
Monro Inc 901
Monroe Medical Foundation Inc 901
Monster Beverage Corp (new) 901
Montana State University 901
Montclair State University 902
Montefiore Medical Center 902
Montefiore Nyack Hospital Foundation, Inc. 902
Monterey Mushrooms, Llc 902
Monument Health Rapid City Hospital, Inc. 902
Moody's Corp. 902
Moog Inc 903
Moore & Van Allen Pllc 903
Moorefield Construction, Inc. 903
Moravian University 903
Morehead Memorial Hospital Inc 903

Morehouse College (inc.) 903
Morgan Stanley 904
Morgan, Lewis & Bockius Llp 904
Morningstar Inc 904
Moro Corp. 904
Morre-tec Industries, Inc. 904
Morris Business Development Co 904
Morris College 905
Morris Hospital 905
Morris Publishing Group, Llc 905
Morristown Star Struck Llc 905
Morse Operations, Inc. 905
Mosaic 905
Mosaic Co (the) 906
Mosaic Health System 906
Mosaic Immunoengineering Inc 906
Mossy Holding Company, Inc 906
Mother Murphy's Laboratories, Inc. 906
Mothers Against Drunk Driving Inc 906
Motion Computing, Inc. 907
Motion Picture Association, Inc. 907
Motor City Electric Co. 907
Motorcar Parts Of America Inc 907
Motorola Solutions Inc 907
Mott Macdonald Group Inc. 907
Mount Carmel Health System 908
Mount Olive Pickle Company, Inc. 908
Mount Sinai Medical Center Of Florida, Inc. 908
Mountain Merger Sub Corporation 908
Mountain States Health Alliance 908
Mountain States Pipe & Supply Co, Inc 908
Mountainwest Pipeline, Llc 909
Movado Group, Inc. 909
Move Solutions, Ltd. 909
Mozilla Foundation 909
Mphase Technologies Inc. 909
Mplx Lp 909
Mpm Capital Limited Partnership 910
Mpm Holdings Inc. 910
Mr Cooper Group Inc 910
Mr. Goodcents, Inc. 910
Mrc Global Inc 910
Mriglobal 910
Mrv Communications, Inc. 911
Ms Foundation For Women Inc 911
Msc Industrial Direct Co Inc 911
Msci Inc 911
Msg Networks Inc. 911
Msgi Security Solutions Inc 911
Msx International, Inc. 912
Mt San Antonio Community College District 912
Mtd Products Inc 912
Mtm Technologies, Inc. 912
Mtr Gaming Group, Inc. 912
Mueller (paul) Co 912
Mueller Industries Inc 913
Mueller Water Products Inc 913
Muhlenberg Regional Medical Center, Inc. 913
Mulesoft, Inc. 913
Multi-color Corporation 913
Multi-fineline Electronix, Inc. 913
Multi-media Tutorial Services, Inc. 914
Multi-shifter, Inc. 914
Multi-state Lottery Association 914
Multicare Health System 914
Multicell Technologies Inc 914
Muncy Columbia Financial Corp 914
Municipal Electric Authority Of Georgia 915
Municipal Utilities Board Of Decatur, Morgan County, Alabama 915
Munroe Regional Medical Center, Inc. 915
Munson Healthcare 915
Murphy Company Mechanical Contractors And Engineers 915
Murphy Oil Corp 915
Murphy Usa Inc 916
Muscular Dystrophy Association, Inc. 916
Museum Of Fine Arts 916

Museum Of The City Of New York, Inc. 916
Mustang Fuel Corporation 916
Mustang Machinery Company, Llc 916
Mutual Of Omaha Insurance Co. (ne) 917
Mv Oil Trust 917
Mv Transportation, Inc. 917
Mvp Health Plan, Inc. 917
Mw Builders, Inc. 917
Mwh Global, Inc. 917
Myers Industries Inc. 918
Mymd Pharmaceuticals Inc 918
Myr Group Inc 918
Myrexis, Inc. 918
Myriad Genetics, Inc. 918
N-viro International Corp 918
Nacco Industries Inc 919
Naismith Memorial Basketball Hall Of Fame, Inc 919
Nami-maine 919
Nan Ya Plastics Corporation, America 919
Nano Magic Inc 919
Nanophase Technologies Corp. 919
Nanostring Technologies Inc 920
Nanthealth Inc 920
Napco International Llc 920
Napco Security Technologies, Inc. 920
Naprotek, Llc 920
Nasb Financial Inc 920
Nasco Healthcare Inc. 921
Nasdaq Inc 921
Nash Produce, Llc 921
Nasland Engineering 921
Nassau Health Care Corporation 921
Nathan's Famous, Inc. 921
National Academy Of Recording Arts & Sciences, Inc. 922
National American University Holdings Inc. 922
National Amusements, Inc. 922
National Association For Stock Car Auto Racing, Inc. 922
National Association For The Advancement Of Colored People 922
National Association Of Broadcasters 922
National Association Of Credit Management, Inc. 923
National Association Of Music Merchants Inc. 923
National Association Of Wholesaler-distributors, Inc 923
National Audubon Society, Inc. 923
National Automobile Dealers Association 923
National Bank Holdings Corp 923
National Bankshares Inc. (va) 924
National Baseball Hall Of Fame And Museum, Inc. 924
National Beef Packing Co. Llc/nb Finance Corp. 924
National Beverage Corp. 924
National Cable Satellite Corp 924
National Cemetery Administration 924
National Center For State Courts 925
National Center For Victims Of Crime, Inc. 925
National Cinemedia Inc 925
National Collegiate Athletic Association 925
National Constitution Center 925
National Cooperative Refinery Association 925
National Council Of Young Men's Christian Associations Of The United States Of America 926
National Council On Aging, Inc. 926
National Council On Alcoholism And Drug Dependence Inc. 926
National Distributing Company, Inc. 926
National Education Association Of The United States 926
National Football League 926
National Football League Players Association 927
National Football Museum, Inc. 927
National Frozen Foods Corporation 927
National Fuel Gas Co. (nj) 927
National Gallery Of Art 927
National Golf Foundation, Inc. 927
National Grape Co-operative Association, Inc. 928
National Grid Usa Service Company, Inc. 928
National Grocers Association 928
National Guardian Life Insurance Co. (madison, Wis.) 928
National Head Start Association 928
National Health Investors, Inc. 928
National Healthcare Corp. 929
National Institutes Of Health 929
National Italian American Foundation, Inc. 929
National Lampoon Inc 929
National Medical Association, Inc. A/k/a National Medical Association 929
National Multiple Sclerosis Society 929
National Organization For Women, Inc 930
National Park Foundation 930
National Park Trust, Inc. 930
National Presto Industries, Inc. 930
National Public Radio, Inc. 930
National Railroad Passenger Corporation 930
National Recreation And Park Association, Incorporated 931
National Research Corp 931
National Retail Federation, Inc. 931
National Review, Inc. 931
National Rifle Association Of America 931
National Rural Electric Cooperative Association 931
National Rural Utilities Cooperative Finance Corp 932
National Safety Council 932
National Space Society 932
National Spinning Co., Inc. 932
National Storage Affiliates Trust 932
National Thoroughbred Racing Association, Inc. 932
National Trust For Historic Preservation In The United States 933
National University 933
National Urban League, Inc. 933
National Van Lines, Inc. 933
National Vision Holdings Inc 933
National Wic Association, Inc. 933
National Wildlife Federation Inc 934
Nationshealth Inc 934
Nationwide Agribusiness Insurance Co. 934
Nationwide Children's Hospital 934
Native Environmental, L.l.c. 934
Natural Alternatives International, Inc. 934
Natural Fruit Corp. 935
Natural Gas Services Group Inc 935
Natural Grocers By Vitamin Cottage Inc 935
Natural Resource Partners Lp 935
Natural Resources Defense Council Inc. 935
Nature's Sunshine Products, Inc. 935
Natus Medical Incorporated 936
Navarro Research And Engineering, Inc. 936
Navicent Health, Inc. 936
Navidea Biopharmaceuticals Inc 936
Navient Corp 936
Navy Exchange Service Command 936
Nbcuniversal Media, Llc 937
Nbhx Trim Usa Corporation 937
Nbl Permian Llc 937
Nbt Bancorp. Inc. 937
Nch Corporation 937
Nch Healthcare System, Inc. 937
Nci, Inc. 938
Ncr Voyix Corp 938
Ncs Multistage Holdings Inc 938
Ncs Technologies, Inc. 938
Nearfield Systems Inc. 938
Nebraska Department Of Labor 938
Nebraska Public Power District 939
Neffs Bancorp Inc. 939
Neighborhood Reinvestment Corporation 939
Nektar Therapeutics 939
Nelnet Inc 939
Nemours Foundation 939
Neogen Corp 940
Neogenomics Inc 940
Neomagic Corp. 940
Neomedia Technologies, Inc. 940
Neos Therapeutics, Inc. 940
Nephros Inc 940
Nes Rentals Holdings, Inc. 941
Nest Technologies Corp. 941
Net Medical Xpress Solutions Inc 941
Netapp, Inc. 941
Netflix Inc 941
Netgear Inc 941
Netlist Inc 942
Netmotion Software, Inc. 942
Netscout Systems Inc 942
Netsol Technologies Inc 942
Netsuite, Inc. 942
Network Management Resources, Inc. 942
Neuberger & Berman, Llc 943
Neuehealth Inc 943
Neulion, Inc. 943
Neumann Systems Group, Inc. 943
Neurocrine Biosciences, Inc. 943
Neurogene Inc 943
Neurometrix Inc 944
Neustar, Inc. 944
Neutral Posture, Inc. 944
Nevada City Hospital (inc) 944
Nevada Gold & Casinos, Inc. 944
Nevada Power Co. 944
Nevada System Of Higher Education 945
New Bedford, City Of (inc) 945
New Braunfels Utilities 945
New Concept Energy, Inc. 945
New Creature Holdings, Inc. 945
New England Patriots Llc 945
New England Power Company 946
New England Realty Associates L.p. 946
New Enterprise Stone & Lime Co., Inc. 946
New Hampshire Electric Co-op Foundation 946
New Harbinger Publications, Inc. 946
New Horizons Worldwide, Llc 946
New Israel Fund 947
New Jersey Devils Llc 947
New Jersey Housing And Mortgage Finance Agency 947
New Jersey Institute Of Technology 947
New Jersey Resources Corp 947
New Jersey Turnpike Authority Inc 947
New Leaf Brands, Inc. 948
New Mexico State University 948
New Milford Hospital, Inc. 948
New Press 948
New Prime, Inc. 948
New Source Energy Partners Lp 948
New Tangram, Llc 949
New Vision Group, Llc 949
New York Academy Of Medicine 949
New York Blood Center, Inc. 949
New York City Health And Hospitals Corporation 949
New York City Transit Authority 949
New York Community Bancorp Inc. 950
New York Convention Center Operating Corporation 950
New York Health Care Inc 950
New York Life Insurance Co. 950
New York Medical College 950
New York Mortgage Trust Inc 950
New York Power Authority 951
New York Public Radio 951
New York Shakespeare Festival 951
New York State Catholic Health Plan, Inc. 951
New York State Energy Research And Development Authority 951
New York Times Co. 951
New York University 952

New York Yankees Partnership 952
Newark Beth Israel Medical Center Inc. 952
Newark Corporation 952
Newaygo County General Hospital Association 952
Newell Brands Inc 952
Newesco, Inc. 953
Newmark & Company Real Estate, Inc. 953
Newmark Group Inc 953
Newmarket Corp 953
Newmarket Technology Inc 953
Newmont Corp 953
Newpark Resources, Inc. 954
Newport Corporation 954
Newport Digital Technologies Inc. 954
News Corp (new) 954
News/media Alliance 954
Newsmax Media, Inc. 954
Newtekone Inc 955
Newton Memorial Hospital (inc) 955
Newton Wellesley Hospital Corp 955
Newyork-presbyterian/brooklyn Methodist 955
Newyork-presbyterian/queens 955
Nexeo Solutions Holdings, Llc 955
Nexpoint Storage Partners, Inc. 956
Nexstar Media Group Inc 956
Next, Inc. 956
Nextera Energy Inc 956
Nextera Energy Partners Lp 956
Neyenesch Printers, Inc. 956
Nfa Corp. 957
Nfi Industries, Inc. 957
Nfinanse Inc 957
Nfp Corp. 957
Ngl Energy Partners Lp 957
Nhl Enterprises, Inc. 957
Nhw Healthcare, Inc. 958
Nibco Inc. 958
Nicholas Financial Inc (bc) 958
Nicolet Plastics Llc 958
Nicolon Corporation 958
Niemann Foods, Inc. 958
Nii Holdings Inc 959
Nike Inc 959
Nimble Storage, Inc. 959
Ninyo & Moore Geotechnical & Environmental Sciences Consultants Corp 959
Niska Gas Storage Partners Llc 959
Nisource Inc. (holding Co.) 959
Nl Industries, Inc. 960
Nmi Health Inc 960
Nmi Holdings Inc 960
Nn, Inc 960
Nnn Reit Inc 960
Nobility Homes, Inc. 960
Noble Investment Group, Llc 961
Noble Roman's, Inc. 961
Nobleworks Inc 961
Noblis, Inc. 961
Noco Energy Corp. 961
Nocopi Technologies Inc Md 961
Nofire Technologies Inc. 962
Nokia Of America Corporation 962
Noland Company 962
Non-invasive Monitoring Systems Inc. 962
Noodles & Co 962
Noranda Aluminum Holding Corp 962
Norcraft Holdings, L.p. 963
Nordicus Partners Corp 963
Nordson Corp. 963
Nordstrom, Inc. 963
Norfolk Iron & Metal Co. 963
Norfolk Southern Corp 963
Norfolk State University 964
Norkus Enterprises, Inc. 964
Norman Regional Hospital Authority 964
Nortech Systems Inc. 964
Nortek, Inc. 964
North American Electric Reliability Corporation 964
North American Lighting, Inc. 965
North American Technologies Group, Inc. 965
North Atlantic Trading Company, Inc. 965
North Baja Pipeline, Llc 965
North Broward Hospital District 965
North Carolina Electric Membership Corporation 965
North Carolina State University 966
North Central Farmers Elevator 966
North Colorado Medical Center Foundation, Inc. 966
North Dakota Mill & Elevator Association 966
North Dakota State University 966
North Dallas Bank & Trust Co (dallas, Tx) 966
North European Oil Royalty Trust 967
North Florida Regional Medical Center, Inc. 967
North Memorial Health Care 967
North Mississippi Health Services, Inc. 967
North Mississippi Medical Center, Inc. 967
North Pacific Canners & Packers, Inc. 967
North Pacific Paper Company, Llc 968
North Park University 968
North Philadelphia Health System 968
North Shore Medical Center, Inc. 968
North Shore University Hospital 968
North Sonoma County Hospital District 968
North Texas Tollway Authority 969
North Wind, Inc. 969
Northeast Bank (me) 969
Northeast Community Bancorp Inc (md) 969
Northeast Georgia Health System, Inc. 969
Northeast Health Systems Inc. 969
Northeast Indiana Bancorp Inc 970
Northeast Iowa Community College 970
Northeastern Supply, Inc. 970
Northeastern University 970
Northern Arizona Healthcare Corporation 970
Northern Arizona University 970
Northern California Power Agency 971
Northern Indiana Public Service Company Llc 971
Northern Inyo Healthcare District 971
Northern Natural Gas Company 971
Northern Oil & Gas Inc (mn) 971
Northern Pride, Inc. 971
Northern Technologies International Corp. 972
Northern Tier Energy Lp 972
Northern Trust Corp 972
Northern Utah Healthcare Corporation 972
Northern Virginia Electric Cooperative 972
Northfield Bancorp Inc (de) 972
Northrim Bancorp Inc 973
Northrop Grumman Corp 973
Northrop Grumman Innovation Systems, Inc. 973
Northside Hospital 973
Northside Hospital, Inc. 973
Northway Financial, Inc. 973
Northwest Bancshares, Inc. (md) 974
Northwest Biotherapeutics Inc 974
Northwest Community Hospital Inc 974
Northwest Dairy Association 974
Northwest Natural Holding Co 974
Northwest Pipe Co. 974
Northwest Texas Healthcare System, Inc. 975
Northwestern Energy Group Inc 975
Northwestern Lake Forest Hospital 975
Northwestern Memorial Healthcare 975
Northwestern Mutual Life Insurance Co. (milwaukee, Wi) 975
Northwestern University 975
Norton Community Hospital Auxiliary, Inc. 976
Norton Laird Trust Company 976
Norwegian Cruise Line Holdings Ltd 976
Norwich University 976
Norwood Financial Corp. 976
Notre Dame Of Maryland University, Inc. 976
Nov Inc 977
Nova Southeastern University, Inc. 977
Novabay Pharmaceuticals Inc 977
Novagold Resources Inc. 977
Novant Health, Inc. 977
Novanta Inc 977
Novartis Pharmaceuticals Corporation 978
Novation Companies Inc 978
Novavax, Inc. 978
Novelis Alr Aluminum Holdings Corporation 978
Novelis Inc. 978
Novelstem International Corp 978
Npc Restaurant Holdings, Llc 979
Nrg Energy Inc 979
Nri, Inc. 979
Nstar Electric Co 979
Ntelos Holdings Corp. 979
Nts Realty Holdings Limited Partnership 979
Nu Skin Enterprises, Inc. 980
Nuclear Fuel Services, Inc. 980
Nucor Corp. 980
Nueske's Meat Products, Inc. 980
Numerex Corp. 980
Nuo Therapeutics Inc 980
Nurx Pharmaceuticals, Inc. 981
Nustar Energy Lp 981
Nustar Gp Holdings, Llc 981
Nutanix Inc 981
Nutra Pharma Corp 981
Nutraceutical International Corporation 981
Nutrisystem, Inc. 982
Nutrition Management Services Co. 982
Nuvera Communications Inc 982
Nuware Tech Corp. 982
Nv5 Global Inc 982
Nve Corp 982
Nvidia Corp 983
Nvr Inc. 983
Nyack College 983
O'brien & Gere Limited 983
O'neal Steel, Llc 983
O'neil Industries, Inc. 983
O'reilly Automotive, Inc. 984
O'reilly Media, Inc. 984
O-i Glass Inc 984
O. C. Tanner Company 984
O.p.e.n. America, Inc. 984
Oak Valley Bancorp (oakdale, Ca) 984
Oakland University 985
Oakridge Global Energy Solutions Inc 985
Oberg Industries, Llc 985
Oberlin College 985
Object Management Group, Inc. 985
Object Technology Solutions, Inc. 985
Objectivity, Inc. 986
Oblong Inc 986
Obocon Inc 986
Occidental College 986
Occidental Petroleum Corp 986
Ocean Beauty Seafoods Llc 986
Ocean Duke Corporation 987
Ocean Power Technologies Inc 987
Ocean Spray Cranberries, Inc. 987
Oceaneering International, Inc. 987
Oceanfirst Financial Corp 987
Ochoco Lumber Company 987
Oci Partners Lp 988
Oclc, Inc. 988
Oconee Regional Health Systems, Inc. 988
Ocular Therapeutix Inc 988
Ocuphire Pharma Inc 988
Ocwen Financial Corp 988
Odom Corporation 989
Odp Corp (the) 989
Odyssey Marine Exploration, Inc. 989
Oewaves, Inc. 989
Office Movers, Inc. 989
Office Properties Income Trust 989
Oge Energy Corp 990
Oglethorpe Power Corp 990
Oha Investment Corporation 990

COMPANIES LISTED ALPHABETICALLY

Ohio Art Co. 990
Ohio Department Of Transportation 990
Ohio Edison Co 990
Ohio Living 991
Ohio Power Company 991
Ohio State University Research Foundation 991
Ohio Turnpike And Infrastructure Commission 991
Ohio Valley Banc Corp 991
Ohio Valley Electric Corp. 991
Ohio Valley General Hospital 992
Ohio Valley Medical Center Incorporated 992
Ohiohealth Corporation 992
Oil States International, Inc. 992
Oil-dri Corp. Of America 992
Okeechobee Hospital, Inc. 992
Oklahoma State University 993
Okta Inc 993
Old Claimco, Llc 993
Old Copper Company, Inc. 993
Old Dominion Electric Cooperative 993
Old Dominion Freight Line, Inc. 993
Old Dominion Tobacco Company Incorporated 994
Old National Bancorp (evansville, In) 994
Old Point Financial Corp 994
Old Republic International Corp. 994
Old Second Bancorp., Inc. (aurora, Ill.) 994
Ole' Mexican Foods, Inc. 994
Olin Corp. 995
Ollie's Bargain Outlet Holdings Inc 995
Olmsted Medical Center 995
Olympic Pipe Line Company 995
Olympic Steel Inc. 995
Omagine Inc 995
Omaha Public Power District 996
Omaha Steaks International, Inc. 996
Omega Flex Inc 996
Omega Healthcare Investors, Inc. 996
Omega Institute For Holistic Studies, Inc. 996
Omega Protein Corporation 996
Omeros Corp 997
Omni Cable, Llc 997
Omni Hotels Corporation 997
Omnicell Inc 997
Omnicom Group, Inc. 997
Omnimax Holdings, Inc. 997
Omnivision Technologies, Inc. 998
Omron Robotics And Safety Technologies, Inc. 998
On Semiconductor Corp 998
On Stage Entertainment Inc 998
On-site Fuel Service, Inc. 998
On-target Supplies & Logistics, Ltd. 998
Oncologix Tech Inc 999
Oncology Services International, Inc. 999
Onconova Therapeutics Inc 999
Oncor Electric Delivery Co Llc 999
Oncotelic Therapeutics Inc 999
Oncternal Therapeutics Inc 999
One Gas, Inc. 1000
One Liberty Properties, Inc. 1000
One Planet Ops Inc. 1000
One Stop Systems Inc 1000
One To One Interactive, Inc. 1000
Oneida Health Systems, Inc. 1000
Onemain Holdings Inc 1001
Oneok Inc 1001
Oneok Partners, L.p. 1001
Onespan Inc 1001
Online Vacation Center Holdings Corp 1001
Onstream Media Corp 1001
Onto Innovation Inc 1002
Ontrak Inc 1002
Onvia, Inc. 1002
Opendoor Technologies Inc 1002
Openlane Inc. 1002
Openlink Financial Llc 1002
Opentv Corp. 1003
Operating Engineers Funds Inc 1003
Operation Smile, Inc. 1003

Operational Technologies Corporation 1003
Opko Health Inc 1003
Opp Liquidating Company, Inc. 1003
Oppenheimer Holdings Inc 1004
Oppenheimerfunds, Inc. 1004
Optical Cable Corp. 1004
Optimumbank Holdings Inc 1004
Optimumcare Corp. 1004
Option Care Health Inc 1004
Opts Ideas, Inc 1005
Oracle Corp 1005
Oragenics Inc 1005
Orange And Rockland Utilities, Inc. 1005
Orange Coast Title Company 1005
Orange County Global Medical Center Auxiliary 1005
Orange County Transportation Authority Scholarship Foundation, Inc. 1006
Orasure Technologies Inc. 1006
Orbcomm Inc. 1006
Orbit International Corp. 1006
Orbital Infrastructure Group Inc 1006
Orbitz Worldwide, Inc. 1006
Orca Bay Seafoods, Inc. 1007
Orchard Enterprises Ny, Inc. 1007
Orchid Island Capital Inc 1007
Orecul, Inc. 1007
Oregon Department Of Transportation 1007
Oregon Health & Science University 1007
Oregon Pacific Bancorp 1008
Oregon State Lottery 1008
Oregon State University 1008
Organically Grown Company 1008
Organics Corporation Of America 1008
Original Impressions, Llc 1008
Orion Energy Systems Inc 1009
Orion Group Holdings Inc 1009
Orion Seafood International, Inc. 1009
Orlando Health, Inc. 1009
Orlando Utilities Commission (inc) 1009
Orleans Homebuilders, Inc. 1009
Ormat Technologies Inc 1010
Orrstown Financial Services, Inc. 1010
Oryx Technology Corp. 1010
Osborn & Barr Communications, Inc. 1010
Osc Sports, Inc. 1010
Oscar De La Renta, Llc 1010
Osceola Regional Hospital, Inc. 1011
Osf Healthcare Saint Clare Medical Center 1011
Osf Healthcare System 1011
Oshkosh Corp (new) 1011
Osi Group, Llc 1011
Osi Systems, Inc. (de) 1011
Otis Worldwide Corp 1012
Ott Hydromet Corp 1012
Otter Products, Llc 1012
Otter Tail Corp. 1012
Ottumwa Regional Legacy Foundation, Inc. 1012
Our Lady Of Lourdes Health Care Services, Inc. 1012
Our Lady Of Lourdes Regional Medical Center, Inc. 1013
Our Lady Of The Lake Hospital, Inc. 1013
Our Lady Of The Lake University Of San Antonio 1013
Outcome Sciences, Inc. 1013
Outdoor Advertising Association Of America, Inc. 1013
Outfront Media Inc 1013
Outward Bound Inc. 1014
Overlake Hospital Medical Center 1014
Overland Contracting Inc. 1014
Overseas Shipholding Group Inc (new) 1014
Ovintiv Exploration Inc. 1014
Ovintiv Inc 1014
Ovintiv Usa Inc. 1015
Owens & Minor, Inc. 1015
Owens Corning 1015

Owensboro Municipal Utilities Electric Light & Power System 1015
Oxbow Corporation 1015
Oxford Industries, Inc. 1015
Ozarks Electric Cooperative Corporation 1016
P And E, Inc. 1016
P.a.m. Transportation Services, Inc. 1016
P.j. Dick Incorporated 1016
Pac Northwest Electric Power & Conservation Planning Council 1016
Paccar Inc. 1016
Pace University 1017
Pacers Basketball, Llc 1017
Pacific Alliance Medical Center, Inc. 1017
Pacific Biosciences Of California Inc 1017
Pacific Building Group 1017
Pacific Cma Inc. 1017
Pacific Coast Oil Trust 1018
Pacific Coast Producers 1018
Pacific Dental Services, Llc 1018
Pacific Financial Corp. 1018
Pacific Hide & Fur Depot 1018
Pacific International Vegetable Marketing, Inc. 1018
Pacific Mutual Holding Co. 1019
Pacific Sands Inc 1019
Pacific Sunwear Of California, Llc 1019
Pacifica Foundation Inc. 1019
Pacifichealth Laboratories, Inc. 1019
Pacificorp 1019
Pacira Biosciences Inc 1020
Packaging Corp Of America 1020
Packaging Machinery Manufacturers Institute, Incorporated 1020
Page Southerland Page, L.l.p. 1020
Paid Inc 1020
Paisano Publications, Llc 1020
Palatin Technologies Inc 1021
Palisade Bio Inc 1021
Pall Corporation 1021
Palms West Hospital Limited Partnership 1021
Palo Alto Networks, Inc 1021
Palomar Community College District 1021
Palomar Health 1022
Pandora Media, Llc 1022
Panduit Corp. 1022
Panera Bread Company 1022
Pangea, Inc. 1022
Panhandle Eastern Pipe Line Company, Lp 1022
Papa John's International, Inc. 1023
Papa's Pizza To Go Inc 1023
Paper Converting Machine Company 1023
Par Pacific Holdings Inc 1023
Par Technology Corp. 1023
Parabel Inc 1023
Paradigm Medical Industries Inc. (de) 1024
Paradise Valley Hospital 1024
Paragon Development Systems, Inc. 1024
Paragon Solutions Inc. 1024
Paragon Technologies Inc 1024
Paramount Global 1024
Paramount Gold Nevada Corp 1025
Parents As Teachers National Center, Inc. 1025
Parents Television Council, Inc. 1025
Parexel International (ma) Corporation 1025
Paric Corporation 1025
Park Aerospace Corp 1025
Park Corporation 1026
Park Hotels & Resorts Inc 1026
Park National Corp (newark, Oh) 1026
Park Nicollet Health Services 1026
Park Nicollet Methodist Hospital 1026
Park-ohio Holdings Corp. 1026
Parke Bancorp Inc 1027
Parke-bell Ltd., Inc. 1027
Parker Drilling Co 1027
Parker Hannifin Corp 1027
Parkervision Inc 1027
Parkridge Medical Center, Inc. 1027

Parkway Plastics, Inc. 1028
Parkwest Medical Center 1028
Parlux Holdings, Inc. 1028
Parma Community General Hospital 1028
Parron-hall Corporation 1028
Parsons Corp (de) 1028
Parsons Environment & Infrastructure Group Inc. 1029
Parsons Government Services Inc. 1029
Partech International, Inc. 1029
Participant Media, Llc 1029
Particle Drilling Technologies, Inc. 1029
Partnership For A Drug-free America, Inc. 1029
Partsbase, Inc. 1030
Party City Holdco Inc 1030
Partylite, Inc. 1030
Pasadena Area Community College District 1030
Pasadena Hospital Association, Ltd. 1030
Passur Aerospace, Inc. 1030
Pathfinder Cell Therapy Inc. 1031
Pathfinder International 1031
Pathward Financial Inc 1031
Patient Satisfaction Plus, Llc 1031
Patriarch Partners, Llc 1031
Patrick Industries Inc 1031
Patriot National Bancorp Inc 1032
Pattern Energy Group Inc. 1032
Patterson Belknap Webb & Tyler Llp 1032
Patterson Companies Inc 1032
Patterson-uti Energy Inc. 1032
Patton Wings, Inc. 1032
Paul Fredrick Menstyle, Llc 1033
Paxton Media Group, Llc 1033
Paychex Inc 1033
Paylocity Holding Corp 1033
Payments Business Corp. 1033
Paypal Holdings Inc 1033
Pbf Energy Inc 1034
Pbf Logistics Lp 1034
Pc Calendar 2010, Llc 1034
Pc Connection, Inc. 1034
Pc Group, Inc. 1034
Pcl Construction Enterprises, Inc. 1034
Pcs Edventures! Inc 1035
Pctel Inc 1035
Pdb Sports, Ltd. 1035
Pdf Solutions Inc. 1035
Pdg-environmental, Inc. 1035
Pdl Biopharma Inc 1035
Pds Defense, Inc. 1036
Peabody Energy Corp (new) 1036
Peacehealth 1036
Peacehealth Southwest Medical Center 1036
Peak Methods, Inc. 1036
Peapack-gladstone Financial Corp. 1036
Pebblebrook Hotel Trust 1037
Peco Energy Company 1037
Pedernales Electric Cooperative, Inc. 1037
Pedevco Corp 1037
Pediatrix Medical Group Inc 1037
Peebles Inc. 1037
Peerless Systems Corporation 1038
Pegasystems Inc 1038
Peirce College 1038
Peirce Enterprises, Inc. 1038
Peloton Interactive Inc 1038
Penbay Technology Group Llc 1038
Pendleton Woolen Mills, Inc. 1039
Pendrell Corp 1039
Penguin Computing, Inc. 1039
Penn Entertainment Inc 1039
Penn Mutual Life Insurance Co. 1039
Penn State Health Holy Spirit Medical Center 1039
Pennichuck Corporation 1040
Pennoni Associates Inc. 1040
Penns Woods Bancorp, Inc. (jersey Shore, Pa) 1040
Pennsylvania - American Water Company 1040
Pennsylvania Electric Co. 1040

Pennsylvania Higher Education Assistance Agency 1040
Pennsylvania Housing Finance Agency 1041
Pennsylvania Power Co. 1041
Pennsylvania Real Estate Investment Trust 1041
Pennsylvania Turnpike Commission 1041
Pennymac Financial Services Inc (new) 1041
Pennymac Mortgage Investment Trust 1041
Penske Automotive Group Inc 1042
Penumbra Inc 1042
People For The Ethical Treatment Of Animals, Inc. 1042
Peoples Bancorp Inc (marietta, Oh) 1042
Peoples Bancorp Of North Carolina Inc 1042
Peoples Bancorp, Inc. (md) 1042
Peoples Educational Holdings, Inc. 1043
Peoples Financial Corp (biloxi, Ms) 1043
Peoples Financial Services Corp 1043
Peoples Natural Gas Company Llc 1043
Pepco Holdings Llc 1043
Pepper Construction Group, Llc 1043
Pepperdine University 1044
Pepsi-cola Bottling Co Of Central Virginia 1044
Pepsico Inc 1044
Peraso Inc 1044
Perceptron, Inc. 1044
Perdoceo Education Corp 1044
Perera Construction & Design, Inc. 1045
Perez Trading Company, Inc. 1045
Perfection Bakeries, Inc. 1045
Perficient Inc 1045
Performance Food Group Co 1045
Performant Financial Corp 1045
Perham Hospital District 1046
Pericom Semiconductor Corporation 1046
Perkins & Marie Callender's, Llc 1046
Perkins Coie Llp 1046
Perma-fix Environmental Services, Inc. 1046
Perma-pipe International Holdings Inc 1046
Permian Basin Royalty Trust 1047
Permianville Royalty Trust 1047
Pernix Group Inc 1047
Pernix Therapeutics Holdings, Inc. 1047
Perry Ellis International Inc 1047
Perspective Therapeutics Inc 1047
Pervasip Corp 1048
Pet Supermarket, Inc. 1048
Petco Health & Wellness Co Inc 1048
Peter Kiewit Sons', Inc. 1048
Peter Pan Bus Lines, Inc. 1048
Petmed Express Inc 1048
Petro Star Inc. 1049
Petroleum Traders Corporation 1049
Petroquest Energy Inc (new) 1049
Petrotal Corp 1049
Pfenex Inc. 1049
Pfg Ventures, L.p. 1049
Pfizer Inc 1050
Pg&e Corp (holding Co) 1050
Pga Tour, Inc. 1050
Pharmacy Buying Association, Inc. 1050
Pharmacyte Biotech Inc 1050
Pharmerica Corporation 1050
Phasebio Pharmaceuticals Inc 1051
Phelps Dunbar, L.l.p. 1051
Phelps Memorial Hospital Association 1051
Phi Group Inc (de) 1051
Phi Group Inc. 1051
Phibro Animal Health Corp. 1051
Philadelphia Consolidated Holding Corp. 1052
Philadelphia University 1052
Philadelphia Workforce Development Corporation 1052
Philip Morris International Inc 1052
Phillips 66 1052
Phillips And Jordan, Incorporated 1052
Phillips Edison & Company Llc 1053
Phoebe Putney Memorial Hospital, Inc. 1053

Phoenix Children's Hospital, Inc. 1053
Phoenix Footwear Group, Inc. 1053
Phoenix Gold International Inc 1053
Photronics, Inc. 1053
Phx Minerals Inc 1054
Physicians For Human Rights, Inc. 1054
Picis Clinical Solutions, Inc. 1054
Piedmont Athens Regional Medical Center, Inc. 1054
Piedmont Hospital, Inc. 1054
Piedmont Municipal Power Agency 1054
Piedmont Natural Gas Company, Inc. 1055
Piedmont Office Realty Trust Inc 1055
Piedmont University, Inc. 1055
Pih Health Good Samaritan Hospital 1055
Pikeville Medical Center, Inc. 1055
Piksel, Inc. 1055
Pilgrims Pride Corp. 1056
Pilkington North America, Inc. 1056
Pillarstone Capital Reit 1056
Pilot Corporation 1056
Pine Grove Manufactured Homes, Inc. 1056
Pine State Trading Co. 1056
Pineapple Energy Inc 1057
Piney Woods Healthcare System, L.p. 1057
Pinnacle Bancshares, Inc. 1057
Pinnacle Bankshares Corp 1057
Pinnacle Financial Partners Inc 1057
Pinnacle West Capital Corp 1057
Pinterest Inc 1058
Pioneer Bankshares Inc 1058
Pioneer Data Systems, Inc. 1058
Pioneer Energy Services Corp. 1058
Pioneer Natural Resources Co 1058
Pioneer Oil & Gas 1058
Pioneer Telephone Cooperative, Inc. 1059
Piper Sandler Companies 1059
Pismo Coast Village, Inc. 1059
Piston Automotive, L.l.c. 1059
Pitney Bowes Inc 1059
Pitt County Memorial Hospital, Incorporated 1059
Pitt-ohio Express, Llc 1060
Pittsburgh Associates 1060
Pittsburgh Steelers Sports, Inc. 1060
Pittsburgh Technical Institute, Inc. 1060
Pixelworks Inc 1060
Pjm Interconnection, L.l.c. 1060
Pjt Partners Inc 1061
Placid Refining Company Llc 1061
Plains All American Pipeline Lp 1061
Plains Cotton Cooperative Association 1061
Plainscapital Corp 1061
Planar Systems, Inc. 1061
Planet Fitness Inc 1062
Planet Payment, Inc. 1062
Planned Parenthood Federation Of America, Inc. 1062
Plantation General Hospital, L.p. 1062
Plastek Industries, Inc. 1062
Plastic Suppliers, Inc. 1062
Platinum Studios, Inc. 1063
Platte River Power Authority (inc) 1063
Playboy Enterprises, Inc. 1063
Players Network (the) 1063
Playtika Holding Corp. 1063
Plexus Corp. 1063
Plexus Installations, Inc. 1064
Plug Power Inc 1064
Plumas Bancorp Inc 1064
Plumb Supply Company, Llc 1064
Plus Therapeutics Inc 1064
Plx Pharma Inc 1064
Ply Gem Holdings, Inc. 1065
Pmi Group, Inc. 1065
Pnc Financial Services Group (the) 1065
Png Builders 1065
Pnm Resources Inc 1065
Poindexter (j.b.) & Co., Inc. 1065

COMPANIES LISTED ALPHABETICALLY

Point Loma Nazarene University Foundation 1066
Point.360 1066
Points Of Light Foundation 1066
Polaris Alpha, Llc 1066
Polaris Inc 1066
Polycom, Inc. 1066
Pomona College 1067
Pomp's Tire Service, Inc. 1067
Poniard Pharmaceuticals Inc 1067
Poof-slinky, Llc 1067
Pool Corp 1067
Pop Warner Little Scholars Inc 1067
Pope Resources (a Delaware Limited Partnership) 1068
Popeyes Louisiana Kitchen, Inc. 1068
Poplar Bluff Regional Medical Center, Llc 1068
Popular Inc. 1068
Population Services International 1068
Port Imperial Ferry Corp. 1068
Port Newark Container Terminal Llc 1069
Port Of Corpus Christi Authority Of Nueces County, Texas 1069
Port Of Houston Authority 1069
Port Of New Orleans 1069
Port Of Seattle 1069
Portland General Electric Co. 1069
Portland State University 1070
Portola Pharmaceuticals, Inc. 1070
Portsmouth Square, Inc. 1070
Positiveid Corp 1070
Positron Corp 1070
Post Holdings Inc 1070
Postal Instant Press Inc. 1071
Postrock Energy Corp 1071
Potbelly Corp 1071
Potlatchdeltic Corp 1071
Potomac Bancshares, Inc. 1071
Potomac Hospital Corporation Of Prince William 1071
Poudre Valley Health Care, Inc. 1072
Powell Electronics, Inc. 1072
Powell Industries, Inc. 1072
Power Construction Company, Llc 1072
Power Integrations Inc. 1072
Powerfleet Inc 1072
Powerlinx, Inc. 1073
Powersouth Energy Cooperative 1073
Ppg Industries Inc 1073
Ppl Corp 1073
Ppl Electric Utilities Corp 1073
Pra Group Inc 1073
Pragmatics, Inc. 1074
Prairie Farms Dairy, Inc. 1074
Prairie View A&m University 1074
Pratt Industries, Inc. 1074
Precigen Inc 1074
Precipio Inc 1074
Precision Castparts Corp. 1075
Precision Data Products, Inc. 1075
Precision Environmental Company 1075
Precision Optics Corp Inc (ma) 1075
Precision Optics Inc. 1075
Preferred Apartment Communities, Llc 1075
Preferred Bank (los Angeles, Ca) 1076
Preferred Utilities Manufacturing Corporation 1076
Preformed Line Products Co. 1076
Premier Ag Co-op, Inc. 1076
Premier Entertainment Iii, Llc 1076
Premier Exhibitions Inc 1076
Premier Financial Corp 1077
Premier Health Partners 1077
Premiere Global Services, Inc. 1077
Premio, Inc. 1077
Premium Beers Of Oklahoma, L.l.c. 1077
Premium Retail Services, Inc. 1077
Presbyterian Healthcare Services 1078
Prescott Aerospace, Inc. 1078
President & Trustees Of Bates College 1078
President & Trustees Of Williams College 1078
President And Board Of Trustees Of Santa Clara College 1078
President And Fellows Of Middlebury College 1078
President And Trustees Of Hampden-sydney College 1079
Presidential Realty Corp. 1079
Presidio, Inc. 1079
Presonus Audio Electronics, Inc. 1079
Pressure Biosciences Inc 1079
Prestige Consumer Healthcare Inc 1079
Prestige Travel Inc 1080
Prevent Cancer Foundation, Inc. 1080
Prevent Child Abuse Of America 1080
Prgx Global, Inc. 1080
Pricesmart Inc 1080
Pridgeon & Clay, Inc. 1080
Prime Healthcare Services - Garden City, Llc 1081
Prime Healthcare Services - Reno, Llc 1081
Prime Healthcare Services - Shasta, Llc 1081
Primecare System, Inc. 1081
Primeenergy Resources Corp 1081
Primemd Inc 1081
Primerica Inc 1082
Primex International Trading Corporation 1082
Primis Financial Corp 1082
Primo Water Corp (canada) 1082
Primo Water Operations Llc 1082
Primoris Services Corp 1082
Primus Builders, Inc. 1083
Primus Software Corporation 1083
Princeton Community Hospital Association, Inc. 1083
Princeton Healthcare System Holding Inc. 1083
Princeton Insurance Company 1083
Princeton Lightwave, Inc. 1083
Princeton National Bancorp, Inc. 1084
Principal Financial Group Inc 1084
Printpack, Inc. 1084
Prism Software Corp. 1084
Prism Technologies Group Inc 1084
Prisma Health-midlands 1084
Prisma Health-upstate 1085
Prison Rehabilitative Industries And Diversified Enterprises, Inc. 1085
Private Export Funding Corp. 1085
Pro Consulting Services Inc. 1085
Pro Farm Group, Inc. 1085
Pro-dex Inc. (co) 1085
Pro-fac Cooperative Inc. 1086
Proassurance Corp 1086
Processa Pharmaceuticals Inc 1086
Procter & Gamble Company (the) 1086
Procyon Corp. 1086
Producers Rice Mill, Inc. 1086
Products (se) Pipe Line Corporation 1087
Professional Disc Golf Association 1087
Professional Diversity Network Inc 1087
Professional Golfers Association Of America Inc 1087
Professional Placement Resources Llc 1087
Professional Project Services, Inc. 1087
Professionals For Non-profits, Inc. 1088
Prog Holdings Inc 1088
Proginet Corporation 1088
Progress Energy, Inc. 1088
Progress Investment Management Company, Llc 1088
Progress Software Corp 1088
Progressive Corp. (oh) 1089
Prohealth Care, Inc. 1089
Project Adventure 1089
Project Enhancement Corp 1089
Prologis Inc 1089
Promedica Health System, Inc. 1089
Promega Corporation 1090
Proof Advertising, Llc 1090
Propellus Inc 1090
Propetro Holding Corp 1090
Prophase Labs Inc 1090
Propper International Sales, Inc. 1090
Pros Holdings Inc 1091
Prosegur Services Group, Inc. 1091
Prosek Llc 1091
Prospect Waterbury, Inc. 1091
Prosperity Bancshares Inc. 1091
Prosys Information Systems, Inc. 1091
Protagenic Therapeutics Inc 1092
Protalex Inc 1092
Protalix Biotherapeutics Inc 1092
Protective Life Insurance Co 1092
Protective Life Insurance Co. (birmingham, Ala.) 1092
Protective Life Insurance Company 1092
Protestant Memorial Medical Center, Inc. 1093
Protext Mobility Inc 1093
Proto Labs Inc 1093
Protosource Corp. 1093
Provectus Biopharmaceuticals Inc 1093
Providence And Worcester Railroad Company 1093
Providence College 1094
Providence Health & Services 1094
Providence Health & Services - Montana 1094
Providence Hospital 1094
Providence St. Joseph Health 1094
Provident Financial Holdings, Inc. 1094
Provident Financial Services Inc 1095
Proxim Wireless Corp. 1095
Prudential Annuities Life Assurance Corp 1095
Prudential Financial Inc 1095
Prudential Overall Supply 1095
Prwt Services, Inc. 1095
Ps Business Parks Inc 1096
Pscu, Llc 1096
Pseg Power Llc 1096
Psi Services Inc. 1096
Psychemedics Corp. 1096
Ptc Inc 1096
Ptc Therapeutics Inc 1097
Pubco Corp. 1097
Public Broadcasting Service 1097
Public Communications Services, Inc. 1097
Public Health Solutions 1097
Public Library Of Science 1097
Public Radio International, Inc. 1098
Public Relations Advertising Company 1098
Public Service Company Of New Hampshire 1098
Public Service Company Of Oklahoma 1098
Public Service Enterprise Group Inc 1098
Public Storage 1098
Public Utilities Board Of The City Of Brownsville, Texas 1099
Public Utility District 1 Of Clark County 1099
Public Utility District 1 Of Snohomish County 1099
Public Utility District 2 Grant County 1099
Public Utility District No 1 Of Cowlitz County 1099
Public Utility District No. 1 Of Chelan County 1099
Publishing Office, Us Government 1100
Publix Super Markets, Inc. 1100
Publix Super Markets, Inc. 1100
Puerto Rican Family Institute, Inc. 1100
Puget Energy, Inc. 1100
Pulmatrix Inc 1100
Pulse Electronics Corporation 1101
Pultegroup Inc 1101
Puradyn Filter Technologies Inc 1101
Pure Bioscience Inc 1101
Pure Cycle Corp. 1101
Pure Fishing, Inc. 1101
Pure Storage Inc 1102
Puresafe Water Systems Inc 1102
Puretek Corporation 1102
Puritan Medical Products Company I Lp 1102
Purity Wholesale Grocers, Inc. 1102
Purple Communications, Inc. 1102
Pvh Corp 1103

Pvs Technologies, Inc. 1103
Pyco Industries, Inc. 1103
Pyxus International Inc 1103
Pzena Investment Management, Inc. 1103
Q-matic Corporation 1103
Q.e.p. Co., Inc. 1104
Qad Inc. 1104
Qc Holdings Inc 1104
Qcept Technologies Inc. 1104
Qcr Holdings Inc 1104
Qf Liquidation, Inc. 1104
Qhg Of South Carolina, Inc. 1105
Qlik Technologies Inc. 1105
Qlogic Llc 1105
Qnb Corp. 1105
Qorvo Inc 1105
Qrs Music Technologies, Inc. 1105
Qst Industries, Inc. 1106
Quabbin Wire & Cable Co., Inc. 1106
Quad/graphics, Inc. 1106
Quaker Valley Foods, Inc. 1106
Qualcomm Inc 1106
Qualitor, Inc. 1106
Quality Consulting, Inc. 1107
Quality Oil Company, Llc 1107
Qualstar Corp 1107
Qualys, Inc. 1107
Quanex Building Products Corp 1107
Quanta Services, Inc. 1107
Quantum Corp 1108
Quantum3d, Inc. 1108
Quarles & Brady Llp 1108
Queen Of The Valley Medical Center Foundation 1108
Quest Diagnostics, Inc. 1108
Quest Media & Supplies, Inc. 1108
Questar Gas Co. 1109
Quick-med Technologies Inc 1109
Quicklogic Corp 1109
Quicksilver Resources Inc. 1109
Quidelortho Corp 1109
Quinn Emanuel Urquhart & Sullivan, Llp 1109
Quinnipiac University 1110
Quinstreet, Inc. 1110
Quorum Health Corporation 1110
Qurate Retail Inc 1110
Qurate Retail Inc - Com Ser A 1110
Qurate Retail Inc - Com Ser B 1110
Qvc, Inc. 1111
R & R Products, Inc. 1111
R. B. Pamplin Corporation 1111
R. E. Michel Company, Llc 1111
R. J. Daum Construction Company 1111
R. L. Jordan Oil Company Of North Carolina, Inc. 1111
R. R. Donnelley & Sons Company 1112
R.c. Willey Home Furnishings 1112
R.j. O'brien & Associates, Llc 1112
R.s. Hughes Company, Inc. 1112
R1 Rcm Inc New 1112
Raani Corporation 1112
Racetrac, Inc. 1113
Rackspace Technology Global, Inc. 1113
Rackspace Technology Inc 1113
Radian Group, Inc. 1113
Radiant Logistics, Inc. 1113
Radiant Power Idc, Llc 1113
Radient Pharmaceuticals Corp 1114
Radisson Hotels International, Inc. 1114
Radisys Corporation 1114
Radius Recycling Inc 1114
Radnet Inc 1114
Rady Children's Hospital-san Diego 1114
Rait Financial Trust 1115
Raley's 1115
Ralph Lauren Corp 1115
Ramboll Holdings, Inc. 1115
Rambus Inc. (de) 1115

Rand Logistics, Llc 1115
Randa Accessories Leather Goods Llc 1116
Range Resources Corp 1116
Rangers Sub I, Llc 1116
Ranken Technical College 1116
Rapid Response Monitoring Services Inc 1116
Rapid7 Inc 1116
Rappahannock Electric Cooperative 1117
Raritan Bay Medical Center, A New Jersey Nonprofit Corporation 1117
Raritan Valley Community College 1117
Rave Restaurant Group Inc 1117
Raven Industries, Inc 1117
Rayburn Country Electric Cooperative, Inc. 1117
Raymond James & Associates Inc 1118
Raymond James Financial, Inc. 1118
Raymours Furniture Company, Inc. 1118
Rayonier Advanced Materials Inc 1118
Rayonier Inc. 1118
Rb Global Inc 1118
Rbc Bearings Inc 1119
Rbc Life Sciences Inc 1119
Rbz Llp 1119
Rci Hospitality Holdings Inc 1119
Rcm Technologies, Inc. 1119
Rcs Corporation 1119
Rdo Construction Equipment Co. 1120
Rdr, Inc. 1120
Re/max, Llc 1120
Reachlocal, Inc. 1120
Reading Hospital 1120
Reading International Inc 1120
Reading Is Fundamental, Inc. 1121
Ready Capital Corp 1121
Real Foundation, Inc. 1121
Real Goods Solar Inc 1121
Reald Inc. 1121
Realnetworks Llc 1121
Realpage, Inc. 1122
Realty Income Corp 1122
Receptos, Inc. 1122
Recommind, Inc. 1122
Recon Environmental, Inc. 1122
Recording Industry Association Of America, Inc. 1122
Rector & Visitors Of The University Of Virginia 1123
Red Blossom Sales, Inc. 1123
Red Jacket Orchards, Inc. 1123
Red Lion Hotels Corporation 1123
Red River Commodities, Inc. 1123
Red River Technology Llc 1123
Red Robin Gourmet Burgers Inc 1124
Red Rock Resorts Inc 1124
Redfin Corp 1124
Redmond Park Hospital, Llc 1124
Redner's Markets, Inc. 1124
Redpoint Bio Corp 1124
Redwood Trust Inc 1125
Reeds Inc 1125
Refocus Group Inc 1125
Regal Entertainment Group 1125
Regal Marketing, Inc. 1125
Regal Rexnord Corp 1125
Regal Ware, Inc. 1126
Regen Biologics Inc 1126
Regency Centers Corp 1126
Regeneron Pharmaceuticals, Inc. 1126
Regenerx Biopharmaceuticals Inc 1126
Regenetp Inc 1126
Regents Of The University Of Idaho 1127
Regents Of The University Of Michigan 1127
Regents Of The University Of Minnesota 1127
Regina Medical Center 1127
Regional Management Corp 1127
Regional Transit Authority 1127
Regions Financial Corp (new) 1128
Regions Hospital Foundation 1128
Regis Corp 1128

Regulus Therapeutics Inc 1128
Rehrig Pacific Company 1128
Rei Systems, Inc. 1128
Reinsurance Group Of America, Inc. 1129
Reis, Inc. 1129
Relax The Back Corporation 1129
Reliability First Corporation 1129
Reliability Inc 1129
Reliable Wholesale Lumber, Inc. 1129
Reliance Inc 1130
Reliv' International Inc 1130
Renaissance Marine Group, Inc. 1130
Renasant Corp 1130
Renesas Electronics America Inc. 1130
Renesas Electronics America Inc. 1130
Renesas Electronics America Inc. 1131
Renewal Fuels Inc 1131
Renfro Llc 1131
Rennova Health Inc 1131
Reno Contracting, Inc. 1131
Rensselaer Polytechnic Institute 1131
Rentech, Inc. 1132
Replacement Parts, Inc. 1132
Replacements, Ltd. 1132
Repligen Corp. 1132
Repositrak Inc 1132
Reproductive Freedom For All 1132
Repros Therapeutics Inc. 1133
Republic Airways Holdings Inc. 1133
Republic Bancorp, Inc. (ky) 1133
Republic First Bancorp, Inc. 1133
Republic Indemnity Co. Of America 1133
Republic Services Inc 1133
Republican Governors Public Policy Committee 1134
Res-care, Inc. 1134
Resaca Exploitation Inc 1134
Research Frontiers Inc. 1134
Research Triangle Institute Inc 1134
Reserve Industries Corp 1134
Reserve Petroleum Co. 1135
Resideo Technologies Inc 1135
Residual Pumpkin Entity, Llc 1135
Resmed Inc. 1135
Resolute Fp Us Inc. 1135
Resonate Blends Inc 1135
Resource America, Inc. 1136
Resources Connection Inc 1136
Respirerx Pharmaceuticals Inc 1136
Restaurant Developers Corp. 1136
Restaurant Technologies, Inc. 1136
Retail Industry Leaders Association, Inc 1136
Retail Opportunity Investments Corp 1137
Retail Properties Of America, Inc. 1137
Retailmenot, Inc. 1137
Retirement Housing Foundation Inc 1137
Retractable Technologies Inc 1137
Reunion Industries Inc. 1137
Rev Group Inc 1138
Reva Medical, Inc. 1138
Revance Therapeutics Inc 1138
Review Publishing Limited Partnership 1138
Revlon Inc 1138
Revolution Lighting Technologies Inc 1138
Revvity Inc 1139
Rex American Resources Corp 1139
Rex Chemical Corporation 1139
Rex Energy Corp 1139
Rex Healthcare, Inc. 1139
Rexford Industrial Realty Inc 1139
Reynolds American Inc. 1140
Rf Binder Partners Inc. 1140
Rf Industries Ltd. 1140
Rfd & Associates, Inc. 1140
Rgc Resources, Inc. 1140
Rh 1140
Rhode Island Housing And Mortgage Finance Corporation 1141

COMPANIES LISTED ALPHABETICALLY

Rhode Island School Of Design Inc 1141
Rhodes College 1141
Rhythm Pharmaceuticals Inc 1141
Ricebran Technologies 1141
Riceland Foods, Inc. 1141
Rich Products Corporation 1142
Richard J. Caron Foundation 1142
Richardson Companies, Inc. 1142
Richardson Electronics Ltd 1142
Richelieu Foods, Inc. 1142
Riechesbaird, Inc. 1142
Rigel Pharmaceuticals Inc 1143
Riley Exploration Permian Inc 1143
Ringcentral Inc 1143
Rio Holdings, Inc. 1143
Riot Platforms Inc 1143
Rip Griffin Truck Service Center, Inc. 1143
Ripon College 1144
Riptide Software, Inc. 1144
Risk George Industries Inc 1144
Rite Aid Corp 1144
Rithm Capital Corp 1144
Rival Technologies Inc 1144
River District Community Hospital Authority 1145
Riverside Community College District Foundation 1145
Riverside Healthcare Association, Inc. 1145
Riverside Hospital, Inc. 1145
Riverview Bancorp, Inc. 1145
Riverview Hospital 1145
Riverview Realty Partners Lp 1146
Rlh Wrap-up, Inc. 1146
Rli Corp 1146
Rm2 International Inc 1146
Roadrunner Transportation Systems Inc 1146
Robert Bosch Llc 1146
Robert Half Inc 1147
Robert Morris University 1147
Robert W Baird & Co Inc 1147
Robert W Woodruff Health Sciences Center 1147
Robert Wood Johnson University Hospital At Rahway 1147
Robert Wood Johnson University Hospital, Inc. 1147
Roberts Dairy Company, Llc 1148
Roberts Wesleyan College 1148
Robertson Global Health Solutions Corp. 1148
Robins Kaplan Llp 1148
Robinson (c.h.) Worldwide, Inc. 1148
Robinson Health System, Inc. 1148
Robinson Oil Corporation 1149
Rochester Gas & Electric Corp 1149
Rochester Institute Of Technology (inc) 1149
Rock Creek Pharmaceuticals Inc 1149
Rock Energy Resources Inc 1149
Rocket Software, Inc. 1149
Rockford Health System 1150
Rockhurst University 1150
Rockview Dairies, Inc. 1150
Rockwell Automation, Inc. 1150
Rockwell Medical, Inc 1150
Rocky Brands Inc 1150
Rocky Mountain Chocolate Factory Inc (de) 1151
Roehl Transport, Inc. 1151
Rofin-sinar Technologies Llc 1151
Rogers Corp. 1151
Roku Inc 1151
Roland Machinery Company 1151
Rollins College 1152
Rollins, Inc. 1152
Ronald Mcdonald House Charities, Inc. 1152
Ronile, Inc. 1152
Roofing Wholesale Co., Inc. 1152
Roosevelt Capital Llc 1152
Root Llc 1153
Root9b Holdings Inc 1153
Roper St. Francis Healthcare 1153
Roper Technologies Inc 1153

Rose International, Inc. 1153
Rose Paving, Llc 1153
Rose's Southwest Papers, Inc. 1154
Rosen Hotels And Resorts, Inc. 1154
Rosetta Stone Inc. 1154
Ross Stores Inc 1154
Rotary International 1154
Rotech Healthcare Inc. 1154
Roth Iga Foodliner Incorporated 1155
Roth Produce Co. 1155
Roth Staffing Companies, L.p. 1155
Round Table Pizza, Inc. 1155
Roundy's, Inc. 1155
Rowan Regional Medical Center, Inc. 1155
Royal Caribbean Group 1156
Royal Gold Inc 1156
Royale Energy Inc 1156
Rpc, Inc. 1156
Rpl International Inc. 1156
Rpm International Inc (de) 1156
Rpx Corporation 1157
Rs Integrated Supply Us Inc. 1157
Rs Legacy Corporation 1157
Rsp Permian, Inc. 1157
Rsr Group, Inc. 1157
Rtw Retailwinds, Inc. 1157
Rtx Corp 1158
Ruan Transportation Management Systems, Inc. 1158
Rubicon Genomics, Inc. 1158
Rubicon Technology Inc 1158
Ruby Tuesday, Inc. 1158
Rudolph And Sletten, Inc. 1158
Rumsey Electric Company 1159
Rural School And Community Trust 1159
Rush Copley Medical Center 1159
Rush Enterprises Inc. 1159
Rush System For Health 1159
Rush Trucking Corporation 1159
Russell County Medical Center Inc 1160
Russell Sigler, Inc. 1160
Rutherford Electric Membership Corporation 1160
Rwj Barnabas Health, Inc. 1160
Ryan Building Group, Inc. 1160
Ryan, Llc 1160
Ryder System, Inc. 1161
Ryerson Holding Corp 1161
Ryman Hospitality Properties Inc 1161
S & B Engineers And Constructors, Ltd. 1161
S & T Bancorp Inc (indiana, Pa) 1161
S C & A, Inc. 1161
S&me, Inc. 1162
S&p Global Inc 1162
S&w Seed Co. 1162
Sabel Steel Service, Inc. 1162
Sabine Royalty Trust 1162
Sabra Health Care Reit Inc 1162
Sabre Corp 1163
Sacramento Municipal Utility District 1163
Sacred Heart Health System, Inc. 1163
Sacred Heart Hospital Of Allentown 1163
Sacred Heart Hospital Of The Hospital Sisters Of The Third Order Of St. Francis 1163
Saddleback Memorial Medical Center 1163
Saddlebrook Resorts, Inc. 1164
Safeco Insurance Company Of America 1164
Safeguard Scientifics, Inc. 1164
Safehold Inc (new) 1164
Safety Insurance Group, Inc. 1164
Saga Communications Inc 1164
Sagarsoft Inc. 1165
Sage Hospitality Resources L.l.c. 1165
Sage Therapeutics Inc 1165
Sagent Pharmaceuticals, Inc. 1165
Saia Inc 1165
Saint Agnes Medical Center 1165
Saint Alphonsus Regional Medical Center, Inc. 1166
Saint Anselm College 1166

Saint Edward's University, Inc. 1166
Saint Elizabeth Medical Center, Inc. 1166
Saint Elizabeth Regional Medical Center 1166
Saint Francis Health System, Inc. 1166
Saint Francis Hospital And Medical Center Foundation, Inc. 1167
Saint Francis University 1167
Saint Joseph Hospital, Inc 1167
Saint Joseph's Hospital Inc 1167
Saint Joseph's University 1167
Saint Louis University 1167
Saint Luke's Health System, Inc. 1168
Saint Luke's Quakertown Hospital 1168
Saint Mary's University Of Minnesota 1168
Saint Peter's University Hospital, Inc. 1168
Saint Thomas Rutherford Hospital 1168
Saint Vincent Health System 1168
Sakar International, Inc. 1169
Salem Health 1169
Salem Media Group, Inc. 1169
Salesforce Inc 1169
Salinas Valley Health 1169
Saline Memorial Hospital Auxiliary 1169
Salisbury Bancorp, Inc. 1170
Sally Beauty Holdings Inc 1170
Salon City Inc 1170
Salon Media Group Inc. 1170
Salt Lake Community College 1170
Salt River Project Agricultural Improvement And Power District 1170
Salve Regina University 1171
Sam Houston State University 1171
Sam Levin Inc. 1171
Sam Swope Auto Group, Llc 1171
Samaritan Pharmaceuticals 1171
Samaritan Regional Health System 1171
Sammons Enterprises, Inc. 1172
Samsung C&t America, Inc. 1172
San Antonio Spurs, L.l.c. 1172
San Antonio Water System 1172
San Antonio Zoological Society 1172
San Diego Christian College Inc 1172
San Diego County Office Of Education 1173
San Diego County Water Authority 1173
San Diego Gas & Electric Company 1173
San Diego State University Foundation 1173
San Diego Unified Port District 1173
San Francisco Bay Area Rapid Transit District 1173
San Francisco Forty Niners 1174
San Francisco Opera Association 1174
San Francisco State University 1174
San Jose Water Company 1174
San Juan Basin Royalty Trust 1174
Sanderson Farms, Llc 1174
Sandler, O'neill & Partners, L.p. 1175
Sandler, Travis & Rosenberg, P.a. 1175
Sandridge Energy Inc 1175
Sandston Corp 1175
Sandusky International Inc. 1175
Sandy Spring Bancorp Inc 1175
Sanfilippo (john B) & Son Inc 1176
Sanford 1176
Sanford Airport Authority 1176
Sanford Burnham Prebys Medical Discovery Institute 1176
Sangamo Therapeutics Inc 1176
Sanmina Corp 1176
Santa Cruz Seaside Company Inc 1177
Santa Fe Gold Corp 1177
Santa Monica Community College District 1177
Santander Holdings Usa Inc. 1177
Sapp Bros. Petroleum, Inc. 1177
Sapp Bros., Inc. 1177
Sara Enterprises, Inc. 1178
Sarah Bush Lincoln Health Center 1178
Sarah Lawrence College 1178
Sarasota County Public Hospital District 1178
Saratoga Resources Inc 1178

Sarcom, Inc. 1178
Sarepta Therapeutics Inc 1179
Sargent Electric Company 1179
Sargento Foods Inc. 1179
Sartori Company 1179
Sas Institute Inc. 1179
Satterfield And Pontikes Construction, Inc. 1179
Saul Centers Inc 1180
Savage Companies 1180
Savannah Health Services, Llc 1180
Savara Inc 1180
Save Mart Supermarkets Llc 1180
Save The Children Federation, Inc. 1180
Sawnee Electric Membership Corporation 1181
Sayers40, Inc 1181
Sb Financial Group Inc 1181
Sba Communications Corp (new) 1181
Scai Holdings, Llc 1181
Scan-optics, Inc. 1181
Scanner Technologies Corp 1182
Scansource, Inc. 1182
Scheels All Sports, Inc. 1182
Scheid Vineyards Inc. 1182
Schein (henry) Inc 1182
Schenectady County Community College 1182
Schenker, Inc. 1183
Schewel Furniture Company Incorporated 1183
Schiff Hardin Llp 1183
Schmitt Industries Inc (or) 1183
Schneider National Inc (wi) 1183
Scholastic Corp 1183
Schonfeld Securities, Llc 1184
School Administrators Association Of Nys (inc) 1184
Schottenstein Stores Corporation 1184
Schulze And Burch Biscuit Co. 1184
Schumacher Electric Corporation 1184
Schurz Communications, Inc. 1184
Schwab (charles) Corp (the) 1185
Schwebel Baking Company 1185
Sciclone Pharmaceuticals, Inc. 1185
Science Applications International Corp (new) 1185
Scientific Industries Inc 1185
Scientific Research Corp 1185
Scl Health - Front Range, Inc. 1186
Scolr Pharma Inc 1186
Scott And White Health Plan 1186
Scott Equipment Company, L.l.c. 1186
Scott Pet Products, Inc. 1186
Scott's Liquid Gold, Inc. 1186
Scottish Rite Cathedral Of San Diego 1187
Scotts Miracle-gro Co (the) 1187
Scripps (ew) Company (the) 1187
Scripps College 1187
Scripps Health 1187
Scripps Networks Interactive, Inc. 1187
Scrypt Inc 1188
Sculptz, Inc. 1188
Scynexis, Inc. 1188
Sdb Trade International, Llc 1188
Sdi Technologies Inc. 1188
Seaboard Corp. 1188
Seabrook Brothers & Sons, Inc. 1189
Seachange International Inc. 1189
Seacoast Banking Corp. Of Florida 1189
Seacor Holdings Inc. 1189
Seagate Cloud Systems, Inc. 1189
Seakr Engineering, Llc 1189
Sealaska Corporation 1190
Sealed Air Corp 1190
Sears Holdings Corp 1190
Sears Hometown Stores, Inc. 1190
Seattle Children's Hospital 1190
Seattle University 1190
Secureworks Corp 1191
Securian Financial Group Inc 1191
Securities Investor Protection Corporation 1191
Security Federal Corp (sc) 1191

Security Finance Corporation Of Spartanburg 1191
Security Health Plan Of Wisconsin, Inc. 1191
Security Industry Association 1192
Security Innovation, Inc. 1192
Security Land & Development Corp. 1192
Security National Financial Corp 1192
Sed International Holdings, Inc. 1192
Sedona Corp 1192
Seelos Therapeutics Inc 1193
Sefton Resources Inc 1193
Sei Investments Co 1193
Seibels Bruce Group, Inc. (the) 1193
Seitel Inc 1193
Select Medical Holdings Corp 1193
Select Water Solutions Inc 1194
Select Water Solutions, Llc 1194
Selectis Health Inc 1194
Selective Insurance Group Inc 1194
Sellas Life Sciences Group Inc 1194
Sematech, Inc. 1194
Semco Energy, Inc. 1195
Semi 1195
Seminole Electric Cooperative, Inc. 1195
Semler Scientific Inc 1195
Sempra 1195
Semtech Corp. 1195
Sendec Corp. 1196
Seneca Foods Corp. 1196
Senior Slr Investment Corp 1196
Senomyx, Inc. 1196
Sense Technologies Inc 1196
Sensei Bio Subsidiary, Inc. 1196
Sensient Technologies Corp. 1197
Sentara Health 1197
Sentara Rmh Medical Center 1197
Sentara Williamsburg Regional Medical Center 1197
Sentry Insurance-a Mutual Co. (stevens Point, Wisc.) 1197
Sentry Technology Corp. 1197
Sequachee Valley Electric Co-operative Inc 1198
Sequenom, Inc. 1198
Serena Software, Inc. 1198
Seres Therapeutics Inc 1198
Serious Fun Children's Network, Inc. 1198
Servatron, Inc. 1198
Servco Pacific Inc. 1199
Service Corp. International 1199
Service Properties Trust 1199
Servicenow Inc 1199
Servicesource International, Inc. 1199
Servisfirst Bancshares Inc 1199
Servotronics, Inc. 1200
Servpro Intellectual Property, Inc. 1200
Seton Ascension 1200
Seton Hall University 1200
Setton's International Foods, Inc. 1200
Seven Seas Technologies Inc. 1200
Sevenson Environmental Services, Inc. 1201
Seventy Seven Energy Llc 1201
Seyfarth Shaw Llp 1201
Sgpa Planning And Architecture San Diego 1201
Sgt, Llc 1201
Shake Shack Inc 1201
Shaklee Corporation 1202
Shamrock Foods Company 1202
Shands Jacksonville Medical Center, Inc. 1202
Shands Teaching Hospital And Clinics, Inc. 1202
Shari's Management Corporation 1202
Sharp Healthcare 1202
Sharp Memorial Hospital 1203
Sharpe Resources Corp. 1203
Sharplink Gaming Inc 1203
Shawmut Woodworking & Supply, Inc. 1203
Shawnee Mission Medical Center, Inc. 1203
Shearman & Sterling Llp 1203
Sheervision Inc 1204
Sheetz, Inc. 1204

Shelco, Llc 1204
Shenandoah Telecommunications Co 1204
Shepherd Center, Inc. 1204
Shepherd Electric Company, Llc 1204
Sheppard, Mullin, Richter & Hampton, Llp 1205
Sheridan Community Hospital (osteopathic) 1205
Sherrill Furniture Company Inc 1205
Sherry Matthews, Inc. 1205
Sherwin-williams Co (the) 1205
Shi International Corp. 1205
Shl Liquidation Industries Inc. 1206
Shoals Provision, Inc. 1206
Shoe Carnival, Inc. 1206
Shoestring Valley Holdings Inc. 1206
Shore Bancshares Inc. 1206
Shore Memorial Hospital 1206
Shorepower Technologies Inc 1207
Shriners Hospitals For Children 1207
Shutterfly, Llc 1207
Shutterstock Inc 1207
Shyft Group Inc (the) 1207
Sid Harvey Industries, Inc. 1207
Sidley Austin Llp 1208
Siebert Financial Corp 1208
Sierra Bancorp 1208
Sierra Club 1208
Sierra Nevada Corporation 1208
Sierra Pacific Power Co. 1208
Sierra View District Hospital League, Inc. 1209
Sierra-cedar, Llc 1209
Sifco Industries Inc. 1209
Siga Technologies Inc 1209
Sigmanet, Inc. 1209
Sigmatron International Inc. 1209
Signature Bank (new York, Ny) 1210
Signature Eyewear Inc. 1210
Sika Corporation 1210
Silgan Holdings Inc 1210
Silicon Graphics International Corp. 1210
Silicon Laboratories Inc 1210
Silicus Technologies, Llc 1211
Silver Bay Realty Trust Corp. 1211
Silver Cross Hospital And Medical Centers 1211
Silverbow Resources Inc 1211
Simmons First National Corp 1211
Simon Property Group, Inc. 1211
Simon Worldwide Inc. 1212
Simply Inc 1212
Simpson Manufacturing Co., Inc. (de) 1212
Simpson Thacher & Bartlett Llp 1212
Simtrol Inc 1212
Simulations Plus Inc 1212
Sinai Health System 1213
Sinai Hospital Of Baltimore, Inc. 1213
Sinclair Inc 1213
Sinclair Television Of Capital District, Inc. 1213
Singing Machine Co., Inc. 1213
Singularity Future Technology Ltd 1213
Sintx Technologies Inc 1214
Sir Speedy, Inc. 1214
Sirius Federal, Llc 1214
Sirius Xm Holdings Inc 1214
Sirva Inc 1214
Sisters Of Charity Of Leavenworth Health System, Inc. 1214
Site Centers Corp 1215
Siteone Landscape Supply Inc 1215
Six Flags Entertainment Corp 1215
Sizmek Inc. 1215
Sjw Group 1215
Skadden, Arps, Slate, Meagher & Flom Llp 1215
Skanska Usa Building Inc. 1216
Skanska Usa Civil Inc. 1216
Skechers Usa Inc 1216
Skf Usa Inc. 1216
Skidmore College 1216
Skidmore, Owings & Merrill Llp 1216
Skillsoft (us) Llc 1217

COMPANIES LISTED ALPHABETICALLY

Skinvisible Inc 1217
Sklar Corp. 1217
Skullcandy, Inc. 1217
Skyline Champion Corp 1217
Skyline Multimedia Entertainment Inc 1217
Skywest Inc. 1218
Skyworks Solutions Inc 1218
Sl Green Realty Corp 1218
Sl Industries, Inc. 1218
Sl Liquidation Llc 1218
Slalom, Inc. 1218
Sleep Number Corp 1219
Sleepmed Incorporated 1219
Slm Corp. 1219
Sloan Implement Company, Inc. 1219
Slumberland, Inc. 1219
Sm Energy Co. 1219
Small Parts Manufacturing Co., Inc. 1220
Smallbizpros, Inc 1220
Smart Move Inc 1220
Smart Sand Inc 1220
Smart Stores Operations Llc 1220
Smartfinancial Inc 1220
Smartronix, Llc 1221
Smc Networks, Inc. 1221
Smc Systems, Inc. 1221
Smg Industries Inc 1221
Smith & Wesson Brands Inc 1221
Smith (a O) Corp 1221
Smith Micro Software Inc 1222
Smith-midland Corp. 1222
Smithfield Foods, Inc. 1222
Smithgroup Companies, Inc. 1222
Smithsonian Institution 1222
Sms Alternatives Inc 1222
Smucker (j.m.) Co. 1223
Snap Inc 1223
Snap-on, Inc. 1223
Snapping Shoals Electric Trust, Inc. 1223
Snappy Popcorn Company 1223
Snavely Forest Products Inc 1223
Snell & Wilmer L.l.p. 1224
Snyder Langston Holdings, Llc 1224
Snyder's-lance, Inc. 1224
Societal Cdmo Inc 1224
Society Of Manufacturing Engineers 1224
Socket Holdings Corporation 1224
Socket Mobile Inc 1225
Soft Computer Consultants Inc. 1225
Softech, Inc 1225
Softheon, Inc. 1225
Software Publishers Assoc (inc) 1225
Software Quality Associates Llc 1225
Solarcraft Services, Inc. 1226
Solaredge Technologies, Inc. 1226
Solaris Oilfield Infrastructure Inc 1226
Solarwinds North America, Inc. 1226
Solco Plumbing Supply, Inc. 1226
Solera Holdings, Llc 1226
Solerity, Inc. 1227
Soligenix Inc 1227
Solitario Resources Corp 1227
Solitron Devices, Inc. 1227
Soluna Holdings Inc 1227
Somalogic Operating Co., Inc. 1227
Somerset Tire Service, Inc. 1228
Sonesta International Hotels Corporation 1228
Sonic Automotive, Inc. 1228
Sonic Foundry, Inc. 1228
Sonic Llc 1228
Sonida Senior Living Inc 1228
Sonim Technologies Inc 1229
Sono-tek Corp. 1229
Sonoco Products Co. 1229
Sonoma Pharmaceuticals Inc 1229
Sonoma State University 1229
Sonomawest Holdings, Inc. 1229
Soros Fund Management Llc 1230

Sotheby's 1230
Sotherly Hotels Inc 1230
Sothys U.s.a., Inc. 1230
Sound Financial Bancorp Inc 1230
Sound Health Solutions Inc 1230
Sourcecorp, Incorporated 1231
South Bend Medical Foundation Inc 1231
South Broward Hospital District 1231
South Carolina Department Of Education 1231
South Carolina Public Service Authority (inc) 1231
South Carolina State Ports Authority 1231
South Central Communications Corporation 1232
South Central Power Company Inc 1232
South Dakota School Of Mines And Technology Foundation 1232
South Dakota Soybean Processors Llc 1232
South Dakota State Medical Holding Company, Inc. 1232
South Dakota State University 1232
South Jersey Gas Co. 1233
South Jersey Industries, Inc. 1233
South Miami Hospital, Inc. 1233
South Peninsula Hospital, Inc. 1233
South Shore Health System, Inc. 1233
South Shore University Hospital 1233
Southco Distributing Company 1234
Southcoast Health System, Inc. 1234
Southcoast Hospitals Group, Inc. 1234
Southcross Energy Partners Llc 1234
Southeast Missouri State University 1234
Southeast Texas Industries, Inc. 1234
Southeastern Banking Corp. (darien, Ga) 1235
Southeastern Freight Lines, Inc. 1235
Southeastern Pennsylvania Transportation Authority 1235
Southeastern Universities Research Association, Inc. 1235
Southern Banc Co., Inc. 1235
Southern Bancshares (nc), Inc. 1235
Southern California Edison Co. 1236
Southern California Gas Co. 1236
Southern California Regional Rail Authority 1236
Southern Community Newspapers, Inc. 1236
Southern Company (the) 1236
Southern Company Gas 1236
Southern Counties Oil Co. 1237
Southern First Bancshares, Inc. 1237
Southern Illinois Healthcare Enterprises, Inc. 1237
Southern Illinois University Inc 1237
Southern Maine Health Care 1237
Southern Management Companies Llc 1237
Southern Methodist University Inc 1238
Southern Michigan Bancorp Inc 1238
Southern Minnesota Beet Sugar Cooperative 1238
Southern Minnesota Municipal Power Agency 1238
Southern Missouri Bancorp, Inc. 1238
Southern Natural Gas Co 1238
Southern Natural Gas Company, L.l.c. 1239
Southern New Hampshire Medical Center 1239
Southern Nuclear Operating Company, Inc. 1239
Southern Pine Electric Cooperative 1239
Southern Pipe & Supply Company, Inc. 1239
Southern Polytechnic State University Foundation, Inc 1239
Southern Power Co 1240
Southern Research Institute 1240
Southern States Cooperative Inc. 1240
Southern Union Gas Company, Inc. 1240
Southland Industries 1240
Southside Bancshares, Inc. 1240
Southstar Bank, S.s.b. 1241
Southstate Corp 1241
Southwest Airlines Co 1241
Southwest Gas Holdings, Inc. 1241
Southwest Louisiana Electric Membership Corporation 1241
Southwest Mississippi Regional Medical Center 1241

Southwest Research Institute Inc 1242
Southwestern Community College District (inc) 1242
Southwestern Electric Power Co. 1242
Southwestern Energy Company 1242
Southwestern University 1242
Southwestern Vermont Health Care Corporation 1242
Sp Plus Corp 1243
Space Coast Health Foundation, Inc. 1243
Space Micro Inc 1243
Spacequest, Ltd. 1243
Spahn & Rose Lumber Co. 1243
Span-america Medical Systems, Inc. 1243
Spang & Company 1244
Spanish Broadcasting System Inc 1244
Spar Group, Inc. 1244
Spark Networks, Inc. 1244
Sparrow Eaton Hospital 1244
Sparrow Health System 1244
Spartanburg Regional Health Services District, Inc. 1245
Spartannash Co 1245
Sparton Corporation 1245
Spaulding Rehabilitation Hospital (srh) Volunteer Services, 1245
Spaw Glass Holding, Llc 1245
Special Olympics, Inc. 1245
Specialized Marketing Services, Inc. 1246
Specialty Rice, Inc. 1246
Spectra Energy, Llc 1246
Spectra Systems Corp 1246
Spectranetics Llc 1246
Spectrum Brands Holdings Inc (new) 1246
Spectrum Brands Legacy, Inc. 1247
Spectrum Group International Inc 1247
Speed Commerce Inc 1247
Speedus Corp 1247
Speedway Motorsports, Llc 1247
Spelman College 1247
Spf Energy, Inc. 1248
Spherotech, Inc. 1248
Spindletop Oil & Gas Co (tex) 1248
Spire Alabama Inc. 1248
Spire Corp. 1248
Spire Inc 1248
Spirit Aerosystems Holdings Inc 1249
Spirit Airlines Inc 1249
Spitzer Management, Inc. 1249
Spok Holdings Inc 1249
Sportsman's Warehouse Holdings Inc 1249
Sportsquest Inc 1249
Spotlight Capital Holdings Inc 1250
Sprague Resources Lp 1250
Sprenger Enterprises, Inc. 1250
Spring Arbor University 1250
Spring Hill College 1250
Spring, O'brien & Company, Inc. 1250
Springfield Electric Supply Company, Llc 1251
Springfield Hospital Inc. 1251
Sprouts Farmers Market Inc 1251
Sps Commerce, Inc. 1251
Spx Flow, Inc. 1251
Spx Technologies Inc 1251
Spy Inc. 1252
Spyr Inc 1252
Squab Producers Of Calif, Inc. 1252
Squar, Milner, Peterson, Miranda & Williamson, Certified Public Accountants, Llp 1252
Sri International 1252
Srt Communications, Inc. 1252
Ss&c Technologies Holdings Inc 1253
Ssht S&t Group Ltd 1253
Ssm Health Care Corporation 1253
Ssr Mining Inc 1253
St Barnabas Medical Center (inc) 1253
St Bonaventure University 1253
St David's South Austin Medical Center 1254

St Davids Healthcare Partnership Llp 1254
St James Healthcare, Inc 1254
St John Fisher College 1254
St John's University, New York 1254
St Joseph's College New York 1254
St Lawrence University (inc) 1255
St Mary's Regional Health Center 1255
St Tammany Parish Hospital Service District No 1 1255
St Thomas Aquinas College 1255
St. Agnes Continuing Care Center 1255
St. Agnes Healthcare, Inc. 1255
St. Alexius Medical Center 1256
St. Anthony's Hospital, Inc. 1256
St. Bernard Hospital 1256
St. Clair Health Corporation 1256
St. Francis Health Services Of Morris, Inc. 1256
St. Francis Hospital, Roslyn, New York 1256
St. Joe Co. (the) 1257
St. John Health System, Inc. 1257
St. John Hospital And Medical Center 1257
St. John Providence 1257
St. John's College 1257
St. John's Hospital Of The Hospital Sisters Of The Third Order Of St. Francis 1257
St. Joseph Health System 1258
St. Joseph Healthcare Foundation 1258
St. Joseph Hospital Of Orange 1258
St. Joseph's Health Partners Llc 1258
St. Joseph's Hospital Health Center 1258
St. Joseph's Hospital, Breese, Of The Hospital Sisters Of The Third Order Of St. Francis 1258
St. Joseph's Wayne Hospital, Inc. 1259
St. Joseph's/candler Health System, Inc. 1259
St. Jude Children's Research Hospital, Inc. 1259
St. Jude Hospital 1259
St. Jude Medical, Llc 1259
St. Lucie Medical Center Auxiliary, Inc. 1259
St. Luke's Episcopal Hospital Physician Hospital Organization, Inc. 1260
St. Luke's Episcopal-presbyterian Hospitals 1260
St. Luke's Health Network, Inc. 1260
St. Luke's Health System, Ltd. 1260
St. Luke's Hospital Of Duluth 1260
St. Mary's Health, Inc. 1260
St. Mary's Hospital, Inc. 1261
St. Mary's Medical Center, Inc. 1261
St. Norbert College, Inc. 1261
St. Olaf College Corp 1261
St. Peter's Health Partners 1261
St. Vincent Health Services, Inc. 1261
St. Vincent's Health Services Corporation 1262
St. Vincent's Health System, Inc. 1262
Staar Surgical Co. 1262
Stabillis Solutions Inc 1262
Stabler Companies Inc. 1262
Staff Force, Inc. 1262
Staff One, Inc. 1263
Stag Industrial Inc 1263
Stage Stores, Inc. 1263
Stagwell Inc 1263
Stamford Health, Inc. 1263
Stampin' Up Inc. 1263
Stamps.com Inc. 1264
Stand Energy Corporation 1264
Standard Avb Financial Corp. 1264
Standard Biotools Inc 1264
Standard Electric Company 1264
Standard Energy Corp. 1264
Standard Motor Products, Inc. 1265
Standex International Corp. 1265
Stanford Health Care 1265
Stanion Wholesale Electric Co., Inc. 1265
Stanley Black & Decker Inc 1265
Stanley Steemer International, Inc. 1265
Stanly Regional Medical Center 1266
Staple Cotton Cooperative Association 1266
Staples Construction Company, Inc. 1266

Star Buffet, Inc. 1266
Star Equity Holdings Inc 1266
Star Group Lp 1266
Star Of The West Milling Company 1267
Starbucks Corp. 1267
Stark Holdings Inc. 1267
Starlight Children's Foundation 1267
Starrett (ls) Co (the) 1267
Starwood Property Trust Inc. 1267
Starz Acquisition Llc 1268
State Of New York Mortgage Agency 1268
State Street Corp. 1268
State University Of Iowa Foundation 1268
State University Of New York 1268
State University Of New York College At Brockport 1268
State Water Resources Control Board 1269
Statehouse Holdings Inc 1269
Staten Island University Hospital 1269
Stater Bros. Holdings Inc. 1269
Statera Biopharma Inc 1269
Statesville Hma, Llc 1269
Steadfast Income Reit, Inc. 1270
Steel Connect Inc 1270
Steel Dynamics Inc. 1270
Steel Of West Virginia, Inc. 1270
Steel Partners Holdings Lp 1270
Steel Technologies Llc 1270
Steel Ventures, L.l.c. 1271
Steelcase, Inc. 1271
Steelcloud Inc 1271
Stein Mart, Inc. 1271
Steiner Electric Company 1271
Stellar Group, Incorporated 1271
Stemline Therapeutics, Inc. 1272
Sten Corp. 1272
Stepan Co. 1272
Stephan Co (the) 1272
Stephen Gould Corporation 1272
Stephens Inc. 1272
Stephenson Wholesale Company, Inc. 1273
Stereotaxis Inc 1273
Stericycle Inc. 1273
Steris Instrument Management Services, Inc. 1273
Sterling Infrastructure Inc 1273
Sterling Sugars, Inc. 1273
Stetson University, Inc. 1274
Stevens Community Medical Center, Inc 1274
Stevens Transport, Inc. 1274
Stevenson University Inc. 1274
Steward Health Care System Llc 1274
Steward Sharon Regional Health System, Inc. 1274
Stewart & Stevenson Inc. 1275
Stewart Builders, Inc. 1275
Stewart Information Services Corp 1275
Stewart's Shops Corp. 1275
Stg Llc 1275
Stifel Financial Corp 1275
Stiles Corporation 1276
Stillwater Mining Company 1276
Stock Yards Bancorp Inc 1276
Stockade Companies, Llc 1276
Stonemor Partners L.p. 1276
Stoneridge Inc. 1276
Stonex Group Inc 1277
Stony Brook University 1277
Storr Office Environments Inc 1277
Stoughton Hospital Association 1277
Stowers Institute For Medical Research 1277
Str Holdings Inc. 1277
Strack And Van Til Super Market Inc. 1278
Strafford Technology, Inc. 1278
Strata Skin Sciences Inc 1278
Strategic Education Inc 1278
Strattec Security Corp. 1278
Stratus Properties Inc. 1278
Streamline Health Solutions Inc 1279
Streck, Inc. 1279

Stride Inc 1279
Strike Operating Company Llc 1279
Strobel Construction Unlimited, Inc. 1279
Strongwell Corporation 1279
Structural Group, Inc. 1280
Stryker Corp 1280
Stuart-dean Co. Inc. 1280
Stupp Bros., Inc. 1280
Sturdy Memorial Hospital, Inc. 1280
Sturgis Bancorp Inc 1280
Sturm, Ruger & Co., Inc. 1281
Stussy, Inc. 1281
Stv Group, Incorporated 1281
Stv Holdings, Inc. 1281
Subjex Corp 1281
Suburban Hospital, Inc. 1281
Suburban Propane Partners Lp 1282
Subzero Constructors, Inc. 1282
Sucampo Pharmaceuticals, Inc. 1282
Suffolk Construction Company, Inc. 1282
Suffolk County Water Authority Inc 1282
Suffolk University 1282
Sukut Construction, Inc. 1283
Sullivan & Cromwell Llp 1283
Summa Health System 1283
Summer Infant, Inc. 1283
Summerlin Hospital Medical Center, Llc 1283
Summit Bancshares, Inc. (ca) 1283
Summit Electric Supply Co., Inc. 1284
Summit Financial Group Inc 1284
Summit Hotel Properties Inc 1284
Summit Materials Inc 1284
Summit Partners, L.p. 1284
Summit State Bank (santa Rosa, Ca) 1284
Sumter Coatings, Inc. 1285
Sumter Electric Cooperative, Inc. 1285
Sun Coast Resources, Llc 1285
Sun Communities Inc 1285
Sun Eagle Corporation 1285
Sun Orchard Fruit Company, Inc. 1285
Sun-maid Growers Of California 1286
Suncast Corporation 1286
Suncliff Inc 1286
Suncoast Post-tension, Ltd. 1286
Suncoke Energy Inc 1286
Sundance Institute 1286
Sunedison Semiconductor Ltd 1287
Sunedison, Inc. 1287
Sunflower Electric Power Corp 1287
Sunkist Growers, Inc. 1287
Sunlink Health Systems Inc 1287
Sunoco Lp 1287
Sunopta Inc 1288
Sunpower Corp 1288
Sunrise Hospital And Medical Center, Llc 1288
Sunrun Inc 1288
Sunrun Installation Services Inc. 1288
Suns Legacy Partners, L.l.c. 1288
Sunset Development Company Inc 1289
Sunsweet Growers Inc. 1289
Suntory International 1289
Suny At Binghamton 1289
Suny At Old Westbury 1289
Suny Cobleskill College Of Agriculture And Technology 1289
Suny Downstate Medical Center 1290
Super Micro Computer Inc 1290
Superior Drilling Products Inc 1290
Superior Energy Services, Inc. 1290
Superior Graphite Co. 1290
Superior Group Of Companies Inc 1290
Superior Industrial Solutions, Inc. 1291
Superior Industries International, Inc. 1291
Supernus Pharmaceuticals Inc 1291
Supershuttle International, Inc. 1291
Supply Chain Consultants Inc 1291
Support.com, Inc. 1291
Supreme Gear Co. 1292

COMPANIES LISTED ALPHABETICALLY

Supreme Industries, Inc. 1292
Surfrider Foundation, Inc 1292
Surgalign Holdings Inc 1292
Surge Components Inc 1292
Surge Global Energy Inc 1292
Surgery Partners Inc 1293
Surgline International Inc. 1293
Surmodics Inc 1293
Surrey Bancorp (nc) 1293
Susquehanna River Basin Commission 1293
Sutter Bay Hospitals 1293
Sutter Bay Medical Foundation 1294
Sutter Central Valley Hospitals 1294
Sutter Health 1294
Sv Labs Corporation 1294
Svb Financial Group 1294
Swarthmore College 1294
Swat.fame, Inc. 1295
Swedish Health Services 1295
Swedishamerican Health System Corporation 1295
Swimwear Anywhere, Inc. 1295
Swinerton Builders 1295
Swinerton Incorporated 1295
Swisher Hygiene Inc. 1296
Switch, Inc. 1296
Sylvania Franciscan Health 1296
Symbion, Inc. 1296
Symbolic Logic Inc 1296
Symbollon Pharmaceuticals Inc. 1296
Symms Fruit Ranch, Inc. 1297
Symvionics, Inc. 1297
Synacor, Inc. 1297
Synaptics Inc 1297
Synarc Inc. 1297
Synchronoss Technologies Inc 1297
Synchrony Financial 1298
Syncora Holdings Ltd 1298
Synergetics Usa, Inc. 1298
Synergy Health North America, Inc. 1298
Synergy It Solutions Of Nys, Inc. 1298
Syniverse Holdings, Inc. 1298
Synopsys Inc 1299
Synovus Financial Corp 1299
Synthesis Energy Systems Inc 1299
Synutra International, Inc. 1299
Sypris Solutions, Inc. 1299
Syracuse University 1299
Sysco Corp 1300
Systems Engineering Technologies Corporation 1300
Systrand Manufacturing Corp 1300
Syzygy Technologies, Inc. 1300
T & G Corporation 1300
T Rowe Price Group Inc. 1300
T-mobile Us Inc 1301
T. D. Williamson, Inc. 1301
T.j.t., Inc. 1301
Tablemax Corp 1301
Taco John's International, Inc. 1301
Tacoma Public Utilities 1301
Taconic Biosciences, Inc. 1302
Tacony Corporation 1302
Tailored Brands, Inc. 1302
Taitron Components Inc. 1302
Take-two Interactive Software, Inc. 1302
Tal International Group, Inc. 1302
Talent Technical Services, Inc. 1303
Tallahassee Memorial Healthcare, Inc. 1303
Tallahassee, City Of (inc) 1303
Tallgrass Energy Partners, Lp 1303
Tallgrass Energy, Lp 1303
Talon International, Inc. 1303
Talos Petroleum Llc 1304
Talphera Inc 1304
Tampa Electric Company 1304
Tandem Diabetes Care Inc 1304
Tandy Leather Factory Inc 1304
Tanger Inc 1304

Tangoe Us, Inc. 1305
Tanner Industries, Inc. 1305
Taos Health Systems, Inc. 1305
Taos Mountain, Llc 1305
Tap Enterprises, Inc. 1305
Tapestry Inc 1305
Targa Resources Corp 1306
Target Corp 1306
Targeted Medical Pharma, Inc. 1306
Tarleton State University 1306
Tarrant County Hospital District 1306
Tas-chfh 1306
Tas-cnh, Inc. 1307
Tata America International Corporation 1307
Tatung Company Of America, Inc. 1307
Tauber Oil Company 1307
Tawa Supermarket, Inc. 1307
Taylor (calvin B.) Bankshares, Inc. (md) 1307
Taylor Corporation 1308
Taylor Devices Inc 1308
Taylor Morrison Home Corp (holding Co) 1308
Taylor Morrison Home Corporation 1308
Taylor Products Inc 1308
Tbc, Inc. 1308
Tcg Family Business Llc 1309
Tcg, Inc. 1309
Td Ameritrade Holding Corporation 1309
Td Ameritrade, Inc. 1309
Td Synnex Corp 1309
Team Air Express, Inc. 1309
Team Health Holdings, Inc. 1310
Team Inc 1310
Team Industries Holding Corporation 1310
Teamquest Corporation 1310
Tech Data Corporation 1310
Technica Corporation 1310
Technical Communications Corp 1311
Technipfmc Plc 1311
Techniscan Inc. 1311
Technology Concepts & Design, Inc. 1311
Technology Service Corporation 1311
Techsmith Corporation 1311
Techtarget Inc 1312
Teco Energy, Inc. 1312
Teco-westinghouse Motor Company 1312
Tecogen Inc 1312
Tecplot, Inc. 1312
Tecumseh Products Company Llc 1312
Tegna Inc 1313
Tejas Office Products, Inc. 1313
Tejon Ranch Co 1313
Teknor Apex Company 1313
Teksystems, Inc. 1313
Tel Instrument Electronics Corp. 1313
Telecommunication Systems, Inc. 1314
Teledyne Lecroy, Inc. 1314
Teledyne Technologies Inc 1314
Teleflex Incorporated 1314
Telenav, Inc. 1314
Telephone & Data Systems Inc 1314
Telephone Electronics Corporation 1315
Telephonics Corporation 1315
Telex Communications, Inc. 1315
Teligent Inc (new) 1315
Telkonet Inc. 1315
Tellurian Inc 1315
Telos Corp. (md) 1316
Tempaco, Inc. 1316
Temple University Health System, Inc. 1316
Temple University-of The Commonwealth System Of Higher Education 1316
Tempur Sealy International, Inc. 1316
Ten Pubco, Inc. 1316
Tenax Therapeutics Inc 1317
Tenenbaum Recycling Group, Llc 1317
Tenerity, Inc. 1317
Tenet Healthcare Corp. 1317
Tenfold Corporation 1317

Tennant Co. 1317
Tenneco Inc. 1318
Tennessee Gas Pipeline Co. 1318
Tennessee State University 1318
Tennessee Technological University 1318
Tennessee Valley Authority 1318
Tension Envelope Corporation 1318
Ter Holdings I, Inc 1319
Teradata Corp (de) 1319
Teradyne, Inc. 1319
Terawulf Inc. 1319
Terex Corp. 1319
Terra Nitrogen Company, L.p. 1319
Terracon Consultants, Inc. 1320
Terracycle, Inc. 1320
Terraform Power, Inc. 1320
Terranext, Llc 1320
Terreno Realty Corp 1320
Territorial Bancorp Inc 1320
Tesla Energy Operations, Inc. 1321
Tesla Inc 1321
Tessera Technologies, Inc. 1321
Teton Energy Corporation 1321
Tetra Tech Inc 1321
Tetra Technologies, Inc. 1321
Tetralogic Pharmaceuticals Corp 1322
Tetraphase Pharmaceuticals, Inc. 1322
Texans For Lawsuit Reform Foundation 1322
Texas A & M Research Foundation Inc 1322
Texas Capital Bancshares Inc 1322
Texas Children's Hospital 1322
Texas Christian University Inc 1323
Texas Department Of Transportation 1323
Texas Gas Transmission Llc 1323
Texas Guaranteed Student Loan Corporation 1323
Texas Health Harris Methodist Hospital Fort Worth 1323
Texas Health Presbyterian Hospital Dallas 1323
Texas Health Resources 1324
Texas Hospital Association 1324
Texas Instruments Inc. 1324
Texas Lutheran University 1324
Texas Medical Association Library 1324
Texas Municipal Power Agency 1324
Texas Pacific Land Corp 1325
Texas Rangers Baseball Foundation 1325
Texas Roadhouse Inc 1325
Texas Southern University 1325
Texas State History Museum Foundation, Inc 1325
Texas State University 1325
Texas Tech University System 1326
Texas Vanguard Oil Company 1326
Texas Workforce Commission 1326
Texas-new Mexico Power Company 1326
Textron Financial Corp 1326
Textron Inc 1326
Textura Corporation 1327
Tfs Financial Corp 1327
Tg Therapeutics Inc 1327
Thanksgiving Coffee Company, Inc. 1327
The A C Houston Lumber Company 1327
The Adt Security Corporation 1327
The Advertising Council Inc 1328
The Advisory Board Company 1328
The Aerospace Corporation 1328
The Africa-america Institute 1328
The American Farmland Trust 1328
The American Kennel Club 1328
The American Museum Of Natural History 1329
The American Society For The Prevention Of Cruelty To Animals 1329
The American Society Of Civil Engineers 1329
The American-scandinavian Foundation 1329
The Andrew W Mellon Foundation 1329
The Anschutz Corporation 1329
The Arc Of Westmoreland 1330
The Art Broad Foundation 1330
The Artery Group Llc 1330

The Arthritis Foundation, Inc. 1330
The Aspen Institute Inc 1330
The Associated Press 1330
The Association Of Junior Leagues International Inc 1331
The Bancorp Inc 1331
The Behler-young Company 1331
The Belting Company Of Cincinnati 1331
The Benecon Group Inc 1331
The Bernd Group Inc 1331
The Bessemer Group Incorporated 1332
The Betty Ford Center 1332
The Bidwell Family Corporation 1332
The Biltmore Company Llc 1332
The Bms Enterprises Inc 1332
The Bradford Exchange Ltd 1332
The Branch Group Inc 1333
The Brigham And Women's Hospital Inc 1333
The Brookdale Hospital Medical Center 1333
The Brookings Institution 1333
The Brother's Brother Foundation 1333
The Burton Corporation 1333
The Cadmus Group Llc 1334
The California Endowment 1334
The Carter-jones Lumber Company 1334
The Catholic University Of America 1334
The Centech Group Inc 1334
The Chair King Inc 1334
The Champaign Telephone Company 1335
The Charles Stark Draper Laboratory Inc 1335
The Charlotte-mecklenburg Hospital Authority 1335
The Chilcote Company 1335
The Children's Health Fund 1335
The Children's Hospital Corporation 1335
The Children's Hospital Of Philadelphia 1336
The Childrens Hospital Los Angeles 1336
The Chimes Inc 1336
The Christ Hospital 1336
The Christian Broadcasting Network Inc 1336
The Christian Coalition 1336
The Cigna Group 1337
The Citadel 1337
The City Of Huntsville 1337
The City Of Seattle-city Light Department 1337
The Claremont Colleges Inc 1337
The Cleveland Clinic Foundation 1337
The Coast Distribution System Inc 1338
The College Network Inc 1338
The College Of Charleston 1338
The College Of William & Mary 1338
The College Of Wooster 1338
The Collegiate School 1338
The Colonial Williamsburg Foundation 1339
The Community Hospital Group Inc 1339
The Computer Merchant Ltd 1339
The Computing Technology Industry Association Inc 1339
The Conference Board Inc 1339
The Connell Company 1339
The Conservation Fund A Nonprofit Corporation 1340
The Cooper Health System A New Jersey Non-profit Corporation 1340
The Cooper Union For The Advancement Of Science And Art 1340
The Corporation Of Haverford College 1340
The Corporation Of Mercer University 1340
The Council Population Inc 1340
The Culinary Institute Of America 1341
The Daston Corporation 1341
The David And Lucile Packard Foundation 1341
The Dch Health Care Authority 1341
The Deaconess Associations Inc 1341
The Depository Trust & Clearing Corporation 1341
The Donohoe Companies Inc 1342
The Dow Chemical Company 1342
The Drees Company 1342

The Dun & Bradstreet Corporation 1342
The Dyson-kissner-moran Corporation 1342
The Earst Foundation Inc 1342
The Electronic Retailing Association 1343
The Empire District Electric Company 1343
The Evangelical Lutheran Good Samaritan Society 1343
The F Dohmen Co 1343
The Finish Line Inc 1343
The Fishel Company 1343
The Floating Hospital Incorporated 1344
The Ford Foundation 1344
The Foundation For Aids Research 1344
The Fox Chase Cancer Center Foundation 1344
The Frederick Gunn School Incorporated 1344
The Fresh Market Inc 1344
The Fulton Dekalb Hospital Authority 1345
The G W Van Keppel Company 1345
The Gap Inc 1345
The Generation Companies Llc 1345
The George J Falter Company 1345
The George Lucas Educational Foundation 1345
The George Washington University 1346
The Georgetown University 1346
The Gettysburg Hospital 1346
The Glik Company 1346
The Global Fund For Women Inc 1346
The Goldfield Corporation Del 1346
The Golub Corporation 1347
The Good Samaritan Hospital Of Md Inc 1347
The Good Shepherd Hospital Inc 1347
The Great Atlantic & Pacific Tea Co Inc 1347
The Griffin Hospital 1347
The H T Hackney Co 1347
The Health Care Authority Of The City Of Huntsville 1348
The Henry Francis Dupont Winterthur Museum Inc 1348
The Heritage Foundation 1348
The Hershey Salty Snacks Sales Company 1348
The Hibbert Company 1348
The Hillman Companies Inc 1348
The Home City Ice Company 1349
The Hopkins Johns University 1349
The Hospital For Sick Children Pediatric Center 1349
The Howard University 1349
The Humane Society Of The United States 1349
The Ingalls Memorial Hospital 1349
The Institute Of Electrical And Electronics Engineers Incorporated 1350
The Institute Of International Finance Inc 1350
The Interfaith Alliance Inc 1350
The International Association Of Lions Clubs Incorporated 1350
The International City Management Association Retirement Corporation 1350
The Jackson Laboratory 1350
The Jamaica Hospital 1350
The Jane Goodall Institute For Wildlife Research Education And Conservation 1351
The Jay Group Inc 1351
The Jewish Federations Of North America Inc 1351
The Jockey Club 1351
The John And Mary R Markle Foundation 1351
The John Gore Organization Inc 1352
The Johns Hopkins Health System Corporation 1352
The Judge Group Inc 1352
The Juilliard School Inc 1352
The Kane Company 1352
The Kenneth T And Eileen L Norris Foundation 1352
The Keyw Holding Corporation 1353
The Kleinfelder Group Inc 1353
The Krystal Company 1353
The Lancaster General Hospital 1353
The Lane Construction Corporation 1353

The Layton Companies Inc 1353
The Legal Aid Society Inc 1354
The Life Is Good Company 1354
The Lightstone Group Llc 1354
The Linux Foundation 1354
The Long & Foster Companies Inc 1354
The Los Angeles Kings Hockey Club L P 1354
The Maids International Llc 1355
The Marcus & Millichap Company 1355
The Marine Mammal Center 1355
The Massachusetts General Hospital 1355
The Maureen And Mike Mansfield Foundation 1355
The Mclean Hospital Corporation 1355
The Medical University Of South Carolina 1356
The Medicines Company 1356
The Memorial Hospital 1356
The Memorial Hospital 1356
The Merchants Company Llc 1356
The Methodist Hospital 1356
The Methodist Hospitals, Inc. 1357
The Metrohealth System 1357
The Metropolitan Museum Of Art 1357
The Michaels Companies Inc 1357
The Middle Tennessee Electric Membership Corporation 1357
The Mill Steel Co 1357
The Mitre Corporation 1358
The Monarch Beverage Company Inc 1358
The Moore Company 1358
The Morganti Group Inc 1358
The Moses H Cone Memorial Hospital Operating Corporation 1358
The National Alliance To End Homelessness Incorporated 1358
The National Association For The Exchange Of Industrial Resources Inc 1359
The National Association Of Professional Baseball Leagues Inc 1359
The National Football Foundation And College Hall Of Fame Inc 1359
The National Parks & Conservation Association 1359
The Natori Company Incorporated 1359
The Nature Conservancy 1359
The Nature's Bounty Co 1360
The Navsys Corporation 1360
The Nead Organization 1360
The Nebraska Medical Center 1360
The New Home Company Inc 1360
The New Jersey Transit Corporation 1360
The New Liberty Hospital District Of Clay County Missouri 1361
The New School 1361
The New York And Presbyterian Hospital 1361
The New York Independent System Operator Inc 1361
The New York Public Library 1361
The Newtron Group L L C 1361
The North Highland Company Llc 1362
The Northern Illinois University 1362
The Ocean Conservancy Inc 1362
The Ogden Newspapers Inc 1362
The Oltmans Construction Co 1362
The Options Clearing Corporation 1362
The Paradies Shops Llc 1363
The Partnership For New York City Inc 1363
The Pennsylvania Hospital Of The University Of Pennsylvania Health System 1363
The Pennsylvania State University 1363
The Penrod Company 1363
The Pep Boys - Manny Moe & Jack 1363
The Pew Charitable Trusts 1364
The Pharmacy At Cmc 1364
The Philadelphia Parking Authority 1364
The Philharmonic-symphony Society Of New York Inc 1364
The Plaza Group, Inc 1364
The Port Authority Of New York & New Jersey 1364

COMPANIES LISTED ALPHABETICALLY

The Poynter Institute For Media Studies Inc 1365
The President And Trustees Of Colby College 1365
The Public Health Trust Of Miami-dade County 1365
The Ralph M Parsons Foundation 1365
The Rdw Group Inc 1365
The Reed Institute 1365
The Regents Of The University Of Colorado 1366
The Research Foundation For The State University Of New York 1366
The Rock And Roll Hall Of Fame And Museum Inc 1366
The Rockefeller Foundation 1366
The Rockefeller University Faculty And Students Club Inc 1366
The Rudolph/libbe Companies Inc 1366
The Rutland Hospital Inc 1367
The Salvation Army 1367
The Salvation Army National Corporation 1367
The Savannah College Of Art And Design Inc 1367
The Scotia Group Inc 1367
The Scott Fetzer Company 1367
The Scoular Company 1368
The Scripps Research Institute 1368
The Segerdahl Corp 1368
The Shamrock Companies Inc 1368
The Sheridan Group Inc 1368
The Shubert Foundation Inc 1368
The Simon Konover Company 1369
The Solomon-page Group Llc 1369
The Southern Poverty Law Center Inc 1369
The Step2 Company Llc 1369
The Sundt Companies Inc 1369
The Susan G Komen Breast Cancer Foundation Inc 1369
The Synergos Institute Inc 1370
The Tech Interactive 1370
The Technology Association Of America 1370
The Texas A&m University System 1370
The Trade Event Resource Management Group Llc 1370
The Trump Organization Inc 1370
The Trustees Of Davidson College 1371
The Trustees Of Grinnell College 1371
The Trustees Of Mount Holyoke College 1371
The Trustees Of Princeton University 1371
The Trustees Of Purdue University 1371
The Trustees Of The Smith College 1371
The Trustees Of The Stevens Institute Of Technology 1372
The Trustees Of The University Of Pennsylvania 1372
The Trustees Of Wheaton College 1372
The Turner Corporation 1372
The Ucla Foundation 1372
The Union Memorial Hospital 1372
The United Methodist Publishing House 1373
The University Of Akron 1373
The University Of Alabama System 1373
The University Of Arizona Foundation 1373
The University Of Central Florida Board Of Trustees 1373
The University Of Chicago 1373
The University Of Chicago Medical Center 1374
The University Of Dayton 1374
The University Of Hartford 1374
The University Of Iowa 1374
The University Of North Carolina 1374
The University Of North Carolina At Charlotte 1374
The University Of North Carolina Health System 1375
The University Of North Florida 1375
The University Of Southern Mississippi 1375
The University Of The South 1375
The University Of Toledo 1375
The University Of Tulsa 1375
The University Of Utah 1376
The University Of Vermont Medical Center Inc 1376

The Unlv Research Foundation 1376
The Urban Institute 1376
The Valley Hospital Inc 1376
The Vanderbilt University 1376
The Vanguard Group Inc 1377
The Viscardi Center Inc 1377
The Wachtell Lipton Rosen & Katz Foundation 1377
The Waldinger Corporation 1377
The Walman Optical Company 1377
The Walsh Group Ltd 1377
The Warrior Group Inc 1378
The Washington And Lee University 1378
The Washington University 1378
The Water Works Board Of The City Of Birmingham 1378
The Watson Institute 1378
The Western & Southern Life Insurance Company 1378
The Whiting-turner Contracting Company 1379
The Will-burt Company 1379
The Willamette Valley Company Llc 1379
The Wills Group Inc 1379
The Wine Group Inc 1379
The Wistar Institute Of Anatomy And Biology 1379
The Workers Compensation Research Institute 1380
The Yates Companies Inc 1380
Thedacare Regional Medical Center - Appleton, Inc. 1380
Thedacare, Inc. 1380
Therapeuticsmd Inc 1380
Theriva Biologics Inc 1380
Thermo Fisher Scientific Inc 1381
Thermodynetics Inc. (nv) 1381
Thermoenergy Corp 1381
Thermogenesis Holdings Inc 1381
Thermon Group Holdings Inc 1381
Thermwood Corp. 1381
Thestreet, Inc. 1382
Third Coast Midstream, Llc 1382
Thirdera, Llc 1382
Thirteen Productions Llc 1382
Thomas Graphics, Inc. 1382
Thomas Jefferson School Of Law 1382
Thomas Jefferson University 1383
Thomas Jefferson University Hospitals, Inc. 1383
Thomas Saint Midtown Hospital 1383
Thomasville Bancshares, Inc. 1383
Thompson Creek Metals Company Usa 1383
Thompson Hospitality Corporation 1383
Thompson Steel Company, Inc. 1384
Thor Industries, Inc. 1384
Thoratec Llc 1384
Thos. S. Byrne, Inc. 1384
Thrustmaster Of Texas, Inc. 1384
Thruway Authority Of New York State 1384
Thryv Holdings Inc 1385
Thunder Mountain Gold, Inc. 1385
Ti Gotham Inc. 1385
Tidewater Inc (new) 1385
Tiffin Motor Homes, Inc. 1385
Tift Regional Medical Center Foundation, Inc. 1385
Tigerlogic Corporation 1386
Tigrent Inc 1386
Timbercon, Inc. 1386
Timberland Bancorp, Inc. 1386
Timberline Resources Corp 1386
Time Warner Entertainment Co., L.p. 1386
Timios National Corporation 1387
Timken Co. (the) 1387
Tiptree Inc 1387
Tis Mortgage Investment Co. 1387
Titan International Inc 1387
Titan Machinery, Inc. 1387
Titan Pharmaceuticals Inc (de) 1388
Titusville Area Hospital 1388
Tivity Health, Inc. 1388

Tivo Corporation 1388
Tivo Solutions Inc. 1388
Tix Corp 1388
Tjx Companies, Inc. 1389
Tlic Worldwide, Inc 1389
Tma Systems, L.l.c. 1389
Tnemec Company, Inc. 1389
Toastmasters International 1389
Tobira Therapeutics, Inc. 1389
Tofutti Brands Inc 1390
Toledo Edison Co 1390
Toledo Promedica Hospital 1390
Toll Brothers Inc. 1390
Tom James Company 1390
Tom Lange Company, Inc. 1390
Tomah Memorial Hospital, Inc. 1391
Tomball Hospital Authority 1391
Tompkins Cortland Community College Alumni Association, Inc. 1391
Tompkins Financial Corp 1391
Tootsie Roll Industries Inc 1391
Top Down Systems Corporation 1391
Topbuild Corp 1392
Topgolf Callaway Brands Corp 1392
Tor Minerals International Inc 1392
Torch Energy Royalty Trust 1392
Toro Company (the) 1392
Torrance Memorial Medical Center 1392
Total Health Care, Inc. 1393
Tote Maritime Puerto Rico, Llc 1393
Touchstone Bankshares Inc 1393
Touchstone Energy Cooperative, Inc. 1393
Touro College 1393
Tower International, Inc. 1393
Tower Tech, Inc. 1394
Towerstream Corp 1394
Town Sports International Holdings Inc 1394
Township High School District 211 Foundation 1394
Townsquare Media Inc 1394
Toyota Motor Credit Corp. 1394
Toyota Motor Sales Usa Inc 1395
Toys "r" Us, Inc. 1395
Tpg Re Finance Trust Inc 1395
Tpi Acquisition, Inc. 1395
Tpi Composites Inc 1395
Track Data Corp. 1395
Track Group Inc 1396
Tractor & Equipment Company Inc 1396
Tractor Supply Co. 1396
Tradeweb Markets Inc 1396
Traditional Medicinals, Inc. 1396
Trail Blazers Inc. 1396
Trailer Bridge, Inc. 1397
Trammo, Inc. 1397
Trandes Corp. 1397
Trans World Corporation 1397
Trans-system, Inc. 1397
Transact Technologies Inc. 1397
Transatlantic Petroleum Ltd. 1398
Transcat Inc 1398
Transchemical Incorporated 1398
Transcontinental Gas Pipe Line Company, Llc 1398
Transcontinental Realty Investors, Inc. 1398
Transdev North America, Inc. 1398
Transdigm Group Inc 1399
Transitcenter, Inc. 1399
Transmontaigne Partners Llc 1399
Transnet Corporation 1399
Transperfect Translations International Inc. 1399
Transportation Insight, Llc 1399
Transtech Industries, Inc. 1400
Transunion 1400
Travel + Leisure Co 1400
Travel Store 1400
Travelers Companies Inc (the) 1400
Travelzoo 1400
Traylor Bros., Inc. 1401

Trc Companies, Inc. 1401
Treaty Energy Corp. 1401
Trecora Llc 1401
Tredegar Corp. 1401
Tree Top, Inc. 1401
Treecon Resources Inc 1402
Treehouse Foods Inc 1402
Trellis Earth Products, Inc. 1402
Trevena Inc 1402
Trex Co Inc 1402
Trg Products, Inc. 1402
Tri Harbor Holdings Corporation 1403
Tri-city Electrical Contractors, Inc. 1403
Tri-city Hospital District (inc) 1403
Tri-cor Industries, Inc. 1403
Tri-s Security Corp 1403
Tri-west, Ltd. 1403
Tribune Publishing Company 1404
Trico Bancshares (chico, Ca) 1404
Trihealth, Inc. 1404
Trilogy Communications, Inc. 1404
Trim-lok Inc 1404
Trimas Corp (new) 1404
Trimble Inc 1405
Trimedyne Inc 1405
Trimega Purchasing Association 1405
Trimol Group, Inc. 1405
Trinet Group Inc. 1405
Trinitas Regional Medical Center 1405
Trinity Christian Center Of Santa Ana, Inc. 1406
Trinity Health Corporation 1406
Trinity Health System 1406
Trinity Industries, Inc. 1406
Trinity University 1406
Trinseo Plc 1406
Tripadvisor Inc 1407
Triple "b" Corporation 1407
Trippe Manufacturing Co 1407
Triumph Apparel Corp 1407
Triumph Group Inc. 1407
Trivascular Technologies, Inc. 1407
Troika Media Group Inc 1408
Tronox Llc 1408
Trout-blue Chelan-magi, Llc 1408
Troy University 1408
Trt Holdings, Inc 1408
Trubridge Inc 1408
True Value Company, L.l.c. 1409
Trueblue Inc 1409
Truecar Inc 1409
Truist Financial Corp 1409
Trujillo & Sons, Inc. 1409
Trulia, Inc. 1409
Truman Arnold Companies 1410
Truman Medical Center, Incorporated 1410
Trustco Bank Corp. (n.y.) 1410
Trustees Of Boston College 1410
Trustees Of Clark University 1410
Trustees Of Dartmouth College 1410
Trustees Of Indiana University 1411
Trustees Of The Colorado School Of Mines 1411
Trustees Of The Estate Of Bernice Pauahi Bishop 1411
Trustees Of Tufts College 1411
Trustees Of Union College In The Town Of Schenectady In The State Of New York 1411
Trustmark Corp 1411
Truth Initiative Foundation 1412
Tsi Holding Company 1412
Tsr Inc 1412
Tsrc, Inc. 1412
Tss Inc De 1412
Ttec Holdings Inc 1412
Ttm Technologies Inc 1413
Ttx Co. 1413
Tubby's Sub Shops, Inc 1413
Tubemogul, Inc. 1413
Tucson Electric Power Company 1413

Tuesday Morning Corp (new) 1413
Tufco Technologies, Inc. 1414
Tumac Lumber Co., Inc. 1414
Tunnell Consulting, Inc. 1414
Tupperware Brands Corp 1414
Turlock Irrigation District Employees Association 1414
Turner Construction Company Inc 1414
Turtle & Hughes, Inc 1415
Turtle Beach Corp 1415
Tutor Perini Corp 1415
Tutor-saliba Corporation 1415
Twilio Inc 1415
Twin Cities Public Television, Inc. 1415
Twin County Community Foundation 1416
Twin Disc Incorporated 1416
Twin Vee Powercats Inc 1416
Twitter, Inc. 1416
Two Harbors Investment Corp 1416
Tyler Technologies, Inc. 1416
Tyndale House Publishers, Inc. 1417
Tyson Foods Inc 1417
U-haul Holding Co 1417
U-swirl Inc. 1417
U.g.n., Inc. 1417
U.s. Equities Realty, Llc 1417
U.s. General Services Administration 1418
U.s. Geothermal Inc. 1418
U.s. Physical Therapy, Inc. 1418
U.s. Shipping Corp 1418
U.s. Venture, Inc. 1418
Uber Technologies Inc 1418
Uc Health, Llc. 1419
Uch-mhs 1419
Uci Medical Affiliates, Inc. 1419
Udr Inc 1419
Ufp Industries Inc 1419
Ufp Technologies Inc. 1419
Ugi Corp. 1420
Ukg Inc. 1420
Uline, Inc. 1420
Ulta Beauty Inc 1420
Ulta Salon, Cosmetics & Fragrance, Inc. 1420
Ultra Clean Holdings Inc 1420
Ultragenyx Pharmaceutical Inc 1421
Ultralife Corp 1421
Ultratech, Inc. 1421
Uluru Inc 1421
Umb Financial Corp 1421
Umh Properties Inc 1421
Unbound Inc 1422
Under Armour Inc 1422
Underwood Jewelers Corp. 1422
Underwriters Laboratories Inc. 1422
Unfi Grocers Distribution, Inc. 1422
Unico American Corp. 1422
Unidosus 1423
Unifi, Inc. 1423
Unifirst Corp 1423
Uniformed Services University Of The Health Sciences 1423
Unihealth Foundation 1423
Union Bank And Trust Company 1423
Union Bankshares, Inc. (morrisville, Vt) 1424
Union Carbide Corporation 1424
Union Health Service Inc 1424
Union Hospital, Inc. 1424
Union Of Concerned Scientists, Inc. 1424
Union Pacific Corp 1424
Union Pacific Railroad Co 1425
Unipro Foodservice, Inc. 1425
Uniroyal Global Engineered Products Inc 1425
Unisys Corp 1425
Unit Corp. 1425
Unitarian Universalist Association, Inc 1425
United Airlines Holdings Inc 1426
United Airlines, Inc. 1426
United Apple Sales, Llc 1426

United Bancorp, Inc. (martins Ferry, Oh) 1426
United Bancshares Inc. (oh) 1426
United Bankshares Inc 1426
United Brass Works, Inc. 1427
United Cerebral Palsy Associations Of New York State, Inc. 1427
United Community Banks Inc (blairsville, Ga) 1427
United Dairy Farmers, Inc 1427
United Dairymen Of Arizona 1427
United Electric Supply Company, Inc. 1427
United Farmers Cooperative 1428
United Fire Group, Inc. 1428
United Gilsonite Laboratories, Inc. 1428
United Hardware Distributing Co 1428
United Health Services Hospitals, Inc. 1428
United Health Services, Inc. 1428
United Maritime Group, Llc 1429
United Mine Workers Of America 1429
United Natural Foods Inc. 1429
United Negro College Fund, Inc. 1429
United Of Omaha Life Insurance Co. 1429
United Online, Inc. 1429
United Parcel Service Inc 1430
United Parks & Resorts Inc 1430
United Performing Arts Fund, Inc. 1430
United Refining Company 1430
United Regional Health Care System, Inc. 1430
United Rentals Inc 1430
United Security Bancshares (ca) 1431
United Services Automobile Association 1431
United Space Alliance, Llc 1431
United Stars, Inc. 1431
United States Antimony Corp. 1431
United States Beef Corporation 1431
United States Cellular Corp 1432
United States Fund For Unicef 1432
United States Golf Association, Inc. 1432
United States Holocaust Memorial Museum 1432
United States Lime & Minerals Inc. 1432
United States Olympic Committee Inc 1432
United States Parachute Association 1433
United States Soccer Federation, Inc. 1433
United States Sports Academy, Inc. 1433
United States Steel Corp. 1433
United States Sugar Corporation 1433
United States Telephone Association 1433
United States Tennis Association Incorporated 1434
United Surgical Partners International, Inc. 1434
United Therapeutics Corp 1434
United Way Worldwide 1434
United Wisconsin Grain Producers, Llc 1434
United-guardian, Inc. 1434
Unitedhealth Group Inc 1435
Unitek Global Services, Inc. 1435
Uniti Group Inc 1435
Unitil Corp 1435
Unity Bancorp, Inc. 1435
Universal Corp 1435
Universal Detection Technology 1436
Universal Display Corp 1436
Universal Electronics Inc. 1436
Universal Health Realty Income Trust 1436
Universal Health Services, Inc. 1436
Universal Insurance Holdings Inc 1436
Universal Logistics Holdings Inc 1437
Universal Manufacturing Co 1437
Universal Power Group, Inc. 1437
Universal Security Instruments, Inc. 1437
Universal Stainless & Alloy Products, Inc. 1437
Universal Technical Institute, Inc. 1437
Universal Wilde, Inc. 1438
Universities Of Wisconsin 1438
Universities Research Association Inc. 1438
University At Albany 1438
University Bancorp Inc. (mi) 1438
University Community Hospital, Inc. 1438
University Corporation For Atmospheric Research 1439

COMPANIES LISTED ALPHABETICALLY

University Health Care, Inc. 1439
University Health Services, Inc. 1439
University Health System Services Of Texas, Inc. 1439
University Health System, Inc. 1439
University Health Systems Of Eastern Carolina, Inc. 1439
University Hospitals Health System, Inc. 1440
University Medical Center Of Southern Nevada 1440
University Of Alaska System 1440
University Of Arizona 1440
University Of Arkansas System 1440
University Of California, Davis 1440
University Of California, Irvine 1441
University Of California, Los Angeles 1441
University Of California, Merced 1441
University Of California, Riverside, Alumni Association 1441
University Of California, San Diego 1441
University Of California, San Francisco 1441
University Of Cincinnati 1442
University Of Colorado Foundation 1442
University Of Colorado Hospital Foundation 1442
University Of Delaware 1442
University Of Denver 1442
University Of Detroit Mercy 1442
University Of Evansville 1443
University Of Florida 1443
University Of Georgia 1443
University Of Hawaii System 1443
University Of Houston System 1443
University Of Kentucky Hospital Auxiliary Inc. 1443
University Of La Verne 1444
University Of Louisville 1444
University Of Lynchburg 1444
University Of Maine Systems Inc 1444
University Of Maryland Medical System Corporation 1444
University Of Maryland St. Joseph Medical Center, Llc 1444
University Of Massachusetts Incorporated 1445
University Of Mississippi 1445
University Of Missouri System 1445
University Of Mobile, Inc. 1445
University Of Montana 1445
University Of New Haven, Incorporated 1445
University Of New Mexico 1446
University Of New Orleans 1446
University Of North Carolina At Chapel Hill 1446
University Of North Carolina At Greensboro 1446
University Of North Dakota 1446
University Of Northern Iowa 1446
University Of Oklahoma 1447
University Of Oregon 1447
University Of Pittsburgh-of The Commonwealth System Of Higher Education 1447
University Of Puget Sound 1447
University Of Redlands 1447
University Of Rhode Island 1447
University Of Richmond 1448
University Of San Diego 1448
University Of San Francisco Inc 1448
University Of Scranton 1448
University Of South Alabama 1448
University Of South Carolina 1448
University Of South Florida 1449
University Of Southern California 1449
University Of St. Thomas 1449
University Of Tennessee 1449
University Of Texas At Austin 1449
University Of Texas At Dallas 1449
University Of Texas At El Paso 1450
University Of Texas System 1450
University Of The Ozarks 1450
University Of The Pacific 1450
University Of Utah Health Hospitals And Clinics 1450
University Of Vermont & State Agricultural College 1450

University Of Washington Inc 1451
University Of West Georgia 1451
University Of Wisconsin Foundation 1451
University Of Wisconsin Hospitals And Clinics Authority 1451
University Of Wisconsin Medical Foundation, Inc. 1451
University Of Wyoming 1451
University System Of Maryland 1452
University System Of New Hampshire 1452
Univest Financial Corp 1452
Univision Communications Inc. 1452
Uniworld Group, Inc. 1452
Unmc Physicians 1452
Unum Group 1453
Upbound Group Inc 1453
Upmc 1453
Upmc Altoona 1453
Upmc Children's Hospital Of Pittsburgh 1453
Upmc Pinnacle 1453
Upp Technology, Inc. 1454
Upper Chesapeake Health Foundation, Inc. 1454
Upson County Hospital, Inc. 1454
Upstate Medical University 1454
Uqm Technologies, Inc. 1454
Urata & Sons Concrete, Inc. 1454
Urban Affairs Coalition 1455
Urban Edge Properties 1455
Urban One Inc 1455
Urban Outfitters, Inc. 1455
Ureach Technologies Inc 1455
Urm Stores, Inc. 1455
Urologix Inc. 1456
Us 1 Industries, Inc. 1456
Us Bancorp (de) 1456
Us China Mining Group Inc 1456
Us Dairy Export Council 1456
Us Energy Corp 1456
Us Foods Holding Corp 1457
Us Foods, Inc. 1457
Us Global Investors Inc 1457
Us Gold Corp (canada) 1457
Us Premium Beef Llc 1457
Us Silica Holdings, Inc. 1457
Us Stem Cell Inc 1458
Us Venture Partners Iii Llc 1458
Usa Environmental Management, Inc. 1458
Usa Hockey, Inc. 1458
Usa Track & Field, Inc. 1458
Usa Truck, Inc. 1458
Usana Health Sciences Inc 1459
Usc Arcadia Hospital 1459
Usfalcon, Inc. 1459
Usg Corporation 1459
Ushio America, Inc. 1459
Usio Inc 1459
Uss-upi, Llc 1460
Ut Medical Group, Inc. 1460
Utah Associated Municipal Power Systems 1460
Utah Medical Products, Inc. 1460
Utah State University 1460
Utg Inc 1460
Utica College 1461
Utilities Telecom Council 1461
Uva Prince William Health System 1461
Uwharrie Capital Corp. 1461
Uwink Inc. Delaware 1461
Vaalco Energy, Inc. 1461
Vail Resorts Inc 1462
Valdosta State University 1462
Valence Technology, Inc. 1462
Valero Energy Corp 1462
Valhi, Inc. 1462
Valley Health System 1462
Valley Health System Llc 1463
Valley Health System Llc 1463
Valley Health System, Inc. 1463
Valley Home & Community Health Care Inc 1463

Valley National Bancorp (nj) 1463
Valley View Community Unit School District 365u 1463
Valmont Industries Inc 1464
Value Drug Company 1464
Value Line Inc 1464
Valvoline Inc 1464
Van Atlas Lines Inc 1464
Van Budd Lines Inc 1464
Van Horn Metz & Co., Inc. 1465
Vanda Pharmaceuticals Inc 1465
Vanderbilt University Medical Center 1465
Vantage Drilling Co 1465
Vantage Drilling International 1465
Vantage Group Inc 1465
Varex Imaging Corp 1466
Variety Children's Hospital 1466
Varonis Systems, Inc 1466
Vartech Systems, Inc. 1466
Vasamed Inc 1466
Vaso Corp 1466
Vasquez & Company Llp 1467
Vassar College 1467
Vaughan Furniture Company, Incorporated 1467
Vaughan-bassett Furniture Company, Incorporated 1467
Vaxart Inc 1467
Vbi Vaccines (delaware) Inc. 1467
Vca Inc. 1468
Vcom3d, Inc. 1468
Vecellio & Grogan, Inc. 1468
Vector Group Ltd 1468
Vector Pipeline L.p. 1468
Vectra Co. 1468
Veeco Instruments Inc (de) 1469
Veeva Systems Inc 1469
Venoco, Llc 1469
Ventas Inc 1469
Ventera Corporation 1469
Venture Construction Company Inc 1469
Vera Bradley Inc. 1470
Veracyte Inc 1470
Veradigm Inc 1470
Verastem Inc 1470
Vericast Corp. 1470
Vericel Corp 1470
Verifone Systems, Inc. 1471
Verifyme Inc 1471
Verint Systems Inc 1471
Veris Residential Inc 1471
Verisign Inc 1471
Verisk Analytics Inc 1471
Veriteq Corp 1472
Verizon Communications Inc 1472
Vermeer Manufacturing Company 1472
Versant Power 1472
Versar, Inc. 1472
Verst Group Logistics, Inc. 1472
Vertex Inc 1473
Vertex Pharmaceuticals, Inc. 1473
Vertical Communications, Inc. 1473
Vertical Computer Systems, Inc. 1473
Vertiv Holdings Co 1473
Veru Inc 1473
Vesco Oil Corporation 1474
Vestar Capital Partners, Inc. 1474
Veterans Of Foreign Wars Of The United States 1474
Vf Corp. 1474
Vhs Acquisition Subsidiary Number 3, Inc. 1474
Vhs Of Illinois, Inc. 1474
Via Renewables Inc 1475
Viad Corp. 1475
Viasat Inc 1475
Viavi Solutions Inc 1475
Vibrantz Corporation 1475
Vicor Corp 1475
Victorias Secret & Co 1476

Victory Packaging, L.p. 1476
Victory Screen Printing, Inc. 1476
Video Display Corp 1476
Videon Central, Inc. 1476
Vietnam Veterans Of America, Inc. 1476
View Systems, Inc. 1477
Viewcast.com Inc. 1477
Viewsonic Corporation 1477
Vifor Pharma, Inc. 1477
Viking Yacht Company 1477
Village Bank & Trust Financial Corp 1477
Village Super Market, Inc. 1478
Villanova University In The State Of Pennsylvania 1478
Vince Holding Corp 1478
Vining-sparks Ibg, Limited Partnership 1478
Vino.com, L.l.c. 1478
Viper Energy Inc 1478
Vira Manufacturing Inc 1479
Viracta Therapeutics Inc 1479
Virbac Corporation 1479
Virco Manufacturing Corp. 1479
Virgin America Inc. 1479
Virginia Commonwealth University 1479
Virginia Electric & Power Co. 1480
Virginia Hospital Center Arlington Health System 1480
Virginia Housing Development Authority 1480
Virginia International Terminals, Llc 1480
Virginia Military Institute 1480
Virginia Polytechnic Institute & State University 1480
Viridian Therapeutics Inc 1481
Virnetx Holding Corp 1481
Virtra Inc 1481
Virtu Financial Inc 1481
Virtua Memorial Hospital Burlington County, Inc 1481
Virtua Our Lady Of Lourdes Hospital, Inc. 1481
Virtual Enterprises, Inc. 1482
Virtualscopics, Inc. 1482
Virtus Investment Partners Inc 1482
Virtusa Corporation 1482
Visa Inc 1482
Vishay Intertechnology, Inc. 1482
Vishay Precision Group Inc. 1483
Visionworks Of America, Inc. 1483
Visiting Nurse Service Of New York 1483
Vista Gold Corp 1483
Vista International Technologies Inc 1483
Vista Outdoor Inc 1483
Visteon Corp 1484
Vistra Corp 1484
Vistronix, Llc 1484
Vita Food Products, Inc. 1484
Vitalant 1484
Vitalsmarts, Lc 1484
Viveve Medical Inc 1485
Vizio Holding Corp 1485
Vizio, Inc. 1485
Vjs Construction Services, Inc. 1485
Volt Information Sciences Inc 1485
Volunteer Bancorp, Inc. 1485
Volunteer Energy Cooperative 1486
Volunteers Of America, Inc. 1486
Von Maur, Inc. 1486
Vonage Holdings Corp. 1486
Vontier Corp 1486
Vornado Realty L.p. 1486
Vornado Realty Trust 1487
Voxware, Inc. 1487
Voxx International Corp 1487
Voyager Digital Ltd 1487
Voyager Entertainment International Inc 1487
Vratsinas Construction Company 1487
Vroom Automotive Finance Corporation 1488
Vroom Inc 1488
Vse Corp. 1488

Vsoft Corporation 1488
Vtv Therapeutics Inc 1488
Vu1 Corp 1488
Vulcan International Corp. 1489
Vulcan Materials Co (holding Company) 1489
Vuzix Corp 1489
Vwr Corporation 1489
Vyant Bio Inc 1489
Vydrotech Inc 1489
Vystar Corp 1490
W & T Offshore Inc 1490
W World Corp 1490
W. C. Bradley Co. 1490
W. E. Aubuchon Co., Inc. 1490
W. K. Kellogg Foundation 1490
W. L. Butler Construction, Inc. 1491
W. M. Keck Foundation 1491
W. R. Grace & Co. 1491
W. Thomas Co. 1491
W.j. Deutsch & Sons Ltd. 1491
W.m.jordan Company, Incorporated 1491
W.p. Carey Inc 1492
W.s. Badcock Llc 1492
Wabash College 1492
Wabash County Hospital 1492
Wabash National Corp 1492
Wabash Power Equipment Co. 1492
Wabco Holdings Inc. 1493
Wada Farms Marketing Group Llc 1493
Wadley Regional Medical Center 1493
Wafd Inc 1493
Wagner Industries, Llc 1493
Wahl Clipper Corporation 1493
Wake Forest University 1494
Wake Forest University Baptist Medical Center 1494
Wakefern Food Corp. 1494
Wakemed 1494
Walgreens Boots Alliance Inc 1494
Walker & Dunlop Inc 1494
Walker Die Casting, Inc. 1495
Walmart Inc 1495
Walsh & Associates, Inc. 1495
Walsh Brothers, Incorporated 1495
Walter Energy, Inc. 1495
Walters-dimmick Petroleum, Inc. 1495
Walton & Post, Inc. 1496
Walton Electric Membership Corporation 1496
War Memorial Hospital, Inc. 1496
Ward Trucking, Llc 1496
Warner Bros Discovery Inc 1496
Warner Media, Llc 1496
Warner Music Group Corp 1497
Warren Resources Inc (md) 1497
Warren Rural Electric Cooperative Corporation 1497
Warrior Met Coal Inc 1497
Washington Hospital Center Corporation 1497
Washington Legal Foundation 1497
Washington Metropolitan Area Transit Authority 1498
Washington Regional Medical Center 1498
Washington Sports & Entertainment, Inc. 1498
Washington Suburban Sanitary Commission (inc) 1498
Washington Trust Bancorp, Inc. 1498
Waste Connections Us, Inc. 1498
Waste Control Specialists Llc 1499
Waste Management, Inc. (de) 1499
Waterfurnace Renewable Energy Inc 1499
Waters Corp. 1499
Watkins And Shepard Trucking, Inc. 1499
Watkins Associated Industries, Inc. 1499
Watonwan Farm Service, Inc 1500
Watsco Inc. 1500
Watts Water Technologies Inc 1500
Waukesha Memorial Hospital, Inc. 1500
Waukesha-pearce Industries, Llc 1500
Wausau Financial Systems, Inc. 1500

Wausau Paper Corp. 1501
Wavedancer Inc 1501
Waxman Industries Inc. 1501
Wayfair Inc 1501
Wayland Baptist University Inc 1501
Wayne J. Griffin Electric, Inc. 1501
Wayne Memorial Health System, Inc. 1502
Wayne Savings Bancshares Inc 1502
Wayne State University 1502
Wbi Energy Transmission, Inc 1502
Wci Communities, Inc. 1502
Wd-40 Co 1502
Weatherford International Plc 1503
Weaver Popcorn Manufacturing, Llc 1503
Web.com Group, Inc. 1503
Webasto Roof Systems Inc. 1503
Webb Chemical Service Corporation 1503
Webco Industries Inc. 1503
Weber Distribution, Llc 1504
Weber State University 1504
Webmd Health Corp. 1504
Webster Financial Corp (waterbury, Conn) 1504
Webster Preferred Capital Corp. 1504
Webster University 1504
Wec Energy Group Inc 1505
Wedbush Securities Inc. 1505
Weeks Marine, Inc. 1505
Wegener Corp. 1505
Wegmans Food Markets, Inc. 1505
Weirton Medical Center, Inc. 1505
Weis Markets, Inc. 1506
Welbilt, Inc. 1506
Welch Foods Inc., A Cooperative 1506
Wellesley College 1506
Wellex Corporation 1506
Wellmont Health System 1506
Wellsky Corporation 1507
Wellstar Health System, Inc. 1507
Welltower Inc 1507
Wendy's Co (the) 1507
Werner Enterprises, Inc. 1507
Wesbanco Inc 1507
Wesco Aircraft Holdings, Inc. 1508
Wesco International, Inc. 1508
Wesleyan University 1508
Wessco International Ltd., A California Limited Partnership 1508
West Bancorporation, Inc. 1508
West Central Cooperative 1508
West Coast Novelty Corporation 1509
West Marine, Inc. 1509
West Pharmaceutical Services, Inc. 1509
West Technology Group, Llc 1509
West Texas Gas, Inc. 1509
West Virginia University Hospitals, Inc. 1509
West Virginia United Health System, Inc. 1510
West Virginia University 1510
West Virginia University Foundation, Incorporated 1510
Westamerica Bancorporation 1510
Westat, Inc. 1510
Westbridge Research Group 1510
Westech Capital Corp 1511
Westell Technologies Inc 1511
Western & Southern Financial Group, Inc 1511
Western Alliance Bancorporation 1511
Western Connecticut Health Network, Inc. 1511
Western Construction Group, Inc. 1511
Western Digital Corp 1512
Western Farmers Electric Cooperative 1512
Western Fuels Association, Inc. 1512
Western Illinois University Inc 1512
Western Magnesium Corp 1512
Western Massachusetts Electric Co. 1512
Western Michigan University 1513
Western Midstream Partners Lp 1513
Western New England Bancorp Inc 1513
Western Pennsylvania Hospital 1513

COMPANIES LISTED ALPHABETICALLY

Western Refining Logistics, Lp 1513
Western Refining, Inc. 1513
Western Summit Constructors, Inc. 1514
Western Switches And Controls Inc. 1514
Western Union Co 1514
Western Washington University 1514
Western Wyoming Community College District 1514
Westinghouse Lighting Corporation 1514
Westlake Chlor-vinyls Corporation 1515
Westlake Corp 1515
Westminster Manor 1515
Westminster University 1515
Westmoreland Resource Partners Lp 1515
Westrock Co 1515
Westrock Company 1516
Westrock Paper And Packaging, Llc 1516
Westside Family Health Center 1516
Westwater Resources Inc 1516
Westwood Group Inc (the) 1516
Westwood Holdings Group, Inc. 1516
Wework Inc 1517
Wex Inc 1517
Wexford Health Sources, Inc. 1517
Weyco Group, Inc 1517
Weyerhaeuser Co 1517
Wgbh Educational Foundation 1517
Wgl Holdings, Inc. 1518
Wgnb Corp. 1518
Whalley Computer Associates, Inc. 1518
Wheaton College 1518
Wheaton Franciscan Services, Inc. 1518
Wheaton Van Lines Inc 1518
Wheeler Real Estate Investment Trust Inc 1519
Wheeling & Lake Erie Railway Company 1519
Wheeling-nippon Steel, Inc. 1519
Whirlpool Corp 1519
White Castle System, Inc. 1519
White County Medical Center 1519
White Memorial Medical Center Inc 1520
White River Health System, Inc. 1520
Whitehead Institute For Biomedical Research 1520
Whitestone Reit 1520
Whitman College 1520
Whitney Museum Of American Art 1520
Whole Foods Market, Inc. 1521
Wholesale Supply Group, Inc. 1521
Whyy, Inc. 1521
Wichita State University 1521
Wichita, City Of (inc) 1521
Widener University 1521
Wideopenwest Inc 1522
Widepoint Corp 1522
Wikimedia Foundation, Inc. 1522
Wikoff Color Corporation 1522
Wilbur Smith Associates, Inc. 1522
Wilbur-ellis Holdings Ii, Inc. 1522
Wildlife Conservation Society 1523
Wiley (john) & Sons Inc. 1523
Wilhelm Construction, Inc. 1523
Wilhelmina International, Inc. 1523
Wilkes-barre Hospital Company, Llc 1523
Wilkinson-cooper Produce Inc 1523
Will County 1524
Willamette University 1524
Willamette Valley Vineyard Inc. 1524
Willbros Group, Inc. 1524
Willdan Group Inc 1524
William Beaumont Hospital 1524
William Blair & Company Llc 1525
William Marsh Rice University Inc 1525
William Paterson University 1525
Williams Industrial Services Group Inc 1525
Williams Partners L.p. 1525
Williams Sausage Company, Inc. 1525
Williams Scotsman Inc 1526
Williams Sonoma Inc 1526
Willis Lease Finance Corp. 1526

Wilmer Cutler Pickering Hale And Dorr Llp 1526
Wilshire Enterprises, Inc. 1526
Wilson Sonsini Goodrich & Rosati, Professional Corporation 1526
Wilson Trucking Corporation 1527
Winchester Healthcare Management, Inc. 1527
Winchester Medical Center Auxiliary, Inc. 1527
Winco Foods, Llc 1527
Window To The World Communications, Inc. 1527
Windsor Distributing, Inc. 1527
Windstream Bv Holdings, Llc 1528
Windstream Holdings, Inc. 1528
Windtree Therapeutics Inc 1528
Windward Consulting Group, Inc. 1528
Wine & Spirits Wholesalers Of America, Inc. 1528
Winland Holdings Corp 1528
Winmark Corp 1529
Winnebago Industries, Inc. 1529
Winston & Strawn Llp 1529
Winter Haven Hospital, Inc. 1529
Winter Sports Inc 1529
Winthrop Nyu Hospital 1529
Winthrop Realty Liquidating Trust 1530
Wintrust Financial Corp (il) 1530
Wireless Xcessories Group, Inc. 1530
Wisconsin Gas Llc 1530
Wisconsin Power And Light Co 1530
Wisetech Global (us) Inc. 1530
Withlacoochee River Electric Cooperative Inc 1531
Wixon Inc. 1531
Wm. Wrigley Jr. Company 1531
Woc, Inc. 1531
Wolf Creek Nuclear Operating Corporation 1531
Wolf Energy Services Inc 1531
Wolfspeed Inc 1532
Wolverine Pipe Line Company 1532
Wolverine Power Supply Cooperative, Inc. 1532
Wolverine World Wide, Inc. 1532
Womack Publishing Company, Inc. 1532
Woman's Hospital Foundation Inc 1532
Women & Childrens Hospital Llc 1533
Woods Hole, Martha's Vineyard And Nantucket Steamship Authority 1533
Woodstock Holdings Inc 1533
Woodward, Inc. 1533
Woolrich, Inc. 1533
Workday Inc 1533
Workforcelogic Llc 1534
Workman Publishing Co. Inc. 1534
World Acceptance Corp. 1534
World Business Chicago 1534
World Finer Foods, Llc 1534
World Kinect Corp 1534
World Point Terminals, Lp 1535
World Surveillance Group Inc 1535
World Vision International 1535
World Wide Technology, Llc 1535
World Wildlife Fund, Inc. 1535
World Wrestling Entertainment, Llc 1535
World's Finest Chocolate, Inc. 1536
Worldwide Media Services Group Inc. 1536
Worldwide Travel Staffing Ltd 1536
Worth Group, Architects, A Professional Corporation 1536
Worthington Enterprises Inc 1536
Wqn Inc 1536
Wright Investors' Service Holdings, Inc. 1537
Wright Medical Group, Inc. 1537
Wright State University 1537
Writers Guild Of America West, Inc. 1537
Wsfs Financial Corp 1537
Wso2 Llc 1537
Wsp Flack + Kurtz, Inc. 1538
Wta Tour, Inc. 1538
Wvs Financial Corp. 1538
Ww International Inc 1538
Wyckoff Heights Medical Center 1538
Wynalda Litho, Inc. 1538

Wynn Resorts Ltd 1539
Wyoming Medical Center, Inc. 1539
Wyse Advertising, Inc. 1539
X Prize Foundation, Inc. 1539
Xavier University 1539
Xcel Energy Inc 1539
Xencor, Inc 1540
Xenonics Holdings Inc 1540
Xenoport, Inc. 1540
Xerox Credit Corp. 1540
Xerox Holdings Corp 1540
Xo Group Inc. 1540
Xo Holdings, Inc 1541
Xoma Corp 1541
Xoriant Corporation 1541
Xplore Technologies Corp. 1541
Xpo Inc 1541
Xponential, Inc. 1541
Xtant Medical Holdings Inc 1542
Xtera Communications Inc 1542
Xwell Inc 1542
Xylem Inc 1542
Yahoo Inc. 1542
Yakima Valley Memorial Hospital Association Inc 1542
Yale New Haven Health Services Corporation 1543
Yale New Haven Hospital, Inc. 1543
Yale University 1543
Yankee Publishing Incorporated 1543
Yash Technologies, Inc. 1543
Yates Group, Inc. 1543
Yavapai County Community College District 1544
Yellow Corp (new) 1544
Yelp Inc 1544
Yeo & Yeo, P.c. 1544
Yeshiva University 1544
Yeti Holdings Inc 1544
Yext Inc 1545
Yield10 Bioscience Inc 1545
Yoakum Community Hospital 1545
York Hospital 1545
York Pennsylvania Hospital Company Llc 1545
York Water Co 1545
Young Broadcasting, Llc 1546
Young Electric Sign Company Inc 1546
Young Life 1546
Youngs Nurseries Incorporated 1546
Youngstown State University Inc 1546
Yum China Holdings Inc 1546
Yum! Brands Inc 1547
Yuma Energy Inc (new) 1547
Yuma Regional Medical Center Inc 1547
Yume, Inc. 1547
Yunhong Green Cti Ltd 1547
Ywca Of The Usa, National Board (inc) 1547
Z Gallerie, Llc 1548
Z Pizza Inc 1548
Zachary Confections, Inc. 1548
Zagg Inc 1548
Zanett, Inc. 1548
Zap 1548
Zayo Group Holdings, Inc. 1549
Zaza Energy Corp. 1549
Zebra Technologies Corp. 1549
Zeeland Community Hospital 1549
Zeltiq Aesthetics, Inc. 1549
Zendesk, Inc. 1549
Zenith Energy Logistics Partners Lp 1550
Zerify Inc 1550
Zero Mountain, Inc. 1550
Zhejiang Dashang Media Co Ltd 1550
Ziegler Cos., Inc. (wi) 1550
Ziegler Inc 1550
Ziff Davis Inc 1551
Zimmer Biomet Holdings Inc 1551
Zimmer Gunsul Frasca Architects Llp 1551
Zinkan Enterprises, Inc. 1551
Zion Oil & Gas Inc 1551

Zions Bancorporation, N.a. 1551
Zoetis Inc 1552
Zoological Society Of San Diego 1552
Zoom Video Communications Inc 1552
Zoomaway Technologies Inc 1552
Zoominfo Technologies Inc 1552
Zovio Inc 1552
Zumiez Inc 1553
Zurn Elkay Water Solutions Corp 1553
Zvelo Inc. 1553
Zyla Life Sciences, Llc 1553

Index by Headquarters

ALABAMA

Andalusia
Powersouth Energy Cooperative 1073

Auburn
Auburn National Bancorp, Inc. 137
Auburn University 137

Birmingham
Alabama Power Co 39
American Cast Iron Pipe Company 70
Associated Grocers Of The South, Inc. 126
B. L. Harbert International, L.l.c. 150
Big Jack Ultimate Holdings Lp 179
Birmingham-southern College Inc 184
Books-a-million, Inc. 198
Brasfield & Gorrie, L.l.c. 205
Bromberg & Company, Inc. 212
City Of Birmingham 300
Consolidated Pipe & Supply Company, Inc. 352
Doster Construction Company, Inc. 423
Encompass Health Corp 465
First Us Bancshares Inc 525
Golden Enterprises, Inc. 584
Hibbett Inc 638
Mayer Electric Supply Company, Inc. 847
Medical Properties Trust Inc 855
O'neal Steel, Llc 983
Proassurance Corp 1086
Protective Life Insurance Co 1092
Protective Life Insurance Co. (birmingham, Ala.) 1092
Protective Life Insurance Company 1092
Regions Financial Corp (new) 1128
Servisfirst Bancshares Inc 1199
Southern Research Institute 1240
Spire Alabama Inc. 1248
Steris Instrument Management Services, Inc. 1273
The Water Works Board Of The City Of Birmingham 1378
Tractor & Equipment Company Inc 1396

Vulcan Materials Co (holding Company) 1489
Walter Energy, Inc. 1495

Brookwood
Warrior Met Coal Inc 1497

Daphne
United States Sports Academy, Inc. 1433

Decatur
Alabama Farmers Cooperative, Inc. 39
Municipal Utilities Board Of Decatur, Morgan County, Alabama 915

Dothan
Aaa Cooper Transportation 7
Houston County Healthcare Authority 657

Fairfield
Miles College, Inc. 885

Florence
Shoals Provision, Inc. 1206

Gadsden
Gadsden Regional Medical Center, Llc 556
Southern Banc Co., Inc. 1235

Hoover
Hanna Steel Corporation 615
Influence Health, Inc. 689
Southern Nuclear Operating Company, Inc. 1239

Hope Hull
Miltope Corporation 888

Huntsville
Adtran Holdings Inc 24
Colsa Corporation 335
Lakeland Industries, Inc. 774
Madison Huntsville County Airport Authority 823
Network Management Resources, Inc. 942
The City Of Huntsville 1337
The Health Care Authority Of The City Of Huntsville 1348

Irondale
Imaging Business Machines, L.l.c. 678

Jasper
Pinnacle Bancshares, Inc. 1057

Mobile
Alabama State Port Authority 40
International Shipholding Corporation 707
Spring Hill College 1250
Trubridge Inc 1408
University Of Mobile, Inc. 1445
University Of South Alabama 1448

Montgomery
Calhoun Enterprises, Inc. 229
City Of Montgomery 307
Dept Of Education Alabama 406
Jackson Hospital & Clinic, Inc. 725
Sabel Steel Service, Inc. 1162
The Southern Poverty Law Center Inc 1369

Muscle Shoals
Johnson Contractors, Inc. 738

Opelika
East Alabama Health Care Authority 439

Rainsville
Farmers Telecommunications Cooperative, Inc. 502

Red Bay
Tiffin Motor Homes, Inc. 1385

Troy
Troy University 1408

Tuscaloosa
The Dch Health Care Authority 1341
The University Of Alabama System 1373

ALASKA

Anchorage
Alaska Communications Systems Group, Inc. 41
Alaska Conservation Foundation 41
Alaska Native Tribal Health Consortium 41
Alaska Railroad Corporation 41
Alyeska Pipeline Service Company 62
Anchorage, Municipality Of (inc) 93
Arctic Slope Regional Corporation 110

Chenega Corporation 277
Chugach Alaska Corporation 289
Chugach Electric Association, Inc. 289
First National Bank Alaska 523
Northrim Bancorp Inc 973
Petro Star Inc. 1049

Fairbanks
University Of Alaska System 1440

Homer
South Peninsula Hospital, Inc. 1233

Juneau
Sealaska Corporation 1190

Palmer
Matanuska Telecom Association, Incorporated 843

ARIZONA

Chandler
City Of Chandler 301
Earnhardt Management Company 438
Everspin Technologies Inc 489
Insight Enterprises Inc. 695
Microchip Technology Inc 878
Rogers Corp. 1151
Sun Eagle Corporation 1285
Viavi Solutions Inc 1475
Virtra Inc 1481
Zovio Inc 1552

Flagstaff
Flagstaff Medical Center, Inc. 527
Northern Arizona Healthcare Corporation 970
Northern Arizona University 970

Glendale
City Of Glendale 304

Mesa
City Of Mesa 307
Empire Southwest, Llc 463
Mitel Networks, Inc. 894

Paradise Valley
Imh Financial Corporation 679
The New Home Company Inc 1360

Peoria
City Of Peoria 309

HOOVER'S MASTERLIST OF U.S. COMPANIES 2024

INDEX BY HEADQUARTERS LOCATION

Phoenix
Apollo Education Group, Inc. 101
Arizona Professional Baseball Lp 112
Arizona Public Service Co. 112
Avnet Inc 147
Banner Health 157
Best Western International, Inc. 176
Blue Cross And Blue Shield Of Arizona, Inc. 191
Cable One Inc 225
Cavco Industries Inc (de) 257
City Of Phoenix 310
Core Construction, Inc. 358
Dbm Global Inc 396
Drivetime Automotive Group Inc 426
Edgio Inc 447
Ewing Irrigation Products, Inc. 491
Freeport-mcmoran Inc 547
Grand Canyon Education Inc 592
Gutierrez-palmenberg, Inc. 609
Innsuites Hospitality Trust 693
John C. Lincoln Health Network 735
Kitchell Corporation 759
Knight Transportation, Inc. 761
Knight-swift Transportation Holdings Inc 761
Linkmont Technologies, Inc. 800
Make-a-wish Foundation Of America 826
Mercy Care 862
Mesa Air Group Inc 867
Native Environmental, L.l.c. 934
O.p.e.n. America, Inc. 984
Phoenix Children's Hospital, Inc. 1053
Pinnacle West Capital Corp 1057
Republic Services Inc 1133
Roofing Wholesale Co., Inc. 1152
Shamrock Foods Company 1202
Snell & Wilmer L.l.p. 1224
Sprouts Farmers Market Inc 1251
Suns Legacy Partners, L.l.c. 1288
Universal Technical Institute, Inc. 1437
Western Alliance Bancorporation 1511

Prescott
Yavapai County Community College District 1544

Prescott Valley
Prescott Aerospace, Inc. 1078

Scottsdale
1399 Internet Technology Application Group Inc 2
Alanco Technologies Inc 41
Alcor Life Extension Foundation 44
Av Homes, Inc. 142
Axon Enterprise Inc 148
Carlisle Companies Inc. 247
Egpi Firecreek Inc 450
Gadsden Properties Inc 556
Giga-tronics Inc 575
Higher One Holdings, Inc. 640
Honorhealth Ambulatory 651
Meritage Homes Corp 865
On Semiconductor Corp 998
Reliance Inc 1130
Resideo Technologies Inc 1135
Star Buffet, Inc. 1266
Supershuttle International, Inc. 1291
Taylor Morrison Home Corp (holding Co) 1308
Taylor Morrison Home Corporation 1308
Tpi Composites Inc 1395
Viad Corp. 1475
Vitalant 1484

Scottsdale
Universal Electronics Inc. 1436

Tempe
Align Technology Inc 47
Amkor Technology Inc. 89
Amtech Systems, Inc. 92
Arizona State University 113
Benchmark Electronics, Inc. 171
Carvana Co 251
Crexendo Inc 372
First Solar Inc 525
Gen Digital Inc 562
Godaddy Inc 583
Mach 1 Global Services, Inc. 821
Maxx Sports Tv Inc 847
Medaire Inc 854
Northern Tier Energy Lp 972
Opendoor Technologies Inc 1002
Salt River Project Agricultural Improvement And Power District 1170
The Sundt Companies Inc 1369
United Dairymen Of Arizona 1427

Tolleson
Russell Sigler, Inc. 1160

Tucson
Accelerate Diagnostics Inc 12
Applied Energetics Inc 104
Asarco Llc 121
Association Of Universities For Research In Astronomy, Inc. 128
Auto Brakes, Inc. 140
Banner-university Medical Center Tucson Campus Llc 157
City Of Tucson 314
R & R Products, Inc. 1111
The University Of Arizona Foundation 1373
Tucson Electric Power Company 1413
University Of Arizona 1440

Yuma
Yuma Regional Medical Center Inc 1547

ARKANSAS

Batesville
Lyon College 818
White River Health System, Inc. 1520

Benton
Saline Memorial Hospital Auxiliary 1169

Bentonville
Walmart Inc 1495

Blytheville
Mississippi County Electric Cooperative, Inc. 892

Brinkley
Specialty Rice, Inc. 1246

Clarksville
University Of The Ozarks 1450

Conway
Conway Regional Medical Center, Inc. 356
Home Bancshares Inc 650

El Dorado
Anthony Forest Products Company, Llc 98
Murphy Usa Inc 916

Fayetteville
Ozarks Electric Cooperative Corporation 1016
Washington Regional Medical Center 1498

Fort Smith
Abf Freight System, Inc. 10
Arcbest Corp 108
Forth Smith Hma, Llc 538
Zero Mountain, Inc. 1550

Holiday Island
Holiday Island Holdings Inc 648

Hot Springs
Saint Joseph's Hospital Inc 1167

Jacksonville
First Electric Co-operative Corporation 520

Jonesboro
Arkansas State University 114
E. C. Barton & Company 436

Little Rock
Arkansas Children's Hospital 113
Arkansas Electric Cooperative Corp. 113
Arkansas Heart Hospital, Llc 113
Bank Ozk 156
Baptist Health 157
Cdi Contractors, Llc 259
Dac Technologies Group International Inc. 387
Dillard's Inc. 414
Entergy Arkansas Llc 473
Heifer Project International Inc 630
Inuvo Inc 711
Replacement Parts, Inc. 1132
St. Vincent Health Services, Inc. 1261
Stephens Inc. 1272
Uniti Group Inc 1435
University Of Arkansas System 1440
Vratsinas Construction Company 1487
Windstream Bv Holdings, Llc 1528
Windstream Holdings, Inc. 1528

Lowell
Hunt (j.b.) Transport Services, Inc. 662

Mountain Home
Baxter County Regional Hospital, Inc. 162

North Little Rock
Bruce Oakley, Inc. 216
Tenenbaum Recycling Group, Llc 1317

Pine Bluff
Jefferson Hospital Association, Inc. 731
Simmons First National Corp 1211

Rogers
America's Car-mart Inc 66
Cooper Communities, Inc. 356
New Creature Holdings, Inc. 945

Russellville
Arkansas Tech University 114

Searcy
White County Medical Center 1519

Siloam Springs
John Brown University 735

Springdale
H.c. Schmieding Produce Company, Llc 611
Moistureshield Inc. 898
Tyson Foods Inc 1417

Stuttgart
Producers Rice Mill, Inc. 1086
Riceland Foods, Inc. 1141

Tontitown
P.a.m. Transportation Services, Inc. 1016

Van Buren
Usa Truck, Inc. 1458

White Hall
Arkansas Department Of Corrections 113

CALIFORNIA

Agoura Hills
Oncotelic Therapeutics Inc 999
Paisano Publications, Llc 1020

Alameda
Exelixis Inc 492
Penumbra Inc 1042
West Coast Novelty Corporation 1509

Alhambra
Emcore Corp. 460

Aliso Viejo
Clarient, Inc. 317

Alviso
Tivo Solutions Inc. 1388

Anaheim
Ahmc Anaheim Regional Medical Center Lp 36
Angels Baseball Lp 95
City Of Anaheim 298
Eaco Corp 436
Pacific Sunwear Of California, Llc 1019
Willdan Group Inc 1524

Arcadia
Symvionics, Inc. 1297

INDEX BY HEADQUARTERS LOCATION

Usc Arcadia Hospital 1459
Atwater
  A.v. Thomas Produce, Inc. 7
  Global Diversified Industries, Inc. 579
Auburn
  Flyers Energy, Llc 532
Azusa
  Azusa Pacific University 149
Bakersfield
  Berry Petroleum Company, Llc 176
  Calcot, Ltd. 228
  City Of Bakersfield 299
  Jaco Oil Company 726
Belmont
  Ringcentral Inc 1143
Berkeley
  Andalay Solar Inc 93
  City Of Berkeley 299
  Vu1 Corp 1488
Beverly Hills
  Academy Of Motion Picture Arts & Sciences 11
  First Physicians Capital Group Inc 524
  Kennedy-wilson Holdings Inc 749
  Live Nation Entertainment Inc 803
  Participant Media, Llc 1029
  Reald Inc. 1121
  Universal Detection Technology 1436
Bishop
  Northern Inyo Healthcare District 971
Brea
  Kprs Construction Services, Inc. 766
  Viewsonic Corporation 1477
  Western Switches And Controls Inc. 1514
Brisbane
  Bi-rite Restaurant Supply Co., Inc. 178
  Caredx Inc 245
  Cutera Inc 382
  Gt Biopharma Inc 603
  Sangamo Therapeutics Inc 1176
Buena Park
  Tawa Supermarket, Inc. 1307
  Trim-lok Inc. 1404
Burbank
  Disney (walt) Co. (the) 416
  Eros Media World Plc 483
Burlingame
  Innoviva Inc 693
  Mills-peninsula Health Services 888
  Virgin America Inc. 1479
Calabasas
  Dts, Inc. 427
  Ixia 720
  Resonate Blends Inc 1135
  Unico American Corp. 1422
Calabasas Hills
  Cheesecake Factory Inc. (the) 276
Calexico
  Altar Produce, Llc 59

Camarillo
  Red Blossom Sales, Inc. 1123
  Semtech Corp. 1195
Campbell
  8x8 Inc 4
  Barracuda Networks, Inc. 160
  Chargepoint, Inc. 273
  Liveworld, Inc. 804
Cardiff
  Viracta Therapeutics Inc 1479
Carlsbad
  Alphatec Holdings Inc 57
  Bergelectric Corp. 173
  Breg, Inc. 207
  Brendan Technologies Inc 207
  Clarocity Corp 318
  Genmark Diagnostics, Inc. 568
  Ionis Pharmaceuticals Inc 713
  Lineage Cell Therapeutics Inc 799
  Maxlinear Inc 846
  National Association Of Music Merchants Inc. 923
  Natural Alternatives International, Inc. 934
  Palisade Bio Inc 1021
  Phoenix Footwear Group, Inc. 1053
  Sound Health Solutions Inc 1230
  Spy Inc. 1252
  Topgolf Callaway Brands Corp 1392
  Viasat Inc 1475
Carson
  Dermalogica, Llc 407
  The Salvation Army 1367
Chatsworth
  Mrv Communications, Inc. 911
Chico
  Ameramex International Inc 65
  Chico State Enterprises 281
  Fafco, Inc. 497
  Trico Bancshares (chico, Ca) 1404
Chula Vista
  City Of Chula Vista 301
  Community Health Group 342
  Hyspan Precision Products, Inc. 667
  Southwestern Community College District (inc) 1242
City Of Industry
  America Chung Nam (group) Holdings Llc 66
  International Building Technologies Group Inc 704
  Markwins Beauty Brands, Inc. 836
  Premio, Inc. 1077
  Swat.fame, Inc. 1295
Claremont
  Claremont Graduate University 316
  Claremont Mckenna College Foundation 317
  Harvey Mudd College 621
  Keck Graduate Institute Of Applied Life Sciences 747
  Pomona College 1067
  Scripps College 1187
  The Claremont Colleges Inc 1337
Colton
  Arrowhead Regional Medical Center 118

Commerce
  99 Cents Only Stores Llc 4
  Amexdrug Corp. 89
  Gibson Overseas, Inc. 574
  Smart Stores Operations Llc 1220
  Unfi Grocers Distribution, Inc. 1422
Concord
  Bay Cities Paving & Grading, Inc. 163
  Brenden Theatre Corporation 207
  Cerus Corp. 269
  Round Table Pizza, Inc. 1155
  Swinerton Builders 1295
Corona
  Index Fresh, Inc. 684
  Monster Beverage Corp (new) 901
Corona Del Mar
  Ecc Capital Corp 444
Corte Madera
  Rh 1140
Costa Mesa
  Chargers Football Company, Llc 273
  Charlies Holdings Inc 274
  Commerce Energy Group Inc 339
  El Pollo Loco Holdings Inc 452
  Experian Information Solutions, Inc. 494
Covina
  Emanate Health Medical Group 459
Culver City
  Westside Family Health Center 1516
  X Prize Foundation, Inc. 1539
Cupertino
  Affymax Inc 31
  Apple Inc 103
  Durect Corp 432
  Inventergy Global Inc 711
Cypress
  Ushio America, Inc. 1459
Davis
  Moller International Inc 898
  University Of California, Davis 1440
Del Mar
  Liquid Investments, Inc. 801
Diamond Bar
  First Mortgage Corp 523
Dixon
  First Northern Community Bancorp 524
Downey
  Rockview Dairies, Inc. 1150
Duarte
  Humangood Norcal 662
  Png Builders 1065
Dublin
  Ross Stores Inc 1154
  Trinet Group Inc. 1405
El Cajon
  Pure Bioscience Inc 1101
  Royale Energy Inc 1156
El Segundo
  A-mark Precious Metals, Inc 5

  Beachbody Co Inc (the) 165
  Belkin International, Inc. 169
  Big 5 Sporting Goods Corp 178
  Guthy-renker Llc 609
  Interdent, Inc. 701
  Mattel Inc 844
  Stamps.com Inc. 1264
  The Aerospace Corporation 1328
Emeryville
  Amyris Inc 92
  Clif Bar & Company, Llc 322
  Dynavax Technologies Corp 434
  Grocery Outlet Holding Corp 601
  Leapfrog Enterprises, Inc. 783
  Nmi Holdings Inc 960
  Novabay Pharmaceuticals Inc 977
  Tubemogul, Inc. 1413
  Xoma Corp 1541
Encino
  Netsol Technologies Inc 942
  Republic Indemnity Co. Of America 1133
Escondido
  California Center For The Arts, Escondido, Foundation 229
  E -pacific I Inc 435
  Gtc Systems Inc. 604
  One Stop Systems Inc 1000
  Palomar Health 1022
Fairfield
  Jelly Belly Candy Company 732
  Tpi Acquisition, Inc. 1395
Folsom
  California Independent System Operator Corporation 230
  Prism Technologies Group Inc 1084
  Workforcelogic Llc 1534
Fontana
  California Steel Industries, Inc. 233
  City Of Fontana 303
Fort Bragg
  Mendocino Coast District Hospital 860
  Thanksgiving Coffee Company, Inc. 1327
Foster City
  Aoxing Pharmaceutical Co Inc 98
  Geron Corp. 573
  Gilead Sciences Inc 576
  Qualys, Inc. 1107
  Quinstreet, Inc. 1110
  Sciclone Pharmaceuticals, Inc. 1185
Fountain Valley
  Memorial Health Services 858
Fremont
  Actelis Networks Inc 17
  Actividentity Corporation 18
  Aehr Test Systems 28
  Asi Computer Technologies Inc 124
  Axt Inc 148
  Biogenex Laboratories 182
  City Of Fremont 303
  Document Capture Technologies, Inc. 420

INDEX BY HEADQUARTERS LOCATION

Elma Electronic Inc. 458
Enphase Energy Inc. 471
Identiv Inc 672
Lam Research Corp 775
Mattson Technology, Inc. 845
Penguin Computing, Inc. 1039
Socket Mobile Inc 1225
Td Synnex Corp 1309
Wellex Corporation 1506

Fresno
California State University, Fresno 232
City Of Fresno 303
Community Hospitals Of Central California 343
Saint Agnes Medical Center 1165
Sun-maid Growers Of California 1286
United Security Bancshares (ca) 1431

Fullerton
Csu Fullerton Auxiliary Services Corporation 378
St. Jude Hospital 1259

Garden Grove
Microsemi Corporation 879
R. J. Daum Construction Company 1111
Southland Industries 1240

Gardena
Z Gallerie, Llc 1548

Gilroy
Christopher Ranch, Llc 287

Glendale
Bowtie, Inc. 202
City Of Glendale 304
Dwa Holdings, Llc 432
Glendale Adventist Medical Center Inc 578
Glendale Community College Dist 578
Hutchinson & Bloodgood Llp 665
Public Storage 1098
Vasquez & Company Llp 1467

Glendora
Citrus Community College District 296
Mcg-hjt, Inc. 850

Goleta
Community West Bancshares 344
Deckers Outdoor Corp. 399
Inogen, Inc 693

Hawthorne
Osi Systems, Inc. (de) 1011

Hayward
Anthera Pharmaceuticals Inc 98
California State University East Bay 231
Ultra Clean Holdings Inc 1420

Healdsburg
North Sonoma County Hospital District 968

Hercules
Bio-rad Laboratories Inc 180

Hermosa Beach
Encore Nationwide, Inc. 465

Huntington Beach
Bj's Restaurants Inc 185

Boardriders, Inc. 194
Reliable Wholesale Lumber, Inc. 1129

Imperial
Imperial Irrigation District 681

Inglewood
Marvin Engineering Co., Inc. 839
Signature Eyewear Inc. 1210

Irvine
Acme Communications, Inc. 16
Advantage Solutions Inc 26
Aeronet Worldwide, Inc. 29
Alliance Healthcare Services, Inc. 52
Alteryx, Inc. 59
Arbitech, Llc 107
Biomerica Inc 183
Bkf Capital Group Inc 185
Calamp Corp 228
California Coastal Communities, Inc. 230
Combimatrix Corporation 338
Edwards Lifesciences Corp 449
Emulex Corporation 464
Endologix, Inc. 466
Five Point Holdings Llc 527
Fox Head, Inc. 542
Gamefly Holdings, Llc 558
Gan Ltd 558
Golden State Foods Corp. 585
Humax Usa, Inc. 662
In-n-out Burgers 682
Ingram Micro Inc. 691
Interlink Electronics Inc 702
Lantronix Inc. 778
Local Corp 805
Masimo Corp. 841
Multi-fineline Electronix, Inc. 913
Netlist Inc 942
Newport Corporation 954
Pacific Dental Services, Llc 1018
Phi Group Inc. 1051
Pro-dex Inc. (co) 1085
Prudential Overall Supply 1095
Qlogic Llc 1105
Qualstar Corp 1107
Resources Connection Inc 1136
Riechesbaird, Inc. 1142
Sabra Health Care Reit Inc 1162
Simon Worldwide Inc. 1212
Skyworks Solutions Inc 1218
Smc Networks, Inc. 1221
Snyder Langston Holdings, Llc 1224
Spectrum Group International Inc 1247
Squar, Milner, Peterson, Miranda & Williamson, Certified Public Accountants, Llp 1252
St. Joseph Health System 1258
Steadfast Income Reit, Inc. 1270
Stussy, Inc. 1281
Trimedyne Inc 1405
Trivascular Technologies, Inc. 1407
University Of California, Irvine 1441
Vizio Holding Corp 1485
Vizio, Inc. 1485

Kentfield
Marin General Hospital 832

La Canada Flintridge
Allen Lund Company, Llc 50

La Jolla
Edgewave, Inc 446
Enterprise Partners Management, Llc 475
Institute Of The Americas 696
John F. Kennedy University 736
Medicinova Inc 855
Sanford Burnham Prebys Medical Discovery Institute 1176
The Scripps Research Institute 1368
University Of California, San Diego 1441

La Mesa
Grossmont Hospital Corporation 602

La Mirada
Biola University, Inc. 182

La Verne
University Of La Verne 1444

Lafayette
Jcm Partners, Llc 730

Laguna Beach
Z Pizza Inc 1548

Laguna Hills
Saddleback Memorial Medical Center 1163

Laguna Niguel
Comarco Inc. 337
I O Interconnect, Ltd. 667
Optimumcare Corp. 1004

Lake Forest
Aura Systems Inc 139
Biolase Inc 182
I/omagic Corporation 668
Liquidmetal Technologies Inc 801
Prism Software Corp. 1084
Qf Liquidation, Inc. 1104
Staar Surgical Co. 1262

Lancaster
Simulations Plus Inc 1212

Livermore
Formfactor Inc 537
G.s.e. Construction Company, Inc. 555
Mcgrath Rentcorp 850
Performant Financial Corp 1045

Lodi
Pacific Coast Producers 1018

Loma Linda
Loma Linda University 807
Loma Linda University Medical Center 808

Long Beach
Alameda Corridor Transportation Authority 40
California Resources Corp 231
California State University System 231
City Of Long Beach 306
K. V. Mart Co. 743
Long Beach Medical Center 808
Molina Healthcare Inc 898
Relax The Back Corporation 1129
Retirement Housing Foundation Inc 1137

The Kenneth T And Eileen L Norris Foundation 1352

Los Altos
The David And Lucile Packard Foundation 1341

Los Angeles
A.b.c. Home Furnishings, Inc. 6
Air Lease Corp 36
American Business Bank (los Angeles, Ca) 70
App Winddown, Llc 102
Ares Management Corp 111
Armata Pharmaceuticals Inc 114
Boingo Wireless, Inc. 196
Breitburn Energy Partners Lp 207
Broadway Financial Corp. (de) 211
Brookfield Oaktree Holdings Llc 213
Cadiz Inc 227
California Community Foundation 230
California State University, Los Angeles 232
California Wellness Foundation 233
Cannabis Global Inc 239
Cathay General Bancorp 255
Cha Hollywood Medical Center Lp 270
Chromadex Corp 288
City Of Los Angeles 306
Colony Capital, Inc. 332
Compumed Inc 345
County Of Los Angeles 365
Daily Journal Corporation 387
Drinks Americas Holdings, Ltd. 426
Fiji Water Company, Llc 515
Fox Bsb Holdco, Inc. 541
Fraser/white, Inc. 545
Gibson, Dunn & Crutcher Llp 575
Grill Concepts, Inc. 601
Gursey, Schneider & Co. Llc 608
Hamagami/carroll, Inc. 613
Hanmi Financial Corp. 615
Harland M. Braun & Co., Inc. 618
Houlihan Lokey Inc 656
Howard Building Corporation 658
Hudson Pacific Properties Inc 661
Innovative Card Technologies Inc 692
Intergroup Corp. (the) 702
International Lease Finance Corp. 706
Internet Corporation For Assigned Names And Numbers 708
Irell & Manella Llp 715
Iw Group 720
Joseph Drown Foundation 740
Kb Home 746
Kilroy Realty Corp 755
Korn Ferry 764
Ladrx Corp 772
Laemmle Theatres, Llc 772
Leonard Green & Partners, L.p. 789
Los Angeles Department Of Water And Power 810
Los Angeles Philharmonic Association 810

INDEX BY HEADQUARTERS LOCATION

Loyola Marymount University 812
Mercury General Corp. 861
Merle Norman Cosmetics, Inc. 866
Mitchell Silberberg & Knupp Llp 894
Mmrglobal Inc 895
Occidental College 986
Parents Television Council, Inc. 1025
Pih Health Good Samaritan Hospital 1055
Platinum Studios, Inc. 1063
Playboy Enterprises, Inc. 1063
Point.360 1066
Portsmouth Square, Inc. 1070
Preferred Bank (los Angeles, Ca) 1076
Primex International Trading Corporation 1082
Public Communications Services, Inc. 1097
Quinn Emanuel Urquhart & Sullivan, Llp 1109
Radnet Inc 1114
Rbz Llp 1119
Rentech, Inc. 1132
Rexford Industrial Realty Inc 1139
Sheppard, Mullin, Richter & Hampton, Llp 1205
Southern California Gas Co. 1236
Southern California Regional Rail Authority 1236
Starlight Children's Foundation 1267
Targeted Medical Pharma, Inc. 1306
The Art Broad Foundation 1330
The California Endowment 1334
The Childrens Hospital Los Angeles 1336
The Los Angeles Kings Hockey Club L P 1354
The Ralph M Parsons Foundation 1365
The Ucla Foundation 1372
Travel Store 1400
Unihealth Foundation 1423
University Of California, Los Angeles 1441
University Of Southern California 1449
Vca Inc. 1468
W. M. Keck Foundation 1491
Wedbush Securities Inc 1505
Wessco International Ltd., A California Limited Partnership 1508
White Memorial Medical Center Inc 1520
Writers Guild Of America West, Inc. 1537

Los Gatos
Infogain Corporation 689
Netflix Inc 941

Madison
Accuray Inc (ca) 14

Malibu
Pepperdine University 1044

Manhattan Beach
Skechers Usa Inc 1216

Marina Del Rey
Adstar, Inc. 23

Menlo Park
Corcept Therapeutics Inc 358
Exponent Inc. 494
Hewlett, William And Flora Foundation (inc) 637
Menlo College 860
Meredith Enterprises Inc 864
Meta Platforms Inc 868
Pacific Biosciences Of California Inc 1017
Robert Half Inc 1147
Rudolph And Sletten, Inc. 1158
Sri International 1252
Us Venture Partners Iii Llc 1458

Merced
University Of California, Merced 1441

Mill Valley
Redwood Trust Inc 1125

Milpitas
Alliance Fiber Optic Products, Inc. 51
Altigen Communications Inc 60
Array Networks, Inc. 117
Devcon Construction Incorporated 408
Integrated Silicon Solution, Inc. 698
Ixys, Llc 720
Jds Uniphase Canada Ltd 730
Kla Corp 760
Linear Technology Llc 800
Nimble Storage, Inc. 959
Pericom Semiconductor Corporation 1046
Proxim Wireless Corp. 1095
Quantum3d, Inc. 1108
Renesas Electronics America Inc. 1130
Semi 1195
Silicon Graphics International Corp. 1210
Solaredge Technologies, Inc. 1226

Mission Viejo
Aeolus Pharmaceuticals Inc 28
Dynatem Inc 434
Elixir Industries 457
Franchise Services, Inc. 542
Postal Instant Press Inc. 1071
Sir Speedy, Inc. 1214

Modesto
City Of Modesto 307
E. & J. Gallo Winery 435
Modesto Irrigation District (inc) 897
Save Mart Supermarkets Llc 1180
Squab Producers Of Calif, Inc. 1252
Sutter Central Valley Hospitals 1294

Monrovia
World Vision International 1535

Montebello
Mexican American Opportunity Foundation 874

Monterey
Community Hospital Of The Monterey Peninsula 343

Morgan Hill
All Sensors Corporation 48

Del Monaco Foods, Llc 400

Mountain View
Alphabet Inc 56
Hansen Medical, Inc. 616
Intuit Inc 710
Iridex Corp. 715
Mereo Biopharma 5 Inc 865
Objectivity, Inc. 986

Napa
Queen Of The Valley Medical Center Foundation 1108

National City
Paradise Valley Hospital 1024

Newport Beach
American Vanguard Corp. 86
California First Leasing Corp 230
Chipotle Mexican Grill Inc 285
Clean Energy Fuels Corp 318
Hoag Hospital Foundation 645
Hoag Memorial Hospital Presbyterian 646
Impac Mortgage Holdings, Inc. 680
Morris Business Development Co 904
Newport Digital Technologies Inc. 954
Pacific Mutual Holding Co. 1019
Vroom Automotive Finance Corporation 1488

Nicasio
The George Lucas Educational Foundation 1345

North Hollywood
Academy Of Television Arts And Sciences 11
Ipc Healthcare, Inc. 714

Northridge
American Soil Technologies Inc 84
California State University, Northridge 232
Ikano Communications, Inc. 675

Norwalk
Cerritos Community College District 269

Novato
Bank Of Marin Bancorp 155
Horizon Pharmaceutical Llc 653
Mosaic Immunoengineering Inc 906
Solarcraft Services, Inc. 1226
Ultragenyx Pharmaceutical Inc 1421

Oakdale
Oak Valley Bancorp (oakdale, Ca) 984

Oakland
Children's Hospital & Research Center At Oakland 283
City Of Oakland 308
Clorox Co (the) 323
Commercial Energy Of Montana Inc. 339
County Of Alameda 365
E.l.f. Beauty Inc 436
East Bay Municipal Utility District, Water System 439
Give Something Back, Inc. 576
Kaiser Foundation Health Plan, Inc. 743

Kaiser Foundation Hospitals Inc 744
New Harbinger Publications, Inc. 946
Pandora Media, Llc 1022
Pg&e Corp (holding Co) 1050
San Francisco Bay Area Rapid Transit District 1173
Sierra Club 1208
Statehouse Holdings Inc 1269
Summit Bancshares, Inc. (ca) 1283

Oceanside
Miracosta Community College District 891
Tri-city Hospital District (inc) 1403

Ojai
Financialcontent Inc 516

Ontario
Blumenthal Distributing, Inc. 193
Cardenas Markets Llc 244
Cvb Financial Corp 382
Eco2 Plastics, Inc. 445
Fullmer Construction 552
Perera Construction & Design, Inc. 1045
Sigmanet, Inc. 1209

Orange
Campbell Lodging, Inc. 237
Chapman University 272
Children's Healthcare Of California 282
D W W Co., Inc. 386
Orange County Transportation Authority Scholarship Foundation, Inc. 1006
Roth Staffing Companies, L.p. 1155
Southern Counties Oil Co. 1237
St. Joseph Hospital Of Orange 1258
Volt Information Sciences Inc 1485

Oxnard
Cdti Advanced Materials Inc 260
City Of Oxnard 309

Pacific Grove
Elegant Illusions Inc 456

Palm Desert
Surge Global Energy Inc 1292

Palo Alto
Applovin Corp 105
Broadcom Inc (de) 211
Eiger Biopharmaceuticals Inc 450
Electric Power Research Institute, Inc. 453
Hereuare, Inc. 634
Hp Inc 659
Ioco 713
Mega Matrix Corp 857
Sutter Bay Medical Foundation 1294
The Marcus & Millichap Company 1355
Wilson Sonsini Goodrich & Rosati, Professional Corporation 1526

Pasadena
Alexandria Real Estate Equities Inc 46

INDEX BY HEADQUARTERS LOCATION

Arrowhead Pharmaceuticals Inc 118
Art Center College Of Design Inc 118
California Institute Of Technology 230
Dine Brands Global Inc 415
East West Bancorp, Inc 440
Fuller Theological Seminary 552
General Finance Corporation 564
Guidance Software, Inc. 605
Oewaves, Inc. 989
Operating Engineers Funds Inc 1003
Pasadena Area Community College District 1030
Pasadena Hospital Association, Ltd. 1030
Tetra Tech Inc 1321
Xencor, Inc 1540

Pico Rivera
Spotlight Capital Holdings Inc 1250

Pismo Beach
Pismo Coast Village, Inc. 1059

Pittsburg
Uss-upi, Llc 1460

Playa Del Rey
Chipton-ross, Inc. 286

Pleasanton
Armanino Foods Of Distinction, Inc. 114
Kinetic Systems, Inc. 756
Natus Medical Incorporated 936
Omron Robotics And Safety Technologies, Inc. 998
Shaklee Corporation 1202
Simpson Manufacturing Co., Inc. (de) 1212
Thoratec Llc 1384
Veeva Systems Inc 1469
Workday Inc 1533
Zeltiq Aesthetics, Inc. 1549

Pomona
California State Polytechnic University Of Pomona 231

Porterville
Sierra Bancorp 1208
Sierra View District Hospital League, Inc. 1209

Poway
Cohu Inc 329
John Hine Pontiac 736

Rancho Cascades
Tutor-saliba Corporation 1415

Rancho Cordova
Thermogenesis Holdings Inc 1381
Urata & Sons Concrete, Inc. 1454

Rancho Cucamonga
Agent Information Software Inc 33
Amphastar Pharmaceuticals Inc (de) 90

Rancho Mirage
Eisenhower Medical Center 451
The Betty Ford Center 1332

Rcho Sta Marg
Subzero Constructors, Inc. 1282

Redding
Prime Healthcare Services - Shasta, Llc 1081

Redlands
University Of Redlands 1447

Redwood City
Abilitypath 10
Adverum Biotechnologies Inc 27
Box Inc 202
Codexis Inc 327
Dpr Construction, Inc. 425
Electronic Arts, Inc. 455
Equinix Inc 480
Finjan Holdings, Inc. 516
Glu Mobile Inc. 582
Informatica Llc 690
Shutterfly, Llc 1207
Vifor Pharma, Inc. 1477
W. L. Butler Construction, Inc. 1491

Richmond
C. Overaa & Co. 224
City Of Richmond 311
Sunpower Corp 1288

Ripon
The Wine Group Inc 1379

Riverside
Bourns, Inc. 201
City Of Riverside 311
Dura Coat Products, Inc. 432
Provident Financial Holdings, Inc. 1094
Riverside Community College District Foundation 1145
University Of California, Riverside, Alumni Association 1441

Rohnert Park
Sonoma State University 1229

Rolling Hills Estates
Sheervision Inc 1204

Rosemead
Edison International 447
Southern California Edison Co. 1236

Roseville
Adventist Health System/west, Corporation 26
Northern California Power Agency 971
Quest Media & Supplies, Inc. 1108

Sacramento
Alston Construction Company, Inc. 58
California Beer And Beverage Distributors 229
California Department Of Water Resources 230
California Pharmacists Association 231
California State University, Sacramento 232
City Of Sacramento 311
Housing Finance Agency, California 657
Jck Legacy Company 730
Macias Gini & O'connell Llp 822
Sacramento Municipal Utility District 1163
State Water Resources Control Board 1269

Sutter Health 1294

Salinas
City Of Salinas 312
Pacific International Vegetable Marketing, Inc. 1018
Salinas Valley Health 1169
Scheid Vineyards Inc. 1182

San Francisco
First Republic Bank (san Francisco, Ca) 524

San Bernardino
Community Hospital Of San Bernardino 343
Stater Bros. Holdings Inc. 1269

San Carlos
General Hardware And Builders Supply, Inc. 564

San Clemente
Caretrust Reit Inc 246
Consolidated Contracting Services, Inc. 351
Icu Medical Inc 671
Micro Imaging Technology Inc 877
Surfrider Foundation, Inc 1292

San Diego
Acadia Pharmaceuticals Inc 12
Ace Relocation Systems, Inc. 14
Ainos Inc 36
All Star Glass, Inc. 48
Alliant International University, Inc. 53
American Assets Trust, Inc. 67
Arcturus Therapeutics Holdings Inc 110
Axesstel Inc 147
Biocept Inc 181
Biocom Institute 181
Biomed Realty Trust, Inc. 183
Bycor General Contractors, Inc. 223
Capricor Therapeutics Inc 242
Carvin Corp. 251
Cdc Small Business Finance Corp. 259
City Of San Diego 312
Coast Citrus Distributors 325
Coleman University 330
Corporate Computer Centers, Inc. 361
Cubic Corporation 379
Cuso Financial Services, L.p. 382
Cymer, Inc. 384
D.r. Systems, Inc. 386
Dare Bioscience Inc 391
Delawie 401
Dexcom Inc 409
Dmk Pharmaceuticals Corp 419
Dunham & Associates Investment Counsel, Inc. 430
E.digital Corp. 436
Encore Capital Group Inc 465
Enterprise Informatics Inc 475
Epsilon Systems Solutions, Inc. 479
Event Network, Llc 487
Evofem, Inc. 490
Fate Therapeutics Inc 504
Franklin Wireless Corp 545
Genasys Inc 562
Gene Biotherapeutics Inc 563

Glenn A. Rick Engineering And Development Co. 578
Guild Mortgage Company 606
Halozyme Therapeutics Inc 613
Hawthorne Machinery Co. 623
Heron Therapeutics Inc 635
Histogen Inc 643
Illumina Inc 677
Imageware Systems Inc 678
Inseego Wireless, Inc. 695
Interact Holdings Group Inc 700
Jack In The Box, Inc. 724
Job Options, Incorporated 734
Johnson & Jennings Inc 737
Ligand Pharmaceuticals Inc 796
Live Current Media Inc 803
Lpl Financial Holdings Inc. 812
Mitek Systems, Inc. 894
Nasland Engineering 921
National University 933
Neurocrine Biosciences, Inc. 943
Neyenesch Printers, Inc. 956
Ninyo & Moore Geotechnical & Environmental Sciences Consultants Corp 959
Oncternal Therapeutics Inc 999
Pacific Building Group 1017
Parron-hall Corporation 1028
Petco Health & Wellness Co Inc 1048
Pfenex Inc. 1049
Point Loma Nazarene University Foundation 1066
Pricesmart Inc 1080
Pulse Electronics Corporation 1101
Qualcomm Inc 1106
Quidelortho Corp 1109
Rady Children's Hospital-san Diego 1114
Realty Income Corp 1122
Receptos, Inc. 1122
Recon Environmental, Inc. 1122
Regulus Therapeutics Inc 1128
Reno Contracting, Inc. 1131
Resmed Inc. 1135
Retail Opportunity Investments Corp 1137
Reva Medical, Inc. 1138
Rf Industries Ltd. 1140
San Diego County Office Of Education 1173
San Diego County Water Authority 1173
San Diego Gas & Electric Company 1173
San Diego State University Foundation 1173
San Diego Unified Port District 1173
Scottish Rite Cathedral Of San Diego 1187
Scripps Health 1187
Sempra 1195
Senomyx, Inc. 1196
Sequenom, Inc. 1198
Sgpa Planning And Architecture San Diego 1201
Sharp Healthcare 1202
Sharp Memorial Hospital 1203
Sonim Technologies Inc 1229
Space Micro Inc. 1243

INDEX BY HEADQUARTERS LOCATION

Syzygy Technologies, Inc. 1300
Tandem Diabetes Care Inc 1304
Teradata Corp (de) 1319
The Kleinfelder Group Inc 1353
Thomas Jefferson School Of Law 1382
University Of San Diego 1448
Wd-40 Co 1502
Zoological Society Of San Diego 1552

San Dimas
American States Water Co 84
Athena Engineering, Inc. 131
Cabral Roofing & Waterproofing Corporation 226

San Fernando
Puretek Corporation 1102

San Francisco
Airbnb Inc 37
American Shared Hospital Services 83
Aradigm Corporation 107
Asura Development Group, Inc 129
Atlassian Corp 134
Autodesk Inc 140
Bank Of The West (san Francisco, Ca) 156
Bebe Stores Inc 167
Big Heart Pet Brands, Inc. 179
Block Inc 189
Blum Capital Partners T, L.p. 193
Business For Social Responsibility 222
Cai International, Inc. 227
Castlight Health, Inc. 254
Charles And Helen Schwab Foundation Inc 273
City & County Of San Francisco 297
Colombia Energy Resources Inc. 332
Dignity Health 414
Docusign Inc 420
Dolby Laboratories Inc 420
Doordash Inc 422
Dropbox Inc 426
Dupont Fabros Technology, Inc. 431
Eastern Light Capital Inc 441
Federal Home Loan Bank Of San Francisco 507
Federal Reserve Bank Of San Francisco, Dist. No. 12 509
Fibrogen Inc 514
First Republic Preferred Capital Corp 524
Foundation For National Progress 540
Futures Without Violence 554
Gemstone Solutions Group, Inc 562
Geopetro Resources Co 570
Global Exchange 579
Golden Gate National Parks Conservancy 584
Golden State Warriors, Llc 585
Gordon Rees Scully Mansukhani, Llp. 589
Henry J Kaiser Family Foundation 633
Hornblower Yachts, Llc 653

Jmp Group Inc. 734
Kkr Financial Holdings Llc 760
Kqed Inc. 766
Levi Strauss & Co. 791
Levi Strauss & Co. 791
Littler Mendelson, P.c. 803
Liveramp Holdings Inc 804
Lyft Inc 817
Marin Software Inc 833
Mechanics' Institute 853
Medivation, Inc. 856
Merriman Holdings Inc. 867
Mozilla Foundation 909
Mulesoft, Inc. 913
Nektar Therapeutics 939
Okta Inc 993
Opentv Corp. 1003
Partech International, Inc. 1029
Pattern Energy Group Inc. 1032
Poniard Pharmaceuticals Inc 1067
Progress Investment Management Company, Llc 1088
Prologis Inc 1089
Public Library Of Science 1097
Recommind, Inc. 1122
Rpx Corporation 1157
Salesforce Inc 1169
Salon Media Group Inc. 1170
San Francisco Opera Association 1174
San Francisco State University 1174
Sunrun Inc 1288
Sunrun Installation Services Inc. 1288
Sutter Bay Hospitals 1293
Swinerton Incorporated 1295
The Gap Inc 1345
The Global Fund For Women Inc 1346
The Linux Foundation 1354
Tis Mortgage Investment Co. 1387
Trulia, Inc. 1409
Twilio Inc 1415
Twitter, Inc. 1416
Uber Technologies Inc 1418
University Of California, San Francisco 1441
University Of San Francisco Inc 1448
Visa Inc 1482
Wikimedia Foundation, Inc. 1522
Wilbur-ellis Holdings Ii, Inc. 1522
Williams Sonoma Inc 1526
Yelp Inc 1544
Yume, Inc. 1547
Zendesk, Inc. 1549

San Francisco
Pinterest Inc 1058

San Jose
8point3 Energy Partners Lp 4
A10 Networks Inc 7
Adeia Inc 21
Adobe Inc 23
Alfa Tech Consulting Engineers, Inc. 46
Altera Corporation 59
Anixa Biosciences Inc 96
Apx, Inc. 106
Aruba Networks, Inc. 120
Atmel Corporation 134
Bloom Energy Corp 189

Brocade Communications Systems Llc 212
Cadence Design Systems Inc 226
California Water Service Group (de) 233
Calix Inc 233
Cisco Systems Inc 292
City Of San Jose 312
Ebay Inc. 443
Echelon Corporation 444
Energous Corp 467
Exar Corporation 491
Firsthand Technology Value Fund, Inc. 526
Forescout Technologies, Inc. 536
Gct Semiconductor, Inc. 561
Globalfluency, Inc. 581
Good Samaritan Hospital, L.p. 587
Harmonic, Inc. 619
Heritage Commerce Corp 634
Human Pheromone Sciences, Inc. 661
Infinera Corp 688
Inphi Corporation 694
Invensense, Inc. 711
Isign Solutions Inc 717
Itron Networked Solutions, Inc. 719
J. Lohr Winery Corporation 722
Lumentum Holdings Inc 815
Mcafee Corp. 849
Naprotek, Llc 920
Neomagic Corp. 940
Netapp, Inc. 941
Netgear Inc 941
Nutanix Inc 981
Oryx Technology Corp. 1010
Paypal Holdings Inc 1033
Peraso Inc 1044
Polycom, Inc. 1066
Power Integrations Inc. 1072
Quantum Corp 1108
Quicklogic Corp 1109
Rambus Inc. (de) 1115
Renesas Electronics America Inc. 1130
Roku Inc 1151
San Jose Water Company 1174
Sanmina Corp 1176
Sjw Group 1215
Super Micro Computer Inc 1290
Synaptics Inc 1297
Tessera Technologies, Inc. 1321
The Tech Interactive 1370
Tivo Corporation 1388
Ultratech, Inc. 1421
Western Digital Corp 1512
Zoom Video Communications Inc 1552

San Juan Capistrano
Cosco Fire Protection, Inc. 363
Ensign Group Inc 471

San Leandro
Energy Recovery Inc 467
International Fleet Sales, Inc. 705

San Luis Obispo
California Polytechnic State University 231
Mindbody, Inc. 889

San Marcos
California State University, San Marcos 232

Palomar Community College District 1021

San Mateo
Armco Metals Holdings Inc 115
Avistar Communications Corp 146
Essex Property Trust Inc 484
Franklin Resources Inc 545
Gopro Inc 588
Guidewire Software Inc 606
Imperva, Inc. 681
Marketo, Inc. 835
Model N, Inc 896
Netsuite, Inc. 942
Synarc Inc. 1297
Talphera Inc 1304
Tesla Energy Operations, Inc. 1321

San Pedro
Tatung Company Of America, Inc. 1307

San Rafael
Biomarin Pharmaceutical Inc 183
Westamerica Bancorporation 1510

San Ramon
Annams Systems Corporation 97
Arc Document Solutions, Inc. 108
Callidus Software Inc. 234
Chevron Corporation 279
Cooper Companies, Inc. (the) 357
Five9, Inc 527
Hill Physicians Medical Group, Inc. 641
Jacobs, Malcolm & Burtt 726
Sunset Development Company Inc 1289

Santa Ana
Banc Of California Inc 154
Brandywine Communications 205
City Of Santa Ana 312
Collectors Universe, Inc. 331
Ducommun Inc. 428
First American Financial Corp 517
Foundation Building Materials, Inc. 540
Moorefield Construction, Inc. 903
Orange Coast Title Company 1005
Orange County Global Medical Center Auxiliary 1005
Specialized Marketing Services, Inc. 1246
Sukut Construction, Inc. 1283
Ttm Technologies Inc 1413

Santa Barbara
Callwave Inc 234
Direct Relief Foundation 415
Qad Inc. 1104

Santa Clara
Actiontec Electronics, Inc. 18
Advanced Micro Devices Inc 25
Affymetrix, Inc. 31
Agilent Technologies, Inc. 34
Ambarella, Inc. 64
Analogix Semiconductor, Inc. 93
Applied Materials, Inc. 104
Applied Micro Circuits Corp 104
Arista Networks Inc 112

INDEX BY HEADQUARTERS LOCATION

Cavium, Llc 257
Chegg Inc 276
Envivio, Inc. 477
Evolveware, Inc. 490
Gigamon Inc. 575
Infoblox Inc. 689
Intel Corp 699
Intevac, Inc. 709
Nvidia Corp 983
Omnivision Technologies, Inc. 998
Palo Alto Networks, Inc 1021
Pdf Solutions Inc. 1035
President And Board Of Trustees Of Santa Clara College 1078
Pure Storage Inc 1102
Renesas Electronics America Inc. 1131
Robinson Oil Corporation 1149
San Francisco Forty Niners 1174
Semler Scientific Inc 1195
Servicenow Inc 1199
Svb Financial Group 1294
Telenav, Inc. 1314
Wso2 Llc 1537

Santa Clara
Ehealth Inc 450

Santa Cruz
Santa Cruz Seaside Company Inc 1177

Santa Fe Springs
Hurlen Corporation 664
New Tangram, Llc 949
Tri-west, Ltd. 1403
Weber Distribution, Llc 1504

Santa Monica
Cornerstone Ondemand, Inc. 361
Douglas Emmett Inc 423
Entravision Communications Corp. 475
Jakks Pacific Inc 727
K-micro, Inc. 742
Kite Pharma, Inc. 759
Leaf Group Ltd. 783
Macerich Co (the) 821
Milken Family Foundation 886
National Academy Of Recording Arts & Sciences, Inc. 922
Nurx Pharmaceuticals, Inc. 981
Santa Monica Community College District 1177
Snap Inc 1223
Truecar Inc 1409

Santa Paula
Calavo Growers, Inc. 228
Limoneira Co 798

Santa Rosa
Democrasoft, Holdings Inc 405
Exchange Bank (santa Rosa, Ca) 492
Keysight Technologies Inc 753
Luther Burbank Corp 816
Summit State Bank (santa Rosa, Ca) 1284
Zap 1548

Santee
San Diego Christian College Inc 1172

Sausalito
The Marine Mammal Center 1355

Seaside
California State University, Monterey Bay 232

Sebastopol
O'reilly Media, Inc. 984
Sonomawest Holdings, Inc. 1229
Traditional Medicinals, Inc. 1396

Sherman Oaks
Apex Global Brands Inc. 99
Golden State Health Centers, Inc. 585

Simi Valley
Intermetro Communications, Inc. (nv) 703
Microblend, Inc. 877

Solana Beach
Clearpoint Neuro Inc 320

Solana Beach
Evoke Pharma Inc 490

Sonora
Front Porch, Inc. 549

South San Francisco
Assembly Biosciences Inc 125
Cytokinetics Inc 385
Gyre Therapeutics Inc 609
Portola Pharmaceuticals, Inc. 1070
Rigel Pharmaceuticals Inc 1143
Standard Biotools Inc 1264
Titan Pharmaceuticals Inc (de) 1388
Tobira Therapeutics, Inc. 1389
Vaxart Inc 1467
Veracyte Inc 1470

Stanford
Leland Stanford Junior University 788
Stanford Health Care 1265

Stockton
California Cedar Products Company 229
City Of Stockton 313
Coastal Pacific Food Distributors, Inc. 325
University Of The Pacific 1450

Studio City
Crown Media Holdings, Inc. 375
Pacifica Foundation Inc. 1019

Sunnyvale
Biocardia Inc 181
Edelman Financial Engines, Llc 446
Egain Corp 449
Fairchild Semiconductor International, Inc. 498
Fortinet Inc 538
Gsi Technology Inc 603
Intuitive Surgical Inc 711
Juniper Networks Inc 741
Linkedin Corporation 800
Logic Devices Inc 806
R.s. Hughes Company, Inc. 1112
Synopsys Inc 1299
Xoriant Corporation 1541

Sylmar
Tutor Perini Corp 1415

Tehachapi
Green St. Energy, Inc 598

Tejon Ranch
Tejon Ranch Co 1313

Temecula
Genica Corporation 568

Thousand Oaks
Amgen Inc 89
Ceres, Inc. 268
Teledyne Technologies Inc 1314

Torrance
American Honda Finance Corporation 76
Carparts.com Inc (new) 249
Convaid Products Llc 355
Emi Holding, Inc. 461
Enova Systems Inc 471
Ledtronics, Inc. 784
Motorcar Parts Of America Inc 907
Nearfield Systems Inc. 938
Ocean Duke Corporation 987
Oncologix Tech Inc 999
Torrance Memorial Medical Center 1392
Virco Manufacturing Corp. 1479

Turlock
Turlock Irrigation District Employees Association 1414

Tustin
Avid Bioservices Inc 146
Radient Pharmaceuticals Corp 1114

Ukiah
Alambic, Inc. 40
Mendocino Brewing Co Inc 859

Union City
Abaxis, Inc. 8

Valencia
Del West Engineering, Inc. 400
Fruit Growers Supply Company Inc 550
Henry Mayo Newhall Memorial Hospital 633
Sunkist Growers, Inc. 1287
Taitron Components Inc. 1302

Van Nuys
Capstone Green Energy Corp 243
Funrise, Inc. 553
Uwink Inc. Delaware 1461

Ventura
Staples Construction Company, Inc. 1266

Vernon
Rehrig Pacific Company 1128

Vista
Amron International, Inc. 91
Dei Holdings Inc 400
Hay House, Llc 623
Javo Beverage Company, Inc. 729
Westbridge Research Group 1510

Walnut
Mt San Antonio Community College District 912
Propellus Inc 1090

Walnut Creek
Central Garden & Pet Co 265
J. Stokes & Assoc., Inc. 722
John Muir Health 736
One Planet Ops Inc. 1000
Pmi Group, Inc. 1065

Watsonville
Granite Construction Inc 594
Monterey Mushrooms, Llc 902
Sv Labs Corporation 1294

West Hollywood
Cedars-sinai Medical Center 261
National Lampoon Inc 929
Salon City Inc 1170

West Sacramento
Raley's 1115

Westlake Village
Aspyra Inc 125
Decision Diagnostics Corp 398
Eom Pharmaceutical Holdings Inc 478
Guitar Center Holdings, Inc. 607
Ipayment, Inc. 714
Ltc Properties, Inc. 814
Pennymac Financial Services Inc (new) 1041
Pennymac Mortgage Investment Trust 1041
Timios National Corporation 1387
United Online, Inc. 1429

Westminster
Biolargo Inc 182

Whittier
The Oltmans Construction Co 1362

Woodland Hills
Blackline Inc 187
Reachlocal, Inc. 1120
Talon International, Inc. 1303

Yorba Linda
Edsi 448

Yuba City
Sunsweet Growers Inc. 1289

COLORADO

Alamosa
Adams State University 20

Aspen
Aspen Skiing Company, L.l.c. 124

Aurora
Children's Hospital Colorado 283
Graebel Companies, Inc. 591
Kolorfusion International Inc 763
Poudre Valley Health Care, Inc. 1072
Sefton Resources Inc 1193

Boulder
American Outdoor Products, Inc. 80
Applied Trust Engineering, Inc. 105
Aurora Organic Dairy Corp. 139
Boulder Brands, Inc. 200
Clovis Oncology Inc 323
Encision Inc. 464
Fresh Tracks Therapeutics Inc 548
Hain Celestial Group Inc 612
Intellabridge Technology Corp 699

INDEX BY HEADQUARTERS LOCATION

Neomedia Technologies, Inc. 940
Somalogic Operating Co., Inc. 1227
Sonoma Pharmaceuticals Inc 1229
The Regents Of The University Of Colorado 1366
University Corporation For Atmospheric Research 1439
Zayo Group Holdings, Inc. 1549

Broomfield
Crocs Inc 373
Danone Us, Inc. 391
Dmc Global Inc 418
Level 3 Parent, Llc 790
Mwh Global, Inc. 917
Noodles & Co 962
Sisters Of Charity Of Leavenworth Health System, Inc. 1214
Vail Resorts Inc 1462
Zvelo Inc. 1553

Castle Rock
Riot Platforms Inc 1143

Centennial
Api Group Life Safety Usa Llc 100
Arrow Electronics, Inc. 117
Dhi Group Inc 410
Haselden Construction, Llc 621
National Cinemedia Inc 925
Seakr Engineering, Llc 1189
Westwater Resources Inc 1516

Centennial
Biomedical Technology Solutions Holdings, Inc. 183

Colorado Springs
Carrio Cabling Corporation 250
Century Casinos Inc. 268
City Of Colorado Springs 302
Colorado College 333
Colorado Springs Utilities 334
Colorado Structures, Inc. 334
Junior Achievement Usa 741
Mountain States Pipe & Supply Co, Inc 908
Neumann Systems Group, Inc. 943
Polaris Alpha, Llc 1066
Public Relations Advertising Company 1098
Root9b Holdings Inc 1153
Spectranetics Llc 1246
The Navsys Corporation 1360
Uch-mhs 1419
United States Olympic Committee Inc 1432
Usa Hockey, Inc. 1458
Young Life 1546

Commerce City
Vista International Technologies Inc 1483

Conifer
Oblong Inc 986

Craig
The Memorial Hospital 1356

Denver
Advanced Energy Industries Inc 24
Advantego Corp 26
Alterra Mountain Company 59
Altex Industries, Inc. 60
American Indian College Fund, The (inc) 76

Angi Inc 95
Antero Midstream Corp 97
Antero Resources Corp 97
Apartment Income Reit, L.p. 99
Apartment Investment & Management Co 99
Asset Acquisition Authority, Inc. 125
Auraria Higher Education Center 139
Birner Dental Management Services, Inc. 184
Black Raven Energy, Inc. 186
Civitas Resources Inc 315
Colorado Rockies Baseball Club, Ltd. 333
Coresite Realty Corporation 360
Davita Inc 395
Dcp Midstream Lp 397
Denver Board Of Water Commissioners 405
Denver Health And Hospitals Authority Inc 406
Emerald Oil, Inc. 460
Ensign-bickford Industries, Inc. 472
Escalera Resources Co 483
Farmland Partners Inc 503
Gasco Energy Inc. 560
Gates Industrial Corp Plc 560
Global Market Development Center 580
Gold Resource Corp 583
Guaranty Bancorp Inc (nh) 605
Healthpeak Properties Inc 627
Heartland Financial Usa, Inc. (dubuque, Ia) 629
Hycroft Mining Corporation 666
Infonow Corp. 689
Intrepid Potash Inc 710
Janus Capital Group Inc. 728
Kroenke Sports Holdings Llc 767
Leprino Foods Company 790
Liberty Energy Inc 793
M.d.c. Holdings, Inc. 820
Markwest Energy Partners, L.p. 836
Medianews Group, Inc. 855
Metropolitan State University Of Denver 872
Modivcare Inc 897
Modivcare Solutions, Llc 897
Newmont Corp 953
Ovintiv Inc 1014
Ovintiv Usa Inc. 1015
Pacific Alliance Medical Center, Inc. 1017
Pcl Construction Enterprises, Inc. 1034
Re/max, Llc 1120
Real Goods Solar Inc 1121
Red Lion Hotels Corporation 1123
Royal Gold Inc 1156
Sage Hospitality Resources L.l.c. 1165
Saint Joseph Hospital, Inc 1167
Sara Enterprises, Inc. 1178
Scl Health - Front Range, Inc. 1186
Sm Energy Co. 1219
Ssr Mining Inc 1253
Summit Materials Inc 1284
Terranext, Llc 1320

Teton Energy Corporation 1321
The Anschutz Corporation 1329
Transmontaigne Partners Llc 1399
University Of Colorado Foundation 1442
University Of Colorado Hospital Foundation 1442
University Of Denver 1442
Venoco, Llc 1469
Vf Corp. 1474
Western Fuels Association, Inc. 1512
Western Union Co 1514
Worth Group, Architects, A Professional Corporation 1536

Durango
Rocky Mountain Chocolate Factory Inc (de) 1151
U-swirl Inc. 1417

Engelwood
Liberty Media Corp (de) - Formula One Group 793

Englewood
Accucode, Inc. 14
American Furniture Warehouse Co. 75
Ampio Pharmaceuticals Inc 91
Centennial Specialty Foods Corp 263
Ch2m Hill Companies Ltd 270
Csg Systems International Inc. 376
Dish Network Corp 416
Echostar Corp 444
Gevo Inc 574
Ihs Inc. 675
Image Software, Inc. 678
Innospec Inc 692
Liberty Media Corp (de) 793
Liberty Media Corp (de) - Common Series B Braves Group 793
Ls Gallegos & Associates Inc 813
Pdb Sports, Ltd. 1035
Qurate Retail Inc 1110
Qurate Retail Inc - Com Ser A 1110
Qurate Retail Inc - Com Ser B 1110
Red Robin Gourmet Burgers Inc 1124
Starz Acquisition Llc 1268
Symbolic Logic Inc 1296
Toastmasters International 1389
Vista Gold Corp 1483
Viveve Medical Inc 1485
Westmoreland Resource Partners Lp 1515
Wideopenwest Inc 1522

Fort Collins
Colorado State University 334
Otter Products, Llc 1012
Platte River Power Authority (inc) 1063
Statera Biopharma Inc 1269
Woodward, Inc. 1533

Golden
American Millennium Inc 80
Golden Minerals Co 585
Good Times Restaurants Inc. 587

Trustees Of The Colorado School Of Mines 1411

Grand Junction
Colorado Mesa University 333

Greeley
Hensel Phelps Construction Co. 633
North Colorado Medical Center Foundation, Inc. 966
Pilgrims Pride Corp. 1056

Greenwood Village
Air Methods Llc 37
Arq Inc 117
Ascent Capital Group, Inc. 122
Century Communities Inc 268
Cmtsu Liquidation Inc 324
Cobank Acb 326
Great West Life & Annuity Insurance Co - Insurance Products 596
National Bank Holdings Corp 923
National Storage Affiliates Trust 932
Scott's Liquid Gold, Inc. 1186
Selectis Health Inc 1194
Smart Move Inc 1220
Ttec Holdings Inc 1412

Highlands Ranch
Udr Inc 1419

Lakewood
American Cannabis Co Inc 70
Boker Usa, Inc. 196
Catamount Constructors, Inc. 254
Christy Sports L.l.c. 288
General Moly, Inc. 565
Jacobs Entertainment, Inc. 726
Mesa Laboratories, Inc. 867
Natural Grocers By Vitamin Cottage Inc 935

Littleton
Cpi Card Group Inc 368
Primemd Inc 1081

Longmont
Enservco Corp 471
S&w Seed Co. 1162
Seagate Cloud Systems, Inc. 1189
Uqm Technologies, Inc. 1454

Louisville
Casey Industrial, Inc. 252
Eldorado Artesian Springs Inc 453
Gaia Inc (new) 556
Globeimmune, Inc 582

Pueblo
Colorado State University-pueblo Foundation 334

Salida
High Country Bancorp, Inc. 638

Thornton
Ascent Solar Technologies Inc 122
Myr Group Inc 918
Virtual Enterprises, Inc. 1482

Watkins
Pure Cycle Corp. 1101

Westminster
Arca Biopharma Inc 108
Ball Corp 153

Genethera, Inc. 568
Trimble Inc 1405
Wheat Ridge
Central City Opera House Association 265
Solitario Resources Corp 1227

CONNECTICUT
Ansonia
Farrel Corporation 504
Berlin
Connecticut Light & Power Co 349
Bethel
Morristown Star Struck Llc 905
Bloomfield
Kaman Corp. 744
The Cigna Group 1337
Bridgeport
Bridgeport Hospital & Healthcare Services Inc 208
St. Vincent's Health Services Corporation 1262
Bristol
Barnes Group Inc. 159
Bristol Hospital Incorporated 210
Brookfield
Photronics, Inc. 1053
Cheshire
Bozzuto's, Inc. 203
The Lane Construction Corporation 1353
Danbury
Ethan Allen Interiors, Inc. 485
Fuelcell Energy Inc 551
Linde Plc (new) 799
Mannkind Corp 829
Preferred Utilities Manufacturing Corporation 1076
The Morganti Group Inc 1358
Western Connecticut Health Network, Inc. 1511
Darien
Genesee & Wyoming Inc. 566
Derby
Griffin Health Services Corporation 600
The Griffin Hospital 1347
Enfield
Str Holdings Inc. 1277
Fairfield
Calmare Therapeutics Inc 234
Fairfield University 498
Save The Children Federation, Inc. 1180
Farmington
Acmat Corp. 15
Acturus, Inc. 18
Mcphee Electric, Ltd 852
Otis Worldwide Corp 1012
Glastonbury
Sagarsoft Inc. 1165
Greenwich
Berkley (wr) Corp 173
Gamco Investors Inc 557
Gxo Logistics Inc 609

Interactive Brokers Group Inc 700
Starwood Property Trust Inc. 1267
Tiptree Inc 1387
Xpo Inc 1541
Hamden
Quinnipiac University 1110
Transact Technologies Inc. 1397
Hartford
Connecticut Children's Medical Center 349
Connecticut State University System 350
Eversource Energy Service Company 489
Hartford Financial Services Group Inc. 619
Hartford Healthcare Corporation 620
Saint Francis Hospital And Medical Center Foundation, Inc. 1167
Virtus Investment Partners Inc 1482
Lakeville
Salisbury Bancorp, Inc. 1170
Manchester
First Hartford Corp 521
Lydall, Inc. 817
Scan-optics, Inc. 1181
Mashantucket
Mashantucket Pequot Tribal Nation 840
Meriden
Midstate Medical Center 883
Middletown
Wesleyan University 1508
Milford
Alinabal Holdings Corporation 47
Eastern Bag And Paper Company, Incorporated 440
New Britain
Hospital Of Central Connecticut 655
Stanley Black & Decker Inc 1265
New Haven
Knights Of Columbus 761
Precipio Inc 1074
Yale New Haven Health Services Corporation 1543
Yale New Haven Hospital, Inc. 1543
Yale University 1543
New London
Connecticut College 349
Lawrence + Memorial Hospital, Inc. 781
New Milford
New Milford Hospital, Inc. 948
Norwalk
After, Inc. 32
Booking Holdings Inc 198
Emcor Group, Inc. 460
Factset Research Systems Inc. 497
Frontier Communications Parent Inc 549
Mbi, Inc. 848
Mecklermedia Corp 854
Reeds Inc 1125
Xerox Credit Corp. 1540

Xerox Holdings Corp 1540
Norwich
Inc.jet Holding Inc 682
Old Greenwich
Ellington Financial Inc 457
Ellington Residential Mortgaging Real Estate Investment Trust 457
Hudson Global Inc 661
Star Equity Holdings Inc 1266
Orange
Avangrid Inc 143
Oxford
Rbc Bearings Inc 1119
Plainville
Carling Technologies, Inc. 247
Pomfret
Loos & Co., Inc. 809
Putnam
Day Kimball Healthcare, Inc. 396
Ridgefield
Boehringer Ingelheim Corporation 195
Boehringer Ingelheim Pharmaceuticals, Inc. 195
Chefs' Warehouse Inc (the) 276
Shelton
Acme United Corp. 16
Doctor's Associates Inc. 419
Eastern Co. 441
Edgewell Personal Care Co 447
Flexiinternational Software, Inc. 528
Hubbell Inc. 660
Southport
Sturm, Ruger & Co., Inc. 1281
Stamford
Aircastle Limited 38
American Banknote Corporation 68
American Institute For Foreign Study, Inc. 77
American Pet Products Association, Inc. 81
Americares Foundation, Inc. 87
Cara Therapeutics Inc 243
Charter Communications Inc (new) 275
Eagle Bulk Shipping Inc 437
Equinor Marketing & Trading (us) Inc. 480
Gartner Inc 559
General Atlantic Llc 563
Hexcel Corp. 637
Information Services Group Inc 690
Itt Inc 719
Patriot National Bancorp Inc 1032
Peerless Systems Corporation 1038
Philip Morris International Inc 1052
Pitney Bowes Inc 1059
Revolution Lighting Technologies Inc 1138
Silgan Holdings Inc 1210
Stamford Health, Inc. 1263
Star Group Lp 1266
Synchrony Financial 1298
Tenerity, Inc. 1317

Tronox Llc 1408
United Rentals Inc 1430
W.j. Deutsch & Sons Ltd. 1491
Webster Financial Corp (waterbury, Conn) 1504
World Wrestling Entertainment, Llc 1535
Uncasville
Mohegan Tribal Gaming Authority 898
Wallingford
Amphenol Corp. 90
Edible International, Llc 447
Vantage Group Inc 1465
Washington
The Frederick Gunn School Incorporated 1344
Waterbury
Prospect Waterbury, Inc. 1091
Webster Preferred Capital Corp. 1504
Waterford
Defender Industries, Inc. 399
Watertown
Crystal Rock Holdings, Inc. 376
West Hartford
Colt Defense Llc 335
The Simon Konover Company 1369
The University Of Hartford 1374
West Haven
University Of New Haven, Incorporated 1445
Westport
Charter Oak Equity, Lp 275
Cloud Peak Energy Inc. 323
Compass Diversified 345
Gsv Inc 603
Serious Fun Children's Network, Inc. 1198
Terex Corp. 1319
Wethersfield
Connecticut Department Of Labor 349
Wilton
Blue Buffalo Pet Products, Inc. 190
Youngs Nurseries Incorporated 1546
Windsor
Ss&c Technologies Holdings Inc 1253
Thermodynetics Inc. (nv) 1381
Trc Companies, Inc. 1401

DELAWARE
Claymont
Golden Star Enterprises Ltd 585
Dover
Chesapeake Utilities Corp. 279
Delaware State University 401
Dover Motorsports, Inc. 424
Jsd Management, Inc. 740
Premier Entertainment Iii, Llc 1076

INDEX BY HEADQUARTERS LOCATION

Lewes
Beebe Medical Center, Inc. 168
Fiorano Software, Inc. 516

New Castle
Planet Payment, Inc. 1062
United Electric Supply Company, Inc. 1427

Newark
Artesian Resources Corp. 119
Atlantic City Electric Co 133
Christiana Care Health System, Inc. 287
Delmarva Power & Light Co. 403
Slm Corp. 1219
University Of Delaware 1442

Wilmington
Acorn Energy Inc 16
Ashland Inc (new) 123
Bancroft Construction Company 154
Barclays Bank Delaware 159
Chemours Co (the) 277
Coinbase Global Inc 329
Dupont De Nemours Inc 431
Enovis Corp 471
Incyte Corporation 683
Marvell Technology Inc 839
Supply Chain Consultants Inc 1291
Support.com, Inc. 1291
The Bancorp Inc 1331
Torch Energy Royalty Trust 1392
Vulcan International Corp. 1489
Wsfs Financial Corp 1537

Winterthur
The Henry Francis Dupont Winterthur Museum Inc 1348

DISTRICT OF COLUMBIA

Washington
Aarp 8
Accion International 13
Africare 32
American Association For The Advancement Of Science 67
American Bankers Association Inc 68
American Bus Association Inc. 69
American Chemical Society 71
American Dental Education Association 72
American Federation Of Labor & Congress Of Industrial Organzation 74
American Federation Of State County & Municipal Employees 74
American Federation Of Teachers Afl-cio Aft Committee On Political 74
American Forests 75
American Gaming Association 75
American Institute Of Architects, Inc 77
American Insurance Association Inc. 78
American Petroleum Institute Inc 81
American Psychological Association, Inc. 82
American Trucking Associations, Inc. 85
American University 86
Appalachian Regional Commission Inc 102
Arcadis Inc. 108
Arnold & Porter Kaye Scholer Llp 116
Bgr Government Affairs, Llc 178
Born Free Usa, United With Animal Protection Institute 199
Bread For The World, Inc. 206
Bsa Business Software Alliance, Inc 217
Carlyle Group Inc (the) 247
Carnegie Institution Of Washington 248
Cato Institute, Inc. 256
Chamber Of Commerce Of The United States Of America 271
Child Welfare League Of America, Inc. 282
Children's National Medical Center 284
Cogent Communications Holdings, Inc. 328
Communications Workers Of America, Afl-cio, Clc 341
Corporation For Public Broadcasting 362
Costar Group, Inc. 363
Counterpart International Inc 364
Crowell & Moring Llp 374
Cssi, Inc. 377
Danaher Corp 390
Defenders Of Wildlife 399
Direct Selling Association (inc) 415
Easterly Government Properties Inc 440
Elme Communities 458
Export-import Bank Of The United States 495
Fannie Mae 500
Federal Agricultural Mortgage Corp 505
Federal Deposit Insurance Corp. 505
Federal Prison Industries, Inc 507
Federal Reserve System 510
Financial Industry Regulatory Authority, Inc. 515
Freedom From Hunger Foundation 546
Fti Consulting Inc. 551
Gallaudet University 557
Gallup, Inc. 557
Government National Mortgage Assn. 590
Government Of District Of Columbia 590
House Of Representatives, United States 657
Ibw Financial Corp 669
Inter-american Development Bank 700
International Brotherhood Of Electrical Workers 704
International Brotherhood Of Teamsters 704
International Center For Research On Women 705
International Finance Corp. (world Corporations Gov't) 705
Jaffe Associates Incorporated 727
John F Kennedy Center For The Performing Arts 736
Legal Services Corporation 786
Library Of Congress 794
Lucy Webb Hayes National Training School For Deaconesses And Missionaries 814
Lutheran Services In America Inc 817
Medstar-georgetown Medical Center, Inc. 857
Metropolitan Washington Airports Authority 873
Miller & Chevalier Chartered 886
Motion Picture Association, Inc. 907
National Association Of Broadcasters 922
National Association Of Wholesaler-distributors, Inc 923
National Cable Satellite Corp 924
National Cemetery Administration 924
National Education Association Of The United States 926
National Football League Players Association 927
National Gallery Of Art 927
National Grocers Association 928
National Italian American Foundation, Inc. 929
National Organization For Women, Inc 930
National Park Foundation 930
National Public Radio, Inc. 930
National Railroad Passenger Corporation 930
National Retail Federation, Inc. 931
National Space Society 932
National Trust For Historic Preservation In The United States 933
National Wic Association, Inc. 933
Neighborhood Reinvestment Corporation 939
New Israel Fund 947
Nri, Inc. 979
Outdoor Advertising Association Of America, Inc. 1013
Pathfinder International 1031
Pepco Holdings Llc 1043
Population Services International 1068
Providence Hospital 1094
Publishing Office, Us Government 1100
Reading Is Fundamental, Inc. 1121
Recording Industry Association Of America, Inc. 1122
Reproductive Freedom For All 1132
Republican Governors Public Policy Committee 1134
Retail Industry Leaders Association, Inc 1136
Rural School And Community Trust 1159
Securities Investor Protection Corporation 1191
Smithsonian Institution 1222
Software Publishers Assoc (inc) 1225
Southeastern Universities Research Association, Inc. 1235
Special Olympics, Inc. 1245
Tcg, Inc. 1309
The Advisory Board Company 1328
The American Farmland Trust 1328
The Aspen Institute Inc 1330
The Brookings Institution 1333
The Catholic University Of America 1334
The Christian Coalition 1336
The George Washington University 1346
The Georgetown University 1346
The Heritage Foundation 1348
The Hospital For Sick Children Pediatric Center 1349
The Howard University 1349
The Humane Society Of The United States 1349
The Institute Of International Finance Inc 1350
The Interfaith Alliance Inc 1350
The International City Management Association Retirement Corporation 1350
The Jane Goodall Institute For Wildlife Research Education And Conservation 1351
The National Alliance To End Homelessness Incorporated 1358
The National Parks & Conservation Association 1359
The Ocean Conservancy Inc 1362
The Technology Association Of America 1370
The Urban Institute 1376
Truth Initiative Foundation 1412
U.s. General Services Administration 1418
Unidosus 1423
United Negro College Fund, Inc. 1429
United States Holocaust Memorial Museum 1432
United States Telephone Association 1433
Universities Research Association Inc. 1438
Vanda Pharmaceuticals Inc 1465
Versar, Inc. 1472
Washington Hospital Center Corporation 1497
Washington Legal Foundation 1497
Washington Metropolitan Area Transit Authority 1498
Washington Sports & Entertainment, Inc. 1498
Wgl Holdings, Inc. 1518
Wilmer Cutler Pickering Hale And Dorr Llp 1526
Wine & Spirits Wholesalers Of America, Inc. 1528
World Wildlife Fund, Inc. 1535

INDEX BY HEADQUARTERS LOCATION

Xylem Inc 1542
Ywca Of The Usa, National Board (inc) 1547

FLORIDA

Alachua
Axogen Inc 148

Altamonte Springs
Adventist Health System/sunbelt, Inc. 26
Tri-city Electrical Contractors, Inc. 1403

Arcadia
Dmh Real Estate Holdings, Inc. 419

Ave Maria
Ave Maria University, Inc. 144

Aventura
Immersion Corp 679

Bartow
American Commerce Solutions Inc 71

Bay Harbor Islands
Clicker Inc 322

Belle Glade
Wilkinson-cooper Produce Inc 1523

Boca Raton
Adt Inc (de) 23
Applied Card Systems Inc. 103
Celsius Holdings Inc 262
Cross Country Healthcare Inc 373
Digitalbridge Group Inc 413
Florida Atlantic University 529
Friendfinder Networks Inc 549
Geo Group Inc (the) (new) 569
Geosyntec Consultants, Inc. 572
Johnson Controls Fire Protection Lp 738
Juniper Group Inc. 741
Newsmax Media, Inc. 954
Newtekone Inc 955
Novelstem International Corp 978
Odp Corp (the) 989
Partsbase, Inc. 1030
Purity Wholesale Grocers, Inc. 1102
Q.e.p. Co., Inc. 1104
Sba Communications Corp (new) 1181
The Adt Security Corporation 1327
Therapeuticsmd Inc 1380
Veriteq Corp 1472

Bonita Springs
Herc Holdings Inc 634
Ten Pubco, Inc. 1316

Boynton Beach
Cubesmart, L.p. 379
Puradyn Filter Technologies Inc 1101

Bradenton
Beall's, Inc. 166
Manatee Memorial Hospital, L.p. 827

Brandon
Prison Rehabilitative Industries And Diversified Enterprises, Inc. 1085

Cape Canaveral
Iap Worldwide Services, Inc. 668

Cape Coral
Genesiscare Usa, Inc. 567
Tigrent Inc 1386

Clearwater
Apyx Medical Corp 107
Baycare Health System, Inc. 163
Eckerd Youth Alternatives, Inc. 445
Fletcher Music Centers, Inc. 528
Marinemax Inc 833
Nicholas Financial Inc (bc) 958
Soft Computer Consultants Inc. 1225
Tech Data Corporation 1310

Clewiston
United States Sugar Corporation 1433

Cocoa
Video Display Corp 1476

Coconut Creek
Food For The Poor, Inc. 534
Willis Lease Finance Corp. 1526

Coconut Grove
Hmg/courtland Properties, Inc. 644

Coral Gables
Aci Worldwide Inc 15
Aura Minerals Inc (british Virgin Islands) 139
Bermello, Ajamil & Partners, Inc. 175
Catalyst Pharmaceuticals Inc 254
Machado/garcia-serra Publicidad, Inc. 821
Mastec Inc. (fl) 842

Coral Springs
Verifone Systems, Inc. 1471

Dade City
Withlacoochee River Electric Cooperative Inc 1531

Davie
Arnet Pharmaceutical Corporation 116
Hard Rock Heals Foundation, Inc. 617
Kellstrom Aerospace, Llc 748
Nova Southeastern University, Inc. 977
Plantation General Hospital, L.p. 1062

Daytona Beach
Bethune-cookman University Inc. 177
Brown & Brown Inc 215
Embry-riddle Aeronautical University, Inc. 459
International Speedway Corporation 707
Ladies Professional Golf Association 772
National Association For Stock Car Auto Racing, Inc. 922
Topbuild Corp 1392

De Leon Springs
Sparton Corporation 1245

Deerfield Beach
Coverall North America, Inc. 367

Deland
Rm2 International Inc 1146
Stetson University, Inc. 1274

Delray Beach
Decisionpoint Systems Inc (new) 398
Levenger Company 791
Morse Operations, Inc. 905
Petmed Express Inc 1048
Positiveid Corp 1070

Doral
Andes Chemical, Llc 94
G.e.c. Associates, Inc. 555
Perry Ellis International Inc 1047
Sothys U.s.a., Inc. 1230
Univision Communications Inc. 1452

Dunedin
The Bernd Group Inc 1331

Englewood
Hca Florida Englewood Hospital 624

Estero
Hertz Global Holdings Inc (new) 636

Fort Lauderdale
Autonation, Inc. 141
Bbx Capital Corporation 165
Citrix Systems, Inc. 296
Edisonlearning, Inc. 447
Element Solutions Inc 456
Flanigan's Enterprises, Inc. 528
Future Tech Enterprise, Inc. 554
Ga Telesis, Llc 556
Holy Cross Hospital, Inc. 649
Interbond Of America, Llc 701
Itg Cigars Inc. 718
National Beverage Corp. 924
North Broward Hospital District 965
Online Vacation Center Holdings Corp 1001
Optimumbank Holdings Inc 1004
Protext Mobility Inc 1093
Seacor Holdings Inc. 1189
Singing Machine Co., Inc. 1213
Stiles Corporation 1276
Swisher Hygiene Inc. 1296
Tcg Family Business Llc 1309
Universal Insurance Holdings Inc 1436
West Marine, Inc. 1509

Fort Myers
Alico, Inc. 47
Data2logistics, Llc 392
Lee Memorial Health System Foundation, Inc. 785
Neogenomics Inc 940
Wci Communities, Inc. 1502

Fort Pierce
Lawnwood Medical Center, Inc. 781
Twin Vee Powercats Inc 1416

Gainesville
Exactech, Inc. 491
Gainesville Regional Utilities 556
Infinite Energy, Llc 688
North Florida Regional Medical Center, Inc. 967
Quick-med Technologies Inc 1109
Shands Teaching Hospital And Clinics, Inc. 1202
University Of Florida 1443

Hialeah
Aerokool Aviation Corporation 29
City Of Hialeah 304
Natural Fruit Corp. 935

Hollywood
Heico Corp 630
Nv5 Global Inc 982
South Broward Hospital District 1231

Homestead
Brooks Tropicals Holding, Inc. 215

Jacksonville
Baptist Health System, Inc. 158
Beaver Street Fisheries, Inc. 167
Black Knight, Inc. 186
City Of Jacksonville 305
Crowley Maritime Corporation 374
Csx Corp 378
Dun & Bradstreet Holdings Inc 430
Elkins Constructors, Inc. 457
Entegee, Inc. 472
Equity One, Inc. 481
Everbank Financial Corp 488
Fidelity National Financial Inc 514
Fidelity National Information Services Inc 514
Florida State College At Jacksonville 531
Frp Holdings Inc 550
Gee Group Inc 561
Genesis Health, Inc. 567
International Baler Corp 703
Jacksonville Electric Authority 725
Jacksonville Jaguars, Llc 725
Jacksonville University 725
Landstar System, Inc. 777
Markmonitor Inc. 835
Mayo Clinic Jacksonville (a Nonprofit Corporation) 848
Miller Electric Company 886
Nemours Foundation 939
Parkervision Inc 1027
Rayonier Advanced Materials Inc 1118
Regency Centers Corp 1126
Shands Jacksonville Medical Center, Inc. 1202
Smc Systems, Inc. 1221
St. Vincent's Health System, Inc. 1262
Stein Mart, Inc. 1271
Stellar Group, Incorporated 1271
The Dun & Bradstreet Corporation 1342
The University Of North Florida 1375
Tote Maritime Puerto Rico, Llc 1393
Trailer Bridge, Inc. 1397
Underwood Jewelers Corp. 1422
Web.com Group, Inc. 1503

INDEX BY HEADQUARTERS LOCATION

Jacksonville Beach
Intrepid Capital Corporation 709
Professional Placement Resources Llc 1087

Juno Beach
Florida Power & Light Co. 531
Nextera Energy Inc 956
Nextera Energy Partners Lp 956

Jupiter
Dyadic International Inc 433
G4s Secure Solutions (usa) Inc. 555
Jupiter Medical Center, Inc. 742
National Golf Foundation, Inc. 927
Town Sports International Holdings Inc 1394

Keystone Heights
Clay Electric Cooperative, Inc. 318

Kissimmee
Kissimmee Utility Authority (inc) 759
Osceola Regional Hospital, Inc. 1011

Lake Mary
Dixon Ticonderoga Company 418
Faro Technologies Inc. 503
Fonon Corp 534
Verifyme Inc 1471

Lake Park
Findex.com, Inc. 516

Lake Wales
Citrus World, Inc. 296

Lakeland
Lakeland Regional Medical Center, Inc. 774
Publix Super Markets, Inc. 1100
Publix Super Markets, Inc. 1100

Lakewood Ranch
Gulf Coast Project Services, Inc. 607

Largo
Bulova Technologies Group, Inc 220
Conmed Corp 349

Las Vegas
Methes Energies International Ltd 869

Longwood
D & A Building Services, Inc. 386

Loxahatchee
Palms West Hospital Limited Partnership 1021

Maitland
Amacore Group Inc 62

Margate
Margate Medical Staff, Inc. 832

Marianna
Jackson County Hospital District 724

Medley
All American Containers, Inc. 48
Community Asphalt Corp. 341
Medley Steel And Supply, Inc. 856
Rex Chemical Corporation 1139
Walton & Post, Inc. 1496

Melbourne
Holiday Builders, Inc. 647

Holmes Regional Medical Center, Inc. 649
L3harris Technologies Inc 770
Parabel Inc 1023
The Goldfield Corporation Del 1346

Merritt Island
World Surveillance Group Inc 1535

Miami
Baptist Hospital Of Miami, Inc. 158
Barry University, Inc. 160
Carnival Corp 248
City Of Miami 307
Edd Helms Group 446
Everglades Steel Corporation 488
Evi Industries Inc 490
Florida International University 530
Foundever Operating Corporation 541
Gancedo Lumber Co., Inc. 558
Gaucho Group Holdings Inc 561
Hackett Group Inc 611
Honshy Electric Co., Inc. 652
Intermark Industries, Inc. 702
Ladenburg Thalmann Financial Services Inc 772
Laureate Education Inc 780
Lennar Corp 789
Miami Jewish Health Systems, Inc. 875
Non-invasive Monitoring Systems Inc. 962
Norwegian Cruise Line Holdings Ltd 976
Ontrak Inc 1002
Opko Health Inc 1003
Perez Trading Company, Inc. 1045
Popeyes Louisiana Kitchen, Inc. 1068
Royal Caribbean Group 1156
Ryder System, Inc. 1161
Sandler, Travis & Rosenberg, P.a. 1175
Spanish Broadcasting System Inc 1244
The Public Health Trust Of Miami-dade County 1365
Trujillo & Sons, Inc. 1409
Variety Children's Hospital 1466
Vector Group Ltd 1468
Veru Inc 1473
Watsco Inc. 1500
World Kinect Corp 1534

Miami
Simply Inc 1212

Miami Beach
Meridian Partners, Llc 865
Millennium Prime Inc 886
Mount Sinai Medical Center Of Florida, Inc. 908

Miami Gardens
El Dorado Furniture Corp 451
Florida Memorial University, Inc. 530

Miami Lakes
Bankunited Inc. 156
Erba Diagnostics 481

Ifx Corp 674

Miramar
Energy Services Providers, Inc. 468
Generex Biotechnology Corp (de) 566
Parlux Holdings, Inc. 1028
Spirit Airlines Inc 1249

Mount Dora
Metwood Inc 873

Mulberry
W.s. Badcock Llc 1492

Naples
American Farms, Llc 74
Beasley Broadcast Group Inc 166
Nch Healthcare System, Inc. 937
Windsor Distributing, Inc. 1527

North Fort Myers
Lee County Electric Cooperative, Inc. 784

Ocala
Aim Immunotech Inc 36
Marion Community Hospital Inc 833
Munroe Regional Medical Center, Inc. 915
Nobility Homes, Inc. 960

Odessa
Allied Universal Electronic Monitoring Us, Inc. 54
Dais Corp 388

Okeechobee
Okeechobee Hospital, Inc. 992

Oldsmar
Cryo-cell International Inc 376
Procyon Corp. 1086

Opa Locka
American Fruit & Produce, Corp. 75

Orlando
Adventist Health System/sunbelt, Inc. 26
City Of Orlando 309
Darden Restaurants, Inc. 391
Enterprise Florida, Inc. 474
Florida Municipal Power Agency 530
Gencor Industries Inc 563
Genelink Inc 563
Greater Orlando Aviation Authority 597
Hilton Grand Vacations Inc 642
Holiday Inn Club Vacations Incorporated 647
Imaging Diagnostic Systems Inc 679
International Association Of Amusement Parks And Attractions 703
Legacy Awc, Inc. 785
Lgl Group Inc (the) 792
Lightpath Technologies, Inc. 797
Marriott Vacations Worldwide Corp. 837
Nnn Reit Inc 960
Orlando Health, Inc. 1009
Orlando Utilities Commission (inc) 1009
Passur Aerospace, Inc. 1030

Rosen Hotels And Resorts, Inc. 1154
Rotech Healthcare Inc. 1154
T & G Corporation 1300
Tempaco, Inc. 1316
The University Of Central Florida Board Of Trustees 1373
Travel + Leisure Co 1400
Tupperware Brands Corp 1414
United Parks & Resorts Inc 1430
Vcom3d, Inc. 1468
Voxx International Corp 1487

Oviedo
A. Duda & Sons, Inc. 5
Riptide Software, Inc. 1144

Palm Bay
Oakridge Global Energy Solutions Inc 985

Palm Beach Gardens
Carrier Global Corp 250
Dycom Industries, Inc. 433
Professional Golfers Association Of America Inc 1087

Palmetto
Jupiter Marine International Holdings, Inc. 742

Panama City
Bay County Health System, Llc 163

Panama City Beach
St. Joe Co. (the) 1257

Pembroke Pines
Mera Pharmaceuticals, Inc. 860

Pensacola
Baptist Health Care Corporation 157
Gulf Power Co 607
Sacred Heart Health System, Inc. 1163

Pinellas Park
Comerton Corp 338

Plantation
Cd International Enterprises Inc 259
Chewy Inc 279
Djsp Enterprises, Inc. 418
Nutra Pharma Corp 981
Payments Business Corp. 1033

Pompano Beach
Baer's Furniture Co., Inc. 151
Onstream Media Corp 1001

Ponte Vedra
Advanced Disposal Services, Inc. 24

Ponte Vedra Beach
Pga Tour, Inc. 1050

Port Saint Lucie
St. Lucie Medical Center Auxiliary, Inc. 1259

Port St. Lucie
Fpb Bancorp Inc 542

Riviera Beach
Consulier Engineering, Inc. 353

Rockledge
American Services Technology, Inc. 83

Health First Shared Services, Inc. 626
Space Coast Health Foundation, Inc. 1243

Saint Petersburg
City Of Saint Petersburg 311
Corporate Fitness Works, Inc. 362
Eckerd College, Inc. 445
Hsn, Inc. 660
Johns Hopkins All Children's Hospital, Inc. 736
Northside Hospital 973
Pscu, Llc 1096
Raymond James & Associates Inc 1118
St. Anthony's Hospital, Inc. 1256
The National Association Of Professional Baseball Leagues Inc 1359
The Poynter Institute For Media Studies Inc 1365
Wta Tour, Inc. 1538

Sanford
Mobile Area Networks Inc 895
Sanford Airport Authority 1176

Sarasota
Helios Technologies Inc 631
Radiant Power Idc, Llc 1113
Rock Creek Pharmaceuticals Inc 1149
Roper Technologies Inc 1153
Sarasota County Public Hospital District 1178
Uniroyal Global Engineered Products Inc 1425

South Miami
Baptist Health South Florida, Inc. 157
Ilg, Llc 675
Larkin Community Hospital, Inc. 778
Magnum Construction Management, Llc 824
South Miami Hospital, Inc. 1233

St. Petersburg
American Coastal Insurance Corp 71
Duke Energy Florida Llc 428
Hydron Technologies, Inc. 667
Jabil Inc 723
Powerlinx, Inc. 1073
Raymond James Financial, Inc. 1118
Superior Group Of Companies Inc 1290

Stuart
Seacoast Banking Corp. Of Florida 1189

Sumterville
Sumter Electric Cooperative, Inc. 1285

Sunny Isles Beach
Icahn Enterprises Lp 669

Sunrise
Fednat Holding Co 511
Florida Panthers Hockey Club, Ltd. 531
Interim Healthcare Inc. 702
Nationshealth Inc 934

Pediatrix Medical Group Inc 1037
Pet Supermarket, Inc. 1048
Us Stem Cell Inc 1458

Tallahassee
Capital City Bank Group, Inc. 241
Florida A & M University 529
Florida Department Of Lottery 529
Florida Housing Finance Corp 530
Florida State University 531
Image Api, Llc 677
Infinity Software Development, Inc. 688
Tallahassee Memorial Healthcare, Inc. 1303
Tallahassee, City Of (inc) 1303

Tampa
Advanzeon Solutions Inc 26
American Fiber Green Products Inc 74
Ameristeel Corp. 88
Autoweb, Inc. 142
Big Brothers Big Sisters Of America Corporation 178
Bloomin' Brands Inc 189
City Of Tampa 313
Connecton, Inc. 350
Crown Holdings Inc 375
Florida Health Sciences Center, Inc. 530
Gulfstream Natural Gas System, L.l.c. 608
H. Lee Moffitt Cancer Center And Research Institute Hospital, Inc. 611
Healthplan Holdings, Inc. 627
Heritage Insurance Holdings Inc 634
Hillsborough County Aviation Authority 642
Inhibitor Therapeutics Inc 691
Innovaro Inc. 692
Innovative Software Technologies Inc 692
Jagged Peak, Inc. 727
Keenan, Hopkins, Schmidt And Stowell Contractors, Inc. 747
Kforce Inc. 754
Mark Master, Inc. 834
Mcnichols Company 852
Mosaic Co (the) 906
Nfinanse Inc 957
Odyssey Marine Exploration, Inc. 989
Oragenics Inc 1005
Overseas Shipholding Group Inc (new) 1014
Pacira Biosciences Inc 1020
Primo Water Corp (canada) 1082
Seminole Electric Cooperative, Inc. 1195
Shriners Hospitals For Children 1207
Syniverse Holdings, Inc. 1298
Tampa Electric Company 1304
Teco Energy, Inc. 1312
United Maritime Group, Llc 1429
University Community Hospital, Inc. 1438
University Of South Florida 1449
Us China Mining Group Inc 1456

Tampa
Hci Group Inc 625

Tavares
Florida Hospital Waterman, Inc. 530

Trinity
Welbilt, Inc. 1506

Vero Beach
Armour Residential Reit Inc. 115
George E. Warren Llc 570
Javelin Mortgage Investment Corp. 729
Marquette Lumber Company, Incorporated 836
Orchid Island Capital Inc 1007

Wesley Chapel
Saddlebrook Resorts, Inc. 1164

West Melbourne
Bk Technologies Corp 185

West Palm Beach
Affiliated Managers Group Inc. 30
Chatham Lodging Trust 275
Columbia Hospital (palm Beaches) Limited Partnership 336
Innovate Corp 692
Ocwen Financial Corp 988
Oxbow Corporation 1015
Rennova Health Inc 1131
Solitron Devices, Inc. 1227
Sportsquest Inc 1249
Surgline International Inc. 1293

Weston
Original Impressions, Llc 1008

Wildlight
Rayonier Inc. 1118

Winter Garden
Knox Nursery, Inc. 761

Winter Haven
Carpenter Contractors Of America, Inc. 249
Southstate Corp 1241
Winter Haven Hospital, Inc. 1529

Winter Park
Cto Realty Growth Inc (new) 378
Lasersight Inc 779
Rollins College 1152
Rsr Group, Inc. 1157

GEORGIA

Albany
Community Capital Bancshares Inc 342
Phoebe Putney Memorial Hospital, Inc. 1053

Alpharetta
Agilysys Inc (de) 34
Alimera Sciences Inc 47
Alithya Usa, Inc. 48
Avanos Medical Inc 143
Colonial Pipeline Company 332
Coolsystems, Inc. 356
Gcp Applied Technologies Inc. 561
Jackson Healthcare, Llc 724
Legend Oil & Gas Ltd 786
Mativ Inc 843
Premiere Global Services, Inc. 1077
Sierra-cedar, Llc 1209

Streamline Health Solutions Inc 1279
Tri-s Security Corp 1403

Appling
Professional Disc Golf Association 1087

Athens
Piedmont Athens Regional Medical Center, Inc. 1054
Smallbizpros, Inc 1220
St. Mary's Hospital, Inc. 1261
University Of Georgia 1443

Atlanta
A-1 Express Delivery Service, Inc. 5
Acuity Brands Inc (holding Company) 19
Alston & Bird Llp 58
American Caresource Holdings Inc 70
American Software Inc 83
Americold Realty Trust Inc 87
Ameris Bancorp 87
Assuranceamerica Corp 128
Assurant Inc 128
Atlanta Clark University Inc 132
Atlanta National League Baseball Club, Llc 132
Atlantic American Corp. 132
Atlanticus Holdings Corp 134
Balfour Beatty Infrastructure, Inc. 153
Beazer Homes Usa, Inc. 167
Boys & Girls Clubs Of America 203
Call2recycle, Inc. 233
Cardtronics, Inc. 245
Carter's Inc 251
Catchmark Timber Trust, Inc. 255
Centerwell Health Services, Inc. 264
Choate Construction Company 286
Citizens Bancshares Corp. (ga) 294
City Of Atlanta 298
Coca-cola Co (the) 326
Cooperative For Assistance And Relief Everywhere, Inc. (care) 357
Corenet Global, Inc. 359
Corplay Inc 361
Cotiviti Holdings, Inc. 363
Cousins Properties Inc 365
Cox Enterprises, Inc. 368
Cumulus Media Inc 380
Davidson Hotel Company Llc 395
Delta Air Lines Inc (de) 403
Dlh Solutions, Inc 418
Equifax Inc 480
Federal Home Loan Bank Of Atlanta 506
Federal Reserve Bank Of Atlanta, Dist. No. 6 508
Floor & Decor Holdings Inc 529
Genuine Parts Co. 569
Georgia Power Co 571
Gf Health Products, Inc. 574
Global Payments Inc 580
Graphic Packaging Holding Co 594

INDEX BY HEADQUARTERS LOCATION

Gray Television Inc 594
H. J. Russell & Company 610
Habitat For Humanity International, Inc. 611
Hardinge Inc. 617
Heartland Payment Systems, Llc 629
Holder Properties, Inc. 647
Home Depot Inc 650
Idi Logistics, Llc 673
Intercontinental Exchange Inc 701
Interdenominational Theological Center, Inc. 701
Interface Inc. 701
Interstate Resources, Inc. 709
Invesco Ltd 712
Invesco Mortgage Capital Inc 712
J.m. Huber Corporation 723
Kwalu Llc 769
Lanier Parking Holdings, Inc. 777
Logility, Inc. 807
Manhattan Associates, Inc. 827
Marine Products Corp 833
Mikart, Llc 884
Miller Zell, Inc. 887
Morehouse College (inc.) 903
Mueller Water Products Inc 913
Municipal Electric Authority Of Georgia 915
National Distributing Company, Inc. 926
Ncr Voyix Corp 938
New Vision Group, Llc 949
Newell Brands Inc 952
Noble Investment Group, Llc 961
Norfolk Southern Corp 963
North American Electric Reliability Corporation 964
Northside Hospital, Inc. 973
Novelis Alr Aluminum Holdings Corporation 978
Novelis Inc. 978
Numerex Corp. 980
Oxford Industries, Inc. 1015
Perma-fix Environmental Services, Inc. 1046
Piedmont Hospital, Inc. 1054
Piedmont Office Realty Trust Inc 1055
Piksel, Inc. 1055
Points Of Light Foundation 1066
Preferred Apartment Communities, Llc 1075
Premier Exhibitions Inc 1076
Prgx Global, Inc. 1080
Primo Water Operations Llc 1082
Printpack, Inc. 1084
Pultegroup Inc 1101
Qcept Technologies Inc. 1104
Racetrac, Inc. 1113
Robert W Woodruff Health Sciences Center 1147
Rollins, Inc. 1152
Rpc, Inc. 1156
Scientific Research Corp 1185
Secureworks Corp 1191
Shepherd Center, Inc. 1204
Southern Company (the) 1236
Southern Company Gas 1236
Southern Power Co 1240
Spelman College 1247
Sunlink Health Systems Inc 1287
The Arthritis Foundation, Inc. 1330

The Fulton Dekalb Hospital Authority 1345
The Monarch Beverage Company Inc 1358
The North Highland Company Llc 1362
The Paradies Shops Llc 1363
Unipro Foodservice, Inc. 1425
United Parcel Service Inc 1430
Vsoft Corporation 1488
Watkins Associated Industries, Inc. 1499
Westrock Co 1515
Westrock Company 1516
Westrock Paper And Packaging, Llc 1516
Williams Industrial Services Group Inc 1525
Xenoport, Inc. 1540

Atlanta
Dlh Holdings Corp 418
First Advantage Corp (new) 517

Augusta
Au Medical Center, Inc. 137
Augusta University 138
Doctors Hospital Of Augusta, Llc 419
Georgia Rehabilitation Institute, Inc. 571
Morris Publishing Group, Llc 905
Security Land & Development Corp. 1192
University Health Services, Inc. 1439

Baldwin
Fieldale Farms Corporation 515

Ball Ground
Chart Industries Inc 274

Baxley
Baxley & Appling County Hospital Authority 162

Blairsville
United Community Banks Inc (blairsville, Ga) 1427

Brookhaven
Autotrader.com, Inc. 142
Children's Healthcare Of Atlanta, Inc. 282
Hlss Management Llc 644

Calhoun
Mohawk Industries, Inc. 897

Carrollton
University Of West Georgia 1451
Wgnb Corp. 1518

Columbus
Aflac Inc 31
Columbus Regional Healthcare System, Inc 337
Synovus Financial Corp 1299
W. C. Bradley Co. 1490

Conyers
Pratt Industries, Inc. 1074

Covington
Snapping Shoals Electric Trust, Inc. 1223

Cumming
Sawnee Electric Membership Corporation 1181

Dalton
Dixie Group Inc. 417

Darien
Southeastern Banking Corp. (darien, Ga) 1235

Decatur
Agnes Scott College, Inc. 34
Dekalb Medical Center, Inc. 400

Demorest
Piedmont University, Inc. 1055

Duluth
Agco Corp. 32
Asap Solutions Group, Llc 120
Asbury Automotive Group Inc 121
Ccur Holdings Inc 258
Delta Apparel Inc. 403
Fox Factory Holding Corp 542
National Vision Holdings Inc 933
Patient Satisfaction Plus, Llc 1031
Primerica Inc 1082
Primus Software Corporation 1083
Q-matic Corporation 1103

Dunwoody
Ants Software Inc. 98
The Krystal Company 1353

Fayetteville
Fayette Community Hospital, Inc. 504

Fitzgerald
Colony Bankcorp, Inc. 332

Forest Park
Dealers Supply Company, Inc. 397

Gainesville
Aeon Global Health Corp 28
America's Home Place, Inc. 66
Mar-jac Poultry, Inc. 830
Northeast Georgia Health System, Inc. 969

Garden City
Georgia Ports Authority 571

Hinesville
Liberty Regional Medical Center Inc. 794

Hiram
Greystone Power Corporation, An Electric Membership Corporation 600

Jefferson
Jackson Electric Membership Corporation 724

Johns Creek
Ebix Inc 443
Saia Inc 1165
Wegener Corp. 1505

Jonesboro
Low Temp Industries, Inc. 811

Kennesaw
Artivion Inc 119
Beaumont Products Incorporated 167
Eau Technologies Inc 443
Kennesaw State University 749

Lawrenceville
Gwinnett Health System, Inc. 609
Richardson Companies, Inc. 1142
Sed International Holdings, Inc. 1192

Southern Community Newspapers, Inc. 1236

Mableton
Atlanta Hardwood Corporation 132

Macon
Blue Bird Corp 190
Georgia Farm Bureau Mutual Insurance Company 571
Navicent Health, Inc. 936
The Corporation Of Mercer University 1340

Marietta
Bluelinx Holdings Inc 193
Cobb Electric Membership Corporation 326
Kennestone Hospital At Windy Hill, Inc. 749
Southern Polytechnic State University Foundation, Inc 1239
Wellstar Health System, Inc. 1507

Martinez
Bwmb, Llc 223

Milledgeville
Oconee Regional Health Systems, Inc. 988

Milton
Exide Technologies 493

Monroe
Walton Electric Membership Corporation 1496

Moultrie
Colquitt Electric Membership Corporation 334

Norcross
Cape Environmental Management Inc. 240
Corecard Corp 359
Galectin Therapeutics Inc 557
Guided Therapeutics Inc 606
Ole' Mexican Foods, Inc. 994
Omnimax Holdings, Inc. 997
Prosys Information Systems, Inc. 1091
Simtrol Inc 1212
Venture Construction Company Inc 1469
Xponential, Inc. 1541

Peachtree Corners
Crawford & Co. 369
Herschend Entertainment Company, Llc 635
Immucor, Inc. 680

Pendergrass
Nicolon Corporation 958

Reynolds
Flint Electric Membership Corporation 529

Rome
Floyd Healthcare Management, Inc. 532
Redmond Park Hospital, Llc 1124

Roswell
Dynamix Group, Inc 433
Siteone Landscape Supply Inc 1215
Vertical Communications, Inc. 1473

INDEX BY HEADQUARTERS LOCATION

Savannah
Citi Trends Inc 293
Savannah Health Services, Llc 1180
St. Joseph's/candler Health System, Inc. 1259
The Savannah College Of Art And Design Inc 1367

Statesboro
Georgia Southern University 571

Stillmore
Crider, Inc. 372

Stockbridge
Henry County Bancshares Inc (stockbridge, Ga) 632

Stone Mountain
Ga Communications, Inc. 555

Suwanee
Arris Group, Inc. 117
Papa's Pizza To Go Inc 1023

Thomaston
Upson County Hospital, Inc. 1454

Thomasville
Flowers Foods, Inc. 532
Thomasville Bancshares, Inc. 1383

Toccoa
1st Franklin Financial Corp. 3

Tucker
Georgia Transmission Corporation (an Electric Membership Corporation) 572
Gms Inc 583
Oglethorpe Power Corp 990

Valdosta
Hospital Authority Of Valdosta And Lowndes County, Georgia 654
Tift Regional Medical Center Foundation, Inc. 1385
Valdosta State University 1462

Woodstock
Primus Builders, Inc. 1083
Woodstock Holdings Inc 1533

HAWAII

Aiea
Diagnostic Laboratory Services, Inc. 410

Hilo
Hawaiian Macadamia Nut Orchards Lp 623

Honolulu
Alexander & Baldwin Inc (reit) 45
Bank Of Hawaii Corp 155
Barnwell Industries, Inc. 160
Central Pacific Financial Corp 266
City & County Of Honolulu 297
First Hawaiian Inc 521
Hawai I Pacific Health 622
Hawai I Pacific University 622
Hawaii Department Of Transportation 622
Hawaiian Electric Industries Inc 622
Hawaiian Holdings Inc 622
Hawaiian Telcom Holdco, Inc. 623

Kuakini Health System 768
L & L Franchise, Inc. 769
Matson Inc 844
Servco Pacific Inc. 1199
Territorial Bancorp Inc 1320
Trustees Of The Estate Of Bernice Pauahi Bishop 1411
University Of Hawaii System 1443

Kailua-kona
Cyanotech Corp. 384

Maui
Maui Land & Pineapple Co., Inc. 845

IDAHO

Boise
Albertsons Companies Inc 43
Amalgated Sugar Company 63
Boise Cascade Co. (de) 196
Boise State University Foundation, Inc. 196
Idacorp Inc 671
Idaho Power Co 672
Micron Technology Inc. 878
Opts Ideas, Inc 1005
Pcs Edventures! Inc 1035
Saint Alphonsus Regional Medical Center, Inc. 1166
St. Luke's Health System, Ltd. 1260
Taos Mountain, Llc 1305
Thunder Mountain Gold, Inc. 1385
Winco Foods, Llc 1527

Caldwell
Symms Fruit Ranch, Inc. 1297

Coeur D Alene
Mines Management, Inc. 889

Coeur D'alene
Hecla Mining Co 630
Idaho Strategic Resources Inc 672
Timberline Resources Corp 1386

Eagle
Lamb Weston Holdings Inc 775

Emmett
T.j.t., Inc. 1301

Fairfield
High Country Fusion Company, Inc. 639

Idaho Falls
International Isotopes Inc 706
Melaleuca, Inc. 858
North Wind, Inc. 969
Wada Farms Marketing Group Llc 1493

Ketchum
The A C Houston Lumber Company 1327

Moscow
Regents Of The University Of Idaho 1127

Pocatello
Idaho State University 672

Rexburg
Amx International, Inc. 92

Sandpoint
Litehouse, Inc. 802

ILLINOIS

Abbott Park
Abbott Laboratories 9

Alsip
Capstone Holding Corp 243
Griffith Foods Group Inc. 601

Arlington Heights
Northwest Community Hospital Inc 974

Assumption
Sloan Implement Company, Inc. 1219

Aurora
Cano Container Corporation 239
Old Second Bancorp., Inc. (aurora, Ill.) 994
Osi Group, Llc 1011
Rush Copley Medical Center 1159
Westell Technologies Inc 1511

Bannockburn
Option Care Health Inc 1004
Stericycle Inc. 1273

Barrington
Yunhong Green Cti Ltd 1547

Batavia
Suncast Corporation 1286

Bedford Park
Lapham-hickey Steel Corp. 778
Raani Corporation 1112

Belleville
Protestant Memorial Medical Center, Inc. 1093

Bensenville
Rubicon Technology Inc 1158
The Trade Event Resource Management Group Llc 1370

Berwyn
Campagna-turano Bakery, Inc. 237

Bloomingdale
Pctel Inc 1035

Bloomington
Country Casualty Insurance Co. (bloomington, Il) 365
Country Investors Life Assurance Co. (bloomington, Il) 365
Evergreen Fs, Inc 488
Growmark, Inc. 602
Illinois Wesleyan University 677

Bolingbrook
Ulta Beauty Inc 1420
Ulta Salon, Cosmetics & Fragrance, Inc. 1420

Braidwood
Drx, Ltd. 427

Breese
St. Joseph's Hospital, Breese, Of The Hospital Sisters Of The Third Order Of St. Francis 1258

Bridgeview
Manitex International Inc 828
Midland Capital Holdings Corp 882
Rose Paving, Llc 1153

Broadview
National Van Lines, Inc. 933

Buffalo Grove
Essex Rental Corp 485

Burr Ridge
Bankfinancial Corp 156
Daubert Industries, Inc. 393
Integrated Project Management Company, Inc. 698

Carbondale
Southern Illinois Healthcare Enterprises, Inc. 1237
Southern Illinois University Inc 1237

Carmi
Martin & Bayley, Inc. 838

Carol Stream
Tyndale House Publishers, Inc. 1417

Caseyville
Earl L. Henderson Trucking Company, Llc 438

Champaign
First Busey Corp 519
Great American Bancorp Inc 595

Chester
Chester Bancorp Inc. 279

Chicago
A. Epstein And Sons International, Inc. 6
Adtalem Global Education Inc 23
Alexian Brothers Health System 46
Alzheimer's Disease And Related Disorders Association, Inc. 62
American Bar Association 68
American College Of Healthcare Executives 71
American Dental Association 72
American Hospital Association 76
American Library Association 78
American Lung Association 79
American Marketing Association Inc 79
American Medical Association Inc 79
Amsted Industries Incorporated 92
Ann & Robert H. Lurie Children's Hospital Of Chicago 96
Apics, Inc. 100
Arch Venture Corporation 109
Archer Daniels Midland Co. 109
Association For Creative Industries 127
Azek Co Inc (the) 149
Benevolent And Protective Order Of Elks 172
Blue Cross & Blue Shield Association 190
Board Of Trustees Of Community College District 508 (inc) 194
Byline Bancorp Inc 224
Cboe Global Markets Inc 258
Ccc Intelligent Solutions Holdings Inc 258
Central Steel And Wire Company, Llc 267

INDEX BY HEADQUARTERS LOCATION

Century Aluminum Co. 268
Chicago Blackhawk Hockey Team, Inc. 280
Chicago Community Trust 280
Chicago Professional Sports Corporation 280
Chicago Review Press Incorporated 280
Chicago Transit Authority (inc) 281
Chicago White Sox, Ltd. 281
Citadel Enterprise Americas Llc 293
City Of Chicago 301
Clayco, Inc. 318
Cme Group Inc 323
Cna Financial Corp 324
Coeur Mining Inc 327
Columbia College Chicago 335
Commonspirit Health 340
Commonwealth Edison Company 340
Conagra Brands Inc 347
Continental Materials Corp. 354
Corcentric, Llc 358
Daniel J. Edelman, Inc. 390
Depaul University 406
Distribution Solutions Group Inc 416
Donnelley Financial Solutions Inc 422
Draper And Kramer, Incorporated 425
Easter Seals, Inc. 440
Echo Global Logistics, Inc. 444
Electronic Knowledge Interchange Inc 455
Enova International Inc 470
Equity Commonwealth 481
Equity Lifestyle Properties Inc 481
Equity Residential 481
Exelon Corp 493
Federal Home Loan Bank Chicago 506
Federal Reserve Bank Of Chicago, Dist. No. 7 508
Field Museum Of Natural History 514
First Industrial Realty Trust Inc 521
First Nonprofit Unemployment Administration Company, Llc 523
Freightcar America Inc 547
Gatx Corp 561
Gelber Group, Llc 562
Groupon Inc 602
Guaranteed Rate, Inc. 604
Harborquest, Inc. 617
Heidrick & Struggles International, Inc. 630
Hinshaw & Culbertson Llp 643
Home Products International Inc. 651
Hometown America, L.l.c. 651
Huron Consulting Group Inc 665
Hyatt Hotels Corp 666
Illinois Housing Development Authority (inc) 676
Illinois Institute Of Technology 676
Inteliquent, Inc. 699
John Bean Technologies Corp 735

John D And Catherine T Macarthur Foundation 735
Jones Lang Lasalle Inc 739
Kellanova 747
Kemper Corp (de) 748
Kingsway Financial Services Inc (de) 757
Leopardo Companies Inc. 790
Lincoln International Llc 799
Littelfuse Inc 802
Lkq Corp 805
Loyola University Of Chicago Inc 812
Luster Products, Inc. 816
Lyric Opera Of Chicago 818
Mack & Associates Ltd. 822
Mattersight Corporation 844
Methode Electronics Inc 869
Mondelez International Inc 899
Morningstar Inc 904
Motorola Solutions Inc 907
Muscular Dystrophy Association, Inc. 916
National Council Of Young Men's Christian Associations Of The United States Of America 926
Nes Rentals Holdings, Inc. 941
Newark Corporation 952
North Park University 968
Northern Trust Corp 972
Northwestern Memorial Healthcare 975
O'neil Industries, Inc. 983
Oil-dri Corp. Of America 992
Old Republic International Corp. 994
Onespan Inc 1001
Orbitz Worldwide, Inc. 1006
Pepper Construction Group, Llc 1043
Potbelly Corp 1071
Power Construction Company, Llc 1072
Prevent Child Abuse Of America 1080
Professional Diversity Network Inc 1087
R. R. Donnelley & Sons Company 1112
Rj. O'brien & Associates, Llc 1112
Riverview Realty Partners Lp 1146
Ronald Mcdonald House Charities, Inc. 1152
Rush System For Health 1159
Ryerson Holding Corp 1161
Schiff Hardin Llp 1183
Schulze And Burch Biscuit Co. 1184
Seyfarth Shaw Llp 1201
Sidley Austin Llp 1208
Sinai Health System 1213
Skidmore, Owings & Merrill Llp 1216
Sp Plus Corp 1243
St. Bernard Hospital 1256
Superior Graphite Co. 1290
Telephone & Data Systems Inc 1314
The Options Clearing Corporation 1362
The University Of Chicago 1373
The University Of Chicago Medical Center 1374

The Walsh Group Ltd 1377
Tootsie Roll Industries Inc 1391
Transunion 1400
Tribune Publishing Company 1404
True Value Company, L.l.c. 1409
Ttx Co. 1413
U.s. Equities Realty, Llc 1417
Union Health Service Inc 1424
United Airlines Holdings Inc 1426
United Airlines, Inc. 1426
United States Cellular Corp 1432
United States Soccer Federation, Inc. 1433
Usg Corporation 1459
Ventas Inc 1469
Veradigm Inc 1470
Vhs Acquisition Subsidiary Number 3, Inc. 1474
Victory Screen Printing, Inc. 1476
Vita Food Products, Inc. 1484
William Blair & Company Llc 1525
Window To The World Communications, Inc. 1527
Winston & Strawn Llp 1529
Wm. Wrigley Jr. Company 1531
World Business Chicago 1534
World's Finest Chocolate, Inc. 1536
Ziegler Cos., Inc. (wi) 1550

Chicago
Mcdonald's Corp 850

Chicago Heights
Chs Acquisition Corp. 288

Cicero
A.l.l. Masonry Construction Co., Inc. 6
Broadwind Inc 212

Collinsville
Ameren Illinois Co 66
The Glik Company 1346

Crystal Lake
Aptargroup Inc. 106
Centegra Health System 263
Curran Group, Inc. 381

Dakota
Berner Food & Beverage, Llc 175

Decatur
Decatur Memorial Hospital 398

Deerfield
Bab Inc 150
Baxter International Inc 163
Cf Industries Holdings Inc 270
Essendant Inc. 484
Fortune Brands Innovations Inc 539
Horizon Pharma, Inc. 653
Magneco/metrel, Inc. 824
Scai Holdings, Llc 1181
Surgalign Holdings Inc 1292
Terra Nitrogen Company, L.p. 1319
Textura Corporation 1327
Walgreens Boots Alliance Inc 1494

Dekalb
Kishhealth System 758
The Northern Illinois University 1362

Des Plaines
Brg Sports, Inc. 208

Frank Consolidated Enterprises, Inc. 543
Institute Of Gas Technology 696

Downers Grove
Advocate Aurora Health Inc. 27
Advocate Charitable Foundation Inc 27
Dover Corp 424
Ftd Companies, Inc. 551
Global Gear & Machining Llc 579
Illinois State Of Toll Highway Authority 677
Mid Ventures Inc. 880
Roadrunner Transportation Systems Inc 1146
The Computing Technology Industry Association Inc 1339
U.g.n., Inc. 1417

East Dubuque
Crescent Electric Supply Company 371

East Moline
Yash Technologies, Inc. 1543

Edwardsville
Prairie Farms Dairy, Inc. 1074

Effingham
Midland States Bancorp Inc 882

Elgin
Illinois Wholesale Cash Register, Inc. 677
Jerry Biggers Chevrolet, Inc. 732
Middleby Corp 881
Sanfilippo (john B) & Son Inc 1176

Elk Grove Village
Biosynergy, Inc. 183
Newesco, Inc. 953
Sigmatron International Inc. 1209
Steiner Electric Company 1271

Elmhurst
Elmhurst Memorial Hospital Inc 459
Mcmaster-carr Supply Company 852

Evanston
Endeavor Health Clinical Operations 465
Northwestern University 975
Rotary International 1154
Underwriters Laboratories Inc. 1422

Forest Park
Farmington Foods, Inc. 503

Franklin Park
Bretford Manufacturing, Inc. 208

Freeport
Freeport Regional Health Care Foundation 547

Galesburg
The National Association For The Exchange Of Industrial Resources Inc 1359

Glenview
Illinois Tool Works, Inc. 677

INDEX BY HEADQUARTERS LOCATION

Ryan Building Group, Inc. 1160
Glenwood
Landauer, Inc. 776
Harvey
Atkore Inc 132
Atkore International Holdings Inc. 132
The Ingalls Memorial Hospital 1349
Hinsdale
Upp Technology, Inc. 1454
Hodgkins
Marietta Corporation 832
Hoffman Estates
Cdk Global, Inc. 260
Sears Holdings Corp 1190
Sears Hometown Stores, Inc. 1190
Homewood
Carl Buddig And Company 246
Itasca
American Academy Of Pediatrics 67
Emkay, Inc. 462
Enable Holdings, Inc. 464
Flexera Software Llc 528
Fundamental Global Inc 553
Hamilton Partners, Inc. 614
Henricksen & Company, Inc. 632
Knowles Corp 761
National Safety Council 932
Joliet
Central Grocers, Inc. 265
Will County 1524
Joppa
Electric Energy, Inc. 453
Kewanee
Boss Holdings, Inc. 199
La Grange
H Group Holding, Inc 610
Lafox
Richardson Electronics Ltd 1142
Lake Forest
Assertio Holdings Inc 125
Chicago Bears Football Club, Inc. 280
Grainger (w.w.) Inc. 592
Hospira, Inc. 654
Lake Forest College 773
Northwestern Lake Forest Hospital 975
Packaging Corp Of America 1020
Spherotech, Inc. 1248
Zyla Life Sciences, Llc 1553
Lake Zurich
Acco Brands Corp 13
Lansing
Land O'frost, Inc. 776
Libertyville
Aldridge Electric, Inc. 44
Intermatic Incorporated 702
Lincolnshire
Camping World Holdings Inc 238
Zebra Technologies Corp. 1549
Lincolnwood
Loeber Motors, Inc. 806
Lisle
Alliance For Audited Media 51

Cts Corp 378
Suncoke Energy Inc 1286
Lombard
Pernix Group Inc 1047
Transdev North America, Inc. 1398
Long Grove
Midwest Air Technologies, Inc. 883
Macomb
Mcdonough County Hospital District 850
Western Illinois University Inc 1512
Mattoon
Consolidated Communications Holdings Inc 351
Fairpoint Communications, Inc. 499
First Mid Bancshares Inc 522
Sarah Bush Lincoln Health Center 1178
Maywood
Mercy Hospital And Medical Center 863
Melrose Park
Gottlieb Memorial Hospital 589
Kreher Steel Company, Llc 767
Mettawa
Brunswick Corp. 217
Milan
Group O, Inc. 602
Moline
Deere & Co. 399
Qcr Holdings Inc 1104
Morris
Morris Hospital 905
Morton Grove
Lifeway Foods, Inc. 796
Naperville
Calamos Asset Management, Inc. 227
Chicago Rivet & Machine Co. 280
Corporate Travel Consultants, Inc. 362
Eby-brown Company, Llc 443
Hearthstone Utilities, Inc. 628
Qst Industries, Inc. 1106
Track Group Inc 1396
New Lenox
Silver Cross Hospital And Medical Centers 1211
Niles
The Bradford Exchange Ltd 1332
Normal
Board Of Trustees Of Illinois State University 194
North Chicago
Abbvie Inc 9
Northbrook
Allstate Corp 55
Idex Corporation 673
Stepan Co. 1272
Northfield
Medline Industries, Lp 856
Oak Brook
Ace Hardware Corp. 14
Advocate Health Care Network 27

Ascent Industries Co 122
Blistex Inc. 188
Carry Transit, Llc 250
Castle (am) & Co 253
Delta Dental Plans Association 404
Federal Signal Corp. 510
Hub Group, Inc. 660
Intellisys Technology, L.l.c. 700
Irc Retail Centers Llc 715
Retail Properties Of America, Inc. 1137
The International Association Of Lions Clubs Incorporated 1350
Treehouse Foods Inc 1402
Oakbrook Terrace
Ach Food Companies, Inc. 15
Joint Commission On Accreditation Of Healthcare Organizations 739
Orland Park
Alliance Shippers Inc. 52
Palatine
Acura Pharmaceuticals Inc 19
Township High School District 211 Foundation 1394
Paris
North American Lighting, Inc. 965
Park Ridge
Advocate Health And Hospitals Corporation 27
Pekin
Alto Ingredients Inc 61
Peoria
Bradley University 204
Central Illinois Light Co 266
Connor Co. 350
Osf Healthcare System 1011
Rli Corp 1146
Plainfield
Harbour Contractors, Inc. 617
Princeton
Osf Healthcare Saint Clare Medical Center 1011
Princeton National Bancorp, Inc. 1084
Quincy
Blessing Hospital 188
Niemann Foods, Inc. 958
Riverwoods
Discover Financial Services 416
Robinson
Crawford Memorial Foundation 369
First Robinson Financial Corp. 524
Rock Island
Augustana College 138
Modern Woodmen Of America 896
Rockford
Bergstrom Inc. 173
Ingersoll Machine Tools, Inc. 690
Rockford Health System 1150
Swedishamerican Health System Corporation 1295
Rolling Meadows
Gallagher (arthur J.) & Co. 557
Icon Identity Solutions, Inc. 671
Kelso-burnett Co. 748

Romeoville
Florstar Sales, Inc. 531
Nanophase Technologies Corp. 919
Valley View Community Unit School District 365u 1463
Rosemont
Mcshane Construction Company Llc 853
Mcshane Development Company Llc 853
Randa Accessories Leather Goods Llc 1116
Trimega Purchasing Association 1405
Us Foods Holding Corp 1457
Us Foods, Inc. 1457
Wintrust Financial Corp (il) 1530
Schaumburg
Associated Equipment Distributors 126
Convergint Technologies Llc 356
Gary Rabine & Sons, Inc. 560
Isco International, Inc. 716
Paylocity Holding Corp 1033
Perdoceo Education Corp 1044
Sagent Pharmaceuticals, Inc. 1165
Wisetech Global (us) Inc. 1530
Skokie
Tenneco Inc. 1318
Springfield
Eei Holding Corporation 449
Horace Mann Educators Corp. 652
Hospital Sisters Health System 655
Illinois Department Of Employment Security 676
Illinois Environmental Protection Agency 676
Illinois Historic Preservation Agency 676
Illinois State Board Of Education 676
Memorial Behavioral Health Center In Springfield 858
Memorial Health System 858
Roland Machinery Company 1151
Springfield Electric Supply Company, Llc 1251
St. John's Hospital Of The Hospital
Sisters Of The Third Order Of St.
Francis 1257
Sterling
Wahl Clipper Corporation 1493
Tinley Park
Goodheart-willcox Co., Inc. 587
Panduit Corp. 1022
Urbana
Carle Foundation Hospital 247
Vernon Hills
Cdw Corp 260
Sayers40, Inc 1181
Warrenville
Excel Railcar Corporation 492

INDEX BY HEADQUARTERS LOCATION

Fuel Tech Inc 551
Watseka
Iroquois Memorial Hospital & Resident Home 716
West Chicago
Ball Horticultural Company 153
Titan International Inc 1387
Westchester
Ingredion Inc 691
Rb Global Inc 1118
Westmont
Positron Corp 1070
Sirva Inc 1214
Wheaton
The Trustees Of Wheaton College 1372
Wheeling
The Segerdahl Corp 1368
Wabash Power Equipment Co. 1492
Winfield
Central Dupage Hospital Association 265
Wood Dale
Aar Corp 8
Woodridge
Trippe Manufacturing Co 1407

INDIANA

Anderson
Community Hospital Of Anderson And Madison County, Incorporated 343
Ener1, Inc. 466
Angola
Henry County Memorial Hospital 632
Batesville
Hillenbrand Inc 642
Bloomington
Hoosier Energy Rural Electric Cooperative Inc 652
Indiana University Foundation, Inc. 685
Indiana University Health Bloomington, Inc. 685
Trustees Of Indiana University 1411
Carmel
Alliance For Cooperative Energy Services Power Marketing Llc 51
Automotive Finance Corporation 141
Cno Financial Group Inc 324
Indiana Municipal Power Agency 685
Itt Educational Services Inc 719
Lauth Properties, Llc 781
Leaf Software Solutions, Inc. 783
Merchants Bancorp (indiana) 861
Midcontinent Independent System Operator, Inc. 881
Openlane Inc. 1002
Columbus
Cummins, Inc. 380

Corydon
First Capital Inc. 519
Crawfordsville
Ceres Solutions, Llp 268
Wabash College 1492
Dale
Thermwood Corp. 1381
Edinburgh
Mac Beath Hardwood Company 820
Elkhart
Asa Electronics Llc 120
Elkhart General Hospital, Inc. 457
Lci Industries 782
Nibco Inc. 958
Patrick Industries Inc 1031
Thor Industries, Inc. 1384
Evansville
Atlas World Group, Inc. 134
Berry Global Group Inc 176
Deaconess Health System, Inc. 397
Deaconess Hospital Inc 397
Escalade, Inc. 483
Fidelity Federal Bancorp 514
First Bancorp Of Indiana Inc 518
Koch Enterprises, Inc. 762
Lewis Brothers Bakeries Inc 791
Old National Bancorp (evansville, In) 994
Onemain Holdings Inc 1001
Shoe Carnival, Inc. 1206
South Central Communications Corporation 1232
St. Mary's Health, Inc. 1260
Traylor Bros., Inc. 1401
University Of Evansville 1443
Van Atlas Lines Inc 1464
Fishers
First Internet Bancorp 522
Fort Wayne
City Of Fort Wayne 303
Do It Best Corp. 419
Franklin Electric Co., Inc. 544
Hagerman Construction Corporation 612
Masterspas, Llc 843
Perfection Bakeries, Inc. 1045
Petroleum Traders Corporation 1049
Steel Dynamics Inc. 1270
Waterfurnace Renewable Energy Inc 1499
Frankfort
Zachary Confections, Inc. 1548
Gary
The Methodist Hospitals, Inc. 1357
Goshen
Liberty Homes Inc 793
Menno Travel Service, Inc. 860
Supreme Industries, Inc. 1292
Greencastle
Depauw University 406
Greenfield
Elanco Animal Health Inc 452
Hammond
Indiana Harbor Belt Railroad Co 684

Hanover
Hanover College 616
Highland
Strack And Van Til Super Market Inc. 1278
Hobart
Indiana Botanic Gardens Inc 684
Huntingburg
Parke-bell Ltd., Inc. 1027
Huntington
Northeast Indiana Bancorp Inc 970
Indianapolis
Allison Transmission Holdings Inc 55
American Red Ball Transit Company, Inc 83
American United Mutual Insurance Holding Company 86
Angie's List, Inc. 95
Apria Healthcare Group Llc 106
Bell Industries Inc (de) 169
Bowen Engineering Corporation 201
Calumet Specialty Product Partners Lp 235
Carbonite, Inc. 244
Celadon Group Inc 261
Citizens Energy Group 295
Community Health Network, Inc. 342
Duke Realty L.p. 429
Duke Realty Llc 429
Eidp, Inc. 450
Elevance Health Inc 456
Emmis Corp 462
Enghouse Networks (us) Inc. 469
Federal Home Loan Bank Indianapolis 506
Future Farmers Of America Incorporated 553
Hhgregg Inc 638
Hurco Companies Inc 664
Indiana Farm Bureau, Inc. 684
Indiana Symphony Society, Inc. 685
Indiana University Health, Inc. 686
Indiana University Research And Technology Corporation 686
Indianapolis Colts, Inc. 686
Indianapolis Motor Speedway Foundation Inc 686
Interactive Intelligence Group, Inc. 700
Ipalco Enterprises, Inc. 714
Kite Realty Group Trust 759
Kiwanis International, Inc. 759
Lilly (eli) & Co 797
Macallister Machinery Co Inc 821
Marian University, Inc. 832
Mid America Clinical Laboratories Llc 880
National Collegiate Athletic Association 925
Noble Roman's, Inc. 961
Pacers Basketball, Llc 1017
Republic Airways Holdings Inc. 1133
Simon Property Group, Inc. 1211
Superior Industrial Solutions, Inc. 1291

Tangoe Us, Inc. 1305
The College Network Inc 1338
The Finish Line Inc 1343
Usa Track & Field, Inc. 1458
Wheaton Van Lines Inc 1518
Wilhelm Construction, Inc. 1523
Jasper
German American Bancorp Inc 573
Kimball Electronics Inc 755
Jeffersonville
First Savings Financial Group Inc 525
Kokomo
Haynes International, Inc. 624
Lafayette
Greater Lafayette Health Services, Inc. 597
Kirby Risk Corporation 758
Wabash National Corp 1492
Logansport
Logansport Financial Corp. 806
Memorial Hospital 859
Madison
Arvin Sango, Inc. 120
Merrillville
Nisource Inc. (holding Co.) 959
Northern Indiana Public Service Company Llc 971
Michigan City
Horizon Bancorp Inc 653
Mishawaka
Franciscan Alliance, Inc. 543
Schurz Communications, Inc. 1184
Muncie
Ball State University 153
First Merchants Corp 522
Indiana University Health Ball Memorial Hospital, Inc. 685
Munster
Finward Bancorp 516
Noblesville
Riverview Hospital 1145
Plainfield
Duke Energy Indiana, Inc. 428
Richmond
Earlham College 438
Roanoke
Vera Bradley Inc. 1470
Rockville
Scott Pet Products, Inc. 1186
Seymour
Premier Ag Co-op, Inc. 1076
Shelbyville
Blue River Bancshares, Inc. 192
South Bend
1st Source Corp 3
Beacon Medical Group, Inc. 165
South Bend Medical Foundation Inc 1231
St. John
Amb Financial Corp 63
Terre Haute
First Financial Corp. (in) 521

Hallador Energy Co 612
Union Hospital, Inc. 1424
Valparaiso
Family Express Corporation 500
Us 1 Industries, Inc. 1456
Vincennes
Good Samaritan Hospital 586
Wabash
Ffw Corp. 513
Next, Inc. 956
Wabash County Hospital 1492
Warsaw
Kosciusko 21st Century Foundation, Inc. 765
Lakeland Financial Corp 774
Zimmer Biomet Holdings Inc 1551
Washington
Daviess County Hospital 395
West Lafayette
Inotiv Inc 693
The Trustees Of Purdue University 1371
Whitestown
Weaver Popcorn Manufacturing, Llc 1503

IOWA

Algona
American Power Group Corp 82
Ames
Ames National Corp. 89
Danfoss Power Solutions Inc. 390
Iowa State University Of Science And Technology 713
Ankeny
Casey's General Stores, Inc. 253
Armstrong
Arts Way Manufacturing Co Inc 119
Boone
Fareway Stores, Inc. 501
Breda
Snappy Popcorn Company 1223
Calmar
Northeast Iowa Community College 970
Cedar Falls
University Of Northern Iowa 1446
Cedar Rapids
Central Iowa Power Cooperative 266
Coe College 327
Crst International, Inc. 376
D. C. Taylor Co. 386
Greatamerica Financial Services Corporation 596
United Fire Group, Inc. 1428
Clear Lake
Teamquest Corporation 1310
Clive
Mercy Health Network, Inc. 863
Multi-state Lottery Association 914
Coralville
Kinseth Hospitality Company, Inc. 757

Creston
Fansteel Inc. 500
Davenport
Genesis Health System 567
Lee Enterprises, Inc. 784
Von Maur, Inc. 1486
Decorah
Luther College 817
Des Moines
Berkshire Hathaway Energy Company 174
Drake University 425
Farmland Mutual Insurance Co 503
Federal Home Loan Bank Of Des Moines 507
Krause Gentle, L.l.c. 767
Nationwide Agribusiness Insurance Co. 934
Plumb Supply Company, Llc 1064
Principal Financial Group Inc 1084
Ruan Transportation Management Systems, Inc. 1158
The Waldinger Corporation 1377
Trg Products, Inc. 1402
Dubuque
Flexsteel Industries, Inc. 528
Spahn & Rose Lumber Co. 1243
Farnhamville
Farmers Cooperative Company 502
Goldfield
Gold-eagle Cooperative 584
Grinnell
The Trustees Of Grinnell College 1371
Harlan
Farm Service Cooperative 501
Hills
Hills Bancorporation 642
Iowa City
Act, Inc. 17
Midwestone Financial Group, Inc. 884
State University Of Iowa Foundation 1268
The University Of Iowa 1374
Marcus
Little Sioux Corn Processors Llc 802
Mason City
Golden Grain Energy, Llc 584
Muscatine
Hni Corp 645
Iowa First Bancshares Corp. 713
New Hampton
Five Star Cooperative 527
North Liberty
Heartland Express, Inc. 629
Ottumwa
Ottumwa Regional Legacy Foundation, Inc. 1012
Pella
Vermeer Manufacturing Company 1472

Radcliffe
Mirenco Inc 892
Ralston
West Central Cooperative 1508
Sioux Center
Farmers Co-operative Society, Sioux Center, Iowa 502
Sioux City
Aalfs Manufacturing, Inc. 7
West Des Moines
American Equity Investment Life Holding Co 73
Heartland Co-op 629
Hy-vee, Inc. 666
Iowa Health System 713
Ita Group, Inc 717
Quality Consulting, Inc. 1107
West Bancorporation, Inc. 1508

KANSAS

Atchison
Benedictine College 171
Blish-mize Co. 188
Mgp Ingredients Inc (new) 875
Burlington
Wolf Creek Nuclear Operating Corporation 1531
Columbus
Crossland Construction Company, Inc. 374
De Soto
Mr. Goodcents, Inc. 910
Emporia
Emporia State University 463
Hays
Fort Hays State University Foundation 538
Hays Medical Center, Inc. 624
Midwest Energy, Inc. 883
Sunflower Electric Power Corp 1287
Humboldt
Monarch Cement Co. 899
Hutchinson
Stockade Companies, Llc 1276
Kansas City
Associated Wholesale Grocers, Inc. 127
Dairy Farmers Of America, Inc. 388
Four B Corp. 541
Gourmet Specialties, Inc. 590
Kansas City Board Of Public Utilities 745
Unbound Inc 1422
Lawrence
Hea Legacy, Inc. 625
Leawood
Amc Entertainment Holdings Inc. 64
Carmike Cinemas, Llc 248
Empire Energy Corp International 462
Euronet Worldwide Inc. 487
Object Technology Solutions, Inc. 985

Tallgrass Energy Partners, Lp 1303
Tallgrass Energy, Lp 1303
Lenexa
American Noble Gas Inc 80
Cboe Bats, Llc 257
Digital Ally Inc (new) 413
Mw Builders, Inc. 917
Manhattan
American Institute Of Baking 77
Kansas State University 745
Landmark Bancorp Inc 776
Mcpherson
Jayhawk Pipeline, L.l.c. 729
National Cooperative Refinery Association 925
Merriam
Seaboard Corp. 1188
New Century
Butler National Corp. 223
Olathe
Psi Services Inc. 1096
Terracon Consultants, Inc. 1320
Overland Park
Black & Veatch Corporation 185
Cartesian, Inc. 251
Compass Minerals International Inc 345
Ealixir Inc 437
Epiq Systems, Inc. 479
Isg Technology, Llc 717
Mmc Corp 895
Npc Restaurant Holdings, Llc 979
Qc Holdings Inc 1104
Wellsky Corporation 1507
Pratt
Stanion Wholesale Electric Co., Inc. 1265
Salina
Blue Beacon, Inc. 190
Great Plains Manufacturing Incorporated 596
Shawnee Mission
Shawnee Mission Medical Center, Inc. 1203
Spring Hill
Tap Enterprises, Inc. 1305
Topeka
Capitol Federal Financial Inc 242
Federal Home Loan Bank Topeka 507
Kansas Department Of Transportation 745
Kansas Electric Power Cooperative, Inc. 745
Wichita
Ageagle Aerial Systems Inc (new) 33
Ascension Via Christi Health, Inc. 122
Berry Companies, Inc. 175
Capps Manufacturing, Incorporated 242
Eby Corporation 443
Intrust Financial Corp. 710
Koch Supply & Trading, Lp 762
Spirit Aerosystems Holdings Inc 1249

INDEX BY HEADQUARTERS LOCATION

Wichita State University 1521
Wichita, City Of (inc) 1521

KENTUCKY

Berea
Berea College 172
Bowling Green
Bayou City Exploration, Inc. 164
Commonwealth Health Corporation, Inc. 340
Houchens Industries, Inc. 656
Warren Rural Electric Cooperative Corporation 1497
Covington
Ashland Llc 123
Crestview Hills
Columbia Sussex Corporation 337
Danville
Centre College Of Kentucky 267
Edgewood
Saint Elizabeth Medical Center, Inc. 1166
Elizabethtown
Kentucky Neighborhood Bank, Inc. 751
Erlanger
Disabled American Veterans 416
Florence
Healthwarehouse.com, Inc. 628
Hazard
Kentucky First Federal Bancorp 750
Henderson
Audubon Metals Llc 138
Gibbs Die Casting Corporation 574
Kenergy Corp. 748
Highland Heights
General Cable Corporation 564
Lexington
Appalachian Regional Healthcare, Inc. 102
Kentucky Medical Services Foundation, Inc. 750
Kentucky Utilities Company Inc 751
Lexmark International, Inc. 792
National Thoroughbred Racing Association, Inc. 932
Tempur Sealy International, Inc. 1316
University Of Kentucky Hospital Auxiliary Inc. 1443
Valvoline Inc 1464
Louisville
Almost Family, Inc. 56
Baptist Healthcare System, Inc. 158
Brown-forman Corp 216
Churchill Downs, Inc. 289
Citizens Financial Corp. (ky) 295
Creative Realities Inc 371
Humana Inc. 662
Louisville-jefferson County Metro Government 810
North Atlantic Trading Company, Inc. 965

Nts Realty Holdings Limited Partnership 979
Papa John's International, Inc. 1023
Pharmerica Corporation 1050
Republic Bancorp, Inc. (ky) 1133
Res-care, Inc. 1134
Residual Pumpkin Entity, Llc 1135
Sam Swope Auto Group, Llc 1171
Steel Technologies Llc 1270
Stock Yards Bancorp Inc 1276
Sypris Solutions, Inc. 1299
Texas Roadhouse Inc 1325
University Health Care, Inc. 1439
University Of Louisville 1444
Yum! Brands Inc 1547
Middlesboro
Hfb Financial Corp. 637
Owensboro
Brescia University 208
Owensboro Municipal Utilities Electric Light & Power System 1015
Texas Gas Transmission Llc 1323
Paducah
Paxton Media Group, Llc 1033
Pikeville
Community Trust Bancorp, Inc. 344
Pikeville Medical Center, Inc. 1055
Prestonsburg
Consolidated Health Systems, Inc. 352
Richmond
Eastern Kentucky University 441
Stanford
Utg Inc 1460
Tompkinsville
Monroe Medical Foundation Inc 901
Walton
Verst Group Logistics, Inc. 1472
Winchester
Delta Natural Gas Company, Inc. 404

LOUISIANA

Alexandria
Christus Health Central Louisiana 287
Baton Rouge
Adhera Therapeutics Inc 22
Amedisys, Inc. 65
Associated Grocers, Inc. 127
Baton Rouge General Medical Center 161
Cajun Industries Holdings, Llc 227
City Of Baton Rouge 299
General Health System 565
H&e Equipment Services Inc 610
Investar Holding Corp 712
Lamar Advertising Co (new) 775
Mmr Group, Inc. 895
Our Lady Of The Lake Hospital, Inc. 1013
Presonus Audio Electronics, Inc. 1079

The Newtron Group L L C 1361
Vartech Systems, Inc. 1466
Woman's Hospital Foundation Inc 1532
Covington
Cgb Enterprises, Inc. 270
Globalstar Inc 581
Loop Llc 809
Pool Corp 1067
St Tammany Parish Hospital Service District No 1 1255
Deridder
Amerisafe Inc 88
Franklin
Sterling Sugars, Inc. 1273
Golden Meadow
Abdon Callais Offshore, Llc 9
Gonzales
Crown Crafts, Inc. 375
Grand Cane
Azure Midstream Partners Lp 149
Houma
Hospital Service District No. 1 655
Jeanerette
M.a. Patout & Son Limited, L.l.c. 820
Jefferson
Entergy Gulf States Louisiana, L.l.c. 473
Entergy Louisiana Llc (new) 473
Lafayette
Acadian Ambulance Service, Inc. 12
Atc Group Services Llc 130
Home Bancorp Inc 650
Lafayette General Medical Center, Inc. 772
Our Lady Of Lourdes Regional Medical Center, Inc. 1013
Petroquest Energy Inc (new) 1049
Phi Group Inc (de) 1051
Southwest Louisiana Electric Membership Corporation 1241
Talos Petroleum Llc 1304
Lake Charles
Ckx Lands Inc 316
Mcneese State University 852
Women & Childrens Hospital Llc 1533
Mandeville
Color Me Mine Enterprises Inc 333
Marrero
Hospital Service District 1 Inc 655
Monroe
Lumen Technologies Inc 814
Scott Equipment Company, L.l.c. 1186
Morgan City
B & G Food Enterprises, Llc 150
Conrad Industries Inc 351
New Orleans
City Of New Orleans 308
Delgado Community College 402
Dillard University 414
Entergy Corp 473
Entergy New Orleans Llc 473
Loyola University, New Orleans 812

Phelps Dunbar, L.l.p. 1051
Port Of New Orleans 1069
Regional Transit Authority 1127
Treaty Energy Corp. 1401
University Of New Orleans 1446
Opelousas
American Bancorp, Inc (la) 68
Pineville
Cleco Corporate Holdings Llc 321
Crest Operations, Llc 372
Ruston
Louisiana Tech University 810
Shreveport
Caddo International Inc 226
City Of Shreveport 313
Correlate Energy Corp 362
Zachary
Hospital Service District 1 Of East Baton Rouge Parish 655

MAINE

Augusta
Central Maine Power Co. 266
Mainegeneral Health 826
Bangor
Husson University 665
St. Joseph Healthcare Foundation 1258
Versant Power 1472
Woc, Inc. 1531
Bar Harbor
Bar Harbor Bankshares 159
The Jackson Laboratory 1350
Biddeford
Biddeford Internet Corp. 178
Southern Maine Health Care 1237
Brewer
Eastern Maine Healthcare Systems 441
Brunswick
Bowdoin College 201
Camden
Camden National Corp. (me) 237
Damariscotta
First Bancorp Inc (me) 518
Miles Health Care, Inc 885
Ellsworth
Maine Coast Regional Health Facilities Inc 825
Farmington
Franklin Community Health Network 544
Gardiner
Pine State Trading Co. 1056
Guilford
Puritan Medical Products Company I Lp 1102
Lewiston
President & Trustees Of Bates College 1078
Lincoln
Larkin Enterprises, Inc. 778
Millinocket
Millinocket Regional Hospital Inc 887

North Berwick
Hussey Seating Company 665

Orono
University Of Maine Systems Inc 1444

Pittsfield
Cianbro Corporation 290

Portland
Covetrus North America, Llc 367
Diversified Communications 417
Hil Technology, Inc. 640
Immucell Corp. 679
Mainehealth 826
Mainehealth Services 826
Mercy Hospital 863
Northeast Bank (me) 969
Wex Inc 1517

Presque Isle
Maine & Maritimes Corporation 825

South Portland
Ciee, Inc. 290

Waterville
The President And Trustees Of Colby College 1365

Westbrook
Idexx Laboratories, Inc. 673
Osc Sports, Inc. 1010

MARYLAND

Adelphi
University System Of Maryland 1452

Annapolis
Davco Restaurants, Inc. 393
Hannon Armstrong Sustainable Infrastructure Capital Inc 615
Luminis Health Anne Arundel Medical Center, Inc 815
St. John's College 1257
Telecommunication Systems, Inc. 1314

Baltimore
Alban Tractor, Llc 42
Associated Catholic Charities Inc. 126
Baltimore Gas And Electric Company 154
City Of Baltimore 299
Cowan Systems, Llc 367
Dla Piper Llp (us) 418
Enerwise Global Technologies, Llc Dba Cpower 469
Franklin Square Hospital Center, Inc. 545
Greater Baltimore Medical Center, Inc. 596
Harbor Bankshares Corp. 616
Harbor Hospital Foundation, Inc. 616
Johns Hopkins Bayview Medical Center, Inc. 737
Kennedy Krieger Institute, Inc. 749
Levindale Hebrew Geriatric Center And Hospital, Inc. 791
Lifebridge Health, Inc. 795

Loyola University Maryland, Inc. 812
Medifast Inc 855
Millennial Media, Inc. 886
Monarch Services Inc. 899
Mymd Pharmaceuticals Inc 918
National Association For The Advancement Of Colored People 922
Northeastern Supply, Inc. 970
Notre Dame Of Maryland University, Inc. 976
Plexus Installations, Inc: 1064
Shepherd Electric Company, Llc 1204
Sinai Hospital Of Baltimore, Inc. 1213
St. Agnes Healthcare, Inc. 1255
T Rowe Price Group Inc 1300
Tbc, Inc. 1308
The Chimes Inc 1336
The Good Samaritan Hospital Of Md Inc 1347
The Hopkins Johns University 1349
The Johns Hopkins Health System Corporation 1352
The Union Memorial Hospital 1372
The Whiting-turner Contracting Company 1379
Under Armour Inc 1422
University Of Maryland Medical System Corporation 1444
Williams Scotsman Inc 1526

Bel Air
Upper Chesapeake Health Foundation, Inc. 1454

Berlin
Taylor (calvin B.) Bankshares, Inc. (md) 1307

Bethesda
Acas, Llc 12
Agnc Investment Corp 34
American Podiatric Medical Association, Incorporated 81
Centrus Energy Corp 268
Clark Construction Group, Llc 317
Clark Enterprises, Inc. 317
Cystic Fibrosis Foundation 385
Diamondrock Hospitality Co. 411
Eagle Bancorp Inc (md) 437
Earth Share 438
Enviva Inc 477
Gov New Oppty Reit 590
Host Hotels & Resorts Inc 656
Invenda Corporation 711
Jbg Smith Properties 730
Liquidity Services Inc 801
Marriott International, Inc. 837
Mountain Merger Sub Corporation 908
National Institutes Of Health 929
Northwest Biotherapeutics Inc 974
Pebblebrook Hotel Trust 1037
Rangers Sub I, Llc 1116
Saul Centers Inc 1180
Suburban Hospital, Inc. 1281
The Artery Group Llc 1330
The Donohoe Companies Inc 1342

Uniformed Services University Of The Health Sciences 1423
Walker & Dunlop Inc 1494

Bowie
Inovalon Holdings, Inc. 694

Chevy Chase
Xo Group Inc. 1540

Clarksburg
Reliability Inc 1129

Cockeysville
Abs Capital Partners Iii, L.p. 11

College Park
American Institute Of Physics Incorporated 77

Columbia
Adelberg, Rudow, Dorf, Hendler, Llc 21
Copt Defense Properties 358
Enterprise Community Partners, Inc. 474
Flavorx, Inc. 528
Hemagen Diagnostics Inc 632
Howard Community College 659
Ibiquity Digital Corporation 669
Igene Biotechnology, Inc. 674
Maxim Healthcare Services, Inc. 846
Medstar Health, Inc. 857
National Association Of Credit Management, Inc. 923
Structural Group, Inc. 1280
W. R. Grace & Co. 1491

Columbia
Gse Systems Inc 603

Crofton
Sirius Federal, Llc 1214

Easton
Easton Bancorp, Inc. 443
Shore Bancshares Inc. 1206
Terawulf Inc. 1319

Elkridge
Office Movers, Inc. 989
The Kane Company 1352

Elkton
Cecil Bancorp Inc 260

Frederick
Frederick Health Hospital, Inc. 546

Gaithersburg
Adventist Healthcare, Inc. 27
Altimmune Inc 60
American Dental Association Foundation 72
Attronica Computers, Inc. 136
Broadsoft, Inc. 211
Emergent Biosolutions Inc 461
Genvec, Inc. 569
Novavax, Inc. 978

Germantown
Precigen Inc 1074
Project Enhancement Corp 1089

Glen Arm
Trandes Corp. 1397

Glen Burnie
Allied International Corporation Of Virginia 54
Glen Burnie Bancorp 577

R. E. Michel Company, Llc 1111

Greenbelt
International Software Systems, Inc. 707
Sgt, Llc 1201
View Systems, Inc. 1477

Hagerstown
Meritus Health, Inc. 866

Halethorpe
The George J Falter Company 1345

Hanover
Aerotek Affiliated Services, Inc. 29
Allegis Group, Inc. 50
Ciena Corp 290
Keller North America, Inc. 747
Maryland Department Of Transportation 840
Processa Pharmaceuticals Inc 1086
Teksystems, Inc. 1313
The Keyw Holding Corporation 1353

Hollywood
Smartronix, Llc 1221

Hughesville
Maryland Southern Electric Cooperative Inc 840

Hunt Valley
Ea Engineering, Science, And Technology, Inc., Pbc 436
Logical Ventures, Inc. 806
Mccormick & Co Inc 849
Omega Healthcare Investors, Inc. 996
Sinclair Inc 1213

Hyattsville
National Center For Victims Of Crime, Inc. 925

La Plata
Charles Regional Medical Center Foundation Inc. 273
The Wills Group Inc 1379

Lanham
2u Inc 3
Hargrove, Llc 618
Luminis Health Doctors Community Medical Center Foundation, Inc. 815

Largo
1 Source Consulting, Inc. 2
Dimensions Health Corporation 414

Laurel
Washington Suburban Sanitary Commission (inc) 1498

Lexington Park
Indyne, Inc. 687

National Harbor
Accelpath Inc 12

North Bethesda
Federal Realty Investment Trust (new) 508

Oakland
First United Corporation (md) 525

Olney
Sandy Spring Bancorp Inc 1175

INDEX BY HEADQUARTERS LOCATION

Owings Mills
Baltimore Ravens Limited Partnership 154
Lsref4 Lighthouse Corporate Acquisitions, Llc 813
Universal Security Instruments, Inc. 1437

Point Of Rocks
Canam Steel Corporation 238

Potomac
Igc Pharma Inc 674

Prince Frederick
Calverthealth Medical Center, Inc. 235

Rockville
Aetea Information Technology, Inc. 30
American Speech-language-hearing Association 84
Argan Inc 111
Association For Financial Professionals, Inc. 127
Ceva Inc 270
Choice Hotels International, Inc. 286
Digicon Corporation 413
Glycomimetics Inc 582
Goodwill Industries International, Inc. 588
Grunley Construction Co., Inc. 603
Macrogenics, Inc 822
Maxcyte Inc 846
Mphase Technologies Inc. 909
National Park Trust, Inc. 930
Regenerx Biopharmaceuticals Inc 1126
Sensei Bio Subsidiary, Inc. 1196
Sucampo Pharmaceuticals, Inc. 1282
Supernus Pharmaceuticals Inc 1291
Synutra International, Inc. 1299
Theriva Biologics Inc 1380
Top Down Systems Corporation 1391
Westat, Inc. 1510

Saint Charles
American Community Properties Trust Inc 71

Silver Spring
A & T Systems, Inc. 5
Association For Intelligent Information Management 127
Fibertower Corporation 513
National Medical Association, Inc. A/k/a National Medical Association 929
Security Industry Association 1192
United Therapeutics Corp 1434
Urban One Inc 1455
Vietnam Veterans Of America, Inc. 1476

Stevenson
Stevenson University Inc. 1274

Towson
University Of Maryland St. Joseph Medical Center, Llc 1444

Upper Marlboro
International Association Of Machinists And Aerospace Workers 703

Westminster
Mcdaniel College, Inc. 850

Williamsport
D.m. Bowman, Inc. 386

MASSACHUSETTS

Marlborough
Ipg Photonics Corp 714

Acton
Insulet Corp 696
Psychemedics Corp. 1096

Allston
Houghton Chemical Corporation 656
New England Realty Associates L.p. 946

Andover
Mercury Systems Inc 861
Mks Instruments Inc 894
Vicor Corp 1475

Arlington
Kala Bio Inc 744

Athol
Starrett (ls) Co (the) 1267

Attleboro
Sturdy Memorial Hospital, Inc. 1280

Auburndale
Alseres Pharmaceuticals Inc 57
Atrius Health, Inc. 136
Parexel International (ma) Corporation 1025

Ayer
American Superconductor Corp. 84
Learning Express, Inc. 784

Babson Park
Babson College 151

Bedford
Anika Therapeutics Inc. 96
Continental Resources, Inc. 354
Ice Data Services, Inc. 670
Irobot Corp 716
Novanta Inc 977
Ocular Therapeutix Inc 988
Pulmatrix Inc 1100
Spire Corp. 1248
The Mitre Corporation 1358

Belmont
The Mclean Hospital Corporation 1355

Beverly
Atn International Inc 135
Axcelis Technologies Inc 147
King Fish Media, Llc 756
Northeast Health Systems Inc. 969
Project Adventure 1089

Billerica
American Science And Engineering, Inc. 83
Bruker Corp 217

Entegris Inc 472

Boston
Action For Boston Community Development, Inc. 17
American Tower Corp (new) 85
Amryt Pharmaceuticals Inc. 91
Athenahealth, Inc. 131
Aveo Pharmaceuticals, Inc. 144
Bain Capital, Lp 151
Berklee College Of Music, Inc. 173
Berkshire Hills Bancorp Inc 174
Berkshire Income Realty, Inc. 174
Beth Israel Deaconess Medical Center, Inc. 176
Boston Beer Co Inc (the) 199
Boston Medical Center Corporation 199
Boston Properties Inc 200
Boston Sand & Gravel Co. 200
Boston Symphony Orchestra, Inc. 200
Brightcove Inc 209
Brookline Bancorp Inc (de) 213
Brown Rudnick Llp 216
Cabot Corp. 225
Caregroup, Inc. 245
Citizen Schools, Inc. 294
City Of Boston 300
Clark Dubin & Company Inc 317
Cognition Financial Corporation 328
Corium, Llc 360
Cra International Inc 369
Dana-farber Cancer Institute, Inc. 390
Elderhostel, Inc. 452
Emerson College 461
Enel X North America, Inc. 466
Fa Finale, Inc. 497
Federal Home Loan Bank Boston 506
Federal Reserve Bank Of Boston, Dist. No. 1 508
First Eagle Private Credit, Llc 520
Foley Hoag Llp 533
Foundation Medicine, Inc. 540
General Electric Co 564
Gordon Brothers Group, Llc 588
Goto Group, Inc. 589
Haemonetics Corp. 611
Helmsman Management Services Llc 631
Houghton Mifflin Harcourt Company 656
Innosight Consulting, Llc 692
Intersections Inc. 709
Ironwood Pharmaceuticals Inc 716
Jenzabar, Inc. 732
Juniper Pharmaceuticals, Inc. 742
Leerink Partners Llc 785
Liberty Mutual Holding Co., Inc. 793
Linkage, Inc. 800
Lub Liquidating Trust. 814
Massachusetts Department Of Transportation 841
Massachusetts Higher Education Assistance Corporation 841
Massachusetts Port Authority 842
Museum Of Fine Arts 916
Northeastern University 970
Nstar Electric Co 979

One To One Interactive, Inc. 1000
Outcome Sciences, Inc. 1013
Physicians For Human Rights, Inc. 1054
Ptc Inc 1096
Rapid7 Inc 1116
Rhythm Pharmaceuticals Inc 1141
Safety Insurance Group, Inc. 1164
Santander Holdings Usa Inc. 1177
Seachange International Inc. 1189
Shawmut Woodworking & Supply, Inc. 1203
Stag Industrial Inc 1263
State Street Corp. 1268
Suffolk Construction Company, Inc. 1282
Suffolk University 1282
Summit Partners, L.p. 1284
The Brigham And Women's Hospital Inc 1333
The Children's Hospital Corporation 1335
The Life Is Good Company 1354
The Massachusetts General Hospital 1355
Trustees Of Dartmouth College 1410
Unitarian Universalist Association, Inc 1425
University Of Massachusetts Incorporated 1445
Vertex Pharmaceuticals, Inc. 1473
Walsh Brothers, Incorporated 1495
Wayfair Inc 1501
Wgbh Educational Foundation 1517
Winthrop Realty Liquidating Trust 1530

Braintree
Heroix Llc 635
Richelieu Foods, Inc. 1142

Brockton
Brockton Hospital, Inc. 212
City Of Brockton 300
Lyne Laboratories, Inc. 818

Burlington
Arqule, Inc. 117
Aware Inc. (ma) 147
Azenta Inc 149
Demandware, Llc 404
Exa Corporation 491
Keurig Dr Pepper Inc 752
Lahey Health System, Inc. 773
Lemaitre Vascular Inc 788
Microfinancial Incorporated 878
Minerva Neurosciences Inc 889
Progress Software Corp 1088

Cambridge
Agios Pharmaceuticals Inc 34
Akamai Technologies Inc 39
Alnylam Pharmaceuticals Inc 56
Ariad Pharmaceuticals, Inc. 112
Biogen Inc 181
Blueprint Medicines Corp 193
Cambridge Bancorp 236
Cambridge Public Health Commission 236

INDEX BY HEADQUARTERS LOCATION

City Of Cambridge 300
Editas Medicine Inc 448
Eterna Therapeutics Inc 485
Farm Aid Inc 501
Forrester Research Inc. 537
Genocea Biosciences Inc 568
Harvard Student Agencies Inc 620
Hubspot Inc 660
Infinity Pharmaceuticals Inc 688
Massachusetts Institute Of Technology 841
Merrimack Pharmaceuticals Inc 866
Moderna Inc 897
Mpm Capital Limited Partnership 910
Pathfinder Cell Therapy Inc. 1031
Pegasystems Inc 1038
Sage Therapeutics Inc 1165
Sarepta Therapeutics Inc 1179
Seres Therapeutics Inc 1198
The Charles Stark Draper Laboratory Inc 1335
The Workers Compensation Research Institute 1380
Union Of Concerned Scientists, Inc. 1424
Vbi Vaccines (delaware) Inc. 1467
Vericel Corp 1470
Whitehead Institute For Biomedical Research 1520

Canton
Destination Xl Group Inc 408
Dunkin' Brands Group, Inc. 430
Medical Information Technology, Inc. 855
Thompson Steel Company, Inc. 1384
Universal Wilde, Inc. 1438

Charlestown
Spaulding Rehabilitation Hospital (srh) Volunteer Services, 1245

Chelmsford
Datacon, Inc. 392
Harte Hanks Inc 619

Chelsea
Kayem Foods, Inc. 746

Chestnut Hill
Trustees Of Boston College 1410

Chicopee
Consumer Product Distributors, Llc 353

Concord
Emerson Hospital 461
Technical Communications Corp 1311
Welch Foods Inc., A Cooperative 1506

Dedham
Atlantic Power Corporation 133

Fairhaven
Acushnet Holdings Corp 19

Fall River
Southcoast Hospitals Group, Inc. 1234

Fiskdale
All Star Premium Products, Inc 49

Fitchburg
Micron Solutions Inc (de) 878

Foxboro
New England Patriots Llc 945

Framingham
Ameresco Inc 66
Asa International Ltd. 120
Heartware International, Inc. 629
J. F. White Contracting Company 722
Tjx Companies, Inc. 1389

Gardner
Precision Optics Corp Inc (ma) 1075
Precision Optics Inc. 1075

Hanover
Independent Bank Corp (ma) 683

Hingham
Hingham Institution For Savings 643
Microbot Medical Inc 878

Holliston
Harvard Bioscience Inc. 620
Wayne J. Griffin Electric, Inc. 1501

Holyoke
Iso New England Inc. 717

Hyannis
Cape Cod Healthcare, Inc. 240
Cape Cod Hospital 240

Lexington
Agenus Inc 33
Aldeyra Therapeutics Inc 44
Curis Inc 381
Dicerna Pharmaceuticals, Inc. 412
Dyax Corp. 433
Ibasis, Inc. 669

Littleton
Dover Saddlery, Inc. 424
Live Microsystems Inc 803

Lowell
Bh Media, Inc. 178
Csp Inc 377
Enterprise Bancorp, Inc. (ma) 474
Lowell, City Of (inc) 811
Macom Technology Solutions Holdings Inc 822
Softech, Inc 1225
Ukg Inc. 1420

Ludlow
Massachusetts Municipal Wholesale Electric Company 842

Marlborough
Bj's Wholesale Club Holdings Inc 185
Boston Scientific Corp. 200
Hologic Inc 649
Intrinsix Corp. 710
Paid Inc 1020

Medfield
Symbollon Pharmaceuticals Inc. 1296

Medford
Melrosewakefield Healthcare Parent Corporation 858

Methuen
Tas-chfh 1306

Middleboro
Ocean Spray Cranberries, Inc. 987

Milford
Milford Regional Medical Center, Inc. 885
Waters Corp. 1499

Natick
Cognex Corp 328
Moro Corp. 904

Needham
Tripadvisor Inc 1407
Verastem Inc 1470

New Bedford
New Bedford, City Of (inc) 945
Southcoast Health System, Inc. 1234

Newburyport
Ufp Technologies Inc. 1419

Newton
Alerislife Inc. 45
City Of Newton 308
Diversified Healthcare Trust 417
Dynasil Corp Of America 434
Environmental Health & Engineering, Inc. 477
Karyopharm Therapeutics Inc 746
Newton Wellesley Hospital Corp 955
Office Properties Income Trust 989
Service Properties Trust 1199
Sonesta International Hotels Corporation 1228
Techtarget Inc 1312

North Andover
Watts Water Technologies Inc 1500

North Attleboro
Mini-systems, Inc. 890

North Reading
Teradyne, Inc. 1319

Northampton
The Trustees Of The Smith College 1371

Northborough
Aspen Aerogels Inc 124
Borgwarner Massachusetts Inc. 199

Norton
Cps Technologies Corp 368
Wheaton College 1518

Norwell
Clean Harbors Inc 319
The Computer Merchant Ltd 1339

Norwood
Apogee Technology, Inc. 101
Elcom International, Inc. 452
National Amusements, Inc. 922
Tas-cnh, Inc. 1307

Peabody
Analogic Corporation 93
Sleepmed Incorporated 1219

Pittsfield
Berkshire Health Systems, Inc. 174

Plymouth
Partylite, Inc. 1030

Quincy
Granite Telecommunications Llc 594

J.jill Inc 723

Raynham
Edi Specialists, Inc. 447

Reading
Mavenir, Inc. 845

Revere
Westwood Group Inc (the) 1516

Rochester
Jonathan Sprouts, Inc. 739

Rockland
Object Management Group, Inc. 985

Salem
North Shore Medical Center, Inc. 968

Somerville
Bluebird Bio Inc 192
Mass General Brigham Health Plan, Inc. 841
Mass General Brigham Incorporated 841
Trustees Of Tufts College 1411

South Easton
Pressure Biosciences Inc 1079

South Hadley
The Trustees Of Mount Holyoke College 1371

South Weymouth
South Shore Health System, Inc. 1233

Southborough
Virtusa Corporation 1482

Southbridge
Harrington Memorial Hospital, Inc. 619
Hyde Group, Inc. 666

Southwick
Whalley Computer Associates, Inc. 1518

Springfield
American Hockey League Inc 76
Baystate Health Inc. 164
Baystate Health System Health Services, Inc. 164
Eversource Energy 489
Massachusetts Mutual Life Insurance Co. (springfield, Ma) 842
Merriam-webster, Incorporated 866
Naismith Memorial Basketball Hall Of Fame, Inc 919
Peter Pan Bus Lines, Inc. 1048
Smith & Wesson Brands Inc 1221
Western Massachusetts Electric Co. 1512

Stoughton
Collegium Pharmaceutical Inc 331

Tewksbury
Avery Design Systems Inc 145
Cambridge Heart Inc. 236
Megatech Corp. 857

Wakefield
Franklin Street Properties Corp 545

INDEX BY HEADQUARTERS LOCATION

Picis Clinical Solutions, Inc. 1054
Waltham
Alere Inc. 45
American Dg Energy Inc. 73
Ardelyx Inc 110
Asg Technologies Group, Inc. 123
Bentley University 172
Bg Medicine Inc 177
Bioverativ Inc. 184
Brandeis University 205
Commonwealth Equity Services, Llc 340
Constant Contact, Inc. 352
Crane Nxt Co 369
Cys Investments, Inc. 385
Deciphera Pharmaceuticals Inc 398
Global Partners Lp 580
Harvey Industries, Llc 620
La Jolla Pharmaceutical Company 771
Lionbridge Technologies, Llc 800
Massachusetts Medical Society Inc 842
National Grid Usa Service Company, Inc. 928
Repligen Corp. 1132
Revvity Inc 1139
Rocket Software, Inc. 1149
Tecogen Inc 1312
Tetraphase Pharmaceuticals, Inc. 1322
The Cadmus Group Llc 1334
Thermo Fisher Scientific Inc 1381
Viridian Therapeutics Inc 1481
Ware
Quabbin Wire & Cable Co., Inc. 1106
Watertown
Als Therapy Development Foundation Inc 57
Eloxx Pharmaceuticals Inc 459
Enanta Pharmaceuticals Inc 464
Wellesley
Wellesley College 1506
Wellesley Hills
American Biltrite Inc. 69
Wenham
Gordon College 589
Westborough
Astellas Institute For Regenerative Medicine 128
Kopin Corp. 764
New England Power Company 946
Westfield
Mestek Inc. 868
Western New England Bancorp Inc 1513
Westford
Cynosure, Llc 384
Kadant Inc 743
Netscout Systems Inc 942
Westminster
W. E. Aubuchon Co., Inc. 1490
Williamstown
President & Trustees Of Williams College 1078
Wilmington
Analog Devices Inc 93

Charles River Laboratories International Inc. 274
Onto Innovation Inc 1002
Security Innovation, Inc. 1192
Unifirst Corp 1423
Winchester
Winchester Healthcare Management, Inc. 1527
Woburn
Bridgeline Digital Inc 208
Monotype Imaging Holdings Inc. 901
Neurometrix Inc 944
Yield10 Bioscience Inc 1545
Woods Hole
Woods Hole, Martha's Vineyard And Nantucket Steamship Authority 1533
Worcester
College Of The Holy Cross (inc) 331
Hanover Insurance Group Inc 616
Imperial Distributors, Inc. 680
Lawrence R. Mccoy & Co., Inc. 781
Providence And Worcester Railroad Company 1093
Thermoenergy Corp 1381
Trustees Of Clark University 1410
Vystar Corp 1490

MICHIGAN

Ada
Access Business Group Llc 13
Alticor Inc. 60
Baker Book House Company 152
Albion
Albion College 43
Allendale
Grand Valley State University 593
Alma
Alma College 55
Medler Electric Company 856
Ann Arbor
Altarum Institute 59
Arotech Corporation 116
Dominos Pizza Inc. 421
Ervin Industries, Inc. 483
Esperion Therapeutics Inc (new) 484
Regents Of The University Of Michigan 1127
Rubicon Genomics, Inc. 1158
Tecumseh Products Company Llc 1312
University Bancorp Inc. (mi) 1438
Auburn Hills
Borgwarner Inc 199
Guardian Glass Company 605
Hirotec America Inc. 643
Spar Group, Inc. 1244
Wabco Holdings Inc. 1493
Webasto Roof Systems Inc. 1503
Battle Creek
Bronson Battle Creek Hospital 212
W. K. Kellogg Foundation 1490
Bay City
Mclaren Bay Region 851

Bear Lake
Blarney Castle Oil Co. 188
Belding
Belleharvest Sales, Inc. 170
Belmont
Wynalda Litho, Inc. 1538
Benton Harbor
Whirlpool Corp 1519
Big Rapids
Ferris State University (inc) 512
Bloomfield Hills
Agree Realty Corp. 35
Penske Automotive Group Inc 1042
Trimas Corp (new) 1404
Brighton
Lowry Holding Company, Inc. 811
Brownstown Twp
Systrand Manufacturing Corp 1300
Cadillac
Wolverine Power Supply Cooperative, Inc. 1532
Canton
Duo-gard Industries, Inc. 430
Charlotte
Sparrow Eaton Hospital 1244
Cheboygan
Cnb Corp (mi) 324
Clinton
Eden Foods, Inc. 446
Clinton Township
Macomb-oakland Regional Center, Inc. 822
Coldwater
Southern Michigan Bancorp Inc 1238
Comstock Park
Nbhx Trim Usa Corporation 937
Dearborn
Carhartt, Inc. 246
Edw. C. Levy Co. 449
Ford Motor Co. (de) 535
Ford Motor Credit Company Llc 535
Detroit
Ajax Metal Processing, Inc. 38
Ally Financial Inc 55
American Axle & Manufacturing Holdings Inc 68
Crain Communications, Inc. 369
Detroit Pistons Basketball Company 408
Diversified Chemical Technologies, Inc. 417
Dte Electric Company 427
Dte Energy Co 427
Faygo Beverages, Inc. 505
General Motors Co 565
Henry Ford Health System 632
Ideal Shield, L.l.c. 672
Ilitch Holdings, Inc. 675
International Union, Untd Autmble, Arspce And Agrcltrl Implmnt Wrkrs Of Amrica 707
Metaldyne Performance Group Inc. 868

Michigan Consolidated Gas Co 877
Motor City Electric Co. 907
Msx International, Inc. 912
Pvs Technologies, Inc. 1103
Smithgroup Companies, Inc. 1222
University Of Detroit Mercy 1442
Wayne State University 1502
East China
River District Community Hospital Authority 1145
East Lansing
Greenstone Farm Credit Services Aca 599
Michigan State University 877
Techsmith Corporation 1311
Farmington Hills
Electro-matic Ventures, Inc. 454
Layne Marx & Company 781
Ocuphire Pharma Inc 988
Robert Bosch Llc 1146
Fenton
Fentura Financial Inc 512
Flint
Hurley Medical Center 664
Kettering University 752
Frankenmuth
Star Of The West Milling Company 1267
Frankfort
Graceland Fruit, Inc. 591
Fraser
Supreme Gear Co. 1292
Fremont
Newaygo County General Hospital Association 952
Garden City
Prime Healthcare Services - Garden City, Llc 1081
Gaylord
Big Buck Brewery & Steakhouse, Inc. 179
Gladstone
Forest Besse Products Inc 536
Grand Blanc
Ascension Genesys Hospital 121
Mclaren Health Care Corporation 851
Grand Haven
Jsj Corporation 740
Grand Rapids
Adac Plastics, Inc. 19
Cascade Engineering, Inc. 252
Corewell Health 360
Crystal Flash, Inc. 376
Davenport University 394
Etna Distributors, Llc 486
Haviland Enterprises, Inc. 622
Independent Bank Corporation (ionia, Mi) 683
Meijer, Inc. 857
Mercantile Bank Corp. 861
Meritage Hospitality Group Inc 866

INDEX BY HEADQUARTERS LOCATION

Pridgeon & Clay, Inc. 1080
Spartannash Co 1245
Steelcase, Inc. 1271
The Mill Steel Co 1357
Total Health Care, Inc. 1393
Ufp Industries Inc 1419

Grosse Pointe Farms
Saga Communications Inc 1164

Hastings
Hastings Manufacturing Co 621

Holland
Holland Community Hospital Auxiliary, Inc. 648
Leanlogistics, Inc. 783
Macatawa Bank Corp. 821

Houghton
Michigan Technological University 877

Howell
Cleary University 320

Ionia
Independent Bank (ionia, Mi) 683

Jackson
Alro Steel Corporation 57
Cdgjl, Inc. 259
Cms Energy Corp 324
Consumers Energy Co. 354

Kalamazoo
Ascension Borgess Hospital 121
Borgess Health Alliance, Inc. 198
Bronson Health Care Group, Inc. 213
Bronson Methodist Hospital Inc 213
Stryker Corp 1280
Western Michigan University 1513

Kentwood
Precision Data Products, Inc. 1075

Lansing
Lansing Board Of Water And Light 777
Neogen Corp 940
Sparrow Health System 1244

Livonia
Accuride Corporation 14
Masco Corp. 840
Tower International, Inc. 1393
Trinity Health Corporation 1406
Vector Pipeline L.p. 1468

Madison Heights
Mcnaughton-mckay Electric Co. 852
Nano Magic Inc 919

Marshall
Walters-dimmick Petroleum, Inc. 1495

Mason
Capital Directions, Inc. 241

Midland
Dow Inc 424
Midland Cogeneration Venture Limited Partnership 882
The Dow Chemical Company 1342

Monroe
La-z-boy Inc. 771

Mount Clemens
Mclaren Macomb 851

Mount Pleasant
Central Michigan University 266

Muskegon
Hackley Hospital 611
Webb Chemical Service Corporation 1503

Northville
Cooper-standard Holdings Inc 357
Gentherm Inc 569

Novi
Berkshire Production Supply Llc 174
Itc Holdings Corp. 718
Michigan Milk Producers Association 877
Miracle Software Systems Inc. 891
Shyft Group Inc (the) 1207
Stoneridge Inc. 1276

Oak Park
Azure Dynamics Corp. 149

Pigeon
Cooperative Elevator Co. 357

Plymouth
Garrett Motion Inc. 559
Perceptron, Inc. 1044
Rofin-sinar Technologies Llc 1151

Pontiac
George W. Auch Company 570

Port Huron
Semco Energy, Inc. 1195

Portage
Wolverine Pipe Line Company 1532

Redford
Bayview Electric Company, Llc 164
Piston Automotive, L.l.c. 1059

Riverview
Ash Stevens Llc 123
Matteson-ridolfi, Inc. 844

Rochester
Ascension Providence Rochester Hospital 122
General Sports And Entertainment, L.l.c. 566
Oakland University 985

Rochester Hills
Dura Automotive Systems Inc 431

Rockford
Wolverine World Wide, Inc. 1532

Romulus
Federal Screw Works 510

Roseville
Tubby's Sub Shops, Inc 1413

Royal Oak
Beaumont Health 167
Harley Ellis Devereaux Corp 618
William Beaumont Hospital 1524

Saginaw
Covenant Medical Center, Inc. 366
Robertson Global Health Solutions Corp. 1148
Standard Electric Company 1264
Yeo & Yeo, P.c. 1544

Saint Clair Shores
P And E, Inc. 1016

Sheridan
Sheridan Community Hospital (osteopathic) 1205

Southfield
Ascension Providence Hospital 122
Atwell, Llc 136
Barton Malow Company 161
Covisint Corporation 367
Credit Acceptance Corp (mi) 371
Epitec, Inc. 479
Hospice Of Michigan, Inc. 654
Lear Corp. 783
Maxitrol Company 846
Society Of Manufacturing Engineers 1224
Sun Communities Inc 1285
Superior Industries International, Inc. 1291
Vesco Oil Corporation 1474

Sparta
Choiceone Financial Services, Inc. 286

Spring Arbor
Spring Arbor University 1250

Spring Lake
Interior Concepts Corporation 702

Sturgis
Sturgis Bancorp Inc 1280

Traverse City
Cherry Central Cooperative, Inc. 278
Munson Healthcare 915
Sandston Corp 1175

Troy
Altair Engineering Inc 58
Atos Syntel Inc. 135
Automation Alley 141
Iconma, L.l.c. 671
Kelly Services, Inc. 748
Logicalis, Inc. 807
Patton Wings, Inc. 1032
Skyline Champion Corp 1217

University Center
Delta College Foundation 403

Utica
Mnp Corporation 895

Van Buren Township
Visteon Corp 1484

Van Buren Twp
Contractors Steel Company 355

Walled Lake
American Plastic Toys, Inc. 81

Warren
Angelo Iafrate Construction Company 95
Madison Electric Company 823
St. John Hospital And Medical Center 1257
St. John Providence 1257
Universal Logistics Holdings Inc 1437

Watervliet
Lakeland Community Hospital, Watervliet 774

Wayne
Rush Trucking Corporation 1159

Whitehall
Hilite International, Inc. 641

Wixom
Integral Vision Inc. 697
Rockwell Medical, Inc 1150

Wyoming
Gordon Food Service, Inc. 589
The Behler-young Company 1331

Ypsilanti
Eastern Michigan University 441

Zeeland
Gentex Corp. 568
Howard Miller Company 659
Millerknoll Inc 887
Zeeland Community Hospital 1549

MINNESOTA

Alexandria
Alexandria Extrusion Company 45

Anoka
Vista Outdoor Inc 1483

Arden Hills
Intricon Corporation 710
Land O' Lakes Inc 775

Austin
Hormel Foods Corp. 653

Bagley
Team Industries Holding Corporation 1310

Baudette
Ani Pharmaceuticals Inc 96

Bayport
Andersen Corporation 94

Bloomington
Granite City Food & Brewery Ltd 593
Toro Company (the) 1392

Brooklyn Park
Clearfield Inc 319

Burnsville
Ames Construction, Inc. 88
Atrix International, Inc. 136
Telex Communications, Inc. 1315

Chaska
Lifecore Biomedical Inc 795

Circle Pines
Northern Technologies International Corp. 972

Detroit Lakes
Btd Manufacturing, Inc. 218
St Mary's Regional Health Center 1255

Duluth
Allete Inc 51
Benedictine Health System 171
St. Luke's Hospital Of Duluth 1260

Eagan
Dynatronics Corp. 434
Norcraft Holdings, L.p. 963

Eden Prairie
Avi Systems, Inc. 145
Datalink Corporation 393
Globalscape, Inc. 581
Legacy Imbds Inc 786

INDEX BY HEADQUARTERS LOCATION

Nve Corp 982
Robinson (c.h.) Worldwide, Inc. 1148
Sunopta Inc 1288
Surmodics Inc 1293
Tennant Co. 1317
Winnebago Industries, Inc. 1529
Farmington
Dakota Electric Association 388
Fergus Falls
Otter Tail Corp. 1012
Fosston
First Care Medical Services 519
Hastings
Regina Medical Center 1127
Hermantown
Miners Incorporated 889
Hibbing
Great Northern Iron Ore Properties 595
Hopkins
Digi International Inc 412
Michael Foods Group, Inc. 876
Hutchinson
Hutchinson Technology Incorporated 665
International Falls
International Falls Memorial Hospital Association 705
Inver Grove Heights
Chs Inc 288
Lakeville
Imagetrend, Llc 678
Mankato
Winland Holdings Corp 1528
Maple Grove
Great River Energy 596
Nortech Systems Inc. 964
Maple Lake
Bernatello's Pizza, Inc. 175
Maple Plain
Proto Labs Inc 1093
Medina
Polaris Inc 1066
Mendota Heights
Restaurant Technologies, Inc. 1136
Minneapolis
Abbott Northwestern Hospital 9
Adolfson & Peterson Inc 23
Agiliti Health, Inc. 34
Alight 47
Allina Health System 55
Ameriprise Financial Inc 87
Apogee Enterprises Inc 101
Autoscope Technologies Corp 141
Bio-techne Corp 181
Biovest International, Inc. 184
Buffalo Wild Wings, Inc. 219
Capella Education Company 241
Caribou Coffee Company, Inc. 246
Ceridian Corporation 269
Children's Health Care 282
City Of Minneapolis 307
Cliftonlarsonallen Llp 322
Datasite Global Corporation 393

Dayforce Inc 396
Dc Group Inc. 396
Deluxe Corp 404
Donaldson Co. Inc. 422
Dorsey & Whitney Llp 423
Entrx Corporation 476
Federal Reserve Bank Of Minneapolis, Dist. No. 9 509
General Mills Inc 565
Graco Inc 591
Groove Botanicals Inc 601
Infinite Graphics Incorporated 688
Kraus-anderson, Incorporated 767
Kurt Manufacturing Company, Inc. 768
Lendway Inc 788
M. A. Mortenson Company 819
Metropolitan Airports Commission 870
Midcontinent Media, Inc. 881
Mocon, Inc. 896
Napco International Llc 920
Neuehealth Inc 943
Piper Sandler Companies 1059
Public Radio International, Inc. 1098
Regents Of The University Of Minnesota 1127
Regis Corp 1128
Robins Kaplan Llp 1148
Scanner Technologies Corp 1182
Sharplink Gaming Inc 1203
Sleep Number Corp 1219
Sps Commerce, Inc. 1251
Subjex Corp 1281
Target Corp 1306
The Walman Optical Company 1377
Urologix Inc. 1456
Us Bancorp (de) 1456
Vasamed Inc 1466
Winmark Corp 1529
Xcel Energy Inc 1539
Ziegler Inc 1550
Minnetonka
Atc Venture Group Inc 130
Cogentix Medical, Inc. 328
Delphax Technologies Inc 403
Electro-sensors, Inc. 454
Imris Inc 681
Northern Oil & Gas Inc (mn) 971
Pineapple Energy Inc 1057
Radisson Hotels International, Inc. 1114
Sten Corp. 1272
Unitedhealth Group Inc 1435
Moorhead
American Crystal Sugar Company 72
Morris
St. Francis Health Services Of Morris, Inc. 1256
Stevens Community Medical Center, Inc 1274
New Brighton
Api Group, Inc. 100
New Prague
Electromed, Inc. 454
New Ulm
Nuvera Communications Inc 982

North Mankato
Taylor Corporation 1308
Northfield
Carleton College 247
St. Olaf College Corp 1261
Oakdale
Atrm Holdings, Inc. 136
Slumberland, Inc. 1219
Owatonna
Federated Mutual Insurance Co. (owatonna, Minn.) 510
Federated Service Insurance Co. (owatonna, Mn) 511
Perham
Perham Hospital District 1046
Plymouth
Charter Solutions, Inc. 275
Christopher & Banks Corp. 287
Eniva Usa, Inc. 470
K-tel International Inc 742
Silver Bay Realty Trust Corp. 1211
United Hardware Distributing Co 1428
Ramsey
Connexus Energy 350
Renville
Southern Minnesota Beet Sugar Cooperative 1238
Richfield
Best Buy Inc 176
Robbinsdale
North Memorial Health Care 967
Rochester
Hmn Financial Inc. 645
Mayo Clinic Hospital-rochester 847
Olmsted Medical Center 995
Southern Minnesota Municipal Power Agency 1238
Roseville
Hawkins Inc 623
Saint Cloud
Centracare Health Foundation 265
Coborn's, Incorporated 326
Saint Joseph
College Of Saint Benedict 331
Saint Louis Park
Park Nicollet Methodist Hospital 1026
Saint Paul
Agribank, Fcb 35
Brown & Bigelow, Inc. 215
Cardiovascular Systems, Inc. 244
Center For Victims Of Torture 264
City Of Saint Paul 311
Fairview Health Services 499
Gillette Children's Specialty Healthcare 576
Green Mill Restaurants, Llc 598
Healtheast Diversified Services, Inc. 627
Healtheast St John's Hospital 627
Macalester College 820
Mcgough Construction Co., Llc 850
Minnesota State Colleges And Universities 890

Minnesota Wild Hockey Club, Lp 891
Regions Hospital Foundation 1128
St. Jude Medical, Llc 1259
Talent Technical Services, Inc. 1303
Twin Cities Public Television, Inc. 1415
University Of St. Thomas 1449
Saint Peter
Gustavus Adolphus College 608
Shakopee
Canterbury Park Holding Corp (new) 240
South St. Paul
Ballistic Recovery Systems, Inc. 153
St Cloud
Ssht S&t Group Ltd 1253
St Louis Park
Park Nicollet Health Services 1026
St. Louis Park
Two Harbors Investment Corp 1416
St. Paul
3m Co 3
Bremer Financial Corp. 207
Ecolab Inc 445
Fuller (hb) Company 552
Patterson Companies Inc 1032
Securian Financial Group Inc 1191
Thief River Falls
Arctic Cat Inc. 110
Northern Pride, Inc. 971
Truman
Watonwan Farm Service, Inc 1500
Winona
Fastenal Co. 504
Miller Waste Mills, Incorporated 887
Saint Mary's University Of Minnesota 1168
Winthrop
United Farmers Cooperative 1428
Woodbury
Broadview Institute, Inc. 211

MISSISSIPPI

Biloxi
Peoples Financial Corp (biloxi, Ms) 1043
Brandon
On-site Fuel Service, Inc. 998
Flowood
Cimarron Mortgage Company 291
Ergon Asphalt Partners, Lp 481
Greenville
Delta Health System 404
Greenwood
Staple Cotton Cooperative Association 1266

INDEX BY HEADQUARTERS LOCATION

Gulfport
Hancock Whitney Corp 614
Memorial Hospital Auxiliary, Inc. 859
Mississippi Power Co 893

Hattiesburg
First Bancshares Inc (ms) 518
Forrest County General Hospital 537
The Merchants Company Llc 1356
The University Of Southern Mississippi 1375

Jackson
Entergy Mississippi Llc 473
Integrated Management Services, P.a. 698
Jackson State University 725
Miller Transportation Services, Inc. 887
Telephone Electronics Corporation 1315
Trustmark Corp 1411
Unitek Global Services, Inc. 1435

Kiln
Coast Electric Power Association 325

Kosciusko
Ivey Mechanical Company, Llc 720

Laurel
Sanderson Farms, Llc 1174

Madison
Mmc Materials, Inc. 895

Mccomb
Southwest Mississippi Regional Medical Center 1241

Meridian
Southern Pipe & Supply Company, Inc. 1239

Mississippi State
Mississippi State University 893

Olive Branch
Edelbrock, Llc 446

Pearl
Trilogy Communications, Inc. 1404

Philadelphia
Citizens Holding Co 296
The Yates Companies Inc 1380

Richland
Irby Construction Company 715

Ridgeland
Cal-maine Foods Inc 227
Eastgroup Properties Inc 442

Taylorsville
Southern Pine Electric Cooperative 1239

Tupelo
Jesco, Inc. 733
North Mississippi Health Services, Inc. 967
North Mississippi Medical Center, Inc. 967
Renasant Corp 1130

University
University Of Mississippi 1445

MISSOURI

Altenburg
Altenburg Hardwood Lumber Co Inc 59

Bridgeton
Tsi Holding Company 1412

Cape Girardeau
Francis Saint Medical Center 543
Southeast Missouri State University 1234

Carthage
Leggett & Platt, Inc. 787

Chesterfield
Aegion Corporation 28
Bunge Global Sa 220
Bunge North America, Inc. 220
Missouri Higher Education Loan Authority 893
Premium Retail Services, Inc. 1077
Reinsurance Group Of America, Inc. 1129
Reliv' International Inc 1130
Rose International, Inc. 1153
Seven Seas Technologies Inc. 1200
St. Luke's Episcopal-presbyterian Hospitals 1260
Vectra Co. 1468

Clayton
Enterprise Financial Services Corp 474
Enterprise Financial Services Group Inc 474
First Banks, Inc. (mo) 518
Olin Corp. 995

Columbia
Boone Hospital Center 198
Mfa Incorporated 874
Mfa Oil Company 874
Socket Holdings Corporation 1224
University Of Missouri System 1445

Des Peres
Jones Financial Companies Lllp 739

Fenton
Cic Group, Inc. 290
Maritz Holdings Inc. 834
Tacony Corporation 1302

Grandview
Nasb Financial Inc 920

Independence
City Of Independence 305

Jefferson City
Missouri Department Of Transportation 893

Joplin
Freeman Health System 547
The Empire District Electric Company 1343

Kansas City
American Century Companies, Inc. 70
Bartlett Agri Enterprises, Inc. 160
Block (h & R), Inc. 188
Bluescope Construction, Inc. 193
Butler Manufacturing Company Inc 223
Commerce Bancshares Inc 339
Corenergy Infrastructure Trust Inc 359
Dst Systems, Inc. 427
Epr Properties 479
Evergy Inc 488
Federal Reserve Bank Of Kansas City, Dist. No. 10 509
J.e. Dunn Construction Company 722
J.e. Dunn Construction Group, Inc. 723
Kansas City Life Insurance Co (kansas City, Mo) 745
Mercy Children's Hospital 862
Midway Ford Truck Center, Inc. 883
Milbank Manufacturing Co. 884
Missouri City Of Kansas City 893
Miriglobal 910
National Beef Packing Co. Llc/nb Finance Corp. 924
Novation Companies Inc 978
Pharmacy Buying Association, Inc. 1050
Rockhurst University 1150
Saint Luke's Health System, Inc. 1168
Steel Ventures, L.l.c. 1271
Stowers Institute For Medical Research 1277
Tension Envelope Corporation 1318
The G W Van Keppel Company 1345
Tnemec Company, Inc. 1389
Truman Medical Center, Incorporated 1410
Umb Financial Corp 1421
Us Premium Beef Llc 1457
Veterans Of Foreign Wars Of The United States 1474

Kearney
Midwest Game Supply Company 884

Lake Saint Louis
American Poolplayers Association, Inc. 81

Liberty
Ferrellgas Partners Lp 512
The New Liberty Hospital District Of Clay County Missouri 1361

Maryland Heights
J. D. Streett & Company, Inc. 721
Sunedison, Inc. 1287

Moberly
Mid-am Building Supply, Inc. 880

Monett
Jack Henry & Associates, Inc. 723

Mountain Grove
First Bancshares Inc. (mo) 518

Nevada
Nevada City Hospital (inc) 944

Nixa
Aire-master Of America, Inc. 38

North Kansas City
Garney Holding Company 559
Henry Wurst, Inc. 633
Maxus Realty Trust Inc 847

Wagner Industries, Llc 1493

O Fallon
Nortek, Inc. 964
Synergetics Usa, Inc. 1298

Poplar Bluff
Poplar Bluff Regional Medical Center, Llc 1068
Southern Missouri Bancorp, Inc. 1238

Saint Charles
American Railcar Industries, Inc. 82
Client Services, Inc. 322
Lmi Aerospace, Inc. 805

Saint Joseph
Heartland Regional Medical Center 629
Mosaic Health System 906

Saint Louis
A-mrazek Moving Systems, Inc. 5
Alberici Corporation 43
Amdocs Ltd. 65
Apex Oil Company, Inc. 100
Ascension Health 121
Baldwin Technology Company, Inc. 152
Barry-wehmiller Group, Inc. 160
Bryan Cave Leighton Paisner Llp 217
Christian Hospital Northeast - Northwest 287
City Of St. Louis 313
Connectria, Llc 350
Csi Leasing, Inc. 377
Edward D. Jones & Co., L.p. 449
Electrical Apparatus Service Association Inc 454
Enterprise Mobility 475
Express Scripts Holding Company 495
Guarantee Electrical Company 604
Hbe Corporation 624
Huttig Building Products, Inc. 666
Inroads, Inc. 694
Isle Of Capri Casinos Llc 717
Korte Construction Company 764
Maryville Consulting Group, Inc. 840
Mccarthy Building Companies, Inc. 849
Mercy Health 862
Mercy Hospital South 864
Metropolitan St. Louis Sewer District 872
Murphy Company Mechanical Contractors And Engineers 915
Osborn & Barr Communications, Inc. 1010
Panera Bread Company 1022
Pangea, Inc. 1022
Parents As Teachers National Center, Inc. 1025
Paric Corporation 1025
Perficient Inc 1045
Ranken Technical College 1116
Saint Louis University 1167
Ssm Health Care Corporation 1253

INDEX BY HEADQUARTERS LOCATION

Stupp Bros., Inc. 1280
Td Ameritrade, Inc. 1309
The Washington University 1378
Tom Lange Company, Inc. 1390
Transchemical Incorporated 1398
Walsh & Associates, Inc. 1495
Webster University 1504
Western Construction Group, Inc. 1511
World Point Terminals, Lp 1535
World Wide Technology, Llc 1535

Saint Peters
Sunedison Semiconductor Ltd 1287

Springfield
Associated Electric Cooperative, Inc. 126
City Utilities Of Springfield Mo 315
Enactus 464
Great Southern Bancorp, Inc. 596
Guildmaster, Inc. 606
Hiland Dairy Foods Company., Llc 640
Incredible Pizza Co., Inc. 683
Lester E. Cox Medical Centers 790
Mercy Hospital Springfield 864
Missouri State University 893
Mueller (paul) Co 912
New Prime, Inc. 948
O'reilly Automotive, Inc. 984

St. Louis
Allied Healthcare Products Inc 53
Ameren Corp 65
Arch Resources Inc (de) 109
Armstrong Energy Inc 115
Belden Inc 169
Build-a-bear Workshop Inc 219
Caleres Inc 228
Cass Information Systems Inc. 253
Centene Corp 263
Emerson Electric Co. 461
Energizer Holdings Inc (new) 466
Esco Technologies, Inc. 483
Federal Reserve Bank Of St. Louis, Dist. No. 8 510
Futurefuel Corp 554
Graybar Electric Co., Inc. 594
Peabody Energy Corp (new) 1036
Post Holdings Inc 1070
Spire Inc 1248
Stereotaxis Inc 1273
Stifel Financial Corp 1275

St. Louis
Core & Main Inc 358

Troy
Cuivre River Electric Cooperative, Inc. 379

Weldon Spring
Propper International Sales, Inc. 1090

MONTANA

Belgrade
Xtant Medical Holdings Inc 1542

Billings
Billings Clinic 180
First Interstate Bancsystem Inc 522

Bozema
Fair Isaac Corp 498

Bozeman
Montana State University 901

Butte
St James Healthcare, Inc 1254

Columbus
Stillwater Mining Company 1276

Glendive
Glendive Medical Center, Inc. 578

Great Falls
Pacific Hide & Fur Depot 1018

Helena
Eagle Bancorp Montana, Inc. 437

Kalispell
Cityservicevalcon, Llc 315
Glacier Bancorp, Inc. 576

Lakeside
Earth Search Sciences Inc. 438

Missoula
Blackfoot Telephone Cooperative, Inc. 187
Providence Health & Services - Montana 1094
The Maureen And Mike Mansfield Foundation 1355
University Of Montana 1445

Thompson Falls
United States Antimony Corp. 1431

Whitefish
Winter Sports Inc 1529

NEBRASKA

Battle Creek
Battle Creek Farmers Cooperative, Non-stock 162
Condor Hospitality Trust Inc 348

Chadron
Chadron State College 271

Clarks
Strobel Construction Unlimited, Inc. 1279

Columbus
Nebraska Public Power District 939

Fremont
Fremont Contract Carriers, Inc. 547
Fremont Health 548

Gothenburg
All Points Cooperative 48

Grand Island
Chief Industries, Inc. 281
Sense Technologies Inc 1196

Kearney
Buckle, Inc. (the) 219
Cash-wa Distributing Co. Of Kearney, Inc. 253

Kimball
Risk George Industries Inc 1144

La Vista
Streck, Inc. 1279

Lincoln
Board Of Regents Of The University Of Nebraska 194
Bryan Medical Center 217
City Of Lincoln 306
Crete Carrier Corporation 372
Landscapes Unlimited, L.l.c. 776
Lincoln Benefit Life Co 798
Lincoln Industries, Inc. 799
Madonna Rehabilitation Hospital 823
National Research Corp 931
Nebraska Department Of Labor 938
Nelnet Inc 939
Saint Elizabeth Regional Medical Center 1166
Union Bank And Trust Company 1423
Universal Manufacturing Co 1437

Norfolk
Affiliated Foods Midwest Cooperative, Inc. 30
Norfolk Iron & Metal Co. 963

Omaha
Ag Processing Inc A Cooperative 32
Alegent Creighton Health 44
Amcon Distributing Company 65
Berkshire Hathaway Inc 174
Children's Hospital & Medical Center 282
City Of Omaha 309
Corporate Travel Management North America, Inc. 362
Creighton University 371
First National Of Nebraska, Inc. 523
G4s Secure Integration Llc 555
Greater Omaha Packing Co., Inc. 597
Green Plains Inc. 598
Hawkins Construction Company 623
Hdr, Inc. 625
Home Instead, Inc. 650
Kutak Rock Llp 768
Leo A. Daly Company 789
Lindsay Corp 799
Lozier Corporation 812
Metropolitan Utilities District Of Omaha 872
Mosaic 905
Mutual Of Omaha Insurance Co. (ne) 917
Northern Natural Gas Company 971
Omaha Public Power District 996
Omaha Steaks International, Inc. 996
Peter Kiewit Sons', Inc. 1048
Roberts Dairy Company, Llc 1148
Sapp Bros. Petroleum, Inc. 1177
Sapp Bros., Inc. 1177
Td Ameritrade Holding Corporation 1309
The Maids International Llc 1355
The Nebraska Medical Center 1360
The Scoular Company 1368
Union Pacific Corp 1424
Union Pacific Railroad Co 1425
United Of Omaha Life Insurance Co. 1429
Unmc Physicians 1452
Valmont Industries Inc 1464
Werner Enterprises, Inc. 1507
West Technology Group, Llc 1509

Winnebago
Ho-chunk, Inc. 645

NEVADA

Boulder City
Amerityre Corporation 88
Fisher Pen Company 526

Carson City
Carson Tahoe Regional Healthcare 251

Elko
Us Gold Corp (canada) 1457

Henderson
Cipherloc Corporation 292
City Of Henderson 304
Playtika Holding Corp. 1063
Rpl International Inc. 1156

Las Vegas
Affinity Interactive 30
Allegiant Travel Company 49
Ault Alliance Inc 138
Axos Financial Inc 148
Boyd Gaming Corp. 202
Cannae Holdings Inc 239
Cardiovascular Biotherapeutics Inc 244
Cirtran Corp 292
City Of Las Vegas 306
Colony Resorts Lvh Acquisitions, Llc 333
Consumer Portfolio Services, Inc. 353
Everi Holdings Inc 489
Full House Resorts, Inc. 552
Global Acquisitions Corp 578
Golden Entertainment Inc 584
Icoa Inc 670
Inova Technology Inc 694
Janone Inc 728
Las Vegas Events, Inc. 779
Las Vegas Sands Corp 779
Las Vegas Valley Water District 779
Light & Wonder Inc 796
Live Ventures Inc 804
Mgm Resorts International 875
Nevada Gold & Casinos, Inc. 944
Nevada Power Co. 944
Nordicus Partners Corp 963
On Stage Entertainment Inc 998
Pharmacyte Biotech Inc 1050
Players Network (the) 1063
Prestige Travel Inc 1080
Red Rock Resorts Inc 1124
Rival Technologies Inc 1144
Samaritan Pharmaceuticals 1171
Skinvisible Inc 1217
Southwest Gas Holdings, Inc. 1241
Summerlin Hospital Medical Center, Llc 1283
Sunrise Hospital And Medical Center, Llc 1288
Switch, Inc. 1296

The Unlv Research Foundation 1376
Tix Corp 1388
University Medical Center Of Southern Nevada 1440
Valley Health System Llc 1463
Valley Health System Llc 1463
Voyager Entertainment International Inc 1487
Wynn Resorts Ltd 1539

Laughlin
Archon Corp 109

North Las Vegas
Gaming Partners International Corporation 558

Reno
Altair Nanotechnologies Inc 58
Brookmount Explorations Inc 214
Caesars Entertainment Inc (new) 227
Circus And Eldorado Joint Venture, Llc 292
Employers Holdings Inc 463
Encompass Holdings, Inc. 465
Itronics Inc. 719
Monarch Casino & Resort, Inc. 899
Nevada System Of Higher Education 945
Nmi Health Inc 960
Ormat Technologies Inc 1010
Pdl Biopharma Inc 1035
Plumas Bancorp Inc 1064
Prime Healthcare Services - Reno, Llc 1081
Sierra Pacific Power Co. 1208
U-haul Holding Co 1417
U.s. Geothermal Inc. 1418
Zoomaway Technologies Inc 1552

Sparks
Sierra Nevada Corporation 1208

Winnemucca
Paramount Gold Nevada Corp 1025

Yerington
Lion Copper & Gold Corp 800

Zephyr Cove
Virnetx Holding Corp 1481

NEW HAMPSHIRE

Berlin
Northway Financial, Inc. 973

Claremont
Red River Technology Llc 1123

Concord
Concord Hospital, Inc. 347
Concord Litho Group Llc 348
Hopto Inc 652
University System Of New Hampshire 1452

Dublin
Yankee Publishing Incorporated 1543

Exeter
Exeter Health Resources, Inc. 493

Hampton
Planet Fitness Inc 1062

Unitil Corp 1435

Hudson
Gt Advanced Technologies Inc. 603

Keene
C&s Wholesale Grocers, Llc 224
Co Holdings, Llc 325
North European Oil Royalty Trust 967

Laconia
Boyd Laconia, Llc 202

Lebanon
Dartmouth-hitchcock Clinic 392

Londonderry
Electronics For Imaging, Inc. 456
Strafford Technology, Inc. 1278

Manchester
Allegro Microsystems, Llc 50
Catholic Medical Center 256
Elliot Hospital Of The City Of Manchester 458
Kid Galaxy, Inc. 754
Minim Inc 890
Public Service Company Of New Hampshire 1098
Saint Anselm College 1166

Merrimack
Pc Connection, Inc. 1034
Pennichuck Corporation 1040

Milford
Hitchiner Manufacturing Co., Inc. 644

Nashua
Icad Inc 669
Skillsoft (us) Llc 1217
Southern New Hampshire Medical Center 1239

Pembroke
Associated Grocers Of New England, Inc. 126

Plymouth
New Hampshire Electric Co-op Foundation 946

Portsmouth
Bottomline Technologies, Inc. 200
Iron Mountain Inc (new) 716
Orion Seafood International, Inc. 1009
Sprague Resources Lp 1250

Rochester
Albany International Corp 42
Frisbie Memorial Hospital 549

Salem
Standex International Corp. 1265

NEW JERSEY

Bridgewater
Amneal Pharmaceuticals Inc 90

Atlantic City
Ter Holdings I, Inc 1319

Basking Ridge
Barnes & Noble Education Inc 159
Lisata Therapeutics Inc 801

Bayonne
Bcb Bancorp Inc 165

Bedminster
Peapack-gladstone Financial Corp. 1036

Berkeley Heights
Cormedix Inc 360
Cyclacel Pharmaceuticals Inc 384
The Connell Company 1339

Blackwood
Mccloskey Mechanical Contractors, Inc. 849

Bloomfield
World Finer Foods, Llc 1534

Bound Brook
Far Technologies Holdings, Inc. 501

Branchburg
Arena 3d Holdings, Inc. 110
Lifecell Corporation 795
Raritan Valley Community College 1117
Transnet Corporation 1399

Branchville
Selective Insurance Group Inc 1194

Bridgeton
Seabrook Brothers & Sons, Inc. 1189

Bridgewater
Brother International Corporation 215
Cyberthink, Inc. 384
Insmed Inc 695
Synchronoss Technologies Inc 1297

Buena
Teligent Inc (new) 1315

Burlington
Burlington Stores Inc 221

Camden
American Water Works Co, Inc. 86
Campbell Soup Co 237
Delaware River Port Authority 401
Nfi Industries, Inc. 957
Our Lady Of Lourdes Health Care Services, Inc. 1012
The Cooper Health System A New Jersey Non-profit Corporation 1340
Virtua Our Lady Of Lourdes Hospital, Inc. 1481

Carlstadt
Coloredge, Inc. 334

Cherry Hill
1st Colonial Bancorp Inc 2
Determine, Inc. 408
Vyant Bio Inc 1489

Clark
Turtle & Hughes, Inc 1415

Clifton
Electronic Control Security Inc. 455

Clinton
Unity Bancorp, Inc. 1435

Cranbury
Innophos Holdings, Inc. 691
Iveric Bio, Inc. 720

Palatin Technologies Inc 1021
Princeton Lightwave, Inc. 1083

Cranford
Enzon Pharmaceuticals Inc 478
Joyce Leslie Inc 740
Metalico, Inc. 868
Paragon Solutions Inc. 1024
Tofutti Brands Inc 1390
Weeks Marine, Inc. 1505

East Hanover
Fgi Industries Ltd 513
Novartis Pharmaceuticals Corporation 978
Wilshire Enterprises, Inc. 1526

East Orange
East Orange General Hospital (inc) 439

East Rutherford
Amber Road, Inc. 64
Cambrex Corporation 236
Tel Instrument Electronics Corp. 1313
The Nead Organization 1360

Eatontown
Climb Global Solutions Inc 322
Laird & Company 773

Edison
Colavita Usa L.l.c. 330
Conti Enterprises Inc. 354
Diaspark Inc. 411
Hmh Hospitals Corporation 645
Jfk Health System, Inc. 733
Sakar International, Inc. 1169
The Community Hospital Group Inc 1339
U.s. Shipping Corp 1418
Zerify Inc 1550

Egg Harbor Township
Atlanticare Health System Inc. 133

Elizabeth
Allied Beverage Group L.l.c. 53
Atalanta Corporation 130
Jacobson & Company, Inc 727
Trinitas Regional Medical Center 1405

Englewood
Englewood Hospital And Medical Center Foundation Inc. 469

Englewood Cliffs
Asta Funding, Inc. 128
Connectone Bancorp Inc (new) 350

Ewing
Church & Dwight Co Inc 289
Delaware River Basin Commission 400
Universal Display Corp 1436

Fairfield
Acuative Corporation 19
Kearny Financial Corp (md) 747

Far Hills
United States Golf Association, Inc. 1432

Farmingdale
Cherry Hill Mortgage Investment Corp 278

INDEX BY HEADQUARTERS LOCATION

Flemington
Hunterdon Healthcare System 663
Florham Park
Conduent Inc 348
Protalex Inc 1092
Folsom
South Jersey Gas Co. 1233
Fort Lee
Immune Pharmaceuticals Inc 680
Franklin Lakes
Becton, Dickinson & Co 168
C. R. Bard, Inc. 225
Freehold
Centrastate Healthcare Partners Limited Liability Company 267
Speedus Corp 1247
Umh Properties Inc 1421
Glen Rock
Respirerx Pharmaceuticals Inc 1136
Hackensack
Champions Oncology Inc 271
Foundation Of Northern New Jersey Inc. 541
Infocrossing, Llc 689
Protalix Biotherapeutics Inc 1092
Regen Biologics Inc 1126
Hammonton
Ag&e Holdings Inc. 32
South Jersey Industries, Inc. 1233
Hampton
Celldex Therapeutics, Inc. 262
Harrison
Laser Master International, Inc 779
Hillside
Integrated Biopharma Inc 697
Ho-ho-kus
Holobeam, Inc. 649
Hoboken
The Trustees Of The Stevens Institute Of Technology 1372
Wiley (john) & Sons Inc. 1523
Holmdel
Icims, Inc. 670
Ureach Technologies Inc. 1455
Vonage Holdings Corp. 1486
Iselin
Careadvantage, Inc. 245
Echo Therapeutics Inc 444
Enherent Corp 470
Middlesex Water Co. 882
Mott Macdonald Group Inc. 907
Nuware Tech Corp. 982
Pioneer Data Systems, Inc. 1058
Jersey City
Atalian Us Northeast, Llc 130
City Of Jersey City 305
Franklin Credit Holding Corporation 544
Goya Foods, Inc. 590
Jackson Hewitt Tax Service Inc. 725
Jersey City Medical Center, Inc. 733
Provident Financial Services Inc 1095

Prudential Annuities Life Assurance Corp 1095
Rand Logistics, Llc 1115
Scynexis, Inc. 1188
The Depository Trust & Clearing Corporation 1341
Veris Residential Llc 1471
Verisk Analytics Inc 1471
Keasbey
Wakefern Food Corp. 1494
Lakewood
Eroom System Technologies Inc 482
Georgian Court University 572
Kimball Medical Center Inc. 755
Lawrenceville
Imunon Inc 682
Iti Tropicals Inc. 718
Little Falls
Cantel Medical Llc 240
Livingston
Formosa Plastics Corporation, U.s.a. 537
Nan Ya Plastics Corporation, America 919
St Barnabas Medical Center (inc) 1253
Long Branch
Monmouth Medical Center Inc. 900
Long Valley
Frazier Industrial Company 545
Lyndhurst
Argo International Corporation 111
Aro Liquidation, Inc. 116
Sika Corporation 1210
Madison
Anywhere Real Estate Group Llc 98
Drew University 425
Stephen Gould Corporation 1272
Mahwah
Koru Medical Systems Inc 765
Mahwah Bergen Retail Group, Inc. 825
Matawan
Hovnanian Enterprises, Inc. 658
Key Food Stores Co-operative, Inc. 753
Pacifichealth Laboratories, Inc. 1019
Mercerville
Congoleum Corp (new) 349
Monroe Township
Ocean Power Technologies Inc 987
Montclair
180 Degree Capital Corp 2
Immtech Pharmaceuticals, Inc. 679
Montclair State University 902
Montvale
Balchem Corp. 152
Berry Global Films, Llc 175
Oncology Services International, Inc. 999
The Great Atlantic & Pacific Tea Co Inc 1347

Moorestown
Destination Maternity Corp 408
Morristown
Artech L.l.c. 118
Atlantic Health System Inc. 133
Avaya Llc 144
Covanta Holding Corporation 366
Cover-all Technologies Inc. 367
Financial Executives International 515
Pernix Therapeutics Holdings, Inc. 1047
Mount Holly
Virtua Memorial Hospital Burlington County, Inc 1481
Mount Laurel
Marlin Business Services Corp. 836
Mountainside
Children's Specialized Hospital Inc 284
Cosi, Inc. 363
Mt. Laurel
Intest Corp. 709
J&j Snack Foods Corp. 721
New Brunswick
Johnson & Johnson 737
Magyar Bancorp Inc 824
Robert Wood Johnson University Hospital, Inc. 1147
Saint Peter's University Hospital, Inc. 1168
New Gretna
Viking Yacht Company 1477
New Providence
Nokia Of America Corporation 962
Newark
City National Bancshares Corp. (newark, N.j.) 297
Genie Energy Ltd 568
Idt Corp 673
Idw Media Holdings Inc 673
New Jersey Devils Llc 947
New Jersey Institute Of Technology 947
Newark Beth Israel Medical Center Inc. 952
Port Newark Container Terminal Llc 1069
Prudential Financial Inc 1095
Pseg Power Llc 1096
Public Service Enterprise Group Inc 1098
The New Jersey Transit Corporation 1360
Newton
Newton Memorial Hospital (inc) 955
Northvale
Adm Tronics Unlimited, Inc. 22
Elite Pharmaceuticals Inc 457
Inrad Optics Inc 694
Oak Ridge
Lakeland Bancorp, Inc. 774
Oakland
Dewey Electronics Corp. 409
Old Bridge
Blonder Tongue Laboratories, Inc. 189

Old Tappan
New Leaf Brands, Inc. 948
Palmyra
Callahan Chemical Company, Llc 234
Paramus
Alexander's Inc 45
Bergen Community College 173
Bergen Pines County Hospital Inc 173
Empire Resources, Inc. 463
Movado Group, Inc. 909
Valley Home & Community Health Care Inc 1463
Parsippany
Advansix Inc 25
Aquis Communications Group, Inc 107
Avis Budget Group Inc 146
B&g Foods Inc 150
Delta Corporate Services, Inc 403
Emerson Radio Corp. 461
Interpace Biosciences Inc 708
Lincoln Educational Services Corp 798
Melinta Therapeutics, Llc 858
Pbf Energy Inc 1034
Pbf Logistics Lp 1034
Skanska Usa Building Inc. 1216
The Medicines Company 1356
Zoetis Inc 1552
Paterson
St. Joseph's Health Partners Llc 1258
Pennsauken
Lattice Inc 780
Rcm Technologies, Inc. 1119
Perth Amboy
Raritan Bay Medical Center, A New Jersey Nonprofit Corporation 1117
Vira Manufacturing Inc 1479
Pine Brook
Ipco Us Llc 714
Piscataway
Aaron And Company, Inc. 8
Intellect Design Arena Inc. 699
Parkway Plastics, Inc. 1028
The Institute Of Electrical And Electronics Engineers Incorporated 1350
Transtech Industries, Inc. 1400
Plainfield
Muhlenberg Regional Medical Center, Inc. 913
Plainsboro
Derma Sciences, Inc. 406
Princeton Healthcare System Holding Inc. 1083
Point Pleasant Beach
Chefs International, Inc. 276
Norkus Enterprises, Inc. 964
Pompton Plains
Chilton Hospital 285

INDEX BY HEADQUARTERS LOCATION

Princeton
Agile Therapeutics Inc 33
Bristol Myers Squibb Co. 210
Clearway Energy Inc 320
Domain Associates L.l.c. 420
Educational Testing Service 449
Integra Lifesciences Holdings Corp 697
Kepner-tregoe, Inc. 751
Learning Ally, Inc. 784
Logicquest Technology Inc 807
Princeton Insurance Company 1083
Soligenix Inc 1227
The Trustees Of Princeton University 1371

Princeton Junction
Mistras Group Inc 894

Rahway
Merck & Co Inc 861
Robert Wood Johnson University Hospital At Rahway 1147
Sdi Technologies Inc. 1188

Red Bank
Oceanfirst Financial Corp 987

Ridgefield Park
Innodata Inc 691
Lifequest World Corp 795
Samsung C&t America, Inc. 1172

Ridgewood
The Valley Hospital Inc 1376
Valley Health System, Inc. 1463

River Vale
Poof-slinky, Llc 1067

Rochelle Park
Can-am Consulting Services, Inc 238
Orbcomm Inc. 1006

Roseland
Automatic Data Processing Inc. 141
Lowenstein Sandler Llp 811
Milestone Scientific Inc. 885

Rutherford
Kid Brands, Inc. 754

Saddle Brook
Peoples Educational Holdings, Inc. 1043

Scotch Plains
Regal Marketing, Inc. 1125

Secaucus
Children's Place Inc (the) 284
Quest Diagnostics, Inc. 1108

Short Hills
Humanigen Inc 662

Shrewsbury
Echl Inc. 444
Intercloud Systems Inc 701

Somers Point
Shore Memorial Hospital 1206

Somerset
Appliedinfo Partners, Inc. 105
Carecloud Inc 245
Catalent Inc 254
Shi International Corp. 1205
Van Budd Lines Inc 1464

Somerville
Conolog Corp 351
Matlen Silver Group, Inc. 844

South Orange
Nephros Inc 940
Seton Hall University 1200

South Plainfield
Ptc Therapeutics Inc 1097

Sparta
High Point Solutions Inc. 639
Plx Pharma Inc 1064

Springfield
Village Super Market, Inc. 1478

Swedesboro
Powell Electronics, Inc. 1072

Teaneck
Cognizant Technology Solutions Corp. 328
Fairleigh Dickinson University 498
Phibro Animal Health Corp. 1051

Teterboro
A & E Stores, Inc. 4

Tinton Falls
Commvault Systems Inc 344

Toms River
Community Medical Center, Inc. 344

Totowa
Ballet Makers, Inc. 153
Organics Corporation Of America 1008

Trenton
Capital Health System, Inc. 241
City Of Trenton 314
New Jersey Housing And Mortgage Finance Agency 947
Terracycle, Inc. 1320
The Hibbert Company 1348
Voxware, Inc. 1487

Union
Bed, Bath & Beyond, Inc. 168
Deep Foods Inc. 399
Morre-tec Industries, Inc. 904

Union City
Nobleworks, Inc 961

Upper Saddle River
Nofire Technologies Inc. 962

Vineland
F&s Produce Company, Inc. 497
Inspira Health Network, Inc. 695

Voorhees
Art Van Furniture, Llc 118
Kennedy Health System, Inc. 749
Sam Levin Inc. 1171
The Africa-america Institute 1328

Wall
Bio-key International Inc 180
New Jersey Resources Corp 947

Wall Township
Coates International Ltd 326
Monmouth-ocean Hospital Service Corporation 900

Warren
Ii-vi Optoelectronic Devices, Inc. 675

Washington Township
Parke Bancorp Inc 1027

Wayne
Building Materials Corp. Of America 220
Metro Packaging & Imaging Inc 870
St. Joseph's Wayne Hospital, Inc. 1259
Toys "r" Us, Inc. 1395
William Paterson University 1525

Weehawken
Port Imperial Ferry Corp. 1068

West Atlantic City
Tablemax Corp 1301

West Deptford
Checkpoint Systems, Inc. 276

West Long Branch
Monmouth University Inc 900

West Orange
Bel Fuse Inc 168
Rwj Barnabas Health, Inc. 1160

West Trenton
Homasote Co. 649

Whippany
Breeze-eastern Llc 206
Suburban Propane Partners Lp 1282

Woodbridge
New Jersey Turnpike Authority Inc 947
Northfield Bancorp Inc (de) 972
The Bessemer Group Incorporated 1332

Woodcliff Lake
Eagle Pharmaceuticals, Inc. 437
Hudson Technologies Inc 661
Party City Holdco Inc 1030
Powerfleet Inc 1072

NEW MEXICO

Albuquerque
Apache Construction Company, Inc. 99
Applied Research Associates, Inc. 105
Bowlin Travel Centers Inc 201
City Of Albuquerque 298
David Montoya Construction, Inc. 394
Integrated Control Systems, Inc. 697
L&m Technologies, Inc. 770
Mckee Wallwork & Company, Llc 851
Net Medical Xpress Solutions Inc 941
Orecul, Inc. 1007
Pnm Resources Inc 1065
Presbyterian Healthcare Services 1078
Reserve Industries Corp 1134
Rose's Southwest Papers, Inc. 1154
Santa Fe Gold Corp 1177
Summit Electric Supply Co., Inc. 1284

University Of New Mexico 1446

Clovis
E.n.m.r. Telephone Cooperative 436

Espanola
Akal Security, Inc. 38

Las Cruces
New Mexico State University 948

Santa Fe
Georgia O'keeffe Museum 571
Mariah Media, Inc. 832
Meridian Technology Group, Inc. 865

Taos
Taos Health Systems, Inc. 1305

NEW YORK

Albany
Albany College Of Pharmacy And Health Sciences 42
Albany Med Health System 42
Capital District Physicians' Health Plan, Inc. 241
Curia Global, Inc. 381
New York State Energy Research And Development Authority 951
Sematech, Inc. 1194
Soluna Holdings Inc 1227
St. Peter's Health Partners 1261
State University Of New York 1268
The Research Foundation For The State University Of New York 1366
Thruway Authority Of New York State 1384
University At Albany 1438

Albertson
The Viscardi Center Inc 1377

Alfred
Alfred University 46

Amherst
Allient Inc 54
Daemen University 387
Fetch Logistics, Inc. 512

Amityville
Napco Security Technologies, Inc. 920

Annandale On Hudson
Bard College 159

Armonk
International Business Machines Corp 704

Ballston Spa
Ballston Spa Bancorp Inc 154
Stewart's Shops Corp. 1275

Batavia
Graham Corp. 591

Bay Shore
South Shore University Hospital 1233

Bethpage
Cablevision Systems Corporation 225

Binghamton
Suny At Binghamton 1289

INDEX BY HEADQUARTERS LOCATION

United Health Services Hospitals, Inc. 1428
United Health Services, Inc. 1428
Bohemia
Andrea Electronics Corp. 94
Carrier Alliance Holdings Inc 250
Global Payment Technologies, Inc. 580
Ilc Industries, Llc 675
Scientific Industries Inc 1185
Briarcliff Manor
Mtm Technologies, Inc. 912
Brockport
State University Of New York College At Brockport 1268
Bronx
Bronxcare Health System 213
Calvary Hospital, Inc. 235
Fordham Preparatory School 535
Fordham University 535
Manhattan College Corp 827
Montefiore Medical Center 902
New York Yankees Partnership 952
Wildlife Conservation Society 1523
Bronxville
Concordia College - New York Foundation, Inc. 348
Sarah Lawrence College 1178
Brooklyn
Bayside Fuel Oil Depot Corp 164
Brooklyn Academy Of Music Inc 214
Brooklyn Hospital Center 214
Brooklyn Institute Of Arts And Sciences 214
Brooklyn Navy Yard Development Corporation 214
Brooklyn Nets, Llc 214
Cazenovia College 257
Etsy Inc 486
Grenadier Realty Corp. 600
Kingsbrook Jewish Medical Center Inc 757
Lupus Research Alliance, Inc. 816
Maimonides Medical Center 825
Mays (j.w.), Inc. 848
Ms Foundation For Women Inc 911
Multi-media Tutorial Services, Inc. 914
New York Health Care Inc 950
Newyork-presbyterian/brooklyn Methodist 955
Solco Plumbing Supply, Inc. 1226
St Joseph's College New York 1254
Suny Downstate Medical Center 1290
The Brookdale Hospital Medical Center 1333
Track Data Corp. 1395
Uniworld Group, Inc. 1452
Wyckoff Heights Medical Center 1538
Buffalo
Catholic Health System, Inc. 256
City Of Buffalo 300
Gibraltar Industries Inc 574
Kaleida Health 744
M & T Bank Corp 819
Medaille College Foundation, Inc. 854

Mod-pac Corp. 896
Rich Products Corporation 1142
Synacor, Inc. 1297
Burt
Sun Orchard Fruit Company, Inc. 1285
Camden
International Wire Group, Inc. 708
Canandaigua
Canandaigua National Corp. 238
Canton
St Lawrence University (inc) 1255
Castleton On Hudson
Hodgson Mill, Inc. 646
Catskill
Greene County Bancorp Inc 599
Central Islip
Brainworks Software Development Corporation 204
Cvd Equipment Corp. 383
Chestnut Ridge
Teledyne Lecroy, Inc. 1314
Clinton
Hamilton College 613
Cobleskill
Suny Cobleskill College Of Agriculture And Technology 1289
Commack
Setton's International Foods, Inc. 1200
Cooperstown
National Baseball Hall Of Fame And Museum, Inc. 924
Corning
Corning Inc 361
Corning Natural Gas Corp 361
Deer Park
Surge Components Inc 1292
Dewitt
Community Bank System Inc 341
Dobbs Ferry
Mercy University 864
Dryden
Tompkins Cortland Community College Alumni Association, Inc. 1391
Dunkirk
Lake Shore Bancorp Inc 773
East Aurora
Astronics Corp 129
East Elmhurst
Skanska Usa Civil Inc. 1216
East Meadow
Nassau Health Care Corporation 921
East Patchogue
Long Island Community Hospital At Nyu Langone Health 808
East Syracuse
Am Opterna Inc 62
D/l Cooperative Inc. 386
Microwave Filter Co., Inc. 879
East Yaphank
Clare Rose, Inc. 316

Edgewood
Cpi Aerostructures, Inc. 368
Globecomm Systems Inc 581
Elma
Servotronics, Inc. 1200
Elmira
Chemung Financial Corp. 277
Elmsford
Afp Imaging Corp. 31
Fairport
Lidestri Foods, Inc. 794
Manning & Napier, Inc. 829
Pro-fac Cooperative Inc. 1086
Seneca Foods Corp. 1196
Farmingdale
Dinewise Inc 415
Enzo Biochem, Inc. 478
Jennifer Convertibles, Inc. 732
Minuteman Press International, Inc. 891
Misonix Opco, Inc. 892
Swimwear Anywhere, Inc. 1295
Telephonics Corporation 1315
Flushing
Judlau Contracting, Inc. 741
Newyork-presbyterian/queens 955
Garden City
Adelphi University 21
Lifetime Brands Inc 796
Proginet Corporation 1088
Prophase Labs Inc 1090
Sid Harvey Industries, Inc. 1207
Geneva
Hobart And William Smith Colleges 646
Red Jacket Orchards, Inc. 1123
Glendale
Independent Chemical Corp 684
Glens Falls
Arrow Financial Corp. 117
Glenville
Trustco Bank Corp. (n.y.) 1410
Gloversville
Taylor Products Inc 1308
Goshen
Media Sciences International, Inc. 854
Gouverneur
Gouverneur Bancorp Inc Md 590
Kph Healthcare Services, Inc. 765
Great Neck
Brt Apartments Corp 216
Manhattan Bridge Capital, Inc. 827
One Liberty Properties, Inc. 1000
Singularity Future Technology Ltd 1213
Greenvale
Long Island University Westchester & Rockland Alumni Association Ltd. 809
Hadley
Sarcom, Inc. 1178
Hamburg
Hilbert College 641
Hamilton
Colgate University 330

Hauppauge
Axis Construction Corp. 148
Dime Community Bancshares Inc (new) 414
Forward Industries, Inc. 539
Hauppauge Digital, Inc. 621
Ivci, Llc 719
Jaco Electronics, Inc. 726
Orbit International Corp. 1006
Tsr Inc 1412
United-guardian, Inc. 1434
Hawthorne
Metric & Multistandard Components Corp. 870
Hempstead
Hofstra University 647
Henrietta
Dss Inc 427
Hicksville
New York Community Bancorp Inc. 950
Huntington
Huntington Hospital Dolan Family Health Center, Inc. 663
Hyde Park
The Culinary Institute Of America 1341
Irvington
Eileen Fisher, Inc. 451
Ithaca
Cornell University 360
Tompkins Financial Corp 1391
Jamaica
Medisys Health Network Inc. 856
Pacific Cma Inc. 1017
St John's University, New York 1254
The Jamaica Hospital 1351
Jamestown
Dawson Metal Company, Inc. 396
Jeffersonville
Jeffersonville Bancorp 731
Jericho
1-800 Flowers.com, Inc. 2
American Learning Corporation 78
Educational & Institutional Cooperative Service, Inc. 448
Kimco Realty Corp 756
Nathan's Famous, Inc. 921
Schonfeld Securities, Llc 1184
Keuka Park
Keuka College 752
Kinderhook
American Bio Medica Corp. 69
Kingston
Kingstone Companies Inc 757
Lagrangeville
Outward Bound Inc. 1014
Lake Success
Broadridge Financial Solutions Inc 211
Lancaster
Ecology And Environment Inc. 445

INDEX BY HEADQUARTERS LOCATION

Latham
Angiodynamics Inc 95
Plug Power Inc 1064
School Administrators Association Of Nys (inc) 1184

Liverpool
Raymours Furniture Company, Inc. 1118

Long Island City
Altice Usa Inc 60
Jetblue Airways Corp 733
Madden (steven) Ltd. 822
Standard Motor Products, Inc. 1265
Stuart-dean Co. Inc. 1280
The Floating Hospital Incorporated 1344

Lyndonville
H. H. Dobbins, Inc. 610
United Apple Sales, Llc 1426

Manhasset
North Shore University Hospital 968

Melville
Comtech Telecommunications Corp. 347
First Of Long Island Corp 524
Fonar Corp 534
Health Diagnostics, Llc 625
Intellicheck Inc 699
Lloyd Staffing, Inc. 805
Marchon Eyewear, Inc. 831
Msc Industrial Direct Co Inc 911
Schein (henry) Inc 1182
Verint Systems Inc 1471

Menands
Health Research, Inc. 626

Millbrook
Bexil Corp 177

Millwood
Somerset Tire Service, Inc. 1228

Milton
Sono-tek Corp. 1229

Mineola
Winthrop Nyu Hospital 1529

Mitchel Field
Frequency Electronics Inc 548

Monticello
Empire Resorts, Inc. 462

Mount Kisco
Wright Investors' Service Holdings, Inc. 1537

Mount Vernon
Defoe Corp. 399

Mt. Vernon
Michael Anthony Jewelers Inc 876

New Hartford
Par Technology Corp. 1023

New Hyde Park
Dealertrack Technologies, Inc. 397
Long Island Jewish Medical Center 808

New York
Abm Industries, Inc. 10
Acacia Research Corp 11
Access Capital, Inc. 13

Acre Realty Investors Inc 17
Affinity Solutions, Inc. 31
Ag Mortgage Investment Trust Inc 32
Age Group Ltd. 33
Agritech Worldwide Inc 35
Alj Regional Holdings Inc 48
Allen & Company Incorporated 50
Altaba Inc. 58
Amalgamated Financial Corp 63
Amanasu Environment Corp 63
Ambac Financial Group, Inc. 64
Amc Networks Inc 64
American Arbitration Association, Inc. 67
American Association Of Advertising Agencies, Inc. 67
American Civil Liberties Union Foundation, Inc. 71
American Express Co. 73
American International Group Inc 78
American Jewish World Service, Inc. 78
American Management Association International, Inc. 79
Anacor Pharmaceuticals, Inc. 92
Anchin, Block & Anchin Llp 93
Annaly Capital Management Inc 97
Anti-defamation League 98
Apogee 21 Holdings Inc 100
Apollo Commercial Real Estate Finance Inc. 101
Apollo Global Management Inc (new) 101
Apollo Residential Mortgage, Inc. 101
Apollo Theatre Foundation Inc 102
Arena Group Holdings Inc Del 111
Ares Commercial Real Estate Corp 111
Aretec Group, Inc. 111
Arista Investors Corp. 112
Ark Restaurants Corp 113
Arrow Resources Development, Inc. 118
Artisanal Brands Inc. 119
Avenue Group Inc 144
Axel Johnson Inc. 147
Bank Of New York Mellon Corp 155
Barnes & Noble, Inc. 159
Bend The Arc A Jewish Partnership For Justice 171
Beth Israel Medical Center 176
Bgc Group Inc 177
Bion Environmental Technologies Inc 183
Blackrock Inc 187
Blackstone Inc 187
Blackstone Mortgage Trust Inc 187
Blue Nile, Inc. 191
Blue Tee Corp. 192
Bollore Logistics Usa Inc. 197
Breaking Ground Housing Development Fund Corporation 206
Brixmor Property Group Inc 210
Buchbinder Tunick & Company L.l.p 218
Cancer Care, Inc. 239

Cancer Research Fund Of The Damon Runyon-walter Winchell Foundation 239
Candid 239
Carver Bancorp Inc. 251
Catalyst, Inc. 254
Catholic Health Care System 255
Center For Constitutional Rights Inc 263
Centric Brands Llc 267
Chimera Investment Corp 285
China Huaren Organic Products Inc 285
China North East Petroleum Holdings Limited 285
Cifc Corp. 290
Cineverse Corp 291
Citigroup Global Markets Holdings Inc 293
Citigroup Global Markets Holdings Inc 293
Citigroup Inc 294
Citrin Cooperman & Company, Llp 296
City Harvest, Inc. 297
City Of New York 308
Cohen & Steers Inc 329
Colgate-palmolive Co. 330
College Entrance Examination Board 331
Compass Inc 345
Consolidated Edison Co. Of New York, Inc. 352
Consolidated Edison Inc 352
Constantin Associates, Llp 352
Cornerstone Agency Inc. 360
Coty, Inc. 364
Council For Economic Education 364
Council On Foreign Relations, Inc. 364
Covenant House 366
Credit Suisse (usa) Inc 371
Ctpartners Executive Search Inc 378
Cypress Bioscience, Inc. 385
Daily News, L.p. 387
David Yurman Enterprises Llc 395
Delcath Systems Inc 401
Derive Technologies Llc 406
Dgt Holdings Corp. 409
Diamond Discoveries International Corp 410
Direct Marketing Association, Incorporated 415
Dominari Holdings Inc 421
Dress For Success Worldwide 425
Dvl, Inc. 432
Earl G. Graves, Ltd. 438
Eisneramper Llp 451
Emerald Holding Inc 460
Emmet, Marvin & Martin, Llp 462
Empire State Realty Op Lp 463
Empire State Realty Trust Inc 463
Environmental Defense Fund, Incorporated 476
Equitable Holdings Inc 480
Ernst & Young Llp 482
Euronav Mi Ii Inc. 487
Evercore Inc 488
Everyday Health, Inc. 489
Excel Interior Construction Corp. 492

Exlservice Holdings Inc 493
Fairway Group Holdings Corp 499
Fashion Institute Of Technology 504
Federal Home Loan Bank New York 506
Federal Reserve Bank Of New York, Dist. No. 2 509
First Manhattan Co 522
Foot Locker, Inc. 534
Fortress Investment Group Llc 539
Fox Corp 541
Fp Acquisition Company 3.5 Llc 542
Frick Collection 548
Ftai Aviation Ltd 550
G-iii Apparel Group Ltd. 554
Genco Shipping & Trading Ltd 562
Genesis Corp. 566
Getty Realty Corp. 573
Girl Scouts Of The United States Of America 576
Girls Incorporated Of New York City 576
Glassbridge Enterprises Inc 577
Global Brokerage Inc 579
Globalworks Group Llc 581
Goldman Sachs Group Inc 585
Granite Broadcasting Corp 593
Granite Point Mortgage Trust Inc 594
Griffon Corp. 601
Guardian Life Insurance Co. Of America (nyc) 605
Handy & Harman Ltd. 615
Harper's Magazine Foundation 619
Hazen And Sawyer, D.p.c. 624
Healthfirst, Inc. 627
Hearst, William Randolph Foundation 628
Helen Keller International 630
Helios & Matheson Analytics Inc 631
Henry Modell & Company, Inc. 633
Hess Corp 636
Hsbc Usa, Inc. 660
Human Rights Watch, Inc. 661
Humanscale Corporation 662
Iac Inc 668
Immunic Inc 680
Infor, Inc. 689
Information Builders, Inc. 690
Inter Parfums, Inc. 700
International Flavors & Fragrances Inc. 705
Interpublic Group Of Companies Inc. 708
Intrepid Museum Foundation, Inc. 709
Iron Eagle Group, Inc. 716
J. Crew Group, Llc 721
Janel Corp 728
Japan Society, Inc. 729
Jefferies Financial Group Inc 730
Jefferies Group Llc 730
Jlm Couture Inc. 734

INDEX BY HEADQUARTERS LOCATION

Jpmorgan Chase & Co 740
Kelso & Company, L.p. 748
Kensington Publishing Corp. 750
Kiwibox.com, Inc. 760
Kkr & Co Inc 760
Kkr Real Estate Finance Trust Inc 760
Kleinknecht Electric Company, Inc. 760
Kohn Pedersen Fox Associates, Pc 762
Kpmg Llp 765
Ladder Capital Corp 771
Lazare Kaplan International Inc. 782
Lehman Brothers Holdings Inc. 787
Lescarden Inc 790
Levcor International Inc. 790
Lhh Corporation 792
Lincoln Center For The Performing Arts, Inc. 798
Liquid Holdings Group Inc 801
Liveperson Inc 804
Livestyle, Inc. 804
Loews Corp. 806
Loral Space & Communications Inc. 809
Lxp Industrial Trust 817
Magnite Inc 824
Major League Baseball Players Association 826
Manhattan School Of Music Inc 828
Marcum Llp 831
Marketaxess Holdings Inc. 835
Marks Paneth Llp 836
Marsh & Mclennan Companies Inc. 837
Martha Stewart Living Omnimedia, Inc. 838
Marymount Manhattan College 840
Medallion Financial Corp 854
Media Storm, Llc 854
Medidata Solutions, Inc. 855
Memorial Sloan-kettering Cancer Center 859
Mesabi Trust 867
Metlife Inc 869
Metro-north Commuter Railroad Co Inc 870
Metropolitan Bank Holding Corp 870
Metropolitan College Of New York 871
Metropolitan Opera Association, Inc. 871
Metropolitan Transportation Authority 872
Mfa Financial, Inc. 874
Midas Medici Group Holdings Inc 881
Milberg Llp 885
Minerals Technologies, Inc. 889
Mongodb Inc 899
Moody's Corp. 902
Moog Inc 903
Morgan Stanley 904
Msci Inc 911
Msg Networks Inc. 911
Msgi Security Solutions Inc 911
Museum Of The City Of New York, Inc. 916

Myrexis, Inc. 918
Nasdaq Inc 921
National Audubon Society, Inc. 923
National Council On Alcoholism And Drug Dependence Inc. 926
National Football League 926
National Multiple Sclerosis Society 929
National Review, Inc. 931
National Urban League, Inc. 933
Natural Resources Defense Council Inc. 935
Nbcuniversal Media, Llc 937
Neuberger & Berman, Llc 943
New Press 948
New York Academy Of Medicine 949
New York Blood Center, Inc. 949
New York City Health And Hospitals Corporation 949
New York City Transit Authority 949
New York Convention Center Operating Corporation 950
New York Life Insurance Co. 950
New York Mortgage Trust Inc 950
New York Public Radio 951
New York Shakespeare Festival 951
New York Times Co. 951
New York University 952
Newmark & Company Real Estate, Inc. 953
Newmark Group Inc 953
News Corp (new) 954
Nfp Corp. 957
Nhl Enterprises, Inc. 957
Nyack College 983
Oha Investment Corporation 990
Omagine Inc 995
Omnicom Group, Inc. 997
Oppenheimer Holdings Inc 1004
Oppenheimerfunds, Inc. 1004
Orchard Enterprises Ny, Inc. 1007
Oscar De La Renta, Llc 1010
Outfront Media Inc 1013
Pace University 1017
Paramount Global 1024
Partnership For A Drug-free America, Inc. 1029
Patriarch Partners, Llc 1031
Patterson Belknap Webb & Tyler Llp 1032
Pc Group, Inc. 1034
Peloton Interactive Inc 1038
Pfizer Inc 1050
Pjt Partners Inc 1061
Planned Parenthood Federation Of America, Inc. 1062
Presidential Realty Corp. 1079
Presidio, Inc. 1079
Private Export Funding Corp. 1085
Professionals For Non-profits, Inc. 1088
Prosek Llc 1091
Protagenic Therapeutics Inc 1092
Ps Business Parks Inc 1096
Public Health Solutions 1097
Puerto Rican Family Institute, Inc. 1100
Puresafe Water Systems Inc 1102
Pvh Corp 1103
Pzena Investment Management, Inc. 1103

Rait Financial Trust 1115
Ralph Lauren Corp 1115
Reading International Inc 1120
Ready Capital Corp 1121
Reis, Inc. 1129
Revlon Inc 1138
Rf Binder Partners Inc. 1140
Rithm Capital Corp 1144
Rtw Retailwinds, Inc. 1157
S&p Global Inc 1162
Safehold Inc (new) 1164
Sandler, O'neill & Partners, L.p. 1175
Scholastic Corp 1183
Seelos Therapeutics Inc 1193
Sellas Life Sciences Group Inc 1194
Senior Slr Investment Corp 1196
Shake Shack Inc 1201
Shearman & Sterling Llp 1203
Shutterstock Inc 1207
Siebert Financial Corp 1208
Siga Technologies Inc 1209
Signature Bank (new York, Ny) 1210
Simpson Thacher & Bartlett Llp 1212
Sirius Xm Holdings Inc 1214
Skadden, Arps, Slate, Meagher & Flom Llp 1215
Skyline Multimedia Entertainment Inc 1217
Sl Green Realty Corp 1218
Sl Industries, Inc. 1218
Soros Fund Management Llc 1230
Sotheby's 1230
Spring, O'brien & Company, Inc. 1250
Stagwell Inc 1263
State Of New York Mortgage Agency 1268
Steel Connect Inc 1270
Steel Partners Holdings Lp 1270
Stemline Therapeutics, Inc. 1272
Stonex Group Inc 1277
Sullivan & Cromwell Llp 1283
Syncora Holdings Ltd 1298
Take-two Interactive Software, Inc. 1302
Tapestry Inc 1305
Tata America International Corporation 1307
Tenfold Corporation 1317
Terraform Power, Inc. 1320
The Advertising Council Inc 1328
The American Kennel Club 1328
The American Museum Of Natural History 1329
The American Society For The Prevention Of Cruelty To Animals 1329
The American-scandinavian Foundation 1329
The Andrew W Mellon Foundation 1329
The Associated Press 1330
The Association Of Junior Leagues International Inc 1331
The Children's Health Fund 1335
The Conference Board Inc 1339
The Cooper Union For The Advancement Of Science And Art 1340

The Council Population Inc 1340
The Earst Foundation Inc 1342
The Ford Foundation 1344
The Foundation For Aids Research 1344
The Jewish Federations Of North America Inc 1351
The Jockey Club 1351
The John And Mary R Markle Foundation 1351
The John Gore Organization Inc 1352
The Juilliard School Inc 1352
The Legal Aid Society Inc 1354
The Lightstone Group Llc 1354
The Metropolitan Museum Of Art 1357
The Natori Company Incorporated 1359
The New School 1361
The New York And Presbyterian Hospital 1361
The New York Public Library 1361
The Partnership For New York City Inc 1363
The Philharmonic-symphony Society Of New York Inc 1364
The Port Authority Of New York & New Jersey 1364
The Rockefeller Foundation 1366
The Rockefeller University Faculty And Students Club Inc 1366
The Shubert Foundation Inc 1368
The Solomon-page Group Llc 1369
The Synergos Institute Inc 1370
The Trump Organization Inc 1370
The Turner Corporation 1372
The Wachtell Lipton Rosen & Katz Foundation 1377
Thestreet, Inc. 1382
Thirteen Productions Llc 1382
Ti Gotham Inc. 1385
Time Warner Entertainment Co., L.p. 1386
Touro College 1393
Tpg Re Finance Trust Inc 1395
Tradeweb Markets Inc 1396
Trammo, Inc. 1397
Trans World Corporation 1397
Transitcenter, Inc. 1399
Transperfect Translations International Inc. 1399
Travelers Companies Inc (the) 1400
Travelzoo 1400
Trimol Group, Inc. 1405
Triumph Apparel Corp 1407
Troika Media Group Inc 1408
Turner Construction Company Inc 1414
United Cerebral Palsy Associations Of New York State, Inc. 1427
United States Fund For Unicef 1432
Urban Edge Properties 1455
Valley National Bancorp (nj) 1463
Value Line Inc 1464
Varonis Systems, Inc 1466

INDEX BY HEADQUARTERS LOCATION

Verizon Communications Inc 1472
Vestar Capital Partners, Inc. 1474
Vince Holding Corp 1478
Virtu Financial Inc 1481
Visiting Nurse Service Of New York 1483
Vornado Realty L.p. 1486
Vornado Realty Trust 1487
Voyager Digital Ltd 1487
W World Corp 1490
W.p. Carey Inc 1492
Warner Bros Discovery Inc 1496
Warner Media, Llc 1496
Warner Music Group Corp 1497
Webmd Health Corp. 1504
Wework Inc 1517
Whitney Museum Of American Art 1520
Workman Publishing Co. Inc. 1534
Worldwide Media Services Group Inc. 1536
Wqn Inc 1536
Wsp Flack + Kurtz, Inc. 1538
Ww International Inc 1538
Xwell Inc 1542
Yahoo Inc. 1542
Yeshiva University 1544
Yext Inc 1545
Young Broadcasting, Llc 1546
Zanett, Inc. 1548
Ziff Davis Inc 1551

Newark
Creation Technologies New York Inc. 370
Ultralife Corp 1421

Niagara Falls
Sevenson Environmental Services, Inc. 1201

North Tonawanda
Taylor Devices Inc 1308

Norwich
Nbt Bancorp. Inc. 937

Nyack
Montefiore Nyack Hospital Foundation, Inc. 902

Oakdale
Dowling College 424
Suffolk County Water Authority Inc 1282

Oceanside
Xenonics Holdings Inc 1540

Old Westbury
Suny At Old Westbury 1289

Olean
Cutco Corporation 382

Oneida
Oneida Health Systems, Inc. 1000

Pearl River
Acorda Therapeutics Inc 16
Active Media Services, Inc. 18
Orange And Rockland Utilities, Inc. 1005

Pittsford
Infinite Group, Inc. 688

Plainview
123greetings.com, Inc. 2
Neulion, Inc. 943

Vaso Corp 1466
Veeco Instruments Inc (de) 1469

Port Chester
Euro Group Of Companies Inc 486
Hop Energy, Llc 652

Port Jefferson
John T. Mather Memorial Hospital Of Port Jefferson, New York, Inc. 736

Port Jefferson Station
Canal Capital Corp. 238

Port Washington
Global Industrial Company 580
Pall Corporation 1021
Tri Harbor Holdings Corporation 1403

Potsdam
Clarkson University 318

Poughkeepsie
Adams Fairacre Farms, Inc. 19
Marist College 834
The Dyson-kissner-moran Corporation 1342
Vassar College 1467

Purchase
Manhattanville College 828
Mastercard Inc 843
Mbia Inc. 848
Pepsico Inc 1044
Tal International Group, Inc. 1302
Townsquare Media Inc 1394

Queensbury
Adirondack Community College (inc) 22

Rego Park
New York State Catholic Health Plan, Inc. 951

Rensselaer
Taconic Biosciences, Inc. 1302
The New York Independent System Operator Inc 1361

Rhinebeck
Omega Institute For Holistic Studies, Inc. 996

Riverhead
Central Suffolk Hospital 267

Rochester
5linx Holdings Inc. 4
Birds Eye Foods Inc 184
Caliber Imaging & Diagnostic Inc 229
Catalyst Direct, Inc. 254
City Of Rochester 311
Curaegis Technologies Inc 381
Eastman Kodak Co. 442
Genesee Valley Group Health Association 566
Indotronix International Corp 687
Monro Inc 901
Paychex Inc 1033
Roberts Wesleyan College 1148
Rochester Gas & Electric Corp 1149
Rochester Institute Of Technology (inc) 1149
St John Fisher College 1254
Synergy It Solutions Of Nys, Inc. 1298

Transcat Inc 1398
Virtualscopics, Inc. 1482
Wegmans Food Markets, Inc. 1505

Rockville Centre
Catholic Health System Of Long Island, Inc. 256
Mercy Medical Center 864
Molloy College 898

Ronkonkoma
Medlink International Inc 856
Sentry Technology Corp. 1197
The Nature's Bounty Co 1360

Roslyn
St. Francis Hospital, Roslyn, New York 1256

Rye
Acadia Realty Trust 12
Lict Corp 794

Saint Bonaventure
St Bonaventure University 1253

Saratoga Springs
Espey Manufacturing & Electronics Corp. 484
Skidmore College 1216

Saugerties
Nasco Healthcare Inc. 921

Schenectady
Ellis Hospital 458
Gaming Commission, New York 558
Mvp Health Plan, Inc. 917
Schenectady County Community College 1182
The Golub Corporation 1347
Trustees Of Union College In The Town Of Schenectady In The State Of New York 1411

Sleepy Hollow
Phelps Memorial Hospital Association 1051

Smithtown
Guide Dog Foundation For The Blind, Inc. 606

Somers
Mcap Inc (new) 849

Southhampton
International Dispensing Corp 705

Sparkill
St Thomas Aquinas College 1255

Staten Island
Adco Electrical Corp. 20
Coffee Holding Co Inc 327
Eger Health Care And Rehabilitation Center 450
Staten Island University Hospital 1269

Stony Brook
Applied Dna Sciences Inc 103
Softheon, Inc. 1225
Stony Brook University 1277

Suffern
Avon Products, Inc. 147

Syracuse
Carrols Restaurant Group Inc 250
City Of Syracuse 313
Cxtec Inc. 383

Le Moyne College 782
O'brien & Gere Limited 983
Rapid Response Monitoring Services Inc 1116
St. Joseph's Hospital Health Center 1258
Syracuse University 1299
Upstate Medical University 1454

Tarrytown
Prestige Consumer Healthcare Inc 1079
Regeneron Pharmaceuticals, Inc. 1126

Tonawanda
Noco Energy Corp. 961
Worldwide Travel Staffing Ltd 1536

Troy
Rensselaer Polytechnic Institute 1131

Uniondale
Acres Commercial Realty Corp 17
Arbor Realty Trust Inc 108
Flushing Financial Corp. 532
Long Island Power Authority 808
Openlink Financial Llc 1002

Utica
Utica College 1461

Valhalla
New York Medical College 950

Valley Cottage
Creditriskmonitor.com, Inc. 371

Valley Stream
Franklin Hospital 544

Victor
Constellation Brands Inc 353

Warsaw
Financial Institutions Inc. 516

Waterford
Mpm Holdings Inc. 910

West Henrietta
Vuzix Corp 1489

West Islip
Good Samaritan Hospital Medical Center 586

Westbury
Park Aerospace Corp 1025

Westfield
National Grape Co-operative Association, Inc. 928

Westhampton Beach
Iconix Brand Group, Inc. 671

White Plains
American Booksellers Association, Inc. 69
Atlas Air Worldwide Holdings, Inc. 134
Burke Rehabilitation Hospital 220
Debt Resolve Inc 398
Golden Krust Caribbean Bakery Inc. 584
Krasdale Foods, Inc. 766
New York Power Authority 951
Northeast Community Bancorp Inc (md) 969

INDEX BY HEADQUARTERS LOCATION

Pervasip Corp 1048
Turtle Beach Corp 1415
United States Tennis Association Incorporated 1434

Williamsville
Evans Bancorp, Inc. 487
Independent Health Association, Inc. 684
Internetarray Inc 708
National Fuel Gas Co. (nj) 927

Woodbury
Research Frontiers Inc. 1134

Woodside
Firecom, Inc. 517

Yonkers
Alpha-en Corp 56
City Of Yonkers 314
Consumer Reports, Inc. 353
Zhejiang Dashang Media Co Ltd 1550

NORTH CAROLINA

Albemarle
Stanly Regional Medical Center 1266
Uwharrie Capital Corp. 1461

Asheville
Ingles Markets Inc 691
Mission Hospital, Inc. 892
The Biltmore Company Llc 1332

Boone
Appalachian State University Inc 102

Burlington
Alamance Regional Medical Center, Inc. 40
Laboratory Corporation Of America Holdings 771

Cary
Cornerstone Building Brands, Inc. 361
Cotton Incorporated 364
Ientertainment Network, Inc. 674
Ply Gem Holdings, Inc. 1065
Sas Institute Inc. 1179
Sms Alternatives Inc 1222
Usfalcon, Inc. 1459

Chapel Hill
Investors Title Co. 712
Tenax Therapeutics Inc 1317
The University Of North Carolina 1374
The University Of North Carolina Health System 1375
University Of North Carolina At Chapel Hill 1446

Charlotte
Abl Management, Inc. 10
Air T Inc 37
Albemarle Corp. 43
Avintiv Specialty Materials Inc. 146
Bank Of America Corp 155
Bojangles', Inc. 196
Brighthouse Financial Inc 209
Carolina Handling, Llc 248
Cato Corp. 256

Charlotte Pipe And Foundry Company 274
City Of Charlotte 301
Coca-cola Consolidated Inc 326
Cogentrix Energy, Inc. 328
Columbus Mckinnon Corp. (ny) 337
Concentric Consumer Marketing, Inc. 347
Cpp International, Llc 368
Crowder Construction Company Inc 374
Dentsply Sirona Inc 405
Duke Energy Carolinas Llc 428
Duke Energy Corp 428
Elevate Textiles, Inc. 456
Enpro Inc 471
Extended Stay America, Inc. 495
Forms & Supply, Inc. 537
Glatfelter Corp 577
Hg Holdings Inc 638
Honeywell International Inc 651
Jeld-wen Holding Inc 731
Johnson C. Smith University, Incorporated 737
Lendingtree Inc (new) 788
Loeffler Associates, Inc. 806
Monogram Food Solutions, Llc 900
Moore & Van Allen Pllc 903
Multi-shifter, Inc. 914
Nn, Inc 960
Nucor Corp. 980
Parsons Environment & Infrastructure Group Inc. 1029
Piedmont Natural Gas Company, Inc. 1055
Rcs Corporation 1119
Sealed Air Corp 1190
Shelco, Llc 1204
Snyder's-lance, Inc. 1224
Sonic Automotive, Inc. 1228
Spx Flow, Inc. 1251
Spx Technologies Inc 1251
The Charlotte-mecklenburg Hospital Authority 1335
The University Of North Carolina At Charlotte 1374
Truist Financial Corp 1409

Clyde
Haywood Health Authority 624

Concord
Speedway Motorsports, Llc 1247

Concord
Hydromer, Inc. 666

Davidson
Curtiss-wright Corp. 381
Ingersoll Rand Inc 690
The Trustees Of Davidson College 1371

Durham
374water Inc 3
American Institute Of Certified Public Accountants 77
Argos Therapeutics, Inc. 112
Avaya Holdings Corp 144
Biocryst Pharmaceuticals Inc 181
Chimerix Inc. 285
Duke University 429
Duke University Health System, Inc. 430

Epi Group, Llc. 479
Family Health International Inc 500
Iqvia Holdings Inc 714
M & F Bancorp Inc 819
Research Triangle Institute Inc 1134
Wolfspeed Inc 1532

Eden
Morehead Memorial Hospital Inc 903

Fayetteville
Cumberland County Hospital System, Inc. 380
Fayetteville Public Works Commission 505

Forest City
Rutherford Electric Membership Corporation 1160

Garner
Overland Contracting Inc. 1014

Gastonia
Caromont Health, Inc. 249
Mann+hummel Filtration Technology Intermediate Holdings Inc. 828

Goldsboro
Southco Distributing Company 1234

Graham
Big Rock Sports, Llc 179

Greensboro
Bell Partners Inc. 170
Bennett College 172
Center For Creative Leadership 263
City Of Greensboro 304
Columbia Forest Products, Inc. 335
Cross Technologies, Inc. 373
Kontoor Brands Inc 764
Market America, Inc. 835
Mother Murphy's Laboratories, Inc. 906
Qorvo Inc 1105
Tanger Inc 1304
Technology Concepts & Design, Inc. 1311
The Fresh Market Inc 1344
The Moses H Cone Memorial Hospital Operating Corporation 1358
Unifi, Inc. 1423
University Of North Carolina At Greensboro 1446

Greenville
Greenville Utilities Commission 599
Pitt County Memorial Hospital, Incorporated 1059
University Health Systems Of Eastern Carolina, Inc. 1439

Hickory
Alex Lee, Inc. 45
Commscope Holding Co Inc 341
Sherrill Furniture Company Inc 1205
Transportation Insight, Llc 1399

High Point
Culp Inc 380

High Point Regional Health 639
Vtv Therapeutics Inc 1488

Huntersville
American Tire Distributors Holdings, Inc. 85

Jacksonville
Sl Liquidation Llc 1218

Lenoir
Blue Ridge Energy Members Foundation 191

Lillington
American Defense Systems Inc 72

Lincolnton
Carolinas Medical Center-lincoln 249

Madison
A. P. Hubbard Wholesale Lumber Corporation 6

Mc Leansville
Replacements, Ltd. 1132

Mooresville
Lowe's Companies Inc 811

Morganton
Blue Ridge Healthcare Hospitals, Inc. 191
Blue Ridge Healthcare System, Inc.. 192

Morrisville
Channeladvisor Corporation 272
Charles & Colvard Ltd 273
Extreme Networks Inc 496
Jaggaer, Llc 727
Pyxus International Inc 1103
Tg Therapeutics Inc 1327

Mount Airy
Insteel Industries, Inc. 696
Renfro Llc 1131
Surrey Bancorp (nc) 1293

Mount Gilead
Mcrae Industries, Inc. 853

Mount Olive
Mount Olive Pickle Company, Inc. 908
Southern Bancshares (nc), Inc. 1235

Nashville
Nash Produce, Llc 921

Newton
Peoples Bancorp Of North Carolina Inc 1042

Pinehurst
Firsthealth Of The Carolinas, Inc. 526

Raleigh
Advance Auto Parts Inc 24
Alliance Of Professionals & Consultants, Inc. 52
Bandwidth Inc 155
Bjt, Inc. 185
City Capital Corp 297
City Of Raleigh 310
Duke Energy Progress, Llc 429
First Citizens Bancshares Inc (de) 519
Fortovia Therapeutics, Inc. 539
Highwoods Properties, Inc. 640

INDEX BY HEADQUARTERS LOCATION

Hurricanes Hockey Limited Partnership 665
L & M Companies Inc. 769
Martin Marietta Materials, Inc. 838
Mgt Capital Investments Inc 875
North Carolina Electric Membership Corporation 965
North Carolina State University 966
Pro Farm Group, Inc. 1085
Progress Energy, Inc. 1088
Rex Healthcare, Inc. 1139
S&me, Inc. 1162
Storr Office Environments Inc 1277
Suntory International 1289
The Generation Companies Llc 1345
Vontier Corp 1486
Wakemed 1494

Randleman
United Brass Works, Inc. 1427

Research Triangle Park
Fennec Pharmaceuticals Inc 511
G1 Therapeutics Inc 555

Rocky Mount
Boddie-noell Enterprises, Inc. 195

Salisbury
Global Contact Services, Llc 579
Livingstone College, Inc. 804
Rowan Regional Medical Center, Inc. 1155

Severn
Meherrin Agricultural & Chemical Co 857

Smithfield
Ks Bancorp Inc 768

Southern Pines
First Bancorp (nc) 518

Statesville
Energyunited Electric Membership Corporation 468
Kewaunee Scientific Corporation 752
Statesville Hma, Llc 1269

Thomasville
Old Dominion Freight Line, Inc. 993

Washington
Flanders Corporation 527
Fountain Powerboat Industries, Inc. 541
National Spinning Co., Inc. 932

West Jefferson
Lifestore Financial Group 796

Wilkesboro
Key City Furniture Company Inc 752

Wilmington
Nhw Healthcare, Inc. 958

Winston Salem
B/e Aerospace, Inc. 150
Forsyth Medical Center Foundation 538
Novant Health, Inc. 977
Quality Oil Company, Llc 1107
Reynolds American Inc. 1140

Wake Forest University 1494
Wake Forest University Baptist Medical Center 1494

Winston-salem
Hanesbrands Inc 615

Winterville
Nanthealth Inc 920

NORTH DAKOTA

Beulah
Dakota Gasification Company Inc 388

Bismarck
Bnccorp Inc 194
Mdu Resources Group Inc 853
St. Alexius Medical Center 1256
Wbi Energy Transmission, Inc 1502

Bismarck,
Basin Electric Power Cooperative 161

Fargo
Blue Cross Blue Shield Of North Dakota 191
Dakota Supply Group, Inc. 389
Eide Bailly Llp 450
North Dakota State University 966
Rdo Construction Equipment Co. 1120
Red River Commodities, Inc. 1123
Sanford 1176
Scheels All Sports, Inc. 1182

Grand Forks
Aatrix Software, Inc. 8
Altru Health System 61
Minnkota Power Cooperative, Inc. 891
North Dakota Mill & Elevator Association 966
University Of North Dakota 1446

Minot
Centerspace 264
Spf Energy, Inc. 1248
Srt Communications, Inc. 1252

Wahpeton
Minn-dak Farmers Cooperative Inc 890

West Fargo
Midnite Express Inc. 883
Titan Machinery, Inc. 1387

OHIO

Akron
Akron General Health System 39
Akron General Medical Center Inc 39
Bit Mining Ltd 184
Childrens Hospital Medical Center Of Akron 284
City Of Akron 298
Cleveland Electric Illuminating Co 321
Firstenergy Corp 525
Goodyear Tire & Rubber Co. 588
Jersey Central Power & Light Co. 732

Metropolitan Edison Company 871
Myers Industries Inc. 918
Ohio Edison Co 990
Pennsylvania Electric Co. 1040
Pennsylvania Power Co. 1041
Summa Health System 1283
The University Of Akron 1373
Toledo Edison Co 1390

Archbold
Mbc Holdings, Inc. 848

Ashland
Samaritan Regional Health System 1171

Avon Lake
Avient Corp 146

Batavia
Multi-color Corporation 913

Beachwood
Cohesant Inc. 329
Datatrak International Inc. 393
Site Centers Corp 1215

Beavercreek
Advant-e Corporation 25

Bedford Heights
Waxman Industries Inc. 1501

Berea
Cleveland Browns Football Company Llc 321
Ohio Turnpike And Infrastructure Commission 991

Blue Ash
Belcan, Llc 169
Indiepub Entertainment Inc. 686

Bowling Green
Bowling Green State University 201

Brewster
Wheeling & Lake Erie Railway Company 1519

Brooklyn Heights
Graftech International Ltd 591

Bryan
Bmc Holdings, Inc. 193
Manufactured Housing Enterprises, Inc. 830
Ohio Art Co. 990

Bucyrus
Community Investors Bancorp, Inc 344

Canfield
Farmers National Banc Corp. (canfield,oh) 502

Canton
Aultman Health Foundation 138
Cleveland Clinic Mercy Hospital 321
Metallus Inc 868
National Football Museum, Inc. 927

Chillicothe
Adena Health System 22
Horizon Telcom, Inc. 653

Cincinnati
American Financial Group Inc 74
Bethesda Hospital, Inc. 177
Bon Secours Mercy Health, Inc. 197

Burke, Inc. 221
Busken Bakery, Inc. 222
Chemed Corp 277
Children's Hospital Medical Center 283
Cincinnati Bell Inc. 291
Cintas Corporation 292
City Of Cincinnati 301
Clark, Schaefer, Hackett & Co. 317
Duke Energy Of Kentucky 429
Duke Energy Ohio, Inc. 429
Enerfab, Inc. 466
Federal Home Loan Bank Of Cincinnati 506
Fifth Third Bancorp (cincinnati, Oh) 515
First Financial Bancorp (oh) 520
Gold Star Chili, Inc. 583
Great American Insurance Co. 595
Healthspan Integrated Care 628
Hickman, Williams & Company 638
Kgbo Holdings, Inc. 754
Kroger Co (the) 767
Lsi Industries Inc. 813
Meridian Bioscience, Inc. 865
Messer Construction Co. 867
Phillips Edison & Company Llc 1053
Procter & Gamble Company (the) 1086
Scripps (ew) Company (the) 1187
Stand Energy Corporation 1264
The Belting Company Of Cincinnati 1331
The Christ Hospital 1336
The Deaconess Associations Inc 1341
The Hillman Companies Inc 1348
The Home City Ice Company 1349
The Western & Southern Life Insurance Company 1378
Trihealth, Inc. 1404
Uc Health, Llc. 1419
United Dairy Farmers, Inc 1427
University Of Cincinnati 1442
Western & Southern Financial Group, Inc 1511
Xavier University 1539

Cleveland
Abeona Therapeutics Inc 9
American Greetings Corporation 75
Applied Industrial Technologies, Inc. 104
Athersys Inc 131
Baker & Hostetler Llp 151
Bearing Distributors, Inc. 166
Buschman Corporation 222
Case Western Reserve University 252
Cavaliers Operating Company, Llc 256
City Of Cleveland 302
Cleveland State University 321
Cleveland-cliffs Inc (new) 322
Crawford United Corp 370
Federal Reserve Bank Of Cleveland,
Dist. No. 4 508

INDEX BY HEADQUARTERS LOCATION

Forest City Enterprises, L.p. 536
Hyster-yale Materials Handling Inc 667
International Management Group (overseas), Llc 706
Keycorp 753
Lincoln Electric Holdings, Inc. 798
Mace Security International, Inc. 821
Nacco Industries Inc 919
Park-ohio Holdings Corp. 1026
Parker Hannifin Corp 1027
Pubco Corp. 1097
Qualitor, Inc. 1106
Reliability First Corporation 1129
Restaurant Developers Corp. 1136
Sherwin-williams Co (the) 1205
Sifco Industries Inc. 1209
Tfs Financial Corp 1327
The Chilcote Company 1335
The Cleveland Clinic Foundation 1337
The Metrohealth System 1357
The Rock And Roll Hall Of Fame And Museum Inc 1366
Transdigm Group Inc 1399
Wyse Advertising, Inc. 1539

Columbus
Aep Texas Central Co 29
Airnet Systems, Inc. 38
American Electric Power Co Inc 73
American Municipal Power, Inc. 80
Appalachian Power Co. 102
Atlas Industrial Contractors, L.l.c. 134
Bath & Body Works Inc 161
Battelle Memorial Institute Inc 162
Big Lots, Inc. 179
Bread Financial Holdings Inc 206
Buckeye Power, Inc. 219
Central Ohio Transit Authority 266
Cf Bankshares Inc 270
City Of Columbus 302
Columbia Gas Of Ohio, Inc. 336
Core Molding Technologies Inc 359
Designer Brands Inc 407
Diamond Hill Investment Group Inc. 410
Express Inc 495
Fahlgren, Inc. 498
Hexion Inc 637
Huntington Bancshares Inc 663
Indiana Michigan Power Company 685
Installed Building Products Inc 695
Kentucky Power Company 751
M/i Homes Inc 820
Mettler-toledo International, Inc. 873
Mount Carmel Health System 908
Nationwide Children's Hospital 934
Northwest Bancshares, Inc. (md) 974
Ohio Department Of Transportation 990
Ohio Power Company 991

Ohio State University Research Foundation 991
Ohiohealth Corporation 992
Plastic Suppliers, Inc. 1062
Public Service Company Of Oklahoma 1098
Roth Produce Co. 1155
Schottenstein Stores Corporation 1184
Southwestern Electric Power Co. 1242
The Fishel Company 1343
White Castle System, Inc. 1519
Worthington Enterprises Inc 1536

Columbus Grove
United Bancshares Inc. (oh) 1426

Concord Township
Lake Hospital System, Inc. 773

Coshocton
Home Loan Financial Corp 650

Cuyahoga Falls
Associated Materials, Llc 127

Dayton
Bob Ross Buick, Inc. 195
City Of Dayton 302
Dpl Inc. 425
Good Samaritan Hospital 586
Kettering Adventist Healthcare 751
Miami Valley Hospital 876
Premier Health Partners 1077
Rex American Resources Corp 1139
The University Of Dayton 1374
Wright State University 1537

Defiance
Premier Financial Corp 1077
Sb Financial Group Inc 1181

Delaware
Greif Inc 600

Dover
Ffd Financial Corp 513

Dublin
Cardinal Health, Inc. 244
Community Choice Financial Inc 342
Navidea Biopharmaceuticals Inc 936
Oclc, Inc. 988
Stanley Steemer International, Inc. 1265
Wendy's Co (the) 1507

Elyria
Invacare Corp 711
Spitzer Management, Inc. 1249

Fairfield
Cincinnati Financial Corp. 291

Findlay
Legacy Farmers Cooperative 786
Marathon Petroleum Corp. 830
Mplx Lp 909

Fremont
Beck Suppliers, Inc. 168
Croghan Bancshares, Inc. 373
Crown Battery Manufacturing Company 375

Gallipolis
Ohio Valley Banc Corp 991

Gambier
Kenyon College 751

Granville
Denison University 405

Heath
Englefield, Inc. 469

Highland Hills
Olympic Steel Inc. 995

Hilliard
Advanced Drainage Systems Inc 24

Hiram
Great Lakes Cheese Co., Inc. 595

Hudson
Diebold Nixdorf Inc 412
Joann Inc 734

Independence
Apple American Group Llc 103
Cbiz Inc 257
Mobilepro Corp. 896
Pfg Ventures, L.p. 1049
Precision Environmental Company 1075

Kent
Davey Tree Expert Co. (the) 394
Kent State University 750
The Carter-jones Lumber Company 1334

Killbuck
Killbuck Bancshares, Inc. 755

Lancaster
Fairfield Medical Center 498
South Central Power Company Inc 1232

Lebanon
Lcnb Corp 782

Lima
East Of Chicago Pizza Inc 439
Mercy Health - St. Rita's Medical Center, Llc 863

Lorain
Sprenger Enterprises, Inc. 1250

Loveland
Cold Jet, Llc 330

Mansfield
Gorman-rupp Company (the) 589

Marietta
Integral Technologies Inc 697
Peoples Bancorp Inc (marietta, Oh) 1042
Peoples Bancorp, Inc. (md) 1042

Martins Ferry
United Bancorp, Inc. (martins Ferry, Oh) 1426

Marysville
Scotts Miracle-gro Co (the) 1187

Mason
Atricure Inc 135

Massillon
Fresh Mark, Inc. 548

Maumee
Andersons Inc 94
Dana Inc 390
Sylvania Franciscan Health 1296

Mayfield Heights
Materion Corp 843

Vibrantz Corporation 1475

Mayfield Village
Preformed Line Products Co. 1076
Progressive Corp. (oh) 1089

Medina
Discount Drug Mart, Inc. 416
Park Corporation 1026
Rpm International Inc (de) 1156

Mentor
Avery Dennison Corp 145
Cleveland Construction, Inc. 321
Synergy Health North America, Inc. 1298

Miamisburg
Danis Building Construction Company 391
Midmark Corporation 882

Middlefield
Hardwood Flooring And Paneling, Inc. 618
Middlefield Banc Corp. 882

Millersburg
Holmes Lumber & Building Center, Inc. 649

Minerva
Consumers Bancorp, Inc. (minerva, Oh) 354

Moraine
Compunet Clinical Laboratories, Llc 345
Noland Company 962

Navarre
Alfred Nickles Bakery, Inc. 46

Nelsonville
Rocky Brands Inc 1150

New Albany
Abercrombie & Fitch Co 9
Bob Evans Farms, Inc. 194
Commercial Vehicle Group Inc 340

New Bremen
Crown Equipment Corporation 375

Newark
Licking Memorial Health Systems 794
Park National Corp (newark, Oh) 1026

Niles
First Niles Financial Inc. 523

North Canton
Timken Co. (the) 1387

Oberlin
Oberlin College 985

Orrville
Smucker (j.m.) Co. 1223
The Will-burt Company 1379

Oxford
Miami University 875

Parma
Parma Community General Hospital 1028

Perrysburg
Mercy Health 862

INDEX BY HEADQUARTERS LOCATION

O-i Glass Inc 984
Pickerington
American Motorcycle Association 80
Piketon
Ohio Valley Electric Corp. 991
Ravenna
Robinson Health System, Inc. 1148
Stv Holdings, Inc. 1281
Reynoldsburg
Victorias Secret & Co 1476
Salem
Blubuzzard Inc 190
Sandusky
Cedar Fair Lp 261
Civista Bancshares Inc 315
Firelands Regional Health System 517
Sandusky International Inc. 1175
Shaker Heights
University Hospitals Health System, Inc. 1440
Solon
Advanced Lighting Technologies, Llc 25
Aurora Wholesalers, Llc 139
Energy Focus Inc 467
Steubenville
Franciscan University Of Steubenville 543
Trinity Health System 1406
Stow
Audio-technica U.s., Inc. 137
Streetsboro
The Step2 Company Llc 1369
Sylvania
Root Llc 1153
Toledo
Block Communications, Inc. 188
City Of Toledo 313
Manor Care, Inc. 829
Marco's Franchising, Llc 831
Mercy Health North Llc 863
N-viro International Corp 918
Owens Corning 1015
Pilkington North America, Inc. 1056
Promedica Health System, Inc. 1089
The University Of Toledo 1375
Toledo Promedica Hospital 1390
Welltower Inc 1507
Trenton
The Bidwell Family Corporation 1332
Twinsburg
Zinkan Enterprises, Inc. 1551
University Heights
John Carroll University 735
Urbana
The Champaign Telephone Company 1335
Valley City
Mtd Products Inc 912
Shl Liquidation Industries Inc. 1206

Vandalia
American Way Van And Storage, Inc. 86
Vienna
Litco International, Inc. 802
Walbridge
The Rudolph/libbe Companies Inc 1366
Warren
Anderson And Dubose, Inc. 94
Avalon Holdings Corp. 143
West Chester
Advancepierre Foods, Inc. 25
Westerville
Ck Construction Group Inc. 315
Kokosing Construction Company, Inc. 763
Lancaster Colony Corp 775
Ohio Living 991
Vertiv Holdings Co 1473
Westlake
Nordson Corp. 963
The Scott Fetzer Company 1367
The Shamrock Companies Inc 1368
Willoughby Hills
Gale's Willoughby Hills Garden Center, Inc. 556
Wilmington
Air Transport Services Group, Inc. 37
Woodville
Luckey Farmers, Inc. 814
Wooster
The College Of Wooster 1338
Wayne Savings Bancshares Inc 1502
Youngstown
Debartolo, Inc. 398
Forge Industries, Inc. 536
Hynes Industries, Inc. 667
Schwebel Baking Company 1185
Youngstown State University Inc 1546
Zanesville
Alc Holdings, Inc. 43
Genesis Healthcare System 567
Mattingly Foods, Inc. 845

OKLAHOMA

Altus
Jackson County Memorial Hospital Authority 724
Anadarko
Western Farmers Electric Cooperative 1512
Chouteau
Grand River Dam Authority 592
Durant
Stephenson Wholesale Company, Inc. 1273
Enid
Hiland Holdings Gp, Lp 641
Johnston Enterprises, Inc. 739

Kingfisher
Pioneer Telephone Cooperative, Inc. 1059
Norman
Norman Regional Hospital Authority 964
University Of Oklahoma 1447
Oklahoma
Energy & Environmental Services Inc 467
Oklahoma
Greenshift Corp 599
Oklahoma City
A-1 Freeman Moving & Storage, L.l.c. 5
Advancia Corporation 25
Ams Health Sciences, Inc. 92
Avalon Correctional Services, Inc. 142
Bancfirst Corp. (oklahoma City, Okla) 154
Cd Warehouse Inc 259
Chesapeake Energy Corp. 278
City Of Oklahoma City 309
Continental Resources, Inc. 355
Devon Energy Corp. 409
Encompass Energy Services Inc 464
Express Services, Inc. 495
Feed The Children, Inc. 511
Fred Jones Enterprises, L.l.c. 546
Fullnet Communications Inc 552
Gulfport Energy Corp. 608
Hobby Lobby Stores, Inc. 646
Hunzicker Brothers, Inc. 664
Integris Baptist Medical Center, Inc. 698
Integris Health, Inc. 698
Long Wave Inc. 809
Lsb Industries, Inc. 813
Mammoth Energy Services Inc 827
Mustang Fuel Corporation 916
New Source Energy Partners Lp 948
Oge Energy Corp 990
Postrock Energy Corp 1071
Premium Beers Of Oklahoma, L.l.c. 1077
Reserve Petroleum Co. 1135
Riley Exploration Permian Inc 1143
Sandridge Energy Inc 1175
Seventy Seven Energy Llc 1201
Sonic Llc 1228
Tower Tech, Inc. 1394
Pryor
Opp Liquidating Company, Inc. 1003
Sand Springs
Webco Industries Inc 1503
Stillwater
Oklahoma State University 993
Stilwell
Cherokee Nation Industries, L.l.c. 278
Sulphur
Chickasaw Holding Company 281
Tulsa
Aaon, Inc. 7

Ahs Hillcrest Medical Center, Llc 36
Alliance Holdings Gp, L.p. 52
Alliance Resource Partners Lp 52
Bok Financial Corp 196
City Of Tulsa 314
Clearsign Technologies Corp 320
Cypress Environmental Partners Lp 385
Daylight Donut Flour Company Llc 396
Educational Development Corp. 448
Enxnet Inc. 477
Greystone Logistics Inc 600
Helmerich & Payne, Inc. 631
Kaiser-francis Oil Company 744
Matrix Service Co. 844
Ngl Energy Partners Lp 957
One Gas, Inc. 1000
Oneok Inc 1001
Oneok Partners, L.p. 1001
Peak Methods, Inc. 1036
Saint Francis Health System, Inc. 1166
St. John Health System, Inc. 1257
T. D. Williamson, Inc. 1301
The University Of Tulsa 1375
Tma Systems, L.l.c. 1389
Unit Corp. 1425
United States Beef Corporation 1431
Williams Partners L.p. 1525

OREGON

Beaverton
Digimarc Corp 413
Formfactor Beaverton, Inc. 537
Nike Inc 959
Serena Software, Inc. 1198
Bend
Deschutes Brewery, Inc. 407
Central Point
Erickson Incorporated 482
Corvallis
Citizens Bancorp (corvallis, Or) 294
Oregon State University 1008
Eugene
Electrical Geodesics, Inc 454
Eugene Water & Electric Board 486
Organically Grown Company 1008
The Willamette Valley Company Llc 1379
University Of Oregon 1447
Florence
Oregon Pacific Bancorp 1008
Hillsboro
Lattice Semiconductor Corp 780
Planar Systems, Inc. 1061
Radisys Corporation 1114
Shorepower Technologies Inc 1207
Klamath Falls
Cell Tech International, Inc. 262
Lake Oswego
Greenbrier Companies Inc (the) 598

INDEX BY HEADQUARTERS LOCATION

Leadventure Inc. 783
Precision Castparts Corp. 1075
Tigerlogic Corporation 1386
Medford
C & K Market, Inc. 224
Falcon Northwest Computer Systems, Inc. 499
Lithia Motors Inc 802
North Plains
Jewett-cameron Trading Co. Ltd. 733
Portland
Allegro Corporation 50
Babcock & Jenkins, Inc. 150
Blount International, Inc. 189
Bonneville Power Administration 198
Calypte Biomedical Corp 235
City Of Portland 310
Columbia Sportswear Co. 337
Fortis Construction, Inc. 538
Hoffman Corporation 646
Legacy Emanuel Hospital & Health Center 785
Legacy Health 786
Lewis & Clark College 791
Mercy Corps 862
North Baja Pipeline, Llc 965
Northwest Natural Holding Co 974
Oregon Health & Science University 1007
Pac Northwest Electric Power & Conservation Planning Council 1016
Pacificorp 1019
Pendleton Woolen Mills, Inc. 1039
Phoenix Gold International Inc 1053
Pixelworks Inc 1060
Portland General Electric Co. 1069
Portland State University 1070
R. B. Pamplin Corporation 1111
Radius Recycling Inc 1114
Schmitt Industries Inc (or) 1183
Shoestring Valley Holdings Inc. 1206
Small Parts Manufacturing Co., Inc. 1220
The Reed Institute 1365
Trail Blazers Inc. 1396
Trellis Earth Products, Inc. 1402
Zimmer Gunsul Frasca Architects Llp 1551
Prineville
Ochoco Lumber Company 987
Salem
Colson & Colson Construction Co 335
North Pacific Canners & Packers, Inc. 967
Oregon Department Of Transportation 1007
Oregon State Lottery 1008
Roth Iga Foodliner Incorporated 1155
Salem Health 1169
Willamette University 1524
Talent
Brammo, Inc. 204
Tualatin
Bioject Medical Technologies Inc 182

Monje, Inc. 900
Timbercon, Inc. 1386
Turner
Willamette Valley Vineyard Inc. 1524
Wilsonville
Mentor Graphics Corporation 860

PENNSYLVANIA
Abington
Abington Memorial Hospital 10
Allentown
Air Products & Chemicals Inc 37
American Bank Inc (pa) 68
Buckeye Pipe Line Company, L P 218
Computer Aid, Inc. 345
Crossamerica Partners Lp 374
Lehigh Valley Health Network, Inc. 787
Ppl Corp 1073
Ppl Electric Utilities Corp 1073
Sacred Heart Hospital Of Allentown 1163
Altoona
Rlh Wrap-up, Inc. 1146
Sheetz, Inc. 1204
Upmc Altoona 1453
Ward Trucking, Llc 1496
Ambler
Bradford White Corporation 203
Audubon
Globus Medical Inc 582
Bala Cynwyd
Larimar Therapeutics Inc 778
Philadelphia Consolidated Holding Corp. 1052
The Pep Boys - Manny Moe & Jack 1363
Beaver
Heritage Valley Health System, Inc. 635
Belleville
Kish Bancorp Inc. 758
Bensalem
Healthcare Services Group, Inc. 626
Orleans Homebuilders, Inc. 1009
Stonemor Partners L.p. 1276
Berwick
First Keystone Corp 522
Berwyn
Ametek Inc 89
Daniel F. Young, Incorporated 390
Envestnet Inc 476
Bethlehem
Artsquest 120
Just Born, Inc. 742
Lehigh University 787
Moravian University 903
Orasure Technologies Inc. 1006
St. Luke's Health Network, Inc. 1260
Bloomsburg
Muncy Columbia Financial Corp 914

Blue Bell
Achillion Pharmaceuticals Inc 15
Brightview Holdings Inc 209
Peirce Enterprises, Inc. 1038
Unisys Corp 1425
Bradford
Control Chief Holdings, Inc. 355
Bridgeville
Universal Stainless & Alloy Products, Inc. 1437
Bristol
Lenox Corporation 789
Bryn Mawr
Bryn Mawr College 217
Essential Utilities Inc 484
Main Line Hospitals, Inc. 825
Butler
Butler Health System, Inc. 222
Camp Hill
Gannett Fleming, Inc. 559
Penn State Health Holy Spirit Medical Center 1039
Canonsburg
Ansys Inc. 97
Centimark Corporation 264
Cnx Resources Corp 325
Carlisle
Daily Express, Inc. 387
Dickinson College 412
Carnegie
Ampco-pittsburgh Corp. 90
Center Valley
Desales University 407
Chambersburg
E-lynxx Corporation 435
Franklin Financial Services Corp 544
Chester
Widener University 1521
Chesterbrook
Jg Wentworth Co (the) 733
Trevena Inc 1402
Clearfield
Clearfield Hospital 319
Cnb Financial Corp. (clearfield, Pa) 324
Colmar
Dorman Products Inc 423
Columbia
Colonial Metals Co. 332
Concordville
La France Corp. 770
Conshohocken
Allied Security Holdings Llc 54
American Society For Testing And Materials 83
Cencora Inc 262
Hamilton Lane Inc 614
Integrated Data Corp 698
New Horizons Worldwide, Llc 946
Rumsey Electric Company 1159
Van Horn Metz & Co., Inc. 1465
Coraopolis
A. Stucki Company 6
Dick's Sporting Goods, Inc 412

Metals Recovery Holdings Llc 869
Robert Morris University 1147
Danville
Geisinger Health 562
Denver
High Concrete Group Llc 638
Douglassville
Stv Group, Incorporated 1281
Doylestown
Delaware Valley University 401
Doylestown Hospital Health And Wellness Center, Inc. 424
Duncansville
Hoss's Steak & Sea House, Inc. 656
Value Drug Company 1464
Dunmore
Fidelity D&d Bancorp Inc 514
Fncb Bancorp Inc 533
United Gilsonite Laboratories, Inc. 1428
Easton
Crayola Llc 370
Lafayette College 772
Paragon Technologies Inc 1024
Erie
Erie Indemnity Co. 482
Hamot Health Foundation 614
Logistics Plus, Inc. 807
Plastek Industries, Inc. 1062
Saint Vincent Health System 1168
Exeter
The Coast Distribution System Inc 1338
Exton
Fibrocell Science, Inc. 513
Innovative Solutions And Support Inc 693
Omega Flex Inc 996
Societal Cdmo Inc 1224
West Pharmaceutical Services, Inc. 1509
Fairview
Api Technologies Corp. 100
Feasterville Trevose
Broder Bros., Co. 212
Data Systems Analysts, Inc. 392
Fort Washington
Acts Retirement-life Communities, Inc. 18
Ditech Holding Corporation 417
Gate 1, Ltd 560
Nutrisystem, Inc. 982
Toll Brothers Inc. 1390
Fredericksburg
Farmers Pride, Inc. 502
Freeport
Oberg Industries, Llc 985
Gettysburg
Acnb Corp 16
Gettysburg College 573
The Gettysburg Hospital 1346
Glen Rock
Adhesives Research, Inc. 22

HOOVER'S MASTERLIST OF U.S. COMPANIES 2024

INDEX BY HEADQUARTERS LOCATION

Greensburg
Allegheny Energy Supply Company, Llc 49
Excela Health Holding Company, Inc. 492
The Arc Of Westmoreland 1330

Grove City
Earth Sun Moon Trading Company, Inc. 439

Gwynedd Valley
Mercy Gwynedd University 862

Hanover
Hanover Health Corporation, Inc. 616
The Sheridan Group Inc 1368

Harleysville
Harleysville Financial Corp 618

Harrisburg
Bravo Group, Inc. 205
Hersha Hospitality Trust 636
Mid Penn Bancorp Inc 880
Ollie's Bargain Outlet Holdings Inc 995
Pennsylvania Higher Education Assistance Agency 1040
Pennsylvania Housing Finance Agency 1041
Rite Aid Corp 1144
Stabler Companies Inc. 1262
Susquehanna River Basin Commission 1293
Upmc Pinnacle 1453

Haverford
The Corporation Of Haverford College 1340

Havertown
Amrep Corp. 91

Hellertown
Protosource Corp. 1093

Hershey
Hershey Company (the) 636
Hershey Entertainment & Resorts Company 636
Milton Hershey School 888
The Hershey Salty Snacks Sales Company 1348

Honesdale
Norwood Financial Corp. 976
Wayne Memorial Health System, Inc. 1502

Horsham
Strata Skin Sciences Inc 1278

Huntingdon
J. C. Blair Memorial Hospital 721
Juniata College 741

Huntingdon Valley
Wireless Xcessories Group, Inc. 1530

Indiana
First Commonwealth Financial Corp (indiana, Pa) 519
Indiana University Of Pennsylvania 686
S & T Bancorp Inc (indiana, Pa) 1161

Johnstown
Ameriserv Financial Inc. 88

Concurrent Technologies Corporation 348
Conemaugh Health Company, Llc 348

Kane
Kane Upmc 745

Kennett Square
Exelon Generation Co Llc 493
Genesis Healthcare Inc 567

Kimberton
Nutrition Management Services Co. 982

King Of Prussia
Amag Pharmaceuticals, Inc. 63
American Future Systems, Inc. 75
Ic Compliance Llc 669
Nocopi Technologies Inc Md 961
Qlik Technologies Inc. 1105
Sedona Corp 1192
Tunnell Consulting, Inc. 1414
Ugi Corp. 1420
Universal Health Realty Income Trust 1436
Universal Health Services, Inc. 1436
Vertex Inc 1473

Lafayette Hill
Hajoca Corporation 612
Merakey Usa 861

Lancaster
Armstrong World Industries Inc 115
Eurofins Lancaster Laboratories, Inc. 486
Franklin And Marshall College 543
Fulton Financial Corp. (pa) 552
High Hotels, Ltd. 639
High Industries Inc. 639
High Steel Structures Llc 639
Irex Corporation 715
The Jay Group Inc 1351
The Lancaster General Hospital 1353

Langeloth
Thompson Creek Metals Company Usa 1383

Langhorne
Pop Warner Little Scholars Inc 1067
Savara Inc 1180
Sculptz, Inc. 1188

Lansdale
Greene, Tweed & Co., Inc. 599
Skf Usa Inc. 1216

Latrobe
Commercial National Financial Corp. (pa) 339

Lewisburg
Bucknell University 219
Evangelical Community Hospital 487

Lititz
The Benecon Group Inc 1331

Loretto
Saint Francis University 1167

Malvern
Cantaloupe Inc 240

Ecovyst Inc 445
Phasebio Pharmaceuticals Inc 1051
Tetralogic Pharmaceuticals Corp 1322
The Vanguard Group Inc 1377
Vishay Intertechnology, Inc. 1482
Vishay Precision Group Inc. 1483

Mansfield
Citizens Financial Services Inc 295

Marietta
Donegal Group Inc. 422

Mc Kees Rocks
Ohio Valley General Hospital 992

Mcsherrystown
Boyds Collection Ltd 203

Meadville
Allegheny College 49
Channellock, Inc. 272

Mechanicsburg
Messiah University 868
Pennsylvania - American Water Company 1040
Select Medical Holdings Corp 1193

Media
Elwyn Of Pennsylvania And Delaware 459

Middletown
Pennsylvania Turnpike Commission 1041

Mifflintown
Juniata Valley Financial Corp 741

Monroeville
Standard Avb Financial Corp. 1264

Moon Township
Calgon Carbon Corporation 228
Mastech Digital Inc 842

Nazareth
Essroc Holdings Llc 485

Neffs
Neffs Bancorp Inc. 939

New Enterprise
New Enterprise Stone & Lime Co., Inc. 946

Newtown
Epam Systems, Inc. 478
Onconova Therapeutics Inc 999

Newtown Square
Mercy Health Foundation Of Southeastern Pennsylvania 863
St. Agnes Continuing Care Center 1255

Norristown
Pjm Interconnection, L.l.c. 1060

Northumberland
Furman Foods, Inc. 553

Nottingham
Herr Foods Incorporated 635

Oakdale
Pittsburgh Technical Institute, Inc. 1060

Oaks
Sei Investments Co 1193

Peach Glen
Knouse Foods Cooperative, Inc. 761

Philadelphia
Alteva, Inc. 60
Amicus Therapeutics Inc 89
Aramark 107
Audacy Inc 137
Avax Technologies, Inc. 143
Bdp International, Inc. 165
Brandywine Realty Trust 205
Campus Apartments, Inc. 238
Carisma Therapeutics Inc 246
Carpenter Technology Corp. 249
Cdi Corp. 259
City Of Philadelphia 309
Cohen & Company Inc (new) 329
Comcast Corp 338
Cozen O'connor 368
Drexel University 426
Enviri Corp 476
Faegre Drinker Biddle & Reath Llp 497
Federal Reserve Bank Of Philadelphia, Dist. No. 3 509
Five Below Inc 527
Fmc Corp. 533
Food Export U S A North East 534
Health Partners Plans, Inc. 626
Hill International, Inc. 641
Jefferson Health - Northeast 731
Kate Spade Holdings Llc 746
Lasalle University 779
Magee Rehabilitation Hospital Foundation 824
Morgan, Lewis & Bockius Llp 904
National Constitution Center 925
North Philadelphia Health System 968
Peco Energy Company 1037
Peirce College 1038
Penn Mutual Life Insurance Co. 1039
Pennoni Associates Inc. 1040
Pennsylvania Real Estate Investment Trust 1041
Philadelphia University 1052
Philadelphia Workforce Development Corporation 1052
Prwt Services, Inc. 1095
Quaker Valley Foods, Inc. 1106
Redpoint Bio Corp 1124
Republic First Bancorp, Inc. 1133
Resource America, Inc. 1136
Review Publishing Limited Partnership 1138
Saint Joseph's University 1167
Southeastern Pennsylvania Transportation Authority 1235
Temple University Health System, Inc. 1316
Temple University-of The Commonwealth System Of Higher Education 1316
The Children's Hospital Of Philadelphia 1336
The Fox Chase Cancer Center Foundation 1344
The Pennsylvania Hospital Of The University Of Pennsylvania Health System 1363
The Pew Charitable Trusts 1364

INDEX BY HEADQUARTERS LOCATION

The Philadelphia Parking Authority 1364
The Trustees Of The University Of Pennsylvania 1372
The Wistar Institute Of Anatomy And Biology 1379
Thomas Jefferson University 1383
Thomas Jefferson University Hospitals, Inc. 1383
Urban Affairs Coalition 1455
Urban Outfitters, Inc. 1455
Usa Environmental Management, Inc. 1458
Wausau Paper Corp. 1501
Westinghouse Lighting Corporation 1514
Whyy, Inc. 1521

Pine Grove
Pine Grove Manufactured Homes, Inc. 1056

Pittsburgh
Alcoa Corporation 44
Allegheny General Hospital Inc 49
Allin Corp 54
American Eagle Outfitters, Inc. 73
Arconic Corporation 110
Automatic Steel, Inc. 141
Babcock Lumber Company 151
Busy Beaver Building Centers, Inc. 222
Cardiacassist, Inc. 244
Carnegie-mellon University 248
Chatham University 275
City Of Pittsburgh 310
Computer Enterprises Inc 346
Duquesne Light Co 431
Duquesne Light Holdings, Inc. 431
Duquesne University Of The Holy Spirit 431
Education Management Corp 448
Eqt Corp 480
Equitrans, L.p. 480
Federal Home Loan Bank Of Pittsburgh 507
Federated Hermes Inc 510
Fnb Corp 533
Foster (l.b.) Co 540
Giant Eagle, Inc. 574
Howmet Aerospace Inc 659
Industrial Scientific Corporation 687
J.j. Gumberg Co. 723
Kennametal Inc. 749
Keystone Dedicated Logistics Co Llc 754
Koppers Holdings Inc 764
Kraft Heinz Co (the) 766
Lemieux Group Lp 788
M. J. Brunner Inc. 819
Marshall Marketing & Communications, Inc. 837
Matthews International Corp 845
Michael Baker International, Inc. 876
Miller Electric Construction, Inc 886
P.j. Dick Incorporated 1016
Pdg-environmental, Inc. 1035
Peoples Natural Gas Company Llc 1043
Pitt-ohio Express, Llc 1060
Pittsburgh Associates 1060

Pittsburgh Steelers Sports, Inc. 1060
Pnc Financial Services Group (the) 1065
Ppg Industries Inc 1073
Reunion Industries Inc. 1137
Sargent Electric Company 1179
Smith Micro Software Inc 1222
Snavely Forest Products Inc 1223
Spang & Company 1244
St. Clair Health Corporation 1256
The Brother's Brother Foundation 1333
United States Steel Corp. 1433
University Of Pittsburgh-of The Commonwealth System Of Higher Education 1447
Upmc 1453
Upmc Children's Hospital Of Pittsburgh 1453
Wesco International, Inc. 1508
Western Pennsylvania Hospital 1513
Wexford Health Sources, Inc. 1517
Wvs Financial Corp. 1538

Pittston
Benco Dental Supply Co. 171

Plymouth Meeting
Adapthealth Corp 20
Css Industries, Inc. 377
Inovio Pharmaceuticals Inc. 694

Port Washington
Cca Industries, Inc. 258

Quakertown
Qnb Corp. 1105
Saint Luke's Quakertown Hospital 1168

Radnor
Actua Corp 18
Airgas, Inc. 38
Avantor Inc 143
Community Energy, Inc. 342
Lincoln National Corp. 799
Main Line Health System 825
Marinus Pharmaceuticals Inc 833
Niska Gas Storage Partners Llc 959
Rs Integrated Supply Us Inc. 1157
Safeguard Scientifics, Inc. 1164
Triumph Group Inc. 1407
Vwr Corporation 1489

Reading
Albright College 43
Alvernia University 61
Brentwood Industries, Inc. 207
Enersys 468
Hofmann Industries, Inc. 647
Paul Fredrick Menstyle, Llc 1033
Reading Hospital 1120
Redner's Markets, Inc. 1124
W. Thomas Co. 1491

Saxonburg
Coherent Corp 329

Scranton
Arlington Industries, Inc. 114
Gerrity's Super Market, Inc. 573
Peoples Financial Services Corp 1043
University Of Scranton 1448

Sellersville
Grand View Hospital 593

Seneca
Qrs Music Technologies, Inc. 1105

Sewickley
The Watson Institute 1378

Sharon
Steward Sharon Regional Health System, Inc. 1274

Shenandoah
Ateeco, Inc. 131

Shippensburg
Orrstown Financial Services, Inc. 1010

Souderton
Univest Financial Corp 1452

Southampton
Environmental Tectonics Corp. 477
Tanner Industries, Inc. 1305

Springfield
Ckhs, Inc. 316

State College
Glenn O. Hawbaker, Inc. 578
Minitab, Llc 890
Rex Energy Corp 1139
Videon Central, Inc. 1476

Stroudsburg
Essa Bancorp Inc 484

Sunbury
Weis Markets, Inc. 1506

Swarthmore
Swarthmore College 1294

Titusville
Titusville Area Hospital 1388

Topton
Diakon 410

Towanda
Guthrie Towanda Memorial Hospital 608

Trevose
Lannett Co., Inc. 777

University Park
The Pennsylvania State University 1363

Villanova
Devereux Foundation 408
Villanova University In The State Of Pennsylvania 1478

Warminster
Arbutus Biopharma Corp 108

Warren
United Refining Company 1430

Warrington
Windtree Therapeutics Inc 1528

Wayne
Escalon Medical Corp 483
Radian Group, Inc. 1113
Teleflex Incorporated 1314
The Judge Group Inc 1352
Trinseo Plc 1406

Wellsboro
Citizens & Northern Corp 294

Wernersville
Richard J. Caron Foundation 1142

West Chester
A. Duie Pyle Inc. 6

Accesslex Institute 13
Communications Test Design, Inc. 341
Omni Cable, Llc 997
Qvc, Inc. 1111
Sklar Corp. 1217

West Conshohocken
Madrigal Pharmaceuticals Inc 823

West Reading
Customers Bancorp Inc 382

Wilkes Barre
King's College 757
Wilkes-barre Hospital Company, Llc 1523

Williamsport
Little League Baseball Inc 802
Penns Woods Bancorp, Inc. (jersey Shore, Pa) 1040
Stephan Co (the) 1272

Windber
Sendec Corp. 1196

Woolrich
Woolrich, Inc. 1533

Worcester
Allan Myers, Inc. 49

Wyomissing
Penn Entertainment Inc 1039

York
Bon-ton Stores Inc 197
Codorus Valley Bancorp, Inc. 327
Industrial Supply Association 687
York Hospital 1545
York Pennsylvania Hospital Company Llc 1545
York Water Co 1545

PUERTO RICO

Guaynabo
Cemex De Puerto Rico, Inc. 262
Lopito, Ileana & Howie Inc. 809

San Juan
Evertec, Inc. 489
Popular Inc. 1068

RHODE ISLAND

Cumberland
Nfa Corp. 957

Exeter
Atrion, Inc. 135
Tlic Worldwide, Inc 1389

Kingston
University Of Rhode Island 1447

Lincoln
Lighthouse Computer Services, Inc. 797

Middletown
Kvh Industries, Inc. 769
Towerstream Corp 1394

Newport
Salve Regina University 1171

Pawtucket
Hasbro, Inc. 621

INDEX BY HEADQUARTERS LOCATION

Teknor Apex Company 1313
Providence
Brown University 216
Capital Properties, Inc. 242
Care New England Health System Inc 245
Citizens Financial Group Inc (new) 295
Dimeo Construction Company 414
Gilbane Building Company 575
Gilbane Development Company 575
Johnson & Wales University Inc 737
Lifespan Corporation 795
Lin Holdings Corp. 798
Providence College 1094
Rhode Island Housing And Mortgage Finance Corporation 1141
Rhode Island School Of Design Inc 1141
Software Quality Associates Llc 1225
Spectra Systems Corp 1246
Textron Financial Corp 1326
Textron Inc 1326
The Rdw Group Inc 1365
United Natural Foods Inc. 1429
Riverside
Ann & Hope, Inc. 96
Warwick
Kent County Memorial Hospital 750
Metropolitan Group Property & Casualty Insurance Co. 871
Metropolitan Property & Casualty Insurance Co. 871
The Memorial Hospital 1356
West Warwick
Arpin Moving, Inc. 116
Astronova Inc 129
Lighting Science Group Corp 797
Westerly
Fenway Partners, Llc 512
The Moore Company 1358
Washington Trust Bancorp, Inc. 1498
Woonsocket
Cvs Health Corporation 383
Multicell Technologies Inc 914
Summer Infant, Inc. 1283

SOUTH CAROLINA

Aiken
Agy Holding Corp. 35
Security Federal Corp (sc) 1191
Anderson
Anmed Health Services, Inc. 96
Beaufort
Beaufort Memorial Hospital 166
Cayce
Dominion Energy South Carolina, Inc. 421
Charleston
Advanced Composite Structures, Llc 24
Bank Of South Carolina Corp 155
Blackbaud, Inc. 186
Marketing Analysts Inc. 835
Roper St. Francis Healthcare 1153
The Citadel 1337
The College Of Charleston 1338
The Medical University Of South Carolina 1356
Clinton
Laurens County Health Care System 780
Columbia
Agfirst Farm Credit Bank 33
Benedict College 171
Bonitz, Inc. 197
Companion Professional Services Llc 344
Integrated Business Systems & Services, Inc. 697
M. B. Kahn Construction Co., Inc. 819
Prisma Health-midlands 1084
Pure Fishing, Inc. 1101
Seibels Bruce Group, Inc. (the) 1193
South Carolina Department Of Education 1231
Uci Medical Affiliates, Inc. 1419
University Of South Carolina 1448
Wilbur Smith Associates, Inc. 1522
Conway
Coastal Carolina University Alumni Association, Inc. 325
Horry Telephone Cooperative, Inc. 654
The Pharmacy At Cmc 1364
Eutawville
Koppers Utility And Industrial Products Inc. 764
Florence
Qhg Of South Carolina, Inc. 1105
Fort Mill
Domtar Corporation 422
Wikoff Color Corporation 1522
Gaffney
Hamrick Mills 614
Gaston
G&p Trucking Company, Inc. 554
Georgetown
Georgetown Memorial Hospital 570
Goose Creek
Hirequest Inc 643
Greenville
Furman University Foundation, Inc. 553
Gerber Childrenswear Llc 572
Grandsouth Bancorporation 593
Prisma Health-upstate 1085
Scansource, Inc. 1182
Southern First Bancshares, Inc. 1237
Span-america Medical Systems, Inc. 1243
World Acceptance Corp. 1534
Greenwood
Greenwood Mills, Inc. 600
Greer
Piedmont Municipal Power Agency 1054
Regional Management Corp 1127
Hartsville
Sonoco Products Co. 1229
Kingstree
Farmers Telephone Cooperative, Inc. 503
Lexington
First Community Corp (sc) 520
Southeastern Freight Lines, Inc. 1235
Moncks Corner
South Carolina Public Service Authority (inc) 1231
Mount Pleasant
South Carolina State Ports Authority 1231
Vino.com, L.l.c. 1478
Myrtle Beach
Grand Strand Regional Medical Center, Llc 592
North Charleston
Ingevity Corp 690
Orangeburg
Claflin University 316
Rock Hill
3d Systems Corp. (de) 3
Spartanburg
Denny's Corp 405
J M Smith Corporation 721
R. L. Jordan Oil Company Of North Carolina, Inc. 1111
Security Finance Corporation Of Spartanburg 1191
Spartanburg Regional Health Services District, Inc. 1245
Summerville
Aeterna Zentaris Inc 30
Sumter
Morris College 905
Sumter Coatings, Inc. 1285
West Columbia
Lexington Medical Center 792

SOUTH DAKOTA

Aberdeen
Agtegra Cooperative 35
Brookings
Daktronics Inc. 389
South Dakota State University 1232
Ipswich
North Central Farmers Elevator 966
Madison
Dakota State University 388
Pierre
Avera St. Mary's 145
Rapid City
Black Hills Corporation 186
Black Hills Power Inc. 186
Monument Health Rapid City Hospital, Inc. 902
National American University Holdings Inc. 922
South Dakota School Of Mines And Technology Foundation 1232
Sioux Falls
Augustana University Association 138
Avera Health 144
Northwestern Energy Group Inc 975
Pathward Financial Inc 1031
Raven Industries, Inc 1117
South Dakota State Medical Holding Company, Inc. 1232
The Evangelical Lutheran Good Samaritan Society 1343
Spearfish
Lehman Trikes Inc 787
Volga
South Dakota Soybean Processors Llc 1232
Wentworth
Lake Area Corn Processors Co-operative 773
Winner
Country Pride Cooperative, Inc. 365

TENNESSEE

Knoxville
Smartfinancial Inc 1220
Brentwood
Brookdale Senior Living Inc 213
Chancelight, Inc. 272
Corecivic Inc 359
Delek Logistics Partners Lp 401
Delek Us Energy, Inc. 402
Delek Us Holdings Inc (new) 402
Diversicare Healthcare Services, Inc. 417
Kirkland's Inc 758
Lifeway Christian Resources Of The Southern Baptist Convention 796
Quorum Health Corporation 1110
Surgery Partners Inc 1293
Symbion, Inc. 1296
Tractor Supply Co. 1396
Bristol
Alpha Natural Resources, Inc. 56
Calhoun
Resolute Fp Us Inc. 1135
Chattanooga
Astec Industries, Inc. 128
Cbl & Associates Properties Inc 257
Covenant Logistics Group Inc 366
Covista Communications Inc. 367
Electric Power Board Of Chattanooga 453
Emj Corporation 462
Hamilton Chattanooga County Hospital Authority 613
Metropolitan Security Services, Inc. 872
Parkridge Medical Center, Inc. 1027

INDEX BY HEADQUARTERS LOCATION

Unum Group 1453
Cleveland
Lee University 785
Life Care Centers Of America, Inc. 795
Wholesale Supply Group, Inc. 1521
Collierville
Helena Agri-enterprises, Llc 630
Mueller Industries Inc 913
Cookeville
Averitt Express, Inc. 145
Cookeville Regional Medical Center 356
Tennessee Technological University 1318
Decatur
Volunteer Energy Cooperative 1486
Erwin
Nuclear Fuel Services, Inc. 980
Franklin
Acadia Healthcare Company Inc. 11
Clarcor Inc. 316
Community Health Systems, Inc. 343
Community Healthcare Trust Inc 343
Famc Subsidiary Company 500
Farmvet.com, Inc. 503
Iasis Healthcare Llc 668
Kaiser Aluminum Corp. 743
Noranda Aluminum Holding Corp 962
Tivity Health, Inc. 1388
Tom James Company 1390
Gallatin
Charles C Parks Co Inc 273
Servpro Intellectual Property, Inc. 1200
Germantown
Mid-america Apartment Communities Inc 880
Goodlettsville
Dollar General Corp 420
Greeneville
Forward Air Corp 539
Jackson
H And M Construction Co., Inc. 609
Jackson Energy Authority 724
Lane College 777
Jefferson City
Jefferson County Hma, Llc 731
Johnson City
East Tennessee State University 440
Johnson City Energy Authority 737
Mountain States Health Alliance 908
Kingsport
Eastman Chemical Co 442
Wellmont Health System 1506
Knoxville
Ackermann Pr, Inc. 15
Covenant Health 366

East Tennessee Children's Hospital Association, Inc. 439
Educational Funding Of The South, Inc. 448
Knoxville Utilities Board 762
Parkwest Medical Center 1028
Phillips And Jordan, Incorporated 1052
Pilot Corporation 1056
Provectus Biopharmaceuticals Inc 1093
Regal Entertainment Group 1125
Scripps Networks Interactive, Inc. 1187
Team Health Holdings, Inc. 1310
Tennessee Valley Authority 1318
The H T Hackney Co 1347
University Health System, Inc. 1439
University Of Tennessee 1449
Lebanon
Cracker Barrel Old Country Store Inc 369
Lewisburg
Walker Die Casting, Inc. 1495
Maryville
Blount Memorial Hospital, Incorporated 190
Ruby Tuesday, Inc. 1158
Memphis
Autozone, Inc. 142
Baptist Memorial Health Care System, Inc. 158
Baptist Memorial Hospital 158
City Of Memphis 307
Ducks Unlimited, Inc. 428
Duncan-williams, Inc. 430
Federal Express Corporation 505
Fedex Corp 511
First Horizon Corp 521
Fred's, Inc. 546
International Paper Co 707
Lemoyne-owen College 788
Methodist Le Bonheur Healthcare 869
Perkins & Marie Callender's, Llc 1046
Rhodes College 1141
St. Jude Children's Research Hospital, Inc. 1259
Ut Medical Group, Inc. 1460
Vining-sparks Ibg, Limited Partnership 1478
Wright Medical Group, Inc. 1537
Morristown
Adams Wood Products, Inc. 20
Mount Juliet
Hohner, Inc. 647
Murfreesboro
Firstfleet, Inc. 526
Middle Tennessee State University 881
National Health Investors, Inc. 928
National Healthcare Corp. 929
Saint Thomas Rutherford Hospital 1168
The Middle Tennessee Electric Membership Corporation 1357
Nashville
Alley-cassetty Companies, Inc. 51

Alliancebernstein Holding L.p. 53
Alliancebernstein Holding Lp 53
American Blue Ribbon Holdings, Llc 69
Beacon Technologies, Inc 166
Caterpillar Financial Services Corp 255
Change Healthcare Holdings, Inc. 272
Cumberland Pharmaceuticals Inc 380
Cynergistek, Inc. 384
Dialysis Clinic, Inc. 410
Electric Power Board Of The Metropolitan Government Of Nashville & Davidson County 453
Enterprise Electric, Llc 474
Envision Healthcare Corporation 477
Fb Financial Corp 505
First Acceptance Corp 517
Fisk University 526
Genesco Inc. 566
Hardaway Construction Corp. 617
Hca Healthcare Inc 625
Healthstream Inc 628
J. Alexander's Holdings, Inc. 721
Lipscomb University 801
Louisiana-pacific Corp 810
Lri Holdings, Inc. 813
Metropolitan Government Of Nashville & Davidson County 871
Pinnacle Financial Partners Inc 1057
Revance Therapeutics Inc 1138
Ryman Hospitality Properties Inc 1161
Servicesource International, Inc. 1199
Tennessee State University 1318
The United Methodist Publishing House 1373
The Vanderbilt University 1376
Thomas Saint Midtown Hospital 1383
Vanderbilt University Medical Center 1465
Yellow Corp (new) 1544
Oak Ridge
Navarro Research And Engineering, Inc. 936
Professional Project Services, Inc. 1087
Ooltewah
Miller Industries Inc. (tn) 887
Rogersville
Volunteer Bancorp, Inc. 1485
Sewanee
The University Of The South 1375
South Pittsburg
Sequachee Valley Electric Co-operative Inc 1198
Springfield
Hollingsworth Oil Company, Inc. 648
Union City
Williams Sausage Company, Inc. 1525
Vonore
Mastercraft Boat Holdings Inc 843

TEXAS
Abilene
Abilene Christian University Inc 10
First Financial Bankshares, Inc. 520
Hendrick Southwestern Health Development Corporation 632
Lauren Engineers & Constructors, Inc. 780
Addison
Affirmative Insurance Holdings Inc 31
Brightland Homes, Ltd. 209
Cadence Mcshane Construction Company Llc 226
Guaranty Bancshares Inc 605
Jani-king International, Inc. 728
Sonida Senior Living Inc 1228
Transatlantic Petroleum Ltd. 1398
Uluru Inc 1421
Airport
Thryv Holdings Inc 1385
Alice
Forbes Energy Services Ltd 535
Allen
Atrion Corp. 135
Xtera Communications Inc 1542
Amarillo
Affiliated Foods, Inc. 30
Baptist/st. Anthony's Health System 158
Church Loans & Investment Trust 289
Hastings Entertainment, Inc. 621
Maxor National Pharmacy Services Llc 846
Northwest Texas Healthcare System, Inc. 975
Anderson
Texas Municipal Power Agency 1324
Arlington
City Of Arlington 298
Forestar Group Inc (new) 536
Horton (dr) Inc 654
Lapolla Industries, Llc 778
Six Flags Entertainment Corp 1215
Texas Health Resources 1324
Texas Rangers Baseball Foundation 1325
Austin
Aac Group Holding Corp. 7
Akela Pharma Inc 39
American Campus Communities Llc 70
Aspira Womens Health Inc 124
Astrotech Corp 129
Asure Software Inc. 130
Attorney General, Texas 136
Austin Community College 140
Austin Task, Inc. 140
Aviat Networks, Inc. 145
Bantam Electronics, Inc. 157

HOOVER'S MASTERLIST OF U.S. COMPANIES 2024

INDEX BY HEADQUARTERS LOCATION

Bazaarvoice, Inc. 165
Bvsn, Llc 223
Capital Metropolitan Transportation Authority 242
Cassava Sciences Inc 253
Chuy's Holdings Inc 289
Cirrus Logic Inc 292
Citizens, Inc. (austin, Tx) 296
City Of Austin 299
Digital Realty Trust Inc 413
Digital Turbine Inc 413
Electric Reliability Council Of Texas, Inc. 454
Entorian Technologies Inc. 475
Enviromedia, Inc. 476
Ex-students Association Of The University Of Texas 491
Falconstor Software Inc 499
Farm Credit Bank Of Texas 501
Fieldpoint Petroleum Corp 515
Fired Up, Inc. 517
Goodwill Industries Of Central Texas 588
Green Dot Corp 598
Greenleaf Book Group, Llc 599
Gts Technology Solutions, Inc. 604
Hanger, Inc. 615
Iteris Inc 718
J.d. Abrams, L.p. 722
Jauregui, Inc. 729
Jive Software, Inc. 734
Latinworks Marketing Llc 780
Ldr Holding Corporation 782
Littlefield Corp 803
Ll&e Royalty Trust Co. 805
Lower Colorado River Authority 811
Luminex Corporation 815
Lumos Pharma Inc 815
Lyris, Inc. 818
Molecular Templates Inc 898
Motion Computing, Inc. 907
Oracle Corp 1005
Plus Therapeutics Inc 1064
Proof Advertising, Llc 1090
Purple Communications, Inc. 1102
Retailmenot, Inc. 1137
Rfd & Associates, Inc. 1140
Rio Holdings, Inc. 1143
Saint Edward's University, Inc. 1166
Saratoga Resources Inc 1178
Scrypt Inc 1188
Seton Ascension 1200
Sherry Matthews, Inc. 1205
Silicon Laboratories Inc 1210
Sizmek Inc. 1215
Solarwinds North America, Inc. 1226
St David's South Austin Medical Center 1254
Stark Holdings Inc. 1267
Stratus Properties Inc. 1278
Summit Hotel Properties Inc 1284
Tesla Inc 1321
Texas Department Of Transportation 1323
Texas Hospital Association 1324
Texas Medical Association Library 1324
Texas State History Museum Foundation, Inc 1325

Texas Vanguard Oil Company 1326
Texas Workforce Commission 1326
Thermon Group Holdings Inc 1381
Thomas Graphics, Inc. 1382
University Of Texas At Austin 1449
University Of Texas System 1450
Valence Technology, Inc. 1462
Westech Capital Corp 1511
Westminster Manor 1515
Whole Foods Market, Inc. 1521
Xplore Technologies Corp. 1541
Yeti Holdings Inc 1544

Bastrop
Bluebonnet Electric Cooperative, Inc. 192

Beaumont
Deli Management, Inc. 402

Bedford
Io Integration Inc. 712

Brownsville
City Of Brownsville 300
Columbia Valley Healthcare System, L.p. 337
Public Utilities Board Of The City Of Brownsville, Texas 1099

Bryan
Neutral Posture, Inc. 944

Buna
Southeast Texas Industries, Inc. 1234

Carrollton
Addvantage Technologies Group, Inc. 21

Cedar Hill
Mjb Wood Group, Llc 894

College Station
Texas A & M Research Foundation Inc 1322
The Texas A&m University System 1370

Conroe
Chca Conroe, L.p. 276

Coppell
Alco Stores, Inc. 44
Container Store Group, Inc 354
Dave & Buster's, Inc. 394
Dave & Busters Entertainment Inc 394
Impreso Inc. 681
Mr Cooper Group Inc 910
Universal Power Group, Inc. 1437

Corinth
Denton County Electric Cooperative, Inc. 405

Corpus Christi
American Medical Technologies Inc 79
Asset Protection & Security Services, Lp 125
Christus Spohn Health System Corporation 288
City Of Corpus Christi 302
Port Of Corpus Christi Authority Of Nueces County, Texas 1069
Tor Minerals International Inc 1392

Cypress
International Center For Entrepreneurial Development Inc 704

Dallas
Adeptus Health Inc. 22
Aecom 28
Alon Usa Partners, Lp 56
American Natural Energy Corp 80
American Realty Investors, Inc. 82
Amn Healthcare Services Inc 90
Applied Digital Corp 103
Army & Air Force Exchange Service 115
Ashford Hospitality Trust Inc 123
At&t Inc 130
Ati Inc (new) 131
Atmos Energy Corp. 135
Balfour Beatty Construction Group, Inc. 152
Baylor Scott & White Health 163
Baylor University Medical Center 164
Berry Corp (bry) 175
Bridgford Foods Corp. 208
Brinker International, Inc. 210
Builders Firstsource Inc. 219
Cambium Learning Group, Inc. 236
Capstead Mortgage Corporation 243
Cbre Group Inc 258
Ceco Environmental Corp. 260
Children's Medical Center Of Dallas 283
City Of Dallas 302
Clubcorp Holdings, Inc. 323
Comerica, Inc. 338
Compx International, Inc. 346
Copart Inc 357
Creative Media & Community Trust Corp 370
Cross Border Resources Inc. 373
Cross Timbers Royalty Trust 373
Crossroads Impact Corp 374
Culinaire International, Inc. 379
Dallas Basketball Limited 389
Dallas County Hospital District 389
Dallasnews Corp 389
Dean Foods Company 397
Dominion Resources Black Warrior Trust 421
Dorchester Minerals Lp 422
Dougherty's Pharmacy Inc 423
Drive Shack Inc 426
Eagle Materials Inc 437
Elah Holdings Inc 452
Energy Future Holdings Corp 467
Energy Transfer Lp 468
Enlink Midstream Llc 470
Enlink Midstream Partners, Lp 470
Entech Sales And Service, Llc 472
Essilor Of America, Inc. 485
Etp Legacy Lp 486
Exco Resources Inc 492
Federal Reserve Bank Of Dallas, Dist. No. 11 508
Foundation Healthcare, Inc. 540
Gilbert May, Inc. 575
Hallmark Financial Services Inc. 613

Harvest Natural Resources, Inc. 620
Hf Sinclair Corp 637
Hilltop Holdings, Inc. 642
Hks, Inc. 644
Hoak Media, Llc 646
Homevestors Of America, Inc. 651
Hugoton Royalty Trust (tx) 661
Income Opportunity Realty Investors Inc 682
Invitation Homes Inc 712
Jacobs Solutions Inc 726
Keystone Consolidated Industries, Inc. 754
Kimberly-clark Corp. 756
Kosmos Energy Ltd (de) 765
Kronos Worldwide Inc 768
Lundy Services, L.l.c. 816
Methodist Hospitals Of Dallas Inc 869
Mv Transportation, Inc. 917
New Concept Energy, Inc. 945
Newmarket Technology Inc 953
Nexpoint Storage Partners, Inc. 956
Nl Industries, Inc. 960
North Dallas Bank & Trust Co (dallas, Tx) 966
Omni Hotels Corporation 997
On-target Supplies & Logistics, Ltd. 998
Oncor Electric Delivery Co Llc 999
Panhandle Eastern Pipe Line Company, Lp 1022
Pc Calendar 2010, Llc 1034
Permian Basin Royalty Trust 1047
Placid Refining Company Llc 1061
Plainscapital Corp 1061
Primoris Services Corp 1082
Real Foundation, Inc. 1121
Refocus Group Inc 1125
Ryan, Llc 1160
Sabine Royalty Trust 1162
Sammons Enterprises, Inc. 1172
Shari's Management Corporation 1202
Southern Methodist University Inc 1238
Southwest Airlines Co 1241
Spindletop Oil & Gas Co (tex) 1248
Stevens Transport, Inc. 1274
Steward Health Care System Llc 1274
Sunoco Lp 1287
Tenet Healthcare Corp. 1317
Texas Capital Bancshares Inc 1322
Texas Health Presbyterian Hospital Dallas 1323
Texas Instruments Inc. 1324
Texas Pacific Land Corp 1325
The Susan G Komen Breast Cancer Foundation Inc 1369
Transcontinental Realty Investors, Inc. 1398
Trinity Industries, Inc. 1406
Trt Holdings, Inc 1408
Truman Arnold Companies 1410
Tuesday Morning Corp (new) 1413

INDEX BY HEADQUARTERS LOCATION

United States Lime & Minerals Inc. 1432
United Surgical Partners International, Inc. 1434
Valhi, Inc. 1462
Vhs Of Illinois, Inc. 1474
Vydrotech Inc 1489
Warren Resources Inc (md) 1497
Waste Control Specialists Llc 1499
Westwood Holdings Group, Inc. 1516
Wilhelmina International, Inc. 1523
Zion Oil & Gas Inc 1551

Denton
City Of Denton 303
Sally Beauty Holdings Inc 1170

Desoto
The Warrior Group Inc 1378

Dfw Airport
American Locker Group, Inc. 79
Dallas-fort Worth International Airport Facility Improvement Corporation 389

Eastland
Eastland Memorial Hospital District 442

Edinburg
J & D Produce, Inc. 720

El Paso
City Of El Paso 303
El Paso County Hospital District 451
El Paso Electric Company 451
Elamex, S.a. De C.v. (mexico) 452
Jordan Cf Investments Llp 740
Miratek Corp. 891
University Of Texas At El Paso 1450
Western Refining Logistics, Lp 1513
Western Refining, Inc. 1513

Farmers Branch
Monitronics International, Inc. 899

Flower Mound
American Healthchoice, Inc. 76
Mannatech Inc 829

Fort Worth
American Airlines Group Inc 67
Atco Rubber Products, Inc. 131
Azz Inc 149
Basic Energy Services Inc 161
Ben E. Keith Company 170
Bent Grass Holdings, Inc. 172
Burlington Northern & Santa Fe Railway Co. (the) 221
Burlington Northern Santa Fe, Llc 221
Cook Children's Health Care System 356
Corvel Corp 362
Dfb Pharmaceuticals, Llc 409
Emerge Energy Services Lp 460
Entech Solar, Inc 472
Firstcash Holdings Inc 525
Freese And Nichols, Inc. 547
Frontier Merger Sub Llc 549
Fts International, Inc. 551

General Motors Financial Co Inc 565
Image Microsystems Inc. 678
Kimbell Art Foundation 755
Omnicell Inc 997
Phx Minerals Inc 1054
Quicksilver Resources Inc. 1109
Range Resources Corp 1116
Rs Legacy Corporation 1157
Schumacher Electric Corporation 1184
Tandy Leather Factory Inc 1304
Tarrant County Hospital District 1306
Texas Christian University Inc 1323
Texas Health Harris Methodist Hospital Fort Worth 1323
Thos. S. Byrne, Inc. 1384
Trinity Christian Center Of Santa Ana, Inc. 1406
Wesco Aircraft Holdings, Inc. 1508

Fredericksburg
Hill Country Memorial Hospital 641

Frisco
Addus Homecare Corp 21
Capillary Brierley Inc 241
Comstock Resources Inc 346
Goodman Networks Incorporated 587
Jamba, Inc. 727

Garland
American Terrazzo Company, Ltd. 85
City Of Garland 304
Electric & Gas Technology, Inc. 453
Micropac Industries, Inc. 878

Georgetown
Embree Construction Group, Inc. 459
Southwestern University 1242

Grand Prairie
Falkenberg Construction Co., Inc. 500
Neos Therapeutics, Inc. 940

Grapevine
Buchanan Technologies, Inc. 218
Gamestop Corp 558

Greenville
Hunt Memorial Hospital District 663

Haltom City
The Bms Enterprises Inc 1332

Hawkins
Jarvis Christian University 729

Houston
Adams Resources & Energy, Inc. 20
Aegis Aerospace, Inc. 28
Alaunos Therapeutics Inc 42
Alta Mesa Resources, Lp 58
Aly Energy Services Inc (de) 62
Aly Energy Services, Inc. 62
American Productivity & Quality Center, Inc. 82
American Spectrum Realty, Inc. 84
Americus Mortgage Corporation 87

Ampco Services, L.l.c. 90
Amplify Energy Corp (new) 91
Amplify Energy Holdings Llc 91
Anr Pipeline Company 97
Apa Corp 99
Aravive Inc 107
Archrock Inc 109
Archrock Partners, L.p. 109
Atwood Oceanics, Inc. 137
Baker Hughes Company 152
Baker Hughes Holdings Llc 152
Battalion Oil Corp 162
Belden & Blake Corporation 169
Black Stone Minerals Lp 186
Blue Dolphin Energy Co. 191
Bpz Resources, Inc. 203
Bristow Group Inc (de) 210
Brothers Produce, Incorporated 215
Buckeye Partners, L.p. 218
Calpine Corporation 235
Camber Energy Inc 236
Camden Property Trust 237
Cameron International Corporation 237
Carbo Ceramics Inc. 243
Carriage Services, Inc. 249
Centerpoint Energy Houston Electric Llc 264
Centerpoint Energy, Inc 264
Challenger International, Inc. 271
Cheniere Energy Inc. 277
Cheniere Energy Partners L P 277
Cheniere Energy Partners Lp Holdings, Llc 278
Chevron Pipe Line Company 279
Chord Energy Corp 286
Citation Oil & Gas Corp. 293
Citgo Petroleum Corp. 293
City Of Houston 305
Civeo U.s. Holdings Llc 315
Colorado Interstate Gas Co. 333
Columbia Gulf Transmission, Llc 336
Columbia Pipeline Group, Inc. 336
Columbia Pipeline Partners Lp 336
Comfort Systems Usa Inc 338
Core Laboratories Inc 359
Coterra Energy Inc 363
Crestwood Midstream Partners Lp 372
Crown Castle Inc 375
Darkpulse Inc 391
David E. Harvey Builders, Inc. 394
Diamond Offshore Drilling Inc (new) 411
Dnow Inc 419
Dril-quip Inc 426
Dxp Enterprises, Inc. 432
Dyonyx, L.p. 434
Englobal Corp. 469
Enterprise Products Partners L.p. 475
Eog Resources, Inc. 478
Ep Energy Corp. 478
Erhc Energy Inc 482
Erin Energy Corp 482
Evolution Petroleum Corp 490
Evolve Transition Infrastructure Lp 490
Expro Group Holdings Nv 495
Farouk Systems, Inc. 504

Florida Gas Transmission Company, Llc 529
Flotek Industries Inc 531
Fmc Technologies, Inc. 533
Forum Energy Technologies Inc 539
Furmanite, Llc 553
Gallery Model Homes, Inc. 557
Gas Transmission Northwest Llc 560
Gateway Energy Corporation 560
Gc Services Limited Partnership 561
Genesis Energy L.p. 567
Geokinetics Inc. 570
Geospace Technologies Corp 572
Glen Rose Petroleum Corp 577
Glori Energy Inc 582
Goodrich Petroleum Corporation 588
Great Lakes Dredge & Dock Corp 595
Group 1 Automotive, Inc. 602
Gulf South Pipeline Company, Llc 607
Gulf United Energy Inc 607
Halliburton Company 612
Harvest Oil & Gas Corp 620
Helix Energy Solutions Group Inc 631
Herborium Group Inc 634
Hess Midstream Lp 636
Hines Interests Limited Partnership 643
Holland Southwest International, Incorporated 648
Hospital Solutions, Inc. 655
Houston American Energy Corp. 657
Houston Community College, Inc. 657
Houston Grand Opera Association, Inc. 657
Houston Livestock Show And Rodeo Educational Fund 658
Houston Museum Of Natural Science 658
Houston Wire & Cable Company Inc 658
Houston Zoo, Inc. 658
Hyperdynamics Corp 667
Ies Holdings Inc 674
Internet America Inc 708
Ion Geophysical Corp 713
Itis Holdings Inc 718
Johnson Supply And Equipment Corporation 738
Kbr Inc 746
Key Energy Services Inc (de) 753
Kinder Morgan Inc. 756
King Ranch, Inc. 756
Kirby Corp. 758
Koil Energy Solutions Inc 763
Kraton Corporation 766
Livanova Usa, Inc. 803
Lrr Energy, L.p. 813
Lyondellbasell Advanced Polymers Inc. 818
M.c.a. Communications, Inc. 820
Marathon Oil Corp. 830
Marker Therapeutics Inc 834

Mattress Firm Holding Corp. 845
Mccoy-rockford, Inc. 849
Memorial Hermann Healthcare System 859
Menil Foundation, Inc. 860
Mesquite Energy, Inc. 867
Metropolitan Transit Authority Of Harris County 872
Michael Merger Sub Llc 876
Midcoast Energy Partners, L.p. 881
Mossy Holding Company, Inc 906
Mrc Global Inc 910
Murphy Oil Corp 915
Mustang Machinery Company, Llc 916
Mv Oil Trust 917
Natural Resource Partners Lp 935
Nbl Permian Llc 937
Ncs Multistage Holdings Inc 938
Nov Inc 977
Nrg Energy Inc 979
Nuo Therapeutics Inc 980
Occidental Petroleum Corp 986
Oceaneering International, Inc. 987
Oil States International, Inc. 992
Orbital Infrastructure Group Inc 1006
Orion Group Holdings Inc 1009
Pacific Coast Oil Trust 1018
Page Southerland Page, L.l.p. 1020
Par Pacific Holdings Inc 1023
Parker Drilling Co 1027
Particle Drilling Technologies, Inc. 1029
Patterson-uti Energy Inc. 1032
Pedevco Corp 1037
Permianville Royalty Trust 1047
Petrotal Corp 1049
Phillips 66 1052
Pillarstone Capital Reit 1056
Plains All American Pipeline Lp 1061
Poindexter (j.b.) & Co., Inc. 1065
Port Of Houston Authority 1069
Powell Industries, Inc. 1072
Primeenergy Resources Corp 1081
Pro Consulting Services Inc. 1085
Products (se) Pipe Line Corporation 1087
Pros Holdings Inc 1091
Prosperity Bancshares Inc. 1091
Quanex Building Products Corp 1107
Quanta Services, Inc. 1107
Rci Hospitality Holdings Inc 1119
Resaca Exploitation Inc 1134
Rock Energy Resources Inc 1149
S & B Engineers And Constructors, Ltd. 1161
San Juan Basin Royalty Trust 1174
Satterfield And Pontikes Construction, Inc. 1179
Sdb Trade International, Llc 1188
Seitel Inc 1193
Select Water Solutions Inc 1194
Select Water Solutions, Llc 1194
Service Corp. International 1199
Silicus Technologies, Llc 1211
Silverbow Resources Inc 1211
Smg Industries Inc 1221
Solaris Oilfield Infrastructure Inc 1226

Southcross Energy Partners Llc 1234
Southern Natural Gas Co 1238
Southern Natural Gas Company, L.l.c. 1239
Southern Union Gas Company, Inc. 1240
Spectra Energy, Llc 1246
St. Luke's Episcopal Hospital Physician Hospital Organization, Inc. 1260
Stabillis Solutions Inc 1262
Stage Stores, Inc. 1263
Stewart & Stevenson Inc. 1275
Stewart Builders, Inc. 1275
Stewart Information Services Corp 1275
Sun Coast Resources, Llc 1285
Suncoast Post-tension, Ltd. 1286
Superior Energy Services, Inc. 1290
Synthesis Energy Systems Inc 1299
Sysco Corp 1300
Tailored Brands, Inc. 1302
Targa Resources Corp 1306
Tauber Oil Company 1307
Technipfmc Plc 1311
Tejas Office Products, Inc. 1313
Tellurian Inc 1315
Tennessee Gas Pipeline Co. 1318
Texans For Lawsuit Reform Foundation 1322
Texas Children's Hospital 1322
Texas Southern University 1325
The Chair King Inc 1334
The Methodist Hospital 1356
The Plaza Group, Inc 1364
The Scotia Group Inc 1367
Third Coast Midstream, Llc 1382
Thrustmaster Of Texas, Inc. 1384
Tidewater Inc (new) 1385
Transcontinental Gas Pipe Line Company, Llc 1398
U.s. Physical Therapy, Inc. 1418
United Space Alliance, Llc 1431
University Of Houston System 1443
Us Energy Corp 1456
Vaalco Energy, Inc. 1461
Vantage Drilling Co 1465
Vantage Drilling International 1465
Via Renewables Inc 1475
Victory Packaging, L.p. 1476
Vroom Inc 1488
W & T Offshore Inc 1490
Waste Management, Inc. (de) 1499
Waukesha-pearce Industries, Llc 1500
Weatherford International Plc 1503
Westlake Chlor-vinyls Corporation 1515
Westlake Corp 1515
Whitestone Reit 1520
Willbros Group, Inc. 1524
William Marsh Rice University Inc 1525
Yuma Energy Inc (new) 1547
Zaza Energy Corp. 1549
Zenith Energy Logistics Partners Lp 1550

Huntsville
Sam Houston State University 1171
Irving
Boy Scouts Of America 202
Caterpillar Inc. 255
Celanese Corp (de) 261
Christus Health 287
City Of Irving 305
Commercial Metals Co. 339
Daegis Inc. 387
Darling Ingredients Inc 392
Envela Corp 476
Federal Home Loan Bank Of Dallas 507
Flowserve Corp 532
Fluor Corp. 532
Gruma Corporation 602
Hms Holdings Llc 645
La Quinta Holdings Inc. 771
Mckesson Corp 851
Mothers Against Drunk Driving Inc 906
Move Solutions, Ltd. 909
Nch Corporation 937
Nexstar Media Group Inc 956
Old Claimco, Llc 993
Pds Defense, Inc. 1036
Pioneer Natural Resources Co 1058
Rbc Life Sciences Inc 1119
Salem Media Group, Inc. 1169
Sourcecorp, Incorporated 1231
Staff One, Inc. 1263
The Michaels Companies Inc 1357
The National Football Foundation And College Hall Of Fame Inc 1359
Vistra Corp 1484
Western Summit Constructors, Inc. 1514
Johnson City
Pedernales Electric Cooperative, Inc. 1037
Katy
Academy Sports & Outdoors Inc 11
Staff Force, Inc. 1262
Us Silica Holdings, Inc. 1457
Kemah
American International Industries Inc 78
Kilgore
Kilgore Junior College District 755
Martin Midstream Partners Lp 839
Martin Resource Management Corporation 839
Wolf Energy Services Inc 1531
Killeen
Metroplex Adventist Hospital, Inc. 870
Kingwood
Insperity Inc 695
Lancaster
Frozen Food Express Industries, Inc. 550
Laredo
City Of Laredo 305
International Bancshares Corp. 704

La India Packing Co. 771
League City
American Homestar Corporation 76
Lewisville
Texas-new Mexico Power Company 1326
Lindale
Mercy Ships International 864
Little Elm
Retractable Technologies Inc 1137
Longview
Friedman Industries, Inc. 548
The Good Shepherd Hospital Inc 1347
Lubbock
City Of Lubbock 306
Covenant Health System 366
Lee Lewis Construction, Inc. 785
Plains Cotton Cooperative Association 1061
Pyco Industries, Inc. 1103
Rip Griffin Truck Service Center, Inc. 1143
Texas Tech University System 1326
Lufkin
Memorial Health System Of East Texas 859
Piney Woods Healthcare System, L.p. 1057
Treecon Resources Inc 1402
Manchaca
Marbridge Foundation, Inc. 830
Marshall
North American Technologies Group, Inc. 965
Mckinney
Collin County Community College District 331
Encore Wire Corp. 465
Globe Life Inc 581
Independent Bank Group Inc. 683
Mesquite
Abatix Corp. 8
Midland
Concho Resources Inc. 347
Dawson Geophysical Co (new) 395
Diamondback Energy, Inc. 411
Legacy Reserves Lp 786
Mexco Energy Corp. 873
Natural Gas Services Group Inc 935
Propetro Holding Corp 1090
Rsp Permian, Inc. 1157
Viper Energy Inc 1478
West Texas Gas, Inc. 1509
Midlothian
Ennis Inc 470
Missouri City
Global Geophysical Services Inc 579
Montgomery
Geneca, L.l.c. 563

INDEX BY HEADQUARTERS LOCATION

Moulton
Southstar Bank, S.s.b. 1241
Nederland
Oci Partners Lp 988
New Braunfels
Dyna Group International, Inc. 433
Guadalupe Valley Telephone Cooperative, Inc. 604
New Braunfels Utilities 945
Rush Enterprises Inc. 1159
North Richland Hills
Calloway's Nursery, Inc. 234
Northlake
Farmer Bros. Co. 501
Pasadena
Dynacq Healthcare Inc 433
Kior, Inc. 758
Pearland
Approach Resources Inc. 105
Pharr
London Fruit, Inc. 808
Plainview
Wayland Baptist University Inc 1501
Plano
Cinemark Holdings Inc 291
City Of Plano 310
Diodes, Inc. 415
Dzs Inc 435
Fogo De Chao, Inc. 533
Foxworth-galbraith Lumber Company 542
Green Brick Partners Inc 597
Integer Holdings Corp 696
Intrusion Inc 710
Kynect, Ltd. 769
North Texas Tollway Authority 969
Old Copper Company, Inc. 993
Toyota Motor Credit Corp. 1394
Toyota Motor Sales Usa Inc 1395
Tyler Technologies, Inc. 1416
Upbound Group Inc 1453
Viewcast.com Inc 1477
Yum China Holdings Inc 1546
Prairie View
Prairie View A&m University 1074
Richardson
Amen Properties Inc 65
Fossil Group Inc 540
Lennox International Inc 789
Lojack Corporation 807
Microwave Transmission Systems, Inc 880
Realpage, Inc. 1122
Speed Commerce Inc 1247
University Of Texas At Dallas 1449
Vertical Computer Systems, Inc. 1473
Rockwall
Channell Commercial Corporation 272
Rayburn Country Electric Cooperative, Inc. 1117
Rollingwood
Ezcorp, Inc. 496
Round Rock
Ayro Inc 148

Dell Inc. 402
Dell Technologies Inc 402
Kratos Defense & Security Solutions, Inc. 766
St Davids Healthcare Partnership Llp 1254
Teco-westinghouse Motor Company 1312
Texas Guaranteed Student Loan Corporation 1323
Tss Inc De 1412
San Angelo
Angelo State University 95
San Antonio
Ads Media Group, Inc. 23
Aiadvertising Inc 36
Alamo Community College District 40
American Payroll Institute, Inc. 81
Andeavor Llc 94
Billing Services Group Ltd. 180
Bolner's Fiesta Products, Inc. 197
Broadway Bancshares, Inc. (tx) 211
Ccc Group, Inc. 258
City Of San Antonio 312
City Public Services Of San Antonio 314
Clear Channel Outdoor Holdings Inc (new) 319
Clearday Inc 319
Cst Brands, Llc 377
Cullen/frost Bankers, Inc. 379
Curtis C. Gunn, Inc. 381
Digerati Technologies Inc 412
H Munoz And Company, Inc. 610
H W D Casings, Inc. 610
Iheartmedia Inc 674
Maldonado Nursery & Landscaping Inc. 826
Mission Pharmacal Company 892
Nustar Energy Lp 981
Nustar Gp Holdings, Llc 981
Operational Technologies Corporation 1003
Our Lady Of The Lake University Of San Antonio 1013
Pioneer Energy Services Corp. 1058
Rackspace Technology Global, Inc. 1113
Rackspace Technology Inc 1113
San Antonio Spurs, L.l.c. 1172
San Antonio Water System 1172
San Antonio Zoological Society 1172
Southwest Research Institute Inc 1242
Trinity University 1406
United Services Automobile Association 1431
University Health System Services Of Texas, Inc. 1439
Us Global Investors Inc 1457
Usio Inc 1459
Valero Energy Corp 1462
Vericast Corp. 1470
Visionworks Of America, Inc. 1483
San Marcos
Texas State University 1325
Seadrift
Union Carbide Corporation 1424

Seguin
Alamo Group, Inc. 40
Texas Lutheran University 1324
Selma
Call Now Inc. 233
Spaw Glass Holding, Llc 1245
Sherman
Austin College 140
Southlake
Align Communications Inc. 47
Geos Communications, Inc. 572
Hkn, Inc. 644
Sabre Corp 1163
Spring
American Bureau Of Shipping 69
Exxon Mobil Corp 496
Exxonmobil Pipeline Company 496
Hewlett Packard Enterprise Co 637
Layne Christensen Company 781
Perma-pipe International Holdings Inc 1046
Smart Sand Inc 1220
Southwestern Energy Company 1242
Stafford
Elgin Separation Solutions Industrials Llc 456
Kitz Corporation Of America 759
Stephenville
Tarleton State University 1306
Sugar Land
Applied Optoelectronics Inc 104
Bluebonnet Nutrition Corporation 192
Cvr Energy Inc 383
Cvr Partners Lp 383
Team Inc 1310
Trecora Llc 1401
Tahoka
Lyntegar Electric Cooperative, Inc. 818
Temple
Mclane Company, Inc. 851
Scott And White Health Plan 1186
Terrell
Madix, Inc. 823
Texarkana
Wadley Regional Medical Center 1493
Yates Group, Inc. 1543
The Colony
Rave Restaurant Group Inc 1117
The Woodlands
Apptech Corp 106
Championx Corp 271
Chevron Phillips Chemical Company Llc 279
Conns Inc 351
Csi Compressco Lp 376
Gulf Island Fabrication, Inc. 607
Howard Hughes Holdings Inc 659
Huntsman Corp 663
Huntsman International Llc 664
Imperial Petroleum Recovery Corp. 681

Lexicon Pharmaceuticals, Inc. 792
Lgi Homes, Inc. 792
Mind Technology Inc 889
Newpark Resources, Inc. 954
Nexeo Solutions Holdings, Llc 955
Ovintiv Exploration Inc. 1014
Repros Therapeutics Inc. 1133
Spyr Inc 1252
Sterling Infrastructure Inc 1273
Strike Operating Company Llc 1279
Tetra Technologies, Inc. 1321
Waste Connections Us, Inc. 1498
Western Midstream Partners Lp 1513
Tomball
Ricebran Technologies 1141
Tomball Hospital Authority 1391
Tyler
Christus-trinity Mother Frances Foundation 288
East Texas Medical Center Regional Healthcare System 440
Southside Bancshares, Inc. 1240
Waco
Baylor University 163
Brazos Electric Power Cooperative, Inc. 205
Brazos Higher Education Service Corporation, Inc. 206
West Lake Hills
The Drees Company 1342
Westlake
Schwab (charles) Corp (the) 1185
Solera Holdings, Llc 1226
Virbac Corporation 1479
Wichita Falls
Midwestern State University 884
Mission Broadcasting, Inc. 892
United Regional Health Care System, Inc. 1430
Willis
Kongsberg Power Products Systems I, Llc 763
Winnsboro
Team Air Express, Inc. 1309
Yoakum
Yoakum Community Hospital 1545

UTAH

Centerville
Management & Training Corporation 827
Draper
Comenity Bank 338
Control4 Corporation 355
Fuelstream, Inc. 551
Healthequity Inc 627
Prog Holdings Inc 1088
Eureka
Applied Minerals Inc 104
Chief Consolidated Mining Co. 281

HOOVER'S MASTERLIST OF U.S. COMPANIES 2024

INDEX BY HEADQUARTERS LOCATION

Hurricane
Dats Trucking, Inc. 393
Lehi
Nature's Sunshine Products, Inc. 935
Spark Networks, Inc. 1244
Lindon
Fonix Corp. (de) 534
Forevergreen Worldwide Corp 536
Logan
Cache Valley Electric Company 226
Icon Health & Fitness, Inc. 670
Utah State University 1460
Midvale
Ally Bank 55
Beyond Inc 177
Savage Companies 1180
Utah Medical Products, Inc. 1460
Zagg Inc 1548
Murray
R1 Rcm Inc New 1112
Repositrak Inc 1132
North Salt Lake
Big West Oil, Llc 179
Ogden
Autoliv Asp, Inc. 140
Columbia Ogden Medical Center, Inc. 336
Weber State University 1504
Park City
Skullcandy, Inc. 1217
Sundance Institute 1286
Provo
Alpine Air Express, Inc. 57
Brigham Young University 209
Nu Skin Enterprises, Inc. 980
Vitalsmarts, Lc 1484
Riverton
Stampin' Up Inc. 1263
Salt Lake City
A & K Railroad Materials, Inc. 4
Allen Communication Learning Services, Inc. 50
Allied Resources Inc 54
Alsco Inc. 57
Arnold Machinery Company 116
Associated Food Stores, Llc 126
Big-d Construction Corp. 180
Bsd Medical Corporation 218
Burton Lumber & Hardware Co. 222
C.r. England, Inc. 225
Caspian Services Inc 253
Celtic Investment, Inc. 262
Children's Miracle Network 284
Clarus Corp (new) 318
Clearone Inc 320
Codale Electric Supply, Inc. 327
Cyrq Energy, Llc 385
Daw Technologies Inc. 395
Dominion Energy Questar Corporation 421
Evans & Sutherland Computer Corporation 487
Extra Space Storage Inc 496
Franklin Covey Co 544
Fx Energy, Inc. 554

Groen Brothers Aviation Inc 601
Intermountain Health Care Inc 703
Joe Granato, Incorporated 735
Mountainwest Pipeline, Llc 909
Myriad Genetics, Inc. 918
Northern Utah Healthcare Corporation 972
Novagold Resources Inc. 977
Nutraceutical International Corporation 981
O. C. Tanner Company 984
Paradigm Medical Industries Inc. (de) 1024
Questar Gas Co. 1109
Regenetp Inc 1126
Salt Lake Community College 1170
Security National Financial Corp 1192
Sintx Technologies Inc 1214
Standard Energy Corp. 1264
Techniscan Inc. 1311
The University Of Utah 1376
University Of Utah Health Hospitals And Clinics 1450
Usana Health Sciences Inc 1459
Utah Associated Municipal Power Systems 1460
Varex Imaging Corp 1466
Westminster University 1515
Young Electric Sign Company Inc 1546
Zions Bancorporation, N.a. 1551
Sandy
Incontact, Inc. 682
Landcar Management, Ltd. 776
The Layton Companies Inc 1353
South Jordan
Deseret Generation And Transmission Co-operative 407
Headwaters Incorporated 625
Merit Medical Systems, Inc. 865
Mobileiron, Inc. 896
Pioneer Oil & Gas 1058
South Salt Lake
Allergy Research Group Llc 51
R.c. Willey Home Furnishings 1112
St. George
Skywest Inc. 1218
Vernal
Superior Drilling Products Inc 1290
West Jordan
Sportsman's Warehouse Holdings Inc 1249
West Valley City
Central Refrigerated Service, Llc 267

VERMONT

Bennington
Bennington College Corporation 172
Southwestern Vermont Health Care Corporation 1242
Burlington
The Burton Corporation 1333

The University Of Vermont Medical Center Inc 1376
University Of Vermont & State Agricultural College 1450
Colchester
Engelberth Construction, Inc. 469
Green Mountain Power Corporation 598
Derby
Community Bancorp. (derby, Vt) 341
Middlebury
President And Fellows Of Middlebury College 1078
Morrisville
Union Bankshares, Inc. (morrisville, Vt) 1424
Northfield
Norwich University 976
Plainfield
Goddard College Corporation 583
Rutland
Casella Waste Systems, Inc. 252
The Rutland Hospital Inc 1367
Springfield
Springfield Hospital Inc. 1251
Waterbury
Keurig Green Mountain, Inc. 752

VIRGIN ISLANDS

Christiansted
Limetree Bay Terminals Llc 797

VIRGINIA

Reston
Leidos Holdings Inc 787
Abingdon
K-va-t Food Stores, Inc. 743
Alexandria
Addx Corporation 21
Alexandria Inova Hospital 46
American Council Of The Blind Inc 72
American Staffing Association 84
Armed Forces Benefit Association 115
Asis International, Inc. 124
Burke Herbert Financial Services Corp 220
Calibre Systems, Inc. 229
Catholic Charities Usa 255
City Of Alexandria 298
Community Health Charities 342
Comtex News Network Inc 347
Cuisine Solutions, Inc. 379
Good360 587
Health Industry Distributors Association 626
Healthy Mothers Healthy Babies Inc 628
Institute For Defense Analyses Inc 696
International Sign Association Inc 707
Milestone Construction Services, Inc. 885

National Head Start Association 928
Prevent Cancer Foundation, Inc. 1080
Spok Holdings Inc 1249
Systems Engineering Technologies Corporation 1300
The Salvation Army National Corporation 1367
United Way Worldwide 1434
Volunteers Of America, Inc. 1486
Vse Corp. 1488
Alexandria
Diamondhead Casino Corp 411
Altavista
Pinnacle Bankshares Corp 1057
Arlington
Access Worldwide Communications, Inc. 13
Aerovironment, Inc. 29
Aes Corp 29
American Diabetes Association 73
American Institutes For Research In The Behavioral Sciences 77
Avalonbay Communities, Inc. 143
Boeing Co. (the) 195
Brc Merger Sub, Llc 206
Calatlantic Group, Inc. 228
Ceb Inc. 260
Conservation International Foundation 351
Consumer Technology Association 353
Council Of Better Business Bureaus, Inc. 364
Del Friscos Of Georgia, Llc 400
E Trade Financial Corporation 435
Experience Works, Inc. 494
Feminist Majority Foundation 511
Graham Holdings Co. 592
Greater Washington Educational Telecommunications Association, Inc. 597
Healthcare Distribution Alliance 626
Hr Policy Association 660
Ids International, Llc 673
Imagine Schools, Inc. 678
In-q-tel, Inc 682
Indus Corporation 687
Leonardo Drs Inc 789
March Of Dimes Inc. 831
Meals On Wheels America 853
Metters Industries, Inc. 873
Nami-maine 919
National Council On Aging, Inc. 926
National Rural Electric Cooperative Association 931
News/media Alliance 954
Public Broadcasting Service 1097
Ramboll Holdings, Inc. 1115
Rtx Corp 1158
S C & A, Inc. 1161
Sinclair Television Of Capital District, Inc. 1213
Technology Service Corporation 1311

1648　HOOVER'S MASTERLIST OF U.S. COMPANIES 2024

INDEX BY HEADQUARTERS LOCATION

The Conservation Fund A Nonprofit Corporation 1340
The Nature Conservancy 1359
Touchstone Energy Cooperative, Inc. 1393
Us Dairy Export Council 1456
Utilities Telecom Council 1461
Virginia Hospital Center Arlington Health System 1480

Ashburn
Computer Sciences Corporation 346
Dxc Technology Co 432
M V M, Inc. 819
National Recreation And Park Association, Incorporated 931
Steelcloud Inc 1271
Telos Corp. (md) 1316

Ashland
Tsrc, Inc. 1412

Bassett
Bassett Furniture Industries, Inc 161

Blacksburg
National Bankshares Inc. (va) 924
Virginia Polytechnic Institute & State University 1480

Bluefield
First Community Bankshares Inc (va) 520

Bristol
Strongwell Corporation 1279

Centreville
Parsons Corp (de) 1028
Parsons Government Services Inc. 1029

Chantilly
America's Charities 66
American Systems Corporation 85
Centauri, Llc 263
Citizant, Inc. 294
Rdr, Inc. 1120
The Centech Group Inc 1334

Charlottesville
Cervomed Inc 269
Kohr Brothers, Inc. 763
Martha Jefferson Health Services Corporation 838
Pepsi-cola Bottling Co Of Central Virginia 1044
Rector & Visitors Of The University Of Virginia 1123

Chatham
Womack Publishing Company, Inc. 1532

Chesapeake
City Of Chesapeake 301
Dollar Tree Inc 420
Schenker, Inc. 1183

Chester
Industrial Turnaround Corporation 687

Culpeper
Jefferson Homebuilders, Inc. 731

Danville
Danville Regional Medical Center, Llc 391

Dulles
Cigital, Inc. 291
National Rural Utilities Cooperative Finance Corp 932

Edinburg
Shenandoah Telecommunications Co 1204

Fairfax
American Wholesale Marketers Assn, Inc 86
Customink, Llc 382
Ecs Federal, Llc 446
George Mason University 570
Guest Services, Inc. 605
Horne International Inc 654
Inova Health System Foundation 693
Kaiser Group Holdings, Inc. 744
National Rifle Association Of America 931
Obocon Inc 986
Spacequest, Ltd. 1243
The Long & Foster Companies Inc 1354
Wavedancer Inc 1501
Widepoint Corp 1522

Falls Church
Csra Inc. 377
Hitt Contracting, Inc. 644
Northrop Grumman Corp 973
Northrop Grumman Innovation Systems, Inc. 973

Farmville
President And Trustees Of Hampden-sydney College 1079

Fishersville
Wilson Trucking Corporation 1527

Fredericksburg
Mary Washington Healthcare 839
Rappahannock Electric Cooperative 1117
United States Parachute Association 1433

Galax
Twin County Community Foundation 1416
Vaughan Furniture Company, Incorporated 1467
Vaughan-bassett Furniture Company, Incorporated 1467

Glen Allen
Asgn Inc 123
Dynex Capital Inc 434
Eastern Gas Transmission And Storage, Inc. 441
Endi Corp 466
Hamilton Beach Brands Holding Co 613
Markel Group Inc 834
Old Dominion Electric Cooperative 993

Hampton
Hampton University 614
Old Point Financial Corp 994

Harrisonburg
James Madison University 728
Rosetta Stone Inc. 1154
Sentara Rmh Medical Center 1197

Heathsville
Sharpe Resources Corp. 1203

Herndon
Apex Data Services, Inc. 99
Apptix, Inc. 106
Artel, Llc 119
Beacon Roofing Supply Inc 166
Brtrc Federal Solutions, Inc. 216
Certainteed Gypsum Products, Inc. 269
Eplus Inc 479
Lancesoft, Inc. 775
Learning Tree International Inc 784
Mantech International Corporation 829
Maryland And Virginia Milk Producers Cooperative Association, Incorporated 839
Navient Corp 936
Packaging Machinery Manufacturers Institute, Incorporated 1020
Prosegur Services Group, Inc. 1091
Strategic Education Inc 1278
Windward Consulting Group, Inc. 1528
Xo Holdings, Inc 1541

Lebanon
Russell County Medical Center Inc 1160

Leesburg
Applied Visual Sciences Inc. 105
Electronic Instrumentation And Technology, Llc 455
The Daston Corporation 1341
Thirdera, Llc 1382

Lexington
The Washington And Lee University 1378
Virginia Military Institute 1480

Lorton
Ctsc, Llc 378

Lynchburg
Bank Of The James Financial Group Inc 156
Bwx Technologies Inc 223
Centra Health, Inc. 265
Schewel Furniture Company Incorporated 1183
University Of Lynchburg 1444

Manakin Sabot
Luck Stone Corporation 814

Manassas
Aurora Flight Sciences Corp 139
Ncs Technologies, Inc. 938
Northern Virginia Electric Cooperative 972
Uva Prince William Health System 1461

Martinsville
Hooker Furnishings Corp 652

Mc Lean
Acentra Health, Llc 14
Belcan Government Solutions, Inc. 169
Corascloud, Inc. 358
Hii Mission Technologies Corp. 640
Icore Networks, Inc. 671

Immixgroup, Inc. 679
Solerity, Inc. 1227
Southern Management Companies Llc 1237
The Electronic Retailing Association 1343

Mclean
Appian Corp 103
Booz Allen Hamilton Holding Corp. 198
Capital One Financial Corp 242
Delta Tucker Holdings Inc 404
Freddie Mac 546
Gannett Co Inc (new) 559
Gladstone Commercial Corp 577
Gladstone Land Corp 577
Gtt Communications, Inc 604
Guidehouse Inc. 606
Hilton Worldwide Holdings Inc 642
Iridium Communications Inc 715
Jer Investors Trust Inc 732
Lcc International Inc. 782
Maximus Inc. 846
Primis Financial Corp 1082
Western Magnesium Corp 1512

Mechanicsville
Owens & Minor, Inc. 1015

Midland
Smith-midland Corp. 1222

Midlothian
Village Bank & Trust Financial Corp 1477

Newport News
City Of Newport News 308
Ferguson Enterprises, Llc 512
Huntington Ingalls Industries, Inc. 663
Primecare System, Inc. 1081
Riverside Healthcare Association, Inc. 1145
Riverside Hospital, Inc. 1145
W.m.jordan Company, Incorporated 1491

Norfolk
Childrens Health System, Inc. 284
City Of Norfolk 308
Eastern Virginia Medical School 442
Norfolk State University 964
People For The Ethical Treatment Of Animals, Inc. 1042
Pra Group Inc 1073
Sentara Health 1197
Virginia International Terminals, Llc 1480

Norton
Norton Community Hospital Auxiliary, Inc. 976

Onancock
Marker 29 Produce, Inc. 834

Prince George
Touchstone Bankshares Inc 1393

Reedville
Omega Protein Corporation 996

Reston
Altum, Incorporated 61
Bechtel Group, Inc. 168

Bowman Consulting Group Ltd 202
Caci International Inc 226
Calnet, Inc. 234
Comscore Inc 346
Comstock Holding Companies, Inc 346
Ellucian Inc. 458
Emerald Dairy Inc 460
General Dynamics Corp 564
Global Infotek, Inc. 580
Icf International Inc 670
Idemia Identity & Security Usa Llc 672
Internap Corp 703
Lightbridge Corp 797
Metrostar Systems, Llc 873
Midwave Wireless, Inc. 883
National Wildlife Federation Inc 934
Nci, Inc. 938
Neustar, Inc. 944
Nii Holdings Inc. 959
Noblis, Inc. 961
Nvr Inc. 983
Pragmatics, Inc. 1074
Science Applications International Corp (new) 1185
Stride Inc 1279
The American Society Of Civil Engineers 1329
Thompson Hospitality Corporation 1383
Tri-cor Industries, Inc. 1403
Ventera Corporation 1469
Verisign Inc 1471
Vistronix, Llc 1484

Richlands
Clinch Valley Medical Center, Inc. 323

Richmond
Altria Group Inc 61
Arko Corp 114
Atlantic Union Bankshares Corp 133
Bon Secours - Richmond Community Hospital, Incorporated 197
Brinks Co (the) 210
Captech Ventures, Inc. 243
Carmax Inc. 248
Cherry Bekaert Llp 278
Childfund International, Usa 282
Children's Hospital Foundation 283
City Of Richmond 310
Desktop Service Center, Inc. 407
Dominion Energy Inc (new) 421
Estes Express Lines 485
Federal Reserve Bank Of Richmond, Dist. No. 5 509
Genworth Financial, Inc. (holding Co) 569
Gpm Investments, Llc 591
James River Coal Company 728
Kbs, Inc. 747
Kinsale Capital Group Inc 757
Ll Flooring Holdings Inc 805
Newmarket Corp 953
Performance Food Group Co 1045
Southern States Cooperative Inc. 1240

The Collegiate School 1338
Tredegar Corp. 1401
Universal Corp 1435
University Of Richmond 1448
Virginia Commonwealth University 1479
Virginia Electric & Power Co. 1480
Virginia Housing Development Authority 1480

Roanoke
Branch Builds, Inc. 204
Carilion Clinic 246
Grand Piano & Furniture Co. 592
Hollins University Corporation 648
Home Energy Savings Corp 650
Luna Innovations Inc 816
Optical Cable Corp. 1004
Rgc Resources, Inc. 1140
The Branch Group Inc 1333

Rocky Mount
Ronile, Inc. 1152

Smithfield
Smithfield Foods, Inc. 1222

South Hill
Peebles Inc. 1037

Springfield
Isomet Corp. 717

Stanley
Pioneer Bankshares Inc 1058

Sterling
Astron Wireless Technologies Inc. 129
Nest Technologies Corp. 941
Ott Hydromet Corp 1012
Rei Systems, Inc. 1128
Technica Corporation 1310

Strasburg
First National Corp. (strasburg, Va) 523

Timberville
F & M Bank Corp. 496

Toano
C & F Financial Corp. 224

Triangle
Marine Toys For Tots Foundation 833
United Mine Workers Of America 1429

Tysons
National Automobile Dealers Association 923
Park Hotels & Resorts Inc 1026
Tegna Inc 1313

Tysons Corner
Cvent, Inc. 383
Microstrategy Inc. 879

Union Hall
Penbay Technology Group Llc 1038

Verona
Dgo Corporation 409

Vienna
Actionet, Inc. 17
Cel-sci Corporation 261
Cleannet U.s.a., Inc. 319
Intellidyne, L.l.c. 699
Microtechnologies Llc 879

Stg Llc 1275

Virginia Beach
Atlantic Diving Supply, Inc. 133
Cedar Realty Trust Inc 261
City Of Virginia Beach 314
Navy Exchange Service Command 936
Old Dominion Tobacco Company Incorporated 994
Operation Smile, Inc. 1003
The Christian Broadcasting Network Inc 1336
The Penrod Company 1363
Wheeler Real Estate Investment Trust Inc 1519

Warrenton
Air Serv International, Inc. 37
Fhi Services 513

Waynesboro
Lumos Networks Corp. 815
Ntelos Holdings Corp. 979

Williamsburg
National Center For State Courts 925
Sentara Williamsburg Regional Medical Center 1197
Sotherly Hotels Inc 1230
The College Of William & Mary 1338
The Colonial Williamsburg Foundation 1339

Winchester
American Woodmark Corp. 87
Trex Co Inc 1402
Valley Health System 1462
Winchester Medical Center Auxiliary, Inc. 1527

Woodbridge
Potomac Hospital Corporation Of Prince William 1071

WASHINGTON

Aberdeen
Pacific Financial Corp. 1018

Bellevue
City Of Bellevue 299
Coinstar, Llc 330
Gly Construction, Inc. 582
Her Interactive, Inc. 633
Itex Corp 718
Odom Corporation 989
Overlake Hospital Medical Center 1014
Paccar Inc. 1016
Puget Energy, Inc. 1100
T-mobile Us Inc 1301
Tecplot, Inc. 1312
Terreno Realty Corp 1320

Bellingham
Exp World Holdings Inc 493
Haggen, Inc. 612
Western Washington University 1514

Bonney Lake
International Market Brands, Inc. 706

Bothell
Achieve Life Science Inc 15

Biolife Solutions Inc 182
Helix Biomedix Inc 631
Lundbeck Seattle Biopharmaceuticals, Inc. 816
Scolr Pharma Inc 1186

Cashmere
Liberty Orchards Company, Inc. 794

Chelan
Trout-blue Chelan-magi, Llc 1408

Cheney
Eastern Washington University Inc 442
Trans-system, Inc. 1397

Clarkston
Renaissance Marine Group, Inc. 1130

Ephrata
Public Utility District 2 Grant County 1099

Everett
Fortive Corp 538
Public Utility District 1 Of Snohomish County 1099

Fife
Brown & Haley 215

Hoquiam
Timberland Bancorp, Inc. 1386

Issaquah
Costco Wholesale Corp 363
Lakeside Industries, Inc. 774

Kennewick
Electronic Systems Technology, Inc. 455

Kent
Alaskan Copper Companies, Inc. 42

Kirkland
Monolithic Power Systems Inc 900
Pendrell Corp 1039

Lacey
I-5 Design Build Inc. 668

Liberty Lake
Itron Inc 719

Longview
North Pacific Paper Company, Llc 968
Public Utility District No 1 Of Cowlitz County 1099

Lynnwood
Zumiez Inc 1553

Mercer Island
Farmers New World Life Insurance Co. 502

Mountlake Terrace
Fs Bancorp Inc (washington) 550

Olympia
Evergreen State College 488
Heritage Financial Corp (wa) 634

Orondo
Auvil Fruit Company, Inc. 142

INDEX BY HEADQUARTERS LOCATION

Poulsbo
Pope Resources (a Delaware Limited Partnership) 1068

Redmond
Data I/o Corp. 392
Maq, Llc 830
Microsoft Corporation 879
Microvision Inc. 879

Renton
Boeing Capital Corp 195
Convergent Outsourcing, Inc. 355
First Financial Northwest Inc 521
Football Northwest Llc 535
National Frozen Foods Corporation 927
Olympic Pipe Line Company 995
Providence Health & Services 1094
Providence St. Joseph Health 1094
Radiant Logistics, Inc. 1113

Richland
Commodore Applied Technologies, Inc. 340
Energy Northwest 467
Kadlec Regional Medical Center 743
Perspective Therapeutics Inc 1047

Seattle
Alaska Air Group, Inc. 41
Amazon.com Inc 63
Bill & Melinda Gates Foundation 180
Bloodworks 189
Carrix, Inc. 250
Cascadian Therapeutics, Inc. 252
City Of Seattle 312
Diamond Parking Services, Llc 411
Expedia Group Inc 494
Expeditors International Of Washington, Inc. 494
Experience Learning Community 494
F5 Inc 497
General Insurance Company Of America 565
Getty Images Holdings Inc 573
Homestreet Inc 651
Icicle Seafoods, Inc. 670
Immune Design Corp. 680
Impinj Inc 681
Jones Soda Co. 739
L&l Energy Inc 770
Lane Powell Pc 777
Marchex Inc 831
Nanostring Technologies Inc 920
Netmotion Software, Inc. 942
Neurogene Inc 943
Nordstrom, Inc. 963
Northwest Dairy Association 974
Norton Laird Trust Company 976
Ocean Beauty Seafoods Llc 986
Omeros Corp 997
Onvia, Inc. 1002
Orca Bay Seafoods, Inc. 1007
Perkins Coie Llp 1046
Port Of Seattle 1069
Realnetworks Llc 1121
Redfin Corp 1124
Safeco Insurance Company Of America 1164

Seattle Children's Hospital 1190
Seattle University 1190
Slalom, Inc. 1218
Sound Financial Bancorp Inc 1230
Starbucks Corp. 1267
Swedish Health Services 1295
The City Of Seattle-city Light Department 1337
Triple "b" Corporation 1407
University Of Washington Inc 1451
Wafd Inc 1493
Weyerhaeuser Co 1517

Selah
Tree Top, Inc. 1401

Shelton
Cascade Forest Corporation 252

Shoreline
Crista Ministries 372

Spokane
Agwest Farm Credit, Flca 35
Ambassador Programs, Inc. 64
Avista Corp 146
Clearwater Paper Corp 320
E Z Loader Boat Trailers, Inc. 435
Gold Reserve Inc 583
Goldrich Mining Co 586
Gonzaga University 586
Potlatchdeltic Corp 1071
Urm Stores, Inc. 1455

Spokane
Kaspien Holdings Inc 746

Spokane Valley
Key Tronic Corp 753
Servatron, Inc. 1198

Tacoma
Burkhart Dental Supply Co. 221
Columbia Banking System Inc 335
Franciscan Health System 543
L.d. Mcfarland Company, Limited 770
Multicare Health System 914
Suncliff Inc 1286
Tacoma Public Utilities 1301
Trueblue Inc 1409
University Of Puget Sound 1447

Toppenish
Heritage University 635

Tukwila
Harnish Group Inc. 619

Vancouver
Barrett Business Services, Inc. 160
Bowflex Inc 201
Calvert Company, Inc. 235
Northwest Pipe Co. 974
Peacehealth 1036
Peacehealth Southwest Medical Center 1036
Public Utility District 1 Of Clark County 1099
Riverview Bancorp, Inc. 1145
Tumac Lumber Co., Inc. 1414
Zoominfo Technologies Inc 1552

Walla Walla
Banner Corp. 156
Key Technology, Inc. 753
Whitman College 1520

Wenatchee
Goodfellow Bros. Llc 587

Public Utility District No. 1 Of Chelan County 1099

Woodinville
Geobio Energy Inc 569
Jit Manufacturing, Inc. 734
Loud Technologies Inc 810

Yakima
Yakima Valley Memorial Hospital Association Inc 1542

WEST VIRGINIA

Beckley
Vecellio & Grogan, Inc. 1468

Berkeley Springs
War Memorial Hospital, Inc. 1496

Charles Town
American Public Education Inc 82
Potomac Bancshares, Inc. 1071

Charleston
Charleston Area Medical Center, Inc. 274
Charleston Hospital, Inc. 274
City Holding Co. 297
Jacobs Financial Group Inc 726
United Bankshares Inc 1426

Chester
Mtr Gaming Group, Inc. 912

Elkins
Citizens Financial Corp. (wv) 295

Fairmont
Monongahela Power Co 901

Follansbee
Wheeling-nippon Steel, Inc. 1519

Gilbert
International Industries, Inc. 706

Huntington
Champion Industries Inc (wv) 271
Energy Services Of America Corp. 468
Marshall University 837
St. Mary's Medical Center, Inc. 1261
Steel Of West Virginia, Inc. 1270

Marlinton
Burns Motor Freight, Inc. 221

Moorefield
Summit Financial Group Inc 1284

Morgantown
West Virginia University Hospitals, Inc. 1509
West Virginia United Health System, Inc. 1510
West Virginia University 1510
West Virginia University Foundation, Incorporated 1510

Petersburg
Highlands Bankshares Inc 640

Point Pleasant
Fruth, Inc. 550

Princeton
Princeton Community Hospital Association, Inc. 1083

Weirton
Weirton Medical Center, Inc. 1505

Wheeling
Ohio Valley Medical Center Incorporated 992
The Ogden Newspapers Inc 1362
Wesbanco Inc 1507

WISCONSIN

Amery
Amery Regional Medical Center, Inc. 88

Appleton
Appvion, Inc. 106
Creative Group, Inc. 370
Thedacare Regional Medical Center - Appleton, Inc. 1380
U.s. Venture, Inc. 1418

Beaver Dam
Beaver Dam Community Hospitals, Inc. 167
Good Karma Broadcasting Llc 586

Beloit
Beloit College 170
Beloit Health System, Inc. 170
Blackhawk Bancorp Inc 187
United Stars, Inc. 1431

Brookfield
Cib Marine Bancshares Inc 290
Fiserv Inc 526
Hunzinger Construction Company 664
Rev Group Inc 1138

Brownsville
Michels Corporation 876

De Pere
St. Norbert College, Inc. 1261

Dodgeville
Lands' End Inc 776

Durand
Bauer Built, Inc. 162

Eau Claire
Citizens Community Bancorp Inc (md) 295
Market & Johnson, Inc. 835
Mayo Clinic Health System - Northwest Wisconsin Region, Inc. 847
National Presto Industries, Inc. 930
Sacred Heart Hospital Of The Hospital Sisters Of The Third Order Of St. Francis 1163

Ellsworth
Ellsworth Cooperative Creamery 458

Fitchburg
Certco, Inc. 269
Promega Corporation 1090

Fond Du Lac
C.d. Smith Construction, Inc. 225

Fort Atkinson
Hard And Soft Fishing, Llc 617

Franklin
Carma Laboratories, Inc. 247

INDEX BY HEADQUARTERS LOCATION

Krones, Inc. 767
Friendship
Adams-columbia Electric Cooperative 20
Friesland
United Wisconsin Grain Producers, Llc 1434
Germantown
Iag Corp. 668
Glendale
Wheaton Franciscan Services, Inc. 1518
Green Bay
Associated Banc-corp 125
Green Bay Packers, Inc. 597
Krueger International, Inc. 768
Paper Converting Machine Company 1023
Pomp's Tire Service, Inc. 1067
Schneider National Inc (wi) 1183
Tufco Technologies, Inc. 1414
Watkins And Shepard Trucking, Inc. 1499
Hudson
Acolad Inc 16
Kenosha
Kenosha Beef International, Ltd. 750
Pacific Sands Inc 1019
Snap-on, Inc. 1223
Kewaskum
Regal Ware, Inc. 1126
Kohler
Kohler Co. 762
La Crosse
Dairyland Power Cooperative 388
Gundersen Lutheran Medical Center, Inc. 608
Kwik Trip, Inc. 769
Mayo Clinic Health System-franciscan Healthcare, Inc. 847
Mcloone Metal Graphics, Inc. 852
La Farge
Cooperative Regions Of Organic Producer Pools 357
Madison
Alliant Energy Corp 53
Ascendium Education Group, Inc. 121
City Of Madison 306
Exact Sciences Corp. 491
First Business Financial Services, Inc. 519
J. H. Findorff & Son Inc. 722
Madison Area Technical College District 823
Meriter Health Services, Inc. 866
Mge Energy Inc 874
National Guardian Life Insurance Co. (madison, Wis.) 928
Sonic Foundry, Inc. 1228
Universities Of Wisconsin 1438
University Of Wisconsin Foundation 1451
University Of Wisconsin Hospitals And Clinics Authority 1451
Wisconsin Power And Light Co 1530

Manitowoc
Orion Energy Systems Inc 1009
Marshfield
Marshfield Clinic Health System, Inc. 837
Marshfield Clinic, Inc. 838
Roehl Transport, Inc. 1151
Security Health Plan Of Wisconsin, Inc. 1191
Mayville
Mayville Engineering Co Inc 848
Menasha
Faith Technologies, Inc. 499
Menomonee Falls
Bradley Company, Llc 203
Enerpac Tool Group Corp 468
Ensync Inc 472
Kohl's Corp. 762
Magnetek, Inc. 824
Menomonie
Chippewa Valley Bean Company, Inc. 286
Mequon
Charter Manufacturing Company, Inc. 275
Middelton
Spectrum Brands Holdings Inc (new) 1246
Middleton
Spectrum Brands Legacy, Inc. 1247
University Of Wisconsin Medical Foundation, Inc. 1451
Milwaukee
Alverno College 61
Artisan Partners Asset Management Inc 119
Badger Meter Inc 151
Brady Corp 204
C. G. Schmidt, Inc. 224
Children's Hospital And Health System, Inc. 283
Commerce Group Corp. 339
Douglas Dynamics, Inc. 423
Fred Usinger, Inc. 546
Froedtert Memorial Lutheran Hospital, Inc. 549
Gardner Denver Investments, Inc. 559
Harley-davidson Inc 618
Johnson Controls, Inc. 738
Komatsu Mining Corp. 763
Koss Corp 765
Luxfer Holdings Plc 817
Manitowoc Company Inc (the) 828
Manpowergroup Inc 829
Marcus Center For The Performing Arts, Inc. 831
Marcus Corp. (the) 832
Marquette University 836
Meyer & Wallis, Inc. 874
Mgic Investment Corp. (wi) 875
Milwaukee Area Technical College Foundation, Inc. 888
Milwaukee Bucks, Llc 888
Milwaukee County War Memorial, Inc. 888
Ministry Health Care, Inc. 890

Northwestern Mutual Life Insurance Co. (milwaukee, Wi) 975
Quarles & Brady Llp 1108
Regal Rexnord Corp 1125
Renewal Fuels Inc 1131
Robert W Baird & Co Inc 1147
Rockwell Automation, Inc. 1150
Roundy's, Inc. 1155
Sensient Technologies Corp. 1197
Smith (a O) Corp 1221
Strattec Security Corp. 1278
The F Dohmen Co 1343
Twin Disc Incorporated 1416
United Performing Arts Fund, Inc. 1430
Wec Energy Group Inc 1505
Weyco Group, Inc 1517
Wisconsin Gas Llc 1530
Wixon Inc. 1531
Zurn Elkay Water Solutions Corp 1553
Mondovi
Marten Transport Ltd 838
Monroe
Colony Brands, Inc. 332
Mount Pleasant
Roosevelt Capital Llc 1152
Mountain
Nicolet Plastics Llc 958
Neenah
Plexus Corp. 1063
Thedacare, Inc. 1380
New Berlin
International Monetary Systems Ltd 706
Oak Creek
Astronautics Corporation Of America 129
Oconomowoc
Paragon Development Systems, Inc. 1024
Oshkosh
Oshkosh Corp (new) 1011
Pewaukee
Vjs Construction Services, Inc. 1485
Pleasant Prairie
Uline, Inc. 1420
Plymouth
Sargento Foods Inc 1179
Sartori Company 1179
Prairie Du Sac
Culver Franchising System, Llc 380
Racine
Johnson Outdoors Inc 738
Milaeger's, Inc. 884
Modine Manufacturing Co 897
Ripon
Alliance Laundry Holdings Llc 52
Ripon College 1144
Schofield
L & S Electric, Inc. 770
Sheboygan Falls
Bemis Manufacturing Company Inc 170

Johnsonville, Llc 738
Stevens Point
Sentry Insurance-a Mutual Co. (stevens Point, Wisc.) 1197
Stoughton
Stoughton Hospital Association 1277
Sun Prairie
General Casualty Co. Of Wisconsin (sun Prairie) 564
Sussex
Quad/graphics, Inc. 1106
Tomah
Tomah Memorial Hospital, Inc. 1391
Waukesha
American Transmission Company, Llc 85
Electronic Tele-communications, Inc. 455
Generac Holdings Inc 563
Grandview Management, Inc. 593
Prohealth Care, Inc. 1089
Telkonet Inc. 1315
Waukesha Memorial Hospital, Inc. 1500
Wausau
Aspirus, Inc. 124
Wausau Financial Systems, Inc. 1500
Wauwatosa
Briggs & Stratton Corporation 209
West Bend
Manitou America Holding, Inc. 828
Westfield
Brakebush Brothers, Inc. 204
Wisconsin Dells
Holiday Wholesale, Inc. 648
Wittenberg
Nueske's Meat Products, Inc. 980
Woodruff
Howard Young Health Care, Inc 659

WYOMING

Buffalo
Crazy Woman Creek Bancorp Inc. 370
Casper
Wyoming Medical Center, Inc. 1539
Cheyenne
Great Lakes Aviation Ltd. 595
Taco John's International, Inc. 1301
Laramie
University Of Wyoming 1451
Rock Springs
Western Wyoming Community College District 1514